McGraw-Hill
networks™
A Social Studies Learning System

CHOOSE how you want to teach

- All print
- All digital
- Your own custom print and digital mix

MEETS YOU ANYWHERE —
TAKES YOU EVERYWHERE

McGraw-Hill
networks™

**MEETS YOU ANYWHERE —
TAKES YOU EVERYWHERE**

MANAGE your classroom anytime

- Use prepared model lessons
- Clear pathway through critical content
- Quick, targeted instruction

From anywhere

- Plan instruction
- Create presentations
- Differentiate instruction

McGraw-Hill
networks™

**MEETS YOU ANYWHERE —
TAKES YOU EVERYWHERE**

MANAGE your classroom anytime

- Use prepared model lessons
- Clear pathway through critical content
- Quick, targeted instruction

From anywhere

- Plan instruction
- Create presentations
- Differentiate instruction

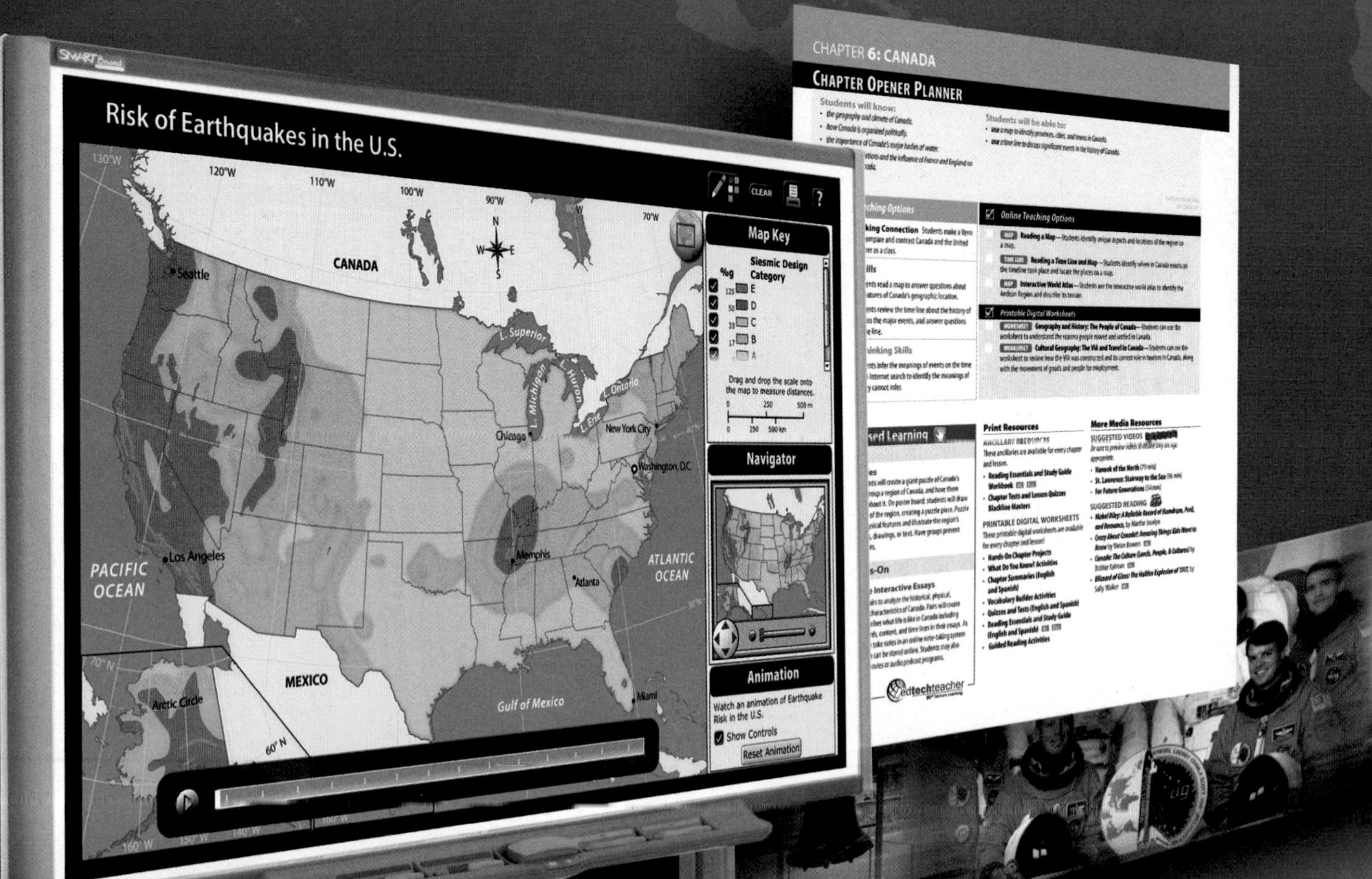

ORGANIZE with everything in one place

- Upload personal resources
- Search Resource Library
- Create class rosters
- File and Save

start networking

McGraw-Hill
networks™

MEETS YOU ANYWHERE — TAKES YOU EVERYWHERE

CUSTOMIZE everything for your students – easy, quick, and efficient

- Personalize lessons
- Create tests
- Modify assignments

DIFFERENTIATE instruction to meet the needs of all your students

- Assign different reading levels
- Access full audio
- Use PDFs or modify worksheets
- Print or assign online

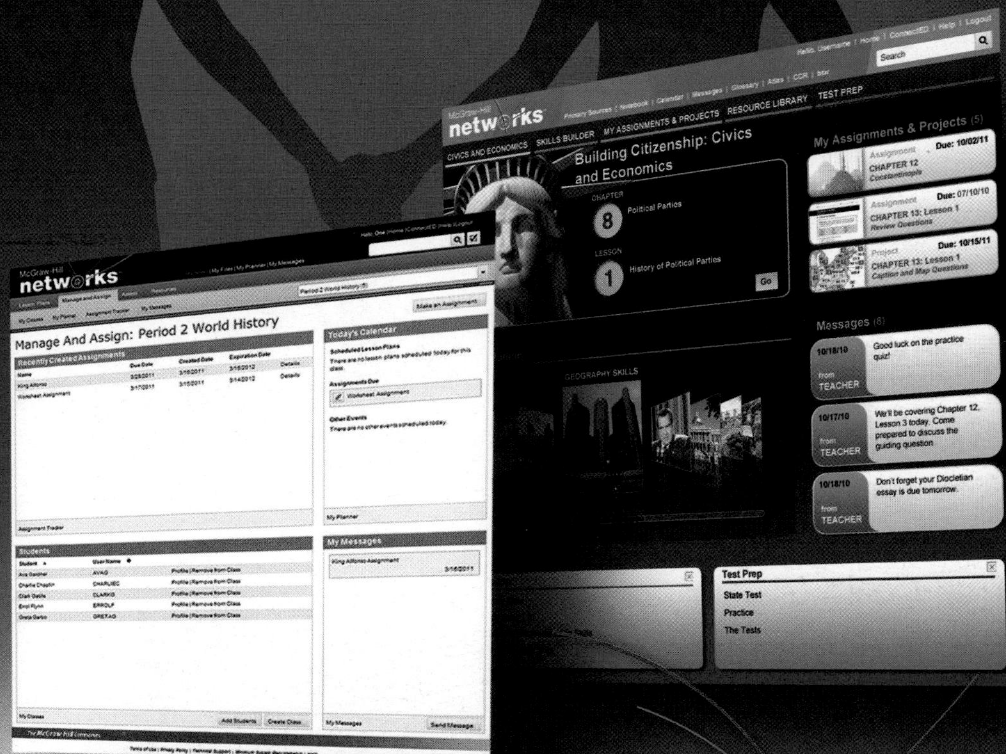

start networking

McGraw-Hill
networks™

MEETS YOU ANYWHERE — TAKES YOU EVERYWHERE

ENGAGE your students for the way they want to learn

- Hands-on projects
- interactive maps, presentations, and primary sources
- Streaming video and games

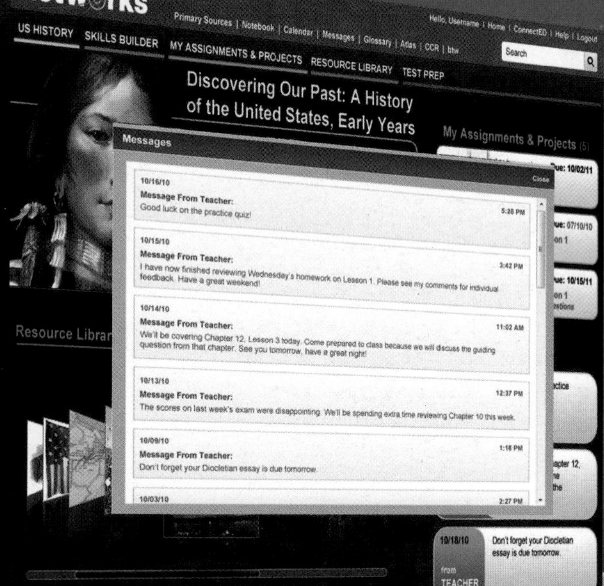

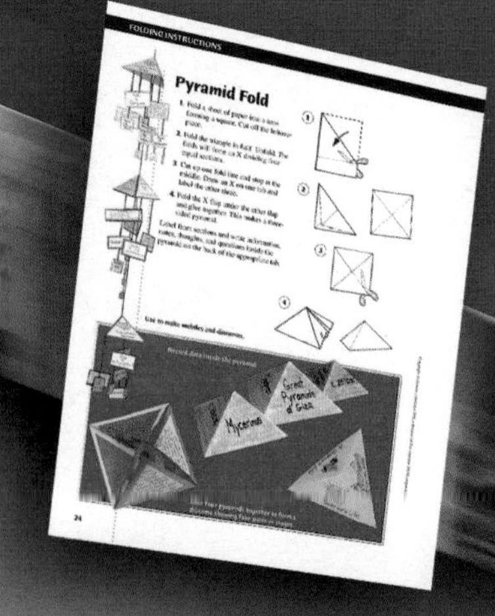

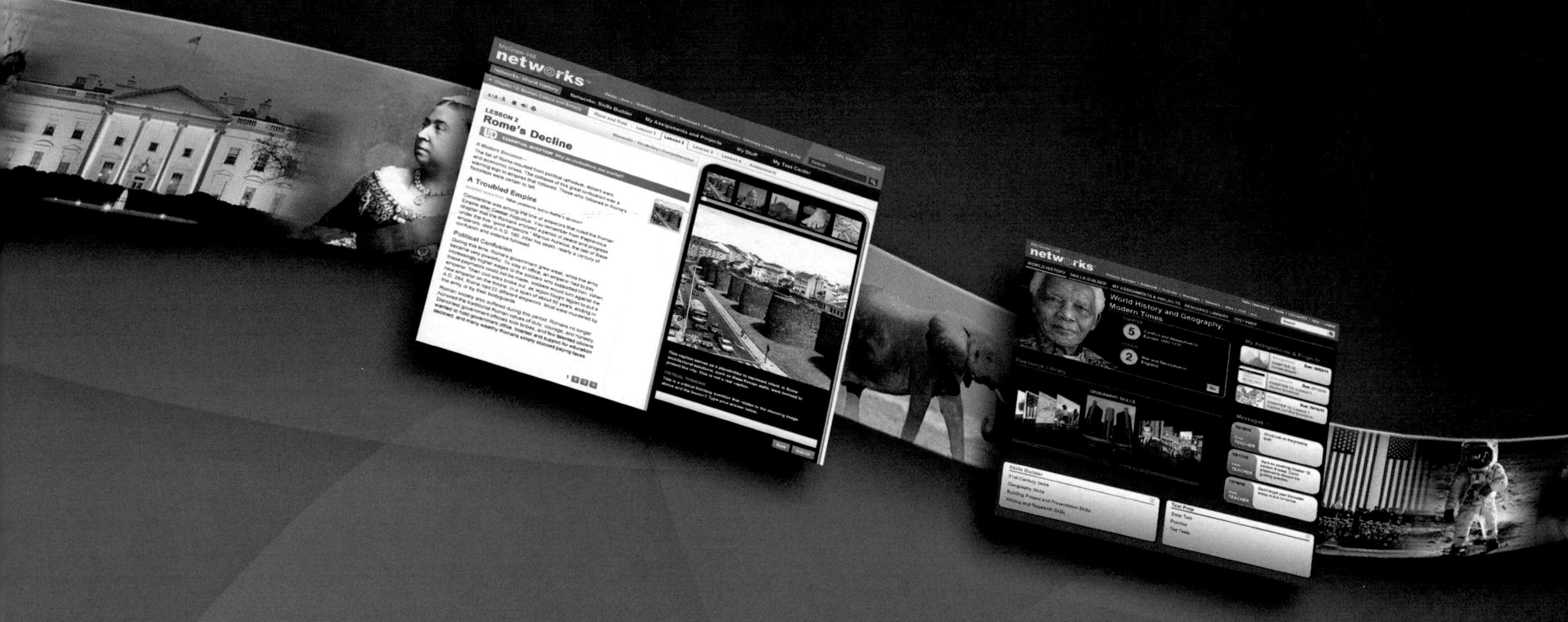

COMMUNICATE with your students

- Assign homework and tests
- Send messages
- Track and print student results

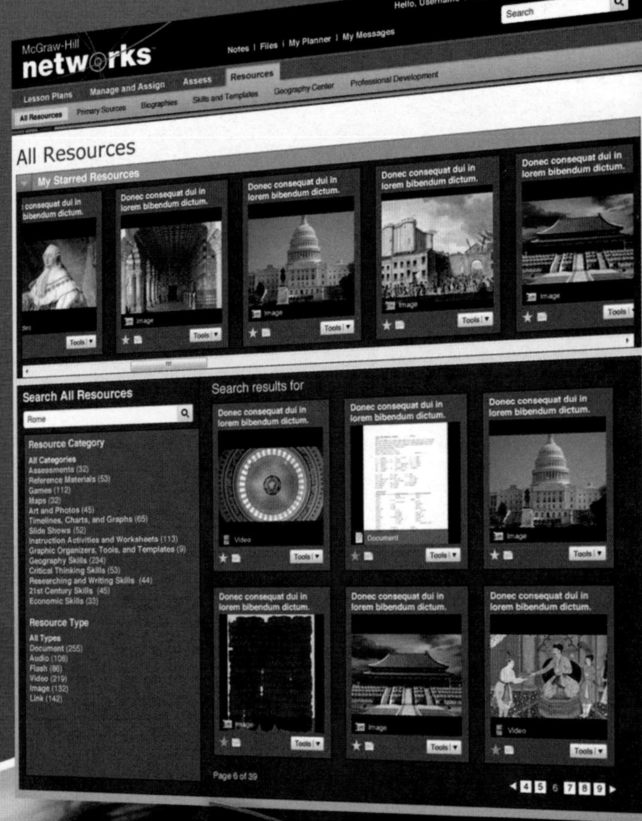

start networking

McGraw-Hill

networks™

MEETS YOU ANYWHERE — TAKES YOU EVERYWHERE

CONNECT with colleagues, students, experts, and content

1. Log on to the Internet and go to ***connected.mcgraw-hill.com***.
2. Enter User Name and Password.
3. Click on your **Networks** book.
4. Select your chapter and lesson.

start networking

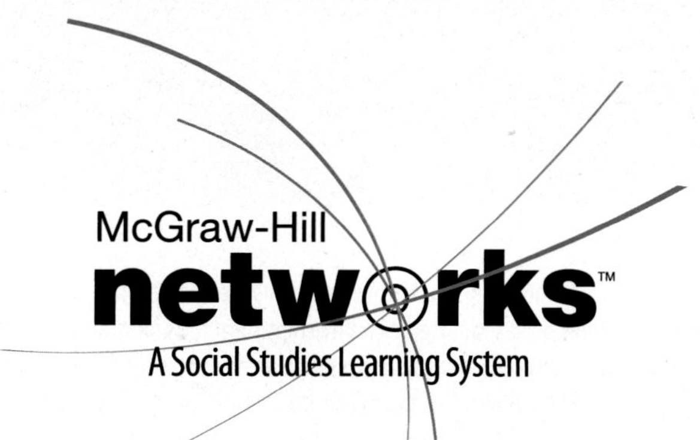

Teacher Edition

DISCOVERING OUR PAST

A HISTORY of the WORLD

Early Ages

Jackson J. Spielvogel, Ph.D.

Bothell, WA • Chicago, IL • Columbus, OH • New York, NY

AUTHORS

Jackson J. Spielvogel is Associate Professor of History Emeritus at The Pennsylvania State University. He received his Ph.D. from The Ohio State University, where he specialized in Reformation history under Harold J. Grimm. His work has been supported by fellowships from the Fulbright Foundation and the Foundation for Reformation Research. At Penn State, Spielvogel helped inaugurate the Western civilization courses, as well as a popular course on Nazi Germany. His book, *Hitler and Nazi Germany,* was published in 1987 (sixth edition, 2010). He is also the author of *Western Civilization,* published in 1991 (eighth edition, 2012). Spielvogel is the coauthor (with William Duiker) of *World History,* first published in 1998 (sixth edition, 2010). Spielvogel has won five major university-wide teaching awards. In 1988–1989, he held the Penn State Teaching Fellowship, the university's most prestigious teaching award. He won the Dean Arthur Ray Warnock Award for Outstanding Faculty Member in 1996 and the Schreyer Honors College Excellence in Teaching Award in 2000.

Cover credits:
(Main image) Emperor Charlemagne, The Gallery Collection/Corbis; (thumbnails l to r, t to b) Renaud Visage/Photographer's Choice/Getty Images, Burke/Triolo/Brand X Pictures/Jupiterimages, The McGraw-Hill Companies, Glen Allison/Photodisc/Getty Images, Library of Congress Prints and Photographs Division (LC-USZC2-2870), C. Sherburne/PhotoLink/Getty Images, Royalty-Free/CORBIS, Fernando Fernandez/age Fotostock, Photographer's Choice RF/Getty Images, Pixtal/age Fotostock, Melba Photo Agency/PunchStock, John Wang/Photodisc/Getty Images, Photodisc/Getty Images, Pixtal/age Fotostock, The McGraw-Hill Companies, Inc./Barry Barker, photographer, Author's Image/PunchStock, Ingram Publishing/SuperStock, Pixtal/age Fotostock.

National Council for the Social Studies, *National Curriculum Standards for Social Studies: A Framework for Teaching, Learning, and Assessment (Silver Spring, MD: NCSS, 2010).*

connected.mcgraw-hill.com

Send all inquiries to:
McGraw-Hill Education
8787 Orion Place
Columbus, OH 43240

Teacher Edition:
ISBN: 978-0-07-664761-3
MHID: 0-07-664761-7

Student Edition:
ISBN: 978-0-07-664757-6
MHID: 0-07-664757-9

Printed in the United States of America.

2 3 4 5 6 7 8 9 QVS 16 15 14 13

CONTRIBUTING AUTHORS

Jay McTighe has published articles in a number of leading educational journals and has coauthored 10 books, including the best-selling *Understanding by Design* series with Grant Wiggins. McTighe also has an extensive background in professional development and is a featured speaker at national, state, and district conferences and workshops. He received his undergraduate degree from the College of William and Mary, earned a master's degree from the University of Maryland, and completed post-graduate studies at the Johns Hopkins University.

Dinah Zike, M.Ed., is an award-winning author, educator, and inventor recognized for designing three-dimensional, hands-on manipulatives and graphic organizers known as Foldables®. Foldables are used nationally and internationally by parents, teachers, and other professionals in the education field. Zike has developed more than 150 supplemental educational books and materials. Her two latest books, *Notebook Foldables®* and *Foldables®, Notebook Foldables®, & VKV®s for Spelling and Vocabulary 4th–12th* were each awarded *Learning Magazine's* Teachers' Choice Award for 2011. In 2004, Zike was honored with the CESI Science Advocacy Award. She received her M.Ed. from Texas A&M, College Station, Texas.

Doug Fisher Ph.D. and Nancy Frey Ph.D. are professors in the School of Teacher Education at San Diego State University. Fisher's focus is on literacy and language, with an emphasis on students who are English Learners. Frey's focus is on literacy and learning, with a concentration in how students acquire content knowledge. Both teach elementary and secondary teacher preparation courses, in addition to their work with graduate and doctoral programs. Their shared interests include supporting students with diverse learning needs, instructional design, and curriculum development. Fisher and Frey are coauthors of numerous articles and books, including *Better Learning Through Structured Teaching, Checking for Understanding, Background Knowledge*, and *Improving Adolescent Literacy*. They are coeditors (with Diane Lapp) of the NCTE journal *Voices From the Middle*.

CONSULTANTS AND REVIEWERS

ACADEMIC CONSULTANTS

David Berger, Ph.D.
Ruth and I. Lewis Gordon Professor of Jewish History
Dean, Bernard Revel Graduate School
Yeshiva University
New York, New York

Albert S. Broussard, Ph.D.
Professor of History
Texas A & M University
College Station, Texas

Sheilah F. Clarke-Ekong, Ph.D.
Associate Professor, Cultural Anthropology
University of Missouri–St. Louis
St. Louis, Missouri

Tom Daccord
Educational Technology Specialist
Co-Director, EdTechTeacher
Boston, Massachusetts

Dr. Kenji Oshiro
Professor Emeritus of Geography
Wright State University
Dayton, Ohio

Justin Reich
Educational Technology Specialist
Co-Director, EdTechTeacher
Boston, Massachusetts

Joseph Rosenbloom, Ph.D.
Adjunct Professor, Jewish and Middle East Studies
Washington University
St. Louis, Missouri

TEACHER REVIEWERS

Mary Kathryn Bishop
Fairhope Middle School
Fairhope, Alabama

Janine Brown
Social Studies Department Chairperson
Discovery Middle School
Orlando, Florida

Carl M. Brownell
Social Studies Department Chairperson
Maine East High School
Park Ridge, Illinois

James Hauf
Berkeley Middle School
St. Louis, Missouri

Amy Kanuck
Morgan Village Middle School
Camden, New Jersey

Kim J. Lapple
Grades 6–12 Social Studies Chairperson
H.C. Crittenden Middle School
Armonk, New York

CONTENTS

How to Use the Teacher Edition **T28**
NCSS Correlations **T37**
Common Core State Standards Correlations **T41**
Professional Development **T52**
Reference Atlas maps **RA1**
Scavenger Hunt **RA28**

Norbert Millauer/AFP/Getty Images

Chapter and Lesson Planner Pages **1A**
Intervention and Remediation Strategies **1F**

What Does a Historian Do? 1

Essential Questions
Why is history important? • How do we learn about the past? • How do you research history?

LESSON 1 **What Is History?** **4**
Biography Heinrich Schliemann 8
Connections to Today How Lucy Got Her Name 9

LESSON 2 **How Does a Historian Work?** **10**
Connections to Today The Census 12
What Do You Think? Should Artifacts Be Returned to Their Countries of Origin? 16

LESSON 3 **Researching History** **18**
Thinking Like a Historian Internet Tips 20

Chip Somodevilla/Getty Images News/Getty Images

Chapter and Lesson Planner Pages **25A**
Intervention and Remediation Strategies **25F**

Studying Geography, Economics, and Citizenship 25

Essential Questions
How does geography influence the way people live? • Why do people trade? • Why do people form governments?

LESSON 1 **Studying Geography** **28**
Connections to Today GIS/GPS 32
Biography Gerardus Mercator 36

LESSON 2 **Exploring Economics** **38**
Thinking Like a Historian Analyzing Primary Sources 41

LESSON 3 **Practicing Citizenship** **44**
Then and Now The American Flag Design 46

This icon indicates where reading skills and writing skills from the *Common Core State Standards for English Language Arts & Literacy in History/Social Studies, Science, and Technical Subjects* are practiced and reinforced.

CONTENTS

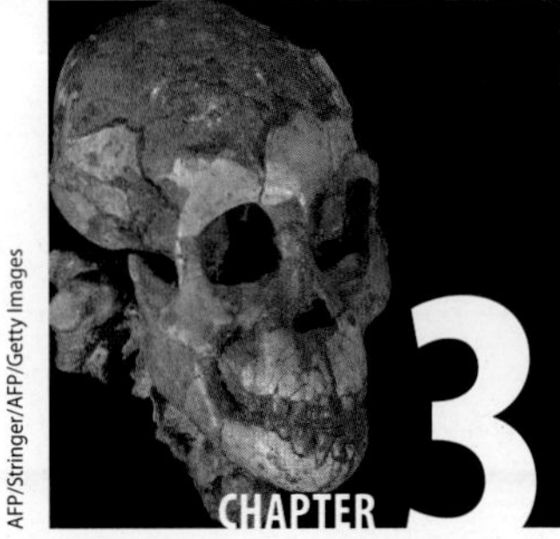

AFP/Stringer/AFP/Getty Images

Chapter and Lesson Planner Pages **51A**

Intervention and Remediation Strategies **51E**

Early Humans and the Agricultural Revolution 51

Essential Question

How do people adapt to their environments?

LESSON 1 Hunter-Gatherers **54**

LESSON 2 The Agricultural Revolution **62**

Biography Ötzi the Iceman 66

Thinking Like a Historian Making Inferences 67

Charles & Josette Lenars/CORBIS

Chapter and Lesson Planner Pages **73A**

Intervention and Remediation Strategies **73E**

Mesopotamia 73

Essential Questions

How does geography influence the way people live? • Why does conflict develop?

LESSON 1 The Sumerians **76**

Thinking Like a Historian Classifying and Categorizing Information 83

The World's Literature *Epic of Gilgamesh*. 84

LESSON 2 Mesopotamian Empires **86**

Biography Sargon 87

Connections to Today Libraries 89

Corbis

Chapter and Lesson Planner Pages **97A**

Intervention and Remediation Strategies **97G**

Ancient Egypt and Kush 97

Essential Questions

How does geography influence the way people live? • What makes a culture unique? • Why do civilizations rise and fall?

LESSON 1 The Nile River **100**

Thinking Like a Historian Researching on the Internet 102

LESSON 2 Life in Ancient Egypt **108**

LESSON 3 Egypt's Empire **120**

Connections to Today Ivory 122

Biography Hatshepsut 123

LESSON 4 The Kingdom of Kush **128**

Lebrecht Music and Arts Photo Library/Alamy

Chapter and Lesson Planner Pages 137A
Intervention and Remediation Strategies 137G

The Israelites 137

Essential Questions

How do religions develop? • What are the characteristics of a leader? • How does religion shape society? • Why does conflict develop?

LESSON 1 Beginnings **140**
Biography Moses 142
Connections to Today Alphabets 145

LESSON 2 The Israelite Kingdom **148**

LESSON 3 The Development of Judaism **154**
Connections to Today Heroes 157

LESSON 4 The Jews in the Mediterranean World **160**
Biography Judas Maccabeus 162
Connections to Today Dead Sea Scrolls 166

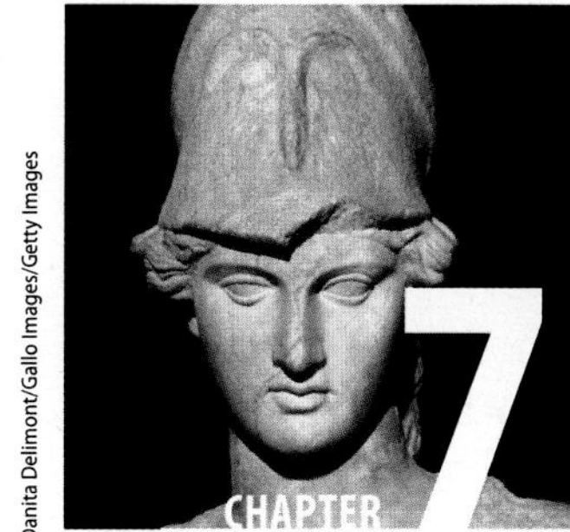

Danita Delimont/Gallo Images/Getty Images

Chapter and Lesson Planner Pages 171A
Intervention and Remediation Strategies 171G

The Ancient Greeks 171

Essential Questions

How does geography influence the way people live? • Why do people form governments? • Why does conflict develop? • How do governments change?

LESSON 1 Rise of Greek Civilization **174**
Thinking Like a Historian Analyzing Primary and Secondary Sources 177
Connections to Today Coins 179

LESSON 2 Sparta and Athens: City-State Rivals **183**
Biography Solon 188
Connections to Today The Olympics 189

LESSON 3 Greece and Persia **190**
Connections to Today Marathons 195

LESSON 4 Glory, War, and Decline **198**
Biography Aspasia 201

CONTENTS

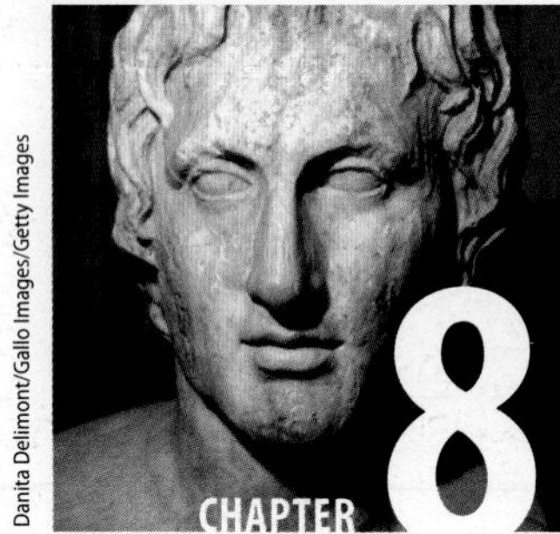

Danita Delimont/Gallo Images/Getty Images

Chapter and Lesson Planner Pages 209A
Intervention and Remediation Strategies 209G

Greek Civilization 209

Essential Questions

What makes a culture unique? • How do new ideas change the way people live? • What are the characteristics of a leader?

LESSON 1 **Greek Culture** 212
Then and Now Greek Theater 217

LESSON 2 **The Greek Mind** 220
Biography Plato 222
What Do You Think? Did Socrates Commit Treason? 228

LESSON 3 **Alexander's Empire** 230
Thinking Like a Historian Researching on the Internet 231

LESSON 4 **Hellenistic Culture** 236
Connections to Today Constant *pi* 240

Dinodia Photo Library/Age fotostock

Chapter and Lesson Planner Pages 245A
Intervention and Remediation Strategies 245F

Ancient India 245

Essential Questions

How does geography influence the way people live? • How do religions develop? • What makes a culture unique?

LESSON 1 **Early Civilizations** 248
Thinking Like a Historian Researching on the Internet 252

LESSON 2 **Religions of Ancient India** 257
Connections to Today Hindu Beliefs 259
Biography The Buddha 260

LESSON 3 **The Mauryan Empire** 265
Connections to Today Math Poems 271

Apic/Hulton Archives/Getty Images

Chapter and Lesson Planner Pages 275A
Intervention and Remediation Strategies 275F

Early China 275

Essential Questions

What makes a culture unique? • How do new ideas change the way people live? • How do governments change?

LESSON 1 **The Birth of Chinese Civilization** 278
Thinking Like a Historian Analyzing Sources 282

LESSON 2 **Society and Culture in Ancient China** 286
Connections to Today Confucianism in Asia 287

LESSON 3 **The Qin and the Han Dynasties** 292
Connections to Today The Great Wall 293
Biography Ban Zhao 295
Then and Now Paper 296

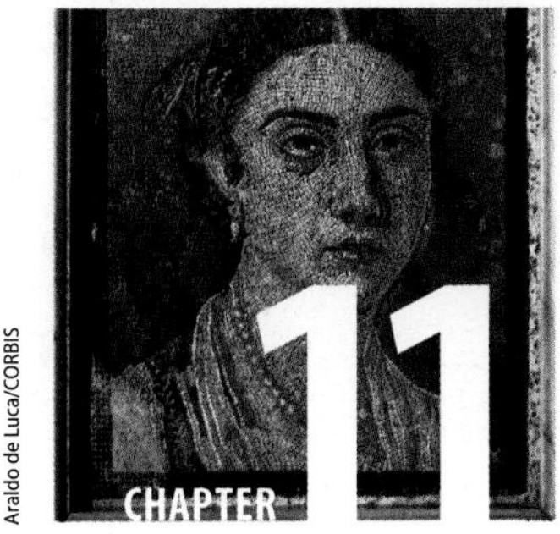

Araldo de Luca/CORBIS

Chapter and Lesson Planner Pages 303A
Intervention and Remediation Strategies 303G

Rome: Republic to Empire 303

Essential Questions

How does geography influence the way people live? • How do governments change? • Why does conflict develop? • What are the characteristics of a leader?

LESSON 1 The Founding of Rome 306
Thinking Like a Historian Analyzing Primary and Secondary Sources 308

LESSON 2 Rome as a Republic 312
Connections to Today Hannibal's Elephants 319

LESSON 3 The End of the Republic 320
Connections to Today Crossing the Rubicon 324
Biography Mark Antony 326
Biography Cleopatra 326

LESSON 4 Rome Builds an Empire 328
Then and Now Pompeii 330

Byzantine School/The Bridgeman Art Library/Getty Images

Chapter and Lesson Planner Pages 337A
Intervention and Remediation Strategies 337F

Roman Civilization 337

Essential Questions

What makes a culture unique? • Why do civilizations rise and fall? • How does geography influence the way people live?

LESSON 1 The Roman Way of Life 340
Thinking Like a Historian Researching on the Internet 342
Biography Livia 343
Then and Now Medical Technology 345
The World's Literature *The Aeneid* 348

LESSON 2 Rome's Decline 350
Connections to Today Vandalism 355
What Do You Think? Did People Benefit from Roman Rule? 358

LESSON 3 The Byzantine Empire 360
Biography Justinian I 362
Biography Empress Theodora 362

Scala/Art Resource, NY

Chapter and Lesson Planner Pages 369A
Intervention and Remediation Strategies 369F

The Rise of Christianity 369

Essential Questions

What are the characteristics of a leader? • How do religions develop? • How do new ideas change the way people live?

LESSON 1 Early Christianity 372
Biography Peter 374
Biography Mary Magdalene 377

LESSON 2 The Early Church 380
Then and Now Roman Catacombs 382

LESSON 3 A Christian Europe 386

CONTENTS

Italian School/The Bridgeman Art Library/Getty Images

Chapter and Lesson Planner Pages **395A**
Intervention and Remediation Strategies **395F**

CHAPTER 14 Islamic Civilization 395

Essential Questions
How do religions develop? • How do new ideas change the way people live?

LESSON 1 A New Faith **398**
Biography Muhammad 401
Thinking Like a Historian Using a Time Line 403

LESSON 2 The Spread of Islam **404**
Biography Suleiman I 410

LESSON 3 Life in the Islamic World **411**
Then and Now Shopping 412
Connections to Today Becoming a Doctor 413

Peter Horree/Alamy

Chapter and Lesson Planner Pages **419A**
Intervention and Remediation Strategies **419F**

CHAPTER 15 African Civilizations 419

Essential Questions
Why do people trade? • How does religion shape society? • How do religions develop?

LESSON 1 The Rise of African Civilizations **422**
Thinking Like a Historian Researching on the Internet 427

LESSON 2 Africa's Governments and Religions **430**
Biography Mansa Musa 435

LESSON 3 African Society and Culture **436**
Connections to Today West African Music Today 441
What Do You Think? Africa's Water Resources: Should Private Companies Control Them? 442

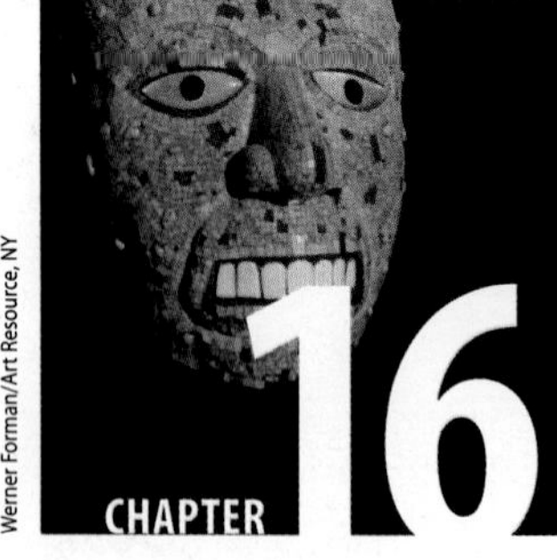
Werner Forman/Art Resource, NY

Chapter and Lesson Planner Pages **447A**
Intervention and Remediation Strategies **447E**

CHAPTER 16 The Americas 447

Essential Questions
How does geography affect the way people live? • What makes a culture unique?

LESSON 1 The First Americans **450**

LESSON 2 Life in the Americas **459**
Connections to Today The Maya Today 460
Biography Pachacuti 464
Thinking Like a Historian Comparing and Contrasting 467

The British Library Heritage/Age fotostock

Chapter and Lesson Planner Pages **471A**
Intervention and Remediation Strategies **471G**

Imperial China 471

Essential Questions

How does geography affect the way people live? • How do new ideas change the way people live? • What are the characteristics of a leader?

LESSON 1 China Reunites **474**
Connections to Today Three Gorges Dam 475
Biography Empress Wu 476
Connections to Today Civil Service Examinations 481

LESSON 2 Chinese Society **482**
Thinking Like a Historian Drawing Conclusions 485

LESSON 3 The Mongols in China **489**
Biography Genghis Khan 492
The World's Literature *Monkey* 496

LESSON 4 The Ming Dynasty **498**

Max Paddler/Flickr/Getty Images

Chapter and Lesson Planner Pages **507A**
Intervention and Remediation Strategies **507G**

Civilizations of Korea, Japan, and Southeast Asia 507

Essential Questions

Why do people form governments? • How does geography influence the way people live? • What makes a culture unique?

LESSON 1 Korea: History and Culture **510**
Then and Now Observatories 512

LESSON 2 Early Japan **516**

LESSON 3 Medieval Japan **520**
Biography Murasaki Shikibu 526

LESSON 4 Southeast Asia: History and Culture **528**
Connections to Today Saving Angkor Wat 531

Chapter and Lesson Planner Pages **537A**
Intervention and Remediation Strategies **537H**

Medieval Europe 537

Essential Questions

Why does conflict develop? • What is the role of religion in government? • What are the characteristics that define a culture? • How do governments change?

LESSON 1 The Early Middle Ages **540**

LESSON 2 Feudalism and the Rise of Towns **548**
Thinking Like a Historian Researching Using Internet Resources 555

LESSON 3 Kingdoms and Crusades **556**

LESSON 4 Culture and the Church **564**
Then and Now Gothic Architecture 565

LESSON 5 The Late Middle Ages **570**
Biography Joan of Arc 574

Chapter and Lesson Planner Pages **579A**
Intervention and Remediation Strategies **579G**

Renaissance and Reformation 579

Essential Questions

Why do people make economic choices? • How do new ideas change the way people live? • Why does conflict develop?

LESSON 1 The Renaissance Begins **582**
Thinking Like a Historian Drawing Conclusions 587

LESSON 2 New Ideas and Art **589**
Biography Michelangelo Buonarroti 594
The World's Literature *Henry V* 596

LESSON 3 The Reformation Begins **598**

LESSON 4 Catholics and Protestants **606**
Biography Catherine de' Medici 610

Chapter and Lesson Planner Pages **615A**
Intervention and Remediation Strategies **615F**

Age of Exploration and Trade 615

Essential Questions

How does technology change the way people live? • Why do civilizations rise and fall? • Why do people make economic choices?

LESSON 1 The Age of Exploration **618**
Then and Now Navigation Tools 619
Thinking Like a Historian Predicting Consequences 623

LESSON 2 Spain's Conquests in the Americas **624**
Biography Hernán Cortés 626

LESSON 3 Exploration and Worldwide Trade **628**
Connections to Today Blending Languages 631

The Art Archive/CORBIS

Chapter and Lesson Planner Pages 639A
Intervention and Remediation Strategies 639E

The Scientific Revolution and the Enlightenment 639

Essential Questions

How do new ideas change the way people live? • How do governments change?

LESSON 1 **The Scientific Revolution** 642
Biography Galileo 646

LESSON 2 **The Enlightenment** 650
Connections to Today Women's Rights Around the World 655

Jacques Louis David/The Bridgeman Art Library/Getty Images

Chapter and Lesson Planner Pages 661A
Intervention and Remediation Strategies 661H

Political and Industrial Revolutions 661

Essential Questions

Why does conflict develop? • How do new ideas change the way people live? • How do governments change?

LESSON 1 **The American Revolution** 664

LESSON 2 **The French Revolution and Napoleon** 672
Connections to Today Political Left and Right 674
Biography Marie Antoinette 675
What Do You Think? Did the French People Have Cause to Rebel Against Their Monarchy? 680

LESSON 3 **Nationalism and Nation-States** 682

LESSON 4 **The Industrial Revolution** 690
Biography The Wright Brothers 695

LESSON 5 **Society and Industry** 696
Biography Albert Einstein 702

Glossary/Glosario 707

Index 736

FEATURES

What Do You Think?

Should Artifacts Be Returned to Their Countries of Origin? **16**
Did Socrates Commit Treason? **228**
Did People Benefit from Roman Rule? **358**
Africa's Water Resources: Should Private Companies Control Them? **442**
Did the French People Have Cause to Rebel Against Their Monarchy? **680**

The World's Literature

Epic of Gilgamesh **84**
The Aeneid **348**
Monkey **496**
Henry V **596**

Biographies

Heinrich Schliemann **8**
Gerardus Mercator **36**
Őtzi the Iceman **66**
Sargon **87**
Hatshepsut **123**
Moses **142**
Judas Maccabeus **162**
Solon **188**
Aspasia **201**
Plato **222**
The Buddha **260**
Ban Zhao **295**
Mark Antony **326**
Cleopatra **326**
Livia **343**
Justinian **362**
Empress Theodora **362**
Peter **374**
Mary Magdalene **377**
Muhammad **401**
Suleiman I **410**
Mansa Musa **435**
Pachacuti **464**
Empress Wu **476**
Genghis Khan **492**
Murasaki Shikibu **526**
Joan of Arc **574**
Michelangelo Buonarroti **594**
Catherine de' Medici **610**
Hernán Cortés **626**
Galileo **646**
Marie Antoinette **675**
The Wright Brothers **695**
Albert Einstein **702**

Connections to TODAY

How Lucy Got Her Name **9**
The Census **12**
GIS/GPS **32**
Libraries **89**
Ivory **122**
Alphabets **145**
Heroes **157**
Dead Sea Scrolls **166**
Coins **179**
The Olympics **189**
Marathons **195**
Constant *pi* **240**
Hindu Beliefs **259**
Math Poems **271**
Confucianism in Asia **287**
The Great Wall **293**
Hannibal's Elephants **319**
Crossing the Rubicon **324**
Vandalism **355**
Becoming a Doctor **413**
West African Music Today **441**
The Maya Today **460**
Three Gorges Dam **475**
Civil Service Examinations **481**
Saving Angkor Wat **531**
Blending Languages **631**
Women's Rights Around the World **655**
Political Left and Right **674**

THEN AND NOW

The American Flag Design **46**
Greek Theater **217**
Paper **296**
Pompeii **330**
Medical Technology **345**
Roman Catacombs **382**
Shopping **412**
Observatories **512**
Gothic Architecture **565**
Navigation Tools **619**

Thinking Like a HISTORIAN

Internet Tips **20**
Analyzing Primary Sources **41**
Making Inferences **67**
Classifying and Categorizing Information **83**
Researching on the Internet **102**
Analyzing Primary and Secondary Sources **177**
Researching on the Internet **231**
Researching on the Internet **252**
Analyzing Sources **282**
Analyzing Primary and Secondary Sources **308**
Researching on the Internet **342**
Using a Time Line **403**
Researching on the Internet **427**
Comparing and Contrasting **467**
Drawing Conclusions **485**
Researching Using Internet Resources **555**
Drawing Conclusions **587**
Predicting Consequences **623**

MAPS, CHARTS, AND GRAPHS

REFERENCE ATLAS MAPS

World: Political **RA2**
World: Physical **RA4**
North America: Political **RA6**
North America: Physical **RA7**
Middle America: Physical/ Political **RA8**
South America: Political **RA10**
South America: Physical **RA11**
Europe: Political **RA12**
Europe: Physical **RA14**
Middle East: Physical/ Political **RA16**
Africa: Political **RA18**
Africa: Physical **RA19**
Asia: Political **RA20**
Asia: Physical **RA22**
Pacific Rim: Physical/ Political **RA24**
Geographic Dictionary **RA26**

CHAPTER MAPS

Chapter 2 Natural Wonders of the Ancient World 26
Hemispheres 29
Latitude and Longitude 30
Goode's Interrupted Equal-Area Projection 30
Mercator Projection 31
Robinson Projection 31
Winkel Tripel Projection 31
Alexander's Empire 323 B.C. 34
Egypt: Population Density 37

Chapter 3 Human Settlements 8000 B.C. to 2000 B.C. 52
Ice Age Migration 60
Early Farming 63
Early Civilizations 3000 B.C. 68

Chapter 4 Mesopotamia 3000 B.C. to 500 B.C. 74
Ancient Mesopotamia 3000 B.C. 78
Assyrian Empire 900 B.C. 89
The Chaldean Empire 605 B.C. 90

Chapter 5 Ancient Egypt c. 1550 B.C.–1070 B.C. 99
Ancient Egypt c. 31 B.C. 101
Early Trade Routes 106
Ancient Egyptian Kingdoms 124
Kush Kingdom c. 250 B.C. 131

Chapter 6 The Israelites 1800 B.C. to A.D. 70 138
Ancient Israel c. 922 B.C. 151
Diaspora 161
Judaea c. A.D. 70 164

Chapter 7 Ancient Greece 2000 B.C. to 400 B.C. 173
Ancient Greece 2000 B.C. 175
Greek Trading Among Colonies 750 B.C.–550 B.C. 180
Sparta and Athens 184
The Persian Empire c. 500 B.C. 191
Persian Wars 499–449 B.C.. 194
The Peloponnesian War 431–404 B.C. 204

Chapter 8 Alexander's Empire c. 331 B.C. 210
Alexander's Empire 323 B.C. 232
Hellenistic World 241 B.C. 234

Chapter 9 Ancient India c. 3000 B.C. 247
The Geography of India 249
Aryan Migration 2000–500 B.C. 253
Mauryan Empire c. 250 B.C. 266
Gupta Empire c. A.D. 600 269

Chapter 10 China c. 1750 B.C. to A.D. 190 276
The Geography of China 279
Shang Empire c. 1750–1045 B.C. 281
Zhou Empire 1045–256 B.C. 284
Qin and Han Empires 221 B.C.–A.D. 220 294
Trading in the Ancient World c. A.D. 100s 298

Chapter 11 Roman Empire at Its Height 304
Growth of the Roman Republic 500 B.C.–146 B.C. 314
The Punic Wars 264 B.C.–146 B.C. 317
Trade Routes of the Roman Empire A.D. 200s 332

Chapter 12 The Roman Empire A.D. 400 338
Roads of the Roman Empire A.D. 117 346
Germanic Migrations c. A.D. 200-500 354
Justinian's Conquests 364

Chapter 13 Spread of Christianity to A.D. 600 370
Spread of Christianity A.D. 325 381
Spread of Christianity A.D. 325–1100 388

Chapter 14 Islamic Empire A.D. 750 396
Southwest Asia c. A.D. 600 399
The Spread of Islam A.D. 632–A.D. 750 405
The Abbasid Empire A.D. 800 408

CHAPTER MAPS (CONTINUED)

Chapter 15 Climate Zones of Africa....................421
Geography and Climate Zones in Africa........423
Trade Routes of North Africa c. 1050–1500.....426
Religion in Africa Today....................433
Bantu Migrations....................437
The Slave Trade c. 1450-1800....................440

Chapter 16 North and South American Groups............449
North America Physical Map....................451
Migration to America....................453
Civilizations of Mesoamerica....................455
People and Food Sources of North America c. 1300–1500....................466

Chapter 17 Mongol Empire c. A.D. 1294....................472
Tang China c. A.D. 700....................475
Song China c. A.D. 1200....................477
Mongol Empire Under Genghis Kahn c. A.D. 1227....................490
Mongol Empire c. A.D. 1294....................491
Ming China 1368-1644....................499
The Voyages of Zheng He 1405–1433..........501

Chapter 18 Early Empires of Korea, Japan, and Southeast Asia....................508
Geography of Korea....................511
Three Kingdoms of Korea c. A.D. 400...........513
Geography of Japan....................517
Southeast Asia Today....................529

Chapter 19 Medieval Europe c. 950–1300....................538
Europe's Geography and People c. A.D. 500.....541
Invasions of Europe c. A.D. 800–1000..........545
European Kingdoms c. 1160....................559
Growth of Moscow 1300–1505....................561
The Crusades 1096–1204....................562
The Black Death in Europe 1350....................571
The Hundred Years' War 1346–1453..........573

Chapter 20 Renaissance Europe A.D. 1500....................580
Italy c. 1500....................583
Holy Roman Empire 1520....................602
Religions in Europe c. 1600....................608

Chapter 21 European Exploration of the World...........616
Portugal and da Gama 1497–1499............620
Spanish Explorations 1500–1600............625
European Trade in Asia c. 1700....................632
The Columbian Exchange....................634

Chapter 22 Centers of Enlightenment 1785....................640
Growth of Prussia and Austria c. 1525–1720....656

Chapter 23 Political Revolutions 1775–1815.............662
Europeans in North America 1750............665
Colonial Trade Routes 1750....................668
Napoleon's Empire....................678
The Rise of Italy and Germany....................685
U.S. Expansion 1783–1898....................687
The Industrial Revolution 1870....................691

MAPS, CHARTS, AND GRAPHS

CHARTS, GRAPHS, AND TIME LINES

Chapter 1 Time Line: World History 2
Time Line: Ancient India 7

Chapter 2 Key Dates in Geography, Economics, and Civics 26
Supply and Demand Curves 39
Model of the Business Cycle 41
U.S. Imports and Exports, 2000–2009 42
Checks and Balances 45

Chapter 3 Time Line: Early Settlements 52

Chapter 4 Time Line: Mesopotamia 74

Chapter 5 Time Line: Ancient Egypt and Kush 98
Inside A Pyramid 114
Social Status In Ancient Egypt 116

Chapter 6 Time Line: The Israelites 138
The Ten Commandments 143
Early Alphabets 145
Israelite Prophets 152

Chapter 7 Time Line: Greece 172
The Greek Alphabet 178
Comparing Governments 200
Athenian Architecture 201

Chapter 8 Time Line: Ancient Greece 210
Greek Gods and Goddesses 213
The Parthenon 218
Greek Philosophers 224
Model of Solar System by Aristarchus 238
Greek Scientists and Their Contributions 239

Chapter 9 Time Line: Ancient India 246
Houses in Mohenjo-Daro 251
The Caste System of India 255

Chapter 10 Time Line: Early China 276
Chinese Philosophers 288
Chinese Village 290

Chapter 11 Time Line: Rome 304
Roman Legionary 310
The "Good Emperors" of the *Pax Romana* 331

Chapter 12 Time Line: Rome 338
Roman Home 341
The Fall of Rome 355

Chapter 13 Time Line: Early Christianity 370
The Beatitudes 375
Early Church Hierarchy 384
The Cyrillic Alphabet 390

Chapter 14 Time Line: Islamic Civilization 396
The First Four Caliphs 406

Chapter 15 Time Line: African Civilizations 420
Comparing Africa to the U.S. 424
African Trading Empires A.D. 100–1600 428
Religion in Africa Today 433

Chapter 16 Time Line: The Americas 448

Chapter 17 Time Line: Imperial China 472

Chapter 18 Time Line: Civilizations of Korea, Japan, and Southeast Asia 508

Chapter 19 Time Line: Medieval Europe 538
Feudal Society 549
A Medieval Manor 552

Chapter 20 Time Line: Europe 580
Florence Cathedral 586

Chapter 21 Time Line: Age of Exploration and Trade 616
The Santa María 621
Important European Explorers 630

Chapter 22 Time Line: Europe 640
Indian-Arabic and Roman Numerals 643
A New View of the Universe 645
The Scientific Revolution 647
The Scientific Method 649

Chapter 23 Time Line: The Western Hemisphere 662
The Three Estates in Prerevolutionary France . . . 673
A Locomotive 693

Videos

Chapter 1 Great Reasons to Learn History
Uncovering the Past
Internet Research Techniques

Chapter 2 Geography Basics: Climate, Water, etc.
Introduction to Economics Part 1
The Seven Dynamics of Citizenship

Chapter 3 How We Know About the Ice Ages
The Ice Man

Chapter 4 Mesopotamia: An Overview
Persepolis

Chapter 5 The Nile River
Life in Ancient Egypt
Ancient Egypt
Kingdom of Axum

Chapter 6 Assignment: Galilee-Israeli Culture
The Middle East: A Region of Contrasts
Temple Mount
Temple of Herod

Chapter 7 Ancient Greece: Geography and Government
Athens
The Early Olympics
Coinage and Democracy in Athens

Chapter 8 Ancient Greece: Farmers and Daily Life
Gods and Heroes
Building Alexander the Great's Empire
Alexander the Great's Empire

Chapter 9 Timelines of Ancient Civilizations: Inda-Indus River Civilizations to Buddhism- Part 1
India's History from the Hindus to the Buddhists
India's History from the Golden Age to Today

Chapter 10 The Chinese Landscape
Chinese History from Peking Man to Confucius
Chinese History from the First Emperor to the Romance of the Three Kingdoms

Chapter 11 Life in Ancient Rome
The Roman Empire: Cultural Contributions
Bread and Circuses
The Roman World

Chapter 12 The Geography of Italy
The Colosseum
Constantinople to Istanbul

Chapter 13 Christianity in Greece
St. Peter's Tomb
The Development of Christianity in Ireland

Chapter 14 Islamic World
Islamic Trade Routes
Islamic Scientific Advances

Chapter 15 Great African Queens
History and Traditions of Mali
The History, Exploration, and Conquest of South Africa

Chapter 16 Aztec, Maya, and Inca Civilizations
Peru: History

Chapter 17 Ming Dynasty
Chinese History from the Grand Canal Waterway to Marco Polo
Marco Polo's Inspiration
Chinese History from the Ming Dynasty to the Three Gorges Dam

Chapter 18 The Korean Landscape
East Asian Religions and Other Cultural Traditions
The Samurai
Religions of Southeast Asia

Chapter 19 Castle Design
Feudalism, Lords and Vassals Video Quiz
Castles: The Center of Power
Religious Architecture
History of Austria from the Late Middle Ages

Chapter 20 Leonardo da Vinci
Chaucer's England
Martin Luther and The Reformation
Britain Arises: England Defeats the Spanish Armada

Chapter 21 Journey to the New World: Christopher Columbus
Hernán Cortés
Age of Discovery: English, French, and Dutch Explorations

Chapter 22 Planetary Motion: Kepler's Three Laws
Reason and the Age of Enlightenment

Chapter 23 Making a Revolution
Napoleon
Napoleon's Early Military Career
The Wright Brothers
The Industrial Revolution

Interactive Charts/Graphs

Chapter 2 Supply and Demand Curves
Model of the Business Cycle
Checks and Balances

Chapter 3 Paleolithic Tools
Neolithic Artifacts

Chapter 5 How Egyptians Made Papyrus
Egyptian Foods

Chapter 6 Early Alphabets
Twelve Tribes of Israel

Chapter 7 Greek Alphabet
Athens Population Graph

Chapter 8 Ancient Greek Writers
The Lincoln Memorial and the Parthenon
Seven Wonders of the World
Winged Victory and Unique Forms of Continuity in Space (sculpture)
Aristarchus' Model of Solar System
Contributions of Greek Scientists
Eratosthenes and Earth's Circumference

Chapter 9 Ancient Indian Number Symbols

Chapter 10 Confucius's Philosophy About Education
World Population Time Line

Chapter 11 Rights of the Accused
Poverty in Rome

Chapter 12 History of Constantinople Time Line
Infographic: The Fall of Rome

Chapter 13 The Beatitudes
Early Church Hierarchy
Cyrillic Alphabet

Chapter 14 The Four Caliphs
Shopping: Then and Now

Chapter 15 Quick Facts: African Kingdoms

Chapter 16 Highest Peaks in the United States

Chapter 17 Buddhists Around the World

Chapter 18 Japanese Feudal Class System

Chapter 19 Pyramid of Classes
Trade in Medieval Marketplaces
Thomas Aquinas
European Population A.D. 1300–1500

Chapter 20 Martin Luther and the Reformation
Sale of Indulgences
De Medici's Family Tree

Chapter 22 Indian-Arabic and Roman Numerals
European Trade in Asia
Scientific Revolution
European Trade in Asia
Columbian Exchange
The Scientific Method

Chapter 23 Marxism, Socialism, & Communism

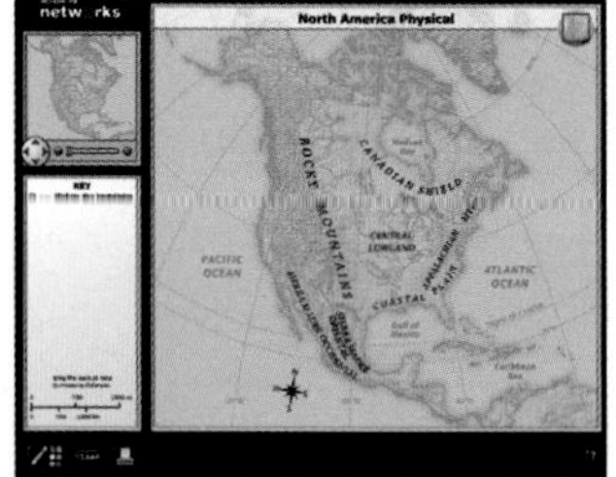

Maps

All maps that appear in your printed textbook are also available in an interactive format in your Online Student Edition.

Slide Shows

Chapter 1 The Terra-cotta Army
Primary Source Artifacts

Chapter 2 Tools of Geography
Good Citizenship

Chapter 3 Woolly Mammoth
Çatalhüyük

Chapter 4 Ancient Irrigation
The Ziggurat
Sumerian Jewelry

Chapter 5 Worlds' Longest Rivers
The Pyramids of Giza

Chapter 6 Locusts
Israelite Prophets
Jewish Heroes
Torah Scrolls
Hanukkah

Chapter 7 Mycenaean Artifacts
The Agora
Battle of Salamis

Chapter 8 Greek Art and Sculpture
Greek Philosophers and Their Ideas
Facts About Thales
Story of *Pi*

Chapter 9 Harappan Crafts
Modern Crafts in India
Upanishads
Representations of Buddha
Gandhi
Ancient Indian Medical Tools

Chapter 10 Zhou Dynasty Art

Chapter 11 Rome: Yesterday and Today
Symbols of Authority
Buildings in Rome
Pompeii and Mt. Vesuvius
The Five Good Emperors

Chapter 12 Roman Homes
The U.S. Capitol
Hagia Sophia
The Hippodrome of Constantinople

Chapter 13 Religious Art
Burial Places
Cyril, Creator of the Cyrillic Alphabet

Chapter 14 Lives of the Bedouin
Sacred Muslim Sites
Islamic Architecture
The Taj Mahal

Chapter 15 Great Rift Valley
Dhows
Mosques in Africa
West African Art

Chapter 16 Amazon Wildlife
Casa Grande
Native American Creation Stories
Mound Builders
Tenochtitlan

Chapter 17 The Tang Dynasty
Silk-making
Chinese Landscape Painting

Chapter 18 Buddhist Temples
Samurai
Japanese Art

Chapter 19 The Manorial System
The Crusades
Medieval Architecture
Medieval Mystics

Chapter 20 Il Duomo
Venice
Leonardo da Vinci
Gutenberg Press and Type

Chapter 21 The Madiera Islands
Atahualpa's Life

Chapter 22 Sir Isaac Newton
Through a Microscope

Chapter 23 The Estates General
The Bastille
Industrial Revolution Inventions
Working Conditions
Monet's Paintings

Interactive Graphic Organizers

Chapter 1 Studying History
The Julian and Gregorian Calendars
How a Historian Works
Understanding Primary and Secondary Sources
Historical Research
Is This Plagiarism?

Chapter 2 Six Essential Elements of Geography
Characteristics of Economic Systems
Citizenship: Rights and Responsibilities

Chapter 3 Paleolithic Inventions
Neolithic Advancements

Chapter 4 Sumerian Inventions
Major Mesopotamian Empires

Chapter 5 Benefits of the Nile
Ancient Egypt
Middle and New Kingdoms
Achievements of the Pharaohs
Kush Conquers Egypt

Chapter 6 The Ancient Israelites
King David and King Solomon
Roles of Synagogues and Scribes
Greek and Roman Rule

Chapter 7 Compare Minoans and Mycenaeans
Compare Sparta and Athens
Persian Kings Attacking Greece and Greek Defenders
Accomplishments: Age of Pericles
Comparing Governments: Direct Democracy and Representative Democracy

Chapter 8 Influence of Greek Culture Today
Greek Thinkers
Accomplishments of Philip II and Alexander the Great
Rise of Alexander the Great
Achievements of Greek Scientists

Chapter 9 The Caste System of India
Ways Aryans Changed India
Religions of Ancient India
Ashoka's Reign
Mauryan and Gupta Empires

Chapter 10 How Life Changed Under Shang Rule
Three Chinese Philosophies
Comparing and Contrasting: Qin and Han Dynasties

Chapter 11 Events in Roman History
Roman Society
Fall of the Roman Republic
Achievements of Emperor Augustus

Chapter 12 The Greeks and the Romans
Roles of Family Members
Why Rome Collapsed
Why the Byzantine Empire Thrived
Justinian's Army

Chapter 13 The Life of Jesus
Reasons Christianity Spread
Honoring Icons
Cooperation Between Byzantine Church and Government

Chapter 14 The Development of Islam
How Islam Spread
Muslim Contributions to Science

Chapter 15 Products of West African Trading Kingdoms
Achievements of African Leaders
African Culture

Chapter 16 Climates and Mountains
Aztec Social Classes

Chapter 17 Accomplishments of Three Dynasties
Chinese Advancements
Mongols in China
Voyages of Zheng He

Chapter 18 Shamans
China Influences Japanese Culture
Angkor Wat

Chapter 19 Achievements of European Leaders
Feudalism
Serfs and Freemen
Causes and Effects of the Crusades
Organizing Information: Medieval Life

Chapter 20 Wealth Grows in City-States
Renaissance Art
Reasons for the Reformation
Reform in the Catholic Church
Effects from the Council of Trent

Chapter 21 Explorers of Asia and the Americas
Conquests by Hernán Cortés and Francisco Pizarro
Crops and Workers in Three Colonies

Chapter 22 Scientists and Their Contributions
Thinkers and Their Ideas

Chapter 23 The American Revolution
Time Line: Major Events of the French Revolution
Uprisings and Outcomes
Causes of the Industrial Revolution
Social Advances During the Industrial Revolution

Presentation Resources

INTERACTIVE WHITEBOARD ACTIVITIES

Chapter 1 It Happened in My Lifetime
Primary and Secondary Sources

Chapter 2 Food Chain
Separation of Powers

Chapter 3 Paleolithic Nomads
Paleolithic Times and the Ice Age

Chapter 4 Bartering
The Akkad, Babylonian, and Assyrian Empires

Chapter 5 The Hyksos and the Egyptians

Chapter 6 Ten Rules for Our School
Kosher Foods

Chapter 7 Ancient Greece
Athens and Spartan Culture

Chapter 8 Greek Influences
Early Greek Scientists' Contributions
Alexander the Great's Achievements

Chapter 9 Community Symbols

Chapter 10 Pictographs
Confucianism, Daoism, Legalism

Chapter 11 Roman Soldier's Equipment
Types of Laws

Chapter 12 Women's Roles
Justinian and Theodora

Chapter 13 Literary Elements of Parables

Chapter 14 Muslim Advancements

Chapter 15 How West Africa Changed Because of Trade

Chapter 16 Mesoamerican Civilizations
Think Like a Historian

Chapter 17 Traveling the Silk Road
Mongol Warriors
Dynasties and Eras

Chapter 18 Sequence of Events, Feudal Japan
Japanese Feudalism

Chapter 19 European Leaders
Monarchy in France
Religious and Political Occurrences in Europe

Chapter 20 Church Leaders

Chapter 21 Spanish Conquest
Explorers in America

Chapter 22 Icons of the Scientific Revolution
Hobbes, Montesquieu, and Locke

Chapter 23 The Bill of Rights
Revolution and Empire in France
The American Civil War

LECTURE SLIDES

Chapter 1 Measuring Time
Types of Historians
Evidence
Facts and Opinions

Chapter 2 Different Types of Maps
Charts, Graphs, and Diagrams
Economic Systems

Chapter 3 Trial and Error Learning
Settled Communities

Chapter 4 Periodic Flooding
City-State
Social Class
Hammurabi's Code

Chapter 5 Ancient Egypt
Social Class
Pharaohs of Ancient Egypt
Cultural Diffusion

Chapter 6 The Phoenicians
Two Kingdoms
The Torah
The Arrival of Greek Rule

Chapter 7 Rise of Greek Civilization
Colonies and Trade
Government in Greece
Persia's Empire
The Persian Wars
Definition of "Golden Age"
Pericles's Achievements
The Delian League

Chapter 8 Greek Art and Architecture
Greek Thinkers
Alexander's Legacy
The Hellenistic Era

Chapter 9 Geography of India
Sanskrit Language
Religions of the Ancient World
Cultural Contributions of Ancient India

Chapter 10 The Land of China
Chinese Life
Han Dynasty Inventions
Buddhism Reaches China

Chapter 11 Greek Influence on Rome
Plebeian and Patrician
Governing Rome
Marius Faces Problems in the Republic
Roman Emperors

Chapter 12 Roman Achievements
Scarcity and Inflation Definitions
The New Rome

Presentation Resources (continued)

LECTURE SLIDES (continued)

Chapter 13 Zealots
Apostles
Issues that Divided the Church

Chapter 14 Beliefs and Practices of Islam
Three Muslim Empires
Division and Growth
Roles of Men and Women in Muslim Society
Major Muslim Contributions

Chapter 15 Trading Empires in Africa
Geographic Zones of Africa
Traditional African Religions
Extended Family
African Arts
African Education

Chapter 16 The First American Civilizations
The Maya
North American Peoples

Chapter 17 Buddhism in China
Revival of Confucian Ideas
Technological Advances
The World's Literature
Ming Dynasty

Chapter 18 Early Korea
Way of the Spirits
The Nara Period
A Divided Japan
Kingdoms and Empires

Chapter 19 Hierarchy of the Catholic Church
The Feudal System
Royal Power in England
Monarchy in France
The Impact of Religion on Society
Famine and Plague
U.S. Populations

Chapter 20 The States of Italy
A New Ruling Class
Renaissance Art Techniques
Italy's Renaissance Artists
Early Calls for Reform
The Reformation of England
Religious Wars

Chapter 21 Early Voyages of Discovery
Spain's Conquests in the Americas
World Trade Changes

Chapter 22 New Ideas About the Universe
The Philosophes of France
Absolute Monarchs

Chapter 23 Britain's American Colonies
A War for Independence
Napoleon Leads France
Coup d'état
Nationalism and Reform
Birth of Industry
Industrialization Changes Political Ideas
Revolution in the Arts

Presentation Resources (continued)

GAMES

Chapter 1 Chronology Terms
Types of Calendars
Historical Evidence
Historical Research
Reliable Web Sites

Chapter 2 Studying Economics

Chapter 3 Paleolithic People

Chapter 4 Mesopotamian Empires
Mesopotamia

Chapter 5 Egyptians and Their Gods
Hyksos and Egyptians
Pharaohs and Their Achievements

Chapter 6 The Ten Commandments
The Development of Judaism

Chapter 7 Athenian and Spartan History
Greek and Persian Wars

Chapter 8 Greek Gods and Goddesses
The Trojan Horse
Philosophers
Socrates-The Greek Mind
The Hellenistic Culture

Chapter 10 Qin Dynasty
Chinese Inventions and Discoveries

Chapter 11 Italy
Patricians and Plebeians
Across Rome
Roman Numerals

Chapter 12 Invaders of the Roman Empire
The Early Roman Empire

Chapter 13 A Christian Europe

Chapter 15 Empire Building
Kingdoms and States of Africa
Africa's Government and Religion
African Society and Culture

Chapter 16 Olmec Statue

Chapter 17 Dynasties, Buddhism, and Confucianism
Chinese Arts and Discoveries
Chinese Exploration

Chapter 18 Korea: History and Culture
Early Japan
Medieval Japan
Southeast Asia

Chapter 19 Medieval Europe
Early Middle Ages
Feudalism
Kingdoms and Crusades
Culture and Church

Chapter 20 Renaissance Begins
Ideas and Art of the Renaissance
The Reformation Begins
Catholics and Protestants

Chapter 21 Age of Exploration
Exploration and Worldwide Trade

Chapter 22 Achievements
Ptolemy and Copernicus
The Enlightenment

Chapter 23 Colonial America
The French Revolution and Napoleon
Nationalism and Nation-States
Society and Industry

Worksheets

These printable worksheets are available for every lesson or chapter and can be edited on eAssessment.

- **What Do You Know? Activities**
- **Guided Reading Activities**
- **Vocabulary Builder Activities**
- **Chapter Summaries**
- **Spanish Chapter Summaries**

These printable worksheets are for point-of-use instruction and can be edited on eAssessment.

Chapter 1 Primary Source Activity | The White House Renovation
21st Century Skills Activity | Critical Thinking and Problem Solving: Recognize Bias
21st Century Skills Activity | Thinking and Problem Solving: Distinguish Facts and Opinions

Chapter 2 Geography and History Activity | Understanding Location: Longitude and Latitude
Geography and History Activity | Understanding Location: Physical Maps
Economics of History Activity | Trade in the Ancient World
21st Century Skills Activity | Leadership and Responsibility: Plan a Service Project

Chapter 3 21st Century Skills Activity | Critical Thinking and Problems Solving: Use Different Types of Reasoning

Chapter 4 Economics of History Activity | Bartering
Primary Source Activity | The Code of Hammurabi

Chapter 5 Geography and History Activity | Understanding Location: Ancient Egypt
Economics of History Activity | Scarcity and Ancient Egyptian Farmers
Primary Source Activity | Ancient Palettes
21st Century Skills Activity | Critical Thinking and Problem Solving: Making Connections
Economics of History Activity | The Kingdom of Kush

Chapter 6 Geography and History Activity | Human-Environment Interaction: The Israelites and Canaan
21st Century Skills Activity | Creativity and Innovation: Problem Solving
Primary Source Activity | The Hebrew Bible
21st Century Skills Activity | Information Literacy: Sequence and Categorize Information

Chapter 7 21st Century Skills Activity | Communication: Outlining
Geography and History Activity | Understanding Location: The Greek Peninsula
Economics of History Activity | Economics and Greek Governments
Primary Source Activity | Herodotus's Account of the Battle of Salamis
Primary Source Activity | Pericles's Funeral Oration

Chapter 8 Economics of History Activity | Support for the Arts in Ancient Greece
Primary Source Activity | The Boy Who Cried Wolf
21st Century Skills Activity | Writing in Expository Style
Primary Source Activity | Alexander the Great: Hero or Villain?
Geography and History Activity | Understanding Location: Greek Migration
Geography and History Activity | Understanding Location: Hellenistic Cities

Chapter 9 Geography and History Activity | Understanding Human-Environment Interaction: Ancient India
21st Century Skills Activity | Communication: Summarizing
Primary Source Activity | Buddhism and Hinduism
21st Century Skills Activity | Communication: Create and Give a Group Presentation

Chapter 10 Geography and History Activity | Understanding Place: China
21st Century Skills Activity | Communication: Create and Give a Presentation
Economics of History Activities | Trade Along the Silk Road

Chapter 11 Geography and History Activity | Understanding Location: Early Rome
21st Century Skills Activity | Critical Thinking: Making Connections

Chapter 12 Primary Source Activity | Women in Protest
Economics of History Activity | Inflation and the Fall of the Roman Empire
Geography and History Activity | Understanding Location: Constantinople

Chapter 13 Primary Source Activity | Jesus and the Jewish Religion
21st Century Skills Activity | Collaboration: Group Project
Geography and History Activity | The Role of Geography in the Spread of Christianity
Economics of History Activity | The Economic Life of Christian Monasteries

Chapter 14 Geography and History Activity | Understanding Places: The Arabian Peninsula
21st Century Skills Activity | Information Literacy: Sequence and Categorize Information
Economics of History Activity | The Use of Credit in the Islamic Empire

Chapter 15 Geography and History Activity | Understanding Location: The Sahara
21st Century Skills Activity | Find Cardinal and Intermediate Directions
Economics of History Activity | The Value of Gold
21st Century Skills Activity | Information and Communication Technologies: Use Presentation Software

Chapter 16 Geography and History Activity | Understanding Movement
21st Century Skills Activity | Critical Thinking and Problem Solving: Compare and Contrast

Chapter 17 Geography and History Activity | Understanding Location: Chan'gan and Hangzhou
Economics of History Activity | Chinese Currency
Primary Source Activity | Two European Views of China During Mongol Rule
Geography and History Activity | Sailing the Western Oceans: The Voyages of Zheng He
21st Century Skills Activity | Creativity and Innovation: Identify Problems and Solutions

Chapter 18 Geography and History Activity | Understanding Borders
21st Century Skills Activity | Use Latitude and Longitude
21st Century Skills Activity | Writing a Poem
Economics and History Activity | The Rise of Angkor

Chapter 19 Geography and History Activity | How Christianity United Europe
Primary Source Activity | From Froissart's *Chronicles:* The Lives of Peasants and Knights
Primary Source Activity | The Frist Crusade
21st Century Skills Activity | Media Literacy: Understanding and Analyzing Media Messages
Economics of History Activity | Famine and Plague

Worksheets (continued)

Chapter 20 Economics of History Activity | The Role of Guilds
21st Century Skills Activity | Critical Thinking and Problem Solving: Analyze Writing, Visuals, Communication
21st Century Skills Activity | Critical Thinking and Problem Solving: Determining Cause and Effect
Primary Source Activity | The Expulsion of the Jews from Spain

Chapter 21 Geography and History Activity | Understanding Location: Europeans and the Known World
Economics of History Activity | Quipu and Inca Society
Primary Source Activity | Cortés Arrives in Tenochtitlán
Economics of History Activity | The Columbian Exchange

Chapter 22 21st Century Skills Activity | Communication: Write a Résumé
Primary Source Activity | The Ideas of Hobbes and Locke

Chapter 23 Economics of History Activity | Tariffs in the American Colonies
21st Century Skills Activity | Leadership and Responsibility: Citizenship
Geography and History Activity | Human-Environment Interaction: Crossing the Andes Mountains
21st Century Skills Activity | Information Literacy: Research on the Internet
Economics of History Activity | Specialization and the Industrial Revolution

Hands-On Chapter Projects and Technology Extensions

Chapter 1 Evaluating Sources: Web sites and Print Resources
Technology Extension: Social Bookmarking

Chapter 2 Simulation: Create a Successful Country
Technology Extension: Google Spreadsheets for Aggregating Country Features Data

Chapter 3 Time Capsule: Cultural Adaptations to a Specific Environment
Technology Extension: Collaborative Time Capsules with Wikis

Chapter 4 Annotated Poster: Sumerian Occupation
Technology Extension: Using Glogster for Online Interactive Multimedia Posters

Chapter 5 Creating a Model: Personal Sarcophagus
Technology Extension: Using Glogster for Online Interactive Multimedia Posters

Chapter 6 Research: Historical Jewish Leaders
Technology Extension: Online Video "Interview"

Chapter 7 Mapping: Creating a Map of Athens, Sparta, or Persia
Technology Extension: Interactive Map of Athens, Sparta, or Persia

Chapter 8 Creating a Model: Greek Architecture
Technology Extension: Voice Thread Exhibit

Chapter 9 Presentation: PowerPoint® on Ancient Indian Culture
Technology Extension: PowerPoint® Projects

Chapter 10 Illustrated Letter: Sharing Cultural Knowledge
Technology Extension: Multimedia Presentation with Images and Narration

Chapter 11 Talk Show Interviews: Roman Conflicts That Led to Change
Technology Extension: Capturing a Roman Talk Show on Video

Chapter 12 Museum Exhibit: Roman Culture
Technology Extension: Online Museum Exhibition with Wikis

Chapter 13 Creating Blogs: Christian Leaders and Christianity
Technology Extension: Early Christian Leadership Blog

Chapter 14 Encyclopedia Entry: Islamic Civilizations
Technology Extension: Islamic Encyclopedia Wiki

Chapter 15 Illustrated Children's Story: African Civilizations
Technology Extension: Children's Story eBook

Chapter 16 Journal Entries: Through the Eyes of Native Americans
Technology Extension: Blogging Historical Fiction Journal Entries

Chapter 17 Illustrated Time Line: Chinese Dynasties
Technology Extension: Online Interactive Time Line

Chapter 18 Travel Itinerary: Korea, Japan, and Southeast Asia
Technology Extension: Virtual Scrapbook

Chapter 19 Writing a Script: Feudal System
Technology Extension: Online Avatar

Chapter 20 Interview: Important People of the Renaissance
Technology Extension: Renaissance Online Chat

Chapter 21 Poster: Famous Explorers
Technology Extension: Hall of Explorers Media Presentation

Chapter 22 Newspaper Article: Scientific Revolution
Technology Extension: Podcast or Role-Play Interview

Chapter 23 Political Cartoon: Political Issues of the Late Eighteenth and Early Nineteenth Centuries
Technology Extension: Online Comic Creation Tools

TO THE TEACHER Welcome to the McGraw-Hill **networks** Teacher Edition—a new approach to the Teacher Edition based on the principles of *Understanding By Design*®.

Planning the Chapter

Understanding By Design®

All Networks programs have been created using the approach developed by Jay McTighe, coauthor of *Understanding By Design*®.

- The main goal is to focus on the desired results before planning each chapter's instruction.
- The Chapter Planner lists the **Enduring Understandings** and the **Essential Questions** that students will learn and use as they study the chapters.
- Identifying the **Predictable Misunderstandings** will help you anticipate misconceptions students might have as they read the chapters.
- Every chapter provides assessment options to help you measure student understanding.

Standards

Each Chapter Planner identifies the National Council for the Social Studies standards that are covered in the chapter.

Pacing Guide

Time management suggestions for teaching the chapter are provided.

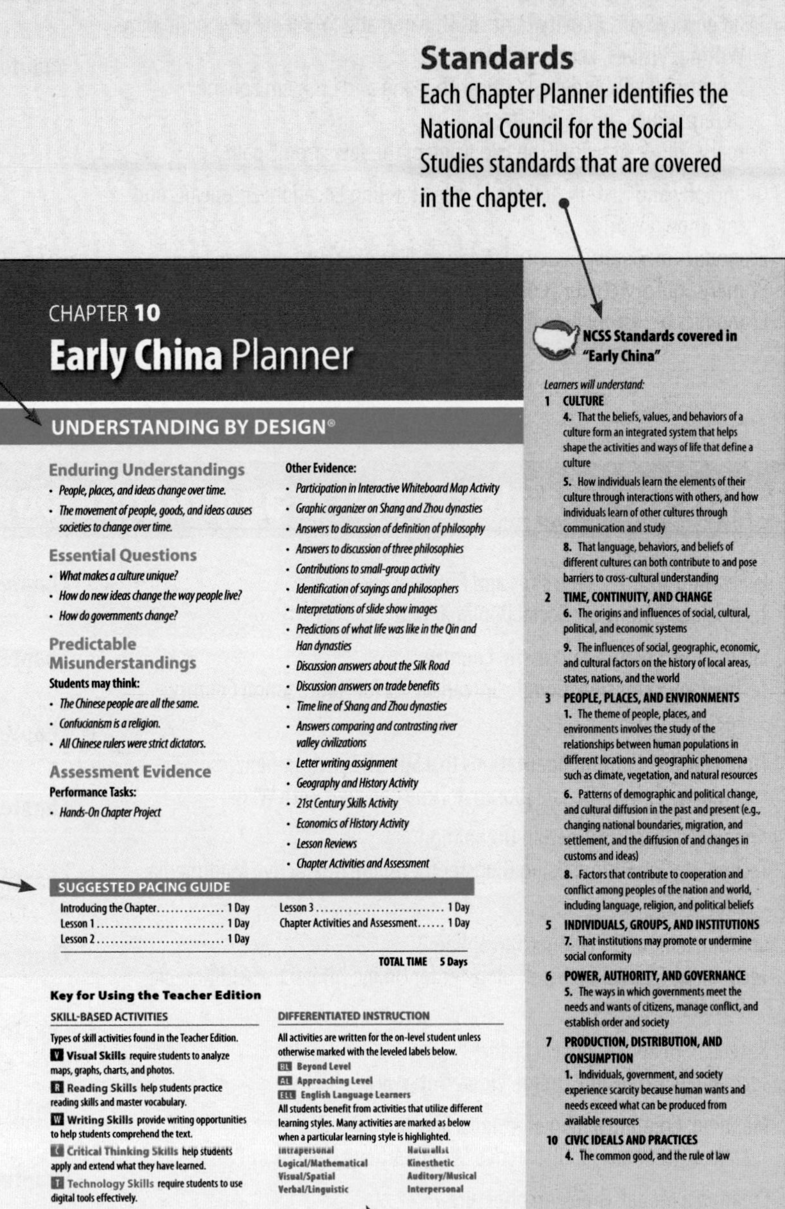

CHAPTER **10**

Early China Planner

UNDERSTANDING BY DESIGN®

Enduring Understandings
- *People, places, and ideas change over time.*
- *The movement of people, goods, and ideas causes societies to change over time.*

Essential Questions
- *What makes a culture unique?*
- *How do new ideas change the way people live?*
- *How do governments change?*

Predictable Misunderstandings

Students may think:
- *The Chinese people are all the same.*
- *Confucianism is a religion.*
- *All Chinese rulers were strict dictators.*

Assessment Evidence

Performance Tasks:
- *Hands-On Chapter Project*

Other Evidence:
- *Participation in Interactive Whiteboard Map Activity*
- *Graphic organizer on Shang and Zhou dynasties*
- *Answers to discussion of definition of philosophy*
- *Answers to discussion of three philosophies*
- *Contributions to small-group activity*
- *Identification of sayings and philosophers*
- *Interpretations of slide show images*
- *Predictions of what life was like in the Qin and Han dynasties*
- *Discussion answers about the Silk Road*
- *Discussion answers on trade benefits*
- *Time line of Shang and Zhou dynasties*
- *Answers comparing and contrasting river valley civilizations*
- *Letter writing assignment*
- *Geography and History Activity*
- *21st Century Skills Activity*
- *Economics of History Activity*
- *Lesson Reviews*
- *Chapter Activities and Assessment*

SUGGESTED PACING GUIDE

Introducing the Chapter .... 1 Day
Lesson 1 .... 1 Day
Lesson 2 .... 1 Day
Lesson 3 .... 1 Day
Chapter Activities and Assessment ...... 1 Day

TOTAL TIME 5 Days

Key for Using the Teacher Edition

SKILL-BASED ACTIVITIES

Types of skill activities found in the Teacher Edition.

V Visual Skills require students to analyze maps, graphs, charts, and photos.

R Reading Skills help students practice reading skills and master vocabulary.

W Writing Skills provide writing opportunities to help students comprehend the text.

C Critical Thinking Skills help students apply and extend what they have learned.

T Technology Skills require students to use digital tools effectively.

*Letters are followed by a number when there is more than one of the same type of skill on the page.

DIFFERENTIATED INSTRUCTION

All activities are written for the on-level student unless otherwise marked with the leveled labels below.

BL Beyond Level
AL Approaching Level
ELL English Language Learners

All students benefit from activities that utilize different learning styles. Many activities are marked as below when a particular learning style is highlighted.

Intrapersonal **Naturalist**
Logical/Mathematical **Kinesthetic**
Visual/Spatial **Auditory/Musical**
Verbal/Linguistic **Interpersonal**

NCSS Standards covered in "Early China"

Learners will understand:

1 **CULTURE**
4. That the beliefs, values, and behaviors of a culture form an integrated system that helps shape the activities and ways of life that define a culture
5. How individuals learn the elements of their culture through interactions with others, and how individuals learn of other cultures through communication and study
8. That language, behaviors, and beliefs of different cultures can both contribute to and pose barriers to cross-cultural understanding

2 **TIME, CONTINUITY, AND CHANGE**
6. The origins and influences of social, cultural, political, and economic systems
9. The influences of social, geographic, economic, and cultural factors on the history of local areas, states, nations, and the world

3 **PEOPLE, PLACES, AND ENVIRONMENTS**
1. The theme of people, places, and environments involves the study of the relationships between human populations in different locations and geographic phenomena such as climate, vegetation, and natural resources
6. Patterns of demographic and political change, and cultural diffusion in the past and present (e.g., changing national boundaries, migration, and settlement, and the diffusion of and changes in customs and ideas)
8. Factors that contribute to cooperation and conflict among peoples of the nation and world, including language, religion, and political beliefs

5 **INDIVIDUALS, GROUPS, AND INSTITUTIONS**
7. That institutions may promote or undermine social conformity

6 **POWER, AUTHORITY, AND GOVERNANCE**
5. The ways in which governments meet the needs and wants of citizens, manage conflict, and establish order and society

7 **PRODUCTION, DISTRIBUTION, AND CONSUMPTION**
1. Individuals, government, and society experience scarcity because human wants and needs exceed what can be produced from available resources

10 **CIVIC IDEALS AND PRACTICES**
4. The common good, and the rule of law

Chapter 10 Planner 275A

Skills-Based Activities

Each lesson includes a variety of print-based and digital activities designed to teach a range of skills, including:

C Critical Thinking Skills
V Visual Skills
R Reading Skills
T Technology Skills
W Writing Skills

Differentiated Instruction

Activities are designed to meet the needs of:

BL Beyond Level
AL Approaching Level
ELL English Language Learners

In addition, activities are designed to address a range of *learning styles.*

networks

Don't forget! You can customize all your Lesson Plans online.

Planning the Chapter *(continued)*

Planners
The Chapter Opener and Lesson Planners provide a snapshot of the resources available to enhance and extend learning. The activities are organized by skill type, level, and learning style.

Student Objectives
Using *Understanding By Design*® as the framework, the planners outline the content and skills that students will be expected to know.

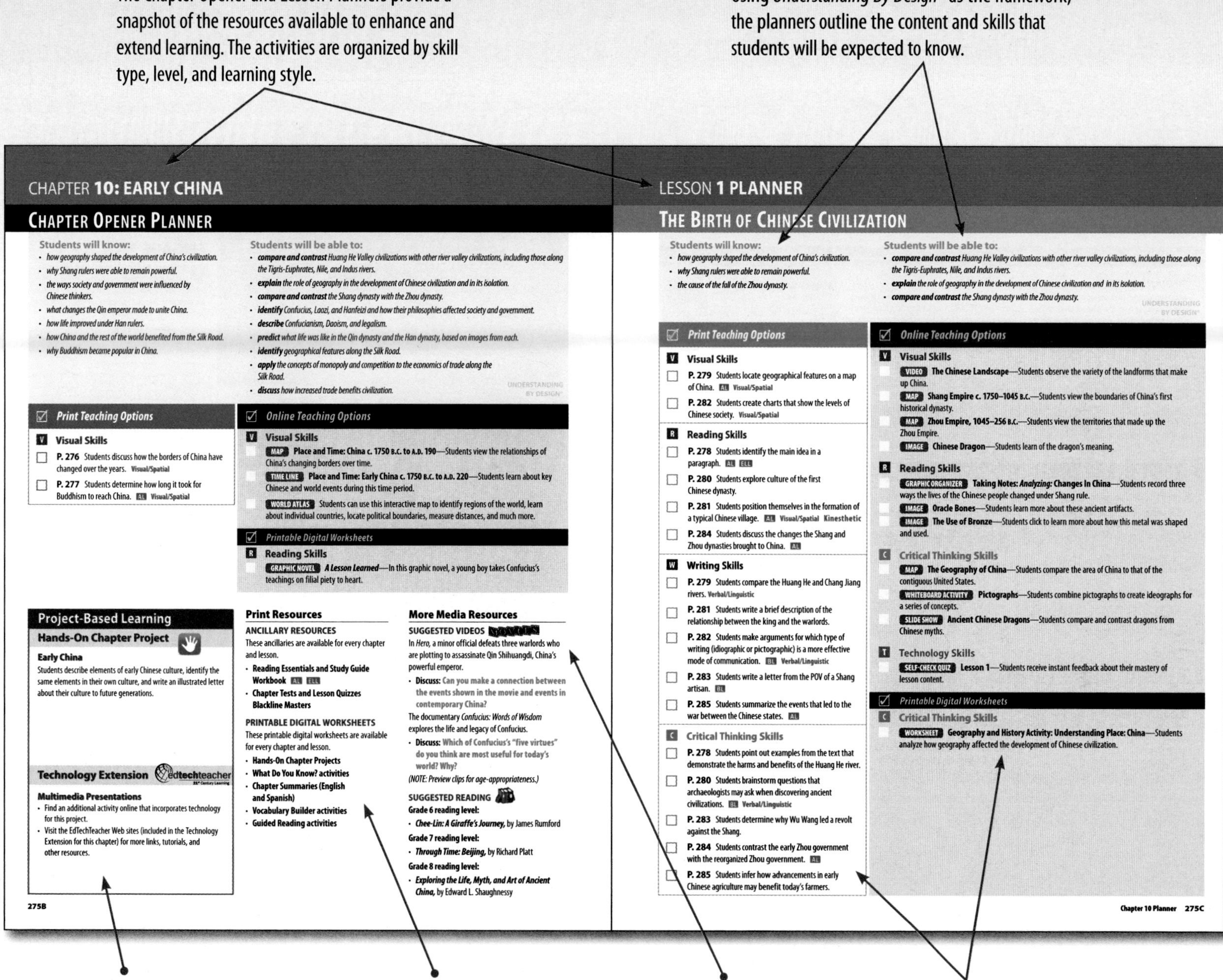

CHAPTER **10: EARLY CHINA**

CHAPTER OPENER PLANNER

Students will know:
- *how geography shaped the development of China's civilization.*
- *why Shang rulers were able to remain powerful.*
- *the ways society and government were influenced by Chinese thinkers.*
- *what changes the Qin emperor made to unite China.*
- *how life improved under Han rulers.*
- *how China and the rest of the world benefited from the Silk Road.*
- *why Buddhism became popular in China.*

Students will be able to:
- ***compare and contrast*** *Huang He Valley civilizations with other river valley civilizations, including those along the Tigris-Euphrates, Nile, and Indus rivers.*
- ***explain*** *the role of geography in the development of Chinese civilization and in its isolation.*
- ***compare and contrast*** *the Shang dynasty with the Zhou dynasty.*
- ***identify*** *Confucius, Laozi, and Hanfeizi and how their philosophies affected society and government.*
- ***describe*** *Confucianism, Daoism, and legalism.*
- ***predict*** *what life was like in the Qin dynasty and the Han dynasty, based on images from each.*
- ***identify*** *geographical features along the Silk Road.*
- ***apply*** *the concepts of monopoly and competition to the economics of trade along the Silk Road.*
- ***discuss*** *how increased trade benefits civilization.*

UNDERSTANDING BY DESIGN®

Print Teaching Options

V Visual Skills
- **P. 276** Students discuss how the borders of China have changed over the years. Visual/Spatial
- **P. 277** Students determine how long it took for Buddhism to reach China. AL Visual/Spatial

Online Teaching Options

V Visual Skills
- MAP **Place and Time: China c. 1750 B.C. to A.D. 190**—Students view the relationships of China's changing borders over time.
- TIME LINE **Place and Time: Early China c. 1750 B.C. to A.D. 220**—Students learn about key Chinese and world events during this time period.
- WORLD ATLAS Students can use this interactive map to identify regions of the world, learn about individual countries, locate political boundaries, measure distances, and much more.

Printable Digital Worksheets

R Reading Skills
- GRAPHIC NOVEL ***A Lesson Learned***—In this graphic novel, a young boy takes Confucius's teachings on filial piety to heart.

Project-Based Learning

Hands-On Chapter Project

Early China
Students describe elements of early Chinese culture, identify the same elements in their own culture, and write an illustrated letter about their culture to future generations.

Technology Extension edtechteacher 21st Century Learning

Multimedia Presentations
- Find an additional activity online that incorporates technology for this project.
- Visit the EdTechTeacher Web sites (included in the Technology Extension for this chapter) for more links, tutorials, and other resources.

Print Resources

ANCILLARY RESOURCES
These ancillaries are available for every chapter and lesson.
- **Reading Essentials and Study Guide Workbook** AL ELL
- **Chapter Tests and Lesson Quizzes Blackline Masters**

PRINTABLE DIGITAL WORKSHEETS
These printable digital worksheets are available for every chapter and lesson.
- **Hands-On Chapter Projects**
- **What Do You Know? activities**
- **Chapter Summaries (English and Spanish)**
- **Vocabulary Builder activities**
- **Guided Reading activities**

More Media Resources

SUGGESTED VIDEOS
In *Hero*, a minor official defeats three warlords who are plotting to assassinate Qin Shihuangdi, China's powerful emperor.
- **Discuss:** Can you make a connection between the events shown in the movie and events in contemporary China?

The documentary *Confucius: Words of Wisdom* explores the life and legacy of Confucius.
- **Discuss:** Which of Confucius's "five virtues" do you think are most useful for today's world? Why?

(NOTE: Preview clips for age-appropriateness.)

SUGGESTED READING

Grade 6 reading level:
- ***Chee-Lin: A Giraffe's Journey,*** by James Rumford

Grade 7 reading level:
- ***Through Time: Beijing,*** by Richard Platt

Grade 8 reading level:
- ***Exploring the Life, Myth, and Art of Ancient China,*** by Edward L. Shaughnessy

275B

LESSON **1 PLANNER**

THE BIRTH OF CHINESE CIVILIZATION

Students will know:
- *how geography shaped the development of China's civilization.*
- *why Shang rulers were able to remain powerful.*
- *the cause of the fall of the Zhou dynasty.*

Students will be able to:
- ***compare and contrast*** *Huang He Valley civilizations with other river valley civilizations, including those along the Tigris-Euphrates, Nile, and Indus rivers.*
- ***explain*** *the role of geography in the development of Chinese civilization and in its isolation.*
- ***compare and contrast*** *the Shang dynasty with the Zhou dynasty.*

UNDERSTANDING BY DESIGN®

Print Teaching Options

V Visual Skills
- **P. 279** Students locate geographical features on a map of China. AL Visual/Spatial
- **P. 282** Students create charts that show the levels of Chinese society. Visual/Spatial

R Reading Skills
- **P. 278** Students identify the main idea in a paragraph. AL ELL
- **P. 280** Students explore culture of the first Chinese dynasty.
- **P. 281** Students position themselves in the formation of a typical Chinese village. AL Visual/Spatial Kinesthetic
- **P. 284** Students discuss the changes the Shang and Zhou dynasties brought to China. AL

W Writing Skills
- **P. 279** Students compare the Huang He and Chang Jiang rivers. Verbal/Linguistic
- **P. 281** Students write a brief description of the relationship between the king and the warlords.
- **P. 282** Students make arguments for which type of writing (idiographic or pictographic) is a more effective mode of communication. BL Verbal/Linguistic
- **P. 283** Students write a letter from the POV of a Shang artisan. BL
- **P. 285** Students summarize the events that led to the war between the Chinese states. AL

C Critical Thinking Skills
- **P. 278** Students point out examples from the text that demonstrate the harms and benefits of the Huang He river.
- **P. 280** Students brainstorm questions that archaeologists may ask when discovering ancient civilizations. BL Verbal/Linguistic
- **P. 283** Students determine why Wu Wang led a revolt against the Shang.
- **P. 284** Students contrast the early Zhou government with the reorganized Zhou government. AL
- **P. 285** Students infer how advancements in early Chinese agriculture may benefit today's farmers.

Online Teaching Options

V Visual Skills
- VIDEO **The Chinese Landscape**—Students observe the variety of the landforms that make up China.
- MAP **Shang Empire c. 1750–1045 B.C.**—Students view the boundaries of China's first historical dynasty.
- MAP **Zhou Empire, 1045–256 B.C.**—Students view the territories that made up the Zhou Empire.
- IMAGE **Chinese Dragon**—Students learn of the dragon's meaning.

R Reading Skills
- GRAPHIC ORGANIZER **Taking Notes: *Analyzing:* Changes In China**—Students record three ways the lives of the Chinese people changed under Shang rule.
- IMAGE **Oracle Bones**—Students learn more about these ancient artifacts.
- IMAGE **The Use of Bronze**—Students click to learn more about how this metal was shaped and used.

C Critical Thinking Skills
- MAP **The Geography of China**—Students compare the area of China to that of the contiguous United States.
- WHITEBOARD ACTIVITY **Pictographs**—Students combine pictographs to create ideographs for a series of concepts.
- SLIDE SHOW **Ancient Chinese Dragons**—Students compare and contrast dragons from Chinese myths.

T Technology Skills
- SELF-CHECK QUIZ **Lesson 1**—Students receive instant feedback about their mastery of lesson content.

Printable Digital Worksheets

C Critical Thinking Skills
- WORKSHEET **Geography and History Activity: Understanding Place: China**—Students analyze how geography affected the development of Chinese civilization.

Chapter 10 Planner 275C

Project-Based Learning
Cumulative projects bring the subject to life for the student and help you assess your students' level of understanding. The program includes Hands-On Projects as well as Digital Hands-On Projects.

Print Resources
Every chapter includes printable worksheets, including tests, quizzes, and materials to build vocabulary and improve reading comprehension.

Make It Relevant
Enrich and extend the content with videos and books.

Print and Digital Options
Each planner has two columns listing print-based activities and online digital assets.

Digital assets include:
- interactive maps
- photos
- animations
- slide shows
- whiteboard activities
- lesson videos
- worksheets

Using the Wraparound Resources and Activities

STUDENT EDITION PAGES AND WRAPAROUND ACTIVITIES

The entire Student Edition appears in the Teacher Edition. Activities and recommended resources appear in the side and bottom margins of the Teacher Edition, at point of use.

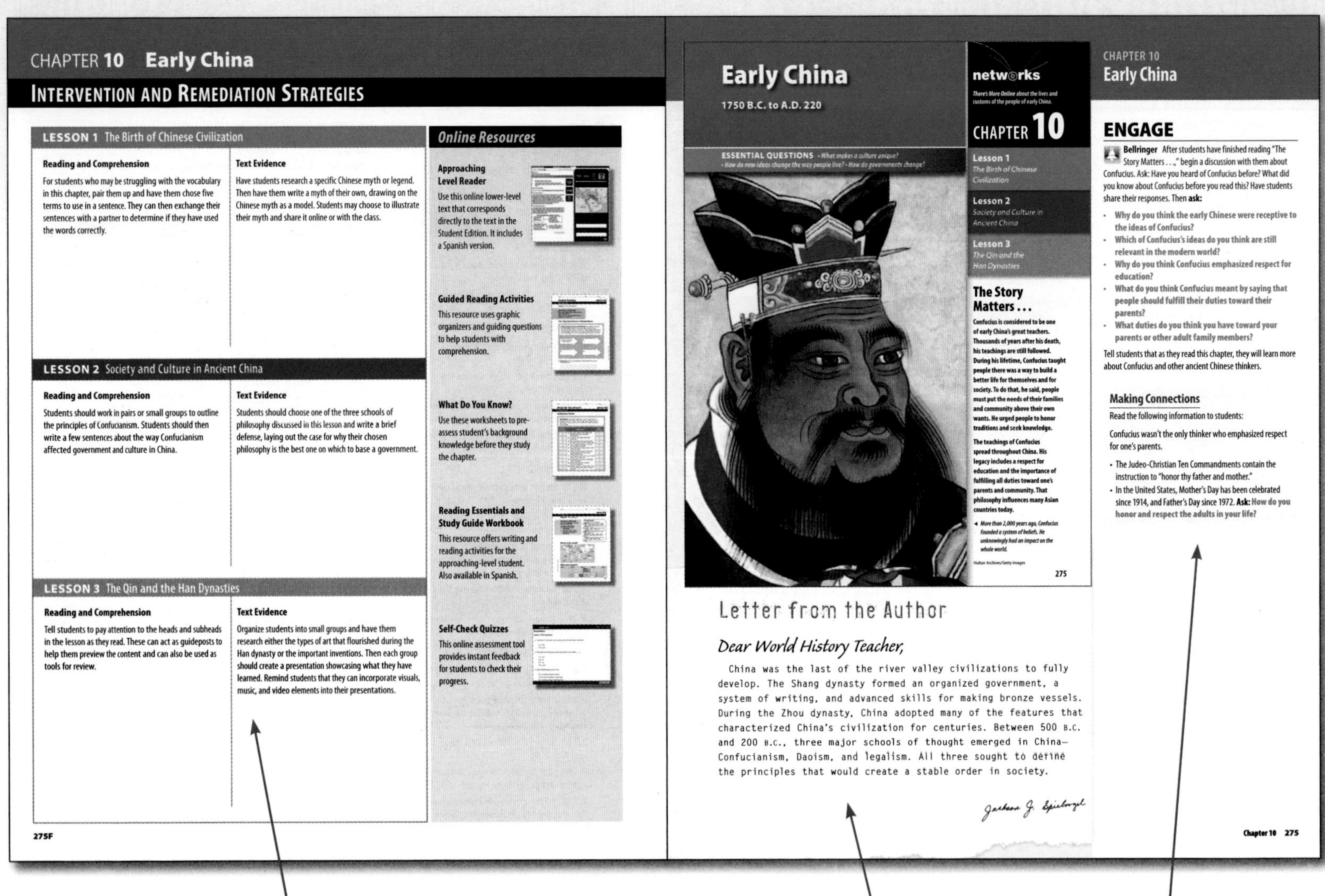

Intervention and Remediation

Each Chapter Planner concludes with intervention and remediation strategies for every lesson, as well as Online Resources that can be used to help students understand the content.

Author Letter

Each chapter begins with the author's perspective about key concepts found in the chapter.

Introduce the Chapter

Each chapter begins with activities to engage students' interest in the chapter's content.

Don't forget! You can customize all your Lesson Plans online.

Using the Wraparound Resources and Activities *(continued)*

Step Into The Place/Step Into The Time

These two pages of the Chapter Opener are designed to help students locate the region in the world that they will learn about, along with important historical events that took place in that region.

The Teacher Edition contains activities and discussion questions for these features.

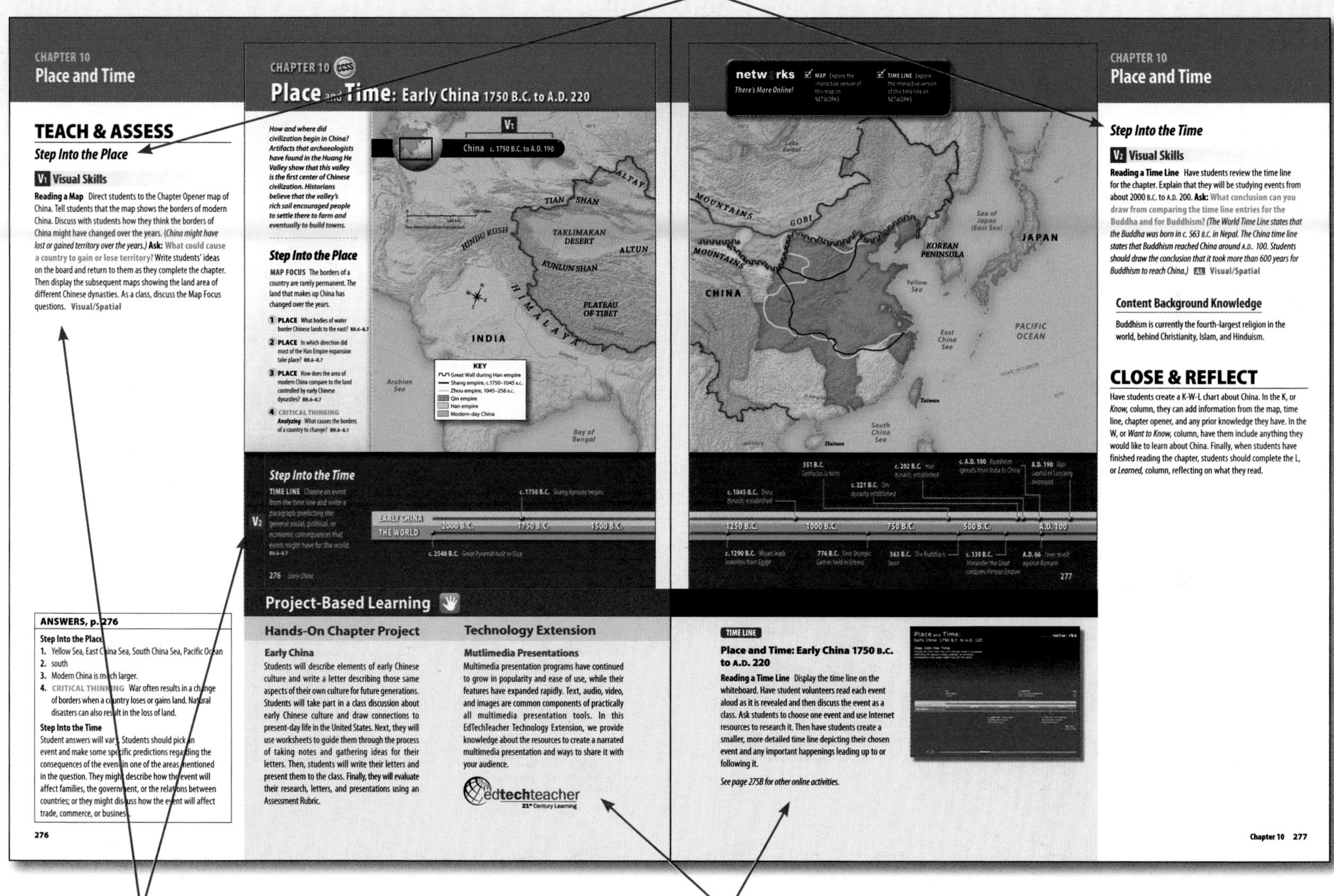

Print-Based Activities

Activities in the margins correspond to the text in the Student Edition. These activities are coded to indicate their level and the learning style they support.

Online Digital Activities

Online digital activities for the lesson appear at the bottom of each page. The gray icon indicates the type of activity available in the online Teacher Center. Activities include interactive whiteboard activities, animations, videos, interactive maps, images, and worksheets. Activities can be projected or used on your classroom whiteboard. Worksheets can be edited and printed, or assigned online, depending on student access to technology.

Using the Wraparound Resources and Activities *(continued)*

ENGAGE

Every lesson begins with an Engage activity designed to motivate students and focus their attention on the lesson topic.

Guiding Questions

Guiding Questions in the Student Edition point out key knowledge that students need to acquire to be able to answer the chapter's Essential Questions.

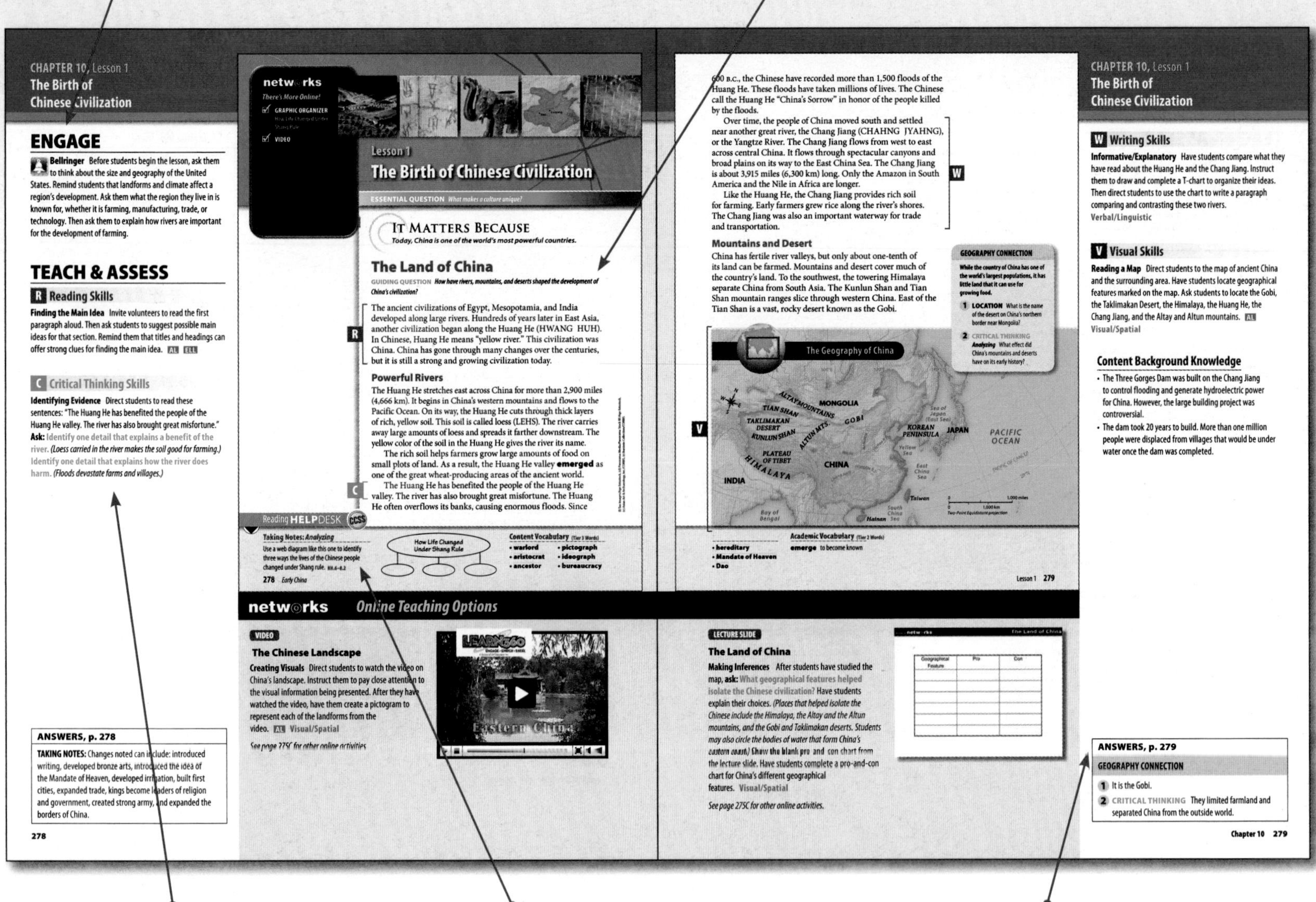

TEACH & ASSESS

Teach & Assess is the core of the lesson. It contains activities, lecture notes, background information, and discussion questions to teach the lesson.

Reading Help Desk

- Content Vocabulary
- Academic Vocabulary
- Note-Taking Activity and Graphic Organizer

Answers

Answers to questions and activities in the Student Edition appear in the bottom corner of the Teacher Edition pages.

Don't forget! You can customize all your Lesson Plans online.

Using the Wraparound Resources and Activities *(continued)*

Brackets

Brackets on the Student Edition page correspond to teaching strategies and activities in the Teacher Edition. As you teach the lesson, the brackets show you where to use these activities and strategies.

Progress Check

A progress check appears at the end of each topic in the Student Edition to help gauge student reading comprehension.

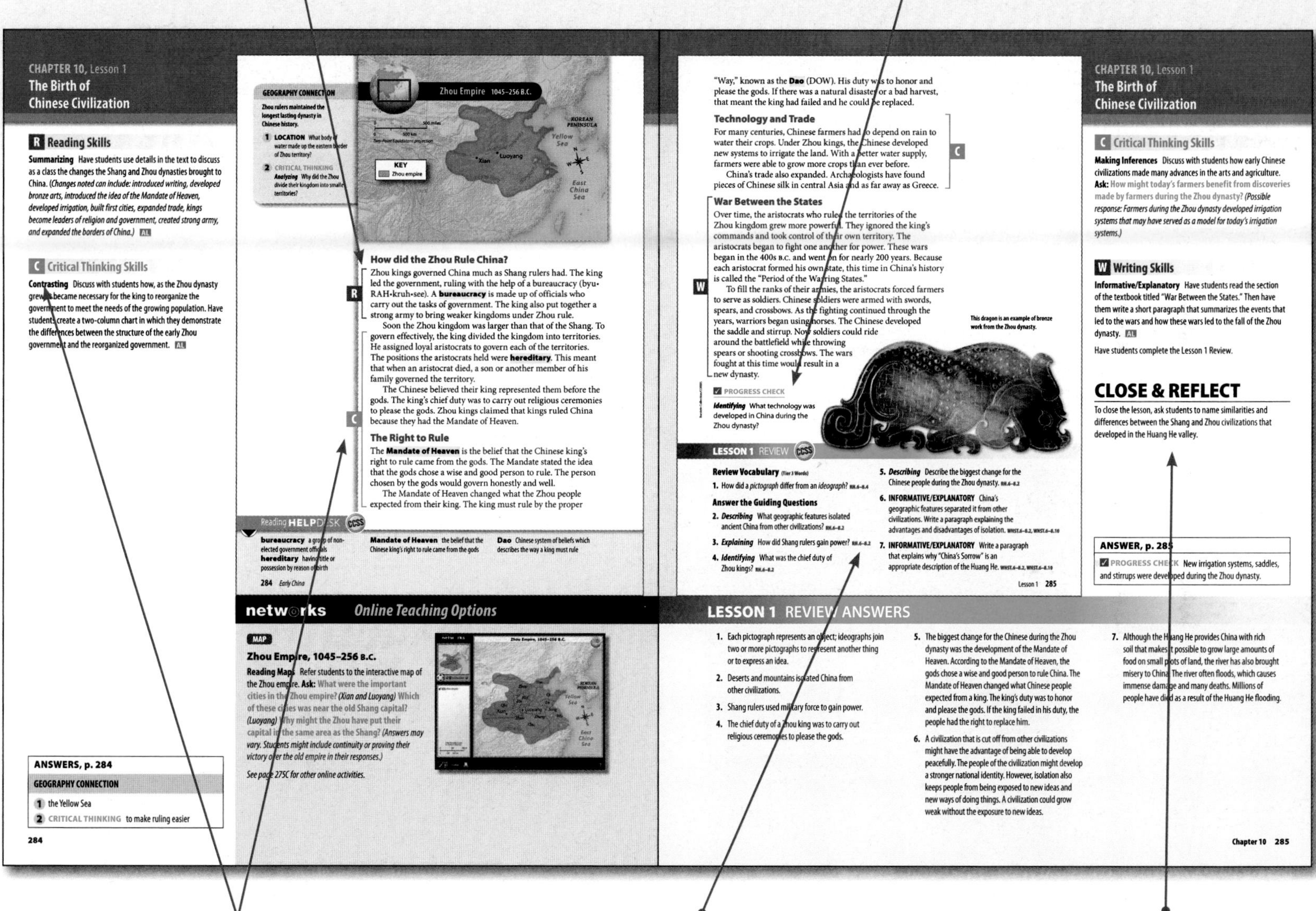

CHAPTER 10, Lesson 1
The Birth of Chinese Civilization

R Reading Skills

Summarizing Have students use details in the text to discuss as a class the changes the Shang and Zhou dynasties brought to China. (*Changes noted can include: introduced writing, developed bronze arts, introduced the idea of the Mandate of Heaven, developed irrigation, built first cities, expanded trade, kings become leaders of religion and government, created strong army, and expanded the borders of China.*) AL

C Critical Thinking Skills

Contrasting Discuss with students how, as the Zhou dynasty grew, it became necessary for the king to reorganize the government to meet the needs of the growing population. Have students create a two-column chart in which they demonstrate the differences between the structure of the early Zhou government and the reorganized government. AL

GEOGRAPHY CONNECTION

Zhou rulers maintained the longest lasting dynasty in Chinese history.

1 LOCATION What body of water made up the eastern border of Zhou territory?

2 CRITICAL THINKING *Analyzing* Why did the Zhou divide their kingdom into smaller territories?

How did the Zhou Rule China?

Zhou kings governed China much as Shang rulers had. The king led the government, ruling with the help of a bureaucracy (byu•RAH•kruh•see). A **bureaucracy** is made up of officials who carry out the tasks of government. The king also put together a strong army to bring weaker kingdoms under Zhou rule.

Soon the Zhou kingdom was larger than that of the Shang. To govern effectively, the king divided the kingdom into territories. He assigned loyal aristocrats to govern each of the territories. The positions the aristocrats held were **hereditary**. This meant that when an aristocrat died, a son or another member of his family governed the territory.

The Chinese believed their king represented them before the gods. The king's chief duty was to carry out religious ceremonies to please the gods. Zhou kings claimed that kings ruled China because they had the Mandate of Heaven.

The Right to Rule

The **Mandate of Heaven** is the belief that the Chinese king's right to rule came from the gods. The Mandate stated the idea that the gods chose a wise and good person to rule. The person chosen by the gods would govern honestly and well.

The Mandate of Heaven changed what the Zhou people expected from their king. The king must rule by the proper

Reading HELPDESK CCSS

bureaucracy a group of non-elected government officials
hereditary having title or possession by reason of birth
Mandate of Heaven the belief that the Chinese king's right to rule came from the gods
Dao Chinese system of beliefs which describes the way a king must rule

284 *Early China*

"Way," known as the **Dao** (DOW). His duty was to honor and please the gods. If there was a natural disaster or a bad harvest, that meant the king had failed and he could be replaced.

Technology and Trade

For many centuries, Chinese farmers had to depend on rain to water their crops. Under Zhou kings, the Chinese developed new systems to irrigate the land. With a better water supply, farmers were able to grow more crops than ever before.

China's trade also expanded. Archaeologists have found pieces of Chinese silk in central Asia and as far away as Greece.

War Between the States

Over time, the aristocrats who ruled the territories of the Zhou kingdom grew more powerful. They ignored the king's commands and took control of their own territory. The aristocrats began to fight one another for power. These wars began in the 400s B.C. and went on for nearly 200 years. Because each aristocrat formed his own state, this time in China's history is called the "Period of the Warring States."

To fill the ranks of their armies, the aristocrats forced farmers to serve as soldiers. Chinese soldiers were armed with swords, spears, and crossbows. As the fighting continued through the years, warriors began using horses. The Chinese developed the saddle and stirrup. Now soldiers could ride around the battlefield while throwing spears or shooting crossbows. The wars fought at this time would result in a new dynasty.

This dragon is an example of bronze work from the Zhou dynasty.

PROGRESS CHECK

Identifying What technology was developed in China during the Zhou dynasty?

LESSON 1 REVIEW CCSS

Review Vocabulary (Tier 3 Words)

1. How did a *pictograph* differ from an *ideograph*? RH.6–8.4

Answer the Guiding Questions

2. *Describing* What geographic features isolated ancient China from other civilizations? RH.6–8.2
3. *Explaining* How did Shang rulers gain power? RH.6–8.2
4. *Identifying* What was the chief duty of Zhou kings? RH.6–8.2
5. *Describing* Describe the biggest change for the Chinese people during the Zhou dynasty. RH.6–8.2
6. INFORMATIVE/EXPLANATORY China's geographic features separated it from other civilizations. Write a paragraph explaining the advantages and disadvantages of isolation. WHST.6–8.2, WHST.6–8.10
7. INFORMATIVE/EXPLANATORY Write a paragraph that explains why "China's Sorrow" is an appropriate description of the Huang He. WHST.6–8.2, WHST.6–8.10

Lesson 1 285

CHAPTER 10, Lesson 1
The Birth of Chinese Civilization

C Critical Thinking Skills

Making Inferences Discuss with students how early Chinese civilizations made many advances in the arts and agriculture. **Ask:** How might today's farmers benefit from discoveries made by farmers during the Zhou dynasty? (*Possible response: Farmers during the Zhou dynasty developed irrigation systems that may have served as a model for today's irrigation systems.*)

W Writing Skills

Informative/Explanatory Have students read the section of the textbook titled "War Between the States." Then have them write a short paragraph that summarizes the events that led to the wars and how these wars led to the fall of the Zhou dynasty. AL

Have students complete the Lesson 1 Review.

CLOSE & REFLECT

To close the lesson, ask students to name similarities and differences between the Shang and Zhou civilizations that developed in the Huang He valley.

ANSWER, p. 285

PROGRESS CHECK New irrigation systems, saddles, and stirrups were developed during the Zhou dynasty.

networks Online Teaching Options

MAP

Zhou Empire, 1045–256 B.C.

Reading Maps Refer students to the interactive map of the Zhou empire. **Ask:** What were the important cities in the Zhou empire? (*Xian and Luoyang*) Which of these cities was near the old Shang capital? (*Luoyang*) Why might the Zhou have put their capital in the same area as the Shang? (*Answers may vary. Students might include continuity or proving their victory over the old empire in their responses.*)

See page 275C for other online activities.

ANSWERS, p. 284

GEOGRAPHY CONNECTION

1 the Yellow Sea
2 CRITICAL THINKING to make ruling easier

284

LESSON 1 REVIEW ANSWERS

1. Each pictograph represents an object; ideographs join two or more pictographs to represent another thing or to express an idea.
2. Deserts and mountains isolated China from other civilizations.
3. Shang rulers used military force to gain power.
4. The chief duty of a Zhou king was to carry out religious ceremonies to please the gods.
5. The biggest change for the Chinese during the Zhou dynasty was the development of the Mandate of Heaven. According to the Mandate of Heaven, the gods chose a wise and good person to rule China. The Mandate of Heaven changed what Chinese people expected from a king. The king's duty was to honor and please the gods. If the king failed in his duty, the people had the right to replace him.
6. A civilization that is cut off from other civilizations might have the advantage of being able to develop peacefully. The people of the civilization might develop a stronger national identity. However, isolation also keeps people from being exposed to new ideas and new ways of doing things. A civilization could grow weak without the exposure to new ideas.
7. Although the Huang He provides China with rich soil that makes it possible to grow large amounts of food on small plots of land, the river has also brought misery to China. The river often floods, which causes immense damage and many deaths. Millions of people have died as a result of the Huang He flooding.

Chapter 10 285

Letters

The letters on the reduced Student Edition page identify the type of activity. See the key on the first planning page of each chapter to learn about the different types of activities.

Common Core State Standards

Questions and activities throughout the Student Edition are correlated to the Reading Standards for Literacy in History/Social Studies 6–8 (RH.6–8) and the Writing Standards for Literacy in History/Social Studies 6–8 (WH.6–8).

CLOSE & REFLECT

Each lesson ends with activities designed to help students link the content to the lesson's Guiding Questions and the chapter's Essential Questions.

Special Features

The World's Literature

This program includes *The World's Literature* features that represent a wide range of time periods. Each of *The World's Literature* features analyzes an excerpt from a famous piece of fiction and describes its historical lessons.

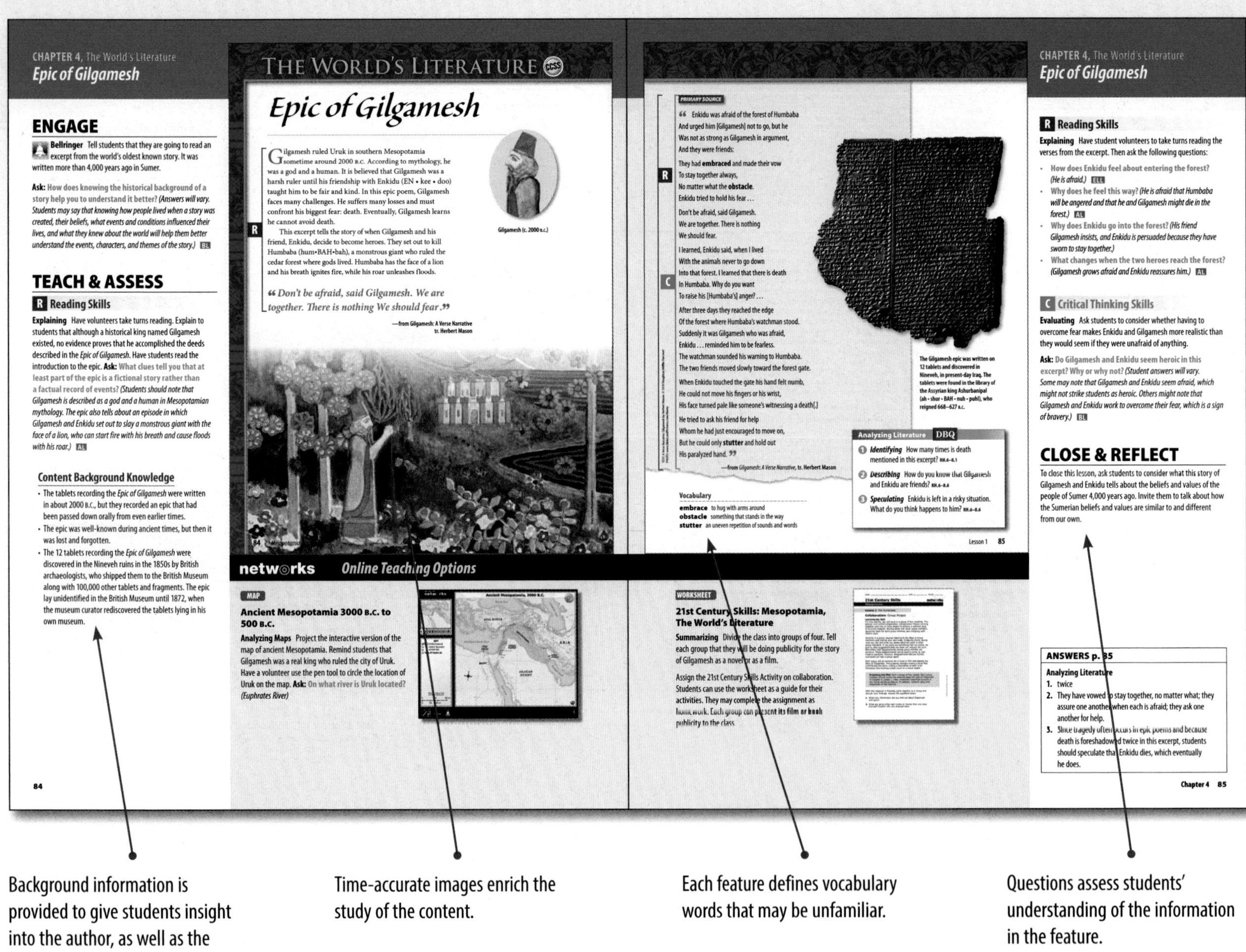

Background information is provided to give students insight into the author, as well as the author's work.

Time-accurate images enrich the study of the content.

Each feature defines vocabulary words that may be unfamiliar.

Questions assess students' understanding of the information in the feature.

Don't forget! You can customize all your Lesson Plans online.

Special Features *(continued)*

What Do You Think?

This program includes a number of *What Do You Think?* features. Students are asked to analyze different points of view on current world issues and events.

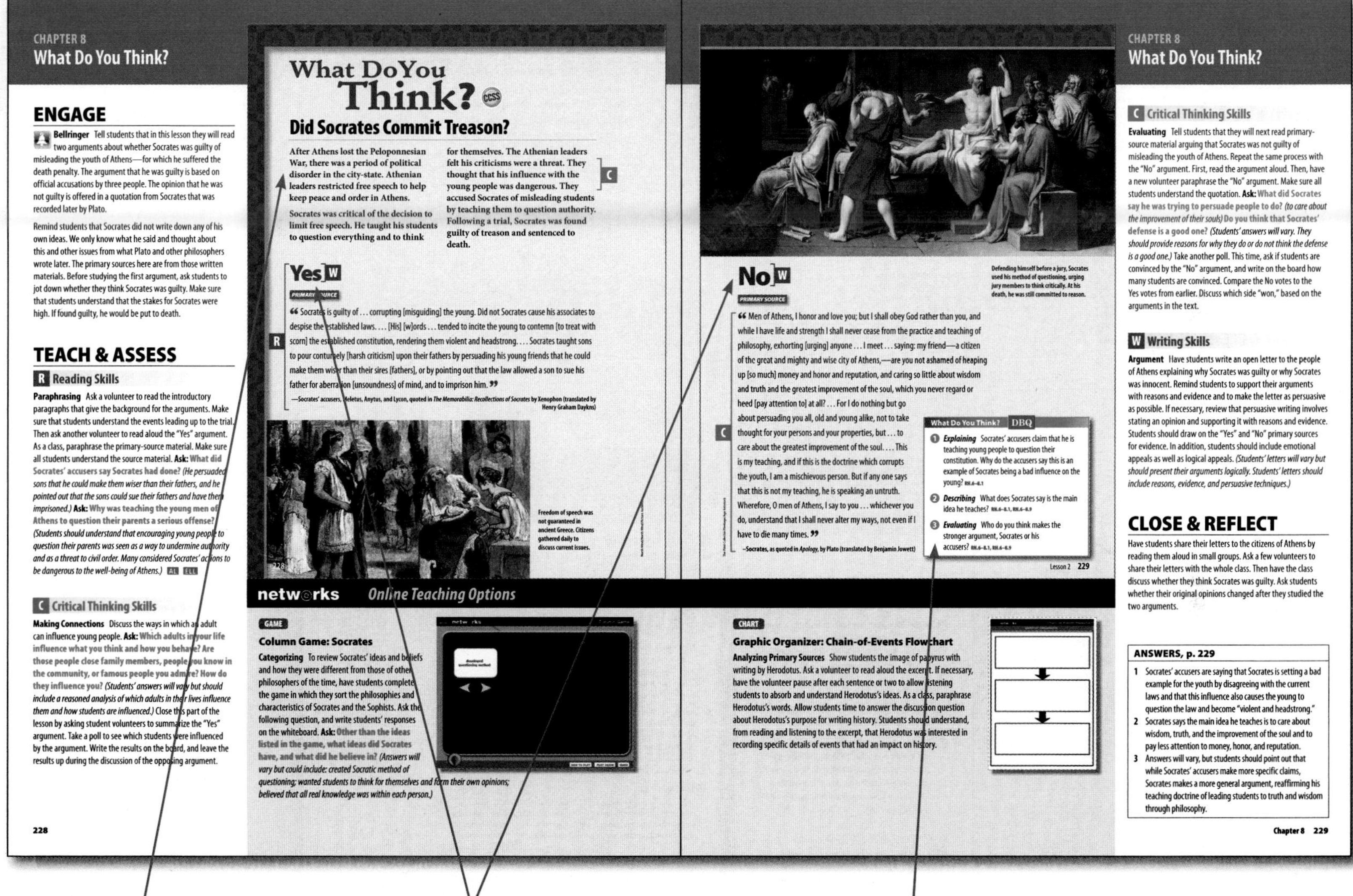

CHAPTER 8
What Do You Think?

ENGAGE

Bellringer Tell students that in this lesson they will read two arguments about whether Socrates was guilty of misleading the youth of Athens—for which he suffered the death penalty. The argument that he was guilty is based on official accusations by three people. The opinion that he was not guilty is offered in a quotation from Socrates that was recorded later by Plato.

Remind students that Socrates did not write down any of his own ideas. We only know what he said and thought about this and other issues from what Plato and other philosophers wrote later. The primary sources here are from those written materials. Before studying the first argument, ask students to jot down whether they think Socrates was guilty. Make sure that students understand that the stakes for Socrates were high. If found guilty, he would be put to death.

TEACH & ASSESS

R Reading Skills

Paraphrasing Ask a volunteer to read the introductory paragraphs that give the background for the arguments. Make sure that students understand the events leading up to the trial. Then ask another volunteer to read aloud the "Yes" argument. As a class, paraphrase the primary-source material. Make sure all students understand the source material. **Ask:** What did Socrates' accusers say Socrates had done? *(He persuaded sons that he could make them wiser than their fathers, and he pointed out that the sons could sue their fathers and have them imprisoned.)* **Ask:** Why was teaching the young men of Athens to question their parents a serious offense? *(Students should understand that encouraging young people to question their parents was seen as a way to undermine authority and as a threat to civil order. Many considered Socrates' actions to be dangerous to the well-being of Athens.)* AL ELL

C Critical Thinking Skills

Making Connections Discuss the ways in which an adult can influence young people. **Ask:** Which adults in your life influence what you think and how you behave? Are those people close family members, people you know in the community, or famous people you admire? How do they influence you? *(Students' answers will vary but should include a reasoned analysis of which adults in their lives influence them and how students are influenced.)* Close this part of the lesson by asking student volunteers to summarize the "Yes" argument. Take a poll to see which students were influenced by the argument. Write the results on the board, and leave the results up during the discussion of the opposing argument.

228

What Do You Think?

Did Socrates Commit Treason?

After Athens lost the Peloponnesian War, there was a period of political disorder in the city-state. Athenian leaders restricted free speech to help keep peace and order in Athens.

Socrates was critical of the decision to limit free speech. He taught his students to question everything and to think for themselves. The Athenian leaders felt his criticisms were a threat. They thought that his influence with the young people was dangerous. They accused Socrates of misleading students by teaching them to question authority. Following a trial, Socrates was found guilty of treason and sentenced to death.

Yes

PRIMARY SOURCE

"Socrates is guilty of . . . corrupting [misguiding] the young. Did not Socrates cause his associates to despise the established laws. . . . [His] [w]ords . . . tended to incite the young to contemn [to treat with scorn] the established constitution, rendering them violent and headstrong. . . . Socrates taught sons to pour contumely [harsh criticism] upon their fathers by persuading his young friends that he could make them wiser than their sires [fathers], or by pointing out that the law allowed a son to sue his father for aberration [unsoundness] of mind, and to imprison him."

—Socrates' accusers, Meletus, Anytus, and Lycon, quoted in *The Memorabilia: Recollections of Socrates* by Xenophon (translated by Henry Graham Dakyns)

Freedom of speech was not guaranteed in ancient Greece. Citizens gathered daily to discuss current issues.

No

PRIMARY SOURCE

"Men of Athens, I honor and love you; but I shall obey God rather than you, and while I have life and strength I shall never cease from the practice and teaching of philosophy, exhorting [urging] anyone . . . I meet . . . saying: my friend—a citizen of the great and mighty and wise city of Athens,—are you not ashamed of heaping up [so much] money and honor and reputation, and caring so little about wisdom and truth and the greatest improvement of the soul, which you never regard or heed [pay attention to] at all? . . . For I do nothing but go about persuading you all, old and young alike, not to take thought for your persons and your properties, but . . . to care about the greatest improvement of the soul. . . . This is my teaching, and if this is the doctrine which corrupts the youth, I am a mischievous person. But if any one says that this is not my teaching, he is speaking an untruth. Wherefore, O men of Athens, I say to you . . . whichever you do, understand that I shall never alter my ways, not even if I have to die many times."

—Socrates, as quoted in *Apology*, by Plato (translated by Benjamin Jowett)

Defending himself before a jury, Socrates used his method of questioning, urging jury members to think critically. At his death, he was still committed to reason.

What Do You Think? DBQ

1. **Explaining** Socrates' accusers claim that he is teaching young people to question their constitution. Why do the accusers say this is an example of Socrates being a bad influence on the young?
2. **Describing** What does Socrates say is the main idea he teaches?
3. **Evaluating** Who do you think makes the stronger argument, Socrates or his accusers?

Lesson 2 229

networks Online Teaching Options

GAME

Column Game: Socrates

Categorizing To review Socrates' ideas and beliefs and how they were different from those of other philosophers of the time, have students complete the game in which they sort the philosophies and characteristics of Socrates and the Sophists. Ask the following question, and write students' responses on the whiteboard. **Ask:** Other than the ideas listed in the game, what ideas did Socrates have, and what did he believe in? *(Answers will vary but could include: created Socratic method of questioning; wanted students to think for themselves and form their own opinions; believed that all real knowledge was within each person.)*

CHART

Graphic Organizer: Chain-of-Events Flowchart

Analyzing Primary Sources Show students the image of papyrus with writing by Herodotus. Ask a volunteer to read aloud the excerpt. If necessary, have the volunteer pause after each sentence or two to allow listening students to absorb and understand Herodotus's ideas. As a class, paraphrase Herodotus's words. Allow students time to answer the discussion question about Herodotus's purpose for writing history. Students should understand, from reading and listening to the excerpt, that Herodotus was interested in recording specific details of events that had an impact on history.

CHAPTER 8
What Do You Think?

C Critical Thinking Skills

Evaluating Tell students that they will next read primary-source material arguing that Socrates was not guilty of misleading the youth of Athens. Repeat the same process with the "No" argument. First, read the argument aloud. Then, have a new volunteer paraphrase the "No" argument. Make sure all students understand the quotation. **Ask:** What did Socrates say he was trying to persuade people to do? *(to care about the improvement of their souls)* Do you think that Socrates' defense is a good one? *(Students' answers will vary. They should provide reasons for why they do or do not think the defense is a good one.)* Take another poll. This time, ask if students are convinced by the "No" argument, and write on the board how many students are convinced. Compare the No votes to the Yes votes from earlier. Discuss which side "won," based on the arguments in the text.

W Writing Skills

Argument Have students write an open letter to the people of Athens explaining why Socrates was guilty or why Socrates was innocent. Remind students to support their arguments with reasons and evidence and to make the letter as persuasive as possible. If necessary, review that persuasive writing involves stating an opinion and supporting it with reasons and evidence. Students should draw on the "Yes" and "No" primary sources for evidence. In addition, students should include emotional appeals as well as logical appeals. *(Students' letters will vary but should present their arguments logically. Students' letters should include reasons, evidence, and persuasive techniques.)*

CLOSE & REFLECT

Have students share their letters to the citizens of Athens by reading them aloud in small groups. Ask a few volunteers to share their letters with the whole class. Then have the class discuss whether they think Socrates was guilty. Ask students whether their original opinions changed after they studied the two arguments.

ANSWERS, p. 229

1. Socrates' accusers are saying that Socrates is setting a bad example for the youth by disagreeing with the current laws and that this influence also causes the young to question the law and become "violent and headstrong."
2. Socrates says the main idea he teaches is to care about wisdom, truth, and the improvement of the soul and to pay less attention to money, honor, and reputation.
3. Answers will vary, but students should point out that while Socrates' accusers make more specific claims, Socrates makes a more general argument, reaffirming his teaching doctrine of leading students to truth and wisdom through philosophy.

Chapter 8 229

Background information is provided to help students understand why there are opposing viewpoints about the issue or event.

Two primary sources are presented that answer the *What Do You Think?* question.

Questions assess students' understanding of both points of view and ask students to make comparisons between the arguments.

Activities and Assessment

Chapter Activities

Each chapter ends with the following:

- Exploring the Essential Question Writing Activity
- 21st Century Skills Activity
- Thinking Like a Historian Activity
- Geography Activity

Chapter Assessment

Each chapter ends with the following:

- Review the Guiding Questions Standardized Test Practice
- Analyzing Documents Questions and Writing Activities

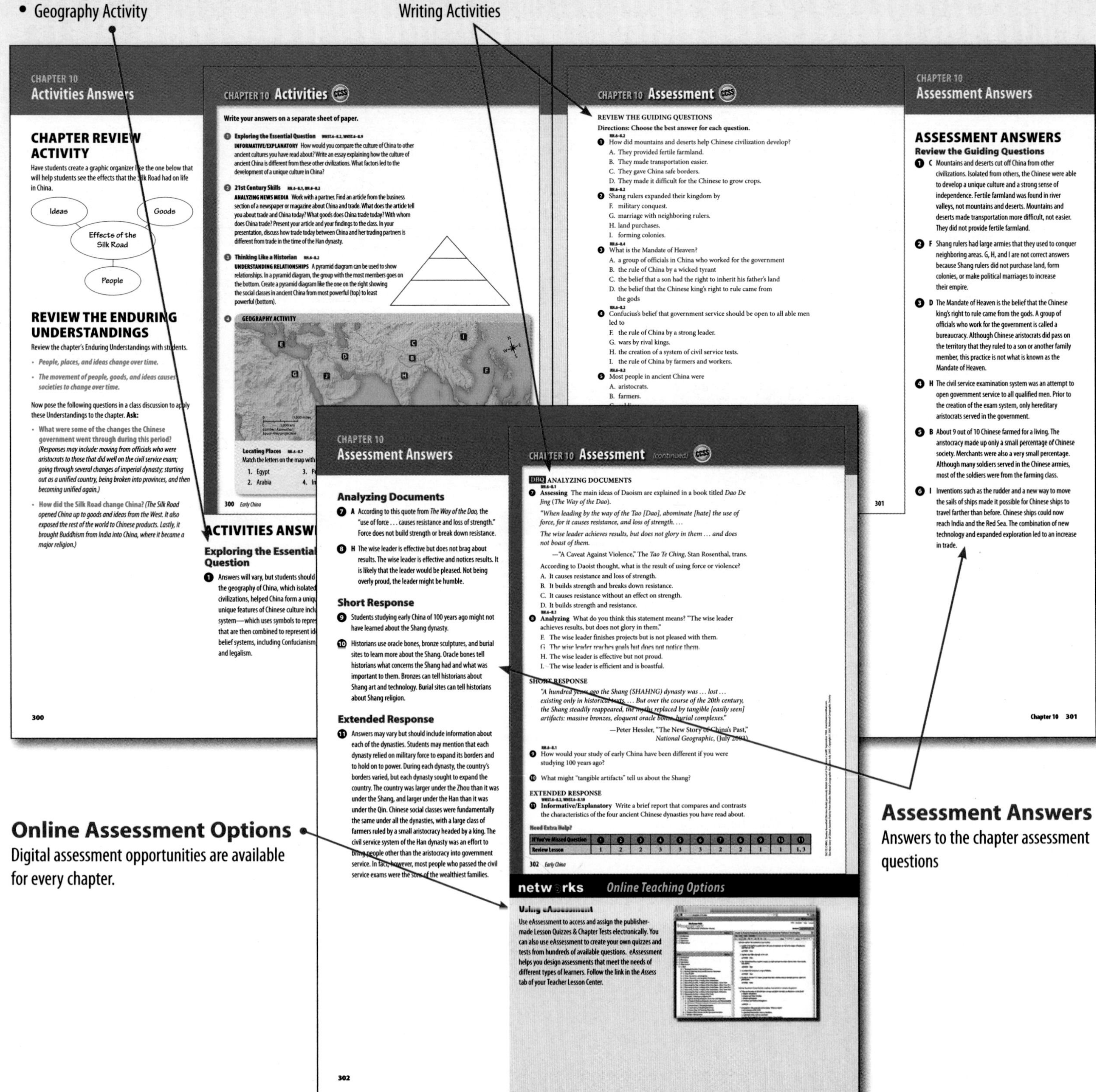

Online Assessment Options

Digital assessment opportunities are available for every chapter.

Assessment Answers

Answers to the chapter assessment questions

Correlation of *Discovering Our Past: A History of the World, Early Ages* to the Revised NCSS Thematic Strands

The revised standards continue to be focused on ten themes, like the original standards. They represent a way of categorizing knowledge about the human experience, and they constitute the organizing strands that should thread through a social studies program.

Theme and Learning Expectation	Student Edition Chapter/Lesson
1. CULTURE	
1. "Culture" refers to the socially transmitted behaviors, beliefs, values, traditions, institutions, and ways of living together for a group of people	**Ch 2** L1; **Ch 8** L1, L4; **Ch 9** L3; **Ch 15** L3; **Ch 16** L2; **Ch 18** L1, L2
2. Concepts such as beliefs, values, institutions, cohesion, diversity, accommodation, adaptation, assimilation, and dissonance	**Ch 2** L1; **Ch 8** L1; **Ch 10** L2; **Ch 11** L1; **Ch 18** L1, L2
3. How culture influences the ways in which human groups solve the problems of daily living	**Ch 3** L1; **Ch 8** L4; **Ch 12** L2; **Ch 16** L2; **Ch 19** L2
4. That the beliefs, values, and behaviors of a culture form an integrated system that helps shape the activities and ways of life that define a culture	**Ch 2** L1; **Ch 3** L1; **Ch 5** L2, L3; **Ch 6** L1, L3; **Ch 8** L1, L2; Ch 10 L2; **Ch 11** L1; **Ch 12** L2, L3; **Ch 13** L1; **Ch 14** L1; **Ch 15** L3; Ch 16 L2; **Ch 17** L1; **Ch 18** L1, L2, L3; **Ch 19** L2
5. How individuals learn the elements of their culture through interactions with others, and how individuals learn of other cultures through communication and study	**Ch 3** L1, L2; **Ch 5** L3; **Ch 6** L1, L3; **Ch 9** L2; **Ch 10** L2; **Ch 12** L2; **Ch 18** L1
6. That culture may change in response to changing needs, concerns, social, political, and geographic conditions	**Ch 3** L1; **Ch 11** L1; **Ch 12** L3; **Ch 13** L2; **Ch 17** L4; **Ch 19** L2
7. How people from different cultures develop different values and ways of interpreting experience	**Ch 7** L2; **Ch 16** L2; **Ch 17** L1; **Ch 18** L2, L3
8. That language, behaviors, and beliefs of different cultures can both contribute to and pose barriers to cross-cultural understanding	**Ch 8** L3; **Ch 10** L3; **Ch 14** L1, L2; **Ch 17** L1; **Ch 18** L2, L3
2. TIME, CONTINUITY, AND CHANGE	
1. The study of the past provides representation of the history of communities, nations, and the world	**Ch 1** L1, L2
2. Concepts such as: chronology, causality, change, conflict, complexity, multiple perspectives, primary and secondary sources, and cause and effect	**Ch 1** L2, L3; **Ch 8** L2; **Ch 11** L3
3. That learning about the past requires the interpretation of sources, and that using varied sources provides the potential for a more balanced interpretive record of the past	**Ch 1** L2, L3; **Ch 8** L2; **Ch 9** L2
4. That historical interpretations of the same event may differ on the basis of such factors as conflicting evidence from varied sources, national or cultural perspectives, and the point of view of the researcher	**Ch 1** L2, L3; **Ch 8** L2
5. Key historical periods and patterns of change within and across cultures (e.g., the rise and fall of ancient civilizations, the development of technology, the rise of modern nation-states, and the establishment and breakdown of colonial systems)	**Ch 3** L1, L2; **Ch 8** L3; **Ch 9** L3; **Ch 11** L3, L4; **Ch 17** L4; **Ch 18** L3; **Ch 20** L1; **Ch 21** L1; **Ch 22** L1, L2; **Ch 23** L2, L3, L4
6. The origins and influences of social, cultural, political, and economic systems	**Ch 3** L1, L2; **Ch 4** L1; **Ch 7** L1; **Ch 9** L1, L3; **Ch 10** L2; **Ch 12** L1; **Ch 13** L2; **Ch 15** L2; **Ch 18** L2, L3; **Ch 19** L2, L3; **Ch 22** L2
7. The contributions of key persons, groups, and events from the past and their influence on the present	**Ch 6** L1, L2; **Ch 8** L2, L3; **Ch 11** L3, L4; **Ch 12** L2, L3; **Ch 13** L1, L2, L3; **Ch 14** L1, L3; **Ch 15** L2; **Ch 17** L3; **Ch 18** L3; **Ch 19** L1, L3, L4; **Ch 20** L2, L3, L4; **Ch 21** L1; **Ch 22** L1, L2; **Ch 23** L3, L4
8. The history of democratic ideals and principles, and how they are represented in documents, artifacts and symbols	**Ch 19** L3; **Ch 22** L2
9. The influences of social, geographic, economic, and cultural factors on the history of local areas, states, nations, and the world	**Ch 10** L1; **Ch 15** L2; **Ch 19** L1, L3

Theme and Learning Expectation	Student Edition Chapter/Lesson
3. PEOPLE, PLACES, AND ENVIRONMENTS	
1. The theme of people, places, and environments involves the study of the relationships between human populations in different locations and geographic phenomena such as climate, vegetation, and natural resources	**Ch 2** L1; **Ch 4** L1; **Ch 5** L1; **Ch 7** L1; **Ch 9** L1; **Ch 10** L1; **Ch 11** L1; **Ch 15** L1; **Ch 16** L1
2. Concepts such as: location, region, place, migration, as well as human and physical systems	**Ch 2** L1; **Ch 4** L1; **Ch 9** L1; **Ch 15** L1; **Ch 16** L1; **Ch 18** L1, L2
3. Past and present changes in physical systems, such as seasons, climate, and weather, and the water cycle, in both national and global contexts	**Ch 3** L1
4. The roles of different kinds of population centers in a region or nation	**Ch 16** L1; **Ch 18** L3; **Ch 19** L1; **Ch 20** L2; **Ch 21** L1; **Ch 23** L5
5. The concept of regions identifies links between people in different locations according to specific criteria (e.g., physical, economic, social, cultural, or religious)	**Ch 10** L1; **Ch 15** L1, L3; **Ch 16** L1, L2; **Ch 18** L1, L2; **Ch 19** L1
6. Patterns of demographic and political change, and cultural diffusion in the past and present (e.g., changing national boundaries, migration, and settlement, and the diffusion of and changes in customs and ideas)	**Ch 9** L3; **Ch 10** L3; **Ch 18** L1, L2; **Ch 20** L2; **Ch 23** L5
7. Human modifications of the environment	**Ch 3** L2; **Ch 4** L1; **Ch 5** L1; **Ch 16** L2; **Ch 23** L5
8. Factors that contribute to cooperation and conflict among peoples of the nation and world, including language, religion, and political beliefs	**Ch 6** L2, L4; **Ch 7** L3; **Ch 10** L3; **Ch 13** L1, L2; **Ch 14** L2; **Ch 17** L1, L4; **Ch 18** L1; **Ch 19** L4; **Ch 20** L2, L4; **Ch 23** L1, L3
9. The use of a variety of maps, globes, graphic representations, and geospatial technologies to help investigate the relationships among people, places, and environments	**Ch 2** L1
4. INDIVIDUAL DEVELOPMENT AND IDENTITY	
1. The study of individual development and identity helps us know that individuals change physically, cognitively, and emotionally over time	**Ch 22** L2
2. Concepts such as: development, change, personality, learning, individual, family, groups, motivation, and perception	**Ch 3** L1; **Ch 10** L2
3. How factors such as physical endowment, interests, capabilities, learning, motivation, personality, perception, and beliefs influence individual development and identity	**Ch 5** L2; **Ch 13** L1; **Ch 14** L3
4. How personal, social, cultural, and environmental factors contribute to the development and the growth of personal identity	**Ch 9** L2; **Ch 10** L2, L3; **Ch 13** L1; **Ch 14** L1, L3
5. That individuals' choices influence identity and development	**Ch 22** L2
6. That perceptions are interpretations of information about individuals and events, and can be influenced by bias and stereotypes	**Ch 1** L2, L3; **Ch 9** L1
5. INDIVIDUALS, GROUPS, AND INSTITUTIONS	
1. This theme helps us know how individuals are members of groups and institutions, and influence and shape those groups and institutions	**Ch 9** L1; **Ch 19** L5
2. Concepts such as: mores, norms, status, role, socialization, ethnocentrism, cultural diffusion, competition, cooperation, conflict, race, ethnicity, and gender	**Ch 4** L2; **Ch 9** L1; **Ch 14** L2, L3
3. Institutions are created to respond to changing individual and group needs	**Ch 3** L2; **Ch 13** L2
4. That ways in which young people are socialized include similarities as well as differences across cultures	**Ch 23** L2
5. That groups and institutions change over time	**Ch 3** L2; **Ch 13** L3; **Ch 19** L1, L5; **Ch 20** L3, L4; **Ch 23** L1, L2
6. That cultural diffusion occurs when groups migrate	**Ch 2** L1; **Ch 9** L1, L2; **Ch 13** L2; **Ch 14** L1, L2; **Ch 18** L1; Ch 20 L2; **Ch 21** L2; **Ch 23** L5

Theme and Learning Expectation	Student Edition Chapter/Lesson
7. That institutions may promote or undermine social conformity	**Ch 5** L2; **Ch 9** L1; **Ch 10** L2; **Ch 18** L3; **Ch 19** L1, L2, L4; Ch 23 L2
8. That when two or more groups with differing norms and beliefs interact, accommodation or conflict may result	**Ch 4** L2; **Ch 6** L2, L4; **Ch 7** L3; **Ch 11** L2; **Ch 13** L3; **Ch 20** L3, L4; **Ch 21** L2; **Ch 23** L1, L2, L5
9. That groups and institutions influence culture in a variety of ways	**Ch 5** L2; **Ch 7** L2; **Ch 14** L1; **Ch 17** L3, L4; **Ch 19** L1, L2, L4, L5
6. POWER, AUTHORITY, AND GOVERNANCE	
1. Rights are guaranteed in the U.S. Constitution, the supreme law of the land	**Ch 23** L1
2. Fundamental ideas that are the foundation of American constitutional democracy (including those of the U.S. Constitution, popular sovereignty, the rule of law, separation of powers, checks and balances, minority rights, the separation of church and state, and Federalism)	**Ch 11** L2; **Ch 12** L1, L2; **Ch 19** L3; **Ch 22** L2; **Ch 23** L1
3. Fundamental values of constitutional democracy (e.g., the common good, liberty, justice, equality, and individual dignity)	**Ch 7** L2, L4; **Ch 19** L3; **Ch 22** L2; **Ch 23** L1, L2
4. The ideologies and structures of political systems that differ from those of the United States	**Ch 7** L2; **Ch 19** L3; **Ch 22** L2
5. The ways in which governments meet the needs and wants of citizens, manage conflict, and establish order and society	**Ch 3** L2; **Ch 4** L1, L2; **Ch 10** L1; **Ch 11** L2, L3; **Ch 12** L1, L2, L3; **Ch 15** L2; **Ch 19** L2, L5; **Ch 22** L2; **Ch 23** L2
7. PRODUCTION, DISTRIBUTION, AND CONSUMPTION	
1. Individuals, government, and society experience scarcity because human wants and needs exceed what can be produced from available resources	**Ch 2** L2; **Ch 10** L3; **Ch 11** L3; **Ch 15** L1, L3; **Ch 17** L2; **Ch 21** L1, L3; **Ch 23** L1
2. How choices involve trading off the expected value of one opportunity gained against the expected value of the best alternative	**Ch 2** L2; **Ch 23** L4
3. The economic choices that people make have both present and future consequences	**Ch 11** L3; **Ch 15** L3; **Ch 21** L1; **Ch 23** L4
4. Economic incentives affect people's behavior and may be regulated by rules or laws	**Ch 19** L2; **Ch 20** L2; **Ch 23** L1
5. That banks and other financial institutions channel funds from savers to borrowers and investors	**Ch 21** L3
6. The economic gains that result from specialization and exchange as well as the trade-offs	**Ch 3** L2; **Ch 4** L1; **Ch 15** L1; **Ch 21** L1, L3; **Ch 23** L1
7. How markets bring buyers and sellers together to exchange goods and services	**Ch 2** L2; **Ch 15** L1, L3; **Ch 20** L2; **Ch 21** L1, L3
8. How goods and services are allocated in a market economy through the influence of prices on decisions about production and consumption	**Ch 2** L2
9. How the overall levels of income, employment, and prices are determined by the interaction of households, firms, and the government	**Ch 2** L2
8. SCIENCE, TECHNOLOGY, AND SOCIETY	
1. Science is a result of empirical study of the natural world, and technology is the application of knowledge to accomplish tasks	**Ch 3** L1; **Ch 22** L1; **Ch 23** L4
2. Society often turns to science and technology to solve problems	**Ch 4** L1; **Ch 5** L1; **Ch 17** L2; **Ch 20** L2; **Ch 21** L1; **Ch 22** L1; Ch 23 L4
3. Our lives today are media and technology dependent	**Ch 1** L3; **Ch 23** L4
4. Science and technology have had both positive and negative impacts upon individuals, societies, and the environment in the past and present	**Ch 3** L2; **Ch 5** L4; **Ch 17** L2; **Ch 22** L1; **Ch 23** L4, L5
5. Science and technology have changed peoples' perceptions of the social and natural world, as well as their relationship to the land, economy and trade, their concept of security, and their major daily activities	**Ch 3** L2; **Ch 5** L4; **Ch 17** L2; **Ch 20** L2; **Ch 21** L1; **Ch 22** L1; Ch 23 L5

Theme and Learning Expectation	Student Edition Chapter/Lesson
6. Values, beliefs, and attitudes that have been influenced by new scientific and technological knowledge (e.g., invention of the printing press, conceptions of the universe, applications of atomic energy, and genetic discoveries)	**Ch 14** L3; **Ch 20** L2; **Ch 22** L1; **Ch 23** L5
7. How media are created and received depends upon cultural contexts	**Ch 1** L2
8. Science and technology sometimes create ethical issues that test our standards and values	**Ch 22** L1; **Ch 23** L5
9. The need for laws and policies to govern scientific and technological applications	**Ch 23** L5
10. That there are gaps in access to science and technology around the world	**Ch 2** L2
9. GLOBAL CONNECTIONS	
1. Global connections have existed in the past and increased rapidly in current times	**Ch 2** L2
2. Global factors such as cultural, economic, and political connections are changing the places in which people live (e.g., through trade, migration, increased travel, and communication)	**Ch 2** L1, L2
3. Spatial relationships that relate to ongoing global issues (e.g., pollution, poverty, disease, and conflict) affect the health and well-being of Earth and its inhabitants	**Ch 15** L3, What Do You Think?
4. Global problems and possibilities are not generally caused or developed by any one nation	**Ch 15** L3, What Do You Think?
5. Global connections may make cultures more alike or increase their sense of distinctiveness	**Ch 21** L1, L2, L3
6. Universal human rights cut across cultures but are not necessarily understood in the same way in all cultures	**Ch 23** L2, What Do You Think?
10. CIVIC IDEALS AND PRACTICES	
1. The theme of civic ideals and practices helps us to learn about and know how to work for the betterment of society	**Ch 7** L2, L4; **Ch 11** L2
2. Concepts and ideals such as: individual dignity, liberty, justice, equality, individual rights, responsibility, majority and minority rights, and civil dissent	**Ch 2** L3; **Ch 7** L1, L2, L4; **Ch 11** L2
3. Key practices involving the rights and responsibilities of citizenship and the exercise of citizenship (e.g., respecting the rule of law and due process, voting, serving on a jury, researching issues, making informed judgments, expressing views on issues, and collaborating with others to take civic action)	**Ch 7** L1, L4; **Ch 11** L2
4. The common good, and the rule of law	**Ch 7** L2, L4; **Ch 10** L2; **Ch 11** L2
5. Key documents and excerpts from key sources that define and support democratic ideals and practices (e.g., the U.S. Declaration of Independence, the U.S. Constitution, the Gettysburg Address, the Letter from Birmingham Jail; and international documents such as the Declaration of the Rights of Man, and the Universal Declaration of the Rights of Children)	**Ch 23** L1, L2
6. The origins and function of major institutions and practices developed to support democratic ideals and practices	**Ch 2** L3
7. Key past and present issues involving democratic ideals and practices, as well as the perspectives of various stakeholders in proposing possible solutions to these issues	**Ch 11** L2
8. The importance of becoming informed in order to make positive civic contributions	**Ch 2** L3

Discovering Our Past: A History of the World, Early Ages Correlated to Common Core State Standards

CCSS

Common Core State Standards for English Language Arts and Literacy in History/Social Studies, Science, and Technical Subjects

The following pages contain correlation charts to the Common Core State Standards. The first chart contains the College and Career Readiness (CCR) Anchor Standards for Reading. The chart that follows the CCR Anchor Standards for Reading chart identifies specifically what students should understand and be able to do by the end of grades 6–8. The CCR and grade-specific standards are necessary complements—the former providing broad standards, the latter providing additional specificity—that together define the skills and understandings that all students must demonstrate.

College and Career Readiness Anchor Standards for Reading	
Key Ideas and Details	
1. Read closely to determine what the text says explicitly and to make logical inferences from it; cite specific textual evidence when writing or speaking to support conclusions drawn from the text.	**Student Edition:** *Step into the Place:* Critical Thinking: 52, 74, 396, 508, 538, 598, 616, 606, 662 *Reading Help Desk:* Reading Strategy: 702 *The World's Literature:* Speculating: 85 *What Do You Think?:* Contrasting: 17; Identifying: 17; Making Inferences: 359, 681; Problem Solving: 17 *Text Features:* Analyzing: 46, 66, 67, 107; Conjecturing: 649; Drawing Conclusions: 34, 88, 123, 180, 218, 237, 254, 294, 332, 346, 351, 373, 374, 401, 437, 475, 514, 529, 532, 546, 583, 602, 620, 653, 673, 685; Hypothesizing: 233, 352; Inferring: 111, 201, 364; Making Generalizations: 375, 621, 691; Making Inferences: 8, 78, 89, 151, 175, 191, 251, 314, 362, 385, 402, 415, 423, 429, 455, 461, 483, 531, 543, 568, 608, 626, 643, 652, 702; Predicting: 56, 105, 188, 249, 324, 454; Speculating: 36, 59, 80, 81, 87, 91, 110, 114, 192, 194, 199, 204, 217, 222, 260, 267, 283, 379, 381, 484, 491, 499, 512, 541, 542, 545, 565, 573, 574, 592, 610, 633, 647, 670, 675; Theorizing: 216, 588, 678, 687, 695; Thinking Like a Historian: 485, 587 *Lesson Review:* Determining Cause and Effect: 21, 61, 189, 197, 205, 271, 299, 403, 410, 527, 595, 605, 689, 695, 703; Drawing Conclusions: 133, 241, 264, 333, 354, 365, 406, 467, 519, 555, 671; Generalizing: 605; Identifying Cause and Effect: 69, 365, 391, 555, 563; Inferring: 69, 219, 627; Making Generalizations: 15, 375; Making Inferences: 37, 47, 343, 385, 391, 595, 605, 611; Speculating: 488 *Chapter Activities & Assessment:* 21st Century Skills: 300, 468; Thinking Like a Historian: 94; Drawing Conclusions: 50, 96, 136, 170, 208, 274, 336, 368, 394, 446, 506, 638, 660, 706; Inferring: 136, 24, 394, 506; Making Inferences: 446, 578, 614, 638; Predicting: 244; *Short Response:* 136, 208, 244, 394, 506, 578, 638, 706 **Teacher Edition:** PLACE & TIME: 173, C641 ENGAGE: 108, 140, 148, 154, 171, 220, 230, 245, 265, 278, 286, 303, 312, 328, 337, 340, 350, 369, 395, 398, 410, 415, 471, 474, 482, 537, 598, 606, 615, 618, 624, 650, 661 TEACH & ASSESS: $R_1$4, $R_2$4, 04, C8, R9, C13, $C_1$19, C34, 035, C44, C55, 058, C59, C60, $C_1$62, 065, C66, C67, 067, $C_1$76, 076, C79, 080, C81, $C_1$82, $C_2$82, C85, C87, 076, $C_1$88, $C_2$88, C89, R90, C93, R100, R101, C103, R103, 0105, C106, R110, 0110, $R_1$114, $R_2$114, R115, C116, R117, 0128, C130, C140, $C_2$142, C143, R144, C144, R147, C149, C150, 0150, R151, $C_1$152, $C_2$152, $C_1$153, C154, C155, 0156, C157, 0157, C159, C161, R162, 0162, R164, 0164, $C_1$166, $C_2$166, $C_1$167, R174, C174, C177, C178, R179, 0179, $C_1$185, C186, R187, 0188, T189, 0190, C191, R193, $C_2$193, 0194, 0196, R199, R202, C202, 0211, $C_2$213, C214, $C_2$216, R218, C218, R220, C220, $C_2$221, R221, C223, C227, V231, C232, R233, C235, C236, C237, C248, C251, R253, R254, R255, R256, $R_1$257, C257, C258, R262, C262, R264, C264, R265, $R_1$266, R267, C270, C278, 0279, C280, $R_2$280, $R_1$281, 0282, C283, C284, C285, C286, R287, C288, $C_1$289, $C_2$289, C290, $C_1$291, C292, 0292, C294, $C_1$295, $C_2$295, 0295, C296, C298, C299, R306, 0306, R307, 0308, $R_2$309, 0309, C315, R315, $R_1$317, 0317, R319, C321, R322, $C_1$322, $C_2$322, C323, $C_2$234, 0326, C237, C329, R331, R340, C343, 0346, R348, R350, 0351, R356, C360, R361, 0361, R372, C373, 0376, R377, C380, C382, C383, $R_2$384, C385, C388, C389, 0390, R391, C398, C399, C400, C401, C402, 0402, C403, R404, R405, $R_1$406, C407, C408, $C_1$409, 0409, R410, R411, R412, 0412, C415, C421, C422, C423, C424, 0424, 0426, R428, C429, R430, C431, R432, 0432, R435, C436, 0437, R438, R439, C440, C450, R451, C452, C454, 0454, C458, R459, R460, C461, 0464, R457, $R_1$476, $R_2$476, R477, R478, C479, R479, C480, R482, C483, $R_1$484, C485, $C_1$486, R486, C487, 0487, R489, R490, R491, R493, R497, R499, R500, R501, $R_2$502, C503, C510, 0510, 0514, R514, C517, C520, $C_1$522, $C_2$522, C524, 0524, C526, C528, C529, C532, C544, C550, C551, C557, 0557, C561, C566, 0568, C571, C572, C574, R582, $C_1$585, R587, 0587, C591, 0593, R594, 0594, C594, 0601, C602, C603, C610, C622, C623, C626, 0628, $C_1$629, C633, $C_2$643, C644, 0645, C646, C647, C648, 0648, R649, C650, 0654, $C_1$655, C657, R664, C665, 0665, $C_2$669, 0674, C677, C685, R686, C689, C693, C698 CLOSE & REFLECT: 93, 107, 187, 205, 241, 285, 349, 357, 385, 403, 441, 551, 555, 623, 635, 657, 671, 703 CHAPTER ASSESSMENT: CRA22, CRA206, CRA242, CRA444 INTERVENTION AND REMEDIATION STRATEGIES: 21F, 51E, 171G, 245F, 303G, 395F, 447E, 471G, 579G, 639E

Codes used for the Teacher Edition pages are the initial caps of the activities.

College and Career Readiness Anchor Standards for Reading	
2. Determine central ideas or themes of a text and analyze their development; summarize the key supporting details and ideas.	**Student Edition:** *Step into the Place:* Critical Thinking: 2, 26, 52, 74, 98, 138, 172, 210, 246, 276, 304, 338, 370, 420, 448, 580, 640 *Reading Help Desk:* Taking Notes: 4, 10, 18, 28, 38, 44, 54, 62, 76, 86, 100, 108, 120, 128, 140, 148, 154, 160, 174, 183, 190, 198, 212, 220, 230, 236, 248, 257, 265, 278, 286, 292, 306, 312, 320, 328, 340, 350, 360, 372, 380, 386, 398, 404, 411, 422, 430, 436, 450, 459, 474, 482, 489, 510, 516, 528, 540, 548, 556, 564, 570, 582, 589, 618, 624, 628, 642, 650, 672, 682, 690, 696; Reading Strategy: 34, 80, 110, 117, 122, 194, 342, 362, 376, 400, 423, 440, 478, 492, 522, 552, 560, 594, 600, 684, 694 *The World's Literature:* Analyzing: 349, 597, 719; Assessing, 597; Describing: 85, 497; Identifying: 85; Interpreting: 349, 597; Speculating: 85; Synthesizing: 497 *What Do You Think?:* Describing: 229, 359; Evaluating: 229; Explaining: 229, 681; Identifying: 359; Identifying Central Issues: 681 *Text Features:* Analyzing: 55, 64, 65, 79, 107, 117, 156, 176, 195, 214, 224, 227, 235, 239, 255, 266, 279, 281, 284, 288, 295, 296, 309, 310, 315, 317, 318, 321, 322, 330, 331, 342, 353, 377, 378, 382, 383, 384, 388, 399, 431, 433, 451, 452, 453, 462, 464, 466, 472, 511, 513, 517, 521, 522, 552, 559, 645, 651, 677, 686, 697; Assessing: 594; Comparing: 115, 152, 159, 477, 562, 647, 657; Comparing and Contrasting: 341; Contrasting: 196, 355, 490, 522, 619; Describing: 104, 477; Differentiating: 121, 144; Document-Based Question: 375; Evaluating: 203, 439, 665; Explaining: 109, 112, 142, 161, 164, 251, 326, 355, 387, 389, 440, 476, 477, 494, 515, 518, 524, 526, 552, 584, 603, 604, 646, 655, 668, 669, 698; Finding the Main Idea, 143, 231; Identifying: 7, 58, 116, 118, 143, 224, 239, 253, 255, 288, 331, 341, 355, 435, 607; Making Connections: 360, 405, 438, 501, 571, 586; Summarizing: 572; Synthesizing: 185, 376; Thinking Like a Historian: 467, 587 *Lesson Review:* Analyzing: 107, 119, 127, 182, 197, 333, 488, 495, 527, 547, 569, 575, 695, 703; Assessing: 15, 21, 291, 679, 689, 703; Categorizing: 256; Comparing: 83, 93, 159, 219, 264, 385, 435, 458, 689; Comparing and Contrasting: 119, 133, 227, 391, 428, 481, 569; Contrasting: 37, 43, 107, 347, 379, 406, 467, 519, 533, 569, 595, 623, 703; Defending: 119; Describing: 9, 61, 83, 93, 119, 127, 147, 189, 205, 227, 235, 241, 256, 271, 285, 299, 347, 357, 365, 379, 385, 403, 410, 415, 429, 435, 441, 467, 481, 488, 503, 515, 555, 563, 627, 657; Determining Cause and Effect: 21, 61, 189, 197, 205, 271, 299, 403, 410, 527, 595, 605, 689, 695, 703; Differentiating: 97, 311, 347, 551, 588, 623, 627, 679; Distinguishing Fact from Opinion: 319; Drawing Conclusions: 15, 47, 133, 241, 264, 333, 365, 467, 519, 555, 671; Explaining: 43, 93, 107, 127, 133, 147, 153, 159, 162, 165, 167, 182, 189, 197, 205, 219, 227, 241, 256, 264, 285, 291, 299, 311, 319, 327, 333, 357, 365, 379, 391, 403, 410, 415, 429, 435, 441, 458, 481, 488, 503, 515, 519, 533, 547, 563, 575, 588, 595, 611, 623, 627, 635, 649, 657; Evaluating: 679, 689; Finding the Main Idea: 37, 47, 695; Generalizing: 605; Identifying: 37, 69, 83, 107, 147, 153, 159, 167, 189, 205, 219, 235, 271, 285, 291, 327, 347, 385, 406, 410, 415, 428, 429, 441, 481, 495, 503, 515, 519, 527, 533, 547, 569, 575, 588, 605, 611, 623, 635, 649, 657; Identifying Cause and Effect: 69, 365, 391, 555, 563; Inferring: 69, 219, 627; Listing: 9, 21, 533; Making Connections: 9, 61, 671; Making Inferences: 37, 47, 385, 391, 595, 605, 611; Naming: 429; Paraphrasing: 281; Review Vocabulary: 9, 15, 21, 37, 43, 47, 61, 69, 83, 93, 107, 119, 127, 133, 147, 153, 159, 167, 182, 189, 197, 205, 219, 227, 235, 241, 256, 264, 271, 285, 291, 299, 311, 319, 327, 333, 347, 357, 365, 379, 385, 391, 403, 410, 415, 429, 435, 441, 458, 467, 481, 488, 495, 503, 515, 519, 527, 533, 547, 555, 563, 569, 575, 588, 595, 605, 611, 623, 627, 635, 649, 657, 671, 679, 689, 695, 703; Sequencing: 441; Stating: 69; Summarizing: 43, 61, 127, 147, 182, 235, 256, 311, 319, 327, 357, 415, 435, 458, 495, 503, 515, 547, 555, 649, 657; Understanding Cause and Effect: 327 *Chapter Activities & Assessment:* 21st Century Skills: 134, 206, 242, 300, 468, 504, 576, 636, 658, 704; Thinking Like a Historian: 48, 70, 134, 168, 206, 272, 300, 334, 392, 416, 444, 468, 504, 534, 576, 612, 636, 658, 704; Review the Guiding Questions: 23, 49, 71, 93, 135, 169, 207, 243, 273, 301, 335, 367, 393, 417, 445, 469, 505, 535, 577, 613, 637, 659, 705 *DBQ: Analyzing:* 302, 470, 536, 706; Assessing: 302; Comparing: 368; Comparing and Contrasting: 274, 418, 536; Drawing Conclusions: 50, 96, 136, 170, 208, 272, 336, 368, 446, 660, 706; Evaluating: 470; Explaining: 96; Finding the Main Idea: 50, 660; Identifying: 24, 72, 208; Identifying Point of View: 24; Making Connections: 72; Summarizing: 170, 336, 418, 578, 614; Short Response: 24, 50, 72, 96, 136, 170, 208, 244, 274, 302, 336, 368, 418, 446, 470, 536, 578, 638, 660, 706; Extended Response: 578 **Teacher Edition:** ENGAGE: 51, 86, 248, 275, 397, 411, 419, 507, 528, 639, 642 TEACH & ASSESS: 04, 06, R7, 08, 010, 013, 014, R17, 018, R18, $C_1$19, $C_2$19, 019, 020, R28, R29, C31, $C_2$32, $C_2$32, R33, $C_2$33, 033, R34, C37, C39, $C_2$40, R40, R41, C41, R42, C43, 044, C45, 045, R46, C46, $R_1$54, R55, 055, R56, C57, R58, R59, 059, 060, R61, C62, 062, $C_2$63, 063, R65, $C_2$76, R77, C77, 077, R78, R79, R80, R81, 082, R83, R84, R85, 085, 086, R88, 088, C92, $R_2$92, 092, 0100, 0101, C102, 0102, 0103, 0104, 0105, R107, 0108, 0109, 0110, 0112, C113, 0114, 0117, C118, 0118, R119, 0120, R121, 0121, R122, C123, 0123, 0125, C125, R128, 0126, 0128, 0129, 0130, R132, 0132, C133, 0139, R142, 0142, 0143, $C_1$145, 0145, R146, 0146, R147, C148, R152, $C_2$153, R155, 0155, R156, R157, 0158, R159, R160, R161, V162, R163, C164, $R_1$165, $R_2$165, R166, $C_1$167, 0171, $R_2$176, 0178, C181, 0181, R183, R185, 0185, 0186, 0187, R188, 0190, 0191, 0192, 0193, R194, 0195, R197, 0198, R201, 0201, 0202, 0203, R204, C204, C212, $C_1$213, 0213, 0214, R215, 0215, $C_1$221, 0221, C222, R222, 0222, 0223, R225, C225, R227, R228, 0228, R230, 0230, 0231, 0236, 0237, R238, C238, 0238, 0239, R240, $C_1$241, $C_2$241, 0248, $R_2$250, 0250, R251, $R_1$252, $R_2$252, R254, 0257, R259, 0259, R260, R261, $C_2$261, R263, 0263, 0265, $R_2$266, $R_1$268, C271, R278, $R_1$280, 0280, $R_2$281, 0287, R283, R284, $C_1$287, 0289, $C_2$291, R292, C293, C294, R296, R297, 0297, R299, 0307, R308, C310, 0312, $C_2$313, 0313, R316, 0318, C320, 0321, 0322, 0323, R325, 0325, C326, R327, 0328, $C_1$330, C331, 0331, R332, R333, 0339, 0340, 0341, R342, C342, C344, 0344, R349, 0349, R350, C351, R353, 0353, 0355, 0360, 0362, 0363, 0372, 0373, R373, C374, 0375, R376, 0377, C379, R380, R381, 0383, 0384, R386, 0386, 0387, 0389, 0397, 0398, R399, 0399, R400, R401, 0401, $R_1$402, $R_2$402, C406, $R_2$406, 0406, R407, C411, 0411, C412, C2413, 0413, R414, R422, 0422, 0423, R425, 0425, R426, R427, R429, 0430, 0431, R434, C434, 0436, 0438, 0439, R440, 0443, 0450, 0453, R454, R456, 0456, 0459, 0460, R461, C463, 0463, R464, 0473, R474, R475, $R_1$480, $R_2$480, 0480, 0482, R483, $R_2$484, 0485, C488, 0489, 0491, R492, C494, 0494, R495, 0497, C498, C500, $R_1$502, R503, R510, 0511, $R_1$512, $R_2$512, C513, 0513, C514, R516, 0516, R517, 0517, C518, 0518, C519, R520, 0520, R521, 0521, 0522, R523, C523, 0523, R524, C525, 0525, C526, C527, 0528, R529, 0529, R530, R532, 0532, C533, $R_2$540, 0540, C541, 0541, R542, 0542, R543, C543, R544, 0544, R545, C546, 0546, R547, 0548, C549, 0549, 0550, 0551, 0552, R553, R554, R555, R556, 0556, R557, R558, 0558, R559, 0559, R560, 0560, 0562, 0564, 0566, $C_1$567, $C_2$567, 0567, C568, $R_1$569, 0570, R573, 0573, R574, 0574, 0583, $C_2$585, $C_1$588, R589, 0589, R590, 0591, R592, $R_1$597, R598, 0598, R599, 0599, $R_2$601, 0602, R603, R604, R605, R606, 0606, R607, 0607, 0608, R610, 0610, R619, 0619, R620, R621, C625, 0625, R626, 0626, R627, R628, R629, 0629, R630, 0630, R631, C631, 0631, C634, R634, 0634, 0641, R642, 0642, $C_1$643, 0644, C645, R646, 0647, R648, 0649, 0650, R651, 0651, C652, 0652, C653, R653, 0653, C654, $C_2$655, R655, 0655, R656, 0656, R657, 0664, C666, C667, R670, R671, C672, 0672, C673, 0673, R674, $R_1$675, $R_2$675, R677, 0677, 0678, R679, R680, R682, 0682, R683, 0683, R684, R687, 0687, 0688, 0690, R692, 0692, R695, C697, R698, 0698, C699, C700, C701, R702

Codes used for the Teacher Edition pages are the initial caps of the activities.

College and Career Readiness Anchor Standards for Reading	
	CLOSE & REFLECT: 37, 43, 61, 69, 127, 133, 147, 167, 227, 235, 256, 264, 271, 277, 311, 327, 347, 379, 391, 443, 458, 467, 503, 519, 527, 533, 547, 563, 569, 585, 611, 627, 641, 696 CHAPTER ASSESSMENT: CRA22, REU22, CRA48, REU48, CRA70, REU70, CRA94, REU94, CRA134, REU134, CRA168, REU168, CRA206, REU206, REU242, CRA272, REU272, CRA300, REU300, CRA334, REU334, CRA366, REU366, CRA392, REU392, CRA416, REU416, REU444, CRA468, REU468, CRA504, REU504, CRA534, REU534, CRA576, REU576, CRA612, REU612, CRA636, REU636, CRA658, REU658, CRA704, REU704 INTERVENTION AND REMEDIATION STRATEGIES: 1F, 25F, 73E,137G, 171G, 209G, 245F, 275F, 303G, 337F, 369F, 395F, 419F, 447E, 471G, 507G, 537H, 579G, 615F, 639E, 661H PROJECT-BASED LEARNING: HOCP580
3. Analyze how and why individuals, events, or ideas develop and interact over the course of a text.	**Student Edition:** *Reading Help Desk:* Taking Notes: 10, 520, 664; Reading Strategy: 532, 630 *Text Features:* Cause and Effect: 620, 625, 630, 632, 634; Determining Cause and Effect: 492 *Lesson Review:* Identifying Cause and Effect: 69 **Teacher Edition:** ENGAGE: 73, 84, 430, 436, 489, 498, 540, 605 TEACH & ASSESS: 05, 064, C90, C106, C116, 0122, C156, C158, $C_1$195, 0220, 0274, 0230, C250, 0267, $R_2$268, 0287, R293, C297, R374, 0400, 0404, $C_1$413, R415, C441, 0512, C516, 0531, R548, C553, C558, C562, C570, 0571, C583, 0600, C618, $C_2$629, C635, $C_1$669, C676, C686, C691, C696, 0696 CLOSE & REFLECT: 292, 320, 386, 435, 481, 595 CHAPTER ASSESSMENT: REU22 INTERVENTION AND REMEDIATION STRATEGIES: 1F, 73E, 615F, 661H
Craft and Structure	
4. Interpret words and phrases as they are used in a text, including determining technical, connotative, and figurative meanings, and analyze how specific word choices shape meaning or tone.	**Student Edition:** *Reading Help Desk:* Build Vocabulary: 8, 116, 178, 250, 262, 325, 361, 390, 457, 558, 683; Reading Strategy: 6, 193 *What Do You Think?:* Describing: 443 *Lesson Review:* Defining: 649; Review Vocabulary: 9, 15, 21, 37, 43, 47, 61, 69, 83, 93, 107, 119, 127, 133, 147, 153, 159, 167, 182, 189, 197, 205, 219, 227, 235, 241, 256, 264, 271, 285, 291, 299, 311, 319, 327, 333, 347, 357, 365, 379, 385, 391, 403, 410, 415, 429, 435, 441, 458, 467, 481, 488, 495, 503, 515, 519, 527, 533, 547, 555, 563, 569, 588, 595, 605, 611, 623, 627, 635, 649, 657, 671, 679, 689, 695, 703 *Chapter Activities & Assessment:* Review the Guiding Questions: 23, 49, 71, 207, 273, 301, 535, 577, 613, 705; Identifying Point of View: 24 **Teacher Edition:** ENGAGE: 44, 128, 257, 471, 520, 664, 672, 682 TEACH & ASSESS: R5, T15, R21, R38, R44, $R_2$54, R62, R64, R68, R86, $R_1$92, R108, 0111, C116, C120, R123, R127, R140, R148, R158, $R_1$176, 0184, $C_2$185, R192, R198, R205, R214, R219, R220, R223, $C_1$226, R256, C240, R249, $R_1$250, $R_3$250, $R_2$257, R269, R282, 0286, 0288, $R_1$309, R312, R313, R314, $R_2$317, R323, 0324, R326, R328, R359, R375, R382, $R_1$384, R387, C435, R437, $R_1$442, $R_2$442, R450, R462, 0474, R488, 0496, $R_2$512, R526, $R_1$540, R546, R551, R561, R564, R565, R566, R568, $R_2$569, R570, R574, 0581, R586, R593, $R_2$597, R624, R632, R633, 0633, R644, R647, R650, R652, R666, 0674, R686, R690, R694, R700 CLOSE & REFLECT: 9, 689 INTERVENTION AND REMEDIATION STRATEGIES: 1F, 25F, 97G, 171G, 209G, 245F, 275F, 303G, 337F, 419F, 507G, 537H, 579G, 615F, 661H
5. Analyze the structure of texts, including how specific sentences, paragraphs, and larger portions of the text (e.g., a section, chapter, scene, or stanza) relate to each other and the whole.	**Student Edition:** *Reading Help Desk:* Taking Notes: 498 *Text Features:* Determining Cause and Effect: 492 *Lesson Review:* Determining Cause and Effect: 21; Understanding Cause and Effect: 327 *Chapter Activities & Assessment:* 21st Century Skills: 366 **Teacher Edition:** TEACH & ASSESS: C132, 0132, $C_2$145, $C_2$409, C461, C498, C500, 0680 CLOSE & REFLECT: 305, 339, 371 INTERVENTION AND REMEDIATION STRATEGIES: 97G, 275F

Codes used for the Teacher Edition pages are the initial caps of the activities.

College and Career Readiness Anchor Standards for Reading	
6. Assess how point of view or purpose shapes the content and style of a text.	**Student Edition:** *Reading Help Desk:* Reading Strategy: 542 *The World's Literature:* Analyzing: 349, 597; Assessing: 597; Identifying: 85; Identifying Points of View: 497; Describing: 85; Evaluating: 719; Interpreting: 349, 597; Speculating: 85; Synthesizing: 497 *Text Features:* Analyzing Primary Sources: 13, 654; Identifying Points of View: 479, 557 *Lesson Review:* Identifying Points of View: 689 *Chapter Activities & Assessment:* DBQ: Analyzing: 302, 470, 536, 706; Assessing: 302; Comparing: 368; Comparing and Contrasting, 274, 418, 536; Drawing Conclusions: 50, 96, 136, 170, 208, 274, 336, 368, 394, 446, 506, 660, 706; Evaluating: 470; Explaining: 96; Finding the Main Idea: 50, 660; Identifying: 24, 72, 208; Identifying Point of View: 24, 50; Inferring: 136, 244, 394, 506; Making Connections: 72; Making Inferences: 446, 614; Predicting: 244; Summarizing: 170, 336, 418, 614; *Short Response:* 24, 50, 72, 96, 136, 170, 208, 244, 274, 302, 336, 368, 394, 418, 446, 470, 506, 536, 614, 660, 706 **Teacher Edition:** **ENGAGE:** 358 **TEACH & ASSESS:** 010, C11, 011, C12, 012, R16, 016, C100, W126, C126, C131, $C_1$142, 0152, 0166, $C_2$167, R182, $C_1$193, $C_2$195, $C_1$216, 0216, 0225, $C_1$226, C229, 0229, 0258, C267, 0269, $C_2$287, C308, C312, $C_2$313, 0315, C319, $C_1$324, C349, 0353, C356, W390, C414, 0414, C427, C439, C443, 0478, $C_2$486, 0492, C495, C531, C563, 0585, $C_2$588, C593, C597, $R_1$601, 0666, 0681, 0686 **CLOSE & REFLECT:** 85, 159 **INTERVENTION AND REMEDIATION STRATEGIES:** 369F, 579G
Integration of Knowledge and Ideas	
7. Integrate and evaluate content presented in diverse formats and media, including visually and quantitatively, as well as in words.	**Student Edition:** *Step into the Place:* Analyzing Visuals: 2; Human-Environment Interaction: 370; Identifying: 2; Location: 52, 74, 98, 138, 172, 210, 246, 304, 338, 370, 396, 420, 448, 508, 538, 616, 640; Movement: 74, 338, 396, 616, 640; Place: 26, 52, 74, 98, 172, 210, 246, 276, 304, 338, 420, 448, 472, 508, 538, 580, 662; Regions: 138, 246, 396, 420, 472, 580, 640, 662 *Step into the Time:* 2, 26, 52, 74, 98, 138, 172, 210, 246, 276, 304, 338, 370, 396, 420, 448, 472, 508, 538, 580, 616, 640, 662 *Reading Help Desk:* Taking Notes: 306; Reading Strategy: 131 *Text Features:* Analyzing: 37, 41, 60, 68, 101, 106, 131, 184, 200, 213, 224, 239, 255, 266, 269, 279, 284, 288, 290, 310, 317, 331, 384, 388, 399, 433, 451, 453, 457, 466, 511, 513, 517, 559; Analyzing Primary Sources: 13; Analyzing Visuals: 232, 234, 298, 456, 554, 561, 566, 572, 656; Applying: 390; Assessing: 693; Calculating: 426; Cause and Effect: 620, 625, 630, 632, 634; Charts and Tables: 45, 143, 145, 152, 178, 200, 213, 224, 239, 288, 331, 355, 384, 390, 406, 424, 428, 549, 630, 643, 645, 647, 649; Comparing: 124, 152, 477, 562, 647; Comparing and Contrasting, 341, 384, 424, 428; Contrasting: 355, 406, 490; Describing: 218, 477; Determining Cause and Effect: 39, 42, 475; Diagrams: 114, 116, 201, 215, 218, 238, 251, 255, 290, 297, 310, 341, 477, 550, 552, 586, 621, 693; Drawing Conclusions: 45, 180, 218, 294, 332, 346, 437, 529, 583, 602, 673, 685; Explaining: 161, 164, 251, 440, 476, 477, 552, 668, 802, 808; Evaluating: 90, 408, 665; Finding the Main Idea, 143; Geography Connection: 34, 37, 60, 63, 68, 78, 89, 90, 100, 106, 124, 131, 151, 161, 164, 175, 180, 184, 191, 194, 204, 232, 234, 249, 251, 253, 266, 269, 279, 281, 284, 294, 298, 314, 317, 332, 346, 354, 381, 388, 399, 405, 408, 423, 426, 433, 437, 440, 451, 453, 455, 466, 475, 477, 490, 491, 499, 501, 511, 513, 517, 529, 541, 545, 559, 561, 562, 571, 573, 583, 602, 608, 620, 625, 632, 634, 656, 665, 668, 678, 685, 687, 691; Graphs: 39, 41, 42, 433, 673; Human-Environment Interaction: 691; Identifying: 41, 42, 45, 143, 200, 213, 224, 239, 253, 255, 288, 331, 341, 355, 390, 406, 424, 428, 634, 693; Inferring: 201; Infographic: 7, 39, 41, 42, 45, 114, 116, 143, 145, 200, 201, 213, 218, 224, 255, 288, 290, 310, 331, 341, 355, 375, 384, 390, 424, 428, 477, 621, 630, 647, 693; Interpreting: 39, 41; Location: 34, 78, 89, 90, 101, 106, 124, 131, 164, 175, 180, 184, 194, 234, 269, 279, 281, 284, 317, 346, 381, 423, 426, 433, 477, 511, 517, 529, 541, 559, 561, 573, 583, 620, 625, 687; Making Connections: 501, 571; Making Generalizations: 621, 691; Making Inferences: 78, 89, 145, 151, 175, 191, 251, 314, 423, 455, 608; Maps: 29, 30, 31, 34, 37, 60, 63, 68, 78, 89, 90, 100, 106, 124, 131, 151, 161, 164, 175, 180, 184, 191, 194, 204, 232, 234, 249, 253, 266, 269, 279, 281, 284, 294, 298, 314, 317, 332, 346, 354, 381, 388, 399, 405, 408, 423, 424, 426, 433, 437, 440, 451, 453, 455, 466, 475, 477, 490, 491, 499, 501, 511, 513, 517, 529, 541, 545, 559, 561, 562, 571, 573, 583, 602, 608, 620, 625, 632, 634, 656, 665, 668, 678, 685, 687, 69; Movement: 106, 151, 161, 191, 253, 354, 405, 437, 440, 453, 490, 545, 562, 571, 668; Place, 68, 124, 204, 232, 249, 314, 332, 399, 405, 451, 455, 466, 475, 499, 501, 608, 632, 665, 678, 685; Predicting, 249; Regions: 37, 60, 63, 266, 294, 298, 399, 408, 491, 501, 513, 602, 656; Speculating: 63, 194, 204, 381, 491, 499, 541, 545, 573; Summarizing: 752, 777; Theorizing: 678, 687; Thinking Like a Historian: 403; Time, 621, 630; Understanding a Map Key: 388 *Lesson Review:* Analyzing Visuals: 299 *Chapter Activities & Assessment:* 21st Century Skills: 48, 392, 534; Thinking Like a Historian: 134, 612; Geography Activity: 22, 48, 70, 94, 134, 168, 206, 242, 272, 300, 334, 366, 392, 416, 444, 468, 504, 534, 576, 612, 636, 658, 704; Review the Guiding Questions: 49; Making Connections: 72; Short Response: 706 **Teacher Edition:** **PLACE & TIME:** V2, V3, V26, V27, V52, V53, V74, V75, 075, V98, V99, C139, V172, V173, V210, V211, V246, V247, V276, V277, 0277, V304, V305, 0305, V338, C339, V370, V371, 0371, C396, C397, V420, C421, 0421, V448, V449, 0449, V472, V473, V508, V509, 0509, V538, V539, V580, V581, V616, V617, 0617, V640, V641, V662, V663, 0663 **ENGAGE:** 76, 100, 120, 160, 174, 190, 212, 236, 306, 360, 372, 404, 421, 422, 430, 450, 459, 470, 516, 540, 556, 579, 589, 628

Codes used for the Teacher Edition pages are the initial caps of the activities.

College and Career Readiness Anchor Standards for Reading	
	TEACH & ASSESS: V7, 07, C10, V12, 021, V28, V29, 029, $V_1$30, $V_2$30, T30, 031, V32, V34, V35, V36, V37, V38, V39, 039, V40, 041, V42, V45, 053, 054, V56, 056, 057, V60, V61, V63, $V_1$64, $V_2$64, V65, V68, 068, V69, V78, 078, 079, V80, 084, V89, 089, R90, 099, 0102, T102, 0104, V105, V106, 0106, V109, T111, V112, 0113, V114, 0115, V116, 0116, C120, 0120, V122, V124, 0124, C130, V131, 0131, 0140, V141, 0141, 0142, 0144, 0146, V147, 0148, V151, 0151, 0154, V156, 0161, 0163, $R_2$165, 0165, 0173, V175, 0175, V177, 0177, V178, V180, V184, 0185, R190, V191, V192, V196, 0200, V201, 0204, 0212, C215, V217, 0217, 0218, V219, C224, 0226, V232, V234, 0234, V235, V239, 0247, V249, 0249, V251, V252, 0252, V253, 0253, V255, 0255, V258, 0261, 0262, V266, 0266, 0268, V269, 0270, 0277, 0278, V279, V282, 0284, V288, V290, 0290, 0293, 0294, V298, 0305, V310, 0310, V314, 0314, V317, V318, V329, 0329, 0330, V332, 0332, V341, V345, 0345, 0354, V355, $V_1$358, $V_2$358, V358, V359, V363, V364, 0371, 0374, V376, V377, V378, 0378, 0380, V381, 0381, V382, V384, V387, V388, 0388, V390, V401, V403, V404, V405, 0405, 0406, 0407, V408, 0408, V414, 0421, V423, V424, V426, V428, 0428, V433, 0433, 0434, V436, V437, 0440, 0442, 0449, 0451, R452, 0452, V453, V455, 0455, V457, 0457, V460, 0461, 0462, V464, 0465, V466, 0466, 0475, 0476, 0477, V479, 0479, 0483, 0484, V487, V490, 0490, V491, 0493, V496, 0498, V499, 0499, 0500, V501, 0501, 0509, V1511, V2511, V513, V521, V523, 0530, V531, 0539, V541, V543, 0543, V545, 0545, V549, V550, V552, 0554, V559, V561, 0561, V562, V565, 0565, V571, V572, 0572, V573, 0582, V583, V586, 0586, V589, V596, 0596, V600, V602, 0603, 0604, V608, 0617, 0618, V620, 0620, 0621, 0622, 0624, V632, 0632, 0643, V644, V645, V647, V653, V654, V656, 0663, V665, V668, 0668, V673, V674, V678, V685, 0685, V687, V688, V691, 0691, 0693, 0697, 0699, 0701, 0702 **CLOSE & REFLECT:** 15, 27, 53, 75, 99, 139, 247, 365, 429, 488, 509, 641 **INTERVENTION AND REMEDIATION STRATEGIES:** 97G, 419F, 579G, 639E, 661H **PROJECT-BASED LEARNING:** HOCP26, HOCP52, HOCP84,HOCP98, HOCP172, TE172, HOCP210, HOCP396, HOCP472, TE472, HOCP616
8. Delineate and evaluate the argument and specific claims in a text, including the validity of the reasoning as well as the relevance and sufficiency of the evidence.	**Student Edition:** *What Do You Think?:* Evaluating: 229 *Text Features:* Defending: 410; Evaluating: 203, 408, 412, 439, 495, 671 *Lesson Review:* Distinguishing Fact from Opinion: 319; Evaluating: 679, 689 *Chapter Activities & Assessment:* Thinking Like a Historian: 366; Extended Response: 24 **Teacher Edition:** **ENGAGE:** 16 **TEACH & ASSESS:** C6, C8, C11, 012, 016, C21, $C_1$33, $C_1$40, C187, T189, 0199, C229, $C_1$261, C307, C311, 0320, C353, C430, C433, C481, C493, 0590, C611, C650, R651, 0667, 0669, 0675, 0684, C703 **CLOSE & REFLECT:** 17, 229, 333, 679, 681, 695 **INTERVENTION AND REMEDIATION STRATEGIES:** 369F
9. Analyze how two or more texts address similar themes or topics in order to build knowledge or to compare the approaches the authors take.	**Student Edition:** *What Do You Think?:* Analyzing: 349, 443; Analyzing Information: 443; Contrasting: 17; Describing: 229, 359, 443; Evaluating: 229; Explaining: 229, 681; Identifying: 17, 359, 443; Identifying Central Issues: 681; Interpreting: 349; Making Inferences: 359, 681; Problem Solving: 17 *Text Features:* Thinking Like a Historian: 308 *Chapter Activities & Assessment:* Geography Activity: 22 **Teacher Edition:** **ENGAGE:** 228, 442 **TEACH & ASSESS:** V12, R16, 016, C124, W126, C200, C229, 0316, R358, R680, R681 **CLOSE & REFLECT:** 182, 229, 359 **INTERVENTION AND REMEDIATION STRATEGIES:** 337F
Range of Reading and Level of Text Complexity	
10. Read and comprehend complex literary and informational texts independently and proficiently.	**Student Edition:** *Reading Help Desk:* Reading Strategy: 145, 204, 426, 432 *The World's Literature:* Analyzing: 597; Assessing: 597; Describing: 85, 497; Identifying: 85; Identifying Points of View: 497; Interpreting: 597; Speculating: 85; Synthesizing: 497 *Text Features:* Infographic: 375 **Teacher Edition:** **ENGAGE:** 348, 496 **TEACH & ASSESS:** R16, 016, R17, 0216, 0218, C228, C229, 0486, R680, R681 **CLOSE & REFLECT:** 85, 497

Codes used for the Teacher Edition pages are the initial caps of the activities.

Discovering Our Past: A History of the World, Early Ages Correlated to Common Core State Standards

Common Core State Standards for English Language Arts and Literacy in History/Social Studies, Science, and Technical Subjects

Reading Standards for Literacy in History/Social Studies 6-8	
Key Ideas and Details	**Student Edition**
RH.6-8.1 Cite specific textual evidence to support analysis of primary and secondary sources.	*Step into the Place:* Critical Thinking: 26, 52, 172, 210, 246, 276, 304, 338, 370, 448; *Reading Help Desk:* Reading Strategy: 126, 194, 492, 702 *The World's Literature:* Analyzing: 597; Assessing: 597; Describing: 497; Identifying: 85; Identifying Point of View: 497; Interpreting: 597; Synthesizing: 497 *What Do You Think?:* Contrasting: 17; Describing: 229; Evaluating: 229; Explaining: 229, 681; Identifying: 17; Identifying Central Issues: 681; Making Inferences: 359, 681; Problem Solving: 17 *Lesson Review:* Analyzing: 107, 119, 127; Assessing: 21; Contrasting: 43; Describing: 147; Determining Cause and Effect: 61; Identifying: 69; Identifying Cause and Effect: 69, 498; Listing: 9, 21; Making Connections: 9, 61; Making Generalizations: 15; Making Inferences: 37 *Chapter Activities & Assessment:* 21st Century Skills: 300, 468; Thinking Like a Historian: 70 *DBQ:* Analyzing: 302, 470, 536, 706; Assessing: 302; Comparing: 368; Comparing and Contrasting: 274, 418, 536; Drawing Conclusions: 96, 136, 170, 208, 274, 368, 394, 446, 506, 638, 660, 706; Evaluating: 470; Finding the Main Idea: 660; Identifying: 208; Inferring: 136, 244, 394, 506; Making Inferences, 446, 578, 614, 638; Predicting: 244; Summarizing: 170, 336, 578, 614; Short Response: 24, 50, 72, 96, 136, 170, 208, 244, 274, 302, 336, 368, 394, 446, 470, 506, 536, 578, 614, 638
RH.6-8.2 Determine the central ideas or information of a primary or secondary source; provide an accurate summary of the source distinct from prior knowledge or opinions.	*Step into the Place:* Critical Thinking: 2, 74, 98, 138, 396, 420, 472, 508, 538, 580, 616, 640, 662 *Reading Help Desk:* Taking Notes: 4, 18, 28, 38, 44, 54, 62, 76, 86, 100, 108, 120, 128, 140, 148, 154, 160, 174, 183, 190, 198, 212, 220, 230, 236, 248, 257, 265, 278, 286, 292, 306, 312, 320, 328, 340, 350, 360, 372, 380, 386, 398, 404, 411, 422, 430, 436, 450, 459, 474, 482, 489, 510, 516, 520, 528, 540, 548, 556, 564, 570, 582, 589, 598, 606, 618, 624, 628, 642, 650, 664, 672, 682, 690, 696; Reading Strategy: 34, 80, 117, 122, 204, 234, 342, 362, 376, 423, 440, 522, 532, 552, 594, 600, 630, 684, 694 *The World's Literature:* Interpreting: 349 *Lesson Review:* Analyzing: 182, 197, 333, 488, 495, 527, 547, 569, 575, 695, 703; Assessing: 291, 679, 689, 703; Categorizing: 256; Comparing: 83, 93, 159, 219, 264, 385, 435, 458, 680; Comparing and Contrasting: 119, 133, 227, 391, 481, 569; Contrasting: 107, 347, 379, 467, 519, 533, 569, 595, 623, 703; Defending: 119; Defining: 649; Describing: 61, 83, 93, 119, 127, 189, 205, 227, 235, 241, 256, 271, 285, 299, 347, 357, 365, 379, 385, 403, 410, 415, 429, 435, 441, 467, 481, 488, 503, 515, 555, 563, 627, 657; Determining Cause and Effect: 21, 189, 197, 205, 271, 299, 403, 410, 527, 595, 605, 689, 695, 703; Differentiating: 197, 311, 347, 588, 623, 627, 679; Drawing Conclusions: 47, 133, 241, 264, 333, 365, 467, 519, 555, 671; Explaining: 93, 107, 127, 133, 147, 153, 159, 167, 182, 189, 197, 205, 219, 227, 241, 256, 264, 285, 291, 299, 311, 319, 327, 333, 357, 365, 379, 391, 403, 410, 415, 429, 435, 441, 458, 481, 488, 503, 515, 519, 533, 547, 563, 575, 588, 595, 611, 623, 627, 635, 649, 657; Evaluating: 495, 671, 679, 689; Finding the Main Idea: 37, 47, 695; Generalizing: 605; Identifying: 37, 83, 107, 147, 153, 159, 167, 189, 205, 219, 235, 271, 285, 291, 327, 347, 385, 415, 429, 441, 481, 495, 503, 515, 519, 527, 533, 547, 569, 575, 588, 605, 611, 623, 635, 649, 657; Identifying Cause and Effect: 365, 391, 410, 555, 563; Identifying Point of View: 689; Inferring: 69, 219, 627; Listing: 9, 533; Making Connections, 671; Making Inferences: 47, 385, 391, 595, 605, 611; Naming: 429; Paraphrasing: 291; Review Vocabulary: 311, 327, 333, 347, 357, 365, 379, 385, 391, 403, 410, 415, 429, 435, 441, 458, 467, 481, 488, 495, 503, 515, 519, 527, 533, 547, 555, 563, 569, 575, 588, 595, 605, 611, 623, 627, 635, 649, 657, 671, 679, 689, 695, 703; Sequencing: 441; Speculating: 488; Stating: 69; Summarizing: 43, 61, 127, 147, 182, 235, 256, 311, 319, 327, 357, 415, 435, 458, 495, 503, 515, 547, 555, 649, 657; Understanding Cause and Effect: 327 *Chapter Activities & Assessment:* 21st Century Skills: 134, 206, 242, 300, 468, 504, 576, 636, 658, 704; Thinking Like a Historian: 22, 48, 94, 134, 168, 206, 272, 300, 334, 392, 416, 444, 468, 504, 534, 576, 612, 636, 658, 704; Review the Guiding Questions: 23, 49, 71, 95, 135, 169, 207, 243, 273, 301, 335, 367, 393, 417, 445, 469, 505, 535, 577, 613, 637, 659, 705 ; DBQ: Drawing Conclusions: 50, 336; Explaining: 96; Finding the Main Idea: 50, 660; Identifying: 24, 72; Summarizing: 336, 418; Short Response: 136, 244, 418, 706; Extended Response: 170, 578
RH.6-8.3 Identify key steps in a text's description of a process related to history/social studies (e.g., how a bill becomes law, how interest rates are raised or lowered).	*Reading Help Desk:* Taking Notes: 10, 128 *Lesson Review:* Describing: 9; Drawing Conclusions: 15
Craft and Structure	
RH.6-8.4 Determine the meaning of words and phrases as they are used in a text, including vocabulary specific to domains related to history/social studies.	*Reading Help Desk:* Reading Strategy: 6, 8, 110, 116, 178, 193, 250, 262, 325, 361, 390, 457, 558, 682 *The World's Literature:* Interpreting: 597 *What Do You Think?:* Describing: 443 *Lesson Review:* Defining: 649; Explaining: 43; Review Vocabulary: 9, 15, 21, 37, 43, 47, 61, 69, 83, 93, 107, 119, 127, 133, 147, 153, 159, 167, 182, 189, 197, 205, 219, 227, 235, 241, 256, 264, 271, 285, 291, 299, 311, 319, 327, 333, 347, 357, 365, 379, 385, 391, 403, 410, 415, 429, 435, 441, 458, 467, 481, 488, 495, 503, 515, 519, 527, 533, 547, 555, 563, 569, 575, 588, 595, 605, 611, 627, 635, 649, 657, 671, 679, 689, 695, 703 *Chapter Activities & Assessment:* Review the Guiding Questions: 23, 49, 71, 207, 273, 301, 335, 367, 535, 577, 613, 705

Reading Standards for Literacy in History/Social Studies 6-8	
RH.6-8.5 Describe how a text presents information (e.g., sequentially, comparatively, causally).	*Reading Help Desk:* Taking Notes 498, 598, 606, 664; Reading Strategy: 560, 630 *Lesson Review:* Determining Cause and Effect: 403, 410, 595, 605, 689, 695, 703; Identifying Cause and Effect: 365, 391, 555, 563; Understanding Cause and Effect: 327 *Chapter Activities & Assessment:* 21st Century Skills: 366
RH.6-8.6 Identify aspects of a text that reveal an author's point of view or purpose (e.g., loaded language, inclusion or avoidance of particular facts).	*Reading Help Desk:* Reading Strategy: 654 *The World's Literature:* Analyzing: 597; Assessing: 597; Describing: 85; Identifying Points of View: 497; Interpreting: 597; Speculating: 85; Synthesizing: 497 *What Do You Think?:* Analyzing: 349, 44; Analyzing Information: 443; Describing: 229, 359; Explaining: 229; Identifying: 359; Interpreting: 349; Making Inferences: 359; Narrative Writing: 443 *Lesson Review:* Identifying Point of View: 689 *Chapter Activities & Assessment:* Thinking Like a Historian: 704 *DBQ:* Analyzing: 302, 470, 536, 706; Assessing: 302; Comparing: 368; Comparing and Contrasting: 274, 418, 536; Drawing Conclusions: 50, 208, 274, 336, 368, 394, 446, 506, 638, 660, 706; Evaluating: 470; Finding the Main Idea: 50, 660; *Identifying Point of View:* 24; Inferring: 136, 244, 394, 506; Making Inferences: 446, 578, 614, 638; Predicting: 244; Summarizing: 336, 418, 578, 614; Short Response: 50, 208, 302, 336, 394, 418, 446, 470, 506, 536, 578, 614, 638, 660, 706
Integration of Knowledge and Ideas	
RH.6-8.7 Integrate visual information (e.g., in charts, graphs, photographs, videos, or maps) with other information in print and digital texts.	*Step into the Place:* Analyzing Visuals: 2; Human-Environment Interaction: 370; Identifying: 2; Location: 52, 74, 98, 138, 172, 210, 246, 304, 338, 370, 396, 420, 448, 508, 538, 616, 640; Movement: 74, 338, 396, 616, 640; Place: 26, 52, 74, 98, 172, 210, 246, 276, 304, 338, 420, 448, 472, 508, 538, 580, 662; Regions: 138, 246, 396, 420, 472, 580, 640, 662 *Step into the Time:* 2, 26, 52, 74, 98, 138, 172, 210, 246, 276, 304, 338, 370, 396, 420, 448, 472, 508, 538, 580, 616, 640, 662 *Reading Help Desk:* Reading in the Content Areas: 354, 432; Reading Strategy: 131, 145 *Lesson Review:* Analyzing Visuals: 299; Explaining: 519; Identifying: 547 *Chapter Activities & Assessment:* 21st Century Skills: 392, 534, 612; Thinking Like a Historian: 612; Geography Activity: 22, 48, 70, 94, 134, 168, 206, 242, 272, 300, 334, 366, 392, 416, 444, 468, 504, 534, 576, 612, 636, 658, 704; Review the Guiding Questions: 49 *DBQ:* Making Connections: 72; Short Response: 706
RH.6-8.8 Distinguish among fact, opinion, and reasoned judgment in a text.	*Reading Help Desk:* Taking Notes: 230 *What Do You Think?:* Contrasting: 17 *Lesson Review:* Distinguishing Fact from Opinion: 319 *Chapter Activities & Assessment:* Thinking Like a Historian: 366; Review the Guiding Questions: 23; DBQ: Short Response: 24
RH.6-8.9 Analyze the relationship between a primary and secondary source on the same topic.	*What Do You Think?:* Describing: 229; Evaluating: 229; Explaining: 681; Identifying: 359; Identifying Central Issues: 681; Making Inferences: 681 *Lesson Review:* Assessing: 15; Making Inferences: 37 *Chapter Activities & Assessment:* Geography Activity: 22
Range of Reading and Level of Text Complexity	
RH.6-8.10 By the end of grade 8, read and comprehend history/social studies texts in the grades 6–8 text complexity band independently and proficiently	*The World's Literature:* Analyzing: 597; Assessing: 597; Describing: 497; Identifying Points of View: 497; Interpreting: 597; Synthesizing: 497

Discovering Our Past: A History of the World, Early Ages Correlated to Common Core State Standards

Common Core State Standards for English Language Arts and Literacy in History/Social Studies, Science, and Technical Subjects

The following pages contain correlation charts to the Common Core State Standards. The first chart contains the College and Career Readiness (CCR) Anchor Standards for Writing. The chart that follows the CCR Anchor Standards for Writing chart identifies specifically what students should understand and be able to do by the end of grades 6–8. The CCR and grade-specific standards are necessary complements—the former providing broad standards, the latter providing additional specificity—that together define the skills and understandings that all students must demonstrate.

College and Career Readiness Anchor Standards for Writing	
Text Types and Purposes	
1. Write arguments to support claims in an analysis of substantive topics or texts using valid reasoning and relevant and sufficient evidence.	**Student Edition:** *Lesson Review:* Argument: 21, 69, 83, 93, 127, 133, 167, 197, 227, 235, 241, 291, 311, 357, 365, 415, 481, 503, 519, 605, 649, 657, 671 *Chapter Activities & Assessment:* Exploring the Essential Questions: 334; 21st Century Skills: 272; Extended Response: 50, 274, 336, 706 **Teacher Edition:** TEACH & ASSESS: 017, W20, W43, W56, W83, W126, W141, W214, W229, W293, W295, W310, W321, W329, W349, 0359, W362, W398, W405, W409, W443, W494, W502, 0597, W598, W606, W698, W669, W692, W700 CLOSE & REFLECT: 189, 575 INTERVENTION AND REMEDIATION STRATEGIES: 73E, 275F, 337F, 419F, 471G PROJECT-BASED LEARNING: HOCP662
2. Write informative/explanatory texts to examine and convey complex ideas and information clearly and accurately through the effective selection, organization, and analysis of content.	**Student Edition:** *Step into the Time:* 210, 338, 370 *Thinking Like a Historian:* 41, 282 *Lesson Review:* Informative/Explanatory: 9, 15, 37, 43, 107, 119, 147, 159, 182, 205, 219, 256, 264, 285, 299, 319, 333, 347, 379, 391, 410, 435, 441, 458, 488, 527, 533, 547, 555, 563, 569, 575, 588, 595, 627, 679, 689, 695, 703 *Chapter Activities & Assessment:* Exploring the Essential Questions: 22, 70, 94, 134, 168, 206, 242, 272, 300, 366, 416, 444, 468, 504, 534, 576, 636, 658, 704; 21st Century Skills: 22, 70, 416, 444, 658; Extended Response: 96, 208, 302, 446, 506, 536, 578 **Teacher Edition:** ENGAGE: 209 TEACH & ASSESS: W13, W14, W18, W32, W47, W61, W69, W79, 091, 0100, W104, W129, W132, W143, 0148, W150, W154, W158, W163, W179, W224, W239, W259, W279, W281, W285, W308, W316, W331, W354, W363, W364, W378, W390, W407, W410, W413, W425, W431, W451, W477, W485, W515, W525, W530, W549, W554, W581, W587, W600, W604, W606, W625, W643, W652, W676, W682 CLOSE & REFLECT: 291, 319, 689 INTERVENTION AND REMEDIATION STRATEGIES: 25F, 73E, 137G, 209G, 245F, 369F, 395F, 419F, 471G, 507G, 537H, 615F PROJECT-BASED LEARNING: HOCP420, HOCP508, HOCP640
3. Write narratives to develop real or imagined experiences or events using effective technique, well-chosen details and well-structured event sequences.	**Student Edition:** *Lesson Review:* Narrative: 47, 61, 153, 189, 271, 327, 385, 403, 429, 467, 495, 515, 527, 533, 611, 623, 635 *Chapter Activities & Assessment:* Exploring the Essential Questions: 392, 612; 21st Century Skills: 48; Extended Response: 24, 72, 136, 170, 244, 368, 394, 418, 470, 614, 638, 660 **Teacher Edition:** TEACH & ASSESS: W31, W58, W65, W112, W118, W149, 0176, W186, T189, W194, W200, W233, W283, W286, W311, W343, W346, 0352, W375, W438, W462, W497, W518, W526, W551, W563, W567, W575, 0584, W590, W606, W621, W667, W697 INTERVENTION AND REMEDIATION STRATEGIES: 209G, 275F, 661H PROJECT-BASED LEARNING: HOCP448, HOCP538

Codes used for the Teacher Edition pages are the initial caps of the activities.

College and Career Readiness Anchor Standards for Writing	
Production and Distribution of Writing	
4. Produce clear and coherent writing in which the development, organization, and style are appropriate to task, purpose, and audience.	**Student Edition:** *Chapter Activities & Assessment:* Extended Response: 24, 50, 72, 96, 136, 170, 208, 244, 274, 302, 336, 368, 394, 418, 446, 470, 506, 536, 614, 638, 660 **Teacher Edition:** TEACH & ASSESS: W13, W14, 017, W18, W20, W31, W32, W43, W47, W56, W58, W61, W65, W69, W79, W83, 091, 0100, W104, W118, W126, W129, W132, W141, W143, 0148, W149, W150, W154, W158, W163, W179, W194, W200, W214, W224, W229, W233, W239, W259, W279, W281, W282, W285, W286, W293, W295, W308, W310, W311, W316, W321, W329, W331, W343, W346, W349, 0352, W354, 0359, W362, W363, W364, W375, W378, W390, W405, W407, W409, W410, W413, W425, W431, W438, W443, W451, W462, W477, W485, W494, W497, W502, W515, W518, W525, W526, W530, W549, W551, W554, W563, W567, W575, 0584, W587, W590, W598, W600, W604, W606, W621, W625, W630, W643, W648, W652, W669, W676, W677, W682, W683, W692, W697, W700 CLOSE & REFLECT: 189 INTERVENTION AND REMEDIATION STRATEGIES: 25F, 73E, 137G, 209G, 225F, 245F, 275F, 337F, 369F, 395F, 419F, 471G, 507G, 537H, 615F, 661H PROJECT-BASED LEARNING: HOCP420, HOCP448, HOCP508, HOCP538, HOCP640, HOCP662
5. Develop and strengthen writing as needed by planning, revising, editing, rewriting, or trying a new approach.	**Student Edition:** *Chapter Activities & Assessment:* Extended Response: 50, 72, 96, 136, 170, 208, 244, 274, 302, 336, 368, 394, 418, 446, 470, 506, 536, 614, 638, 660 **Teacher Edition:** PLACE & TIME: 0448 TEACH & ASSESS: W13, W14, 017, W18, W20, W31, W32, W43, W47, W56, W58, W61, W65, W69, W79, W83, 091, 0100, W104, W118, W126, W129, W132, W141, W143, 0148, W149, W150, W154, W158, W163, W179, W194, W200, W214, W224, W229, W233, W239, W259, W279, W281, W282, W285, W286, W293, W295, W308, W310, W311, W316, W321, W329, W331, W343, W346, W349, 0352, W354, 0359, W362, W363, W364, W375, W378, W390, W405, W407, W409, W410, W413, W425, W431, W438, W443, W451, W462, W477, W485, W494, W497, W502, W515, W518, W525, W526, W530, W549, W551, W554, W563, W567, W575, 0584, W587, W590, W598, W600, W604, W606, W621, W625, W630, W643, W648, W652, W669, W676, W677, W682, W683, W692, W697, W700 CLOSE & REFLECT: 189 INTERVENTION AND REMEDIATION STRATEGIES: 25F, 73E, 137G, 209G, 225F, 245F, 275F, 337F, 369F, 395F, 419F, 471G, 507G, 537H, 615F, 661H PROJECT-BASED LEARNING: HOCP420, HOCP448, HOCP508, HOCP538, HOCP640, HOCP662
6. Use technology, including the Internet, to produce and publish writing and to interact and collaborate with others.	**Student Edition:** *Thinking Like a Historian:* 67, 102, 177, 231, 252, 282, 342, 427, 555, 623 *Chapter Activities & Assessment:* 21st Century Skills: 94, 168, 242, 334, 392, 416, 504, 534, 612, 636, 658, 704; Thinking Like a Historian: 242; Review the Guiding Questions: 23 **Teacher Edition:** ENGAGE: 447 TEACH & ASSESS: T8, T15, T20, 029, W31, 034, T36, T41, T47, T59, T67, T91, T102, T105, T111, T115, T121, T126, T132, T143, 0144, T146, 0149, T153, T157, 0160, T162, T189, T293, T217, T234, 0260, T262, T267, T270, 0283, T289, T309, T318, T325, T330, 0343, T347, T385, T389, T400, T408, T412, T415, 0427, T441, T456, T465, T475, T526, T544, T552, T560, T564, T572, T584, T591, 0592, T593, T609, T622, T627, T646, T654, T668, T675, T687, T692 INTERVENTION AND REMEDIATION STRATEGIES: 25F, 51E, 419F, 471G, 507G, 537H, 579G, 615F PROJECT-BASED LEARNING: TE2, TE26, TE52, TE74, TE98, HOCP138, TE138, TE210, HOCP246, TE246, TE276, HOCP304, TE304, HOCP338, TE338, HOCP370, TE370, TE396, HOCP420, TE420, TE472, HOCP508, TE508, HOCP538, TE538, TE580, HOCP616, TE616, HOCP640, TE640, TE662

Codes used for the Teacher Edition pages are the initial caps of the activities.

College and Career Readiness Anchor Standards for Writing	
Research to Build and Present Knowledge	
7. Conduct short as well as more sustained research projects based on focused questions, demonstrating understanding of the subject under investigation.	**Student Edition:** *Thinking Like a Historian:* 41, 67, 102, 177, 231, 252, 282, 342, 427, 555, 623, 774 *Chapter Activities & Assessment:* 21st Century Skills: 22, 392, 416, 534, 612, 658, 740, 784; Thinking Like a Historian: 242, 334 **Teacher Edition:** TEACH & ASSESS: W14, R14, T15, W18, T20, 028, W31, T36, T41, T47, T59, 066, T67, T91, T105, T115, T121, T126, W126, W132, T146, T157, C160, T162, T217, $C_2$226, 0260, T262, T267, T270, 0283, T289, T309, T318, T330, 0343, T347, T385, T387, T400, T412, T415, 0427, T441, T465, T475, T526, T544, T552, T560, T564, T572, T584, T593, T609, 0609, T622, T627, T646, 0646, T654, T668, T675, T687, 0694, T702 CLOSE & REFLECT: 211 INTERVENTION AND REMEDIATION STRATEGIES: 25F, 51E, 245F, 275F, 303G, 337F, 369F, 419F, 471G, 507G, 537H, 579G, 615F PROJECT-BASED LEARNING: TE2, TE74, TE138, HOCP246, HOCP276, HOCP304, HOCP338, HOCP396, HOCP420, HOCP508, HOCP616, HOCP640
8. Gather relevant information from multiple print and digital sources, assess the credibility and accuracy of each source, and integrate the information while avoiding plagiarism.	**Student Edition:** *Thinking Like a Historian:* 20, 41, 67, 102, 177, 231, 252, 282, 308, 342, 427, 555, 623 *Chapter Activities & Assessment:* 21st Century Skills: 22, 334, 392, 416, 534, 612, 658; Thinking Like a Historian: 242; Review the Guiding Questions: 23 **Teacher Edition:** ENGAGE: 18 TEACH & ASSESS: 05, T8, R14, T15, $C_2$19, T20, C21, W31, T36, T41, T47, T59, T67, T91, C102, T192, 0102, T105, 0110, T111, 0114, T115, T121, T126, W126, W132, T146, T157, T162, T217, 0260, T267, T270, 0283, T289, T309, T318, T330, 0343, T385, T389, T400, T412, T415, 0427, T441, T456, T465, T475, T526, T544, T552, T560, T564, T572, T584, T593, T609, 0609, T622, T627, T646, C649, T654, T668, T675, T687, T702 INTERVENTION AND REMEDIATION STRATEGIES: 25F, 51E, 419F, 471G, 507G, 537H, 579G, 615F PROJECT-BASED LEARNING: HOCP2, TE74, TE138, HOCP246, HOCP276, HOCP304, HOCP338, TE396, HOCP420, HOCP508, HOPC616, HOCP640
9. Draw evidence from literary or informational texts to support analysis, reflection, and research.	**Student Edition:** *Thinking Like a Historian:* 41, 67, 102, 177, 231, 252, 282, 342, 427, 555, 623 *Chapter Activities & Assessment:* 21st Century Skills: 48, 334, 392, 416, 504, 534, 576, 612, 658; Thinking Like a Historian: 22, 70, 242, 416, 612, 704 **Teacher Edition:** TEACH & ASSESS: T15, W31, T36, T41, T47, T59, T67, T91, T105, T121, T126, W132, T146, T157, T162, T189, T217, T264, T270, 0283, T289, T309, T318, T330, 0343, T385, T389, T400, T412, T415, 0427, T441, T456, T465, T475, T526, T544, T552, T560, T564, T572, T584, T593, T609, 0609, T622, T627, T646, T654, T668, T675, T687, T702 CLOSE & REFLECT: 119 INTERVENTION AND REMEDIATION STRATEGIES: 25F, 51E, 209G, 419F, 471G, 507G, 537H, 579G, 615F PROJECT-BASED LEARNING: TE74, TE138, HOCP246, HOCP276, HOCP304, HOCP338, TE396, HOCP420, HOCP508, HOCP616, HOCP640

Codes used for the Teacher Edition pages are the initial caps of the activities.

College and Career Readiness Anchor Standards for Writing	
Range of Writing	
10. Write routinely over extended time frames (time for research, reflection, and revision) and shorter time frames (a single sitting or a day or two) for a range of tasks, purposes, and audiences.	**Student Edition:** *Step into the Time:* 210, 338, 370, 396, 448, 472, 508, 538, 580, 616, 640, 708 What Do You Think?: Read to Write: Personal: 443 *Thinking Like a Historian:* 41, 282 *Lesson Review:* Argument: 21, 69, 83, 93, 127, 133, 167, 197, 227, 235, 241, 291, 311, 357, 365, 415, 481, 503, 519, 605, 649, 657, 671; Informative/Explanatory: 9, 15, 37, 43, 107, 119, 147, 159, 182, 205, 219, 256, 264, 285, 299, 319, 333, 347, 379, 391, 410, 435, 441, 458, 488, 533, 547, 555, 563, 569, 575, 588, 595, 627, 679, 689, 695, 703; Narrative: 47, 61, 153, 189, 271, 327, 385, 403, 429, 467, 495, 515, 527, 611, 623, 635 *Chapter Activities & Assessment:* Exploring the Essential Questions: 22, 48, 70, 94, 134, 168, 206, 242, 272, 300, 334, 366, 392, 416, 444, 468, 504, 534, 576, 612, 636, 658, 704 *21st Century Skills:* 22, 70, 94, 134, 272, 334, 366, 416, 444, 576, 612, 658, 704; Thinking Like a Historian: 242; Extended Response: 24, 50, 72, 96, 136, 170, 208, 244, 274, 302, 336, 368, 394, 418, 446, 470, 506, 536, 578, 614, 638, 660, 706 **Teacher Edition:** **ENGAGE:** 44 **TEACH & ASSESS:** W13, W14, O17, W18, W20, W31, W32, W43, W47, W56, W58, W61, W65, W69, W79, W83, O91, O100, W104, W112, W118, W126, W129, W132, W141, W143, O148, W149, W150, W154, W158, W163, O176, W179, W186, W194, W200, W214, W224, W229, W233, W239, W259, W279, W281, W282, W283, W285, W286, W293, W295, W308, W310, W311, W316, W321, W329, W331, W343, W346, W349, O352, W354, O359, W362, W363, W364, W375, W378, W390, O597, W398, W405, W407, W409, W410, W413, W425, W431, W438, W443, W451, W462, W477, W485, W494, W497, W502, W515, W518, W525, W526, W530, W549, W551, W554, W563, W567, W575, O584, W587, W590, W598, W600, W604, W606, W621, W625, W630, W643, W648, W652, W669, W676, W677, W682, W683, W692, W697, W700 **CLOSE & REFLECT:** 189, 291, 319, 575 **INTERVENTION AND REMEDIATION STRATEGIES:** 25F, 73E,137G, 209G, 225F, 245F, 275F, 337F, 369F, 395F, 419F, 471G, 507G, 537H, 615F, 661H **PROJECT-BASED LEARNING:** HOCP276, HOCP420, HOCP488, HOCP508, HOCP538, HOCP662

Codes used for the Teacher Edition pages are the initial caps of the activities.

Discovering Our Past: A History of the World, Early Ages Correlated to Common Core State Standards

Common Core State Standards for English Language Arts & Literacy in History/Social Studies, Science, and Technical Subjects

Writing Standards for Literacy in History/Social Studies, Science, and Technical Subjects 6–8	
Text Types and Purposes	**Student Edition**
WHST.6-8.1 Write arguments focused on *discipline-specific content.*	*Lesson Review:* Argument: 21, 69, 83, 93, 127, 133, 167, 197, 227, 235, 241, 291, 311, 357, 365, 415, 481, 503, 519, 605, 649, 657, 671 *Chapter Activities & Assessment:* Exploring the Essential Questions: 334; Extended Response: 50, 274, 336, 706
WHST.6-8.2 Write informative/explanatory texts, including the narration of historical events, scientific procedures/ experiments, or technical processes.	*Step into the Time:* 370, 538, 616, 640 *Lesson Review:* Informative/Explanatory: 9, 15, 37, 43, 107, 119, 147, 159, 182, 205, 219, 256, 264, 285, 299, 319, 333, 347, 379, 391, 410, 435, 441, 458, 488, 533, 547, 555, 563, 569, 575, 588, 595, 627, 679, 689, 695 *Chapter Activities & Assessment:* Exploring the Essential Questions: 22, 48, 70, 94, 134, 168, 206, 242, 300, 366, 416, 444, 468, 504, 534, 576, 636, 658, 704 *21st Century Skills:* 416, 444, 658 *Thinking Like a Historian:* 242 *DBQ:* Extended Response: Informative/Explanatory: 96, 208, 302, 446, 506, 536 *Outlining a Reference Article:* 578
WHST.6-8.3 (See note; not applicable as a separate requirement)	**Note:** Students' narrative skills continue to grow in these grades. The Standards require that students be able to incorporate narrative elements effectively into arguments and informative/explanatory texts. In history/social studies, students must be able to incorporate narrative accounts into their analyses of individuals or events of historical import. In science and technical subjects, students must be able to write precise enough descriptions of the step-by-step procedures they use in their investigations or technical work that others can replicate them and (possibly) reach the same results.
Production and Distribution of Writing	
WHST.6-8.4 Produce clear and coherent writing in which the development, organization, and style are appropriate to task, purpose, and audience.	*Chapter Activities & Assessment:* Extended Response: 24, 50, 72, 96, 136, 170, 208, 244, 274, 302, 336, 368, 394, 418, 446, 470, 506, 536, 614, 638, 660, 706
WHST.6-8.5 With some guidance and support from peers and adults, develop and strengthen writing as needed by planning, revising, editing, rewriting, or trying a new approach, focusing on how well purpose and audience have been addressed.	*Chapter Activities & Assessment:* Extended Response: 24, 50, 72, 96, 136, 170, 208, 244, 274, 302, 336, 368, 394, 418, 446, 470, 506, 536, 614, 638, 660, 706
WHST.6-8.6 Use technology, including the Internet, to produce and publish writing and present the relationships between information and ideas clearly and efficiently.	*Chapter Activities & Assessment:* 21st Century Skills: 94, 168, 242, 416, 504, 612, 636, 658, 704; Thinking Like a Historian: 242
Research to Build and Present Knowledge	
WHST.6-8.7 Conduct short research projects to answer a question (including a self-generated question), drawing on several sources and generating additional related, focused questions that allow for multiple avenues of exploration.	*Chapter Activities & Assessment:* 21st Century Skills: 22, 334, 392, 416, 534, 612, 658
WHST.6-8.8 Gather relevant information from multiple print and digital sources, using search terms effectively; assess the credibility and accuracy of each source; and quote or paraphrase the data and conclusions of others while avoiding plagiarism and following a standard format for citation.	*Chapter Activities & Assessment:* 21st Century Skills: 22, 334, 392, 416, 534; Review the Guiding Questions: 23
WHST.6-8.9 Draw evidence from informational texts to support analysis, reflection, and research.	*Reading Help Desk:* Taking Notes: 372, 380, 386 *Chapter Activities & Assessment:* 21st Century Skills: 48, 134, 334, 392, 416, 504, 534, 576, 612, 658; Thinking Like a Historian: 70, 416, 612, 704; Short Response: 706

Writing Standards for Literacy in History/Social Studies, Science, and Technical Subjects 6–8	
Range of Writing	
WHST.6-8.10 Write routinely over extended time frames (time for reflection and revision) and shorter time frames (a single sitting or a day or two) for a range of discipline-specific tasks, purposes, and audiences.	*Step into the Time:* 210, 338, 370, 396, 448, 472, 508, 538, 580, 616, 640 *What Do You Think?:* Read to Write: Narrative: 443 *Lesson Review:* Argument: 21, 69, 83, 93, 127, 133, 167, 197, 227, 235, 241, 291, 311, 357, 365, 415, 481, 503, 519, 605, 649, 657, 671; Informative/ Explanatory: 9, 15, 37, 43, 107, 119, 147, 159, 182, 205, 219, 256, 264, 285, 299, 319, 333, 347, 379, 391, 410, 435, 441, 458, 488, 533, 547, 555, 563, 569, 575, 588, 595, 627, 679, 689, 695; Narrative: 47, 61, 153, 189, 271, 327, 385, 403, 429, 467, 495, 527, 611, 623, 635, 703 *Chapter Activities & Assessment:* Exploring the Essential Questions: 22, 48, 70, 94, 134, 168, 206, 242, 272, 300, 334, 366, 392, 416, 444, 468, 504, 534, 576, 612, 636, 658, 704; 21st Century Skills: 70, 94, 134, 272, 334, 366, 416, 444, 476, 612, 658, 704; Thinking Like a Historian: 242; Extended Response: 24, 50, 72, 96, 136, 170, 208, 244, 274, 302, 336, 368, 394, 418, 446, 470, 506, 536, 570, 614, 638, 660, 706

professional development

UNDERSTANDING BY DESIGN®

by Jay McTighe

Understanding by Design® (UbD™) offers a planning framework to guide curriculum, assessment, and instruction. Its two key ideas are contained in the title: 1) focus on teaching and assessing for understanding and transfer, and 2) design curriculum "backward" from those ends.

UbD is based on seven key tenets:

1. UbD is a way of thinking purposefully about curricular planning, not a rigid program or prescriptive recipe.
2. A primary goal of UbD is developing and deepening student understanding: the ability to make meaning of learning via "big ideas" and transfer learning.
3. Understanding is revealed when students autonomously make sense of and transfer their learning through authentic performance. Six facets of understanding—the capacity to explain, interpret, apply, shift perspective, empathize, and self assess—serve as indicators of understanding.
4. Effective curriculum is planned "backward" from long-term desired results though a three-stage design process (Desired Results, Evidence, Learning Plan). This process helps to avoid the twin problems of "textbook coverage" and "activity-oriented" teaching in which no clear priorities and purposes are apparent.
5. Teachers are coaches of understanding, not mere purveyors of content or activity. They focus on ensuring learning, not just teaching (and assuming that what was taught was learned); they always aim and check for successful meaning making and transfer by the learner.
6. Regular reviews of units and curriculum against design standards enhance curricular quality and effectiveness.
7. UbD reflects a continuous improvement approach to achievement. The results of our designs —student performance—inform needed adjustments in curriculum as well as instruction.

Three Stages of Backward Design

In UbD, we propose a 3-stage "backward design" process for curriculum planning. The concept of planning "backward" from desired results is not new. In 1949 Ralph Tyler described this approach as an effective process for focusing instruction. More recently, Stephen Covey, in the best selling book, *Seven Habits of Highly Effective People*, reports that effective people in various fields are goal-oriented and plan with the end in mind. Although not a new idea, we have found that the deliberate use of backward design for planning curriculum units and courses results in more clearly defined goals, more appropriate assessments, more tightly aligned lessons, and more purposeful teaching.

Backward planning asks educators to consider the following three stages:

Stage 1 – Identify Desired Results

What should students know, understand, and be able to do? What content is worthy of understanding? What "enduring" understandings are desired? What essential questions will be explored?

In the first stage of backward design we consider our goals, examine established Content Standards (national, state, province, district), and review curriculum expectations. Since there is typically more "content" than can reasonably be addressed within the available time, teachers must make choices. This first stage in the design process calls for setting priorities.

More specifically, Stage 1 of UbD asks teachers to identify the "big ideas" that we want students to come to understand, and then to identify or craft companion essential questions. Big ideas reflect transferable concepts, principles and processes that are key to understanding the topic or subject. Essential questions present open-ended, thought-provoking inquiries that are explored over time.

More specific knowledge and skill objectives, linked to the targeted Content Standards and Understandings, are also identified in Stage 1. An important point in UbD is to recognize that factual knowledge and skills are not taught for their own sake, but as a means to larger ends. Ultimately, teaching should equip learners to be able to use or transfer their learning; i.e., meaningful performance with content. This is the "end" we always want to keep in mind.

Stage 2 – Determine Acceptable Evidence

How will we know if students have achieved the desired results? What will we accept as evidence of student understanding and proficiency? How will we evaluate student performance?

Backward design encourages teachers and curriculum planners to first "think like an assessor" before designing specific units and lessons. The assessment evidence we need reflects the desired results identified in Stage 1. Thus, we consider in advance the assessment evidence needed to document and validate that the targeted learning has been achieved. Doing so invariably sharpens and focuses teaching.

In Stage 2, we distinguish between two broad types of assessment—Performance Tasks and Other Evidence. The performance tasks ask students to apply their learning to a new and authentic situation as means of assessing their understanding. In UbD, we have identified six facets of understanding for assessment purposes[1]. When someone truly understands, they:

- Can **explain** concepts, principles and processes; i.e., put it in their own words, teach it to others, justify their answers, show their reasoning.
- Can **interpret**; i.e., make sense of data, text, and experience through images, analogies, stories, and models.
- Can apply; i.e., effectively use and adapt what they know in new and complex contexts.
- Demonstrate **perspective**; i.e., can see the big picture and recognize different points of view.
- Display **empathy**; i.e., perceive sensitively and "walk in someone else's shoes."
- Have **self-knowledge**; i.e., show metacognition, use productive habits of mind, and reflect on the meaning of their learning and experience.

These six facets do not present a theory of how people come to understand something. Instead, the facets are intended to serve as indicators of how understanding is revealed, and thus provide guidance as to the kinds of assessments we need to determine the extent of student understanding. Here are two notes regarding assessing understanding through the facets:

1) All six facets of understanding need not be used all of the time in assessment. In social studies, Empathy and Perspective may be added when appropriate.

2) Performance Tasks based on one or more facets are not intended for use in daily lessons. Rather, these tasks should be seen as culminating performances for a unit of study.

In addition to Performance Tasks, Stage 2 includes Other Evidence, such as traditional quizzes, tests, observations, and work samples to round out the assessment picture to

Examples of Essential Questions in Social Studies	
Understandings or Big Ideas	**Essential Questions**
History involves interpretation, and different people may interpret the same events differently.	*Whose "story" is this? How do we know what really happened in the past?*
The geography, climate, and natural resources of a region influence the culture, economy, and lifestyle of its inhabitants.	*How does where we live influence how we live?*
History often repeats itself. Recognizing the patterns of the past can help us better understand the present and prepare for the future.	*Why study the past? What does the past have to do with today?*
Governments can change based on the changing needs of their people, the society, and the world.	*What makes an effective government? Why do/should governments change?*

[1] Wiggins, G. and McTighe, J. and (1998, 2005). *Understanding by Design.* Alexandria, VA: The Association for Supervision and Curriculum Development.

professional development

UNDERSTANDING BY DESIGN®

(continued)

determine what students know and can do. A key idea in backward design has to do with alignment. In other words, are we assessing everything that we are trying to achieve (in Stage 1) or only those things that are easiest to test and grade? Is anything important slipping through the cracks because it is not being assessed? Checking the alignment between Stages 1 and 2 helps insure that *all* important goals are appropriately assessed.

Stage 3 – Plan Learning Experiences and Instruction

How will we support learners in coming to an understanding of important ideas and processes? How will we prepare them to autonomously transfer their learning? What enabling knowledge and skills will students need in order to perform effectively and achieve desired results? What activities, sequence, and resources are best suited to accomplish our goals?

In Stage 3 of backward design, teachers now plan the most appropriate learning activities to help students acquire important knowledge and skills, come to understand important ideas and processes, and transfer their learning in meaningful ways. When developing a plan for learning, we propose that teachers consider a set of instructional principles, embedded in the acronym W.H.E.R.E.T.O. These design elements provide the armature or blueprint for instructional planning in Stage 3 in support of our goals of understanding and transfer.

Each of the W.H.E.R.E.T.O. elements is presented in the form of questions to consider.

W = *How will I help learners know – What they will be learning? Why this is worth learning? What evidence will show their learning? How will their performance be evaluated?*

Learners of all ages are more likely to put forth effort and meet with success when they understand the learning goals and see them as meaningful and personally relevant. The "W" in W.H.E.R.E.T.O. reminds teachers to clearly communicate the goals and help students see their relevance. In addition, learners need to know the concomitant performance expectations and assessments through which they will demonstrate their learning so that they have clear learning targets and the basis for monitoring their progress toward them.

H = *How will I hook and engage the learners?*

There is wisdom in the old adage: "Before you try to teach them, you've got to get their attention." The best teachers have always recognized the value of "hooking" learners through introductory activities that "itch" the mind and engage the heart in the learning process, and we encourage teachers to deliberately plan ways of hooking their learners to the topics they teach. Examples of effective hooks include provocative essential questions, counter-intuitive phenomena, controversial issues, authentic problems and challenges, emotional encounters, and humor. One must be mindful, of course, of not just coming up with interesting introductory activities that have no carry-over value. The intent is to match the hook with the content and

PHOTO: Banana Stock/Picture Quest

the experiences of the learners—by design—as a means of drawing them into a productive learning experience.

E = *How will I equip students to master identified standards and succeed with the transfer performances? What learning experiences will help develop and deepen understanding of important ideas?*

Understanding cannot be simply transferred like a load of freight from one mind to another. Coming to understand requires active intellectual engagement on the part of the learner. Therefore, instead of merely covering the content, effective educators "uncover" the most enduring ideas and processes in ways that engage students in constructing meaning for themselves. To this end, teachers select an appropriate balance of constructivist learning experiences, structured activities, and direct instruction for helping students acquire the desired knowledge, skill, and understanding. While there is certainly a place for direct instruction and modeling, teaching for understanding asks teachers to engage learners in making meaning through active inquiry.

R = *How will I encourage the learners to rethink previous learning? How will I encourage on-going revision and refinement?*

Few learners develop a complete understanding of abstract ideas on the first encounter. Indeed, the phrase "coming to understand" is suggestive of a process. Over time, learners develop and deepen their understanding by thinking and re-thinking, by examining ideas from a different point of view, from examining underlying assumptions, by receiving feedback and revising. Just as the quality of writing benefits from the iterative process of drafting and revising, so to do understandings become more mature. The "R" in W.H.E.R.E.T.O. encourages teachers to explicitly include such opportunities.

E = *How will I promote students' self-evaluation and reflection?*

Capable and independent learners are distinguished by their capacity to set goals, self-assess their progress, and adjust as needed. Yet, one of the most frequently overlooked aspects of the instructional process involves helping students to develop the metacognitive skills of self-evaluation, self-regulation, and reflection. The second "E" of WHERETO reminds teachers to build in time and expectations for students to regularly self-assess, reflect on the meaning of their learning, and set goals for future performance.

T = *How will I tailor the learning experiences to the nature of the learners I serve? How might I differentiate instruction to respond to the varied needs of students?*

"One size fits all teaching" is rarely optimal. Learners differ significantly in terms of their prior knowledge and skill levels, their interests, talents, and preferred ways of learning. Accordingly, the most effective teachers get to know their students and tailor their teaching and learning experiences to connect to them. A variety of strategies may be employed to differentiate *content* (e.g., how subject matter is presented), *process* (e.g., how students work), and *product* (e.g., how learners demonstrate their learning). The logic of backward design offers a cautionary note here: the Content Standards and Understandings should *not* be differentiated (except for students with Individualized Education Plans —I.E.P.s). In other words, differentiate means keeping the end in mind for all.

O = *How will I organize the learning experiences for maximum engagement and effectiveness? What sequence will be optimal given the understanding and transfer goals?*

When the primary educational goals involve helping students acquire basic knowledge and skills, teachers may be comfortable "covering" the content by telling and modeling.

However, when we include understanding and transfer as desired results, educators are encouraged to give careful attention to how the content is organized and sequenced. Just as effective story tellers and filmmakers often don't begin in the "beginning," teachers can consider alternatives to sequential content coverage. For example, methods such as the Case Method, Problem or Project-Based Learning, and Socratic Seminars immerse students in challenging situations, even before they may have acquired all of the "basics." They actively engage students in trying to make meaning and apply their learning in demanding circumstances without single "correct" answers.

Conclusion

Many teachers who are introduced to the backward design process have observed that while the process makes sense in theory, it often feels awkward in use. This is to be expected since the principles and practices of UbD often challenge conventional planning and teaching habits. However, with some practice, educators find that backward design becomes not only more comfortable, but a way of thinking. The resources found in this program support teaching and assessing for understanding and transfer.

professional development

WHY TEACH WITH TECHNOLOGY?

by Tom Daccord and Justin Reich, EdTechTeacher

✓ **Technology is transforming the practice of historians and should transform history classrooms as well.** While printed documents, books, maps, and artwork constitute the bulk of the historical record before 1900, the history of the last century is also captured in sound and video recording and in Web sites and other Internet resources. Today's students need to learn how to analyze and build arguments using these multimedia records as well as traditional primary sources.

✓ **So many of the sources that helped historians and history teachers fall in love with the discipline are now available online.** In recent decades, universities, libraries, archives, and other institutions have scanned and uploaded many vast treasure troves of historical sources. The Internet-connected classroom increasingly has access to the world's historical record, giving students a chance to develop critical thinking skills as well as learning historical narratives.

✓ **Whoever is doing most of the talking or most of the typing is doing most of the learning, and the more people listening the better.** Technology allows us to transfer the responsibility for learning from teachers to students, and to put students in the driver's seat of their own learning. Students who are actively engaged in creating and presenting their understandings of history are learning more than students passively listening. Technology also allows students to publish their work to broader audiences of peers, parents, and even the entire Internet-connected world. Students find the opportunities challenging, exciting, and engaging.

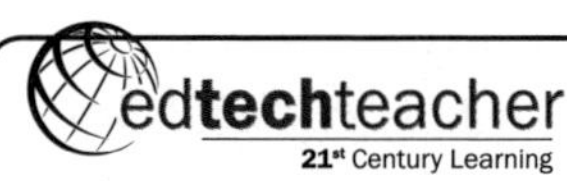

Technology Extension

- Find an additional activity online that incorporates technology for this project.
- Visit the EdTechTeacher Web sites (included in the Technology Extension for this chapter) for more links, tutorials, and other resources.

Teaching With Technology

In addition to the many other online resources embedded in this program, EdTechTeacher Technology Extensions are provided for every Hands-On Chapter Project. These detailed instructions and inspiration help history teachers creatively and effectively integrate technology in their classrooms. Each Technology Extension describes a technology project, explains the rationale for the suggested technology, and provides guidelines for classroom teachers to help conduct and facilitate the activity. Each Technology Extension also provides links to pages on Teaching History with Technology (www.thwt.org) with up-to-date tutorials, guides, links to examples, and exemplary projects.

✓ **The more ways students have to engage with content, the more likely they are to remember and understand that content.** The Internet can provide students and teachers with access to text documents, images, sounds and songs, video, simulations, and games. The more different ways students engage with historical content, the more likely they are to make meaning of that material.

✓ **Students live in a technology-rich world, and classrooms should prepare students for that world.** When students spend most of their waking hours connected to a worldwide, online network of people, resources, and opportunities, they experience dissonance and disappointment in entering a "powered-down" school. Many students will leave school to go on to workplaces completely transformed by technology, and teachers have a responsibility to prepare students for these environments.

Integrating Technology Effectively

Ben Shneiderman, in his book *Leonardo's Laptop,* lays out a four-part framework for teaching with technology: Collect-Relate-Create-Donate. This framework is a helpful blueprint for designing projects and learning experiences with technology.

Collect Students should begin a project by collecting the resources necessary to produce a meaningful presentation of their understanding. In some cases, students might collect these resources through textbook reading and teacher lecture, but students should also collect resources from online collections, school library Web sites, and online searches.

Relate Technology greatly facilitates the process of students working together socially. The ability to collaborate is essential to the workplace and civic sphere of the future. In creating technology projects, students should have the chance to work together, or at least comment on each other's work, using blogs, wikis, podcasts, and other collaborative publishing tools.

Create Using multimedia publishing tools, students should have the opportunity to design presentations and performances of their historical understanding. They should make historical arguments in linear text, as well as through images, audio and video recordings, and multimedia presentations.

Donate Finally, students should create work not just for their teachers, but for broader audiences. Students who have a chance to share their work with their peers, their families, their community, and the Internet-connected world find that opportunity rewarding. Today's students experience very few barriers to expression in their networked lives, and they crave these opportunities in schools.

Guidelines for Successful Technology Projects

1) **Plan for problems.** Things can go wrong when working with technology, and learning how to deal with these challenges is essential for students, and for their teachers. As you start using technology in the classroom, try to have an extra teacher, aide, student-teacher, or IT staff member in the room with you to help troubleshoot problems. When things do go wrong, stay calm, and ask your students to help you resolve challenges and make the most of class time. Always have a back up, "pencil and paper" activity prepared in case there are problems with computers or networks. Over time, teachers who practice teaching with technology experience fewer and fewer of these problems, but they can be very challenging the first time you experience them!

2) **Practice from multiple perspectives.** Whenever you develop a technology project, try to do everything that students will do from a student's perspective. If you create a blog or wiki with a teacher account, create a student account to test the technology.

3) **Adapt to your local technology resources, but don't let those resources keep you from using technology.** Some schools have excellent and ample technology resources—labs and laptop carts—that make completing technology projects straightforward. Other schools have fewer resources, but virtually every student can get access to a networked computer in school, at the library or at home, especially if you give them a few nights to do so. Many technology activities are described as if you could complete them in a few class periods, but if resources are limited, you might consider spreading the activity out over a few days or weeks to give students the chance to get online.

4) **Plan with a partner.** Going it alone can be scary. If possible, have another teacher in your department or on your team, design and pilot technology projects with you to help solve the challenges that crop up whenever trying out new pedagogies.

5) **It's harder, then it gets easier.** Learning new teaching strategies is always hard. With technology, however, once you get past the initial learning curve there are all sorts of ways technology can make teaching more efficient and simultaneously make learning more meaningful for students.

Learn More about Teaching History with Technology

EdTechTeacher has several Web sites designed to help social studies and history teachers learn more about teaching with technology. The Best of History Web Sites (www.besthistorysites.net) is the Internet's authoritative directory of history-related resources, Web sites, games, simulations, lesson plans, and activities. Teaching History with Technology (www.thwt.org) has a series of white papers, tutorials, and guides for enriching history teaching strategies (lecturing, discussion, presentations, assessments, and so forth) with educational technology. EdTechTeacher (www.edtechteacher.org) has additional teaching resources and information about learning opportunities such as free webinars and other professional development workshops.

Tom Daccord and Justin Reich are co-Directors of EdTechTeacher. Together they authored Best Ideas for Teaching With Technology: A Practical Guide for Teachers by Teachers.

BACKGROUND KNOWLEDGE: THE KEY TO UNDERSTANDING

by Douglas Fisher, Ph.D., and Nancy Frey, Ph.D.

Mention background knowledge and most middle school educators will tell you that it is an essential component of history and social studies learning. They will discuss the importance of activating it in their students and building it when there are gaps. Yet most will also confess to being unsure of how to accomplish this in a systematic way beyond asking some questions about prior experiences. As for the gaps, how can anyone find the time to build it when there is so much new information to be covered?

The answer is to integrate background knowledge activation, building, and assessment into the heart of the lesson, not just as bookends to new learning. The reasons for this are pretty striking. Background knowledge directly influences a learner's ability to understand new information and act upon it (RAND Reading Study Group, 2002). In addition, background knowledge is demonstrated through the use of academic vocabulary and academic language, an important measure of content learning (Cromley & Azevedo, 2007). Finally, students with strong background knowledge about a topic process text better, especially in their ability to monitor and correct comprehension difficulties (Cakir, 2008).

Cultivating Background Knowledge

The key to understanding new information is to link it to what is already known. A feature of initial learning is that we aren't very good at doing so. Our efforts to focus on what is unfamiliar temporarily blind us to what we already know. It is helpful to have well-placed reminders about what is already known, because it assists us in marshalling the familiar in order to understand the new.

When we ask questions of students about prior experiences, or invite them to engage in a quickwrite about a previously taught topic, we are activating their background knowledge. More importantly, we are providing the signposts they need to direct them to the most salient information they will need to learn the new material. For example, a study of ancient Rome doesn't merely begin with the legendary founding of a great city by two boys raised by wolves. It also requires knowledge of the influence of ancient Greek civilization on Rome's governance, military, art, and culture. It is easy, however, for students to temporarily forget everything they have learned about Greece in their effort to assimilate new information. Well-placed questions, writing opportunities, and graphic organizers can remind them of what they have previously learned.

Another means for cultivating background knowledge is to assess what students know (or think they know) about a topic. This shouldn't be a quiz of isolated facts, but instead should focus on the anticipated misconceptions that a learner is likely to hold about a new topic. For instance, it is easy for students to confuse what they have learned about Greek mythology when learning about Roman gods and goddesses. Those terms (gods and goddesses) alone suggest that for Romans this was at the heart of their religious beliefs. But Roman mythology differs from Greek mythology. For Greeks, mythology formed the heart of religion. For Romans, the gods and goddesses made for good stories, but weren't necessarily worshiped. Posing questions that are designed to surface misconceptions such as this help to rectify incorrect perceptions before they are ingrained.

Assessing Background Knowledge

Despite the efforts of caring educators, families, and communities, students come to us with gaps in their background knowledge. This can be due to a variety of causes, including frequent moves, second language acquisition, lack of experience with a topic, or difficulty with the content itself. Students at the middle school level face the additional well-documented challenges of transitioning from elementary school, where one teacher made connections for them to background knowledge, to a middle school schedule with many teachers and content areas. These changes require them to make more of their own connections across subjects.

In addition, a middle school schedule leaves us with less time across the day to get to know our students and the background knowledge they possess. It is useful to have formative assessment embedded into lessons in order to gauge where gaps might exist.

Activities that draw on core background knowledge necessary for deep understanding of new information provide these opportunities. Lessons that invite students to construct graphic organizers using both new knowledge and background knowledge give us such a window. A well-placed question invites students to consider what they already know.

If and when students have difficulty with activities like this, the teacher can pause to supply missing background knowledge. This may be done through direct explanation, by drawing their attention to features in the text, and even to returning to a previous chapter to revisit information. These need not be seen as delays, but rather as time well spent to solidify foundational knowledge.

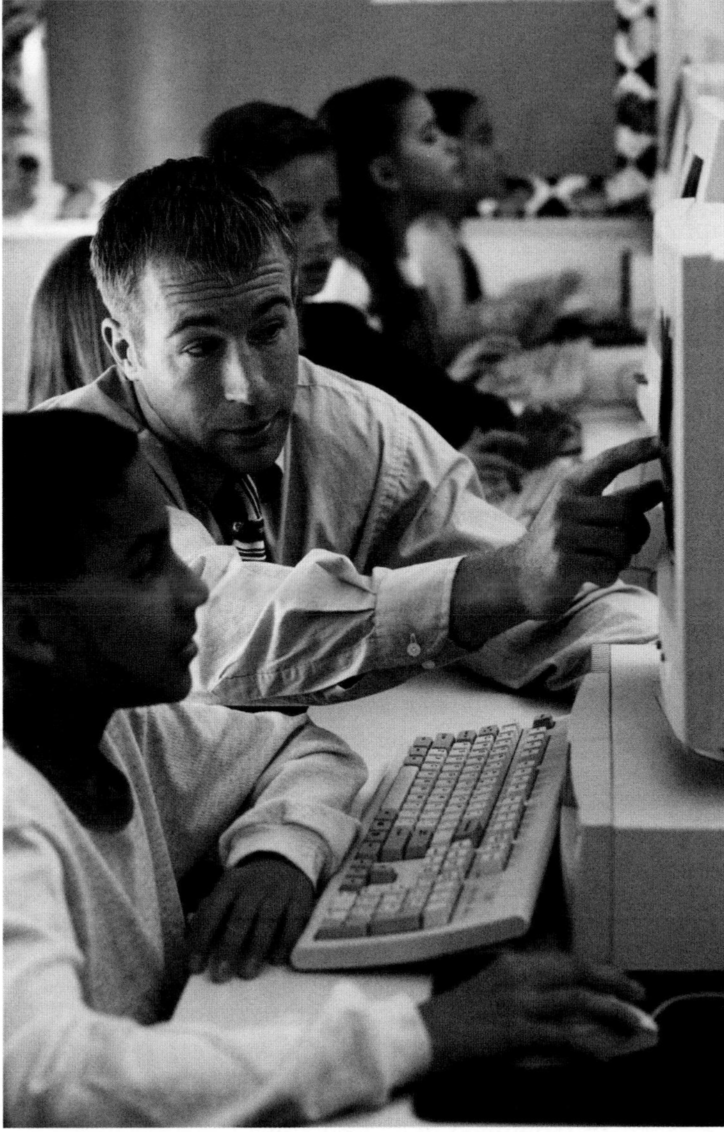

PHOTO: SW Productions/Getty Images

Building Background Knowledge

Effective middle school educators take a proactive stance to building background knowledge by creating opportunities to do so. They conduct read alouds and shared readings of text and provide visual information to build students' mental image banks. Texts and images related to necessary background knowledge are especially useful in history and social studies, where students are required to understand and use primary source documents. A challenge is that many of these are hard for students to make sense of on their own, as they often use archaic language and represent ideas that are not contemporary to adolescent lives. Texts and images carefully selected with middle school students in mind can build their background knowledge of the people and times being studied, and help them more fully appreciate the influences one culture has upon another. For example, illustrations of Greek and Roman architecture invite comparison. Maps of the ancient world highlight why empires fought over land.

Student background knowledge is also built through deeper understanding of the academic vocabulary and language that lies at the heart of history and social studies. By using a think aloud technique, teachers build their students' background knowledge about the derivation of the term, as well as the way they approach an unfamiliar word. This ensures that students will recall the term more precisely while also equipping them with a problem-solving strategy to apply to other new words.

Conclusion

McGraw-Hill **networks** learning system offers middle school educators the tools needed to activate, assess, and build student background knowledge by infusing approaches like this into the lesson design. The habit of mind of drawing on what one already knows and seeking information to fill in knowledge gaps begins with educators like you who show students how this is done.

Douglas Fisher, Ph.D., and Nancy Frey, Ph.D., are professors in the School of Teacher Education at San Diego State University.

Cakir, O. (2008). The effect of textual differences on children's processing strategies. *Reading Improvement, 45*(2), 69-83.

Cromley, J. G., & Azevedo, R. (2007). Testing and refining the direct and inferential mediation model of reading comprehension. *Journal of Educational Psychology, 99*(2), 311-325.

RAND *Reading Study Group. (2002). Reading for understanding: Toward an R&D program in reading comprehension.* Office of Educational Research and Improvement. Santa Monica, CA: RAND.

USING FOLDABLES® IN THE CLASSROOM

by Rhonda Meyer Vivian, Ph.D., and Nancy F. Wisker, M.A.

Graphic Organizers

Current research shows that graphic organizers are powerful teaching and learning tools. Most of us are familiar with common graphic organizers such as diagrams, maps, outlines, and charts, all of which are two-dimensional. Foldables® are three-dimensional, interactive graphic organizers that were created more than 30 years ago by educator Dinah Zike.

Graphic organizers are visual representations combining line, shape, space, and symbols to convey facts and concepts or to organize information. Graphic organizers, when designed and used appropriately:

- Speed up communication
- Help organize information
- Are easy-to-understand
- Show complex relationships
- Clarify concepts with few words
- Convey ideas and understanding
- Assess comprehension

Graphic organizers help students organize information in a visual manner. This is a profound concept, especially as the number of non-native English-speaking students increases. A student is able to use graphic organizers to clarify concepts or to convey ideas and understandings with fewer words.

Graphic organizers also make complex relationships or concepts easier to understand, particularly for visual learners. Foldables take that process to the next level, most notably, for tactile/kinesthetic learners.

When to Use Graphic Organizers

Graphic organizers may be used at any point during instruction, but just as with any other instructional strategy, they are most successful when they are built into the instructional plan, rather than presented as an 'extra' activity.

Graphic organizers may work better than outline notes in helping students discover or understand relationships between concepts. Foldables help teach students how to take notes by visually and kinesthetically chunking information into sections.

Foldables may be used as an alternative form of assessment in the classroom. Because the Foldable has readily identifiable sections, a teacher can quickly see gaps in student knowledge.

Reading, Writing, and Social Studies

Graphic organizers have been shown to be highly effective in literacy development. In numerous studies, graphic organizers help improve the development of literacy skills—including oral, written, and comprehension.

Graphic organizers have been found to help students organize information from expository social studies texts and comprehend content area reading. They also help students develop critical thinking skills and help transfer these skills to new situations and content areas.

Students With Special Needs

Graphic organizers may help English language learners improve higher-order thinking skills.

Because of their visual organization, graphic organizers seem to be quite beneficial for use with learning disabled students. They appear to help students understand content area material, to organize information, and to retain and recall content.

Conclusions

Graphic organizers may lead to improved student performance, whether measured by classroom-based observation, textbook assessments, or standardized assessments, when compared with more traditional forms of instruction.

When students construct their own graphic organizers, as they do with Foldables, they are active participants in their learning.

Our goal as educators is to help students glean important information and understand key concepts and to be able to relate these concepts or apply them to real-world situations. Graphic organizers help support and develop students' note-taking skills, summarizing skills, reading comprehension, and vocabulary development, which leads to better understanding and application of social studies content.

Dinah Zike is an award-winning author, educator, educational consultant, and inventor, known internationally for graphic organizers known as Foldables®. Based outside of San Antonio, Texas, Zike is a frequent keynote speaker and conducts seminars for over 50,000 teachers and parents annually.

Rhonda Myer Vivian, Ph.D., is CEO of Dinah-Might Adventures, LP, and Nancy F. Whisker, M.A., is Director of Math and Science for Dinah-Might Adventures, L.P.

FOLDABLES®

Notebook Foldables®

Using Foldables® in the *Reading Essentials and Study Guide* will help your students develop note-taking and critical thinking skills while directly interacting with the text.

Templates allow students to make their own Notebook Foldables®.

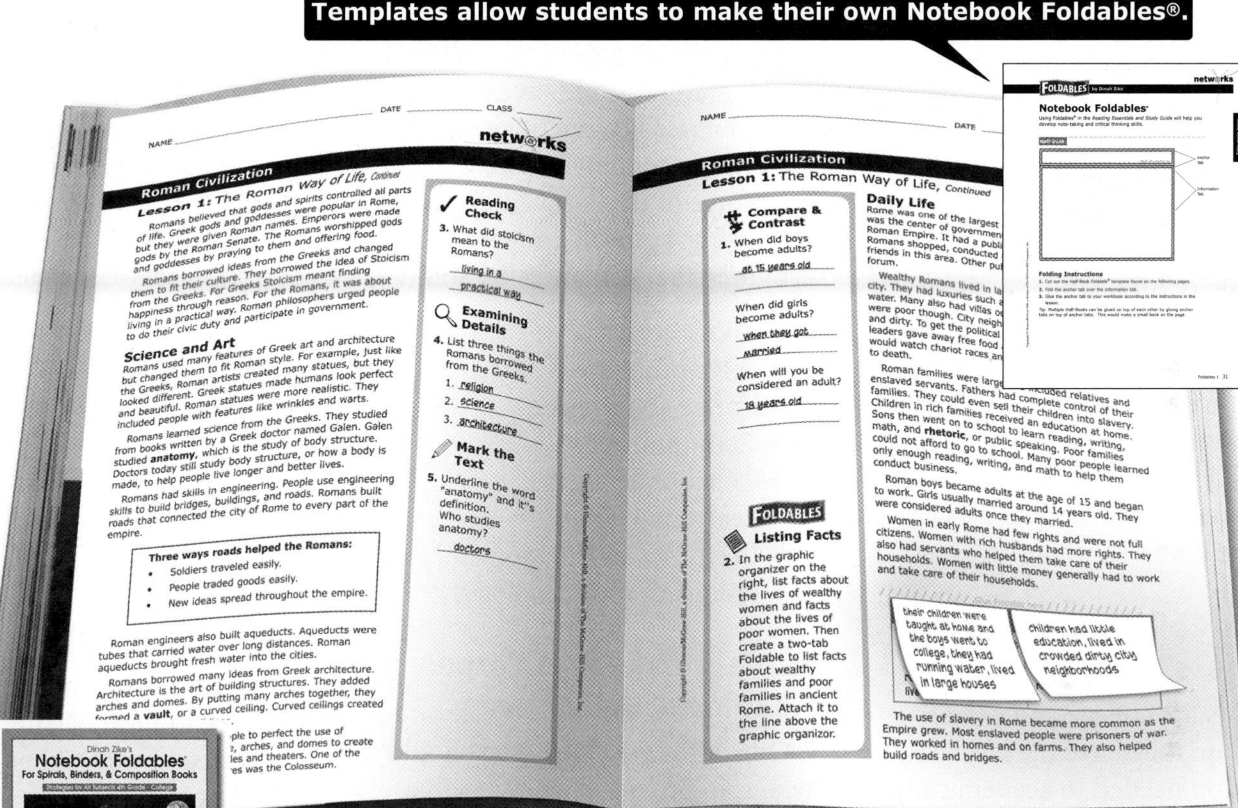

The *Reading Essentials and Study Guide* extends learning with Dinah Zike's award winning Notebook Foldables®. Notebook Foldables are specially designed to fit in workbooks and composition books. In partnership with Dinah, McGraw-Hill has developed the *Reading Essentials and Study Guide* with Notebook Foldables® to engage students more fully in social studies content.

It is easy to make Notebook Foldables®

1. **FOLD** an anchor tab and the desired number of information tabs.
2. **GLUE** the anchor tab.
3. **CUT** information tabs.

Students will master social studies concepts, ideas, and facts as they complete the side margin activities in this workbook, along with the many Notebook Foldables® activities placed within the pages.

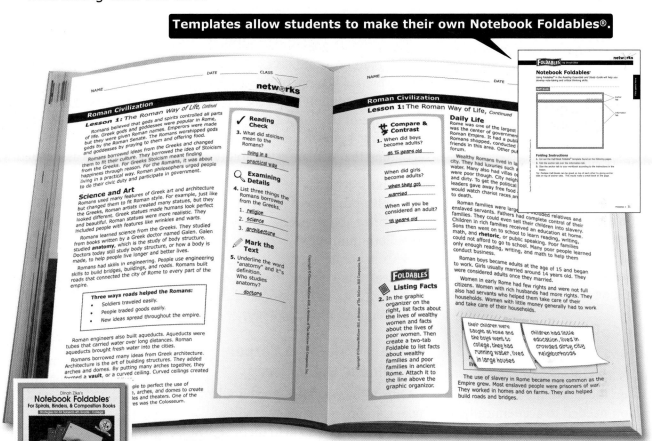

COLLEGE AND CAREER READINESS

Why Is College & Career Readiness Crucial?

- Only 70% of American students receive a high school diploma.
- Of that 70% of high school graduates, 53% of those who make it to college require remedial help.
- Over 90% of new jobs that will be available to students in the 21st century will require some postsecondary education.
- Most employers today cannot compete successfully without a workforce that has solid academic skills.
- The average difference in salary between someone with a high school degree and someone with postsecondary credentials can be $1 million over their lifetimes.

What Is College & Career Readiness?

Students are college and career ready when they have the level of preparation needed to academically, socially, and cognitively complete a postsecondary course of study without remediation. Students are prepared when they can enter the workforce at a level at which they are in line for promotion and career enhancement.

The ultimate goal of the college & career readiness initiative is to maintain America's competitive edge in the global economy of today. The workforce of the 21st century is an increasingly global, knowledge-based economy that demands the ability to:

- Think critically
- Solve problems
- Create and innovate
- Communicate
- Collaborate
- Learn new skills
- Use ICT (information and communications technology)

Explain College & Career Readiness to Students

One of the first steps you should take is to provide students with a framework that will help them see the relevancy of what they do in school. The three principal elements of College & Career Readiness (CCR) are:

- an understanding of core academic skills and the ability to apply them in educational and employment settings
- familiarity with skills valued by a broad range of employers such as communication, critical thinking, and responsibility
- mastery of the technologies and skill sets associated with a career pathway

Once students have been exposed to these elements, it is critical for them to see how they relate to their own plans for continuing education and career choice. Mention that CCR is more than just a personal issue, and it affects the country and our quality of life.

Most students—as well as many adults—consider work to be an obligation that they must perform in order to have money. Earning a salary is, of course, a central benefit of working, but so is the sense of satisfaction that comes from doing a job well. Moreover, every job contributes to the quality of life in our communities and our nation. Being prepared to pursue an education or get a job after high school is the hallmark of a good citizen.

Recognize That All Careers Are Important

Without question, the greatest challenge faced by educators, parents, and the public is recognizing that all jobs are important. When you discuss careers, be generous with your reflections and encourage your students to do the same. Be sure to mention the enormous variety of opportunities

PHOTO: Mark Scott/Photographer's Choice/Getty Images

available to them in diverse fields. The more that students can recognize the rich possibilities of whatever career they pursue, the more likely they will be to enjoy success and personal satisfaction.

Students typically have a relatively narrow perspective on the careers and jobs available to them. As part of the discussion of careers, broaden this perspective by reviewing some opportunities that your students might not be aware of. An interesting place to start is in the high profile industries of sports and entertainment.

Many students dream of being celebrities and have no idea about how unlikely this is. What they don't realize is that for every professional athlete, singer, or movie star, there are a hundred or more fascinating careers including sports trainers, writers, administrative assistants, drivers, and a seemingly endless list of other jobs. Not surprisingly, students usually respond positively when they learn that just in case they are not the next superstar in sports or entertainment, there are other opportunities that will allow them to achieve their dream in a slightly different way.

Students can explore careers in many ways; one way is by reviewing the 16 career clusters. Career clusters are groups of similar occupations and industries. They were developed by the U.S. Department of Education as a way to organize career planning. Students can visit the Career Center at http://ccr.mcgraw-hill.com/ to begin their explorations.

Make It Clear That There Are Various Paths To Success

A surprisingly small percentage of adults reach their careers through a direct and well-planned strategy. Familiarizing students with the various paths to success provides them with a realistic view of what life is like after high school and college. It may also give them an anchor in their own lives in the future when they find that they are wandering, which most of them will inevitably do.

Divergence from a direct path to a career is almost inevitable, and in many cases, is a desirable and enriching experience. Helping students to recognize this will make their future challenges seem less intimidating.

Have students investigate and discuss the career paths of people they know personally and by reputation, including celebrities. This discussion will promote engagement while showing the twists and turns that usually lead to success. Be sure to include some common but less-known paths, like the college benefits associated with military service or the arrangements nurses might make with a hospital to exchange tuition payments for a commitment of several years.

Make College & Career Readiness a regular part of interactive classroom discussions.

Unlike many other school subjects, a critical aspect of College & Career Readiness is its focus is on the future of each student, not the content of a course. Perhaps the best way to have students recognize this is to be sure that the time you spend discussing students' future pathways is truly interactive, with at least as much commentary from students as there is from you or other adult participants.

Because students are more willing to participate in discussions that have personal meaning to them, consider using these questions as starting points. These are "self-mentoring" questions that will help students clarify their thinking.

- What is something you really want to do in the next 10 years?
- How do you plan to get there?
- What is your back-up plan?
- What is something that you have done that made you proud?
- In which postsecondary courses do you think you would do best? Why do you think this?
- Imagine that you are going into the military. This choice involves activities that are hard physically and mentally. How would you handle these challenges?
- When you can't make up your mind about something important, what do you do?

Have students explore college & career readiness on their own at http://ccr.mcgraw-hill.com/ .

professional development

MEETING THE DIVERSE NEEDS OF OUR STUDENTS

by Douglas Fisher, Ph.D.

Today's classroom contains students from a variety of backgrounds with a variety of learning styles, strengths, and challenges. As teachers we are facing the challenge of helping students reach their educational potential. With careful planning, you can address the needs of all students in the social studies classroom. The basis for this planning is universal access. When classrooms are planned with universal access in mind, fewer students require specific accommodations.

What Is a Universal Access Design for Learning?

Universal design was first conceived in architectural studies when business people, engineers, and architects began making considerations for physical access to buildings. The idea was to plan the environment in advance to ensure that everyone had access. As a result, the environment would not have to be changed later for people with physical disabilities, people pushing strollers, workers who had injuries, or others for whom the environment would be difficult to negotiate. The Center for Universal Design at www.design.ncsu.edu/cud defines Universal Design as:

The design of products and environments to be usable by all people, to the greatest extent possible, without the need for adaptation or specialized design.

Universal Design and Access in Education

Researchers, teachers, and parents in education have expanded the development of built-in adaptations and inclusive accommodations from architectural space to the educational experience, especially in the area of curriculum.

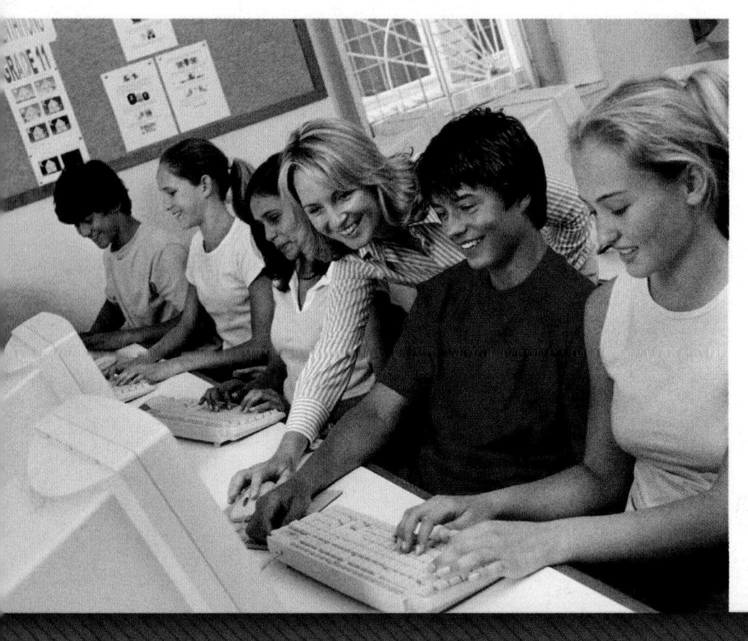

In 1998, the National Center to Improve the Tools of Educators (NCITE), with the partnership of the Center for Applied Special Technology (CAST), proposed an expanded definition of universal design focused on education:

In terms of learning, universal design means the design of instructional materials and activities that allows the learning goals to be achievable by individuals with wide differences in their abilities to see, hear, speak, move, read, write, understand English, attend, organize, engage, and remember.

How Does Universal Design Work in Education?

Universal design and access, as they apply to education and schooling, suggest the following:

✓ **Inclusive Classroom Participation**
Curriculum should be designed with all students and their needs in mind. The McGraw-Hill social studies print and online texts and materials were designed with a wide range of students in mind. For example, understanding that English learners and students who struggle with reading would be using this text, vocabulary is specifically taught and reinforced. Similarly, the teacher-support materials provide multiple instructional points to be used depending on the needs of the students in the class. Further, the text is written such that essential questions and guiding questions are identified for all learners.

✓ **Maximum Text Readability**
In universally designed classrooms that provide access for all students, texts use direct language, clear noun-verb agreements, and clear construct-based wording. In addition to these factors, the McGraw-Hill social studies texts use embedded

PHOTO: BananaStock/PictureQuest

definitions for difficult terms, provide for specific instruction in reading skills, use a number of visual representations, and include note-taking guides.

✓ **Adaptable and Accommodating**
The content in this textbook can be easily translated, read aloud, or otherwise changed to meet the needs of students in the classroom. The lesson and end-of-chapter activities and assessments provide students with multiple ways of demonstrating their content knowledge while also ensuring that they have practice with thinking in terms of multiple-choice questions. Critical thinking and analysis skills are also practiced.

How Is Differentiated Instruction the Key to Universal Access?

To differentiate instruction, teachers must acknowledge student differences in background knowledge and current reading, writing, and English language skills. They must also consider student learning styles and preferences, interests, and needs, and react accordingly. There are a number of general guidelines for differentiating instruction in the classroom to reach all students, including:

✓ **Link Assessment With Instruction**
Assessments should occur before, during, and after instruction to ensure that the curriculum is aligned with what students do and do not know. Using assessments in this way allows you to plan instruction for whole groups, small groups, and individual students. Backward planning, where you establish the assessment before you begin instruction, is also important.

✓ **Clarify Key Concepts and Generalizations**
Students need to know what is essential and how this information can be used in their future learning. In addition, students need to develop a sense of the big ideas—ideas that transcend time and place.

✓ **Emphasize Critical and Creative Thinking**
The content, process, and products used or assigned in the classroom should require that students think about what they are learning. While some students may require support, additional motivation, varied tasks, materials, or equipment, the overall focus on critical and creative thinking allows for all students to participate in the lesson.

✓ **Include Teacher- and Student-Selected Tasks**
A differentiated classroom includes both teacher- and student-selected activities and tasks. At some points in the lesson or day, the teacher must provide instruction and assign learning activities. In other parts of the lesson, students should be provided choices in how they engage with the content. This balance increases motivation, engagement, and learning.

How Do I Support Individual Students?

The vast majority of students will thrive in a classroom based on universal access and differentiated instruction. However, wise teachers recognize that no single option will work for all students and that there may be students who require unique systems of support to be successful.

Classroom Activity

Display a map of imperialism in Africa around 1914. Discuss with students the map's general information and have them list each country under the European power that controlled it.

To differentiate this activity:

- Have students imagine they are living in the early 1900s. Have them write a letter to a British newspaper about colonial rule in Africa.
- Have students record the number of African countries under European rule. Have them take the data and create a bar graph that shows which European powers were the most active colonizers at the time.
- Have students compose a song or poem about European rule in Africa, from an African's point of view.
- Have students choose a country of modern Africa to research. Have them write a three-page paper discussing how that country was affected by colonialism and how it has changed since the days of European rule.

professional development

MEETING THE DIVERSE NEEDS OF OUR STUDENTS

(continued)

Tips For Instruction

The following tips for instruction can support your efforts to help all students reach their maximum potential.

- ✓ Survey students to discover their individual differences. Use interest inventories of their unique talents so you can encourage contributions in the classroom.
- ✓ Be a model for respecting others. Adolescents crave social acceptance. The student with learning differences is especially sensitive to correction and criticism, particularly when it comes from a teacher. Your behavior will set the tone for how students treat one another.
- ✓ Expand opportunities for success. Provide a variety of instructional activities that reinforce skills and concepts.
- ✓ Establish measurable objectives and decide how you can best help students who meet them.
- ✓ Celebrate successes and make note of and praise "work in progress."
- ✓ Keep it simple. Point out problem areas if doing so can help a student effect change. Avoid overwhelming students with too many goals at one time.
- ✓ Assign cooperative group projects that challenge all students to contribute to solving a problem or creating a product.

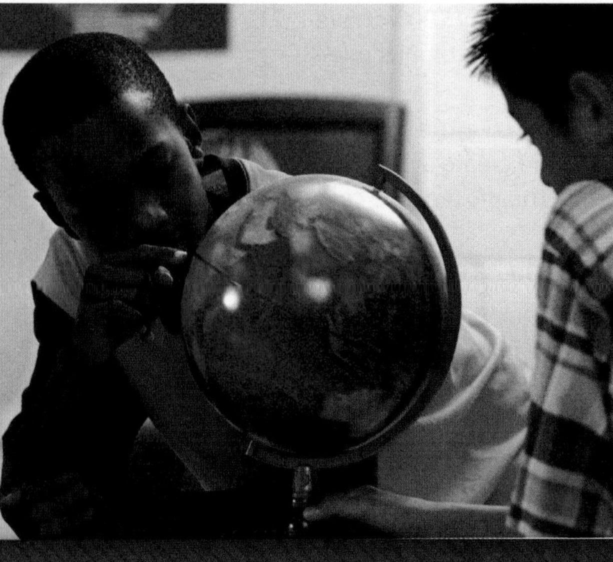

How Do I Reach Students With Learning Disabilities?

- ✓ Provide support and structure. Clearly specify rules, assignments, and responsibilities.
- ✓ Practice skills frequently. Use games and drills to help maintain student interest.
- ✓ Incorporate many modalities into the learning process. Provide opportunities to say, hear, write, read, and act out important concepts and information.
- ✓ Link new skills and concepts to those already mastered.
- ✓ If possible, allow students to record answers on audio.
- ✓ Allow extra time to complete assessments and assignments.
- ✓ Let students demonstrate proficiency with alternative presentations, including oral reports, role plays, art projects, and musical presentations.
- ✓ Provide outlines, notes, or recordings of lecture material.
- ✓ Pair students with peer helpers, and provide class time for pair interaction.

How Do I Reach Students With Behavioral Challenges?

- ✓ Provide a structured environment with clear-cut schedules, rules, seat assignments, and safety procedures.
- ✓ Reinforce appropriate behavior and model it for students.
- ✓ Cue distracted students back to the task through verbal signals and teacher proximity.
- ✓ Set goals that can be achieved in the short term. Work for long-term improvement in the big areas.

How Do I Reach Students With Physical Challenges?

- ✓ Openly discuss with the student any uncertainties you have about when to offer aid.
- ✓ Ask parents or therapists and students what special devices or procedures are needed and whether any special safety precautions need to be taken.
- ✓ Welcome students with physical challenges into all activities, including field trips, special events, and projects.
- ✓ Provide information to assist class members and adults in their understanding of support needed.

How Do I Reach Students With Visual Impairments?

- ✓ Facilitate independence. Modify assignments as needed.
- ✓ Teach classmates how and when to serve as visual guides.
- ✓ Limit unnecessary noise in the classroom if it distracts the student with visual impairments.
- ✓ Provide tactile models whenever possible.

- Foster a spirit of inclusion. Describe people and events as they occur in the classroom. Remind classmates that the student with visual impairments cannot interpret gestures and other forms of nonverbal communication.
- Provide recorded lectures and reading assignments for use outside the classroom.
- Team the student with a sighted peer for written work.

How Do I Reach Students With Hearing Impairments?

- Seat students where they can see your lip movements easily and where they can avoid any visual distractions.
- Avoid standing with your back to the window or light source.
- Use an overhead projector so you can maintain eye contact while writing information for students.
- Seat students where they can see speakers.
- Write all assignments on the board, or hand out written instructions.
- If the student has a manual interpreter, allow both student and interpreter to select the most favorable seating arrangements.
- Teach students to look directly at each other when they speak.

How Do I Reach English Learners?

- Remember, students' ability to speak English does not reflect their academic abilities.
- Try to incorporate the students' cultural experience into your instruction. The help of a bilingual aide may be effective.
- Avoid any references in your instruction that could be construed as cultural stereotypes.
- Preteach important vocabulary and concepts.
- Encourage students to preview text before they begin reading, noting headings.
- Remind students not to ignore graphic organizers, photographs, and maps since there is much information in these visuals.
- Use memorabilia and photographs whenever possible to build background knowledge and understanding. An example of this would be coins in a foreign currency or a raw cotton ball to reinforce its importance in history.

How Do I Reach Gifted Students?

- Make arrangements for students to take selected subjects early and to work on independent projects.
- Ask "what if" questions to develop high-level thinking skills. Establish an environment safe for risk taking in your classroom.
- Emphasize concepts, theories, ideas, relationships, and generalizations about the content.
- Promote interest in the past by inviting students to make connections to the present.
- Let students express themselves in alternate ways such as creative writing, acting, debates, simulations, drawing, or music.
- Provide students with a catalog of helpful resources, listing such things as agencies that provide free and inexpensive materials, appropriate community services and programs, and community experts who might be called upon to speak to your students.
- Assign extension projects that allow students to solve real-life problems related to their communities.

Classroom Activity

Students respond eagerly to a subject when they can relate it to their own experiences. With the growing number of students who come from other world regions, explaining geography through a global theme (such as volcanoes) can give them a worldwide as well as a regional perspective. To develop this awareness, display a large world map. Have students use the library or the Internet to research the latitude and longitude of 15 major volcanoes around the world. Ask them to mark these locations on the map and answer the following questions:

- What patterns do you see in volcanic activity?
- What causes volcanic activity?
- Where in the world are volcanoes most active?

As a follow-up, suggest students go to http://volcano.und.nodak.edu/vwdocs/kids/legends.html to find legends about the origins of some of the world's volcanoes. Encourage students to share what they find with the class.

professional development

ACADEMIC VOCABULARY

How Can I Help My Students Learn Academic Vocabulary?

What Is Academic English?

Academic English is the language used in academics, business, and courts of law. It is the type of English used in textbooks, and contains linguistic features associated with academic disciplines like social studies. Proficiency in reading and using academic English is especially related to long-term success in all parts of life.

By reinforcing academic English, teachers can help learners to access authentic, academic texts—not simplified texts that dummy down the content. In this way, they can provide information that will help build their students' background knowledge rapidly.

What Is Academic Vocabulary?

Academic vocabulary is based on academic English. By the time children have completed elementary school, they must have acquired the knowledge needed to understand academic vocabulary. How many words should they acquire to be able to access their texts? A basic 2,000-word vocabulary of high-frequency words makes up 87% of the vocabulary of academic texts. Eight hundred other academic words comprise an additional 8% of the words. Three percent of the remaining words are technical words. The remaining 2% are low-frequency words. There may be as many as 123,000 low-frequency words in academic texts.

Why Should Students Learn Academic Vocabulary?

English learners who have a basic 2,000-word vocabulary are ready to acquire most general words found in their texts.

Knowledge of academic words and general words can significantly boost a student's comprehension level of academic texts. Students who learn and practice these words before they graduate from high school are more likely to master

PHOTO: BananaStock/PictureQuest

academic material with increased confidence and speed. They waste less time and effort in guessing words or consulting dictionaries than those who only know the basic 2,000 words that characterize general conversation.

How Do I Include Academic Vocabulary and Academic English in My Teaching?

Teachers can provide students with academic vocabulary and help students understand the academic English of their text.

To develop academic English, learners must have already acquired basic proficiency in everyday English.

Academic English should be taught within contexts that make sense. In terms of instruction, teaching academic English includes providing students with access to core curriculum—in this case social studies.

Academic English arises in part from social practices in which academic English is used. The acquisition of academic vocabulary and grammar is necessary to advance the development of academic English.

Tips for Teaching Academic Vocabulary

- ✓ **Expose Students to Academic Vocabulary** You do not need to call attention to words students are learning because they will acquire them subconsciously.
- ✓ **Do Not Correct Students' Mistakes When Using the Vocabulary Words** All vocabulary understanding and spelling errors will disappear once the student reads more.
- ✓ **Help Students Decode the Words Themselves** Once they learn the alphabet, they should be able to decode words. Decoding each word they don't recognize will help them more than trying to focus on sentence structure. Once they can recognize the words, they can read "authentic" texts.
- ✓ **Do Not Ignore the English Learner in This Process** They can learn academic vocabulary before they are completely fluent in oral English.
- ✓ **Helping Students Build Academic Vocabulary Leads to Broader Learning** Students who have mastered the basic academic vocabulary are ready to acquire words from the rest of the groups. To help determine which words are in the 2,000-word basic group, refer to *West's General Service List of English Words,* 1953. The list is designed to serve as a guide for teachers and as a checklist and goal list for students.

Guidelines for Teaching Academic Vocabulary

1. Direct and planned instruction
2. Models—that have increasingly difficult language
3. Attention to form—pointing out linguistic features of words

Classroom Activity

Writing About Modern America

Give students a brief writing assignment. Ask them to write a short essay about one of the topics listed below in the left column. Have students use as many of the academic vocabulary words in the right column as they can in their essay. When completed, ask student volunteers to share their writing. Note what academic vocabulary words they use.

Topic	Academic Vocabulary
The challenges of reducing poverty in America	sufficient minimum medical income
Recent technological advances	innovate technology media potential data transmit

NASA Earth Observatory/image by Robert Simmon with data courtesy of the NASA/NOAA GOES Project Science team

Reference Atlas

World: Political RA2

World: Physical RA4

North America: Political. RA6

North America: Physical RA7

Middle America: Physical/Political. . . .RA8

South America: Political. RA10

South America: Physical RA11

Europe: Political RA12

Europe: Physical RA14

Middle East: Physical/Political. RA16

Africa: Political RA18

Africa: Physical RA19

Asia: Political RA20

Asia: Physical RA22

Pacific Rim: Physical/Political. RA24

Geographic Dictionary. RA26

ATLAS KEY

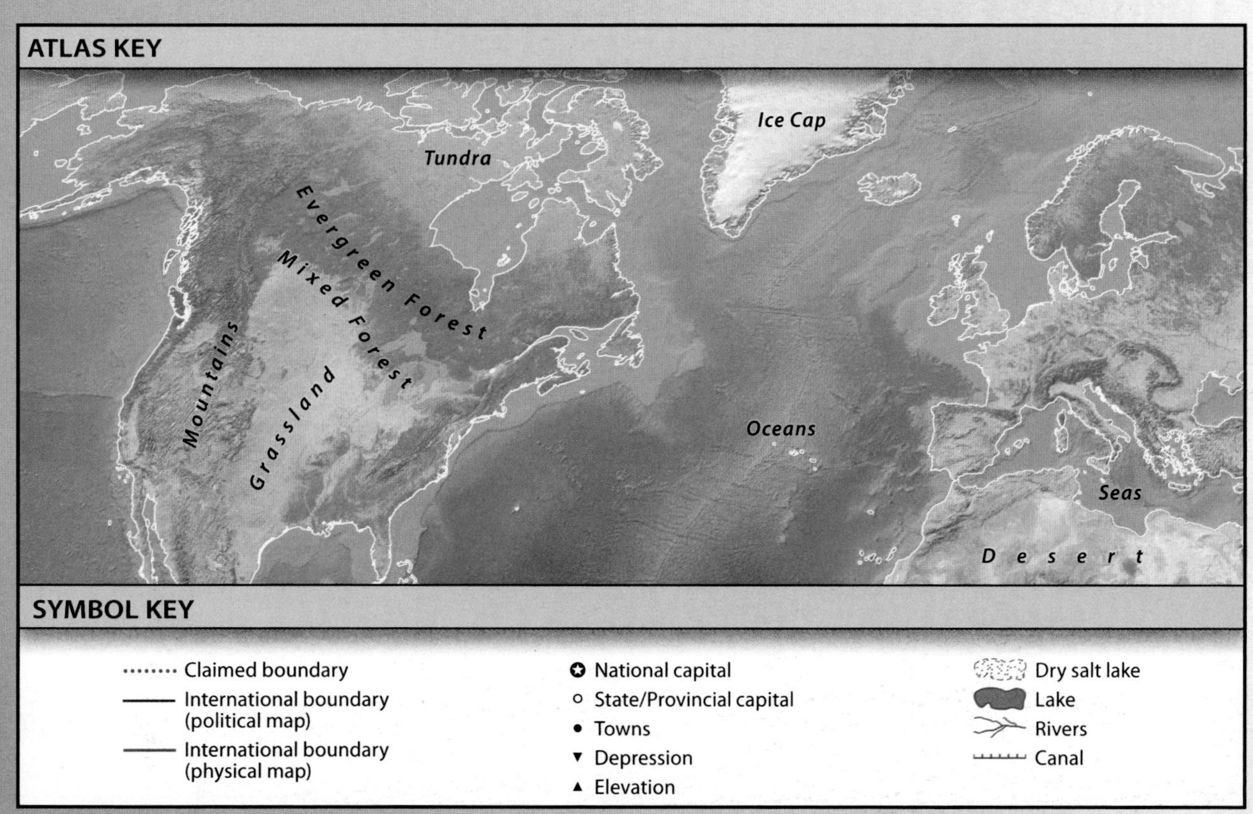

SYMBOL KEY

- Claimed boundary
- International boundary (political map)
- International boundary (physical map)
- National capital
- State/Provincial capital
- Towns
- Depression
- Elevation
- Dry salt lake
- Lake
- Rivers
- Canal

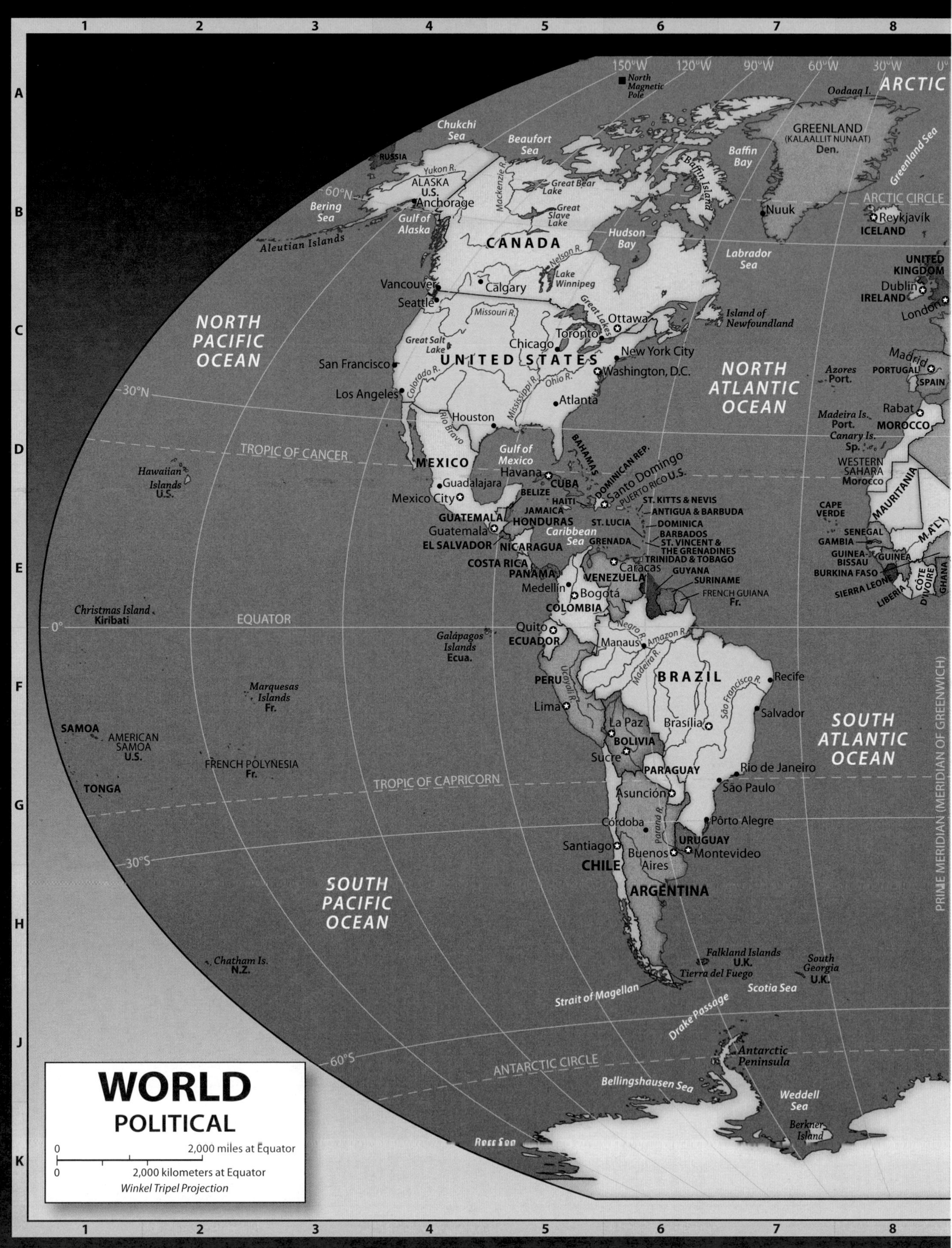
WORLD
POLITICAL
0
2,000 miles at Equator
0
2,000 kilometers at Equator
Winkel Tripel Projection
1
2
3
4
5
6
7
8
A
B
C
D
E
F
G
H
J
K
150°W
120°W
90°W
60°W
30°W
North Magnetic Pole
ARCTIC
Oodaaq I.
GREENLAND
(KALAALLIT NUNAAT)
Den.
Greenland Sea
Baffin Bay
Baffin Island
Nuuk
ARCTIC CIRCLE
Reykjavík
ICELAND
Chukchi Sea
Beaufort Sea
RUSSIA
Yukon R.
ALASKA
U.S.
Anchorage
Mackenzie R.
Great Bear Lake
Great Slave Lake
60°N
Bering Sea
Gulf of Alaska
Aleutian Islands
Hudson Bay
CANADA
Nelson R.
Labrador Sea
UNITED KINGDOM
Dublin
IRELAND
London
Vancouver
Calgary
Lake Winnipeg
Seattle
Missouri R.
Great Lakes
Ottawa
Island of Newfoundland
NORTH PACIFIC OCEAN
Great Salt Lake
Chicago
Toronto
New York City
San Francisco
UNITED STATES
Washington, D.C.
NORTH ATLANTIC OCEAN
Colorado R.
Ohio R.
Mississippi R.
Azores
Port.
PORTUGAL
Madrid
SPAIN
Los Angeles
30°N
Atlanta
Houston
Rio Bravo
Madeira Is.
Port.
Rabat
MOROCCO
Canary Is.
Sp.
TROPIC OF CANCER
Gulf of Mexico
BAHAMAS
MEXICO
Havana
CUBA
DOMINICAN REP.
Santo Domingo
PUERTO RICO U.S.
WESTERN SAHARA
Morocco
Hawaiian Islands
U.S.
Guadalajara
BELIZE
HAITI
Mexico City
JAMAICA
ST. KITTS & NEVIS
ANTIGUA & BARBUDA
DOMINICA
CAPE VERDE
MAURITANIA
GUATEMALA
HONDURAS
ST. LUCIA
Guatemala
Caribbean Sea
BARBADOS
ST. VINCENT & THE GRENADINES
SENEGAL
GAMBIA
MALI
EL SALVADOR
NICARAGUA
GRENADA
TRINIDAD & TOBAGO
GUINEA-BISSAU
GUINEA
COSTA RICA
Caracas
GUYANA
BURKINA FASO
PANAMA
VENEZUELA
SURINAME
SIERRA LEONE
Medellín
FRENCH GUIANA
Fr.
LIBERIA
CÔTE D'IVOIRE
GHANA
Bogotá
COLOMBIA
Christmas Island
Kiribati
EQUATOR
0°
Quito
ECUADOR
Negro R.
Amazon R.
Manaus
Galápagos Islands
Ecua.
Madeira R.
PERU
Ucayali R.
BRAZIL
São Francisco R.
Recife
Marquesas Islands
Fr.
Lima
Salvador
SOUTH ATLANTIC OCEAN
PRIME MERIDIAN (MERIDIAN OF GREENWICH)
SAMOA
AMERICAN SAMOA
U.S.
La Paz
Brasília
BOLIVIA
Sucre
FRENCH POLYNESIA
Fr.
PARAGUAY
Rio de Janeiro
TONGA
TROPIC OF CAPRICORN
São Paulo
Asunción
Pôrto Alegre
Córdoba
Paraná R.
URUGUAY
Santiago
Buenos Aires
Montevideo
30°S
CHILE
ARGENTINA
SOUTH PACIFIC OCEAN
Falkland Islands
U.K.
Chatham Is.
N.Z.
Tierra del Fuego
South Georgia
U.K.
Scotia Sea
Strait of Magellan
Drake Passage
60°S
Antarctic Peninsula
ANTARCTIC CIRCLE
Bellingshausen Sea
Weddell Sea
Ross Sea
Berkner Island

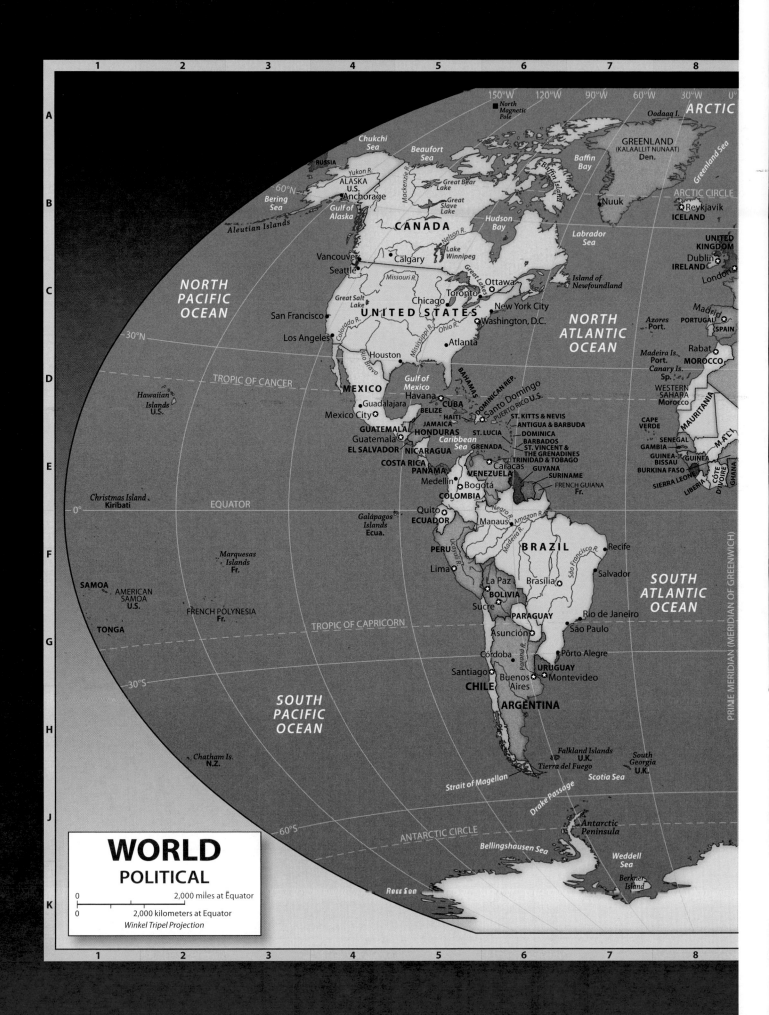

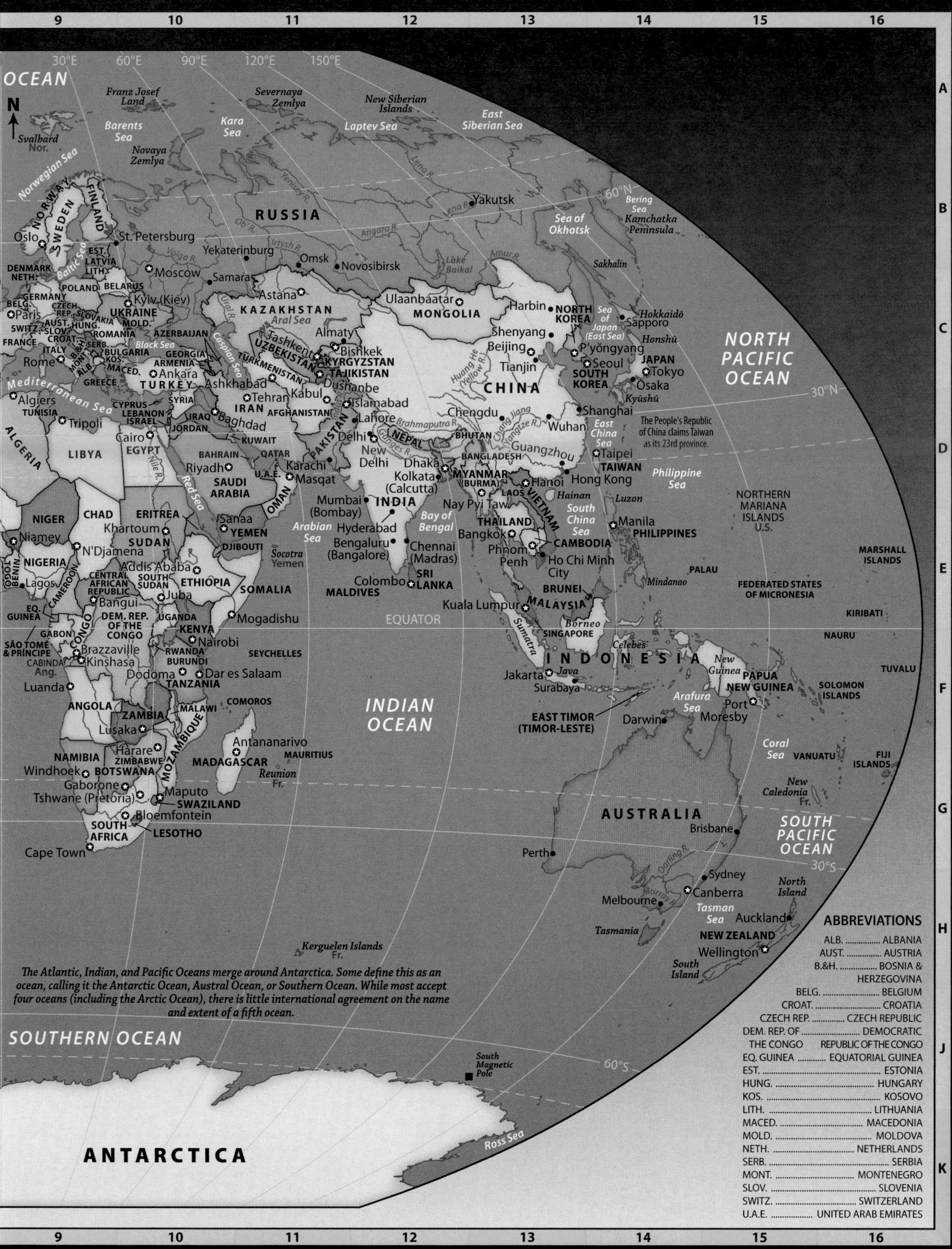
9
10
11
12
13
14
15
16
A
B
C
D
E
F
G
H
J
K
30°E
60°E
90°E
120°E
150°E
60°N
30°N
EQUATOR
30°S
60°S
OCEAN
N
Franz Josef Land
Severnaya Zemlya
New Siberian Islands
East Siberian Sea
Laptev Sea
Kara Sea
Barents Sea
Svalbard Nor.
Novaya Zemlya
Norwegian Sea
NORWAY
SWEDEN
FINLAND
Oslo
St. Petersburg
RUSSIA
Yakutsk
Bering Sea
Sea of Okhotsk
Kamchatka Peninsula
Sakhalin
Yenisey R.
Lena R.
Ob' R.
Angara R.
Irtysh R.
Volga R.
Amur R.
Lake Baikal
Yekaterinburg
Omsk
Novosibirsk
EST.
LATVIA
LITH.
Baltic Sea
DENMARK
NETH.
Moscow
Samara
POLAND
BELARUS
GERMANY
BELG.
Paris
CZECH REP.
SLOVAKIA
UKRAINE
Kyiv (Kiev)
SWITZ.
SLOV.
AUST.
HUNG.
MOLD.
ROMANIA
FRANCE
CROAT.
SERB.
B.&H.
MONT.
KOS.
ITALY
BULGARIA
Black Sea
Rome
MACED.
ALB.
GREECE
Ankara
TURKEY
GEORGIA
ARMENIA
AZERBAIJAN
Caspian Sea
Ural R.
Astana
KAZAKHSTAN
Aral Sea
Ulaanbaatar
MONGOLIA
Harbin
NORTH KOREA
Sea of Japan (East Sea)
Hokkaidō
Sapporo
Honshū
Shenyang
Beijing
Tianjin
P'yŏngyang
Seoul
SOUTH KOREA
JAPAN
Tokyo
Osaka
Kyūshū
NORTH PACIFIC OCEAN
Tashkent
UZBEKISTAN
Almaty
Bishkek
KYRGYZSTAN
TAJIKISTAN
TURKMENISTAN
Ashkhabad
Dushanbe
Tehran
Kabul
IRAN
AFGHANISTAN
Islamabad
Lahore
PAKISTAN
Huang He (Yellow R.)
CHINA
Chengdu
Wuhan
Shanghai
Chang Jiang (Yangtze R.)
Brahmaputra R.
NEPAL
BHUTAN
East China Sea
The People's Republic of China claims Taiwan as its 23rd province.
Mediterranean Sea
Algiers
TUNISIA
CYPRUS
SYRIA
LEBANON
ISRAEL
IRAQ
Baghdad
JORDAN
KUWAIT
Tripoli
Cairo
ALGERIA
LIBYA
EGYPT
Nile R.
BAHRAIN
QATAR
Riyadh
SAUDI ARABIA
U.A.E.
Masqat
OMAN
Karachi
Delhi
New Delhi
Ganges R.
Dhaka
BANGLADESH
Kolkata (Calcutta)
Guangzhou
Taipei
TAIWAN
Hong Kong
MYANMAR (BURMA)
LAOS
Hanoi
VIETNAM
Hainan
Philippine Sea
Luzon
Red Sea
NIGER
CHAD
ERITREA
Sanaa
YEMEN
Khartoum
SUDAN
Mumbai (Bombay)
INDIA
Arabian Sea
Bay of Bengal
Hyderabad
Nay Pyi Taw
THAILAND
Bangkok
South China Sea
Manila
PHILIPPINES
NORTHERN MARIANA ISLANDS U.S.
Niamey
N'Djamena
DJIBOUTI
Socotra Yemen
Bengaluru (Bangalore)
Chennai (Madras)
Phnom Penh
CAMBODIA
Ho Chi Minh City
MARSHALL ISLANDS
NIGERIA
BENIN
TOGO
Lagos
CAMEROON
CENTRAL AFRICAN REPUBLIC
SOUTH SUDAN
Juba
Addis Ababa
ETHIOPIA
SOMALIA
Colombo
SRI LANKA
MALDIVES
PALAU
Mindanao
FEDERATED STATES OF MICRONESIA
BRUNEI
MALAYSIA
Kuala Lumpur
EQ. GUINEA
Bangui
DEM. REP. OF THE CONGO
UGANDA
KENYA
Mogadishu
KIRIBATI
GABON
CONGO
Nairobi
Sumatra
SINGAPORE
Borneo
NAURU
SÃO TOMÉ & PRÍNCIPE
Brazzaville
Kinshasa
CABINDA Ang.
RWANDA
BURUNDI
SEYCHELLES
Celebes
INDONESIA
New Guinea
Dodoma
Dar es Salaam
TANZANIA
Jakarta
Java
Surabaya
PAPUA NEW GUINEA
TUVALU
Luanda
SOLOMON ISLANDS
ANGOLA
COMOROS
INDIAN OCEAN
ZAMBIA
MALAWI
Arafura Sea
Port Moresby
EAST TIMOR (TIMOR-LESTE)
Darwin
Lusaka
MOZAMBIQUE
Antananarivo
Coral Sea
VANUATU
FIJI ISLANDS
Harare
ZIMBABWE
NAMIBIA
MAURITIUS
MADAGASCAR
Windhoek
BOTSWANA
Reunion Fr.
New Caledonia Fr.
Gaborone
Tshwane (Pretoria)
Maputo
SWAZILAND
AUSTRALIA
Bloemfontein
SOUTH PACIFIC OCEAN
SOUTH AFRICA
LESOTHO
Brisbane
Cape Town
Perth
Darling R.
Sydney
Murray R.
Canberra
North Island
Melbourne
Tasman Sea
Auckland
Tasmania
NEW ZEALAND
Wellington
South Island
Kerguelen Islands Fr.
The Atlantic, Indian, and Pacific Oceans merge around Antarctica. Some define this as an ocean, calling it the Antarctic Ocean, Austral Ocean, or Southern Ocean. While most accept four oceans (including the Arctic Ocean), there is little international agreement on the name and extent of a fifth ocean.
SOUTHERN OCEAN
South Magnetic Pole
Ross Sea
ANTARCTICA
ABBREVIATIONS
ALB. .... ALBANIA
AUST. .... AUSTRIA
B.&H. .... BOSNIA & HERZEGOVINA
BELG. .... BELGIUM
CROAT. .... CROATIA
CZECH REP. .... CZECH REPUBLIC
DEM. REP. OF THE CONGO .... DEMOCRATIC REPUBLIC OF THE CONGO
EQ. GUINEA .... EQUATORIAL GUINEA
EST. .... ESTONIA
HUNG. .... HUNGARY
KOS. .... KOSOVO
LITH. .... LITHUANIA
MACED. .... MACEDONIA
MOLD. .... MOLDOVA
NETH. .... NETHERLANDS
SERB. .... SERBIA
MONT. .... MONTENEGRO
SLOV. .... SLOVENIA
SWITZ. .... SWITZERLAND
U.A.E. .... UNITED ARAB EMIRATES

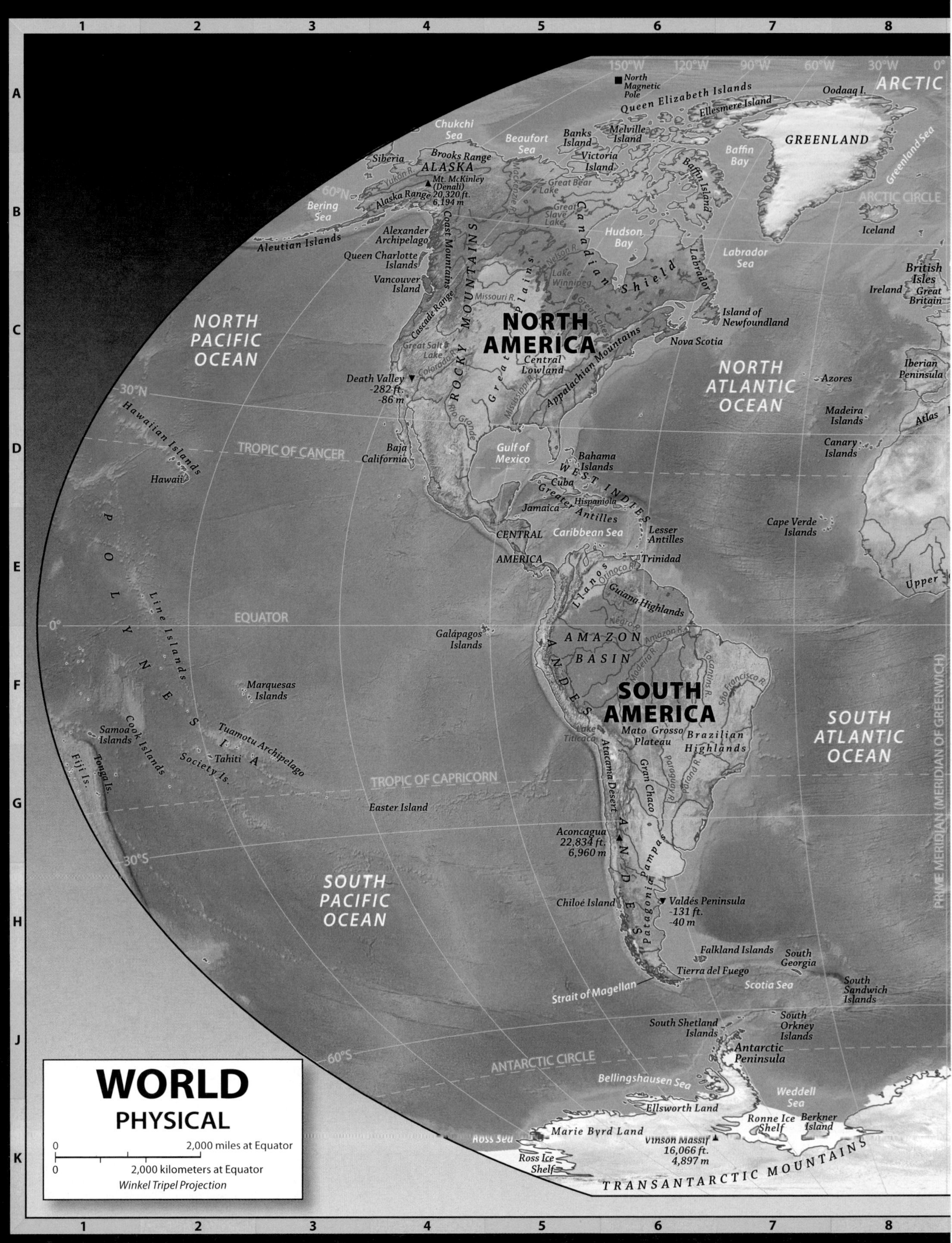

WORLD
PHYSICAL
0
2,000 miles at Equator
0
2,000 kilometers at Equator
Winkel Tripel Projection
150°W
120°W
90°W
60°W
30°W
0°
ARCTIC
North Magnetic Pole
Queen Elizabeth Islands
Ellesmere Island
Oodaaq I.
GREENLAND
Greenland Sea
ARCTIC CIRCLE
Iceland
Chukchi Sea
Beaufort Sea
Banks Island
Melville Island
Victoria Island
Baffin Bay
Baffin Island
Siberia
Brooks Range
ALASKA
Yukon R.
Mt. McKinley (Denali) 20,320 ft. 6,194 m
Alaska Range
60°N
Bering Sea
Great Bear Lake
Great Slave Lake
Mackenzie R.
Canadian Shield
Hudson Bay
Labrador Sea
Labrador
Aleutian Islands
Alexander Archipelago
Coast Mountains
Queen Charlotte Islands
Vancouver Island
Nelson R.
Lake Winnipeg
Missouri R.
Cascade Range
ROCKY MOUNTAINS
Great Plains
Great Lakes
NORTH AMERICA
Island of Newfoundland
British Isles
Ireland
Great Britain
NORTH PACIFIC OCEAN
Great Salt Lake
Colorado R.
Central Lowland
Appalachian Mountains
Nova Scotia
NORTH ATLANTIC OCEAN
Iberian Peninsula
Azores
Death Valley -282 ft. -86 m
30°N
Mississippi R.
Rio Grande
Madeira Islands
Atlas
Hawaiian Islands
TROPIC OF CANCER
Baja California
Gulf of Mexico
Bahama Islands
Canary Islands
Hawaii
WEST INDIES
Cuba
Greater Antilles
Hispaniola
Jamaica
Cape Verde Islands
CENTRAL AMERICA
Caribbean Sea
Lesser Antilles
Trinidad
POLYNESIA
Line Islands
Llanos
Orinoco R.
Guiana Highlands
Upper
EQUATOR
0°
Galápagos Islands
Negro R.
Amazon R.
AMAZON BASIN
ANDES
Madeira R.
Tocantins R.
São Francisco R.
PRIME MERIDIAN (MERIDIAN OF GREENWICH)
Marquesas Islands
SOUTH AMERICA
SOUTH ATLANTIC OCEAN
Samoa Islands
Cook Islands
Tuamotu Archipelago
Tahiti
Society Is.
Lake Titicaca
Mato Grosso Plateau
Brazilian Highlands
Fiji Is.
Tonga Is.
Atacama Desert
Gran Chaco
Paraguay R.
Paraná R.
TROPIC OF CAPRICORN
Easter Island
Aconcagua 22,834 ft. 6,960 m
Pampas
30°S
SOUTH PACIFIC OCEAN
Chiloé Island
Patagonia
Valdés Peninsula -131 ft. -40 m
Falkland Islands
South Georgia
Tierra del Fuego
Scotia Sea
South Sandwich Islands
Strait of Magellan
South Shetland Islands
South Orkney Islands
Antarctic Peninsula
60°S
ANTARCTIC CIRCLE
Bellingshausen Sea
Weddell Sea
Ellsworth Land
Ronne Ice Shelf
Berkner Island
Ross Sea
Marie Byrd Land
Vinson Massif 16,066 ft. 4,897 m
Ross Ice Shelf
TRANSANTARCTIC MOUNTAINS

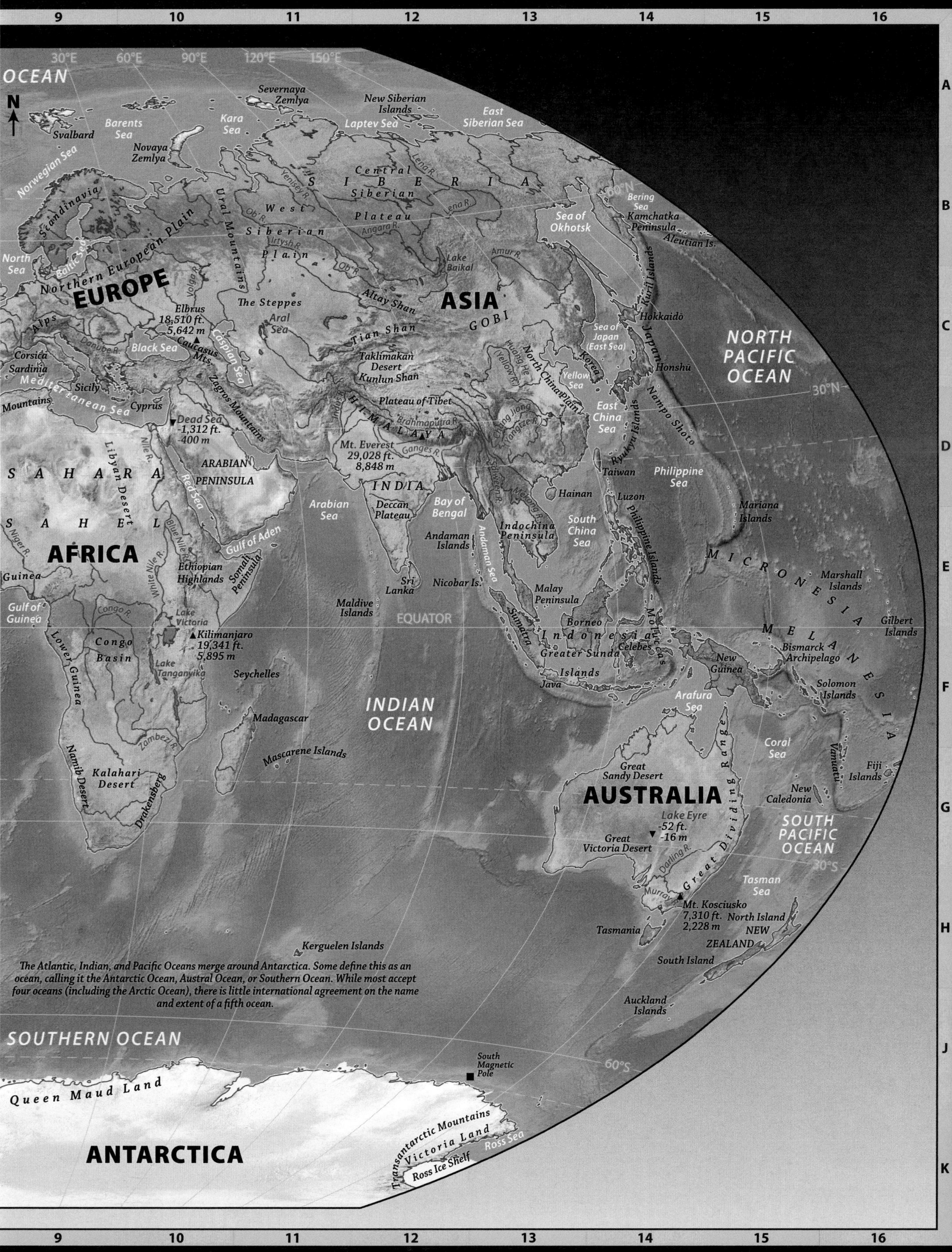

9
10
11
12
13
14
15
16
A
B
C
D
E
F
G
H
J
K
30°E
60°E
90°E
120°E
150°E
OCEAN
N
Svalbard
Barents Sea
Kara Sea
Severnaya Zemlya
New Siberian Islands
Laptev Sea
East Siberian Sea
Novaya Zemlya
Norwegian Sea
Scandinavia
Ural Mountains
Central Siberian Plateau
S I B E R I A
Lena R.
Yenisey R.
West Siberian Plain
Ob R.
Irtysh R.
Angara R.
60°N
Bering Sea
Kamchatka Peninsula
Aleutian Is.
Sea of Okhotsk
North Sea
Baltic Sea
Northern European Plain
EUROPE
Volga R.
Lake Baikal
Amur R.
Kuril Islands
Altay Shan
ASIA
GOBI
Tian Shan
The Steppes
Aral Sea
Elbrus 18,510 ft. 5,642 m
Caucasus Mts.
Caspian Sea
Alps
Danube R.
Black Sea
Sea of Japan (East Sea)
Hokkaido
Japan
Honshu
NORTH PACIFIC OCEAN
Corsica
Sardinia
Sicily
Mediterranean Sea
Taklimakan Desert
Kunlun Shan
Huang He (Yellow R.)
North China Plain
Korea
Yellow Sea
30°N
Mountains
Cyprus
Zagros Mountains
Plateau of Tibet
H I M A L A Y A
Brahmaputra R.
Chang Jiang (Yangtze R.)
East China Sea
Ryukyu Islands
Nampo Shoto
Dead Sea -1,312 ft. -400 m
Mt. Everest 29,028 ft. 8,848 m
Ganges R.
Indus R.
S A H A R A
Libyan Desert
Nile R.
ARABIAN PENINSULA
Red Sea
INDIA
Taiwan
Philippine Sea
Arabian Sea
Deccan Plateau
Bay of Bengal
Hainan
Luzon
Mariana Islands
S A H E L
Blue Nile R.
Gulf of Aden
Andaman Islands
Andaman Sea
Indochina Peninsula
Mekong R.
Salween R.
South China Sea
Philippine Islands
Niger R.
AFRICA
Ethiopian Highlands
Somali Peninsula
White Nile R.
M I C R O N E S I A
Guinea
Sri Lanka
Nicobar Is.
Marshall Islands
Malay Peninsula
Gulf of Guinea
Congo R.
Lake Victoria
Maldive Islands
EQUATOR
Sumatra
Borneo
Moluccas
Gilbert Islands
M E L A N E S I A
Congo Basin
Lower Guinea
Kilimanjaro 19,341 ft. 5,895 m
Indonesia
Celebes
Greater Sunda Islands
New Guinea
Bismarck Archipelago
Lake Tanganyika
Seychelles
Java
Solomon Islands
Arafura Sea
INDIAN OCEAN
Madagascar
Zambezi R.
Mascarene Islands
Great Dividing Range
Coral Sea
Vanuatu
Fiji Islands
Namib Desert
Kalahari Desert
Drakensberg
Great Sandy Desert
AUSTRALIA
New Caledonia
Lake Eyre -52 ft. -16 m
Great Victoria Desert
Darling R.
SOUTH PACIFIC OCEAN
30°S
Tasman Sea
Murray R.
Mt. Kosciusko 7,310 ft. 2,228 m
North Island
Tasmania
NEW ZEALAND
South Island
Kerguelen Islands
The Atlantic, Indian, and Pacific Oceans merge around Antarctica. Some define this as an ocean, calling it the Antarctic Ocean, Austral Ocean, or Southern Ocean. While most accept four oceans (including the Arctic Ocean), there is little international agreement on the name and extent of a fifth ocean.
Auckland Islands
SOUTHERN OCEAN
South Magnetic Pole
60°S
Queen Maud Land
Transantarctic Mountains
Victoria Land
Ross Sea
Ross Ice Shelf
ANTARCTICA

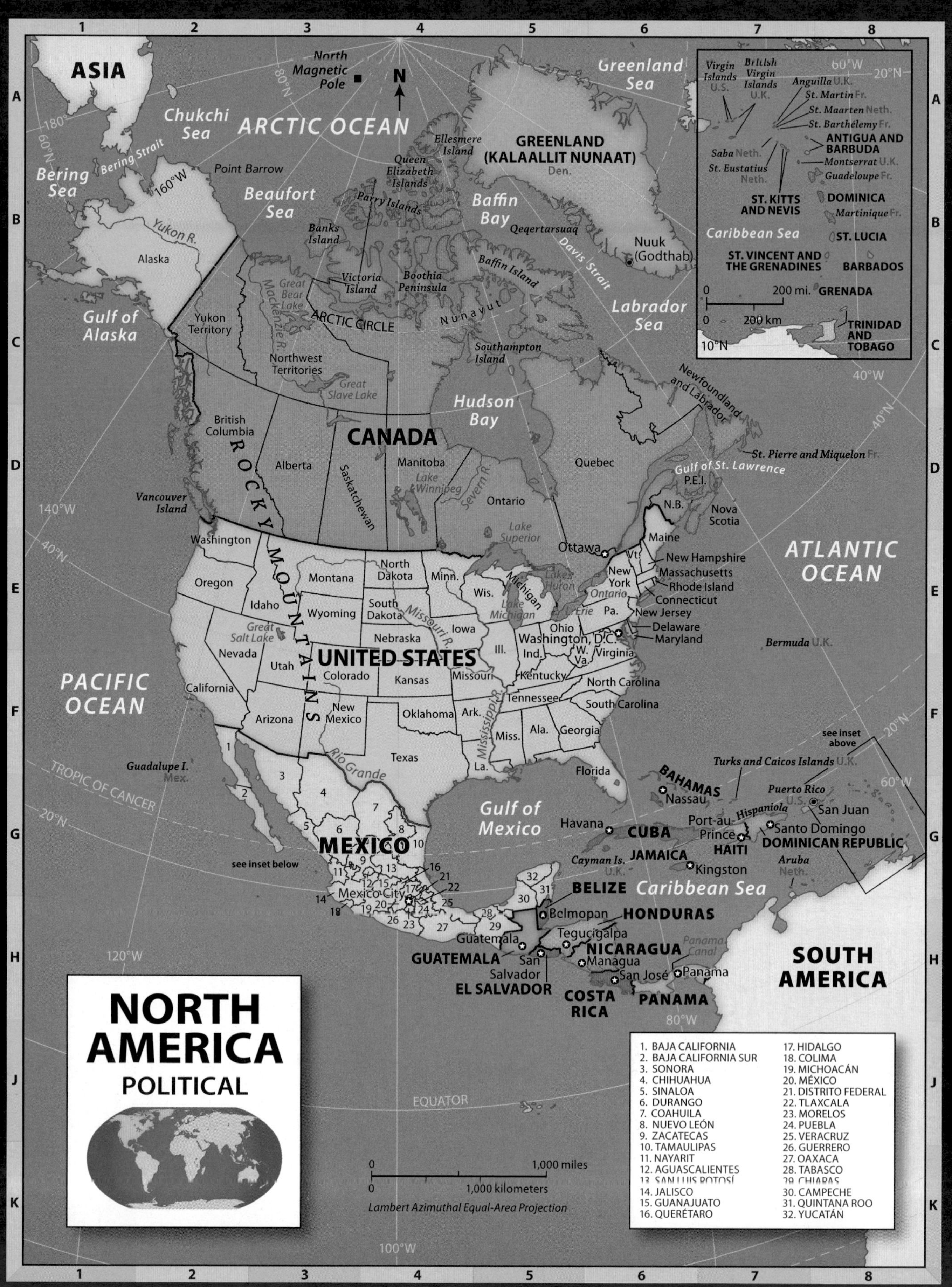
NORTH AMERICA
POLITICAL
ASIA
Chukchi Sea
ARCTIC OCEAN
North Magnetic Pole
N
Bering Sea
Bering Strait
Point Barrow
Beaufort Sea
Alaska
Yukon R.
Gulf of Alaska
Yukon Territory
Northwest Territories
Great Bear Lake
Mackenzie R.
Great Slave Lake
ARCTIC CIRCLE
Banks Island
Victoria Island
Parry Islands
Queen Elizabeth Islands
Ellesmere Island
Boothia Peninsula
Nunavut
Baffin Bay
Baffin Island
Southampton Island
GREENLAND (KALAALLIT NUNAAT) Den.
Greenland Sea
Qeqertarsuaq
Davis Strait
Nuuk (Godthab)
Labrador Sea
Hudson Bay
Newfoundland and Labrador
CANADA
British Columbia
Alberta
Saskatchewan
Manitoba
Lake Winnipeg
Severn R.
Ontario
Quebec
Vancouver Island
ROCKY MOUNTAINS
Gulf of St. Lawrence
St. Pierre and Miquelon Fr.
P.E.I.
N.B.
Nova Scotia
Lake Superior
Ottawa
ATLANTIC OCEAN
Washington
Oregon
Idaho
Montana
Wyoming
North Dakota
South Dakota
Minn.
Wis.
Lake Michigan
Michigan
Lake Huron
Lake Ontario
Lake Erie
Maine
Vt.
New Hampshire
Massachusetts
Rhode Island
Connecticut
New York
Pa.
New Jersey
Delaware
Maryland
Ohio
Washington, D.C.
W. Va.
Virginia
Iowa
Nebraska
Missouri R.
Ill.
Ind.
Great Salt Lake
Nevada
Utah
Colorado
Kansas
Missouri
Kentucky
UNITED STATES
California
PACIFIC OCEAN
North Carolina
Tennessee
South Carolina
Arizona
New Mexico
Oklahoma
Ark.
Mississippi R.
Miss.
Ala.
Georgia
Texas
La.
Florida
Rio Grande
Bermuda U.K.
Guadalupe I. Mex.
TROPIC OF CANCER
MEXICO
Mexico City
see inset below
Gulf of Mexico
BAHAMAS
Nassau
Havana
CUBA
Cayman Is. U.K.
JAMAICA
Kingston
Port-au-Prince
HAITI
Hispaniola
Santo Domingo
DOMINICAN REPUBLIC
Turks and Caicos Islands U.K.
Puerto Rico U.S.
San Juan
Aruba Neth.
see inset above
BELIZE
Belmopan
Caribbean Sea
HONDURAS
Tegucigalpa
GUATEMALA
Guatemala
San Salvador
EL SALVADOR
NICARAGUA
Managua
San José
COSTA RICA
Panama Canal
Panama
PANAMA
SOUTH AMERICA
EQUATOR
Virgin Islands U.S.
British Virgin Islands U.K.
Anguilla U.K.
St. Martin Fr.
St. Maarten Neth.
St. Barthélemy Fr.
ANTIGUA AND BARBUDA
Saba Neth.
St. Eustatius Neth.
Montserrat U.K.
Guadeloupe Fr.
ST. KITTS AND NEVIS
DOMINICA
Martinique Fr.
Caribbean Sea
ST. LUCIA
ST. VINCENT AND THE GRENADINES
BARBADOS
GRENADA
TRINIDAD AND TOBAGO
200 mi.
200 km
1,000 miles
1,000 kilometers
Lambert Azimuthal Equal-Area Projection
1. BAJA CALIFORNIA
2. BAJA CALIFORNIA SUR
3. SONORA
4. CHIHUAHUA
5. SINALOA
6. DURANGO
7. COAHUILA
8. NUEVO LEÓN
9. ZACATECAS
10. TAMAULIPAS
11. NAYARIT
12. AGUASCALIENTES
13. SAN LUIS POTOSÍ
14. JALISCO
15. GUANAJUATO
16. QUERÉTARO
17. HIDALGO
18. COLIMA
19. MICHOACÁN
20. MÉXICO
21. DISTRITO FEDERAL
22. TLAXCALA
23. MORELOS
24. PUEBLA
25. VERACRUZ
26. GUERRERO
27. OAXACA
28. TABASCO
29. CHIAPAS
30. CAMPECHE
31. QUINTANA ROO
32. YUCATÁN

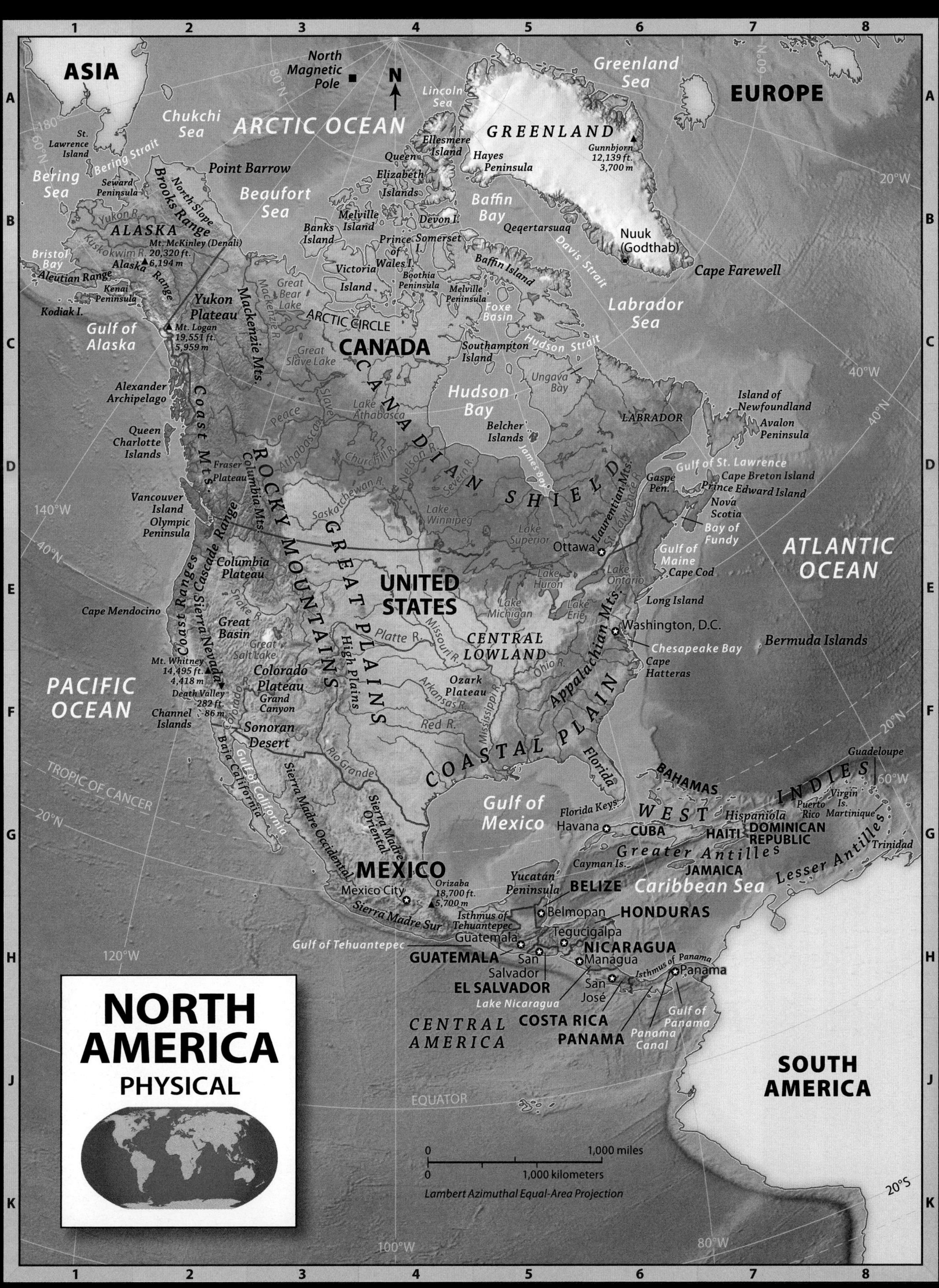
NORTH AMERICA
PHYSICAL
ASIA
EUROPE
GREENLAND
CANADA
UNITED STATES
MEXICO
SOUTH AMERICA
ARCTIC OCEAN
PACIFIC OCEAN
ATLANTIC OCEAN
North Magnetic Pole
N
Chukchi Sea
Bering Sea
Bering Strait
St. Lawrence Island
Seward Peninsula
Point Barrow
Beaufort Sea
Brooks Range
North Slope
ALASKA
Yukon R.
Kuskokwim R.
Bristol Bay
Mt. McKinley (Denali) 20,320 ft. 6,194 m
Alaska Range
Aleutian Range
Kenai Peninsula
Kodiak I.
Gulf of Alaska
Mt. Logan 19,551 ft. 5,959 m
Yukon Plateau
Mackenzie Mts.
Mackenzie R.
Great Bear Lake
Great Slave Lake
ARCTIC CIRCLE
Lincoln Sea
Ellesmere Island
Queen Elizabeth Islands
Hayes Peninsula
Gunnbjorn 12,139 ft. 3,700 m
Greenland Sea
Banks Island
Melville Island
Devon I.
Baffin Bay
Qeqertarsuaq
Davis Strait
Nuuk (Godthab)
Cape Farewell
Prince of Wales I.
Somerset I.
Victoria Island
Boothia Peninsula
Melville Peninsula
Baffin Island
Foxe Basin
Labrador Sea
Southampton Island
Hudson Strait
Ungava Bay
Hudson Bay
Belcher Islands
James Bay
LABRADOR
Island of Newfoundland
Avalon Peninsula
CANADIAN SHIELD
Lake Athabasca
Peace
Slave
Athabasca
Churchill R.
Nelson R.
Severn R.
Saskatchewan R.
Lake Winnipeg
Alexander Archipelago
Queen Charlotte Islands
Coast Mts.
Fraser Plateau
Columbia Mts.
ROCKY MOUNTAINS
GREAT PLAINS
Vancouver Island
Olympic Peninsula
Cascade Range
Columbia Plateau
Gulf of St. Lawrence
Gaspe Pen.
Cape Breton Island
Prince Edward Island
Nova Scotia
Bay of Fundy
Laurentian Mts.
St. Lawrence R.
Lake Superior
Ottawa
Gulf of Maine
Cape Cod
Lake Huron
Lake Ontario
Lake Michigan
Lake Erie
Long Island
Washington, D.C.
Chesapeake Bay
Cape Hatteras
Bermuda Islands
Cape Mendocino
Coast Ranges
Sierra Nevada
Snake R.
Great Basin
Great Salt Lake
Mt. Whitney 14,495 ft. 4,418 m
Death Valley -282 ft. -86 m
Colorado Plateau
Grand Canyon
High Plains
Platte R.
Missouri R.
CENTRAL LOWLAND
Ohio R.
Ozark Plateau
Arkansas R.
Mississippi R.
Appalachian Mts.
Red R.
Channel Islands
Colorado R.
Sonoran Desert
Baja California
Gulf of California
Rio Grande
COASTAL PLAIN
Florida
TROPIC OF CANCER
Sierra Madre Occidental
Sierra Madre Oriental
Gulf of Mexico
Florida Keys
Havana
CUBA
BAHAMAS
WEST INDIES
Hispaniola
HAITI
DOMINICAN REPUBLIC
Puerto Rico
Virgin Is.
Guadeloupe
Martinique
Trinidad
Cayman Is.
Greater Antilles
JAMAICA
Lesser Antilles
Yucatán Peninsula
BELIZE
Caribbean Sea
Orizaba 18,700 ft. 5,700 m
Mexico City
Sierra Madre Sur
Isthmus of Tehuantepec
Belmopan
HONDURAS
Gulf of Tehuantepec
Guatemala
Tegucigalpa
GUATEMALA
San Salvador
NICARAGUA
Managua
EL SALVADOR
Lake Nicaragua
San José
Isthmus of Panama
Panama
Gulf of Panama
CENTRAL AMERICA
COSTA RICA
PANAMA
Panama Canal
EQUATOR
0 1,000 miles
0 1,000 kilometers
Lambert Azimuthal Equal-Area Projection
180°
160°W
140°W
120°W
100°W
80°W
60°W
40°W
20°W
80°N
60°N
40°N
20°N
20°S
1 2 3 4 5 6 7 8
A B C D E F G H J K

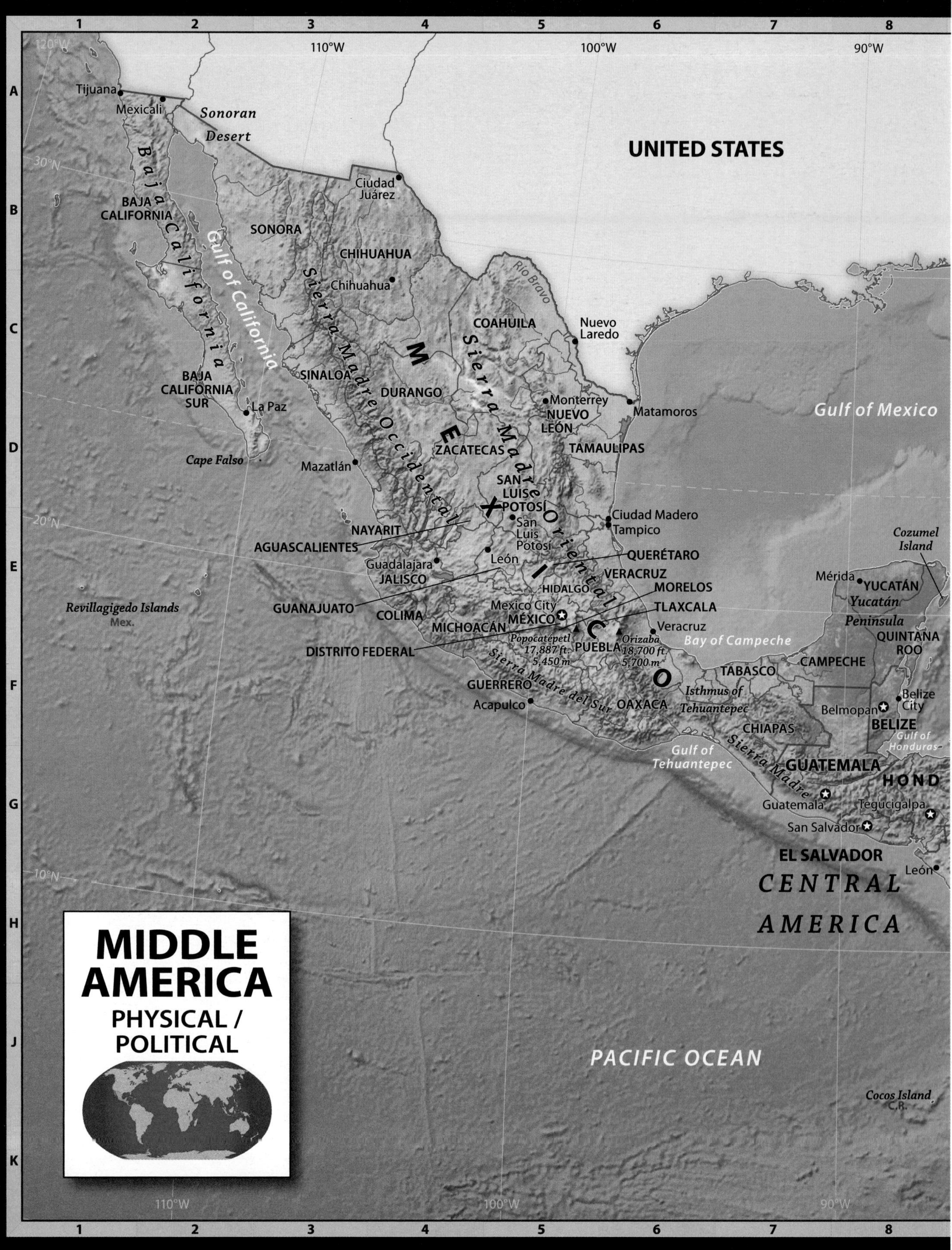
MIDDLE AMERICA
PHYSICAL / POLITICAL
UNITED STATES
MEXICO
Gulf of Mexico
PACIFIC OCEAN
CENTRAL AMERICA
Tijuana
Mexicali
Sonoran Desert
Ciudad Juárez
Baja California
BAJA CALIFORNIA
SONORA
Gulf of California
CHIHUAHUA
Chihuahua
Sierra Madre Occidental
Rio Bravo
COAHUILA
Nuevo Laredo
Sierra Madre Oriental
BAJA CALIFORNIA SUR
La Paz
SINALOA
DURANGO
Monterrey
NUEVO LEÓN
Matamoros
ZACATECAS
TAMAULIPAS
Cape Falso
Mazatlán
SAN LUIS POTOSÍ
San Luis Potosí
Ciudad Madero
Tampico
NAYARIT
AGUASCALIENTES
Guadalajara
JALISCO
León
QUERÉTARO
VERACRUZ
HIDALGO
MORELOS
TLAXCALA
GUANAJUATO
Revillagigedo Islands
Mex.
COLIMA
MICHOACÁN
Mexico City
MÉXICO
Veracruz
DISTRITO FEDERAL
Popocatépetl
17,887 ft.
5,450 m
PUEBLA
Orizaba
18,700 ft.
5,700 m
Bay of Campeche
Sierra Madre del Sur
GUERRERO
Acapulco
OAXACA
Isthmus of Tehuantepec
TABASCO
CAMPECHE
Cozumel Island
Mérida
YUCATÁN
Yucatán Peninsula
QUINTANA ROO
Belize City
Belmopan
BELIZE
Gulf of Honduras
CHIAPAS
Gulf of Tehuantepec
Sierra Madre
GUATEMALA
HOND
Guatemala
Tegucigalpa
San Salvador
EL SALVADOR
León
Cocos Island
C.R.
110°W
100°W
90°W
120°W
30°N
20°N
10°N
1
2
3
4
5
6
7
8
A
B
C
D
E
F
G
H
J
K

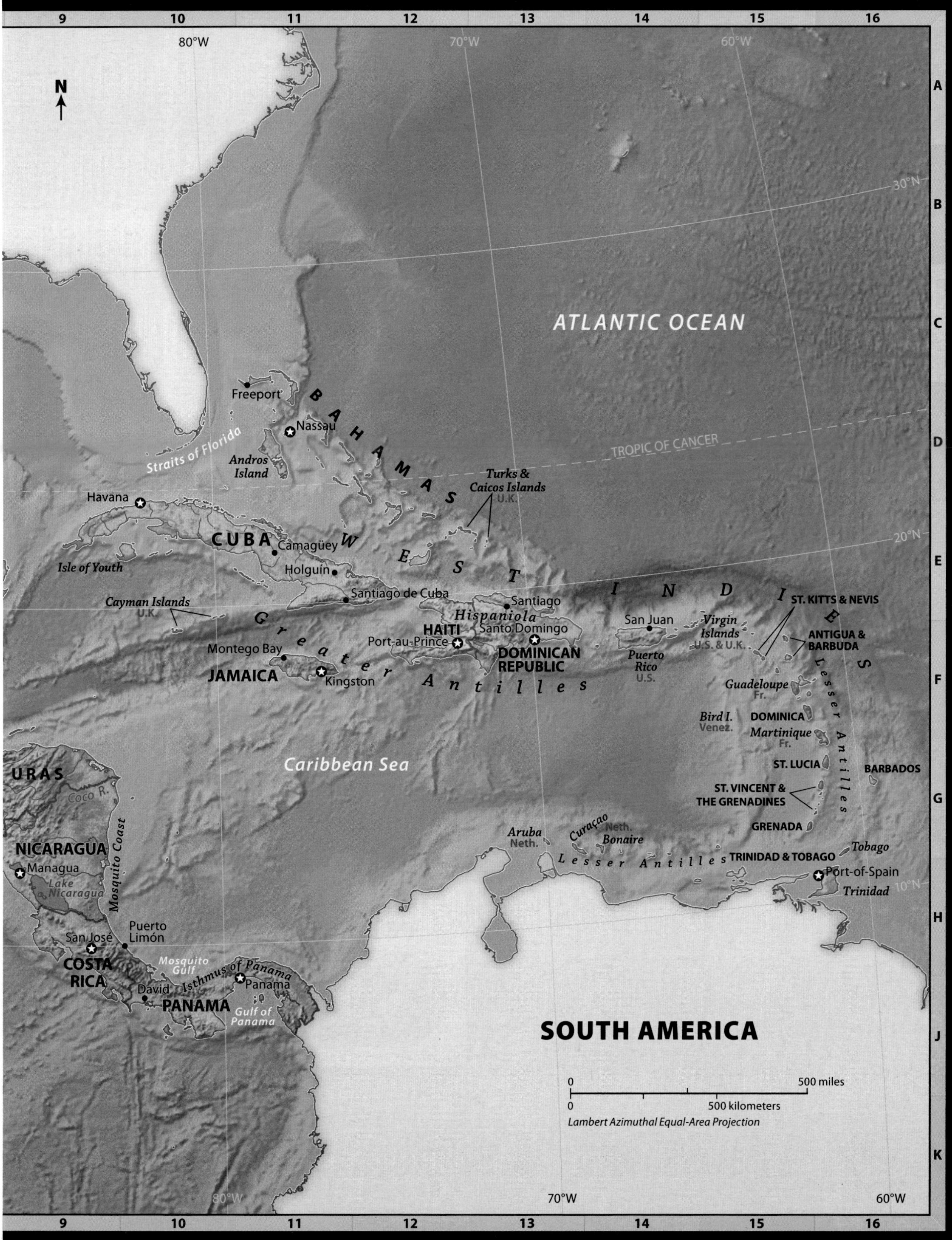

ATLANTIC OCEAN
Freeport
Nassau
BAHAMAS
Straits of Florida
Andros Island
TROPIC OF CANCER
Turks & Caicos Islands
U.K.
Havana
CUBA
Camagüey
Isle of Youth
Holguín
WEST INDIES
Santiago de Cuba
Santiago
Cayman Islands
U.K.
Hispaniola
HAITI
Santo Domingo
Port-au-Prince
DOMINICAN REPUBLIC
San Juan
Puerto Rico
U.S.
Virgin Islands
U.S. & U.K.
ST. KITTS & NEVIS
ANTIGUA & BARBUDA
Montego Bay
JAMAICA
Kingston
Greater Antilles
Guadeloupe
Fr.
Bird I.
Venez.
DOMINICA
Martinique
Fr.
ST. LUCIA
BARBADOS
Lesser Antilles
Caribbean Sea
ST. VINCENT & THE GRENADINES
GRENADA
Aruba
Neth.
Curaçao
Neth.
Bonaire
Lesser Antilles
TRINIDAD & TOBAGO
Tobago
Port-of-Spain
Trinidad
URAS
Coco R.
NICARAGUA
Managua
Lake Nicaragua
Mosquito Coast
Puerto Limón
San José
COSTA RICA
Mosquito Gulf
Isthmus of Panama
Panama
David
PANAMA
Gulf of Panama
SOUTH AMERICA
0
500 miles
0
500 kilometers
Lambert Azimuthal Equal-Area Projection
N
80°W
70°W
60°W
30°N
20°N
10°N
9
10
11
12
13
14
15
16
A
B
C
D
E
F
G
H
J
K

SOUTH AMERICA
POLITICAL
Lambert Azimuthal Equal-Area Projection
0 1,000 miles
0 1,000 kilometers
Caribbean Sea
PACIFIC OCEAN
ATLANTIC OCEAN
VENEZUELA
GUYANA
SURINAME
FRENCH GUIANA
Fr.
COLOMBIA
ECUADOR
PERU
BRAZIL
BOLIVIA
PARAGUAY
CHILE
ARGENTINA
URUGUAY
AMAZON BASIN
ANDES
Caracas
Maracaibo
Valencia
Ciudad Guayana
Georgetown
Paramaribo
Cayenne
Santa Marta
Barranquilla
Cartagena
Bucaramanga
San Cristóbal
Medellín
Bogotá
Cali
Malpelo I.
Col.
Esmeraldas
Quito
Guayaquil
Iquitos
Boa Vista
Boundary claimed by Suriname
Marajó Island
Manaus
Santarém
Belém
São Luís
Fortaleza
Teresina
Natal
Campina Grande
Recife
Rio Branco
Pôrto Velho
Callao
Lima
Machu Picchu
Cuzco
Ayacucho
Lake Titicaca
Arequipa
La Paz
Trinidad
Santa Cruz
Oruro
Sucre
Arica
Iquique
Tarija
Salvador
Brasília
Goiânia
Uberlândia
Uberaba
Campo Grande
Belo Horizonte
Londrina
Campinas
Nova Iguaçu
São Paulo
Santos
Rio de Janeiro
Curitiba
Antofagasta
Salta
Asunción
San Félix I.
San Ambrosio I.
Chile
San Miguel de Tucumán
Uruguaiana
Santa Maria
Pôrto Alegre
La Serena
Coquimbo
Córdoba
Valparaíso
Santiago
Mendoza
Rosario
Juan Fernández Is.
Buenos Aires
Montevideo
La Plata
Río de la Plata
Concepción
Mar del Plata
Bahía Blanca
Puerto Montt
Comodoro Rivadavia
Falkland Islands (Islas Malvinas)
Stanley
Administered by United Kingdom
Claimed by Arg.
Río Gallegos
Punta Arenas
Ushuaia
Strait of Magellan
Cape Horn
South Georgia Island
U.K.
Lake Maracaibo
Orinoco R.
Rio Negro
Amazon R.
Marañón R.
Ucayali R.
Purus R.
Madeira R.
Tapajós R.
Xingu R.
Araguaia R.
Tocantins R.
São Francisco R.
Paraguay R.
Paraná R.
Uruguay R.
Colorado R.
Negro R.
EQUATOR
TROPIC OF CAPRICORN
0°
20°S
40°S
80°W
60°W
40°W
100°W
20°W
1 2 3 4 5 6 7 8
A B C D E F G H J K
N

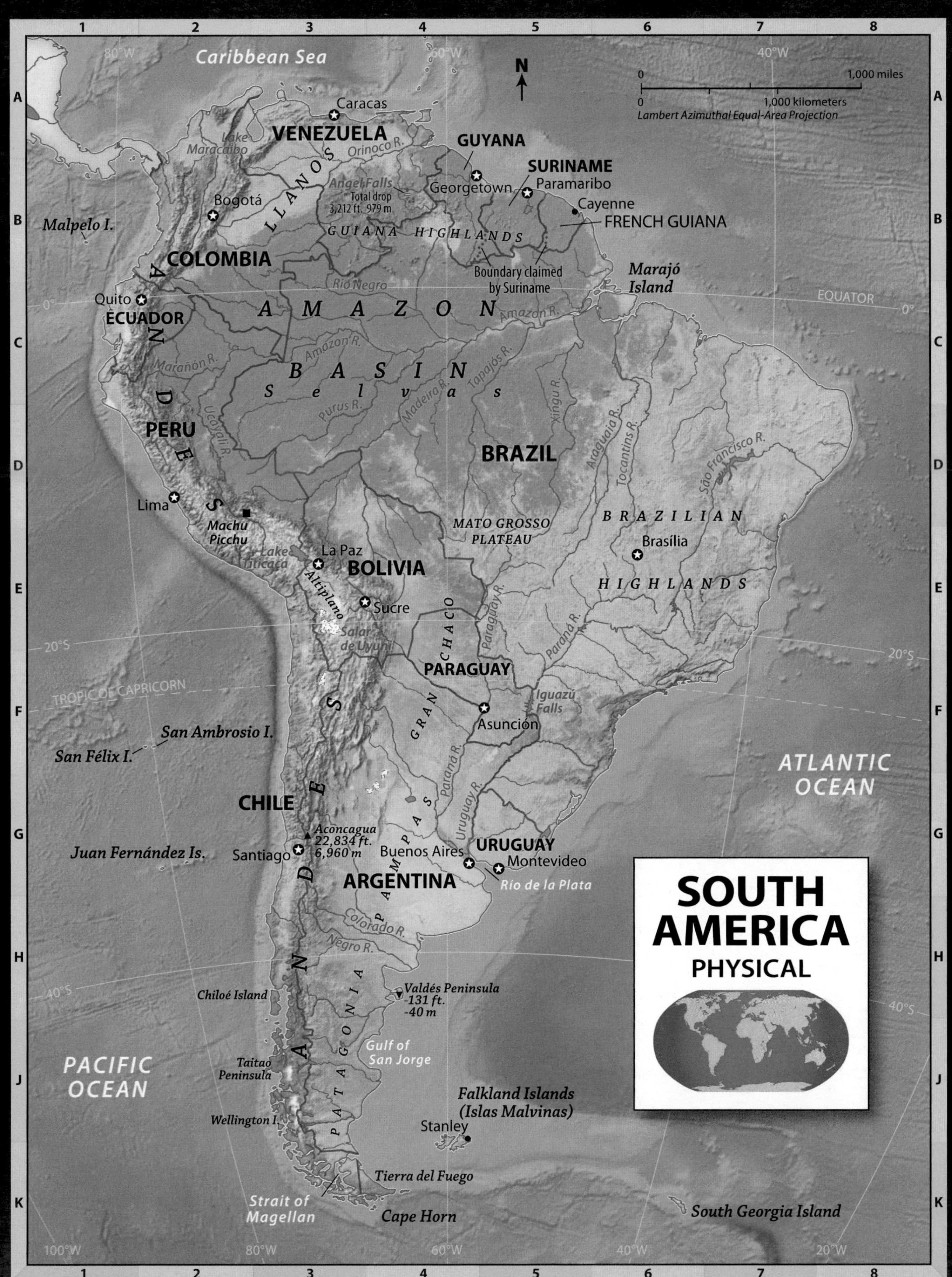

SOUTH AMERICA
PHYSICAL
Caribbean Sea
Lambert Azimuthal Equal-Area Projection
Caracas
VENEZUELA
Lake Maracaibo
Orinoco R.
LLANOS
Angel Falls Total drop 3,212 ft. 979 m
GUYANA
Georgetown
SURINAME
Paramaribo
Cayenne
FRENCH GUIANA
Bogotá
Malpelo I.
GUIANA HIGHLANDS
Boundary claimed by Suriname
COLOMBIA
Marajó Island
Quito
ECUADOR
Río Negro
AMAZON BASIN
Selvas
Amazon R.
EQUATOR
Marañón R.
Purus R.
Madeira R.
Tapajós R.
Xingu R.
Ucayali R.
PERU
BRAZIL
Araguaia R.
Tocantins R.
São Francisco R.
Lima
Machu Picchu
MATO GROSSO PLATEAU
BRAZILIAN HIGHLANDS
Brasília
Lake Titicaca
La Paz
BOLIVIA
Altiplano
Sucre
Salar de Uyuni
GRAN CHACO
Paraguay R.
Paraná R.
PARAGUAY
TROPIC OF CAPRICORN
Iguazú Falls
Asunción
San Ambrosio I.
San Félix I.
ATLANTIC OCEAN
CHILE
ANDES
Aconcagua 22,834 ft. 6,960 m
Juan Fernández Is.
Santiago
Buenos Aires
URUGUAY
Uruguay R.
Montevideo
ARGENTINA
PAMPAS
Río de la Plata
Colorado R.
Negro R.
Chiloé Island
Valdés Peninsula -131 ft. -40 m
PATAGONIA
Gulf of San Jorge
PACIFIC OCEAN
Taitao Peninsula
Falkland Islands (Islas Malvinas)
Wellington I.
Stanley
Tierra del Fuego
Strait of Magellan
Cape Horn
South Georgia Island

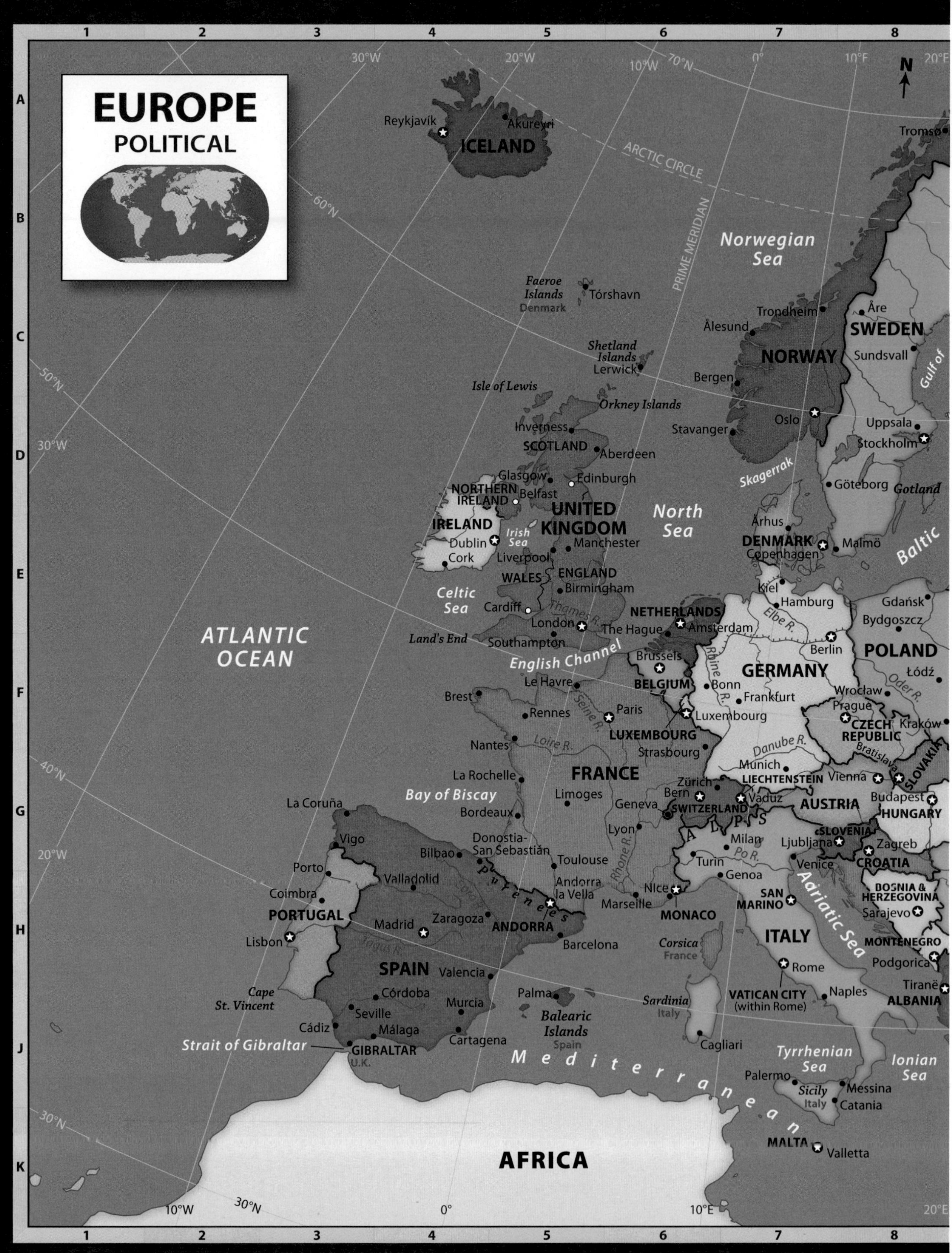
EUROPE
POLITICAL
ICELAND
Reykjavík
Akureyri
ARCTIC CIRCLE
Norwegian Sea
PRIME MERIDIAN
Faeroe Islands
Denmark
Tórshavn
Shetland Islands
Lerwick
Isle of Lewis
Orkney Islands
NORWAY
SWEDEN
Trondheim
Ålesund
Bergen
Oslo
Stavanger
Åre
Sundsvall
Uppsala
Stockholm
Göteborg
Gotland
Tromsø
Inverness
SCOTLAND
Aberdeen
Glasgow
Edinburgh
NORTHERN IRELAND
Belfast
UNITED KINGDOM
IRELAND
Dublin
Cork
Irish Sea
Manchester
Liverpool
ENGLAND
WALES
Birmingham
Celtic Sea
Cardiff
London
Thames R.
Southampton
Land's End
North Sea
Skagerrak
Århus
DENMARK
Copenhagen
Malmö
Baltic
Kiel
Hamburg
Gdańsk
Bydgoszcz
POLAND
Łódź
Elbe R.
NETHERLANDS
The Hague
Amsterdam
Berlin
English Channel
Brussels
BELGIUM
GERMANY
Bonn
Frankfurt
Rhine R.
Oder R.
Wrocław
Prague
CZECH REPUBLIC
Kraków
Le Havre
Brest
Rennes
Paris
Seine R.
Luxembourg
LUXEMBOURG
Nantes
Loire R.
Strasbourg
Danube R.
Munich
Bratislava
SLOVAKIA
ATLANTIC OCEAN
FRANCE
La Rochelle
Zürich
LIECHTENSTEIN
Vienna
Bern
Vaduz
AUSTRIA
Budapest
HUNGARY
Bay of Biscay
Limoges
Geneva
SWITZERLAND
ALPS
La Coruña
Bordeaux
Lyon
Milan
Ljubljana
SLOVENIA
Zagreb
CROATIA
Vigo
Donostia-San Sebastián
Bilbao
Toulouse
Rhone R.
Turin
Po R.
Venice
Porto
Valladolid
Pyrenees
Andorra la Vella
Nice
Genoa
BOSNIA & HERZEGOVINA
Sarajevo
Coimbra
PORTUGAL
Madrid
Zaragoza
ANDORRA
Marseille
MONACO
SAN MARINO
Adriatic Sea
Lisbon
Tagus R.
Barcelona
Corsica
France
ITALY
MONTENEGRO
Podgorica
SPAIN
Valencia
Rome
Tiranë
ALBANIA
Cape St. Vincent
Córdoba
Seville
Murcia
Palma
Balearic Islands
Spain
Sardinia
Italy
VATICAN CITY (within Rome)
Naples
Cádiz
Málaga
Cartagena
Strait of Gibraltar
GIBRALTAR
U.K.
Mediterranean
Cagliari
Tyrrhenian Sea
Ionian Sea
Palermo
Sicily
Italy
Messina
Catania
MALTA
Valletta
AFRICA
N
30°W
20°W
10°W
0°
10°E
20°E
70°N
60°N
50°N
40°N
30°N
1
2
3
4
5
6
7
8
A
B
C
D
E
F
G
H
I
J
K

Barents Sea
White Sea
Kola Peninsula
LAPLAND
URAL MOUNTAINS
A commonly accepted division between Asia and Europe—here marked by a gray line—is formed by the Ural Mountains, Ural River, Caspian Sea, Caucasus Mountains, and the Black Sea with its outlets, the Bosporus and the Dardanelles.
Europe/Asia boundary
ASIA
FINLAND
RUSSIA
ESTONIA
LATVIA
LITHUANIA
BELARUS
UKRAINE
MOLDOVA
ROMANIA
SERBIA
KOSOVO
BULGARIA
MACEDONIA
GREECE
TURKEY
CYPRUS
GEORGIA
AZERBAIJAN
KAZAKHSTAN
Caspian Sea
Black Sea
Sea of Azov
Caucasus Mountains
Carpathian Mts.
Balkan Mts.
Sea of Marmara
Aegean Sea
Bosporus
Dardanelles
Crimea
Peloponnese
Rhodes
Crete
Greece
Lake Onega
Lake Ladoga
Northern Dvina R.
Volga R.
Don R.
Dnieper R.
Dniester R.
Vistula R.
Ural R.
Bothnia
Sea
Tobseda
Murmansk
Ivalo
Kirovsk
Umba
Kiruna
Kemi
Luleå
Oulu
Umeå
Kem'
Arkhangel'sk
Severodvinsk
Pechora
Syktyvkar
Vaasa
Kuopio
Pori
Tampere
Turku
Helsinki
St. Petersburg
Tallinn
Novgorod
Yaroslavl'
Perm'
Kirov
Ufa
Kazan'
Nizhniy Novgorod
Tver'
Moscow
Samara
Orenburg
Riga
Daugavpils
Smolensk
Ryazan'
Penza
Vilnius
Vitsyebsk
Kaunas
Kaliningrad
Minsk
Bryansk
Saratov
Oral
Homyel'
Kursk
Warsaw
Chernihiv
Sumy
Kharkiv
Volgograd
Kyiv (Kiev)
Poltava
L'viv
Vinnytsya
Donets'k
Astrakhan
Dnipropetrovs'k
Rostov
Stavropol'
Chişinău
Odessa
Kerch
Grozny
Simferopol'
Sevastopol'
Yalta
Baku
Belgrade
Bucharest
Constanța
Varna
Priština
Sofia
Skopje
İstanbul
Thessaloniki
Athens
Nicosia
Iraklion
60°E
70°E
80°E
30°E
40°E
50°E
60°N
50°N
40°N
30°N
0
400 miles
400 kilometers
Lambert Azimuthal Equal-Area Projection

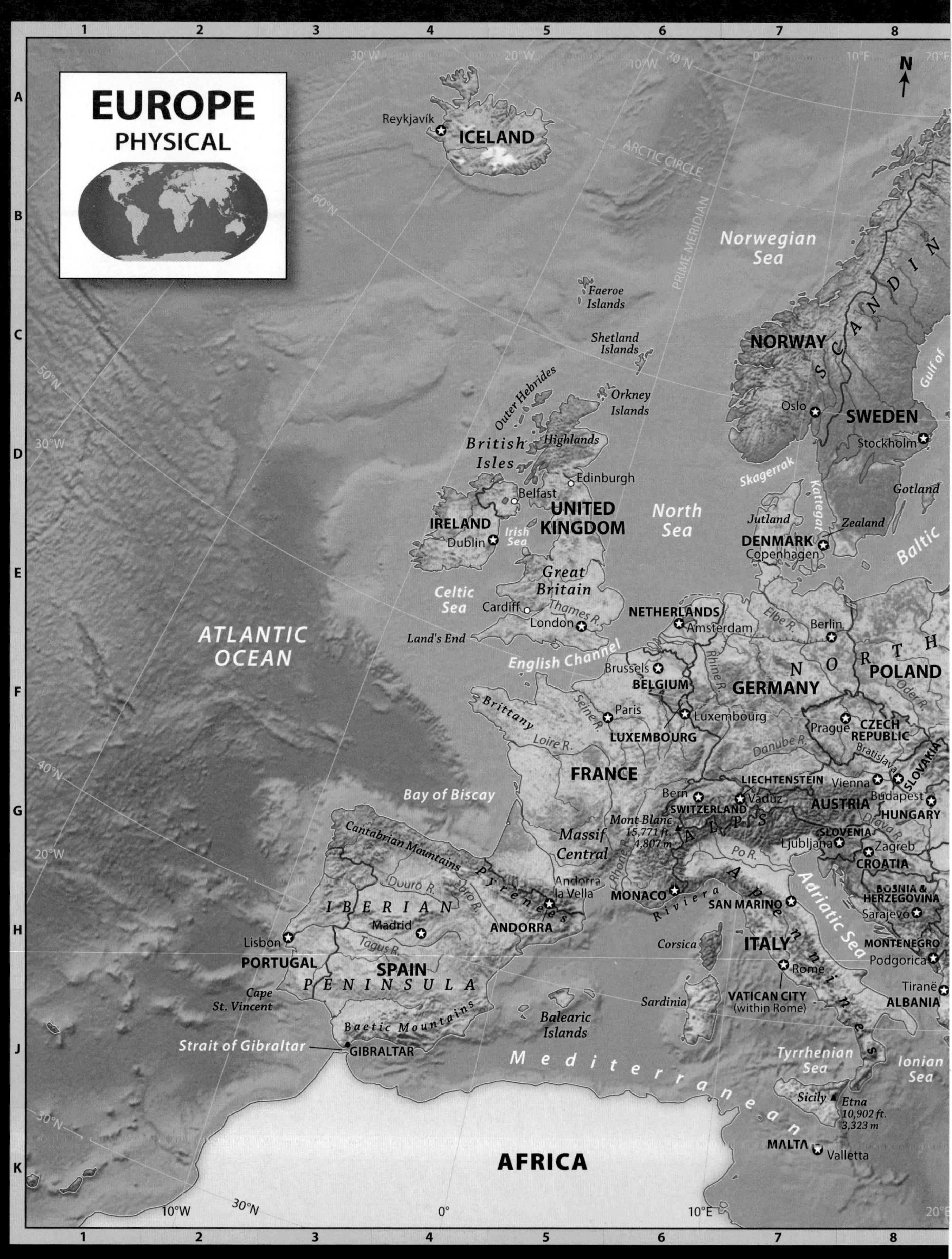
EUROPE
PHYSICAL
ICELAND
Reykjavík
Norwegian Sea
Faeroe Islands
Shetland Islands
Orkney Islands
Outer Hebrides
British Isles
Highlands
Edinburgh
Belfast
UNITED KINGDOM
IRELAND
Dublin
Irish Sea
North Sea
Great Britain
Celtic Sea
Cardiff
London
Thames R.
Land's End
English Channel
ATLANTIC OCEAN
NORWAY
Oslo
SWEDEN
Stockholm
Skagerrak
Kattegat
Jutland
Zealand
DENMARK
Copenhagen
Gotland
Baltic
NETHERLANDS
Amsterdam
Berlin
Elbe R.
Brussels
BELGIUM
GERMANY
POLAND
Oder R.
Rhine R.
Paris
Seine R.
Luxembourg
LUXEMBOURG
Brittany
Loire R.
Prague
CZECH REPUBLIC
Danube R.
Bratislava
SLOVAKIA
FRANCE
LIECHTENSTEIN
Vienna
Vaduz
Bern
SWITZERLAND
AUSTRIA
Budapest
HUNGARY
Bay of Biscay
Mont Blanc 15,771 ft. 4,807 m
ALPS
Massif Central
SLOVENIA
Ljubljana
Zagreb
CROATIA
Po R.
Cantabrian Mountains
Pyrenees
Andorra la Vella
ANDORRA
MONACO
Riviera
SAN MARINO
Adriatic Sea
BOSNIA & HERZEGOVINA
Sarajevo
Douro R.
Ebro R.
IBERIAN PENINSULA
Madrid
Lisbon
PORTUGAL
Tagus R.
SPAIN
Corsica
ITALY
Rome
Apennines
MONTENEGRO
Podgorica
Tiranë
ALBANIA
Cape St. Vincent
Sardinia
VATICAN CITY (within Rome)
Balearic Islands
Baetic Mountains
Strait of Gibraltar
GIBRALTAR
Mediterranean
Tyrrhenian Sea
Ionian Sea
Sicily
Etna 10,902 ft. 3,323 m
MALTA
Valletta
AFRICA
ARCTIC CIRCLE
PRIME MERIDIAN
Gulf of
30°W
20°W
10°W
0°
10°E
20°E
70°N
60°N
50°N
40°N
30°N
N

Barents Sea
North Cape
Kola Peninsula
White Sea
LAPLAND
Bothnia
FINLAND
Lake Region
Lake Onega
Lake Ladoga
Helsinki
Gulf of Finland
Tallinn
ESTONIA
LATVIA
Riga
LITHUANIA
Vilnius
RUSSIA
Minsk
BELARUS
Warsaw
Vistula R.
Moscow
RUSSIA
Northern Dvina R.
Pechora R.
EUROPEAN PLAIN
CENTRAL RUSSIAN UPLAND
Don R.
Volga R.
(Kyiv) Kiev
Dnieper R.
Dniester R.
UKRAINE
Carpathian Mts.
Tisza R.
MOLDOVA
Chișinău
ROMANIA
Belgrade
Bucharest
Danube R.
SERBIA
BALKAN PENINSULA
KOSOVO
Priština
Sofia
Balkan Mts.
BULGARIA
Skopje
MACEDONIA
Sea of Azov
Crimea
Black Sea
Bosporus
TURKEY
Sea of Marmara
Dardanelles
GREECE
Aegean Sea
Athens
Peloponnese
Rhodes
Crete
Sea
Nicosia
CYPRUS
URAL MOUNTAINS
Europe/Asia boundary
ASIA
Ural R.
KAZAKHSTAN
Caspian Depression
Caspian Sea
Mt. Elbrus 18,510 ft. 5,642 m
Caucasus Mountains
GEORGIA
AZERBAIJAN
Baku
ASIA
0 400 miles
0 400 kilometers
Lambert Azimuthal Equal-Area Projection
30°E 40°E 50°E 60°E 70°E 80°E
60°N 50°N 40°N 30°N

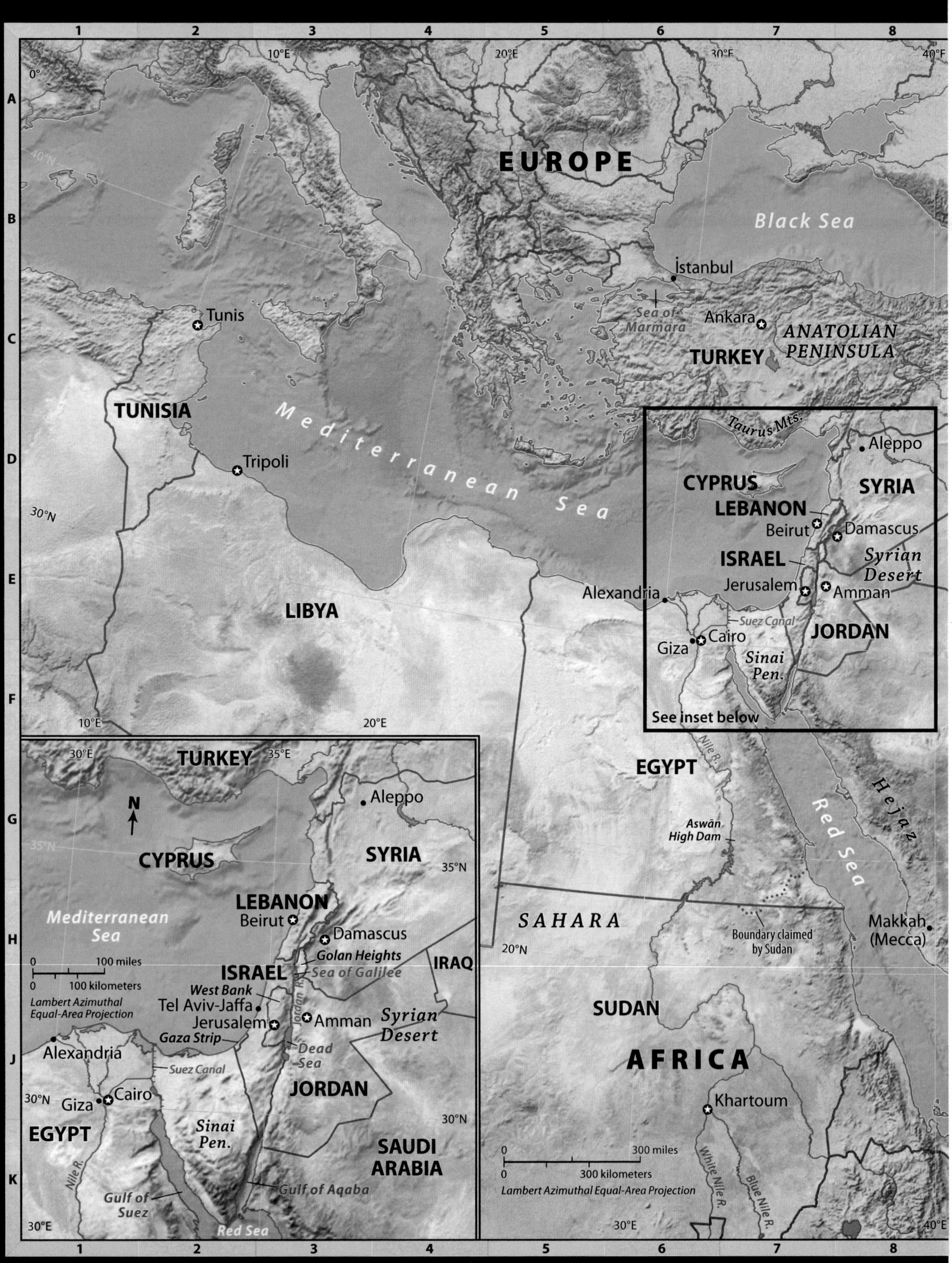

EUROPE
Black Sea
İstanbul
Sea of Marmara
Ankara
ANATOLIAN PENINSULA
TURKEY
Tunis
TUNISIA
Mediterranean Sea
Tripoli
Taurus Mts.
Aleppo
CYPRUS
SYRIA
LEBANON
Beirut
Damascus
ISRAEL
Syrian Desert
Jerusalem
Amman
Alexandria
Suez Canal
LIBYA
JORDAN
Giza
Cairo
Sinai Pen.
See inset below
EGYPT
Nile R.
Hejaz
Red Sea
Aswān High Dam
SAHARA
Makkah (Mecca)
Boundary claimed by Sudan
SUDAN
AFRICA
Khartoum
300 miles
300 kilometers
Lambert Azimuthal Equal-Area Projection
White Nile R.
Blue Nile R.
TURKEY
Aleppo
CYPRUS
SYRIA
Mediterranean Sea
LEBANON
Beirut
Damascus
100 miles
100 kilometers
Lambert Azimuthal Equal-Area Projection
ISRAEL
Golan Heights
Sea of Galilee
IRAQ
West Bank
Tel Aviv-Jaffa
Jordan R.
Jerusalem
Amman
Syrian Desert
Gaza Strip
Dead Sea
Alexandria
Suez Canal
JORDAN
Giza
Cairo
EGYPT
Sinai Pen.
SAUDI ARABIA
Nile R.
Gulf of Suez
Gulf of Aqaba
Red Sea

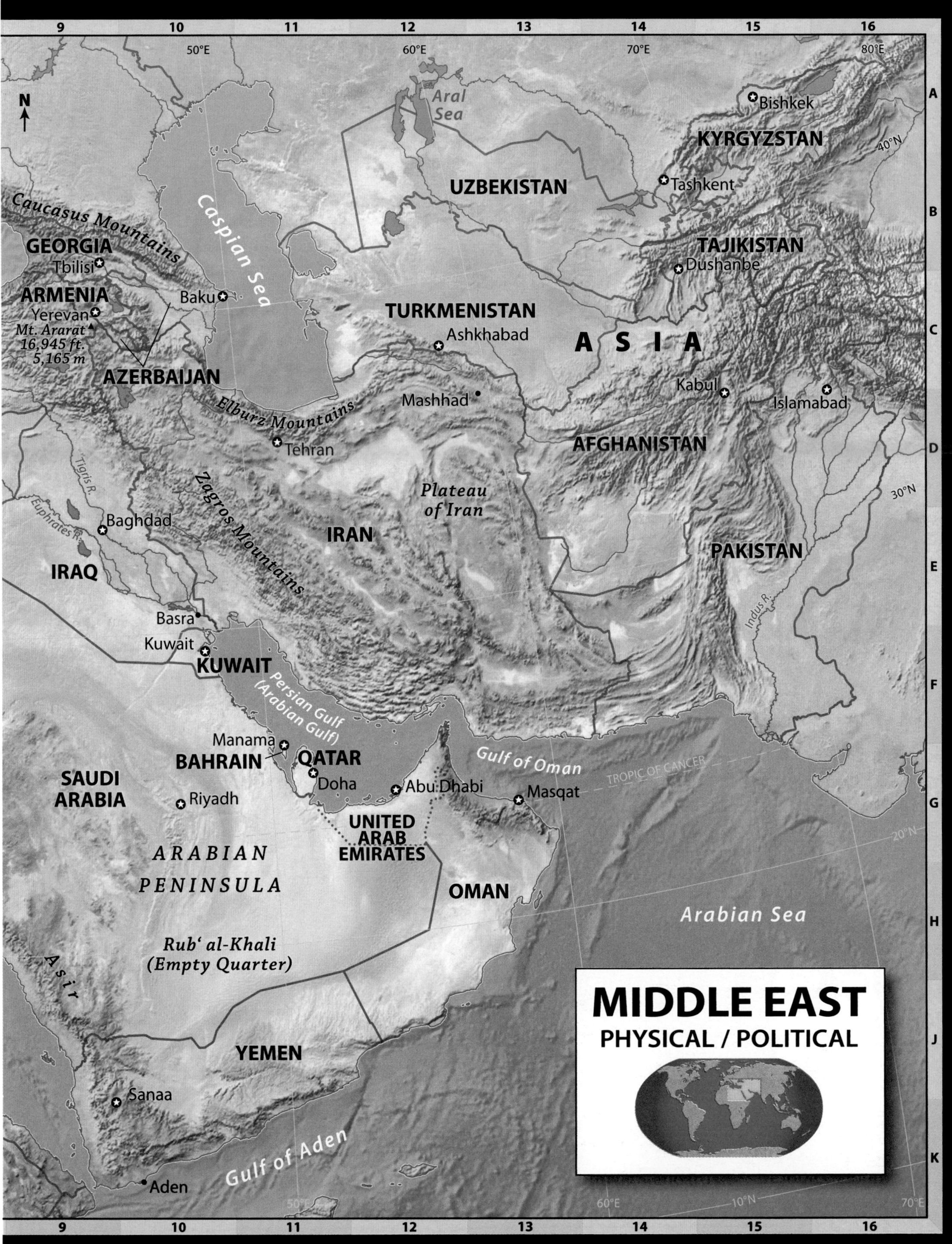
MIDDLE EAST
PHYSICAL / POLITICAL
ASIA
Caspian Sea
Aral Sea
Caucasus Mountains
Elburz Mountains
Zagros Mountains
Plateau of Iran
Persian Gulf (Arabian Gulf)
Gulf of Oman
Arabian Sea
Gulf of Aden
ARABIAN PENINSULA
Rub' al-Khali (Empty Quarter)
Asir
Mt. Ararat 16,945 ft. 5,165 m
GEORGIA
ARMENIA
AZERBAIJAN
UZBEKISTAN
KYRGYZSTAN
TAJIKISTAN
TURKMENISTAN
AFGHANISTAN
PAKISTAN
IRAN
IRAQ
KUWAIT
BAHRAIN
QATAR
SAUDI ARABIA
UNITED ARAB EMIRATES
OMAN
YEMEN
Tbilisi
Yerevan
Baku
Bishkek
Tashkent
Dushanbe
Ashkhabad
Mashhad
Kabul
Islamabad
Tehran
Baghdad
Basra
Kuwait
Manama
Doha
Abu Dhabi
Masqat
Riyadh
Sanaa
Aden
Tigris R.
Euphrates R.
Indus R.
TROPIC OF CANCER
N

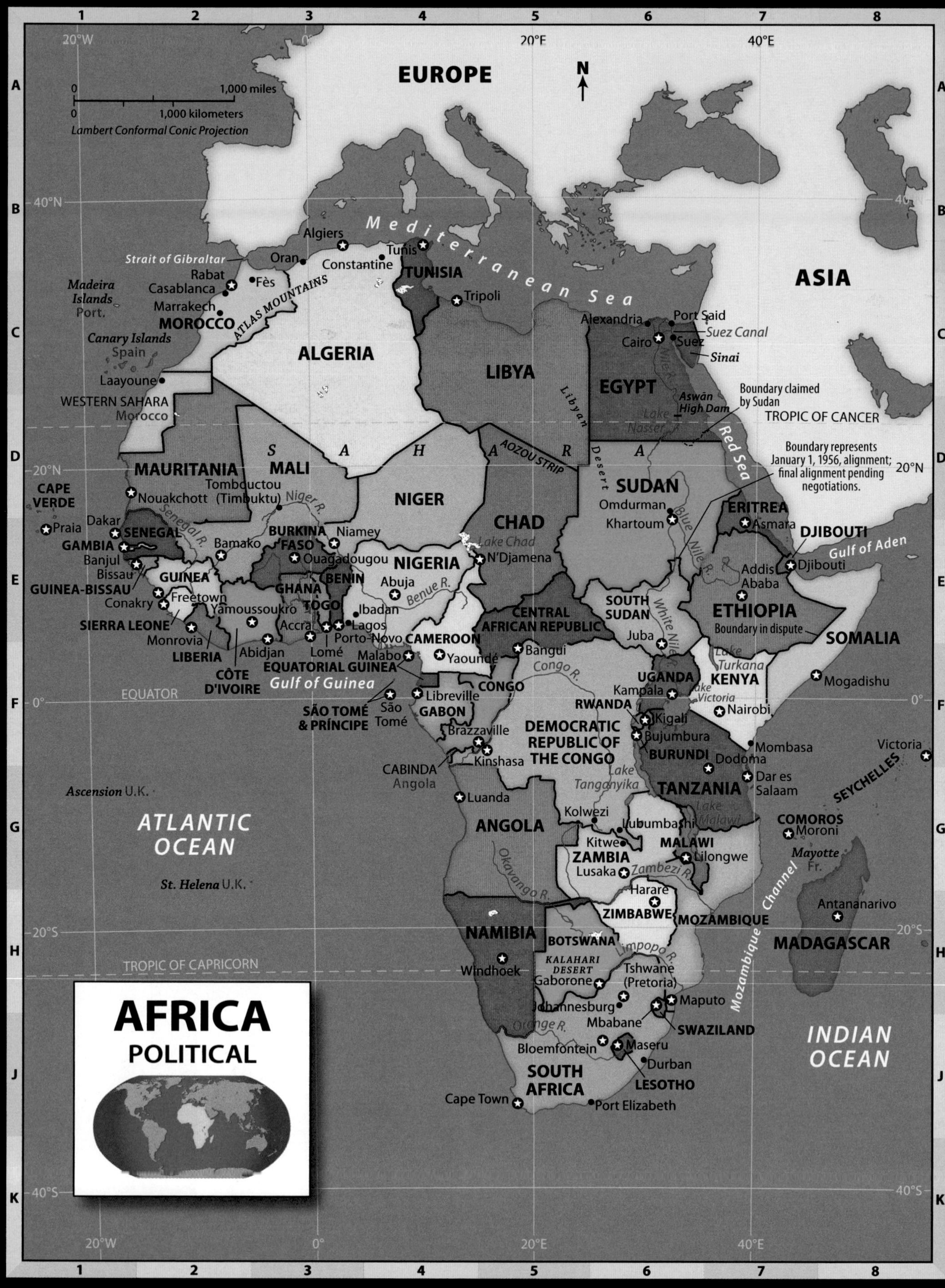

AFRICA
POLITICAL
EUROPE
ASIA
ATLANTIC OCEAN
INDIAN OCEAN
Mediterranean Sea
Red Sea
Gulf of Aden
Gulf of Guinea
Mozambique Channel
Lambert Conformal Conic Projection
1,000 miles
1,000 kilometers
TROPIC OF CANCER
TROPIC OF CAPRICORN
EQUATOR
MOROCCO
ALGERIA
TUNISIA
LIBYA
EGYPT
MAURITANIA
MALI
NIGER
CHAD
SUDAN
SOUTH SUDAN
ERITREA
DJIBOUTI
ETHIOPIA
SOMALIA
KENYA
UGANDA
RWANDA
BURUNDI
TANZANIA
DEMOCRATIC REPUBLIC OF THE CONGO
CONGO
GABON
CAMEROON
CENTRAL AFRICAN REPUBLIC
NIGERIA
BENIN
TOGO
GHANA
BURKINA FASO
CÔTE D'IVOIRE
LIBERIA
SIERRA LEONE
GUINEA
GUINEA-BISSAU
GAMBIA
SENEGAL
CAPE VERDE
EQUATORIAL GUINEA
SÃO TOMÉ & PRÍNCIPE
ANGOLA
ZAMBIA
MALAWI
MOZAMBIQUE
ZIMBABWE
BOTSWANA
NAMIBIA
SOUTH AFRICA
LESOTHO
SWAZILAND
MADAGASCAR
COMOROS
SEYCHELLES
WESTERN SAHARA Morocco
CABINDA Angola
Madeira Islands Port.
Canary Islands Spain
Ascension U.K.
St. Helena U.K.
Mayotte Fr.
Strait of Gibraltar
ATLAS MOUNTAINS
SAHARA
Libyan Desert
AOZOU STRIP
KALAHARI DESERT
Suez Canal
Sinai
Aswān High Dam
Lake Nasser
Lake Chad
Lake Turkana
Lake Victoria
Lake Tanganyika
Lake Malawi
Nile R.
Blue Nile R.
White Nile R.
Niger R.
Senegal R.
Benue R.
Congo R.
Zambezi R.
Okavango R.
Limpopo R.
Orange R.
Boundary claimed by Sudan
Boundary represents January 1, 1956, alignment; final alignment pending negotiations.
Boundary in dispute
Algiers
Tunis
Constantine
Oran
Rabat
Casablanca
Fès
Marrakech
Tripoli
Alexandria
Port Said
Cairo
Suez
Laayoune
Nouakchott
Tombouctou (Timbuktu)
Dakar
Praia
Banjul
Bissau
Conakry
Freetown
Monrovia
Bamako
Niamey
Ouagadougou
Yamoussoukro
Abidjan
Accra
Lomé
Porto-Novo
Lagos
Ibadan
Abuja
N'Djamena
Omdurman
Khartoum
Asmara
Djibouti
Addis Ababa
Juba
Mogadishu
Bangui
Yaoundé
Malabo
Libreville
São Tomé
Brazzaville
Kinshasa
Luanda
Kampala
Nairobi
Kigali
Bujumbura
Mombasa
Dodoma
Dar es Salaam
Victoria
Moroni
Kolwezi
Lubumbashi
Kitwe
Lusaka
Lilongwe
Harare
Antananarivo
Windhoek
Gaborone
Tshwane (Pretoria)
Johannesburg
Maputo
Mbabane
Bloemfontein
Maseru
Durban
Cape Town
Port Elizabeth
20°W
0°
20°E
40°E
40°N
20°N
0°
20°S
40°S
N

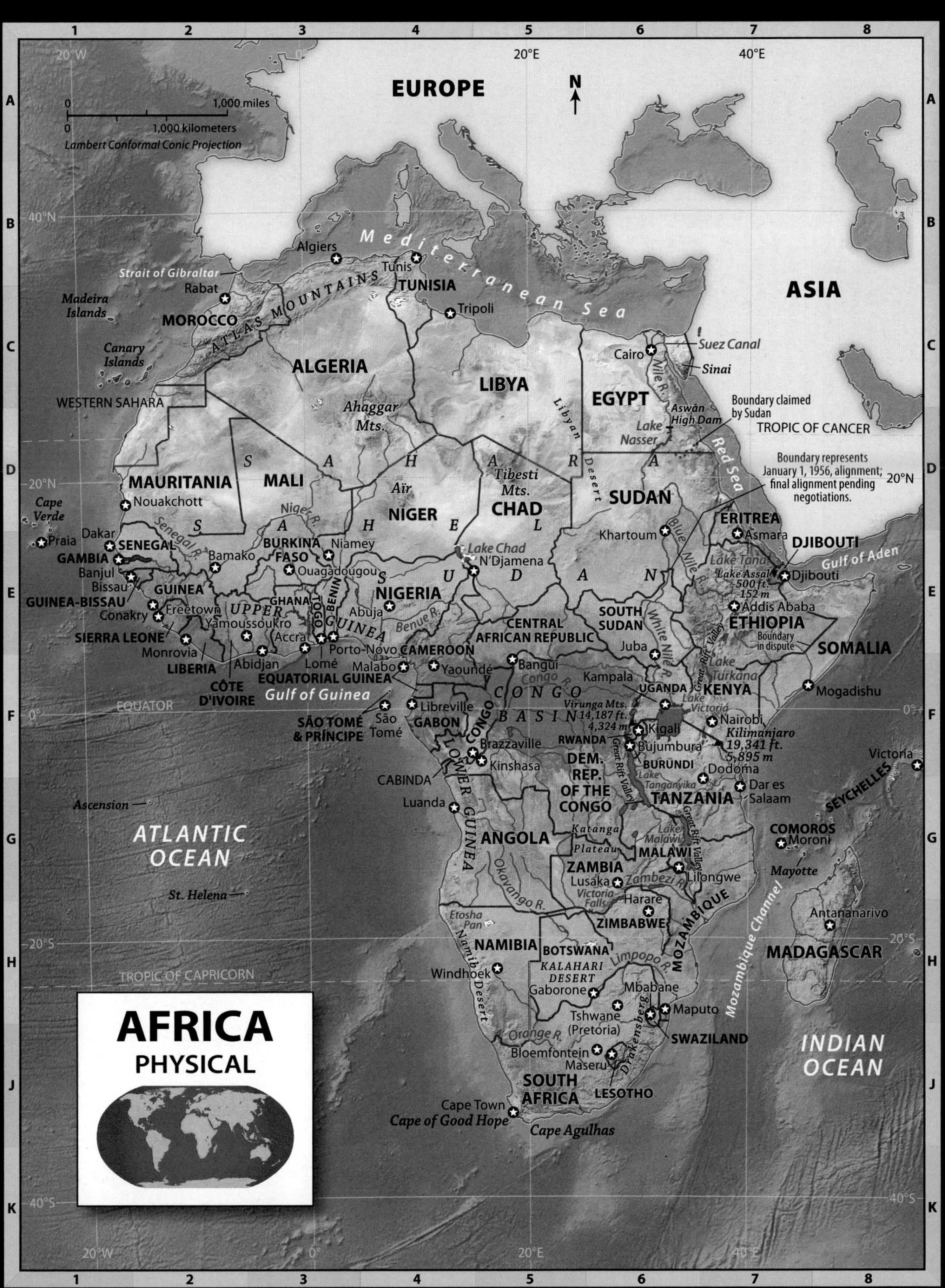

AFRICA
PHYSICAL
EUROPE
ASIA
ATLANTIC OCEAN
INDIAN OCEAN
0 1,000 miles
0 1,000 kilometers
Lambert Conformal Conic Projection
Mediterranean Sea
Strait of Gibraltar
Madeira Islands
Canary Islands
ATLAS MOUNTAINS
Algiers
Tunis
TUNISIA
Rabat
MOROCCO
Tripoli
ALGERIA
LIBYA
EGYPT
Cairo
Suez Canal
Sinai
Nile R.
Aswân High Dam
Lake Nasser
Boundary claimed by Sudan
TROPIC OF CANCER
Red Sea
Boundary represents January 1, 1956, alignment; final alignment pending negotiations.
WESTERN SAHARA
Ahaggar Mts.
Libyan Desert
SAHARA
Tibesti Mts.
MAURITANIA
Nouakchott
MALI
Aïr
NIGER
CHAD
SUDAN
Cape Verde
Praia
Dakar
SENEGAL
Senegal R.
Niger R.
GAMBIA
Banjul
Bamako
BURKINA FASO
Niamey
Ouagadougou
Lake Chad
N'Djamena
Khartoum
Blue Nile R.
ERITREA
Asmara
DJIBOUTI
Djibouti
Gulf of Aden
Lake Tana
Lake Assal 500 ft. 152 m
SUDAN
Bissau
GUINEA-BISSAU
GUINEA
Conakry
Freetown
SIERRA LEONE
Monrovia
LIBERIA
UPPER GUINEA
GHANA
TOGO
BENIN
Yamoussoukro
Accra
Porto-Novo
Lomé
Abidjan
CÔTE D'IVOIRE
NIGERIA
Abuja
Benue R.
CENTRAL AFRICAN REPUBLIC
SOUTH SUDAN
Juba
White Nile R.
Addis Ababa
ETHIOPIA
Boundary in dispute
SOMALIA
Great Rift Valley
Lake Turkana
CAMEROON
Malabo
Yaoundé
EQUATORIAL GUINEA
Gulf of Guinea
Bangui
Congo R.
CONGO BASIN
Kampala
UGANDA
KENYA
Mogadishu
EQUATOR
SÃO TOMÉ & PRÍNCIPE
São Tomé
Libreville
GABON
CONGO
Virunga Mts. 14,187 ft. 4,324 m
Lake Victoria
Nairobi
Kilimanjaro 19,341 ft. 5,895 m
Kigali
RWANDA
Bujumbura
BURUNDI
Brazzaville
Kinshasa
DEM. REP. OF THE CONGO
Lake Tanganyika
Dodoma
Dar es Salaam
TANZANIA
Victoria
SEYCHELLES
CABINDA
Luanda
LOWER GUINEA
Ascension
ANGOLA
Katanga Plateau
Lake Malawi
MALAWI
Lilongwe
COMOROS
Moroni
Mayotte
ZAMBIA
Lusaka
Zambezi R.
Victoria Falls
Harare
St. Helena
Okavango R.
Etosha Pan
ZIMBABWE
MOZAMBIQUE
Mozambique Channel
Antananarivo
MADAGASCAR
NAMIBIA
BOTSWANA
Limpopo R.
TROPIC OF CAPRICORN
Windhoek
KALAHARI DESERT
Namib Desert
Gaborone
Mbabane
Maputo
Tshwane (Pretoria)
SWAZILAND
Drakensberg
Orange R.
Bloemfontein
Maseru
SOUTH AFRICA
LESOTHO
Cape Town
Cape of Good Hope
Cape Agulhas
20°W
0°
20°E
40°E
40°N
20°N
20°S
40°S

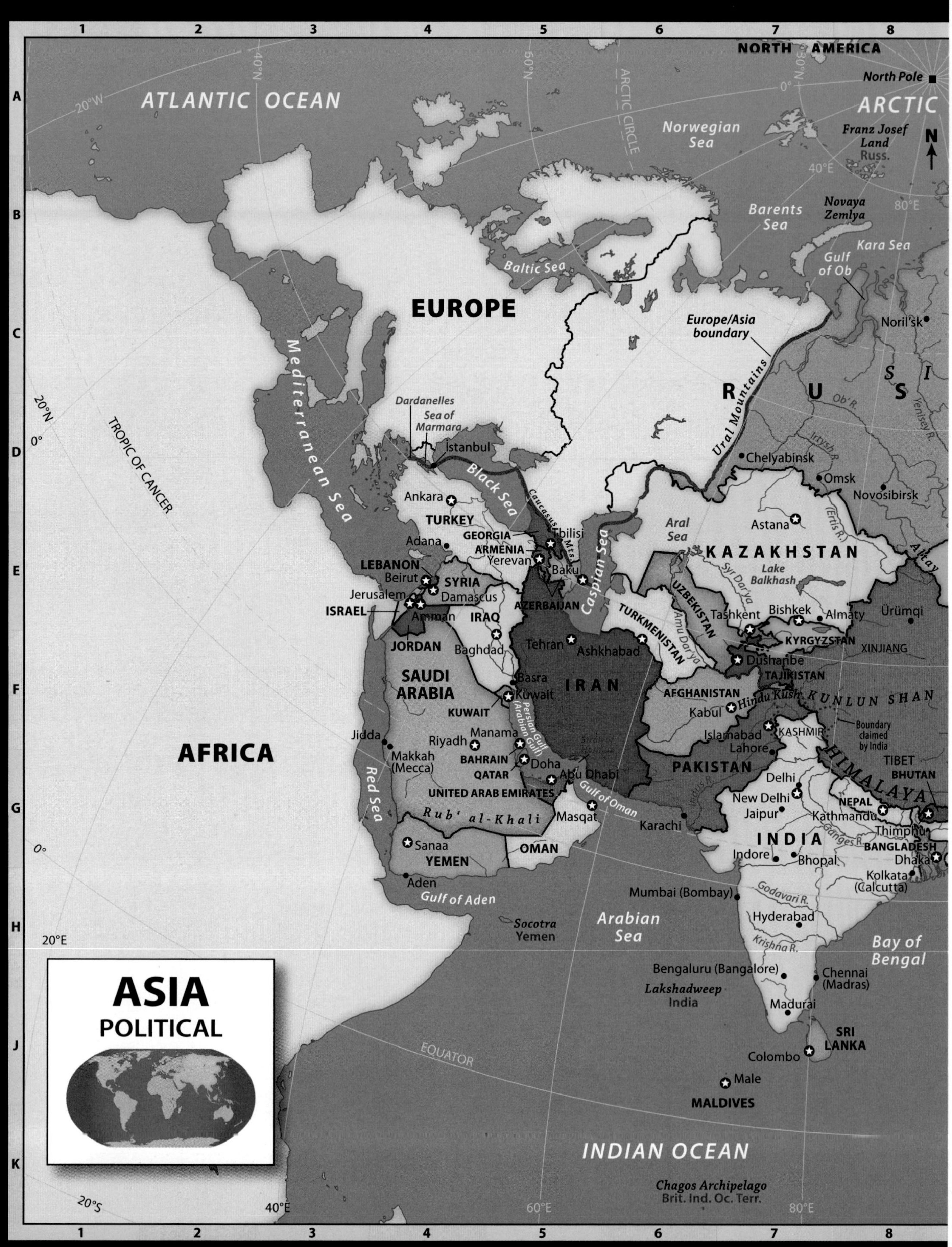
ASIA
POLITICAL
ATLANTIC OCEAN
ARCTIC
NORTH AMERICA
North Pole
Franz Josef Land Russ.
Norwegian Sea
Barents Sea
Novaya Zemlya
Kara Sea
Gulf of Ob
Baltic Sea
EUROPE
Europe/Asia boundary
Ural Mountains
Noril'sk
Mediterranean Sea
Dardanelles
Sea of Marmara
Istanbul
Black Sea
Chelyabinsk
Omsk
Novosibirsk
Ankara
TURKEY
Caucasus Mts.
Tbilisi
GEORGIA
ARMENIA
Yerevan
Baku
AZERBAIJAN
Caspian Sea
Aral Sea
KAZAKHSTAN
Astana
Lake Balkhash
Adana
LEBANON
Beirut
SYRIA
Damascus
Jerusalem
ISRAEL
Amman
JORDAN
IRAQ
Baghdad
Tehran
IRAN
TURKMENISTAN
Ashkhabad
UZBEKISTAN
Tashkent
Bishkek
Almaty
Ürümqi
KYRGYZSTAN
XINJIANG
Dushanbe
TAJIKISTAN
AFGHANISTAN
Kabul
Hindu Kush
KUNLUN SHAN
Basra
Kuwait
KUWAIT
SAUDI ARABIA
Persian Gulf (Arabian Gulf)
Manama
BAHRAIN
Riyadh
Doha
QATAR
Abu Dhabi
UNITED ARAB EMIRATES
Gulf of Oman
Masqat
Jidda
Makkah (Mecca)
Red Sea
Rub' al-Khali
OMAN
Sanaa
YEMEN
Aden
Gulf of Aden
Socotra Yemen
Arabian Sea
AFRICA
KASHMIR
Islamabad
Lahore
PAKISTAN
Boundary claimed by India
TIBET
BHUTAN
HIMALAYA
Delhi
New Delhi
Jaipur
Karachi
NEPAL
Kathmandu
Thimphu
INDIA
Indore
Bhopal
BANGLADESH
Dhaka
Kolkata (Calcutta)
Mumbai (Bombay)
Godavari R.
Hyderabad
Krishna R.
Bay of Bengal
Bengaluru (Bangalore)
Chennai (Madras)
Lakshadweep India
Madurai
SRI LANKA
Colombo
Male
MALDIVES
EQUATOR
INDIAN OCEAN
Chagos Archipelago Brit. Ind. Oc. Terr.
TROPIC OF CANCER
ARCTIC CIRCLE

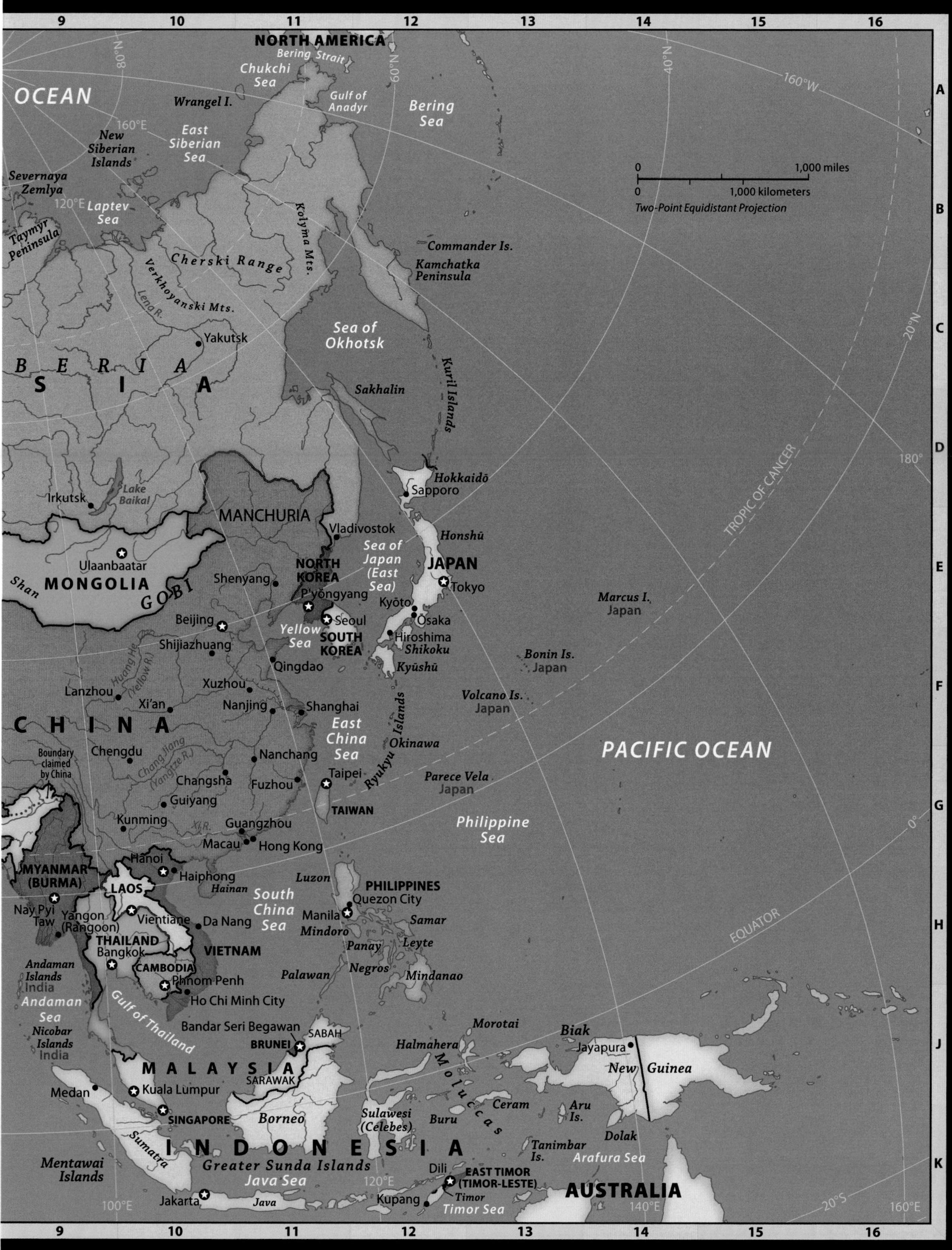
NORTH AMERICA
Bering Strait
Chukchi Sea
OCEAN
Wrangel I.
Gulf of Anadyr
Bering Sea
New Siberian Islands
East Siberian Sea
Severnaya Zemlya
Laptev Sea
Taymyr Peninsula
Kolyma Mts.
Commander Is.
Kamchatka Peninsula
Cherski Range
Verkhoyanski Mts.
Lena R.
Yakutsk
Sea of Okhotsk
Kuril Islands
Sakhalin
S I B E R I A
Hokkaidō
Sapporo
Irkutsk
Lake Baikal
MANCHURIA
Vladivostok
Honshū
Sea of Japan (East Sea)
JAPAN
Ulaanbaatar
MONGOLIA
GOBI
Shenyang
NORTH KOREA
Tokyo
P'yŏngyang
Kyōto
Marcus I. Japan
Beijing
Seoul
Osaka
Yellow Sea
SOUTH KOREA
Hiroshima
Shikoku
Shijiazhuang
Qingdao
Kyūshū
Bonin Is. Japan
Lanzhou
Huang He (Yellow R.)
Xuzhou
Volcano Is. Japan
Xi'an
Nanjing
Shanghai
CHINA
East China Sea
Ryukyu Islands
Okinawa
PACIFIC OCEAN
Chengdu
Nanchang
Boundary claimed by China
Chang Jiang (Yangtze R.)
Changsha
Fuzhou
Taipei
Parece Vela Japan
Guiyang
TAIWAN
Kunming
Xi R.
Guangzhou
Philippine Sea
Macau
Hong Kong
Hanoi
MYANMAR (BURMA)
Haiphong
Hainan
Luzon
PHILIPPINES
LAOS
South China Sea
Quezon City
Nay Pyi Taw
Yangon (Rangoon)
Vientiane
Da Nang
Manila
Samar
Mindoro
THAILAND
Bangkok
VIETNAM
Panay
Leyte
EQUATOR
Andaman Islands India
CAMBODIA
Negros
Phnom Penh
Palawan
Mindanao
Andaman Sea
Ho Chi Minh City
Gulf of Thailand
Bandar Seri Begawan
Morotai
Nicobar Islands India
BRUNEI
SABAH
Halmahera
Biak
Jayapura
MALAYSIA
Moluccas
SARAWAK
New Guinea
Medan
Kuala Lumpur
Ceram
Aru Is.
SINGAPORE
Borneo
Sulawesi (Celebes)
Buru
Sumatra
INDONESIA
Tanimbar Is.
Dolak
Arafura Sea
Mentawai Islands
Greater Sunda Islands
Java Sea
Dili
EAST TIMOR (TIMOR-LESTE)
Jakarta
Java
Kupang
Timor
AUSTRALIA
Timor Sea
TROPIC OF CANCER
0 1,000 miles
0 1,000 kilometers
Two-Point Equidistant Projection
80°N
60°N
40°N
20°N
0°
20°S
160°E
120°E
100°E
140°E
160°W
180°
9 10 11 12 13 14 15 16
A B C D E F G H J K

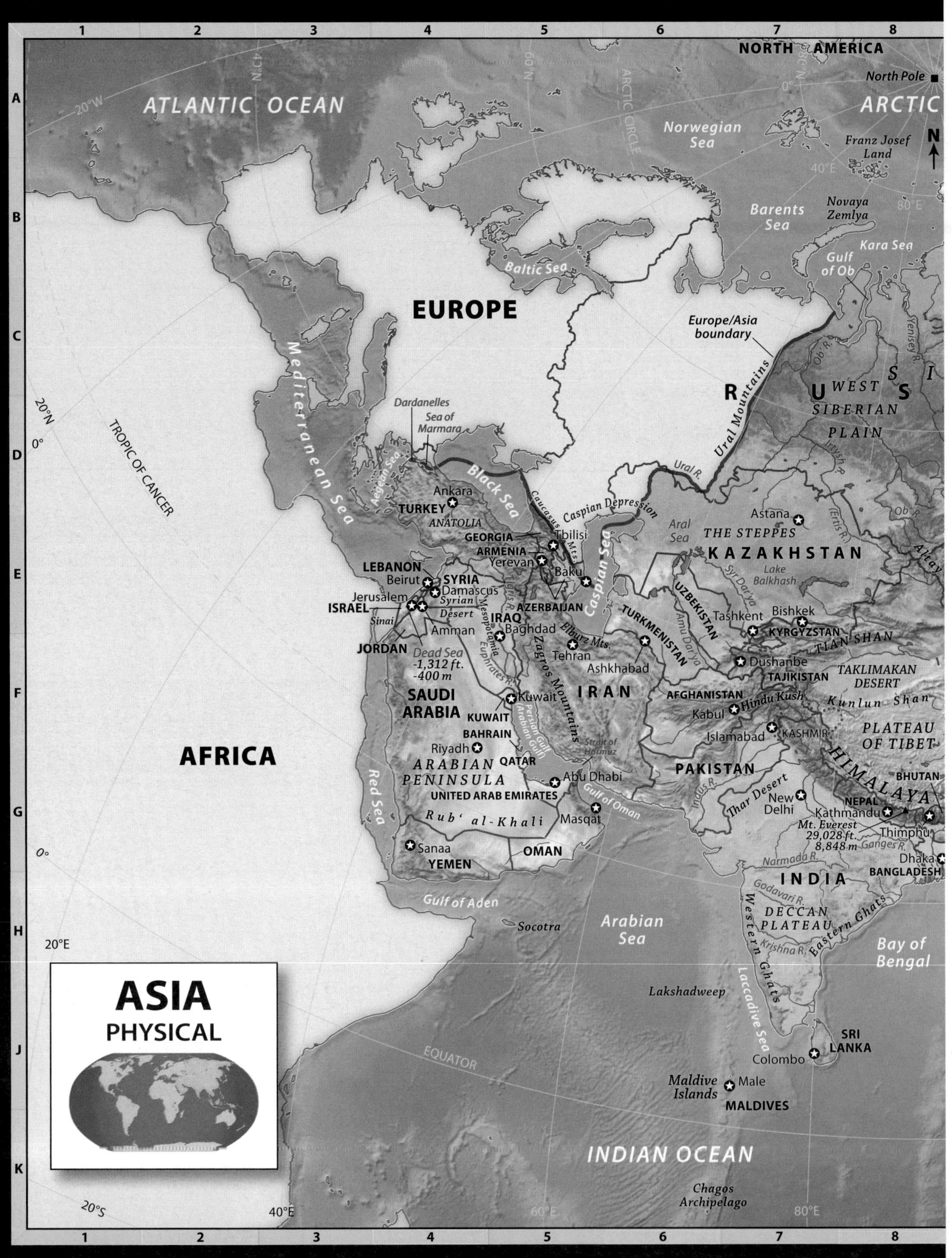
ASIA
PHYSICAL
ATLANTIC OCEAN
ARCTIC
NORTH AMERICA
North Pole
Norwegian Sea
Franz Josef Land
Barents Sea
Novaya Zemlya
Kara Sea
Gulf of Ob
Baltic Sea
EUROPE
Europe/Asia boundary
Ural Mountains
WEST SIBERIAN PLAIN
Mediterranean Sea
Dardanelles
Sea of Marmara
Aegean Sea
Black Sea
Caspian Depression
Caucasus Mts.
Caspian Sea
Ural R.
TROPIC OF CANCER
Ankara
TURKEY
ANATOLIA
GEORGIA
Tbilisi
ARMENIA
Yerevan
Baku
AZERBAIJAN
LEBANON
Beirut
SYRIA
Damascus
Syrian Desert
Jerusalem
ISRAEL
Sinai
Amman
JORDAN
Dead Sea -1,312 ft. -400 m
IRAQ
Baghdad
Mesopotamia
Euphrates R.
Elburz Mts.
Tehran
Zagros Mountains
IRAN
Kuwait
KUWAIT
SAUDI ARABIA
BAHRAIN
Persian Gulf
Arabian Gulf
Strait of Hormuz
Riyadh
QATAR
ARABIAN PENINSULA
Abu Dhabi
UNITED ARAB EMIRATES
Gulf of Oman
Masqat
Rub' al-Khali
OMAN
Red Sea
Sanaa
YEMEN
Gulf of Aden
Socotra
Arabian Sea
AFRICA
Astana
Aral Sea
THE STEPPES
KAZAKHSTAN
Lake Balkhash
Syr Darya
UZBEKISTAN
TURKMENISTAN
Amu Darya
Ashkhabad
Tashkent
Bishkek
KYRGYZSTAN
TIAN SHAN
Dushanbe
TAJIKISTAN
TAKLIMAKAN DESERT
AFGHANISTAN
Hindu Kush
Kabul
Kunlun Shan
Islamabad
KASHMIR
PLATEAU OF TIBET
PAKISTAN
HIMALAYA
BHUTAN
Indus R.
Thar Desert
New Delhi
NEPAL
Kathmandu
Mt. Everest 29,028 ft. 8,848 m
Thimphu
Ganges R.
Dhaka
BANGLADESH
Narmada R.
INDIA
Godavari R.
DECCAN PLATEAU
Western Ghats
Eastern Ghats
Krishna R.
Bay of Bengal
Lakshadweep
Laccadive Sea
SRI LANKA
Colombo
Maldive Islands
Male
MALDIVES
INDIAN OCEAN
Chagos Archipelago
EQUATOR
ARCTIC CIRCLE
Irtysh R.
Ob R.
Yenisey R.
Altay
20°W
20°N
0°
20°E
40°E
60°E
80°E
20°S
1 2 3 4 5 6 7 8
A B C D E F G H J K

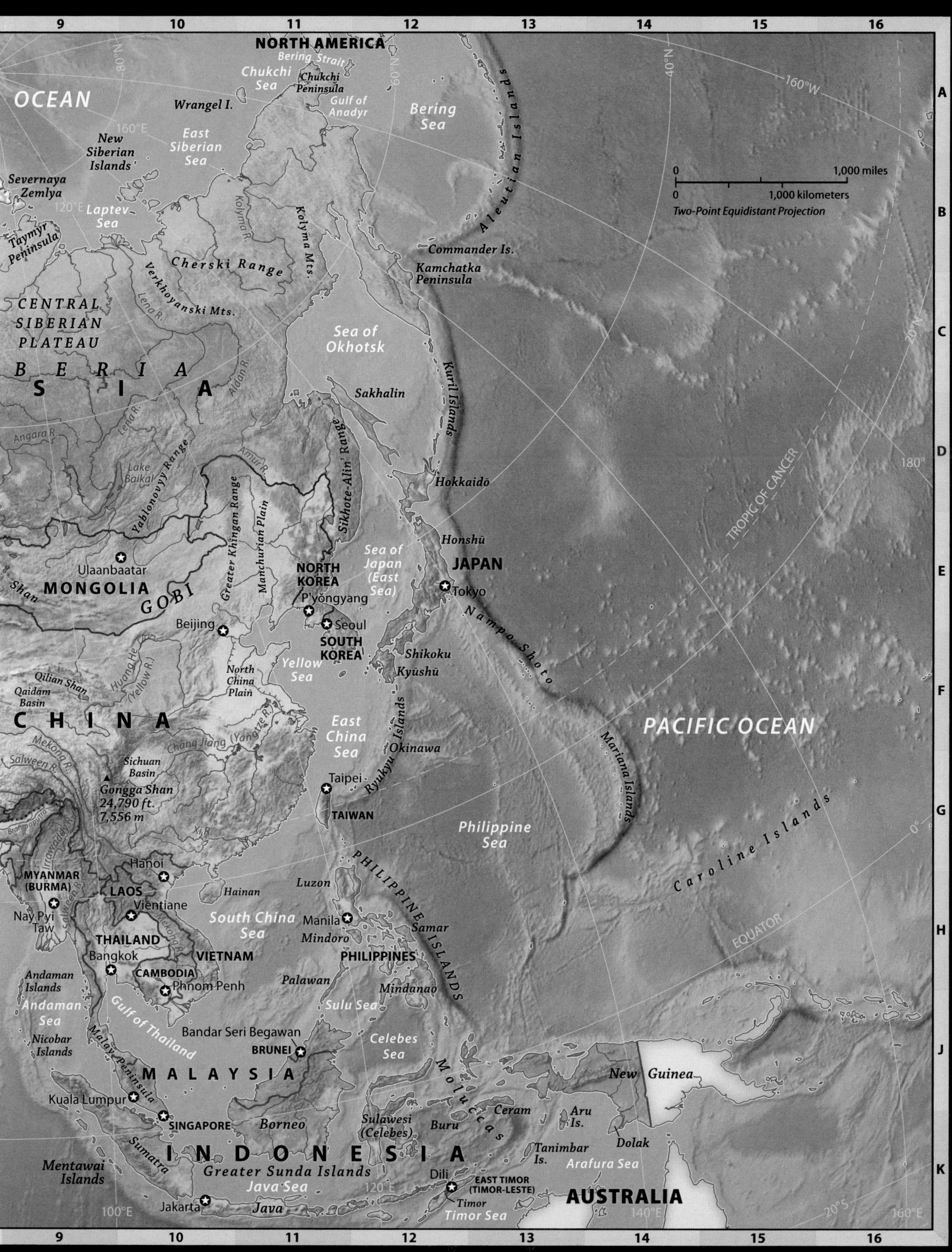
NORTH AMERICA
Bering Strait
Chukchi Sea
Chukchi Peninsula
Gulf of Anadyr
Bering Sea
OCEAN
Wrangel I.
New Siberian Islands
East Siberian Sea
Severnaya Zemlya
Laptev Sea
Taymyr Peninsula
Aleutian Islands
Commander Is.
Kamchatka Peninsula
Cherski Range
Kolyma Mts.
Verkhoyanski Mts.
CENTRAL SIBERIAN PLATEAU
SIBERIA
ASIA
Sea of Okhotsk
Kuril Islands
Sakhalin
Sikhote-Alin' Range
Lake Baikal
Yablonovyy Range
Greater Khingan Range
Manchurian Plain
Hokkaidō
Honshū
JAPAN
Sea of Japan (East Sea)
NORTH KOREA
P'yŏngyang
Seoul
SOUTH KOREA
Tokyo
Nampo Shoto
Ulaanbaatar
MONGOLIA
GOBI
Beijing
North China Plain
Yellow Sea
Shikoku
Kyūshū
Qilian Shan
Qaidam Basin
CHINA
East China Sea
Okinawa
Ryukyu Islands
Sichuan Basin
Gongga Shan 24,790 ft. 7,556 m
Taipei
TAIWAN
PACIFIC OCEAN
Mariana Islands
Philippine Sea
Caroline Islands
TROPIC OF CANCER
EQUATOR
Hanoi
MYANMAR (BURMA)
LAOS
Nay Pyi Taw
Vientiane
Hainan
Luzon
PHILIPPINE ISLANDS
South China Sea
Manila
Mindoro
Samar
THAILAND
Bangkok
VIETNAM
PHILIPPINES
CAMBODIA
Phnom Penh
Andaman Islands
Andaman Sea
Palawan
Mindanao
Sulu Sea
Gulf of Thailand
Nicobar Islands
Bandar Seri Begawan
BRUNEI
Celebes Sea
MALAYSIA
Malay Peninsula
Moluccas
New Guinea
Kuala Lumpur
SINGAPORE
Borneo
Sulawesi (Celebes)
Buru
Ceram
Aru Is.
Sumatra
INDONESIA
Tanimbar Is.
Dolak
Arafura Sea
Mentawai Islands
Greater Sunda Islands
Java Sea
Dili
EAST TIMOR (TIMOR-LESTE)
Timor
Timor Sea
AUSTRALIA
Jakarta
Java
0 1,000 miles
0 1,000 kilometers
Two-Point Equidistant Projection

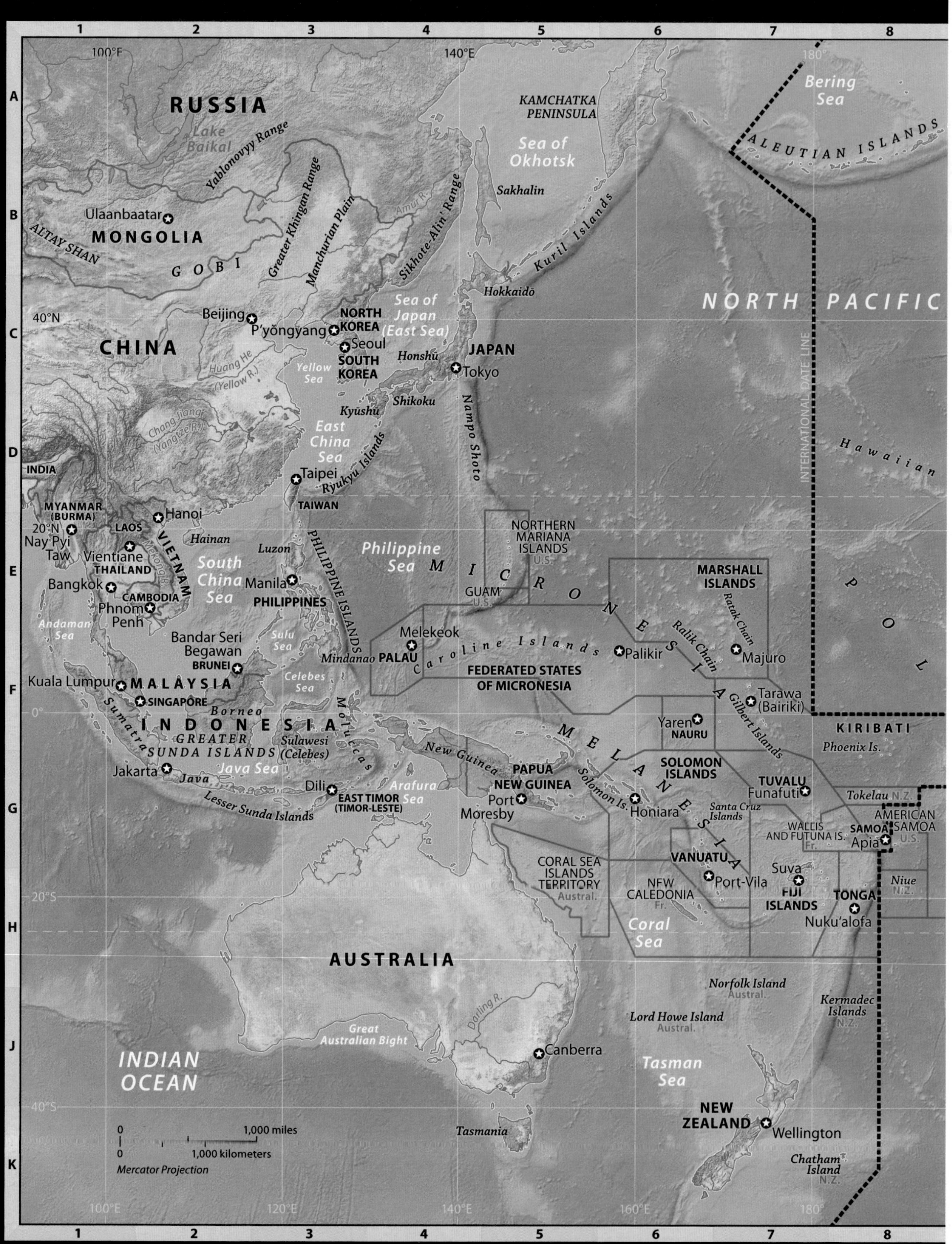
RUSSIA
Lake Baikal
Yablonovyy Range
Greater Khingan Range
Manchurian Plain
Sikhote-Alin' Range
KAMCHATKA PENINSULA
Sea of Okhotsk
Sakhalin
Kuril Islands
Bering Sea
ALEUTIAN ISLANDS
Ulaanbaatar
MONGOLIA
ALTAY SHAN
GOBI
Hokkaido
NORTH PACIFIC
Beijing
NORTH KOREA
P'yŏngyang
Seoul
SOUTH KOREA
Sea of Japan (East Sea)
CHINA
Huang He (Yellow R.)
Yellow Sea
Honshu
JAPAN
Tokyo
Kyushu
Shikoku
Chang Jiang (Yangtze R.)
East China Sea
Nampo Shoto
Ryukyu Islands
INTERNATIONAL DATE LINE
Hawaiian
INDIA
Taipei
TAIWAN
MYANMAR (BURMA)
Nay Pyi Taw
Hanoi
LAOS
Vientiane
VIETNAM
THAILAND
Bangkok
CAMBODIA
Phnom Penh
Hainan
South China Sea
Luzon
Manila
PHILIPPINES
PHILIPPINE ISLANDS
Philippine Sea
NORTHERN MARIANA ISLANDS U.S.
GUAM U.S.
MICRONESIA
MARSHALL ISLANDS
Ratak Chain
Ralik Chain
Majuro
POLYNESIA
Andaman Sea
Bandar Seri Begawan
BRUNEI
Sulu Sea
Mindanao
Melekeok
PALAU
Caroline Islands
Palikir
FEDERATED STATES OF MICRONESIA
Kuala Lumpur
MALAYSIA
SINGAPORE
Celebes Sea
Borneo
Sumatra
INDONESIA
GREATER SUNDA ISLANDS
Sulawesi (Celebes)
Moluccas
Tarawa (Bairiki)
Gilbert Islands
KIRIBATI
Phoenix Is.
Yaren
NAURU
MELANESIA
Jakarta
Java
Java Sea
New Guinea
PAPUA NEW GUINEA
SOLOMON ISLANDS
TUVALU
Funafuti
Tokelau N.Z.
Dili
EAST TIMOR (TIMOR-LESTE)
Arafura Sea
Lesser Sunda Islands
Port Moresby
Solomon Is.
Honiara
Santa Cruz Islands
WALLIS AND FUTUNA IS. Fr.
SAMOA
Apia
AMERICAN SAMOA U.S.
CORAL SEA ISLANDS TERRITORY Austral.
VANUATU
Port-Vila
NEW CALEDONIA Fr.
Suva
FIJI ISLANDS
TONGA
Nuku'alofa
Niue N.Z.
Coral Sea
AUSTRALIA
Norfolk Island Austral.
Kermadec Islands N.Z.
Lord Howe Island Austral.
Darling R.
Great Australian Bight
Canberra
Tasman Sea
INDIAN OCEAN
NEW ZEALAND
Wellington
Tasmania
Chatham Island N.Z.
0 1,000 miles
0 1,000 kilometers
Mercator Projection
100°E
120°E
140°E
160°E
180°
40°N
20°N
0°
20°S
40°S
1 2 3 4 5 6 7 8
A B C D E F G H J K

PACIFIC RIM
PHYSICAL / POLITICAL
Gulf of Alaska
Kodiak I.
Alexander Archipelago
Queen Charlotte Islands
Vancouver Island
Coast Mountains
ROCKY MOUNTAINS
Cascade Range
CANADA
CANADIAN SHIELD
Hudson Bay
GREAT PLAINS
Great Lakes
Ottawa
APPALACHIAN MTS.
CENTRAL LOWLAND
UNITED STATES
Missouri R.
Mississippi R.
Washington, D.C.
COASTAL PLAIN
ATLANTIC OCEAN
OCEAN
MEXICO
Baja California
Gulf of California
Sierra Madre Occidental
Sierra Madre Oriental
Gulf of Mexico
TROPIC OF CANCER
Hawaiian Islands
HAWAII U.S.
Mexico City
Nassau
BAHAMAS
Havana
CUBA
JAMAICA
HAITI
DOMINICAN REPUBLIC
Santo Domingo
BELIZE
HONDURAS
Tegucigalpa
GUATEMALA
Guatemala
San Salvador
EL SALVADOR
NICARAGUA
Managua
Caribbean Sea
San José
COSTA RICA
Panama
PANAMA
Caracas
LLANOS
VENEZUELA
Bogotá
COLOMBIA
Kiritimati
Line Islands
EQUATOR
Galápagos Islands Ecua.
Quito
ECUADOR
AMAZON BASIN
BRAZIL
PERU
Lima
ANDES
La Paz
BOLIVIA
POLYNESIA
Marquesas Is.
Tuamotu Archipelago
Society Is.
COOK ISLANDS N.Z.
FRENCH POLYNESIA Fr.
Austral Is.
Pitcairn Island U.K.
Easter Island Chile
TROPIC OF CAPRICORN
Santiago
CHILE
ARGENTINA
PATAGONIA
Chiloé Island
SOUTH PACIFIC OCEAN
100°W
140°W
120°W
160°W
80°W
40°N
20°N

GEOGRAPHIC DICTIONARY

archipelago a group of islands

basin area of land drained by a given river and its branches; area of land surrounded by lands of higher elevations

bay part of a large body of water that extends into a shoreline, generally smaller than a gulf

canyon deep and narrow valley with steep walls

cape point of land that extends into a river, lake, or ocean

channel wide strait or waterway between two landmasses that lie close to each other; deep part of a river or other waterway

cliff steep, high wall of rock, earth, or ice

continent one of the seven large landmasses on the Earth

delta flat, low-lying land built up from soil carried downstream by a river and deposited at its mouth

divide stretch of high land that separates river systems

downstream direction in which a river or stream flows from its source to its mouth

escarpment steep cliff or slope between a higher and lower land surface

glacier large, thick body of slowly moving ice

gulf part of a large body of water that extends into a shoreline, generally larger and more deeply indented than a bay

harbor a sheltered place along a shoreline where ships can anchor safely

highland elevated land area such as a hill, mountain, or plateau

hill elevated land with sloping sides and rounded summit; generally smaller than a mountain

island land area, smaller than a continent, completely surrounded by water

isthmus narrow stretch of land connecting two larger land areas

lake a sizable inland body of water

lowland land, usually level, at a low elevation

mesa broad, flat-topped landform with steep sides; smaller than a plateau

mountain land with steep sides that rises sharply (1,000 feet or more) from surrounding land; generally larger and more rugged than a hill

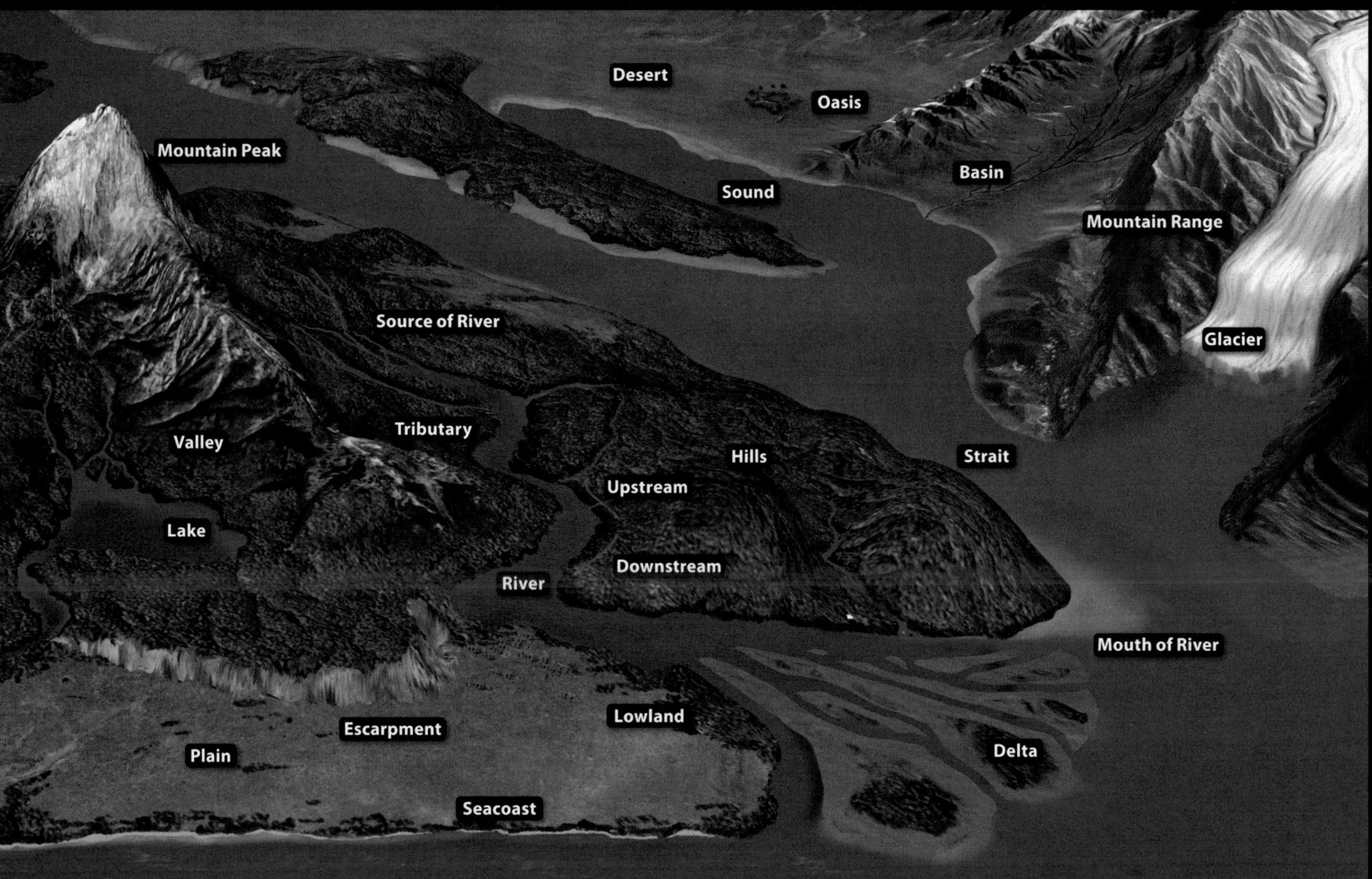

mountain peak pointed top of a mountain

mountain range a series of connected mountains

mouth (of a river) place where a stream or river flows into a larger body of water

oasis small area in a desert where water and vegetation are found

ocean one of the four major bodies of salt water that surround the continents

ocean current stream of either cold or warm water that moves in a definite direction through an ocean

peninsula body of land jutting into a lake or ocean, surrounded on three sides by water

physical feature characteristic of a place occurring naturally, such as a landform, body of water, climate pattern, or resource

plain area of level land, usually at low elevation and often covered with grasses

plateau area of flat or rolling land at a high elevation, about 300 to 3,000 feet (90 to 900 m) high

reef a chain of rocks, coral or sand at or near the surface of the water

river large natural stream of water that runs through the land

sea large body of water completely or partly surrounded by land

seacoast land lying next to a sea or an ocean

sound broad inland body of water, often between a coastline and one or more islands off the coast

source (of a river) place where a river or stream begins, often in highlands

strait narrow stretch of water joining two larger bodies of water

tributary small river or stream that flows into a large river or stream; a branch of the river

upstream direction opposite the flow of a river; toward the source of a river or stream

valley area of low land usually between hills or mountains

volcano mountain or hill created as liquid rock and ash erupt from inside the Earth

SCAVENGER HUNT

NETWORKS contains a wealth of information. The trick is to know where to look to access all the information in the book. If you complete this scavenger hunt exercise with your teachers or parents, you will see how the textbook is organized and how to get the most out of your reading and studying time. Let's get started!

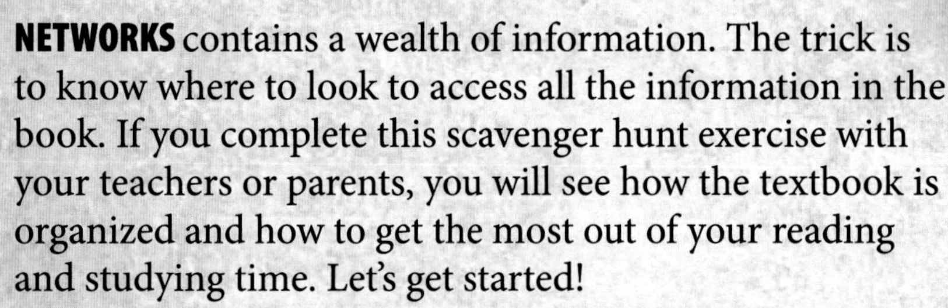

1. **How many chapters are in this book?** 23
2. **Where in the front of the book can you find page numbers for each lesson?** Table of Contents
3. **What is the title of Chapter 2?** Studying Geography, Economics, and Citizenship
4. **What Essential Questions will you answer in Chapter 5?** How does geography influence the way people live? What makes a culture unique? Why do civilizations rise and fall?
5. **Who is discussed in the biography feature of Chapter 6, Lesson 1?** Moses
6. **What is the *Thinking Like a Historian* activity for Chapter 8?** **Researching on the Internet.** Students should use reliable sources to learn what Philip's goals were and why he wanted to conquer the Greeks as opposed to being their allies.
7. **What time period does Chapter 11 cover?** 500 B.C. to A.D. 180
8. **What is the title of Lesson 2 in Chapter 12?** Rome's Decline
9. **Where in the back of the book can you find the meaning of vocabulary words such as *ephor*?** Glossary
10. **Where in the back of the book can you find page numbers for information about citizenship?** Index

CHAPTER 1

What Does a Historian Do? Planner

UNDERSTANDING BY DESIGN®

Enduring Understanding

- *Learning about the past helps us understand the present and make decisions about the future.*

Essential Questions

- *Why is history important?*
- *How do we learn about the past?*
- *How do you research history?*

Predictable Misunderstandings

Students may think:

- *It is unnecessary to learn about the past.*
- *It is acceptable to copy information from sources, especially those they find on the Internet.*
- *All sources are equally reliable.*

Assessment Evidence

Performance Tasks:

- *Hands-On Chapter Project*

Other Evidence:

- *Primary Source Activity*
- *21st Century Skills Activities*
- *Answers to identifying names for the current time period*
- *Identification of classroom artifacts*
- *What Do You Think? questions*
- *Interactive Graphic Organizers*
- *Responses to place mat cooperative learning activity*
- *Participation in class discussion about primary and secondary sources*
- *Participation in a discussion about where to find answers*
- *Responses to Interactive Whiteboard Activities*
- *Lesson Reviews*
- *Chapter Activities and Assessment*

SUGGESTED PACING GUIDE

Introducing the Chapter	1 day	*What Do You Think?*	1 day
Lesson 1	1 day	Lesson 3	1 day
Lesson 2	1 day	Chapter Wrap-Up and Assessment	1 day

TOTAL TIME 6 Days

Key for Using the Teacher Edition

SKILL-BASED ACTIVITIES

Types of skill activities found in the Teacher Edition.

V Visual Skills require students to analyze maps, graphs, charts, and photos.

R Reading Skills help students practice reading skills and master vocabulary.

W Writing Skills provide writing opportunities to help students comprehend the text.

C Critical Thinking Skills help students apply and extend what they have learned.

T Technology Skills require students to use digital tools effectively.

*Letters are followed by a number when there is more than one of the same type of skill on the page.

DIFFERENTIATED INSTRUCTION

All activities are written for the on-level student unless otherwise marked with the leveled labels below.

BL Beyond Level

AL Approaching Level

ELL English Language Learners

All students benefit from activities that utilize different learning styles. Many activities are marked as below when a particular learning style is highlighted.

Intrapersonal	**Naturalist**
Logical/Mathematical	**Kinesthetic**
Visual/Spatial	**Auditory/Musical**
Verbal/Linguistic	**Interpersonal**

NCSS Standards covered in "What Does a Historian Do?"

Learners will understand:

2 **TIME, CONTINUITY, AND CHANGE**

1. The study of the past provides representation of the history of communities, nations, and the world.

2. Concepts such as: chronology, causality, change, conflict, complexity, multiple perspectives, primary and secondary sources, and cause and effect.

3. That learning about the past requires the interpretation of sources, and that using varied sources provides the potential for a more balanced interpretive record of the past.

4. That historical interpretations of the same event may differ on the basis of such factors as conflicting evidence from varied sources, national or cultural perspectives, and the point of view of the researcher.

4 **INDIVIDUAL DEVELOPMENT AND IDENTITY**

6. That perceptions are interpretations of information about individuals and events, and can be influenced by bias and stereotypes.

8 **SCIENCE, TECHNOLOGY, AND SOCIETY**

3. Our lives today are media and technology dependent.

CHAPTER OPENER PLANNER

Students will know:

- *why people study history.*
- *what artifacts historians use to understand the past.*
- *guidelines for researching.*
- *how to work safely using the Internet.*

Students will be able to:

- ***contribute*** *to a group activity about why people study history.*
- ***understand*** *and recall concepts of time.*
- ***synthesize*** *their understanding of how eras are named and apply this understanding to naming today.*
- ***analyze*** *what makes a source reliable.*
- ***categorize*** *by primary or secondary source.*
- ***evaluate*** *reliable sources.*
- ***distinguish*** *fact from opinion.*
- ***recognize*** *bias.*

UNDERSTANDING BY DESIGN®

☑ *Print Teaching Options*

V Visual Skills

- ☐ **P. 2** Students discuss images of historians at work.
- ☐ **P. 3** Students examine the elements of a time line.

☑ *Online Teaching Options*

V Visual Skills

- **IMAGE** **Historians in the 21st Century**—Students contrast archaeologists and paleontologists.
- **WORLD ATLAS** Students can use this interactive map to identify regions of the world, learn about individual countries, locate political boundaries, measure distances, and much more.

W Writing Skills

- **TIME LINE** **Place and Time: What Does a Historian Do?**—Students are introduced to the ages of history, choose one age, and write a paragraph.

☑ *Printable Digital Worksheets*

R Reading Skills

- **GRAPHIC NOVEL** ***The Eruption of Mt. Vesuvius***—The experiences of one citizen during the eruption of Mt. Vesuvius are told.

Project-Based Learning

Hands-On Chapter Project

What Does a Historian Do?

Students will research and investigate both Web sites and print sources and demonstrate the ability to distinguish fact from opinion, identify primary and secondary sources, understand bias, and determine the reliability of sources.

Technology Extension

Social Bookmarking

- Find an additional activity online that incorporates technology for this project.
- Visit the EdTechTeacher Web sites (included in the Technology Extension for this chapter) for more links, tutorials, and other resources.

Print Resources

ANCILLARY RESOURCES

These ancillaries are available for every chapter and lesson.

- **Reading Essentials and Study Guide Workbook** AL ELL
- **Chapter Tests and Lesson Quizzes Blackline Masters**

PRINTABLE DIGITAL WORKSHEETS

These printable digital worksheets are available for every chapter and lesson.

- **Hands-On Chapter Projects**
- **What Do You Know? activities**
- **Chapter Summaries (English and Spanish)**
- **Vocabulary Builder activities**
- **Guided Reading activities**

More Media Resources

SUGGESTED READING 

Grade 6 reading level:

- ***Ancient Celts: Archaeology Unlocks the Secrets of the Celts' Past,*** by Jen Green

Grade 7 reading level:

- ***Archaeology,*** by Trevor Barnes

Grade 8 reading level:

- ***Take Me Back: A Trip through History from the Stone Age to the Digital Age,*** by DK Publishing

LESSON 1 PLANNER

WHAT IS HISTORY?

Students will know:

- *why people study history.*

Students will be able to:

- ***contribute*** *to a group activity about why people study history.*
- ***understand and recall*** *concepts of time.*
- ***synthesize*** *their understanding of how eras are named and apply this understanding to naming today.*

UNDERSTANDING BY DESIGN®

Print Teaching Options

V Visual Skills

- [ ] **P. 7** Students use a time line to show a sequence of events. Logical/Mathematical

R Reading Skills

- [ ] **P. 4** Students identify tools for keeping track of time. AL ELL
- [ ] **P. 4** Students examine reasons for studying history. AL ELL
- [ ] **P. 5** Students review and define terms used to organize time. ELL
- [ ] **P. 7** Students summarize the main idea of a section of text.
- [ ] **P. 9** Students contrast types of historians. AL ELL

C Critical Thinking Skills

- [ ] **P. 6** Students contrast the Julian and Gregorian calendars.
- [ ] **P. 8** Students consider the impact of the invention of writing on history.

T Technology Skills

- [ ] **P. 6** Students determine what today's date would be using the Julian and Gregorian calendar systems.
- [ ] **P. 8** Students use presentation software to produce a slide show about heroes of the Trojan War.

Online Teaching Options

V Visual Skills

VIDEO **Great Reasons to Learn History**—Students view a video that identifies ten reasons why people should study history.

IMAGE **Lucy**—Students analyze information scientists have discovered about Lucy's skeleton.

R Reading Skills

GRAPHIC ORGANIZER **Taking Notes: *Categorizing:* The Julian and Gregorian Calendars**—Students use a Venn diagram to organize information about these two calendars.

BIOGRAPHY **Heinrich Schliemann**—Students read about this archaeologist, who is considered the founder of prehistoric Greek archaeology.

C Critical Thinking Skills

WHITEBOARD ACTIVITY **It Happened in My Lifetime**—Students create a time line of important historical events that have occurred during their lifetime.

T Technology Skills

GAME **Chronology Terms Concentration Game**—Students match important terms with their definitions.

GAME **Types of Calendars Concentration Game**—Students match calendars and facts.

SELF-CHECK QUIZ **Lesson 1**—Students receive instant feedback of their mastery of lesson content.

Printable Digital Worksheets

W Writing Skills

WORKSHEET **Primary Source Activity: What Does a Historian Do?**—Students respond to two primary sources as they look for clues to the past.

How Does a Historian Work?

Students will know:
- *what artifacts historians use to understand the past.*

Students will be able to:
- ***analyze** what makes a source reliable.*
- ***categorize** by primary or secondary source.*

UNDERSTANDING BY DESIGN®

Print Teaching Options

V Visual Skills
- [ ] **P. 12** Students analyze two maps. **Visual/Spatial**

R Reading Skills
- [ ] **P. 14** Students categorize sample research subjects as narrow or broad.

W Writing Skills
- [ ] **P. 13** Students work together to describe a cave painting in a short paragraph. **Interpersonal**
- [ ] **P. 14** Students research and write a brief article and evaluate their partner's article on the same topic. **Interpersonal**

C Critical Thinking Skills
- [ ] **P. 10** Students analyze present-day artifacts and explain what historians in the future might learn from these objects. **AL**
- [ ] **P. 11** Students identify bias in written materials. **AL**
- [ ] **P. 12** Students analyze different points of view.
- [ ] **P. 13** Students practice making inferences.

T Technology Skills
- [ ] **P. 15** Students create a brief presentation on a chosen history-related career.

Online Teaching Options

V Visual Skills
- **VIDEO** **Uncovering the Past**—Students watch a video in which they explore ruins, caves, and ancient cities to understand how archaeology contributes to our understanding of human history.

R Reading Skills
- **GRAPHIC ORGANIZER** **Taking Notes: *Sequencing:* How a Historian Works**—Students Identify the steps in finding and evaluating evidence.

C Critical Thinking Skills
- **SLIDE SHOW** **Primary Source Artifacts**—Students analyze photos of art for clues the art reveals about past cultures.
- **SLIDE SHOW** **Terra-Cotta Warriors**—Students analyze photos of the Terra-cotta Army found in Xi'an China.
- **WHITEBOARD ACTIVITY** **Types of Evidence**—Students sort examples of research materials into primary and secondary sources.
- **IMAGE** **History Magazines**—Students contrast narrow focus and broad focus publications.

T Technology Skills
- **SELF-CHECK QUIZ** **Lesson 2**—Students receive instant feedback of their mastery of lesson content.
- **GAME** **Historical Evidence Crossword Puzzle**—Students complete the puzzle using terms that relate to types of historical evidence.
- **GAME** **Historical Research Fill in the Blank**—Students complete sentences describing how historians work.

Printable Digital Worksheets

C Critical Thinking Skills
- **WORKSHEET** **21st Century Skills Activity: Critical Thinking and Problem Solving: Recognize Bias**—Students analyze primary sources for bias and write their conclusions.

LESSON 3 PLANNER

Researching History

Students will know:
- *guidelines for researching.*
- *how to work safely using the Internet.*

Students will be able to:
- ***evaluate** reliable sources.*
- ***distinguish** fact from opinion.*
- ***recognize** bias.*

UNDERSTANDING BY DESIGN®

☑ Print Teaching Options

R Reading Skills

- ☐ **P. 18** Students read and summarize a section of text.
- ☐ **P. 21** Students define plagiarism and determine whether given scenarios are examples of plagiarism. ELL

W Writing Skills

- ☐ **P. 18** Students discuss methods of generating a topic for a research project.
- ☐ **P. 20** Students write a short letter on the importance of writing without bias. BL Verbal/Linguistic

C Critical Thinking Skills

- ☐ **P. 19** Students distinguish fact from opinion. AL
- ☐ **P. 19** Students practice taking and organizing notes.
- ☐ **P. 21** Students practice making generalizations.

T Technology Skills

- ☐ **P. 20** Students evaluate Web sources for reliability. BL

☑ Online Teaching Options

V Visual Skills

- ☐ VIDEO **Internet Research Techniques**—Students view a video that shows how to use the Internet when researching reports.

R Reading Skills

- ☐ GRAPHIC ORGANIZER **Taking Notes: *Finding the Main Idea:* Researching History**—Students identify and record the main idea and supporting details of each section of the lesson.

C Critical Thinking Skills

- ☐ CHART **Is This Plagiarism?**—Students analyze several scenarios and determine whether each represents plagiarized material.
- ☐ GAME **Reliable Web Sites Column Game: Researching History**—Students sort Web sites into those that are reliable and those that are not.

T Technology Skills

- ☐ SELF-CHECK QUIZ **Lesson 3**—Students receive instant feedback of their mastery of lesson content.

☑ Printable Digital Worksheets

C Critical Thinking Skills

- ☐ WORKSHEET **21st Century Skills Activity: Critical Thinking and Problem Solving: Distinguish Facts and Opinions**—Students analyze primary sources and write about the facts and opinions they identify.

Intervention and Remediation Strategies

LESSON 1 What Is History?

Reading and Comprehension

In small groups, have students read the third paragraph under "Why Study History?" that traces the invention of the wheel all the way through the development of the car. Have each student take one step in that process and describe it more fully based on prior knowledge. Then have students combine their descriptions into a sequence.

Text Evidence

To help students understand the different measures of time, use visual or manipulable examples. You might write *day, month, year, decade, century,* and *millennium* in increasingly larger text, or use counting objects to show the relative differences. Have students create their own visual model of time measures.

LESSON 2 How Does a Historian Work?

Reading and Comprehension

To make sure students understand how to draw conclusions, have them paraphrase the section titled "Drawing Conclusions." Remind students that to paraphrase means to restate in your own words. Organize students into pairs and have one explain it to the other.

Text Evidence

Organize students into small groups. Have each group create a list of the types of evidence that historians use. The groups should rank their list based on which they think is most important. In a class discussion, have the groups share and defend their rankings.

LESSON 3 Researching History

Reading and Comprehension

To ensure comprehension of the concepts in this lesson, have students look up synonyms for *bias* and *plagiarism.* Then have students offer real-world examples of where each of these may occur.

Text Evidence

Students may need help clarifying the difference between nonfiction and persuasive writing. Explain that both will be found in the nonfiction section of the library, but that persuasive writing will contain bias. Students should make a list of the characteristics of persuasive writing and then compare several popular books or Web sites against the list.

Online Resources

Approaching Level Reader

Use this online lower-level text that corresponds directly to the text in the Student Edition. It includes a Spanish version.

Guided Reading Activities

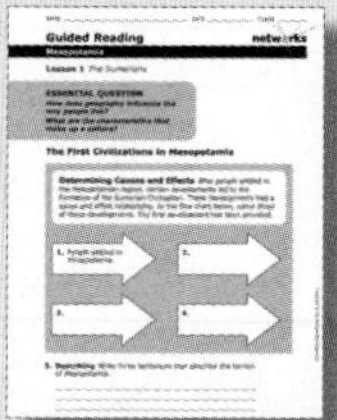

This resource uses graphic organizers and guiding questions to help students with comprehension.

What Do You Know?

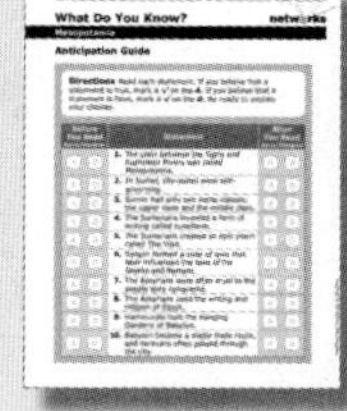

Use these worksheets to pre-assess student's background knowledge before they study the chapter.

Reading Essentials and Study Guide Workbook

This resource offers writing and reading activities for the approaching-level student. Also available in Spanish.

Self-Check Quizzes

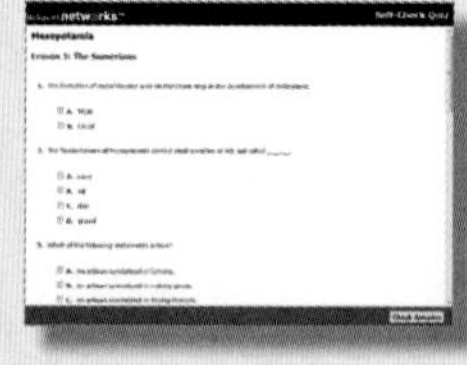

This online assessment tool provides instant feedback for students to check their progress.

What Does a Historian Do?

networks

There's More Online about historians and how they work.

CHAPTER 1

ESSENTIAL QUESTIONS • *Why is history important?* • *How do we learn about the past?* • *How do you research history?*

Lesson 1 *What Is History?*

Lesson 2 *How Does a Historian Work?*

Lesson 3 *Researching History*

The Story Matters . . .

Hundreds of terra-cotta warriors stood, silent and without expression, in the empty exhibit hall. They were replicas of the original statues found in China in 1974. Since their discovery, the warriors, dating from 210 B.C., had fascinated historians. Why were they created? How had they remained a buried secret for centuries?

The mystery of the warriors captured the imaginations of people all over the world. Museums asked for a chance to show the statues in their cities. Researchers carefully created exact replicas of the statues that would be strong enough to travel around the world. Museum workers like this one in Dresden, Germany, assembled heads, arms, and bodies in exactly the correct order. Thousands of visitors came to marvel at the beautiful and mysterious warriors.

◄ *A museum employee places the head on a statue in the Terra-cotta Warriors exhibit at the Dresden Energy Museum.*

Norbert Millauer/AFP/Getty Images

1

Letter from the Author

Dear World History Teacher,

People have said that history is everything that has happened since the beginning of time. This definition, however, is so broad that it is ineffective. History has a more common meaning as a record of the past. To create this record, historians use documents; artifacts such as pottery, tools, and weapons; and even artworks. History, according to this definition, really began more than 5,000 years ago when people first started to keep records. Historians today not only uncover factual evidence, but also use critical thinking to explain the cause-and-effect relationships among facts.

Jackson J. Spielvogel

ENGAGE

Bellringer Have students study the photograph of the museum employee assembling a terra-cotta warrior. Then invite a volunteer to read aloud "The Story Matters . . ." Next, challenge students to brainstorm a list of people who would have worked to make the museum exhibit possible. **Ask:** **Who would have to work on this project to make it happen?** *(Answers will vary. Responses may include curators, art historians, government officials, fundraisers, and donors.)* Remind students that someone had to find and clean the original terra-cotta warriors. Others had to replicate, transport, reassemble, and advertise the museum exhibit. Then **ask:** **Why do you think people would be interested in learning more about the terra-cotta warriors?** *(Answers may vary. Students might cite curiosity about another culture or an appreciation for the statues as works of art.)*

Explain to students that the terra-cotta warriors were part of an elaborate burial ceremony for China's first emperor. Compare them to the pyramids in Egypt, which are also part of elaborate burial rituals.

Explain that just as people all over the world are interested in learning about the Egyptian pyramids, so too are they interested in the warriors of China. People are interested in the customs of people throughout history.

Making Connections

Read the following information to students.

- Burial sites are some of the best sources for information about cultures of the past. Tombs and the objects inside them can indicate what was important to people in a particular time and place.
- The burial places of former U.S. presidents are important historic sites. These including Grant's Tomb in New York City and the McKinley Mausoleum in Canton, Ohio. Presidents Washington and Jefferson were both buried near their homes in Virginia.
- Many nations, including the United States, Japan, Brazil, and Australia, honor those fallen in war with a Tomb of the Unknown Soldier.

TEACH & ASSESS

Step Into the Place

V1 Visual Skills

Analyzing Images Direct students' attention to the Chapter Opener images of historians at work. Ask volunteers to read the captions. Have students identify the activities in each picture and then explain how the images relate to history. **Ask:** **Where have you found information about events that have happened in the past?** *(Possible responses: museums, Internet, books, movies, TV shows, talking to people)*

Find images of archaeologists at work, and show them to students. Have students consider what it might be like to be part of a research team digging for artifacts. Have them discuss what the job might involve. Encourage them to use details from the images to support their answers. **Ask:** **Is this the kind of work you would expect a historian to do?**

As a class, discuss the Image Focus questions.

Content Background Knowledge

Three noteworthy archaeological finds include:

- Howard Carter excavated the tomb of the Egyptian boy-king Tutankhamen in 1923. The tomb was remarkable for being largely intact and a rich source of artifacts and information about life in ancient Egypt.
- Mary Leakey was an archaeologist who discovered some of the earliest known fossils of human ancestors in Africa.
- Robert Ballard used deep-sea diving and unmanned submersibles to discover the wreck of the *Titanic* in 1985.

ANSWERS, p. 2

Step Into the Place

1. People find information about the past in the ground, in books and documents, in museums, and online.
2. People use digging tools and computers.
3. CRITICAL THINKING Students should identify local libraries and museums as sources of local history.

Step Into the Time

Prehistory

CHAPTER 1 CCSS

Place and Time: Historians in the 21st Century

Many people are historians. Some study written records of a war that happened decades ago. Some study dinosaur bones and other ancient artifacts from millions of years in the past. Family historians may be the ones you are most familiar with. They are the relatives who remember when everyone's birthday is and can tell you what your great-grandparents did for a living.

V1

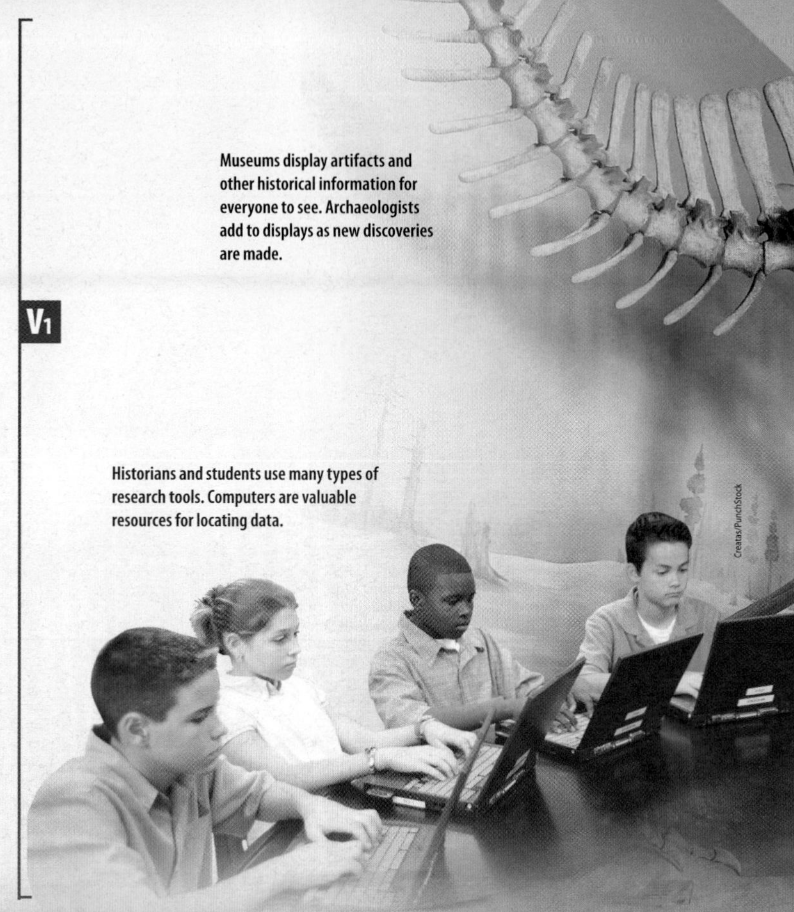

Museums display artifacts and other historical information for everyone to see. Archaeologists add to displays as new discoveries are made.

Historians and students use many types of research tools. Computers are valuable resources for locating data.

Creatas/PunchStock

Step Into the Place

IMAGE FOCUS There are many ways to study the past. Look at the photos.

1. **ANALYZING VISUALS** Where do people find information about the past? RH.6–8.7
2. **IDENTIFYING** What tools do people use to study the past? RH.6–8.7
3. **CRITICAL THINKING** *Making Connections* Where could you go to learn about the history of your community? RH.6–8.2

Step Into the Time

V2

TIME LINE The time line shows different periods in history. What name is given to the first time period in history? RH.6–8.7

WORLD HISTORY

Prehistory up to 3500 B.C.

Ancient History 3500 B.C. to A.D. 500

B.C. 4000 | B.C. 3000 | B.C. 2000

Project-Based Learning 

Hands-On Chapter Project

What Does a Historian Do?

Students will learn how to evaluate sources and determine their reliability and credibility. Through class discussion, review the definitions of primary and secondary sources, the concept of bias, and methods for determining whether a Web site is reliable. Choose a topic of interest and research it, using at least one Web site and one print resource. In a small group, discuss the quality and reliability of the sources used for individual research. Use an Assessment Rubric to evaluate students' research, understanding of reliable and unreliable sources, and collaboration in small groups.

Technology Extension

Social Bookmarking

Students will practice using social bookmarking platforms as an extension of the Hands-On Chapter Project. They will bookmark reliable and unreliable sites, tag them, and share them with the class via a social bookmark site.

Bookmarking Web sites has become a common practice in order to revisit useful resources in the future without searching.

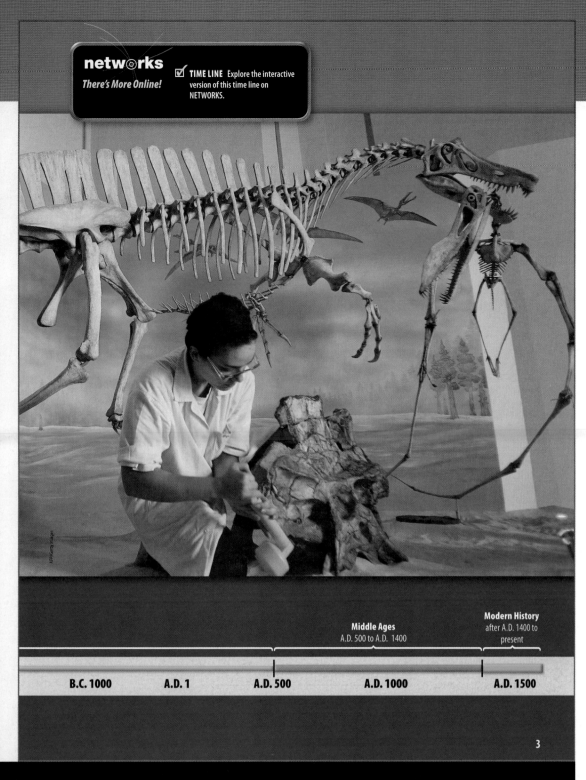

networks
There's More Online!

☑ **TIME LINE** Explore the interactive version of this time line on NETWORKS.

AFP/Getty Images

Middle Ages
A.D. 500 to A.D. 1400

Modern History
after A.D. 1400 to present

B.C. 1000 **A.D. 1** **A.D. 500** **A.D. 1000** **A.D. 1500**

3

CHAPTER 1

Place and Time

Step Into the Time

V2 Visual Skills

Have students review the time line for the chapter. Point out elements that are common to many time lines, including the letters b.c. and a.d., the numbers and brackets that indicate a range of years, and the benchmark dates. Have students explain what each element of the time line indicates. Explain that they will learn about the parts of a time line in this chapter. **Ask:** On the time line, what is the period in which you live? *(Modern History)*

Content Background Knowledge

Modern history, the era we live in today, is characterized by the scientific method of drawing conclusions from observations. This began during the European Renaissance and continues today.

CLOSE & REFLECT

Making Predictions Have each student write two or three sentences explaining what he or she thinks a historian's job is. Students may write these in their notebooks—or on a separate sheet of paper to be collected by the teacher. At the end of the chapter, students can revisit their predictions to see how accurate the predictions were.

TIME LINE

Place and Time: What Does a Historian Do?

Predicting Have students choose an event or time period from the time line and write a paragraph predicting the general social, political, or economic consequences that event might have for the world.

See page 1B for other online activities.

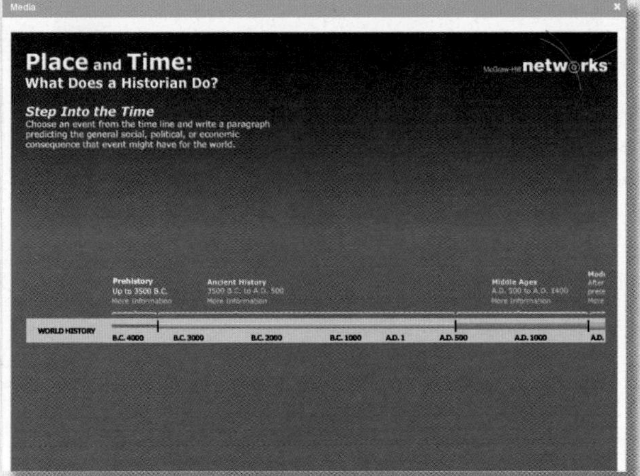

ENGAGE

Bellringer Before students begin the lesson, invite them to remember some significant events in their own lives. Tell them that these events are part of their personal history. **Ask: What are some important events in the lives of family members?** *(Answers may include births, marriages, deaths, or perhaps emigrating from one country to another.)* Explain that such events are part of their family history. **Ask: What are some other kinds of histories?** *(Students may cite the history of a school, neighborhood, community, city, state, nation, or the world.)*

TEACH & ASSESS

R1 Reading Skills

Identifying As students read, introduce the idea that historians keep track of time. **Ask: How do we keep track of time during the day?** *(a watch or clock)* **How do we keep track of time during a month? A year?** *(a calendar, an organizer, the computer)* **More than a year?** *(a calendar, a history textbook, an organizer, the computer)*

Explain that many historians study long time periods and they use a variety of tools to organize their work. AL ELL

R2 Reading Skills

Explaining Organize students into groups of four. Give each group a place mat made out of butcher paper. Ask each group to draw an oval in the center of the paper. Out of the center oval, have them draw four rules that extend to the corners of the paper. These divide the paper into four sections, one section for each student to write on. Pose a question to the group. **Ask: Why do people study history?** Have one student write this question in the center oval. Then, each group member should write answers to that question in his or her section of the place mat. Students should use details from the text in their answers. The team should compare their answers and circle or highlight any answers that all four team members have in common. Finally, have each group share its ideas with the class as a whole. AL ELL

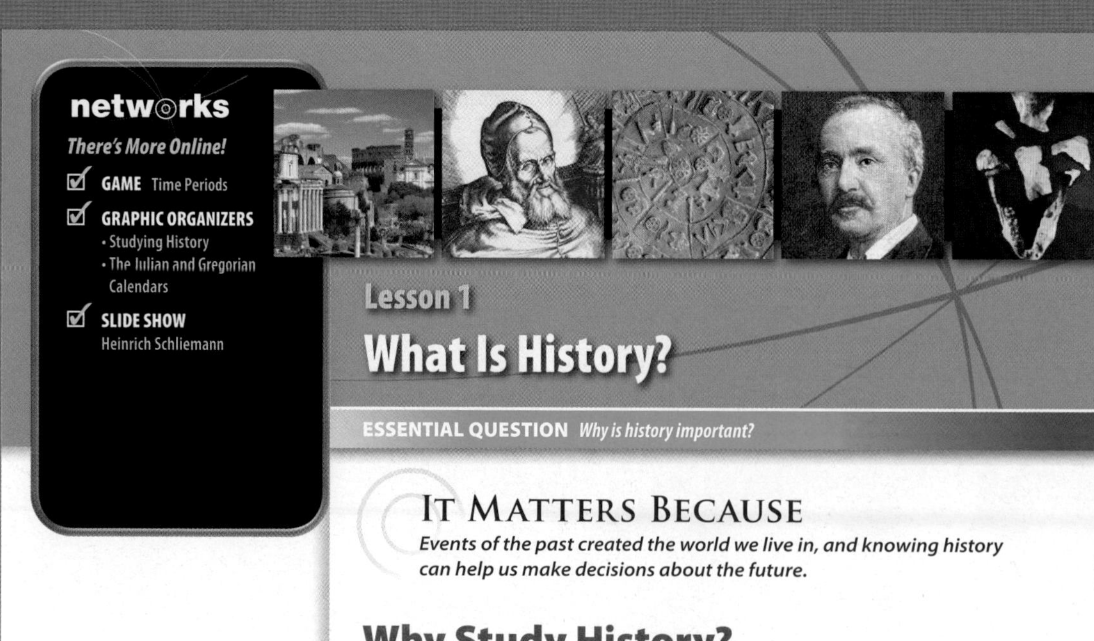

Lesson 1

What Is History?

ESSENTIAL QUESTION *Why is history important?*

IT MATTERS BECAUSE

Events of the past created the world we live in, and knowing history can help us make decisions about the future.

Why Study History?

GUIDING QUESTION *What types of things can history reveal about the past?*

History is the study of the people and events of the past. History explores both the way things change and the way things stay the same. History tells the story of the ways that cultures change over time.

R1 People who study history are called historians. A historian's job is to examine the causes, or reasons, that something happened in the past. They also look for the effects, or results, of the event. They ask, "What happened?" and "Why did it happen?" They ask, "How did things change?" and "How has it influenced today?" Sometimes they ask, "What would have happened if . . . ?"

R2 History explains why things are the way they are. The invention of the wheel in prehistoric times paved the way for the use of horse-drawn carts in later time periods. The carts were a step toward the invention of the automobile in modern times. Today, cars are an **integral** part of our culture.

Learning about the past helps us understand the present. It helps us make decisions about the future. Historical instances of conflict and cooperation are examples we can learn from. We can use that knowledge when we face similar choices.

(l) Jean-Pierre Lescourret/Corbis, (cl) Bettmann/CORBIS, (c) Nimatallah/Art Resource, NY (cr) North Wind Picture Archives/North Wind Picture Archives (r) Kevin Fujii/Associated Press

Reading HELPDESK CCSS

Taking Notes: ***Categorizing***

Use a graphic organizer like the one shown here to list the important details about studying history. WHST.6–8.9

Studying History		
Reasons to Study History	Measuring Historical Time	People Who Study Time

Content Vocabulary (Tier 3 Words)

- **era**
- **archaeology**
- **artifact**
- **paleontology**
- **fossil**
- **anthropology**
- **species**

networks Online Teaching Options

VIDEO

Great Reasons to Learn History

Paraphrasing Have students watch the Great Reasons to Learn History video. Ask students to paraphrase each of the reasons given in the video and provide an example supporting each reason.

See page 1C for other online activities.

ANSWER, p. 4

TAKING NOTES: Reasons to Study History: to find causes and effects; **Measuring Historical Time:** time lines, calendars, A.D. and B.C.; **People Who Study Time:** anthropologist, archaeologist, paleontologist

Studying history helps us understand how we fit into the human story. Some of the clues are the languages we speak, the technologies we use, and the pastimes we enjoy. All these are results of events that happened in the past. History teaches us who we are.

✓ PROGRESS CHECK

Explaining Why is it important to understand cause and effect when studying the past?

Measuring Time

GUIDING QUESTION *What are historical periods?*

To study the past, historians must have a way to identify and describe when things happened. They do that by measuring and labeling time in different ways.

Periods of History

One way to measure time is to label groups of years. For example, a group of 10 years is called a **decade**. A group of 100 years is known as a *century.* Centuries are grouped into even longer time periods. Ten centuries grouped together is called a *millennium,* which is a period of 1,000 years. **R**

Historians also divide the past into larger blocks of time known as **eras.** *Prehistory* is the first of these long periods. Prehistory is the time before people developed writing.

Jean-Pierre Lescourret/Corbis

The ancient Roman Forum has been called the most important meeting place in all of history. Today, it stands next to the buildings of modern Rome. Different historical eras are represented by both ancient and modern buildings.

era a large division of time

Academic Vocabulary (Tier 2 Words)

integral essential; necessary

decade a group or set of 10 years

R Reading Skills

Defining Review the terms related to accounting for time: *A.D., B.C., periods, decades, centuries, epoch, era, millennia, Prehistory, Ancient History, Middle Ages,* and *Modern History.* Explain that the words we use to describe the passing of time are simply tools to organize the way we think about history.

For extra practice with these words, have students write each word on a note card. Then write the definition of each word on separate note cards. Have students play a game of concentration where they pair the words with their definitions. ELL

Content Background Knowledge

Ancient historians used different methods to track eras. Here are two examples.

- The Roman historian Tacitus divided his record of history according to the reign of different emperors.
- The Anglo-Saxon Chronicle was a history written by monks in England that recorded important events year by year.

WORKSHEET

Primary Source Activity: What Does a Historian Do?

Evaluating Explain to students that one of the most important jobs for a historian is to determine the causes and effects of a historical event. Remind students that a cause is the reason an event happens and an effect is the result, or consequence, of the event. Provide examples from daily life, such as "The car stopped because it ran out of gas"; "The alarm did not go off, so Joey overslept"; and "Olivia scored high on the test because she studied." Have students give more examples of cause and effect. Assign the Primary Source Activity on the White House renovation for homework. Instruct students to evaluate the primary sources, looking for causes and effects of the event.

See page 1C for other online activities.

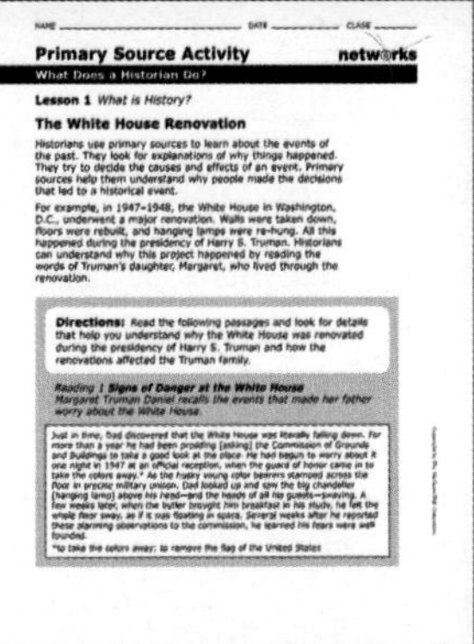

ANSWER, p. 5

✓ PROGRESS CHECK Learning about the causes and effects of past events helps us understand the present and anticipate the future.

What Is History?

C Critical Thinking Skills

Identifying Problems Review the similarities and differences between the Julian and the Gregorian calendars. **Ask:**

- **Who was the Julian calendar named for?** *(Julius Caesar)*
- **Who was the Gregorian calendar named for?** *(Pope Gregory)*
- **What problem did both calendars share?** *(losing time)*
- **How did each calendar deal with this problem?** *(Julian: leap years; Gregorian: also leap years, but more spread out)*

Lead a short discussion about leap years in the present and whether a leap year presents advantages or disadvantages for people in modern society.

T Technology Skills

Researching on the Internet Remind students that many civilizations and cultures have developed calendars. Ask students to research two calendar systems mentioned in the text. For each calendar, have students determine what today's date would be using that calendar system. Ask students to provide evidence for their determinations.

Writing was invented about 5,500 years ago. The period known as *Ancient History* comes next. It ends c. A.D. 500 (c., or circa, means "about"). Historians call the time period between about A.D. 500 and about A.D. 1400 the *Middle Ages*, or the medieval period. *Modern History* begins about A.D. 1400. It continues to the present day.

The Gregorian calendar is named for its creator, Pope Gregory XIII. Why is it important that most of the world uses a form of the calendar he developed?

Bettmann/CORBIS

Calendars

A *calendar* is a system for arranging days in order. Different cultures in the world have developed about 40 different calendars. T

Some cultures developed calendars based on nature, such as the cycle of the moon. The Chinese and Jewish calendars base their months on the appearance of the new moon. The ancient Egyptians also based one of their calendars on the moon.

Julian Calendar

The calendar we use today is based in part on a calendar developed by Julius Caesar, a Roman leader. This calendar is called the Julian calendar, and it started counting years at the **founding** of Rome. A year on the Julian calendar was 365¼ days long. The calendar added an extra day every four years. The year with the extra day was called a leap year. However, the Julian calendar was still not **precisely,** or exactly, right. It lost several minutes each year, which added up to about one lost day every 128 years. C

Gregorian Calendar

By A.D. 1582, the Julian calendar was losing time—about 10 days. Pope Gregory XIII decided to create a new calendar. First, he started counting from the birth of Jesus. Next, he ordered that the days between October 4th and October 15th of that year be dropped from the calendar. Like the Julian calendar, the Gregorian calendar includes leap years. However, in the Gregorian calendar, no century year will be a leap year unless it is divisible by 400, such as the years 1600 or 2000. That way, it will take thousands of years before there is another lost day.

Reading HELPDESK CCSS

Academic Vocabulary (Tier 2 Words)

found to create or set up something, such as a city

precise exact

Reading Strategy: *Context Clues*

Context clues are words or phrases that give hints about the meaning of another word. Which phrase provides a clue about the meaning of the word *precisely?*

6 *What Does a Historian Do?*

ANSWERS, p. 6

Caption: It is important for people to use the same calendar so that there is a universal system for dating events that can be used and understood by people of all backgrounds. The Gregorian calendar is the one used in most of the world.

Reading Strategy The phrase "lost several minutes each year" provides a clue about the meaning of the word *precisely.*

networks *Online Teaching Options*

LECTURE SLIDE

Measuring Time

Making Connections Display on the board the lecture slide with the words *decade, century,* and *millennium.* **Ask: Tell me something that happened in the past decade.** *(Students should name a recent event.)* **Name a person who lived in the last century.** *(Possible answers: Ronald Reagan, John F. Kennedy, Michael Jackson)* **Now name an event that happened about a millennium ago.** *(Accept any reasonable answer.)*

See page 1C for other online activities.

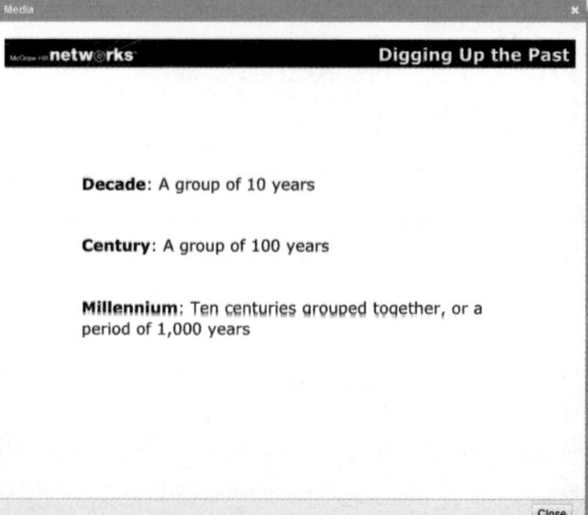

Media
networks
Digging Up the Past
Decade: A group of 10 years
Century: A group of 100 years
Millennium: Ten centuries grouped together, or a period of 1,000 years
Close

Not all countries accepted the Gregorian calendar right away. It took more than three centuries for the calendar to be recognized around the world. Today, most of the world uses this calendar. Like the Gregorian calendar, other calendars are also based on events of religious importance. The Jewish calendar begins about 3,760 years before the Gregorian calendar. According to Jewish tradition, that is when the world was created. Muslims date their calendar from the time that Muhammad, their first leader, left the city of Makkah (Mecca) to go to Madinah (Medina). This was the year A.D. 622 in the Gregorian calendar.

This stone calendar was made by the Minoans, people who lived on ancient Crete.

Dating Events

In the Gregorian calendar, the years before the birth of Jesus are known as "B.C.," or "before Christ." The years after are called "A.D.," or *anno domini*. This phrase comes from the Latin language and means "in the year of the Lord."

To date events before the birth of Jesus, or "B.C.," historians count backwards from A.D. 1. There is no year "0." The year before A.D. 1 is 1 B.C. (Notice that "A.D." is written before the date and "B.C." is written after the date.) For example, on the time line below, the founder of Buddhism was born about 563 B.C., or 563 years before the birth of Jesus. To date events after the birth of Jesus, or "A.D.," historians count forward, starting at A.D. 1. A date in the first 100 years after the birth of Jesus is between A.D. 1 and A.D. 100. Therefore, on the time line below, Buddhism spread to China in A.D. 100, or 100 years after the birth of Jesus. **R**

To avoid a religious reference in dating, many historians prefer to use the initials B.C.E. ("before the common era") and C.E. ("common era"). These initials do not change the numbering of the years.

Using Time Lines

A time line is another way to track the passage of time. Time lines show the order of events within a period of time. They also show the amount of time between events. Most time lines are divided into even sections of time. Events are placed on a time line at the date when the event occurred. **V**

INFOGRAPHIC

Time lines can trace the growth and decline of civilizations. This time line tracks the events of ancient India.

1. **IDENTIFYING** Around what year did the Mauryan Empire's Golden Age begin?
2. **CRITICAL THINKING** ***Analyzing*** Which dates and events on this time line give information about the Aryans?

ANCIENT INDIA

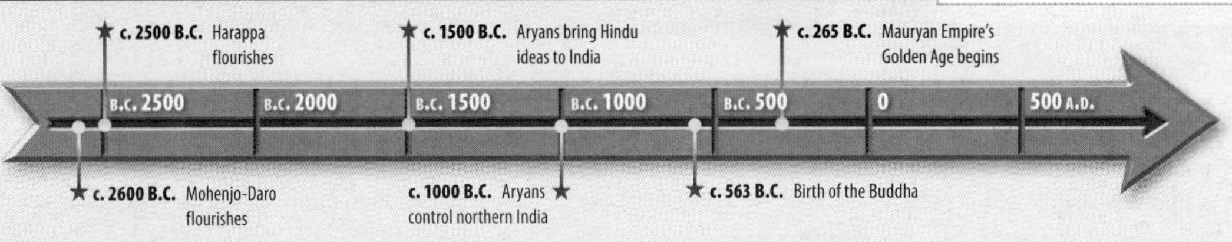

R Reading Skills

Finding the Main Idea Direct students to the section titled "Dating Events." Explain that they can use the subheads to help them determine the main idea for a section. Instruct students to write a sentence that uses the words in the title to express the main idea of this section. Then have each student choose a partner to exchange sentences with another student. If time permits, lead a class discussion and ask pairs to share their sentences.

V Visual Skills

Creating Time Lines Explain to students that any set of events can be plotted on a time line. Ask students to identify five different activities they undertook in the last week. Instruct students to create a time line to visually depict those activities and their relationships to each other. **Logical/Mathematical**

WHITEBOARD ACTIVITY

It Happened in My Lifetime

Applying Guide students through the Interactive Whiteboard Activity about time lines. Before having students create their individual time lines, work as a class to create a time line of the school year. **Ask: When did school start? When does the term end? What big events happen during each school term?** **AL** Have volunteers mark each event on the class time line. Then, have students create time lines of their lives as described in the Interactive Whiteboard Activity. Guide students by **asking: When were you born? When did you start going to school? Did you ever move to a new home? If so, when?**

networks
Important Historical Events That Have Happened in My Lifetime

Directions: Create a time line of events that have occurred during your lifetime.

To create the time line:
- Fill in the list of important events to add to your time line.
- Add date labels to the time line to show how much time each section represents.
- Finally, drag and drop the number of each entry onto the correct spot on the time line.

Important events to add to time line
1. Year of birth: ______ 6. ______
2. ______ 7. ______
3. ______ 8. ______
4. ______ 9. ______
5. ______ 10. Present year/date: ______

Close

See page 1C for other online activities.

ANSWERS, p. 7

INFOGRAPHIC

1. 265 B.C.
2. **CRITICAL THINKING** c. 1500 B.C. Aryans bring Hindu ideas to India; c. 1000 B.C. Aryans control northern India.

T Technology Skills

Making Presentations Have students reflect on Schliemann's discovery of ancient Troy. Then have students complete the following assignment for homework.

Heinrich Schliemann was inspired by stories of the heroes of the Trojan War, as told in the stories of the Greek poet Homer. Find images and stories on the Internet about the Greeks and Trojans who fought in this war. Create a slideshow presentation of these people, and close by explaining why they might be inspiring. Students may want to include music in the presentation.

C Critical Thinking Skills

Making Connections Point out to students that the invention of writing has had an immeasurable impact on virtually all areas of study. Reading and writing are among the most important tools for learning. **Ask: How would the study of history differ without the invention of writing?** *(It would be significantly less detailed and more speculative without written records of any type.)*

ANSWERS, p. 8

CRITICAL THINKING Uncovering evidence of an entire city would give archaeologists a more complete picture of how people in earlier eras lived.

✓ PROGRESS CHECK A historian would use a calendar to find out when something happened and a time line to figure out the order in which things happened.

Build Vocabulary Archaeologists are people who study artifacts to learn about the past. Paleontologists are people who study fossils. Anthropologists are people who study the history of human culture.

BIOGRAPHY

Heinrich Schliemann
(A.D. 1822–1890)

As a boy, Heinrich Schliemann (SHLEE • MAHN) loved stories about ancient Greece. He dreamed of finding Troy, an ancient city destroyed during the Trojan War.

In 1871, Schliemann began to dig through a human-made mound in Hissarlik (HIH • suhr • LIHK), Turkey. Two years later, he uncovered the remains of a mysterious ancient city in the area where Troy had stood. Some archaeologists believe that Schliemann actually found Troy. Others are unsure. Nevertheless, his work led to the discovery of many ancient Greek treasures. Because of his work, Schliemann is considered the founder of prehistoric Greek archaeology.

T

▶ **CRITICAL THINKING**
Making Inferences Archaeologists study and catalog evidence they find. What might be the historical value of uncovering evidence of an entire city?

Usually, the dates on a time line are evenly spaced. Sometimes, however, a time line covers events over too many years to show on one page. In this case, a slanted or jagged line might be placed on the time line. This shows that a certain period of time is omitted from the time line.

Time lines help historians make sense of the flow of events. A time line can be a single line, or it can be two or more lines stacked on top of each other. Stacked time lines are called multilevel time lines.

✓ PROGRESS CHECK

Applying When would a historian use a calendar? When would a historian use a time line?

Digging Up the Past

GUIDING QUESTION *What do students of prehistory look for?*

C

Since the invention of writing, people have recorded important events. These written records give historians a window to the past. Students of prehistory look into an even deeper past, one without writing. They must find a different kind of window.

History and Science

These historians use science to study history. As scientists, they study physical evidence to learn about our ancestors.

Archaeology (ahr•kee•AHL•luh•jee) is the study of the

North Wind Picture Archives/North Wind Picture Archives

Reading HELPDESK CCSS

archaeology the study of objects to learn about past human life
artifact an object made by people
paleontology the study of fossils

fossil plant or animal remains that have been preserved from an earlier time
anthropology the study of human culture and how it develops over time
species a class of individuals with similar physical characteristics

Build Vocabulary: *Word Parts*
The suffix *-ology* means "the study of." The suffix *-ist* means "a person who." For example, *biology* is the study of life. A *biologist* is a person who studies life. What are archaeologists, paleontologists, and anthropologists?

networks *Online Teaching Options*

BIOGRAPHY

Heinrich Schliemann

Paraphrasing Have students read the biography of Heinrich Schliemann, the German archaeologist who discovered the ancient city of Troy. Then ask them to retell Schliemann's biography in their own words. **Ask: Who was this man? What do you know about him? What was his most important achievement?** *(Sample response: Heinrich Schliemann was an archaeologist. He loved the stories of ancient Greece and Troy. He discovered the ruins of Troy and is considered the founder of prehistoric Greek archaeology.)*

See page 1C for other online activities.

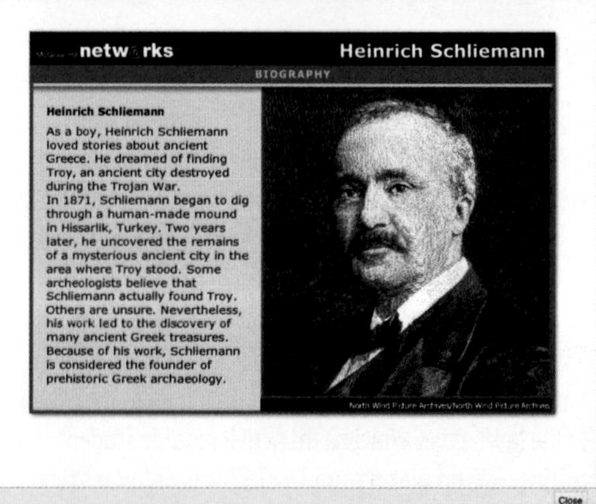

past by looking at what people left behind. Archaeologists dig in the earth for places where people once lived. They never know what they will find. They often discover **artifacts** (AHR•tih•FAKTS)—objects made by people. Common artifacts include tools, pottery, weapons, and jewelry. Archaeologists study artifacts to learn what life was like in the past.

Paleontology (PAY•lee•AHN•TAH•luh•jee) also looks at prehistoric times. Paleontologists study fossils to learn what the world was like long ago. **Fossils** are the remains of plant and animal life that have been preserved from an earlier time.

Anthropology (AN•thruh•PAH•luh•jee) is the study of human culture and how it develops over time. Anthropologists study artifacts and fossils, too. They look for clues about what people valued and believed.

Connections to TODAY

How Lucy Got Her Name

R The night that Lucy was discovered, the team that found her was listening to the song "Lucy in the Sky with Diamonds" by the singing group the Beatles. They nicknamed the skeleton "Lucy," which was more attractive than her official name, AL 288-1.

Human Discoveries

In 1974, a team led by paleontologist Donald Johanson made an exciting find in Ethiopia in Africa. They discovered a partial skeleton of a human ancestor who lived more than 3.2 million years ago. Lucy, as she was called, was about three and a half feet tall (1.07 m) and weighed about 60 pounds (27.2 kg). She had long arms and short legs, and she walked upright.

Lucy belonged to the species *Australopithicus afarensis*. A **species** is a class of individuals with similar physical characteristics. Lucy lived long before the species called *Homo sapiens* evolved. All modern human beings belong to this species. The term *Homo sapiens* is Latin for "wise man." Scientists believe that Homo sapiens probably developed about 150,000 to 195,000 years ago.

Scientists have found and pieced together about 40 percent of Lucy's skeleton.

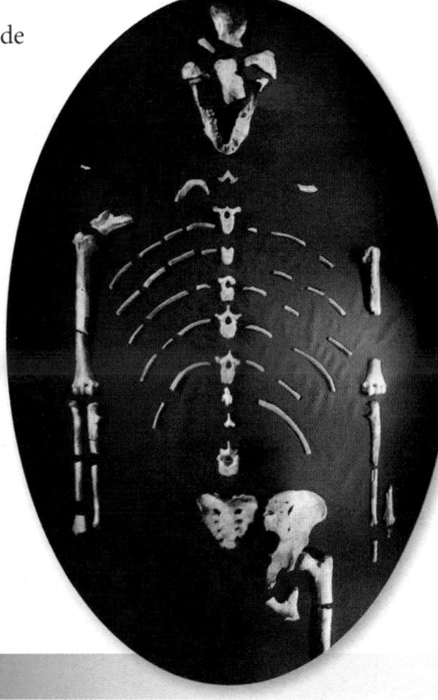

Kevin Fujii/Associated Press

PROGRESS CHECK

Comparing How are archaeologists, paleontologists, and anthropologists like detectives?

LESSON 1 REVIEW (CCSS)

Review Vocabulary (Tier 3 Words)

1. Explain what a historical *era* is. RH.6–8.4
2. Compare and contrast *artifacts* and *fossils*. RH.6–8.4

Answer the Guiding Questions

3. ***Making Connections*** Name one example of how the past influences daily life today. RH.6–8.1
4. ***Listing*** Identify different ways that historians measure time. RH.6–8.1, RH.6–8.2
5. ***Describing*** How do historians learn about people who lived in the earliest historical eras? RH.6–8.3
6. **INFORMATIVE/EXPLANATORY** How would a historian describe your life? Write a short essay that identifies the era in which you live and the artifacts that tell about your culture. WHST.6–8.2, WHST.6–8.10

LESSON 1 REVIEW ANSWERS

1. A *historical era* is a large block of time.
2. *Artifacts* are human-made objects, such as tools and jewelry. *Fossils* are evidence of early animal or plant life that has been preserved from an earlier time. Both help historians understand life in the past.
3. Students might say that the writing of the U.S. Constitution gave them the freedoms they enjoy, or they might identify a more personal historical event, such as a relocation that required them to go to a new school and make new friends.
4. Historians measure time in small blocks such as decades and centuries and larger blocks such as millennia and eras.
5. They look for physical evidence such as fossils and artifacts that tell how people lived.
6. Students should recognize that they live in the era of Modern History. They might also identify that they've lived longer than a decade. They should identify artifacts such as cell phones, computers, backpacks, electronic music players, and so forth as indicative of their culture.

R Reading Skills

Discussing Have students read the textbook to explain how each historian is similar to and different from the others. **Ask:** Which type of historian would you most like to be? Have students explain why they made their choices. AL ELL

Content Background Knowledge

Prehistoric findings are evident throughout the United States. For example, the land near Koshkonong, Wisconsin, is hilly and wooded. The Wisconsin Department of Transportation planned to pave the area for a highway-expansion project to be completed in 2013. As the land was dug, a large, ancient dumping ground for artifacts that spans several eras was discovered. The land contains more than 100,000 prehistoric Native American artifacts. Artifacts include broken cookware, knife points, and even a 1,200-year-old deer bone with markings on it from an ancient tool. In addition to the findings in Wisconsin, housing developers in Sandusky, Ohio, discovered prehistoric artifacts in 2003. Construction workers discovered skeletal remains and cooking pots from an ancient Native American group that occupied the region about 5,000 years ago.

Have students complete the Lesson 1 Review.

CLOSE & REFLECT

Making Connections Explain to students that historians often name periods in history after achievements or events relating to the people who defined that period—such as the Stone Age, the Industrial Age, the Victorian Age. To close, have students speculate about appropriate names we might use to describe the period in which we live. Students may refer to current events or the president who is in office.

ANSWER, p. 9

PROGRESS CHECK Each uncovers and analyzes evidence of past events.

ENGAGE

Bellringer As a class, have students brainstorm as many different kinds of historical evidence as they can think of. You can either list these ideas on the board or have a student write them down for the class.

C Critical Thinking Skills

Making Connections Bring in a variety of present-day artifacts, including newspapers, magazines, photos, and other objects such as an electronic music player, a microwave popcorn bag, and a cell phone. **Ask:** What do these objects reflect about our culture? Explain that these objects are artifacts that tell about our society. In the future, historians will study these objects to learn about our lives. **Ask:** If a historian finds a saddle and horseshoes, what does that tell him or her about the culture? *(that the people rode horses)*

Point out that historians use documents and artifacts from the past to learn about cultures from long ago. AL

networks
There's More Online!

☑ **GRAPHIC ORGANIZER**
- How a Historian Works
- Understanding Primary and Secondary Sources

☑ **SLIDE SHOW**
- Ancient Art
- Terra-cotta Army

Lesson 2
How Does a Historian Work?

ESSENTIAL QUESTION *How do we learn about the past?*

IT MATTERS BECAUSE
Knowing how historians work helps us understand historical information.

What Is the Evidence?

GUIDING QUESTION *What types of evidence do historians use to understand the past?*

Historians ask questions about the information they find from the past. Why did some nations go to war? How were the people affected by that war? How did events of the past change people's lives? These questions help us focus on historical problems.

C To learn the answers to the historical questions, historians look for **evidence** (EH•vuh•duhnts). Evidence is something that shows proof or an indication that something is true. Evidence could be in the form of material objects, such as a soldier's uniform or scraps of pottery from an archaeological dig.

Other evidence may appear in documents or written materials that were created during a historical event. Historians use the evidence they read in historical **sources** to interpret what happened in the past.

Primary and Secondary Sources

Historians look for clues about the past in primary and secondary sources. **Primary sources** are firsthand pieces of evidence. They were written or created by the people who saw or experienced an event. Primary sources include letters, diaries, or government records. Literature or artwork from a particular time

Reading HELPDESK CCSS

Taking Notes: *Sequencing*
As you read, think about the steps in finding and evaluating evidence. Use the sequence chart to note the steps in the process. RH.6–8.3, WHST.6–8.9

Step 1 → Step 2 → Step 3

Content Vocabulary (Tier 3 Words)
- **evidence**
- **primary source**
- **secondary source**
- **point of view**
- **bias**
- **conclusion**
- **scholarly**

networks ***Online Teaching Options***

VIDEO

Uncovering the Past

Integrating Visual Information Remind students that archaeologists use clues from the past to learn about our ancestors. As they watch the video, ask students to take notes on what they learn. At the end of the video, work with students to create a job description for an archaeologist. ELL

See page 1D for other online activities.

ANSWER, p. 10

TAKING NOTES: **Step 1:** Collect sources. **Step 2:** Compare sources to known facts. **Step 3:** Make an inference or draw a conclusion.

and place is a primary source. Spoken interviews and objects, such as tools or clothing, are also primary sources. Primary sources help historians learn what people were thinking while the events took place. They use the sources to find evidence that explains historical events.

C

Historians also use **secondary sources**. Secondary sources are created after an event. They are created by people who were not part of the historical event. The information in secondary sources is often based on primary sources. Examples of secondary sources are biographies, encyclopedias, history books, and textbooks.

A secondary source contains background information. Secondary sources also offer a broad view of an event. However, a historian must use primary sources to find new evidence about a subject.

Reliable Sources

Suppose you were studying the history of England and you wanted to know how ancient people lived. You might look in a book called the *Domesday Book*. This book was created in A.D. 1086 by administrators under William I. The book is a primary source from the period. It contains information about the people of England at the time it was written.

These sculptures of warriors are evidence of life in China during the Qin Dynasty. They give archaeologists and historians information about China's culture and its first emperor.

evidence something that shows proof that something is true
primary source firsthand evidence of an event in history
secondary source a document or written work created after an event

Academic Vocabulary (Tier 2 Words)

source document or reference work

TEACH & ASSESS

C Critical Thinking Skills

Evaluating Remind students that some sources contain a bias—an unreasoned, emotional opinion about something. **Ask:** **Are primary or secondary sources more likely to contain bias?** *(Primary sources are more likely to contain the bias of the eyewitness. Reliable secondary sources should not contain bias, but sometimes they do.)*

Historians should recognize the bias as they study each source. Ask students to identify written materials they have read recently that contain biased information.

Ask: **Why would bias in sources be a danger for historians?** *(If historians accepted a biased source, they could draw the wrong conclusions about a time or event.)* AL

Content Background Knowledge

- Libraries and museums are excellent places to look for primary sources. Many important primary sources are available online. Students can find primary sources about the history of their own community in local libraries, universities, and historical societies.
- Libraries are also home to many secondary sources, in the form of books, movies, and even artwork.

WORKSHEET

21st Century Skills Activity: Critical Thinking and Problem Solving: Recognize Bias

Analyzing Primary Sources Explain that students will read two primary sources about Genghis Khan and evaluate whether the sources contain bias. Point out that the writers of the sources have different opinions about the historical figure. **Ask:** **How do primary sources lead historians to disagree about how to interpret historical events?** *(The authors of primary sources take different positions on events. This sometimes leads historians to draw different conclusions.)*

See page 1D for other online activities.

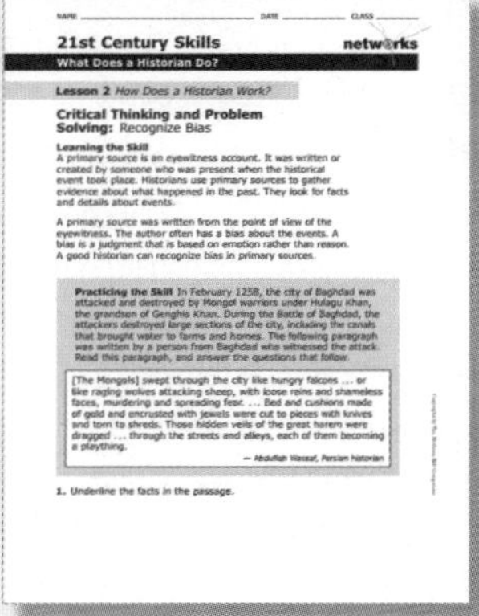

How Does a Historian Work?

V Visual Skills

Analyzing Maps Ask students to analyze the two maps at the top of the page. **Ask:**

- **How are these maps similar?** *(They both show all of the continents and oceans.)*
- **How are the maps different?** *(The size and shapes of the continents on the earlier map do not match what we know today.)*
- **What might account for the differences?** *(Mapmakers today have more accurate tools and a better understanding of the world's geography than mapmakers in A.D. 1500.)* **Visual/Spatial**

C Critical Thinking Skills

Identifying Points of View Tell students that primary and secondary sources about the same time period or event might have different points of view. **Ask:**

- **What might be the point of view of a historian hired by a ruler?** *(He might tend to have a positive point of view about the ruler's actions.)*
- **What might be the point of view of one of the king's enemies?** *(An enemy would probably have a negative point of view about the king's actions.)*

ANSWERS, p. 12

Caption: The map from A.D. 1500 shows different land shapes than the modern map. By comparing these maps, historians can learn what people of the past knew about the world.

✓ PROGRESS CHECK When a historian looks at a primary source, he or she must identify point of view, detect bias, and determine the credibility of the source.

Maps can be primary sources. The map on the left was created around A.D. 1500. How does it compare with the modern world map on the right? What can historians learn by comparing these maps?

The *Domesday Book* is a long list of manors and the names of their owners. It includes details about how many workers worked the land. It lists the number of fishponds, mills, and animals owned by each person. It also estimated the value of each property. The historian's job is to analyze and interpret the information from primary sources. They consider where and when a source was created. They also look for the reasons that the source was created. Was it a secret letter? Was it a document created for the king, such as the *Domesday Book*? Was it written so that all the people in a town or country would read it?

Connections to **TODAY**

The Census

In A.D. 1086, King William I of England decided to collect information about the land and people in his country. Today, our government collects similar data every ten years in the U.S. Census. Questions in the census do not include details about mills and animals as in the *Domesday Book*. They instead focus on age, race, and living arrangements. The census information is a primary source about the people who live in the United States.

What is Point of View?

Historians interpret the document and the reasons it was created. Then they form an opinion about whether the source is trustworthy and reliable in its facts. This step is important since each source was written with a particular **point of view** or general attitude about people or life. The authors of primary sources use their points of view to decide what information is important and what to include in the document. Historians evaluate a primary source to find its point of view. They decide if it has a trustworthy viewpoint.

Sometimes a point of view is expressed as a **bias** or an unreasoned, emotional judgment about people and events. Sources with a bias cannot always be trusted.

✓ PROGRESS CHECK

Explaining What is a historian's job when looking at primary sources?

Reading HELPDESK (CCSS)

point of view a personal attitude about people or life

bias an unreasoned, emotional judgment about people and events

networks Online Teaching Options

WHITEBOARD ACTIVITY

Types of Evidence: Primary and Secondary Sources

Evaluating Review with students what they know about reliable sources and the difference between primary and secondary sources. Then guide the Interactive Whiteboard Activity as students sort sources for a research paper about Ancient Greece. **Ask: Are all of these sources reliable? How do you know?** *(The primary sources include ancient artifacts, maps, literature, and an essay. Some students may note that these might include bias or inaccuracies. The secondary sources include standard references that are assumed to be reliable, such as an atlas, an encyclopedia, and a history book.)*

See page 1D for other online activities.

Writing About History

GUIDING QUESTION *How do we write about history?*

When historians write about an event, they interpret the information from primary sources to draw conclusions and make inferences.

Making an inference means choosing the most likely explanation for the facts at hand. Sometimes the inference is simple. For example, if you see a person who is wearing a raincoat walk into a room with a dripping umbrella, you can infer that it is raining outside. The dripping umbrella and the raincoat are the evidence that combine with your prior knowledge about weather to infer that it is raining.

Making inferences about historical events is more complex. Historians check the evidence in primary sources and compare it to sources already known to be trustworthy. Then, they look at secondary sources that express different points of view about an event. In this way, historians try to get a clear, well-rounded view of what happened. The inference they make is how they explain what happened in the past. This explanation is based on the evidence in primary and secondary sources.

For example, you might read the *Domesday Book* to analyze the types of animals raised in 1086. You could add this knowledge to additional evidence from another source about grain that was planted. Then, you could think about what you know to be true about food. You might use all of this information to make an inference about the types of food people ate in eleventh-century England.

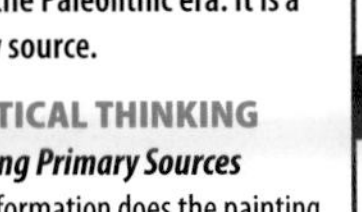

This cave painting was made during the Paleolithic era. It is a primary source.

▶ CRITICAL THINKING
Analyzing Primary Sources
What information does the painting give historians?

Yoko Aziz/Age fotostock

Lesson 2 13

networks

GAME

Historical Evidence Crossword Puzzle

Naming Allow students who want to test their knowledge of historical evidence to complete this online crossword puzzle.

See page 1D for other online activities.

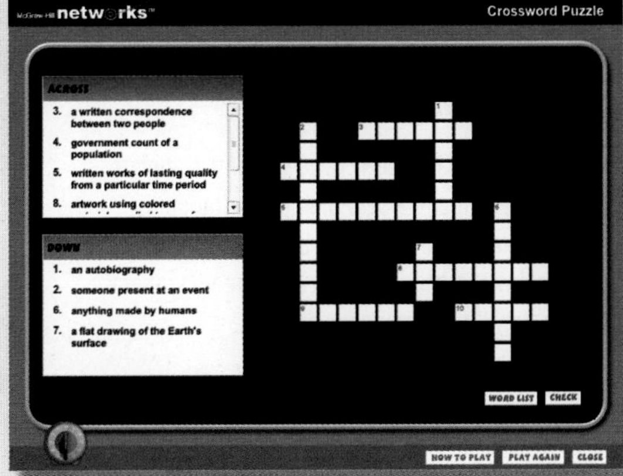

C Critical Thinking Skills

Making Inferences Tell students that prior knowledge is an important part of making inferences. Explain that prior knowledge is everything that students already know. They may have learned some of it in school, and they may have learned some of it simply as part of living and growing. Build on the example in the book by asking students to practice making inferences by looking at the items in the classroom or in the immediate environment. Some appropriate examples might be inferring from the books on a shelf what subjects are taught here, or inferring from the environment visible through a window what type of area this is and where most students live—i.e., rural or urban.

W Writing Skills

Informative/ Explanatory Direct students' attention to the cave painting. In small groups, have students describe what is shown in the painting. They should answer these questions: **Who or what is shown in this painting? What is happening?** Then have each group write a short paragraph, clearly explaining their interpretation of the painting. Invite groups to share their paragraphs. **Interpersonal**

ANSWER, p. 13

CRITICAL THINKING Paintings like this one provide information about methods the artists used and about subjects that were important to them. This painting tells historians that the people who created it hunted animals with bows and arrows.

How Does a Historian Work?

W Writing Skills

Informative/Explanatory Organize the class into pairs, and ask each pair of students to determine a topic for research. Explain to students that each partner should work on his or her own to conduct research and write a brief article on the topic. Then students will switch papers with their partner, who has researched and written about the same topic, to review their partner's work for accuracy. Interpersonal

R Reading Skills

Labeling Ask a volunteer to read the section titled "Focusing Research" aloud. As a class, have students brainstorm different subjects a historian might choose to research. When they have ten or so, ask students to label each one as "narrow" or "broad." Invite one student to come to the whiteboard and write the appropriate letter after each area of research.

Looking at History

W

Professional historians become experts on their historical subject. Historians gather artifacts and data about a subject and then write what they have learned from the study. Such writing may become an article in a **scholarly** (SKAH•luhr•lee) journal, or magazine. It may become a book on the specific subject.

In most cases, historical books and articles are reviewed by other scholars for accuracy. Experts in the field will review the sources and write their own articles. They evaluate how the historian has interpreted the facts. This study of historical interpretations is called historiography. Historians must keep accurate notes and be careful that their inferences are reasonable.

If you were researching World War I, this photo of American soldiers could help you. Using photos as evidence is a good way to expand information. What do you think these soldiers are waiting for?

Hulton Archive/Getty Images

Focusing Research

R

Some historians keep their areas of study very narrow. For example, someone could spend an entire career investigating the events that occurred on a single day, such as the day in the year A.D. 79 that Mount Vesuvius, a volcano in the region that is now Italy, erupted and destroyed the city of Pompeii. This subject is a **finite** place and time. Other historians focus on broader subjects. For example, some historians study the economic history of a period. Others study the political history of a country during a certain period of time. Still others might study military history, the history of medicine, or the history of technology in a certain place.

Drawing Conclusions

A **conclusion** (kuhn•KLOO•zhun) is a final decision that is reached by reasoning. You draw conclusions all the time. For example, you may notice that a friend often wears T-shirts from music concerts that he has attended. You might also remember he can never get together on Thursday nights because he has guitar lessons on Thursdays. Based on these two clues, you could draw the conclusion that your friend is really interested in music. Historians draw conclusions in the same way. They look for facts and evidence in their primary and secondary sources. Then, they use reasoning to make a judgment or draw a conclusion.

Reading HELPDESK (CCSS)

scholarly concerned with academic learning or research

conclusion a decision reached after examining evidence

Academic Vocabulary (Tier 2 Words)

finite limited; having boundaries

interpretation an explanation of the meaning of something

networks Online Teaching Options

GAME

Historical Research Fill-in-the-Blank Game

Finding the Main Idea Have students complete the online game to assess their understanding of historical research and the main ideas in this lesson. Instruct students to review the text for any terms they do not use correctly.

See page 1D for other online activities.

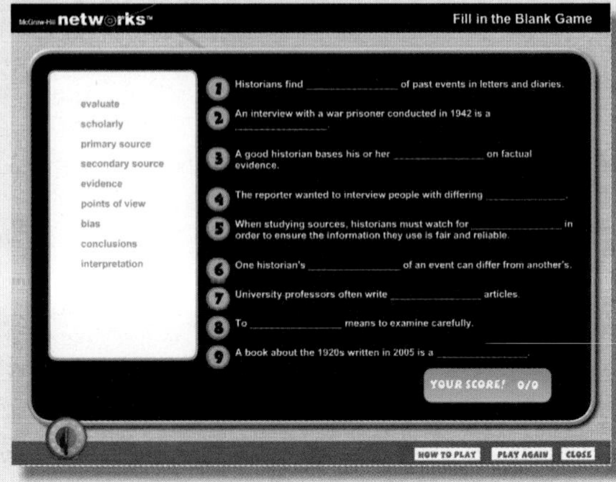

ANSWER, p. 14

They are waiting for orders to fire their guns at the enemy.

Historical Interpretations

Sometimes historians disagree about their **interpretations** of the facts. For example, historians disagree about how to evaluate the historical figure of Genghis Khan. There are historians who argue that Genghis Khan was a fierce and bloodthirsty warrior. Some have expressed horror at the tremendous destruction that Genghis Khan's fierce soldiers brought as they conquered new lands. Yet some historians see Genghis Khan differently. They look at the way Genghis Khan ruled his great Mongol empire. Sources show that this was a time of peace, prosperity, and stability in a huge portion of central and eastern Asia. The people living in the Mongol empire enjoyed a remarkable degree of religious tolerance, higher learning, and consistent laws.

Which conclusion is correct? Was Genghis Khan a ruthless warrior or a strong, intelligent leader of a great land? A historian may rely on evidence to support either position. However, it is the job of the historian to evaluate the primary sources and explain why both interpretations can be argued.

Genghis Khan and his Mongol warriors expanded the Mongol Empire. The violence of their invasions contrasted with the peace inside the empire.

PROGRESS CHECK

Analyzing Why do historians draw different conclusions about events of the past?

LESSON 2 REVIEW 

Review Vocabulary (Tier 3 Words)

1. Name one way a *primary source* is different from a *secondary source.* RH.6–8.4
2. Why does a historian have to understand what *point of view* is? RH.6–8.4

Answer the Guiding Questions

3. ***Drawing Conclusions*** Why does drawing a conclusion come at the end of a research process? RH.6–8.3
4. ***Making Generalizations*** How does a primary source help a historian understand the past? RH.6–8.1
5. ***Assessing*** Explain why some historians differ in their interpretations of historical events. WHST.6–8.9
6. **INFORMATIVE/EXPLANATORY** Think of the reading you do every day. In a short paragraph, give an example of one primary source and one secondary source that you have read recently. Explain why each example fits into the category you have chosen. WHST.6–8.2, WHST.6–8.10

LESSON 2 REVIEW ANSWERS

1. A primary source is a firsthand piece of evidence created by a person who experienced an event. A secondary source is created after the event took place by an individual who did not experience the event.
2. Historians should know what a point of view is because identifying a source's point of view will help them determine the reliability of the source and recognize bias.
3. Drawing conclusions comes at the end of the process because a historian first needs to find and evaluate sources.
4. A primary source contains details about a historical time period. Although it is written from a potentially biased point of view, a primary source contains concrete evidence from which to draw conclusions.
5. Historians use different historical sources to find evidence for their positions. Their interpretations may differ based on the facts in their sources.
6. Students should write a paragraph in which they identify at least two reading materials from their everyday lives, such as textbooks, social media, graphic novels, or young adult fiction. They should accurately identify the reading materials as primary or secondary sources and explain why each source fits in the designated category.

T Technology Skills

Making Presentations Review the following history-related careers with students. Then ask students select one of the careers to research. Have students provide more information about the type of work a person in each career might undertake, as well as the education required to pursue the career. Students should create a brief presentation using their findings.

- **Anthropologist** Scientists work to uncover clues to learn about early human life. Anthropologists focus on human society. They study how humans developed and related to one another.
- **Archivist** Archivists are responsible for cataloguing and preserving collections of historical artifacts and manuscripts so that these materials can be used for research or public display.
- **Archaeologist** When digging begins for the construction of a new building, workers sometimes find artifacts or ruins of earlier societies. Officials will usually call an archaeologist to study the discoveries before the work continues.
- **Genealogist** Many people are curious about their own families' past. Genealogists help people trace their roots in order to learn more about their families.
- **Historian** Historians are people who study and write about the human past to learn about important people and events. Historians work for many types of institutions—from the government to professional football's Hall of Fame—to study and record history.
- **Paleontologist** Man's earliest history has no written records and few artifacts for historians to study. Paleontologists find clues about prehistoric humans by studying bones and fossils.

Have students complete the Lesson 2 Review.

CLOSE & REFLECT

Giving Examples To close the lesson, have students identify objects in the classroom that would make appropriate artifacts for future historians. Have students speculate about what these artifacts would reveal about the class to people in the future.

ANSWER, p. 15

PROGRESS CHECK Historians use different primary sources for their research. They decide which sources to use to support their conclusions. Sometimes historians make different choices about how to interpret a historical event.

ENGAGE

Bellringer Ask students to consider the following list of artifacts from American history: the original Declaration of Independence, the original flag sewn by Betsy Ross, and the furniture owned by George Washington. **Ask:**

- **Where should these historical items be kept?**
- **Should they remain in the United States?**
- **What if people from Europe or Asia purchased one of these objects?**
- **Should they display the item in their country?**
- **Would that object still be American?**

TEACH & ASSESS

R Reading Skill

Citing Text Evidence Direct students to the two primary sources in this feature. Explain that the quotation marks are a way to show, or *cite,* that these are a direct quote from a source. In the "Yes" argument, **ask**: **What are two sources that the author is citing to support his point?** *(The Oxford English Dictionary and the U.S. courts)* AL

Content Background Knowledge

One of the most famous controversies around the return of artifacts is that of the so-called Elgin Marbles. The Elgin Marbles are sculptures that were removed from the Parthenon and other buildings on the Acropolis in Athens, Greece. The Earl of Elgin, the British ambassador in the early 1800s, organized the removal of these artifacts. Elgin believed that the sculptures, which were carved in the 5th century B.C. and had already been damaged by vandalism and neglect, were in danger from a regional civil war. Today, the marbles reside in the British Museum. The Greek government has been pressing for the return of the artworks. However, so far, the government of the United Kingdom has refused, citing the global significance of the carvings and the millions of visitors from around the world who see them every year.

What Do You Think? CCSS

Should Artifacts Be Returned to Their Countries of Origin?

Imagine you were an archaeologist who found an important ancient artifact in another country. You would want to take that artifact home with you and display it in a museum. The country where you found the artifact might raise a protest. They may want the object to stay in their own country. Many such artifacts are displayed in museums far away from their country of origin. Who has the biggest claim to them? Should artifacts be returned to the countries in which they were found?

Yes

PRIMARY SOURCE

R "The Oxford English Dictionary defines "repatriate" as "to restore (an artifact or other object) to its country of origin." Many artifacts. . . have special cultural value for a particular community or nation. When these works are removed from their original cultural setting, they lose their context and the culture loses a part of its history. A request for repatriation of an artifact. . .usually has a strong legal basis. The antiquity was exported illegally, probably also excavated [dug up] illegally, and most importantly, it is now defined by U.S. courts as stolen property. Even in the United States, where private property rights are greatly respected, the government claims ownership of antiquities from federal lands—and would request their repatriation if they were to be privately excavated and exported."

—Malcolm Bell III, professor emeritus, University of Virginia

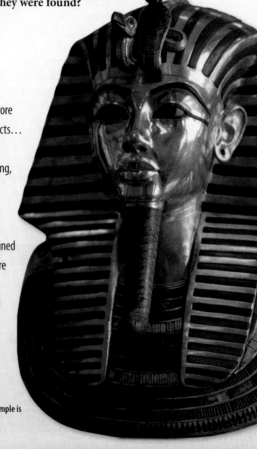

The Cairo Museum holds countless artifacts from Egypt's long history. An example is this famous golden burial mask of Pharaoh Tutankhamen.

TEXT: "Who's Right? Repatriation of Cultural Property," Malcolm Bell III, america.gov, October 2010.
PHOTO: Tim Graham/Getty Images

16 *What Does a Historian Do?*

networks Online Teaching Options

SLIDE SHOW

Critical Thinking Skills: How to Recognize Historical Perspectives

Evaluating Explain to students that two speakers may have very different perspectives on the same topic. Explain to students that as they study current or historical events, they will have to analyze the actions taking place or the beliefs being expressed. To understand statements like the ones in this feature, students must carefully consider the time period and perspective, or the experiences and viewpoints, of the people involved.

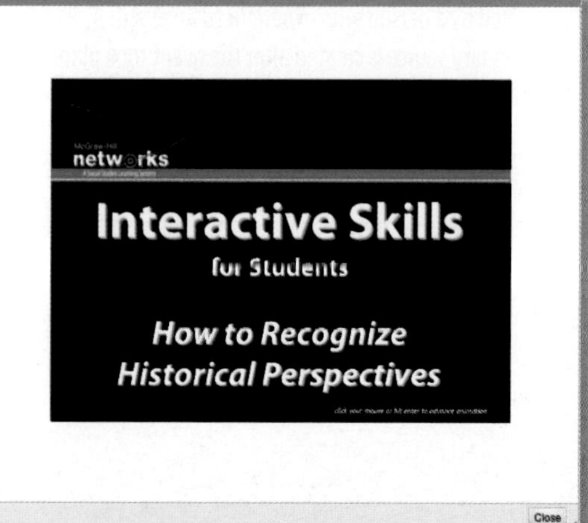

Media
networks
Interactive Skills
for Students
How to Recognize
Historical Perspectives
Close

PHOTO: (t) Yoko Aziz/Age fotostock, (b) The Print Collector/Heritage/Age fotostock

The Metropolitan Museum of Art in New York is visited by millions of people every year. The museum's collection includes treasures from all over the world, including this sphinx of the Egyptian pharaoh Amenhotep II.

No

PRIMARY SOURCE

> "History is long and untidy. Territory held today by a given nation-state in the past likely belonged to a different political entity [unit], one with other descendents. Does ancient Hellenistic [Greek] art made and found in Afghanistan, once on the edge of the Greek empire, belong to Greece or to Afghanistan? To which modern nation do they belong? The lines designating [assigning] claims to art and culture are not clear-cut.
>
> I would argue that within the limits of the law, museums, wherever they are, should be encouraged to acquire works of art representative of the world's many and diverse cultures. This can be through purchase or long-term loan and working in collaboration [cooperation] with museums and nations around the world. These collections encourage a cosmopolitan [international] view of the world and promote a historically accurate understanding of the fluidity [constantly changing] of culture."

R —James Cuno, president and Eloise W. Martin Director of the Art Institute of Chicago

What Do You Think? DBQ

1. ***Identifying*** Why is repatriation a legal issue according to Bell? RH.6–8.1
2. ***Contrasting*** How do the arguments of Bell and Cuno differ? RH.6–8.1

CRITICAL THINKING RH.6–8.1

3. ***Problem Solving*** Describe a compromise that might solve a conflict over ownership of artifacts.

R Reading Skill

Summarizing Have students read the two primary source passages on their own. Review challenging words with students. ELL

Then have volunteers summarize the main argument in each passage. **Ask:** **Do you think the United States has the right to reclaim all the American artifacts in museums around the world? Do you think American museums should return artifacts to other countries, where they originated?** *(Students who support the "NO" argument in the feature should argue that American artifacts abroad belong to the museum where they are being kept. They should point out that such artifacts help others around the world appreciate and learn about American culture. Students who support the "YES" argument should argue that artifacts represent part of a unique cultural heritage that belongs to the people of those countries.)* Have students support their answers with explanations and details from the text. BL

Finally, have students complete the *What Do You Think?* questions.

CLOSE & REFLECT

Drawing Conclusions To close this feature, point out that many ancient artifacts were smuggled out of the country of origin by historians or researchers. These historians and researchers believed they could better care for the artifacts than the people in that country. Many also were seeking fame and fortune. **Ask:** **Should the way an artifact was originally obtained play a role in the decision to return the artifact?** *(Responses will vary. Students may think that whether an artifact was stolen is an important criterion for returning it.)*

WORKSHEET

Writing Process Strategies: Persuasive Writing

Persuasive Writing Ask students to create a short piece taking a stance on repatriating antiquities. Students should state which side of the argument they agree with, and they should use several facts to back up their reasoning.

networks — Writing Process Strategies

Persuasive Writing

Persuasive writing is similar to an argument. It provides an opinion and then supports that opinion with facts. The goal of persuasive writing is to convince the reader to agree with you. Examples of persuasive writing include a letter of complaint, most forms of advertising, an opinion piece from a newspaper columnist or a letter to the editor, and political campaign pamphlets.

Follow these strategies for successful persuasive writing.

- **Know your audience:** Understand your audience so you know how to make a convincing appeal.
- **Sympathize:** Imagine how your audience may feel and offer to help. Relate to your audience by showing you understand their point of view.
- **Use facts:** Provide your opinion and back up your point of view with facts. Statistics and data are most convincing. Use reliable sources.
- **Appeal to emotions:** Provide personal examples or an anecdote. Your audience will be more attached to your point of view.
- **Explain:** Show that you are knowledgeable and have a reasoned point of view. Convince your audience that you know better than the opposition or the competition.
- **Conclude:** Provide a plan of action by letting the audience know what to do next.

CHECKLIST FOR YOUR WRITING

The following checklist will help you do your best work. Make sure you:

- ❑ Support and develop your ideas with specific details and examples.
- ❑ Organize your writing with a strong introduction, body, and conclusion.
- ❑ Use precise language that is best-suited to your audience and purpose.
- ❑ Vary your sentences to add interest to your writing.
- ❑ Check for errors in grammar, spelling, punctuation, and sentence structure.

ANSWERS, p. 17

1. Bell argues that the U.S. court system considers antiquities stolen property when they are acquired from other countries illegally.
2. Bell argues that countries lose part of their culture when artifacts are taken from them, and it is considered illegal in U.S. courts. Cuno, however, argues that one country cannot own artifacts since numerous cultures in that country of origin have influenced the creation of them.
3. Students might suggest that museums work out loan programs or compensate countries for displaying their artifacts.

ENGAGE

Bellringer Point out a few reference books in the classroom. **Ask:**

- **Where do you go to find answers to questions?**
- **Do you look up the answers? If so, where?**
- **If you use a book, what type of book?**
- **Or do you use the Internet? If so, what type of site?**
- **Do you ask someone for help? If so, whom do you ask?**
- **How do you know if you have found the correct answer to your question?**

(Answers should show an understanding of the types of reliable places students should use to start a research project.)

TEACH & ASSESS

R Reading Skills

Summarizing Pair up students and have one member of the pair read the section about project planning and the other read the section on choosing research materials. Then have each student summarize the section he or she read for their partner.

As a whole class, ask volunteers to share their partner's summaries.

W Writing Skills

Informative/Explanatory Share with students that there are many ways to generate ideas for their research projects. These include:

- Brainstorming
- Mind mapping
- Listing interests

Ask: Which of these have students used in the past? Do they feel that those approaches have been successful? *(Answers will vary.)*

ANSWER, p. 18

TAKING NOTES: The main idea should contain a broad concept about interpreting research materials accurately. Detail boxes should contain facts that support the main idea.

networks *There's More Online!*

- **GAME** Reliable Sources
- **GRAPHIC ORGANIZER**
  - Historical Research
  - Is This Plagiarism?

Lesson 3

Researching History

ESSENTIAL QUESTION *How do you research history?*

It Matters Because

Knowing where to find information about your subject will make it easier to complete research projects and other schoolwork.

Planning Your Project

GUIDING QUESTION *How do you begin a research project?*

W The first step in a history research project is to identify your topic. A topic should not be too broad (The Middle Ages) or too narrow (Middlebury, England, 1535). To test your topic, try looking it up in an encyclopedia. If there is no entry for your topic, it may be too small. If there are many entries, or a very long entry, the topic may be too large. Selecting a topic that is workable is the most important part of the project.

R After you choose a topic, you need to decide what you want to learn about it. Create six questions to help you find out *who, what, when, where, why,* and *how.* Then write each question at the top of a note card. These cards will become your research tools. You may need to add additional cards as you research.

Choosing Research Materials

After selecting a topic and creating your question cards, the next step is to gather your research materials. Begin with general reference books, such as encyclopedias and textbooks, or your notes from class. Next, try looking for books about your subject at the library. Your research material must be nonfiction, rather than fiction or persuasive writing.

Reading HELPDESK CCSS

Taking Notes: *Finding the Main Idea*

As you read, look for the main idea of each section. Use a graphic organizer like this one to write the details that support the main idea. RH.6–8.2, WHST.6–8.9

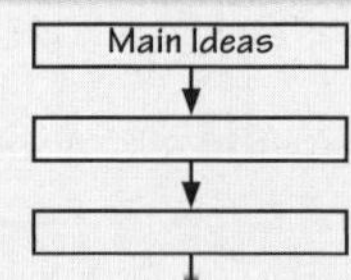

Content Vocabulary (Tier 3 Words)

- **credentials**
- **URL**
- **.gov**
- **.edu**
- **.org**
- **plagiarize**

networks *Online Teaching Options*

VIDEO

Internet Research Techniques

Differentiating Review the details about researching on the Internet. You may choose to show the short video "Internet Research Techniques." Then have students differentiate between the sites they may encounter while they research a topic. Create an idea web on the board using students' ideas about Internet research.

See page 1E for other online activities.

Distinguishing Fact From Opinion

Scan each possible source to determine if the source is trustworthy. Look for opinion statements in the text. This will give you a clue that a resource could be biased or untrustworthy. Remember, a statement of fact expresses only what can be proven by evidence. A statement of opinion expresses an attitude. It is a conclusion or judgment about something that cannot be proven true or false. Historical research should rely on facts and primary sources rather than opinions. G1

Making Notes

As you find information, make a note about it on your cards. Your notes should be in your own words and in complete sentences. On the back of each card, make notes about the books in which you found the information.

PROGRESS CHECK

Explaining Why is it important to distinguish fact from opinion in historical writing?

G2

Researching on the Internet

GUIDING QUESTION *How do you safely research on the Internet?*

Looking for information on the Internet is quick and rewarding. However, it can be a challenge to find out if the information you located is true. Good historians follow a few important guidelines as they gather information.

Authorship

Many articles on the Internet are unsigned. A reader has no way of knowing who wrote the content and whether the author is an expert on the subject. However, reliable articles will be signed by well-known experts on the subject. The authors will include details about their **credentials** (kreh•DEN•shulz), or evidence that they are experts.

Web sites such as these may be reliable for certain subjects. There are many clues on a Web site to let you know if it will have reliable information.

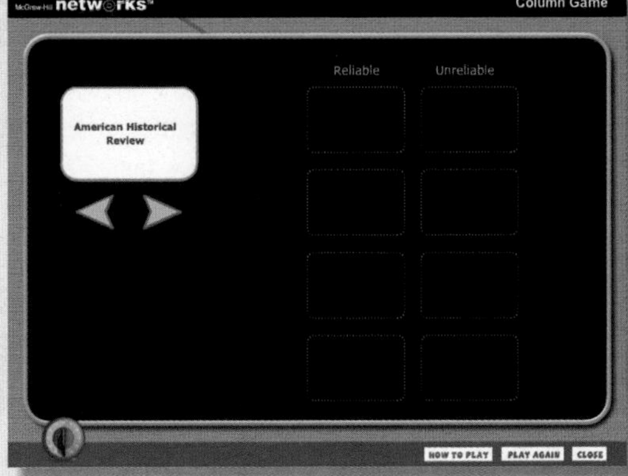

(t) Library of Congress (c) NASA, (b) National Archives

credentials something that gives confidence that a person is qualified for a task

G1 Critical Thinking Skills

Distinguishing Fact from Opinion Remind students that facts can be proven; opinions cannot. Offer several examples of opinions, such as *"The most interesting period of history is Ancient Egypt"* and *"The worst leader in history was Genghis Khan."* Remind students that these are opinions. They cannot be proven. Then have students write down two facts and one opinion about a topic of your choice. Ask volunteers to read their examples aloud, and have classmates identify which statements are facts and which are opinions. AL

G2 Critical Thinking Skills

Organizing As students proceed with their research projects, they will need to organize all the information they find. Distribute note cards and have students spend ten minutes practicing note-taking skills. Direct them to the section on Researching on the Internet. **Ask:** What is the main idea from this section? Direct students to write that on a card and label it "main idea." Then **ask:** What are some details that support the main idea? Direct students to write those details on the card beneath the main idea.

Ask: What facts or details from this section were the most interesting to you? What would you like to know more about? Tell students that their responses to these questions might be good candidates for a research project.

Content Background Knowledge

- The Internet was created in 1980s as a way for scholars and scientists to exchange information rapidly and efficiently.
- In 1990, the British computer scientist Sir Tim Berners-Lee used a hypertext system that he developed to connect information in a way that the user could browse. This became the World Wide Web. This is why every Web site begins with *www*—they exist on the World Wide Web.

GAME

Reliable Web Sites Column Game: Researching History

Differentiating Review with students how to determine which sources were reliable and which were unreliable. Launch the interactive game about reliable Web sites. Have students play the game as a class or in groups in which they sort the Web sites according to reliability.

See page 1E for other online activities.

networks Column Game
Reliable Unreliable
American Historical Review
HOW TO PLAY PLAY AGAIN CLOSE

ANSWER, p. 19

PROGRESS CHECK If a source contains opinions, it might be biased or untrustworthy.

T Technology Skills

Researching on the Internet Ask students to read the section titled Web URLs. Then have students pick a research topic and find one example of a possible source for each URL type, including *.com*. Remind students what each of the endings of a URL mean. Have students evaluate each of their sources to determine which ones are likely to be the most reliable sources. BL

W Writing Skills

Argument Review the content about writing without bias. Then have students write a short letter to a friend, arguing the importance of writing about history but without bias. Remind them to use facts from the reading to support their argument. BL **Verbal/Linguistic**

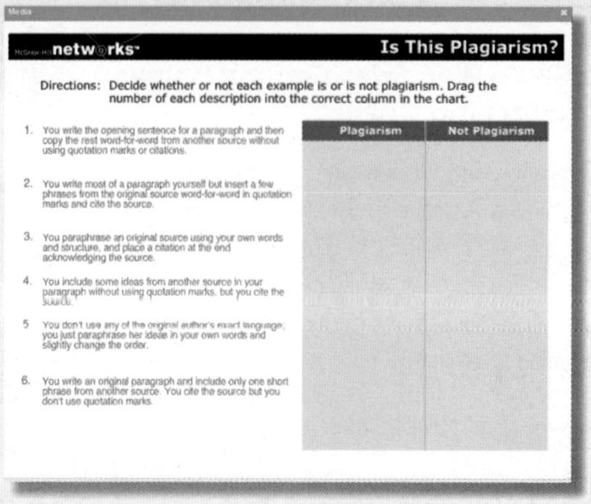

ANSWER, p. 20

✓ PROGRESS CHECK A biased resource would alter the interpretation of historical events. Conclusions will be inaccurate if historians do not use reliable sources for their research.

Thinking Like a HISTORIAN

Internet Tips

Check it Out!

If you answer NO to any of the questions below, the Web page or Web site is probably not a reliable resource.

- Is the authorship of the article clear?
- Can you easily find out who is responsible for the Web site?
- Has the Web page been updated recently?
- Does the writing seem balanced or does it contain a bias toward one point of view?

There are other ways to decide if an article is worth using for research. You can look at the homepage for the article. If the article is on the site of a university, government office, or museum, it is probably reliable. For example, suppose you find a signed article about the foods eaten by American colonists. You find that the article is published by an academic journal at a university. You can assume that this page is a better source than an unsigned article about the same subject by a blogger on a cooking Web site.

Web URLs

T A uniform resource locator, or **URL,** is the address of an online resource. The ending on a URL tells a great deal about the content. A URL that ends in **.gov** is most likely a government entity. This site probably contains accurate **data.** This data is usually as up to date as possible.

A URL that ends in **.edu** is usually a site for an educational institution, such as a college or university. Most .edu sites pride themselves on accuracy. However, it is possible that documents on these sites may contain opinions in addition to facts.

Nonprofit organizations usually use **.org** at the end of their URLs. These sites may be very accurate. However, these groups often gather information to support their cause. Their sites may contain biased information, and they often contain opinions.

You have gathered information and answered the questions on your note cards. Then organize your cards into categories. Once your cards are sorted, you can use them as an outline for writing your research paper.

✓ PROGRESS CHECK

Speculating What are the consequences of using an Internet resource with biased information?

Writing Without Bias

GUIDING QUESTION *How do you interpret historical events accurately?*

W You have chosen a good topic. You have created your question cards and used them while reading encyclopedia articles and library books. You have also used your cards while reviewing reliable Internet resources about your topic. You have turned the answers on your question cards into an outline. Now you are ready to write your research report. As you work, be aware of some important guidelines for writing about history.

Reading HELPDESK CCSS

URL abbreviation for *uniform resource locator;* the address of an online resource

.gov the ending of a URL for a government Web site

.edu the ending of a URL for a Web site for an educational institution

.org the ending of a URL for an organization

plagiarize to present someone's work as your own without giving that person credit

Academic Vocabulary (Tier 2 Words)

data information, usually facts and figures

violate to disobey or break a rule or law

networks Online Teaching Options

CHART

Is This Plagiarism?

Categorizing Students can use the interactive chart to review six hypothetical circumstances and decide whether those circumstances represent plagiarism. Students may do this independently, or you can organize a full-class activity on the interactive whiteboard.

See page 1E for other online activities.

Plagiarism

To **plagiarize** (PLAY•juh•RYZ) is to present the ideas or words of another person as your own without offering credit to the source. Plagiarism is similar to forgery, or copying something that is not yours. It also **violates** copyright laws. These laws prevent the unauthorized use of a writer's work. If you copy an idea or a written text exactly word-for-word, that is plagiarism. Some scholars have ruined their careers through plagiarism. They used content from books or the Internet without citing the source or giving credit.

To avoid plagiarism, follow these rules:

- Put information in your own words.
- When you restate an opinion from something you read, include a reference to the author: "According to Smith and Jones, ..."
- Always include a footnote when you use a direct quotation from one of your sources.

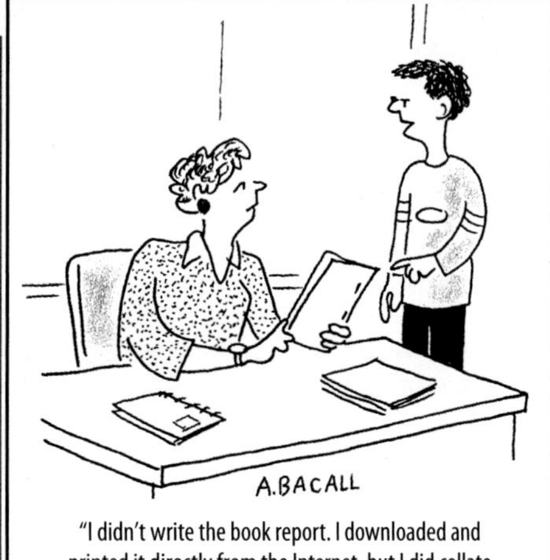

"I didn't write the book report. I downloaded and printed it directly from the Internet, but I did collate and staple it myself."

Cartoons can make plagiarism seem humorous, but it is illegal and can lead to serious consequences.

Ancient History and Modern Values

Avoid using modern ideas to evaluate a historical event. For example, a scholar of women's history may want to apply modern ideas to women's rights in historical settings. Ideas have changed over time. Drawing conclusions about women's attitudes in the Middle Ages using modern ideas would be a mistake. Your evaluations of history should be based on the evidence, not on today's understanding of rights and society.

 PROGRESS CHECK

Listing What is one way to avoid plagiarism when writing about history?

LESSON 3 REVIEW (CCSS)

Review Vocabulary (Tier 3 Words)

1. Why is it against the law to *plagiarize*? RH.6–8.4
2. Which URL ending would identify a Web site for a charity? RH.6–8.4

   a. .org b. .gov c. .edu

Answer the Guiding Questions

3. ***Assessing*** How do you know if a resource in a library book can be trusted? RH.6–8.1
4. ***Listing*** Identify the clues you would look for to decide if an online resource is trustworthy. RH.6–8.1
5. ***Determining Cause and Effect*** What is one negative effect that can come from applying modern values to a historical event? RH.6–8.2
6. **ARGUMENT** Your teacher does not want students to use the Internet for research. Write two paragraphs in which you persuade the teacher that the Internet can be a reliable source of information. WHST.6–8.1, WHST.6–8.10

R Reading Skills

Determining Word Meanings Ask students to define *plagiarism.* Have a student volunteer record the answers on the whiteboard. Present students with scenarios such as "Jane copied Johnny's homework" and "Lupe used her own words to describe the terra-cotta soldiers." Have students give a thumbs-down sign if the example is plagiarism and a thumbs-up sign if it is not. ELL

Then have students create a two-column chart. Label the first column "Plagiarism" and the second column "Not Plagiarism." Have students complete the chart by categorizing the examples used earlier in this activity. Have them add two examples of their own to the chart.

C Critical Thinking Skill

Making Generalizations Explain the class policy on plagiarism to students. Offer examples of how to avoid plagiarizing material they read in an encyclopedia or other research material. **Ask:** **Can you make any generalizations about historians or history students who plagiarize the work of others?** *(Sample answer: Historians who plagiarize are careless or dishonest about their work.)*

Have students complete the Lesson 3 Review.

CLOSE & REFLECT

Evaluating To close the lesson, have students think about people they trust in real life. Then ask them to think about Web sites they have visited. Do they feel that those websites are trustworthy? How do they know? BL

LESSON 3 REVIEW ANSWERS

1. Plagiarism is against the law because it is a form of stealing.
2. A is the correct answer. A charity would most likely have a URL that ends with *.org*.
3. A resource should not be trusted if it contains statements of opinion about a subject that are not backed up by verifiable facts.
4. Three clues are the authorship of the article, the ending of the URL, and the level of scholarship of the journal from which the article comes.
5. When modern values are used to evaluate an event in history, a writer may draw incorrect conclusions about the event.
6. Students' paragraphs should demonstrate an understanding of evaluating credible resources, especially as it applies to Internet sources.

ANSWER, p. 21

PROGRESS CHECK Students may cite any of the following: put the ideas you read in your own words, give credit to the sources of ideas, and footnote direct quotations.

CHAPTER REVIEW ACTIVITY

Draw a sample flowchart on the whiteboard. Explain that a flowchart shows a sequence of events. Organize students into small groups. Have each group work together to create a flowchart of how historians work. Each group should present its flowchart to the class. *(Flowcharts should include choosing a topic, finding evidence, evaluating sources, drawing conclusions/making inferences, and presenting findings.)*

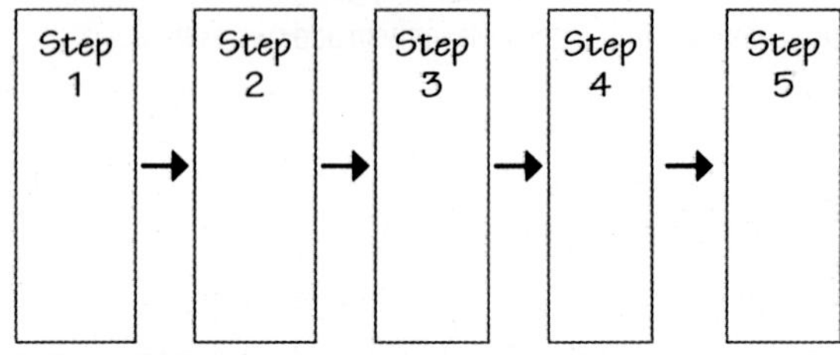

REVIEW THE ENDURING UNDERSTANDING

Review this chapter's Enduring Understanding with students.

- *Learning about the past helps us understand the present and make decisions about the future.*

Now pose the following questions in a class discussion to apply it to the chapter.

What are some of the sources that can teach us about history? *(Answers may include: written records, artifacts uncovered by archaeologists, fossils and tombs, primary sources, secondary sources, scholarly journals.)*

Why is it important to learn about the past? *(Students might include ideas about understanding either their own culture or other cultures. Students may also discuss how understanding the conflicts of the past can help prevent conflicts in the future.)*

What are some important things to keep in mind while researching history? *(Answers may include: choosing an appropriate topic, selecting the appropriate research material, and writing without bias.)*

CHAPTER 1 Activities CCSS

Write your answers on a separate piece of paper.

1. **Exploring the Essential Question** WHST.6–8.2
INFORMATIVE/EXPLANATORY Using information you have read in this chapter, give three reasons why we study history.

2. **21st Century Skills** WHST.6–8.7, WHST.6–8.8
ANALYZE AND INTERPRET MEDIA Research a historical subject of your choice. Find three reliable sources and at least one source that would not be considered reliable. Write a paragraph that analyzes the online resources you discovered. Describe why each source is reliable or unreliable.

3. **Thinking Like a Historian** WHST.6–8.9
SEQUENCING Create a personal time line using the terms *before my birth* and *after my birth*. Fill in the time line with three key events that happened before and three key events that happened after you were born.

4. **GEOGRAPHY ACTIVITY**

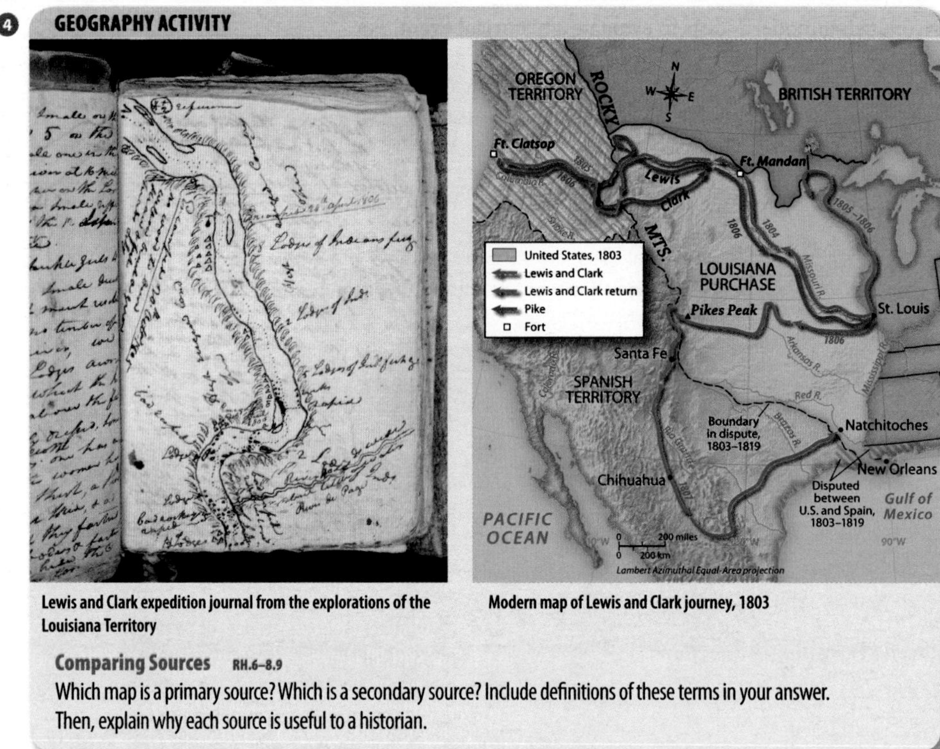

Lewis and Clark expedition journal from the explorations of the Louisiana Territory

Modern map of Lewis and Clark journey, 1803

Comparing Sources RH.6–8.9
Which map is a primary source? Which is a secondary source? Include definitions of these terms in your answer. Then, explain why each source is useful to a historian.

ACTIVITIES ANSWERS

Exploring the Essential Question

1. Possible answer: Reason 1: Historians who know about ancient peoples have been able to explain the meaning of the cave paintings discovered in Europe and to help preserve them for the future. Reason 2: Historians who study early religious documents are able to reveal the significance of early religious doctrines for modern worshipers. Reason 3: Historians who study wars can explain how events of the past led to wars in the present.

21st Century Skills

2. Students should be able to identify three reliable sources and explain why they should be trusted, using criteria such as credible authorship, scholarly journal, and appropriateness of the URL. Students should identify three unreliable resources and be able to point out why they are biased or lack credibility.

Thinking Like a Historian

3. Student time lines should reflect understanding of how time lines work, with events prior to students' birth and since their birth placed chronologically on the time line and clearly labeled.

Comparing Sources

4. The hand-drawn map created by Lewis and Clark when they explored the Louisiana Territory is a primary source. It shows details and evidence of their experience. The second map is a secondary source. It offers after-the-fact information about where the Lewis and Clark expedition traveled on their journey and how the land surrounding the Louisiana Territory was organized.

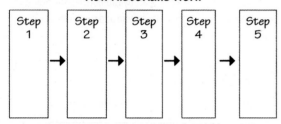

CHAPTER 1 Assessment CCSS

REVIEW THE GUIDING QUESTIONS

Directions: Choose the best answer for each question.

RH.6–8.2

1. How does the Gregorian calendar label events that happened after the birth of Jesus?
   A. B.C.E
   B. C.E.
   C. A.D.
   D. B.C.

RH.6–8.4

2. An anthropologist is a historian who studies
   F. fossils found in sea beds.
   G. ancient plant life.
   H. animal behavior.
   I. the history of human culture.

WHST.6–8.8

3. A historian looks for firsthand evidence about an event in which type of resource?
   A. a secondary source
   B. a primary source
   C. the Internet
   D. an online scholarly journal

RH.6–8.8

4. A work of scholarly history can be identified by
   F. its lively writing style.
   G. its biased point of view.
   H. its accuracy and lack of bias.
   I. its relevance to current events.

WHST.6–8.8

5. If you were researching data on the population of India, which online source would most likely contain reliable information?
   A. www.tourism-india.com
   B. www.cia.gov/india
   C. www.beautiful-people-of-india.org
   D. www.population.com

WHST.6–8.8

6. What is one way to avoid plagiarism?
   F. Always give credit to someone else for their ideas.
   G. Never use the Internet for research.
   H. Read a source three times.
   I. Always use the library for research.

23

CHAPTER 1

Assessment Answers

ASSESSMENT ANSWERS

Review the Guiding Questions

1. **C** Some historians use the designations C.E. and B.C.E., but the Gregorian calendar does not. The Gregorian calendar uses B.C. to identify events that occurred before the birth of Jesus and A.D. to identify events that occurred after Jesus's birth. Therefore, C is the correct answer.

2. **I** An anthropologist is interested in human beliefs and culture, not the history of sealife, plants, or animals. Thus, I is the correct answer.

3. **B** Firsthand evidence is found in primary sources, which were written by people who experienced an event. A scholarly journal is a secondary source, and the Internet is not always trustworthy. Thus, B is the correct answer.

4. **H** Historians who write scholarly history try to avoid bias, or a decided point of view. They focus instead on accuracy. Although the material may be relevant to current events, the focus of the writing does not have to be relevant to today. Therefore, H is the correct answer.

5. **B** Web sites such as "beautiful-people-of-india.org" and "population.com" do not have reliable URLs. Government (.gov) Web sites are usually considered reliable for population statistics. Thus, B is the correct answer.

6. **F** Plagiarism is not determined by which sources are used or how many times a source is read, but rather by how the sources are used. Sources from the library can be plagiarized as easily as sources from the Internet. Plagiarism is best avoided by giving credit where it is due. Therefore, F is the correct answer.

Analyzing Documents

7 **C** According to McNeill, learning about people of the past teaches us more about ourselves. He says that educated guesses, not truth, emerge from the study of history. It is this result, he says, that does not seem good. Thus, C is the correct answer.

8 **G** McNeill sees benefits in studying history so he would not see the effort as a waste of time, nor would he believe that history has no influence on the present. Because he believes there is no absolute truth in history, McNeill probably would not agree with statement I. Therefore, G is the correct answer.

Short Response

9 The first sentence in the passage ("Historians do not perform heart transplants . . .") is a fact. The second sentence ("History is in fact very useful . . .") is an opinion.

10 The usefulness of history is difficult to identify because studying history does not produce immediate, visible results the way work in other occupations does.

Extended Response

11 Students should mention primary sources, such as their letters, text messages, and diaries and secondary sources, such as school yearbooks and descriptions of them written by others. They might indicate that diaries and letters could show a bias.

DBQ ANALYZING DOCUMENTS

RH.6–8.2

7 **Identifying** Historian William H. McNeill wrote an essay explaining why people should study history.

"[We] can only know ourselves by knowing how we resemble and how we differ from others. Acquaintance [familiarity] with the human past is the only way to such self knowledge. . . .

In [studying history], eternal and unchanging truth does not emerge. Only inspired, informed guesses about what mattered and how things changed through time. . . . Not very good, perhaps; simply the best we have in the unending effort to understand ourselves and others . . ."

—Excerpt from "Why Study History?" by William H. McNeill

According to McNeill, what do people gain from the study of history?

A. They discover absolute truth.
B. They discover that the past was not very good.
C. They learn more about themselves.
D. They learn to give their best effort in what they do.

RH.6–8.6

8 **Identifying Point of View** With which statement would McNeill agree?

F. Studying history is a waste of time.
G. We have much to learn from history.
H. History has no influence on the present time.
I. We should look to history for the answers to all of our questions.

SHORT RESPONSE

"Historians do not perform heart transplants, improve highway design, or arrest criminals. . . . History is in fact very useful, actually indispensable [necessary], but the products of historical study are less tangible [physical], sometimes less immediate, than those that stem from some other disciplines."

—Excerpt from "Why Study History?" by Peter N. Stearns

RH.6–8.8

9 Which part of this passage is fact? Which part is opinion?

RH.6–8.1

10 According to Stearns, why is the usefulness of history difficult to identify?

EXTENDED RESPONSE

WHST.6–8.10

11 **Narrative** Write two paragraphs that identify primary sources and secondary sources about your life. Would these sources be biased? Explain.

Need Extra Help?

If You've Missed Question	1	2	3	4	5	6	7	8	9	10	11
Review Lesson	1	1	2	2	3	3	1	1	2	1	3

networks Online Teaching Options

Using eAssessment

Use eAssessment to access and assign the publisher-made Lesson Quizzes & Chapter Tests electronically. You can also use eAssessment to create your own quizzes and tests from hundreds of available questions. eAssessment helps you design assessments that meet the needs of different types of learners. Follow the link in the *Assess* tab of your Teacher Lesson Center.

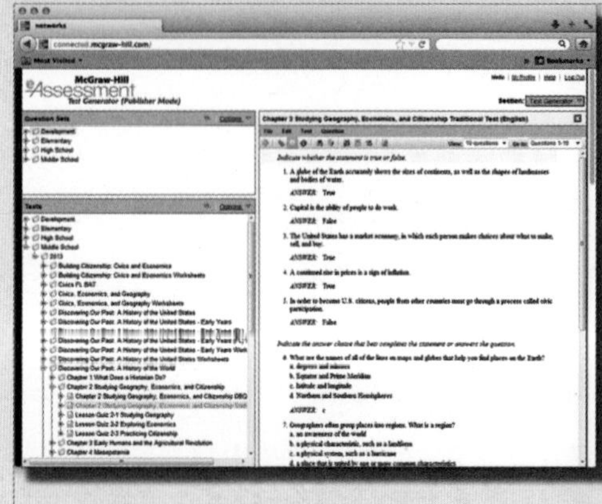

CHAPTER 2
Studying Geography, Economics, and Citizenship Planner

UNDERSTANDING BY DESIGN®

Enduring Understandings
- *People, places, and ideas change over time.*
- *Resources are limited, so people must make choices.*
- *The value that a society places on individual rights is often reflected in that society's government.*

Essential Questions
- *How does geography influence the way people live?*
- *Why do people trade?*
- *Why do people form governments?*

Predictable Misunderstandings
Students may think:
- *The study of geography and economics will not help them understand history.*
- *Maps and globes show the same information about Earth.*
- *Geographers study only the locations of places on Earth.*
- *Economics has little to do with their daily lives.*
- *Citizenship relates to rights but not duties or responsibilities.*

Assessment Evidence
Performance Tasks:
- *Hands-On Chapter Project*

Other Evidence:
- *Responses to Interactive Whiteboard Activities*
- *Comparing and contrasting different map projections*
- *Responses to economics simulation activity*
- *Class discussion answers*
- *Interactive Graphic Organizers*
- *Economics of History Activity*
- *Geography and History Activities*
- *21st Century Skills Activity*
- *Written Paragraphs*
- *Lesson Reviews*
- *Chapter Activities and Assessment*

SUGGESTED PACING GUIDE
Introducing the Chapter . . . . 1 day
Lesson 1 . . . . 2 days
Lesson 2 . . . . 1 day
Lesson 3 . . . . 1 day
Chapter Wrap-Up and Assessment . . . . . . 1 day

TOTAL TIME 6 DAYS

Key for Using the Teacher Edition

SKILL-BASED ACTIVITIES

Types of skill activities found in the Teacher Edition.

V Visual Skills require students to analyze maps, graphs, charts, and photos.

R Reading Skills help students practice reading skills and master vocabulary.

W Writing Skills provide writing opportunities to help students comprehend the text.

C Critical Thinking Skills help students apply and extend what they have learned.

T Technology Skills require students to use digital tools effectively.

*Letters are followed by a number when there is more than one of the same type of skill on the page.

DIFFERENTIATED INSTRUCTION

All activities are written for the on-level student unless otherwise marked with the leveled labels below.

BL Beyond Level
AL Approaching Level
ELL English Language Learners

All students benefit from activities that utilize different learning styles. Many activities are marked as below when a particular learning style is highlighted.

Intrapersonal	Naturalist
Logical/Mathematical	Kinesthetic
Visual/Spatial	Auditory/Musical
Verbal/Linguistic	Interpersonal

NCSS Standards covered in "Studying Geography, Economics, and Citizenship"

Learners will understand:

1 CULTURE

1. "Culture" refers to the socially transmitted behaviors, beliefs, values, traditions, institutions, and ways of living together for a group of people.

2. Concepts such as beliefs, values, institutions, cohesion, diversity, accommodation, adaptation, assimilation, and dissonance

4. That the beliefs, values, and behaviors of a culture form an integrated system that helps shape the activities and ways of life that define a culture

3 PEOPLE, PLACES, AND ENVIRONMENTS

1. The theme of people, places, and environments involves the study of the relationships between human populations in different locations and geographic phenomena such as climate, vegetation, and natural resources.

2. Concepts such as: location, region, place, migration, as well as human and physical systems

9. The use of a variety of maps, globes, graphic representations, and geospatial technologies to help investigate the relationships among people, places, and environments

5 INDIVIDUALS, GROUPS, AND INSTITUTIONS

6. That cultural diffusion occurs when groups migrate

7 PRODUCTION, DISTRIBUTION, AND CONSUMPTION

1. Individuals, government, and society experience scarcity because human wants and needs exceed what can be produced from available resources.

2. How choices involve trading off the expected value of one opportunity gained against the expected value of the best alternative

7. How markets bring buyers and sellers together to exchange goods and services

8. How goods and services are allocated in a market economy through the influence of prices on decisions about production and consumption

10 CIVIC IDEALS AND PRACTICES

2. Concepts and ideals such as: individual dignity, liberty, justice, equality, individual rights, responsibility, majority and minority rights, and civil dissent

6. The origins and function of major institutions and practices developed to support democratic ideals and practices

CHAPTER OPENER PLANNER

Students will know:

- *the Six Essential Elements of Geography and how geography relates to history.*
- *the uses for longitude and latitude, map projections, and types of maps.*
- *basic principles of economics and trade.*
- *the meaning of representative government and the responsibilities of citizenship.*

Students will be able to:

- ***apply** their understanding of geography to the interpretation of maps.*
- ***synthesize** information about geography and its relationship with history.*
- ***identify** basic economic systems.*
- ***explore** the role of trade in world history.*
- ***compare and contrast** the advantages and disadvantages of trade.*
- ***recall** key facts about the United States government.*
- ***summarize** important facts about the rights, duties, and responsibilities of United States citizens.*
- ***discuss** ways in which people can practice good citizenship in their communities.*
- ***compare** their roles as American citizens with their roles as global citizens.*

UNDERSTANDING BY DESIGN®

Print Teaching Options

V Visual Skills

- ☐ **P. 26** Students discuss how geography may be either a resource for or a barrier to development. Visual/Spatial
- ☐ **P. 27** Students identify important historical events related to geography. Visual/Spatial

Online Teaching Options

V Visual Skills

MAP **Natural Wonders of the Ancient World**—Students use the interactive map to learn more about the location and characteristics of the natural wonders of the world.

WORLD ATLAS Students can use this interactive map to identify regions of the world, learn about individual countries, locate political boundaries, measure distances, and much more.

W Writing Skills

TIME LINE **Place and Time: Key Dates in Geography, Economics, and Civics**—Students reflect and write about a the social, political, or economic consequences of a key historical event.

Printable Digital Worksheets

R Reading Skills

GRAPHIC NOVEL ***The Golden Caravan***—A young boy describes how Mansa Musa's visit to Egypt personally affects him.

Project-Based Learning

Hands-On Chapter Project

Geography, Economics, and Citizenship

Students participate in a simulation in order to learn how physical geography influences the way people live and trade.

Technology Extension

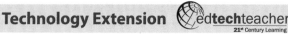

Google Spreadsheets for Aggregating Country Features Data

- Find an additional activity online that incorporates technology for this project.
- Visit the EdTechTeacher Web sites (included in the Technology Extension for this chapter) for more links, tutorials, and other resources.

Print Resources

ANCILLARY RESOURCES

These ancillaries are available for every chapter and lesson.

- **Reading Essentials and Study Guide Workbook** AL ELL
- **Chapter Tests and Lesson Quizzes Blackline Masters**

PRINTABLE DIGITAL WORKSHEETS

These printable digital worksheets are available for every chapter and lesson.

- **Hands-On Chapter Projects**
- **What Do You Know? activities**
- **Chapter Summaries (English and Spanish)**
- **Vocabulary Builder activities**
- **Guided Reading activities**

More Media Resources

SUGGESTED READING 

Grade 6 reading level:

- ***Show Me the Money: How to Make Sense of Economics,*** by Alvin Hall

Grade 7 reading level:

- ***A Tugging String: A Novel About Growing Up in the Civil Rights Era,*** by David T. Greenberg

Grade 8 reading level:

- ***Earth Matters,*** by David de Rothschild

LESSON 1 PLANNER

STUDYING GEOGRAPHY

Students will know:

- *the Six Essential Elements of Geography and how geography relates to history.*
- *the uses for longitude and latitude, map projections, and types of maps.*

Students will be able to:

- ***recall** information about the study of geography.*
- ***apply** their understanding of geography to the interpretation of maps.*
- ***synthesize** information about geography and its relationship with history.*
- ***reflect** on their understanding of geography.*

UNDERSTANDING BY DESIGN®

☑ *Print Teaching Options*

V Visual Skills

- ☐ **P. 28** Students examine a globe and consider the benefits of the Panama Canal. **Visual/Spatial**
- ☐ **P. 29** Students locate countries and continents along the Equator or Prime Meridian. **BL** **Verbal/Linguistic**
- ☐ **P. 30** Students find locations using latitude and longitude. **Visual/Spatial**
- ☐ **P. 30** Students attempt to peel an orange and produce a flat result. **AL** **ELL** **Kinesthetic**
- ☐ **P. 34** Students compare maps of Alexander the Great's empire in 323 B.C. and the region today.
- ☐ **P. 36** Students graph the same data in multiple ways. **BL** **Logical/Mathematical**

R Reading Skills

- ☐ **P. 29** Students discuss why imaginary lines are used in geography. **AL** **ELL**
- ☐ **P. 34** Students use a graphic organizer to summarize types of maps. **Verbal/Linguistic**

W Writing Skills

- ☐ **P. 31** Students write a journal entry as if they are a sailor in the 1600s sailing from Europe to the New World.
- ☐ **P. 32** Students write about increasing their awareness of their immediate physical environment.

C Critical Thinking Skills

- ☐ **P. 31** Students contrast map projections with sizes and shapes of continents on a globe. **BL**
- ☐ **p. 32** Students discuss GPS systems.
- ☐ **p. 33** Students evaluate whether changes humans make to the environment are positive or negative.
- ☐ **p. 33** Students speculate which tools of geography would make a map easier to make and more accurate.

T Technology Skills

- ☐ **p. 30** Students use online resources to identify cities by their latitude and longitude. **Interpersonal**
- ☐ **p. 31** Students research the Mercator, Robinson, and Winkel Tripel projections.
- ☐ **p. 36** Students use presentation software to produce a slide show about a famous geographer.

☑ *Online Teaching Options*

V Visual Skills

- ☐ **VIDEO** **Geography Basics: Climate, Water, etc.**—Students learn that the world's six primary climate regions are the product of latitude, altitude, topography, bodies of water, and global wind patterns.
- ☐ **IMAGE** **Environment and Society**— Reinforces how human actions positively and negatively impact the environment.
- ☐ **MAP** **Hemispheres**—Students use the interactive map to explore the hemispheres.
- ☐ **MAP** **Latitude and Longitude**—Students use the map to explore latitude and longitude.
- ☐ **MAP** **Alexander's Empire 323 B.C.**—Students examine the extent of the empire, identify sites of major battles, and trace Alexander's routes.
- ☐ **SLIDE SHOW** **Tools of Geography**—Students examine the sextant, satellite images, and GPS imaging.

R Reading Skills

- ☐ **GRAPHIC ORGANIZER** **Taking Notes: *Identifying:* Six Essential Elements of Geography**—Students identify and record the six essential elements of geography in the graphic organizer.
- ☐ **BIOGRAPHY** **Gerardus Mercator**—Students learn more about this geographer's background.

C Critical Thinking Skills

- ☐ **WHITEBOARD ACTIVITY** **Food Chain**—Students drag and drop photos and arrows to make their own food chain or food web.

T Technology Skills

- ☐ **SELF-CHECK QUIZ** **Lesson 1**—Students receive instant feedback of their mastery of lesson content.

☑ *Printable Digital Worksheets*

W Writing Skills

- ☐ **WORKSHEET** **Geography and History Activity: Studying Geography, Economics, and Citizenship - Studying Geography: Longitude and Latitude**—Students use longitude and latitude to determine location and reflect on what they have learned.

C Critical Thinking Skills

- ☐ **WORKSHEET** **Geography and History Activity: Studying Geography, Economics, and Citizenship - Studying Geography: Physical Maps**—Students read about and examine a physical map and answer questions about its uses.

Exploring Economics

Students will know:
- *basic principles of economics and trade.*

Students will be able to:
- ***identify** basic economic systems.*
- ***explore** the role of trade in world history.*
- ***compare and contrast** the advantages and disadvantages of trade.*

UNDERSTANDING BY DESIGN®

☑ Print Teaching Options

V Visual Skills

- ☐ **P. 39** Students analyze supply and demand curves. BL **Visual/Spatial**
- ☐ **P. 42** Students analyze import/export data. **Visual/Spatial**

R Reading Skills

- ☐ **P. 38** Students review the terms used in discussing economics. AL ELL
- ☐ **P. 40** Students contrast different economic systems.
- ☐ **P. 41** Students describe the business cycle.
- ☐ **P. 42** Students identify the main idea of a passage. AL

W Writing Skills

- ☐ **P. 43** Students write an editorial stating their point of view regarding globalization. **Verbal/Linguistic**

C Critical Thinking Skills

- ☐ **P. 39** Students analyze supply and demand. AL ELL
- ☐ **P. 40** Students analyze advertisements and identify phrases that indicate scarcity. **Interpersonal**
- ☐ **P. 40** Students give examples of opportunity cost. BL
- ☐ **P. 41** Students discuss the country's current economic conditions.
- ☐ **P. 42** Students identify examples of bartering in their own lives. BL

T Technology Skills

- ☐ **p. 41** Students research current economic data.

☑ Online Teaching Options

V Visual Skills

- VIDEO **Introduction to Economics, Part 1**—Students view a video that shows how an economy functions and provides examples of economic characteristics.
- GRAPH **Supply and Demand**—Students learn about a supply and demand graph by clicking on its parts.
- GRAPH **U.S. Trade With China: 1999–2009**—Students see how export and import totals change over time.
- CHART **Business Cycle**—Students click on terms to learn about the parts of the business cycle.

R Reading Skills

- IMAGE **Hunter-Gatherer Societies**—Students read about this traditional economic system.
- GRAPHIC ORGANIZER **Taking Notes: *Describing:* Economic Systems and Their Characteristics**—Students use a chart to describe two types of economic systems and their key elements.

C Critical Thinking Skills

- GAME **Studying Economics Matching Game**—Students match phrases and descriptions that describe key economic concepts.

T Technology Skills

- SELF-CHECK QUIZ **Lesson 2**—Students receive instant feedback of their mastery of lesson content.

☑ Printable Digital Worksheets

W Writing Skills

- WORKSHEET **Economics of History Activity: Studying Geography, Economics, and Citizenship - Exploring Economics**—Students respond to an extended passage that describes trade in the ancient world.

LESSON 3 PLANNER

Practicing Citizenship

Students will know:

- *the meaning of representative government and the responsibilities of citizenship.*

Students will be able to:

- ***recall key** facts about the United States government.*
- ***summarize** important facts about the rights, duties, and responsibilities of United States citizens.*
- ***discuss** ways in which people can practice good citizenship in their communities.*
- ***compare** their roles as American citizens with their roles as global citizens.*

UNDERSTANDING BY DESIGN®

Print Teaching Options

V Visual Skills

- [ ] **P. 45** Students examine and interpret a graphic on checks and balances. **Visual/Spatial**

R Reading Skills

- [ ] **P. 44** Students define lesson vocabulary. AL ELL
- [ ] **P. 46** Students explain how duties and responsibilities of citizenship improve quality of life and ensure freedom.

W Writing Skills

- [ ] **P. 47** Students write paragraphs about U.S. and global citizenship.

C Critical Thinking Skills

- [ ] **P. 44** Students speculate as to why voting is an important responsibility of citizenship. AL
- [ ] **P. 45** Students categorize examples of duties and responsibilities. AL BL ELL
- [ ] **P. 46** Students connect what they have learned about our system of government to what they have learned about citizenship. AL

T Technology Skills

- [ ] **P. 47** Students research and present information on different forms of government.

Online Teaching Options

V Visual Skills

- [ ] SLIDE SHOW **Good Citizenship**—Students view images that reinforce the rights and responsibilities of citizens.
- [ ] VIDEO **The Seven Dynamics of Citizenship**—Students view a video that explains the seven dynamics of citizenship.
- [ ] CHART **A System of Checks and Balances**—Students learn more about how our government functions by clicking on different areas of the chart.

R Reading Skills

- [ ] IMAGE **United States Flag**—Students read about how the flag has changed over time.
- [ ] GRAPHIC ORGANIZER **Taking Notes: *Summarizing:* Rights and Responsibilities of Citizens**—Students use a graphic organizer to show the rights and responsibilities of citizenship.

C Critical Thinking Skills

- [ ] WHITEBOARD ATIVITY **Separation of Powers**—Students analyze a list of terms and categorize them by judicial, executive, or legislative branch.

T Technology Skills

- [ ] SELF-CHECK QUIZ **Lesson 3**—Students receive instant feedback of their mastery of lesson content.

Printable Digital Worksheets

C Critical Thinking Skills

- [ ] WORKSHEET **21st Century Skills Activity: Studying Geography, Economics, and Citizenship - Practicing Citizenship**—Students learn how to plan a service project, and then they read about a proposed project and analyze it for the characteristics of a good plan.

INTERVENTION AND REMEDIATION STRATEGIES

LESSON 1 Studying Geography

Reading and Comprehension

Have students write sentences using each of the Lesson 1 content vocabulary words. Sentences should show a clear understanding of the words' meanings.

Text Evidence

Ask students to choose one of the Six Essential Elements of Geography and one specific place on Earth. Have them do research and then write two or three paragraphs describing their chosen place in terms of the essential element.

LESSON 2 Exploring Economics

Reading and Comprehension

Ask students to create an outline of Lesson 2. They can use the major heads as outline topics. They should include all main ideas for each topic.

Text Evidence

Have students choose one decade from the past 100 years of U.S. history and do research to learn about the business cycles of that period. Ask students to write a summary of the cycles, identifying peaks and troughs, recessions, booms, and other major elements of the cycles.

LESSON 3 Practicing Citizenship

Reading and Comprehension

Have students review the lesson and list five responsibilities or duties of citizenship. Then have them write one or two sentences for each, explaining how fulfilling those responsibilities and duties help to protect the rights and freedoms of all U.S. citizens.

Text Evidence

Ask students to do research to learn about naturalization. Have them list the steps required to become a citizen, and describe the process.

Online Resources

Approaching Level Reader

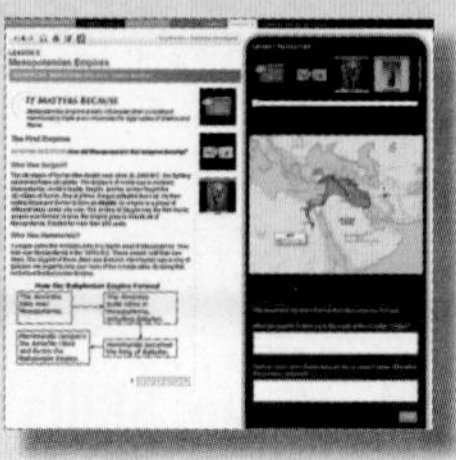

Use this online lower-level text that corresponds directly to the text in the Student Edition. It includes a Spanish version.

Guided Reading Activities

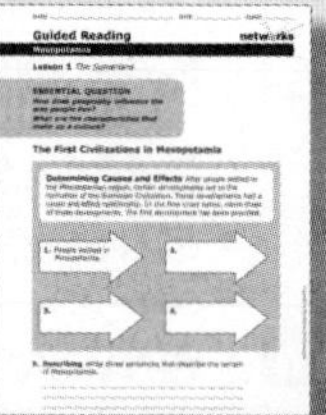

This resource uses graphic organizers and guiding questions to help students with comprehension.

What Do You Know?

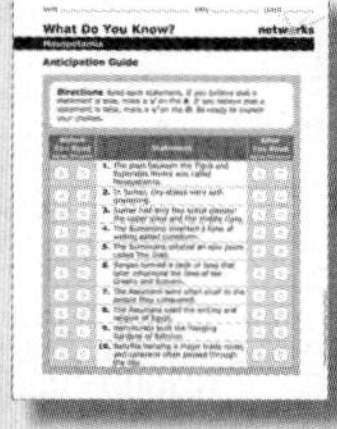

Use these worksheets to pre-assess student's background knowledge before they study the chapter.

Reading Essentials and Study Guide Workbook

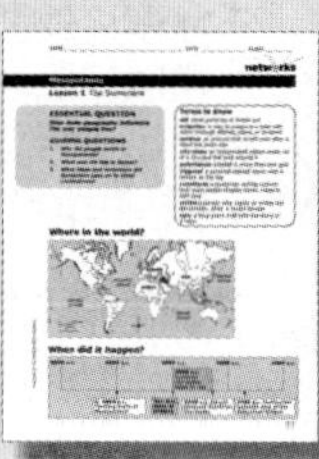

This resource offers writing and reading activities for the approaching-level student. Also available in Spanish

Self-Check Quizzes

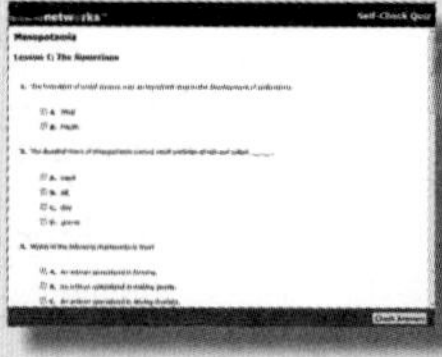

This online assessment tool provides instant feedback for students to check their progress.

Studying Geography, Economics, and Citizenship

ESSENTIAL QUESTIONS • *How does geography influence the way people live?* • *Why do people trade?* • *Why do people form governments?*

networks

There's More Online about the key ideas of geography, economics, and citizenship.

CHAPTER 2

Lesson 1 *Studying Geography*

Lesson 2 *Exploring Economics*

Lesson 3 *Practicing Citizenship*

The Story Matters . . .

Why is this woman smiling? She has just become a citizen of the United States. Though she was born in another country, she now enjoys all the rights and responsibilities of U.S. citizenship. Her last step toward gaining citizenship was taking the Oath of Allegiance. In this oath, people swear to "support and defend the Constitution against all enemies, foreign and domestic."

Whether you have taken this oath or not, as a U.S. citizen, you share this duty to defend the laws of your nation. Being a good citizen also means staying informed about the world around you. Understanding history, geography, and economics can help you fulfill this responsibility.

◄ *For many people, citizenship comes with being born in a certain country. For others, like this woman, citizenship is a matter of choice.*

25

Letter from the Author

Dear World History Teacher,

When people meet for the first time, they usually ask each other where they are from. People recognize that the environment in which we live greatly influences our development, opportunities, and even belief systems. Likewise, historians must be aware of Earth's physical geography and how people interact with their environment. Also, the way people accumulate, distribute, and use resources, which are central to the study of economics, might be the most powerful gauge of people's beliefs, traditions, and actions. The study of history is also crucial to being a good citizen.

Jackson J. Spielvogel

ENGAGE

Bellringer Read aloud "The Story Matters" in class or ask for a volunteer to read it aloud. Explain that the process of becoming a U.S. citizen is called naturalization. Discuss the reasons a person might want to become a citizen of the United States. **Ask:** What sorts of rights and responsibilities do U.S. citizens have? Do you know anyone who has become a naturalized U.S. citizen? Have a few students share their ideas about citizenship or their stories of naturalized citizens. List their ideas on the board in a web graphic organizer, with Citizenship written in the center.

Ask: If you do not understand your duties and responsibilities as a citizen, what might happen? Who would protect your rights and freedoms?

Discuss with students how their experiences as citizens or naturalized citizens are similar to or different from one another. Then tell students that they will be learning more about the concept of citizenship later in this chapter.

Making Connections

Read the following information to students:

One of the responsibilities of citizenship is being informed about key issues. The countries of the world are more connected now than ever before, so it is even more important to understand geography. It is also important to learn about economics so that we can understand the dynamics of trade and how to manage our own money.

TEACH & ASSESS

Step Into the Place

V1 Visual Skills

Analyzing Maps Have students study the Chapter Opener map. Tell students that major geographic features, such as large rivers and mountain ranges, can shape the development of civilizations. In some cases, such features provide valuable resources. In other situations, geography may be a barrier to travel and can limit contact between different peoples. **Ask:** **How might some of the landmarks shown on the map provide benefits or disadvantages to the people living near them?**

Have student volunteers categorize the different natural wonders of the ancient world shown on the map, identifying them as rivers, mountains, deserts, and so on. As a class, discuss the Map Focus questions. **Visual/Spatial**

Content Background Knowledge

- Arizona's Grand Canyon is more than a mile deep in spots and spans more than 277 river miles.
- The semicircular Iguazú Falls bordering Argentina and Brazil measures approximately 262 feet high. A subtropical wet forest containing more than 2,000 known plant species surrounds it.
- Matterhorn is one of the tallest mountain peaks in the Pennine Alps. It lies on the border of Italy and Switzerland.
- Uluru, or "Ayers Rock," is a massive sandstone rock formation in central Australia. Archaeological evidence shows that people have inhabited the area near Uluru for more than 30,000 years.

ANSWERS, p. 26

Step Into the Place

1. Mount Kilimanjaro, Matterhorn, Himalaya
2. Asia: Gobi and Himalaya; Africa: Great Rift Valley, Mount Kilimanjaro, Victoria Falls, Sahara, Nile River
3. **CRITICAL THINKING** Mountains and deserts often form barriers to trade and to the exchange of ideas.

Step Into the Time

The right to vote was expanded to include people of all races, women, and 18-year-old citizens.

CHAPTER 2 CCSS

Place and Time: Geography, Economics, and Citizenship

Where in the world are you? How should you spend your money? What are your responsibilities as a citizen? Geography helps us understand the places around us. Economics explores the exchange of goods. Civics explains citizenship. These topics help us understand history.

Step Into the Place

V1 **MAP FOCUS** Scholars sometimes talk about the natural wonders of the ancient world. These are natural landmarks that helped shape the history around them.

1. **PLACE** Look at the map. Which of the natural wonders shown are mountains? RH.6–8.7
2. **PLACE** What natural wonders are located in Asia? In Africa? RH.6–8.7
3. **CRITICAL THINKING** *Analyzing* How do mountains and deserts affect trade and the exchange of ideas? RH.6–8.1

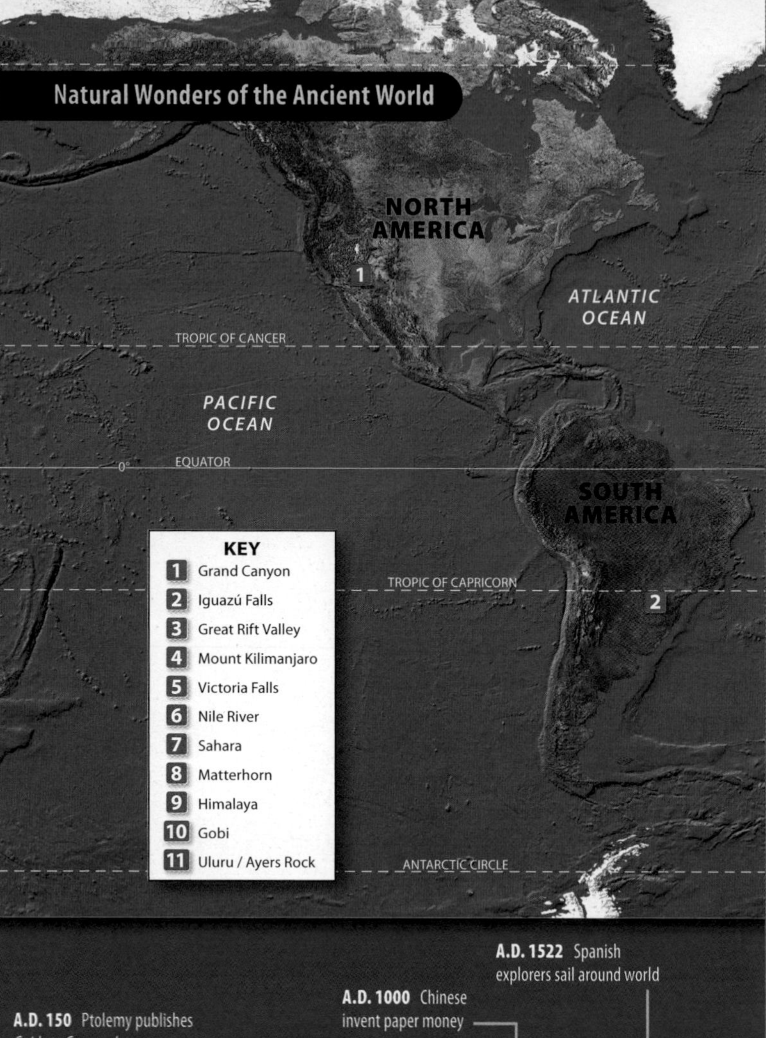

Step Into the Time

V2 **TIME LINE** Voting is a duty of U.S. citizens. How did the voting rights of U.S. citizens change over time? RH.6–8.7

KEY DATES IN GEOGRAPHY, ECONOMICS, AND CIVICS

A.D. 100 A.D. 500 A.D. 1000 A.D. 1500

A.D. 150 Ptolemy publishes *Guide to Geography*

A.D. 1000 Chinese invent paper money

A.D. 1522 Spanish explorers sail around world

A.D. 1569 Mercator introduces map projection

Project-Based Learning 

Hands-On Chapter Project

Geography, Economics, and Citizenship

Students will work in small groups to invent a country and create a map of it. Through discussion and worksheets, they will name the country, identify its physical geographic features, specify its population and population distribution, identify its animals and vegetation, and specify its goods and services. After watching other presentations, students will meet again with their group to decide what and how their country will trade and with whom.

Technology Extension

Google Spreadsheets for Aggregating Country Features Data

Using Google Docs, student groups will create a collaborative spreadsheet in which they record information from their country simulation to facilitate communication, comparison, and analysis. Students will then present a "global" overview of the fictional world they have created for analysis.

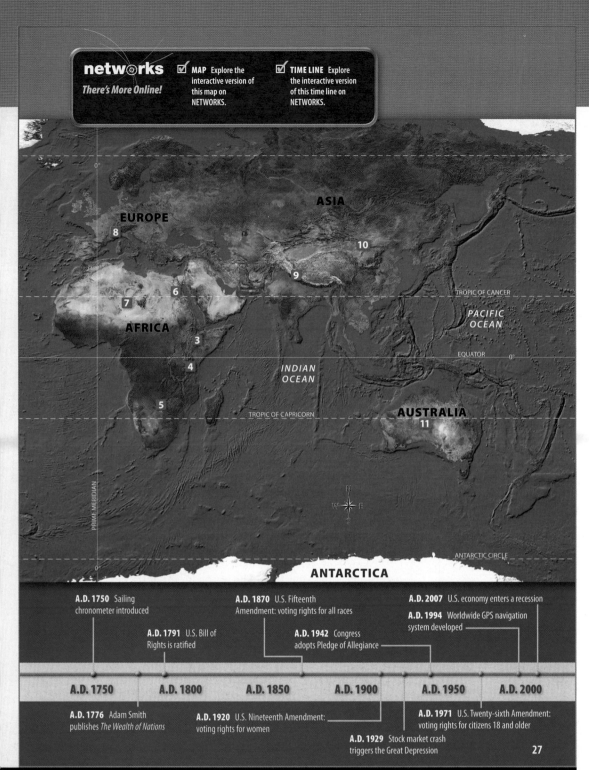

networks *There's More Online!*

☑ **MAP** Explore the interactive version of this map on NETWORKS.

☑ **TIME LINE** Explore the interactive version of this time line on NETWORKS.

EUROPE · ASIA · AFRICA · INDIAN OCEAN · PACIFIC OCEAN · AUSTRALIA · ANTARCTICA · TROPIC OF CANCER · EQUATOR · TROPIC OF CAPRICORN · ANTARCTIC CIRCLE · PRIME MERIDIAN

A.D. 1750 Sailing chronometer introduced

A.D. 1776 Adam Smith publishes *The Wealth of Nations*

A.D. 1791 U.S. Bill of Rights is ratified

A.D. 1870 U.S. Fifteenth Amendment: voting rights for all races

A.D. 1920 U.S. Nineteenth Amendment: voting rights for women

A.D. 1929 Stock market crash triggers the Great Depression

A.D. 1942 Congress adopts Pledge of Allegiance

A.D. 1971 U.S. Twenty-sixth Amendment: voting rights for citizens 18 and older

A.D. 1994 Worldwide GPS navigation system developed

A.D. 2007 U.S. economy enters a recession

A.D. 1750 · A.D. 1800 · A.D. 1850 · A.D. 1900 · A.D. 1950 · A.D. 2000

27

Step Into the Time

V2 Visual Skills

Analyzing Time Lines Have students review the time line for the chapter and pick out events related to geography. Advise them to look for key words like *map, globe,* and *world.* **Ask:** **Based on the information on the time line, what can you conclude about how our knowledge of geographic locations has changed?** *(Our knowledge of geographic locations has increased greatly. First, the world has been and is still being explored. Then, tools such as Mercator's map projection and the sailing chronometer were invented. Now, satellite imagery and GPS technology provide even more specific information about Earth's surface.)* **Visual/Spatial**

Content Background Knowledge

- *Guide to Geography* by Ptolemy (A.D. 90–168) appeared in eight volumes. It provides the most detailed geographic information we have of the Roman Empire during its peak.
- The Mercator projection shows parallel lines of latitude and longitude, making it ideal for navigation because sailors can plot straight-line courses.
- *The Wealth of Nations* is regarded as the first work on political economy. It established the foundation for *laissez-faire capitalism.*
- The sailing chronometer allowed sailors to determine longitude accurately. By estimating speed and knowing the time, sailors could determine longitude. Ordinary clocks were unreliable on ships.

CLOSE & REFLECT

Informative/Explanatory Explain that this chapter will draw together three main topics: geography, economics, and citizenship. These topics will form a foundation for much of what follows in this textbook. Ask students to choose one of the events from the time line or a landform from the map and then write a paragraph describing how they think that landform or event affected events in world history.

MAP

Natural Wonders of the Ancient World

Analyzing Maps Have students explore the map. They can read more about the natural wonders by clicking on the numbered locations that appear on the map. Ask students to choose one location and to research on the Internet to learn more about it. Have them write a brief description of the place.

See page 25B for other online activities.

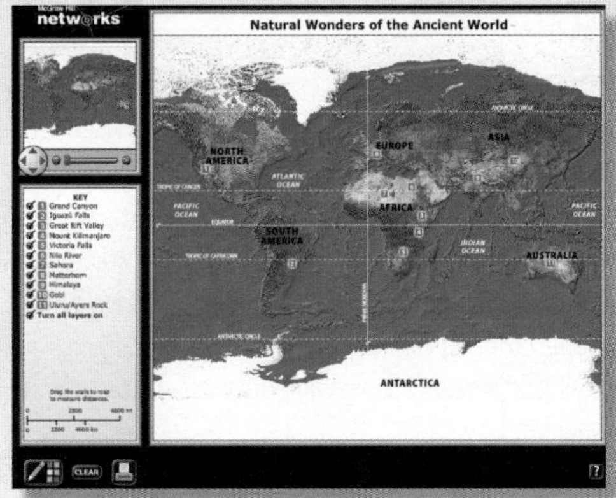

ENGAGE

Bellringer Encourage students to think about the geography of their immediate area. Ask them what major cities or towns their school is located near. Have students list the physical characteristics of the landscape in which they live *(mountainous, flat, heavily forested, coastal)*, and then have them describe an area of the country or the world that has a very different geography from their own.

TEACH & ASSESS

R Reading Skills

Contrasting After students have read the text, have them make a two-column chart. Have them use the first column to list the ways a map would be more informative than a globe, and to use the second column to list the ways a globe would be more informative than a map. *(Students might state that a map would be better for showing small details or a lot of information about a particular location. A globe, on the other hand, would be better for identifying the relationship of one location to another and for showing the geography of the entire Earth.)* AL ELL

V Visual Skills

Problem Solving Have students locate North and South America on a globe. Encourage them to think about how a ship in the Atlantic Ocean would have had to travel to reach the Pacific Ocean before the building of the Panama Canal. **Ask:** **Why would a ship need to sail all the way south of South America before the Panama Canal was built?** *(There was no waterway connecting the Atlantic and Pacific oceans.)* **What were some of the benefits of human beings changing the land in this way?** *(The canal provided easier and faster travel between the two oceans.)* **Visual/Spatial**

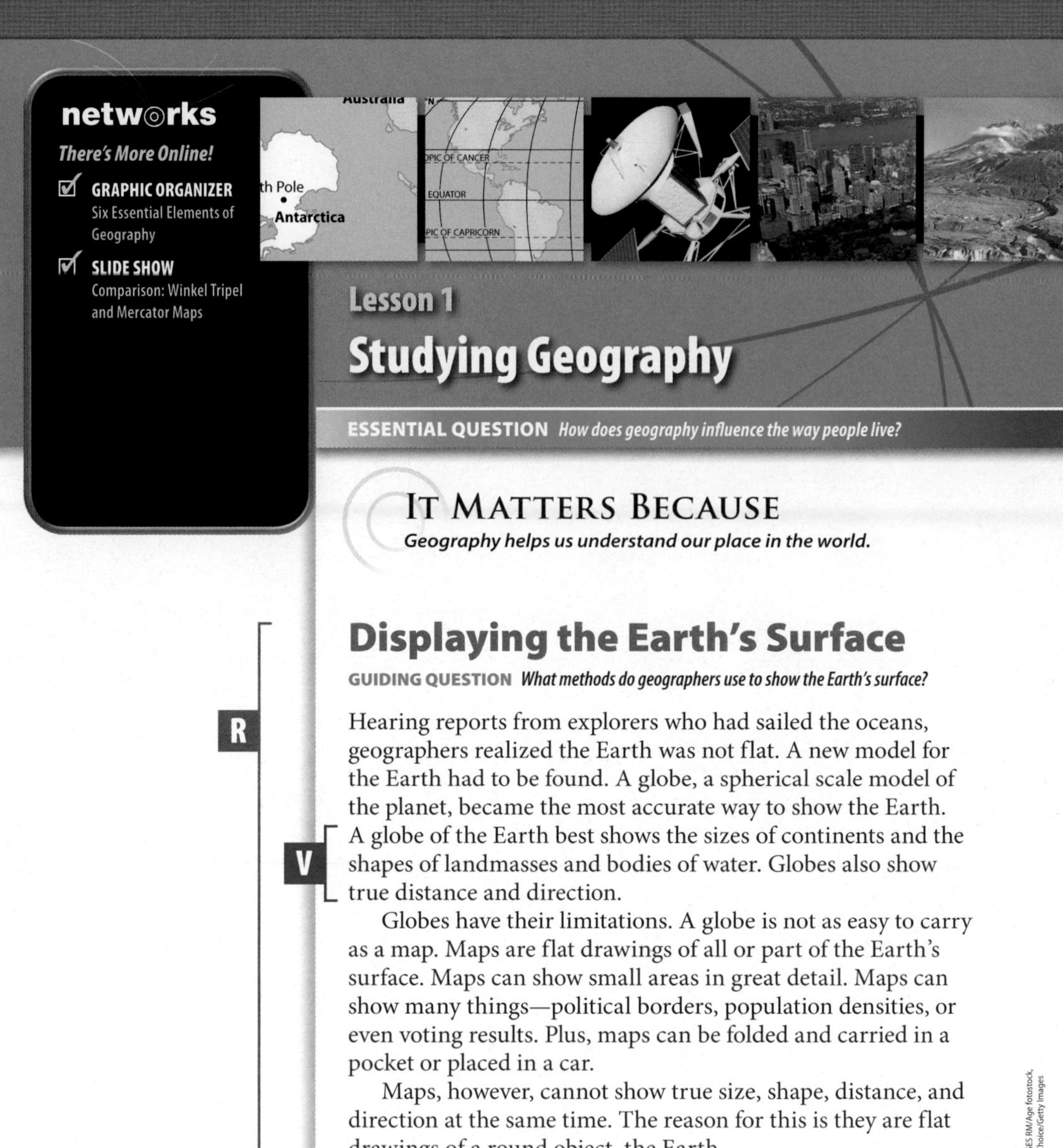

networks
There's More Online!
- GRAPHIC ORGANIZER Six Essential Elements of Geography
- SLIDE SHOW Comparison: Winkel Tripel and Mercator Maps

Lesson 1
Studying Geography

ESSENTIAL QUESTION *How does geography influence the way people live?*

IT MATTERS BECAUSE
Geography helps us understand our place in the world.

Displaying the Earth's Surface

GUIDING QUESTION *What methods do geographers use to show the Earth's surface?*

Hearing reports from explorers who had sailed the oceans, geographers realized the Earth was not flat. A new model for the Earth had to be found. A globe, a spherical scale model of the planet, became the most accurate way to show the Earth. A globe of the Earth best shows the sizes of continents and the shapes of landmasses and bodies of water. Globes also show true distance and direction.

Globes have their limitations. A globe is not as easy to carry as a map. Maps are flat drawings of all or part of the Earth's surface. Maps can show small areas in great detail. Maps can show many things—political borders, population densities, or even voting results. Plus, maps can be folded and carried in a pocket or placed in a car.

Maps, however, cannot show true size, shape, distance, and direction at the same time. The reason for this is they are flat drawings of a round object, the Earth.

Globes and maps have some features in common. Both are marked with imaginary lines that geographers use to locate places on Earth's surface. These lines divide the Earth into halves called hemispheres.

Reading HELPDESK CCSS

Taking Notes: *Identifying*
Use a diagram like the one shown here to list the Six Essential Elements of Geography. RH.6–8.2

Six Essential Elements of Geography

Content Vocabulary (Tier 3 Words)
- hemisphere
- latitude
- longitude
- projection
- physical map
- political map

networks Online Teaching Options

VIDEO

Geography Basics: Climate, Water, etc.

Formulating Questions Play the video for the class. Explain that this video illustrates how the Earth's six primary climates are the product of latitude, altitude, topography, and other geographic features. Ask students to pay attention to the ways in which water and wind affect the different climates and to record several questions they have after viewing the video. Discuss the questions in class.

See page 25C for other online activities.

ANSWER, p. 28

TAKING NOTES: The Six Essential Elements of Geography are the World in Spatial Terms, Places and Regions, Physical Systems, Human Systems, Environment and Society, and the Uses of Geography.

Hemispheres

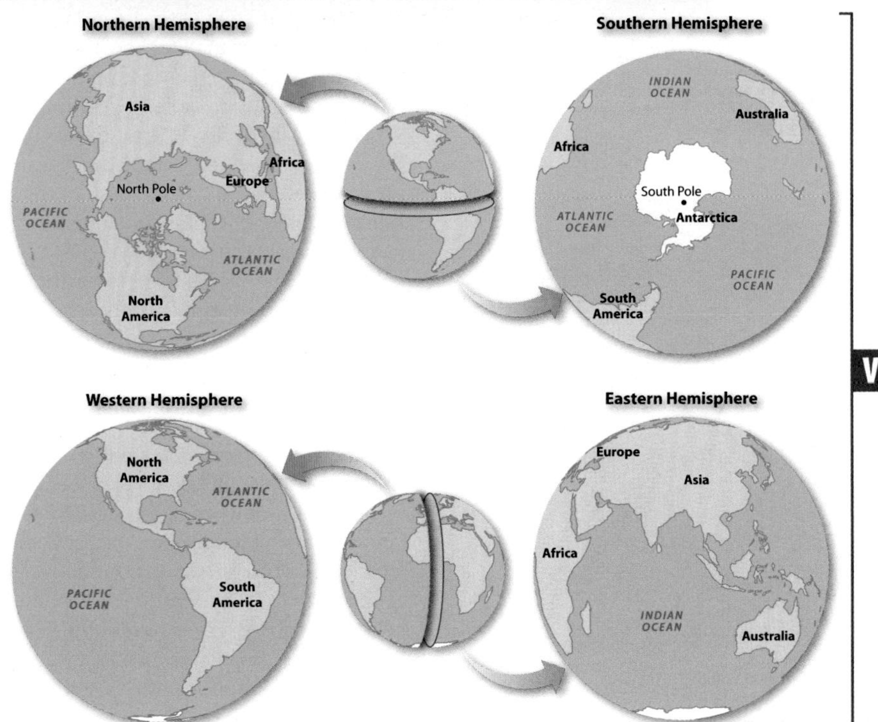

Dividing the Earth into hemispheres helps geographers locate places on the planet's surface. Which oceans are located in the Western Hemisphere? Which oceans are in the Eastern Hemisphere?

V

Hemispheres

To find a place on the Earth, geographers use a system of imaginary lines that crisscross the globe. The Equator (ih•KWAY•tuhr) is one of these lines. It circles the middle of the Earth like a belt. It divides the Earth into "half spheres," or **hemispheres** (HEH•muh•sfihrz). Everything north of the Equator is in the Northern Hemisphere. Everything south of the Equator is in the Southern Hemisphere. In which of these hemispheres do you live?

R

Another imaginary line divides the Earth into Eastern and Western Hemispheres. This line is called the Prime Meridian. Generally, the area east of the Prime Meridian is in the Eastern Hemisphere. Everything west of the Prime Meridian is in the Western Hemisphere.

Content Vocabulary (Tier 3 Words)

- **special-purpose map**
- **scale**
- **cardinal directions**
- **choropleth**
- **migration**
- **culture**

hemisphere a "half sphere," used to refer to one-half of the globe when divided into North and South or East and West

Studying Geography

V Visual Skills

Analyzing Globes Allow pairs or small groups time to study the image on the page. Then have them study a globe. Ask them to locate both the Equator and the Prime Meridian on the globe. **Ask:**

- **Which continents does the Equator pass through?** *(South America, Africa, and Asia)*
- **What are some countries that the Equator passes through?** *(Answers may include South America: Ecuador, Colombia, and Brazil; Africa: Uganda, Kenya, and Somalia; Asia: Indonesia)*
- **Which continents does the Prime Meridian pass through?** *(Europe, Africa, and Antarctica)*
- **What are some countries that the Prime Meridian passes through?** *(Answers may include Europe: U.K., France, and Spain; Africa: Algeria, Mali, and Ghana.)* **Visual/Spatial**

Ask students if they can identify the country that takes its name from its location on either the Equator or the Prime Meridian. *(Ecuador)* BL **Verbal/Linguistic**

R Reading Skills

Finding the Main Idea After reading "Hemispheres," **ask:** **Why do geographers use imaginary lines when showing Earth's surface?** *(so they can precisely identify regions and specific locations on Earth)* **What is the significance of the Equator and the Prime Meridian?** *(They divide Earth into hemispheres.)* AL ELL

MAP

Hemispheres

Using Digital Tools Ask students to study the interactive diagrams illustrating Earth's Northern, Southern, Eastern, and Western Hemispheres. Using the digital pen, have students attempt to draw approximate representations of both the Equator and the Prime Meridian.

See page 25C for other online activities.

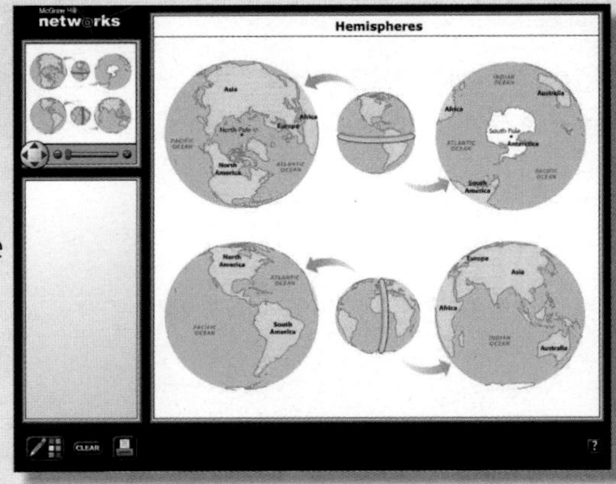

ANSWER, p. 29

Caption: The Pacific Ocean and the Atlantic Ocean are in the Western Hemisphere. The Indian Ocean is in the Eastern Hemisphere.

Studying Geography

V1 Visual Skills

Reading a Map Provide students with several locations *(expressed in terms of latitude and longitude)*, and have them find these locations on a globe or map. Ask students to locate the city or major geographic feature that is closest to those coordinates. **Visual/Spatial**

- **What city is located at latitude 41° 52′ North, longitude 87° 37′ West?** *(Chicago, Illinois)*
- **What island is located at latitude 18° 55′ South, longitude 47° 31′ East?** *(Madagascar)*
- **What continent is located at latitude 90° South, longitude 0° West?** *(Antarctica)*

T Technology Skills

Analyzing Data For a whole-class activity, select a volunteer to call out coordinates. The rest of the class will search online to find a city on or near the coordinates. The first student to identify the city then selects the next coordinates for the class to find. **Interpersonal**

V2 Visual Skills

Visualizing Provide students with oranges, and instruct them to re-create the orange peel experiment described in the text on the next page. See if students can remove the peel in a single piece and lay it flat on a table. They may wish to use markers to draw representations of the various continents, following Goode's Interrupted Equal-Area projection as a guide. Then ask them to restore the peel to a spherical shape and compare their "globe" to an actual one. AL ELL **Kinesthetic**

ANSWER, p. 30

The Prime Meridian is at 0° longitude.

Latitude and Longitude

V1

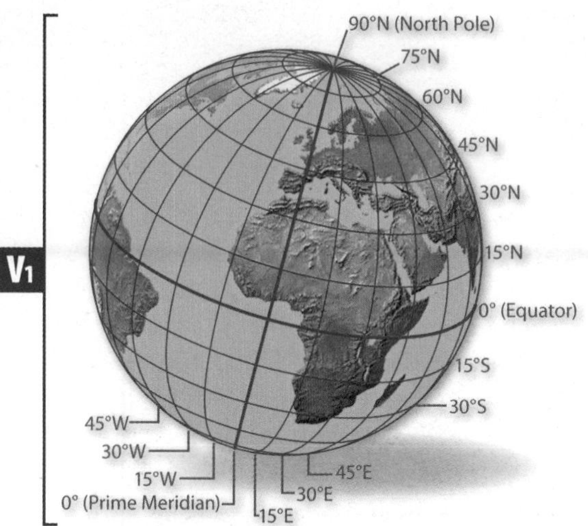

Finding the intersection of latitude and longitude allows geographers to pinpoint absolute location. At what degree point is the Prime Meridian?

Finding Places on the Earth

The Equator and Prime Meridian are two of the lines on maps and globes that help you find places on the Earth. All the lines together are called latitude and longitude. Latitude and longitude lines cross one another, forming a pattern called a grid system.

Lines of **latitude** (LA•tuh•tood) circle the Earth parallel to the Equator. They measure distance north or south of the Equator in degrees. The Equator is at 0° (zero degrees) latitude, while the North Pole is at latitude 90° N (90 degrees north).

Lines of **longitude** (LAHN•juh•tood) circle the Earth from Pole to Pole. These lines measure distances east or west of the Prime Meridian, which is at 0° longitude.

T

The grid system formed by lines of latitude and longitude makes it possible to find the absolute location of a place. This is the exact spot where a line of latitude crosses a line of longitude. An absolute location is written in special symbols called degrees (°) and minutes (') (points between degrees). For example, the Empire State Building in New York City is located at a latitude of 40° 44' North and a longitude of 73° 59' West (40 degrees 44 minutes North and 73 degrees 59 minutes West).

Goode's Interrupted Equal-Area Projection

Goode's Interrupted Equal-Area projection shows a realistic representation of continents' sizes and shapes.

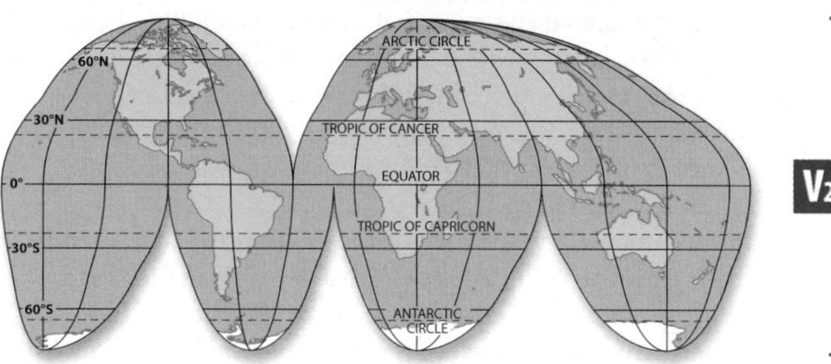

V2

Reading **HELP**DESK 

latitude imaginary lines that circle the Earth parallel to the Equator
longitude imaginary lines that circle the Earth from Pole to Pole, measuring distance east or west of the Prime Meridian
projection a way of showing the round Earth on a flat map

Academic Vocabulary (Tier 2 Words)
distort to twist out of shape or change the size of

networks Online Teaching Options

MAP

Latitude and Longitude

Analyzing Data Allow students to explore the interactive latitude and longitude maps of the various hemispheres. **Ask:**

- **What are the latitude and longitude coordinates for Moscow, Russia?** *(latitude 55° 45′ N, longitude 37° 36′ E)*
- **What are the coordinates for Tokyo, Japan?** *(latitude 35° 41′ N, longitude 139° 44′ E)*
- **What city is found at latitude 34° S, longitude 151° E?** *(Sydney, Australia)*

See page 25C for other online activities.

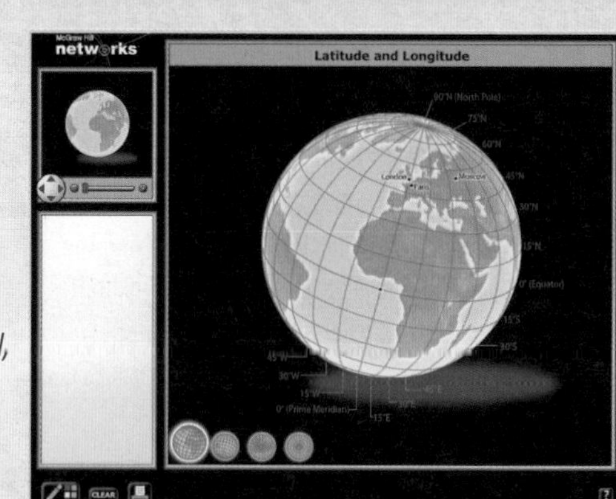

From Globes to Maps

C When the curves of a globe become straight lines on a map, the size, shape, distance, or area can change. Imagine taking an orange peel and trying to flatten it on a table. You would either have to cut it or **distort**, or stretch, parts of it. Mapmakers face a similar problem in showing the surface of the Earth on a map. Using mathematics, they have created different types of map **projections** (pruh•JEK•shuhnz), or ways of showing the Earth on a flat sheet of paper. Each kind of projection shows the Earth's surface in a slightly different way.

Flattening Out the Planet

When you take an image of the Earth and flatten it, big gaps open up. To fill in the gaps, mapmakers stretch parts of the Earth. They show either the correct shapes of places or their correct sizes. It is impossible to show both. As a result, mapmakers use different map projections depending on their goals.

Map Projections

Take another look at that flattened orange peel. You might see something that looks like a map based on Goode's Interrupted Equal-Area projection. A map made using this projection shows continents close to their true shapes and sizes. This projection is helpful for comparing land areas among continents.

The map on the top right was made using the Mercator projection. It shows true direction and land shapes fairly accurately. However, it does not show correct size or distance. Areas located far from the Equator are distorted on this projection. Alaska, for example, appears much larger on a Mercator map than it does on a globe.

A map using the Robinson projection is less distorted. Land on the western and eastern sides of the Robinson map appears much as it does on a globe. Areas near the North and South Poles are distorted the most on this projection.

The Winkel Tripel projection gives a good overall view of the continents' shapes and sizes. You can see that land areas in this projection are not as distorted near the Poles.

PROGRESS CHECK

Analyzing What are an advantage and a disadvantage to using a map rather than a globe to study the Earth's geography?

Mercator Projection

On a Mercator projection, land size and distance appear quite distorted.

W

Robinson Projection

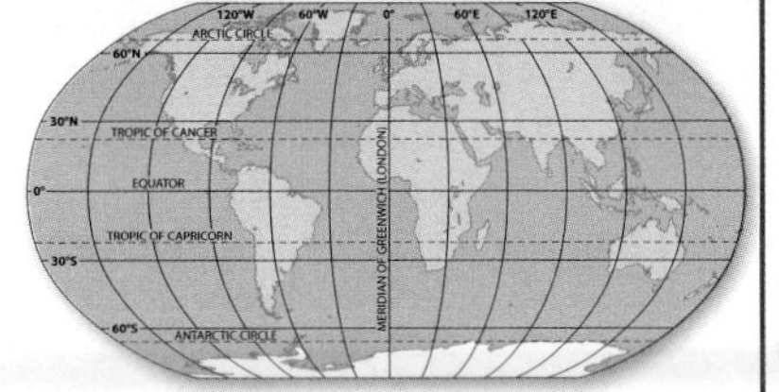

The Robinson projection shows a truer picture of land size and shape. However, the North and South Poles show a great deal of distortion.

T

Winkel Tripel Projection

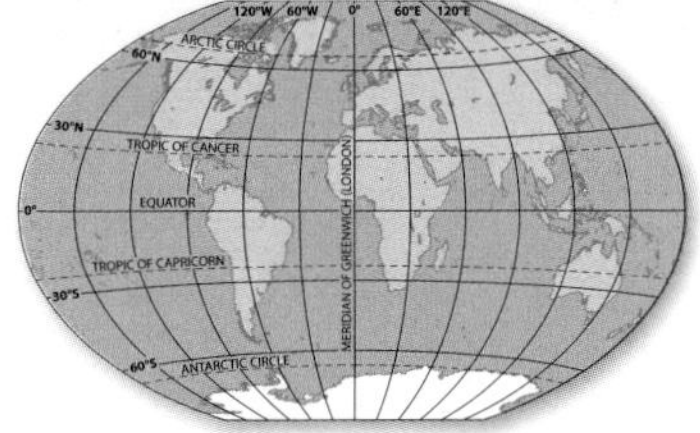

The representation of land areas on the Winkel Tripel projection most closely resembles the globe model.

C Critical Thinking Skills

Contrasting Have students contrast the sizes and shapes of the continents shown on the map projections on these pages with the sizes and shapes of continents on a globe. **Ask:** **Why do landmasses on maps look different from those on globes?** *(Maps are flat representations of a round object. Each type of map distorts the view of Earth in some way.)* **Why do these map projections look different from each other?** *(Each map projection distorts the view of Earth in a different way. A map can show correct shapes or correct sizes, but not both.)* BL

W Writing Skills

Narrative Ask students to imagine they are a sailor in the 1600s sailing from Europe and trying to reach the New World. Instruct them to write a journal entry about their experiences at sea, including descriptions of their different locations expressed in terms of latitude and longitude.

T Technology Skills

Researching on the Internet Have students conduct online research to learn about the origins of the Mercator, Robinson, and Winkel Tripel projections. Have students share their findings with the class.

Content Background Knowledge

The oldest known map was discovered in 1993 by archaeologists in a cave in northern Spain. The small stone tablet measures only seven inches by five inches and is engraved with what appear to be symbolic representations of landscape features such as mountains and rivers. Scientists estimate the map to be almost 14,000 years old.

WORKSHEET

Geography and History Activity: Studying Geography, Economics, and Citizenship - Studying Geography: Longitude and Latitude

Locating Have students complete the Geography and History Activity on latitude and longitude. Review the meaning of the terms *hemisphere, longitude,* and *latitude.* Direct students to complete the questions at the end of the worksheet, either individually or in groups. As students look at the map in the worksheet, **ask:** **Between which lines of latitude and longitude is our community located?** *(Students should identify your community's lines of latitude and longitude.)*

See page 25C for other online activities.

ANSWER, p. 31

PROGRESS CHECK An advantage is that maps are portable. A disadvantage is that maps distort either the size or the shape of Earth's landmasses and bodies of water.

C1 Critical Thinking Skills

Making Connections Ask students to read the sidebar on GIS/GPS systems. **Ask:** Where do we commonly find a GPS system these days? *(Many cars have onboard GPS systems. Smart phones also include GPS features.)* How is a GPS system in a car able to tell the driver where to go? *(It is receiving information about the landscape from a satellite in orbit.)*

C2 Critical Thinking Skills

Identifying Ask students to describe or identify what they think geographers study. Many students are likely to think that geography involves finding places on Earth and making maps. Explain that geography deals with much more than just location. Tell students that geographers use their tools to show us what the world looks like and to describe how people, plants, animals, physical forces, and the environment interact with one another. Point out that the study of geography can also help us understand the past. AL

W Writing Skills

Informative/Explanatory Have students think about the term *awareness* as it relates to geography and the physical world in which they live. Have students interview one another about ways they might improve their awareness of the world around them. For example, students may say that they could broaden their awareness of the geography of their area by taking nature walks, studying local maps, or using the Internet to study satellite imagery of their location. Students should summarize their interviews in a written paragraph or blog entry.

Connections to TODAY

GIS/GPS

C1 Technology has changed the way we make maps. Most mapmakers use software programs called geographic information systems (GIS). This software combines information from satellite images, printed text, and statistics. A Global Positioning System (GPS) helps people locate places based on data broadcast by satellites.

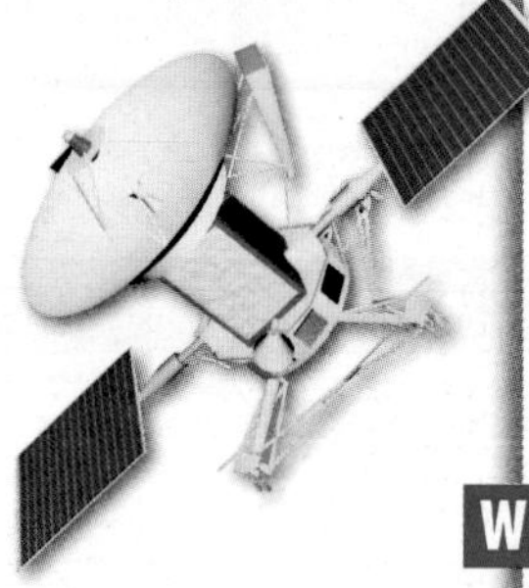

Five Themes and Six Essential Elements of Geography

GUIDING QUESTION *How do geographers use the five themes and six essential elements of geography?*

To understand how our world is connected, some geographers have broken the study of geography into five **themes** or six essential elements.

Five Themes of Geography

The Five Themes of Geography are (1) location, (2) place, (3) human-environment interaction, (4) movement, and (5) regions. You will see these themes highlighted in the geography skills questions throughout the book.

Six Essential Elements

Recently, geographers have begun to divide the study of geography into Six Essential Elements. Understanding these elements will help you build your knowledge of geography. 

W **THE WORLD IN SPATIAL TERMS** What do geographers do when studying a certain place? They first take a look at where the place is located. Location is a useful starting point. By asking "Where is it?" you begin to develop an **awareness** of the world around you.

PLACES AND REGIONS Place has a special meaning in geography. It refers to more than where a place is. It also describes what a place is like. It might describe physical characteristics such as landforms, climate, and plant or animal life. Or it might describe human characteristics, such as language and way of life.

To help organize their study, geographers often group places into regions. Regions are united by one or more common characteristics.

PHYSICAL SYSTEMS When geographers study places and regions, they analyze how physical systems—such as hurricanes, volcanoes, and glaciers—shape the Earth's surface. They also look at the communities of livings things. The populations of plants and animals depend upon one another and their surroundings for survival.

Stockbyte/Alamy

Reading HELPDESK 

Academic Vocabulary (Tier 2 Words)

theme a topic that is studied or a special quality that connects ideas
awareness the state of having understanding or knowledge

networks *Online Teaching Options*

WHITEBOARD ACTIVITY

Food Chain

Diagramming For the geography theme "Physical Systems," show students the Lesson 1 Interactive Whiteboard Activity on food chains. Guide them through making the connections among the different parts to construct food chains or food webs.

See page 25C for other online activities.

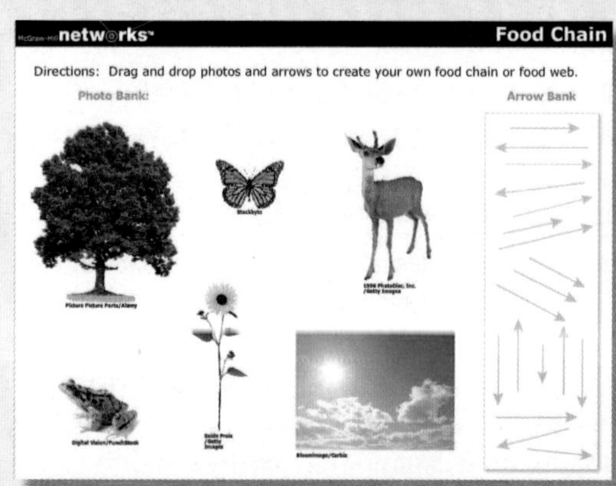

HUMAN SYSTEMS Geographers are interested in human systems. Human systems refer to how people have shaped our world. Geographers look at how borders are decided and why people settle in certain places and not in others. A basic theme in geography is the movement of people, ideas, and goods.

ENVIRONMENT AND SOCIETY How does the relationship between people and their natural surroundings influence the way we live? The theme of human-environment interaction investigates this. It also shows how people use the environment and how their actions affect the environment.

Central Park in New York covers 843 acres of open land. People use the park for recreation. A yearlong study recorded about 35 million visits by people from the city and from around the world.

THE USES OF GEOGRAPHY Geography helps us understand the relationships among people, places, and environments. Mastering the tools and technology used for studying geography can also help us in our daily lives.

✓ PROGRESS CHECK

Identifying Which Essential Elements of Geography might be involved in the study of an area's landforms and how they affect people living there?

The 1980 eruption of Mount St. Helens in Washington state removed the top 1,314 feet (400 meters) of the volcano's peak and leveled nearly 230 square miles (595 square km) of surrounding forest. The destruction happened in a matter of minutes.

▶ CRITICAL THINKING

Analyzing What does this photo suggest about the wildlife living in the region?

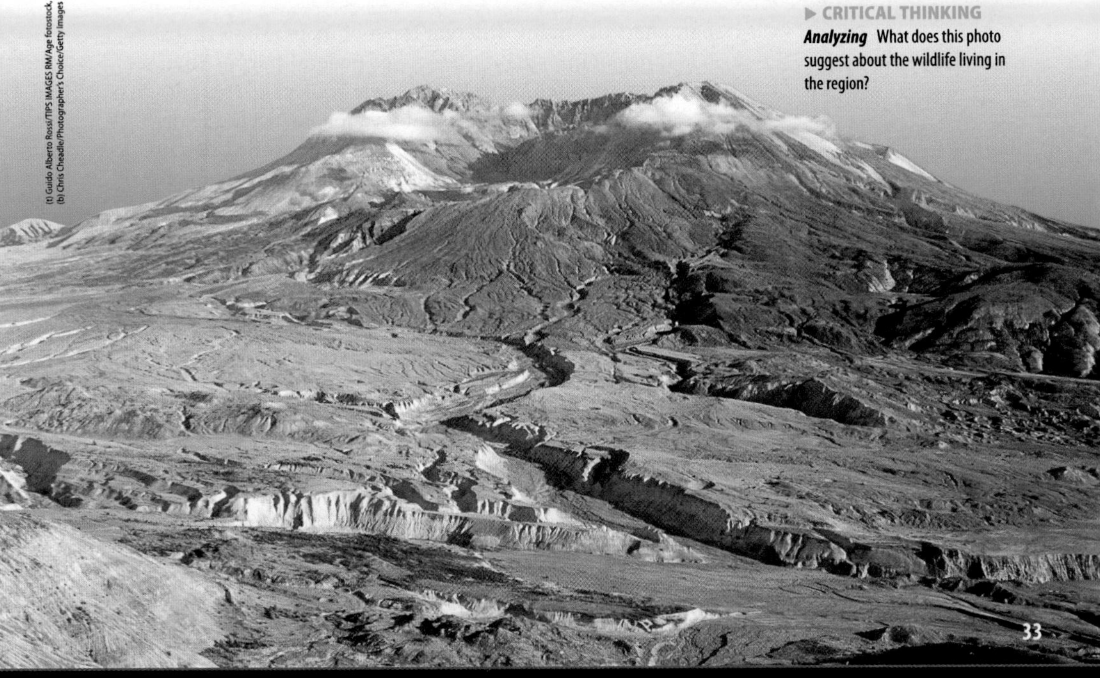

G1 Critical Thinking Skills

Evaluating Have students brainstorm ways in which humans change the physical environment. Give them five minutes to list several of their ideas on a sheet of paper, and then ask students to share their ideas. Ask students to consider whether each is a "positive" or "negative" change, and to explain why they think so.

R Reading Skills

Locating Have students study the images of both Central Park and Mount St. Helens and read the photo captions carefully. **Ask:**

- How many acres of land does Central Park cover? *(843 acres)*
- How many square miles of forest were destroyed when Mount St. Helens erupted in 1980? *(230 square miles)* AL

G2 Critical Thinking Skills

Making Connections Have students draw from memory a simple map from their homes to the school. Then ask them to consider and write down some tools of geography that would make their map easier to create, and more accurate. Have students save their maps for use later in the lesson.

GRAPHIC ORGANIZER

Taking Notes: *Identifying:* Six Essential Elements of Geography

Identifying Briefly review the Five Themes of Geography with students. Then show students the interactive graphic organizer on the Six Essential Elements of Geography. Enter each of the elements into the organizer. Then prompt students to provide an example for each element.

See page 25C for other online activities.

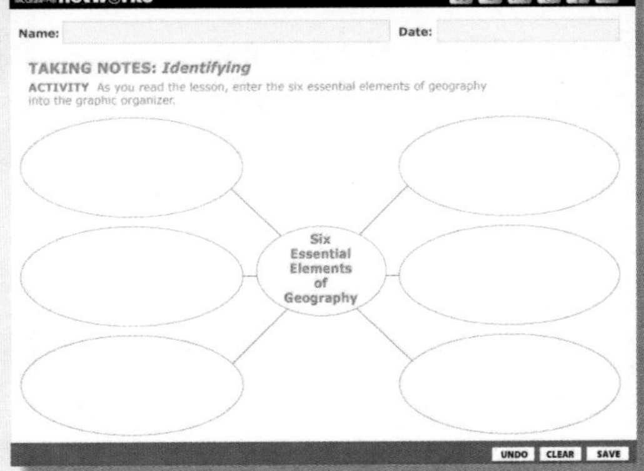

ANSWERS, p. 33

CRITICAL THINKING The area around Mount St. Helens is not populated, perhaps because of the volcano, which has scarred the landscape. There would be little food for wildlife.

✓ **PROGRESS CHECK** Places and Regions would be involved in the description of the landforms. Environment and Society could be involved in studying how people have changed the landforms and adapted to them. The Uses of Geography could address the impact on the landforms over time.

V Visual Skills

Analyzing Maps Direct students to study the map of Alexander the Great's empire in 323 B.C. and compare it to the region as it appears on a modern political map, seen in the inset. Help students recognize that despite the changes in place names and borders, the landmasses remain unchanged. **Ask:**

- **In the place named Asia Minor in Alexander's time, what country can be found today?** *(Turkey)*
- **Which place names can be found on both the ancient map and the modern map?** *(Egypt and Syria)*
- **In what country can the site of the Battle of Gaugamela be found today?** *(Iraq)*

C Critical Thinking Skills

Speculating Point out to students that the map of Alexander's empire shows one example of how geography can be used to help understand history. By seeing the size of Alexander's empire, it is easier to understand the scale and importance of his conquests. Ask students to consider other ways in which the tools of geography might be used to help understand historical events. BL

R Reading Skills

Summarizing After students read the information on types of maps, help them summarize the information using a Web graphic organizer. Label the center *Types of Maps,* and put *Physical, Political,* and *Special Purpose* in three separate circles connected to the center circle by spokes. Challenge students to provide details about each category of map as you record their ideas. **Verbal/Linguistic**

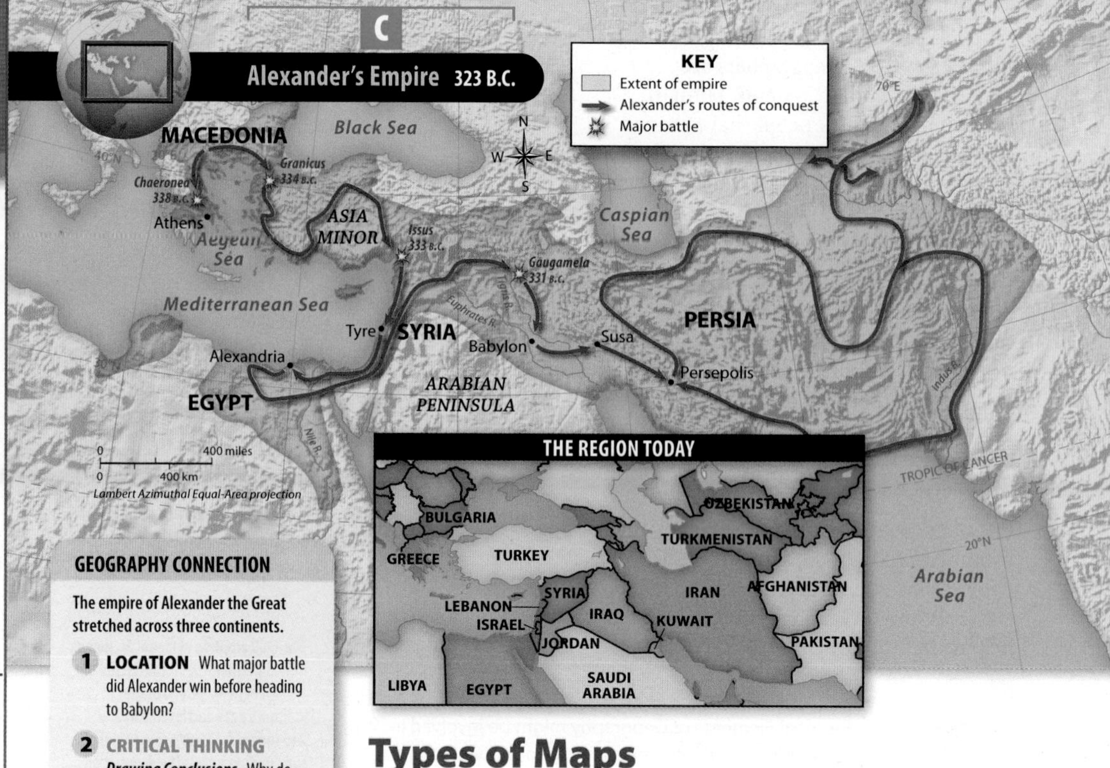

GEOGRAPHY CONNECTION

The empire of Alexander the Great stretched across three continents.

1. **LOCATION** What major battle did Alexander win before heading to Babylon?
2. **CRITICAL THINKING** ***Drawing Conclusions*** Why do you think Alexander circled the Mediterranean Sea but did not cross it?

Types of Maps

GUIDING QUESTION ***What are some of the key ways that maps are used?***

Geographers use many different types of maps. Maps that show a wide range of information are called general-purpose maps. These maps are often collected into one book called an atlas. An atlas may be a collection of special area maps—such as North America maps—or general maps of the entire world. Two of the most common general-purpose maps found in an atlas are physical and political maps.

Physical maps show land and water features. The colors used on physical maps include brown or green for land and blue for water. Physical maps may also use colors to show elevation. Elevation is the height of an area above sea level. A key explains the meaning of each color. **Political maps** show the names and borders of countries. They also show the location of cities and other human-made features of a place. Often they identify major physical features of a land area.

Reading HELPDESK CCSS

physical map a map that shows land and water features
political map a map that shows the names and borders of countries

special-purpose map a map that shows themes or patterns such as climate, natural resources, or population

Reading Strategy: *Summarizing*

How do you read a map? Summarize how to read a map by identifying map parts and the information they provide.

ANSWERS, p. 34

GEOGRAPHY CONNECTION

1. He won the Battle of Gaugamela.
2. **CRITICAL THINKING** Students might say that the Mediterranean Sea provided too big a barrier or that Alexander did not have the ships to cross it.

Reading Strategy: To read a map, study the symbols that tell what the map shows, the scale that tells the distances on the map, and the compass rose that tells where the cardinal directions are.

networks Online Teaching Options

MAP

Alexander's Empire 323 B.C.

Using Digital Tools Have students familiarize themselves with the various interactive tools on the digital map of Alexander the Great's empire at the height of his power. Have students make approximate measurements using the drag-and-drop scale. **Ask:**

- **How long, in miles, was the distance between the cities of Babylon and Susa?** *(approximately 350 miles)*
- **How long, in kilometers, was the distance between the cities of Athens and Alexandria?** *(approximately 1,350 kilometers)*

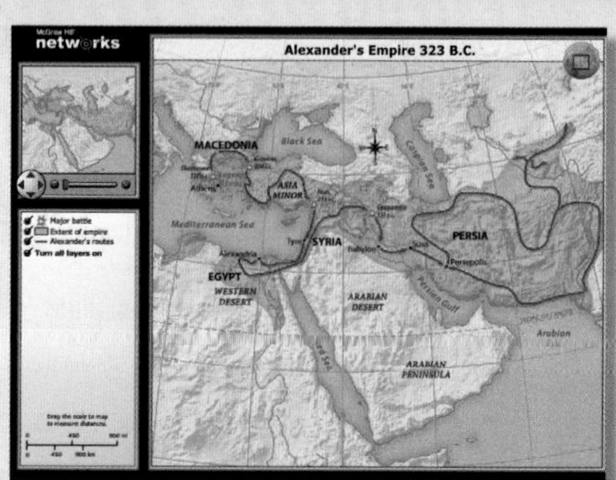

See page 25C for other online activities.

Special-Purpose Maps

Some maps show specific kinds of information. These are called **special-purpose maps.** They usually show patterns such as climate, natural resources, or population. A road map is another example of a special-purpose map. Like this map of Alexander's empire, special-purpose maps may also display historical information, such as battles or territorial changes.

Reading Maps

An important step in reading a map is to study the map key. The key explains the lines and colors used on a map. It also explains any **symbols,** or signs and pictures, used on a map. For example, the map of Alexander's empire details the size of the empire, the route of Alexander's conquest, and some important battles. Cities are usually shown as a solid circle (•), like the one for Athens.

The map **scale** is a measuring line that tells you the distances represented on the map. Suppose you wanted to know the approximate distance from Tampa, Florida to New York City. Using the scale bar will help you calculate this distance.

A map has a symbol called a compass rose that tells you the position of the **cardinal directions**—north, south, east, and west. Cardinal directions help you explain the relative location of any place on Earth. Some maps also have a locator map, a small inset map. This shows where the region on the large map is located.

V

✓ PROGRESS CHECK

Drawing Conclusions Why is reading the map key important when looking at a special-purpose map?

Using Charts, Graphs, and Diagrams

GUIDING QUESTION *What are the uses of charts, graphs, and diagrams?*

Charts, graphs, and diagrams are tools for showing information. The first step to understanding these visual aids is to read the title. This tells you the subject.

Charts show facts in an organized way. They arrange information in rows and columns. To read a chart, look at the labels at the top of each column and on the left side of the chart. The labels explain what the chart is showing.

scale a measuring line that shows the distances on a map

cardinal directions north, south, east, and west

Academic Vocabulary (Tier 2 Words)

symbol a sign or image that stands for something else

V Visual Skills

Creating Maps Tell students to look at their "home to school" maps that they drew earlier in the lesson. Ask them to describe the types of features and landmarks that they showed on their maps. It is likely that students chose certain buildings or locations to use as reference points. Then ask students if they used any symbols or labels to make their maps easier to read. For example, students might have labeled street names, included a scale, or indicated cardinal directions.

Explain to students that they will be learning about different types of maps and the types of information that they display.

Help students understand the challenges faced by early mapmakers who did not have access to the technology that makes modern cartography so precise, such as the use of airplanes and satellites to view landscapes from high above. Distribute paper, clipboards, and pencils to student pairs or groups, and explore the school grounds as a class. Ask students to try to draw accurate maps that show the correct size and shape of the school building as well as key natural or human-made features on the immediate school grounds.

After students have completed their maps, ask them to compare them to a satellite image of the school building and school grounds. Have students share what they were able to draw accurately and what on their maps differs greatly from the satellite image. Students should discuss why the two versions might be different. ELL **Kinesthetic**

SLIDE SHOW

Tools of Geography

Citing Text Evidence Have students use the slide show to learn about some ancient and modern tools of geography, such as the sextant, satellite, and Global Positioning System (GPS). **Ask:**

- **What must a user focus on to use a sextant?** *(a star)*
- **What kinds of things can be seen in satellite images of Earth?** *(Answers could include geographic features such as mountains, rivers, or forests; and human-made features such as roads or buildings.)*

See page 25C for other online activities.

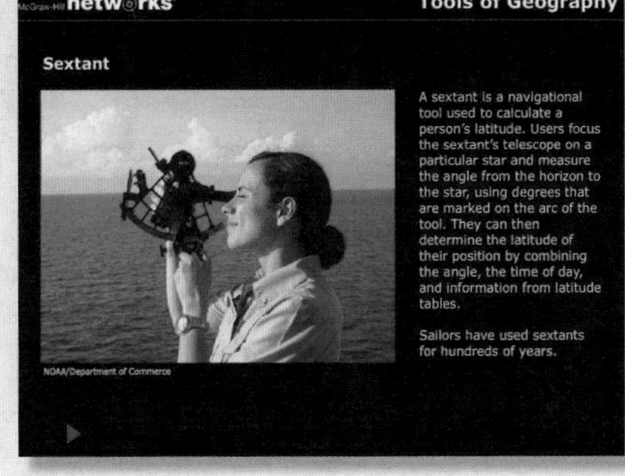

McGraw-Hill networks
Tools of Geography
Sextant
A sextant is a navigational tool used to calculate a person's latitude. Users focus the sextant's telescope on a particular star and measure the angle from the horizon to the star, using degrees that are marked on the arc of the tool. They can then determine the latitude of their position by combining the angle, the time of day, and information from latitude tables.
Sailors have used sextants for hundreds of years.
NOAA/Department of Commerce

ANSWER, p. 35

✓ PROGRESS CHECK The map key contains information about the symbols, lines, and colors used on a special-purpose map. Without this information, such maps might be difficult to understand.

V Visual Skills

Creating Graphs Gather a number of data points together as a class and practice displaying the information using various forms of graphs. For example, identify the birth month of each student and write the information on the board (three students in January, five students in February, and so on). Then place students in pairs and have them work together to graph the information using a bar graph, a line graph, and a circle graph. Students can draw graphs by hand or use spreadsheet software. BL Logical/Mathematical

T Technology Skills

Making Presentations Divide students into teams and ask them to choose one of the two historical figures introduced in this lesson (Alexander the Great and Gerardus Mercator) and do some basic research on their biographies. Alternatively, you could ask students to choose a famous geographer, cartographer, or explorer to research. Examples include Ptolemy, Amerigo Vespucci, and Sir Francis Drake. Students should prepare short presentations using presentation software, incorporating text, images, and possibly music to illustrate the life of their chosen figure. Have students present their finished projects to the class.

ANSWERS, p. 36

CRITICAL THINKING Before Mercator's map was available, sailors used the stars to guide them. They probably also drew their own maps of their travels.

✓ **PROGRESS CHECK** A line graph best shows changes over time.

BIOGRAPHY

Gerardus Mercator (A.D. 1512 to A.D. 1594)

Gerardus Mercator was a European mapmaker. He is best known for creating the Mercator projection, the first map to show longitude and latitude as straight lines. His map helped sailors navigate at sea. Mercator was also the first person to call a collection of maps an *atlas*. Many people think Mercator was the greatest geographer of the 1500s.

▶ **CRITICAL THINKING**
Speculating Before sailors had a map such as Mercator's, how do you think they were able to find their way on the sea?

Graphs come in different types. Bar graphs use thick, wide lines to compare data. They are useful for comparing amounts. Line graphs show changes over a particular period of time. A climate graph, or climograph (KLY•muh•graf), combines a line graph and a bar graph. It shows the long-term weather patterns in a place.

To read a bar graph, line graph, or climograph, look at the labels along the side and bottom. The vertical line along the left side of the graph is the y-axis. The horizontal line along the bottom is the x-axis. One axis tells you what is being measured. The other axis tells what units of measurement are being used.

Pie graphs are circular graphs that show how the whole of something is divided into parts. Each "slice" shows a part or percentage of the whole "pie." The entire pie totals 100 percent.

Diagrams are special drawings. They show steps in a process, point out the parts of an object, or explain how something works. An elevation profile is a diagram that shows a piece of land as if it were sliced open. This shows changes in height.

✓ **PROGRESS CHECK**

Identifying What type of graph shows changes over time?

Population and Culture

GUIDING QUESTION ***How do geographers study population and culture?***

Like geographers, historians study population, culture, and the movement of people, ideas, and goods. Historians are interested in how these things change over time.

Population Shifts

Population refers to how many people live in a specific area or place. Geographers study this in great detail. They look at what sorts of people make up a population. They examine how fast a population grows or shrinks over time. They also measure population density. This is the average number of people living in a square mile or square kilometer. A **choropleth** (KAWR•uh•plehth) uses colors to show population density.

Populations can also change location. The movement of people from one place to settle in another place is called **migration** (my•GRAY•shuhn). Throughout history there have been many migrations of human beings.

Reading HELPDESK (CCSS)

choropleth a special-purpose map that uses color to show population density

migration the movement of people from one place to settle in another place

culture the set of beliefs, behaviors, and traits shared by a group of people

networks *Online Teaching Options*

WORKSHEET

Geography and History Activity: Studying Geography, Economics, and Citizenship—Studying Geography: Physical Maps

Summarizing Have students complete the Geography and History Activity on physical maps. As students read about the importance of water, **ask:** **What physical features does the activity discuss?** *(water features such as oceans, seas, rivers, and lakes)* AL **What water features are shown on the map?** *(the Mediterranean Sea, Caspian Sea, Black Sea, Red Sea, Persian Gulf, Arabian Sea, and the Nile, Tigris, and Euphrates Rivers)*

Point out that the worksheet describes one example of how geography affects history. The water features shown on the map shaped the development of nearby civilizations in significant ways. Ask students to consider other ways in which physical geography might shape history.

See page 25C for other online activities.

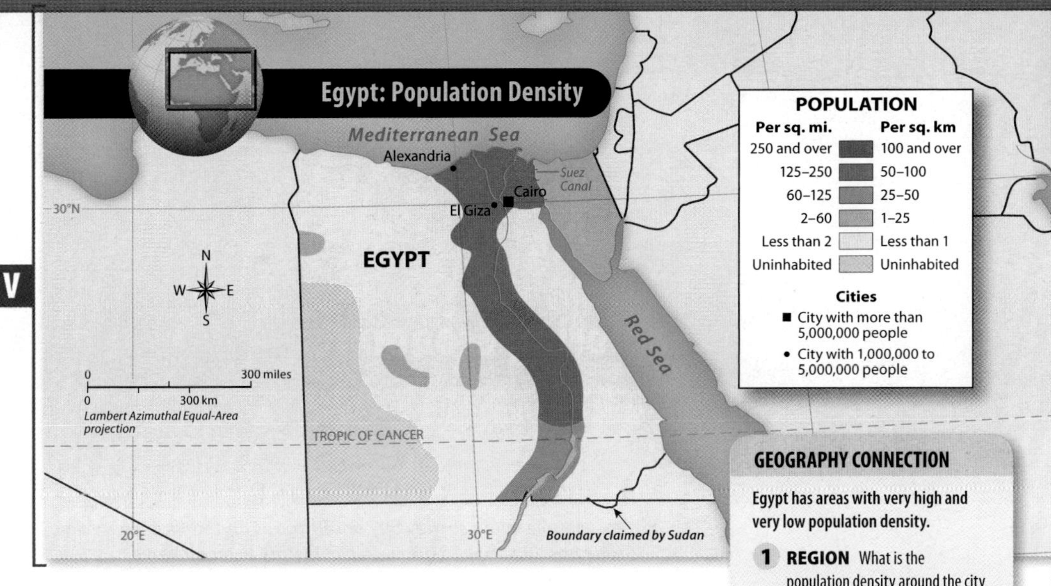

GEOGRAPHY CONNECTION

Egypt has areas with very high and very low population density.

1. **REGION** What is the population density around the city of Cairo?
2. **CRITICAL THINKING** *Analyzing* Around what physical feature is Egypt's population the densest?

Culture and Change

Culture is the set of beliefs, behaviors, and traits shared by the members of a group. Scholars study cultures by examining the language, religion, government, and customs of different groups.

Throughout history, different peoples have met through exploration, migration, and trade. These meetings often lead to cultural diffusion. In cultural diffusion, each group shares part of its culture with the other. Sometimes a completely new culture is formed. Many historians believe this happened in India as a result of the Aryan migrations.

PROGRESS CHECK

Analyzing Why are geographers interested in contact between cultures?

LESSON 1 REVIEW (CCSS)

Review Vocabulary (Tier 3 Words)

1. How do *latitude* and *longitude* help identify your exact location on the Earth? RH.6–8.4
2. Why would a *scale* be helpful when trying to determine distances on a *physical map*? RH.6–8.4

Answer the Guiding Questions

3. ***Identifying*** What type of map would you choose to find the borders between countries? Why? RH.6–8.2
4. ***Finding the Main Idea*** Why do mapmakers have to choose between showing the correct land shapes or distances on the Earth? RH.6–8.2
5. ***Contrasting*** What is the difference between a chart and a diagram? RH.6–8.9
6. ***Making Inferences*** How might migration lead to the spread and mixing of cultures? RH.6–8.1
7. **INFORMATIVE/EXPLANATORY** Write a paragraph explaining which Essential Elements of Geography you would use to study the weather in an area. WHST.6–8.2, WHST.6–8.10

LESSON 1 REVIEW ANSWERS

1. A person must know where latitude and longitude intersect to know an absolute location on Earth's surface.
2. The scale shows proportional distances displayed on the map, which helps people measure the size of large physical features.
3. a political map because it displays country borders
4. Because maps are a flat representation of a round object, they distort either size or shape.
5. A chart is a type of table that displays data in an organized way. A diagram is a drawing that shows steps in a process, points out the parts of an object, or explains how something works.
6. Migration brings a new group of people to settle in an area. If other people are already living there, then one or both cultures might take on the characteristics of the other.
7. Student answers will vary. The study of weather might involve Physical Geography. Environment and Society could be involved in studying how the weather of the region affects people's activities.

V Visual Skills

Reading a Map Explain that studying population and culture is an important part of geography and history. Draw students' attention to the choropleth map showing Egypt's population density. **Ask:** **What type of map is a choropleth?** *(a special-purpose map)* **What does this choropleth map show?** *(population density or distribution)* BL

C Critical Thinking Skills

Making Connections Ask students to think of examples of culture in their own lives. Note that music, fashion, language, and education vary from one culture to another. Encourage students to think about how cultures influence each other and to consider what other cultures have influenced their taste in music, clothing, food, and so forth. AL

Have students complete the Lesson 1 Review.

CLOSE & REFLECT

Lead a discussion with students about the importance of geography in history. Draw the connection between the role of geography in their daily lives, which they have already discussed, and the role that geography played in the lives of people in the past. For example, people in the past interacted with their environment as do people in the present.

ANSWERS, p. 37

GEOGRAPHY CONNECTION

1. Around the city of Cairo, there are more than 250 people per square mile, or 100 per square kilometer.
2. **CRITICAL THINKING** Egypt's population is concentrated along the Nile River.

PROGRESS CHECK Contact between cultures and the sharing of ideas often leads to changes in those cultures.

ENGAGE

Bellringer Invite students to talk about things they like to buy. Explore these questions with students:

- Can you buy everything you want? *(no)* Explain. *(Students should acknowledge they can't afford everything they want.)*
- Do you sometimes shop around for items you want? Why? *(to find the best price)*
- Do you always buy the brand you want? Explain. *(The brand they want may be too expensive.)*

Encourage students to give examples as they respond to these questions. Help them recognize that when they shop, they are making economic decisions. Explain that in this lesson, they will learn about some of the underlying ideas and relationships that govern what they buy and how much they pay.

TEACH & ASSESS

R Reading Skills

Defining As students read this paragraph, ensure that they understand the terms used in discussing economics. Ask them to define these terms and to give examples of each:

- Resources *(the things needed to produce goods and services, such as buildings, land, money, and workers)*
- Labor *(the effort given to produce goods and services, such as farming, driving a taxi, fixing a leaking pipe, and filming a movie)*
- Capital *(money and goods needed to produce other goods and services, including money to pay salaries and rent as well as to buy or lease the buildings, machinery, tools, and equipment needed to produce products and services to sell)*
- Entrepreneurship *(starting and running a business, such as a car dealership, a bakery, a home-based business, or a babysitting business)* AL ELL

ANSWER, p. 38

TAKING NOTES: In a traditional economy, people produce goods for their local group and typically use barter to trade. In a command economy, rulers decide what is made and how it is distributed.

networks *There's More Online!*

GRAPHIC ORGANIZER Characteristics of Economic Systems

GRAPH Supply and Demand Model of the Business Cycle

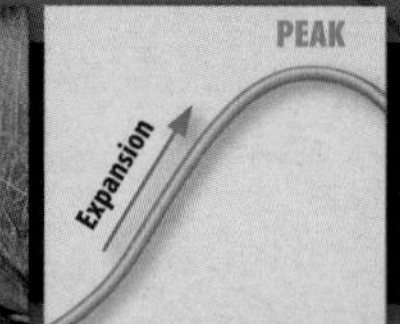

Lesson 2

Exploring Economics

ESSENTIAL QUESTION *Why do people trade?*

IT MATTERS BECAUSE

Most people in our society buy or sell goods and services every day. Trade has also shaped the course of history in major ways.

What Is Economics?

GUIDING QUESTION *What are the basic ideas of economics?*

There are three key questions to ask about any economy: *What* goods and services should we offer? *How* should we create and distribute these goods and services? *Who* will use these goods and services?

Resources and Production

R In order to make goods and offer services, people need **resources.** There are four major kinds of resources: land, labor, capital, and entrepreneurship. Land includes the surface of the Earth and its natural resources, such as minerals and water. **Labor** is the ability of people to do work. You need labor to make goods and provide services. **Capital** is money and goods used to help people make or do things. You need capital to run a business. **Entrepreneurship** (ahn•truh•pruh•NUHR•shihp) is the act of running a business and taking on the risks of that business. Entrepreneurship usually describes individual or small businesses. Another kind of resource is **technology**. Technology is using knowledge in a practical way to accomplish a task. Technology can make it easier and cheaper to create goods.

Reading **HELP**DESK CCSS

Taking Notes: *Describing*

Use a chart like this one to list these two types of economic systems and their key elements. RH.6–8.2

Traditional	Command

Content Vocabulary (Tier 3 Words)

- capital
- entrepreneurship
- supply
- demand
- scarcity
- opportunity cost
- traditional economy
- command economy
- recession

networks *Online Teaching Options*

VIDEO

Introduction to Economics, Part 1

Integrating Visual Information Explain that this video provides an introduction to some basic ideas about economics, including what economics is and why it is important. Ask students to write questions as they view the video about any points or concepts raised. Discuss the questions in class.

See page 25D for other online activities.

All of these resources were important to early civilizations. Good land and freshwater were very important to farmers. Early rulers needed many workers for large projects. They gathered capital by collecting taxes. Merchants showed entrepreneurship. They traded goods to earn a profit, or an increase in the value of what they owned.

Supply and Demand

Getting the resources needed to offer a good or service is a first step to providing that good or service. Next, you need to know how much of that good or service to offer. You will also want to decide how much money to charge for the good or service. These choices are affected by the laws of supply and demand.

Supply is the amount of a good or service that a producer wants to sell. The law of supply says that the higher the price you can charge for a good or service, the more of it you will want to sell. **Demand** is the amount of something that a consumer wants to buy. The law of demand says that the lower the price of a good or service, the more of it people will want to buy.

C

You can see the supply and demand curves in the graph on this page. Look at the supply curve. It shows that people want to make more goods when the price is high. The demand curve shows that buyers want to buy less when the price is high. In a free market, these forces balance each other over time. The seller and buyer will agree on a price and amount that satisfies both.

Academic Vocabulary (Tier 2)

resource something that is useful
labor the ability of people to do work
technology the use of advanced methods to solve problems

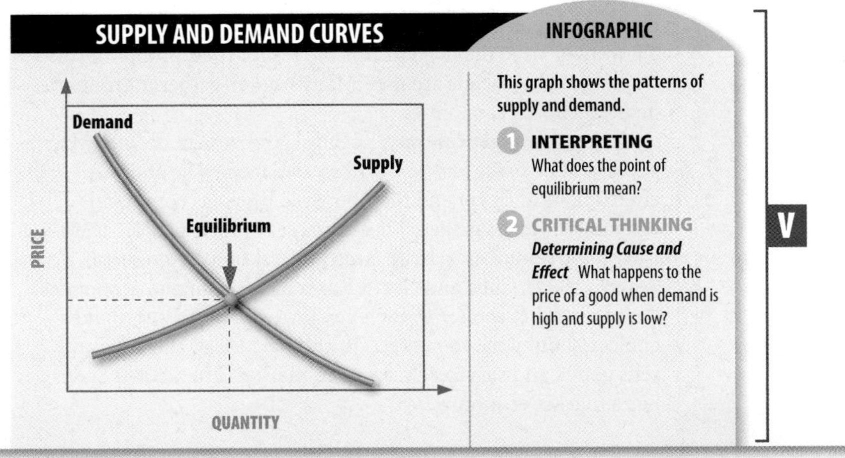

This graph shows the patterns of supply and demand.

1. **INTERPRETING** What does the point of equilibrium mean?
2. **CRITICAL THINKING** ***Determining Cause and Effect*** What happens to the price of a good when demand is high and supply is low?

V

Content Vocabulary (Tier 3 Words)
- **inflation**
- **barter**
- **exports**
- **globalization**
- **imports**

capital money and goods used to help people make or do things
entrepreneurship the act of running a business and taking on the risks of that business
supply the amount of a good or service that a producer wants to sell
demand the amount of something that a consumer wants to buy

C Critical Thinking Skills

Analyzing Discuss how an entrepreneur goes about producing a good or service. **Ask:** What are three of the first decisions an entrepreneur must make before producing a good or service? *(what kinds of resources are needed; how many goods or services to provide; how much to charge customers for the good or service)* **Ask:**

- What is supply? *(how much of a good or service is produced and available for sale)* What is demand? *(how many goods or services customers want to buy)* AL ELL
- How will an entrepreneur know how much of a good or service to produce? *(The entrepreneur must estimate how many customers there are and how much they will pay for the good.)*

Prompt students to provide examples of actual situations that illustrate supply and demand. **Ask:**

- Do you know of instances in which many people wanted a good but few of those items were available? What happened? *(Students might cite examples of customers standing in line before a store opened.)* Explain that the high demand often pushes up the price of the item.
- What will a store do if it cannot sell a particular item it has on the shelves? *(It will lower the price.)* Ask students to give an example.

V Visual Skills

Analyzing Graphs Explain the graph to students, pointing out how it illustrates the relationship between supply and demand. On the board, draw some alternative graphs that show what happens when demand or supply goes higher or lower, shifting the point of equilibrium. **Ask:** What does the point of equilibrium tell an entrepreneur? *(This is the optimum price at which a good should be sold and produced)* BL
Visual/Spatial

GRAPH

Supply and Demand

Analyzing Graphs Have students view the interactive graph on supply and demand. Click on parts of the graph to reveal information explaining the graph. **Ask:** What happens when the supply of an item increases? *(The price decreases.)* What happens when the demand increases? *(The price increases.)* Discuss how equilibrium is reached.

See page 25D for other online activities.

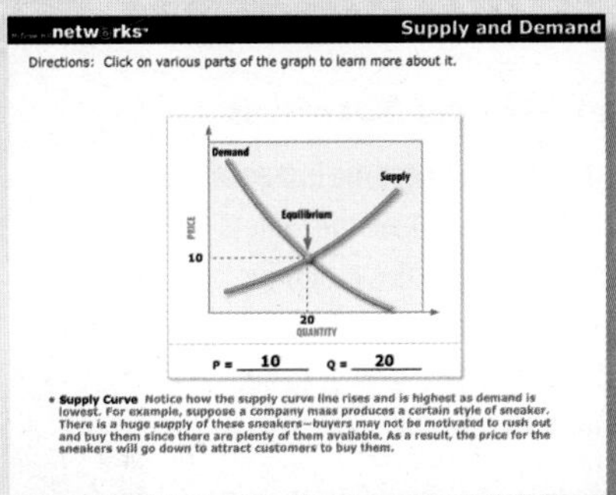

ANSWERS, p. 39

INFOGRAPHIC

1. The point of equilibrium means that the amounts of items that consumers demand and that producers sell are the same.
2. **CRITICAL THINKING** The price of the good will increase.

C1 Critical Thinking Skills

Analyzing Information Reinforce that the relationship between supply and demand is influenced by a third factor—scarcity. **Ask:** What does *scarcity* mean? *(the lack of a resource)*

Explain that demand for goods usually increases as the price of those goods decreases. Also note that when an item is perceived to be rare, it is often thought to be more desirable.

Distribute several newspaper sale inserts. Have pairs of students look for phrases that imply a scarcity of goods such as *while supplies last, at least one per store,* and *this week only.* Discuss how these phrases imply a scarcity, either real or imagined, of goods, and how the phrases help entice people to stock up. Interpersonal

C2 Critical Thinking Skills

Giving Examples Discuss opportunity cost. Point out that the example in the text explains the opportunity cost for the producer of a good. **Ask:** What is an example of opportunity cost for a customer? *(Sample answer: A customer has a limited number of dollars. He or she has enough money to buy a smart phone or tablet computer, but not both. Buying the smart phone means giving up the opportunity to buy the tablet.)* BL

R Reading Skills

Contrasting After students have read the text, guide a discussion of the different economic systems. Explain to students that in a traditional economy, they would have to barter one kind of good for another. Each family would make a few kinds of goods for itself. Anything extra could be traded for different types of goods. **Ask:** How does using money make it simpler to get the goods you want? *(Money can be exchanged for a wide variety of goods. You don't have to find someone who is willing to trade for what you have.)*

ANSWER, p. 40

PROGRESS CHECK According to the law of supply, producers will want to make fewer of the goods in order to maintain high prices. The law of demand states that consumers will want to buy more goods if prices are low.

In a hunter-gatherer community, some members might provide food by hunting for meat or gathering vegetables. Others might turn furs into clothing.

Fabio Chironi/Workbook Stock/Getty Images

C1 There are other things that affect supply and demand. One is **scarcity** (SKEHR•suh•tee), or lack of a resource. When not much of a needed resource is available, then the demand for it will grow. The higher demand will raise the price. This may force people to seek replacements for that resource. Another factor is opportunity cost. C2 The **opportunity cost** of something is what you give up to make it or buy it. Suppose you are a farmer. You choose to grow wheat on your land. You spend time and resources to grow the wheat. While you are growing wheat, you cannot use the land to grow beans. You are giving up the chance to grow something else when you grow wheat. The time, resources, and choices that you gave up are all part of the opportunity cost of growing wheat. People are always weighing the opportunity costs of their choices about what to make or buy.

PROGRESS CHECK

Predicting How will the people who make goods and those who buy the goods react if the price goes down?

Managing and Measuring Economies

GUIDING QUESTION *What are the different types of economic systems?*

Dealing with resources, supply, and demand can be very hard. Each society organizes its economy using an economic system.

Economic Systems

A **traditional economy** is based on custom. In such an economy, children often do the same work as their parents. Members of a family or tribe make goods for the rest of their group. In this way, everyone's needs are met. Many hunter-gatherer groups had traditional economies.

R In a **command economy,** a central government decides what goods will be made and who will receive them. The ancient civilizations of Egypt and Mesopotamia began as command economies. Rulers gathered the resources of their people. They used these resources to build large projects or raise powerful armies. Today, Cuba and North Korea have command economies.

In a market economy, each person, or **individual,** makes choices about what to make, sell, and buy. He or she buys and sells goods and services on an open market. The United States has a market economy.

Reading HELPDESK (CCSS)

scarcity the lack of a resource
opportunity cost what is given up, such as time or money, to make or buy something

traditional economy an economic system in which custom decides what people do, make, buy, and sell

command economy an economic system in which a central government decides what goods will be made and who will receive them

networks Online Teaching Options

IMAGE

Hunter-Gatherer Societies

Analyzing Images Project the image of hunter-gatherers and click on the bullets to reveal information about this economic system. Have students describe how a hunter-gatherer society is similar to and different from their own.

See page 25D for other online activities.

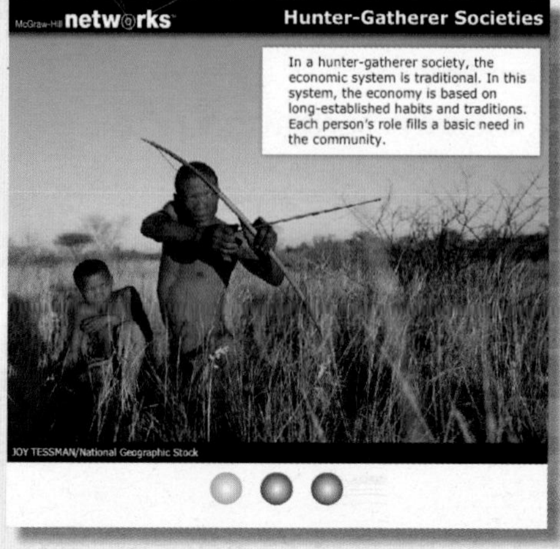

McGraw-Hill networks
Hunter-Gatherer Societies
In a hunter-gatherer society, the economic system is traditional. In this system, the economy is based on long-established habits and traditions. Each person's role fills a basic need in the community.
JOY TESSMAN/National Geographic Stock

In a mixed economy, the government has some control over what and how much is made. Individuals make the rest of the economic choices. Some countries in Europe are mixed economies.

Measuring Economies

Economies grow and shrink over time. This pattern is called the business cycle. When the economy grows quickly, it is often called a boom. When the economy grows very slowly or shrinks, it is called a **recession** (rih•SEH•shuhn). In a recession, companies often close and people lose their jobs. The United States entered a recession in December 2007. **R**

Governments try to keep their economies growing and avoid recessions. One way they do this is by watching prices. Rising prices are a sign of **inflation** (ihn•FLAY•shuhn). High inflation means that money buys less. This raises the cost of living. Say the yearly rate of inflation is 10 percent. This means that something that cost you $10 last year costs you $11 this year. Sometimes inflation can get very high. In Argentina in the 1980s, the yearly rate of inflation hit 1,000 percent. The same goods and services cost 10 times more than they did the year before. **T**

Governments want to avoid having too much inflation. However, **experts** who study economics disagree about what causes inflation. So finding the right government policies is difficult.

☑ PROGRESS CHECK

Identifying In which type of economic system are all decisions made by a central government?

Thinking Like a HISTORIAN

Analyzing Primary Sources

In 1929, the United States and much of the world entered a long, painful depression. This period is called the Great Depression. Prices in the United States deflated by nearly one-third, and one in five Americans was unemployed. Historians still argue about the causes of this serious dip in the business cycle. Use your library to locate two primary sources dealing with the depression of the 1930s. Write a brief report analyzing the information and present your findings to the class. For more information about analyzing primary source material, read the chapter *What Does a Historian Do?*

MODEL OF THE BUSINESS CYCLE

PEAK
Contraction or Recession
Expansion
TROUGH
(LOWEST POINT)
PEAK
Expansion
Contraction or Recession

INFOGRAPHIC **C**

This graph shows the pattern of a business cycle. This cycle shows when businesses expand or contract.

1. **IDENTIFYING** What kind of graph is this?
2. **INTERPRETING** What is a trough?
3. **CRITICAL THINKING** ***Analyzing*** Why is there no end to the business cycle?

recession a period of slow economic growth or decline
inflation a continued rise in prices or the supply of money

Academic Vocabulary (Tier 2 Words)
individual a single human being
expert a skilled person who has mastered a subject

R Reading Skills

Describing Have a volunteer read the text. Then, discuss the business cycle by asking these questions:

- **What happens when the country goes into a recession?** *(The economy shrinks; people lose jobs; companies close.)*
- **What happens when there is an economic boom?** *(The economy grows quickly; unemployment drops; companies prosper.)*

T Technology Skills

Researching on the Internet Explain that current economic data is readily available so everyone can know how our economy is doing. Have students use the Internet to learn what the inflation rate is and what experts are predicting for the economy. Have students discuss their findings in class.

C Critical Thinking Skills

Making Connections Discuss the country's current economic conditions. Prompt students to identify where the current economy is in the business cycle by asking questions such as the following:

- **Has our economy been expanding or contracting?** *(Answers will vary.)*
- **Do you think it will continue its current trend? Why?** *(Answers will vary.)*
- **What part of the business cycle are we now in?** *(Answers will vary depending on present conditions.)*

CHART

Business Cycle

Analyzing Images Have students view the interactive chart. Direct them to click on words on the chart to reveal definitions and explanations of the business cycle. Ask students to define the terms in their own words and to explain how the business cycle works.

See page 25D for other online activities.

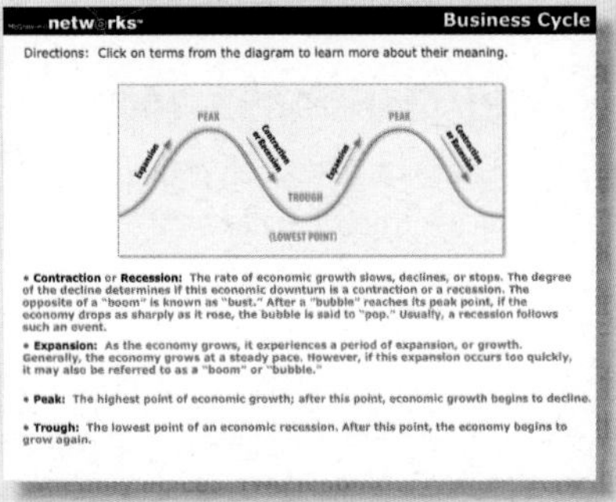

ANSWERS, p. 41

☑ PROGRESS CHECK All decisions are made by a central government in a command economy.

INFOGRAPHIC

1. a line graph
2. a low point in the business cycle
3. CRITICAL THINKING The business cycle repeats continually.

R Reading Skills

Finding the Main Idea After students have read the text, discuss trading in world history. Point out that traders from ancient civilizations often traveled great distances to exchange goods. **Ask:** **Why do countries trade with each other?** *(They trade goods they produce to get goods they don't have or can't produce.)* **What kinds of goods did Europeans export?** *(wool, gold, silver)* **What kinds of goods did they import?** *(silk, spices)* AL

C Critical Thinking Skills

Making Connections Discuss bartering with students. Point out that bartering was the usual method of exchange long ago and that although it has been largely replaced with money, bartering still occurs. **Ask:** **What are some examples of bartering you have participated in or know about?** *(Answers will vary but should clearly demonstrate understanding of the practice.)*

Discuss barriers to trade. **Ask:** **What sorts of barriers did ancient traders have to overcome?** *(conflicts between countries; geographic features such as mountains, deserts, and seas; countries closed to trade)* **What are some modern barriers to trade?** *(Possible answers: conflict, tariffs, political disruptions between nations)* BL

V Visual Skills

Analyzing Graphs Review how to read a graph with students by explaining the grid, the key, and the x-axis and y-axis. **Ask:** **About how much did the U.S. export in 2001?** *(about $1 trillion)* **About how much more did the U.S. import in 2003 than it exported?** *(about $0.5 trillion)* **Visual/Spatial**

Trade in World History

GUIDING QUESTION *What are the benefits and disadvantages of trade?*

Trade has been important to many different civilizations. What makes trade between different peoples so common?

Why Do People Trade?

R Two countries trade with each other when both sides can gain something from the exchange. **Exports** are goods shipped out of a country and sold somewhere else. **Imports** are the goods and services that a country buys from other countries.

Countries want to export goods of which they have a large supply. They want to import goods that are hard to find in their own lands. For hundreds of years, Europeans traded wool, gold, and silver with Asians for rare goods such as silk and spices.

C Early civilizations often traded by bartering. When people **barter,** goods and services are traded for other goods and services. For example, a merchant might trade fish for furs. Eventually, some ancient peoples invented money. Money had a set value, could be traded for anything, and was easier to carry.

Barriers to Trade

Barriers can make international trade difficult. Conflict can stop trade. Geography can make it hard to travel between two places. Sometimes a country chooses to cut off contact with other peoples. In the 1600s, Japan limited trade with European countries. The Japanese wanted to limit European influence on Japanese society.

V

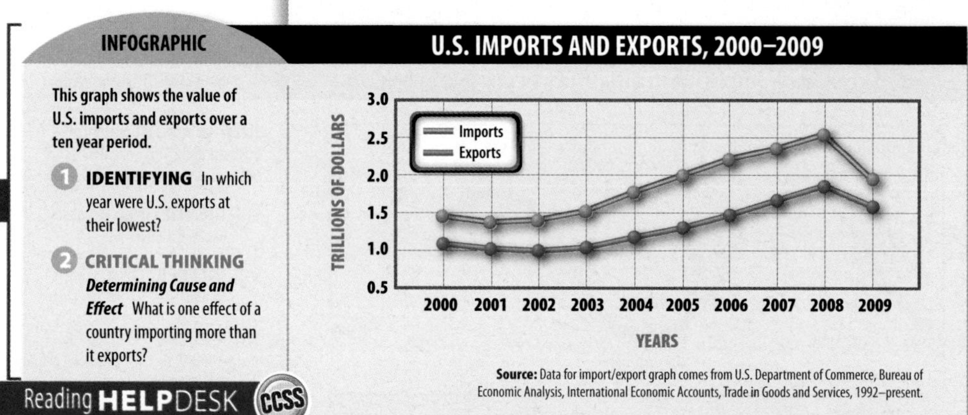

INFOGRAPHIC
U.S. IMPORTS AND EXPORTS, 2000–2009
This graph shows the value of U.S. imports and exports over a ten year period.
1 IDENTIFYING In which year were U.S. exports at their lowest?
2 CRITICAL THINKING Determining Cause and Effect What is one effect of a country importing more than it exports?
Imports
Exports
TRILLIONS OF DOLLARS
3.0
2.5
2.0
1.5
1.0
0.5
2000 2001 2002 2003 2004 2005 2006 2007 2008 2009
YEARS
Source: Data for import/export graph comes from U.S. Department of Commerce, Bureau of Economic Analysis, International Economic Accounts, Trade in Goods and Services, 1992–present.

Reading **HELP**DESK (CCSS)

export a good sent from one country to another in trade
import a good brought into a country from another country
barter to trade by exchanging one good or service for another
globalization the growth in free trade between countries

networks Online Teaching Options

GRAPH

U.S. Trade With China: 1999–2009

Analyzing Graphs Have students analyze this graph that shows the trend of U.S. trade with China from 1999 to 2009. Ask students to summarize what happened during this ten-year period. Invite them to discuss whether this trend is good or bad and to explain their reasoning.

See page 25D for other online activities.

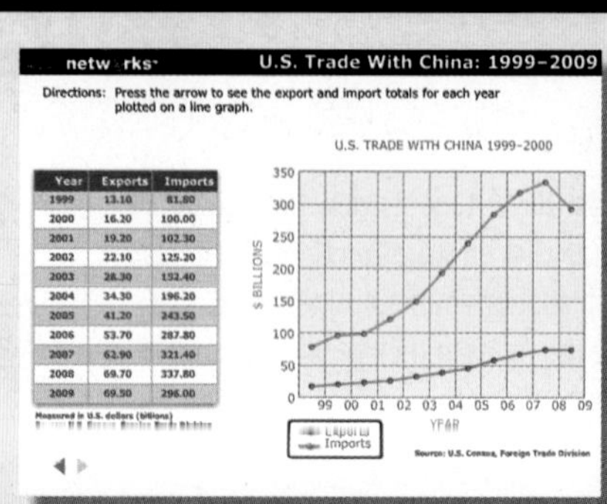

Year	Exports	Imports
1999	13.10	81.80
2000	16.20	100.00
2001	19.20	102.30
2002	22.10	125.20
2003	28.30	152.40
2004	34.30	196.20
2005	41.20	243.50
2006	53.70	287.80
2007	62.90	321.40
2008	69.70	337.80
2009	69.50	296.00

ANSWERS, p. 42

INFOGRAPHIC

1. 2002
2. CRITICAL THINKING The country will spend more money than it earns.

Finally, nations may try to limit or ban trade that hurts producers in their own country. For example, in the Great Depression, U.S. farmers were worried about food imports from Europe. They feared that European farmers might drive them out of business. So they asked the U.S. government to raise taxes on imported European crops. The government did so to protect American farmers. This led other countries to tax U.S. goods to protect their own farmers and businesses.

Shipping through international ports is an important method of transporting goods. This global trade may help the economies of different countries grow.

▶ CRITICAL THINKING
Analyzing Where do you fit into the process of global trade?

Ian Murphy/Stone/Getty Images

Global Trade

W Today, most of the world's countries take part in some form of international trade. The process is called **globalization** (gloh•buh•luh•ZAY•shuhn). Countries like the United States have numerous trade partners. Many large companies also have business branches in more than one country.

Much of this growth has come from efforts to increase free trade. The goal of free trade is a world market where people are free to choose what to buy and sell. People who favor free trade say that it boosts trade. It also cuts the prices of goods. These changes help economies grow. Those against free trade say that it makes imports and foreign labor costs too cheap. They fear that a country will lose companies and jobs to other countries.

Globalization has increased the ties among the world's economies. In 2009, the United States had the largest economy in the world. The U.S. economy was bigger than that of the next two leading countries, Japan and China, added together. Every day, Americans buy and use goods made in other countries. At the same time, American goods and services are sold around the world. When the U.S. economy struggles, it affects the entire world. The questions about what to make, how to make it, and who should buy it are no longer just national issues.

✓ PROGRESS CHECK

Finding the Main Idea Why do countries agree to trade with one another?

LESSON 2 REVIEW (CCSS)

Review Vocabulary (Tier 3 Words)

1. Why are *capital* and *labor* needed to make goods? RH.6–8.4
2. How does *demand* relate to buyers of a good? RH.6–8.4

Answer the Guiding Questions

3. ***Explaining*** What is opportunity cost? RH.6–8.4
4. ***Contrasting*** Describe the differences between a command economy and a traditional economy. RH.6–8.1
5. ***Summarizing*** What types of barriers might prevent trade between countries? RH.6–8.2
6. **INFORMATIVE/EXPLANATORY** Write a paragraph describing how countries decide what goods to export and what goods to import. WHST.6–8.2, WHST.6–8.10

W Writing Skills

Argument Discuss globalization with students. Ask them to explain the reasons some people favor free trade and some oppose it. Encourage students to express their opinions on the subject, telling why they think one view is more valid than the other. Finally, ask students to write a brief editorial stating their point of view and giving their reasons. Urge them to consider the different opinions they have heard in class when expressing their own views. **Verbal/Linguistic**

Have students complete the Lesson 2 Review.

CLOSE & REFLECT

To close the lesson, lead a discussion about the importance of economics in students' daily lives. Have them give examples of economic activities they have participated in during the past week. Then invite students to consider how those activities would change under these circumstances:

- Inflation sharply increases
- The country falls into a recession.
- The United States turns to isolation and no longer participates in world trade.

LESSON 2 REVIEW ANSWERS

1. Capital is the investment needed to start a business and pay its costs, while labor is needed to make things.
2. Demand is the amount of a good that consumers want to buy. When demand is high, prices are usually high. When demand is low, prices are generally low.
3. Opportunity cost is what a person gives up when he or she chooses to produce or buy a particular good or service.
4. Command economies rely on central government control; traditional economies rely on custom.
5. Geographical barriers or violent conflicts might discourage trade. Countries might also choose to limit trade.
6. Students should note that countries choose what to trade based on the scarcity of their own resources, their ability to make certain items, and which items offer them the greatest competitive advantage.

ANSWERS, p. 43

CRITICAL THINKING Students may say that their role in global trade is that of a consumer because they buy goods made in many different countries.

✓ PROGRESS CHECK Countries agree to trade because they benefit from the exchange of goods and services.

ENGAGE

Bellringer Introduce the term *citizen* to students. Ask them what they think it means to be a citizen of their local community, their state, and the United States. Following this discussion, have students write a short paragraph describing what citizenship means to them. AL

Ask volunteers to share their paragraphs. Then tell students to save their paragraphs for the end of the lesson. Explain to students that they will be learning about the structure of our government. They will also be learning about the rights and responsibilities of U.S. citizenship.

TEACH & ASSESS

R Reading Skills

Defining After students have read "Principles of Government," write the content vocabulary terms on the board and call on volunteers to explain each term in their own words.
AL ELL

C Critical Thinking Skills

Speculating Remind students that we have a federal republic, in which people elect their representatives and power is divided between the federal government and the state governments. **Ask: What responsibility do citizens have in a representative government?** *(Citizens have the responsibility to vote for their representatives.)* **Why is voting an important responsibility for citizens in a democracy?** *(Democracies are representative governments. Citizens should use their right to vote so they can choose officials to protect their rights.)* AL

ANSWER, p. 44

TAKING NOTES: ***Rights:*** seek life, liberty, happiness; freedom of expression; attend peaceful gatherings; petition the government; worship; fair trial by jury; vote and serve ***Responsibilities:*** stay informed; vote; respect the rights and views of others; take part in the community

networks *There's More Online!*
- GRAPHIC ORGANIZER Citizenship: Rights and Responsibilities
- SLIDE SHOW Citizens' Duties and Responsibilities
- VIDEO

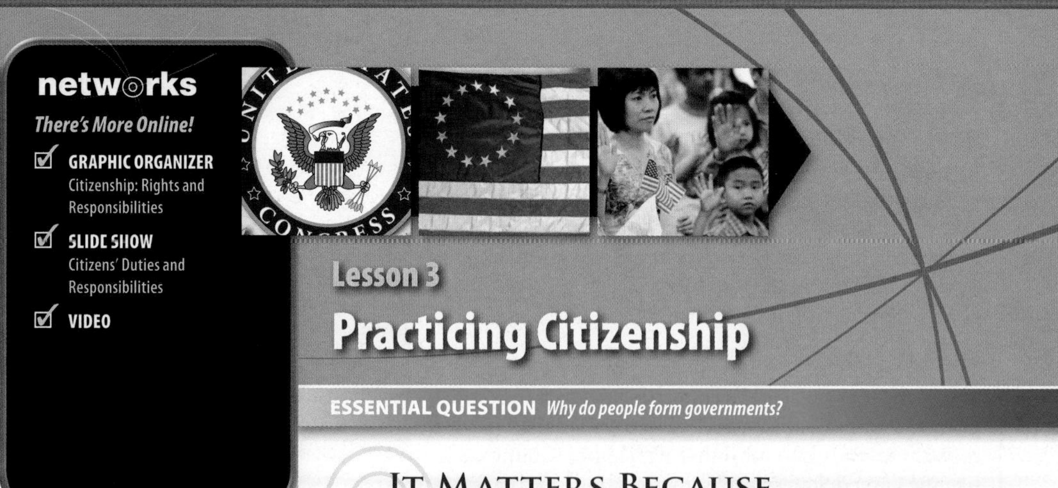

Lesson 3
Practicing Citizenship

ESSENTIAL QUESTION *Why do people form governments?*

IT MATTERS BECAUSE
Our system of government needs active citizens who understand their rights and responsibilities.

Principles of Government

GUIDING QUESTION *What are the key principles of the U.S. government?*

The U.S. Constitution is the highest law in the United States. It contains the key ideas of America's government. Many of these ideas came from ancient Greece and Rome. The United States has a **representative government.** This means that citizens vote for officials who serve the will of the people. The government must act in the people's interests and protect their rights.

The Constitution created a **federal system** of government. The central, or federal, government is the highest authority. However, it also shares some powers with the state governments.

The federal government is split into three equal parts, or branches. Each branch has its own specific powers, an idea called **separation of powers.** This concept was adopted so that no one branch could become too powerful. An overly powerful government could harm its citizens. Each branch limits the power of the other branches. The diagram shows this system of **checks and balances.**

What do the three branches of government do? The **legislative** (LEH•juhs•lay•tihv) **branch** is known as the U.S. Congress. It passes laws for the whole country. The **executive branch** includes the office of the U.S. president. The president and other members of the executive branch ensure that the nation's laws are carried out.

Reading HELPDESK CCSS

Taking Notes: *Summarizing*
Use a graphic organizer like this one to show the rights and responsibilities of citizenship. RH.6–8.2

Citizenship → Rights | Responsibilities

Content Vocabulary (Tier 3 Words)
- representative government
- federal system
- separation of powers
- checks and balances

networks ***Online Teaching Options***

VIDEO

The Seven Dynamics of Citizenship

Discussing As students watch the video, urge them to take notes on the main points and to record any questions they have. When they finish, discuss students' questions. Then ask students to write a short essay stating their reactions to the ideas presented in the video.

See page 25E for other online activities.

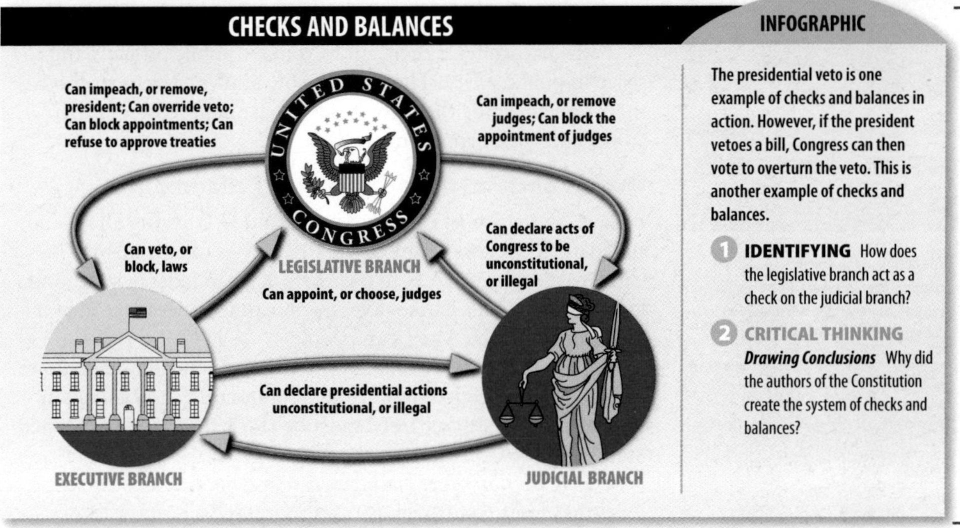

INFOGRAPHIC

The presidential veto is one example of checks and balances in action. However, if the president vetoes a bill, Congress can then vote to overturn the veto. This is another example of checks and balances.

1 **IDENTIFYING** How does the legislative branch act as a check on the judicial branch?

2 **CRITICAL THINKING** ***Drawing Conclusions*** Why did the authors of the Constitution create the system of checks and balances?

V

The **judicial** (joo•DIH•shuhl) **branch** includes the U.S. Supreme Court and various lesser courts. The judges in the judicial branch use the Constitution to interpret laws. They can strike down laws that violate the Constitution.

legislative branch part of government that passes laws
executive branch part of government that enforces laws
judicial branch part of government that interprets laws

 PROGRESS CHECK

Identifying What type of government does the United States have?

What Is Citizenship?

GUIDING QUESTION *What are the civic rights, duties, and responsibilities of U.S. citizens?*

The system of government in the United States provides many freedoms. However, it also needs citizens to carry out certain duties and responsibilities. This idea, called civic participation, comes from ancient Greece and Rome. Good citizenship helps our government and communities work as well as possible.

C

Rights of Citizenship

All Americans have the right to **seek** life, liberty, and happiness. All Americans have the right to freedom of expression. This means that they can speak and write openly. They can attend peaceful gatherings. They can petition the government to address their needs. The Constitution also protects the right of people to worship as they choose. People who are accused of a crime have the right to receive a fair trial by a **jury** of their peers.

Content Vocabulary (Tier 3 Words)
- **legislative branch**
- **executive branch**
- **judicial branch**

representative government government in which citizens elect officials who govern
federal system government which divides power between central and state governments
separation of powers the division of power among the branches of government
checks and balances system in which each branch of government limits the power of another branch

CHART

A System of Checks and Balances

Discussing Ask students to view the interactive chart. Explain that they can click on the icon for each branch of government to read examples of how the checks and balances system works to balance the powers of the three branches of government. Afterward, guide a discussion of how this system helps preserve our democracy.

See page 25E for other online activities.

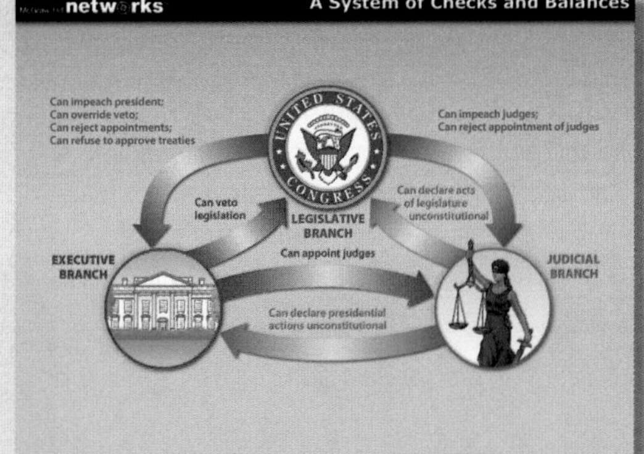

Practicing Citizenship

V Visual Skills

Interpreting Point out the diagram on checks and balances. **Ask**:

- **How can Congress contain the actions of the president?** *(Congress can impeach the president.)*
- **How can the Supreme Court limit the actions of Congress and the president?** *(The Court can declare acts of Congress and the president unconstitutional.)*
- **How can the president limit the power of the courts?** *(The president appoints judges.)*
- **What is the purpose of having separation of powers and checks and balances?** *(Each of these prevents any one branch of government from becoming powerful enough to dominate the other branches of the government.)* **Visual/Spatial**

C Critical Thinking Skills

Categorizing Have a student read the opening paragraph of "What Is Citizenship?" aloud. **Ask:**

- **What is the difference between a duty and a responsibility?** *(A duty is an action required by law. A responsibility is an act that society does not require by law but expects people to carry out for their own good and for the good of others.)* AL ELL
- **Give one example of a duty and one example of a responsibility.** *(Sample responses: Serving on a jury when called is a duty. Voting in an election is a responsibility.)* BL
- **Why do citizens need to obey the law?** *(Our government is based on rule of law. Everyone must follow the laws to keep order and to ensure that the rights of everyone are protected.)* ELL

Content Background Knowledge

The discussion of the judiciary in this lesson refers to federal courts. Each state also has its own court system. The dual system arises because the Constitution gives certain powers to the federal government and reserves others for the states. Two court systems, therefore, help adjudicate the laws specific to the two levels of government.

ANSWERS, p. 45

INFOGRAPHIC

1. A federal system is a strong central government that shares power with the states.
2. **CRITICAL THINKING** to prevent any one branch from becoming too powerful

✓ **PROGRESS CHECK** The United States has a federal, representative government.

R Reading Skills

Applying Explain that citizens have duties and responsibilities in their local community, as well as in their state and country. Emphasize that these duties and responsibilities are meant to improve the quality of life and ensure the freedom of all citizens. Have students read the text. Then, **ask:** **How does paying taxes improve the quality of life and ensure the freedom of Americans?** *(Taxes pay for government services, such as roads and schools; they pay for our military, which protects our freedom.)* **How does serving on a jury help ensure our freedom?** *(It guarantees that citizens are involved in the process of deciding on guilt and innocence, which protects our freedom from authoritarian rule.)*

Point out that taking part in their community is another responsibility of citizens. People should stay informed about important issues. **Ask:** **Why is it important for citizens to stay informed?** *(Only by being informed can citizens vote wisely and support actions to improve the common good or oppose actions that will harm it.)*

C Critical Thinking Skills

Making Connections Connect what students have learned about our system of government to what they have learned about citizenship. Ask students to describe the different ways in which citizens participate in government. *(Students should note that citizens vote, serve in public office, and petition members of government with their concerns.)* AL

The design of the American flag has changed over the years. However, its red and white stripes still honor the country's thirteen original states.

▶ CRITICAL THINKING

Analyzing Like the flags of other countries, the U.S. flag contains symbols. Each of the 50 stars represents a state. If the U.S. wanted a new flag to represent the country today, what symbols would you suggest, and why?

Citizens also have the right to vote for public officials and to serve in public office. The right to vote allows citizens to choose their leaders, while the right to serve lets them represent their fellow citizens in government.

Duties and Responsibilities of Citizenship

By law, citizens must carry out some duties. Obeying all federal, state, and local laws is one of the first duties of citizenship. Citizens also have a duty to pay their taxes to federal, state, and local governments. These taxes pay for the services provided by government to the American people.

Citizens must serve on a jury if the government asks them to. This service is needed in order to honor people's right to a fair trial by jury. Finally, citizens must be ready to defend the United States and the Constitution.

People born in other countries can also become U.S. citizens. First, they must go through naturalization. This is a process of applying for, and being granted, citizenship. To qualify, they have to have lived in the United States for a certain amount of time. They also need to show good moral character. They must be able to use basic English and must know about U.S. history and government. In addition, they must swear to uphold all duties of citizenship. R

In addition to their duties, citizens also have responsibilities. Citizens should stay informed about important **issues,** or topics. An awareness of critical issues—such as concern for the global environment—will help them make wise choices when they vote in federal, state, and local elections. Voting is a powerful right and a key responsibility of citizenship. If people do not vote, they give away part of their voice in government.

Citizens should also respect the rights and views of other people. The United States welcomes people of many different backgrounds. They all share the same freedoms. Before you deny a right to someone else, put yourself in that person's place. Think how you would feel if someone tried to take away your rights.

C Finally, citizens should take part in their local community. By working with one another, we help make our neighborhoods and towns better places to live. There are different ways to keep our communities strong. We can volunteer our time. We can join neighborhood groups, and we can serve in public office.

☑ PROGRESS CHECK

Summarizing What duties do citizens have?

Reading **HELP**DESK CCSS

Academic Vocabulary (Tier 2 Words)

seek to look for or try to achieve
jury a group of people sworn to make a decision in a legal case
issue a concern or problem that has not yet been solved

networks *Online Teaching Options*

SLIDE SHOW

Good Citizenship

Discussing This slideshow describes a number of ways that people can demonstrate good citizenship. After students view the slides, ask them to offer more examples and to explain how these examples contribute to the betterment and support of our country.

See page 25E for other online activities.

ANSWERS, p. 46

CRITICAL THINKING Students should identify relevant symbols that could be used to represent the United States.

☑ **PROGRESS CHECK** Citizens have a duty to obey laws, to pay taxes, to serve on juries, and to defend the country.

Being a Global Citizen

GUIDING QUESTION *What does it mean to be a global citizen?*

Today the world faces many problems that go beyond the borders of any one country. Threats to the health of the environment, such as pollution or the destruction of a tropical rain forest, affect people living in many different places. Many countries also have close economic ties to other nations. Because of these ties, economic problems in one country affect other countries. In addition, the idea is growing around the world that all people should have certain basic human rights. World leaders must often work together to deal with these issues. **T**

W Being a global citizen means learning about the different issues that affect the world as a whole. It means taking care of the environment. It also means understanding how people live in other countries. We are all affected by drought and hunger or economic troubles in other countries. Once we understand one another's ways of life, we can work together more easily to solve big problems.

Being a global citizen does not mean giving up your duties and responsibilities as a citizen of the United States. It means thinking about how you can make the world a better place by your actions. Making the effort to stay informed and to respect the views of others helps all Americans. Through that same effort, you can also help the rest of the world.

This family is taking the Oath of Allegiance. It is the final step in becoming a U.S. citizen through naturalization.

Getty Images News/Getty Images

PROGRESS CHECK

Finding the Main Idea What are some of the ways in which you could become a better global citizen?

LESSON 3 REVIEW (CCSS)

Review Vocabulary (Tier 3 Words)

1. What is a *federal system* of government? RH.6–8.4
2. How are *checks and balances* related to the idea of *separation of powers*? RH.6–8.4

Answer the Guiding Questions

3. ***Finding the Main Idea*** What is the main purpose of a representative government? RH.6–8.2
4. ***Drawing Conclusions*** Why do citizens have duties and responsibilities as well as rights? RH.6–8.2
5. ***Making Inferences*** What are some of the challenges of being a global citizen? RH.6–8.2
6. **NARRATIVE** Write a paragraph describing how you can fulfill two of the responsibilities of citizenship in your daily life. WHST.6–8.10

Practicing Citizenship

W Writing Skills

Informative/Explanatory Discuss our role as citizens of the United States compared with our roles as citizens of the world. Then organize the class into two groups. Provide each group with one of the following prompts. Have students in each group work together to outline, write, edit, and present their ideas to the class.

- **How is being a global citizen similar to being a United States citizen?** *(Students should include the idea that respecting the rights of others and staying informed are responsibilities for both types of citizenship.)*
- **How is being a global citizen different from being a U.S. citizen?** *(Students should include the idea that U.S. citizens have duties to the U.S., but they do not have duties to the rest of the world. They also cannot vote for world leaders and so cannot participate in government in the same way.)*

T Technology Skills

Using and Citing Information Have pairs of students work together to research information on the Internet on forms of government different from that of the United States. Suggest that they focus on the basic human rights each type of government promotes. Challenge students to organize the information so that others can easily compare and contrast two or three different forms. Require students to cite the Internet sites they use.

Have students complete the Lesson 3 Review.

CLOSE & REFLECT

Have students return to the paragraphs they wrote for the Engage activity. Invite students to compare their ideas about citizenship now to their views before starting the lesson. **Ask: How have your views about citizenship changed?** *(Student answers will vary but should reflect an understanding of the rights and duties of citizenship.)*

LESSON 3 REVIEW ANSWERS

1. A federal system of government is a government in which the central government has the highest authority but shares power with state governments.
2. Separation of powers gives each branch its own specific authority, but checks and balances limit the power of any one branch over another branch. Together they keep government from becoming too powerful.
3. The main purpose of a representative government is to act in the people's interest and protect the people's rights.
4. Citizens have duties and responsibilities to ensure that rights are respected, that the voice of the people is heard in government, and that communities can be protected and strengthened.
5. Learning about global issues and other cultures takes effort, and some topics may be hard to understand. U.S. citizens must also remember that they have specific duties and responsibilities to the United States.
6. Student answers will vary. Students will not be able to vote, but they can stay informed on issues, respect the rights of others, and be active in their community.

ANSWER, p. 47

PROGRESS CHECK People can become better global citizens by staying informed about world issues, learning about other cultures, and respecting the rights of others.

CHAPTER REVIEW ACTIVITY

Have students create a three-column chart as shown. Then guide a class discussion reviewing the main points of the chapter. Have students list the main ideas and important details for each lesson in their charts.

Geography	Economics	Citizenship

REVIEW THE ENDURING UNDERSTANDINGS

Review the chapter's Enduring Understandings with students.

- *People, places, and ideas change over time.*
- *Resources are limited, so people must make choices.*
- *The value that a society places on individual rights is often reflected in that society's government.*

How did geographers respond to the need to depict and describe Earth's surface more thoroughly? *(Answers should include a description of the new ways of mapping Earth's surface, including different map projections and different types of maps to fit the different needs of people studying and traveling over Earth. They should also include the development of ways to plot latitude and longitude.)*

How does economics affect your daily life? Give examples. *(Students should recognize that economics plays a crucial part in their daily lives. They might provide examples such as how much they must pay for the things they want; whether or not a product they want is available and affordable; and how unemployment affects those around them.)*

How does our government protect the rights you most value? *(Answers will vary, but students should identify some rights they value, such as the right to speak freely, to have a secure and safe life, and to enjoy some degree of privacy. They should then cite ways in which their local, state, or federal government acts to protect those rights, such as through enforcement of the right to freedom of speech, through armed forces that protect the country's security, and by laws that limit how much others can investigate personal information.)*

CHAPTER 2 Activities CCSS

Write your answers on a separate piece of paper.

1. **Exploring the Essential Question** WHST.6–8.10
NARRATIVE Think about the role of the Six Essential Elements of Geography in your daily life. How do you affect the environment where you live? How does it affect you? Write a short essay answering these questions. Be sure to include descriptive details.

2. **21st Century Skills** WHST.6–8.9
ANALYZING INFORMATION Imagine that the price of a gallon of gasoline has varied in the following way: January—$2.50, March—$2.45, May—$2.75, July—$3. Create a line graph that shows the rise and fall in gas prices over this period. According to the laws of supply and demand, when would gasoline producers want to sell the most gas?

3. **Thinking Like a Historian** RH.6–8.2
CITIZENSHIP AND SOCIETY Imagine that you are teaching a class of people seeking citizenship. What are the three topics you would be sure to include in your teaching?

4. **GEOGRAPHY ACTIVITY**

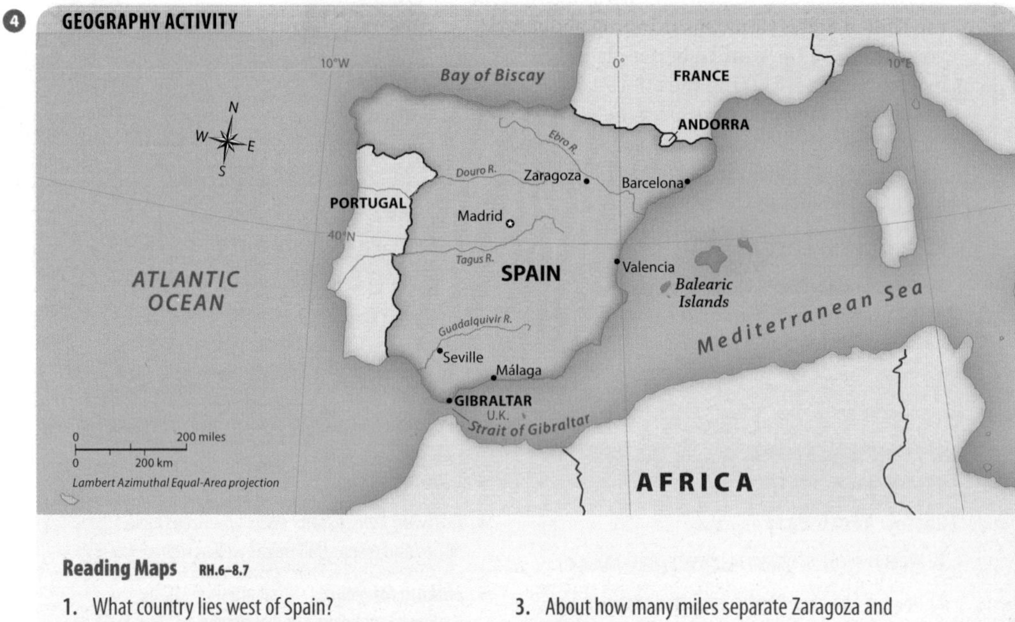

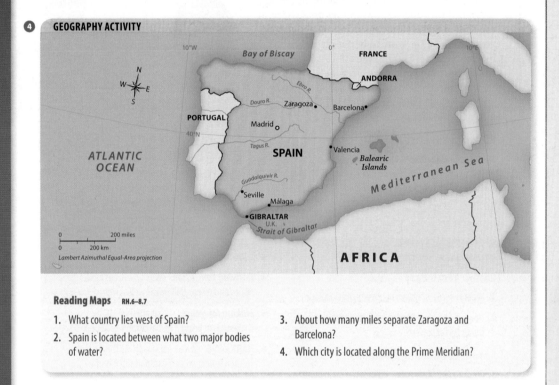

Reading Maps RH.6–8.7

1. What country lies west of Spain?
2. Spain is located between what two major bodies of water?
3. About how many miles separate Zaragoza and Barcelona?
4. Which city is located along the Prime Meridian?

ACTIVITIES ANSWERS

Exploring the Essential Question

1. Students' essays will vary. They should discuss some of the features of the environment in which they live, such as its weather patterns, its physical features, or the living things in the area. They may note how they and the people around them interact with this environment.

21st Century Skills

2. Student graphs should show the proper dates and prices, with a low in March and a peak in July. The law of supply states that gasoline producers would want to sell the most gas when the price is highest, which would be in July.

Thinking Like a Historian

3. Students might identify the duties, responsibilities, and rights of citizens. They may also want to teach about the structure of the government of the United States.

Reading Maps

4. **1.** Portugal; **2.** the Atlantic Ocean and Mediterranean Sea; **3.** about 200 miles (322 km); **4.** Valencia

REVIEW THE GUIDING QUESTIONS

Directions: Choose the best answer for each question.

RH.6–8.7
1. Which map projection shows correct direction and shape, but not size and distance?
   A. Goode's Interrupted Equal-Area
   B. Mercator
   C. Robinson
   D. Winkel Tripel

RH.6–8.2
2. The line that divides the Earth into eastern and western halves is called the
   F. Equator.
   G. latitude.
   H. hemisphere.
   I. Prime Meridian.

RH.6–8.4
3. A map showing population density would be considered a
   A. general-purpose map.
   B. political map.
   C. physical map.
   D. special-purpose map.

RH.6–8.4
4. In a ______ economy, all decisions are made by a central government.
   F. command
   G. market
   H. mixed
   I. traditional

RH.6–8.4
5. In economics, capital is
   A. how much of something someone wants to make.
   B. the price charged for goods or services.
   C. money or goods used to produce things.
   D. the willingness of people to take risks.

RH.6–8.2
6. The ______ branch of the United States government interprets the laws.
   F. judicial
   G. federal
   H. executive
   I. legislative

ASSESSMENT ANSWERS

Review the Guiding Questions

1. **B** The Mercator projection distorts size and distance but is still used because it shows directions and shapes accurately. The other map projections listed provide a more accurate representation of the size and distance of objects on Earth's surface. Therefore, the correct answer is B.

2. **I** A hemisphere is one-half of the globe, not a line. The Equator divides Earth into the Northern and Southern Hemispheres. The Prime Meridian divides the globe into the Eastern and Western Hemispheres. Greenwich is the name of the town that the Prime Meridian passes through. Thus, I is the correct answer.

3. **D** Physical maps show physical features rather than population. Political maps show borders and locations of cities. Population density is shown by choropleth maps, which are a type of special-purpose map. Therefore, D is the correct answer.

4. **F** Command economies are controlled by central governments. In mixed economies, only some economic decisions are controlled by the central government. In market economies, individuals make economic choices for themselves. Traditional economies are based on custom. Therefore, the correct answer is F.

5. **C** Capital is money or goods used to produce items. It is a type of investment. Answer A refers to the idea of supply, answer B deals with costs, and answer D deals with entrepreneurship. So C is the correct answer.

6. **F** The judicial branch interprets laws, the executive branch enforces laws, and the legislative branch makes laws. The term *federal* describes the division of power between the state governments and the national government. Thus, the correct answer is F.

Assessment Answers

Analyzing Documents

7 **B** Students should understand Smith's argument that people trade goods to get items they want in return for those goods. One of the traders might want money, while the other trader might want goods. The trading partners are not giving or receiving gifts. Trading is done for self-interest, not kindness. Therefore, B is the correct answer.

8 **H** The passage says that people provide these goods out of self-interest because they get something in return. The passage does not indicate that the government tells anyone to do anything and states that trade is not done out of kindness. The passage does not indicate that they provide food because we want it. Thus, H is the correct answer.

Short Response

9 The passage explains that citizens should participate in the democratic process to protect freedom and liberty.

10 The American democracy is based on the will of the people, shown by the votes and actions of its citizens. The justice is suggesting that this is a great responsibility and that honoring it deserves high praise.

Extended Response

11 The content of student letters will vary. Students should note that our representative form of government needs an informed, active set of voters so that the will of the people can be expressed. They should also note that our way of life includes many freedoms that are made possible when people carry out their duties and responsibilities.

CHAPTER 2 Assessment *(continued)* 

DBQ ANALYZING DOCUMENTS

RH.6–8.2
7 **Drawing Conclusions** Adam Smith wrote about reasons people trade in his 1776 economics book, *The Wealth of Nations*:

> *"Whoever offers to another a bargain of any kind, proposes to do this [trade]. Give me that which I want, and you shall have this which you want, is the meaning of every such offer. . . . It is not from the benevolence [kindness] of the butcher, the brewer, or the baker that we expect our dinner, but from their regard [attention] to their own interest."*
>
> —from *The Wealth of Nations*

According to this passage, why do people trade with each other?

A. to get something illegally
B. to get something that they want
C. to offer gifts
D. to be benevolent

RH.6–8.2
8 **Finding the Main Idea** According to the passage, what convinces the butcher, baker, or brewer to provide food for us?

F. They do it because the government tells them to do it.
G. They do it out of kindness.
H. They do it because it serves their self-interest.
I. They do it because we want the food.

SHORT RESPONSE

> *"Former Supreme Court Justice Louis Brandeis once said, 'The only title in our democracy superior to that of President [is] the title of citizen.' In the United States, the power of government comes directly from people like you. To protect freedom and liberty, U.S. citizens must participate in the democratic process and in their communities."*
>
> —from the *Citizen's Almanac*, U.S. Citizenship and Immigration Services

RH.6–8.1
9 According to the passage, why do citizens need to take part in the democratic process?

RH.6–8.1
10 Why does Brandeis say the title of citizen is greater than the title of President?

EXTENDED RESPONSE

WHST.6–8.1, WHST.6–8.10
11 **Argument** You are a new American citizen. Write a letter to the editor explaining why citizens must fulfill their duties and responsibilities.

Need Extra Help?

If You've Missed Question	1	2	3	4	5	6	7	8	9	10	11
Review Lesson	1	1	1	2	2	3	2	2	3	3	3

networks *Online Teaching Options*

More Assessment Resources

The *Assess* tab in the online Teacher Lesson Center includes resources to help students improve their test-taking skills. It also contains many project-based rubrics to help you assess students' work.

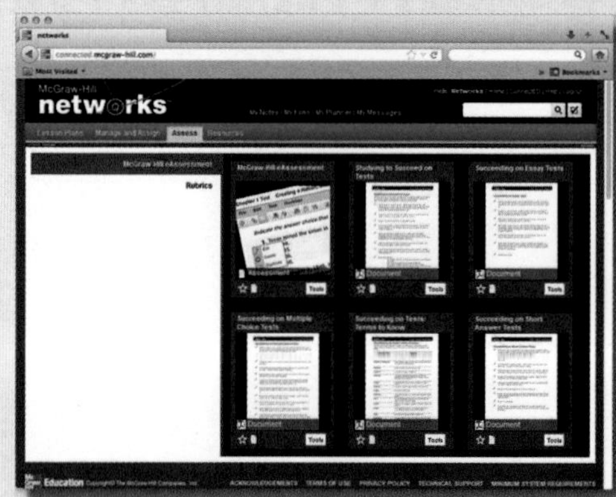

CHAPTER 3

Early Humans and the Agricultural Revolution Planner

UNDERSTANDING BY DESIGN®

Enduring Understanding

- *People, places, and ideas change over time.*

Essential Question

- *How do people adapt to their environment?*

Predictable Misunderstandings

Students may think:

- *The Paleolithic and Neolithic ages were short spans of time.*
- *People during this time were not smart.*
- *People made few advances during this time.*
- *People did not live together as families.*

Assessment Evidence

Performance Tasks:

- *Hands-On Chapter Project*

Other Evidence:

- *Responses to Interactive Whiteboard Activities*
- *Answers to questions about Neolithic Age shelters*
- *Class discussion answers*
- *Writing activity in which students describe the relationship between trial and error and survival during the Paleolithic Age*
- *Brainstorming activity of phrases and adjectives that describe what life was like during the Paleolithic Age*
- *Concept Web creation*
- *Whiteboard drag-and-drop activity*
- *21st Century Skills Activity*
- *Lesson Reviews*
- *Chapter Activities and Assessment*

SUGGESTED PACING GUIDE

Introducing the Chapter	1 day	Lesson 2	1 day
Lesson 1	1 day	Chapter Wrap-Up and Assessment	1 day

TOTAL TIME 4 Days

Key for Using the Teacher Edition

SKILL-BASED ACTIVITIES

Types of skill activities found in the Teacher Edition.

V Visual Skills require students to analyze maps, graphs, charts, and photos.

R Reading Skills help students practice reading skills and master vocabulary.

W Writing Skills provide writing opportunities to help students comprehend the text.

C Critical Thinking Skills help students apply and extend what they have learned.

T Technology Skills require students to use digital tools effectively.

*Letters are followed by a number when there is more than one of the same type of skill on the page.

DIFFERENTIATED INSTRUCTION

All activities are written for the on-level student unless otherwise marked with the leveled labels below.

BL Beyond Level

AL Approaching Level

ELL English Language Learners

All students benefit from activities that utilize different learning styles. Many activities are marked as below when a particular learning style is highlighted.

Intrapersonal	**Naturalist**
Logical/Mathematical	**Kinesthetic**
Visual/Spatial	**Auditory/Musical**
Verbal/Linguistic	**Interpersonal**

NCSS Standards covered in "Early Humans and the Agricultural Revolution"

Learners will understand:

1 **CULTURE**

3. How culture influences the ways in which human groups solve the problems of daily living

4. That the beliefs, values, and behaviors of a culture form an integrated system that helps shape the activities and ways of life that define a culture

5. How individuals learn the elements of their culture through interactions with others, and how individuals learn of other cultures through communication and study

6. That culture may change in response to changing needs, concerns, social, political, and geographic conditions

2 **TIME, CONTINUITY, AND CHANGE**

5. Key historical periods and patterns of change within and across cultures (e.g., the rise and fall of ancient civilizations, the development of technology, the rise of modern nation-states, and the establishment and breakdown of colonial systems)

6. The origins and influences of social, cultural, political, and economic systems

7. Human modifications of the environment

4 **INDIVIDUAL DEVELOPMENT AND IDENTITY**

2. Concepts such as: development, change, personality, learning, individual, family, groups, motivation, and perception

5 **INDIVIDUALS, GROUPS, AND INSTITUTIONS**

3. Institutions are created to respond to changing individual and group needs

5. That groups and institutions change over time

6 **POWER, AUTHORITY, AND GOVERNANCE**

5. The ways in which governments meet the needs and wants of citizens, manage conflict, and establish order and society

7 **PRODUCTION, DISTRIBUTION, AND CONSUMPTION**

6. The economic gains that result from specialization and exchange as well as the trade-offs

8 **SCIENCE, TECHNOLOGY, AND SOCIETY**

1. Science is a result of empirical study of the natural world, and technology is the application of knowledge to accomplish tasks

CHAPTER OPENER PLANNER

Students will know:

- *how Paleolithic humans adapted to their environments to survive.*
- *how advances during the Paleolithic Age made it possible for humans to survive the Ice Ages.*
- *why some historians consider the Agricultural Revolution the most important event in human history.*
- *why people created permanent settlements when they began to farm.*
- *how tools and roles changed as a result of permanent communities.*

Students will be able to:

- ***analyze** photographs of shelters used in the Paleolithic Age.*
- ***use** trial-and-error methods to solve a problem.*
- ***write** a descriptive paragraph on how trial and error helped humans survive.*
- ***analyze** photographs of shelters used in the Neolithic Age.*
- ***connect** farming to their daily lives.*
- ***draw conclusions** about why the Agricultural Revolution was a revolution.*

UNDERSTANDING BY DESIGN®

☑ *Print Teaching Options*

V Visual Skills

- ☐ **P. 52** Students study, discuss, and calculate distances on a map of early human settlements. **Logical/Mathematical**
- ☐ **P. 53** Students study and answer questions about a time line of early human settlements.

☑ *Online Teaching Options*

V Visual Skills

MAP **Human Settlements 8000 B.C. to 2000 B.C.**—Students identify the locations of early human settlements and the physical features of the land that surrounds them.

TIME LINE **Place and Time: Early Humans and the Agricultural Revolution, 8000 B.C. to 2000 B.C.**—Students learn about key historical events that occurred between 8000 and 2000 B.C.

WORLD ATLAS Students can use this interactive map to identify regions of the world, learn about individual countries, locate political boundaries, measure distances, and much more.

☑ *Printable Digital Worksheets*

R Reading Skills

GRAPHIC NOVEL ***Fire and Error***—This humorous graphic novel speculates how some discoveries may have been by chance, leading to larger discoveries and improved ways of living.

Project-Based Learning

Hands-On Chapter Project

Early Humans and the Agricultural Revolution

Students will create a time capsule in order to identify and compare cultural adaptations to a geographic environment.

Technology Extension

Collaborative Time Capsules with Wikis

- Find an additional activity online that incorporates technology for this project.
- Visit the EdTechTeacher Web sites (included in the Technology Extension for this chapter) for more links, tutorials, and other resources.

Print Resources

ANCILLARY RESOURCES

These ancillaries are available for every chapter and lesson.

- **Reading Essentials and Study Guide Workbook** AL ELL
- **Chapter Tests and Lesson Quizzes Blackline Masters**

PRINTABLE DIGITAL WORKSHEETS

These printable digital worksheets are available for every chapter and lesson.

- **Hands-On Chapter Projects**
- **What Do You Know? activities**
- **Chapter Summaries (English and Spanish)**
- **Vocabulary Builder activities**
- **Guided Reading activities**

More Media Resources

SUGGESTED VIDEOS MOVIES

Watch *Cave of Forgotten Dreams.* To make this film, director Werner Herzog was given unprecedented access to the Chauvet Cave in southern France, where some of the oldest artistic creations of humans are found. *(NOTE: Preview any clips for age-appropriateness.)*

SUGGESTED READING 

Grade 6 reading level:

- ***Exploring the Ice Age,*** by Margaret Cooper

Grade 7 reading level:

- ***Bodies from the Ice: Melting Glaciers and the Recovery of the Past,*** by James M. Deem

Grade 8 reading level:

- ***A Bone from a Dry Sea,*** by Peter Dickinson

HUNTER-GATHERERS

Students will know:
- *how Paleolithic humans adapted to their environments to survive.*
- *how advances during the Paleolithic Age made it possible for humans to survive the Ice Ages.*

Students will be able to:
- ***analyze*** *photographs of shelters from the Paleolithic Age.*
- ***use*** *trial-and-error methods to solve a problem.*
- ***write*** *a descriptive paragraph on how trial and error helped humans survive.*

UNDERSTANDING BY DESIGN®

☑ *Print Teaching Options*

V Visual Skills

- ☐ **P. 56** Students study the image of a Paleolithic ax and discuss how it was made.
- ☐ **P. 60** Students read and analyze a map about the land bridge connecting Asia and North America. **Visual/Spatial**
- ☐ **P. 61** Students study and discuss an image of early people gathered around a fire. **Visual/Spatial**

R Reading Skills

- ☐ **P. 54** Students calculate the number of years ago people began recording time and when the Paleolithic Age ended. **AL** **Logical/Mathematical**
- ☐ **P. 55** Students identify traits of hunters and gatherers and the division of labor in the Paleolithic Age. **ELL**
- ☐ **P. 56** Students define *technology* and discuss the technology of the Paleolithic Age and today. **ELL**
- ☐ **P. 58** Students discuss the different ways people communicate. **ELL**
- ☐ **P. 61** Students use text evidence to discuss the Ice Age and the land bridge. **BL**

W Writing Skills

- ☐ **P. 56** Students write a paragraph arguing how people in the Paleolithic Age would have benefited from working in pairs vs. working in a group. **ELL** **BL**
- ☐ **P. 58** Students write and role-play an incident that could have promoted the development of language during the Paleolithic Age. **Kinesthetic**

C Critical Thinking Skills

- ☐ **P. 55** Students discuss how Paleolithic people met their basic human needs.
- ☐ **P. 57** Students compare and contrast the shelters that Paleolithic people lived in with the homes people live in today. **AL**
- ☐ **P. 59** Students express opinions about the reasons Paleolithic people created cave paintings.
- ☐ **P. 60** Students make inferences about why the ocean levels lowered as glaciers grew larger. **BL**

T Technology Skills

- ☐ **P. 59** Students research Paleolithic art online. **BL**

☑ *Online Teaching Options*

V Visual Skills

- **SLIDE SHOW** **Paleolithic-Era Animals**—Students compare pictures of modern animals with pictures drawn by early humans.
- **VIDEO** **How We Know About the Ice Ages**—Students examine evidence that a thick ice sheet once covered much of Earth's surface.
- **MAP** **Ice Age Migration**—Students explore the extent of the Ice Age land bridge and compare it with modern-day land boundaries.
- **CHART** **Paleolithic Tools**—Students click on images to learn more about a variety of tools.

R Reading Skills

- **IMAGE** **Cueva de las Manos, Río Pinturas**—Students read more about "The Cave of the Hands."
- **IMAGE** **Cave Paintings**—Students explore techniques involved in cave painting.
- **GRAPHIC ORGANIZER** **Taking Notes: *Sequencing:* Paleolithic Inventions**—Students identify the importance of two major inventions of Paleolithic people.

C Critical Thinking Skills

- **WHITEBOARD ACTIVITY** **Paleolithic Nomads**—Students analyze a scene showing Paleolithic life and categorize tools as those that belong and those that do not belong in the scene.
- **WHITEBOARD ACTIVITY** **Paleolithic Time and the Ice Ages**—Students compare and contrast characteristics of the Paleolithic Age and the Ice Ages.

T Technology Skills

- **SELF-CHECK QUIZ** **Lesson 1**—Students receive instant feedback about their mastery of lesson content.

☑ *Printable Digital Worksheets*

C Critical Thinking Skills

- **WORKSHEET** **21st Century Skills Activity: Early Humans and the Agricultural Revolution: Hunter-Gatherers**—Students review the concept of trial-and-error problem solving, analyze scenarios where problem solving may or may not work, and write a description of how a particular problem might be solved.

THE AGRICULTURAL REVOLUTION

Students will know:

- *why some historians consider the Agricultural Revolution the most important event in human history.*
- *why people created permanent settlements when they began to farm.*
- *how tools and roles changed as a result of permanent communities.*

Students will be able to:

- ***analyze** photographs of shelters from the Neolithic Age.*
- ***connect** farming to their daily lives.*
- ***draw conclusions** about why the Agricultural Revolution was a revolution.*

UNDERSTANDING BY DESIGN®

☑ Print Teaching Options

V Visual Skills

- ☐ **P. 63** Students study a map about early farming. AL
- ☐ **P. 64** Student groups create Neolithic Age time lines. BL
- ☐ **P. 65** Students analyze and discuss an image of the excavation of Çatalhüyük.
- ☐ **P. 68** Students analyze and answer questions about a map of the four great river valley civilizations. BL
- ☐ **P. 69** Students diagram social class structure in early civilizations. **Visual/Spatial**

R Reading Skills

- ☐ **P. 62** Students use the root *-lithic* to determine the meaning of Paleolithic and Neolithic. AL
- ☐ **P. 64** Students define *economy* and discuss systematic agriculture. AL ELL
- ☐ **P. 65** Students list the characteristics of a perfect place to build a Neolithic village. AL

W Writing Skills

- ☐ **P. 66** Students write a journal entry about life in Çatalhüyük. **Verbal/Linguistic**
- ☐ **P. 69** Students work in groups to write a paragraph about a specific characteristic of early civilizations. **Verbal/Linguistic**

C Critical Thinking Skills

- ☐ **P. 62** Students evaluate the uses and usefulness of domestic animals. AL ELL
- ☐ **P. 63** Students work in pairs to create concept webs on the effects of agriculture on civilization and then create menus of food grown in early civilizations. AL
- ☐ **P. 66** Students draw conclusions about the benefits and drawbacks of living in settled communities. AL
- ☐ **P. 67** Students discuss and compare the roles of men and women in the Neolithic settlements. BL **Verbal/Linguistic**

T Technology Skills

- ☐ **P. 67** Students use the Internet to research Bronze Age pottery and create a presentation for the class. AL

☑ Online Teaching Options

V Visual Skills

- VIDEO **The Ice Man**—Students view the first part of a video that describes the importance of the Ice Man and the technology he carried.
- MAP **Early Civilizations, 3000 B.C.**—Students get an overview of the location of the earliest civilizations.
- CHART **Neolithic Artifacts**—Students click on images to learn more about Neolithic artifacts.

R Reading Skills

- BIOGRAPHY **Ötzi the Iceman**—Students read more about the discovery of this Neolithic man.
- IMAGE **Neolithic Farming Communities**—Students click on the image to explore life in a Neolithic farming community.
- GRAPHIC ORGANIZER **Taking Notes: *Identifying:* Neolithic Advancements**—Students identify three advancements made during the Neolithic Age.

C Critical Thinking Skills

- MAP **Early Farming**—Students explore the map to identify crops grown in different areas of the world.
- SLIDE SHOW **Çatalhüyük**—Students explore this ancient village to learn more about it and the people who lived there.

T Technology Skills

- SELF-CHECK QUIZ **Lesson 2**—Students receive instant feedback about their mastery of lesson content.

INTERVENTION AND REMEDIATION STRATEGIES

LESSON 1 Hunter-Gatherers

Reading and Comprehension

Have students make an outline of the lesson, using the larger red headings as the first level and the smaller red headings as the second level of the outline. Explain that they should add third and fourth levels to their outlines by finding details in the lesson to support each of the headings.

Text Evidence

Have students use the Internet to research cave paintings created by Paleolithic artists. Have them write a description of one of the paintings they find. Ask them to include their thoughts on why early artists created the images in that painting.

LESSON 2 The Agricultural Revolution

Reading and Comprehension

To ensure comprehension of the lesson as they read, have students write one central idea for each subsection under a smaller red heading. Tell students they should remember to consider both the text and the illustrations of a subsection before writing the central idea.

Text Evidence

Remind students that historians call the growth of systematic farming during the Neolithic Age the Agricultural Revolution. Ask each student to defend the use of the word *revolution* in this context by making a list of evidence in the lesson that supports the idea that a revolution occurred during the Neolithic Age.

Online Resources

Approaching Level Reader

Use this online lower-level text that corresponds directly to the text in the Student Edition. It includes a Spanish version.

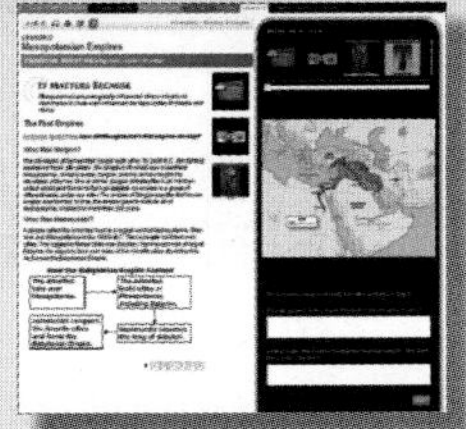

Guided Reading Activities

This resource uses graphic organizers and guiding questions to help students with comprehension.

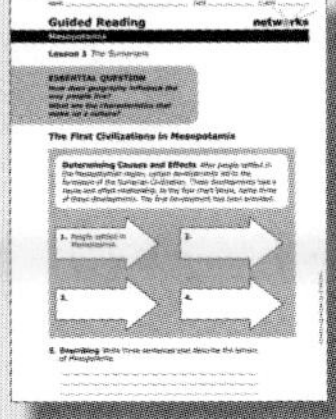

What Do You Know?

Use these worksheets to pre-assess student's background knowledge before they study the chapter.

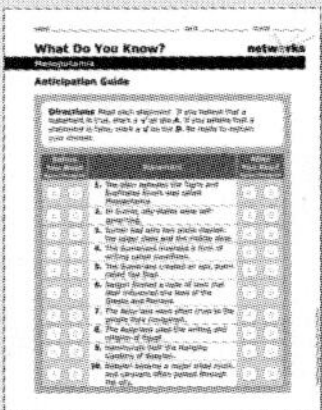

Reading Essentials and Study Guide Workbook

This resource offers writing and reading activities for the approaching-level student. Also available in Spanish.

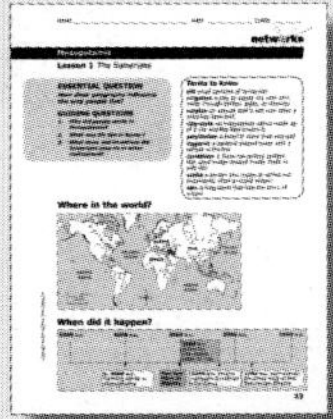

Self-Check Quizzes

This online assessment tool provides instant feedback for students to check their progress.

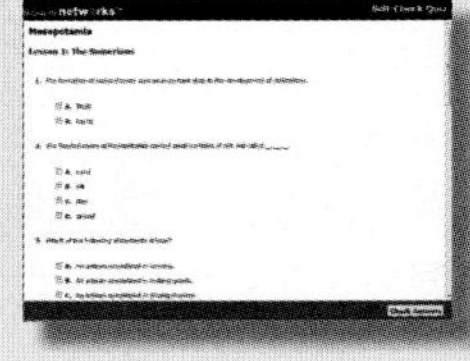

How Do I Apply
Understanding By Design®?

All materials developed for this program incorporate Understanding By Design® (UBD™) as a planning framework to guide content development, assessment, and instruction. Often referred to as "backward design," the goal of Understanding By Design is to plan with the end in mind. This ensures more clearly defined goals, more appropriate assessments, more tightly aligned lessons, and more purposeful teaching. Consider these three stages as you integrate UBD into your planning.

Stage 1 Identify Desired Results

- What should students know, understand, and be able to do?
- Identify the "big ideas" that you want students to understand and then craft companion "essential questions." Big ideas are transferable concepts, principles, and processes that are key to understanding the topic or subject. Essential questions present open-ended, thought-provoking inquiries that are explored over time.
- Consider the appropriate teaching goals, examine relevant content standards, and make choices on what content to emphasize during teaching.

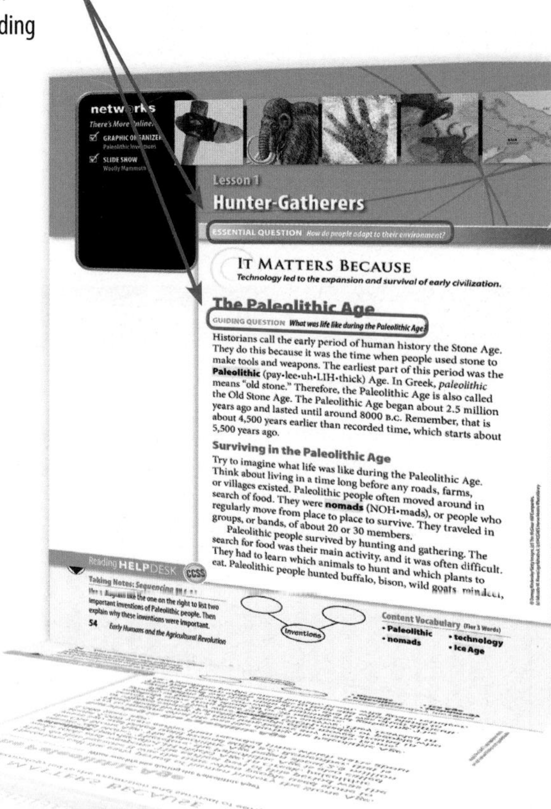
networks
There's More Online!
GRAPHIC ORGANIZER Paleolithic Inventions
SLIDE SHOW Woolly Mammoth

Lesson 1
Hunter-Gatherers

ESSENTIAL QUESTION *How do people adapt to their environment?*

IT MATTERS BECAUSE
Technology led to the expansion and survival of early civilization.

The Paleolithic Age
GUIDING QUESTION *What was life like during the Paleolithic Age?*

Historians call the early period of human history the Stone Age. They do this because it was the time when people used stone to make tools and weapons. The earliest part of this period was the **Paleolithic** (pay•lee•uh•LIH•thick) Age. In Greek, *paleolithic* means "old stone." Therefore, the Paleolithic Age is also called the Old Stone Age. The Paleolithic Age began about 2.5 million years ago and lasted until around 8000 B.C. Remember, that is about 4,500 years earlier than recorded time, which starts about 5,500 years ago.

Surviving in the Paleolithic Age
Try to imagine what life was like during the Paleolithic Age. Think about living in a time long before any roads, farms, or villages existed. Paleolithic people often moved around in search of food. They were **nomads** (NOH•mads), or people who regularly move from place to place to survive. They traveled in groups, or bands, of about 20 or 30 members.

Paleolithic people survived by hunting and gathering. The search for food was their main activity, and it was often difficult. They had to learn which animals to hunt and which plants to eat. Paleolithic people hunted buffalo, bison, wild goats, reindeer,

Reading HELPDESK CCSS
Taking Notes: Sequencing
Use a diagram like the one on the right to list two important inventions of Paleolithic people. Then explain why these inventions were important.
Inventions
Content Vocabulary
• Paleolithic
• nomads
• technology
• Ice Age
54 Early Humans and the Agricultural Revolution

Stage 2 Determine Acceptable Evidence

- How will you know if students have achieved the desired results? What will you accept as evidence of student understanding and proficiency? How will you evaluate student performance?
- Identify in advance the evidence that will verify that expected levels of learning and content mastery have been achieved.
- There are two types of UBD assessment: Performance Tasks and Other Evidence. "Performance Tasks" require students to apply their learning to an authentic situation to assess their understanding. "Other Evidence" includes traditional assessment materials, such as quizzes, tests, observations, and daily work. Examples of "Assessment Evidence" can be found in the Chapter Planners of your print and online Teacher Editions.

Stage 3 Plan Learning Experiences and Instruction

- What knowledge and skills will students need to perform effectively and achieve desired results? What activities, sequence, and resources are best suited to accomplish these goals?
- The McGraw-Hill Networks Learning System offers a variety of print and digital teaching materials to help your students acquire important knowledge and skills, understand important ideas and processes, and transfer their learning in meaningful ways. Choose from any of these teaching resources with the confidence that you will create a learning plan that meets your students' needs and matches your teaching goals.

Early Humans and the Agricultural Revolution

8000 B.C. to 2000 B.C.

ESSENTIAL QUESTION • *How do people adapt to their environment?*

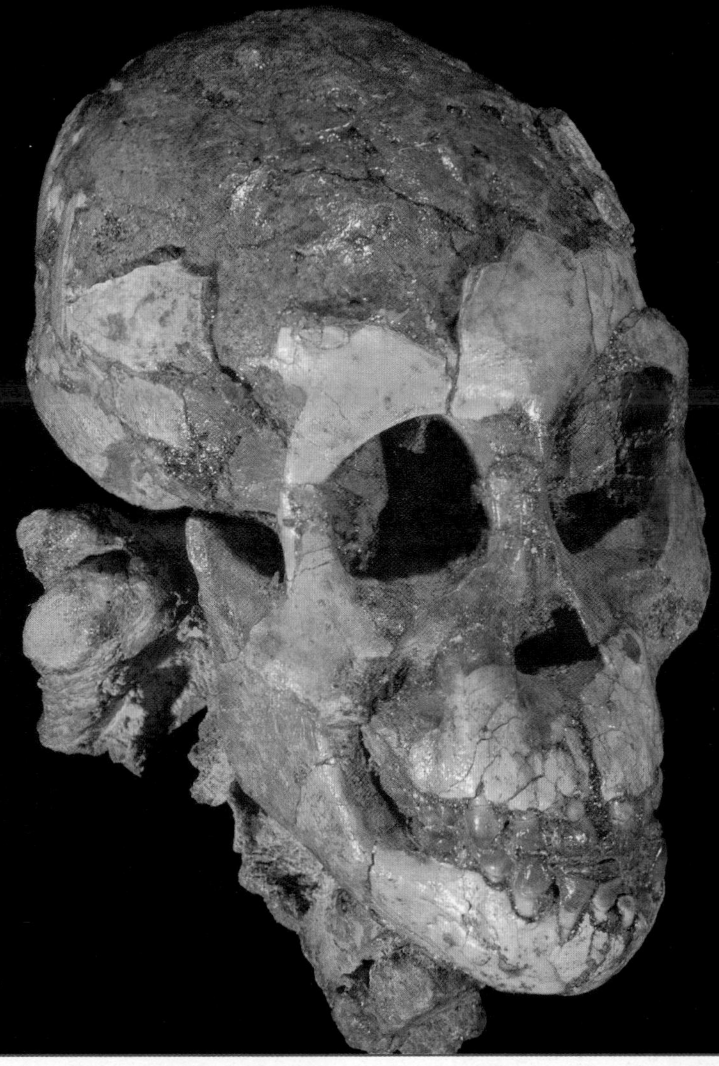

networks

There's More Online about the lives and customs of early humans.

CHAPTER 3

Lesson 1
Hunter-Gatherers

Lesson 2
The Agricultural Revolution

The Story Matters . . .

Was eastern Africa the home of the earliest humans? Many scientists believe that is where the first group of human-like beings lived. Some early human skeletons found in Africa are over six million years old. Scientists estimate that this skull may be more than 3.2 million years old. It may have belonged to a three-year-old child who lived in eastern Africa. Fossils like this one tell us a lot about early humans.

Some early people may have begun moving from Africa to other regions about 1.8 million years ago. Over a period of time humans were found in Europe and as far away as China. Everywhere early humans went, they left behind clues about their lives. By studying these clues, scientists can tell us about our past.

◄ *Ancient human-like fossils tell us about our early ancestors.*

AFP/Getty Images

51

Letter from the Author

Dear World History Teacher,

Over a long period of time, Paleolithic people created sophisticated tools, used fire for lighting and cooking, and adapted to and changed their physical environment. Paleolithic people were nomads who hunted animals and gathered wild plants. The Agricultural Revolution of the Neolithic Age dramatically changed human patterns of living. Growing food and taming animals made it possible for humans to live in more permanent settlements. An increase in food production led to a significant growth in human population and the growth of cities.

Jackson J. Spielvogel

ENGAGE

Bellringer After students have carefully read "The Story Matters . . .," begin a discussion with them about why archaeologists are excited about fossil finds such as the skull shown here. **Ask:**

- What do archaeologists hope to learn by studying the bones and artifacts of prehistoric people?
- Is the information that archaeologists learn from these artifacts important to contemporary life?
- What clues do you think we will leave behind for archaeologists to find 3 million years from now?

Have students share their ideas. Tell students that the movement of early people out of Africa is one of the earliest examples we have of the migration, or movement, of a large group of people.

Begin a discussion with students about migration. **Ask:**

- Have you ever moved from one house to another?
- Why do individuals or families move?
- What causes a large number of people to leave one place and move to another?
- What might have caused early people to migrate out of Africa?
- How do you think these early migrations of people compare to the movement of people from one place to another that we see today?

Tell students that as they continue their study of history, they will learn about other times when large groups of people moved from one place to another.

Making Connections

Read the following information to students.

Most of ancient Mesopotamia, often called the cradle of civilization, is now contained within the modern country of Iraq.

The modern city of Baghdad is situated on the banks of the Tigris River. From there, the Euphrates River is just 25 miles to the west of the Tigris.

TEACH & ASSESS

Step Into the Place

V1 Visual Skills

Analyzing Maps Review the parts of the map with the students, including the title, compass rose, and scale. **Ask:** Which continent appears in the southwest portion of this map? *(Africa)* Which rivers are shown on this map? *(Nile, Jordon, Tigris, and Euphrates)* What is the region called in the river valley between the Tigris and Euphrates rivers? *(Mesopotamia)*

Remind students of information in "The Story Matters..." about human migration out of Africa. Ask students how people might have traveled from Africa to the region shown on the map. *(They probably walked over the thin strip of land that connects Africa to Asia.)* Have students find Jericho and Çatalhüyük on the map. Explain that these were both locations of settlements by early humans.

Have pairs use the map scale to calculate the approximate distances early humans had to walk from the Nile River to these locations:

- Jericho *(about 150 miles)*
- Çatalhüyük *(about 450 miles)*
- Mesopotamia *(about 300 miles)*

Ask volunteers to give the distances they determined. Then, as a class, discuss the Map Focus questions. **Logical/ Mathematical**

Content Background Knowledge

- The Nile River is the longest river in the world, with a length of about 4,132 miles.
- The name for the region that includes the Tigris and Euphrates river valleys—Mesopotamia—comes from a Greek word meaning "between rivers." The earliest settlements in Mesopotamia date from about 7000 B.C.
- Evidence of a thriving agriculture in Egypt dates back to about 8000 B.C.

ANSWERS, p. 52

Step Into the Place

1. They are near the Mediterranean Sea.
2. The land appears to be hilly.
3. Jericho is located near the Jordan River, which is northwest of the Nile River and southeast of the Tigris and Euphrates rivers.
4. **CRITICAL THINKING** Answers will vary but may include access to water for drinking, irrigation, and transportation.

Step Into the Time

Answers will vary but should demonstrate knowledge of early civilizations and the Agricultural Revolution.

CHAPTER 3 CCSS

Place and Time: Early Humans 8000 B.C. to 2000 B.C.

During the Paleolithic Age, people began to develop technology, or knowledge that is applied to help people. They created tools that helped them survive in different locations.

Step Into the Place

MAP FOCUS By about 8000 B.C., people in Southwest Asia began to stay in one place and grow crops. They also raised animals for food and clothing.

1. **LOCATION** Look at the map. Near what major body of water are Çatalhüyük and Jericho located? RH.6–8.7
2. **PLACE** Based on the map, what is the land around both settlements like? RH.6–8.7
3. **LOCATION** Describe Jericho's location in relation to the three major rivers on the map. RH.6–8.7
4. **CRITICAL THINKING** *Drawing Conclusions* Why do you think the earliest settlements developed along rivers? RH.6–8.1

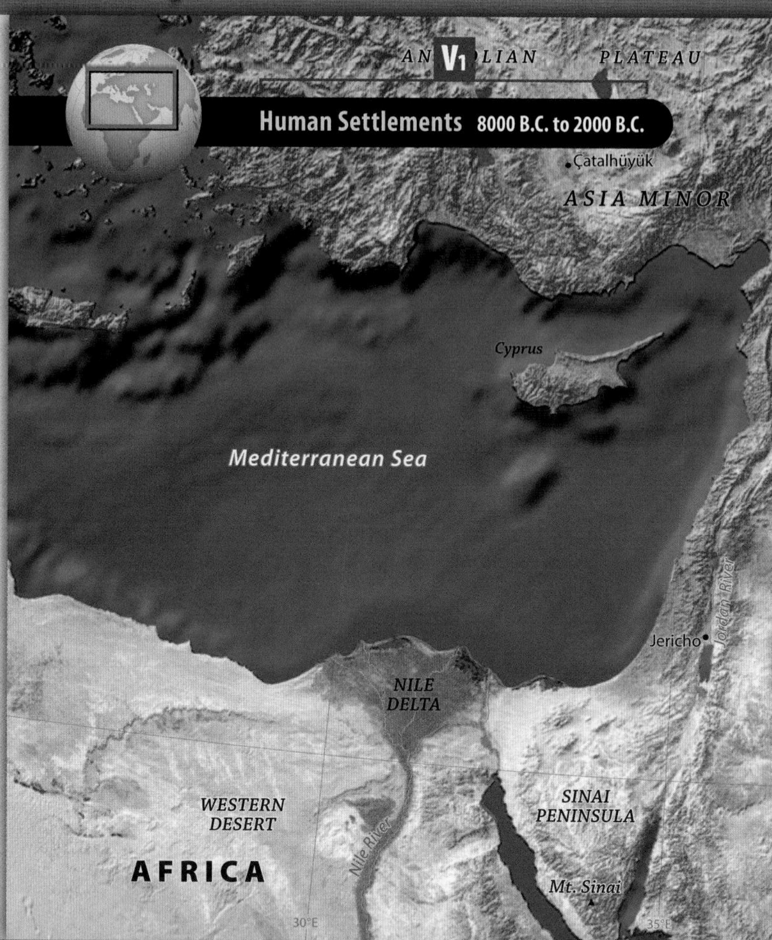

Step Into the Time

V2 **TIME LINE** Choose an event from the Early Settlements time line and write a paragraph predicting the general social or economic effects that event might have had on the world. RH.6–8.7

EARLY SETTLEMENTS
THE WORLD
2.5 MILLION B.C. — c. 2.5 million B.C. Paleolithic Age begins
100,000 B.C. — c. 100,000 B.C. Last Ice Age begins

Project-Based Learning

Hands-On Chapter Project

Early Humans and the Agricultural Revolution

Students will create a time capsule in order to identify and compare cultural adaptations to a geographic environment. Students will work in small groups to create a time capsule. They will participate in a class discussion about the cultural regions of the United States, then choose a region for their time capsule. After researching items to include in the time capsule, students will present their completed time capsules to the class and discuss and self-evaluate their work.

Technology Extension

Collaborative Time Capsules with Wikis

A wiki is a Web site where students can write, gather, and share information. Students will use a wiki to organize their regional time capsule from the Hands-On Chapter Project. Each group will set up a wiki page for each cultural element they investigate, such as buildings, food, transportation, government, and so on. Students can gather photos and other online elements on their wiki pages. Physical objects can be photographed or scanned.

networks *There's More Online!*

☑ **MAP** Explore the interactive version of this map on NETWORKS.

☑ **TIME LINE** Explore the interactive version of this time line on NETWORKS.

Caspian Sea

MESOPOTAMIA

Euphrates River

Tigris River

ASIA

SYRIAN DESERT

ARABIAN DESERT

Persian Gulf

N W E S

0 100 miles
0 100 km
Albers Equal-Area Conic projection

40°E 45°E 50°E

c. 8000 B.C. Farming begins in Southwest Asia

c. 6700 B.C. Çatalhüyük established

c. 6000 B.C. Farming begins in Nile Valley in Egypt and in China

c. 4000 B.C. Farming established in Europe

c. 3000 B.C. River valley civilizations emerge

8000 B.C. | 7000 B.C. | 6000 B.C. | 5000 B.C. | 4000 B.C. | 3000 B.C. | 2000 B.C. | 1000 B.C.

c. 8000 B.C. Neolithic Age begins

c. 8000 B.C. Last Ice Age ends

c. 4000 B.C. Neolithic Age ends

c. 3000–1200 B.C. Bronze Age begins

53

TIME LINE

Place and Time: Early Humans and the Agricultural Revolution, 8000 B.C. to 2000 B.C.

Reading a Time Line Display the time line on the whiteboard, and have student volunteers read each event as it is revealed. Discuss each event as a class, noting questions that students have. Tell students they will learn more about each of these events as they read the chapter.

See page 51B for other online activities.

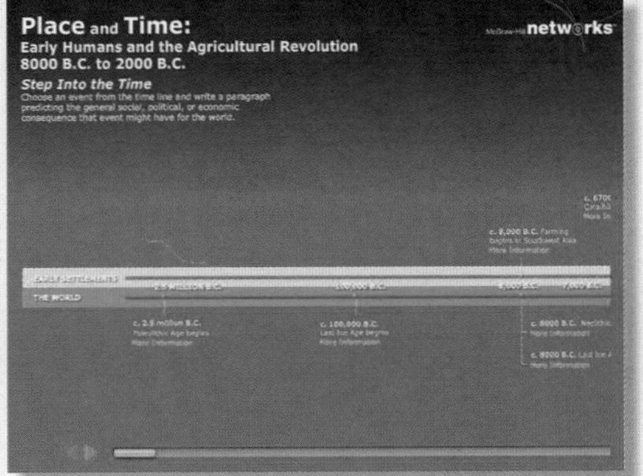

CHAPTER 3

Place and Time

Step Into the Time

V2 Visual Skills

Analyzing Time Lines Remind students that a time line sequences events that took place over a period of time. Have students read through the events included in the time line, reminding them to read both above and below the line. Then discuss the time line's major points as a class. **Ask:**

- **When does the time line begin and when does it end?** *(2,500,000 B.C., 1000 B.C.)*
- **What major development took place before the creation of settlements such as Jericho and Çatalhüyük?** *(farming)*
- **When does the Neolithic Age begin and when does it end?** *(8000 B.C., 4000 B.C.)*
- **What emerged in 3000 B.C.?** *(the river valley civilizations)*

Ask students if they have any questions about reading the time line or the information it presents. Write their questions on the board, and ask that students write these questions in their notebooks. As a class, answer as many as you can. Tell students that reading the chapter will answer many of their remaining questions.

Content Background Knowledge

- During the Paleolithic Age, fully modern human beings *(Homo sapiens)* first appeared about 150,000 years ago in Africa and Asia.
- The Paleolithic humans who lived in Europe beginning about 40,000 years ago were once often referred to as Cro-Magnons, after the location where the first fossil skeletons were discovered. The cave paintings in Lascaux, France, are sometimes called Cro-Magnon paintings.
- Some archaeologists consider Jericho to be the oldest known human settlement, dating to 8000 B.C. or earlier.
- Archaeologists have pinpointed when the domestication of common farm animals occurred during the Neolithic Age: goats in about 7000 B.C., sheep in about 6700 B.C., pigs in about 6500 B.C., and cattle in about 6000 B.C.
- Çatalhüyük is one of the largest Neolithic communities ever discovered. Evidence shows that its economy was likely based on the growing of crops, with some cattle-raising.

CLOSE & REFLECT

Have each student write a question based on the map, time line, or class discussion about the settlements of early humans. Then call on volunteers to read their questions, and have students answer as many as they can. Tell students that they will be learning more about early humans as they study the chapter.

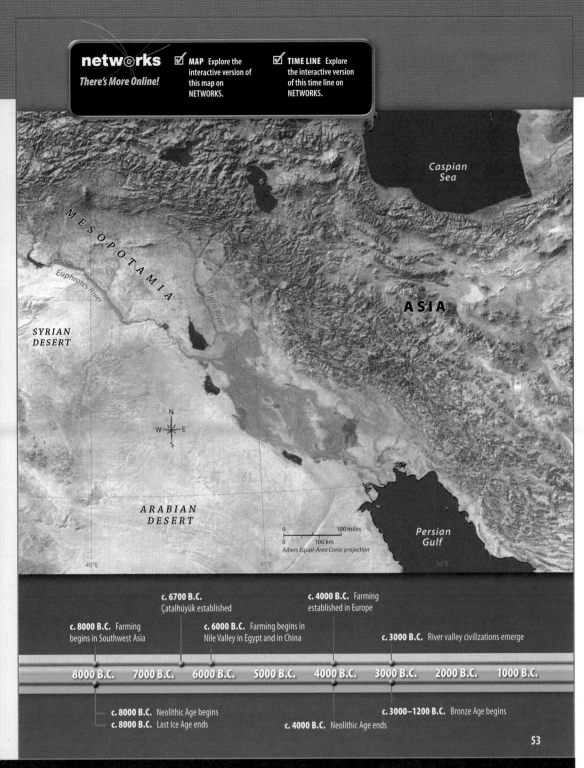

ENGAGE

Bellringer Show students a photo of an ax or a hatchet that might be used on a camping trip. Discuss how such a tool would be useful when going camping in the wilds of a national park or forest. **Ask:** **What other tools would you want to take with you when going camping?** *(Answers will vary. Students might mention a knife, a shovel, and a hammer.)* Point out that such tools would also have been useful for people in the Paleolithic Age, but there were no modern tools available. **Ask:** **If you had to make an ax, a knife, or a shovel—and you had no modern machinery to help you—how would you go about it?** *(Answers will vary. Students might suggest breaking apart stones to produce sharp edges and then strapping those sharp stones onto wooden handles.)* Tell students that in this lesson, they'll learn how Paleolithic people made tools.

TEACH & ASSESS

R1 Reading Skills

Calculating Have students read the text. Help them associate the current year with the time frame of the period they are now studying. **Ask:** **How many thousands of years ago was the year A.D. 1?** *(about 2,000 years ago)* AL Direct students' attention to the text, which says that the Paleolithic Age ended around 8000 B.C. **Ask:** **How many years ago was that?** *(10,000 years ago)* Explain that recorded time began when people started writing. **Ask:** **If recorded time started 5,500 years ago, about what year was it?** *(about 3500 B.C.)* **Logical/Mathematical**

R2 Reading Skills

Defining Have students skim the text. **Ask:** **What are nomads?** *(people who regularly move from place to place to survive)* Prompt students to recognize that the lives of nomadic peoples are very different from those of people who live in one place for most or all of their lives. As a class, discuss some basic characteristics of a nomadic lifestyle. **Ask:** **Why did Paleolithic people have to move regularly?** *(Answers will vary, but students might suggest that the people had to move to find food sources, including following herds of animals and moving with the seasons to find fruits and vegetables.)* AL ELL

ANSWER, p. 54

TAKING NOTES: Answers should include the use of fire, scraping tools, harpoons, spears, and the bow and arrow; all were important because they allowed the users of the tools to live and hunt more efficiently.

networks
There's More Online!
GRAPHIC ORGANIZER
Paleolithic Inventions
SLIDE SHOW
Woolly Mammoth
ASIA

Lesson 1
Hunter-Gatherers

ESSENTIAL QUESTION *How do people adapt to their environment?*

IT MATTERS BECAUSE
Technology led to the expansion and survival of early civilization.

The Paleolithic Age

GUIDING QUESTION *What was life like during the Paleolithic Age?*

Historians call the early period of human history the Stone Age. They do this because it was the time when people used stone to make tools and weapons. The earliest part of this period was the **Paleolithic** (pay•lee•uh•LIH•thick) Age. In Greek, *paleolithic* means "old stone." Therefore, the Paleolithic Age is also called R1 the Old Stone Age. The Paleolithic Age began about 2.5 million years ago and lasted until around 8000 B.C. Remember, that is about 4,500 years earlier than recorded time, which starts about 5,500 years ago.

Surviving in the Paleolithic Age

Try to imagine what life was like during the Paleolithic Age. Think about living in a time long before any roads, farms, or villages existed. Paleolithic people often moved around in R2 search of food. They were **nomads** (NOH•mads), or people who regularly move from place to place to survive. They traveled in groups, or bands, of about 20 or 30 members.

Paleolithic people survived by hunting and gathering. The search for food was their main activity, and it was often difficult. They had to learn which animals to hunt and which plants to eat. Paleolithic people hunted buffalo, bison, wild goats, reindeer,

Reading **HELP**DESK CCSS

Taking Notes: ***Sequencing*** RH.6–8.2
Use a diagram like the one on the right to list two important inventions of Paleolithic people. Then explain why these inventions were important.

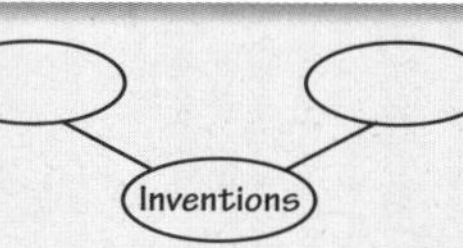

Content Vocabulary (Tier 3 Words)
- **Paleolithic**
- **nomads**
- **technology**
- **Ice Age**

networks Online Teaching Options

VIDEO

How We Know About the Ice Ages

Using Visual Tools Play the video titled How We Know About the Ice Ages. After watching the video, discuss what glaciers are made of and then, as a class, create a list of the components. *(ice and snow—with dirt, sand, and rock on the bottom)* **Ask:** **What evidence did John Muir find to support his idea that the Yosemite Valley was shaped by glaciers?** *(rock surfaces polished by the movement of ice; boulders in places they shouldn't be; granite scarred by moving ice; paths left by glaciers; and small glaciers among the higher peaks nearby)* **During the Ice Ages, how many times did the glaciers move down across what are now Canada and parts of the United States?** *(at least four times)*

See page 51C for other online activities.

and other animals, depending on where they lived. Along coastal areas, they fished. These early people also gathered wild nuts, berries, fruits, wild grains, and green plants.

Finding Food

Paleolithic men and women performed different tasks within the group. Men—not women—hunted large animals. They often had to search far from their camp. Men had to learn how animals behaved and how to hunt them. They had to develop tracking methods. At first, men used clubs or drove the animals off cliffs to kill them. Over time, however, Paleolithic people developed tools and weapons to help them hunt. The traps and spears they made increased their chances of killing their prey.

C

Women stayed close to the camp, which was often located near a stream or other body of water. They looked after the children and searched nearby woods and meadows for berries, nuts, and grains. Everyone worked to find food, because it was the key to the group's survival.

R

Paleolithic people traveled in bands to hunt and gather food. Bands lived together in the open, under overhangs such as the one pictured here, or in caves.

▶ CRITICAL THINKING

Analyzing Why did these people live together in groups?

Paleolithic relating to the earliest period of the Stone Age

nomads people who move from place to place as a group to find food for themselves

CHAPTER 3, Lesson 1
Hunter-Gatherers

R Reading Skills

Identifying Remind students that the title of Lesson 1 is Hunter-Gatherers. Have a volunteer read the text. Then, **ask:**

- **Why are the Paleolithic people called "Hunter-Gatherers"?** *(Paleolithic people survived by hunting and gathering.)* ELL
- **What did they hunt?** *(buffalo, bison, wild goats, reindeer, and other animals)*
- **What did they gather?** *(fruits, wild grains, and green plants)*
- **Did everybody hunt and gather equally?** *(No. Men hunted and women gathered.)*
- **Why do you think there was a division in the tasks that men and women did?** *(Answers will vary. Students may suggest that men are generally larger and stronger than women, so they would be better at attacking and killing large animals. The women had small children to take care of and, as a result, had to stay close to the camp.)*

C Critical Thinking Skills

Reasoning Discuss with students how Paleolithic people met their basic human needs. **Ask: What are the basic needs that people have to meet in order to survive?** *(Answers will vary, although students should mention food, water, and shelter.)* **How did Paleolithic people meet these basic needs?** *(They hunted for and gathered food, camped by a stream or other body of water, and lived together under rock overhangs or in caves.)*

WHITEBOARD ACTIVITY

Paleolithic Nomads

Categorizing Ask students to examine the scene of the Paleolithic nomads and imagine what these people's lives were like. Then have students categorize each item in the Object Bank as objects that belong or do not belong in the scene by clicking on and dragging the names of the objects into the correct columns. After all objects are categorized, discuss with students how Paleolithic people could have accomplished necessary tasks without the objects that do not belong in the scene. **Logical/Mathematical**

See page 51C for other online activities.

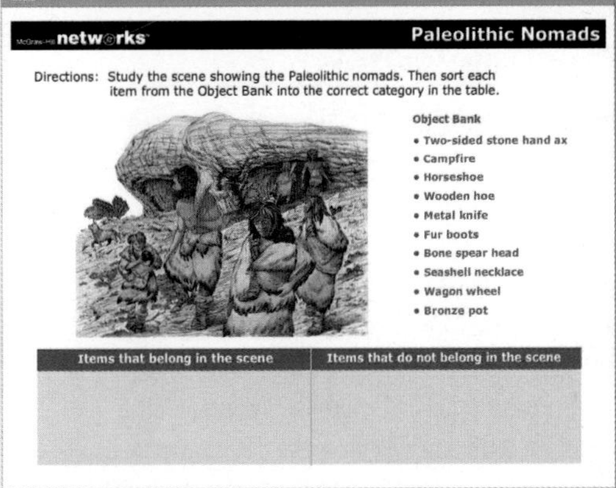

ANSWER, p. 55

CRITICAL THINKING A group of people can gather more food and provide safety for one another better than individuals living alone can.

Hunter-Gatherers

W Writing Skills

Argument Briefly discuss with students that some Paleolithic men and women may have hunted in monogamous pairs. **Ask:** What is a monogamous pair? *(a man and woman who are in an exclusive relationship together)* ELL

Then have each student write a paragraph which argues either that people in the Paleolithic Age would have benefited from pairing off or that they would have been better off working as a group, without men and women in monogamous pairs. Call on volunteers to read their paragraph to the class. Discuss the reasons cited for each position. BL

R Reading Skills

Describing From the text, discuss with students the definition of the word *technology*. *(tools and methods to perform tasks)* **Ask:** What first comes to mind when a friend tells you she has bought some new technology? *(Answers will vary, but most students will mention a device that depends on computer technology, such as a smart phone.)*

Explain that *technology* actually includes both very complicated devices and the simplest tools, such as a knife or a hammer. Emphasize that *technology* also includes methods, not just things. **Ask:** What are some examples of technology that the Paleolithic people used? *(Answers will vary but should include some of the following: flint, hand axes, spears, bows, arrows, harpoons, needles)* ELL

V Visual Skills

Analyzing Images Direct students to the image of the Paleolithic tool. Ask: What two main materials do you think a Paleolithic person used in making this ax? *(wood for the handle and stone for the blade)* What do you think the material is that holds the blade in place on the handle? *(Answers will vary. The ropelike material was probably made from flexible plant stems.)*

ANSWER, p. 56
CRITICAL THINKING Answers will vary. Possible uses include as a weapon, as a tool to chop down a tree, and as a digging tool.

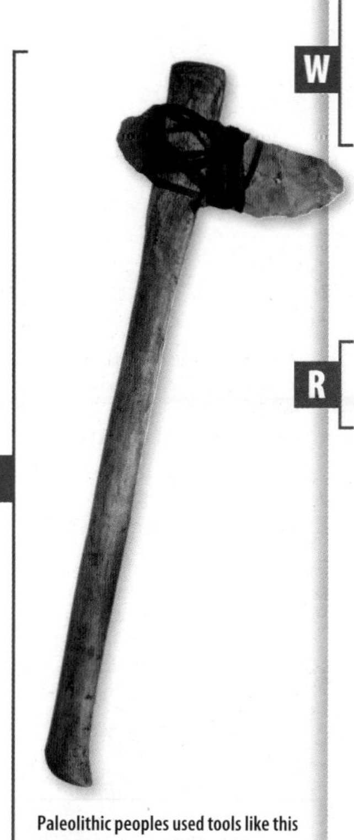

Paleolithic peoples used tools like this for many purposes. Look at this ax and decide what materials it was made of.

▶ CRITICAL THINKING

Predicting What do you think this tool was used for?

Some scientists believe that an equal relationship existed between Paleolithic men and women. It is likely that both made decisions that affected the band or group. Some evidence suggests that some men and women may have hunted in monogamous pairs. This means that a man and a woman worked together to find food for themselves and their children. Such groupings became the first families.

The Invention of Tools

Culture is the way of life for a group of people who share similar beliefs and customs. The **methods** Paleolithic people used to hunt and gather their food were part of their culture, as were the tools they used.

Technology (tehk•NAHL•uh•jee)—tools and methods to perform tasks—was first used by Paleolithic people. Before this time, sticks, stones, and tree branches served as tools. Later, people made devices from a hard stone called flint. Have you ever imagined how difficult it would be to prepare or eat food without a cutting tool? Paleolithic people learned that by hitting flint with another hard stone, the flint would flake into pieces. These pieces had very sharp edges that could be used for cutting. Hand axes, for example, were large pieces of flint tied to wooden poles. Flint technology was a major breakthrough for early peoples.

Over time, early people made better, more complex tools. Spears and bows and arrows made killing large animals easier. Harpoons, or spears with sharp points, and fishhooks increased the number of fish caught. Early humans used sharp-edged tools to cut up plants and dig roots. They used scraping tools to clean animal hides, which they used for clothing and shelter.

By the end of the Paleolithic Age, people were making smaller and sharper tools. They crafted needles from animal bones to make nets and baskets and to sew hides together for clothing. This technology had a far-reaching effect. It drove the development of more advanced farming tools and influenced where people settled.

Changing to Survive

Climate affected how Paleolithic people lived. Some early people lived in cold climates and made clothing from animal skins to stay warm. They sought protection in **available** natural shelters, such as caves and rock overhangs. Remember, there

Reading HELPDESK (CCSS)

technology an ability gained by the practical use of knowledge

Academic Vocabulary (Tier 2 Words)

method a way of doing something
available ready to be used
construct to build by putting parts together

networks Online Teaching Options

CHART

Paleolithic Tools

Analyzing Visuals Have students look closely at the images of each of the Paleolithic tools listed in the left-hand column of the chart. For each tool, call on volunteers to describe how Paleolithic people might have used it to accomplish a necessary task. After speculating about the use of a tool, students can click on the image of that tool to access a description of its purpose. Clicking on the image a second time will place the description in the right-hand column, and students can move on to the next tool.

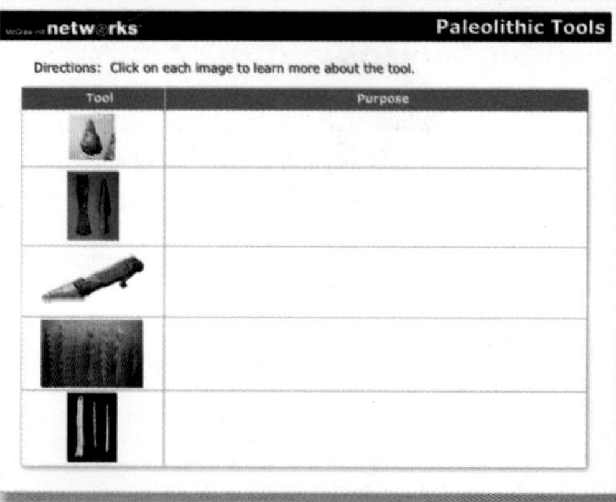

See page 51C for other online activities.

were no houses or apartment buildings as we know them in the Paleolithic Age. Gradually, humans learned to make their own shelters. People **constructed** tents and huts of animal skins, brush, and wood. In very cold climates, some people made shelters from ice and snow. In regions where wood was scarce, Paleolithic people used the large bones from dead woolly mammoths, or hairy elephant-like animals, to build frames for shelters. They then covered the bones with animal hides. C

People living in warmer climates, on the other hand, needed little clothing or shelter. For the purposes of safety and comfort, however, many lived in caves and huts. These shelters provided protection against attacks by large animals.

Fire Sparks Changes

Life became less difficult for Paleolithic people once they discovered how to make fire. People learned that fire provided warmth in cold caves. It provided light when it was dark and could be used to scare away wild animals. Armed with spears, hunters could also use fire to chase animals from bushes to be killed. Eventually, people gathered around fires to share stories and to cook. Cooked food, they discovered, tasted better and was easier to chew and digest. In addition, meat that was smoked by fire did not have to be eaten right away and could be stored.

How did people learn to use fire? Archaeologists believe early humans produced fire by friction. They learned that by rubbing two pieces of wood together, the wood became heated and charred. When the wood became hot enough, it caught fire. Paleolithic people continued rubbing wood together, eventually developing drill-like wooden tools to start fires. They also discovered that a certain stone, iron pyrite, gave off sparks when struck against another rock. The sparks could then ignite dry grass or leaves—another way to start a fire.

Visual Vocabulary

woolly mammoth a large, hairy, extinct animal related to modern-day elephants

C Critical Thinking Skills

Comparing and Contrasting Discuss the differences and similarities of the shelters Paleolithic people lived in and the homes people live in today. **Ask:**

- **What are some things Paleolithic people used to make their shelters?** *(animal skins, wood, ice, large bones, animal skins)*
- **What materials do builders use in making frames and coverings for modern houses and apartment buildings?** *(wood, steel, aluminum, bricks)*
- **How did the climate of a region affect the types of shelters Paleolithic people built?** *(People used available resources to help protect them from animal attacks and from the weather.)* AL

Content Background Knowledge

Ice Age Architecture Found in Ukraine

In 1965 a farmer was digging in the ground to expand his cellar in Mezhirich, Ukraine, and struck a bone—a huge lower jawbone of a mammoth. After excavation, nearly 149 bones were discovered. The bones indicated that the site dated back to the Ice Age of 15,000 years ago. These huge, heavy bones were formed into four oval-shaped dwellings. The jaw bones were interlocked, forming a solid, circular base. Also, there were roof supports made of giant tusks. Scientists guess that animal hides covered the buildings. The site at Mezhirich is the oldest example of architecture in the world.

SLIDE SHOW

Paleolithic-Era Animals

Analyzing Visuals Present the slide show about Paleolithic animals. Begin a discussion with students about how the animals adapted to their environment. **Ask:** **In what kind of climate would this animal live? What kind of food do you think it ate? How would this animal protect itself? How would speed be important to an animal? Why do you think some slow animals were able to survive?** *(Responses will vary. Accept all answers that can be supported.)* Ask students to predict what kinds of adaptations early humans made to survive in harsh environments. AL **Visual/Spatial**

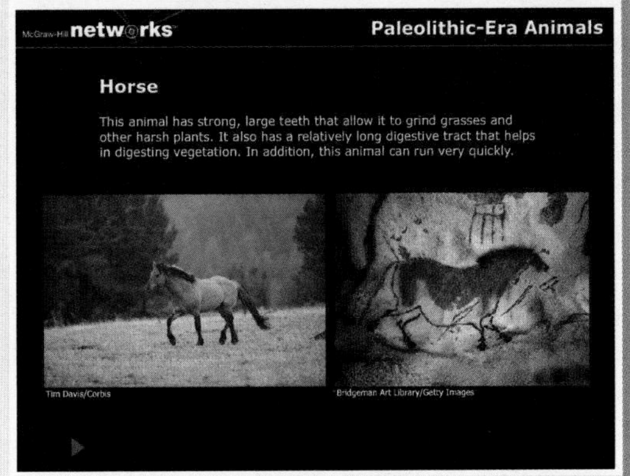

networks
Paleolithic-Era Animals
Horse
This animal has strong, large teeth that allow it to grind grasses and other harsh plants. It also has a relatively long digestive tract that helps in digesting vegetation. In addition, this animal can run very quickly.

See page 51C for other online activities.

R Reading Skills

Discussing Have a volunteer read the text. Then, as a class, discuss the different ways people communicate. **Ask:** What does the word communication mean? *(an act of transmitting, or a verbal or written message)* ELL Call on volunteers to describe ways that people have of communicating with one another. *(verbal and written language, gestures, body position, facial expression)* Point out that many animals communicate with one another about dangers, food sources, and courtship. Discuss reasons that the development of language would have benefited Paleolithic people.

W Writing Skills

Narrative Explain that the Paleolithic people developed a language for a reason—people needed language to communicate about important events in their lives. Divide the class into small groups, and ask each group to write a role-play of an incident that could have occurred during the Paleolithic Age that spurred on the development of language, including the creation of new words. Allow these role-plays to be humorous as long as the basic premise is a reasonable explanation of why language developed during the Paleolithic Age. Invite groups to perform their role-plays. After each performance, discuss how the incident presented could have been the impetus for the development of language. Kinesthetic

ANSWER, p. 58

CRITICAL THINKING Human handprints and the animals that people hunted were common subjects.

Paleolithic art has been found in caves in Argentina. Early people left a message that remains today.

▶ CRITICAL THINKING
Identifying What subjects were most common in cave paintings?

Eduardo M. Rivero/age fotostock

Language and Art

R Other advancements took place during the Paleolithic Age. One important advancement was the development of spoken language. Up until this time, early people **communicated** through sounds and physical gestures. Then they began to develop language.

W Ancient peoples started to express themselves in words for the same reasons we do. We use language to communicate information and emotions. Language makes it easier for us to work together and to pass on knowledge. We also use words to express our thoughts and feelings. The spoken language of early people was **constantly** growing and changing. New technology and more complicated experiences, for example, required new words.

Early people also expressed themselves through art. Some of this art can still be seen today, even though it is thousands of years old. For example, in 1879 a young girl named Maria de Sautuola wandered into a cave on her grandfather's farm near Altamira, Spain. She was startled by what she discovered on the walls of that cave:

PRIMARY SOURCE

> "Maria entered the cave . . . and suddenly reappeared all excited, shouting 'Papa, mira, toros pintados! [Papa, look, painted bulls!]' Maria had discovered one of the most famous animal-art galleries in the world."
>
> —from *Hands: Prehistoric Visiting Cards?* by August Gansser

Reading **HELP**DESK (CCSS)

Academic Vocabulary (Tier 2 Words)

communicate to share information with someone

constant always happening

networks *Online Teaching Options*

IMAGE

Cueva de las Manos, Río Pinturas

Interpreting Explain to students that Patagonia is a region in the southern part of Argentina. Then have students look at the image of a cave painting found in Patagonia. **Ask:** Why do you think Paleolithic people painted this image on a cave wall? *(Accept any reasonable answer that reflects an understanding of the lives of Paleolithic people, including references to available resources and important events in their daily lives.)* After thinking about the painting's purpose, students can click below the image to access more information about the painting.

networks
Cueva de las Manos, Río Pinturas
Eduardo M. Rivero/Age Fotostock
This striking painting of early human hands was discovered in Patagonia, Argentina. The Cueva de las Manos, Río Pinturas, is known as "The Cave of the Hands." Early humans likely traced and made impressions of their own hands after dipping them in different colored pigments. The artwork was probably created around 9500 years ago. The site also features illustrations of animals. It has been declared a UNESCO World Heritage Site. Tourists can visit the site to admire the pre-historic artwork.

See page 51C for other online activities.

About ten thousand years before Maria's visit, Paleolithic artists had painted mysterious signs, including what looked like a herd of animals—horses, boars, bison, and deer—on the cave's ceiling. In 1940, a cave with similar paintings to those in Spain was discovered near Lascaux (lah•SKOH) in southern France. **R**

Paleolithic cave paintings have been found all around the world. Early artists crushed yellow, black, and red rocks and combined them with animal fat to make their paints. They used twigs and their fingertips to apply these paints to the rock walls. They later used brushes made from animal hair. Early people created scenes of lions, oxen, panthers, and other animals. Few humans, however, appear in these paintings.

Historians are not sure why early artists chose to make cave paintings. Early people may have thought that painting an animal would bring hunters good luck. Some scholars believe, however, that the paintings may have been created to record the group's history. They may have been created simply to be enjoyed. **C**

✓ PROGRESS CHECK

Explaining Why was fire important for Paleolithic people?

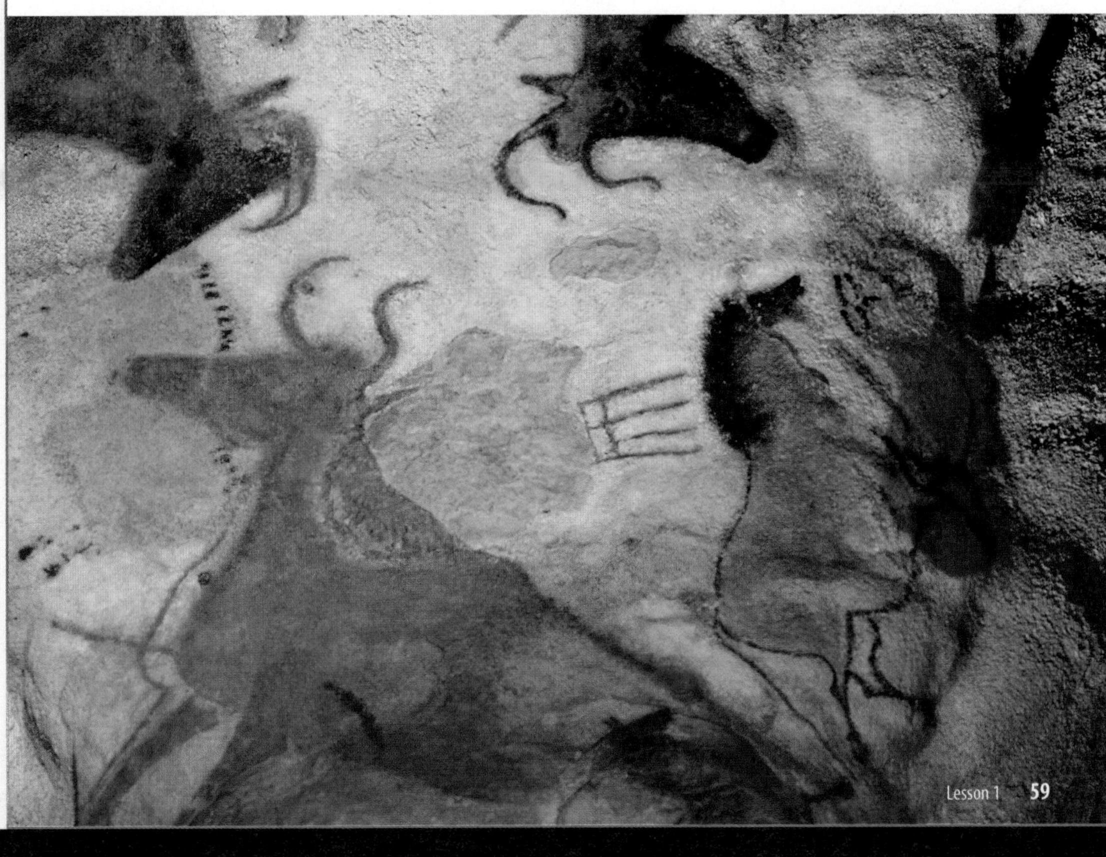

HUGHES Herve/Hemis/Photolibrary

The paintings in the Lascaux caves are the most famous examples of Paleolithic art. Scientists now believe that such paintings took thousands of years, and hundreds of generations, to produce. **T**

▶ **CRITICAL THINKING**

Speculating Why do you think these paintings lasted so long?

R Reading Skills

Locating After students have read the text, have them find Lascaux, France, on an atlas or an online map. **Ask:** **What are large bodies of water near Lascaux?** *(the Atlantic Ocean and the Mediterranean Sea)* Have students recall where the people came from at the beginning of the Paleolithic Age. *(Africa)* **When did people first leave Africa?** *(about 1.8 million years ago)* **About when were the paintings in the Lascaux caves painted?** *(about ten thousand years ago, or in about 8000 B.C.)* Point out that these cave paintings were created near the end of the Paleolithic Age.

C Critical Thinking Skills

Speculating Invite students to express an opinion about the reasons Paleolithic people created cave paintings. **Ask:** **Why did early people create scenes of lions, oxen, panthers, and other animals?** *(Answers will vary. Some students might suggest that such animals were central to early people's lives. They hunted oxen and similar animals; humans were hunted by lions, panthers, and other predators.)* **Why do you think few humans are shown in cave paintings?** *(Answers will vary. Students might suggest that such images would have been feared as some kind of magic. There may have been religious reasons for not painting human images.)*

T Technology Skills

Researching on the Internet Ask a small group of interested students to do a quick search on the Internet for examples of art from the Paleolithic Age. Explain that they could use a search engine to search for images related to terms such as *Paleolithic* or *cave painting*. If possible, display the images they find through a projector for the rest of the class to see. (An alternative is to print out some of the images.) Discuss each image with the whole class, emphasizing what each image tells us about the Paleolithic people. Make sure the students who found the images can cite the location and approximate time for each image. BL

IMAGE

Cave Paintings

Explaining Have students study the cave painting and identify images they recognize. *(a horse, boar, bison, deer, and a forklike weapon)* Call on volunteers to respond to each question, then have students click on the buttons (left to right) to access answers to the first three questions. **Ask:** **1. About when do you think people painted these images? 2. How do you think Paleolithic people made the paints? 3. How do you think Paleolithic people applied paint to cave walls? 4. What does this image tell us about the lives of the Paleolithic people?**

See page 51C for other online activities.

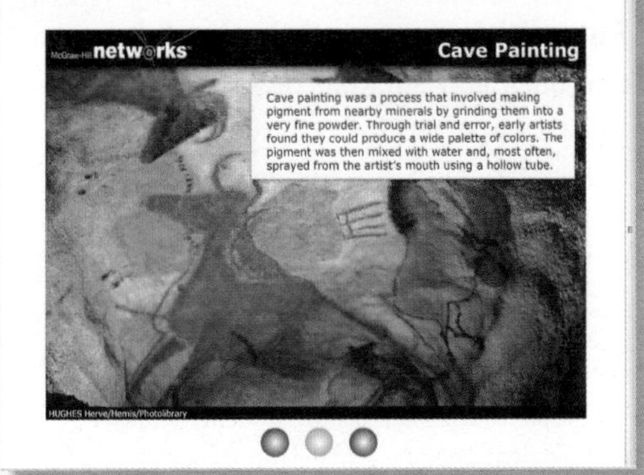

ANSWERS, p. 59

CRITICAL THINKING They lasted so long because they were located in and protected by caves.

✓ PROGRESS CHECK It offered protection, warmth, cooking, and a social element.

C Critical Thinking Skills

Making Inferences Point out that the students' text says that the water level of oceans was lowered as glaciers grew larger. **Ask:** **Why did the oceans' levels drop as glaciers grew larger?** *(The extreme cold caused more and more water on Earth to freeze, creating huge sheets of ice. As water froze, there was less liquid water in the oceans.)* BL

V Visual Skills

Reading a Map Review the parts of the map with students, including the title, the compass rose, the scale, and the key. **Ask:**

- **What does the purple region on the map represent?** *(the land bridge connecting Asia and North America)*
- **What bodies of water bordered the land bridge?** *(the Arctic Ocean and the Bering Sea)*
- **How far would early people have had to walk to travel from Asia to North America during the most recent Ice Age?** *(Answers will vary. Using the scale to measure the distance across the Bering Strait, students should determine that early people had to walk about 50 miles.)* **Visual/Spatial**

Content Background Knowledge

Ice Ages Ice ages have occurred naturally at various times in the last 3 million years. There is evidence that the fluctuations in the climate that have caused huge sheets of ice to form are the result of changes in Earth's orbit around the sun. A change in orbit can decrease the amount of solar radiation that reaches Earth, causing the climate to get colder. The next time that conditions will be right for another ice age to begin will be in about 30,000 years.

ANSWERS, p. 60

GEOGRAPHY CONNECTION

1. When the most recent Ice Age ended, sea levels rose and the land bridge disappeared underwater.
2. **CRITICAL THINKING** Answers will vary but should include the idea that regions to the south would be warmer and more hospitable to humans than the area near the land bridge.

The Ice Ages

GUIDING QUESTION *How did people adapt to survive during the ice ages?*

Tools and fire were two important technological developments of Paleolithic people. Throughout history, people have used new technology to help them survive when the environment changes. The ice ages were major environmental disturbances. The changes they brought about threatened the very survival of humans.

What Changes Came With the Ice Ages?

The **ice ages** were long periods of extreme cold that affected all of Earth. The most recent Ice Age began about 100,000 years ago. Thick sheets of ice moved across large parts of Europe, Asia, and North America. As the ice sheets, or glaciers, grew larger, the water level of the oceans was lowered. The low sea

GEOGRAPHY CONNECTION

During the most recent Ice Age, a strip of land connected the continents of Asia and North America.

1. **REGIONS** How did the geography of this region change when the most recent Ice Age ended?
2. **CRITICAL THINKING** *Analyzing* After people arrived in North America, what is a likely reason they moved south rather than staying near the land bridge?

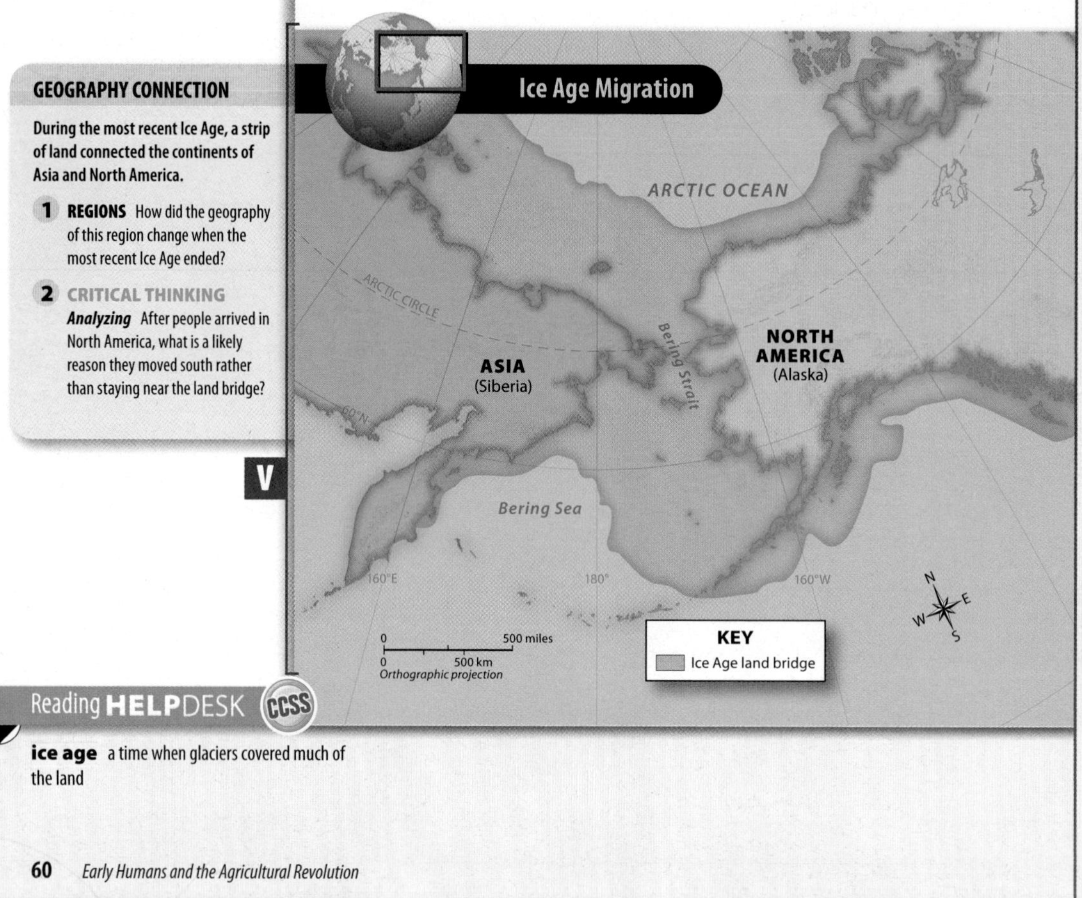

Reading HELPDESK (CCSS)

ice age a time when glaciers covered much of the land

networks Online Teaching Options

WHITEBOARD ACTIVITY

Paleolithic Time and the Ice Ages

Comparing and Contrasting Have students compare and contrast the Paleolithic Age with the Ice Ages. **Ask:**

- **How were the Ice Ages different from the Paleolithic Age?**
- **How were they the same?**

Then show Venn diagram for the Paleolithic and Ice Age on the whiteboard. Have students drag and drop words and phrases into the correct location on the diagram. **Logical/Mathematical**

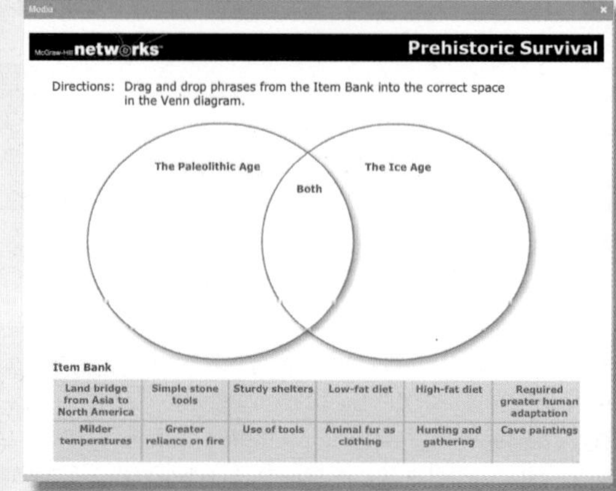

See page 51C for other online activities.

levels exposed a strip of dry land connecting the continents of Asia and North America. This strip of land was known as a land bridge. The land bridge acted as a natural highway that allowed people to travel from Asia into North America. From there, Paleolithic peoples moved southward to settle in different regions.

How Did the Ice Ages Affect Humans?

Ice age conditions posed a grave threat to human life. To survive in the cold temperatures, humans had to adapt, or change, many areas of their lives. One way they adapted their diets was by enriching meals with fat. To protect themselves from the harsh environment, they learned to build sturdier shelters. They also learned to make warm clothing using animal furs. Paleolithic people used fire to help them stay warm in this icy environment.

The last Ice Age lasted about 90,000 years, ending between about 9000 and 8000 B.C.

✓ PROGRESS CHECK

Explaining How were land bridges formed?

After early people controlled fire, they brought it into their shelters. At the site of some Stone Age huts, scientists have discovered an early form of a fireplace—a shallow hole lined with blackened stones.

LESSON 1 REVIEW (CCSS)

Review Vocabulary (Tier 3 Words)

1. What is another name for the *Paleolithic* Age? RH.6–8.4

Answer the Guiding Questions

2. ***Describing*** By what methods did Paleolithic people get food? RH.6–8.2
3. ***Summarizing*** How did fire help Paleolithic people survive? RH.6–8.2
4. ***Determining Cause and Effect*** How did the ice ages affect where people settled in the Americas? RH.6–8.1
5. ***Making Connections*** How does climate affect the type of house you live in or the clothes you wear? RH.6–8.1
6. **NARRATIVE** You are a mother or father who lives in the early Paleolithic Age. In a few paragraphs, describe your daily life. WHST.6–8.10

LESSON 1 REVIEW ANSWERS

1. The Paleolithic Age is also called the Old Stone Age. People used stones to make tools and weapons.
2. They got food by hunting, gathering, and fishing.
3. Fire provided warmth, helped scare away animals, and lit the darkness. It was also used for cooking.
4. The ice ages created a land bridge from Asia to the Americas. When the Ice Ages ended, people were able to migrate to different regions.
5. Answers will vary. Accept all reasonable answers.
6. Students' writings should be consistent with the lesson content. Students should mention hunting and gathering as well as the types of shelters in which Paleolithic people lived.

Hunter-Gatherers

R Reading Skills

Discussing Discuss with students the events of the last Ice Age. Have them use information from the text to answer the following questions. **Ask:** **Why would early people have crossed the land bridge from Asia to North America?** *(Answers will vary. Students might suggest that early people were nomadic, and so they probably crossed the land bridge in search of food and better living conditions.)* BL **Where did early people go when they moved southward from the land bridge?** *(into the rest of North America and down through Central America and South America)* **When did the last Ice Age end?** *(between about 9000 and 8000 B.C.)* Point out that the end of the last Ice Age is about the same as the end of the Paleolithic Age.

V Visual Skills

Analyzing Images Discuss with students how people were able to adapt to survive after the Ice Ages. Have them examine the image of the group of early people gathered around a fire. **Ask:** **Using the clues you can see in this picture, what technology had people developed since the early Paleolithic Age that helped them adapt to the colder conditions of the most recent Ice Age?** *(Answers will vary, but students should mention the ability to make fire, warmer clothing, and sturdier shelters.)* **Why do you think early people made a shallow hole lined with stones to hold a fire?** *(for safety reasons; so that the fire wouldn't spread to ignite the wood and other materials that composed the shelter)* Ask students how they think humans today might adjust if there were another drastic change in Earth's climate. **Visual/Spatial**

Have students complete the Lesson 1 Review.

CLOSE & REFLECT

Have each student write a summary of one section of this lesson. After all students finish, call on volunteers to read their summaries to the class. For each summary read, other students can suggest important information that should be added to the summary or corrections that should be made.

ANSWER, p. 61

✓ PROGRESS CHECK The ice lowered water levels in the oceans so the land that had been under water became visible.

ENGAGE

Bellringer Have each student write down his or her favorite lunch food. Begin a discussion about where the foods come from that make up their lunch. Prompt students with questions such as the following. **Ask:**

- Where does the bread come from for your sandwich?
- Where is the wheat from?
- How do we get wheat?

Continue with other questions of this sort. Lead students to understand that their food is the result of agriculture. AL ELL Then, **ask:** How did people obtain food before agriculture? *(They hunted, fished, and gathered wild food.)* Ask students to speculate on how agriculture might change people's lives. Write students' ideas on the board. Discuss which ideas are correct, which ideas might need to be changed, and which ideas they would like to add to the list. BL

TEACH & ASSESS

C Critical Thinking Skills

Classifying Make sure students understand what it means to domesticate animals. **Ask:** What domesticated animals do you have in your life at home? *(Answers will vary, but students should mention dogs, cats, and various other pets.)* What animals around you are not domesticated? *(all wild animals, including birds, rabbits, and squirrels)* What domesticated animals do you or your friends use for food? *(Answers will vary but should include cattle, milk cows, chickens, and sheep.)* Explain that these same kinds of animals were domesticated by early people, but the types of animals that were domesticated varied from region to region around the world. AL ELL

R Reading Skills

Defining Using the text, point out that the words *Paleolithic* and *Neolithic* both have the same root, *-lithic,* which means "stone." **Ask:** If pale- means "old," then what does neo- mean? *(new)* Why is that name somewhat misleading? *(The real change from the Paleolithic to the Neolithic Age was a shift to systematic agriculture.)* Discuss the meaning of systematic agriculture. **Ask:** Does systematic agriculture, which began in the Neolithic Age, continue today? *(Yes. Almost all agriculture around the world focuses on growing food on a regular basis.)* AL

ANSWER, p. 62

TAKING NOTES: Answers include systematic agriculture, domesticated animals, and settled communities.

networks *There's More Online!*

- **BIOGRAPHY** Ötzi the Iceman (c. 3300 B.C.)
- **GRAPHIC ORGANIZER** • Neolithic Advancements • Ancient Religions
- **MAP** • Early Farming • Early Civilizations 3000 B.C.
- **SLIDE SHOW** Çatalhüyük

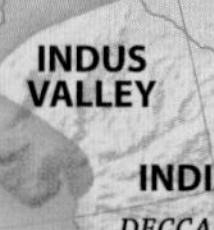

Lesson 2
The Agricultural Revolution

ESSENTIAL QUESTION *How do people adapt to their environment?*

IT MATTERS BECAUSE
The Agricultural Revolution allowed people to set up permanent settlements.

Neolithic Times

GUIDING QUESTION *How did farming change people's lives?*

The earliest people were nomads who moved from place to place to hunt animals and gather plants. After the last Ice Age ended, Earth's temperatures rose. As the climate warmed, many nomads moved into areas with a mild climate and fertile land.

Another historical revolution then occurred. For the first time, people began staying in one place to grow grains and vegetables. Gradually, farming replaced hunting and gathering as the main source of food. At the same time, people began to **domesticate** (duh•MEHS•tih•kayt), or tame, animals for human use. Animals transported goods and provided meat, milk, and wool.

The Neolithic Age

This change in the way people lived marked the beginning of the **Neolithic Age** (nee•uh•LIH•thick). It began about 8000 B.C. and lasted until around 4000 B.C.—about 4,000 years. The word *neolithic* is Greek for "new stone." Calling this time period the New Stone Age, however, is somewhat misleading. Although new stone tools were made, the real change in the Neolithic Age was the shift from hunting and gathering to **systematic agriculture**. This is growing food on a regular basis.

Reading **HELP**DESK CCSS

Taking Notes: ***Identifying***
Use a diagram like this to identify three advancements made during the Neolithic Age. RH.6–8.2

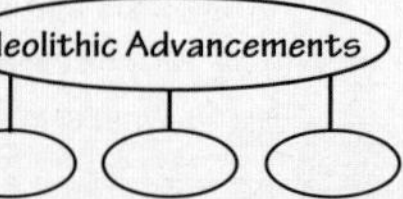

Content Vocabulary (Tier 3 Words)
- **domesticate**
- **Neolithic Age**
- **systematic agriculture**
- **shrine**
- **specialization**
- **Bronze Age**
- **monarchy**

networks ***Online Teaching Options***

VIDEO

The Ice Man

Comparing and Contrasting Play the first segment of the video about the Paleolithic man found frozen in the Austrian Alps. Ask students to write down what they learned from the video about the life and times of Ötzi the Iceman. Then have students work in small groups to make lists of similarities and differences between life in Otzi's time and life today. In a whole-class discussion, call on a member of each group to compare and contrast Paleolithic culture with modern culture.

See page 51D for other online activities.

This shift from hunting and gathering to food production, however, did not happen quickly. Even during the Mesolithic Age, or Middle Stone Age, some people continued to hunt and gather, while others began to grow their own food.

Big Changes for Humankind

Historians call this settled farming during the Neolithic Age the Agricultural Revolution. The word *revolution* refers to any change that has an enormous effect on people's ways of life. While hunter-gatherers ate wild grains that they collected, early farmers saved some of the grains to plant. Humans lived differently once they learned how to grow crops and tame animals that produced food. They now could produce a constant food supply. This allowed the population to grow at a faster rate. Nomads gave up their way of life and began living in settled communities. Some historians consider the Agricultural Revolution the most important event in human history.

GEOGRAPHY CONNECTION

Between about 7000 and 2000 B.C., farming developed on different continents.

1. **REGIONS** What crops were grown south of the Equator?
2. **CRITICAL THINKING** *Speculating* Why do you think so many different crops were grown in Central America?

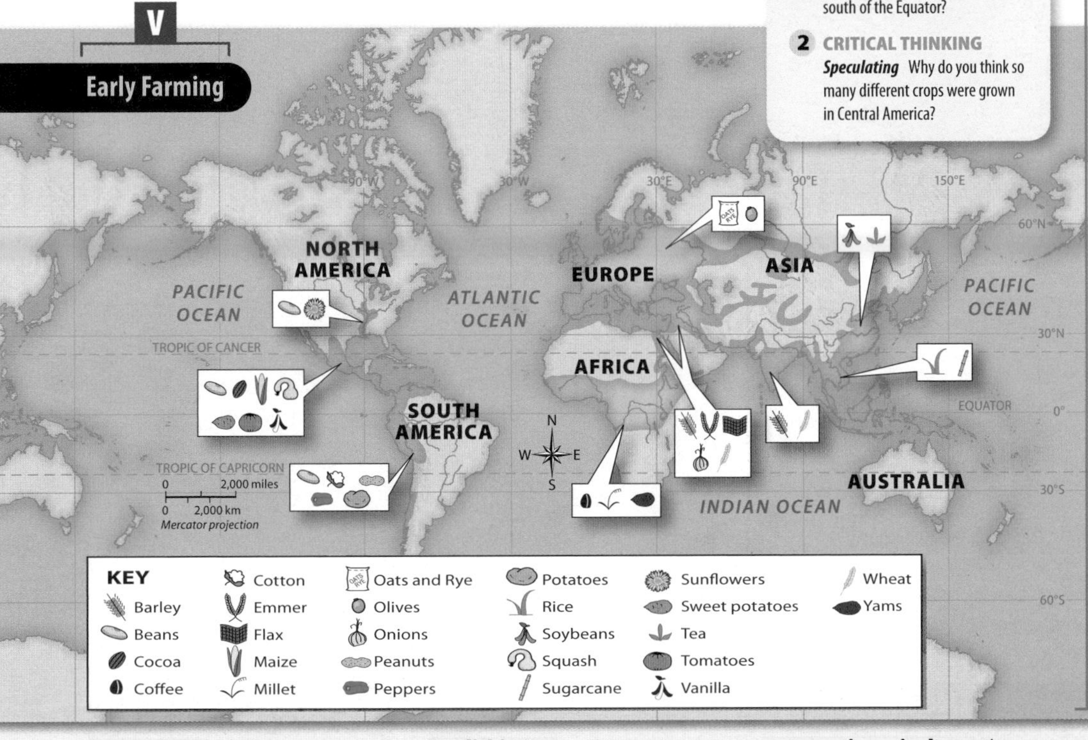

domesticate to adapt an animal to living with humans for the advantage of humans

Neolithic Age relating to the latest period of the Stone Age

systematic agriculture the organized growing of food on a regular schedule

V Visual Skills

Analyzing Maps Have students study the "Early Farming" Map. Ask a volunteer to describe what the map shows. *(where different crops were grown by early farmers around the world)* After students study the map, pose the following questions. **Ask:**

- **How can you tell where early farmers grew different crops?** *(by finding the symbols shown for each continent in the key at the bottom of the map)* AL
- **Where did early farmers grow coffee?** *(in Africa)*
- **What crops were grown in North America?** *(beans, sunflowers)*
- **Which continent had the largest amount of land dedicated to crops?** *(Europe)*

C Critical Thinking Skills

Making Inferences Have pairs of students create concept webs showing the effects of agriculture on civilization. **Ask: How is the agricultural revolution really a revolution?** *(A revolution is any change that has an enormous effect on how people live. The move from hunting and gathering to systematic agriculture brought changes to all aspects of life. People lived in different kinds of houses; they ate different kinds of food. They no longer had to move from place to place, so they could build sturdier buildings. The people were safer, and better food made them healthier.)* AL

Next, tell students about the different crops that early farmers grew: beans, corn, potatoes, squash, rice, tomatoes, soybeans, and peanuts. Have students create menus using these types of foods. **Ask: Which of these foods do you eat? In what form do you eat each one?** *(Accept all reasonable responses.)* When students have completed their menus, have them share their menus with the class. Then begin a discussion with students about the source of the food they eat. AL **Ask:**

- **Do you have a garden?**
- **Do you grow your own food?**
- **Do you know any people who grow most of the food they eat?**
- **Why would people choose to grow their own food?**

Tell students that in this lesson, they will find out that early people had to learn how to farm and that doing so changed human history. AL

MAP

Early Farming

Identifying Have students click on each of the different kinds of crops in the map key to the left to see where Neolithic farmers grew each type of food. Explain that some foods, which are now eaten by people all over the world, were once limited to certain regions. Neolithic people in different parts of the world domesticated different kinds of plants. Have students answer questions by finding the crop in the list and clicking on its symbol. **Ask: Where did Neolithic farmers grow potatoes?** *(South America)* **Where did Neolithic farmers grow tea?** *(Asia)* Discuss how these familiar crops spread throughout the world.

See page 51D for other online activities.

ANSWERS, p. 63

GEOGRAPHY CONNECTION

1. Crops grown south of the Equator included beans, cotton, peanuts, peppers, potatoes, coffee, millet, and yams.
2. **CRITICAL THINKING** Answers will vary but should include the idea that the region's warm and rainy climate would allow a wide variety of crops to be grown.

The Agricultural Revolution

R Reading Skills

Defining After students have read the first paragraph, ask a student to read aloud the definition of *economy* at the bottom of this page. **Ask:** What are parts of our economy today? *(Answers will vary, though students should mention important areas of modern commerce, such as manufacturing, retail sales, banking, and agriculture.)* Point out that systematic agriculture would always be considered as part of a region's economy. **Ask:** Where and when did early people first grow wheat and barley as part of systematic agriculture? *(Southeast Asia, by 8000 B.C.)* Note that this was at the beginning of the Neolithic Age. AL ELL

V1 Visual Skills

Analyzing Images Have students study the image of the Neolithic family in front of a house. Ask a volunteer to read the caption aloud. **Ask:** How can you tell this is a Neolithic group of people and not a Paleolithic group? *(Neolithic people settled in one area and built homes, made clothing, and domesticated animals. A Paleolithic group would have been nomadic.)* What domesticated animals does this group keep? *(sheep and a dog)*

V2 Visual Skills

Creating Time Lines Divide the class into groups, and ask each group to create a time line of the Neolithic Age. **Ask:** When did the Neolithic Age begin and end? *(It began around 8000 B.C. and lasted until around 4000 B.C.)* Have each group create a time line to match the length of the Neolithic Age. Students should add entries for each of the dates they find in the Widespread Farming section in their textbooks. After groups have completed their time lines, ask students to use the time lines to create a larger time line of the Neolithic Age for a classroom wall. Have these students add more entries to the time line as they read the rest of the chapter. BL

ANSWERS, p. 64

✓ PROGRESS CHECK It allowed people to settle and form communities.

CRITICAL THINKING Different materials, such as wood, stone, or clay (for bricks), would be available in different geographical locations. These different materials require different construction methods.

Widespread Farming

R By 8000 B.C., people in Southwest Asia began growing wheat and barley. They also domesticated pigs, cows, goats, and sheep. From there, farming spread into southeastern Europe. By 4000 B.C., farming was an established **economic** activity in Europe.

V2 At about the same time, around 6000 B.C., people had begun growing wheat and barley in the Nile Valley in Egypt. Farming soon spread along the Nile River and into other regions in Africa. In Central Africa, different types of crops emerged. There, people grew root crops called tubers, which included yams. They also grew fruit crops, such as bananas. Wheat and barley farming moved eastward into India between 8000 and 5000 B.C.

By 6000 B.C., people in northern China were growing a food grain called millet and were domesticating dogs and pigs. By 5000 B.C., farmers in Southeast Asia were growing rice. From there, rice farming spread into southern China.

In the Western Hemisphere, between 7000 and 5000 B.C., people in Mexico and Central America were growing corn, squash, and potatoes. They also domesticated chickens and dogs.

✓ PROGRESS CHECK

Explaining How did the spread of farming change the lives of nomads?

V1 

Originally, Neolithic people built large dwelling places that housed a small clan, or family group, along with their cattle and grain stores. Eventually, these were replaced by one- or two-room houses, which were usually clustered in groups.

▶ CRITICAL THINKING

Analyzing Why would construction methods vary depending on geographical location?

Reading HELPDESK CCSS

Academic Vocabulary (Tier 2 Words)

economy the system of economic life in an area or country; an economy deals with the making, buying, and selling of goods or services

networks Online Teaching Options

IMAGE

Neolithic Farming Communities

Determining Cause and Effect Have students read the paragraphs about the effect that the development of agriculture had on culture and society in the Neolithic Age. Make sure students know to scroll down to read the material to the end. **Ask:** How did the development of agriculture result in the creation of the first cities? *(As farming knowledge and technology improved and spread, farming communities could feed larger populations. Larger populations led to the creation of cities.)* What were some of the specialized jobs that were created during the Neolithic Age? *(pottery-making, tool-making, weaving)*

McGraw-Hill networks
Neolithic Farming Communities
The development of agriculture was the main reason early humans gave up their nomadic lifestyles. Nomads hunted and gathered, moving from place to place based wherever food sources were most plentiful. Instead, Neolithic peoples settled into communities that were located near the land that they farmed and the animals they raised.
As farming knowledge and technology improved and spread, farming communities were able to feed larger populations. Before this, farming communities would have to split into smaller groups if the population grew higher than could be sustained, or kept alive. This change led to the creation of the first cities.

See page 51D for other online activities.

▶ CRITICAL THINKING
Analyzing The village of Çatalhüyük grew into a large community. These ruins reveal well thought out construction. ***Why do you think some people were happy to settle in villages?***

Life in the Neolithic Age

GUIDING QUESTION *What was life like during the Neolithic Age?*

During the Neolithic Age, people settled in villages where they built permanent homes. They **located** villages near fields so people could plant, grow, and harvest their crops more easily. People also settled near water sources, especially rivers.

Neolithic Communities

Neolithic farming villages developed throughout Europe, India, Egypt, China, and Mexico. The biggest and earliest known communities have been found in Southwest Asia. One of the oldest communities was Jericho (JAIR•ih•koh). This farming village grew in an area between present-day Israel and Jordan called the West Bank. The village of Jericho was well established by about 8000 B.C. It extended across several acres. The area of sun-dried-brick houses was surrounded by walls that were several feet thick.

Academic Vocabulary (Tier 2 Words)
locate to set up in a particular place

V Visual Skills

Analyzing images Have students look at the image of the excavation in the village of Çatalhüyük. **Ask:** Why would these ruins be described as well-thought-out construction? *(Answers will vary, but students should mention the right angles formed by the walls as well as the regular pattern formed by the wooden beams that would support a floor or ceiling.)* Have students look back at the picture on the previous page. **Ask:** How does the construction in this picture differ from the shelters built by Paleolithic people? *(Students should compare the simple mud-and-hide structures of the Paleolithic Age with the well-designed structures shown in the image.)*

R Reading Skills

Listing Have a volunteer read the text. Then, ask students to imagine that they live in the Neolithic Age and they want to build a village. **Ask:** What are the characteristics of the perfect place to start your village? *(Answers will vary, but students should mention such characteristics as nearness to a river or another body of water and nearness to good farmland. Some might also suggest characteristics associated with defense against enemies, such as some kind of natural fortifications.)* Why would Neolithic people want to build a settlement near a river? *(for transportation purposes and for easy access to water for food and drink)* AL

SLIDE SHOW

Çatalhüyük

Making Inferences Direct students' attention to the slide show about Çatalhüyük, and encourage them to read the text that accompanies each image. Then, as a class, discuss what daily life might have been like in this ancient city. As students share their thoughts, have them describe how the work of archaeologists helped them draw these conclusions. .

See page 51D for other online activities.

networks
Çatalhüyük
The people here grew mainly wheat, barley, and peas. The main source of meat came from raised cattle, but inhabitants also relied on hunting. Bright murals were painted on many of the village walls. Figurines of animals and goddesses were mounted on many walls. No one knows what happened to this ancient city.

ANSWER, p. 65

CRITICAL THINKING Living in a community meant security and an easier life.

W Writing Skills

Narrative As a class, discuss what life may have been like in the Neolithic community of Çatalhüyük. Then have students imagine they were living 6,000 years ago, and ask them to write a journal entry about their life in Çatalhüyük. Allow students to write from the point of view of a person of any age or gender they choose. *(Students' diary entries can be imaginative but should reflect an understanding of the information provided about this specific community as well as what students have learned in general about Neolithic communities.)* Ask volunteers to read their entries to the class. **Verbal/Linguistic**

C Critical Thinking Skills

Drawing Conclusions Have students draw conclusions about the benefits and drawbacks of living in settled communities rather than living as nomads or living in small family groups. **Ask:** **What were the benefits of living in settled communities?** *(Answers will vary. Students may suggest that people could be safer and healthier. They could form governments and build cities.)* **What were the drawbacks of living in settled communities?** *(Answers will vary. Some students might not see any drawbacks. Others might point out that staying in one place is not as exciting or as interesting as moving from place to place. It might be harder for some people to live in a community and follow the rules than to be free to do as they want.)* **AL**

Content Background Knowledge

The mummified remains of Ötzi the Iceman were discovered by two German hikers in 1991. They thought they had found the body of a person who had fairly recently met an accidental death.

Since this discovery, we have learned that when Ötzi died, he was wearing a hide coat, a loincloth, a bearskin cap, leggings, shoes, a belt with a pouch, and a mat made of swamp grass on his head.

After discovering his remains, scientists developed special instruments to examine Ötzi's body. Among many discoveries, scientists determined that Ötzi's lungs were blackened as a consequence of sitting by open fires. Scientists were also able to determine Ötzi's last meal: a grain porridge, meat, and vegetables. Today, Ötzi the Iceman's body is on display at the South Tyrol Museum of Archaeology in Bolzano, Italy.

ANSWER, p. 66

CRITICAL THINKING He probably used clothing made of hides, tools made of flint and wood, and a bow along with arrows.

BIOGRAPHY

Ötzi the Iceman (c. 3300 B.C.)

Mystery Man Ötzi was a Neolithic man whose remains were discovered in 1991 in the Austrian Alps. Also called the "Iceman," Ötzi presented a mystery. Did he live where he died? Did he spend his life in another location? What did he do for a living? Scientists found the same form of oxygen in Ötzi's teeth as in the water of the southern Alpine valleys. They have concluded that, even though Ötzi was found in the mountains, he lived most of his life in the valleys south of the Alps. Scientists believe Ötzi was either a shepherd or a hunter who traveled from the valleys to the mountains.

▶ **CRITICAL THINKING**
Analyzing What types of clothing or tools do you think Ötzi used?

Another well-known Neolithic community was Çatalhüyük (chah•tahl•hoo•YOOK) in present-day Turkey. Although little evidence of the community remains, historians know that between 6700 and 5700 B.C., it covered 32 acres and was home to about 6,000 people. The people lived in simple mud-brick houses that were built close together. What if, instead of a front door, your house had a roof door? In Çatalhüyük, the houses did not have front doors. Instead of going through a door in the wall, people entered their homes through holes in the rooftops. They could also walk from house to house across the roofs. People decorated the inside of their homes with wall paintings.

In addition to homes, Çatalhüyük had special buildings that were **shrines** (SHREYENZ), or holy places. These shrines were decorated with images of gods and goddesses. Statues of women giving birth have also been found in the shrines. Both the shrines and the statues show that the role of religion was growing in the lives of Neolithic people.

Farmers grew fruits, nuts, and different grains on land outside Çatalhüyük. People grew their own food and kept it in storerooms within their homes. They raised sheep, goats, and cattle that provided milk and meat. They ate fish and bird eggs from nearby low-lying wetlands called marshes. Scenes drawn on the walls of the city's ruins show that the people of Çatalhüyük also hunted.

What Were the Benefits of a Settled Life?

Neolithic people needed protection from the weather and wild animals. A settled life provided greater security. Steady food supplies created healthier, growing populations. As the population increased, more workers became available. Those individuals could grow more crops. Villagers produced more than they could eat, so they began to trade their food for supplies they could not produce themselves.

Because an abundant amount of food was produced, fewer people were needed in the fields. Neolithic people began to take part in economic activities other than farming. **Specialization** (speh•shuh•leh•ZAY•shun) occurred for the first time. People took up specific jobs as their talents allowed. Some people became artisans, or skilled workers. They made weapons and jewelry that they traded with neighboring communities. People made pottery from clay to store grain and food. They made

Reading HELPDESK 

shrine a place where people worship

specialization the act of training for a particular job

networks Online Teaching Options

BIOGRAPHY

Ötzi the Iceman

Analyzing Information Have students read the biography of Ötzi the Iceman. Make sure they know to scroll down to read all the material. After reading, ask students to imagine that they are reporters covering the discovery of Ötzi's body. Have them write a list of questions they would like to ask the hikers who discovered him and the scientists who studied his body.

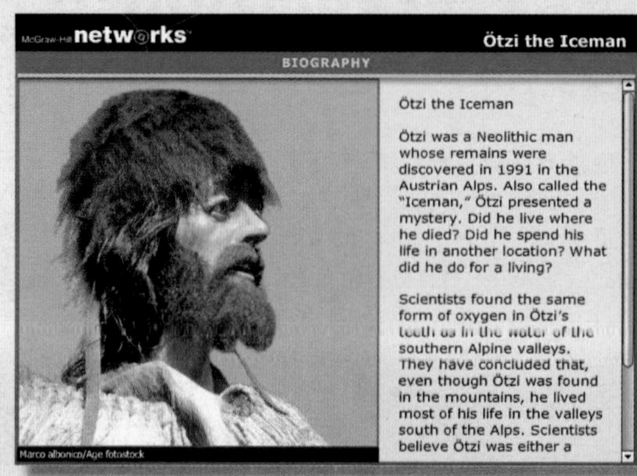

See page 51D for other online activities.

baskets from plant fibers. They also used plant fibers to weave cloth. Ötzi, the Neolithic Iceman, wore a cape made from woven grass fibers. These craftspeople, like farmers, also exchanged the goods they produced for other things they did not have.

The roles of men and women changed when people moved into settlements. Men worked in the fields to farm and herd animals. They gradually became more responsible for growing food and protecting the village. Men emerged as family and community leaders. Women bore the children and stayed in the villages. They wove cloth, using the wool from their sheep. They also used bone needles to make clothing from cloth and animal skins. In addition, women managed food supplies and performed other tasks.

The growth of communities did not always bring benefits. In some places, such as settlements in present-day Jordan, rapid population growth caused resources such as wood supplies to be used up quickly. On occasion, this loss of forestation caused desert-like conditions to spread. Where this type of ecological damage occurred, many settlements were abandoned.

The End of the Neolithic Age

During the late Neolithic Age, people made more technological advances. Toolmakers created better farming tools as the need for them arose. These included hoes for digging soil, sickles for cutting grain, and millstones for grinding flour. In some regions, people began to work with metals, including copper. Workers heated rocks and discovered melted copper inside them. They then experimented with making the copper into tools and weapons. These proved to be easier to make and use than those made of stone.

Craftspeople in western Asia discovered that mixing copper and tin formed bronze. This was a technological breakthrough because bronze was stronger than copper. Bronze became widely used between 3000 and 1200 B.C. This period is known as the **Bronze Age**. Few people, however, could afford bronze and continued to use tools and weapons made of stone.

✓ PROGRESS CHECK

Explaining How did the spread of agriculture affect trade?

Bronze Age the period in ancient human culture when people began to make and use bronze

(l) Barbara Heller/Heritage/Age fotostock, (r) De Agostini/Getty Images

Thinking Like a HISTORIAN

Making Inferences

In Çatalhüyük the homes were built very close together. Each house had a door in its roof. People climbed into their homes using ladders. Use the Internet to research why the people of Çatalhüyük used this style of building. Then make an inference about the reason for the roof doors and present it to the class. For more information about making inferences, read the chapter *What Does a Historian Do?*

Bronze Age pottery shows fine details. The use of bronze for tools and weapons was another step forward for ancient peoples.

▶ CRITICAL THINKING

Analyzing Why do you think bronze tools and weapons would have been an important achievement?

C Critical Thinking Skills

Making Inferences Ask students to consider how the roles of men and women changed when people moved into settlements. **Ask:** **What became the primary roles of men and women in settlements?** *(Men emerged as family and community leaders; women bore the children and stayed in the villages.)* **How did these roles compare to the roles of men and women among nomads during the Paleolithic Age?** *(Answers will vary. Some students might suggest that during the Paleolithic Age, women had to stay close to camp to take care of children while the men went hunting. Their roles in the settlements were different but in some ways followed the patterns already set.)* Invite students to debate whether these roles for men and women were a natural consequence of biology or simply accidents of how things developed. BL **Verbal/Linguistic**

T Technology Skills

Making Presentations Ask interested students to go online to find images of Bronze Age pottery, tools, and weapons. Give these students a set amount of time to gather images. Remind them that they can use a search engine to look for such images, and they should focus on Web sites of prominent museums. Then have students transfer the images they find to a presentation software, such as Microsoft PowerPoint, and make a presentation to the class. Make sure that, for each object, students know where each object originally came from. AL

CHART

Neolithic Artifacts

Making Inferences Have students click on each Neolithic artifact to identify it and learn about when it was made. **Ask:** **What makes these objects more advanced than the tools of the Paleolithic Age?** *(Answers will vary. Students might mention that these Neolithic artifacts look much better crafted, both in design and the kind of materials.)* Point out that at least some of these objects are made of bronze. **Ask:** **Why was working with bronze a technological advance?** *(Bronze is stronger than copper, the material that people previously used to make tools and weapons.)* **Visual/Spatial**

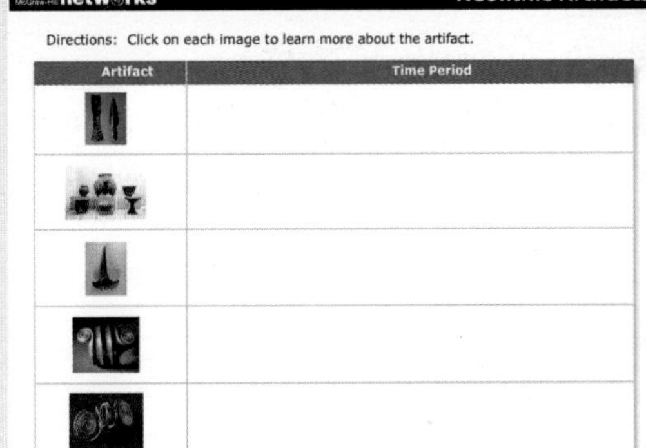

See page 51D for other online activities.

ANSWERS, p. 67

CRITICAL THINKING Stronger tools would have made farming more efficient. Stronger weapons would give one people an advantage over nearby peoples if a battle were to be fought.

✓ PROGRESS CHECK People had an abundance of food and could trade for what they needed.

R Reading Skills

Defining After students have read the text, ask them to come up with a definition for *civilization*. **Ask:** What makes a civilization? *(Students should mention characteristics such as government, laws, art, and religion.)* Write students' ideas on the board.

V Visual Skills

Reading a Map Ask a volunteer to read aloud the names of the four great river valley civilizations. **Ask:** When did these civilizations begin? *(around 3000 B.C.)* Then turn students' attention to the map on this page, and ask them the following questions.

- Which early civilization settled the farthest north? *(China)*
- What geographic feature did all of these civilizations settle near? *(rivers)*
- What continents are each of these civilizations part of? *(Egypt is part of Africa, and the Indus Valley, Mesopotamia, and China are all part of Asia.)* BL

Point out that early people had spread throughout the world since emerging from Africa during the Paleolithic Age. Have students use the scale to determine about how far the China civilization was from the Egypt civilization. *(about 5,000 miles or about 8,000 km)*

ANSWERS, p. 68

GEOGRAPHY CONNECTION

1. In Mesopotamia, civilization developed along the Tigris and Euphrates rivers. Civilization developed along the Nile River in Egypt.
2. CRITICAL THINKING As cultures became more complex, the need for organization—in the form of government—led to the development of civilizations.

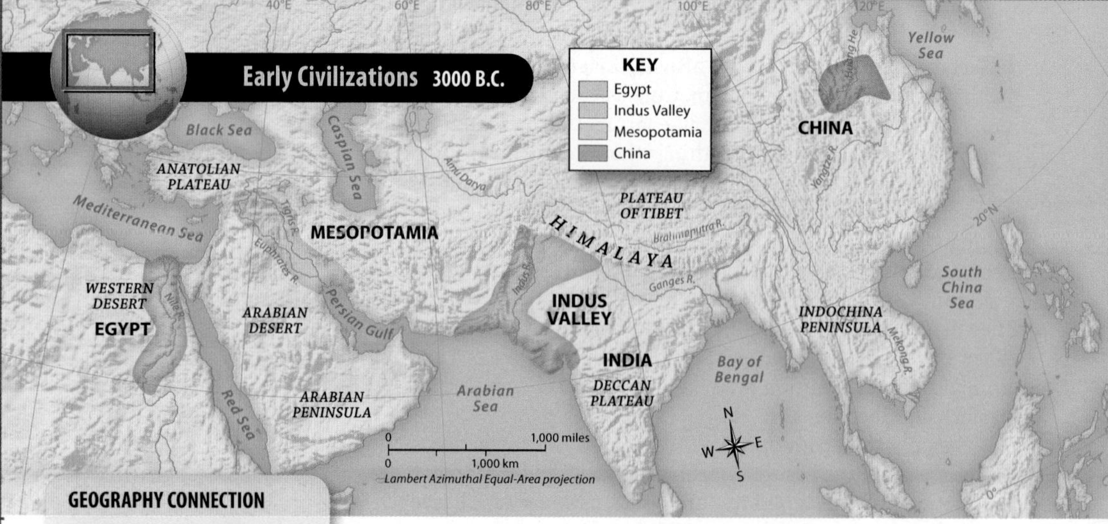

V

GEOGRAPHY CONNECTION

Civilizations developed in the river valleys of Mesopotamia, Egypt, India, and China.

1. **PLACE** Along which rivers did the early civilizations of Mesopotamia and Egypt develop?
2. **CRITICAL THINKING** *Analyzing* As these cultures became more complex, what characteristics set some of them apart as civilizations?

Civilizations Emerge

GUIDING QUESTION *What characteristics did early civilizations share?*

Humans continued to develop more complex cultures, or ways of life. By the beginning of the Bronze Age, communities were widespread. More complex cultures called civilizations began to develop in these communities. Four of the great river valley civilizations—Mesopotamia, Egypt, India, and China—emerged around 3000 B.C. All civilizations share similar characteristics.

Cities and Government

One characteristic of these early civilizations was that they developed cities and formed governments. The first civilizations developed in river valleys, where fertile land made it easy to grow crops and feed large numbers of people. The rivers provided fish and water. They also encouraged trade, which allowed the exchange of both goods and ideas. The cities that developed in these valleys became the centers of civilizations.

R

People formed governments to protect themselves and their food supplies. In these early civilizations, the first governments were monarchies. A **monarchy** is a type of government led by a king or queen. Monarchs created armies to defend against enemies and made laws to keep order. They also appointed government officials who managed food supplies and building projects.

Reading **HELP**DESK 

monarchy a government whose ruler, a king or queen, inherits the position from a parent

networks Online Teaching Options

MAP

Early Civilizations, 3000 B.C.

Analyzing Maps Using the interactive key on the left, students can turn on and off the areas included for each of the great river valley civilizations. **Ask:**

- Which of these early civilizations was the largest? *(Indus Valley)*
- The Huang He River runs through the land of which early civilization? *(China)*
- Which of these early civilizations borders the Mediterranean Sea? *(Egypt)*
- Two large rivers run nearly parallel through the land of which early civilization? *(Mesopotamia)*

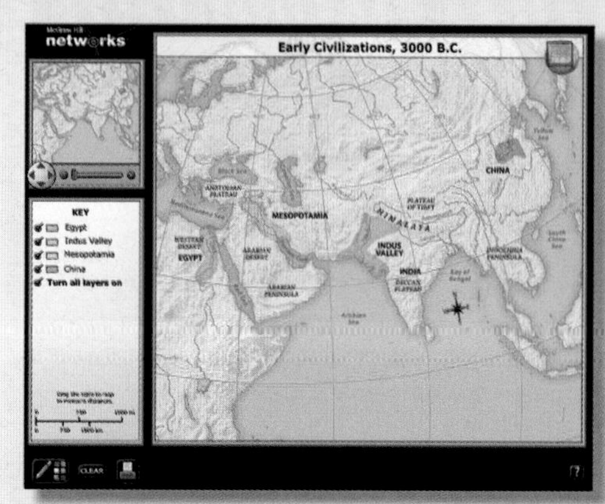

See page 51D for other online activities.

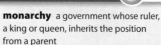

Religions

Religions emerged in the new civilizations to help people explain their lives. For example, religions helped explain the forces of nature and the role of humans in the world.

Early people believed that gods were responsible for a community's survival. Priests performed religious ceremonies to try to win the support of the gods. Rulers claimed that their own power was based on the approval of the gods.

W

Social Structure

Early civilizations had social class structures. That is, people in society were organized into groups. These groups were defined by the type of work people did and the amount of wealth or power they had. Generally, rulers and priests, government officials, and warriors made up the highest social class. They set the rules and made the important decisions. Below this class was a large group of free people, including farmers, artisans, and craftspeople. At the bottom of the class structure were enslaved people, most of whom were captured from enemies during war.

V

Writing and Art

To pass on information, people invented ways of writing. These early systems used symbols in place of letters and words. Writing became an important feature of these new civilizations. People used writing to keep accurate records and to preserve stories.

Civilizations also created art for enjoyment and practical purposes. Artists created paintings and sculptures portraying gods and forces of nature. People designed massive buildings that served as places of worship or burial tombs for kings.

✓ PROGRESS CHECK

Speculating Why did early peoples form governments?

LESSON 2 REVIEW (CCSS)

Review Vocabulary (Tier 3 Words)

1. What was *systematic agriculture?* RH.6–8.4
2. How did *specialization* affect the lives of Neolithic peoples? RH.6–8.4

Answer the Guiding Questions

3. ***Stating*** What was the Agricultural Revolution? RH.6–8.2
4. ***Identifying Cause and Effect*** How did farming lead to new types of economic activities? RH.6–8.1
5. ***Inferring*** What are the advantages and disadvantages when a community grows? RH.6–8.2
6. ***Identifying*** Which groups made up the largest social class in early civilizations? RH.6–8.1
7. **ARGUMENT** You are the leader of a band of hunter-gatherers. You have seen other bands settle in river valleys and begin to farm. Write a speech to persuade your own band to settle and begin farming. WHST.6–8.1, WHST.6–8.10

LESSON 2 REVIEW ANSWERS

1. At first, humans relied on hunting and gathering for their daily food. With the shift to systematic agriculture, humans grew their own food on a regular basis.
2. People took up specific jobs as their talents allowed. Some farmed, and others became artisans.
3. The Agricultural Revolution was a major change in the way people lived. They turned from hunting and gathering their food in nomadic communities to farming and herding in established, settled communities.
4. A steady food supply and food surplus meant that not all people had to farm. Some people became skilled workers who produced goods.
5. When a community grows, one advantage is that more people are available to do work. Also, there may be more security and a steadier food supply for people. A disadvantage is that a larger population means the resources and goods must be shared among more people.
6. The largest social group in early civilizations was made up of free people, including farmers, artisans, and craftspeople.
7. Answers will vary. Speeches should provide persuasive reasoning when discussing settling in communities and farming.

W Writing Skills

Information/Explanatory Conduct a brief review discussion in preparation for a writing activity. **Ask: What are the characteristics that the four early civilizations shared?** *(They developed cities and formed governments. Religions emerged in the civilizations. They had social class structures. Writing and art became important in the early civilizations.)* Divide the class into four groups, and assign one of the four characteristics to each group. Ask each group to discuss its characteristic and compose a paragraph that explains why that characteristic was important to the development of these early civilizations. Then have each group read its paragraph to the whole class. After each presentation, invite the rest of the class to ask questions or suggest additions. **Verbal/Linguistic**

V Visual Skills

Creating Visuals As a class, review the definition of *social class structures. (groups defined by the type of work that people did and the amount of wealth or power that they had).* Then have students sketch a diagram showing the social class structure of the early civilizations. The design of the diagram may be unique to each student but should show rulers, priests, government officials, and warriors as the highest class; free people (farmers, artisans, and craftspeople) at the next level; and enslaved people in the lowest class. **Visual/Spatial**

Have students complete the Lesson 2 Review.

CLOSE & REFLECT

Comparing To close the lesson, have students think about the Agricultural Revolution and the people of the Neolithic Age. Ask students to think about what aspects of lifestyles of the early civilizations are still evident in our lives today. Have them work in small groups to compile a list of these characteristics. As a class, review the lists and describe how the characteristics can be seen in modern life. **Interpersonal**

ANSWER, p. 69

✓ PROGRESS CHECK They wanted to protect themselves and bring order to their lives.

CHAPTER REVIEW ACTIVITY

Have students create a Venn diagram like the one below and write "Paleolithic Age" in one oval, "Neolithic Age" in the other, and "Both" in the area where the two ovals intersect. Then lead a discussion that allows students to recall characteristics of the two periods. Have a student write these characteristics in the correct area on the diagram. *(Answers will vary, but students should include much of the following in their Venn diagrams. In the "Paleolithic Age" oval: hunter-gatherers; nomads; stone tools; overhangs, caves, tents, and huts for shelter; cave paintings. In the "Neolithic Age" oval: domesticated animals; systematic agriculture; widespread farming; permanent homes in villages, large communities, and cities; religious shrines; specialization; copper tools and weapons; bronze pottery, tools and weapons. In the "Both" oval: Women cared for children, and men worked away from home; fire; adapted to change.)*

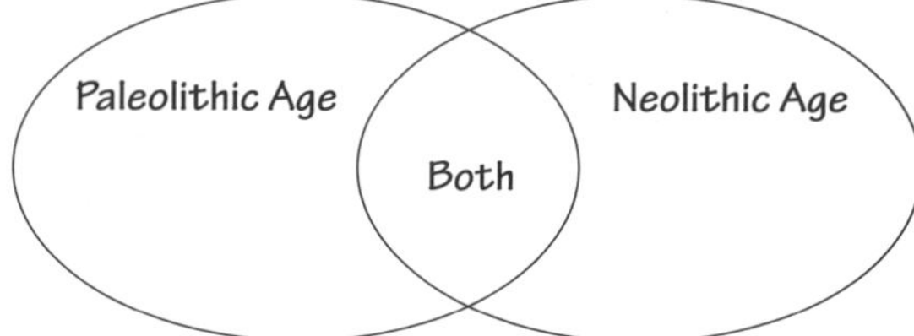

REVIEW THE ENDURING UNDERSTANDING

Review the chapter's Enduring Understanding with students.

- ***People, places, and ideas change over time.***

Now pose the following questions in a class discussion to apply this enduring understanding to the chapter.

How did Paleolithic people adapt to new environments after they left Africa and went to other parts of the world? *(The Paleolithic people survived as nomads. They traveled regularly from place to place to survive. The men hunted animals, including buffalo, bison, wild goats, and reindeer. Women gathered food, such as nuts, berries, fruits, wild grains, and green plants. They lived in small groups or bands, and sought shelter in overhangs or caves. Eventually, the Paleolithic people developed new technology to hunt and gather food, including stone tools. Flint technology was a major breakthrough. Over time, they made more complex weapons and tools, including bows and arrows and sharp-edged tools to cut up plants and dig roots. Paleolithic people's lives improved when they learned how to make fire. The warmth of fire helped early people survive through the ice ages. In addition to fire, they adapted to the cold with changes in diet, sturdier shelters, and warmer clothes.)*

CHAPTER 3 Activities

Write your answers on a separate piece of paper.

1 Exploring the Essential Question WHST.6–8.2

INFORMATIVE/EXPLANATORY How would you describe the ways people adapted to a colder environment during the Ice Age? Write an essay telling how some changes people made may have led to the development of agriculture when the last Ice Age was over.

2 21st Century Skills WHST.6–8.10

ANALYZING AND MAKING JUDGMENTS Early humans made several technical advancements during the Paleolithic Age. These included the use of fire, flint tools and weapons, spoken language, and tents and wooden structures. Write a paragraph telling which of these helped them most to become more efficient hunters and why.

3 Thinking Like a Historian RH.6–8.1, WHST.6–8.9

COMPARING AND CONTRASTING Create a diagram like the one shown to compare and contrast the technological advancements of the Paleolithic Age with those of the Neolithic Age.

Paleolithic Age Advancements	Neolithic Age Advancements

4 GEOGRAPHY ACTIVITY

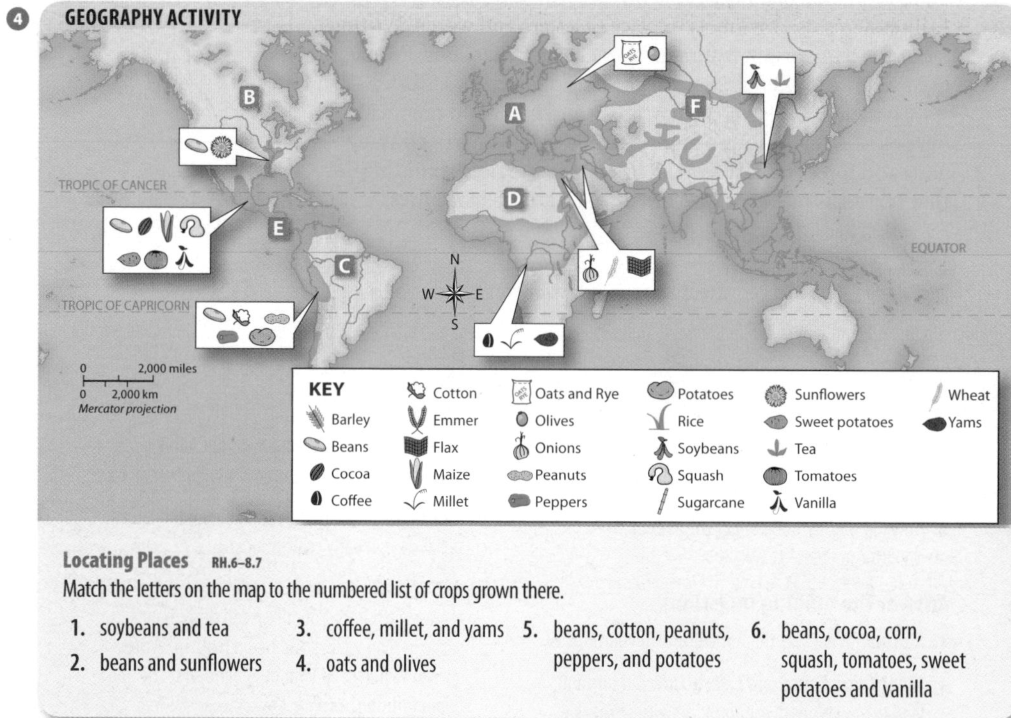

Locating Places RH.6–8.7

Match the letters on the map to the numbered list of crops grown there.

1. soybeans and tea
2. beans and sunflowers
3. coffee, millet, and yams
4. oats and olives
5. beans, cotton, peanuts, peppers, and potatoes
6. beans, cocoa, corn, squash, tomatoes, sweet potatoes and vanilla

How did the Agricultural Revolution change people's lives? *(The Agricultural Revolution resulted in a constant supply of food, which allowed for a greater rate of population growth. People were able to live in settled communities. Neolithic farming communities developed throughout Europe, India, Egypt, China, and Mexico. The steady food supplies created healthier, growing populations. As a result, Neolithic people began to take part in activities other than farming and specialization occurred for the first time. By the end of the Neolithic Age, toolmakers were producing better farming tools. All of these benefits were the result of the Agricultural Revolution.)*

ACTIVITIES ANSWERS

Exploring the Essential Question

1 Students should note that people had to adapt their lives to survive the Ice Age. They changed their diets. They built sturdier shelters and made warm clothing. They used fire to help them survive. Sturdier shelters made moving from place to place harder, so permanent settlements began to develop. With permanent settlements, domesticating animals and plants became more practical.

CHAPTER 3 Assessment

REVIEW THE GUIDING QUESTIONS

Directions: Choose the best answer for each question.

RH.6–8.2
1. Paleolithic people first used tools made of
   A. bronze.
   B. copper.
   C. sticks, stones, and tree branches.
   D. flint.

RH.6–8.2
2. Which of the following developed after the Paleolithic Age?
   F. language
   G. farming
   H. art
   I. tools

RH.6–8.2
3. What major change took place during the Neolithic Age?
   A. People built sturdier shelters.
   B. People began farming in a systematic way.
   C. People began to use spoken language to communicate.
   D. People learned to use fire to survive in cold environments.

RH.6–8.2
4. Where did farming first develop?
   F. Southwest Asia
   G. southeastern Europe
   H. India
   I. China

RH.6–8.4
5. Çatalhüyük had special buildings that were holy places, or
   A. fortresses.
   B. lofts.
   C. shrines.
   D. cathedrals.

RH.6–8.2
6. Which of the following groups was at the bottom of early social class structures?
   F. farmers
   G. enslaved people
   H. craftspeople
   I. artisans

CHAPTER 3 Assessment Answers

ASSESSMENT ANSWERS

Review the Guiding Questions

1. **C** The first tools were sticks, stones, and tree branches. Copper tools and bronze tools did not come into use until the Neolithic Era. Flint tools were used during the Paleolithic Age.

2. **G** Farming did not develop during the Paleolithic Age, but during the Agricultural Revolution of the Neolithic Age. The use of tools and the development of spoken language and art took place during the Paleolithic Age.

3. **B** The shift to systematic farming occurred during the Agricultural Revolution of the Neolithic Age. During the Ice Age of the Paleolithic Age, people built sturdier shelters, developed spoken language, and discovered how to use fire.

4. **F** Farming first developed in Southwest Asia around 8000 B.C. It developed later in India around 7000 B.C., in China around 6000 B.C., and in southeastern Europe around 4000 B.C.

5. **C** Cathedrals and shrines are holy places, but of these two, only shrines existed in Çatalhüyük. A fortress is not a holy place. A loft is part of a barn and is not a holy place.

6. **G** Enslaved people were at the bottom of the class structure. Farmers, craftspeople, and artisans were all members of a large group of free people.

21st Century Skills

2. Learning to shape flint into sharp-edged tools and weapons helped Paleolithic people become more efficient hunters. Flint arrowheads and spears were more efficient for bringing down prey.

Thinking Like a Historian

3. Paleolithic Age Advancements: nomadic life; hunters and gatherers; women gathered food, and men hunted; primitive tools made of stone; developed spoken language; cave paintings.

   Neolithic Age Advancements: settled life; farmers; men herded, farmed, and served as leaders, while women bore children, stayed in the villages, and wove cloth; more advanced tools made of copper and bronze; developed written language; art was for enjoyment and practical purposes.

Locating Places

4. **1.** F, **2.** B, **3.** D, **4.** A, **5.** C, **6.** E

Analyzing Documents

7 **B** The animals in the painting have horns and resemble modern cattle. Woolly mammoths and horses do not have horns. Reindeer have antlers rather than horns.

8 **I** Twigs were one of the first tools used in cave painting. F, G, and H are incorrect because they are more modern tools and would not have been used in the cave paintings.

Short Response

9 The change was probably gradual, with a period of intensive food gathering before farming actually began.

10 Answers will vary but may mention that more suitable species were discovered, that changes in the environment made raising a particular species more difficult, or that people's tastes changed and made certain species less desirable.

Extended Response

11 Answers will vary but should reflect what the student has learned from the chapter. Some historians believe that the Paleolithic hunters were seeking good luck by painting a particular animal. Others believe the paintings might have had religious significance or that they were done for enjoyment.

CHAPTER 3 Assessment *(continued)*

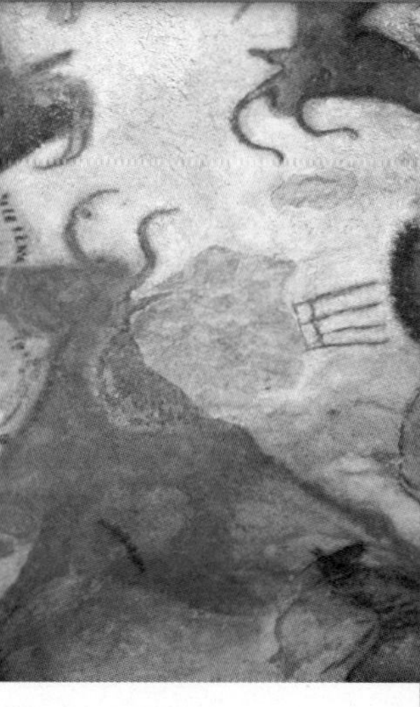

DBQ ANALYZING DOCUMENTS

RH.6–8.7
7 **Making Connections** Study this example of one of the oldest Paleolithic cave paintings.

What kind of animals does this painting appear to represent?

A. woolly mammoths
B. cattle
C. horses
D. reindeer

RH.6–8.2
8 **Identifying** What type of tools did Paleolithic people use for painting on the cave walls?

F. wood blocks
G. paint rollers
H. pencils
I. twigs

SHORT RESPONSE

Write your answers on a separate piece of paper.

"Agriculture developed at different times and in different places. . . . Over the years, people have domesticated many different plants and animals. Domestication of some species has been abandoned. Following the last Ice Age, people began to cultivate rice, wheat, potatoes, and corn. However, herding of reindeer declined because of the climate changes."

—from "History of Agriculture," *Encyclopaedia Britannica*

RH.6–8.1
9 Was the change from hunting and gathering to agriculture sudden? Explain.

RH.6–8.1
10 What are some possible reasons that people stopped raising some domesticated species?

EXTENDED RESPONSE

Write your answer on a separate piece of paper.

WHST.6–8.10
11 **Narrative** You are a member of a Paleolithic group of hunter-gatherers. Write a letter to a friend describing the hunting stories you are recording in cave paintings. Explain how you think your stories might help other hunters improve their skills.

Need Extra Help?

If You've Missed Question	1	2	3	4	5	6	7	8	9	10	11
Review Lesson	1	1, 2	2	2	2	2	1	1	2	2	1

networks *Online Teaching Options*

Help students use the Skills Builder resources

Your students can practice important 21st Century skills such as geography, reading, writing, and critical thinking by using resources found in the *Skills Builder* tab of the online Student Learning Center. Resources include templates, handbooks, and slide shows. These same resources are also available in the Resource Library of the Teacher Lesson Center.

CHAPTER 4

Mesopotamia Planner

UNDERSTANDING BY DESIGN®

Enduring Understandings

- *People, places, and ideas change over time.*
- *Cultures are held together by shared beliefs and common practices and values.*

Essential Questions

- *How does geography influence the way people live?*
- *Why does conflict develop?*

Predictable Misunderstandings

Students may think:

- *The wheel was invented before Sumer existed.*
- *The Mesopotamians had no laws before the Code of Hammurabi.*
- *There was only one Babylonian Empire.*

Assessment Evidence

Performance Task:

- *Hands-On Chapter Project*

Other Evidence:

- *Interactive Graphic Organizers*
- *The World's Literature questions*
- *21st Century Skills Activity*
- *Economics of History Activity*
- *Primary Source Activity*
- *Interactive Guided Reading Activities*
- *Written paragraphs*
- *Lesson Reviews*
- *Chapter Activities and Assessments*

SUGGESTED PACING GUIDE

Introducing the Chapter	1 day	Lesson 2	1 day
Lesson 1	2 days	Chapter Wrap-Up and Assessment	1 day
The World's Literature	1 day		

TOTAL TIME 6 DAYS

Key for Using the Teacher Edition

SKILL-BASED ACTIVITIES

Types of skill activities found in the Teacher Edition.

C Critical Thinking Skills help students apply and extend what they have learned.

V Visual Skills require students to analyze maps, graphs, charts, and photos.

R Reading Skills help students practice reading skills and master vocabulary.

T Technology Skills require students to use digital tools effectively.

W Writing Skills provide writing opportunities to help students comprehend the text.

*Letters are followed by a number when there is more than one of the same type of skill on the page.

DIFFERENTIATED INSTRUCTION

All activities are written for the on-level student unless otherwise marked with the leveled labels below.

BL Beyond Level
AL Approaching Level
ELL English Language Learners

All students benefit from activities that utilize different learning styles. Many activities are marked as below when a particular learning style is highlighted.

Intrapersonal	**Naturalist**
Logical/Mathematical	**Kinesthetic**
Visual/Spatial	**Auditory/Musical**
Verbal/Linguistic	**Interpersonal**

NCSS Standards covered in "Mesopotamia"

Learners will understand:

2 TIME, CONTINUITY, AND CHANGE

6. The origins and influences of social, cultural, political, and economic systems

3 PEOPLE, PLACES, AND ENVIRONMENTS

1. The theme of people, places, and environments involves the study of the relationships between human populations in different locations and geographic phenomena such as climate, vegetation, and natural resources

2. Concepts such as: location, region, place, migration, as well as human and physical systems

7. Human modifications of the environment

5 INDIVIDUALS, GROUPS, AND INSTITUTIONS

2. Concepts such as: mores, norms, status, role, socialization, ethnocentrism, cultural diffusion, competition, cooperation, conflict, race, ethnicity, and gender

8. That when two or more groups with differing norms and beliefs interact, accommodation or conflict may result

6 POWER, AUTHORITY, AND GOVERNANCE

5. The ways in which governments meet the needs and wants of citizens, manage conflict, and establish order and society

7 PRODUCTION, DISTRIBUTION, AND CONSUMPTION

6. The economic gains that result from specialization and exchange as well as the trade-offs

8 SCIENCE, TECHNOLOGY, AND SOCIETY

2. Society often turns to science and technology to solve problems

CHAPTER OPENER PLANNER

Students will know:

- *how Gilgamesh relates to modern-day literature pieces.*
- *what it was like to live in Sumer.*
- *the Sumerian ideas and inventions that have been passed on to other civilizations.*
- *the themes found in the epic poem genre.*
- *how civilizations developed in Mesopotamia.*
- *what contributions the Assyrians made to Southwest Asia.*
- *why Babylon was an important city in the ancient world.*

Students will be able to:

- ***explain*** *how floods sometimes helped the farmers of Mesopotamia.*
- ***draw conclusions*** *about why the Sumerians built cities with walls around them.*
- ***analyze*** *why the Sumerians invented a writing system .*
- ***describe*** *where the Fertile Crescent is located.*
- ***compare*** *the social classes of Sumer.*
- ***describe*** *why scribes were important in Sumerian society.*
- ***find*** *the main reason why Hammurabi's Code was important.*
- ***summarize*** *why Assyria's army was so strong.*
- ***identify*** *the wonder of the ancient world that was located in Babylon.*
- ***describe*** *how the Assyrians ruled their empire.*
- ***explain*** *why the Chaldeans overthrew the Assyrians.*

UNDERSTANDING BY DESIGN®

Print Teaching Options

V Visual Skills

- [ ] **P. 74** Students use a map to gain familiarity with the Fertile Crescent. AL ELL
- [ ] **P. 75** Students examine events leading to the rise of the city-state.

Online Teaching Options

V Visual Skills

MAP **Mesopotamia, 3000 B.C. to 500 B.C.**—Students identify the locations of several cities in ancient Mesopotamia.

TIME LINE **Place and Time: Mesopotamia, 3000 B.C. to 500 B.C.**—Students learn about key historical events in ancient Mesopotamia.

WORLD ATLAS Students can use this interactive map to identify regions of the world, learn about individual countries, locate political boundaries, measure distances, and much more.

Project-Based Learning

Hands-On Chapter Project

Mesopotamia

Students will work in pairs or small groups to create a poster of a person performing one of the occupations of Sumerian society.

Technology Extension

edtechteacher 21st Century Learning

Using Glogster for Online Interactive Multimedia Posters

- Find an additional activity online that incorporates technology for this project.
- Visit the EdTechTeacher Web sites (included in the Technology Extension for this chapter) for more links, tutorials, and other resources.

Print Resources

ANCILLARY RESOURCES

These ancillaries are available for every chapter and lesson.

- **Reading Essentials and Study Guide Workbook** AL ELL
- **Chapter Tests and Lesson Quizzes Blackline Masters**

PRINTABLE DIGITAL WORKSHEETS

These printable digital worksheets are available for every chapter and lesson.

- **Hands-On Chapter Projects**
- **What Do You Know? activities**
- **Chapter Summaries (English and Spanish)**
- **Vocabulary Builder activities**
- **Guided Reading activities**

More Media Resources

SUGGESTED VIDEOS MOVIES

Watch clips of documentaries about ancient Mesopotamia, such as Time Life's *Lost Civilizations or Ancient Mysteries: Seven Wonders of the Ancient World.*

Discuss: **Do documentaries convey different information about a topic than books convey?**

(NOTE: Preview any clips for age-appropriateness.)

SUGGESTED READING

Grade 6 reading level:

- ***Seven Wonders of the Ancient World,*** by Lynn Curlee

Grade 7 reading level:

- ***Ten Kings and the Worlds They Ruled,*** by Milton Meltzer

Grade 8 reading level:

- ***Archaeology,*** by Trevor Barnes

THE SUMERIANS

Students will know:

- *what it was like to live in Sumer.*
- *the Sumerian ideas and inventions that have been passed on to other civilizations.*
- *the themes found in the epic poem genre.*

Students will be able to:

- ***explain** how floods sometimes helped the farmers of Mesopotamia.*
- ***draw conclusions** about why the Sumerians built cities with walls around them.*
- ***analyze** why the Sumerians invented a writing system and why scribes were important in Sumerian society.*
- ***compare** the social classes of Sumer.*
- ***describe** why scribes were important in Sumerian society.*

UNDERSTANDING BY DESIGN®

Print Teaching Options

V Visual Skills

- [ ] **P. 78** Students use a map to quickly access information about land and river features. AL ELL **Visual/Spatial**
- [ ] **P. 80** Students draw conclusions about the ziggurat. AL **Visual/Spatial**

R Reading Skills

- [ ] **P. 77** Students review unfamiliar words and names. AL ELL **Auditory/Musical**
- [ ] **P. 78** Students relate irrigation to advancement of civilization.
- [ ] **P. 79** Students define *city-state*. AL ELL
- [ ] **P. 80** Students explore Sumerian class and social groups. BL **Verbal/Linguistic**
- [ ] **P. 81** Students discuss the importance of farming in Sumer. AL BL

W Writing Skills

- [ ] **P. 79** Students compare and contrast Sumerian city-states with modern cities. **Verbal/Linguistic**
- [ ] **P. 83** Students argue the importance of a specific Sumerian invention. **Verbal/Linguistic**

C Critical Thinking Skills

- [ ] **P. 76** Students infer how living in cities affected the development of early civilizations. BL
- [ ] **P. 76** Students make connections between the presence of rivers and the development of civilizations. AL
- [ ] **P. 77** Students relate the Mesopotamian flood cycles to those of the present.
- [ ] **P. 78** Students infer military and political advantages from geography. BL
- [ ] **P. 81** Students draw conclusions about Sumerian society from an image of an expensive necklace.
- [ ] **P. 82** Students consider how writing affected ancient people. BL **Verbal/Linguistic**
- [ ] **P. 82** Students contrast the technologies of paper and clay tablets for writing.

Online Teaching Options

V Visual Skills

- [ ] VIDEO **Mesopotamia: An Overview**—Students view a video that provides an overview of Mesopotamian cultures.
- [ ] MAP **Ancient Mesopotamia, 3000 B.C.**—Students identify the Fertile Crescent and important early cities.
- [ ] SLIDE SHOW **Ancient Irrigation**—Students view photos of irrigation systems to learn how they work.
- [ ] SLIDE SHOW **The Ziggurat**—Students examine these tall, religious structures.
- [ ] SLIDE SHOW **Sumerian Jewelry**—Students view photos of the uncut gems and finished works of Sumerian artisans.
- [ ] IMAGE **Sumerian Products**—Students examine an image from a tapestry that shows some of the products Sumerians made and traded.
- [ ] IMAGE **Everyday Life in Sumer**—Students examine an image of a cuneiform tablet that shows scenes of everyday Sumerian life.
- [ ] IMAGE **Cuniform Writing**—Students examine an image of an Assyrian tablet and click to reveal text that describes how these tablets were made and identifies the images shown.

R Reading Skills

- [ ] GRAPHIC ORGANIZER **Taking Notes: *Identifying*: Sumerian Inventions**—Students identify major inventions of the Sumerians.

C Critical Thinking Skills

- [ ] WHITEBOARD ACTIVITY **Bartering**—Students evaluate the relative value of a variety of items and determine which items they would trade for something else.

T Technology Skills

- [ ] SELF-CHECK QUIZ **Lesson 1**—Students receive instant feedback about their mastery of lesson content.

Printable Digital Worksheets

W Writing Skills

- [ ] WORKSHEET **Economics of History Activity: Mesopotamia, The Sumerians**—Students read information on bartering, participate in a bartering activity, and reflect on what they have learned.

C Critical Thinking Skills

- [ ] WORKSHEET **21st Century Skills Activity: Mesopotamia, The World's Literature**—Students collaborate to create publicity for the story of Gilgamesh as a film or book."

Mesopotamian Empires

Students will know:
- *how civilizations developed in Mesopotamia.*
- *what contributions the Assyrians made to Southwest Asia.*
- *why Babylon was an important city in the ancient world.*

Students will be able to:
- ***find** the main reason why Hammurabi's Code was important.*
- ***summarize** why Assyria's army was so strong.*
- ***describe** how the Assyrians ruled their empire.*
- ***explain** why the Chaldeans overthrew the Assyrians.*

UNDERSTANDING BY DESIGN®

☑ Print Teaching Options

V Visual Skills

- ☐ **P. 89** Students use a map to identify geographic features that limited the Assyrian Empire. AL Visual/Spatial

R Reading Skills

- ☐ **P. 86** Students define *empire.* AL ELL
- ☐ **P. 88** Students evaluate the advantages of the Assyrian army. AL
- ☐ **P. 90** Students cite evidence from the text that supports a description of Babylon's wealth. AL
- ☐ **P. 92** Students define *tax* and *tribute.* AL ELL
- ☐ **P. 92** Students examine the root of the word *astronomer* and consider the significance of the stars to ancient people.

C Critical Thinking Skills

- ☐ **P. 87** Students draw conclusions about the influence of Hammurabi's Code. BL
- ☐ **P. 88** Students discuss the benefits of how Assyrian kings governed.
- ☐ **P. 88** Students compare and contrast the laws and punishments of Assyrians with other civilizations. AL
- ☐ **P. 89** Students infer challenges the Assyrians faced in obtaining building supplies.
- ☐ **P. 90** Students relate events to outcomes in the Chaldean defeat of the Assyrians. AL
- ☐ **P. 93** Students infer the wisdom of the Persians in preserving elements of Chaldean culture.

T Technology Skills

- ☐ **P. 91** Students identify features of the ancient world among the Seven Wonders. Verbal/Linguistic

☑ Online Teaching Options

V Visual Skills

- VIDEO **Persepolis**—Students view a video that describes this capital city of ancient Persia, which was a pre-Christian rival with Athens for the title of "crowning achievement" of ancient civilization.
- MAP **Assyrian Empire, 900 B.C.**—Students identify the location of important cities in the Assyrian Empire.
- MAP **The Chaldean Empire, 605 B.C.**—Students examine the intersection of the Assyrian and Chaldean empires.
- IMAGE **Caravans**—Students explore the image to find out what ancient caravan travelers had to take on their desert journeys.
- IMAGE **The Hanging Gardens of Babylon**—Students explore what is known of this ancient wonder.

R Reading Skills

- GRAPHIC ORGANIZER **Taking Notes: *Identifying*: Major Mesopotamian Empires**—Students use a graphic organizer to identify the major Mesopotamian empires covered in the lesson.
- PRIMARY SOURCE **Hammurabi's Code**—Students read partial translations of the first six laws of the Code of Hammurabi.
- BIOGRAPHY **Sargon**—Students learn more about the king of the world's first empire.

C Critical Thinking Skills

- WHITEBOARD ACTIVITY **The Akkad, Babylonian, and Assyrian Empires**—Students sort unique characteristics into the correct empire.

T Technology Skills

- SELF-CHECK QUIZ **Lesson 2**—Students receive instant feedback about their mastery of lesson content.
- GAME **Mesopotamian Empires Crossword Puzzle**—Students complete the puzzle using key chapter vocabulary.
- GAME **Mesopotamia Fill in the Blank Game**—Students complete sentences using key chapter vocabulary.

☑ Printable Digital Worksheets

W Writing Skills

- WORKSHEET **Primary Source Activity: Mesopotamia, Mesopotamian Empires**—Students analyze and write about several of the laws in Hammurabi's Code.

INTERVENTION AND REMEDIATION STRATEGIES

LESSON 1 The Sumerians

Reading and Comprehension

Listing Ask students to skim the lesson and list ways in which the Tigris and Euphrates rivers made the development of the Sumer civilization possible and ways in which the Sumerians used the rivers.

Text Evidence

Informative/Explanatory Have students do research to learn how the Sumer civilization influenced later peoples. Ask them to write a brief essay telling what they learned.

LESSON 2 Mesopotamian Empires

Reading and Comprehension

Determining Cause and Effect Have students review the lesson and locate sentences or words that indicate cause-and-effect relationships among events. Have them list the events and tell which is the cause and which is the effect.

Text Evidence

Argument Have students work in pairs and create a chart comparing major events or accomplishments of three of the Mesopotamian Empires. Students should list two or three items for each empire. They should then write a short paragraph explaining why the items listed for each empire are important.

Online Resources

Approaching Level Reader

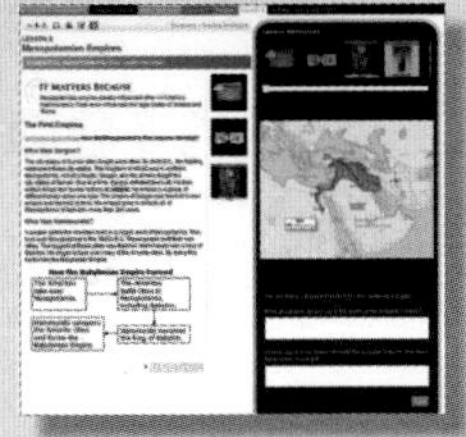

Use this online lower-level text that corresponds directly to the text in the Student Edition. It includes a Spanish version.

Guided Reading Activities

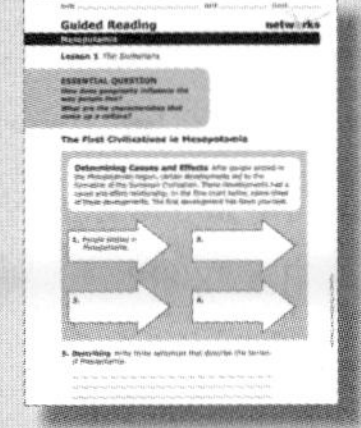

This resource uses graphic organizers and guiding questions to help students with comprehension.

What Do You Know?

Use these worksheets to pre-assess student's background knowledge before they study the chapter.

Reading Essentials and Study Guide Workbook

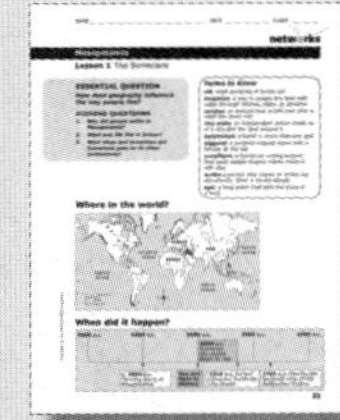

This resource offers writing and reading activities for the approaching-level student. Also available in Spanish.

Self-Check Quizzes

This online assessment tool provides instant feedback for students to check their progress.

How Do I Use the btw: Stuff You Should Know Current Events Web Site?

Using social media in the classroom sounds like a great idea. But where do you start?

The articles on McGraw-Hill's btw Web site offer engaging, student-centric coverage of current events. These articles can be used in your classroom in a number of ways.

Option 1 Use as a Bellringer Activity

- Start your class by having students read an article on *btw*. Then, launch a discussion by having students respond to the questions that accompany that article.
- Or, post the article on your classroom blog or discussion board and have the students respond to the questions as homework before you teach the content.

Option 2 Activate Critical Thinking

- Assign an article and the accompanying questions to encourage analysis of a specific topic.
- Use accompanying activities for group work during class time.

Option 3 Engage Students in High-Interest Projects

- Ask students to analyze different points of view and take a stand on current domestic and world issues in the "You Decide" feature.
- In the "Be an Active Citizen!" section, encourage students to link to the iCivics Web site inspired by Justice Sandra Day O'Connor.
- Tap into the btw "Teacher Page" to find tools to help you create more digitally-driven projects.

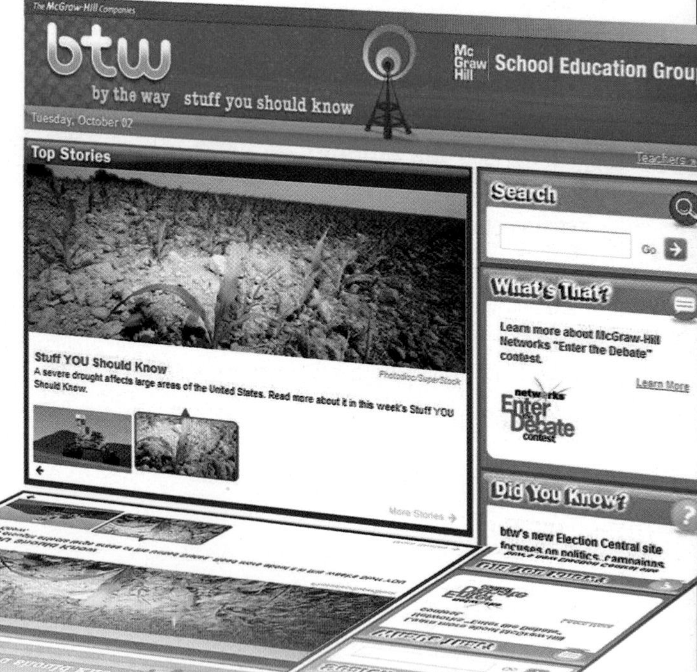

Visit **http://blog.glencoe.com** to keep up to date with the btw Current Events Web site.

Mesopotamia

3000 B.C. to 500 B.C.

ESSENTIAL QUESTIONS
• *How does geography influence the way people live?* • *Why does conflict develop?*

networks

There's More Online about the lives and customs of the Sumerians.

CHAPTER 4

Lesson 1
The Sumerians

Lesson 2
Mesopotamian Empires

The Story Matters . . .

Have you ever watched a large subdivision of homes being built? Did you notice solid structures beginning to appear on what was once only flat land? Assyrian King Ashurnasirpal II built such a project during his reign from 883–859 B.C. He took the small town of Nimrud and made it his capital. When he was finished, the city occupied about 900 acres. Around it, Ashurnasirpal II built a wall 120 feet thick, 42 feet high, and 5 miles long. The gates were guarded by two huge human-headed winged bulls. Parts of these gates can be seen in the New York Metropolitan Museum today. When he finished the city, the king held a festival attended by about 70,000 people. Here, he said, were "the happy people of all lands together. . . ."

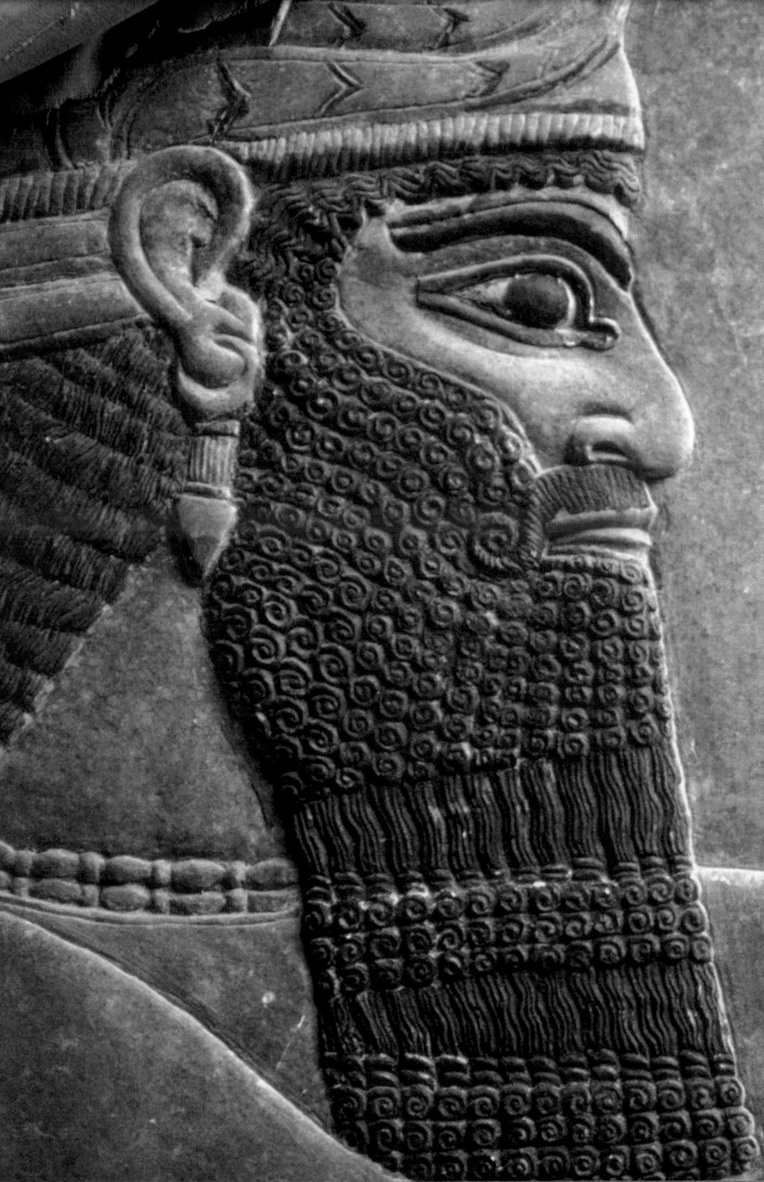

◄ *Relief sculpture of Ashurnasirpal II, Assyrian king from 883-859 B.C.*

Charles & Josette Lenars/Corbis

73

ENGAGE

Bellringer Ask a student to read aloud "The Story Matters. . . ." Then guide the class in a discussion of what it might have been like to live in the palace in Nimrud during the time of the Assyrian Empire. **Ask:** **Have you ever been inside a palace or mansion? Have you seen programs on television or movies that take place in a palace or mansion? What were they like?** Have a few students share their thoughts. Then **ask:** **Do you think historic buildings, like palaces or mansions, should be preserved? In what ways might these historic buildings benefit the community? Are there any examples of historic buildings in our community?** Tell the class that the history of Mesopotamia at this time is well documented because of the many Assyrian artifacts that have been found. Explain to interested students that they can learn more about the artifacts of Assyria online.

Making Connections

Read the following information to students.

Like Nimrud, the city of Washington, D.C., was purposely built to be a national capital. Congress designated the area where the city would be located, and George Washington selected the exact site. He set aside 82 acres for a "President's Park" where the White House would be built.

- The White House was once called the President's Palace; it was not officially named the White House until 1901, when President Theodore Roosevelt gave it that name.
- The White House has 132 rooms and 35 bathrooms.
- Until the Civil War, the White House was the largest house in the United States.

Letter from the Author

Dear World History Teacher,

The peoples of Mesopotamia built one of the first civilizations. They developed cities and struggled with organization as they moved from individual communities to larger territorial units and then to empires. They invented writing to keep records, and they created literature. They constructed monumental buildings and developed new political, military, social, and religious structures. The Mesopotamians left detailed records that allow us to view how they wrestled with three fundamental problems that humans have pondered: the nature of human relationships, the nature of the universe, and the role of divine forces in that universe.

Jackson J. Spielvogel

TEACH & ASSESS

Step Into the Place

V1 Visual Skills

Reading a Map Review the locator map, map key, compass rose, and scale with students. **Ask:**

- Why is a locator map included? *(to indicate where in the world the region in the larger map is located)*
- About how many miles across is Sumer at its widest point? *(about 170 miles)*
- In what general direction do the Tigris and Euphrates rivers flow on their way to the Persian Gulf? *(southeastern)*
- What large body of water borders the western portion of the Fertile Crescent? *(the Mediterranean Sea)*

As a class, discuss the Map Focus questions.

Explain to students that many areas of this region are arid or semi-arid. Ask students to name the deserts in this region and describe their locations on the map. Then discuss why people decided to settle in the Fertile Crescent rather than in other regions shown on the map. Tell students that civilizations developed where large numbers of people settled. **Ask:** What other area shown on the map might have become a center of civilization? *(Nile Delta)* AL ELL

Content Background Knowledge

- The Persian Gulf, Mediterranean Sea, and Caspian Sea are salty; only the rivers and a few smaller lakes provided water that could be used for agriculture.
- The Arabian Desert covers about 900,000 square miles; it averages just 4 inches of rain per year.
- The Syrian Desert receives fewer than 5 inches of rain a year.
- Most people in this region have always lived near the rivers.

ANSWERS, p. 74

Step Into the Place

1. the Euphrates River
2. about 500 miles
3. the Persian Gulf
4. CRITICAL THINKING The rivers would provide water for farming and transportation for goods and people.

Step Into the Time

Sumerians invent cuneiform, settlements develop along the Indus River, Assyrians control Mesopotamia, first Olympic Games

CHAPTER 4 

Place and Time: Mesopotamia 3000 B.C. to 500 B.C.

Mesopotamia extended from the Tigris River to the Euphrates. The Sumerians were the first settlers in the region. They are the people who developed the world's first civilization. Soon several civilizations appeared in Mesopotamia. This area was called the fertile crescent because of its shape.

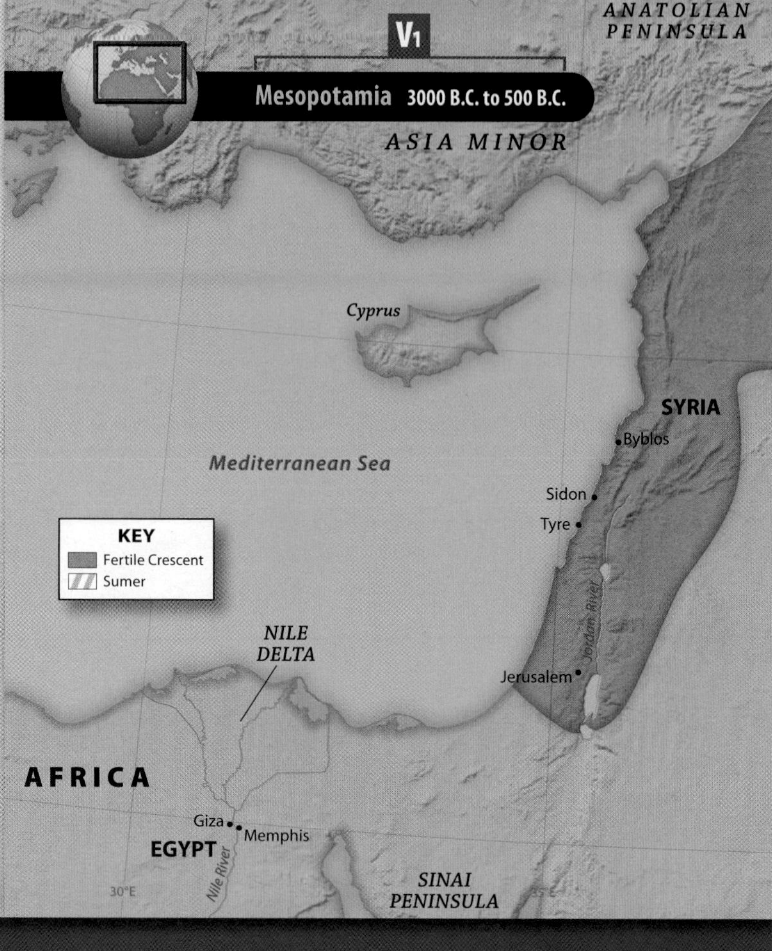

Step Into the Place

MAP FOCUS There were many Mesopotamian cities that arose along the Tigris and Euphrates Rivers.

1. **PLACE** What river flowed through the western side of Mesopotamia? RH.6–8.7
2. **LOCATION** What is the approximate distance from Nineveh to Ur? RH.6–8.7
3. **MOVEMENT** To what larger body of water did the people living along these rivers sail? RH.6–8.7
4. **CRITICAL THINKING** *Making Inferences* Why do you think many cities in Mesopotamia developed near rivers? RH.6–8.2

Step Into the Time

V2

TIME LINE Place these events in order, starting with the earliest: Assyrians control Mesopotamia, settlements develop along the Indus River, Sumerians invent cuneiform, and first Olympic Games. RH.6–8.7

MESOPOTAMIA
- c. 3200 B.C. Sumerians invent cuneiform writing system
- c. 3000 B.C. City-states arise in Sumer
- c. 2340 B.C. Sargon conquers Sumer
- c. 1792 B.C. Hammurabi becomes king of Babylonian Empire

3000 B.C. — 2000 B.C.

THE WORLD
- c. 2700 B.C. Chinese master art of silk weaving
- c. 2500 B.C. Settlements develop along Indus River
- c. 2300 B.C. Ceramics are produced in Central America
- c. 1800 B.C. Egyptians use mathematics for architecture

74 *Mesopotamia*

Project-Based Learning 

Hands-On Chapter Project

Mesopotamia

Students will create a poster showing one of the occupations of Sumerian society. Students will work in pairs to choose an occupation, conduct research, take notes, and document sources. Then team members will share information and create the poster and a bibliography. Pairs will present their posters to the class. Finally, both you and your students will complete the Rubric Assessment for each poster.

Technology Extension

Using Glogster for Online Interactive Multimedia Posters

Tell students they will be creating multimedia posters using Glogster. Organize small groups of students. Have them brainstorm Sumerian occupations, occupational tasks, and images that represent these occupations. Have students choose an occupation and begin researching. When the Glogs are completed, they can be shared via blog, wiki, or email, or by embedding them into a Web site.

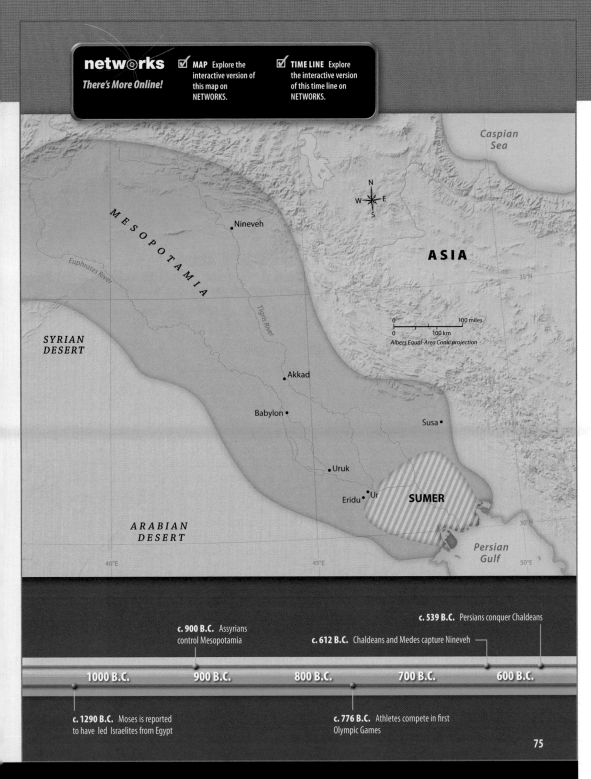

networks There's More Online!

MAP Explore the interactive version of this map on NETWORKS.

TIME LINE Explore the interactive version of this time line on NETWORKS.

Caspian Sea

MESOPOTAMIA

Nineveh

ASIA

Euphrates River

Tigris River

SYRIAN DESERT

0 100 miles
0 100 km
Albers Equal-Area Conic projection

Akkad

Babylon

Susa

Uruk

Eridu

Ur

SUMER

ARABIAN DESERT

Persian Gulf

40°E 45°E 50°E 35°N 30°N

c. 900 B.C. Assyrians control Mesopotamia

c. 612 B.C. Chaldeans and Medes capture Nineveh

c. 539 B.C. Persians conquer Chaldeans

1000 B.C. | 900 B.C. | 800 B.C. | 700 B.C. | 600 B.C.

c. 1290 B.C. Moses is reported to have led Israelites from Egypt

c. 776 B.C. Athletes compete in first Olympic Games

75

CHAPTER 4

Place and Time

Step Into the Time

V2 Visual Skills

Analyzing Time Lines Have students review the time line for the chapter. Explain that they will be studying events from about 3000 B.C. to 500 B.C. Ask these questions:

- **Based on the information in the time line, what was happening in Mesopotamia beginning around 3000 B.C.?** *(Sumerians developed an advanced civilization and formed city-states. Sargon conquered Sumer and all of Mesopotamia. Then a series of peoples took control of Mesopotamia: the Babylonians, the Assyrians, the Chaldeans and Medes, and finally the Persians.)*
- **What was happening elsewhere in the world at about the time Sargon conquered Sumer?** *(Ceramics were being produced in Central America.)*
- **How many years after the city-states arose in Sumer did the first settlements develop along the Indus River?** *(about 500 years)*

Content Background Knowledge

The Fertile Crescent provided the setting for the development of numerous early civilizations, beginning with the city-states of Sumer. These civilizations were dependent upon the Tigris and Euphrates rivers. Other early civilizations, likewise, grew up in river valleys. These included the Egyptian civilization along the Nile, the Harappan civilization along the Indus River on the Indian subcontinent, and the first Chinese civilization along the Wei River.

CLOSE & REFLECT

Formulating Questions Ask students to work in pairs and write two or three questions about the map and time line. Have them briefly discuss possible answers to their questions. Then, as a class, discuss some of the questions and proposed answers.

TIME LINE

Place and Time: Mesopotamia 3000 B.C. to 500 B.C.

Reading a Time Line Have students explore the interactive time line by opening and reading more details about each event. Then have students choose one event to investigate further online. Ask students to write a paragraph predicting the social, political, or economic consequences that the event may have had for the world.

See page 73B for other online activities.

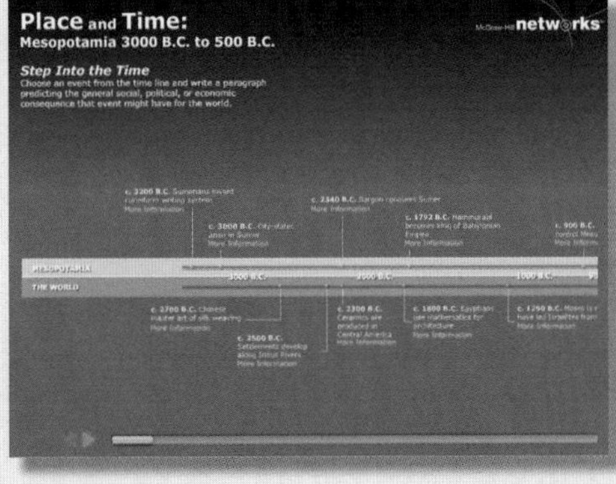

ENGAGE

Bellringer Have students skim "The First Civilizations in Mesopotamia," noting the headings, key terms, and images. Explain that archaeologists have found many artifacts that provided information about early Mesopotamian civilization. **Ask:**

- What do you think some of these artifacts might have been? *(Answers will vary, but students might mention pottery, cuneiform tablets, and religious statues.)*
- How does studying these artifacts help us learn more about these ancient people? *(Possible answers: They tell us what skills and technologies these people had, how they lived, and what they may have thought about and believed in.)*

TEACH & ASSESS

C1 Critical Thinking Skills

Making Inferences Explain that civilizations developed as people congregated into towns and cities. **Ask:**

- Why did living in towns lead to the development of social classes? *(Some people naturally took leadership positions; others were followers; some made more valuable goods and became wealthier; and so on.)*
- How did living in a city allow people to engage in specialized occupations? *(When people lived in isolated groups, people had to do many tasks to live. When people lived in cities, they could divide up the work, each doing specific jobs.)* BL

C2 Critical Thinking Skills

Making Connections Remind students what they have learned about the geography of the region. **Ask:** Why would people choose to build a civilization on the plain between the two rivers? *(There would be plenty of water for irrigating crops, drinking, and other uses. The flat landscape was easier to build on and to farm on.)* AL

ANSWER, p. 76

TAKING NOTES: Answers might include writing, the wheel, a number system based on 60, and the wooden plow.

networks *There's More Online!*

- GRAPHIC ORGANIZER Sumerian Inventions
- IMAGE Cuneiform
- SLIDE SHOW
  - Ancient Irrigation Methods
  - The Ziggurat
  - Sumerian Jewelry

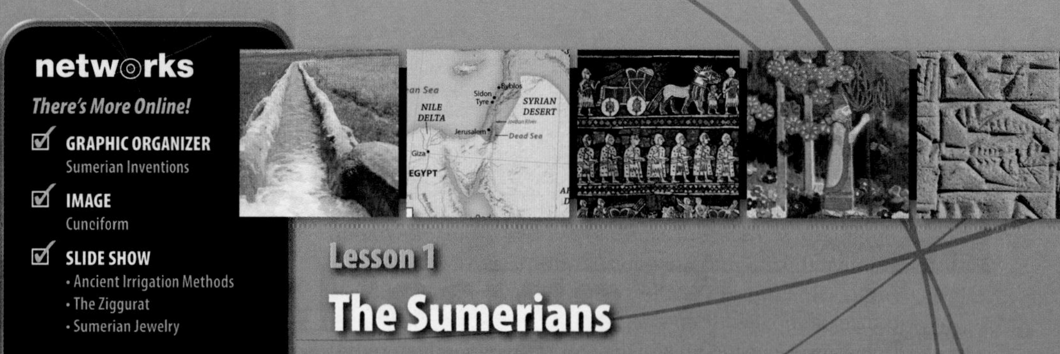

Lesson 1

The Sumerians

ESSENTIAL QUESTION *How does geography influence the way people live?*

IT MATTERS BECAUSE

The Sumerians made important advances in areas such as farming and writing that laid the foundation for future civilizations.

The First Civilizations in Mesopotamia

GUIDING QUESTION *Why did people settle in Mesopotamia?*

C1 Civilizations first developed about 3000 B.C. in the river valleys of Mesopotamia (MEH • suh • puh • TAY • mee • uh), Egypt, India, and China. Throughout history, the need to have water for drinking and growing crops influenced where people settled. Although there were differences among the early civilizations, they were alike in many ways. As these early civilizations developed, people formed social classes. The social class people belonged to partly depended on their occupations. They did specialized types of work. Using improved technology, they made more and better goods. They set up governments to pass laws, defend their land, and carry out large building projects. The people of these civilizations also developed systems of values and beliefs that gave meaning to their lives.

The Two Rivers

C2 Mesopotamia, the earliest known civilization, developed in what is now southern Iraq (ih•RAHK). Mesopotamia means "the land between the rivers" in Greek. The civilization began on the plain between the Tigris (TY•gruhs) and the Euphrates (yu•FRAY•teez) rivers.

Reading HELPDESK CCSS

Taking Notes: ***Identifying***

On a diagram like this one, identify two major inventions of the Sumerians. RH.6–8.2

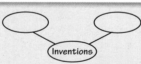

Inventions

Content Vocabulary (Tier 3 Words)

- silt
- irrigation
- surplus
- city-state
- polytheism
- ziggurat
- cuneiform
- scribe
- epic

76 *Mesopotamia*

networks ***Online Teaching Options***

VIDEO

Mesopotamia: An Overview

Drawing Conclusions Explain to students that this video will give them an overview of Sumer, an early Mesopotamian civilization. Ask them to take notes as they view the video. Then organize students into small groups, and ask them to discuss which achievements of the Sumerians are left, even though the Sumerian civilization itself disappeared and left few clues to its existence. AL **Visual/Spatial**

See page 73C for other online activities.

These rivers run about **parallel** to each other and flow more than 1,000 miles (1,600 km). They run southeast from the mountains of southeastern Asia to the Persian (PUR•zhuhn) Gulf.

Mesopotamia itself was located in the eastern part of the larger Fertile Crescent. This curving strip of good farmland extends from the Mediterranean (mehd•uh•tuh•RAY•nee•uhn) Sea to the Persian Gulf. The Fertile Crescent includes parts of the modern countries of Turkey, Syria, Iraq, Lebanon, Israel, and Jordan.

Early Valley Dwellers

For thousands of years, clues to Mesopotamia's history lay buried among its ruins and piles of rubble. In the 1800s, archaeologists began to dig up many buildings and artifacts. These finds revealed much about early Mesopotamia.

R

Historians believe that people first settled Mesopotamia about 7000 B.C. The first settlers were hunters and herders. By about 4000 B.C., some of these groups had moved to the plain of the Tigris-Euphrates valley. They built farming villages along the two rivers.

Irrigation canals help farmers grow crops in areas that would otherwise be dry and not suitable for farming.

FLPA/Alamy

Taming the Rivers

Early Mesopotamian farmers used water from the Tigris and Euphrates Rivers to water their fields. However, the farmers could not always rely on the rivers for their needs. Little or no rain fell in the summer. As a result, the rivers were often low. The farmers did not have enough water to plant crops in the fall.

C

During the spring harvest, rains and melting snow from the northern mountains caused rivers to overflow their banks. This flooded the plains. Sometimes, unexpected and violent floods swept away crops, homes, and livestock.

Yet farmers in Mesopotamia knew that the floods were also helpful. Flooded rivers were filled with **silt**, or small particles of soil. When the floods ended, silt was left on the banks and plains. The silt proved to be a very good soil for farming.

Over time, people in Mesopotamia learned to build dams to control the seasonal floods. They dug canals that let water flow from a water source to their fields. This method of watering crops is called **irrigation** (IHR • uh • GAY • shuhn).

silt fine particles of fertile soil

irrigation a system that supplies dry land with water through ditches, pipes, or streams

Academic Vocabulary (Tier 2 Words)

parallel moving or lying in the same direction and the same distance apart

R Reading Skills

Applying From the text, review the pronunciations and meanings of unfamiliar words and names, paying particular attention to *Persian Gulf, Mediterranean Sea, silt,* and *irrigation.* Ask volunteers to pronounce the words and offer meanings if they know them. AL ELL **Auditory/Musical**

Have students summarize the text. **Ask:** How did the lives of the first settlers change when they settled the Tigris-Euphrates valley? *(They changed from relying upon hunting and herding animals to farming and raising crops.)* How were the rivers both a benefit and a disadvantage to these people? *(The rivers made agriculture possible, but they also destroyed homes and fields when they flooded.)* AL

C Critical Thinking Skills

Making Connections Point out that the cycle of flooding and drought occurs in other river systems around the world. **Ask:** Where does such a cycle occur in the United States? *(Possible answers: the Mississippi, Ohio, and Missouri river valleys)* How are these cycles like the cycle experienced by the Mesopotamians? *(Both caused loss of crops, homes, and sometimes human life.)*

Content Background Knowledge

- The Euphrates is 2,235 miles (3,596 km.) long.
- The Tigris River is 1,180 miles (1,899 km.) long.
- Both rivers originate in the high mountains of what is now eastern Turkey.
- Although shorter, the Tigris River carries more water and is a swifter river than the Euphrates. It also tends to be more unpredictable and to have larger floods.
- The Euphrates is located above the plain and so is easier to tap for irrigation. The Tigris has cut more deeply into the land, and so its water is more difficult to access.

SLIDE SHOW

Ancient Irrigation

Summarize a Process Review how irrigation works, reminding students that the great civilizations of Mesopotamia could not have existed without the development of irrigation. Then have students watch the interactive slide show about irrigation. Have students describe in their own words how irrigation works and how it changes a civilization.

See page 73C for other online activities.

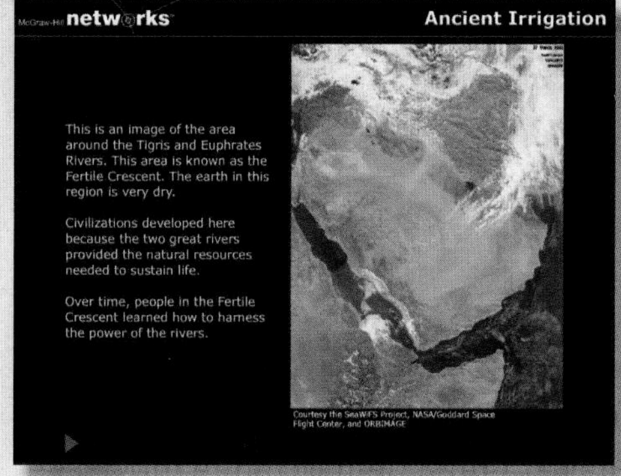

networks
Ancient Irrigation
This is an image of the area around the Tigris and Euphrates Rivers. This area is known as the Fertile Crescent. The earth in this region is very dry.
Civilizations developed here because the two great rivers provided the natural resources needed to sustain life.
Over time, people in the Fertile Crescent learned how to harness the power of the rivers.

V

V Visual Skills

Analyzing Maps Remind students that maps can provide certain kinds of information much more clearly and quickly than a written description. Tell students to study the map, and then ask them these questions:

- **How would you describe the landscape where the Tigris and Euphrates rivers originated?** *(mountainous)*
- **What cities developed along the lower parts of the Tigris and Euphrates rivers?** *(Uruk, Ur, and Eridu)*
- **Where do the Tigris and Euphrates join?** *(in southern Mesopotamia, about 100 miles before the combined rivers reach the Persian Gulf)* AL ELL **Visual/Spatial**

R Reading Skills

Discussing After students have read the text, lead a discussion about the advantages of rivers and irrigation for a civilization. **Ask: How did the two rivers and irrigation technology make it possible for the Mesopotamian civilization to arise?** *(They allowed greater production of food, so that some people could spend time on activities besides farming. People were able to develop the goods, technology, trade, and skills that gave rise to the civilization.)*

C Critical Thinking Skills

Making Inferences Call students' attention to the locations of the Sumerian cities of Babylon, Ur, and Uruk. **Ask: What political and military advantages might these locations have given to the city-states?** *(The city-states could control travel up and down the rivers. They would have easy access to river transportation for trade.)* BL

ANSWERS, p. 78

GEOGRAPHY CONNECTION

1. Nineveh
2. **CRITICAL THINKING** The Tigris and Euphrates rivers provided water for drinking and for crops. Also, the flooding of these two rivers made the soil fertile. As a result, agriculture flourished, allowing people to specialize in crafts and other activities.

✓ **PROGRESS CHECK** Rich silt, which helped crops grow, was left behind by floodwaters.

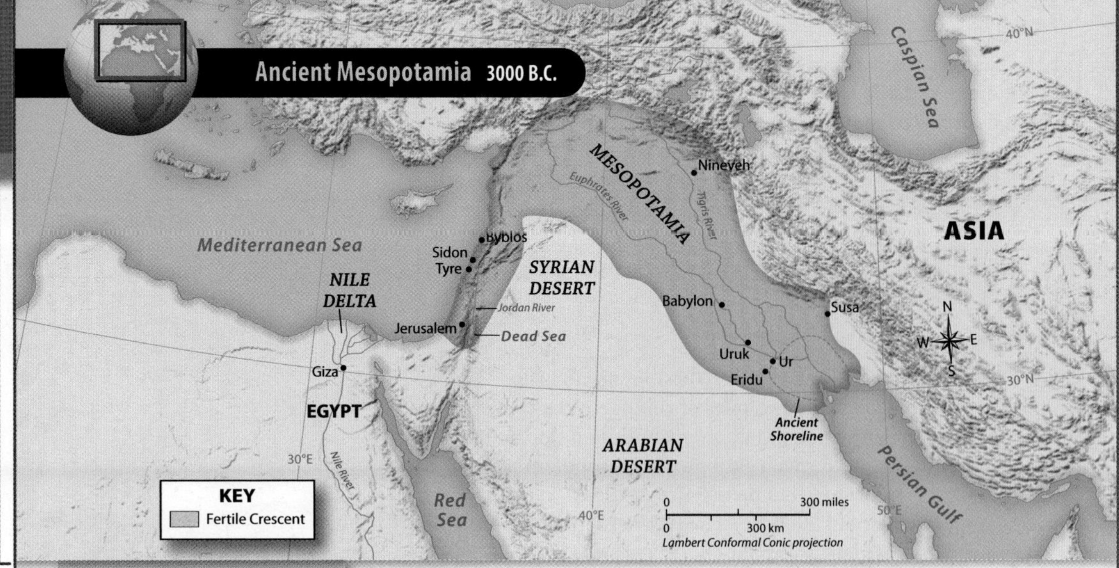

GEOGRAPHY CONNECTION

A number of great civilizations developed in Mesopotamia.

1. **LOCATION** What city was located in northern Mesopotamia?
2. **CRITICAL THINKING** *Making Inferences* Why do you think Mesopotamia was a good location for the growth of civilization?

Irrigation let these early farmers grow **surpluses** (SUHR•plus•ehz)—or extra amounts—of food. Farmers stored the surpluses for later use.

When food was plentiful, not all people needed to farm. Some became artisans, or skilled workers. They specialized in weaving cloth and making pottery, tools, and weapons.

As artisans made more goods, people's lives changed. People began to live together in places that favored trade. Small farming villages grew into cities. By 3000 B.C., several cities developed in Sumer (SOO•mer), a region in southern Mesopotamia. R

✓ **PROGRESS CHECK**

Explaining How did floods sometimes help farmers?

Sumer's Civilization

GUIDING QUESTION *What was life like in Sumer?*

C Sumer's people were known as Sumerians. They built the first cities in Southwest Asia, including Ur (uhr), Uruk (OO•rook), and Eridu (ER•i•doo). These cities became centers of civilization that controlled the lower part of the Tigris and Euphrates valleys.

Reading HELPDESK CCSS

surplus an amount that is left over after a need has been met

city-state a city that governs itself and its surrounding territory

polytheism a belief in more than one god

networks *Online Teaching Options*

MAP

Ancient Mesopotamia, 3000 B.C.

Analyzing Maps Have students click to reveal the location of the Fertile Crescent, as well as the main city-states of this region of the ancient world. Then ask them to listen to audio that provides background on Mesopotamia.

See page 73C for other online activities.

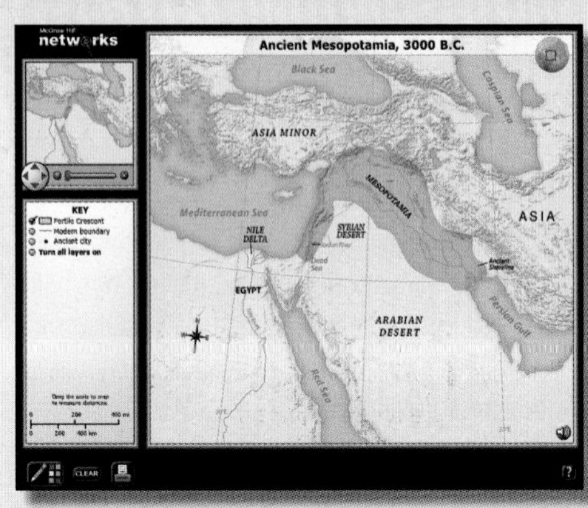

City-States Arise

Sumer's cities were surrounded by mudflats and patches of scorching desert. The harsh landscape made it hard to travel by land and communicate with other groups. This meant that each city was largely cut off from its neighbors.

As a result, Sumerian cities became independent. The people of each city raised their own crops and made their own goods. As the cities grew, they gained political and economic control over the lands around them. By doing this, they formed **city-states**. Each city-state had its own government and was not part of any larger governing state. The population of the city-states ranged from about 5,000 to 20,000 people.

Historians think that each Sumerian city-state was protected by a large city wall. Ruins and artifacts have been found by archaeologists that support this theory. Because stone and wood were in short supply, the Sumerians used mud from the rivers as their main building material. They mixed mud with crushed reeds, formed bricks, and left them in the sun to dry. The gates of the wall stayed open during the day but were closed at night for protection. The ruler's palace, a large temple, and other public buildings were located in the center of the city.

Often, these city-states went to war with one another over resources and political borders. Sometimes, they fought to win glory or to gain more territory. During times of peace, city-states traded with each other. They also agreed to help each other by forming alliances (uh•LY•uhns•uhs) to protect their common interests.

Gods, Priests, and Kings

The Sumerian people worshipped many gods, a type of belief known as **polytheism** (PAH•lee•thee•ih•zuhm). These multiple gods played different roles in Sumerian life. The Sumerians thought that some gods had power over parts of nature, such as the rain or the wind. They also believed that some gods guided the things that people did, such as plowing or brick-making. They honored whatever god would help their activity.

Although Sumerians honored all the gods, each city-state claimed one as its own.

In areas where there was little rainfall, farmers watered their fields using irrigation channels.

▶ CRITICAL THINKING
Analyzing What other water sources were available in addition to the river?

R Reading Skills

Explaining Have students find text evidence to explain how the environment contributed to the development of the Sumer civilization and to the formation of the city-states. **Ask: What is a city-state?** *(a city that governs itself and its surrounding territory)* Discuss how archaeologists have come to know about the city-states, then **ask:**

- **What is an archaeologist?** *(someone who studies ancient peoples and their cultures by looking at artifacts and ruins)*
- **What are ruins?** *(the decayed remnants of homes, cities, and other structures)* **What are artifacts?** *(things that people have made)* AL ELL

W Writing Skills

Informative/Explanatory As you discuss city-states, have students list the characteristics of the Sumerian city-states. Then have them write a paragraph comparing those ancient cities with modern American cities. **Verbal/Linguistic**

When students finish, guide a discussion on this question: **Are the Sumerian city-states and modern American cities more alike or more different than one another?**

IMAGE

Everyday Life in Sumer

Analyzing Visuals Students can click on "more information" to read text that describes the everyday life of Sumerians in more detail. After students read the text, have them look closely at the tapestry. Ask them to write a paragraph describing in detail what these images tell them about life in ancient Sumer.

See page 73C for other online activities.

McGraw-Hill networks
Everyday Life in Sumer
People lived in villages in Sumer, and clusters of villages formed larger cities. The cities usually had a temple to a chosen god in the form of a ziggurat. With cuneiform, their form of writing, laws were recorded, as well as property sales. If a farmer bought some cows, for example, the sale was recorded on clay tablets. Clay was also used to make bowls for eating and serving food. Farmers grew crops with the help of their new irrigation systems. People's jobs included fishing, building the large temple buildings, raising date palms, and breeding animals. Others built ships, created pottery, and wove fabric. Goods produced in large amounts, like dates, were often traded in other villages and cities.
Michael Holford

ANSWER, p. 79

CRITICAL THINKING rain and canals

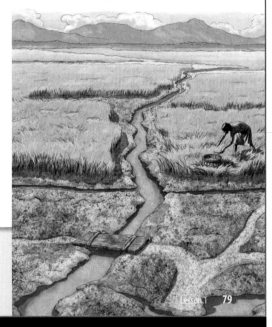

V Visual Skills

Analyzing Images Have students read the text about the ziggurat and then compare what they have read to the picture. Ask the following questions:

- **What are some key characteristics of the ziggurat shown in the picture?** *(It is the highest place in the city. It is surrounded by a wall. It is shaped like a pyramid with five levels.)* AL
- **What can you infer about Sumerian society from the wall around the ziggurat?** *(Possible answers: The ziggurat was a holy place, and the wall kept out people who were not allowed to enter. This might show that ziggurat priests were a special group in the society.)* **Visual/Spatial**

R Reading Skills

Discussing After students have read the text, discuss the social groups of Sumer. Ask students to describe the kinds of people who made up each class. **Ask: How do the social classes in Sumer compare with those in our society?** *(We also have three classes, but ours are defined by wealth rather than strictly by social status. We do not have royalty or enslaved persons; instead we have the upper class, middle class, and poor.)*

Invite students to try to explain how the Sumer social classes developed, and why.  BL **Verbal/Linguistic**

The ziggurat was built to be visible throughout the city-state. The walls of the ziggurat enclosed the royal warehouses and the city's treasury.

▶ CRITICAL THINKING
Speculating Why do you think the Sumerians would want the ziggurat to be highly visible?

To honor its god, a city-state often included a large temple called a **ziggurat** (ZIG•oo•rat). The word *ziggurat* means "to rise high" in the ancient Akkadian (uh•KAY•dee•uhn) language. The very top of the ziggurat was a holy place. It was the god's home, and only special priests were allowed to go there. In the early days, priests of the ziggurat ruled the city-states. Groups of important men helped them govern. Later, Sumerian city-states became monarchies. V

Sumerian kings claimed they received their power to rule from the city's god. The first kings were most likely war heroes. Over time, their rule became hereditary. This meant that after a king died, his son took over. In most cases, the wives of kings did not have political power. However, some controlled their own lands.

Social Groups

People in Sumer were divided into social classes. Generally, people remained in the social class into which they were born. Kings, priests, warriors, and government officials belonged to the upper class. The middle class **consisted** of merchants, farmers, fishers, and artisans. The middle class was Sumer's largest social group. Enslaved people made up Sumer's lowest class. Most of these workers had been captured in war. Also, criminals and people who could not pay their debts often were enslaved. Enslaved men and women worked for the upper class. R

Women and men had different roles in Sumerian society. The basic unit of society was the family. Men were the head of the home. Boys went to school and were trained for a specific job. Sumerian women ran the home, taught their daughters to do the same, and cared for the children. Women had a few civil rights. Some owned businesses. Sumerian law required parents to care for their children. The law also required adult children to care for their parents if their parents needed help.

Reading HELPDESK CCSS

ziggurat a pyramid-shaped structure with a temple at the top

Academic Vocabulary (Tier 2)
consist to be made up of

Reading Strategy: *Summarizing*
When you summarize, you find the main idea of a passage and restate it in your own words. Read the paragraph under the heading "Social Groups." On a separate sheet of paper, summarize the paragraph in one or two sentences.

networks *Online Teaching Options*

SLIDE SHOW

The Ziggurat

Making Inferences Have students watch the interactive slide show to help them make connections between ziggurats and modern structures. **Ask: Do you think ziggurats were important to the Sumerians? Explain.** *(Yes, ziggurats were huge, so they must have been important. Also, Sumerians worshiped their gods at the ziggurats. Since their gods were important to them, so too were the ziggurats.)* **Are there any buildings in the United States that are as important to American culture as the ziggurat was to Sumerian culture? Explain.** *(Answers will vary. For example, a student might say that the White House is important because the president lives there.)*

networks
The Ziggurat
The ziggurat in each city-state was built to stand out in the city's skyline.

See page 73C for other online activities.

ANSWERS, p. 80

CRITICAL THINKING Answers will vary but may include the idea that they wanted to emphasize the importance of the temple.

Reading Strategy The Sumerian social structure included an upper class, a middle class, and a lower class that was made up of enslaved people. Most Sumerians belonged to the middle class.

Farmers and Traders

R If you lived in Sumer, you were most likely a farmer. Each farmer had a plot of land located in the area around a city-state. Dams and waterways ran through this farmland. Wheat, barley, and dates were the major crops. Farmers also raised sheep, goats, and pigs.

Trade was another key part of Sumer's economy. The Sumerians did not have some of the goods that they needed. **C** For example, even though many Sumerians were skilled metalworkers, they had to trade with other peoples to obtain most of their metals. Trade routes linked Sumer to places as far away as India and Egypt.

Sumerian merchants went to other lands. They traded wheat, barley, and tools for timber, minerals, and metals. The minerals and metals were then used to make jewelry or tools. For jewelry making, Sumerians valued a red stone called carnelian from India's Indus Valley. They also searched for a blue stone known as lapis lazuli from what is now Afghanistan. Traders returned with iron and silver from present-day Turkey.

Sumerian artisans produced a variety of goods, including jewelry. This piece is made of gold and lapis lazuli.

▶ CRITICAL THINKING

Speculating If you were an artisan in ancient times, what would you produce?

✓ PROGRESS CHECK

Analyzing Why do you think the Sumerians built cities with walls around them?

Sumerian Contributions

GUIDING QUESTION *What ideas and inventions did Sumerians pass on to other civilizations?*

The Sumerians created the first civilization that had a great influence on history. Later civilizations copied and improved many of the ideas and inventions that began in Sumer. As a result, Mesopotamia has been called the "cradle of civilization." It was the beginning of organized human society.

Writing

Of all the contributions made by Sumerians to the world, writing is perhaps the most important. The writing system they developed was the earliest known system in the world.

This Royal Standard of Ur —the royal design—shows scenes of everyday life in Sumer. *Which methods of travel are shown on this standard?*

R Reading Skills

Explaining Have volunteers take turns reading the text aloud. Lead a discussion on the role and importance of farming in Sumer. Invite students to explain why most people in this society were probably farmers. Ask and discuss these questions:

- What are some foods that Sumerian farmers planted? *(wheat, barley, dates)* AL
- What livestock did farmers raise? *(sheep, goats, pigs)* AL
- What would the daily life of a Sumerian farmer have been like? *(Possible answer: Farmers would have had to tend their crops and livestock. They would have had to maintain their irrigation ditches, waterways, and dams.)* BL

C Critical Thinking Skills

Drawing Conclusions Direct students to look at the necklace shown on the page and to read the caption. **Ask:**

- People from what class would most likely have worn a piece of jewelry like this? Why do you think so? *(It was probably worn by someone of the upper class because the necklace is made of gold and lapis, valuable materials that would have been brought from far away. Only a highly skilled artisan could have made it. So the piece was costly, and probably only someone from the upper class could have afforded it.)*
- What can you conclude about Sumerian society from this piece? *(It was a prosperous society with skilled craftspeople and an extensive trading system.)*

WORKSHEET

Economics of History Activity: Mesopotamia, The Sumerians

Applying Introduce students to the Economics of History activity to help them understand the bartering system used in Sumer. Students may complete the worksheet as homework.

See page 73C for other online activities.

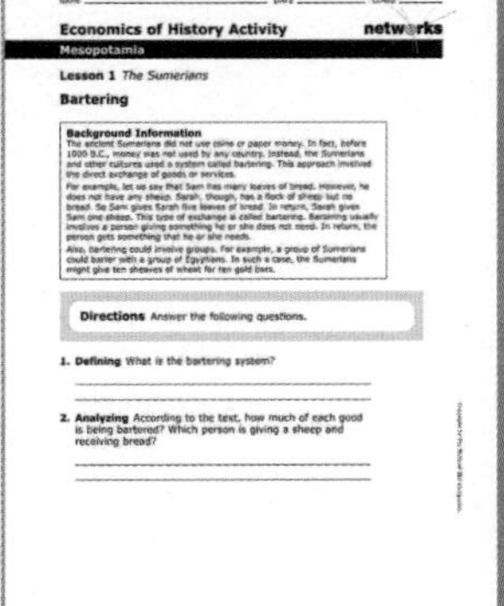

NAME ______ DATE ______ CLASS ______

Economics of History Activity networks

Mesopotamia

Lesson 1 *The Sumerians*

Bartering

Background Information
The ancient Sumerians did not use coins or paper money. In fact, before 1000 B.C., money was not used by any country. Instead, the Sumerians and other cultures used a system called bartering. This approach involved the direct exchange of goods or services.

For example, let us say that Sam has many loaves of bread. However, he does not have any sheep. Sarah, though, has a flock of sheep but no bread. So Sam gives Sarah five loaves of bread. In return, Sarah gives Sam one sheep. This type of exchange is called bartering. Bartering usually involves a person giving something he or she does not need. In return, the person gets something that he or she needs.

Also, bartering could involve groups. For example, a group of Sumerians could barter with a group of Egyptians. In such a case, the Sumerians might give ten sheaves of wheat for ten gold bars.

Directions Answer the following questions.

1. **Defining** What is the bartering system?

2. **Analyzing** According to the text, how much of each good is being bartered? Which person is giving a sheep and receiving bread?

ANSWERS, p. 81

CRITICAL THINKING Answers will vary, but students should try to identify various crafted goods produced in Sumer.

Caption: The standard shows people riding in chariots and walking.

✓ PROGRESS CHECK They built walled cities for defense.

C1 Critical Thinking

Reasoning Emphasize to students that the Sumerian cuneiform writing is the earliest known form of writing. Before the development of this technology, people would have had to depend entirely on their memories or oral history. **Ask:** **How would the lives of ancient people have been different if they had not developed writing?** *(Answers will vary. Students may say that people could not have kept records of business transactions or recorded their history or stories. They could not have recorded directions or methods of doing things.)* Guide a discussion of how the invention of writing would have changed people's lives. **BL Verbal/Linguistic**

C2 Critical Thinking

Speculating Point out that paper was a later technology, so Sumerians had to find another material on which to write. **Ask:** **Compared with paper, what were the disadvantages of clay tablets as a writing material?** *(Possible answers: The clay would have had to be prepared each time; it would have had to be kept damp while records were being made; it was heavy and cumbersome to store.)*

Point out that clay tablets were also durable. **What might have happened to Sumerian writing if Sumerians had used paper?** *(We might not have any record of it.)*

Sumerians needed materials for building and making tools. They sailed to other lands to trade for wood logs to take home.

Gianni Dagli Orti/CORBIS

C1 Writing was a way for Sumerians to keep records of their lives and their history. Writing was also a way to share information. They could pass on their ideas to later generations.

Sumerians created a way of writing called **cuneiform** (kyoo•NEE•uh•FAWRM). The cuneiform writing system was made up of about 1,200 different characters. Characters represented such things as names, physical objects, and numbers. Cuneiform was written by cutting wedge-shaped marks into damp clay with a sharp reed. The name *cuneiform* comes from a Latin word meaning "wedge." C2 Sumerians wrote on clay because they did not have paper. Archaeologists have found cuneiform tablets that have provided important information about Mesopotamian history.

Only a few people—mostly boys from wealthy families—learned how to read and write cuneiform. After years of training, some students became **scribes** (SKRYBS), or official record keepers. Scribes wrote documents that recorded much of the everyday life in Mesopotamia, including court records, marriage contracts, business dealings, and important events. Some scribes were judges and government officials.

Sumerians told stories orally for centuries. After developing writing, they were able to record these stories. Their tales praised the gods and warriors for doing great deeds. The world's oldest known story is from Sumer. Written more than

Reading HELPDESK CCSS

cuneiform a system of writing developed by the Sumerians that used wedge-shaped marks made in soft clay

scribe a person who copies or writes out documents; often a record keeper

epic a long poem that records the deeds of a legendary or real hero

networks Online Teaching Options

IMAGE

Cuneiform Writing

Comparing Have students click on the first bullet to reveal text that describes the process of cuneiform writing. Have them write a summary of the process in their own words. Ask them to consider any special skills required to write in this medium compared with writing on paper.

See page 73C for other online activities.

4,000 years ago and still studied today, this story is called the *Epic of Gilgamesh* (GIHL•guh•MEHSH). An **epic** is a long poem that tells the story of a hero.

Technology and Mathematics

The people of Mesopotamia also made many useful inventions. For example, the Sumerians were the first people to use the wheel. The earliest wheels were solid wood circles made from carved boards that were clamped together. A Sumerian illustration from about 3500 B.C. shows a wheeled vehicle. They built the first carts, which were pulled by donkeys. They also introduced vehicles into military use with the development of the chariot.

R

For river travel, Sumerians developed the sailboat. They invented a wooden plow to help them in the fields. Artisans made the potter's wheel, which helped to shape clay into bowls and jars. Sumerians were also the first to make bronze out of copper and tin. They used bronze to craft stronger tools, weapons, and jewelry.

The Sumerians also studied mathematics and astronomy. They used geometry to measure the size of fields and to plan buildings. They created a place-value system of numbers based on 60. They also devised tables for calculating division and multiplication. The 60-minute hour, 60-second minute, and 360-degree circle we use today are ideas that came from the Sumerians. Sumerians watched the positions of the stars. It showed them the best times to plant crops and to hold religious ceremonies. They also made a 12-month calendar based on the cycles of the moon.

W

✓ PROGRESS CHECK

Explaining Why did the Sumerians invent a writing system?

Sumerian writing etched on stone has been found by archaeologists.

Louvre, Paris/Bridgeman Art Library

Thinking Like a HISTORIAN

Classifying and Categorizing Information

The Sumerians invented or improved many items and methods. To classify these, look for topics with broad characteristics, such as *farming* or *communication*. Under each broad classification, you can divide the topic into narrower categories. Under farming, for example, include the category *irrigation*. Create a chart to organize broad topics and categories for the Sumerians' inventions and present your information to the class. For more about classifying and categorizing, read the chapter *What Does a Historian Do?*

LESSON 1 REVIEW (CCSS)

Review Vocabulary (Tier 3 Words)

1. How were *polytheism* and *ziggurats* related in Sumerian civilization? RH.6–8.4

Answer the Guiding Questions

2. ***Describing*** Where is the Fertile Crescent located? Where is Mesopotamia located? RH.6–8.7
3. ***Comparing*** How were the social classes of Sumer organized? RH.6–8.2
4. ***Identifying*** What was the most common role for women in Sumerian society? RH.6–8.2
5. ***Describing*** Why were scribes important in Sumerian society? RH.6–8.2
6. **ARGUMENT** Sumerians developed many inventions. Choose the invention that you think is the most significant and explain why you made this choice. WHST.6–8.1, WHST.6–8.10

LESSON 1 REVIEW ANSWERS

1. The Sumerian people practiced polytheism, or the worship of many gods and goddesses. The ziggurat was the temple in a Sumerian city that was dedicated to the chief god or goddess of the city.
2. The Fertile Crescent is an area of land extending from the Mediterranean Sea to the Persian Gulf. Mesopotamia is the name for the region between the Tigris and Euphrates rivers. Mesopotamia lies within the Fertile Crescent.
3. The upper class consisted of kings, priests, warriors, and government officials. The middle class included merchants, farmers, fishers, and artisans. Enslaved people made up the lower class.
4. Most women ran their households and cared for and raised their children.
5. There were few scribes, so their skill was special. Their important work included recording business transactions and documenting Sumerian history and literature.
6. Answers will vary, but students should demonstrate knowledge of the invention they chose and support its importance.

R Reading Skills

Discussing After students have read the text, ask them to consider the importance of inventions to a particular culture. **Ask:** **What inventions did the Sumerians develop?** *(the wheel, cart, chariot, sailboat, plow, potter's wheel, bronze, the place-value system of numbers, tables for calculating division and multiplication, the 60-minute hour, the 360-degree circle, and the 12-month calendar)*

Discuss ways in which these inventions changed ancient people's lives as well as benefited our own. AL

W Writing Skills

Argument Ask students to write a short essay explaining which of the Sumerian inventions was ultimately the most important. Remind them to give reasons and facts to support their conclusion **Verbal/Linguistic**

Have students complete the Lesson 1 Review

CLOSE & REFLECT

Making Connections To close the lesson, have students consider the effect of the environment and geography on the rise of civilization in Mesopotamia. Ask them to think about how, as a result of this civilization, crucial developments occurred, such as the invention of writing, the wheel, and bronze. Invite students to predict how these developments may have affected people in other parts of the ancient world.

ANSWER, p. 83

✓ PROGRESS CHECK They invented a writing system to record business dealings and other important information.

ENGAGE

Bellringer Tell students that they are going to read an excerpt from the world's oldest known story. It was written more than 4,000 years ago in Sumer.

Ask: **How does knowing the historical background of a story help you to understand it better?** *(Answers will vary. Students may say that knowing how people lived when a story was created, their beliefs, what events and conditions influenced their lives, and what they knew about the world will help them better understand the events, characters, and themes of the story.)* BL

TEACH & ASSESS

R Reading Skills

Explaining Have volunteers take turns reading. Explain to students that although a historical king named Gilgamesh existed, no evidence proves that he accomplished the deeds described in the *Epic of Gilgamesh*. Have students read the introduction to the epic. **Ask:** **What clues tell you that at least part of the epic is a fictional story rather than a factual record of events?** *(Students should note that Gilgamesh is described as a god and a human in Mesopotamian mythology. The epic also tells about an episode in which Gilgamesh and Enkidu set out to slay a monstrous giant with the face of a lion, who can start fire with his breath and cause floods with his roar.)* AL

Content Background Knowledge

- The tablets recording the *Epic of Gilgamesh* were written in about 2000 B.C., but they recorded an epic that had been passed down orally from even earlier times.
- The epic was well-known during ancient times, but then it was lost and forgotten.
- The 12 tablets recording the *Epic of Gilgamesh* were discovered in the Nineveh ruins in the 1850s by British archaeologists, who shipped them to the British Museum along with 100,000 other tablets and fragments. The epic lay unidentified in the British Museum until 1872, when the museum curator rediscovered the tablets lying in his own museum.

THE WORLD'S LITERATURE CCSS

Epic of Gilgamesh

Gilgamesh (c. 2000 B.C.)

R Gilgamesh ruled Uruk in southern Mesopotamia sometime around 2000 B.C. According to mythology, he was a god and a human. It is believed that Gilgamesh was a harsh ruler until his friendship with Enkidu (EN • kee • doo) taught him to be fair and kind. In this epic poem, Gilgamesh faces many challenges. He suffers many losses and must confront his biggest fear: death. Eventually, Gilgamesh learns he cannot avoid death.

This excerpt tells the story of when Gilgamesh and his friend, Enkidu, decide to become heroes. They set out to kill Humbaba (hum•BAH•bah), a monstrous giant who ruled the cedar forest where gods lived. Humbaba has the face of a lion and his breath ignites fire, while his roar unleashes floods.

"Don't be afraid, said Gilgamesh. We are together. There is nothing We should fear."

—from Gilgamesh: A Verse Narrative
tr. Herbert Mason

Mary Evans Picture Library

networks Online Teaching Options

MAP

Ancient Mesopotamia 3000 B.C. to 500 B.C.

Analyzing Maps Project the interactive version of the map of ancient Mesopotamia. Remind students that Gilgamesh was a real king who ruled the city of Uruk. Have a volunteer use the pen tool to circle the location of Uruk on the map. **Ask:** **On what river is Uruk located?** *(Euphrates River)*

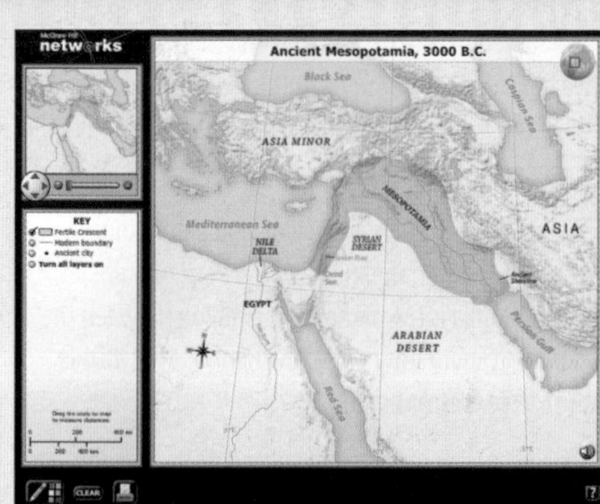

Epic of Gilgamesh

PRIMARY SOURCE

"Enkidu was afraid of the forest of Humbaba
And urged him [Gilgamesh] not to go, but he
Was not as strong as Gilgamesh in argument,
And they were friends:

They had **embraced** and made their vow
R To stay together always,
No matter what the **obstacle**.
Enkidu tried to hold his fear . . .

Don't be afraid, said Gilgamesh.
We are together. There is nothing
We should fear.

I learned, Enkidu said, when I lived
With the animals never to go down
Into that forest. I learned that there is death
C In Humbaba. Why do you want
To raise his [Humbaba's] anger? . . .

After three days they reached the edge
Of the forest where Humbaba's watchman stood.
Suddenly it was Gilgamesh who was afraid,
Enkidu . . . reminded him to be fearless.
The watchman sounded his warning to Humbaba.
The two friends moved slowly toward the forest gate.

When Enkidu touched the gate his hand felt numb,
He could not move his fingers or his wrist,
His face turned pale like someone's witnessing a death[.]

He tried to ask his friend for help
Whom he had just encouraged to move on,
But he could only **stutter** and hold out
His paralyzed hand."

—from *Gilgamesh: A Verse Narrative*, tr. Herbert Mason

The Gilgamesh epic was written on 12 tablets and discovered in Nineveh, in present-day Iraq. The tablets were found in the library of the Assyrian king Ashurbanipal (ah • shur • BAH • nuh • puhl), who reigned 668–627 B.C.

Vocabulary

embrace to hug with arms around
obstacle something that stands in the way
stutter an uneven repetition of sounds and words

Analyzing Literature DBQ

1. ***Identifying*** How many times is death mentioned in this excerpt? RH.6–8.1
2. ***Describing*** How do you know that Gilgamesh and Enkidu are friends? RH.6–8.6
3. ***Speculating*** Enkidu is left in a risky situation. What do you think happens to him? RH.6–8.6

R Reading Skills

Explaining Have student volunteers take turns reading the verses from the excerpt. Then ask the following questions:

- **How does Enkidu feel about entering the forest?** *(He is afraid.)* ELL
- **Why does he feel this way?** *(He is afraid that Humbaba will be angered and that he and Gilgamesh might die in the forest.)* AL
- **Why does Enkidu go into the forest?** *(His friend Gilgamesh insists, and Enkidu is persuaded because they have sworn to stay together.)*
- **What changes when the two heroes reach the forest?** *(Gilgamesh grows afraid and Enkidu reassures him.)* AL

C Critical Thinking Skills

Evaluating Ask students to consider whether having to overcome fear makes Enkidu and Gilgamesh more realistic than they would seem if they were unafraid of anything.

Ask: **Do Gilgamesh and Enkidu seem heroic in this excerpt? Why or why not?** *(Student answers will vary. Some may note that Gilgamesh and Enkidu seem afraid, which might not strike students as heroic. Others might note that Gilgamesh and Enkidu work to overcome their fear, which is a sign of bravery.)* BL

CLOSE & REFLECT

To close this lesson, ask students to consider what this story of Gilgamesh and Enkidu tells about the beliefs and values of the people of Sumer 4,000 years ago. Invite them to talk about how the Sumerian beliefs and values are similar to and different from our own.

WORKSHEET

21st Century Skills: Mesopotamia, The World's Literature

Summarizing Divide the class into groups of four. Tell each group that they will be doing publicity for the story of Gilgamesh as a novel or as a film.

Assign the 21st Century Skills Activity on collaboration. Students can use the worksheet as a guide for their activities. They may complete the assignment as homework. Each group can present its film or book publicity to the class.

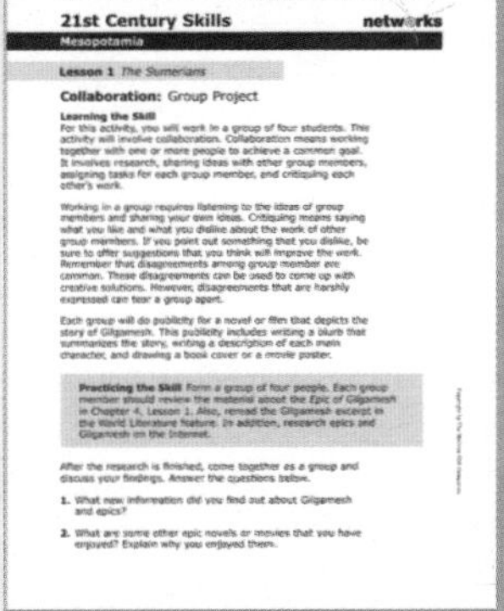

NAME ______ DATE ______ CLASS ______

21st Century Skills networks

Mesopotamia

Lesson 1 *The Sumerians*

Collaboration: Group Project

Learning the Skill
For this activity, you will work in a group of four students. This activity will involve collaboration. Collaboration means working together with one or more people to achieve a common goal. It involves research, sharing ideas with other group members, assigning tasks for each group member, and critiquing each other's work.

Working in a group requires listening to the ideas of group members and sharing your own ideas. Critiquing means saying what you like and what you dislike about the work of other group members. If you point out something that you dislike, be sure to offer suggestions that you think will improve the work. Remember that disagreements among group member are common. These disagreements can be used to come up with creative solutions. However, disagreements that are harshly expressed can tear a group apart.

Each group will do publicity for a novel or film that depicts the story of Gilgamesh. This publicity includes writing a blurb that summarizes the story, writing a description of each main character, and drawing a book cover or a movie poster.

Practicing the Skill Form a group of four people. Each group member should review the material about the *Epic of Gilgamesh* in Chapter 4, Lesson 1. Also, reread the Gilgamesh excerpt in the World Literature feature. In addition, research epics and Gilgamesh on the Internet.

After the research is finished, come together as a group and discuss your findings. Answer the questions below.

1. What new information did you find out about Gilgamesh and epics?
2. What are some other epic novels or movies that you have enjoyed? Explain why you enjoyed them.

ANSWERS p. 85

Analyzing Literature

1. twice
2. They have vowed to stay together, no matter what; they assure one another when each is afraid; they ask one another for help.
3. Since tragedy often occurs in epic poems and because death is foreshadowed twice in this excerpt, students should speculate that Enkidu dies, which eventually he does.

Mesopotamian Empires

ENGAGE

Bellringer Ask students to turn back to the Place and Time feature. Point out that so far, they have been learning about Sumer. Have students find Sumer on the map and then compare it with the rest of the Fertile Crescent. **Ask:**

- **Why is this region called the Fertile Crescent?** *(The land is very fertile because of the water from the Tigris and Euphrates rivers, and the region is in a crescent shape.)*
- **What do you think was happening in other parts of this fertile region while Sumer was evolving in the south?** *(Students may suggest that other Fertile Crescent peoples were growing crops, building towns, and developing their own kingdoms and civilizations.)*

Tell students that eventually, these other kingdoms became powerful rivals of the Sumerian city-states. In this lesson, students will learn about some of the major ones.

TEACH & ASSESS

R Reading Skills

Defining As students read the text, discuss with them that Sargon was king of Akkad and that he conquered Sumer. He became known as the King of Sumer and Akkad. He had formed an empire. **Ask:** **What is an empire?** *(a group of lands or kingdoms that are governed by one ruler)* Invite students to name other empires they know about. Discuss why their suggestions are or are not empires. AL ELL

networks
There's More Online!
- GRAPHIC ORGANIZER Major Mespotamian Empires
- BIOGRAPHY Hammurabi (c. 1800 B.C.)
- PRIMARY SOURCE Code of Hammurabi
- GAMES
- VIDEO

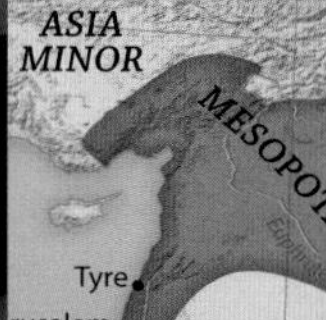

Lesson 2
Mesopotamian Empires

ESSENTIAL QUESTION *Why does conflict develop?*

IT MATTERS BECAUSE
Mesopotamia's empires greatly influenced other civilizations. Hammurabi's Code even influenced the legal codes of Greece and Rome.

The First Empires

GUIDING QUESTION *How did Mesopotamia's first empires develop?*

By 2400 B.C., Sumer's city-states were weakened by conflict. As the strength of Sumer faded, powerful kingdoms arose in northern Mesopotamia and in neighboring Syria. Seeking new lands, rulers of these kingdoms built empires. An **empire** (EHM•PYR) is a group of many different lands under one ruler. Through conquest and trade, these empires spread their cultures over a wide region.

R

Who Was Sargon?

The kingdom of Akkad (AK•ad) developed in northern Mesopotamia. Sargon (SAHR•GAHN) was an ambitious leader who ruled the people of Akkad, known as Akkadians (uh•KAY•dee•uhnz). About 2340 B.C., Sargon moved his well-trained armies south. He conquered the remaining Sumerian city-states one by one. Sargon united the conquered territory with Akkad and became known as the king of Sumer and Akkad. In doing so, he formed the world's first empire. Eventually, Sargon extended this empire to include all of the peoples of Mesopotamia. His Mesopotamian empire lasted for more than 200 years before invaders conquered it.

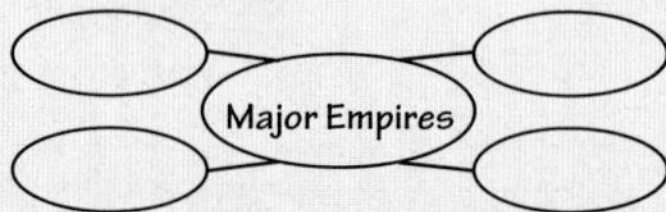

Taking Notes: ***Identifying***
On a diagram like this one, identify the major Mesopotamian empires from this lesson. RH.6–8.2

Major Empires

Content Vocabulary (Tier 3 Words)
- **empire**
- **tribute**
- **province**
- **caravan**
- **astronomer**

networks Online Teaching Options

VIDEO

Persepolis

Assessing Explain to students that this video will give them a close-up look at one of the later empires to rule Mesopotamia, that of the Persian Empire. The video focuses on the extraordinary ancient city of Persepolis. Have students view the video and then, with a partner, discuss these questions:

- **What is most impressive about the city?**
- **Does it surprise you to know such a city existed 2,600 years ago? Why or why not?**
- **How would the city compare to a modern city?**

See page 73D for other online activities.

ANSWERS, p. 86

TAKING NOTES: Akkad, Babylonia, Assyria, Chaldea

Who Was Hammurabi?

A people called the Amorites lived in the region west of Mesopotamia. In the 1800s B.C., they conquered Mesopotamia and built their own cities. Babylon (BA•buh•luhn) was the grandest of these cities. It was located on the eastern bank of the Euphrates River in what is now Iraq. Around 1792 B.C., the Babylonian king, Hammurabi (HA•muh•RAH•bee), began conquering cities controlled by the Amorites to the north and south. By adding these lands he created the Babylonian Empire. This new empire stretched north from the Persian Gulf through the Tigris-Euphrates valley and west to the Mediterranean Sea.

Hammurabi's Code

Hammurabi was thought to be a just ruler. He is best known for creating a set of laws for his empire. He posted this law **code** for all to read. The code dealt with crimes, farming, business, marriage, and the family—almost every area of life. The code listed a punishment for each crime. C

The Code of Hammurabi was stricter than the old Sumerian laws. The code demanded what became known as "an eye for an eye, and a tooth for a tooth." This means that the punishment for a crime should match the seriousness of the crime. It was meant to limit punishment and do away with blood feuds.

The code also protected the less powerful. For example, it protected wives from abuse by their husbands. Hammurabi's Code influenced later law codes, such as those of Greece and Rome.

✓ PROGRESS CHECK

Finding the Main Idea Why was Hammurabi's Code important?

The Assyrian Empire

GUIDING QUESTION *How did the Assyrians influence Southwest Asia?*

The Assyrian Empire arose about 1,000 years after the empire of Hammurabi. Assyria (uh•SIHR•ee•uh) was a large empire, extending into four present-day countries: Turkey, Syria, Iran, and Iraq.

The Assyrians built a large and powerful **military** to defend their hills and fertile valleys. Around 900 B.C., their army began taking over the rest of Mesopotamia.

BIOGRAPHY

Sargon (c. 2300 B.C.)

What king created the world's first empire? Sargon united Akkad with Sumer in the region between the Tigris and Euphrates Rivers. Sargon's Akkadian name, Sharrum-kin, means "the true king."

Under Sargon's rule, the cultures of Akkad and Sumer mixed. The people of Mesopotamia spoke the Akkadian language, but they wrote in Sumerian cuneiform. They also worshipped Sumerian gods. Sargon's empire grew wealthy through its many trade routes.

▶ CRITICAL THINKING

Speculating What made Sargon a "true king"?

empire a large territory or group of many territories governed by one ruler

Academic Vocabulary (Tier 2 Words)

code a set of official laws

military having to do with soldiers, weapons, or war

C Critical Thinking Skills

Drawing Conclusions Discuss Hammurabi's Code and its influence. Ask the following questions:

- **How did the code make clear what actions were crimes?** *(Hammurabi's Code was the first set of laws that was posted for all to read. The Code made clear exactly what actions were crimes. It also let people know that criminal activity would be punished, and what those punishments would be.)*
- **What was the guiding principle for the laws in Hammurabi's Code?** *(The guiding principle behind Hammurabi's Code was "an eye for an eye and a tooth for a tooth," which means that for every wrong done, there should be a similar measure of justice. Also, the code helped people who were less powerful, such as women.)*
- **How do you think Hammurabi's Code helped the development of the Babylonian Empire?** *(Answers will vary. Students might mention that the code probably established more order throughout the empire, so there was less conflict, and fewer uprisings occurred.)* BL

Content Background Knowledge

- Hammurabi reigned from about 1792 to 1750 B.C.
- He was personally involved in many details of governing his kingdom. Day-to-day tasks involved restoring and building temples, public buildings, city walls, canals, and other waterways, and conducting warfare.
- Hammurabi's rule shifted the center of Mesopotamian society and culture from the south, where it had been focused since the time of the Sumerians, to the north, where it remained for the next 1,000 years.

PRIMARY SOURCE

Hammurabi's Code

Integrating Visual Information Display students the primary source slide showing translations of the introduction and several excerpts from Hammurabi's Code. **Ask: Why do you think Hammurabi created a code of laws?** *(Answers will vary. Students might say that Hammurabi wanted to create a just system of laws that was fair for all people. Also, he probably wanted to maintain order in his empire.)*

See page 73D for other online activities.

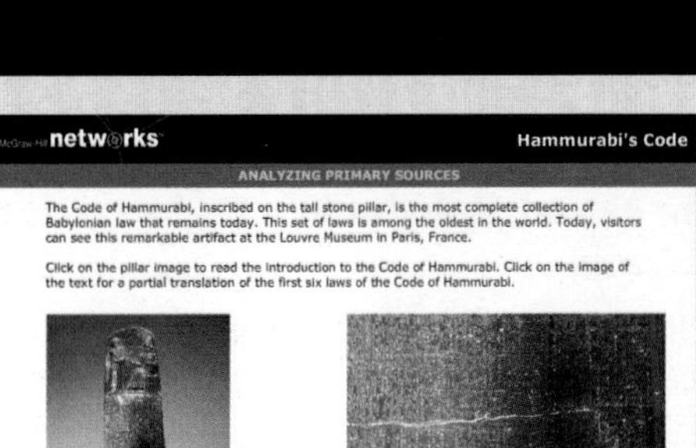

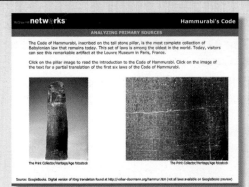

ANSWERS, p. 87

✓ **PROGRESS CHECK** Hammurabi's Code created a new set of stricter, standard punishments for crimes in his empire. It thus affected all his people. It also influenced the law codes of later societies.

CRITICAL THINKING He created the first empire. Under Sargon, the empire grew and became wealthy.

R Reading Skills

Explaining Have students read the text. Point out that Assyria was already a powerful empire when it invaded and conquered southern Mesopotamia. **Ask:**

- **What factors made the Assyrian army so successful?** *(It had 50,000 soldiers. They were well-trained; included infantry, cavalry, and charioteers; were brutal toward enemies; and had iron weapons.)* AL
- **How did iron contribute to the Assyrian army's effectiveness?** *(Iron weapons would remain sharper, break less frequently, and last longer. They could penetrate shields and armor more effectively than weapons made of bronze or tin.)*

G1 Critical Thinking Skills

Reasoning Guide a discussion of the methods the Assyrian kings used in governing their empire. **Ask: Did these methods benefit the citizens of the empire? How?** *(Roads enabled trade; local officials understood local issues while representing the empire's interests; guard stations made the roads safe for travelers and traders so they could transport goods.)*

G2 Critical Thinking Skills

Comparing and Contrasting Emphasize that the Assyrians adopted many elements of the other Mesopotamian societies. **Ask: How was the Assyrian civilization similar to and different from these other civilizations?** *(The Assyrians followed laws, although they imposed harsher punishments. They used the same form of writing and worshipped the same gods. They built temples and palaces and wrote and collected stories, as other Mesopotamian people did.)* AL

ANSWER, p. 88

CRITICAL THINKING Displaying the code helped Babylonians understand which actions broke the law and what the punishments were for various criminal acts. It also made it less likely that some people might receive lesser or greater punishments for the same crime.

The Assyrian Army

The army of Assyria was well trained and disciplined. In battle, the troops numbered around 50,000 soldiers. This army was made up of infantry, or foot soldiers; cavalry, or horse soldiers; and charioteers. The Assyrians fought with slingshots, bows and arrows, swords, and spears.

R The Assyrians robbed people, set crops on fire, and destroyed towns and dams. They took **tribute**, or forced payments, from conquered people. The Assyrian army also drove people from their homes. Stories of Assyrian brutality spread. Sometimes people were so afraid of the Assyrians that they would surrender to them without a fight.

One of the key factors in the Assyrian successes was iron weapons. The Hittites (HIH•tyts), a people to the north, had mastered iron production, making iron stronger than tin or copper. The Assyrians learned from Hittite technology.

Hammurabi's Code was carved on stone slabs that were placed where the most people would see them. Sometimes a statue of the king was placed with it.

▶ **CRITICAL THINKING**
Drawing Conclusions Why was displaying the code important for Babylonians?

Kings and Government

Assyria extended from the Persian Gulf in the east to the Nile River in the west. The capital was located at Nineveh (NIH•nuh•vuh), along the Tigris River.

G1 Assyrian kings had to be powerful leaders to rule such a large area. They divided their empire into **provinces** (PRAH•vuhn•suhs), or political districts. The government built roads that connected these provinces. The kings chose officials to govern, collect taxes, and carry out the laws in each province. Soldiers stood guard at stations along the roads to protect traders from bandits. Messengers on government business used the stations to rest and change chariot horses.

Life in Assyria

The lives of the Assyrians were built on what they learned from other Mesopotamian peoples. The Assyrians had law codes, but their punishments were harsher. Assyrians based their writing on Babylonian writing. They worshipped many of the same gods. G2

Assyrians built large temples and palaces filled with wall carvings and statues. They also wrote and collected stories. An ancient Assyrian king named Ashurbanipal (ah•shur•BAH•nuh•puhl) built one of the world's first libraries in Nineveh. It held 25,000 tablets of stories and songs to the gods. Historians have learned much about ancient civilizations from this library.

Reading HELPDESK CCSS

tribute a payment made to a ruler or state as a sign of surrender

province a territory governed as a political district of a country or empire

networks *Online Teaching Options*

WHITEBOARD ACTIVITY

The Akkad, Babylonian, and Assyrian Empires

Differentiating This activity allows students to understand the differences between the three empires studied so far: Akkad, Babylon, and Assyria. Guide the class in completing the whiteboard activity. If students are unsure, have them review the text to find the answer.

See page 73D for other online activities.

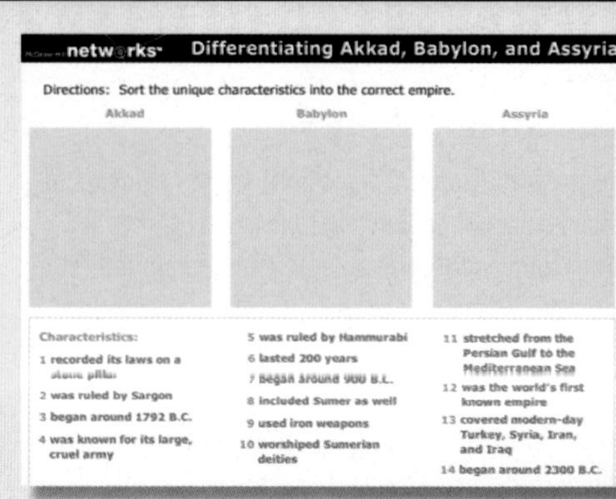

networks Differentiating Akkad, Babylon, and Assyria
Directions: Sort the unique characteristics into the correct empire.
Akkad
Babylon
Assyria
Characteristics:
1 recorded its laws on a
2 was ruled by Sargon
3 began around 1792 B.C.
4 was known for its large, cruel army
5 was ruled by Hammurabi
6 lasted 200 years
7 began around 900 B.C.
8 included Sumer as well
9 used iron weapons
10 worshiped Sumerian deities
11 stretched from the Persian Gulf to the Mediterranean Sea
12 was the world's first known empire
13 covered modern-day Turkey, Syria, Iran, and Iraq
14 began around 2300 B.C.

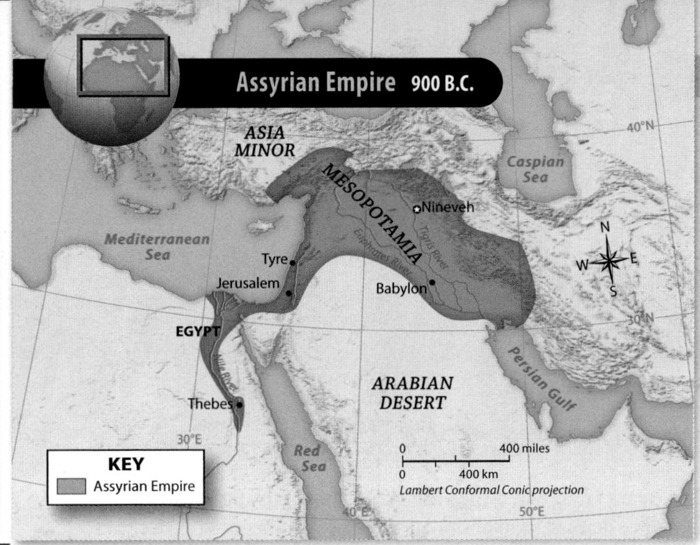

GEOGRAPHY CONNECTION

The Assyrians conquered lands from Mesopotamia to Egypt.

1. **LOCATION** What geographic feature lay to the south of the Assyrian Empire?
2. **CRITICAL THINKING** ***Making Inferences*** Several major rivers flowed through the Assyrian Empire. Why were these rivers important?

Farming and trade were both important to the Assyrians. They brought in wood and metal from far away to supply their empire with material for building and for making tools and weapons.

PROGRESS CHECK

Summarizing Why was Assyria's army so strong?

Connections to TODAY

Libraries

The United States Library of Congress in Washington, D.C., ranks as the largest library in the world. It holds millions of books, photographs, and other documents.

The Chaldean Empire

GUIDING QUESTION ***Why was Babylon an important city in the ancient world?***

For 300 years, Assyria ruled the area from the Persian Gulf to Egypt. Because they were harsh rulers, people often rebelled. In about 650 B.C., fighting broke out over who would be the next Assyrian ruler. With the Assyrians in turmoil, a group of people called the Chaldeans (kal•DEE•uhns) took power.

A New Empire

Centuries before, about 1000 B.C., the Chaldean people had moved into southern Mesopotamia. At that time, the Assyrians had quickly conquered the Chaldeans' small kingdom. The Chaldeans hated their harsh new rulers and were never completely under Assyrian control.

Visual Vocabulary

slingshot a weapon that is used to throw stones or other objects

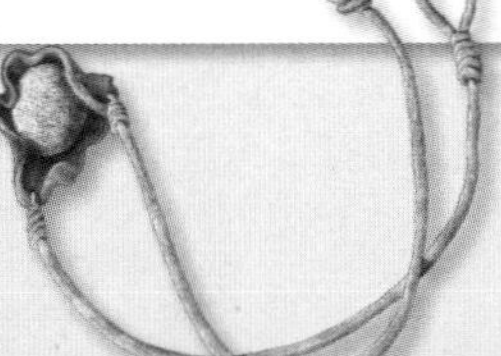

V Visual Skills

Analyzing Maps Tell students to look closely at the shape of the Assyrian Empire. **Ask: What natural geographic features limited the extent of the Assyrian Empire?** *(Mediterranean Sea, Arabian Desert, mountains to the north and east, the Persian Gulf)* **AL** **Visual/Spatial**

C Critical Thinking Skills

Making Inferences Explain to students that the Assyrians had to bring in building supplies from far away. Point out that building supplies, such as wood and stone, are very heavy. **Ask: Why did the Assyrians bring building materials from great distances?** *(Mesopotamia was an arid land with several deserts. Few trees grew there, and the land evidently did not have a supply of stone suitable to the Assyrians' building needs.)*

Content Background Knowledge

Point out that many of the early empires of Mesopotamia existed for hundreds of years. Assyria ruled Mesopotamia for 300 years. Tell students that the United States is often described as the world's oldest democracy, and yet it will not celebrate its 300th birthday as a nation until 2076.

MAP

Assyrian Empire, 900 B.C.

Analyzing Maps Have students look at the map of the Assyrian Empire and explore the tools for studying it more closely. Then ask students to use the tools to complete the following tasks:

- **Measure how far the empire extended from east to west.** *(about 1,230 miles)*
- **Circle the capital of Assyria with a red marker.** *(Nineveh)*
- **Circle in blue the geographic feature that marked the limit of the Assyrian Empire in the north.** *(mountains of Asia Minor)*

See page 73D for other online activities.

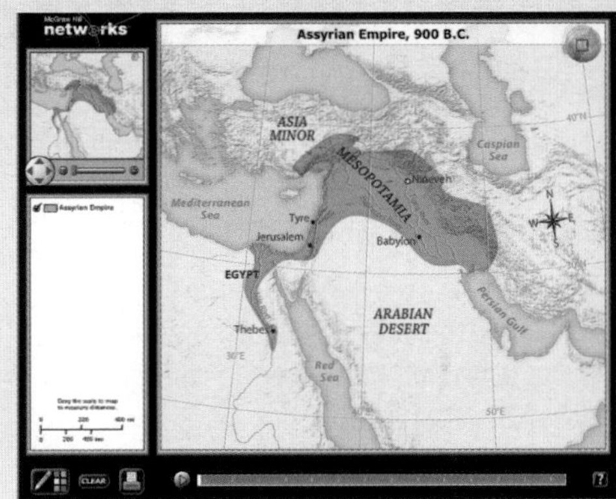

ANSWERS, p. 89

GEOGRAPHY CONNECTION

1. the Arabian Desert
2. **CRITICAL THINKING** They provided water for drinking, farming, and trading.

PROGRESS CHECK Its soldiers were well-trained and had advanced weapons.

C Critical Thinking

Determining Cause and Effect Ask students the following questions and discuss their responses as a class.

- **What happened that allowed the Chaldeans to overcome their Assyrian rulers?** *(The Assyrians were fighting each other over who would be their next ruler, which created an opportunity for the Chaldeans to rise up against them.)*
- **Why do you think the Chaldeans burned Nineveh to the ground?** *(Possible answers: They may have hated the Assyrians and wanted revenge; they may have believed that burning Nineveh was the surest way of preventing the Assyrians from rebuilding their empire and attacking the Chaldeans again.)* AL
- **Why is the Chaldean Empire sometimes called the New Babylonian Empire?** *(The Chaldeans were descendants of the Babylonians who created the first Babylonian Empire, and they made the city of Babylon their new capital.)* AL

R Reading Skills

Citing Text Evidence Have a volunteer read the text. Then, point out that the text describes Babylon as the richest city in the world. **Ask: What supporting details in the text can you find that support that statement?** *("huge brick walls surrounded the city"; "soldiers kept watch in towers"; "grand palaces and temples"; "a huge ziggurat stood more than 300 feet tall": "its gold roof could be seen for miles.")* AL

GEOGRAPHY CONNECTION

1. **LOCATION** In which direction would someone travel from Sidon to reach the Persian Gulf?
2. **CRITICAL THINKING** *Evaluating* Why do you think the Chaldeans naturally became traders?

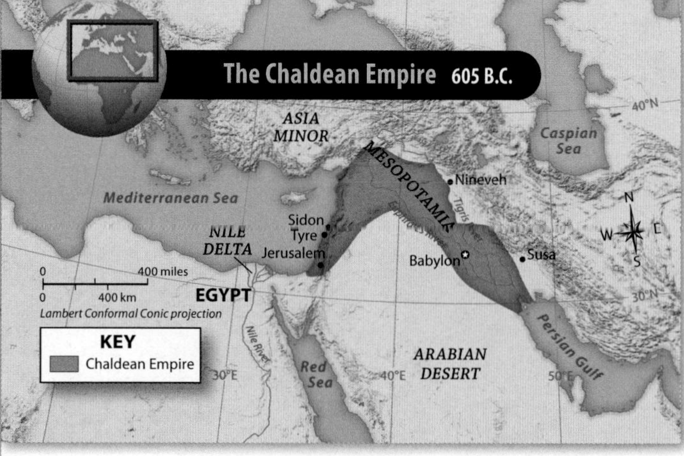

Years later, when the Assyrians were fighting each other, the Chaldean king Nabopolassar (NAH•buh•puh•LAH•suhr) decided to reclaim his kingdom.

In 627 B.C., Nabopolassar led a revolt against the Assyrians. Within a year, he had forced the Assyrians out of Uruk and was crowned king of Babylonia. The Medes, another people in the **region** who wanted to break free from Assyrian rule, joined the Chaldeans. Together, they defeated the Assyrian army. In 612 B.C., they captured the Assyrian capital of Nineveh and burned it to the ground. The hated Assyrian Empire quickly crumbled. C

Nabopolassar and his son, Nebuchadnezzar (NEH•byuh•kuhd•NEH•zuhr), created a new empire. Most of the Chaldeans were descendants of the Babylonians who made up Hammurabi's empire about 1,200 years earlier. Through conquest, the Chaldeans gained control of almost all of the lands the Assyrians had once ruled. The city of Babylon served as their capital. Because of this, the Chaldean Empire is sometimes called the New Babylonian Empire.

The Greatness of Babylon

King Nebuchadnezzar rebuilt Babylon, making it the largest and richest city in the world. Huge brick walls surrounded the city. Soldiers kept watch in towers that were built into the walls. R

Grand palaces and temples were located in the center of Babylon. A huge ziggurat stood more than 300 feet (92 m) tall. When the sun shone, its gold roof could be seen for miles.

Reading HELPDESK CCSS

Academic Vocabulary (Tier 2 Words)
region a geographic area

Academic Vocabulary (Tier 2 Words)
complex having many parts, details, or ideas

networks *Online Teaching Options*

MAP

The Chaldean Empire, 605 B.C.

Analyzing Maps Have students analyze the map of the Chaldean Empire and explore the tools that reveal additional information. Then **ask:**

- **Which empire, the Assyrian or the Chaldean, controlled the largest area?** *(the Assyrian Empire)*
- **About how many miles was Nineveh from Babylon?** *(about 250 miles)*
- **Circle the capital of Assyria with an orange marker.** *(Nineveh)*
- **Circle the capital of the Chaldean Empire with a purple marker.** *(Babylon)*

See page 73D for other online activities.

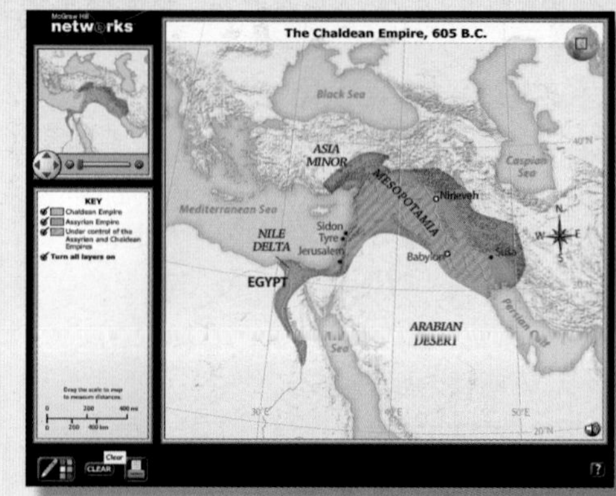

ANSWERS, p. 90

GEOGRAPHY CONNECTION

1. To reach the Persian Gulf from Sidon, people would travel south and east.
2. **CRITICAL THINKING** The Chaldeans became traders because they had easy access to other regions by way of the Mediterranean Sea and the Persian Gulf, which their empire bordered.

The richness of the ziggurat was equaled by that of the king's palace. The palace had a giant staircase of greenery known as the Hanging Gardens.

Babylon's Hanging Gardens were considered one of the Seven Wonders of the Ancient World. These terraced gardens—built like huge steps—included large trees, masses of flowering vines, and other beautiful plants. A **complex** irrigation system brought water from the Euphrates River to water the gardens. It is believed that Nebuchadnezzar built the gardens to please his wife. She missed the mountains and plants of her homeland in the northwest.

For his people, Nebuchadnezzar built a beautiful street near the palace that they could visit. It was paved with limestone and marble, and lined with walls of blue glaze tile.

These ruins of the original gardens stand today as a reminder of Babylon's glory.

The grand Hanging Gardens of Babylon were watered from the top down using irrigation. Water flowed from one level to the next.

▶ CRITICAL THINKING
Speculating Why do you think ancient cities had at least one magnificent building?

T Technology Skills

Classifying Remind students that the Hanging Gardens of Babylon are considered one of the Seven Wonders of the Ancient World. **Ask:** **Can you name any of the other six?** *(Students may correctly guess that the pyramids of Egypt are another of the Seven Wonders.)*

Have students use the Internet to research the Seven Wonders of the Ancient World. Ask each student to write a paragraph describing one of the Seven Wonders and to explain why it was considered so important. Suggest that students illustrate their reports. **Verbal/Linguistic**

Content Background Knowledge

Nebuchadnezzar lavished great effort on rebuilding Babylon. Besides building the ziggurat, the Hanging Gardens, and the impressive street near his palace that was known as the Processional Way, he rebuilt temples and built a new waterway. He also reinforced and completed the city's fortifications, which included the building of a new wall around the city and a great moat. His purpose behind his building projects was partly to bring glory for himself, but also as a way of honoring the gods.

The Seven Wonders of the Ancient World:

- Hanging Gardens of Babylon
- Great Pyramids of Egypt
- Statue of Zeus at Olympia
- Mausoleum at Halicarnassus
- Temple of Artemis at Ephesus
- Colossus of Rhodes
- Pharos—Lighthouse—of Alexandria

IMAGE

The Hanging Gardens of Babylon

Formulating Questions Have students learn more about the Hanging Gardens of Babylon by clicking on the bullets to reveal additional text. Ask students to write a list of three questions they have about the Hanging Gardens and then to do research to find answers to as many of the questions as they can. Have students share their findings with the class.

networks
The Hanging Gardens of Babylon
The Hanging Gardens of Babylon were watered with irrigation from the top down. Each level cascaded water to the next level.

See page 73D for other online activities.

ANSWER, p. 91

CRITICAL THINKING People built large structures to honor their rulers or their gods.

Mesopotamian Empires

R1 Reading Skills

Defining After students have read the text, remind them that familiar concepts of today have origins in earlier civilizations but may have changed over time. **Ask:**

- What is a tax? *(a payment a government collects from people to pay government expenses)*
- What is a tribute? *(a forced payment from a conquered people)* AL ELL
- Why did Nebuchadnezzar collect such high taxes and tributes? *(He needed to pay for all the work being done on Babylon and for his wars.)*

Discuss with students how Nebuchadnezzar's subjects must have felt about the taxes and tributes. Encourage them to speculate on whether they would have felt that the wars and the new temples, the Hanging Gardens, the streets, and the canals were worth such high taxes.

Making Connections

Discuss both positive and negative sentiments that people in modern society have about taxes. **Ask:** How do Americans feel about high taxes to pay for such expenses? *(Students should recognize that some people in every age dislike taxes, while others value the benefits that come from the taxes.)*

R2 Reading Skills

Explaining Point out the word *astronomer.* Explain that its root word is *astro-,* from the Greek word *astron,* which means "star." Point out that although the stars were linked to the gods, the Chaldeans—as well as other ancient peoples—studied astronomy for very practical reasons. **Ask:** What practical value would mapping the movement of heavenly bodies have had for ancient peoples? *(Sample answer: The movements of the sun, moon, and stars helped ancient peoples keep track of the passing of time and of seasons, which enabled them to know when to plant crops, when the rivers might flood, and when to celebrate their various religious ceremonies.)*

King Nebuchadnezzar in the Hanging Gardens.

Stapleton Collection/Corbis

Each spring, thousands of people crowded into Babylon to watch a gold statue of the god Marduk (MAHR•dook) as it was wheeled along the street. Chaldeans believed that the ceremony would bring peace and bigger crops to their empire.

R1 The Babylonians built many new canals, making the land even more fertile. To pay for his building projects and to maintain his army, Nebuchadnezzar had to collect very high taxes and tributes. Because his empire stretched as far as Egypt, it had to have an efficient system of government.

One Greek historian in the 400s B.C. described the beauty of Babylon. He wrote, "In magnificence, there is no other city that approaches it." Outside the center of Babylon stood houses and marketplaces. There artisans made pottery, cloth, and baskets. The major trade route between the Persian Gulf and the Mediterranean Sea passed through Babylon. Merchants came to the city in traveling groups called **caravans** (KAR•uh•VANZ). They bought Babylonian goods —pottery, cloth, baskets, and jewelry. Babylon grew wealthy from this trade; under the Assyrians, the area had been fairly poor.

R2 The people of Babylon also made many scientific advancements. The Chaldeans, like other people in Mesopotamia, believed that the gods showed their plans in the changes in the sky. Chaldean **astronomers** (uh•STRAH•nuh•muhrs)—people who study the heavenly bodies—mapped the stars, the planets, and the phases of the moon as it changed. The Chaldeans invented one of the first sundials to measure time. They also were the first to follow a seven-day week.

The Fall of the Empire

After Nebuchadnezzar died, a series of weak kings ruled the Chaldean empire. Poor harvests and slow trade further weakened the empire. In 539 B.C., the Persians recognized

Reading HELPDESK CCSS

caravan a group of merchants traveling together for safety, usually with a large number of camels

astronomer a person who studies planets and stars

networks Online Teaching Options

IMAGE

Caravans

Applying Have students learn more about caravans and the role that caravans played in ancient times by clicking on the bullets to read additional information. In a class discussion, have students explain why caravans were especially useful for the Mesopotamians. Invite them to name some of the trade goods these caravans might have brought into Babylon and other parts of Mesopotamia.

networks
Caravans
Explore this illustration to find out more about what ancient caravan travelers had to take on their desert journeys. People today use camels in the desert for travel, just as they did in ancient times. They need to carry similar supplies with them when crossing the desert as were needed back then.
Sylvain Grandadam/Age fotostock

See page 73D for other online activities.

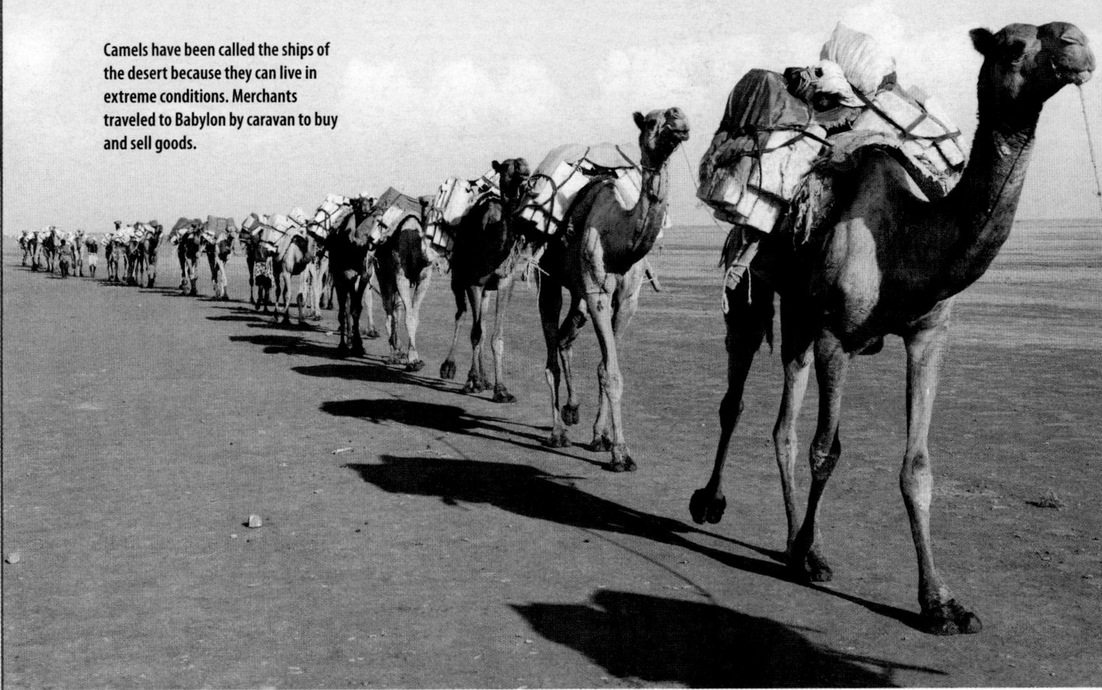

Camels have been called the ships of the desert because they can live in extreme conditions. Merchants traveled to Babylon by caravan to buy and sell goods.

Christopher Boisvieux /agefotostock

that the Chaldeans had lost their strength and leadership. The Persians took advantage and captured Babylon and made Mesopotamia part of their empire. However, they allowed their newly captured land to keep its distinct culture. The Persians wisely did not want to destroy all the Chaldeans had accomplished. C

✓ PROGRESS CHECK

Identifying Which wonder of the ancient world was located in Babylon?

LESSON 2 REVIEW CCSS

Review Vocabulary (Tier 3 Words)

1. How could *caravans* passing through Babylon be helped by *astronomers*? RH.6–8.4
2. How might conquered people feel about paying *tribute* to the Assyrians? RH.6–8.4

Answer the Guiding Questions

3. ***Comparing*** How did Hammurabi's Code differ from earlier Sumerian laws? RH.6–8.2
4. ***Describing*** How did the Assyrians rule their empire? RH.6–8.2
5. ***Explaining*** Why did the Chaldeans overthrow the Assyrians? RH.6–8.2
6. **ARGUMENT** You live in an area that the Assyrian army is attempting to conquer. Write a speech that you might give to your neighbors to persuade them either to defend themselves or to surrender without a fight. WHST.6–8.1, WHST.6–8.10

LESSON 2 REVIEW ANSWERS

1. Babylon was a trading center, and astronomers could help merchants traveling in caravans with scheduling and weather predictions.
2. People might feel upset. Paying tribute to the Assyrians meant the Assyrians had conquered them.
3. Hammurabi's Code provided the first written rule of law, forcing all people to follow the law in how they treated others.
4. The Assyrians divided their empire into provinces and chose officials to collect taxes and enforce laws.
5. The Assyrians were merciless to those they defeated. When the Assyrians fought among themselves, the Chaldeans rebelled and destroyed the Assyrian Empire.
6. The speeches should be informative and persuasive and reflect accurate details based on the description of Assyrian warfare in the text.

C Critical Thinking Skills

Making Inferences Remind students that when one empire conquered another, it did not always result in the complete destruction of the conquered civilization. **Ask:** **Why were the Persians wise not to destroy what the Chaldeans had accomplished?** *(The Chaldeans achieved many important things; the Persians understood that they would benefit more from preserving them than from destroying them.)*

Have students complete the Lesson 2 Review.

CLOSE & REFLECT

Making Inferences To close the lesson, have students make inferences about the influence of the Tigris and Euphrates rivers on the empires of Mesopotamia. **Ask:**

- **How do you think the Tigris and Euphrates rivers helped the formation of the empires of Mesopotamia?** *(Answers will vary. Students might answer that the rivers helped with the movement of troops.)*
- **How did these rivers help unify these empires?** *(Answers will vary. Students might mention that the rivers could have been used to send messages and goods, which would help trade and communication.)*

ANSWER, p. 93

✓ PROGRESS CHECK the Hanging Gardens

CHAPTER REVIEW ACTIVITY

Have students create a three-column chart with six rows, like the one shown below. Then lead a review of the chapter during which students recall important details about the economy and key events of each civilization. Students should record these details in their charts.

	Economy	Key Events
Sumer		
Akkad		
Babylon		
Assyria		
Chaldea		

REVIEW THE ENDURING UNDERSTANDINGS

Review this chapter's Enduring Understandings with students:

- ***People, places, and ideas change over time.***
- ***Cultures are held together by shared beliefs and common practices and values.***

Now pose the following questions in a class discussion to apply the Enduring Understandings to the chapter.

How did civilization survive in Mesopotamia despite the rise and fall of a series of kingdoms and empires? *(Students should recognize that once civilization developed among the Sumerians, it did not die just because that society declined and was overthrown. Rather, new groups of people replaced them, building their own civilizations in part on the remnants of the one that preceded them.)*

How did the advances and developments made by one civilization continue to influence later civilizations? *(Students should recognize that the advances of one civilization do not always disappear when that civilization comes to an end. They may cite examples, such as the laws originated by Hammurabi that reappeared in the Assyrian Empire, the continued use of iron that began with the Hittites and was adopted by the Assyrians and subsequent civilizations, the survival of writing, the wheel, and sailboats that have remained part of civilizations to the present.)*

CHAPTER 4 Activities CCSS

Write your answers on a separate piece of paper.

1 Exploring the Essential Question WHST.6–8.2, WHST.6–8.10

INFORMATIVE/EXPLANATORY How would you describe the influence of Mesopotamia's physical geography on the region? Write an expository essay about how geography influenced the way people lived in Mesopotamia. Think about the Tigris River and the Euphrates River and the effect of flooding on the region. Include information about how geography influenced the formation of city-states in your essay.

2 21st Century Skills WHST.6–8.6, WHST.6–8.10

CREATING A COMMUNICATIONS PRODUCT Write a script for a documentary about the technological and mathematical contributions made by the Sumerians. Divide your script into two columns. The left column should include the narration for your documentary. The right column should describe the images that will be shown. These images should match with the narration in the left column. Read your script to the class, or, if you have access to a video camera, shoot a short film based on your script.

3 Thinking Like a Historian RH.6–8.2

IDENTIFYING Create a diagram like the one here to identify types of archeological evidence that researchers might search for to learn about ancient Mesopotamia.

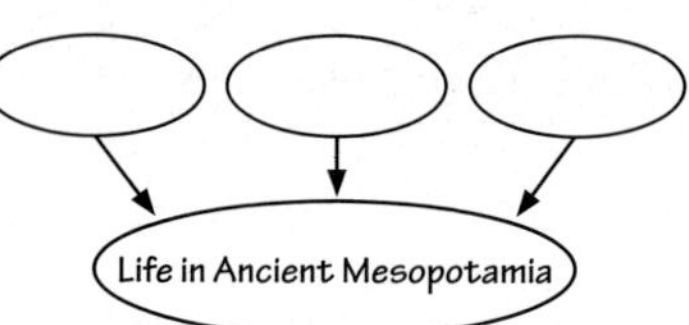

4 GEOGRAPHY ACTIVITY

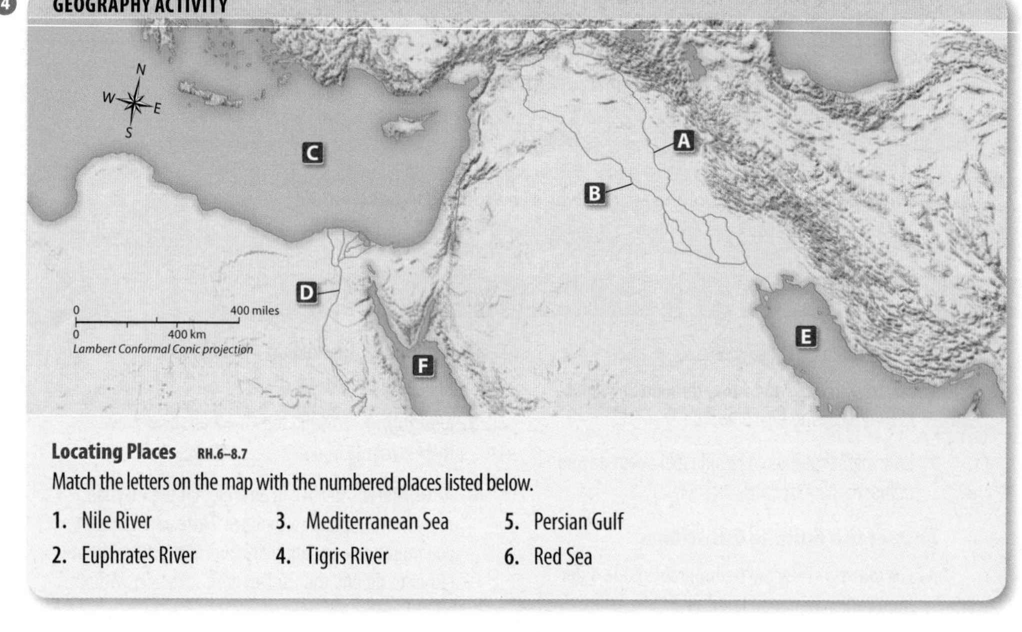

Locating Places RH.6–8.7

Match the letters on the map with the numbered places listed below.

1. Nile River
2. Euphrates River
3. Mediterranean Sea
4. Tigris River
5. Persian Gulf
6. Red Sea

94 *Mesopotamia*

ACTIVITIES ANSWERS

Exploring the Essential Question

1 Students' essays should note the effect of the Tigris and Euphrates rivers on Mesopotamians. They should discuss how these rivers affected transportation and farming. They might also include how Mesopotamians dealt with flooding, and why city-states became independent units.

21st Century Skills

2 Students' scripts or videos should have narration that describes the major technological and mathematical contributions of the Sumerians. Key contributions include the wheel, the calendar, bronze, the cuneiform system of writing, and the creation of a system of numbers. The visuals should be compelling and match the narration.

Thinking Like a Historian

3 Graphic organizers might contain responses such as: archaeological evidence from ancient cities; uncovered artifacts such as pottery or tools; or writings on clay tablets.

Locating Places

4 Letters should match the correct geographic locations. **1.** D, **2.** B, **3.** C, **4.** A, **5.** E, **6.** F

CHAPTER 4 Assessment CCSS

REVIEW THE GUIDING QUESTIONS

Directions: Choose the best answer for each question.

RH.6–8.2
1 In Mesopotamia, floods deposited silt, which made the soil
A. rocky. C. dry.
B. fertile. D. barren.

RH.6–8.2
2 Which of the following groups belonged to the Sumerian middle class?
F. government officials H. merchants
G. warriors I. enslaved people

RH.6–8.2
3 Sumerians developed a 12-month calendar by recording the
A. position of planets and stars. C. amount of flooding.
B. length of the seasons. D number of days with rainfall.

RH.6–8.2
4 Who developed the first empire in Mesopotamia?
F. Hammurabi H. Ashurbanipal
G. Sargon I. Nabopolassar

RH.6–8.2
5 What did Assyrians often demand from the people they conquered?
A. leaving their homes C. volunteers for the army
B. participation in elections D. the worship of gods

RH.6–8.2
6 The astronomers of Babylon mapped
F. the irrigation canals. H. the nearby mountains.
G. the ocean currents. I. the stars and the planets.

DBQ ANALYZING DOCUMENTS

This excerpt comes from a poem called "The Mesopotamian View of Death" that was written by an unknown Mesopotamian mother.

Hark the piping!

My heart is piping in the wilderness
where the young man once went free.

He is a prisoner now in death's kingdom
lies bound where once he lived.

The ewe gives up her lamb
and the nanny goat her kid

My heart is piping in the wilderness,
an instrument of grief.

—"The Mesopotamian View of Death," *Poems of Heaven and Hell from Ancient Mesopotamia*, N. K. Sanders, trans

95

ASSESSMENT ANSWERS

Review the Guiding Questions

1 **B** Silt has small particles of soil. It does not contain rocks. Silt would not make the soil drier or wetter. It does not damage the soil and would not make the soil barren. When silt is deposited on the land, it makes the soil more fertile. Thus, choice B is the correct answer.

2 **H** Merchants belonged to the middle class. Government officials and warriors belonged to the upper class, and enslaved people belonged to the lower class. So choice H is the correct answer.

3 **A** The amount of flooding and the number of days with rainfall are not relevant. The length of seasons might vary and is not precise enough to use for a calendar. By recording the positions of the planets and the stars, Sumerians developed a 12-month calendar based on the phases of the moon. The correct answer is choice A.

4 **G** Hammurabi, Ashurbanipal, and Nabopolassar lived centuries after Sargon. As leader of Akkad, Sargon developed the first Mesopotamian empire when he conquered the Sumerian cities. So G is the correct answer.

5 **A** The Assyrians often forced the people they conquered to leave their homes. They did not hold elections and did not force captives to join their army. They worshiped many of the same gods that people they conquered worshiped and did not force conquered people to worship. Thus, choice A is the correct answer.

6 **I** Astronomers do not map Earth's geographic features. Babylonian astronomers mapped the stars and the planets. Choice I is the correct answer.

Analyzing Documents

7 **A** Although the young man is imprisoned, it is in "death's kingdom," not a physical jail. The excerpt does not address his skills as a warrior and does not say whether he has been a shepherd. It does say that he is dead, so choice A is the correct answer.

8 **I** The excerpt does not address the mother's desire to hug her son and does not suggest that she assigns blame for his death. She speaks of sheep and goats giving up their young, not of tending sheep. She feels that her heart cries out her grief in the keening tones of a musical instrument. Choice I is the correct answer.

Short Response

9 Student responses should mention that the trader might make a lucky deal, prosper through hard work, or benefit from a combination of the two.

10 No, wealth was shown by owning land. The author states that most people in the Mesopotamian empires were poor and had no political power, which suggests that few people had high social status and that improving it was not a common occurrence.

Extended Response

11 Students' reports should contain phrases that describe the design of the city, the ziggurat, the wall and moat, and the Hanging Gardens. Students should give their opinion as a visitor from Egypt.

 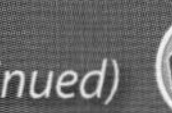

RH.6–8.1
7 **Drawing Conclusions** What has happened to the young man in the poem?

A. He has died.
B. He is in prison for life.
C. He is a successful warrior.
D. He tends a flock of sheep.

RH.6–8.2
8 **Explaining** How does the mother react to what has happened?

F. She wants a chance to hug her son again.
G. She blames the king for what has happened.
H. She says she should have been tending her sheep.
I. She believes that her body is acting out her feelings.

SHORT RESPONSE

"The vast majority of the inhabitants of Babylonia, Assyria, and other Mesopotamian empires were poor and had no political power. . . .

"Under some circumstances a person could change his or her social status. . . . a trader or merchant who was uncommonly diligent or lucky in business might . . . be able to afford his own plots of land."

—from *Empires of Mesopotamia* by Don Nardo

RH.6–8.1
9 How might a trader improve his social status?

RH.6–8.1
10 How did a person show their wealth at this time? Do you think people often improved their social status in ancient Mesopotamia? Explain your answer.

EXTENDED RESPONSE

WHST.6–8.10
11 **Informative/Explanatory** You are a diplomat from Egypt who is visiting Babylon around 565 B.C. The leader of your country wants information about the city, including the Hanging Gardens. How is the city organized? What do the Hanging Gardens look like? Write a report that describes Babylon, and give your opinion about the city.

Need Extra Help?

If You've Missed Question	1	2	3	4	5	6	7	8	9	10	11
Review Lesson	1	1	1	2	2	2	2	1, 2	1	1	2

networks Online Teaching Options

Using eAssessment

Use eAssessment to access and assign the publisher-made Lesson Quizzes & Chapter Tests electronically. You can also use eAssessment to create your own quizzes and tests from hundreds of available questions. eAssessment helps you design assessments that meet the needs of different types of learners. Follow the link in the Assess tab of your Teacher Lesson Center.

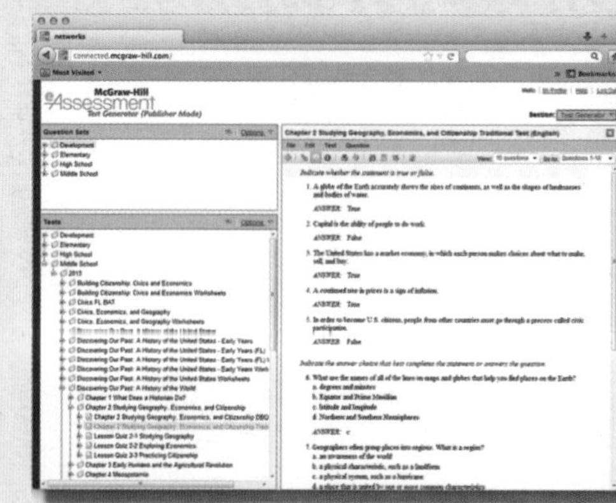

CHAPTER 5

Ancient Egypt and Kush Planner

UNDERSTANDING BY DESIGN®

Enduring Understanding

- *People, places, and ideas change over time.*
- *Cultures are held together by shared beliefs and common practices and values.*

Essential Questions

- *How does geography influence the way people live?*
- *What makes a culture unique?*
- *Why do civilizations rise and fall?*

Predictable Misunderstandings

Students may think:

- *Egypt is not part of Africa.*
- *All of Egypt is desert.*
- *The Nile River flows south from the Mediterranean Sea.*

Assessment Evidence

Performance Tasks:

- *Hands-On Chapter Project*

Other Evidence:

- *Class discussion answers*
- *Class simulation participation*
- *Whiteboard activity responses*
- *Brainstorming activity*
- *Geography and History Activity*
- *Economics of History Activities*
- *21st Century Skills Activities*
- *Evaluation of class simulation*
- *Writing activities*
- *Lesson Reviews*
- *Chapter Activities and Assessment*

SUGGESTED PACING GUIDE

Introducing the Chapter	1 day	Lesson 3	2 days
Lesson 1	2 days	Lesson 4	1 day
Lesson 2	2 days	Chapter Wrap-Up and Assessment	1 day

TOTAL TIME 9 Days

Key for Using the Teacher Edition

SKILL-BASED ACTIVITIES

Types of skill activities found in the Teacher Edition.

V Visual Skills require students to analyze maps, graphs, charts, and photos.

R Reading Skills help students practice reading skills and master vocabulary.

W Writing Skills provide writing opportunities to help students comprehend the text.

C Critical Thinking Skills help students apply and extend what they have learned.

T Technology Skills require students to use digital tools effectively.

*Letters are followed by a number when there is more than one of the same type of skill on the page.

DIFFERENTIATED INSTRUCTION

All activities are written for the on-level student unless otherwise marked with the leveled labels below.

BL Beyond Level
AL Approaching Level
ELL English Language Learners

All students benefit from activities that utilize different learning styles. Many activities are marked as below when a particular learning style is highlighted.

Intrapersonal	**Naturalist**
Logical/Mathematical	**Kinesthetic**
Visual/Spatial	**Auditory/Musical**
Verbal/Linguistic	**Interpersonal**

NCSS Standards covered in "Ancient Egypt and Kush"

Learners will understand:

1 **CULTURE**

4. That the beliefs, values, and behaviors of a culture form an integrated system that helps shape the activities and ways of life that define a culture

3 **PEOPLE, PLACES, AND ENVIRONMENTS**

1. The theme of people, places, and environments involves the study of the relationships between human populations in different locations and geographic phenomena such as climate, vegetation, and natural resources

7. Human modifications of the environment

4 **INDIVIDUAL DEVELOPMENT AND IDENTITY**

3. How factors such as physical endowment, interests, capabilities, learning, motivation, personality, perception, and beliefs influence individual development and identity

5 **INDIVIDUALS, GROUPS, AND INSTITUTIONS**

7. That institutions may promote or undermine social conformity

9. That groups and institutions influence culture in a variety of ways

8 **SCIENCE, TECHNOLOGY, AND SOCIETY**

2. Society often turns to science and technology to solve problems

4. Science and technology have had both positive and negative impacts upon individuals, societies, and the environment in the past and present

5. Science and technology have changed peoples' perceptions of the social and natural world, as well as their relationship to the land, economy and trade, their concept of security, and their major daily activities

CHAPTER OPENER PLANNER

Students will know:

- *why the Nile River was important to the ancient Egyptians.*
- *characteristics of ancient Egyptian religion and society.*
- *factors that led to the rise and fall of the ancient Egyptian empire.*
- *how Egypt influenced other kingdoms.*

Students will be able to:

- ***compare*** *information on populations of the Fertile Crescent and Nile River valley.*
- ***describe*** *a main agricultural product and its economic effect on ancient Egypt.*
- ***analyze*** *how the Nile River affected Egyptian life.*
- ***analyze*** *how belief in the afterlife influenced ancient Egyptian life.*
- ***describe*** *ancient Egyptian social classes.*
- ***organize*** *information on a pharaoh's responsibilities.*
- ***analyze*** *visuals from Egypt's golden age.*
- ***describe*** *an empire and how it is built.*
- ***identify*** *reasons Egypt reached the height of its power.*
- ***explain*** *how the pharaoh contributed to the rise and fall of the Egyptian empire.*
- ***identify*** *how Nubia and Kush were influenced by Egyptian culture.*

UNDERSTANDING BY DESIGN®

☑ *Print Teaching Options*

V Visual Skills

☐ **P. 98** Students discuss physical characteristics of the location of ancient Egypt. **Visual/Spatial**

☐ **P. 99** Students identify important historical events related to ancient Egypt. **AL** **Logical/Mathematical**

☑ *Online Teaching Options*

V Visual Skills

MAP **Ancient Egypt c. 5000 B.C. to 1070 B.C.**—Students observe the extent of ancient Egypt and some features of the area.

TIMELINE **Place and Time: Ancient Egypt and Kush 5000 B.C. to A.D. 350**—Students compare present-day boundaries with those of ancient Egypt.

WORLD ATLAS **World Atlas**—Students can use this interactive map to identify regions of the world, learn about individual countries, locate political boundaries, measure distances, and more.

☑ *Printable Digital Worksheets*

R Reading Skills

GRAPHIC NOVEL ***Floating Along the Nile***—This story illustrates the transmission of culture between Egypt and Kush.

Project-Based Learning

Hands-On Chapter Project

Create Maps

In order to understand the function of the sarcophagus in ancient Egypt, students will create a personal sarcophagus that represents themselves and their interests. Students will plan and construct the sarcophagus, explain its designs in writing, and present their finished project to the class.

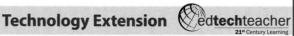

Technology Extension

Create Online Interactive Maps

- Find an additional activity online that incorporates technology for this project.
- Visit the EdTechTeacher Web sites (included in the Technology Extension for this chapter) for more links, tutorials, and other resources.

Print Resources

ANCILLARY RESOURCES

These ancillaries are available for every chapter and lesson.

- **Reading Essentials and Study Guide Workbook** **AL** **ELL**
- **Chapter Tests and Lesson Quizzes Blackline Masters**

PRINTABLE DIGITAL WORKSHEETS

These printable digital worksheets are available for every chapter and lesson.

- **Hands-On Chapter Projects**
- **What Do You Know? activities**
- **Chapter Summaries (English and Spanish)**
- **Vocabulary Builder activities**
- **Guided Reading activities**

More Media Resources

SUGGESTED VIDEOS MOVIES

Watch clips of popular culture films about Ancient Egypt, such as Cecil B. DeMille's *The Ten Commandments* (1956) or Warner Brothers' *The Prince of Egypt* (1998). Alternatively, view documentaries about Egyptian civilization, such as National Geographic's *The Mysteries of Egypt* (1998).

Dicsuss: **Can fictional movies capture historical events accurately?**

(NOTE: Preview any clips for age-appropriateness.)

SUGGESTED READING 

Grade 6 reading level:

- ***Voices of Ancient Egypt,*** by Kay Winters

Grade 7 reading level:

- ***Ancient Egypt,*** by Andrew Haslam and Alexandra Parsons

Grade 8 reading level:

- ***Curse of the Pharaohs: My Adventures with Mummies,*** by Zahi Hawass

THE NILE RIVER

Students will know:
- *why the Nile River was important to the ancient Egyptians.*

Students will be able to:
- ***compare** information on populations of the Fertile Crescent and Nile River valley.*
- ***describe** a main agricultural product and its economic effect on ancient Egypt.*
- ***analyze** how the Nile River affected Egyptian life.*

UNDERSTANDING BY DESIGN®

Print Teaching Options

V Visual Skills
- [ ] **P. 105** Students create their own hieroglyphics. ELL AL Verbal/Linguistic
- [ ] **P. 106** Students trace different trading routes used by ancient Egyptians. Visual/Spatial

R Reading Skills
- [ ] **P. 100** Students describe the Nile River and the land around it.
- [ ] **P. 101** Students brainstorm ways in which the Nile affected Egyptian life.
- [ ] **P. 103** Students explain how Nile flooding helped farmers. AL
- [ ] **P. 106** Students describe the expanding government of Egypt. BL
- [ ] **P. 107** Students review the characteristics of a dynasty. AL ELL

W Writing Skills
- [ ] **P. 104** Students write recipes using ingredients grown in Ancient Egypt. ELL Interpersonal Verbal/Linguistic

C Critical Thinking Skills
- [ ] **P. 101** Students analyze an excerpt from "Hymn to the Nile."
- [ ] **P. 102** Students compare and contrast the Nile to a local river. Naturalist
- [ ] **P. 103** Students compare the rise and fall of the Nile to human breathing. AL ELL Naturalist
- [ ] **P. 106** Students discuss how Egypt's natural resources aided in building trade. AL

T Technology Skills
- [ ] **P. 102** Students examine satellite images of the Nile delta. Visual/Spatial
- [ ] **P. 105** Students research and present slide shows on 10 amazing ancient Egyptian inventions. BL Interpersonal

Online Teaching Options

V Visual Skills
- VIDEO **The Nile River**—Students discover how the world's longest river affects the people that live along its bank.
- MAP **Ancient Egypt, c. 31 B.C.**—Students locate important landmarks along the Nile River.
- MAP **Early Trade Routes**— Students trace early trade routes.
- IMAGE **Farming on the Nile**—Students view an image of Egyptian wall art and click to learn about farming along the Nile.
- IMAGE **Shadoof**—Students explore how to use this water-lifting tool.
- SLIDE SHOW **World's Longest Rivers**—Students click and compare data on the world's 15 longest rivers.

R Reading Skills
- GRAPHIC ORGANIZER **Taking Notes: *Identifying:* Benefits of the Nile—**Students identify benefits of the Nile River.
- IMAGE **Historic Use of the Sahara—**Students view an image of an oasis in the Sahara and read about the desert's uses over time.
- PRIMARY SOURCE **Ancient Palettes**—Students examine and read about the Narmer Palette, one of the oldest examples of hieroglyphics.

C Critical Thinking Skills
- CHART **How Egyptians Made Papyrus**—Students explore the steps in the making of papyrus.

T Technology Skills
- SELF-CHECK QUIZ **Lesson 1**—Students receive instant feedback of their mastery of lesson content.

Printable Digital Worksheets

W Writing Skills
- WORKSHEET **Geography and History Activity: Understanding Location: Ancient Egypt**—Students write responses after reading a passage and analyzing a map.

C Critical Thinking Skills
- WORKSHEET **Economics of History Activity: Scarcity and Ancient Egyptian Farmers**—Students write responses to critical thinking questions after reading a passage about scarcity.

LIFE IN ANCIENT EGYPT

Students will know:
- *characteristics of ancient Egyptian religion and society.*

Students will be able to:
- ***analyze** how belief in the afterlife influenced ancient Egyptian life.*
- ***describe** ancient Egyptian social classes.*
- ***organize** information on a pharaoh's responsibilities.*

UNDERSTANDING BY DESIGN®

☑ *Print Teaching Options*

V Visual Skills

- ☐ **P. 109** Students interpret a painting to infer how the Pharaoh was treated. ELL Visual/Spatial
- ☐ **P. 112** Students interpret an artist's rendering of a pharaoh's burial preparation. BL Visual/Spatial
- ☐ **P. 114** Students analyze the structure of a pyramid. AL ELL Visual/Spatial
- ☐ **P. 116** Students interpret a graphic depicting Egyptian society. AL Visual/Spatial Logical/Mathematical

R Reading Skills

- ☐ **P. 108** Students define lesson vocabulary. AL ELL
- ☐ **P. 110** Students use a T-chart to organize information about the pharaoh's roles. AL ELL Verbal/Linguistic
- ☐ **P. 114** Students Identify scientific knowledge needed to build the pyramids.
- ☐ **P. 115** Students consider the mathematical knowledge needed to build the pyramids. BL Logical/Mathematical
- ☐ **P. 117** Students use text and graphic evidence to order the classes of Egyptian society. AL Logical/Mathematical

W Writing Skills

- ☐ **P. 112** Students write narratives detailing how belief in the afterlife might have affected Egyptians in their daily work. Interpersonal Verbal/Linguistic
- ☐ **P. 118** Students write "day in the life" stories. AL ELL Verbal/Linguistic

C Critical Thinking Skills

- ☐ **P. 110** Students translate the role of Egyptian gods into modern-day roles. BL
- ☐ **P. 113** Students identify items they would need in the afterlife. ELL AL Intrapersonal
- ☐ **P. 116** Students generalize about how what a person does for a living affects his or her place in society. AL
- ☐ **P. 118** Students categorize the classes of Egyptian society using a graphic organizer. AL ELL

T Technology Skills

- ☐ **P. 111** Students make a slide show of Egyptian artifacts used for embalming. AL Visual/Spatial
- ☐ **P. 115** Students research Egyptian artifacts. BL

☑ *Online Teaching Options*

V Visual Skills

- ☐ VIDEO **Life in Ancient Egypt**—Students view a video that Identifies what kinds of crops were grown along the Nile Delta and that examines crafts from artisans.
- ☐ SLIDE SHOW **Pyramids**—Students learn additional information on the pharaohs and the pyramids.
- ☐ IMAGE **Pyramids of Giza**—Students click to learn more about these three pyramids.
- ☐ IMAGE **Family Roles**— Students view an ancient painting and click to learn more about roles of men and women in ancient Egypt.
- ☐ IMAGE **Feluccas**—Students click to learn about the parts of these narrow, flat-bottom sailboats.

R Reading Skills

- ☐ GRAPHIC ORGANIZER **Taking Notes: *Organizing:* Ancient Egypt**—Students use this graphic organizer to record information on the ruler, religion, and social groups of ancient Egypt.

C Critical Thinking Skills

- ☐ CHART **Egyptian Society**—Students compare the duties and privileges of each tier of Egyptian society.
- ☐ CHART **Role of Women**—Students compare the roles of women in ancient Egypt with roles of American women today.
- ☐ CHART **Foods of the Egyptians**—Students click to learn about food consumed by the Egyptians.

T Technology Skills

- ☐ SELF-CHECK QUIZ **Lesson 2**—Students receive instant feedback about their mastery of lesson content.
- ☐ GAME **Egyptians and Their Gods Concentration Game**—Students match the names of Egyptian gods to their descriptions.

☑ *Printable Digital Worksheets*

R Reading Skills

- ☐ WORKSHEET **Primary and Secondary Sources Activity: Old Kingdom and Ancient Egypt**—Students respond to a passage from *Papyrus Lansing: A Schoolbook.*

C Critical Thinking Skills

- ☐ WORKSHEET **21st Century Skills Activity: Critical Thinking and Problem Solving: Making Connections**—Students explore the qualities of good leaders and analyze a hero of their own choosing as to whether that hero exhibits these qualities.

LESSON 3 PLANNER

Egypt's Empire

Students will know:
- *factors that led to the rise and fall of the ancient Egyptian empire.*
- *how Kush and Egypt influenced each other.*

Students will be able to:
- ***analyze** visuals from Egypt's golden age.*
- ***describe** an empire and how it is built.*
- ***identify** reasons Egypt reached the height of its power.*
- ***explain** how the pharaoh contributed to the rise and fall of the Egyptian empire.*

UNDERSTANDING BY DESIGN®

☑ Print Teaching Options

V Visual Skills
- ☐ **P. 120** Students make a time line that they will add to throughout the lesson.
- ☐ **P. 122** Students analyze representations of Hatshepsut. AL **Visual/Spatial**
- ☐ **P. 124** Students interpret a map of ancient Egyptian kingdoms. AL **Visual/Spatial**

R Reading Skills
- ☐ **P. 121** Students identify the characteristics of the Hyksos that allowed them to overthrow the Egyptians. AL ELL
- ☐ **P. 122** Students summarize Egypt's growth into an empire.
- ☐ **P. 123** Students use decoding techniques to determine the meanings of content vocabulary. AL ELL **Verbal/Linguistic**
- ☐ **P. 127** Students define *incline* and *decline*. ELL **Visual/Spatial**

W Writing Skills
- ☐ **P. 126** Students discover the controversy over the building of the Aswan Dam. BL **Verbal/Linguistic**

C Critical Thinking Skills
- ☐ **P. 120** Students classify events during the Golden Age as internal or external. ELL **Verbal/Linguistic**
- ☐ **P. 123** Students discuss the increase in trade during the New Kingdom. BL
- ☐ **P. 124** Students compare the rights of enslaved peoples in Egypt to those of enslaved Africans in the United States.
- ☐ **P. 125** Students discuss how changes in religion affected Egypt. BL
- ☐ **P. 126** Students analyze a quote by Ramses II.

T Technology Skills
- ☐ **P. 121** Students research musical instruments used by the ancient Egyptians. **Auditory/Musical**
- ☐ **P. 126** Students read several accounts of Carter's discovery of King Tut's tomb and identify the primary source. **Verbal/Linguistic**

☑ Online Teaching Options

V Visual Skills
- VIDEO **Ancient Egypt**—Paintings, sculptures, carvings, and ruins serve as a backdrop for a discussion of the customs and lifestyles of ancient Egyptians.
- MAP **Ancient Egyptian Kingdoms**—Students explore the extent of the lands of the Old, Middle, and New Kingdoms.
- IMAGE **Art of the Middle Kingdom**—Students click to learn about the type of art created during the Middle Kingdom.
- IMAGE **Karnak**—Students click to learn about this temple built by Ramses II.
- IMAGE **Abu Simbel**—Students click to learn about the statues of Ramses II built at this temple complex.

R Reading Skills
- GRAPHIC ORGANIZER **Taking Notes: *Organizing:* The Middle and New Kingdoms**—Students record details about the Middle and New Kingdoms.
- IMAGE **Elephants**—Students read about the effects of the ivory trade on elephant populations.
- BIOGRAPHY **Hatshepsut**—Students read additional background about this successful ruler of Egypt.

C Critical Thinking Skills
- WHITEBOARD ACTIVITY **The Hyksos and the Egyptians**—Students identify defining characteristics of each group.
- CHART **Pharaohs and Their Achievements**—Students drag and drop to match each pharaoh to his or her achievements.

T Technology Skills
- SELF-CHECK QUIZ **Lesson 3**—Students receive instant feedback of their mastery of lesson content.
- GAME **Hyksos and Egyptians True-or-False Game**—Students identify facts about these two groups.

☑ Printable Digital Worksheets

R Reading Skills
- WORKSHEET **Primary and Secondary Sources Activity: The New Kingdom**—Students respond to a passage from Great Captains of Antiquity.

W Writing Skills
- WORKSHEET **21st Century Skills Activity: Communication: Writing in Various Styles: Expository**—Students write a job description for position of pharaoh.

LESSON 4 PLANNER

THE KINGDOM OF KUSH

Students will know:
- *how Egypt influenced other kingdoms.*

Students will be able to:
- ***identify** how Nubia and Kush were influenced by Egyptian culture.*

UNDERSTANDING BY DESIGN®

☑ Print Teaching Options

V Visual Skills

- ☐ **P. 129** Students create time lines of the events discussed in the lesson. **Visual/Spatial**
- ☐ **P. 130** Students analyze a painting of Kushite and Egyptian royalty. **Visual/Spatial**
- ☐ **P. 131** Students speculate about the size of the Kush kingdom. **AL** **Visual/Spatial**

R Reading Skills

- ☐ **P. 128** Students find the main ideas in the first section of the lesson. **AL** **ELL**
- ☐ **P. 132** Students identify how iron changed the lives of the Kushites.

W Writing Skills

- ☐ **P. 129** Students write paragraphs about the rise of Kerma. **Verbal/Linguistic**
- ☐ **P. 132** Students research and write a report about changes brought about by technology. **Interpersonal** **Verbal/Linguistic**

C Critical Thinking Skills

- ☐ **P. 130** Students discuss important points about the Kushite kingdom.
- ☐ **P. 131** Students interpret a Kushite primary source. **AL** **BL** **Interpersonal**
- ☐ **P. 132** Students compare and contrast Meroë with an Egyptian city.
- ☐ **P. 133** Students organize information about Kushite trade relations. **AL** **ELL** **Visual/Spatial**

T Technology Skills

- ☐ **P. 132** Students convert their reports on technological innovations into slide shows. **Auditory/Musical**

☑ Online Teaching Options

V Visual Skills

- **VIDEO** **Kingdom of Axum**—Students view a video about this city and the archaeological relics that remain there.
- **MAP** **Kush Kingdom, c. 250 B.C.**—Students examine the extent of the Kush Kingdom.
- **CHART** **Savanna and Desert**—Students click to compare the characteristics of these two biomes.
- **IMAGE** **Kushite Pyramids**—Students click to learn about the pyramids the Kushites built.
- **IMAGE** **Nubian Trade**—Students examine an image in which Nubian royalty offer gifts to an Egyptian pharaoh.

R Reading Skills

- **GRAPHIC ORGANIZER** **Taking Notes: *Sequencing:* Kush Conquers Egypt**—Students sequence events that led up to the Kush conquest of Egypt.
- **PRIMARY SOURCE** **Shabaka Stone**—Students examine an excerpt from the text on this stone, which underscores the cultural ties between Egypt and Nubia.

T Technology Skills

- **SELF-CHECK QUIZ** **Lesson 4**—Students receive instant feedback of their mastery of lesson content.
- **GAME** **Kingdom of Kush Crossword Puzzle**—Students complete a puzzle using key vocabulary terms.

☑ Printable Digital Worksheets

C Critical Thinking Skills

- **WORKSHEET** **Economics of History Activity: Ancient Egypt and Kush**—Students explore the exchange of both goods and ideas among Egypt, Assyria, and Kush.

INTERVENTION AND REMEDIATION STRATEGIES

LESSON 1 The Nile River

Reading and Comprehension

Have students skim the lesson to find new or unfamiliar words and then use dictionaries to define the terms. In small groups, have each student read one of the definitions. The other students should guess the word and explain how it is used in the lesson.

Text Evidence

To help students understand the importance of the Nile to a desert people, have them list all the times they use water during a day. As a class, combine all the examples into one list. Discuss whether it would be feasible to use water for all these purposes if one lived in a desert environment.

LESSON 2 Life in Ancient Egypt

Reading and Comprehension

Call students' attention to the large and small red headings in the chapter. Have them list each of these on index cards. In small groups, have students brainstorm what they might learn under each heading.

Text Evidence

Direct students to the photos of the Sphinx and Great Pyramid in their textbooks. Have students write a paragraph describing what they think it would be like to see these monuments in person. Encourage students to use information from their text and a variety of descriptive words or phrases as they write their paragraphs.

LESSON 3 Egypt's Empire

Reading and Comprehension

Preview the lesson by having students take turns reading the photo captions and titles of the other visual elements. Spend some time with each visual, saying how it fits in with the lesson's content.

Text Evidence

Organize the class into several small groups. Have each group create a list of reasons why the period from 2055 B.C. to about 1200 B.C. was considered Egypt's golden age. Have each group present their lists and defend their arguments.

LESSON 4 The Kingdom of Kush

Reading and Comprehension

To ensure comprehension of concepts in this lesson, have students write sentences using the new lesson vocabulary. Sentences should show an understanding of the meaning of each word and how it applies to the lesson content.

Text Evidence

Students may not fully grasp the importance of cultural diffusion. Organize the class into groups, and assign each a cultural group such as the Egyptians, the Kush, the Phoenicians, and the Assyrians. Have students review the text for goods and ideas that their cultural group traded with others. Have groups write a poem, song, or rap describing these interactions that they can present to the class.

Online Resources

Approaching Level Reader

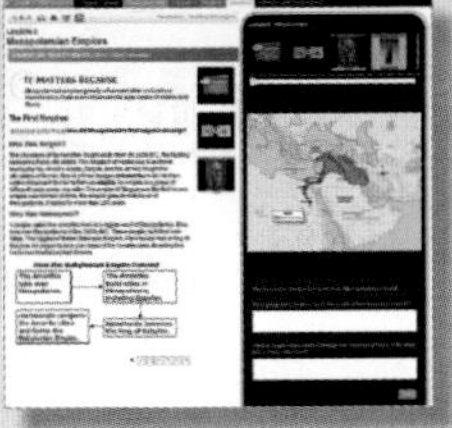

Use this online lower-level text that corresponds directly to the text in the Student Edition. It includes a Spanish version.

Guided Reading Activities

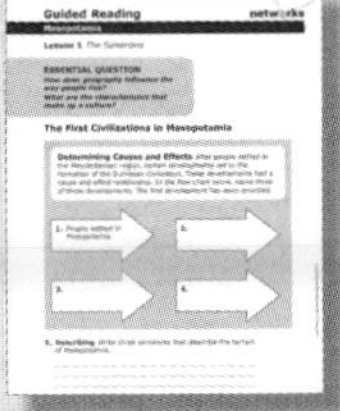

This resource uses graphic organizers and guiding questions to help students with comprehension.

What Do You Know?

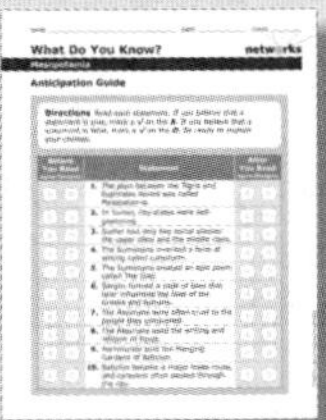

Use these worksheets to pre-assess student's background knowledge before they study the chapter.

Reading Essentials and Study Guide Workbook

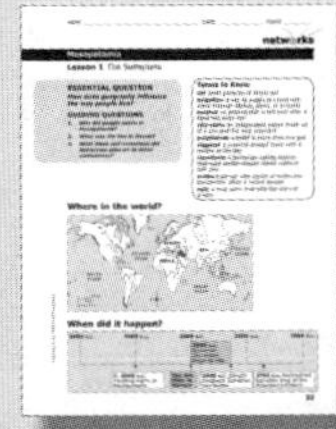

This resource offers writing and reading activities for the approaching-level student. Also available in Spanish.

Self-Check Quizzes

This online assessment tool provides instant feedback for students to check their progress.

How Do I Incorporate the Common Core State Standards in My Lessons?

The Common Core State Standards (CCSS), are national standards focused on ensuring that students master language arts skills by the time they complete high school. In grades 6 through 12, the standards require that some of this skill development and skill practice be part of other subjects, such as social studies.

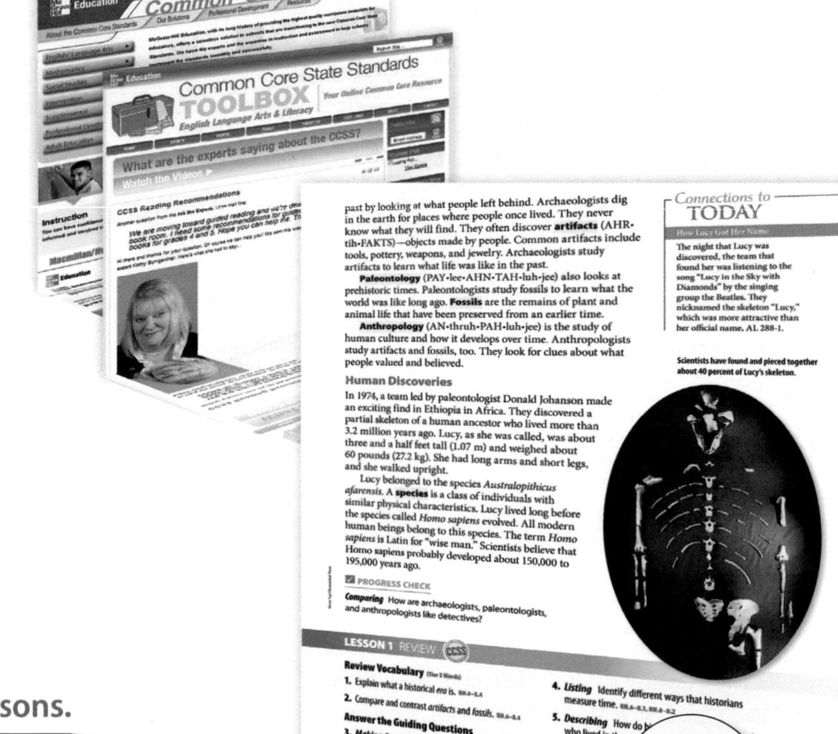

Step 1 Familiarize Yourself with the Standards.

- The Common Core Solutions Web site, **http://www.commoncoresolutions.com**, has several free training modules on the CCSS.
- The Common Core State Standards Toolbox Web site, **http://www.mhecommoncoretoolbox.com**, has articles and tips from other teachers and professionals that you can refer to throughout the year.

Step 2 Incorporate the Standards into Your Lessons.

- Common core activities are clearly marked in the McGraw-Hill print teacher and student editions and online teacher lesson plans to help you incorporate the standards into your lessons.
- Activities are correlated to the Common Core State Standards.

Step 3 Use Resources in the Online Resource Library to Promote Student Skill Mastery.

Slide Shows that help students learn how to:

- Identify main ideas
- Understand cause and effect
- Compare and contrast
- Draw conclusions
- Analyze visuals, documents, videos

Writing and Analyzing Templates to help students:

- Write drafts
- Evaluate writing samples
- Write persuasive text
- Create expository text
- Compose narrative

Ancient Egypt and Kush

5000 B.C. to A.D. 350

ESSENTIAL QUESTIONS • *How does geography influence the way people live?* • *What makes a culture unique?* • *Why do civilizations rise and fall?*

networks

There's More Online about the cultures of ancient Egypt and Kush.

CHAPTER 5

Lesson 1
The Nile River

Lesson 2
Life in Ancient Egypt

Lesson 3
Egypt's Empire

Lesson 4
The Kingdom of Kush

The Story Matters . . .

When you think of the most powerful person in your country, who is it? Is it the president? For ancient Egyptians, one of the most important beings was the god Osiris. Osiris controlled the power of life and death. As the god of agriculture, he controlled the very food Egyptians ate. He allowed the Nile River to flood its banks and bring fertile soil and water to the Egyptian desert. Osiris also knew death. In the underworld, the souls of the dead met the god Osiris. He did not have the power to return the dead to life, but he was a symbol of ongoing life. As you read this chapter, you will learn how the forces of life and death shaped the daily life of the ancient Egyptians and Kushites.

◄ *The god Osiris was respected because he represented new life and new crops.*

97

Letter from the Author

Dear World History Teacher,

Of central importance to the development of Egyptian civilization was the Nile River. Of equal importance in Egyptian history was the pharaoh, who was, in theory, a god who maintained order and harmony within the kingdom. Egyptian technical achievements, especially visible in the construction of the pyramids, demonstrated skills unique to the world at that time. The Egyptians also made an impact in the south in Nubia, which became the independent state of Kush. Kushite culture borrowed elements from Egypt, including hieroglyphs, religious beliefs, and the practice of interring kings in pyramids.

Jackson J. Spielvogel

ENGAGE

Bellringer Read "The Story Matters . . ." aloud in class. Then have students work with a partner to discuss what it might have been like to be a young person living in ancient Egypt, where death was the focus of daily life. Have students focus on the following questions:

- **How do you honor your ancestors or the people who came before you?**
- **How would you like to be remembered by the generations that follow you? What stories or memories of your life would you like people to share?**

Bring the class back together, and have a few students share their stories. Then tell the class that Egypt's dry, sandy climate helped preserve ancient artifacts and monuments for thousands of years. Well-preserved carvings and other artifacts from the ancient pyramids tell us most of what we know about this ancient culture and its history. Tell students that they can view the rediscovered treasures of ancient Egypt online. **Interpersonal**

Making Connections

Read the following information to students. **BL**

There are similarities between the development of ancient Egypt and the development of the United States as governments and nations.

- Egyptian kings/pharaohs concluded that a strong central government was essential to keeping a kingdom running smoothly and profitably.
- George Washington also came to this conclusion and worked diligently to form a central government in the newly made United States of America. Other founders thought that a central government would become all-powerful, as it was in the England they had just defeated.
- The main departments of the U.S. government, the cabinet, parallel the activities of ancient Egyptian government—labor, commerce, defense, international relations, agriculture, and so on.
- Isolation and waterways were as important to the development of the United States as they were to the development of ancient Egypt.
- The United States was also rich in natural resources important at the time—codfish, wood, ores. The United States also had what seemed like infinite space, which Egypt lacked.

TEACH & ASSESS

Step Into the Place

V1 Visual Skills

Analyzing Maps Review the parts of the map with students such as the title, compass rose, scale, and key. **Ask:**

- **What does the area shown in orange represent?** *(the extent of ancient Egypt between 1550 and 1070 B.C.)*
- **About how far would you have to travel to go from the northern end of Phoenecia** *(near Mesopotamia)* **to the southern end of Kush?** *(about 5400 miles, or 11,350 km)*
- **Is the Nile Delta north or south of Kush?** *(north)*

As students continue to analyze the map, **ask:**

- **What large bodies of water bordered Ancient Egypt?** *(Mediterranean Sea, Red Sea)*
- **What river runs the length of Egypt in Africa?** *(Nile River)*

Explain that in this chapter, students will learn the importance of the Nile River to the development of Egypt and the surrounding kingdoms. **Visual/Spatial**

Content Background Knowledge

The Nile River Today The Nile River valley remains the most important region in modern Egypt. It is home to most of the country's economic activity. As in ancient Egypt, agriculture plays a key part of the Egyptian economy. It is the country's single largest source of employment. In the modern era, Egyptians have built dams to control the Nile. These dams regulate the Nile's flow and allow control of the river's flooding. The Aswan High Dam, in addition to controlling irrigation waters, also provides electric power for Egypt. However, the dam has also reduced the fertility of Egyptian soil. Many of the nutrients that were once delivered by the Nile's annual flooding are now captured by the dam system. Egypt's use of fertilizers has not been enough to compensate, and the productivity of farmland along the Nile has suffered.

ANSWERS, p. 98

Step Into the Place

1. south
2. the Nile River, the Red Sea, and the Mediterranean Sea
3. Egypt is south of the Mediterranean Sea and west of the Red Sea.
4. CRITICAL THINKING A waterway provides a trade route and water for drinking and for growing crops.

Step Into the Time

Students may cite: Narmer unites Egypt, the Egyptians develop hieroglyphics, and the Great Pyramid is built.

CHAPTER 5 

Place and Time: Egypt and Kush: 5000 B.C. to A.D. 350

The Egyptian Empire covered the northeastern corner of Africa. It centered on the mysterious Nile River valley. Egypt extended from central Africa to coastal areas along the Red and the Mediterranean Seas. Despite periods of weakness, the empire expanded over the centuries of the Middle Kingdom and the New Kingdom.

The hot, dry climate of Egypt allowed ancient Egyptians to preserve the bodies of their dead as mummies.

These jars were used for storage during the process of making mummies. The tops of the jars show the heads of Egyptian gods.

Step Into the Place

MAP FOCUS Egypt's location in a river valley surrounded by deserts helped it become powerful.

1. **LOCATION** Look at the map. Is Egypt located north or south of the Mediterranean Sea? **RH.6–8.7**
2. **PLACE** What physical features made it possible for Egyptians to travel and trade? **RH.6–8.7**
3. **LOCATION** Describe the location of Egypt using cardinal directions. **RH.6–8.7**
4. **CRITICAL THINKING** ***Analyzing*** How does location near a waterway contribute to the success of a civilization? **RH.6–8.2**

Step Into the Time

V2

TIME LINE What events in the time line suggest that the Egyptians were unified, organized, and determined to build an empire? **RH.6–8.7**

ANCIENT EGYPT AND KUSH
- c. 3100 B.C. Narmer unites Egypt
- c. 3000 B.C. Egyptians develop hieroglyphics
- c. 2600 B.C. Old Kingdom period begins
- c. 2540 B.C. Great Pyramid built

3000 B.C.

THE WORLD
- c. 3000 B.C. India's early civilization begins
- c. 2700 B.C. Chinese begin making bronze artifacts
- c. 2500 B.C. Mesopotamia sets up world's first libraries

Project-Based Learning 

Hands-On Chapter Project

Create Maps

Students will individually create "shoe box" sarcophagi that represent their identity and personal interests. Each student will write an explanation of their sarcophagi and its contents for them to present with their work to the class.

Technology Extension

Create Online Interactive Maps

Students will gather materials found online and from personal sources in order to tell the story of their lives. Glogster posters, or Glogs, provide students a dynamic way to reflect their unique lives and personal interests. The Glogs can easily be published and made viewable for friends, family, and classmates. Students may work with text, audio clips, video files, and images to fulfill their vision.

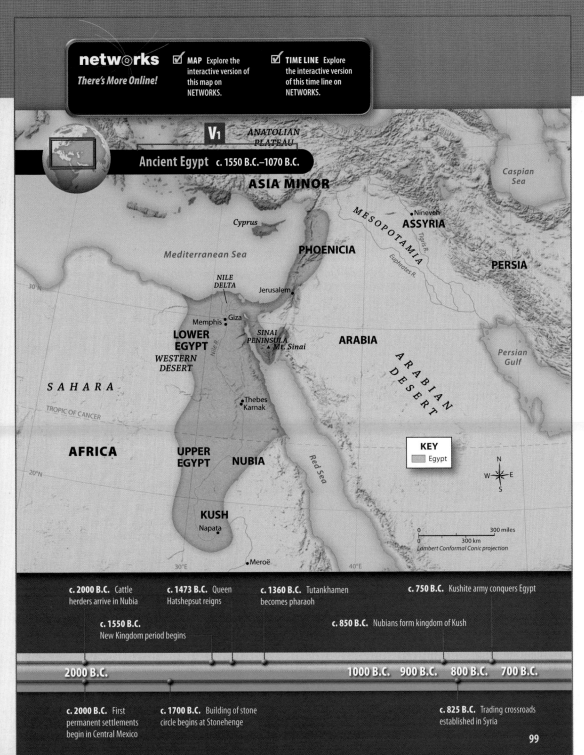

networks *There's More Online!*

☑ **MAP** Explore the interactive version of this map on NETWORKS.

☑ **TIME LINE** Explore the interactive version of this time line on NETWORKS.

V1 **Ancient Egypt** c. 1550 B.C.–1070 B.C.

ANATOLIAN PLATEAU
ASIA MINOR
Caspian Sea
Cyprus
Nineveh
ASSYRIA
MESOPOTAMIA
Tigris R.
Euphrates R.
Mediterranean Sea
PHOENICIA
PERSIA
NILE DELTA
Jerusalem
30°N
Giza
Memphis
LOWER EGYPT
SINAI PENINSULA
Mt. Sinai
ARABIA
Persian Gulf
Nile R.
WESTERN DESERT
ARABIAN DESERT
SAHARA
Thebes
Karnak
TROPIC OF CANCER
AFRICA
UPPER EGYPT
NUBIA
Red Sea
KEY
Egypt
N W E S
20°N
KUSH
Napata
0 300 miles
0 300 km
Lambert Conformal Conic projection
30°E
Meroë
40°E

c. 2000 B.C. Cattle herders arrive in Nubia

c. 1473 B.C. Queen Hatshepsut reigns

c. 1360 B.C. Tutankhamen becomes pharaoh

c. 750 B.C. Kushite army conquers Egypt

c. 1550 B.C. New Kingdom period begins

c. 850 B.C. Nubians form kingdom of Kush

2000 B.C. 1000 B.C. 900 B.C. 800 B.C. 700 B.C.

c. 2000 B.C. First permanent settlements begin in Central Mexico

c. 1700 B.C. Building of stone circle begins at Stonehenge

c. 825 B.C. Trading crossroads established in Syria

99

CHAPTER 5

Place and Time

Step Into the Time

V2 Visual Skills

Analyzing Time Lines Have students review the time line for the chapter. Explain that they will be studying events from about 3000 B.C. to 700 B.C. Use the time line to remind students how B.C. dates are arranged from higher to lower numerals. Help students by suggesting that they think of B.C. dates as a countdown, beginning around 3000 and counting down to zero. **Ask:** **Was the year 1250 B.C. before or after 1400 B.C.?** *(after)* **Was the year 825 B.C. before or after 750 B.C.?** *(before)* Continue to quiz students, using random dates until they demonstrate command of the concept. **AL** **Logical/ Mathematical**

As students continue to analyze the time line, have them identify any events that they are familiar with and share what they know about those events with the class.

CLOSE & REFLECT

Have students write clues to the location of places shown on the map, but without giving the name of the place. Have students share their clues with the class and have others guess the place. Discuss differences in how various students identified the same location. Tell students that the places shown on the map will be important in the chapter to come.

WORLD ATLAS

World Atlas

Locating Project the Interactive Atlas on the whiteboard. Focus on the region of North Africa and Southwest Asia. Remind students about the rise and fall of the Mesopotamians. Discuss as a class how geographical features of a place or region provided protection from enemies as well as opportunities for farming and trade. Have student volunteers analyze the map and draw circles around the deserts in the region. Then ask students what impact the deserts might have had on the development of ancient Egypt. **AL** **Visual/Spatial**

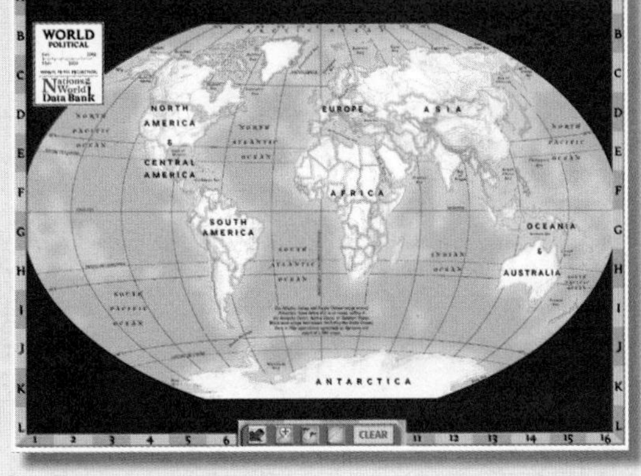

See page 97B for other online activities.

ENGAGE

 **Bellringer** You'll need:

- 1-inch-wide blue painter's tape
- strips of green paper, such as crepe paper, or green packing tape two inches wide
- sheets of yellow or tan paper

Tell students you are going to use tape and paper to make a river—the Nile River. Ask students to move their desks to make a center aisle. Have volunteers help you use blue tape to make a stripe down the center of the room. Then add a stripe of green on each side of the blue "river." If you are using crepe paper, you will want to securely tape it to the floor. Have students write "desert" on sheets of yellow paper and tape them on either side of this model.

Explain to students that the blue line is the Nile. Along it on both sides are narrow areas of fertile land, represented by the green strips. Make sure they understand that the yellow paper represents large areas of desert. Tell students that all the action described in this lesson (and in this chapter) takes place in the narrow band of blue and green. **ELL** **Kinesthetic**

To further extend the activity, have students help you make a Nile model to scale, with one inch representing 100 miles, for example. You might need to use a hallway, gymnasium, or playground. **Logical/Mathematical**

TEACH & ASSESS

R Reading Skills

Describing Discuss as a class why people originally settled near the Nile River. Have students use details from the text to describe the Nile River and the land around it. Ask them to identify how the characteristics in their descriptions contribute to the area being an inviting place for the people to settle and live.

networks
There's More Online!

- **DIAGRAM** How Egyptians Made Papyrus
- **GRAPHIC ORGANIZER** Benefits of the Nile
- **MAP**
  - Ancient Egypt
  - Early Trade Routes

Lesson 1
The Nile River

ESSENTIAL QUESTION *How does geography influence the way people live?*

IT MATTERS BECAUSE
The Nile River was the most important factor in the development of ancient Egypt.

The Nile River Valley

GUIDING QUESTION *Why was the Nile River important to the ancient Egyptians?*

While empires flourished and fell in Mesopotamia, two other civilizations developed along the Nile River in northeastern Africa. One of these civilizations was Egypt (EE•jihpt). It developed in the northern part of the Nile River valley. The other civilization, Kush (CUSH), emerged in the far southern part of the Nile River valley. Although Egypt and Kush were **unique** civilizations, they influenced one another throughout their long histories.

Valley Civilization

R The Nile River valley was ideal for human settlement because of its fertile land. As early as 5000 B.C., hunters and gatherers from the drier areas of Africa and Southwest Asia began to move into the Nile River valley. Permanent settlements were created by early groups who farmed the land and built villages along the Nile's banks. These people were the earliest Egyptians and Kushites.

The early Egyptians lived in the northern region of the Nile River valley. They called their land *Kemet* (KEH•meht), which means "black land," after the dark, rich soil. Later, this northern Nile area would be called *Egypt*. Of the world's early river valley

Reading **HELP**DESK 

Taking Notes: ***Identifying***
Use a web diagram like this one to identify three reasons why most ancient Egyptians lived near the Nile River. RH.6–8.2

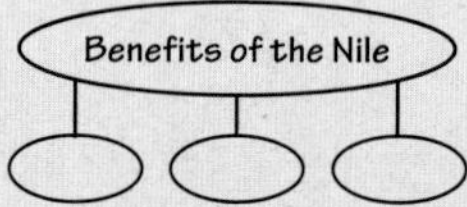

Content Vocabulary (Tier 3 Words)
- **cataract**
- **delta**
- **shadoof**
- **papyrus**
- **hieroglyphics**
- **dynasty**

networks Online Teaching Options

VIDEO

The Nile River

Finding the Main Idea After students view the video, have them write a paragraph summarizing the video's main idea. Remind students to include a topic sentence and 3–4 supporting details in their paragraphs.

See page 97C for other online activities.

ANSWER, p. 100

TAKING NOTES: The Nile provided water for crops, drinking, and bathing; rich soil for farming; a means of transportation; and security against attack.

civilizations, you probably are most familiar with ancient Egypt. People still marvel at its ruins located in present-day Egypt. These ruins include the enormous stone Sphinx that has the body of a lion and a human head. Archaeologists also study the wondrous pyramids and the mummies found buried in tombs once full of riches.

The Gift of the River

Many of ancient Egypt's structures survived because Egypt has a hot, dry climate. Since the region receives little rainfall, ancient Egyptians depended on the Nile for drinking and bathing. The river also supplied water to grow crops. To the Egyptians, the Nile was the "creator of all good." They praised it in a hymn: **R**

PRIMARY SOURCE

> "You create the grain, you bring forth the barley,
> Assuring perpetuity [survival] to the temples.
> If you cease your toil and your work,
> Then all that exists is in anguish [suffering]."
>
> —from "Hymn to the Nile"

C

GEOGRAPHY CONNECTION

The Nile carries its life-giving water the length of Egypt.

1. **LOCATION** Describe the relative locations of Upper Egypt and Lower Egypt.
2. **CRITICAL THINKING** *Analyzing* Why do you think the location of Giza made it an early thriving city in ancient Egypt?

Academic Vocabulary (Tier 2 Words)

unique one of a kind; different from all others

Lesson 1 101

GRAPHIC ORGANIZER

Taking Notes: *Identifying:* Benefits of the Nile

Identifying Discuss as a class why people originally settled near the Nile River. Have students describe the Nile River and the land around it. Then have students complete the Taking Notes interactive graphic organizer. If necessary, review the meanings of key terms such as *crops, drinking, soil,* and *transportation.* ELL AL

See page 97C for other online activities.

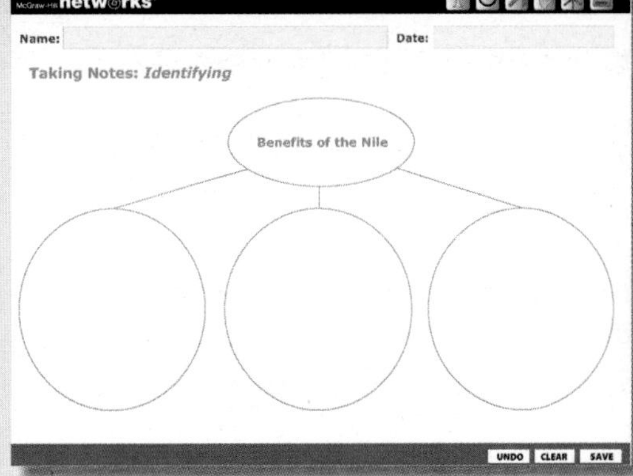

The Nile River

R Reading Skills

Identifying As a class, use details from the text to brainstorm a list of ways in which the Nile River affected Egyptian life. **Ask:** What important resources did the Nile provide to settlers? *(water for drinking, bathing, cooking, and farming; fertile soil for growing crops)*

C Critical Thinking Skills

Analyzing Primary Sources Have a volunteer read the excerpt from "Hymn to the Nile." **Ask:**

- What is this poem about? *(the Nile River)*
- What important work does the Nile do? *(provides crops)*
- What does the author say will happen if the Nile ceases in its work? *(All will suffer.)*

Point out to students that this poem is a metaphor that compares the Nile to a person. **Ask:** What human characteristics are attributed to the Nile? *(working in the fields to produce grain)*

Making Connections

Share this information with students about locations on the map:

- The Egyptian capital of Thebes is designated as a United Nations World Heritage Site.
- The magnificent temple of Karnak is on the eastern bank of the city of Thebes—the city was located on both sides of the Nile.
- Memphis is about 14 miles south of Egypt's current capital, Cairo. It is also a World Heritage Site.
- Memphis and its surrounding area were home to many of the best-preserved pyramids. The pyramids are part of a great cemetery called a Necropolis (Greek for "city of the dead").

ANSWERS, p. 101

GEOGRAPHY CONNECTION

1. Lower Egypt is located north of Upper Egypt.
2. **CRITICAL THINKING** Giza's location near the Nile Delta made trade easier. Its location along the Nile River would have made agriculture easier too.

The Nile River

C Critical Thinking Skills

Comparing and Contrasting Have students make a table to compare and contrast the Nile with a creek, stream, or river in their area. They may need to do some research into their local waterway as well as the Nile. A sample table is given below. **Naturalist**

Characteristic	Nile	Local River
Length		
Drop (from origin to sea level)		
Rate of flow		
Used for recreation?		
Used for agriculture?		
Used for fishing?		
Used for defense?		
Used for transportation?		

T Technology Skills

Researching on the Internet Have students look on the Internet to find satellite photographs of the Nile Delta. The demarcation between arable and barren land often is easily visible, as is the fan-shaped delta. **Visual/Spatial Ask:**

- **How did the delta serve Egypt as a barrier to invasion?** *(It had no clear channels for ships of war to sail through.)*
- **What could be done to make the delta easier to navigate?** *(A channel could be dug through the delta.)* In fact, later Egyptians dredged a channel through the delta to get better access to the Mediterranean.

Thinking Like a HISTORIAN

Researching on the Internet

As the "lifeblood" of Egypt, the Nile River was and continues to be essential to daily life in Egypt. It is also important to the other places through which it flows. Use the Internet to find reliable sources about the lands through which the Nile River and its tributaries run. Identify three facts that you discover about the Nile River from your research and present them to the class. For more information about using the Internet for research, read the chapter *What Does a Historian Do?*

Narrow cataracts on the Nile limit river travel, especially for larger ships.

Do you know which is the world's longest river? It is the Nile that flows north about 4,000 miles (6,437 km) from central Africa to the Mediterranean Sea. It has been called the "lifeblood" of Egypt. **C**

At its source, the Nile is two separate rivers: the Blue Nile and the White Nile. The Blue Nile begins in the snowy mountains of eastern Africa. The White Nile starts in the tropics of central Africa. The two rivers join just south of Egypt to form the Nile River. There, steep cliffs and large boulders form dangerous, fast-moving waters called **cataracts** (KA•tuh•RAKTS). Cataracts make traveling by ship along the Nile difficult.

A Protected Land

T As with many rivers, the Nile's flow throughout the centuries has created a valley. You can see on the map on the previous page that the Nile looks like the long winding root of a plant. Shortly before the Nile reaches the Mediterranean Sea, it splits into many branches that resemble a plant's bloom. These waterways form a fan-shaped area of fertile marshland called a **delta** (DEHL•tuh).

In the Nile River valley, we see the effect that water has on the landscape. The lush, green Nile valley and delta contrast sharply with the barren deserts that stretch out on either side of the river. The change in landscape can be so sudden that a person can stand with one foot in fertile soil and one foot in barren sand.

The Nile borders the largest deserts in the world. To the west of the Nile River is the Libyan Desert, which forms part of the Sahara (suh•HAR•uh). To the river's east lies the Eastern Desert that extends to the Red Sea. The ancient Egyptians called these deserts the "Red Land" because of their scorching heat. These large desert areas were not favorable to humans or animals. They kept Egypt **isolated,** however, from outside invaders.

In addition to the deserts, other physical features protected Egypt. To the far south, the Nile's dangerous cataracts prevented enemy ships from attacking Egypt. In the north, delta marshes stopped invaders who sailed from the Mediterranean Sea. These physical features gave the Egyptians advantages that Mesopotamians lacked. The Egyptians rarely faced the danger of invasion. As a result, Egyptian civilization developed peacefully.

The Egyptians, though isolated, were not completely cut off from other peoples. The Mediterranean Sea to the north and the Red Sea to the east provided routes for trade.

Reading HELPDESK (CCSS)

cataract a waterfall or rapids in a river

delta a fan-shaped area of silt near where a river flows into the sea

Academic Vocabulary (Tier 2 Words)

isolate to separate from others

networks Online Teaching Options

SLIDE SHOW

World's Longest Rivers

Comparing and Contrasting Remind students that the Nile is the longest river in the world. Advance the slide show to display the interactive chart. Have students share what they know about any of the rivers listed. Then click to reveal the continents on which the rivers flow and the lengths of the rivers. You may wish to have students make a bar graph to help them visualize the differences in length.

See page 97C for other online activities.

The stark contrast between watered and not watered land can be seen along the banks of the Nile.

Michel Gounot /Godong/Corbis

Egyptians took advantage of the region's wind patterns so that they could travel and trade. Although the natural flow of the Nile's currents carried boats north, winds from the north pushed sailboats south.

✓ PROGRESS CHECK

Explaining How were the Egyptians protected by their physical environment?

People of the River

GUIDING QUESTION *How did the ancient Egyptians depend on the Nile River to grow their crops?*

We know that the Mesopotamians controlled the floods of the Tigris and Euphrates Rivers to grow crops. They developed the technology to do so, but the unpredictable rivers constantly challenged them. In Egypt, however, the flooding of the Nile River was seasonal and consistent from year to year. So the Egyptians did not face the same challenge.

Predictable Floods

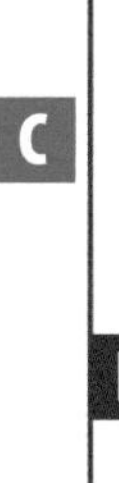

As in Mesopotamia, flooding along the Nile in Egypt was common. The Nile floods, however, were more predictable and less destructive than those of the Tigris and the Euphrates. As a result, the Egyptians were not afraid that heavy floods would destroy their homes and crops. Each year, during late spring, heavy tropical rains in central Africa and melting mountain snow in eastern Africa added water to the Nile. Around the middle of summer, the Nile overflowed its banks and flooded the land. Egyptian farmers were ready to take advantage of this cycle. When the waters returned to their normal level in late fall, thick deposits of fertile soil remained.

C Critical Thinking Skills

Making Comparisons Draw an analogy between the lungs in the human body and the seasonal expansion and contraction of a river. Both the lungs and the river expand and contract *(get larger and smaller)*. The Nile and the lungs follow a predictable pattern of increase and decrease and expand and contract to the same distance. Other rivers, such as the Euphrates, expand and contract unpredictably in terms of timing and extent. **Ask: Could you survive if your lungs were more like the Euphrates than the Nile?** *(No; the body would go too long without oxygen to survive.)* Note that, like human breathing, life along the Nile also depended on a regular "inhale" and "exhale" of water. AL ELL **Naturalist**

R Reading Skills

Explaining Direct students to read the text to explain how the Nile was beneficial to Egyptian farmers. **Ask: How did the flooding of the Nile River help farmers?** *(Regular and predictable flooding meant that Egyptians knew when floodwaters would come and could plan their farming methods around such increases in water in the soil. The floods left fertile soil behind, which was good for growing crops.)* Remind students to cite evidence from the text to support their responses. AL

Making Connections

Carrying Capacity of Water Pour water into a clear plastic cup. Add two tablespoons of sand or soil. Put your hand over the cup and shake. Point out that moving water can hold a great deal of soil and debris. Set the cup back on the table. The sand or soil will start to settle out. Point out that soil and debris will start to sink in still or slow-moving water. Slowly pour off the water, leaving the sand/soil in the bottom of the cup. Point out that when waters flow on or evaporate, they leave behind the soil and debris they were carrying. Discuss with students that this is how the land along the Nile stayed fertile. Each year, the swollen Nile slowed down and dropped its load of nutrients and soil. AL ELL **Kinesthetic**

IMAGE

Historic Use of the Sahara

Identifying Direct students' attention to the interactive image of the Sahara. Have volunteers read the two paragraphs as you reveal the text. If displaying the image on a whiteboard, have students come to the board and underline the ways people used the Sahara long ago. Suggest that students do research to determine if the Sahara is used in the same way today.

See page 97C for other online activities.

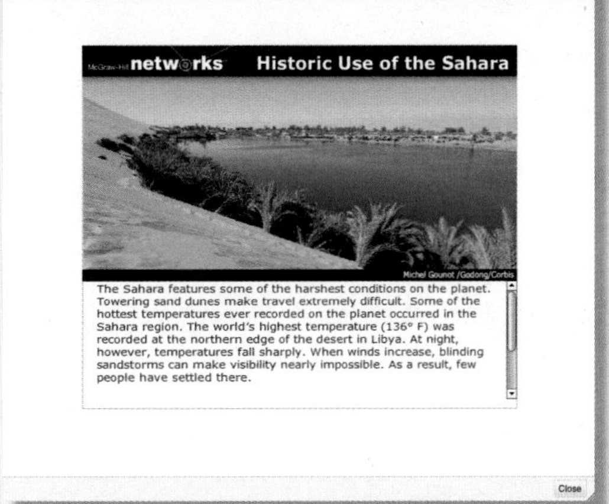

networks
Historic Use of the Sahara
Michel Gounot /Godong/Corbis
The Sahara features some of the harshest conditions on the planet. Towering sand dunes make travel extremely difficult. Some of the hottest temperatures ever recorded on the planet occurred in the Sahara region. The world's highest temperature (136° F) was recorded at the northern edge of the desert in Libya. At night, however, temperatures fall sharply. When winds increase, blinding sandstorms can make visibility nearly impossible. As a result, few people have settled there.
Close

ANSWER, p. 103

✓ PROGRESS CHECK The Nile River's cataracts and its marshy delta kept invaders out of Egypt. The hot, sandy deserts also prevented outsiders from reaching Egypt.

W Writing Skills

Informative/Explanatory The plant crops that were grown by the ancient Egyptians along the Nile included barley, beans, cabbages, figs, flax, garlic, grapes, leeks, lettuce, lentils, onions, plums, radishes, turnips, and wheat. Egyptians also raised cattle, chickens, ducks, goats, oxen, and pigs. Have students work in pairs to make meal plans that include as many of the foods from ancient Egypt as they can. Many online recipe sites let you search for different combinations of foods. Have students write out recipes that they use and make an *Ingredients of Ancient Egypt* cookbook. ELL **Interpersonal Verbal/Linguistic**

Making Connections

Writing Then and Now Remind students that the paper they use every day—and on which their books are printed—is made from plants, just like the paper made from the papyrus plant in Egypt. Most paper today is made from pine trees, with recycled paper commonly included.

Content Background Knowledge

Shadoofs To build a shadoof, two poles are put in the ground about two feet apart. A connecting board fastens them together. A long pole is balanced on the crosspiece like a seesaw, but with one piece extending out farther than the other. A rope with a bucket is attached to the long end; a weight is attached to the short end. An operator lowers and raises the bucket into and out of the water by raising and lowering the weighted end.

Special techniques and tools—such as this shadoof—helped farmers grow crops in the dry season.

How Did Egyptians Farm?

Farmers planted wheat, barley, and flax seeds while the soil was still wet. Over time, they grew enough food to feed themselves and the animals they raised. W

During the dry season, Egyptian farmers irrigated their crops. They scooped out basins, or bowl-shaped holes, in the earth to store river water. They then dug canals that extended from the basins to the fields, allowing water to flow to their crops. Raised areas of soil provided support for the basin walls.

In time, Egyptian farmers developed new tools to make their work easier. For example, farmers created a **shadoof** (shuh•DOOF), which is a bucket attached to a long pole that lifts water from the Nile and empties it into basins. Many Egyptian farmers still use this method today.

Egyptian farmers also needed a way to measure the area of their lands. When floods washed away boundary markers that divided one field from another, farmers used geometry to help them recalculate where one field began and the other ended.

Egyptians gathered **papyrus** (puh•PY•ruhs), a reed plant that grew wild along the Nile. They used the long, thin reeds to weave rope, sandals, baskets, and river rafts. Later, they used

We learn about ancient farming methods from Egyptian art murals such as this.

▶ CRITICAL THINKING

Describing What details about ancient farming methods can you find in this painting of farmers?

Reading HELPDESK CCSS

shadoof a bucket attached to a long pole used to transfer river water to storage basins

networks Online Teaching Options

CHART

How Egyptians Made Papyrus

Sequencing Explain that papyrus was used for writing. Show students the sequence chart about papyrus. **Ask:** **Why did Egyptians develop a system of writing?** *(They wanted a way to document their ideas and record information about their crops.)* If time permits, allow students to make their own recycled paper from torn, used paper and water, which you can blend together and strain onto a screen fitted into a flat tray. Then drain the water and allow to dry. Have students compare this process with that used to make papyrus. AL ELL **Kinesthetic**

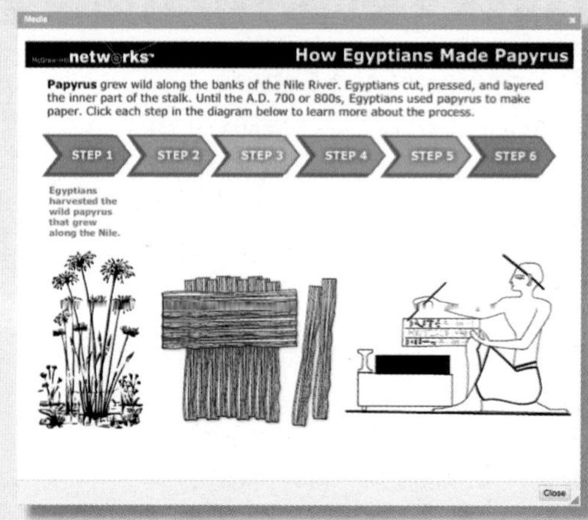

networks
How Egyptians Made Papyrus
Papyrus grew wild along the banks of the Nile River. Egyptians cut, pressed, and layered the inner part of the stalk. Until the A.D. 700 or 800s, Egyptians used papyrus to make paper. Click each step in the diagram below to learn more about the process.
STEP 1
STEP 2
STEP 3
STEP 4
STEP 5
STEP 6
Egyptians harvested the wild papyrus that grew along the Nile.
Close

See page 97C for other online activities.

ANSWER, p. 104

CRITICAL THINKING The painting shows that ancient Egyptians used plows and animals to help them farm.

papyrus to make paper. To do this, the Egyptians cut strips from the stalks of the papyrus plant and soaked them in water. Next, the strips were laid side by side and pounded together. They were then set out to dry, forming a large sheet of papyrus on which the Egyptians could write. **T**

Papyrus reeds grow wild along rivers. From harvesting the reeds to final product, the process of making paper from papyrus took many days.

▶ CRITICAL THINKING

Predicting If Egyptians had not developed papyrus, what other material could they have used to write on?

How Did the Egyptians Write?

Like the Mesopotamians, the Egyptians developed their own writing system. At first, Egyptian writing was made up of thousands of picture symbols that represented objects and ideas. A house, for example, would be represented by a drawing of a house. Later, Egyptians created symbols that represented sounds, just as the letters of our alphabet do. The combination of pictures and sound symbols created a complex writing system called **hieroglyphics** (hy•ruh•GLIH•fihks). **V**

Few ancient Egyptians could read and write hieroglyphics. Some Egyptian men, however, attended special schools to prepare for careers as scribes in government or business. The Egyptians did not write on clay tablets like the Mesopotamians. For their daily tasks, Egyptian scribes developed a simpler script that they wrote or painted on papyrus. These same scribes carved hieroglyphics onto stone walls and monuments.

☑ PROGRESS CHECK

Identifying What kind of writing system did the Egyptians develop?

papyrus a reed plant that grew wild along the Nile

hieroglyphics a writing system made up of a combination of pictures and sound symbols

T Technology Skills

Making Presentations The Web site "HowStuffWorks" lists 10 Amazing Ancient Egyptian Inventions: (1) toothpaste; (2) the door lock; (3) barbering; (4) bowling; (5) breath mints; (6) the plow; (7) the calendar; (8) paper made from papyrus; (9) written language; and (10) eye makeup. Have pairs of students research each of these inventions and prepare slideshows on them. **BL** **Interpersonal**

V Visual Skills

Simulating Find examples of hieroglyphics online or in reference books. Display these examples to the class and explain the meaning of each hieroglyph. Explain that Egyptians used hieroglyphics to record their stories and histories. **Ask:** **Do you think a picture-based alphabet would be easier or harder to learn?** *(Answers may include that pictures would be easier to read than letters; handwriting would be easier than drawings; and so on. Have students go online to find the spelling of their own names in various alphabets. Some names, such as Joy or Charity, might be spelled with a single symbol to represent the definition.)*

Work with the class to create an alphabet of hieroglyphics. Have each student write two or three simple sentences using the class's hieroglyphic alphabet. In these sentences, students should introduce themselves ("My name is . . .") and share one or two interesting facts about themselves. Ask student volunteers to share their hieroglyphic sentences with the class. **ELL** **AL** **Verbal/Linguistic**

WORKSHEET

Geography and History Activity: Understanding Location: Ancient Egypt

Describing Have students work with a partner to complete the Geography and History activity. Remind students to refer to their textbook for details as they complete the map and answer questions about the physical features of the Nile River. **Ask:**

- **Where does the Nile River flow?** *(north from Central Africa to the Mediterranean Sea)*
- **What is the land like around the Nile River?** *(Most is hot, sandy desert.)*
- **How has the Nile River affected the land in which it flows?** *(It has produced a valley of fertile land in the desert.)*

See page 97C for other online activities.

NAME ______ DATE ______ CLASS ______

Geography and History Activity networks

Ancient Egypt and Kush

Lesson 1 *The Nile River*

Understanding Location: Ancient Egypt

Geography helped the ancient Egyptian civilization succeed. Egypt is located in a desert region with a hot and dry climate. Ancient Egyptians settled in a narrow strip of fertile land called the Nile River Valley. The valley was surrounded on both sides by large deserts. Life in the Nile River Valley had its challenges. Flooding of the Nile River was followed by periods of drought, or lack of rain. Yet the Nile River and nearby deserts also provided protection that helped the Egyptians survive.

The river and deserts provided natural defenses for the Egyptians. The Nile River has a marshy delta. As a result, Egyptians could not build a port at the mouth of the Nile. This made it difficult for invaders to reach Egyptian settlements along the river. In addition, the rough waters, or cataracts, in the southern part of the river made travel and invasion difficult. The deserts that surrounded the Nile River Valley were hot, dry, and sandy. They made invasion over land nearly impossible. With these natural defenses, the ancient Egyptians did not have to build fortifications for their settlements. In addition, ancient Egyptians could travel and trade along the Nile River. Friendly relations among the villages helped create a sense of unity. Protected from enemies, the Egyptians could focus on developing trade and culture instead of defending themselves.

ANSWERS, p. 105

CRITICAL THINKING If the ancient Egyptians had not developed papyrus, they could have written on cloth, wood, stone, or animal skin (vellum).

☑ **PROGRESS CHECK** The Egyptians developed hieroglyphics, a system of symbols that represent sounds.

V Visual Skills

Analyzing Maps Direct students to study the map of early trade routes. Ask: **What route did a trader probably follow to get from Nubia to Crete?** *(A trader would likely float goods down the Nile, join a caravan traveling along the south coast of the Mediterranean Sea, and then sail from north Africa to Crete.)*

Continue asking similar questions to point out how arduous the work of trading was, and how dangerous. **Visual/Spatial**

C Critical Thinking Skills

Making Inferences Lead students in a discussion of how Egypt's natural resources helped Egyptians grow surpluses of food and goods and develop a system of trade. **Ask: How did the Nile River help relations among Egyptian villages?** *(The river allowed for trade and travel among the villages.)* **How did the Egyptians get their goods to areas outside Egypt?** *(Egyptians used caravans to carry their goods.)* AL

R Reading Skills

Explaining After students read the text, help them relate the role of government leadership to the changes that occur in a growing civilization. **Ask: Why was a united government necessary as ancient Egypt grew?** *(A government was needed to oversee the farming, trading, and land ownership in a growing Egypt.)*

Have students compare the role of Egyptian government with what they know of the role of the U.S. government. Point out that while the role of government has grown, both governments had several of the same functions. BL

Content Background Knowledge

Camels: Ships of the Desert

- The domestication of dromedaries, African camels, made invasions of the Nile valley possible from the deserts east and west of the Nile.
- Camels are related to llamas, alpacas, vicunas, and guanacos—animals of South America. They are well suited to desolate areas. Their humps are made of fibrous tissue and fat and are used as a food source, not as a storage place for water.
- Dromedaries can carry humans and cargo for up to 20 hours at a time, allowing large stretches of desert to be covered quickly. They can go without water for about four days.

ANSWERS, p. 106

GEOGRAPHY CONNECTION

1 Cyprus and Crete

2 Petra and Damascus

3 **CRITICAL THINKING** Travel is faster on water than on land; it was easier to carry large loads on a boat.

GEOGRAPHY CONNECTION

Trade routes brought new ideas to Egypt as well as money and goods.

1 **LOCATION** What two islands were the farthest north on Egyptian trade routes?

2 **MOVEMENT** A trader traveling from Memphis to Babylon might stop in which cities?

3 **CRITICAL THINKING** *Analyzing* Why do so many trade routes run along waterways?

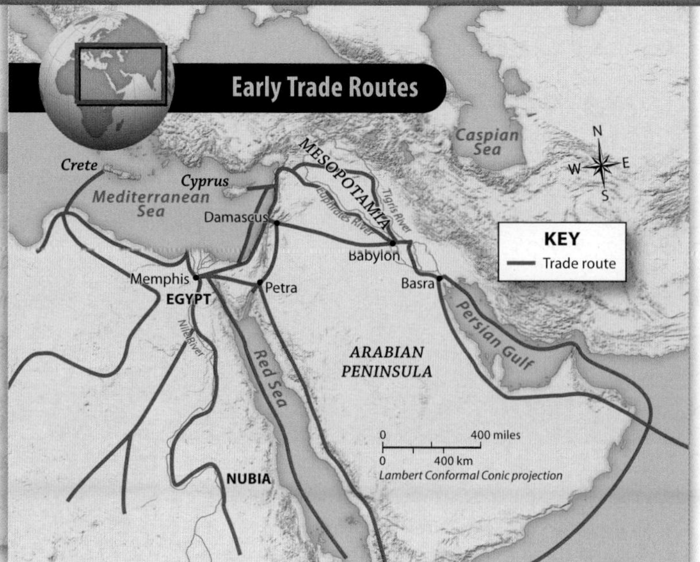

Uniting Egypt

GUIDING QUESTION *How did Egypt become united?*

Protected from outside attacks by desert barriers, Egyptian farmers were able to grow surpluses—extra amounts—of food. In Egypt, as in Mesopotamia, extra food meant that some people could leave farming to work in other occupations. Artisans, merchants, and traders began to play an important role in Egypt's economy. As more goods became available, villages along the Nile traded with one another. Before long, Egyptian caravans were carrying goods to Nubia (NOO•bee•uh) to the south, Mesopotamia to the northeast, and other places outside Egypt's borders. Along with the exchange of goods, Egyptian traders learned about the ways of life and governments of other societies.

Forming Kingdoms

The need for organized government became increasingly important as farming and trade increased. A government was necessary to oversee the construction and repair of irrigation ditches and dams. A government was needed to develop a process for storing and distributing grain during famines. In addition, conflicts over land ownership had to be settled.

Reading HELPDESK CCSS

dynasty a line of rulers from one family

Academic Vocabulary (Tier 2 Words)

unify to unite; to bring together into one unit

networks Online Teaching Options

MAP

Early Trade Routes

Interpreting Maps Display the interactive map of early trade routes, and play the audio for students. Have them use the distance tools to measure the length of several of the routes. Compare these distances to distances students may be familiar with. For example, the distance from Damascus to Babylon was about 500 miles. This is about the same as the distance from Columbus, Ohio, to New York City.

See page 97C for other online activities.

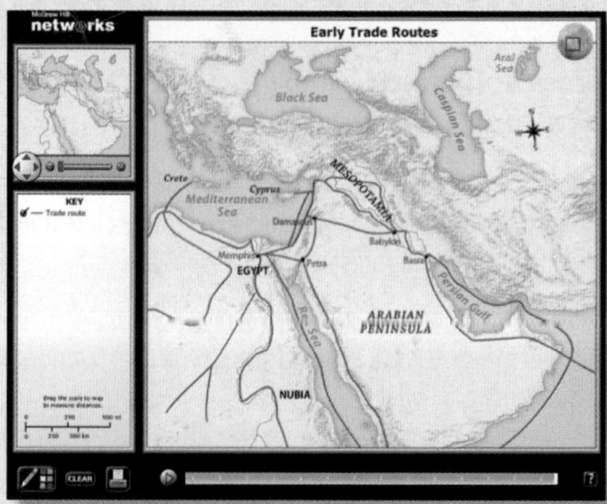

Over time, groups of villages merged to form small kingdoms. Each of these kingdoms was ruled by a king. The weaker kingdoms eventually fell under the control of the stronger ones. By 4000 B.C., Egypt was made up of two large kingdoms. One was Upper Egypt, which was located in the south-central part of the Nile River valley. The other was Lower Egypt, which was located along the Nile River's north delta.

Who Was Narmer?

Narmer (NAHR•mer) was a king of Upper Egypt. About 3100 B.C., he led his armies from the valley north into the delta. Narmer conquered Lower Egypt and married one of Lower Egypt's princesses, which **unified** the kingdoms. For the first time, all of Egypt was ruled by one king.

R Narmer established a new capital at Memphis, a city on the border between Upper Egypt and Lower Egypt. He governed both parts of Egypt from this city. Memphis began to flourish as a center of government and culture along the Nile.

Narmer's kingdom lasted long after his death. The right to rule was passed from father to son to grandson. Such a line of rulers from one family is called a **dynasty** (DY•nuh•stee). When one dynasty died out, another took its place.

From about 3100 B.C. to 332 B.C., a series of 30 dynasties ruled Egypt. These dynasties are organized into three time periods: the Old Kingdom, the Middle Kingdom, and the New Kingdom. Throughout these three time periods, Egypt was usually united under a single ruler and enjoyed stable government.

Egyptian art often glorified rulers. The man in the center of this carving is Narmer.

▶ CRITICAL THINKING
Analyzing How does the carving show that Narmer was a powerful leader?

☑ PROGRESS CHECK

Explaining How did the separate kingdoms of Egypt unite?

LESSON 1 REVIEW (CCSS)

Review Vocabulary (Tier 3 Words)

1. Why did the Egyptians need *hieroglyphics*? RH.6–8.2
2. How does a *dynasty* work? RH.6–8.2

Answer the Guiding Questions

3. ***Identifying*** What physical feature is to the east and west of the Nile River? How did this feature help Egyptians? RH.6–8.2
4. ***Contrasting*** How did the flooding of major rivers affect both the Mesopotamians and the Egyptians? RH.6–8.2
5. ***Explaining*** What was significant about the joining of the two kingdoms under Narmer? RH.6–8.2
6. ***Analyzing*** How did the Nile River help the ancient Egyptians develop as a well-governed civilization? RH.6–8.1
7. **INFORMATIVE/EXPLANATORY** Why has the Nile River been described as the "lifeblood" of Egypt? Why was the river essential to the Egyptians? Explain your answer in the form of a short essay. WHST.6–8.2, WHST.6–8.10

R Reading Skills

Summarizing Have a volunteer read the section about Narmer, the ruler who united Egypt and established a system of family rule called a dynasty. **Ask:**

- **What is a dynasty?** *(a line of rulers, all of which come from one family)*
- **Why was the dynasty system important?** *(It created a stable and united system of government.)*
- **How many dynasties ruled Egypt?** *(30)*
- **How have historians organized these dynasties?** *(into the Old, Middle, and New Kingdoms)* AL ELL

Have students complete the Lesson 1 Review.

CLOSE & REFLECT

Have students predict the effect of the dynasty system on Egypt. Ask students to consider the benefits of such a system *(long-term political stability)* and the potential problems. *(A pharaoh might not have children to inherit the throne. A family that is corrupt or weak could damage Egypt.)*

LESSON 1 REVIEW ANSWERS

1. They needed hieroglyphics in order to communicate and record ideas and facts.
2. A dynasty is a system of rule in which power is handed down from grandfather to father to son.
3. The deserts that lie east and west of the river provided Egypt with a natural defense against intruders. The heat and sand kept outsiders from crossing lands that separated Egypt from other places.
4. The Mesopotamians could not predict or control the flooding of their rivers, and as a result, property and lives were often lost. The floods in Egypt were regular and predictable, so people could plan their lives around them.
5. The unification of the two kingdoms was the first time that Egypt was united under one ruler. Unification represented an important step in the development of Egypt as a powerful civilization.
6. Students should explain that the Nile River provided resources and natural defenses to the ancient Egyptians. This allowed them to grow and develop a civilization.
7. Answers will vary but should include the idea that the Nile was an essential, life-giving resource that provided water for crops, drinking, and bathing; rich soil for farming; a means of transportation; and security against attack.

ANSWERS, p. 107

CRITICAL THINKING Narmer is bigger than the other figures, and he is holding up a weapon.

☑ PROGRESS CHECK The weaker villages fell to the stronger ones until two powerful kingdoms remained—Upper Egypt and Lower Egypt. Both were united under Narmer, who, as king of Upper Egypt, conquered Lower Egypt and married one of its princesses.

Life in Ancient Egypt

ENGAGE

Bellringer Have a brainstorming session with students about things they have to do every week. Write their ideas on the board. Suggestions might include eating, grooming, bathing, doing chores, going to church, visiting, playing, or listening to music. Invite students to come up and circle items that they think people in ancient Egypt also had to do. Ask students how early Egyptians might have carried out the circled activities. Tell them that they'll find some of the answers in this lesson.

TEACH & ASSESS

R Reading Skills

Defining Ensure that students understand the terms used in this lesson. Suggest that students skim the text for definitions of words they do not know.

- theocracy *(government by religious leaders)*
- pharaoh *(a ruler of ancient Egypt)*
- bureaucrat *(a government official)*
- embalming *(the process of treating a dead body to keep it from decaying)*
- pyramid *(a great stone tomb built for an Egyptian pharaoh)* AL ELL

networks
There's More Online!
- CHART/GRAPH Egyptian Foods
- GRAPHIC ORGANIZER Ancient Egypt
- SLIDE SHOW The Pyramids of Giza
- VIDEO

Lesson 2
Life in Ancient Egypt

ESSENTIAL QUESTION *What makes a culture unique?*

IT MATTERS BECAUSE

The Egyptian pharaohs were all-powerful rulers. Egyptians built such gigantic and sturdy pyramids in their honor that the pyramids still stand today.

Egypt's Early Rulers

GUIDING QUESTION *How was ancient Egypt governed?*

Around 2600 B.C., Egyptian civilization entered the period known as the Old Kingdom. The Old Kingdom lasted until about 2200 B.C. During these years, the Egyptians built magnificent cities and increased trade. They also formed a unified government. The Egyptians prized unity. They understood the importance of everyone working and living according to similar principles and beliefs. Therefore, they developed a government under an all-powerful ruler who controlled both religious and political affairs. R A government in which the same person is both the political leader and the religious leader is called a **theocracy** (thee•AH•kruh•see).

A Political Leader

At first, the Egyptian ruler was called a king. Later, he was known as **pharaoh** (FEHR•oh). The word *pharaoh* originally meant "great house." It referred to the grand palace in which the king and his family lived.

The Egyptians were fiercely loyal to the pharaoh because they believed that a strong ruler unified their kingdom. The pharaoh held total power. He issued commands that had to

Reading HELPDESK CCSS

Taking Notes: ***Organizing***

Use a diagram like this one to list information about ancient Egypt by adding one or more facts to each of the boxes. RH.6–8.2

Ancient Egypt: Ruler | Religion | Social Groups

Content Vocabulary (Tier 3 Words)
- theocracy
- pharaoh
- bureaucrat
- embalming
- pyramid

networks Online Teaching Options

VIDEO

Life in Ancient Egypt

Discussing As students view the video, have them take notes on the roles played by farmers and craftspeople in ancient Egypt. Have students circle on their lists any new facts they learned. **Ask: What did the video reveal was a technology that the Egyptians used quite early?** *(the wheel)* **How was this technology shown being used in the video?** *(to make pottery)*

LEARN360 ENGAGE • ENRICH • EXCEL

See page 97D for other online activities.

ANSWER, p. 108

TAKING NOTES: Ruler: The pharaoh had total power in Egypt. **Religion:** Religion guided every part. **Social Groups:** People could move between groups.

be obeyed. Egyptians believed that a pharaoh's wise and far-reaching leadership would help their kingdom survive such disasters as war and famine.

The pharaoh appointed **bureaucrats** (BYUR•uh•kratz), or government officials, to carry out his orders. Bureaucrats supervised the construction and repair of dams, irrigation canals, and brick granaries. Granaries (GRAY•nuh•reez) were used to store grain from bountiful harvests so people would not starve during times of poor harvests.

The pharaoh owned all the land in Egypt and could use it as he pleased. The pharaoh's officials collected tax payments of grain from farmers. The pharaoh also **distributed** land to officials, priests, and wealthy Egyptians whom he favored.

A Religious Leader

Egyptians were also loyal to the pharaoh because they thought he was the son of Re (RAY), the Egyptian sun god. They believed their pharaoh was a god on earth who protected Egypt. Whenever the pharaoh appeared in public, people played music on flutes and cymbals and bowed their heads.

The pharaoh (left) had many servants to wait on him and provide him with all his needs.

▶ CRITICAL THINKING
Explaining What role did the pharaoh play as a political leader?

INTERFOTO/Alamy

theocracy government by religious leaders
pharaoh ruler of ancient Egypt
bureaucrat a government official

Academic Vocabulary (Tier 2 Words)
distribute to divide into shares and deliver the shares to different people

V Visual Skills

Interpreting Visual Information Tell students that paintings often tell stories beyond the actual items shown. Have students look carefully at the illustration on this page. Ask them to point to parts of the illustration as they answer the following questions. **Ask:**

- **How do you know the pharaoh had servants?** *(They are shown fanning him and serving him.)*
- **What did the pharaoh eat?** *(fruits, as shown on plates of blue and red items)*
- **What did the pharaoh sit on?** *(a throne)*
- **What did he wear?** *(He wore special clothing, including special headgear.)*
- **Was he worshipped by his people?** *(Yes; worshipers are shown at the right edge of the picture.)*
- **Could people get to the pharaoh directly?** *(No; it looks like they must apply to servants to gain access to the pharaoh.)* **ELL Visual/Spatial**

Making Connections

Powers of the President Versus Powers of the Pharaoh The president of the United States has far less power than a pharaoh had. The president does not represent or serve any particular religion and shares power with the judiciary and legislative branches of government. Citizens of the U.S. do not think their president is a god.

CHART

Foods of the Egyptians

Classifying Display the opening image of the servants waiting on the pharaoh. Remind students that people treated the pharaoh as a god. Then advance to the interactive chart, and click to reveal the kinds of foods consumed by the Egyptians. Point out that all of these foods would have been raised by farmers who would have been required to give part of their crops to the pharaoh for his use.

See page 97D for other online activities.

Media
networks
Foods of the Egyptians
Directions: Click each column to learn more about food consumed by the Egyptians.
Food grown
Food hunted/gathered
Animals raised for food
Barley Wheat Beans Onions Figs Dates Leeks Lettuce Turnips Cabbage Grapes Garlic
Fish Ducks Geese Antelope Ibex Honey
Sheep Goats Pigs
Close

ANSWER, p. 109

CRITICAL THINKING The pharaoh issued commands that had to be obeyed and appointed bureaucrats to carry out his orders.

R Reading Skills

Organizing As students answer the Progress Check question, draw a T-chart on the board. Have volunteers take turns providing examples of the pharaoh as a religious leader *(represented gods, participated in ceremonies)* and a political leader *(apportioned land and appointed bureaucrats).* AL ELL Verbal/Linguistic

C Critical Thinking Skills

Interpreting Have students choose people they know to represent the sun god Re, river god Hapi, life/death gods Osiris and Isis, and god of learning Thoth. For example, a parent might be Re, since the mother or father might be the one who wakes a child up. Hapi might be represented by swimmer Michael Phelps. Osiris might be a school principal. Thoth would be represented by a teacher. BL

As Egypt's religious leader, the pharaoh participated in ceremonies to help the kingdom thrive. For example, the pharaoh rode a bull around Memphis because the Egyptians believed that this would help keep the soil fertile. The pharaoh was also the first person to cut the ripened grain at harvest time. Egyptians believed this action would produce abundant crops.

R **PROGRESS CHECK**

Analyzing How was the pharaoh a political leader and a religious leader?

Religion in Egypt

GUIDING QUESTION ***What kind of religion did the ancient Egyptians practice?***

Religion influenced every aspect of Egyptian life. Like the people of Mesopotamia, ancient Egyptians worshipped many gods and goddesses. The people of Egypt, however, thought their gods were more powerful. The Egyptians believed these deities (DEE•uh•teez) controlled natural forces as well as human activities.

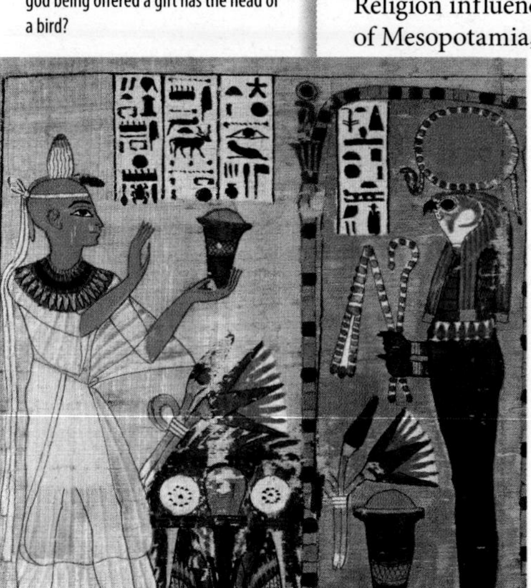

The Egyptians gave offerings to their gods, whom they believed controlled their lives.

▶ CRITICAL THINKING

Speculating Why do you think the god being offered a gift has the head of a bird?

Gianni Dagli Orti/CORBIS

The Egyptians depended on the sun to grow their crops and on the Nile River to make the soil fertile. Thus, two of the most **crucial** gods were the sun god Re and the river god Hapi (HAH•pee). Another important god was Osiris (oh•SY•ruhs). According to legend, Osiris was an early pharaoh who gave the Egyptian people laws and taught them farming. His wife Isis (EYE•suhs) represented the faithful wife and mother. Osiris and Isis together ruled over the world of the dead. Thoth (THOHTH) was the god of learning. He could take human or animal form—or both—as did most gods and goddesses. C

The Afterlife

The Egyptians had a positive view of the afterlife. They believed that life after death would be even better than the present life. After a long journey, the dead arrived at a place of peace.

Reading **HELP**DESK (CCSS)

Reading Strategy: *Contrasting*

Look for clue words such as *however, but,* and *although.* These words tell you that the author is contrasting two ideas. Which sentence on this page uses a contrasting clue word? What ideas are being contrasted?

Academic Vocabulary (Tier 2 Words)

crucial important or significant

networks Online Teaching Options

WORKSHEET

21st Century Skills Activity: Critical Thinking and Problem Solving: Making Connections

Identifying Place students into small groups. Tell them they will complete a graphic organizer that identifies pharaohs' political and religious responsibilities. Remind them to return to their textbooks for details to fill in the graphic organizer. If students need help, **ask: How did Egypt's rulers unify and lead the country?** *(politically and through religion)* **How did the rulers serve as religious leaders?** *(The pharaohs participated in religious ceremonies and were considered to be gods.)*

See page 97D for other online activities.

ANSWERS, p. 110

PROGRESS CHECK Pharaohs had total control over all aspects of life. As political leaders, they both issued commands about how land would be used and appointed bureaucrats to carry out their orders. They protected and led the people during times of trouble. As religious leaders, pharaohs represented the gods and participated in ceremonies that affected crops and farming.

CRITICAL THINKING Students might speculate that the god is the god of the sky and, thus, takes the shape of a bird.

Reading Strategy The contrasting clue word *however* is used in the sentence "The Egyptians, however, believed their gods were more powerful." The sentence is contrasting the religious beliefs of the Egyptians with the religious beliefs of the Mesopotamians.

One of the most important writings of ancient Egypt was *The Book of the Dead*. Egyptians studied its prayers and magic spells to prepare for the afterlife. They believed that Osiris greeted those who had just died at the gate to the next world. If people had led good lives and knew the spells, Osiris would give them eternal life. This passage from *The Book of the Dead* explains what a person who enters the happy afterlife can expect:

PRIMARY SOURCE

"Wheat and barley . . . shall be given unto him therein, and he shall flourish there just as he did upon earth."

—from *Papyrus of Ani—The Egyptian Book of the Dead*

The earliest Egyptians believed that only the pharaohs could enjoy the afterlife. They thought that the pharaoh's soul **resided** in his body, and that the body had to be protected in order for the soul to complete the journey to the afterlife. There, the pharaoh would continue to protect Egypt. If the pharaoh's body decayed after death, his soul would not have a place to live. The pharaoh would not survive in the afterlife. As the centuries passed, however, Egyptians came to believe that the afterlife was not only for pharaohs. All people—rich and poor—could hope for eternal life with the help of the god Osiris. As a result, the process of **embalming** (ihm•BAHLM•ihng) emerged so that Egyptians could protect bodies for the afterlife.

Before a body was embalmed, priests removed the body's organs. The organs were stored in special jars that were buried with the body. Then the priests covered the body with a salt called natron and stored it for several days. The natron dried up the water in the body, causing it to shrink. The shrunken, dried body was then filled with burial spices and tightly wrapped with long strips of linen. The wrapped body was then known as a mummy (MUH•mee). The mummy was sealed in a coffin and placed in a decorated tomb.

The goddess Isis was the wife of the god Osiris. She was a powerful god respected on her own.

▶ CRITICAL THINKING

Inferring Why do you think the Egyptians worshipped some powerful gods that were men and others that were women?

embalming the process of treating a body to keep it from decaying

Academic Vocabulary (Tier 2 Words)

reside to be present continuously or have a home in a particular place

Life in Ancient Egypt

T Technology Skills

Researching on the Internet Have students research to find pictures of the jars used by embalmers to hold particular body organs, such as the liver, brain, heart, lungs, kidneys, and gall bladder. Have students make a slide show of their results, labeling each jar and including a picture of the organ itself. Discuss how Egyptians felt that each part of the body would be important in the afterlife. AL Visual/Spatial

Making Connections

Afterlife Most cultures have a central text in which the path to an afterlife of some kind is presented through sacred texts. Ancient Egyptians had The Book of the Dead. Modern religions use the Quran (Islam), early biblical texts (Judaism), the Bible (Christianity), the Upanishads (Hinduism), and the Book of Mormon (Latter-Day Saints). Have students research the similarities among and differences among these sacred texts. BL Verbal/Linguistic

GAME

Egyptians and Their Gods Concentration Game

Defining Organize the class into two teams. Click on one of the squares. Ask Team 1 to click on a second card. If they get a match, they play again. If they do not, play moves to Team 2. Continue until all the cards have been matched.

As an alternative, have each team work to match all the cards. Use the timing option to determine the winner.

See page 97D for other online activities.

ANSWER, p. 111

CRITICAL THINKING Students might say that some things were seen as "male" and others as "female." They might also note that the gods were seen as part of Egyptian history, so they would have taken male and female forms, like the Egyptians themselves.

V Visual Skills

Interpreting Return to the list of associations students generated in the lesson's Bellringer activity. Explain that many of the images or objects that most people associate with ancient Egyptians, such as mummies and pyramids, are related to the topic of religion. **Ask:** **How are mummies and pyramids related to the religion of the ancient Egyptians?** *(Egyptians mummified bodies so the bodies could travel to the afterlife. Pyramids were meant to protect the pharaohs from floods, robbers, and wild animals during the afterlife.)*

Lead a discussion of how the lives of ancient Egyptians were focused on the afterlife. **Ask:** **What did the ancient Egyptians think the afterlife would be like?** *(They thought it was even better than the present life.)* **Who was allowed to reach the afterlife?** *(At first, Egyptians believed only the pharaohs could reach the afterlife, but later, Egyptians believed everyone could.)* **BL** **Visual/Spatial**

W Writing Skills

Narrative Explain that ancient Egyptians' belief in the afterlife influenced all areas of their lives. Then organize the class into four groups. Assign each group an area of Egyptian life—science, religion, daily activities, and medicine. Ask each group to make connections between Egyptians' belief in the afterlife and the area they were assigned. Groups should work together to write a narrative in which a person in their assigned career discusses his work and beliefs. To help students, **ask:**

- **If you were a scientist or a doctor, how would your belief in the afterlife affect your work?** *(A scientist might think the afterlife would provide answers to all questions. A doctor might hope the next life would have less suffering than this one.)*
- **If you were an Egyptian priest, how would your belief in the afterlife affect your work?** *(You knew that your work was important in helping people reach the afterlife.)*
- **If you were an ordinary worker, how would your belief in the afterlife affect you?** *(You would try to make good decisions so you could achieve eternal life.)* **Interpersonal** **Verbal/Linguistic**

ANSWERS, p. 112

CRITICAL THINKING Embalming taught the Egyptians about anatomy, internal organs, and blood circulation.

✓ PROGRESS CHECK The Egyptians protected the body in order to preserve the person's soul so that it would have a successful journey through the afterlife.

V

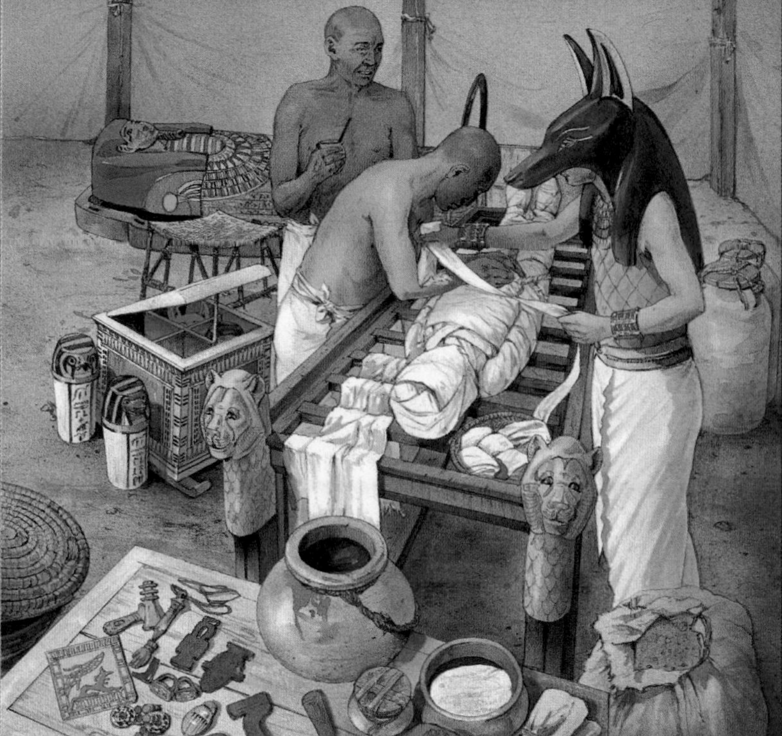

Preparing the pharaoh's body for burial involved a mix of science and religion. Special priests performed the process.

▶ CRITICAL THINKING
Explaining What do you think Egyptians learned about the human body by embalming?

W

Wealthy people had their mummies placed in coffins and buried in tombs. Poorer people had their mummies buried in caves or in the sand. Even animals were embalmed. Egyptians viewed animals not only as pets, but also as sacred creatures. As a result, they buried the mummies of cats, birds, and other animals at temples honoring their gods and goddesses.

Medical Skills

The Egyptians learned much about the human body from embalming. This knowledge helped them to develop basic medical skills. Egyptian doctors sewed up cuts and set broken bones. They were the first to use splints, bandages, and compresses. Egyptians also wrote down medical information on papyrus scrolls. These records were the world's first medical books.

✓ PROGRESS CHECK

Analyzing Why did Egyptians protect a person's body after death?

Reading **HELP**DESK (CCSS)

pyramid great stone tomb built for an Egyptian pharaoh

Academic Vocabulary (Tier 2 Words)
labor work

networks *Online Teaching Options*

GRAPHIC ORGANIZER

Taking Notes: *Organizing:* Ancient Egypt

Organizing Work as a class to generate a list of the responsibilities of early Egyptian rulers. Then return to the graphic organizer as you continue working through the lesson. You may wish to have students work in pairs to complete the remainder of the activity.

See page 97D for other online activities

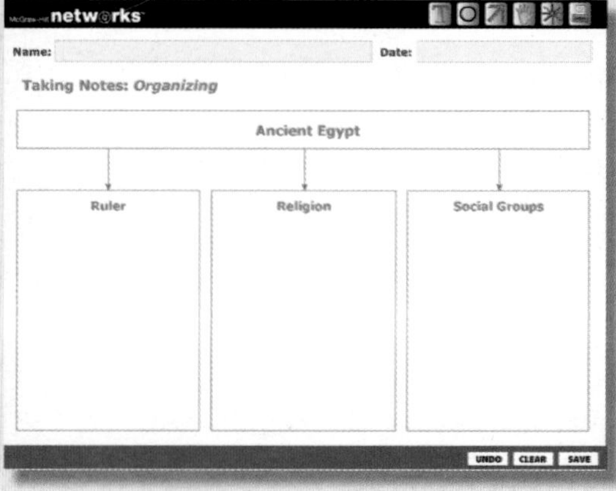

Pyramid Tombs

GUIDING QUESTION *Why and how were pyramids built?*

The Egyptians honored their pharaohs in a special way. They built great tombs called **pyramids** (PIHR•uh•mihds) for the pharaohs. These enormous structures were made of stone and covered the area of several city blocks. Centuries after they were built, these monuments still tower over the desert sands. The pyramids protected the bodies of dead pharaohs from floods, wild animals, and robbers. The Egyptians believed the pharaohs would be happy after death if they had their personal belongings. For that reason, they placed the pharaoh's clothing, weapons, furniture, and jewelry in the pyramids. C

The pyramids preserved, or saved, these objects in relatively good condition for centuries. Today, archaeologists are able to study the pyramids and the treasures they hold to learn about life in ancient Egypt.

How Were Pyramids Built?

Thousands of workers spent years of hard **labor** to build the pyramids. Farmers did much of the work during the summer months when the Nile River flooded and they could not farm.

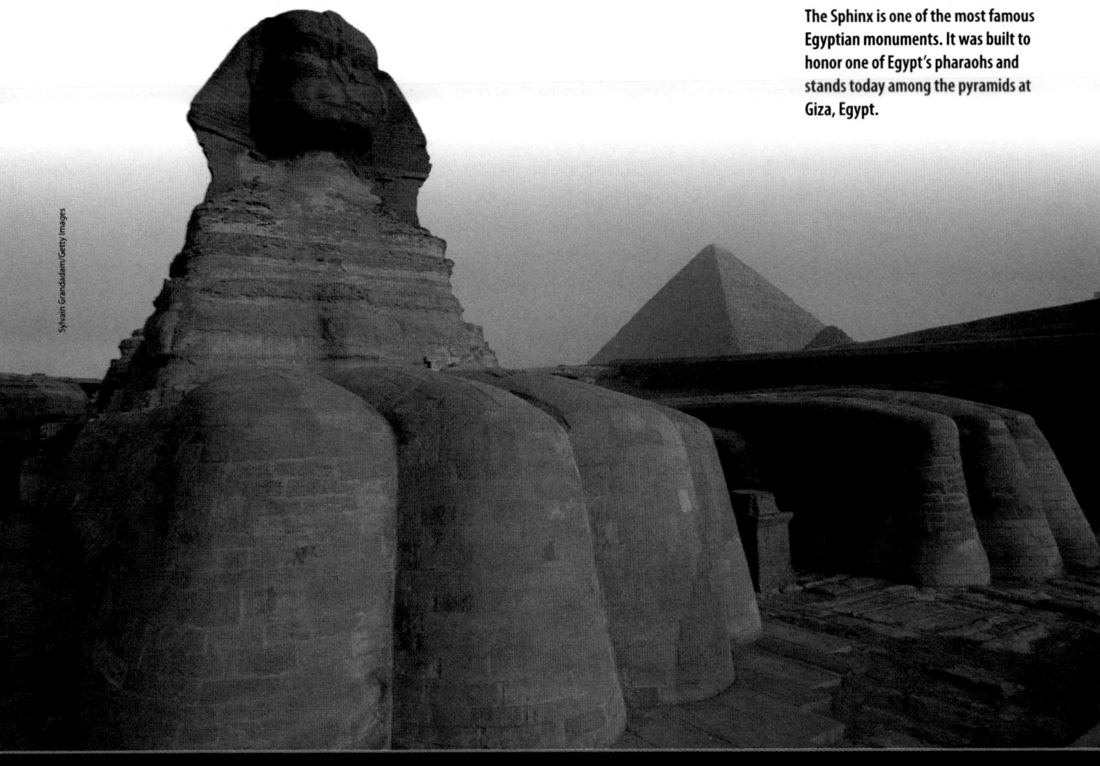

Sylvain Grandadam/Getty Images

The Sphinx is one of the most famous Egyptian monuments. It was built to honor one of Egypt's pharaohs and stands today among the pyramids at Giza, Egypt.

C Critical Thinking Skills

Categorizing Have students fold a piece of paper into fourths and label the sections "Food," "Furnishings," "Clothing," and "Entertainment." Instruct them to make lists of the items they think they would like to have with them in their pyramid to use in the afterlife. Less able readers or ELL students could use a catalogue to find and categorize their lists. Have student volunteers share their lists and discuss similarities and differences. ELL AL Intrapersonal

Making Connections

Have students find out where presidents of the United States have been buried—from Grant's Tomb to Arlington National Cemetery. Play a video of the funeral of President Ronald Reagan or John F. Kennedy to demonstrate that rituals for fallen leaders are important, even today. Remind students how important death rituals were to the Egyptians. AL Visual/Spatial Verbal/Linguistic

Content Background Knowledge

The Sphinx The Sphinx is one of the most recognizable landmarks in the world. Carved from limestone found in Giza, the monument shows a creature with the body of a lion and the head of a pharaoh. The sculpture is 240 feet (73 m) long and 66 feet (20 m) high. It is believed to be more than 4,600 years old. The face of the Sphinx once had a nose and a beard. The nose was probably removed in the 8th century A.D., but it is not known for certain why . The beard was worn away by wind and erosion. Historians are not certain which pharaoh is depicted by the Sphinx. However, because the monument faces Khafre's pyramid, some historians think the Sphinx has some connection to Khafre.

SLIDE SHOW

Pyramids

Analyzing Visuals Display the slideshow about the pyramids. Tell students that today there are over 90 pyramids in Egypt. Click though the images, stopping at the passage that leads down into the Great Pyramid. Explain that these passages are very short. If you were to go inside the pyramid, you would have to bend down until you reached the burial chamber. Click again to reveal the queen's burial chamber. Have students discuss what the artwork reveals about the life of Egyptian royalty and religion.

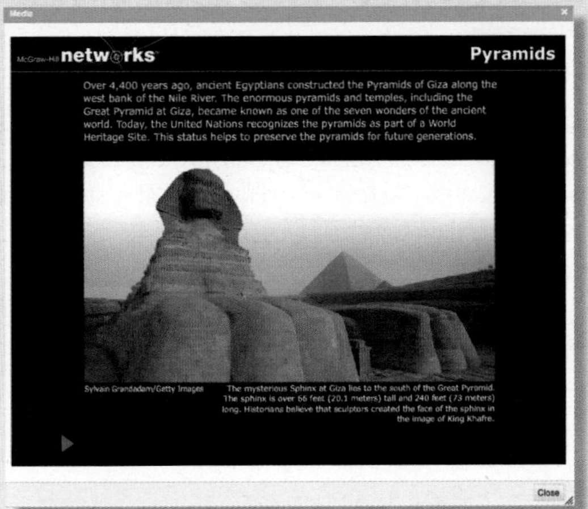

See page 97D for other online activities.

V Visual Skills

Analyzing Visuals Have students trace with their fingers the path from the numbered feature of the pyramid shown on this page and the number label to which it corresponds. Then have them read the label and follow a path back to the item. **Ask: If the number 1 stood for the most important part of the pyramid, what feature would be #1?** *(burial chamber)* Compare the size of the pharaoh's pyramid with the size of the queen's pyramid (number 7 on the illustration). **Ask: What do the sizes of these pyramids say about the importance of queens compared with pharaohs?** *(The pharaoh was absolutely the most important, which shows in the size of his pyramid.)* AL ELL **Visual/Spatial**

R1 Reading Skills

Explaining As students read the text, point out that the pyramids were tombs built by Egyptian workers so the pharaohs would be happy after death. **Ask:**

- **Why did ancient Egyptian farmers, engineers, and stonecutters build tombs for their leaders?** *(to protect the bodies of the pharaohs)*
- **Why was it important to protect the bodies of the pharaohs?** *(They believed the pharaohs needed their bodies so the pharaohs could move on to and live in the afterlife.)* AL
- **Where did workers find the stone that made up the pyramids, and how did they cut the stones?** *(They used copper tools to cut stones found throughout the Nile River valley and Upper Egypt.)*

R2 Reading Skills

Identifying After students have read the text, ask them to identify the types of scientific knowledge that Egyptians needed to build the pyramids. **Ask: Why did the Egyptians need to better understand astronomy and study the skies in order to build a pyramid?** *(They needed astronomy to find north so the pyramid entrance could face north.)*

INSIDE A PYRAMID

V

❶ **Air Shaft**

❷ **King's Burial Chamber** The king's mummified body was placed in a room at the pyramid's center.

❸ **Grand Gallery** This tall, sloping hall held large granite blocks that sealed the tomb.

❹ **Queen's Burial Chamber** This chamber held a statue of the king, not the queen's body.

❺ **Entrance**

❻ **Underground Burial Chamber** Sometimes kings were buried here instead.

❼ **Queen's Pyramids** These smaller pyramids are believed to be tombs for the kings' wives.

❽ **Mastaba** These tombs surrounding the pyramids held royal family members and other nobles.

❾ **Valley Temple** This temple may have been used for rituals before the king was buried.

INFOGRAPHIC

The pyramids contained many rooms, each used for a different purpose.

▶ **CRITICAL THINKING**
Speculating Why was the king's burial chamber constructed in the middle of the pyramid and not at the top?

Surveyors, engineers, carpenters, and stonecutters also helped build the pyramids. The first great engineer who built pyramids was Imhotep (ihm•HOH•tehp). He also served as an official for the pharaoh.

R1 Workers searched for stone in places throughout the Nile River valley or in Upper Egypt. After locating the stone, skilled artisans used copper tools to cut the stone into huge blocks. Next, workers used rope to fasten the blocks onto wooden sleds. The sleds were pulled along a path made of logs to the Nile River. There, the stones were moved onto barges that carried them to the building site. Workers unloaded the blocks and dragged or pushed them up ramps to be set in place at each new level of the pyramid.

R2 The Egyptians faced many challenges as they built the pyramids. These challenges, however, led to important discoveries. For example, each pyramid rested on a square-shaped foundation, with an entrance facing north. To find north, the Egyptians studied the skies and developed an understanding of astronomy. With this knowledge, they invented a 365-day calendar with 12 months divided into three seasons. This calendar became the basis for our modern calendar.

Reading **HELP**DESK CCSS

networks *Online Teaching Options*

WORKSHEET

Web Diagram: Graphic Organizer

Organizing Provide small groups of students with a copy of the Web diagram. Have students use the diagram to record facts about the pyramids, their uses, how they were built, and their size. After students finish reading this section of the lesson, have groups compare the information they recorded and discuss any differences they discover.

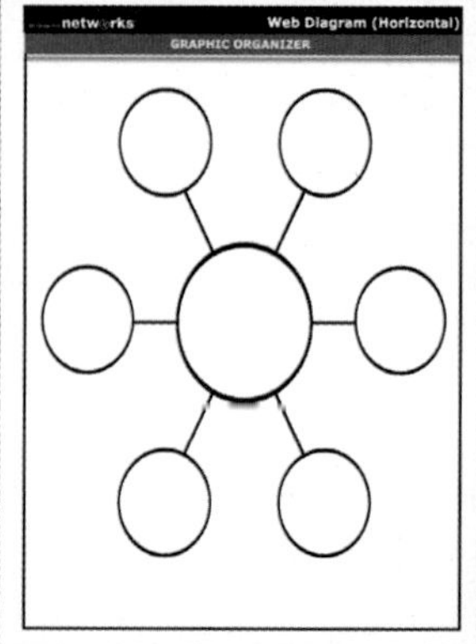

See page 97D for other online activities.

ANSWER, p. 114

INFOGRAPHIC

CRITICAL THINKING The king's burial chamber was in the middle of the pyramid so the pharaoh's body and his treasures would be safe.

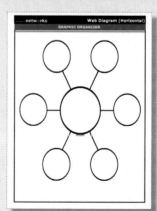

Egyptians also made advancements in mathematics. Egypt's pyramid builders had to calculate how much stone was needed to build a pyramid. They had to measure angles in order to **construct** a pyramid's walls. To do this, they invented a system of written numbers based on 10. They also created fractions, using them with whole numbers to add, subtract, and divide. **R**

An Egyptian Wonder

About the mid-2000s B.C., the Egyptians built the biggest and grandest of the pyramids—the Great Pyramid. It lies about 10 miles (16.1 km) from the modern city of Cairo. Built for King Khufu (KOO•foo), the Great Pyramid is one of three pyramids **T** still standing at Giza on the Nile's west bank. It is about the height of a 48-story building, towering nearly 500 feet (153 m) above the desert. It extends over an area equal in size to nine football fields. More than 2 million stone blocks were used in the pyramid's construction, each weighing an average of 2.5 tons (2.3 metric tons). For more than 4,000 years, the Great Pyramid stood as the tallest structure in the world.

✓ PROGRESS CHECK

Explaining Why did the Egyptians build the pyramids?

Free Agents Limited/CORBIS

In this photo of the Great Pyramid, the pyramid in the center belongs to King Khafre, son of Khufu. Khafre's pyramid has a width (at its base) to height ratio of about 708:471 ft (216:143 m). Khufu's pyramid has a ratio of about 756:481 ft (230:147 m).

▶ CRITICAL THINKING

Comparing Which pyramid is larger?

Academic Vocabulary (Tier 2 Words)

construct to build

R Reading Skills

Interpreting As students read the text, remind them that in order to construct pyramids, Egyptians needed to make calculations and measure angles. Ask students to count to 100 by tens. Remind them that this task is made easy because our number system is based on 10. **Ask: What did the Egyptians develop in mathematics to help them make calculations, such as how much stone was needed to make a pyramid?** *(They invented a number system based on 10; they created fractions; and they used whole numbers and fractions to add, subtract, and divide.)* BL **Logical/Mathematical**

Making Connections

How Tall *Were* the Pyramids? The tallest pyramids were nearly 500 feet high. Compare that to today's five tallest buildings without spires: Burj Khalifa (Dubai, United Arab Emirates, 2,217 feet); Tapei 101 (Taipei, Taiwan, 1,667 feet); Shanghai World Financial Center, Shanghai, China (1,614 feet); International Commerce Center, Hong Kong, China, 1,588 feet); tied for fifth, Petronas Towers 1 and 2 (Kuala Lumpur, 1,483 feet). Still, most buildings in the world today would be dwarfed by the Great Pyramids. **Logical/Mathematical**

T Technology Skills

Researching on the Internet Have students explore more about Egyptian artifacts online. Many museums throughout the world display Egyptian art and artifacts. Challenge students to conduct research and share their findings with the class. Remind students of the appropriate safety guidelines as well as guidelines for quality research sources. BL

IMAGE

Pyramids of Giza

Describing Display the interactive image of the Pyramids of Giza. Click on the three active areas, one at a time, to reveal the extended captions. Have volunteers read the information presented. Have students record the heights of the two tallest pyramids, and share that the smallest pyramid, built for Menkaure—the fifth king of the fourth dynasty—was 218 feet tall. Have students draw diagrams that represent the relative heights of these structures. Discuss the manpower needed to quarry, move, and erect this amount of stone.

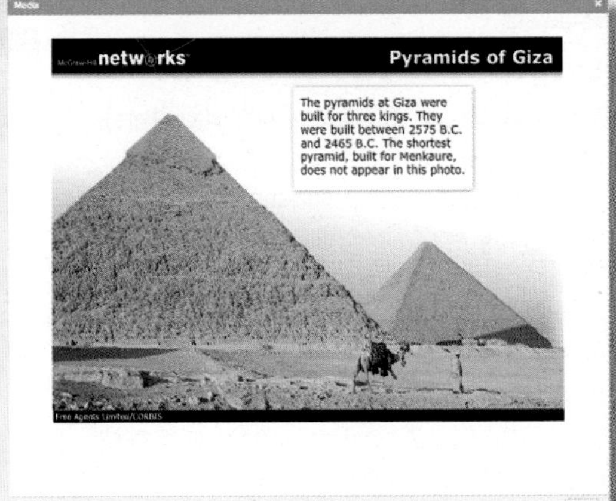

See page 97D for other online activities.

ANSWERS, p. 115

✓ PROGRESS CHECK They built the pyramids to provide tombs that would honor deceased pharaohs and protect them and all their belongings from floods, wild animals, and robberies.

CRITICAL THINKING Khufu's pyramid is larger.

C Critical Thinking Skills

Making Generalizations Explain to students that most societies have different social classes. A person's social class or status is mostly defined by the work he or she does. Introduce the term *division of labor* and explain that the jobs people do may affect their place in society. To illustrate this point, ask students to name different kinds of work or professions. Write their answers on the board. Then have students consider whether these jobs can be sorted by social status. **Ask:**

- Why do you think some jobs have a higher status than others? *(They require more training or education. They are difficult or admired.)*
- Which jobs do you think had the highest status in ancient Egypt? *(pharaoh, bureaucrat, priest, scribe, pyramid architect)* AL

V Visual Skills

Interpreting Point out to students that this pyramid graphic is divided into five layers. **Ask:**

- What do you see people doing on the bottom level? *(carrying food and water, serving)*
- What are people doing on the second level? *(farming, taking care of animals)*

Continue to the top level of the pyramid. **Ask:** At which level do you think people need to have the most education? *(third, fourth)* AL **Visual/Spatial**

Point out that the pyramid shows the numbers of people in each group. Unskilled workers in the widest level of the chart were the largest percentage of the Egyptian population. The narrowest level at the top holds only one person, the pharaoh. **Logical/Mathematical**

ANSWER, p. 116

INFOGRAPHIC

CRITICAL THINKING A teacher would be in the middle level of society.

Daily Life

GUIDING QUESTION *How was Egyptian society organized?*

At its peak, ancient Egypt was home to about 5 million people. This would be about equal to the number of people living today in the state of Colorado. Most ancient Egyptians lived in the fertile Nile valley and delta. The delta is found at the mouth of the river. These two areas, which make up only 3 percent of Egypt's land, are densely populated even today.

Egypt's Social Groups

C The **roles** of the people in ancient Egypt reflected their social status, or position in society. Look at the diagram of the different social groups, or classes, in ancient Egypt. The king or pharaoh and his family held the highest social position in Egypt, followed by a small upper class of army commanders, nobles, and priests. The priests served as government officials and supervised people who worked as clerks and scribes. A larger group of traders, artisans, and scribes made up the middle class. The lowest but largest groups in Egyptian society

V

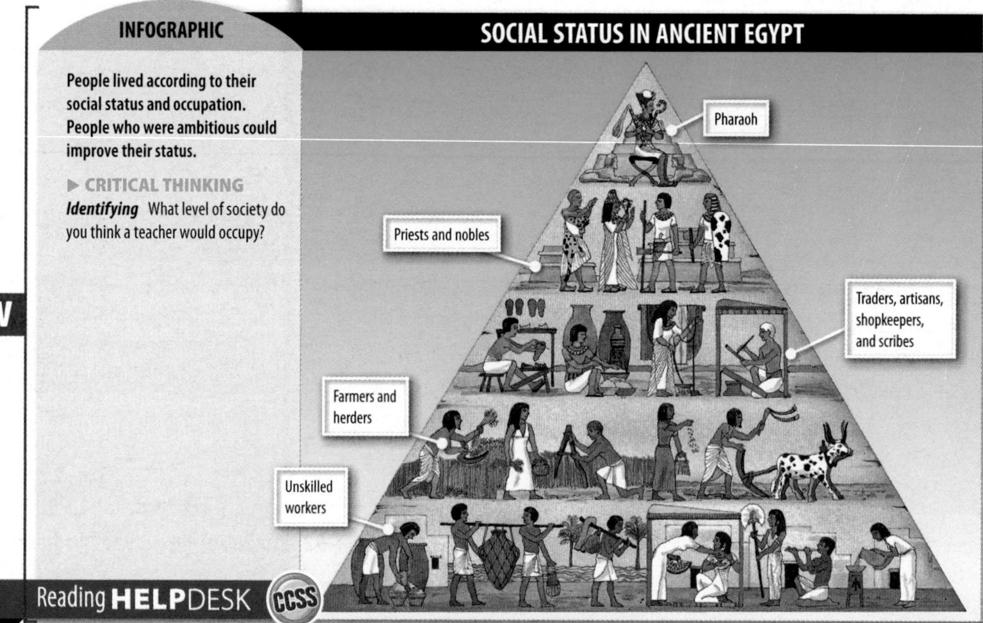

People lived according to their social status and occupation. People who were ambitious could improve their status.

▶ CRITICAL THINKING
Identifying What level of society do you think a teacher would occupy?

Reading **HELP**DESK CCSS

Academic Vocabulary (Tier 2 Words)

role the function or part an individual fills in society

Build Vocabulary: *Word Forms*

As a noun, *official* means "someone who holds an office or who manages the rules of a game." As an adjective, it means "authorized." The verb *officiate* means "to act in an official role."

networks Online Teaching Options

CHART

Egyptian Society

Analyzing Visuals Display the interactive chart of Egyptian society. As you discuss each societal layer, click on the label to reveal more information. **Ask:** How is a pyramid an accurate representation of Egyptian society? *(The higher up in society you go, the fewer people there are.)* Have students think back to the chapter's video. **Ask:** Which levels would agricultural workers occupy? What about artisans? *(Agricultural workers are farmers; artisans are part of the middle class.)*

See page 97D for other online activities.

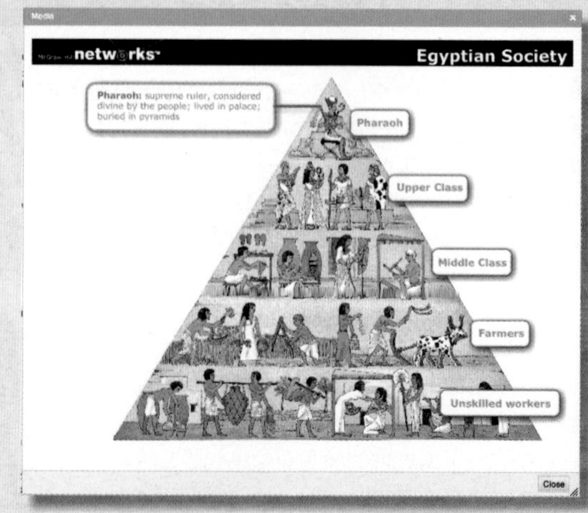

Life in Ancient Egypt

These ancient Egyptian women are chemists. Women were educated and valued for their special skills.

▶ CRITICAL THINKING

Analyzing What social class would these women belong to?

Bettmann/CORBIS

was made up of farmers and unskilled workers. Even though there were divisions in Egyptian class structures, ambitious people in the lower classes were able to improve their social position.

How People Lived

Egypt's upper class lived in elegant homes and on estates along the Nile River. Their homes were constructed of wood and sun-dried mud bricks, and some were two or three stories tall. Surrounding their homes were lush gardens and pools filled with fish and water lilies. Men and women from the upper class dressed in fashionable white linen clothes and wore dark eye makeup and jewelry. Servants waited on them and performed household tasks.

The middle class of ancient Egyptian society was made up of people who owned businesses and held skilled jobs. These jobs included trading and working as a scribe. Artisans were also important members of the middle class. These craft-makers produced linen cloth, jewelry, pottery, and metal goods. The middle class lived in smaller homes and dressed more simply than the upper class.

Reading Strategy: *Finding the Main Idea*

Remember that each paragraph contains ideas that are related. Usually one sentence summarizes the main idea of a paragraph. Find the main idea in the last paragraph on this page.

R Reading Skills

Drawing Conclusions Tell students that they will figure out the classes of ancient Egypt from the text and the visuals on these pages. **Ask:**

- Can you put the classes in order from richest to poorest? *(pharaoh, nobility, craftspeople and traders, farmers, unskilled workers)*
- From which class would you find someone to repair your sandals? *(middle)*
- From which class would you buy seeds? *(farmers)*
- From which class would you find someone to write out a contract for you? *(middle)*
- To whom would you turn for resolution of a dispute? *(nobility)*
- From which class would you hire someone to move your belongings to a new house? *(unskilled labor)* **AL** **Logical/Mathematical**

Content Background Knowledge

Scribes Scribes had a very important job in Egypt. They copied down almost every official communication in the government, meaning that they had access to a wide range of significant or secret information. They also wrote out wills, tax records, and personal letters, to name a few. Many hieroglyphs show scribes at work or with their pens and ink pots. They were present at every rite and ceremony.

Scribes started as apprentices and were often treated cruelly. In some texts, you can see where their work was corrected—in red ink. The word scribe comes from the word *seba,* which meant both "teach" and "beat."

CHART

Role of Women

Comparing and Contrasting Display the first screen of the interactive chart, which shows two women chemists. Explain that in this time period, many women were restricted to household duties. Then advance to the chart and click to reveal the roles of women in ancient Egypt. After discussing, **ask:** What additional roles do American women have? After discussion, click to reveal the text. Challenge students to add more examples to the chart.

See page 97D for other online activities.

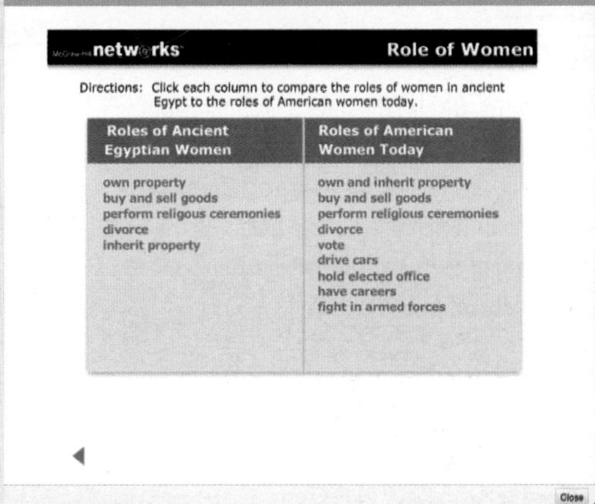

ANSWERS, p. 117

CRITICAL THINKING The women chemists would belong to the middle social class.

Reading Strategy The middle class of ancient Egyptian society was made up of business owners and skilled workers.

Life in Ancient Egypt

C Critical Thinking Skills

Categorizing As students continue to read "How People Lived," have them work together to identify each social class, its members, and their jobs. Model how to draw a three-column chart with the headings "Class," "Members," and "Their Jobs." Then ask students to identify each social class, starting with the most powerful. Direct them to write their responses in the first column. *(Ruling, Upper, Middle, Working)* Next, under "Members," have students identify which people belonged to each class. *(Ruling: pharaoh; Upper: priests, army commanders, and nobles; Middle: merchants and artisans; Working: farmers, unskilled workers, and slaves)* Finally, ask students to tell what jobs each group did. Record their answers under "Their Jobs." *(Ruling: rule Egypt; Upper: run the army and the government; Middle: run shops; Working: grow food and build things)* After students complete the organizer, **ask: What does each social class contribute to Egyptian society as a whole?** *(Each class performs a different role that helps society run smoothly.)* AL ELL

W Writing Skills

Narrative Assign or have students choose a member of ancient Egyptian society, such as a pharaoh, scribe, farmer, priest, merchant, doctor, or laborer. Have each student write a paragraph or two that describes a day in that person's life. Remind students to write using "I" and to include details from the chapter about the person's social class. AL If necessary, have students meet with you or a partner to share a few phrases or sentences orally. ELL **Verbal/Linguistic**

The felucca, an ancient Egyptian river craft, sailed the Nile. Sailors today still use the same ship and sail design.

▶ CRITICAL THINKING

Identifying Into what Egyptian social class would fishers fit?

The largest Egyptian social classes included farmers, unskilled workers, and enslaved people. Most farmers worked on land that was owned by wealthy nobles. They paid rent to the landowners, usually with a portion of their crops. Farmers lived in houses that were made of mud brick. The houses generally had only one room and a roof made of palm leaves. Farmers ate a simple diet of bread, vegetables, and fruit.

C

Unskilled workers performed **manual** labor, such as unloading cargo from boats and transporting it to markets. Some were fishers. Most unskilled workers settled in crowded city neighborhoods. They lived in small mud-brick houses with hard-packed dirt floors. Their houses sometimes included a courtyard. Families often gathered on the flat rooftops to socialize, play games, and sleep. Because of the hot Egyptian climate, they also did their cooking on the rooftop. This helped their homes stay cooler.

W

Some of these unskilled workers were enslaved people. Many of them had been captured in war, and they could earn their freedom over time. Some of these enslaved people helped build the pyramids.

Egyptian Families

The family was the most important group in ancient Egyptian society. Even the gods and goddesses were arranged in family groupings. The father was the head of the family in ancient Egypt, but women had more rights than women in other early civilizations had. Egyptian women held a legal status similar to that of men. They could own property, buy and sell goods, and **obtain** divorces.

Wealthy women even served as priests, managing temples and performing religious ceremonies. Wives of farmers often worked in the fields with their husbands. Women of the higher social classes were more likely to stay at home while their husbands worked at their jobs.

Reading HELPDESK CCSS

Academic Vocabulary (Tier 2 Words)

manual involving physical effort

obtain to gain something through a planned effort

networks Online Teaching Options

IMAGE

Feluccas

Describing Display the interactive image of feluccas—boats used in both ancient and modern Egypt. Click on the arrows to reveal information about the different parts of the boat. Discuss how the design of these narrow, flat-bottom boats is appropriate for river travel.

See page 97D for other online activities.

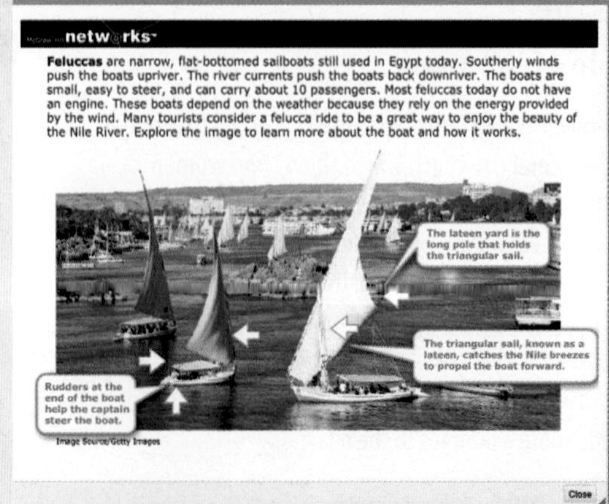

Media
networks
Feluccas are narrow, flat-bottomed sailboats still used in Egypt today. Southerly winds push the boats upriver. The river currents push the boats back downriver. The boats are small, easy to steer, and can carry about 10 passengers. Most feluccas today do not have an engine. These boats depend on the weather because they rely on the energy provided by the wind. Many tourists consider a felucca ride to be a great way to enjoy the beauty of the Nile River. Explore the image to learn more about the boat and how it works.
The lateen yard is the long pole that holds the triangular sail.
The triangular sail, known as a lateen, catches the Nile breezes to propel the boat forward.
Rudders at the end of the boat help the captain steer the boat.
Image Source/Getty Images
Close

ANSWER, p. 118

CRITICAL THINKING Fishers would fall into the same working class as farmers.

Few Egyptian children attended school. Egyptian children had time for fun, playing with board games, dolls, spinning tops, and stuffed leather balls. As in many other cultures, Egyptian children were expected to respect their parents. Mothers taught their daughters to sew, cook, and run a household. Boys learned farming or other trades from their fathers. Learning their father's trade was important, because very often the oldest son would inherit his father's business. **R**

When boys and girls became teenagers, they were expected to get married and start families of their own. In Egyptian cities and among the upper class, people usually lived in nuclear families. A nuclear family is made up of two parents and their children. Some farm families and others in the lower class lived as extended families. In an extended family, older adults, along with their married children and their families, live together. For farm families, this provided more people to work the fields.

Egyptian sons learned their fathers' trades, such as fishing or farming. This ancient art piece shows fishers hauling nets.

The oldest son, and sometimes the oldest daughter, were also responsible for taking care of their parents when the parents became too old or sick to take care of themselves. This responsibility included making sure the parents were given a proper burial after they died.

✓ **PROGRESS CHECK**

Identifying What types of people made up Egypt's upper class?

LESSON 2 REVIEW 

Review Vocabulary (Tier 3 Words)

1. Explain the role a *pharaoh* played in a *theocracy*. RH.6–8.4
2. What was the social status of a *bureaucrat* in ancient Egypt? RH.6–8.4

Answer the Guiding Questions

3. ***Describing*** What kind of religion did the ancient Egyptians practice? Describe at least one way that their religion was tied to agriculture. RH.6–8.2
4. ***Analyzing*** What was the most important purpose of the pyramids? Explain your reasoning. RH.6–8.1
5. ***Comparing and Contrasting*** How was life for Egyptian children similar to or different from that of children today? RH.6–8.2
6. ***Defending*** Why did the Egyptians spend years and many resources to build enormous tombs for their dead pharaohs? RH.6–8.2
7. **INFORMATIVE/EXPLANATORY** If you could be anyone in ancient Egypt except the pharaoh, who would you choose to be? Explain the reasons for your choice. Make sure to include the advantages and disadvantages of your social position. WHST.6–8.2, WHST.6–8.10

Life in Ancient Egypt

R Reading Skills

Summarizing Have students answer the following questions about what they learned about ancient Egyptian class structure. Students can answer the questions orally in small groups, or they can jot down and submit their answers on paper.

- **Why did Egypt have different social classes?** *(The social classes helped society run smoothly and made sure all work got done.)*
- **What roles did Egyptian social classes play in society?** *(Social classes dictated what you wore, where and how you lived, and what you did for a living.)*
- **Based on what you learned, how are the social classes of ancient Egypt similar to or different from social classes in the modern world?** *(Answer will vary. Students should cite evidence from the text as well as their own opinions when responding.)* BL

Have students complete the Lesson 2 Review.

CLOSE & REFLECT

Simulating Have students use what they learned in the lesson to plan skits in which they portray members of ancient Egypt's social classes. Student groups of four should choose a social class to portray and then work together to present information about the classes in a skit. Debrief with students by discussing the importance of people performing different roles in society. Point out examples from students' skits of social classes having contact with each other, such as a scribe recording a grain harvest or a doctor treating a farmer's injury.

ANSWERS, p. 119

✓ **PROGRESS CHECK** The nobles, army commanders, and priests made up the upper class.

LESSON 2 REVIEW ANSWERS

1. The pharaoh served as the religious leader. The pharaoh represented the gods and participated in religious ceremonies.
2. A bureaucrat was a member of the upper class. It was the bureaucrat's job to carry out the orders of the pharaoh.
3. The ancient Egyptians believed the gods controlled nature and human activities. Students should point out that an agricultural society would consider gods who were connected to the elements, such as sun and rain, to be most important.
4. The pyramid was important because it served as a tomb for the pharaoh and provided a place where the body would safely pass into the afterlife. Although the pyramid also protected the body from robbers, floods, and wild animals, the journey of the pharaoh's soul was important to the beliefs of the Egyptians, and therefore was a priority.
5. Like children of today, Egyptian children played games. Unlike children of today, Egyptian youngsters did not attend school. Also, Egyptian girls learned housekeeping skills from their mothers. Today, both boys and girls learn how to take care of their homes.
6. Students may suggest that building tombs provided an opportunity for Egyptians to work together to preserve their culture and to follow their religious beliefs.
7. Students will probably suggest that life in the upper class was easier and more interesting than life in the other classes. Students who prefer the upper class should mention the benefits of wealth and power but also the drawbacks of having big responsibilities, such as fighting battles. Those who prefer the middle class may point to the ability of those people to make and sell things and to have a comfortable life without the responsibilities of power.

ENGAGE

Bellringer Explain that a golden age is the period in which a civilization is at its greatest political, cultural, and economic power. Have students skim Lesson 3 for images of artifacts from Egypt's golden age. Guide students toward understanding that the objects represent ancient Egypt at its height. To make a connection to the modern world, **ask: What objects today suggest that we are living in a golden age?** *(Students may suggest that handheld computers and other technology represent a culture at its height.)* Tell students that in this lesson they will be learning about ancient Egypt at its most powerful. They will also learn about several leaders who caused the growth and decline of the Egyptian empire.

TEACH & ASSESS

C Critical Thinking Skills

Classifying Introduce the terms *internal* and *external* and define them. Have students list the events from the section "Conquests" as either internal or external. ELL **Verbal/Linguistic**

V Visual Skills

Creating Time Lines Direct students to the opening paragraph of this lesson. Have them identify the dates that this lesson encompasses. Have them make a time line showing these dates. As students progress through the chapter, have them add dates of different rulers and other important events to their time lines.

As an extension, you may wish to have students refer back to the time line in the chapter opener and note the items in the "World" part of the time line. **Ask: What other civilizations were developing at the same time as ancient Egypt?** *(Civilizations were developing in Europe, China, India, Mesopotamia, and Central America.)* Tell students that they will be learning about these other civilizations in this course.

ANSWER, p. 120

TAKING NOTES: Middle Kingdom—Dates: c. 2055 B.C.–c. 1650 B.C. Government: Pharaohs increased farm acreage and improved irrigation. Economy: Trade expanded. **New Kingdom**—Dates: 1550 B.C.–1070 B.C. Government: Ahmose established new dynasty; Hatshepsut expanded Egypt through trade; Thutmose III expanded the kingdom; and Ramses II expanded the kingdom and formed political ties with neighboring kingdoms. Economy: Trade increased; the building of temples under Ramses II helped the economy grow.

networks *There's More Online!*

- GRAPHIC ORGANIZER
  - Middle and New Kingdoms
  - Achievements of the Pharaohs
- MAP Ancient Egyptian Kingdoms

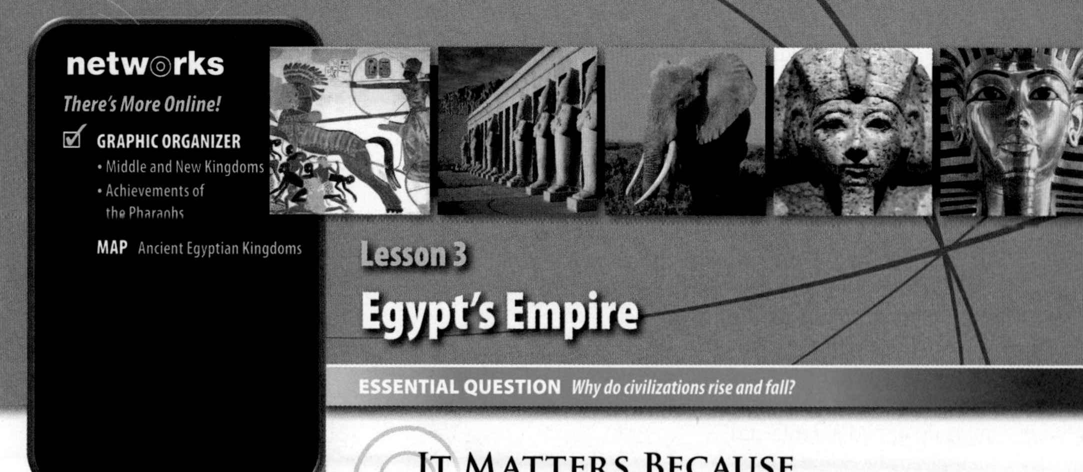

Lesson 3

Egypt's Empire

ESSENTIAL QUESTION *Why do civilizations rise and fall?*

IT MATTERS BECAUSE

The leaders during the golden age of Egypt expanded the empire through war and trade. Although Egypt later declined, it greatly influenced other civilizations.

A Golden Age

GUIDING QUESTION *Why was the Middle Kingdom a "golden age" for Egypt?*

C Around 2200 B.C., the ruling pharaohs in Memphis began to weaken. Ambitious nobles fought for control of Egypt. For more than 200 years, disorder and violence swept through the region. Finally, a new dynasty of pharaohs came to power. They moved V the capital south to a city called Thebes (THEEBZ). These new pharaohs began a period of peace and order called the Middle Kingdom that lasted from about c. 2055 B.C. to c. 1650 B.C.

Conquests

During the Middle Kingdom, Egypt conquered new territories. Egyptian armies gained control of Nubia to the south and expanded northeast into present-day Syria. The Egyptian pharaohs added to their kingdom's wealth. They required tribute, or forced payments, from the peoples their armies had conquered.

Within Egypt, the pharaohs made many improvements. They added thousands of acres to the land already being farmed to increase crop production. They had more irrigation dams and channels built to supply more water to the population. The pharaohs also ordered the construction of a canal between the

(l) Jon Bower/LOOP IMAGES/CORBIS, (cl) Juergen Ritterbach/The Image Bank/Getty Images, (c) Royalty-Free/CORBIS, (cr) Iain Masterton/Age fotostock, (r) Egyptian National Museum, Cairo/SuperStock

Reading HELPDESK CCSS

Taking Notes: *Organizing*

As you read this lesson, complete a chart like this one about the Middle Kingdom and the New Kingdom. RH.6–8.2

	Middle Kingdom	New Kingdom
Date		
Government		
Economy		

Content Vocabulary (Tier 3 Words)
- incense
- envoy

networks *Online Teaching Options*

VIDEO

Ancient Egypt

Classifying As students view the paintings, carvings, sculptures and ruins that serve as a backdrop for this video, have them record the customs described by the narrator. When they have viewed the entire video, have them classify the customs by type religious customs, social customs, and so on.

See page 97E for other online activities.

Nile River and the Red Sea. As a result, Egyptian traders were able to send goods south by ship through the Red Sea. From there, the ships sailed to ports along the coasts of Arabia and East Africa.

The Arts Flourish

Egyptian arts and architecture thrived during the Middle Kingdom. Painters decorated the walls of tombs and temples with colorful scenes. These tomb paintings illustrated stories about the deities, as well as scenes from everyday life. Sculptors carved hunting, fishing, and battle scenes on large stone walls. They created statues of the pharaohs, showing them as ordinary humans rather than gods. **T**

During the Middle Kingdom, the Egyptians developed a new kind of architecture. Pharaohs no longer had pyramids built. Instead, they had their tombs cut into limestone cliffs west of the Nile River. This area became known as the Valley of the Kings.

Artisans produced jewels for pharaohs and decorative objects from gold, such as this chair.

▶ CRITICAL THINKING

Differentiating What about this chair makes you think it was made for royalty?

The Hyksos

R During the 1600s B.C., some Egyptian nobles challenged the power of the pharaohs. Civil war divided Egypt, ending an era of peace and prosperity. As the Middle Kingdom weakened, outsiders invaded Egypt. A people from western Asia known as the Hyksos (HIHK•sahs) swept across the desert into Egypt.

The Hyksos were powerful warriors who used methods of warfare unknown to the Egyptians. The Hyksos rode in horse-drawn chariots and fought with sturdy weapons made of bronze and iron. As a result, they overwhelmed the Egyptian soldiers and took control of the land.

For more than 100 years, Hyksos kings ruled Egypt. The Hyksos borrowed some Egyptian customs but remained separate from the Egyptian people. Meanwhile, most Egyptians hated the Hyksos and planned to overthrow them. The Egyptians learned how to steer horse-drawn chariots and use Hyksos weapons. Around 1550 B.C., an Egyptian prince named Ahmose (AH•mohs) formed an army and drove the Hyksos out of Egypt.

☑ PROGRESS CHECK

Analyzing How were the Egyptians able to defeat the Hyksos?

The Hyksos introduced chariots to Egypt. Battle scenes show the advantage a soldier on a chariot has over those on foot.

T Technology Skills

Researching on the Internet Egyptians were also fluent in the musical arts. They had a variety of musical instruments similar to ones we use today. They played harps, shakers (such as the *sistrum*), lyres, and flutes. Have students research ancient Egyptian musical instruments and download samples of the sounds they made. Discuss with students which instruments today are like the ones used by the Egyptians. **Auditory/Musical**

R Reading Skills

Identifying As students read the passage on the Hyksos, have them identify the reasons this group was able to overwhelm the Egyptians and rule them for more than 100 years. **Ask:**

- **What methods of warfare did the Hyksos use?** *(They rode in horse-drawn chariots and fought with weapons made of bronze and iron.)*
- **How did the intermingling of the Egyptians and the Hyskos eventually lead to the overthrowing of the Hyskos?** *(The Egyptians learned the Hyskos' art of warfare, and eventually defeated them.)* AL ELL

Content Background Knowledge

The Hyksos

- The word *Hyksos* was a combination of Egyptian words *heqa-khase,* which meant "rulers of foreign lands."
- In addition to the horse and chariot and weapons of bronze and iron, the Hyksos introduced the compound bow and new techniques in building defensive earthworks.
- The Hyksos drew on several cultural sources. At their ruling city of Avaris, articles were found that suggested interaction with Palestine, Crete, and Canaan.

WHITEBOARD ACTIVITY

The Hyksos and the Egyptians

Interpreting Project the activity on your whiteboard. Have students take turns choosing a characteristic and dropping it into the proper column to describe either the Hyksos or the Egyptians at the end of the Middle Kingdom. **Ask: How did the Hyksos help the Egyptians?** *(They provided knowledge that ultimately made the Egyptians more powerful.)*

See page 97E for other online activities.

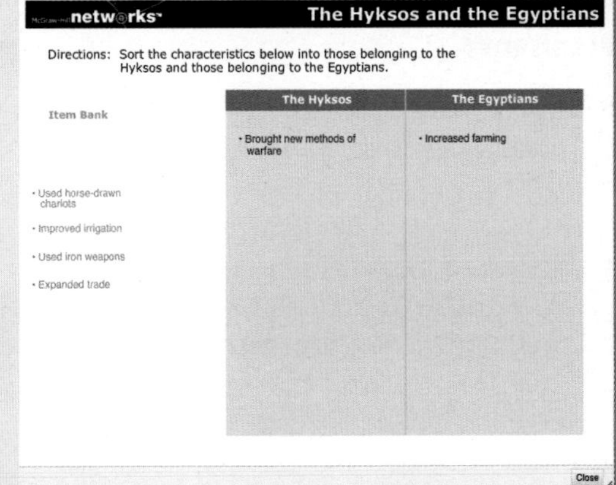

ANSWERS, p. 121

CRITICAL THINKING The chair is decorated with great detail and with lion heads.

☑ PROGRESS CHECK During the Hyksos' rule, the Egyptians improved their fighting skills by learning to drive chariots and to use new weapons. Later, these skills helped the Egyptians, under the leadership of Ahmose, drive out the Hyksos.

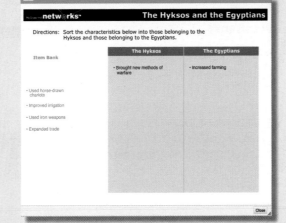

R Reading Skills

Summarizing Have students examine the passage that details Egypt's growth into an empire. Then ask students to summarize what they have read. **Ask:** **How did the ancient Egyptians increase the power and wealth of their empire during the Middle and New Kingdoms?** *(They conquered and developed lands, took resources and goods, enslaved their enemies, built more farms and canals, developed new artistic and architectural methods, and increased their trade with other places.)* Remind students to support their answers using details from the text.

V Visual Skills

Analyzing Images Have students examine the statues of Hatshepsut on this page and the image of her on the facing page **Ask:** **What do you notice about images of Hatshepsut?** *(She is shown with a beard.)* AL
Visual/Spatial Explain to students that the beard was a symbol of leadership in ancient Egypt.

Making Connections

Women Leaders Remind students of other women who served as leaders of their countries, such as Angela Merkel, Margaret Thatcher, Golda Meir, Catherine the Great, and Elizabeth I, among others. Have interested students research these and other female rulers. BL

Connections to TODAY

Ivory

Ivory comes from mammals with tusks, such as elephants and walruses.

Building an Empire

GUIDING QUESTION *Why was the New Kingdom a unique period in ancient Egypt's history?*

R Ahmose founded a new dynasty. It began a period known as the New Kingdom, which lasted from about 1550 B.C. to 1070 B.C. During this time, Egypt prospered through trade, gained more lands through conquest, and reached the height of its power. No longer isolated, Egyptians benefited from the spread of goods, ideas, and cultures within their empire.

A Woman Pharaoh

A queen named Hatshepsut (hat•SHEHP•soot) was one of the few women to rule Egypt. She came to power in about 1473 B.C. and governed with her husband. Then, after his death, she made herself pharaoh and ruled on behalf of her young nephew.

Because the title of pharaoh was usually passed from father to son, Hatshepsut had to prove that she was a good leader. In order for the people to accept her, Hatshepsut dressed in the clothes of a male pharaoh. She even wore the false beard to copy the one worn by male Egyptian kings. She built magnificent temples and restored old monuments. Her tomb in the Valley of the Kings contains large wall carvings that illustrate some of the major events of her reign.

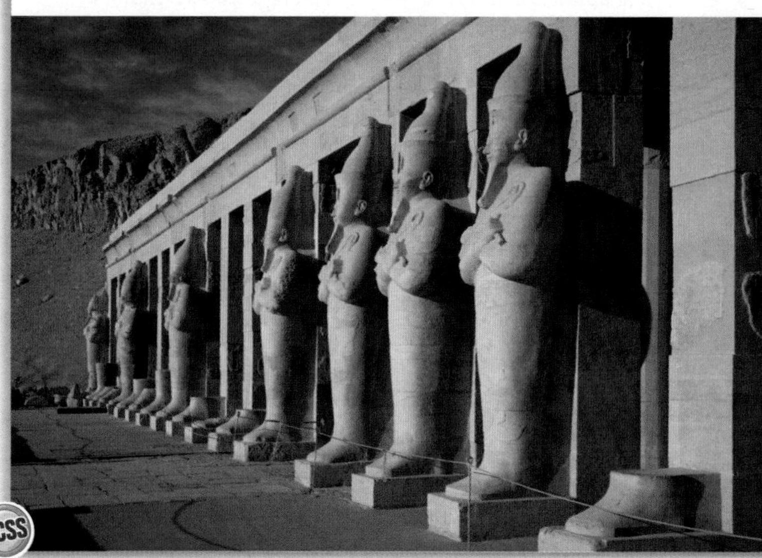

V One of the few women to govern Egypt, Hatshepsut ruled with the support of her subjects. This enormous tomb stands today in honor of her reign.

Reading HELPDESK (CCSS)

Reading Strategy: *Sequencing*

Key words such as *then, later,* and *after* are clues to the order in which events happened. Which of these key words is used on this page?

networks Online Teaching Options

IMAGE

Elephants

Determining Cause and Effect Have volunteers read aloud the information on modern elephant hunting. As a class, discuss why these animals are hunted. You may wish to use a cause-and-effect graphic organizer to record student ideas. Have students suggest ways in which the hunting of these endangered animals could be better curtailed.

See page 97E for other online activities.

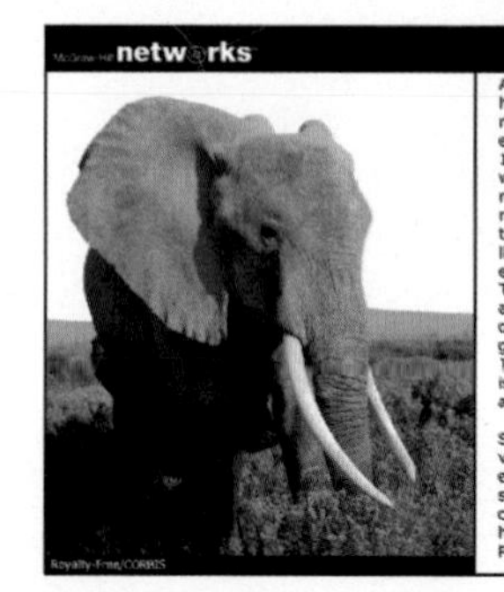

ANSWER, p. 122

Reading Strategy The key words *then* and *after* are used in the first paragraph under the heading "A Woman Pharaoh."

Growth of Trade

Hatshepsut was more interested in promoting trade than starting wars. She made great efforts to restore trade relations that had been interrupted by the Hyksos invasion.

During the rule of Hatshepsut, Egyptian seafarers sailed to ports in Arabia and East Africa. There, Egyptian traders exchanged beads, metal tools, and weapons for gold, ivory, ebony wood, and **incense** (IN•sens), a material burned for its pleasant smell. **R**

The Egyptians valued wood products because the Nile River valley had few trees. They needed wood to build boats, furniture, and other items. To find wood, Egyptian traders traveled to the east coast of the Mediterranean Sea where the present-day country of Lebanon is located. The people in this region were called the Phoenicians (fih•NEE•shuns). The Phoenicians had a great impact on other cultures in the region. Their invention of an alphabet and a system of writing influenced others. Phoenician trade routes and settlements also encouraged the spread of goods and ideas across a large part of the ancient world. **C**

Trade and Politics

The Egyptians traded wheat, paper, gold, copper, tin and tools to the Phoenicians for purple dye, wood and furniture. The traders exchanged goods they had for supplies they needed, rather than selling goods for money. The Phoenicians in turn traded Egyptian goods to other people. By trading with the Phoenicians, Egyptians spread their food and goods across Southwest Asia. Trade in the eastern Mediterranean helped make the Egyptian kingdom wealthier. Hatshepsut used some of this wealth to build monuments.

In addition to trade, New Kingdom pharaohs developed political ties between Egypt and nearby kingdoms. For example, the Egyptian dynasty became joined by treaty or marriage with ruling families in the Babylonian Empire in Mesopotamia, the Mittani (mih•TAH•nee) in Syria, and the Hittite Empire in Anatolia (ah•nuh•TOH•lee•uh).

To maintain close ties, pharaohs and the other rulers also exchanged **envoys** (EHN•voyz), or representatives. These actions marked the first time in history that a group of nations tried working together to reach common goals.

Iain Masterton/age fotostock

BIOGRAPHY

Hatshepsut (reigned 1473–1458 B.C.)

Hatshepsut was one of the most successful rulers of Egypt. Hatshepsut chose people who were loyal to her to serve in government positions. She valued the opinions of common Egyptians and sought their support for decisions she made. After her death, Thutmose III, Hatshepsut's nephew, had her name removed from royal texts and monuments. Historians believe that he did this to show that no female ruler interrupted the royal line of males.

▶ CRITICAL THINKING
Drawing Conclusions What actions of hers helped make Hatshepsut a successful ruler?

incense a material that produces a pleasant smell when burned

envoy a government representative to another country

R Reading Skills

Defining Bring in a set of nested dolls or show a photograph of them. Tell students that the content words used in social studies are often big and look hard, but usually there are less difficult words that have similar meanings—until you get to short, common English words. As you discuss this, open the dolls in order to reveal the smallest doll. Organize the class into small groups. Challenge students to find simpler words to replace the difficult vocabulary on the page. For example, in the first line, *promoting* is an abstract word. *Promoting* means "encouraging," which means "helping." Provide each group with a thesaurus, if possible. After groups have completed the task, read the page aloud and have students call out their substitute words when you come across them in the text. AL ELL **Verbal/Linguistic**

C Critical Thinking Skills

Analyzing Discuss how trade changed during the reign of the New Kingdom pharaohs. **Ask:**

- **Why were the Egyptians interested in trading for wood?** *(The Nile River valley and the surrounding desert had few trees.)*
- **What impact did the Phoenecians have on cultures they traded with?** *(They introduced the idea of an alphabet and writing. Their extensive trade routes also encouraged the spread of goods and ideas.)*
- **Think back to what you know about systems of trade. In what type of trade did the Egyptians and Phoenecians participate?** *(Barter; they traded goods for goods. They did not use money.)* BL

BIOGRAPHY

Hatshepsut

Discussing Have volunteers take turns reading the extended biographical information on Hatshepsut. Remind students to note important details from her life as the text is read. Then lead a discussion centering on women's roles in this time period. You may wish to review the section on women's roles in the last lesson. Have students identify ways that Hatshepsut exhibited the characteristics of a good ruler.

See page 97E for other online activities.

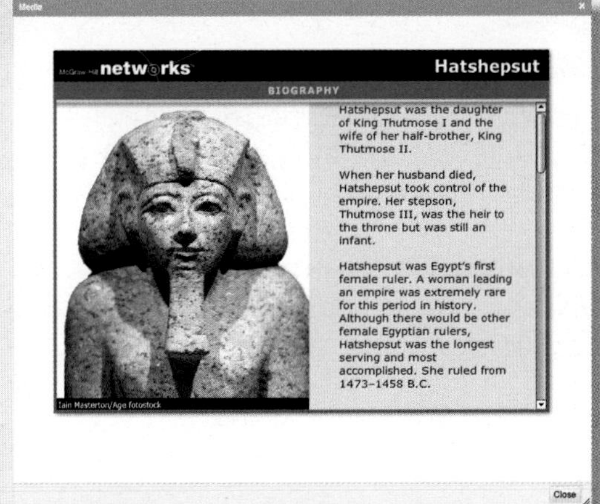

ANSWER, p. 123

CRITICAL THINKING Hatshepsut was successful because she chose loyal government officials and paid attention to common Egyptians.

Egypt's Empire

V Visual Skills

Making Generalizations Have students identify the shaded areas on the map that indicate the borders of the Old Kingdom, the Middle Kingdom, and the New Kingdom. Challenge students to make a generalization about how Egypt changed over time, based on the details on the map. *(Egypt grew in size over time, covering more territory.)* AL **Ask:** **How did the ancient Egyptians increase the size and power of their empire?** *(They conquered and developed lands, took resources and goods, enslaved their enemies, and increased their trade with other people.)* Remind students that Egypt's territorial expansion helped increase Egyptian political power, wealth, and cultural influence.

Have students compare the map on this page to the map of this region in the Atlas at the end of this book. Have them list the present-day countries through which the Egyptian kingdoms passed. These include Turkey, Syria, Lebanon, Israel, Jordan, Saudi Arabia, Sudan, Libya, and Cyprus. AL **Visual/Spatial**

C Critical Thinking Skills

Contrasting Direct students to read the description of the rights of enslaved people in the New Kingdom. Have students contrast these rights with what they know about the rights of enslaved Africans in the United States before 1862. *(Students should understand that while not free, people enslaved by the Egyptians did enjoy many rights that were not given to enslaved Africans in the United States.)*

GEOGRAPHY CONNECTION

During the Middle Kingdom, the capital of Egypt was moved from Memphis to Thebes.

1. **LOCATION** Identify the relative location of Thebes.
2. **PLACE** Describe the borders of the New Kingdom.
3. **CRITICAL THINKING** *Comparing* Which kingdom added the most territory?

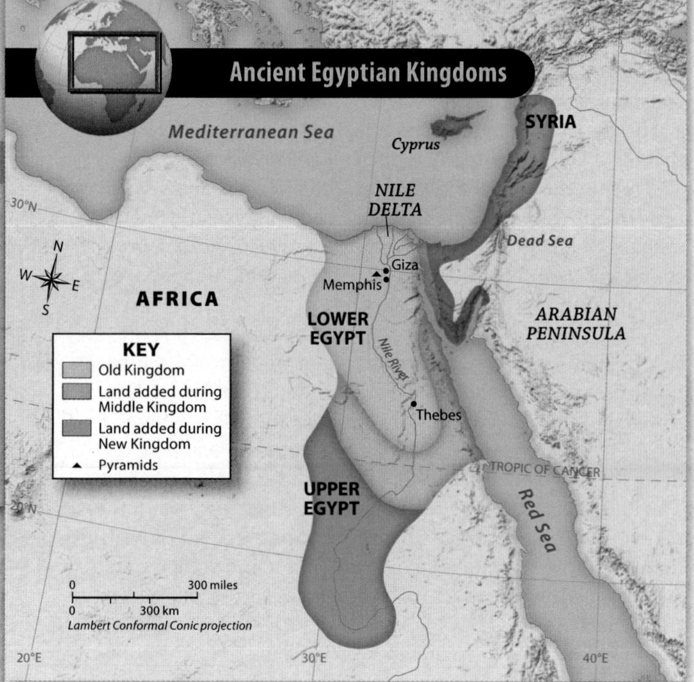

Expanding the Empire

When Hatshepsut died, her nephew, Thutmose III (thoot•MOH•suh), became pharaoh. Thutmose was a strong leader and general who expanded Egypt's control north to the Euphrates River in Mesopotamia. His troops also moved south far up the Nile and conquered Nubia, which had once thrown off Egyptian rule. Egyptian armies captured nearly 350 cities during Thutmose's reign.

As Thutmose and his armies conquered more areas, the Egyptian empire grew wealthy, and slavery became more common. Egypt **acquired** gold, copper, ivory and other valuable goods from conquered peoples. Egyptians captured and enslaved many prisoners of war. Enslaved people had some rights, however, including the right to own land, marry, and eventually gain their freedom.

✓ **PROGRESS CHECK**

Explaining Why did the Egyptians want to trade with the Phoenicians?

Reading HELPDESK (CCSS)

Academic Vocabulary (Tier 2 Words)

acquire to get possession of something

ANSWERS, p. 124

GEOGRAPHY CONNECTION

1. Thebes is south of Memphis but north of the Tropic of Cancer.
2. The New Kingdom was bordered by the Mediterranean Sea, the Dead Sea, and the Red Sea.
3. **CRITICAL THINKING** The New Kingdom added the most territory.

✓ **PROGRESS CHECK** They traded with the Phoenicians in order to obtain goods they could not make or grow for themselves, especially furniture and wood for building ships.

networks Online Teaching Options

MAP

Ancient Egyptian Kingdoms

Analyzing Maps Turn off all the layers, and then click on the buttons one at a time to help students visualize the growing extent of Ancient Egypt. As the extent of the kingdom is revealed over time, have students describe the events that lead this expansion. Point out the location of the pyramids near Giza and Memphis.

See page 97E for other online activities.

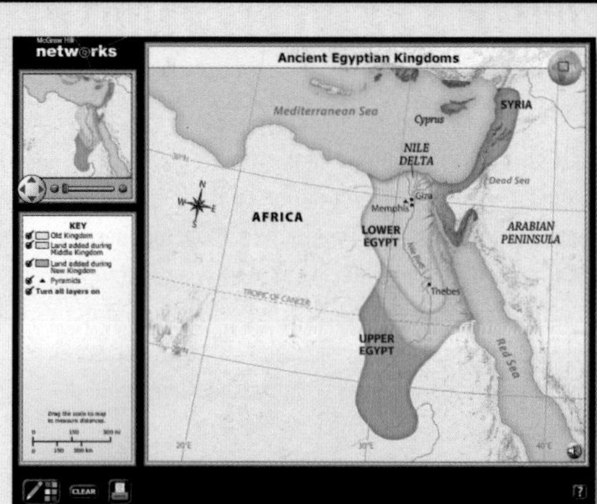

Two Unusual Pharaohs

GUIDING QUESTION *How did two unusual pharaohs change ancient Egypt?*

During the New Kingdom, two remarkable pharaohs came to power. One pharaoh, Amenhotep IV, tried to make dramatic changes, and one, Tutankhamen, was very young. Their actions set them apart from other rulers in Egypt's long history.

A Religious Founder

A new pharaoh named Amenhotep IV (ah•muhn•HOH•tehp) came to power in about 1370 B.C. Supported by his wife, Nefertiti (nehf•uhr•TEE•tee), Amenhotep tried to change Egypt's religion, which was based on the worship of many deities.

Amenhotep believed that Egypt's priests had grown too powerful and wealthy. He felt threatened by their power. To lessen the priests' **authority,** Amenhotep started a new religion. He introduced the worship of Aton (AHT•n), the sun god, as Egypt's only god. When Egypt's priests opposed this change, Amenhotep removed many of them from their posts, took their lands, and closed temples. He then changed his name to Akhenaton (ahk•NAH•tuhn), meaning "Spirit of Aton." The capital was moved to a new city north of Thebes called Akhetaton (ahk•heh•TAH•tuhn).

These changes unsettled Egypt. Most Egyptians rejected Aton and continued to worship many deities. In addition, the priests of the old religion resisted their loss of power. The discontent with Akhenaton's rule spread to the army leaders. They believed Akhenaton, devoted to his new religion, neglected his duties as pharaoh. Under Akhenaton's weak rule, Egypt lost most of its lands in western Asia to outside invaders.

Who Was "King Tut"?

When Akhenaton died about 1360 B.C., his son, 10-year-old Tutankhamen (too•tang•KAH•muhn), became pharaoh. The young pharaoh relied on advice from priests and officials to rule Egypt. Tutankhamen quickly restored the worship of many deities. Tutankhamen's short rule ended after only nine years, when he died unexpectedly. The cause of his death is still a mystery to historians, and he remains a fascinating figure.

King Tut is shown wearing the false beard worn by all pharaohs. Tut was a child when he became pharaoh. He died at the age of 19.

Academic Vocabulary (Tier 2 Words)

authority the right or power to give orders, make decisions, or control people

C Critical Thinking Skills

Discussing Remind students that the pharaohs were all-powerful and influenced all aspects of Egyptians' daily life. Ask:

- **What are two specific examples of how the pharaohs of the New Kingdom used their power over Egyptian religious life?** *(Amenhotep IV, also called Akhenaton, was able to change the religion; Tut restored the worship of many deities.)* BL
- **What was the effect of Amenhotep's new religion on the priests, army leaders, and Egyptian citizens?** *(They were unhappy with the change. Citizens kept worshiping their many deities, and the priests and army leaders became discontent.)*
- **What was the final result of Akhenaton's rule?** *(Egypt lost most of its lands in western Asia to outside invaders.)*

Content Background Knowledge

Amenhotep IV and Tut

- Amenhotep IV's new name may be spelled Akhenaton, Akhenaten, Akhnaton, and Ikhnaton.
- The religion introduced by Akhenaton is often seen as monotheistic. However, Akhenaton was promoting one god over the others instead of having only one. The people of Egypt were uncomfortable when the god Aton was elevated even over the pharaoh himself. Many statues and depictions of other gods have been found in excavations of Akhetaton, the city founded by Akhenaton.
- An article published in 2010 in *National Geographic* reported the results of a study of the Boy-King Tutankhamun's DNA. King Tut's mother and father were identified, as well as relatives going back several generations.

GRAPHIC ORGANIZER

Taking Notes: *Organizing:* The Middle and New Kingdoms

Organizing Use the interactive Graphic Organizer to help students organize facts about the time span, the role of government, and the economy of the Middle and New Kingdoms of ancient Egypt. You may wish to have students work in pairs or small groups to complete the chart. Have groups share their results with the class. Then combine all of the information into one master chart that students can use as they study for tests.

networks

Name: Date:

TAKING NOTES: *Organizing*

	Middle Kingdom	New Kingdom
Date		
Government		
Economy		

UNDO CLEAR SAVE

See page 97E for other online activities

Egypt's Empire

T Technology Skills

Researching on the Internet Have students go online to find an assortment of accounts of Howard Carter's discovery of Tutankhamen's tomb, including Carter's own account. Read three or four different accounts, including Carter's, aloud to students. **Ask:** **Which of these reports is a primary source?** *(Most students will identify Carter's account as a primary source.)* Ask students if that means Carter's account is true. Remind students that primary sources let us hear the voices of history, but their words may reflect ego or political or other aims. **Verbal/Linguistic**

W Writing Skills

Argument One of the temples built by Ramses was Abu Simbel, located about 40 miles south of the Aswan Dam in southern Egypt. Have students work in pairs and find articles about how the building of the dam affected the temple complex and the fertility of the soil along the Nile. After reading, have students use separate sheets of paper for each article to (1) record the topic sentences of each paragraph in the article and (2) list on the left side of the paper the benefits of having the dam and list on the right side the drawbacks of the dam. Are they able to tell which perspective the author of a particular article has taken? Discuss how writers can select facts to present one point of view more strongly than another. BL **Verbal/Linguistic**

C Critical Thinking Skills

Analyzing Primary Sources Have students read the quote carved on the Karnak temple wall. **Ask:** **To what is this quote referring?** *(a victory of Ramses over one of his foes)* **What does Ramses say he will do to his foes?** *(kill them by cutting them into pieces)* **How might the ability of the Egyptians to use chariots have aided Ramses in his victories?** *(Sample answer: Ramses could ride quickly into a group of enemies. Being on a chariot would give him a height advantage so that he could more easily "hew them into pieces" and "dash them into dust.")*

ANSWERS, p. 126

PROGRESS CHECK Akhenaton took the unusual step of changing the Egyptian religion to the worship of one deity. Tutankhamen is well known today for the riches found in his tomb, but he was an unusually young pharaoh who died after ruling for only nine years.

Caption: The length of Ramses' reign can be calculated using the mathematical expression 63 + 3.

Reading Strategy The cause is that most Egyptians prayed in their homes.

T Even though "King Tut" played a small role in the history of Egypt, he is the most famous of the pharaohs. British archaeologist Howard Carter attracted public attention when he discovered Tut's tomb in 1922. Carter's find was amazing because most tombs of the pharaohs had been robbed by thieves. Tut's tomb, however, contained the pharaoh's mummy and many treasures, including a brilliant gold mask of the young ruler's face.

PROGRESS CHECK

Evaluating Why are Akhenaton and Tutankhamen considered unusual pharaohs?

Recovery and Decline

GUIDING QUESTION ***Why did the Egyptian empire decline in the late 1200s B.C.?***

During the 1200s B.C., the pharaohs worked to restore Egypt's greatness. They fought battles for more territory, increased Egypt's wealth through trade, and built large temples and monuments.

Ramses II

The most successful of these pharaohs was Ramses II (RAM•seez), who ruled from 1279 B.C. to 1213 B.C. Ramses conquered the region of Canaan and moved north into Syria. To get this territory, he fought the Hittites, who lived in present-day Turkey. After many battles, Ramses and the Hittite king signed a peace treaty.

Few rulers reigned as long as Ramses. He reigned three years longer than England's Queen Victoria, who ruled for 63 years. What mathematical expression would tell you the length of Ramses' reign?

Sandro Vannini/CORBIS

Age of Temples

W During his 66-year reign, Ramses also devoted himself to peaceful activities. Ramses II and other New Kingdom rulers had many temples built throughout Egypt. One of the most magnificent was Karnak (KAHR•nack) at Thebes. Its huge columned hall still impresses visitors today. A poem celebrating a victory by Ramses is carved in the temple. In part of the poem, Ramses says this to his chariot driver:

> "Halt! take courage, charioteer, As a sparrow-hawk swoops down upon his prey,
> So I swoop upon the foe, and I will slay, I will hew [cut] them into pieces,
> I will dash them into dust." C
>
> —from *Pen-ta-tur: The Victory of Ramses II Over the Khita*

Most Egyptians prayed in their homes, so temples were used only for special occasions. Egyptians saw the temples as the

Academic Vocabulary (Tier 2 Words)

decline to become weaker

Reading Strategy: *Understanding Cause and Effect*

The word *so* indicates the effect of an event. Read the first sentence in the last paragraph above. The *effect* is that temples were used only for special occasions. What is the cause?

networks *Online Teaching Options*

CHART

Pharaohs and Their Achievements

Categorizing Use this interactive chart to aid students in reviewing the major achievements of the pharaohs discussed in this lesson. Have volunteers take turns choosing a pharaoh and matching an achievement to that ruler.

See page 97E for other online activities.

networks **Pharaohs and Their Achievements**

Directions: Match each pharaoh to his or her achievements. Drag the correct number into the second column of the chart.

Item Bank

1. Became king at the age of 10
2. Started a new religion in which people worshiped only Aton, the sun god
3. Founded a new dynasty (the New Kingdom)
4. A female ruler of Egypt
5. Worked to restore Egypt's in the 1200s B.C.
6. This ruler's armies captured 350 cities.

Ahmose	
Hatshepsut	
Thutmose III	
Amenhotep IV	
Tutankhamen	
Ramses II	

Egypt's Empire

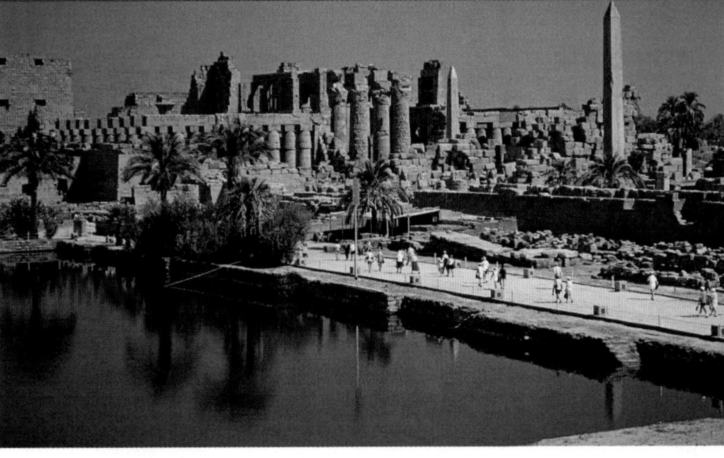

Still in use after more than 3,000 years, Karnak remains to honor Ramses' many achievements.

Gavin Hellier/Getty Images

homes of their deities. Priests and priestesses performed daily rituals, washed the statues of the deities, and brought them food.

Temples were important to Egypt's economy. Priests hired people to work in temple workshops and granaries. Temples also served as banks. Egyptians used them to store valuable items, such as gold jewelry, fragrant oils, and finely woven textiles.

Why Did Egypt Decline?

After Ramses II died, Egypt **declined.** Pharaohs fought costly wars. Armies from the eastern Mediterranean attacked Egypt. By 1150 B.C., the Egyptian empire controlled only the Nile delta. **R**

In the 900s B.C., the Libyans conquered Egypt. Then, the people of Kush seized power. Finally, in 670 B.C., Egypt was taken over by the Assyrians from Mesopotamia.

✓ PROGRESS CHECK

Summarizing What were the accomplishments of Ramses II?

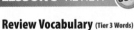

LESSON 3 REVIEW

Review Vocabulary (Tier 3 Words)

1. Why would someone want to buy *incense*? RH.6–8.4
2. What might have been the duties of an ancient Egyptian *envoy*? RH.6–8.4

Answer the Guiding Questions

3. ***Describing*** Discuss two reasons why the Middle Kingdom period was a "golden age" for Egypt. RH.6–8.2
4. ***Explaining*** Why was the New Kingdom a unique period in ancient Egypt's history? RH.6–8.2
5. ***Summarizing*** Describe the religious changes brought about by Akhenaton and Tutankhamen. RH.6–8.2
6. ***Analyzing*** In what ways were temples important to Egypt's economy? RH.6–8.1
7. **ARGUMENT** You are a scribe who works for Queen Hatshepsut. Write a brief report that explains why she is a good pharaoh and deserves the support of the people. WHST.6–8.1, WHST.6–8.10

R Reading Skills

Defining Write the word *declined* on the board both at an upward slant and at a downward slant. **Ask:** Which of these shows the meaning of the word *declined?* *(the downward slant)* Erase the upward slanted version. Then add the word *incline* at an upward slant so that, with *decline,* it makes a peak. Ask students to infer what the word *incline* means. Note that an incline/decline also makes a slope or a ramp, many of which were used to build the pyramids. ELL **Visual/Spatial**

Have students complete the Lesson 3 Review.

CLOSE & REFLECT

Read aloud the actions taken by Egyptian pharaohs listed below. As you read each item, ask students to give a thumbs-up sign if the activity helped strengthen Egypt and a thumbs-down sign for activities that led to the empire's decline. Make sure students are in agreement in their answers. AL ELL **Kinesthetic**

- Building new temples and restoring old tombs *(thumbs-up) (Hatshepsut, Ramses II)*
- Seeking the opinions of common Egyptians *(thumbs-up) (Hatshepsut)*
- Promoting trade *(thumbs-up) (Hatshepsut)*
- Removing a pharaoh's name from public records *(thumbs-down) (Thutmose III)*
- Conquering new territories *(thumbs-up) (Thutmose III, Ramses II)*
- Acquiring resources and valuables *(thumbs-up) (Thutmose III)*
- Founding a new religion and removing priests from power *(thumbs-down) (Amenhotep/Akhenaton)*
- Neglecting duties as a pharaoh *(thumbs-down) (Amenhotep/ Akhenaton)*
- Signing a peace agreement with neighbors *(thumbs-up) (Ramses II)*

LESSON 3 REVIEW ANSWERS

1. Someone would want to buy incense to make his or her home smell better or to use in a religious ceremony.
2. An envoy's duties may have included representing the Egyptian empire by meeting with political leaders in other places and sending reports back to the pharaoh.
3. Egypt acquired new territory and reached the height of its power. With the building of great tombs and statues, arts and architecture flourished.
4. During the New Kingdom, two remarkable pharaohs came to power. Amenhotep IV tried to change Egypt's religion. Tutankhamen was only a boy.
5. Akhenaton tried to change Egypt's religion. The changes unsettled the people and the Egyptian social structure. The pharaoh's interest in religion made him ineffective, and Egypt lost territory. Tutankhamen restored the religion but was too young and died too soon to become a ruler who made much impact.
6. Priests hired people to work in the temples' storage buildings and workshops. People also used temples as banks.
7. Students' answers should take the form of a letter and point out that Hatshepsut was a peaceful leader who valued loyalty and believed that trading relations could help maintain the empire better than war could. She also solicited the opinions of ordinary Egyptians before making decisions that affected the empire.

ANSWER, p. 127

✓ PROGRESS CHECK Ramses II regained lost territory in western Asia and signed a peace treaty with the Hittite king. He also had temples built, which helped the Egyptian economy.

ENGAGE

Bellringer Share with students the definition of cultural diffusion: the process of spreading ideas, languages, and customs from one culture to another. Lead students in a discussion of how cultures interact and shape one another. Ask students for examples of how their lives are affected or influenced by other cultures. **Ask:** **Do you enjoy music, food, clothing, or games that are from other cultures? How or why do certain cultures "rub off" on each other?** Students should understand that cultures that are close geographically often influence each other. Explain that the ancient Egyptians influenced many civilizations in the region. Tell students that in this lesson they will learn how Nubia and Egypt influenced each other and why the kingdom of Kush rose to power. AL ELL

TEACH & ASSESS

R Reading Skills

Finding the Main Idea Go through each paragraph on this page and the following one with students to determine the main ideas. List these on the board. For example, the first paragraph's main idea is, "Other civilizations, such as Nubia, flourished in Africa." **Ask:** **How are these pages organized—big to little, oldest to newest, or important to unimportant?** Put dates from each paragraph next to its topic. Lead students to see that this section is organized by oldest to newest—or chronologically. "Unpack" this word: *chrono-* means "time"; *-ology* means "study of." Inform students that history books are usually organized chronologically, or from the earliest event that happened to the most recent. AL ELL

Making Connections

Have interested students research and report on conflicts occurring in Sudan in the twenty-first century. BL

ANSWER, p. 128

TAKING NOTES: New Kingdom declines; Nubians rebel and found Kush; Kush grows rich from trade; Kush conquers Egypt.

---

netw◎rks
There's More Online!

☑ **GRAPHIC ORGANIZER** Kush Conquers Egypt

☑ **MAP** Kush Kingdom, c. 250 B.C.

Lesson 4

The Kingdom of Kush

ESSENTIAL QUESTION *Why do civilizations rise and fall?*

It Matters Because

The kingdoms of Nubia and Kush were influenced by Egyptian culture, and they continued many Egyptian traditions.

The Nubians

GUIDING QUESTION ***How did Nubia and Egypt influence each other?***

In addition to Egypt, other civilizations flourished in Africa. One of these African civilizations was Nubia, later known as Kush. Nubia was located south of Egypt along the Nile River in present-day Sudan.

Cattle herders were the first people to settle in this region, arriving about 2000 B.C. They herded long-horned cattle on the **savannas** (suh•VA•nuhs), or grassy plains, that stretch across Africa south of the Sahara. Later, people settled in farming villages along the Nile River.

R Unlike the Egyptians, the Nubians did not **rely** on the Nile floods to create fertile soil. Their land had fertile soil and received rainfall all year long. Nubian villagers grew crops such as beans, yams, rice, and grains. The Nubians also hunted for food. Their hunters and warriors excelled at using the bow and arrow.

The Rise of Kerma

Gradually, the stronger Nubian villages took over the weaker ones and formed the kingdom of Kerma (KAR•muh). The Nubians of Kerma grew wealthy from agriculture and the mining of gold. Their kingdom developed a close relationship

Reading **HELP**DESK CCSS

Taking Notes: *Sequencing*

Use a diagram like this one to list events that led up to the Kush conquest of Egypt. RH.6–8.2, RH.6–8.3

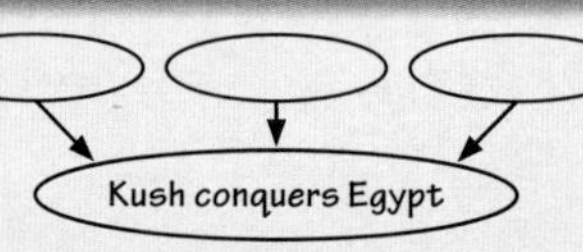

Content Vocabulary (Tier 3 Words)
- **savanna**
- **textile**

netw◎rks ***Online Teaching Options***

VIDEO

Kingdom of Axum

Describing Have students view this video about the city of Axum. Discuss the archaeological relics that remain there today and what they suggest about the history of that city over the last 3000 years.

See page 97F for other online activities.

with Egypt in the north. Kerma's central location in the Nile valley benefited the Nubians. It made Kerma an important trade link between Egypt and the tropical areas of southern Africa. From Kerma, the Egyptians acquired cattle, gold, incense, ivory, giraffes, leopards, and enslaved people. They also hired Nubians to serve in their armies because of their skills in warfare.≈Kerma's artisans produced fine pottery, jewelry, and metal goods. **W**

Workers built tombs for Kerma's kings, usually on a smaller scale than Egyptian tombs. Like the Egyptian pharaohs, the kings of Kerma were buried with their personal belongings, including valuable gems, gold, jewelry, and pottery. These artifacts were as magnificent as those found in Egypt's royal tombs that were built during the same time period.

Egyptian Invasion

Egyptian armies invaded Nubia in the 1400s B.C. After a 50-year war, the Egyptians conquered the kingdom of Kerma and ruled it for the next 700 years. **V**

As a result of Egyptian rule, the Nubians adopted many of the beliefs and customs of Egyptian culture. For example, the Nubians worshipped Egyptian gods and goddesses along with their own Nubian deities. They learned to use copper and bronze to make tools. The Nubians adapted Egyptian hieroglyphs to fit their own language and created an alphabet.

☑ PROGRESS CHECK

Analyzing Why did Kerma become an important center for trade?

The savannas of Africa are grassy and dotted with trees and herds of wildlife. The grasses can withstand long, hot periods without rain. These broad plains covered much of Nubia.

Mike D. Kock/Gallo Images/Getty Images

savanna a flat grassland, sometimes with scattered trees, in a tropical or subtropical region

Academic Vocabulary (Tier 2 Words)

rely to depend on someone or something

W Writing Skills

Informative/Explanatory After students read about the rise of the Nubian kingdom of Kerma and its time under Egyptian rule, ask them to make a generalization about how the two cultures interacted. **Ask:** Why was Egypt an influence on the Nubians? *(Nubia traded with Egypt and later was under Egyptian rule.)* In what ways did Egypt shape Nubian culture? *(Nubians adopted Egyptian religious practices as well as hieroglyphics and tool-making skills.)* Have students use the information they discussed to write a paragraph on this topic. Verbal/Linguistic

V Visual Skills

Creating Time Lines As students read the lesson, have them make notes of the dates of each important event and convert that list into a time line. They should include a short description of the event as well as the date for each entry. Visual/Spatial

Content Background Knowledge

Savanna Savanna-like areas typically have (or had) large herds of hoofed animals, such as wildebeest and zebra. Climate change and habitat loss due to human activities are reducing the number and biodiversity of animals in this biome.

CHART

Savanna and Desert

Compare and Contrast Use the interactive chart to aid students in comparing and contrasting savanna and desert environments. Start by clicking on the rows beneath "Desert" to reveal its characteristics. As you move from row to row, ask volunteers whether the characteristics of the savanna are the same or different from those of the desert. Click on the "Savanna" rows to check students' answers.

See page 97F for other online activities.

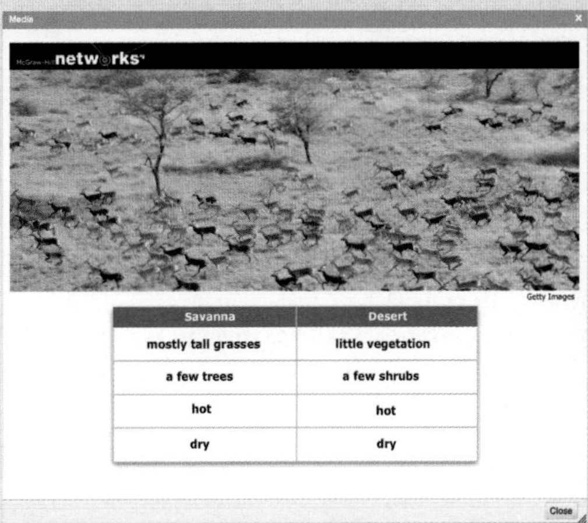

Savanna	Desert
mostly tall grasses	little vegetation
a few trees	a few shrubs
hot	hot
dry	dry

ANSWER, p. 129

☑ PROGRESS CHECK Kerma was centrally located in Nubia and had close relations with Egypt.

The Kingdom of Kush

C Critical Thinking Skills

Discussing Use these questions to help students understand important points about the Kushite Kingdom. **Ask:**

- **How did southern Africans influence the Kushites?** *(The Kushites adopted ankle and ear jewelry worn by southern Africans.)*
- **Why would the Kushites continue to admire the ancient Egyptians even after conquering them?** *(The Kushites had lived with the Egyptians for many years and had adopted their customs and culture.)*

V Visual Skills

Analyzing Visuals Direct students to the painted scene at the bottom of the page. **Ask: What are some of the differences between the Nubian royalty and the pharaoh and his escort depicted in the painting?** *(Students may point out the style of dress, the different headdresses, and the differences in skin color.)* Explain that the Nubian pharaohs, including Piye, are known as "The Black Pharaohs" because their skin was considerably darker than that of Egyptian pharaohs. They ruled Egypt during the 25th dynasty. Skin color was not an issue to the Egyptians and Nubians. They each accepted each other's rule without question. **Visual/Spatial**

Content Background Knowledge

- Archaeological exploration of the area of the Kushite Kingdom reveals a thriving and complex society, active in trade, religion, and the arts—both fine arts and military arts.
- In 2003, a team led by archaeologist Charles Bonnet discovered statues of seven ancient kings of Kush. The statues reflect the complexity and longevity of the Kushite culture.
- A proposed dam 600 miles upriver from the Aswan Dam threatens to swamp hundreds of newly excavated Nubian archaeological sites and thousands of undiscovered sites.

The Kushite Kingdom

GUIDING QUESTION *Why did the kingdom of Kush prosper?*

By the end of the Middle Kingdom, Egypt was weak. It could no longer govern its conquered peoples effectively, and the Nubians were able to break away from Egyptian rule.

The Rise of Kush

By 850 B.C., the Nubians had formed an independent kingdom known as Kush. Powerful kings ruled the country from its capital at Napata (NA•puh•tuh).

The city of Napata was located where trade caravans crossed the upper part of the Nile River. Caravans came from central Africa, bringing ivory and other goods. They stopped at Napata for Kushite products and then continued on to Egypt. The Egyptians traded with Kush for goods the Egyptians could not make. Such trade brought wealth to the traders and kings of Kush.

C

Kush Conquers Egypt

In time, Kush became powerful enough to **challenge** Egypt. About 750 B.C., a Kushite king named Kashta (KAHSH•tuh) invaded Egypt. His soldiers reached the city of Thebes. After Kashta died, his son Piye (PY) became king and completed the conquest of Egypt in 728 B.C. Piye founded the Twenty-fifth Dynasty that governed Egypt and Kush from Napata.

The kings and wealthy people of Kush continued to admire Egyptian culture. Kushites built white sandstone temples and monuments similar to those in Egypt. The Kushites also believed

V In this scene, Nubian royalty offer gifts to an Egyptian pharaoh. The procession shows respect for the pharaoh.

Reading HELPDESK (CCSS)

Academic Vocabulary (Tier 2 Words)

challenge to invite the start of a competition

networks Online Teaching Options

GRAPHIC ORGANIZER

Taking Notes: *Sequencing:* Kush Conquers Egypt

Sequencing As students read the information presented on this page, have them work with a partner to complete the graphic organizer. Have them record events, in order, that led to the conquering of Egypt by the Kushite king Kashta.

See page 97F for other online activities.

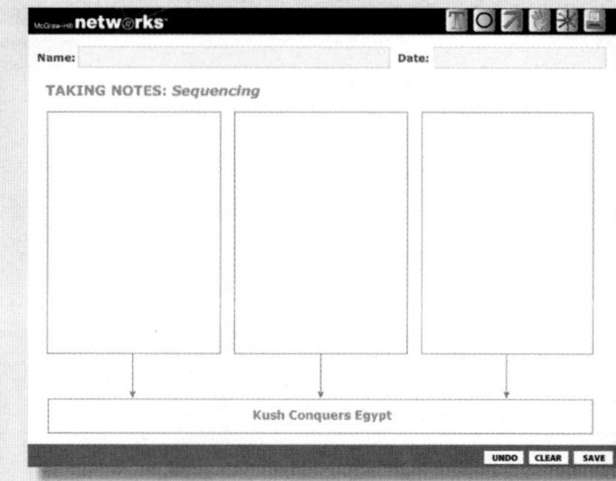

Kush Kingdom c. 250 B.C.

Mediterranean Sea
Memphis
EGYPT
Thebes
ARABIA
SAHARA
Nile River
Red Sea
Persian Gulf
Napata
Meroë
KEY
Kush
20°N
10°N
20°E
40°E
50°E
0 400 miles
0 400 km
Lambert Conformal Conic projection

GEOGRAPHY CONNECTION

Trade caravans crossed the Nile near Napata, which made the city a busy trading center.

1. **LOCATION** In what direction would traders travel to get from Napata to Meroë?
2. **CRITICAL THINKING** ***Analyzing*** How is the Nile different south of Meroë?

V

Kushite artisans worked in gold, creating objects such as this statue of Amon-Re. They also made fine pottery.

in a close relationship between their rulers and their deities, many of whom were Egyptian. For example, when a king died, Kushite officials met at the temple to ask the Egyptian god Amon-Re to appoint a new leader:

PRIMARY SOURCE

> “So the commanders of His Majesty and the officials of the palace . . . [found] the major priests waiting outside the temple. They said to them, “Pray, may this god, Amon-Re . . . give us our lord. . . . We cannot do a thing without this god. It is he who guides us. . . .” Then the commanders . . . and the officials . . . entered into the temple and put themselves upon their bellies before this god. They said, “We have come to you, O Amon-Re, . . . that you might give to us a lord, to revive us, to build the temples of the gods, . . .”
>
> —from *The Selection of Aspalta as King of Kush*

C

The Kushites also built small, steeply-sloped pyramids as tombs for their kings. Some people in Kush, however, adopted customs and styles similar to those worn by southern Africans. This included wearing ankle and ear jewelry. By this time, the people of Kush also had developed their own style of painted pottery. The elephant, a sacred animal in Kush, was used as a theme in sculpture and other arts.

Reading Strategy: *Reading a Map*

When reading a map, first locate the key. It will help you identify what is being shown on the map. What is the key identifying on the map above?

The Kingdom of Kush

V Visual Skills

Speculating Have students study the map of the Kush kingdom. **Ask:** **Why do you think the Kush kingdom was able to extend farther away from the Nile river than the Egyptian kingdom?** You may wish to have students review the map in Lesson 3 showing the ancient Egyptian kingdoms before answering this question. *(Sample answer: The Kush kingdom was in an area of savanna. Its southern reaches were not surrounded by desert, like the Egyptian kingdom.)* AL **Visual/Spatial**

C Critical Thinking Skills

Analyzing Primary Sources Read aloud the quote from The Selection of Aspalta as King of Kush. **Ask:** **What does this passage describe?** *(the ceremony undertaken by Kushite officials when they needed to appoint a new king)* AL **How does this passage illustrate cultural diffusion?** BL *(The Kushites are asking an Egyptian god for guidance.)* Have students work together to make a mural showing the series of events described in this passage. **Interpersonal**

Making Connections

After students read the description of the influence of cultures in southern Africa on the Kushites, draw students into a discussion of where their own cultural influences come from. To begin, have them list ten of their favorite movies. **Ask:** **Were they all made by U.S. studios? Were all of the characters American?**

MAP

Kush Kingdom, c. 250 B.C.

Analyzing Maps Display the interactive map, Kush Kingdom, c. 250 B.C., with the layers turned off. Then click to reveal the extent of the kingdom. Point out the location of the kingdom in relation to Egypt. Have students use the interactive scale to measure the width and length of the kingdom.

See page 97F for other online activities.

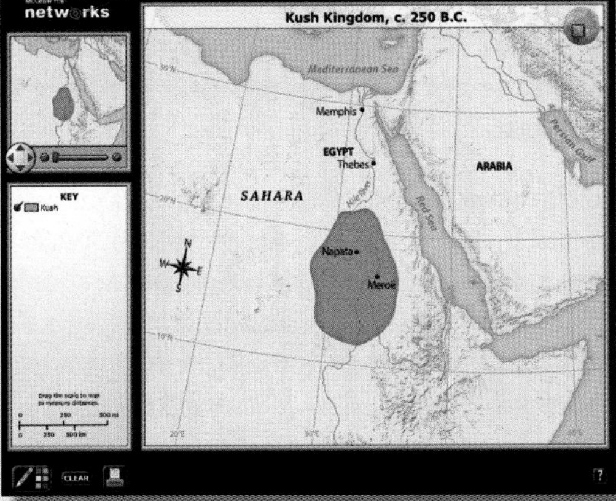

ANSWERS, p. 131

GEOGRAPHY CONNECTION

1. Traders would travel southeast to get from Napata to Meroë.
2. **CRITICAL THINKING** South of Meroë, the Nile is two rivers instead of one.

The Kingdom of Kush

R Reading Skills

Identifying After students read the passage, ask them to identify how the use of iron changed the lives of the Kushites. **Ask:**

- **What caused the defeat of the Kushites by the Assyrians?** *(Kushite bronze weapons and tools were not as strong as iron ones.)*
- **What did the Kushites learn from the Assyrians, and how did this benefit the Kushites?** *(Kushites learned how to use iron to make tools and weapons. Iron tools allowed them to grow more food, and iron weapons boosted the Kushites' military strength.)*

W Writing Skills

Informative/Explanatory To further explore the effect of new technologies, such as the Assyrians' use of iron, have small groups of students write reports that describe how changes in technology affect culture. The topics could include the steam engine, the Bessemer process (steel-making), antibiotics, airplanes, cell phones, the automobile, wireless technology, the Internet. Each report should include (1) important dates; (2) a brief description; (3) life before the invention; (4) life after the invention. **Interpersonal Verbal/Linguistic**

T Technology Skills

Making Presentations Have students convert their report on technological innovations into a slide presentation. Presentations should include narration or background music. **Auditory/Musical**

C Critical Thinking Skills

Compare and Contrasting After students read the description of the capital city of Meroë, **ask: How was the city of Meroë like and unlike an Egyptian city?** *(Its layout was like an Egyptian city, and it contained tombs and monuments. Unlike Egypt's cities, Meroë had many iron furnaces, and there were many trees nearby.)*

Using Iron

Kush ruled Egypt for about 60 years. In 671 B.C., the Assyrians invaded Egypt. Armed with iron weapons, the Assyrians defeated the Kushites, who only had bronze weapons, which were not as strong. The Kushites fled Egypt and returned to their homeland in the south.

Despite their defeat in Egypt, the Kushites learned how to make iron from the Assyrians. Farmers in Kush used iron to make their hoes and plows instead of copper or stone. With better tools, they were able to grow more grain and other crops. Kushite warriors also created iron weapons, which boosted their military strength.

The Capital of Meroë

About 540 B.C., Kush's rulers moved their capital to the city of Meroë (MEHR•oh•ee), near one of the Nile's cataracts. This move made them safer from Assyrian attacks. The Nile River continued to provide a means for trade and transportation for the Kushites. Large deposits of iron ore and trees were nearby and were used to fuel furnaces for making iron. As a result, Meroë became a major center for iron production as well as a busy trading city.

Kushite kings modeled the layout and design of Meroë after Egypt's great cities. A temple dedicated to the god Amon-Re stood at the end of a long avenue lined with sculptures of rams. The walls of palaces and houses were decorated with paintings. Small pyramids stood in the royal graveyard, modeled on the larger pyramids of Egypt. Meroë, however, was different from a typical Egyptian city because it contained iron furnaces. Huge columns of smoke poured out of iron furnaces. Heaps of shiny black slag, or waste from iron making, lay around the furnaces.

The Kushites adopted pyramids as tombs. They usually built tombs that were smaller than those of the Egyptians, however.

Reading HELPDESK (CCSS)

textile woven cloth

networks Online Teaching Options

WORKSHEET

Economics of History Activity: Ancient Egypt and Kush

Making Connections Have students work with a partner to complete the activity describing the exchange of goods and ideas among Egypt, Kush, and Assyria. **Ask: What ideas or goods were exchanged among the Egyptians, Kushites, and Assyrians?** *(Egypt gave Kush its religion and the idea to build pyramids and monuments; the Assyrians gave the Kushites the technology to make iron tools and weapons; Kush traded goods with Egypt.)*

See page 97F for other online activities.

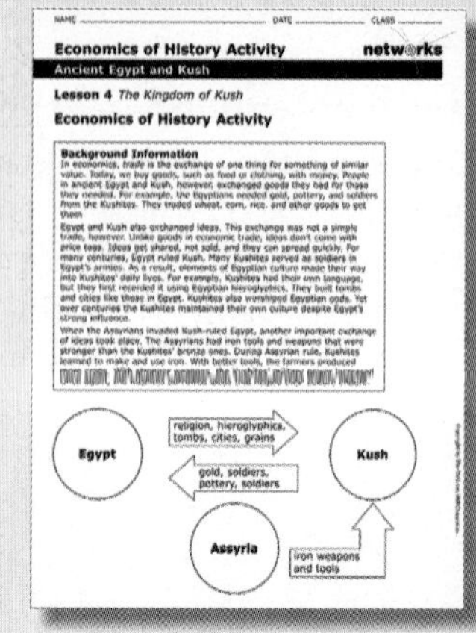

Economics of History Activity — networks
Ancient Egypt and Kush
Lesson 4 The Kingdom of Kush
Economics of History Activity
Background Information

Modeled on Egyptian cities, Meroë had a special purpose. It was an iron-making city with smokestacks and soot.

A Trading Center

Meroë was at the heart of a large web of trade that ran north to Egypt's border and south into central Africa. Kush's merchants received leopard skins and valuable woods from the tropical interior of Africa. They traded these items, along with enslaved workers and their own iron products, to places as far away as Arabia, India, China, and Rome. In return, they brought back cotton, **textiles** (TEHK•styls), or woven cloth, and other goods. Kush's merchants used their wealth to build fine houses and public baths like ones they had seen in Rome. C

Kush remained a great trading kingdom for nearly 600 years. Then, another kingdom called Axum (AHK•soom) emerged near the Red Sea in eastern Africa. Axum is located in the present-day country of Ethiopia. Axum gained its strength from its location on the Red Sea. Goods from Africa flowed into Axum. Over time, it served as a trading center for the ancient Mediterranean and East African worlds. Around A.D. 350, the armies of Axum invaded Kush and destroyed Meroë.

✓ PROGRESS CHECK

Explaining How did the use of iron affect Kush?

LESSON 4 REVIEW (CCSS)

Review Vocabulary (Tier 3 Words)

1. What are the characteristics of a *savanna*? RH.6–8.4
2. What are *textiles* used to make? RH.6–8.4

Answer the Guiding Questions

3. ***Explaining*** How did Nubia and Egypt influence one other? RH.6–8.2
4. ***Comparing and Contrasting*** How were the cities of Kush similar to and different from those of Egypt? RH.6–8.2
5. ***Drawing Conclusions*** How did natural resources help make Meroë a great trading city? RH.6–8.2
6. **ARGUMENT** Create an advertisement that could have been used in ancient Egypt and Kush to encourage people to use iron. WHST.6–8.1, WHST.6–8.10

C Critical Thinking Skills

Identifying Discuss as a class the best graphic organizer for identifying the trade relationships between the Kushites and other peoples. Suggest that students draw a Web diagram with the center circle labeled "Kush." Have students work in small groups to draw satellite circles and label them with the names of Kushite trading partners. *(Egypt, southern Africa, India, Arabia, China, and Rome)* Students should then draw arrows to and from the center circle to each smaller one. On the arrows, students should write the goods that were traded or exchanged. For example, the Kushites sent leopard skins, wood, slaves, and iron products to Rome. They received woven cloth and other goods in return. AL ELL **Visual/Spatial**

Have students complete the Lesson 4 Review.

CLOSE & REFLECT

Comparing and Contrasting Have students work in small groups to examine Egyptian and Nubian culture, institutions, and ways of life. Tell students first to brainstorm categories, such as religion, agriculture, and art. Have them consult their textbooks or do research in the library or on the Internet. After they gather their data, ask students to create a Venn diagram that identifies similarities and differences between Egyptian and Nubian civilizations. Have students share their findings with the class.

LESSON 4 REVIEW ANSWERS

1. Savannas are grassy plains that stretch across Africa south of the Sahara.
2. Textiles are used to make clothes and other items, such as sheets and towels.
3. Egypt admired the Nubians' skills in warfare and traded for goods that they needed. Nubian leaders were buried in tombs, much like the pharaohs of Egypt. Nubians also worshiped Egyptian gods and adopted hieroglyphics.
4. Kushite cities had a design and layout similar to the design of cities in Egypt. Like Egyptian cities, Kushite cities contained temples and pyramid tombs. Unlike Egyptian cities, the Kush capital of Meroë contained wood-fueled iron furnaces.
5. The land contained rich deposits of iron ore. The city had access to the Nile River for trade and transportation.
6. Students' advertisements should point out that iron has many uses, including weapons and tools. Iron tools and weapons helped people become more productive farmers and more effective soldiers.

ANSWER, p. 133

✓ PROGRESS CHECK Tools and weapons made from iron were stronger than those made from copper. As a result, the Kushites had stronger weapons for fighting and stronger tools for growing more crops. With these tools, Kush grew militarily and economically.

CHAPTER REVIEW ACTIVITY

Have students create a three-column chart like the one below and write "Ancient Egypt" in one column and "Ancient Kush" in the other. Then lead a discussion that allows students to recall features of daily life, the economy, and key events for each empire. AL

	Ancient Egypt	Ancient Kush
Daily Life		
Economy		
Key Events		

As an alternative, have students make three time lines, one each for the Old Kingdom, Middle Kingdom, and New Kingdom. You may need to assist them with the scale. A data table like the one below may help them organize all of the dates given in the chapter. Make sure students understand that the years get smaller from left to right because they are B.C. dates.

Event	Date

REVIEW THE ENDURING UNDERSTANDINGS

Review the chapter's Enduring Understandings with students.

- *People, places, and ideas change over time.*
- *Cultures are held together by shared beliefs and common practices and values.*

Now pose the following questions in a class discussion to apply this enduring understanding to the chapter.

What features of the geography of the Nile valley influenced the way the people lived? *(Answers may include but are not limited to the following: flooding made farming successful, river provided transportation, river unified the people into one culture and one religion, deserts to the west and east kept out invaders allowing the culture to develop freely, Nile Delta kept out invaders, Mediterranean and Red Sea opened up trade, deposits of iron ore facilitated development of weaponry.)*

What factors made the Egyptian and Kushite culture different from one another? *(location—Nubia's location upriver gave access to cultural traditions from civilizations in central Africa; Egypt was more exposed to Mediterranean cultures; the people of Kush did not experience annual flooding and had access to surrounding land for hunting and farming.)*

CHAPTER 5 Activities 

Write your answers on a separate piece of paper.

1. **Exploring the Essential Question** WHST.6–8.2, WHST.6–8.10
INFORMATIVE/EXPLANATORY Why did ancient Egyptian civilization fail? Write an essay that explains the events and decisions that led to the end of Egypt's role as a political, economic, and cultural power.

2. **21st Century Skills** RH.6–8.2, WHST.6–8.9, WHST.6–8.10
GIVING A PRESENTATION Prepare a presentation that identifies the key events and achievements of Egypt's Old Kingdom, Middle Kingdom, and New Kingdom. Compare and contrast the developments in each time period. End your presentation with a brief statement about the importance of the Egyptian civilization.

3. **Thinking Like a Historian** RH.6–8.2
UNDERSTANDING PROS AND CONS Create a chart like the one here to identify the pros and cons of living along the Nile River. Then write a sentence that tells why early Egyptians settled there.

Characteristics of the Nile River	Pros	Cons
Regular flooding		
Cataracts		
Downhill flow		

4. **GEOGRAPHY ACTIVITY**

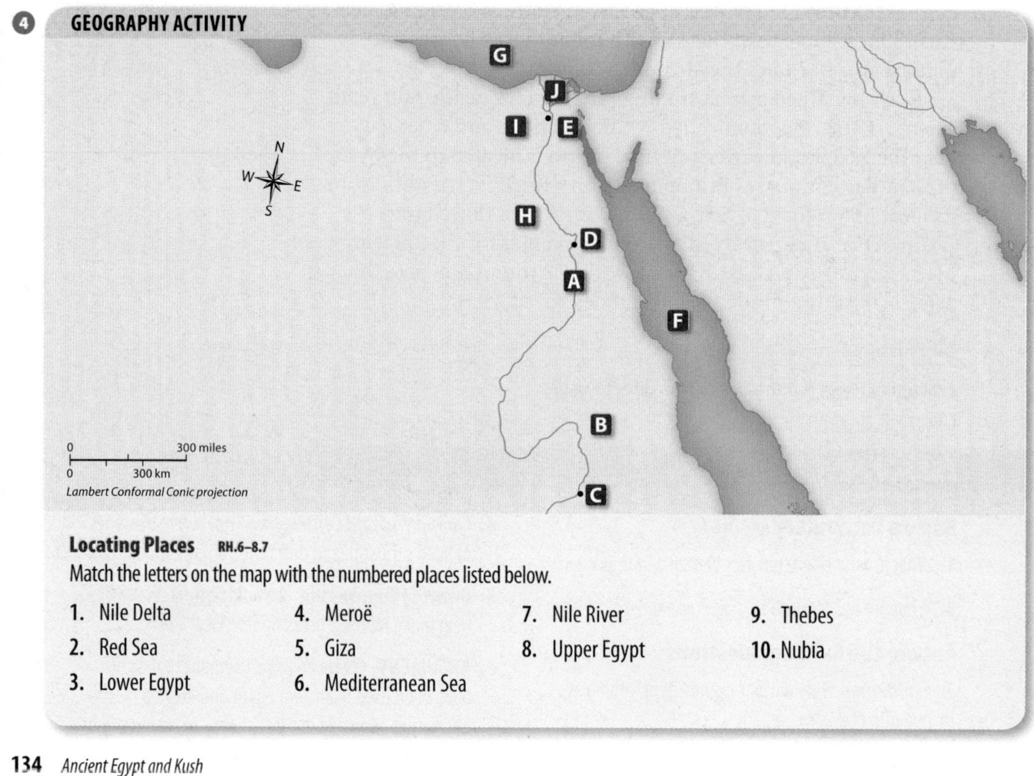

Locating Places RH.6–8.7
Match the letters on the map with the numbered places listed below.

1. Nile Delta
2. Red Sea
3. Lower Egypt
4. Meroë
5. Giza
6. Mediterranean Sea
7. Nile River
8. Upper Egypt
9. Thebes
10. Nubia

Compare and contrast the fall of Egypt with the fall of Kush. *(Kush fell because a culture closer to the Red Sea—Axum—took away most of its trade and eventually invaded and destroyed the Kushite capital of Meroë. Egypt lost its wealth paying for wars, and other regions took advantage of Egypt's weakness to attack and conquer it—the Libyans from the west and the Assyrians from Mesopotamia.)*

ACTIVITIES ANSWERS

Exploring the Essential Question

1. Students should note that Egyptian civilization lasted many centuries and experienced several declines or downturns, but it usually recovered and entered a new period of prosperity and influence. They should identify factors that caused ancient Egypt to decline, such as weak leadership, costly wars, and loss of land, as well as the arrival of other powerful groups, such as the Kushites and Assyrians, who had superior weapons.

CHAPTER 5 Assessment

REVIEW THE GUIDING QUESTIONS

Directions: Choose the best answer for each question.

RH.6–8.2
1. What did the delta of the Nile River provide Egyptians?
   A. trade route to the Mediterranean Sea
   B. protection from invaders
   C. fertile soil for growing crops
   D. regular rainfall

RH.6–8.2
2. Who was responsible for uniting and governing Egypt?
   F. bureaucrats
   G. priests
   H. workers
   I. pharaohs

RH.6–8.2
3. Egyptians built pyramids because they
   A. wished to honor the achievements of their leaders.
   B. desired to please the gods.
   C. hoped to impress later civilizations with their buildings.
   D. wanted to protect the dead pharaohs' bodies.

RH.6–8.2
4. The largest group in Egyptian society was made up of
   F. farmers and workers.
   G. scribes and traders.
   H. artisans and merchants.
   I. army commanders and nobles.

RH.6–8.2
5. What was the main focus of Queen Hatshepsut's rule?
   A. building pyramids
   B. developing trade
   C. preparing for the afterlife
   D. conquering new territory

RH.6–8.2
6. How were Kushites different from the Egyptians?
   F. They produced large amounts of iron.
   G. They built temples and tombs for their kings.
   H. They used a system of writing with hieroglyphics.
   I. They sailed the Nile to reach faraway trading partners.

135

21st Century Skills

2. Students should highlight the historical and cultural events of each time period and be able to compare them. For example, students should mention the establishment of the dynastic system of rule, the development during the Old Kingdom of a religion based on belief in an afterlife, and the empire-building of Hatshepsut, Thutmose III, and Ramses II. Students' presentations should include a statement that summarizes the contributions of Egyptian civilization to world history.

Thinking Like a Historian

3. Graphic organizers should identify advantages and disadvantages. For example, regular flooding meant being displaced, but it also enriched the soil for growing crops. Cataracts provided a natural defense but made travel on the Nile difficult. A northward, downhill flow meant that using the Nile to travel to the Nile Delta and Mediterranean Sea was easy, but traveling to southern Africa on the Nile was difficult.

Locating Places

4. **1.** J **2.** F **3.** I **4.** C **5.** E **6.** G **7.** A **8.** H **9.** D **10.** B

CHAPTER 5 Assessment Answers

ASSESSMENT ANSWERS

Review the Guiding Questions

1. **B** The marshy delta of the Nile prevented invaders from entering Egypt. It did not provide a trade route, fertile soil for growing crops, or regular rainfall. Thus, B is the correct answer.

2. **I** Workers were members of Egypt's lowest social class. They could not be responsible for the government. Priests and bureaucrats performed vital tasks in the Egyptian empire, but ultimately it was the pharaoh's job to unite and govern Egypt. Therefore, I is the correct answer.

3. **D** Egyptians believed in the afterlife; therefore, it was important to preserve a pharaoh's body so that his soul, which resided in his body, could complete the journey through the afterlife. As a result, they built pyramids to protect the pharaohs' bodies from floods, dust and heat, and robbers. Thus, the correct answer is D.

4. **F** Farmers and workers made up the lowest and largest group in Egyptian society. Scribes, traders, artisans, merchants, army commanders, and nobles belonged to groups that made up a smaller percentage of the population. Thus, F is the correct answer.

5. **B** Unlike leaders before and after, Hatshepsut was more interested in improving trading ties with neighboring lands than with starting wars to gain more territory. Trade increased during her reign. Thus, B is correct..

6. **F** Students should understand that the Kushites were greatly influenced by the Egyptians even after Kush had conquered Egypt. The Kushites built cities and burial grounds like those of the Egyptians and adapted the Egyptian writing system. Unlike the Egyptians, however, the Kushites had access to wood and iron ore and built furnaces to produce iron. Therefore, F is correct.

Analyzing Documents

7 **D** In addition to references to sparrows and swooping, the king's speech contains strong words about fighting and courage. He speaks as a person who is confident in his leadership abilities and unafraid of battle. D is the best answer.

8 **H** The poem speaks of strength and victory, so Egyptians probably felt pride when they read or heard it. Thus, H is the correct answer.

Short Response

9 Students should understand that building the pyramids required the labor of many people working together to cut and move large objects and fit them together. As the excerpt suggests, they would have had to cooperate and coordinate their efforts in order to get the work done.

10 Students should understand that the pyramids were massive projects that involved many different structures and required many people to build them. In order to get the pyramids built properly, workers would have needed to organize themselves and plan how and when to work.

Extended Response

11 Students' journal entries should contain descriptive phrases that indicate that Meroë was a busy trading city that was influenced by Egyptian culture. Their entries should include specific details about the layout and design of the city, including the presence of wood-burning iron furnaces.

CHAPTER 5 Assessment (continued)

DBQ ANALYZING DOCUMENTS

RH.6–8.1
7 **Drawing Conclusions** An epic poem describes the victory of King Ramses II over the Hittites.

Then the King spake [spoke] to his squire,
"Halt! take courage, charioteer,
As a sparrow-hawk swoops down on his prey
So I swoop upon the foe [enemy], and I will slay."

—from *Pen-ta-tur: The Victory of Ramses II Over the Khita*

Which word best describes Ramses as he is depicted in the poem?

A. bird-like
B. innocent
C. uncertain
D. courageous

RH.6–8.1
8 **Inferring** How might the Egyptians have reacted to this poem?

F. It made them afraid of their king.
G. It made them regret going to war.
H. It made them feel proud to be Egyptian.
I. It made them worry about losing to the enemy.

SHORT RESPONSE

"To build such monumental structures, the Egyptians needed a highly organized workforce. From tomb inscriptions and from laborers' instructions on walls, [. . .] researchers can now draw something close to a modern personnel chart for the ancient workers. 'Every project like a pyramid had a crew of workers,' explains Ann Roth, an Egyptologist who has studied the groups of workers in detail. 'And each group was responsible for one part of the pyramid complex.'"

— from "The Pyramid Builders" by Virginia Morell

RH.6–8.1
9 How did Egyptian workers cooperate to build the pyramids?

RH.6–8.2
10 Why did workers need to be organized to build the pyramids?

EXTENDED RESPONSE

WHST.6–8.10
11 **Narrative** You are an Egyptian trader visiting the Kush city of Meroë. Write a journal entry in which you describe the city and compare it to your Egyptian home.

Need Extra Help?

If You've Missed Question	1	2	3	4	5	6	7	8	9	10	11
Review Lesson	1	2	2	2	3	4	3	3	2	2	4

networks Online Teaching Options

More Assessment Resources

The *Assess* tab in the online Teacher Lesson Center includes resources to help students improve their test-taking skills. It also contains many project-based rubrics to help you assess students' work.

CHAPTER 6

The Israelites Planner

UNDERSTANDING BY DESIGN®

Enduring Understandings

- *People, places, and ideas change over time.*
- *The value that a society places on individual rights is often reflected in that society's government.*
- *Countries have relationships with each other.*

Essential Questions

- *How do religions develop?*
- *What are the characteristics of a leader?*
- *How does religion shape society?*
- *Why does conflict develop?*

Predictable Misunderstandings

Students may think:

- *Judaism did not influence other world religions.*
- *The Phoenicians made no lasting contributions to world culture.*
- *All the Jewish people supported Roman rule over their homeland.*

Assessment Evidence

Performance Tasks:

- *Hands-On Chapter Project*

Other Evidence:

- *Interactive Graphic Organizer Activities*
- *Geography and History Activity*
- *21st Century Skills Activities*
- *Primary Source Activities*
- *Interactive Whiteboard Activities*
- *Classroom discussions*
- *Summary paragraph*
- *Lesson Reviews*
- *Chapter Activities and Assessment*

SUGGESTED PACING GUIDE

Introducing the Chapter	1 Day	Lesson 3	2 Days
Lesson 1	2 Days	Lesson 4	2 Days
Lesson 2	2 Days	Chapter Wrap-Up and Assessment	1 Day

TOTAL TIME 10 Days

Key for Using the Teacher Edition

SKILL-BASED ACTIVITIES

Types of skill activities found in the Teacher Edition.

V Visual Skills require students to analyze maps, graphs, charts, and photos.

R Reading Skills help students practice reading skills and master vocabulary.

W Writing Skills provide writing opportunities to help students comprehend the text.

C Critical Thinking Skills help students apply and extend what they have learned.

T Technology Skills require students to use digital tools effectively.

*Letters are followed by a number when there is more than one of the same type of skill on the page.

DIFFERENTIATED INSTRUCTION

All activities are written for the on-level student unless otherwise marked with the leveled labels below.

BL Beyond Level

AL Approaching Level

ELL English Language Learners

All students benefit from activities that utilize different learning styles. Many activities are marked as below when a particular learning style is highlighted.

Intrapersonal	**Naturalist**
Logical/Mathematical	**Kinesthetic**
Visual/Spatial	**Auditory/Musical**
Verbal/Linguistic	**Interpersonal**

NCSS Standards covered in "The Israelites"

Learners will understand:

1 CULTURE

4. That the beliefs, values, and behaviors of a culture form an integrated system that helps shape the activities and ways of life that define a culture

5. How individuals learn the elements of their culture through interactions with others, and how individuals learn of other cultures through communication and study

2 TIME, CONTINUITY, AND CHANGE

7. The contributions of key persons, groups, and events from the past and their influence on the present

3 PEOPLE, PLACES, AND ENVIRONMENTS

8. Factors that contribute to cooperation and conflict among peoples of the nation and world, including language, religion, and political beliefs

5 INDIVIDUALS, GROUPS, AND INSTITUTIONS

8. That when two or more groups with differing norms and beliefs interact, accommodation or conflict may result

CHAPTER OPENER PLANNER

Students will know:

- *the differences between monotheism and polytheism.*
- *the beliefs of the ancient Israelites.*
- *the key leaders of the ancient Israelites.*
- *the role of religion in everyday life.*
- *about the Jewish exile in Babylon and the Jews' return to Judah.*
- *what life was like for Jews during Greek and Roman rule.*

Students will be able to:

- ***contrast** religious concepts.*
- ***identify** leaders and key historical figures.*
- ***read** a historical map of Southwest Asia/Canaan.*
- ***analyze** how geography contributes to settlement.*
- ***draw** a map of Canaan or of a dwelling in Canaan.*
- ***analyze** the role of kings in ancient Israel.*
- ***summarize** information about the ancient Israelites.*
- ***read** a map depicting the Jewish exile to Babylon.*
- ***identify** the role of scribes in spreading ideas.*
- ***demonstrate** understanding of Jewish culture and interpret what they learned.*
- ***analyze** how conflicts develop.*
- ***read and interpret** primary sources.*
- ***make** the connection between historical events and religious holidays.*
- ***differentiate** four different Jewish groups under Roman rule.*

UNDERSTANDING BY DESIGN®

☑ Print Teaching Options

V Visual Skills

☐ **P. 138** Students study map and suggest alternate locations for ancient capital of Israelites.

C Critical Thinking Skills

☐ **P. 139** Students study time line and make inferences about Jewish history

☑ Online Teaching Options

V Visual Skills

☐ MAP **The Israelites 1800 B.C. to A.D. 70**—Students examine the political boundaries of important empires that interacted with the Israelites during this time period.

☐ TIME LINE **Place and Time: The Israelites 1800 B.C. to A.D. 70**—Students learn about key historical events that occurred as Judaism grew.

☐ WORLD ATLAS Students can use this interactive map to identify regions of the world, learn about individual countries, locate political boundaries, measure distances, and much more.

☑ Printable Digital Worksheets

R Reading Skills

☐ GRAPHIC NOVEL **The Festival of Lights**—In this graphic novel, a family recounts the events that Hanukkah commemorates and shows how the holiday is celebrated.

Project-Based Learning

Hands-On Chapter Project

Create Presentations

Students research a historical Jewish leader to discover the qualities and experiences that made that person successful. Students will prepare presentations to share with the class.

Technology Extension

Record Multimedia Interviews

- Find an additional activity online that incorporates technology for this project.
- Visit the EdTechTeacher Web sites (included in the Technology Extension for this chapter) for more links and tutorials, and other resources.

Print Resources

ANCILLARY RESOURCES

These ancillaries are available for every chapter and lesson.

- **Reading Essentials and Study Guide Workbook** AL ELL
- **Chapter Tests and Lesson Quizzes Blackline Masters**

PRINTABLE DIGITAL WORKSHEETS

These printable digital worksheets are available for every chapter and lesson.

- **Hands-On Chapter Projects**
- **What Do You Know? activities**
- **Chapter Summaries (English and Spanish)**
- **Vocabulary Builder activities**
- **Guided Reading activities**

More Media Resources

SUGGESTED VIDEOS MOVIES

Watch clips of popular culture films about the Israelites, such as *The Ten Commandments* (1956, Paramount).

Discuss: Can fictional movies accurately capture historical events?

(NOTE: Preview any clips for age-appropriateness.)

SUGGESTED READING

Grade 6 reading level:

- ***Exodus,*** by Brian Wildsmith

Grade 7 reading level:

- ***Words and Miracles: A Passover Companion,*** by Eric A. Kimmel

Grade 8 reading level:

- ***It's a Miracle! A Hanukkah Storybook,*** by Stephanie Spinner

BEGINNINGS

Students will know:
- *the differences between monotheism and polytheism.*
- *the beliefs of the ancient Israelites.*
- *the key leaders of the ancient Israelites.*

Students will be able to:
- ***read** a historical map of Southwest Asia/Canaan.*
- ***analyze** how geography contributes to settlement.*
- ***draw** a map of Canaan or of a dwelling in Canaan.*

UNDERSTANDING BY DESIGN®

Print Teaching Options

V Visual Skills
- [ ] **P. 141** Students evaluate an image of Abraham leading his family to Canaan. AL Visual/Spatial
- [ ] **P. 147** Students create a visual based on the text's description of homes of the Israelites. Visual/Spatial

R Reading Skills
- [ ] **P. 140** Students break down and analyze key vocabulary words. ELL Verbal/Linguistic
- [ ] **P. 142** Students summarize the events leading up to the Exodus. Verbal/Linguistic
- [ ] **P. 144** Students assess the effectiveness of the text describing the Phoenicians. Verbal/Linguistic
- [ ] **P. 146** Students list three ideas that summarize what they read about the Battle of Jericho. Verbal/Linguistic
- [ ] **P. 147** Students analyze a passage from the Hebrew Bible as a primary source.

W Writing Skills
- [ ] **P. 141** Students consider how Judaism influenced other cultures and societies. Intrapersonal
- [ ] **P. 143** Students summarize the main idea or ideas behind the Ten Commandments. AL Verbal/Linguistic

C Critical Thinking Skills
- [ ] **P. 140** Students analyze how Judaism is both ancient and modern. BL
- [ ] **P. 142** Students compare the leadership qualities of Moses and Abraham. BL
- [ ] **P. 143** Students consider the influence of the Ten Commandments. BL
- [ ] **P. 144** Students consider how Canaan's dry climate would affect farming.
- [ ] **P. 145** Students consider factors that made the Phoenicians skilled sailors, traders, and shipbuilders.
- [ ] **P. 145** Students compare the Phoenicians' and Israelites' motivation for settlement in new lands. Intrapersonal

T Technology Skills
- [ ] **P. 143** Students develop presentations about school rules to parallel the Ten Commandments. AL

Online Teaching Options

V Visual Skills
- VIDEO **Assignment Galilee-Israeli Culture**—Students follow a photojournalist who seeks to humanize the land of Israel to promote better understanding.
- CHART **Early Alphabets**—Students click to read how the Phoenician idea of an alphabet has influenced other cultures.
- IMAGE **Jericho**—Students learn more about the Jewish account of the destruction of walls of this city.
- IMAGE **The Ark of the Covenant**—Students click to explore the significance of the chest that held the tablets on which the Ten Commandments were written.
- CHART **History of Phoenician Sailors**—Students click to learn more about the builders of small, sturdy ships.
- SLIDE SHOW **Locusts**—Students are shown how locusts could be considered a plague.
- MAP **The Israelites 1800 B.C. to A.D. 70**—Students learn more about where the Israelites lived.

R Reading Skills
- GRAPHIC ORGANIZER **Taking Notes: *Summarizing:* Ancient Israelites**—Students summarize facts about the ancient Israelites in a graphic organizer.
- BIOGRAPHY **Moses**—Students learn more about this leader of the Israelites.
- PRIMARY SOURCE **The Tabernacle**—Students read an excerpt from Exodus that describes how the tabernacle was supposed to be built.

C Critical Thinking Skills
- WHITEBOARD ACTIVITY **Ten Rules for Our School**—Students work in groups to create a list of 10 rules that they think students should follow.

T Technology Skills
- SELF-CHECK QUIZ **Lesson 1**—Students receive instant feedback of their mastery of lesson content.
- GAME **The Ten Commandments Concentration Game**—Students match descriptions to key vocabulary terms.

Printable Digital Worksheets

W Writing Skills
- WORKSHEET **Geography and History Activity: Human–Environment Interaction: The Israelites and Canaan**—Students respond after reading a description of the land of Canaan and examining a physical map of the area.

LESSON **2 PLANNER**

THE ISRAELITE KINGDOM

Students will know:

- *the key leaders of the ancient Israelites.*
- *the role of religion in everyday life.*

Students will be able to:

- ***identify*** *the role of scribes in spreading ideas.*
- ***demonstrate*** *understanding of Jewish culture and interpret what they learned.*

UNDERSTANDING BY DESIGN®

☑ *Print Teaching Options*

V Visual Skills

- ☐ **P. 151** Students draw flowcharts chronicling the separation between Israel and Judah. **BL** **Visual/Spatial**

R Reading Skills

- ☐ **P. 148** Students use context clues to define the word *anointed.* **ELL**
- ☐ **P. 149** Students analyze the grammatical structure of the David and Goliath story as it appears in their text. **Verbal/Linguistic**
- ☐ **P. 151** Students consider reasons for the split between Israelite tribes.
- ☐ **P. 152** Students find the main idea of the text. **ELL** **Verbal/Linguistic**

W Writing Skills

- ☐ **P. 149** Students describe how they imagine King David's return unfolded. **BL** **Intrapersonal**
- ☐ **P. 150** Students write sentences to practice use of prepositional phrases. **Verbal/Linguistic**

C Critical Thinking Skills

- ☐ **P. 148** Students compare the arguments for and against choosing a king as a leader. **BL** **Intrapersonal**
- ☐ **P. 149** Students infer qualities of King David's character from his story.
- ☐ **P. 150** Students list ways in which both David and Solomon were great kings. **Verbal/Linguistic**
- ☐ **P. 152** Students compare the Israelites and the Samaritans. **AL** **ELL**
- ☐ **P. 152** Students hypothesize roots of conflict between Israelites and Chaldeans. **BL**
- ☐ **P. 153** Students consider the effects of the failed revolt of Judah against Chaldean rule.
- ☐ **P. 153** Students discuss the role of prophets in Judean life and try to think of modern examples. **AL** **Intrapersonal**

T Technology Skills

- ☐ **P. 153** Students create a PowerPoint that shows the role of the prophets in Judean life. **Visual/Spatial**

☑ *Online Teaching Options*

V Visual Skills

- **VIDEO** **The Middle East: A Region of Contrasts**—Students view a video that describes the contrasting landscapes and religious beliefs found in the Middle East.
- **MAP** **Ancient Israel, c. 922 B.C.**—Students explore the political boundaries and locations of cities.
- **CHART** **Twelve Tribes of Israel**—Students click to learn about Jacob's twelve sons, whose descendants became known as the Twelve Tribes of Israel.

R Reading Skills

- **GRAPHIC ORGANIZER** **Taking Notes: *Listing:* King David and King Solomon**—Students list the achievements of King David and King Solomon.
- **BIOGRAPHY** **King David**—Students learn more about this famous king of Israel.
- **IMAGE** **Solomon's Temple**—Students learn about the temple that this king built.
- **SLIDE SHOW** **The Prophets**—Students learn more about four important prophets.

T Technology Skills

- **SELF-CHECK QUIZ** **Lesson 2**—Students receive instant feedback of their mastery of lesson content.

☑ *Printable Digital Worksheets*

W Writing Skills

- **WORKSHEET** **21st Century Skills Activity: Creativity and Innovation: Problem Solving**—Students review the problem-solving process in the context of King David's reign, and then apply the skill to a problem of their own.

THE DEVELOPMENT OF JUDAISM

Students will know:

- *the role of religion in everyday life.*
- *about the Jewish exile in Babylon and the Jews' return to Judah.*

Students will be able to:

- ***demonstrate** understanding of Jewish culture and interpret what they learned.*
- ***identify** the role of scribes in spreading ideas.*

UNDERSTANDING BY DESIGN®

Print Teaching Options

V Visual Skills

- [ ] **P. 156** Students examine a painting of Daniel and consider what it represents.

R Reading Skills

- [ ] **P. 155** Students summarize the paragraph describing the Torah scrolls. **Verbal/Linguistic**
- [ ] **P. 156** Students read a passage from the Hebrew Bible and determine the main idea. **ELL** **Verbal/Linguistic**
- [ ] **P. 157** Students identify the sequence of events in the story of Naomi and Ruth. **Verbal/Linguistic**
- [ ] **P. 158** Students consider synonyms for the word *kosher.* **ELL** **Verbal/Linguistic** **Interpersonal**
- [ ] **P. 159** Students read a passage about Passover and determine the main idea of the text. **AL** **Verbal/Linguistic**

W Writing Skills

- [ ] **P. 154** Students write a short explanation of the likely origins of the words *Jews* and *Judaism.* **Interpersonal**
- [ ] **P. 158** Students write an essay about rules that affect their own lives. **Verbal/Linguistic**

C Critical Thinking Skills

- [ ] **P. 154** Students predict the main idea of the section based on the header. **ELL**
- [ ] **P. 155** Students evaluate the text explaining the importance of the Torah scrolls.
- [ ] **P. 156** Students share examples of communication challenges in their own lives. **AL** **Interpersonal**
- [ ] **P. 157** Students consider how teachings of the Torah affected Jewish behavior.
- [ ] **P. 158** Students suggest reasons why Ruth became a role model for Jewish girls.
- [ ] **P. 159** Students hypothesize why the ritual nature of Passover is important. **BL**

T Technology Skills

- [ ] **P. 157** Students use the Internet to research information about the Torah.

Online Teaching Options

V Visual Skills

- [ ] **VIDEO** **Temple Mount**—Students view a video that explains the significance of the Temple Mount in the old city of Jerusalem.
- [ ] **SLIDE SHOW** **Jewish Heroes**—Students study art and read text to learn about Jewish heroes.
- [ ] **IMAGE** **Jewish Clothing**— Students learn about the significance of certain items of Jewish clothing.

R Reading Skills

- [ ] **GRAPHIC ORGANIZER** **Taking Notes: *Identifying the Main Idea:* Roles of Synagogues and Scribes**—Students describe the roles of synagogues and scribes in the survival of Judaism.
- [ ] **PRIMARY SOURCE** **The Story of Esther**—Students read an extended passage from Esther.
- [ ] **SLIDE SHOW** **Torah Scrolls**—Students examine pictures and read extended text to learn about rituals associated with these holy scrolls.
- [ ] **SLIDE SHOW** **Five Books of the Torah**—Students examine pictures and read extended text to learn about the five books that comprise the Torah.

C Critical Thinking Skills

- [ ] **WHITEBOARD ACTIVITY** **Kosher Foods**—Students classify foods as kosher and non-kosher.

T Technology Skills

- [ ] **SELF-CHECK QUIZ** **Lesson 3**—Students receive instant feedback about their mastery of lesson content.
- [ ] **GAME** **The Development of Judaism Crossword Puzzle**—Students use clues to complete the puzzle with key vocabulary terms.

Printable Digital Worksheets

C Critical Thinking Skills

- [ ] **WORKSHEET** **Primary Source Activity: The Hebrew Bible**—Students read and interpret several passages from the Hebrew Bible.

LESSON 4 PLANNER

THE JEWS IN THE MEDITERRANEAN WORLD

Students will know:

- *what life was like for Jews during Greek and Roman rule.*

Students will be able to:

- ***make** the connection between historical events and religious holidays.*
- ***differentiate** four different Jewish groups under Roman rule.*

UNDERSTANDING BY DESIGN®

☑ Print Teaching Options

V Visual Skills

- ☐ **P. 162** Students create a time line showing the key events in the life of Judas Maccabeus. ELL Visual/Spatial
- ☐ **P. 165** Students create a cause-effect chart based on information from the text. BL

R Reading Skills

- ☐ **P. 160** Students find the main idea in the text. ELL Verbal/Linguistic
- ☐ **P. 161** Students contemplate the influence of Jewish culture on other peoples. ELL
- ☐ **P. 162** Students investigate the origins of Hanukkah and link it to the story of Judas Maccabeus.
- ☐ **P. 163** Students find the main idea of the text. AL Verbal/Linguistic
- ☐ **P. 164** Students predict the outcome of battle between the Zealots and Romans. Verbal/Linguistic
- ☐ **P. 165** Students answer questions about the Western Wall based on their reading. AL
- ☐ **P. 166** Students explain ways in which ben Zaccai helped the Jewish religion to survive to present day.

W Writing Skills

- ☐ **P. 163** Students write short essay on the Essenes and other Jewish groups. Verbal/Linguistic

C Critical Thinking Skills

- ☐ **P. 160** Students develop questions about what might happen when two cultures combine. Interpersonal
- ☐ **P. 161** Students compare Greek rule over Judah with similar situations throughout human history.
- ☐ **P. 164** Students create an idea web about the Dead Sea Scrolls. Verbal/Linguistic
- ☐ **P. 166** Students state central issues behind the actions of Yohanan ben Zaccai. Verbal/Linguistic
- ☐ **P. 166** Students consider reasons for the importance of rabbis during Jewish struggles against the Romans.
- ☐ **P. 167** Students consider the purpose of wording found in the Talmud. Verbal/Linguistic

T Technology Skills

- ☐ **P. 162** Students research the Internet for information about King Herod. Interpersonal

☑ Online Teaching Options

V Visual Skills

- VIDEO **The Temple of Herod**—Students learn about the expansion made by Herod to the Second Temple in Jerusalem.
- MAP **Diaspora**—Students view the extent of the Diaspora.
- IMAGE **The Talmud**—Students click to learn the evolution of this collection of Jewish traditions and teachings.

R Reading Skills

- GRAPHIC ORGANIZER **Taking Notes: *Comparing and Contrasting:* Greek and Roman Rule**—Students complete a Venn diagram by identifying similarities and differences between Greek rule and Roman rule.
- BIOGRAPHY **Judas Maccabeus**—Students learn about this Jewish priest who led the fight against Seleucid rule.
- SLIDE SHOW **Hanukkah**—Students learn the elements of this celebration.
- IMAGE **Battle at Masada**—Students learn of the Zealots' battle against the Romans.
- IMAGE **Dead Sea Scrolls**—Students learn the history of the discovery of the scrolls and hypotheses as to why they were hidden.
- IMAGE **The Western Wall**—Students learn of the importance of the only wall that remains of Herod's temple.

T Technology Skills

- SELF-CHECK QUIZ **Lesson 4**—Students receive instant feedback about their mastery of lesson content.

☑ Printable Digital Worksheets

C Critical Thinking Skills

- WORKSHEET **21st Century Skills: Information Literacy: Sequence and Categorize Information**—Students use a time line as an organizing tool.

INTERVENTION AND REMEDIATION STRATEGIES

LESSON 1 Beginnings

Reading and Comprehension

Instruct students to retell in their own words the journey of the Israelites in this lesson. Where did they begin their journey and with whom? Where were they at the end of the lesson?

Text Evidence

Ask students to work in small groups to answer this question: How did each place where the early Jews lived affect the development of their religion? Have groups share their answers, citing evidence from the text to support their findings.

LESSON 2 The Israelite Kingdom

Reading and Comprehension

Have students explain how the kingdoms of Israel and Judah developed and summarize what happened in each kingdom.

Text Evidence

Have students think of the Israelite kings they've read about in this lesson and make a list of the things the kings had in common, and the things that made each king different and unique, citing evidence from the text as support.

LESSON 3 The Development of Judaism

Reading and Comprehension

Have students write a paragraph using the lesson vocabulary, in which they summarize the content of the lesson.

Text Evidence

Ask students to analyze the role of religion in the Jews' everyday life. Have them list as many reasons as they can from the text that explain and support the different elements of Judaism which come into play each day in the lives of Jews.

LESSON 4 The Jews in the Mediterranean World

Reading and Comprehension

Ask small groups of students to discuss the similarities and differences between the Greeks' and Romans' rule over the Jews. Have them share what they find as a class.

Text Evidence

Have pairs of students summarize what happened during Greek and Roman rule by creating a time line, including dates and events as cited from the text.

Online Resources

Approaching Level Reader

Use this online lower-level text that corresponds directly to the text in the Student Edition. It includes a Spanish version.

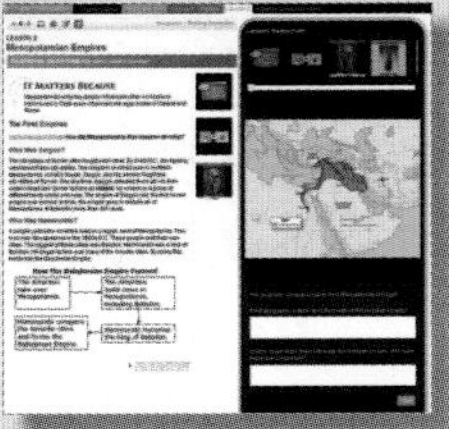

Guided Reading Activities

This resource uses graphic organizers and guiding questions to help students with comprehension.

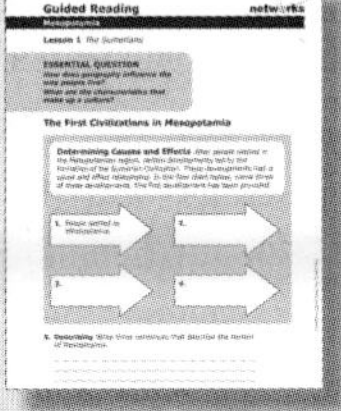

What Do You Know?

Use these worksheets to pre-assess student's background knowledge before they study the chapter.

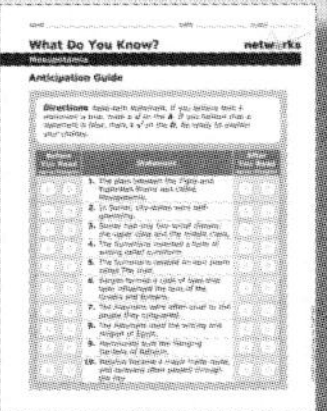

Reading Essentials and Study Guide Workbook

This resource offers writing and reading activities for the approaching-level student. Also available in Spanish.

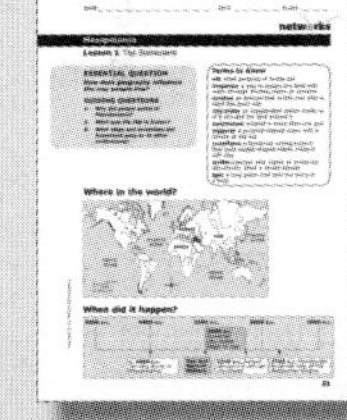

Self-Check Quizzes

This online assessment tool provides instant feedback for students to check their progress.

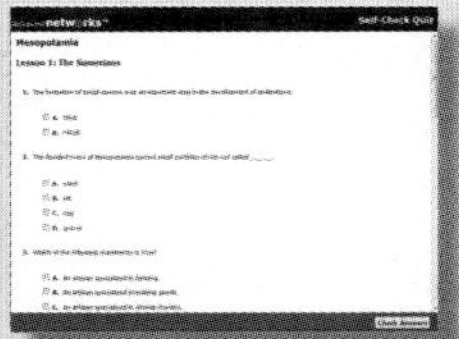

How Do I Teach with
Graphic Novels?

Graphic novels cannot replace reading for content, but they can be used effectively to build a student's background knowledge, to motivate students, to provide a different access route to the content, and to allow students to check and review their work. A variety of graphic novels can be found in the online Teacher and Student Resource Libraries of each McGraw-Hill program.

Teaching Strategy 1 Previewing Content

- Before reading textbook narrative, assign appropriate graphic novels to activate background knowledge.
- Project the digital graphic novel on the classroom whiteboard and discuss it with the class.

Teaching Strategy 2 Narrative and Summary Writing

- Ask students to read one of the graphic novels, paying attention to details and imagery presented in the story.
- Then ask students to write their own summary of the story being told in the graphic novel. This strategy can be especially useful in the graphic novels that are very illustrative and don't use much character dialogue.

Teaching Strategy 3 Improving Content Analysis Skills

- Graphic novels often have a thematic strand that illustrates a specific point about the content being studied. This may take the form of irony, humor, or a more direct and formal approach to an event.
- Have students read a graphic novel with the intention of trying to understand the main point the author is trying to convey. This approach is particularly useful after students have covered the content in the main textbook. Pose these questions to help students uncover the main points:

  a) Why did the author choose this topic?

  b) What does the graphic novel tell me about the people or events we have studied?

  c) Does the author portray the characters in a positive or a negative way?

  d) Is the tone of the story humorous or serious?

  e) What conclusions can I draw about the author's intentions in creating this graphic novel?

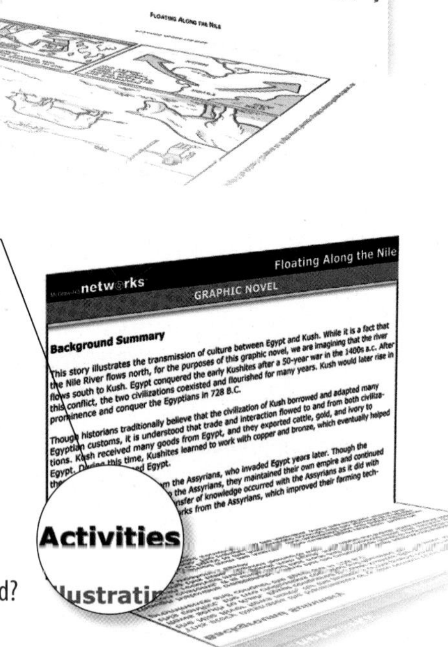

The Israelites

1800 B.C. to A.D. 70

ESSENTIAL QUESTIONS *• How do religions develop? • What are the characteristics of a leader? • How does religion shape society? • Why does conflict develop?*

networks

There's More Online about the lives and customs of the Israelites.

CHAPTER 6

Lesson 1 *Beginnings*

Lesson 2 *The Israelite Kingdom*

Lesson 3 *The Development of Judaism*

Lesson 4 *The Jews in the Mediterranean World*

The Story Matters . . .

David is regarded as the greatest Israelite king, yet he was not born into royalty. David, a shepherd, became a leader of the Israelite people. As their king, he united the Israelites and expanded their lands. He was also the author of the Psalms, or poems often used in prayer and song. David stands as the greatest among many important leaders who guided the Israelites throughout their history.

◄ *As a young man, David was known for his bravery and his skill in playing the lyre, a type of harp.*

137

Letter from the Author

Dear World History Teacher,

Scholars today agree that between 1200 B.C. and 1000 B.C., the Israelites emerged as a distinct group of people. Three leaders—Saul, David, and Solomon—were influential in establishing Israelite control over Canaan. After Solomon's death, tensions between tribes in Israel led to the formation of the kingdom of Israel in the north and the southern kingdom of Judah. The Assyrians conquered Israel in 722 B.C., and Judah fell to the Chaldeans in 586 B.C. Judeans were exiled in Babylon. Later, the Judeans, now known as the Jews, were allowed to return to Jerusalem and rebuild their city.

Jackson J. Spielvogel

ENGAGE

Bellringer Read "The Story Matters . . ." aloud in class or ask for a volunteer to read it aloud. Discuss with students David's rise to greatness.

Ask: Who are some other important historical leaders who rose to power from humble beginnings? Have students share examples with which they are familiar, such as Abraham Lincoln or Andrew Jackson. Then **ask: How do the life stories of historical figures affect how we think about them?** Guide the class in a discussion of this question. Point out that knowing about a historical figure's life can make learning about the events involving that person more interesting or easier to understand. Tell students that they can learn more online about the story of David's life.

Making Connections

Read the following information to students:

It is interesting to know the stories behind the world's great leaders.

- Abraham Lincoln, who served as the 16th president of the United States, was born in a small home in Kentucky, moved to a farm in Indiana, and attended school for less than one year. He educated himself by reading books, and he later studied law and moved into politics. He lost many political races before he became president.
- Mahatma Gandhi, who freed India from British rule, was born into a fairly well-to-do family and was educated in England as a lawyer. Once back in India, he chose to give up his material possessions so that he could connect with the common people and fight for their rights.

TEACH & ASSESS

Step Into the Place

V Visual Skills

Analyzing Maps Project the chapter opener map on the whiteboard and then point to the homelands of the ancient Israelites. Remind students of some geographic features that people might look for when choosing the location of a capital city. Students might suggest features such as a central location or access to water and transportation routes. Have student volunteers analyze the map and identify alternate locations for a capital of the ancient Israelites. Ask each volunteer to explain why Jerusalem might have been chosen over these alternate locations. Next, discuss the Map Focus questions.

Content Background Knowledge

- The land of Canaan lies at the junction of three continents: Asia, Europe, and Africa.
- Canaan's lowest point is the Dead Sea, which lies 1339 feet (408 meters) below sea level.
- It has a Mediterranean climate, which is hot and dry with short, warm, and wet winters. In the desert areas, the high temperatures can reach 114 degrees Fahrenheit (46 degrees C).

CHAPTER 6 CCSS

Place and Time: The Israelites 1800 B.C. to A.D. 70

The ancient Israelites struggled for centuries to build a secure homeland. This was difficult because their location in the eastern Mediterranean region was surrounded by more powerful empires. Their religion, Judaism, became a world religion. It would later influence Christianity and Islam.

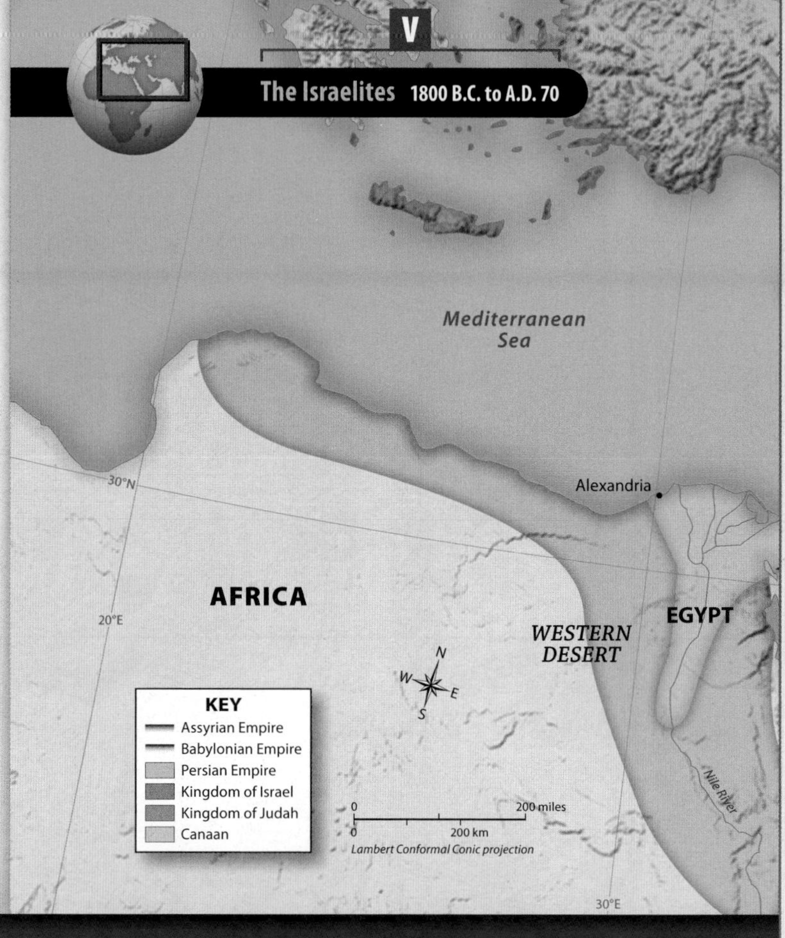

Step Into the Place

MAP FOCUS The Israelites constructed the city of Jerusalem atop seven hills.

LOCATION Look at the map. Where is Jerusalem located relative to the Mediterranean Sea?

1. **REGIONS** Which geographic features surround Jerusalem? RH.6–8.7
2. **LOCATION** Where is Jerusalem located relative to Egypt? RH.6–8.7
3. **CRITICAL THINKING** *Analyzing* Why might the Israelites have chosen Jeruselem for their capital city? RH.6–8.2

Step Into the Time

TIME LINE What was happening to new ideas all over the world as Judaism grew? RH.6–8.7

C

THE ISRAELITES

THE WORLD

3000 B.C.

2000 B.C.

c. 1290 B.C. Moses is reported to lead Israelites from Egypt

c. 1800 B.C. Abraham is said to travel to Canaan

c. 2540 B.C. Egyptians complete building of Great Pyramid

Project-Based Learning

Hands-On Chapter Project

Create Presentations

Students will research a historical Jewish leader to discover the qualities and experiences that made that person successful. Students will participate in a class discussion to identify key qualities possessed by successful leaders. Then students will choose a leader to research. They will use worksheets to help them plan and prepare a presentation on their chosen leader. Next, students will deliver their completed presentations to the class. Finally, students will evaluate their research and presentations using an Assessment Rubric.

Technology Extension

Record Multimedia Interviews

Have students work in pairs to record "interviews" in which they nominate their historical figure for an award. Have them create a video interview with an authentic voice, using the information they gather about their influential Jewish leader. Afterward, students can embed the video in an online page, such as a classroom Web site, classroom newspaper, or a video-sharing site.

ANSWERS, p. 138

Step Into the Place

1. Jerusalem is surrounded by hills and desert. The Dead Sea lies to the east. The Mediterranean Sea lies to the west.
2. Jerusalem is northeast of Egypt.
3. CRITICAL THINKING The hilltops of Jerusalem allowed residents to see approaching attackers.

Step Into the Time

Civilizations in the rest of the world also experienced political changes and the development of religious beliefs.

CHAPTER 6

Place and Time

networks *There's More Online!*

☑ **MAP** Explore the interactive version of this map on NETWORKS.

☑ **TIME LINE** Explore the interactive version of this time line on NETWORKS.

Caspian Sea
Nineveh
Tigris River
CANAAN
Euphrates River
Tyre
Babylon
PERSIA
Yavneh
Samaria
Jericho
Jerusalem
Bethlehem
Dead Sea
Mt. Sinai
ARABIA
Persian Gulf
Red Sea
ARABIAN DESERT
40°E
50°E

- **c. 1000 B.C.** King David rules in Jerusalem
- **c. 722 B.C.** Assyrians destroy northern kingdom of Israel
- **c. 586 B.C.** Chaldeans destroy Jerusalem
- **c. 168 B.C.** Maccabean revolt
- **c. A.D. 66** Jews revolt against Rome
- **c. A.D. 70** Romans destroy temple in Jerusalem

1000 B.C. | 750 B.C. | 500 B.C. | 250 B.C. | A.D. 100 | A.D. 1000

- **c. 700 B.C.** Homer writes the *Iliad* and *Odyssey*
- **c. 530 B.C.** Confucius develops his philosophy in China
- **c. 530 B.C.** Buddhism arises in India
- **c. 330 B.C.** Alexander the Great conquers Persian Empire
- **c. A.D. 55** Paul preaches Christianity in Asia Minor

139

Step Into the Time

C Critical Thinking Skills

Analyzing Time Lines Have students review the time line for the chapter. Point out the beginning and ending dates and several major events, and have students describe how world history and Israeli history coincide. Explain to students that they will be studying events from about 1800 B.C. to A.D. 70. **Ask:**

- **Based on the information listed in the time line, what can you infer about the history of the Israelites after the reign of David?** *(After the reign of David, the history of the Israelites was marked by conflict with various other groups.)*
- **What can you infer about what happened after the Romans destroyed the temple in Jerusalem, based on what you know about Israel and the Jewish people?** *(They probably came back and rebuilt the temple, based on the fact that the Jews have regained footing in Israel, but the temple was never rebuilt, because only the Western Wall was left.)*

CLOSE & REFLECT

Have pairs of students formulate several questions based on the map, the time line, or class discussions about Israel and the Jewish people. Tell students that they will be learning more about the Israelites as they study this chapter.

CHART

The Israelites: What Do You Know?

Assessing Have students complete the What Do You Know? activity, a concept ladder about the Israelites, before they study the chapter. Direct students to read each question. Explain that they will use their prior knowledge to write an answer or a prediction for each question. Encourage students to use these questions as a guide to important themes found in this chapter. After students complete the chapter, have them reread their answers and make any changes or corrections they believe are needed. Ask students who changed their responses to explain why they did so. *(Students should cite facts from the chapter.)*

See page 137B for other online activities.

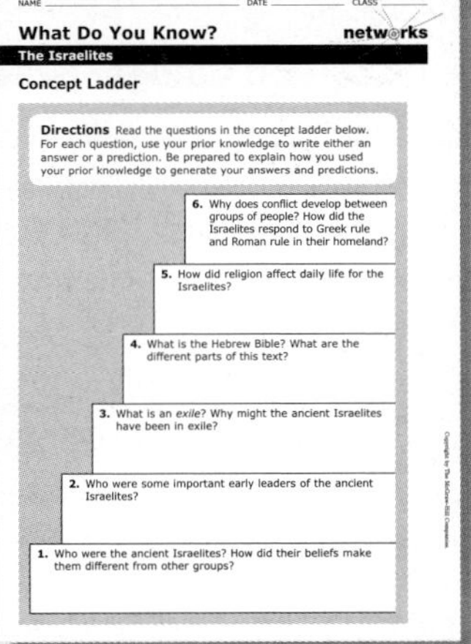

NAME ________ DATE ________ CLASS ________

What Do You Know? networks

The Israelites

Concept Ladder

Directions Read the questions in the concept ladder below. For each question, use your prior knowledge to write either an answer or a prediction. Be prepared to explain how you used your prior knowledge to generate your answers and predictions.

6. Why does conflict develop between groups of people? How did the Israelites respond to Greek rule and Roman rule in their homeland?
5. How did religion affect daily life for the Israelites?
4. What is the Hebrew Bible? What are the different parts of this text?
3. What is an *exile*? Why might the ancient Israelites have been in exile?
2. Who were some important early leaders of the ancient Israelites?
1. Who were the ancient Israelites? How did their beliefs make them different from other groups?

ENGAGE

Bellringer Show students the picture of Moses as a baby on page 142. Have volunteers read aloud the text below the picture. **Ask:** **How do you think Moses was able to preserve his Israelite heritage while living in an Egyptian palace as a prince?** *(Possible answer: He may have heard stories about the Israelites while growing up and may have felt a bond with the people.)* Tell students they will be learning about the religious beliefs of the ancient Israelites as well as the Israelites' settlement in Canaan. Explain that they will also examine how the Israelites' religious beliefs differed from those of earlier groups.

TEACH & ASSESS

C Critical Thinking Skills

Hypothesizing As a class, discuss the idea that Judaism is both an ancient and modern religion. Then, with students in small groups, **ask:**

- **How might a religion change between ancient times and modern times?** *(Students may say that the way it is practiced could become more modern, or that different branches or versions may develop over time.)*
- **What factors might influence those changes?** *(There may be pressure to adapt practices to align with modern society; branches may develop to accommodate different ways of interpreting the religion.)* Have the groups discuss their answers. BL

R Reading Skills

Determining Word Meanings On the board, write the terms *monotheism* and *polytheism.* Discuss the meaning of the root word, *-theism (belief in the existence of a god or gods),* and the prefixes *mono- (one)* and *poly- (many).* Ask students to name other words that use the prefixes *mono-* and *poly- (monogamy, polyglot).* Have students work in small groups to make up several words beginning with *mono-* and *poly- (for example, polycycle)* and share their words' meanings with the class.

ELL **Verbal/Linguistic**

ANSWER, p. 140

TAKING NOTES: Answers may vary. Sample answers: Hebrew Bible: The Torah is the first part of the Hebrew Bible. The Ten Commandments are part of the Torah. The Promised Land: Canaan was the promised land. According to Jewish tradition, God told Abraham to take his family to Canaan, which God promised would belong to Abraham and his descendants forever. Twelve Tribes: The 12 sons of Jacob were the ancestors of the Twelve Tribes. Each son became a leader of one of the tribes.

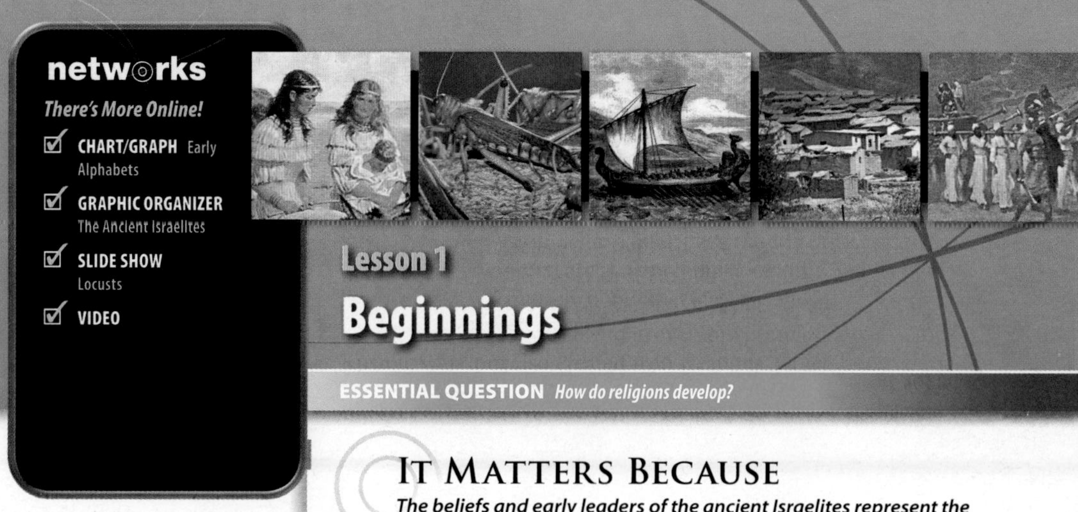

networks *There's More Online!*

- **CHART/GRAPH** Early Alphabets
- **GRAPHIC ORGANIZER** The Ancient Israelites
- **SLIDE SHOW** Locusts
- **VIDEO**

Lesson 1

Beginnings

ESSENTIAL QUESTION *How do religions develop?*

IT MATTERS BECAUSE

The beliefs and early leaders of the ancient Israelites represent the foundations of Judaism.

Beginnings

GUIDING QUESTION *What did the ancient Israelites believe?*

C You probably have heard of the religion of Judaism (JOO•dee•ih•zuhm). You may not know, however, that it is both an ancient and modern religion. Many ancient societies worshipped many deities, or gods. The worship of more than one god is called polytheism. A group of people in Southwest Asia known as the Israelites (IHZ•ree•ah•lites) were different. Unlike other **cultures** of the day, they worshipped only one God.

The Israelites believed that God sent **prophets** (PRAH•fehts), or messengers, to share God's word with the people. The prophets communicated to the Israelites that their God created and ruled the world. They argued that God is very powerful but also just and good. The prophets wanted the Israelites to understand that God expects goodness from his people.

The prophets also believed that every individual could connect personally to God through prayer, religious study, and good and just acts. The belief in one all-powerful, just, R and personal God is called **monotheism** (MAH•nuh•thee•ih•zuhm). The practice of monotheism made Judaism unique among ancient religions.

Reading **HELP**DESK 

Taking Notes: ***Summarizing***

Use a diagram like this one to list at least two facts about each category. RH.6–8.2

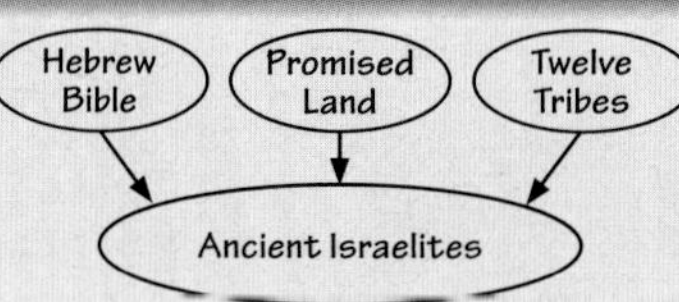

Content Vocabulary (Tier 3 Words)

- **prophet**
- **monotheism**
- **tribe**
- **Exodus**
- **covenant**
- **Torah**
- **commandment**
- **alphabet**

networks ***Online Teaching Options***

VIDEO

Assignment: Galilee–Israeli Culture

Analyzing Visuals Follow a photojournalist who is helping the world understand the people of Israel. On her journey, she photographs a religious celebration of Hasidic Jews and brings light to their traditions, devotion, and rituals.

Point out the photograph in the video of the Hasidic Jew dancing by the fire. Discuss with the class what makes that picture a good representation of the traditions and spirituality of Judaism.

See page 137C for other online activities.

The Hebrew Bible

The Israelites recorded their beliefs and history. These writings became known as the Hebrew Bible or Tanakh (TAH•nahk). Through the Hebrew Bible, the beliefs and faith of the ancient Israelites lived on to become the religion of Judaism. The followers of Judaism are today known as Jews.

Although the original Israelite population was small, their influence was great. Judaism played an important part in the development of two other major monotheistic religions—Christianity and Islam. Christians call the Hebrew Bible the Old Testament. Christianity grew directly out of Judaism. Islam also accepted many of Judaism's beliefs and practices. Through the Hebrew Bible, Judaism influenced the values, ethics, and principles of many other societies.

Abraham

Around 1200 B.C. great changes took place in the Mediterranean region. Egypt's empire ended, and new peoples, including the Israelites, created kingdoms in the region. The early Israelites depended on herding and trading to survive. According to the Hebrew Bible, Abraham and his family migrated from Mesopotamia and settled in Canaan (KAY•nuhn) along the Mediterranean Sea. Today, the countries of Lebanon, Israel, and Jordan occupy the land that was once Canaan.

According to Jewish belief, the ancestors of the ancient Israelites were a man named Abraham and his family. The Hebrew Bible gives this account of Abraham's family and the early history of the Israelites. The Hebrew Bible states that God told Abraham to journey to Canaan, which would belong to Abraham and his descendants forever. According to the Hebrew Bible, Abraham, his wife Sarah, and their entire household accepted God's promise and settled in Canaan. The land is often called the Promised Land because of God's promise to Abraham.

V The Hebrew Bible says that Abraham led his family to Canaan. In addition to his role in Judaism, Abraham is regarded as an important figure in Christianity and Islam.

Tom Lovell/National Geographic Society Image Collection

prophet a messenger sent by God to share God's word with people
monotheism a belief in one God

Academic Vocabulary (Tier 2 Words)
culture the beliefs and behaviors of a group of people

MAP

Israelites 1800 B.C. to A.D. 70

Reading a Map Point out to students that the city of Ur in Mesopotamia, one of the cities where Abraham lived, was located between Babylon and what we now call the Persian Gulf. Have students find that location on the map. Then point out the area by the Mediterranean Sea where Abraham and his family arrived at the end of their journey to Canaan. Tell them that one of the places Abraham lived was in Shechem, not far from where the city of Jerusalem is on the map. Have students drag the map scale to estimate the approximate distance between Ur and Shechem. *(approximately 600–700 miles)*

See page 137C for other online activities.

W Writing Skills

Argument The text says that throughout the Hebrew Bible, Judaism influenced the values, ethics, and principles of many other societies. Have students each write an argument telling whether they believe this assertion is true and, if so, how they think this influence of other societies occurred. Have students support their claims with what they know about the ethics and principles in the stories of the Bible and those of societies and cultures with which they are familiar. **Intrapersonal**

V Visual Skills

Analyzing Images Have students study the painting that depicts Abraham leading his family to Canaan. **Ask:**

- From this image, what can you tell about Abraham and his family? Did they have wealth and possessions, or were they poor? *(fairly wealthy)*
- Were they rushing to escape from something or moving toward something of promise? *(moving toward something)*
- How might they have made their living? *(perhaps by raising animals and herding)*
- What type of land did they travel through? *(desert)*
- What may the temperature have been like? *(hot)*
- What types of problems might they have encountered? *(heat, lack of shelter, not enough food, exhaustion)* **AL** **Visual/Spatial**

Content Background Knowledge

- According to the Hebrew Bible, Abraham was probably a semi-nomadic tent dweller, meaning he had a base camp where he grew crops but he moved around throughout the year, living in a tent. He owned flocks, silver, gold, and slaves.
- According to the Hebrew Bible, Abraham lived in the city of Ur in Mesopotamia. Upon leaving Mesopotamia, Abraham and his family walked hundreds of miles to Canaan, along the Mediterranean Sea.

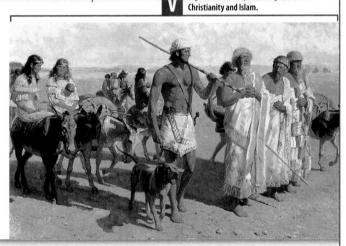

C1 Critical Thinking Skills

Analyzing Primary Sources The text cites several of the 10 plagues sent by God, as described in the Hebrew Bible. Other plagues include water turning to blood and darkness descending upon the Egyptians. These may seem more miraculous than based on science. **Ask: Do you accept the Hebrew Bible as a factual source of information? Why or why not?** Lead a discussion about the different interpretations of the Hebrew Bible—as hard facts, as teachable stories, or a combination.

C2 Critical Thinking Skills

Comparing Discuss with students the qualities Moses showed (1) as he listened to the call from God to tell the pharaoh to let the Israelites go and (2) when he led the Jews out of Egypt. Review Abraham's qualities as a leader. **Ask: How were Abraham and Moses similar?** *(Possible answer: They were prophets who led people to settle in new lands.)* BL

R Reading Skills

Explaining Direct students to read the section titled "Moses and the Exodus." As they read, ask students to list the events that led to the Israelites' flight from Egypt. Once students have compiled their lists, ask them to use the list to explain how these events led to the Exodus. **Verbal/Linguistic**

BIOGRAPHY

Moses (c. 14th–13th century B.C.)

According to the Hebrew Bible, Moses, as a baby, was floated down the Nile River. He was born in Egypt to an Israelite woman enslaved by the pharaoh. After the pharaoh demanded all newborn Israelite boys be killed, Moses's mother hid him in a basket to float on the Nile. The pharaoh's daughter rescued him and adopted him.

▶ **CRITICAL THINKING**
Explaining What important leadership traits did Moses show?

Isaac and Jacob

After Abraham died, his son Isaac and later his grandson Jacob headed the family. An angel gave Jacob the new name of Israel, which means "one who struggles with God." Later Jacob's descendants were called "Israelites." As stated in the Hebrew Bible, Jacob's 12 sons became the leaders of **tribes** (TRYBS), or separate family groups. Jacob's sons were the ancestors of the Twelve Tribes of Israel.

After living in Canaan for many years, Jacob's family left because of a famine. They migrated to Egypt and lived there in peace for several generations. As the Israelite population increased, however, the Egyptian pharaoh grew uneasy. He feared that one day the Israelites would rebel. To prevent this, the Egyptians reduced the Israelites to slavery.

Moses and the Exodus

The Israelites were forced to work at hard labor, so they prayed to God to be set free. According to the Hebrew Bible, an Israelite prophet named Moses turned out to be their deliverer. While tending sheep in the wilderness outside Egypt, Moses saw a bush in flames. God called to Moses from the burning bush. He told Moses to tell the pharaoh to let the Israelites go.

C1 Moses went before the pharaoh to demand the release of the Israelites. When the pharaoh refused, the Hebrew Bible says that God sent 10 plagues upon Egypt. These plagues were events that caused problems for the Egyptians, such as **locusts** devouring the fields or outbreaks of disease. The plagues convinced the pharaoh to free the Israelites. After the Israelites left Egypt for Canaan, the pharaoh decided to send his army to pursue them. C2 R

When the Israelites reached the Red Sea, there was no way to cross the waters. According to the Hebrew Bible, God parted the Red Sea to let his people cross to the other side. When the pharaoh's army tried to follow, the waters flooded back and drowned them. The departure of the Israelites out of slavery in Egypt is known as the **Exodus** (EHK•suh•duhs). Jews celebrate a holy festival called Passover to remember their freedom from slavery.

The Covenant

On their way from Egypt, according to the Hebrew Bible, the Israelites received a **covenant** (KUHV • uh • nuhnt), or agreement with God. In the agreement, God promised to return the Israelites

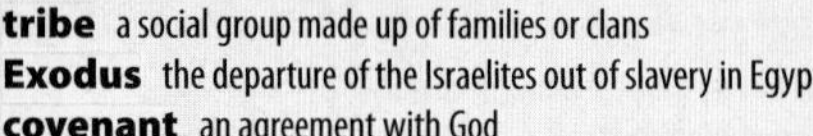

Reading HELPDESK CCSS

tribe a social group made up of families or clans
Exodus the departure of the Israelites out of slavery in Egypt
covenant an agreement with God

Visual Vocabulary
locust a grasshopper that often migrates in large numbers

networks Online Teaching Options

SLIDE SHOW

Locusts

Discussing Present the interactive feature on locusts. Ask volunteers to share their responses to the discussion question. Point out that a plague of locusts can completely destroy crops. Loss of crops would have been extremely disruptive in a society such as ancient Egypt in which agriculture was an important economic activity. ELL

See page 137C for other online activities.

ANSWER, p. 142

CRITICAL THINKING He showed courage by demanding the Israelites' release from the pharaoh.

THE TEN COMMANDMENTS

W

1. Do not worship any god except me.
2. Do not . . . bow down and worship idols.
3. Do not misuse my name.
4. Remember the Sabbath Day and keep it holy.
5. Honor your father and your mother.
6. Do not murder.
7. Be faithful in marriage.
8. Do not steal.
9. Do not testify falsely [tell lies] about others.
10. Do not want anything that belongs to someone else.

—**Paraphrased** from Exodus 20:3-17

The Hebrew Bible says Mount Sinai is where Moses received the tablets containing the Ten Commandments and other teachings.

INFOGRAPHIC

FINDING THE MAIN IDEA What is the main idea of the fourth commandment?

CRITICAL THINKING
Identifying Which commandments address family relationships?

safely to Canaan and they promised to follow God's teachings. Moses climbed to the top of Mount Sinai (SY • ny). There, as God's chosen leader, he received teachings from God. Known as the **Torah** (TAWR • uh), these teachings later became part of the Hebrew Bible.

The Torah made clear what God considered to be right and wrong. One important part of the Torah is the Ten **Commandments** (kuh•MAND•muhnts).

Loyalty to God is the central idea of the Ten Commandments. The name of God was never to be misused. The Israelites were not to worship any other gods or images. This belief that there is only one God became the basis for both Christianity and Islam. T

In addition, the Ten Commandments later helped shape the moral principles of many nations. Think about the laws and rules we have today and how they might relate to these commandments. For example, the principles on which many laws are based, such as rules against stealing or killing, come from the Ten Commandments. The Ten Commandments also promoted social justice and a feeling of community. They contribute to the democratic belief that laws should apply equally to all. C

The Ark of the Covenant was a wooden chest, overlaid in gold, that held the tablets on which the Ten Commandments—part of God's covenant with the Israelites—appeared.

✔ PROGRESS CHECK

Comparing and Contrasting How did the Israelites' beliefs differ from the beliefs of most other ancient peoples?

Torah teachings that Moses received from God; later became the first part of the Hebrew Bible
commandment a rule that God wanted the Israelites to follow

W Writing Skills

Informative/Explanatory Ask students to read the Ten Commandments listed and write a paragraph explaining what they believe to be the main idea or ideas behind the Commandments. Have them include at least three reasons to support their thesis and write a strong concluding statement. **AL Verbal/Linguistic**

T Technology Skills

Collaborating Review with students that the central idea of the Ten Commandments is loyalty to God. **Ask: What would be the central idea of the 10 rules that you write for your school?** *(Answers may vary but could include that the central idea of these rules should be school safety and/or success.)* Have students create a list of 10 rules that they think students at their school should follow. Encourage students to refer to the central idea they have chosen as they write their rules for the school. Discuss the list and determine the order in which each rule should be listed. Have students create a PowerPoint presentation listing their 10 school rules. Discuss how these rules could help make their school a better place to study and learn. **AL**

C Critical Thinking Skills

Drawing Conclusions Ask: Why are the Ten Commandments considered an influential list of rules? *(Possible answer: The ideas in the Ten Commandments shaped the principles on which many laws, rules, and morals are based even today. For example, many places have laws against stealing and killing. Laws such as these originate in the Ten Commandments. Other important principles such as justice, community, and equality also have roots in the Ten Commandments.)* **BL**

GAME

The Ten Commandments—The Israelites

Applying Allow students to play this concentration game as a timed activity in order to practice reading quickly and to reinforce their knowledge of the text.

See page 137C for other online activities.

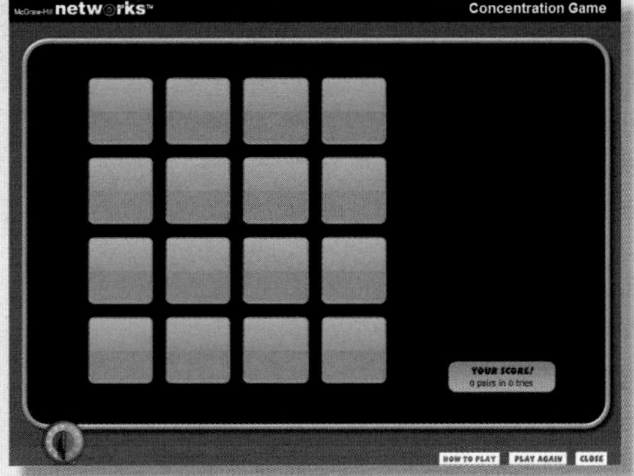

ANSWERS, p. 143

INFOGRAPHIC

1. The main idea of the fourth commandment is that the Israelites were to set aside the Sabbath for worship and not use the day for other activities.
2. **CRITICAL THINKING** The fifth commandment instructs children to honor their parents. The seventh commandment tells people to be faithful to their husbands and wives.

✔ PROGRESS CHECK The Israelites believed in a single, just, all-powerful God. Many other ancient peoples believed in worshiping many deities.

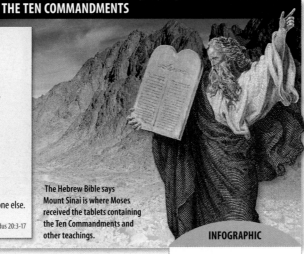

C Critical Thinking Skills

Determining Cause and Effect Explain that Canaan was very rocky and dry and that most people there were herders. Remind students that many Israelites were farmers. **Ask:** **How do you think the environment of Canaan shaped the way the Israelites farmed?** *(Possible answers include: The lack of water required the farmers to adapt and conserve water. Farmers may have raised crops that could grow in very dry climates.)*

R Reading Skills

Listing Review the text that introduces the Phoenicians. **Ask:** **Does the text answer the questions *who, what, when, where, why,* and *how* as it gives us information about the Phoenicians?** Have students list the answers to each of these questions. Discuss whether they think the text was effective in conveying this information. **Verbal/Linguistic**

The Phoenicians' small, yet durable, ships influenced shipbuilding for centuries. Phoenician sailors also helped advance the use of astronomy in navigation.

▶ CRITICAL THINKING
Differentiating How do the Phoenician ships appear to be similar to and different from contemporary ships?

North Wind/North Wind Picture Archives

The Land of Canaan

GUIDING QUESTION ***How did the Israelites settle Canaan?***

The Hebrew Bible states that Moses died before the Israelites reached the land God had promised them. A new leader named Joshua guided the Israelites into Canaan, but they found other people living there. These peoples included the Canaanites (KAY•nuh•NYTS) and—somewhat later—the Philistines (FIH•luh•STEENS). Unlike the Israelites, these people of Canaan worshipped many gods and goddesses. They also had different ways of life.

Who Were the Canaanites?

C Nomadic tribes probably settled in Canaan as early as 3000 B.C. At first, most of the people were herders. They journeyed with their flocks of sheep and other animals from pasture to pasture. Later, they settled in villages, farmed the land, and learned to trade.

R Many different groups lived in Canaan. One Canaanite group was the Phoenicians (fih•NEE•shuhns). The Phoenicians lived in cities along the Mediterranean Sea in northern Canaan. Located near a major waterway, the Phoenicians were skilled sailors and talented traders. They used the sun and the stars to plot long sea voyages. Well-built Phoenician ships with oars and sails carried trade goods across the Mediterranean Sea to Greece, Spain, and even western Africa. Phoenician sailors may even have traveled as far as the British Isles in northwestern Europe.

Reading HELPDESK (CCSS)

alphabet a set of letters or other characters used to write a language

networks Online Teaching Options

CHART

History of Phoenician Sailors

Using Digital Tools Have students use this interactive flowchart to learn more about the history of Phoenician sailors. **Ask:** **What characteristics of the Phoenicians indicate that they were skilled sailors?** *(The Phoenicians used the sun and stars to plot long voyages. They also built ships that had oars and sails that were able to travel great distances.)* BL

See page 137C for other online activities.

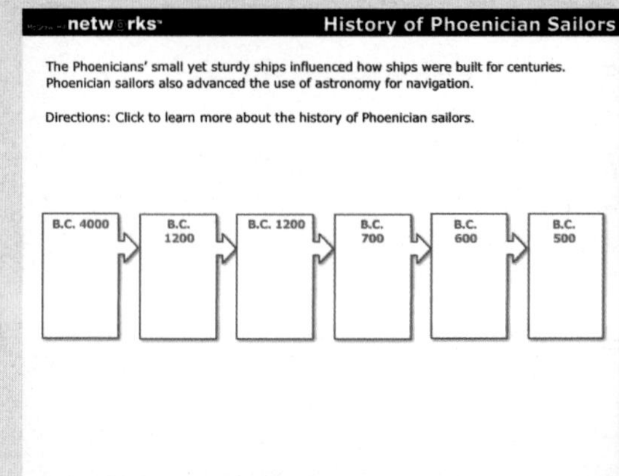

ANSWER, p. 144

CRITICAL THINKING Answers will vary, but students should correctly identify features of the ship in the image to highlight similarities to and differences from modern ships.

The Phoenicians soon controlled Mediterranean shipping and trade. At various ports, they exchanged cedar logs, glass, and jewelry for tin and other precious metals. One of the most valued Phoenician products was cloth colored with a beautiful purple dye. This dye was **extracted** from shellfish along the Phoenician coast.

As they traded, the Phoenicians founded settlements throughout the Mediterranean world. Carthage, a settlement on the coast of North Africa, in time became the most powerful city in the western Mediterranean.

As a result of these settlements, Phoenician ideas and goods spread to other peoples. Think what your life might be like without written language. One of the Phoenicians' important contributions was an **alphabet** (AL•fuh•beht), or a group of letters that stand for sounds. The letters could be used to spell out the words in their language. The alphabet made writing simpler and helped people keep better records.

Philistines

Another group in Canaan, the Philistines, migrated from near present-day Greece. They were one of the groups known as the "Sea People" who invaded the Mediterranean area about 1200 B.C. The Philistines set up five walled towns in southern Canaan along the Mediterranean coast. They were skilled in making iron tools and weapons, which helped them create the strongest army in Canaan. The Philistines kept their own language and religion. Still, they accepted many ideas and practices from their neighbors in Canaan.

Connections to **TODAY**

Alphabets

The Phoenicians began using the alphabet as a way to keep track of trade. Later, the Greeks adapted the Phoenician alphabet. From the Greek alphabet, the Romans created their alphabet. The Roman alphabet is the most widely used writing system in the world today.

EARLY ALPHABETS

INFOGRAPHIC

Modern Characters	Ancient Phoenician	Ancient Hebrew	Ancient Greek	Early Roman
A	≮ ⊬	⊀	ᗅ A A	ᗰ ᐱ A
B	ᒧ 9	ϥ 9	9 Ƀ	B B
G	7 ʒ	7 1	‹ Γ 7 1	C G
D	◁ ɑ	9 ◁	Δ ◁ A	ᐅ D
E	Ǝ	Ǝ	Ǝ ₣ Є	E
F		Y	Ƭ F Ꮯ	F
Z	Z		I	Z
TH	⊗		⊙	
I	Ր ᙁ	ᘔ	ʅ ƨ	I

The Phoenician alphabet contained 22 letters. Unlike our alphabet today, it was written from right to left.

▶ **CRITICAL THINKING**

Making Inferences How would the lack of written language have made trade more difficult for ancient people?

Academic Vocabulary (Tier 2 Words)

extract to remove by a physical or chemical process

Reading in the Content Area

Tables organize information in a way that helps you remember it. To read a table, look first at the title and headings. Ask yourself questions such as "How is the information organized? What is the table trying to show me?"

G1 Critical Thinking Skills

Analyzing Tell students that the Phoenicians were known as skilled sailors, talented traders, and excellent ship builders. **Ask: What geological feature of Canaan contributed to these skills?** *(access to the Mediterranean Sea)*

G2 Critical Thinking Skills

Making Comparisons Ask students to compare the Phoenicians' motivation in founding new settlements with that of the Israelites who were settling in Canaan. **Ask: What did each group want, and why? How were the Israelites different from the Phoenicians in their motivations and how were they the same?** *(Students may say the Phoenicians were more motivated by accruing material goods and wealth and the Israelites were more motivated by finding a place in which they could survive and practice their religion.)* **Intrapersonal**

Making Connections

Discuss with students the variety of reasons that people move and settle into new places. Have students make a list of the reasons their family or other families they know have moved to new places. Then have them list the reasons other groups in history have moved. These may include conquest, survival, increased trade, and freedom to practice religion. Ask students how many of these reasons are similar in concept and how many of them are different.

CHART

Early Alphabets

Discussing Show students the interactive chart that includes the Phoenician alphabet. Click on the visual to learn more about the meaning of the term *alphabet.* Encourage students to share and discuss their responses to the discussion question. **Ask: Which of the alphabets shown do you think most closely resembles the modern alphabet? What might this resemblance suggest about the alphabet you chose?** *(Possible answers: The early Roman alphabet most closely resembles the modern alphabet. This likely suggests that the early Roman alphabet is the most recent of the other alphabets shown. It might also suggest that the modern alphabet evolved most directly from this alphabet.)* **AL** **ELL**

See page 137C for other online activities.

networks — Alphabet

EARLY ALPHABETS

Modern Characters	Ancient Phoenician	Ancient Hebrew	Ancient Greek	Early Roman
A	≮ ⊬	⊀	ᗅ A A	ᗰ ᐱ A
B	ᒧ 9	ϥ 9	9 Ƀ	B B
G	7 ʒ	7 1	‹ Γ 7 1	C G
D	◁ ɑ	9 ◁	Δ ◁ A	ᐅ D
E	Ǝ	Ǝ	Ǝ ₣ Є	E
F	/	Y	Ƭ F Ꮯ	F
Z	Z		I	Z
TH	⊗		⊙	
I	Ր ᙁ	ᘔ	ʅ ƨ	I

ANSWER, p. 145

INFOGRAPHIC

CRITICAL THINKING The lack of written language would have made it difficult to identify or label items being traded. It would have made communication about things like shipping and prices challenging.

R Reading Skills

Summarizing Ask students to list three important ideas that would allow them to summarize what they have read on this page. *Sample answer:*

1. *The Israelites believed it was God's will that they fight for the land.*
2. *Joshua helped the Israelites take the city of Jericho in battle.*
3. *Other leaders, called judges, helped their tribes fight, and together they destroyed other forces in Canaan.*

Have students provide answers in their own words but also indicate specific passages in the text that they are paraphrasing. **Verbal/Linguistic**

T Technology Skills

Researching on the Internet Ask students to formulate a question about Joshua and the battle of Jericho. Then have students use the Internet to research and find the answer to their question. An example of a question to research might be: *How many people lived in the city of Jericho at the time of the battle?* Instruct students to explore multiple sources to substantiate the answers that they find.

Military Conquest

Because other groups lived in the region, the Israelites faced a challenge establishing Canaan as their new homeland. They believed, however, that it was God's will that they claim the land. Joshua led them in a series of battles to conquer Canaan.

The Hebrew Bible tells about the battle at the city of Jericho. There, Joshua told the Israelites to march around the city walls. For six days, they marched while priests blew their trumpets. On the seventh day, according to the account:

PRIMARY SOURCE

> “Joshua commanded the people, "Shout, for the LORD has given you the city. . . . At the sound of the trumpet, when the people gave a loud shout, the wall collapsed.”
>
> —from the Hebrew Bible, the book of Joshua, 6: 16–20

The Israelites took control of the city after the walls of Jericho crumbled.

According to the Hebrew Bible, Joshua led the Israelites in other battles. Any land they seized was divided among the 12 tribes. After Joshua died, political and military leaders called judges ruled the tribes. The judges settled disputes. They also led troops into battle. The Hebrew Bible tells of a woman judge named Deborah, who was admired for her wisdom and bravery. She told the commander Barak (Buh•RAHK) to attack the army of the Canaanite king Jabin. Deborah went to the battlefield as an adviser. With her help, Barak and 10,000 Israelites destroyed the Canaanite forces.

Jericho is one of the oldest continuously inhabited sites in the world. Here we see an illustration of the Hebrew Bible story of Joshua bringing down the walls of the city.

Reading HELPDESK (CCSS)

Academic Vocabulary (Tier 2 Words)

ensure to make certain or make sure of

networks Online Teaching Options

IMAGE

Jericho

Summarizing Have pairs of students look at the text and image in this feature and summarize to each other all that they know about Jericho. **Interpersonal**

See page 137C for other online activities.

Life in Canaan

After many battles, the Israelite tribes won control of the hilly region of central Canaan and settled there. Most Israelites farmed and herded animals. The land was rocky and dry, with little water. So during the rainy season, farmers collected the rainwater. They stored it in small caves or under the ground. They used the stored water to irrigate crops such as olives, flax, barley, and grapes.

V Imagine a rocky countryside dotted by square white houses. Most Israelites lived in houses with two levels. The walls of the houses were made of mud-brick or stone plastered with mud and white-washed. Floors were made of clay. Wooden beams supported a flat, thatched roof, covered with clay. During the day, people cooked and did household chores in the home's lower level. At night, donkeys and goats bedded down there. The family slept on the upper level.

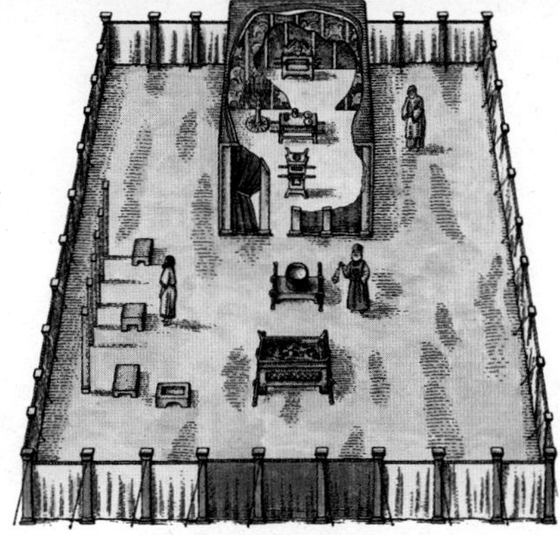

The ancient tabernacle was a tent constructed from beautiful tapestries, or woven fabric, that were decorated with angels. It was an elaborate structure, containing a courtyard and two rooms. The measurements of the structure were said to have come directly from God, according to the Hebrew Bible.

Dorling Kindersley/Getty Images

The Tabernacle

R According to the Hebrew Bible, the Israelite tribes worshipped God in a large tent-like structure called the tabernacle (TA•buhr•na•kuhl). The Israelites believed that the tabernacle housed God's presence. This structure was taken down and put away as the Israelites moved from place to place. In Canaan, they erected the tabernacle at a religious center called Shiloh.

The Hebrew Bible says that the tabernacle housed a sacred object called the Ark of the Covenant. The ark, a gold-covered wooden chest, held tablets, or stone slabs. The Israelites believed that the Ten Commandments were written on these tablets. The Israelites believed the ark was a sign of God's presence and that having it with them in battle would **ensure** victory.

✓ PROGRESS CHECK

Identifying Who were the Phoenicians, and what was their major contribution to world civilization?

LESSON 1 REVIEW (CCSS)

Review Vocabulary (Tier 3 Words)

1. Describe the difference between *monotheism* and *polytheism*. RH.6–8.4

Answer the Guiding Questions

2. ***Describing*** What subjects are covered in the Hebrew Bible? RH.6–8.1
3. ***Explaining*** How did the Israelites settle Canaan? RH.6–8.2
4. ***Summarizing*** What is the central theme of the Ten Commandments? RH.6–8.2
5. ***Identifying*** Which group living in Canaan included skilled sailors and traders? RH.6–8.2
6. **INFORMATIVE/EXPLANATORY** Moses was chosen to lead the Israelites out of Egypt. Write a paragraph to explain the qualities you think Moses possessed to undertake this difficult task. WHST.6–8.2, WHST.6–8.10

LESSON 1 REVIEW ANSWERS

1. Monotheism is the worship of one god. Polytheism is the worship of two or more gods.
2. The history and religious beliefs of the Israelites are covered in the Hebrew Bible.
3. They fought the Canaanites to return to their promised land.
4. Loyalty to God is the central theme of the Ten Commandments.
5. The Phoenicians were the group living in Canaan, and they included skilled sailors and traders.
6. Answers will vary, but students might note that Moses was a strong, brave, and fair leader; his faith in God was unique.

V Visual Skills

Creating visuals Read aloud the second paragraph on this page and ask students to visualize the countryside and homes described. Have students draw (or construct three-dimensionally, using art supplies) the setting and home described in the paragraph. AL Visual/Spatial

R Reading Skills

Describing Direct students to read the section titled "The Tabernacle." Discuss the tabernacle's importance to the Israelites. Then read the following quotations from the Hebrew Bible:

"Make the tabernacle with ten curtains of finely twisted linen and blue, purple and scarlet yarn, with cherubim woven into them by a skilled worker. All the curtains are to be the same size. . . . Join five of the curtains together, and do the same with the other five. Make loops of blue material along the edge of the end curtain in one set, and do the same with the end curtain in the other set.

. . . Make curtains of goat hair for the tent over the tabernacle—eleven altogether."
From Exodus 26:1–5,7, Christian Old Testament translation (NIV)

Ask: **How would you describe the tabernacle based on this quotation? Explain its purpose.** *(The tabernacle was a large, tent-like structure that served as the place of worship for the Israelites and as the place where they believed God's presence was found.)* **What does this quote tell about the importance of the tabernacle?** *(Because the instructions are so detailed, the tabernacle must be very important.)*

Remind students that they should complete the lesson's Taking Notes graphic organizer.

Have students complete the Lesson 1 Review.

CLOSE & REFLECT

Lead students in a brief discussion in which they summarize the places where the Israelites lived during this period of history and how their experience in each place affected the development of Judaism.

ANSWER, p. 147

✓ PROGRESS CHECK The Phoenicians were skilled shipbuilders and traders who lived in northern Canaan; their major contribution to the world was their alphabet.

ENGAGE

Bellringer Direct students' attention to the Taking Notes graphic organizer on the first page of Lesson 2. Point out the names of the Israelite leaders. **Ask:** **Based on the information in the graphic organizer, what do you think will be the main ideas of this lesson?** *(Answers may include that the focus will be the early kings of the Israelites as well as the divisions that grew among the Israelites over time.)* Ask students why good leaders are important. *(Leaders can help groups through difficult challenges and periods of change.)* AL

TEACH & ASSESS

C Critical Thinking Skills

Comparing and Contrasting Compare the arguments the Israelites may have used for choosing a king as a leader with those that Samuel used in warning the Israelites they should not have a king as a leader. **Ask:** **Which argument do you think is stronger? Why? Do you think the Israelites made the right choice in deciding to have a king?** *(Answers will vary, but students should be able to back their opinions with reasonable arguments.)* BL **Intrapersonal**

R Reading Skills

Using Context Clues Ask students to define the word *anointed* as it is used in the text. Have them find context clues in the sentence to help them define the word. *(The sentence states that Samuel poured holy oil on Saul to show that God blessed him. Therefore this must be what it means to anoint.)* ELL

ANSWER, p. 148

TAKING NOTES: King David drove the Philistines out, created an empire, built Jerusalem, and wrote many psalms. King Solomon built the Temple in Jerusalem and brought peace to the region.

networks
There's More Online!
- CHART/GRAPH — Twelve Tribes of Israel
- GRAPHIC ORGANIZER — King David and King Solomon
- SLIDE SHOW — Israelite Prophets

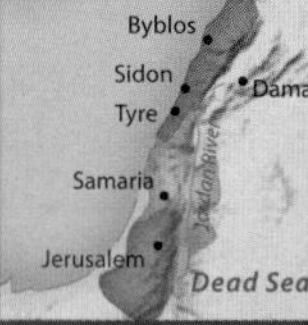

Lesson 2
The Israelite Kingdom

ESSENTIAL QUESTION *What are the characteristics of a leader?*

IT MATTERS BECAUSE

The Israelites were ruled by several important kings. After this time, they were divided into two kingdoms and faced threats from neighboring empires.

Early Kings

GUIDING QUESTION *What was the role of kings in Israelite history?*

By 1100 B.C., the Israelites had settled much of the land of Canaan. They developed a prosperous culture, creating an alphabet and a calendar based on Canaanite ideas. Yet one powerful enemy—the Philistines—remained. When the Philistines moved inland from the Mediterranean Sea, they came into conflict with the Israelites. Many Israelites called for a king to unite the Twelve Tribes and lead them in battle against the Philistines.

Saul: The First King

C According to the Hebrew Bible, the Israelites asked the judge Samuel to choose a king. Samuel, though, warned that a king would tax them and enslave them. The Israelites, however, still demanded a king so Samuel chose a young man named Saul R (SAWL). Samuel anointed Saul as king, pouring holy oil on him to show that God had blessed him.

Under Saul's leadership, the Israelites won many battles against the Philistines. With each victory, Saul gained greater fame. Later, however, Saul lost the support of the people. According to the Hebrew Bible, Saul disobeyed some of God's commands.

Reading HELPDESK CCSS

Taking Notes: *Listing*

Use a chart like this one to list the achievements of King David and King Solomon. RH.6–8.2

King David	King Solomon

Content Vocabulary (Tier 3 Words)
- psalm
- exile
- proverb

networks *Online Teaching Options*

VIDEO

The Middle East: A Region of Contrasts

Informative/Explanatory Play the video for students. This video shows the Middle East as the birthplace of the Western religions of Christianity, Judaism, and Islam as well as a land of many cultures and contrasts: deserts; lush, green hills and valleys; ultramodern cities; and ancient towns.

Discuss the video with students. Then ask them to write a short analysis of why the Middle East has so many different cultures, religions, and contrasts. **Verbal/Linguistic**

See page 137D for other online activities.

The Twelve Tribes of Israel were family groups. According to the Hebrew Bible, each family descended from a son of Jacob. Scholars note that family connections and a common religion bound the tribes together long before they united under David.

C God then instructed Samuel to choose and anoint another king. Samuel chose a young shepherd named David.

King David

Even before he became Israel's king, David had won praise for his bravery. The Hebrew Bible provides an account of David and his victory over Goliath, a giant Philistine warrior. In a bragging fashion, Goliath dared any Israelite to **R** fight him one-on-one. Young David stepped forward with his shepherd's staff, a slingshot, and five smooth stones. With a heavy spear in hand, Goliath rushed forward. David hurled one stone straight at the giant's forehead. Goliath dropped dead.

Impressed by David's skill, King Saul placed his army under David's command. As David won more and more victories, the women of Israel sang his praises: "Saul has slain his thousands, and David his tens of thousands." Then, seized by jealousy, Saul tried to kill David, but David escaped. When Saul died in battle against the Philistines, David returned and became king. **W**

According to the Hebrew Bible, once David was in power, he united the Israelite tribes. David and his army defeated the Philistines. He then established a capital city for Israel at Jerusalem (juh•ROO•suh•lehm). The Israelites built their capital in the hill country away from the coast. A fine musician and poet, David is believed to have written many of the sacred songs found in the Hebrew Bible's Book of **Psalms** (SALMZ)—also found in the Christian Bible. One of the most famous is Psalm 23, which begins:

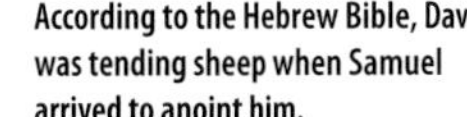
According to the Hebrew Bible, David was tending sheep when Samuel arrived to anoint him.

PRIMARY SOURCE

> "The LORD is my shepherd, I shall not be in want.
> He makes me lie down in green pastures,
> he leads me beside quiet waters,
> he restores my soul.
> He guides me in the paths of righteousness [fairness]
> for his name's sake."
>
> —Psalm: 23:1–3

psalm a sacred song or poem used in worship

C Critical Thinking Skills

Making Inferences Tell students that according to the Hebrew Bible, David had to be called in from the fields where he was tending his sheep when Samuel arrived to anoint him as king. Review the information about David's background and achievements, as well as life in Israel under his rule. **Ask: How would you describe David before he was king?** *(Possible answer: David was courageous when he fought Goliath, and he came from humble beginnings.)*

R Reading Skills

Identifying Ask students to identify the verbs used in the description of David's battle with Goliath. **Ask:**

- **Are most of these verbs active verbs or passive verbs?** *(active)*
- **How does the use of active verbs affect the way this section sounds when you read it?** *(It makes the section more exciting to read because of the sense of action.)* **Verbal/Linguistic**

W Writing Skills

Narrative Ask students to imagine what the scene might have been like when David returned home to become king after Saul died in battle. Have them write a paragraph describing the scene. Ask them to use strong action verbs in their sentences, as were used in the scene describing the battle between David and Goliath. **BL** **Intrapersonal**

Making Connections

- By 1100 B.C., many Israelites called for a king to unite the Twelve Tribes. David eventually became the second king of the Israelites and became known as the greatest king of the Israelites.
- One thing King David was known for was his ability to solve problems. For example, when he became king, the Israelite tribes were divided, and the kingdom also faced a threat from the Philistines. David gained recognition by uniting the Israelites and defeating the Philistines. **Ask: Why would the ability to solve large problems be important for a successful leader?** *(Answers may vary but should include that leadership is about helping others reach a common goal. Large obstacles usually surface along the way to any significant goal. Therefore, the ability to solve problems and remove obstacles is essential for any successful leader.)* **BL**
- Tell students that the ability to solve problems can lead to success in many areas of life, and that they probably solve problems every day at home, at school, and elsewhere. Have students think about the steps they take to solve problems.

IMAGE

Twelve Tribes of Israel

Using Digital Tools Jacob, the grandson of Abraham, had twelve sons. The descendants of these sons later became known as the Twelve Tribes of Israel. Have students click on each box to reveal Jacob's descendants.

See page 137D for other online activities.

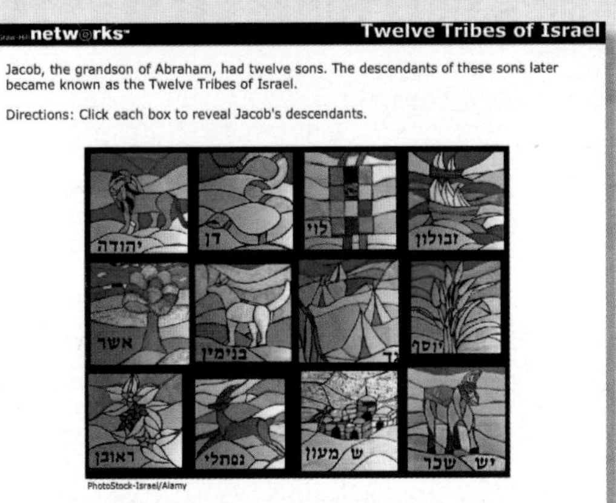

The Israelite Kingdom

C Critical Thinking Skills

Identifying Evidence Ask students to identify the evidence given in the text that shows David and Solomon to be good kings. Have students create a two-column chart, writing in each column the evidence they've found that supports each king being great. **Verbal/Linguistic**

W Writing Skills

Informative/Explanatory Remind students that writing is a way of learning and demonstrating understanding. Read the sentence beginning with *Through trade and treaties . . .* Have students identify the prepositional phrase *(Through trade and treaties)* and the main part of the sentence *(Solomon brought a long period of peace to the region).* Ask students to rewrite the sentence putting the prepositional phrase at the end. Have students create three sentences in which they practice both beginning and ending with the prepositional phrase. Point out that the exercise not only requires students to exercise writing skills but also causes them to consider the relationship between ideas in the text and conditions and events in the historic period. **Verbal/Linguistic**

Solomon built the First Temple on a site David had selected, the Temple Mount. The spot had religious significance. It was the place, according to the Hebrew Bible, where Abraham had tried to sacrifice Isaac.

Under David's rule, the Israelites enjoyed prosperous times. Farmers cultivated the tough, dry land by building terraces on the steep hillsides. Terraced fields are strips of land cut out of a hillside like stair steps. Terraces prevented soil from washing down the hillside when it rained. After David's death, the Israelites honored him as their greatest king, as do Jews today. King David's son Solomon (SAH•luh•muhn) became the next Israelite king around 970 B.C. **C** **W** Through trade and treaties with other peoples, Solomon brought a long **period** of peace to the region. He constructed many cities and, according to the Hebrew Bible, built the first temple in Jerusalem. Built of fragrant cedar wood and costly stone, Solomon's temple—also called the First Temple—held the Ark of the Covenant and other sacred objects.

King Solomon was also known for his wisdom. He is believed to be the author of **proverbs** (PRAHV•uhrbz), or wise sayings, that are recorded in the Hebrew Bible. Solomon shared his proverbs in hopes of helping his people:

PRIMARY SOURCE

> "Whoever walks in integrity walks securely,
> but whoever takes crooked paths will be found out."
>
> —Proverbs: 10:9

Despite Solomon's accomplishments, many Israelites turned against him. They did not like working on his building projects or paying the high taxes he demanded. After Solomon's death around 922 B.C., the Israelites entered a troubled period in their history. Deep disagreements split their kingdom. In addition, powerful neighbors threatened their survival.

✓ PROGRESS CHECK

Evaluating Why did the Israelites believe David was their greatest king?

Reading HELPDESK (CCSS)

proverb a wise saying

Academic Vocabulary (Tier 2 Words)

period a division of time that is shorter than an era

networks Online Teaching Options

IMAGE

Solomon's Temple

Drawing Conclusions Present the interactive feature on King Solomon. Click the image to read the information provided. **Ask:** Why was Solomon considered wise? *(Solomon used unusual methods to find the truth.)*

See page 137D for other online activities.

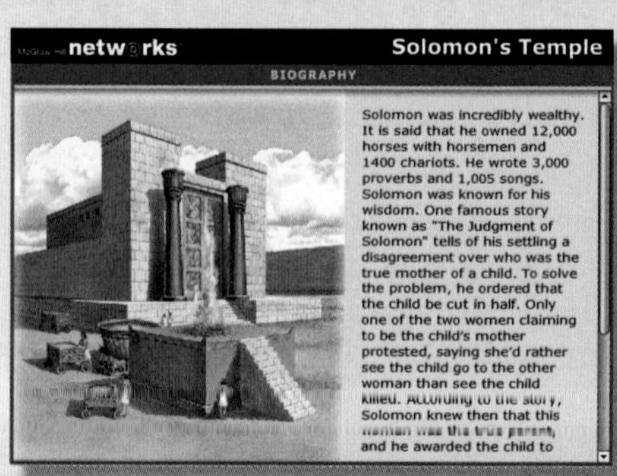

ANSWER, p. 150

✓ PROGRESS CHECK David united the Twelve Tribes of Israel, defeated the Philistines, and established Jerusalem as the capital city of his kingdom.

Two Kingdoms

GUIDING QUESTION *How did neighboring empires respond to the Israelites?*

After Solomon's death, the ten northern tribes rebelled against the government in Jerusalem. These tribes **founded** a separate kingdom, Israel. Its capital was Samaria. The two tribes in the south founded the smaller kingdom of Judah (JOO•duh). Judah's capital was Jerusalem. Although split politically, the people of Israel and Judah preserved the Israelite religion.

R

During this time, large empires formed around Israel and Judah. As you read previously, the Assyrians and the Chaldeans built powerful empires. Their rulers wanted to control the trade routes that ran through the Israelite kingdoms. Small and weak, the kingdoms of Israel and Judah felt threatened by their powerful neighbors.

V

The Fall of Israel

The Assyrians spread fear throughout the region. They forced conquered peoples to pay tribute. If they did not receive tribute, the Assyrians destroyed towns, burned estates, and carried away all valuable goods. Then they forced the conquered people to move to different areas to start new settlements.

When the kingdom of Israel refused to pay tribute, the Assyrians invaded Israel in 722 B.C. The Assyrians captured major cities, including the capital at Samaria. They wanted absolute control.

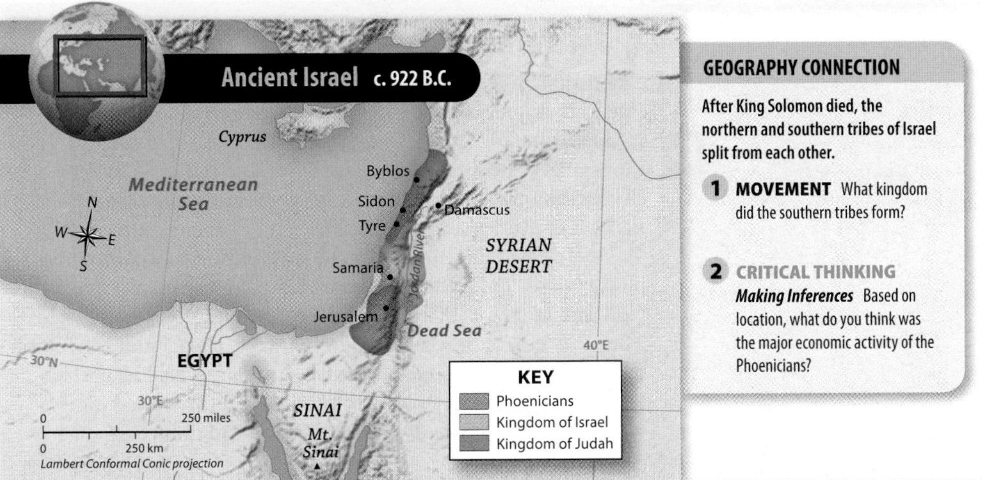

GEOGRAPHY CONNECTION

After King Solomon died, the northern and southern tribes of Israel split from each other.

1. **MOVEMENT** What kingdom did the southern tribes form?
2. **CRITICAL THINKING** ***Making Inferences*** Based on location, what do you think was the major economic activity of the Phoenicians?

Academic Vocabulary (Tier 2 Words)

found to set up or establish

R Reading Skills

Describing Direct students' attention to the text about the split between the Israelite tribes. **Ask: How did this split occur?** *(After Solomon's death, the 10 northern tribes rebelled against the government in Jerusalem. The northern tribes founded a separate kingdom called Israel. The two southern tribes established a smaller kingdom called Judah.)*

V Visual Skills

Creating Visuals Ask students to draw a flow chart that chronicles the separation of Israel and Judah through the time when Israel is conquered by the Assyrians. *(Charts should include the formation of the Assyrian and Chaldean empires, attempts to control trade routes, spreading of fear and destruction of towns by the Assyrians, the Israelites' refusal to pay tribute, and the final conquering of Israel by the Assyrians.)* Have students share their flow charts with a partner. BL **Visual/Spatial**

MAP

Ancient Israel, c. 922 B.C.

Analyzing Visuals Remind students that the Israelites split into two kingdoms following the death of their third king, Solomon. Show students the map of ancient Israel. Click on the map key to view the locations of the different kingdoms of Israel. **Ask:**

- **To which Israelite kingdom would the Phoenicians have posed a greater threat?** *(Israel)*
- **What body of water was east of Judah?** *(the Dead Sea)* Ask students to use the information on the map to draw their own simple outline map of the split between Israel and Judah. Tell students to add labels for Israel, Judah, Jerusalem, and Samaria to their maps. AL ELL

See page 137D for other online activities.

ANSWERS, p. 151

GEOGRAPHY CONNECTION

1. They formed Judah.
2. **CRITICAL THINKING** The Mediterranean was important to the tribes for trade and transportation.

R Reading Skills

Finding the Main Idea Have students carefully read the second paragraph on this page. **Ask:**

- **What is the main idea of the text in the second paragraph?** *(The Samaritans and Israelites had different religious practices.)*
- **What structure does the text use to show this? Is it arranged mainly in a sequence structure, a cause-and-effect structure, or a compare/contrast structure?** *(compare/contrast)*
- **What word in the paragraph gives us a clue to the structure?** *(however)* ELL **Verbal/Linguistic**

C1 Critical Thinking Skills

Comparing and Contrasting Direct students to review the final paragraph in the section on the fall of Israel. **Ask: How were the Israelites and the Samaritans alike and different?** *(Like the Israelites, the Samaritans worshiped the God of Israel, read the Torah, and followed religious teachings. However, the Samaritans also adopted religious practices that the Israelites did not accept. Over time, the two groups grew more and more different.)* AL ELL

C2 Critical Thinking Skills

Hypothesizing Ask students why they think the conflicts may have developed between the Chaldeans and the Israelites and why the Chaldeans forced the Israelites to leave Jerusalem and move to Babylon. *(The Chaldeans may have wanted to show their control over Jerusalem, and they saw the Israelites as a threat.)* BL

ANSWER, p. 152

CRITICAL THINKING Both deal with the nature, or behavior, of God.

CHART

ISRAELITE PROPHETS

Jeremiah was one of several prophets. The Israelites believed the prophets brought them the word of God.

▶ **CRITICAL THINKING**
Comparing What do the teachings of Hosea and Jeremiah have in common?

Name	Time Periods	Teachings
Elijah	874–840 B.C.	Only God should be worshipped—not idols or false gods.
Amos	780–740 B.C.	The kingdom of King David will be restored and will prosper.
Hosea	750–722 B.C.	God is loving and forgiving.
Isaiah	738–700 B.C.	God wants us to help others and promote justice.
Micah	735–700 B.C.	Both rich and poor have to do what is right and follow God.
Jeremiah	626–586 B.C.	God is just and kind—he rewards as well as punishes.
Ezekiel	597–571 B.C.	Someone who has done wrong can choose to change.

So they forced some of the Israelites to resettle in the Assyrian Empire. Assyrians then brought in people from other parts of their empire to live in Israel. These settlers mixed with the Israelites still living there. A new mingled culture developed. These people became known as Samaritans.

R C1 The Samaritans adopted many of the Israelites' religious beliefs. They worshipped the God of Israel, read the Torah, and followed the Israelites' religious laws. The Samaritans, however, adopted religious practices that the Israelites did not accept. In time, the Samaritans and the people of Israel had little in common. Today's Judaism developed from the religious practices preserved mainly in the kingdom of Judah.

The Fall of Judah

C2 The people of Judah **survived** the Assyrian conquests, but their freedom did not last. In 597 B.C., the Chaldeans under King Nebuchadnezzar (NEHB•uh•kuhd•NEHZ•zuhr), forced thousands of people to leave Jerusalem and live in Babylon (BAB•uh•lahn), the Chaldean capital. Nebuchadnezzar chose a new king, a Judean, to rule Judah.

At first, Judah's king did as he was told. Soon, however, he plotted to set Judah free. A prophet named Jeremiah warned that God did not want Judah to rebel, but the king refused to listen. The king led the people of Judah to revolt. The Chaldeans retook Jerusalem in 586 B.C. Nebuchadnezzar then leveled Jerusalem to the ground. He destroyed the temple, captured the king, and took him and thousands of Judah's people to Babylon.

Reading **HELP**DESK CCSS

exile a forced absence from one's home or country

Academic Vocabulary (Tier 2 Words)

survive to continue to live; to live through a dangerous event

networks ***Online Teaching Options***

IMAGE

The Prophets

Identifying Points of View Have students view the interactive slide show. Discuss with the class why the prophets' teachings might remain relevant today. Guide students to understand that the prophets' belief in a just society remains an important topic of discussion and debate. **Ask: What was the prophets' point of view on being faithful to God?** *(The prophets argued that being faithful to God meant more than going to a temple to worship. They also believed that it was important to live a moral life and help others connect with God.)*

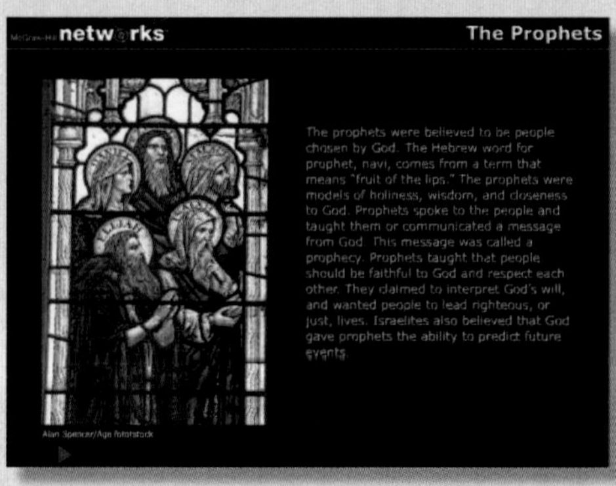

See page 137D for other online activities.

In Jewish history, this time became known as the Babylonian **Exile** (EHG•zyl). When people are exiled, they are forced to leave their home or country. Psalm 137 in the Hebrew Bible describes the sadness many of Judah's people felt in living far away from their homeland:

PRIMARY SOURCE

"By the rivers of Babylon we sat and wept. . . .
How can we sing the songs of the LORD while in a foreign land?
If I forget you, O Jerusalem, may my right hand forget its skill.
May my tongue cling to the roof of my mouth if I do not remember you,
if I do not consider Jerusalem my highest joy . . ."

—Psalm 137:1–6

What Was the Prophets' Message?

The prophets had an important role in Judean life. They offered words of hope in times of despair. At other times, the prophets explained that the people were not obeying God. They urged people to change their ways and make the world a better place.

The prophet Amos said, "But let justice roll on like a river, righteousness like a never-failing stream!" This means that all people should work for a just society in which everyone is treated fairly. Dr. Martin Luther King, Jr. quoted the prophet's words in the 20th century in his "I Have a Dream" speech. The goal of a just society later became a primary part of the teachings of Christianity and Islam. Jewish prophets also stressed the importance of leading a moral life and helping others in order to connect with God.

✓ PROGRESS CHECK

Identifying What empires conquered Israel and Judah?

LESSON 2 REVIEW (CCSS)

Review Vocabulary (Tier 3 Words)

1. How might reading a series of *proverbs* affect people? RH.6–8.4

Answer the Guiding Questions

2. ***Explaining*** Why was it important that King David united the tribes of Israel? RH.6–8.2
3. ***Explaining*** How did Solomon's death affect the Israelites? RH.6–8.2
4. ***Identifying*** Which group mixed with the Israelites to form the Samaritan culture? RH.6–8.2
5. ***Identifying*** What was the Babylonian Exile? RH.6–8.2
6. **NARRATIVE** The Jews were exiled and forced to spend 70 years in Babylon. If you were forced to live far away from your homeland, how would you react to your situation? Write a journal entry describing your thoughts about being forced to live away from your homeland. WHST.6–8.10

LESSON 2 REVIEW ANSWERS

1. Proverbs are short, wise sayings meant to reinforce good behavior. Reading a series of proverbs might cause people to examine their behavior and possibly change.
2. By uniting the Israelites, King David led them into a new and prosperous era in which they defeated the Philistines and established a capital city in Jerusalem.
3. After Solomon's death, the Israelite tribes split into two separate kingdoms—Israel and Judah.
4. The Assyrians mixed with the Israelites to form the Samaritan culture.
5. The Babylonian Exile was the deportation, or forced move, of as many as 10,000 Jews to Babylon.
6. Answers will vary, but students should demonstrate thoughtful consideration of the experience of living in exile. They might refer to living in an unfamiliar place, facing difficult conditions, or confronting intolerance.

G1 Critical Thinking Skills

Determining Cause and Effect Ask students to consider not only the sequence of events of the exile of Judah's people, but also how the people were affected by it. **Ask:** **How did Judah's failed revolt against Chaldean rule affect the people of Judah?** *(After the revolt failed, Nebuchadnezzar destroyed Jerusalem and took many of Judah's people to live in the Chaldean capital of Babylon.)*

G2 Critical Thinking Skills

Making Comparisons Discuss with students the role of the prophets in Judean life. **Ask:** **In our life today, do we have people who are like the prophets, offering hope in times of despair? Who are those people in our lives today?** *(some political leaders, and people who take on roles as Dr. Martin Luther King, Jr. did in our history)* AL **Intrapersonal**

T Technology Skills

Making Presentations Guide students to recognize that today's Judaism developed from the religious practices preserved mainly in the kingdom of Judah. Explain that the prophets played an important role in Judean life. Have students use the information from the text and from online research to create a PowerPoint presentation that shows the role they believe the prophets played in Judean life. If time allows, have students share their presentations with the class. **Visual/Spatial**

Have students complete the Lesson 2 Review.

CLOSE & REFLECT

Have students write a paragraph summarizing what they have learned from this lesson about the important people and events of the early Israelites. Ask volunteers to read their summary paragraphs aloud to the class. Invite the class to discuss whether these summaries differ, and if so, students should consider which facts are essential to include in a summary. Summaries should focus on which facts are essential to understanding the lesson content. BL

ANSWER, p. 153

✓ PROGRESS CHECK First the Assyrians conquered the Jewish people, and then the Chaldeans did.

The Development of Judaism

ENGAGE

Bellringer Remind students that in Lesson 2 they learned that the people of Judah were sent to live in exile in Babylon after being captured by the Chaldeans. Discuss with students some of the reasons that groups of people might be forced into exile. Guide students to understand that exile is usually the result of political factors. Explain that in this lesson they will learn about the important figures and events surrounding the movements of the Jews into and out of exile in Babylon.

TEACH & ASSESS

W Writing Skills

Informative/Explanatory Review the first paragraph of text on this page. **Ask: How do you think the terms *Jews* and *Judaism* came about during this period?** Assign students to write a paragraph explaining how they believe the Jews came to be called Jews. Remind students to make their explanations clear and informative. *(Possible answer: When the people were away from Judah, the Babylonians referred to them as* Judeans *and the word* Judean *may have become shortened to* Jew.*)* Have students pair up and critique each other's writing for clarity. **Interpersonal**

C Critical Thinking Skills

Analyzing Focus students' attention on the section titled "Rebuilding Judah." Discuss with students that during the period of Babylonian exile, Judaism spread in the ancient world. Guide students to recognize that although many Jews eventually returned to Judah, others stayed in Babylon, thereby spreading their belief system in this area.

Ask: Based on the title of the section and chapter, what do you think the focus of the chapter will be on? *(the life of the Jews in Judah)* ELL

ANSWER, p. 154

TAKING NOTES: Synagogues were houses of worship where Jews met, each Sabbath, to pray and discuss their faith. Scribes included religious scholars who recorded the Torah and other Jewish writings for future generations.

networks *There's More Online!*

GRAPHIC ORGANIZER Roles of Synagogues and Scribes

Lesson 3

The Development of Judaism

ESSENTIAL QUESTION *How does religion shape society?*

It Matters Because

Religion served as the basis for all daily activities for the ancient Israelites. Many of their religious beliefs and practices continue today.

Return to Judah

GUIDING QUESTION *How did the people of Judah practice their religion while in exile and in their homeland?*

W The families of Judeans who were exiled to Babylon spent 70 years away from Judah. During their exile, they became known as the Jews. We call their religion Judaism.

While in Babylon, the Jews no longer had a temple in which to worship God. It is believed that small groups of Jews began to meet at **synagogues** (SIHN•uh•GAHGS), or Jewish houses of worship. They worshipped on the **Sabbath** (SA•buhth). According to **tradition**, the Sabbath lasts from sundown Friday to nightfall Saturday. During this weekly day of worship and rest, Jews prayed and talked about their religion and history. Jews still observe the Sabbath today.

Rebuilding Judah

C While some Jews accepted Babylon as their permanent home, others hoped to return to Judah some day. This hope was achieved when a group of people called the Persians swept across Southwest Asia. The Persians defeated the Chaldeans and took over Babylon. In 538 B.C., the Persian king Cyrus II let Jews return to Judah.

Reading **HELP**DESK CCSS

Taking Notes: ***Identifying the Main Idea***

As you read, complete a graphic organizer like this one to describe the roles of both synagogues and scribes in the survival of Judaism. RH.6–8.2

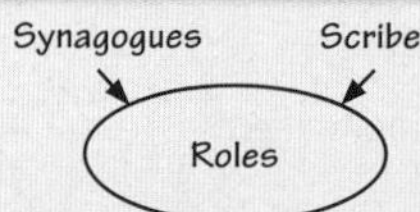

Content Vocabulary (Tier 3 Words)

- synagogue
- Sabbath
- scroll
- kosher

networks ***Online Teaching Options***

VIDEO

Temple Mount

Interpreting In the old city of Jerusalem, the Temple Mount, also known as the noble sanctuary, is the holiest religious site for Judaism, but it also holds great significance in the Muslim and Christian world. Today, visitors can visit the site and see a high-tech digitalized video, showing the Temple as archaeologists believe it once looked.

Discuss with students the benefits of creating this type of video and showing it to visitors at the site. How many benefits can the class list?

See page 137E for other online activities.

Some Jews stayed in Babylon, but many returned to Judah. They rebuilt Jerusalem and constructed a new temple to replace the one destroyed by the Chaldeans. This new place of worship became known as the Second Temple.

Meanwhile, the Persians chose officials to rule the country and collect taxes from the people. They did not allow the Jews to have their own government or king. The Jews depended on religious leaders—the temple priests and scribes—to guide their society.

Many priests were religious scholars. These priests had a deep understanding of the Jewish faith. Scribes often lectured in the synagogues and taught in the schools. Led by a scribe named Ezra, the Jews wrote the five books of the Torah on pieces of parchment. They sewed the pieces together to make long **scrolls** (SKROHLZ). The Torah and writings that were added later make up the Hebrew Bible. **R**

What Is In the Hebrew Bible?

Isn't it easier to follow rules when they are clearly explained? That is what the Hebrew Bible provided for the ancient Jews. Three parts—the Torah, the Prophets, and the Writings—make up the Hebrew Bible. It contains a series of 24 books written and collected over many centuries. The Hebrew Bible presents the laws and rules of the Israelites. It also reflects the culture of the people. Jewish history, art, literature, poetry, and proverbs are also part of the Hebrew Bible.

C Genesis, the first book of the Torah, presents the Israelite view of human beginnings. It tells how God created the Earth in six days and rested on the seventh day. Genesis also describes how God punished the world for wicked behavior. In this book, God warns a man named Noah that a flood is coming and commands him to build an ark, or large boat. As the rains poured and flood waters rose, Noah, his family, and two of every animal on Earth boarded the ark. The Earth flooded and many perished. Only those on the ark escaped drowning. After the rain stopped, God placed a rainbow in the sky as a sign that the world would never again be destroyed by a flood.

Genesis also explains why the people of the world speak many different languages. It tells how the citizens of the city of Babel tried to build a tower to reach heaven.

In Jewish synagogues, the Torah is read from scrolls kept in a cabinet called the Ark of the Law. These scrolls are handled with great respect and care during worship.

Richard T. Nowitz/CORBIS

synagogue a Jewish house of worship
Sabbath a weekly day of worship and rest
scroll a long document made from pieces of parchment sewn together

Academic Vocabulary (Tier 2 Words)

tradition a custom, or way of life, passed down from generation to generation

R Reading Skills

Summarizing Review the paragraph about the Torah scrolls. Ask students to work in pairs to summarize this paragraph in one or two sentences. Have students share their summaries with the class. Discuss what makes a good summary. **Verbal/Linguistic**

C Critical Thinking Skills

Evaluating Help students to evaluate the text that explains about the Torah by **asking: Why do you think the Jews wrote the Torah? What did they include in the Torah, and why do you think they included it?** *(Possible answer: They wanted to record their history and their views so that their history and religion would be carried on.)*

Content Background Knowledge

- When the Jews returned to Judah, they rebuilt King Solomon's temple on the same site as the first one, doing the best they could to make it look like the original. Many of the artifacts had been stolen, including the Ark of the Covenant. Also, two ornamental columns were missing from this temple. These columns had been symbols of royal authority, and now this group of Jews did not have their own king.
- This Second Temple was dedicated in the year 516 B.C.

SLIDE SHOW

Five Books of the Torah

Comparing and Contrasting Have students read through the information about each of the five books of the Torah and then compare this text with that of their own religions or other religions they know. **Ask: Which concepts are the same? Which are different?** BL

See page 137E for other online activities.

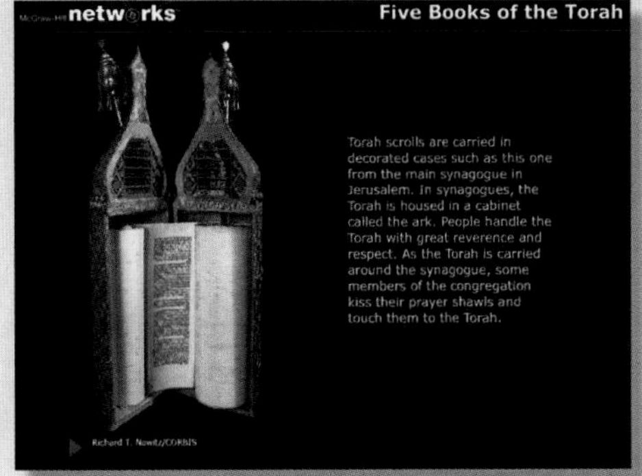

networks
Five Books of the Torah
Torah scrolls are carried in decorated cases such as this one from the main synagogue in Jerusalem. In synagogues, the Torah is housed in a cabinet called the ark. People handle the Torah with great reverence and respect. As the Torah is carried around the synagogue, some members of the congregation kiss their prayer shawls and touch them to the Torah.
Richard T. Nowitz/CORBIS

The Development of Judaism

V Visual Skills

Interpreting Discuss the painting of Daniel in the lion's den. Ask students to look at the details of the lions and of Daniel and tell everything they can about Daniel's character traits, his attitude and emotion, and about the situation he is in. **Ask:** **How have Daniel's religious beliefs affected how he is behaving in this situation?** *(His faith in God has made him unafraid, even while in extreme danger.)*

C Critical Thinking Skills

Making Connections Discuss the Tower of Babel story with students. **Ask:** **Have there been times in your life when an inability to communicate has prevented people from being able to accomplish something?** Have small groups of students discuss this question and share their answers with the class. **AL** **Interpersonal**

R Reading Skills

Paraphrasing Read the Primary Source quotation with students and have them paraphrase the quote, telling the main idea. **Ask:** **Which words in this quotation make it particularly strong or memorable? Would it have been as strong if the main idea were stated in another way?** *(Student answers may vary.)* **ELL** **Verbal/Linguistic**

ANSWERS, p. 156

CRITICAL THINKING The story reminds Jewish people to believe in God because God will protect them during difficult times.

✓ **PROGRESS CHECK** Because the Persians who ruled Judah did not allow Jews to be government leaders, the Jewish people depended on religious leaders—the temple priests and scribes—to guide them.

Daniel's faith in God protected him from the lions. As a result, Daniel became a model of faith and strength to Jews facing difficult challenges.

▶ **CRITICAL THINKING**

Analyzing What lesson does the story of Daniel provide for Jewish people, especially during hard times?

God disapproved and made the people speak in different languages. The people could not **communicate** with one another. As a result, they could not work together to complete the tower. God then scattered the people across the Earth.

Later parts of the Hebrew Bible describe Jewish hopes for the future. The book of Isaiah describes what the Jews believed to be God's plan for a peaceful world. It says that the nations:

PRIMARY SOURCE

> " [W]ill beat their swords into plowshares and their spears into pruning hooks. Nation will not take up sword against nation, nor will they train for war anymore. "
>
> — Isaiah 2:4 (New International Version)

The book of Daniel explains that the Jews also believed that evil and suffering would eventually be replaced by goodness. Daniel was a trusted adviser to a Babylonian king. As a Jew, however, he refused to worship Babylonian gods. For punishment, the Chaldeans threw Daniel into a lions' den. God, however, protected Daniel from the wild beasts. The story of Daniel reminds Jews that God will rescue them. Christians and Muslims share with the Jews the hope of a better world in which good triumphs over evil.

✓ **PROGRESS CHECK**

Explaining Why did religious leaders guide Jewish society after the Jews returned from exile?

Reading HELPDESK CCSS

Academic Vocabulary (Tier 2 Words)

communicate to exchange knowledge or information

networks Online Teaching Options

SLIDE SHOW

Jewish Heroes

Evaluating Explain that the book of Daniel in the Hebrew Bible uses the story of a heroic figure to express hope for a better world. **Ask:** **What heroic qualities did Daniel demonstrate?** *(Possible answer: Daniel demonstrated heroic qualities such as courage, faith, and goodness.)* Then present the interactive slide show about other Jewish heroes. Discuss with students the qualities they associate with each of these heroes and which qualities these heroes have in common. Students may suggest characteristics such as courage, strength, and determination.

See page 137E for other online activities.

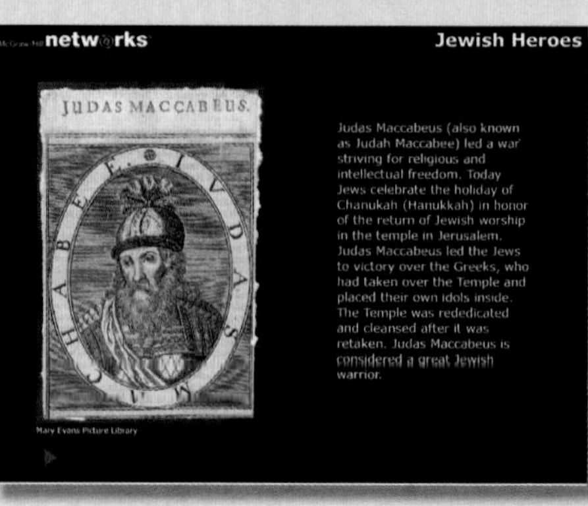

Jewish Daily Life

GUIDING QUESTION *How did religion shape the Jewish way of life?*

The Torah provides teachings for daily living. These teachings shaped the family life of the early Jews. The teachings gave instructions about what foods to eat and what clothes to wear. They also required Jews to help the poor, deal honestly with their neighbors, and apply laws fairly. Jewish teachings emphasized individual worth and responsibility, as well as self-discipline. It also reminded Jews of their loyalty to God.

C

The Jewish Family

The ancient Israelites stressed the importance of family life. The Torah identifies specific roles for the father and the mother of the house. If a father died, his sons would take his place to lead the family.

The Jewish family also stressed education—especially for young men. When sons grew old enough, fathers taught them to worship God and to learn a trade. Later, under the guidance of religious teachers, boys learned to read the Torah. Everything the students learned—from the alphabet to Jewish history—they learned from the Torah. Because reading the Torah was central to Jewish life, religious teachers became important **community** leaders.

T

Daughters, who were educated at home by their mothers, learned to be wives, mothers, and housekeepers. This included learning Jewish teachings about food, the Sabbath, and holidays. They also learned about the women of ancient Israel. Two of these women were Ruth and her mother-in-law, Naomi.

According to the Hebrew Bible, Naomi's husband and her two sons died. One of the sons was married to Ruth. Ruth, who was not a Jew herself, made a difficult decision. To help Naomi, Ruth chose to leave her Moabite homeland. She moved to Bethlehem to be with Naomi. Naomi had urged Ruth to stay with her own people, but Ruth responded:

R

Connections to TODAY

Heroes

Stories of brave leaders like Daniel have inspired Jews to maintain their faith during times of trial and trouble. Brainstorm a list of present-day individuals or groups who inspire others with their bravery in the face of great difficulty or danger.

Richard T. Nowitz/Age fotostock

Sabbath comes from the Hebrew word *Shabbat*, which means "cease or desist." The Sabbath is the day of the week when, according to Jewish tradition, people stop working in order to worship. In traditional Jewish homes, the Sabbath begins with a prayer and a family meal.

Academic Vocabulary (Tier 2 Words)

community a group of people with common interests living in an area

Lesson 3 157

C Critical Thinking Skills

Making Inferences Direct students to read the introductory text under the heading "Jewish Daily Life." Remind students that the Torah was written over centuries and provided clear rules for ancient Jews. It also gives instructions about how individuals and families should act, such as what clothes to wear and what foods to eat. Point out to students the ways in which the teachings of the Torah shaped the behaviors of early Jews. **Ask:** **How did the teachings of the Torah encourage Jews to behave responsibly?** *(Possible answer: The teachings of the Torah encouraged Jews to help the poor, to deal honestly with other people, and to apply laws fairly. The Torah also encouraged them to show self-discipline in their daily lives.)*

T Technology Skills

Researching on the Internet Explain to students that because of the Torah's importance to Jewish life, Israelite families stressed the value of education. Ask students to formulate questions about how the values of the Torah affect the everyday life of Jews today regarding education, clothing, helping the poor, and applying laws fairly. Have students look up the answers to their questions on the Internet.

R Reading Skills

Identifying Read the story of Ruth and Naomi. Have students identify the sequence of events in the story. Have the students list this sequence in steps. *(Possible answer: 1. Naomi's husband and sons die. 2. One son's wife, Ruth, tells Naomi she will leave her homeland to live with her. 3. Naomi argues that Ruth should stay with her own people. 4. Ruth insists on staying with Naomi to help her.)* **Verbal/Linguistic**

GAME

The Development of Judaism

Making Generalizations Have students complete the crossword puzzle. **Ask:** **What statements can you make about Jewish daily life based on the information in the crossword puzzle? What elements come into play in the daily lives of Jewish people?**

See page 137E for other online activities.

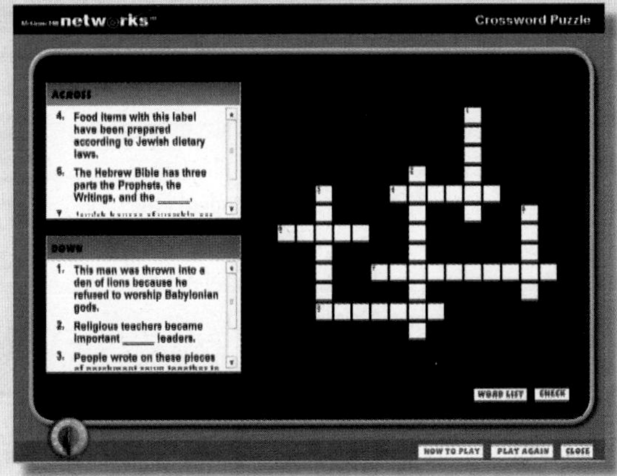

C Critical Thinking Skills

Making Connections Lead students in a discussion about why the story of Ruth and Naomi is important. **Ask:** **What traits did Ruth demonstrate that made her a role model for Jewish girls?** *(Ruth showed courage and devotion to her family in her decision to remain with Naomi. These traits made her a leader on which Jewish girls could model their actions.)*

W Writing Skills

Informative/Explanatory Discuss with students the statement in the text that by following laws related to food, Jews believed they were showing obedience to God. Have students write an essay about an area of their own lives in which they must follow certain rules in order to show that they are obedient toward somebody or something. Do they believe that this is important? Why? **Verbal/Linguistic**

R Reading Skills

Determining Word Meanings Have students read the word *kosher* and its definition in the text. Ask students to state the meaning of *kosher* in their own words, using a synonym or phrase. *(for example, substituting the word* proper *for* kosher*)* Then have students rewrite one of the sentences in the text using their word or phrase in place of *kosher*. Have students work in pairs to determine whether their definitions were correct. **ELL** **Verbal/Linguistic** **Interpersonal**

Because Ruth was Naomi's daughter-in-law, she was accepted with kindness in Bethlehem.

(t) Peter Willi/SuperStock

PRIMARY SOURCE

> "Where you go I will go, and where you stay I will stay. Your people will be my people and your God my God. Where you die I will die, and there I will be buried."
>
> —The Book of Ruth 1:16-17 (New International Version)

C

Ruth's courage and devotion to her family provided an example for Jewish girls to follow.

Dietary Laws

W

Jewish law tells Jews what they can eat. Ancient Jews could eat the meat of only certain animals. For example, they could eat beef and lamb but not pork. Laws about food are known as *kashrut*, which means "that which is proper." By following laws related to food, Jews believed they were showing obedience to God.

R

Today, food that is prepared according to Jewish dietary laws is called **kosher** (KOH•shuhr). Many items you see in a grocery store have the symbol for kosher on the label. Animals used for kosher meat must be killed in a certain way. The meat must

K

This symbol can be found on some food packages. It indicates that foods have been prepared according to Jewish dietary laws.

kosher prepared according to Jewish dietary law

158 *The Israelites*

networks Online Teaching Options

WHITEBOARD ACTIVITY

Kosher Foods

Categorizing Clarify for students that, just as with education, Jewish families emphasized following Jewish dietary laws. Then review with students the types of foods that are considered kosher and not kosher. Next, present the Interactive Whiteboard Activity on kosher foods. Assist students as they categorize each type of food as kosher or not kosher. When students have completed the activity, discuss as a class any other types of laws that might affect what people eat. **ELL**

See page 137E for other online activities.

networks Kosher Foods

Directions: Drag the label for each food into the appropriate column on the chart.

Food Bank: Green beans, French fries, Cheeseburger, Hamburger bun, Baked potato, Eggs, Bacon, Cucumber, Lettuce, Chicken, Salmon, Rice, Shrimp, Salted corned beef, Lobster

Kosher Foods	Non-Kosher Foods

The Development of Judaism

be inspected, salted, and soaked in water. Foods that are not kosher are considered to be unclean. Dietary law prohibits Jews from eating meat and dairy products together. Jews also cannot eat shellfish, such as crab or shrimp.

R Specific foods with religious significance are eaten during some meals. For example, the seder (SAY•duhr) is a special meal eaten during the festival of Passover. It is a holiday that celebrates the Exodus of the Jewish people from Egypt. Foods such as lamb, hardboiled eggs, vinegar, salt water, herbs, and flat bread called matzoh, are served at the seder. During the meal, the youngest child at the table asks a series of questions about the food and the meaning of Passover. The adults and older children at the table recite the answer to the question together. For example, they tell how the bitter herbs reflect the bitter experience of the Jews living in exile. The tradition of eating special foods at Passover and reflecting on history is sacred to the Jewish people. **C**

The foods of the seder are symbolic. For example, the egg is a symbol of God's kindness. Bitter herbs are dipped in fruit juice or honey to symbolize the sweetness and bitterness of life.

▶ CRITICAL THINKING

Comparing What is a particular food your friends or family include when you have a special dinner?

Mitch Hedlicka/Getty Images

✓ PROGRESS CHECK

Evaluating Why did religious teachers become important leaders in Jewish communities?

LESSON 3 REVIEW 

Review Vocabulary (Tier 3 Words)

1. Use the terms *synagogue*, *Sabbath*, and *kosher* to describe traditional Jewish practices. RH.6–8.4

Answer the Guiding Questions

2. *Identifying* What are the three parts of the Hebrew Bible? RH.6–8.2
3. *Explaining* How did the people of Judah practice their religion while in exile? RH.6–8.2
4. *Comparing* How were Jewish sons and daughters educated differently? RH.6–8.2
5. *Identifying* What is one type of food that is considered unclean according to Jewish dietary laws? RH.6–8.2
6. **ARGUMENT** What do you think is the main lesson to be learned from the story of Daniel in the lions' den? Write a paragraph describing your thoughts. WHST.6–8.2, WHST.6–8.10

R Reading Skills

Summarizing Have students read the section about Passover. Together, determine the central idea of the paragraph. Ask students to write a one- or two-sentence summary, stating the central idea in their own words. AL **Verbal/Linguistic**

C Critical Thinking Skills

Hypothesizing Read the last sentence of text on this page, about the tradition of eating special foods on Passover and reflecting on Passover history being sacred to the Jewish people. Ask students to hypothesize why this type of reflection each year would be important to the survival of any religion. *(Remembering important events and continuing rituals would be important to the survival of any religion because it would help ensure that the teachings, history, beliefs, and practices of the religion were passed down to younger generations.)* BL

Have students complete the Lesson 3 Review.

CLOSE & REFLECT

Remind students of the primary sources they have learned about in this lesson, including the Hebrew Bible and the Torah scrolls. Discuss with students why sources such as these documents can prove valuable when learning about the ancient Israelites. Note the information that such sources provide about the rules that governed daily life. AL

LESSON 3 REVIEW ANSWERS

1. Jews worship in *synagogues,* or houses of worship, on the weekly religious holiday called the *Sabbath.* Many Jews eat foods that are *kosher,* prepared according to Jewish dietary laws.
2. The Torah, the Prophets, and the Writings are the three parts of the Hebrew Bible.
3. Small groups of Jews met at synagogues to worship.
4. Sons learned how to read the Torah and to worship. They also learned a trade. Daughters learned how to be wives, mothers, and housekeepers.
5. Students may respond that pork and shellfish are considered unclean under Jewish dietary law.
6. Answers will vary but might include the following: God will rescue good people from evil; good eventually will triumph.

ANSWERS, p. 159

CRITICAL THINKING Answers will vary.

✓ PROGRESS CHECK Religious teachers became important leaders because of the Torah's great influence on daily life in Jewish communities.

ENGAGE

Bellringer Show several pictures of people celebrating Hanukkah. Invite students to tell what they know about Hanukkah and its traditions. Ask volunteers to describe similar traditions from their backgrounds that commemorate important historical events. Inform students that in this lesson they will learn about this holiday's origins as well as about other key events in Jewish history. AL

TEACH & ASSESS

C Critical Thinking Skills

Formulating Questions Read the section that tells about Alexander the Great introducing Greek culture to Judah. Discuss with students the things that may happen when two cultures mix. Ask small groups of students to formulate a list of five questions each about what may happen when two cultures mix. *(For example: What would happen to the foods the people eat? Which language would people speak?)* Have groups exchange questions and try to give answers. **Interpersonal**

R Reading Skills

Paraphrasing Have students paraphrase the information in the first four sentences of the section titled "How Did Jewish Ideas Spread?" Challenge them to find the main idea and write it in only one sentence. ELL **Verbal/Linguistic**

networks
There's More Online!
- GRAPHIC ORGANIZER Greek and Roman Rule
- MAP Diaspora
- SLIDE SHOW Hanukkah

Lesson 4
The Jews in the Mediterranean World

ESSENTIAL QUESTION *Why does conflict develop?*

IT MATTERS BECAUSE
The Jews experienced many significant changes under Greek and Roman rule.

The Arrival of Greek Rule

GUIDING QUESTION *What was life like for the Jews in Greek-ruled lands?*

The Jews of Judah remained under Persian rule for nearly 200 years. That is about the same amount of time as the entire history of the United States. Then, in 331 B.C., a king from Macedonia, who had conquered Greece, defeated the Persians. C This king was Alexander the Great. Alexander admired Greek ways and wanted to spread them. He introduced the Greek language and culture to Judah. Alexander allowed the Jews to stay in Judah.

How Did Jewish Ideas Spread?

R Under Alexander, Judah remained the center of Judaism. Many Jews at that time, however, had long lived outside Judah. Thousands had been exiled to Babylon in 586 B.C. When in 538 B.C. the conquering Persians gave them permission to return to Judah, many chose to stay in Babylon or go to other Mediterranean lands instead. These groups of Jews living outside of the Jewish homeland became known as the **Diaspora** (deye•AS•puh•ruh). *Diaspora* is a Greek word that means

Reading **HELP**DESK 

Taking Notes: ***Comparing and Contrasting***
As you read, complete a diagram like this one by identifying similarities and differences between Greek rule and Roman rule. RH.6–8.2

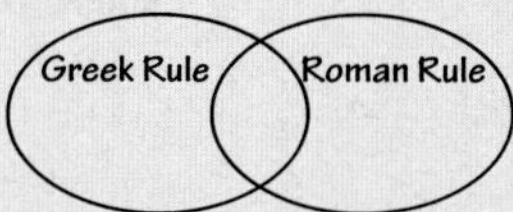

Content Vocabulary (Tier 3 Words)
- **Diaspora**
- **rabbi**

networks Online Teaching Options

VIDEO

Temple of Herod

Analyzing Images King Herod set out to win the hearts and minds of the Jews by expanding the Second Temple in Jerusalem. Herod's tomb was built under the Temple, but it wasn't discovered until archaeologist Ehud Netzer and his team made an amazing discovery. Show this video and then ask students to discuss and record the evidence archaeologists found that led them to believe they'd found King Herod's tomb.

See page 137F for other online activities.

ANSWER, p. 160

TAKING NOTES: Similarities—Both conquered Judah and introduced their culture to Judah. Differences—Greeks allowed Jews to stay in Judah, but many Jews settled in other parts of the Greek Empire as part of the Diaspora.

"scattered." Where these Jews settled, they practiced their customs, and Jewish ideas spread.

The Jews of the Diaspora remained loyal to Judaism. At the same time, many learned the Greek language and adopted features of Greek culture. A group of Jewish scholars in Egypt copied the Hebrew Bible into Greek. This Greek **version**, called the Septuagint (sehp•TOO•uh•juhnt), helped people who were not Jews to read and understand the Hebrew Bible. As a result, Jewish ideas spread throughout the Mediterranean world.

C R

The Revolt of Maccabeus

After Alexander's death, four of his generals divided his empire into separate kingdoms. One kingdom covered much of Southwest Asia. A family known as the Seleucids (suh•LOO•suhds) ruled this kingdom. By 200 B.C., Judah was under the control of Seleucid kings.

In 176 B.C., Antiochus IV (an•TEE•uh•kuhs) came to power as the Seleucid king. As ruler of Judah, Antiochus required the Jews to worship the many Greek gods and goddesses.

GEOGRAPHY CONNECTION

The Diaspora continued throughout Alexander's Greek empire. During the first century A.D., Jews represented about 40 percent of the empire's population.

1 **MOVEMENT** How did the Diaspora help spread Jewish ideas?

2 CRITICAL THINKING *Explaining* How can the interaction of two cultures create benefits for both groups?

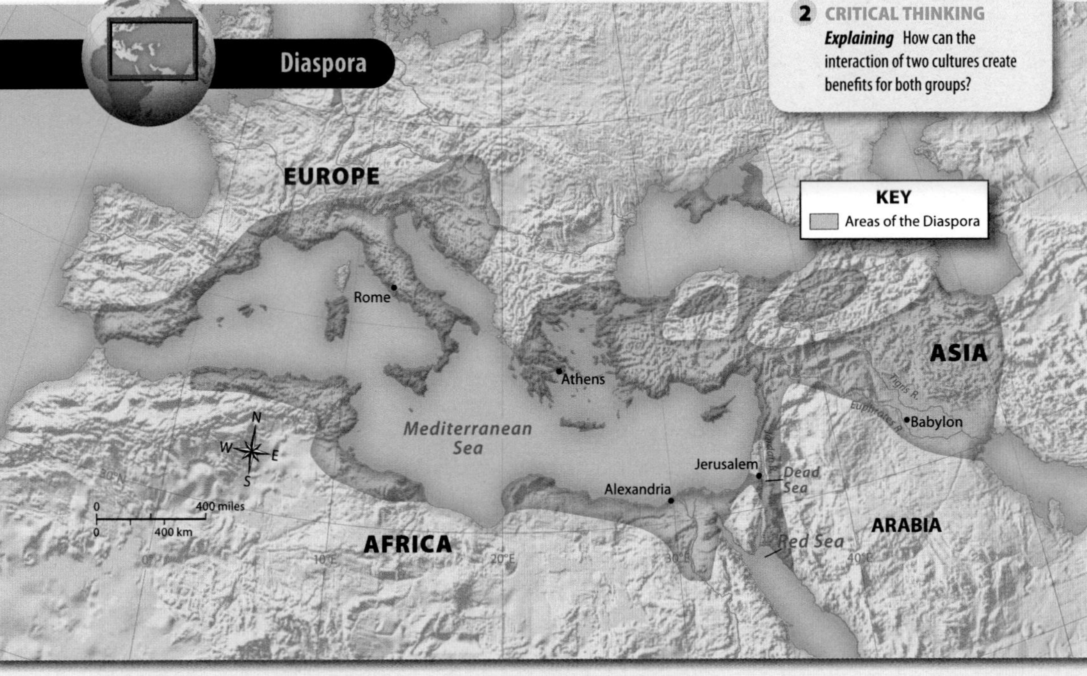

Diaspora the groups of Jews living outside the Jewish homeland

Academic Vocabulary (Tier 2 Words)

version a different form or edition; a translation of the Bible

C Critical Thinking Skills

Comparing and Contrasting Discuss with students the beginning of Greek rule in Judah. Have students compare and contrast (1) what happened when the Greeks began to rule Judah with (2) what has happened when nations have taken over the rule of other countries. *(For example: Native Americans were forced to change and move after the arrival of Europeans.)*

R Reading Skills

Explaining After students have read the text, discuss the Diaspora, and how Jews settled and thrived in major cities outside Judah, such as Alexandria. Help students to understand how the Jews influenced other cultures. **Ask:** **What was the Septuagint? Why was it important to the spread of Jewish ideas in the Mediterranean world?** *(The Septuagint was a version of the Hebrew Bible that had been copied into Greek. It helped people who were not Jewish read and understand the ideas in the Hebrew Bible.)* ELL

MAP

Diaspora

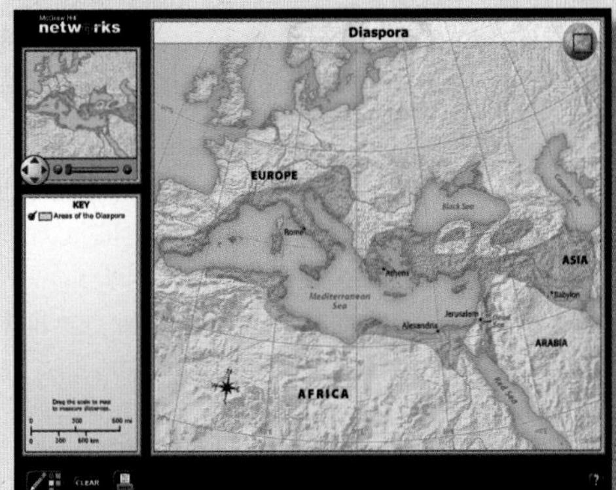

Analyzing Visuals Discuss with students the meaning of the word *empire*. Guide them to understand that empires often controlled huge areas of land and included people of many different cultures. Then present the interactive maps of the Diaspora. Click on the maps and read the information provided. Help students answer the discussion question by pointing out the concentration of dense Jewish settlements along the Mediterranean coast. **Ask:** **How do you think the settlement patterns of the Diaspora might have changed over time?** *(Possible answer: The Diaspora probably moved gradually outward from Judah. Those areas located farther away from Judah might have become more populated by Jews over time.)* BL

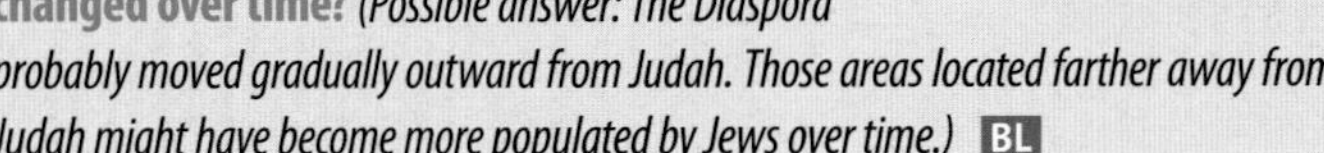

See page 137F for other online activities.

ANSWERS, p. 161

GEOGRAPHY CONNECTION

1 As Jews moved and settled around the world, they practiced their beliefs. Other cultures learned from them.

2 CRITICAL THINKING Each culture can learn from the knowledge, customs, and beliefs of the other group.

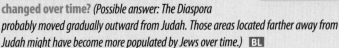

V Visual Skills

Creating Time Lines Discuss the sequence of events from the time of Judas Maccabeus until after Herod's death. Have students create a time line that shows the key events and when they happened. ELL **Visual/Spatial**

R Reading Skills

Identifying Show the picture of Judas Maccabeus, and have a volunteer read the information below it. **Ask: How do you think guerrilla warfare helped the Maccabees beat the Seleucids?** *(The Seleucids may not have been prepared for the surprise attacks, and the constant strain of being on guard may have taken its toll.)* Review with students the connection between the victory of the Maccabees and the annual festival of Hanukkah. **Ask: Who wrote the First Book of Maccabees?** *(a Jewish historian who lived in Judah during the second century B.C.)*

T Technology Skills

Researching on the Internet Ask students to work in groups to find out more about King Herod by doing research on the Internet. Have each student in the group choose one aspect of Herod's life to research, such as family, childhood, early life events, or later life events. Ask groups to present the information orally that they've found. **Interpersonal**

BIOGRAPHY

Judas Maccabeus (c. 190 B.C.–160 B.C.)

Judas Maccabeus and his followers engaged in guerrilla warfare against the Greek armies. Guerrilla warfare is irregular combat carried out by small groups of independent soldiers. This strategy helped the Maccabees succeed in battle against the Seleucids. The family of Judas Maccabeus ruled Judah and expanded its lands. With more territory protecting it, Judah remained free until the Roman conquest.

▶ **CRITICAL THINKING**
Explaining Why is Judas Maccabeus considered a hero?

A large number of Jews, however, refused to abandon their religion. In 167 B.C., Judas Maccabeus (JOO•duhs MAK•uh•BEE•uhs), a Jewish priest, led the fight against Seleucid rule. He and his followers fled to the hills. They formed a rebel army known as the Maccabees.

After many battles, the Maccabees succeeded in capturing the Temple. They cleared it of all statues of Greek gods and goddesses. They then rededicated the temple to the worship of God. Each year, Jews recall the cleansing of the Temple when they celebrate the festival of Hanukkah (HAH•nuh•kuh).

✓ **PROGRESS CHECK**

Analyzing How did Alexander and later the Seleucids affect the people of Judah?

Roman Rule in Judaea

GUIDING QUESTION *How did the Jews react to Roman rule of their homeland?*

By 100 B.C., the Romans controlled much of the eastern Mediterranean lands. The name *Roman* came from Rome, their capital. Rome was located far to the west in what is known today as Italy. Led by powerful generals, the Romans **expanded** their empire. In 63 B.C., Roman forces conquered Judah and renamed it Judaea (joo•DEE•uh).

At first, the Romans chose a follower of the Jewish religion, Herod (HEHR•uhd), to rule as king of Judaea. Herod built many forts and cities in Judaea. The Second Temple in Jerusalem, rebuilt during Herod's reign, served as the center of Jewish worship.

Jewish Groups

After Herod's death, Roman officials ruled Judaea. At that time, disagreement grew about how Judaism should be practiced. Jews also had different views on how to deal with the Romans.

One group of Jews was known as the Pharisees (FEH•ruh•seez). The Pharisees gained the support of the common people. They taught in the synagogues and applied the teachings of the Torah to daily life. Through their teachings, the Pharisees helped to make Judaism a religion of the home and family. The Pharisees wanted to help people obey the commandments. To do this, they stressed both written and oral law. Oral law is the unwritten interpretations passed down over time by word of mouth.

Hulton Archives/Getty Images

Reading HELPDESK CCSS

Academic Vocabulary (Tier 2 Words)
expand to enlarge

networks ***Online Teaching Options***

SLIDE SHOW

Hanukkah

Creating Charts Have students watch the slide show about Hanukkah and then create a two-column chart with the headings "Past" and "Present." Have them fill in the columns with information from the text and slide show, and ask them to cite how many connections they can find between past and present. Have them draw lines connecting past events with present traditions.

See page 137F for other online activities.

ANSWERS, p. 162

✓ **PROGRESS CHECK** Under Alexander, Judah remained the center of Judaism; the Diaspora took place; and a Greek version of the Hebrew Bible was written, which helped spread Jewish ideas in the Mediterranean world. Under the Seleucid kings, Jews had to worship other gods, leading to a revolt by the Maccabees.

CRITICAL THINKING Judas Maccabeus is considered a hero because he led the Maccabees as they defeated the Seleucids. This began a period of growth and freedom in Judah.

Herod was primarily responsible for developing the fortress at Masada. It was the scene of a major Roman and Jewish battle. Visitors may tour its mountainous ruins today.

Francesco Dazzi/Flickr/Getty Images

The Pharisees wanted Judaea free of Roman rule. However, they did not urge Jews to fight the Romans. Instead, they told people to resist Roman control. They urged the people to practice the Torah's teachings with greater **devotion**.

Another Jewish group made up of wealthy noble families was the Sadducees (SA•juh•SEEZ). Many of them served as priests and scribes in the Temple. The Sadducees accepted the laws of the Torah. They were more concerned, however, with applying the laws to temple ceremonies. They also did not agree with many of the Pharisees' teachings. For example, the Sadducees emphasized the written law but rejected oral law. The Sadducees favored **cooperation** with the Romans. They wanted to keep peace and order in Judaea.

A third group was called the Essenes (ih•SEENZ). They were priests who broke away from the Temple in Jerusalem. Many Essenes lived at Qumrān, an area in the desert near the Dead Sea. They spent their lives praying and waiting for God to deliver the Jews from Roman rule. The Essenes followed only the written law of the Torah.

Centuries later, in A.D. 1947, ancient scrolls were found in caves at Qumrān. Because the caves were near the Dead Sea, the scrolls became known as the Dead Sea Scrolls. Many of the scrolls were most likely written by Essenes. The scrolls are important to historians because they provide a window into a particular place and time.

R

W

Academic Vocabulary (Tier 2 Words)

devotion dedication, a strong commitment
cooperation working together

R Reading Skills

Finding the Main Idea Assign small groups of students one of the paragraphs on this page. Each group should write the main idea and several supporting details for their paragraph. Then groups should share their findings as a class.
AL Verbal/Linguistic

W Writing Skills

Informative/Explanatory Discuss the Essenes as well as the other two groups of Jews featured in the text about Jewish groups under Roman rule. Ask students to write a short explanatory essay to explain what made each group unique. Guide them to determine the types of people that made up each group. **Ask:** Which group probably had the support of common families? *(the Pharisees)* Which group was made up of wealthy noble families? *(the Sadducees)*

Have students critique each other's work, looking for clarity in the writing. Verbal/Linguistic

IMAGE

Battle At Masada

Analyzing Visuals Present the interactive image on the fortress at Masada, and have students take turns reading the informational text aloud. **Ask:** Why is Masada considered an important historic site? *(It is the site of an ancient fortress that was developed primarily by Herod. It was also the location of an important battle between Jewish and Roman forces in the Jewish struggle for independence.)*

See page 137F for other online activities.

networks
Battle at Masada
Masada, an ancient Jewish fortress near the Dead Sea, is a dramatic example of the relationship between geography and history. Jewish leaders ordered the construction of the fortress on top of a mesa. It featured aqueducts to bring water to its citizens and defense towers to protect the people. The remote location and steep hills of Masada

CHAPTER 6, Lesson 4

The Jews in the Mediterranean World

C Critical Thinking Skills

Determining Central Ideas Together as a class, determine the central idea of the section about the Dead Sea Scrolls. Create an idea web and have students fill it in with the evidence in the text that supports that central idea. **Verbal/Linguistic**

R Reading Skills

Predicting Consequences Have students read the section about the Zealots. **Ask:**

- **Given this information, what do you predict that the Zealots in Judea will do?** *(fight against the Romans)*
- **What evidence do you have to back up your prediction?** *(Tensions were rising, they wanted to fight, and they were preparing to act.)*
- **What are your predictions about the outcome of a fight if there is one? What evidence do you base this on? Verbal/Linguistic**

GEOGRAPHY CONNECTION

There are rocky cliffs along the shores of the Dead Sea. Caves in these cliffs contained the Dead Sea scrolls.

1 **LOCATION** Describe the location of the Dead Sea in relation to the Mediterranean Sea.

2 **CRITICAL THINKING** *Explaining* Why would the discovery of the Dead Sea Scrolls be considered so significant?

Locating the Dead Sea Scrolls is considered to be one of the most significant modern archaeological discoveries.

They let historians see that Judaism was not always an established religion. They show that not all followers practiced Judaism in the same way during Roman times.

Some of the scrolls tell a story about a group of Jews who, in exile, developed their own beliefs about good and evil. They saw themselves as alone in the world, surrounded by enemies. They were waiting for someone to lead them. Some scrolls describe the beliefs, holy days, and practices of other Jewish groups. The variety of the scrolls makes some historians believe that the writings were perhaps the contents of a library. The reasons for hiding the scrolls are unclear. Someone may have wanted to protect them from destruction during times of conflict with the Romans. Since their discovery, however, the scrolls have helped historians understand more about Judaism during Roman times. C

R A fourth Jewish group, the Zealots, lived in Judaea. They wanted to fight for their freedom against the Romans. During the A.D. 60s, Jewish hatred of Roman rule reached its peak. Hope remained in the Jewish faith, however. Many Jews were waiting for God to send a deliverer to free them from Roman rule. As **tensions** between Romans and Jews in Judaea increased, the Zealots prepared to act.

Reading HELPDESK CCSS

Academic Vocabulary (Tier 2 Words)

tensions opposition between individuals or groups; stress

networks Online Teaching Options

IMAGE

Dead Sea Scrolls

Explaining Present the interactive image of the Dead Sea Scrolls. Click on the image and read the information provided. **Ask: Why might the Dead Sea Scrolls have been placed in caves?** *(The documents might have been placed in caves to hide them from Roman armies.)*

See page 137F for other online activities.

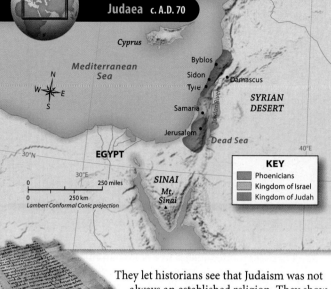

networks
Dead Sea Scrolls
• The Dead Sea Scrolls, found in caves near the Dead Sea, are one of the most significant modern archaeological discoveries ever made. The Scrolls are ancient writings that were found in 1947 in caves high above the shore of the Dead Sea. Study of the scrolls has led to changes in understanding of Middle East history and religious events, including the history of Israel from the 400 B.C. to A.D. 135, and the

ANSWERS, p. 164

GEOGRAPHY CONNECTION

1 The Dead Sea is east of the Mediterranean Sea.

2 **CRITICAL THINKING** The discovery of the Dead Sea Scrolls would provide first-hand information about Judaism during the period of Roman rule.

Jewish-Roman Wars

In A.D. 66, the Zealots revolted. They overpowered the small Roman army in Jerusalem. Four years later, Roman forces retook the city. They killed thousands of Jews and forced many others to leave. The Romans also destroyed the Second Temple in Jerusalem. Today the Western Wall still stands in Jerusalem. This structure is all that remains of the Temple complex. It is a long-standing Jewish custom to come to this spot to pray.

After a number of years passed, some Jews rebelled once again. In A.D. 132, a military leader named Simon ben Kosiba, known as Bar Kochba, led the Jews in the battle for freedom. However, three years later, Roman forces crushed the revolt. They killed Bar Kochba and many other Jewish leaders during the fighting.

With the revolt put down, the Romans imposed stricter controls and did not allow Jews to live in or even visit Jerusalem. The Romans renamed Judaea and called it Palestine. This name refers to the Philistines, whom the Israelites had conquered centuries before.

The ancient Western Wall is the only remaining structure of the Temple of Jerusalem. Coming here to pray has been a Jewish custom for hundreds of years. Those who visit the wall often leave prayers on paper stuffed into its cracks.

▶ CRITICAL THINKING

Explaining Why might people still come to this site to pray?

V Visual Skills

Creating Charts Have students create a cause-and-effect chart, organizing the sequence of events on this page into cause-and-effect relationships. Go over their charts as a class. BL

R1 Reading Skills

Identifying Point students to the section titled "Jewish-Roman Wars." **Ask: Which Jewish group led a revolt against Roman rule?** *(the Zealots)* Discuss with students the outcome of Jewish revolts against Roman rule. Help them understand that the Romans eventually put down these revolts, leading to stricter controls and harsh penalties on the Jews.

R2 Reading Skills

Finding the Main Idea Tell students to focus on the text about the Romans' destruction of the Second Temple in Jerusalem. Then point to the picture of the Western Wall of the Temple and read the information next to it. **Ask: Why is the Western Wall still important to modern Jews?** *(It is the only part of the Temple complex available to Jews for prayer. It is a monument to their faith. It is a symbol of how their faith has outlasted their enemies.)* AL

IMAGE

The Western Wall

Analyzing Visuals Present the interactive image and text about the Western Wall and ask students to write a list of words that describe the image. Then have them find words in the text that correspond with the list inspired by the image. How many words can the students find? **Ask: How does this image convey the meaning of the text?**

See page 137F for other online activities.

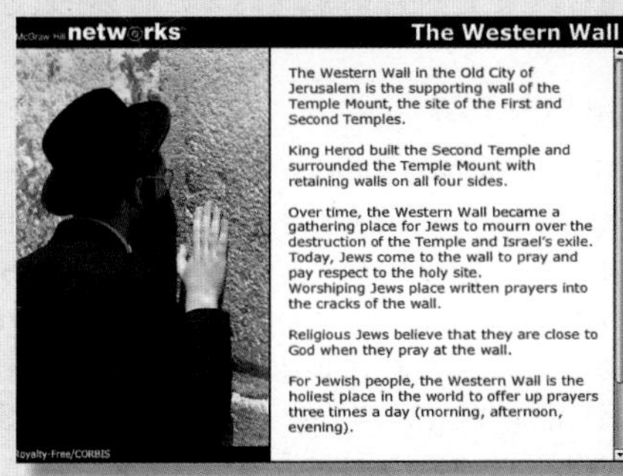

networks
The Western Wall
The Western Wall in the Old City of Jerusalem is the supporting wall of the Temple Mount, the site of the First and Second Temples.
King Herod built the Second Temple and surrounded the Temple Mount with retaining walls on all four sides.
Over time, the Western Wall became a gathering place for Jews to mourn over the destruction of the Temple and Israel's exile. Today, Jews come to the wall to pray and pay respect to the holy site. Worshiping Jews place written prayers into the cracks of the wall.
Religious Jews believe that they are close to God when they pray at the wall.
For Jewish people, the Western Wall is the holiest place in the world to offer up prayers three times a day (morning, afternoon, evening).
Royalty-Free/CORBIS

ANSWER, p. 165

CRITICAL THINKING The Western Wall is not only the former site of the Temple, it is also an important location in the history of Judaism. The people who come to pray there probably view it as a sacred site.

R Reading Skills

Explaining Help students locate the text on rabbis, and discuss with them how the rabbis helped the Jewish people regroup after their unsuccessful struggle for independence. Guide this discussion to focus on the rabbis' roles as religious leaders and teachers. **Ask:** **How did Yohanan ben Zaccai help the Jewish religion survive?** *(ben Zaccai persuaded the Romans to spare the city of Yavneh. He also founded a school that continued to teach the Torah and preserve the basic beliefs of Judaism.)*

G1 Critical Thinking Skills

Drawing Conclusions Review with students the changes that took place after the Jews lost their struggle for independence from the Romans. **Ask:** **Why do you think the rabbis became important during this time?** *(Possible answer: During this time, the Jewish people no longer had the Temple or priests. This helped the rabbis become important. The Jewish people also might have been looking for guidance during this difficult period. The rabbis provided this guidance. The work of the rabbis to preserve Judaism also probably helped give them a leadership role among the Jewish people.)*

G2 Critical Thinking Skills

Identifying Central Issues Have students read the information about Rabbi Yohanan ben Zaccai and identify the central issues behind his actions. **Ask:** **What did Yohanan ben Zaccai want for the Jews?** *(He wanted to ensure that the basic beliefs of Judaism were preserved.)* **Verbal/Linguistic**

Connections to TODAY

Dead Sea Scrolls

In A.D. 1947, a shepherd in the Judaean desert entered a cave along the shore of the Dead Sea. There he discovered several large clay jars. Some jars were empty, but in others he found ancient scrolls of leather, papyrus, and copper. These **documents**, written between 200 B.C. and A.D. 68, are called the Dead Sea scrolls. The scrolls found in several caves in the area include the oldest complete copy of the Book of Isaiah and pieces of many other books of the Hebrew Bible. Among the documents are works in ancient Hebrew, Greek, and Aramaic. Most scholars believe that the scrolls were part of a library that belonged to an early Jewish community.

The Rabbis

G1 Despite losing their struggle for independence, the Jews regrouped with the help of their **rabbis** (RA•byz), or religious leaders. The Jewish people no longer had a temple or priests. Instead, the synagogues and rabbis gained importance. The rabbis taught and explained the Torah. They provided moral guidance—accepted notions of right and wrong—to the people.

G2 One of the most famous rabbis was Yohanan ben Zaccai (YOH•kah•nahn behn zah•KY). Ben Zaccai lived in Judaea when Jerusalem fell to the Romans in A.D. 70. He persuaded the Romans to spare the Jewish city of Yavneh. There, he founded a school to continue teaching the Torah.

Ben Zaccai helped the Judaic spirit survive the destruction of the temple and the loss of Jerusalem. He placed great importance on the study of the Torah. He also stressed acts of loving kindness and community service. Because of ben Zaccai's efforts, the school at Yavneh became a center of Torah studies and a model for other schools. Other rabbis founded Torah schools in places as far away as Babylon and Egypt. R

Through the efforts of ben Zaccai and other rabbis, the basic beliefs of Judaism were preserved. Eventually, the rabbis gathered their oral discussions about Jewish law and recorded them in a work known as the Mishnah. Later, the Mishnah was combined with other Jewish legal traditions into an authoritative collection of Jewish tradition known as the Talmud. The word *Talmud* is a Hebrew term that means "instruction." The Talmud became the basis for Jewish teachings throughout the ages.

Godong/Robert Harding World Imagery/Getty Images

A part of the Talmud called the Mishnah began as an oral history of Jewish law passed from one generation of rabbis to another.

Reading HELPDESK (CCSS)

rabbi the official leader of a Jewish congregation

Academic Vocabulary (Tier 2 Words)

document an official paper used as proof or support of something

networks Online Teaching Options

IMAGE

The Talmud

Analyzing Primary Sources Show students the interactive image with text describing the Mishnah and the Talmud. Make sure students understand that rabbis developed these works to preserve important ideas about Jewish law. Click on the image to read the information provided, and then click again to hear quotes from the Talmud. Have students reflect on the quotations from the Talmud. **Ask:** **How do these quotations reflect what you know about the purpose of the Talmud?** *(Possible answer: The Talmud discusses issues faced in daily life. These quotations offer practical advice that could be applied to everyday situations.)* BL

See page 137F for other online activities.

CHAPTER 6, Lesson 4
The Jews in the Mediterranean World

Rabbis continue to educate students today. They might also perform charity or social functions for their congregations. C1

To this day, the Talmud remains central to Jewish teaching and is the ultimate authority on Jewish law. A prayer at the end of part of the Talmud reveals the Jewish reverence for the Torah:

PRIMARY SOURCE

"Make sweet, O Lord, our God, the words of Thy Law in our mouths, and in the mouth of Thy people the house of Israel; and may we, our children, and the children of Thy people the house of Israel, all know Thy Name and learn Thy Law." C2

—from *The Babylon Talmud, Book 1: Tract Sabbath*

SAFRA Sylvain/Age fotostock

✓ PROGRESS CHECK

Explaining How did the rabbis help Judaism survive after the Roman conquest?

LESSON 4 REVIEW (CCSS)

Review Vocabulary (Tier 3 Words)

1. In what way did *rabbis* help the Jews during the period of Roman rule? RH.6–8.4

Answer the Guiding Questions

2. ***Explaining*** What was life like for the Jews in Greek-ruled lands? RH.6–8.2
3. ***Identifying*** Which group gained control of Judah following Alexander's death? RH.6–8.2
4. ***Explaining*** How did the Jews react to Roman rule of their homeland? RH.6–8.2
5. ***Identifying*** Who established a school for teaching the Torah at Yavneh? RH.6–8.2
6. **ARGUMENT** Imagine you are living in Judaea during the Roman conquest. Write a letter to a friend describing what action you would like to see taken to make Judaea free again. WHST.6–8.1, WHST.6–8.10

C1 Critical Thinking Skills

Comparing and Contrasting Point out the picture of the rabbi educating students. Remind students of the many elements of Jewish life and law shown in the picture, such as the focus on education and the wearing of head coverings. Ask volunteers to describe important characteristics of life for Jews under Roman rule. Then discuss with the class how these characteristics were similar or different under Greek rule. Record students' responses in a Venn diagram. *(Possible answers include the following. Greek rule: Jews were forced to worship Greek gods. Hebrew texts were translated into Greek. Jewish rebellion overthrew Greek rule. Both: Jews opposed foreign rule. Some Jews fought against Greek and Roman rulers. Roman rule: Romans defeated Jewish rebellions and cast Jews out of Jerusalem.)*

C2 Critical Thinking Skills

Analyzing Primary Sources After reading the quotation on this page from the Talmud, ask students what purpose the quotation serves and why they think it was included as part of the Talmud. **Ask: What was the intention of the rabbis who wrote the Talmud when they included these words?** *(Possible answer: They wanted to ensure that the teachings would be passed down over generations.)* **Verbal/Linguistic**

Have students complete the Lesson 4 Review.

CLOSE & REFLECT

Sequencing Have the class review Lesson 4 and, together, create a time line of events featured in the text.

LESSON 4 REVIEW ANSWERS

1. The rabbis helped by explaining and teaching the Torah and providing moral guidance.
2. The Jews were allowed to stay in Judah. The Greek language and Greek ways were introduced to Judah.
3. The Seleucids gained control of Judah following Alexander's death.
4. They rebelled against Roman rule.
5. The rabbi Yohanan ben Zaccai established this school at Yavneh.
6. Letters will vary but should show thoughtful consideration of the difficulties of Jewish life under Roman rule.

ANSWER, p. 167

✓ PROGRESS CHECK Rabbis taught and explained the Torah. They also provided moral guidance to others. Some rabbis founded schools that preserved the basic beliefs of Judaism.

CHAPTER REVIEW ACTIVITY

Have students create a web like the one below and write the phrase "Individual Rights of the Israelites" in the center. Then have volunteers from each group add to the diagram the key ideas they discussed about individual rights and freedoms related to the Israelites.

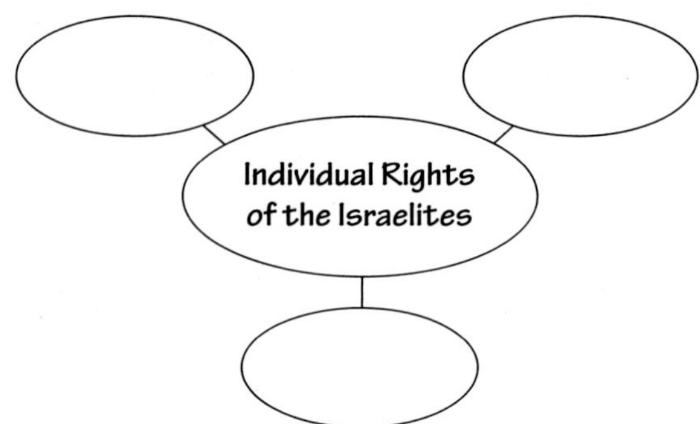

Guide students in small-group discussions about the ways in which the individual rights of the Israelites changed during the time period of this chapter. Ask them to consider what these changes might suggest about the various groups that governed the Israelites. Guide students to recognize that governments that sought to limit the Israelites' freedom to practice their beliefs did not place great value on individual rights.

REVIEW THE ENDURING UNDERSTANDINGS

Review the chapter's Enduring Understandings with students.

- *People, places, and ideas change over time.*
- *The value that a society places on individual rights is often reflected in that society's government.*
- *Countries have relationships with each other.*

Now pose the following questions in a class discussion to apply these to the chapter.

How did conflict with other nations affect the Israelites and their religion? *(Conflicts with the Egyptians, Romans, Greeks, and others forced the Israelites to move, spread their religion to many places, and merge it with other cultures. The victories of the Israelites against opposing forces led to many of the observances and celebrations of Jews today.)*

CHAPTER 6 Activities

Write your answers on a separate piece of paper.

1. **Exploring the Essential Question** WHST.6–8.2, WHST.6–8.10
   INFORMATIVE/EXPLANATORY Write an expository essay about how key leaders influenced the Israelites during the time periods discussed in this chapter. Identify specific leaders who had the most significant effect. Explain how they led during times of conflict.

2. **21st Century Skills** WHST.6–8.6
   CREATING A SLIDE SHOW Create a slide show about an aspect of Jewish culture that you have studied in this chapter. When presenting, briefly introduce each image, and offer a clear interpretation of why it is significant.

3. **Thinking Like a Historian** WHST.6–8.2
   COMPARING AND CONTRASTING Create a diagram like the one shown to compare and contrast the Jewish groups that existed under Roman rule.

4. **GEOGRAPHY ACTIVITY**

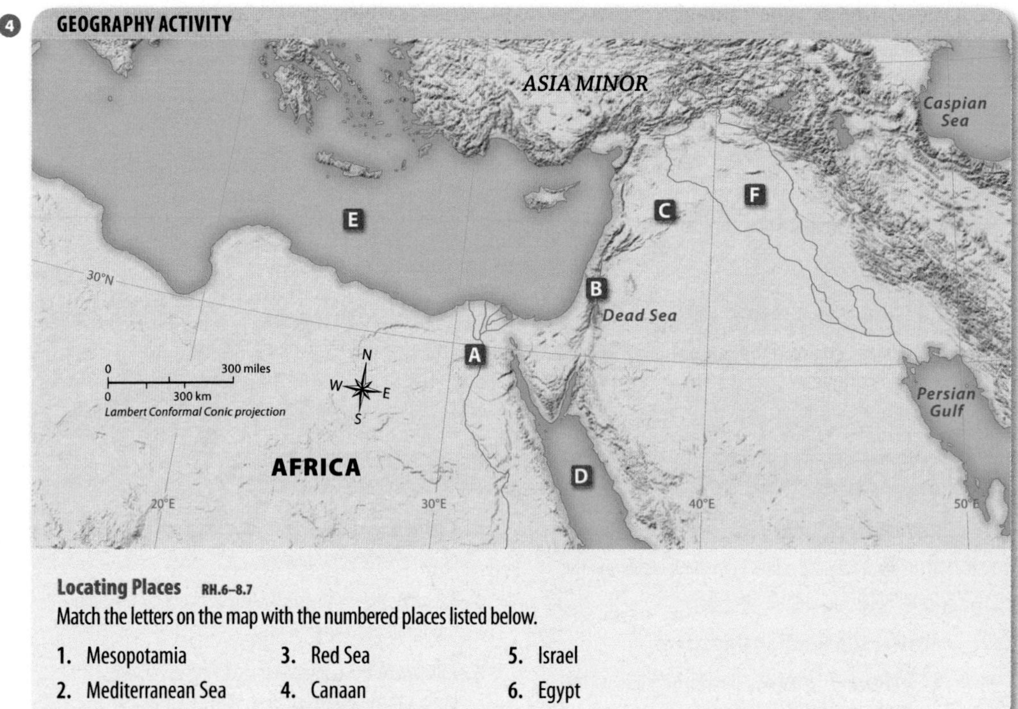

Locating Places RH.6–8.7
Match the letters on the map with the numbered places listed below.

1. Mesopotamia
2. Mediterranean Sea
3. Red Sea
4. Canaan
5. Israel
6. Egypt

What were some of the traits the Jewish kings and prophets had in common? How did they affect the Israelites' history? *(Kings such as David and Solomon and prophets such as Elijah were wise and courageous. They showed leadership and helped the Jewish people stay united during difficult times.)*

What has stayed the same about Jewish ideas and religion and what has changed over time? *(The emphasis on learning and education and following the laws of Torah have stayed the same, but the interpretation of how to follow those laws, such as following the rules for staying kosher, varies in different areas and among different groups of Jews.)*

ACTIVITIES ANSWERS

Exploring the Essential Questions

1. Students' essays should correctly identify key leaders discussed in the chapter. Their writing should clearly explain the roles of these leaders in the development of Judaism and the conflicts that arose during this time period. Students may highlight leaders such as Abraham, Moses, Joshua, David, Daniel, Judas Maccabeus, and Yohanan ben Zaccai in their essays.

CHAPTER 6 Assessment (CCSS)

REVIEW THE GUIDING QUESTIONS

Directions: Choose the best answer for each question.

RH.6–8.2
1. The Israelites differed from many other ancient civilizations by
   A. battling neighboring civilizations.
   B. settling in Canaan.
   C. worshiping only one God.
   D. creating written documents.

RH.6–8.2
2. According to the Hebrew Bible, from which location did the Israelites migrate to Canaan?
   F. Mesopotamia
   G. Egypt
   H. Lebanon
   I. Jordan

RH.6–8.2
3. Which of the following is considered the greatest king in Israelite history?
   A. David
   B. Alexander
   C. Solomon
   D. Samuel

RH.6–8.2
4. Though it had survived earlier conquests, in 586 B.C., Jerusalem was destroyed by the
   F. Chaldeans.
   G. Assyrians.
   H. Samaritans.
   I. Israelites.

RH.6–8.2
5. While in exile in Babylon, Jews began to
   A. believe in one God.
   B. construct new temples.
   C. join the Maccabees.
   D. worship in synagogues.

RH.6–8.2
6. Which group overpowered the Romans and captured Jerusalem in 66 B.C.?
   F. Sadducees
   G. Essenes
   H. Pharisees
   I. Zealots

169

CHAPTER 6
Assessment Answers

ASSESSMENT ANSWERS

Review the Guiding Questions

1. **C** Unlike many other ancient civilizations that practiced polytheism, the Israelites practiced monotheism, or the worship of only one god.

2. **F** The Hebrew Bible indicates that the Israelites migrated to Canaan from Mesopotamia.

3. **A** Because of factors such as David's successes in battle, his construction of a capital city, and the prosperous economic conditions during his reign, David is considered the greatest king in Israelite history.

4. **F** Despite having withstood earlier Assyrian conquests, Jerusalem was captured by the Chaldeans in 597 B.C. and then destroyed by them in 586 B.C.

5. **D** During the Babylonian Exile, Jews did not have a temple in which to worship. As a result, they began meeting at synagogues to worship on the Sabbath.

6. **I** The Zealots wanted to be free from Roman rule and rebelled in 66 B.C., capturing Jerusalem

21st Century Skills

2. Students should select relevant, informative images and clearly explain how each image relates to their selected topics.

Thinking Like a Historian

3. Graphic organizers might include the following information: Pharisees—resisted by practicing the Torah's teachings with greater devotion; Sadducees—disagreed with Pharisees, favored cooperation with Romans; Essenes—rebellious priests broke away from Temple and only followed the Torah; Zealots—wanted to fight Romans for freedom.

Locating Places

4. **1.** Mesopotamia F; **2.** Mediterranean Sea E; **3.** Red Sea D; **4.** Canaan C; **5.** Israel B; **6.** Egypt A

Assessment Answers

Analyzing Documents

7 **D** The main purpose of the Ten Commandments is to provide rules for living, not to suggest ways to observe the Sabbath, describe qualifications for kings, or reveal warnings.

8 **I** Modern laws incorporate the moral principles of the Ten Commandments by punishing bad behavior (murder and theft, for example) and promoting a fair society. Modern biology and geography are based on scientific fact, not moral principles. Modern politics do not consistently uphold moral principles.

Short Response

9 Students should explain that Solomon's power was weakened by his decisions to tax the people heavily and to expect them to serve as soldiers, officers, and commanders of his army. Also, he favored the tribe of Judah over the other tribes.

10 Students' responses should indicate that Solomon's granting of favors to only one tribe likely made the other tribes feel they were being treated unfairly.

Extended Response

11 Students' essays should detail the conditions of Jewish life under Greek and Roman rule. For instance, they might suggest that under the Greek rule of Alexander, Judah remained the center of Judaism. Greek culture spread into Judah, and many Jews also moved to other parts of the Greek Empire. This helped spread Jewish ideas throughout the Mediterranean region. Later, Greek rulers ordered Jews to give up their beliefs, which led to conflict. Disagreements also grew during the period of Roman rule. Several Jewish groups suggested different responses to Roman policies, including a revolt. The Romans eventually defeated several Jewish rebellions.

CHAPTER 6 Assessment *(continued)*

DBQ ANALYZING DOCUMENTS

RH.6–8.1

7 **Summarizing** Which of the following best states the main purpose of the Ten Commandments?

A. to suggest ways to observe the Sabbath
B. to describe the qualifications for kings
C. to reveal warnings to Israelites
D. to provide rules for living

RH.6–8.1

8 **Drawing Conclusions** The message found in the Ten Commandments can best be seen today in

F. modern biology.
G. modern geography.
H. modern politics.
I. modern law.

The Ten Commandments

1. Do not worship any god except me.
2. Do not . . . bow down and worship idols.
3. Do not misuse my name.
4. Remember the Sabbath Day and keep it holy.
5. Honor your father and your mother.
6. Do not murder.
7. Be faithful in marriage.
8. Do not steal.
9. Do not testify falsely [tell lies] about others.
10. Do not want anything that belongs to someone else.

—**Paraphrased** from Exodus 20:3-17

SHORT RESPONSE

"The biblical King Solomon was known for his wisdom, his wealth and his writings. . . . Solomon's downfall came in his old age. . . . Within Solomon's kingdom, he placed heavy taxation on the people, who became bitter. He also had the people work as soldiers, chief officers and commanders of his chariots and cavalry. He granted special privileges to the tribes of Judah and this alienated [angered] the northern tribes."

—from "Solomon" by Shira Schoenberg

RH.6–8.1

9 What is believed to have weakened Solomon as a king?

RH.6–8.1

10 Why might Solomon granting special privileges to the tribes of Judah have displeased the other tribes?

EXTENDED RESPONSE

RH.6–8.2, WHST.6–8.2, WHST.6–8.10

11 **Narrative** Write a short essay in which you compare and contrast the daily life of Jews under Greek and Roman rule. Consider how Greek and Roman rule affected the Jewish peoples' ability to practice their religion. Describe how conflicts eventually developed between the Jews and the ruling groups.

Need Extra Help?

If You've Missed Question	1	2	3	4	5	6	7	8	9	10	11
Review Lesson	1	1	2, 4	2, 3	2	4	1	1	2	2	4

networks Online Teaching Options

Help Students Use the Skills Builder Resources

Your students can practice important 21st Century skills such as geography, reading, writing, and critical thinking by using resources found in the Skills Builder tab of the online Student Learning Center. Resources include templates, handbooks, and slide shows. These same resources are also available in the Resource Library of the Teacher Lesson Center.

CHAPTER 7

The Ancient Greeks Planner

UNDERSTANDING BY DESIGN®

Enduring Understandings

- *People, places, and Ideas change over time.*
- *The value that a society places on individual rights is often reflected in that society's government.*
- *Countries have relationships with each other.*

Essential Questions

- *How does geography influence the way people live?*
- *Why do people form governments?*
- *Why does conflict develop?*
- *How do governments change?*

Predictable Misunderstandings

Students may think:

- *Democracy was the same in Athens as in the United States.*
- *The Greek city-states were friendly to one another because they were all located in Greece.*

Assessment Evidence

Performance Tasks:

- *Hands-On Chapter Project*

Other Evidence:

- *Responses to Interactive Whiteboard Activities*
- *Comparing and Contrasting Photos of Greek culture*
- *Class Discussions of the Peloponnesian War*
- *Economics of History Activity*
- *21st Century Skills Activity*
- *Geography and History Activity*
- *Primary Source Activities*
- *Written Essay*
- *Lesson Reviews*
- *Chapter Activities and Assessment*

SUGGESTED PACING GUIDE

Introducing the Chapter	1 day	Lesson 3	1 day
Lesson 1	2 days	Lesson 4	2 days
Lesson 2	2 days	Chapter Wrap-Up and Assessment	1 day

TOTAL TIME 9 DAYS

Key for Using the Teacher Edition

SKILL-BASED ACTIVITIES

Types of skill activities found in the Teacher Edition.

V Visual Skills require students to analyze maps, graphs, charts, and photos.

R Reading Skills help students practice reading skills and master vocabulary.

W Writing Skills provide writing opportunities to help students comprehend the text.

C Critical Thinking Skills help students apply and extend what they have learned.

T Technology Skills require students to use digital tools effectively.

*Letters are followed by a number when there is more than one of the same type of skill on the page.

DIFFERENTIATED INSTRUCTION

All activities are written for the on-level student unless otherwise marked with the leveled labels below.

BL Beyond Level

AL Approaching Level

ELL English Language Learners

All students benefit from activities that utilize different learning styles. Many activities are marked as below when a particular learning style is highlighted.

Intrapersonal	**Naturalist**
Logical/Mathematical	**Kinesthetic**
Visual/Spatial	**Auditory/Musical**
Verbal/Linguistic	**Interpersonal**

NCSS Standards covered in "The Ancient Greeks"

Learners will understand:

1 CULTURE

4. That the beliefs, values, and behaviors of a culture form an integrated system that helps shape the activities and ways of life that define a culture

8. That language, behaviors, and beliefs of different cultures can both contribute to and pose barriers to cross-cultural understanding

2 TIME, CONTINUITY, AND CHANGE

7. The contributions of key persons, groups, and events from the past and their influence on the present

3 PEOPLE, PLACES, AND ENVIRONMENTS

8. Factors that contribute to cooperation and conflict among peoples of the nation and world, including language, religion, and political beliefs

4 INDIVIDUAL DEVELOPMENT AND IDENTITY

3. How factors such as physical endowment, interests, capabilities, learning, motivation, personality, perception, and beliefs influence individual development and identity

4. How personal, social, cultural, and environmental factors contribute to the development and the growth of personal identity

5 INDIVIDUALS, GROUPS, AND INSTITUTIONS

2. Concepts such as: mores, norms, status, role, socialization, ethnocentrism, cultural diffusion, competition, cooperation, conflict, race, ethnicity, and gender

6. That cultural diffusion occurs when groups migrate

9. That groups and institutions influence culture in a variety of ways

8 SCIENCE, TECHNOLOGY, AND SOCIETY

6. Values, beliefs, and attitudes that have been influenced by new scientific and technological knowledge (for example, invention of the printing press, conceptions of the universe, applications of atomic energy, and genetic discoveries)

CHAPTER OPENER PLANNER

Students will know:

- *how geography affected the early Greeks.*
- *what contributed to the development of the Minoan civilization.*
- *how the Mycenaeans became a powerful military force.*
- *how Greek culture spread to other parts of the world.*
- *the different types of government that developed among the Greek city-states.*
- *why Sparta became a military society.*
- *what characteristics made Athens unique.*
- *how the Persians successfully ruled their large empire.*
- *what the Greeks did to defeat the Persians.*
- *what it was like to live in Athens during the rule of Pericles.*

Students will be able to:

- ***explain*** *how geography affected the settlement of Greece.*
- ***identify*** *similarities and differences between the rights and responsibilities of ancient Greek citizens and U.S. citizens today.*
- ***describe*** *the characteristics of tyranny, oligarchy, and democracy.*
- ***explain*** *differences between Sparta and Athens.*
- ***identify*** *the location of the Persian Empire.*
- ***explain*** *how the Greeks won the Persian Wars.*
- ***explain*** *differences between Athenian democracy and American democracy.*
- ***identify*** *characteristics of life in Athens.*

UNDERSTANDING BY DESIGN®

☑ *Print Teaching Options*

V **Visual Skills**

- ☐ **P. 172** Students locate Greece on a map and discuss its location and how its geography affected people in ancient times.
- ☐ **P. 173** Students study and discuss a time line covering major events from about 2000 B.C. to about 400 B.C.

☑ *Online Teaching Options*

V **Visual Skills**

- MAP **Ancient Greece 2000 B.C. to 400 B.C.**—Students observe the extent of ancient Greece and locate important cities in the area.
- TIME LINE **Place and Time: The Ancient Greeks: 2000 B.C. to 400 B.C.**—Students learn about key historical events related to the rise and fall of ancient Greece.
- WORLD ATLAS Students can use this interactive map to identify regions of the world, learn about individual countries, locate political boundaries, measure distances, and much more.

☑ *Printable Digital Worksheets*

R **Reading Skills**

- GRAPHIC NOVEL ***Peloponnesian Strangers!*** In this graphic novel, Draco of Sparta and Cylon of Athens discuss their differing outlooks on life.

Project-Based Learning

Hands-On Chapter Project

Create Maps

To understand how the strengths and weaknesses of Athens, Sparta, and Persia contributed to conflicts among their governments, students will create maps that show how each army could conquer another.

Technology Extension

Create Interactive Maps

- Find an additional activity online that incorporates technology for this project.
- Visit the EdTechTeacher Web sites (included in the Technology Extension for this chapter) for more links and tutorials, and other resources.

Print Resources

ANCILLARY RESOURCES

These ancillaries are available for every chapter and lesson.

- **Reading Essentials and Study Guide Workbook** AL ELL
- **Chapter Tests and Lesson Quizzes Blackline Masters**

PRINTABLE DIGITAL WORKSHEETS

These printable digital worksheets are available for every chapter and lesson.

- **Hands-On Chapter Projects**
- **What Do You Know? activities**
- **Chapter Summaries (English and Spanish)**
- **Vocabulary Builder activities**
- **Guided Reading activities**

More Media Resources

SUGGESTED VIDEOS MOVIES

Watch clips of popular films and shows such as *The Odyssey,* a television miniseries based on Homer's epic poem about the Greek hero Ulysses's 10-year voyage home following the Trojan War. This retelling of one of the greatest adventures of all time was produced by the Hallmark Channel.

- **Ask:** **Why do you think stories written by the Greeks so many years ago are still popular today?**

(NOTE: Preview clips for age-appropriateness.)

SUGGESTED READING

Grade 6 reading level:

- ***Mythological Creatures: A Classical Bestiary,*** written and illustrated by Lynn Curlee

Grade 7 reading level:

- ***Eyewitness Books: Olympics,*** by Chris Oxlade and David Ballheimer

Grade 8 reading level:

- ***Troy,*** by Adele Geras

Rise of Greek Civilization

Students will know:
- *how geography affected the early Greeks.*
- *what contributed to the development of the Minoan civilization.*
- *how the Mycenaeans became a powerful military force.*
- *how Greek culture spread to other parts of the world.*

Students will be able to:
- ***explain*** *how geography affected the settlement of Greece.*
- ***identify*** *similarities and differences between the rights and responsibilities of ancient Greek citizens and U.S. citizens today.*

UNDERSTANDING BY DESIGN®

☑ Print Teaching Options

V Visual Skills

- ☐ **P. 175** Students use a map to answer questions about the geography of Ancient Greece. **Visual/Spatial**
- ☐ **P. 177** Students study the Mask of Agamemnon to learn about life of the Mycenaean people.
- ☐ **P. 178** Students use a chart to learn about and practice writing the Greek alphabet. **Visual/Spatial**
- ☐ **P. 180** Students study a map about Greek trading in ancient times and use the map to answer questions. **AL** **BL**

R Reading Skills

- ☐ **P. 174** Students discuss why fishing was more popular in ancient Greece than farming.
- ☐ **P. 176** Students use context clues to understand the work of archaeologists. **AL** **ELL**
- ☐ **P. 176** Students use the ruins discovered by archaeologists to describe what life may have been like in an ancient Greek palace, and then draw a palace map.
- ☐ **P. 179** Students explain the role geography played in developing the concept of Greek citizenship. **BL** **ELL**
- ☐ **P. 182** Students read a primary-source quotation and restate the content in their own words. **Linguistic/Verbal**

W Writing Skills

- ☐ **P. 179** Students write a paragraph about the effects of trading in ancient Greece.

C Critical Thinking Skills

- ☐ **P. 174** Students speculate on how people living on a peninsula today might earn a living.
- ☐ **P. 177** Students create a Venn diagram to compare and contrast the Minoans and the Mycenaeans. **AL**
- ☐ **P. 178** Students discuss the effects of having a surplus of food.
- ☐ **P. 181** Student create a chart to show the rights and responsibilities of ancient Greek citizens.

☑ Online Teaching Options

V Visual Skills

- **VIDEO** **Ancient Greece: Geography and Government**—Students view a video that explains how the Greek landscape affected the development of government.
- **MAP** **Ancient Greece c. 2000 B.C.**—Students examine the extent of ancient Greece in 2000 B.C.
- **MAP** **Greek Trading Among Colonies, 750 B.C.–550 B.C.**—Students examine the routes followed by traders between the Greek colonies.
- **SLIDE SHOW** **Greece**—Students view images and read text that describes Greece today.
- **IMAGE** **Knossos Palace**—Students click to learn facts about this ancient Minoan structure.
- **SLIDE SHOW** **Agora**—Students view images and read text that describes the structure and uses of these public spaces.
- **IMAGE** **Hoplites**—Students learn more about these citizen soldiers.

R Reading Skills

- **GRAPHIC ORGANIZER** **Taking Notes: *Comparing:* Minoans and Mycenaeans**—Students complete a Venn diagram to compare and contrast the Minoans and Mycenaeans.
- **SLIDE SHOW** **Mycenaean Artifacts**—Students explore Mycenaean artifacts through visuals and text.

C Critical Thinking Skills

- **CHART** **Greek Alphabet**—Students spell vocabulary terms using the Greek alphabet.
- **WHITEBOARD ACTIVITY** **Ancient Greece**—Students sequence events in ancient Greek history.
- **IMAGE** **Greek and American Coins**—Students identify similarities among coins from both countries.

T Technology Skills

- **SELF-CHECK QUIZ** **Lesson 1**—Students receive instant feedback about their mastery of lesson content.

☑ Printable Digital Worksheets

R Reading Skills

- **WORKSHEET** **21st Century Skills Activity: Communication: Outlining**—Students practice this important reading and organizational skill.

C Critical Thinking Skills

- **WORKSHEET** **Geography and History Activity: Understanding Location: The Greek Peninsula**—Students analyze how the physical characteristics of the Greek landscape affected the development of its civilization.

SPARTA AND ATHENS: CITY-STATE RIVALS

Students will know:

- *the different types of government that developed among the Greek city-states.*
- *why Sparta became a military society.*
- *what characteristics made Athens unique.*

Students will be able to:

- ***describe** the characteristics of tyranny, oligarchy, and democracy.*
- ***explain** differences between Sparta and Athens.*

UNDERSTANDING BY DESIGN®

☑ Print Teaching Options

V Visual Skills

- ☐ **P. 184** Students study a map and answer questions about ancient Athens and Sparta. **Visual/Spatial**

R Reading Skills

- ☐ **P. 183** Students review conditions that ancient Greek farmers faced and discuss why the farmers wanted to change their government.
- ☐ **P. 185** Students read a primary-source quotation and determine the main idea of the passage.
- ☐ **P. 186** Students discuss the government of ancient Sparta. **AL**
- ☐ **P. 187** Students explain why many Spartans were resistant to change and how this affected their economy. **AL**
- ☐ **P. 188** Students discuss three leaders of ancient Athens and discuss the influence each had on the government of the city-state.

W Writing Skills

- ☐ **P. 186** Students write a journal entry from the point of view of an ancient Spartan.

C Critical Thinking Skills

- ☐ **P. 185** Students compare Spartan education to education in the United States today. **AL** **BL**
- ☐ **P. 185** Students learn the modern-day definition of the word *spartan* and explain how the definition ties back to ancient times.
- ☐ **P. 186** Students discuss the role of women in ancient Sparta.
- ☐ **P. 187** Students give a brief speech defending the education system in either Sparta or Athens. **Verbal/Linguistic**

T Technology Skills

- ☐ **P. 189** Students write and produce a short video about four characters living in ancient Athens. **Interpersonal** **Verbal/Linguistic**

☑ Online Teaching Options

V Visual Skills

- **VIDEO** **Athens**—Students learn about the Greek city-state of Athens, the birth of theater and Greek tragedy, and the goddess Athena.
- **MAP** **Sparta and Athens**—Students locate the areas controlled by these two city-states.
- **IMAGE** **Life of a Spartan Soldier**—Students click to learn about the training of Spartan soldiers.
- **IMAGE** **Greeks Elections**—Students learn that Greek officials were chosen by lottery, not by voting.
- **IMAGE** **The Reforms of Solon**—Students read about how Solon reformed Athens' strict code of laws.
- **IMAGE** **Athenian Education**—Students click to learn details of the public education offered to boys in Athens.

R Reading Skills

- **GRAPHIC ORGANIZER** **Taking Notes: *Comparing:* Sparta and Athens**—Students use a Venn diagram to compare and contrast Sparta and Athens.
- **BIOGRAPHY** **Solon**—The accomplishments of this Athenian civilian head-of-state are recounted.
- **IMAGE** **The Lives of Spartan Women**—Students read extended text to learn about the roles of Spartan women.

C Critical Thinking Skills

- **WHITEBOARD ACTIVITY** **Athens and Sparta Culture**—Students match terms with definitions in a tic-tac-toe format.

T Technology Skills

- **SELF-CHECK QUIZ** **Lesson 2**—Students receive instant feedback about their mastery of lesson content.
- **GAME** **Athenian and Spartan History eFlashcards**—Students practice key vocabulary by quizzing themselves with flashcards.

☑ Printable Digital Worksheets

W Writing Skills

- **WORKSHEET** **Economics of History Activity: Economics and Greek Governments**—Students write responses to passages about trade in Sparta and Athens.

LESSON 3 PLANNER

GREECE AND PERSIA

Students will know:
- *how the Persians successfully ruled their large empire.*
- *what the Greeks did to defeat the Persians.*

Students will be able to:
- ***identify** the location of the Persian Empire.*
- ***explain** how the Greeks won the Persian Wars.*

UNDERSTANDING BY DESIGN®

☑ Print Teaching Options

V Visual Skills

- ☐ **P. 191** Students study a map of the Royal Road in ancient Persia and use the information to answer questions. AL **Logical/Mathematical**
- ☐ **P. 192** Students analyze an image of a building in Persepolis and reenact a scene in the picture. **Kinesthetic**
- ☐ **P. 196** Students study an image and imagine they are in Salamis, watching the ships, to answer discussion questions.

R Reading Skills

- ☐ **P. 190** Students identify the Persian Empire on a modern-day map.
- ☐ **P. 192** Students discuss Zoroastrianism and define the terms *monotheistic* and *polytheism*. BL
- ☐ **P. 193** Students explain how Zoroastrianism related to the rule of Persian kings. AL
- ☐ **P. 194** Students summarize the events of the battle of Marathon.
- ☐ **P. 197** Students discuss and explain why the Greek army ultimately defeated the Persians.

W Writing Skills

- ☐ **P. 194** Students write a speech that a messenger from Marathon might have given before his death.

C Critical Thinking Skills

- ☐ **P. 190** Students discuss how Cyrus ruled the people he conquered. BL
- ☐ **P. 191** Students compare and contrast the system of provinces in the Persian Empire to states in the U.S. today. BL
- ☐ **P. 193** Students read a primary-source quotation aloud and rewrite the statement in their own words. **Auditory**
- ☐ **P. 193** Students discuss why Darius invaded Greece in 490 B.C. and discuss what may have happened if the Athenians had not chosen to help the rebels. AL
- ☐ **P. 195** Students use information they learned about the Spartans to discuss the soldiers that King Leonides selected for battle.
- ☐ **P. 195** Students read a primary-source description of a battle scene and then use the information to draw a sketch of what they think the battle may have looked like. **Visual/Spatial**

☑ Online Teaching Options

V Visual Skills

- VIDEO **The Early Olympics**—Students learn about these ancient events.
- MAP **The Persian Empire, c. 500 B.C.**—Students trace the route of the Royal Road across the Persian Empire.
- MAP **Persian Wars 499–449 B.C.**—Students trace the routes of the two Persian invasions and identify the location of important battles.

R Reading Skills

- GRAPHIC ORGANIZER **Taking Notes: *Identifying:* Persian and Greek Leaders**—Students record the names of Persian kings who attacked Greece and the names of the Greek defenders.
- PRIMARY SOURCE **Behistun Monument to Darius**—Students view images and read text carved in the cliffs of this monument.
- BIOGRAPHY **Zoroaster**—Students learn the background of this Persian religious leader.

C Critical Thinking Skills

- SLIDE SHOW **The Battle of Salamis**—Students view a diagram of the military deployments of this battle and examine a model of a Greek warship.

T Technology Skills

- SELF-CHECK QUIZ **Lesson 3**—Students receive instant feedback about their mastery of lesson content.
- GAME **Greek–Persian Wars Concentration Game**—Students match names with events.

☑ Printable Digital Worksheets

W Writing Skills

- WORKSHEET **Primary Source Activity: Herodotus's Account of the Battle of Salamis**—Students analyze and respond to two passages.

LESSON 4 PLANNER

Glory, War, and Decline

Students will know:
- *what it was like to live in Athens during the rule of Pericles.*

Students will be able to:
- ***explain** differences between Athenian democracy and American democracy.*
- ***identify** characteristics of life in Athens.*

UNDERSTANDING BY DESIGN®

☑ Print Teaching Options

V Visual Skills

- ☐ **P. 201** Students study and discuss an infographic about Athenian homes and home life. **Visual/Spatial**

R Reading Skills

- ☐ **P. 198** Students review and discuss the meaning of the terms *direct democracy* and *representative democracy.* AL ELL
- ☐ **P. 199** Students identify ways Athens became a center of learning and the arts during the rule of Pericles.
- ☐ **P. 201** Students summarize the role of slavery in ancient Athens. BL
- ☐ **P. 202** Students discuss the formation and purposes of the Delian League. AL ELL
- ☐ **P. 204** Students explain why Athens's army was not as powerful as the Spartan army.
- ☐ **P. 205** Students define the term *blockade* and discuss the results of a military blockade.

W Writing Skills

- ☐ **P. 200** Students write a dialogue from the point of view of a person living in ancient Athens. **Verbal/Linguistic**

C Critical Thinking Skills

- ☐ **P. 200** Students compare and contrast Athenian and American democracy.
- ☐ **P. 202** Students predict how other city-states would respond to Athens's gaining power. BL
- ☐ **P. 204** Students create a living time line to sequence the events of the Peloponnesian War.

T Technology Skills

- ☐ **P. 203** Students use the Internet and PowerPoint to create presentations about speeches and monuments designed to honor the military. **Interpersonal**

☑ Online Teaching Options

V Visual Skills

- ☐ **VIDEO** **Coinage and Democracy in Athens**—Students view a video that explains the economic and political processes of ancient Athens.
- ☐ **MAP** **The Peloponnesian War, 431–404 B.C.**—Students identify areas occupied by the city-states and their allies, as well as locations of important battles.
- ☐ **IMAGE** **Athenian Assembly**— Students click to learn more about the Ecclesia.
- ☐ **IMAGE** **Delos**—Students click to learn more about this small Greek island.

R Reading Skills

- ☐ **GRAPHIC ORGANIZER** **Taking Notes: *Identifying:* Age of Pericles**—Students list the accomplishments during the age of Pericles.
- ☐ **BIOGRAPHY** **Aspasia**—Students learn the background of this foreign companion of Pericles.
- ☐ **BIOGRAPHY** **Pericles**—Students learn the background of this leader of Athens during its golden age.

C Critical Thinking Skills

- ☐ **GRAPH** **Athens Population Graph**—Students compare the numbers of people in the social groups that made up the population of Athens.

T Technology Skills

- ☐ **SELF-CHECK QUIZ** **Lesson 4**—Students receive instant feedback about their mastery of lesson content.

☑ Printable Digital Worksheets

W Writing Skills

- ☐ **WORKSHEET** **Primary Source Activity: Pericles's Funeral Oration**—Students respond to an excerpt from a speech made by Pericles at a funeral for slain soldiers.

INTERVENTION AND REMEDIATION STRATEGIES

LESSON 1 Rise of Greek Civilization

Reading and Comprehension

To ensure understanding of concepts, have students work in pairs to write sentences using new vocabulary in this lesson. Sentences should use the words correctly and demonstrate an understanding of each word and how it relates to the Guiding Questions.

Text Evidence

Ask students to analyze how the Hellenes adopted aspects of other cultures and spread their own culture throughout the Mediterranean. They should use evidence about trade and colonization from the text.

LESSON 2 Sparta and Athens: City-State Rivals

Reading and Comprehension

Have students work in groups to summarize the events that led to Athens's becoming a democracy. Ask them to include a description of the limits of Athenian democracy.

Text Evidence

Have students complete a Venn diagram to compare and contrast Athens and Sparta. Diagrams should provide evidence from the text about education, government, and social structure in each city-state.

LESSON 3 Greece and Persia

Reading and Comprehension

Have students describe the strengths and weaknesses of the Persian Empire. They should use as many vocabulary words from the lesson as possible.

Text Evidence

Have students work in small groups to create time lines that identify the major events in the war between Greece and Persia. Groups should use evidence from the text to write one to two sentences about each event.

LESSON 4 Glory, War, and Decline

Reading and Comprehension

Ask students to skim the lesson to find new or unfamiliar words and then use a dictionary to define them. Students can share the definitions with others and let the rest of the class identify what words are being defined.

Text Evidence

Have students write a description of life in Athens for men, women, and children. They should use specific evidence from the text to show that in this "democracy," people at different levels of society had very different rights and privileges.

Online Resources

Approaching Level Reader

Use this online lower-level text that corresponds directly to the text in the Student Edition. It includes a Spanish version.

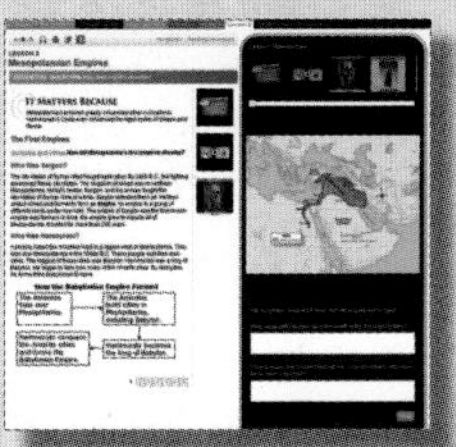

Guided Reading Activities

This resource uses graphic organizers and guiding questions to help students with comprehension.

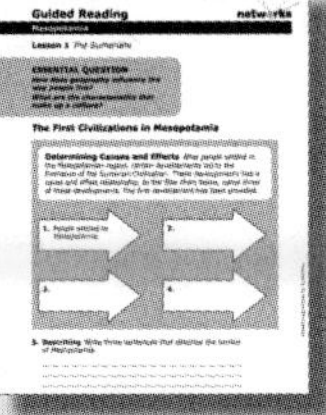

What Do You Know?

Use these worksheets to pre-assess student's background knowledge before they study the chapter.

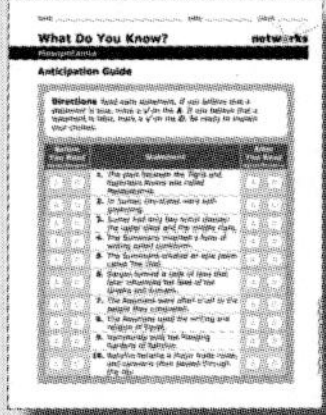

Reading Essentials and Study Guide Workbook

This resource offers writing and reading activities for the approaching-level student. Also available in Spanish.

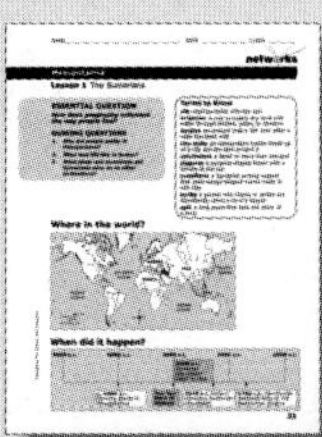

Self-Check Quizzes

This online assessment tool provides instant feedback for students to check their progress.

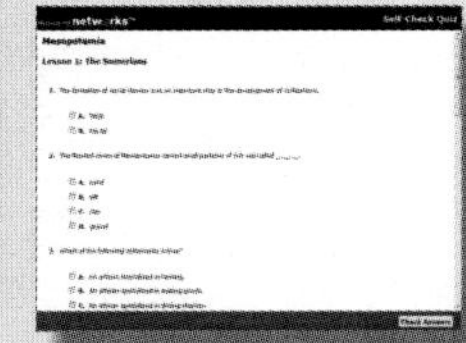

How Do I Teach with
Hands-On Chapter Projects?

Would you like your students to explore a more complicated bit of chapter content that could take more than a class period? Do you want to teach group work rather than assign individual homework? The Hands-On Chapter Project option can help you meet such teaching goals. Each chapter features a cumulative project that brings the content to life for students in different ways. Here are some steps for running project-based teaching more effectively.

Step 1 Gather the right resources

- Projects require student research outside of the student textbook. Familiarize them with the proper tools and research techniques.
- Sources could include online collections, reference materials in your school library, or additional Web sites.

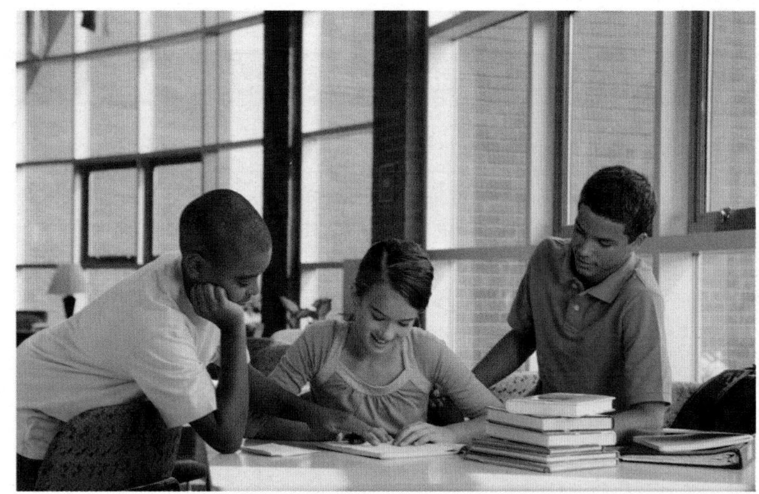

Blend Images/Getty Images

Step 2 Collaboration Skills

- Students need to be aware that group projects require interaction with classmates and review of each other's work.
- Build in time and methods for group members to review the assigned product throughout the project. This may be done in class, digitally outside of school, or in another agreed-upon method.

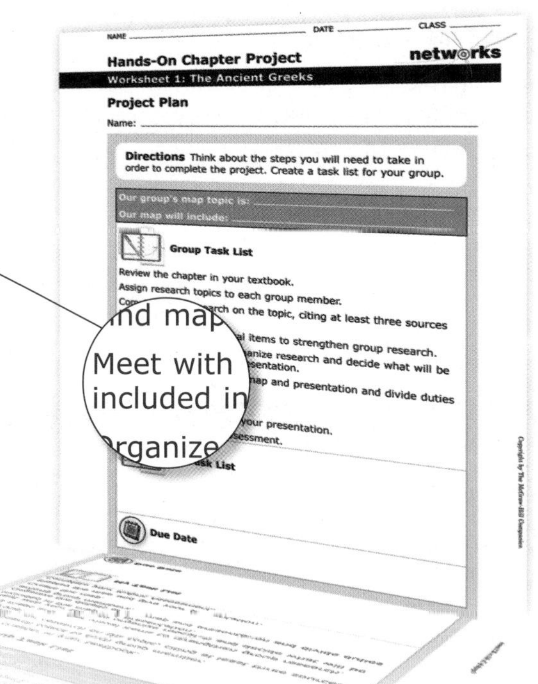

NAME DATE CLASS

Hands-On Chapter Project networks

Worksheet 1: The Ancient Greeks

Project Plan

Name:

Directions Think about the steps you will need to take in order to complete the project. Create a task list for your group.

Our group's map topic is:

Our map will include:

Group Task List

Review the chapter in your textbook.

Assign research topics to each group member.

...rch on the topic, citing at least three sources

...nd map...

...l items to strengthen group research.

Meet with ...anize research and decide what will be included in ...sentation.

...ap and presentation and divide duties

...rganize...

...your presentation.

...sessment.

...sk List

Due Date

Step 3 Producing the Final Project

- Students may choose to utilize technology for the final project. Today's students are skilled creators. Provide them with the tools and the opportunity to be as creative in class as they can.

The Ancient Greeks

2000 B.C. to 400 B.C.

ESSENTIAL QUESTIONS • *How does geography influence the way people live?* • *Why do people form governments?* • *Why does conflict develop?* • *How do governments change?*

networks

There's More Online about the lives and the culture of the ancient Greeks.

CHAPTER 7

Lesson 1 *Rise of Greek Civilization*

Lesson 2 *Sparta and Athens: City-State Rivals*

Lesson 3 *Greece and Persia*

Lesson 4 *Glory, War, and Decline*

The Story Matters . . .

In ancient times, Greek language, culture, and mythology spread throughout the Mediterranean region. Traditional figures, such as the goddess Athena, were featured in art and on pottery and other household objects.

In time, ancient Greek civilization was absorbed by the more powerful Romans. Because the Romans imitated Greek culture in many ways, the achievements of the Greeks in politics, philosophy, and literature were passed on through the centuries. In this way, the ancient Greeks continue to influence Western civilization.

◄ *The gods and goddesses of Greek mythology are part of our most enduring literature. As shown here, the goddess Athena is usually depicted with a helmet ready for battle.*

Letter from the Author

Dear World History Teacher,

The earliest Greek-speaking people migrated from Asia into Greece and established the Mycenaean civilization. After the civilization's collapse in the 1100s B.C., Greece entered its Dark Age. With the end of the Dark Age around 800 B.C., the era of the polis, or city-state, began. The polis was a community of people ruled by its male citizens. The two most famous city-states were Sparta and Athens. Many of our political terms are Greek in origin. Our concepts of the rights and duties of citizenship were also conceived in Athens.

Jackson J. Spielvogel

ENGAGE

Bellringer Read "The Story Matters . . ." aloud in class, or ask a volunteer to read it aloud. Then discuss what it might have been like living in Greece as a young person when Greek culture was a strong influence in the Mediterranean area. **Ask:** What are the effects of American cultural influence in the world? Ask a few students to share their views. Then **ask:** Does living in a dominant culture affect the way people in that culture live and view the rest of the world? Tell the class that Greek civilization developed from the Minoans and Mycenaeans. By the 700s B.C., Greek city-states and colonies flourished in the Mediterranean region. The Persian Empire attempted unsuccessfully to invade Greece. However, by the end of the 400s B.C., Greek culture declined after a bitter war between the two most powerful city-states, Athens and Sparta.

Making Connections

Discuss with students some of the ways in which American society today is influenced by ancient Greece.

- Athens, Greece, had one of the earliest forms of democracy in the world. The founders of the United States government were influenced by Greek ideas about government and citizenship.
- Greek architecture influenced American architecture in the early 1800s, and many of the buildings of Washington, D.C., in particular, have elements of Greek architecture in them.
- Many popular modern forms of literature, including dramas and epic poems, were first created by the ancient Greeks. Characters and themes from Greek mythology have been used throughout Western literature.

TEACH & ASSESS

Step Into the Place

V1 Visual Skills

Reading a Map Display a current world map, and ask students how many of them know where Greece is and what present-day countries are close to Greece. Then have students find ancient Greece on the chapter opener map. Ask questions such as:

- **What can you tell about the geography of ancient Greece by looking at this map?** *(It is on a peninsula and has many small islands. It is also a mountainous region)*
- **How might the geography of ancient Greece have affected its people?** *(With so much coastline, the Greeks were probably sailors and traders. The mountains may have made it difficult to travel on land.)*

Content Background Knowledge

- Today, the nation of Greece is about 51,000 square miles, which is smaller than the area of ancient Greece.
- In spite of the many achievements of ancient Greece, modern-day Greece faced numerous political and economic problems. These problems have occurred in part because Greece has many mountains and few natural resources.
- The nation of Greece has a population of more than 10 million, and more than half of its people live in cities. Greece's capital is Athens.

CHAPTER 7 CCSS

Place and Time: Greece 2000 B.C. to 400 B.C.

Greek city-states developed after the civilizations of the Minoans and Mycenaeans. By the 700s B.C., city-states and colonies flourished in the Mediterranean region. The Persian Empire attempted unsuccessfully to invade Greece. By the late 400s, however, all of Greece had been weakened during a bitter war between Athens and Sparta.

The city-state of Sparta was a military society. Spartan boys began training for the military at the age of seven. Between the ages of 20 and 60, Spartan men served as soldiers in the city-state's army. Discipline was strict, and in battle soldiers were expected to win—or die trying. Sparta's differences with Athens made it impossible for ancient Greece to become a politically unified state.

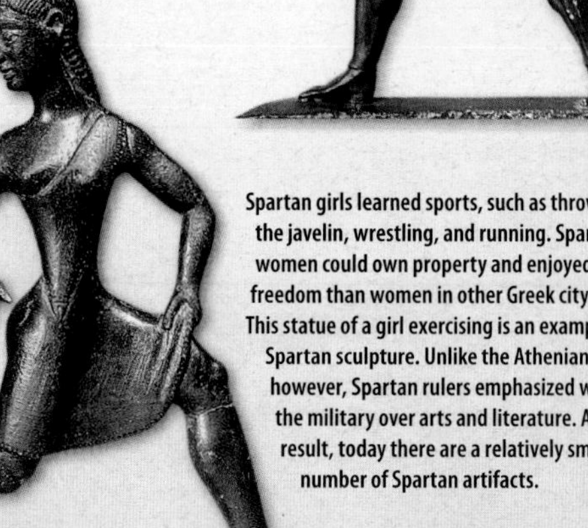

Spartan girls learned sports, such as throwing the javelin, wrestling, and running. Spartan women could own property and enjoyed more freedom than women in other Greek city-states. This statue of a girl exercising is an example of Spartan sculpture. Unlike the Athenians, however, Spartan rulers emphasized war and the military over arts and literature. As a result, today there are a relatively small number of Spartan artifacts.

(t) Foto Marburg/Art Resource, NY; (b) Figurine of a girl running, (bronze), Greek, (6th century BC)/British Museum, London, UK/The Bridgeman Art Library

Step Into the Place

MAP FOCUS The location of Greece put it at the crossroads of Europe, Africa, and Asia.

1. **LOCATION** Is Greece located east or west of Asia Minor? RH.6–8.7
2. **PLACE** What influence would the Greeks' location on the Mediterranean Sea have on the way they earned a living and traveled? RH.6–8.7
3. **PLACE** What type of geographic landform is mainland Greece as a whole? RH.6–8.7
4. **CRITICAL THINKING** *Analyzing Visuals* What makes the area occupied by the ancient Greeks a crossroads between three continents? RH.6–8.1

Step Into the Time

V2 **TIME LINE** What events in Greece point out that conflict was often a part of ancient Greek life? RH.6–8.7

GREECE
- c. 2000 B.C. Minoans control eastern Mediterranean
- c. 1450 B.C. Mycenaeans conquer Minoans; control Aegean
- c. 1200 B.C. Mycenaean civilization declines

2000 B.C. — 1000 B.C.

THE WORLD
- c. 1792 B.C. Hammurabi becomes king of Babylonian Empire
- c. 1500 B.C. Queen Hatshepsut reigns in Egypt
- c. 1390 B.C. Writing appears in China
- c. 1020 B.C. Saul chosen as first king of Israel

ANSWERS, p. 172

Step Into the Place

1. Greece is west of Asia Minor.
2. The location of Greece in the Mediterranean Sea would encourage its people to fish for a living. A major form of transportation would be by boat.
3. The mainland is a peninsula. Greece also has several nearby islands.
4. CRITICAL THINKING Greece lies at the crossroads of Europe, Africa, and Asia. Its location increased the likelihood of contact between Greeks and people from the other continents.

Step Into the Time

Students will note the uprising and wars listed on the time line. Their answers would include the following: Greek revolt of 499 B.C., invasion by Xerxes in 480 B.C., Peloponnesian War beginning in 431 B.C.

Project-Based Learning

Hands-On Chapter Project

Create Maps

To understand how the strengths and weaknesses of Athens, Sparta, and Persia contributed to conflicts among their governments, students will create maps that show how the advantages of each army had helped them conquer others. Students will participate in a class discussion about conflicts between governments or cultures. In small groups, they will study Athens, Sparta, or Persia. Each group will plan, research, and create their maps. Then groups will present their completed maps to the class and discuss what they have learned.

Technology Extension

Create Interactive Maps

Students will create interactive maps of Athens, Sparta, or Persia online. They will work in groups to learn about their assigned locations and then insert text, images, links to Web sites, and videos in their Interactive maps. Students will then explore and critique each other's maps and hold a class discussion about what they have learned from the activity.

networks
There's More Online!

☑ **MAP** Explore the interactive version of this map on NETWORKS.

☑ **TIME LINE** Explore the interactive version of this time line on NETWORKS.

V1

Ancient Greece 2000 B.C. to 400 B.C.

Black Sea
MACEDONIA
Sea of Marmara
Mt. Olympus
BALKAN PENINSULA
Troy
KEY
Ancient Greece
GREECE
Aegean Sea
ASIA MINOR
Ionian Sea
Delphi
Gulf of Corinth
Thebes
Corinth
Athens
Mycenae
PELOPONNESUS
Miletus
Sparta
Mediterranean Sea
Knossos
Crete
0 100 miles
0 100 km
Lambert Azimuthal Equal-Area projection
20°E
25°E
30°E
35°N
40°N

c. 650 B.C. Greeks colonize shores of the Mediterranean

c. 480 B.C. Xerxes invades Greece

499 B.C. Greeks revolt against Persian rulers

c. 431 B.C. Peloponnesian War begins

c. 330 B.C. Alexander the Great conquers Persian Empire

800 B.C. | 600 B.C. | 400 B.C. | 200 B.C.

c. 680 B.C. Iron-making skills spread in East Africa

c. 575 B.C. India adopts the caste system

486 B.C. Xerxes becomes king of Persia

c. 241 B.C. Rome defeats Carthage in First Punic War

173

TIME LINE

Place and Time: The Ancient Greeks: 2000 B.C. to 400 B.C.

Reading a Time Line Display the interactive time line and have volunteers read each event. Then have students make K-W-L charts for each event on the top half of the time line. They can write what they *know (K)* and want to *learn (W)* about the event now. As they read the chapter, they can fill in what they have *learned (L)*.

See page 171B for other online activities.

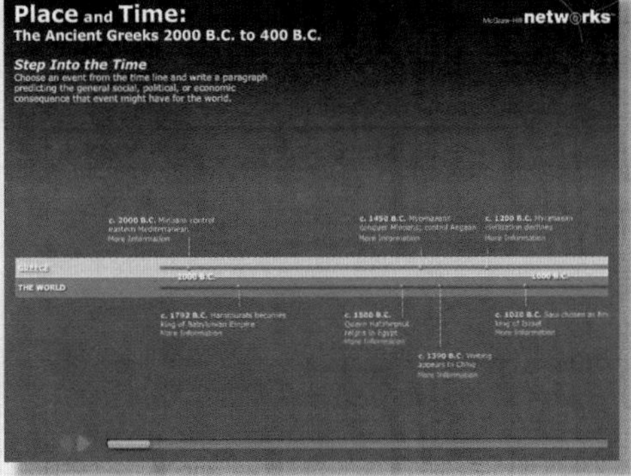

CHAPTER 7

Place and Time

Step Into the Time

V2 Visual Skills

Analyzing Time Lines Have students review the time line for the chapter. Point out that the top half of the time line focuses on events in Greece and the bottom half of the time line covers events in other parts of the world at the same time. Explain that they will be studying events from about 2000 B.C. to about 400 B.C. **Ask:** **What are some events you already know about that happened during those years?** *(Students might answer that Hammurabi became the king of the Babylonian Empire and that Saul was chosen as the first king of Israel.)*

Have students review the time line and discuss its major event as a class. Ask questions such as these:

- **Who controlled Greece around 2000 B.C.?** *(the Minoans)*
- **How many years passed between the year that Xerxes became king of Persia and the year he invaded Greece?** *(6 years)*
- **What was happening in Greece around the time that iron-making skills were spreading in East Africa?** *(The Greeks were colonizing the shores of the Mediterranean.)*

Content Background Knowledge

- Greeks were organized into city-states, which were geographically small political units that had their own form of government. Important city-states included Athens, Sparta, Thebes, and Corinth.
- At times, the city-states formed alliances to fight against others, such as when they joined forces to fight against the Persian Empire.
- At other times, the city-states fought against one another. The best example of this is the Peloponnesian War, in which Athens and its allies fought against Sparta and its allies.

CLOSE & REFLECT

Formulating Questions Have each student write a question based on the map, time line, or class discussion about ancient Greece. Collect the questions and answer them as a class. Tell students they will be learning more about ancient Greece as they study this chapter.

Rise of Greek Civilization

ENGAGE

Bellringer Project the interactive map of Greece, Crete, and the Mediterranean Sea from the chapter opener. Discuss as a class how geography affected the lives of the early Greeks. **Ask:**

- **What three major bodies of water surround the Greek peninsula?** *(the Ionian Sea, the Mediterranean Sea, and the Aegean Sea)*
- **Though Greece is surrounded by water on three sides, what is most of the land like on the Greek peninsula?** *(Most of the land is rugged and mountainous.)*

Tell students they will be learning how geography affected the development of the first civilizations in Greece.

TEACH & ASSESS

R Reading Skills

Discussing After students read the text, discuss with them why people who live on a peninsula would be likely to earn their living from trading and fishing. **Ask: Why might fishing and trading have been easier than farming in some parts of Greece?** *(The mountains would have made farming difficult, and the coastline would have been good for fishing and trading.)*

C Critical Thinking Skills

Speculating Explain that the geography of Greece continues to affect the way people live there today. **Ask: In addition to fishing and trading, can you think of other ways that people living on a peninsula might earn a living today? To help, think about peninsulas such as Florida in the United States.** *(Greece's beautiful coastline makes tourism an important part of Greece's economy today.)*

ANSWER, p. 174

TAKING NOTES: Answers for Minoans include island civilization and mysterious collapse. Answers for Mycenaeans include mainland civilization, warfare, and detailed records. Answers for both include kings, large palaces, and trade.

There's More Online!

- CHART/GRAPH: Greek Alphabet
- GRAPHIC ORGANIZER: Compare Minoans and Mycenaeans
- SLIDE SHOW: • Mycenaean Artifacts • The Agora

Lesson 1

Rise of Greek Civilization

ESSENTIAL QUESTION *How does geography influence the way people live?*

IT MATTERS BECAUSE

The early Greeks developed important settlements, trade routes, and political ideas in the Mediterranean region.

Mountains and Seas

GUIDING QUESTION *How did physical geography influence the lives of the early Greeks?*

Greece was the first civilization to develop in Europe and the westernmost part of Asia. In other early civilizations, people first settled in river valleys that had rich soil. Greek civilization began in an area **dominated** by mountains and seas.

If you flew over this region today, you would see rugged landscapes and beautiful seas. The Greek mainland is on the southern part of Europe's Balkan Peninsula. A **peninsula** (puh•NIHN•suh•luh) is a body of land with water on three sides. Far to the east of the Greek mainland is another peninsula called Anatolia. It is part of present-day Turkey.

Between these two land areas are the dazzling blue waters of the Aegean Sea. The Aegean Sea is part of the larger Mediterranean Sea. There are hundreds of islands in the Aegean Sea. They look like stepping stones between the Greek mainland and Anatolia.

The Greeks traded goods and ideas between islands and along the area's coastlines. Today many Greeks fish and trade for a living, much as the ancient Greeks did before them. Other ancient Greeks settled in farming **communities**. These settlements began on narrow, fertile plains that ran along the

(tl) GUIZIOU Franck/Hemis/Age fotostock, (tcl) The Print Collector/Heritage/Age fotostock, (tc) Georgios Kollidas/Panther Media/Age fotostock, (tcr) Jeff Greenberg/Age fotostock, (tr) North Wind/North Wind Picture Archives

Reading **HELP**DESK 

Taking Notes: ***Comparing***

Use a Venn diagram like the one here to compare the Minoans and Mycenaeans. RH.6–8.2

Minoans | Both | Mycenaeans

Content Vocabulary (Tier 3 Words)

- **peninsula**
- **bard**
- **colony**
- **polis**
- **agora**
- **phalanx**

networks *Online Teaching Options*

VIDEO

Ancient Greece: Geography and Government

Determining Cause and Effect/Comparing and Contrasting Watch this video as a class. It describes how the geography of ancient Greece created isolated communities that in turn developed into city-states, with their own forms of government. Have students take notes on how the geography led to the growth of city-states, and then ask them to compare and contrast the different city-states.

See page 171C for other online activities.

coast and between the mountains. In the area's mild climate, farmers grew crops, such as wheat, barley, olives, and grapes. They also raised sheep and goats.

Even though some Greek communities were near the sea, others were far from the coast. Inland communities were separated from each other by rugged mountains and deep valleys. As a result, communities in many parts of ancient Greece became fiercely independent. They came to think of their communities almost as small separate countries.

✓ PROGRESS CHECK

Understanding Cause and Effect How did seas influence the way many ancient Greeks lived?

GEOGRAPHY CONNECTION

All parts of ancient Greece were near water.

1. **LOCATION** Which body of water lies east of the Balkan Peninsula?
2. **CRITICAL THINKING** ***Making Inferences*** What type of transportation was probably most useful to the early Greeks?

V

peninsula a piece of land nearly surrounded by water

Academic Vocabulary (Tier 2 Words)

dominate to control or influence something or someone

community people with common interests living in a particular area; the area itself

V Visual Skills

Analyzing Maps Have students study the map of ancient Greece. To familiarize students with major regions and city-states, **ask:**

- **What three city-states were located on the Peloponnesus peninsula?** *(Corinth, Mycenae, and Sparta)*
- **Where was the city-state Knossos located?** *(on the island of Crete)*
- **Which two city-states were located across the Aegean Sea from the main peninsula of Greece?** *(Troy and Miletus)* **Visual/Spatial**

Content Background Knowledge

The Geography of Greece

- About 70% of Greece is covered by mountains, and most of these are mountain chains that run from the northwest to the southeast. The country's highest mountain is Mount Olympus, in Thessaly.
- Greece's coast is made up of hundreds of small peninsulas that create many inlets, gulfs, and bays,
- The islands of Greece make up about 20% of its total land area.
- Greece has a Mediterranean climate, which means that it has hot, dry summers and mild, rainy winters.

MAP

Ancient Greece c. 2000 B.C.

Reading a Map Share the map of ancient Greece, and have students use the "zoom" tool to examine areas of the map more closely. Have them use the interactive scale to measure distances between Athens and the following city-states:

Delphi *(about 80 miles/130 km)*
Sparta *(about 100 miles/160/km)*
Crete *(about 240 miles/380 km)*

See page 171C for other online activities.

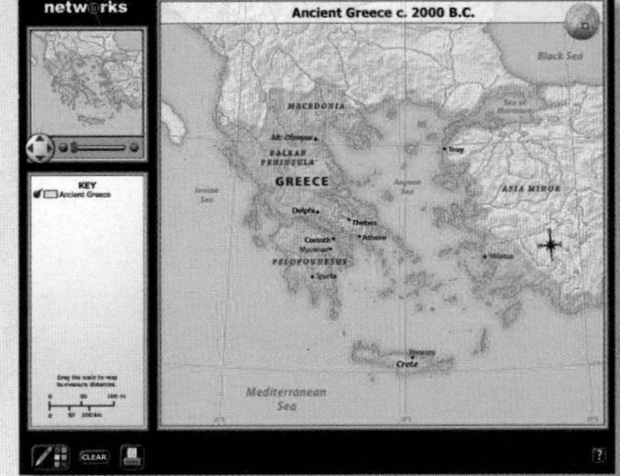

ANSWERS, p. 175

✓ PROGRESS CHECK Seas provided a living for many Greek fishers and traders.

GEOGRAPHY CONNECTION

1. The Aegean Sea lies east of the Balkan Peninsula.
2. **CRITICAL THINKING** Ships were probably most useful.

R1 Reading Skills

Determining Word Meanings Point out the text about the work of Arthur Evans. **Ask:** What is an archaeologist? *(a person who studies physical objects, such as fossil artifacts, to learn about past societies)* AL ELL

R2 Reading Skills

Describing As students read the text, explain that, like other archaeologists, Evans drew conclusions from the physical evidence he found. **Ask:** Based on the ruins that Evans found, what was the palace like where Minos and his family lived? *(It had numerous rooms that were connected by twisting passageways. The rooms had many different functions.)* After your discussion, have students draw a map of what they think the palace may have looked like in ancient times. Remind students to use details from the text when creating their maps.

The palace at Knossos included a large outdoor theater. Colorful wall paintings decorated the palace, both inside and outside.

▶ CRITICAL THINKING

Analyzing What kind of activities do the ruins of the palace suggest?

An Island Civilization

GUIDING QUESTION *How did the civilization of the Minoans develop?*

Greek myths describe an early civilization that developed on Crete (KREET), an island southeast of the Greek mainland. About A.D. 1900, a British archaeologist named Arthur Evans discovered a site on Crete called Knossos (NAH•suhs). He unearthed the amazing palace of a legendary king named Minos (MY•nuhs). R1

Evans **concluded** that Minos and his family lived in the palace. The palace had numerous rooms that were connected by twisting passageways. Some of these rooms were used to store oil, wine, and grain. Other rooms were workshops where people made jewelry, vases, and statues. There were even bathrooms in the palace. R2

An ancient people called the Minoans (muh•NOH•uhnz) built the palace at Knossos. The Minoan civilization was the first to develop in the Aegean region, but they were not Greeks. Their civilization lasted from about 2500 B.C. to 1450 B.C.

Trade was an important **economic** activity for the Minoans. They built ships using the wood from Crete's forests of oak and cedar trees. The Minoans sailed to Egypt and Syria. There they traded pottery and stone vases for ivory and metals. Minoan ships also patrolled the eastern Mediterranean Sea to protect Minoan trade from pirates.

Sometime around 1450 B.C., however, the Minoan civilization collapsed. Historians do not know why this happened. One theory for the collapse is that undersea earthquakes caused huge waves that destroyed Minoan cities. Other historians think that people from the Greek mainland, known as Mycenaeans (my•suh•NEE•uhns), invaded Crete.

☑ PROGRESS CHECK

Explaining What did the discovery at Knossos reveal about the Minoans?

A Mainland Civilization

GUIDING QUESTION *How did the Mycenaeans gain power in the Mediterranean?*

About 2000 B.C., the Mycenaeans left their homeland in central Asia. They moved into mainland Greece. There, they gradually mixed with the local people and set up several kingdoms.

Reading **HELP**DESK CCSS

Academic Vocabulary (Tier 2 Words)

conclude to reach an understanding; to make a decision

economic the system in a country that involves making, buying, and selling goods

networks Online Teaching Options

IMAGE

Knossos Palace

Narrative Share the image of Knossos Palace, and have students read the different callouts to learn more about the typical home of the rulers of the Minoans. After they have studied the images, ask them to imagine they are living in the palace in ancient times. Have them write a letter to a friend describing their home.

See page 171C for other online activities.

ANSWERS, p. 176

CRITICAL THINKING The ruins suggest that the inhabitants enjoyed activities that related to the arts.

☑ PROGRESS CHECK It revealed that the Minoans were economically prosperous and artistically talented.

Mycenaean Kingdom

Little was known about the Mycenaeans until the late 1800s. That was when a German archaeologist named Heinrich Schliemann (HYN•rihk SHLEE•mahn) discovered the ruins of a palace in Mycenae (my•SEE•nee). He named the people of this civilization the Mycenaeans.

Each Mycenaean king lived in a palace built on a hill. Thick stone walls circled the palace and protected the kingdom's people. Nobles lived outside the walls on large farms, called estates. The workers and enslaved people who farmed the land lived in villages on these estates.

Mycenaean palaces were centers of government. Artisans there made leather goods, clothes, and jars for wine and olive oil. Other workers made swords and ox-hide shields. Government officials recorded the wealth of the kingdom's residents. They also collected wheat, livestock, and honey as taxes.

Thinking Like a HISTORIAN

Analyzing Primary and Secondary Sources

German historian Heinrich Schliemann is considered the modern discoverer of the Mycenaean world. Schliemann (1822–1890) discovered several palaces and the ancient city of Troy. Research a biography or articles about Schliemann to create a short report about the archaeologist. Present your report to the class. For more information about using primary and secondary sources, read the chapter *What Does a Historian Do?*

Traders and Warriors

Minoan traders from Crete visited the Greek mainland. Gradually, the Mycenaeans adopted features of Minoan culture. They built ships and worked with bronze. They used the sun and stars to navigate the seas. The Mycenaeans also worshipped the Earth Mother, the Minoans' chief god.

By the mid-1400s B.C., the Mycenaeans had conquered the Minoans and controlled the Aegean area. This brought new wealth to the Mycenaeans, which they used to expand their military strength. The Mycenaeans were proud of their military successes in the Trojan War.

C

A Dark Age

However, the Mycenaean civilization **declined** over time. Mycenaean kingdoms fought one another, and earthquakes destroyed their palace fortresses. By 1100 B.C., the Mycenaean civilization had crumbled.

About this time, groups of warring peoples moved from place to place throughout the eastern Mediterranean region.

Mycenaean artisans made golden masks to cover the faces of their dead kings. This is known as the Mask of Agamemnon.

V

GUIZIOU Franck/Hemis/Age fotostock

Academic Vocabulary (Tier 2 Words)

decline to move toward a weaker condition

C Critical Thinking Skills

Comparing and Contrasting Have students use a Venn diagram or other graphic organizer to compare and contrast the Minoans and the Mycenaeans. To guide them, **ask:**

- **Where were the cultures located?** *(The Mycenaeans settled on mainland Greece, and the Minoans were on the island of Crete.)* AL
- **How did the civilizations interact with each other?** *(They traded with each other. The Mycenaeans adopted several features of the Minoan culture.)*
- **How did each civilization end?** *(The Minoans collapsed for unknown reasons, although the Mycenaeans might have conquered them. The Mycenaean civilization grew weaker due to internal conflict and ended after earthquakes destroyed their buildings.)*

V Visual Skills

Analyzing Images Point out the Mask of Agamemnon on this page. **Ask:** **What does this image tell you about the Mycenaeans?** *(It tells me that they had enough wealth to make and decorate gold objects such as this one. It also tells me that worshipping their dead kings was important and might have been part of their religious beliefs.)*

SLIDE SHOW

Mycenaean Artifacts

Analyzing Primary Sources Display the slide show of Mycenaean artifacts. Then divide the class into small groups, and have them discuss (1) what they think the artifacts were used for and (2) what the artifacts say about the culture of the Mycenaeans.

See page 171C for other online activities.

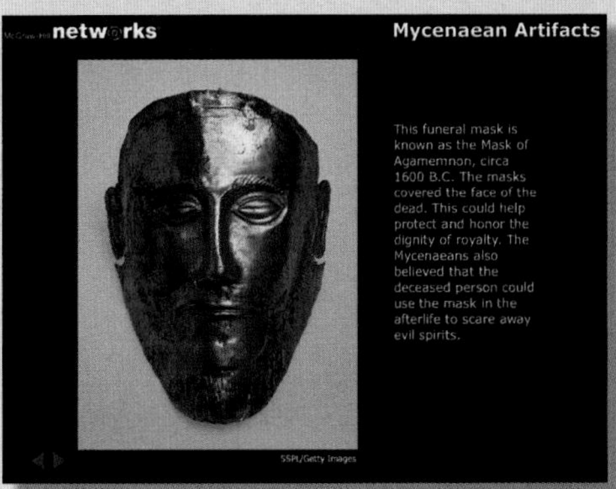

networks
Mycenaean Artifacts
This funeral mask is known as the Mask of Agamemnon, circa 1600 B.C. The masks covered the face of the dead. This could help protect and honor the dignity of royalty. The Mycenaeans also believed that the deceased person could use the mask in the afterlife to scare away evil spirits.

Rise of Greek Civilization

V Visual Skills

Reading a Chart Point out the table of the Greek alphabet on the left side of the page. Ask students if they have heard of any of the names of these letters and, if so, where. **Ask: Look at the names of the first two letters. What English word comes from those letters?** *(alphabet)* If you have time, you may wish to have students write their names using the Greek alphabet. **Visual/Spatial**

C Critical Thinking Skills

Determining Cause and Effect Remind students that the Hellenes grew more food than they needed. **Ask: What was an important effect of having a surplus of food?** *(Since the Hellenes had extra food, they could trade it with each other and with nearby peoples. In this way, they got new products and also adopted new ideas, such as the alphabet, from people with whom they traded.)*

THE GREEK ALPHABET

Greek Letter	Written Name	English Sound
Α	alpha	a
Β	beta	b
Γ	gamma	g
Δ	delta	d
Ε	epsilon	e
Ζ	zeta	z
Η	eta	e
Θ	theta	th
Ι	iota	i
Κ	kappa	c,k
Λ	lambda	l
Μ	mu	m
Ν	nu	n
Ξ	xi	x
Ο	omicron	o
Π	pi	p
Ρ	rho	r
Σ	sigma	s
Τ	tau	t
Υ	upsilon	y,u
Φ	phi	ph
Χ	chi	ch
Ψ	psi	ps
Ω	omega	o

One of these groups was a Greek-speaking people known as the Dorians (DOHR•ee•uhns). They invaded the Greek mainland from the north and took control of most of the region.

Historians call the next 300 years of Greek history a Dark Age. During this difficult time, trade slowed down, people made fewer things to sell, and most were very poor. Farmers grew only enough food to feed their families. Many people also stopped writing and keeping records.

In Greece, several positive developments also happened during this time. Dorian warriors introduced iron weapons and the skill of iron making. Iron weapons and farm tools were stronger and cheaper than the bronze ones used by the Mycenaeans. As the Dorians pushed into Greece, thousands of people fled the Greek mainland. They settled on the Aegean islands and the western shore of Anatolia.

The Hellenes

By 750 B.C., many descendants of the people who ran away returned to the Greek mainland. They brought back new ideas, crafts, and skills. Small independent communities developed under local leaders who became kings. These people called themselves Hellenes, or Greeks. Farmers in these communities grew more food than their families could use. The Greeks traded their surplus food with each other and with neighboring peoples, such as the Egyptians and Phoenicians. As trade increased, a new need for writing developed. The Greeks adopted an alphabet from Phoenician traders who sailed from the Mediterranean coast.

The Greek alphabet had 24 letters that represented different sounds. It greatly simplified reading and writing in the Greek language. Record keeping became easier. Soon, people wrote down the tales that had been told by **bards**, or storytellers. Previously, these tales had been passed down from generation to generation orally. Now they could finally be kept in written form.

✔ PROGRESS CHECK

Determining Cause and Effect How did the Dorian invasion help spread Greek culture?

Reading **HELP**DESK 

bard someone who writes or performs epic poems or stories about heroes and their deeds

Build Vocabulary: ***Word Origins***

Geographers call the place where a large river divides into smaller rivers near the ocean a *delta*. Deltas often form in the shape of a triangle, like the Greek letter delta. Try writing a word using the Greek alphabet.

networks Online Teaching Options

WHITEBOARD ACTIVITY

Ancient Greece

Sequencing Show students the Interactive Whiteboard Activity. Have them place the key events in Greek history in the proper order. When they are finished, review the activity as a class, answering any questions students may have about these events.

See page 171C for other online activities.

networks Ancient Greece

Directions: Sort the events below into the correct order.

Item Bank

- Greek colonies settle outside the Aegean Sea.
- Minoans build the Palace at Knossos.
- The Dark Ages begin, and trade and achievements slow down.
- Dorians invade the Greek mainland.
- The Mycenaeans conquer the [illegible] Aegean Sea.
- Hellenes reestablish trade and record-keeping.

1.
2.
3.
4.
5.
6.

ANSWER, p. 178

✔ PROGRESS CHECK The Dorians introduced iron weapons and farm tools. As a result of the invasions, Greek communities spread throughout the Aegean and into Anatolia.

Colonies and Trade

GUIDING QUESTION *How did early Greeks spread their culture?*

As Greece recovered from the Dark Age, its population increased rapidly. By 700 B.C., local farmers could not produce enough grain to feed the growing population. To solve this problem, Greek communities began to send people outside the Aegean area to establish **colonies** (KAH•luh•nees). A colony is a settlement in a new territory that has close ties to its homeland.

The Greeks founded many colonies along the coasts of the Mediterranean Sea and the Black Sea between 750 B.C. and 550 B.C. Greek culture spread into new areas, such as southern Italy, Sicily, France, Spain, North Africa, and western Asia.

The colonies traded with their "parent" cities on the Greek mainland. They shipped grains, metals, fish, timber, and enslaved people to Greece. In return, the Greek mainland sent wine, olive oil, and pottery to the colonies. As the Greeks began to make coins from metal, this **affected** their trade. Trade expanded as merchants traded money for goods rather than bartered for goods. This system increased a colony's wealth. As the demand for goods grew, artisans made more goods to meet the demand. People in different colonies specialized in making certain products. For example, in colonies where farmers raised sheep, people began to make cloth from the sheep's wool.

Connections to TODAY

Coins

The Greeks began making coins from silver in the 600s B.C. Current American quarters and dimes are made of layers of copper and nickel and covered with a copper-nickel alloy or blend. Many American coins have symbols similar to ones used on ancient Greek coins. If you could create a new American coin, whose image would you place on it?

PROGRESS CHECK

Determining Cause and Effect How did the colonies affect trade and industry in the Greek world?

The Greek City-State

GUIDING QUESTION *How did Greek city-states create the idea of citizenship?*

Mountains and seas separated Greek communities from each other. As a result, people developed a loyalty to the community in which they lived. Communities became fiercely independent. By the end of the Dark Age, nobles who owned large estates had overthrown the Greek kings. Across Greece, nobles ruled numerous city-states.

Georgios Kollidas/Panther Media/Age fotostock

colony a group of people living in a new territory who have ties to their homeland; the new territory itself

Academic Vocabulary (Tier 2 Words)

affect to influence; to cause a change

W Writing Skill

Informative/Explanatory Have students write a paragraph about the effects of trading with colonies. Students should cite evidence from the text about the effect of trade on both Greece and its colonies.

R Reading Skill

Explaining As students read, discuss how geography influenced the concept of citizenship in Greek city-states. Remind students to cite details from the text as support for their answers. **Ask:**

- **What role did mountains and the sea play in developing the concept of Greek citizenship?** *(These geographic features isolated Greek city-states from each other and from other nations, leading Greeks to think of their communities as small, independent countries.)* BL
- **What did the city-states consist of?** *(a town or city and the surrounding countryside)*
- **Who ruled the Greek city-state?** *(nobles)* ELL

MAP

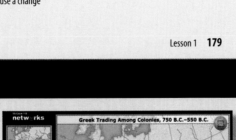

Greek Trading Among Colonies, 750 B.C.–550 B.C.

Drawing Conclusions Show the map of trade between Greece and her colonies from the lecture slide. Point out to students that Greece had trading colonies in Europe, Asia, and Africa. **Ask: Did trade increase or decrease the spread of Greek culture and ideas?** *(Greek trade increased the spread of their culture and ideas.)*

See page 171C for other online activities.

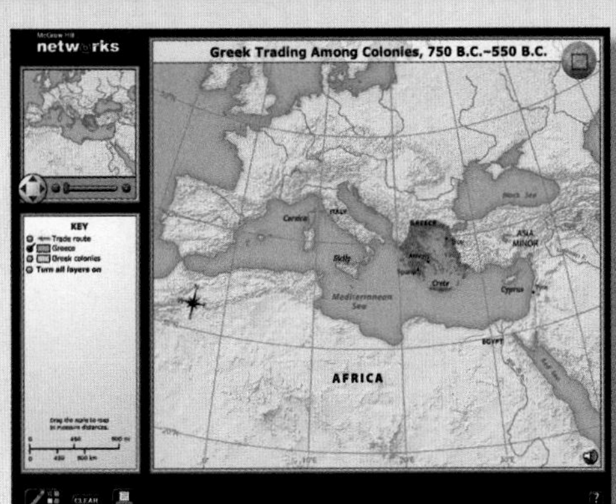

ANSWER, p. 179

PROGRESS CHECK Trade expanded between the colonies and their "parent" cities.

Rise of Greek Civilization

V Visual Skills

Reading a Map Direct students' attention to the map of this page. **Then ask:**

- **What do the red arrows on the map show?** *(trade routes)* AL
- **The Greeks traded with people on how many different continents?** *(three)*
- **In what modern-day country was Greek's most remote colony located?** *(Spain)* BL

Making Connections

Discuss with students the places in your community that are similar to an agora, where people gather to do business or discuss issues. Depending on the type of community you live in, this could be a mall, a town hall, or some other location. Discuss how technology and other aspects of modern life have made these kinds of meeting places less common than they once were.

Greek Trading Among Colonies 750 B.C.–550 B.C.

Black Sea
ITALY
Corsica
GREECE
Troy
ASIA MINOR
Tigris R.
Euphrates R.
Sicily
Athens
Sparta
Crete
Cyprus
Tyre
Mediterranean Sea
AFRICA
EGYPT
Nile R.
Red Sea

KEY
Trade route
Greece
Greek colonies

0 600 miles
0 600 km
Lambert Azimuthal Equal-Area projection

GEOGRAPHY CONNECTION

Greece set up trading posts and colonies north to the Black Sea.

1. **LOCATION** On which islands were Greek colonies located?
2. **CRITICAL THINKING** ***Drawing Conclusions*** In addition to the buying and selling of goods, what effect would Greece have on the people of its colonies and surrounding lands?

As in Mesopotamia, the Greek city-states were made up of a town or city and the surrounding area. Each city-state or **polis** (PAH•luhs), was like an independent country. Today, English words such as *police* and *politics* come from the Greek word *polis*.

What Did a Polis Look Like?

The polis was the basic political unit of Greek civilization. At the center of each polis was a fort built on a hilltop. The hilltop that a fort stood on was called an acropolis (uh•KRAH•puh•luhs). Local people could take refuge in the acropolis when invaders attacked. The Greeks built temples on the acropolis to honor local gods.

Outside the acropolis was an open area called an **agora** (A•guh•ruh). This space was used as a marketplace. It was also an area where people could gather and debate issues, choose officials, pass laws, and carry out business. City neighborhoods surrounded the agora. Just beyond the city were the villages and farmland that also were part of the polis.

Reading HELPDESK CCSS

polis a Greek city-state

agora a gathering place; marketplace in ancient Greece

180 *The Ancient Greeks*

networks Online Teaching Options

SLIDE SHOW

Agora

Analyzing Images Discuss the three different images and the captions about the Agora. Ask students to describe what they see, what activities they think would have taken place in them, and what they think it would have been like to meet in this kind of space.

See page 171C for other online activities.

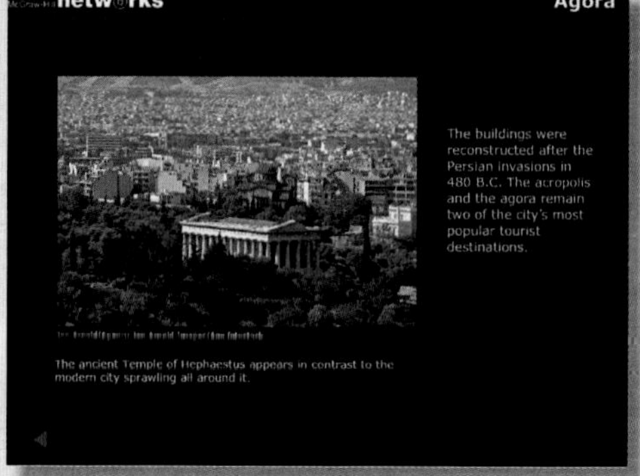

ANSWERS, p. 180

GEOGRAPHY CONNECTION

1. Cyprus, Sicily, and Corsica were home to Greek colonies.
2. **CRITICAL THINKING** Greek ideas and customs would spread to people in Greece's colonies and in the surrounding lands.

Because most city-states were surrounded by mountains and seas, they were usually small. Some were only a few square miles in area, while others covered hundreds of square miles. By 500 B.C., nearly 300,000 people lived in the city-state of Athens. Most city-states, however, were much smaller.

What Did Citizenship Mean to the Greeks?

Today, in the United States, a person who is born here is considered a citizen. We owe many of our ideas about citizenship to the ancient Greeks.

C Who was a Greek citizen? Citizens were members of a political community with rights and responsibilities. In Greece, male citizens had the right to vote, hold public office, own property, and defend themselves in court. In return, citizens had the responsibility to serve in government and to fight for their polis as citizen soldiers. Ancient Greek citizenship was very different from that of ancient Mesopotamia or Egypt, where most people were subjects. They had no rights, no voice in government, and no choice but to obey their rulers.

In most Greek city-states, only free, land-owning men born in the polis could be citizens. They believed the responsibility to run the city-state was theirs because the polis was made up of their property. Some city-states later ended the requirement of owning land for a person to be a citizen. Women and children might qualify for citizenship, but they had none of the rights that went with it.

When people today take the American oath of citizenship, a new life of rights and responsibilities begins.

In the agora at Athens, people of different professions met in different parts of the space. Theatrical performances were also held here.

(t) Jeff Greenberg/Age fotostock, (b) The Print Collector/Heritage/Age fotostock

C Critical Thinking Skills

Categorizing Have students create a two-column chart with the headings "Rights" and "Responsibilities." Then ask them to complete the chart by listing the rights and responsibilities of ancient Greek citizens.

Content Background Knowledge

Ancient Greek Politics and Citizenship

- The English word *idiot* is derived from the Greek *idiotes*, which means "private person or individual"—in other words, someone who does not get involved in politics.
- Citizens were obligated to take an intelligent and active role in governing Athens. They voted for legislation, made decisions on war or peace, elected officials, and spoke in the Assembly.
- Losing citizenship was a punishment for crimes such as bribery, cowardice in battle, violence against your parents, and anti-democratic activity.
- After 451 B.C., only males with a father who had Athenian citizenship and a mother whose father had Athenian citizenship could themselves be citizens.
- Very rarely, it was possible for a foreigner, a free Greek, a woman, or an enslaved person to receive citizenship by vote as a reward for extraordinary service to the democracy.

SLIDE SHOW

Greece

Describing After watching the interactive slide show, discuss how geography affected the lives of the early Greeks. **Ask:** **How did the many islands in the Aegean Sea affect life in Greece?** *(The Greeks traded goods and ideas among islands.)* **What made inland communities in ancient Greece so fiercely independent?** *(Inland communities were fiercely independent because they were separated by rugged mountains and deep valleys.)* **How do you think these geographical features might have affected life in ancient Greece?** *(Geography influenced how people earned a living, what they ate, and how they traveled and communicated.)*

networks
Greece
The large island of Crete is home to the ruins of the Mycenaean civilization. Today the island features popular tourist spots, beautiful beaches, and bustling trade. This photograph of the north-central city of Rethymno shows Crete's modern landscape. Two of Crete's major agricultural cash crops are olives and olive oil.

See page 171C for other online activities.

Rise of Greek Civilization

R Reading Skills

Paraphrasing Point to the primary-source quotation on this page. Ask students to think about what it means, and then have them put the quotation into their own words. *(Answers will vary but should reflect the idea that soldiers believed it was their duty to act honorably and to follow the laws, and that they were proud of their role in society.)* You may wish to have students come to the front of the classroom and share their interpretation with the rest of the class. **Linguistic/Verbal**

Have students complete the Lesson 1 Review.

CLOSE & REFLECT

To close the lesson, moderate a class discussion comparing and contrasting the rights and responsibilities of Greek citizens with those of U.S. citizens. Guide students to realize that many of the rights and responsibilities we have today can be traced back to the Greeks.

North Wind/North Wind Picture Archives

Citizen Soldiers

In Greece, wars were fought by wealthy nobles riding horses and driving chariots. By 700 B.C., citizens called hoplites (HAHP•lyts) made up the city-state armies. The hoplites fought on foot. Each heavily armed soldier carried a round shield, a short sword, and a spear. During battles, rows of hoplites marched forward together, shoulder to shoulder. They raised their shields above them to protect them from the enemy's arrows. This unified formation is called a **phalanx** (FAY•langks).

The success of the hoplites came from their pride in fighting as brave warriors. In Athens, for example, soldiers took this oath:

PRIMARY SOURCE

> "I will not disgrace my sacred arms nor desert my comrade, [fellow soldier] wherever I am stationed [located]. . . And I will observe the established laws and whatever laws in the future may be reasonably established. If any person seek to overturn the laws . . . I will oppose him. I will honor the religion of my fathers."
>
> —from *Athenian Ephebic Oath*, tr. Clarence A. Forbes

R

phalanx a group of armed foot soldiers in ancient Greece arranged close together in rows

The polis gave Greek citizens a sense of belonging. This is similar to how people feel about their home states today. The citizens put the needs of the polis above their own. Such strong loyalty to their own city-state divided the Greeks. They were not as unified as a whole country. This lack of unity weakened Greece, making it easier to conquer.

☑ PROGRESS CHECK

Explaining What were the rights and responsibilities of Greek citizens?

LESSON 1 REVIEW (CCSS)

Review Vocabulary (Tier 3 Words)

1. Explain the difference between a *colony* and a *polis*. RH.6–8.4

Answer the Guiding Questions

2. ***Analyzing*** What were the ancient Greeks' most important economic activities? RH.6–8.2
3. ***Explaining*** How did the Minoans develop wealth? RH.6–8.2
4. ***Summarizing*** What happened to Mycenaean civilization during the Dark Age? RH.6–8.2
5. ***Explaining*** Why did the Greeks establish colonies? RH.6–8.2
6. **INFORMATIVE/EXPLANATORY** How did Greek city-states apply democracy? How did they limit democracy? Write a short essay explaining your answers. WHST.6–8.2, WHST.6–8.10

LESSON 1 REVIEW ANSWERS

1. A colony is a settlement in a new territory that keeps close ties to its homeland. A polis is an ancient Greek city-state.
2. Their most important economic activities were farming and trading.
3. The Minoans prospered because of their overseas trade.
4. The Mycenaean civilization collapsed. People became poor, Greece was invaded by the Dorians, and the art of writing was lost during the Dark Age.
5. The Greeks established colonies because farmers could not grow enough grain to feed the increasing population.
6. Answers will vary. Students should point out that city-states extended democracy by including more diverse social classes in government. However, they limited democracy by excluding noncitizens, women, and enslaved people from government.

ANSWER, p. 182

☑ PROGRESS CHECK Citizens had the right to vote, hold public office, own property, and defend themselves in court. Their responsibilities included serving in government and fighting for their polis.

networks
There's More Online!
☑ GRAPHIC ORGANIZER
Compare Sparta and Athens

Lesson 2
Sparta and Athens: City-State Rivals

ESSENTIAL QUESTION *Why do people form governments?*

IT MATTERS BECAUSE
The city-states of Athens and Sparta had two quite different governments. Athenian democracy strongly influenced later forms of democracy.

Political Changes

GUIDING QUESTION *Which types of government did the Greek city-states have?*

As Greek city-states grew, wealthy nobles seized power from kings. They did not rule very long, however. Owners of small farms resented the nobles' power. Many of the farm owners had borrowed money from the nobles to buy land. When the farmers could not repay the loans, the nobles often took their land. The farmers then had to work for the nobles or move to the city to find jobs. In some cases, they even had to sell themselves into slavery.

By 650 B.C., small farmers wanted political change and a greater voice in government. Merchants and artisans also called for reforms. Merchants and artisans had earned a good living in the growing city-states. However, because they did not own land, they were not **considered** citizens. That meant they had no role in ruling the polis. **R**

The growing unrest led to the rise of tyrants. A **tyrant** (TY•ruhnt) is someone who seizes power and rules with total authority. Most tyrants who commanded city-states ruled fairly.

Reading **HELP**DESK (CCSS)

Taking Notes: ***Comparing***
Use a Venn diagram like this one to compare life in Sparta and Athens. **RH.6–8.2**

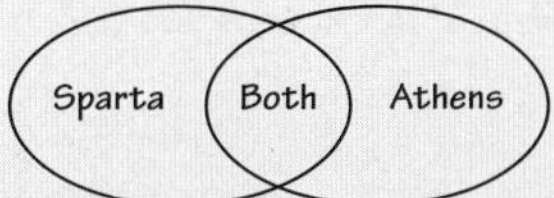

Content Vocabulary (Tier 3 Words)
- **tyrant**
- **oligarchy**
- **democracy**
- **helot**
- **ephor**

ENGAGE

Bellringer Divide the class into pairs. Explain that you are going to ask a question and each student will write an answer. Then have the students share their responses with their partners. After they have had time to compare answers, pairs will share their answers with the class.

Tell students that the United States is a democracy. **Ask: What other forms of government can you name?** *(Answers might include dictatorship and monarchy.)*

TEACH & ASSESS

R Reading Skills

Finding Main Idea Ask students to cite evidence in the text that shows why farmers in many Greek city-states were unhappy with their rulers. **Ask: What conditions did farmers face that made them want to change the government?** *(Many farmers had borrowed money from nobles, and when they couldn't pay back their loans, they had to give the nobles their farms. That meant that they no longer owned land and were no longer citizens. They had no role in governing the polis, and they were unhappy about it.)*

VIDEO

Athens

Describing Show students the Athens video and discuss how the culture of ancient Athens is visible in Athens today. Then have students work in small groups to create a travel brochure, urging visitors to come explore the culture of present-day Athens.

See page 171D for other online activities.

ANSWER, p. 183

TAKING NOTES: Answers for Sparta include warlike society, strict military training, comparative freedom for women, oligarchic government. Answers for Athens include diverse culture, seclusion of women, democratic government. Answers for both include successful city-state.

V Visual Skills

Analyzing Maps Direct students' attention to the map on this page, and ask following questions about Sparta and Athens.

- **What is different about the location of the two city-states?** *(Athens is closer to the coast and Sparta is inland, near a river.)*
- **What might be the advantages and disadvantages of these locations?** *(Answers will vary but may include that Athens might have easier access to the water, so it would be more likely to trade with other city-states. It might also be more likely to be attacked by other city-states as well.)* **Visual/Spatial**

Content Background Knowledge

- The word *democracy* comes from the Greek words *demos,* which means "people," and *kratos*, which means "rule."
- Ancient Greece is believed to be one of the world's first democracies, although it was not the same kind of democracy that exists in many places today.
- During the 20th century, the number of countries with democratic governments increased significantly. By the beginning of the 21st century, more than one-third of the world's countries were generally considered democratic and another one-sixth of them had some democratic institutions. In total, about half of the world's people live under democratic or near-democratic governments today.

ANSWERS, p. 184

GEOGRAPHY CONNECTION

1. They were about 100 miles apart.
2. **CRITICAL THINKING** Answers will vary, but students should refer to physical barriers, such as mountains and water, in their answers.

✓ **PROGRESS CHECK** Tyrants could hold power because they had the support of the hoplites, or citizen soldiers, in the army.

GEOGRAPHY CONNECTION

Sparta and Athens were the dominant city-states in ancient Greece.

1. **LOCATION** About how many miles apart were Sparta and Athens?
2. **CRITICAL THINKING** *Analyzing* Which city-state's geography might make it more open to attack in a military battle? Explain.

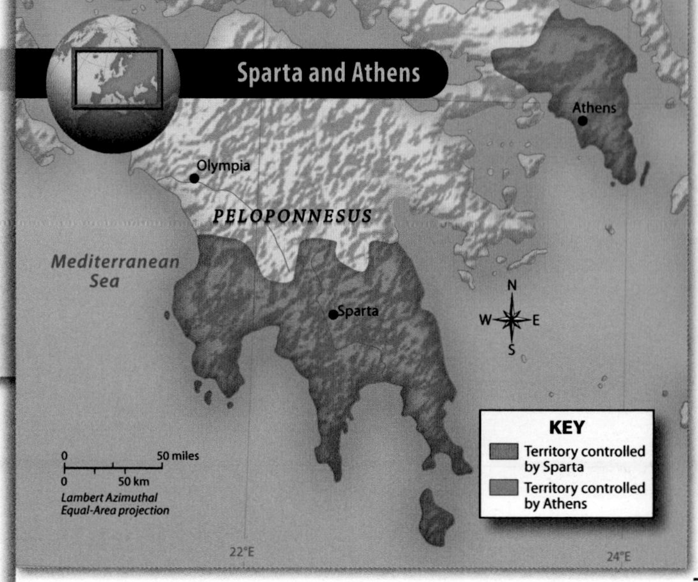

However, the harsh rule of a few tyrants gave the word *tyranny* its current meaning; that is, rule by a cruel and unjust person.

The common people of Greece supported the tyrants when they overthrew the nobles during the 600s B.C. Tyrants also gained support from the hoplites, or citizen soldiers, in the army. Tyrants strengthened their popularity by building new temples, fortresses, and marketplaces. Nevertheless, most Greeks objected to rule by a single person. They wanted a government in which all citizens could participate.

Tyrants ruled many of the Greek city-states until about 500 B.C. From then until 336 B.C., most city-states developed into either oligarchies or democracies. In an **oligarchy** (AH•luh•gahr•kee), a few wealthy people hold power over the larger group of citizens. In a **democracy** (dih•MAH•kruh•see), all citizens share in running the government. Two of the major city-states, Sparta and Athens, were governed differently and created very different societies.

✓ **PROGRESS CHECK**

Evaluating Why were tyrants able to hold power in various Greek city-states?

Reading HELPDESK (CCSS)

tyrant an absolute ruler unrestrained by law
oligarchy a government in which a small group has control
democracy a government by the people

Academic Vocabulary (Tier 2 Words)
consider to give careful thought

networks Online Teaching Options

WHITEBOARD ACTIVITY

Athens and Sparta Culture

Determining Word Meanings Review the meanings of the terms *tyrant, oligarchy,* and *democracy* with the class. Using the interactive whiteboard, create a three-column graphic organizer. Label columns "Tyranny," "Oligarchy," and "Democracy." Label the four horizontal rows "Ruled By," "Citizenship," "Advantages," and "Disadvantages." Have students begin filling in the horizontal columns for each of the three types of governments as they read this page. You may wish to have them continue completing the table as they read the rest of the lesson.

networks Athens and Sparta Culture

Directions: Drag the correct answer to its corresponding question. Try to answer three questions across, down, or diagonally to win the game.

Item Bank: oligarchy, iron bars, coins, democracy, military training, math and culture, Athens, Sparta, Solon

Athens was ruled by which kind of government?	Sparta was ruled by which kind of government?	In which city-state were citizens over 30 years old allowed to be part of the assembly?
Which city-state considered itself a population of free thinkers?	What form of money did the Spartans use?	What form of money did the Athenians use?
What kind of education did the Athenians receive?	What kind of education did the Spartans receive?	Who helped free the Athenian farmers from debt and enslavement?

See page 171D for other online activities.

Sparta: A Military Society

GUIDING QUESTION *Why did the Spartans focus on military skills?*

The city-state of Sparta was located on the Peloponnesus (peh•luh•puh•NEE•suhs) Peninsula in southern Greece. The Spartans were descended from the Dorians who invaded Greece in the Dark Age. Like other city-states, Sparta's economy was based on agriculture.

Sparta did not set up overseas colonies. Instead, Sparta invaded neighboring city-states and enslaved the local people. The Spartans called their enslaved laborers **helots** (HEH•luhts), a word that comes from the Greek word for "capture."

A Strong Military

G1 About 650 B.C., the helots revolted against their Spartan masters. The Spartans crushed that uprising. Sparta's leaders wanted to prevent future revolts. They decided to make Sparta a **military** society that stressed discipline. They also believed in simplicity, and strength through self-denial. The leaders thought that a military society created more obedient and loyal citizens.

G2 Sparta's government prepared all boys and men for a life of war. Boys left their homes at age seven to join the military. In military camps, they learned to read, write, and use weapons. They also were treated harshly. The military leaders believed that harsh treatment would turn the young boys into adults who would survive the pain of battle. The Greek historian Plutarch (PLOO•tahrk) described life for Spartan boys:

Spartan warriors depended on their training to help them survive.

▶ CRITICAL THINKING
Synthesizing What types of weapons were used in hand-to-hand combat?

PRIMARY SOURCE

R "They were enrolled in certain companies . . ., where they all lived under the same order and discipline, doing their exercises and taking play together. Of these he who showed the most conduct and courage was made captain; they . . . obeyed his orders and underwent patiently whatsoever punishment he inflicted [delivered]; so that the whole course of their education was one continued exercise of a ready and perfect obedience."

—from *Plutarch: The Lives of the Noble Grecians and Romans*

North Wind/North Wind Picture Archives

helots enslaved people in ancient Sparta

Academic Vocabulary (Tier 2 Words)

military relating to soldiers, arms, or war

R Reading Skills

Finding the Main Idea Direct students' attention to the primary source at the bottom of the page. **Ask:** Based on this description, what quality was most important in Spartan boys? *(obedience)*

G1 *Critical Thinking Skills*

Making Connections Explain to students that today, one definition of the word *spartan* is "having a lot of self-discipline." Another meaning is "very plain and having nothing luxurious or comfortable." For example, a room might be described as spartan. **Ask:** What do these meanings have to do with ancient Sparta? *(The Spartans had great self-discipline and did not believe in excess luxury or comfort. They believed that harsh conditions were good training for young men who would go into battle.)*

G2 Critical Thinking Skills

Contrasting Spartans tried to develop obedience and strength in all young men. **Ask:** Why was this important to the government? *(They wanted to turn the young boys into adults who would survive the pain of battle.)* AL **Ask:** How is that different from the goals of your education today? *(Answers will vary but should mention that today's education is designed to develop well-rounded individuals and that thinking for one's self, not just obeying others, is important.)* BL

IMAGE

Life of a Spartan Soldier

Analyzing Have students click on the buttons at the bottom of the screen to read additional information about Spartan soldiers. Then ask them to create a chart listing the pros and cons of the Spartan system of education and warfare.

See page 171D for other online activities.

ANSWER, p. 185

CRITICAL THINKING Spears and knives were used in hand-to-hand combat.

C Critical Thinking Skills

Determining Cause and Effect Discuss the role of women in Sparta. **Ask:** Why did women have more freedom in Sparta than in some other Greek city-states? *(The men were away from home much of the time.)* **Ask:** What are some examples of the freedoms that Spartan women had? *(They could own property and travel; girls were trained in sports and were expected to be physically fit.)*

W Writing Skills

Narrative Have each student write a journal entry from the perspective of a Spartan boy, girl, man, or woman. Entries should describe a typical day and should use include factual details from the text, as well as fictional events in the life of the character.

R Reading Skills

Identifying As students read, ask them to identify key elements of the Spartan government. **Ask:**

- Who was in the Spartan assembly? *(all male citizens over the age of 30)* AL
- What was the most powerful body in the government *(the council of elders)*
- What did the Spartan government discourage? *(It discouraged change and new ideas, and it outlawed travel outside the city-state.)*

Making Connections

Women in Sparta had more freedom than they did in most other city-states, but they still had less freedom than many women have today, especially women in the United States. Women in Sparta did not have the right to vote, but today, women have the right to vote in most, though not all, countries of the world.

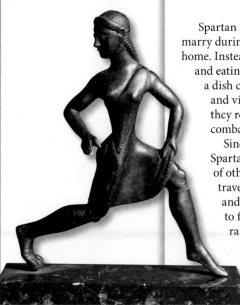

Physical fitness was important for Spartan women. Girls trained in sports to increase their athletic abilities.

Spartan men entered the regular army at age 20. Men could marry during their twenties, but they were not allowed to live at home. Instead, they stayed in military camps, sharing barracks and eating meals with other soldiers. A typical army meal was a dish called black broth—pork boiled in animal blood, salt, and vinegar. Spartan men could live at home again when they reached the age of 30, but they continued to train for combat. They finally retired from the army at age 60. W

Since many Spartan men lived away from home, Spartan women enjoyed more freedom than the women of other Greek city-states. They could own property and travel. Girls were trained in sports, such as wrestling and throwing the javelin. They remained physically fit to fulfill their roles as mothers. Their main goal was to raise sons who were brave, strong Spartan soldiers. C

Spartan women expected their men to either win or die in battle. Spartan soldiers must never surrender. One Spartan mother ordered her son to "Come home carrying your shield or being carried on it."

How Was Sparta Governed?

Sparta's government was an oligarchy. Two kings ruled jointly, but they had little power. Their only duties were to lead the army and carry out religious ceremonies. In addition to the kings, Sparta had two other governing bodies, the assembly and the council of elders.

R The assembly included all male citizens over the age of 30. The assembly made decisions about war and peace. However, the council of elders was the most powerful body in the government. Council members served as judges. They were the only officials who could order executions or exile. Each year, the council elected five people to be **ephors** (EH•fuhrs). The ephors enforced the laws and managed the collection of taxes.

Sparta's strict government brought **stability**. But that stability cost the people of Sparta. Because the government feared losing the helots, it discouraged free thinking and new ideas. Officials believed learning could lead to unrest. As a result, Sparta did not welcome foreign visitors and prevented citizens from traveling outside the city-state except for military reasons. It even discouraged people from studying literature and the arts.

Reading HELPDESK CCSS

ephor a high-ranked government official in Sparta who was elected by the council of elders

Academic Vocabulary (Tier 2 Words)

stability the condition of being steady and unchanging

networks Online Teaching Options

IMAGE

The Lives of Spartan Women

Discussing Have students look at the image and read the accompanying text about Spartan women. Moderate a discussion about what Spartan women's lives were like and the ways in which they were similar to and different from men's lives in Sparta. If time permits, you may wish to continue the discussion by comparing and contrasting the lives of Spartan women with the lives of women in the United States today.

networks
The Lives of Spartan Women
Spartan girls were trained and partially educated in schools called "sisterhoods." They were taught physical education, including wrestling, gymnastics, and fighting skills. The Spartans wanted girls to be strong so that they would have healthy children, especially sons who could serve in the military.
At age 18, a Spartan woman had to pass a fitness test. She was then assigned a husband and allowed to return home. Spartan women were expected to train their sons to be fearless soldiers, and to teach them that it was shameful to surrender. They trained their daughters to run the household. A Spartan woman was expected to endure long absences of her husband while he was away serving on military assignments.

See page 171D for other online activities.

In addition, Sparta resisted other types of change. For example, Spartans continued to use heavy iron bars for money when other Greeks used coins. This discouraged trade and isolated Sparta from the rest of Greece. While other city-states built up business and trade and improved their standard of living, Sparta remained a poor farming society. **R**

For Sparta's strong, well-trained army, the only important goals were military power and victory. The Spartans **achieved** Greece's greatest military strength and power. Sparta would play a key role in defending Greece against invaders.

✓ PROGRESS CHECK

Determining Cause and Effect Why did Sparta fall behind other Greek city-states in many areas?

Athens: A Young Democracy

GUIDING QUESTION *How did the culture in Athens differ from other Greek city-states?*

Another great Greek city-state was Athens. It was located northeast of Sparta, about a two-day trip away. Athens was founded by the descendants of the Mycenaeans and differed from Sparta in its ideas about society and government.

An Athenian Education

Athenians received an education far different from that of the Spartans. Athens educated its males, as Sparta did. In Athenian schools, boys studied subjects such as arithmetic, geometry, drawing, music, and public speaking. They also participated in sports. The Athenians believed that this type of education produced young people with strong minds and bodies. At age 18, when boys finished school, they were expected to take an active role in public affairs. **C**

The Italian artist Raphael painted this picture, *School of Athens*, in 1510–11. This shows younger students mixing with teachers and older students.

The Print Collector/Heritage/Age fotostock

Academic Vocabulary (Tier 2 Words)

achieve to succeed; to gain something as the result of work

R Reading Skills

Explaining Point out the text that describes Spartans' resistance to change. **Ask:** What economic change did the Spartans resist? *(They resisted using coins and used heavy bars instead.)* **AL** **Ask:** How did this action contribute to Sparta remaining poor? *(Other city-states did not want to trade for the heavy bars, so they did not trade with Sparta. Sparta's economy did not grow the way other city-states' economies did.)*

C Critical Thinking Skills

Defending Ask students to choose one city-state, either Athens or Sparta, and speak for 30 to 60 seconds in defense of that city-state's system of education. Students should relate the method of education to the goal of education in the city-state they choose. Verbal/Linguistic

GRAPHIC ORGANIZER

Taking Notes: *Comparing:* Sparta and Athens

Comparing and Contrasting Have students complete a Venn diagram for Athens and Sparta. In the middle, note that both were powerful city-states that allowed slavery. Ask students how the two differed in terms of government, the military, trade, and education. *(Students should note that Sparta was a militaristic oligarchy that discouraged trade and focused education on military preparedness. Athens was a democracy that encouraged trade and a broad education. Males in Athens were educated in arithmetic, geometry, drawing, music, and public speaking. They also participated in sports.)*

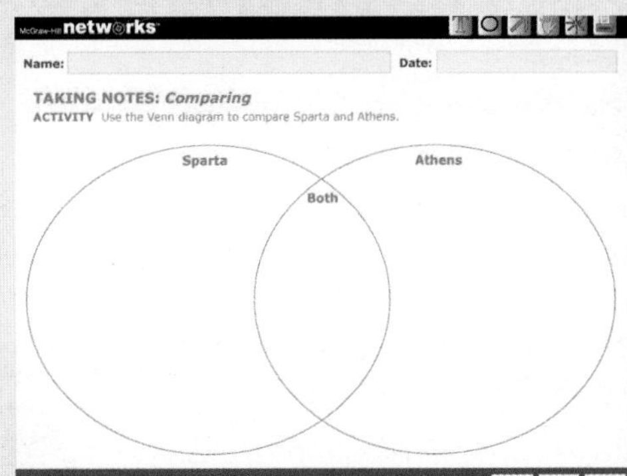

See page 171D for other online activities.

ANSWER, p. 187

✓ PROGRESS CHECK Spartans were basically conservative. They thought free thinking and learning might lead to unrest and weaken their control over the helots, so they resisted change.

R Reading Skills

Identifying Tell students that one of the reasons Sparta and Athens developed so differently is that from 600 B.C. to 500 B.C., Athens had three leaders who moved Athens from an oligarchy to more of a democracy. Review the "Early Reforms" section in the textbook. Then **ask:**

- **What are three changes Solon made in Athens?** *(He opened up the governing assembly to all male citizens. He promoted trade by farmers and rewrote the Athenian constitution.)*
- **What are two changes Peisistratus made in Athens?** *(He divided large estates among farmers and gave citizenship to people who did not own land.)*
- **What was the major change made by Cleisthenes?** *(He brought Athens even closer to a democracy by making the assembly the city-state's major governing body.)*

BIOGRAPHY

Solon (c. 630 B.C.–560 B.C.)

The great reformer Solon was the son of a well-to-do family, but he did not live the life of a rich Greek. Solon was a poet and a lawmaker. His goal was to find agreement between nobles and farmers who needed to be able to work together. He improved the economy by requiring all sons to continue in the same job their fathers had. He promoted trade by farmers and rewrote the Athenian constitution.

▶ **CRITICAL THINKING**
Predicting How do you think people today would accept Solon's ruling that sons follow fathers in their life's work?

Athenian mothers educated their daughters at home. Girls were taught spinning, weaving, and other household duties. In some wealthy families, they learned to read, write, and play music. Women were expected to marry and care for their children. For the most part, women were not active in business or government in Athens.

Early Reforms

The history of Athens was much like that of the other Greek city-states. By about 600 B.C., most Athenian farmers owed money to the nobles. Some farmers were forced to sell themselves into slavery to repay their debts. Athenians began to rebel. Farmers called for an end to all debts. They also asked that land be distributed to the poor.

To avoid an uprising, the nobles agreed to make some changes. They turned to a respected merchant named Solon (SOH•luhn) for leadership. In 594 B.C., Solon ended the farmers' debts and freed those who were enslaved. He also opened the assembly and the law courts to all male citizens. The assembly was responsible for passing laws written by a council of 400 wealthy citizens.

R

The common people praised Solon's reforms. Still, many Athenians were unhappy. Wealthy people felt Solon had gone too far, while poor people thought he had not gone far enough. By the time Solon left office, he had lost much of his support.

In 560 B.C., a tyrant named Peisistratus (py•SIHS•truht•uhs) took over the government. A relative of Solon, Peisistratus made reforms that went even further than those that Solon had made. Peisistratus divided large estates among farmers who had no land. He provided loans to help farmers buy equipment to work their farms. He gave citizenship to Athenians who did not own land. He also hired the poor to **construct** temples and other public works. Since religion was important in Athens, Peisistratus built additional shrines to different gods. He also encouraged the worship of the goddess Athena. Under Peisistratus, festivals held to honor Athena were expanded by the addition of athletic contests.

This clay ballot was used to select jurors for Athenian courts. How different is the ballot voters use today?

Reading **HELP**DESK CCSS

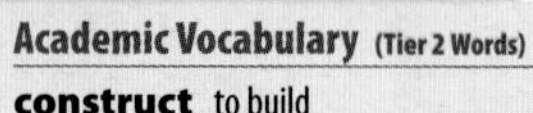

Academic Vocabulary (Tier 2 Words)
construct to build

networks Online Teaching Options

IMAGES

The Reforms of Solon and Greeks Choose Officials

Discussing Have students scroll down the side of the text about Solon's reforms to learn how he changed the political structure in Athens. Students can then click on the *Greeks Choose Officials* image to find out more about how leaders were chosen in the city-state.

After reviewing both interactive activities, facilitate a class discussion on democracy in Greece, focusing on how Greek rulers tried to make their government fair for everyone.

See page 171D for other online activities.

networks
The Reforms of Solon
In 594 B.C. Greece's government was unable to maintain power. As a result, the oligarchy chose Solon to serve as the civilian head-of-state (archon), and gave him great power so that he could help to restore order to Greece. Solon was selected for this role because of his reputation for wisdom and honor. Solon had previously advised Greek rulers in important military and political matters.
Solon is known as one of the first law-makers in Greece. He reformed Athens' code of strict laws, established by the previous ruler Draco (The term Draconian has come to mean
made it illegal for Athenians to sell themselves or their families into slavery to get out of debt,
networks
Greeks Choose Officials
Gianni Dagli Orti/CORBIS
The ancient Greeks preferred to elect their officials by lottery rather than by voting. Qualified citizens could meet with the assembly and add their name to the lottery drawing. Athenians believed that drawing by lottery discouraged politicians from trying to influence a vote.

ANSWERS, p. 188

CRITICAL THINKING Answers will vary. Most people would disagree with such a ruling.

Caption: Most will say ballots today are paper or electronic.

Toward Democracy

After the death of Peisistratus, a noble named Cleisthenes (KLYS•thuh•neez) became the next leader of Athens. Prizing democracy, Cleisthenes made the assembly the city-state's major governing body. As before, all male citizens could participate in the assembly and vote on laws. Assembly members could now discuss issues freely, hear legal cases, and appoint army officials.

Cleisthenes also created a new council of 500 citizens. They were to help the assembly manage daily government affairs. The council introduced laws and controlled the treasury. They also managed relations with other city-states. Each year Athenian citizens held a lottery to choose the council members. Athenians preferred the lottery system over an election. In their view, an election might unfairly favor the rich, who were well-known. Terms on the council were limited to one year, and no one could serve on the council for more than two terms. Thus, every citizen had a chance to be a council member.

While Cleisthenes's reforms made the government of Athens more democratic, many residents were still excluded from the political process. People who were not citizens still could not participate in the government. This group included all Athenian women, foreign-born men, and enslaved people.

Connections to TODAY

The Olympics

The ancient Olympic Games were held every four years at Olympia, in the western part of Greece, in honor of the god Zeus. The first Olympics were organized in 776 B.C. According to one legend, the founder of the games was the hero Hercules. The modern Olympics began in 1896 in Athens.

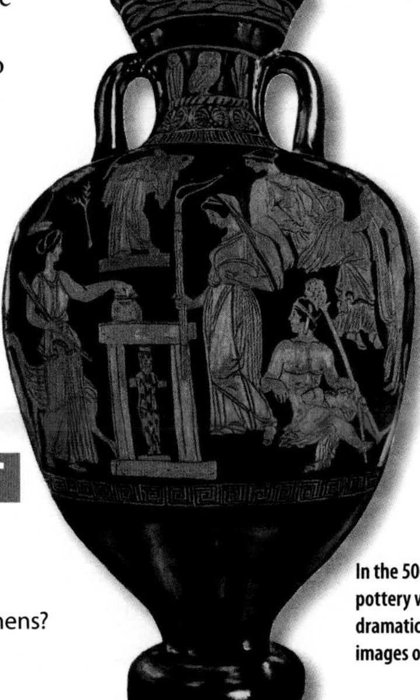

In the 500s B.C., Athenian pottery was decorated with dramatic black and red images of heroes and gods.

SuperStock/Getty Images

✓ PROGRESS CHECK

Explaining Why was Solon chosen to be leader of Athens?

LESSON 2 REVIEW (CCSS)

Review Vocabulary (Tier 3 Words)

1. What might a *tyrant* say to citizens who are asking for democracy? RH.6–8.4

Answer the Guiding Questions

2. ***Explaining*** Why were the tyrants able to seize control in Athens? RH.6–8.2
3. ***Determining Cause and Effect*** Why did the Spartans emphasize military training? RH.6–8.2
4. ***Describing*** How did Athenians feel about the changes Solon put in place? RH.6–8.2
5. ***Identifying*** What was a major accomplishment of Cleisthenes? RH.6–8.2
6. **NARRATIVE** You are a student living in ancient Sparta or Athens. Write a journal entry that describes a day in your life. WHST.6–8.10

LESSON 2 REVIEW ANSWERS

1. A tyrant would probably reply that public order demanded the rule of a single person.
2. They were able to seize power because of civic unrest, which led to demands for political change.
3. They emphasized military training because they feared an uprising by the helots, whom they had enslaved.
4. Some wealthy Athenians believed Solon had gone too far, but poor Athenians thought he had not gone far enough.
5. One of Cleisthenes's major accomplishments was to make the city-state's assembly in Athens the city's major governing body. He also created a new council of citizens.
6. Answers will vary. Students should point out that daily life in Athens involved diverse activities, but life in Sparta had an almost exclusively military focus.

T Technology Skills

Collaborating Divide students into small groups and have them imagine they were living in Athens in ancient times. Ask them to write and create a video for a short play with four characters: a man who is a citizen, a woman, a foreign-born man, and an enslaved person. Each character should describe what he or she thinks of the political system. Those who are not citizens should make a case for why they think they should be included in the political process. **Interpersonal Verbal/Linguistic**

Have students complete the Lesson 2 Review.

CLOSE & REFLECT

Argument Have students write short essays stating whether they would have wanted to live in Sparta or Athens. Ask students to explain why they might favor one form of government over the other. Remind them to cite specific evidence from the text to support their point of view. After they have completed the essays, you may want to hold a classroom debate on this topic.

ANSWER, p. 189

✓ PROGRESS CHECK Solon was chosen because he was a wealthy merchant who was respected by all classes of Athenians.

Greece and Persia

ENGAGE

Bellringer Show students the map of the Persian Empire on the facing page. Tell students that while political changes were occurring in Greek city-states, Persia was building an empire that grew as large as what is now the continental United States. **Ask:** **Why might the ancient Greeks and the Persians have come into conflict? Where might such conflict have taken place first?**

Moderate a class discussion, reminding students that the Greeks were expanding and founding overseas colonies. Note that Asia Minor was a region that lay between both civilizations. Tell students that in this lesson they will be learning about the rise of the Persian Empire and its conflict with the Greek city-states.

TEACH & ASSESS

R Reading Skills

Identifying As students read the text, talk with them about where the Persian empire was located. Then have them find Southwest Asia on a world map. **Ask:** **What is Persia called today?** *(Iran)*

C Critical Thinking Skills

Making Inferences Discuss with students how Cyrus ruled the peoples that he conquered. **Ask:** **Why do you think Cyrus allowed the people he conquered to keep their own languages and customs?** *(Allowing people to keep their customs might make them less angry about being conquered and less likely to rebel against Persian rule.)* BL

ANSWER, p. 190

TAKING NOTES: Persian Kings Attacking Greece: Darius I and Xerxes; Greek Defenders: King Leonidas of Sparta and Themistocles of Athens

networks *There's More Online!*
- GRAPHIC ORGANIZER Persian Kings Attacking Greece & Greek Defenders
- VIDEO
- SLIDE SHOW Battle of Salamis

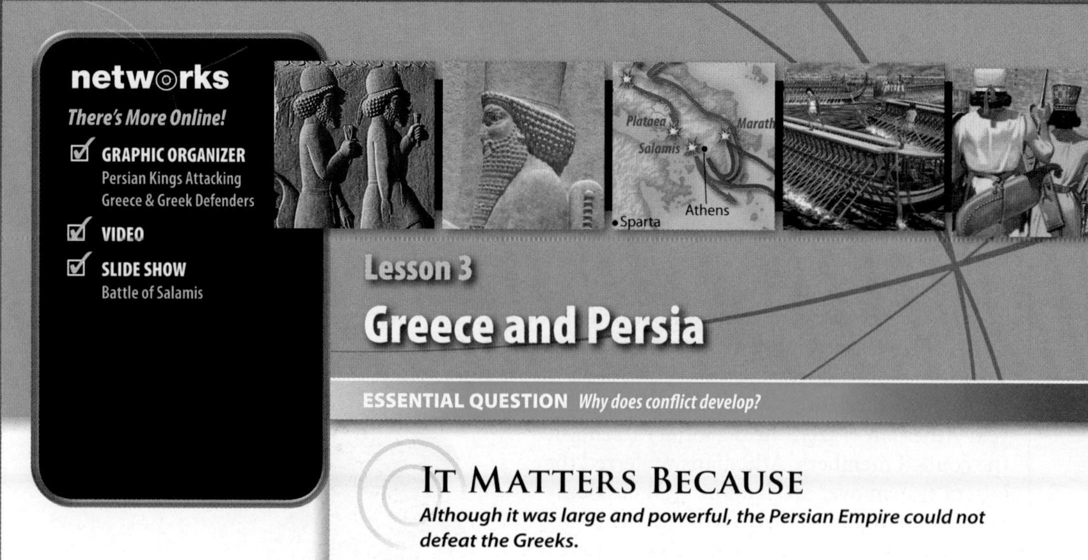

Lesson 3

Greece and Persia

ESSENTIAL QUESTION *Why does conflict develop?*

IT MATTERS BECAUSE

Although it was large and powerful, the Persian Empire could not defeat the Greeks.

Persia's Empire

GUIDING QUESTION ***How did the Persians rule a vast empire?***

R About the time that the government in Athens was undergoing political changes, the Persians were building a powerful empire in Southwest Asia. Persia (PUHR•zhuh), the homeland of the Persians, was located in what is today southwestern Iran.

Early Persians were warriors and cattle herders from the grasslands of central Asia. After settling in the highlands of Persia, they came under the control of other peoples. Then a dynasty of kings brought the Persians together into a powerful kingdom. In the 500s B.C., a talented king named Cyrus (SY•ruhs) the Great built a strong Persian army. With that army, he began creating an empire that became the largest in the ancient world.

Creating an Empire

C During the 540s B.C., Persian troops swept into neighboring lands. They brought Mesopotamia, Syria, Judah, and the Greek city-states of the area of Anatolia under Persian rule. King Cyrus held his growing empire together by treating conquered peoples fairly. He allowed them to keep their own languages, religions, and laws. In addition, Cyrus decided that the Jews exiled in Babylon would be allowed to return to their homeland.

Reading HELPDESK CCSS

Taking Notes: *Identifying*

As you read the lesson, fill in a chart like this one with the names of participants. RH.6–8.2

Persian Kings Attacking Greece	Greek Defenders

Content Vocabulary (Tier 3 Words)
- **satrapy**
- **satrap**
- **Zoroastrianism**

networks ***Online Teaching Options***

VIDEO

The Early Olympics

Comparing and Contrasting Show the video *The Early Olympics* and ask students to take notes on what they learn. Then moderate a discussion about how the early Olympics were similar to and different from the Olympic Games today.

See page 171E for other online activities.

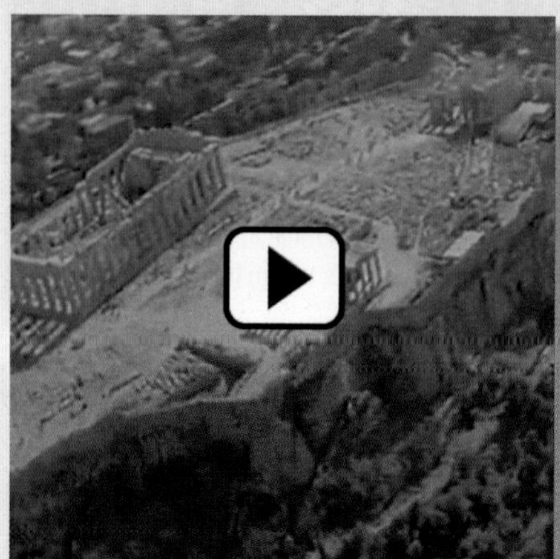

After Cyrus, other Persian rulers continued to expand the empire. Their armies took over Egypt, western India, and lands to the northeast of Greece. From west to east, the Persian Empire stretched a distance of some 3,000 miles (4,800 km). This is about the size of the continental United States today.

To link this large territory, the Persians improved the network of roads begun by the Assyrians. The most important route, the Royal Road, ran more than 1,500 miles (2,400 km) from Persia to Anatolia. Travelers could **obtain** food, water, and fresh horses at roadside stations along the route. Using the Royal Road, messengers could travel from Persia to Anatolia in just seven days. That same journey had taken three months before the road was built.

Persian Government

As the Persian Empire expanded, its increasing size made it more difficult to manage. Darius I (duh•RY•uhs), who ruled Persia from 522 to 486 B.C., reorganized the government to make it more efficient. He divided the empire into provinces called **satrapies** (SAY•truh•peez). Each satrapy was ruled by a governor called a **satrap** (SAY•trap), which means "defender of the kingdom." The satrap collected taxes, judged legal cases, managed the police, and recruited soldiers for the Persian army. C

V

GEOGRAPHY CONNECTION

Persian kings built the Royal Road to connect the areas of their large empire.

1 **MOVEMENT** About how far was the shortest distance from Greece to the western end of the Royal Road?

2 **CRITICAL THINKING** ***Making Inferences*** Based on the map, why might the Persian Empire have posed a danger to Greece?

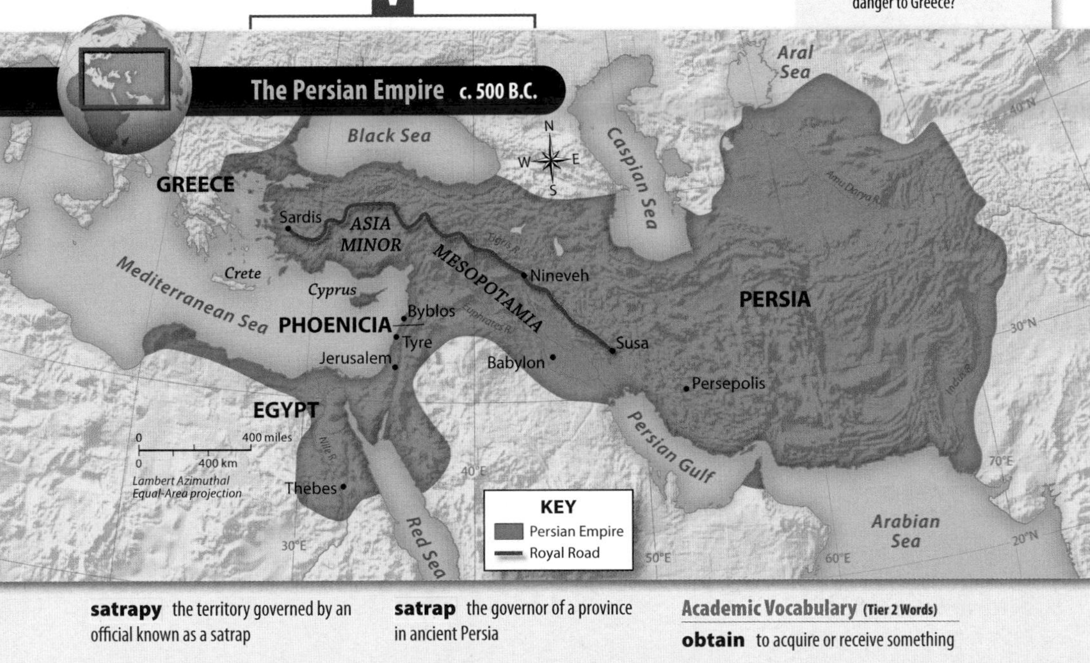

satrapy the territory governed by an official known as a satrap

satrap the governor of a province in ancient Persia

Academic Vocabulary (Tier 2 Words)

obtain to acquire or receive something

C Critical Thinking Skills

Comparing and Contrasting Tell students that as the Persian Empire grew, it became more difficult to manage. Darius I reorganized the government to make it easier to rule the empire. He divided the empire into provinces called *satrapies*. Each province was ruled by a governor called a *satrap*. **Ask:** **How was this system of provinces similar to and different from the system of states in the United States today?** *(Answers will vary. Among other points of comparison, students might note that Persian provinces and American states have governors. However, the Persian satraps were appointed, but U.S. governors are elected.)* BL

V Visuals Skills

Reading a Map Point to the Royal Road on the map of the Persian Empire. **Ask:** **What were the two cities at the ends of the Royal Road?** *(Sardis and Susa)* AL Ask students to use the map scale to estimate the length of the Royal Road. *(approximately 1600 miles long)* **Logical/Mathematical**

Content Background Knowledge

- Share the following information with students about Darius the Great and his rule.
- Darius was the son of a satrap and gained power after assassinating a king of the Empire. Darius said that the man was an imposter, but most historians disagree.
- To keep control of the empire, Darius set up a strong government with tax rates, standard coins, and a written code of laws.
- During his reign, Darius had many new buildings built, including forts and palaces. Persian architecture developed a unique style during his reign.

MAP

The Persian Empire, c. 500 B.C.

Summarizing Keep the map of the Persian Empire projected on the interactive whiteboard. Discuss as a class what happened in Persia that led to the establishment of a large empire. **Ask:** **Which king first expanded the Persian Empire?** *(Cyrus)* **How did Cyrus rule?** *(He ruled fairly. He let the conquered peoples keep their own languages, religions, and laws.)* **How did Darius I reorganize the Persian Empire?** *(He divided the empire into provinces. Each province was ruled by a governor, or satrap, who collected taxes, judged legal cases, managed the police, and recruited soldiers for the Persian army.)*

See page 171E for other online activities.

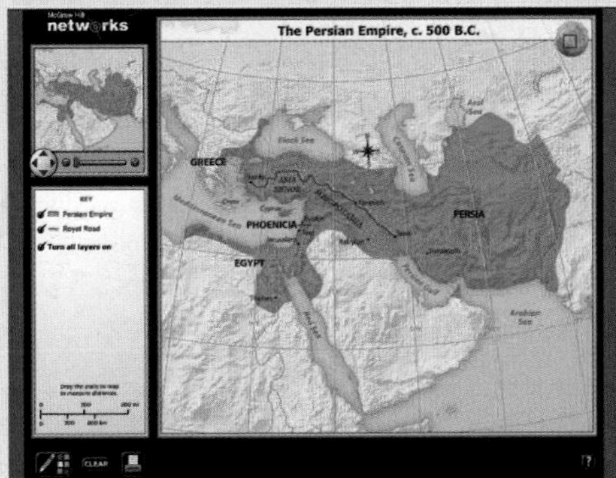

ANSWERS, p. 191

GEOGRAPHY CONNECTION

1 Greece was about 311 miles (500 km) away.

2 **CRITICAL THINKING** The Persian Empire was within easy striking distance of Greece on two fronts. It bordered the Greek mainland in the northeast and was less than 100 miles (161 km) from Greece across the Mediterranean.

V Visual Skills

Analyzing Images Discuss with students the image of the building in Persepolis. Explain that Persepolis was a city that served as the capital of the Persian Empire. **Ask:** **What does this photograph tell you about Darius and the Persian Empire?** *(Answers will vary but should include that the structure looks large, and its artistic elements, such as the sculpture of the nobles, might have been intended to show Darius's power and the strength of the empire.)* You may wish to have students come to the front of the class and pose like the nobles in this image. If possible, take a picture of the students in this position and compare it with the image in the book. **Kinesthetic**

R Reading Skills

Defining Direct students to read the section titled "Who Was Zoroaster?" Discuss with students the tenets of Zoroastrianism. **Ask:** **What is a monotheistic religion?** *(a religion based on a belief in a single god)* **Ask:** **What is the term for a religion in which people believe in many gods?** *(polytheism)* BL

V King Darius I of Persia established Persepolis as the center of his government. This sculpture from one of the main buildings in Persepolis shows a line of nobles and dignitaries waiting to speak with the king.

▶ **CRITICAL THINKING**
Speculating The artist shows all of the nobles, except one, facing forward. Why do you think the artist chose to show one person looking back?

Persia maintained a full-time, paid, professional army. In comparison, the Greek army consisted of citizens called to serve only during times of war. The best fighters in the Persian army were the 10,000 soldiers who were trained to guard the king. They were known as the Immortals because when a member died, another soldier immediately took his place.

Who Was Zoroaster?

R The Persians at first worshipped many gods. Then, sometime in the 600s B.C., a religious teacher named Zoroaster (ZOHR•uh•WAS•tuhr) preached a new monotheistic religion. Most Persians accepted his religion, which was called **Zoroastrianism** (zohr•uh•WAS•tree•uh•nih•zuhm).

Zoroaster taught that there was one supreme god. This deity was called Ahura Mazda, or "Wise Lord." Ahura Mazda was the creator of all things and the leader of the forces of good. Zoroaster believed that evil existed in the world. People were free to choose between good and evil, but at the end of time, goodness would be victorious. Zoroastrian teachings, prayers, and hymns (sacred songs) were written down in a holy book. Because of Zoroastrianism, the Persians began to view their monarchy as a sacred institution or role.

This Zoroastrian holy site is in present-day Iran.

Reading HELPDESK CCSS

Zoroastrianism a Persian religion based on the belief of one god

networks Online Teaching Options

BIOGRAPHY

Zoroaster

Identifying Show the beliefs of Zoroastrians from the lecture slide. Tell students that in the 600s B.C., a religious teacher named Zoroaster taught Persians to follow a single god, named Ahura Mazda. Most Persians accepted this religion, called Zoroastrianism. **Ask:** **How was Zoroastrianism related to the rule of Persian kings?** *(Persian kings believed they ruled by the power of Ahura Mazda and were responsible only to him.)*

See page 171E for other online activities.

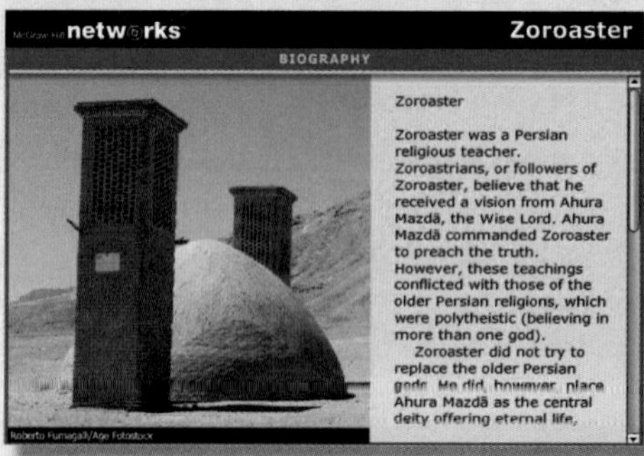

ANSWER, p. 192

CRITICAL THINKING Answers will vary. Perhaps he has turned to discuss something with the person behind him.

R

Persian kings believed that they ruled by the power of Ahura Mazda and were responsible to him alone. Darius I had the following statement carved on a cliff:

C1

PRIMARY SOURCE

> "For this reason Ahura Mazda [the Zoroastrian god] bore me aid . . . because I was not an enemy, I was not a deceiver, I was not a wrong-doer, neither I nor my family; according to rectitude [righteousness] I ruled."
>
> —from Darius I, *Behistun Inscription*, column 4, line 4.13

After Darius's rule ended, the Persians continued to practice Zoroastrianism for centuries. The religion has about 200,000 followers today. Most of them live in South Asia.

✓ **PROGRESS CHECK**

Explaining How did Persian rulers unite their vast empire?

King Darius I, shown in this carving, believed that the Zoroastrian god approved of his rule.

Gianni Dagli Orti/CORBIS

The Persian Wars

GUIDING QUESTION ***How did the Greeks defeat the Persians?***

As the 400s B.C. began, the Persians were ready to expand into Europe. However, they soon clashed with the Greeks, who had colonies in the Mediterranean area. Persia and Greece were very different civilizations. While the Persians obeyed an all-powerful king, many of the Greeks believed that citizens should choose their own rulers and government.

As a result of the conquests made by Cyrus, the Persians already controlled the Greek cities in Anatolia. In 499 B.C., these Greeks revolted against their Persian rulers. The Athenians sent warships to help the rebels, but the Persians crushed the uprising. The Persian king Darius was angry that the Athenians interfered. He decided to punish the mainland Greeks for meddling in his empire.

How Did the Greeks Win at Marathon?

In 490 B.C., Darius sent a fleet of 600 ships and an army to invade Greece. The Persians landed at Marathon (MAR•uh•thahn), which was a plain about 25 miles (40 km) northeast of Athens. The Persians waited there for several days. They expected the Greeks to come there and fight them. However, the Athenians did not come forward. They had only 10,000 troops compared to the Persians' 20,000 soldiers.

Build Vocabulary: *Words With Multiple Meanings*

One word can have many meanings, depending on how the word is used in a sentence. The noun *fleet*, for example, means "a group of vehicles operated under one control." As an adjective, *fleet* means "fast" or "temporary."

R Reading Skills

Explaining After reading the text, ask students to explain the role of Zoroastrianism in Persia's government. **Ask:** How was Zoroastrianism related to the rule of Persian kings? *(Persian kings believed they ruled by the power of Ahura Mazda and were responsible only to him.)* AL

C1 Critical Thinking Skills

Analyzing Primary Sources Direct students' attention to the primary source at the top of the page, and ask for a volunteer to read the passage aloud. Then have students restate this quotation from Darius in their own words. *(Students' responses will vary but should make the point that Darius believed that Ahura Mazda, the god of Zoroastrianism, helped him to be successful because he was a just and righteous man.)* **Auditory**

C2 Critical Thinking Skills

Speculating Discuss with students why Darius invaded Greece in 490 B.C. **Ask:** Why was Darius angry at the Athenians? *(He was angry because they sent warships to help people in Anatolia who were rebelling against the Persian Army.)* AL **Ask:** What do you think would have happened if the Athenians had not chosen to help those rebels? *(Answers will vary. Some students may say that Darius would have left them alone; others might say that he would have invaded anyway, since he was so intent on expanding.)*

LECTURE SLIDE

The Persian Wars

Comparing and Contrasting Show the blank Venn diagram about the Persian Wars from the lecture slide. Have students work in small groups to complete Venn diagrams comparing and contrasting ancient Greece and ancient Persia during the Persian Wars. Tell students to focus on the following points of comparison: geography, government, religion, and daily life. After students have finished their diagrams, ask them to speculate about why conflict might have developed between the Greeks and the Persians.

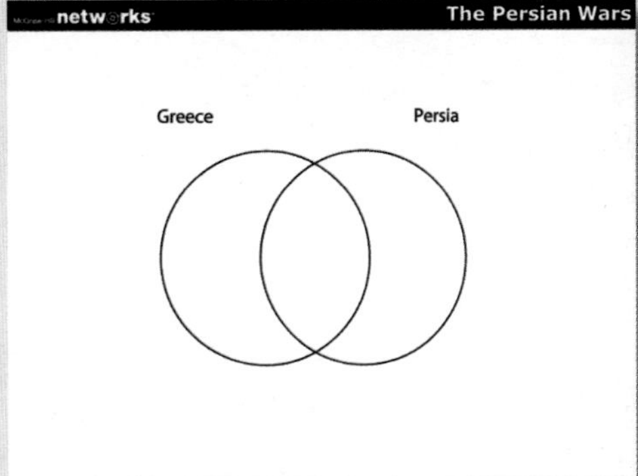

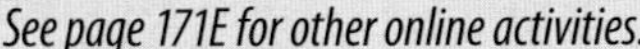

See page 171E for other online activities.

ANSWER, p. 193

✓ **PROGRESS CHECK** They divided the empire into satrapies and assigned important government responsibilities to each satrap. They also treated their conquered peoples fairly.

Greece and Persia

R Reading Skills

Summarizing Have students use details from the text to summarize the battle of Marathon. **Ask:** **Although the Athenians were outnumbered, they defeated the Persians at Marathon. How were they able to win this battle?** *(The Athenians tricked the Persians into thinking that they were not going to attack, so the Persians began putting their troops back on ships. Therefore, the Persian army was not prepared to fight when the Athenians finally attacked, so the Athenians defeated them.)*

W Writing Skills

Narrative Have students write a short speech that might have been given by the messenger from Marathon before his death. The speech should include information about the battle of Marathon as well as some emotional comments that the messenger may have said at the time.

Persian Wars 499–449 B.C.

1 Athenian army defeats Persian army.

2 Greek force, led by Spartans, falls to Persian army.

3 Greek fleet defeats Persian navy.

4 Greeks defeat Persians, ending the war.

Black Sea, Sea of Marmara, Aegean Sea, Thermopylae, Plataea, Salamis, Marathon, Athens, Sparta, Sardis, Miletus, Crete, 40°N, 20°E, 25°E, 30°E

KEY
- Greek states
- Persian Empire
- 1st Persian invasion, 490 B.C.
- 2nd Persian invasion, 480 B.C.
- Major battle

0 – 100 miles
0 – 100 km
Lambert Azimuthal Equal-Area projection

GEOGRAPHY CONNECTION

The Greek city-states successfully defended their territory against two invasions by the Persian Empire.

1. **LOCATION** Which Greek city-state defeated the Persian army in a major battle?
2. **CRITICAL THINKING** ***Speculating*** Why might the Greek city-states have had an advantage over the Persians?

When their enemy refused to fight, the Persians decided to sail directly to Athens and attack it by sea. The Persians began loading their ships with their strongest units—the cavalry. As soon as the Persian horsemen were on the ships, the Athenians charged down the hills and onto the plain of Marathon. The Athenians caught the Persian foot soldiers standing in the water, out of formation. They were without any help from their cavalry. **R**

The Persians suffered a terrible defeat. According to Greek legend, a young messenger raced 25 miles from Marathon to Athens with news of the victory. When the runner reached Athens, he cried out "Victory" and then **collapsed** and died from exhaustion. Today's marathon races are named for that famous run and are just over 26 miles (41.8 km) long. **W**

Land and Sea Battles

After the defeat at Marathon, the Persians vowed revenge against the Athenians. In 480 B.C., a new Persian king named Xerxes (ZUHRK•seez) invaded Greece with about 200,000 troops and thousands of warships and supply vessels. The Greek city-states banded together to fight the Persians.

Reading HELPDESK (CCSS)

Academic Vocabulary (Tier 2 Words)

collapse to break down; to lose effectiveness

Reading Strategies: *Ask Questions*

Asking questions as you read helps you understand what you read. Ask questions with the words *who, what, why, where, when,* and *how.*

networks *Online Teaching Options*

MAP

Persian Wars 499–449 B.C.

Identifying Show students the image of the naval battle between the Greek and Persian fleets at Salamis. **Ask:**

- **Who won the battle of Salamis?** *(The Greek navy destroyed almost the entire Persian fleet.)*
- **How did the Greeks win even though their navy ships were smaller?** *(The Greek ships were smaller in size but faster, and they could be maneuvered more easily.)*

See page 171E for other online activities.

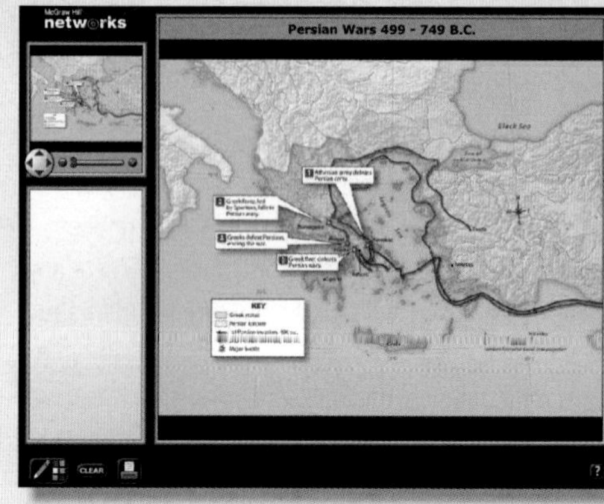

ANSWERS, p. 194

GEOGRAPHY CONNECTION

1. Athens defeated the Persian army at Marathon.
2. **CRITICAL THINKING** The armies of the city-states were fighting in their home territories, while the Persians were in unfamiliar territory and far from supply bases.

King Leonidas (lee•AH•nuh•duhs) of Sparta supplied the most soldiers. Themistocles (thuh•MIHS•tuh•kleez) of Athens directed the Greek naval forces and devised a battle plan.

Persian ships supplied the invaders with food. Themistocles wanted to attack the Persians' ships and cut off the army's supplies. To do this, the Greeks had to stop the Persian army from reaching Athens. Sparta's King Leonidas led 7,000 soldiers into a battle that lasted for three days. The Spartans' bravery at Thermopylae (thur•MAH•puh•lee) was much celebrated.

C1

The Greeks, however, could not stop the Persians at Thermopylae. A traitor showed the Persians a trail leading around the Greek line, allowing them to attack from behind. Realizing that his Greek army would soon be surrounded, Leonidas dismissed most of the troops. He and 300 Spartans remained and fought to the death. The Greek historian Herodotus (hair•RAH•deh•tuhs) gave this description of the battle:

PRIMARY SOURCE

> "They [the Spartans] defended themselves to the last, those who still had swords using them, and the others resisting with their hands and teeth; till the barbarians [Persians], who in part . . . had gone round and now encircled them upon every side, overwhelmed and buried the remnant [remainder] which was left beneath showers of missile weapons."
>
> —from *The Histories* by Herodotus

C2

akg-images/Peter Connolly

Connections to TODAY

Marathons

The first marathon runner is said to have been a Greek soldier. He is thought to have run from Athens to Sparta.

The first Olympic marathon—which took its name from that battle—was held when the modern games began in 1896. In 1924, the Olympic marathon distance was set at 26 miles and 385 yards (42.195 km).

At the Battle of Salamis, smaller, faster Greek ships defeated the Persian fleet.

▶ **CRITICAL THINKING**

Analyzing Why were the Persians at a disadvantage in the battle?

C1 Critical Thinking Skills

Making Connections Remind students of what they learned about the Spartans in Lesson 2. **Ask:** **Why do you think King Leonides of Sparta supplied the most soldiers when Persia invaded in 480 B.C.?** *(The Spartans were trained to be excellent warriors, so King Leonides probably believed they would be more successful than troops from any other city-states in fighting against the Persians.)*

C2 Critical Thinking Skills

Analyzing Primary Sources Read aloud the primary-source quote on this page to the class. Then ask students to draw a sketch of what they think the battle scene looked like, based on this account. When they are finished, have them share their drawings with the class, and ask them to point out the specific words in the passage that helped them create their image. **Visual/Spatial**

Content Background Knowledge

- Share the following information with students about Thermopylae.
- Thermopylae is a narrow pass between the ocean and a large mountainous region. It is about four miles long.
- The battle of Thermopylae has been celebrated in Greek literature and history for thousands of years.
- In 1955, a large marble-and-bronze monument commemorating the battle of Thermopylae was built in Thermopylae.

GAME

Greek–Persian Wars Concentration Game

Identifying Have students click on squares and match the event or person to the description to check students' understanding of important events of the Greek and Persian wars.

See page 171E for other online activities.

ANSWER, p. 195

CRITICAL THINKING It was difficult to maneuver the large Persian ships in the narrow Strait of Salamis.

V Visual Skills

Analyzing Images Have students look at the illustration and imagine that they are Greeks in Salamis, watching the Persian ships arrive. **Ask:** **What might the Greeks have felt upon seeing the ships?** *(Answers will vary. Some students might say that seeing so many large ships would have been frightening. Other might say that those who lived in the region might have known that the large Persian ships would have trouble moving in such a narrow strait.)* Ask students to explain which clues in the picture helped them come up with their answers.

The Persian king Xerxes watches his fleet battle the Greeks at the Battle of Salamis.

▶ **CRITICAL THINKING**

Contrasting Xerxes led his armies into battle. How is his role in wartime different from that played by most modern political leaders?

V

National Geographic Society/Corbis

The Spartans' heroic stand gave Themistocles time to carry out his plan to attack Persia's ships. The Athenian fleet of ships lured the Persian fleet into the strait of Salamis (SA•luh•muhs), near Athens. A strait is a narrow **channel** of water between two pieces of land. The Greeks hoped this move would give them an advantage in battle. Themistocles believed that the heavy Persian ships would crowd together in the strait, making them difficult to move. His assumption proved to be correct. Vigorous fighting

Academic Vocabulary (Tier 2 Words)

channel a strait or narrow sea between two landmasses

networks *Online Teaching Options*

SLIDE SHOW

The Battle of Salamis

Explaining Have students view the images and read the text on the slide show. Then ask them to explain why the Greeks were able to win the battle of Salamis even though they were greatly outnumbered.

See page 171E for other online activities.

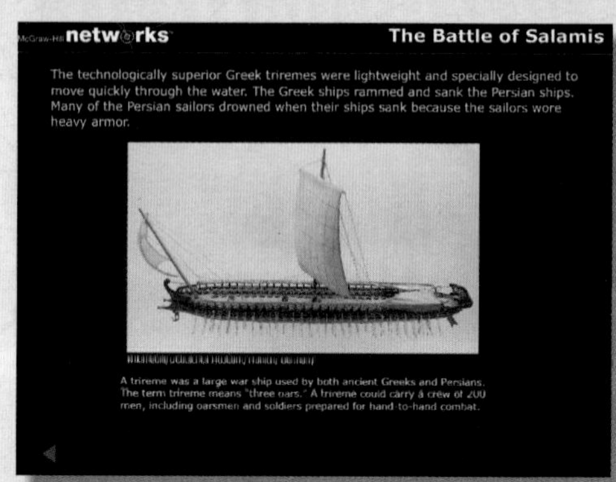

McGraw-Hill networks
The Battle of Salamis
The technologically superior Greek triremes were lightweight and specially designed to move quickly through the water. The Greek ships rammed and sank the Persian ships. Many of the Persian sailors drowned when their ships sank because the sailors wore heavy armor.
A trireme was a large war ship used by both ancient Greeks and Persians. The term trireme means "three oars." A trireme could carry a crew of 200 men, including oarsmen and soldiers prepared for hand-to-hand combat.

ANSWER, p. 196

CRITICAL THINKING Most modern political leaders do not take an active part in battles.

took place between the two navies. The Greeks had fewer ships, but their boats were smaller and faster, and could outmaneuver the Persian ships. The plan worked. The Greeks sank about 300 Persian ships and lost only about 40 ships of their own. The Persian fleet was almost entirely destroyed. Still, the Persian foot soldiers marched on to Athens. Finding the city almost deserted, the Persians set it on fire.

The combined forces of the Greek city-states in 479 B.C. formed their largest army yet. They had improved their fighting forces with better armor and weapons. At Plataea (pluh•TEE•uh), northwest of Athens, the Greek army again faced the Persians. In numbers, the two sides were evenly matched. Each fielded a force of about 100,000 men. This time, however, the Greeks defeated the Persian army. Fighting continued as the Greeks went on the defensive to free the city-states in Anatolia from Persian rule. Peace between the Greek allies and the Persians did not come until 449 B.C. **R**

Decline of Persia

After its losses in Greece, Persia faced many challenges. The Persian army was no longer strong enough to defend the entire empire. Also, the Persian people grew unhappy with their government. The kings taxed the people heavily to pay for magnificent palaces and other luxuries. Members of the royal family disagreed about who should rule.

As Persia weakened, it became open to outside attacks. In the 300s B.C., Persia could not resist the invasion of an army led by a young and powerful ruler named Alexander. The Persian Empire ended, and a new Greek empire emerged that extended beyond even Persia's boundaries.

✓ **PROGRESS CHECK**

Explaining After the losses in Greece, why did the Persians grow unhappy with their government?

LESSON 3 REVIEW 

Review Vocabulary (Tier 3 Words)

1. What were the responsibilities of the *satrap?* RH.6–8.4

Answer the Guiding Questions

2. ***Explaining*** Why did Darius I create satrapies? RH.6–8.2
3. ***Determining Cause and Effect*** What brought Sparta and Athens together as allies? RH.6–8.2
4. ***Analyzing*** Why did Persia invade Greece? RH.6–8.2
5. ***Differentiating*** Which Persian leader do you think made the biggest contribution? Why? RH.6–8.2
6. **ARGUMENT** You are an officer in the Athenian army. The Persians have just landed at Marathon to invade Greece. Write a letter to a friend explaining why the Athenian army did not go out to fight the Persians when they arrived at Marathon. WHST.6–8.1, WHST.6–8.10

LESSON 3 REVIEW ANSWERS

1. The satrap collected taxes, judged legal cases, managed the police, and recruited soldiers for the army.
2. He created satrapies to make the government more efficient.
3. Sparta and Athens formed an alliance to fight off Persian invasions.
4. Persia invaded in order to punish Greece for aiding the rebellious cities of Anatolia.
5. Answers will vary but should be supported by valid reasons.
6. Letters will vary. Students may mention that the Athenians had far fewer troops than the Persians. They may also mention the Athenians' decision to wait and catch the Persians off-guard without the protection of their cavalry.

R Reading Skills

Explaining Ask a volunteer to use details from the text to explain why the Greek army ultimately defeated the Persians. **Ask:** **What do you think was the one factor that allowed the Greeks to succeed?** *(Students may say that by combining forces, the Greek city-states formed their largest army yet, which defeated the Persians. Other students may say that the Greeks had better armor and weapons. Others might describe the successful battle strategies of the Greeks as well.)*

Have students complete the Lesson 3 Review.

CLOSE & REFLECT

Speculating Hold a class discussion on the war between the Greeks and the Persians. Ask students what happened to Persia as a result of the war. Then have them predict what happened to Greece after the war. **Ask:** **Did Greece become more united or less united, or did it remain the same?**

ANSWER, p. 197

✓ **PROGRESS CHECK** Persians were unhappy because the kings taxed the people heavily.

ENGAGE

Bellringer Tell students they will learn how Athens started to dominate other city-states, which helped lead to war among the city-states. Ask students if they have ever seen a movie or TV show in which a character tries to take charge of a group. Have a class discussion about how people felt toward this person in the movie or TV program. Explain to students that Athens tried to take charge of a group that the Greek city-states had formed. Athens also interfered with Sparta's allies. This eventually led to war among the Greek city-states.

TEACH & ASSESS

R Reading Skill

Defining Review with students the meaning of the terms *direct democracy* and *representative democracy.* ELL **Ask:**

- **What form of government was practiced in Athens during its golden age?** *(direct democracy)*
- **How does direct democracy work?** *(All citizens meet to debate and vote on government matters.)* AL
- **How does representative democracy work?** *(Citizens elect a smaller group of people to represent them and govern on their behalf.)*

networks *There's More Online!*

GRAPHIC ORGANIZER
- Accomplishments: Age of Pericles
- Comparing Governments

GRAPH
- Athens Population Graph

Lesson 4
Glory, War, and Decline

ESSENTIAL QUESTION *How do governments change?*

IT MATTERS BECAUSE

The Peloponnesian War had a decisive effect on Greece. Greek culture declined after the Athenian loss to Sparta.

The Rule of Pericles

GUIDING QUESTION *How did Pericles influence government and culture in Athens?*

As the Persian Wars ended, Athens became a powerful and self-confident city-state. From 461 B.C. to 429 B.C., the Athenians, under their new leader Pericles (PEHR•uh•kleez), enjoyed a golden age of prosperity and achievement. Their city-state became the economic and cultural center of Greece. Athens also practiced democratic government.

Democracy in Athens

R Athenians took great pride in their democratic system. The form of government practiced by the Athenians is called **direct democracy** (dih•MAH•kruh•see). In a direct democracy, all citizens meet to debate and vote on government matters. In a **representative democracy**, such as the one we have in the United States today, citizens elect a smaller group of people. This group represents them, makes laws, and governs on their behalf.

In ancient Athens, direct democracy worked because of its relatively small number of citizens. The assembly consisted of some 43,000 male citizens over the age of 18. Often, however, fewer than 6,000 participated in the meetings, which were held

Reading **HELP**DESK 

Taking Notes: ***Identifying***

Use a chart like this one to list the accomplishments during the age of Pericles. RH.6–8.2

Age of Pericles

Content Vocabulary (Tier 3 Words)
- **direct democracy**
- **representative democracy**
- **philosopher**

networks ***Online Teaching Options***

VIDEO

Coinage and Democracy in Athens

Analyzing Show the video *Coinage and Democracy in Athens.* Ask students to take notes on the economic and political processes shown in the video. Then discuss what these concepts tell about life in ancient Athens and draw comparisons with the present day.

See page 171F for other online activities.

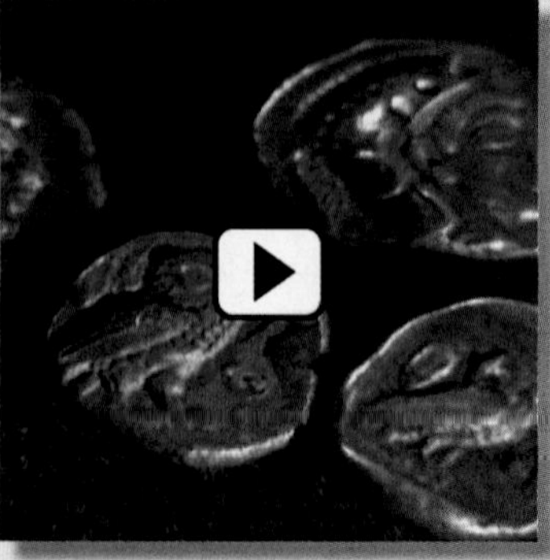

ANSWER, p. 198

TAKING NOTES: Answers should include rebuilding of Athens; political leadership during the period of the Delian League; support of writers, artists, and philosophers; expansion of democratic government.

every 10 days. At those meetings, participating citizens passed laws, elected officials, and made policy on war and foreign affairs. The ten top officials, elected each year, were known as generals.

Pericles in Charge

After the Persian Wars, the most important general in Athenian government was Pericles. His wise rule guided the city-state for more than 30 years.

Pericles made Athens a more democratic city-state. He appointed people to positions because of their abilities, not because they were members of a certain social class. Pericles brought more ordinary Athenians into government. As a result, even shopkeepers and laborers could, for the first time, share in the government along with nobles and farmers.

Under Pericles's rule, Athens became a center of learning and the arts. The Persians had burned much of the city during the Persian Wars. Under Pericles, Athens was rebuilt. He erected new temples, monuments, and statues throughout the city.

Pericles also supported writers, artists, teachers, sculptors, and architects. **Philosophers** (fuh•LAH•suh•fuhrs) also flourished during the rule of Pericles. Philosophers are thinkers who reflect on the meaning of life. Athens became a great center for knowledge. Pericles called the city "the school of Greece."

R

✓ **PROGRESS CHECK**

Explaining How was Athens able to become a direct democracy?

National Geographic Society/Corbis

Political discussion was highly popular in Athens.

▶ **CRITICAL THINKING**

Speculating Citizens in Athens would meet on a hill in the city set aside for political discussion. What issues do you think Athenian citizens might have debated there?

direct democracy a form of democracy in which all citizens can participate firsthand in the decision-making process

representative democracy a form of democracy in which citizens elect officials to govern on their behalf

philosopher a person who searches for wisdom or enlightenment

Glory, War, and Decline

R Reading Skills

Identifying After students read the text, ask them to explain how, under Pericles's rule, Athens became a center of learning and the arts. *(Students should note that he supported writers, artists, teachers, sculptors, and architects. They should also note that people who reflected on the meaning of life, called philosophers, also flourished.)* **Ask:**

- **What did Pericles call Athens?** *(the school of Greece)*
- **What did he mean by that phrase?** *(Answers will vary, but students should recognize that Athens was the center of learning in Greece.)*

Content Background Knowledge

Biography of Pericles

- Pericles was born about 495 B.C. to a wealthy and powerful family just outside of Athens. He was educated by philosophers.
- When he became ruler, Pericles strongly supported democracy. He was from a wealthy family, but he believed that citizenship should not be limited to the wealthy and powerful. He made changes to take power from the few and give it to the many.
- Pericles wanted Athens to be a model for the world. He hired hundreds of workers to construct public buildings in Athens. The best-known building is the Parthenon. Workers hauled 20,000 tons of marble from a nearby mountain and spent almost 15 years completing it.
- Pericles avoided being in public as much as possible. He spent most of his time alone, with family, or with close friends. He married and had three sons. In 429 B.C. Pericles died from the plague.

BIOGRAPHY

Pericles

Evaluating Have students scroll through the text about Pericles to learn more about the Athenian leader. Ask students which of Pericles' achievements they think was most important, and have them support their answer with specific details. You may want to revisit this question at the end of this lesson.

See page 171F for other online activities.

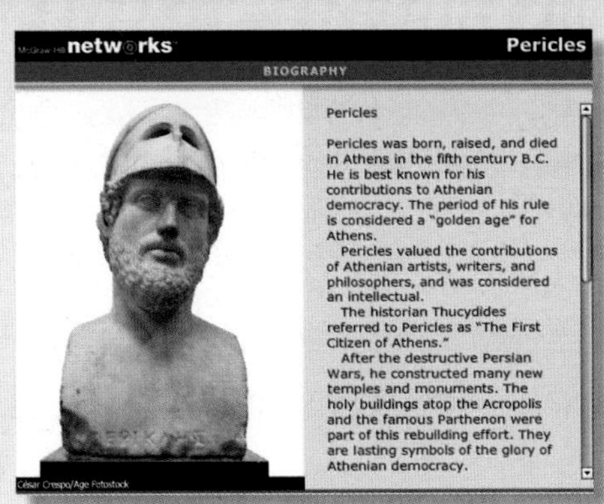

McGraw-Hill networks
Pericles
BIOGRAPHY
Pericles
Pericles was born, raised, and died in Athens in the fifth century B.C. He is best known for his contributions to Athenian democracy. The period of his rule is considered a "golden age" for Athens.
Pericles valued the contributions of Athenian artists, writers, and philosophers, and was considered an intellectual.
The historian Thucydides referred to Pericles as "The First Citizen of Athens."
After the destructive Persian Wars, he constructed many new temples and monuments. The holy buildings atop the Acropolis and the famous Parthenon were part of this rebuilding effort. They are lasting symbols of the glory of Athenian democracy.
César Crespo/Age Fotostock

ANSWERS, p. 199

CRITICAL THINKING Answers will vary but may include politics or philosophy.

✓ **PROGRESS CHECK** The population of Athenian citizens attending the assembly meetings was relatively small, making direct democracy possible. In addition, Pericles, the most important leader in Athens, encouraged direct democracy and participation in government by all classes of citizens.

Glory, War, and Decline

C Critical Thinking Skills

Making Connections Show the class the infographic at the top of the page comparing the direct democracy of Athens with the representative democracy of the United States. Then guide students through a comparison and contrast of the two democratic systems. Ask them to consider the strengths and weaknesses of each form of democracy.

W Writing Skills

Narrative Have students write a dialogue in which an Athenian man and woman describe their daily lives to someone from another city. Students can make up some details about the specific people they are describing, but they should include factual details from the text in their narratives. After they have finished, ask volunteers to read their dialogues aloud. **Verbal/Linguistic**

ANSWERS, p. 200

INFOGRAPHIC

1. Citizens who had voting rights could vote directly for or against all laws.
2. **CRITICAL THINKING** A broader segment of the population has the right to vote in the United States than the population did under Athenian democracy.

INFOGRAPHIC

COMPARING GOVERNMENTS

Athens was able to have a direct democracy because it had a low number of citizens.

1. **IDENTIFYING** In Athens, what involvement could citizens have in the passage of laws?
2. **CRITICAL THINKING** *Analyzing* Under which government does a broader segment of the population have the right to vote?

	Athenian Democracy	American Democracy
Type of Democracy	Direct	Representative
Right to Vote	Only adult males born in Athens	All citizens, male and female age 18 or over
Laws	Proposed by the council and approved by a majority in the assembly	Approved by both houses of Congress and signed by the president
Citizen Involvement	Citizens with voting rights can vote for or against any law	Citizens with voting rights can vote for or against the officials who make the laws

Athenian Life

GUIDING QUESTION *What was life like for Athenians under the rule of Pericles?*

At its height in the 400s B.C., Athens was the largest Greek city-state. Its population numbered about 285,000. Of this number, about 150,000 were citizens. Only 43,000 of these citizens, however, were males who had political rights. Athens was home to about 35,000 foreigners and 100,000 enslaved people.

Athenian Men and Women

Athenian men worked as farmers, artisans, and merchants. They often finished their daily work in the morning. They spent afternoons exercising at the gymnasium. In the evening, upper-class men enjoyed all-male gatherings where they ate, drank, and discussed philosophy or politics.

Athenian women focused on their homes and families. Girls married at a young age, often in their mid-teens. Their duties centered on having children and taking care of their households. Women of poor families helped with the farm work or sold goods in the local marketplace. Most upper-class women rarely left their houses except to attend funerals and festivals. Even then, they had to be **accompanied** by a male relative. Upper-class women generally supervised the servants and spun, dyed, or wove cloth.

Athenian women could not attend school, but many learned to read and to play music. However, Athenian society did not consider educated women as equal to men. Women could not participate in political activities or own property. Greek women

Reading HELPDESK CCSS

Academic Vocabulary (Tier 2 Words)

accompany to go with someone as a companion

networks Online Teaching Options

GRAPH

Athens Population Graph

Analyzing Graphs Have students click on arrows at the bottom of the graph to see the number of people who took part in Athenian government. **Ask: How many people had political rights?** *(43,000)* **About what percentage of the population was that?** *(about 15%)*

See page 171F for other online activities.

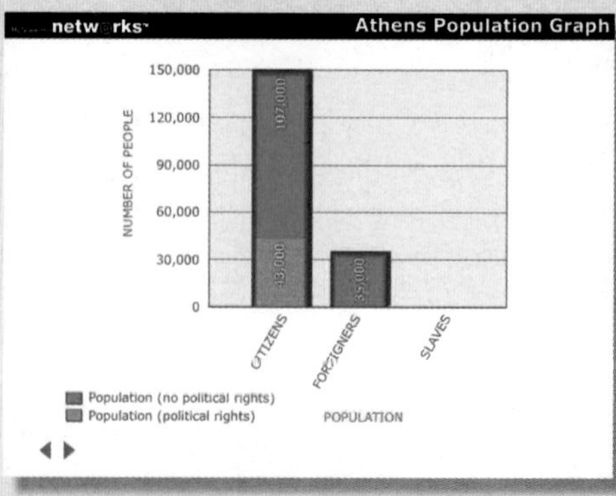

were always under the care of a male family member. Husbands were responsible for their wives and unmarried daughters. Sons looked after their widowed mothers.

A few women had more freedom, especially foreigners, who were regarded differently than Athenian-born women. One well-regarded woman was Aspasia (as•PAY•zhuh). She was known for her intelligence and charm. Aspasia taught public speaking, and her ideas were popular among Athenians. Both Plato (PLAY•toh), the famous Greek philosopher, and Pericles were influenced by her.

What Was the Role of Slavery in Athens?

Slavery was common in ancient civilizations. It was often considered to be a normal part of life, even by enslaved people themselves. Even in a democracy like Athens, slavery was common. Most Athenian households had at least one enslaved person. Wealthy Athenian families often had several.

Many enslaved people were prisoners who had been captured in battle. These included both Greeks and non-Greeks. Enslaved men worked on farms, in the shops of artisans, or at hard labor. Enslaved women were cooks and servants in wealthy homes and sometimes taught upper-class children. The treatment of enslaved people varied. Those who labored in mines often died very young. Slaves who worked as craftspeople had easier lives. Sometimes, enslaved people could earn money and, in rare cases, buy their freedom. Slavery might have helped Athens develop its prosperous economy. **R**

BIOGRAPHY

Aspasia (c. 470–400 B.C.)

Aspasia originally came from the Greek-speaking city of Miletus in Asia Minor. Her beauty and intellect made her a democratic symbol to many Greeks who treated her like a modern rock star.

She aggressively entered into the male-dominated society and government of Greece. She was one of the first women to encourage other females to participate in government and demand their rights.

ATHENIAN ARCHITECTURE

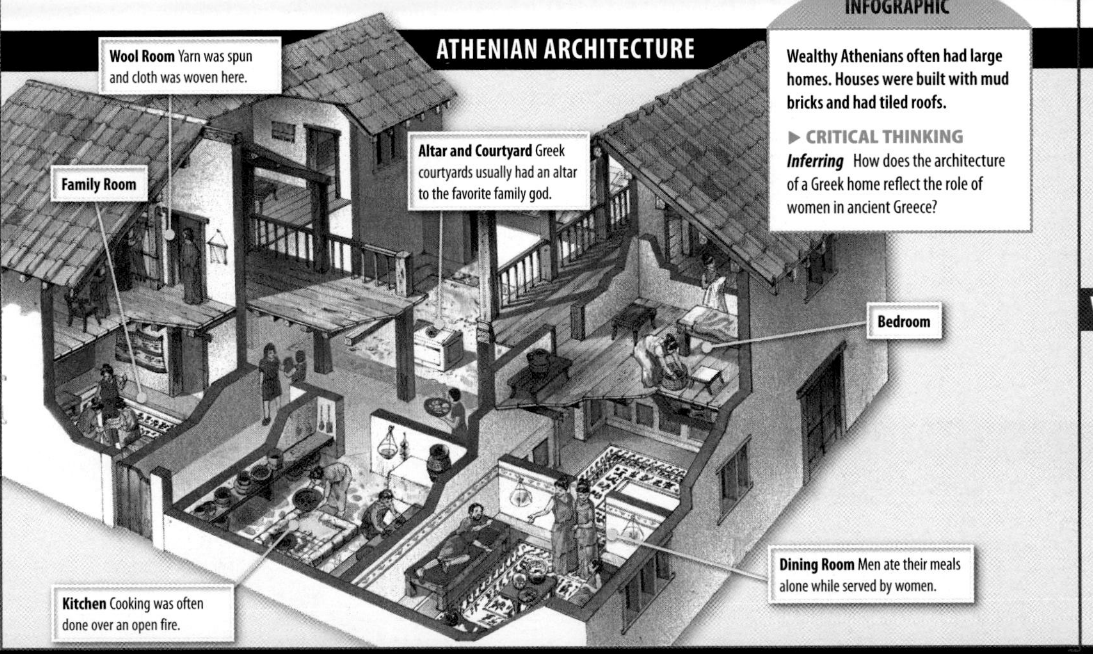

INFOGRAPHIC

Wealthy Athenians often had large homes. Houses were built with mud bricks and had tiled roofs.

▶ **CRITICAL THINKING**

Inferring How does the architecture of a Greek home reflect the role of women in ancient Greece? **V**

R Reading Skills

Summarizing After they finish reading, ask students to summarize the role of slavery in Athens. Remind them that unlike in the United States, slavery was not race-based in Athens. **Ask:** **Who was enslaved in Athens?** *(Most enslaved people were prisoners who had been captured in battle.)* **What jobs did enslaved people have?** *(They worked on farms, in shops, and at hard labor.)* **How did slavery help Athens's economy?** *(The slave contributed to the productivity of the city by doing manual labor and producing artisan goods.)* **BL**

V Visual Skills

Analyzing Images Have students look closely at the infographic at the bottom of the page. **Ask:** **What does this diagram tell you about the home life of Athenians?** *(Answers will vary but may include that Athenians worshipped in their homes, did work—such as weaving—at home, and had other separate rooms for specific functions than students might have expected.)* **Visual/Spatial**

Making Connections

Ask students to discuss the division of labor between men and women in the United States today. Have them discuss roles both inside and outside of the home. Remind students that while women today perform most of the same roles that men do, this change did not take place for many American women until the second half of the twentieth century.

BIOGRAPHY

Aspasia

Describing Have students scroll through the text to learn about the life of Aspasia. Then have the class describe her role in Athenian society. Lead a discussion about how Aspasia was ahead of her time in many aspects of her life. Ask students to share some examples of the privileges she was granted, and have them explain how this differed from the actions of most Athenian women at this time.

See page 171F for other online activities.

McGraw-Hill networks
Aspasia
BIOGRAPHY
Aspasia
Aspasia was a unique woman in ancient Greece. She was the unmarried, foreign companion of Pericles. He showed respect for her in ways most women never experienced. The commoners of Athens were suspicious of Aspasia. Throughout her lifetime with Pericles, she was allowed to attend meetings that were usually just attended by men. Pericles is said to have consulted her on important decisions, and she likely advised him in matters of state.
Notable scholars, philosophers, and thinkers, including Socrates, were known to visit Aspasia and Pericles for conversations at their home.
Hulton Archive/Getty Images

ANSWER, p. 201

INFOGRAPHIC

CRITICAL THINKING Rooms were set aside for tasks such as spinning and cooking, which were women's work. Only men ate in the dining room, where they were served by women.

Glory, War, and Decline

R Reading Skills

Discussing Ask students to read the section titled "War Between Athens and Sparta." Discuss with students the creation of the Delian League and its contribution to the start of the Peloponnesian War. Remind students to support their answers with details from the text. **Ask:**

- **In its early years, what did the Delian League accomplish?** *(The Delian League drove the Persians from the Greek territories in Anatolia.)*
- **Did the Delian League succeed?** *(No, it failed.)* ELL
- **Why did it fail?** *(Athens, the strongest city-state, began to control the other member city-states.)*
- **How was Athens able to take control of the Delian League?** *(Athens provided the league with most of its soldiers and sailors and eventually controlled the other members.)* AL

C Critical Thinking Skills

Speculating Ask students to think about how other city-states would have responded to Athens's gaining so much power. **Ask: How do you think the Spartans would react to Athens gaining control of the Delian League?** *(Students might predict that because Spartans prided themselves on their strength, they might resent Athens's gaining so much power. A conflict may occur between the two city-states.)* BL

Marble lions like this one guarded the way from the harbor to the temples in Delos.

The Athenian Economy

Farming was a common occupation among Athenians. Local farmers grew grains, vegetables, and fruits, including grapes and olives to make wine and olive oil for shipment to foreign markets.

Athenian farms lacked **sufficient** land to grow enough food to support the city-state. Although Athenians grew some grain, they had to import more from other places. Athens built a large fleet of ships to trade with colonies and other city-states in the Mediterranean world. During the 400s B.C., Athens led the Greek world in trade. Important goods made and traded in Athens included pottery and leather products.

☑ PROGRESS CHECK

Comparing and Contrasting How did the roles of Athenian men and women differ?

War Between Athens and Sparta

GUIDING QUESTION *How did the Peloponnesian War affect the Greek city-states?*

As time passed, the Greek city-states learned that their survival depended on cooperation. Even after the Persian Wars ended, the Persian threat against Greece remained. In 478 B.C., Athens joined with other city-states to form a defensive league, or protective group, to defend its members against the Persians. Because the league at first had its headquarters on the island of Delos (DEE•LAHS), it became known as the Delian League.

Athens provided the Delian League with most of its sailors and soldiers, while the other city-states supplied money and ships. During the next several **decades**, the league drove Persia out of the remaining Greek territories in Anatolia. Free of Persian domination, Greece grew richer through increased overseas trade.

The Athenian Empire

In spite of its successes, the Delian League failed. Athens was the strongest city-state, and the league's officials and commanders and most of the troops were Athenian. Over time, Athens began to use its influence to control the other member city-states. The league was no longer an alliance of equal city-states fighting Persia. It had become a group of city-states controlled by Athens.

Reading HELPDESK CCSS

Academic Vocabulary (Tier 2 Words)

sufficient enough
decade a period of ten years

networks Online Teaching Options

IMAGE

Delos

Categorizing Have students click on the buttons below the image of Delos to learn more about this island. Ask them to create a three-column chart with the following headings: Religion, Literature, Politics. Then ask them to fill in the chart and explain the importance of Delos in each of the categories.

See page 171F for other online activities.

networks
Delos
Delos went on to become a flourishing port and it remained a major religious center. It gained even greater importance after it was mentioned in The Odyssey by Homer. The Delian League placed its headquarters on the holy island, and took its name from it as well.
The tiny island of Delos has a long history, dating back over 4,000 years. Tourists flock to Delos to visit the many religious ruins there.

ANSWER, p. 202

☑ PROGRESS CHECK Men did farm work, exercised at the gymnasium, and attended gatherings in the evening to talk about politics and philosophy. Women did housework and raised families.

Pericles's leadership helped Athens dominate the Delian League. He treated the other city-states like subjects, demanding strict loyalty and regular payments from them. He even insisted that they use Athenian coins and measures. In 454 B.C., the Athenians moved the Delian League's treasury from Delos to Athens. They also sent troops to other Greek city-states to help the common people rebel against the nobles in power.

War Breaks Out

As the economic and political power of Athens grew, other city-states, especially Sparta, became alarmed. Politically and socially, Sparta and Athens were quite different. Neither trusted the other. Both wanted to be the major power in the Greek world.

Sparta became the leader of an alliance of city-states opposed to Athens. In 433 B.C., Athens began interfering with some of Sparta's allies. These allies pressured Sparta to attack Athens. War broke out in 431 B.C. and continued until 404 B.C. The possibility of future cooperation among the Greek city-states disappeared as a result of this war. Historians call this **conflict** the Peloponnesian War because Sparta was located in the Peloponnesus.

Pericles's Funeral Oration

During the war's first winter, Athens held a public funeral to honor soldiers who had died in battle. Afterward, the Athenian families gathered to mourn their losses. In a famous speech, called the *Funeral Oration*, Pericles talked about the greatness of Athens and reminded the people that they made their government strong. He reminded them that citizens had to obey the rules in their constitution—their framework of government. They accepted certain duties, such as paying taxes and defending the city. They were also awarded certain rights, such as the ability to vote and run for office.

T

PRIMARY SOURCE

"Our constitution is called a democracy because power is in the hands not of a minority but of the whole people. When it is a question of settling private disputes, everyone is equal before the law. . . ."

—Pericles, *Funeral Oration*, quoted in *History of the Peloponnesian War*

In his speech, Pericles **emphasized** that the democratic way of life is worth protecting. He urged his listeners to have the courage to continue fighting. The ideas Pericles expressed are still valued by citizens of democratic countries today.

The historian Thucydides described Pericles as "the first citizen" of Athens.

▶ CRITICAL THINKING

Evaluating Pericles was not an emperor, a king, or even a president, yet he was able to lead Athens to the greatest glories the city would ever know. How do you think he was able to accomplish what he did?

César Crespo/Age fotostock

Academic Vocabulary (Tier 2 Words)

conflict a battle or war

emphasize to attach a sense of importance to something; to express the importance of something

T Technology Skills

Using Digital Tools Pericles's *Funeral Oration* is part of a tradition of honoring soldiers who have died in battle. Ask students to research speeches (such as the Gettysburg Address) and monuments that honor members of the military who have died serving the United States. Then have small groups work together to create PowerPoint presentations about the speeches and monuments. **Interpersonal**

Content Background Knowledge

- The Peloponnesian War began in 431 B.C. and lasted for 27 years. It is often divided into three phases.
- The first phase was from 431 B.C. to 421 B.C. During these years, there was intermittent fighting between Sparta and Athens. Sparta attacked Attica, the territory around Athens, but because Sparta did not have a navy, it could not defeat its rival. Pericles died during these years.
- The second phase was a truce that lasted until 415. It is known as the "Peace of Nicias" and was named for the Athenian general Nicias.
- The third phase began when Athens attacked Sicily and lost, greatly weakening their navy. With help from Persia, Sparta built up a navy during these years and participated in a number of successful naval battles. The fighting ended in 404 B.C.

LECTURE SLIDE

War Between Athens and Sparta: The Delian League

Making Connections Show the slide to students and ask volunteers to read each of the bulleted points. As a class, discuss the purposes of the Delian League and whether the League succeeded in achieving these goals. Then ask students to think of organizations in your community today that were formed to help protect a cause or support a specific group of citizens. Have students compare and contrast these groups with the Delian League.

See page 171F for other online activities.

networks — War Between Athens and Sparta

The Delian League

- Athens formed a league with other city-states.
- The Delian League's headquarters was located on the island of Delos.
- The league was formed to defend its city-states against the Persians.

ANSWER, p. 203

CRITICAL THINKING Answers will vary. Pericles expanded Athenian democracy, which helped broaden his base of support. He was able to maintain power for more than 30 years, which allowed him to carry out his plans to rebuild Athens and make it a great center for knowledge.

R Reading Skills

Finding the Main Idea Ask students to find details in the text that explain how Athens, despite a smaller army, initially was able to withstand Sparta's attacks. **Ask:** **What was Pericles's strategy early in the war?** *(Pericles's strategy was to keep the army and people of Athens inside the walls of the city, so that the Spartan army could not enter and fight in an open battle.)* **Was this strategy successful?** *(It was successful for several years, but then a deadly disease wiped out a large number of Athenians in the city. The two sides then continued fighting.)*

C Critical Thinking Skills

Sequencing Divide the class into two or three groups, and give each group sheets of paper with events from the Peloponnesian War written on them. You may wish to include the following events: War begins in 431 B.C.; Sparta and its allies surround Athens; Disease breaks out in Athens; Each side wins victories over the next 25 years; Sparta makes a deal with Persia and builds a fleet; Sparta's navy destroys the Athenian fleet; Athens surrenders; the Spartans knock down the walls of Athens. Then ask each group to create a time line to put the events in proper sequence in the front of the classroom.

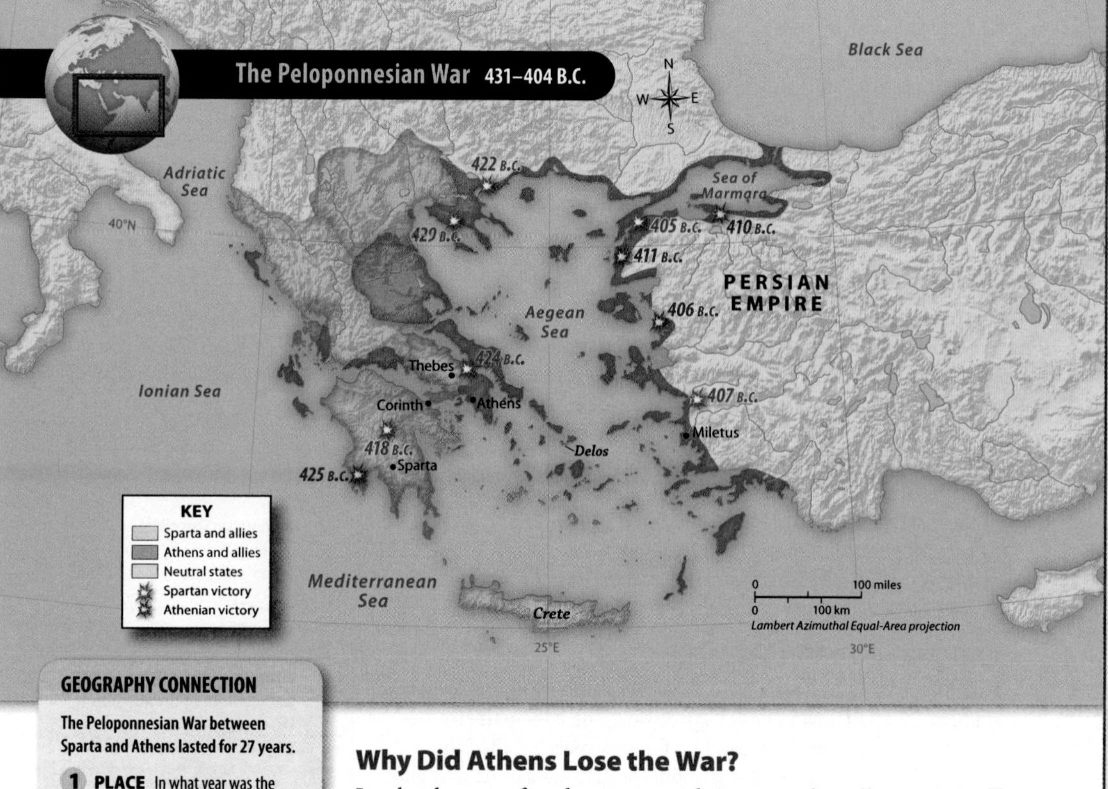

GEOGRAPHY CONNECTION

The Peloponnesian War between Sparta and Athens lasted for 27 years.

1. **PLACE** In what year was the final battle of the war? In whose territory was it fought?
2. **CRITICAL THINKING** *Speculating* Which cities were on the side of Athens? Why do you think having those allies was not enough help for Athens to win the war?

Why Did Athens Lose the War?

In a battle soon after the war started, Sparta and its allies surrounded Athens. They knew that, in an open battle, they could easily defeat the Athenian army. Pericles understood the weakness of the Athenian troops. He chose to keep his army and the people within the walls of the surrounded city. The powerful Athenian navy would bring supplies to the city from its colonies and allies. Sparta lacked a navy and could not stop the Athenian ships. R

C For almost two years, Athens remained safe. Then a deadly disease broke out within the overcrowded city's population. More than a third of the people died, including Pericles. During the next 25 years, each side won some victories but was unable to defeat its opponent.

Finally, Sparta made a deal with the Persian Empire. The Spartans agreed to give the Persians some Greek territory in Anatolia. In return, Sparta received enough Persian gold to build its own navy.

Reading **HELP**DESK CCSS

Reading Strategy: *Rereading*

When a paragraph is difficult to understand, try reading it again. Read it once to understand the main idea. Read it again to understand the details.

networks *Online Teaching Options*

MAP

The Peloponnesian War, 431–404 B.C.

Reading a Map Have students use the interactive map key to identify territory that was allied with Athens, allied with Sparta, or neutral in the Peloponnesian War. **Ask:**

- **Which city-state had more allies along the coasts?** *(Athens)*
- **Which had more allies on the main peninsula of Greece?** *(Sparta)*
- **Which city-state won the last major battle?** *(Sparta)*
- **Which side of the war did Crete support?** *(neither; Crete was neutral.)*

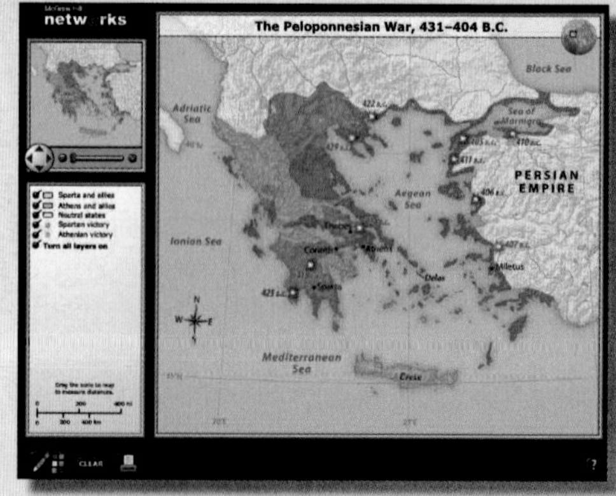

See page 171F for other online activities.

ANSWERS, p. 204

GEOGRAPHY CONNECTION

1. The final battle was fought in 405 B.C. in the territory of Athens.
2. **CRITICAL THINKING** Miletus and the Island of Delos were allied with Athens. These cities were much farther away than Sparta and Sparta's allies. It would be more difficult for Miletus and Delos to provide aid to Athens than it was for Sparta's allies to aid Sparta.

As the war dragged on, Athens fell into a state of unrest. The democracy had been overthrown. The government that replaced it was then overthrown. By the end of 411 B.C., democracy had been restored. The war, however, continued. In 405 B.C., Sparta's newly built navy destroyed the Athenian fleet. Sparta then placed a blockade around Athens, preventing food and other supplies from entering the city. Starving, the Athenians finally surrendered a year later. The Spartans and their allies then knocked down the city walls. The Athenian empire collapsed. **R**

The Effects of the War

The Peloponnesian War brought disaster to the Greek city-states. The governments were left divided and weak. Many people had died in battle or from disease. Fighting had destroyed farms and left many people with no way to earn a living. As a result, thousands of young Greeks left Greece to join the Persian army.

After the conflict, Sparta ruled its newly acquired empire, much as Athens had ruled its empire before. This harsh treatment angered Sparta's former allies. An uneasy political situation developed. During the next 30 years, Sparta tried to put down rebellions and fought Persia again. Finally, in 371 B.C., the city-state of Thebes seized Sparta and ended the Spartan empire. About 10 years later, Thebes also collapsed.

As the city-states fought, they failed to notice the growing threat from the kingdom of Macedonia to the north. Macedonia's strength and desire for expansion would eventually cost the Greek city-states their independence.

✓ PROGRESS CHECK

Explaining Why was Sparta's deal with Persia so important in the war against Athens?

LESSON 4 REVIEW 

Review Vocabulary (Tier 3 Words)

1. Explain why a group taking a vote on something is an example of a *direct democracy*. RH.6–8.4

Answer the Guiding Questions

2. ***Describing*** How did Pericles choose people for positions in the government in Athens? RH.6–8.2
3. ***Explaining*** What jobs did Athenian slaves do? RH.6–8.2
4. ***Determining Cause and Effect*** Why did the Delian League break apart? RH.6–8.2
5. ***Identifying*** What was the most important accomplishment of Pericles? RH.6–8.2
6. **ARGUMENT** Ancient Athens was a direct democracy. The United States Constitution provides for a representative democracy. Do you think the United States should change to a direct democracy? Why or why not? WHST.6–8.1, WHST.6–8.10

LESSON 4 REVIEW ANSWERS

1. The group is an example of direct democracy because everyone in the group has a vote.
2. Pericles appointed people to government positions because of their abilities rather than their social class.
3. Enslaved Athenians worked on farms or in the shops of artisans. They also performed hard labor. Enslaved women worked as cooks, servants, and tutors.
4. It broke apart because Athens assumed an increasingly oppressive role, demanding tribute from league members.
5. Pericles's most important accomplishments were leading the city of Athens, expanding democratic government there, and helping Athens dominate the Delian League.
6. Answers will vary. Many students will say that the population of the United States is too large for the country to function effectively as a direct democracy.

R Reading Skills

Defining Ask students to use context clues to define the word *blockade*. **Ask:** What is a blockade? *(A blockade is the isolation of an enemy area by troops or warships to prevent the passage of people or supplies.)* What were the results of the blockade? *(The Athenians were starving because they could not get food, so they were forced to surrender.)*

Have students complete the Lesson 4 Review.

CLOSE & REFLECT

Determining Cause and Effect Have students work in small groups to create cause-and-effect chains that illustrate the fall of Athenian power. Remind students that some effects have more than one cause and some causes have more than one effect. Challenge groups to make their chains as detailed as possible. Then ask groups to explain their cause-and-effect chains to the class. BL English language learners might benefit from writing paragraphs to describe the cause-and-effect relationships listed in their chains. Paragraphs should include words such as *as a result of, because,* or *then* that identify cause-and-effect relationships. ELL Once students have written their paragraphs, they should underline any of these clue words to see if their paragraphs accurately describe the relationships found in their chains.

ANSWER, p. 205

✓ PROGRESS CHECK The alliance gave Sparta enough money to build its own navy.

Activities Answers

CHAPTER REVIEW ACTIVITY

Lead the class in a discussion of how Greece has provided examples of change and unity.

Ask questions such as these: **How does geography influence the way people live? Why do people form governments? Why does conflict develop? How do governments change?**

You might want to have one or more student volunteers record the best examples for each topic on a three-column chart like the one below.

Major Changes in Greek History	Times When Greeks United	Times When Greeks Were Divided

REVIEW THE ENDURING UNDERSTANDINGS

Review the chapter's Enduring Understandings with students.

- *People, places, and ideas change over time.*
- *The value that a society places on individual rights is often reflected in that society's government.*
- *Countries have relationships with each other.*

Now pose the following questions in a class discussion to apply these to the chapter.

How did the physical geography of Greece affect its development and political structures? *(Answers may include that the mountains and islands of Greece isolated different parts of the region, which led to the development of city-states, which did not all have the same political structures.)*

How did the governments of Sparta and Athens reflect the values of those societies? *(Answers may include that the values of Sparta were mostly to remain strong and powerful in relation to other city-states. Its government was an oligarchy, in which only a few people held power. The rulers did not worry about extending the right to rule to everyone, because they did not see it as essential to remaining powerful. In Athens, individual rights were more highly valued, so the government was a democracy in which all citizens participated. Only men who owned property were citizens, but this was still a greater level of participation than in other city states.)*

What wars were fought in ancient Greece, and why were they fought? *(The city-states of Greece fought a long war against the Persian Empire, and Athens and its allies fought against Sparta and its allies in the Peloponnesian Wars. The war against the Persian Empire was fought because Persia's rulers wanted to expand and because Greeks had aided rebels who fought against Persian rule. The Peloponnesian War was fought because Athens took control of the Delian League and Sparta, and other city-states in Greece resented Athens's growing political power.)*

CHAPTER 7 Activities 

Write your answers on a separate piece of paper.

1 Exploring the Essential Question WHST.6–8.2, WHST.6–8.10

INFORMATIVE/EXPLANATORY Why does conflict develop? Write an essay describing the ways that conflict played an important role in the lives of the ancient Greeks. In your writing, discuss such examples as Mycenaeans versus Minoans, Persia versus Greece, and Athens versus Sparta.

2 21st Century Skills RH.6–8.2

ANALYZING AND MAKING JUDGMENTS Which of these experiences would help you to better understand the meaning of *democracy*?

A. running for class president
B. trading CDs with your friend
C. picking up litter in your neighborhood
D. checking out a book at a library

3 Thinking Like a Historian RH.6–8.2

COMPARING AND CONTRASTING Create a diagram like the one below to compare and contrast the causes and effects of the Persian War with those of the Peloponnesian War.

Persian War	Peloponnesian War

4 GEOGRAPHY ACTIVITY

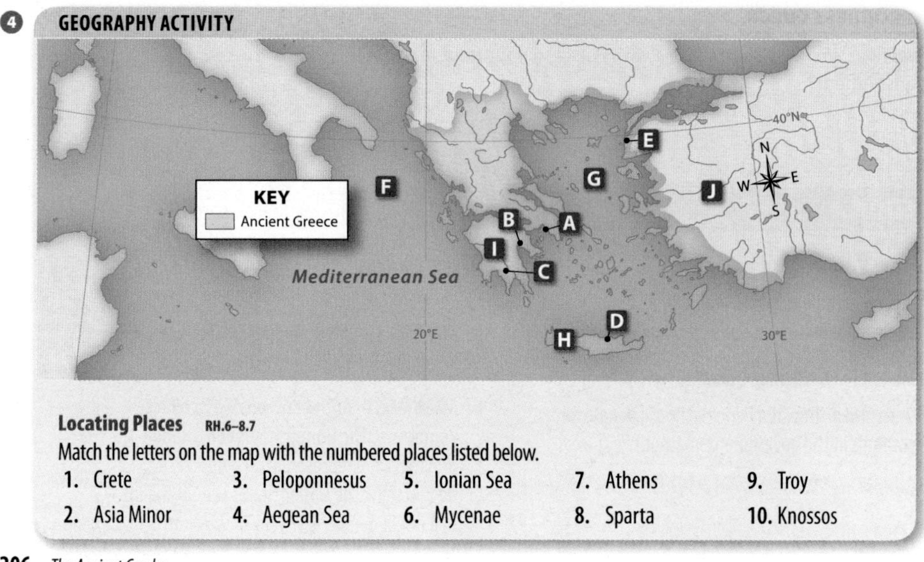

Locating Places RH.6–8.7

Match the letters on the map with the numbered places listed below.

1. Crete
2. Asia Minor
3. Peloponnesus
4. Aegean Sea
5. Ionian Sea
6. Mycenae
7. Athens
8. Sparta
9. Troy
10. Knossos

ACTIVITIES ANSWERS

Exploring the Essential Question

1 Students should note that the Mycenaeans took aggressive action to gain supremacy in the Mediterranean world, first by subduing the Minoans and then through their military successes in the Trojan War. Students may also mention economic conflicts such as the debts of farmers to the nobles in Greek city-states; political friction resulting from the concentrated power of tyrants; international tensions resulting from Greek aid to the Anatolian cities that revolted against the Persians; and Spartan resentment of the Athenian buildup of power as a result of Athens's leadership of the Delian League.

21st Century Skills

2 **A** A democracy is a type of political system, and running for class president would provide political experience. Answers B, C, and D are not good choices because these activities are not necessary to a democracy.

Thinking Like a Historian

3 **Persian War:** vast extent of Persian Empire; Persian resentment when Greek city-states aided Greek revolts in western Anatolia; Persian defeats at Marathon and Salamis; Greek recovery under the leadership of Athens; Athenian buildup of power in the Delian League
Peloponnesian War: resentment of Athens by other Greek city-states, especially Sparta; leadership of Pericles; Pericles' death from the plague; Spartan alliance with Persia; Spartan defeat of Athenian navy; decline of Athens and Sparta after the war

CHAPTER 7 Assessment CCSS

REVIEW THE GUIDING QUESTIONS

Directions: Choose the best answer for each question.

RH.6–8.2
1 Where was Knossos located?
A. Sparta
B. Persia
C. Athens
D. Crete

RH.6–8.2
2 Why did Greek colonies spread throughout the Mediterranean region?
F. Tyrants created many of them.
G. Population pressures caused them to develop.
H. Persia attacked mainland Greece.
I. Pericles founded them.

RH.6–8.4
3 What is the rule of a few wealthy people called?
A. tyranny
B. direct democracy
C. oligarchy
D. representative democracy

RH.6–8.4
4 The officials who enforced the law and collected taxes in ancient Sparta were called
F. kings.
G. generals.
H. ephors.
I. helots.

RH.6–8.2
5 Which of the following was a Persian king?
A. Xerxes
B. Alexander the Great
C. Pericles
D. Leonidas

RH.6–8.2
6 About how long did the Peloponnesian War last?
F. 10 years
G. 17 years
H. 27 years
I. 50 years

207

Locating Places

4 **1.** H, **2.** J, **3.** I, **4.** G, **5.** F, **6.** B, **7.** A, **8.** C, **9.** E, **10.** D

CHAPTER 7 Assessment Answers

ASSESSMENT ANSWERS

Review the Guiding Questions

1 **D** Knossos was located on the island of Crete. Sparta is located on the Peloponnesus, and Athens lies about 100 miles east of Sparta on the Greek mainland. Persia is on the Asian continent. Therefore, D is the correct answer.

2 **G** The population grew, and city-states needed colonies to grow food for the increased population. Tyrants did not create colonies, although they sometimes governed them. Pericles lived after the great age of Greek colonization. The Persian attack had no influence on the formation of Greek colonies. Thus, the correct answer is G.

3 **C** The rule of a few wealthy people is called an oligarchy. Tyranny is the rule of a single, all-powerful individual. Direct democracy and representative democracy are systems in which the majority of the citizens have a role in government. Thus, C is the correct answer.

4 **H** Men called ephors were the officials who enforced the law. Kings ruled Mycenaean states, while generals were the highest-ranked public officials in Athens. Helots were enslaved people in Sparta. Therefore, H is the correct answer.

5 **A** Xerxes was king of Persia and fought the Persian war against Greek city-states. Alexander was from Macedon, north of Greece, and he later built an empire. Pericles was an Athenian statesman during its golden age. Leonidas was a Spartan king. Thus, A is the correct answer.

6 **H** The Peloponnesian War broke out in 431 B.C. and ended in 404 B.C., for a total span of 27 years. The war continued longer than 10 and 17 years but did not last as long as 50 years.

Assessment Answers

Analyzing Documents

7 **C** Although Spartan boys might go on to become teachers, lawyers, or doctors, the purpose of their education was to train them for the military, so the correct choice is C.

8 **G** Spartan boys were expected to later be victorious in battle. Although they were taught to read and write, reading and writing not emphasized. Students were strictly disciplined, and rejecting discipline was not allowed. Serving in the assembly was not the prime expectation. Therefore, G is the correct answer.

Short Response

9 Whereas the Spartans's lifestyle was centered almost exclusively on physical fitness and military training, the Athenian lifestyle included a diverse education, physical activity, discussions of politics and philosophy, and the exploration of new ideas.

10 Answers will vary but may mention the concepts of pluralism, diversity, prosperity, and innovation.

Extended Response

11 Essays should discuss topics such as education and mention activities that girls do today that they were not permitted to do in ancient Athens, such as go to school and go out unaccompanied by a male family member.

CHAPTER 7 Assessment *(continued)*  

DBQ ANALYZING DOCUMENTS

Greek historian Plutarch describes the state-run education of boys in Sparta:

"Reading and writing they gave them, just enough to serve their turn; their chief care was to make them good subjects, and to teach them to endure pain and conquer in battle."

—from Plutarch, *The Lives of the Noble Grecians and Romans*

RH.6–8.1

7 **Identifying** Spartans were educated and trained to be

A. lawyers.
B. politicians.
C. soldiers.
D. doctors.

RH.6–8.1

8 **Drawing Conclusions** According to Plutarch, what Spartan educators most wanted from students was for them to

F. write epics.
G. win wars.
H. reject discipline.
I. serve in the assembly.

SHORT RESPONSE

"Further, we [Athenians] provide plenty of means [ways] for the mind to refresh itself from business. We celebrate games and sacrifices all the year round, and the elegance of our private establishments forms a daily source of pleasure . . . while the magnitude [large size] of our city draws the produce of the world into our harbor."

—from Pericles' Funeral Oration, quoted in *The Complete Writings of Thucydides*

RH.6–8.1

9 How did Athenians live a more varied lifestyle than Spartans?

RH.6–8.1

10 In what ways might a modern city want to imitate ancient Athens?

EXTENDED RESPONSE

WHST.6–8.2, WHST.6–8.10

11 **Informative/Explanatory** The lives of Athenian girls were very different from the lives of girls today. Write a brief essay that explains the differences, giving real-life examples.

Need Extra Help?

If You've Missed Question	1	2	3	4	5	6	7	8	9	10	11
Review Lesson	1	1	2	2	3	4	1	1	2	2	2

208 *The Ancient Greeks*

networks Online Teaching Options

Using eAssessment

Use eAssessment to access and assign the publisher-made Lesson Quizzes & Chapter Tests electronically. You can also use eAssessment to create your own quizzes and tests from hundreds of available questions. eAssessment helps you design assessments that meet the needs of different types of learners. Follow the link in the Assess tab of your Teacher Lesson Center.

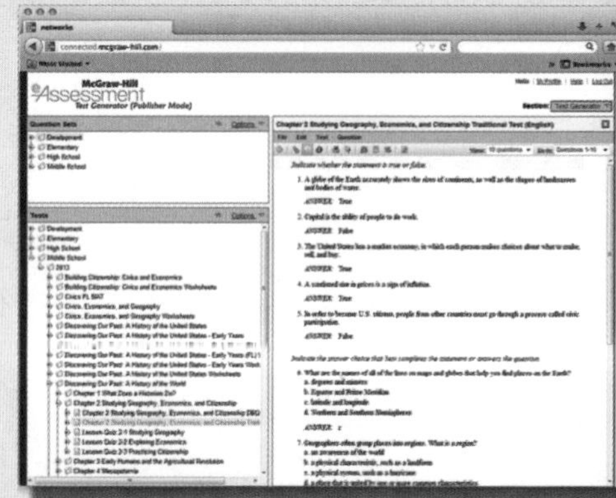

CHAPTER 8

Greek Civilization Planner

UNDERSTANDING BY DESIGN®

Enduring Understandings

- *Cultures are held together by shared beliefs and common practices and values.*
- *People, places, and ideas change over time.*
- *Leaders can bring about change in society.*

Essential Questions

- *What makes a culture unique?*
- *How do new ideas change the way people live?*
- *What are the characteristics of a leader?*

Predictable Misunderstandings

Students may think:

- *The Greeks and Greek culture remained in a remote area.*
- *There is little or no connection between the Greeks and life in the United States today.*
- *The Greeks excelled mostly in the arts and not in math and science.*

Assessment Evidence

Performance Tasks:

- *Hands-On Chapter Project*

Other Evidence:

- *Answers to class discussion comparing beliefs*
- *Discussion answers about ancient Greek thinkers*
- *Participation in a small-group activity*
- *Newspaper article on idea of Hellenistic Era*
- *Economics of History Activity*
- *21st Century Skills Activity*
- *Booklet on philosophical ideas*
- *Primary Source Activity*
- *Geography and History Activities*
- *Graphic Organizer Activities*
- *Interactive Whiteboard Activity responses*
- *Lesson Reviews*
- *Chapter Activities and Assessment*

SUGGESTED PACING GUIDE

Introducing the Chapter	1 Day
Lesson 1	1 Day
Lesson 2	1 Day
Feature: What Do You Think?	1 Day
Lesson 3	1 Day
Lesson 4	1 Day
Chapter Wrap-Up and Assessment	1 Day
TOTAL TIME	**7 Days**

Key for Using the Teacher Edition

SKILL-BASED ACTIVITIES

Types of skill activities found in the Teacher Edition.

V Visual Skills require students to analyze maps, graphs, charts, and photos.

R Reading Skills help students practice reading skills and master vocabulary.

W Writing Skills provide writing opportunities to help students comprehend the text.

C Critical Thinking Skills help students apply and extend what they have learned.

T Technology Skills require students to use digital tools effectively.

*Letters are followed by a number when there is more than one of the same type of skill on the page.

DIFFERENTIATED INSTRUCTION

All activities are written for the on-level student unless otherwise marked with the leveled labels below.

BL Beyond Level

AL Approaching Level

ELL English Language Learners

All students benefit from activities that utilize different learning styles. Many activities are marked as below when a particular learning style is highlighted.

Intrapersonal	**Naturalist**
Logical/Mathematical	**Kinesthetic**
Visual/Spatial	**Auditory/Musical**
Verbal/Linguistic	**Interpersonal**

NCSS Standards covered in "Greek Civilization"

Learners will understand:

1 CULTURE

1. "Culture" refers to the socially transmitted behaviors, beliefs, values, traditions, institutions, and ways of living together for a group of people

2. Concepts such as beliefs, values, institutions, cohesion, diversity, accommodation, adaptation, assimilation, and dissonance

3. How culture influences the ways in which human groups solve the problems of daily living

4. That the beliefs, values, and behaviors of a culture form an integrated system that helps shape the activities and ways of life that define a culture

8. That language, behaviors, and beliefs of different cultures can both contribute to and pose barriers to cross-cultural understanding

2 TIME, CONTINUITY, AND CHANGE

2. Concepts such as: chronology, causality, change, conflict, complexity, multiple perspectives, primary and secondary sources, and cause and effect

3. That learning about the past requires the interpretation of sources, and that using varied sources provides the potential for a more balanced interpretive record of the past

4. That historical interpretations of the same event may differ on the basis of such factors as conflicting evidence from varied sources, national or cultural perspectives, and the point of view of the researcher

5. Key historical periods and patterns of change within and across cultures (e.g., the rise and fall of ancient civilizations, the development of technology, the rise of modern nation-states, and the establishment and breakdown of colonial systems)

7. The contributions of key persons, groups, and events from the past and their influence on the present

CHAPTER OPENER PLANNER

Students will know:

- *the ideas that the ancient Greeks expressed in their literature, drama, art, and architecture.*
- *ancient Greek beliefs about history and science.*
- *how successful Alexander was in achieving his goals.*
- *how Hellenistic kingdoms spread Greek culture.*
- *ideas developed during the Hellenistic Era.*

Students will be able to:

- ***organize*** *information about Greek gods and goddesses.*
- ***compare*** *ancient and modern Greek beliefs.*
- ***describe*** *ancient Greek philosophy.*
- ***discuss*** *the philosophy and life of Socrates.*
- ***compare*** *and contrast Socrates, Plato, and Aristotle.*
- ***interpret*** *ancient Greek philosophical ideas.*
- ***compare and contrast*** *the qualities of a great military leader and an effective ruler.*
- ***categorize*** *Alexander's leadership qualities and military achievements.*
- ***analyze*** *images of culture from the Hellenistic Era.*
- ***explain*** *the meaning of Hellenistic.*
- ***identify*** *contributions from the Hellenistic Era.*

UNDERSTANDING BY DESIGN®

☑ *Print Teaching Options*

V Visual Skills

- ☐ **P. 210** Students locate places to be covered in the chapter. **AL** **Visual/Spatial**
- ☐ **P. 211** Students answer questions based on the time line. **AL** **Verbal/Linguistic**

☑ *Online Teaching Options*

V Visual Skills

- **MAP** **Alexander's Empire c. 331 B.C.**—Students see the relationships between the boundaries of Ancient Greece, the Persian Empire, and Alexander's empire.
- **TIME LINE** **Place and Time: Ancient Greece 700 B.C. to 212 B.C.**—Students learn about key Greek and world events related to this period of history.
- **WORLD ATLAS** Students can use this interactive map to identify regions of the world, learn about individual countries, locate political boundaries, measure distances, and much more.

☑ *Printable Digital Worksheets*

R Reading Skills

- **GRAPHIC NOVEL** ***Sophocles Presents: Oedipus Rex***—This graphic novel presents a comedic view of the actors and directors involved in a production of the play *Oedipus Rex* in ancient Greece.

Project-Based Learning

Hands-On Chapter Project

Greek Architecture Model

Students groups will create models of Greek-styled buildings to learn about Greek architecture.

Technology Extension

VoiceThread Exhibit

- Find an additional activity online that incorporates technology for this project.
- Visit the EdTechTeacher Web sites (included in the Technology Extension for this chapter) for more links, tutorials, and other resources.

Print Resources

ANCILLARY RESOURCES

These ancillaries are available for every chapter and lesson.

- **Reading Essentials and Study Guide Workbook** **AL** **ELL**
- **Chapter Tests and Lesson Quizzes Blackline Masters**

PRINTABLE DIGITAL WORKSHEETS

These printable digital worksheets are available for every chapter and lesson.

- **Hands-On Chapter Projects**
- **What Do You Know? activities**
- **Chapter Summaries (English and Spanish)**
- **Vocabulary Builder activities**
- **Guided Reading activities**

More Media Resources

SUGGESTED VIDEOS 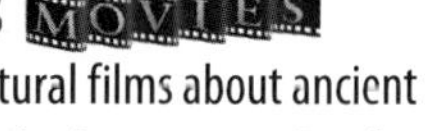

Watch clips of popular cultural films about ancient Greece, such as *Jason and the Argonauts* or *Barefoot in Athens*. Or view documentaries about the civilization such as *The Greeks: Crucible of Civilization.*

- **Discuss: Can fictional movies capture historical events accurately?**

(NOTE: Preview clips for age-appropriateness.)

SUGGESTED READING 

Grade 6 reading level:

- ***Everyday Life in the Ancient World,*** by Sally Tagholm, Julie Ferris, Jonathan Stroud, and Sue Nicholson

Grade 7 reading level:

- ***Alexander the Great: The Legend of a Warrior King,*** by Peter Chrisp

Grade 8 reading level:

- ***The Library of Alexandria,*** by Kelly Trumble

GREEK CULTURE

Students will know:
- *the ideas that the ancient Greeks expressed in their literature, drama, art, and architecture.*

Students will be able to:
- ***organize** information about Greek gods and goddesses.*
- ***compare** ancient and modern Greek beliefs.*

UNDERSTANDING BY DESIGN®

Print Teaching Options

V Visual Skills

- ☐ **P. 217** Students compare/contrast diagrams of Greek and modern theaters. ELL Visual/Spatial
- ☐ **P. 219** Students connect ancient Greek architecture to the Lincoln Memorial. Visual/Spatial

R Reading Skills

- ☐ **P. 212** Students define the word myth. AL ELL
- ☐ **P. 215** Students summarize the plots of the *Iliad* and *Odyssey*. AL ELL
- ☐ **P. 218** Students give the names of particular Greek playwrights.
- ☐ **P. 219** Students determine the meaning of conflict in drama. ELL Verbal/Linguistic

W Writing Skills

- ☐ **P. 214** Students write a paragraph about a favorite Greek deity, giving reasons for the choice.

C Critical Thinking Skills

- ☐ **P. 212** Compare/contrast Greek deities to humans.
- ☐ **P. 213** Students read a diagram and categorize the information. Logical/Mathematical
- ☐ **P. 213** Students compare modern and Greek explanations of nature. BL
- ☐ **P. 214** Students consider what kinds of advice state leaders wanted from the Oracle at Delphi. AL
- ☐ **P. 215** Students connect the Iliad and Odyssey to modern works.
- ☐ **P. 216** Students discuss the cultural value of Homer and interpret the meaning of an excerpt. BL Verbal/Linguistic
- ☐ **P. 216** Students connect Greek fables to modern-day storytelling.
- ☐ **P. 218** Students compare Greek playwrights to modern playwrights. AL

T Technology Skills

- ☐ **P. 217** Students do Internet research to find other cultures with an oral tradition. BL Interpersonal Verbal/Linguistic

Online Teaching Options

V Visual Skills

- VIDEO **Ancient Greece: Farmers and Daily Life**—Students view a video that examines the role of the farmer and Greek dependency on trade.
- SLIDE SHOW **Greek Art and Sculpture**—Students examine a bronze sculpture and a fragment of a water pot.

R Reading Skills

- GRAPHIC ORGANIZER **Taking Notes: *Summarizing:* Greek Influences**—Students identify three ways Greek culture influences our world today.
- PRIMARY SOURCE **The Boy Who Cried Wolf**—Students read and analyze an Aesop fable.
- IMAGE **The Oracle of Delphi**—Students read extensive background about this temple and its priestess.

C Critical Thinking Skills

- CHART **The Lincoln Memorial and the Parthenon**—Students compare and contrast these two structures.
- CHART **Greek Writers**—Students compare and contrast the backgrounds of four Greek writers and the genres of writing they produced.

T Technology Skills

- SELF-CHECK QUIZ **Lesson 1**—Students receive instant feedback about their mastery of lesson content.
- GAME **Greek Gods and Goddesses Fill-in-the-Blank Game**—Students match gods and goddesses with their individual powers.
- GAME **Classical Greek Culture Concentration Game**—Students match items and descriptions to review lesson content.

Printable Digital Worksheets

C Critical Thinking Skills

- WORKSHEET **Economics of History Activity: Support for the Arts in Ancient Greece**—Students respond to a reading passage.

LESSON **2 PLANNER**

THE GREEK MIND

Students will know:

- *ancient Greek beliefs about history and science.*

Students will be able to:

- ***describe*** *ancient Greek philosophy.*
- ***discuss*** *the philosophy and life of Socrates.*
- ***compare and contrast*** *Socrates, Plato, and Aristotle.*
- ***interpret*** *ancient Greek philosophical ideas.*

UNDERSTANDING BY DESIGN®

☑ *Print Teaching Options*

R Reading Skills

- ☐ **P. 220** Students use dates in the text to calculate the length of the Golden Age. **Logical/Mathematical**
- ☐ **P. 221** Students explain the effects of the Peloponnesian War on freedoms in Athens and why Socrates was considered dangerous.
- ☐ **P. 222** Students specify the traits of Plato's ideal government.
- ☐ **P. 223** Students explore the different meanings of the word "mean." **ELL** **Verbal/Linguistic**
- ☐ **P. 225** Students identify the main idea in a paragraph.
- ☐ **P. 227** Students list parts of the Hippocratic Oath. **AL**

W Writing Skills

- ☐ **P. 224** Students write a paragraph about Aristotelian ideas in the U.S. Government.

C Critical Thinking Skills

- ☐ **P. 220** Students speculate on the types of questions about the world ancient Greek philosophers might have asked. **BL**
- ☐ **P. 221** Students compare the Sophists to other Greek thinkers.
- ☐ **P. 221** Students discuss the life and teachings of Socrates and his views on the Sophists.
- ☐ **P. 222** Students fill in a social structure diagram. **AL** **Visual/Spatial**
- ☐ **P. 223** Students draw conclusions about which modern sciences might depend on Aristotle.
- ☐ **P. 224** Students analyze a chart and answer a question about Greek philosophers. **BL**
- ☐ **P. 225** Students compare/contrast Herodotus and Thucydides.
- ☐ **P. 226** Students interpret an excerpt from Thucydides' *History of the Peloponnesian War.* **AL** **ELL**
- ☐ **P. 226** Students formulate questions about Thales. **BL**
- ☐ **P. 227** Students draw conclusions about Hippocrates.

☑ *Online Teaching Options*

V Visual Skills

- **VIDEO** **Gods and Heroes**—Students explore the roles of the pantheon of Greek gods that were a key part of daily life and culture.
- **IMAGE** **Facts About Thales**—Students explore the ideas of this mathematician.

R Reading Skills

- **GRAPHIC ORGANIZER** **Taking Notes: *Identifying:* Greek Thinkers**—Students identify Greek thinkers and their ideas.
- **PRIMARY SOURCE** **Herodotus**—Students read an extended excerpt from *The History of Herodotus.*
- **BIOGRAPHY** **Plato**—Students learn more about the background of this philosopher.
- **BIOGRAPHY** **Thucydides**—Students learn more about the background of this historian.

C Critical Thinking Skills

- **WHITEBOARD ACTIVITY** **Early Greek Scientists' Contributions**—Students sort a list of contributions into the correct column.
- **PRIMARY SOURCE** **Plato's *Republic***—Students analyze an excerpt from *Republic* in which Socrates questions the philosopher Polemarchus on justice, personal judgment, and friendship.
- **SLIDE SHOW** **Philosophers and Their Ideas**—Students compare and contrast the philosophies of Plato, Aristotle, and Socrates.

T Technology Skills

- **SELF-CHECK QUIZ** **Lesson 2**—Students receive instant feedback about their mastery of lesson content.
- **GAME** **The Greek Mind Column Game**—Students test their knowledge of Greek philosophy.
- **GAME** **Socrates and the Sophists Column Game**—Students classify statements into two categories.

☑ *Printable Digital Worksheets*

W Writing Skills

- **WORKSHEET** **21st Century Skills Activity: Communication: Writing in Expository Style**—Students write a short expository essay explaining how Aristotle's ideas were used in creating the original government of the United States.

ALEXANDER'S EMPIRE

Students will know:

- *the ideas that the ancient Greeks how successful Alexander was in achieving his goals.*

Students will be able to:

- ***compare and contrast** the qualities of a great military leader and an effective ruler.*
- ***categorize** Alexander's leadership qualities and military achievements.*

UNDERSTANDING BY DESIGN®

Print Teaching Options

V Visual Skills

- [ ] **P. 231** Students use an image and text about Demosthenes to answer questions.
- [ ] **P. 232** Students locate various places on a map of Alexander's empire.
- [ ] **P. 234** Students read a map to identify the largest territory after Alexander's death. AL **Visual/Spatial**
- [ ] **P. 235** Students analyze an image of the Pharos for Greek and Egyptian influences. AL **Visual/Spatial**

R Reading Skills

- [ ] **P. 230** Students summarize changes in Greece under Philip.
- [ ] **P. 233** Students use dates in the text to figure out spans of time during Alexander's conquests. AL ELL **Logical/Mathematical**

W Writing Skills

- [ ] **P. 233** Students write paragraphs from the point of view of one of Alexander's soldiers.

C Critical Thinking Skills

- [ ] **P. 230** Students determine how the Peloponnesian War helped Philip conquer the Greeks. AL
- [ ] **P. 231** Students interpret an excerpt from Demosthenes. AL ELL **Verbal/Linguistic**
- [ ] **P. 232** Students make a hypothesis about Alexander and his father v. modern children and parents. BL
- [ ] **P. 235** Students debate whether or not Alexander achieved his goals. BL

T Technology Skills

- [ ] **P. 234** Students work in groups to design an Alexander Web page. **Interpersonal Visual/Spatial**

Online Teaching Options

V Visual Skills

- [ ] VIDEO **Building Alexander the Great's Empire**—Students view a video that explains how Alexander became a great commander after the death of his father, a Macedonian king.
- [ ] MAP **Alexander's Empire c. 331 B.C.**—Students see the relationships between the boundaries of Ancient Greece, the Persian Empire, and Alexander's empire and identify sites of major battles.
- [ ] MAP **Hellenistic World 241 B.C.**—Students identify the four separate kingdoms made from Alexander's empire after his death.

R Reading Skills

- [ ] GRAPHIC ORGANIZER **Taking Notes: *Summarizing:* Alexander and Philip II**—Students use a web to summarize how Philip II and Alexander changed Greece.
- [ ] CHART **Rise of Alexander the Great**—Students click to reveal the sequence of events that led to the rise of Alexander the Great.

C Critical Thinking Skills

- [ ] WHITEBOARD ACTIVITY **The Achievements of Alexander the Great**—Students match achievements of this leader with the location where each occurred.

T Technology Skills

- [ ] SELF-CHECK QUIZ **Lesson 3**—Students receive instant feedback about their mastery of lesson content.

Printable Digital Worksheets

R Reading Skills

- [ ] WORKSHEET **Primary Source Activity: Alexander the Great: Hero or Villain?**—Students analyze an excerpt from *Description of the Battle at Tyre* by Diodorus of Sicily.

C Critical Thinking Skills

- [ ] WORKSHEET **Geography and History Activity: Understanding Location: Greek Migration**—Students analyze a reading and a map and answer questions about the movement of people in the Mediterranean area.

LESSON 4 PLANNER

HELLENISTIC CULTURE

Students will know:

- *how Hellenistic kingdoms spread Greek culture.*
- *ideas developed during the Hellenistic Era.*

Students will be able to:

- ***analyze** images of culture from the Hellenistic Era.*
- ***explain** the meaning of Hellenistic.*
- ***identify** contributions from the Hellenistic Era.*

UNDERSTANDING BY DESIGN®

☑ Print Teaching Options

V Visual Skills

- ☐ **P. 237** Students analyze the image of Winged Victory. **Visual/Spatial**
- ☐ **P. 239** Students do a mini-version of Eratosthenes' experiment. **Kinesthetic** **Logical/Mathematical**

R Reading Skills

- ☐ **P. 236** Students learn the roots and meaning of *Hellenistic* and related words. AL ELL
- ☐ **P. 238** Students state the basic philosophy of the Epicureans.
- ☐ **P. 240** Students write a summary about Archimedes saving Syracuse.

W Writing Skills

- ☐ **P. 239** Students write an article about a "new" experiment/discovery during the Hellenistic Age. BL

C Critical Thinking Skills

- ☐ **P. 236** Students explore how Hellenistic rulers viewed Greek culture.
- ☐ **P. 237** Students contrast Golden Age and Hellenistic cultures. BL
- ☐ **P. 238** Students contrast the Epicureans and Stoics.
- ☐ **P. 240** Students differentiate between plane and solid geometry. AL ELL
- ☐ **P. 241** Students create a flowchart to show the sequence of events that led to Rome conquering Greece. AL
- ☐ **P. 241** Students synthesize several events to understand comprehensively why the Hellenistic Age ended.

☑ Online Teaching Options

V Visual Skills

- VIDEO **Alexander the Great's Empire**—Students view a video that describes the huge empire Alexander created after eleven years of battle, and the effect that Alexander's death had on the empire.
- CHART **Contributions of Greek Scientists**—Students click to learn about Greek scientists' contributions to science, math, and technology.
- IMAGE **Aristarchus' Model of the Solar System**—Students view a moving model of a heliocentric solar system.

R Reading Skills

- GRAPHIC ORGANIZER **Taking Notes: *Describing:* Greek Scientists and Their Achievements**—Students describe the achievements of three Greek scientists.
- BIOGRAPHY **Hypatia**—Students read the story of this fourth-century Greek scholar.

C Critical Thinking Skills

- CHART **The *Winged Victory* and *Unique Forms***—Students compare and contrast these two sculptures.
- SLIDE SHOW **The Story of *Pi***—Students discover how this constant is determined and used.

T Technology Skills

- SELF-CHECK QUIZ **Lesson 4**—Students receive instant feedback about their mastery of lesson content.
- GAME **Hellenistic Culture Crossword Puzzle**—Students complete the puzzle with key terms, using clues from the lesson.

☑ Printable Digital Worksheets

C Critical Thinking Skills

- WORKSHEET **Geography and History Activity: Understanding Location: Hellenistic Cities**—Students analyze a passage and a map in order to respond to questions about the locations of Hellenistic cities.

INTERVENTION AND REMEDIATION STRATEGIES

LESSON 1 Greek Culture

Reading and Comprehension

Defining Direct students to create flashcards showing the vocabulary words and definitions from this lesson. Have partners use the flashcards to quiz each other.

Text Evidence

Narrative Have students write a short fable in the style of the legendary writer Aesop. Tell them to refer to the textbook to identify the elements that should be included in their writing.

LESSON 2 The Greek Mind

Reading and Comprehension

Comparing and Contrasting Tell students to select one major topic studied by Greek philosophers, such as government. Have them create a graphic organizer to show how different philosophers viewed that topic over time.

Text Evidence

Informative/Explanatory Direct students to select one of the philosophers discussed in the lesson and conduct research using reliable print or online resources to learn more about that person's life. Have them write a short biography based on their research. Tell them to make at least one connection between the lesson content and their writing.

LESSON 3 Alexander's Empire

Reading and Comprehension

Summarizing Have students write several sentences to summarize the expansion of the Macedonian Empire during the reigns of Philip and Alexander.

Text Evidence

Organizing Have students create a web graphic organizer showing the kingdoms that made up the Hellenistic world after the death of Alexander the Great. Then direct them to use the text and map on pp. 234–235 in the textbook to help them add details to their web.

LESSON 4 Hellenistic Culture

Reading and Comprehension

Analyzing Information Invite students to create an outline using the headings and subheadings of the lesson.

Text Evidence

Argument Write this claim on the board: *The thinkers and artists of the Hellenistic Era were more skillful than those of the Golden Age of Greece.* Have students search the text to locate evidence to support or oppose this argument.

Online Resources

Approaching Level Reader

Use this online lower-level text that corresponds directly to the text in the Student Edition. It includes a Spanish version.

Guided Reading Activities

This resource uses graphic organizers and guiding questions to help students with comprehension.

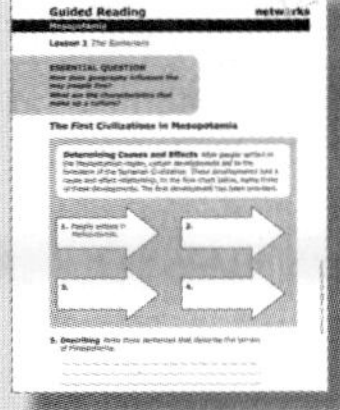

What Do You Know?

Use these worksheets to pre-assess student's background knowledge before they study the chapter.

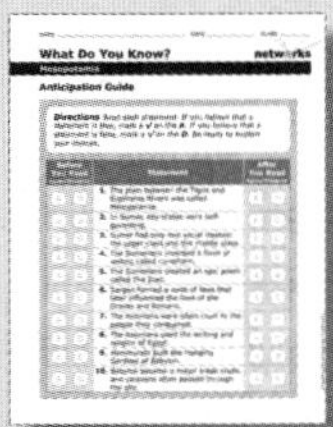

Reading Essentials and Study Guide Workbook

This resource offers writing and reading activities for the approaching-level student. Also available in Spanish.

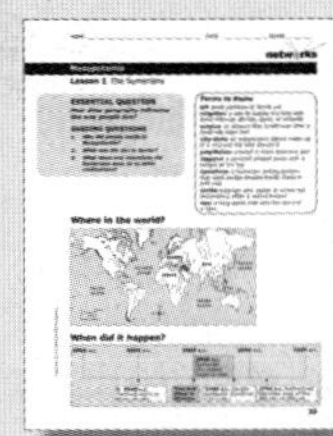

Self-Check Quizzes

This online assessment tool provides instant feedback for students to check their progress.

How Do I Teach with
Technology Extensions?

Each Hands-On Chapter Project in this program includes an online Technology Extension to help you integrate technology into your classroom projects. Visit the EdTechTeacher Web sites (included in the Technology Extension for each chapter) for more links, tutorials, and other resources. Before you assign the Technology Extensions:

Strategy 1 Plan Ahead

- Be prepared to troubleshoot technology and connectivity problems. Ask for assistance from a teacher's aide or a member of your school's IT staff or do preliminary research online.
- Don't be afraid to ask your tech-savvy students for their help in fixing a problem.
- Have an alternative plan ready to avoid wasting classroom time and to keep students engaged in learning.
- Record any problems you encountered to avoid delays on future projects.

Creatas/PunchStock

Strategy 2 Practice the Activity Ahead of Time

- Do a trial run to make sure that the project requirements can be completed in the amount of time that you have allotted.
- Look at the project from the student's point of view. Do the instructions make sense? Walk through each step yourself, so that you can clearly explain those steps to your class.

Strategy 3 Use Your Technology Resources Flexibly and Creatively

- Not every school has top-of-the-line equipment, but that shouldn't stop you from using technology to the fullest. Investigate what your school offers and plan accordingly.
- Your students can access computers in your school computer lab or school library, at the community library, or at home. Many of the technology extension activities are designed to be done over multiple class periods, so students can take advantage of using computers in multiple places if necessary.
- Technology resources are not just machines and screens. Plan with other tech-savvy teachers and learn from their expertise. And remember that integrating technology is at first a challenge, but gets easier over time and with repetition.

Greek Civilization

700 B.C. to 212 B.C.

networks

There's More Online about the lives and customs of the ancient Greeks.

CHAPTER 8

ESSENTIAL QUESTIONS • *What makes a culture unique?* • *How do new ideas change the way people live?* • *What are the characteristics of a leader?*

Lesson 1 *Greek Culture*

Lesson 2 *The Greek Mind*

Lesson 3 *Alexander's Empire*

Lesson 4 *Hellenistic Culture*

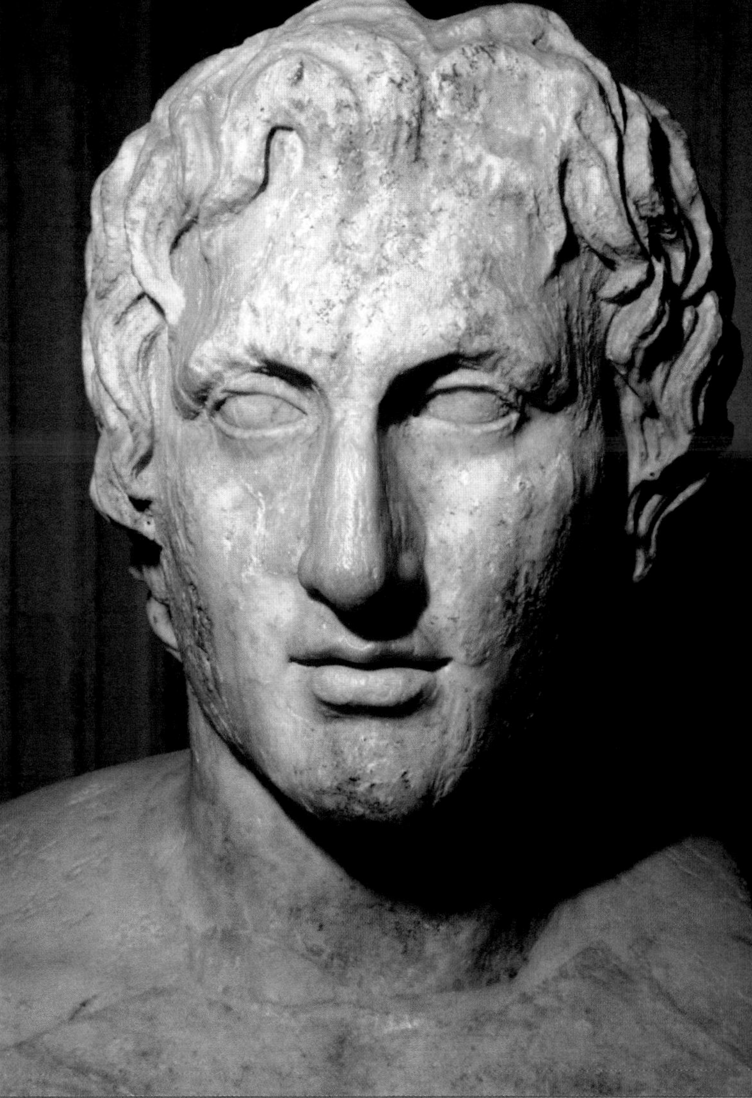

The Story Matters . . .

Alexander became king of Macedonia when he was only 20 years old. Before his death at age 32, he built the largest empire the world had known. His strong will and personality enabled him to lead armies to victory. He is considered one of the greatest generals who ever lived.

Alexander's childhood tutor was the Greek philosopher Aristotle, who encouraged Alexander's interest in philosophy, medicine, and science. As an adult, Alexander spread Greek art, ideas, language, and architecture into all the lands he conquered. The impact of his rule lasted for centuries.

◄ *This marble bust of Alexander the Great, carved in 330 B.C., is in the Louvre, a famous museum located in Paris, France.*

Danita Delimont/Gallo Images/Getty Images

209

Letter from the Author

Dear World History Teacher,

Socrates, Plato, and Aristotle established the foundations of Western philosophy. Herodotus and Thucydides created the discipline of history. Our Western literary forms are derived from Greek poetry and drama. Greek notions of harmony and proportion have remained the standards for Western art and architecture. Despite these achievements, the Greeks were unable to rise above rivalries that caused them to fight and undermine their own civilization. The independent Greek city-states were conquered by the Macedonians. Greek culture survived, but in a new form.

Jackson J. Spielvogel

ENGAGE

Bellringer Read "The Story Matters . . ." aloud in class. Tell students that Alexander was tutored by Aristotle, the famous philosopher. **Ask:** **How do you think Aristotle's teachings affected Alexander?** *(Answers will vary, but students may mention that Aristotle taught Alexander to be interested in many different fields of study. This teaching probably influenced Alexander to want to spread many different Greek ideas and aspects of Greek culture to the lands he conquered.)* Tell students that Alexander was a commander in his father's armies by the time he was 16 years old. **Ask:** **How do you think childhood and the teenage years were different in the time of Alexander from how they are now?** *(Answers will vary, but students may mention that children had to grow up and take responsibility at a much younger age than they do now.)*

Tell the class that Alexander became king at a young age, after his father, Philip II, was assassinated. Alexander went on to fulfill his father's dream of conquering the Persian Empire and creating a new Hellenistic, or Greek-influenced, empire. Alexander also died at a young age, but the influence of Greek culture lived on throughout the lands he conquered. Even after the end of the Hellenistic Era, the Romans, who conquered much of Alexander's former empire, were strongly influenced by Greek culture.

Making Connections

Read the following information to students: There are countless ways in which the influences of ancient Greek culture are still important today. Americans were especially interested in ancient Greek culture because of the shared concept of democracy. Classical Greek architecture was just one influence on modern American culture. Important national buildings, such as the U.S. Treasury and Boston's historic Quincy Market, use Greek-style columns and other features. In fact, historians have called Greek-style architecture the "Greek Revival"—the first truly national American style.

TEACH & ASSESS

Step Into the Place

V1 Visual Skills

Reading a Map Direct students' attention to the map. Invite volunteers to point out locations of some civilizations they may have already studied. *(Mesopotamia, Egypt, Kush, and the area that is now modern-day Israel)* Point out that their locations helped these civilizations thrive. Discuss how the locations of these civilizations gave them opportunities for trade and access to the spread of ideas but also made them vulnerable to attack.

Next, point out the mainland and islands of Greece. Explain that Greece's location helped it become a powerful civilization. As a class, discuss the Map Focus questions. AL **Visual/Spatial**

Content Background Knowledge

- During his lengthy period of conquest, Alexander the Great visited the famous Oracle at Delphi. There, the priestess said that Alexander was "invincible."
- Alexander traveled with a huge army on his conquests. He alone commanded some 30,000 foot soldiers and more than 5,000 mounted troops. His generals oversaw thousands more.
- Like many Greeks, Alexander was inspired by the stories of Homer. He visited the city of Troy, the location of Homer's famous epic poem the *Iliad,* just before invading Persia.

V2

ANSWERS, p. 210

Step Into the Place

1. Africa
2. A major battle took place.
3. CRITICAL THINKING Bodies of water such as the Mediterranean Sea connected the seagoing Greeks with lands throughout the region.

Step Into the Time

Students should pick an event and make specific predictions regarding its consequences. They might tell how the event will affect the government or the relations between empires, or they might tell how the event will affect trade, commerce, or business.

CHAPTER 8 CCSS

Place and Time: Ancient Greece 700 B.C. to 212 B.C.

The Greeks are remembered for their advances in the study of science, philosophy, mathematics, and the arts. When Alexander the Great conquered the Persian Empire, he spread Greek culture and ideas throughout southwest Asia and the Mediterranean world.

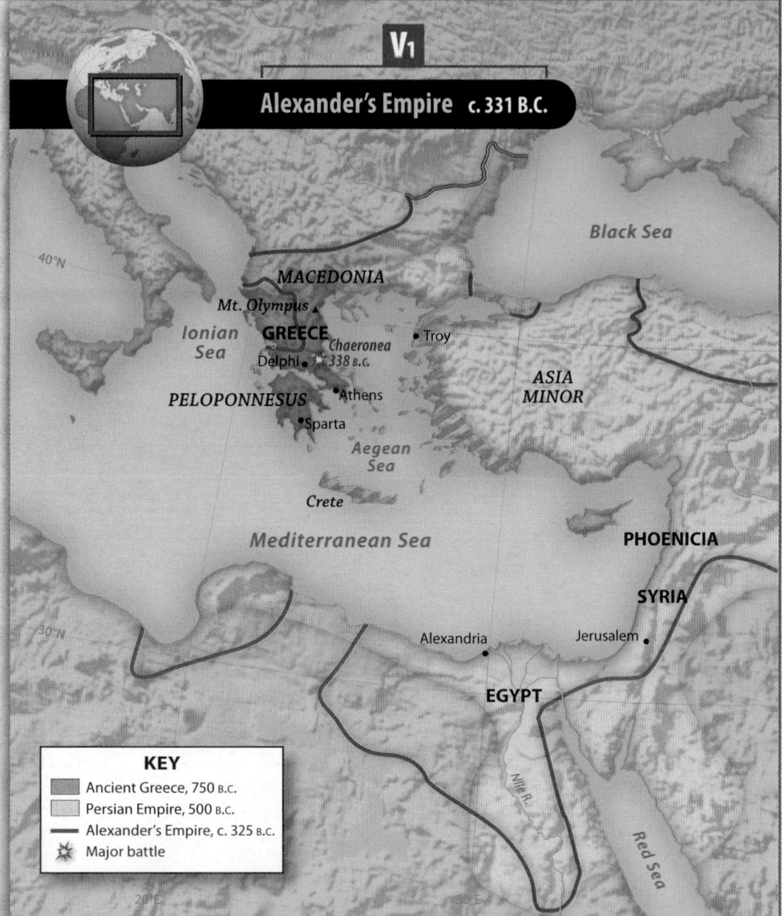

Step Into the Place

MAP FOCUS By 100 B.C., Alexandria was the largest city in the Mediterranean world. Alexandria included two excellent harbors, a towering lighthouse, and a library with the largest collection of writings in ancient times.

1. **LOCATION** Look at the map. On which continent is Alexandria located? RH.6–8.7
2. **PLACE** What happened at Chaeronea? RH.6–8.7
3. **CRITICAL THINKING** **Analyzing** How might the region's physical features allow Greek culture to spread to other areas? RH.6–8.1

Step Into the Time

TIME LINE Choose an event from the time line and write a paragraph predicting the general social, political, or economic consequences that event might have on the world. RH6–8.7, WHST.6–8.10

ANCIENT GREECE
776 B.C. First Olympic Games
c. 700s B.C. Homer writes the *Iliad* and the *Odyssey*

800 B.C. — 650 B.C.

THE WORLD
c. 728 B.C. Kush conquers Egypt
c. 530 B.C. Confucius develops his philosophy in China

Project-Based Learning

Hands-On Chapter Project

Greek Architecture Model

Students will create a model of a Greek-styled building to learn about Greek architecture. Before the activity, have students discuss the ideas that the Greeks expressed in their architecture. Students' small groups will each work on a certain type of building. Groups will use discussion to guide their project plan and research. Next, each group will create a model of its chosen building. Then, students will present their models to the class. Finally, students will evaluate their research, presentation, and collaboration using a class-developed assessment rubric. BL **Kinesthetic**

Technology Extension

VoiceThread Exhibit

Once students construct their Greek-styled buildings, they can present their exhibits using VoiceThread. To describe their design choices, groups record an audio commentary that is synced with photos or a video of the model. Have students take six detailed digital photos or a short video of their completed model and upload to VoiceThread. Then, have students view their show multiple times and write a script to accompany the presentation. **Auditory/Musical**

networks
There's More Online!

MAP Explore the interactive version of this map on NETWORKS.

TIME LINE Explore the interactive version of this time line on NETWORKS.

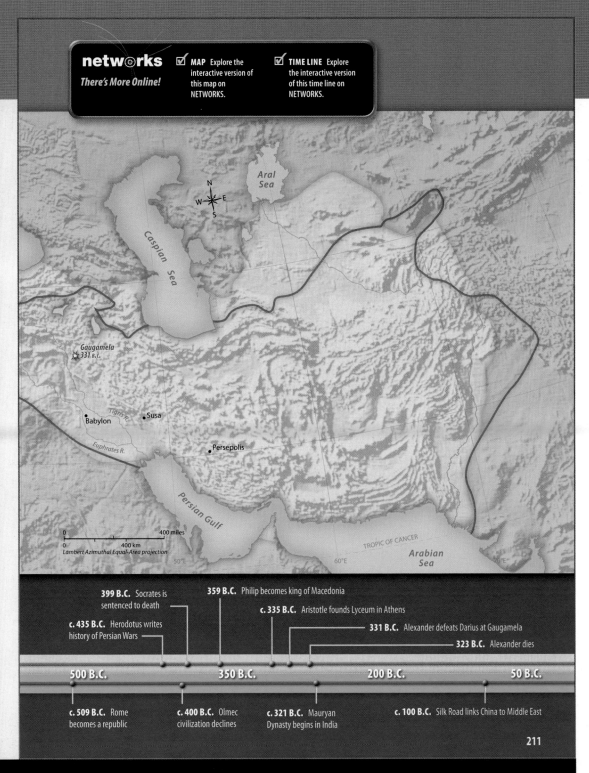

Aral Sea
Caspian Sea
Gaugamela 331 B.C.
Babylon
Tigris R.
Susa
Euphrates R.
Persepolis
Persian Gulf
TROPIC OF CANCER
Arabian Sea
0 400 miles
0 400 km
Lambert Azimuthal Equal-Area projection
50°E
60°E

399 B.C. Socrates is sentenced to death

c. 435 B.C. Herodotus writes history of Persian Wars

359 B.C. Philip becomes king of Macedonia

c. 335 B.C. Aristotle founds Lyceum in Athens

331 B.C. Alexander defeats Darius at Gaugamela

323 B.C. Alexander dies

500 B.C. | 350 B.C. | 200 B.C. | 50 B.C.

c. 509 B.C. Rome becomes a republic

c. 400 B.C. Olmec civilization declines

c. 321 B.C. Mauryan Dynasty begins in India

c. 100 B.C. Silk Road links China to Middle East

211

CHAPTER 8
Place and Time

Step Into the Time

V2 Visual Skills

Analyzing Visuals Call students' attention to the time line for this chapter. Explain that between about 800 B.C. and 200 B.C., Greece became a thriving kingdom. Draw students' attention to the entries on the ancient Greece time line that refer to Alexander the Great. Note that Alexander was born in 356 B.C. **Ask:** How might Alexander's age have made his accomplishments seem more impressive? *(Answers will vary, but students should note that Alexander was only 25 when he defeated Darius, and he conquered all the lands shown on the map by the time of his death at age 33.)* AL Verbal/Linguistic

Content Background Knowledge

Have students locate the Battle of Gaugamela on the map. Explain that it was one of the most important tests of Alexander's conquests because it determined who would control the enormous Persian Empire. Darius's troops greatly outnumbered Alexander's when the two forces met in what is now Iraq. But Alexander's approximately 47,000 soldiers were well-trained and had a good battle strategy. Alexander and some cavalry troops who fought with him managed to break through Persian lines to attack the rear. Darius fled from the battleground and his army quickly fell apart. Alexander became the ruler of what had been the massive, powerful Persian Empire.

CLOSE & REFLECT

Formulating Questions Have students work in pairs to formulate at least three questions about Alexander the Great or Hellenistic culture that they would like to learn answers to as they read the chapter.

MAP

Alexander's Empire c. 331 B.C.

Predicting Consequences Display the interactive map. Point out the relative sizes of Greece and the Persian Empire. Discuss with students the expansion of the Greek empire under Alexander. Invite students to predict how the massive expansion of the Greek empire might have affected both Greece and the regions and peoples who came under its political control.

See page 209B for other online activities.

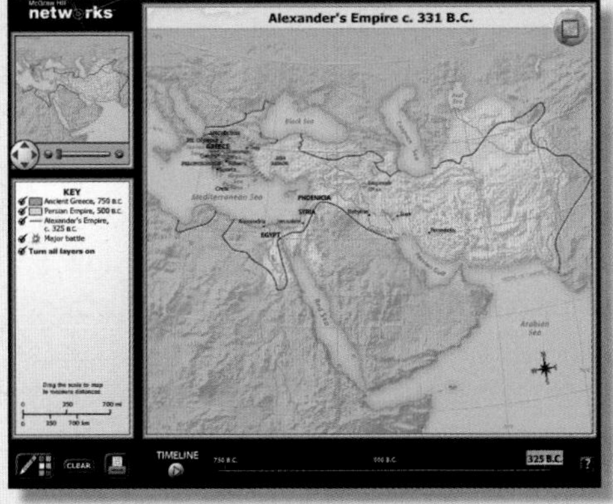

ENGAGE

Bellringer Display a common U.S. cultural artifact, such as a magazine or DVD. Discuss with students how the artifact relates to modern U.S. culture. **Ask: What else might a person study to learn about U.S. culture?** *(Sample answers: television shows, movies, books, art, clothing)* Invite students to suggest ways in which historians might use one of the cultural artifacts that they listed to learn about U.S. culture. Then tell students that in this lesson, they will learn about cultural artifacts made by the ancient Greeks to discover information about those people's ideas, beliefs, and lives.

TEACH & ASSESS

R Reading Skills

Defining Point out the definition of *myth* in the text. Have a volunteer read it aloud. **Ask: What are some other words you know that mean about the same thing as myth?** *(legend, tall tale, fairy tale)* **Ask: How might you define myth in your own words?** *(Sample answer: an old story that tells about important gods and early people in a culture)* AL ELL

C Critical Thinking Skills

Comparing and Contrasting Point out to students that the Greeks viewed their gods and goddesses as imperfect beings, like humans. Have students make a compare/contrast chart to identify how the Greek gods and goddesses were similar to and different from humans. *(Similar: looked and acted like human beings, married and had children, acted like children by playing tricks; Different: had great powers, some lived on Mount Olympus)*

ANSWER, p. 212

TAKING NOTES: Answers will vary but may include the following: Aristotle's ideas influenced European and American governmental systems; *pi;* Pythagorean theorem; Hippocratic Oath; Socratic method; Greek classical architecture—columns; Olympic Games; Greek plays and writings served as models for more modern writers; term *Trojan horse* describes computer viruses; Aesop's fables used to teach morals.

networks
There's More Online!

- **CHART**
  - Ancient Greek Writers
  - The Lincoln Memorial and the Parthenon
- **GRAPHIC ORGANIZER**
  Influence of Greek Culture Today
- **SLIDESHOW**
  Greek Art and Sculpture

Lesson 1

Greek Culture

ESSENTIAL QUESTION *What makes a culture unique?*

IT MATTERS BECAUSE

The Greeks made many advancements that continue to shape our world.

Greek Beliefs

GUIDING QUESTION *How did the ancient Greeks honor their gods?*

You have learned that the ancient Greeks formed city-states. These are independent states made up of a city and the land that surrounds it. Although city-states separated Greece politically, the Greek people were united by a common culture. They spoke the Greek language. They shared many beliefs and customs. The Greek people also believed many of the same **R** **myths**, or traditional stories about gods and heroes. Greek myths expressed the religious beliefs of the ancient Greeks.

Who Were the Greek Gods?

Like other people of the ancient world, the Greeks believed in gods and goddesses. The Greeks, however, did not think of their gods as all-powerful beings. In Greek myths, the gods have great powers, but they look and act like human beings. In Greek **C** mythology, they marry and have children. At times, they act like children, playing tricks on each other. Because the gods showed human qualities, the Greek people did not fear them. Greeks believed that the 12 most important gods and goddesses lived on Mount Olympus (uh•LIHM•puhs), Greece's highest mountain.

Reading HELPDESK CCSS

Taking Notes: *Summarizing*
Use a diagram like this one to identify three ways Greek culture influences our world today. RH.6–8.2

Greek Influences

Content Vocabulary (Tier 3 Words)
- myth
- ritual
- oracle
- fable
- oral tradition
- drama
- tragedy
- comedy

networks ***Online Teaching Options***

VIDEO

Ancient Greece: Farmers and Daily Life

Synthesizing Play the video about daily life in ancient Greece. Tell students that this video describes the everyday activities, concerns, and interactions of ancient Greeks. As students watch, have them pay close attention to how geographic location and available resources influenced daily life. Display a physical map of ancient Greeks for students as they discuss their observations. Invite them to connect information from the map to facts and details about daily life from the video.

See page 209C for other online activities.

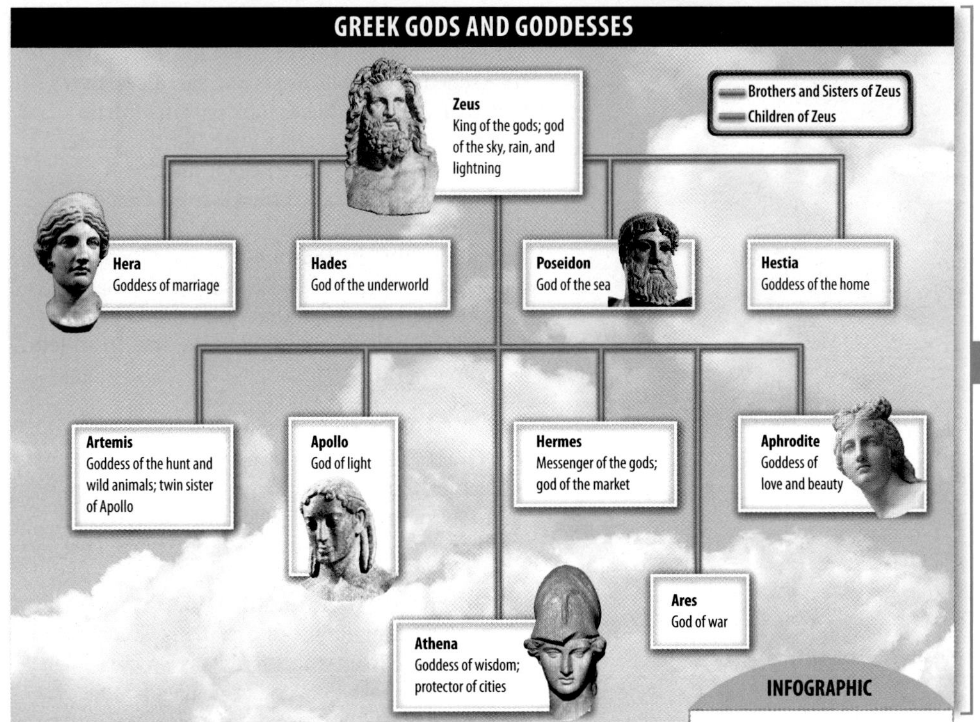

INFOGRAPHIC

1. **IDENTIFYING** Which god or goddess protected the city of Athens?
2. **CRITICAL THINKING** ***Analyzing*** How were Athena and Hera related?

A gate of clouds protected Olympus. The gods could come and go as they pleased, but humans were stopped from entering through the gate of clouds.

Zeus was the king of the Olympian gods, while Athena was the goddess of wisdom and crafts. Apollo was worshipped as the god of the sun and poetry. People looked up to Aphrodite, the goddess of love. Two fierce gods were Ares, the god of war, and Poseidon, the god of the seas and earthquakes. C2

All Greeks worshipped Zeus as their chief god. Each city-state also chose one god or goddess as its protector. To win the favor of their god, the people of the city-state performed rituals. A **ritual** (RIH•chuh•wuhl) is an action that is part of a religious ceremony. The people worshipped the god in temples and at home. They prayed and offered gifts to the god. Through these rituals, the Greeks hoped the god would reward them.

myth a traditional story that explains the practices or beliefs of a people, or something in the natural world

ritual words or actions that are part of a religious ceremony

C1 Critical Thinking Skills

Categorizing Have students study the infographic. Remind students that Greeks believed their gods and goddesses were responsible for nature, as well as for other areas of life. Draw a two-column graphic organizer on the board with the headings *Nature* and *Life.* Direct students to categorize each god and goddess from the infographic into the correct column. *(Nature: Zeus, Poseidon, Artemis, Apollo; Life: Hera, Hades, Hestia, Athena, Hermes, Ares, Aphrodite)* **Logical/Mathematical**

C2 Critical Thinking Skills

Hypothesizing Point out that the ancient Greeks believed the gods and goddesses controlled nature. **Ask:** How do modern people explain nature? *(Modern people explain nature by using science.)* Why do you think the ancient Greeks believed that gods and goddesses controlled nature? *(Students should understand that modern scientific techniques for understanding the world had not yet been developed, so the Greeks based their beliefs on religion instead.)* BL

GAME

Greek Gods and Goddesses Game—Greek Culture

Giving Examples Have students complete the game in which they match the gods' and goddesses' functions to their names. Then have students provide examples of a specific person, place, or activity with which a Greek god or goddess would have been associated.

See page 209C for other online activities.

ANSWERS, p. 213

INFOGRAPHIC

1. Athena was the protector of cities.
2. **CRITICAL THINKING** As the sister and wife of Zeus, Athena's father, Hera was Athena's aunt. Athena was Hera's niece.

W Writing Skills

Argument Have students write a paragraph for homework about their favorite Greek god or goddess. Have them explain why that one is their favorite, and include information they learned in the lesson. When writing is complete, have pairs of students exchange papers and read them. Students can ask their partners questions about anything in the paragraph that is not clear. Ask volunteers to share their paragraphs with the class.

C Critical Thinking Skills

Identifying Central Issues Have students reread the paragraphs about the Oracle of Delphi, as the priestess there was known. **Ask:** What kinds of advice do you think state leaders wanted from the Oracle? *(Students may say that state leaders might want advice about when to go to war, about making laws, and other important decisions.)* AL

Content Background Knowledge

The Temple of Delphi The ancient Greeks considered the site of the Temple of Delphi to be the center of the world. Legend said that Zeus, the king of the gods, released two eagles. One flew from the east, and the other flew from the west. They met at Delphi, on the slopes of Mount Parnassus, indicating the location's importance. A stone marking the spot where the eagles met was called the *omphalos,* or navel. The influential Oracle of Apollo was known all over the Greek world. People around the ancient world consulted the oracle, a woman over the age of 50, about matters of political, military, and even personal importance.

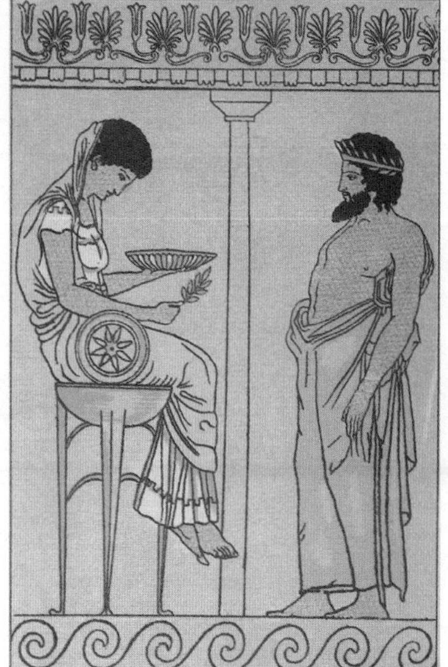

Greeks visited oracles for predictions and advice about their futures.
CRITICAL THINKING
Analyzing Why do you think people sometimes misunderstood the oracles' predictions?

Festivals honoring the gods and goddesses were an important part of Greek life. Each city-state scheduled public feasts and sacrifices. Every four years, Greek athletes took part in athletic competitions. These games were "for the greater glory of Zeus." They were held at the city of Olympia and were called the Olympic Games. Beginning in 776 B.C., the ancient Olympic Games took place for more than 1,000 years. The first modern Olympics were held in 1896 in Athens. W

The Greeks believed their gods would be pleased if people showed skill in the arts, in athletic games, or in thinking.

Greek Oracles

The Greeks believed that each person had a fate or destiny. Certain events were going to happen no matter what they did. They also believed in prophecy, or a prediction about the future. The Greeks believed that the gods gave prophecies to warn people about the future in time to change it.

To find out about the future, many Greeks visited an **oracle** (AWR•uh•kuhl). This was a sacred shrine where a priest or priestess spoke for a god. The most famous was the oracle at the Temple of Apollo at Delphi (DEHL•fy). The oracle chamber was deep inside the temple. The room had an opening in the floor where volcanic smoke hissed from a crack in the earth. C

There a priestess sat on a stool and listened to questions. The priests translated her answers. State leaders or their messengers traveled to Delphi to ask advice from the Oracle of Apollo.

 PROGRESS CHECK

Explaining Why did the ancient Greeks seek advice from oracles?

Epics and Fables

GUIDING QUESTION ***Why were epics and fables important to the ancient Greeks?***

Greek poems and stories are some of the oldest literature in Western civilization. For hundreds of years, Europeans and Americans used ancient Greek works as models for writing their own literature. England's William Shakespeare is an example.

Reading HELPDESK CCSS

oracle a sacred shrine where a priest or priestess spoke for a god or goddess

Academic Vocabulary (Tier 2 Words)

construct to build

networks *Online Teaching Options*

IMAGE

The Oracle of Delphi

Making Connections Show students the image of the Oracle of Delphi. Read the accompanying text with students. Ask students to explain what a *ritual* is in their own words. Then have volunteers describe religious rituals they may know of in the United States, such baptisms, weddings, church services, and so on. **Ask:** Why do people perform rituals? *(Students may say that people perform rituals to honor religious beliefs or to create a feeling of community among the members of a religion.)*

See page 209C for other online activities.

ANSWERS, p. 214

CRITICAL THINKING The oracles often gave their answer in the form of riddles, which were open to different interpretations.

PROGRESS CHECK They believed oracles could speak for the gods, see into the future, and give wise advice.

He borrowed Greek plots and settings for his many dramas. He also organized his plays similarly to the way Greek dramas were organized.

C The first Greek stories were epics. Two great epics of ancient Greece were the *Iliad* and the *Odyssey*. The poet Homer (HOH•muhr) composed them during the 700s B.C. Homer based these epics on stories about a war between Greece and the city of Troy. Troy once existed in the area that is today northwestern Turkey.

The Trojan Horse

R In the *Iliad*, a prince of Troy falls in love with Helen, the wife of a Greek king, and kidnaps her. The kidnapping angers the Greeks, who attack Troy in revenge. The Greeks, however, cannot break through the thick walls surrounding the city. In order to get into the city, the Greeks trick the Trojans and **construct** a huge, hollow wooden horse. The finest Greek soldiers hide inside the horse. All the other Greek soldiers board ships and sail away.

The Trojans think they have won the war and that the horse is a victory prize from the Greeks. The Trojans roll the giant horse into the city. That night, the Greeks creep out of the horse and open the city gates. They allow the rest of the Greek army, who have sailed back to Troy after dark, to enter the city. The Greeks then capture the city, rescue Helen, and take her home.

The *Odyssey* tells the story of Odysseus (oh•DYS•ee•uhs), a Greek hero of the Trojan War. It describes his long trip home after the fall of Troy. He faces storms, monsters, and witches along the way. Odysseus finally returns to his wife. According to the poem, it takes Odysseus 10 years to accomplish his arrival in Greece. Today, people use the word *odyssey*—a word taken from his name—to describe a long, exciting journey.

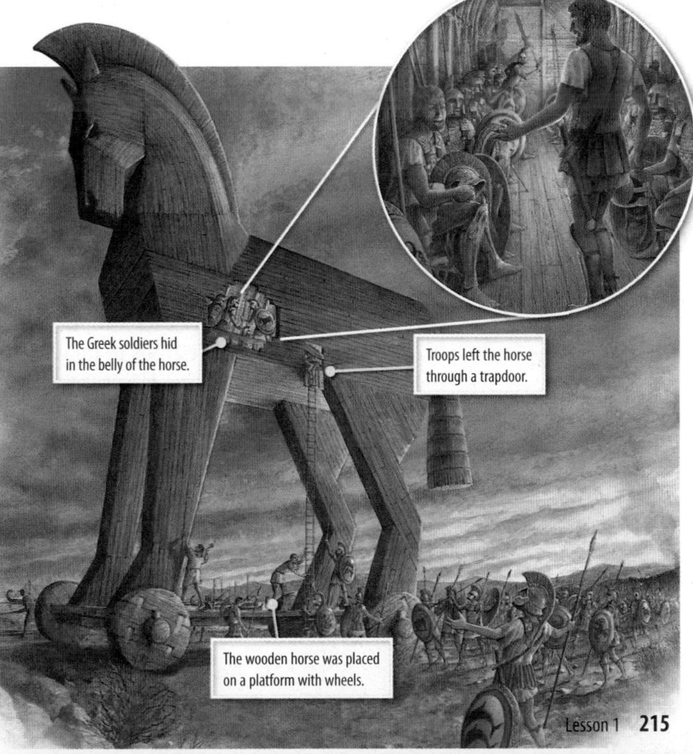

The Greek soldiers hid in the belly of the horse.
Troops left the horse through a trapdoor.
The wooden horse was placed on a platform with wheels.

The epic the *Iliad* tells how the Greeks built the Trojan Horse as a way to get a small group of soldiers into Troy. The term "Trojan Horse" is still used today to mean the use of deception.

Greek Culture

C Critical Thinking Skills

Making Connections Remind students that an epic is a long narrative poem that tells of a hero's great adventures. After discussing the epics of the *Iliad* and the *Odyssey,* ask students to think of movies, stories, or even video games that draw on the themes or elements of the Greek epics. *(Students' responses will vary, but students should understand that almost any story that involves a long journey toward home is derived in part from Homer's* Odyssey.)

R Reading Skills

Summarizing Have students reread the information about the *Iliad* and the *Odyssey* and then, in their own words, write a paragraph or outline describing the main events to summarize the plot of each story. AL ELL

WORKSHEET

Guided Reading Activity: Greek Civilization—Greek Culture

Identifying/Classifying Have students access the Guided Reading Worksheet for this lesson. Direct their attention to the section *Epics and Fables.* If time permits, invite student volunteers to complete the Classifying activity on this page in class. Assign the complete worksheet as homework.

See page 209C for other online activities.

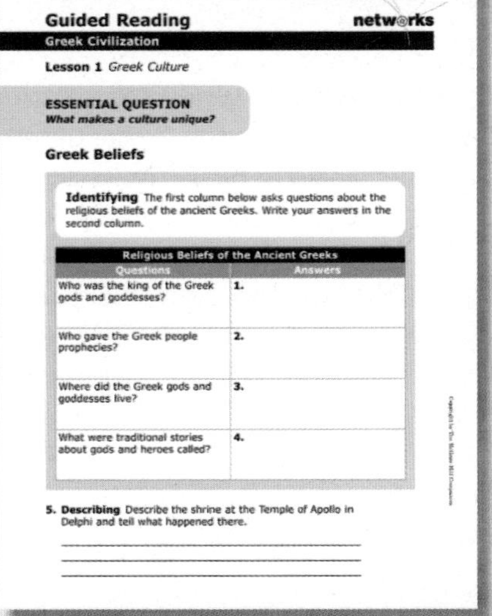
NAME DATE CLASS

Guided Reading networks

Greek Civilization

Lesson 1 *Greek Culture*

ESSENTIAL QUESTION
What makes a culture unique?

Greek Beliefs

Identifying The first column below asks questions about the religious beliefs of the ancient Greeks. Write your answers in the second column.

Religious Beliefs of the Ancient Greeks	
Questions	Answers
Who was the king of the Greek gods and goddesses?	1.
Who gave the Greek people prophecies?	2.
Where did the Greek gods and goddesses live?	3.
What were traditional stories about gods and heroes called?	4.

5. **Describing** Describe the shrine at the Temple of Apollo in Delphi and tell what happened there.

C1 Critical Thinking Skills

Analyzing Primary Sources Read aloud the quotation from an ancient Athenian to the class. **Ask:** What does this quote tell about ancient Greeks' opinion of Homer's poems? *(Students may suggest that the ancient Greeks believed that the poems were very important as a source of cultural values.) Refer students to the excerpt from the* Iliad. **Ask:** What does this excerpt encourage people to do? *(It tells them to act in a way that will not shame themselves, their families, their nation, and their ancestors.)* BL **Verbal/Linguistic**

C2 Critical Thinking Skills

Making Connections After students have discussed epics and fables, ask them to consider the impact of both forms on the stories we tell today. Point out that many of our stories have morals, like fables, and many of our stories feature heroes doing great deeds, as in Greek epics.

Greeks believed the *Iliad* and the *Odyssey* were more than stories. They looked on the epics as real history. These poems gave the Greeks an ideal past with a cast of heroes. One Athenian wrote, "My father, in his pains to make me a good man, compelled me to learn the whole of Homer's poems."

Homer's stories taught courage and honor. They also taught that it was important to be loyal to your friends and to value the relationship between husband and wife. The stories showed heroes striving to be the best they could be. Heroes fought to protect their own honor and their family's honor. Homer's heroes became role models for Greek boys.

PRIMARY SOURCE

"O friends, be men; so act that none may feel
Ashamed to meet the eyes of other men.
Think each one of his children and his wife,
His home, his parents, living yet or dead."

— from *The Iliad* by Homer,

Aesop's Fables

Have you heard the stories "The Fox and the Grapes" or "The Boy Who Cried Wolf"? These stories have traditionally been credited to a man named Aesop (EE•sahp). He is supposed to have lived and told his stories around 550 B.C. Historians now know that Aesop probably never existed. However, the stories he is supposed to have told certainly do exist. They are known as Aesop's fables. A **fable** (FAY•buhl) is a short tale that teaches a lesson. In most of Aesop's fables, animals speak and act like people. These stories are often funny and show human weaknesses and strengths. Each fable ends with a moral, or useful truth.

One of Aesop's popular fables is "The Hare and the Tortoise." In this fable, a slow-moving tortoise, or turtle, and a speedy hare, or rabbit, race each other. Soon, the hare is far ahead. Sure of victory, the hare stops to take a nap. Meanwhile, the tortoise keeps slowly moving. He passes the sleeping rabbit and wins the race.

The moral of the story is "slow and steady wins the race." Many phrases from Aesop's fables are still in use, including: "It is easy to dislike something you cannot have," and "Appearances can be deceiving."

Aesop's fables teach moral lessons in an entertaining way.

▶ CRITICAL THINKING
Theorizing Why might Aesop have used animal characters to tell his fables?

Alinari/Art Resource, NY

Reading HELPDESK CCSS

fable a story meant to teach a lesson

oral tradition the custom of passing along stories by speech

networks Online Teaching Options

PRIMARY SOURCE

The Boy Who Cried Wolf

Citing Text Evidence Ask students how many of them know the story about the boy who cried wolf. Explain that this story is one of Aesop's fables. Assign the Primary Source activity, "The Boy Who Cried Wolf" for this lesson. Have students take turns reading the fable out loud, paragraph by paragraph. **Ask:** What clues within the text tell you that this story is a fable? *(None of the characters have names; the story has a moral.)* **Ask:** How are the characters in this fable different from those in many other fables? *(The main characters in this fable are people, not animals.)*

See page 209C for other online activities.

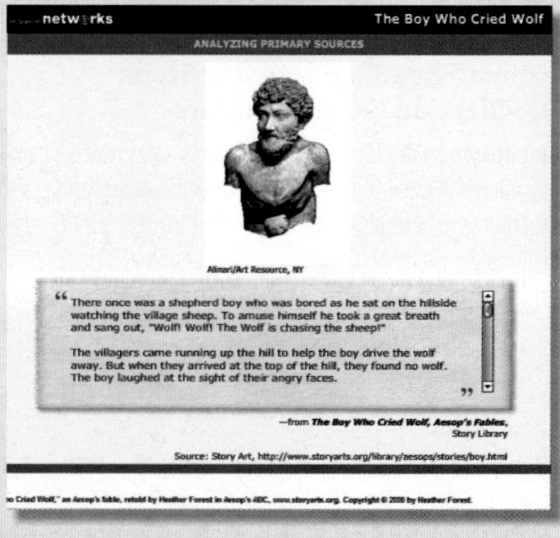

networks
The Boy Who Cried Wolf
ANALYZING PRIMARY SOURCES
Alinari/Art Resource, NY
There once was a shepherd boy who was bored as he sat on the hillside watching the village sheep. To amuse himself he took a great breath and sang out, "Wolf! Wolf! The Wolf is chasing the sheep!"
The villagers came running up the hill to help the boy drive the wolf away. But when they arrived at the top of the hill, they found no wolf. The boy laughed at the sight of their angry faces.
—from The Boy Who Cried Wolf, Aesop's Fables, Story Library
Source: Story Art, http://www.storyarts.org/library/aesops/stories/boy.html

ANSWER, p. 216

CRITICAL THINKING Using animals was a nonthreatening way to get the message across without forcing listeners to see themselves in the story.

Aesop's fables were told during the time that is known as the Golden Age of Greece. During this period, art, philosophy, architecture, and literature flourished.

For 200 years, Aesop's fables were a part of Greek **oral tradition**. This means that the stories were passed from generation to generation by word of mouth. It took many years before these tales were written down. Since then, Aesop's fables have been translated into many languages. They are still read by people around the world today.

PROGRESS CHECK

Describing How do fables usually end?

The Impact of Greek Drama

GUIDING QUESTION *How did Greek dramas develop?*

The ancient Greeks created and performed the first dramas (DRAH•muhs). A **drama** is a story told mainly through the words and actions of a cast of characters. A drama is performed by actors. In ancient Greece, they were performed on stage. Many of today's movies, plays, and television shows are dramas.

Think about your favorite movie. How would you describe it? Is it humorous? Is it a serious story? Greek drama can be divided into two categories: tragedy and comedy. In a **tragedy** (TRA•juh•dee), the main character struggles to overcome hardships but does not succeed. As a result, the story has a tragic, or unhappy, ending. The earliest Greek plays were tragedies. Later, the Greeks also wrote comedies. In a **comedy** (KAH•muh•dee), the story ends happily. Today, the word *comedy* means a story filled with humor.

During the fifth century B.C., four writers emerged as the greatest Greek dramatists, or writers: Aeschylus, Sophocles, Euripides, and Aristophanes. These four dramatists wrote their plays during the Golden Age of Greece, which was from about 500 to 350 B.C.

Aeschylus (EHS•kuh•luhs) was the earliest Greek dramatist. One of his dramas is a set of three plays called the *Oresteia* (ohr•eh•STY•uh). This drama tells about a Greek king's return from the Trojan War and the troubles that strike his family. The Oresteia is a story about revenge and murder. It shows how one evil action can lead to another. Although the play ends tragically, good triumphs over evil in the end.

Theaters in ancient Greece were often located outside. Plays took place in a level semicircle partially surrounded by stepped seating.

Today, most plays are performed in enclosed theaters like the one below. However, you can still attend plays at outdoor theaters in Greece and in other parts of the world.

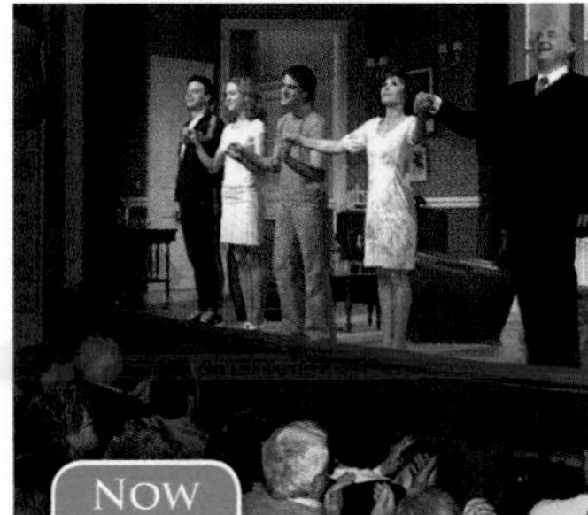

▶ CRITICAL THINKING
Speculating Why do you think Greek plays were performed outside?

drama a story written in the form of a play

tragedy a play or film in which characters fail to overcome serious problems

comedy a play or film that tells a humorous story

T Technology Skills

Researching on the Internet Organize students into small groups. Tell them that they will work together to find out about other cultures with strong oral traditions. Have each group spend 10–15 minutes conducting research on the topic, using reliable online resources. Then invite groups to share their findings with the class. BL **Interpersonal Verbal/Linguistic**

V Visual Skills

Analyzing Images Have students study the photographs of the ancient Greek and modern-day theaters. Read the captions aloud with students, and encourage them to describe each feature in their own words. Have students identify specific features that appear in both ancient Greek and modern theaters. *(stage, actors, seating)* ELL **Visual/Spatial**

CHART

Greek Writers

Using Visual Aids Give students the interactive chart on ancient Greek writers. Have them work alone or in pairs to complete the activity, matching the names of the four most important writers in ancient Greece with their themes and stories. Remind students to skim their textbooks for information about the writers to help them complete the chart.

See page 209C for other online activities.

networks — Greek Writers

Ancient Greek Writer	Title / Genre	Fast Facts
Aeschylus		
Sophocles		
Euripides		
Aristophanes		

ANSWERS, p. 217

PROGRESS CHECK Many fables end with a moral, or useful truth.

CRITICAL THINKING Outside areas could hold the most people; the climate in Greece is warm, which allows outside theater.

Greek Culture

R Reading Skills

Naming After students have read the text, review the differences between tragedy and comedy with them. Point out that Greek playwrights usually wrote just one type of drama **Ask:** **Which Greek playwright was known for showing ordinary people in realistic situations?** *(Euripides)* **Ask:** **Which Greek playwright wrote plays that poked fun at leaders and events?** *(Aristophanes)*

C Critical Thinking Skills

Contrasting Reread the first three sentences of the last paragraph with students. **Ask:** **How were Greek performers different from modern performers?** *(All Greek performers were men. Men, women, and children all perform today.)* AL

Content Background Knowledge

The Parthenon The Parthenon was built on the Acropolis, the fortified center of Athens. It was a holy site. Many other temples were built there, including the Erechtheum—a small temple dedicated to Athena and Poseidon; the Temple of Athena Nike—dedicated to the goddess of victory; and the Sanctuary of Zeus—where burnt offerings were made to the chief god. The Parthenon stood as the grandest of all temples on the hill. It was built to honor the goddess Athena, the patron goddess of the city, with money collected from Athens's empire. High walls surrounding the rocky hill protected the temples there. The Athenians fled to the Acropolis for shelter during times of war.

THE PARTHENON

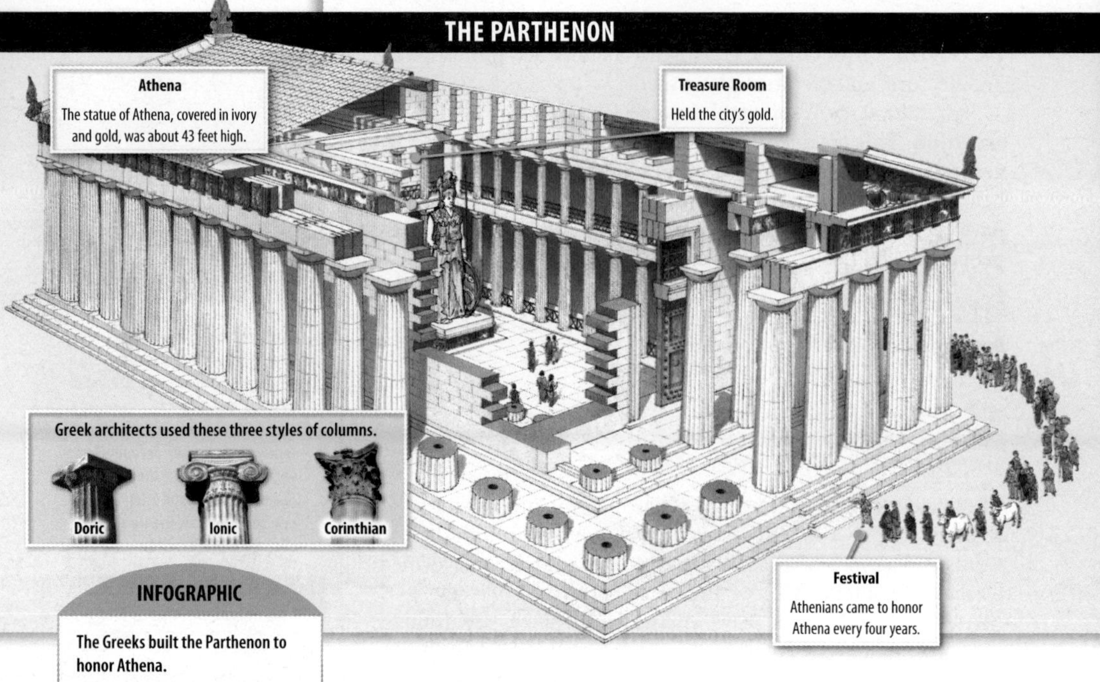

INFOGRAPHIC

The Greeks built the Parthenon to honor Athena.

1. **DESCRIBING** What features of the temple tell you that it was built by the Greeks?
2. **CRITICAL THINKING** ***Drawing Conclusions*** Why were temples the most important buildings in Greek city-states?

Sophocles (SAH•fuh•kleez) was a great Athenian writer. In his plays, Sophocles accepted suffering as a real part of life. He also stressed courage and understanding. In his play *Antigone* (an•TIH•guh•nee), Sophocles questions whether it is better to obey orders or to do what one believes to be right.

Another leading Greek dramatist was Euripides (yuh•RIH•puh•deez). Unlike Aeschylus and Sophocles, Euripides wrote about ordinary human beings in realistic situations. His plays often show the suffering caused by war.

In theaters today, the actors include men, women, and children. In ancient Greece, however, only men could be actors. Even female characters were played by male actors. The most famous writer of Greek comedies was Aristophanes (ar•uh•STAH•fuh•neez). His works poked fun at the leaders and issues of his day. He encouraged people to think and laugh. Many of Aristophanes' comedies included jokes, just as television comedy shows do today.

Reading HELPDESK CCSS

Academic Vocabulary (Tier 2 Words)

conflict a fight or disagreement
style a distinctive form or type of something

networks Online Teaching Options

WORKSHEET

Economics of History Activity: Support for the Arts in Ancient Greece

Assessing Display the worksheet and ask volunteers to read aloud paragraphs of the Background Information. Make sure students understand the concepts and specialized vocabulary. After reading, students should be able to identify the main idea—that the government and wealthy patrons supported the arts in order to glorify ancient Greek culture. **Ask:** **Why might a Hellenistic king or a famous athlete want to have a large marble statue carved in his or her likeness?** *(to show his or her greatness and importance, or so his or her fame will live on even after death.)* Have students complete the activity for homework.

See page 209C for other online activities.

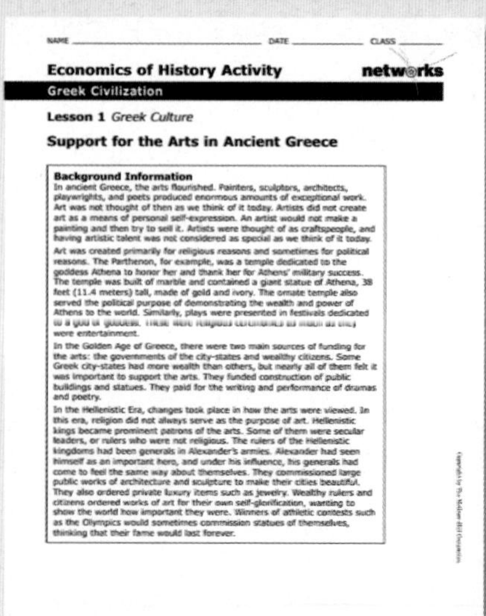

NAME ______ DATE ______ CLASS ______

Economics of History Activity networks

Greek Civilization

Lesson 1 *Greek Culture*

Support for the Arts in Ancient Greece

Background Information

In ancient Greece, the arts flourished. Painters, sculptors, architects, playwrights, and poets produced enormous amounts of exceptional work. Art was not thought of then as we think of it today. Artists did not create art as a means of personal self-expression. An artist would not make a painting and then try to sell it. Artists were thought of as craftspeople, and having artistic talent was not considered as special as we think of it today.

Art was created primarily for religious reasons and sometimes for political reasons. The Parthenon, for example, was a temple dedicated to the goddess Athena to honor her and thank her for Athens' military success. The temple was built of marble and contained a giant statue of Athena, 38 feet (11.4 meters) tall, made of gold and ivory. The ornate temple also served the political purpose of demonstrating the wealth and power of Athens to the world. Similarly, plays were presented in festivals dedicated [illegible] were entertainment.

In the Golden Age of Greece, there were two main sources of funding for the arts: the governments of the city-states and wealthy citizens. Some Greek city-states had more wealth than others, but nearly all of them felt it was important to support the arts. They funded construction of public buildings and statues. They paid for the writing and performance of dramas and poetry.

In the Hellenistic Era, changes took place in how the arts were viewed. In this era, religion did not always serve as the purpose of art. Hellenistic kings became prominent patrons of the arts. Some of them were secular leaders, or rulers who were not religious. The rulers of the Hellenistic kingdoms had been generals in Alexander's armies. Alexander had seen himself as an important hero, and under his influence, his generals had come to feel the same way about themselves. They commissioned large public works of architecture and sculpture to make their cities beautiful. They also ordered private luxury items such as jewelry. Wealthy rulers and citizens ordered works of art for their own self-glorification, wanting to show the world how important they were. Winners of athletic contests such as the Olympics would sometimes commission statues of themselves, thinking that their fame would last forever.

ANSWERS, p. 218

INFOGRAPHIC

1. The large, graceful columns indicate that the structure was built by ancient Greeks.
2. **CRITICAL THINKING** They were important because they were the places where ancient Greeks worshiped.

How Greek Drama Developed

Drama was more than entertainment for the people of ancient Greece. It was part of religious festivals and a way to show loyalty to their city-state.

In early Greek dramas, a group of performers, called the chorus, presented the story through singing and dancing. Later, dramas used several actors on stage. Then, stories were created using action and **conflicts** among the characters.

✓ PROGRESS CHECK

Determining Cause and Effect How did Greek drama influence how people are entertained today?

Greek Art and Architecture

GUIDING QUESTION *What ideas did the Greeks express in their art and architecture?*

The ancient Greeks excelled in the arts and architecture. They created works that expressed the ideals of reason, balance, and harmony. The characteristics of Greek art became the artistic **style** that we now call classical. Classical Greek art set standards of beauty that people still admire today.

The Greeks constructed beautiful buildings. Every Greek city-state had a temple dedicated to a god or goddess. Temples such as the Parthenon included a central room that housed statues of the gods. Large, graceful columns supported many Greek buildings. Some famous buildings in Washington, D.C., such as the White House and the Capitol, have Greek columns.

Sculpture decorated many Greek temples. The human body was the favorite subject of Greek artists. Greek sculptors tried to show ideal beauty in perfect human forms.

The design of the Lincoln Memorial in Washington, D.C., is similar to the Parthenon. Its 36 columns represent the number of states in the union at the time President Lincoln died.

V

✓ PROGRESS CHECK

Explaining How did the Greeks design their buildings?

LESSON 1 REVIEW (CCSS)

Review Vocabulary (Tier 3 Words)

1. How is a *fable* part of an *oral tradition?* RH.6–8.4

Answer the Guiding Questions

2. ***Explaining*** Why was Mount Olympus important to the Greeks? RH.6–8.2
3. ***Identifying*** What epic included the story of the Trojan horse? RH.6–8.2
4. ***Comparing*** What two types of drama did the Greeks create? How do they differ? RH.6–8.2
5. ***Inferring*** Why are some computer viruses called Trojan horses? RH.6–8.2
6. **INFORMATIVE/EXPLANATORY** Compare Greek theater actors to modern theater actors. How are they alike and different? Write a paragraph or two that compares these types of actors. WHST.6–8.2, WHST.6–8.10

LESSON 1 REVIEW ANSWERS

1. A fable is a short story that teaches a lesson. A fable is an example of the oral tradition because it can be passed down from generation to generation by word of mouth, as was the case for Aesop's fables.
2. The ancient Greeks considered Mount Olympus the home of their 12 most important gods and goddesses.
3. The *Iliad* includes the story of the Trojan horse.
4. The ancient Greeks created tragedy and comedy. In a tragedy, a person tries but fails to overcome hardships; the story has a tragic, or sad, ending. In contrast, a comedy is a story with funny parts, and it ends happily.
5. Trojan horse viruses are put into a computer in a sneaky way in order to cause harm. This process is similar to the way the original Trojan horse was put into Troy in a deceitful way in order to destroy the city.
6. Students should suggest that modern and ancient Greek actors are similar in that they act out stories on the stage. They are different in that ancient Greek actors usually told stories through speeches or singing and dancing. Modern actors usually tell stories through realistic actions and by exchanging words with other actors. Another difference is that ancient Greek actors were always men. Modern actors can be men, women, or children.

R Reading Skills

Determining Word Meanings As students read the text, explain that Greek dramas told stories about events and conflicts using acting, singing, and dancing. **Ask:** **What do you think a conflict is, in drama?** *(Students may suggest that the conflict is when characters disagree, argue, or fight.)* ELL **Verbal/Linguistic**

V Visual Skills

Making Connections Point out the photograph of the Lincoln Memorial to students. **Ask:** **How are public buildings, especially in our nation's capital, influenced by Greek architecture?** *(Students should note that many public buildings use elements of Greek architecture, such as columns.)* **Visual/Spatial**

Have students complete the Lesson 1 Review.

CLOSE & REFLECT

To close, have a class discussion comparing our beliefs today to the beliefs of ancient Greeks. Base the discussion on the Essential Question: *What makes a culture unique?* Have students suggest ways in which ancient Greek culture was unique in its time.

ANSWERS, p. 219

✓ **PROGRESS CHECK** The two types of Greek drama—comedy and tragedy—are still the basis for most modern entertainment. Modern plays, movies, and television shows almost always have elements of comedy or tragedy, or both.

✓ **PROGRESS CHECK** They used a mathematical formula that helped them design buildings with attractive proportions.

The Greek Mind

ENGAGE

Bellringer Have students read "It Matters Because" in their textbooks and preview the illustrations, captions, and headings in the lesson. Explain that ancient Greece was remarkable for the many new fields of study that were being explored then. Challenge students to make a list of the fields of study, based on their preview of the lesson. Write their answers on the board. *(Answers should include philosophy, history, and science.)* Make sure students understand that many of the subjects taught in schools today were first developed and studied in ancient Greece. Ask students what they know about Greek thinkers, or philosophers. Remind them that they may have learned about these philosophers in other classes, such as science or math. Have students share their information with the class. *(Some students may know something about the Socratic method, Plato, Aristotle, the Pythagorean theorem, or the Hippocratic Oath.)* Tell students that in this lesson they will learn about some of the first philosophers and scientists in the world.

TEACH & ASSESS

R Reading Skills

Calculating After students read the paragraph, discuss the Golden Age of Greece. **Ask:** **Why was this period known as the "Golden Age"?** *(because it was a time of great artistic achievement and because gold is a valuable metal, symbolic of something valuable or wonderful)* The Golden Age of Greece took place between 500 B.C. and 350 B.C. **Ask:** **About how long did the Golden Age of Greece last?** *(about 150 years)* Direct students to cite support from the text in their responses. **Logical/Mathematical**

C Critical Thinking Skills

Speculating Help students understand that philosophers were thinkers who were interested in a variety of subjects. Tell them that philosophers studied history, politics, and the natural world to try to understand how things work or how to improve them. **Ask:** **What is one question that a philosopher might have tried to answer?** *(Answers will vary. Sample answer: What is the best way to govern?)* BL

ANSWER, p. 220

TAKING NOTES: Students may suggest any six of the following thinkers and facts about them: Socrates: Socratic method; Plato: ideal government; Aristotle: golden mean, classified living things; Herodotus: historian, father of history, wrote history of Persian wars; Thucydides: historian, did careful research, wrote History of the Peloponnesian Wars; Thales: first scientist, studied astronomy and math; Pythagoras: Pythagorean theorem; Hippocrates: Hippocratic Oath, developed cures for diseases.

networks *There's More Online!*

- GRAPHIC ORGANIZER
  Greek Thinkers
- SLIDE SHOW
  • Greek Philosophers and Their Ideas
  • Facts About Thales

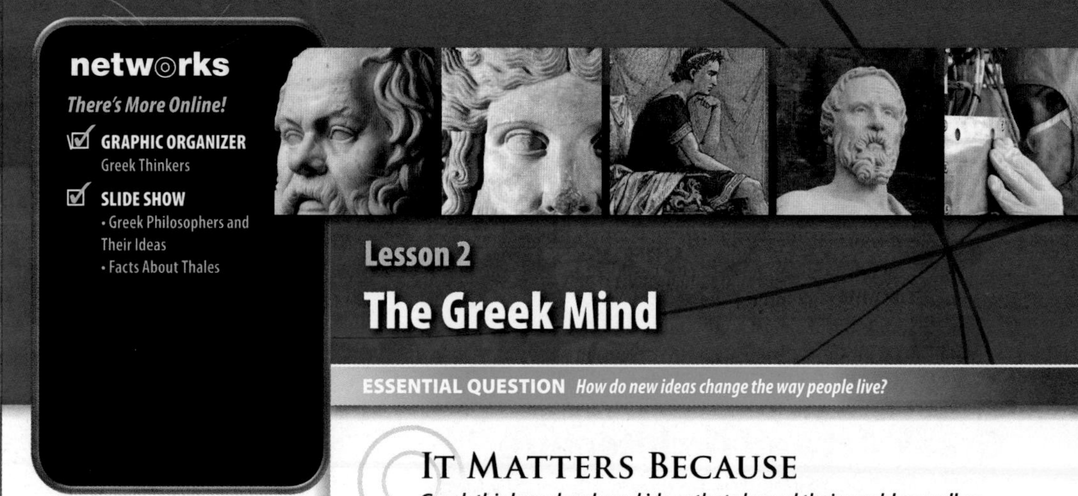

Lesson 2

The Greek Mind

ESSENTIAL QUESTION *How do new ideas change the way people live?*

IT MATTERS BECAUSE

Greek thinkers developed ideas that shaped their world as well as ours today. The Greeks created the study of history, political science, biology, and logic.

Greek Thinkers

GUIDING QUESTION ***What ideas did the Greeks develop to explain the world around them?***

R The Greeks believed the human mind was capable of great understanding. During the Golden Age of Greece, from approximately 500 B.C. to 350 B.C., art, architecture, and literature all flourished. This was also a very fertile time for the life of the mind. Most of the thinkers discussed in this chapter were part of that exciting time. They were pondering deep questions about truth and also developing the study of science and mathematics. Greek thinkers produced some of the most remarkable ideas the world has ever known.

One type of thinker was involved in creating a new body of knowledge. These thinkers were known as philosophers. The body of knowledge they created is called philosophy (fih•LAH•suh•fee). Philosophy is a Greek word that means "love of wisdom." C Through philosophy, Greek philosophers helped develop the study of many subjects, including history, political science, biology, and logic, or the study of reasoning.

Reading **HELP**DESK CCSS

Taking Notes: *Identifying*

Use a diagram like the one here to list the Greek thinkers you read about in this lesson. With each name you list, write down one thing the person is known for. RH.6–8.2

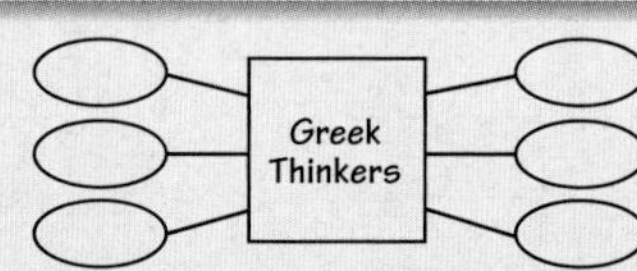

Content Vocabulary (Tier 3 Words)
- **Sophists**
- **rhetoric**
- **Socratic method**
- **Hippocratic Oath**

networks ***Online Teaching Options***

VIDEO

Gods and Heroes

Making Connections Play the video about the gods and heroes of ancient Greece. Point out that the video connects modern figures, such as superheroes, to ancient Greek heroes. Invite students to brainstorm a list of modern stories, television shows, comic books, or films that feature characters who seem to connect to gods or heroes of ancient Greece.

See page 209D for other online activities.

The Sophists

Many Greek philosophers were teachers. A group of philosophers known as the **Sophists** (SAH•fihsts) traveled from polis to polis. They made a living by teaching. The Sophists taught many subjects, including mathematics, science, and history. However, they were best known for teaching **rhetoric**, or the art of public speaking and debate.

Sophists did not believe that the gods influenced human actions. They also **rejected** the idea of absolute right or wrong. For the Sophists, a way of life that was right for one person might be wrong for another.

The Sophists not only challenged Greek traditions, but they also accepted money for their teaching. Other Greek philosophers did not approve of this practice. Many Greeks also thought that the Sophists lacked ideals and values. Critics claimed the Sophists taught students to win arguments rather than seek truths. C1

Who Was Socrates?

Although a sculptor by training, Socrates (SAH•kruh•teez) loved philosophy. He lived in Athens and spent most of his time teaching. Socrates did not leave a written record of his beliefs. Information about him is found in his students' writings. These writings **reveal** that Socrates was a harsh critic of the Sophists.

Unlike the Sophists, Socrates believed in absolute truth and that all real knowledge was within each person. In his search for truth, Socrates created a new way of questioning called the **Socratic** (suh•KRA•tihk) **method**. Today, many university professors use the Socratic Method when they teach. Socrates did not lecture. Instead, he asked pointed questions and waited for his students to respond. He wanted students to find the answers for themselves and form their own opinions. C2

Some Athenian leaders believed that the Socratic method was dangerous. At one time, Athens had allowed its people to speak freely. They could publicly question their leaders. However, when Athens lost the Peloponnesian War, its new rulers limited this freedom. The Athenians no longer trusted open debate. This method of discussion, however, was exactly what Socrates thought was necessary. He continued to teach his students. R

Socrates believed that obeying the law was more important than his own life. Rather than leave Athens, he accepted a sentence of death.

Araldo de Luca/CORBIS

rhetoric the art of public speaking and debate
Sophists Greek teachers of philosophy, reasoning, and public speaking
Socratic method philosophical method of questioning to gain truth

Academic Vocabulary (Tier 2 Words)
reject to refuse to accept or consider
reveal to make information public; to tell a secret

C1 Critical Thinking Skills

Contrasting Reiterate the main characteristics of the Sophists with students. **Ask:** **What was one way in which the Sophists differed from other Greek philosophers?** *(Sample answer: They took money for their teaching.)*

C2 Critical Thinking Skills

Making Inferences Talk with students about the life and teachings of Socrates. **Ask:** **Why was Socrates critical of the Sophists?** *(Students may suggest that because he believed that truth and knowledge are within each person, he did not think it was right for the Sophists to charge money for teaching.)* **Do you agree with Socrates' view of the Sophists? Why or why not?** *(Answers will vary; students should support their reasoning with a logical argument.)*

R Reading Skills

Explaining After students read, ask them to consider the consequences of Socrates' decision to continue teaching after the Peloponnesian War. **Ask:** **What was the effect of the Peloponnesian War on political and intellectual freedom in Athens?** *(It limited freedoms greatly. The government had much more control over what people could say and do publicly. Thinkers such as Socrates died for their beliefs.)* **Why do you think the new leaders thought Socrates was dangerous?** *(Students may suggest that because he sought knowledge by questioning and thinking freely, Socrates was a threat to the city's rulers.)*

GRAPHIC ORGANIZER

Greek Thinkers

Identifying Tell students to write in the Taking Notes graphic organizer the names of any Greek thinkers they know and the accomplishment(s) that made them famous. Have students continue to fill in the graphic organizer as they read the lesson. **Ask:** **If you could spend a day with one of the thinkers you learned about here, which one would you choose? Explain why.** *(Students' responses should state a definite choice, and the reasons for their choices should include details from the text about the thinker they chose.)*

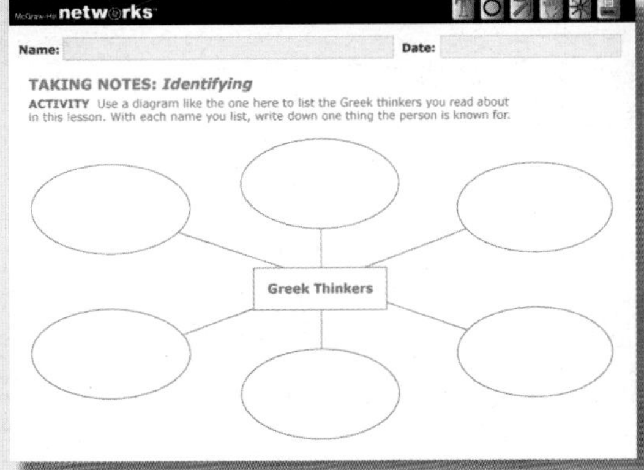

See page 209D for other online activities.

C Critical Thinking Skills

Organizing Draw a social structure diagram on the board using a large triangle, and divide it into three sections, with the smallest section at the top and the largest section at the bottom. Have students review Plato's ideal social structure as presented in *The Republic.* With students, filling the diagram to show Plato's ideal social structure. *(Top: philosopher kings; Middle: warriors; Bottom: all others)* **Ask: Why did Plato dislike democracy and want the government to be run by philosopher kings?** *(Plato distrusted the common people, whom he thought could not think for themselves. He believed that intelligent, educated thinker-kings were the only people who were fit to rule.)* AL **Visual/Spatial**

R Reading Skills

Specifying After students have read the passage, discuss the main ideas that Plato presented in *The Republic.* **Ask: Which type of government did Plato think was best?** *(monarchy)* **Which type of government did Plato think was worst?** *(democracy)*

ANSWER, p. 222

CRITICAL THINKING Plato did not want to participate in a government that put his teacher, Socrates, to death.

BIOGRAPHY

Plato (c. 428–347 B.C.)

Plato had planned a career in government. However, he was horrified by the death of his teacher, Socrates. As a result, Plato left politics and spent many years traveling and writing. When Plato returned to Athens in 387 B.C., he started the Academy, which was a school where students learned using Socrates' method of questioning. His academy attracted young people from Athens and other Greek city-states. He believed that by training the mind, people could discover truth. Plato's teachings and writings would influence the Western world for centuries.

▶ **CRITICAL THINKING**
Speculating Why do you think Plato felt he could not have a career in government?

In 399 B.C., city leaders—fearing his influence— arrested Socrates. They charged that he had urged young people to rebel against the government. A jury found Socrates guilty and sentenced him to death.

Following the verdict of the court, Socrates was given the opportunity to leave Athens and live. Instead, he stayed. Surrounded by his students and friends, Socrates gave his last speech.

He said that he was living under the city's laws. As a result, he stated, he was committed to obeying them. Socrates then drank poison to carry out the jury's sentence, and died.

Plato's Ideas

The two Greek philosophers you may have heard of are Plato and Aristotle. The philosopher Plato (PLAY•toh) was one of Socrates' students. Plato became a teacher and founded a school in Athens called the Academy. Unlike Socrates, Plato recorded his ideas in writing. One work Plato wrote was *The Republic*. It presented his plan for an ideal society and government.

C In *The Republic*, Plato organized society into three groups. At the top were philosopher kings. They ruled through logic and wisdom. Warriors, the second group, defended society from attack, using force. The third group included the rest of the people. Their role was to produce society's food, clothing, and shelter. They lacked the wisdom of the kings and the courage of the warriors.

R Plato believed that an ideal society must have a just and reasonable government. In *The Republic*, Plato noted his dislike of Athenian democracy. He wrote that the common people did not think for themselves and that they could be easily influenced into making foolish decisions. Plato believed that "philosopher kings" were intelligent and well-educated. He felt these kings would place the needs of the community ahead of their own needs. Plato wanted only these philosopher kings to govern the citizens of Greece.

Despite his distrust of the common people, Plato was willing to grant more rights to women. He believed that women should have the same opportunities for education and jobs that men have.

SEF/Art Resource, NY

Reading **HELP**DESK 

Academic Vocabulary (Tier 2 Words)

despite in spite of, regardless of

networks *Online Teaching Options*

PRIMARY SOURCE

Plato's *Republic*

Paraphrasing Show students the excerpt from Plato's *Republic.* Ask volunteers to read the parts of the dialogue aloud for the class. Make sure that students understand the ideas expressed in the dialogue. Ask students to work with partners to paraphrase the dialogue.

See page 209D for other online activities.

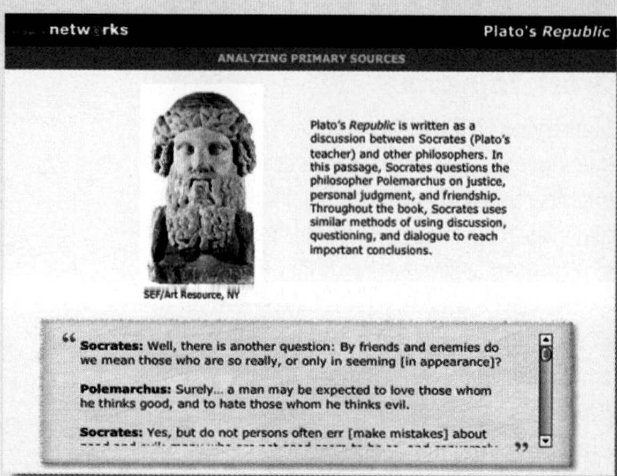

networks
Plato's Republic
ANALYZING PRIMARY SOURCES
Plato's Republic is written as a discussion between Socrates (Plato's teacher) and other philosophers. In this passage, Socrates questions the philosopher Polemarchus on justice, personal judgment, and friendship. Throughout the book, Socrates uses similar methods of using discussion, questioning, and dialogue to reach important conclusions.
SEF/Art Resource, NY
Socrates: Well, there is another question: By friends and enemies do we mean those who are so really, or only in seeming [in appearance]?
Polemarchus: Surely... a man may be expected to love those whom he thinks good, and to hate those whom he thinks evil.
Socrates: Yes, but do not persons often err [make mistakes] about

Before starting his own school, the Lyceum, Aristotle taught at Plato's Academy. Here he tutors a young man who soon would be called Alexander the Great.

Who Was Aristotle?

Another great thinker of ancient Greece was Aristotle (AR•uh•stah•tuhl). He wrote more than 200 works on topics such as government, astronomy, and political science. In 335 B.C., Aristotle started a school called the Lyceum. At this school, he taught his students the "golden mean." The mean is the middle position between two extremes. The idea of the golden mean is that people should live moderately. For example, **individuals** should not eat too little or too much. Instead, they should eat just enough to stay well. **R**

Aristotle had many interests, including science. He studied the stars, plants, and animals and carefully recorded what he observed. Aristotle classified living things according to their similarities and differences. Aristotle's methods were an important step in the development of modern science. **C**

Like Plato, Aristotle also wrote about government. He studied and compared the governments of different city-states and hoped to find the best political system. In his book *Politics*, Aristotle divided governments into three types.

Academic Vocabulary (Tier 2 Words)

individuals human beings, persons

R Reading Skills

Determining Word Meanings Have students locate the word *mean* in the second paragraph. Tell them that the word *mean* is a homonym. A *homonym* is a word that is spelled the same, but has different meanings. Here, the word *mean* describes the balance between two extremes. As students may know, *mean* is also an adjective, describing someone who is unfriendly and rude. Also, *mean* is a verb that describes what something expresses or stands for—what it "means." Ask students to write one sentence using each version of the word *mean*.

ELL Verbal/Linguistic

C Critical Thinking Skills

Drawing Conclusions Discuss with students the parts of the natural world that Aristotle studied. Point out that scientists today study these same parts of the natural world. **Ask: In which fields might scientists today build on studies done long ago by Aristotle?** *(astronomy and biology)*

Content Background Knowledge

Point out to students that Socrates was the teacher of Plato, that Plato was the teacher of Aristotle, and that Aristotle was the teacher of Alexander the Great. These connections represent what many historians consider to be the greatest teacher-student chain in history.

SLIDE SHOW

Philosophers and Their Ideas

Sequencing Have students review the section "Greek Thinkers," and then show them the slide show of Socrates, Plato, and Aristotle. Have students identify the order in which these three philosophers lived, and who taught whom. *(Socrates was the oldest, and he taught Plato. Plato was the next one, and he taught Aristotle. Aristotle was the last of the three.)* Point out that the relationship between the three thinkers is important. Because Socrates taught Plato and Plato taught Aristotle, each thinker used the previous one as a foundation for his ideas. Students should also understand that without Plato and his writings, we would have no first-hand account of Socrates' life and ideas.

networks
Philosophers and Their Ideas
Plato presents his ideas in the form of dialogues between his teacher (Socrates) and other philosophers. In these discussions, he encourages his readers to develop their own thoughts and beliefs. Plato's writings about the ideal government suggest that he believed that only people in the ruling and educated class are able to make decisions that are for the common good.
Fact: Plato was not this philosopher's given name. People called him "Plato" because of his wide forehead, which meant he had knowledge about many different things.

See page 209D for other online activities.

C Critical Thinking Skills

Analyzing Visuals Have students study the infographic "Greek Philosophers." **Ask:** **Which Greek philosopher do you think is the most important, overall? Why?** *(Answers will vary; some students may suggest that Aristotle is the most important because his ideas have influenced so many institutions and thinkers since his time.)* BL

W Writing Skills

Informative/Explanatory Invite students to share their ideas about how Aristotle's ideal government resembled the U.S. government. If necessary, remind students that the U.S. government is divided into branches. Tell them that the president leads one branch and the U.S. Congress leads another. **Ask:** **Is the U.S. government a monarchy, oligarchy, or democracy?** *(democracy)* Have students write a paragraph in which they tell how the U.S. government reflects Aristotle's ideas.

GREEK PHILOSOPHERS

	Sophists	Socrates	Plato	Aristotle
Thinker Or Group				
Main Idea	Sophists like Libanius (above) thought that people should use knowledge to improve themselves. They believed that there is no absolute right or wrong.	Socrates was a critic of the Sophists. He believed that there was an absolute truth.	Plato rejected the idea of democracy as a form of government. He believed that philosopher-kings should rule society.	Aristotle taught the idea of the "golden mean." He believed observation and comparison were necessary to gain knowledge.
Important Contribution	They developed the art of public speaking and debate.	He created the Socratic method of teaching.	He described his vision of the ideal government in his work the *Republic*.	He wrote over 200 books on philosophy and science. He divided all governments into three basic types.
Influence on Today	The importance of public speaking can be seen in political debates between candidates.	His methods influenced the way teachers interact with their students.	He introduced the idea that government should be fair and just.	His political ideas still shape political ideas today.

INFOGRAPHIC

The influence of Greek thinkers is felt today in education and politics.

1. **IDENTIFYING** What did the Sophists believe?
2. **CRITICAL THINKING** ***Analyzing*** Would Plato approve or disapprove of the American system of government? Why?

The first was monarchy, or rule by one person. The second was oligarchy (OHL•uh•gahr•kee), which is rule by a few people. The third type was democracy, or rule by many.

Aristotle believed the best government had features of all three. A chief executive would serve as head of state. A council or legislature would assist this leader and be supported by the people.

Aristotle's ideas influenced the way Europeans and Americans thought about government. The authors of the United States Constitution, like Aristotle, believed that no one person or group should have too much power.

✓ PROGRESS CHECK

Explaining Why did Plato dislike Athenian democracy?

Reading HELPDESK CCSS

Academic Vocabulary (Tier 2 Words)

investigate to observe or study by examining closely and questioning systematically

networks Online Teaching Options

LECTURE SLIDE

Greek Thinkers

Discussing Explain to students that today, great thinkers who are likely to be famous are usually people who have made advances in technology or science. Show the lecture slide about the great Greek thinkers. Then have students make connections with modern thinkers. **Ask:** **Who are some of the great thinkers of the past 75 years? What are they known for?** *(Answers may include Albert Einstein, theory of relativity; Francis Crick and James Watson, structure of DNA molecule; Jane Goodall, tool-making abilities in chimpanzees; Stephen Hawking, physicist and astronomer; Steve Jobs and Bill Gates, advances in computer technology.)* Ask students to identify ancient Greece's thinkers and explain their key contributions to philosophy.

networks — Greek Thinkers

- **Socrates** was a philosopher that believed in absolute truth. He used a questioning method so that students would find the answers for themselves. He also thought public debate was an important type of expression.
- **Plato** was a teacher who wanted a just and reasonable government. He believed that women should have the same opportunities as men.
- **Aristotle** was a thinker who wrote about government, astronomy, and political science. He believed people should follow the "golden mean" and live moderately.

See page 209D for other online activities.

ANSWERS, p. 224

✓ PROGRESS CHECK Plato believed the common people were too easily persuaded to make poor decisions. He believed that only the "philosopher-kings," the best-educated citizens, would place the people's best interests above personal goals.

INFOGRAPHIC

1. Sophists believed people should use knowledge to improve themselves and that there is no absolute right or wrong.
2. **CRITICAL THINKING** He would disapprove, because he rejected democracy in favor of rule by philosopher-kings.

New History and Science Ideas

GUIDING QUESTION *What did the Greeks believe about history and science?*

The Greeks used their thinking skills to write history. They also **investigated** the natural world. They developed new ways of studying science and history.

The Greeks and History

In many ways, the ancient Greeks were like most people living at that time. They believed that legends and myths were true. People did not analyze events in order to explain the past. Then, in 435 B.C., the Greek thinker Herodotus (hih•RAH•duh•tuhs) wrote a history of the Persian Wars. Herodotus wrote that the gods played a role in historical events. However, he made a great effort to separate fact from fiction. Like a news reporter, he questioned many people to get information, but then he investigated the truthfulness of these sources. Because of Herodotus's careful research, many European and American historians consider him "the father of history." **R**

Another famous historian of ancient Greece was Thucydides (thoo•SIH•duh•deez). He was a general in the Peloponnesian War. The two great Greek city-states of Athens and Sparta fought in this conflict, which lasted nearly 30 years. Thucydides considered this war to be a major event in world history. After the war, he wrote *The History of the Peloponnesian War.* **C**

Unlike Herodotus, Thucydides rejected the idea that the gods affected human history. Thucydides believed that only people made history. In his writing, Thucydides tried hard to be accurate and impartial. Thucydides acted like a modern roving reporter. He visited battle sites, and he also carefully examined documents. In addition, he accepted only actual eyewitness reports of events.

Herodotus was careful about any information he recorded. He wanted to be sure of the accuracy of what he wrote.

Michele Falzone/age fotostock

R Reading Skills

Finding the Main Idea Remind students that the main idea of a paragraph is the most important idea. Explain that students can find the main idea of a paragraph by summarizing all the details within it. Point out that the main idea is often stated in the first or last sentence of a paragraph. **Ask:** **Which sentence gives the main idea of the first paragraph in the section The Greeks and History?** *(the last sentence)*

C Critical Thinking Skills

Comparing and Contrasting Review with students the details about the work of Herodotus and Thucydides. Tell them that both historians lived and worked at about the same time. **Ask:** **How were the methods of both historians similar?** *(Both conducted careful research and interviewed many people to find out the truth about the past.)* **How were these historians different?** *(Herodotus believed that the gods affected human history, but Thucydides did not. They also wrote about different historical events.)*

PRIMARY SOURCE

Herodotus

Analyzing Primary Sources Show students the image of papyrus with writing by Herodotus. Ask a volunteer to read aloud the excerpt. If necessary, have the volunteer pause after each sentence or two to allow listening students to absorb and understand Herodotus's ideas. As a class, paraphrase Herodotus's words. Allow students time to answer the discussion question about Herodotus's purpose for writing history. Students should understand, from reading and listening to the excerpt, that Herodotus was interested in recording specific details of events that had an impact on history.

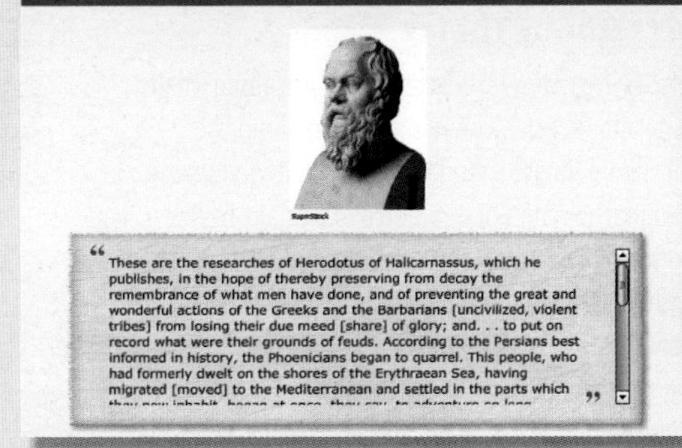

See page 209D for other online activities.

C1 Critical Thinking Skills

Analyzing Primary Sources Read aloud the primary-source excerpt from Thucydides' *History of the Peloponnesian War* with students. Ensure that students understand complex vocabulary terms such as *injustice* and *innovation.* Point out that Thucydides intended this excerpt as a warning. Work with students to restate the excerpt in their own words. *(Sample answer: Sparta cannot have peace because it is old-fashioned and unjust. Athens is more advanced and more just, and therefore has peace.)* AL ELL

C2 Critical Thinking Skills

Formulating Questions Refer students to the paragraph about Thales. **Ask:** **Why do historians consider Thales to be a "scientist"?** *(He studied the natural world and mathematics by observing and thinking.)* **What is one possible research question that you might ask to learn more about Thales?** *(Answers will vary. Sample answer: How did Thales gather the observations for his theories?)* BL

Thales was one of the first scientists to explain the physical world using examples from nature. He is pictured here with some of the tools he used to develop his theories.

Thucydides did not just state the facts. He also explored the causes and effects of events. He believed that future generations could learn from the past. Moreover, as a historian, he wanted to leave behind ideas and commentary so that others could learn.

For example, in *The History of the Peloponnesian War,* Thucydides wrote of a warning to Sparta:

PRIMARY SOURCE C1

"And yet, [Sparta], you still delay. You fail to see that peace stays longest with those who . . . show their determination not to submit to injustice. . . . Your habits are old-fashioned as compared with [those of Athens]. It is the law as in art, so in politics, that improvements [will win out]. . . . Athens has [made greater progress] than you on the path of innovation."

— from *The History of the Peloponnesian War,* by Thucydides, c. 431 B.C.

The First Scientists

The ancient Greeks developed many scientific ideas. These ideas have influenced scientific thinking for centuries. In ancient times, most people thought that their gods controlled nature. Early Greek scientists had a different idea. They thought that natural events could be explained logically and that people could discover the causes of these events by using reason.

C2 The first important Greek scientist was Thales (THAY•leez) of Miletus. Born in the mid-600s B.C., Thales studied astronomy and mathematics. He did not have telescopes and other instruments that scientists use today. Thales made discoveries and developed theories by observing and thinking.

Another Greek scientist, Pythagoras (puh•THA•guh•ruhs), taught his pupils that the universe followed the same laws that governed music and numbers. He believed that all relationships could be expressed in numbers. As a result, he developed many new ideas about mathematics. Most people know his name because of the Pythagorean Theorem that is still used in geometry today. It is a way to determine the length of the sides of a triangle.

Reading HELPDESK 

Hippocratic Oath a set of promises about patient care that new doctors make when they start practicing medicine

networks Online Teaching Options

IMAGE

Facts About Thales

Identifying Show students the image about Thales. If time allows, ask a volunteer to read aloud the information. Invite a student who is knowledgeable about mathematics or geometry to explain Thales's diagram of a triangle inside a circle. **Ask:** **What is a hypothesis?** *(an educated guess)* **What is the scientific method?** *(It is a way of using observation, logic, and educated guesses to explain things in the natural world.)* **What was new about the way Greek scientists thought?** *(They did not believe that everything in nature was caused by the gods. They thought natural events could be explained logically.)*

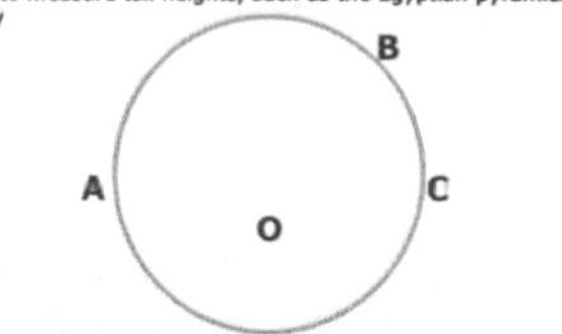

networks
Facts About Thales
Facts About Thales:
• Known as the "father of science"
• Looked for ways to explain things in the natural world without relying on superstition or mythology
• Started a new method of scientific inquiry: he would form a hypothesis, or educated guess, and then experiment to try to prove or disprove it. (This process was an early form of the standard scientific method used by all scientists today.)
• Was one of the first true mathematicians
• Invented a way to measure tall heights, such as the Egyptian pyramids, by using simple geometry
A
B
C
O

See page 209D for other online activities.

Today's scientist have the use of many tools that were not available to Thales and other ancient Greeks.

▶ CRITICAL THINKING
Analyzing What might Thales have discovered about water if he had been able to use a modern microscope?

Alessandro Della Bella/Keystone/Corbis

Ancient Greek Medicine

Greek scientists also studied medicine, or the science of treating diseases. Hippocrates (hih•PAH•kruh•TEEZ) was a physician in ancient Greece who is regarded as the "father of medicine." He believed diseases came from natural causes. Most people at that time thought evil spirits caused diseases. Hippocrates traveled all over Greece to help the sick. He used his new ideas to diagnose different illnesses. He also discovered his own treatments to help cure sick people.

Hippocrates created a list of rules about how doctors should use their skills to help patients. His rules are listed in the **Hippocratic Oath** (HIH•puh•KRAT•ihk). The oath says that doctors should do their best to help the patient. It also says that they should protect the patient's privacy. Today, doctors around the world still promise to honor the Hippocratic Oath. R

✔ PROGRESS CHECK

Explaining Why is Herodotus called "the father of history"?

LESSON 2 REVIEW (CCSS)

Review Vocabulary (Tier 3 Words)

1. How would someone use *rhetoric* in everyday life? RH.6–8.4

Answer the Guiding Questions

2. ***Comparing and Contrasting*** What was one important similarity between Plato and Aristotle? What was one major difference? RH.6–8.2
3. ***Describing*** What is the Hippocratic Oath? RH.6–8.2
4. ***Explaining*** Who are the three most important and famous philosophers from ancient Greece? Explain the teacher-student relationships among the three of them. What do all three have in common? RH.6–8.2
5. **ARGUMENT** Think about the people you read about in this lesson. Whose ideas are still important to us today? Why? Express your opinion in a one-page paper. WHST.6–8.1, WHST.6–8.10

Lesson 2 227

C Critical Thinking Skills

Drawing Conclusions Discuss the achievements of Hippocrates with students. Point out that people today still consider him to be the "father of medicine." **Ask: Why is Hippocrates known as the father of medicine?** *(He was the first doctor to believe that diseases came from natural causes rather than from evil spirits or other supernatural causes.)*

R Reading Skills

Listing After students read, ask them to explain the importance of the Hippocratic Oath. **Ask: What are some of the rules in the Hippocratic Oath?** *(Doctors should do their best to help patients. They should protect patients' privacy.)* AL

Have students complete the Lesson 2 Review.

CLOSE & REFLECT

Have each student make a booklet about the three ideas he or she likes best from Socrates, Plato,and Aristotle. In their booklets, students should explain the ideas and discuss how the ideas apply to their own lives. AL

LESSON 2 REVIEW ANSWERS

1. A person could use rhetoric when giving presentations in class or in debates, or when participating in various club or volunteer activities.
2. Similarity: Plato and Aristotle were both interested in government. Differences: Plato didn't believe in democracy; he believed in rule by philosopher-kings. Aristotle believed that the best government has elements of monarchy, oligarchy, and democracy.
3. The oath is a code of ethics and behavior that physicians agree to uphold in their professional lives.
4. The three most important and famous philosophers in ancient Greece were Socrates, Plato, and Aristotle. Socrates was the teacher of Plato. Plato was the teacher of Aristotle. Answers may vary on what the three have in common, but students may say they all used the Socratic method, they all sought to find the truth about life and the world, and they all enjoyed teaching their ideas.
5. Answers will vary but may include Socrates, Plato, Aristotle, Herodotus, Thucydides, Thales, Pythagoras, and Hippocrates. Students should note at least one key idea the thinker is known for and explain why they think that contribution is important or valuable.

ANSWERS, p. 227

CRITICAL THINKING Answers will vary but should include that he probably would have discovered that water contains living organisms.

✔ PROGRESS CHECK Herodotus is considered the "father of history" because he was the first historian to distinguish fact from fiction. He questioned many people to get his information, and he investigated the truthfulness of his sources.

ENGAGE

Bellringer Tell students that in this lesson they will read two arguments about whether Socrates was guilty of misleading the youth of Athens—for which he suffered the death penalty. The argument that he was guilty is based on official accusations by three people. The opinion that he was not guilty is offered in a quotation from Socrates that was recorded later by Plato.

Remind students that Socrates did not write down any of his own ideas. We only know what he said and thought about this and other issues from what Plato and other philosophers wrote later. The primary sources here are from those written materials. Before studying the first argument, ask students to jot down whether they think Socrates was guilty. Make sure that students understand that the stakes for Socrates were high. If found guilty, he would be put to death.

TEACH & ASSESS

R Reading Skills

Paraphrasing Ask a volunteer to read the introductory paragraphs that give the background for the arguments. Make sure that students understand the events leading up to the trial. Then ask another volunteer to read aloud the "Yes" argument. As a class, paraphrase the primary-source material. Make sure all students understand the source material. **Ask:** **What did Socrates' accusers say Socrates had done?** *(He persuaded sons that he could make them wiser than their fathers, and he pointed out that the sons could sue their fathers and have them imprisoned.)* **Ask:** **Why was teaching the young men of Athens to question their parents a serious offense?** *(Students should understand that encouraging young people to question their parents was seen as a way to undermine authority and as a threat to civil order. Many considered Socrates' actions to be dangerous to the well-being of Athens.)* AL ELL

C Critical Thinking Skills

Making Connections Discuss the ways in which an adult can influence young people. **Ask:** **Which adults in your life influence what you think and how you behave? Are those people close family members, people you know in the community, or famous people you admire? How do they influence you?** *(Students' answers will vary but should include a reasoned analysis of which adults in their lives influence them and how students are influenced.)* Close this part of the lesson by asking student volunteers to summarize the "Yes" argument. Take a poll to see which students were influenced by the argument. Write the results on the board, and leave the results up during the discussion of the opposing argument.

What Do You Think? CCSS

Did Socrates Commit Treason?

After Athens lost the Peloponnesian War, there was a period of political disorder in the city-state. Athenian leaders restricted free speech to help keep peace and order in Athens.

Socrates was critical of the decision to limit free speech. He taught his students to question everything and to think for themselves. The Athenian leaders felt his criticisms were a threat. They thought that his influence with the young people was dangerous. They accused Socrates of misleading students by teaching them to question authority. Following a trial, Socrates was found guilty of treason and sentenced to death.

Yes W

PRIMARY SOURCE

"Socrates is guilty of . . . corrupting [misguiding] the young. Did not Socrates cause his associates to despise the established laws. . . . [His] [w]ords . . . tended to incite the young to contemn [to treat with scorn] the established constitution, rendering them violent and headstrong. . . . Socrates taught sons to pour contumely [harsh criticism] upon their fathers by persuading his young friends that he could make them wiser than their sires [fathers], or by pointing out that the law allowed a son to sue his father for aberration [unsoundness] of mind, and to imprison him."

—Socrates' accusers, Meletus, Anytus, and Lycon, quoted in *The Memorabilia: Recollections of Socrates* by Xenophon (translated by Henry Graham Daykns)

Freedom of speech was not guaranteed in ancient Greece. Citizens gathered daily to discuss current issues.

North Wind/North Wind Picture Archives

228

networks Online Teaching Options

GAME

Column Game: Socrates

Categorizing To review Socrates' ideas and beliefs and how they were different from those of other philosophers of the time, have students complete the game in which they sort the philosophies and characteristics of Socrates and the Sophists. Ask the following question, and write students' responses on the whiteboard. **Ask:** **Other than the ideas listed in the game, what ideas did Socrates have, and what did he believe in?** *(Answers will vary but could include: created Socratic method of questioning; wanted students to think for themselves and form their own opinions; believed that all real knowledge was within each person.)*

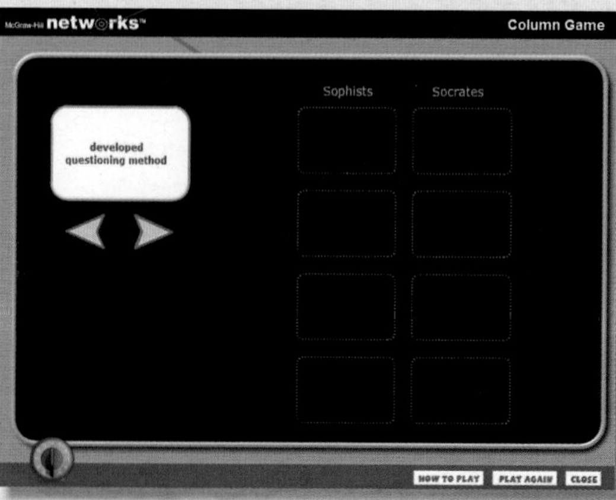

No W

PRIMARY SOURCE

Defending himself before a jury, Socrates used his method of questioning, urging jury members to think critically. At his death, he was still committed to reason.

C

" Men of Athens, I honor and love you; but I shall obey God rather than you, and while I have life and strength I shall never cease from the practice and teaching of philosophy, exhorting [urging] anyone . . . I meet . . . saying: my friend—a citizen of the great and mighty and wise city of Athens,—are you not ashamed of heaping up [so much] money and honor and reputation, and caring so little about wisdom and truth and the greatest improvement of the soul, which you never regard or heed [pay attention to] at all? . . . For I do nothing but go about persuading you all, old and young alike, not to take thought for your persons and your properties, but . . . to care about the greatest improvement of the soul. . . . This is my teaching, and if this is the doctrine which corrupts the youth, I am a mischievous person. But if any one says that this is not my teaching, he is speaking an untruth. Wherefore, O men of Athens, I say to you . . . whichever you do, understand that I shall never alter my ways, not even if I have to die many times. "

—Socrates, as quoted in *Apology*, by Plato (translated by Benjamin Jowett)

The Print Collector/Heritage/Age fotostock

What Do You Think? DBQ

1. ***Explaining*** Socrates' accusers claim that he is teaching young people to question their constitution. Why do the accusers say this is an example of Socrates being a bad influence on the young? RH.6–8.1
2. ***Describing*** What does Socrates say is the main idea he teaches? RH.6–8.1, RH.6–8.9
3. ***Evaluating*** Who do you think makes the stronger argument, Socrates or his accusers? RH.6–8.1, RH.6–8.9

What Do You Think?

C Critical Thinking Skills

Evaluating Tell students that they will next read primary-source material arguing that Socrates was not guilty of misleading the youth of Athens. Repeat the same process with the "No" argument. First, read the argument aloud. Then, have a new volunteer paraphrase the "No" argument. Make sure all students understand the quotation. **Ask:** **What did Socrates say he was trying to persuade people to do?** *(to care about the improvement of their souls)* **Do you think that Socrates' defense is a good one?** *(Students' answers will vary. They should provide reasons for why they do or do not think the defense is a good one.)* Take another poll. This time, ask if students are convinced by the "No" argument, and write on the board how many students are convinced. Compare the No votes to the Yes votes from earlier. Discuss which side "won," based on the arguments in the text.

W Writing Skills

Argument Have students write an open letter to the people of Athens explaining why Socrates was guilty or why Socrates was innocent. Remind students to support their arguments with reasons and evidence and to make the letter as persuasive as possible. If necessary, review that persuasive writing involves stating an opinion and supporting it with reasons and evidence. Students should draw on the "Yes" and "No" primary sources for evidence. In addition, students should include emotional appeals as well as logical appeals. *(Students' letters will vary but should present their arguments logically. Students' letters should include reasons, evidence, and persuasive techniques.)*

CLOSE & REFLECT

Have students share their letters to the citizens of Athens by reading them aloud in small groups. Ask a few volunteers to share their letters with the whole class. Then have the class discuss whether they think Socrates was guilty. Ask students whether their original opinions changed after they studied the two arguments.

CHART

Graphic Organizer: Chain-of-Events Flowchart

Analyzing Primary Sources Show students the image of papyrus with writing by Herodotus. Ask a volunteer to read aloud the excerpt. If necessary, have the volunteer pause after each sentence or two to allow listening students to absorb and understand Herodotus's ideas. As a class, paraphrase Herodotus's words. Allow students time to answer the discussion question about Herodotus's purpose for writing history. Students should understand, from reading and listening to the excerpt, that Herodotus was interested in recording specific details of events that had an impact on history.

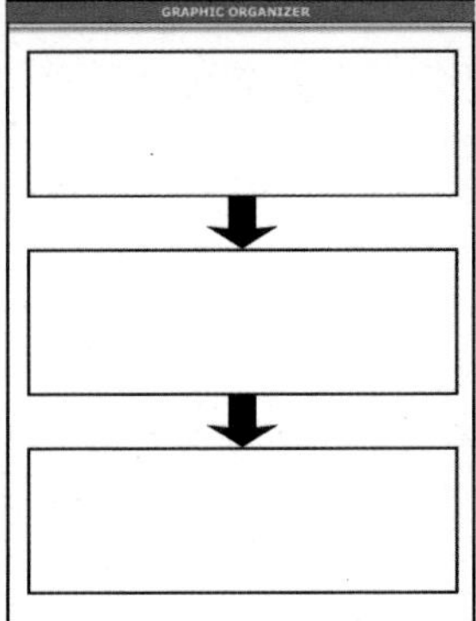

ANSWERS, p. 229

1. Socrates' accusers are saying that Socrates is setting a bad example for the youth by disagreeing with the current laws and that this influence also causes the young to question the law and become "violent and headstrong."
2. Socrates says the main idea he teaches is to care about wisdom, truth, and the improvement of the soul and to pay less attention to money, honor, and reputation.
3. Answers will vary, but students should point out that while Socrates' accusers make more specific claims, Socrates makes a more general argument, reaffirming his teaching doctrine of leading students to truth and wisdom through philosophy.

Alexander's Empire

ENGAGE

Bellringer Divide the class into four groups. For two of the groups, **ask:** What are some traits of a great military leader? Have these groups write their answers on a sheet of paper. *(Answers will vary but may include the following: must be brave, intelligent, able to inspire people to follow you, good at military strategy, and good at choosing generals.)* For the other two groups, **ask:** What are some traits of an effective ruler? *(Answers will vary but may include the following: must be able to inspire people to follow you, be good at choosing advisers, be able to get people to trust you, and be fair and just.)* Have groups share their responses and discuss the similarities and differences between the responses to each question. Tell students that in this lesson they will study the life of Alexander the Great and learn about his achievements as a ruler and a military leader. Review with students the traits of a great military leader compared with a great ruler.

TEACH & ASSESS

R Reading Skills

Summarizing After they read, ask students to summarize what Macedonia was like before King Philip II. **Ask:** How did Macedonia change under King Philip II? *(The kingdom became a major superpower for the first time.)*

C Critical Thinking Skills

Determining Cause and Effect Remind students that Athens, Sparta, and other Greek city-states fought one another during the Peloponnesian War. Point out that although the war was over by the time of Philip II, the city-states refused to work together. **Ask:** How did the Peloponnesian War help Philip conquer Greece? *(The city-states did not work together, so his army could defeat them more easily.)* AL

Lesson 3

Alexander's Empire

ESSENTIAL QUESTION *What are the characteristics of a leader?*

IT MATTERS BECAUSE

Strong leaders can bring change to society. Philip II and Alexander the Great, as strong leaders, spread many Greek ideas to conquered lands.

Philip II of Macedonia

GUIDING QUESTION *Why did Macedonia become powerful?*

As you learned earlier, the Persians set out to conquer the Greek city-states but failed. The Macedonians (ma•suh•DOH•nee•uhnz) were people who lived north of Greece. In the 300s B.C., they conquered Greece.

Conquering Greece

R The Macedonians were farmers. They raised sheep and horses and grew crops in their river valleys. For much of its history, Macedonia was not a very strong kingdom. Under King Philip II, however, Macedonia became a superpower in the ancient world.

As a young man, Philip had lived in Greece. He came to admire Greek culture and military skill. Philip became king of Macedonia in 359 B.C. He **created** a strong army. Philip planned to unite the Greek city-states under his rule and destroy the mighty Persian Empire. Philip trained a vast army of foot soldiers to fight like the Greeks. At this time, the Greek city-states were weak. C They had been divided by the Peloponnesian War. As a result, they could not defend themselves against Philip's powerful army.

Reading **HELP**DESK CCSS

Taking Notes: *Summarizing*

Use a diagram like this one to describe how Philip II and Alexander changed Greece. RH.6–8.2, RH.6–8.8

Content Vocabulary (Tier 3 Words)
- **cavalry**
- **Hellenistic Era**

networks Online Teaching Options

VIDEO

Building Alexander the Great's Empire

Summarizing Play the video about the life and achievements of Alexander the Great. As students watch, encourage them to note important details about Alexander and his efforts. Then have students work in small groups to write summaries of their notes. Invite student volunteers to share their summaries with the class.

See page 209E for other online activities.

ANSWER, p. 230

TAKING NOTES: ended freedom of Greek city-states, defeated Persian Empire, expanded the economy, spread Greek culture, exposed Greece to Eastern cultures

Philip took control of the city-states one by one. He defeated some city-states in battle, and he bribed the leaders of others to surrender. A few city-states **voluntarily** agreed to join with Macedonia.

V Many Greeks worried about Philip's plans. Demosthenes (dih•MAHS•thuh•neez) was an Athenian who opposed Philip. He was a lawyer and one of Athens's great public speakers. Demosthenes warned the Athenians that Philip was a threat to Greek freedom. He urged all the city-states to join together to fight the Macedonians:

C PRIMARY SOURCE

> "Remember only that Philip is our enemy, that he has long been robbing and insulting us . . . that the future depends on ourselves, and that unless we are willing to fight him there we shall perhaps be forced to fight here. . . . You need not speculate [guess] about the future except to assure yourselves that it will be disastrous unless you face the facts and are willing to do your duty."
>
> —Demosthenes, "The First Philippic" in *Orations of Demosthenes*

By the time the Greeks tried to unite, it was too late. The Athenians joined with Thebes and a few other free city-states. They battled Philip's army, but they could not stop his invasion. In 338 B.C., the Greeks and the Macedonians fought one last major battle. At the Battle of Chaeronea (kehr•uh•NEE•uh), Philip's army crushed the Greeks. Philip now ruled most of Greece.

☑ PROGRESS CHECK

Summarizing How was Philip II able to gain control over most of Greece?

Alexander Takes Over

GUIDING QUESTION *What were Alexander's goals as a ruler?*

After conquering Greece, Philip hoped to lead the Greeks and Macedonians to war against the Persian Empire. Before Philip could carry out his plans, however, he was killed. His son Alexander became king.

Alexander was only 20 when he became ruler of Macedonia and Greece, but Philip had carefully prepared his son for the job. By age 16, Alexander was serving as a commander in the Macedonian army. He quickly won the respect of his soldiers.

Thinking Like a HISTORIAN

Researching on the Internet

Philip II of Macedonia admired the art and ideas of the Greeks—and their armies. Philip set out to take over the Greek city-states. Why do you think Philip wanted to conquer the Greeks rather than be allies with them? Use the Internet to find reliable sources about Philip's goals. Then present them to your class. For more information about using the Internet for research, read *What Does a Historian Do?*

▶ CRITICAL THINKING

Finding the Main Idea Demosthenes spoke out against Philip. Why was Demosthenes opposed to Philip's plans?

Academic Vocabulary (Tier 2 Words)

create to make or produce something; to bring something into existence

voluntarily by choice or free will; willingly

V Visual Skills

Integrating Visual Information Point out the image of Demosthenes to students. Explain to the class that when Demosthenes was a boy, he spoke with a stammer and had bad pronunciation. He practiced speaking with pebbles in his mouth and recited verses when he was running out of breath or already out of breath. He also practiced speaking in front of a large mirror. He is considered to be one of the most famous orators of all time. **Ask:** **What characteristics did Demosthenes display that helped make him a great orator and leader?** *(Answers may include that he displayed perseverance, the willingness to work hard, and ingenuity [cleverness].)*

C Critical Thinking Skills

Analyzing Primary Sources Read the primary-source excerpt from Demosthenes' speech aloud for students. Work with the class to paraphrase Demosthenes' words in modern language. **Ask:** **What main warning did Demosthenes want listeners to understand?** *(The city-states needed to work together against Philip now, or they would all be conquered.)*

AL **ELL** **Verbal/Linguistic**

GRAPHIC ORGANIZER

Taking Notes: *Summarizing:* Alexander and Philip II

Summarizing Have students fill in the Taking Notes graphic organizer on how Phillip II and Alexander changed Greece. Remind students that they may consult their textbooks for details and information for their organizers.

See page 209E for other online activities.

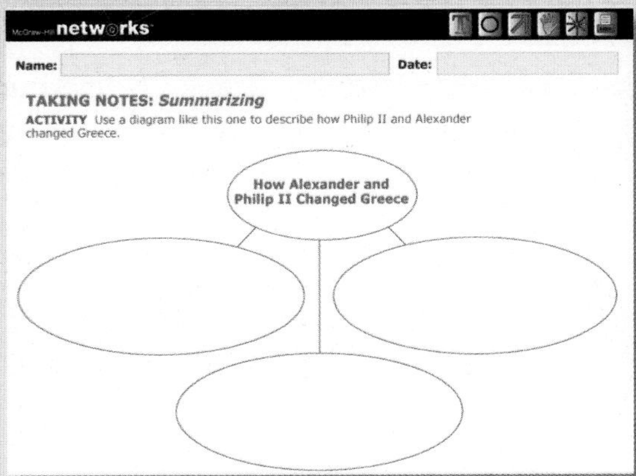

ANSWERS, p. 231

Thinking Like a Historian Answers will vary, but most students should mention that the Greek city-states were not unified and their armies were weak, so they were an easy target; Philip was an empire-builder; Philip's ambitions to be a ruler made him more interested in conquering Greece than in being a friendly ally and neighbor; and Philip needed to conquer Greece so he could topple the Persian Empire.

CRITICAL THINKING Demosthenes was worried about the Greeks' loss of freedom.

☑ **PROGRESS CHECK** The Greek city-states were not unified, and they were weakened by the Peloponnesian War. Philip conquered some city-states and bribed others. Some willingly joined him.

Alexander's Empire

V Visual Skills

Reading a Map Have students find the map "Alexander's Empire" in their textbooks. **Ask:**

- What do the arrows and red lines represent? *(the path Alexander and his armies took)*
- What modern countries make up the eastern borders of the empire? *(Afghanistan, Pakistan, Uzbekistan, Turkmenistan)*
- What geographic feature marks the eastern reach of Alexander's empire? *(the Indus River)*
- Near what river was the Battle of Gaugamela fought? *(the Tigris River)*

C Critical Thinking Skills

Hypothesizing Point out that Alexander was strongly influenced by his father. **Ask:** Do you think that following in the footsteps of one's parents was more common in Alexander's day than it is now? Why? *(Answers will vary. Possible answer: Yes, it was probably more common in Alexander's day. In those days, most people did the same kind of work their parents did. Young people now have many more choices than people did in Alexander's time.)* BL

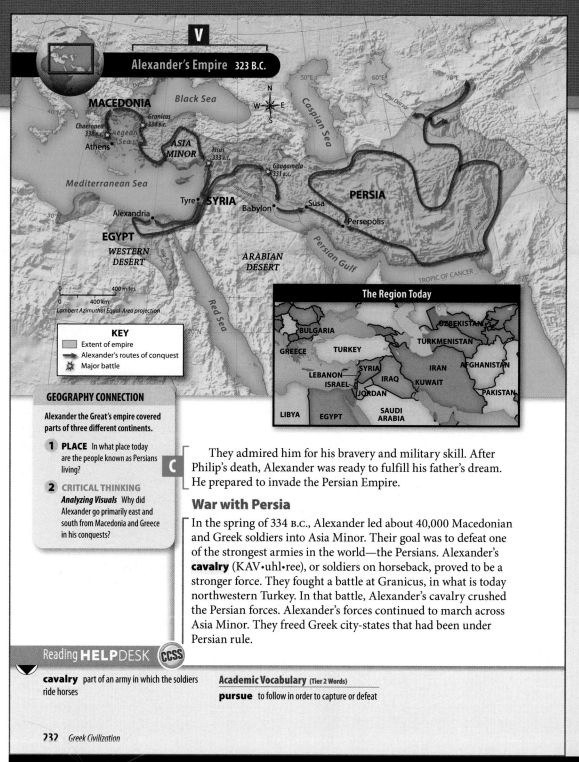

V

Alexander's Empire 323 B.C.

MACEDONIA
Black Sea
Caspian Sea
Danube R.
Granicus 334 B.C.
Chaeronea 338 B.C.
Aegean Sea
Athens
ASIA MINOR
Issus 333 B.C.
Gaugamela 331 B.C.
Mediterranean Sea
Tyre
SYRIA
Babylon
Susa
PERSIA
Persepolis
Alexandria
EGYPT
WESTERN DESERT
Nile R.
ARABIAN DESERT
Persian Gulf
Red Sea
Amu Darya
Indus R.
Euphrates R.
Tigris R.
TROPIC OF CANCER
40°N
30°N
20°N
50°E
60°E
70°E
0 400 miles
0 400 km
Lambert Azimuthal Equal-Area projection

KEY
Extent of empire
Alexander's routes of conquest
Major battle

The Region Today

BULGARIA
GREECE
TURKEY
UZBEKISTAN
TURKMENISTAN
SYRIA
LEBANON
ISRAEL
IRAQ
IRAN
AFGHANISTAN
KUWAIT
JORDAN
PAKISTAN
LIBYA
EGYPT
SAUDI ARABIA

GEOGRAPHY CONNECTION

Alexander the Great's empire covered parts of three different continents.

1. **PLACE** In what place today are the people known as Persians living?
2. **CRITICAL THINKING** ***Analyzing Visuals*** Why did Alexander go primarily east and south from Macedonia and Greece in his conquests?

C They admired him for his bravery and military skill. After Philip's death, Alexander was ready to fulfill his father's dream. He prepared to invade the Persian Empire.

War with Persia

In the spring of 334 B.C., Alexander led about 40,000 Macedonian and Greek soldiers into Asia Minor. Their goal was to defeat one of the strongest armies in the world—the Persians. Alexander's **cavalry** (KAV•uhl•ree), or soldiers on horseback, proved to be a stronger force. They fought a battle at Granicus, in what is today northwestern Turkey. In that battle, Alexander's cavalry crushed the Persian forces. Alexander's forces continued to march across Asia Minor. They freed Greek city-states that had been under Persian rule.

Reading **HELP**DESK CCSS

cavalry part of an army in which the soldiers ride horses

Academic Vocabulary (Tier 2 Words)

pursue to follow in order to capture or defeat

232 *Greek Civilization*

ANSWERS, p. 232

GEOGRAPHY CONNECTION

1. People in Iran are known as Persians because Iran is the modern name for the main area that was known as Persia.
2. **CRITICAL THINKING** Alexander wanted to invade and conquer the Persian Empire, which was located to the east and to the south of Greece and Macedonia.

networks *Online Teaching Options*

WORKSHEET

Guided Reading Activity: Greek Civilization—Alexander's Empire

Speculating Have students access the Guided Reading Worksheet for this lesson. Review the section *Alexander Takes Over* with the class. Have students predict how successful Alexander the Great was likely to be at fulfilling his father's goals. Assign the complete worksheet as homework.

See page 209E for other online activities.

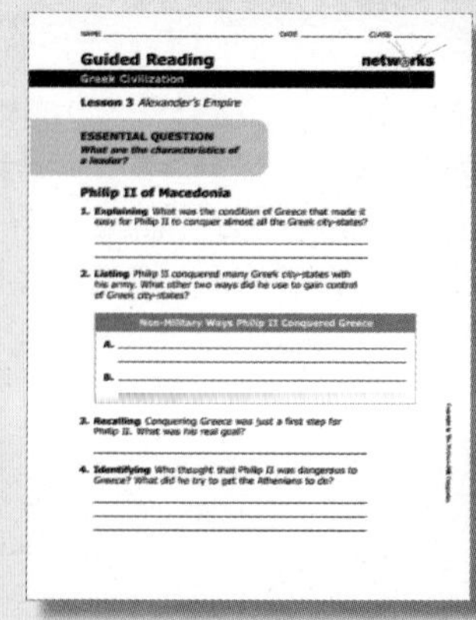
Guided Reading
Greek Civilization
Lesson 3 Alexander's Empire
ESSENTIAL QUESTION
Philip II of Macedonia

A year and a half later, in November 333 B.C., Alexander fought the next major battle against the Persians at Issus (IH•suhs), in Syria. Once again, Alexander's military skills resulted in a victory. The Persian king Darius III was forced to flee from Issus.

Alexander and his troops did not **pursue** Darius, though. Instead, they moved south along the Mediterranean coast. In early 331 B.C., they conquered Egypt. Alexander built a new city in Egypt and named it Alexandria (a•lihg•ZAN•dree•uh) after himself. As a center of business and trade, Alexandria became one of the most important cities of the ancient world. It remains a vital city in the Mediterranean region today. R

In late 331 B.C., Alexander's army headed back north. He turned eastward and invaded Mesopotamia, now ruled by the Persians. Alexander's army smashed Darius's forces at Gaugamela (gaw•guh•MEE•luh), near the Tigris River. After this victory, Alexander's army took over the rest of the Persian Empire.

After he conquered Persia, Alexander did not stop. In 327 B.C., he marched his army into northwestern India. There he fought a number of bloody battles. His soldiers were tired of constant fighting and refused to go farther. Alexander agreed to lead them home.

On the return march, the troops crossed a desert in what is now southern Iran. Heat and thirst killed thousands of soldiers. At one point, a group of soldiers found a little water and scooped it up in a helmet. They offered the water to Alexander. According to a Greek historian:

PRIMARY SOURCE

> "Alexander, with a word of thanks for the gift, took the helmet, and, in full view of his troops, poured the water on the ground. So extraordinary was the effect of this action that the water wasted by Alexander was as good as a drink for every man in the army." W
>
> —*The Campaigns of Alexander* by Arrian, tr. by Aubrey De Sélincourt

At the far left of this battle scene is Alexander the Great, who fought alongside his soldiers.

▶ CRITICAL THINKING
Hypothesizing What was Alexander trying to show when he threw water on the ground in front of his thirsty soldiers?

R Reading Skills

Calculating Have a volunteer read about Alexander the Great's conquests. Remind students that dates shown with *B.C.* count down toward zero. **Ask:**

- **In what year did Alexander begin his conquests?** *(334 B.C.)*
- **In what year did Alexander end his conquests?** *(327 B.C.)*
- **How many years did Alexander's campaign last?** *(seven years)* AL ELL **Logical/Mathematical**

W Writing Skills

Narrative Read with the class the primary-source description of Alexander's actions in the desert. Invite volunteers to share how they would have felt about Alexander's actions if they had been members of his army. Remind students of the leadership traits that they discussed at the beginning of the lesson. Have them share their ideas about whether or not Alexander was a good leader. Then have students write a paragraph or two in which they retell the story of Alexander's army in the desert from the perspective of a soldier. Tell them to include details about what the soldier might have thought about the quality of Alexander's leadership.

CHART

Rise of Alexander the Great

Organizing Begin by drawing a two-column chart on the board. Have students suggest facts and details about Alexander the Great. Categorize them under either "Military Achievements" or "Leadership Qualities." Allow students to refer to their textbooks. Then have students use the chart to complete the flowchart titled "Rise of Alexander the Great."

See page 209E for other online activities.

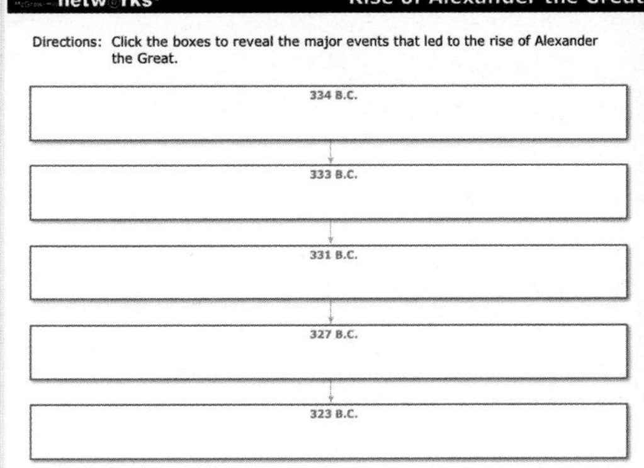

ANSWER, p. 233

CRITICAL THINKING He was showing that he was no better than his soldiers; if they did not have enough water for everyone to drink, then he would not drink either. He inspired them to continue, despite the hardships.

Alexander's Empire

V Visual Skills

Reading a Map Point out the map key and the scale to students. Have them identify the regions controlled by each kingdom on the map. **Ask:** Which kingdom controlled the most territory? *(the Seleucid kingdom)* AL Visual/Spatial

T Technology Skills

Making Presentations Have students work in small groups to design a Web site home page for Alexander the Great. The page should explain why Alexander is considered "great" and should include images, drawings, and text that represent his achievements. Have students present their designs to the class. Interpersonal Visual/Spatial

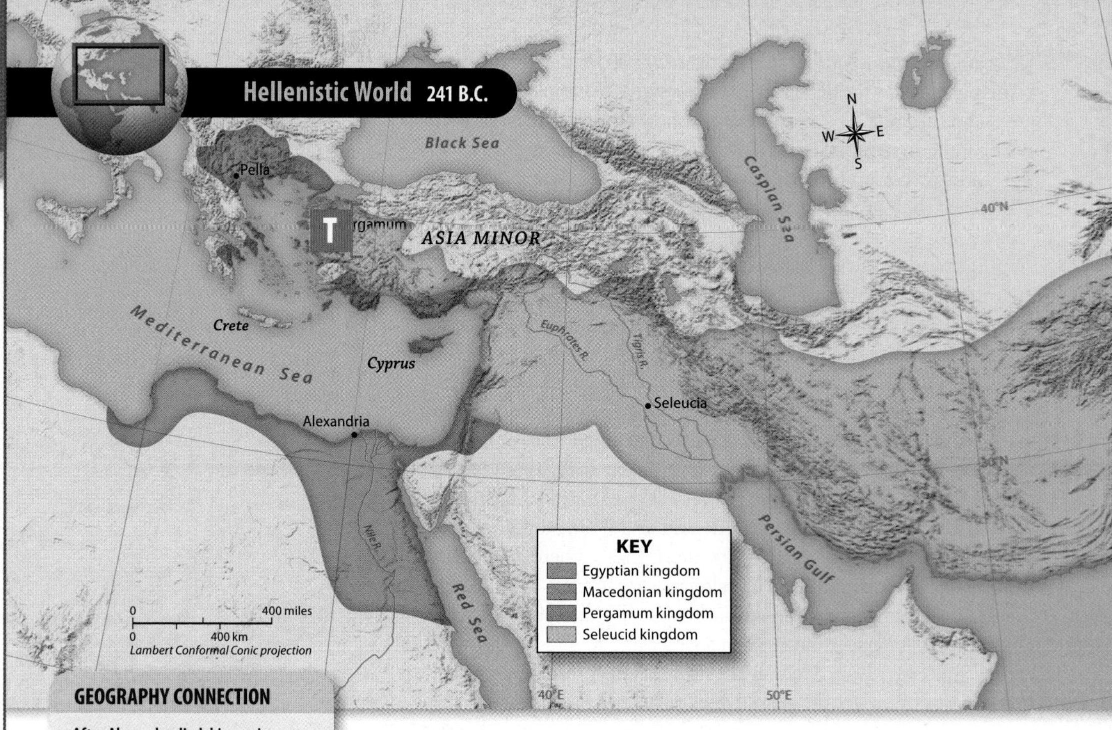

GEOGRAPHY CONNECTION

After Alexander died, his empire was divided up into four separate kingdoms, which were all part of the Hellenistic World.

1. **LOCATION** In which kingdom was Greece mostly located?
2. **CRITICAL THINKING** ***Analyzing Visuals*** How many different continents was Alexander's empire on, and which continents were they?

In 323 B.C., Alexander returned to Babylon, one of the Persian cities now under his control. The hardships of the journey had wrecked his health. Suffering from wounds and worn out by fever, Alexander died. He was only 32 years old.

✓ PROGRESS CHECK

Explaining Why was the Battle of Gaugamela so important to Alexander?

Alexander's Legacy

GUIDING QUESTION *How successful was Alexander in achieving his goals?*

Alexander was a great general who feared nothing. He rode into battle ahead of his soldiers and marched into unknown lands. The key to Alexander's courage may have been his early education. As a boy, Alexander read the Greek epics. His role model was Homer's warrior-hero Achilles. Today, Alexander is called Alexander the Great.

Alexander's armies extended Greek rule over a vast region. They

Reading HELPDESK (CCSS)

Hellenistic Era the time period following the death of Alexander during which Greek culture spread through the known world

Reading Strategy: *Summarizing*

When you finish reading a section of text about an important person or event in history, write a paragraph that tells what the person did or what happened. Use your own words. Then compare your summary to the text and check any facts.

ANSWERS, p. 234

✓ PROGRESS CHECK It was the battle in which his forces defeated the Persians and gave Alexander control of the Persian Empire.

GEOGRAPHY CONNECTION

1. Greece was mostly located in the Macedonian kingdom.
2. CRITICAL THINKING Alexander's empire was on three continents: Europe, Asia, and Africa.

READING STRATEGY Students' paragraphs should have a topic sentence and contain facts to support it.

networks *Online Teaching Options*

WHITEBOARD ACTIVITY

The Achievements of Alexander the Great

Analyzing Maps Have students complete the activity "The Achievements of Alexander the Great" to match Alexander's achievements with the places on the map where the achievements were accomplished.

See page 209E for other online activities.

networks The Achievements of Alexander the Great

Directions: Drag the number for an achievement of Alexander the Great onto the correct spot on the map.

1. Becomes king of Greece and Macedonia
2. Frees Greek city-states under Persian rule
3. Forces Darius to flee
4. Conquers Egypt
5. Founds major city that becomes important center of ancient world
6. Defeats Darius in Mesopotamia
7. Conquers remainder of Persia
8. Expands his empire to its easternmost point

spread Greek language, ideas, art, and architecture throughout Southwest Asia and Egypt. Alexander's successes marked the beginning of the **Hellenistic Era** (heh•luh•NIHS•tihk EHR•uh). *Hellenistic* means "like the Greeks." The Hellenistic Era refers to when Greek culture spread to the non-Greek peoples that Alexander had conquered.

A Divided Empire

C Alexander planned to unite Macedonians, Greeks, Egyptians, and Asians in his new empire. His dream of creating one great empire, however, didn't last. After Alexander died, his generals divided the empire into four separate kingdoms. These kingdoms were Macedonia, Pergamum (PUHR•guh•muhm), Egypt, and the Seleucid (suh•LOO•suhd) Empire.

The Hellenistic Kings

People who served in the governments of the Hellenistic kings had to speak Greek. The Hellenistic kings preferred to give jobs to Greeks and Macedonians. In this way, they were able to keep control of the governments.

By 100 B.C., Alexandria, in Egypt, was the largest city in the Mediterranean world. It included two excellent harbors and a towering lighthouse. It stood on a harbor island with a burning flame at its top. The library at Alexandria had the largest collection of writings in ancient times.

The Hellenistic kings also created new cities and military posts. These new Greek communities needed architects, artists, engineers, and philosophers. Hellenistic rulers encouraged Greeks and Macedonians to settle in the conquered lands. These colonies spread Greek culture widely—into Egypt and India.

V **The lighthouse at Alexandria was one of the Seven Wonders of the Ancient World. It was completed about 280 B.C. and stood on an island in the harbor.**

▶ **CRITICAL THINKING**

Analyzing Why was a fire kept burning on top of the lighthouse at night?

Archives Charmet/Bridgeman Art Library

 **PROGRESS CHECK**

Explaining What happened to Alexander's empire after he died?

LESSON 3 REVIEW (CCSS)

Review Vocabulary (Tier 3 Words)

1. Why was the *cavalry* an important part of Alexander's army? RH.6–8.4

Answer the Guiding Questions

2. ***Summarizing*** What did Demosthenes want the Greek city-states to do about the Macedonians? Did they follow his advice? RH.6–8.2
3. ***Describing*** What is the Hellenistic Era? RH.6–8.2
4. ***Identifying*** What were some of the policies of Alexander and the Hellenistic kings that helped to spread Greek culture throughout the empire? RH.6–8.2
5. **ARGUMENT** Alexander admired the heroes of the Trojan War so much that he traveled with a copy of Homer's *Iliad*. What book would you carry if you traveled as Alexander did? Write a description of your choice and explain your reasons for it. WHST.6–8.10

LESSON 3 REVIEW ANSWERS

1. Alexander's soldiers on horseback—his cavalry—were a strong force. At Granicus, they crushed the local Persian forces, leading to the final downfall of the Persian Empire.
2. Demosthenes wanted the Greek city-states to unite to fight Philip and the Macedonians. The Athenians finally did try to unite, but it was too late.
3. The Hellenistic Era refers to a time when Greek language and ideas spread to the non-Greek peoples that Alexander had conquered.
4. Alexander and the Hellenistic rulers had ambitious building programs, creating new cities and military posts. They recruited Greeks and Macedonians to settle in the conquered lands and work as artists, architects, engineers, writers, philosophers, government officials, and soldiers.
5. Answers will vary, but students should name a book they value or admire and clearly state the reasons they would find it valuable to have it with them all the time and in different life situations they encounter.

C Critical Thinking Skills

Evaluating Discuss with students Alexander's goals and what happened to his empire after he died. Lead students in a debate over whether Alexander's goals were truly achieved. Encourage students to support their ideas with facts and evidence from the text. BL

V Visual Skills

Analyzing Images Direct students' attention to the image of the lighthouse of Alexandria. **Ask: How does this building show Greek influences? What about it seems more Egyptian than Greek?** *(Students may note the columns and the style of the urn at the top; students may see Egyptian style in the plain, large stones at the base and the pyramid shape.)* AL **Visual/Spatial**

Have students complete the Lesson 3 Review.

CLOSE & REFLECT

Ask volunteers to summarize the impact of Alexander the Great on the ancient world. Suggest that students first summarize Alexander's military exploits and then his impact as a ruler of a great empire.

ANSWERS, p. 235

CRITICAL THINKING to guide ships into the harbor

PROGRESS CHECK It was divided into four kingdoms: Egypt, Macedonia, Pergamum, and the Seleucid Empire.

Hellenistic Culture

ENGAGE

Bellringer Have students look at the images in this lesson in the sections on the arts and writers in the Hellenistic Era. **Ask:** **How are the sculptures of human figures different from those in the Golden Age of Greece?** *(The figures are more realistic. They show more emotion and movement.)* Tell students that a similar change occurred in the writing of the Hellenistic Era. For example, dramas told stories about ordinary people, not gods and heroes. Discuss with the class how the arts were supported in the Hellenistic Era by the rulers of the kingdoms and by wealthy citizens who were eager to import Greek culture to their lands and especially to the new cities they were building. Explain to students that in this lesson they will learn about artists, writers, playwrights, philosophers, scientists, and mathematicians in the Hellenistic world.

TEACH & ASSESS

R Reading Skills

Determining Word Meanings Clarify the meaning of the word *Hellenistic* with students. Tell the class that the Greeks called their peninsula *Hellas* and called themselves the Hellenes. Point out that the word *Hellenistic* is an adjective that shares the same root as these words. Students should understand that the Hellenistic Era was a continuation and extension of the Classical Greek Era that they have been studying. AL ELL

C Critical Thinking Skills

Identifying Points of View Tell students that Greek culture spread over a large region during the Hellenistic Era. Explain that one way historians can see evidence of this spread today is by studying the Greek-style buildings that Hellenistic rulers built in their cities. **Ask:** **What point of view did Hellenistic rulers have about Greek culture?** *(They admired Greek culture and Greek cities, such as Athens, and wanted their cities to reflect that culture.)*

ANSWER, p. 236

TAKING NOTES: Eratosthenes: determined that Earth is round; measured Earth's circumference, distance to sun, distance to moon; concluded that the sun is larger than the moon. **Euclid:** described plane geometry. **Archimedes:** worked on solid geometry, established the science of physics, calculated the value of *pi*, invented machinery and weapons.

networks *There's More Online!*

- **CHART**
  - *Winged Victory* and *Unique Forms of Continuity in Space* (sculpture)
  - Aristarchus' Model of Solar System
  - Contributions of Greek Scientists
  - Eratosthenes and Earth's Circumference
- **GRAPHIC ORGANIZER** Achievements of Greek Scientists
- **SLIDE SHOW** Story of *Pi*

Moon
90°
x°
Earth

Lesson 4

Hellenistic Culture

ESSENTIAL QUESTION *How do new ideas change the way people live?*

It Matters Because

Hellenistic cities became centers of learning and culture. Philosophy and the arts flourished, and new discoveries that were made are still important to us today.

Hellenistic Arts

GUIDING QUESTION *How did Greek culture spread during the Hellenistic Era?*

R During the Hellenistic Era, philosophers, scientists, poets, and writers moved to the new Greek cities of Southwest Asia and Egypt. Alexandria, for example, served as the Greek capital of Egypt and was a major center of learning. Many scholars were attracted to Alexandria's library. It contained more than 500,000 scrolls. Alexandria also had a museum that attracted scholars to do research. The city's reputation as a place of learning and its location on the Mediterranean Sea contributed to Alexandria's economic growth. Today, Alexandria remains a vital city in Egypt where nearly 4 million people live and work.

Buildings and Statues

Greek architects served an important role in expanding Alexander's empire. They planned public building projects for new cities that were being founded and for old cities that C were being rebuilt. Hellenistic kings wanted to make these cities like Athens and other cultural centers in Greece. They were willing to spend huge amounts of money to do so. These

Reading **HELP**DESK CCSS

Taking Notes: *Describing*

Use a chart like this one to describe the achievements of the Greek scientists. RH.6–8.2

Greek Scientist	Achievements
Eratosthenes	
Euclid	
Archimedes	

Content Vocabulary (Tier 3 Words)

- **Epicureanism**
- **Stoicism**
- **circumference**
- **plane geometry**
- **solid geometry**

networks ***Online Teaching Options***

VIDEO

Alexander the Great's Empire

Speculating Play for students the video about Alexander the Great's conquests. Ask students what they recall about Alexander the Great's achievements. Invite students to speculate about how Alexander was personally responsible for the spread of Greek culture far from the original Greek city-states.

See page 209F for other online activities.

kings wanted to line the streets with Greek temples, theaters, and baths.

Hellenistic kings and other wealthy citizens hired Greek sculptors, who created thousands of statues for towns and cities. Hellenistic sculptors proved as talented as the sculptors of Greece's Golden Age. These sculptors, however, developed new styles. They did not carve ideal figures to reflect beauty and harmony. Instead, they showed people in a more realistic style. They even created statues that looked angry or sad.

Hellenistic Writers

Hellenistic rulers also supported talented writers. As a result, poets and writers produced a large amount of literature during the Hellenistic Era. Very little of this writing has survived today.

One work that we do know about is an epic poem called *Argonautica*. Written by Appolonius (a•puh•LOH•nee•uhs) of Rhodes (ROHDZ), the poem tells the story of Jason and his band of heroes. You may have read or seen a modern version of this poem, often called *Jason and the Argonauts*. Jason and his band sail the seas **seeking** a ram with a golden fleece. Along the way, they have many adventures. Another poet, Theocritus (thee•AH•kruh•tuhs), wrote short poems about the beauty of nature.

C

Athens remained the center for Greek theater. There, writers of plays produced comedies, not tragedies. These comedies are known as Greek New Comedy. However, the comedies of the Hellenistic Era were not like the comedies of Greece's Golden Age. Those of the Hellenistic Era did not poke fun at political leaders. Instead, the plays told stories about love and relationships of ordinary people. One of the best known of the new playwrights was Menander (muh • NAN • duhr). He lived from 343 B.C. to 291 B.C. and is considered the most important poet of Greek New Comedy. The temple of Apollo at Delphi had an inscription that read "Know thyself." Making a humorous comment on that inscription, Menander said "This 'Know Yourself' is a silly proverb in some ways; To know the man next door is a much more useful rule." His works were later adapted by Roman writers. Through his works, Menander influenced the development of European comedy during the Renaissance (reh • nuh • ZAHNTS) and even comedy today.

✓ PROGRESS CHECK

Explaining How did Greek sculpture and drama change during the Hellenistic Era?

V

Hellenistic artists were masters at capturing movement and emotion. This statue, *Winged Victory*, seems to be walking forcefully forward.

▶ CRITICAL THINKING

Drawing Conclusions Washington D.C.'s buildings showcase many statues in the Greek style. Why do you think so many of them are in this style?

Academic Vocabulary (Tier 2 Words)

seek to search for

V Visual Skills

Analyzing Images Point out to the class the image of the sculpture *Winged Victory at Samothrace*. Have a volunteer read aloud the caption that accompanies the image. **Ask:** **How does *Winged Victory at Samothrace* reflect the Hellenistic culture of its time?** *(Answers will vary but may include that it has a heroic feel and it portrays strength and powerful, dynamic movement.)* **Visual/Spatial**

C Critical Thinking Skills

Contrasting Have students reread the section on Greek theater during the Hellenistic Era. **Ask:** **How was the theater different in the Hellenistic Era from the way it was during Greece's Golden Age?** *(Playwrights did not write tragedies, only comedies, known collectively as Greek New Comedy; the comedies did not make fun of political leaders; they were about ordinary people.)* BL

GRAPHIC ORGANIZER

Taking Notes: *Describing:* Greek Scientists and Their Achievements

Identifying Tell students they will complete the Taking Notes graphic organizer by adding the achievements of the three scientists listed. Students may draw on what they already know to begin filling in the chart. Later, they may add details from their textbooks and the information they learn from the chart "Contributions of Greek Scientists."

See page 209F for other online activities.

networks

Name: Date:

TAKING NOTES: *Describing*

ACTIVITY Use a chart like this one to describe the achievements of the Greek scientists.

Greek Scientist	Achievements
Eratosthenes	
Euclid	
Archimedes	

ANSWERS, p. 237

CRITICAL THINKING The classical style is associated with formality and realism.

✓ PROGRESS CHECK Sculpture became more realistic, showing people as they really are. Dramas were not produced—only comedies, which were written about ordinary people rather than about political leaders.

R Reading Skills

Stating After students read, ask them to state the philosophy of Epicureanism. Remind students that Epicureanism was one way in which people tried to live a good life. **Ask: What were the two main lessons that Epicurus taught about life?** *(The goal of life is finding happiness. This can be done by avoiding pain.)*

C Critical Thinking Skills

Contrasting Discuss with students the philosophy of Stoicism versus Epicureanism. **Ask: How did Stoicism differ from Epicureanism?** *(Stoics thought happiness came from using reason, but Epicureans believed that it come from avoiding pain.)*

Thinkers and Scientists

GUIDING QUESTION *What ideas and discoveries emerged during the Hellenistic Era?*

During the Hellenistic Era, Athens continued to support Greek philosophers. These philosophers tried to answer questions such as, "What is a good life?" and "How can people find peace of mind in a troubled world?" The two most important Hellenistic philosophers were Epicurus and Zeno.

Who Was Epicurus?

R Epicurus founded a philosophy known as **Epicureanism** (eh•pih•kyu•REE•uh•nih•zuhm). He taught his students that finding happiness was the goal of life. He believed that the way to be happy was to avoid pain.

Today the word *epicurean* means the love of physical pleasure, such as good food or comfortable surroundings. For Epicurus, however, pleasure meant spending time with friends. It meant learning not to be upset about problems in life. Epicureans avoided worry. They limited their wants and lived simply.

Other astronomers would not believe Aristarchus when he stated that the solar system moved around the sun. This diagram shows his idea.

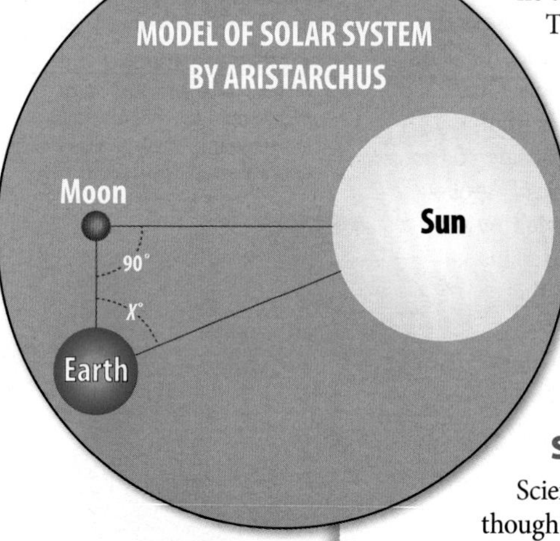

The Stoics

C A Phoenician thinker named Zeno developed a philosophy called **Stoicism** (STOH•uh•sih•zuhm). Zeno did not have the money to rent a lecture hall in which to teach. Instead, he taught at a building called the "painted porch". The Greek word for *porch* was *stoa*. The term "Stoicism" thus comes from the Greek word *stoa*.

The Stoics claimed that people who were guided by their emotions lived unhappy lives. They believed that happiness resulted from using reason. Sound thinking, they thought, should guide decisions. Today, the word *stoic* is used to describe someone who seems not affected by joy or sadness. Unlike Epicureans, Stoics thought people had a duty to serve their **community**. The ideas of the Stoics would later influence Roman thinkers.

Science and Mathematics

Science also flourished during the Hellenistic Era. Even though Hellenistic scientists used simple instruments, they performed many experiments and developed new theories.

Reading **HELP**DESK (CCSS)

Epicureanism the philosophy of Epicurus, stating that the purpose of life is to look for happiness and peace

Stoicism the philosophy of the Stoics who believed that people should not try to feel joy or sadness

Academic Vocabulary (Tier 2 Words)

community a group of various kinds of people living in a particular area or a common location

networks *Online Teaching Options*

WORKSHEET

Guided Reading Activity: Civilization—Hellenistic Culture

Categorizing Have students access the Guided Reading Worksheet for this lesson. Review the section *Thinkers and Scientists* with the class. Work with the whole class to begin the categorization chart about Hellenistic philosophies. Assign any remaining part of the worksheet as homework.

See page 209F for other online activities.

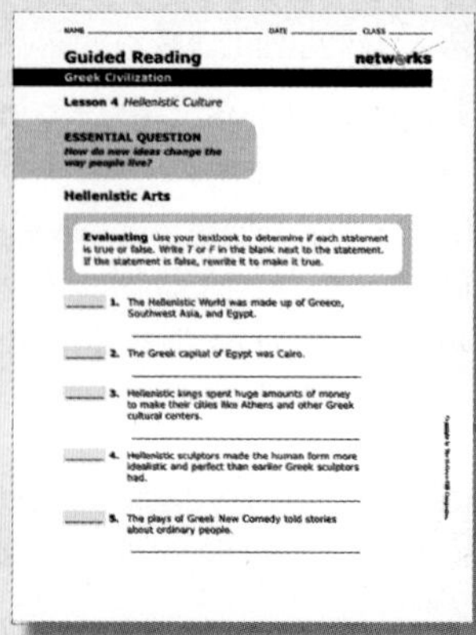

Aristarchus (ar•uh•STAHR•kuhs) claimed that the sun was at the center of the universe. He said that Earth circled the sun. At the time, other astronomers rejected his ideas. They thought that Earth was the center of the universe. Euclid taught others his theories about geometry. If you study geometry today, you will be learning about the same topics studied by ancient Greeks.

Another scientist, Eratosthenes (ehr•uh•TAHS•thuh•neez), was the chief librarian at the library at Alexandria. After study and research, Eratosthenes concluded that Earth was round. He then used his knowledge to measure Earth's **circumference** (suhr•KUHM•fuhr•ens)—the distance around Earth.

The modern age owes a great debt to the Hellenistic thinkers. Here the mathematician Euclid is immortalized in "The School of Athens," a painting by sixteenth-century artist Raphael. The work can be viewed today at the Vatican in Rome.

In order to measure the Earth's circumference, Eratosthenes put two sticks in the ground far apart from each other. When the sun was directly over one stick, he measured its shadow. By measuring the shadows, he was able to calculate the curve of Earth's surface. **V**

Using his measurements, Eratosthenes tried to figure the distance around Earth. Remarkably, his estimate was within 185 miles (298 km) of the actual distance. Using similar **methods**, he tried to determine how far it was to the sun and to the moon. Although his measurements were not **accurate**, he concluded that the sun was much larger than Earth and the moon.

W

GREEK SCIENTISTS AND THEIR CONTRIBUTIONS

Scientist	Scientific "Firsts"
Archimedes	Established the science of physics Explained the lever and compound pulley
Aristarchus	Established that Earth revolves around the sun
Eratosthenes	Figured out that Earth is round
Euclid	Wrote a book that organized information about geometry
Hipparchus	Created a system to explain how planets and stars move
Hippocrates	Known as the "Father of Medicine" First to write a medical code of good behavior
Hypatia	Expanded knowledge of mathematics and astronomy
Pythagoras	First to establish the principles of geometry

CHART

The ancient Greeks made advances in science.

1. **IDENTIFYING** How was Euclid's achievement important for the study of geometry?
2. **CRITICAL THINKING** ***Analyzing*** Why did Aristarchus' ideas upset some people?

Joseph Sohm/Visions of America/Corbis

circumference the outer border of a circle; the measurement of that border

Academic Vocabulary (Tier 2 Words)

method a procedure or process; a way of doing something

accurate free from error; in agreement with truth

V Visual Skills

Simulating Demonstrate Eratosthenes' work by using two pencils or rulers, a piece of string, and a lightweight ball. Have two students hold the pencils or rulers several inches apart on a low surface. Then have another student hold the ball above them. Ask a third student to use the string to measure the resulting shadow on the surface. **Kinesthetic Logical/Mathematical**

W Writing Skills

Informative/Explanatory Have students review the chart "Greek Scientists and Their Contributions." Tell students to choose one idea or discovery that emerged during the Hellenistic Era and to write a newspaper article about it. Students should describe the idea or discovery as if it were new, and to "predict" what might happen in the future because of this new idea or discovery. BL

BIOGRAPHY

Hypatia

Specifying Show students the image about Hypatia. Ask a volunteer or volunteers to read the text aloud to the class. **Ask: Where did Hypatia work?** *(She taught philosophy and advanced mathematics in Alexandria.)* **How does Hypatia's scholarly work stand out from the work of other thinkers and teachers you have learned about?** *(She is the only female scholar. She is considered the first female scholar to study and teach higher mathematics.)*

See page 209F for other online activities.

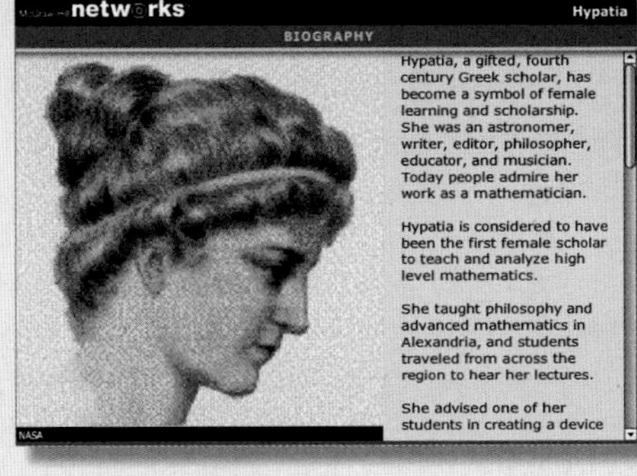

networks
Hypatia
BIOGRAPHY
Hypatia, a gifted, fourth century Greek scholar, has become a symbol of female learning and scholarship. She was an astronomer, writer, editor, philosopher, educator, and musician. Today people admire her work as a mathematician.
Hypatia is considered to have been the first female scholar to teach and analyze high level mathematics.
She taught philosophy and advanced mathematics in Alexandria, and students traveled from across the region to hear her lectures.
She advised one of her students in creating a device
NASA

ANSWERS, p. 239

CHART

1. His book, *Elements,* organized information on geometry in a way that made it easier to teach.
2. **CRITICAL THINKING** His ideas required people to consider the idea that Earth was not the center of the universe.

Hellenistic Culture

C Critical Thinking Skills

Differentiating Help students understand the difference between plane geometry and solid geometry. Explain that students can think of plane geometry as any type of measurement that can be done on a flat surface, or plane. Tell them that solid geometry describes shapes that have three dimensions—height, width, and depth. If necessary, demonstrate the difference by comparing a flat paper circle to a baseball, or something similar. AL ELL

R Reading Skills

Summarizing Invite volunteers to take turns reading aloud the paragraphs about Archimedes's work to protect the city of Syracuse. Help students understand that Archimedes was a skilled inventor and a scientist. Have students write a summary explaining how Archimedes protected his community from the Romans. *(Archimedes invented catapults that could throw weapons over long distances. This helped Syracuse resist the Romans for three years.)*

Connections to TODAY

Constant *pi*

Astronomers in the Hellenistic Era made amazing discoveries. Many of the measurements they made were very accurate. Even though scientists today can measure more accurately, no one has ever been able to improve on Archimedes' calculation of *pi*. The number *pi* (π) is a ratio. When the circumference of a circle is divided by its diameter, you get *pi*. *Pi* is always the same for every circle—about 3.1416.

Archimedes' calculation of *pi* is used daily in mathematics, more than 2,000 years after he worked it out.

Euclid (YOO•kluhd) of Alexandria advanced the field of mathematics. His best-known book *Elements* describes plane geometry. **Plane geometry** is one branch of mathematics. It shows how points, lines, angles, and surfaces relate to one another. Around 300 B.C., Egypt's King Ptolemy I (TAH• luh• mee) asked Euclid if he knew a faster way to learn geometry. Euclid answered that "there is no royal way" to learn geometry. In other words, if the king wanted to understand Euclid's ideas, he would have to study. Euclid's theories still influence mathematicians today.

The most famous scientist of the Hellenistic Era was Archimedes (ahr • kuh• MEE• deez). Archimedes worked on **solid geometry**. He studied ball-like shapes, called spheres, and tube-like shapes, called cylinders. He also figured out the value of *pi*. This number is used to measure the area of circles. It is represented by the Greek symbol π.

Archimedes was also an inventor. He developed machinery and weapons of war. Archimedes was known as a modest man. According to one story, however, he boasted, "Give me a lever and a place to stand on . . . and I will move the earth."

The king of Syracuse heard of Archimedes' boast. He asked Archimedes to build a machine to defend the city, so Archimedes designed catapults. These machines could throw rocks, arrows, and spears over long distances.

When the Romans attacked Syracuse in 212 B.C., the catapults drove them back. It took the Romans three years to capture the city. During the massacre that followed, Archimedes was killed.

Hellenistic thought and culture had long-lasting effects. The mathematician Hypatia (hy• PAY• shuh) lived in Alexandria in Egypt around A.D. 400, more than 700 years after the Hellenistic Era. She kept up the Greek tradition of studying philosophy and mathematics. Like the great Greek thinkers of the past, Hypatia also championed the use of reason over superstition:

> "To teach superstitions as truth is a most terrible thing."
> "Reserve your right to think, for even to think wrongly is better than not to think at all."
> —from Hypatia, *Encyclopaedia Britannica Profiles, 300 Women Who Changed the World*

PROGRESS CHECK

Comparing and Contrasting How were Epicureanism and Stoicism similar? How were they different?

Reading **HELP**DESK 

plane geometry a branch of mathematics centered around measurement and relationships of points, lines, angles, and surfaces of figures on a plane

solid geometry a branch of mathematics about measurement and relationships of points, lines, angles, surfaces, and solids in three-dimensional space

240 *Greek Civilization*

networks Online Teaching Options

SLIDE SHOW

The Story of *Pi*

Problem-Solving Show students the slide show about *pi*. Read the text on the slides aloud. Tell students that Archimedes figured out the value of *pi* (about 3.1416). That contribution helped mathematicians make great advances in geometry. Lead the class in finding the circumference of a circle drawn on a piece of paper by measuring the circle's diameter and multiplying that by *pi*. They could check their work by carefully putting a piece of string around the circumference of the circle and then measuring the string.

See page 209F for other online activities.

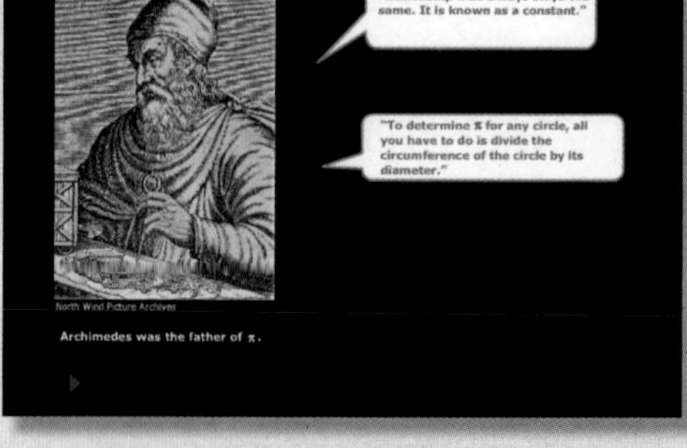

ANSWER, p. 240

PROGRESS CHECK Epicureans and Stoics wanted to have simple and happy lives, but their ideas about how to achieve that goal were different. Epicureans saw happiness as a goal of life. They thought the way to happiness was to avoid pain and worry and to spend time with friends. Stoics believed they had a duty to serve their community, that their lives should be ruled by reason and sound thinking, and that emotions could cause unhappiness. Therefore, they believed they should be indifferent to joy or sadness.

Greece and Rome

GUIDING QUESTION *How did Greece fall under Roman rule?*

The four kingdoms that formed from Alexander's empire shared Hellenistic culture. Despite their common culture, the kingdoms were unable to work together. They often fought wars with one another.

Macedonia held power over Greece for a time. It could not keep the Greek city-states permanently under control, though. Sparta and some other city-states regained their independence. These city-states had Hellenistic cultures, but they did not have strong armies. They remained free for only a short time.

Rome was a city-state in central Italy. In the late 200s B.C., Rome conquered the entire Italian Peninsula. Greece lost its lands in southern Italy. The Greeks now feared that Rome would take control of Greece.

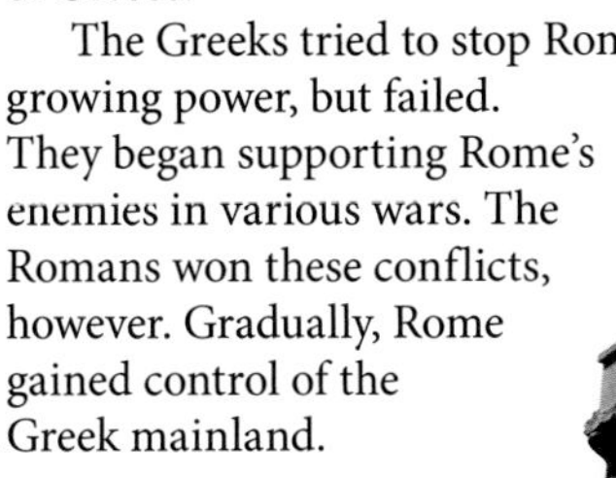

The Greeks tried to stop Rome's growing power, but failed. They began supporting Rome's enemies in various wars. The Romans won these conflicts, however. Gradually, Rome gained control of the Greek mainland.

Sicily is a beautiful island in the Mediterranean. Ruled by ancient Greeks and then the Romans, it is the home today of many historic ruins of both cultures.

✓ PROGRESS CHECK

Explaining How did the Greek city-states react to Rome's growing power?

LESSON 4 REVIEW (CCSS)

Review Vocabulary (Tier 3 Words)

1. Why did Greek scientists study the *circumference* of Earth? RH.6–8.4

Answer the Guiding Questions

2. ***Explaining*** Why did Alexandria become a major center of learning? RH.6–8.2
3. ***Describing*** What contributions did Archimedes make to science? RH.6–8.2
4. ***Explaining*** How did the Greeks attempt to stop Rome's invasion of Greece? RH.6–8.2
5. ***Drawing Conclusions*** What beliefs about Earth and the heavens were proved by the discoveries of Aristarchus and Eratosthenes? RH.6–8.2
6. **ARGUMENT** Compare the Stoic and Epicurean views about life. Which of these views appeals to you? Write a paragraph that explains the reasons for your choice. WHST.6–8.2, WHST.6–8.10

Hellenistic Culture

C1 Critical Thinking Skills

Sequencing Have students reread the text on this page. Tell them to work in pairs to create a flowchart that shows the steps that led to Roman domination over Greece. Review the steps as a class, and have students make any necessary corrections to their charts. *(Hellenistic kingdoms fought one another; Macedonia lost control of some city-states; Rome conquered all of Italy; the Greeks started to support Rome's enemies, but the Romans won these conflicts; Rome gradually took over Greece.)* AL

C2 Critical Thinking Skills

Synthesizing Point out that the Hellenistic Era ended as Roman armies conquered Greek cities in Italy and Greece. On the board, write the reasons—as students identify them—why the Hellenistic Era came to an end. **Ask: Which reason seems the most important or the most likely to have caused the end of the Hellenistic Era?** *(Answers will vary, but students should point out that the Greeks were divided and had weak armies. They could not hold off the Romans.)*

Have students complete the Lesson 4 Review.

CLOSE & REFLECT

The Hellenistic world included many different cultural and ethnic groups. Have students explain how this diversity was both a strength and a weakness. *(Diversity could have led to many different and good ideas, but it also could have led to conflict among the groups.)* Then have them compare the diversity of the Greek world after Alexander's death to the diversity in the United States today. Write students' responses on the board.

LESSON 4 REVIEW ANSWERS

1. Studying the circumference of Earth was part of the studies of astronomy and geography. The Greek scientists used that measurement to calculate the size of the sun and the moon and the distance from Earth to the sun and to the moon.
2. Alexandria was a central port on the Mediterranean coast. It had the largest library in the world and a museum that many researchers used for their work.
3. Archimedes established the science of physics, explained the lever and compound pulley, worked on solid geometry, calculated the value of *pi,* and invented weapons of war.
4. The Greeks supported Rome's enemies in various wars.
5. Aristarchus proved that the sun, not Earth, is the center of the universe. Eratosthenes proved that Earth is round, not flat.
6. In their comparisons, students should mention several characteristics of both groups. The Epicureans believed that happiness was the goal of life and that the way to happiness was to seek pleasure, spend time with friends, not worry, and live simply. The Stoics believed happiness came from following reason, not emotions, and that everyone had a duty to serve their community. Students' responses to which view appeals to them will vary, but students should state their preferences clearly and support them with specific reasons related to Epicureanism and Stoicism.

ANSWER, p. 241

✓ PROGRESS CHECK They were afraid; they tried to stop Rome by supporting Rome's enemies in wars, but they were not successful and were defeated by the Romans.

CHAPTER REVIEW ACTIVITY

Have a student volunteer create a three-column chart on the board and write "Golden Age" in the middle column and "Hellenistic Era" in the far right column. Then lead a discussion that allows students to recall philosophers, writers and playwrights, and scientists from each period and identify what their main accomplishments were. The student volunteer should record names of the Greek thinkers in the chart.

	Golden Age	Hellenistic Era
Philosophers		
Writers and playwrights		
Scientists		

REVIEW THE ENDURING UNDERSTANDINGS

Review the chapter's Enduring Understandings with students.

- ***Cultures are held together by shared beliefs and common practices and values.***
- ***People, places, and ideas change over time.***
- ***Leaders can bring about change in society.***

Now pose the following questions in a class discussion to apply the understandings to the chapter. **Ask:**

How did Greek culture unite the diverse Greek city-states? *(Students should note that Greek city-states were politically independent but were held together by: a shared cultural background, including beliefs in gods, goddesses, and a shared mythology; a common literary and oral tradition; connections through trade; and common philosophical and scientific advances.)*

How did the conquests of Philip and Alexander the Great spread Greek culture? *(Students should understand that the conquests of Macedonian rulers, especially Alexander the Great, brought about widespread Hellenistic kingdoms that modeled their cultures after that of Classical Greece. These conquests thus spread Greek ideas and culture far beyond the borders of the Greek peninsula.)*

What are some elements of ancient Greek culture that influenced later cultures? *(Students may suggest elements including the ideas of philosophers such as the Sophists, Socrates, Plato, Aristotle, Epicurus, and Zeno; politics and government; literature, especially the epic poems of Homer, the fables of Aesop, and the tragedies and comedies of dramatists; theater-production practices; historical research methods; art, sculpture, and architecture.)*

CHAPTER 8 Activities CCSS

Write your answers on a separate piece of paper.

1. **Exploring the Essential Question** WHST.6–8.2, WHST.6–8.10
INFORMATIVE/EXPLANATORY Write an expository essay about what made the Greek people and their culture unique. Think of the new ideas they developed in philosophy and the sciences. Think of the new forms of art and architecture that they created. Include in your essay a discussion of the lasting influences that Greece has had on the world.

2. **21st Century Skills** RH.6–8.2, WHST.6–8.6
APPLY TECHNOLOGY EFFECTIVELY Create a blog entry to compare and contrast the sculpture and architecture of the Hellenistic Era with that of the modern world. Choose photos that show the general differences and details. Write copy that analyzes the styles and points out the differences. Include your personal opinions of the two styles.

3. **Thinking Like a Historian** RH.6–8.7, WHST.6–8.2, WHST.6–8.6, WHST.6–8.10
COMPARING AND CONTRASTING Select one of the historical maps from the chapter. Then search the Internet for maps of the same area today. Write one or two paragraphs explaining how the area has changed or remained the same between the time of ancient Greece and now.

4. **GEOGRAPHY ACTIVITY**

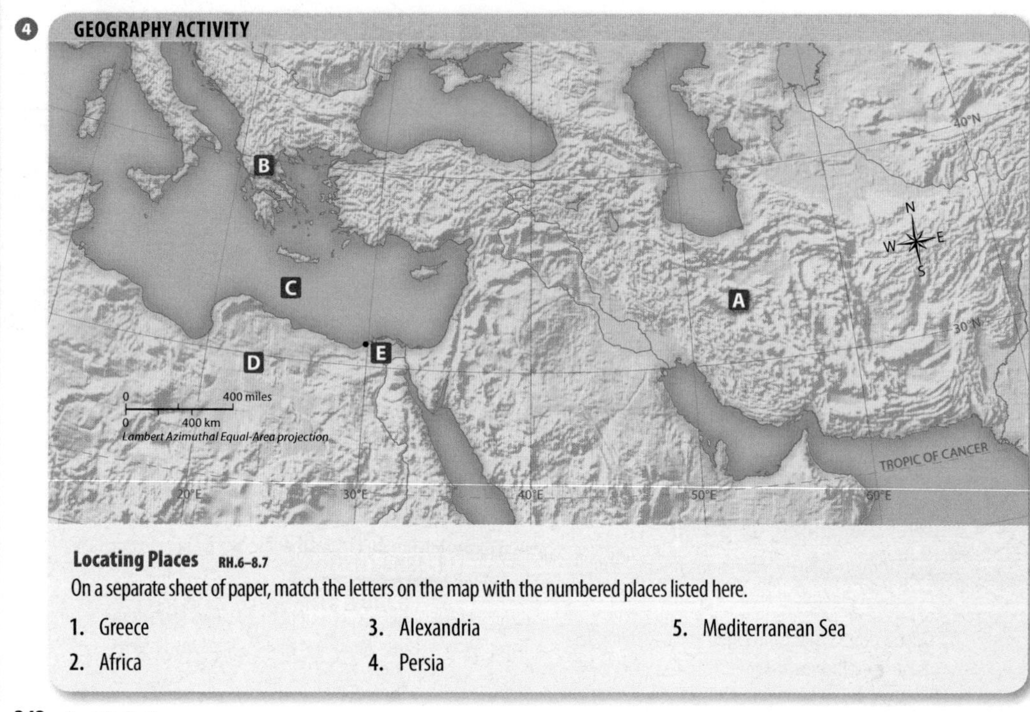

Locating Places RH.6–8.7
On a separate sheet of paper, match the letters on the map with the numbered places listed here.

1. Greece
2. Africa
3. Alexandria
4. Persia
5. Mediterranean Sea

242 *Greek Civilization*

ACTIVITIES ANSWERS

Exploring the Essential Question

1. **EXPOSITORY WRITING** Students should note the ideas of some of the Greek philosophers and the discoveries of some of the Greek astronomers and mathematicians. There should be mention of Greek theater, writing, art, and sculpture. Their answer should discuss the importance that gods and goddesses played in the lives of Greek citizens. Lasting influences could include art, architecture, and political ideas.

21st Century Skills

2. **APPLY TECHNOLOGY EFFECTIVELY** The blog entry should include photos and written descriptions that illustrate the way in which statues of the human form were idealized in theGolden Age and how they became more realistic and emotional in the Hellenistic Era. The illustration and description of architecture could show the evolution of styles of columns and the same changes in human figures as part of friezes and bas-reliefs that occurred in statues. The blog entry should also include the writer's opinions and preferences. The visuals should be compelling and match the print copy.

CHAPTER 8 Assessment

Directions: Choose the best answer for each question.

RH.6–8.2
1. The original Olympic games were held
   A. to honor the goddess Aphrodite.
   B. to appease the god Poseidon, king of the sea.
   C. for the greater glory of the god Zeus.
   D. for the god Ares to make the people strong in war.

RH.6–8.2
2. Socrates was sentenced to death because
   F. some people thought his teaching was dangerous.
   G. he did not believe in absolute right and wrong.
   H. he accepted money for his teaching.
   I. some people did not like his ideas about philosopher kings.

RH.6–8.2
3. Who taught the idea of the golden mean?
   A. Socrates
   B. Aristotle
   C. the Sophists
   D. Plato

RH.6–8.2
4. Alexander's plan to unite a great empire didn't last because
   F. the Persians reconquered their lost lands.
   G. his generals divided the kingdom after his death.
   H. his armies grew frustrated and wished to return home.
   I. the Romans rose to power and conquered his weakened empire.

RH.6–8.2
5. Sculptors in the Hellenistic Era carved figures that
   A. appeared abstract, only partly looking like real people.
   B. showed the beauty and harmony of the ideal human.
   C. represented people realistically, with emotions.
   D. emphasized the humorous side of life.

RH.6–8.2
6. Who was the first scientist to calculate the value of *pi*?
   F. Aristarchus
   G. Eratosthenes
   H. Hypatia
   I. Archimedes

243

CHAPTER 8 Assessment Answers

ASSESSMENT ANSWERS

Review the Guiding Questions

1. **C** Zeus was the head of all the gods and goddesses and the most powerful. The Olympic Games were held to honor him, so C is the correct answer. Other gods and goddesses were honored in ceremonies, but the Olympics were always held in honor of Zeus.

2. **F** Socrates was sentenced to death because many Athenians thought he was encouraging the youth to rebel. Thus, they thought his teachings were dangerous. The answer is F. It was the Sophists, not Socrates, who did not believe in absolute right and wrong. The Sophists also accepted money for their teaching, but Socrates did not. Socrates did not teach about philosopher-kings; Plato did.

3. **B** Aristotle taught his students the principle of the golden mean—that a person should live moderately and avoid extremes in behavior. Choice B is the correct answer.

4. **G** After Alexander the Great's death, his generals divided the empire among themselves. Thus, choice G is the correct answer. Much of Alexander's empire was eventually conquered by Romans and others, but those takeovers took place many years after the empire was established. Alexander's troops threatened to rebel during the general's lifetime; their threats, however, did not cause the breakup of the empire.

5. **C** By the time of the Hellenistic Era, sculptors were carving the human figure more realistically and even depicting strong emotions. Thus, the correct answer is C. Sculptures showing the beauty and harmony of the ideal human were from the Golden Age of Greece.

6. **I** Archimedes first calculated the value of *pi.* Aristarchus claimed the sun was the center of the solar system, Eratosthenes discovered that Earth was round, and Hypatia lived after the Hellenistic Era.

Thinking Like a Historian

3. **COMPARING AND CONTRASTING** Students should identify places and explain why the historical and modern maps do not exactly correspond—for example, where an area that used to be one country is now two countries. They also should comment generally on the changes that have taken place—for instance, noting whether there have been many changes or just a few.

Locating Places

Letters should match the correct geographic locations.

4. **1.** B; **2.** D; **3.** E; **4.** A; **5.** C

Analyzing Documents

7 **C** Choice C is the correct answer. Demosthenes told the Athenians they need not speculate about the future, that the future was certain "unless they were willing to fight him there," and that they should not wait until he comes to Athens.

8 **I** Choice I is the correct answer. Demosthenes says "the future . . . will be disastrous" if the Athenians don't "do [their] duty" and conquer Philip.

Short Response

9 Students' responses should mention that the lake provided freshwater for drinking and watering crops, and the harbor made the city a major port for ships sailing on the Mediterranean Sea.

10 Students should note that Alexandria was able to thrive and grow because the Hellenistic Era (following Alexander's death) was a flourishing time for commerce and trade, the arts, building, science, and scholarship. Alexandria's location and the library, museum, and lighthouse made it a main center in that region of the world.

Extended Response

11 Students' reports should contain a description of an ideal city that reflects the values of Hellenistic culture. They should include some specific details about how they would plan the city's layout and buildings. Students may say they would encourage people to live there by paying them to work on building the city (for example, architects and sculptors) and by providing good library facilities, support for the arts, and beautiful, open public spaces.

 **Assessment** *(continued)* 

DBQ ANALYZING DOCUMENTS

RH.6–8.1
7 **Inferring** This excerpt is from a speech by Demosthenes. He spoke to the people of Athens about Philip II of Macedonia.

"Remember only that Philip is our enemy, that he has long been robbing and insulting us, . . . that the future depends on ourselves, and that unless we are willing to fight him there we shall perhaps be forced to fight here [our homeland]. . . . You need not speculate [guess] about the future except to assure yourselves that it will be disastrous unless you face the facts and are willing to do your duty."

—from "The First Philippic," *Orations of Demosthenes*

Demosthenes says the Athenians must "do their duty." What is their duty?

A. to fight Philip when he comes to Athens
B. to speculate about what will happen in the future
C. to go fight Philip now
D. to seek aid from other city-states

RH.6–8.1
8 **Predicting** What does Demosthenes predict?

F. If the Athenians are not good to Philip, he will rob them.
G. It is still possible to make peace with Philip.
H. There are others who will help the Athenians fight Philip.
I. If the Athenians ignore Philip, there will be disaster.

SHORT RESPONSE

"The choice of the site . . . was determined by the abundance of water from [the lake] . . . and by the good anchorage [harbor]. . . . Alexandria became, within a century of its founding, one of the Mediterranean's largest cities and a centre of Greek scholarship and science."

—from *Encyclopaedia Britannica Online*, "Alexandria."

RH.6–8.1
9 How did Alexandria's physical features help make it a great city?

RH.6–8.2
10 Why do you think the city flourished, even after the death of Alexander?

EXTENDED RESPONSE

WHST.6–8.10
11 **Narrative** You are a citizen in a new city of the Hellenistic Era. Write a description of the ideal Hellenistic city.

Need Extra Help?

If You've Missed Question	1	2	3	4	5	6	7	8	9	10	11
Review Lesson	1	2	2	3	4	4	3	3	3, 4	4	4

networks ***Online Teaching Options***

More Assessment Resources

The *Assess* tab in the online Teacher Lesson Center includes resources to help students improve their test-taking skills. It also contains many project-based rubrics to help you assess students' work.

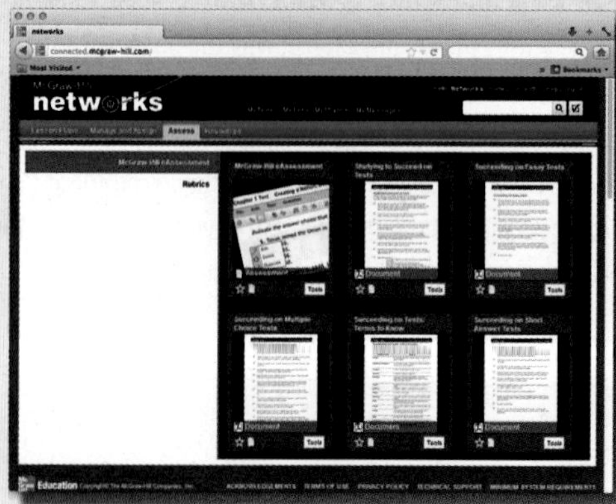

CHAPTER 9

Ancient India Planner

UNDERSTANDING BY DESIGN®

Enduring Understandings

- *People, places, and ideas change over time.*
- *Religion can influence a society's beliefs and values.*

Essential Questions

- *How does geography influence the way people live?*
- *How do religions develop?*
- *What makes a culture unique?*

Predictable Misunderstandings

Students may think:

- *Early civilizations were primitive and completely unlike ours.*
- *It only took a few hundred years for the early Indian societies to form, develop, and disappear.*
- *Indian culture had no influence on Western people.*

Assessment Evidence

Performance Tasks:

- *Hands-On Chapter Project*

Other Evidence:

- *Interactive Graphic Organizers*
- *Primary Source Activity*
- *21st Century Skills Activities*
- *Geography and History Activity*
- *Answers to Guided Reading activity sheets*
- *Classroom discussion and group activity answers*
- *Answers from Analyzing Visuals*
- *Interactive Whiteboard Activity responses*
- *What Do You Think? questions*
- *Written paragraphs*
- *Lesson Reviews*
- *Chapter Activities and Assessment*

SUGGESTED PACING GUIDE

Introducing the Chapter	1 Day	Lesson 3	2 Days
Lesson 1	1 Day	Chapter Wrap-Up and Assessment	1 Day
Lesson 2	1 Day		

TOTAL TIME 6 Days

Key for Using the Teacher Edition

SKILL-BASED ACTIVITIES

Types of skill activities found in the Teacher Edition.

V Visual Skills require students to analyze maps, graphs, charts, and photos.

R Reading Skills help students practice reading skills and master vocabulary.

W Writing Skills provide writing opportunities to help students comprehend the text.

C Critical Thinking Skills help students apply and extend what they have learned.

T Technology Skills require students to use digital tools effectively.

*Letters are followed by a number when there is more than one of the same type of skill on the page.

DIFFERENTIATED INSTRUCTION

All activities are written for the on-level student unless otherwise marked with the leveled labels below.

BL Beyond Level
AL Approaching Level
ELL English Language Learners

All students benefit from activities that utilize different learning styles. Many activities are marked as below when a particular learning style is highlighted.

Intrapersonal	**Naturalist**
Logical/Mathematical	**Kinesthetic**
Visual/Spatial	**Auditory/Musical**
Verbal/Linguistic	**Interpersonal**

NCSS Standards covered in "Ancient India"

Learners will understand:

1 CULTURE

1. "Culture" refers to the socially transmitted behaviors, beliefs, values, traditions, institutions, and ways of living together for a group of people.

5. How individuals learn the elements of their culture through interactions with others, and how individuals learn of other cultures through communication and study;

2 TIME, CONTINUITY, AND CHANGE

3. That learning about the past requires the interpretation of sources, and that using varied sources provides the potential for a more balanced interpretive record of the past;

5. Key historical periods and patterns of change within and across cultures (e.g., the rise and fall of ancient civilizations, the development of technology, the rise of modern nation-states, and the establishment and breakdown of colonial systems);

6. The origins and influences of social, cultural, political, and economic systems;

3 PEOPLE, PLACES, AND ENVIRONMENTS

1. The theme of people, places, and environments involves the study of the relationships between human populations in different locations and geographic phenomena such as climate, vegetation, and natural resources;

2. Concepts such as: location, region, place, migration, as well as human and physical systems;

6. Patterns of demographic and political change, and cultural diffusion in the past and present (e.g., changing national boundaries, migration, and settlement, and the diffusion of and changes in customs and ideas);

4 INDIVIDUAL DEVELOPMENT AND IDENTITY

4. How personal, social, cultural, and environmental factors contribute to the development and the growth of personal identity;

6. That perceptions are interpretations of information about individuals and events, and can be influenced by bias and stereotypes.

5 INDIVIDUALS, GROUPS, AND INSTITUTIONS

1. This theme helps us know how individuals are members of groups and institutions, and influence and shape those groups and institutions;

2. Concepts such as: mores, norms, status, role, socialization, ethnocentrism, cultural diffusion, competition, cooperation, conflict, race, ethnicity, and gender;

6. That cultural diffusion occurs when groups migrate;

7. That institutions may promote or undermine social conformity;

CHAPTER OPENER PLANNER

Students will know:

- *how the Indus Valley civilization developed.*
- *the origins of the caste system in India.*
- *fundamental concepts of Hinduism and Buddhism.*
- *what Ashoka accomplished during his rule.*
- *the achievements of the Golden Age of the Gupta Empire.*
- *the contributions of Indian culture to literature, art, math, and science.*

Students will be able to:

- ***recognize*** *why people settle by rivers.*
- ***describe*** *early civilizations in India.*
- ***recall*** *the names of the castes in India.*
- ***distinguish*** *among the terms* varna, jati, *and* caste.
- ***identify*** *key terms in Hindu beliefs.*
- ***analyze*** *religious concepts.*
- ***compare and contrast*** *Ashoka's rule before and after he embraced Buddhism.*
- ***compare and contrast*** *ancient Indian rule during Ashoka with modern-day government.*
- ***synthesize*** *information to form opinions and make observations about ancient Indian culture.*

UNDERSTANDING BY DESIGN®

Print Teaching Options

V Visual Skills

- ☐ **P. 246** Students identify features on the map and identify places where people might settle. **Visual/Spatial**
- ☐ **P. 247** Students identify civilizations and other events located on the time line. **Visual/Spatial**

Online Teaching Options

V Visual Skills

- **MAP** **Ancient India c. 3000 B.C.**—Students examine the borders of ancient and modern-day India.
- **TIME LINE** **Place and Time: Ancient India c. 3000 B.C. to A.D. 500**—Students learn about key Indian and world events during this time period.
- **WORLD ATLAS** Students can use this interactive map to identify regions of the world, learn about individual countries, locate political boundaries, measure distances, and much more.

Printable Digital Worksheets

R Reading Skills

- **GRAPHIC NOVEL** **Much Ado About Zero**—In this graphic novel, a student creates a symbol to represent zero as her science fair project.

Project-Based Learning

Hands-On Chapter Project

Ancient India Slide Show

Students work in groups to research different aspects of Indian life, and then groups collaborate to create a single PowerPoint® presentation.

Technology Extension

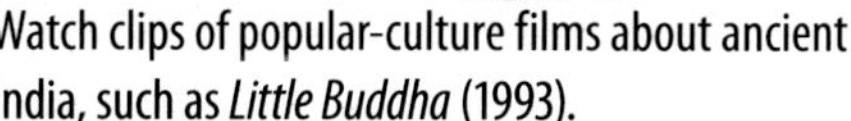

Published Online Projects

- Find an additional activity online that incorporates technology for this project.
- Visit the EdTechTeacher Web sites (included in the Technology Extension for this chapter) for more links and tutorials, and other resources.

Print Resources

ANCILLARY RESOURCES

These ancillaries are available for every chapter and lesson.

- **Reading Essentials and Study Guide Workbook** AL ELL
- **Chapter Tests and Lesson Quizzes Blackline Masters**

PRINTABLE DIGITAL WORKSHEETS

These printable digital worksheets are available for every chapter and lesson.

- **Hands-On Chapter Projects**
- **What Do You Know? activities**
- **Chapter Summaries (English and Spanish)**
- **Vocabulary Builder activities**
- **Guided Reading activities**

More Media Resources

SUGGESTED VIDEOS 

Watch clips of popular-culture films about ancient India, such as *Little Buddha* (1993).

- **Discuss: From the information given in the film, what do you think Buddhists believe?**

(NOTE: Preview clips to ensure age-appropriateness.)

SUGGESTED READING

Grade 6 reading level:

- ***I Remember India,*** by Anita Ganeri

Grade 7 reading level:

- ***Archaeology,*** by Trevor Barnes

Grade 8 reading level:

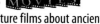

- ***India: People, Place, Culture, History,*** DK Publishing

LESSON 1 PLANNER

EARLY CIVILIZATIONS

Students will know:

- *how the Indus Valley civilization developed.*
- *the origins of the caste system in India.*

Students will be able to:

- ***recognize** why people settle by rivers.*
- ***describe** early civilizations in India.*
- ***recall** the names of the castes in India.*
- ***distinguish** among the terms* varna, jati, *and* caste.

UNDERSTANDING BY DESIGN®

☑ Print Teaching Options

V Visual Skills

- ☐ **P. 249** Students locate the monsoons on the map and answer questions about them. **Visual/Spatial**
- ☐ **P. 251** Students analyze the diagram of the Mohenjo-Daro buildings. **AL** **Visual/Spatial**
- ☐ **P. 252** Students analyze the visual of a seal and speculate on why scholars think these seals show a form of written language. **BL**
- ☐ **P. 253** Students find parts of India where Aryans migrated to. **Visual/Spatial**
- ☐ **P. 255** Students analyze the pyramid shape of the organizer and draw conclusions. **AL** **ELL** **Visual/Spatial**

R Reading Skills

- ☐ **P. 248** Students identify the geographic features of India. **AL**
- ☐ **P. 249** Students explain the effects of seasonal monsoons. **AL**
- ☐ **P. 250** Students define and discuss content vocabulary used in the lesson. **AL** **ELL**
- ☐ **P. 250** Students explain why the Indus Valley civilization is called the cradle of ancient India. **AL** **ELL**
- ☐ **P. 251** Students explain the characteristics of the cities of Mohenjo-Daro and Harappa.
- ☐ **P. 252** Students explain elements of life in the Indus Valley. **AL**
- ☐ **P. 252** Students explain the events that led to the end of the Indus Valley civilization.
- ☐ **P. 254** Students summarize the Aryan way of life and the development and use of written language.
- ☐ **P. 255** Students explain Indian class structure. **AL** **ELL**
- ☐ **P. 256** Students name the four varnas and explain the difference between a *varna* and a *jati*.

C Critical Thinking Skills

- ☐ **P. 250** Students connect the floods and droughts of ancient India and similar events in the United States today.
- ☐ **P. 251** Students draw conclusions about how the ability to grow large crops enabled them to build a civilization.

☑ Online Teaching Options

V Visual Skills

- **VIDEO** **Timelines of Ancient Civilizations: Inda-Indus River Civilizations to Buddhism–Part 1**—Students learn about the Indian subcontinent and the people who came to settle there.
- **MAP** **The Geography of India**—Students visualize how the wet and dry seasons affect the country.
- **MAP** **Aryan Migration, 2000–500 B.C.**—Students click on arrows to trace the movement of Aryans throughout India.
- **SLIDE SHOW** **Deccan Plateau**—Students view pictures of this extensive Indian landform.
- **SLIDE SHOW** **Harappan Crafts**—Students view some of the Harappan artifacts archaeologists have found in the Indus Valley.
- **IMAGE** **Harappan Unicorn Seal**—Students click to learn about the meanings of the symbols on this ancient seal.

R Reading Skills

- **GRAPHIC ORGANIZER** **Taking Notes: *Summarizing:* Ways Aryans Changed India**—Students summarize the three ways the Aryans changed India.
- **SLIDE SHOW** **Modern Crafts in India**—Students view and read about the types of crafts made in different parts of India.

C Critical Thinking Skills

- **WHITEBOARD ACTIVITY** **City Symbols**—Students analyze symbols and match them with the type of community they would likely represent.
- **CHART** **Early India's Social System**—Students click to see India's social classes and an example of a job that someone from that class might have.
- **SLIDE SHOW** **Daily Life in Mohenjo-Daro**—Students learn about life in Mohenjo-Daro and then explore parts of a typical structure.

T Technology Skills

- **SELF-CHECK QUIZ** **Lesson 1**—Students receive instant feedback about their mastery of lesson content.

☑ Printable Digital Worksheets

C Critical Thinking Skills

- **WORKSHEET** **Geography and History Activity: Understanding Human-Environment Interaction: Ancient India**—Students respond after reading text and studying a map.

LESSON 2 PLANNER

RELIGIONS OF ANCIENT INDIA

Students will know:
- *fundamental concepts of Hinduism and Buddhism.*

Students will be able to:
- ***identify** key terms in Hindu beliefs.*
- ***analyze** religious concepts.*

UNDERSTANDING BY DESIGN®

☑ Print Teaching Options

V Visual Skills

- ☐ **P. 258** Students examine the image of Brahma and then do research to learn about symbolism associated with him.

R Reading Skills

- ☐ **P. 257** Students explain the origin of Hinduism.
- ☐ **P. 257** Students discuss content vocabulary words. ELL
- ☐ **P. 258** Students discuss the *Upanishads* and the core Hindu beliefs. **Verbal/Linguistic**
- ☐ **P. 259** Students how karma and dharma support the caste system and how Hindu beliefs shaped the way of life of ancient India. BL AL ELL
- ☐ **P. 260** Students discuss what they know about meditation and the life of Buddha. AL
- ☐ **P. 261** Students paraphrase the Four Noble Truths and the steps of the Eightfold Path.
- ☐ **P. 262** Students discuss the effect on Buddhism on the lives of ancient Indians.
- ☐ **P. 263** Students explain details about Jainism and Mahavira.
- ☐ **P. 264** Students discuss ahimsa, how it is practiced by Jains, and how Jainism is similar to Buddhism. AL ELL

W Writing Skills

- ☐ **P. 259** Students will create a graphic organizer to record answers to questions about Hinduism.

C Critical Thinking Skills

- ☐ **P. 261** Students speculate about the challenges of following the Eightfold Path. BL
- ☐ **P. 261** Students contrast attitudes of the Buddha with attitudes of Hindus at the time.
- ☐ **P. 262** Students hypothesize about the decrease of Buddhism within India and its spread outside India. BL
- ☐ **P. 264** Students theorize about the effectiveness of nonviolence.

T Technology Skills

- ☐ **P. 262** Students will research Tibetan Buddhism and the Dalai Lama and create a multi-media presentation. BL **Interpersonal**

☑ Online Teaching Options

V Visual Skills

- VIDEO **India's History from the Hindus to the Buddhists**—The video recalls the accomplishments, migrations, and caste system of the Hindus and then describes the life and impact of the Buddha on East Indian culture.
- SLIDE SHOW **Upanishads**—Students learn more about these ancient texts that describe the search for Brahman.
- IMAGE **Buddhist Monk**—Students click to learn about the lives and customs of these followers of the Buddha.

R Reading Skills

- GRAPHIC ORGANIZER **Taking Notes: *Describing:* Three Religions**—Students describe important facts about the religions of ancient India.
- PRIMARY SOURCE **Mahavira, Founder of Jainism**—Students read a passage from Majjhima Nikaya, in which Mahavira speaks of the goal of achieving Enlightenment.
- BIOGRAPHY **The Buddha**—Highlights of the life of Siddhartha Gautama are shared.
- SLIDE SHOW **Gandhi**—Students learn about the life and accomplishments of this modern Indian leader.

C Critical Thinking Skills

- SLIDE SHOW **Representations of Buddha**—Students compare representations of the Buddha from different countries.

T Technology Skills

- SELF-CHECK QUIZ **Lesson 2**—Students receive instant feedback of their mastery of lesson content.

☑ Printable Digital Worksheets

W Writing Skills

- WORKSHEET **21st Century Skills Activity: Communication: Summarizing**—Students practice note-taking and summarizing techniques.

THE MAURYAN EMPIRE

Students will know:

- *what Ashoka accomplished during his rule.*
- *the achievements of the Golden Age of the Gupta Empire.*
- *the contributions of Indian culture to literature, art, math, and science.*

Students will be able to:

- ***compare and contrast*** *Ashoka's rule before and after he embraced Buddhism.*
- ***compare and contrast*** *ancient Indian rule during Ashoka with modern-day government.*
- ***synthesize*** *information to form opinions and make observations about ancient Indian culture.*

UNDERSTANDING BY DESIGN®

Print Teaching Options

V Visual Skills

- [ ] **P. 266** Students will examine the map and answer questions about it. AL ELL **Visual/Spatial**
- [ ] **P. 269** Students examine the map and compare the area of the Gupta Empire with that of the Mauryan Empire. AL **Visual/Spatial**

R Reading Skills

- [ ] **P. 265** Students explain why Chandra Gupta built a large army and conquered surrounding kingdoms; they explain how those conquered people felt.
- [ ] **P. 266** Students discuss Chandra Gupta's rule and what he did to stay in power.
- [ ] **P. 266** Students explain why Ashoka changed and why Buddhism brought about the change.
- [ ] **P. 267** Students explain the kind of leader Ashoka became and how he helped the people. AL
- [ ] **P. 268** Students summarize events that brought about the end of the Mauryan Empire.
- [ ] **P. 268** Students make connections between India's golden age, trade, and Samudra Gupta's leadership.
- [ ] **P. 269** Students define *epic* and give examples. AL ELL

C Critical Thinking Skills

- [ ] **P. 267** Students interpret text on one of Ashoka's pillars and compare it to what they know of Buddhism. BL
- [ ] **P. 270** Students demonstrate the importance and use of the concept of zero. BL **Logical/Mathematical**
- [ ] **P. 270** Students speculate on what would happen if there were no zero. BL **Logical/Mathematical**
- [ ] **P. 271** Students discuss the kinds of surgical instruments surgeons use today and tell how they are similar to and different from those used in ancient India.

T Technology Skills

- [ ] **P. 267** Students create a multimedia presentation on stupas.
- [ ] **P. 270** Students do online research to learn about ancient India musical instruments and music and then share recordings with the class. **Kinesthetic, Interpersonal Auditory/Musical**

Online Teaching Options

V Visual Skills

- VIDEO **India's History from the Golden Age to Today**—Students view a video that explains the foundation of the Mauryan Empire in the Ganges River Valley by Chandra Gupta.
- MAP **Mauryan Empire c. 250 B.C.**— Students explore the extent of this empire at its height.
- MAP **Gupta Empire c. A.D. 600**—Students view the location of this empire in northern India.
- SLIDE SHOW **Mural from the Caves at Ajanta**—Students view sculptures and murals created during the Gupta Empire.

R Reading Skills

- GRAPHIC ORGANIZER **Taking Notes: *Identifying:* Mauryan and Gupta Empires**—Students identify and organize information about the Mauryan and Gupta Empires.
- PRIMARY SOURCE **Bhagavad Gita**—Students analyze a passage from this famous section of the *Mahabharata*.

C Critical Thinking Skills

- CHART **Ashoka's Reign**—Students identify causes and effects related to Ashoka's leadership.
- CHART **Ancient Indian Number Symbols**—Students compare and contrast how digits were written in nine ancient languages.
- SLIDE SHOW **Surgical Instruments**—Students compare ancient surgical instruments with those in use today.

T Technology Skills

- SELF-CHECK QUIZ **Lesson 3**—Students receive instant feedback about their mastery of lesson content.

Printable Digital Worksheets

W Writing Skills

- WORKSHEET **21st Century Skills Activity: Communication: Create and Give a Group Presentation**—Students work together to research, write, and present information on medical methods and equipments from the Gupta Empire.

C Critical Thinking Skills

- WORKSHEET **Primary Source Activity: Buddhism and Hinduism**—Students read two passages and then compare and contrast points of view.

Intervention and Remediation Strategies

LESSON 1 Early Civilizations

Reading and Comprehension

List the Content Vocabulary words on the board. Ask students to write sentences using each of the terms correctly. The sentences should refer to the content of the lesson.

Text Evidence

Have students do research to learn about an archaeological discovery from the Indus civilization. Have students write an essay describing the discovery and explaining both why it is important and what it tells us about the civilization.

LESSON 2 Religions of Ancient India

Reading and Comprehension

Have students review the lesson and identify one principal text or person associated with each of the three religions. Ask them to create a word web with details showing how the person or text contributed to the religion.

Text Evidence

Have students review the lesson and identify one principal text or person associated with each of the three religions. Ask them to create a word web with details showing how the person or text contributed to the religion.

LESSON 3 The Mauryan Empire

Reading and Comprehension

Ask students to summarize the development and accomplishments of the Mauryan and Gupta empires by creating an outline of the lesson. Students can use the section headings to organize their ideas and then fill in the most important details.

Text Evidence

Organize students into pairs or small groups. Assign each group one of the emperors of the Mauryan or Gupta empires. Have them do research and present an oral biography of the ruler.

Online Resources

Approaching Level Reader

Use this online lower-level text that corresponds directly to the text in the Student Edition. It includes a Spanish version.

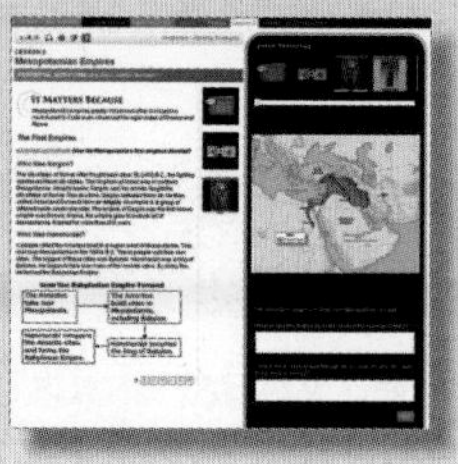

Guided Reading Activities

This resource uses graphic organizers and guiding questions to help students with comprehension.

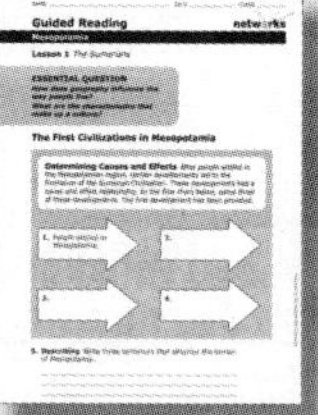

What Do You Know?

Use these worksheets to pre-assess student's background knowledge before they study the chapter.

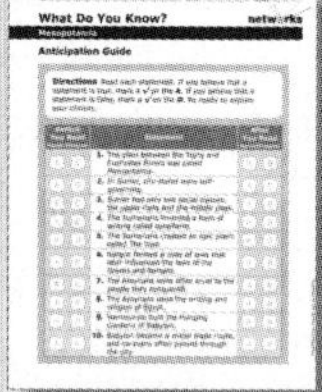

Reading Essentials and Study Guide Workbook

This resource offers writing and reading activities for the approaching-level student. Also available in Spanish.

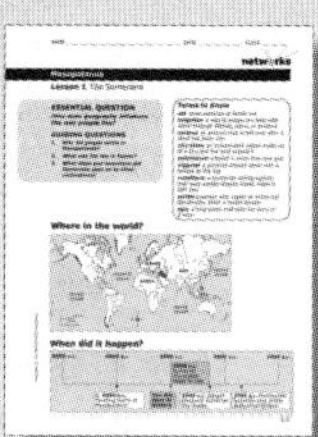

Self-Check Quizzes

This online assessment tool provides instant feedback for students to check their progress.

Ancient India

c. 3000 B.C. to A.D. 500

ESSENTIAL QUESTIONS • *How does geography influence the way people live?* • *How do religions develop?* • *What makes a culture unique?*

networks

There's More Online about the culture of ancient India.

CHAPTER 9

Lesson 1 *Early Civilizations*

Lesson 2 *Religions of Ancient India*

Lesson 3 *The Mauryan Empire*

The Story Matters . . .

Have you ever read a love story? Some of the earliest immortal love stories are found in ancient Indian writing. Radha is the supreme deity featured in many of these stories. She is the Hindu deity with a special companion—Krishna. Together they appear in many tales with happy events and beautiful descriptions. Radha and Krishna represent examples of true love, beauty, loyalty, and devotion. The early Hindu culture honored these qualities as necessary for a good life. The love of Radha and Krishna is said to go on for eternity.

◄ *This picture of Radha emphasizes her eternal beauty. The ornate jewelry is typical of ancient Indian art.*

245

ENGAGE

Bellringer Read "The Story Matters . . ." aloud in class. Then lead a discussion about Radha and Krishna. **Ask:** **Why do you think people held up Radha and Krishna as examples of true love and loyalty?** *(Responses will vary. Students might point out that early Hindus valued the emotion of love and honored their deities.)* **Why is it important to know about deities such as Radha and Krishna?** *(Responses will vary. Students may suggest that knowing about deities such as Radha and Krishna will provide insight into ancient Indian culture and help them see connections between modern and ancient cultures and beliefs.)* To help students answer these questions, encourage them to think about what they know of the deities and gods honored by other cultures. Encourage students to apply this knowledge to help them think about Hindu culture. Explain how knowledge of another culture's beliefs helps lead toward cultural understanding. Then tell them they can learn more about Radha and Krishna online.

Making Connections

Krishna is one of the most popular Hindu gods. As a child, he was threatened by another god and was secretly sent away to live with cowherds. It was during this time that he met Radha, a milkmaid. The love of the two has been the source of innumerable poems and stories in many Indian languages. In certain literature, Radha is a symbol of the human soul, while Krishna represents the divine.

Letter from the Author

Dear World History Teacher,

The first civilization in India arose in the Indus River valley during the fourth millennium B.C. Around 1500 B.C., the Aryans established political control throughout all of India and created a new Indian civilization. A caste system, in which people were divided into distinct social classes, became a chief feature of the new Indian civilization. Two of the world's great religions, Hinduism and Buddhism, began in India. Between 325 B.C. and A.D. 500, India was a land of many different states, but two major empires emerged. The Mauryan Empire in northern India lasted from 321 B.C. until 183 B.C. The Gupta Empire lasted from A.D. 320 until the late fifth century.

Jackson J. Spielvogel

TEACH & ASSESS

Step Into the Place

V1 Visual Skills

Analyzing Maps Review the map with students. Point out that India sticks out into the Indian Ocean. It is a large landmass and is called "the Indian subcontinent." Guide a discussion of the topography of the region. **Ask:** What are some major rivers shown on the map? *(Indus, Ganges, and Brahmaputra)* Where are the mountain ranges? *(to the north of India)* Point out that the mountains cut off India from the rest of Asia to the north and northeast. **Visual/Spatial**

Remind students of other civilizations they have studied. **Ask:** What are some of the geographic features that people might look for when choosing a place to settle? *(Answers will vary but may include ample freshwater and fertile soil.)* Have volunteers identify places where civilizations have formed and places where civilizations might have formed. Ask each volunteer to explain his or her choice. As a class, discuss the Map Focus questions.

Content Background Knowledge

There are many myths about the birth of Gnesha. One of them tells that his mother, Parvati, was taking a bath and scraped together some mud. She formed it into the shape of a child, which came to life. Just then Shiva, her consort, entered and saw the child. He flew into a fit of rage and cut off the child's head. Gnesha's head was finally replaced with the head of an elephant. In the process of providing the elephant head, one of the tusks was broken off, as shown in the image on this page.

ANSWERS, p. 246

Step Into the Place

1. The Himalaya run along India's northern border.
2. The Indus and Ganges rivers flow from the Himalaya.
3. Mount Everest is more than 29,000 feet (8,839 m) tall.
4. CRITICAL THINKING The Himalaya made travel into India difficult. The mountains also presented a barrier to trade with other countries.

Step Into the Time

The Aryans introduced Hindu beliefs around 1500 B.C., which was before the Buddha's birth.

CHAPTER 9 CCSS

Place and Time: Ancient India 3000 B.C. to A.D. 500

The first civilizations of ancient India developed in the Indus Valley. The arrival of the Aryans brought great changes to India, including the caste system and beliefs that would become Hinduism. By the rise of the Mauryan and Gupta Empires, Buddhism had joined Hinduism as a major world religion that began in ancient India.

One of the most honored deities by Hindus is Gnesha. Representing education, wisdom, and wealth, Gnesha is called upon in many Hindu ceremonies. His popularity also stems from the belief that he can solve problems for his worshippers.

Indian emperor Ashoka (c. 273–233 B.C.) was a powerful ruler and Buddhist. He believed humans and animals should be treated with compassion. This carving of lions sits atop a pillar built by Ashoka. The sides of the pillar are covered with Buddhist teachings and Ashoka's laws.

Step Into the Place

MAP FOCUS The history of India has been affected greatly by the Himalaya mountain ranges.

1. **LOCATION** Look at the map. Where are the Himalaya located? RH.6–8.7
2. **REGION** What rivers shown on the map flow from the Himalaya? RH.6–8.7
3. **PLACE** How tall is Mount Everest? RH.6–8.7
4. **CRITICAL THINKING** *Making Inferences* How would the Himalaya have affected the settlement of India or its trade with other countries? RH.6–8.1

Step Into the Time

TIME LINE Look at the time line. Which philosophy appeared in India first—Hinduism or Buddhism? RH.6–8.7

V2

Project-Based Learning 

Hands-On Chapter Project

Ancient India Slide Show

Students will create a slide-show presentation about life in ancient India. Have them participate in a class discussion about how physical geography has influenced the development of ancient civilizations. Then divide into small groups, to research topics about ancient Indian life. Each group will plan, research, and create a software-produced presentation on its chosen topic. Students will work as a team to combine the slide shows into a single class presentation. Finally, students will evaluate their work using a class-developed assessment rubric.

Technology Extension

Published Online Projects

Once students have completed their slide show project, have them save their work on a computer or flash drive. Choose a Web site, wiki, blog, or slide-sharing service to which you may upload the presentations. Then have students create a login and password to upload their work, or alternatively create one class account and upload the student projects yourself. Finally, make the project publicly viewable on the Internet.

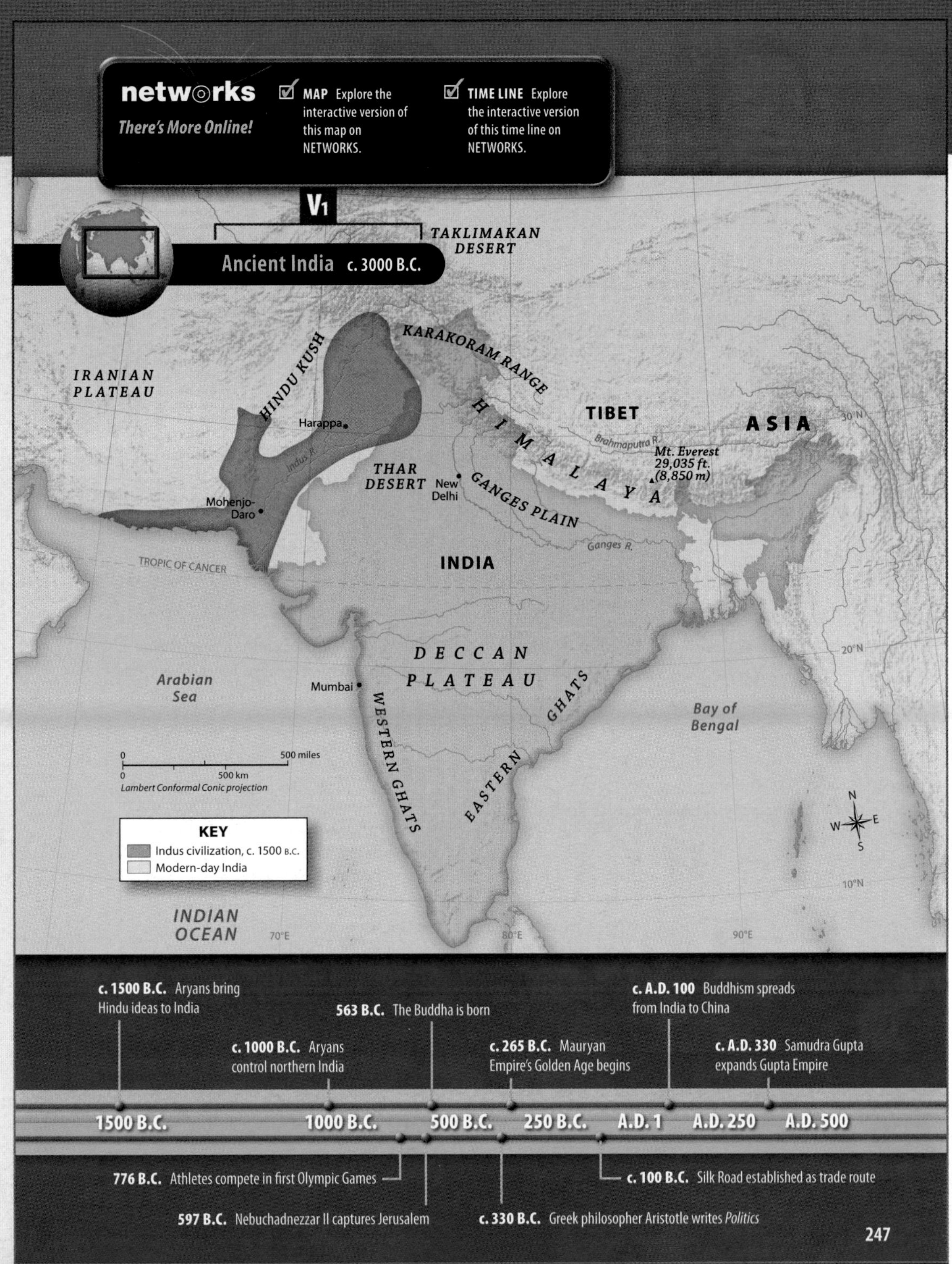

CHAPTER 9

Place and Time

Step Into the Time

V2 Visual Skills

Analyzing Time Lines Have students review the time line for the chapter. Explain that they will be studying events from about 3000 B.C. to 500 A.D. Point out that several civilizations are shown in the time line. Explain that some of these lasted longer than others. **Ask:** What are possible reasons why some civilizations last longer than others? *(Answers may include for longer-lasting civilizations: good leadership, successful farming, no invasions or natural disasters; for shorter-lasting civilizations: natural disasters, war and conquest, and the gradual weakening of society and leadership)* Point out that Hinduism was very old when it was first introduced into India. **Ask:** When was Buddhism founded? *(about 563 B.C., when Buddha was born)* **Visual/Spatial**

Content Background Knowledge

- Buddhism began in northern India and later spread to central and southeast Asia, China, and Korea, and eventually to Japan. Today, it has followers worldwide.
- Hinduism dates back to at least the second millennium B.C. and maybe even earlier. It may be the world's oldest extant religion. Today, about one billion people practice Hinduism.

CLOSE & REFLECT

Have students review on their own the time line, map, and other material on these two pages. Ask them to write three questions based on these materials that they would like to find answers to as they study this chapter.

MAP

Ancient India c. 3000 B.C.

Analyzing Maps Have students explore the interactive map by moving the pointer around the map to highlight certain features and reveal more information. Discuss details that students discover. **Ask:** Where does the Ganges River originate? *(the Himalaya)* **What religious group thinks the Ganges is sacred?** *(Hindus)* Where do Indians get much of their timber? *(the Eastern and Western Ghats)* Have students locate the area occupied by the Indus civilization. Point out that this civilization developed mainly in what is now Pakistan.

See page 245B for other online activities.

ENGAGE

Bellringer Read "It Matters Because . . ." aloud to students, and then review what they have learned about the influence of geography on where people live. Tell them that in this lesson they will learn how geography shaped one of the world's earliest civilizations and discover why that civilization is considered to be the cradle of ancient India.

TEACH & ASSESS

C Critical Thinking Skills

Making Inferences Discuss the Himalaya, reminding students that these mountains form a formidable barrier to people who might travel to or from parts of Asia to the north of India. **Ask:** **How might these mountains have affected the early Indian civilizations?** *(Elicit that the Himalaya helped to protect India from invasion but also isolated it from trade and the exchange of ideas.)*

R Reading Skills

Identifying Ask students to read about the geography of India. Have students identify key geographical features. **Ask:** **What made India an ideal location for early civilizations to grow?** *(It has three great river systems that helped build rich soil for agriculture.)* **What are India's three great rivers?** *(Indus, Ganges, and Brahmaputra)* AL

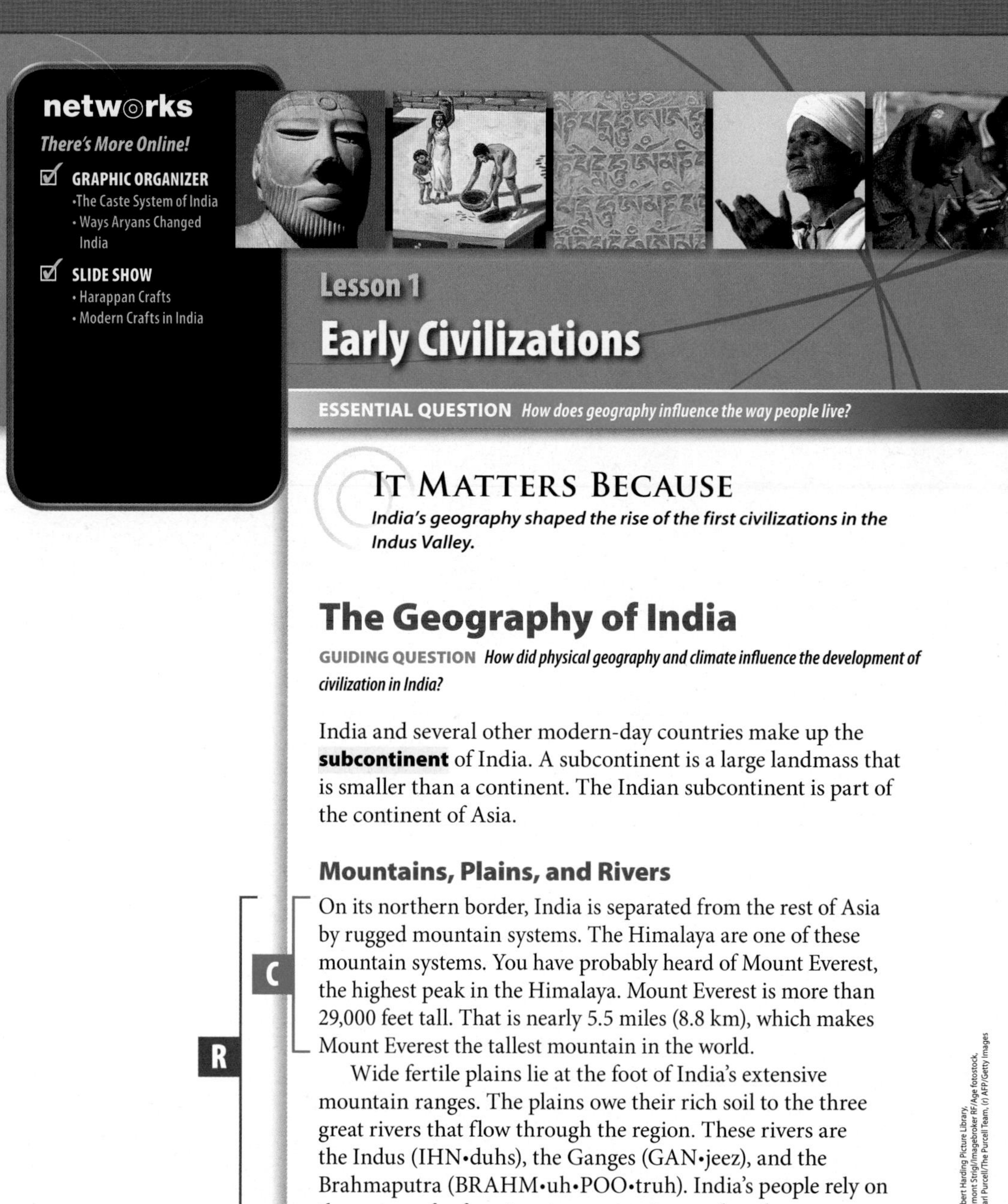

networks
There's More Online!
- GRAPHIC ORGANIZER
  - The Caste System of India
  - Ways Aryans Changed India
- SLIDE SHOW
  - Harappan Crafts
  - Modern Crafts in India

Lesson 1
Early Civilizations

ESSENTIAL QUESTION *How does geography influence the way people live?*

IT MATTERS BECAUSE
India's geography shaped the rise of the first civilizations in the Indus Valley.

The Geography of India

GUIDING QUESTION *How did physical geography and climate influence the development of civilization in India?*

India and several other modern-day countries make up the **subcontinent** of India. A subcontinent is a large landmass that is smaller than a continent. The Indian subcontinent is part of the continent of Asia.

Mountains, Plains, and Rivers

On its northern border, India is separated from the rest of Asia by rugged mountain systems. The Himalaya are one of these mountain systems. You have probably heard of Mount Everest, the highest peak in the Himalaya. Mount Everest is more than 29,000 feet tall. That is nearly 5.5 miles (8.8 km), which makes Mount Everest the tallest mountain in the world.

Wide fertile plains lie at the foot of India's extensive mountain ranges. The plains owe their rich soil to the three great rivers that flow through the region. These rivers are the Indus (IHN•duhs), the Ganges (GAN•jeez), and the Brahmaputra (BRAHM•uh•POO•truh). India's people rely on these rivers for farming, transportation, and trade.

(l) Robert Harding Picture Library, (c) Egmont Strigl/imagebroker RF/Age fotostock, (cr) Carl Purcell/The Purcell Team, (r) AFP/Getty Images

Reading HELPDESK CCSS

Taking Notes: ***Summarizing***
Using a diagram like this one, describe three ways the Aryans changed India. RH.6–8.2

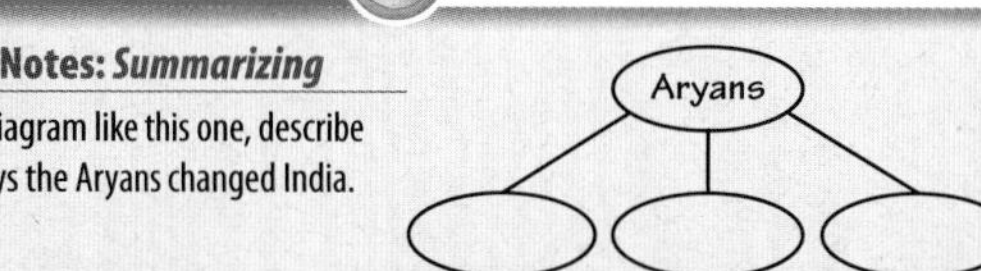

Content Vocabulary (Tier 3 Words)
- subcontinent
- monsoon
- language family
- raja
- Sanskrit
- Vedas
- caste
- guru

248 *Ancient India*

networks *Online Teaching Options*

VIDEO

Timelines of Ancient Civilizations: Inda-Indus River Civilizations to Buddhism–Part 1

Discussing Have students take notes as they view the video time line. Then guide a discussion of the history of the subcontinent. Discuss the reasons why the early civilizations developed along major rivers. **Ask:** **How long have people lived on the subcontinent?** *(as long as 50,000 years ago)* **What were the early people of the subcontinent known as?** *(Munda)* **Where do archaeologists believe the first people of India came from?** *(the east or the west, although it is uncertain which of these was first)*

See page 245C for other online activities.

ANSWER, p. 248

TAKING NOTES: Possible answers include: introducing the Vedas, introducing the caste system, developing a written language, and introducing new agricultural techniques.

V

The Geography of India

KARAKORAM RANGE
HINDU KUSH
Harappa
HIMALAYA
Mt. Everest 29,035 ft. (8,850 m)
GANGES PLAIN
Indus R.
Mohenjo-Daro
INDIA
Ganges R.
TROPIC OF CANCER
DECCAN PLATEAU
WESTERN GHATS
EASTERN GHATS
Arabian Sea
Bay of Bengal
INDIAN OCEAN
0 800 miles
0 800 km
Albers Equal-Area projection
30°N
20°N
10°N
70°E
80°E
90°E

KEY
Winter monsoon (dry winds)
Summer monsoon (wet winds)
▲ Mountain peak

GEOGRAPHY CONNECTION

The mighty Himalaya and major bodies of water border the Indian subcontinent.

1. **PLACE** Which two rivers are found in northern India?
2. **CRITICAL THINKING** ***Predicting*** What might happen to India's farmers if the summer monsoons did not occur?

The landforms in central and southern India are much different from the landforms in the north. Along the west and east coasts of the subcontinent are lush fertile lands. Farther inland, there are two chains of mountains that have worn down over time. As the mountains eroded, they left areas of rugged hills. Between the mountains is a dry highland known as the Deccan Plateau (DEH•kuhn pla•TOH). The southern two-thirds of India is part of this huge **plateau**.

India's civilization has been shaped by its climate as well as by its physical landscape. Seasonal winds called **monsoons** (mahn•SOONZ) have a large influence on India's climate.

During winter, monsoon winds blow cold, dry air from the Himalaya east to west across India. During summer, warmer land temperatures cause the winds to change direction. Summer monsoon winds blow west to east from the Arabian Sea. They bring warm, wet air and pouring rains.

R

subcontinent a large landmass that is smaller than a continent
monsoon seasonal wind, especially in the Indian Ocean and southern Asia

Visual Vocabulary (Tier 2 Words)
plateau a broad flat area of high land

V Visual Skills

Analyzing Maps Discuss the physical map of India. **Ask: Where do the winter monsoons come from?** *(the Himalaya)* **In which direction do the summer monsoons blow?** *(from west to east)* **How might these winds have affected human life in the river valley?** *(They would bring rain for crops, but this extra rain might also bring floods. If the monsoons didn't come, drought could result.)* **Visual/Spatial**

R Reading Skills

Explaining Be sure all students understand the meaning of *monsoons.* Then **ask: Why do the summer monsoons bring warm, wet air?** *(They originate in the Arabian Sea.)* Ask students to explain, in their own words, the effects of the winter and summer monsoons. AL

Content Background Knowledge

Explain to students that the subcontinent of India was once a large island south of Asia. About 200 million years ago, the Indian landmass began drifting north. About 40 or 50 million years ago, it collided with Asia. The resulting forces caused the uplift of Earth's crust, which formed the Himalaya.

MAP

The Geography of India

Analyzing Maps Have students explore the interactive map of India independently. Then discuss the geography with students. **Ask: Where do the winter monsoons come from?** *(the Himalaya)* Point out that the Himalaya are the highest mountains in the world, and Mount Everest is the world's highest peak. **Ask: How high is Mount Everest?** *(29,035 feet)*

See page 245C for other online activities.

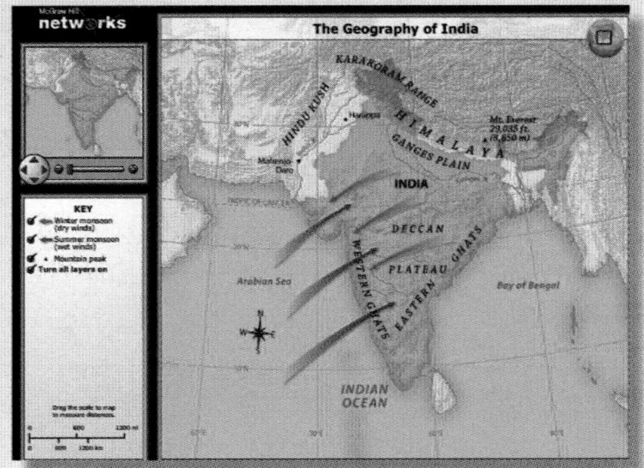

ANSWERS, p. 249

GEOGRAPHY CONNECTION

1. The Indus and Ganges rivers are found in northern India.
2. **CRITICAL THINKING** The farmers would be lacking the water needed for crops.

R1 Reading Skills

Defining Ensure that students have a clear understanding of the terms discussed in this section. **Ask:** What is a drought? *(a long period without rain)* AL ELL

C Critical Thinking Skills

Making Connections Point out to students that floods and drought occur in many parts of the world. Guide a discussion of floods and drought that have occurred in the United States. Help students recall the severe damage and other consequences of these natural disasters.

R2 Reading Skills

Explaining After students have read the section on the Indus Valley civilization, ask volunteers to give reasons why the people who established many of the early civilizations chose to settle in river valleys. **Ask:** Why is the Indus Valley civilization called the cradle of ancient India? *(It was the first civilization in India; all later civilizations developed from this one.)* What are nomads? *(people who do not live in one place for long but wander about)* When did the first people settle in the Indus Valley? *(about 5,000 years ago)* AL ELL

The summer rains bring farmers water that they need for their crops. With good rainfall, farmers can grow large amounts of food. Because of this, people celebrate the arrival of the monsoon rains. However, monsoon rains can also cause damage. Very heavy rains sometimes cause floods that destroy crops. Floods can even kill people and animals.

Too little rain can also be a problem. If the rains come late, there may be a long dry period called a drought. A serious drought can bring disaster to farmers. If lots of farm crops are ruined, many people may go hungry or starve.

PROGRESS CHECK

Explaining How do monsoon winds affect life in India?

Archaeologists have studied the ruins of Mohenjo-Daro (below) and found many artifacts. These include statues of priest-kings, jewelry, and pottery.

The Indus Valley Civilization

GUIDING QUESTION *How did the people of the Indus River Valley build cities?*

Thousands of years ago, India's first civilization began in the valley around the Indus River. The Indus Valley civilization is called the cradle of ancient India. Like the early civilizations in Mesopotamia and Egypt, the Indus Valley civilization developed near a great river system.

About 5,000 years ago, nomads settled in valleys along the Indus River in an area that is now Pakistan. The first settlements were built on the shores of the river. The soil was rich there, and farmers grew large crops of wheat, barley, and beans.

(t) Corbis Art/Corbis, (b) Borromeo/Art Resource, NY

Reading HELPDESK CCSS

Build Vocabulary: *Word Forms*

The word *celebrate* exists in several forms. The verb form means "to honor a person or a holiday with festivities." The noun *celebration* means "an event held to honor a holiday or person." The adjective used to describe a celebration is *celebratory*.

networks Online Teaching Options

SLIDE SHOW

Harappan Crafts

Analyzing Images Have students view the slide show on Harappan crafts. By clicking on the arrows, they will see and read about other examples of their crafts and art. Discuss what these crafts reveal about the Harappan civilization.

See page 245C for other online activities.

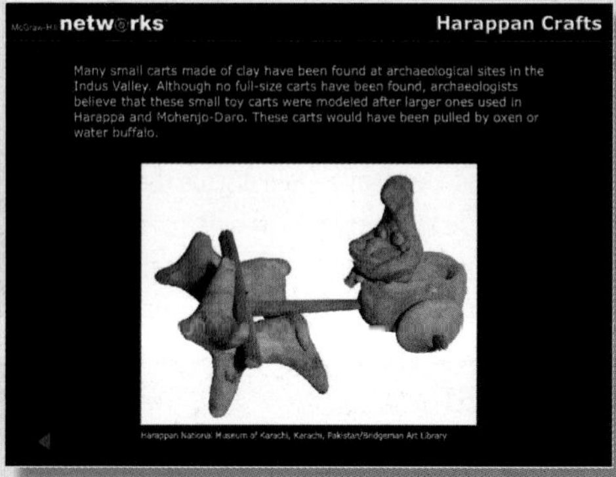

networks
Harappan Crafts
Many small carts made of clay have been found at archaeological sites in the Indus Valley. Although no full-size carts have been found, archaeologists believe that these small toy carts were modeled after larger ones used in Harappa and Mohenjo-Daro. These carts would have been pulled by oxen or water buffalo.

ANSWER, p. 250

PROGRESS CHECK The summer monsoon winds bring rains that can help farmers produce more crops but can also cause destructive floods.

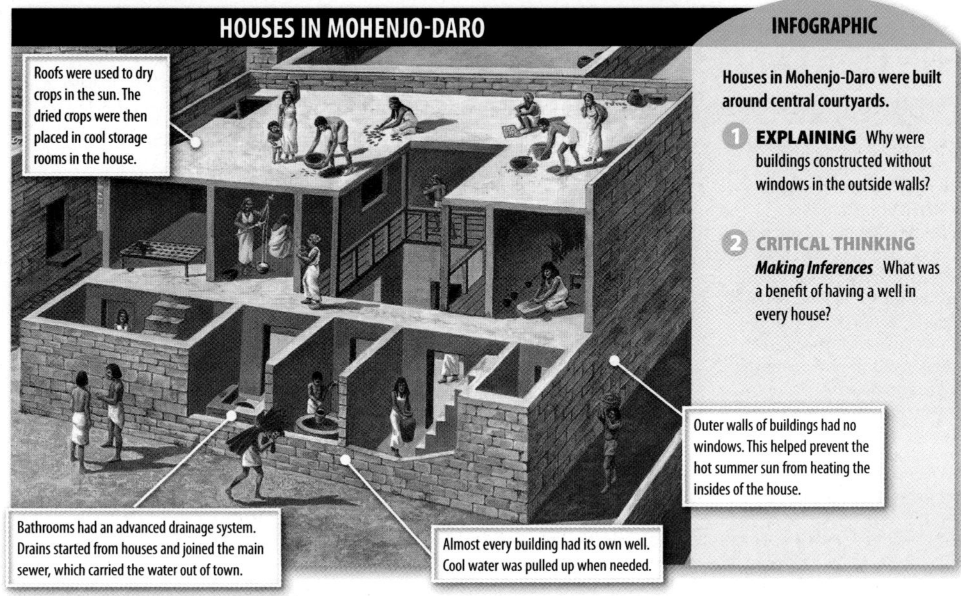

HOUSES IN MOHENJO-DARO
INFOGRAPHIC
Roofs were used to dry crops in the sun. The dried crops were then placed in cool storage rooms in the house.
Houses in Mohenjo-Daro were built around central courtyards.
1 EXPLAINING Why were buildings constructed without windows in the outside walls?
2 CRITICAL THINKING Making Inferences What was a benefit of having a well in every house?
Outer walls of buildings had no windows. This helped prevent the hot summer sun from heating the insides of the house.
Bathrooms had an advanced drainage system. Drains started from houses and joined the main sewer, which carried the water out of town.
Almost every building had its own well. Cool water was pulled up when needed.

V

With abundant crops, not all the people needed to farm. Many people made tools and constructed houses. Some supported themselves by trading extra food and goods. The Indus people prospered and built cities. The Indus civilization spread over much of western India and Pakistan.

C

Mohenjo-Daro and Harappa

R

The Indus culture flourished between 2600 B.C. and 1900 B.C. We know about the Indus culture from studying the ruins of two major cities, Mohenjo-Daro (moh•HEHN•joh DAHR•oh) and Harappa (huh•RA•puh).

At their peak, both Mohenjo-Daro and Harappa had more than 35,000 residents. The cities were designed almost exactly alike. Each city had dozens of streets. Larger streets were paved with tan-colored bricks. The smaller streets that crossed them were often left unpaved. At the west end of each city stood a fortress built on a brick platform and surrounded by strong, thick walls.

The Indus Valley people used oven-baked bricks to build their homes. Most houses had flat wooden roofs. The houses had enclosed courtyards, and some were several stories tall.

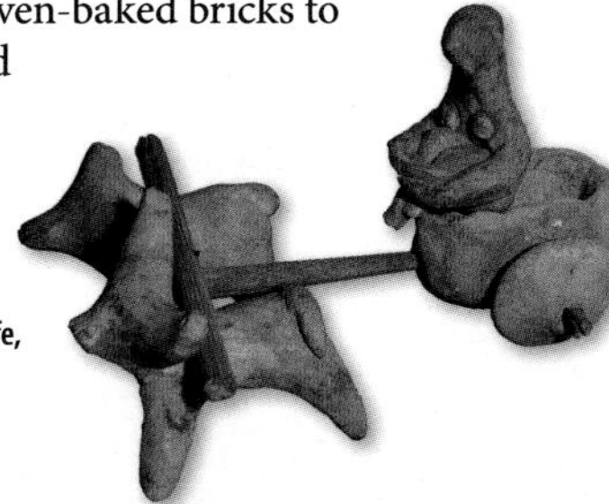

Ancient Indian art portrays daily life, such as driving this ox cart.

V Visual Skills

Analyzing Images Direct students to study the diagram of the Mohenjo-Daro building. Guide them to an understanding of how well planned these buildings were. Discuss the features of the houses, including the construction with bricks, the drainage systems, the wells, and the walls without windows. **Ask:** **How did the people use the flat roofs of their houses?** *(to dry crops for storage)* **How did building with bricks help to keep homes cool in the summer?** *(Bricks insulated the homes from the heat.)* **What did the river supply for building the cities?** *(mud for bricks; water for plumbing)*

AL Visual/Spatial

C Critical Thinking Skills

Drawing Conclusions Point out that the rivers and ample rainfall meant that the Indus Valley people could grow large amounts of crops. As a result, not everyone had to work at farming. **Ask:** **Why was this important for people to build a civilization?** *(It freed up some people's time so they could devote themselves to crafts and the construction of elaborate homes and cities.)*

R Reading Skills

Explaining After students have read the text, ask them to explain the characteristics of the cities of Mohenjo-Daro and Harappa. **Ask:** **How do we know that Mohenjo-Daro was a city rather than a rural village?** *(It had more than 35,000 residents and dozens of streets, and was guarded by a fort surrounded by thick walls)* **What were the houses like?** *(They were made of oven-baked bricks and had flat wooden roofs and enclosed courtyards; many were several stories high.)* Remind them to support their answers using details from the text.

SLIDE SHOW

Daily Life in Mohenjo-Daro

Analyzing Images Have students view the slide show on Mohenjo-Daro. Clicking on the arrows will reveal more information about this civilization. Clicking on the white dots will provide details about the structure. Have students explain what made the buildings highly functional. Point out that indoor plumbing was highly unusual in the ancient world and was not common in many modern cities until fairly recent times.

See page 245C for other online activities.

ANSWERS, p. 251

INFOGRAPHIC

1. Buildings without windows were cooler because windows let in the intense summer heat.
2. **CRITICAL THINKING** Households with their own wells had a steady source of water. Wells made a household more efficient because people did not have to take time to find and collect water.

V Visual Skills

Analyzing Visuals Call students' attention to the image of the Harappan seal, called the Unicorn Seal. Ask a volunteer to read aloud the text about these ancient Indian seals. As a class, answer the discussion questions. Then **ask:** **Why do you think scholars believe these seals may show a form of written language?** *(Answers may include: The pictographs on the seal resemble a form of writing.)* BL

R1 Reading Skills

Explaining After students have read the text, ask them to explain what daily life in the Indus Valley civilization was like. **Ask:** **Where did most people live?** *(in farming villages)* **What crops did they grow?** *(rice, barley, wheat, peas, cotton)* **What kinds of objects did artisans make?** *(copper and bronze tools, clay pottery, cotton cloth, and jewelry made of shells, ivory, and gold)* AL

How do archaeologists know so much about these people? *(Answers will vary. Students may say archaeologists have excavated ruins of cities and farming villages and can infer from the evidence where the people lived and what they did.)*

R2 Reading Skills

Explaining Direct students to the section titled "Aryan Migrations and Settlements." Ask students to explain the events that led to the end of the Indus Valley civilization. **Ask:** **What brought about the end of this civilization?** *(Possible causes include drought, earthquakes, and floods.)* Point out that although floods and drought had always been part of life for people of the Indus River valley, these events may have been especially severe during this period, and they may have brought about the end of this civilization.

ANSWER, p. 252

☑ **PROGRESS CHECK** Most were farmers who lived in villages surrounding the cities.

Thinking Like a HISTORIAN

Researching on the Internet

V Historians have found many clay seals and stamps in Harappa. These objects are covered in writing and pictures. Historians have not determined the meaning of these writings. Use the Internet to find images of some of these seals. Create a list of what you think each might mean. Then discuss your theories with your class. For more information about using the Internet for research, read the chapter *What Does a Historian Do?*

The civilization's engineers and builders were highly skilled. Large buildings stored grain for the entire population. Wells supplied water, and every house had at least one indoor bathroom. Wastewater flowed through pipes to pits outside the city walls. Houses also had garbage chutes connected to bins in the streets.

What was life like?

Archaeologists have learned much about Indus Valley culture by studying its city ruins. For example, the ruins show that cities' royal palaces and temples may have been enclosed in a fortress. This shows the importance of both religion and government in the settlements of the Indus Valley.

Most Indus Valley people **resided** in farming villages surrounding the cities. They grew rice, barley, wheat, peas, and cotton. City residents were merchants, shopkeepers, and artisans. R1 They made and sold copper and bronze tools, clay pottery, and cotton cloth. Artisans also made jewelry from shells, ivory, and gold. Archaeologists have even found toys among the ruins.

Indus Valley merchants traveled as far as Mesopotamia to trade. Some traders made the difficult trip through the mountains to Mesopotamia. Others probably sailed to Mesopotamia along the southern coast of Asia.

☑ **PROGRESS CHECK**

Describing How did most Indus Valley people earn a living?

Aryan Migrations and Settlements

GUIDING QUESTION ***How did the Aryans influence early India?***

Sometime around 1900 B.C., the people of the Indus Valley began to **abandon** their cities and villages. Why did the people leave? Archaeologists have found several possible causes. There was a severe drought that lasted for hundreds of years. R2 It destroyed crops and caused people to starve. Earthquakes and floods killed many more people and changed the course of the Indus River. Meanwhile, groups of people called the Aryans (AR•ee•uhnz) **migrated** to India. Soon a new civilization **emerged**.

Reading HELPDESK CCSS

Academic Vocabulary (Tier 2 Words)

reside to live
abandon to leave and not return
migrate to move from one place to another
emerge to come into being or become known

networks Online Teaching Options

IMAGE

Harappan Unicorn Seal

Analyzing Visuals Students can click on different parts of the image to reveal text that explains the image. Invite students to tell whether they think this seal is of a unicorn or a bull. Then discuss how and why seals were used, pointing out that we still use seals today, especially in government, to show that documents are official.

See page 245C for other online activities.

The Indo-Europeans

The Aryans were not a race or ethnic group. Many historians believe that the Aryan people's language was part of a large language family known as Indo-European. A **language family** is a group of similar languages. Many modern Indian languages, like Hindi, are part of the Indo-European family. So are many European languages, including English. The Aryans were speakers of Indo-European languages.

Indo-European people lived in central Asia but began migrating to other places. Some moved west to Europe or south to Iran. The Aryans went to India. Like most Indo-Europeans, the Aryans raised cattle for meat, milk, and butter. They moved from place to place to find pastures and water for their cattle. The Aryans were expert horse riders and hunters, as well as fierce warriors. As they moved about, the Aryans sometimes raided nearby villages for food.

R

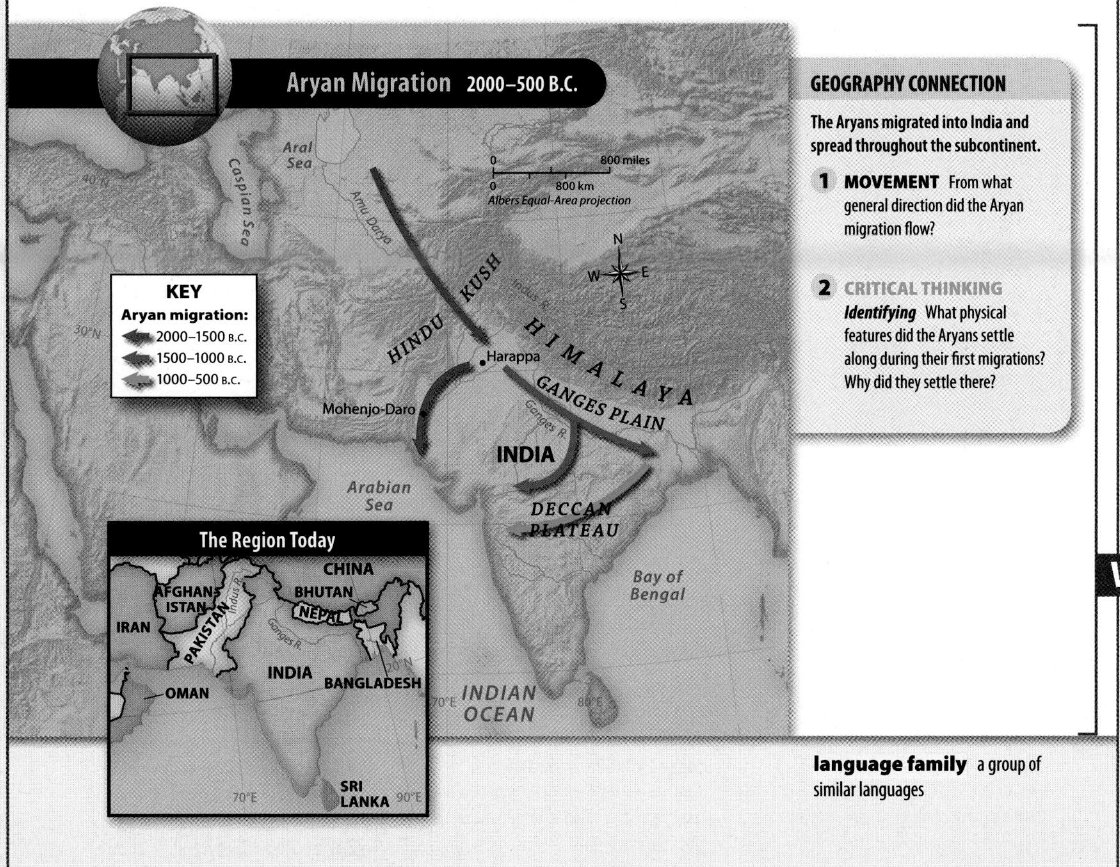

GEOGRAPHY CONNECTION

The Aryans migrated into India and spread throughout the subcontinent.

1. **MOVEMENT** From what general direction did the Aryan migration flow?
2. **CRITICAL THINKING** ***Identifying*** What physical features did the Aryans settle along during their first migrations? Why did they settle there?

V

language family a group of similar languages

MAP

Aryan Migration, 2000–500 B.C.

Analyzing Maps Have students use the interactive map to learn about the Aryan migration into India. By clicking on the arrows, students will see when and where the Aryans migrated during each period. **Ask:** **Where did the Aryan migration begin?** *(near the Aral Sea)* **When did theAryans reach the Deccan Plateau?** *(between 1,000 and 500 B.C.)*

See page 245C for other online activities.

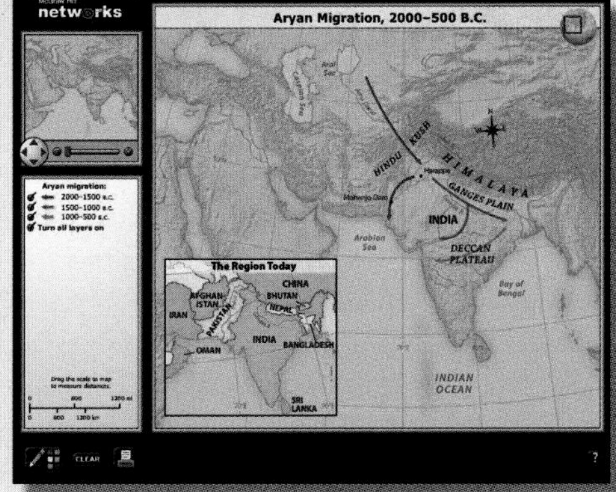

R Reading Skills

Identifying Ask students to read the text and have them explain who the Aryans were and how they made their way to India. Students should understand that the Aryans are a new group of people who moved into ancient India. Emphasize to students that the term *Aryan* refers specifically to the language these people spoke when they arrived in India, not to their racial or ethnic makeup. Aryan is a form of the Indo-European language family. **Ask:** **Where did these Indo-Europeans originate?** *(central Asia)* **Where did they migrate to?** *(Europe, Iran, India)* Point out that these people were nomads who followed their herds from place to place. Ask students to describe the way of life of these people. AL

V Visual Skills

Analyzing Maps Review the map key with students. **Ask:** **To what parts of India did the Aryan people migrate?** *(northern and central India, including what is now Pakistan)* **How many separate periods of migrations are shown on the map?** *(3)* Point out that the Aryans' first period of migration brought them down the Indus Valley to the ancient cities of Harappa and Mohenjo-Daro. **Visual/Spatial**

ANSWERS, p. 253

GEOGRAPHY CONNECTION

1. from the northeast
2. **CRITICAL THINKING** They settled first along the Indus River and then along the Ganges River. The rivers provided water for drinking, farming, and transportation.

Early Civilizations

R Reading Skills

Summarizing Have a volunteer read the text aloud. As a class, discuss the impact of the Aryans on life in India. **Ask:** What became of the earlier Indus Valley people? *(They mixed with the Aryans.)* How did the Aryan way of living change India? *(After migrating and rising to power in India, the Aryans introduced new farming techniques, a written language, and a social class system, among other things.)* Mention to students that the Aryans were the first Indians to develop written language. **Ask:** Why do you think written language did not come about until the Aryans settled down as farmers? *(Possible answer: Prosperity brought about by farming allowed the people more time to develop writing. A writing system was needed to keep records, as an organized society would do.)* **Ask:** What other uses does written language have, other than record-keeping? *(Possible answer: to preserve ideas)*

Content Background Knowledge

- *Sanskrit* remains a living language in India, where it is one of 22 official languages.
- The word *Sanskrit* means "refined" and "sanctified."
- *Sanskrit* is used primarily in religious discussions.
- Some efforts are being made to revive *Sanskrit* for use as an everyday language.

Hindi, India's national language, developed over time from ancient Sanskrit. The Aryans used Sanskrit to record many things.

CRITICAL THINKING

Drawing Conclusions Why did early people develop a system of writing once they settled in groups?

From about 1500 to 1000 B.C., bands of Aryans moved throughout India. These groups mixed with the descendants of the Indus Valley people. Together, they created a new culture. Over time, the Aryans in India adopted a new way of life. They settled down in one place and became farmers, though they still raised cattle. Eventually, the Aryans saw their herds as sacred and banned the use of cattle as food.

The Aryans began to make iron tools to clear forests so they could farm the land. They also built irrigation systems. Gradually, they turned the Ganges River valley into productive farmland. In the north, farmers grew grains such as wheat, millet, and barley. Millet is a grain that is still an important food in many parts of the world. Farmers planted rice in the fertile river valleys. In the south, farmers grew crops such as cotton, vegetables, pepper, ginger, and cinnamon. R

The Aryans lived in tribes. Each tribe was led by a **raja** (RAH•jah), or prince. The rajas created their own small kingdoms, which often fought each other over cattle, treasure, and land.

Like most nomadic people, the early Aryans had no written language. After they settled in villages, they developed a written language called **Sanskrit** (SAN•skriht). Sanskrit gave people a way to record sales, trade, and land ownership. Eventually, Aryan hymns, stories, poems, and prayers were also written in Sanskrit. Later, they were recorded and collected into sacred **texts** known as the **Vedas** (VAY•duhs). Examples of the Vedas remain today. This prayer in the Vedas asks for divine help in offering sacrifices:

PRIMARY SOURCE

> "Let us invoke [call upon] today, to aid our labour, the Lord of Speech, . . . May he hear kindly all our invocations [prayers] who gives all bliss for aid, whose works are righteous."
>
> —from Visvakarman," *Rig-Veda*, Book 10, Hymn LXXXI

✓ PROGRESS CHECK

Identifying How did the Aryans change their way of life after they settled in India?

Reading HELPDESK 

raja an Indian prince
Sanskrit the first written language of India
Vedas ancient sacred writings of India

caste an Indian social class whose members are restricted in the jobs they may take and in their association with members of other castes
guru a teacher

Academic Vocabulary (Tier 2 Words)

text words written down in a particular form, such as a book
manual work done by hand

networks Online Teaching Options

IMAGE

Sanskrit Translation

Analyzing Images Have students view the image. Clicking on the Sanskrit text will cause an English translation to appear. Tell students that *Sanskrit* is still used today. Urge students to discuss why written lanquaqe is important. You might tell students that the Universal Declaration of Human Rights is a declaration adopted by the United Nations in 1948. It resulted from the atrocities of World War II and a determination by the international community to never allow such events to occur again.

networks Sanskrit Translation

Directions: Click on the Sanskrit below to see the translation.

अलल हुमान बेनिगस रे बखरन डरे ानदे ट्राल नि दगिनतिय ानद रगिहतस ॥ त्हेय रें नदखथेद णगविनक्ष थतिह रेासखन ानद चखनसचेंनिचे ानद सहखुलद ाचत तखथारदस खने ानखतहेर नि । सपरिति खड बरखतहेरहखखद ॥

Translation:

All human beings are born free and equal in dignity and rights. They are endowed [given] with reason and conscience and should act towards one another in a spirit of brotherhood.

(Article 1 of the Universal Declaration of Human Rights)

Stotram 1, Sri Vishnu Sahasranama. As viewed on Swami Krishnananda's website, www.swami-krishnananda.org

See page 245C for other online activities.

ANSWERS, p. 254

CRITICAL THINKING Once they settled in groups, early peoples needed a way to record sales, trade, and land ownership.

✓ PROGRESS CHECK The Aryans settled down and became farmers rather than nomads. They also developed a written language, *Sanskrit*.

Ancient Indian Society

GUIDING QUESTION ***How was society in ancient India organized?***

As the Aryans settled into India, people set up towns along India's Ganges River. Most people still farmed for a living. Some workers specialized in crafts such as carpentry or weaving. Others took part in trade. As India's economy grew, a system of social classes gradually developed.

What were the *Varnas*?

The four social classes of ancient India are called *varnas* (VUR•nehs). People were considered members of the *varna* into which they were born. The most powerful *varnas* were the Brahmins (BRAH•mihns) and Kshatriyas (KSHA•tree•uhs). The Brahmins were the priests—the people who performed religious ceremonies. The Kshatriyas were warriors who ran the government and army.

R

(l) Carl Purcell/Encyclopedia/Corbis, (r) AFP/Getty Images

INFOGRAPHIC

Indian society was divided into four major castes.

1. **IDENTIFYING** Which caste was the largest? Which was the smallest?
2. **CRITICAL THINKING** ***Analyzing*** Why do you think unskilled workers and servants were grouped in the Sudra caste?

THE CASTE SYSTEM OF INDIA

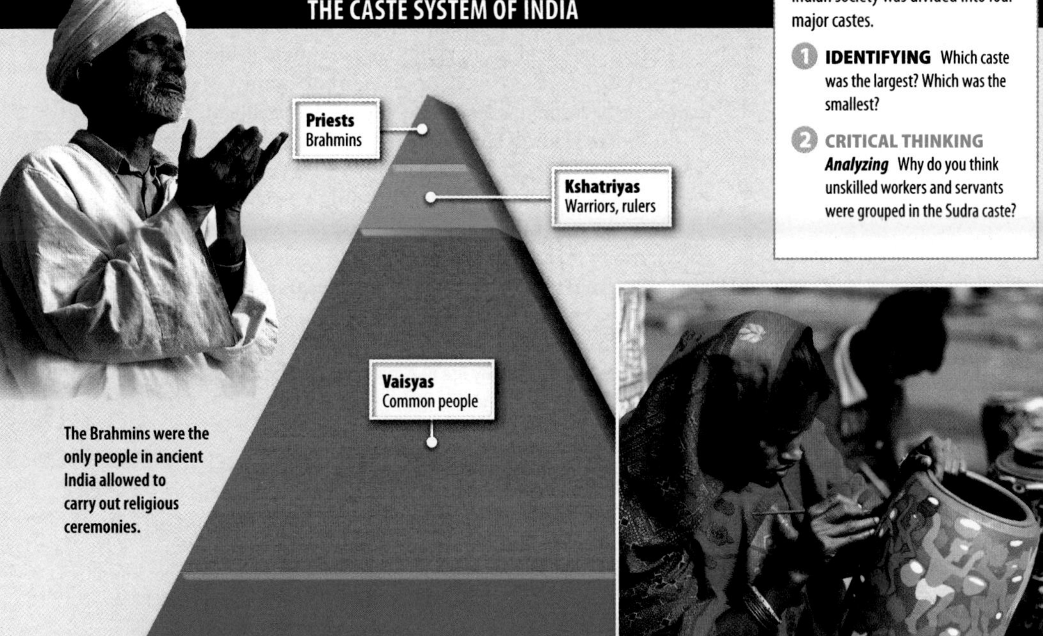

The Brahmins were the only people in ancient India allowed to carry out religious ceremonies.

Craftspeople in India belonged to the Vaisyas *varna*.

R Reading Skills

Discussing Direct students to read the text. Ask them to explain the development of the class system in ancient India. **Ask:** **How did the classes develop?** *(People specialized in different kinds of work, which formed the basis for the classes.)* AL

Ask: **What were the *varnas*?** *(social classes)* **What people made up the two most powerful *varnas*?** *(priests and warriors)* ELL

V Visual Skills

Analyzing Images Direct students' attention to the images depicting the caste system. **Ask:** **What is a caste?** *(a social class)*

Tell students to study the pyramid graphic organizer. **Ask:** **What does the pyramid shape of the organizer suggest about the class divisions in ancient India?** *(It suggests that there were few priests or Brahmins, a larger number of Kshatriyas, many Vaisyas, and a great many Sudras.)* AL ELL **Visual/Spatial**

Refer to the image of a man in prayer. **Ask:** **If you didn't read the caption, would you think this man was of an upper or lower caste? Explain.** *(Possible answer: Upper—the Brahmin caste was dedicated to religion, and he could be leading a ceremony here.)* AL

V

GRAPHIC ORGANIZER

Early India's Social System

Analyzing Charts Have students click on portions of the chart to reveal the hierarchy of early India's social system, along with an example of and more information about someone in each caste.

See page 245C for other online activities.

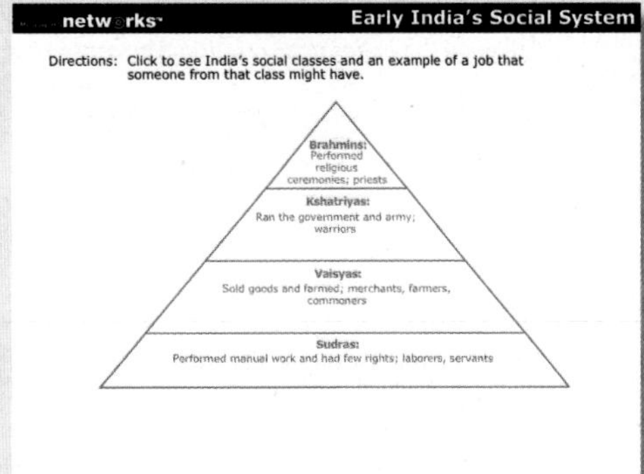

ANSWERS, p. 255

INFOGRAPHIC

1. The Sudra caste was the largest; the Brahmin caste was the smallest.
2. **CRITICAL THINKING** Students may note that these people have the fewest skills and the lowest status in society and so were placed in the Sudra caste.

R Reading Skills

Explaining Continue the discussion of the class system. **Ask:** **What were the four varnas?** *(priests, warriors and rulers, commoners, unskilled laborers and servants)* **What is the difference between a varna and a jati?** *(A jati is a smaller division within a varna. Jatis divided people based on specific types of work.)* Remind students of the roles that the Vaisyas and the Sudras played in ancient Indian society.

Remind students that the Untouchables were not considered part of the caste system. Ask students to explain the roles of the Untouchables in daily life.

Have students complete the Lesson 1 Review.

CLOSE & REFLECT

Discuss the achievements of the Indus Valley and Aryan civilizations with students. Ask them if they were surprised by the relative sophistication of cities like Mohenjo-Daro. Encourage them to consider the lasting impact that the Aryan migration has had on the culture and society of India.

Next were the Vaisyas (VYSH•yuhs), or commoners. Vaisyas were usually farmers, craftspeople, and merchants. Below the Vaisyas came the Sudras (SOO•druhs). Sudras were **manual** workers and servants who had few rights. Most Indians were in the Sudra *varna*. The four *varna* were divided into thousands of smaller groups known as *jati* (JAH•tee). Many *jati* were based on the type of work a person did. These *jati* had their own strict rules for diet, marriage, and social customs.

Scholars refer to the *varna* system as a **caste** (KAST) system. In such a system, people remain in the same caste or social group for life. People's castes determine the jobs they may take. Caste also affects people's choice of marriage partners.

At the lowest level of society were the Untouchables. The Untouchables were not part of the *varna* system. They did work that *varna* Indians would not do, such as collecting trash, skinning animals, and carrying dead bodies.

In ancient India, the family was the center of life. Grandparents, parents, and children lived together in an extended family. Elder family members were respected. The oldest male in the family was in charge of the entire household.

Indian men had more rights than women. Males inherited property, unless there were no sons in the family. Men attended school or became priests, while women were educated at home.

In India's leading families, a boy had a **guru** (GUR•oo), or teacher, until he attended school in the city. Young men from these families could marry only after finishing 12 years of education.

In India, parents arranged marriages for their children. Even today, many marriages are arranged. In early India, boys and girls often married in their teens. People could not get divorced.

PROGRESS CHECK

Explaining What was family life like in ancient India?

LESSON 1 REVIEW

Review Vocabulary (Tier 3 Words)

1. Why was the development of *Sanskrit* important to making the *Vedas* last? RH.6–8.4

Answer the Guiding Questions

2. ***Explaining*** Although the monsoons may bring severe storms, they are considered necessary in India. Why? RH.6–8.2
3. ***Summarizing*** What characteristics did the Indus Valley cities have in common? RH.6–8.2
4. ***Describing*** How did the Aryans interact with the Indus Valley people? RH.6–8.2
5. ***Categorizing*** What are the four major social groups in the *varna* system? RH.6–8.2
6. **ARGUMENT** What is the most important way the Aryans affected India? Write a brief essay that summarizes your ideas about their impact. WHST.6–8.2, WHST.6–8.10

LESSON 1 REVIEW ANSWERS

1. The development of the written language *Sanskrit* allowed the *Vedas* to be preserved in written form.
2. The summer monsoons bring much-needed rain to the Indus Valley region, making farming more productive.
3. Cities such as Harappa and Mohenjo-Daro were well planned and organized, with paved streets, sewer systems, and garbage collection, in addition to their fortified walls.
4. The Aryans began as migrants but eventually mixed with the descendants of the Indus Valley people to form a new culture.
5. The four main groups are: Brahmins, or priests; Kshatriyas, or warriors and rulers; Vaisyas, or commoners who were farmers, craftspeople, and merchants; and the Sudras, or manual laborers and servants.
6. Student answers will vary, but they should note that the Aryans established new kingdoms, introduced the *varna* system to India, and created a new culture that introduced the *Vedas*.

ANSWER, p. 256

PROGRESS CHECK The family was the center of daily life. Many generations lived together in a household controlled by the oldest male.

networks
There's More Online!
- GRAPHIC ORGANIZER
  Religions of Ancient India
- SLIDE SHOW
  - Upanishads
  - Representations of Buddha
  - Gandhi
- VIDEO

Lesson 2
Religions of Ancient India

ESSENTIAL QUESTION *How do religions develop?*

IT MATTERS BECAUSE
Millions of people around the world today follow the beliefs of religions that began in ancient India.

Origins of Hinduism

GUIDING QUESTION *What are the basic beliefs of Hinduism? How did Hinduism develop?*

R1 **Hinduism** (HIHN•doo•ih•zuhm) is one of the world's oldest religions. It is also the third largest religion, after Christianity and Islam. Hinduism developed from the faith of the Aryans. The sacred writings, called the Vedas, teach the key ideas of Aryan religion.

C At first, the Vedas had to be memorized by Brahmin priests and spoken out loud. Much later, they were written down in Sanskrit. Over time, the Aryan religion changed as it blended with the ideas of other people of India. This mix of beliefs eventually became Hinduism.

What is Hinduism?

R2 Hinduism includes many beliefs and practices. A core belief of Hinduism is that there is one universal spirit called **Brahman** (BRAH•muhn).

Ancient texts known as the Upanishads (oo•PAH•nih•SHADZ) describe the search for Brahman. These writings say that every living thing has a soul that is part of Brahman. The body is part of life on Earth. At death, the soul leaves the body and joins with Brahman.

Reading **HELP**DESK (CCSS)

Taking Notes: ***Describing***
Use a diagram like this one to identify three important facts about the religions of ancient India. **RH.6–8.2**

Hinduism | Buddhism | Jainism

Content Vocabulary (Tier 3 Words)
- **Hinduism**
- **Brahman**
- **reincarnation**
- **karma**
- **dharma**
- **Buddhism**
- **nirvana**
- **Jainism**

ENGAGE

Bellringer Explain to students that people in most cultures of the world practice some form of religion. Write the words *monotheism* and *polytheism* on the board, and make sure students know their meanings. Then **ask:** **Based on your knowledge of ancient cultures, which of them believed in many gods?** *(Sumerians, most of the Egyptians, Greeks, Romans)* **Which ancient cultures believed in one God?** *(Israel and, briefly, Egypt)* Explain to students that in this lesson they are going to learn about some religions with roots in India. Tell students that, as they read, they should look for ways in which these religions differ from—and are similar to—those they have studied previously.

TEACH & ASSESS

R1 Reading Skills

Describing Have students read the opening section. **Ask:** **What was the origin of Hinduism?** *(It developed from the faith of Aryans and in particular from the Vedas.)* Have students support their answers with evidence from the text.

C Critical Thinking Skills

Reasoning Point out that the Brahmin priests originally had to memorize the Vedas. **Ask:** **Why didn't they write them down until later?** *(Until they settled into villages in India, the Aryans did not have a written language.)*

R2 Reading Skills

Defining Work with students to clarify the content vocabulary words that they will need to understand in this chapter.
Ask: **What is Brahman?** *(the universal spirit)* **What are the Upanishads?** *(ancient texts that describe the search for Brahman)* If necessary, pronounce each term for students. ELL

VIDEO

India's History from the Hindus to the Buddhists

Formulating Questions Have students view the video on the history of Hinduism, the caste system, geographic changes that influenced the course of Indian history, and Buddhism. Tell students to take notes and to write questions about what they watch. You may wish to pause the video at 5:35 and 7:25 to discuss what students have learned in these major sections.

See page 245D for other online activities.

ANSWER, p. 257

TAKING NOTES: Answers may include: Hinduism: Belief in one universal spirit, reincarnation and karma, support for caste system; Buddhism: Belief in reincarnation, importance of karma, opposition to caste system, search for nirvana; Jainism: Belief in *ahimsa*

V Visual Skills

Analyzing Images Ask students to examine the image of Brahma. Read, or have a volunteer read, the caption for the image. Explain to students that Brahma is holding prayer beads in one hand, which he uses to count the passage of time. In another hand he holds a vase of water, which symbolizes the water from which the universe emerged. Have students do additional research to learn about other symbols associated with Brahma. Have them present their findings in a class discussion.

R Reading Skills

Discussing Call students' attention to the Sanskrit text from the *Upanishads*. **Ask:** **Why were the Upanishads important to Hinduism?** *(The Upanishads are an ancient Hindu text that tells about the search for Brahman.)* Explain that this belief in Brahman is one of the three core beliefs of Hinduism. List the following core Hindu beliefs on the board:

- All souls are connected to one great soul, known as Brahman.
- People are reincarnated, or reborn, again and again in a cycle.
- The cycle ends when the soul is united with Brahman.

Direct students to connect these beliefs to all three of the religions they will study in this lesson.
Verbal/Linguistic

V

The Upanishads (upper right) present basic Hindu views about the universe. Many Hindus regard the deity Brahma as the creator of the universe. Images of Brahma show him with four heads. Each head is believed to have delivered one of the four Vedas, or early sacred texts.

The Upanishads say that a soul that becomes one with Brahman is like a lump of salt thrown into water. The lump of salt is gone, but the water tastes salty. The salt has become part of the water.

R

Most ancient Indians, however, could not easily understand the idea of Brahman. They believed in many different deities that were more like people. Hindus built temples and statues and held ceremonies for these deities. Eventually, three deities became the most important: *Brahma* the Creator, *Vishnu* the Preserver, and *Shiva* the Destroyer. Over time, many Hindus came to think of all the deities as different parts of Brahman, the one universal spirit.

Another part of Hinduism is the belief in **reincarnation** (REE•ihn•kahr•NAY•shuhn), or the rebirth of the soul. Hindus strive for *moksha*, the ultimate peace. Hindus believe that most souls do not reunite with Brahman immediately after death. Instead, each soul must first pass through many lives. The Upanishads describe reincarnation as a process in this way:

PRIMARY SOURCE

> "As a caterpillar, having reached the end of a blade of grass, takes hold of another blade, then draws its body from the first, so the Self having reached the end of his body, takes hold of another body, then draws itself from the first."
>
> —from *Brihadaranyaka Upanishad, Fourth Brahmana*, line 3

TEXT: 'The Sacred Books of the East' translated by various Oriental scholars and edited by F. Max Müller. Oxford: Clarendon Press, 1879. PHOTO: (l) Louise Batalla Duran / Alamy; (r) The Print Collector/Photolibrary

Reading HELPDESK (CCSS)

Hinduism a major religion that developed in ancient India
Brahman the universal spirit worshipped by Hindus
reincarnation the rebirth of the soul
karma a force that decides the form that people will be reborn into in their next lives
dharma a person's personal duty, based on the individual's place in society

Academic Vocabulary (Tier 2 Words)
status a person's rank compared to others

networks Online Teaching Options

SLIDE SHOW

Upanishads

Explaining Have students view the slide show. The first slide tells about the Upanishads, the focus of the meditations, and the meaning of the word *Upanishad.* By clicking on the arrow, another slide provides a translation of a verse from the Upanishads. Ask students to explain the concept of Brahman in their own words.

See page 245D for other online activities.

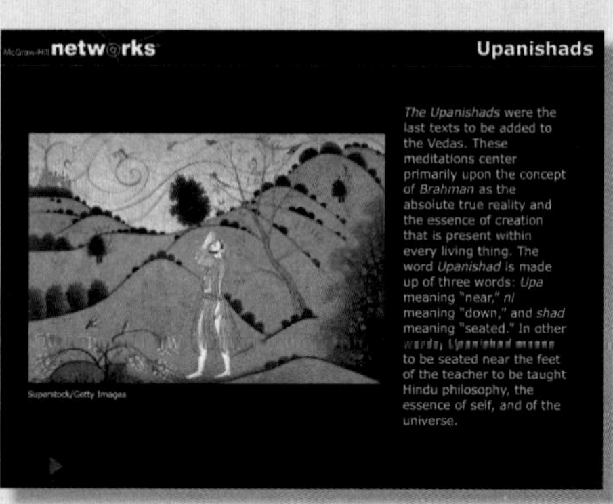

In Hinduism, the idea of reincarnation is closely related to another idea known as **karma** (KAHR•muh). According to karma, people's **status** in life is not an accident. It is based on what they did in past lives. In addition, the things people do in this life decide how they will be reborn. If someone leads a bad life, that person is reborn into a lower form of life. When good people die, their souls are reborn into a higher form of life.

R

Hindus believe they have to earn a better existence in the next life. To do that, they must follow **dharma** (DAHR•muh), or their personal duty. People's duties are different, depending on their place in society. A farmer has different duties than a priest. Men have different duties than women.

How did Hindu beliefs shape the way of life in ancient India? For one thing, Indians accepted the Hindu idea that all life is sacred. Animals as well as people were treated with kindness and respect.

W

Beliefs such as reincarnation also made many Indians more accepting of the *varna* system. A devout Hindu believed that the people in a higher *jati* were superior and deserved their status. At the same time, the belief in reincarnation gave hope to people from every walk of life. A person who leads a good life is reborn into a higher *jati*.

✓ PROGRESS CHECK

Understanding Cause and Effect How did Hinduism affect the way ancient Indians lived day to day?

Hindu Beliefs

Many Hindus today believe that a man should go through four stages in his life: a student (preparing to live in the world), a married man (accepting worldly responsibilities), a forest dweller (retirement from the world), and finally, a wandering monk (completely renouncing the world).

Indian Hindus believe the Ganges River is sacred. They believe that the river is the physical form of a female deity, and they bathe in the river to purify themselves. What tells you this photo shows Hindus in modern times?

Martin Harvey/Gallo Images/Getty Images

R Reading Skills

Explaining Have students cite details from the text to explain the importance of Hinduism in the development of the culture and society of ancient India. **Ask: How did the Hindu beliefs of karma and dharma support the caste system?** *(*Karma, *the good or evil a person creates by doing good or evil deeds, is what determines the caste a person is in. The only way to rise to a different caste is to follow* dharma *[duty] and create better* karma *for the next life.)* BL **How did Hindu beliefs shape the life and culture in ancient India?** *(Hindu beliefs taught acceptance of the caste system and dharma, the necessity of rituals for every part of life, and the importance of living a good life.)* AL ELL

W Writing Skills

Informative/Explanatory Have students work individually, in pairs, or in small groups to summarize what they have learned about Hinduism. Students should use a graphic organizer for their answers:

- **What was Aryan culture like when the Vedas were written?** *(The Aryans were gradually becoming settled farmers instead of wandering nomads.)*
- **Which Hindu practices developed with a more settled life?** *(Rituals, music, temple-building, and reading developed with a settled life. The caste system arose around varieties of work that developed in settled areas.)*
- **How did life under Hinduism change Aryan culture?** *(The caste system became more rigid; rituals were complicated.)*

Examples of graphic organizers include a three-column chart or a cause-and-effect diagram, such as a box (cause) with arrows to several circles (effects). You may choose to provide students with a pre-made graphic organizer, such as a sequence chart or flowchart.

GRAPHIC ORGANIZER

Taking Notes: *Describing:* Three Religions

Describing Have students open the Taking Notes graphic organizer. They can type in words and phrases describing each of the major religions. Allow students time in class to begin completing the organizer with facts about Hinduism. Students should continue to fill in the organizer as they study Buddhism and Jainism later in the lesson.

See page 245D for other online activities.

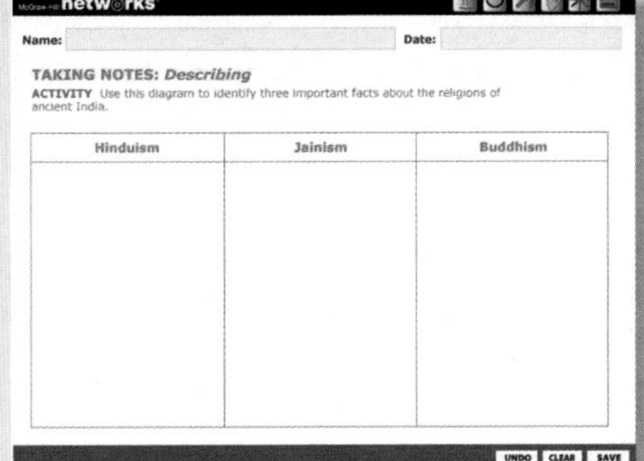

ANSWERS, p. 259

Caption: the style of construction, that the photo is in color, that men and women are together in the river

✓ **PROGRESS CHECK** Hinduism guided most aspects of people's lives through such systems as the *varnas* and the belief in reincarnation and karma.

R Reading Skills

Discussing After they have read the text, ask students what they know about meditation. Students may know that meditation is a mental exercise that uses a variety of methods to achieve relaxation and spiritual awareness. It is commonly used in many religions and for non-spiritual purposes as well. AL

Then, guide a discussion of the life of Buddha.Ask students to support their responses using text evidence. **Ask:** **What was his early life like?** *(He grew up as a prince and was given everything. He was rich, and had a wife and child.)* **Why did Siddhartha become inspired to seek the meaning of life?** *(He saw the misery and poverty of common people and realized that the world was full of suffering.)*

Content Background Knowledge

It is said that Siddhartha chose the color yellow for his robe because it was the color worn by criminals, and he wanted to debase himself and live a humble life apart from society. It is now worn by many monks as a symbol of their humility and renunciation of materialism, but other colors are seen as well.

ANSWER, p. 260

CRITICAL THINKING Students should note that he sought a simple way of life because he did not want his worldly possessions to distract him from his meditations.

BIOGRAPHY

The Buddha (c. 563 B.C.–c. 483 B.C.)

In his search for wisdom, Siddhartha Gautama lived a very simple life. He lived apart from people and slept on the ground. To clear his mind, he stopped eating for a time.

Still, after years, he felt he was no closer to the truth. One day he sat down in the shade of a tree to meditate. At last, Buddhist texts say, he learned the truth he had been seeking. Once he began teaching, he became known to his followers as the Buddha, or "Enlightened One."

▶ **CRITICAL THINKING**
Speculating Why do you think Siddhartha Gautama sought wisdom by living in such a simple way?

Rise of Buddhism

GUIDING QUESTION *Why did Buddhism appeal to many people in various parts of Asia?*

During the 500s B.C., some Indians felt unhappy with the many ceremonies of the Hindu religion. They wanted a simpler, more spiritual faith. They left their homes and looked for peace in the hills and forests. Many trained their minds to **focus** and think in positive ways. This training was called meditation. Some seekers developed new ideas and became religious teachers.

One of these teachers was Siddhartha Gautama (sih•DAHR•tuh GOW•tah•muh). He became known as the Buddha (BOO•dah). He founded a new religion called **Buddhism** (BOO•dih•zuhm).

The Buddha

Today, Buddhism is one of the major world religions. Most Buddhists live in Southeast Asia and East Asia. Only a few live in India, Buddhism's birthplace.

Siddhartha Gautama was born around the year 563 B.C. The exact date of his birth is not known. He grew up as a prince in a small kingdom near the Himalaya. Today, this area is in southern Nepal (nuh • PAWL).

R

As a young man, Siddhartha seemed to have everything. He was rich, handsome, and happily married with a newborn son. Then one day he left his palace to explore the life of ordinary people in the kingdom. As he traveled, Siddhartha was shocked at the misery and poverty around him. He saw beggars, people who were sick, and aged people with nowhere to live. For the first time, he understood that the world was filled with suffering.

Siddhartha gave up all he had and became a monk. Saying goodbye to his wife and son, he began his journey to find the meaning of life. Dressed in a yellow robe, he traveled the country, stopping to **meditate**, or think deeply. As he preached his message to people, he gathered followers. His teachings became known as Buddhism.

What did the Buddha teach?

Some of the Buddha's ideas were not new to India. He followed some Hindu ideas and changed others. Like Hindus, the Buddha believed that the world of the spirit was more important than the everyday world. He felt that one reason people suffered in life was that they cared too much about the wrong things. These included fame, money, and personal possessions. Wanting such

Reading **HELP**DESK CCSS

Buddhism a religion founded in ancient India by the religious teacher Buddha

Academic Vocabulary (Tier 2 Words)

focus to place all of one's attention on something
meditate to focus one's thoughts to gain a higher level of spiritual awareness

networks ***Online Teaching Options***

BIOGRAPHY

The Buddha

Analyzing Images Have students view the image of Buddha and read his biography. Explain to students that this statue presents the Buddha in a pose of meditation. After they read the biography, have students use the Internet to find more facts about the life of Siddhartha. Have them share what they learn with the class.

See page 245D for other online activities.

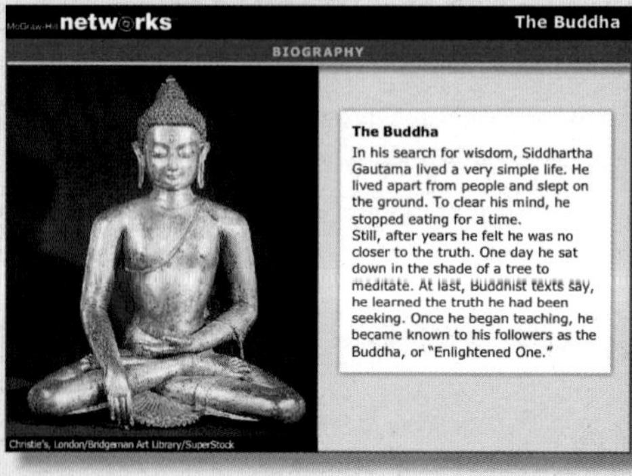

things could fill people with bad emotions like greed or anger. But seeking spiritual truth, he believed, led to inner peace.

The Buddha taught his followers the Four Noble Truths. He believed these would help people seek spiritual truth.

R

The Four Noble Truths:

1. Life is full of suffering.
2. People suffer because they desire worldly things and want to satisfy themselves.
3. The way to end suffering is to stop desiring things.
4. The only way to stop desiring things is to follow the Eightfold Path.

The Buddha's fourth truth says that people can end suffering by following eight steps.

The Eightfold Path:

G1

1. Know and understand the Four Noble Truths.
2. Give up worldly things and do not harm others.
3. Tell the truth, do not gossip, and do not speak badly of others.
4. Do not **commit** evil acts, such as killing, stealing, or living an unclean life.
5. Do rewarding work.
6. Work for good and oppose evil.
7. Make sure your mind keeps your senses under control.
8. Practice meditation to see the world in a new way.

When people were finally free from all earthly concerns, they would reach **nirvana** (nihr•VAH•nuh). According to Buddhist teaching, nirvana is not a physical place. It is an emotional or spiritual state, a feeling of perfect peace and happiness.

G2

Buddhism spread because it welcomed people from all walks of life. The Buddha placed little importance on the *varna* system. He believed people's place in life did not depend on the *varna* into which they were born. The Buddha explained that the success of life depended on peoples' behavior now.

Like Hindus, the Buddha believed in reincarnation, but in a different way. He taught that people could end the cycle of rebirth by following the Eightfold Path rather than their dharma.

Buddhist monks devote their lives to honoring the Buddha through prayer and gifts. Monks are considered to be on a higher spiritual level than other people, and they serve as spiritual teachers.

Martin Puddy/Corbis

nirvana a state of perfect happiness and peace

Academic Vocabulary (Tier 2 Words)
commit to carry out or do

R Reading Skills

Paraphrasing Ask volunteers to read aloud the section in their textbooks about the Four Noble Truths. Model for students how to paraphrase each of the truths in their own words. For example, say: "This is one way to restate the first Truth: 'There is a lot of pain in the world.'" Then ask volunteers to restate the other three truths. Write their paraphrases on the board. Then present the Eightfold Path one step at a time. Ask students to paraphrase each step.

G1 Critical Thinking Skills

Evaluating Ask: Do you think following the Eightfold Path is difficult for people in today's modern world? Why or why not? *(Possible answers: Yes; it probably is hard because our society is so fast-paced. No; if people truly believe, then they will dedicate themselves to following the path's steps.)* BL

G2 Critical Thinking Skills

Contrasting Discuss the role of varna in the Buddha's teachings. **Ask: How did the Buddha's attitude toward varna compare to the attitude of Hindus at this time?** *(The Buddha did not think the varna system was important; people's success in life depended on their behavior. Hindus thought the varna was very important and that it dictates one's success in life.)*

IMAGE

Buddhist Monk

Analyzing Images Have students view the interactive image of the Buddhist monk. Clicking on the bullets reveals additional information about Buddhist monks. Have students use the Internet to learn what kinds of lives Buddhist monks live today.

See page 245D for other online activities.

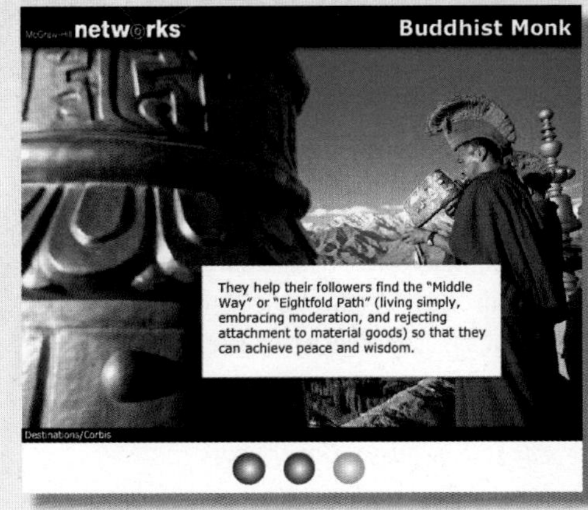

networks
Buddhist Monk
They help their followers find the "Middle Way" or "Eightfold Path" (living simply, embracing moderation, and rejecting attachment to material goods) so that they can achieve peace and wisdom.
Destinations/Corbis

R Reading Skills

Contrasting As they read, direct students to consider how the tenets of Buddhism contrast with what they have read to date. **Ask:** How do you think Buddhism changed life for followers who had converted from Hinduism? *(Everyone was now equal. Anyone could reach enlightenment. Meditation, not ritual, was the key to spiritual growth.)* Why were Untouchables and people in the lower jati more willing to accept the teachings of the Buddha? *(He held out hope to them that they could improve their lives and reach enlightenment and not be forever condemned to poverty and suffering.)* What is the main difference between Theravada Buddhism and Mahayana Buddhism? *(Followers of Theravada Buddhism do not believe Buddha is a god; followers of Mahayana Buddhism believe Buddha is a god.)* Discuss Bodhisattvas and the spread of Buddhism into China, Korea, and Japan.

T Technology Skills

Making Presentations Have students work together in small groups and do research into Tibetan Buddhism, the Dalai Lama, and the Dalai Lama's role as political leader (in exile) of Tibet. Have students investigate the relationship between the Tibetan monks and the government of China. Have groups create a multimedia presentation that they will present to the class.
BL Interpersonal

C Critical Thinking Skills

Speculating Point out to students that although Buddhism originated in India and spread widely, there are few practicing Buddhists in India today. **Ask:** Why do you think Buddhism died out in Indian culture but grew in other parts of Asia? *(Students' speculations will vary but should be reasonable. Possible answers: Hinduism and the caste system were already in place and hard to change. The more powerful castes might not have wanted to convert. The more powerful castes might have suppressed Buddhism. Buddhism does not stress winning converts.)* BL

ANSWERS, p. 262

Build Vocabulary Students should list six words with the suffix *-ward.*
Examples may include: *southward, windward, downward, eastward, westward, leeward,* and *toward.*

✓ PROGRESS CHECK Buddhism is widely practiced in Eastern and Southeastern Asian countries such as Myanmar, Thailand, Cambodia, Laos, and Tibet. It is divided into the Theravada and Mahayana forms.

Many people accepted the Buddha's message, especially Untouchables and Indians in the lower *jati*. For the first time, these groups heard that they, too, could reach enlightenment.

For more than 40 years, the Buddha taught his ideas. After his death, Buddha's followers disagreed over the meaning of the Buddha's ideas. Eventually, the Buddhists divided into two groups: Theravada (ther•uh•VAH•duh) Buddhists and Mahayana (mah•huh•YAH•nuh) Buddhists.

Theravada Buddhism

Theravada means "teachings of the elders." Followers of Theravada view the Buddha as a great teacher, but not a god. Theravada Buddhism is the major religion of the modern-day country of Sri Lanka (sree LAHN•kuh). Buddhist teachers spread the ideas of Theravada to Myanmar (MEEAHN•mahr), Thailand (TEYE•land), Cambodia (kam•BOH•dee•uh), and Laos (LAH•ohs).

Mahayana Buddhism

Mahayana Buddhism teaches that the Buddha is a god. Followers of Mahayana Buddhism believe that the Eightfold Path is too difficult for most people. By worshipping the Buddha, people will go to a heaven after they die. There, they can follow the Eightfold Path and reach nirvana.

Bodhisattvas (BOH•dih•SUHT•vuhz) hold a special place in Mahayana Buddhism. Bodhisattvas are enlightened people who do not enter heaven. Instead, they stay on Earth to do good deeds and help others on the path to nirvana.

Mahayana Buddhism spread northward into China and from there to Korea and Japan. A special kind of Mahayana Buddhism arose in the central Asian country of Tibet (tih•BEHT).

Buddhist leaders called lamas led the government of Tibet. The Dalai Lama (DAH•ly LAH•muh) led Tibet's government, and the Panchen Lama led the religion. Tibetans considered both leaders to be reincarnations of the Buddha.

Today, few Buddhists live in India where the Buddha first preached. Buddhism, however, is widely practiced in Southeast Asia and East Asia. There are an **estimated** 376 million Buddhists in the world today.

✓ PROGRESS CHECK

Identifying Where is Buddhism practiced today and in what forms?

Reading HELPDESK CCSS

Build Vocabulary: *Suffixes*
The suffix *-ward* means "in the direction of" or "toward." It is used in many words that indicate direction, such as *northward, upward, forward,* or *outward*. Create a list of six directional words using the suffix *-ward*.

Academic Vocabulary (Tier 2 Words)
estimate to determine an approximate value, size, or nature of something

networks *Online Teaching Options*

SLIDE SHOW

Representations of Buddha

Analyzing Images Have students view the slide show. By clicking on the arrow, additional images of the Buddha will appear, along with information about each particular image. Have students talk about what these representations have in common. Ask students to use the Internet to find additional representations of the Buddha to share with the class.

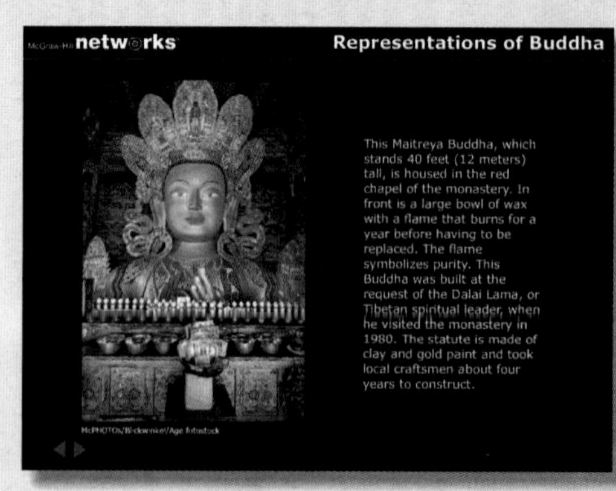

See page 245D for other online activities.

It is a tradition for Buddhist monks in Tibet to create geometric patterns using brightly colored powders, stones, or pieces of metal. The shapes in the patterns represent the cosmos, or universe, and are believed to have special powers.

AFP/Getty Images

Jainism

GUIDING QUESTION *What are the teachings of Jainism?*

Along with Hinduism and Buddhism, another Indian faith known as **Jainism** (JEYE•nih•zihm) arose about 500 B.C. Today, there are 6 million followers of Jainism. Most of them live in India.

Who is Mahavira?

The exact origins of Jainism are unknown. Its current form was developed by a religious leader named Mahavira. Mahavira lived in India at about the same time as Siddhartha Gautama.

Like Siddhartha, Mahavira came from a wealthy royal family in northern India. After his parents died, Mahavira gave up his wealth and property. He owned nothing and begged for his food.

Mahavira became known as the Jina, or the conqueror. His followers came to be known as Jains. Many of Mahavira's teachings were like those of the Buddha. Both taught that people needed to stop wanting worldly things. Only by doing so could they escape the cycle of rebirth and reach nirvana. The Jains practiced strict poverty.

R

Jainism a religion of ancient India that does not believe in a supreme being. It emphasizes nonviolence and respect for all living things.

R Reading Skills

Discussing Tell students that Jainism is the third major Indian religion. Have them add details about this religion to the charts they started at the beginning of this lesson. Discuss the following questions:

- Where do most followers of Jainism live? *(India)*
- Who was Mahavira? *(a religious leader who lived at about the same time as Siddhartha Gautama, and who helped develop Jainism as it is now practiced)*
- What did Mahavira have in common with Siddhartha Gautama? *(Both gave up their wealth and position; both began religions that still exist today; both taught their followers to reject worldly things.)*
- What does Jainism teach will be the reward of giving up worldly possessions? *(the attainment of nirvana)*

Content Background Knowledge

Explain to students that the monks in the image are creating a mandala, which is a symbolic representation of the universe. Its purpose is to concentrate universal forces in the vicinity of the mandala. The mandala is believed to help individuals find their way to enlightenment. Tibetan monks sometimes create them in different-colored sands. When the ceremony is complete, they sweep up these beautiful works of colored sand and spread them into a stream.

PRIMARY SOURCE

Mahavira, Founder of Jainism

Interpreting Have students view the primary-source image of Mahavira, and read what he says about enlightenment. Students can read his exact words by scrolling through the text. Ask students to paraphrase what Mahavira says in the text. Guide a discussion of their responses.

See page 245D for other online activities.

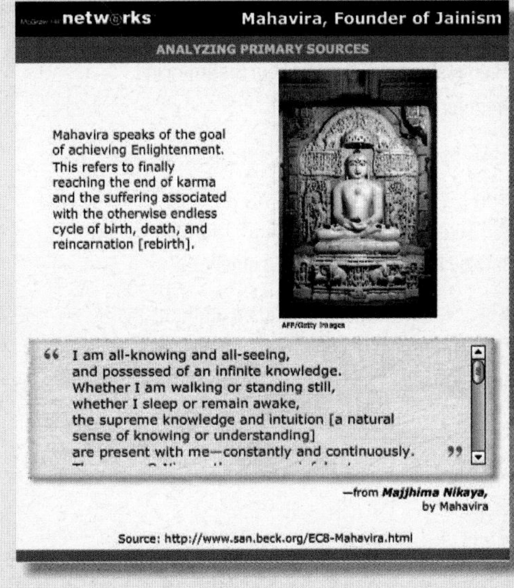

networks
Mahavira, Founder of Jainism
ANALYZING PRIMARY SOURCES
Mahavira speaks of the goal of achieving Enlightenment. This refers to finally reaching the end of karma and the suffering associated with the otherwise endless cycle of birth, death, and reincarnation [rebirth].
AFP/Getty Images
" I am all-knowing and all-seeing,
and possessed of an infinite knowledge.
Whether I am walking or standing still,
whether I sleep or remain awake,
the supreme knowledge and intuition [a natural sense of knowing or understanding]
are present with me—constantly and continuously. "
—from Majjhima Nikaya, by Mahavira
Source: http://www.san.beck.org/EC8-Mahavira.html

Religions of Ancient India

R Reading Skills

Specifying After students read, ask them to provide details on Jainism. **Ask:** **What is ahimsa?** *(the main belief of Jainism—practicing nonviolence toward all living things)* **How do Jains practice this belief?** *(They are careful not to kill even insects or worms.)* **How is Jainism similar to Buddhism?** *(Both share beliefs in giving up worldly things and not harming others.)* AL ELL

C Critical Thinking Skills

Making Connections Provide historical context, as necessary, about Gandhi's life and his impact on the politics of the twentieth century. Explain that he was greatly influenced by the idea of ahimsa. **Ask:** **How might acts of nonviolence help people who are seeking freedom?** *(Possible answer: It gets the attention of those in power who are used to people using only force, and it continues to remind them of what the freedom-fighters want.)*

Have students complete the Lesson 2 Review.

CLOSE & REFLECT

Lead a discussion in which students compare the three Asian religions—Hinduism, Buddhism, and Jainism—to other religions they have studied or know about, such as Christianity, Judaism, and Islam. **Ask:** **How are these religions similar and how are they different?** *(Responses will vary but should be reasonable and based on details from the text.)* Guide students to have a respectful attitude toward all religions.

ANSWER, p. 264

✓ **PROGRESS CHECK** It is the practice of nonviolence toward all living things.

Gandhi (center) used nonviolence as an effective protest tool. He often protested by fasting, or not eating, to show support for a cause.

Dinodia Images/Alamy

What is *Ahimsa*?

The key value of Jainism is *ahimsa* (ah•HIM•sah). This means practicing nonviolence toward all living things. Believing that all life is sacred, Mahavira's followers tried to avoid harming any living creature. For example, they used brooms to sweep away insects so that they would not step on them. Jains did not farm because they were afraid of plowing under worms and other living things in the soil. R

The idea of *ahimsa* has long influenced India's culture and politics. In the 1900s, the Indian leader Mohandas Gandhi (MOE•han•dahs GANH•dee) wanted to free India from Great Britain. He led a nonviolent struggle against British rule. Thousands would come to hear Gandhi speak or to simply sit with him while he prayed. At the time, Indians refused to pay taxes or buy British goods as a show of protest. Many protesters were jailed, but India eventually gained its independence. Gandhi himself was jailed many times. C

Gandhi's method of nonviolent resistance influenced many others. In the United States, Dr. Martin Luther King, Jr., led nonviolent protests to gain rights for African Americans. Like Gandhi, Dr. King was able to use nonviolence to bring about great change in his country.

✓ **PROGRESS CHECK**

Identifying What is the belief of *ahimsa*?

LESSON 2 REVIEW CCSS

Review Vocabulary (Tier 3 Words)

1. What do the ideas of *reincarnation* and *karma* have in common? RH.6–8.4
2. How would practicing *Buddhism* affect people's daily lives? RH.6–8.4

Answer the Guiding Questions

3. ***Explaining*** What do Hindus believe about Brahman? RH.6–8.2
4. ***Drawing Conclusions*** How did the Buddha say people should live? RH.6–8.2
5. ***Comparing*** What beliefs do Buddhism and Jainism share? RH.6–8.2
6. **INFORMATIVE/EXPLANATORY** Write a paragraph comparing Hindu and Buddhist beliefs about reincarnation and how one should live. WHST.6–8.2, WHST.6–8.10

264 *Ancient India*

LESSON 2 REVIEW ANSWERS

1. The karma one earns in life determines the type of life he or she will be reborn into as part of the cycle of reincarnation.
2. Buddhism teaches people to give up worldly desires and possessions, so it would make people live simpler, more spiritual, and less material lives.
3. Hindus believe that Brahman is a universal spirit. Many Hindus believe that the major deities of the Hindu faith are incarnations of Brahman in different forms.
4. The Buddha said that people should follow the Eightfold Path, which involves steps, such as giving up worldly things and avoiding doing harm to others, in order to gain enlightenment and inner peace.
5. Both believe in reincarnation and meditation, and that the attainment of enlightenment will lead to nirvana.
6. Students should note that Buddhists and Hindus believe in reincarnation, the concept that souls are reborn after the body dies. Hindus support the caste system, but Buddhists believe it is not of great importance. Hindus believe that people must follow their dharma, or duty, to earn good karma in life. This dharma is different for each person. Buddhists believe that, instead of living by the dharma of a caste, all people can earn good karma by following the Eightfold Path.

networks
There's More Online!

- GRAPHIC ORGANIZER
  - Ashoka's Reign
  - Mauryan and Gupta Empires
- MAP Gupta Empire
- SLIDE SHOW Ancient Indian Medical Tools

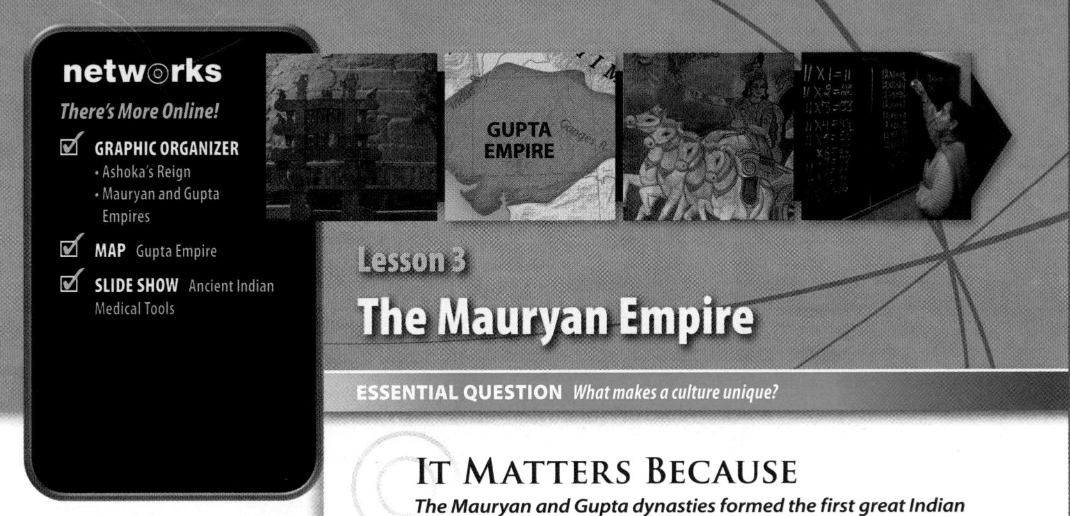

Lesson 3
The Mauryan Empire

ESSENTIAL QUESTION *What makes a culture unique?*

It Matters Because

The Mauryan and Gupta dynasties formed the first great Indian empires. Their cultures were the basis for civilizations that followed.

Origin of an Empire

GUIDING QUESTION *How did religion affect the development of the Mauryan Empire?*

By the 500s B.C., India was divided into many small kingdoms. Conflict over land and trade weakened the kingdoms, leaving them open to foreign invasion. Persian armies conquered the Indus Valley in the 500s B.C. and made it part of the Persian Empire. The Greeks, under Alexander the Great, then defeated the Persians. Alexander entered India but turned back in 325 B.C., when his homesick troops threatened to rebel.

India's First Empire

After Alexander left India, an Indian military officer named Chandra Gupta Maurya (CHUHN•druh GUP•tuh MAH•oor•yuh) built a strong army. He knew that only a large and powerful empire could defend India against invasion. In 321 B.C., Chandra Gupta set out to conquer northern India and unify the region under his rule.

Chandra Gupta was the first ruler of the Mauryan dynasty. He was a skilled administrator. He set up a well-run government in his capital city of Pataliputra (PAH•tah•lih•POO•truh). One of his major achievements was an efficient postal system. The system improved communications throughout his empire.

R

Reading HELPDESK CCSS

Taking Notes: *Identifying*

Use a chart like this one to identify important information about the Mauryan and Gupta Empires. RH.6–8.2

Mauryan	Gupta

Content Vocabulary (Tier 3 Words)
- **stupa**
- **pilgrim**
- ***Bhagavad Gita***

ENGAGE

Bellringer As a class, discuss the qualities that make an effective leader. Have students list the names of some of the leaders from the past that they know about or have studied, such as King David, the ancient Egyptian pharaohs, Pericles, and Alexander the Great. Talk about the accomplishments of each and whether he or she was a good leader, a bad leader, or both. **Ask: What qualities does a good leader need?** *(Positive qualities might include wisdom and concern for people as well as the ability or desire to treat everyone fairly, solve problems, and listen.)* **What qualities does a bad leader have?** *(Negative qualities might include greed, dishonesty, giving certain people special favors, and not solving problems.)* Tell students that they will learn about several different leaders in ancient India and how these leaders influenced their people. Encourage students to look for examples in the text of positive effects and negative effects of each leader's actions.

TEACH & ASSESS

R Reading Skills

Explaining After students have read the text, ask a volunteer to review the history of the invasions that swept through India immediately before Chandra Gupta's rise to power. **Ask: Why did Chandra Gupta build an army and conquer the kingdoms of India?** *(He wanted to unite India as one strong empire that could defend itself against invasion.)* **How do you think the people of these kingdoms felt about Chandra Gupta's plan?** *(Answers will vary. Guide students to understand that many probably opposed the plan, preferring their independence and disliking the war and suffering that resulted from Chandra Gupta's plan.)*

Review with students what an empire is.

VIDEO

India's History from the Golden Age to Today

Sequencing This video recounts the story of Alexander the Great's attempt to conquer India. It tells about Chandra Gupta's actions in throwing out the Greek warriors that Alexander left behind while in building his empire. After students watch the video, have them construct a time line showing the sequence of these events. They may need to view the video more than once.

See page 245E for other online activities.

ANSWER, p. 265

TAKING NOTES: Possible answers: Mauryan: India's first empire, founded by Chandra Gupta Maurya, reached its height during the reign of Ashoka—a soldier who became a Buddhist. Gupta: a power in the Ganges River valley, led by rulers who practiced Hinduism and built temples

The Mauryan Empire

V Visual Skills

Analyzing Maps Have students examine the map of the Mauryan Empire and notice the cities that are marked. **Ask:**

- What do the locations of the cities have in common? *(They are next to rivers.)*
- What does the symbol next to each city mean? *(Ashoka placed a pillar there.)* AL ELL **Visual/Spatial**

R1 Reading Skills

Discussing As they read, ask students to note the tactics used by Chandra Gupta. **Ask:** What tactics did Chandra Gupta use to stay in power? *(He used his army to crush resistance and spies to report disloyalty; he had servants taste his food, and he never slept in the same bed two nights in a row.)* Guide a discussion of modern leaders who used similar tactics to stay in power.

R2 Reading Skills

Explaining After students have read the text, call on volunteers to describe Ashoka when he first came to power. **Ask:** What made him change? *(He was horrified by the deaths and injuries of battle; he decided to become a Buddhist.)* Discuss why Buddhism might have brought about a change in Ashoka.

GEOGRAPHY CONNECTION

The Mauryan dynasty built the first great Indian empire.

1. **REGION** Which part of India was not in the Mauryan Empire?
2. CRITICAL THINKING ***Analyzing*** What does the map key tell you about the religion of the Mauryan Empire?

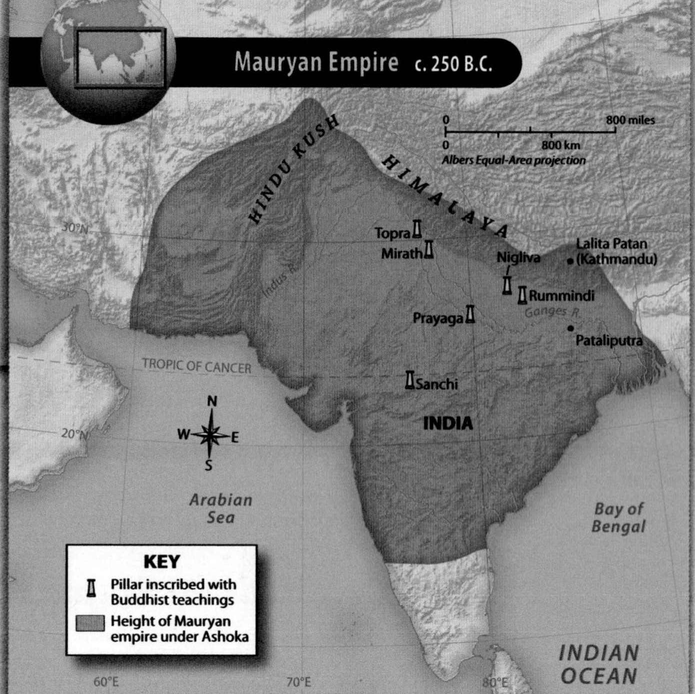

V

R1 Chandra Gupta's powerful army crushed any resistance to his rule. He also used spies to report any disloyalty among his subjects. While he was a strong ruler, Chandra Gupta was very cautious. He was afraid of being poisoned, so he had servants taste his food before he ate it. He was so concerned about being attacked that he never slept two nights in a row in the same bed.

What Did Ashoka Accomplish?

R2 The Mauryan Empire reached the height of its glory under Chandra Gupta's grandson Ashoka (uh•SOH•kuh). Ashoka governed most of northern and central India from about 273 B.C. to 232 B.C.

Ashoka was an unusual king. Like many rulers, Ashoka began his rule with fierce wars of conquest. **Eventually**, he came to hate killing. After one battle, he looked at the fields covered with dead and wounded soldiers. He was horrified by what he saw. He decided that he would follow Buddhist teachings and become a man of peace.

Reading HELPDESK (CCSS)

stupa a Buddhist shrine, usually dome-shaped

Academic Vocabulary (Tier 2 Words)

eventual taking place at an unnamed later time
promote to encourage the doing of something

networks Online Teaching Options

MAP

Mauryan Empire c. 250 B.C.

Analyzing Maps Students can click on each of the items in the map key to reveal those symbols on the map. After they explore the map, ask them to turn off all the layers except the modern boundaries. Ask them to identify the modern countries shown by the boundaries. They can check their work in an atlas.

See page 245E for other online activities.

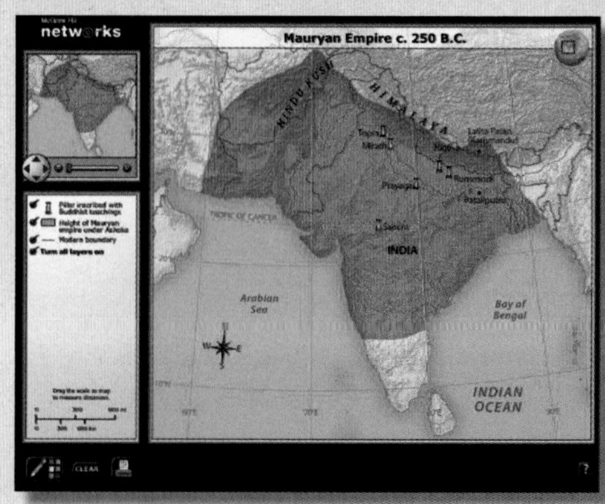

ANSWERS, p. 266

GEOGRAPHY CONNECTION

1. The southern tip of the Indian subcontinent was not part of the Mauryan Empire.
2. CRITICAL THINKING The symbols for pillars inscribed with Buddhist teachings show that Buddhism was important in the empire.

Ashoka kept his promise. During the rest of his life, he tried to improve the lives of his people. Ashoka made laws that encouraged people to do good deeds, practice nonviolence, and respect others. He created hospitals for people and for animals. He built fine roads, with rest houses and shade trees for the travelers' comfort.

Ashoka was the first ruler to **promote** Buddhism. He sent teachers to spread the religion throughout India and other parts of Asia. Buddhist teachings and the laws of Ashoka were carved on rocks and tall stone pillars for all the people to read. Carved on one rock is the idea that:

PRIMARY SOURCE

> "Father and mother must be hearkened [listened to]; similarly, respect for living creatures must be firmly established; truth must be spoken. These are the virtues of the Law of Piety [devotion] which must be practiced."
>
> —from "Summary of the Law of Piety," The Edicts of Ashoka

Ashoka also had thousands of **stupas** (stoo•puhs) built throughout India. Stupas are Buddhist shrines shaped like a dome or burial mound. The stupas contained religious objects and served as a place of worship. Although he was a devout Buddhist, Ashoka was tolerant of all beliefs and allowed his Hindu subjects to practice their religion.

Ashoka's able leadership helped the Mauryan Empire prosper. India's good roads helped it become the center of a large trade network that stretched to the Mediterranean Sea.

Ashoka—shown here—made regular visits to rural people of his empire to spread Buddhist ideas and learn about their needs. He also had this "Great Stupa" built in honor of Buddha.

▶ CRITICAL THINKING

Speculating Why do you think Ashoka had so many stupas built?

R Reading Skills

Explaining After students have read the section on Ashoka, lead a discussion to help them understand the transformation of Ashoka's leadership. **Ask:** What kind of leader did Ashoka become after he converted to Buddhism? *(He became a good leader who was concerned about the welfare of his people.)* What did he do to help them? *(He encouraged people to do good deeds, practice nonviolence, and respect others. He built hospitals, roads and rest houses. He promoted Buddhism, created stone pillars with his laws carved on them, and built stupas. He was tolerant of all religions.)* AL

C Critical Thinking Skills

Interpreting Ask a volunteer to read the primary-source text from one of Ashoka's pillars. Then ask them to paraphrase and explain it. **Ask:** How does this edict compare to what you already know about Buddhism? *(Students should recognize that it follows the laws of the Buddha in calling for respect and responsibility for all living things.)* BL

T Technology Skills

Researching on the Internet Ask volunteers to research stupas on the Internet. Have them learn about the different kinds of stupas, how they are used for worship, and their shared characteristics. Ask them to compile pictures of a variety of stupas to illustrate their information, and then prepare and present a multimedia presentation to the class.

CHART

Ashoka's Reign

Determining Cause and Effect By clickin g on each box, students will reveal a text describing causes and effects relating to Ashoka's leadership. Have students discuss the significance of these causes and effects for the people of the Mauryan Empire. Then have them create a similar chart and add additional causes and effects of events during Ashoka's reign that they read about in the text.

See page 245E for other online activities.

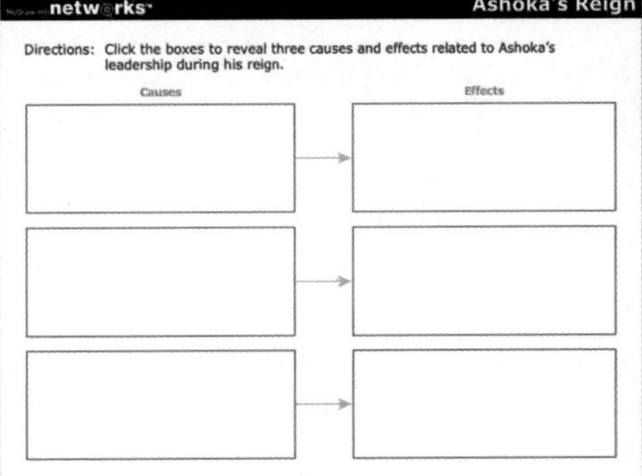

networks
Ashoka's Reign
Directions: Click the boxes to reveal three causes and effects related to Ashoka's leadership during his reign.
Causes
Effects

ANSWER, p. 267

CRITICAL THINKING Ashoka wanted to spread Buddhist teachings, and the stupas provided places for Buddhists to worship and learn.

The Mauryan Empire

R1 Reading Skills

Summarizing After students have read the paragraph, ask a volunteer to summarize the events that brought an end to the Mauryan Empire. **Ask: What happened to the Mauryan Empire after Ashoka's death? Why?** *(The empire declined and split into warring kingdoms because the rulers that followed Ashoka were not as wise or as unselfish as he had been. They raised taxes and seized land.)* **How did the Mauryan Empire finally end?** *(The last king was murdered by one of his generals, and the empire split into small kingdoms.)*

R2 Reading Skills

Making Connections Direct students to read the section titled "The Gupta Empire." Asks students to justify the assertion that India experienced a golden age under the first Gupta rulers. **Ask: What is a "golden age"?** *(Possible answer: a time of prosperity and creativity)* **How is trade connected to India's golden age?** *(The success of trade made India's rulers wealthy. They used this money from trade to pay for projects in the arts and literature.)* **Do you think Samudra Gupta was a good leader or a bad leader?** *(Most students will say he was a good leader because, under his leadership, India entered a golden age.)* Have students provide evidence from the text to support their opinions.

ANSWERS, p. 268

PROGRESS CHECK Ashoka witnessed bloodshed on a battlefield and became a devout Buddhist. This led him to achieve many good works and to promote religious tolerance among his people.

PROGRESS CHECK Trade routes enabled trade within India to flourish and brought goods from other countries to India. In addition, cities grew along trade routes and benefited from pilgrimages and shrines.

The End of the Mauryan Empire

R1 After Ashoka died in 232 B.C., the Mauryan Empire **declined**. The kings who came after Ashoka lacked his kindness and skills. The new rulers made merchants pay heavy taxes and took lands from the peasants. The Indian people rebelled against the harsh treatment. In 183 B.C., the last Mauryan king was murdered by one of his own generals. The land of the Mauryan Empire split into many small warring kingdoms.

PROGRESS CHECK

Explaining What caused Ashoka to denounce violence? What was the result?

The Gupta Empire

GUIDING QUESTION ***Why did the Gupta Empire become powerful?***

R2 For 500 years, the small warring kingdoms fought one another for control of India. Then, in A.D. 320, the Gupta dynasty came to power in the Ganges River valley. The city of Pataliputra had been the capital of the old Mauryan Empire. It now became the capital of the Gupta Empire. Chandra Gupta I, the first Gupta ruler, had the same name as the first ruler of the Mauryan dynasty.

Chandra Gupta I ruled for 10 years. He chose his son, Samudra Gupta (suh•MOO•druh GUP•tuh), to rule after him. Samudra Gupta expanded the Gupta Empire in northern India. He was a great military leader and a patron of arts and literature. Under Samudra Gupta, India entered a golden age.

Gupta rulers practiced the Hindu religion like many of their subjects did. They donated money to support Hindu scholars and build Hindu temples. Many temples had brightly painted sculptures of deities and images from Hindu sacred writings.

Trade helped the Gupta Empire thrive. Salt, cloth, and iron were common goods traded in India. Indian merchants also traded with China and with lands in Southeast Asia and the Mediterranean area. The Gupta rulers benefited from their control of much of the trade. They owned silver and gold mines and large estates.

Cities arose along trade routes. People called **pilgrims** (PIHL•gruhms) used the trade routes to journey to holy sites. Cities with famous temples grew wealthy from visiting pilgrims.

PROGRESS CHECK

Explaining How did the Gupta Empire profit from trade routes?

Reading HELPDESK (CCSS)

pilgrim a person who travels to holy sites

Academic Vocabulary (Tier 2 Words)

decline to become smaller or weaker

networks Online Teaching Options

SLIDE SHOW

Mural from the Caves at Ajanta

Analyzing Visuals During the time of the early Gupta rulers, India experienced a golden age. The murals in the Caves at Ajanta are some of the lasting evidence from that period. Ask students to view the slide show and read the associated text to learn more about this age and the mural. **Ask: How can the art in these caves help us to understand this period in Indian history?** *(The caves show scenes from everyday life, helping us understand how people lived. The art also helps us understand what the people valued and what they believed.)*

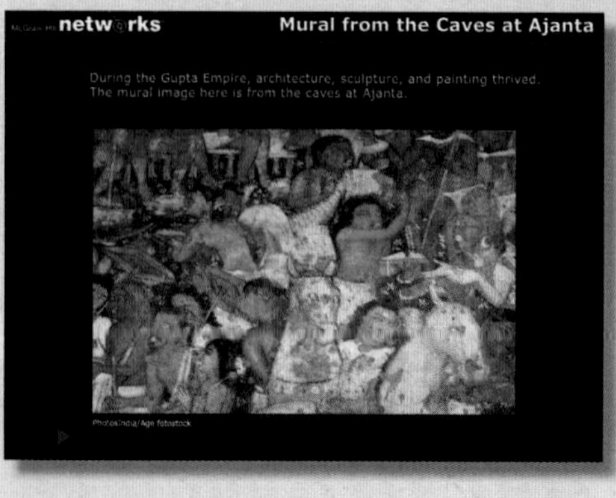

networks
Mural from the Caves at Ajanta
During the Gupta Empire, architecture, sculpture, and painting thrived. The mural image here is from the caves at Ajanta.

See page 245E for other online activities.

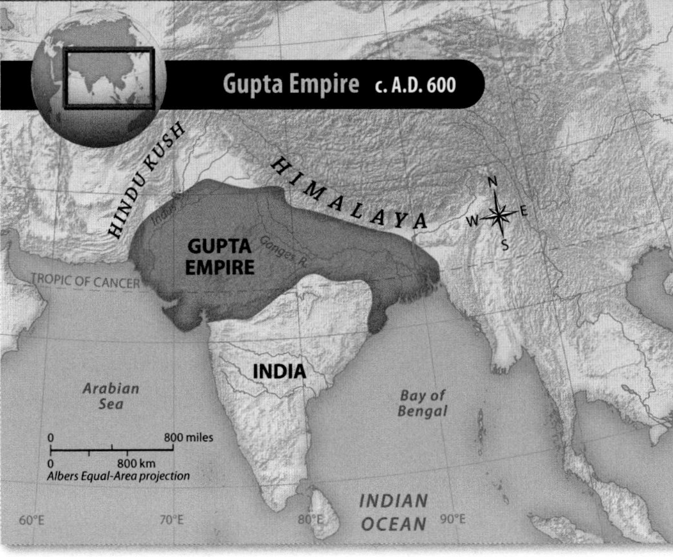

GEOGRAPHY CONNECTION

The Gupta dynasty founded the second great Indian empire.

1 **LOCATION** Where was the Gupta Empire located? Around what river valleys was it formed?

2 **CRITICAL THINKING** ***Analyzing*** What does this map suggest about the power of the Gupta Empire?

V

Culture in Ancient India

GUIDING QUESTION *What were the cultural contributions of the Mauryan and Gupta Empires?*

Ancient India produced a brilliant culture. Artists, builders, writers, and scientists made many **contributions** while the Mauryan and Gupta kings ruled.

The Literature of India

The Vedas were among the first works written in the Sanskrit language. The literature of ancient India also includes epics. Hindu epics are sacred texts that teach important moral lessons. The people could learn the correct and acceptable behavior through interesting stories.

The *Mahabharata* (muh•HAH•BAH•ruh•tuh) is an ancient religious epic. It is also the longest poem in any written language, with about 90,000 verses. The *Mahabharata* describes a struggle for control of an Indian kingdom that took place about 1100 B.C. Its exciting stories about great heroes influenced Hindus then and now.

The best-known section of the *Mahabharata* is the ***Bhagavad Gita*** (BAH•guh•VAHD GEE•tuh), or "Song of the Lord." In it, the deity Krishna goes with a prince into battle. The prince does not want to fight because members of his family are on the other side.

R

Bhagavad Gita a section of the Indian epic the *Mahabharata*

Academic Vocabulary (Tier 2 Words)

contribute to give or donate something

Lesson 3 **269**

V Visual Skills

Analyzing Maps Have students examine the map of the Gupta Empire. **Ask:** How is the area of the Gupta Empire similar to that of the Mauryan Empire? *(Both empires controlled the land around the Indus and Ganges rivers.)* How are the two empires different? *(The Mauryan Empire was much larger than the Gupta Empire.)* AL Visual/Spatial

R Reading Skills

Defining Direct students to read the text and discuss the literature of ancient India. **Ask:** What is an epic? *(a long poetic narration that usually involves a hero)* What are some examples of epics? *(Students might mention* The Lord of the Rings *or another modern epic; the* Odyssey*; the* Iliad*; the* Aeneid*;* Beowulf*; the* Epic of Gilgamesh*; or the* Mahabharata*.)* Ask students to share the basic plot of one of the epics they may know. AL ELL

Content Background Knowledge

- The *Mahabharata* was written in couplets.
- It is about seven times as long as the combined *Iliad* and *Odyssey.*
- The characters in the epic date as far back as 1000 B.C., but the form in which we have it was written about 400 B.C.

PRIMARY SOURCE

Bhagavad Gita

Analyzing Primary Sources This interactive primary source shows an image of Lord Krishna from the *Bhagavad Gita.* Have students examine the art and read the translation below it. Ask students to paraphrase the text and discuss its meaning with a partner.

See page 245E for other online activities.

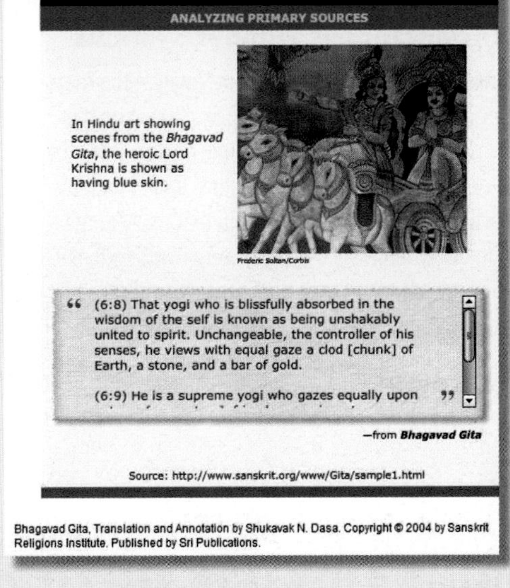

networks
Bhagavad Gita
ANALYZING PRIMARY SOURCES
In Hindu art showing scenes from the *Bhagavad Gita*, the heroic Lord Krishna is shown as having blue skin.
"(6:8) That yogi who is blissfully absorbed in the wisdom of the self is known as being unshakably united to spirit. Unchangeable, the controller of his senses, he views with equal gaze a clod [chunk] of Earth, a stone, and a bar of gold.
(6:9) He is a supreme yogi who gazes equally upon"
—from *Bhagavad Gita*
Source: http://www.sanskrit.org/www/Gita/sample1.html
Bhagavad Gita, Translation and Annotation by Shukavak N. Dasa. Copyright © 2004 by Sanskrit Religions Institute. Published by Sri Publications.

ANSWERS, p. 269

GEOGRAPHY CONNECTION

1 in northern India, in the Indus and Ganges river valleys

2 **CRITICAL THINKING** The Gupta Empire was significantly smaller than the Mauryan Empire, which suggests that it was less powerful.

T Technology Skills

Transferring Knowledge Ask volunteers to do online research to learn more about the instruments and music of ancient India. They might locate images, in audio clips of performances, showing tambourines, flutes, drums, and lutes like those used in ancient India. Ask students to work as a group to compile a multimedia presentation to share with the class. Encourage students who know how to play an instrument to play a piece for the class. **Kinesthetic, Interpersonal, Auditory/Musical**

C Critical Thinking Skills

Analyzing Demonstrate the importance of the concept of zero by asking students to identify written numbers with and without zero. For example, write the numeral one and then add a numeral zero to make the numeral ten, and ask what has changed. *(The number is now a ten.)* Indian mathematicians were the first to invent a symbol for the concept of nothing, or zero. **Ask: In what way is zero important to computers?** *(Possible answer: Computer codes are written in ones and zeroes, which represent on/off or yes/no. Some students might know the word binary.)* **BL Logical/Mathematical**

Ask: What would happen to our understanding of numbers if there were no zero? *(We might not be able to read or write numbers in as easy a way as we do. We could not do higher mathematics, which would limit advances in science.)* **BL Logical/Mathematical**

Content Background Knowledge

The *Ramayana* is perhaps the most popular Sanskrit text. More than 2,000 years old, it was most likely written by a poet named Valmiki around 300 B.C. It is an epic poem that is nearly 50,000 lines long (24,000 couplets), and it tells the story of Rama, the Hindu deity and prince. In the centuries since it was written, the *Ramayana* has been translated into many languages. The events of the poem are, even today, acted out in festivals around India. Many Indians still make an effort to memorize and recite the poem aloud for entertainment, and to much acclaim.

Hindu artists tried to depict the deities. This picture shows Krishna and Prince Arjuna.

(t) Frederic Soltan/Corbis

Krishna reminds the prince to obey his duty as a warrior. The prince makes the painful choice to fight his family.

A second epic, the *Ramayana* (rah•mah•YAH•nah), is a poem that grew to about 25,000 verses before it was written down. It tells the story of Rama, the perfect king, and Sita, his faithful wife. When Sita is kidnapped by an evil king, Rama rushes to her rescue with the help of friends.

The Arts and Architecture

T The ancient Hindus believed that music was a gift from the gods. Many sacred texts, such as the Bhagavad Gita, were probably sung. At yearly festivals, people danced, sang, and played music. Musical instruments included tambourines, flutes, drums, and lutes.

Much of early India's art was created on fragile materials, such as paper, and has not survived. What is left today is mostly religious art—elaborate sculptures carved in stone. Sculptors 270, carved images of the Buddha as early as the A.D. 100s.

The most important **structures** in early India were the rulers' palaces and the temples used for religious worship. During Ashoka's reign, many stone pillars carved with Buddhist messages were placed alongside roads.

Mathematics

C Indian mathematicians of the Gupta period made important contributions. Aryabhata (AHR•yuh•BUHT•uh) was one of the first scientists known to have used algebra. Indian mathematicians explained the idea of infinity—something without an end. They also invented the symbol "0" and connected it with the idea of nothing. The Indians' invention of zero affected the study of mathematics and science. Modern technology, such as computers, would not be possible without the concept of zero.

Reading HELPDESK CCSS

Academic Vocabulary (Tier 2 Words)

structure a building or other built object

networks Online Teaching Options

CHART

Ancient Indian Number Symbols

Analyzing Charts Have students analyze the chart of ancient Indian number symbols. By clicking on the name of the language, the row will be populated. By clicking on numbers in the columns, Indian symbols for each number will appear. Explain that many of the number symbols we use today were first developed by the ancient Indians. Ask students to identify those numbers that most closely resemble ours.

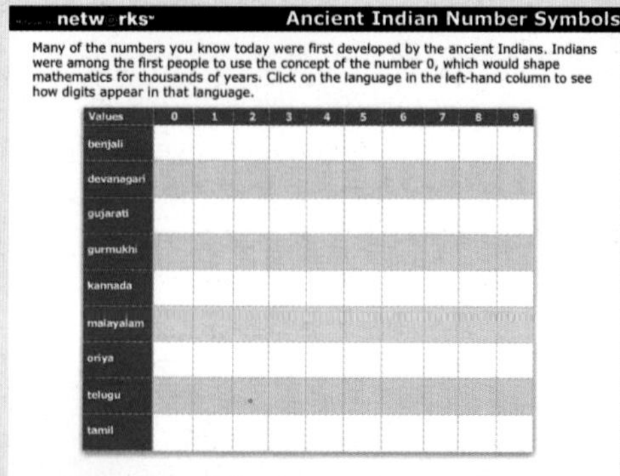

Ancient Indian Number Symbols
Many of the numbers you know today were first developed by the ancient Indians. Indians were among the first people to use the concept of the number 0, which would shape mathematics for thousands of years. Click on the language in the left-hand column to see how digits appear in that language.
Values
0 1 2 3 4 5 6 7 8 9
bengali
devanagari
gujarati
gurmukhi
kannada
malayalam
oriya
telugu
tamil

See page 245E for other online activities.

Gupta mathematicians developed symbols for the numbers 1 to 9 that we use today. In the A.D. 700s, Arab traders adopted these number symbols, or numerals. European traders later borrowed them from the Arabs. In the A.D. 1200s, use of these numbers spread though Europe and replaced Roman numerals. Today, this system of number symbols is known as the Indian-Arabic numerical system.

Advances in Science

Scientists and scholars in ancient India also made important advances in astronomy and technology. Indian astronomers mapped the movements of planets and stars. They proposed the theory that the Earth was round and revolved around the sun. During the Gupta period, scientists advanced metalworking. Among their most impressive constructions is the pillar of iron of Delhi, dating from around A.D. 400. It is still standing, and, in spite of its age, it has hardly rusted.

Advances in Medicine

Can you imagine doctors performing dental surgery 1600 years ago? Indian doctors treated dental problems using tools such as the bow drill. The doctors used this tool, which was usually used to make fire, to drill teeth.

Doctors during the Gupta era were advanced for their time. They could set broken bones, sew wounds, and perform complicated surgeries. They also were skilled in making medical instruments, such as scalpels and needles.

A doctor named Shushruta (shoosh•ROO•tah) repaired damaged noses in an early type of plastic surgery. Indian doctors used herbs to cure illnesses. They also believed in healing the causes of a disease, not just treating the disease itself.

C

Connections to TODAY

Math Poems

Some writings about mathematics from the Gupta dynasty have survived. The math formulas are written as poems. Scholars had to find ways to fit numbers into the poems so that they would sound correct. Imagine having to turn in your math homework in the form of a poem.

Ancient Indian contributions to mathematics made much of today's math-based technology possible.

John Birdsall/agefotostock

✓ **PROGRESS CHECK**

Analyzing What lasting achievement did Indian mathematicians make?

LESSON 3 REVIEW (CCSS)

Review Vocabulary (Tier 3 Words)

1. How would a *pilgrim* in ancient India use a *stupa*? RH.6–8.4
2. What is the *Bhagavad Gita*? RH.6–8.4

Answer the Guiding Questions

3. ***Determining Cause and Effect*** How did religion influence the Mauryan Empire? RH.6–8.2
4. ***Describing*** How did the Gupta Empire grow powerful? RH.6–8.2
5. ***Identifying*** What were the written epics of the Mauryan and Gupta period? RH.6–8.2
6. **NARRATIVE** You are living in India during the rule of Ashoka. Write a letter to a friend describing the things Ashoka is doing as a leader. In your letter, explain whether you think Ashoka is a great ruler. WHST.6–8.10

The Mauryan Empire

C Critical Thinking Skills

Making Connections Discuss the kinds of tools that surgeons use today. List some on the board. *(Examples include various kinds of scalpels; separators and clamps; machines such as X-ray machines and CAT scans.)* Then ask students to identify the surgical tools that ancient Indians developed and the procedures they were able to perform. **Ask: How are ancient and modern surgical instruments alike and different?** *(Similar—some are still used for cutting or sewing; Different—today's tools can give surgeons more information, can do more complicated tasks, and are more precise.)*

Have students complete the Lesson 3 Review.

CLOSE & REFLECT

Ask each student to create a two-column chart and to label the columns *Mauryan Empire* and *Gupta Empire*. Then guide a review of the lesson. Have students fill in important details in the appropriate columns of their chart.

LESSON 3 REVIEW ANSWERS

1. A Buddhist pilgrim might visit a stupa because of its religious significance as a shrine.
2. It is a well-known segment of the *Mahabharata*, an ancient religious epic.
3. Ashoka, the leader of the Mauryan Empire, became a devoted Buddhist and put many Buddhist principles into practice, including the humane treatment of people and animals and tolerance for other religions. This helped the empire prosper during his reign.
4. The Gupta were skilled in battle and prospered from wide-ranging trade networks, becoming powerful through a mixture of military strength and trade.
5. The *Mahabharata*, its subsection the Bhagavad Gita, and the Ramayana were the major literary epics of the period.
6. Student answers will vary. They should note the tolerance of Ashoka's reign, as well as the many public works he undertook and the Buddhist stupas that he erected around the empire. Students should also express an opinion about Ashoka as a leader.

ANSWER, p. 271

✓ **PROGRESS CHECK** Indian mathematicians made many breakthroughs, including the creation of algebra and the use of what we call Arabic numerals, including the mathematical concept of nothing, or zero.

CHAPTER REVIEW ACTIVITY

Organize students into four groups. Then make a chart on the board with rows for the Indus Valley civilization, Aryan civilization, Mauryan Empire, and Gupta Empire. Assign one group to review the accomplishments of each culture. Have each group identify on the chart the two greatest accomplishments of their assigned culture and explain their reasons for choosing those accomplishments.

Culture	Major Accomplishments
Indus Valley Civilization	
Aryan Civilization	
Mauryan Empire	
Gupta Empire	

REVIEW THE ENDURING UNDERSTANDINGS

Review the chapter's Enduring Understandings with students.

- *People, places, and ideas change over time.*
- *Religion can influence a society's beliefs and values.*

Now pose the following questions in a class discussion to apply these to the chapter.

How did the Aryans change after they came into India? *(The Aryans had been nomads, moving from place to place to find pastures and water for their cattle. When they arrived in the Indus Valley, they settled down in one place and became farmers. They established small kingdoms and made many cultural advances, including the development of Sanskrit. They wrote down the Vedas and wrote hymns, stories, poems, and prayers.)*

How did Buddhism influence the values and beliefs of the Mauryan Empire under Ashoka? *(Ashoka was at first a fierce ruler who led wars of conquest. After becoming horrified by the killing, he became a Buddhist and worked to improve the lives of people, making laws that encouraged people to do good deeds, practice nonviolence, and respect others. He actively promoted Buddhism and spread the teachings throughout Asia.)*

ACTIVITIES ANSWERS

Exploring the Essential Question

1. Student answers will vary, but they should note factors such as the sophisticated planning seen in the city of Mohenjo-Daro and the evidence of religion and trade. They should comment on the architecture, dress, and visible art and compare these to modern-day life.

CHAPTER 9 Activities

Write your answers on a separate piece of paper.

1. **Exploring the Essential Question** WHST.6–8.9
   NARRATIVE You are a scholar living in India among the descendants of the Aryans. One day you stumble across a great mural that shows what life was like in the city of Mohenjo-Daro at its height. Write a description to your friends of what the art shows about people and daily life in the city. How does it compare to your life?

2. **21st Century Skills** WHST.6–8.9
   MANAGE INFORMATION Create a poster that displays what you have learned about the Hindu religion. Include the concepts of karma and dharma, with pictures and captions that help show the meaning of each.

3. **Thinking Like a Historian** RH.6–8.2
   GEOGRAPHY AND CIVILIZATION Use a graphic organizer like the one shown here to show why river valleys were the best locations for early civilizations. Write "River" in the center circle and the advantages of living by a river in the surrounding circles. Refer back to the way the citizens of Harappa and Mohenjo-Daro --and later the Aryans-- used the river in their daily lives.

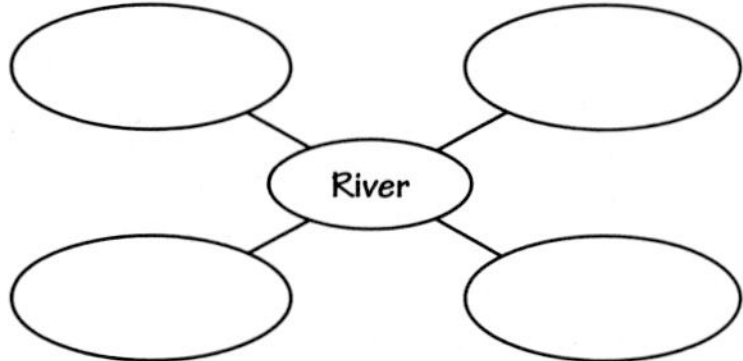

4. **GEOGRAPHY ACTIVITY**

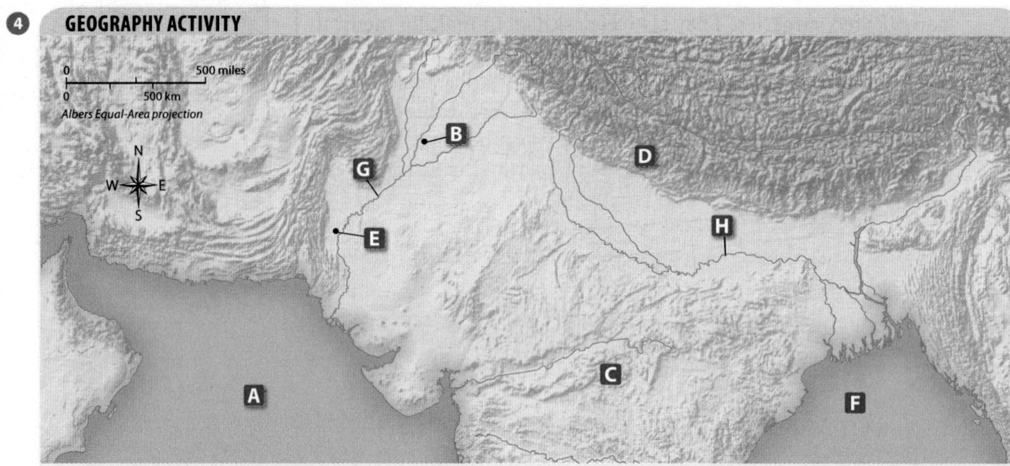

Locating Places RH.6–8.7
Match the letters on the map with the numbered places listed below.

1. Himalaya
2. Arabian Sea
3. Ganges River
4. Harappa
5. Bay of Bengal
6. Deccan Plateau
7. Mohenjo-Daro
8. Indus River

21st Century Skills

2. Student displays will vary but should indicate all levels of the caste system and demonstrate an understanding that one's karma in this life helps determine the form that one will be reincarnated into in the next life. They should also demonstrate an understanding that it is important to follow one's dharma in order to behave in a proper fashion.

Thinking Like a Historian

3. Students should note that the rivers provided water for drinking and for irrigating crops during the dry season. In addition, the presence of the rivers helped make the soil in the area fertile and productive for crops. People also used the rivers for trade and transportation.

Locating Places

4. **1.** Himalaya, D; **2.** Arabian Sea, A; **3.** Ganges River, H; **4.** Harappa, B; **5.** Bay of Bengal, F; **6.** Deccan Plateau, C; **7.** Mohenjo-Daro, E; **8.** Indus River, G

CHAPTER 9 Assessment CCSS

REVIEW THE GUIDING QUESTIONS

Directions: Choose the best answer for each question.

RH.6–8.2
1. Farming, transportation, and trade in the Indus Valley were all dependent on
   A. mountains.
   B. rivers.
   C. monsoons.
   D. lakes.

RH.6–8.2
2. The Aryans were the first Indians to develop
   F. foreign trade.
   G. indoor plumbing.
   H. major cities.
   I. written language.

RH.6–8.2
3. In the Indian caste system, your karma was largely decided by
   A. whether you were reincarnated.
   B. whether you followed your dharma.
   C. whether you learned the Four Noble Truths.
   D. whether you belonged to a *jati*.

RH.6–8.2
4. Buddhism appealed to a wider range of people than Hinduism because
   F. Buddhists believed in many gods.
   G. The Buddha traveled to many places.
   H. Buddhism treated all people equally.
   I. Buddhist poetry was so beautiful.

RH.6–8.4
5. If a mosquito lands on my hand and I refuse to kill it, I am practicing
   A. ahimsa.
   B. the Eightfold Path.
   C. Theravada.
   D. dharma.

RH.6–8.4
6. The *Ramayana* is
   F. a beautiful temple.
   G. an epic poem.
   H. a sacred city.
   I. a metalworking technique.

273

CHAPTER 9 Assessment Answers

ASSESSMENT ANSWERS

Review the Guiding Questions

1. **B** The correct choice is B. The Indus and Ganges rivers were the lifeblood of the region and supported farming, transportation, and trade. The monsoons benefited farming but would not benefit trade or transportation. The mountains could present barriers to trade and transportation and would not affect farming. India's lakes were of less use for farming, transportation, or trade than its rivers, as they do not span the country as the rivers do.

2. **I** The correct choice is I. Aryans developed the written language Sanskrit. Before the Aryans arrived, Indus Valley people were trading as far away as Mesopotamia. Indoor plumbing and grid-based city layouts were developed in the earlier Indus Valley civilization.

3. **B** The correct choice is B. In the caste system, people must follow the dharma, or duty, associated with their caste in order to gain good karma. People's karma would influence how they were reincarnated. People's *jati* would not have an effect on their karma. The Four Noble Truths are a part of Buddhism.

4. **H** The correct choice is H. Buddha treated people equally and offered an end to the cycle of reincarnation, which appealed to those of lower castes. The Buddha's travels would not greatly influence followers, nor would Buddhist poetry. Buddhists did not believe in many gods.

5. **A** The correct choice is A. *Ahimsa* is the principle of nonviolence toward all living things. The Eightfold Path is a Buddhist concept. Theravada is a sect of Buddhism. *Dharma* is the duty associated with a person's caste.

6. **G** The correct choice is G. The *Ramayana* is an epic poem about Prince Rama.

CHAPTER 9
Assessment Answers

Analyzing Documents

7 **D** The passage says that a Buddhist should wait until something is given, rather than asking for it or taking it.

8 **F** The line "He avoids the killing of living beings" is the definition of *ahimsa*.

Short Response

9 Monasteries served as religious centers and sometimes as centers of education. They accepted people who were willing to center their lives on religion.

10 Monks, particularly in Buddhism, helped spread the beliefs of the religion by wandering the land.

Extended Response

11 Student answers will vary, but they should emphasize the idea that following Buddhist principles will promote the greater good of the people by encouraging good behavior and nonviolence.

 **Assessment** *(continued)* 

DBQ ANALYZING DOCUMENTS

RH.6–8.1

7 **Drawing Conclusions** This passage is from the text *The Word of the Buddha*:

"He avoids the killing of living beings. . . . He avoids stealing and abstains from [avoids] taking what is not given to him. Only what is given to him he takes, waiting till it is given; and he lives with a heart honest and pure."

According to the passage, what is the correct way to obtain something?

A. by taking whatever one needs
B. by giving something in return
C. by demanding what one wants
D. by waiting for it to be given

RH.6–8.1

8 **Comparing and Contrasting** The first line of the passage expresses a view similar to what belief?

F. ahimsa
G. karma
H. varna
I. jati

SHORT RESPONSE

"There were a number of similarities [between Buddhism and Jainism]. Religious rituals were essentially congregational [performed in groups]. [M]onasteries [groups of men—monks—who center their lives entirely on religion] [were] organized on democratic lines, and initially accepting persons from all strata [walks] of life. Such monasteries were dependent on their neighborhoods for material support. Some of the monasteries developed into centres of education. The functioning of monks in society was greater, however, among the Buddhist orders. Wandering monks, preaching and seeking alms, gave the religions a missionary flavour. The recruitment of nuns signified a special concern for the status of women."

— Encyclopaedia Britannica Online

RH.6–8.1

9 Buddhism and Jainism both established monasteries. Why were these groups called monasteries and how did they choose their members?

RH.6–8.1

10 What purpose did a monk serve in the Buddhist religion and in the Jain religion?

EXTENDED RESPONSE

WHST.6–8.1, WHST.6–8.10

11 **Argument** You are the ruler Ashoka. You have converted to Buddhism and want to tell your people why. You also want to persuade people to practice acceptance of others. Write a speech that tells why you believe converting to Buddhism would be a positive step in their lives.

Need Extra Help?

If You've Missed Question	1	2	3	4	5	6	7	8	9	10	11
Review Lesson	1	1	2	2	2	3	2	2	2	2	2, 3

networks Online Teaching Options

Help students use the Skills Builder resources

Your students can practice important 21st Century skills such as geography, reading, writing, and critical thinking by using resources found in the Skills Builder tab of the online Student Learning Center. Resources include templates, handbooks, and slide shows. These same resources are also available in the Resource Library of the Teacher Lesson Center.

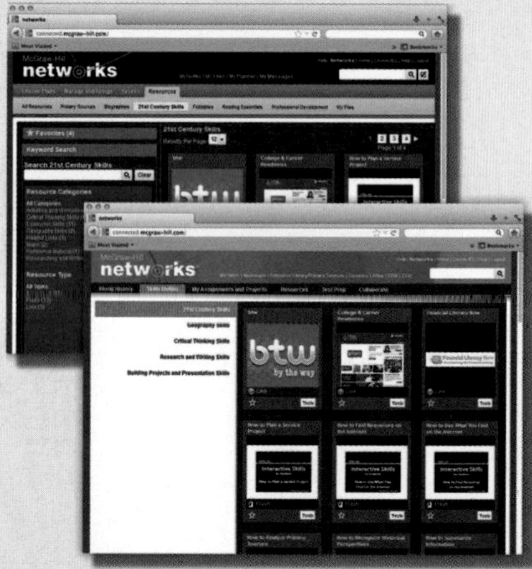

CHAPTER 10

Early China Planner

UNDERSTANDING BY DESIGN®

Enduring Understandings

- *People, places, and ideas change over time.*
- *The movement of people, goods, and ideas causes societies to change over time.*

Essential Questions

- *What makes a culture unique?*
- *How do new ideas change the way people live?*
- *How do governments change?*

Predictable Misunderstandings

Students may think:

- *The Chinese people are all the same.*
- *Confucianism is a religion.*
- *All Chinese rulers were strict dictators.*

Assessment Evidence

Performance Tasks:

- *Hands-On Chapter Project*

Other Evidence:

- *Participation in Interactive Whiteboard Map Activity*
- *Graphic organizer on Shang and Zhou dynasties*
- *Answers to discussion of definition of philosophy*
- *Answers to discussion of three philosophies*
- *Contributions to small-group activity*
- *Identification of sayings and philosophers*
- *Interpretations of slide show images*
- *Predictions of what life was like in the Qin and Han dynasties*
- *Discussion answers about the Silk Road*
- *Discussion answers on trade benefits*
- *Time line of Shang and Zhou dynasties*
- *Answers comparing and contrasting river valley civilizations*
- *Letter writing assignment*
- *Geography and History Activity*
- *21st Century Skills Activity*
- *Economics of History Activity*
- *Lesson Reviews*
- *Chapter Activities and Assessment*

SUGGESTED PACING GUIDE

Introducing the Chapter	1 day
Lesson 1	1 day
Lesson 2	1 day
Lesson 3	2 days
Chapter Wrap-Up and Assessment	1 day
TOTAL TIME	**6 DAYS**

Key for Using the Teacher Edition

SKILL-BASED ACTIVITIES

Types of skill activities found in the Teacher Edition.

V Visual Skills require students to analyze maps, graphs, charts, and photos.

R Reading Skills help students practice reading skills and master vocabulary.

W Writing Skills provide writing opportunities to help students comprehend the text.

C Critical Thinking Skills help students apply and extend what they have learned.

T Technology Skills require students to use digital tools effectively.

*Letters are followed by a number when there is more than one of the same type of skill on the page.

DIFFERENTIATED INSTRUCTION

All activities are written for the on-level student unless otherwise marked with the leveled labels below.

BL Beyond Level

AL Approaching Level

ELL English Language Learners

All students benefit from activities that utilize different learning styles. Many activities are marked as below when a particular learning style is highlighted.

Intrapersonal	**Naturalist**
Logical/Mathematical	**Kinesthetic**
Visual/Spatial	**Auditory/Musical**
Verbal/Linguistic	**Interpersonal**

NCSS Standards covered in "Early China"

Learners will understand:

1 CULTURE

4. That the beliefs, values, and behaviors of a culture form an integrated system that helps shape the activities and ways of life that define a culture

5. How individuals learn the elements of their culture through interactions with others, and how individuals learn of other cultures through communication and study

8. That language, behaviors, and beliefs of different cultures can both contribute to and pose barriers to cross-cultural understanding

2 TIME, CONTINUITY, AND CHANGE

6. The origins and influences of social, cultural, political, and economic systems

9. The influences of social, geographic, economic, and cultural factors on the history of local areas, states, nations, and the world

3 PEOPLE, PLACES, AND ENVIRONMENTS

1. The theme of people, places, and environments involves the study of the relationships between human populations in different locations and geographic phenomena such as climate, vegetation, and natural resources

6. Patterns of demographic and political change, and cultural diffusion in the past and present (e.g., changing national boundaries, migration, and settlement, and the diffusion of and changes in customs and ideas)

8. Factors that contribute to cooperation and conflict among peoples of the nation and world, including language, religion, and political beliefs

5 INDIVIDUALS, GROUPS, AND INSTITUTIONS

7. That institutions may promote or undermine social conformity

6 POWER, AUTHORITY, AND GOVERNANCE

5. The ways in which governments meet the needs and wants of citizens, manage conflict, and establish order and society

7 PRODUCTION, DISTRIBUTION, AND CONSUMPTION

1. Individuals, government, and society experience scarcity because human wants and needs exceed what can be produced from available resources

10 CIVIC IDEALS AND PRACTICES

4. The common good, and the rule of law

CHAPTER OPENER PLANNER

Students will know:

- *how geography shaped the development of China's civilization.*
- *why Shang rulers were able to remain powerful.*
- *the ways society and government were influenced by Chinese thinkers.*
- *what changes the Qin emperor made to unite China.*
- *how life improved under Han rulers.*
- *how China and the rest of the world benefited from the Silk Road.*
- *why Buddhism became popular in China.*

Students will be able to:

- ***compare and contrast*** *Huang He Valley civilizations with other river valley civilizations, including those along the Tigris-Euphrates, Nile, and Indus rivers.*
- ***explain*** *the role of geography in the development of Chinese civilization and in its isolation.*
- ***compare and contrast*** *the Shang dynasty with the Zhou dynasty.*
- ***identify*** *Confucius, Laozi, and Hanfeizi and how their philosophies affected society and government.*
- ***describe*** *Confucianism, Daoism, and legalism.*
- ***predict*** *what life was like in the Qin dynasty and the Han dynasty, based on images from each.*
- ***identify*** *geographical features along the Silk Road.*
- ***apply*** *the concepts of monopoly and competition to the economics of trade along the Silk Road.*
- ***discuss*** *how increased trade benefits civilization.*

UNDERSTANDING BY DESIGN®

☑ *Print Teaching Options*

V Visual Skills

- ☐ **P. 276** Students discuss how the borders of China have changed over the years. **Visual/Spatial**
- ☐ **P. 277** Students determine how long it took for Buddhism to reach China. **AL** **Visual/Spatial**

☑ *Online Teaching Options*

V Visual Skills

- **MAP** **Place and Time: China c. 1750 B.C. to A.D. 190**—Students view the relationships of China's changing borders over time.
- **TIME LINE** **Place and Time: Early China c. 1750 B.C. to A.D. 220**—Students learn about key Chinese and world events during this time period.
- **WORLD ATLAS** Students can use this interactive map to identify regions of the world, learn about individual countries, locate political boundaries, measure distances, and much more.

☑ *Printable Digital Worksheets*

R Reading Skills

- **GRAPHIC NOVEL** ***A Lesson Learned***—In this graphic novel, a young boy takes Confucius's teachings on filial piety to heart.

Project-Based Learning

Hands-On Chapter Project

Early China

Students describe elements of early Chinese culture, identify the same elements in their own culture, and write an illustrated letter about their culture to future generations.

Technology Extension

edtechteacher 21st Century Learning

Multimedia Presentations

- Find an additional activity online that incorporates technology for this project.
- Visit the EdTechTeacher Web sites (included in the Technology Extension for this chapter) for more links, tutorials, and other resources.

Print Resources

ANCILLARY RESOURCES

These ancillaries are available for every chapter and lesson.

- **Reading Essentials and Study Guide Workbook** **AL** **ELL**
- **Chapter Tests and Lesson Quizzes Blackline Masters**

PRINTABLE DIGITAL WORKSHEETS

These printable digital worksheets are available for every chapter and lesson.

- **Hands-On Chapter Projects**
- **What Do You Know? activities**
- **Chapter Summaries (English and Spanish)**
- **Vocabulary Builder activities**
- **Guided Reading activities**

More Media Resources

SUGGESTED VIDEOS MOVIES

In *Hero,* a minor official defeats three warlords who are plotting to assassinate Qin Shihuangdi, China's powerful emperor.

- **Discuss: Can you make a connection between the events shown in the movie and events in contemporary China?**

The documentary *Confucius: Words of Wisdom* explores the life and legacy of Confucius.

- **Discuss: Which of Confucius's "five virtues" do you think are most useful for today's world? Why?**

(NOTE: Preview clips for age-appropriateness.)

SUGGESTED READING 

Grade 6 reading level:

- ***Chee-Lin: A Giraffe's Journey,*** by James Rumford

Grade 7 reading level:

- ***Through Time: Beijing,*** by Richard Platt

Grade 8 reading level:

- ***Exploring the Life, Myth, and Art of Ancient China,*** by Edward L. Shaughnessy

LESSON 1 PLANNER

THE BIRTH OF CHINESE CIVILIZATION

Students will know:

- *how geography shaped the development of China's civilization.*
- *why Shang rulers were able to remain powerful.*
- *the cause of the fall of the Zhou dynasty.*

Students will be able to:

- ***compare and contrast*** *Huang He Valley civilizations with other river valley civilizations, including those along the Tigris-Euphrates, Nile, and Indus rivers.*
- ***explain*** *the role of geography in the development of Chinese civilization and in its isolation.*
- ***compare and contrast*** *the Shang dynasty with the Zhou dynasty.*

UNDERSTANDING BY DESIGN®

☑ Print Teaching Options

V Visual Skills

- ☐ **P. 279** Students locate geographical features on a map of China. AL **Visual/Spatial**
- ☐ **P. 282** Students create charts that show the levels of Chinese society. **Visual/Spatial**

R Reading Skills

- ☐ **P. 278** Students identify the main idea in a paragraph. AL ELL
- ☐ **P. 280** Students explore culture of the first Chinese dynasty.
- ☐ **P. 281** Students position themselves in the formation of a typical Chinese village. AL **Visual/Spatial** **Kinesthetic**
- ☐ **P. 284** Students discuss the changes the Shang and Zhou dynasties brought to China. AL

W Writing Skills

- ☐ **P. 279** Students compare the Huang He and Chang Jiang rivers. **Verbal/Linguistic**
- ☐ **P. 281** Students write a brief description of the relationship between the king and the warlords.
- ☐ **P. 282** Students make arguments for which type of writing (idiographic or pictographic) is a more effective mode of communication. BL **Verbal/Linguistic**
- ☐ **P. 283** Students write a letter from the POV of a Shang artisan. BL
- ☐ **P. 285** Students summarize the events that led to the war between the Chinese states. AL

C Critical Thinking Skills

- ☐ **P. 278** Students point out examples from the text that demonstrate the harms and benefits of the Huang He river.
- ☐ **P. 280** Students brainstorm questions that archaeologists may ask when discovering ancient civilizations. BL **Verbal/Linguistic**
- ☐ **P. 283** Students determine why Wu Wang led a revolt against the Shang.
- ☐ **P. 284** Students contrast the early Zhou government with the reorganized Zhou government. AL
- ☐ **P. 285** Students infer how advancements in early Chinese agriculture may benefit today's farmers.

☑ Online Teaching Options

V Visual Skills

- ☐ VIDEO **The Chinese Landscape**—Students observe the variety of the landforms that make up China.
- ☐ MAP **Shang Empire c. 1750–1045 B.C.**—Students view the boundaries of China's first historical dynasty.
- ☐ MAP **Zhou Empire, 1045–256 B.C.**—Students view the territories that made up the Zhou Empire.
- ☐ IMAGE **Chinese Dragon**—Students learn of the dragon's meaning.

R Reading Skills

- ☐ GRAPHIC ORGANIZER **Taking Notes: *Analyzing:* Changes In China**—Students record three ways the lives of the Chinese people changed under Shang rule.
- ☐ IMAGE **Oracle Bones**—Students learn more about these ancient artifacts.
- ☐ IMAGE **The Use of Bronze**—Students click to learn more about how this metal was shaped and used.

C Critical Thinking Skills

- ☐ MAP **The Geography of China**—Students compare the area of China to that of the contiguous United States.
- ☐ WHITEBOARD ACTIVITY **Pictographs**—Students combine pictographs to create ideographs for a series of concepts.
- ☐ SLIDE SHOW **Ancient Chinese Dragons**—Students compare and contrast dragons from Chinese myths.

T Technology Skills

- ☐ SELF-CHECK QUIZ **Lesson 1**—Students receive instant feedback about their mastery of lesson content.

☑ Printable Digital Worksheets

C Critical Thinking Skills

- ☐ WORKSHEET **Geography and History Activity: Understanding Place: China**—Students analyze how geography affected the development of Chinese civilization.

SOCIETY AND CULTURE IN ANCIENT CHINA

Students will know:
- *the ways society and government were influenced by Chinese thinkers.*

Students will be able to:
- ***identify** Confucius, Laozi, and Hanfeizi and how their philosophies affected society and government.*
- ***describe** Confucianism, Daoism, and legalism.*

UNDERSTANDING BY DESIGN®

☑ Print Teaching Options

V Visual Skills
- ☐ **P. 288** Students locate information in a chart. Visual/Spatial
- ☐ **P. 290** Students interpret a drawing of a typical Chinese village. Visual/Spatial

R Reading Skills
- ☐ **P. 287** Students discuss why the aristocrats were resistant to opening up their government to Confucius's ideas.

W Writing Skills
- ☐ **P. 286** Students write a journal entry from the POV of a young man or woman living in China during the Warring States period. BL Interpersonal

C Critical Thinking Skills
- ☐ **P. 286** Students draw conclusions about why the Chinese would be open to new philosophies.
- ☐ **P. 287** Students prioritize Confucius's duties. AL Verbal/Linguistic
- ☐ **P. 287** Students rewrite a quote in their own words. ELL
- ☐ **P. 288** Students compare and contrast Daoism and Confucianism. Verbal/Linguistic
- ☐ **P. 289** Students discuss the concept of legalism.
- ☐ **P. 289** Students predict the possible effects of sons having less land and wealth with each generation.
- ☐ **P. 290** Students offer examples of the hardships Chinese farmers faced. BL
- ☐ **P. 291** Students discuss whether the concept of filial piety is still common today. BL
- ☐ **P. 291** Students determine the effects of Confucius thought on Chinese families.

T Technology Skills
- ☐ **P. 289** Small groups of students create mini-presentations about one of the three philosophies. BL Verbal/Linguistic

☑ Online Teaching Options

V Visual Skills
- VIDEO **Chinese History from Peking Man to Confucius**—Students learn about the beginning of Chinese civilization over 7,000 years ago, Chinese inventions and philosophies through the Spring and Autumn Period, and the impact of feudal states and Confucian thought on Chinese culture.
- IMAGE **Confucius's Philosophy About Education**—Students click to learn about the interrelationship of the goals of learning and teaching.
- SLIDE SHOW **Zhou Dynasty Art**—Students view examples of Zhou dynasty art.
- IMAGE **Chinese Feudalism**—Students click on an image to learn about a Chinese village.

R Reading Skills
- GRAPHIC ORGANIZER **Taking Notes: *Identifying:* Three Philosophies**—Students identify the three Chinese philosophies that emerged after the fall of the Zhou dynasty.
- IMAGE **Daodejing and Laozi**—Students learn of the development of the book that describes the tenets of Daoism.
- PRIMARY SOURCE **Quotations of Confucius**—Students analyze an excerpt from *Quotes from The Analects* by Confucius.

C Critical Thinking Skills
- WHITEBOARD ACTIVITY **Confucianism, Daoism, Legalism**—Students classify the characteristics of these three schools of thought.

T Technology Skills
- SELF-CHECK QUIZ **Lesson 2**—Students receive instant feedback about their mastery of lesson content.

☑ Printable Digital Worksheets

W Writing Skills
- WORKSHEET **21st Century Skills Activity: Communication: Create and Give a Presentation**—Using a digital-presentation program, students create a slide show about one of the three Chinese philosophies they have read about.

LESSON 3 PLANNER

THE QIN AND THE HAN DYNASTIES

Students will know:
- *what changes the Qin emperor made to unite China.*
- *how life improved under Han rulers.*
- *how China and the rest of the world benefited from the Silk Road.*
- *why Buddhism became popular in China.*

Students will be able to:
- ***predict** what life was like in the Qin dynasty and the Han dynasty, based on images from each.*
- ***identify** geographical features along the Silk Road.*
- ***apply** the concepts of monopoly and competition to the economics of trade along the Silk Road.*
- ***discuss** how increased trade benefits civilization.*

UNDERSTANDING BY DESIGN®

☑ Print Teaching Options

V Visual Skills
- ☐ **P. 293** Students create campaign posters for the revolt that brought down the Qin dynasty. BL **Visual/Spatial**
- ☐ **P. 298** Students interpret a map showing trade routes during the Han Dynasty. AL ELL **Visual/Spatial**

R Reading Skills
- ☐ **P. 292** Students summarize how the Qin emperor came to power.
- ☐ **P. 296** Students identify the main idea and supporting details in a paragraph. AL ELL
- ☐ **P. 297** Students identify three hazards that travelers and traders faced on the Silk Road.
- ☐ **P. 299** Students summarize the arrival of Buddhism in China. ELL

W Writing Skills
- ☐ **P. 295** Students write a letter to the emperor to persuade him to make education accessible to all citizens.

C Critical Thinking Skills
- ☐ **P. 292** Students discuss why Qin would want to unify China. BL
- ☐ **P. 293** Students discuss how the changes Qin made helped unify the country. AL ELL
- ☐ **P. 294** Students discuss how the Warring States period helped Qin rise to power.
- ☐ **P. 295** Students discuss how the system of land inheritance in China eventually led to farmers becoming very poor. BL
- ☐ **P. 295** Students connect the peaceful period during the Han dynasty with the flourishing of the arts. BL
- ☐ **P. 296** Students determine why it was important for farmers to expand land for growing food.
- ☐ **P. 297** Students contrast advancements made under Han Wudi to periods in China's past.
- ☐ **P. 298** Students discuss how the Silk Road benefited China.
- ☐ **P. 299** Students discuss the reasons for the fall of the Han Dynasty.

☑ Online Teaching Options

V Visual Skills
- ☐ VIDEO **Chinese History from the First Emperor to the Romance of the Three Kingdoms**—Students learn about the Great Wall, the Silk Road, Chinese Buddhism, and the Three Kingdoms.
- ☐ MAP **Qin and Han Empires**—Students explore the borders of these empires and the expansion of the Great Wall.
- ☐ SLIDE SHOW **Terra-Cotta Warriors**—Students view images from Qin Shihuangdi's burial complex.
- ☐ IMAGE **Acupuncture**—Students click to learn about this Chinese medical technique.

R Reading Skills
- ☐ GRAPHIC ORGANIZER **Taking Notes: *Comparing:* Qin and Han Dynasties**—Students use a Venn diagram to compare and contrast these two dynasties.
- ☐ BIOGRAPHY **Ban Zhao**—Students learn about the first female Chinese historian.

C Critical Thinking Skills
- ☐ CHART **World Population**—Students compare the times when certain countries reached populations of 60 million or more.
- ☐ MAP **Trading in the Ancient World c. A.D. 100s**—Students trace the Silk Road and other trade routes that extended from China to the Mediterranean Sea.

T Technology Skills
- ☐ SELF-CHECK QUIZ **Lesson 3**—Students receive instant feedback about their mastery of lesson content.
- ☐ GAME **Chinese Invention Identification Game—the Qin and Han Dynasties**—Students play a game to learn more about Chinese inventions.
- ☐ GAME **Chinese Arts and Discoveries Concentration Game**—Students play a concentration game in which they match important terms and concepts.
- ☐ GAME **Qin Dynasty Concentration Game**—Students identify characteristics of the Qin and Han dynasties.

☑ Printable Digital Worksheets

C Critical Thinking Skills
- ☐ WORKSHEET **Economics of History Activity: Trade Along the Silk Road**—Students gain insight into the concept of a monopoly.

INTERVENTION AND REMEDIATION STRATEGIES

LESSON 1 The Birth of Chinese Civilization

Reading and Comprehension

For students who may be struggling with the vocabulary in this chapter, pair them up and have them choose five terms to use in a sentence. They can then exchange their sentences with a partner to determine if they have used the words correctly.

Text Evidence

Have students research a specific Chinese myth or legend. Then have them write a myth of their own, drawing on the Chinese myth as a model. Students may choose to illustrate their myth and share it online or with the class.

LESSON 2 Society and Culture in Ancient China

Reading and Comprehension

Students should work in pairs or small groups to outline the principles of Confucianism. Students should then write a few sentences about the way Confucianism affected government and culture in China.

Text Evidence

Students should choose one of the three schools of philosophy discussed in this lesson and write a brief defense, laying out the case for why their chosen philosophy is the best one on which to base a government.

LESSON 3 The Qin and the Han Dynasties

Reading and Comprehension

Tell students to pay attention to the heads and subheads in the lesson as they read. These can act as guideposts to help them preview the content and can also be used as tools for review.

Text Evidence

Organize students into small groups and have them research either the types of art that flourished during the Han dynasty or the important inventions. Then each group should create a presentation showcasing what they have learned. Remind students that they can incorporate visuals, music, and video elements into their presentations.

Online Resources

Approaching Level Reader

Use this online lower-level text that corresponds directly to the text in the Student Edition. It includes a Spanish version.

Guided Reading Activities

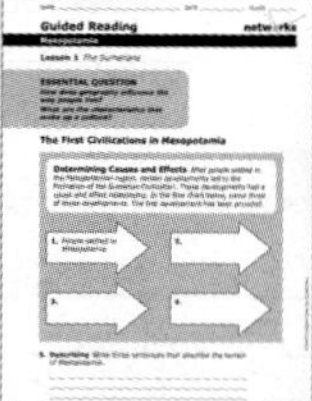

This resource uses graphic organizers and guiding questions to help students with comprehension.

What Do You Know?

Use these worksheets to pre-assess student's background knowledge before they study the chapter.

Reading Essentials and Study Guide Workbook

This resource offers writing and reading activities for the approaching-level student. Also available in Spanish.

Self-Check Quizzes

This online assessment tool provides instant feedback for students to check their progress.

Early China

1750 B.C. to A.D. 220

ESSENTIAL QUESTIONS • *What makes a culture unique?* • *How do new ideas change the way people live?* • *How do governments change?*

networks

There's More Online about the lives and customs of the people of early China.

CHAPTER 10

Lesson 1
The Birth of Chinese Civilization

Lesson 2
Society and Culture in Ancient China

Lesson 3
The Qin and the Han Dynasties

The Story Matters . . .

Confucius is considered to be one of early China's great teachers. Thousands of years after his death, his teachings are still followed. During his lifetime, Confucius taught people there was a way to build a better life for themselves and for society. To do that, he said, people must put the needs of their families and community above their own wants. He urged people to honor traditions and seek knowledge.

The teachings of Confucius spread throughout China. His legacy includes a respect for education and the importance of fulfilling all duties toward one's parents and community. That philosophy influences many Asian countries today.

◄ *More than 2,000 years ago, Confucius founded a system of beliefs. He unknowingly had an impact on the whole world.*

275

ENGAGE

Bellringer After students have finished reading "The Story Matters . . .," begin a discussion with them about Confucius. Ask: Have you heard of Confucius before? What did you know about Confucius before you read this? Have students share their responses. Then **ask:**

- **Why do you think the early Chinese were receptive to the ideas of Confucius?**
- **Which of Confucius's ideas do you think are still relevant in the modern world?**
- **Why do you think Confucius emphasized respect for education?**
- **What do you think Confucius meant by saying that people should fulfill their duties toward their parents?**
- **What duties do you think you have toward your parents or other adult family members?**

Tell students that as they read this chapter, they will learn more about Confucius and other ancient Chinese thinkers.

Making Connections

Read the following information to students:

Confucius wasn't the only thinker who emphasized respect for one's parents.

- The Judeo-Christian Ten Commandments contain the instruction to "honor thy father and mother."
- In the United States, Mother's Day has been celebrated since 1914, and Father's Day since 1972. **Ask: How do you honor and respect the adults in your life?**

Letter from the Author

Dear World History Teacher,

China was the last of the river valley civilizations to fully develop. The Shang dynasty formed an organized government, a system of writing, and advanced skills for making bronze vessels. During the Zhou dynasty, China adopted many of the features that characterized China's civilization for centuries. Between 500 B.C. and 200 B.C., three major schools of thought emerged in China—Confucianism, Daoism, and legalism. All three sought to define the principles that would create a stable order in society.

Jackson J. Spielvogel

TEACH & ASSESS

Step Into the Place

V1 Visual Skills

Reading a Map Direct students to the Chapter Opener map of China. Tell students that the map shows the borders of modern China. Discuss with students how they think the borders of China might have changed over the years. (*China might have lost or gained territory over the years.*) **Ask:** What could cause a country to gain or lose territory? Write students' ideas on the board and return to them as they complete the chapter. Then display the subsequent maps showing the land area of different Chinese dynasties. As a class, discuss the Map Focus questions. **Visual/Spatial**

ANSWERS, p. 276

Step Into the Place

1. Yellow Sea, East China Sea, South China Sea, Pacific Ocean
2. south
3. Modern China is much larger.
4. CRITICAL THINKING War often results in a change of borders when a country loses or gains land. Natural disasters can also result in the loss of land.

Step Into the Time

Student answers will vary. Students should pick an event and make some specific predictions regarding the consequences of the event in one of the areas mentioned in the question. They might describe how the event will affect families, the government, or the relations between countries; or they might discuss how the event will affect trade, commerce, or business.

CHAPTER 10 CCSS

Place and Time: Early China 1750 B.C. to A.D. 220

How and where did civilization begin in China? Artifacts that archaeologists have found in the Huang He Valley show that this valley is the first center of Chinese civilization. Historians believe that the valley's rich soil encouraged people to settle there to farm and eventually to build towns.

Step Into the Place

MAP FOCUS The borders of a country are rarely permanent. The land that makes up China has changed over the years.

1. **PLACE** What bodies of water border Chinese lands to the east? RH.6–8.7
2. **PLACE** In which direction did most of the Han Empire expansion take place? RH.6–8.7
3. **PLACE** How does the area of modern China compare to the land controlled by early Chinese dynasties? RH.6–8.7
4. CRITICAL THINKING *Analyzing* What causes the borders of a country to change? RH.6–8.1

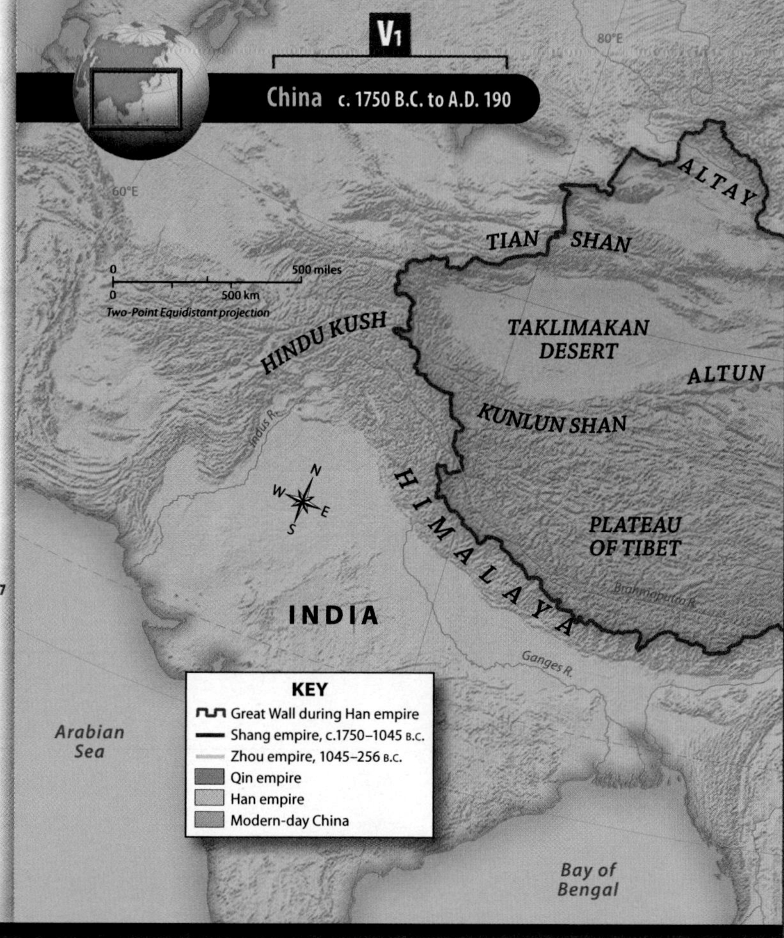

Step Into the Time

V2 **TIME LINE** Choose an event from the time line and write a paragraph predicting the general social, political, or economic consequences that event might have for the world. RH.6–8.7

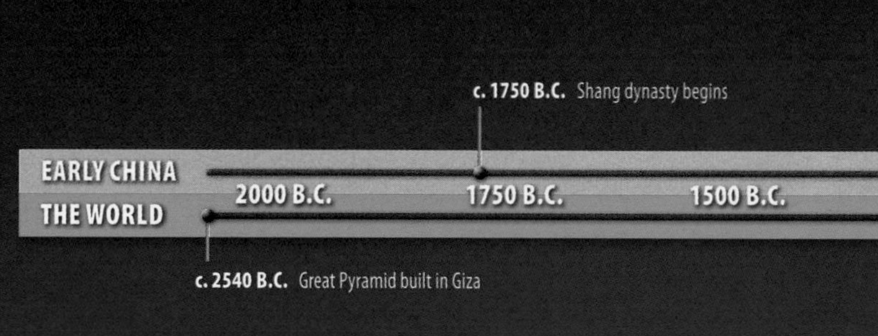

Project-Based Learning

Hands-On Chapter Project

Early China

Students will describe elements of early Chinese culture and write a letter describing those same aspects of their own culture for future generations. Students will take part in a class discussion about early Chinese culture and draw connections to present-day life in the United States. Next, they will use worksheets to guide them through the process of taking notes and gathering ideas for their letters. Then, students will write their letters and present them to the class. Finally, they will evaluate their research, letters, and presentations using an Assessment Rubric.

Technology Extension

Mutlimedia Presentations

Multimedia presentation programs have continued to grow in popularity and ease of use, while their features have expanded rapidly. Text, audio, video, and images are common components of practically all multimedia presentation tools. In this EdTechTeacher Technology Extension, we provide knowledge about the resources to create a narrated multimedia presentation and ways to share it with your audience.

networks *There's More Online!*

☑ **MAP** Explore the interactive version of this map on NETWORKS.

☑ **TIME LINE** Explore the interactive version of this time line on NETWORKS.

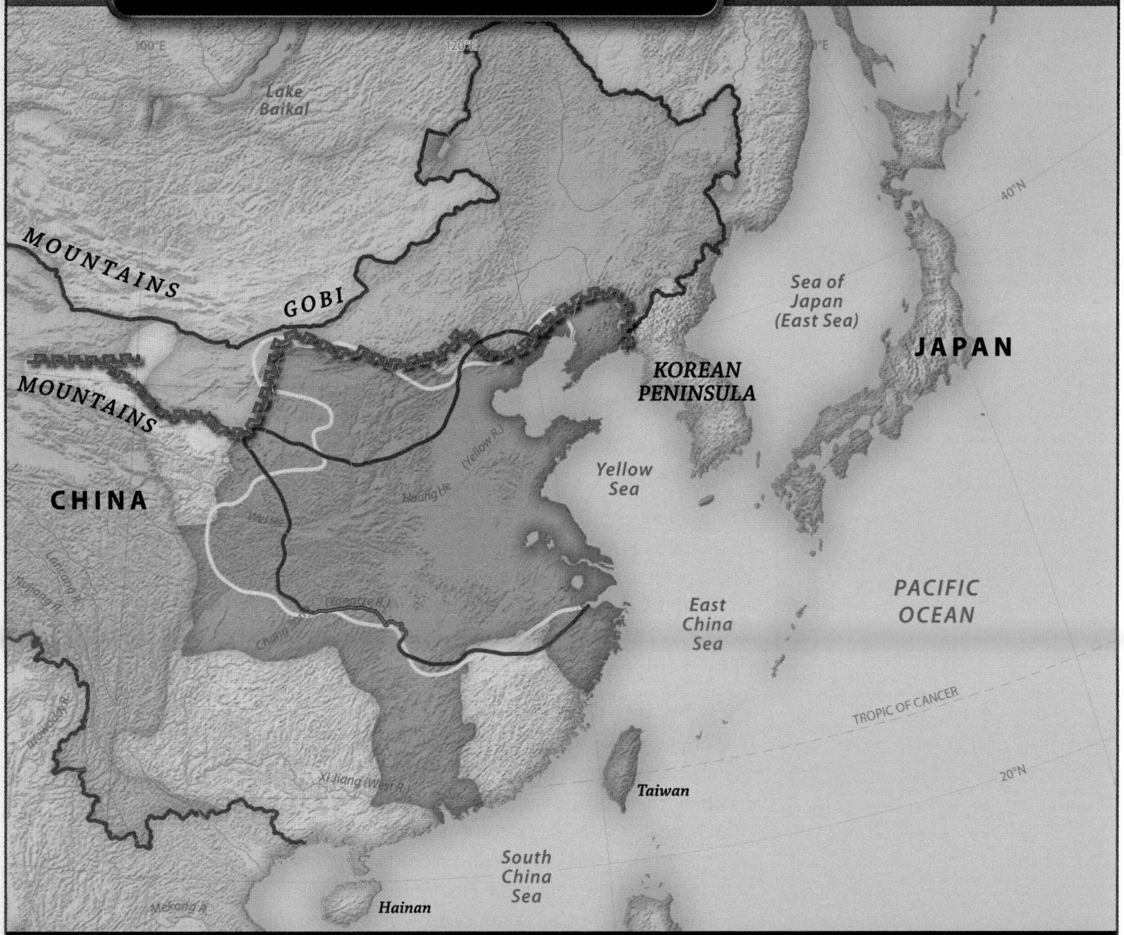

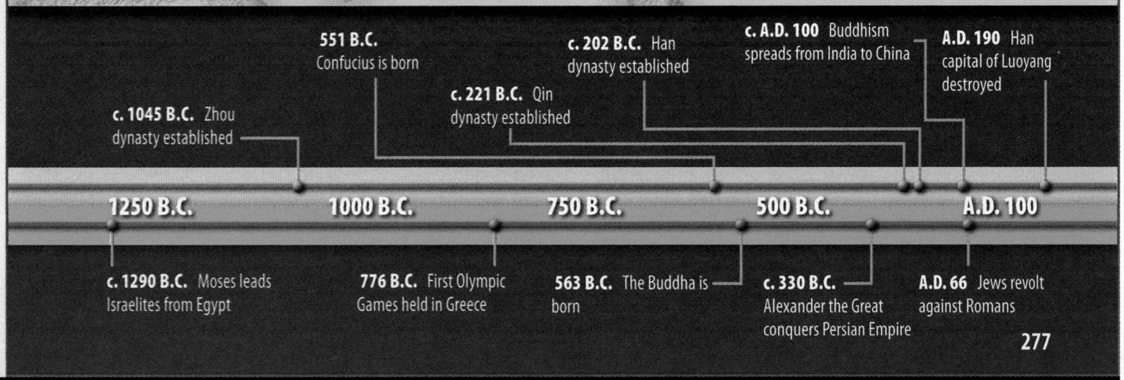

Lake Baikal

MOUNTAINS

GOBI

MOUNTAINS

CHINA

Sea of Japan (East Sea)

JAPAN

KOREAN PENINSULA

Yellow Sea

East China Sea

PACIFIC OCEAN

TROPIC OF CANCER

Taiwan

South China Sea

Hainan

c. 1045 B.C. Zhou dynasty established

551 B.C. Confucius is born

c. 221 B.C. Qin dynasty established

c. 202 B.C. Han dynasty established

c. A.D. 100 Buddhism spreads from India to China

A.D. 190 Han capital of Luoyang destroyed

1250 B.C. | 1000 B.C. | 750 B.C. | 500 B.C. | A.D. 100

c. 1290 B.C. Moses leads Israelites from Egypt

776 B.C. First Olympic Games held in Greece

563 B.C. The Buddha is born

c. 330 B.C. Alexander the Great conquers Persian Empire

A.D. 66 Jews revolt against Romans

277

CHAPTER 10
Place and Time

Step Into the Time

V2 Visual Skills

Reading a Time Line Have students review the time line for the chapter. Explain that they will be studying events from about 2000 B.C. to A.D. 200. **Ask:** **What conclusion can you draw from comparing the time line entries for the Buddha and for Buddhism?** *(The World Time Line states that the Buddha was born in c. 563 B.C. in Nepal. The China time line states that Buddhism reached China around A.D.. 100. Students should draw the conclusion that it took more than 600 years for Buddhism to reach China.)* **AL** **Visual/Spatial**

Content Background Knowledge

Buddhism is currently the fourth-largest religion in the world, behind Christianity, Islam, and Hinduism.

CLOSE & REFLECT

Have students create a K-W-L chart about China. In the K, or *Know,* column, they can add information from the map, time line, chapter opener, and any prior knowledge they have. In the W, or *Want to Know,* column, have them include anything they would like to learn about China. Finally, when students have finished reading the chapter, students should complete the L, or *Learned,* column, reflecting on what they read.

TIME LINE

Place and Time: Early China 1750 B.C. to A.D. 220

Reading a Time Line Display the time line on the whiteboard. Have student volunteers read each event aloud as it is revealed and then discuss the event as a class. Ask students to choose one event and use Internet resources to research it. Then have students create a smaller, more detailed time line depicting their chosen event and any important happenings leading up to or following it.

See page 275B for other online activities.

ENGAGE

Bellringer Before students begin the lesson, ask them to think about the size and geography of the United States. Remind students that landforms and climate affect a region's development. Ask them what the region they live in is known for, whether it is farming, manufacturing, trade, or technology. Then ask them to explain how rivers are important for the development of farming.

TEACH & ASSESS

R Reading Skills

Finding the Main Idea Invite volunteers to read the first paragraph aloud. Then ask students to suggest possible main ideas for that section. Remind them that titles and headings can offer strong clues for finding the main idea. AL ELL

C Critical Thinking Skills

Identifying Evidence Direct students to read these sentences: "The Huang He has benefited the people of the Huang He valley. The river has also brought great misfortune." **Ask:** Identify one detail that explains a benefit of the river. *(Loess carried in the river makes the soil good for farming.)* Identify one detail that explains how the river does harm. *(Floods devastate farms and villages.)*

networks *There's More Online!*
- GRAPHIC ORGANIZER How Life Changed Under Shang Rule
- VIDEO

Lesson 1

The Birth of Chinese Civilization

ESSENTIAL QUESTION *What makes a culture unique?*

IT MATTERS BECAUSE
Today, China is one of the world's most powerful countries.

The Land of China

GUIDING QUESTION *How have rivers, mountains, and deserts shaped the development of China's civilization?*

The ancient civilizations of Egypt, Mesopotamia, and India developed along large rivers. Hundreds of years later in East Asia, another civilization began along the Huang He (HWANG HUH). In Chinese, Huang He means "yellow river." This civilization was China. China has gone through many changes over the centuries, but it is still a strong and growing civilization today.

Powerful Rivers

The Huang He stretches east across China for more than 2,900 miles (4,666 km). It begins in China's western mountains and flows to the Pacific Ocean. On its way, the Huang He cuts through thick layers of rich, yellow soil. This soil is called loess (LEHS). The river carries away large amounts of loess and spreads it farther downstream. The yellow color of the soil in the Huang He gives the river its name.

The rich soil helps farmers grow large amounts of food on small plots of land. As a result, the Huang He valley **emerged** as one of the great wheat-producing areas of the ancient world.

The Huang He has benefited the people of the Huang He valley. The river has also brought great misfortune. The Huang He often overflows its banks, causing enormous floods. Since

Reading **HELP**DESK CCSS

Taking Notes: ***Analyzing***
Use a web diagram like this one to identify three ways the lives of the Chinese people changed under Shang rule. RH.6–8.2

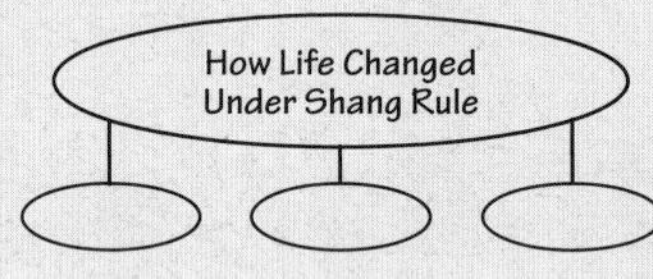

Content Vocabulary (Tier 3 Words)
- warlord
- aristocrat
- ancestor
- pictograph
- ideograph
- bureaucracy

networks ***Online Teaching Options***

VIDEO

The Chinese Landscape

Creating Visuals Direct students to watch the video on China's landscape. Instruct them to pay close attention to the visual information being presented. After they have watched the video, have them create a pictogram to represent each of the landforms from the video. AL Visual/Spatial

See page 275C for other online activities.

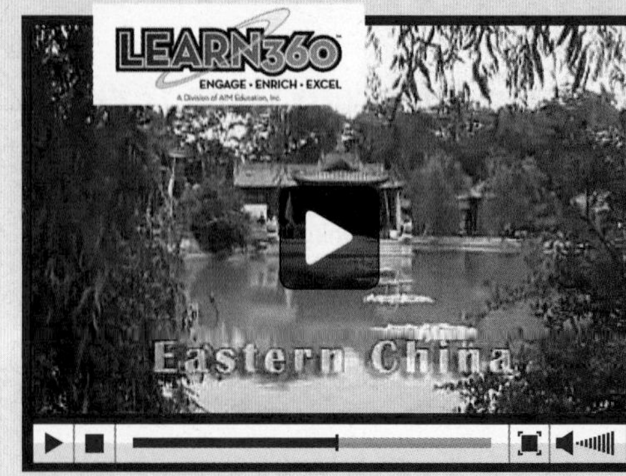

ANSWERS, p. 278

TAKING NOTES: Changes noted can include: introduced writing, developed bronze arts, introduced the idea of the Mandate of Heaven, developed irrigation, built first cities, expanded trade, kings become leaders of religion and government, created strong army, and expanded the borders of China.

600 B.C., the Chinese have recorded more than 1,500 floods of the Huang He. These floods have taken millions of lives. The Chinese call the Huang He "China's Sorrow" in honor of the people killed by the floods.

Over time, the people of China moved south and settled near another great river, the Chang Jiang (CHAHNG JYAHNG), or the Yangtze River. The Chang Jiang flows from west to east across central China. It flows through spectacular canyons and broad plains on its way to the East China Sea. The Chang Jiang is about 3,915 miles (6,300 km) long. Only the Amazon in South America and the Nile in Africa are longer. **W**

Like the Huang He, the Chang Jiang provides rich soil for farming. Early farmers grew rice along the river's shores. The Chang Jiang was also an important waterway for trade and transportation.

Mountains and Desert

China has fertile river valleys, but only about one-tenth of its land can be farmed. Mountains and desert cover much of the country's land. To the southwest, the towering Himalaya separate China from South Asia. The Kunlun Shan and Tian Shan mountain ranges slice through western China. East of the Tian Shan is a vast, rocky desert known as the Gobi.

GEOGRAPHY CONNECTION

While the country of China has one of the world's largest populations, it has little land that it can use for growing food.

1. **LOCATION** What is the name of the desert on China's northern border near Mongolia?
2. **CRITICAL THINKING** ***Analyzing*** What effect did China's mountains and deserts have on its early history?

V

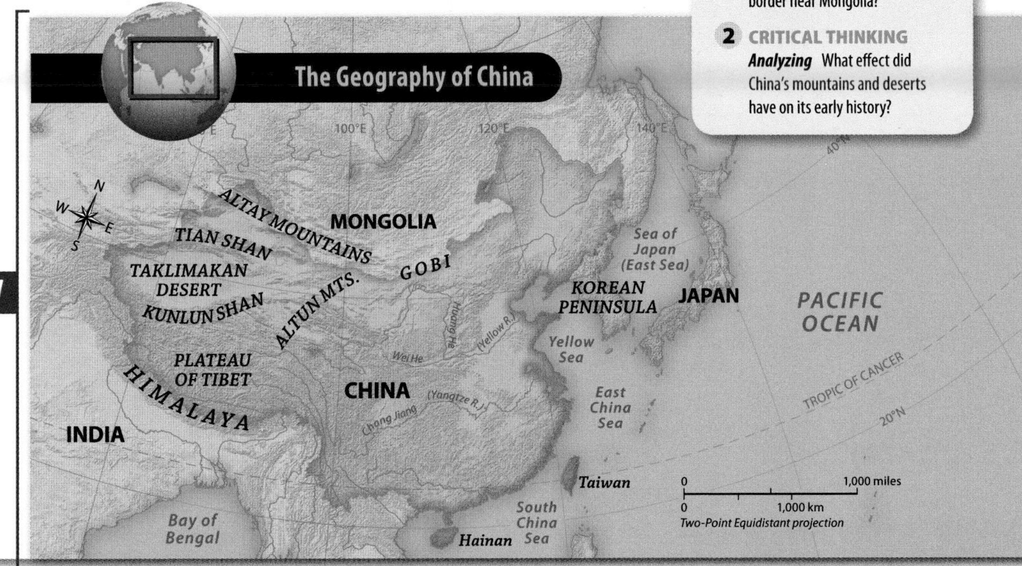

- **hereditary**
- **Mandate of Heaven**
- **Dao**

Academic Vocabulary (Tier 2 Words)

emerge to become known

W Writing Skills

Informative/Explanatory Have students compare what they have read about the Huang He and the Chang Jiang. Instruct them to draw and complete a T-chart to organize their ideas. Then direct students to use the chart to write a paragraph comparing and contrasting these two rivers. **Verbal/Linguistic**

V Visual Skills

Reading a Map Direct students to the map of ancient China and the surrounding area. Have students locate geographical features marked on the map. Ask students to locate the Gobi, the Taklimakan Desert, the Himalaya, the Huang He, the Chang Jiang, and the Altay and Altun mountains. AL **Visual/Spatial**

Content Background Knowledge

- The Three Gorges Dam was built on the Chang Jiang to control flooding and generate hydroelectric power for China. However, the large building project was controversial.
- The dam took 20 years to build. More than one million people were displaced from villages that would be under water once the dam was completed.

LECTURE SLIDE

The Land of China

Making Inferences After students have studied the map, **ask:** **What geographical features helped isolate the Chinese civilization?** Have students explain their choices. *(Places that helped isolate the Chinese include the Himalaya, the Altay and the Altun mountains, and the Gobi and Taklimakan deserts. Students may also circle the bodies of water that form China's eastern coast.)* Show the blank pro-and-con chart from the lecture slide. Have students complete a pro-and-con chart for China's different geographical features. **Visual/Spatial**

See page 275C for other online activities.

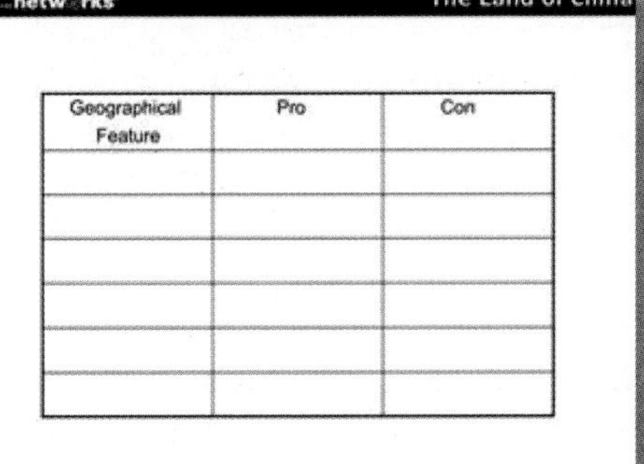

ANSWERS, p. 279

GEOGRAPHY CONNECTION

1. It is the Gobi.
2. **CRITICAL THINKING** They limited farmland and separated China from the outside world.

R1 Reading Skills

Explaining After students have read the passage, ask them to explain why China was isolated from other cultures through much of its early history. Remind them that the Chinese called their land "The Middle Kingdom."

C Critical Thinking Skills

Formulating Questions After students have read about the archaeological evidence for early Chinese civilization, organize them into small groups and instruct them to brainstorm questions that archaeologists and historians might have. Invite a volunteer from each group to share their list of questions with the class. BL **Verbal/Linguistic**

R2 Reading Skills

Discussing Direct students to read the section on Yü the Great. Have students discuss why Yü the Great was the subject of many myths and legends in ancient China. **Ask:** **What were some of the things attributed to Yü the Great?** *(controlling the floods of the Huang He and founding China's first dynasty)*

Why do you think the myths about Yü the Grxeat involved creating flood-control channels for the Huang He? *(Answers may vary. Possible responses: because the river was so important to daily life in ancient China; because floods were so dangerous)*

ANSWER, p. 280

✓ **PROGRESS CHECK** Rivers provided fertile soil and irrigation that made it easier to grow food. They provided waterways for trade and transportation.

Terraced farming, shown here, helps overcome the difficult landscape in China. Farmers plant every strip of land they can, even in the mountains.

For centuries, these rugged mountains and the barren desert acted like walls around the country. These barriers limited contacts between China and other civilizations. The Chinese developed a unique culture and a strong sense of independence. They called their land "the Middle Kingdom." To them, it was the center of the world. R1

✓ **PROGRESS CHECK**

Identifying How did rivers help civilization develop in China?

The First Chinese Dynasty

GUIDING QUESTION *Why did China's Shang rulers become powerful?*

What we know about the early people of China comes from the things they left behind. Archaeologists have unearthed clay pots and cups in the Huang He valley that date back thousands of years. These artifacts show that the Huang He valley was the birthplace of Chinese civilization. C

Archaeologists think that people settled in the valley because of its rich soil. Early settlers farmed the land. As in other early civilizations, people here also used the river for travel and trade. As the population grew, the Chinese began building towns.

Myths and Legends

Like other early peoples, the ancient Chinese created myths to explain the creation of their world. Many Chinese myths celebrate the deeds of great heroes. Yü the Great was one of these heroes. According to myths, Yü dug the first **channels** to control the floodwaters of the Huang He. Yü chased away the dragon that caused the floods. Then, he started digging the channels.

According to the myth, Yü was aided in his task by other dragons. One dragon used its tail to help dig the channels. Still, it took 13 long years to complete the work. After the channels were finished, the flood waters could flow safely away to the sea.

Legend has it that Yü founded China's first dynasty. That dynasty, named the Xia (SHYAH), began about 2000 B.C.

Reading **HELP**DESK

Academic Vocabulary (Tier 2 Words)

channel a canal; a narrow body of water between two landmasses

networks *Online Teaching Options*

IMAGE

Ancient Chinese Dragons

Making Connections After organizing students in pairs, direct them to study the four different dragons from Chinese myth and legend. Have them list the qualities of each dragon, including its appearance and any powers it was perceived to have. Finally, have students write a sentence about each dragon in which they infer the importance of these powers to early Chinese people. BL

networks Ancient Chinese Dragons

Dragons played an important role in ancient Chinese myths and culture. Most dragons were associated with water, probably because rainfall was vital to the survival of crops and people. Dragons were a type of rain god in early Chinese religion, and their images were used in rituals performed to call the rain.

Tianlong

Tianlong: This dragon was thought to protect the heavenly dwellings of the gods.

See page 275C for other online activities.

Archaeologists, however, have not found any historical evidence of the Xia. Based on written records, China's first dynasty is the Shang. Shang kings ruled China from about 1750 B.C. to 1045 B.C. **R1**

Who Were the Shang?

Archaeologists have unearthed long-buried walls and buildings. These ruins show that the Shang built the first cities in China. Among these cities was the royal capital of Anyang (AHN• YAHNG). A palace and temple stood at the center of the city. Public buildings and the homes of government officials circled this central area. Beyond the city's center stood workshops and other homes. **R2**

The king was the most powerful person, serving as the political, religious, and military leader of Shang China. At first, Shang kings controlled only a small area of northern China. In time, the Shang conquered neighboring areas. They ruled over most of the people of the Huang He valley.

As the Shang kingdom grew, kings sent out large armies to defend the kingdom's borders. They appointed people called warlords to govern local territories. **Warlords** are **military** leaders who lead their own armies. Shang kings **relied** on the warlords to stay in power. **W**

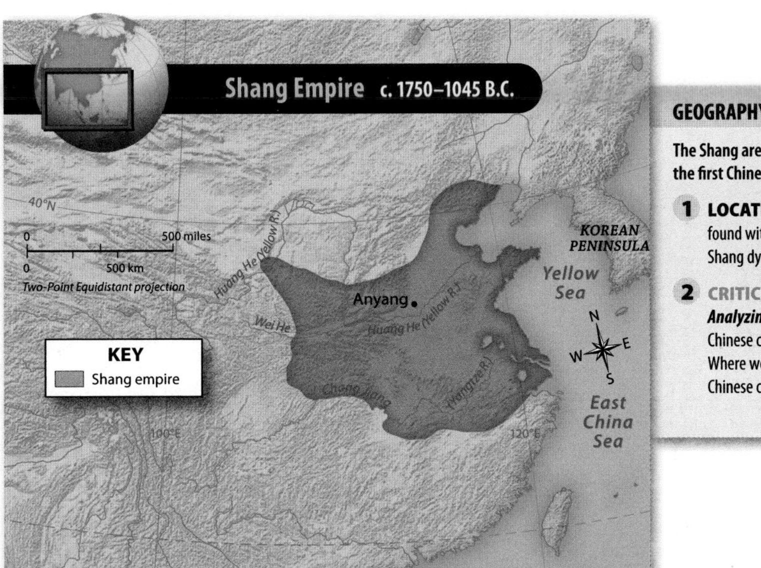

GEOGRAPHY CONNECTION

The Shang are thought to have built the first Chinese cities.

1. **LOCATION** What rivers were found within the borders of the Shang dynasty?
2. **CRITICAL THINKING** ***Analyzing*** Anyang is the only Chinese city shown on the map. Where would you expect other Chinese cities to be located?

warlord a military commander exercising civil power by force, usually in a limited area

Academic Vocabulary (Tier 2 Words)

military related to soldiers, arms, or war

rely to be dependent

R1 Reading Skills

Calculating After students finish reading the section about myths and legends, **ask:** How long did the Shang dynasty rule China? *(about 700 years)* How long before the beginning of the Shang dynasty was the Xia dynasty established? *(about 250 years)* **Logical/Mathematical**

R2 Reading Skills

Depicting Instruct students to make signs for each of the buildings found in the Shang capital of Anyang. Organize students into small groups and give one sign to each group. Using information from the textbook, have the groups arrange themselves based on what archaeologists discovered about the layout of the city. **Ask:** Why would the palace and temple have been in the center of the city? *(Answers may vary but should include a reference to the importance of the king and the religion.)* What conclusions can you draw about the importance of other social classes based on this layout? *(Students may answer that government officials were more important than craftsmen and farmers.)* **AL** **Visual/Spatial Kinesthetic**

W Writing Skills

Informative/Explanatory Have students write one or two sentences explaining the relationship between the king and the warlords. It may help students to make a list that shows the hierarchy of Chinese society during the period of the Shang dynasty.

MAP

Shang Empire c. 1750–1045 B.C.

Interpreting Have students use the interactive map of the Shang Empire to write a short descriptive paragraph that describes the empire's location, geographic features, and relative size compared with modern-day China. **BL**

See page 275C for other online activities.

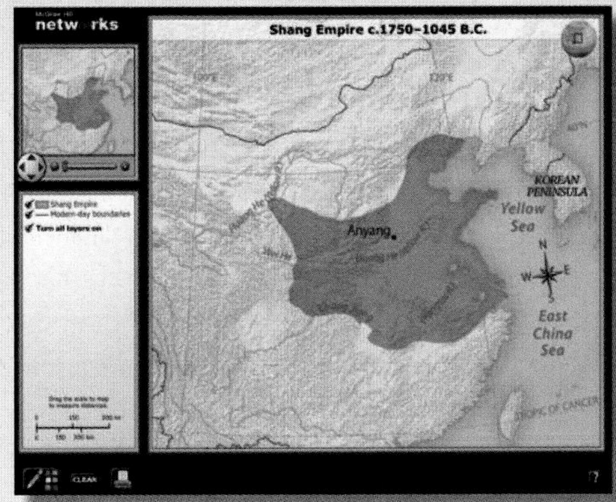

ANSWERS, p. 281

GEOGRAPHY CONNECTION

1. Huang He and Chang Jiang
2. **CRITICAL THINKING** Students will most likely expect other cities to have been built along China's rivers or along its coastline.

R Reading Skills

Defining To demonstrate their understanding of the highlighted terms on this page, have students choose one term and then use it in a sentence. Remind students to use context clues in their own sentences that would help convey the meaning of the word to a reader. ELL

V Visual Skills

Creating Charts Organize students into pairs or small groups and direct them to create charts that show the levels of Chinese society. Encourage students to incorporate visual images into their charts to help convey the information. **Visual/Spatial**

W Writing Skills

Argument Organize the class into two groups. Have each group of students prepare a short speech, arguing for either pictographic or ideographic writing as a more effective, superior form of communication. Invite the groups to share their ideas with the class. BL **Verbal/Linguisitic**

Thinking Like a HISTORIAN

Analyzing Sources

Archaeologists study what ancient societies have left behind. Some of what we know about early China and Chinese writing comes from the study of oracle bones. They are a primary source. Suppose you were an archaeologist who dug up a collection of oracle bones. You would want to analyze them. Use the library to find secondary sources about oracle bones. Write a brief report summarizing your findings and present it to the class. For more information about analyzing sources, read the chapter *What Does a Historian Do?*

Under the king, warlords and other royal officials formed the upper class. They were **aristocrats** (uh•RIHS•tuh•krats), people of noble birth whose wealth came from the land they owned. Aristocrats passed their land and power to their children or to younger family members.

V

Most people of Shang China were farmers. There were much smaller groups of merchants, artisans, and slaves. The farmers lived in rural villages and worked the land that belonged to the aristocrats. They raised cattle, sheep, and chickens and grew grains, such as millet, wheat, and rice.

R

People in Shang China worshipped many gods. The god Shang Ti ruled as supreme god over the lesser gods. According tolegend, the gods lived in the mountains, rivers, and seas.

The early Chinese both admired and feared the gods. They believed the gods could bring good or bad fortune. They attempted to please the gods by offering gifts of food and other goods.

The Chinese also honored their **ancestors**, or long-dead family members. They made offerings to their ancestors. They hoped that their ancestors would bring good luck and help in difficult times. Today, many Chinese still pay respect to their ancestors by going to temples and burning small paper copies of food, clothing, and other items. These copies represent things that departed relatives need in the afterlife.

Seeking Guidance from Ancestors

Shang kings believed that they received their power to rule from the gods and their wisdom from their ancestors. For this reason, religion and government were closely linked. For the kings, an important duty was to contact the gods and the ancestors before making important decisions.

The kings asked for help by using oracle (AWR•uh•kuhl) bones. They instructed priests to scratch questions on the bones, such as "Will I win the battle?" or "Will there be an abundant harvest?" Priests heated the oracle bones over a fire until they cracked. The pattern of cracks provided answers from the gods and ancestors to the king's questions.

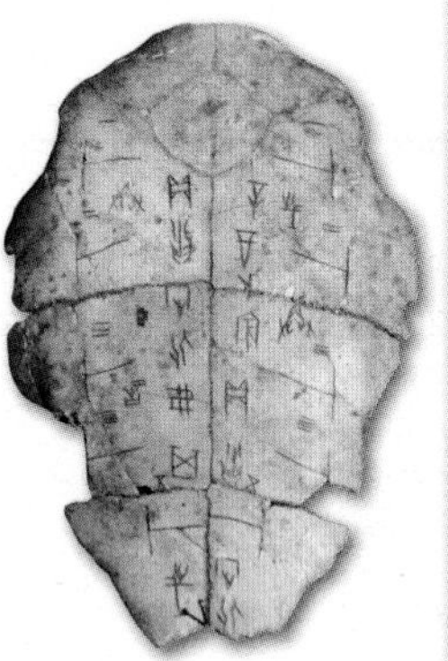

Messages written on animal bones show that the Chinese language originated with pictures representing words.

Panorama Media/Panorama Stock RF/Age fotostock

W

The ancient Chinese wrote in pictographs and ideographs. **Pictographs** (PIKH•tuh•grafs) are characters that represent objects. For example, the Chinese characters for the sun and the moon are pictographs. **Ideographs** (IH•dee•uh•grafs) are another kind of character used in Chinese writing. They link

Reading HELPDESK CCSS

aristocrat a member of an upper class of society, usually made up of hereditary nobility

ancestor a person that someone is descended from

pictograph a symbol in a writing system based on pictures

ideograph a symbol in a writing system that represents a thing or an idea

---

networks Online Teaching Options

IMAGE

Oracle Bones

Analyzing Present the Interactive Whiteboard activity on Chinese writing. Point out to students that one of the achievements of the early Chinese was the development of a writing system. **Ask: How is the writing system developed by the early Chinese different from the writing system used in English?** *(Chinese writing uses pictographs and ideographs. English has 26 characters representing sounds that are put together to form words.)* BL

networks Oracle Bones

Writing was significant to the creation of the Chinese culture. In fact, *wenhau*, the word for *culture*, means "to become literate" in Chinese. The written messages on oracle bones usually contained between 10 and 60 Chinese characters. People of the Shang dynasty used the bones as calendars. As early as 1400 B.C., the Shang calculated months that were 29½ days long and years that included 365¼ days. Shang calendars were almost the same as those we use today.

See page 275C for other online activities.

ANSWER, p. 282

Thinking Like a Historian Answers will vary but should reflect an understanding of the importance of this archaeological find and how oracle bones were used in the Shang dynasty.

two or more pictographs to express an idea. For example, the ideograph that stands for "forest" combines three pictographs of the word "tree."

Unlike the Chinese language, English and many other languages have writing systems based on an alphabet. An alphabet uses characters that represent sounds. Most characters in the Chinese language represent entire words.

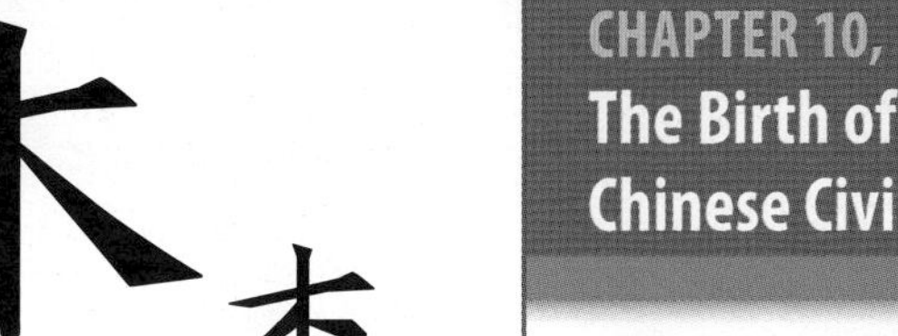

Chinese ideographs combine the pictographs of single items to form a more complex word.

▶ CRITICAL THINKING

Speculating Why do you think many Chinese today practice the ancient craft of pictographs?

Shang Arts

During the Shang dynasty, the Chinese created objects made of bronze. These works of art are some of the finest bronzes ever made. To make bronze objects, artisans made clay molds in several parts. Then they carved designs into the clay. Finally, they joined the parts of the mold together and poured in melted bronze. When the bronze cooled, the artisans removed the mold. The finished object was a beautifully decorated work of art.

Shang bronze objects included sculptures, daggers, vases, cups, and urns—or large ceremonial containers. The Shang used bronze urns to prepare and serve food for ceremonies to honor their ancestors.

Chinese artists and artisans made many other important advances. Farmers raised silk worms that produced silk. Weavers then made the silk into colorful clothing for wealthy people. Artisans crafted vases and dishes from kaolin (KAY•eh•lehn), a fine, white clay. They also carved statues from ivory and a green stone called jade.

✓ PROGRESS CHECK

Explaining Why did Shang kings have questions scratched on oracle bones?

The Zhou: China's Longest Dynasty

GUIDING QUESTION *How did the Zhou claim the right to rule China?*

According to legend, the last of the Shang rulers was a wicked tyrant. Many Chinese turned against him. In 1045 B.C., rebels led by an aristocrat named Wu Wang (WOO WAHNG) overthrew the Shang government. When his victory was complete, Wu declared a new dynasty called the Zhou (JOH). The Zhou ruled China for more than 800 years—longer than any other dynasty in Chinese history.

The Chinese made bronze objects for many uses. What do you think this elephant might have been used for?

(b) Asian Art & Archaeology, Inc./CORBIS

R Reading Skills

Sequencing Using details from the text, have students create numbered lists that explain the process Shang artisans used to cast bronze objects. Remind students that signal words such as *first, next, then,* and *finally* are often used in a paragraph to show an order of events and may help them decipher the steps that Chinese artisans followed as they worked.

W Writing Skills

Narrative Instruct students to write a short letter from the point of view of a Shang artisan. The letter should describe what medium they work in, what types of objects they make, and what purposes these objects serve. BL

C Critical Thinking Skills

Determining Cause and Effect Have students read the section about the Zhou. **Ask:** **Why did Wu Wang lead a revolt against the Shang?** *(because the king was an evil tyrant)* Remind students that this is "according to legend." **Why would that legend be useful to the new Zhou dynasty?** *(Answers may vary. Students might say that it legitimizes the new rulers' acts or that it makes them look like the "good guys.")*

IMAGE

The Use of Bronze

Researching on the Internet Have students use the interactive image of a bronze elephant as a starting point for an Internet research project about the Bronze Age. Students should formulate two or three questions that they would like answered. Remind them about the importance of paraphrasing and citing sources in order to avoid plagiarism. BL

See page 275C for other online activities.

networks
The Use of Bronze
Casting is a process where the melted form of the alloy is poured into a mold, or form. The mixture hardens as it expands, and completely fills the mold, which may result in fine artistic details, depending on how intricate the mold is.

ANSWERS, p. 283

CRITICAL THINKING Pictographs are still part of the Chinese culture.

Caption: Answers will vary but should give a reasonable use for the bronze elephant.

✓ PROGRESS CHECK They had priests scratch questions on oracle bones as a way of asking questions of the gods and ancestors.

R Reading Skills

Summarizing Have students use details in the text to discuss as a class the changes the Shang and Zhou dynasties brought to China. (*Changes noted can include: introduced writing, developed bronze arts, introduced the idea of the Mandate of Heaven, developed irrigation, built first cities, expanded trade, kings become leaders of religion and government, created strong army, and expanded the borders of China.*) AL

C Critical Thinking Skills

Contrasting Discuss with students how, as the Zhou dynasty grew, it became necessary for the king to reorganize the government to meet the needs of the growing population. Have students create a two-column chart in which they demonstrate the differences between the structure of the early Zhou government and the reorganized government. AL

GEOGRAPHY CONNECTION

Zhou rulers maintained the longest lasting dynasty in Chinese history.

1. **LOCATION** What body of water made up the eastern border of Zhou territory?
2. **CRITICAL THINKING** ***Analyzing*** Why did the Zhou divide their kingdom into smaller territories?

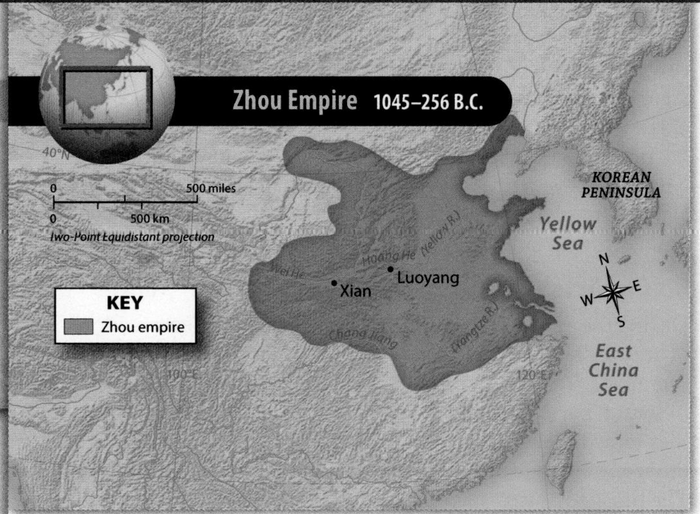

How did the Zhou Rule China?

R Zhou kings governed China much as Shang rulers had. The king led the government, ruling with the help of a bureaucracy (byu•RAH•kruh•see). A **bureaucracy** is made up of officials who carry out the tasks of government. The king also put together a strong army to bring weaker kingdoms under Zhou rule.

Soon the Zhou kingdom was larger than that of the Shang. To govern effectively, the king divided the kingdom into territories. He assigned loyal aristocrats to govern each of the territories. The positions the aristocrats held were **hereditary**. This meant that when an aristocrat died, a son or another member of his family governed the territory.

The Chinese believed their king represented them before the gods. The king's chief duty was to carry out religious ceremonies to please the gods. Zhou kings claimed that kings ruled China C because they had the Mandate of Heaven.

The Right to Rule

The **Mandate of Heaven** is the belief that the Chinese king's right to rule came from the gods. The Mandate stated the idea that the gods chose a wise and good person to rule. The person chosen by the gods would govern honestly and well.

The Mandate of Heaven changed what the Zhou people expected from their king. The king must rule by the proper

Reading HELPDESK 

bureaucracy a group of non-elected government officials
hereditary having title or possession by reason of birth
Mandate of Heaven the belief that the Chinese king's right to rule came from the gods
Dao Chinese system of beliefs which describes the way a king must rule

networks Online Teaching Options

MAP

Zhou Empire, 1045–256 B.C.

Reading Maps Refer students to the interactive map of the Zhou empire. **Ask:** What were the important cities in the Zhou empire? (*Xian and Luoyang*) Which of these cities was near the old Shang capital? (*Luoyang*) Why might the Zhou have put their capital in the same area as the Shang? (*Answers may vary. Students might include continuity or proving their victory over the old empire in their responses.*)

See page 275C for other online activities.

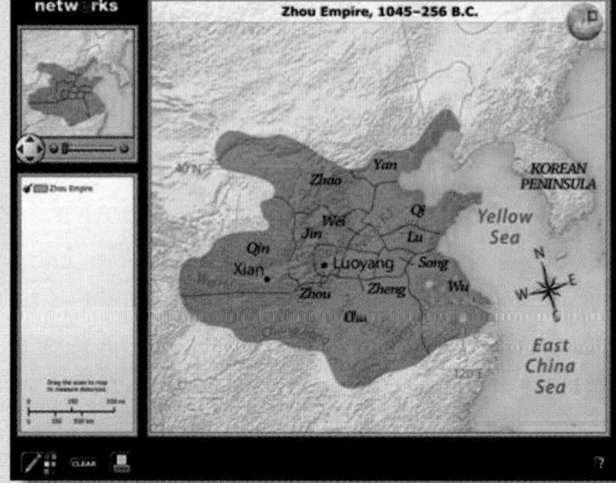

ANSWERS, p. 284

GEOGRAPHY CONNECTION

1. the Yellow Sea
2. **CRITICAL THINKING** to make ruling easier

"Way," known as the **Dao** (DOW). His duty was to honor and please the gods. If there was a natural disaster or a bad harvest, that meant the king had failed and he could be replaced.

Technology and Trade

C

For many centuries, Chinese farmers had to depend on rain to water their crops. Under Zhou kings, the Chinese developed new systems to irrigate the land. With a better water supply, farmers were able to grow more crops than ever before.

China's trade also expanded. Archaeologists have found pieces of Chinese silk in central Asia and as far away as Greece.

War Between the States

W

Over time, the aristocrats who ruled the territories of the Zhou kingdom grew more powerful. They ignored the king's commands and took control of their own territory. The aristocrats began to fight one another for power. These wars began in the 400s B.C. and went on for nearly 200 years. Because each aristocrat formed his own state, this time in China's history is called the "Period of the Warring States."

To fill the ranks of their armies, the aristocrats forced farmers to serve as soldiers. Chinese soldiers were armed with swords, spears, and crossbows. As the fighting continued through the years, warriors began using horses. The Chinese developed the saddle and stirrup. Now soldiers could ride around the battlefield while throwing spears or shooting crossbows. The wars fought at this time would result in a new dynasty.

This dragon is an example of bronze work from the Zhou dynasty.

Burstein Collection/CORBIS

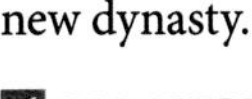

✓ PROGRESS CHECK

Identifying What technology was developed in China during the Zhou dynasty?

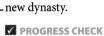

LESSON 1 REVIEW (CCSS)

Review Vocabulary (Tier 3 Words)

1. How did a *pictograph* differ from an *ideograph*? RH.6–8.4

Answer the Guiding Questions

2. ***Describing*** What geographic features isolated ancient China from other civilizations? RH.6–8.2
3. ***Explaining*** How did Shang rulers gain power? RH.6–8.2
4. ***Identifying*** What was the chief duty of Zhou kings? RH.6–8.2
5. ***Describing*** Describe the biggest change for the Chinese people during the Zhou dynasty. RH.6–8.2
6. **INFORMATIVE/EXPLANATORY** China's geographic features separated it from other civilizations. Write a paragraph explaining the advantages and disadvantages of isolation. WHST.6–8.2, WHST.6–8.10
7. **INFORMATIVE/EXPLANATORY** Write a paragraph that explains why "China's Sorrow" is an appropriate description of the Huang He. WHST.6–8.2, WHST.6–8.10

C Critical Thinking Skills

Making Inferences Discuss with students how early Chinese civilizations made many advances in the arts and agriculture. **Ask:** **How might today's farmers benefit from discoveries made by farmers during the Zhou dynasty?** *(Possible response: Farmers during the Zhou dynasty developed irrigation systems that may have served as a model for today's irrigation systems.)*

W Writing Skills

Informative/Explanatory Have students read the section of the textbook titled "War Between the States." Then have them write a short paragraph that summarizes the events that led to the wars and how these wars led to the fall of the Zhou dynasty. AL

Have students complete the Lesson 1 Review.

CLOSE & REFLECT

To close the lesson, ask students to name similarities and differences between the Shang and Zhou civilizations that developed in the Huang He valley.

ANSWER, p. 285

✓ PROGRESS CHECK New irrigation systems, saddles, and stirrups were developed during the Zhou dynasty.

LESSON 1 REVIEW ANSWERS

1. Each pictograph represents an object; ideographs join two or more pictographs to represent another thing or to express an idea.
2. Deserts and mountains isolated China from other civilizations.
3. Shang rulers used military force to gain power.
4. The chief duty of a Zhou king was to carry out religious ceremonies to please the gods.
5. The biggest change for the Chinese during the Zhou dynasty was the development of the Mandate of Heaven. According to the Mandate of Heaven, the gods chose a wise and good person to rule China. The Mandate of Heaven changed what Chinese people expected from a king. The king's duty was to honor and please the gods. If the king failed in his duty, the people had the right to replace him.
6. A civilization that is cut off from other civilizations might have the advantage of being able to develop peacefully. The people of the civilization might develop a stronger national identity. However, isolation also keeps people from being exposed to new ideas and new ways of doing things. A civilization could grow weak without the exposure to new ideas.
7. Although the Huang He provides China with rich soil that makes it possible to grow large amounts of food on small plots of land, the river has also brought misery to China. The river often floods, which causes immense damage and many deaths. Millions of people have died as a result of the Huang He flooding.

ENGAGE

Bellringer Before students begin the lesson, ask them to think about how their actions affect or influence others. Lead students into a discussion of why laws are created. Then discuss how a society's values might be reflected in its laws. Ask volunteers to cite a law. Then discuss whether it reflects a value of our society, and if so, identify what that value is.

TEACH & ASSESS

W Writing Skills

Narrative Ask students to think about what life was like in China during the Period of the Warring States. Have them write a brief journal entry from the point of view of a young man or woman living in China during this time, describing the living conditions and what is going on there. Invite students to share their entries with a partner. BL **Interpersonal**

C Critical Thinking Skills

Drawing Conclusions Based on what students have read, **ask: Why would the Chinese people have been open to new philosophies during this time?** *(They wanted a way to create a peaceful society instead of the violent one they had.)*

networks
There's More Online!
- **CHART/GRAPH** Confucius's Philosophy About Education
- **GRAPHIC ORGANIZER** Three Chinese Philosophies
- **SLIDE SHOW** Zhou Dynasty Art

Lesson 2

Society and Culture in Ancient China

ESSENTIAL QUESTION *How do new ideas change the way people live?*

IT MATTERS BECAUSE
Ideas that started in early China continue to influence today's world.

Chinese Philosophies

GUIDING QUESTION *How did Chinese thinkers influence society and government?*

W During the Period of the Warring States, rulers of rival states fought each other. Armies wiped out entire villages of men, women, and children. Many Chinese looked for ways to stop the killing. They wanted to bring order to society.

Between 500 B.C. and 200 B.C., Chinese thinkers developed three major **philosophies**. They were Confucianism, Daoism, and legalism. These philosophies were different from one C another. However, the philosophies had the same goal. Each philosophy aimed to create a well-run and peaceful society. After decades of war, Chinese people welcomed these new ideas.

What Ideas Did Confucius Teach?

Confucianism (kuhn•FYOO•shuh•nih•zuhm) was based on the teachings of a man named Confucius (kuhn•FYOO•shuhs). Born about 550 B.C. to a farming family, Confucius lived when rival kings fought each other for power. Confucius criticized the misrule of these kings. He urged the people to follow the beliefs of their ancestors. If people would do that, Confucius believed, it would bring peace and harmony to China.

Reading HELPDESK CCSS

Taking Notes: *Identifying* RH.6–8.2
Use a graphic organizer like the one shown here to identify the three Chinese philosophies that emerged after the fall of the Zhou dynasty.

Three Chinese Philosophies

Content Vocabulary (Tier 3 Words)
- **Confucianism**
- **Daoism**
- **legalism**
- **filial piety**

networks Online Teaching Options

VIDEO

Chinese History from Peking Man to Confucius

Recognizing Relationships Show students the video for this lesson, tracing Chinese history through Confucianism. Lead students to understand that philosophy is the study of the beliefs and laws that rule life. **Ask: How does philosophy shape the way we live?** *(Students might say that what people consider true and important will determine how they act.)* Ask students if they think philosophies differ from culture to culture. AL

See page 275D for other online activities.

ANSWERS, p. 286
TAKING NOTES: Confucianism, Daoism, legalism

Duty is a central idea of Confucianism. Duty means that a person places the needs of family and community above his or her own needs. Each **individual** has certain duties to fulfill. It is the duty of parents to love their children, and it is the children's duty to respect their parents. Husbands should support their wives, and wives should obey their husbands. Above all, a ruler had a duty to rule justly and to set an example of right living. In return, subjects should be loyal and obey the law.

Confucius believed that if each individual carried out his or her duties, society would do well. He urged people to be good. This meant behaving moderately, keeping one's promises, honoring traditions, and respecting the elderly. Confucius also advised people to seek knowledge:

PRIMARY SOURCE

"By extensively ... studying all learning, and keeping himself under the restraint [control] of the rules of propriety [correct behavior], one may thus likewise not err ... from what is right."

— Confucius, *Analects*, XII, 15

To Confucius, the right way to live was **similar** to the idea known as the Golden Rule: "Do unto others as you would have others do unto you."

The Influence of Confucius

Confucius believed that government service should be open to all men of ability and merit and not limited to those of noble birth. The aristocrats did not want to open government to more people. They did not want to lose their power. However, over time Chinese emperors developed the practice of choosing government officials through civil service tests.

Many people honored Confucius as a great teacher. His followers wrote down his sayings and collected them in a work called the *Analects*. After Confucius died in 479 B.C., his teachings spread throughout China. Confucianism continued to shape Chinese society and government until the early A.D. 1900s.

Connections to TODAY

Confucianism in Asia

Confucianism still has millions of followers today. Most of these followers are in China. Over the centuries, however, the basic teachings of Confucius spread across Asia. The concepts he handed down—a belief in duty and correct behavior and respect for education—are a part of the culture in many Asian countries today.

The Chinese philosopher Confucius taught that people should do their duty and keep promises.

Keren Su/China Span/Corbis

Confucianism a system of beliefs based on the teachings of Confucius

Academic Vocabulary (Tier 2 Words)

philosophy the study of the basic ideas about society, education, and right and wrong
individual a single human being as contrasted with a group
similar having things in common

C1 Critical Thinking Skills

Prioritizing Organize students into small groups and have them read the passage about Confucianism and duty aloud. Then have each group list the types of duty that Confucius wrote about and prioritize them, based on the group's opinions. Have each group share their lists, and lead the class in discussion about why each group prioritized its list the way it did. AL **Verbal/Linguistic**

C2 Critical Thinking Skills

Analyzing Primary Sources Have students read the quote from Confucius about right behavior. Then have them rewrite the quote in their own words. ELL

R Reading Skill

Applying After students have read about the influence of Confucius, **ask: Why did the aristocrats resist opening up the government?** *(They wanted to protect their power.)* **Why might the emperors have adopted civil service tests anyway?** *(because it made their governments stronger)*

IMAGE

Confucius's Philosophy About Education

Determining Cause and Effect Use the interactive image to guide students in a discussion of Confucius's ideas about education and how Confucius believed that better education would improve society. Ask students whether they agree with Confucius's ideas. Have them support their opinions with reasoning. BL

See page 275D for other online activities.

networks Confucius's Philosophy About Education

- Confucius valued education. He spent most of his life learning and teaching. He believed that education should be available to everyone, not just wealthy people.
- Confucius also believed that the goals of learning and teaching were to improve and transform society. He thought it was the duty of citizens to perform public service.
- According to Confucius, in learning to better one's self, a student will improve society from the inside. This will then lead to the *student* becoming the *teacher* in order to further improve society. This is a *circular* idea. Click on the diagram to learn about the idea.

Goals of Learning and Teaching

V Visual Skills

Reading a Chart Direct students' attention to the chart titled *Chinese Philosophers*. Explain that this chart is organized to compare three philosophers *(one in each column)* across three categories *(one in each row)*. Ask students to identify where they would find Hanzei's picture. *(first row, third column)* Then ask them to locate where they would find Daoism's influence on modern life. *(third row, second column)* **Visual/Spatial**

C Critical Thinking Skills

Comparing and Contrasting Remind students that Daoism is both similar to and different from Confucianism. As a class, have students list the similarities among and differences between the two philosophies. Invite two volunteers to record the lists on the interactive whiteboard. **Verbal/Linguistic**

Content Background Knowledge

Because the Daoists sought to live in harmony with nature, many of the scientific advances in ancient China came about because of Daoist philosophers seeking to understand nature and humanity better. This is the foundation of Chinese advances in medicine, chemistry, and even early geography.

ANSWERS, p. 288

INFOGRAPHIC

1. Confucianism
2. **CRITICAL THINKING** Answers will vary but should be logical.

INFOGRAPHIC

CHINESE PHILOSOPHERS

Three philosophies developed in early China. Each had a strong leader.

1. **IDENTIFYING** Which philosophy encourages followers to concentrate on duty and humanity?
2. **CRITICAL THINKING** *Analyzing* Which of these philosophies do you think would be most popular in the world today? Explain.

	Confucianism	Daoism	Legalism
Founder	Confucius	Laozi	Hanfeizi
Main Ideas	People should put the needs of their family and community first.	People should give up worldly desires in favor of nature and the Dao.	Society needs a system of harsh laws and strict punishment.
Influence on Modern Life	Many Chinese today accept his idea of duty to family. His ideas helped open up government jobs to people with talent.	Daoism teaches the importance of nature and encourages people to treat nature with respect and reverence.	Legalists developed laws that became an important part of Chinese history.

The Philosophy of Daoism

Another Chinese philosophy, known as **Daoism** (DOW•ih•zuhm) also promoted a peaceful society. The word *Dao* means "path" and is often translated as "the Way." Daoism began with the ideas of Laozi (LOW•DZUH). Laozi is believed to have lived during the same time as Confucius.

Like Confucianism, Daoism teaches people how to live a good life. Daoists believed that people should free themselves from worldly desires and live simply. They should turn to nature and the Dao—the spiritual force that guides all things. In this way, they would enjoy a happy life.

Daoism is different from Confucianism in some ways. Followers of Confucius taught that people should work hard to make the world better. Daoism taught people to turn away from worldly affairs and live in harmony with nature. Many Chinese followed both Confucianism and Daoism. They believed that the two philosophies supported each other.

Reading HELPDESK (CCSS)

Daoism a Chinese philosophy concerned with obtaining long life and living in harmony with nature

networks *Online Teaching Options*

CHART

Confucianism, Daoism, Legalism

Identifying Points of View Have students complete the chart, matching sayings of Chinese philosophers to the correct school of philosophy. Then organize students into three groups. One group will be Confucians, another will be Daoists, and the third will be legalists. Students in each group should write sayings representing something that followers of their group's philosophy may have believed. For example, students in the Daoist group might write "Put aside your desire for money." Each group should prepare a list of several sayings. After collecting the lists, read the sayings aloud to the class. AL ELL

See page 275D for other online activities.

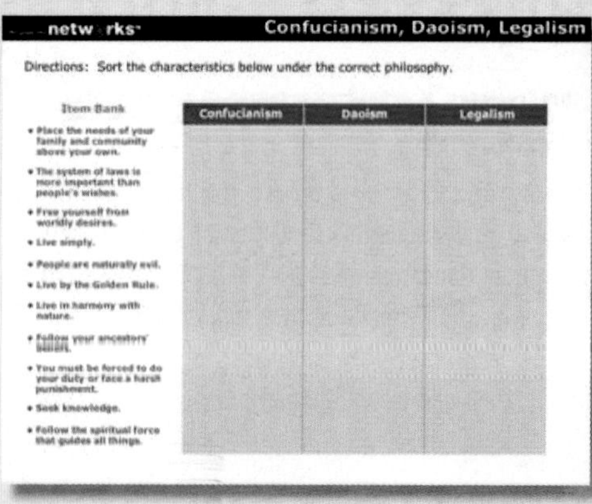

Legalism

A third philosophy stressed the importance of a system of laws. This philosophy became known as **legalism** (lee•guh•lih•zuhm), or the "School of Law."

G1 T A thinker named Hanfeizi (HAN•fay•DZOO) introduced the ideas of legalism during the 200s B.C. Unlike Confucius or Laozi, Hanfeizi believed that humans are naturally evil. Strict laws and harsh punishments were necessary to force people to do their duty.

Many aristocrats supported legalism because it emphasized force. Legalism did not require rulers to consider the needs or wishes of their people. Its ideas led to cruel punishments for even the smallest crimes.

✔ PROGRESS CHECK

Comparing and Contrasting How are the ideas of Confucius and Laozi similar? How are they different?

Chinese Life

GUIDING QUESTION *How was early Chinese society organized?*

Early Chinese society was made up of four social classes. A **social class** includes people who have the same economic and social position. In ancient China, these social classes were landowning aristocrats, farmers, artisans, and merchants.

Lives of the Aristocrats

China's aristocratic families were wealthy. They owned large estates and lived in tile-roofed houses with courtyards and gardens. Walls surrounded their homes as protection against bandits. Inside, fine furniture and carpets filled the rooms.

C2 Aristocratic families owned large plots of land. After the father died, a family's land was divided equally among all of the male heirs. As a result, sons and grandsons owned much less land than their fathers and grandfathers owned.

Lives of the Farmers

About nine out of ten Chinese farmed for a living. The farmers lived in rural villages surrounded by mud walls. Beyond the village walls were fields owned by the aristocrats. The farmers rented the fields by turning over part of their crops to the owners.

The ideas of Laozi became popular in China between around 500 B.C. and 300 B.C. Here he is shown riding a water buffalo into the desert.

Giraudon/Art Resource, NY

legalism a Chinese philosophy that stressed the importance of laws

Academic Vocabulary (Tier 2 Words)

social class a group of people who are at a similar cultural, economic, or educational level

G1 Critical Thinking Skills

Making Connections Guide the class in a discussion about the underlying belief of legalism—that people are fundamentally evil and require laws to make them behave. Solicit student points of view on whether they believe this to be true. Encourage students to offer examples of a time when they have done something without being told and a time when they have been forced to do something because of a certain rule.

T Technology Skills

Making a Presentation Organize students into three small groups. Have each group create a slide show presentation about one of the three philosophies, including legalism, that they have studied in this lesson. Provide time in class for students to research, develop, and deliver their presentations.
BL Verbal/Linguistic

C2 Critical Thinking Skills

Predicting Consequences Ask students to predict what the consequences will be of sons having less land and wealth with each generation. *(Sample answer: The power of the aristocrats will diminish.)*

WORKSHEET

Guided Reading Activity: Chinese Life

Describing Have students read the section of the textbook titled "Chinese Life." Students can use the interactive worksheet to help them gather information that describes life in China during this period. AL

See page 275D for other online activities.

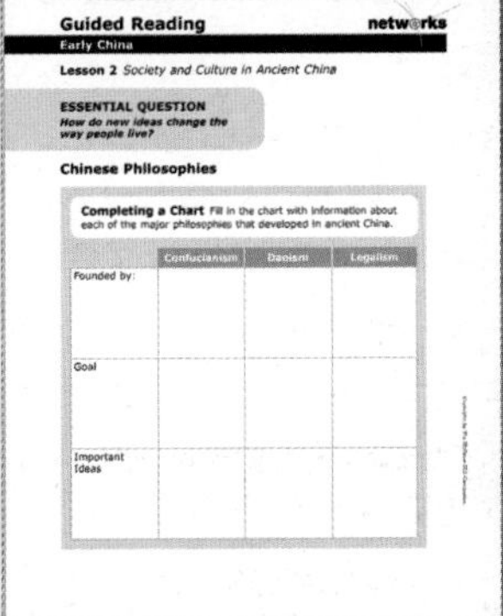

Guided Reading networks
Early China
Lesson 2 Society and Culture in Ancient China
ESSENTIAL QUESTION How do new ideas change the way people live?
Chinese Philosophies
Completing a Chart Fill in the chart with information about each of the major philosophies that developed in ancient China.

	Confucianism	Daoism	Legalism
Founded by:			
Goal			
Important Ideas			

ANSWER, p. 289

✔ PROGRESS CHECK Confucius and Laozi offered people a guide on how to live a good life. Confucius believed that to live a good life, people should work hard to make the world better. Laozi, on the other hand, believed that to have a good life, people should turn away from the material world and focus on nature.

V Visual Skills

Interpreting Have students study the illustration in the textbook of an early Chinese village. **Ask:** **How were early Chinese villages protected?** *(They were surrounded by tall walls; there was only one way in and one way out.)* **Why do you think farming was done in the land surrounding the villages?** *(Possible responses: There was not enough room inside the villages; farmers could expand their fields if needed.)* **Visual/Spatial**

C Critical Thinking Skills

Giving Examples Ask students to give some examples of the hardships faced by Chinese farmers. Then **ask:** **Why do you think people became farmers if it was such a difficult life?** *(Answers will vary. Possible responses: Some people may have been second- or third-generation farmers who had inherited their family's land; people knew that farmers were important to the survival of the Chinese people.)* **What was one indication that merchants were not well thought of in Chinese society?** *(They weren't allowed to serve in government jobs.)* BL

ANSWER, p. 290

INFOGRAPHIC

CRITICAL THINKING One disadvantage is that farmers who do not own the land they farm cannot enjoy all the profits because they must pay rent. Another disadvantage is that farmers might not take good care of the land because they do not own it.

CHINESE VILLAGE

Villagers built walls that surrounded and protected the town.

Foot-pedaled hammers were used to remove grain and rice from their stalks.

Since horses were more valuable as war animals, farmers used oxen and water buffalo to pull plows and carts.

Peasants planted and cultivated rice plants in large flooded fields.

INFOGRAPHIC

Chinese farmers lived in small villages made up of several families. They farmed fields outside the village walls.

▶ **CRITICAL THINKING**
Analyzing What are some possible disadvantages for farmers of working on land they do not own?

In northern China, farmers grew wheat and a grain called millet. In the south, where the climate was warmer and wetter, they grew rice. Most farmers also owned a small plot of land where they grew food for their own use.

The government required farmers to pay taxes and to work one month each year on projects such as building roads. In wartime, farmers were forced to serve as soldiers. In addition, farmers had to face constant threats from famine and floods.

Lives of the Artisans and Merchants

Artisans are skilled workers who make useful objects. The artisans of Zhou China crafted iron tools and weapons, silk cloth, and vessels made of bronze or jade. Many were architects, artists, and woodworkers. Most artisans learned their skills from their fathers and, in turn, passed them along to their sons.

Shopkeepers, traders, and bankers made up the merchant class. Merchants lived in towns and provided goods and services to the aristocrats.

Some merchants became wealthy, but they were not respected members of society. People believed that merchants worked only for their own gain, not for the good of society.

Reading HELPDESK (CCSS)

filial piety the responsibility children have to respect, obey, and care for their parents

networks Online Teaching Options

SLIDE SHOW

Zhou Dynasty Art

Analyzing Visuals Present the slide show on art produced by Chinese artisans. **Ask:** **What do these images tell you about the wealth of ancient China?** *(The quality of the art and the expensive materials suggest that ancient China had great wealth.)* **How did art styles change during the Zhou dynasty?** *(Zhou artists experimented with new styles in forms such as jade carving and bronze work.)* AL

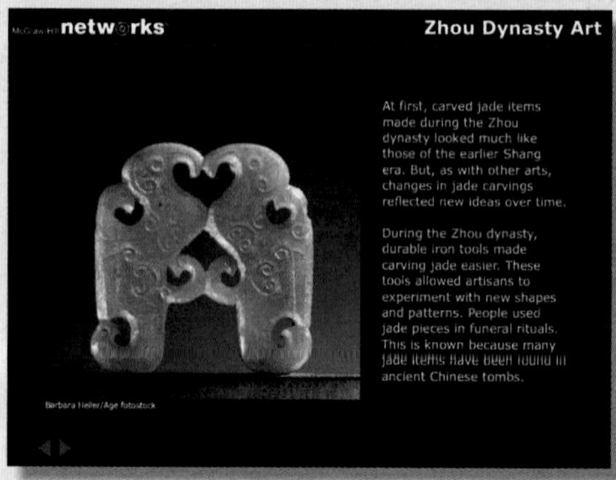

networks
Zhou Dynasty Art
At first, carved jade items made during the Zhou dynasty looked much like those of the earlier Shang era. But, as with other arts, changes in jade carvings reflected new ideas over time.
During the Zhou dynasty, durable iron tools made carving jade easier. These tools allowed artisans to experiment with new shapes and patterns. People used jade pieces in funeral rituals. This is known because many jade items have been found in ancient Chinese tombs.

See page 275D for other online activities.

While artisans made useful goods and farmers grew food for all, merchants made money for themselves. Merchants were also barred from government jobs.

What Were Chinese Families Like?

The family was at the center of early Chinese society. Farming in ancient China required many workers, so parents had many children to help them with the work. Even young children worked in the fields. Chinese families took care of those members in need—the aged, the young, and the sick.

C2 Chinese families practiced **filial piety** (FIH•lee•uhl PY•uh•tee). Filial refers to a son or daughter. Piety refers to duty or devotion. Therefore, *filial piety* refers to people's responsibility to respect and obey their parents. C1

It also requires people to take care of their parents as they grow older. Family members placed the needs of the head of the family before their own. The head of the family was the oldest male, usually the father. Respect for parents and the elderly were central to the teachings of Confucius. Even today, filial piety is an important part of Chinese culture.

Roles of Men and Women

Men and women had very different roles in early China. Men were respected because of the jobs they did—growing crops, attending school, running the government, and fighting wars. The Chinese considered these jobs more important than the work carried out by women. Most women raised children and saw to their education. They also managed the household and family finances.

The man and woman here are shown in brightly colored dress. The colors on these ancient Chinese figures have lasted thousands of years. Why do you think there is such attention to detail?

✓ PROGRESS CHECK

Explaining Why were merchants not respected in ancient China?

LESSON 2 REVIEW (CCSS)

Review Vocabulary (Tier 3 Words)

1. Describe a situation in which you might show *filial piety*. RH.6–8.4

Answer the Guiding Questions

2. ***Explaining*** Why did many aristocrats support legalism? RH.6–8.2
3. ***Identifying*** What were the main social classes of early China? RH.6–8.2
4. ***Assessing*** Which philosophy do you most strongly agree with—Confucianism, Daoism, or legalism? Why? RH.6–8.2
5. ***Paraphrasing*** Read the following quotation by Confucius. Then restate the quotation in your own words: "A journey of a thousand miles begins with a single step." RH.6–8.2
6. **ARGUMENT** Which system of belief—Confucianism, Daoism, or legalism—would lead to the best government? Write a paragraph expressing your opinion in order to convince others. WHST.6–8.1, WHST.6–8.10

LESSON 2 REVIEW ANSWERS

1. Students' answers will vary but should reflect an understanding that filial piety involves the obligation of children to respect, obey, and take care of their parents.
2. Many aristocrats supported legalism because it did not require rulers to consider the needs or wishes of their people, but rather it allowed them to rule by force.
3. The main social classes of early China were aristocrats, farmers, artisans, and merchants.
4. Answers may vary but should demonstrate an understanding of the philosophy students chose to write about.
5. Answers may vary but should state something like "The hardest part of doing something difficult can be getting started. Start off with something small and keep going."
6. Answers may vary but should reflect an understanding of the role of government and the belief system students chose to write about.

C1 Critical Thinking Skills

Making Connections Guide students in a discussion about the early Chinese family. **Ask: What is filial piety?** *(people's responsibility to obey and respect their parents and take care of them when they are older)* Have students discuss whether filial piety is a common practice today in American families. BL

C2 Critical Thinking Skills

Determining Cause and Effect Guide students in a discussion of the effects the teachings of Confucius had on Chinese family life. **Ask: How were the teachings of Confucius reflected in the lives of Chinese families?** *(Confucius stressed the importance of respect for parents and the elderly. In Chinese families, children put the wants of their parents, especially their fathers, above their own wants.)*

Have students complete the Lesson 2 Review.

CLOSE & REFLECT

To close the lesson, have students choose one of the three philosophies (Confucianism, Daoism, legalism) that they believe would make school better if everyone followed it. Have students write a short letter to the principal describing one or more key changes their chosen philosophy could make at the school.

ANSWERS, p. 291

Caption: Possible answer: because the Chinese valued art and made their art as realistic as possible

✓ PROGRESS CHECK Merchants were not respected because most people believed merchants were only interested in making money for themselves, not in improving society.

ENGAGE

Bellringer Before students begin the lesson, ask them to remember a time when government changed, such as after a presidential election. Ask volunteers to share what they know about how the process of changing government works today, and invite students to speculate about how that process was different in the past.

TEACH & ASSESS

R Reading Skills

Summarizing After they have read the opening paragraph, have students summarize how the first Qin emperor came to power. **Ask:** **How did the conflict of the Period of the Warring States help the Qin rise to power?** *(Answers may vary but may include: A weak emperor was easier to overcome; warring states were not unified and therefore were easier to overtake.)*

C Critical Thinking Skills

Identifying Problems Remind students that the Zhou rulers had divided China into provinces ruled by governors. **Ask:** **Why would Qin Shihuangdi want to unify the country again?** *(Answers will vary but could include: to avoid the problems of the Zhou; to weaken the governors and local warlords; to end the chaos that had erupted during the Period of the Warring States.)* BL

ANSWERS, p. 292

TAKING NOTES: Possible answers for Qin: appointed censors, ruled harshly, created a uniform currency, simplified writing system, large building projects, lasted 15 years; Possible answers for Han: civil service system, growth of Confucianism, artists created works for more people, lasted 400 years; Possible answers for both: wanted to strengthen and unify China, expanded China's borders, most people were poor farmers, had social classes.

networks
There's More Online!
- GAME — Qin Dynasty
- GRAPHIC ORGANIZER — Comparing and Contrasting: Qin and Han Dynasties
- CHART — World Population Time Line

Lesson 3
The Qin and the Han Dynasties

ESSENTIAL QUESTION *How do governments change?*

IT MATTERS BECAUSE
Stable government builds solid growth and strength in a civilization.

The Qin Emperor

GUIDING QUESTION *How did the Qin Emperor unite China?*

R You have read about the fighting in China from about 400 B.C. to 200 B.C. During the Period of the Warring States, the strong rulers of local states fought one another and ignored the weak Zhou kings. One of these states was called Qin (CHIHN). In 221 B.C., the ruler of Qin sent a large cavalry force to defeat the other states and end the Zhou dynasty. The Qin then controlled China from the Huang He to the Chang Jiang.

To mark a new beginning for China, the Qin ruler declared himself Qin Shihuangdi (CHIHN SHEE•hwahng•dee), which means "the First Qin Emperor." Qin brought changes to Chinese government that would last for many centuries.

How Did Qin Change China?

C Qin wanted to strengthen and **unify** China. To do that, he took direct control of China's provinces. Under the Zhou rulers, the governors of the provinces had passed on their positions to sons or relatives. Now, only Qin had the power to appoint the governors.

Qin ruled China with absolute control and swift, harsh punishment. Anyone who disagreed with him was punished or killed. Writings that displeased Qin were burned.

Reading HELPDESK CCSS

Taking Notes: ***Comparing***
Use a Venn diagram like the one shown here to compare and contrast the Qin and Han dynasties. RH.6–8.2

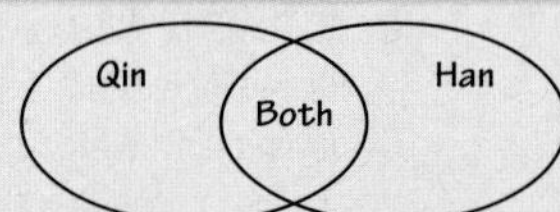

Content Vocabulary (Tier 3 Words)
- censor
- currency
- civil service
- tenant farmer
- acupuncture

networks *Online Teaching Options*

VIDEO

Chinese History from the First Emperor to the Romance of the Three Kingdoms

Analyzing Have students watch the video for this lesson and analyze the ways in which China has changed since the Shang dynasty. AL

See page 275E for other online activities.

Qin also increased the power of his government by appointing officers known as **censors**. The censors' job was to make sure government workers did their work.

Qin developed other policies and projects to unify the empire. He created a **currency**, or type of money, that everyone had to use. He hired scholars to simplify and set rules for the Chinese writing system. Qin also undertook building projects, including the construction of his own tomb. Qin's tomb was so large that it housed an army of life-sized clay soldiers and horses. Qin also ordered tens of thousands of farmers to build palaces, roads, dams, and a huge canal. The canal connected the Chang Jiang in central China to what is today the city of Guangzhou (GWAHNG•JOH) in southern China. The government transported supplies on the canal to soldiers in distant territories.

C

Why Was the Great Wall Built?

Qin united the different parts of China into one empire. He wanted to keep the empire safe from invasion. A vast desert known as the Gobi was on the edge of China's northern border. Nomads, people who move from place to place with herds of animals, lived in the Gobi. The Chinese knew them as the Xiongnu (SYEHN•NOO). The Xiongnu were skilled warriors who fought on horseback and often attacked Chinese settlements. Earlier Chinese rulers had constructed separate walls in the north to keep out the Xiongnu. Qin planned to have the walls joined and strengthened.

R

The End of Qin Rule

V

In 221 B.C., Qin boasted that his dynasty would rule China forever. The Qin dynasty actually ended soon after Qin's death in 210 B.C. Both aristocrats and farmers revolted against the harsh Qin rule. Fighting erupted throughout China. By 206 B.C. the Qin dynasty was over and a new dynasty arose.

Connections to TODAY

The Great Wall

Many things get built and rebuilt over time. Building the Great Wall in China took several years. Qin forced hundreds of thousands of farmers to leave their fields to work on the wall. Thousands of laborers died before the project was completed. The finished wall, the Great Wall of China, was built mainly on the northern slopes of mountains, using stone, sand, and rubble. However, Qin did not build the wall that stands today. The Great Wall today consists of a series of walls and towers built during the Ming dynasty beginning in the late 1400s.

R

Qin Shihuangdi had a large goal: to organize and strengthen the country.

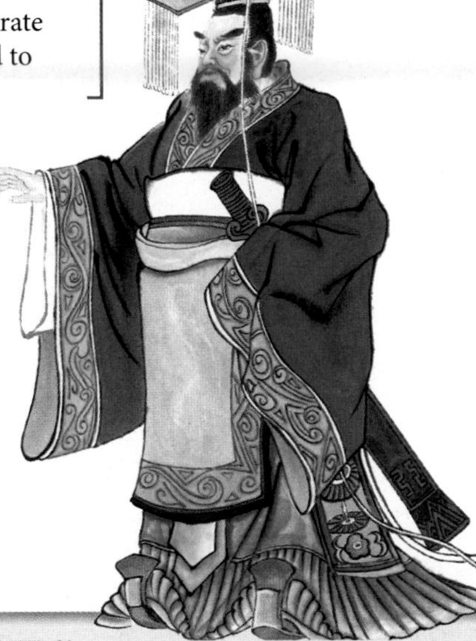

PROGRESS CHECK

Explaining How would you describe Qin as a ruler?

censor an official who watches others for correct behavior

currency something, such as coins or paper money, that is used as a medium of exchange

Academic Vocabulary (Tier 2 Words)

unify to make into a single unit

SLIDE SHOW

Terra-Cotta Warriors

Integrating Visual Information Present the slide show about the Qin tomb, and discuss the information given there. Have students draw conclusions about what life was like under this dynasty, based on what they saw. Invite volunteers to write their conclusions on the interactive whiteboard. Discuss the conclusions, asking students what they based their conclusions on and whether they agree with the conclusions others have drawn.

See page 275E for other online activities.

networks
Terra-Cotta Warriors
Qin Shihuangdi's burial complex is 20 square miles (51.8 square km). It houses 8,000 life-sized terra-cotta, or clay, soldiers arranged in a military formation.

C Critical Thinking Skills

Drawing Conclusions Remind students that one of Qin Shihuangdi's goals was to unify China. Organize the class into small groups, and have each group discuss one of Qin's many changes. Then have each group write a short explanation of how that change helped unify the country. AL ELL

R Reading Skills

Assessing After students have read about the Great Wall, **ask:** **Why was the Great Wall built?** *(to keep the empire safe from nomadic warriors)* **Was this the first wall built for this purpose?** *(No, earlier rulers had built walls in the North.)* **Who built the Great Wall we see today?** *(Ming rulers in the 1400s)*

V Visual Skills

Creating Visuals Have students create campaign posters for the revolt that brought down the Qin dynasty. Students may write slogans and use images that emphasize harsh Qin rule or that seek to draw both farmers and aristocrats together. BL **Visual/Spatial**

ANSWER, p. 293

PROGRESS CHECK Qin was a harsh ruler. He was ambitious and had a vision of China that he was intent on achieving.

C Critical Thinking Skills

Evaluating Tell students that the idea for civil service examinations had begun with Confucius, hundreds of years before Han Wudi. **Ask:** **Why might earlier rulers have relied on family members and loyal aristocrats?** *(Answers will vary but may include: so that the ruler could better control them.)* **How would competitive tests help Han Wudi be a strong ruler?** *(It would help him find the best people to work for his government.)*

R Reading Skills

Identifying After students have read the text, have them imagine that they are the new emperor of China, Han Wudi. **Ask:** **As the new emperor, what teachings of Confucius will help you govern? How will they help?** *(Answers will vary. Students may say they would choose to follow Confucius's rules for good conduct. As the new emperor, they might also want to spread the ideal of filial piety, encouraging their subjects to look upon the emperor as the father of the entire nation, who should be respected and obeyed.)*

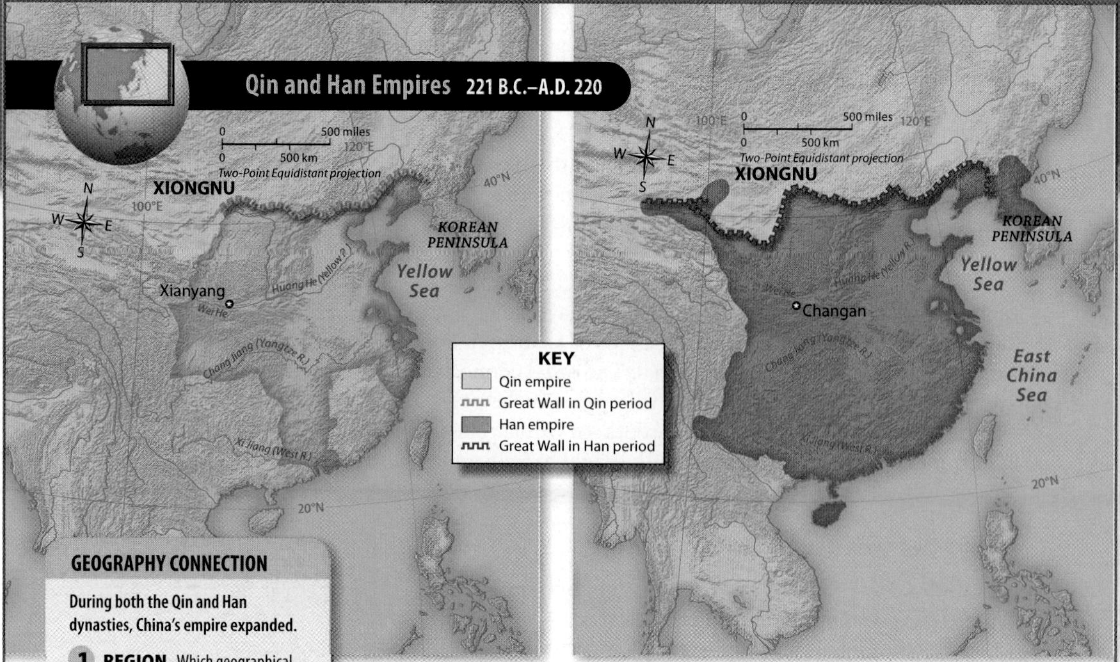

Qin and Han Empires 221 B.C.–A.D. 220
0 500 miles
0 500 km
Two-Point Equidistant projection
XIONGNU
100°E
120°E
40°N
20°N
KOREAN PENINSULA
Yellow Sea
East China Sea
Xianyang
Wei He
Huang He (Yellow R.)
Chang Jiang (Yangtze R.)
Xi Jiang (West R.)
Changan
KEY
Qin empire
Great Wall in Qin period
Han empire
Great Wall in Han period

GEOGRAPHY CONNECTION

During both the Qin and Han dynasties, China's empire expanded.

1. **REGION** Which geographical areas did both empires include?
2. **CRITICAL THINKING** ***Drawing Conclusions*** Why do you think the Han empire was able to expand farther west than the Qin?

Han Rulers

GUIDING QUESTION ***What improvements did the Chinese make under Han rulers?***

In 202 B.C., a new dynasty known as the Han dynasty came to power in China. Its founder was Liu Bang (LYOO BAHNG), a farmer turned soldier. His family began the powerful Han dynasty that would rule China for more than 400 years.

Han Wudi

R C The first strong emperor of the Han dynasty was Han Wudi (HAHN WOO•DEE), who ruled from 141 B.C. to 87 B.C. Han Wudi took important steps to improve China's government. Earlier emperors chose family members and loyal aristocrats to help them run the government. Han Wudi wanted to end this practice. He recruited dedicated and talented people for **civil service**, government workers who were chosen on the basis of competitive tests.

First, scholars and officials recommended qualified candidates. Then, the candidates took long, difficult written examinations. Finally, officials graded the tests, and the emperor reviewed the results. The candidates with the highest scores got the jobs.

Reading HELPDESK (CCSS)

civil service the administrative service of a government

networks Online Teaching Options

MAP

Qin and Han Empires

Comparing and Contrasting Students can use the interactive map, showing both the Qin and Han empires, to compare and contrast the two dynasties. Have students create a Venn diagram to help them show how the dynasties were alike and different. Remind students that the area where the two circles overlap is where similarities should be listed. **BL Visual/Spatial**

See page 275E for other online activities.

networks
Qin and Han Empires
XIONGNU
KOREAN PENINSULA
Yellow Sea
Changan (Han)
Xianyang (Qin)
East China Sea
South China Sea

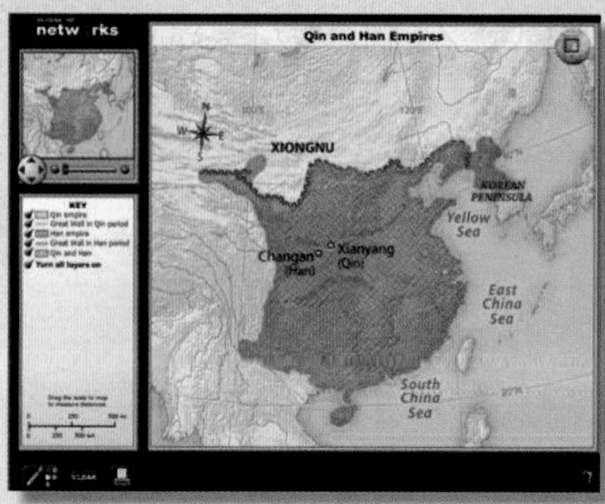

ANSWERS, p. 294

GEOGRAPHY CONNECTION

1. Huang He and Chang Jiang valleys, and much of the eastern coast and western mountains
2. **CRITICAL THINKING** Students may answer that the Han empire had a stronger army and could therefore conquer more land. Accept other reasonable answers that students can support.

Although this system of selecting government officials raised the quality of government, the system also had its faults. Supposedly, government work was open to anyone with talent and ability. Realistically, the system actually favored the rich. Only wealthy families could afford to educate their sons for the difficult civil service tests.

W

Education

The Han government created schools to prepare students for civil service. Students prepared for the exams by studying law, history, and the ideas of Confucius. After many years of schooling, the students took the civil service examinations. If they passed, they earned jobs as government workers or teachers. They also won great respect in society because they were well educated.

The Empire Expands

During the years of Han rule, China's population rose to about 60 million. To meet the needs of China's growing population, farmers needed to produce more food. However, China's farmers faced special challenges in doing so.

When farmers died, their land was divided among their sons. Gradually, over several **generations**, the amount of land farmed by a family became smaller and smaller. By the middle of the Han dynasty, the average farmer owned only about one acre of land.

Farmers could not raise enough food to feed their families on such small plots of land. They had no choice but to sell their land and work as tenant farmers. **Tenant farmers** work land owned by someone else. Eventually, wealthy landlords owned thousands of acres. The tenant farmers remained very poor.

C1

As China's population grew, the Han Empire took in new territory. Han armies conquered lands to the north, including Korea. They moved south into Southeast Asia and west as far as northern India. After Han Wudi's armies pushed back the Xiongnu—the nomads to the north—the Chinese lived in peace for almost 150 years.

Han Culture

During this era of peace, literature and the arts blossomed. Writers wrote about current events. They made copies of old historical works. In the arts, painters and sculptors reached out to new audiences.

C2

BIOGRAPHY

Ban Zhao (c. A.D. 45–A.D. 116)

Ban Zhao was the first female Chinese historian. She served as the imperial historian during the Han dynasty. Along with her historical pieces, she wrote poems and essays. One well-known work is a guide for women titled *Nu Jie* (*Lessons for Women*). It details how women should behave and encourages education for females. The Chinese followed her teachings for hundreds of years, though her emphasis on education was largely ignored.

▶ **CRITICAL THINKING**

ANALYZING Why do you think Ban Zhao emphasized education for women?

tenant farmer a farmer who works land owned by someone else and pays rent in cash or as a share of the crop

Academic Vocabulary (Tier 2 Words)

generation a group of individuals born and living at the same time

W Writing Skills

Argument Tell students that China did not have free public education during this period, which is why the civil service was mainly open to wealthier families. Have students write a letter to the emperor to persuade him to make the system fairer for everyone, including support for changes that should be made to allow equal access to education.

C1 Critical Thinking Skills

Determining Cause and Effect Direct students to create a diagram showing how the system of land inheritance eventually led to most farmers becoming very poor. Then **ask:** How could this problem have been avoided? *(Answers will vary. Possible response: Rather than divide land equally among all of their sons, farmers should have left the land undivided and instructed their sons to farm it together.)* BL

C2 Critical Thinking Skills

Speculating Remind students that the Han empire was large and secure and had strong government, all of which led to peace. Ask them to speculate about the relationship between this peaceful period and the flowering of the arts. BL

BIOGRAPHY

Ban Zhao

Making Generalizations Tell students that Ban Zhao lived from around A.D. 45 to around A.D. 116. Have them read her biography and then write one or two sentences that make generalizations about the lives of women during the Han dynasty.

See page 275E for other online activities.

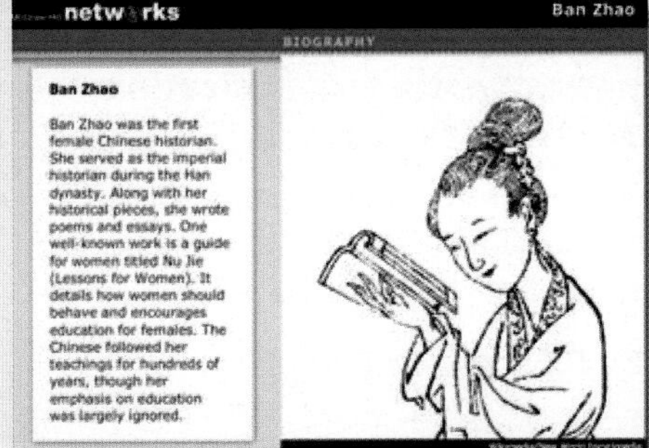

ANSWER, p. 295

CRITICAL THINKING Answers may vary. Students might say that she emphasized the need for education for women because she was a woman and probably had experienced first-hand the difficulty women had in getting an education.

C Critical Thinking Skills

Identifying Problems Tell students that several inventions during this period helped farmers open up more land for growing food. **Ask:** Why was this important? *(China's population was growing quickly, and there was a greater need for food.)*

R Reading Skills

Finding the Main Idea Direct students to read the second paragraph of the section of the textbook titled "Chinese Inventions." **Ask:** In your own words, what is the main idea of this paragraph? *(that Chinese inventors made advancements in areas other than farming)* What are two details that support the main idea? *(Answers will vary. Possible responses: The invention of the wheelbarrow helped move heavy materials on building sites; waterwheels helped grind grain more efficiently.)* AL ELL

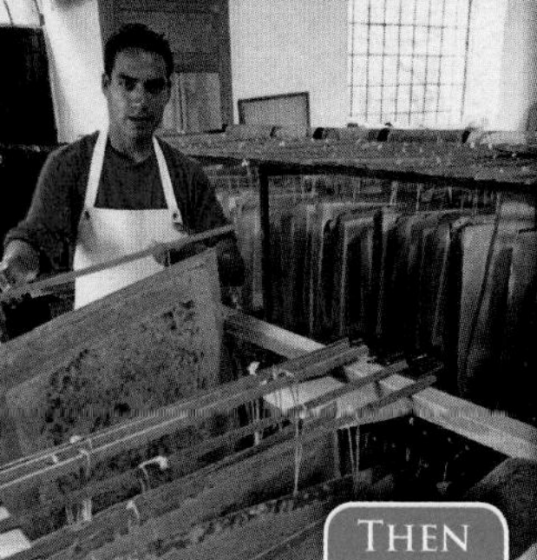

In early China, people made paper one sheet at a time from hemp or rag pulp. This modern artist (above) makes paper the ancient way. Today's paper mills (below) manufacture huge rolls of paper on machines like this one.

▶ CRITICAL THINKING
Analyzing What would be the effect on today's publishing industry if all paper were once again made by hand?

In earlier times, artists had created religious works for rulers and aristocrats. Now, under Han rule, artists created beautiful works of art for less prominent families.

Under the Han, the ideas of Confucius gained influence. The idea of filial piety became very strong. The stability of the government also helped strengthen family ties. The new class of scholarly civil servants greatly influenced government, but other social classes in China remained the same. Daily life also was very similar to what it had been before.

Chinese Inventions

During the Han dynasty, new technology helped Chinese farmers and workers produce more than ever before. One major development was the cast-iron plow, which could break up the soil more easily than wooden plows could. New iron tools and techniques were used to drain swamps and direct water to parched fields. As a result, land that was once unfit for farming now produced food and other crops. C

Improvements took place in areas besides farming. Millers invented **waterwheels** to grind more grain, and miners fashioned iron drill bits to mine more salt. Another Chinese invention, the wheelbarrow, was first used to carry heavy material on building sites. Artisans developed silk manufacturing and invented paper. Used first for wrapping, paper became an ideal writing material. Like Egyptian papyrus, paper provided a way to keep written records. R

Two remarkable achievements of Han inventors were the rudder and a new way to move the sails of ships. With these inventions, ships could sail against the wind for the first time. They could also travel farther than ever before. As a result, China's merchants shipped their goods to areas as far away as India and the Red Sea.

Medical Advances

Chinese medicine advanced under the Han. Doctors discovered that certain foods prevented disease. They used a variety of herbs to treat illnesses. Doctors also relieved pain by piercing patients' skin at vital points with thin needles. This treatment is known as **acupuncture** (A•kyuh•puhngk•chuhr). Acupuncture renews the body by increasing the flow of energy.

☑ PROGRESS CHECK

Explaining Why did Han rulers create civil service examinations?

Reading HELPDESK CCSS

Visual Vocabulary

waterwheel a wheel made to turn by the water flowing against it

networks Online Teaching Options

GAME

Chinese Invention Identification Game—the Qin and Han Dynasties

Present the interactive matching game on Chinese inventions to students. Call on students to provide the correct responses. AL Verbal/Linguistic

See page 275F for other online activities.

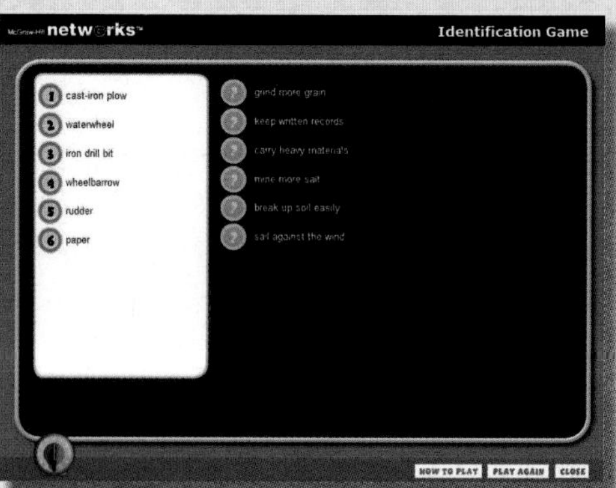

ANSWERS, p. 296

CRITICAL THINKING If all paper were still made by hand, it would be extremely scarce and expensive. The publishing industry would be able to produce very few books. Those books they did produce would be so expensive that not many people could afford them. Most publishing companies would probably go out of business.

☑ PROGRESS CHECK Han rulers created civil service examinations to stop the practice of having royal family members and other aristocrats run the government. Up to this point, government jobs were used as a reward for loyalty to the government. The civil service exam system opened government service to other people with talent and ability.

On the Silk Road

GUIDING QUESTION *How did the Silk Road benefit China and the rest of the world?*

During the Han period, Chinese traders grew rich by sending expensive goods to other parts of the world. Over time, both sea and land trade routes led to an exchange of many different goods and ideas between China and other areas.

New Contacts With the West

China's trade increased in part as a result of Chinese exploration. In 139 B.C., the emperor Han Wudi sent out a general named Zhang Qian (JAHNG CHYEHN) to explore areas west of China. Zhang's mission was to recruit allies to help China fight against its enemies, especially the Xiongnu to the north.

Thirteen years later, Zhang returned to China. He had failed to find allies. He had learned, however, about the people, geography, and culture of the areas west of China. He also visited a kingdom far to the west, probably in the area of present-day Kazakhstan. There, he saw horses of great strength and size.

Emperor Han Wudi was delighted to hear this report. He wanted horses for his soldiers, so he encouraged trade between China and western regions.

In exchange for the horses, Chinese merchants traded silk, spices, and other luxury goods. The trade route to the west was later called the Silk Road in honor of China's most famous export.

Trade Expands

The Silk Road was not just one road. It was a **network** of trade routes. When the road was completed in the A.D. 100s, it was 4,000 miles (6,436 km) long and stretched from western China to the Mediterranean. The distance, rough terrain, and bandits along the road made travel difficult and dangerous.

Over the years, merchants traded many items in addition to luxury goods. These included fruits, vegetables, flowers, and grains. For example, China sent peaches and pears to India, while India sent cotton and spinach to China. In time, Chinese inventions, such as paper, would also travel to other regions along the Silk Road.

Acupuncture is based on finding pressure spots in the human body to help ease pain. Chinese doctors detected certain places on the body that correspond to spots on the foot. Needles can be applied to these spots to help the pain.

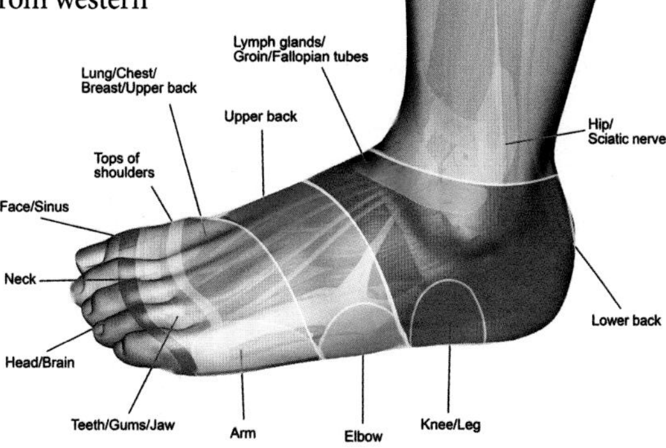

3D4Medical.com/Getty Images

acupuncture originally, a Chinese practice of inserting fine needles through the skin at specific points to treat disease or relieve pain

Academic Vocabulary (Tier 2 Words)

network a connected group or system

C Critical Thinking Skills

Contrasting Have a volunteer read the first paragraph aloud. **Ask:** **How was this development different from China's past?** *(In the past, China had been isolated, both by geography and by the emperor's will.)* After students have read the section about new contacts with the West, **ask:** **How did Han Wudi's military ambitions help China expand trade?** *(He sent out exploration missions to find allies, and he also wanted horses for his soldiers. Both of these led to expanded trade.)*

R Reading Skills

Labeling After students have read the text, discuss with them the establishment of the network of trade routes known as the Silk Road. **Ask:** **What were three hazards to traders and travelers on the Silk Road?** *(distance, rough terrain, and bandits)* **Why was it called the Silk Road?** *(Silk was one of China's main exports.)* Remind students to use text evidence to support their answers.

IMAGE

Acupuncture

Summarizing Direct students to the interactive image about acupuncture, and have them use the information there to write a short summary of how Chinese doctors of this period believed acupuncture worked. AL

See page 275E for other online activities.

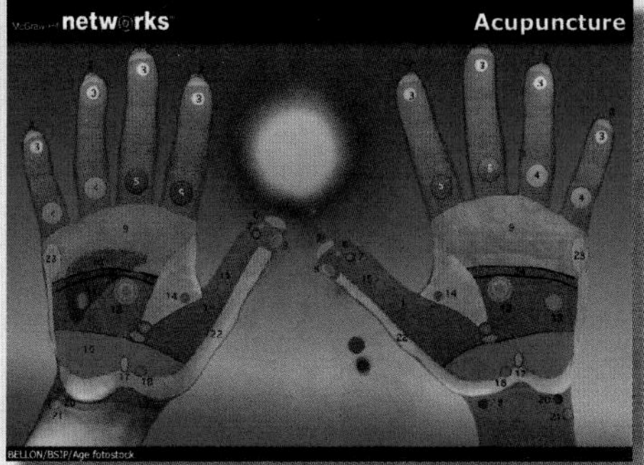

V Visual Skills

Reading Maps Have students study the map of the Silk Road and the trade routes that connected to it. **Ask:** **How far south did the connected trade routes go?** *(Java)* **What kind of goods came from that region?** *(spices)* Then **ask:** **Where did the Silk Road begin?** *(Luoyang)* **Where did it end?** *(Antioch)* AL ELL **Visual/Spatial**

C Critical Thinking Skills

Making Connections Remind students to think about how the Silk Road benefited China and the rest of the world. **Ask:** **What were two ways that China benefited from the Silk Road?** *(China was able to encounter other civilizations and gain access to a wider variety of goods.)*

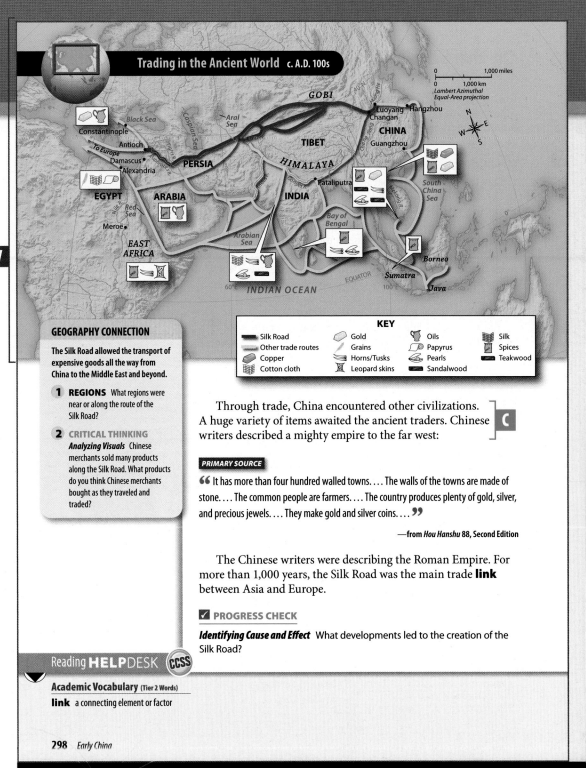

Trading in the Ancient World c. A.D. 100s

0 1,000 miles
0 1,000 km
Lambert Azimuthal Equal-Area projection

GOBI, Luoyang, Hangzhou, Changan, CHINA, Guangzhou, TIBET, HIMALAYA, Pataliputra, INDIA, Bay of Bengal, South China Sea, Aral Sea, Caspian Sea, Black Sea, Constantinople, Antioch, To Europe, Damascus, Alexandria, PERSIA, EGYPT, ARABIA, Red Sea, Meroë, EAST AFRICA, Arabian Sea, INDIAN OCEAN, EQUATOR, Sumatra, Borneo, Java, 60°E, 100°E

KEY

Silk Road	Gold	Oils	Silk
Other trade routes	Grains	Papyrus	Spices
Copper	Horns/Tusks	Pearls	Teakwood
Cotton cloth	Leopard skins	Sandalwood	

GEOGRAPHY CONNECTION

The Silk Road allowed the transport of expensive goods all the way from China to the Middle East and beyond.

1. **REGIONS** What regions were near or along the route of the Silk Road?
2. **CRITICAL THINKING** ***Analyzing Visuals*** Chinese merchants sold many products along the Silk Road. What products do you think Chinese merchants bought as they traveled and traded?

Through trade, China encountered other civilizations. A huge variety of items awaited the ancient traders. Chinese writers described a mighty empire to the far west: C

PRIMARY SOURCE

> “It has more than four hundred walled towns. . . . The walls of the towns are made of stone. . . . The common people are farmers. . . . The country produces plenty of gold, silver, and precious jewels. . . . They make gold and silver coins. . . .”
>
> —from *Hou Hanshu* 88, Second Edition

The Chinese writers were describing the Roman Empire. For more than 1,000 years, the Silk Road was the main trade **link** between Asia and Europe.

PROGRESS CHECK

Identifying Cause and Effect What developments led to the creation of the Silk Road?

Reading HELPDESK CCSS

Academic Vocabulary (Tier 2 Words)

link a connecting element or factor

networks ***Online Teaching Options***

MAP

Trading in the Ancient World c. A.D. 100s

Analyzing Visuals Show the interactive map "Trading in the Ancient World" on the whiteboard. Then **ask:**

- **What does this map show?** *(trading routes across Asia)*
- **How might you group the items that were traded? To what categories do the different items belong?** *(Students might mention that one group of trade items are spices: pepper, cardamom, cloves, cinnamon, nutmeg, and ginger. Other groups might mention metals, including gold and copper, and wood, including teakwood and sandalwood.)*

See page 275E for other online activities.

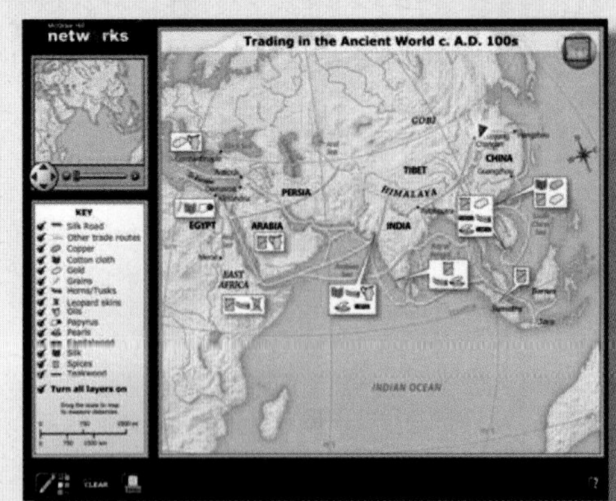

ANSWERS, p. 298

GEOGRAPHY CONNECTION

1. China, Tibet, India, Persia, Arabia, Egypt
2. **CRITICAL THINKING** Students' answers can include any product that the map indicates China did not produce, such as pearls, leopard skins, and horns and tusks.

PROGRESS CHECK Chinese exploration and Emperor Han Wudi's desire for horses for his army helped lead to the creation of the Silk Road.

Buddhism Reaches China

GUIDING QUESTION *Why did Buddhism become a popular religion in China?*

The Silk Road served as a way to spread knowledge, culture, and religions. Buddhism, in particular, spread across the Silk Road from India to China. Buddhism won few followers in China at first. The fall of the Han dynasty and the long period of unrest that followed, however, spurred the spread of Buddhism.

Why Did the Han Dynasty Collapse?

Many of the emperors who succeeded Han Wudi were weak and dishonest. Corrupt officials and greedy aristocrats took over more of the land, forcing many farmers to give up their property. People began to rise up and rebel against the Han rulers.

Rebel armies destroyed the Han capital, Luoyang (LWAW• YAHNG) in A.D. 190. By A.D. 220, civil war divided China. For the next 400 years, China remained divided into many small kingdoms.

Buddhism Wins Followers

The fall of the Han dynasty and the long years of civil war frightened many Chinese. Feeling anxious, fearful, and unsafe, many people turned to Buddhist ideas. Followers of Confucius and Daoists also admired Buddhist ideas, which influenced their own religious rituals and moral ideas. By the A.D. 400s, Buddhism had become one of China's major religions.

PROGRESS CHECK

Determining Cause and Effect Why did the fall of the Han dynasty help Buddhism spread in China?

LESSON 3 REVIEW

Review Vocabulary (Tier 3 Words)

1. What are the advantages of having a *civil service* system to select government workers? RH.6–8.4

Answer the Guiding Questions

2. ***Describing*** How did Qin rulers unite China? RH.6–8.2
3. ***Explaining*** How did the civil service system change China's government? RH.6–8.2
4. ***Determining Cause and Effect*** What was one result of the building of the Great Wall? RH.6–8.2
5. ***Explaining*** What caused the downfall of the Han dynasty? RH.6–8.2
6. ***Analyzing Visuals*** What was one fact that you put in the "Both" part of the Venn diagram comparing the Qin and Han? RH.6–8.7
7. **INFORMATIVE/EXPLANATORY** How do you think early China's history would be different if the Silk Road had never developed? Write a paragraph expressing your view. WHST.6–8.2, WHST.6–8.10

LESSON 3 REVIEW ANSWERS

1. The civil service helped ensure that government officials were qualified for their jobs.
2. Qin rulers united China by taking direct control of the provinces. The Qin created a currency that everyone in the empire had to use. They also built roads as well as a canal that joined central and southern China.
3. The civil service made it possible for bright and talented people to serve in the government. Before the civil service system, those in power appointed government employees.
4. One result of the building of the Great Wall under the Qin was that the forced labor of hundreds of thousands of farmers turned the farming class against their rulers.
5. Many of the emperors who ruled after Han Wudi were dishonest and weak, which led people to rebel against them.
6. Answers may vary. One possible answer is that they both wanted to strengthen and unify China.
7. Without the Silk Road, China might not have come into contact with other countries and civilizations when it did. Without this contact, new ideas and philosophies might not have come to the country. China might never have embraced Buddhism. Without trade, China would have had less wealth.

R Reading Skills

Summarizing Have students read the first paragraph on this page. Discuss with students how the Silk Road allowed for the movement not only of goods, but also of ideas. Ask volunteers to summarize how Buddhism reached China and why it was so widely accepted once it arrived there. Clarify any unfamiliar terms or ideas as needed. ELL

C Critical Thinking Skills

Determining Cause and Effect Be sure to point out to students that Buddhism is one of the ideas that was exchanged along the Silk Road. Then discuss with students the reasons for the fall of the Han dynasty and the rise in popularity of Buddhism in China. **Ask:** **What caused the Han dynasty to fall?** *(Many of the emperors who succeeded Han Wudi were weak. Corrupt and greedy officials stole land; people began to rebel against the Han leaders.)* **What caused the Chinese people to embrace Buddhism?** *(The years of civil war and instability resulting from the decline of the Han dynasty frightened the Chinese people. Buddhism provided comfort to people who were facing fear and anxiety.)*

Have students complete the Lesson 3 Review.

CLOSE & REFLECT

To close the lesson, remind students that the fear and chaos of the Period of the Warring States led to the rise of new philosophies in China. Now, after the fall of the Han dynasty, the Chinese people were ready to look towards Buddhism. Guide a discussion about how difficult times can lead people to look inward.

ANSWER, p. 299

PROGRESS CHECK The fall of the Han dynasty led to many years of civil war in China. The disorder made people feel unsafe. Buddhist ideas helped people overcome their anxiety and fear.

Activities Answers

CHAPTER REVIEW ACTIVITY

Have students create a graphic organizer like the one below that will help students see the effects that the Silk Road had on life in China.

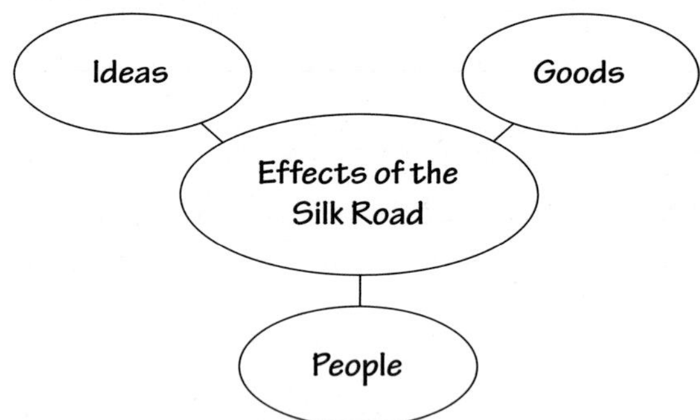

REVIEW THE ENDURING UNDERSTANDINGS

Review the chapter's Enduring Understandings with students.

- *People, places, and ideas change over time.*
- *The movement of people, goods, and ideas causes societies to change over time.*

Now pose the following questions in a class discussion to apply these Understandings to the chapter. **Ask:**

- **What were some of the changes the Chinese government went through during this period?** *(Responses may include: moving from officials who were aristocrats to those that did well on the civil service exam; going through several changes of imperial dynasty; starting out as a unified country, being broken into provinces, and then becoming unified again.)*
- **How did the Silk Road change China?** *(The Silk Road opened China up to goods and ideas from the West. It also exposed the rest of the world to Chinese products. Lastly, it brought Buddhism from India into China, where it became a major religion.)*

CHAPTER 10 Activities (CCSS)

Write your answers on a separate sheet of paper.

1 Exploring the Essential Question WHST.6–8.2, WHST.6–8.9
INFORMATIVE/EXPLANATORY How would you compare the culture of China to other ancient cultures you have read about? Write an essay explaining how the culture of ancient China is different from these other civilizations. What factors led to the development of a unique culture in China?

2 21st Century Skills RH.6–8.1, RH.6–8.2
ANALYZING NEWS MEDIA Work with a partner. Find an article from the business section of a newspaper or magazine about China and trade. What does the article tell you about trade and China today? What goods does China trade today? With whom does China trade? Present your article and your findings to the class. In your presentation, discuss how trade today between China and her trading partners is different from trade in the time of the Han dynasty.

3 Thinking Like a Historian RH.6–8.2
UNDERSTANDING RELATIONSHIPS A pyramid diagram can be used to show relationships. In a pyramid diagram, the group with the most members goes on the bottom. Create a pyramid diagram like the one on the right showing the social classes in ancient China from most powerful (top) to least powerful (bottom).

4 GEOGRAPHY ACTIVITY

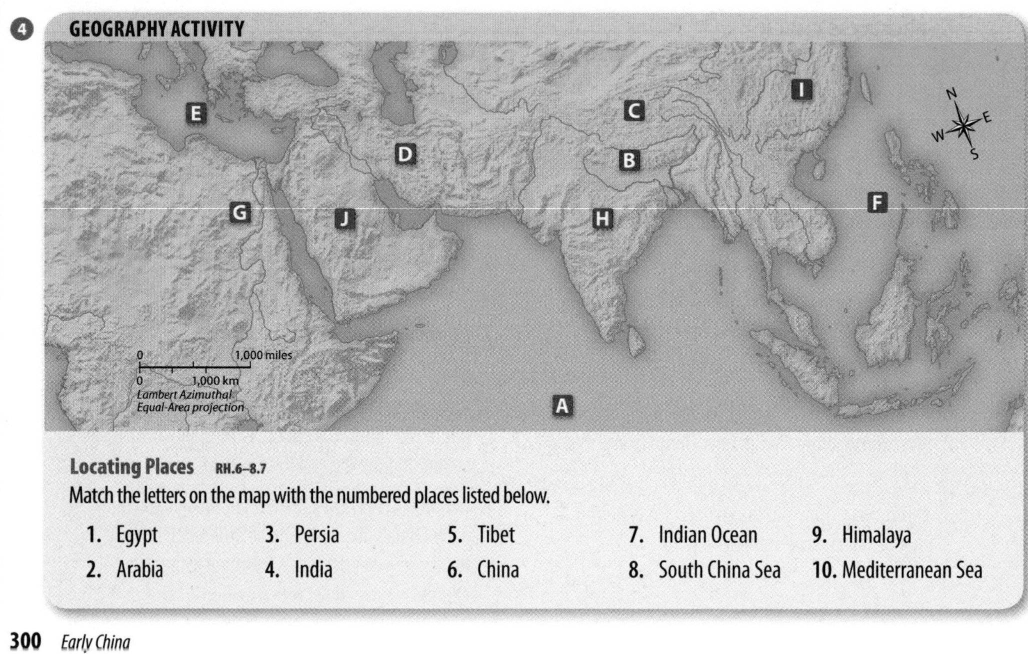

Locating Places RH.6–8.7
Match the letters on the map with the numbered places listed below.

1. Egypt	**3.** Persia	**5.** Tibet	**7.** Indian Ocean	**9.** Himalaya
2. Arabia	**4.** India	**6.** China	**8.** South China Sea	**10.** Mediterranean Sea

ACTIVITIES ANSWERS

Exploring the Essential Question

1 Answers will vary, but students should mention how the geography of China, which isolated it from other civilizations, helped China form a unique culture. Some unique features of Chinese culture include its writing system—which uses symbols to represent objects that are then combined to represent ideas—and its belief systems, including Confucianism, Daoism, and legalism.

21st Century Skills

2 Answers may vary depending on the article that students select. Answers may include that the goods that China trades and the way the goods are traded today are different. Also, China today has different trading partners from those of early China.

Thinking Like a Historian

3 Students' pyramids should show farmers at the bottom of the pyramid, artisans and merchants in the center, and the aristocracy at the top.

Locating Places

4 **1.** G, **2.** J, **3.** D, **4.** H, **5.** C, **6.** I, **7.** A, **8.** F, **9.** B, **10.** E

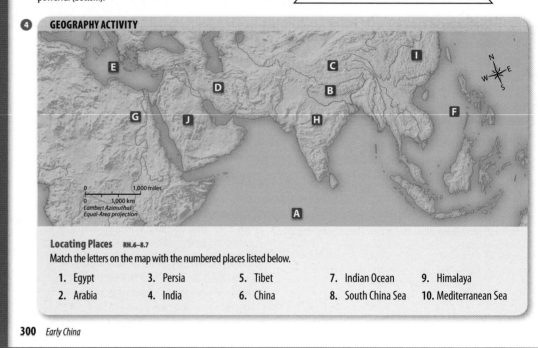

CHAPTER 10 Assessment CCSS

REVIEW THE GUIDING QUESTIONS

Directions: Choose the best answer for each question.

RH.6–8.2
1 How did mountains and deserts help Chinese civilization develop?
A. They provided fertile farmland.
B. They made transportation easier.
C. They gave China safe borders.
D. They made it difficult for the Chinese to grow crops.

RH.6–8.2
2 Shang rulers expanded their kingdom by
F. military conquest.
G. marriage with neighboring rulers.
H. land purchases.
I. forming colonies.

RH.6–8.4
3 What is the Mandate of Heaven?
A. a group of officials in China who worked for the government
B. the rule of China by a wicked tyrant
C. the belief that a son had the right to inherit his father's land
D. the belief that the Chinese king's right to rule came from the gods

RH.6–8.2
4 Confucius's belief that government service should be open to all able men led to
F. the rule of China by a strong leader.
G. wars by rival kings.
H. the creation of a system of civil service tests.
I. the rule of China by farmers and workers.

RH.6–8.2
5 Most people in ancient China were
A. aristocrats.
B. farmers.
C. soldiers.
D. merchants.

RH.6–8.2
6 Trade increased during the Han dynasty because of
F. the expansion of the Roman Empire into China.
G. lower taxes and better roads.
H. food surpluses in China.
I. Chinese exploration and improved technology.

CHAPTER 10 Assessment Answers

ASSESSMENT ANSWERS

Review the Guiding Questions

1 **C** Mountains and deserts cut off China from other civilizations. Isolated from others, the Chinese were able to develop a unique culture and a strong sense of independence. Fertile farmland was found in river valleys, not mountains and deserts. Mountains and deserts made transportation more difficult, not easier. They did not provide fertile farmland.

2 **F** Shang rulers had large armies that they used to conquer neighboring areas. G, H, and I are not correct answers because Shang rulers did not purchase land, form colonies, or make political marriages to increase their empire.

3 **D** The Mandate of Heaven is the belief that the Chinese king's right to rule came from the gods. A group of officials who work for the government is called a bureaucracy. Although Chinese aristocrats did pass on the territory that they ruled to a son or another family member, this practice is not what is known as the Mandate of Heaven.

4 **H** The civil service examination system was an attempt to open government service to all qualified men. Prior to the creation of the exam system, only hereditary aristocrats served in the government.

5 **B** About 9 out of 10 Chinese farmed for a living. The aristocracy made up only a small percentage of Chinese society. Merchants were also a very small percentage. Although many soldiers served in the Chinese armies, most of the soldiers were from the farming class.

6 **I** Inventions such as the rudder and a new way to move the sails of ships made it possible for Chinese ships to travel farther than before. Chinese ships could now reach India and the Red Sea. The combination of new technology and expanded exploration led to an increase in trade.

Analyzing Documents

7 **A** According to this quote from *The Way of the Dao,* the "use of force . . . causes resistance and loss of strength." Force does not build strength or break down resistance.

8 **H** The wise leader is effective but does not brag about results. The wise leader is effective and notices results. It is likely that the leader would be pleased. Not being overly proud, the leader might be humble.

Short Response

9 Students studying early China of 100 years ago might not have learned about the Shang dynasty.

10 Historians use oracle bones, bronze sculptures, and burial sites to learn more about the Shang. Oracle bones tell historians what concerns the Shang had and what was important to them. Bronzes can tell historians about Shang art and technology. Burial sites can tell historians about Shang religion.

Extended Response

11 Answers may vary but should include information about each of the dynasties. Students may mention that each dynasty relied on military force to expand its borders and to hold on to power. During each dynasty, the country's borders varied, but each dynasty sought to expand the country. The country was larger under the Zhou than it was under the Shang, and larger under the Han than it was under the Qin. Chinese social classes were fundamentally the same under all the dynasties, with a large class of farmers ruled by a small aristocracy headed by a king. The civil service system of the Han dynasty was an effort to bring people other than the aristocracy into government service. In fact, however, most people who passed the civil service exams were the sons of the wealthiest families.

CHAPTER 10 Assessment  

DBQ ANALYZING DOCUMENTS

RH.6–8.1

7 **Assessing** The main ideas of Daoism are explained in a book titled *Dao De Jing* (*The Way of the Dao*).

"When leading by the way of the Tao [Dao], abominate [hate] the use of force, for it causes resistance, and loss of strength. . . .

The wise leader achieves results, but does not glory in them . . . and does not boast of them.

—"A Caveat Against Violence," The *Tao Te Ching*, Stan Rosenthal, trans.

According to Daoist thought, what is the result of using force or violence?

A. It causes resistance and loss of strength.
B. It builds strength and breaks down resistance.
C. It causes resistance without an effect on strength.
D. It builds strength and resistance.

RH.6–8.1

8 **Analyzing** What do you think this statement means? "The wise leader achieves results, but does not glory in them."

F. The wise leader finishes projects but is not pleased with them.
G. The wise leader reaches goals but does not notice them.
H. The wise leader is effective but not proud.
I. The wise leader is efficient and is boastful.

SHORT RESPONSE

"A hundred years ago the Shang (SHAHNG) dynasty was . . . lost . . . existing only in historical texts. . . . But over the course of the 20th century, the Shang steadily reappeared, the myths replaced by tangible [easily seen] artifacts: massive bronzes, eloquent oracle bones, burial complexes."

—Peter Hessler, "The New Story of China's Past," *National Geographic*, (July 2003)

RH.6–8.1

9 How would your study of early China have been different if you were studying 100 years ago?

10 What might "tangible artifacts" tell us about the Shang?

EXTENDED RESPONSE

WHST.6–8.2, WHST.6–8.10

11 **Informative/Explanatory** Write a brief report that compares and contrasts the characteristics of the four ancient Chinese dynasties you have read about.

Need Extra Help?

If You've Missed Question	1	2	3	4	5	6	7	8	9	10	11
Review Lesson	1	2	2	3	3	3	2	2	1	1	1, 3

networks Online Teaching Options

Using eAssessment

Use eAssessment to access and assign the publisher-made Lesson Quizzes & Chapter Tests electronically. You can also use eAssessment to create your own quizzes and tests from hundreds of available questions. eAssessment helps you design assessments that meet the needs of different types of learners. Follow the link in the *Assess* tab of your Teacher Lesson Center.

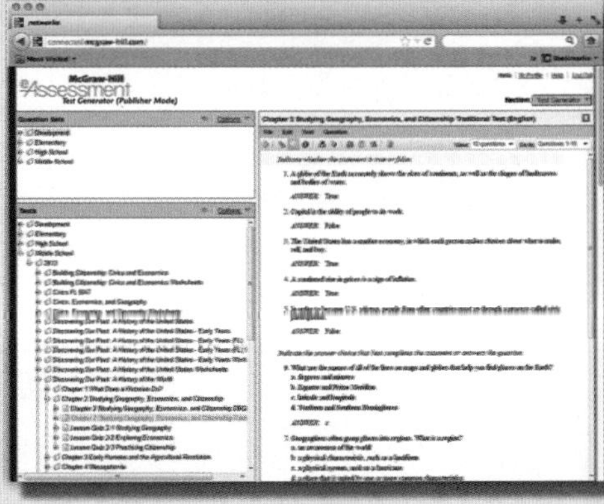

CHAPTER 11

Rome: Republic to Empire Planner

UNDERSTANDING BY DESIGN®

Enduring Understandings

- *People, places, and ideas change over time.*
- *Conflict can lead to change.*
- *Leaders can bring about change in society.*

Essential Questions

- *How does geography influence the way people live?*
- *How do governments change?*
- *Why does conflict develop?*
- *What are the characteristics of a leader?*

Predictable Misunderstandings

Students may think:

- *The Romans enslaved everyone they conquered.*
- *All Roman emperors were cruel dictators.*
- *The Roman Republic was a strong democracy that gave equal power to all citizens.*

Assessment Evidence

Performance Tasks:

- *Hands-On Chapter Project*

Other Evidence:

- *Responses to Think-Pair-Share activity*
- *Journal entries*
- *Brainstorming situations of unequal treatment*
- *Discussion responses*
- *Flowchart on Punic Wars*
- *Family Tree Activity*
- *Explanations of Julius Caesar quotation*
- *Completion of time line activity*
- *Debate on emperors during Pax Romana*
- *Writing assignments and activities*
- *Interactive Graphic Organizers*
- *Geography and History Activities*
- *21st Century Skills Activity*
- *Primary Source Activity*
- *Class discussion answers*
- *Lesson Reviews*
- *Chapter Activities and Assessment*

SUGGESTED PACING GUIDE

Introducing the Chapter	1 Day	Lesson 3	2 Days
Lesson 1	1 Day	Lesson 4	1 Day
Lesson 2	2 Days	Chapter Wrap-Up and Assessment	1 Day

TOTAL TIME 8 Days

Key for Using the Teacher Edition

SKILL-BASED ACTIVITIES

Types of skill activities found in the Teacher Edition.

V Visual Skills require students to analyze maps, graphs, charts, and photos.

R Reading Skills help students practice reading skills and master vocabulary.

W Writing Skills provide writing opportunities to help students comprehend the text.

C Critical Thinking Skills help students apply and extend what they have learned.

T Technology Skills require students to use digital tools effectively.

*Letters are followed by a number when there is more than one of the same type of skill on the page.

DIFFERENTIATED INSTRUCTION

All activities are written for the on-level student unless otherwise marked with the leveled labels below.

BL Beyond Level
AL Approaching Level
ELL English Language Learners

All students benefit from activities that utilize different learning styles. Many activities are marked as below when a particular learning style is highlighted.

Intrapersonal **Naturalist**
Logical/Mathematical **Kinesthetic**
Visual/Spatial **Auditory/Musical**
Verbal/Linguistic **Interpersonal**

NCSS Standards covered in "Rome: Republic to Empire"

Learners will understand:

1 CULTURE

2. Concepts such as beliefs, values, institutions, cohesion, diversity, accommodation, adaptation, assimilation, and dissonance

4. That the beliefs, values, and behaviors of a culture form an integrated system that helps shape the activities and ways of life that define a culture

6. That culture may change in response to changing needs, concerns, social, political, and geographic conditions

2 TIME, CONTINUITY, AND CHANGE

2. Concepts such as: chronology, causality, change, conflict, complexity, multiple perspectives, primary and secondary sources, and cause and effect

5. Key historical periods and patterns of change within and across cultures (e.g., the rise and fall of ancient civilizations, the development of technology, the rise of modern nation-states, and the establishment and breakdown of colonial systems)

7. The contributions of key persons, groups, and events from the past and their influence on the present

3 PEOPLE, PLACES, AND ENVIRONMENTS

1. The theme of people, places, and environments involves the study of the relationships between human populations in different locations and geographic phenomena such as climate, vegetation, and natural resources

5 INDIVIDUALS, GROUPS, AND INSTITUTIONS

8. That when two or more groups with differing norms and beliefs interact, accommodation or conflict may result

6 POWER, AUTHORITY, AND GOVERNANCE

2. Fundamental ideas that are the foundation of American constitutional democracy (including those of the U.S. Constitution, popular sovereignty, the rule of law, separation of powers, checks and balances, minority rights, the separation of church and state, and Federalism)

5. The ways in which governments meet the needs and wants of citizens, manage conflict, and establish order and society

7 PRODUCTION, DISTRIBUTION, AND CONSUMPTION

1. Individuals, government, and society experience scarcity because human wants and needs exceed what can be produced from available resources

3. The economic choices that people make have both present and future consequences

10 CIVIC IDEALS AND PRACTICES

1. The theme of civic ideals and practices helps us to learn about and know how to work for the betterment of society

2. Concepts and ideals such as: individual dignity, liberty, justice, equality, individual rights, responsibility, majority and minority rights, and civil dissent

3. Key practices involving the rights and responsibilities of citizenship and the exercise of citizenship (e.g., respecting the rule of law and due process, voting, serving on a jury, researching issues, making informed judgments, expressing views on issues, and collaborating with others to take civic action)

4. The common good, and the rule of law

7. Key past and present issues involving democratic ideals and practices, as well as the perspectives of various stakeholders in proposing possible solutions to these issues

CHAPTER OPENER PLANNER

Students will know:
- *the effect that geography had on the rise of Rome.*
- *how Rome gained control of the Mediterranean region.*
- *how conflict between Rome's social classes led to change in its government.*
- *the rivalry that led to the Punic Wars.*
- *what caused the decline of the Roman Republic.*
- *the events that enabled Rome to become an empire.*
- *what caused the Roman Empire to prosper.*

Students will be able to:
- ***explain** how geographic features contributed to the settlement and growth of Rome.*
- ***analyze** how the policies of the Roman conquerors led to an increase in power.*
- ***discuss** the perspective of the Roman social classes.*
- ***explain** how conflict was resolved between patricians and plebeians.*
- ***describe** the events of the Punic Wars.*
- ***identify** the causes of the Roman Republic's decline.*
- ***determine** the impact of Julius Caesar.*
- ***identify** the events and people that led to the establishment of the Roman Empire.*
- ***determine** the impact of Augustus.*
- ***describe** the empire's economy.*

UNDERSTANDING BY DESIGN®

☑ Print Teaching Options

V Visual Skills

☐ **P. 304** Students study a map of the Roman Empire and use the details to answer questions.

☐ **P. 305** Students review the chapter time line and read it to answer questions. BL

☑ Online Teaching Options

V Visual Skills

MAP **Roman Empire at its Height**—Students compare the extent of Roman territory in 500 B.C with the extent of the Roman Empire in A.D. 200.

TIME LINE **Place and Time: Rome: Republic to Empire 500 B.C. to A.D. 180**—Students learn about key Roman and world events during this time period.

WORLD ATLAS Students can use this interactive map to identify regions of the world, learn about individual countries, locate political boundaries, measure distances, and much more.

☑ Printable Digital Worksheets

R Reading Skills

GRAPHIC NOVEL ***The Eruption of Mt. Vesuvius***—This graphic novel tells the story of one citizen during the eruption of Mt. Vesuvius.

Project-Based Learning

Hands-On Chapter Project

Roman Talk Show Interview

Using a talk-show interview format, students will interview "guests" from ancient Rome who will discuss conflicts that led to changes in the Roman government.

Technology Extension

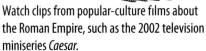

edtechteacher 21st Century Learning

Roman Talk Show Video
- Find an additional activity online that incorporates technology for this project.
- Visit the EdTechTeacher Web sites (included in the Technology Extension for this chapter) for more links, tutorials, and other resources.

Print Resources

ANCILLARY RESOURCES

These ancillaries are available for every chapter and lesson.
- **Reading Essentials and Study Guide Workbook** AL ELL
- **Chapter Tests and Lesson Quizzes Blackline Masters**

PRINTABLE DIGITAL WORKSHEETS

These printable digital worksheets are available for every chapter and lesson.
- **Hands-On Chapter Projects**
- **What Do You Know? activities**
- **Chapter Summaries (English and Spanish)**
- **Vocabulary Builder activities**
- **Guided Reading activities**

More Media Resources

SUGGESTED VIDEOS

Watch clips from popular-culture films about the Roman Empire, such as the 2002 television miniseries *Caesar.*
- **Discuss:** What can we learn about historical events from fictional movies?

(NOTE: Preview clips to ensure age-appropriateness.)

SUGGESTED READING

Grade 6 reading level:
- ***The Romans and Their Empire,*** by Trevor Cairns

Grade 7 reading level:
- ***Bodies from the Ash: Life and Death in Ancient Pompeii,*** by James M. Deem

Grade 8 reading level:
- ***Galen: My Life in Imperial Rome,*** by Marissa Moss

LESSON 1 PLANNER

THE FOUNDING OF ROME

Students will know:

- *the effect that geography had on the rise of Rome.*
- *how Rome gained control of the Mediterranean region.*

Students will be able to:

- ***explain** how geographic features contributed to the settlement and growth of Rome.*
- ***analyze** how the policies of the Roman conquerors led to an increase in power.*

UNDERSTANDING BY DESIGN®

Print Teaching Options

V Visual Skills

- ☐ **P. 310** Students analyze the image of a Roman legionary and discuss the clothing and weapons illustrated. BL Visual/Spatial

R Reading Skills

- ☐ **P. 306** Students explain how Italy's geography and geographic location allowed people and goods to easily travel to and from the region. AL
- ☐ **P. 307** Students work in pairs to discuss how geographic features influenced Rome's development.
- ☐ **P. 308** Students discuss the influence that Greek culture had on Roman civilization. AL
- ☐ **P. 309** Students define the word *devoted* and discuss the Etruscans' devotion to the arts. ELL AL
- ☐ **P. 309** Students discuss the influence the Etruscans had on the Romans.
- ☐ **P. 310** Students learn about Roman legions and calculate how the groups were divided. Logical/Mathematical

W Writing Skills

- ☐ **P. 308** Students write a newspaper article for a Roman newspaper that would have been published in 700 B.C.
- ☐ **P. 310** Students work in small groups to debate the pros and cons of a republic as a form of government. AL ELL Interpersonal Verbal/Linguistic
- ☐ **P. 311** Students write a journal entry from the perspective of a person whose community was recently conquered by Rome.

C Critical Thinking Skills

- ☐ **P. 307** Students determine which legend about Rome is more likely to have been based on facts. BL
- ☐ **P. 308** Students read a primary-source quote and summarize its meaning. BL
- ☐ **P. 310** Students create a graphic organizer to identify things that helped Rome become powerful.
- ☐ **P. 311** Students contrast giving conquered peoples citizenship with making them allies of Rome. BL

T Technology Skills

- ☐ **P. 309** Students use the Internet to research Etruscan art, architecture, clothing, and temples and create a presentation using the images they find.

Online Teaching Options

V Visual Skills

- ☐ VIDEO **Life in Ancient Rome**—Students view a video that describes daily life in ancient Rome, including the food and eating habits and a typical Roman banquet.
- ☐ MAP **Roman Empire at its Height**—Students compare the extent of Roman territory in 500 B.C with the extent of the Roman Empire in A.D. 200.
- ☐ IMAGE **Etruscan Mural**—Students learn about a section of an ancient Etruscan wall painting.

R Reading Skills

- ☐ GRAPHIC ORGANIZER **Taking Notes: *Creating a Time Line:* Events in Roman History**—Students use a time line to order events in Roman history.
- ☐ IMAGE **Roman Soldiers**—Students explore Roman soldiers, their equipment, organization, and daily life.

C Critical Thinking Skills

- ☐ WHITEBOARD ACTIVITY **Roman Soldier's Equipment**—Students identify the elements of a Roman soldier's uniform and equipment.
- ☐ SLIDE SHOW **Rome: Yesterday and Today**—Students compare and contrast ancient and modern Roman street scenes.

T Technology Skills

- ☐ SELF-CHECK QUIZ **Lesson 1**—Students receive instant feedback about their mastery of lesson content.
- ☐ GAME **Italy Crossword Puzzle**—Students complete a puzzle to show their knowledge of lesson vocabulary.

Printable Digital Worksheets

C Critical Thinking Skills

- ☐ WORKSHEET **Geography and History Activity: Understanding Location: Early Rome**—Students consider how the combination of physical features, climate, and location made Rome an ideal place for civilization to develop.

LESSON 2 PLANNER

ROME AS A REPUBLIC

Students will know:

- how conflict between Rome's social classes led to change in its government.
- the rivalry that led to the Punic Wars.

Students will be able to:

- ***discuss*** *the perspective of the Roman social classes.*
- ***explain*** *how conflict was resolved between patricians and plebeians.*
- ***describe*** *the events of the Punic Wars.*

UNDERSTANDING BY DESIGN®

☑ Print Teaching Options

V Visual Skills

- ☐ **P. 314** Students study and answer questions about a map showing the growth of the Roman Republic. **BL** **Visual/Spatial**
- ☐ **P. 317** Students examine a map of the Punic Wars and answer questions about the information presented. **AL** **Visual/Spatial**
- ☐ **P. 318** Students analyze an image of a battle scene and use clues in the picture to answer questions. **AL**

R Reading Skills

- ☐ **P. 312** Students discuss the terms *patricians* and *plebeians* and discuss the characteristics of each group. **ELL**
- ☐ **P. 313** Students define and discuss terms related to the Roman government. **ELL**
- ☐ **P. 314** Students define the word *dictator* and discuss the role of a dictator in early Roman government. **ELL**
- ☐ **P. 315** Students explore the reasons laws need to be written down and also discuss the Twelve Tables. **BL** **AL**
- ☐ **P. 317** Students discuss Rome's preparations for battle with Carthage. **BL**
- ☐ **P. 319** Students identify leaders and events of the Second Punic War. **BL**

W Writing Skills

- ☐ **P. 316** Students write a blog post to young people about legal issues relating to the rule of law. **AL**

C Critical Thinking Skills

- ☐ **P. 312** Students describe points of view of both plebeians and patricians in the Roman Republic. **BL**
- ☐ **P. 313** Students role-play plebeians and patricians in a gathering at the Forum. **BL** **Kinesthetic**
- ☐ **P. 315** Students discuss civic duty and give examples of ways people can perform their civic duty in the United States today. **Verbal/Linguistic**
- ☐ **P. 319** Students read and discuss a primary-source quotation from Polybius. **BL** **Verbal/Linguistic**

T Technology Skills

- ☐ **P. 325** Students use the Internet to research Hannibal's elephants and present their findings to the class. **Interpersonal**

☑ Online Teaching Options

V Visual Skills

- **VIDEO** **The Roman Empire: Cultural Contributions**—Students discover that the impact of Roman rule is still felt today in languages, architecture, sports, and relaxation.
- **MAP** **The Punic Wars, 264 B.C.–146 B.C.**—Students learn the events of these wars that led to the decline of Carthage and dominance of Rome.
- **MAP** **Growth of the Roman Republic, 500 B.C.–146 B.C.**—Students explore the expanding Roman territory during this time period.
- **SLIDE SHOW** **Symbols of Authority**—Students view symbols of authority, both ancient and modern.

R Reading Skills

- **GRAPHIC ORGANIZER** **Taking Notes: *Categorizing Information:* Roman Society**—Students organize facts about the roles of patricians and plebeians in Roman government.
- **PRIMARY SOURCE** **Cincinnatus**—Students analyze an excerpt from *The History of Rome* by Livy.
- **PRIMARY SOURCE** **The Twelve Tables**—Students analyze excerpts from these tablets that record Roman law.

C Critical Thinking Skills

- **WHITEBOARD ACTIVITY** **Types of Laws**—Students match the type of law to examples from the Twelve Tables.
- **CHART** **Legal Systems of Rome and the United States: Rights of the Accused**—Students compare the major features shared by the Roman and U.S. legal systems.

T Technology Skills

- **SELF-CHECK QUIZ** **Lesson 2**—Students receive instant feedback about their mastery of lesson content.
- **GAME** **Patricians and Plebeians Column Game**—Students classify characteristics of these two groups.
- **WORKSHEET** **21st Century Skills Activity: Critical Thinking: Making Connections**—Students explore how making connections between different times and places helps us understand both historical and present-day events.

LESSON 3 PLANNER

THE END OF THE REPUBLIC

Students will know:
- *what caused the decline of the Roman Republic.*
- *the events that enabled Rome to become an empire.*

Students will be able to:
- ***identify*** *the causes of the Roman Republic's decline.*
- ***determine*** *the impact of Julius Caesar.*
- ***identify*** *the events and people that led to the establishment of the Roman Empire.*

UNDERSTANDING BY DESIGN®

☑ Print Teaching Options

R Reading Skills

- ☐ **P. 322** Students identify the reforms that Marius and Sulla put in place to solve some of Rome's problems. AL
- ☐ **P. 323** Students discuss the word *triumvirate* and the prefix *tri-*. ELL
- ☐ **P. 325** Students discuss Caesar's actions once he became a dictator. AL BL
- ☐ **P. 326** Students read biographies of Mark Antony and Cleopatra and discuss the term *alliance*. ELL
- ☐ **P. 327** Students discuss and explain why the Roman Republic ended at the end of the civil wars. BL

W Writing Skills

- ☐ **P. 321** Students imagine they are one of the Gracchus brothers and write a persuasive letter to a wealthy Roman landowner.

C Critical Thinking Skills

- ☐ **P. 320** Students create a flowchart to illustrate why farmers in ancient Rome were struggling to pay back loans. BL
- ☐ **P. 321** Students discuss and analyze the ancient Roman policy of "bread and circuses." BL
- ☐ **P. 322** Students summarize the reasons the Gracchus brothers suffered for trying to help the poor.
- ☐ **P. 322** Students discuss whether or not it is dangerous for military leaders to have political power.
- ☐ **P. 323** Students learn about Julius Caesar and make inferences about what type of leader he was. BL
- ☐ **P. 324** Students read a primary-source quotation from Suetonius and discuss its meaning. AL ELL BL
- ☐ **P. 326** Students create a chart to show the sequence of events surrounding the Second Triumvirate.
- ☐ **P. 327** Students evaluate Octavian's decision to voice his support for the republic while taking steps to become emperor. BL

T Technology Skills

- ☐ **P. 325** Students work together to create a digital mockup of a newspaper reporting Caesar's death. BL **Interpersonal**

☑ Online Teaching Options

V Visual Skills

- VIDEO **Bread and Circuses**—Students view a video that examines the role of sporting events and public entertainment in ancient Rome.
- CHART **Poverty in Rome**—Students click on arrows to read about poverty in Roman society.

R Reading Skills

- GRAPHIC ORGANIZER **Taking Notes: *Sequencing:* Fall of the Roman Republic**—Students identify the events that led to the fall of the Roman Republic.
- BIOGRAPHY **Julius Caesar**—Students read about the life and accomplishments of this important Roman leader.
- SLIDE SHOW **Antony and Cleopatra**—The relationship of these two leaders is told through illustration and text.
- IMAGE **Assassination of Julius Caesar**—Students click to learn the origin of the famous Shakespearean phrase, "Et tu, Brute?"

C Critical Thinking Skills

- GAME **Roman Numerals Identification Game**—Students match Roman and Arabic numerals.
- PRIMARY SOURCE **Caesar Crossing the Rubicon**—Students examine a painting and read a description of this historic event.
- PRIMARY SOURCE **Octavian**—Students read a description of Octavian from the *Aeneid*, written by the poet Virgil.

T Technology Skills

- SELF-CHECK QUIZ **Lesson 3**—Students receive instant feedback of their mastery of lesson content.
- GAME **End of the Republic Crossword**— Students complete a puzzle to show their knowledge of lesson vocabulary.
- GAME **Roman Numerals Identification Game**—Students match Roman numerals with their Arabic counterparts.

☑ Printable Digital Worksheets

R Reading Skills

- WORKSHEET **Primary Source Activity: Julius Caesar**—Students read and respond to an excerpt from Shakespeare's *Julius Caesar.*

ROME BUILDS AN EMPIRE

Students will know:
- *what caused the Roman Empire to prosper.*

Students will be able to:
- ***determine** the impact of Augustus.*
- ***describe** the empire's economy.*

UNDERSTANDING BY DESIGN®

☑ Print Teaching Options

V Visual Skills

- ☐ **P. 329** Students analyze a picture of Rome under Augustus's rule. **Visual/Spatial**
- ☐ **P. 332** Students use a map of trade routes of the Roman Empire to answer questions. **Visual/Spatial**

R Reading Skills

- ☐ **P. 328** Students define and discuss the term *Pax Romana*. **ELL**
- ☐ **P. 331** Students read the excerpt from Tertullian and discuss his point of view.
- ☐ **P. 333** Students discuss the economy of the Roman Empire in the *Pax Romana* era. **AL**

W Writing Skills

- ☐ **P. 329** Students write a slogan that Augustus could have used to promote his accomplishments.
- ☐ **P. 331** Students write profiles of the five "good emperors" of Rome.

C Critical Thinking Skills

- ☐ **P. 329** Students discuss the changes Augustus made to local government. **BL**
- ☐ **P. 330** Students discuss the Roman emperors that ruled after Augustus. **AL**
- ☐ **P. 330** Students discuss disasters and their effect on both ancient Rome and the present-day United States. **AL**
- ☐ **P. 331** Students identify similarities between the actions of the Roman emperors with those of modern governments. **BL**

T Technology Skills

- ☐ **P. 330** Students use the Internet to research Pompeii and create a presentation with the information they find. **Visual/Spatial**
- ☐ **P. 332** Students discuss the engineering and use of aqueducts. **BL**

☑ Online Teaching Options

V Visual Skills

- **VIDEO** **The Roman World**—Students view a fast-paced montage representing Roman contributions to the world.
- **MAP** **Trade Routes of the Roman Empire, A.D. 200s**—Students identify goods produced in different areas and the routes by which those goods were traded.
- **IMAGE** **Aqueducts**—Students click to learn more about these water-transport systems.
- **SLIDE SHOW** **Buildings in Rome**—Students view the ruins of and read about important ancient Roman buildings.

R Reading Skills

- **GRAPHIC ORGANIZER** **Taking Notes: *Identifying:* Achievements of Emperor Augustus**—Students use a diagram to organize the important achievements of Emperor Augustus.
- **SLIDE SHOW** **The Five Good Emperors**—Students read biographical information about the "Good Emperors" of the *Pax Romana*.

C Critical Thinking Skills

- **SLIDE SHOW** **Pompeii and Mount Vesuvius**—Students view artifacts and read descriptions of this city destroyed by a volcanic eruption.

T Technology Skills

- **SELF-CHECK QUIZ** **Lesson 4**—Students receive instant feedback of their mastery of lesson content.

☑ Printable Digital Worksheets

C Critical Thinking Skills

- **WORKSHEET** **Geography and History Activity: Roman Roads**—Students discover how roads built by the Romans helped the spread of people and ideas that lasted into the Middle Ages.

INTERVENTION AND REMEDIATION STRATEGIES

LESSON 1 The Founding of Rome

Reading and Comprehension

To ensure comprehension of the concepts of this lesson, have students write a summary sentence for each of the lesson's subsections. Sentences should reflect the main ideas of the subsections.

Text Evidence

Ask pairs of students to work together to make a two-column chart to organize information about the influence the Greeks and Etruscans had on Roman civilization.

LESSON 2 Rome as a Republic

Reading and Comprehension

Have students skim the lesson to find new or unfamiliar words and then use dictionaries to write definitions of these words. Then have students work in pairs to quiz each other on the words they've defined.

Text Evidence

Have students make an outline of the lesson, using the larger red headings as the first level of the outline and the smaller red headings as the second level. Students can then find supporting details in the text to make third and fourth levels of the outline.

LESSON 3 The End of the Republic

Reading and Comprehension

To ensure comprehension of the sections of the lesson, have students write a new heading for each of the major sections and subsections. The new headings should reflect what the students consider the main idea of the section.

Text Evidence

Ask students to do further research on the life of Julius Caesar, including his military successes before he became dictator, his rise to power, and his murder in the Senate. Then have them suggest what they would have added to the textbook descriptions of these events.

LESSON 4 Rome Builds an Empire

Reading and Comprehension

Have students skim the lesson to make a list of new or unfamiliar words. Then ask them to use each word in the list in a sentence about life under *Pax Romana*.

Text Evidence

Organize students into small groups. Have each group create a list of reasons why *Pax Romana* should be considered one of the most impressive periods in world history. Have each group present its list and defend its arguments.

Online Resources

Approaching Level Reader

Use this online lower-level text that corresponds directly to the text in the Student Edition. It includes a Spanish version.

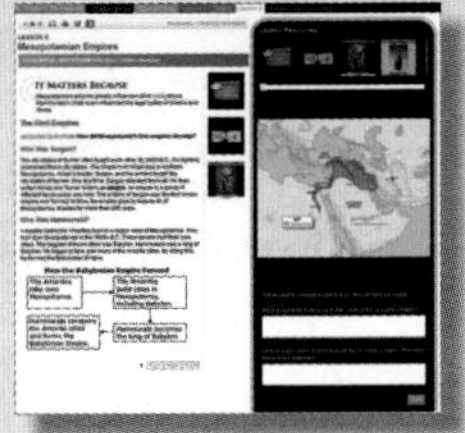

Guided Reading Activities

This resource uses graphic organizers and guiding questions to help students with comprehension.

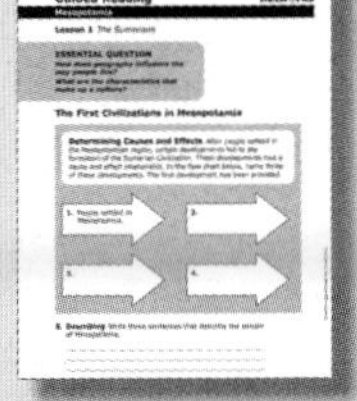

What Do You Know?

Use these worksheets to pre-assess student's background knowledge before they study the chapter.

Reading Essentials and Study Guide Workbook

This resource offers writing and reading activities for the approaching-level student. Also available in Spanish.

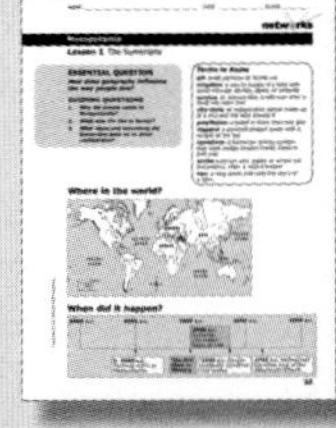

Self-Check Quizzes

This online assessment tool provides instant feedback for students to check their progress.

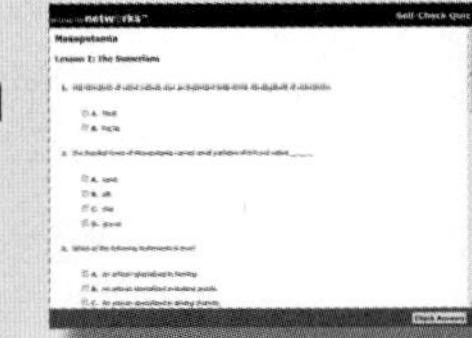

How Do I Help My Students
Review Skills Independently?

Students need to learn and implement a variety of skills in order to master social studies content. These skills include critical thinking; research and writing; reading maps, charts, and graphs; how to find resources on the Internet; how to create presentations, and so on. McGraw-Hill Education's networks™ platform enables students to choose a particular skill to practice or reinforce, at their own pace.

You can individualize your instruction by assigning a specific skill to a student who needs to learn or practice that skill. The networks™ Resource Library offers a series of Interactive Skill Lessons that guides your students independently through the process.

Step 1 Log in to the Networks Student Center Dashboard

- Tell your students to enter the ConnectEd portal and sign in to their social studies book.
- Use the username and password assigned to the student.

Step 2 Look Through the Resource Library and the Skills Builder Section

Step 3 Choose Your Skill

- Within the Resource library and the Skills Builder area are many different kinds of skills-related assets: Geography Skills, Economics Skills, Critical Thinking Skills, Research and Writing Skills, 21st Century Skills, and Building Projects and Presentation Skills.
- Select the asset that best suits your needs.

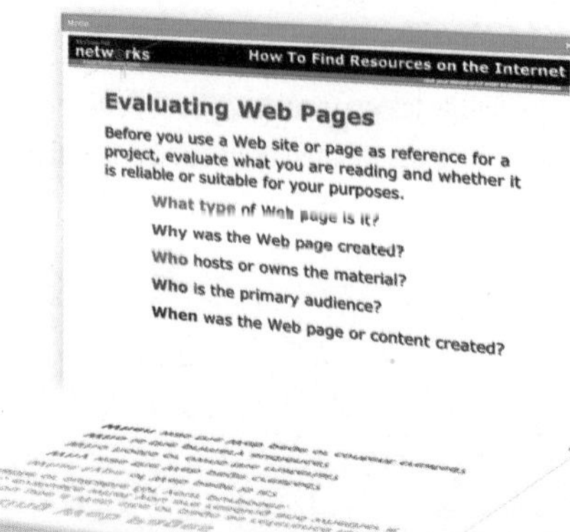

Step 4 Open the Asset and Start Learning

- Students click through the screens one at a time.
- The digital assets lead the user step-by-step through the skill being taught.

Rome: Republic to Empire

500 B.C. to A.D. 180

ESSENTIAL QUESTIONS • *How does geography influence the way people live?* • *How do governments change?* • *Why does conflict develop?* • *What are the characteristics of a leader?*

networks

There's More Online about the cultures of the Roman Republic and Roman Empire.

CHAPTER 11

Lesson 1 *The Founding of Rome*

Lesson 2 *Rome as a Republic*

Lesson 3 *The End of the Republic*

Lesson 4 *Rome Builds an Empire*

The Story Matters . . .

When the volcano Vesuvius erupted in A.D. 79, it covered the Roman city of Pompeii with a thick layer of burning ash. As many as 20,000 people were killed, and the buried city was lost for centuries. When explorers dug into its remains in the early 1700s, they discovered a time capsule of Roman times, with buildings, art, and everyday objects all perfectly preserved.

This mosaic, which is an image of a woman created out of small stones and glass, was discovered in one of the homes of Pompeii. Historians have learned much about the daily life of Romans from artifacts unearthed at Pompeii and other archaeological sites.

◄ *Goddesses were depicted in Roman mosaics, but this woman was most likely a wealthy woman of Pompeii.*

Letter from the Author

Dear World History Teacher,

In the eighth century B.C., a group of Latin-speaking people built Rome, a small community along the Tiber River in Italy. This city expanded to include almost all of the Italian Peninsula. Between 264 and 133 B.C., Rome expanded west and east and became master of the Mediterranean Sea. The Roman Republic was one of the largest empires in antiquity. Its republican institutions proved inadequate for ruling such a vast empire. After bloody civil wars, Augustus created the Roman Empire, now led by a series of autocratic rulers.

Jackson J. Spielvogel

ENGAGE

Bellringer Read "The Story Matters . . ." aloud in class. Discuss with students the importance of understanding lost civilizations. **Ask:** **Why do you think people like archaeologists were interested in unearthing Pompeii? What did they want—or expect—to learn?** Have students suggest reasons why scientists and others want to know about past times and people. Students should point out that scientists can learn about how people lived long ago from studying the remains of past cities and homes. Explain to the class that the history of Pompeii and its destruction has been pieced together since the discovery of the city's ruins. You may wish to tell interested students that they can explore the ruins of Pompeii online.

Then have students look closely at the mosaic of the woman from Pompei on this page. Explain that a mosaic is a kind of decorative art made by inlaying small pieces of colored materials into a surface to form a picture. **Ask:** **What can you learn about this woman from studying the mosaic?** *(She was probably wealthy because she's wearing a beautiful necklace and earrings and fine clothes. Her hair and makeup are also tastefully done.)* Point out that the woman shown in this mosaic would likely stand out as someone of wealth and status even in today's society. Tell students that in this chapter they will be learning about a great empire characterized by many cultural achievements.

Making Connections

Share the following information with students to show them how ancient Roman culture is still alive today:

- The remains of the Roman Colosseum is one of the great tourist attractions in modern Rome. It was built as an oval, with four stories of marble seats, and could hold about 45,000 spectators for gladiator fights and other spectacles. Despite being damaged several times by earthquakes, most of the original structure stands today.
- Latin, the language of the Roman Empire, originated as the language of Latium, a region of central Italy. Because of the reach of the Roman Empire, Latin spread throughout much of Europe. Even after the fall of the empire, Latin remained the language of diplomacy and science. Latin is still used today as the language of the Roman Catholic Church. It is also used for naming biological species—the genus and species names of organisms are usually in Latin.

TEACH & ASSESS

Step Into the Place

V1 Visual Skills

Analyzing Maps Project the Chapter Opener map on the whiteboard. Review the parts of the map with students, including the title, the compass rose, the scale, and the key. **Ask:**

- What cities were part of the Roman territory in 500 B.C.? *(Rome and Ostia)*
- What was the northernmost point of the Roman Empire at the height of the empire? *(Hadrian's Wall, in Britain)*

Point out the Italian peninsula. Discuss, in a general way, how Italy's geographic features (climate, location, natural resources, physical features, and so on) can provide advantages and disadvantages for settlement and expansion. Ask students to brainstorm advantages and disadvantages of Rome's location. Invite them to write their responses on the whiteboard. *(Advantages: mild climate; proximity to the sea provides access to trading; protected by water. Disadvantages: isolated; vulnerable to invasion by sea)* Then, as a class, discuss the Map Focus questions.

Content Background Knowledge

V2

- Rome was built on seven main hills on the east bank of the Tiber River. The central hill of the city is called the Palatine.
- The Tiber River begins in the Apennine Mountains in central Italy and runs mostly south through Rome before emptying into the Tyrrhenian Sea.
- The Mediterranean Sea is about 2,400 miles long and is about 1,000 miles wide at its greatest width. It connects with the Atlantic Ocean through the Strait of Gibraltar. Its largest islands include Sicily, Sardinia, Corsica, Crete, Cyprus, Malta, and Rhodes.

ANSWERS, p. 304

Step Into the Place

1. Rome's boundaries expanded north, east, west, and south.
2. the Mediterranean Sea
3. CRITICAL THINKING Answers may include that Romans wanted to spread their ideas and culture or that they desired power over the region.

Step Into the Time

about 480 years

CHAPTER 11 CCSS

Place and Time: Rome 500 B.C. to 180 A.D.

Rome grew from a small farming village into one of the world's greatest empires. The factors that linked the empire together—a common language, a common money, and massive public works projects—influence Western civilization even today.

Step Into the Place

MAP FOCUS In 500 B.C., Rome was just a small city on the Italian peninsula's Tiber River. By A.D. 200, the Roman Empire had conquered an area roughly the size of the continental United States.

1. **LOCATION** Using cardinal directions, compare and contrast the boundaries of Rome in 500 B.C. with the boundaries in A.D. 200. RH.6–8.7
2. **PLACE** Look at the map. What body of water might have aided the growth of Rome? RH.6–8.7
3. CRITICAL THINKING *Analyzing* Why do you think Romans desired to expand their territory? RH.6–8.1

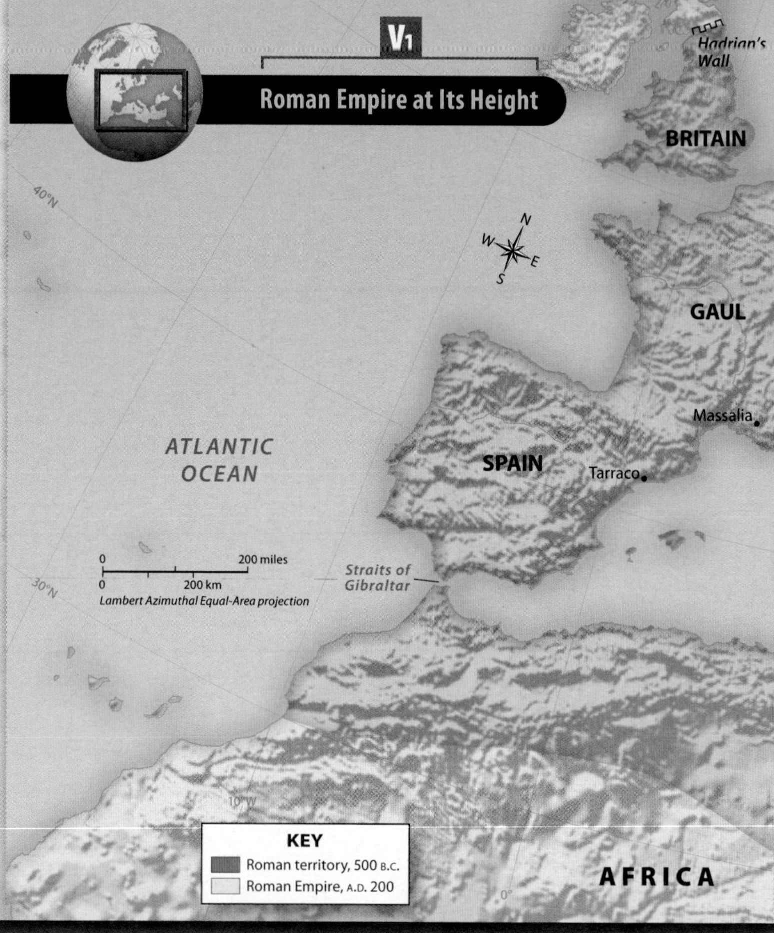

Step Into the Time

TIME LINE Rome changed greatly during the years shown on the time line. About how many years passed between the Republic being established and Rome having its first emperor? RH.6–8.7

ROME
509 B.C. Rome becomes a republic
c. 451 B.C. Romans adopt Twelve Tables

500 B.C. | 400 B.C. | 300 B.C.

THE WORLD
c. 490 B.C. Greeks at war with Persians
323 B.C. Alexander the Great dies
c. 321 B.C. Mauryan Dynasty begins in India

304 *Rome: Republic to Empire*

Project-Based Learning

Hands-On Chapter Project

Roman Talk Show Interview

Students will learn why conflicts developed in ancient Rome and how the conflicts changed the government of Rome over time. Then they will present their ideas to the class in a talk-show forum. Have students meet in groups to discuss a project plan. They will distribute and select conflicts, conduct research, and formulate questions. Then, groups will plan and gather props for a talk-show forum. Finally, students in their groups will act out the talk show, filming it with an audience.

Technology Extension

Roman Talk Show Video

Students will create professional-level videos of their Roman Talk Show from the Hands-On project, using green screen technology—a Web cam, a smartphone, or a digital camera. After following the Hands-On Chapter Project plan, students will be well prepared to video-record their talk-show forum. Once the videos are complete, students can upload the files to a video-sharing service, save their videos to a shared folder on the school network, or embed the videos in a wiki, blog, or class Web site.

networks There's More Online!

☑ **MAP** Explore the interactive version of this map on NETWORKS.

☑ **TIME LINE** Explore the interactive version of this time line on NETWORKS.

North Sea
Rhine R.
Danube R.
ASIA
Caspian Sea
ITALY
Corsica
Rome
Ostia
Adriatic Sea
Black Sea
Byzantium
Sardinia
Puteoli
GREECE
ASIA MINOR
Sicily
Athens
Carthage
Tigris R.
SYRIA
Crete
Cyprus
Sidon
Mediterranean Sea
PALESTINE
Euphrates R.
Jerusalem
Alexandria
EGYPT
ARABIA
10°E 20°E 30°E 40°E

c. 267 B.C. Rome controls most of Italy

264 B.C. Punic Wars begin

27 B.C. Octavian becomes Rome's first emperor

A.D. 66 Jews revolt against Romans

A.D. 96 Rule of Good Emperors begins

c. A.D. 180 *Pax Romana* ends

200 B.C. | 100 B.C. | A.D. 1 | A.D. 100 | A.D. 200

c. 221 B.C. Qin Dynasty begins in China

c. A.D. 100 Silk Road is established

c. A.D. 200 Kush Kingdom begins decline

305

CHAPTER 11
Place and Time

Step Into the Time

V2 Visual Skills

Analyzing Time Lines Remind students that a time line helps illustrate a sequence of events that occurred over a specific period of time. Begin by reviewing the basic elements of a time line, such as the title and the start and end dates. Point out that there are events both above and below the time line. **Ask:** How are the events above and below the time line different? *(The events above the time line focus on Rome and the Romans, while the events below the time line focus on events in other parts of the world.)*

Have students review the time line. Explain that in this chapter they will be studying events from about 500 B.C. to A.D. 180. **Ask:**

- What happened in Rome in 509 B.C.? *(Rome became a Republic.)* Ask if anyone knows what *republic* means. Tell students they will learn the definition of *republic* by reading the chapter.
- When did the Jews revolt against the Romans? *(in A.D. 66)*
- Based on the information in the time line, which event do you think represents Rome's transition from republic to empire? *(27 B.C.—Octavian becomes Rome's first emperor. The word emperor is similar to the word empire. This event likely represents the transition from republic to empire.)* BL

Then have students answer the time line question on the facing page and share their answers with the class.

Content Background Knowledge

- At the height of the empire, there were more than 1 million people living in the city of Rome.
- The Romans built 50,000 miles (80,000 kilometers) of hard-surface roads throughout the empire, most for military needs.
- The Appian Way was the most famous road of the Roman Empire. It was almost 400 miles long and ran from Rome south to the Adriatic Sea, through what is often called the heel of Italy.

TIME LINE

Place and Time: Rome: Republic to Empire 500 B.C. to A.D. 180

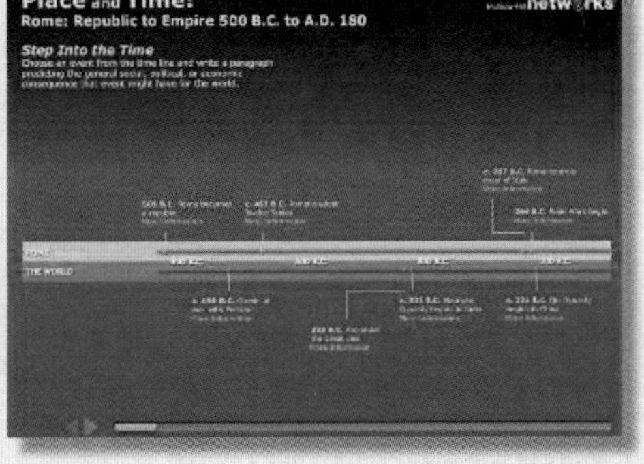

Reading a Time Line The interactive time line allows a user to scroll from the beginning of the time line on the left to the end on the right. Clicking on *More Information* for an event opens a window of details about that event. Display the time line on the whiteboard and slowly scroll from one end to the other, stopping to click on *More Information* for each event. Ask student volunteers to read the information for an event as it is revealed. For many students, this will be their first time hearing of these events. Tell students that they will learn more about Rome as they study the chapter.

See page 303B for other online activities.

CLOSE & REFLECT

Ask each student to write three questions that come to mind after examining both the map and the time line. Call on volunteers to read one of their questions to the class. Invite volunteers to try to answer each question from what they already know. Return to these questions periodically as students read the chapter. If any questions remain unanswered at the end of the chapter, interested students may wish to use the Internet to research the topic or topics.

The Founding of Rome

ENGAGE

Bellringer Before beginning the lesson, display images of the ruins of the Roman Colosseum. Without identifying the structure, have students study the image(s). **Ask:** **What would you compare this ancient structure to in the modern world?** *(Answers will vary; students might mention a football or baseball stadium.)* **What do you think happened in here?** *(Answers will vary. Students may suggest that it was probably used for sporting events or concerts.)* **What does this stadium tell you about the culture that built it?** *(Answers will vary, though students might suggest that such a large and sophisticated structure had to have been built by a rich and powerful people, in a time of peace and prosperity.)* BL After your discussion, tell students that the pictures are of the ruins of the Roman Colosseum in Rome, Italy, and that the Colosseum was one product of a great empire. Rome didn't start as a great empire, however. Tell students that in this lesson they will learn about the beginnings of Rome.

TEACH & ASSESS

R Reading Skills

Explaining After reading the text, have students explain how the location of Italy would have attracted people over time. **Ask:** **How do you think people from Africa and Asia traveled to Italy?** *(People from Asia and Africa could travel to Italy by boat on the Mediterranean Sea.)* **Did the rugged mountains in Northern Italy prevent people from other parts of Europe from getting to Italy?** *(No, because the mountains have passes in them that people and goods have little difficulty moving through to get to their destination.)* **How did Italy's land allow the region to support a large population?** *(large flat plains ideal for growing crops)* AL

ANSWER, p. 306

TAKING NOTES: Answers may vary.
c. 753 B.C. Latins establish the community of Rome;
c. 750 B.C. Greeks settle in southern Italy;
650 B.C. Etruscans take control of Rome;
509 B.C. Roman Republic is established;
267 B.C. Rome rules most of Italy.

networks
There's More Online!
- ☑ **GRAPHIC ORGANIZER** Events in Roman History
- ☑ **SLIDE SHOW** Rome: Yesterday and Todsy
- ☑ **VIDEO**

Lesson 1

The Founding of Rome

ESSENTIAL QUESTION *How does geography influence the way people live?*

IT MATTERS BECAUSE

Rome's location, especially its nearby farmlands and easy access to the Mediterranean Sea, enabled it to grow and influence the world.

The Beginning of Rome

GUIDING QUESTION ***What effect did geography have on the rise of Roman civilization?***

Greek culture did not die when Greece's power declined. Parts of it were adapted and used by the Romans. The Romans had been mostly isolated from the great civilizations of the eastern Mediterranean region. Over time, however, they learned from these civilizations and used their new knowledge to build a vast and powerful empire. Roman rule extended throughout much of present-day Europe, Africa, and Asia.

The Settling of Italy

R Italy's location has attracted people for thousands of years. Italy is centrally located in the Mediterranean region. People can easily travel to it from Africa, Asia, and Europe. In addition, people and goods moved with little difficulty through passes in Italy's rugged mountains. These mountain passes also linked settlements together.

There is another key reason why Italy has attracted settlers. Italy has a sunny, mild climate and fertile farmland. Its mountain slopes level off to large flat plains that are ideal for growing crops. With the ability to grow plenty of food, Italy could support a large population.

Reading HELPDESK CCSS

Taking Notes: *Creating a Time Line* RH.6–8.2

Use a time line like this one to order events from the founding of Rome through the Roman Republic's conquest of most of Italy.

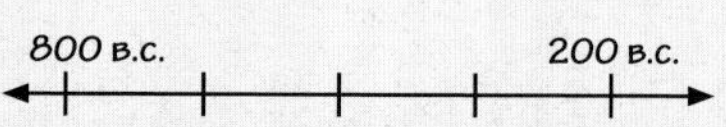

Content Vocabulary (Tier 3 Words)
- **republic**
- **legion**

networks ***Online Teaching Options***

VIDEO

Life in Ancient Rome

Making Comparisons Play the video about life in ancient Rome. Explain that we know a lot about ancient Rome both from the work of archaeologists studying ruins and artifacts of the time and from the many writings from ancient Rome that have survived until today. After the video, divide the class into small groups and have them compare life in ancient Rome and life today. What are obvious differences and similarities? Then bring the class together, and ask each group to share one or two of its conclusions. Invite comment and discussion from the rest of the class.

See page 303C for other online activities.

Rome's Location

The Romans made their home on the Italian Peninsula. This long, thin peninsula juts out from central Europe into the Mediterranean Sea. On a map, Italy looks like a high-heeled boot. The boot's heel points to Greece. The toe points to the island of Sicily (SIH•suh•lee). The Alps are like shoelaces that are strung across the top of the boot. These rugged mountains separate Italy from northern Europe. Another mountain range in Italy is the Apennines (A•puh•NYNZ). These mountains extend from north to south. Volcanoes dot southern Italy's landscape. Italy has long been affected by volcanic eruptions and earthquakes.

R

Physical features influenced Rome's development. Rome was **founded** about 15 miles (24 km) up the Tiber (TY•buhr) River from the Mediterranean Sea. People used the river to move goods easily between northern and southern Italy. Merchants could also ship their goods out to the Mediterranean Sea using the river. In addition, Rome was far enough up the Tiber River to escape raids by sea-going pirates. Rome's location across seven steep hills made it easy to defend against enemy attacks.

Roman Origins

C

Several different legends describe how Rome began. One legend about the founding of Rome is contained in *The Aeneid* (ih•NEE•ihd), written by the Roman poet Virgil. He described what took place after the Greeks captured the city of Troy. First, the Trojan Aeneas (ih•NEE•uhs) and his soldiers escaped from Troy to find a new homeland. The Trojans settled in Italy and waged war. Then Aeneas married a local king's daughter. Their marriage united the Trojans with a group of Latin-speaking people who lived in this region. Because of this, Aeneas is known as the "father" of the Romans.

Another legend describes the founding of Rome much differently. This tale **involves** twin brothers, Romulus (RAHM•yuh•luhs) and Remus (REE•muhs). After they were born, they were left beside the Tiber River. A female wolf discovered the boys and cared for them. A shepherd and his wife found and raised the twins.

According to legend, Romulus and Remus were the sons of the Roman war god, Mars. The historian Livy tells of the brothers' argument about how to build Rome's first walls. As depicted here, Romulus killed Remus in the conflict.

Academic Vocabulary (Tier 2 Words)

found to establish or create
involve to include

R Reading Skills

Drawing Conclusions Have students review the Chapter Opener map and the text related to Rome's location. Then use the following question to conduct a Think-Pair-Share activity with students. **Ask: What geographic features do you think influenced Rome's development?** *(Rome's location along a river, its central location in the Mediterranean region, its mild climate, its large flat plains and fertile farmlands, its good passes through rugged mountains, and its proximity to Greeks and Etruscans)* Have students break into pairs to discuss the question for a few moments. Then ask each pair to share their conclusions with the class.

C Critical Thinking Skills

Evaluating Discuss the two legends of Rome's founding. **Ask: Which legend of Rome's origins is more likely to be based on fact? Why?** *(Answers may vary, but students might identify the legend told in* The Aeneid *as more likely to have a factual basis because it is more realistic and based on actual history. The Remus and Romulus story is less likely to be factual because the idea of two boys being raised by wolves seems unlikely.)* BL

Content Background Knowledge

Aeneas was a mythic figure long before he became the hero of the Latin classic *The Aeneid*. According to legend, Aeneas was the son of the Greek goddess Aphrodite. The mythical Aeneas survived the Trojan War and then made it to the Italian peninsula. Various families of the Latium area claimed a connection to this legendary Trojan hero. Virgil (70–30 B.C.) gave the many strands of the Aeneas legend a narrative form in the epic poem *The Aeneid*.

SLIDE SHOW

Rome: Yesterday and Today

Comparing and Contrasting The interactive image of Rome provides images and information about the city of Rome in two eras—today and in ancient times. Use these images to help introduce students to the story of ancient Rome. Have students click back and forth between the two images, and call on volunteers to read the descriptions. **Ask: What is similar about the ancient city and the modern city?** *(Both contain large buildings, both are bustling with people, both have merchants selling items.)* **What is different about the city then and now?** *(The city then was without modern inventions, and the people depended on horses and wagons to get around. The city today has both historic and modern buildings and hosts tourists from all over the world.)*

See page 303C for other online activities.

The Founding of Rome

C Critical Thinking Skills

Analyzing Primary Sources Ask a volunteer to read aloud Livy's description of the death of Remus. **Ask:** **How does Livy describe Romulus's attitude in this passage?** *(Livy writes that Romulus was "enraged," which means he was very angry.)* **Does this passage tell us how the story ends?** *(Yes; it tells us that Romulus killed his brother and became the only ruler of Rome.)* BL

W Writing Skills

Informative/Explanatory Ask each student to take the role of a local reporter in Italy in 700 B.C. and write a short article about the Latins and the birth of Rome. Tell students to write as though the story would appear in a local paper of the time. After they have finished, invite volunteers to read their articles to the class.

R Reading Skills

Discussing After students read the passage, discuss the influence that Greek culture had on Roman civilization. Review what students have previously learned about the Greeks and their ideas and culture. **Ask:** **When did Greek settlers come to Italy?** *(from about 750 to 500 B.C.)* **In what kinds of communities did the Greeks settle?** *(Greeks settled in farming communities.)* **How did the Greeks influence the Romans?** *(Greek settlers introduced grape farming and olive farming and also passed on the Greek alphabet. The Romans would also be influenced by Greek architecture, sculpture, and literature.)* AL

Thinking Like a HISTORIAN

Analyzing Primary and Secondary Sources

The Roman historian Livy wrote about the history of Rome. What were his sources? What other sources about these events do we have that are as reliable as Livy's? For example, is a fresco an historical source? If so, is it a primary or secondary source? Which type of source is more trustworthy? Write a brief explanation of how you would compare sources if sources were reliable, such as Livy's writing and images painted on a wall. For more information about analyzing primary and secondary sources, read the chapter *What Does a Historian Do?*

When the brothers grew up, they planned to build a city along the Tiber River. However, the two boys argued about the construction of the city. Remus made fun of the walls that Romulus built. The Roman historian Livy (LIH•vee) tells what happened next:

C

PRIMARY SOURCE

"Then followed an angry altercation [argument]; heated passions [emotions] led to bloodshed; in the tumult [uproar] Remus was killed. The more common report is that Remus contemptuously [spitefully] jumped over the newly raised walls and was forthwith killed by the enraged Romulus, . . . Romulus thus became sole ruler, and the city [Rome] was called after him, its founder."

—from *History of Rome*, by Livy

Historically, little is known about the first people to settle in Italy. Archaeological artifacts (AHR•tih•fakts) suggest that Neolithic people might have settled in Italy as early as 5000 B.C. These early groups built farming villages but moved after they had used up the nutrients in the soil. Between 2000 B.C. and 1000 B.C., other groups of people settled permanently in the hills and on the plains. Latin-speaking people, called Latins, settled on the plain of Latium (LAY•shee•uhm) in central Italy.

W

One group of Latins built straw-roofed huts on Rome's hills. They tended animals and grew crops. This settlement, which **occurred** (uh•KUHRD) between 800 B.C. and 700 B.C., marks the birth of Rome. The people living there became known as Romans.

Influences of Greeks and Etruscans

After 800 B.C., other groups moved into the region where the Romans lived. Two of these groups, the Greeks and the Etruscans (ih•TRUHS•kuhnz), would greatly influence Roman civilization.

R

From about 750 B.C. to 500 B.C., Greeks settled in farming villages in southern Italy. The Greeks introduced grape and olive farming to the region. The Greeks also passed on the Greek alphabet to the Romans. Later, the Romans would model their buildings, sculpture, and literature after those of the Greeks.

The Etruscans had an even greater influence on Roman civilization. The Etruscans settled north of Rome in Etruria (ih•TROOR•ee•uh). After 650 B.C., they moved south. The Etruscans **eventually** (ee•VEN•choo•uh•lee) took control of Rome and its surrounding area.

Reading HELPDESK CCSS

Academic Vocabulary (Tier 2 Words)

occur to happen
eventual final or ultimate

networks Online Teaching Options

WORKSHEET

Geography and History Activity: Understanding Location: Early Rome

Making Connections Have students complete the Geography and History Activity for Lesson 1. After students have filled in the graphic organizer at the end of the worksheet, ask them to share their responses with the class. Write their responses on the board in a cause-and-effect format similar to the worksheet. Be sure to point out any geographic features of the area that students did not note.

See page 303C for other online activities.

NAME ______ DATE ______ CLASS ______

Geography and History Activity networks

Rome: Republic to Empire

Lesson 1 *The Founding of Rome*

Understanding Location: Early Rome

The combination of physical features, climate, and location made Rome an ideal place for civilization to develop. Roman civilization first began along the Tiber River, in central Italy, about 15 miles (24 km) upriver from the Mediterranean Sea. The sunny, warm climate and good farmland made this area an attractive place to settle. In addition, Rome's central location provided better protection than coastal settlements but still made it easy to travel to and from other places. As a result, people were readily able to exchange goods and ideas.

As you read in your textbook, the first Romans were probably Latins who grew crops and tended animals in the hills around Rome. Several other civilizations surrounded this early community. To the south, the Greeks lived in farming villages where they grew olives and grapes. To the north, the Etruscans lived in Etruria. Eventually, the Etruscans moved south and took control of Rome. The Greeks and Etruscans both had a great deal of influence over Roman civilization. Other people, the Carthaginians, lived just across the Mediterranean Sea in northern Africa. Carthage eventually became one of Rome's biggest rivals. Because of the nearness of these civilizations to Rome, they greatly affected Rome's development and history.

Etruscan wall paintings were frescoes, meaning they were painted on wet plaster. Many Etruscan frescoes show people enjoying music or dance.

▶ **CRITICAL THINKING:**
Analyzing What does the image suggest about how the Etruscans lived?

The Etruscans were ruled by nobles, who grew wealthy from trade and mining. Other Etruscans **devoted** themselves to the study of the arts. Skilled Etruscan artisans worked with copper, iron, lead, and tin. They turned these metals into weapons, tools, and jewelry. Etruscan artists covered the walls of tombs with colorful paintings. They painted men and women feasting, dancing, and playing music. Some wall paintings also displayed violent battle scenes. These images showed that the Etruscans were proud of their powerful army. R1 T

The Etruscans taught the Romans to build with brick and to roof their homes with tiles. They drained the water from marshes that lay between Rome's hills. They laid out city streets. The Etruscans built temples, passing on their religious rituals to the Romans. They even influenced the style of clothing that the Romans wore. Roman men adopted the Etruscan fashion of wearing short cloaks and togas. Finally, the Etruscan army served as the model for the mighty army that the Romans would later create. R2

✓ PROGRESS CHECK

Explaining How did the Etruscans influence early Rome?

Academic Vocabulary (Tier 2 Words)

devote to give one's time, effort, or attention earnestly

The Founding of Rome

R1 Reading Skills

Explaining Direct students to the passage in the text. Then ask students to explain how Etruscans devoted themselves to the arts. **Ask:** What does devoted mean? *(to be loyal and dedicated to someone or something)* ELL What types of materials did Etruscan artisans use for their works? *(copper, iron, lead, and tin)* What did they do with these metals? *(They made jewelry, weapons, and tools.)* AL

T Technology Skills

Researching on the Internet Ask interested students to use an Internet search engine to search for images related to the Etruscans. Students might begin by simply using "Etruscans" as the search term, but they might also narrow the search to various topics, including Etruscan art, Etruscan architecture, Etruscan clothing, or Etruscan temples. Ask the students to choose a variety of images that they consider representative of the Etruscans. If possible, have students use a projector to share their selections with the class. As an alternative, students could print selected images and create a display for others to see.

R2 Reading Skills

Identifying After students have read the text, ask them to discuss the influence the Etruscans had on the Romans. **Ask:** What did the Romans learn from the Etruscans? *(Etruscans taught Romans how to build with brick and tiles, how to drain marshes, and how to lay out city streets. Etruscans also influenced the Romans' religious rituals, styles of clothing, and army.)* Remind students to support their answers with information from the text.

IMAGE

Etruscan Mural

Drawing Conclusions Show students the image of the Etruscan mural. Then discuss with the class the different ways cultures can influence one another—as a result of living in close proximity and exchanging ideas or as a result of the power one culture holds over another. **Ask:** Why did the Etruscans have a greater influence over Roman civilization than the Greeks? *(The Greeks' influence resulted mainly from living near the Romans in southern Italy, whereas the Etruscans took control of Rome and its surrounding area.)*

See page 303C for other online activities.

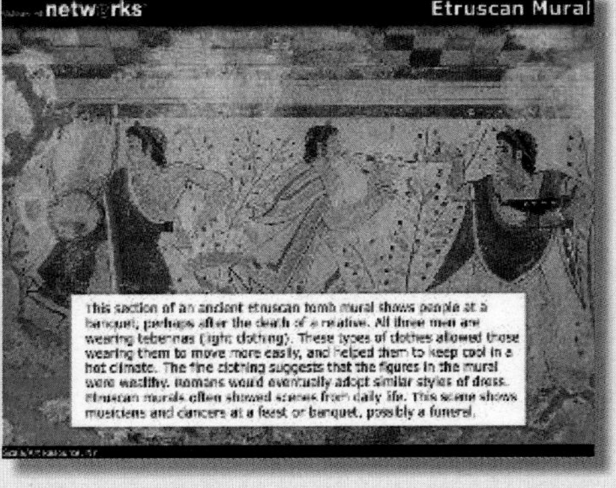

ANSWERS, p. 309

CRITICAL THINKING The Etruscans enjoyed the arts, especially music and dance. They had leisure time for appreciating the arts.

✓ PROGRESS CHECK The Etruscans influenced Roman architecture, religious rituals, clothing styles, and the Roman military.

The Founding of Rome

V Visual Skills

Analyzing Images Have students examine the image of the Roman legionary. Call on volunteers to read aloud each of the descriptions. **Ask:** **What protection did a Roman legionary have when going into battle?** *(body armor, a shield, and a weapon)* **Why would these items give a Roman soldier the advantage in many fights at that time?** *(Answers will vary, but students should mention that most other armies at the time probably wouldn't have armor or such well-made weapons.)* BL **Visual/Spatial**

W Writing Skills

Argument **Ask:** **What is a republic?** *(a form of government in which citizens elect their leaders)* AL ELL Divide the class into small groups, and assign to each group one of two positions—a republic is the best form of government or a republic is a poor form of government. Ask that each group write a series of talking points to support its assigned position. Remind students to put aside their personal feelings and opinions and work to find evidence to support their side of the debate. When students have finished, lead a class debate on the question of whether a republic is the best form of government. **Interpersonal** **Verbal/Linguistic**

C Critical Thinking Skills

Organizing Discuss as a class what type of graphic organizer would be best to identify the general categories of things that helped Rome become powerful. For instance, categories could include "geographic advantages," "military strength," and "leadership." Then have students work in pairs to create a graphic organizer to organize information about Rome's becoming more powerful.

R Reading Skills

Calculating Point out to students that Roman legions usually had 6,000 men. In turn, each legion was divided into groups of 60 to 120 soldiers. **Ask:** **Into how many 60-soldier groups could a Roman legion be divided?** *(100)* **Into how many 120-soldier groups could one legion be divided?** *(50)* **Logical/Mathematical**

ANSWER, p. 310

INFOGRAPHIC

CRITICAL THINKING A professional army would be well trained, disciplined, and focused only on defending Rome, whereas a volunteer army would be trained only when volunteers could take time away from their work.

ROMAN LEGIONARY

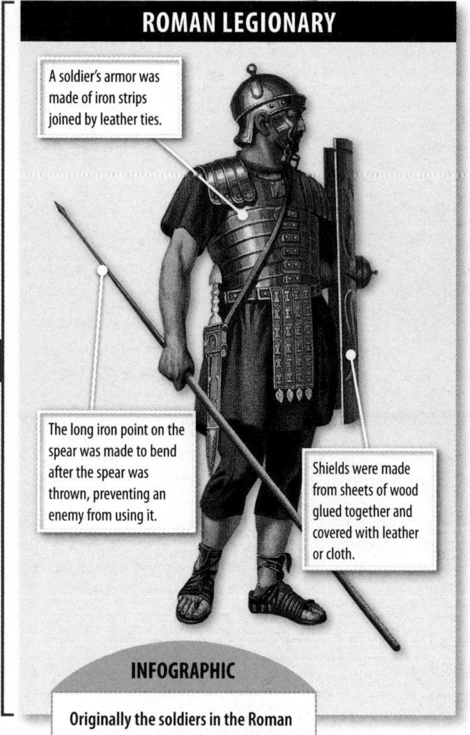

A soldier's armor was made of iron strips joined by leather ties.
The long iron point on the spear was made to bend after the spear was thrown, preventing an enemy from using it.
Shields were made from sheets of wood glued together and covered with leather or cloth.

INFOGRAPHIC

Originally the soldiers in the Roman army were untrained citizens. Through harsh training, the Roman army became known as one of the world's best.

▶ **CRITICAL THINKING**
Analyzing Why was it an advantage to Rome to have a professional army?

Becoming a Republic

GUIDING QUESTION ***How did Rome become a great power?***

The Romans greatly **benefited** from the contributions of the Etruscans. However, they grew weary of Etruscan rulers. According to Roman tradition, in 509 B.C., the Romans overthrew Tarquin the Proud, the Etruscan king, and established a **republic** (rih•PUH•blihk). A republic is a form of government in which citizens elect their leaders. The creation of a republic began a new era in Rome's history. When Rome became a republic, it was still a small city. It was also still surrounded by different groups of people. These groups included Etruscans, Greeks, and other Latins. Over the next 200 years, the Romans fought many wars against these neighbors. By 267 B.C., Rome controlled almost all of Italy. The Roman Republic was able to **acquire** land because of its strong army. During the early years of the republic, every male citizen who owned land had to serve in the army. Roman soldiers were well trained, and deserters were punished by death. This strict discipline ensured soldiers stayed loyal to Rome.

The Romans also developed new battle strategies. In the early days of the republic, the Romans fought like the Greeks. Rows of soldiers moved in a single large group. They attacked from only one direction. Roman generals realized that this way of fighting was slow and hard to control. They reorganized their soldiers into smaller groups, called **legions** (LEE•juhnz). Each legion had about 6,000 men. A legion was further divided into groups of 60 to 120 soldiers. These smaller groups could move quickly around the battlefield to wherever they were most needed.

Roman soldiers were also well armed. Most soldiers carried a short, double-edged iron sword called a *gladius* (GLAY•dee•uhs) and an iron spear called a *pilum* (PY•luhm). Each of the small groups in a legion carried its own standard into battle. The standard was a tall pole topped with a symbol, such as an eagle.

Reading HELPDESK CCSS

republic a form of government in which citizens elect their leaders
legions large groups of Roman soldiers

Academic Vocabulary (Tier 2 Words)
benefit to receive help; to gain
acquire to get as one's own

networks ***Online Teaching Options***

WHITEBOARD ACTIVITY

Roman Soldier's Equipment

Identifying Display the image of the Roman soldier in the Interactive Whiteboard Activity. Have students identify the components of the soldier's uniform and arms and then drag and drop the terms to the correct spot on the image. AL ELL **Ask:**

- **How did legionnaires identify different groups on the battlefield?** *(by looking at the standards, or battle flags)*
- **Why would this have been important?** *(to find each other on the battlefield)* AL ELL

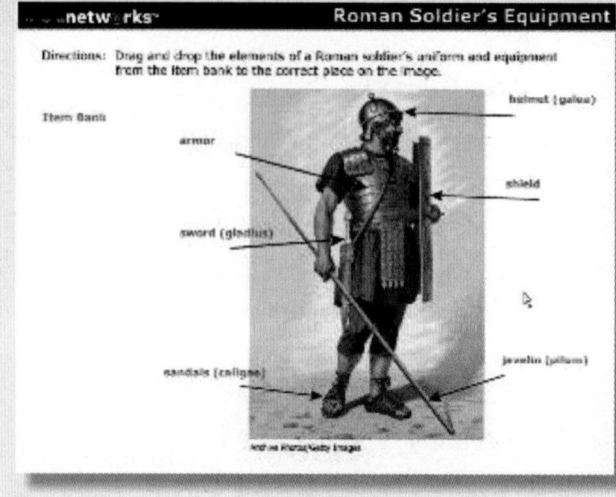

See page 303C for other online activities.

Because the standard could be seen above the action, it showed soldiers where they were supposed to be on the battlefield.

Who Ruled Rome?

In addition to having a strong army, the Romans ruled effectively. After they conquered a region, they built permanent military outposts to protect it. These settlements were built at strategic locations, such as on a high hill or at a river crossing. They also built roads between settlements. As a result, troops and supplies could move quickly within the conquered lands.

W

The Romans stressed the need to treat conquered people fairly. If conquered people were treated well, the Romans believed, the people would become loyal subjects. To encourage fair treatment, the Romans created the Roman Confederation. This system gave some conquered peoples, especially other Latins, full Roman citizenship. They could vote and serve in the government of Rome. They were treated the same as other citizens under the law.

The Roman soldiers, called legionaries, were disciplined and well trained. In groups called legions, they developed new battle strategies.

Other conquered peoples became allies, or friends, of Rome. As allies, they paid Roman taxes. In addition, they were required to supply soldiers to fight for Rome. Allies, however, were free to manage their own local affairs. C

With these policies, the Romans hoped to maintain the peace in their conquered lands. If conquered peoples turned against Rome, its rulers were ready to crush any revolts. Rome's generosity paid off. The republic grew stronger and more unified.

SuperStock/SuperStock

PROGRESS CHECK

Analyzing Why were the Romans able to expand their control of Italy?

LESSON 1 REVIEW (CCSS)

Review Vocabulary (Tier 3 Words)

1. How was the growth of the *republic* aided by the Roman army's use of *legions* in warfare? RH.6–8.2, RH.6–8.4

Answer the Guiding Questions

2. ***Explaining*** How did Rome's location affect its development? RH.6–8.2
3. ***Summarizing*** How did the Roman government maintain control over conquered territories? RH.6–8.2
4. ***Differentiating*** How did the attitude of Romans toward the Etruscans change over time? RH.6–8.2
5. **ARGUMENT** You are a Roman living about 650 B.C. The Etruscans have taken over, and your friends are worried about the new rulers. Write a persuasive speech in which you encourage them to adopt Etruscan ways. Tell what Romans may learn from the Etruscans and why they should not turn against the new rulers. WHST.6–8.1, WHST.6–8.10

LESSON 1 REVIEW ANSWERS

1. The use of legions helped the Roman army fight battles more effectively, which allowed the Romans to conquer more areas and expand the Roman republic, a form of government in which citizens elect their leaders.
2. Rome's location along the Tiber River allowed for movement of goods in and out of the area. Its distance from the Mediterranean Sea provided protection from seagoing pirates, and the steep hills across which Rome extended provided protection from other enemies.
3. The Roman government controlled conquered territories by governing fairly and allowing conquered peoples to become full citizens or allies of the republic. They also crushed any revolts.
4. Etruscans had a lot of influence over Roman life, and over time, Romans tired of being ruled by the Etruscans.
5. Answers will vary. Speeches should mention that the Etruscans are educated, cultured, and wealthy. They know and can teach the Romans many skills, such as how to build better houses and cities and how to farm more effectively. They can teach the Romans about the arts and how to make better weapons. The Romans can learn skills from the Etruscans.

W Writing Skills

Narrative Have students write a journal entry from the perspective of a person whose community was recently conquered by Rome. Have students explain whether this is a positive or negative and why they think this way. Ask volunteers to read aloud from their journal entries. Use these as a starting point to discuss the concept of being "conquered" and why it can be tolerable in some situations.

C Critical Thinking Skills

Evaluating Discuss with students the differences between giving conquered peoples citizenship and making them allies of Rome. **Ask:** **What were the advantages and disadvantages of being a citizen of Rome compared to being an ally?** *(Answers will vary. Students might say that citizenship was preferable, because as citizens they were given the rights and responsibilities of other Roman citizens. Others might argue that it was better for groups to be allies and to continue to govern their own affairs.)* BL

Have students complete the Lesson 1 Review.

CLOSE & REFLECT

To close the lesson, have students think about how the Romans began as a small group of Latin-speaking people and then grew to become rulers of the area. Ask students to give reasons for how and why this transformation occurred.

ANSWER, p. 311

PROGRESS CHECK The Romans were disciplined and fair. They built a strong army, used effective military strategies, and ruled the people they conquered fairly. As a result, they were able to expand control of Italy.

ENGAGE

Bellringer Ask students to brainstorm examples from history of situations in which people have not been treated equally, such as slavery, women not being allowed to vote, or segregated schools. Write their responses on the board and discuss with students why they think inequality exists. **Ask:** What methods have groups in the United States used to try to gain equal treatment under the law? *(Examples include organizing marches and rallies, taking cases to court, strikes and boycotts, and pressuring lawmakers.)* In countries where the leaders did not have the opportunity of reacting fairly to protests, what methods might people use to address unequal treatment? *(Students might suggest that in other countries, people might resort to violence to gain their rights.)* Tell students that in this lesson, they will be learning about the rights of people living in the Roman Republic.

TEACH & ASSESS

R Reading Skills

Defining After students have read the text, discuss the difference between patricians and plebeians in the Roman Republic. **Ask:** What kinds of people were considered to be plebeians? *(artisans, shopkeepers, small farmers, and the very poor)* What kinds of people were considered to be patricians? *(wealthy landowners, members of Rome's oldest and most prominent families)* Explain that the terms are sometimes still used today. Who in this society might be called a patrician? *(Answers will vary, though students should mention people who are prominent or wealthy, or both.)* ELL

C Critical Thinking Skills

Identifying Points of View Ask students to describe the positions of plebeians and patricians in the Roman Republic. Then have students consider the points of view of both sides. **Ask:** What did the plebeians want? *(to participate in the government equally with patricians)* Did the patricians want the plebeians to have the same rights as they did? Why or why not? *(Possible answer: No, because the patricians wanted to hold onto their power in the government; if plebeians had equal rights, they might take control of the republic.)* BL

ANSWER, p. 312

TAKING NOTES: Patricians: ruling class, landowners, prominent families, men were citizens; Role in Roman Government: men were citizens, paid taxes, served in the army, could hold public office and lead public ceremonies. **Plebeians:** majority of Romans, poor artisans, shopkeepers, farmers, illegal to marry patricians; Role in Roman Government: men were citizens, paid taxes, served in the army, Council of the Plebs represented plebeians in government.

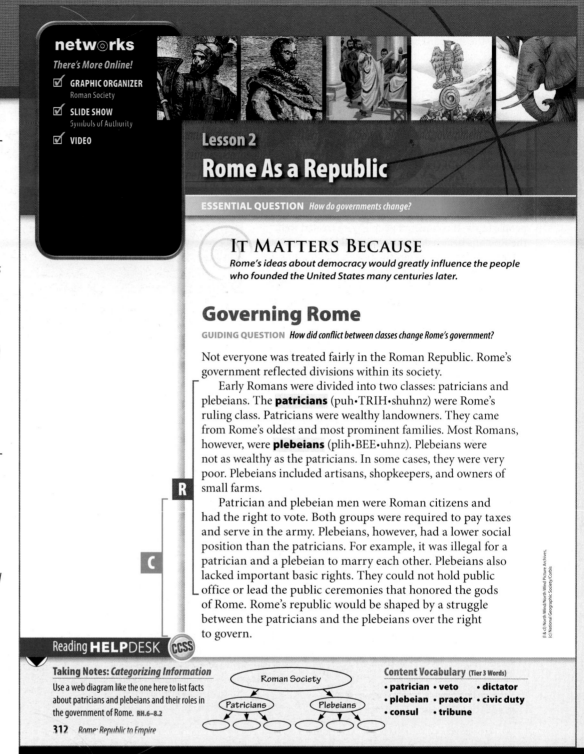

networks *There's More Online!*
- GRAPHIC ORGANIZER Roman Society
- SLIDE SHOW Symbols of Authority
- VIDEO

Lesson 2
Rome As a Republic

ESSENTIAL QUESTION *How do governments change?*

IT MATTERS BECAUSE
Rome's ideas about democracy would greatly influence the people who founded the United States many centuries later.

Governing Rome

GUIDING QUESTION *How did conflict between classes change Rome's government?*

Not everyone was treated fairly in the Roman Republic. Rome's government reflected divisions within its society.

R Early Romans were divided into two classes: patricians and plebeians. The **patricians** (puh•TRIH•shuhnz) were Rome's ruling class. Patricians were wealthy landowners. They came from Rome's oldest and most prominent families. Most Romans, however, were **plebeians** (plih•BEE•uhnz). Plebeians were not as wealthy as the patricians. In some cases, they were very poor. Plebeians included artisans, shopkeepers, and owners of small farms.

C Patrician and plebeian men were Roman citizens and had the right to vote. Both groups were required to pay taxes and serve in the army. Plebeians, however, had a lower social position than the patricians. For example, it was illegal for a patrician and a plebeian to marry each other. Plebeians also lacked important basic rights. They could not hold public office or lead the public ceremonies that honored the gods of Rome. Rome's republic would be shaped by a struggle between the patricians and the plebeians over the right to govern.

Reading **HELP**DESK CCSS

Taking Notes: *Categorizing Information*
Use a web diagram like the one here to list facts about patricians and plebeians and their roles in the government of Rome. RH.6–8.2

Roman Society → Patricians, Plebeians

Content Vocabulary (Tier 3 Words)
- patrician
- plebeian
- consul
- veto
- praetor
- tribune
- dictator
- civic duty

networks *Online Teaching Options*

VIDEO

The Roman Empire: Cultural Contributions

Identifying Evidence Play the video about the impact of Ancient Rome on today's world. Have students take notes during the video about the cultural contributions of the Romans evident in our culture today. **Ask:** What three terms for sports facilities originated with the Romans? *(stadium, gymnasium, arena)* Continue the discussion by asking about what Roman architectural innovations can be seen today or what influence Latin has had on modern languages, including English.

See page 303D for other online activities.

Rome as a Republic

Government of the Republic

The government of the Roman Republic was organized into three branches. One branch made laws; another ran the daily affairs of government; a third branch acted as judges. The republic had a system of checks and balances. This system was designed to prevent one branch from becoming too strong. It did not separate powers like the United States government does today, however. Judges helped run the government and could lead armies. Some leaders who ran the government also helped make laws.

R

Two patrician **consuls** (CAHN•suhlz) headed the government. The consuls were administrators and army leaders. Each consul served one year in office. Their terms of office were short so that they would not become too powerful. Each consul could **veto** (VEE•toh), or reject, the other's decision. The word veto is Latin for "I forbid." Rome also had other major government officials called **praetors** (PREE•tuhrz). They interpreted the law and served as judges in court. They could also lead armies.

The Senate was Rome's **legislature.** The Senate was a group of 300 patrician men. These senators served the republic for life. During the early republic, the Senate only advised the consuls. By the 200s B.C., however, senators debated foreign policy, proposed laws, and approved the construction of roads and temples.

The Assembly of Centuries was another legislative body in Rome. It elected consuls and praetors and passed laws. The Assembly of Centuries was, like the Senate, controlled by patricians.

This plebeian strike to gain a voice in government turned violent. The Roman plebeians went on at least five strikes in order to establish their rights.

Conflict Between Classes

As time passed, the plebeians grew frustrated. They had to serve in the army and pay taxes, yet they had no power in the government.

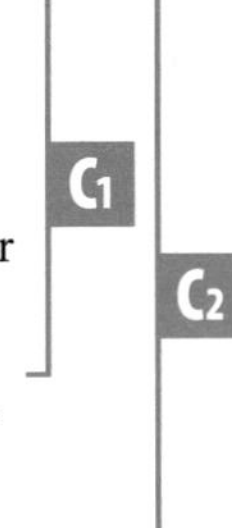

In 494 B.C., many plebeians went on strike, refusing to fight in the army. They even left Rome to create a government of their own. The patricians feared that the republic was in danger of collapsing, so they agreed to share power with the plebeians.

The patricians allowed the plebeians to have their own body of representatives, called the Council of the Plebs. The Council of the Plebs elected officials called **tribunes** (TRIH•byoonz). Tribunes voiced plebeian concerns to the government.

patricians the ruling class
plebeians ordinary citizens
consul head of government, usually with a limited term in office
veto to reject
praetors government officials who interpret the law and serve as judges
tribune an elected official who protects the rights of ordinary citizens

Academic Vocabulary (Tier 2 Words)
legislature a group of people who make the laws

R Reading Skills

Defining Call on volunteers to correctly pronounce each term of the following terms pertaining to Roman government: *consul, veto, praetor, legislature,* and *tribune.* Discuss the meanings of each of the terms related to the Roman government. **Ask:** What was Rome's legislature called? *(the Senate)* Who headed Rome's government? *(two patrician consuls)* What Roman officials acted as judges? *(praetors)* What was the Assembly of Centuries? *(another legislative body in Rome)* ELL

C1 Critical Thinking Skills

Identifying Points of View Have students do a role-playing activity in which one group plays the role of plebeians and another group plays the patricians. Tell students that it is 494 B.C. and the plebeians are on strike against serving in the army. A group of plebeians has gathered at the Forum, ancient Rome's central market area, and encountered a group of patricians. **Ask:** How would each side explain its point of view? Allow a few minutes for the groups to prepare a response before guiding them to role-play a debate or discussion. BL Kinesthetic

C2 Critical Thinking Skills

Categorizing After the role-play, have students share and discuss the feelings they might have experienced as patricians or plebeians. Create a two-column chart on the whiteboard. Label one column "Patricians" and the other "Plebeians." Write students' responses in the appropriate columns on the chart. *(Possible answers: Patricians—They feel threatened, concerned about losing control of the government, and worried that plebeians will try to take their land and wealth. They feel determined to maintain their higher status and power in society. Plebeians—They feel frustrated with their lack of rights, are hopeful that a strike will work, and are determined to seek an equal role in government to improve the lot of all plebeians.)*

GAME

Patricians and Plebeians Column Game

Classifying Before students play the game, make sure they understand the terminology. **Ask:** Who were the plebeians and patricians? *(Possible answer: The plebeians were working-class artisans, shopkeepers, and small farmers. Many of them were very poor. The patricians were Rome's ruling class and were wealthy landowners.)* To reinforce students' understanding of the differences between the two groups, allow students to play the column game, in which they drag and drop terms and phrases into the correct column, either *patrician* or *plebeian.*

See page 303D for other online activities.

Rome as a Republic

V Visual Skills

Analyzing Maps Turn students' attention to the map of the growth of the Roman Republic. Make sure they understand the parts of the map, including the title, the compass rose, the scale, and the key. **Ask:** **What does the key tell about this map?** *(It shows the colors that indicate the extent of the Roman Republic at three different times.)*

- **How would you describe the extent of Rome's control by 264 B.C.?** *(Rome controlled the Italian peninsula.)*
- **By 146 B.C., Rome controlled the lands on both sides of what sea?** *(the Adriatic Sea)*
- **Which mountains formed the northern border of Roman territory in 146 B.C.?** *(the Alps)*
- **Why do you think Rome was able to expand so greatly?** *(Answers will vary, but students should mention the organization, training, and equipment of the Roman legions.)* **BL Visual/Spatial**

R Reading Skills

Defining Before students read the text, ask them to define the word *dictator.* Then direct them to the text to learn the Roman meaning of the word. **Ask:** **What is a dictator?** *(a person granted absolute authority)* **Why did the Romans believe they needed a dictator?** *(They wanted a strong leader.)* **During what kind of circumstances would Rome appoint a dictator?** *(during a crisis)* **What are examples of dictators today or in the recent past?** *(Answers will vary, although students should identify a current or recent leader with absolute power over a country.)* **ELL**

ANSWERS, p. 314

GEOGRAPHY CONNECTION

1. Corsica, Sardinia, Sicily
2. **CRITICAL THINKING** Rome did not want to conquer lands too far from the coast. Roman forces probably could not support efforts to conquer more areas.

GEOGRAPHY CONNECTION

Within 350 years, the Roman Republic conquered territory along much of the Mediterranean Sea's northern coast.

1. **PLACE** What major islands did Rome conquer?
2. **CRITICAL THINKING** ***Making Inferences*** Why do you think Rome did not expand farther north?

Tribunes could also veto government decisions. Later, plebeians were even allowed to become consuls, and marriages between plebeians and patricians were made legal.

In 287 B.C., the plebeians won another important political victory. The Council of the Plebs was given the right to pass laws for all Romans. Politically, all male citizens were now considered equal. In practice, however, a few wealthy patrician families still held most of the power. Women did not have any political rights. The Roman Republic had become more representative, but it was still not democratic.

Cincinnatus and Civic Duty

R The Romans believed that there were times when the republic needed a strong leader. To lead Rome, the Romans created the office of **dictator** (DIHK•tay•tuhr). Today, this word is used to describe an oppressive ruler who has total control over a country. In the Roman Republic, however, the consuls resigned during difficult or dangerous times, and the senate appointed a dictator to lead the republic. During a crisis, the dictator had complete control over Rome. After the crisis was over, the dictator was expected to give up his power, and the regular government's power would then be restored.

One of the most famous Roman dictators was Cincinnatus (SIHN•suh•NA•tuhs). Cincinnatus had been a respected Roman consul who was known for his loyalty to Rome. In

Reading HELPDESK (CCSS)

dictator a person granted absolute power

networks Online Teaching Options

MAP

Growth of the Roman Republic, 500 B.C.–146 B.C.

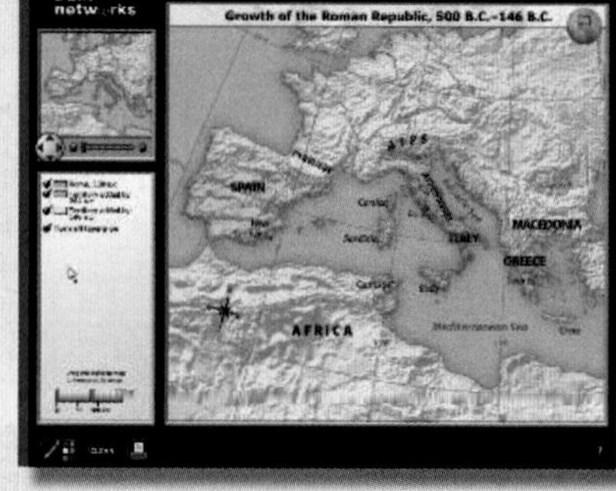

Reading a Map Display the interactive map on the whiteboard, and begin with all layers off. Show students how to turn the layers on and off and how to use the zoom button to magnify the area around Rome. After giving students time to experiment with the map features, **ask:** **What river runs through Rome?** *(the Tiber River)* **How far is it from Rome to Carthage?** *(about 125 miles/200 km)* **When was most of modern-day Italy added to the Roman Republic?** *(264 B.C.)* **On which continent was the southernmost part of the Roman Republic?** *(Africa)* **Visual/Spatial**

See page 303D for other online activities.

458 B.C., a powerful enemy of Rome threatened to destroy the Roman army. The Senate appointed Cincinnatus as dictator to handle this emergency. Messengers were sent to his farm to tell him about his appointment. They found him plowing his fields. Cincinnatus accepted the role of dictator, and he immediately created an army. Then, he led it into battle, easily defeating the enemy. Next, Cincinnatus marched his army back to Rome and resigned as dictator. Just 16 days after taking control of the republic, Cincinnatus returned to his farm.

When called to serve, Cincinnatus willingly left his farm to fulfill his civic duty.

▶ **CRITICAL THINKING**
Analyzing What role did Cincinnatus play in government to fulfill his civic duty?

C Cincinnatus was widely admired because he fulfilled his **civic duty**. Civic duty is the idea that citizens have a responsibility to help their country. This idea was important to the Romans and has been valued by other people as well. George Washington, for example, was inspired by Cincinnatus. Like Cincinnatus, Washington was a farmer who was asked to lead an army: the Continental Army in the American War for Independence. After leading the Americans to victory, Washington returned to his farm in Virginia. Later, he **reluctantly** agreed to become the first president of the United States.

Rome's System of Law

One of Rome's greatest contributions to later civilizations was its system of law. Roman law has influenced the legal systems of the United States and other countries.

R At first, Roman laws were not written down. This sparked criticism from the plebeians. They believed that patrician judges would always rule in favor of the upper classes if therewere no written laws. The plebeians demanded that laws be put into writing. Thus, the judges would have to refer to the laws when they made a legal decision. The patricians eventually agreed.

In 451 B.C., Rome adopted its first written code of laws known as the Twelve Tables. The laws were carved on twelve bronze tablets and placed in Rome's marketplace, called the Forum (FOHR•uhm). These laws served as the foundation for all future Roman laws. The Twelve Tables supported the ideal that all free citizens—patrician and plebeian alike—had the right to be treated equally in the Roman legal system.

These bundles of rods and axes, called fasces, were carried by Roman officials as a symbol of legal authority.

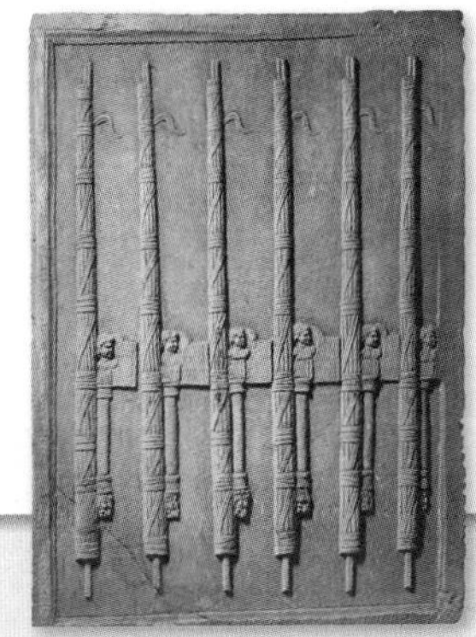

civic duty the idea that citizens have a responsibility to help their country

Academic Vocabulary (Tier 2 Words)
reluctantly hesitantly or unwillingly

CHAPTER 11, Lesson 2

Rome as a Republic

C Critical Thinking Skills

Making Connections Discuss the concept of civic duty with students. **Ask:** **What is civic duty?** *(the idea that citizens have a responsibility to help their country)* **ELL** **What are some ways people can perform their civic duty in the United States today?** Write their responses on the whiteboard. *(Possible answers: voting, doing volunteer work, serving in government office, serving in the military)* Ask each student to share a brief explanation about how he or she sees him- or herself fulfilling a civic duty as an adult and why the student thinks this is important. **Verbal/Linguistic**

R Reading Skills

Explaining Have a volunteer read the text aloud. Ask the class to explain why the plebeians in the Roman Republic had problems with Roman laws not being written down. **Ask:**

- **Suppose a plebeian was arrested for stealing, and the plebeian thought he was completely innocent. Why would it be a problem that no laws were written down?** *(Answers will vary. Students might suggest that a judge might ignore any sense of fairness and rule against the plebeian for no good reason. Without written laws, the plebeian would have nowhere to appeal.)* **BL**
- **What did the plebeians demand as a consequence of this problem?** *(a written code of laws)*
- **What was Rome's first code of laws called?** *(the Twelve Tables)* **AL**
- **What did Roman officials carry as a symbol of legal authority?** *(a bundle of rods and axes called fasces)*

PRIMARY SOURCE

Cincinnatus

Analyzing Primary Sources Project the primary-source information about Cincinnatus on a whiteboard or screen in the classroom. Ask volunteers to read aloud the informative text and the quotation. Take time to have students paraphrase the quotation. Make sure students understand what qualities Livy is emphasizing in his description of Cincinnatus. **Ask:** **Why was Cincinnatus an important figure?** *(He fulfilled his civic duty by leaving his farm to become dictator, but then he returned to his farm when the crisis was over, rather than staying in power.)*

See page 303D for other online activities.

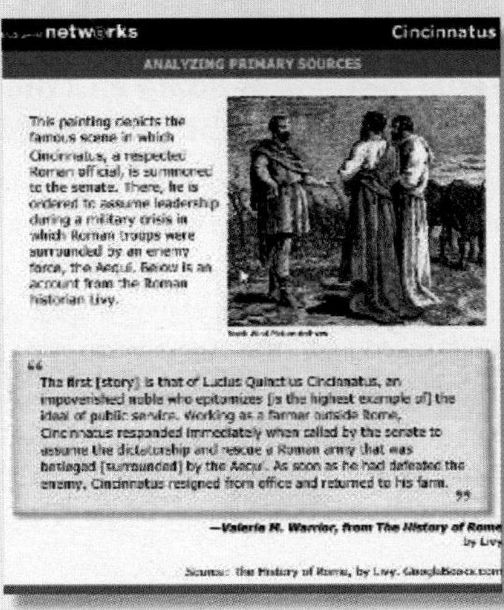

networks
Cincinnatus
ANALYZING PRIMARY SOURCES
This painting depicts the famous scene in which Cincinnatus, a respected Roman official, is summoned to the senate. There, he is ordered to assume leadership during a military crisis in which Roman troops were surrounded by an enemy force, the Aequi. Below is an account from the Roman historian Livy.
"The first [story] is that of Lucius Quinctius Cincinnatus, an impoverished noble who epitomizes [is the highest example of] the ideal of public service. Working as a farmer outside Rome, Cincinnatus responded immediately when called by the senate to assume the dictatorship and rescue a Roman army that was beleaguered [surrounded] by the Aequi. As soon as he had defeated the enemy, Cincinnatus resigned from office and returned to his farm."
—Valerie M. Warrior, from The History of Rome by Livy

ANSWER, p. 315

CRITICAL THINKING He served as Rome's leader during a time of crisis.

W Writing Skills

Informative/Explanatory Discuss the rule of law as one of the key ideas that the Romans passed on to the rest of the world. **Ask: What is the rule of law?** *(the idea that laws apply to everyone equally)* AL Explain that the rule of law is often contrasted with the "rule of force" or, in the past, the "rule of men." Ask each student to write a blog post about the rule of law that could be uploaded to the Internet that would provide information to young people about legal issues. Tell students that this paragraph should explain where the idea of the rule of law came from and why it is beneficial for everyone

R Reading Skills

Describing Before students read about the Punic Wars, set the stage with a discussion of Carthage. **Ask: What was Carthage, and where was it based?** *(Carthage was a trading empire in the Mediterranean region that was based along the north coast of Africa.)* **What made Carthage a rich and powerful force in the Mediterranean region?** *(trade)* **How far did Carthage's territory extend?** *(to parts of northern Africa and southern Europe)* **Why might the Roman Republic have seen Carthage as a threat?** *(Answers will vary. Some students might suggest that Rome was continuing to grow in the region, and Carthage was a growing empire in the same region. Rome would have feared that Carthage might strike Rome to prevent it from growing into areas that Carthage wanted to control.)*

The Roman court system shared many similarities with the legal system in the United States today. Judges heard cases before an audience of citizens.

As the Romans conquered more people, they expanded their system of laws. They created laws that would apply to people who were not Roman citizens. These new laws were known as the Law of Nations. The Law of Nations identified the laws and rights that applied to all people everywhere in the Roman lands.

Roman Justice

The ideas found in Roman laws are woven throughout the American legal system today. For example, the American legal system, like the Roman legal system, **assumes** that a person is innocent until proven guilty. People accused of crimes have the right to defend themselves before a judge. Judges must carefully consider all the evidence in a case before making a decision.

W The *rule of law* is one of the key ideas that the Romans passed on to the world. The rule of law means that laws apply to everyone equally. It also means that the legal system should treat everyone the same way. Before the Romans, the rule of law was unfamiliar to people.

In many regions, people of the upper classes enjoyed special privileges. They often had different laws and courts from the lower classes. People in the lower classes, however, had few legal rights or none at all. The Romans extended the idea of the rule of law to all their lands. Today, the rule of law is the guiding principle of the American legal system.

PROGRESS CHECK

Explaining What was the emergency that caused Cincinnatus to be appointed dictator?

The Punic Wars

GUIDING QUESTION *How did Rome conquer the Mediterranean region?*

R Rome continued to grow as a republic. Its power, however, was threatened by another civilization in the Mediterranean region. Carthage (KAHR•thihj) was a powerful trading empire based along the north African coast. Carthage traced its beginnings to the Phoenicians, who created a trading colony there about 800 B.C. Carthage became the largest and wealthiest city in the western Mediterranean area because of trade. Its territory included parts of northern Africa and southern Europe.

Reading **HELP**DESK CCSS

Academic Vocabulary (Tier 2 Words)

assume to take for granted to be true
intensify to become stronger
innovation the introduction of something new

networks Online Teaching Options

CHART

Legal Systems of Rome and the United States: Rights of the Accused

Making Connections Have students look at the graphic organizer that makes connections between the Roman and U.S. legal systems. **Ask: How were the two systems similar and different?** *(In both systems, the accused have a right to a trial, are innocent until proven guilty, and are protected by the rule of law. However, the Roman system did not separate powers, as the U.S. government does. Roman judges helped run the government and run the armies. U.S. judges may not do such things.)*

See page 303D for other online activities.

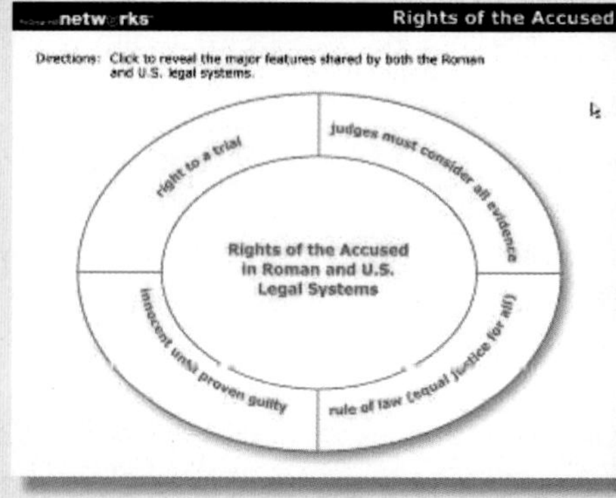

ANSWER, p. 316

PROGRESS CHECK The Roman Senate appointed Cincinnatus as dictator because Rome was under threat from a powerful enemy.

Carthage became Rome's main rival. Each wanted to control the entire Mediterranean world. In 264 B.C., their rivalry **intensified**. It grew into a series of wars that took place over a period of nearly 120 years.

The Punic Wars Begin

War between the Romans and the Carthaginians, or the people of Carthage, erupted in 264 B.C. The original conflict is known as the First Punic War. The First Punic War began when Rome sought control of the fertile island of Sicily. The Carthaginians had already established colonies on the island. So they were determined to stop the Roman invasion.

Carthage used its strong navy to protect its trading empire. Although Rome had a powerful army, it did not have a navy. It was forced to build a fleet quickly in order to fight Carthage. The Romans modeled their new warships after those of Carthage. They made one key **innovation**. They built a small moveable bridge on the front of each ship. This bridge allowed Roman soldiers to board a Carthaginian ship and fight hand-to-hand on its decks. In a way, it changed a sea war into a land war.

R1

R2

For more than 20 years, the Romans and Carthaginians fought each other at sea. Finally, in 241 B.C., a Roman fleet badly defeated Carthage's navy off the coast of Sicily. Carthage was forced to give up Sicily and pay a huge fine to the Romans. Rome then took control of the island.

GEOGRAPHY CONNECTION

After defeating Carthage in the Second Punic War, Rome was the strongest power in the Mediterranean region.

1. **LOCATION** From what direction did Hannibal of Carthage attack Rome?
2. **CRITICAL THINKING** ***Analyzing*** Why did Hannibal take the route he did instead of sailing directly to Rome?

V

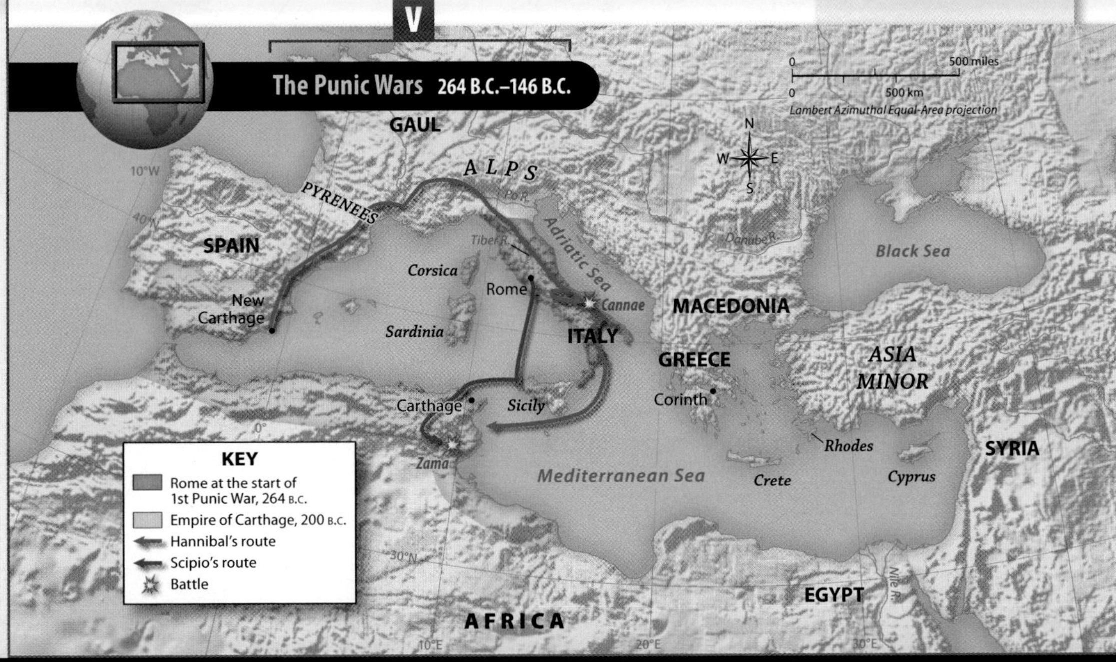

MAP

The Punic Wars, 264 B.C.–146 B.C.

Speculating Direct students to write a short response to the following question: **Why do you think the Romans were so determined to beat the Carthaginians?** *(Possible response: The Romans were determined to beat the Carthaginians because the Romans wanted control over Carthage's territory.)* AL Ask students to share their responses with the class. Then present the interactive map "Growth of the Roman Republic." Invite students to revise their responses after studying the map. *(Possible response: By defeating the Carthaginians, the Romans would greatly increase their control over most of the Mediterranean region.)* BL

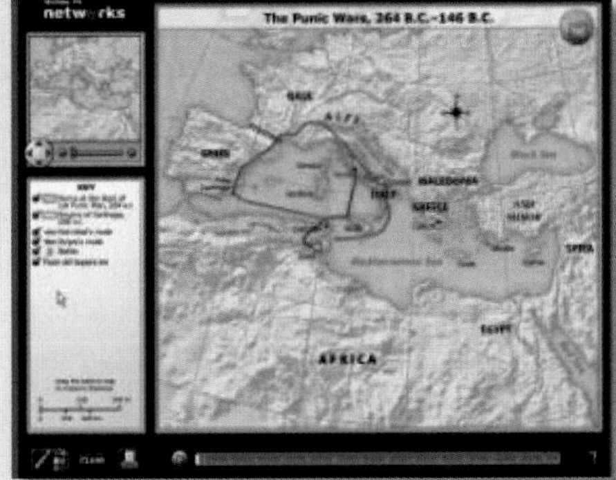

See page 303D for other online activities.

R1 Reading Skills

Identifying After students read the text, prompt them to identify the different components of an effective military force during the period of the Punic Wars. **Ask: What did Rome need to do to prepare to fight Carthage for control of Sicily?** *(Rome needed to build a naval fleet because Carthage was protecting Sicily with its navy.)* Ask students to consider why Carthage might have had a strong navy in the first place. *(because of its location near the sea)* BL

R2 Reading Skills

Defining Call on a volunteer to pronounce the word *innovation,* and explain that an innovation is a new idea, method, or device. **Ask: What was the innovation that the Romans made to their ships?** *(The Romans built a small moveable bridge at the front of each ship that allowed Roman soldiers to board Carthaginian ships, changing a sea war into a type of land war.)* AL ELL

V Visual Skills

Analyzing Maps Have students examine the map of the Punic Wars at the bottom of this page. Call students' attention to the title. **Ask: When did the Punic Wars take place?** *(between 264 B.C. and 146 B.C.)* **How far did the empire of Carthage extend?** *(along the northern coast of Africa and into the southern part of Spain)* Have students locate the main battle sites of the Punic Wars on the map. *(Cannae in southern Italy, Zama in northern Africa)* **Ask: Whose route was longer, Hannibal's or Scipio's?** *(Hannibal's)* AL **Visual/Spatial**

ANSWERS, p. 317

GEOGRAPHY CONNECTION

1. Hannibal attacked Rome from the northwest.
2. **CRITICAL THINKING** Hannibal wanted to surprise the Romans, who would have expected him to make a direct attack from the southwest, from Carthage, across the Mediterranean Sea. Instead, he took a longer, indirect route.

V Visual Skills

Analyzing Images Have students look at the image of the battle, and ask a volunteer to read the caption to the class. **Ask:** **On which side of the picture are the Roman soldiers? The Carthaginians? How can you tell?** *(The Romans are on the left and the Carthaginians are on the right. It's clear because the Carthaginians had elephants while the Romans did not.)* **In what kind of area did this battle take place?** *(the mountains)* **What mountains did Hannibal's army cross to reach Italy?** *(the Alps)* AL

T Technology Skills

Collaborating Ask interested students to collaborate in searching the Internet for information about Hannibal's elephants. Point out that Hannibal lived in Carthage, which was on the Mediterranean Sea north of the Sahara. This area was not where elephants would normally live. Ask students to work together to find reliable Web sites that discuss where Hannibal got his elephants and what kind of elephants they were. Have students present the information they find to the rest of the class. **Interpersonal**

Content Background Knowledge

The Second Punic War During the Second Punic War, Hannibal's army, traveling in the Alps, was far from Carthage and, thus, far from needed supplies and fresh troops. Hannibal wasn't worried, though. He had confidence that he would find allies in Italy to join him in his fight against Rome. These "allies," however, remained loyal to Rome. Hannibal would need to acquire more supplies and troops from Carthage's territory in Spain. The Romans set about conquering Spain to cut off Hannibal. After conquering Spain, the Romans traveled to Carthage. Hannibal was forced to retreat from the Italian peninsula to defend Carthage.

ANSWER, p. 318

CRITICAL THINKING It was the first encounter between Carthaginian forces and the Roman army during the Second Punic War, and Hannibal's army won.

Hannibal Attacks: The Second Punic War

After losing Sicily, Carthage tried to expand its empire into Spain. They wanted to make up for the losses caused by Rome taking over Sicily. Spain had valuable resources of silver, copper, gold, lead, and iron.

The Romans bitterly opposed Carthage's attempt to establish territory so near to Rome. So the Romans encouraged the Spanish to rebel against Carthage. In response, Carthage sent its greatest general, Hannibal (HA•nuh•buhl), to attack Rome. This event, in 218 B.C., started the Second Punic War.

Hannibal planned to fight the Romans in Italy. To do this he gathered an army of about 46,000 men and 37 elephants. He sailed from Carthage to Spain. Then, his soldiers marched through southern Gaul, or present-day France.

Next, they crossed the Alps into Italy. The Carthaginians crossed the Alps with their elephants, hoping to overpower the Roman army. Instead, the bitter cold and attacks by mountain tribes killed almost half of the Carthaginian soldiers and most of the elephants. The remaining army, however, was still a powerful fighting force when it reached Italy.

In December 218 B.C., the Carthaginian forces defeated the Romans in northern Italy. Hannibal made good use of his elephants in the attack. Unfortunately, most of the animals died after the conflict.

▶ CRITICAL THINKING
Analyzing Why was this battle important?

Reading HELPDESK CCSS

networks Online Teaching Options

WORKSHEET

Guided Reading Activity: The Punic Wars

Sequencing Have students work in pairs or small groups to complete the flowchart on page 3 of the lesson's Guided Reading Activity. Explain that when students are finished, their chart will illustrate the sequence of events in the Punic Wars. After pairs have worked to complete the flowchart, come back together as a large group and review each of the events to be sure students have organized them correctly.

See page 303D for other online activities.

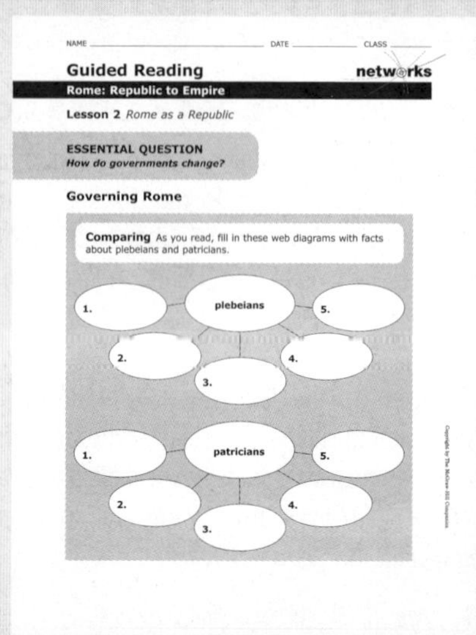
NAME DATE CLASS
Guided Reading networks
Rome: Republic to Empire
Lesson 2 Rome as a Republic
ESSENTIAL QUESTION
How do governments change?
Governing Rome
Comparing As you read, fill in these web diagrams with facts about plebeians and patricians.
plebeians
1. 2. 3. 4. 5.
patricians
1. 2. 3. 4. 5.

As Hannibal and his army grew closer and closer to Italy and the Roman forces, Roman military leaders looked to the Senate for advice.

PRIMARY SOURCE

> “They [the Roman commanders] therefore sent frequent messages to Rome asking for instructions, . . .in view of the fact that the country was being plundered, . . . The Senate passed a resolution . . .give the enemy battle.”
>
> —from *The Histories of Polybius*, by Polybius

C

In 216 B.C., Hannibal defeated the Romans at the Battle of Cannae (KA•nee) in southern Italy. Following the battle, Hannibal's army raided the country. In response, the Romans assembled another army to stop the Carthaginians. In 206 B.C. Roman forces, led by Scipio (SIH•pee•oh), captured Spain and then attacked the city of Carthage. Hannibal returned home to North Africa to defend his people. Scipio's troops defeated the Carthaginians in 202 B.C. at the Battle of Zama (ZAY•muh). Carthage was forced to give up its navy and pay Rome a large sum of money. It also had to give its Spanish territory to Rome. As a result, Rome became the supreme power in the western Mediterranean.

R

Connections to TODAY

Hannibal's Elephants

Historians have wondered how Hannibal obtained elephants for his march. Were they Indian or African elephants? Indian elephants are easier to train. In fact, most circus elephants today are Indian elephants. However, it would have been very difficult for Hannibal to obtain elephants from India. Even African elephants are not native to North Africa, where Hannibal started his march. Historians continue to question which type of elephant Hannibal used—or how he obtained them.

The Third Punic War

Rome still considered Carthage a military threat. In 146 B.C., Rome finally destroyed it in the Third Punic War. At the same time, Rome also waged war against other states in the eastern Mediterranean region. In the 140s B.C., all of Greece fell under Roman rule. About twenty years later, Rome acquired its first province in Asia.

✓ **PROGRESS CHECK**

Describing How did Hannibal lose the Second Punic War?

LESSON 2 REVIEW (CCSS)

Review Vocabulary (Tier 3 Words)

1. Why were Roman *consuls* awarded the power of the *veto?* RH.6–8.2, RH.6–8.4

Answer the Guiding Questions

2. ***Explaining*** How did plebeians gain power in the republic? For what changes were they responsible? RH.6–8.2

3. ***Summarizing*** Describe how Rome defeated Carthage to become the ruler of the Mediterranean region. RH.6–8.2

4. ***Distinguishing Fact from Opinion*** Identify whether the following statement is a fact or an opinion: "At first, patricians had more rights than plebeians." RH.6–8.8

5. **INFORMATIVE/EXPLANATORY** In an essay, describe what the idea of "rule of law" meant to the average Roman. WHST.6–8.2, WHST.6–8.10

LESSON 2 REVIEW ANSWERS

1. The veto prevented any one consul from becoming too powerful. Answers should demonstrate an understanding that the consuls were the heads of the government and that a veto is a rejection of another's decision.
2. The plebeians went on strike from serving in the army and left Rome to create their own government. The patricians then allowed the plebeians to form the Council of the Plebs and gave them the right to elect their own officials, to become consuls, and to pass laws.
3. Rome used its military power to fight the Punic Wars and eventually defeat Carthage and take control of the Mediterranean region.
4. The statement is a fact.
5. Answers will vary, but students should explain that Roman law emphasized the right of all free citizens to be treated equally under the law.

C Critical Thinking Skills

Analyzing Primary Sources Have students read the primary-source excerpt from *The Histories of Polybius*. **Ask:** What did the Senate instruct the Roman commanders to do? *(The Senate ordered the Roman commanders to battle Hannibal's forces.)* **Ask:** What does "being plundered" mean in this statement? *(Answers will vary, but students should convey the idea that the country was being attacked and robbed forcefully by its enemies.)* BL **Verbal/Linguistic**

R Reading Skills

Identifying Direct students to read the text, then identify the events that occurred in the Second Punic War and the leaders who were involved. **Ask:**

- Who commanded the army of the Carthaginians in the Second Punic War? *(Hannibal)*
- Where did Hannibal's army defeat the Romans? *(at the Battle of Cannae in southern Italy)*
- Who led the Roman forces? *(Scipio)*
- Where did Rome finally defeat the Carthaginian army? *(They defeated the Carthaginians at the Battle of Zama.)* BL

Have students complete the Lesson 2 Review.

CLOSE & REFLECT

To close the lesson, have students write a paragraph describing one aspect of government in the Roman Republic. For example, students may wish to focus on the justice system, the types of rulers that led the government, or the Roman military. After students have finished, encourage volunteers to share their paragraphs with the rest of the class.

ANSWER, p. 319

✓ **PROGRESS CHECK** Hannibal tried to overpower the Roman army by marching through southern Gaul into Italy while riding on elephants.

ENGAGE

Bellringer Tell students that in this lesson they will be learning about an unstable period in Rome's history. During this time, Rome was in transition from a republic to an empire. **Ask:** **What problems can cause the decline or instability of a government or a nation?** Have students think about this question on their own for a few moments. Then have them partner with a classmate to discuss it and write down their responses. Each pair can share their responses with the class. *(Possible responses: poverty, crime, unemployment, corruption, violence)* Have students discuss examples of these problems that they are familiar with from world history and U.S. history and how these problems affected the country's stability today. BL

TEACH & ASSESS

C Critical Thinking Skills

Determining Cause and Effect Tell students that as a class, they will be creating a flowchart on the board. Instead of beginning with the first step, though, write the last step on the board: *Farmers could not pay back loans they owed.* Draw an arrow to that step. **Ask:** **What is the cause of that effect?** *(Farmers did not have crops to harvest.)* Write that step on the board and draw an arrow to it. **Why didn't farmers have crops to harvest?** *(Either they had gone to war and neglected their crops or the Carthaginians had destroyed their fields.)* AL Write both reasons as beginning steps to the flowchart. **If you had been part of the Roman upper class, what advice would you have given the government to solve this problem?** *(Answers will vary, although students should suggest reasonable solutions, such as the wealthy could pay off the farmers' debts.)* BL

ANSWER, p. 320

TAKING NOTES: Answer to graphic organizer: Marius elected consul —> Creates professional army —> Sulla becomes dictator —> First Triumvirate rules Rome —> Caesar takes power —> Caesar is killed —> Second Triumvirate fails —> Octavian becomes emperor

networks *There's More Online!*

- GRAPHIC ORGANIZER Fall of the Roman Republic
- PRIMARY SOURCE
  - Crossing the Rubicon
  - Octavian
- VIDEO
- GAMES

Lesson 3

The End of the Republic

ESSENTIAL QUESTION *Why does conflict develop?*

IT MATTERS BECAUSE

Without a strong system of checks and balances, a powerful individual or group can easily take control of a representative government.

Problems in the Republic

GUIDING QUESTION ***What factors led to the decline of the Roman Republic?***

The Roman army won victories abroad, but the republic faced mounting economic troubles at home. The gap between the rich and the poor grew wider. Many farmers faced financial ruin. The cities of the republic were becoming overcrowded and dangerous.

Romans—Rich and Poor

Most Romans were plebeians who farmed small plots of land. The plebeians had made some political gains in the Roman Republic, but they lacked real power. Power was still held by the patricians. The upper class still made up most of the Senate and served in key government positions. They also managed Rome's finances and directed its wars.

C In the 100s B.C., farmers began to fall into poverty and debt. Why? Many small farmers had neglected their fields while fighting in Roman wars. Others had their farms destroyed by the Carthaginians. Now, the farmers did not have crops to harvest. As a result, they could not pay back loans they owed.

Reading **HELP**DESK CCSS

Taking Notes: ***Sequencing***

Complete a diagram like this one to identify the events that led to the fall of the Roman Republic. You may add more boxes if necessary. RH.6–8.2

[ ] → [ ] → Republic Falls

Content Vocabulary (Tier 3 Words)

- **latifundia**
- **triumvirate**

networks ***Online Teaching Options***

VIDEO

Bread and Circuses

Drawing Conclusions Play the video for students and then divide the class into small groups. Have each group discuss this question: **Did Roman leaders of this time make good governing decisions in addressing the needs of the poor?** Ask members of each group to draw a conclusion based on sound reasoning and to be prepared to defend their conclusion. Then bring the class together and call on groups to share their answers and the details that led them to this conclusion.

See page 303E for other online activities.

In addition, small farmers could not compete with wealthy Romans, who owned **latifundia** (la•tuh•FUHN•dee•uh), or large farming estates. Farmers could not even find jobs on these huge farms. Those jobs went to a new source of labor—the thousands of prisoners captured in the Roman wars. Wealthy landowners did not have to pay wages to enslaved workers. Instead, they bought more land for their latifundia. Small farms were pushed out of business.

As small farms shut down, thousands of poor unemployed people left the countryside. They poured into Rome's cities looking for jobs. Even in the cities, however, enslaved people did most of the work. Paying jobs were hard to find. If free people could find a paying job, it was generally for a low wage.

Desperate economic conditions created mounting anger among the poor. Roman leaders worried about a rebellion. To prevent a revolt, Roman leaders began offering cheap food and free entertainment to the poor. Numerous Roman rulers used this policy of "bread and circuses" to acquire or stay in power.

Roman Reformers

Not all wealthy Romans ignored the problems of the poor. Two government officials, who were also brothers, worked for reforms. Tiberius and Gaius Gracchus (GRA•kuhs) thought that Rome's problems were caused by the actions of wealthy landowners. The brothers wanted to stop the wealthy from taking over small farms to create their latifundia. They urged the Senate to take some land from the latifundia and return it to the poor.

Stone carvings such as this show that artists felt farming was an important topic to include. Oxen did the heavy work for farmers.

▶ CRITICAL THINKING

Analyzing How did the reforms of the Gracchus brothers affect Roman farmers?

latifundia large farming estates

C Critical Thinking Skills

Analyzing Explain that the Roman circus referred to in the policy of "bread and circuses," and the Roman circus was not like circuses of today. A Roman circus was a great arena that held spectators who came to see chariot races, footraces, and gladiator fights. In fact, the circuses were more like sporting events than the child-oriented fun of clowns, acrobats, and wild animals performing under a big tent. **Ask: Why did Roman leaders believe the policy of "bread and circuses" would help them acquire or stay in power?** *(Answers will vary, although students should suggest that the poor people of Rome would be so preoccupied and calmed by the free food and entertainment that they wouldn't think of revolting against the leaders of Rome.)* BL

W Writing Skills

Argument Point out that the Gracchus brothers were leaders of Rome, and they could have simply ignored the problems of Rome's poor, as the wealthy landowners did. The Gracchus brothers, though, stood for reform. Ask students to imagine they are one of the Gracchus brothers, and have them write a letter to a wealthy Roman landowner of the time. Explain that this letter should include a description of the problems of the poor, what they would do to address those problems, and how such reforms would benefit everyone in Rome, poor and rich alike. Call on volunteers to read their letters to the class.

CHART

Poverty in Rome

Analyzing Discuss with students the factors that made life difficult for the plebeians. Show students the graphic organizer on poverty in Rome. Guide them in a discussion about why life became so hard for this particular group. AL

See page 303E for other online activities.

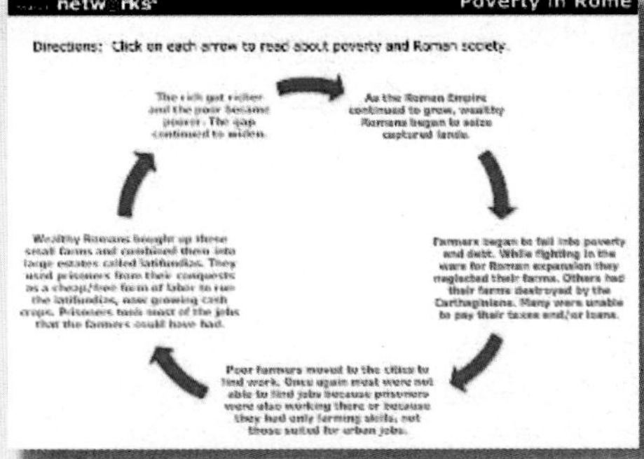

ANSWER, p. 321

CRITICAL THINKING Some farmers neglected their land to fight in the wars; other farms were destroyed.

The End of the Republic

C1 Critical Thinking Skills

Speculating Tell students that martyrs are people who are so committed to a certain cause or belief that they are willing to suffer or die defending it. **Ask:** **In what ways do you think the Gracchus brothers suffered for trying to help the poor?** *(Possible answers: They might have been hated and shunned by other senators and patricians.)*

C2 Critical Thinking Skills

Evaluating Point out that political leaders are elected officials, but military leaders rise through the ranks by appointment of their superiors. **Ask:** **Is it dangerous for military leaders to have political power? Why or why not?** *(Possible response: It is dangerous because military leaders can use their troops to take power by force, which weakens the democracy.)*

R *Reading Skills*

Identifying After students have read the text, prompt them to identify the reforms that Marius and Sulla put in place to solve some of Rome's problems. **Ask:** **What reforms did Marius make to solve Rome's economic problems?** *(He recruited soldiers from the landless poor and he paid them wages.)* **How did Marius's reforms weaken the republican form of government?** *(Soldiers felt more loyalty to Marius than to the republic.)* **When Sulla took power, what reforms did he make?** *(He reduced the power of the tribunes and gave more power to the Senate.)* AL

The Gracchus brothers tried to help the poor farmers who had lost their land to latifundia.

▶ CRITICAL THINKING

Analyzing What does the murder of these brothers tell us about the Roman government at this time?

The Senate was made up of wealthy Romans, some of whom owned the latifundia. They fought the Gracchus brothers' proposals. A group of senators even killed Tiberius in 133 B.C. Gaius was also murdered 12 years later. Dark days had fallen on the Roman Republic. The people charged with making and upholding the laws repeatedly broke them. C1

Roman Politics and the Army

The republic soon faced more challenges. Rome's military leaders began to seek political power. In 107 B.C., a general named Marius (MARE•ee•uhs) became consul. Marius, the son of a worker, was not a patrician.

Marius believed that he could solve Rome's economic problems. He **transformed** the army in order to provide opportunities for the poor. Until then, only property owners served in the military. Marius, however, recruited soldiers from the landless poor. In return for their service, he paid them wages—and promised them land. The Roman army was no longer a force of citizen volunteers. It was now a force of **professional** soldiers.

C2 The plan that Marius put into action provided work for many jobless, landless Romans. However, it also weakened the republican form of government. Soldiers felt more loyalty to the general who hired and paid them than to the republic. As a result, military generals grew enormously powerful. Some generals sought political office. This allowed them to pass laws that gave land to their soldiers—and increased their power. R

The creation of a professional army led to new power struggles. Marius was soon opposed by another general, named Sulla (SUH•luh), who commanded his own army. In 82 B.C., Sulla drove his enemies out of Rome and named himself dictator. It marked the first time a Roman general had led his army into the capital.

Over the next three years, Sulla made changes to the government. He reduced the power of the tribunes and gave the senators more responsibilities. Sulla then stepped down as dictator. Sulla hoped that his reforms would restore the Roman Republic to its earlier days of glory. Instead, Rome plunged into conflict that lasted for the next 50 years. Some Romans took notice of how Sulla had used an army to achieve his goals. Those who were eager for power decided that they would do the same thing.

✓ PROGRESS CHECK

Analyzing What was the purpose of "bread and circuses"?

Reading HELPDESK CCSS

Academic Vocabulary (Tier 2 Words)

transform to change the structure of

professional relating to a type of job that usually requires training and practice

networks *Online Teaching Options*

LECTURE SLIDE

Problems in the Republic

Identifying Show students the lecture slide, which provides an overview of the challenges Marius faced as consul and how he solved those challenges. Ask students to list on the interactive whiteboard the changes that Marius made to the Roman army. *(The army became a paid force; many jobless Romans joined the army; military generals grew powerful.)*

See page 303E for other online activities.

networks — Problems in the Republic

Challenges Faced by Marius	Solutions
Military leaders began to seek political power.	Marius, a general, transforms the army as consul.
Only property owners served in the army, while many others were poor.	The landless poor are given paid positions in the army.
New power struggles emerged with powerful army generals.	General Sulla named himself dictator.

ANSWERS, p. 322

CRITICAL THINKING Senators broke the law in order to silence someone they disagreed with.

✓ **PROGRESS CHECK** They provided bread (food) and circuses (entertainment) to the urban poor in order to win their support and prevent a rebellion.

The End of the Republic

The Rise of Julius Caesar

GUIDING QUESTION *How did Julius Caesar rise to power in Rome?*

After Sulla left office, different Roman leaders fought among themselves for power. Many of them were military officials who relied on their loyal armies to support them. In 60 B.C., three men ruled the Roman Republic: Crassus, Pompey (PAHM•pee), and Julius Caesar (JOOL•yuhs SEE•zuhr). Crassus was a general and one of Rome's wealthiest men. Pompey and Caesar were also rich and known for their military accomplishments. These three men formed the First Triumvirate to rule Rome. A **triumvirate** (try•UHM•vuh•ruht) is a political group of three people who share equal power. R

Caesar's Conquests

C Each Triumvirate member commanded a military post in an outlying area of the Roman Republic. Pompey led in Spain, Crassus in Syria, and Caesar in Gaul. Gaul was made up mostly of what are now France and Belgium. While serving in Gaul, Caesar fought the Celts and invaded Britain. He won the admiration and support of the poorer classes. Roman senators grew uneasy with Caesar, however. They feared that he was becoming too popular and would seek power as Sulla had.

By 50 B.C., the First Triumvirate no longer existed. Crassus had died in battle, and Pompey emerged as Caesar's main rival. In 49 B.C., the Senate gave its support to Pompey. It ordered Caesar to give up his army and return to Rome. Caesar, however, refused. He knew that if he returned to Rome, he might be imprisoned or killed by his rivals. Caesar gathered his loyal troops and crossed the Rubicon (ROO•bih•KAHN) River.

Julius Caesar made himself Rome's first dictator for life in 44 B.C. As dictator, Caesar was greatly admired by the poor for his reforms. But he was hated by his enemies for his ambition.

triumvirate three rulers who share equal political power

R Reading Skills

Defining Once students have read the text, discuss with them the First Triumvirate of Crassus, Pompey, and Caesar. **Ask:** What is a triumvirate? *(a political group of three people who share power equally)* Explain that the prefix *tri-* comes from a Latin word for "three." Can you think of other words beginning with the prefix *tri-* that indicate three of something? *(Answers will vary, though many students might mention the words* trio, triple, triplet, *or* tripod.*)* ELL

C Critical Thinking Skills

Making Inferences Write the phrase "Veni, vidi, vici" on the board. Tell students that it is a Latin phrase. Then write the English translation on the board: "I came, I saw, I conquered." Ask students if they can guess who might have said this. If students have not already guessed, reveal that Julius Caesar was the speaker of the quotation. Explain that Caesar uttered the phrase after a quick military victory over an enemy army near the Black Sea. **Ask:** What does this statement by Caesar tell you about the kind of leader he was? *(Answers will vary, although students should infer that a man who would make that statement was probably supremely confident in himself and his ability to lead.)* BL

Content Background Knowledge

Julius Caesar (c. 100 B.C.–44 B.C.) was born into one of Rome's patrician families, although from early on, he identified with the party of the common people. He became a military tribune before he was 30 years old, and he was a quaestor in Spain by 69 B.C. Caesar proved to be a great military leader. He won victories in the Gallic Wars in Gaul (now France and Belgium). In 47 B.C. Caesar led an army against an enemy near the Black Sea (an area now part of Turkey). His military campaign there was so swift and decisive that he reported his victory with the words *"Veni, vidi, vici"*—"I came, I saw, I conquered." Within three years, Caesar had consolidated power in Rome and was made dictator for life.

BIOGRAPHY

Julius Caesar

Analyzing Show students the image of Julius Caesar before he ruled Rome. Ask a volunteer to read the information aloud. Then challenge the class to think of adjectives that describe Caesar and his life. *(Possible answers:* noble, intellectual, physically fit, ambitious*)* Write students' responses on the whiteboard. **Ask:** What leadership qualities did Caesar possess? *(He was both physically strong and intellectual. He had a strong drive to survive and succeed.)*

See page 303E for other online activities.

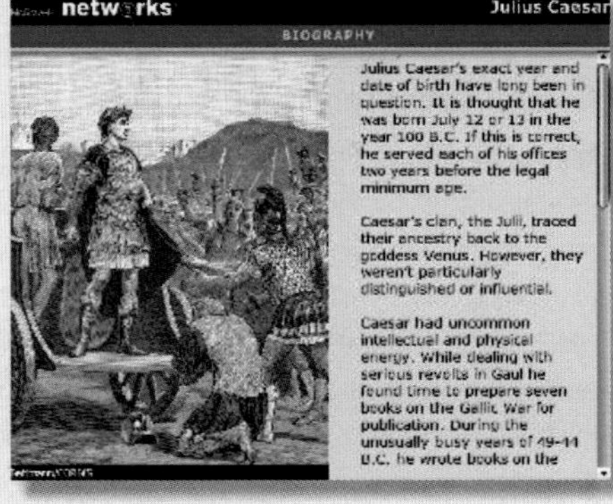

The End of the Republic

C1 Critical Thinking Skills

Analyzing Have students discuss the pros and cons of Caesar's decision to cross the Rubicon. Create a two-column chart on the interactive whiteboard to record students' responses. *(Possible responses: Pros to crossing Rubicon: chance to rule Rome, chance to achieve goals for Rome. Cons to crossing: risk being killed or imprisoned. Pros to turning back: chance to maintain position he already had and to remain safe. Cons to turning back: his enemies already knew his goals, so they might kill him anyway; he would be giving up his chance to rule Rome.)* After students share their responses, challenge them to draw a conclusion about whether Caesar was right to cross the Rubicon and take Rome. AL

C2 Critical Thinking Skills

Analyzing Primary Sources Ask a volunteer to read aloud the quotation from Suetonius. **Ask:** What is a die? *(a small cube marked on each face with one to six spots; usually used in pairs in various games)* Explain that the plural of *die* is *dice*. AL ELL What is Caesar literally saying when he says that "the die is cast"? *(The die has already been thrown.)* Explain that he did not literally mean he'd thrown a die. Rather, he was using the casting of a die as a metaphor. What was Caesar really saying when he said "the die is cast"? *(Answers will vary, although some students will understand that when a die is cast in a game, there's no undoing what has already been done. In this case, Caesar was saying that the actions of his foes and the signs of the gods were like a die being cast—there was no turning back.)* BL

ANSWER, p. 324

CRITICAL THINKING If Caesar had not crossed the Rubicon, he might not have become Rome's leader.

Connections to TODAY

Crossing the Rubicon

Caesar crossed the Rubicon at great risk. Even today, the phrase "crossing the Rubicon" is used when a person makes a decision that cannot be undone.

C1

Caesar crossed the Rubicon even though he knew it would lead to civil war.

▶ CRITICAL THINKING

Predicting What might have happened if Caesar had not decided to cross the Rubicon?

SuperStock

This small river separated Caesar's military command area from Roman Italy. According to legend, Caesar saw a vision that inspired him to cross the Rubicon. He exclaimed to his troops:

PRIMARY SOURCE

C2

"Even yet we may draw back; but once cross yon little bridge, and the whole issue is with the sword. . . . Take we the course which the signs of the gods and false dealing of our foes point out. The die is cast."

—from *Life of Julius Caesar* by Suetonius

Caesar had refused to obey the Senate and was now marching on Rome. He realized that he was starting a **civil** war. His decision, however, could not be reversed.

Caesar and his soldiers swiftly captured all of Italy. They drove Pompey's forces out of the country. The fighting then spread eastward, with Caesar finally crushing Pompey's army in Greece in 48 B.C.

Reading **HELP**DESK CCSS

Academic Vocabulary (Tier 2 Words)

civil of or relating to citizens

networks Online Teaching Options

PRIMARY SOURCE

Caesar Crossing the Rubicon

Making Decisions Present Plutarch's description of Caesar crossing the Rubicon. Discuss the idiom "crossing the Rubicon," which refers to that event. **Ask:** What does this phrase mean? *(making a decision that cannot be undone)* Discuss how people make important decisions—by weighing the risks and benefits of each choice. Explain that all decisions carry some risk because the outcome is unknown. Challenge students to think of their own personal "Rubicon moments" and to share their thoughts with the class, if they wish. Alternately, have students think of other "Rubicon moments" in history, such as Alexander's decision to turn back from India or Moses's decision to lead the ancient Israelites from Egypt. Ask students to recall the risks and benefits of each decision. AL ELL

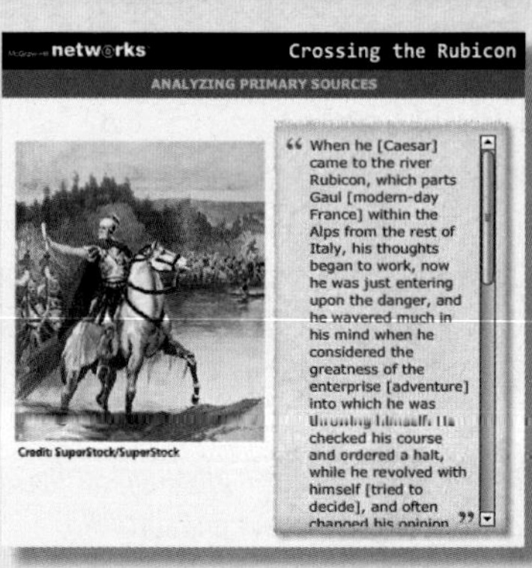

networks
Crossing the Rubicon
ANALYZING PRIMARY SOURCES
"When he [Caesar] came to the river Rubicon, which parts Gaul [modern-day France] within the Alps from the rest of Italy, his thoughts began to work, now he was just entering upon the danger, and he wavered much in his mind when he considered the greatness of the enterprise [adventure] into which he was
checked his course and ordered a halt, while he revolved with himself [tried to decide], and often
Credit: SuperStock/SuperStock

See page 303E for other online activities.

Caesar Takes Power

In 44 B.C., Caesar took over the Roman government. He ended the practice of dictators serving in office for short terms by declaring himself dictator for life. To strengthen his power, Caesar appointed people to the Senate who supported him.

Meanwhile, Caesar introduced reforms that made him popular with Romans, especially the poor. He gave citizenship to many people living in Roman territories. He created jobs for the unemployed. In the countryside, he organized new settlements for landless laborers. He ordered landowners using slave labor to hire more free workers.

One of the most famous reforms that Caesar introduced was the creation of a new calendar. It had 12 months, 365 days, and a leap year. Known as the Julian calendar, it was used throughout Europe until A.D. 1582. Then it was changed slightly to become the Gregorian calendar. The Gregorian calendar is based on the date of the birth of Jesus. This calendar is still used by most countries in the world today.

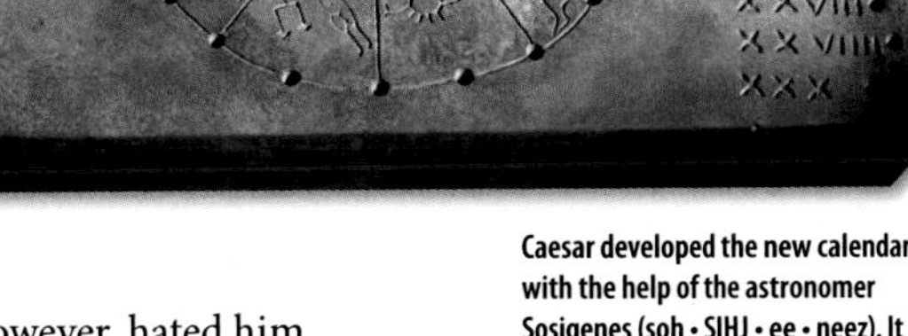

Caesar developed the new calendar with the help of the astronomer Sosigenes (soh • SIHJ • ee • neez). It has movable pegs to allow for changing days.

Many Romans praised Caesar as a wise ruler because he brought peace and good government to Rome. Others, however, hated him. They believed that he wanted to be a king. Caesar's enemies, led by the senators Brutus and Cassius, plotted to kill him. In 44 B.C., Caesar's opponents gathered around him as he entered the Senate and stabbed him to death. Caesar was killed on March 15, also known as the "Ides of March" in the Julian calendar. His murder was made famous in the play *Julius Caesar*, by William Shakespeare. In the play, Caesar was warned to "Beware the Ides of March."

AAAC/Topham/The Image Works

PROGRESS CHECK

Explaining Why did some Romans oppose Caesar?

Build Vocabulary: *Words With Multiple Meanings*

plot: a secret plan

plot: (verb) to plan; to locate; to invent a story line

IMAGE

Assassination of Julius Caesar: "Et tu, Brute?"

Analyzing Present the interactive image of Julius Caesar and his assassination. Ask students for their reactions to the image. They should observe that Caesar is wearing dark robes that match the color of his spilled blood, while his attackers are dressed in white. Challenge students to draw conclusions about the guilt and innocence of the figures based on the use of color. Then ask a volunteer to read aloud the text accompanying the image. **Visual/Spatial**

See page 303E for other online activities.

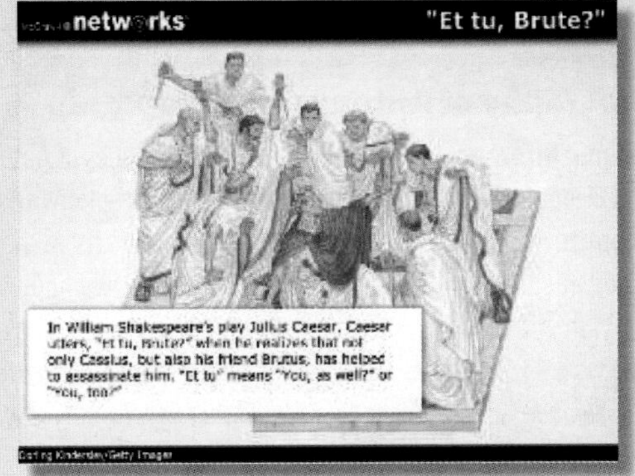

networks
"Et tu, Brute?"
In William Shakespeare's play Julius Caesar, Caesar utters, "Et tu, Brute?" when he realizes that not only Cassius, but also his friend Brutus, has helped to assassinate him. "Et tu" means "You, as well?" or "You, too?"

The End of the Republic

R Reading Skills

Discussing Direct students to read the entire page. Discuss the actions Caesar took once he became dictator. **Ask: What reforms did Caesar introduce to Rome?** *(He gave citizenship to people in the territories, created jobs for the unemployed, organized new settlements for landless laborers, ordered landowners to hire more free workers, and introduced a new calendar.)* AL **Who would likely have been in favor of these reforms and who likely would have opposed them?** *(Answers will vary, although students should suggest that the reforms mainly benefited the poor and not the wealthy Romans.)* BL

T Technology Skills

Using Digital Tools Ask interested students to work together to create a digital mockup of the front page of a modern newspaper that reports the death of Caesar as he entered the Senate. Students may have to do some research to find details about the death of Caesar. Have them use a word processing program to create a mock newspaper page, with various sizes and types of fonts. Students should write at least two articles for this front page, an article reporting the murder and an editorial commenting on the death. Students might also include a sidebar with the observations of a witness to the act. Students can either project the page onto a wall or whiteboard for the class to see or print the page and attach it to the classroom wall. BL **Interpersonal**

Content Background Knowledge

The Julian calendar, named after Julius Caesar's first name, was adopted at the start of 45 B.C., when Caesar added 90 days to 46 B.C. before starting the new year. The Julian calendar was a great improvement on previous calendars, but it had a problem: it assumed the solar year to be about 11 minutes shorter than it actually is. This made no real difference for many centuries, but by the sixteenth century A.D., the Julian calendar was about 10 days off. Pope Gregory XIII appointed an astronomer to fix the problem. The calendar that the astronomer developed, the Gregorian calendar, is the one we still use today. It was named after Pope Gregory XIII.

ANSWER, p. 325

PROGRESS CHECK They thought he had become too powerful and that he wanted to be king.

The End of the Republic

R Reading Skills

Defining Have students read the biographies of Mark Antony and Cleopatra. **Ask: What does *alliance* mean?** *(a union between persons, families, or parties)* ELL **Why do you think Mark Antony and Cleopatra formed an alliance?** *(Answers will vary, but students should suggest that the pair wanted to gain power and rule Rome.)* **Can you think of an example of a modern-day alliance?** *(Answers will vary, but students may describe an incident with their friends or cite an example from a reality television show.)*

C Critical Thinking Skills

Sequencing Explain to students that you are going to make a chart showing the sequence of events surrounding the Second Triumvirate. Begin by writing the name of Julius Caesar on the left. Draw an arrow from the name. **Ask: How did his rule end?** *(Caesar was killed.)* **Who took power after Julius Caesar died?** *(the Second Triumvirate)*

Have students complete the flowchart by writing the names of each of the members *(Mark Antony, Marcus Lepidus, and Octavian).* Then have students complete the chart showing which territories each man ruled and what happened to each after the Second Triumvirate fell apart.

(Lepidus ⟶ North Africa ⟶ retired from politics

Antony ⟶ Greece and east ⟶ formed an alliance with Cleopatra ⟶ went to war with Octavian

Octavian ⟶ Italy and the west ⟶ declared war on Antony)

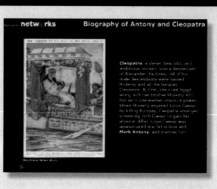

ANSWER, p. 326

CRITICAL THINKING They were supporters of Caesar and wanted to avenge his death. Octavian accused Antony of plotting to take over Rome with Cleopatra's help.

BIOGRAPHIES

R

Mark Antony
(83 B.C. – 30 B.C.)

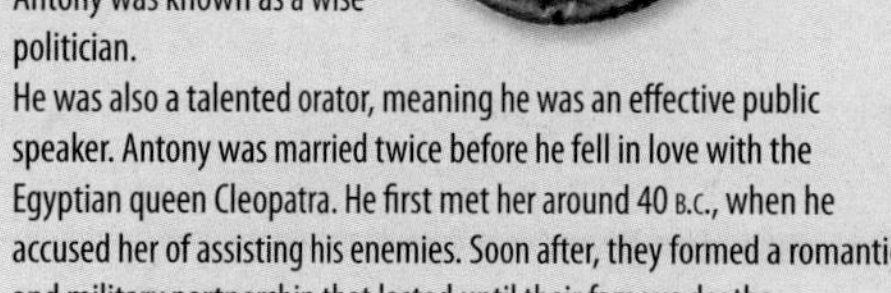

Mark Antony, a Roman, supported Caesar during the civil war between Caesar and Pompey. Antony was known as a wise politician. He was also a talented orator, meaning he was an effective public speaker. Antony was married twice before he fell in love with the Egyptian queen Cleopatra. He first met her around 40 B.C., when he accused her of assisting his enemies. Soon after, they formed a romantic and military partnership that lasted until their famous deaths.

Cleopatra
(69 B.C. – 30 B.C.)

Cleopatra was the daughter of an Egyptian king. When her father died in 51 B.C., Cleopatra took the throne with her brother. They soon became rivals. To hold onto the throne, Cleopatra formed an alliance with Julius Caesar. After Caesar died, Cleopatra allied herself with Mark Antony. When they fled to Egypt, Antony, it is said, heard a false report that Cleopatra had died. Deeply saddened, he killed himself. After Cleopatra buried him, she then took her own life.

▶ **CRITICAL THINKING**
Explaining Why did Mark Antony and Octavian first join forces? Why did Mark Antony and Octavian become divided?

From Republic to Empire

GUIDING QUESTION ***How did Rome become an empire?***

After Caesar's death, civil war broke out. Caesar's 18-year-old grandnephew Octavian (ahk•TAY•vee•uhn) joined two of Caesar's top generals, Mark Antony (AN•tuh•nee) and Marcus Lepidus (LEH•puh•duhs). The three leaders' forces defeated those who killed Caesar. In 43 B.C., they formed the Second Triumvirate. Next, they divided the Roman Empire among themselves. Octavian took command of Italy and the west. Antony ruled in Greece and the east. Lepidus took charge in North Africa.

C Antony and Cleopatra

The Second Triumvirate, however, did not last long. Lepidus retired from politics. Soon Octavian and Antony became rivals. Antony fell in love with the Egyptian queen Cleopatra. Together, they formed an alliance. Octavian accused Antony and Cleopatra of plotting against Rome. According to Octavian, Antony planned to make himself the sole ruler of the republic with Cleopatra's help. Many Romans grew alarmed at this news. Their support **enabled** Octavian to declare war on Antony.

In 31 B.C., Octavian and Antony's navies clashed off the coast of Greece. At the Battle of Actium (AK•shee•uhm), Octavian's forces defeated those of Antony and Cleopatra. Within a year,

Reading HELPDESK CCSS

Academic Vocabulary (Tier 2 Words)

enable to make possible

networks ***Online Teaching Options***

SLIDE SHOW

Biography of Antony and Cleopatra

Making Inferences Present the interactive images of Antony and Cleopatra. Ask volunteers to read aloud the captions and informative text from the slides. Invite students to share their observations and thoughts about the lives of the two figures. **Ask: Why do you think the Romans wanted to stop Antony and Cleopatra from ruling Rome?** *(Possible response: Cleopatra was not a Roman, so they might have feared that Egypt would take control of Rome.)*

See page 303E for other online activities.

The End of the Republic

R Octavian captured Alexandria and made Egypt Roman territory. Antony and Cleopatra killed themselves to avoid being captured by Octavian. Octavian became the supreme ruler of Rome. The civil wars had ended and so, too, did the Roman Republic.

Octavian—a New Direction

Octavian could have made himself a life-long dictator. However, he knew that many Romans favored a republic. These Romans were influenced by Cicero (SIH•suh•ROH) who was a well-known political leader and writer in Rome. Cicero strongly supported the representative, republican government. Cicero also did not trust dictators.

Throughout Rome's civil wars, Cicero had argued that a representative government should be restored to Rome. He died before Octavian rose to power. Cicero's ideas, however, would influence the writers of the United States Constitution centuries later.

C Publicly, Octavian voiced his support for a republic. Privately, however, Octavian felt differently. He believed that a republican government was too weak to solve Rome's problems. Octavian felt that Rome needed a strong leader. With a strong and loyal army supporting Octavian, the Senate consented to his wishes. It declared Octavian consul, tribune, and commander-in-chief for life in 27 B.C. Octavian, however, took the title *Augustus* (aw•GUHS•tuhs), or "the majestic one." Caesar Augustus, as Octavian was now called, became Rome's first emperor, or all-powerful ruler.

Octavian overcame many obstacles to become emperor of Rome.

▶ CRITICAL THINKING

Analyzing How did Octavian's leadership differ from Caesar's?

PROGRESS CHECK

Predicting How do you think Cicero might have reacted when the Senate named Octavian the first emperor of Rome?

LESSON 3 REVIEW

Review Vocabulary (Tier 3 Words)

1. Why did the creation of *latifundia* cause poor people to move to cities? RH.6–8.2, RH.6–8.4

Answer the Guiding Questions

2. ***Understanding Cause and Effect*** How did the election of Marius as consul reflect a change in Rome's government? RH.6–8.2, RH.6–8.5
3. ***Summarizing*** What changes did Julius Caesar bring about as ruler of Rome? RH.6–8.2
4. ***Explaining*** How did Octavian's rule serve as a transition from Roman republic to empire? RH.6–8.2
5. ***Identifying*** Who was Caesar Augustus? RH.6–8.2
6. **NARRATIVE** You own a small Roman farm in the 100s B.C. Write a letter to a friend describing the changes you have witnessed in agriculture and the Roman government. Describe how those changes have affected you personally. WHST.6–8.10

R Reading Skills

Explaining Before students read the paragraph, have them recall the definition of *republic. (a form of government in which citizens elect their leaders)* **Ask:** Why was there no Roman Republic when the civil wars ended? *(Octavian became the supreme ruler of Rome. Since he hadn't been elected as leader, by definition Rome was no longer a republic.)* BL

C Critical Thinking Skills

Evaluating Discuss with students the way Octavian voiced his support for the republic while taking steps to become emperor. **Ask:** Why didn't Octavian just declare himself emperor? *(By voicing support for the republic, Octavian was able to gain support of the Romans and the senators, who then agreed to name him emperor anyway.)* BL

Have students complete the Lesson 3 Review.

CLOSE & REFLECT

To close the lesson, go around the room and call on students to briefly describe each of the following Roman leaders: the Gracchus brothers, Marius, Sulla, Crassus, Pompey, Julius Caesar, Mark Antony, Marcus Lepidus, and Octavian. For each leader, allow time for other students to add important details to the initial description. **Verbal/Linguistic**

LESSON 3 REVIEW ANSWERS

1. Latifundia were large estates whose owners used slaves and would not hire farmers. As a result, farmers lost their land and moved to the city for work.
2. Marius was the first military general to become consul, which led to more military leaders seeking control of the government.
3. Caesar expanded citizenship and introduced reforms that helped the poor, but he also ended the republic by becoming Rome's first dictator for life.
4. Octavian's rule served as a transition because he came to power at the end of the republic, but then the Senate declared him commander-in-chief for life. In addition, Octavian took the title of emperor.
5. Octavian was the Roman general who captured Egypt and later became emperor.
6. Responses will vary. Letters should reflect the changes in farming and government described in the lesson.

ANSWERS, p. 327

CRITICAL THINKING Octavian did not believe in the republic. He favored one all-powerful ruler.

PROGRESS CHECK He might have spoken out against the decision to make Octavian an emperor because he favored a republic, with elected leaders, rather than a dictatorship.

Rome Builds an Empire

ENGAGE

Bellringer Ask students to choose the most important accomplishment they have learned about so far in this chapter and identify two reasons the accomplishment is the most important. Have students share their ideas in a Think-Pair-Share activity. Begin by leading a short class discussion to help students brainstorm examples of important Roman accomplishments. Then divide the class into small groups, and ask each group to come to a consensus about *the* most important accomplishment they've learned about and to write down two reasons for their choice. Then invite groups to share their conclusions with the class. As each group identifies its selection, invite comments from the rest of the class. Finally, explain that in this lesson, students will learn about the events and accomplishments that marked the rule of Augustus and his successors.

TEACH & ASSESS

R Reading Skills

Defining Ask a volunteer to pronounce *Pax Romana*. Explain that this is a Latin phrase. **Ask:** What does the Latin word *pax* mean? *(peace)* ELL When did *Pax Romana* begin and end? *(It began when Caesar Augustus became emperor—in 27 B.C.—and ended in about A.D. 180.)* How would you characterize the Roman Empire in general terms during the *Pax Romana*? *(It was a time of peace and prosperity.)*

ANSWER, p. 328

TAKING NOTES: created permanent professional army; established defendable boundaries; built many public buildings and palaces; established proconsuls; reformed tax system; reformed legal system

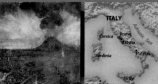

networks
There's More Online!
- GRAPHIC ORGANIZER
  Achievements of Emperor Augustus
- SLIDE SHOW
  - Buildings in Rome
  - Pompeii and Mt. Vesuvius
  - The Five Good Emperors
- VIDEO

Lesson 4

Rome Builds an Empire

ESSENTIAL QUESTION *What are the characteristics of a leader?*

IT MATTERS BECAUSE
The achievements of the Roman Empire influenced the Western world for centuries and continued to affect the modern world today.

The Rule of Augustus

GUIDING QUESTION *How did Augustus create a new age of prosperity for Rome?*

The rule of Caesar Augustus (formerly called Octavian) marked the beginning of a new era. For nearly two hundred years, the Roman world enjoyed peace and prosperity. This time period lasted until about A.D. 180. It is known as the ***Pax Romana*** (PAHKS roh•MAH•nah), or "Roman Peace." During this time, Rome reached the height of its power.

What Reforms Did Augustus Make?

As emperor, Augustus was determined to protect the empire. To do this, he created a permanent professional army. About 150,000 soldiers—all Roman citizens—made up this powerful military force. In addition, Augustus created a special unit known as the Praetorian Guard. The 9,000 men in this select unit guarded the emperor.

Augustus thought that Rome's borders should be easier to defend. He established the empire's boundaries along natural physical features. These included the Rhine (RYN) River and Danube (DAN•yoob) River to the north, the Atlantic Ocean to the west, the Sahara to the south, and near the Euphrates River to the east. Troops were stationed along these frontier areas to protect the empire from invaders.

Reading HELPDESK CCSS

Taking Notes: *Identifying*
Use a web diagram like this one to identify the important achievements of Emperor Augustus. RH.6–8.2

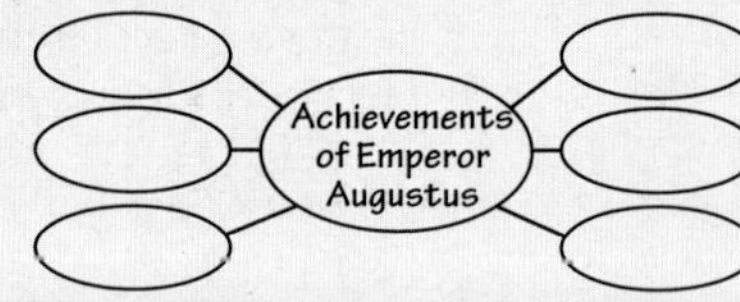

Content Vocabulary (Tier 3 Words)
- ***Pax Romana***
- **proconsul**

networks ***Online Teaching Options***

VIDEO

The Roman World

Summarizing Have students watch the video about the Roman world. Then divide the class into small groups, and ask each group to create a list of five Roman inventions or ideas that can be seen in modern-day life. *(Answers will vary but may include some of the following: language, law, government, architecture, military, art, theater, entertainment venues, calendar, coins.)* After they have finished, invite each group to read its list to the class. After all have been read, invite discussion of other aspects of ancient Rome that can be seen in our world today.

See page 303F for other online activities.

Rome Builds an Empire

Augustus rebuilt many of Rome's buildings in marble to reflect the city's grandeur.

Victoria & Albert Museum, London/Bridgeman Art Library

V

In addition to protecting the empire, Augustus wanted to display the power of Rome. Augustus had many public buildings, fountains, and palaces rebuilt to reflect the greatness of Rome. "I found Rome a city of brick," he boasted, "and left it a city of marble."

Augustus also worked to improve Rome's government. Duringhis reign, more than 50 million people lived within the empire's borders. This is slightly fewer than the number of people living in Italy today. To maintain control over his empire, Augustus named an official called a **proconsul** (PROH•KAHN•suhl), or governor, to oversee each of Rome's provinces. These new local officials replaced the politicians who had been appointed by the Senate. Augustus himself often visited the provinces to **inspect** the work of the proconsuls. C

W

With new leaders in place, Augustus changed the empire's tax system. Before Augustus, tax collectors paid the government for the right to collect taxes. Tax collectors could keep some of what they collected from the people. Many tax collectors, however, were dishonest and took too much from the people. To solve this problem, Augustus made tax collectors permanent government officials and paid them regular wages.

Augustus also changed Rome's legal system. He created a code of laws for people living in the provinces who were not Roman citizens. As time passed, most of these people became citizens, so eventually, the laws were applied to everyone. However, the legal system often favored the authority of the empire over individual citizens' rights.

Pax Romana Roman peace
proconsul governor

Academic Vocabulary (Tier 2 Words)
inspect to look over carefully

V Visual Skills

Analyzing Images Have students examine the image of Rome under Augustus. **Ask:** As you look at the panorama of ancient Rome under Augustus, what comes to mind about this city? *(Answers will vary, although students should mention how large the city is and the number of large buildings.)* Why would Augustus boast about changing a "city of brick" into a "city of marble"? (Answer will vary, but students should suggest that the beauty of marble would be a symbol of greatness and elegance.) **Visual/Spatial**

W Writing Skills

Argument Have students work in small groups to come up with a slogan that Augustus could have used to promote his accomplishments throughout the land. Explain to students that this slogan would be Augustus's way to tell the Roman people that his reforms are justified and beneficial for all. Have groups present their slogans to the rest of the class. Discuss how, even though he was dictator, Augustus still made efforts to keep the public's opinion of him favorable.

C Critical Thinking Skills

Making Inferences Ask students to discuss the changes Augustus made to local government. *(He replaced the local politicians appointed by the Senate with proconsuls that he appointed.)* **Ask:** How did the changes made by Augustus affect Rome's representative government? *(It weakened it because local officials were now appointed by a dictator instead of elected by the people.)* BL

SLIDE SHOW

Buildings in Rome

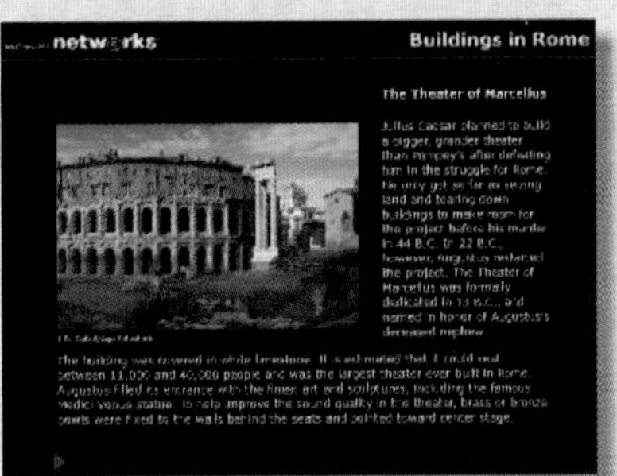

Analyzing Visuals Present the interactive slide show on the Roman Colosseum, the Roman Forum, and the Theater of Marcellus. Explain that these structures were public projects that were also architectural wonders of their time. Ask students to brainstorm examples of other large structures that are considered wonders today. Then **ask:** How did these buildings serve the people of Rome? *(The theater held performances and displayed art and sculptures. The Forum was a center of Roman government. The Colosseum was a massive stadium that hosted contests for the public's entertainment.)* Make sure students understand that the buildings were not only prized for their functionality but also for their grandeur. They made Rome look like a sophisticated and wealthy place.

See page 303F for other online activities.

G1 Critical Thinking Skills

Contrasting Have students discuss the section "Emperors After Augustus." **Ask:** **What was the sequence of Roman emperors after Augustus died?** *(Tiberius, Caligula, Claudius, Nero)* **How were all these emperors connected with one another?** *(They were all from Augustus's family.)* **How did Caligula and Nero differ from Tiberius and Claudius?** *(Caligula and Nero were cruel rulers; Tiberius and Claudius ruled effectively.)* AL

G2 Critical Thinking Skills

Making Connections As a class, discuss the disasters that struck Rome while Titus was emperor. **Ask:** **What destroyed the city of Pompeii?** *(a volcano—Mt. Vesuvius—erupting)* **What damaged Rome?** *(a bad fire)* AL **Can you think of disasters that have struck the United States in recent years?** *(Answers will vary, but students may mention hurricanes, tornadoes, wildfires, or severe snowstorms or rainstorms.)* To close the discussion, ask how cities or regions recover from these types of disasters.

T Technology Skills

Making Presentations Have students examine the illustrations of Pompeii then and now. Ask a volunteer to read the caption aloud. Then have students turn back to the chapter-opening mosaic of the wealthy woman of Pompeii. Explain that the remains of Pompeii, discovered in the 1700s, have provided wonderful details about life in the Roman Empire. Ask for volunteers to use an Internet search engine to find images of buildings, art, and artifacts from the ruins of Pompeii. Suggest that they use search terms such as "Pompeii ruins," "Pompeii art," and "Pompeii artifacts." Have them select a variety of images from their search results and put together a presentation for the class using Microsoft PowerPoint or another presentation software. **Visual/Spatial**

Natural disasters can shape people's interactions with their environment. In August A.D. 79 the volcano Mt. Vesuvius erupted and destroyed the city of Pompeii, in what is now Italy. Several thousand people escaped, while thousands more died. Today, about 600,000 people live near the volcano, although scientists warn it may be due to erupt again soon.

▶ **CRITICAL THINKING**
Analyzing Why might people live in an area where a natural disaster has happened?

Despite all of his reforms, Augustus feared that people might still be unhappy with his leadership. To preserve his rule and the empire, Augustus imported grain from Africa and **distributed** it to the poor. Augustus believed that a well-fed population would be less likely to revolt against him.

Emperors After Augustus

Augustus ruled Rome for almost 40 years. After Augustus died in A.D. 14, his adopted son, Tiberius, became emperor. After Tiberius, three other emperors from Augustus's family ruled Rome—Caligula (kuh•LIH•gyuh•luh), Claudius, and Nero (NEE•roh). They are known as the Julio-Claudian emperors. Tiberius and Claudius governed the empire effectively. In **contrast**, Caligula and Nero proved to be cruel rulers.

Caligula murdered many people and spent money recklessly. He even appointed his favorite horse as consul. The Praetorian Guard murdered him and made Claudius emperor.

Nero was also a brutal emperor who killed many people. Among his victims were his mother and two wives. Nero committed suicide after the Senate had sentenced him to death for treason.

☑ **PROGRESS CHECK**

Explaining How did Augustus protect Rome's borders?

The Roman Peace

GUIDING QUESTION *How did the Roman Empire become rich and prosperous?*

After Nero died, violence erupted throughout the Roman Empire. Then, in A.D. 69, a general named Vespasian (veh•SPAY•zhee•uhn), became emperor. Vespasian restored order, but he treated harshly anyone who opposed Roman rule. Vespasian crushed several uprisings throughout the empire. One such uprising was the Jewish revolt in the eastern province of Judaea. Vespasian's son, Titus, commanded troops that defeated the Jewish rebels. Roman soldiers also destroyed the Jewish temple in Jerusalem in A.D. 70.

Vespasian began the construction of the Colosseum, the huge amphitheater located in central Rome. After Vespasian died, his sons Titus and Domitian each governed Rome. While Titus was emperor, two disasters struck the empire. In A.D. 79, the volcano Mount Vesuvius erupted, destroying the city of Pompeii. A year later, a great fire badly damaged Rome. Both sons, however, ruled during an era of relative growth and prosperity.

Reading HELPDESK CCSS

Academic Vocabulary (Tier 2 Words)

distribute to give or deliver to members of a group
contrast the act of comparing by looking at differences

networks Online Teaching Options

SLIDE SHOW

Pompeii and Mount Vesuvius

Discussing Present the slide show about Pompeii and Mount Vesuvius. After a volunteer reads aloud the informational text, ask students for their reactions to the images. Allow students time to answer the discussion question on the last slide. **Auditory**

See page 303F for other online activities.

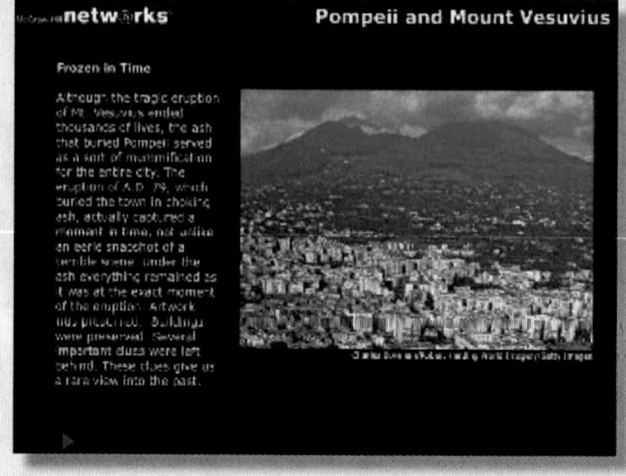

ANSWERS, p. 330

☑ **PROGRESS CHECK** He established them along natural boundaries and stationed troops along the borders to fight off invaders.

CRITICAL THINKING Answers will vary but may include: jobs and family are nearby; the area is "home"; people might think the natural disaster will not happen again.

THE "GOOD EMPERORS" OF THE *PAX ROMANA*

Nerva
A.D. 96–A.D. 98
Revised taxes; land reforms helped the poor

Trajan
A.D. 98–A.D. 117
Greatly expanded the empire; gave money for education

Hadrian
A.D. 117–A.D. 138
Made Roman law easier to understand and apply

Antoninus Pius
A.D. 138–A.D. 161
Enacted laws that assisted orphans

Marcus Aurelius
A.D. 161–A.D. 180
Reformed Roman law; assisted in uniting empire's economy

INFOGRAPHIC

These emperors, who earned the title the Five Good Emperors, together ruled for almost 75 years.

1. **IDENTIFYING** Under which emperor did the empire grow significantly?
2. **CRITICAL THINKING** ***Analyzing*** How would the contributions of Hadrian and Marcus Aurelius affect the empire's legal system?

Five Good Emperors

During the early A.D. 100s, several emperors who were not related to Augustus or Vespasian ruled the empire. Nerva, Trajan, Hadrian, Antoninus Pius, and Marcus Aurelius are known as the "good emperors." The five "good emperors" did not abuse their power. They were among the most **capable** rulers in Rome's history.

The five emperors governed during a time of economic growth. Agriculture and trade flourished during this period, which lasted from A.D. 96 to A.D. 180. Tertullian, a Roman writer, described this time:

PRIMARY SOURCE

> "All places are now accessible [easy to reach], all are well known, all open to commerce . . . cultivated fields have subdued [tamed] forests . . . marshes are drained; and where once were . . . solitary cottages, there are now large cities. . . everywhere are houses, and inhabitants, and settled government, and civilized life."
>
> —from *Treatise on the Soul* by Tertullian

The five emperors introduced programs to help the empire's people. For example, Trajan made money available so that poor children could receive an education. Hadrian made Roman laws easier for ordinary citizens to understand.

Academic Vocabulary (Tier 2 Words)

capable able, competent

W Writing Skills

Informative/Explanatory Ask students to write a brief profile of each of the five "good emperors" featured in the infographic at the top of this page. Have them use what they read in the text as well as the caption under the portrait of each of the emperors. Each profile should contain two or three sentences. Remind students this will give them good practice taking notes and will serve as an excellent study guide for this section.

R Reading Skills

Citing Text Evidence Ask a volunteer to read the excerpt from Tertullian to the class. Then have students assess Tertullian's point of view based on his description. **Ask: Is he positive or negative about trade in the Roman Empire? How can you tell?** *(Answers may vary, but most students will say that Tartullian is positive. He does not use negative words or images. The words he chose, such as* open, subdued, settled, *and* civilized, *are positive.)*

C Critical Thinking Skills

Making Connections Have students identify similarities between the actions of the Roman emperors covered in this lesson with the actions made by modern governments. *(Possible answers include the concept that both governments used or use tax money for building projects, for education, to improve roads, and so on.)* Discuss how effective these actions were in creating or maintaining wealth, prosperity, and stability in the Roman Empire. Then discuss how students see the effectiveness of similar actions in modern times. BL

SLIDE SHOW

The Five Good Emperors

Listing Play the interactive slide show about the Five Good Emperors. Have students identify the accomplishments of each emperor. Then have students discuss this question. **Ask: Which of these five emperors do you think did the most for Rome? Provide examples to support your opinion.** *(Sample response: I think Hadrian did the most for Rome. He strengthened Rome's borders and kept the empire safe from invaders.)* Next, ask for volunteers to read their responses to the class. Allow students to discuss any differences in their opinions. Then ask students if they have changed their opinions as a result of listening to others presenting their responses. AL

See page 303F for other online activities.

ANSWERS, p. 331

INFOGRAPHIC

1. Trajan
2. **CRITICAL THINKING** Under Hadrian, more people would understand the law. Marcus Aurelius reformed the law.

Rome Builds an Empire

V Visual Skills

Analyzing Maps Direct students' attention to the map showing the trade routes of the Roman Empire at the top of this page. After students have had time to study the details on the map and the key, **ask:**

- **What goods came to Rome from Britain?** *(metals and wool)*
- **What goods came to Rome from northern Africa?** *(wild animals and timber)*
- **From where did Rome receive spices and silk?** *(China)*

Tell students that there is an old saying: "All roads lead to Rome." **Ask: Does this map support that saying?** *(Yes, because all the trade routes on this map lead to the city of Rome.)* **Visual/Spatial**

T Technology Skills

Researching on the Internet Ask students to use the Internet to locate an image of an aqueduct. Discuss the technical achievement of building such a massive structure to carry water. Ask students what skills and types of labor might have been required to build an aqueduct. *(excellent engineering skills, as well as the efforts of many people)* **Ask: Why was the aqueduct system important to Rome?** *(It provided the city with water.)* **How would Rome have been different without the aqueduct system in place?** *(Rome would not have been such an efficient city because people would have had to spend a lot of time finding and carrying water instead of focusing on business, politics, or the arts.)* BL

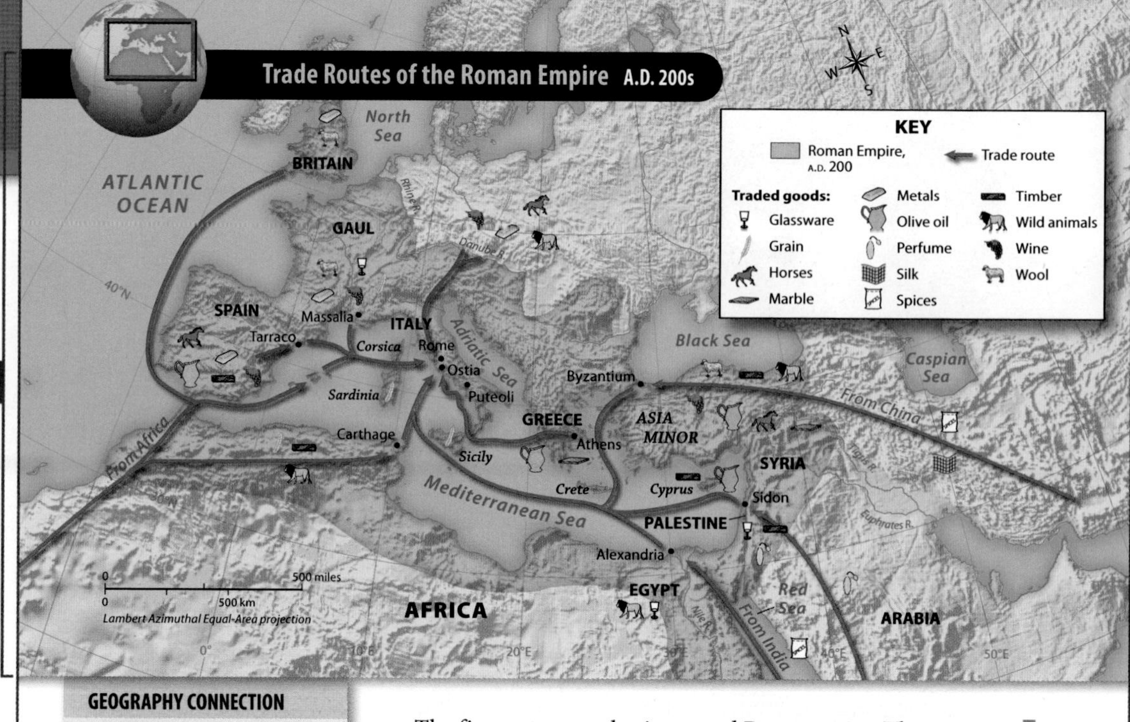

GEOGRAPHY CONNECTION

Trade goods flowed to Rome and kept the city well supplied.

1. **PLACE** Which areas of the empire shipped timber to Rome?
2. **CRITICAL THINKING** ***Drawing Conclusions*** Why do you think Romans traded for horses and wild animals?

The five emperors also improved Roman cities. They spent tax money to build arches and monuments, bridges, roads, and harbors. They also built extensive **aqueducts** (A•kwuh•duhkts) to bring water from the country to the city.

A United Empire

The Emperor Trajan expanded the Roman Empire to its maximum size. The empire's borders extended to Britain in the northwest and Mesopotamia in the east.

Trajan's **successors** believed that the empire had become too large to rule effectively. They withdrew Roman forces from regions they could not defend and reinforced areas that were easier to protect. Hadrian pulled troops from Mesopotamia but strengthened defenses at the Rhine and Danube rivers.

By the A.D. 100s, the Roman Empire was one of the largest empires in history. Its land area was about 3.5 million square miles (9.1 million square km), almost the size of the United States.

Reading HELPDESK CCSS

Academic Vocabulary (Tier 2 Words)

successor one that comes after

Visual Vocabulary

aqueduct a human-made channel that carries water long distances

networks Online Teaching Options

MAP

Trade Routes of the Roman Empire, A.D. 200s

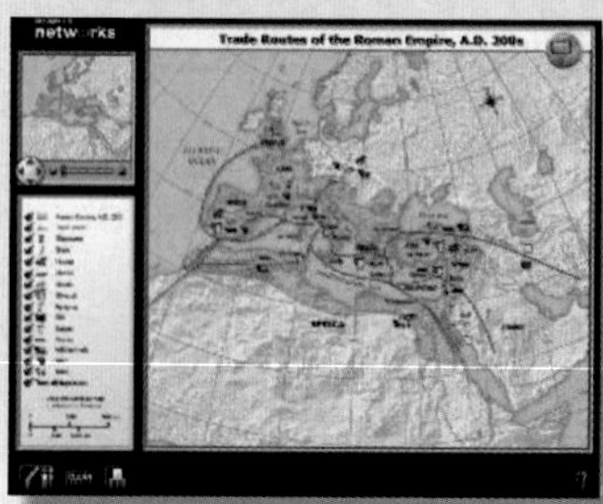

Reading a Map Students can reveal and hide the map's information by clicking on the icon next to each item, including all the trade goods, the trade routes, and the territory of the empire in A.D. 200. Students can also use the zoom function at the upper left to scroll the map to the right or left and then zoom into a specific area. Display the interactive map on the whiteboard and begin with all the layers off. Then have students click on the various elements one by one. **Ask: What color are the trade routes on this map?** *(red)* ELL **What goods came to Rome from Arabia?** *(perfume)* **Good from India traveled through which port city on their way to Rome?** *(Alexandria)* **Which countries shipped marble to Rome?** *(Greece and Syria)* **Visual/Spatial**

See page 303F for other online activities.

ANSWERS, p. 332

GEOGRAPHY CONNECTION

1. Spain, Africa, Cyprus, and Asia Minor shipped timber to Rome.
2. **CRITICAL THINKING** Horses and wild animals were probably not native to Rome. They had to be imported.

Many groups of people lived in the Roman Empire. Roman law, Roman rule, and a shared Roman identity united them all. By A.D. 212, every free person within the empire was considered a Roman citizen. All citizens were treated equally under Roman laws.

The Empire's Economy

Agriculture remained the most important economic activity in the Roman Empire. Most people were farmers. Farmers in northern Italy and in the provinces of Gaul and Spain grew grapes and olives to make wine and olive oil. Grain from Britain, Sicily, and Egypt supplied Rome's people with food.

Industry thrived in the cities. Potters, weavers, and jewelers produced pottery, cloth, and jewelry. Other artisans made glass, bronze, and brass. These goods were exported throughout the Mediterranean region.

Trade flourished. By A.D. 100, a common Roman system of money was used within the empire. Merchants used the same money in Gaul, Greece, or Egypt as they did in Rome. People also used a standard system of weights and measurements.

A network of paved roads extended throughout the empire. The roads allowed the Romans to communicate and move armies and goods easily. The Roman navy eliminated piracy on the Mediterranean Sea and other waterways. As a result, goods could be shipped safely to and from the empire's ports.

Traders from all over the empire arrived in Rome's port cities. Traders sold luxury goods to wealthy Romans. The Romans also imported raw materials, such as British tin and Spanish silver and lead. Roman workshops turned them into different goods.

Trade made many people wealthy. The wealth, however, did not extend to all Romans. Most city dwellers and farmers remained poor, and many other people remained enslaved.

✓ PROGRESS CHECK

Analyzing Why were five of Rome's rulers known as the "good emperors"?

LESSON 4 REVIEW (CCSS)

Review Vocabulary (Tier 3 Words)

1. What was the role of a *proconsul* under Augustus? RH.6–8.2, RH.6–8.4

Answer the Guiding Questions

2. ***Explaining*** How did the changes that Augustus made to the Roman tax system reduce government corruption? RH.6–8.2
3. ***Analyzing*** How did roads contribute to the empire's success? RH.6–8.2
4. ***Drawing Conclusions*** What do you think was the greatest achievement of Augustus? RH.6–8.2
5. **INFORMATIVE/EXPLANATORY** You are a Roman living around A.D. 215. Write an essay about how the Roman Empire has changed since the reign of Trajan. As an ordinary citizen, which change affects you most? WHST.6–8.2, WHST.6–8.10

Lesson 4 333

LESSON 4 REVIEW ANSWERS

1. The proconsul acted as a governor over the province.
2. Augustus converted tax collectors into paid government employees.
3. Roads made trading, communication, and military movement easier.
4. Answers will vary. Sample answer: Augustus's greatest achievement was stabilizing the Roman government, which led to the formation of the Roman Empire.
5. Essays should mention that the empire began to shrink since the reign of Trajan, when it was at its maximum size. Roman forces withdrew from places they could not easily defend. Also, all free people were treated equally under Roman law. Students may suggest that legal reforms would have had the most impact on their lives as ordinary citizens. Because of these changes, a judge would have to treat ordinary citizens fairly.

Rome Builds an Empire

R Reading Skills

Discussing Have students read the section on the Roman Empire's economy. Discuss what made up the economy of the Roman Empire in the *Pax Romana* era. **Ask: Where did Rome get its food if the farmers of Italy mainly grew grapes and olives?** *(Other parts of the empire sent food to Rome, including Britain, Sicily, and Egypt.)* **Did people from different parts of the empire become confused with different kinds of money?** *(No, because merchants used the same money in Gaul, Greece, or Egypt as they did in Rome.)* **Did the trade in the empire make everyone wealthy?** *(No. Most city dwellers and farmers remained poor, and many other people remained enslaved.)* AL

Have students complete the Lesson 4 Review.

Content Background Knowledge

Romance Languages Many European languages are called Romance languages, including Portuguese, Spanish, French, Italian, and Romanian. These languages are not called Romance languages because they sound romantic when spoken. They are considered Romance languages because they derive from Latin, the language of the Romans. Today, more than 900 million people speak Romance languages.

CLOSE & REFLECT

To close the lesson, ask students to reflect on whether they would have wanted to live in the Roman Empire during the *Pax Romana*. Call on students to share their thoughts and opinions. Be sure to challenge them to back up their opinions with information learned in this lesson.

ANSWER, p. 333

✓ PROGRESS CHECK They were known as the "good emperors" because they ruled competently and did not abuse their power.

CHAPTER REVIEW ACTIVITY

Have students create a chain of events (sequence) graphic organizer. Ask for volunteers to write one key event in the organizer. Then ask another volunteer to write the event that followed from the previous event. Continue until you have reached the Pax Romana. *(Answers should be factually and chronologically correct, based on the text.)*

REVIEW THE ENDURING UNDERSTANDINGS

Review the chapter's Enduring Understandings with students.

- *People, places, and ideas change over time.*
- *Conflict can lead to change.*
- *Leaders can bring about change in society.*

Now pose the following questions in a class discussion to review the chapter.

- **Ask: How did Rome's location affect the development of the Roman Republic?** *(Answers will vary, but students should mention Italy's central location in the Mediterranean region as well as its mild climate and fertile farmland. Students should also mention location on the Tiber River, which was good for merchants to ship their goods but far enough from the sea to be protected from pirates.)*
- **How did Julius Caesar come to power?** *(After the dictator Sulla stepped down, three men formed the First Triumvirate to rule Rome—Crassus, Pompey, and Julius Caesar. After Crassus died in battle, Pompey became Caesar's main rival. The Senate backed Pompey, but Caesar crossed the Rubicon with his army, marched on Rome, swiftly captured all of Italy, and crushed Pompey's army. Caesar declared himself Rome's dictator for life in 44 B.C.)*
- **What reforms did Augustus make as Rome's first emperor?** *(Augustus created a permanent professional army, named officials called proconsuls to oversee Rome's provinces, changed the empire's tax system, and created a new code of laws.)*

CHAPTER 11 Activities (CCSS)

Write your answers on a separate piece of paper.

1. **Exploring the Essential Question** WHST.6–8.1, WHST.6–8.10
   ARGUMENT Suppose you support the efforts of Tiberius and Gaius Gracchus to reform Rome. Write a letter or speech to other Romans that explains why reform is needed and what types of reforms should occur.

2. **21st Century Skills** WHST.6–8.7, WHST.6–8.8, WHST.6–8.9, WHST.6–8.10
   COLLABORATE WITH OTHERS Use the Internet and your local library to research the Twelve Tables of Rome. Work with your classmates to design a similar series of laws that are needed in society today. Record them, using modern language. How is your law code similar to and different from the Twelve Tables?

3. **Thinking Like a Historian** RH.6–8.2
   PROBLEM SOLVING Roman leaders faced many problems and obstacles in expanding the empire and creating a peaceful society. Using a chart like this one, list some of the major problems they faced and how they solved these problems.

Problem	Solution

4. **GEOGRAPHY ACTIVITY**

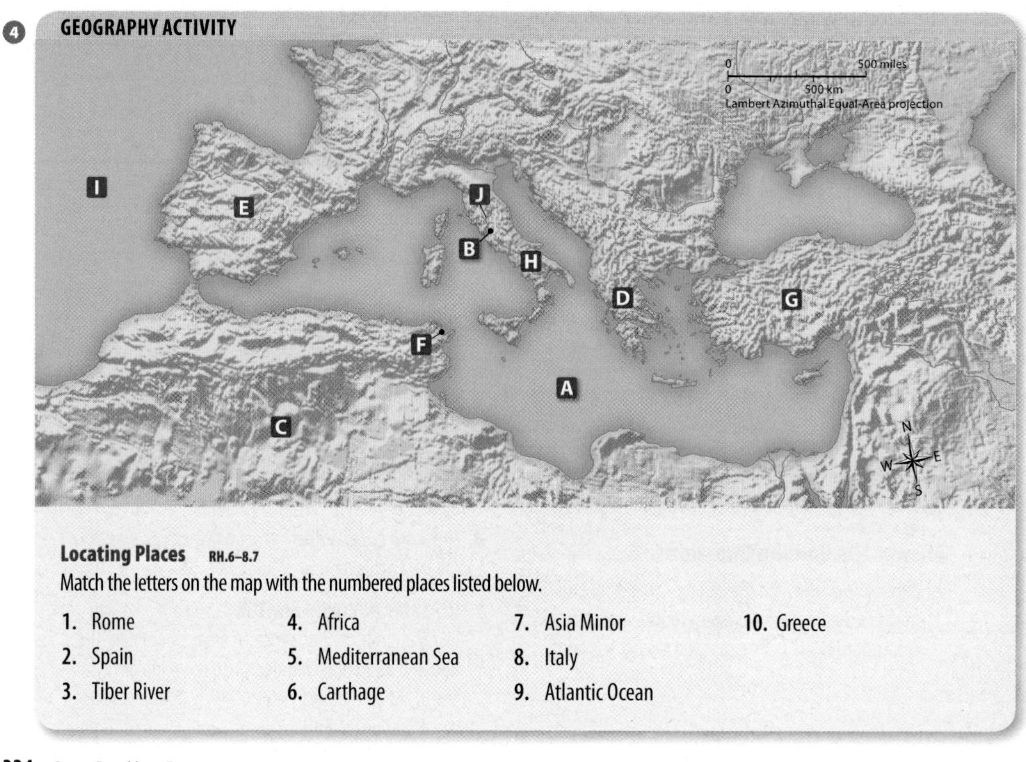

Locating Places RH.6–8.7
Match the letters on the map with the numbered places listed below.

1. Rome
2. Spain
3. Tiber River
4. Africa
5. Mediterranean Sea
6. Carthage
7. Asia Minor
8. Italy
9. Atlantic Ocean
10. Greece

ACTIVITIES ANSWERS

Exploring the Essential Question

1. Suggestions for reform will vary, but students should mention the plan of Tiberius and Gaius Gracchus to provide more land for farmers.

21st Century Skills

2. Students' laws should reflect modern times and situations. Students should compare and contrast their laws to the Twelve Tables, explaining similarities and differences.

Thinking Like a Historian

3. Answers may vary, but some examples might include:

Problem	Solution
Greek battle strategies too slow	Develop legions
Plebeians go on strike	Give them the right to pass laws
Carthage threatens Rome	Fight Punic Wars and defeat Carthage
Urban poor become desperate and angry	Use "bread and circuses" to maintain peace

CHAPTER 11 Assessment

REVIEW THE GUIDING QUESTIONS

Directions: Choose the best answer for each question.

RH.6–8.2
1 Rome conquered Italy by
A. modeling their army after the Greeks.
B. treating everyone fairly.
C. creating an alliance with the Etruscans.
D. developing a flexible, strong army.

RH.6–8.2
2 Early Rome was protected from pirate raids because
F. it had a strong army.
G. pirates were afraid of Romulus, the founder of Rome.
H. it was located far enough from the Mediterranean Sea.
I. there was no treasure in Rome.

RH.6–8.2
3 Plebeians forced the patricians to treat them more equally by
A. vetoing the law that did not allow plebeians and patricians to marry.
B. refusing to serve in the army.
C. electing more plebeians to the Senate.
D. demanding that women be allowed to vote.

RH.6–8.2
4 What was the body of laws that served as the foundation for all future Roman laws called?
F. Twelve Tables
G. Roman Constitution
H. Law of Nations
I. Rule of Law

RH.6–8.2
5 Caesar took control of the republic by
A. making peace with his rivals.
B. starting a civil war with Pompey.
C. winning support of the poor Romans.
D. taking control of the Rubicon River.

RH.6–8.2, RH.6–8.4
6 During the *Pax Romana*
F. textiles became the empire's most important industry.
G. agriculture, industry, and trade flourished.
H. the Empire decreased in power.
I. Emperor Hadrian built the Colosseum.

335

Locating Places

4 **1.** B Rome; **2.** E Spain; **3.** J Tiber River; **4.** C Africa; **5.** A Mediterranean Sea; **6.** F Carthage; **7.** G Asia Minor; **8.** H Italy; **9.** I Atlantic Ocean; **10.** D Greece

CHAPTER 11
Assessment Answers

ASSESSMENT ANSWERS

Review the Guiding Questions

1 **D** Rome developed a disciplined and loyal army. Romans also created more flexible battle strategies, which allowed them to fight more effectively and conquer more territory. Although the Romans treated conquered peoples fairly, they did not find success in modeling their army after the Greeks, and they did not form an alliance with the Etruscans.

2 **H** Rome's location along the Tiber River, about 15 miles from the Mediterranean Sea, helped protect it from pirate raids. Early Rome did not have a strong army, a scary founder, or a lack of treasure.

3 **B** It was the plebeians' strike against serving in the military that prompted the patricians to give them more equal rights under the law.

4 **F** The Twelve Tables were the original foundation of Roman Law. None of the other statements apply to the question.

5 **B** Caesar started and won a civil war with Pompey, which led to him becoming dictator for life. He crossed but did not control the Rubicon. He won the support of poor Romans after becoming dictator. He did not make peace with his rivals.

6 **G** It is true that during the *Pax Romana*, agriculture, industry, and trade flourished. None of the other statements are true about the *Pax Romana*.

Assessment Answers

Analyzing Documents

7 **D** It is clear from the quote that Augustus rewarded his soldiers well—with money and land—and that is why citizens wanted to serve in the Roman army.

8 **H** The most likely benefit to Augustus was troops' loyalty.

Short Response

9 They were more courageous under Caesar's leadership than under the leadership of others.

10 Students' answers may vary but might include that Caesar's soldiers were inspired by their leader's bravery and the fact that he would not use his rank to get out of doing any type of work.

Extended Response

11 Responses will vary. Students should cite their chosen leader's accomplishments. They should use evidence from the text to explain why that leader was better than the other Roman leaders.

CHAPTER 11 Assessment (continued)

DBQ ANALYZING DOCUMENTS

RH.6–8.2, RH.6–8.6

7 **Drawing Conclusions** Augustus wrote a historical document describing his accomplishments. This passage is about his military leadership:

"About 500,000 Roman citizens were under military oath to me. Of these, when their terms of service were ended, I settled in colonies . . . and to all these I allotted lands or granted money as rewards for military service.
" —Augustus, *Res Gestae*, from *Aspects of Western Civilization, Vol. I*

Why would Roman citizens have wanted to serve in Augustus's army?

A. for the opportunity to travel and see new places
B. for the chance to show off Rome's military strength
C. for the honor of serving under a great military leader
D. for the benefits of land and money after serving

RH.6–8.1, RH.6–8.2

8 **Summarizing** How did rewarding retired soldiers benefit Augustus?

F. It made the soldiers want to hurry through their time in service.
G. It caused the soldiers to become ambitious and daring.
H. It ensured the soldiers would always remain loyal to Augustus.
I. It improved Augustus's reputation as a kind-hearted leader.

SHORT RESPONSE

The historian Plutarch wrote of Julius Caesar's leadership:

"He was so much master of the good-will and hearty service of his soldiers that those who in other expeditions [special trips] were but ordinary men displayed a courage past defeating . . . when they went upon any danger where Caesar's glory was concerned. . . . there was no danger to which he [a soldier] did not willingly expose himself, no labour from which he pleaded an exemption [asked to be excused]."

—from *Caesar* by Plutarch

RH.6–8.1

9 How did Caesar's soldiers perform under his leadership?

RH.6–8.1

10 What aspect of Caesar's leadership inspired his soldiers' actions?

EXTENDED RESPONSE

WHST.6–8.1, WHST.6–8.10

11 **Argument** Who do you think was the greatest leader of Rome? Write a persuasive essay in support of your candidate.

Need Extra Help?

If You've Missed Question	1	2	3	4	5	6	7	8	9	10	11
Review Lesson	1	1	2	2	3	4	4	4	3	3	3, 4

336 *Rome: Republic to Empire*

networks Online Teaching Options

More Assessment Resources

The *Assess* tab in the online Teacher Lesson Center includes resources to help students improve their test-taking skills. It also contains many project-based rubrics to help you assess students' work.

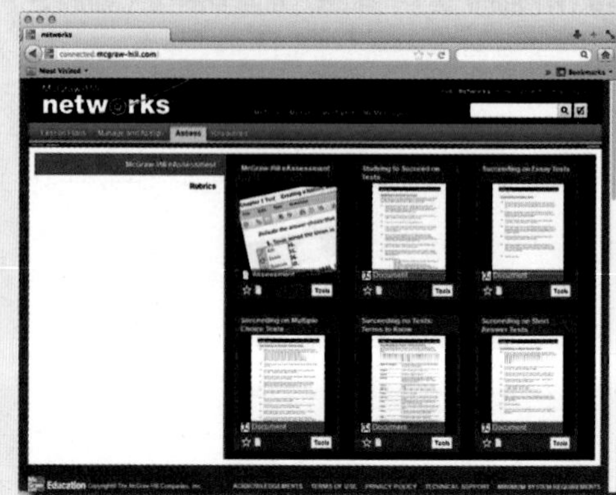

CHAPTER 12

Roman Civilization Planner

UNDERSTANDING BY DESIGN®

Enduring Understandings

- *People, places, and ideas change over time.*

Essential Questions

- *What makes a culture unique?*
- *Why do civilizations rise and fall?*
- *How does geography influence the way people live?*

Predictable Misunderstandings

Students may think:

- *All Romans were gladiators.*
- *The Roman Empire collapsed because it was invaded.*
- *Rome was the only capital of the empire.*

Assessment Evidence

Performance Tasks:

- *Hands-On Chapter Project*

Other Evidence:

- *Economics of History Activity*
- *Geography and History Activity*
- *Primary Source Activity*
- *Responses to Interactive Whiteboard Activities*
- *Interactive Graphic Organizers*
- *Interactive Self-Check Quizzes*
- *The World's Literature questions*
- *Graphic Organizer Activities*
- *What Do You Think? questions*
- *Written paragraphs*
- *Lesson Reviews*
- *Participation in class discussions*

SUGGESTED PACING GUIDE

Introducing the Chapter	1 Day
Lesson 1	2 Days
Feature: The World's Literature	1 Day
Lesson 2	1 Day
Feature: What Do You Think?	1 Day
Lesson 3	2 Days
Chapter Wrap-Up and Assessment	1 Day
TOTAL TIME	**10 Days**

Key for Using the Teacher Edition

SKILL-BASED ACTIVITIES

Types of skill activities found in the Teacher Edition.

V Visual Skills require students to analyze maps, graphs, charts, and photos.

R Reading Skills help students practice reading skills and master vocabulary.

W Writing Skills provide writing opportunities to help students comprehend the text.

C Critical Thinking Skills help students apply and extend what they have learned.

T Technology Skills require students to use digital tools effectively.

*Letters are followed by a number when there is more than one of the same type of skill on the page.

DIFFERENTIATED INSTRUCTION

All activities are written for the on-level student unless otherwise marked with the leveled labels below.

BL Beyond Level
AL Approaching Level
ELL English Language Learners

All students benefit from activities that utilize different learning styles. Many activities are marked as below when a particular learning style is highlighted.

Intrapersonal	**Naturalist**
Logical/Mathematical	**Kinesthetic**
Visual/Spatial	**Auditory/Musical**
Verbal/Linguistic	**Interpersonal**

NCSS Standards covered in "Roman Civilization"

Learners will understand:

1 CULTURE

3. How culture influences the ways in which human groups solve the problems of daily living

4. That the beliefs, values, and behaviors of a culture form an integrated system that helps shape the activities and ways of life that define a culture

5. How individuals learn the elements of their culture through interactions with others, and how individuals learn of other cultures through communication and study

6. That culture may change in response to changing needs, concerns, social, political, and geographic conditions

2 TIME, CONTINUITY, AND CHANGE

6. The origins and influences of social, cultural, political, and economic systems

7. The contributions of key persons, groups, and events from the past and their influence on the present

6 POWER, AUTHORITY, AND GOVERNANCE

2. Fundamental ideas that are the foundation of American constitutional democracy (including those of the U.S. Constitution, popular sovereignty, the rule of law, separation of powers, checks and balances, minority rights, the separation of church and state, and Federalism)

5. The ways in which governments meet the needs and wants of citizens, manage conflict, and establish order and society

CHAPTER OPENER PLANNER

Students will know:
- *how the Greeks influenced Roman religion, science, art, architecture, and literature.*
- *the reasons for the decline of the Roman Empire.*
- *why the Byzantine Empire became powerful.*

Students will be able to:
- ***compare and contrast*** *information about Roman women and women today.*
- ***identify*** *what life was like in Rome.*
- ***analyze*** *how the Greeks influenced the Romans.*
- ***identify and evaluate*** *Rome's contributions to our society today.*
- ***draw conclusions*** *about the success of Diocletian's reforms.*
- ***analyze*** *how the economy influenced the fall of the Roman Empire.*
- ***discuss*** *the effect of Germanic invaders on the decline of Rome.*
- ***identify and evaluate*** *legacy.*
- ***analyze*** *a map of the Byzantine Empire's trade routes.*
- ***identify*** *the cultural influences that shaped the Byzantines.*
- ***discuss*** *the roles of Justinian and Theodora.*

UNDERSTANDING BY DESIGN®

☑ *Print Teaching Options*

V Visual Skills

☐ **P. 338** Students study a map of the Roman Empire and answer questions.

C Critical Thinking Skills

☐ **P. 339** Students study a time line of ancient Rome and make predictions based on key events.

☑ *Online Teaching Options*

V Visual Skills

☐ MAP **The Roman Empire c. 73 B.C.–A.D. 200**—Students view the extent of the Roman Empire and identify locations of Roman architectural and engineering feats.

☐ TIME LINE **Roman Civilization**—Students learn about key events in Roman history between 73 B.C. and A.D. 550.

☐ WORLD ATLAS Students can use this interactive map to identify regions of the world, learn about individual countries, locate political boundaries, measure distances, and much more.

☑ *Printable Digital Worksheets*

R Reading Skills

☐ GRAPHIC NOVEL **Theodora**—Students read how Theodora persuaded her husband Justinian to fight a rebellion in Rome.

Project-Based Learning

Hands-On Chapter Project

Roman Culture Museum Exhibit

Student groups will create museum exhibits that display information about an aspect of Roman culture.

Technology Extension

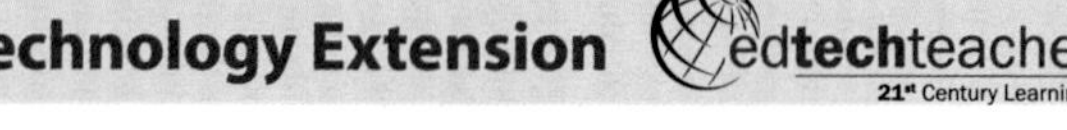

Online Museum Exhibition with Wikis
- Find an additional activity online that incorporates technology for this project.
- Visit the EdTechTeacher Web sites (included in the Technology Extension for this chapter) for more links, tutorials, and other resources.

Print Resources

ANCILLARY RESOURCES

These ancillaries are available for every chapter and lesson.
- **Reading Essentials and Study Guide Workbook** AL ELL
- **Chapter Tests and Lesson Quizzes Blackline Masters**

PRINTABLE DIGITAL WORKSHEETS

These printable digital worksheets are available for every chapter and lesson.
- **Hands-On Chapter Projects**
- **What Do You Know? activities**
- **Chapter Summaries (English and Spanish)**
- **Vocabulary Builder activities**
- **Guided Reading activities**

More Media Resources

SUGGESTED VIDEOS

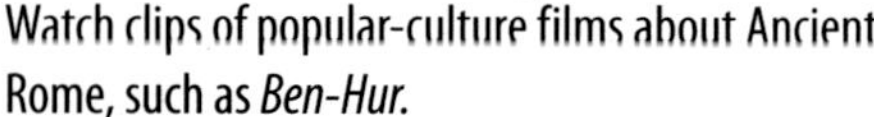

Watch clips of popular-culture films about Ancient Rome, such as *Ben-Hur.*
- **Ask:** **Can fictional movies capture historically accurate events?**

(Note: Preview clips for age-appropriateness.)

SUGGESTED READING

Grade 6 reading level:
- ***Pompeii: Lost and Found,*** by Mary Pope Osborne

Grade 7 reading level:
- ***What Do We Know About the Romans?*** by Mike Corbishley

Grade 8 reading level:
- ***Bodies From the Ash: Life and Death in Ancient Pompeii,*** by James M. Deem

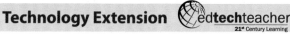

THE ROMAN WAY OF LIFE

Students will know:

- *how the Greeks influenced Roman religion, science, art, architecture, and literature.*

Students will be able to:

- ***compare and contrast** information about Roman women and women today.*
- ***identify** what life was like in Rome.*
- ***analyze** how the Greeks influenced the Romans.*
- ***identify and evaluate** Rome's contributions to our society today.*

UNDERSTANDING BY DESIGN®

Print Teaching Options

V Visual Skills

- ☐ **P. 341** Students identify rooms in a diagram of a Roman house. AL ELL **Visual/Spatial**
- ☐ **P. 345** Students draw a picture that illustrates a Roman style of art or architecture.

R Reading Skills

- ☐ **P. 340** Students name three facts about Rome they learn from text. **Verbal/Linguistic**
- ☐ **P. 342** Students organize information about daily life in ancient Rome.

W Writing Skills

- ☐ **P. 343** Students write diary entries or letters from the perspective of an ancient Roman. **Verbal/Linguistic**
- ☐ **P. 346** Student pairs compose an ode or satirical piece of writing. **Verbal/Linguistic** **Interpersonal**

C Critical Thinking Skills

- ☐ **P. 342** Students compare and contrast their lives with those of ancient Romans. **Intrapersonal**
- ☐ **P. 343** Students discuss effects of slavery on Roman society. BL
- ☐ **P. 344** Students match biographic info with either Galen or Ptolemy. AL ELL

T Technology Skills

- ☐ **P. 347** Students create a slide show about Greek influence on the Romans. BL

Online Teaching Options

V Visual Skills

- VIDEO **The Geography of Italy**—Students view a video describing the geographical regions of this boot-shaped nation.
- IMAGE **Ancient Roman Glassmaking**—Students learn techniques Romans used in making mosaic and blown glass.
- MAP **Roads of the Roman Empire A.D. 117**—Students click to view the system of roads built by the Romans.
- SLIDE SHOW **Roman Architecture**—Students view the ruins of Roman aqueducts, the Colosseum, and the Pantheon.

R Reading Skills

- GRAPHIC ORGANIZER **Taking Notes: *Identifying:* The Greeks and the Romans**—Students identify the ideas the Romans borrowed from the Greeks.
- SLIDE SHOW **Roman House**—Students view how wealthy Romans lived.
- BIOGRAPHY **Livia**—Students read a biography of Caesar Augustus's wife.

C Critical Thinking Skills

- WHITEBOARD ACTIVITY **Life of Roman Women**—Students sort activities and privileges into those enjoyed by wealthy women and less-wealthy women.
- CHART **Roles of Family Members**—Students click to explore the family roles of Romans.
- IMAGE **Roman and Modern Medicine**—Students analyze how Roman medicine affected modern medicine.

T Technology Skills

- SELF-CHECK QUIZ **Lesson 1**—Students receive instant feedback on their mastery of lesson content.

Printable Digital Worksheets

C Critical Thinking Skills

- WORKSHEET **Primary Source Activity: Women in Protest**—Students analyze opinions about the Oppian law, which limited the amount of gold that women could own.

ROME'S DECLINE

Students will know:

- *the reasons for the decline of the Roman Empire.*

Students will be able to:

- ***draw conclusions*** *about the success of Diocletian's reforms.*
- ***analyze*** *how the economy influenced the fall of the Roman Empire.*
- ***discuss*** *the effect of Germanic invaders on the decline of Rome.*
- ***identify and evaluate*** *Rome's legacy.*

UNDERSTANDING BY DESIGN®

☑ *Print Teaching Options*

V Visual Skills

- ☐ **P. 355** Students compare an infographic with an earlier graphic organizer. AL ELL **Visual/Spatial**

R Reading Skills

- ☐ **P. 350** Students identify key reasons the Roman Empire began to decline.
- ☐ **P. 353** Students describe traits of various invaders of Rome.
- ☐ **P. 356** Students name beliefs of the U.S. legal system that come from Roman ideas.

W Writing Skills

- ☐ **P. 354** Students write Q&A or a short essay on the effects of invasions on Rome. **Verbal/Linguistic**

C Critical Thinking Skills

- ☐ **P. 351** Students match causes with effects for the decline of the empire. AL ELL
- ☐ **P. 352** Student groups argue for or against Diocletian's reforms. BL **Verbal/Linguistic Interpersonal**
- ☐ **P. 356** Students read Pope Gregory I's account of the fall of Rome.
- ☐ **P. 357** Students match terms with definitions based on reading passage. AL

☑ *Online Teaching Options*

V Visual Skills

- VIDEO **The Coliseum**—Students view a video that describes the world's most advanced sporting stadium of its time.
- IMAGE **Roman Wall**—Students view the wall that the Romans built around Lugo, Spain.
- MAP **Germanic Migrations c. A.D. 200–500**—Students trace the routes of the invading Angles and Saxons, Franks, Huns, Ostrogoths, Vandals, and Visigoths.
- SLIDE SHOW **Roman Architecture Influenced the U.S. Capitol**—Students identify Roman influence on the architecture of the U.S. Capitol.

R Reading Skills

- GRAPHIC ORGANIZER **Taking Notes: *Organizing:* The Empire Collapses**—Students identify why the Roman Empire collapsed.
- BIOGRAPHY **Constantine**—Students read biographical information about this Roman emperor.

C Critical Thinking Skills

- WHITEBOARD ACTIVITY **History of Constantinople**—Students drag and drop events to build a time line.
- CHART **The Fall of Rome**—Students click to reveal the chain of events that led to economic weakness in the Roman Empire.

T Technology Skills

- SELF-CHECK QUIZ **Lesson 2**—Students receive instant feedback on their mastery of lesson content.
- GAME **Early Roman Empire Crossword Puzzle**—Students test their knowledge of lesson vocabulary.
- GAME **Invaders of the Roman Empire Concentration Game**—Students match invaders with invasions.

☑ *Printable Digital Worksheets*

C Critical Thinking Skills

- WORKSHEET **Economics of History Activity: Inflation and the Fall of the Roman Empire**—Students analyze how changes to Roman currency led to inflation.

LESSON 3 PLANNER

THE BYZANTINE EMPIRE

Students will know:
- *why the Byzantine Empire became powerful.*

Students will be able to:
- ***analyze** a map of the Byzantine Empire's trade routes.*
- ***identify** the cultural influences that shaped the Byzantines.*
- ***discuss** the roles of Justinian and Theodora.*

UNDERSTANDING BY DESIGN®

Print Teaching Options

V Visual Skills

- [ ] **P. 363** Students draw an element of the Hagia Sophia's architecture that interests them visually. AL ELL Visual/Spatial
- [ ] **P. 364** Students create mosaic portraits of Byzantine leaders. AL ELL Visual/Spatial

R Reading Skills

- [ ] **P. 361** Students identify cultural influences of Rome on the Byzantine Empire.

W Writing Skills

- [ ] **P. 362** Students write about their opinions of Empress Theodora. Verbal/Linguistic Intrapersonal
- [ ] **P. 363** Students craft their own code of laws.
- [ ] **P. 364** Students write a short essay based on their chosen Byzantine leader. Verbal/Linguistic Intrapersonal

C Critical Thinking Skills

- [ ] **P. 360** Students craft questions based on their reading.

T Technology Skills

- [ ] **P. 365** Students use PowerPoint® to develop tourist materials for Constantinople.

Online Teaching Options

V Visual Skills

- VIDEO **Constantinople to Istanbul**—Students view a video that shows the evolution of this ancient city.
- MAP **Justinian's Conquests**—Students view the extent of holdings added to the Byzantine Empire by Justinian.
- SLIDE SHOW **Hippodrome**—Students view images of Constantine's Hippodrome.
- SLIDE SHOW **Hagia Sophia**—Students view images of one of Turkey's most important cultural sites.

R Reading Skills

- GRAPHIC ORGANIZER **Taking Notes: *Listing:* Why the Byzantine Empire Thrived**—Students list reasons why the Byzantine Empire thrived.

C Critical Thinking Skills

- WHITEBOARD ACTIVITY **Emperor Justinian I and Empress Theodora**—Students match descriptions with the correct leader.
- CHART **Justinian's Army**—Students click to learn about the six types of troops in Justinian's army.

T Technology Skills

- SELF-CHECK QUIZ **Lesson 3**—Students receive instant feedback on their mastery of lesson content.

Printable Digital Worksheets

R Reading Skills

- WORKSHEET **Geography and History Activity: Understanding Location: Constantinople**—Students interpret maps and text to answer questions about the city of Constantinople.

INTERVENTION AND REMEDIATION STRATEGIES

LESSON 1 The Roman Way of Life

Reading and Comprehension

Have students use a thesaurus to explore how the choice of synonyms and related words can shape meaning and tone of vocabulary terms (poem vs. ode; gladiator vs. fighter; arch vs. curve).

Ask students to use less descriptive words to rewrite sentences that contain vocabulary terms. Discuss how the meaning of the sentence or paragraph may be altered or changed.

Text Evidence

To help students develop further awareness and understanding of Roman life and contributions in science and the arts, have them explore how other texts present the subject matter. Place students in pairs or groups. Have them make lists or take notes that compare and contrast what types of information are included in their textbook and in the other texts. Some questions to consider:

- Is the same information included in each text?
- What topics are different?
- Are any topics included in one text but not the other?
- How is the information presented in each text (use of charts, diagrams, graphs, illustrations, tables, etc.)?
- Which text do you think presents the information in the best way? Explain your answer.

You may also wish to discuss with students how these questions can help them determine the accuracy of a text.

LESSON 2 Rome's Decline

Reading and Comprehension

To help students summarize the information in this lesson, place them in pairs. Give pairs time to review the lesson. Then have each student give a 5– to 6–sentence oral summary to their partner about how and why Rome declined. Tell students that their summaries will be similar, but they shouldn't match verbatim.

Ask volunteers to talk about the ways they thought the summaries they gave were the same as the ones they heard and the ways they thought they were different.

Text Evidence

Have students use research skills to become familiar with information presented in diverse formats. Tell them to pick one topic from this lesson (such as Roman influence on law and government; the use of Latin; Roman writers) and find one or two sources about that topic that aren't in the textbook. Suggest formats like articles (both print and digital), interviews (both written and spoken), and videos. Ask students to

- summarize two or three interesting pieces of information that were in the sources but not in the textbook.
- identify whether students thought it was easier or more difficult to read the sources than to read the textbook, and to explain their thinking.

LESSON 3 The Byzantine Empire

Reading and Comprehension

Group students or place them in pairs. Have students list only nouns, verbs, or adjectives to describe the Byzantine Empire, Constantinople, Constantine, Justinian, Theodora, the Hagia Sophia, and Belisarius. See how many of each part of speech can be used to describe each term.

Text Evidence

Point out to students that one of the purposes of the textbook is to tell about Justinian's rule of the Byzantine Empire. Tell them that talking about Justinian as leader is one point of view. Ask students to write a paragraph or make a list of ways in which they think the purpose or point of view of the textbook might be different if Theodora had ruled the Byzantine Empire.

Online Resources

Approaching Level Reader

Use this online lower-level text that corresponds directly to the text in the Student Edition. It includes a Spanish version.

Guided Reading Activities

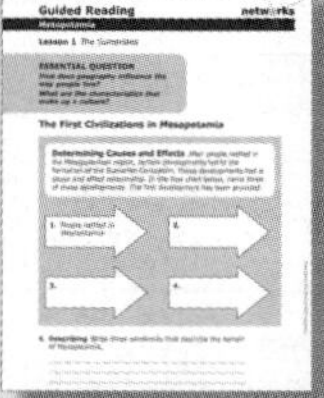

This resource uses graphic organizers and guiding questions to help students with comprehension.

What Do You Know?

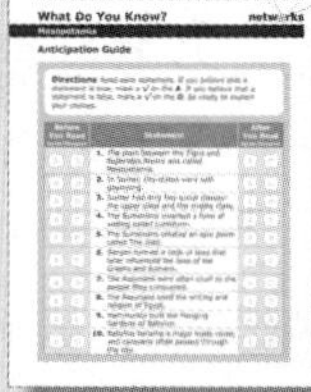

Use these worksheets to pre-assess student's background knowledge before they study the chapter.

Reading Essentials and Study Guide Workbook

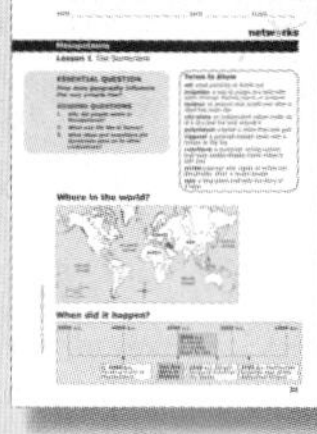

This resource offers writing and reading activities for the approaching-level student. Also available in Spanish.

Self-Check Quizzes

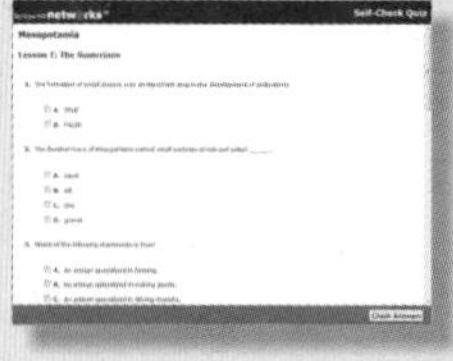

This online assessment tool provides instant feedback for students to check their progress.

Roman Civilization

50 B.C. to A.D. 600

ESSENTIAL QUESTIONS • *What makes a culture unique?* • *Why do civilizations rise and fall?* • *How does geography influence the way people live?*

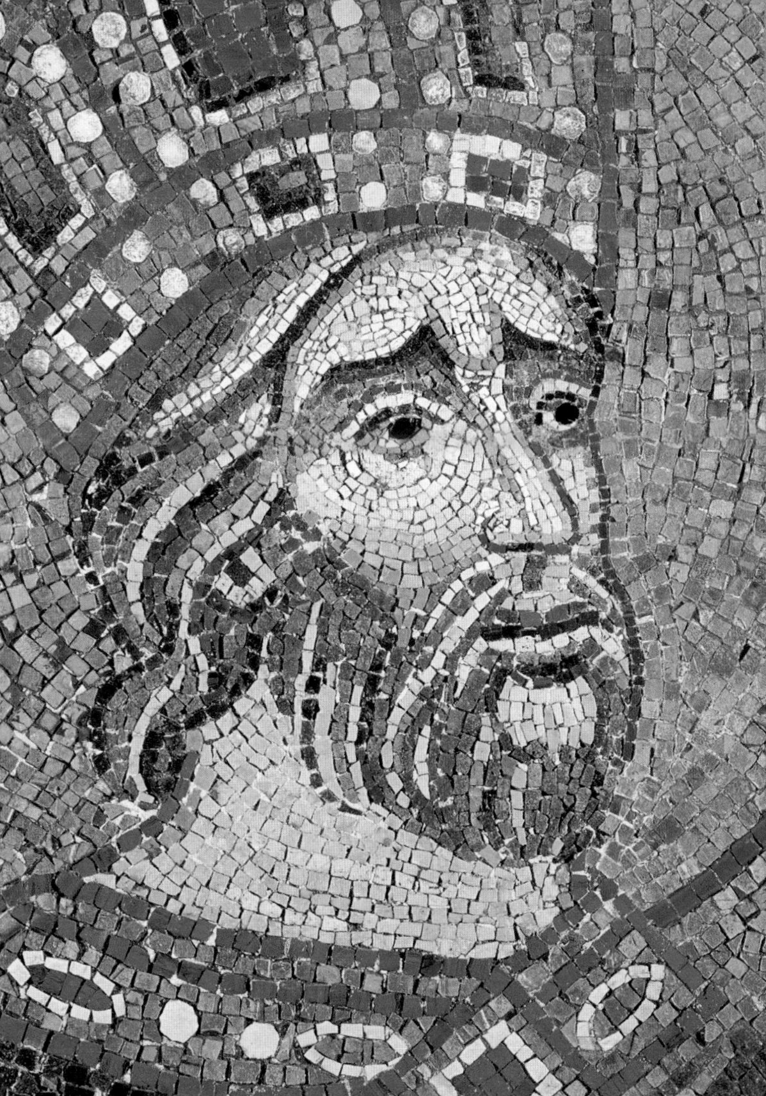

networks

There's More Online about the lives and customs of the ancient Romans.

CHAPTER 12

Lesson 1 *The Roman Way of Life*

Lesson 2 *Rome's Decline*

Lesson 3 *The Byzantine Empire*

The Story Matters . . .

When Constantine defeated his brother-in-law in battle, he became emperor of the Western Roman Empire. At that time, Christians were persecuted in Rome, but Constantine thanked "the God of the Christians" for his victory.

This mosaic shows more than just how Constantine looked. The crown on his head represents his power. This reminds us that Constantine granted religious freedom to Christians and made it possible for Christianity to become widespread in the Roman Empire.

Constantine's influence was so great that 10 other Roman emperors were named after him.

◄ *This mosaic depicts Emperor Constantine I. Mosaics like this one can be seen covering the inside walls of Hagia Sophia, a mosque in the present-day city of Istanbul.*

337

ENGAGE

Bellringer Read "The Story Matters . . ." aloud in class, or ask a volunteer to read it aloud. **Ask:**

- **Why do you think this mosaic of Constantine was created?** *(Possible answer: to honor him because he was the emperor)*

Remind students that Constantine's crown represents his power in the mosaic.

- **What other details in this mosaic of Constantine do you notice? Do you think the artist made good choices for a mosaic of an emperor? What colors might they choose instead, and why?** Discuss details like the use of the color red and the inclusion of jewel shapes in Constantine's collar. As part of the discussion, consider asking students if they would change the colors if they were creating the mosaic.

Tell the class that Constantine did many things to help the Roman Empire survive during a time of great trouble. In fact, he is also called "Constantine the Great." One of the things he did as emperor was to show support for the Christians. Christians were still persecuted in Rome, so Constantine risked persecution himself. The things Constantine accomplished helped the Roman Empire survive, and they influence our lives even today.

Making Connections

Tell students that a mosaic is a picture or design that is made from small pieces of material like glass, stone, or clay (ceramics). The pieces are often brightly colored, and artists arrange them to create a specific pattern or picture, like the mosaic pictured here.

Letter from the Author

Dear World History Teacher,

Crises in the third century and the rise of Christianity gradually brought a transformation of the Roman Empire in the fourth and fifth centuries. Diocletian and Constantine had restored an aura of stability in the late empire. Constantine moved the capital from Rome to Byzantium in the east in an attempt to save the empire. The efforts of these emperors, however, proved to be in vain. As the western part of the Roman Empire disintegrated, the Eastern Roman Empire, also known as the Byzantine Empire, flourished.

Jackson J. Spielvogel

TEACH & ASSESS

Step Into the Place

V Visual Skills

Reading a Map Project the Interactive World Atlas map of Europe, Asia, and North Africa on the whiteboard. Invite volunteers to point out the locations of civilizations they have already studied this year. *(Mesopotamia, Egypt, Israel, and Greece)* Discuss how the locations of these civilizations gave them opportunities for trade and access to the spread of ideas but also made them vulnerable to attack. Next, project the Chapter Opener map and point out the Italian peninsula and Rome. Explain that like some of the civilizations they studied earlier, Rome's location helped it become a powerful civilization. As a class, discuss the Map Focus questions.

Guide students to look at the map's key. Then **ask:** What area is shaded in green on the map? *(Western Roman Empire)* What area is shaded in pink? *(Eastern Roman Empire)*

Remind students of the definition of a border. Then **ask:**

- What are three major bodies of water that can be found along the borders or within the borders of the Roman Empire? *(Answers will vary but should demonstrate accurate use of the map.)*
- Today, the country north of Spain is known as France. What was France called when it was part of the Roman Empire? *(Gaul)*
- The country east of Greece is known today as Turkey. What was Turkey called when it was part of the Roman Empire? *(Asia Minor)*

C

Content Background Knowledge

- The Romans called the area that is now France *Gallia Transalpina,* or "Gaul Across the Alps." This was to distinguish it from the different area called *Gallia Cisalpina,* or "Gaul This Side of the Alps," which was in northern Italy.
- The legendary city of Troy was located in Asia Minor. Troy was originally a Greek city until it came under Roman control. The Romans called Troy by the Latin name *Ilium.*

ANSWERS, p. 338

Step Into the Place

1. west
2. the Mediterranean Sea
3. the Mediterranean Sea and the Adriatic Sea
4. CRITICAL THINKING Sample answer: When people travel on a waterway to trade, they come into contact with other people and learn new ideas from one another.

Step Into the Time

Sample answer: The division of the Roman Empire in A.D. 395 will lead to the end of the Roman Empire because countries are weaker when they are not united.

CHAPTER 12 CCSS

Place and Time: Rome 50 B.C. to A.D. 600

The Roman Empire extended throughout the Mediterranean region. As the empire grew, however, Roman emperors found it more difficult to rule. Political corruption, economic challenges, and invasions by Germanic groups brought about the division of the empire.

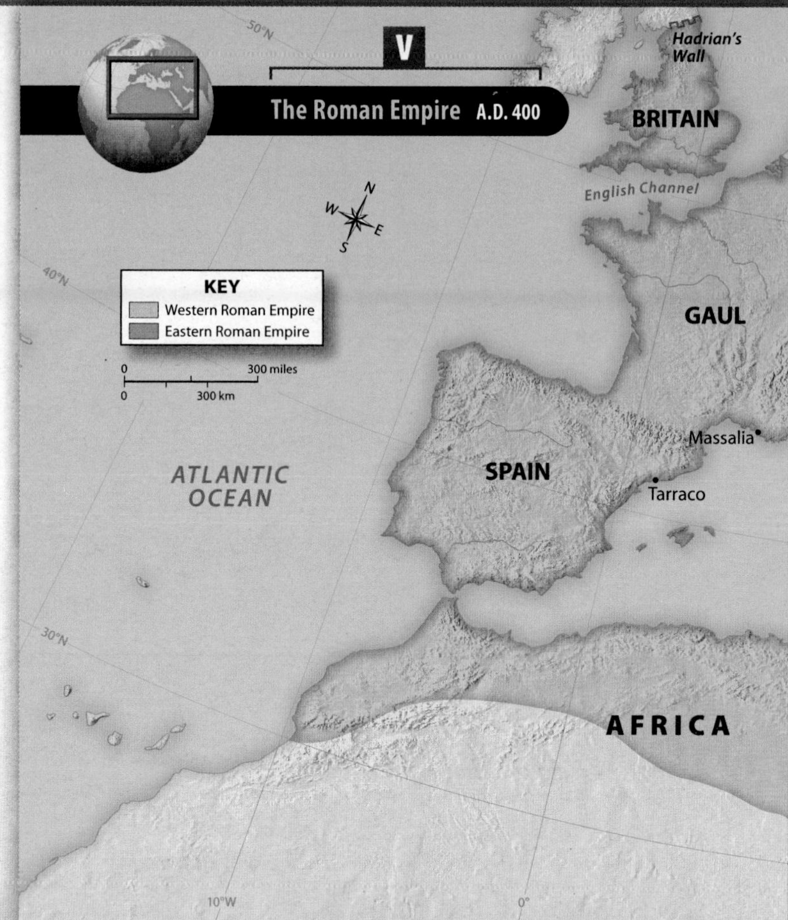

Step Into the Place

MAP FOCUS Rome's location in the center of the long, narrow Italian peninsula helped it become a powerful civilization.

1. **LOCATION** Look at the map. Is Rome located east or west of Greece? RH.6–8.7
2. **MOVEMENT** What physical feature made it possible for Rome to extend its influence to Africa? RH.6–8.7
3. **PLACE** What major bodies of water form the boundaries of Italy? RH.6–8.7
4. CRITICAL THINKING *Drawing Conclusions* How does location near a waterway contribute to the spread of ideas? RH.6–8.1

Step Into the Time

TIME LINE Choose an event from the time line and write a paragraph predicting the effect of that event on the future of the Roman Empire. RH.6–8.7, WHST.6–8.10

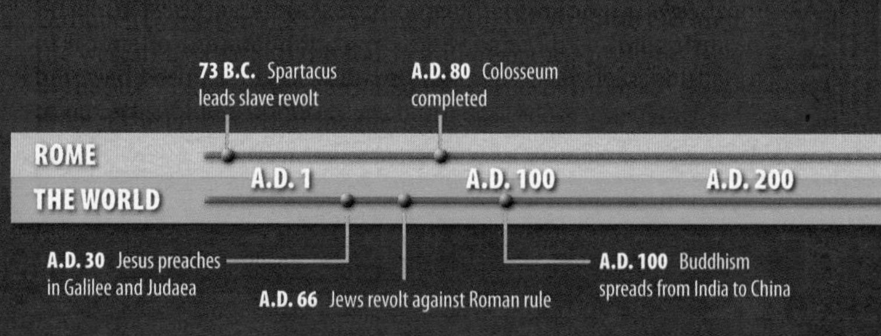

Project-Based Learning

Hands-On Chapter Project

Roman Culture Museum Exhibit

Students will create a museum exhibit displaying information about an aspect of Roman culture. Begin with a class discussion about the different features that help define a culture. Next, divide students into small groups to create plans for their exhibit. Then, each group will research and create an exhibit on its chosen cultural subject. Students will share their exhibits with the rest of the class. Finally, students will evaluate their research, exhibit presentation, and collaboration, using a class-developed assessment rubric.

Technology Extension

Online Museum Exhibition with Wikis

Using Digital Tools Students will use a wiki to create and share a museum exhibition piece that focuses on an aspect of Roman culture. Students will use one wiki page to plan the organization of their exhibition piece and the information that will be referenced in it. A second page will be used for students to publish and share their final pieces with classmates, family members, and their communities.

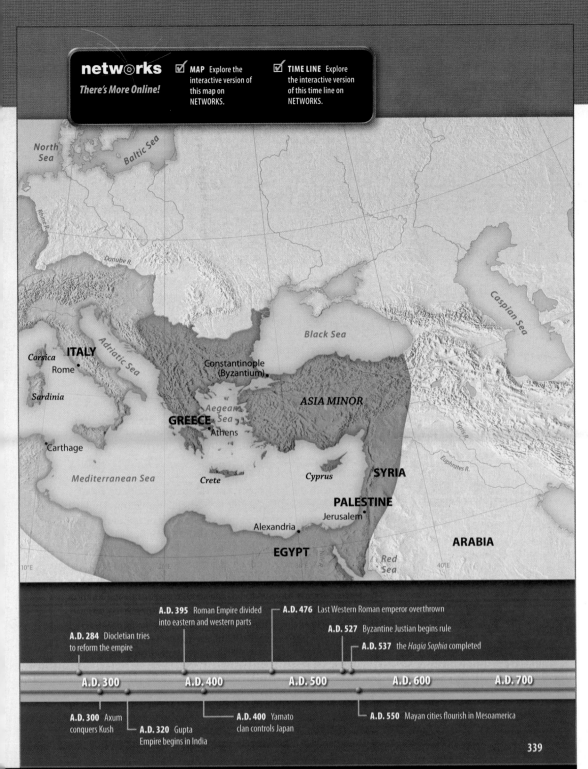

networks *There's More Online!*

MAP Explore the interactive version of this map on NETWORKS.

TIME LINE Explore the interactive version of this time line on NETWORKS.

A.D. 284 Diocletian tries to reform the empire

A.D. 300 Axum conquers Kush

A.D. 320 Gupta Empire begins in India

A.D. 395 Roman Empire divided into eastern and western parts

A.D. 400 Yamato clan controls Japan

A.D. 476 Last Western Roman emperor overthrown

A.D. 527 Byzantine Justian begins rule

A.D. 537 the *Hagia Sophia* completed

A.D. 550 Mayan cities flourish in Mesoamerica

A.D. 300 A.D. 400 A.D. 500 A.D. 600 A.D. 700

339

CHAPTER 12
Place and Time

Step Into the Time

C Critical Thinking Skills

Hypothesizing Place students in pairs or groups, and call their attention to the time line for this chapter. Explain that between 73 B.C. and A.D. 550, Rome flourished but also faced difficult times. Draw students' attention to the event "A.D. 476 Last Western Roman emperor overthrown" on the Rome time line. **Ask:** **How might other events on the Rome time line have helped cause this event?** *(Sample answer: A slave revolt and the splitting of the empire might have helped weaken the empire, making it easier to take over.)*

Review what it means to make a prediction. Have each group choose an event from the time line and write a paragraph or list of reasons why each group or pair predicts that this event will affect the future of the Roman Empire.

After each group or pair has shared its predictions, **ask:** **What are one or two things that you talked about with your partner or in your group that helped all of you make your predictions?** *(Answers will vary.)* Have students compare their predictions to what actually happened in history at the end of the chapter.

Content Background Knowledge

- In A.D. 326, Constantine traveled to Rome. However, he refused to participate in a procession to honor pagan gods. The people of Rome were offended, and Constantine never returned to the city again.
- Constantine was not baptized into Christianity until near the end of his life, in A.D. 337. He died that year and was buried in the Church of the Holy Apostles in Constantinople.

CLOSE & REFLECT

Have each student write a question that they would like to know the answer to by the time they've completed this chapter. Questions can be based on the map, the time line, or the class discussions about Constantine and the Roman Empire. Post the questions in a place where they can easily be seen and reviewed.

At the end of each class session during the chapter, move any of the questions that have been answered during that day's session under a header that reads "Answered." At the end of the chapter, students will have a visual record of the amount of information that they have studied and the number of questions that remain unanswered. These unanswered questions can be researched as an enrichment or extension option.

WORKSHEET

What Do You Know? Activity: Roman Civilization

Making Connections Have students complete the What Do You Know? matching game about Roman civilization before they study the chapter. Direct students to cut out the cards and match each term to its definition. Tell students that the cards review terms and ideas from the previous chapter about Rome. You may choose to have students work in pairs. After students have matched the cards, review with them the correct answers. Then have students mix up and match the cards again.

See page 337B for other online activities.

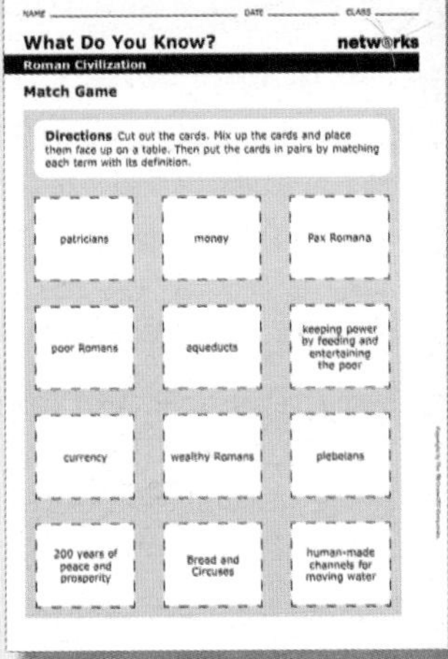
What Do You Know? networks
Roman Civilization
Match Game
Directions Cut out the cards. Mix up the cards and place them face up on a table. Then put the cards in pairs by matching each term with its definition.

patricians	money	Pax Romana
poor Romans	aqueducts	keeping power by feeding and entertaining the poor
currency	wealthy Romans	plebeians
200 years of peace and prosperity	Bread and Circuses	human-made channels for moving water

ENGAGE

Bellringer Tell students that civilizations usually have customs that affect how people in that civilization live their daily lives. For example, many civilizations have rules about how citizens are educated. **Ask:** How do you think the education of young people affects a civilization? *(Possible answer: Education might make a civilization more prosperous because young people would learn basic skills such as mathematics.)*

TEACH & ASSESS

R Reading Skills

Stating After reading "The Empire's Chief City" with students, **ask:** Name three facts about the city of Rome. *(Possible answers: Rome was one of the largest cities in the ancient world; more than a million people lived there in about A.D. 1; Rome was carefully planned; it was laid out in a square, and the main streets crossed at right angles; the emperor lived in Rome in a palace on the top of a hill; the Forum was in Rome; the Forum was a large open space that was Rome's marketplace and public square.)* **Verbal/Linguistic**

networks *There's More Online!*

- GRAPHIC ORGANIZERS
  - The Greeks and the Romans
  - Roles of Family Members
- SLIDE SHOW
  Roman Homes
- VIDEO

Lesson 1

The Roman Way of Life

ESSENTIAL QUESTION *What makes a culture unique?*

IT MATTERS BECAUSE

The Romans have influenced our science, art, architecture, and literature.

Daily Life

GUIDING QUESTION *What was daily life like for the Romans?*

Many Romans lived in cities throughout the Roman Empire. Like cities and towns of today, Roman cities were centers for culture, business, and government. We know quite a lot about life in places like Rome and Pompeii from studying the archaeological ruins. Even though the Roman Empire was widespread, the heart of the empire was on the Italian Peninsula in the city of Rome.

The Empire's Chief City

Rome was one of the largest cities in the ancient world. By about A.D. 1, more than a million people lived there. People traveled to Rome from every part of the empire. Like many other Roman cities, Rome was carefully planned. It was laid out in a square with the main streets crossing at right angles.

The emperor lived in Rome in a splendid palace on the top of a hill. At the foot of the hill was the Forum (FOHR•uhm). This was a large open space that served as a marketplace and public square, much like the malls we visit today. In the Forum marketplace, Romans shopped for food and luxury items, played games, and chatted with their friends. Temples and other public buildings surrounded the Forum.

Reading HELPDESK CCSS

Taking Notes: *Identifying*

Use a table like the one here to list the ideas the Romans borrowed from the Greeks to create their own culture. RH.6–8.2

Greeks Ideas Borrowed by Romans

Greeks	Romans

Content Vocabulary (Tier 3 Words)

- **gladiator**
- **satire**
- **anatomy**
- **ode**
- **vault**

networks Online Teaching Options

VIDEO

The Geography of Italy

Listing Play the video for students. This video discusses the geography of Italy, including the geography of the peninsula and major regions, mountains, and rivers within the country. The political geography of Europe as it relates to Italy is another topic covered in the video.

After playing the video once, play it a second time. Have students write a list of 5-10 geographic facts from the video that they found interesting or that were pieces of information they didn't know. **Verbal/Linguistic**

See page 337C for other online activities.

ANSWERS, p. 340

TAKING NOTES: Greeks: Statues were made to look perfect; bodies were young and healthy. Homer's *Odyssey* served as the basis for Roman literature's ideas; Greeks identified themes to be used in plays. **Romans:** Statues were more realistic; they showed wrinkles, warts, and other less attractive features. Virgil took ideas from Greece's *Odyssey* to create the *Aeneid;* Horace used Greek ideas to create satires and odes.

The Roman Way of Life

Like the emperor, wealthy Romans lived in large, comfortable houses on the city's hills. Their homes had marble walls, tiled floors, and running water. Houses were built around a courtyard called an atrium, which was open to the sky. The atrium often had a garden. Wealthy Romans also had homes called villas on large farms outside the city.

Romans who were less wealthy worked as shopkeepers or artisans. Most Romans, however, were poor. Many did not have jobs, while others performed unskilled labor, such as delivering goods. Poor Romans lived in crowded, noisy, dirty neighborhoods in wooden apartment buildings six or seven stories tall. These buildings often collapsed or caught fire. People tossed garbage into the streets, and thieves prowled the areas at night.

To gain the support of Rome's poor, political leaders offered "bread and circuses." On some days, teams of chariot racers competed in the Circus Maximus, an arena seating more than 150,000 people. On other days, crowds watched **gladiators** (GLA•dee•ay•tuhrz) fight each other to the death or battle wild animals in stadiums such as the Colosseum. Most gladiators were enslaved people, criminals, prisoners of war, or poor people. Romans admired the gladiators' skills and bravery.

INFOGRAPHIC

Many wealthy Romans lived in homes built around courtyards.

1. **IDENTIFYING** In which part of the home did Romans entertain guests?
2. **CRITICAL THINKING** ***Comparing and Contrasting*** How is a Roman home similar to homes in your neighborhood? How is it different?

ROMAN HOME

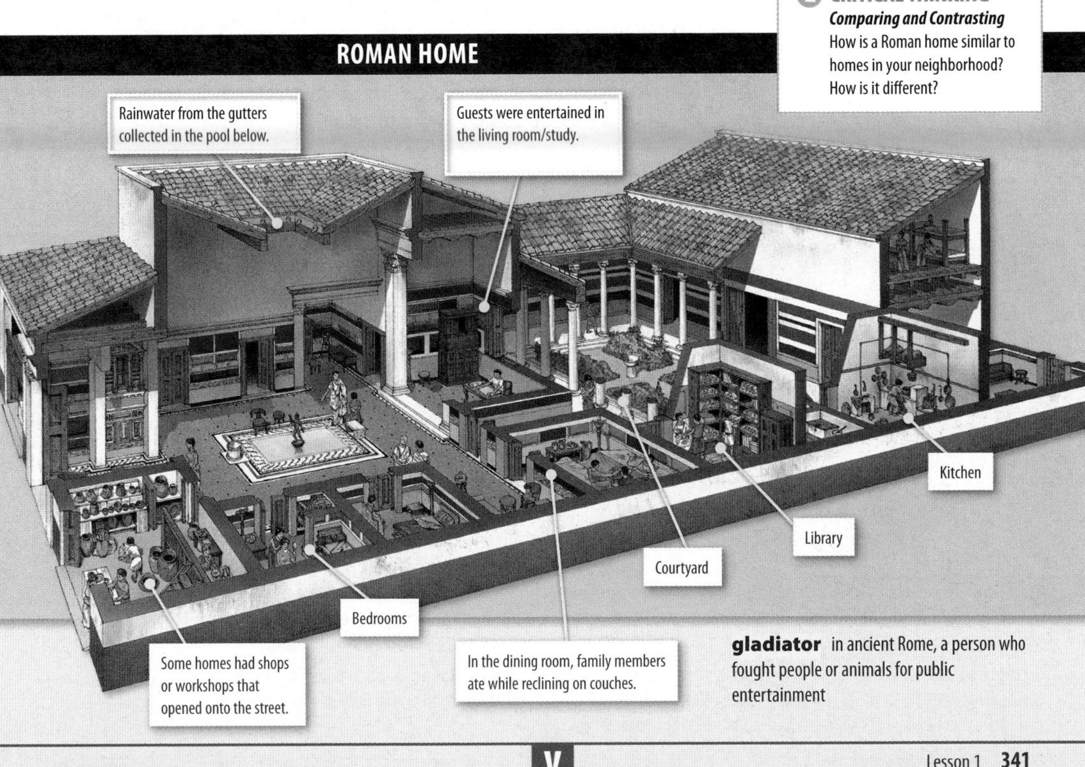

Rainwater from the gutters collected in the pool below.
Guests were entertained in the living room/study.
Kitchen
Library
Courtyard
Bedrooms
Some homes had shops or workshops that opened onto the street.
In the dining room, family members ate while reclining on couches.

gladiator in ancient Rome, a person who fought people or animals for public entertainment

V

V Visual Skills

Diagramming On the board, draw an outline of the Roman Home infographic. Replace the labels with the numbers 1, 2, 3, and so on. Give students a blank numbered copy of the outline.

Then have students look at the Infographic as you ask questions about the location or purpose of each part of a Roman home. *(The Identifying question in the Infographic is one example. Other questions might be: What number identifies where the bedrooms are? Which area of a Roman home is located at number 4?)* Label each area on the board diagram, and have students do the same on their diagrams.

Colors can also be used instead of numbers. *(Find the courtyard. Color this area purple.)* Then work with students to make a color key for their diagrams that tells the color used to designate each area. AL ELL **Visual/Spatial**

Content Background Knowledge

Roman Food

- Soldiers brought Lucanian sausage to Rome when they returned from Lucania, an area of southern Italy. The Roman chef Apicius prepared the sausage by stuffing it with a mixture of meat, the herb cumin, parsley, pepper, and pine nuts. All of these ingredients were ground together, and fat and a salty fish sauce known as garum were also added. Finally, the sausages were hung to be smoked.
- The Romans called dessert *mensa secunda,* or "second meal." Pear patina was a custard made from pears, wine, honey, raisins, cumin, oil, eggs, and garum.
- Libum was a cake made of ricotta cheese, flour, and eggs. The cake would sometimes be offered as a gesture of sacrifice to the Roman gods who protected a household.

SLIDE SHOW

Roman House

Comparing Have students explore a Roman home by viewing the slide show. Ask them to list details that this home has in common with their own modern house. *(For example, students may note that both Roman and modern homes may have dining rooms.)* AL

See page 337C for other online activities.

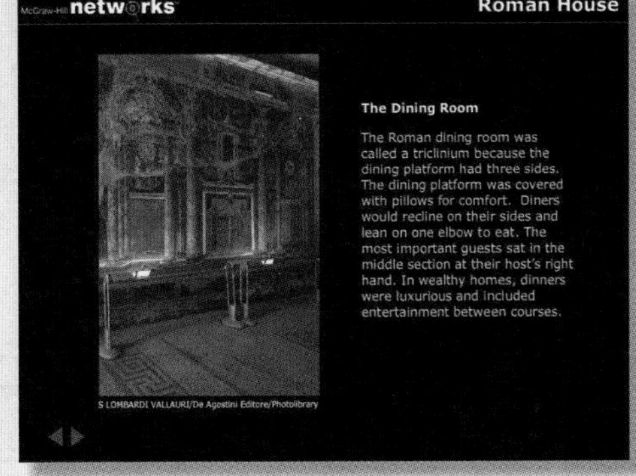

ANSWERS, p. 341

INFOGRAPHIC

1. Romans entertained guests in the living room/study.
2. CRITICAL THINKING Students should note similarities and differences between their homes and Roman homes. These similarities may include the use of a living room to entertain guests. The differences may include the absence of an attached shop and a courtyard in modern homes.

The Roman Way of Life

R Reading Skills

Identifying and Summarizing Have students create a chart like the one below to organize and summarize the information about daily life in the Roman Empire. Students will answer each question by writing information on the right side of the chart. This activity can be completed

- as a class activity in which students read information and fill in the chart.
- as a Think-Pair-Share activity in which students work with a partner, read information together, and fill in the chart.
- as a group activity in which each group is assigned one of the four questions. Groups are responsible for reading information that answers their assigned question and for filling in the chart. Then each group is responsible for sharing what they have learned with the rest of the class so that students are able to complete their charts with the remaining information.

What Was Daily Life Like . . .	
in the city of Rome?	
in a Roman family?	
for Roman women?	
for Roman slaves?	

C Critical Thinking Skills

Comparing and Contrasting At the conclusion of the daily-life chart activity, discuss the following questions with students. **Ask:** Think about your daily life. What do you have in common with the Romans? How is your daily life different from the Romans? *(Answers will vary.)* **Intrapersonal**

ANSWERS, p. 342

CRITICAL THINKING Men were the heads of the household, were responsible for their children's education, and ran the family's business. They could work outside the home and own property. Women had a strong influence on their families and often advised their husbands in private. They did housework or worked in the family business. Few women worked outside their homes.

Reading Strategy Summaries should include the idea that enslaved people led hard lives but that they played an important role in Roman society.

Thinking Like a HISTORIAN

Researching on the Internet

Spartacus--a gladiator— has been portrayed as a hero in literature and in the movies. Use the Internet to find reliable sources about what his life was like and what he tried to accomplish. Identify three facts that you discover from your research and present them to the class. For more about using the Internet for research, read *What Does a Historian Do?*

The Roman Family

At the heart of Roman society was the family. When Rome was a republic, large families were common. Married children often lived in the same house with their parents and other relatives. The father closely watched over his wife and her activities. The law even allowed fathers to sell children into slavery or have them put to death. In later times, fathers lost some of this power, and wives gained some legal rights. Families had fewer children, and Romans were more likely to divorce and remarry.

Fathers in upper-class families were responsible for the education of their children. When they were young, wealthy boys and girls learned from private lessons at home. As they grew older, boys from wealthy families went to schools where they studied reading, writing, arithmetic, and rhetoric, or public speaking. Older girls continued to study at home. Poorer Romans could not afford to go to school, but some of them learned enough reading, writing, and arithmetic to help them conduct business.

R C At about the age of 15, a Roman boy celebrated becoming an adult. He would burn his toys as offerings to the household gods. Then he would put on a white toga, a loose-fitting robe that Roman men wore. Once he became an adult, a man might work at his family's business, join the army, or get a job in the government. Men tended to marry later, but women usually married around the age of 14. Once they married, Roman women were considered adults.

Upper-class Roman women were often educated and expected to teach their children about Roman culture.

▶ CRITICAL THINKING
Analyzing How were the roles of Roman men and women different?

Roman/The Bridgeman Art Library/Getty Images

What Was Life Like for Roman Women?

Women in early Rome were not full citizens and had few rights. They had a strong influence on their families, however, and often advised their husbands in private. When Rome was an empire, the wives of emperors began to exercise more power. For example, while the emperor Septimius fought rebels in distant parts of the empire, the empress Julia Domna **administered,** or was in charge of, political affairs in Rome.

The freedoms a Roman woman enjoyed depended on her husband's wealth and position. By the A.D. 100s, wealthy women had more independence.

Reading HELPDESK (CCSS)

Reading Strategy: *Summarizing*

When you summarize, you find the main idea of a passage and restate it in your own words. Read how the Romans treated enslaved people. On a separate sheet of paper, summarize the passage in one or two sentences.

Academic Vocabulary (Tier 2 Words)

administer to be lawfully in charge of
protect to defend from trouble or harm

networks Online Teaching Options

WHITEBOARD ACTIVITY

Life of Roman Women

Comparing and Contrasting As a class, brainstorm a list of responses that answer this question: What types of rights and freedoms do women in the United States have today? **Ask:** Are women allowed to vote? Can they serve in the military? Can they own property? Can they go to college? Can they pursue any career? *(yes to all)* Point out that in early Rome, wealthy women had more freedoms than women who had less money. Project the Interactive Whiteboard Activity. Have volunteers drag items from the Item Bank to the correct column in the interactive chart. Next, have students circle the freedoms that women have today. *(Students may circle all items.)* AL ELL

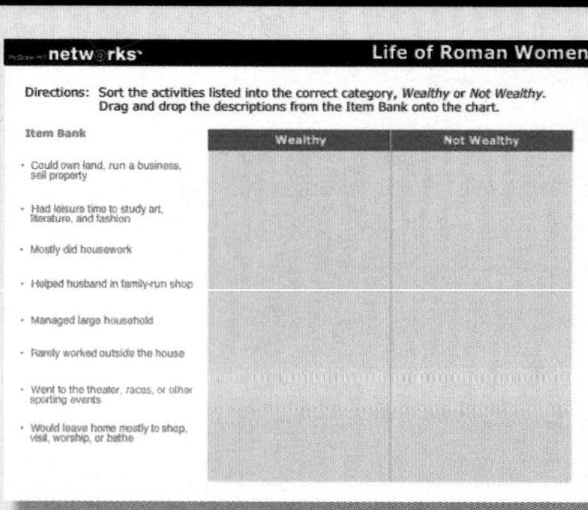

See page 337C for other online activities.

They could own land, run businesses, and sell property. They managed the household while enslaved people did the housework. This left women free to study literature, art, and fashion. Outside the home, they could go to the theater or attend races and fights, but they had to sit in areas separate from men.

Women with less money had less freedom. They spent their time doing housework or helping their husbands in family-run shops. They were allowed to leave home to shop, visit friends, worship at temples, or go to the baths. A few women worked independently outside the home. Some served as priestesses, carrying out religious rituals in temples, while others worked as hairdressers and even doctors.

Rome and Slavery

Slavery was a part of Roman life from early times. The use of slave labor grew, however, as Rome acquired more territory. Roman soldiers took conquered peoples as prisoners. These captives were brought to Rome and sold into slavery. By 100 B.C., about 40 percent of the people in Italy were enslaved.

Enslaved people performed many different jobs. They worked in homes and harvested crops. They mined ore and helped build roads, bridges, and aqueducts throughout the empire. Many enslaved Greeks, though, were well educated. They served as teachers, doctors, and artisans. **C**

For most enslaved people, life was miserable. They were often forced to work long hours and could be sold at any time. They were punished severely for poor work or for running away. To escape their hardships, enslaved people often rebelled.

In 73 B.C., a gladiator named Spartacus (SPAHR•tuh•kuhs) led a slave rebellion. As Spartacus and his forces moved through Italy, their numbers swelled to 70,000. Spartacus planned to reach the Alps. From there, the enslaved people could return to their homelands. The Roman army, however, crushed the revolt. Spartacus was killed in battle and 6,000 of his followers were crucified, or put to death by being nailed to a cross. **W**

Religion and Philosophy

Romans believed that gods controlled all parts of life. Household spirits protected the home and family. Gods **protected** the entire empire. Greek gods and goddesses were given Roman names. For example, Zeus became Jupiter, the sky god, and Aphrodite became Venus, the goddess of love and beauty. Beginning with Augustus, emperors were officially made gods by the Roman Senate.

Romans worshipped their gods and goddesses by praying and offering food to them. Every Roman home included an altar for its household gods. At altars, the head of the family made offerings of incense, wine, honey, and the family meal.

BIOGRAPHY

Livia (58 B.C.–A.D. 29)

Livia Augustus, as she was later called, stood out among Roman women. As the wife of Caesar Augustus for 52 years, she was a symbol of Roman marriage and family. She was also seen as a model of Roman morality. When her grandson, Claudius, became emperor, she took the title of Augustus and held a position of high honor.

▶ **CRITICAL THINKING**
Making Inferences What does the honoring of Livia tell us about the beliefs of the Roman people?

The Roman Way of Life

C Critical Thinking Skills

Explaining Have students consider the role of slavery in Roman society. **Ask:**

- **How much of the Roman population was made up of enslaved people?** *(By 100 B.C., it included about 40 percent of the population.)*
- **Where did enslaved people work?** *(Enslaved people worked in homes, on farms, and in mines.)*
- **How do you think the dependence on slavery might have affected Rome's economy?** *(Answers will vary. Students might say that slave owners could keep more profits since enslaved people did not receive payment for their work. On the other hand, slave rebellions could bring the economy to a halt since many industries were so dependent on slave labor.)* BL
- **Who was Spartacus, and why was he significant?** *(Spartacus was a gladiator who led an unsuccessful slave revolt in 73 B.C.)*

W Writing Skills

Narrative Have students write a series of diary entries or letters about Roman daily life. Students will choose a type of person discussed in this chapter and use information from the chapter to describe who they were and the types of things that they did in daily life. Entries should include specific details about:

- the city of Rome
- the Roman family
- the lives of women or slaves
- religion and philosophy

You may wish to pair students to work together for this activity so that the entries take on a conversational or responsive style in which the two students tell, ask, or respond to one another within their writing. **Verbal/Linguistic**

BIOGRAPHY

Livia

Researching on the Internet Allow students to read the interactive biography of Livia. Then ask students to come up with several additional questions they have about her life that were not mentioned in the biography. Have students research the answers to their questions on the Internet and share their findings later with the class.

See page 337C for other online activities.

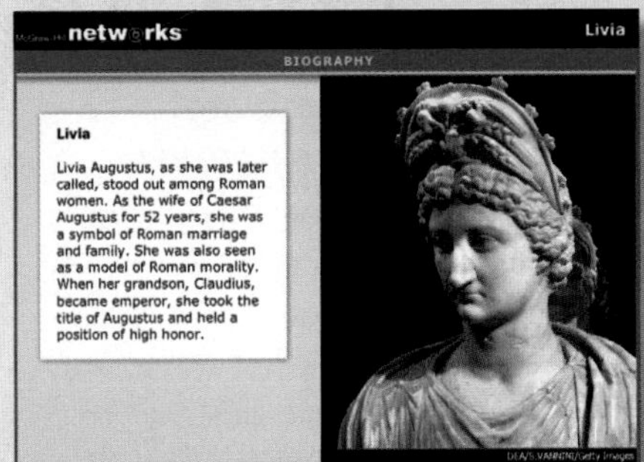

ANSWER, p. 343

CRITICAL THINKING The honoring of Livia tells us that the Roman people respected women who were loyal to their families.

C Critical Thinking Skills

Categorizing On the board, draw a two-column chart. Head one column with *Galen* and the other column with *Ptolemy.* Read each of these descriptive phrases and have students indicate the person to whom the phrase refers. Write—or have volunteers write—each phrase in the correct column. AL ELL

- cut open dead animals to learn about inner organs
- studied the motion of planets and created rules to explain their movements
- scientist who lived in Alexandria
- doctor who was Greek
- mapped over 1,000 different stars
- emphasized the importance of anatomy

Galen	Ptolemy
doctor who was Greek	scientist who lived in Alexandria
cut open dead animals to learn about inner organs	mapped over 1,000 different stars
emphasized the importance of anatomy	studied the motion of planets and created rules to explain their movements

Government officials made offerings in temples where important gods and goddesses of Rome were honored. Temples were open to all people.

The Romans also adapted ideas from Greek **philosophy,** such as the philosophy of Stoicism. For the Greeks, Stoicism was about finding happiness through reason. Romans, however, believed Stoicism was about learning to live in a practical way. Stoic philosophers urged people to participate in public affairs, to do their civic duty, and to treat conquered peoples well.

As the empire grew, Romans came into **contact** with people who practiced different religions. Rome allowed these people to practice their religions if they did not threaten the government.

✓ PROGRESS CHECK

Explaining Why was the family important in Roman society?

Science and Art

GUIDING QUESTION ***How did the Greeks influence Roman culture?***

As a republic and later as an empire, Rome was influenced by Greek civilization. The Romans admired and studied Greek art, architecture, and philosophy. They copied the Greeks in many ways but changed, or adapted, what they borrowed to match their own needs.

This urn is an example of the glass objects that were made and traded throughout the Roman Empire. Just as people recycle glass today, so did ancient Roman glass workers.

Science

C

The Romans learned from Greek science. A Greek doctor named Galen introduced many **medical** ideas to Rome. He emphasized the importance of **anatomy** (uh•NA•tuh•mee), the study of body structure. To learn about inner organs, Galen cut open dead animals and recorded his findings. Doctors in the Western world studied Galen's work for more than 1,500 years.

An important scientist of the Roman Empire was Ptolemy (TAH•luh•mee). Ptolemy lived in the city of Alexandria, in Egypt. He studied the sky and carefully mapped over 1,000 different stars. He studied the motion of planets and stars and created rules to explain their movements. Educated people in Europe accepted his ideas for centuries.

The Romans developed practical engineering skills. They built roads that connected Rome to every part of the empire. The first major Roman road, the Appian Way, linked Rome to southeastern Italy. The roads allowed Roman soldiers to travel quickly to different regions. Merchants used the roads, to trade their goods in different regions throughout the empire.

Reading HELPDESK CCSS

anatomy the study of the body's structure

Academic Vocabulary (Tier 2 Words)

philosophy basic beliefs, concepts, and attitudes
contact communication or connection
medical relating to the practice of medicine

networks Online Teaching Options

GRAPHIC ORGANIZER

Taking Notes: *Identifying:* The Greeks and the Romans

Comparing and Contrasting Show the graphic organizer titled "The Greeks and the Romans" for this lesson. After students have learned about how the Romans adapted Greek ideas, have them list these developments in the graphic organizer.

See page 337C for other online activities.

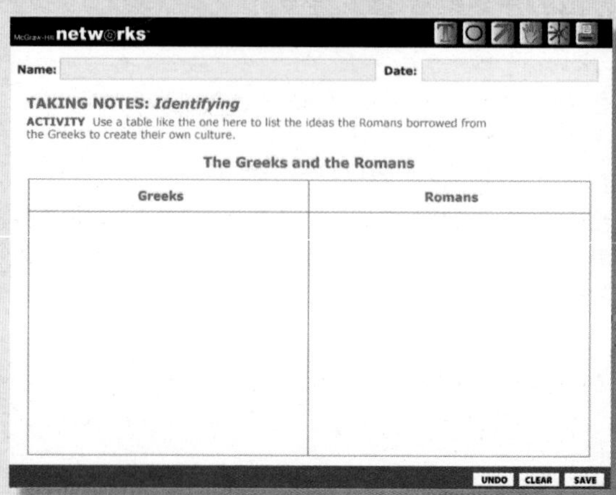

ANSWER, p. 344

✓ PROGRESS CHECK The family was the center of Roman life. A family's wealth determined the level of education available to the children and the amount of freedom available to the women in the family.

Roman engineers supplied cities with fresh water using aqueducts. They built aqueducts to bring water from the hills into the cities. Aqueducts were long troughs supported by rows of high **arches.** Aqueducts carried water over long distances. One Roman-built aqueduct in Segovia, Spain, is still used today—nearly 1,900 years after it was completed.

The Roman system of numbers, also called numerals, helped business people with their accounting. The system used letter-like symbols borrowed from the Greeks and the Etruscans. We still use Roman numerals to show dates on buildings, to create outlines, and to count items in a series, like Super Bowl games.

Art and Architecture

The Romans also adopted many features of Greek art and architecture. Roman artists, however, developed their own styles. The Greeks made statues that showed perfect-looking people with beautiful bodies. Roman statues were more realistic and included wrinkles, warts, and other less attractive features.

Roman builders also introduced their own features to Greek ideas. They used arches in bridges, aqueducts, and buildings. Rows of arches were often built against one another to form a **vault,** or curved ceiling. Using this method, the Romans were able to create domes from many rings of shaped stone.

The Romans were the first people to master the use of concrete, a mixture of volcanic ash, lime, and water. When it dried, this mix was as hard as rock. The Romans used concrete, domes, and arches to build many different structures. One of the most famous Roman structures is the Colosseum, a huge arena completed about A.D. 80. Another example is the Pantheon (PAN•thee•AHN), a temple built to honor Rome's gods. The Pantheon's domed roof was the largest of its time. Today, it is one of the oldest undamaged buildings in the world.

V

Literature

Like the Greeks, Romans respected writers and philosophers. The Romans were also idealists searching for the meaning of life. Roman writers, however, went beyond the Greek myths and plays to create their own style. They honored their gods but also wrote comedies about them. The Romans praised military successes but also wrote about failures in battle.

The Greeks and Romans used medical tools they designed themselves. Greek physicians passed medical knowledge to the Romans, who advanced it further. The Romans then passed medical techniques to the Western world that are still used today.

▶ CRITICAL THINKING

Making Connections What are some of the medical ideas the Romans learned from the Greeks? How are these ideas in use today?

(t) DEA/A.DAGLI ORTI/Getty Images,
(c) Peter Dazeley/Getty Images,
(b) Buena Vista Images/The Image Bank/Getty Images

vault a curved ceiling made of arches

Visual Vocabulary

arch a curved part of a structure that serves as a support

V Visual Skills

Drawing After students have read "Art and Architecture," have students choose one of the following activities:

- Draw a friend, family member, or fictional character in the Roman style of art.
- Draw a room in an actual or fictional location that has two of these Roman architectural features: arch, dome, vault.

Content Background Knowledge

Roman Roads

- The roads in the Roman Empire all connected to Rome. At the center of the capital city was a "golden milestone" *(milliareum aureum)* from which the Roman road system extended. The first of the Roman roads was the Appian Way, built in 312 B.C. to connect Rome and the city of Brundisium (modern Brindisi) on the Adriatic coast. By A.D. 200, the Roman Empire featured 50,000 miles (80,000 km) of roadways stretching from Britain to Mesopotamia and from the Danube River to Spain and northern Africa.
- The Roman roads were noted for being straight, having solid foundations and sufficient drainage, and being built using concrete. Though Roman engineers adapted to local terrain and resources, they followed basically the same principles in building abroad as they did in Italy. The Roman road system made it easier to conquer and administer far-flung territories and later provided a means for great migrations into the empire. The roads also served as a means for the spread of Christianity. Despite deterioration from neglect, Roman roads continued to serve Europe throughout the Middle Ages, and many fragments of the roads—including the Appian Way—survive today.

SLIDE SHOW

Roman Architecture

Analyzing Visuals Share the slide show featuring Roman architecture for Lesson 1, and discuss the developments illustrated in each photo. Help students notice how the Greeks influenced the Romans in each structure. AL ELL

See page 337C for other online activities.

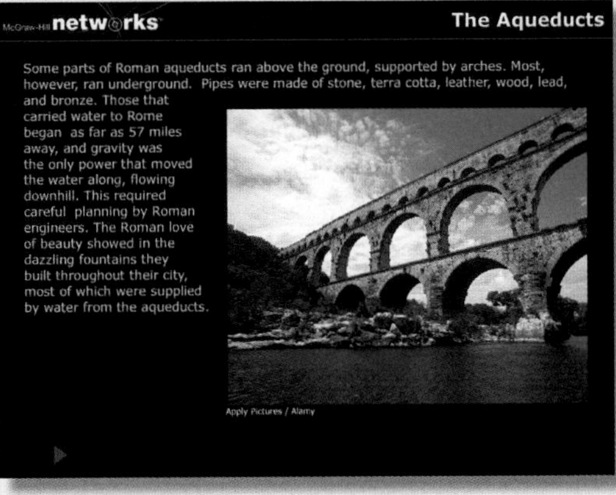

McGraw-Hill networks
The Aqueducts
Some parts of Roman aqueducts ran above the ground, supported by arches. Most, however, ran underground. Pipes were made of stone, terra cotta, leather, wood, lead, and bronze. Those that carried water to Rome began as far as 57 miles away, and gravity was the only power that moved the water along, flowing downhill. This required careful planning by Roman engineers. The Roman love of beauty showed in the dazzling fountains they built throughout their city, most of which were supplied by water from the aqueducts.
Apply Pictures / Alamy

ANSWER, p. 345

CRITICAL THINKING The Romans learned the study of the body's anatomy from Galen, a Greek who learned about the body's structure by dissecting dead animals and documenting his findings. We still use the same knowledge of anatomy to examine and treat people.

W Writing Skills

Narrative Select several texts that contain satirical prose, poetry, or lyric poems that are or could be considered examples of an ode. Place students in pairs and allow them to spend part of one class session exploring the selections.

In the following class session, brainstorm ideas with students that can be used to write a modern-day ode or piece of satire that reflects some aspect of their daily lives. Have the same pairs work together to plan and produce one piece of writing.

Have students write their ode or satire during a third class session. You might consider creating a display or staging a class talent show as ways for students to share their work.
Verbal/Linguistic Interpersonal

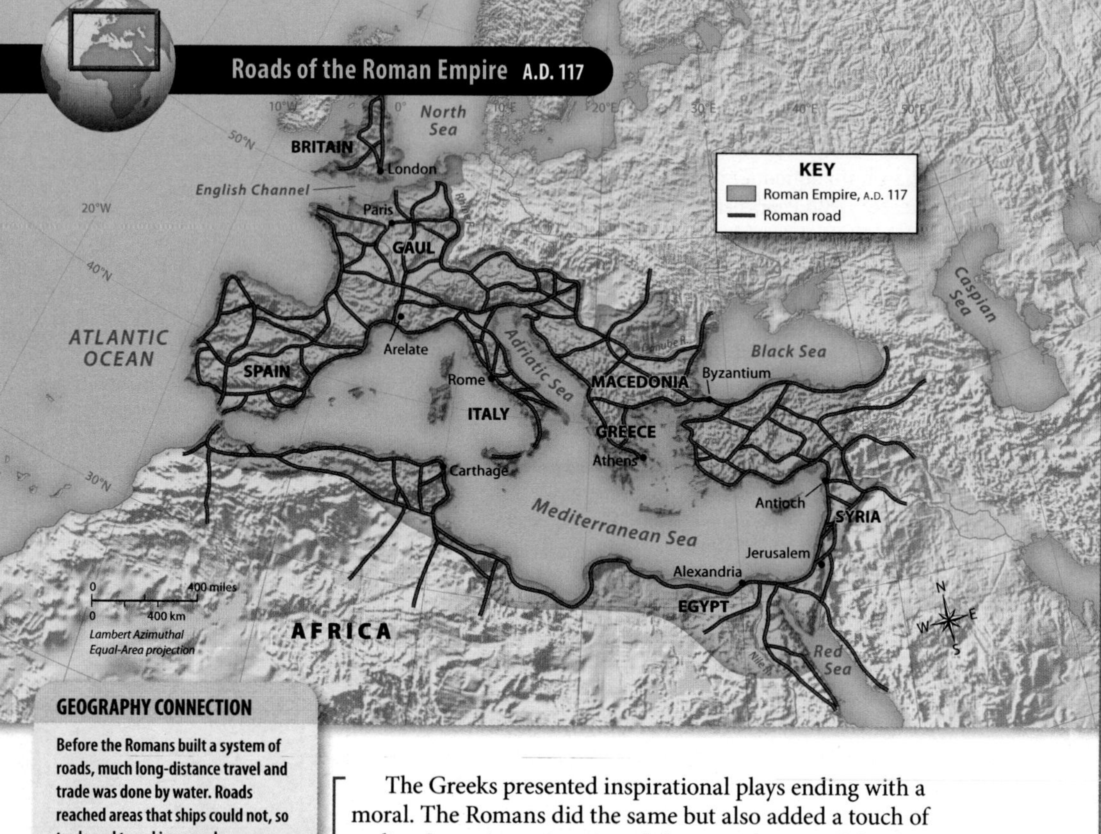

GEOGRAPHY CONNECTION

Before the Romans built a system of roads, much long-distance travel and trade was done by water. Roads reached areas that ships could not, so trade and travel improved.

1 **LOCATION** In relation to the rest of the empire, where is Rome located?

2 **CRITICAL THINKING** ***Drawing Conclusions*** Why were so many Roman roads built along waterways?

The Greeks presented inspirational plays ending with a moral. The Romans did the same but also added a touch of reality. Sometimes situations did not work out well for their characters. The Romans added a twist to their writing, revealing a more human side to people. They were not afraid to poke fun at the gods, political leaders, and heroes.

The Roman poet Virgil (VUHR•juhl) drew ideas from the *Odyssey*, an epic poem by a Greek writer named Homer. Virgil's epic poem, the *Aeneid* (uh•NEE•uhd), tells the story of the founding of Rome. In the *Aeneid*, Virgil expresses the values that he believed should guide Rome:

W

PRIMARY SOURCE

❝ But you, remember, are to be a Roman. . . . Your task is to impose peace by law and order: to protect the downtrodden, and to crush the arrogant [very proud] in war. ❞

—from the *Aeneid*, Book VI. 1151–1154, by Virgil

Reading HELPDESK CCSS

satire verse or prose that pokes fun at human weaknesses

ode a lyric poem that expresses strong emotions about life

networks Online Teaching Options

MAP

Roads of the Roman Empire A.D. 117

Reasoning As a class, view the interactive map that shows the expansion of Roman roads. Students may wish to use the digital pencils to re-create the network of Roman roads on the map in the textbook. **Ask:** How could a reliable road system help extend and maintain an empire? *(Students might explain that a reliable road system makes trade easier and allows troops to move quickly throughout an empire.)*

See page 337C for other online activities.

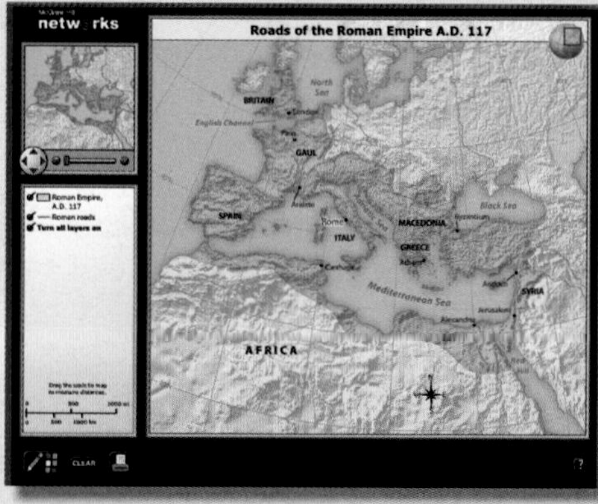

ANSWERS, p. 346

GEOGRAPHY CONNECTION

1 Rome is located in the center of the empire.

2 **CRITICAL THINKING** Roads were built near waterways to connect towns that were already established along the waterways.

Using Greek models, the Roman poet Horace (HAWR•uhs) wrote **satires** (SA•tyrs). These works poked fun at human weaknesses, much like comedians do today. Horace also wrote **odes,** or poems that express strong emotions about life.

Inspired by the Greek historian Herodotus (hih•RAH•duh•tuhs), Livy and Tacitus (TA•suh•tuhs) wrote about Roman history. In his *History of Rome*, Livy describes Rome's rise to power. He said that history had moral lessons to teach people.

While Livy celebrated Rome's greatness, Tacitus took a more critical view. He believed that Rome's emperors had taken away people's freedom. Tacitus also thought Romans were losing the values that made them strong. He accused them of wasting time on sports and other pleasures.

Theater and Language

One of the most popular pastimes in Rome was attending plays. Roman plays were staged as part of religious celebrations or national festivals. The actors wore masks to represent the characters. Masks allowed actors to play different roles. For most of Rome's history, men and boys played all the roles in a play. Women were allowed to act only in comedy plays called mimes.

Latin, the language of the Romans, had an even bigger impact than Roman writings. Latin became Europe's language for government, trade, and learning until about A.D. 1500. Latin is the basis of many modern European languages, such as Italian, French, and Spanish. It shaped several others as well. Some of the English words we use today come from Latin.

Romans attending the theater sat in stadiums much like those in sports arenas today.

Richard Hamilton Smith/CORBIS

✓ PROGRESS CHECK

Explaining Describe Roman improvements to Greek architecture.

LESSON 1 REVIEW (CCSS)

Review Vocabulary (Tier 3 Words)

1. What is the difference between a *satire* and an *ode*?
2. Why would a doctor today need to study *anatomy*? RH.6–8.2, RH.6–8.4

Answer the Guiding Questions

3. ***Identifying*** What were the different roles a father played in the Roman family? RH.6–8.2
4. ***Describing*** What was daily life like for Roman women? Describe two differences that existed between women who were wealthy and those who were poor. RH.6–8.2
5. ***Contrasting*** How did the Romans differ from the Greeks in their art that shows the human body? RH.6–8.2
6. ***Differentiating*** How did the Greeks influence Roman writers? RH.6–8.2
7. **INFORMATIVE/EXPLANATORY** Why do civilizations borrow elements from earlier civilizations? Think of two elements of American culture that have been borrowed from ancient Roman cultures. Explain what they are in a short essay. WHST.6–8.2, WHST.6–8.10

LESSON 1 REVIEW ANSWERS

1. Students should indicate that satire is a free-form piece of writing meant to poke fun at someone or something, and an ode is a poem that expresses strong emotions about life.
2. By studying anatomy, a doctor learns about the structure of the human body.
3. A father was the head of his household. He was responsible for his children's education and his family's business.
4. Women advised their husbands in private, did the housework, shopped, and helped in the family business. Unlike poor women, wealthy women had enslaved people do their housework and were free to study and engage in leisure activities.
5. Greek statues showed perfect-looking people with beautiful bodies. Roman sculpture was more realistic, often showing less attractive details.
6. Greek myths honored their gods and praised military successes. Romans honored their gods but also wrote comedies about their mishaps, and they praised the success of their military generals but also wrote about their failures in battle.
7. Student essays should reflect an awareness that people learn from past generations and from the cultures with which they have interacted. They should mention two or more specific cultural elements—such as language and architectural styles—that Americans have borrowed from Roman civilization.

The Roman Way of Life

T Technology Skills

Making Presentations Have students use the Internet to find photos and information to create their own short slide-show presentations that illustrate one example of how the Greeks influenced Roman science, art, architecture, literature, or theater.

For example, students might find photos of the Greek Parthenon and compare this to the Roman Pantheon. Students should first describe the Greek example and then explain how the Romans adapted it to meet their needs. BL

Have students complete the Lesson 1 Review.

CLOSE & REFLECT

To close the lesson, write the following list on the board: home, family, religion, philosophy, science, art, architecture, literature, theater, language. Then ask students to brainstorm a list of adjectives that describe each aspect of life in the Roman Empire. Write their responses on the board.

ANSWER, p. 347

✓ PROGRESS CHECK The Romans created domes and arches so they could build structures that were more useful for their own purposes. They also used new materials such as concrete.

ENGAGE

Bellringer Remind the class that understanding historical context can help them understand historical literature. List the following names on the board: *The Aeneid*, Virgil, and Augustus. Read the introduction. **Ask:**

- **What is *The Aeneid*?** *(an epic poem)*
- **Who was Virgil?** *(a Roman poet)*
- **Who was Augustus?** *(a Roman emperor)* AL
- **Why is it important to know that Virgil served in the court of Emperor Augustus?** *(Virgil's writings might have been influenced by Augustus. Virgil might have been writing to impress or please Augustus.)*

TEACH & ASSESS

R Reading Skills

Citing Text Evidence Have the class read the quotation chorally (aloud, in unison) as you lead them, using a slightly louder voice. Tell students they have just read the words of a father, Anchises, to his son, Aeneas. **Ask: How do you think Anchises feels about Rome?** *(Sample responses: Anchises is proud because Rome will be his son's city. Anchises sees Rome as a benevolent guardian of its people.)* BL **Auditory/Musical**

Content Background Knowledge

- *The Aeneid* is written in dactylic hexameter. A *dactyl* is a metered foot of classical verse that consists of one long syllable followed by two short syllables. Poetry written in dactylic hexameter is the oldest type of Greek poetry.
- Virgil never completed the *Aeneid*. Approximately 60 lines of the epic poem were unfinished at his time of his death in 19 B.C.

THE WORLD'S LITERATURE CCSS

The Aeneid

by Virgil (70 B.C. –19 B.C.)

Virgil (70 B.C.–19 B.C.), the author of the epic *The Aeneid*

Virgil is one of ancient Rome's greatest poets. He grew up on a farm and spent much of his life away from Rome. Virgil also served as a member in the court of Emperor Augustus.

After Emperor Augustus defeated his rivals and took power, he asked the poet Virgil to write a poem to honor Rome. Virgil wrote the *Aeneid*. It is an epic that retells the Greek legend of the battle of Troy from a Roman point of view.

In writing the *Aeneid*, Virgil did what many Roman artists did—he modeled his work on the earlier works of the Greeks. In the *Aeneid*, Virgil echoed the words of the Greek poet Homer.

In this excerpt, Aeneas (ih • NEE • uhs) is visiting the Underworld, the mythical world of the Dead, where he finds his father, Anchises (an • KEE • seez). There, Anchises explains some of the mysteries of the Underworld and predicts that future members of Aeneas's family will found Rome.

> ***"But you, remember, are to be a Roman. . . . Your task is to impose peace by law and order: to protect the downtrodden, and to crush the arrogant in war."***
>
> —from *Aeneid*, Book VI, by Virgil

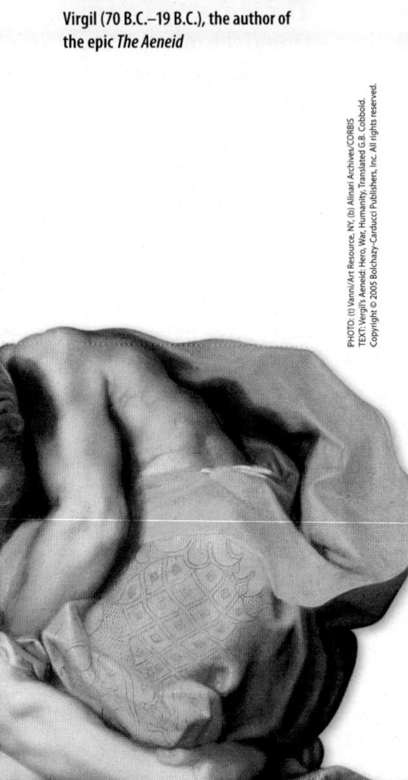

Aeneas carries Anchises—his father—from burning Troy.

networks *Online Teaching Options*

CHART

Roles of Family Members

Creating Charts Have students view the interactive chart to learn about roles of family members in Rome. Explain that a genealogy chart is a flowchart with the eldest known relatives at the top. Read only the first paragraph of the primary source aloud. Next, write *Anchises* in the upper-left corner of the whiteboard. As you ask the following questions, add each name in the proper position, below and slightly to the right, with a line connecting it to the relative(s). **Ask: Who is Anchises's son?** *(Aeneas)* **Who is Aeneas's son?** *(Silvius)* **Who is Silvius's son?** *(Silvius Aeneas)* **Who is Aeneas's wife, and where does she belong on the diagram?** *(Lavinia; she belongs next to Aeneas, with a line connecting down to her son, Silvius.)* BL

networks — Roles of Family Members

Directions: Click the boxes to explore the family roles of Romans.

Family Member	Roles of Romans
Father	
Mother	
Son	
Daughter	

PRIMARY SOURCE

"Now: I will describe to you the glory that will come upon the future generations of Trojans. I will tell you who our Italian **descendants** (dih • SEHN • duhnts) will be, and what distinction they will bring to our name. Do you see that young man leaning on a simple spear? He . . . will be the first to have in his veins a mixture of Trojan and Italian blood. He will be your son, Silvius. His mother will be called Lavinia. . . . She will bring him up in the woods to be a king and the father of kings. . . . And there are his glorious successors, next to him. Look especially at Silvius Aeneas, who will share your name: if ever he comes to the throne, he will be remembered equally for his devotion to the gods and for his courage in war. What excellent young men they are—don't you think?

"Next comes Romulus: he will be the son of Mars and Rhea Silvia, herself descended from my grandfather. Do you see the double **plume** (PLOOM) on the crest of his helmet? And how he is marked out by his father to be a god himself? He will be the founder of Rome—a wall will enclose her seven hills, but her empire will reach to the farthest edges of the world, her fame to the heights of Olympus. She will be fortunate in the race that she will nurture [care for]. . . .

"To sum up: there are some places where **smiths** and sculptors will shape bronze more subtly, or carve more lifelike portraits out of marble; in others, **orators** (AWR • uh • tuhrs) will argue more persuasively, and astronomers will observe more accurately the motion of the heavenly bodies and predict the rising stars. But you, remember, are to be a Roman, and the Romans' art is to be art of a different kind: the art of government, of ruling nations. Your task is to impose peace by law and order: to protect the **downtrodden**, and to crush the arrogant in war."

—from Vergil's* *Aeneid: Hero, War, Humanity*. tr. G.B. Cobbold.

*Vergil is an alternate spelling of Virgil

PHOTO: Nik Keevil/Alamy

Vocabulary

descendant
future member of a family

smith
craftsperson who works with metal

orator
public speaker

downtrodden
people who are poor or suffering

Visual Vocabulary

A **plume** is a group of feathers or horse hair often worn on the top of a headpiece.

Analyzing Literature DBQ

1. ***Analyzing*** What is the purpose of Anchises's speech to Aeneas? What parts of the passage show that purpose? RH.6–8.6
2. ***Interpreting*** What does Anchises describe as the "Romans' art"? RH.6–8.2, RH.6–8.6

C Critical Thinking Skills

Analyzing Primary Sources Review the third paragraph with students. **Ask:**

- **Does Anchises think that people in Rome will do everything better than people in other places?** *(No; he says that in some places, people will do a variety of things better.)*
- **What will Rome do best?** *(rule nations)*

R Reading Skills

Finding the Main Idea Have students review the final paragraph for the main idea behind Anchises's conversation with his son. **Ask: How do you think Emperor Augustus might have felt about Virgil's poem? Why?** *(Sample answer: He might have been pleased because the poem gives a positive view of Rome and identifies how Rome will treat its people.)* BL

W Writing Skills

Argument Anchises tells Aeneas that his task is to impose peace by law and order, protect the downtrodden, and crush the arrogant in war. Have students choose one part of the task and write a paragraph that tells why they think that part of the task is the most important of the three. **Intrapersonal**

CLOSE & REFLECT

To close the lesson, tell students that many great pieces of literature feature a hero who does brave deeds. Ask students to tell who the hero might be and explain why. *(Sample answers: Anchises—because he is guiding his son to make Rome great; Aeneas—because he will return from the Underworld to lead Rome to greatness)*

At the end of the discussion, have students complete the Analyzing Literature questions.

CHART

Web Graphic Organizer

Organizing Have students use a Web graphic organizer to organize the information that Anchises gives to Aeneas. Students can write a phrase like "What Anchises says to Aeneas" in the middle of the Web. One part of the Web should contain information about the descendants of Aeneas.

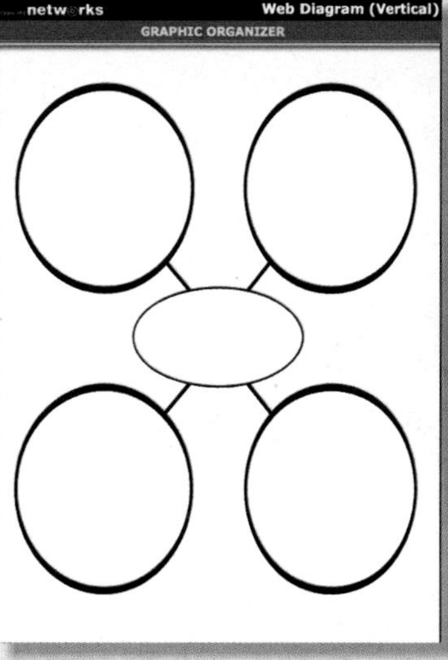

ANSWERS, p. 349

1. He wants to show Aeneas that his descendants will have an important future in Italy. "I have long wished to show you, to let you see for yourself, the generations of our family that are yet to come, so that when you have made your mark in Italy, you may share my pride in them; Now: I will describe to you the glory that will come upon the future generations of Trojans. I will tell you who our Italian descendants will be, and what distinction they will bring to our name."
2. Roman art is to be the art of government, of ruling nations. The Romans are to impose peace by law and order, and to protect the downtrodden, and to crush the arrogant in war.

ENGAGE

Bellringer Tell students that in this lesson they are learning why the Roman Empire collapsed. They will also learn about the actions that emperors took to prevent the Roman Empire from collapsing and why those actions were unsuccessful. **Ask:**

- **What factors might cause an empire like Rome to collapse?** *(Students might identify economic problems, political scandals, or military invasions.)* Write these factors on the board under "Reasons an Empire Might Collapse."
- **If you were a Roman emperor, what are some things you would do to prevent a collapse from happening?** *(Students might identify collecting taxes, passing laws, or strengthening the military.)* List these things on the board under "Ways to Prevent an Empire From Collapsing."
- **Do you think your actions would have prevented the collapse of the Roman Empire? Why or why not?** *(Answers will vary.)* Discuss with students how their ideas might be successful or unsuccessful.

TEACH & ASSESS

R Reading Skills

Specifying Write *politics, economy,* and *invasion* on the board. Tell students to look for and list the reasons in "A Troubled Empire" that these three issues led to Rome's decline. *(Sample answers: politics: the army became powerful and the government became weak; economy: food prices were high and people had less money; invasion: the Roman Empire was invaded from the east and the west.)*

ANSWERS, p. 350

TAKING NOTES: political confusion, economic weakness, invasions

networks *There's More Online!*

- **GRAPHIC ORGANIZER** Why RomeCollapsed
- **CHART/GRAPH**
  - History of Constantinople Time Line
  - Infographic: The Fall of Rome
- **MAP** Germanic Migrations A.D. 200–500
- **SLIDE SHOW** The U.S. Capitol

Lesson 2

Rome's Decline

ESSENTIAL QUESTION *Why do civilizations rise and fall?*

IT MATTERS BECAUSE

The fall of Rome resulted from political uproar, distant wars, and economic crises.

A Troubled Empire

GUIDING QUESTION *What problems led to Rome's decline?*

Marcus Aurelius was the last of five emperors who reigned during the *Pax Romana*, a time of peace and progress. Nearly a century of confusion and violence followed.

Political Confusion

During this time, Rome's government grew weak, while the army became very powerful. To stay in office, an emperor had to pay increasingly higher wages to the soldiers who supported him. **R** When these payments could not be made, soldiers would turn against the emperor. Then civil wars broke out, as legion fought legion to put a new emperor on the throne. In a span of about 50 years, ending in A.D. 284, Rome had 22 different emperors. Most were murdered by the army or by their bodyguards.

Roman society also suffered during this period. Many Romans no longer honored the traditional values of duty, courage, and honesty. Dishonest government officials took bribes, and few talented citizens wanted to hold government office. Interest and support for education declined, and many wealthy Romans simply stopped paying taxes. Enslaved laborers now made up a large part of the empire's population.

Reading **HELP**DESK CCSS

Taking Notes: *Organizing*

Use a graphic organizer like the one shown here to identify reasons the Roman Empire collapsed. RH.6–8.2

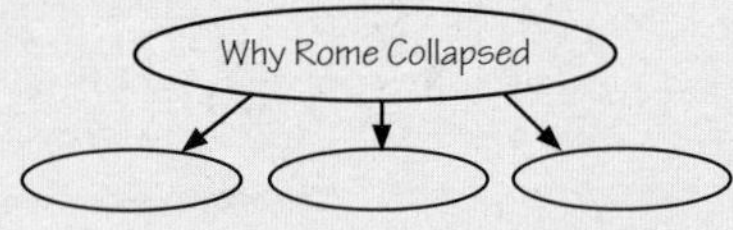

Content Vocabulary (Tier 3 Words)

- **reforms**

networks *Online Teaching Options*

VIDEO

The Coliseum

Comparing and Contrasting Point out to students that *coliseum* and *colosseum* are both common and accepted spellings of the word. They refer to the same structure. ELL Play the video for students. It discusses the archaeological importance and grandeur of the Coliseum along with its notorious history.

Discuss with students some of the reasons that the Coliseum is considered to be one of the world's greatest landmarks. Then contrast that by discussing some of the reasons that the Coliseum's history also has negative aspects.

See page 337D for other online activities.

Economic Weaknesses

Rome's weakened government led to a weakened economy during the A.D. 200s. Roman soldiers and foreign invaders attacked farms and disrupted trade. These attacks led to food shortages, and food prices soared. People had less money to spend, so they bought fewer goods. The price of wheat from Egypt rose from seven or eight drachmae (DRAYK•muh) per unit to 120,000. Merchants saw their profits decline, forcing many out of business. Many workers lost their jobs.

To stop this economic decline, the government produced more coins. The government, however, did not have a large supply of gold and silver. As a result, the new coins had less of these precious metals in them, which reduced their value. In order to get the same profit for their goods, farmers and merchants continued to raise their prices. These actions led to inflation, or a steep rise in prices with a matching decline in the value of money. As the value of Roman coins decreased, people began to barter, or to exchange goods instead of money. C

Invasions

While Rome continued to struggle, Germanic tribes raided the western empire, and Persian armies invaded in the east. People living in cities built protective walls around them. With less money to use, the government started to hire Germanic soldiers. Germanic soldiers, however, had no loyalty to the empire.

When Roman coins were made, they were imprinted with the image of the ruling emperor.

These well-preserved walls were built by the Romans in the late A.D. 200s to protect the town of Lugo, Spain.

▶ CRITICAL THINKING

Drawing Conclusions Why did Roman towns require protection in the A.D. 200s?

C Critical Thinking Skills

Determining Cause and Effect Display the sentences from the chart below on the board in a random order. Then, have students sort the sentences into a two-column cause-and-effect chart. You might also choose to write selected sentences in the chart and have students tell where the remaining sentences should be written. AL ELL

Cause	Effect
Roman soldiers and foreign invaders disrupted trade.	There were food shortages and soaring prices.
People had less money.	People bought fewer goods.
Merchants saw profits decline.	Merchants went out of business.
The government produced coins with less gold and silver in them.	The new coins had a reduced value.
Farmers and merchants raised prices to make profits.	There was a steep rise in prices and a decline in the value of money.
The value of Roman coins decreased.	People began to barter instead of using money.

Content Background Knowledge

- In the Roman Empire, a gold coin was known as an *aureus.* Emperors gave these coins as gifts or used them to make large monetary payments. The average Roman would probably never even have the chance to hold a single *aureus* in his or her lifetime because the coins were so valuable.
- A denarius was a silver coin with a lower weight standard than previous silver coins. The Romans started to mint the *denarius* because the Second Punic War began to cause financial stress on the empire.
- A *sestertius* was a brass coin that was larger in size than a denarius but had less value.

GRAPHIC ORGANIZER

Taking Notes: *Organizing:* The Empire Collapses

Citing Text Evidence Direct students to the graphic organizer. **Ask:** **What three major factors led to the Roman Empire's decline?** *(political confusion, economic weaknesses, invasions)* **What are three reasons that political confusion led to the decline?** *(Sample answers: The army became powerful and the government weak. Many Romans no longer honored traditional values. Support for education declined.)* Have students list reasons under each major factor. AL ELL Repeat with the remaining major factors discussed in "A Troubled Empire."

See page 337D for other online activities.

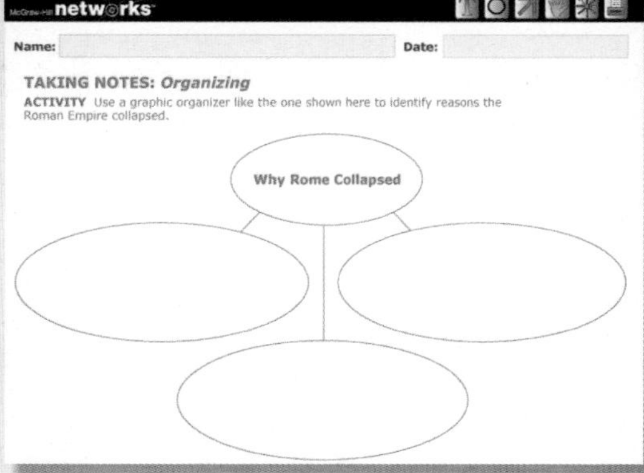

TAKING NOTES: *Organizing*

ACTIVITY Use a graphic organizer like the one shown here to identify reasons the Roman Empire collapsed.

ANSWER, p. 351

CRITICAL THINKING Roman towns required protection because more groups were invading the empire.

C Critical Thinking Skills

Defending Place students into at least two groups. Tell them that one group will argue in favor of Diocletian's reforms and the other group will argue against them. You may need to have more than one of each type of group; make sure each *For* group has a corresponding *Against* group. Instruct students to meet in their groups and read "Who was Diocletian?" Guide students to think about the following questions as they read. **Ask:**

- **What were some of the reforms Diocletian made?** *(Diocletian built forts along the frontiers to defend Rome's borders; divided the empire into four parts; set maximum prices for wages and goods to stop prices from rising; ordered workers to remain in their jobs to increase productivity; held local officials responsible for the taxes their communities had to pay.)*
- **What problem was Diocletian trying to solve by enacting these reforms?** *(Diocletian was trying to bring about political and economic reforms to help the empire survive.)*
- **Which of Diocletian's reforms do you think might have been more successful? Which might have been less successful? Explain.** *(Sample answers: Dividing the Roman Empire into four parts might have been more successful because the empire was so large. Ordering workers to stay at their jobs until they died might have been less successful because everyone might not have wanted to have the same job for their entire life.)*

Tell students that they will be debating in favor of or against Diocletian's reforms, and students must debate the point of view of their assigned group. Do not allow students to change their group assignments. Have each corresponding pair of groups present their arguments to the class. Ensure that all group members are participants in the debate.

At the conclusion of the debate, discuss the following questions with students. **Ask:**

- **Did the reforms solve the empire's problems? Why or why not?** *(No; the reforms were ineffective because people ignored them, and Diocletian's power was weak.)*
- **What do you think were some positive effects of the reforms even though they weren't successful?** *(Answers will vary. Sample answers: Having forts built along the empire's border was positive because the empire was protected from invading Germanic groups. Setting maximum prices on goods was positive so goods wouldn't be too expensive to buy.)* **BL Verbal/Linguistic Interpersonal**

ANSWERS, p. 352

✓ PROGRESS CHECK Diocletian set maximum prices for wages and goods to prevent prices from rising. He ordered workers to remain in the same job until they died. Also, he made local officials personally responsible for the taxes their communities had to pay.

CRITICAL THINKING Students might say the damage was too great to be fixed by Constantine's reforms or that Constantine's reforms did not address the problems facing the empire.

Who Was Diocletian?

A general named Diocletian (DY•uh•KLEE•shuhn) became emperor in A.D. 284. He introduced **reforms,** or political changes to make things better. To defend the empire against invasions, Diocletian built forts along its frontiers. To rule the large empire more efficiently, he divided it into four parts, each with its own ruler. He held ultimate authority over all of them.

C Diocletian also tried to strengthen the economy. He set maximum prices for wages and goods in order to prevent prices from rising further. To improve productivity, he ordered workers to remain at the same jobs until they died. Diocletian also made local officials personally responsible for the taxes their communities had to pay. Despite these efforts, Diocletian's reforms did not succeed. People ignored his rules, and Diocletian was not a strong enough emperor to enforce them.

✓ PROGRESS CHECK

Explaining How did Diocletian try to improve Rome's economy?

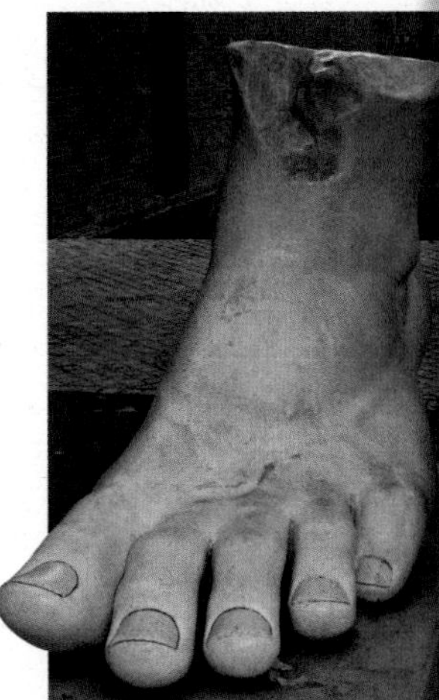

A giant's foot? No, it is actually a replica of a foot from a statue of the Roman Emperor Constantine. This 30-foot (9.1-m) statue once stood in a public building in the Roman Forum.

▶ CRITICAL THINKING

Hypothesizing Why do you think Constantine's reforms did not end Rome's decline?

The Fall of Rome

GUIDING QUESTION *What effect did Germanic invaders have on the Roman Empire?*

When Diocletian left office in A.D. 305, conflict again broke out in the empire. Fighting continued until another general named Constantine (KAHN•stuhn•TEEN) became emperor in A.D. 312.

Constantine's Rule

To improve the economy, Constantine issued several orders to **reinforce** the rules of Diocletian. Constantine also wanted a stable workforce and military. For example, the sons of workers had to follow their fathers' trades. The sons of farmers had to work their fathers' lands. The sons of soldiers served in the army.

In spite of Constantine's reforms, the empire continued to decline. In A.D. 330, Constantine moved the capital from a failing Rome to a new city in the east—the Greek city of Byzantium (buh•ZAN•tee•uhm) in present-day Turkey. This city became known as Constantinople (kahn•stan•tuh•NOH•puhl). After Constantine died a few years later, Theodosius (THEE•uh•DOH•shuhs) took power in Constantinople.

Reading HELPDESK CCSS

reforms changes to bring about improvement

Academic Vocabulary (Tier 2 Words)

reinforce to strengthen
expand to spread out

networks Online Teaching Options

TIME LINE

Place and Time: Roman Civilization

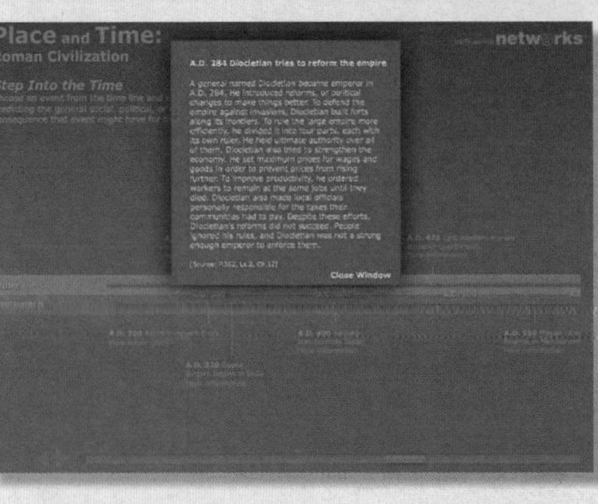

Narrative Show students the information about Diocletian on the *Place and Time: Roman Civilization* time line. Remind them that Diocletian divided the Roman Empire into four parts when he became emperor, and each part had its own ruler. Have students write a letter to Diocletian in Rome as though they were one of the four rulers. Students should write about how politics, the economy, inflation, or invasions are affecting their area of the empire and should offer an opinion about Diocletian's reforms. Have students also include the reasons they feel the way they do. **Intrapersonal**

See page 337D for other online activities.

After taking power, Theodosius found the empire difficult to govern. The empire covered a vast area and faced threats from both inside and outside its borders. Theodosius realized the empire had become too large to control from one seat of government. Theodosius decided that—when he died—the eastern and western parts should become separate empires. This division took place in A.D. 395. One empire was the Western Roman Empire, with its capital remaining at Rome. The other was the Eastern Roman Empire, with its capital city at Constantinople.

Following their rebellion and victory at Adrianople, the Visigoths invaded Rome.

Germanic Invaders

During the late A.D. 300s and 400s, many Germanic tribes migrated from northern Europe and fought to **expand** their hold over Roman territory. Some were looking for better land for raising livestock and farming. Many, however, were fleeing the Huns, a fierce group of warriors from Mongolia in Asia.

In the late A.D. 300s, the Huns entered Eastern Europe. Fearing a Hun attack, one Germanic tribe, the Visigoths (VIH•zuh•gahths), asked the Roman government for protection. The Romans let them settle just inside the empire's border. Here they were under the protection of the Roman army. In return, the Visigoths promised to be loyal to the empire. They promised not to attack the empire from the inside.

The Romans, however, treated the Visigoths badly. They charged them high prices for food and enslaved some of their people. Tired of Roman demands, the Visigoths finally rebelled. In≈A.D. 378, they fought and defeated the Roman legions at Adrianople (AY•dree•uh•NOH•puhl).

R

(t) Mary Evans Picture Library, (b) Travelbox Ltd/Photographers Choice/Getty Images

The modern city of Istanbul was known as Byzantium during the last days of the Western Roman Empire. When Emperor Constantine moved the capital of the empire there from Rome, Byzantium became Constantinople.

▶ **CRITICAL THINKING**
Analyzing Why did Constantine move the capital to Byzantium?

R Reading Skills

Describing On the board, draw a three-column chart or a graphic organizer with three areas. After students read "Germanic Invaders," **ask:** **How are the Huns, Visigoths, and Vandals described?** *(**Huns:** a fierce group of warriors from Mongolia; feared by many Germanic tribes; entered Eastern Europe in the late A.D. 300s; **Visigoths:** a Germanic tribe; feared the Huns; asked the Roman government for protection; settled just inside the empire's border so they were protected by the Roman army; promised to be loyal to the empire and not attack it from inside; were enslaved and treated badly by the Romans; rebelled and defeated the Roman legions at Adrianople in A.D. 378; captured Rome in A.D. 410; looted Rome's government buildings and private homes; **Vandals:** a Germanic group; attacked Roman lands in Spain and northern Africa; entered Rome in A.D. 455; spent almost two weeks seizing valuables and burning buildings in Rome.)*

Write the information in the chart or graphic organizer to help students organize the information as they discuss each group of invaders.

GAME

Invaders of the Roman Empire Concentration Game

Making Connections Allow students to play the concentration game "Invaders of the Roman Empire." Instruct them to match the names of the groups that invaded the Roman Empire from the lesson "Rome's Decline."

See page 337D for other online activities.

ANSWER, p. 353

CRITICAL THINKING Constantine moved the capital to Byzantium to escape the political unrest, economic problems, and invasions in the western part of the empire.

W Writing Skills

Informative/Explanatory Ask students to write about how invasions affected the collapse of the Roman Empire. They can write their answers to these questions in question-answer format, or you may choose to have students use them as the basis for a short essay.

- **Why might a vast—and larger—empire be more likely to be invaded than a smaller empire?** *(Sample answer: A larger empire would be more difficult to defend because it would need many more soldiers to protect it.)*
- **How did the way the Romans treated the Visigoths affect the stability of the empire?** *(Sample answer: After the Romans allowed the Visigoths to settle within the empire's borders, Rome treated them poorly. The Visigoths were charged high prices for food, and some of them were enslaved by the Romans. Tensions between the two groups increased, and the Visigoths rebelled.)*
- **What harmful actions did the Vandals take against the Roman Empire?** *(Sample answer: The Vandals attacked Roman lands in Spain and northern Africa. Then they sailed to Italy and entered Rome. The Vandals spent two weeks in Rome taking valuables and burning buildings.)*
- **Which English word comes from the actions of the Vandals, and what does this word mean in your own words?** *(Sample answer: The English word* vandalism *comes from the actions of the Vandals. Vandalism refers to the action of damaging or destroying property on purpose.)* **Verbal/Linguistic**

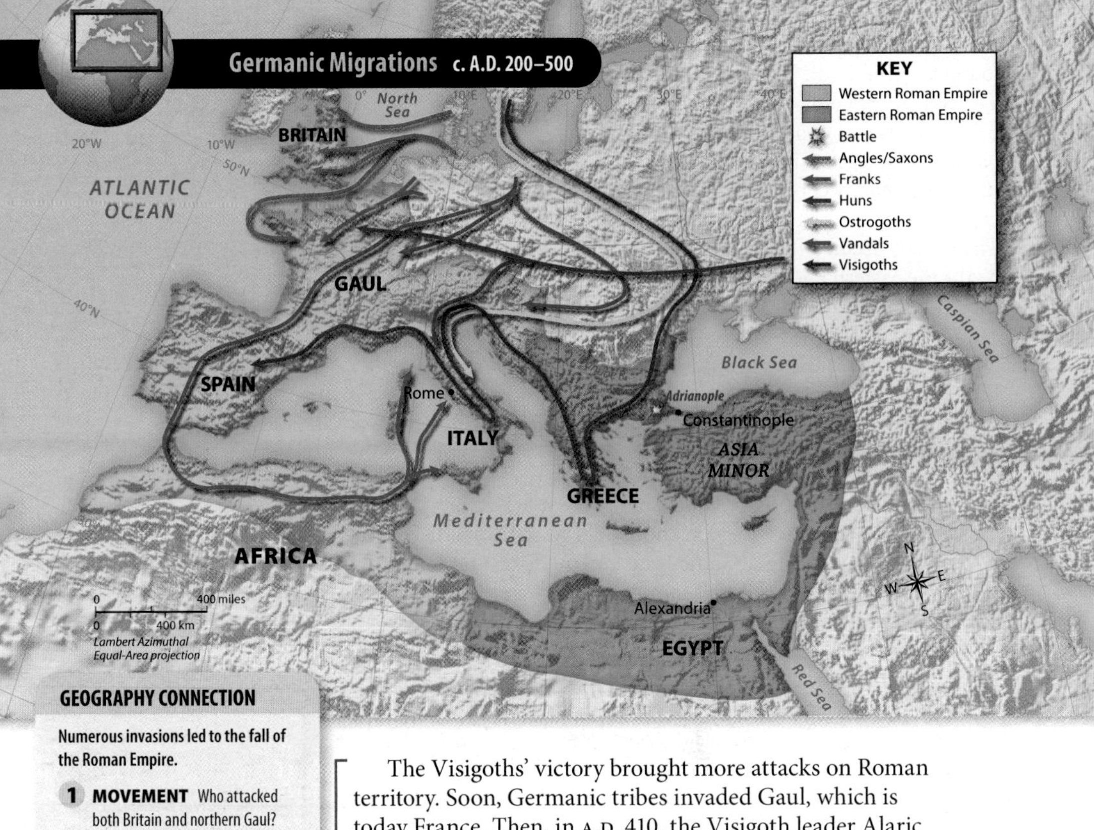

GEOGRAPHY CONNECTION

Numerous invasions led to the fall of the Roman Empire.

1. **MOVEMENT** Who attacked both Britain and northern Gaul?
2. **CRITICAL THINKING** ***Drawing Conclusions*** Why do you think the Eastern Roman Empire experienced very few invasions?

The Visigoths' victory brought more attacks on Roman territory. Soon, Germanic tribes invaded Gaul, which is today France. Then, in A.D. 410, the Visigoth leader Alaric (A•luh•rihk) led his people into Italy and captured Rome itself. The Visigoths looted the city's government buildings and private homes. Rome's conquest by Alaric made it clear that the empire would not, as many Romans believed, last forever.

W The Vandals, another Germanic group, attacked Roman lands in Spain and northern Africa. Then they sailed to Italy, and in A.D. 455, entered Rome. They were able to overcome the Romans living there. The Vandals spent almost two weeks seizing valuables and burning buildings. The English word *vandalism*, meaning "the willful destruction of property," comes from the actions of the Vandals.

The Germanic people had entered every part of Rome's organization. By the mid-A.D. 400s, Germanic soldiers had been working for the Roman government for centuries.

Reading HELPDESK (CCSS)

Reading in the Content Area: *Charts*

Flowcharts can show a chain of events. To read a flowchart, follow the arrows. Ask yourself questions such as, "What are the steps in this event? How does one event lead to another?"

networks *Online Teaching Options*

MAP

Germanic Migrations c. A.D. 200–500

Analyzing Visuals Show students the interactive map. **Ask:** **What do the arrows represent?** *(the paths that the Germanic tribes took)* **Which invaders traveled the farthest south?** *(Vandals)* **Who attacked both Britain and northern Gaul?** *(Angles, Saxons)* **Which groups captured Rome?** *(Vandals, Visigoths)* **Why do you think the Eastern Roman Empire experienced few invasions?** *(Many invading Germanic tribes traveled westward to escape the Huns in the east. Also, mountains and rivers made traveling eastward more difficult.)* AL ELL

See page 337D for other online activities.

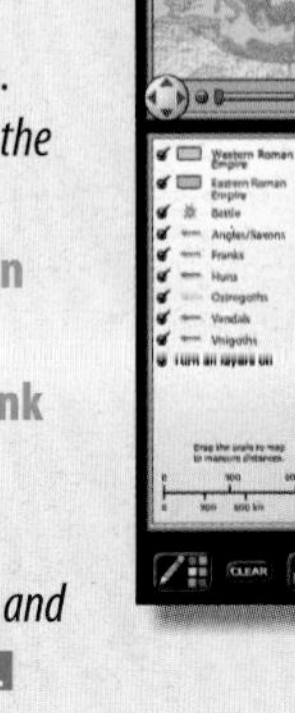

ANSWERS, p. 354

GEOGRAPHY CONNECTION

1. The Angles/Saxons attacked Britain and northern Gaul.
2. **CRITICAL THINKING** Possible answer: Physical barriers made the eastern part of the empire harder to reach.

Roman Emperor Forced Out

As a result, several Germanic leaders held high posts in Rome's government and army. In A.D. 476, the Germanic general named Odoacer (OH•duh•WAY•suhr) had enough support from soldiers that he was able to take control. Odoacer overthrew the western emperor, a 14-year-old boy named Romulus Augustulus (RAHM•yuh•luhs aw•GUHS•chah•luhs).

After Odoacer seized control, no Roman emperor ever again ruled from Rome. From then on, foreign powers ruled what had been the Roman Empire. Historians often use this event to mark the end of the Western Roman Empire. It was a major turning point in history.

Odoacer controlled Rome for almost 15 years. The Germanic peoples, however, continued to fight amongst themselves. During Odoacer's rule, a group of Visigoths attacked the city of Rome. After much fighting, they seized the city and killed Odoacer. They set up their new kingdom in Italy under their leader, Theodoric (thee•AH•duh•rihk). Elsewhere in Europe, other Germanic kingdoms arose and came to power.

The Western Roman Empire ceased to exist. Pope Gregory I wrote about the fall of Rome and how it affected people who had lived within its borders.

Connections to TODAY

Vandalism

Vandalism is a word with Roman origins. It means "the intentional destruction or damage to property." Graffiti is a type of vandalism. It involves writing, drawing, or carving words or symbols on any surface without the permission of the owner. A person who destroys or damages property on purpose is called a *vandal.*

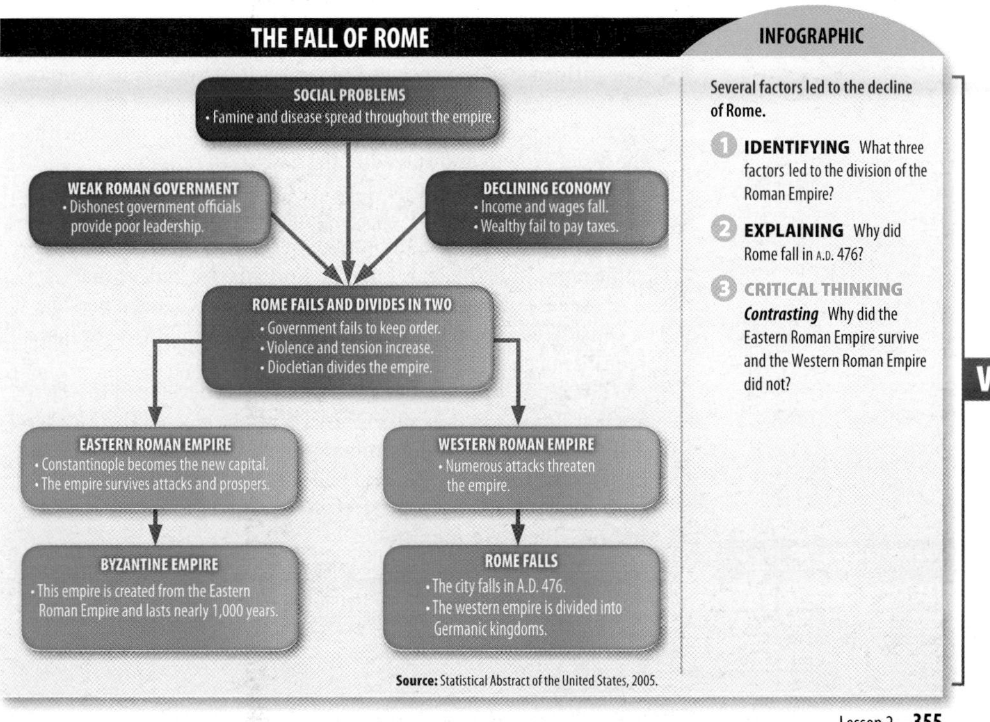

Source: Statistical Abstract of the United States, 2005.

INFOGRAPHIC

Several factors led to the decline of Rome.

1. **IDENTIFYING** What three factors led to the division of the Roman Empire?
2. **EXPLAINING** Why did Rome fall in A.D. 476?
3. **CRITICAL THINKING** ***Contrasting*** Why did the Eastern Roman Empire survive and the Western Roman Empire did not?

GAME

Early Roman Empire Crossword Puzzle

Collaborating Place students in pairs and have them attempt to complete the crossword puzzle about the Early Roman Empire. If necessary, tell students that they may use their textbooks to help them solve the puzzle. **Interpersonal**

See page 337D for other online activities.

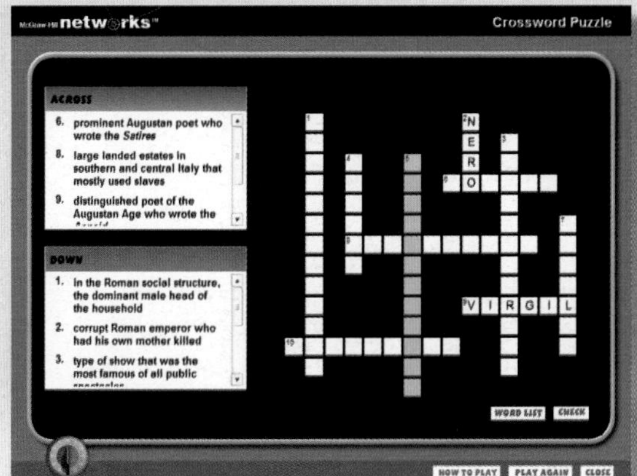

networks
Crossword Puzzle
ACROSS
6. prominent Augustan poet who wrote the Satires
8. large landed estates in southern and central Italy that mostly used slaves
9. distinguished poet of the Augustan Age who wrote the
DOWN
1. In the Roman social structure, the dominant male head of the household
2. corrupt Roman emperor who had his own mother killed
3. type of show that was the most famous of all public
NERO
VIRGIL
WORD LIST
CHECK
HOW TO PLAY
PLAY AGAIN
CLOSE

V Visual Skills

Analyzing Charts Ask the questions in the Infographic "The Fall of Rome." Review the information about flowcharts in the Reading HelpDesk. Then have students compare and contrast the Infographic to their graphic organizers "The Empire Collapses" that they completed earlier.

Ask: How are these two graphics the same? How do they differ? *(Answers will vary. Sample answers: Both graphics have information about trouble in the Roman Empire, and both list reasons why Rome fell. The Infographic is different because it is a flowchart and it has details about the Eastern Roman Empire and the Western Roman Empire.)* **AL** **ELL** **Visual/Spatial**

Content Background Knowledge

- Odoacer thought of himself as a king. During his reign, he gave land to those who supported him and aided in attempts to overthrow Zeno, the emperor of the Eastern Roman Empire. Odoacer also conquered regions in what is now Croatia and took control of the area now known as Sicily away from the Vandals.
- Theodoric invaded Italy in A.D. 489 and had almost taken control of the entire peninsula by A.D. 490. In A.D. 493, Theodoric told Odoacer that he wanted them to rule the empire together. However, a few days later, Theodoric invited Odoacer to a banquet and killed him instead.

ANSWERS, p. 355

INFOGRAPHIC

1. Weak Roman government, social problems, and a declining economy led to the division of the Roman Empire.
2. Numerous attacks threatened the empire.
3. **CRITICAL THINKING** The Eastern Roman Empire survived the attacks against it. The Western Roman Empire did not.

C Critical Thinking Skills

Analyzing Primary Sources Have students read the primary-source quote from Pope Gregory I. **Ask:**

- **How does Pope Gregory I feel about the fall of the Western Roman Empire?** *(Pope Gregory I is displeased and unhappy that the Western Roman Empire has fallen.)*
- **What context clues from the text support the idea that Pope Gregory I is displeased and unhappy that the Western Roman Empire fell?** *(Pope Gregory I talks about sorrows and groans. He also uses words like* destroyed, devastated, *and* ruined. *These words do not describe happy actions or events. Pope Gregory also says that few people are left in the cities.)*
- **What does Pope Gregory I mean when he calls Rome "the Mistress of the World"?** *(Rome was once one of the greatest cities in the world.)*

R Reading Skills

Naming Have students read "Rome's Influence on Law and Government." Then **ask: Which three beliefs of the American legal system come from Roman ideas?** *(Everyone is equal under the law; a person is considered innocent until proven guilty; and judges are required to decide cases fairly.)*

ANSWER, p. 356

PROGRESS CHECK The Germanic general Odoacer invaded Rome and overthrew the emperor. Afterward, no emperor ever ruled the empire from Rome again.

PRIMARY SOURCE

C

> "We see on all sides sorrows; We hear on all sides groans. Cities are destroyed, fortifications razed [forts destroyed] to the ground, fields devastated [left in ruin], land reduced to solitude. No husbandman [farmer] is left in the fields, few inhabitants remain in the cities. . . . What Rome herself, once deemed [regarded as] the Mistress of the World, has now become, we see—wasted away with . . . the loss of citizens, the assaults of enemies, the frequent fall of ruined buildings."
>
> —from *Homiliarum in Ezechielem*, by Pope Gregory I

By A.D. 550, a group of Germanic-ruled territories had replaced the Western Roman Empire, yet Roman culture did not completely disappear. Western Europe's new Germanic rulers adopted the Latin language, Roman laws, and Christianity. In the eastern Mediterranean, the Eastern Roman Empire thrived. It became known as the Byzantine Empire and lasted nearly 1,000 more years.

PROGRESS CHECK

Identifying Why do historians consider A.D. 476 an important date?

Rome's Legacies

GUIDING QUESTION *What are the key achievements and contributions of Roman civilization?*

The influence of the ancient Romans still surrounds us. Roman achievements live on in our system of laws and government today. The peace and order created by Roman rule helped with the rapid growth and spread of the Christian religion.

Rome's Influence on Law and Government

R

Many beliefs about law and justice in the American legal system come from Roman ideas. Like the Romans, we believe that everyone is equal under the law. We also believe that a person is considered innocent until proven guilty. We, like the Romans, require our judges to decide cases fairly.

The republican form of government was developed in ancient Rome. Certain citizens in a republic elected their leaders. The United States and a number of other countries today are democratic republics. We also believe that a republic works best if all adult citizens vote, **participate** in government, and help to improve their communities.

Reading HELPDESK (CCSS)

Academic Vocabulary (Tier 2 Words)

participate to take part

networks Online Teaching Options

SLIDE SHOW

Roman Architecture Influenced the U.S. Capitol

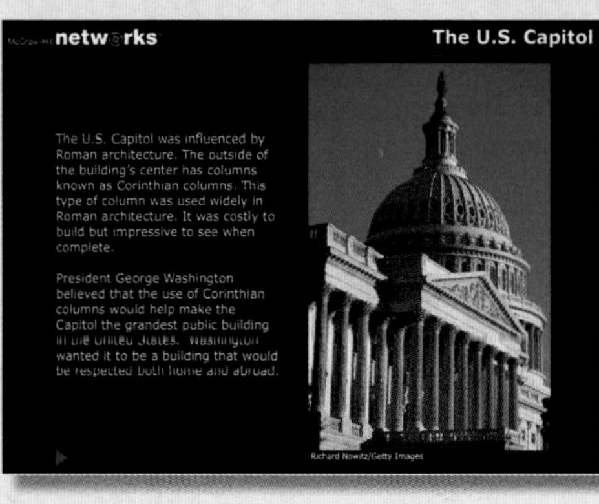

networks
The U.S. Capitol
The U.S. Capitol was influenced by Roman architecture. The outside of the building's center has columns known as Corinthian columns. This type of column was used widely in Roman architecture. It was costly to build but impressive to see when complete.
Richard Nowitz/Getty Images

Making Connections Show students the slide show about Roman influences on the architecture of the U.S. Capitol building. Then discuss how Rome has influenced American culture today. **Ask: Based on what you have learned about Rome, how has Rome influenced the type of government we have in the United States?** *(a republic, though a democratic one)* **The ideas Americans have about laws?** *(innocent until proven guilty; everyone is equal under the law; judges decide legal cases.)* **The language we speak and write?** *(the use of the Latin alphabet; Latin basis of many words we use)* **The architecture of buildings?** *(the use of concrete, arches, vaults, and domes)*

See page 337D for other online activities.

Rome's Cultural Impact

Many Western countries use the Latin alphabet, which has expanded from 22 to 26 letters. The Italian, French, Spanish, Portuguese, and Romanian languages are derived from Latin—the language of the Romans. Many English words have Latin roots. Latin phrases are part of the vocabulary of scientists, doctors, and lawyers. The Romans continue to influence the literature we read and enjoy. The great Roman writers such as Virgil, Horace, Livy, and Tacitus are still admired and studied. Architecture and construction also owe much to the ancient Romans. Government buildings in Washington, D.C. and the capital cities of many states often use domes and arches inspired by Roman architecture. Concrete, a Roman development, remains a major building material today.

Ancient Rome and Christianity

Christianity is a major world religion. It began in the eastern part of the Roman Empire and was adopted by Rome's emperors in the A.D. 300s. Those emperors helped the new religion grow and spread.

The Roman road system allowed the early Christians to travel throughout the empire safely and quickly. As a result, Christian ideas were easily shared with other groups of people. After the fall of the Western Roman Empire, Christianity continued to attract new believers.

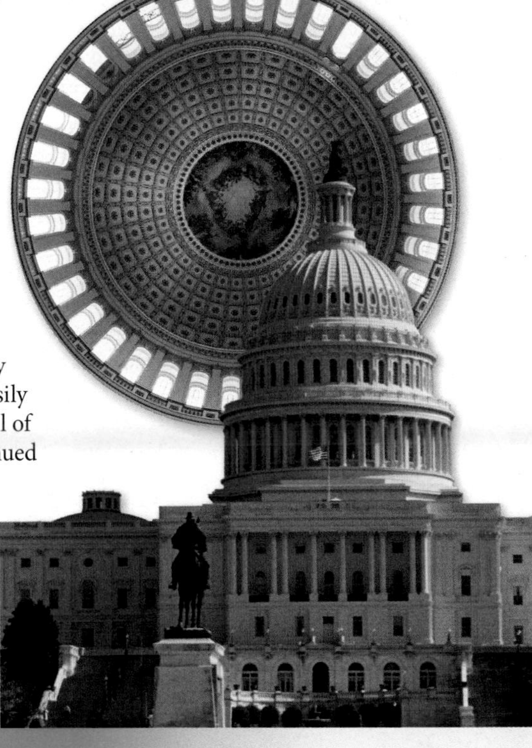

The Roman arch can support large domes. The design of our U.S. Capitol Building was influenced by the Romans. The image above shows what the U.S. Capitol dome looks like on the interior.

✓ PROGRESS CHECK

Comparing What Roman contributions still influence our lives today?

C

LESSON 2 REVIEW (CCSS)

Review Vocabulary (Tier 3 Words)

1. Why were Diocletian's *reforms* unsuccessful? RH.6–8.2, RH.6–8.4

Answer the Guiding Questions

2. ***Describing*** Discuss two problems that led to Rome's decline. RH.6–8.2
3. ***Explaining*** How did the division of the Roman Empire make it easy for people to invade it? RH.6–8.2
4. ***Summarizing*** Describe how Rome contributed to the development of world languages. RH.6–8.2
5. **ARGUMENT** What do you think was the greatest accomplishment of Roman civilization? Write a one-page essay that describes the accomplishment and why you feel it was the civilization's greatest. WHST.6–8.1, WHST.6–8.10

C Critical Thinking Skills

Categorizing List the following words on the board:

A. Barter
B. Constantine
C. Diocletian
D. Inflation
E. Constantinople
F. Rome

Then write the following phrases. As you read each of these phrases aloud, ask volunteers to respond with the matching word.

1. Established maximum prices for wages and goods to stop prices from rising *(C)*
2. A rise in prices and a decline in the value of money *(D)*
3. To exchange using goods instead of money *(A)*
4. Capital of the Western Roman Empire *(F)*
5. Moved capital of empire to Byzantium *(B)*
6. Present-day Istanbul *(E)* AL

Have students complete the Lesson 2 Review.

CLOSE & REFLECT

To close the lesson, remind students that the Roman Empire was one of the largest empires in history. Ask students to think about how history might have changed if the empire had survived. Have students describe one way they think the world might be different if the Roman Empire existed today.

LESSON 2 REVIEW ANSWERS

1. Diocletian's reforms were unsuccessful because people ignored his new rules. He was also too weak as an emperor to enforce them.
2. Students could discuss two of the following three: the weak Roman government, social problems, and the declining economy.
3. The invasions focused on the Western Roman Empire, which was far too extended; and with fewer soldiers, it was too weak to defend itself.
4. The language of the Romans, Latin, shaped other languages, including Italian, French, Spanish, Portuguese, and Romanian. These languages, like English, use the Latin alphabet. Many English words have Latin roots.
5. Essay topics might focus on Roman contributions to law, justice, government, language, architecture, or religion.

ANSWER, p. 357

✓ PROGRESS CHECK Students might say that the Romans have influenced our beliefs about law, justice, government, and citizenship; our use of the Latin alphabet and language; our modern languages; literature, architecture, and the use of concrete in construction; and our religious beliefs.

ENGAGE

Bellringer Prepare two columns on the board headed "Benefit" and "Did Not Benefit." **Ask:** **Now that you have read about the Roman Empire, in what ways do you think people benefited from or did not benefit from Roman rule?** List responses on the chart. *(Answers may include: Benefit: culture, law, engineering, arts; Did Not Benefit: slavery, poverty)*

Students will return to this list to compare their responses with those of the writers of the quotations.

TEACH & ASSESS

V1 Visual Skills

Interpreting Ask students to review the introductory paragraphs. Have the class focus on the background illustration featuring Roman architectural ruins. **Ask:** **What do these ruins tell us about Roman skills?** *(The Romans were skilled in architecture.)*

R Reading Skills

Explaining Have students read the contrasting accounts of Rome from Aelius Aristides and Flavius Josephus. **Ask:**

- **Which writer do you think would have most appreciated the beauty of this architecture? Why?** *(Aelius Aristides, because it shows off the Romans' skill)* BL
- **What kinds of benefits does Aelius Aristides mention?** *(the availability of agricultural and manufactured products from far away; all known skills)*

V2 Visual Skills

Analyzing Images Call students' attention to the round mosaic illustration. **Ask:** **Why was this mosaic a good choice to illustrate Aristides's opinion?** *(It shows men unloading products, which represents the main benefit Aristides mentions: the availability of many trade goods that enter Roman ports.)*

Content Background Knowledge

The Roman Limes was a series of walls, ditches, forts, fortresses, towers, and settlements. It was used to fortify the expansive border of the Roman Empire during the second century, and it spanned over 5,000 kilometers. The Roman Limes stretched from northern Britain, through Europe to the Black Sea, down to the Red Sea, and then across North Africa to the coast of the Atlantic Ocean. Some parts of the Limes have been reconstructed and still exist today.

What Do You Think? CCSS

Did People Benefit from Roman Rule?

V1 Throughout their vast empire, the Romans built roads, bridges, and irrigation systems. These improvements allowed trade and agriculture to flourish. To accomplish these changes, however, the Romans had to sail to other lands to obtain materials. With the traders came Roman soldiers.

Some people, however, did not want to be ruled by the Romans. Many died fighting against the Roman invaders. V2

Mosaic of Romans unloading a boat

Yes

PRIMARY SOURCE

"From neighboring continents far and wide a ceaseless [endless] flow of goods pours into Rome. From every land and every sea come each season's crops, the produce of countryside, rivers, and lakes, and articles skillfully made by Greeks and foreigners.

. . . So many merchants arrive from all points of the compass with their cargoes throughout the year, and with each return of harvest, that the city is like the common warehouse of the world . . . clothing from Babylonia, luxuries from barbarian lands beyond. . . . Egypt, Sicily and Africa are your farms. . . . Everything converges [comes together] here—trade, shipping, agriculture, metallurgy [making products from metals], all the skills that exist and have existed, everything that is bred or grown. Anything that cannot be seen in Rome does not exist." R

—Aelius Aristides, *To Rome*

networks Online Teaching Options

IMAGE

Ancient Roman Glassmaking

Analyzing Images Have students look at the interactive image depicting Roman glassmaking. Explain that the Romans perfected mosaic glass, which was used in murals instead of stones because glass was more colorful. Ask students to consider what the glass decanter in the picture might have been used for.

networks
Ancient Roman Glassmaking
The Romans perfected mosaic glass, which was used instead of stone in murals because glass was brighter and more colorful. Thin slices of glass were cut to make complex and brightly colored patterns, such as flowers.
The Romans also molded glass into different shapes, and developed glassblowing techniques. The first glassblowing took place in Syria around 100 B.C. The art form, as well as the finished objects, spread throughout the Roman Empire.
At first, glassblowers would heat the glass until it was a semi-solid mass that could be shaped. They poured the heated glass into decorative molds, or forms. The mixture cooled and hardened, taking on the shape of the mold. Over time, glassblowers stopped using molds. Instead, they shaped the semi-solid glass with metal tools. Blowing glass allowed for endless possible shapes and sizes of vessels, urns, vases, bowls, jewelry, and other items.
DEA/A DAGLI ORTI/De Agostini Picture Library/Getty Images

The Destruction of the Temple in Jerusalem by the Emperor Titus, a painting by Nicolas Poussin

R

No

PRIMARY SOURCE

"As the legions [soldiers] charged in, neither persuasion nor threat could check [stop] their impetuosity [impulsive behavior]: passion [frenzy] alone was in command. . . . Most of the victims were peaceful citizens, weak and unarmed, butchered [killed] wherever they were caught. While the Sanctuary [Temple] was burning, looting went on right and left and all who were caught were put to the sword. There was no pity for age, no regard for rank; little children and old men, laymen and priests alike were butchered; every class was held in the iron embrace of war, whether they defended themselves or cried for mercy . . . They also burnt the treasuries which housed huge sums of money, huge quantities of clothing, and other precious things."

—(Flavius) Josephus describing the destruction of the Jewish temple by the Romans in A.D. 70, *The Jewish War*

What Do You Think? DBQ

1. ***Identifying*** Which person has a favorable view of Rome? RH.6–8.6, RH.6–8.9
2. ***Describing*** Does (Flavius) Josephus believe the Romans were merciful when they conquered people? How does he try to persuade the reader to support his belief? RH.6–8.6
3. ***Making Inferences*** What do you think Aristides meant when he said, "Anything that cannot be seen in Rome does not exist"? RH.6–8.6

CHART

Graphic Organizer: Tree Diagram

Argument Discuss with students how the two primary sources they will read in this section could be considered editorials. Define what an editorial is *(writing that offers an opinion on a topical issue)*, and have students use the graphic organizer to write their own editorials for or against Roman rule. Students should include specific reasons in the three rectangles for why they feel the way they do. **Intrapersonal**

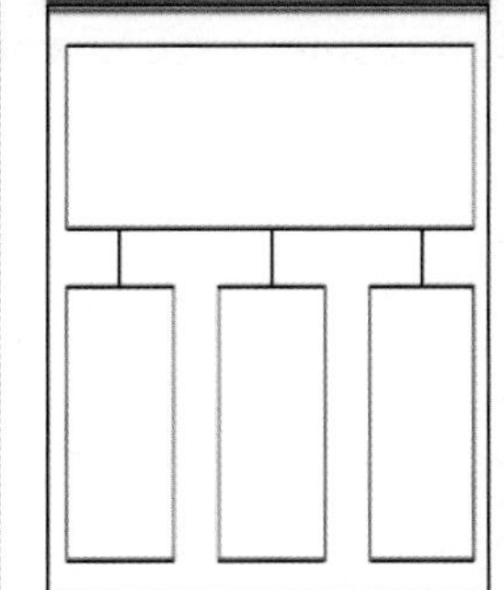

What Do You Think?

R Reading Skills

Using Context Clues Call students' attention to the "No" primary source. **Ask:**

- **Which three words describe the citizens?** *(peaceful, weak, unarmed)*
- **Which words and phrases describe the actions of the soldiers?** *(passion alone was in command, butchered, burning, looting, put to the sword, burnt the treasuries)* ELL

Tell students to think about the different perspectives of the two writers featured in this section. **Ask: Based on what each author writes, what can you guess about their lives within the Roman Empire?** *(Aelius Aristides might have been a merchant or a wealthy buyer. Josephus might have witnessed the destruction of the Jewish temple and escaped.)* BL

V Visual Skills

Analyzing Images Call students' attention to the painting *The Destruction of the Temple in Jerusalem by the Emperor Titus.* **Ask:**

- **What seems to be happening here?** *(Roman soldiers are killing people.)*
- **How does this image support Flavius Josephus's argument?** *(It shows that Romans could be violent and destructive.)* AL ELL

Content Background Knowledge

Hadrian's Wall was built by order of Emperor Hadrian in A.D. 122 in the Roman province of Britannia, now known as England. It was one of the most northern points of the Roman Limes.

CLOSE & REFLECT

To close the lesson, return to the "Benefit" and "Did Not Benefit" lists that students created in the Bellringer activity. Invite volunteers to circle the items on their lists that were mentioned by the writers. Have volunteers add more items, if needed, to the lists.

Have students complete the *What Do You Think?* questions in class or as a homework assignment.

ANSWERS, p. 359

1. Aelius Aristides
2. Flavius Josephus believes the Romans had no mercy. He wrote that they destroyed or stole items from those they conquered and killed children and old people.
3. This statement reflects Aristides's belief that Rome was the center of civilization. Any new trend could be seen in Rome.

The Byzantine Empire

ENGAGE

Bellringer Remind students that the Eastern Roman Empire thrived and became known as the Byzantine Empire. It existed for nearly 1,000 years after the fall of Rome, and its capital was Constantinople.

Display a map of the United States from the Interactive World Atlas. **Ask:** **What does this map show?** *(the United States)* Ask students to locate New York City. Tell them that New York is a large city known for being a center of trade. **Ask:**

- **Before railroads, trucks, and airplanes, how do you think merchants in New York City sent and received products to trade?** *(by ship)*
- **What characteristic do you think New York and Constantinople, also a center of trade in its time, might have in common?** *(Students should note that both cities are, or were, located near bodies of water.)*

Next, ask students

- **What is a peninsula?** *(a piece of land surrounded on three sides by water, connected to the mainland)* AL

Tell students that Constantinople had a great advantage, being located on a peninsula. Tell them that, like New York City, Constantinople developed by benefiting from nearby physical features. These developments spurred economic growth.

TEACH & ASSESS

C Critical Thinking Skills

Formulating Questions Have students read the introductory paragraph about the Byzantine Empire and the section on Constantinople. Then have them write five questions about these sections of text for which they can locate the answers. *(Answers will vary. Sample questions: How large was the Byzantine Empire? What types of people lived there? Which cultural group made up the largest part of the population? Did people like the arts? Who gave Constantinople its name? Why was Constantinople a successful and thriving city? Was Constantinople a city that could be attacked easily? How was the city protected?)*

networks *There's More Online!*

- GRAPHIC ORGANIZERS
  - Why the Byzantine Empire Thrived
  - Justinian's Army
- MAP Justinian's Conquests
- SLIDE SHOWS
  - The Hippodrome of Constantinople
  - Hagia Sophia
- VIDEO

Lesson 3

The Byzantine Empire

ESSENTIAL QUESTION *How does geography influence the way people live?*

It Matters Because

At the height of its power, the Byzantine Empire united people on three continents. Its system of laws and its strong leadership helped the empire flourish.

The New Rome

GUIDING QUESTION *How did the Byzantine Empire become rich and powerful?*

After the Roman Empire was divided in A.D. 395, the eastern half eventually became known as the Byzantine Empire. At the height of its power in the A.D. 500s, the Byzantine territory extended west to Italy, south to Egypt, and east to the Arabian border. A variety of peoples lived within the empire's borders. Greeks made up the largest population. Egyptians, Syrians, Arabs, Armenians, Jews, Persians, Slavs, and Turks also lived in the empire. Under Emperor Justinian, the laws improved, the arts flourished, and the empire grew dramatically.

C

Constantinople

Constantine moved the capital of the Roman Empire from Rome to the Greek city of Byzantium and renamed the city Constantinople. The new capital thrived. By the A.D. 500s, multicultural Constantinople had become one of the world's most advanced cities.

Constantinople's location was a major factor in the city's success. Located on a peninsula between the Black Sea and the Aegean Sea, the city's excellent harbors attracted fishing

Reading HELPDESK CCSS

Taking Notes: *Listing*

Use a graphic organizer like this one to list reasons why the Byzantine Empire thrived. RH.6–8.2

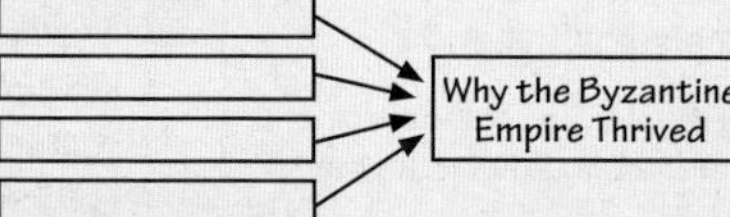

Content Vocabulary (Tier 3 Words)

- mosaics
- saints

networks *Online Teaching Options*

VIDEO

Constantinople to Istanbul

Identifying Watch the video "Constantinople to Istanbul" together as a class. **Ask:**

- **How many names has the city had?** *(three names: Byzantium, Constantinople, and Istanbul)*
- **Where did the name Constantinople come from?** *(It was named after Emperor Constantine.)*
- **What group was the first to conquer the city?** *(Christian crusaders)*

Discuss the question that appears at the end of the film: **What is Istanbul's place in the world today?** *(Students should recognize that Istanbul represents a meeting place of many world cultures.)*

See page 337E for other online activities.

ANSWERS, p. 360

TAKING NOTES: Constantinople's location; wide variety of cultural influences; great leaders such as Constantine and Justinian; the Justinian Code boats, trading ships, and warships. Because of its location at the crossroads of trade routes between Europe and Asia, Constantinople became the wealthiest part of the Roman Empire.

Constantinople was also easy to defend. Lying on a peninsula, the city was protected on three sides by the sea, and a large wall protected it on the fourth side. Later, a huge chain was strung across the city's harbor for greater protection. Surprise attacks were not easily carried out on Constantinople.

What Cultural Influences Shaped the Byzantines?

Constantinople at first resembled other cities in the Roman Empire. The "New Rome," as it was called, had government buildings and palaces built in the Roman style. The city also had an oval arena called the Hippodrome (HIHP•uh•drohm) where chariot races and other events were held.

R

Rome influenced the political and social life of the Byzantine Empire. Emperors spoke Latin and enforced Roman laws. Many wealthy Roman families traveled east to the Byzantine Empire and lived in towns or on large farming estates. Similarly to how things were done in Rome, the government gave the empire's poor people free bread and entertainment shows.

Over time, the Roman influence on the Byzantine Empire faded, while Greek influence in the area increased. Most Byzantines spoke Greek, and Byzantine emperors and officials also began to speak Greek instead of Latin. The ideas of non-Greek peoples, like the Egyptians and the Slavs, also shaped Byzantine life. Still other customs came from Persia to the east. All of these cultures blended together to form the Byzantine civilization.

Between A.D. 500 and A.D. 1200, the Byzantines developed one of the world's most advanced civilizations. They preserved and passed on Greek culture and Roman law to other peoples. As you will learn, they also brought Christianity to people in Eastern Europe.

Sculptures of horses, such as the one above, greeted people who enjoyed chariot races at the Hippodrome.

▶ **CRITICAL THINKING**

Making Connections Why did Greek culture gradually influence the Byzantine Empire more than Roman culture?

Image Club

✓ PROGRESS CHECK

Explaining Why was Constantinople important to the Byzantine Empire?

Build Vocabulary: *Word Origins*

The word *hippodrome* comes from the Greek words *hippos*, meaning "horse," and *dromos*, meaning "race" or "course."

R Reading Skills

Stating Once students have read the section titled "New Rome," **ask: What are three cultural influences that Rome first had on the Byzantine Empire?** *(Answers will vary but should demonstrate accurate recall of the information. Sample answers: Government buildings and palaces were built in the Roman style; emperors spoke Latin and enforced Roman laws; wealthy Roman families lived in towns or on farming estates in the Byzantine Empire; the Byzantine government gave poor people free bread and entertainment shows, as Rome did; chariot races were held in Constantinople just as they were in Rome.)*

Content Background Knowledge

- The official language of the Byzantine Empire was Latin, but students were also educated in Greek culture, history, and literature. The type of Greek that was spoken in the Byzantine Empire is still used today as the language spoken during liturgies in the Greek Orthodox Church.
- In A.D. 451, the Council of Chalcedon divided the parts of the world that practiced Christianity into five areas, or patriarchates. Each one was ruled by a patriarch. The patriarch of Rome would later be called a pope by the Roman Catholic Church. The Byzantine emperor became the patriarch of Constantinople and the spiritual leader for most of Eastern Christianity. The three remaining patriarchates of Alexandria, Antioch, and Jerusalem came under Islamic control in the seventh century.

SLIDE SHOW

Hippodrome

Speculating Explain that emperors used wealth generated by trade to build large projects as a demonstration of their success and prosperity. **Ask: What were some large projects built in Rome?** *(the Colosseum, the Forum)* Show students the slide show of the Hippodrome. **Why might Constantine have chosen to build the Hippodrome instead of a church or other public building?** *(to provide "bread and circuses," as Julius Caesar and the earlier Western Roman emperors did)* Have students think of attending a sports event. Invite volunteers to speculate what the Byzantines would have experienced when they visited the Hippodrome. **AL** **ELL**

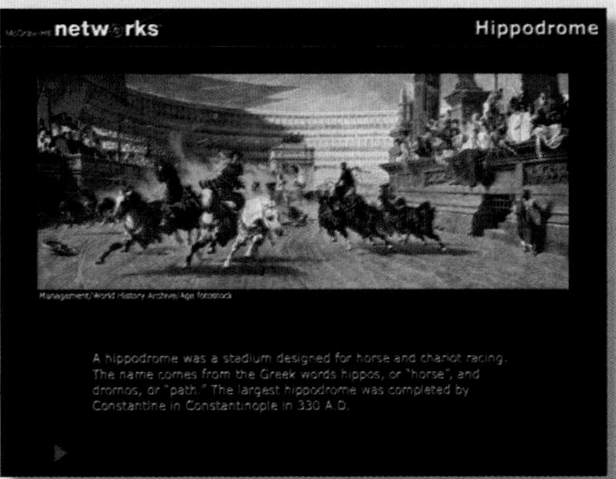

networks
Hippodrome
Management/World History Archive/Age fotostock
A hippodrome was a stadium designed for horse and chariot racing. The name comes from the Greek words hippos, or "horse", and dromos, or "path." The largest hippodrome was completed by Constantine in Constantinople in 330 A.D.

See page 337E for other online activities.

ANSWERS, p. 361

CRITICAL THINKING Roman influence faded, and Greek influence increased. Most Byzantines spoke Greek, and Roman rulers began to speak it.

✓ PROGRESS CHECK Constantinople became the center of political, economic, and social life in the Roman Empire.

W Writing Skills

Argument After reading about Justinian and Theodora, have students imagine that they are a citizen living in the Byzantine Empire. Write a paragraph that tells their opinion about Empress Theodora. Have students consider these questions as the basis for their paragraphs:

- Do you think Empress Theodora's thoughts and ideas were more important than, equally as important as, or not as important as Justinian's thoughts and ideas? Explain why you feel the way that you do.
- What are two or three pieces of advice that you would give Justinian? **Verbal/Linguistic Intrapersonal**

ANSWERS, p. 362

CRITICAL THINKING Students may say that the nobles probably wanted to preserve their power and not share it with members of the lower classes.

Reading Strategy Sample answers:
- persuaded Justinian to make laws that helped women
- persuaded Justinian to stay and fight against rebels

BIOGRAPHY

Justinian I (A.D. 483–565)

Justinian's uncle, Justin, provided Justinian with an excellent education at a school in Byzantium. When Justin became emperor, he adopted Justinian and made him his chief advisor and, later, co-ruler. In A.D. 527, Justin died, and Justinian became emperor.

Empress Theodora (A.D. 500–548)

Theodora was a member of a lower social class. Justinian could not marry her: it was illegal for people of lower classes to marry nobles. Justinian's uncle Justin, who was the emperor, changed the law so that the couple could marry.

▶ **CRITICAL THINKING**
Making Inferences Why do you think there were laws preventing people from the lower classes from marrying nobles?

Justinian's Rule

GUIDING QUESTION ***How did Emperor Justinian and Empress Theodora strengthen the Byzantine Empire?***

Justinian (juh•STIH•nee•uhn) ruled the Byzantine Empire at the height of its power. A skilled general and a strong leader, Justinian ruled from A.D. 527 until A.D. 565. He governed with supreme power and controlled the military and all of the **legal** decisions made within the empire. Many historians view Justinian as the greatest Byzantine emperor.

Who Was Theodora?

Justinian's wife, the empress Theodora (THEE•uh•DOHR•uh), was a beautiful, intelligent, and ambitious woman. She participated actively in government and helped Justinian choose government officials. Theodora helped Byzantine women win more legal rights. At her urging, Justinian changed Byzantine law so that a wife could own land. If a woman became a widow, her land would provide the income she needed to take care of her children. **W**

Theodora showed her political wisdom during a crisis in A.D. 532. When angry taxpayers in Constantinople threatened the government, Justinian's advisers urged Justinian to flee the city. Theodora, however, told her husband to stay and fight. According to one Byzantine historian, Theodora told Justinian that she would rather die as an empress than escape and live as an outlaw:

PRIMARY SOURCE

> "May I never be separated from this purple [royal color], and may I not live that day on which those who meet me shall not address me as mistress. If, now, it is your wish to save yourself, O Emperor, there is no difficulty. For we have much money, and there is the sea, here the boats. However consider whether it will not come about after you have been saved that you would gladly exchange that safety for death. For as for myself, I approve a certain ancient saying that royalty is a good burial-shroud."
>
> —from "The Nika Riot," by Procopius

Taking Theodora's advice, Justinian stayed in the city and fought back. His army crushed the rebels. By doing this, Justinian was able to **restore** order and strengthen his power as emperor.

Reading HELPDESK CCSS

Academic Vocabulary (Tier 2 Words)
legal of or relating to the law
restore to bring back to an original state

Reading Strategy: *Listing*
Listing information you have read about helps you remember it. Create a bulleted list that shows the ways Theodora influenced or helped the Byzantine Empire.

networks ***Online Teaching Options***

WHITEBOARD ACTIVITY

Emperor Justinian I and Empress Theodora

Comparing Have students compare the characteristics and achievements of Justinian with those of Theodora. When students have completed the Interactive Whiteboard Activity, have the class discuss the answers. **Ask:** **What is Justinian most remembered for?** *(Most students will probably say he is most remembered for the creation of a simpler law code.)* **Why is Theodora an important person in the history of the Byzantine Empire?** *(Possible answers: She was known for intelligence. She helped women gain more rights. She helped choose government officials. She was willing to die in power rather than live as an outlaw.)*

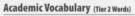

networks Emperor Justinian I and Empress Theodora

Directions: Drag and drop to match the correct descriptions to the leader.

Emperor Justinian I	Descriptions	Empress Theodora
Archiv Gerstenberg/ullstein bild/The Image Works	• Became ruler in 527 • Revived glory of Rome's past through architecture and engineering • Criticized for ruthless manner and disposition • Developed simpler code of laws • Ordered 10,000 workers to build the Hagia Sophia • Strengthened Byzantine army • Refused to flee when threatened by rebellion • Skilled general and strong leader • Helped choose government officials • Helped women gain more rights • Had to cope with terrible effects of bubonic plague on empire • Willing to die in power rather than live as an outlaw • Known for intelligence	Hulton Archive/Getty Images

See page 337E for other online activities.

Justinian's Legal Reforms

One of Justinian's lasting contributions to future civilizations was in the area of law. Shortly after he became emperor, Justinian realized that the empire's laws were disorganized and confusing. He ordered a group of legal scholars headed by Tribonian (truh•BOH•nee•uhn) to create a simpler and better code of laws.

The group's new legal code became known as the Justinian Code. The code helped officials and businesspeople better understand the empire's laws. Throughout the centuries, the Justinian Code has been the basis for the legal systems of almost every country in the Western world.

Byzantine Arts

Justinian, along with other Byzantine emperors, was interested in arts and architecture. The emperors ordered the construction of churches, forts, and government buildings throughout the Byzantine Empire. Among the hundreds of beautiful churches and palaces in Constantinople was the church called Hagia Sophia (HAH•jee•uh soh•FEE•uh), or "Holy Wisdom." **V**

R. Matina/Age fotostock

The dome of the Hagia Sophia towers more than 180 feet above the ground. For more than 1,000 years, the Hagia Sophia was the largest cathedral in the world. When the Ottoman Turks conquered Constantinople in A.D. 1453, the cathedral was converted to a mosque. Today, Hagia Sophia is a museum.

W Writing Skills

Informative/Explanatory Have students write their own code of five laws that they would pass if they ruled the Byzantine Empire. Have students write one sentence for each law that explains why they would pass it.

- Tell them to consider all of the laws and reforms that they have read about in this chapter.
- Remind them that Justinian's Code made laws simpler so that people could understand them, and so students should write laws that are simple and easy to understand as well.

V Visual Skills

Drawing Have students look at the large photo of the interior of the Hagia Sophia. **Ask:**

- **Do you think that this building is an example of art or architecture?** *(Ask a few volunteers to explain their answers.)*
- **Do you think it's possible for a building to be a work of art?** Discuss how one person's perception of art can sometimes be different from what someone else might think. Have students create simple sketches of two or three things in the photo that they consider to be examples of art. Encourage them to focus on the parts of the photo that seem to catch their attention in some way. *(Students might sketch something like the curve of large dome, the shape of the windows, or the arched doorways.)* Ask a few volunteers to share their sketches and explain why they chose these examples of art.

AL ELL Visual/Spatial

SLIDE SHOW

Hagia Sophia

Identifying Remind students that it was Justinian who ordered the building of the Hagia Sophia. Show the slide show about the Hagia Sophia, and have students point out examples of a mosaic, an arch, and a dome.

McGraw-Hill networks
Hagia Sophia
Harvey Lloyd/Taxi/Getty Images
The Hagia Sophia is one of Turkey's most important cultural sites. Its name means "Holy Wisdom of God." Emperor Justinian ordered its construction in 532 A.D. Unfortunately, he was in such a hurry to have the architects complete it that it was not stable enough. Parts of the building had to be replaced after an earthquake in 558. For over 900 years it was one of the most important Christian churches in the world. Its design and complex artwork showed the wealth and importance of the Byzantine Empire.

Ask: Have you seen any buildings as old as the Hagia Sophia that are still standing? After students' responses, point out that even though earthquakes collapsed the Hagia Sophia's dome three times, each collapse took place hundreds of years apart. This allowed time for rebuilding the dome. AL ELL

See page 337E for other online activities.

V Visual Skills

Creating Visuals Review the definition of mosaic with students. *(patterns or pictures made from small pieces of colored glass or stone)* Organize students into pairs. Allow each pair to choose an important Byzantine leader from the lesson: Constantine, Justinian, Theodora, or Belisarius.

Provide construction paper or other colored scrap paper. Have students use this paper to create mosaics that illustrate their chosen leader. Students may first wish to research images of their chosen leader to help guide them as they create their mosaics.

When students have completed their mosaics, you may choose to have volunteers present their work to the class. You may also choose to display all student mosaics in the classroom.
AL ELL Visual/Spatial

W Writing Skills

Informative/Explanatory Have students write a short essay from the point of view of their chosen Byzantine leader, using the questions below to frame their writing:

- Two of my greatest achievements are...
- These achievements are considered to be great because...

Verbal/Linguistic Intrapersonal

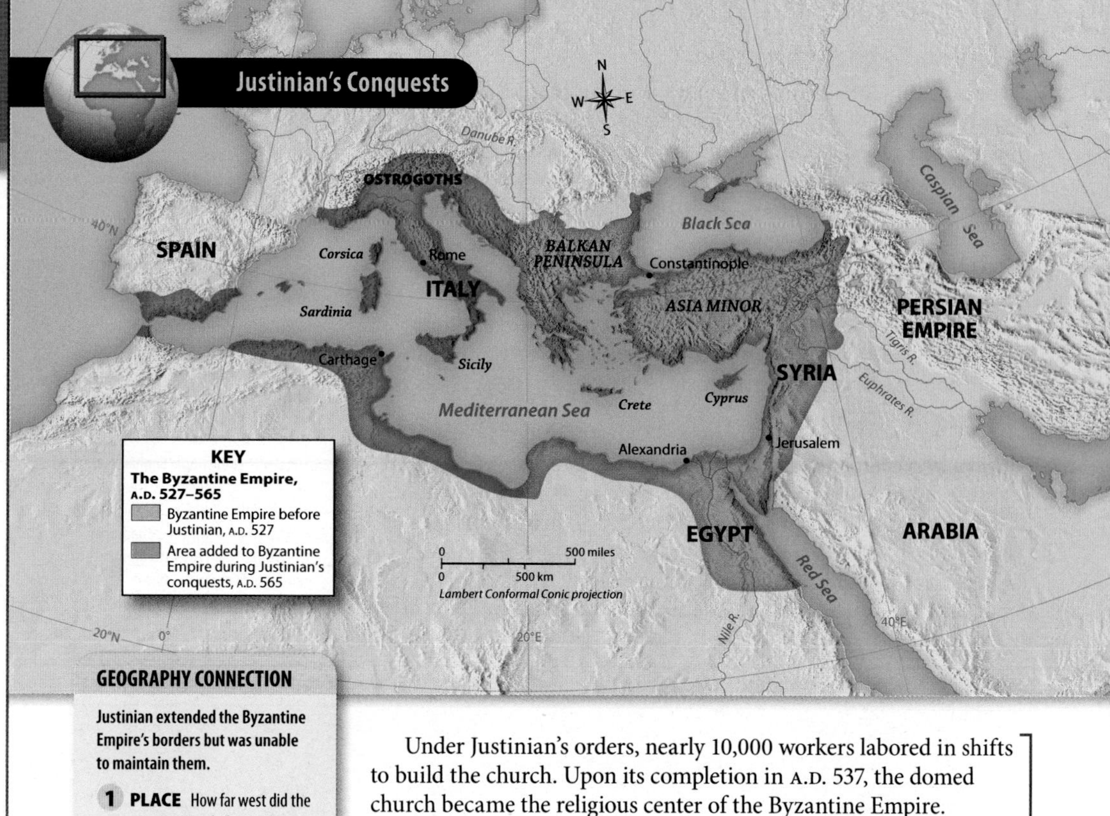

GEOGRAPHY CONNECTION

Justinian extended the Byzantine Empire's borders but was unable to maintain them.

1 **PLACE** How far west did the empire extend after Justinian's conquests?

2 **CRITICAL THINKING** *Inferring* Why might a cavalry be useful for defending this large empire?

Under Justinian's orders, nearly 10,000 workers labored in shifts to build the church. Upon its completion in A.D. 537, the domed church became the religious center of the Byzantine Empire. The interior of Hagia Sophia contains walls of polished marble and beautiful gold and silver ornaments. This unique building still stands in Istanbul today.

Numerous mosaics also decorated the interior walls of Hagia Sophia. **Mosaics** (moh•ZAY•ihks) are patterns or pictures made from small pieces of colored glass or stone. Popular in the Byzantine Empire, most mosaics showed figures of **saints**, or Christian holy people. Other mosaics, such as the one at the beginning of the chapter, honored Byzantine emperors.

In addition to the arts and architecture, Emperor Justinian was concerned about education. Learning was highly respected in the Byzantine culture. In Byzantine schools, boys studied religion, medicine, law, arithmetic, grammar, and other subjects. Some were schooled by private tutors. Girls did not generally attend schools and received any teaching at home.

Reading HELPDESK CCSS

mosaics motifs or images created by an arrangement of colored glass or stone

saints people considered holy by followers of the Christian faith

networks Online Teaching Options

MAP

Justinian's Conquests

Using Digital Tools Have students investigate the interactive map detailing Emperor Justinian's conquests. Have a student volunteer call out two different cities and ask the class to drag the scale onto the map to measure the distances between them. For example: **How many miles is Rome from Constantinople?**

See page 337E for other online activities.

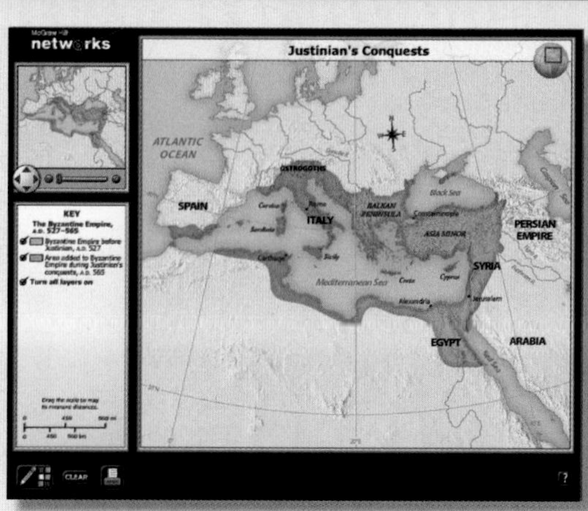

ANSWERS, p. 364

GEOGRAPHY CONNECTION

1 to southern Spain

2 **CRITICAL THINKING** Cavalry soldiers could travel quickly and defend large areas.

Military Conquests

Justinian wanted to restore the Roman Empire and bring back the glory of Rome. Led by a general named Belisarius (BEH•luh•SAR•ee•uhs), the Byzantine army was strengthened and reorganized. Instead of relying on foot soldiers, the new army used cavalry—soldiers mounted on horses. Byzantine cavalry wore armor and carried bows and lances, which were long spears.

Between A.D. 533 and A.D. 555, the Byzantine military conquered territories that were once part of the great Roman Empire. These territories included Italy and parts of Spain and northern Africa. They also defeated the Persians, which increased the security of the eastern borders of the empire. However, the conquests of Justinian's army were short-lived. During the mid-500s, a deadly disease known to historians as "Justinian's Plague" swept through Asia and Europe. The plague killed millions of people, including many men in Justinian's army. The loss of so many soldiers severely weakened the Byzantine Empire's ability to fight wars.

In addition, the Byzantines did not have the money to support an army large enough to defend against the Persians in the east and protect the lands in the west. Most of the western territories that Justinian conquered were lost after his death.

✓ PROGRESS CHECK

Understanding Cause and Effect What effect did Theodora have on Justinian's rule?

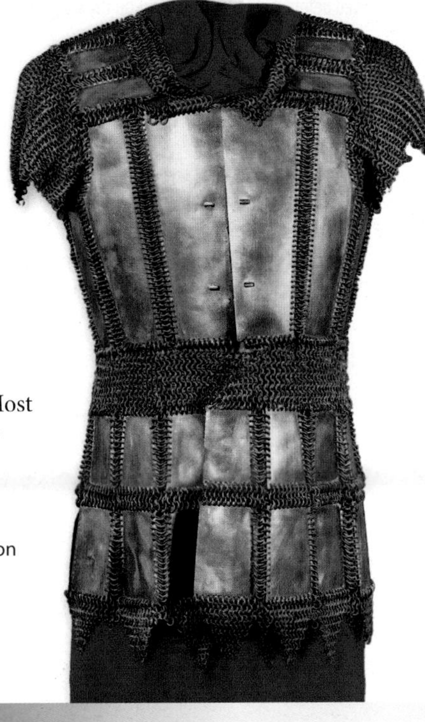

In addition to body armor such as this, Byzantine cavalry soldiers also wore plumed helmets. Cavalry made the Byzantine army a formidable fighting force.

▶ CRITICAL THINKING

Explaining How did Belisarius strengthen the army of the Byzantine Empire?

The Art Archive/Superstock

T

LESSON 3 REVIEW CCSS

Review Vocabulary (Tier 3 Words)

1. How were *saints* shown in *mosaics*? RH.6–8.2, RH.6–8.4

Answer the Guiding Questions

2. ***Explaining*** How did Constantinople's location help it become a wealthy city? RH.6–8.2
3. ***Describing*** How did the advancements made by Greek and Roman civilizations influence the Byzantine Empire? RH.6–8.2
4. ***Identifying Cause and Effect*** What effect did the Justinian Code have on the Byzantine Empire? RH.6–8.2, RH.6–8.5
5. ***Drawing Conclusions*** Why did the Byzantine military grow weaker? RH.6–8.2
6. **ARGUMENT** Write a speech that Theodora might have given to Justinian to convince him to stay in Constantinople during the rebellion in A.D. 532. WHST.6–8.1, WHST.6–8.10

LESSON 3 REVIEW ANSWERS

1. Images of saints were created by using small pieces of cut glass and stone.
2. Constantinople was located between the Black Sea and the Aegean Sea. It was at the crossroads between Asia and Europe, making it an important center for trade.
3. Rome influenced the political and social life of the Byzantine Empire. Emperors spoke Latin and enforced Roman laws. Architecture reflected the Roman style. Chariot races were held, and free bread and entertainment were provided for the poor, similar to what had been done in Rome. Over time, the Byzantine Empire became more heavily influenced by the Greeks. For example, emperors and officials began speaking Greek instead of Latin.
4. Justinian's Code organized laws more clearly and simplified them. Laws were more easily understood by officials and businesspeople.
5. Disease wiped out much of the empire's army. Also, the Byzantines did not have enough money to defend their eastern and western lands.
6. Speeches might include the argument that if Justinian fled, he would not like his new life, but if he stayed in Constantinople and faced his enemies, it would show that he was strong and fearless.

T Technology Skills

Making Presentations Show students examples of tourism posters and brochures. Explain that these documents are meant to encourage people to visit the places being shown. **Ask:** **What is it about the posters and brochures that makes these places seem appealing?** *(Students might note the use of bright colors, the photographs of sun and sand, the images of happy people, and so on.)* Tell students they are going to create their own posters or brochures for the city of Constantinople during the era of the Byzantine Empire. Work as a class to brainstorm images and places that students might use and write about in their projects. *(Possible answers: Hagia Sophia, the Hippodrome, the Black Sea and Mediterranean Sea, and so on.)*

Then have students use PowerPoint or a word processing program and this list of ideas to create their own tourism materials inviting people to visit Constantinople.

Have students complete the Lesson 3 Review.

CLOSE & REFLECT

To close the lesson, show the map of the United States again. Ask students to locate where they live. Then ask them to describe the area and identify the geographic factors and features that determined how and where their community developed. **Ask:**

- **What is our community's major economic activity?**
- **Is trade important to our community? What physical features make trade easy or difficult?**

Have students write a paragraph describing their area's economic resources and how they have been influenced by geography. Have them share their paragraphs with the class.

ANSWERS, p. 365

CRITICAL THINKING He reorganized the army and used armored cavalry.

✓ PROGRESS CHECK Because of Theodora, Justinian gave women more legal rights. Theodora also strengthened his power by helping him stop a revolt.

CHAPTER REVIEW ACTIVITY

Summarizing Conduct a summary discussion to wrap up the chapter. **Ask:** **Summarize three or four things about how the Roman Empire has influenced the art, architecture, language, or government of other cultures.** *(Answers will vary. Sample answers: Roman statues were more realistic than Greek statues. Romans built buildings using arches, domes, and vaults. The Romans were the first people to use concrete. Roman poets and writers wrote odes and satires. Odes are poems that express strong emotions, and satires poke fun at human weaknesses. The design of the U.S. Capitol Building was influenced by the Romans. The languages Italian, French, and Spanish are based on Latin. Like Americans today, Romans believed that everyone is equal under the law.)*

On the board, have a student volunteer create a three-column chart. Use the first column to label the rows. Write "Roman Empire" at the top of the second column and "Byzantine Empire" at the top of the third. Then lead a discussion in which students recall features of daily life, the economy, and key events for each empire. Ask a student volunteer to note these features in the chart.

	Roman Empire	Byzantine Empire
Daily Life		
Economy		
Key Events		

REVIEW THE ENDURING UNDERSTANDING

Review the chapter's Enduring Understanding with students.

- ***People, places, and ideas change over time.***

Now pose the following questions in a class discussion to apply these to the chapter.

- **What key event marked the end of the Western Roman Empire?** *(The Western Roman Empire ended when Odoacer seized power by overthrowing Romulus Augustulus.)*
- **How was the Byzantine Empire's economy able to thrive?** *(Constantinople was located on a peninsula, and fishing boats, trading ships, and warships came to the city's harbor to do business. Constantinople was also easy to defend.)*

CHAPTER 12 Activities CCSS

Write your answers on a separate piece of paper.

1 Exploring the Essential Question WHST.6–8.2, WHST.6–8.10

INFORMATIVE/EXPLANATORY How would you describe the Romans compared to people who lived before them? Write a summary of what made the Romans a unique people. Think of the many ways they were different from the Greeks and other people who lived before them. Include what you think their strongest characteristic was and why.

2 21st Century Skills RH.6–8.5, WHST.6–8.10

DETERMINING CAUSE AND EFFECT Create a poster or other visual aid about the division of the Roman Empire in A.D. 395. Identify two causes and two effects of the split.

3 Thinking Like a Historian RH.6–8.8

DISTINGUISHING FACT FROM OPINION Review the primary source in Lesson 2, *Homiliarum in Ezechielem*, by Pope Gregory I. Decide which statements in the source are facts and which statements are opinions. List the statements of fact and the statements of opinion from the source in a chart like this one.

FACT	OPINION

4 GEOGRAPHY ACTIVITY

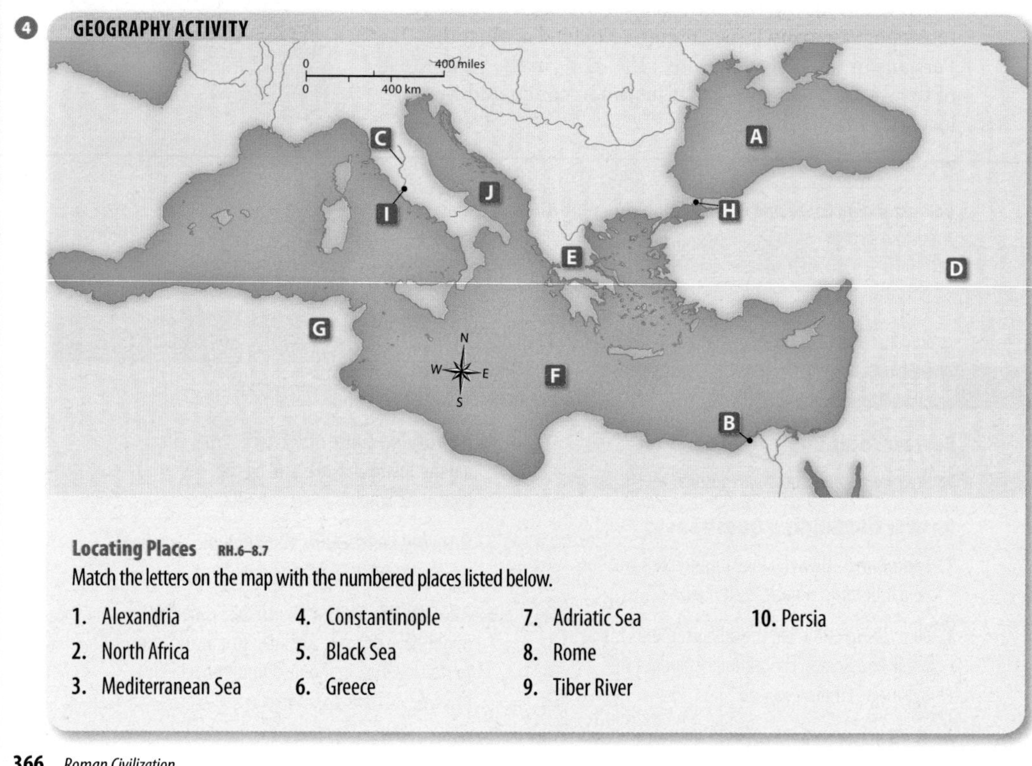

Locating Places RH.6–8.7

Match the letters on the map with the numbered places listed below.

1. Alexandria
2. North Africa
3. Mediterranean Sea
4. Constantinople
5. Black Sea
6. Greece
7. Adriatic Sea
8. Rome
9. Tiber River
10. Persia

ACTIVITIES ANSWERS

Exploring the Essential Question

1 Students should note that the lives of the Greeks were more self-contained. Their lives were spent mostly in conflict, either warring with other people or fighting among themselves over government or power. The Greeks were not as interested in interacting with the outside world as the Romans were. Once the Romans conquered a people, they allowed them to maintain their culture and way of life.

21st Century Skills

2 Student posters should indicate causes, such as the size of the empire and the threats it faced, and effects, such as the collapse and conquest of the Western Roman Empire and the prosperity of the Eastern Roman Empire.

Thinking Like a Historian

3 Facts might include: Cities are destroyed; fortifications are torn down to the ground; few inhabitants remain in the cities. Opinions might include: We see on all sides sorrows. What Rome herself, once deemed the Mistress of the World, has now become, we see—wasted away.

Locating Places

4 **1.** B, **2.** G, **3.** F, **4.** H, **5.** A, **6.** E, **7.** J, **8.** I, **9.** C, **10.** D

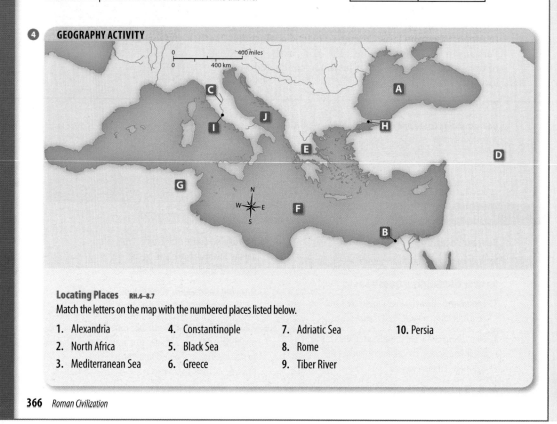

CHAPTER 12 Assessment (CCSS)

REVIEW THE GUIDING QUESTIONS

Directions: Choose the best answer for each question.

RH.6–8.2
1. Which is an example of Greek influence on Roman culture?
   A. arches and domes in Roman architecture
   B. Roman plays that told stories of military failures
   C. letter-like symbols in the Roman number system
   D. Roman statues that showed people's wrinkles and warts

RH.6–8.2
2. Which is a true statement about the lives of Roman women?
   F. Roman women had the same rights as Roman men.
   G. Roman women did not participate in Roman society.
   H. Roman women had less power when Rome was an empire.
   I. Roman women had more freedom if their husbands were wealthy.

RH.6–8.2
3. An increase in prices and a decline in the value of Roman money created
   A. reforms.
   B. inflation.
   C. food shortages.
   D. Germanic invasions.

RH.6–8.2
4. Which of the following is a lasting cultural impact made by the Romans?
   F. the pyramids
   G. the canal lock system
   H. Buddhism
   I. the modern alphabet

RH.6–8.2
5. As emperor, Justinian changed the legal system by
   A. creating a more organized code of laws.
   B. putting his wife, Theodora, in charge.
   C. taking away the rights of women.
   D. building new churches.

RH.6–8.2, RH.6–8.4
6. During the Byzantine Empire
   F. world trade expanded greatly.
   G. education was not considered important.
   H. Christianity was lost.
   I. the development of art and architecture stopped.

367

CHAPTER 12

Assessment Answers

ASSESSMENT ANSWERS

Review the Guiding Questions

1. **C** The Romans created a unique culture by using arches and domes in their architecture, writing plays about military failures, and creating sculptures of realistic-looking people. Thus, choice C, the use of letter-like symbols, is the correct answer.

2. **I** Roman women were not citizens and did not have full rights, but they participated in Roman society. When Rome was an empire, the wives of emperors began to exercise more power. Women's freedom was determined by the wealth and position of their husbands. Therefore, choice I is the correct answer.

3. **B** Reforms were a response to the increased prices and devalued money that created inflation, but they were not enough to end the food shortages that led to higher prices or to stop the foreign invasions that helped weaken the empire. Choice B is the correct answer.

4. **I** The Egyptians built the pyramids; canal lock systems were developed by other cultures; and Buddhism developed in the East. The Romans gave us the modern alphabet, choice I.

5. **A** Although Justinian listened to Theodora's advice, he never put her in charge. Justinian increased women's rights and improved Byzantine law by simplifying and reorganizing the legal system. Choice A is the correct answer.

6. **F** The location of Constantinople between Europe and Asia expanded world trade. Choice F is the correct answer.

Analyzing Documents

❼ **A** Students might use the clue word *victor* to help them answer this question.

❽ **I** Students should know the definitions of *womb* and *tomb*. If not, have them look up the words in the dictionary. Choice I is the correct answer.

Short Response

❾ Student responses should include military control, trade, and communication. The roads signaled that an area belonged to the Roman Empire.

❿ Roman engineers had to construct long bridges over deep valleys and tunnel through mountains of solid rock.

Extended Response

⓫ Students' letters should contain descriptive phrases that would indicate that Constantinople was a busy trading city. They should point out that, like Rome, it was the seat of power and had beautiful buildings and artworks. Unlike Rome, Constantinople's economy was strong, and it was populated by a variety of people from many parts of the world, trading and living within the city.

DBQ ANALYZING DOCUMENTS

Christian leader Jerome wrote this in a letter about attacks on Rome:

"Who would believe that Rome, victor over all the world would fall, that she would be to her people both the tomb [grave] and the womb [birthplace]."

—from The Epistles of St. Jerome, tr. Roland Bainton

RH.6–8.1, RH.6–8.6

❼ **Drawing Conclusions** Which statement best summarizes what Jerome thinks about Rome before its fall?

A. Jerome sees Rome as strong.
B. Jerome sees a bright future for Rome.
C. Jerome sees Rome as weak.
D. Jerome sees that Rome is in danger.

RH.6–8.1

❽ **Comparing** Why does Jerome compare Rome to a womb [birthplace] and a tomb [grave] for its people?

F. He has seen Rome on the decline from its beginning.
G. There have been many births and deaths in Rome.
H. The birth of Rome has meant the death of her people.
I. The words *womb* and *tomb* represent a beginning and an end.

SHORT RESPONSE

"[The] Romans were proud of making their roads go straight even when this meant constructing long bridges over deep valleys or tunneling through solid rock mountains. . . . As the Roman Empire expanded . . . [t]hey helped the Romans . . . by enabling troops to be rushed to trouble spots . . . facilitated [made easier] long-distance trade and . . . sped up communication among the different regions."

—from *Daily Life in the Roman City* by Gregory Aldrete

RH.6–8.1

❾ What advantages did the system of roads provide to Romans?

RH.6–8.1

❿ What obstacles to building the network of roads did the Romans face?

EXTENDED RESPONSE

WHST.6–8.10

⓫ **Narrative** You are a citizen of Rome who recently moved to Constantinople. Write a letter to a friend in Rome about your new home. Explain the differences and similarities between the two cities.

Need Extra Help?

If You've Missed Question	❶	❷	❸	❹	❺	❻	❼	❽	❾	❿	⓫
Review Lesson	1	1	2	2	3	3	2	2	1	1	1, 3

networks *Online Teaching Options*

Help students use the Skills Builder resources

Your students can practice important 21st Century skills such as geography, reading, writing, and critical thinking by using resources found in the Skills Builder tab of the online Student Learning Center. Resources include templates, handbooks, and slide shows. These same resources are also available in the Resource Library of the Teacher Lesson Center.

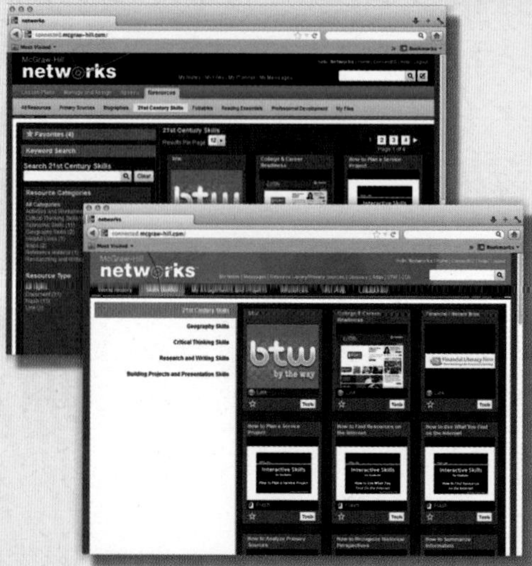

CHAPTER 13

The Rise of Christianity Planner

UNDERSTANDING BY DESIGN®

Enduring Understanding

- *People, places, and ideas change over time.*

Essential Questions

- *What are the characteristics of a leader?*
- *How do religions develop?*
- *How do new ideas change the way people live?*

Predictable Misunderstandings

Students may think:

- *Jesus was not a Jew.*
- *Christianity was not shaped by politics or history.*
- *The Roman Empire never adopted Christianity.*
- *The Roman Catholic Church was the only Christian church in Europe.*

Assessment Evidence

Performance Task:

- *Hands-On Chapter Project*

Other Evidence:

- *Interactive Graphic Organizers*
- *21st Century Skills Activity*
- *Primary Source Activity*
- *Geography and History Activity*
- *Economics of History Activity*
- *What Do You Think? questions*
- *Written paragraphs*
- *Lesson Reviews*
- *Responses to Interactive Whiteboard Activities*
- *Classroom discussion of Christianity's effect on the Roman Empire*
- *Lesson Activities and Assessment*

SUGGESTED PACING GUIDE

Introducing the Chapter............... 1 Day
Lesson 1............................ 1 Day
Lesson 2............................ 1 Day
Lesson 3............................ 1 Day
Chapter Wrap-Up and Assessment...... 1 Day

TOTAL TIME 5 Days

Key for Using the Teacher Edition

SKILL-BASED ACTIVITIES

Types of skill activities found in the Teacher Edition.

V Visual Skills require students to analyze maps, graphs, charts, and photos.

R Reading Skills help students practice reading skills and master vocabulary.

W Writing Skills provide writing opportunities to help students comprehend the text.

C Critical Thinking Skills help students apply and extend what they have learned.

T Technology Skills require students to use digital tools effectively.

*Letters are followed by a number when there is more than one of the same type of skill on the page.

DIFFERENTIATED INSTRUCTION

All activities are written for the on-level student unless otherwise marked with the leveled labels below.

BL Beyond Level
AL Approaching Level
ELL English Language Learners

All students benefit from activities that utilize different learning styles. Many activities are marked as below when a particular learning style is highlighted.

Intrapersonal | **Naturalist**
Logical/Mathematical | **Kinesthetic**
Visual/Spatial | **Auditory/Musical**
Verbal/Linguistic | **Interpersonal**

NCSS Standards covered in "The Rise of Christianity"

Learners will understand:

1 CULTURE

4. That the beliefs, values, and behaviors of a culture form an integrated system that helps shape the activities and ways of life that define a culture

6. That culture may change in response to changing needs, concerns, social, political, and geographic conditions

2 TIME, CONTINUITY, AND CHANGE

6. The origins and influences of social, cultural, political, and economic systems

7. The contributions of key persons, groups, and events from the past and their influence on the present

3 PEOPLE, PLACES, AND ENVIRONMENTS

8. Factors that contribute to cooperation and conflict among peoples of the nation and world, including language, religion, and political beliefs

4 INDIVIDUAL DEVELOPMENT AND IDENTITY

3. How factors such as physical endowment, interests, capabilities, learning, motivation, personality, perception, and beliefs influence individual development and identity

4. How personal, social, cultural, and environmental factors contribute to the development and the growth of personal identity

5 INDIVIDUALS, GROUPS, AND INSTITUTIONS

3. Institutions are created to respond to changing individual and group needs

5. That groups and institutions change over time

6. That cultural diffusion occurs when groups migrate

8. That when two or more groups with differing norms and beliefs interact, accommodation or conflict may result

CHAPTER OPENER PLANNER

Students will know:

- *the message of Jesus and its connection to Jewish thought.*
- *why Christianity spread in the Roman Empire.*
- *the role Constantine played in the acceptance of Christianity in the Roman Empire.*
- *the causes of the split of the Christian church into eastern and western branches.*

Students will be able to:

- ***synthesize** the geographic theme of movement and its importance to spreading Christianity in the Roman Empire.*
- ***summarize** the life of Jesus and basic Christian beliefs.*
- ***identify** the role played by the apostles in the growth of Christianity.*
- ***synthesize** the geographic theme of movement and its importance to spreading Christianity in the Roman Empire.*
- ***draw conclusions** about Christianity's expansion and eventual acceptance in the Roman Empire.*
- ***synthesize** information about the rise and spread of Christianity.*
- ***analyze** the split of the Christian church.*

UNDERSTANDING BY DESIGN®

Print Teaching Options

V Visual Skills

- ☐ **P. 370** Students answer questions about the spread of Christianity as shown on a map. **Visual/Spatial**
- ☐ **P. 371** Students review the time line and make inferences about what was happening in ancient Judaea around A.D. 1. **Visual/Spatial**

Online Teaching Options

V Visual Skills

- **MAP** **Place and Time: Spread of Christianity to A.D. 600**—Students click to reveal Christian areas in A.D. 325, A.D. 400, and A.D. 600.
- **TIME LINE** **Place and Time: The Rise of Christianity A.D. 30 to A.D. 600**—Students see the relationships between key events during this time period.
- **WORLD ATLAS** Students can use this interactive map to identify regions of the world, learn about individual countries, locate political boundaries, measure distances, and much more.

Printable Digital Worksheets

R Reading Skills

- **GRAPHIC NOVEL** ***The Vision***—Constantine has a vision that he will defeat Maxentius if he fights under the sign of Christ. After defeating Maxentius's army, Constantine is declared emperor of Rome. In A.D. 313, Constantine grants religious freedom to all people in the Empire, including Christians.

Project-Based Learning

Hands-On Chapter Project

Rise of Christianity

Student groups will create blogs describing the characteristics and actions of early Christian leaders. Group members will take turns writing blog entries for each leader and responses to those blog entries.

Technology Extension

edtechteacher 21st Century Learning

Early Christian Leadership Blog

- Find an additional activity online that incorporates technology for this project.
- Visit the EdTechTeacher Web sites (included in the Technology Extension for this chapter) for more links, tutorials, and other resources.

Print Resources

ANCILLARY RESOURCES

These ancillaries are available for every chapter and lesson.

- **Reading Essentials and Study Guide Workbook** AL ELL
- **Chapter Tests and Lesson Quizzes Blackline Masters**

PRINTABLE DIGITAL WORKSHEETS

These printable digital worksheets are available for every chapter and lesson.

- **Hands-On Chapter Projects**
- **What Do You Know? activities**
- **Chapter Summaries (English and Spanish)**
- **Vocabulary Builder activities**
- **Guided Reading activities**

More Media Resources

SUGGESTED VIDEOS MOVIES

Watch portions of *The Gospel According to Saint Matthew*, a faithful retelling of Matthew's gospel by Italian filmmaker Pier Paolo Pasolini. Also watch clips from the Frontline documentary *From Jesus to Christ: The First Christians*, produced for PBS.

- **Discuss:** Do documentaries convey different information about a topic than books?

(NOTE: Preview clips to ensure age-appropriateness.)

SUGGESTED READING

Grade 6 reading level:

- ***Ancient Celts: Archaeology Unlocks the Secrets of the Celts' Past,*** by Jen Green

Grade 7 reading level:

- ***Wonders and Miracles: A Passover Companion,*** by Eric A. Kimmel

Grade 8 reading level:

- ***The Treasury of Saints and Martyrs,*** by Margaret Mulvihill

LESSON 1 PLANNER

EARLY CHRISTIANITY

Students will know:
- *the message of Jesus and its connection to Jewish thought.*

Students will be able to:
- ***summarize*** *the life of Jesus and basic Christian beliefs.*
- ***identify*** *the role played by the apostles in the growth of Christianity.*

UNDERSTANDING BY DESIGN®

Print Teaching Options

V Visual Skills

- [ ] **P. 376** Students analyze paintings that illustrate two parables. Visual/Spatial
- [ ] **P. 377** Students examine an image of Mary Magdalene and learn about the use of halos. Visual/Spatial
- [ ] **P. 378** Students examine the painting of the Last Supper. They speculate on and explain what is going on in the painting. BL Visual/Spatial

R Reading Skills

- [ ] **P. 372** Students learn how the Romans tightened control over Judaea and how the Jews responded.
- [ ] **P. 373** Students discuss the Jewish revolts and learn about the Zealots. AL
- [ ] **P. 374** Students discuss the sequence of events and clarify the meaning of *preach* and *disciples*. ELL
- [ ] **P. 375** Students discuss the Beatitudes and explain each one. ELL
- [ ] **P. 376** Students explain what the Romans thought of Jesus and why there was tension between the Romans and the Jews.
- [ ] **P. 377** Students describe the betrayal of Jesus and explain what was unusual about his death. AL ELL

W Writing Skills

- [ ] **P. 375** Students write a parable. BL Interpersonal
- [ ] **P. 378** Students do research to learn about the apostles and prepare a multimedia presentation. Verbal/Linguistic

C Critical Thinking Skills

- [ ] **P. 373** Students assess the outcome of the rebellions against Rome. BL
- [ ] **P. 374** Students determine the central ideas of Jesus' teachings.
- [ ] **P. 379** Students discuss Christian beliefs and compare and contrast them to the beliefs of the Romans and of the Jews. AL

Online Teaching Options

V Visual Skills

- VIDEO **Christianity in Greece**—Students view a video that explains the development of Christianity in Greece.
- BIOGRAPHY **Paul of Tarsus**—Students read about this great Christian missionary.
- IMAGE **Masada**—Students view an image of this fortress defended by Jews against the Romans.
- IMAGE **Jesus and His Disciples**—Students view da Vinci's famous painting *The Last Supper.*

R Reading Skills

- GRAPHIC ORGANIZER **Taking Notes: *Identifying:* Life of Jesus**—Students list three things known about the life of Jesus.
- BIOGRAPHY **Mary Magdalene**—Students read biographical information about this follower of Jesus.
- BIOGRAPHY **Peter**—What we know of Peter from the Christian Bible is summarized.

C Critical Thinking Skills

- WHITEBOARD ACTIVITY **Literary Elements of Parables**—Students sort story elements (setting, plot, lesson) of three different parables.
- SLIDE SHOW **Religious Art**—Students compare several depictions of the Sermon on the Mount.

T Technology Skills

- SELF-CHECK QUIZ **Lesson 1**—Students receive instant feedback on their mastery of lesson content.

Printable Digital Worksheets

W Writing Skills

- WORKSHEET **21st Century Skills Activity: Collaboration: Group Project**—Students collaborate to write their own parable.

C Critical Thinking Skills

- WORKSHEET **Primary Source Activity: Jesus and the Jewish Religion**—Students analyze points of view after reading excerpts from the Torah and the Christian Bible.

THE EARLY CHURCH

Students will know:
- *why Christianity spread in the Roman Empire.*
- *the role Constantine played in the acceptance of Christianity in the Roman Empire.*

Students will be able to:
- ***synthesize** the geographic theme of movement and its importance to spreading Christianity in the Roman Empire.*
- ***draw conclusions** about Christianity's expansion and eventual acceptance in the Roman Empire.*

UNDERSTANDING BY DESIGN®

☑ Print Teaching Options

V Visual Skills

- ☐ **P. 381** Students analyze a map showing the spread of Christianity through A.D. 325. **Visual/Spatial**
- ☐ **P. 382** Students study the image of the Roman Catacombs and contrast them with today's cemeteries. **Visual/Spatial**
- ☐ **P. 384** Students analyze a chart and explain the roles of each person in this hierarchy. **Visual/Spatial**

R Reading Skills

- ☐ **P. 380** Students explain factors that helped the spread of Christianity. AL
- ☐ **P. 381** Students explain why the Romans distrusted Christianity. AL
- ☐ **P. 382** Students discuss the term *martyr.*
- ☐ **P. 384** Students define and discuss key terms relating to the church hierarchy. AL ELL
- ☐ **P. 384** Students discuss the impact early writings had on the establishment of the Christian religion.

W Writing Skills

- ☐ **P. 382** Students write a letter from the point of view of a soldier in Constantine's army. **Interpersonal**

C Critical Thinking Skills

- ☐ **P. 380** Students compare Christianity to the Roman religion.
- ☐ **P. 382** Students consider why Constantine's support was important. BL
- ☐ **P. 383** Students make connections between the church hierarchy and modern day hierarchies. BL **Verbal/Linguistic**
- ☐ **P. 385** Students consider why the Christians called the accounts of Jesus' life the gospels.

T Technology Skills

- ☐ **P. 385** Small groups of students research the writers of the four gospels – Matthew, Mark, Luke, and John. **Interpersonal**

☑ Online Teaching Options

V Visual Skills

- VIDEO **St. Peter's Tomb**—Students explore the development of Christianity in the first century and the place of Vatican City in the modern world.
- MAP **Spread of Christianity A.D. 325**—Students compare the routes Paul followed on his journeys in the first century with the spread of Christianity by A.D. 325.
- SLIDE SHOW **Burial Places**—Students view catacombs, mausoleums, and cemeteries.

R Reading Skills

- GRAPHIC ORGANIZER **Taking Notes: *Listing:* Reasons Christianity Spread**—Students list the major reasons that Christianity spread.
- PRIMARY SOURCE **The Edict of Milan**—Students read an excerpt from this edict, which ordered toleration of Christianity within the Roman Empire.

C Critical Thinking Skills

- CHART **Early Church Hierarchy**—Students click to learn the roles of different people in the church.
- PRIMARY SOURCE **Augustine's *Confessions***—Students analyze an excerpt from Augustine's autobiography.

T Technology Skills

- SELF-CHECK QUIZ **Lesson 2**—Students receive instant feedback on their mastery of lesson content.

☑ Printable Digital Worksheets

C Critical Thinking Skills

- WORKSHEET **Geography and History Activity: The Role of Geography in the Spread of Christianity**—Students analyze cultural and geographic factors that affected the spread of Christianity.

LESSON 3 PLANNER

A CHRISTIAN EUROPE

Students will know:
- *the causes of the split of the Christian church into eastern and western branches.*

Students will be able to:
- ***synthesize** information about the rise and spread of Christianity.*
- ***analyze** the split of the Christian church.*

UNDERSTANDING BY DESIGN®

Print Teaching Options

V Visual Skills

- [ ] **P. 387** Students analyze a painting of the angel Gabriel. BL Visual/Spatial
- [ ] **P. 388** Students explain the use of color highlighting on a map and identify when areas became Christian. Visual/Spatial
- [ ] **P. 390** Students analyze iconography of Cyril and Methodius. BL Visual/Spatial

R Reading Skills

- [ ] **P. 386** Students describe the role of the emperor in the Eastern Orthodox Church.
- [ ] **P. 387** Students define key terms. AL ELL
- [ ] **P. 391** Students describe events that brought Christianity to Ireland and Britain.

W Writing Skills

- [ ] **P. 390** Students rewrite a quote in their own words. AL ELL

C Critical Thinking Skills

- [ ] **P. 388** Students determine causes and effects that affected the relationship between the pope and the patriarch of Constantinople. AL
- [ ] **P. 389** Students discuss monasteries and draw conclusions about their need for isolated locations.

T Technology Skills

- [ ] **P. 389** Students use the Internet to research a religious community and then share their findings with the class. BL

Online Teaching Options

V Visual Skills

- [ ] VIDEO **The Development of Christianity in Ireland**—Students consider how the introduction of Christianity to Ireland influenced the entire British region.
- [ ] MAP **Spread of Christianity A.D. 325–1100**—Students observe the spread of Christianity across Europe and East Asia.
- [ ] SLIDE SHOW **Religious Communities**—Students examine how monks live in communities.

R Reading Skills

- [ ] GRAPHIC ORGANIZER **Taking Notes: *Listing:* Honoring Icons**—Students list arguments for and against honoring icons.
- [ ] IMAGE **The Pope and the Emperor**—Students examine one of the issues that split the eastern and western Christian churches.

C Critical Thinking Skills

- [ ] CHART **The Church and the Empire**—Students click to see how the Eastern Orthodox Church and the Byzantine Empire worked together.
- [ ] SLIDE SHOW **Cyril, Creator of the Cyrillic Alphabet**—Students learn about Cyril, who developed an alphabet to help Slavs understand the Eastern Orthodox faith.

T Technology Skills

- [ ] SELF-CHECK QUIZ **Lesson 3**—Students receive instant feedback on their mastery of lesson content.
- [ ] GAME **A Christian Europe Crossword**—Students complete the puzzle to review lesson vocabulary.

Printable Digital Worksheets

C Critical Thinking Skills

- [ ] WORKSHEET **Economics of History Activity: The Economic Life of Christian Monasteries**—Students analyze the economic ties between monasteries and the local towns and villages.

INTERVENTION AND REMEDIATION STRATEGIES

LESSON 1 Early Christianity

Reading and Comprehension

Ask students to create an outline of Lesson 1. They can use the major heads for the outline topics and should include all main ideas for each topic.

Text Evidence

Have students learn about one of Jesus' parables that has not been presented in the lesson. Then have them explain how that parable illustrates the teachings of Jesus. They should cite evidence from the text to back up their statements.

LESSON 2 The Early Church

Reading and Comprehension

Ask students to write two or three paragraphs describing the relationship between Christianity and the Roman Empire.

Text Evidence

Have students work in pairs and do research to learn more about how and why the Roman emperor Nero blamed Christians for burning Rome and what the consequences were for the Christians.

LESSON 3 A Christian Europe

Reading and Comprehension

Have students create a time line of events discussed in this lesson. Tell them to allow enough space to write one or two sentences explaining each event.

Text Evidence

Organize students into small groups. One group should take the position of the Eastern Orthodox Church, with the other taking the position of the Roman Catholic Church. Have them debate their views of the issues that separated them. Tell them to include facts and details to support their views.

Online Resources

Approaching Level Reader

Use this online lower-level text that corresponds directly to the text in the Student Edition. It includes a Spanish version.

Guided Reading Activities

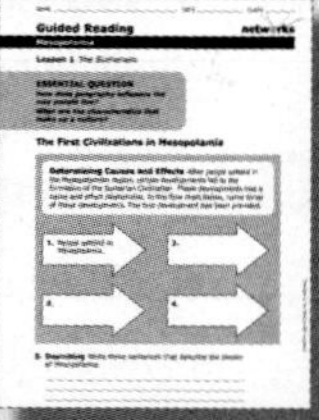

This resource uses graphic organizers and guiding questions to help students with comprehension.

What Do You Know?

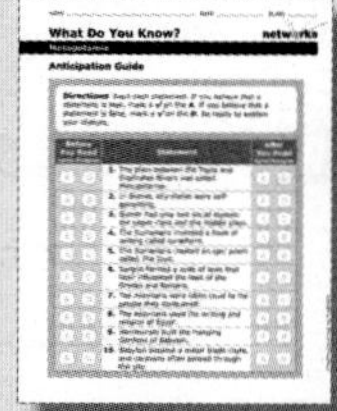

Use these worksheets to pre-assess student's background knowledge before they study the chapter.

Reading Essentials and Study Guide Workbook

This resource offers writing and reading activities for the approaching-level student. Also available in Spanish.

Self-Check Quizzes

This online assessment tool provides instant feedback for students to check their progress.

The Rise of Christianity

A.D. 30 to A.D. 600

ESSENTIAL QUESTIONS • *What are the characteristics of a leader?* • *How do religions develop?* • *How do new ideas change the way people live?*

networks

There's More Online about the beginnings and development of Christianity.

CHAPTER 13

Lesson 1
Early Christianity

Lesson 2
The Early Church

Lesson 3
A Christian Europe

The Story Matters . . .

One of the chosen apostles of Jesus, Simon Peter of Galilee, was called "the rock "of the Christian church. He brought many followers to the Christian faith.

Soon after the death of Jesus, Peter, as he was called, became a leader of the early Christian church. He played an important role in spreading the teachings of Jesus and in contributing to the rise of Christianity. This painting imagines Peter as an older man.

◄ *This image of Peter was painted by the Greek artist El Greco around 1600. St. Peter's Basilica, or church, in the city of Rome, Italy is named in his honor.*

Letter from the Author

Dear World History Teacher,

By the third century, Christianity was spreading throughout the Roman Empire. Christianity began among the followers of Jesus of Nazareth and gained acceptance throughout the empire. After the collapse of the Roman Empire in the West, the Roman Catholic Church, as the Christian church was called, developed an organized government under the leadership of the Bishop of Rome, who became known as the pope. In the east, the Byzantine Empire developed its own form of worship known as the Eastern Orthodox Church.

Jackson J. Spielvogel

ENGAGE

Bellringer Ask a volunteer to read "The Story Matters . . ." aloud, or read it aloud to the students. Then discuss what it might have been like to have lived in ancient Judaea during the lifetime of Jesus of Nazareth. **Ask:** **Have you ever been inside a Christian church or listened to a priest or a minister speak to a group of people about religious matters? Have you seen programs on television or in a movie that depict the life of Jesus or explain how Christianity developed?** Have a few students share their experiences. Then **ask:** **What do you think are some connections between Judaism, the religion of the Jews, and Christianity? If Christianity began in ancient Galilee and Judaea, how do you think it became the worldwide religion it is today?** Tell the class that the beginning of Christianity 2,000 years ago can be well documented because of the many artifacts that have been found and the writings that have been preserved. Tell interested students that they can find more about the development of Christianity online.

Making Connections

Tell students that most names have specific meanings, and that the name *Peter* comes from the Latin *petra*, meaning "rock." Have students read the information about Peter in the textbook. Then ask them to draw connections between the meaning of Peter's names and his successes during his lifetime. If time allows, have students research the origins of their own names.

TEACH & ASSESS

Step Into the Place

V1 Visual Skills

Analyzing Maps Remind students that Christianity began in the Mediterranean region. Direct students to look at the map key and find the corresponding areas on the map. **Ask:** **When did the region around the city of Nazareth become Christian and spread into Rome?** *(by A.D. 325)* **When did it spread to eastern and southern Britain?** *(by A.D. 600)* Point out to students that Christianity was in Ireland and western Britain by A.D. 400, and that there were also pockets of Christianity in parts of Gaul and southern Europe that became Christian hundreds of years earlier than surrounding areas. **Visual/Spatial**

Discuss with the class why the Roman Empire wanted to control the Mediterranean region and why the Mediterranean Sea was important to the spread of Christianity.

Content Background Knowledge

- Many of the areas of Europe shown on the map, such as Spain and Italy, were not nations as they are today. During the period depicted in this map, they were fragmented regions with many small tribal units or kingdoms.
- Gaul was an early name for what became France.

CHAPTER 13 CCSS

Place and Time: The Rise of Christianity A.D. 30 to A.D. 600

As Jesus gained followers, he alarmed Rome's rulers. They feared his growing influence and eventually executed him. Jesus' followers carried his message to many lands, and what began as a Jewish group developed into a separate religion.

Step Into the Place

MAP FOCUS Christianity began in Judaea, an area that was part of the Roman Empire. From Judaea, Christianity spread through the Mediterranean region and beyond.

1. **LOCATION** Look at the map. Is Rome located northwest or southeast of Jerusalem? **RH.6–8.7**
2. **HUMAN-ENVIRONMENT INTERACTION** What physical feature made it challenging for early Christians to expand their faith from Judaea to Britain? **RH.6–8.7**
3. **CRITICAL THINKING** *Analyzing* How did the Mediterranean Sea make it easier for Christianity to spread? **RH.6–8.1**

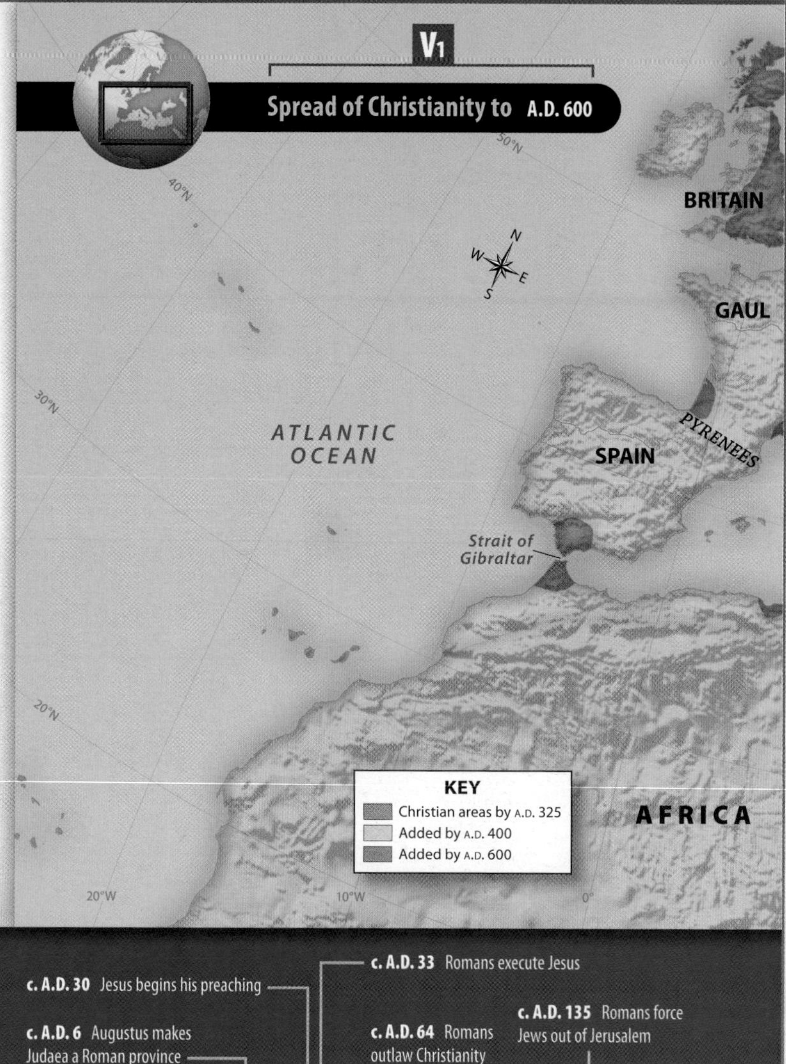

Step Into the Time

TIME LINE Choose an event from the time line and write two or three sentences explaining how the ancient Romans dealt with Christianity during that time. **RH.6–8.7, WHST.6–8.2, WHST.6–8.10**

V2

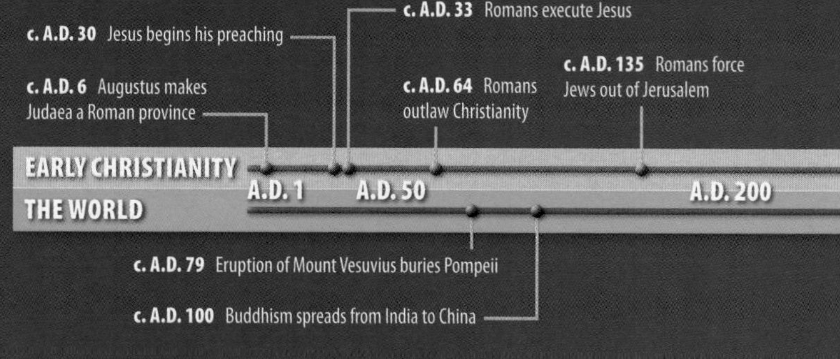

370 *The Rise of Christianity*

Project-Based Learning

Hands-On Chapter Project

Rise of Christianity

Students will create blogs describing the characteristics and actions of early Christian leaders. They will discuss religious leaders and the qualities that make them successful and then work in groups to plan their blogging project.Each group will research its topic and take turns writing blog entries and responses. Students will then share their blogs with the class. Students will evaluate their research, presentation, and collaboration using an Assessment Rubric.

Technology Extension

Early Christian Leadership Blog

Students will publish on the Web their blogs on early Christian Leadership. Blogging is a great way for students to practice literacy skills in an authentic environment. Having your students turn their written work into published blogs will provide them with a sense of accomplishment while opening up individual student work to the entire class for peer editing and instruction.

ANSWERS, p. 370

Step Into the Place

1. Rome is located northwest of Jerusalem.
2. the Mediterranean Sea
3. **CRITICAL THINKING** Answers may vary. Possible answers should include the fact that the Mediterranean Sea allowed followers of Jesus to travel by ship to many seaside cities and from there to travel inland to preach Jesus' message.

Step Into the Time

Sample answer for c. A.D. 33: The Romans crucified Jesus, and after his death they began to persecute his followers.

networks *There's More Online!*

☑ **MAP** Explore the interactive version of this map on NETWORKS.

☑ **TIME LINE** Explore the interactive version of this time line on NETWORKS.

North Sea
EUROPE
ALPS
ITALY
Corsica
Rome
Sardinia
Sicily
GREECE
Constantinople
Black Sea
ASIA MINOR
Tarsus
Antioch
SYRIA
Damascus
Aegean Sea
Mediterranean Sea
Nazareth
Jerusalem
Alexandria
JUDAEA
EGYPT
Red Sea
Caspian Sea
Aral Sea
ASIA
Persian Gulf
0 400 miles
0 400 km
Lambert Azimuthal Equal-Area projection

c. A.D. 312 Constantine accepts Christianity

c. A.D. 392 Christianity becomes official religion of Rome

c. A.D. 597 Monks bring Christianity to Britain

A.D. 300 | A.D. 400 | A.D. 500 | A.D. 600

c. A.D. 320 Gupta Empire begins in India

c. A.D. 395 Roman Empire divides

c. A.D. 400 Yamato clan controls Japan

c. A.D. 550 Mayan cities flourish in Mesoamerica

c. A.D. 600 China prints first books

371

CHAPTER 13

Place and Time

Step Into the Time

V2 Visual Skills

Analyzing Time Lines Have students review the time line for the chapter. Explain that they will be studying events from about A.D. 1 to A.D. 600. **Ask:** **Based on the information in the time line, what can you infer about what was happening in ancient Judaea beginning around A.D. 1?** *(The Romans governed the people who lived there, who were known as Jews and had their own religion. The Romans persecuted the Jews and later the Christians. Eventually, the Roman Empire accepted Christianity and made it the official religion of the empire.)* **Visual/Spatial**

Content Background Knowledge

In the first century A.D., Christianity was just beginning to spread through the Mediterranean region, although a significant number of Christians were already present in Rome. Among most non-Christians, this new religion had a questionable reputation. Many wild accusations were made against Christians, so they were easy targets for politicians seeking to shift blame to a scapegoat. In A.D. 64, the city of Rome caught fire and burned to the ground. Citizens of Rome blamed Nero, the emperor. He was not at fault, but to shift the accusations away from himself, he blamed the fire on Christians. Christians were then persecuted as Nero tried to throw them out of Rome.

CLOSE & REFLECT

Formulating Questions Guide a review of this opening material. Ask students to ask questions based on the material that they would like answered as they study the chapter. Write three or four of the questions on the board, and have students rewrite them on a sheet of paper. Tell them to look for the answers as they read and discuss the chapter.

MAP

Spread of Christianity to A.D. 600

Analyzing Maps Have students explore the map. When they click on items in the map key, those areas will be highlighted on the map. Ask students to analyze the map and discover when particular regions and cities became Christian. Ask them to indicate areas where they think geographical features might have helped or hindered the spread of Christianity. Invite students to make other observations about the information on the map.

See page 369B for other online activities.

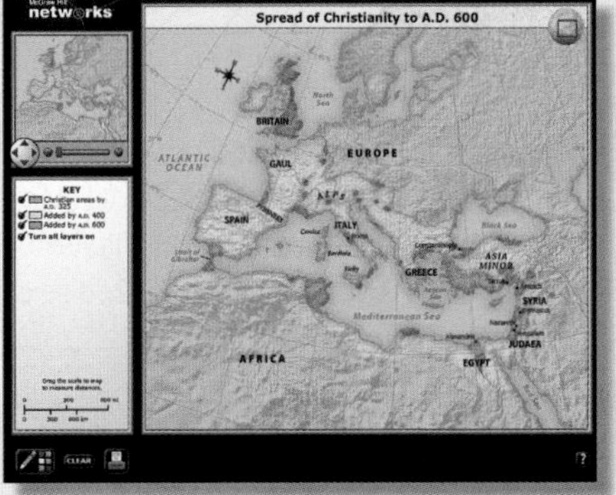

ENGAGE

Bellringer Explain to students that Christianity arose in the Middle East in what is now Palestine and Israel. It grew out of Judaism. Tell students that they will learn about the early days of Christianity in this lesson. For now, ask students to preview the lesson by skimming the lesson and reading the headings, looking at the images, and reading the captions.

TEACH & ASSESS

R Reading Skills

Discussing Introduce the content by reviewing what students know about Judaism. Then direct students to read the text and discuss the Jews' hope and expectation that God would send a deliverer to save them from the Romans and to restore the kingdom of Israel. **Ask:**

- How did the Romans tighten their control over Judaea in A.D. 6? *(They replaced the Jewish king with a Roman procurator and made Judaea into a Roman province.)*
- How did the Jews respond to the tight control of Judaea by the Romans? *(Some cooperated; some limited their contact and continued their traditions; some withdrew to distant settlements and ignored the Romans.)*

ANSWERS, p. 372

TAKING NOTES: Jesus traveled throughout Galilee and Judaea, preaching to people; Roman rulers feared the growing influence of Jesus; Jesus was arrested, charged with treason, and executed.

networks *There's More Online!*

- **BIOGRAPHY**
  - Peter
  - Mary Magdalene
- **CHART/GRAPH** The Beatitudes
- **GRAPHIC ORGANIZER** The Life of Jesus
- **SLIDE SHOW** Religious Art

Lesson 1

Early Christianity

ESSENTIAL QUESTION *What are the characteristics of a leader?*

IT MATTERS BECAUSE

Christianity is one of the world's major religions and continues to influence people around the globe.

Judaism and Rome

GUIDING QUESTION *How did the Jews respond to Roman rule?*

The Romans allowed Judaism (JOO•dee•IH•zuhm) to be practiced throughout the empire. In Judaea and Galilee, however, Romans ruled the Jews with an iron hand. Many Jews hoped that God would send a deliverer to rescue them from Roman rule. They wanted the kingdom of Israel to be restored.

Control by Romans

R The Romans had taken over Judah in 63 B.C., but they allowed Jewish kings to rule it. In A.D. 6, Augustus made Judah a Roman province and called it by the Roman name of Judaea (joo•DEE•uh). Augustus replaced the Jewish ruler with a Roman governor, called a procurator (PRAH•kyuh•RAY•tuhr). Judaea was now more tightly controlled by the Roman Empire.

The Jews disagreed among themselves over how to deal with the Romans. Some Jews wanted to avoid conflict with their rulers. They preferred to cooperate with them. Others limited their contact with Roman officials and continued to practice Jewish traditions. Some Jews completely ignored the Romans. They established communities in remote places, away from Roman rule. Jerusalem, however, remained their holy city.

Reading HELPDESK CCSS

Taking Notes: ***Identifying***

On a graphic organizer like this one, list three things we know about the life of Jesus. RH.6–8.2, WHST.6–8.9

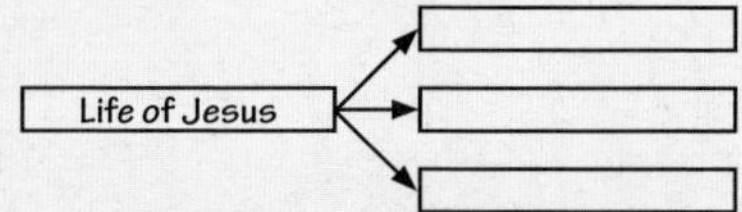

Content Vocabulary (Tier 3 Words)

- **parable**
- **apostle**
- **resurrection**
- **salvation**

networks ***Online Teaching Options***

VIDEO

Christianity in Greece

Analyzing Images Have students view the video to learn more about how Christianity was introduced in Greece. Have students take notes as they watch the video. When they finish, guide the class in creating an outline of the most important ideas.

See page 369C for other online activities.

Jewish Revolts

One group of Jews believed that they should fight the Romans for their freedom. These people, called Zealots (ZEH•luhtz), rebelled against Roman rule in A.D. 66. The Romans, however, brutally crushed the uprising. They destroyed the Jewish temple in Jerusalem and killed thousands of Jews.

The ruins of an ancient Jewish fortress called Masada (muh•SAH•duh) stand on a mountaintop in southeastern Israel. After Jerusalem fell to the Romans in A.D 70, about 1,000 Jewish defenders overtook the Masada fortress. For almost two years, these defenders held off an army of 15,000 Roman soldiers.

R

In A.D. 73, the Romans broke through the walls of the fortress but found only a few Jewish survivors—two women and five children. The others had taken their own lives rather than surrender to the Romans. The fortress is now recognized as a symbol of Jewish heroism.

The Jews organized another unsuccessful rebellion in A.D. 132. In response, the Romans forced all Jews to leave Jerusalem. The Romans then declared that no Jews could ever return to the city. Many Jews, mourning the loss of their city, established communities elsewhere.

C

By A.D. 700, the Jews had settled in regions as far west as Spain and as far east as Central Asia. In later centuries, they settled throughout Europe and the Americas.

An armed group of Jews captured this mountain fortress of Masada from the Romans. They defended it against a Roman army that outnumbered them 15 to one.

▶ CRITICAL THINKING

Drawing Conclusions Why do you think the Jews wanted to control Masada?

R Reading Skills

Discussing Ask a volunteer to read the text aloud. Then lead a discussion of the Jewish revolts. **Ask:**

- Who were the Zealots? *(a group of Jews who wanted to fight the Romans for their freedom)*
- What was the result of the Jewish rebellions? *(The Jewish rebellions failed to achieve their goal of driving out the Romans.)*
- Why do you think these rebellions failed? *(Students might note the superior military strength of Rome and divisions within the Jewish community as reasons.)* AL

C Critical Thinking Skills

Assessing Point out that the outcome of the rebellions against the Romans was devastating for Jews. **Ask:** How do you think the Jews who remained passive felt about the Zealots' failed rebellions? *(Possible response: They were angry with the Zealots and blamed them when the Jews were driven out of Rome.)* BL

Content Background Knowledge

Masada was more than a bleak mountaintop. It was first settled in about 900 B.C. Then, between 37 B.C. and 4 B.C., Herod the Great developed it as a royal citadel with two ornate royal palaces and elaborate fortifications. There were also storehouses and a synagogue, among other structures.

LECTURE SLIDE

Judaism and Rome

Summarizing The lecture slide defines the term *Zealots,* and it outlines the main ideas regarding the rebellions organized by the Zealots. Have students create a cause-and-effect graphic organizer that summarizes the information in the lecture slide. AL

See page 369C for other online activities.

networks Judaism and Rome

Zealots a group of Jews who fought the Romans for their freedom

The zealots led a series of rebellions:

- In response the Romans destroyed the Jewish temple in Jerusalem and killed thousands of people in A.D. 66.
- Jewish defenders held off Roman soldiers for almost two years at the fortress of Masada until the Romans broke through in A.D. 73.
- In A.D. 132, the Jews unsuccessfully rebelled again. All Jews were forced to leave Jerusalem.

ANSWER, p. 373

CRITICAL THINKING Answers should point out that the location of Masada in the mountains would give the Jews added protection from attack.

R Reading Skills

Identifying Clarify for students the time line of events they have read about so far, pointing out that the Jewish rebellions began in 66 A.D. Jesus was born in about 1 A.D. and began preaching in about 30 A.D. **Ask:**

- What does it mean to preach? *(to instruct others about religious beliefs)*
- Who were the disciples? *(the followers of Jesus)* ELL

C Critical Thinking Skills

Determining Central Ideas Explain to students that Jesus drew upon many ideas of the Jewish faith in his teachings. **Ask:** What were the central ideas that Jesus taught? *(God created all people and loves them like a father loves his children. He is coming soon to rule the world. People should love one another the way they love God.)* Have a volunteer read the primary source aloud, and then ask a second volunteer to paraphrase it.

BIOGRAPHY

Peter

Most of what we know about the disciple Peter comes from the Christian Bible. According to tradition, Peter deserted Jesus when Jesus was arrested in the garden outside Jerusalem. Later, Peter felt ashamed and regretted his lack of courage. In the years following the death of Jesus, Peter emerged as a respected leader of the earliest Christian community.

► CRITICAL THINKING
Drawing Conclusions Why do you think Peter deserted Jesus when Jesus was arrested?

Although the Jews were scattered around the world, they kept their faith alive. They did this by studying and following their religious laws and traditions.

✓ PROGRESS CHECK

Identifying Cause and Effect How did the A.D. 132 revolt affect the Jews of Judaea?

Jesus of Nazareth

GUIDING QUESTION ***Why were the life and death of Jesus of Nazareth important to his followers?***

R A few decades before the first Jewish revolt, a Jew named Jesus (JEE•zuhs) grew up in a small town called Nazareth (NA•zuh•ruhth) in Galilee (GA•luh•LEE), the region just north of Judaea. In about A.D. 30, Jesus began to travel throughout Galilee and Judaea, preaching to people about his ideas. A group of 12 close followers called disciples (dih•SY•puhlz) traveled with Jesus.

What Was the Message of Jesus?

According to the Christian Bible, Jesus preached that God was coming soon to rule the world. Jesus urged people to turn from their selfish ways and welcome the kingdom of heaven. In the excerpt below, Jesus calls on his followers to joyfully accept God's coming as a precious gift:

PRIMARY SOURCE

> "The kingdom of heaven is like a treasure buried in a field, which a person finds and hides again, and out of joy goes and sells all that he has and buys that field."
>
> —Matthew 13:54, *New American Bible*

C Jesus preached that God **created** all people and loved them the way a father loves his children. Therefore, people should love God and one another. In this way, they would be obeying God.

The message of Jesus reinforced the Jewish teachings: "Love the Lord your God with all your heart and with all your soul and with all your mind and with all your strength" and "Love your neighbor as yourself."

The teachings of Jesus are summarized in his Sermon on the Mount. Jesus preached on a mountainside to a crowd of thousands.

Alan Spencer/Age fotostock

Reading HELPDESK CCSS

Academic Vocabulary (Tier 2 Words)

create to bring into existence; to produce by a course of action

networks Online Teaching Options

SLIDE SHOW

Religious Art

Analyzing Images Tell students that the core teachings of Jesus can be found in the Sermon on the Mount. Present the interactive slide show, which depicts the Sermon on the Mount through the interpretations of various artists. Tell students they will be learning about Christianity, including how it began and how it spread.

See page 369C for other online activities.

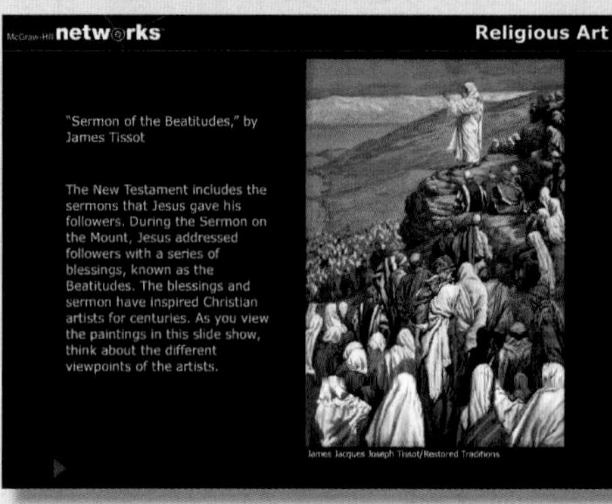

ANSWERS, p. 374

✓ PROGRESS CHECK Roman authorities forced all Jews to leave the city of Jerusalem and told them they could never return.

CRITICAL THINKING Possible answer: because Peter was afraid that he would be tried for being a friend of Jesus

In it Jesus gave the people simple rules to live by called "The Beatitudes." He told people that it was not enough to follow religious laws. People had to love God and forgive others from the heart.

Jesus spoke using everyday language. He often preached using **parables** (PA•ruh•buhlz). These were stories about things his listeners could understand, using events from everyday life. They helped people **interpret**, or explain, the ideas Jesus taught.

In one parable, Jesus told of a Samaritan man who saw an injured traveler by the side of the road. Even though the injured man was not a Samaritan, the passerby helped him. In another parable, Jesus told the story of a father who forgave his son's mistakes. He welcomed his prodigal—or wasteful—son back into the family. Both parables taught that God is like the concerned Samaritan or the forgiving father. He loves people who have erred and will forgive them if they trust in him. **W**

How Did Christianity Begin?

Jesus and his message sparked strong reactions from people. His followers spoke of times in which he healed the sick and performed other miracles. Stories about him were widely told.

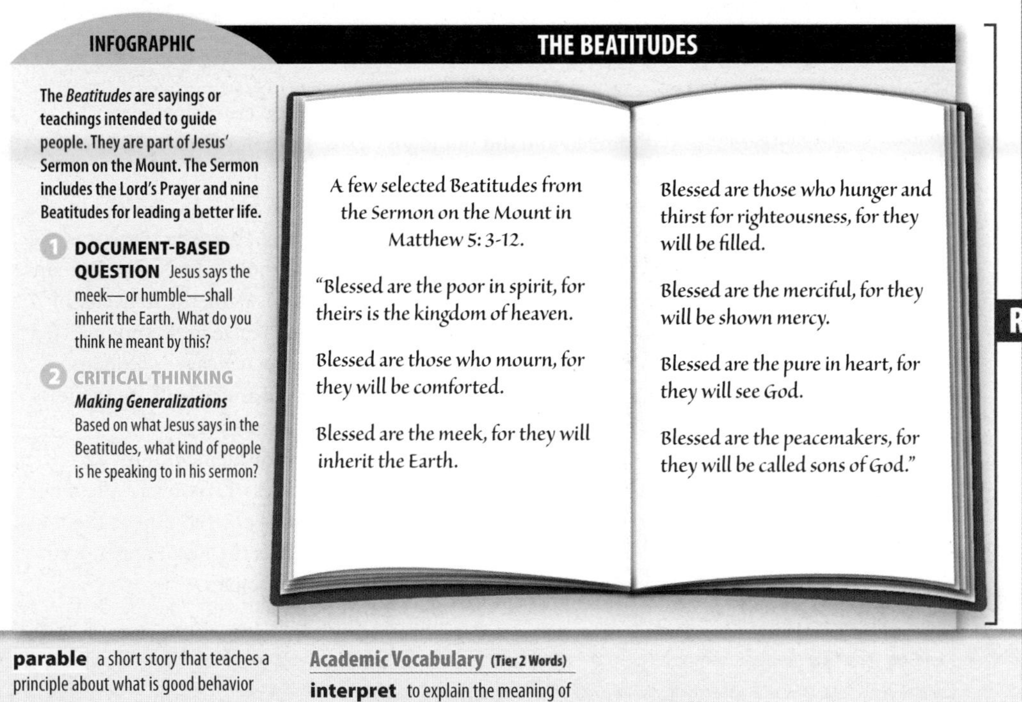

INFOGRAPHIC
THE BEATITUDES
The *Beatitudes* are sayings or teachings intended to guide people. They are part of Jesus' Sermon on the Mount. The Sermon includes the Lord's Prayer and nine Beatitudes for leading a better life.
1 DOCUMENT-BASED QUESTION Jesus says the meek—or humble—shall inherit the Earth. What do you think he meant by this?
2 CRITICAL THINKING *Making Generalizations* Based on what Jesus says in the Beatitudes, what kind of people is he speaking to in his sermon?
A few selected Beatitudes from the Sermon on the Mount in Matthew 5: 3-12.
"Blessed are the poor in spirit, for theirs is the kingdom of heaven.
Blessed are those who mourn, for they will be comforted.
Blessed are the meek, for they will inherit the Earth.
Blessed are those who hunger and thirst for righteousness, for they will be filled.
Blessed are the merciful, for they will be shown mercy.
Blessed are the pure in heart, for they will see God.
Blessed are the peacemakers, for they will be called sons of God."

R

parable a short story that teaches a principle about what is good behavior

Academic Vocabulary (Tier 2 Words)
interpret to explain the meaning of

CHAPTER 13, Lesson 1
Early Christianity

W Writing Skills

Narrative Invite a volunteer to explain what a parable is. Then read or tell the parables of the Good Samaritan and the Prodigal Son. Guide students in explaining the meaning of these parables. Then have pairs of students work together to write their own parables in which they teach an important lesson. Have students share their parables with the class.
BL Interpersonal

R Reading Skills

Listing Have students read the Beatitudes on this page. Then discuss with students what they have read. **Ask:** What are beatitudes? *(sayings or teachings intended to guide people in how they live their lives)* Invite volunteers to read each of the Beatitudes aloud. Discuss each one, calling on students to offer explanations on their meanings. **ELL**

WHITEBOARD ACTIVITY

Literary Elements of Parables

Categorizing Remind students that Jesus used stories called parables to make it easier for his listeners to understand his ideas. Discuss with students the literary elements in parables. Then organize students into teams. Have teams compete to see which one can correctly place the most bulleted items into the columns.

See page 369C for other online activities.

networks — Literary Elements of Parables

Directions: Each parable has characters, a setting, a plot, and a lesson. Drag and drop each story element from the item bank into the chart.

1. **The Good Samaritan** A traveler on a road is robbed and injured. Two people pass without helping. The third, a Samaritan, helps.

2. **The Prodigal Son** A man's youngest son takes his inheritance and spends it wastefully. He realizes how foolish he has been and returns home to ask forgiveness. The love of a father is like God's love.

3. **The Lost Sheep** A man has 100 sheep. One gets lost. He leaves the 99 sheep to find the lost sheep. When he finds the lost sheep, he celebrates.

Item Bank
- a home
- Love your neighbor.
- a traveler and a Samaritan
- a father and son
- Finding a lost soul is cause for celebration.
- the countryside
- A Samaritan helps an injured traveler.
- a road
- a sheepherder
- A man finds his lost sheep and celebrates.
- A son returns home and the father celebrates
- Admitting mistakes and returning home is cause for celebration.

	The Good Samaritan	The Prodigal Son	The Lost Sheep
Characters			
Setting			
Plot Summary			
Lesson			

ANSWERS, p. 375

INFOGRAPHIC

1. Answers may vary. A plausible answer is that people who are meek will do a better job of caring for the Earth than those who are aggressive or warlike.
2. CRITICAL THINKING In the Beatitudes, Jesus seems to be addressing the powerless ("poor in spirit" and "meek") and the oppressed ("those who hunger and thirst for righteousness"). He also says that those who are good on Earth will be rewarded after death.

V Visual Skills

Analyzing Images Have students analyze the painting on the left side of the textbook page. Point out that the injured man is nearly naked. **Ask:**

- **What does this suggest about the man?** *(He has lost everything; even his clothes have been taken.)*
- **What has the Samaritan done to help him?** *(He has bandaged his leg and head; he seems to be helping him to stand.)*

Point out the two men in the background, and explain that these men are used in the parable as contrasts to the Good Samaritan, who has stopped to help. **Visual/Spatial**

R Reading Skills

Explaining Remind students that the people of Judaea were restless under Roman rule and that the Romans were mistrustful of the people. Then direct students to read the passage. **Ask:**

- **What did the Romans think of Jesus?** *(They feared him; he was popular, and they viewed him as a threat to law and order.)*
- **What caused the tension between the Jews and the Romans?** *(The Romans brought statues of the emperor into Jerusalem, and they wanted the Jews to bow down and worship the statues. The Jews refused because they considered them false idols.)*

ANSWER, p. 376

CRITICAL THINKING A good samaritan is a person who helps someone who is in trouble. The term is often used to describe someone who helps a stranger.

V

The parables of the Good Samaritan (left) and the Prodigal Son (right) are shown here. In each case, one person is helping another.

▶ **CRITICAL THINKING**

Synthesizing What do you think of today when you hear that someone is a "good samaritan"?

R

Many believed he was the promised deliverer. Most Jews disagreed and did not follow Jesus. Roman rulers feared his preaching and growing influence and popularity. They viewed Jesus as a threat to law and order.

At the time of the Jewish holy days of Passover, there was growing tension between the Romans and the Jews. The Romans brought statues of the emperor into Jerusalem, the holy city of the Jews. Many Jews saw these statues as false idols and objected to their presence. The Jews had also grown weary of Roman rule and high taxes. Many Romans were angry because the Jews refused to worship statues of the Roman emperor.

In about A.D. 33, Jesus traveled to Jerusalem with his 12 disciples to celebrate the Jewish holy days of Passover. When he arrived in the city, an enthusiastic crowd greeted him as their promised deliverer. In an event known as the Last Supper, Jesus celebrated the Passover meal with his disciples.

Reading **HELP**DESK CCSS

Reading Strategy: *Paraphrasing*

Paraphrasing is restating what you read using your own words. Paraphrasing is a good way to check that you really understood what you read. As you finish reading a paragraph or a passage, ask yourself, "What is the main idea?" Then try to restate the main idea using your own words.

networks *Online Teaching Options*

GRAPHIC ORGANIZER

Taking Notes: *Identifying:* Life of Jesus

Summarizing Have students complete the interactive graphic organizer on the life of Jesus to assess their understanding of the lesson so far.

See page 369C for other online activities.

Betrayal of Jesus

After the meal, however, one of Jesus' closest followers betrayed him. Leaders in Jerusalem arrested Jesus to prevent trouble from erupting in the city. They may have charged Jesus with treason, or disloyalty to the government. He was questioned by the Roman governor and sentenced to death.

According to the Christian Bible, Jesus was crucified, or hung from a wooden cross, and died. Romans regularly crucified criminals and political rebels. The followers of Jesus were greatly saddened by his death. According to Christian belief, Jesus rose from the dead three days after his death and appeared to some of his disciples.

Early Christian writings state that Mary Magdalene, one of Jesus' followers, was the first to see him alive again. The message of Jesus' **resurrection** (REH•zuh•REHK•shuhn), or rising from the dead, led to the birth of Christianity. During this very early period, Christians were still one of the many groups that made up Judaism.

R

PROGRESS CHECK

Explaining How did Jesus reinforce traditional Jewish teachings?

Who Were the Apostles?

GUIDING QUESTION ***How did early Christianity spread throughout the Roman Empire?***

The early Christian leaders who spread the message of Jesus were called **apostles** (uh•PAH•suhlz). The apostles first spoke to the Jews in Judaea and Galilee. The apostles then traveled to other parts of the Mediterranean region. Small groups of Jews and non-Jews in the Greek-speaking cities of the eastern Mediterranean believed the message about Jesus.

Those who accepted Jesus and his teachings became known as "Christians" and referred to Jesus as "Jesus Christ." The word *Christ* comes from *Christos*, which is a Greek term that means "the anointed one."

The first Christians formed churches, or local groups for worship and teaching. Early Christians met in homes of men and women. At these gatherings, Christians prayed and studied the Hebrew Bible and early Christian writings. They also ate a meal similar to the Last Supper to remember the death and resurrection of Jesus.

BIOGRAPHY

V

Mary Magdalene

A practical, down-to-earth woman, Mary Magdalene went with Jesus during his travels throughout Galilee. Biblical accounts of the life of Jesus maintain that she was present during his crucifixion and burial. These accounts also say she and two other women went to his tomb a few days after he was placed there. Finding it empty, Mary hurried to tell the other followers. She then returned to the tomb with Peter, also a follower of Jesus.

▶ **CRITICAL THINKING**

Analyzing What risks did Mary Magdalene face by being loyal to Jesus?

resurrection the act of rising from the dead
apostle Christian leader chosen by Jesus to spread his message

R Reading Skills

Describing Ask students to describe the betrayal of Jesus and his resulting death and resurrection using details from the text. **Ask:**

- **When was Jesus betrayed?** *(after finishing a supper with his disciples to celebrate the Passover)*
- **What was he likely charged with?** *(treason or disloyalty to the government)*
- **According to the Christian Bible, what was unusual about Jesus' death?** *(He was resurrected three days after his death.)*
- **What did the apostles do?** *(spread the message of Jesus after his death)* AL ELL

V Visual Skills

Analyzing Visuals Ask students to examine the image of Mary Magdalene. Point out the orange-red circle around her head. **Ask:**

- **What do you think this circle represents?** *(Answers will vary. Possible responses: a halo; a crown)*
- **What might it signify about Mary Magdalene?** *(that she is holy or sacred)* **Visual/Spatial**

LECTURE SLIDE

Who Were the Apostles?

Identifying Show students the lecture slide defining the early apostles of Christianity. **Ask:** **How did the apostles spread the message of Jesus?** *(They spoke to Jews in Judaea and Galilee before traveling to other parts of the Mediterranean region, carrying the message.)*

See page 369C for other online activities.

networks — Who Were the Apostles?

apostles early Christian leaders who spread the message of Jesus
- The apostles played an important role in the growth of Christianity.
- They traveled around the Mediterranean region teaching and speaking to people about Jesus.
- Peter and Paul were two important apostles in the early Christian church.

ANSWERS, p. 377

PROGRESS CHECK His message reinforced Jewish commandments to "Love the Lord your God with all your heart and with all your soul and with all your strength and with all your mind" and to "Love your neighbor as yourself."

CRITICAL THINKING Mary faced possible persecution and arrest.

V Visual Skills

Analyzing Images Have students examine the painting and describe what they see. Ask students to find Jesus in the picture. **Ask:** **What do Jesus' gestures and body language suggest about what is going on in the painting?** *(He seems to be gesturing toward the bread and inviting those at the table to share it with him.)*

Explain that one interpretation of the painting is that Jesus has just told the disciples that one of them will soon betray him. **What might the other figures be discussing?** *(Possible response: They may be denying that they will betray Jesus or blaming one another for the future betrayal.)* BL **Visual/Spatial**

W Writing Skills

Informative/Explanatory Ask students to work in small groups and do research to learn more about the apostles. Have them answer these questions:

- **Who were the apostles?**
- **What did the apostles do?**
- **Who was Peter? What did he do?**
- **Who was Paul? What did he do?**

Ask students to prepare a multimedia presentation to share what they have learned. **Verbal/Linguistic**

ANSWER, p. 378

CRITICAL THINKING Answers may vary. Possible answers: Jesus and his followers are sharing the Passover meal somewhere in Jerusalem.

At the end of the 1400s, the Italian artist Leonardo da Vinci created this famous painting of Jesus. Called *The Last Supper*, it was painted on a wall in Milan, Italy.

▶ CRITICAL THINKING
Analyzing What do you think is happening in this illustration of Jesus and his followers?

Leonardo da Vinci/The Bridgeman Art Library/Getty Images

Early Christian Leaders

Apostles played an important part in the growth of Christianity. Peter and Paul were two important apostles in the early Christian church. Peter was a Jewish fisher from Galilee. He had known Jesus while he was alive and had been one of the 12 disciples Jesus had chosen to preach his message. According to Christian tradition, Peter helped set up a Christian church in Rome after the death of Jesus. Today, the center of the Catholic branch of Christianity is still located there.

Paul of Tarsus was another important Christian apostle. He was a well-educated Jew and a Roman citizen. He was raised as a loyal Roman who, as an adult, distrusted the Christians. Saul—his Hebrew name—at first tried to stop Christian ideas from spreading in Judaea and Galilee. The chief Jewish priest in Jerusalem then sent him to Damascus, a city in neighboring Syria. There, he was supposed to stop Christians in the city from spreading their ideas.

According to Christian belief, while he was traveling to Damascus in Syria, Paul saw a great light and heard the voice of Jesus. As a result of this encounter, Paul soon became a Christian and devoted his life to spreading the message of Jesus.

Reading HELPDESK CCSS

salvation the act of being saved from the effects of sin

networks Online Teaching Options

IMAGE

Leonardo da Vinci

Interpreting Have students analyze the painting. Before clicking on "more information," **ask:** **Which figure in the painting is Jesus?** *(the one in the center)* **Why do you think he is in the center of the painting?** *(He is the focus of the painting; he is the most important figure in the painting.)* Now have students click on "more information" and read the accompanying text. BL

See page 369C for other online activities.

McGraw-Hill networks
Leonardo da Vinci
Leonardo da Vinci was a true Renaissance man: artist, writer, and scientist. His creativity even led him to write several papers about painting—backwards! Although he may be most famous for his paintings, such as The Last Supper and the Mona Lisa, da Vinci also studied nature and the human body. He left behind a host of writings and sketches. Study the painting above. Jesus is in the center. Look at how the perspective draws the eye toward the center of the work.

Paul traveled throughout the eastern Mediterranean region and founded numerous Christian churches. Many of his important letters to churches in Rome, Greece, and Asia Minor are found in the Christian Bible.

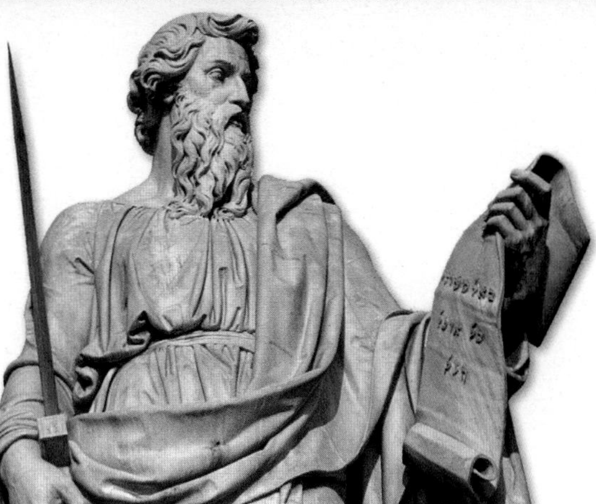

Before becoming an apostle, Paul of Tarsus tried to stop the spread of Christian ideas. After he came to believe in Jesus, Paul became one of the most influential leaders of the early Christian movement.

▶ CRITICAL THINKING

Speculating Why do you think Paul at first tried to stop the spread of the message of Jesus?

What Are Basic Christian Beliefs?

C

The early Christians believed in one God, not the many gods of Rome. They believed that Jesus was the Son of God. They believed he had come to save people. By becoming Christians and by accepting Jesus and his teachings, people could gain **salvation** (sal•VAY•shuhn). They would be saved from their sins, or wrongdoings, and allowed to enter heaven. Like Jesus, people would be resurrected after death and join God in everlasting life.

Because of their faith in Jesus, Christians began to believe in God in a new way. Like the Jews, Christians believed in the God of Israel and studied the Hebrew Bible. However, they also believed in the Christian Trinity, which comes from a word meaning "three." In Christian belief, the Trinity refers to the three persons of God: the Father, Son, and Holy Spirit. These teachings became the basis of the Christian faith.

During the 100 years after Jesus' death, Christianity won followers throughout the world. The peace and order established by the Roman Empire gave people the ability to spread the Christian religion.

✓ PROGRESS CHECK

Identifying Why were the apostles important to early Christianity?

LESSON 1 REVIEW (CCSS)

Review Vocabulary (Tier 3 Words)

1. Why did Jesus preach using *parables*? RH.6–8.2, RH.6–8.4
2. How did the *apostles* spread the message of Jesus? RH.6–8.2, RH.6–8.4

Answer the Guiding Questions

3. ***Explaining*** How did Jewish traditions survive after A.D. 132? RH.6–8.2
4. ***Describing*** When Jesus said "love your neighbor as yourself," what was his message? RH.6–8.2
5. ***Contrasting*** How did some Jews differ in their beliefs about Jesus? RH.6–8.2
6. ***Explaining*** Why did Jesus have disciples? RH.6–8.2
7. **INFORMATIVE/EXPLANATORY** In a paragraph, explain why there were growing tensions between the Romans and the early Christians. WHST.6–8.2, WHST.6–8.10

C Critical Thinking Skills

Comparing and Contrasting Discuss the basic Christian beliefs with students, and help them understand how these beliefs were similar to and different from the beliefs of the Romans and the Jews. **Ask:**

- What did Christians believe? *(They believed in Jesus as the Son of God and felt that by believing in him, they would be saved and join God in everlasting life.)*
- How was the Christian religion different from that of the Roman religion? *(Christians believed in one God; Romans believed in many gods.)*
- How was the Christian religion similar to and different from that of the Jews? *(Both Christians and Jews believed in the one God of Israel, and both studied the Hebrew Bible. Unlike Jews, Christians believed in the Trinity: they believed that the one God was made up of three persons: the Father, Son, and Holy Spirit.)* AL

Have students complete the Lesson 1 Review.

CLOSE & REFLECT

Finding the Main Idea Allow students a few minutes to glance back through the lesson. Ask each of them to identify one main idea. Then call on volunteers to explain their main idea and to tell why they think it is important.

LESSON 1 REVIEW ANSWERS

1. Jesus used parables because they made it easier for people to understand his teachings.
2. Apostles spread the message of Jesus by traveling across the Mediterranean region setting up churches and telling people about Jesus.
3. Over a period of several centuries, Jews established communities outside of Jerusalem as far east as Central Asia and as far west as Spain. They kept their faith alive by studying and practicing their religious laws and traditions.
4. We should treat others the same way we want others to treat us: with respect, kindness, and even love.
5. Some Jews believed that Jesus was their promised deliverer. Most Jews did not believe this. They expected the deliverer to be a political leader who would liberate them from Roman rule.
6. Jesus needed disciples to spread his message after he was gone.
7. One reason for the growing tensions between the Romans and the early Christians was the fact that Christians refused to worship statues of the Roman gods. They also had grown tired of Roman rule and resented having to pay high taxes. Roman authorities, on the other hand, were wary of Jesus and his growing influence, which they feared might threaten law and order.

ANSWERS, p. 379

CRITICAL THINKING Answers may vary. A possible response is that Paul thought followers of Jesus were not being faithful Jews.

✓ **PROGRESS CHECK** They were able to spread his message and the story of his resurrection throughout the Mediterranean region.

ENGAGE

Bellringer Invite students to tell about any long car or bus trips they've taken. **Ask:** What were the roads like? Where did you stay? Did any problems arise along the way? Inform students that the Romans built thousands of miles of roads that connected cities as well as bordered regions of the empire. These roads provided comfort and security, and they enabled people to travel long distances. Because of this network of roads, Christianity was able to spread fairly easily throughout the empire.

TEACH & ASSESS

R Reading Skills

Explaining After students read the text, ask them to explain the conditions in the Roman world that helped Christianity spread. **Ask:**

- What conditions helped support the spread of Christianity? *(peace in most parts of the empire, good roads, common languages)*
- How did these conditions making sharing Christianity easier? *(Peace in the empire helped apostles and others who wanted to share Christianity travel safely from place to place. Good roads made travel easy. Common languages helped people communicate.)* AL

C Critical Thinking Skills

Contrasting Discuss the differences between the official religion promoted by the Roman state and Christianity. **Ask:** Why did Christianity appeal to people? *(It offered people comfort and hope for a better life after death.)*

ANSWERS, p. 380

TAKING NOTES: Because the Romans maintained peace and order over all the lands they ruled, Christians could easily travel safely from one region to another. Christianity had enormous appeal because it provided comfort to people and gave them hope for a better life after death, plus Christians helped those in need. Most people in the Roman Empire spoke Latin or Greek, so Christians could easily communicate the message of Jesus.

networks *There's More Online!*
- CHART/GRAPH Early Church Hierarchy
- GRAPHIC ORGANIZER Reasons Christianity Spread
- MAP Spread of Christianity A.D. 325
- SLIDE SHOW Buial Places
- VIDEO

Lesson 2
The Early Church

ESSENTIAL QUESTION *How do religions develop?*

IT MATTERS BECAUSE
The Roman Empire's system of roads, shared languages, and stability made it easier for Christianity to spread.

Christianity and the Empire

GUIDING QUESTION *How did Christianity change over time?*

As the apostles spread the message of Jesus, many people in the Mediterranean world became Christians. The Roman Empire contributed to this growth.

Christianity Spreads

R Several factors helped Christianity spread throughout the empire. Areas controlled by the Romans were generally peaceful. Well-constructed roads meant Christians could easily travel from one **region** to another. Most people in the empire spoke Latin or Greek. This allowed Christians to communicate with them about the message of Jesus.

C Another reason Christianity spread throughout the empire was that it had an attractive message. The official religion of Rome required people to honor the emperor and the state. This religion did not offer help to people when they experienced personal or economic problems. Christianity, however, provided comfort to people during difficult times. Christianity gave people hope that even if life was bad on Earth, there was the promise of a better afterlife.

Reading HELPDESK CCSS

Taking Notes: *Listing*
Use a graphic organizer like this one to list the major reasons that Christianity spread. RH.6–8.2, WHST.6–8.9

Reasons Christianity Spread
•
•
•
•

Content Vocabulary (Tier 3 Words)
- martyr
- hierarchy
- clergy
- doctrine
- gospel
- pope
- laity

networks *Online Teaching Options*

VIDEO

St. Peter's Tomb

Analyzing Images The development of Christianity in the first century is examined through the lens of the discovery of St. Peter's tomb. Have students view the video and discuss the details that the video adds to their understanding of the spread of Christianity.

See page 369D for other online activities.

Christianity also spread quickly throughout the empire because it provided its followers with security. Christians lived in **communities** where each member was responsible for taking care of the needs of others.

Why Did Romans Mistreat Christians?

R

As the number of Christians grew, some Romans believed that they were dangerous. They thought Christians were a threat to the empire. Romans expected everyone to worship the emperor as a god. The Christians, like the Jews, however, believed that only God could be worshipped. Christians criticized popular Roman festivals that honored the numerous Roman gods. Also, Christians did not support warfare as a way to resolve problems. As a result, they refused to serve in the Roman army. Furthermore, Christians buried their dead outside Rome in catacombs, or underground burial places. Christians could also meet there to hold memorial services.

GEOGRAPHY CONNECTION

Even though the Romans persecuted the Christians, the Christian religion continued to grow and spread its influence.

1. **LOCATION** What areas did Paul visit during his second journey?
2. **CRITICAL THINKING** ***Speculating*** What might have prevented Christianity from spreading to more places during its first three centuries?

V

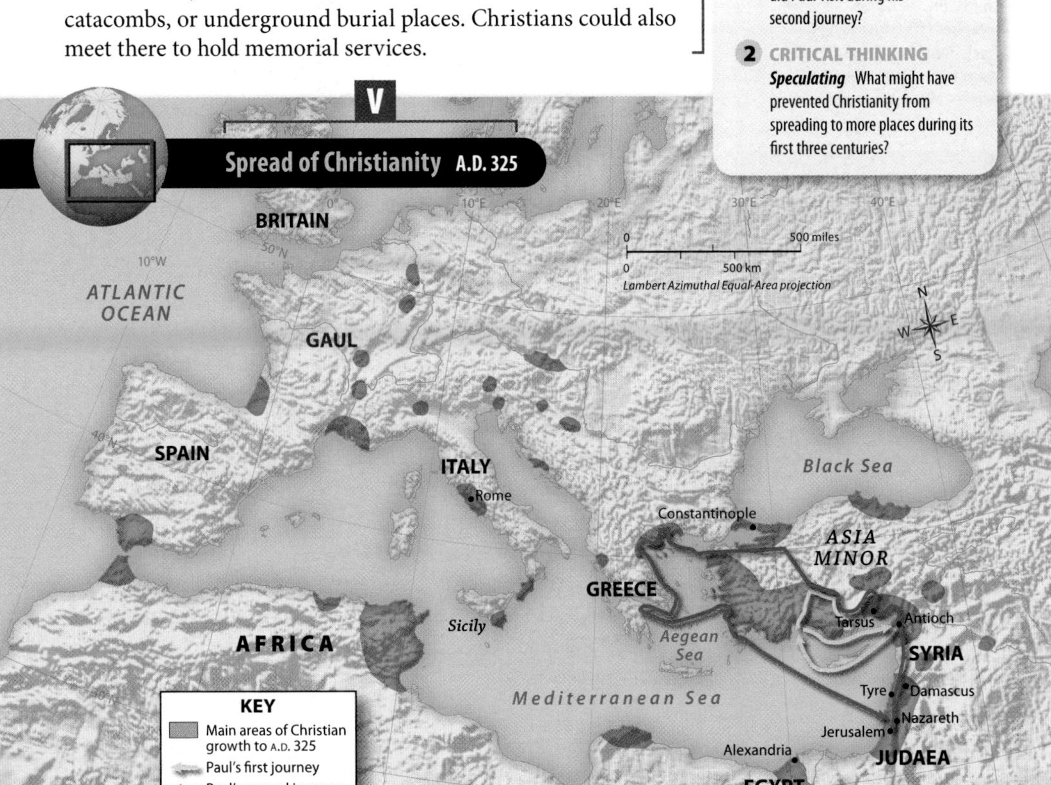

Academic Vocabulary (Tier 2 Words)

region a broad geographic area
community people living in a particular area; the area itself

R Reading Skills

Summarizing Direct students to summarize the passage that details the Roman opposition to Christianity. **Ask:** Why did the Romans distrust Christians? *(Christians would not worship the Roman emperor, and they insisted there was only one God. They ridiculed Roman festivals celebrating the Roman gods. They opposed war and refused to serve in the Roman army.)* AL

V Visual Skills

Analyzing Maps Direct students' attention to the map. **Ask:**

- What does this map show? *(The map shows the main areas of Christianity's growth to A.D. 325.)*
- How far west had Christianity spread by A.D. 325? *(Christianity had spread as far west as the southern coast of Spain and the northern coast of Africa.)*
- How could Paul carry Jesus' message over such a great distance during his second journey? *(The Roman system of roads meant he could easily travel from place to place.)* **Visual/Spatial**

MAP

Spread of Christianity A.D. 325

Analyzing Maps Ask students to explore the map. By clicking on items in the map key, they will highlight information on the map. **Ask:** What did many of the areas where Christianity had spread have in common? *(They are on the sea.)* How did the sea make it easier to spread the ideas of Christianity? *(Traveling to some places by sea was easier and quicker than by road. Traveling by sea helped the ideas of Christianity reach more people.)*

See page 369D for other online activities.

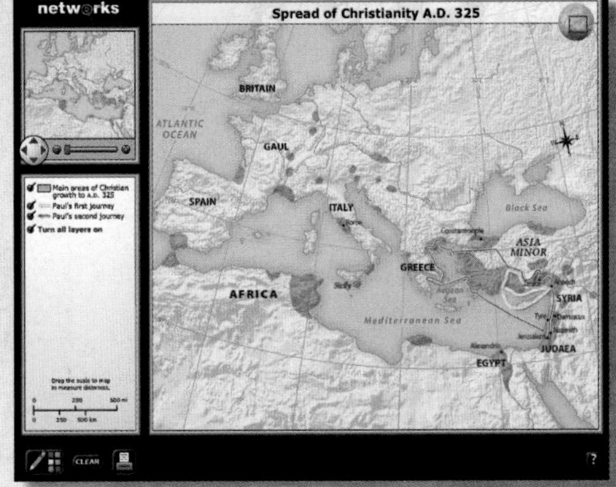

ANSWERS, p. 381

GEOGRAPHY CONNECTION

1. During his second journey, Paul traveled through Judaea, Syria, Asia Minor, and Greece.
2. **CRITICAL THINKING** Continued persecution of Christians, language barriers, and conflict with other religions are some of the factors that might have prevented Christianity from spreading to more places.

The Early Church

R Reading Skills

Defining Work with students to use details from the text to understand the concept of martyrs. **Ask:** What is a martyr? *(someone who dies for his or her beliefs)* Ask students to provide other examples of martyrs.

V Visual Skills

Interpreting Direct students to the picture of the Roman Catacombs. **Ask:** Based on the photo, how would you define the term "catacomb"? *(A catacomb is a series of underground burial vaults.)* Then **ask:** How are cemeteries different today? *(Today's cemeteries are no longer underground. They are out in the open and more easily accessible.)* **Visual/Spatial**

W Writing Skills

Narrative Review the series of events that led Constantine to become a supporter of Christianity. Then have students consider what it must have been like to be a soldier in Constantine's army. Have students write a letter from one of the soldiers to his family, detailing the events and his reaction to them. **Intrapersonal**

C Critical Thinking Skills

Drawing Conclusions Remind students that, for many years, Christians in Rome had been punished and treated as outcasts because of what they believed. **Ask:** Why was Constantine's support of Christianity important? *(Constantine ended the persecution of Christians and allowed them to serve in government. He built churches and provided aid. These measures allowed Christianity to grow stronger and become more accepted by the Roman people.)* BL

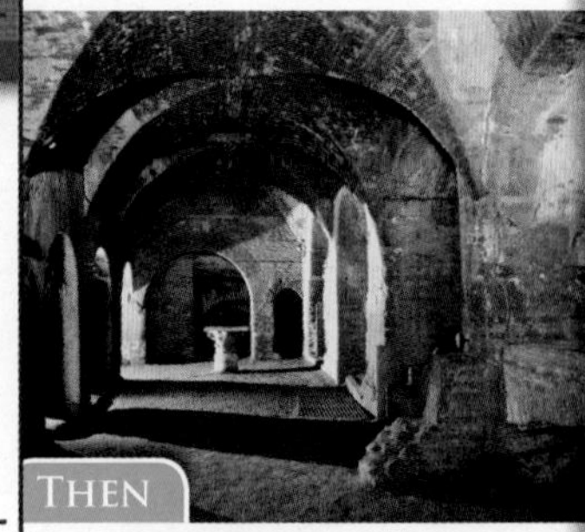

THEN

During the early centuries of Christianity, the Roman Catacombs were used for burials and funeral meals. Today, cemeteries are still places where we go to honor our families, experience shared history, and reflect on the sacrifices of others.

NOW

▶ CRITICAL THINKING

Analyzing Why do you think early Christians buried their dead in hidden catacombs?

People who thought the Christians were dangerous believed that they should be punished. Some Romans blamed Christians for causing natural disasters. In A.D. 64, the emperor Nero falsely accused Christians of starting a fire that burned most of Rome. As a result, Christianity was outlawed.

Christians were often mistreated. They were arrested and beaten. Some Christians became **martyrs** (MAHR•tuhrz), or people who were willing to die rather than give up their beliefs. Despite the mistreatment, Christianity continued to flourish.

The Empire Accepts Christianity

In the early A.D. 300s, the emperor Diocletian carried out the last great persecution of Christians. But his attempt failed. Christianity had grown too strong to be destroyed by force.

In A.D. 312, the Roman emperor Constantine (KAHN•stuhn•TEEN) prepared to lead his **military** forces into battle. According to some early Christian writers, Constantine had a remarkable dream the night before the battle. In the dream he saw a flaming cross in the sky. Written beneath the cross were the Latin words that meant "In this sign you will conquer."

The next day, Constantine ordered his soldiers to paint the Christian cross on their battle shields. Constantine won the battle and believed the Christian God had helped him.

Constantine became a strong supporter of Christianity. In A.D. 313, he issued the Edict of Milan. This decree allowed all religious groups in the empire, including Christians, to practice their religions freely. Constantine attended religious meetings of Christian leaders and gave government aid to Christians. With the help of his mother, Helena (HEH•luh•nuh), he built Christian churches in Rome and Jerusalem. Christians were allowed to serve in government and were excused from paying taxes. They started to serve in the army.

One of Constantine's successors, the emperor Theodosius (THEE•uh•DOH•shuhs), banned Greek and Roman religions. In A.D. 392, he made Christianity the official religion of the Roman Empire.

✓ PROGRESS CHECK

Evaluating How did Constantine support Christianity?

Reading HELPDESK CCSS

martyr a person who is willing to die for his or her beliefs

Academic Vocabulary (Tier 2 Words)

military relating to armed forces

(t) DEA/G CARGAGNA/De Agostini Editore/Age fotostock, (b) Eyewire (Photodisc)/PunchStock

networks Online Teaching Options

SLIDE SHOW

Burial Places

Comparing and Contrasting Have students click on the arrow to reveal additional images and more information about burial places. Ask students to discuss how these various burial places are alike and different and what insights they provide about the various cultures.

See page 369D for other online activities.

networks
Burial Places
Today people in the United States are often buried in mausoleums (above-ground buildings for burial) and cemeteries. In New Orleans, many tombs sit above ground so that rains and underground water will not destroy them.
Craig S. Thrasher/Age fotostock
James Lemass/SuperStock
Eyewire (Photodisc)/PunchStock

ANSWERS, p. 382

CRITICAL THINKING By hiding their burial places, early Christians could make sure their graves would not be disturbed.

✓ **PROGRESS CHECK** Constantine issued the Edict of Milan, which gave religious freedom to all religious groups in the empire, including Christians. He also gave financial aid to Christians and established Christian churches in Rome and Jerusalem.

Constantine led his troops to victory at the Battle of Milvian Bridge near Rome. This triumph led Constantine to convert to Christianity.

▶ CRITICAL THINKING

Analyzing Do you think the Romans could have destroyed Christianity if Constantine hadn't been converted? Explain.

Richard Bonson/Wildlife Art, LTD

Organizing the Church

GUIDING QUESTION *How did early Christians organize their church and explain their beliefs?*

As the number of Christians grew, the church had to become more organized to unite its followers. After the time of the apostles, separate Christian communities began to practice Christianity differently. In order to ensure one form of Christianity, early Christian leaders decided to clarify their beliefsby writing them down.

Church Leadership

Early Christians were familiar with how the Roman Empire was ruled. They used the empire as their model for organizing the church. Like the empire, the church came to be ruled by a **hierarchy** (HY•uh•RAHR•kee). A hierarchy is an organization with different levels of authority.

C

The **clergy** (KLUHR•jee), or church officials, were the leaders of the church. In the early church, only men were allowed to be members of the clergy. The role of the clergy was different from that of the **laity** (LAY•uh•tee), or regular church members. Although women were not allowed to serve in the clergy, they were members of the church. Women cared for sick and needy church members.

hierarchy an organization with different levels of authority
clergy church officials
laity regular church members

CHAPTER 13, Lesson 2

The Early Church

C Critical Thinking Skills

Making Connections Discuss why the Christians began to get organized. **Ask: Why did the church need a hierarchy of officials?** *(Possible answer: The church had grown large and needed to be managed so all churches practiced the same beliefs and ceremonies.)*

Have students offer examples of groups or organizations today that use the same sort of system of hierarchy—for example, students may mention a sports or scouting organization. Ask them to draw and label a diagram (similar to the one in the textbook) that shows the hierarchy. Then invite students to share their examples with the class and explain why the system in place is important to the overall function of the organization. BL **Verbal/Linguistic**

LECTURE SLIDE

Christianity and the Empire

Explaining Project the slide and guide students in discussing Constantine's contributions to the spread of Christianity. After the discussion, ask students to do research to learn more about Constantine. Have them share their findings in a class discussion.

See page 369D for other online activities.

networks — Christianity and the Empire

Constantine's Contributions to the Spread of Christianity:

- Roman general Constantine converted to Christianity after winning an important military victory.
- When he became emperor, Constantine issued the Edict of Milan which gave all religious groups the freedom to practice their religions.
- Constantine provided financial support to Christians, built churches, and permitted Christians to serve in government positions.

ANSWER, p. 383

CRITICAL THINKING Answers may vary. A possible response is that the Christian movement had grown too strong and could not be stopped, even by the Romans.

The Early Church

V Visual Skills

Reading a Chart Review the chart by asking students to explain the roles of each person in the hierarchy. **Ask:**

- **Who did the bishop oversee?** *(priests)*
- **Who did the archbishops go to for guidance?** *(patriarchs)*
- **What role did the laity have in the hierarchy?** *(The laity were regular church members who supported the priests and helped manage and work for individual churches.)* **Visual/Spatial**

R1 Reading Skills

Defining Discuss terms that students will need to understand as they study this section. **Ask:**

- **What is a diocese?** *(several churches and their members)*
- **Who were the patriarchs?** *(archbishops who were in charge of the churches in important cities: Rome, Constantinople, Antioch, Jerusalem)*
- **What is church doctrine?** *(accepted teachings of the church)* AL ELL

R2 Reading Skills

Discussing Direct students to read the section about the early writings of Christianity. Discuss the impact these writings had on the Christian religion. **Ask: How did these writings help Christianity become a unified religion?** *(Answers may vary but should note that these writings became popular and influential, allowing many Christians to begin sharing the same beliefs about what it meant to be a Christian.)*

ANSWERS, p. 384

INFOGRAPHIC

1. Answers may vary but should point out that priests were responsible for just one church, while the patriarchs had power over all churches and made all the rules.
2. **CRITICAL THINKING** Answers may vary but should include something about the need to unify its followers.

EARLY CHURCH HIERARCHY — INFOGRAPHIC

Patriarchs
↓
Archbishops
↓
Bishops
↓
Priests
↓
Laity

1. **COMPARING/CONTRASTING** What are some differences between the status of the patriarchs and priests?
2. **CRITICAL THINKING** ***Analyzing*** Why did the early church have to become more organized as it grew and developed?

By A.D. 300, individual churches were headed by clergy called priests. Priests led worship services and managed local church activities. Clergy called bishops supervised the dioceses (DY•uh•suh•suhz), or several churches grouped together. Bishops explained Christian beliefs to other clergy and laity and managed regional church affairs. A bishop who was in charge of an entire region was known as an archbishop. The five leading archbishops—in charge of the cities of Rome, Constantinople, Alexandria, Antioch, and Jerusalem—were known as patriarchs (PAY•tree•AHRKS).

The bishops met together in councils to define the teachings of the Church. They wanted to make sure that Christians practiced the same beliefs. The decisions they reached at these councils were accepted as **doctrine** (DAHK•truhn), or official church teaching. The ideas that the bishops rejected were heresies (HER•uh•seez), or teachings that did not support the Christian faith.

What Writings Shaped Christianity?

Church leaders also preserved stories about Jesus and the writings of the apostles. Jesus did not write down what he said or did. His followers, however, wrote down and passed on what they remembered about him. By A.D. 300, four accounts of the life and teachings of Jesus were widely known. Christians believed that four apostles of Jesus—Matthew, Mark, Luke, and John—wrote these accounts.

Reading HELPDESK (CCSS)

doctrine official church teaching
gospel the accounts that apostles wrote of Jesus' life
pope the title given to the Bishop of Rome

networks *Online Teaching Options*

CHART

Early Church Hierarchy

Analyzing Charts Students can click on each religious title to reveal text describing its position and role in the hierarchy. **Ask: What was the difference between the roles of bishops and priests?** *(Bishops had authority over more than one church and were responsible for determining Church doctrine. Priests were responsible for a single church and led daily worship.)*

See page 369D for other online activities.

Each account of Jesus' life was called a **gospel** (GAHS• puhl), which means "good news." Christians later included the four gospels with the writings of Paul and other early Christian leaders. Together, these works became known as the New Testament. The New Testament was added to the Greek version of the Jewish sacred writings, which Christians called the Old Testament. Together, these works formed the Christian Bible.

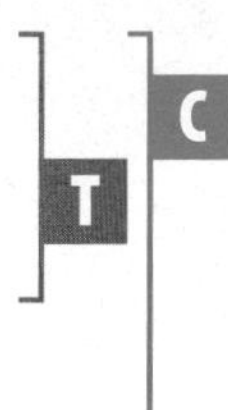

Other writings influenced the early church. Christian thinkers who explained church teachings became known as the Church Fathers. One of the most important Church Fathers was Augustine, a bishop in North Africa. In his writings, Augustine defended Christianity against its critics. Augustine wrote *The City of God*. This was one of the first history books written from the viewpoint of a Christian.

The Bishop of Rome

As the church grew, the bishop of Rome claimed power over the other bishops. He believed that he had received the authority of the apostle Peter. Also, his diocese was in Rome, the capital of the Roman Empire. By A.D. 600, people began to call the bishop of Rome by a special title—**pope** (POHP). The title is from a Latin word, *papa*, related to the word *pater*, meaning "father." Latin-speaking Christians in the western part of the empire accepted the pope as head of all the churches. The Latin churches as a group became known as the Roman Catholic Church. Greek-speaking Christians, however, would not accept the authority of the pope over them. Also claiming a link to the apostles, their churches became known as the Eastern Orthodox Church.

Augustine was one of the most important writers and thinkers in the history of Christianity. Even today, his books continue to inform and inspire.

▶ CRITICAL THINKING
Making Inferences Why do you think Augustine is remembered as one of the Church Fathers?

PROGRESS CHECK

Identifying What writings are included in the New Testament?

LESSON 2 REVIEW 

Review Vocabulary (Tier 3 Words)

1. How did church *doctrine* help to unify early Christians? RH.6–8.2, RH.6–8.4
2. How is the *pope* similar to and different from other bishops? RH.6–8.2, RH.6–8.4

Answer the Guiding Questions

3. ***Identifying*** What were two main reasons Christianity spread during Roman times? RH.6–8.2
4. ***Describing*** Why were early Christians considered traitors to the Roman Empire? RH.6–8.2
5. ***Comparing*** Compare the responsibilities of a priest and a bishop in the early Christian church. RH.6–8.2
6. ***Making Inferences*** Why did bishops meet in councils? RH.6–8.2
7. **NARRATIVE** Write a journal entry that Constantine might have written after the battle he believed God helped him win. WHST.6–8.10

The Early Church

C Critical Thinking Skills

Drawing Conclusions Invite a volunteer to read the definition for the word *gospel* aloud to the class. **Ask:** **Why do you think the Christians referred to the four accounts of Jesus' life as the gospels?** *(Christians recognized the accounts as the foundation of the church that declared the good news that Jesus promised for all believers.)*

T Technology Skills

Collaborating Organize the class into four small groups and assign each group one of the four gospels—Matthew, Mark, Luke, or John. Have groups use the Internet and other resources to find out as much as they can about the writer of their assigned gospel and then assemble the information into a brief report that uses at least one visual aid. Have students present their reports to the class. **Interpersonal**

Have students complete the Lesson 2 Review.

CLOSE & REFLECT

Identifying Central Issues Note to students that Christianity has many active branches today. Add that in the second and third centuries A.D., Christianity was similarly diverse. **Ask:** **What do you think are some of the issues that divided early Christians as they tried to organize themselves after Jesus' death?** *(Possible response: Early Christians probably debated about which Jewish practices to keep and which to discard. They might also have differed about how to relate to the Romans and Roman political authority, how to explain certain Christian beliefs to critics, how the church should be organized, and who should have final authority in the church.)*

LESSON 2 REVIEW ANSWERS

1. Church doctrine helped ensure that Christians lived by the same beliefs.
2. The pope is the bishop of Rome and is also the leader of the other bishops.
3. Answers may vary. Good roads meant Christians could easily travel from one region to another to spread the word. Most people in the empire spoke Latin or Greek, which made it easier to communicate. Also, Christianity had a more attractive message than the official religion of Rome.
4. Some early Christians refused to serve in the Roman army and were seen as traitors.
5. Priests led worship services and managed local church activities. Bishops oversaw several churches instead of one and managed the affairs of these different churches.
6. Bishops met in councils to define the teachings of the church, deciding which particular beliefs were correct and which were wrong.
7. Answers may vary, but students' journal entries might include Constantine's expression of gratitude for the divine assistance he believed he had received. They might also include any changes Constantine expects to make (or promises to God that he will make) in his character or behavior, now that he has become a Christian. Another possibility is for students to recall some of the highlights of the battle and of the specific ways in which God helped Constantine defeat the enemy.

ANSWERS, p. 385

CRITICAL THINKING His writings helped define Christian beliefs and defended Christianity from its critics.

PROGRESS CHECK The New Testament includes the four gospels and the writings of Paul and other early Christian leaders.

ENGAGE

Bellringer Show students an image of Charlemagne as Holy Roman Emperor, and read the accompanying text. Explain that the crowning of Charlemagne angered the leaders of the Byzantine Church because it favored the church leaders in Western Europe. Tell students that this lesson explores some of the reasons early Christianity split into two main branches—the Roman Catholic Church and the Eastern Orthodox Church.

TEACH & ASSESS

R Reading Skills

Describing Before students read the passage, emphasize that the Roman Catholic and Eastern Orthodox churches were both Christian and shared many common traditions, ceremonies, and beliefs. Then ask students to describe the differences in the two churches. Studnts should note that the churches had different leadership, however, and differed in some of their practices.
Ask: **What role did the emperor of the Byzantine Empire have in the Eastern Orthodox Church?** *(He was considered God's representative on Earth and was crowned in religious ceremonies. He appointed church leaders, defined how people worshiped, controlled the church's wealth, and was guardian of the Eastern Orthodox Church.)*

networks *There's More Online!*
- MAP Spread of Christianity A.D. 325–1100
- SLIDE SHOW Cyril, Creator of the Cyrillic Alphabets
- VIDEO

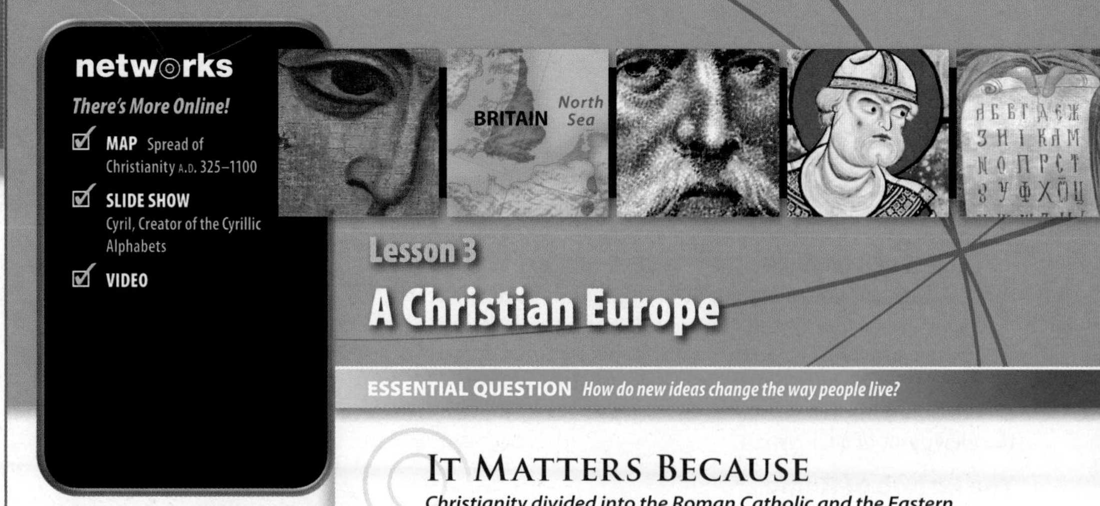

Lesson 3
A Christian Europe

ESSENTIAL QUESTION *How do new ideas change the way people live?*

IT MATTERS BECAUSE
Christianity divided into the Roman Catholic and the Eastern Orthodox branches. Despite this division, all Christians share core beliefs that go back to Jesus of Nazareth.

Two Christian Churches

GUIDING QUESTION *What issues divided the western and eastern Christian churches?*

The Roman Catholic Church was based in Rome, the capital of the Western Roman Empire. The church was led by the verypowerful pope. As the Western Roman Empire declined, the Christian church of Rome survived. At the same time, the Roman Empire in the east, which soon became known as the Byzantine Empire, thrived. The Byzantines developed their own Christian church. Their church reflected their Greek heritage. This church became known as the Eastern Orthodox Church.

R Byzantine Government and Religion

The emperor of the Byzantine Empire and the officials of the Eastern Orthodox Church worked closely together. The Byzantines believed their emperor was God's representative on Earth. Beginning in the A.D. 400s, emperors were crowned in a religious ceremony. They also took an oath to defend Eastern Orthodox Christianity. They believed it was their duty to unite the empire under one Christian faith. Thus, the emperors controlled the Eastern Orthodox Church. Emperors appointed church leaders and defined how people would worship. They also controlled the wealth of the church and helped settle disputes about church beliefs.

Reading HELPDESK (CCSS)

Taking Notes: ***Listing***
Create a chart like this one and use it to list arguments for and against honoring icons. RH.6–8.2, WHST.6–8.9

Honoring Icons	
For	Against

Content Vocabulary (Tier 3 Words)
- icon
- iconoclast
- excommunicate
- schism
- monastery

networks ***Online Teaching Options***

VIDEO

The Development of Christianity in Ireland

Analyzing Images Have students view the video, which tells of the establishment of Christianity in Ireland by St. Patrick. It describes the work of monks in transcribing important Christian manuscripts. Have students take notes as they watch the video.

See page 369E for other online activities.

ANSWERS, p. 386

TAKING NOTES: FOR: These images represent the presence of God in a person's or family's daily life; icons help people understand Christian teachings. AGAINST: Honoring icons is a form of idol worship that is forbidden by God; icons distract Christians from thinking about spiritual matters.

What Are Icons?

Both Byzantine clergy and the Byzantine people discussed and often argued about religious matters. These arguments frequently became political issues and led to fights and riots.

R In the A.D. 700s, a heated dispute about **icons** (EYE•KAWNZ) divided the Eastern Orthodox Church. Icons are paintings of Jesus, Mary (the mother of Jesus), and the saints, or Christian holy people. Many Byzantines **displayed** icons in their homes. They also covered the walls of their churches with them.

People who displayed icons claimed that these images symbolized the presence of God in their lives. They also believed that the images helped people understand Christian teachings. The thinker John of Damascus was the leading defender of icons.

Some Byzantines, however, did not approve of the use of icons. They thought it was a form of idol worship forbidden by God. In A.D. 726, Emperor Leo III ordered that all icons be removed from the churches. Government officials who carried out his orders were called **iconoclasts** (eye•KAH•nuh•KLASTS), or image breakers. Today, this word refers to someone who criticizes traditional beliefs or practices.

Most Byzantines, many church leaders, and even the pope in Rome disapproved of Emperor Leo's actions. The dispute over icons severely damaged the relationship between the Roman Catholic Church and the Eastern Orthodox Church. Over the next century, the argument became less heated, and icons were used once again. They are still important today.

V

This icon painted on wood shows the angel Gabriel. According to the Christian Bible, Gabriel was a messenger sent from God.

▶ CRITICAL THINKING

Explaining Why do you think some Byzantine people were against the use of icons?

The Great Split

Icons were only one of the issues that divided the eastern and western Christian churches. The most serious disagreement was about church authority. The pope claimed to be head of all Christian churches. He believed he was a successor, or person who follows another person, to Peter, disciple of Jesus. Peter was the first bishop of Rome. The Byzantines **rejected** the claim of the pope. They believed the patriarch of Constantinople and other bishops were equal to the pope.

icon a representation of an object of worship

iconoclast *originally:* a person who destroys icons; *today:* a person who criticizes traditional beliefs

Academic Vocabulary (Tier 2 Words)

display to place an object where people can view it

reject to refuse to accept

R Reading Skills

Determining Word Meanings Discuss the meaning of the key terms in the bracketed passage. **Ask:** What are some examples of icons? *(images of Jesus, Mary, the saints)* Discuss how the icons were displayed. What is an iconoclast? *(someone who destroys or criticizes icons or images)* AL ELL

V Visual Skills

Analyzing Images Direct students to the painting in the textbook of the angel Gabriel. **Ask:** How is this image similar to other religious images you have seen, either in person or in this textbook? How is it different? *(Answers will vary. Some students may point out the tilting of the head, the large eyes, and the halo of color around Gabriel's head.)* BL Visual/Spatial

GRAPHIC ORGANIZER

Taking Notes: *Listing:* Honoring Icons

Contrasting Show students the interactive graphic organizer. Have student volunteers make suggestions for each category, and then display the completed graphic organizer to the class. *(Reasons for the use of icons: These images represent the presence of God in one's daily life; icons help people understand Christian teachings. Reasons against the use of icons: Honoring icons is a form of idol worship, which is forbidden by God; icons distract Christians from thinking about spiritual matters.)*

See page 369E for other online activities.

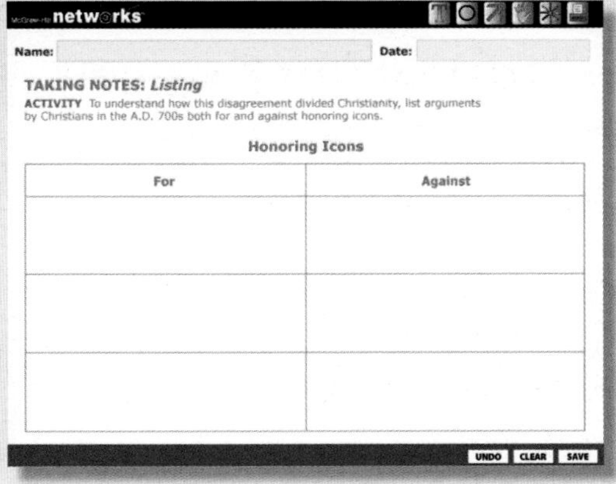

networks
Name:
Date:
TAKING NOTES: Listing
ACTIVITY To understand how this disagreement divided Christianity, list arguments by Christians in the A.D. 700s both for and against honoring icons.
Honoring Icons
For
Against
UNDO
CLEAR
SAVE

ANSWER, p. 387

CRITICAL THINKING Answers may vary. A possible response is that some Byzantines might have thought icons were too much like images of the old Roman gods.

A Christian Europe

V Visual Skills

Analyzing Maps Direct students' attention to the map and invite them to identify and explain the different colors highlighting the map. **Ask:** **Which area was the last to become Christian?** *(the areas shaded in dark green)* **When did Christianity reach northern Africa?** *(by A.D. 400)* **Visual/Spatial**

C Critical Thinking Skills

Determining Cause and Effect Discuss the political events that strained relations between the pope and the patriarch of Constantinople. **Ask:**

- **Why did the pope ask the Frankish king for help against invaders?** *(because the Byzantine emperor refused to help)*
- **Why did the pope crown the Frankish king as emperor?** *(The king had helped save Italy when it was invaded, so the pope rewarded him by crowning him emperor.)*
- **Why did this make the patriarch angry?** *(He believed that the only Roman Emperor was their own ruler in Constantinople.)* AL

Content Background Knowledge

Point out that the pope still has both religious and political power. He is the head of the Roman Catholic Church and also heads the ecclesiastical state of the Vatican. He has absolute political jurisdiction within the city. He also has political influence in many international affairs due to his position as head of the Roman Catholic Church, but not because of a specific political position. In recent years, his political role has diminished.

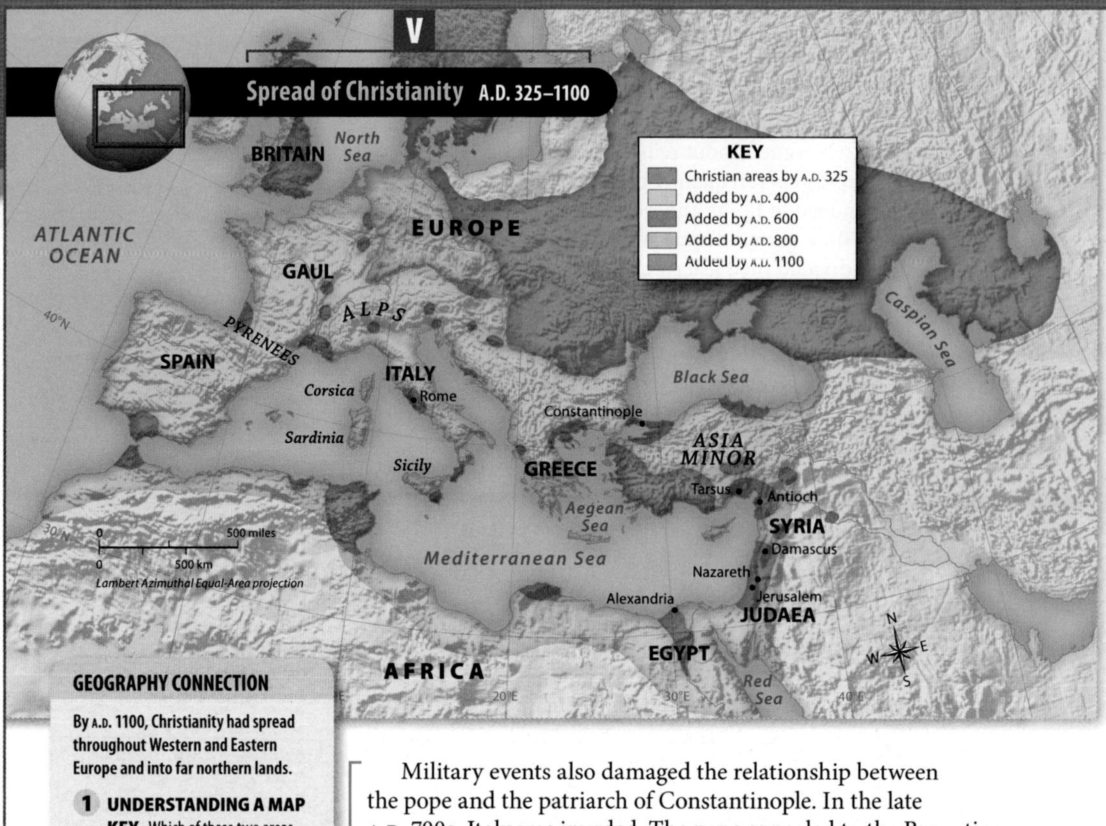

GEOGRAPHY CONNECTION

By A.D. 1100, Christianity had spread throughout Western and Eastern Europe and into far northern lands.

1. **UNDERSTANDING A MAP KEY** Which of these two areas became Christian first: Britain or Syria?
2. **CRITICAL THINKING** *Analyzing* Why do you think some areas took longer to convert to Christianity than others?

Military events also damaged the relationship between the pope and the patriarch of Constantinople. In the late A.D. 700s, Italy was invaded. The pope appealed to the Byzantine emperor for help, but the emperor refused. The pope then asked the Franks to help defend Rome. The Franks were a Germanic people that supported the pope as head of the Christian church.

The Franks successfully defended Italy against the invaders. To show his gratitude, the pope crowned the Frankish king, Charlemagne (SHAHR•luh•MAYN), emperor in A.D. 800. The pope's actions upset the Byzantines. They believed their ruler was the only Roman emperor.

The eastern and western churches also viewed their roles in government differently. In the Byzantine Empire, the emperor controlled both church and government. Byzantine church leaders supported the decisions of the emperor. In the West, the pope claimed he had religious and political authority over all of Europe. He often quarreled with kings about church and government affairs.

Reading HELPDESK CCSS

networks Online Teaching Options

MAP

Spread of Christianity A.D. 325–1100

Analyzing Maps Have students view the map. Ask them to turn on the layers one at a time by clicking on the items in the map key. **Ask:** **When did most of Spain and Gaul become Christian?** *(by A.D. 400)* **When did Christianity reach most of northern Europe?** *(by A.D. 1100)*

See page 369E for other online activities.

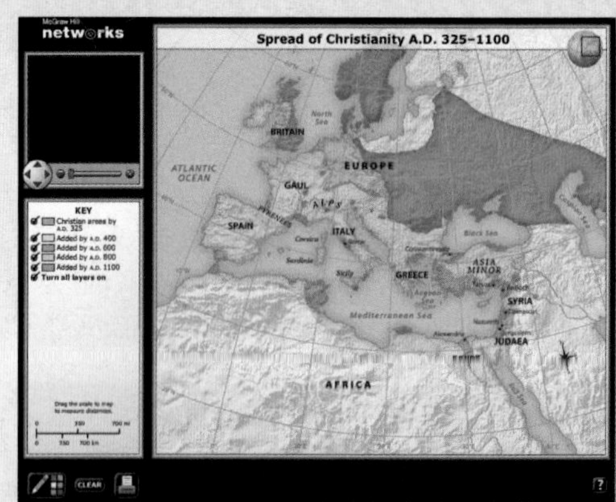

ANSWERS, p. 388

GEOGRAPHY CONNECTION

1. Syria became Christian before Britain did.
2. **CRITICAL THINKING** Answers will vary. Christianity spread quickly around the Mediterranean, which provided transportation. Some far northern lands were separated from the mainland by water, while mountains cut off Eastern Europe.

Finally, in A.D. 1054, after centuries of bitterness, the patriarch of Constantinople and the pope **excommunicated** (EHK•skuh•MYOO•nuh•KAY•tuhd) each other. To excommunicate means to declare that a person or group no longer belongs to the church. This created a **schism** (SIH•zuhm), or separation, between the two major churches of Christianity. The split between the Eastern Orthodox Church and the Roman Catholic Church still exists today.

PROGRESS CHECK

Identifying What issues divided the eastern and western Christian churches?

The Spread of Christianity

GUIDING QUESTION *How did Christianity spread across Europe?*

After the fall of the Western Roman Empire, people in many parts of Europe faced disorder and violence. Many looked to the Christian church for help. They hoped that Christianity would bring peace, order, and unity.

New Christian Communities

C During the A.D. 300s, devout Christians in the Eastern Roman Empire formed religious communities called **monasteries** (MAH•nuh•STEHR•eez). In the monasteries, men called monks lived apart from the world. At the same time, they performed good deeds and modeled how Christians should live.

Christian women established religious communities of their own. These women were called nuns, and they lived in convents. During this time, one of the best known nuns was a Roman widow named Paula. In the early A.D. 400s, Paula helped a scholar named Jerome translate the Christian Bible into Latin.

T The Greek bishop Basil (BAY•zuhl) created a list of rules for monks and nuns. Known as the Basilian (buh•ZIH•lee•uhn) Rule, this list told people how to live and pray in Eastern Orthodox monasteries and convents.

In the West, religious communities followed another set of regulations called the Benedictine Rule. An Italian monk named Benedict (BEH•nuh•DIHKT) wrote these rules about A.D. 529. Benedictines gave up material goods. They devoted their days to work and prayer. One of their major duties was to serve as missionaries. Missionaries teach their religion to those who are not followers.

Charlemagne believed his authority to rule came from God. Inspired by the teachings of St. Augustine, he considered both the spiritual and material needs of his subjects.

▶ CRITICAL THINKING

Explaining Why do you think Charlemagne, a Frankish king, defended Rome?

Popperfoto/Getty Images

excommunicate to declare that a person or group is no longer a member of the church
schism a separation or division from a church
monastery a religious community

C Critical Thinking Skills

Drawing Conclusions Discuss the religious communities that became established beginning in the A.D. 300s. **Ask:**

- **What kind of lives did monks live?** *(They devoted their days to work and prayer. They performed good deeds and modeled how Christians should live.)*
- **Why do you think many monasteries were built in isolated locations?** *(The monks were better able to focus on their religious work and studies without outside distractions.)*

T Technology Skills

Making Presentations Point out that the religious communities that formed in the early years of the church continue to play a role in the church today. Monasteries and convents are found in almost every state. Ask students to work individually to do Internet research on one of the monasteries or convents in their state or region. Have students determine where the community is located, what services it offers in the area, and other activities it engages in. Invite students to share their findings with the class. BL

SLIDE SHOW

Religious Communities

Identifying Show students the slide show on monasteries and monks. Have them identify the various roles played by monks and nuns in Christian Europe. *(Answers should include some or all of the following: Monks and nuns ran hospitals and schools, served the poor, preserved ancient Greek and Roman writings, and served as missionaries.)*

See page 369E for other online activities.

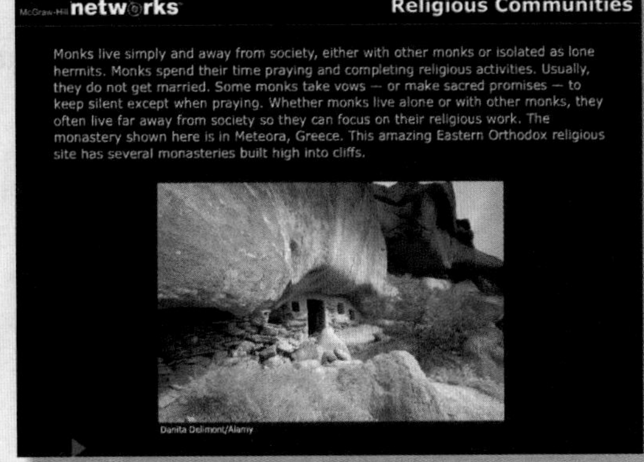

networks
Religious Communities
Monks live simply and away from society, either with other monks or isolated as lone hermits. Monks spend their time praying and completing religious activities. Usually, they do not get married. Some monks take vows — or make sacred promises — to keep silent except when praying. Whether monks live alone or with other monks, they often live far away from society so they can focus on their religious work. The monastery shown here is in Meteora, Greece. This amazing Eastern Orthodox religious site has several monasteries built high into cliffs.
Danita Delimont/Alamy

ANSWERS, p. 389

PROGRESS CHECK Three main issues divided the eastern and western churches. First, whether to worship using icons was an issue. The second issue was the authority of the pope. Western churches believed the pope was the head of all Christian churches; the Byzantines claimed that the patriarch of Constantinople and other bishops were equal to the pope. Finally, a third issue was the relationship of the church to the central government. In the East, the emperor controlled both church and government. In the West, the pope often quarreled with political leaders, including the European kings.

CRITICAL THINKING Answers may vary. A possible response is that Charlemagne wanted the title of emperor in exchange for helping Pope Leo III.

A Christian Europe

V Visual Skills

Analyzing Images Discuss the chart in the textbook and explain that it gives examples of the Cyrillic alphabet and compares it to the English alphabet. Then indicate the iconography at the top of the page. **Ask: How can you tell from the painting that Cyril and Methodius were considered holy figures?** *(Possible responses: They have halos around their heads; they are wearing robes; they are carrying crosses.)* BL **Visual/Spatial**

W Writing Skills

Informative/Explanatory Invite a volunteer to read aloud the quote in the textbook from Chapter 53 of the Benedictine Rule. Discuss with students what they think it means. Then have students rewrite the quote in their own words. AL ELL

ANSWERS, p. 390

INFOGRAPHIC

1. The Cyrillic letters *pey* and *ef* sound like the English *p* and *f*.
2. **CRITICAL THINKING** By inventing a new alphabet, Cyril and his brother Methodius were able to communicate the message of Jesus to Slavic peoples.

V

THE CYRILLIC ALPHABET

Cyrillic Letter	Written Name	English Sound
Б	beh	B
Г	gey	G
Ж	zheh	ZH
М	em	M
П	pey	P
С	ess	S
Ф	ef	F
Ч	cheh	CH

Cyril and Methodius quarreled with German church leaders who opposed the use of Slavic languages for preaching and worship. The Germans wanted only Latin to be used.

INFOGRAPHIC

Cyril, a Byzantine missionary, developed the Cyrillic alphabet, part of which is shown here. The original alphabet, based on Greek, had 43 letters.

1. **IDENTIFYING** Which Cyrillic letters make the same sounds as the letters "p" and "f" in the English alphabet?
2. **CRITICAL THINKING** ***Applying*** Why did Cyril create a new alphabet for people who spoke Slavic languages?

In addition, the Rule stated that monks were to welcome outsiders who were in need of food and shelter:

PRIMARY SOURCE

> "All guests who present themselves are to be welcomed as Christ, for he himself will say: I was a stranger and you welcomed me. . . . Once a guest has been announced, the superior and the brothers are to meet him with all the courtesy of love. . . . All humility [being humble] should be shown in addressing a guest on arrival or departure."
>
> —Benedictine Rule, Chapter 53: The Reception of Guests

W

Monks and nuns had important roles in Christian Europe. They helped the poor and ran hospitals and schools. They also helped preserve ancient Greek and Roman writings.

Christianity and the Slavs

The Byzantines wanted to bring their religion and culture to groups who lived north of their empire. Two brothers, Cyril (SIHR•uhl) and Methodius, were among the most dedicated Byzantine missionaries. Their mission was to deliver the Christian message to the Slavs, a people in Eastern Europe.

Cyril and Methodius believed that the Slavs would be more interested in Christianity if they heard about it in their own languages. About A.D. 863, Cyril invented an alphabet for the Slavic languages. It is known today as the Cyrillic (suh•RIH•lihk)

TEXT: Chapter 53: The Reception of Guests from Study the Holy Rule of St. Benedict. Commentary by Philip Lawrence, OSB, Abbot of Christ in the Desert. Monastery of Christ in the Desert, New Mexico. PHOTO: José F. Poblete/CORBIS

Reading **HELP**DESK CCSS

Build Vocabulary: *Word Origins*

The English word *slave* comes from the word *Slav*. In the early Middle Ages, so many Slavic people were taken into slavery that their name came to be used for anyone who was treated as the property of another and forced to work.

networks Online Teaching Options

WORKSHEET

Economics of History Activity: The Economic Life of Christian Monasteries

Drawing Conclusions Before students complete the worksheet on the economic life of Christian monasteries, **ask: Do you think monasteries were wealthy? Why or why not?** *(Answers will vary.)* **Which resources do you think monasteries used to help them increase their wealth?** *(Answers will vary, but students may point out that they might have used the land surrounding the monasteries; they may have offered religious education.)*

See page 369E for other online activities.

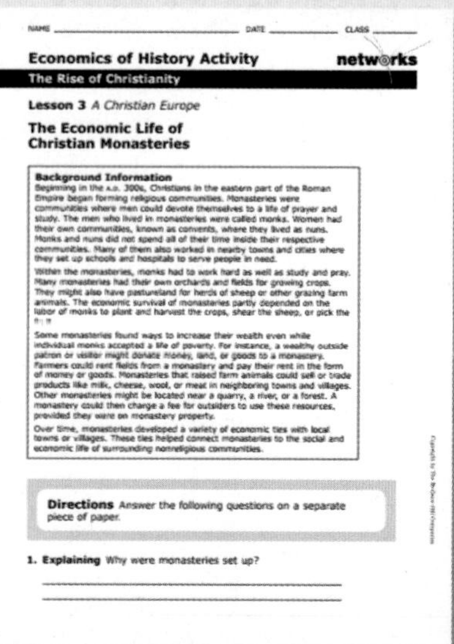

NAME ______ DATE ______ CLASS ______

Economics of History Activity networks

The Rise of Christianity

Lesson 3 *A Christian Europe*

The Economic Life of Christian Monasteries

Background Information

Beginning in the A.D. 300s, Christians in the eastern part of the Roman Empire began forming religious communities. Monasteries were communities where men could devote themselves to a life of prayer and study. The men who lived in monasteries were called monks. Women had their own communities, known as convents, where they lived as nuns. Monks and nuns did not spend all of their time inside their respective communities. Many of them also worked in nearby towns and cities where they set up schools and hospitals to serve people in need.

Within the monasteries, monks had to work hard as well as study and pray. Many monasteries had their own orchards and fields for growing crops. They might also have pastureland for herds of sheep or other grazing farm animals. The economic survival of monasteries partly depended on the labor of monks to plant and harvest the crops, shear the sheep, or pick the [illegible]

Some monasteries found ways to increase their wealth even while individual monks accepted a life of poverty. For instance, a wealthy outside patron or visitor might donate money, land, or goods to a monastery. Farmers could rent fields from a monastery and pay their rent in the form of money or goods. Monasteries that raised farm animals could sell or trade products like milk, cheese, wool, or meat in neighboring towns and villages. Other monasteries might be located near a quarry, a river, or a forest. A monastery could then charge a fee for outsiders to use these resources, provided they were on monastery property.

Over time, monasteries developed a variety of economic ties with local towns or villages. These ties helped connect monasteries to the social and economic life of surrounding nonreligious communities.

Directions Answer the following questions on a separate piece of paper.

1. **Explaining** Why were monasteries set up?

alphabet in honor of its inventor. The Cyrillic alphabet was based on Greek letters. It is still used today by Russians, Ukrainians, Serbs, and Bulgarians.

Christianity in Western Europe

In Western Europe, Christian missionaries sought to convert the peoples of Britain and Ireland to Christianity. Roman soldiers were stationed there also. In the A.D. 300s, Roman soldiers left Britain to defend the empire against Germanic invaders.

Beginning in the A.D. 400s, Germanic tribes from present-day Germany and Denmark invaded much of Britain. Over time, these groups united to become known as the Anglo-Saxons. They built farming villages and founded several small kingdoms. Southern Britain soon became known as Angleland, or England. The people became known as the English.

In Britain, the Anglo-Saxons pushed aside the Celts (KEHLTS), the people already living there. Some Celts fled to remote, mountainous areas of Britain. Others crossed the sea to Ireland. In the A.D. 400s, a priest named Patrick brought Christianity to Ireland. He set up churches and monasteries where monks helped preserve Christian and Roman learning.

In A.D. 597, Pope Gregory I sent about 40 monks from Rome to bring Christianity to the Anglo-Saxons of Britain. They converted King Ethelbert of Kent to Christianity. Ethelbert allowed the missionaries to build a church in his capital city of Canterbury. In about 100 years, most of England had accepted the Christian faith. Monasteries were built throughout England. As in Ireland, they became centers of religion and culture.

R Pope Gregory I is also known as Gregory the Great. A former monk, he was an excellent administrator. As pope, he continued to live as a monk and tried to bring about reforms in the church.

▶ CRITICAL THINKING

Analyzing How might Pope Gregory's background have affected the spread of Christianity?

PROGRESS CHECK

Analyzing Why were monasteries and convents important in Christian Europe?

LESSON 3 REVIEW

Review Vocabulary (Tier 3 Words)

1. Is an *iconoclast* someone who believes in using icons in worship or someone who opposes this practice? RH.6–8.2, RH.6–8.4
2. When the early church underwent a *schism*, does that mean it changed its most important doctrines? RH.6–8.2, RH.6–8.4

Answer the Guiding Questions

3. ***Comparing and Contrasting*** What different views of the role of the church in government did the Eastern and Western churches have? RH.6–8.2
4. ***Explaining*** What were monasteries and what purpose did they serve? RH.6–8.2
5. ***Identifying Cause and Effect*** How did the Cyrillic alphabet help the spread of Christianity? RH.6–8.2, RH.6–8.5
6. ***Making Inferences*** Why do you think the Byzantine emperor refused to help the pope defend Rome from invaders? RH.6–8.2
7. **INFORMATIVE/EXPLANATORY** Write a paragraph to describe what happened to Ireland once Patrick brought Christianity to its lands. WHST.6–8.10

A Christian Europe

R Reading Skills

Specifying Call on students to describe events that eventually brought Christianity to Ireland and Britain. **Ask:** **Who were the Anglo-Saxons?** *(Germanic tribes that invaded Britain and pushed out the Celts)* **Who were the Celts?** *(early residents of Britain and Ireland)* **How did Christianity finally reach Britain?** *(Pope Gregory I sent 40 monks to Britain, where they converted King Ethelbert of Kent to Christianity. He allowed the monks to build a church and spread their religious ideas.)*

Have students complete the Lesson 3 Review.

CLOSE & REFLECT

Synthesizing To allow students to synthesize and analyze what they have learned about the split in the Christian church, brainstorm with them a list of questions that might appear on a test. Examples of such questions include:

- What was the role of Charlemagne in the split?
- Are icons a form of idol worship?
- Did the pope have the authority to crown Charlemagne?

Have students form pairs or small groups. Assign one question from the list to each pair or group. Students will then answer their questions in the form of a short essay, which they can write in class or for homework. Volunteers can read their essays aloud.

ANSWERS, p. 391

CRITICAL THINKING One of the major duties of monks was to serve as missionaries. As a former monk, Pope Gregory would have been interested in spreading Christianity.

✓ PROGRESS CHECK Monasteries and convents were important in Christian Europe because monks and nuns helped the poor and ran hospitals and schools. They also preserved ancient Greek and Roman writings, and they spread their religion by serving as missionaries.

LESSON 3 REVIEW ANSWERS

1. An *iconoclast* is someone who opposes the use of icons in worship.
2. No; a schism is what happens when something divides or splits. The early church divided into western and eastern branches.
3. In Eastern churches, church leaders usually supported the decisions of the emperor and recognized the emperor as having authority over the church and the government. In the West, the pope was not content to live under the authority of emperors or kings and often quarreled with political leaders.
4. Monasteries were religious communities in which men called monks tried to live a purely Christian life, away from the distractions of the world. Monks as well as nuns served as missionaries, helped those in need, and ran schools and hospitals.
5. The Cyrillic alphabet made it possible for Byzantine missionaries to bring their religion and culture to people living in what is now Eastern Europe, including the Slavs.
6. Answers may vary but should point out that the Byzantines believed the head of the Eastern church in Constantinople was equal to the pope in Rome. One possible inference from this is that the emperor wanted the pope to be defeated.
7. After Patrick arrived in Ireland, he converted many of the Irish to Christianity. These Irish Christians went on to set up monasteries and churches. Irish monks copied valuable manuscripts from Christian and Roman sources. Ireland eventually became a center of learning where scholars, monks, and artists from Europe could come to study and work.

CHAPTER REVIEW ACTIVITY

On the board, have a volunteer create a two-column chart and write "Roman Catholic Church" in one column and "Eastern Orthodox Church" in the other. Then lead a discussion that allows students to compare and contrast the two churches according to how they related to political authority and how they viewed the authority of the pope, the religious communities the Church established, and the role of missionaries. The student volunteer should note this information in the chart.

	Roman Catholic Church	Eastern Orthodox Church
Relationship with Political Authority		
Religious Communities		
Missionary Work		

REVIEW THE ENDURING UNDERSTANDING

Review the chapter's Enduring Understanding with students.

- *People, places, and ideas change over time.*

Now pose the following question in a class discussion to apply this to the chapter.

How did Christianity grow into a world-wide religion? *(Christianity grew out of the ancient religion of Judaism. It began with the birth of Jesus, who taught that God was coming to rule the world and that people should turn from their selfish ways and accept the coming of God. Jesus offered hope to all people, no matter how desperate their lives on earth. The message slowly took root as Jesus traveled and spread his teachings. After Jesus' death on the cross, his apostles traveled more widely throughout the Mediterranean world. A peaceful Roman empire and good roads allowed them to carry the Christian message to many regions. At first, they and those who came after them were met with opposition from the Roman government, which felt threatened by Christianity, but in the A.D. 300s, the Roman emperor Constantine accepted Christianity and aided its spread. Gradually, over the centuries, Christianity spread more widely through Europe, northern Africa, and western Asia.)*

CHAPTER 13 Activities (CCSS)

Write your answers on a separate piece of paper.

1 Exploring the Essential Question WHST.6–8.10

NARRATIVE Imagine you are Paul of Tarsus. You want to write your thoughts about how Christianity has developed and spread. You decide to do this in the form of a letter to church leaders. What part did you play in helping Christianity develop? What challenges did you personally face? Which accomplishments are you most proud of?

2 21st Century Skills RH.6–8.7, WHST.6–8.7, WHST.6–8.8, WHST.6–8.9

ANALYZING IMAGES Create a presentation to compare and contrast Byzantine (Eastern Orthodox) churches and religious artifacts with Roman Catholic churches and religious artifacts. Use photos to show how Byzantine icons, for instance, are usually painted on flat surfaces. In Roman Catholic churches, however, religious symbols include more statues and other three-dimensional art works. Make sure you cite the source for your images. Present your findings to the class.

3 Thinking Like a Historian RH.6–8.2

COMPARING AND CONTRASTING Create a diagram like the one shown here. Fill it in to identify the major differences and similarities between the eastern and western Christian churches.

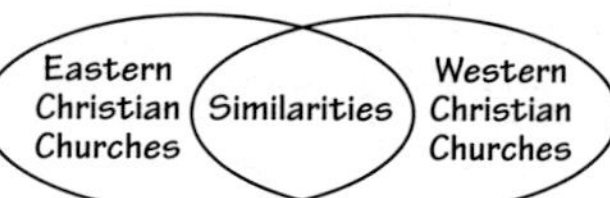

4 GEOGRAPHY ACTIVITY

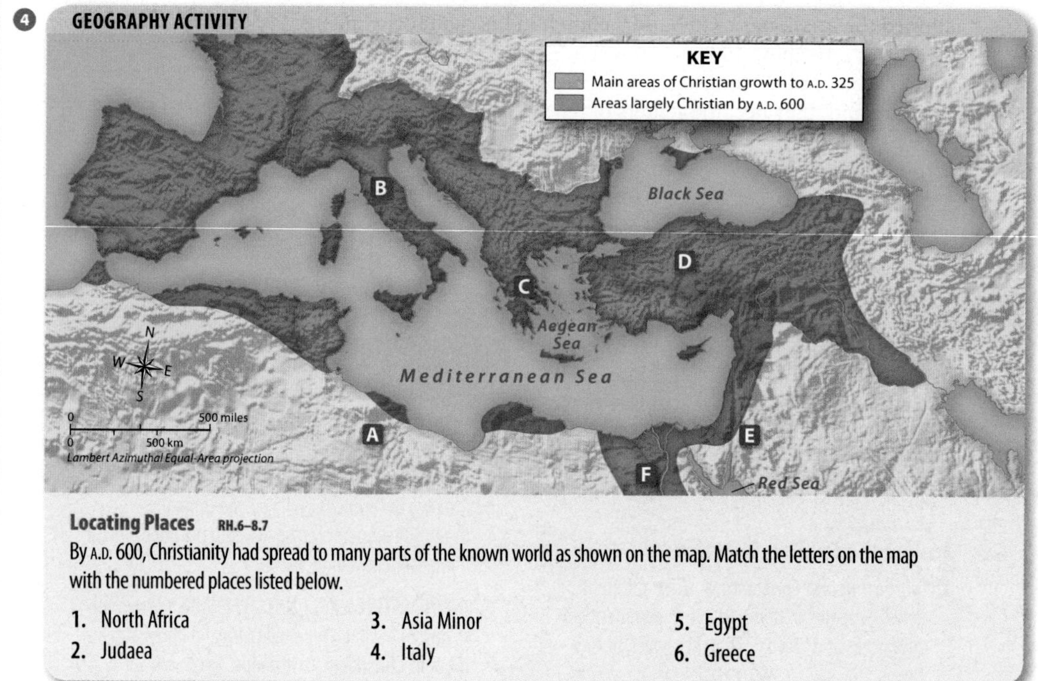

Locating Places RH.6–8.7

By A.D. 600, Christianity had spread to many parts of the known world as shown on the map. Match the letters on the map with the numbered places listed below.

1. North Africa
2. Judaea
3. Asia Minor
4. Italy
5. Egypt
6. Greece

ACTIVITIES ANSWERS

Exploring the Essential Question

1 Answers may vary. Responses might include an account of Paul's earlier opposition to Christianity and his later conversion. Students could also describe imagined accounts of Paul's many travels around the Mediterranean region, including sights he saw, people he met, how those people responded to his message, and problems he had.

21st Century Skills

2 Students' slide show presentations will differ. However, the presentations should emphasize the stylistic differences between the Byzantine and Roman Catholic churches and their respective forms of religious art. Students' slides should be clear and engaging, and they should support the narration.

CHAPTER 13 Assessment CCSS

REVIEW THE GUIDING QUESTIONS

Directions: Choose the best answer for each question.

RH.6–8.2
1. How did the Jews respond to Roman rule?
   A. The Jews tried to be at peace with the Romans.
   B. The Jews had mixed feelings about the Romans.
   C. The Jews disliked everything about the Romans.
   D. The Jews only wanted to please the Romans.

RH.6–8.2
2. Why were the life and death of Jesus important to his followers?
   F. The followers of Jesus were able to profit from his life and death.
   G. His life and death proved that Roman gods were inferior.
   H. They inspired his followers to carry his message to other lands.
   I. They made it easier for his followers to get along with the Romans.

RH.6–8.2
3. How did early Christianity spread throughout the Roman Empire?
   A. Roman soldiers who believed in Jesus brought his message to others.
   B. Jewish religious leaders traveled around the Mediterranean with stories of Jesus.
   C. Christian leaders called apostles spread the message of Jesus.
   D. Christian leaders forced other people to accept Christianity.

RH.6–8.2
4. How did Christianity change over time?
   F. It switched from Latin to Greek as its official language.
   G. It allowed church members to worship the old Roman gods.
   H. It became less and less organized.
   I. Christianity split into eastern and western churches.

RH.6–8.2
5. What issues divided the western and eastern Christian churches?
   A. the authority of the pope and the use of icons
   B. the failure of the Franks to help defend Rome from invaders
   C. the dress code for important officials of the church
   D. whether Latin or Greek should be spoken during church services

RH.6–8.2
6. How did Christianity continue to spread across Europe after the fall of the Western Roman Empire?
   F. Christian missionaries traveled to different parts of Europe.
   G. Christian monasteries converted people to Christianity.
   H. Germanic tribes brought Christianity to Western Europe.
   I. Saint Patrick spread Christianity across Europe.

393

CHAPTER 13 Assessment Answers

ASSESSMENT ANSWERS

Review the Guiding Questions

1. **B** The text clearly states that some Jews wanted nothing to do with the Romans. Nothing in the text supports answer C. Some Jews left Jerusalem in order to avoid contact with Romans.

2. **H** The followers of Jesus were not interested in exploiting his fame. The life and death of Jesus had nothing to do with the Roman gods. After the death of Jesus, his followers were often mistreated by Roman authorities.

3. **C** Roman soldiers would have been deemed traitors if they had converted to Christianity. Many Jewish leaders did not believe that Jesus was the promised deliverer. The use of force would have been against the teachings of Jesus.

4. **I** Latin remained the official language of the Roman Catholic Church, although the Byzantine Church adopted Greek as its official language. The worship of any gods, except the Christian God, was forbidden and went against the teachings of Christianity. Christianity began with people worshiping in private homes and developed into a highly organized system with an official hierarchy.

5. **A** The Franks intervened to defend Rome from invaders. Answers C and D are incorrect because nothing in the text suggests that these were divisive issues.

6. **F** The apostles were mainly responsible for spreading the message of Jesus. People who joined monasteries were already Christian. Germanic tribes were not missionaries. They invaded Britain and conquered the people living there. The focus of Saint Patrick's missionary work was the land we now call Ireland.

Thinking Like a Historian

3. Many eastern Christian churches approved of having icons, but for the most part, western Christian churches did not approve of them. In the west, the pope believed he was the head of all Christian churches. The Byzantines strongly disagreed. They believed the patriarch of Constantinople and various bishops were the pope's equals. The eastern and western churches also disagreed about how the church should relate to political authority. Similarities between the two branches of Christianity include the belief in Jesus as the Son of God, the belief in his teachings, and the use of the Christian Bible, among other religious books.

Locating Places

4. **1.** A, **2.** E, **3.** D, **4.** B, **5.** F, **6.** C

Analyzing Documents

7 **D** The quoted passage does not speak of pity for the dead monk. Answers B and C are close, but they refer only to the punishment of the dead monk and not to the purpose behind this punishment.

8 **H** The quoted passage does not suggest that monks were expected to be cruel and hard-hearted. Answer G could be inferred, but the introduction to the quote states that the sin of the monk was the fact that he had not shared his wealth. I is close, but it is not necessarily true that monks would be severely punished for any misbehavior.

Short Response

9 Answers may vary but should at a minimum include some of the reasons that many Jews, not just Zealots, were opposed to Roman rule: Jews were expected to honor Roman gods; the Emperor Augustus made Judah a Roman province and replaced a Jewish king with a Roman governor; and the Romans treated the Jews cruelly.

10 Answers may vary. Because Zealots used violent means, students could infer that many Romans were afraid for their lives while also feeling angry. Some Jews might have secretly approved of the tactics used by Zealots, while others might have condemned the use of violence.

Extended Response

11 Answers may vary. Students might decide to focus on the Sermon on the Mount and include references to some of the beatitudes in the Sermon. They might also describe the setting in which they (as first-century Jews) first heard Jesus preach. Answers should explain what students have learned about Jesus' teachings.

CHAPTER 13 Assessment *(continued)* 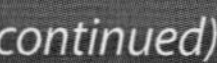 

DBQ ANALYZING DOCUMENTS

Drawing Conclusions Before becoming pope, Gregory I wrote this account of a monk who had not shared three gold coins with his fellow monks:

"When he was dead his body was not placed with the bodies of the brethren, but a grave was dug in the dung pit, and his body was flung down into it, and the three pieces of gold he had left were cast upon him, while all together cried, 'Thy money perish with thee!'"

—"Life in a Christian Monastery, ca. 585"

RH.6–8.1, RH.6–8.6
7 Which statement best captures the attitude of Gregory toward monks who hold on to personal property?

A. They should be pitied for their selfishness.
B. They deserve to die alone, with no one to comfort them.
C. They must be treated with scorn, even when they are dead.
D. Their sins must be punished severely to keep others from sinning.

RH.6–8.1, RH.6–8.6
8 **Inferring** What does Gregory's way of treating the dead monk reveal about life in an early Christian monastery?

F. Monks were expected to be cruel and hard-hearted.
G. Money was thought of as sinful and wicked.
H. Life was lived in common; all personal wealth was to be shared.
I. Monks paid a high price if they broke the rules.

SHORT RESPONSE

"Extremists among the Zealots turned to terrorism and assassination. . . . They frequented [went to] public places with hidden daggers to strike down persons friendly to Rome. . . . [A]t Masada in [A.D. 73] they committed suicide rather than surrender the fortress."

—Encyclopaedia Britannica, "Zealot," 2011

RH.6–8.1, RH.6–8.6
9 Why do you think the Zealots were so against Roman rule?

RH.6–8.1, RH.6–8.6
10 What effect do you think Zealot tactics had on other Jews and Romans?

EXTENDED RESPONSE

WHST.7–8.10
11 **Narrative** You are a young person who lives in Judaea during the time of Jesus' ministry. You have attended his Sermon on the Mount. Write a letter to your grandparents telling them about it.

Need Extra Help?

If You've Missed Question	1	2	3	4	5	6	7	8	9	10	11
Review Lesson	1	1	1	2	2	3	2	3	1	1	1

networks Online Teaching Options

Using eAssessment

Use eAssessment to access and assign the publisher-made Lesson Quizzes & Chapter Tests electronically. You can also use eAssessment to create your own quizzes and tests from hundreds of available questions. eAssessment helps you design assessments that meet the needs of different types of learners. Follow the link in the Assess tab of your Teacher Lesson Center.

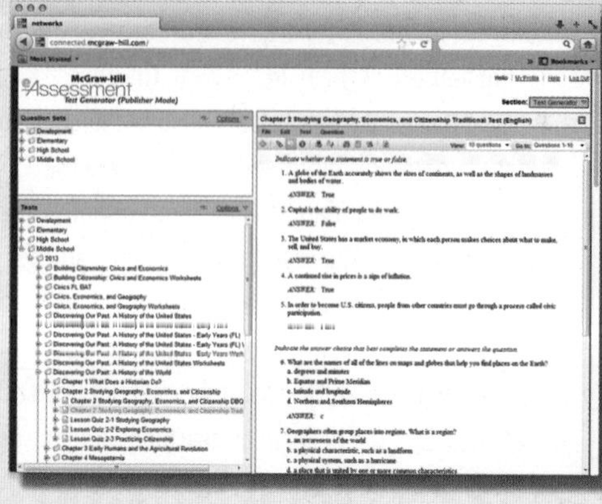

CHAPTER 14

Islamic Civilization Planner

UNDERSTANDING BY DESIGN®

Enduring Understandings

- *People, places, and ideas change over time.*
- *Religion can influence a society's beliefs and values.*

Essential Questions

- *How do religions develop?*
- *How does religion shape society?*
- *How do new ideas change the way people live?*

Predictable Misunderstandings

Students may think:

- *All Muslims are violent extremists or terrorists.*
- *Islam was spread only by conquering armies.*
- *All Muslims are Arabs.*

Assessment Evidence

Performance Tasks:

- *Hands-On Chapter Project*

Other Evidence:

- *Class discussion answers*
- *Compare and Contrast activity*
- *Map activities*
- *Graphic organizer activities*
- *Written activities*
- *Economics of History Activity*
- *21st Century Skills Activity*
- *Geography and History Activity*
- *Lesson Reviews*
- *Written paper to dispel misconception that all Muslims are Arabs*
- *Time line of Muslim contributions*
- *Chapter Activities and Assessment*

SUGGESTED PACING GUIDE

Introducing the Chapter............... 1 day
Lesson 1............................ 1 day
Lesson 2............................ 1 day
Lesson 3............................ 1 day
Chapter Wrap-Up and Assessment...... 1 day

TOTAL TIME 5 DAYS

Key for Using the Teacher Edition

SKILL-BASED ACTIVITIES

Types of skill activities found in the Teacher Edition.

V Visual Skills require students to analyze maps, graphs, charts, and photos.

R Reading Skills help students practice reading skills and master vocabulary.

W Writing Skills provide writing opportunities to help students comprehend the text.

C Critical Thinking Skills help students apply and extend what they have learned.

T Technology Skills require students to use digital tools effectively.

*Letters are followed by a number when there is more than one of the same type of skill on the page.

DIFFERENTIATED INSTRUCTION

All activities are written for the on-level student unless otherwise marked with the leveled labels below.

BL Beyond Level
AL Approaching Level
ELL English Language Learners

All students benefit from activities that utilize different learning styles. Many activities are marked as below when a particular learning style is highlighted.

Intrapersonal **Naturalist**
Logical/Mathematical **Kinesthetic**
Visual/Spatial **Auditory/Musical**
Verbal/Linguistic **Interpersonal**

NCSS Standards covered in "Islamic Civilization"

Learners will understand:

1 CULTURE

4. That the beliefs, values, and behaviors of a culture form an integrated system that helps shape the activities and ways of life that define a culture

8. That language, behaviors, and beliefs of different cultures can both contribute to and pose barriers to cross-cultural understanding

2 TIME, CONTINUITY, AND CHANGE

7. The contributions of key persons, groups, and events from the past and their influence on the present

3 PEOPLE, PLACES, AND ENVIRONMENTS

8. Factors that contribute to cooperation and conflict among peoples of the nation and world, including language, religion, and political beliefs

4 INDIVIDUAL DEVELOPMENT AND IDENTITY

3. How factors such as physical endowment, interests, capabilities, learning, motivation, personality, perception, and beliefs influence individual development and identity

4. How personal, social, cultural, and environmental factors contribute to the development and the growth of personal identity

5 INDIVIDUALS, GROUPS, AND INSTITUTIONS

2. Concepts such as: mores, norms, status, role, socialization, ethnocentrism, cultural diffusion, competition, cooperation, conflict, race, ethnicity, and gender

6. That cultural diffusion occurs when groups migrate

9. That groups and institutions influence culture in a variety of ways

8 SCIENCE, TECHNOLOGY, AND SOCIETY

6. Values, beliefs, and attitudes that have been influenced by new scientific and technological knowledge (for example, invention of the printing press, conceptions of the universe, applications of atomic energy, and genetic discoveries)

CHAPTER OPENER PLANNER

Students will know:

- *how physical geography influenced Arab civilization.*
- *the message that Muhammad preached.*
- *how Islam provides guidance to its followers.*
- *how an empire was created with the spread of Islam.*
- *how a split among Muslims led to a change in the Arab Empire.*
- *the ways in which the Turks, Safavids, and Moguls ruled their empires.*
- *what life was like in the Islamic world.*
- *what contributions Muslims have made in mathematics, science, and the arts.*

Students will be able to:

- ***identify*** *key tenets of Islam.*
- ***discuss*** *the significance of key components of Islam.*
- ***distinguish*** *the methods of how Islam was spread through various events and people.*
- ***determine*** *how the Turks, Safavids, and Moguls incorporated Islam into their empires.*
- ***discuss*** *the role that prayer plays in the lives of Muslims.*
- ***identify*** *the contributions made by Muslims.*
- ***explain*** *how discoveries and inventions affected the lives of Muslims.*

UNDERSTANDING BY DESIGN®

Print Teaching Options

C Critical Thinking Skills

- ☐ **P. 396** Students pose questions about the relationship between geography and culture on the Arabian Peninsula.
- ☐ **P. 397** Students predict chapter contents using the time line and map.

Online Teaching Options

V Visual Skills

- MAP **Islamic Empire, c A.D. 750**—Students compare the extents of the Islamic and Byzantine empires and trace the routes of military campaigns.
- TIME LINE **Islamic Civilization A.D. 600 to A.D. 1629**— Students learn about key events related to the birth and spread of Islam during this time period.
- WORLD ATLAS Students can use this interactive map to identify regions of the world, learn about individual countries, locate political boundaries, measure distances, and much more.

Project-Based Learning

Hands-On Chapter Project

Islamic Civilization

Student groups will create and present to the class an illustrated encyclopedia article about a topic related to Islamic civilization.

Technology Extension

Islamic Encyclopedia Wiki

- Find an additional activity online that incorporates technology for this project.
- Visit the EdTechTeacher Web sites (included in the Technology Extension for this chapter) for more links, tutorials, and other resources.

Print Resources

ANCILLARY RESOURCES

These ancillaries are available for every chapter and lesson.

- **Reading Essentials and Study Guide Workbook** AL ELL
- **Chapter Tests and Lesson Quizzes Blackline Masters**

PRINTABLE DIGITAL WORKSHEETS

These printable digital worksheets are available for every chapter and lesson.

- **Hands-On Chapter Projects**
- **What Do You Know? activities**
- **Chapter Summaries (English and Spanish)**
- **Vocabulary Builder activities**
- **Guided Reading activities**

More Media Resources

SUGGESTED READING 

Grade 6 reading level:

- ***Salaam: A Muslim American Boy's Story,*** by Tricia Brown

Grade 7 reading level:

- ***Mosque,*** by David Macaulay

Grade 8 reading level:

- ***From the Rubayat—Selection From the Poem,*** by Omar Khayyam

LESSON 1 PLANNER

A New Faith

Students will know:

- *how physical geography influenced Arab civilization.*
- *the message that Muhammad preached.*
- *how Islam provides guidance to its followers.*

Students will be able to:

- ***identify** key tenets of Islam.*
- ***discuss** the significance of key components of Islam.*

UNDERSTANDING BY DESIGN®

Print Teaching Options

V Visual Skills

- **P. 401** Students produce graphic organizers of information on the life and work of Muhammad. Visual/Spatial
- **P. 403** Student groups produce graphic organizers about the Five Pillars of Islam. AL ELL

R Reading Skills

- **P. 399** Students evaluate bedouin tribal interaction. AL
- **P. 400** Students summarize the text on life in Arab towns. Verbal/Linguistic
- **P. 401** Students begin to form an understanding of Muhammad as a historical figure.
- **P. 402** Students explain Muhammad's opponents. AL
- **P. 402** Students write a short summary of the concept of the Islamic State. Verbal/Linguistic

W Writing Skills

- **P. 398** Students write anticipatory explanations about the spread of Islam. Verbal/Linguistic

C Critical Thinking Skills

- **P. 398** Students theorize about factors in the development of Arabian civilization. AL
- **P. 399** Students evaluate the physical geography of Arabia.
- **P. 400** Students hypothesize about Arab lifestyles.
- **P. 401** Students compare and contrast Islam with other religions. ELL
- **P. 402** Students determine reasons for support or opposition of political leadership.
- **P. 403** Students connect the tenets of the Quran with Islamic lifestyle expectations. ELL Interpersonal

T Technology Skills

- **P. 400** Students conduct independent research about Makkah. BL

Online Teaching Options

V Visual Skills

- VIDEO **Islamic World**—Students travel with millions of Muslims to Mecca for the sacred pilgrimage of the Hajj.
- DIAGRAM **The Kaaba**—Students click to reveal information about the elements that make up Islam's holiest site.
- MAP **Southwest Asia c. A.D. 600**—Students compare the extent of the Byzantine and Persian empires.

R Reading Skills

- GRAPHIC ORGANIZER **Taking Notes: *Describing*: The Development of Islam**—Students describe the importance of Arabia, Makkah, and Madinah to Islam.
- BIOGRAPHY **Muhammad**—Students read biographical information about Islam's founder.

C Critical Thinking Skills

- SLIDE SHOW **Sacred Muslim Sites**—Students compare images of the Mosque of the Prophet and the Dome of the Rock.
- SLIDE SHOW **Bedouin Life**—Students analyze scenes from bedouin life.

T Technology Skills

- SELF-CHECK QUIZ **Lesson 1**—Students receive instant feedback on their mastery of lesson content.

Printable Digital Worksheets

C Critical Thinking Skills

- WORKSHEET **Geography and History Activity: Understanding Place: The Arabian Peninsula**—Students compare the ancient and modern-day peninsula.

LESSON 2 PLANNER

THE SPREAD OF ISLAM

Students will know:
- *how an empire was created with the spread of Islam.*
- *how a split among Muslims led to a change in the Arab Empire.*
- *the ways in which the Turks, Safavids, and Moguls ruled their empires.*

Students will be able to:
- ***distinguish*** *the methods of how Islam was spread through various events and people.*
- ***determine*** *how the Turks, Safavids, and Moguls incorporated Islam into their empires.*

UNDERSTANDING BY DESIGN®

☑ Print Teaching Options

V Visual Skills

- ☐ **P. 404** Students produce cause-effect charts to organize historical events. **Visual/Spatial**
- ☐ **P. 405** Students use a map to make predictions about the spread of Islam. **Visual/Spatial**
- ☐ **P. 408** Students examine a map for clues about the fall of the Abbasids. **Visual/Spatial**

R Reading Skills

- ☐ **P. 405** Students list qualities of Muslims. **AL** **Verbal/Linguistic**
- ☐ **P. 406** Students explain the effect of Muslim expansion in Spain on other religions. **BL**
- ☐ **P. 406** Students extract the main idea and supporting details about preachers and traders. **AL** **Verbal/Linguistic**
- ☐ **P. 407** Students provide reasons for the Shia rebellion. **Verbal/Linguistic**
- ☐ **P. 410** Students explain interactions of Muslims within the Ottoman Empire. **AL**

W Writing Skills

- ☐ **P. 405** Students defend opinions about consequences of the Muslim method of spreading the empire.
- ☐ **P. 407** Students use multiple sources to prepare essays. **BL** **Verbal/Linguistic**
- ☐ **P. 409** Students write short arguments about inferences regarding Suleiman's rule. **Verbal/Linguistic**
- ☐ **P. 410** Students write essays to explain why all Muslims are not Arab. **ELL** **Verbal/Linguistic**

C Critical Thinking Skills

- ☐ **P. 406** Students compare the first four caliphs. **ELL**
- ☐ **P. 408** Students infer the power of the Abbasids versus the Turks.
- ☐ **P. 409** Students assess the end of the Arab Empire. **AL**
- ☐ **P. 409** Students analyze the development of Ottoman rule. **AL**

T Technology Skills

- ☐ **P. 408** Students develop a time line presentation outlining the rule of the Abbasids. **BL** **Visual/Spatial**

☑ Online Teaching Options

V Visual Skills

- **VIDEO** **Islamic Trade Routes**—Students focus on the role of traders in the world of medieval Islamic civilization.
- **MAP** **The Abbasid Empire A.D. 800**—Students view the extent of the Abbasid Empire during the reign of Harun ar-Rashid.
- **MAP** **The Spread of Islam A.D. 632–A.D. 750**—Students examine Islamic expansion after Muhammad's death.

R Reading Skills

- **GRAPHIC ORGANIZER** **Taking Notes: *Summarizing*: How Islam Spread**—Students describe three ways in which the religion of Islam spread.
- **SLIDE SHOW** **Islamic Architecture**—Students view buildings in Spain that show elements of the country's Islamic past.
- **BIOGRAPHY** **Suleiman I**—Students read of the life and accomplishments of this sultan of the Ottoman Empire.

C Critical Thinking Skills

- **CHART** **The Four Caliphs**—Students click to learn more about four important Islamic rulers.
- **IMAGE** **The Shah Mosque**—Students analyze an image of the Shaw Mosque, considered one of the finest examples of Islamic and Persian architecture.

T Technology Skills

- **SELF-CHECK QUIZ** **Lesson 2**—Students receive instant feedback on their mastery of lesson content.

☑ Printable Digital Worksheets

C Critical Thinking Skills

- **WORKSHEET** **21st Century Skills Activity: Information Literacy: Sequence and Categorize Information**—Students categorize and then sequence information about Suleiman I and the Ottoman Empire.

LESSON 3 PLANNER

LIFE IN THE ISLAMIC WORLD

Students will know:

- *what life was like in the Islamic world.*
- *what contributions Muslims have made in mathematics, science, and the arts.*

Students will be able to:

- ***discuss*** *the role that prayer plays in the lives of Muslims.*
- ***identify*** *the contributions made by Muslims.*
- ***explain*** *how discoveries and inventions affected the lives of Muslims.*

UNDERSTANDING BY DESIGN®

Print Teaching Options

V Visual Skills

- [ ] **P. 414** Students infer characteristics of Omar Khayyam from the illustration. **ELL** **Visual/Spatial**

R Reading Skills

- [ ] **P. 411** Students tell why Muslims were so successful as traders.
- [ ] **P. 412** Students discuss the organization of Muslim society.
- [ ] **P. 414** Students produce an idea web about medical discoveries. **ELL** **Visual/Spatial**
- [ ] **P. 415** Students detail ways that geography and climate shape human activity.

W Writing Skills

- [ ] **P. 413** Students further research related topics of personal interest. **BL**

C Critical Thinking Skills

- [ ] **P. 411** Students determine the main idea in a passage about Muslim trade. **AL** **Verbal/Linguistic**
- [ ] **P. 412** Students compare and contrast early and modern-day bazaars. **AL** **Interpersonal**
- [ ] **P. 413** Students compare and contrast the roles of Muslim men and women.
- [ ] **P. 413** Students classify Muslim contributions to science, art, and other disciplines. **AL**
- [ ] **P. 414** Students interpret the Rubaiyat.
- [ ] **P. 415** Students consider the void of depiction of living creatures in Muslim art.

T Technology Skills

- [ ] **P. 412** Students develop and deliver presentations about Muslim cities or farms. **ELL** **Visual/Spatial**
- [ ] **P. 415** Students develop visual presentations about mosques. **Visual/Spatial**

Online Teaching Options

V Visual Skills

- [ ] **VIDEO** **Islamic Scientific Advances**—Architecture, pictorial representations, and music convey the breadth of early Islamic learning and scientific advances.
- [ ] **SLIDE SHOW** **The Taj Mahal**—Students examine interior and exterior images of this beautiful example of Mughal architecture.
- [ ] **SLIDE SHOW** **Mosques**—Students compare and contrast architectural elements of different mosques.

R Reading Skills

- [ ] **GRAPHIC ORGANIZER** **Taking Notes: *Organizing*: Muslim Contributions to Science**—Students record information on Muslim contributions to science.
- [ ] **PRIMARY SOURCE** **The Rubaiyat**—Students read an excerpt from this collection of poems.

C Critical Thinking Skills

- [ ] **WHITEBOARD ACTIVITY** **Muslim Advancements**—Students categorize data as pertaining to science, architecture, the economy, or literature and art.
- [ ] **IMAGE** **Abu Musa Jabir ibn Hayyan**—Students learn of this scientist's accomplishments.
- [ ] **SLIDE SHOW** **Shopping Then and Now**—Students analyze images of ancient and modern bazaars.

T Technology Skills

- [ ] **SELF-CHECK QUIZ** **Lesson 3**—Students receive instant feedback on their mastery of lesson content.

Printable Digital Worksheets

C Critical Thinking Skills

- [ ] **WORKSHEET** **Economics of History Activity: The Use of Credit in the Islamic Empire**—Students analyze how the use of credit contributed to the expansion of trade in the Islamic Empire.

INTERVENTION AND REMEDIATION STRATEGIES

LESSON 1 A New Faith

Reading and Comprehension

Have students explain how the location of the Arabian Peninsula protected the people there, including the bedouins, the settlers of early towns, and the city of Makkah.

Text Evidence

Ask students to work in small groups to answer these questions: *What qualities did Muhammad have that led to his ability to spread Islam all over the Arabian Peninsula? How did Islam spread under Muhammad's leadership?* Have students cite evidence from the text to support their answers.

LESSON 2 The Spread of Islam

Reading and Comprehension

Have students list the people and groups who were most responsible for the spread of Islam during this period. Ask students to tell in their own words how each person or group contributed to the spread of Islam.

Text Evidence

Draw two columns on the board with the headings "Umayyads" and "Abbasids." Have students use information from their textbooks to provide details in each column about each group.

LESSON 3 Life in the Islamic World

Reading and Comprehension

Have students write a paragraph, using the lesson vocabulary, in which they summarize the content of the lesson.

Text Evidence

Ask students to analyze the role of religion in the Muslims' everyday lives. Have them also discuss what aspects of the Muslim religion may have factored into the many Muslim contributions to art, architecture, science, medicine, and literature. Ask students to support their statements with evidence from the text.

Online Resources

Approaching Level Reader

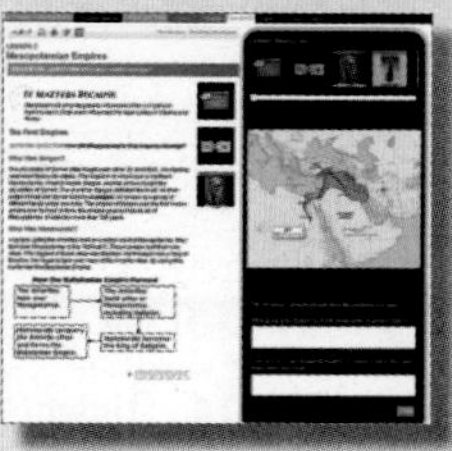

Use this online lower-level text that corresponds directly to the text in the Student Edition. It includes a Spanish version.

Guided Reading Activities

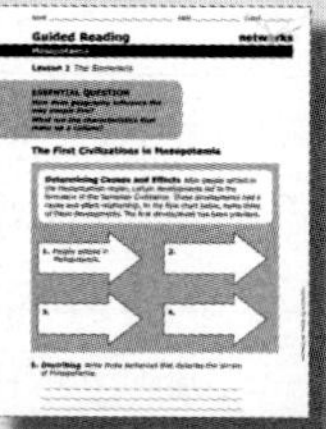

This resource uses graphic organizers and guiding questions to help students with comprehension.

What Do You Know?

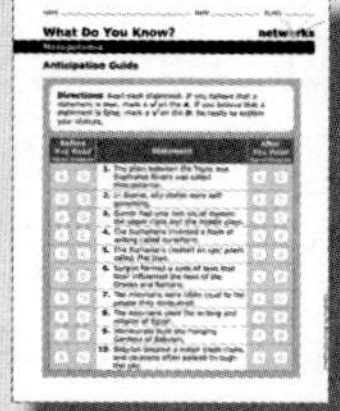

Use these worksheets to pre-assess student's background knowledge before they study the chapter.

Reading Essentials and Study Guide Workbook

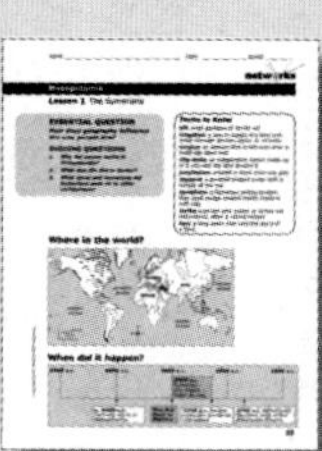

This resource offers writing and reading activities for the approaching-level student. Also available in Spanish.

Self-Check Quizzes

This online assessment tool provides instant feedback for students to check their progress.

Islamic Civilization

A.D. 600 to A.D. 1629

ESSENTIAL QUESTIONS • *How do religions develop?* • *How do new ideas change the way people live?*

networks

There's More Online about Islam and its impact on the world.

CHAPTER 14

Lesson 1 *A New Faith*

Lesson 2 *The Spread of Islam*

Lesson 3 *Life in the Islamic World*

The Story Matters . . .

In the 1300s, in the area now known as Turkey, a Muslim tribal chieftain named Osman gained power. He gradually took control of more lands and established the Ottoman Empire. The Ottoman Empire lasted for nearly six centuries and was ruled by Muslim leaders called sultans.

This painting of Suleiman II, sultan of the Ottoman Empire from 1687-1691, shows the elegant clothes worn by the sultan. The large turban, or headdress, indicates his status and position. For centuries, turbans were a part of dress throughout the Islamic world. An elaborate turban and richly decorated robes showed a person's high rank in society.

◄ *Portrait paintings of leaders such as Suleiman II are important historical artifacts that tell us about the cultures in which the leaders lived.*

Letter from the Author

Dear World History Teacher,

In the seventh century, a new religion called Islam arose in the Arabian Peninsula from the teachings of Muhammad. After Muhammad's death, his successors organized a great Arab expansion westward, across North Africa and into Spain, and eastward into the Persian Empire. Two powerful Muslim states—the Ottoman Empire in the Middle East and the Mogul Empire in India—rose during the early 1500s. The military and political talents of these empires helped protect much of the Muslim world.

Jackson J. Spielvogel

ENGAGE

Bellringer Ask a volunteer to read aloud "The Story Matters . . .," or read it aloud to the class. Then discuss what it might have been like to be a young person living in the Islamic Empire when Osman took control of the land and government. **Ask: Do changes in government affect students and how they live?** Have a few students share their views.

Then **ask:**

- **Have you seen a change in government in your lifetime?**
- **How did it affect you and how you live?**
- **What events happened when the government changed?**

Tell the class that the Islamic Empire was first ruled by various groups that included the Arabs, Persians, and Mongols. Later, it was ruled by Turkish people who called their empire the Ottoman Empire. Muslim accomplishments—such as spreading the faith of Islam, the code of law developed by Ottoman ruler Suleiman I, and many advancements in science and medicine—are well documented and tell us most of what we know about the Islamic Empire's culture and its history.

Making Connections

Read the following information to students:

- Governments that recognize the power of a deity or deities and incorporate this recognition into their rule are called theocracies. The word *theocracy* means "rule by God."
- There are fewer religion-based governments today than there were in the past, and many present Islamic theocracies are currently moving toward becoming democracies.
- Other democratic nations have tried to encourage these governments' transitions toward democracy, but this difficult change has involved much conflict and struggle.

Step Into the Place

C1 Critical Thinking Skills

Formulating Questions Direct students' attention to the Chapter Opener map that displays the Islamic Empire in A.D. 750. Ask students what they know about life in Arabia at that time. Explain that trading was an important livelihood of people in Arabia. **Ask:** What effect would trading have on Arabian culture? *(Arabians would be exposed to many new ideas.)* What other questions would you ask, as you look at this map, about life in Arabia, about Arabian culture, and about the effect of trade? Have students write down several questions and share them as a class. Tell students that reading the chapter may help to answer their questions.

As a class, discuss the Map Focus questions.

Content Background Knowledge

- The area shown on the map includes parts of three different continents—Asia, Africa, and Europe.
- The region in which these three continents come together, where Arabia is located, is referred to as Southwest Asia. It is often called the Middle East in contemporary media.
- Because of their location at the intersection of three continents, Arabians were exposed to people from many diverse cultures and backgrounds.

ANSWERS, p. 396

Step Into the Place

1. Arabia is west of India.
2. Arabia's location made it a connector between East and West through which trade routes often passed.
3. South of Arabia is the Arabian Sea. North of Arabia is the Mediterranean Sea. West of Arabia is the Red Sea, bordered by Africa. East of Arabia are the Persian Gulf, Persia (Iran), and India.
4. CRITICAL THINKING People from many countries pass through a trading center. They share their ideas and values with the people they meet.

Step Into the Time

Students' answers will vary but will likely include the birth of Muhammad or the Vikings reaching North America.

CHAPTER 14 CCSS

Place and Time: Islamic Civilization A.D. 600 to A.D. 1629

Islamic civilization extended across Southwest Asia, North Africa, and parts of Europe. It later spread into India and Southeast Asia. Over time, Islamic rule was challenged by rivalries within Islam and by invasions of outside groups. A series of Islamic empires ruled until the early 1900s.

Step Into the Place

MAP FOCUS Arabia was a crossroads of trade and culture between East and West in the first century A.D.

1. **LOCATION** Look at the map. Is Arabia east or west of India? RH.6–8.7
2. **MOVEMENT** How did Arabia's location make it a trading crossroads between the East and the West? RH.6–8.7
3. **REGIONS** Describe all of the boundaries of Arabia. RH.6–8.2
4. CRITICAL THINKING *Determining Cause and Effect* How does a trading center contribute to the spread of culture and ideas? RH.6–8.7

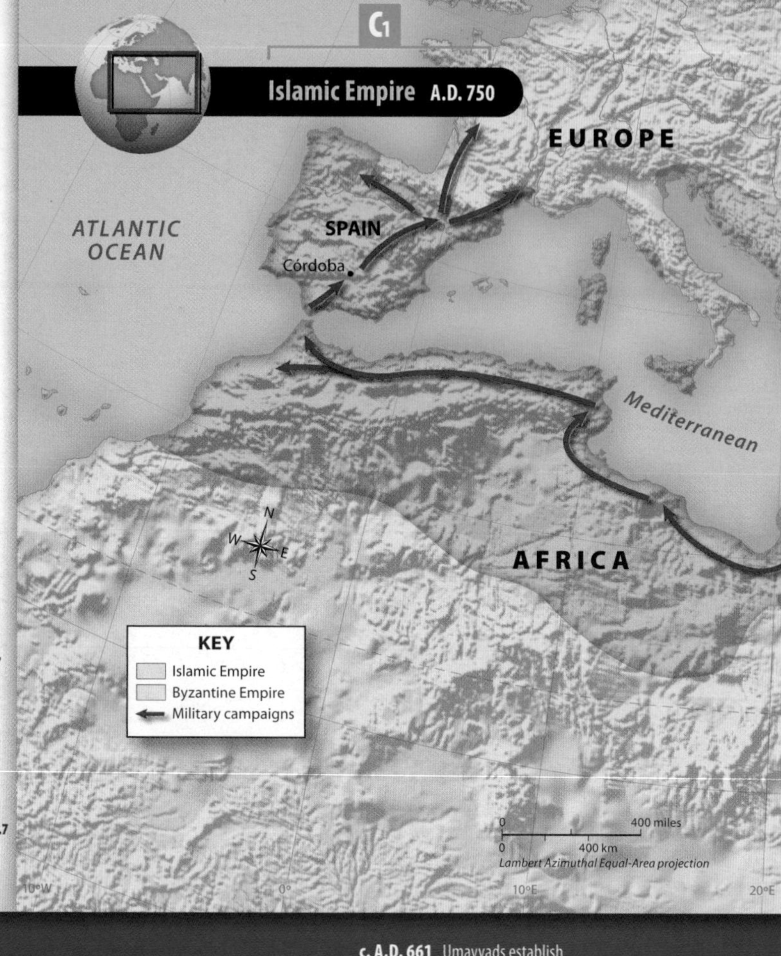

Step Into the Time

C2 **TIME LINE** Choose an event from the time line and write a paragraph predicting the consequences that event might have for the world. RH.6–8.2, WHST.6–8.10

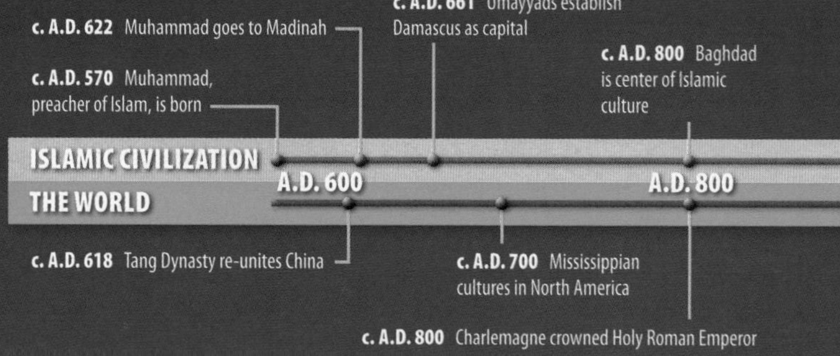

Project-Based Learning

Hands-On Chapter Project

Islamic Civilization

Students will create an illustrated encyclopedia article about a topic related to Islamic civilization. Assign students into small groups to choose a topic, do research, and write and illustrate an article. Have students present their articles to the class.

Technology Extension

Islamic Encyclopedia Wiki

Small groups will create an illustrated encyclopedia online, in a wiki format, about Islamic civilization. Students will work together to research the article, create a research page with links for each topic, publish their article online, and share it with the class. To learn more about creating and setting up wikis, visit the Wiki page at EdTechTeacher's Teaching History with Technology site: http://thwt.org/historywikis.html.

Place and Time

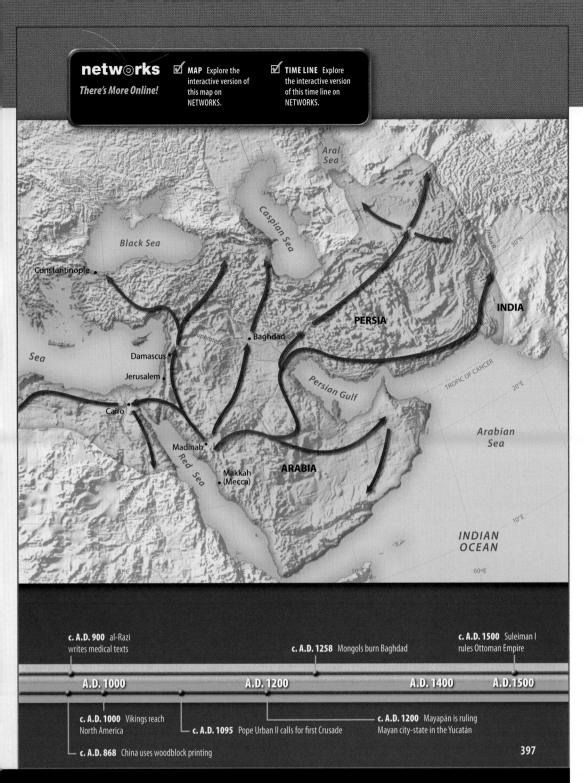

networks
There's More Online!

MAP Explore the interactive version of this map on NETWORKS.

TIME LINE Explore the interactive version of this time line on NETWORKS.

Aral Sea
Caspian Sea
Black Sea
Constantinople
Sea
Damascus
Jerusalem
Baghdad
Euphrates R.
Cairo
Madinah
Red Sea
Makkah (Mecca)
ARABIA
PERSIA
INDIA
Indus R.
Persian Gulf
TROPIC OF CANCER
Arabian Sea
INDIAN OCEAN
Nile R.
30°N
20°E
10°E
60°E

c. A.D. 900 al-Razi writes medical texts

c. A.D. 1258 Mongols burn Baghdad

c. A.D. 1500 Suleiman I rules Ottoman Empire

A.D. 1000 — A.D. 1200 — A.D. 1400 — A.D. 1500

c. A.D. 1000 Vikings reach North America

c. A.D. 1095 Pope Urban II calls for first Crusade

c. A.D. 1200 Mayapán is ruling Mayan city-state in the Yucatán

c. A.D. 868 China uses woodblock printing

397

Step Into the Time

C2 Critical Thinking Skills

Sequencing Have students review the time line for the chapter. Explain that they will be studying events from about A.D. 600 up to about A.D. 1500. **Ask:** What are some events you already know about that happened during those years? *(Student answers might include that Europeans discovered cultures in North America.)* Are there events listed here which give you an idea about what may be discussed in this chapter? What are some of those events? *(war, writing of a medical text, establishing a center of Islamic culture)*

Remind students to use the time lines in their books to help them think of other events that occurred during this time period.

CLOSE & REFLECT

Summarizing Discuss the map, time line, and other information presented in the Chapter Opener. Have students summarize what they've learned and predict what they may learn in the upcoming chapter.

WORKSHEET

What Do You Know? Activity: Islamic Civilization

Assessing Background Knowledge Have students complete the What Do You Know? Anticipation Guide about Islamic civilization before they study the chapter. Direct students to read each statement and, in the "Before" column, check whether they agree or disagree with the statement. After students complete the chapter, have them reread the statements and note in the "After" column whether they agree or disagree with each statement. Ask students who changed their responses to explain why they did so, citing facts from the chapter.

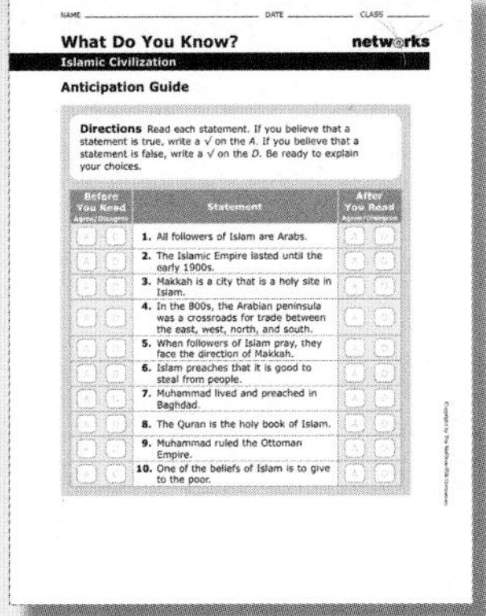
NAME ______ DATE ______ CLASS ______

What Do You Know? networks

Islamic Civilization

Anticipation Guide

Directions Read each statement. If you believe that a statement is true, write a √ on the *A*. If you believe that a statement is false, write a √ on the *D*. Be ready to explain your choices.

Before You Read	Statement	After You Read
A D	1. All followers of Islam are Arabs.	A D
A D	2. The Islamic Empire lasted until the early 1900s.	A D
A D	3. Makkah is a city that is a holy site in Islam.	A D
A D	4. In the 800s, the Arabian peninsula was a crossroads for trade between the east, west, north, and south.	A D
A D	5. When followers of Islam pray, they face the direction of Makkah.	A D
A D	6. Islam preaches that it is good to steal from people.	A D
A D	7. Muhammad lived and preached in Baghdad.	A D
A D	8. The Quran is the holy book of Islam.	A D
A D	9. Muhammad ruled the Ottoman Empire.	A D
A D	10. One of the beliefs of Islam is to give to the poor.	A D

See page 395B for other online activities.

A New Faith

ENGAGE

Bellringer Show the map of Southwest Asia in A.D. 600. Tell students that the Arabian Peninsula was mostly a desert area that was a center of trading and the center of the Islamic faith. **Ask:** **What happens when people from different places meet and trade?** *(They share their ideas and cultures.)* Have students locate Makkah, where Muhammad—the prophet of Islam—was born, and Madinah, where Muhammad was accepted as a prophet. Tell students that they will be learning about Muhammad and the spread of the Islamic religion as they read this chapter.

TEACH & ASSESS

W Writing Skills

Argument Point out that the religion of Islam spread very quickly. **Ask:** **How do you think this quick spread of Islam occurred?** *(perhaps through trading, travel by individuals to other lands, military conquest, or exile)* Discuss the possible answers. Have students think of three possible reasons for this spread and write an essay making a clear argument to explain how this spread may have occurred. They can check these essays later to compare with the information they learn in the chapter. **Verbal/Linguistic**

C Critical Thinking Skills

Hypothesizing As a class, discuss the features of Arabia, including the heat, the oases, and how it is surrounded by different civilizations. **Ask:** **How do you think these factors will affect how Arabia is populated when people begin to settle there and build towns?** *(Arabia may be populated by a variety of people from the surrounding nations, and they may build their towns near the water.)* AL

ANSWER, p. 398

TAKING NOTES: Islam first spread in Arabia, and because it is a peninsula between Africa and western Asia, Islam spread both west and east. Muhammad was born in Makkah and first preached Islam in Makkah. Fearing for their safety in Makkah, Muhammad and his followers fled to Madinah, and the people there received him as a prophet of God.

networks
There's More Online!

- GRAPHIC ORGANIZER The Development of Islam
- DIAGRAM The Kaaba
- MAP Southwest Asia c. A.D. 600
- SLIDE SHOW
  - Lives of the Bedouin
  - Sacred Muslim Sites
- VIDEO

Lesson 1

A New Faith

ESSENTIAL QUESTION *How do religions develop?*

IT MATTERS BECAUSE

Islam is one of the most widely practiced religions in the world today. Approximately 25 percent of the people in the world are Muslim.

Arab Life

GUIDING QUESTION *How did physical geography influence the Arab way of life?*

W Beginning in the A.D. 630s, people called Arabs created a new empire in Southwest Asia. The driving force behind their empire was the religion of **Islam** (IS•lahm). Within a century, Islam spread throughout parts of Asia, northern Africa, and Europe.

The Land of Arabia

C The Arabian Peninsula, also called Arabia, is the homeland of the Arab people. It is also the center of Islam. Arabia is a huge wedge of land between the Red Sea and the Persian Gulf. Very dry plains and deserts cover most of the land. The desert heat can be intense. Summer temperatures can rise above 122° F (50° C). Water is available only at scattered springs and water holes. Such a spot is called an **oasis** (oh•AY•suhs). At an oasis, trees and other plants grow. Not all of Arabia is desert, however. There are mountains and valleys in the southwestern region. Enough rain falls in these locations for juniper and olive trees to grow.

In ancient times, the Arabian Peninsula was surrounded by many different civilizations. At various times, the Egyptian civilization was to the west, the Mesopotamian and Persian

Reading HELPDESK CCSS

Taking Notes: *Describing* RH.6–8.2

On a chart like this one, describe the importance of these places to the development of the religion of Islam.

The Development of Islam

Place	Importance
Arabia	
Makkah	
Madinah	

Content Vocabulary (Tier 3 Words)

- **Islam**
- **oasis**
- **sheikh**
- **caravan**
- **Quran**
- ***shari'ah***

networks ***Online Teaching Options***

VIDEO

Islamic World

Comparing and Contrasting Play the video in which millions of Muslims journey to Mecca for the sacred pilgrimage of the Hajj. Followers from around the world converge in Saudi Arabia to share their Islamic beliefs and traditions. **Ask:** **What purpose does the pilgrimage serve for Muslims?** *(to trace the footsteps of their prophet, Muhammad, and to feel closer to their religion)* **What special things do people of other religions do to feel closer to their religion, prophets, or God?** Have students compare the Muslim's pilgrimage to Mecca with similar aspects of other religions. **Visual/Spatial**

See page 395C for other online activities.

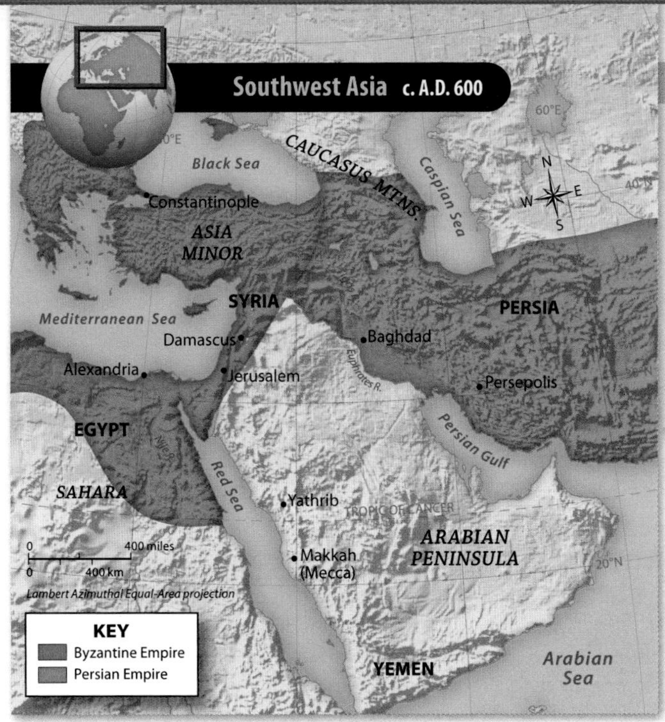

GEOGRAPHY CONNECTION

The prophet Muhammad brought the message of Islam to the people of Arabia.

1. **REGIONS** Which empire was located north and west of the Arabian Peninsula?
2. **PLACE** About how far is it from Makkah to Yathrib?
3. **CRITICAL THINKING** ***Analyzing*** How did Makkah's location make it a center for trade?

civilizations were to the north and east, and farther north were the civilizations of the Israelites, Greeks, and Romans. Long distances and the severe Arabian climate had kept these civilizations from invading the peninsula. This **isolation,** however, was not absolute, as trade brought some outside ideas and practices to the Arab civilization.

Life in the Desert

Long ago, many Arabs were nomads who herded animals and lived in tents. These nomads are called bedouin. The bedouin raised camels, goats, and sheep and traveled from oasis to oasis. The bedouin ate mainly fresh or dried dates and drank milk. On very special occasions they ate goat or sheep meat. **C**

To survive the harsh desert climate, early Arabs formed tribes whose members were loyal to one another. The leader of each tribe was called a **sheikh** (SHAYK). Arab tribes raided other tribes to take camels and horses. Rival tribes battled one another over land and water. **R**

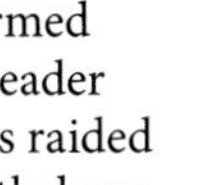

Islam a religion based on the teachings of Muhammad
oasis a green area in a desert fed by underground water
sheikh the leader of an Arab tribe

Academic Vocabulary (Tier 2 Words)
isolation separation from other populated areas

A New Faith

C Critical Thinking Skills

Reasoning Discuss how the physical geography of the area affected life in Arabia. **Ask:** **How did the geography influence the Arab way of life—where they lived, how they survived, and what they ate?** *(It affected where they lived—being nomads traveling from oasis to oasis and living in tents—and what they ate—dates and milk.)* **What type of clothing do you think the bedouins wore, given their surroundings?** *(clothing that protected them from the sun and blowing sand)*

R Reading Skills

Explaining After students read the text, ask them to explain how the geography of the desert impacted the people living there. **Ask:** **How did people living in the desert depend on one another?** *(They formed tribes and were loyal to their tribal members.)* **How did the different tribes get along?** *(Though the tribes helped one another, they also often battled each other.)* **Why did the tribes battle each other?** *(They fought over land and water.)* AL

Content Background Knowledge

- At its widest point, the Arabian Peninsula measures about 1,300 miles (2,090 km).
- Along the Red Sea, it measures about 1,200 miles (1,900 km).
- The Arabian Peninsula has no rivers, but there are some oases and many short wadis, which are dry riverbeds that catch rain when it falls.

SLIDE SHOW

Bedouin Life

Making Connections Have students think about how the physical features of the region might have affected the way Arabs lived and how they relied on one another. Invite them to draw on their own experiences such as watching a movie or a television program about the desert. Show students the interactive slide show about bedouin life.

See page 395C for other online activities.

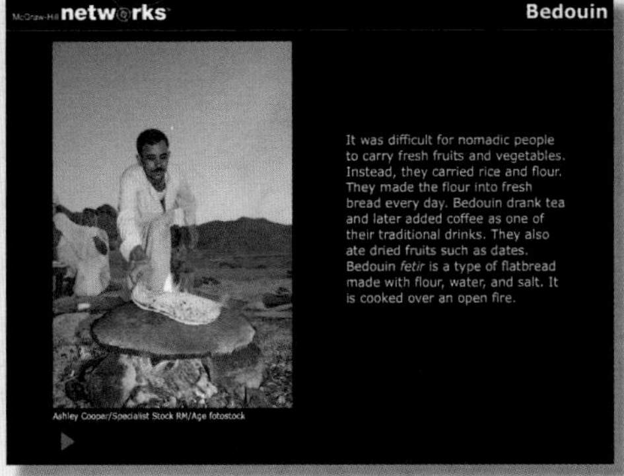

networks
Bedouin
It was difficult for nomadic people to carry fresh fruits and vegetables. Instead, they carried rice and flour. They made the flour into fresh bread every day. Bedouin drank tea and later added coffee as one of their traditional drinks. They also ate dried fruits such as dates. Bedouin fetir is a type of flatbread made with flour, water, and salt. It is cooked over an open fire.

ANSWERS, p. 399

GEOGRAPHY CONNECTION

1. the Byzantine Empire
2. about 200 miles (320 km)
3. **CRITICAL THINKING** Makkah's location gave it access to the trade routes that passed through the Red Sea. It also connected trade routes that passed across the Arabian Desert with the Red Sea trade routes.

R Reading Skills

Summarizing Ask students to use the information in the "Life in Towns" section of the lesson to summarize how the Arabs lived in these new towns. *(Summaries may include information about the bedouins, about caravans arriving with trade goods, and about Makkah and its importance as a trading center and the location of the Kaaba.)* **Verbal/Linguistic**

C Critical Thinking Skills

Hypothesizing Discuss with students how trade became a bustling industry in the town of Makkah. **Ask:** **What might a day have been like in the life of a trader who lived in the new town of Makkah?** *(Maybe a caravan of goods is late and the trader is worried that it has been raided by bedouins, or maybe the trader is going to pray at the Kaaba.)* Discuss the factors that may have affected everyday life.

T Technology Skills

Researching on the Internet Have students use the Internet to find pictures and information about Makkah and the Kaaba. **Ask:** **What made Makkah an important religious center?** *(The Kaaba, a religious site with statues of the Arabian gods and goddesses, was located in Makkah.)* Ask students each to choose two or three details to share. BL

Bedouins value the camel as a reliable carrier. Their wide, flat feet allow the camel to move very quickly across the dunes.

Can you imagine what a camel race might be like? The bedouin enjoyed camel and horse races and other games that improved their battle skills. In the evenings, they told stories around campfires. Poets wrote and recited poems about battles, camels, horses, and love. The lines below are about an Arab warrior and a battle he must fight. He describes his reliable camel.

PRIMARY SOURCE

> "My riding-camels are tractable [obedient],
> they go wherever I wish;
> while my intellect is my helper,
> and I drive it forward with a firm order."
>
> —from *The Poem of Antar*

Life in Towns

By the A.D. 500s, many Arab tribes had settled around oases or in fertile mountain valleys. They set up villages, farmed or raised animals, and traded goods. Merchants carried goods by camel across the desert to different markets. For protection against bedouin raids, some made journeys in **caravans** (KEHR•uh•vanz), or groups of traveling merchants and animals.

C As trade grew, Arab merchants built towns along the trade routes in Arabia. The most important town was Makkah (MAH•kuh), also known as Mecca. Makkah was located about 50 miles (80 kilometers) inland from the Red Sea. The town became a crossroads of trade. Large caravans from southwestern Arabia passed through Makkah on their way to Syria and Mesopotamia. Some caravans traveled as far away as China. R

T Makkah was also an important religious site. In the center of the city was the Kaaba (KAH•buh). This was a low, block-like building surrounded by statues of Arabian gods and goddesses. The people of Arabia worshipped many deities, but the most important was Allah. They believed that Allah was the creator. Arabs believed that a large stone inside the Kaaba came from heaven. Many pilgrims, people who travel to a holy place, visited the Kaaba.

Michael Runkel/Robert Harding World Imagery/Getty Images

✓ PROGRESS CHECK

Contrasting How did the lives of desert Arabs and town Arabs differ?

Reading HELPDESK CCSS

caravan a group of traveling merchants and animals

Reading Strategy: *Formulating Questions*

Asking questions can help you understand and remember what you read. Read about the life of Muhammad. On a separate sheet of paper, write down two or three questions that you would like answered.

Academic Vocabulary (Tier 2 Words)

authority power over thoughts, opinions, and behavior

networks Online Teaching Options

WORKSHEET

Geography and History Activity: Islamic Civilization: A New Faith

Interpreting Tell students that the way people live in the Arabian Peninsula has changed over time. The people of Arabia once depended on trade for their livelihood, but today the economy of the peninsula depends on oil.

Assign the Geography and History Activity worksheet as homework.

See page 395C for other online activities.

ANSWERS, p. 400

✓ PROGRESS CHECK Desert Arabs were nomads who traveled from oasis to oasis. The town Arabs were farmers or merchants who stayed in one place.

Reading Strategy Students may ask questions about Muhammad's personal life, such as the following: *Was he married? Did he have children? What did Muhammad look like? How did he feel about being called to preach?*

Muhammad and His Message

GUIDING QUESTION *What message did Muhammad preach to the people of Arabia?*

Trade increased the contact between Arabs and other civilizations. Life in Arabia changed as people were exposed to new ideas. Arabs searched for ways to deal with these new challenges. Their search paved the way for the rise of Islam.

Who Was Muhammad?

V

The religion of Islam arose in the Arabian Peninsula in the A.D. 600s. Islam grew from the preachings of a man named Muhammad (moh•HAH•muhd). Muhammad was born into a merchant family in Makkah in A.D. 570. He was orphaned at the age of five or six. As a teenager, Muhammad worked as a caravan leader and eventually became a merchant.

R

Despite his success, Muhammad was troubled by many things he saw around him, including the greed of Makkah's wealthy citizens. He despised their dishonesty, neglect of the poor, and disregard for family life. Seeking guidance, he spent time alone praying in a cave outside the city.

Muslim tradition says that in A.D. 610, Muhammad had a vision in which a voice called him to preach Islam. Islam means "surrendering [to the will of Allah]." In the Arabic language, Allah is the word for "God." Three times the voice said, "Recite!" When Muhammad asked what he should recite, the voice said:

PRIMARY SOURCE

> “Recite in the name of your Lord Who created, created man from a clot of congealed [thickened] blood. Recite: and your Lord is Most Generous, Who taught by the pen, taught man what he did not know.”
>
> —*Quran*, Surah 96:1-5

C

Muhammad returned to Makkah and began preaching. He told people that there was only Allah to worship, the one true God. He said they must destroy their statues of fake gods.

Muhammad also preached that people were equal in God's sight, and the rich should share their wealth with the poor. Everywhere he went, Muhammad preached that God valued good deeds. Muhammad urged people to prepare for the Day of Judgment, when God would punish evildoers and reward the just.

Muhammad's Opponents

The first people to become Muslims, or followers of Islam, were Muhammad's family members. Slowly, Muhammad won the support of the poor, who were attracted to his message of sharing. Most wealthy merchants and religious leaders, however, thought Muhammad was trying to destroy their **authority.**

BIOGRAPHY

Muhammad (A.D. 570–632)

The tomb of the prophet Muhammad is a holy place to Muslims. During Muhammad's lifetime, he was well known for fairly resolving disputes among his followers. According to Islamic tradition, when Muhammad was asked to resolve which tribe would have the honor to place the holy black stone in the corner of the rebuilt Kaaba, Muhammad put his cloak on the ground with the stone in the center and had each tribe lift a corner to bring the stone to the correct height to be placed in the Kaaba. Muhammad's legacy has made a major impact on the world.

▶ CRITICAL THINKING

Drawing Conclusions Why do you think Muhammad had each tribe carry his cloak with the holy black stone?

R Reading Skills

Explaining After reading the passage, ask students to explain why Muhammad was uneasy about some things that were happening in Makkah. **Ask:** What troubled Muhammad about the things he saw around him in Makkah? *(that there was greed and dishonesty, neglect of the poor, and disregard for family life)* How did this relate to the message he preached to the people of Arabia? *(His message said that people were equal in God's sight, that the rich should share with the poor, and that God valued good deeds.)*

C Critical Thinking Skills

Comparing and Contrasting Discuss with students the things that Muhammad preached and the main ideas of his message. Tell students to think about the other religions they know about or have read about. **Ask:** What are some of the things that Islam has in common with the precepts, or main ideas, behind these other religions? *(The focus on one God, on the importance of family and good deeds, and on helping the poor are similar to Judaism.)* What makes Islam different from other religions? *(Muslims call their God* Allah*; there is a day of judgment.)* ELL

V Visual Skills

Creating Flowcharts Have students create a flowchart that outlines the sequence of events on this page, from Muhammad's birth through his preaching of Islam. Instruct students to include dates on their flowcharts. **Visual/Spatial**

SLIDE SHOW

Sacred Muslim Sites

Explaining Show students the interactive slide show about sacred Muslim sites. **Ask:** Why is the Mosque of the Prophet important? *(It was built by the prophet Muhammad after his Hijrah to Madinah.)* What is significant about the Dome of the Rock? *(It is sacred to Muslims and Jews.)* Discuss with students the different sites and what makes each important. **Visual/Spatial**

See page 395C for other online activities.

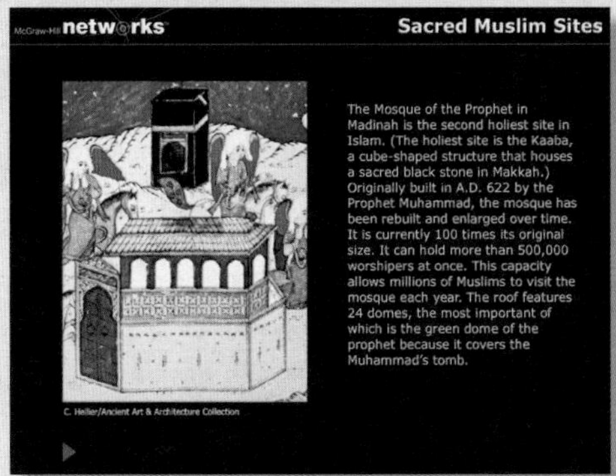

McGraw-Hill networks
Sacred Muslim Sites
The Mosque of the Prophet in Madinah is the second holiest site in Islam. (The holiest site is the Kaaba, a cube-shaped structure that houses a sacred black stone in Makkah.) Originally built in A.D. 622 by the Prophet Muhammad, the mosque has been rebuilt and enlarged over time. It is currently 100 times its original size. It can hold more than 500,000 worshipers at once. This capacity allows millions of Muslims to visit the mosque each year. The roof features 24 domes, the most important of which is the green dome of the prophet because it covers the Muhammad's tomb.
C. Heller/Ancient Art & Architecture Collection

ANSWER, p. 401

CRITICAL THINKING Muhammad wanted to show that the tribes were all equal in status and honor.

A New Faith

R1 Reading Skills

Explaining Ask students to use what they read on the previous page to answer this question. **Ask:** **Why did Makkah become too dangerous for Muhammad and his followers to stay?** *(because there were opponents there who did not like him)* **Why did some people not like Muhammad?** *(Rich merchants and religious leaders felt that he was threatening their authority.)* AL

C Critical Thinking Skills

Making Connections Ask students to share their reactions to the results of recent elections or any experiences they have had when joining or taking part in a religion that was new to them. **Ask:** **What are some reasons that people would support a new religious and political leader or a new religion?** *(They may feel inspired by the person and their new ideas, experience a sense of hope and a connection with others, and feel that they belong to an exciting new cause.)* **What are some reasons they might oppose a new religious and political leader or a new religion?** *(They may feel threatened by the new ideas or the person, may feel that their wealth or power is in jeopardy, or may be afraid of change.)* Have students compare these reactions with the reactions of people in modern situations who are faced with new things.

R2 Reading Skills

Summarizing Ask students to state the main idea of the section called "The Islamic State" and to identify three supporting details in the section. Have students use the main idea and details in writing a short summary of the section. **Verbal/Linguistic**

Thousands of Muslim pilgrims surround the Kaaba in Makkah. A call to worship on special days draws thousands of people.

▶ **CRITICAL THINKING**

Making Inferences Why do you think the Muslim calendar begins with the year of the Hijrah?

R1 In A.D. 622, Muhammad and his followers believed Makkah had become too dangerous. They moved to Yathrib (YA•thruhb). Muhammad's departure to Yathrib became known as the Hijrah (HIHJ•ruh). This Arabic word means "breaking off relationships." The year of the Hijrah later became the first year of the Muslim calendar. The people of Yathrib accepted Muhammad as God's prophet and their ruler. They renamed their city Madinah (mah•DEE•nah), which means "the city of the prophet."

The Islamic State

C R2 Muhammad was a skilled political and religious leader. He applied the laws he believed God had given him to all areas of life. He used these laws to settle disputes among the people. Muhammad also established the foundation for an Islamic state. The government of the state used its political power to uphold Islam. Muhammad required all Muslims to place loyalty to the Islamic state above loyalty to their tribes.

Muhammad formed an army to protect his new state. In a series of battles, Muhammad's soldiers regained Makkah and made it a holy city of Islam. The Muslims then began to expand into new areas. When Muhammad died in A.D. 632, the entire Arabian Peninsula was part of the Islamic state.

☑ **PROGRESS CHECK**

Analyzing Why did Makkah's merchants and religious leaders oppose Muhammad and his message?

(l) Marwan Naamani/AFP/Getty Images, (r) AFP/Getty Images

Reading HELPDESK CCSS

Quran the holy book of Islam

shari'ah Islamic code of law

networks Online Teaching Options

DIAGRAM

The Kaaba

Identifying Allow students to explore the interactive diagram about the Kaaba. **Ask:** **What is the significance of the black stone?** *(Some Muslims believe it was given to Adam when he left the Garden of Eden, and it turned black when it absorbed the sins of the many pilgrims.)* Discuss with students what they believe are the most significant aspects of the Kaaba. **Visual/Spatial**

See page 395C for other online activities.

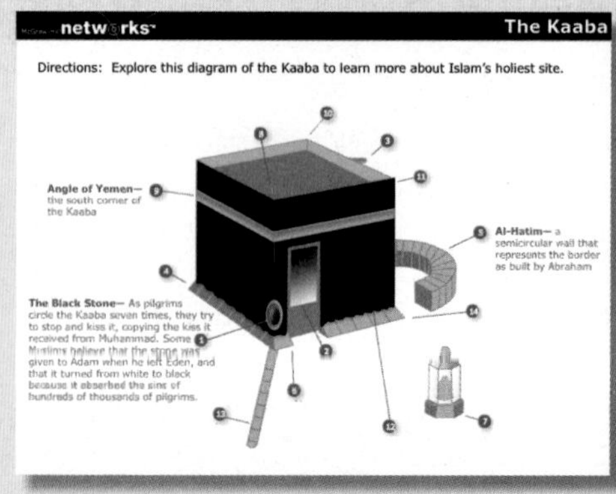

ANSWERS, p. 402

CRITICAL THINKING Students may say the Muslim calendar begins with the year of the Hijrah because the Hijrah marks the beginning of the Islamic state or the beginning of the spread of Islam outside of Makkah.

☑ **PROGRESS CHECK** Makkah's merchants and religious leaders thought Muhammad was trying to destroy their authority.

Beliefs and Practices of Islam

GUIDING QUESTION *How does Islam provide guidance to its followers?*

Islam shares some beliefs with Judaism and Christianity. Like Jews and Christians, Muslims are monotheists. Muslims believe in one all-powerful God who created the universe. They believe that God decides what is right and wrong.

Like Jews and Christians, Muslims believe that God spoke to people through prophets. For Muslims, these prophets include Adam, Abraham, Moses, Jesus, and Muhammad. In Islam, Muhammad is seen as the last and the greatest of the prophets.

The Quran

C

According to Muslim belief, Muhammad received messages from Allah for more than 20 years. These messages were not gathered into a written collection until after Muhammad died. This collection became the **Quran** (kuh•RAN), or holy book of Islam. Muslims believe the Quran is the written word of God. It contains accounts of events, teachings, and instructions.

For Muslims, the Quran provides guidelines for how to live. For example, the Quran instructs Muslims to be honest and treat others fairly. Muslims must respect their parents and be kind to their neighbors. The Quran forbids murder, lying, and stealing.

Islam stresses the need to obey the will of Allah. This means practicing acts of worship known as the Five Pillars of Islam. The Five Pillars are belief, prayer, charity, fasting, and pilgrimage.

Over centuries, Islamic scholars created a code of law called the ***shari'ah*** (shuh•REE•uh). *Shari'ah* is based on the Quran. According to *shari'ah*, Muslims may not gamble, eat pork, or drink alcoholic beverages. The *sunna* also guides Muslims. It is a set of customs based on Muhammad's words and deeds.

PROGRESS CHECK

Evaluating Why is the Quran important in the daily life of Muslims?

Thinking Like a HISTORIAN

Using a Time Line

Many important events led Muhammad to establish Islam. Select three events from his life that you consider important to his founding of Islam. Sequence them on a time line, and present your time line to the class. Be sure to explain your choices in your presentation. For more information about time lines, read *What Does a Historian Do?*

LESSON 1 REVIEW (CCSS)

Review Vocabulary (Tier 3 Words)

1. Why would the people in a *caravan* be glad to see an *oasis*? RH.6–8.2, RH.6–8.4

Answer the Guiding Questions

2. ***Determining Cause and Effect*** How did physical geography shape life in Arabia? RH.6–8.2, RH.6–8.5
3. ***Explaining*** Why did Muhammad and his followers move to Madinah? RH.6–8.2
4. ***Describing*** What is the *shari'ah* and what is it based on? RH.6–8.2
5. ***NARRATIVE*** Imagine that you are a bedouin. Write a letter to a friend who lives in Makkah describing a day in your life. WHST.6–8.10

LESSON 1 REVIEW ANSWERS

1. Caravans travel through the hot, dry desert, and an oasis is a place where water is available.
2. The terrain of the desert was extremely harsh, and it was necessary to join with others in groups in order to survive. The Arabs formed tribes in which people were loyal to one another and helped one another. Tribes are still important to the Arab way of life.
3. Muhammad and his followers moved to Madinah because they believed it was too dangerous for them to stay in Makkah.
4. The shari'ah is a code of law that provides Muslims with a set of practical laws for daily life. It is based on the Quran.
5. Students' letters should mention the bedouin way of living as well as the heat of the desert.

C Critical Thinking Skills

Making Connections Review the Five Pillars of Islam and the guidelines for how to live provided by the Quran. Point out to students that all religions have traditions, rules, and ways of worshiping. **Ask:** **How does Islam provide guidance to its followers? Do other religions have similar guidelines for religious practice? What are they?** *(Students may mention the Ten Commandments in Judaism and Christianity, the Eightfold Path in Buddhism, and so on.)* ELL **Interpersonal**

V Visual Skills

Collaborating Divide students into groups of five, and give each group a poster board or a large piece of butcher paper. Have each group create a graphic organizer or other visual representation of the Five Pillars of Islam. AL ELL

Have students complete the Lesson 1 Review.

CLOSE & REFLECT

Have students discuss how the spread of a religion can change people's way of life. Ask students to predict how the spread of Islam will change the way of life in and around the Arabian Peninsula. Guide students to use what they already learned about the spread of Judaism, Christianity, Hinduism, and Buddhism, as well as their knowledge of Arabia, as the basis of their predictions. Moderate a class discussion.

ANSWER, p. 403

PROGRESS CHECK The Quran provides guidelines on how to live.

ENGAGE

Bellringer Show a world map. Tell students that Islam spread from the Arabian Peninsula to countries throughout the world. Ask students to name a country that is not on the Arabian Peninsula but where people follow Islam. Have students brainstorm how Islam could have spread to so many places. Record their ideas. Tell students that in this lesson they are going to learn that the Arabs spread Islam and created an empire through teaching, trade, and conquest.

TEACH & ASSESS

V Visual Skills

Creating Charts Discuss the sequence of historical events listed that caused other events to happen, such as Muhammad's death leading to the Arabians' choosing a new type of leader, called the caliph. Have students develop a cause-and-effect chart, listing in one column the events that occurred on this page and, in the other column, their effects. Challenge students to list at least four events and four effects. **Visual/Spatial**

R Reading Skills

Citing Text Evidence Have students cite evidence from the text to answer the following question. **Ask: How did the Arabs spread Islam and create an empire?** *(The text states that military forces carried Islam beyond the Arabian Peninsula. It then states that the Umayyads extended Muslim rule farther into Asia and Africa.)*

ANSWER, p. 404

TAKING NOTES: Teaching, Trade, and Conquest

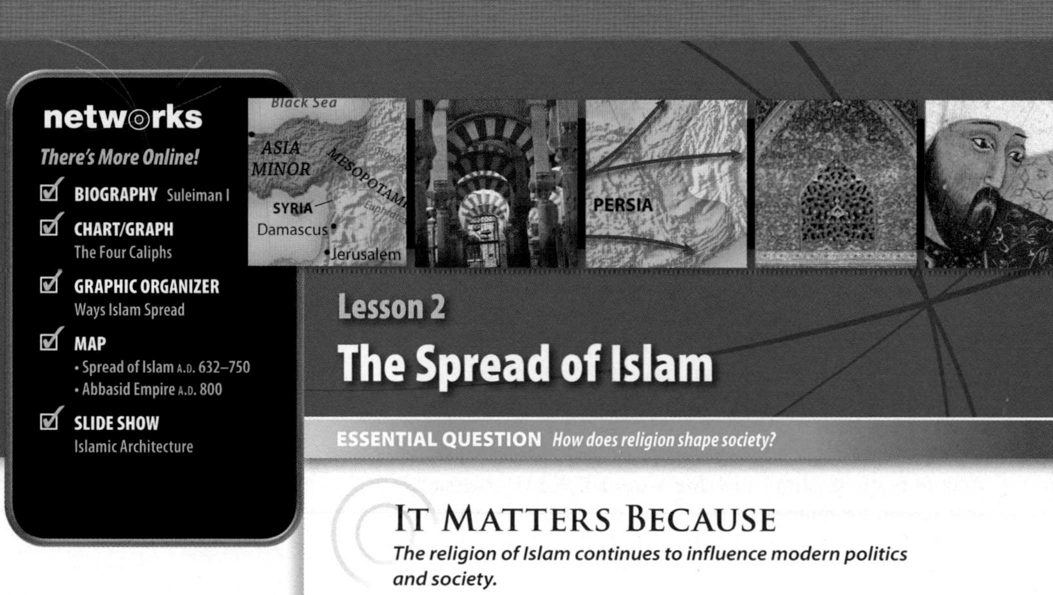

networks
There's More Online!

- **BIOGRAPHY** Suleiman I
- **CHART/GRAPH** The Four Caliphs
- **GRAPHIC ORGANIZER** Ways Islam Spread
- **MAP** • Spread of Islam A.D. 632–750 • Abbasid Empire A.D. 800
- **SLIDE SHOW** Islamic Architecture

Lesson 2

The Spread of Islam

ESSENTIAL QUESTION *How does religion shape society?*

It Matters Because

The religion of Islam continues to influence modern politics and society.

Founding an Empire

GUIDING QUESTION *How did the Arabs spread Islam and create an empire?*

When Muhammad died in A.D. 632, he left no instructions about who should be the next leader of Islam. Muslims knew that no person could take Muhammad's role as a prophet. They realized, however, that the Islamic state needed a strong leader to keep it united. A group of Muslim leaders chose a new type of leader called the **caliph** (KAY•luhf), or "successor."

The First Caliphs

The first four caliphs were close friends or relatives of Muhammad. The goal of the caliphs was to protect and spread Islam. Their military forces carried Islam beyond the Arabian Peninsula. Because the Muslim conquerors were Arab, the territory became known as the Arab Empire. By the 660s, the Arab Empire included all of southwest Asia and northeast Africa.

The Umayyads

Expansion continued under new caliphs known as the Umayyads (oo•MY•uhds). The Umayyads governed the Arab Empire from the city of Damascus (duh•MAS•kuhs) in Syria. They ruled from 661 to 750. Under the Umayyads, Muslim rule extended farther into Asia and Africa.

Reading HELPDESK (CCSS)

Taking Notes: *Summarizing*

On a diagram like this one, describe the ways in which the religion of Islam spread. RH.6–8.2

Ways Islam Spread

Content Vocabulary (Tier 3 Words)

• caliph • Sunni • Shia • sultan

caliph a Muslim leader

networks Online Teaching Options

VIDEO

Islamic Trade Routes

Explaining Show students the video *Islamic Trade Routes,* which depicts medieval Islamic civilization, focusing on the activities of Islamic traders who were part of the Golden Web. **Ask: What are some financial practices still used today that were begun by Muslim merchants?** *(banking, coins, checks)* **What does the term the Golden Web refer to?** *(the web of trade routes)* **Why do you think they termed the trade routes the Golden Web?** *(perhaps because it related to money)* **Visual/Spatial**

See page 395D for other online activities.

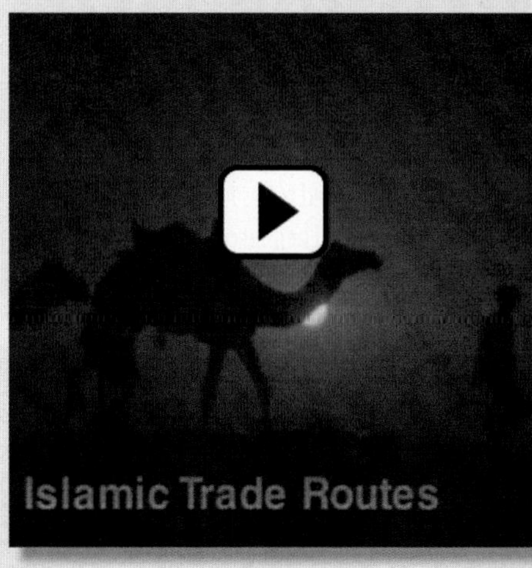

R
A century after the death of Muhammad, Muslims had created a large and powerful empire. Arab soldiers were experienced horse riders and warriors, having raided rival tribes in the past. Now they used those same skills to fight large armies. In addition, Arab soldiers believed they had a religious duty to spread Islam.

The policies of their opponents also helped the Muslims. Byzantine and Persian rulers had tried to unite their peoples under an official religion. They often mistreated those who practiced other faiths. When Muslim armies attacked, many of these people were willing to accept Muslim rule.

W
After the Arabs gained control, they usually let conquered peoples practice their own religions. Islam teaches that Christians and Jews are "People of the Book," people who believe in one God and follow sacred writings. Therefore, many Muslims respect their beliefs and practices. As time passed, many of the conquered peoples in the Arab Empire became Muslims and learned the Arab language. The customs of the conquered peoples also influenced the Arab rulers. Eventually, the term *Arab* meant a speaker of Arabic, not a resident of Arabia.

Islamic Spain

Muslim warriors entered Spain from North Africa in the early 700s. They brought their religion, customs, and traditions. Spanish Muslims made the city of Córdoba a center of Islam.

Spain was home to many of Islam's greatest thinkers. Ibn Rushd (IH•buhn RUHSHT), also known as Averroës (uh•VEHR•uh•weez), practiced law and medicine in Córdoba.

GEOGRAPHY CONNECTION

After Muhammad's death, the territory of the Arab Empire expanded.

1. **MOVEMENT** What area of Europe came under Muslim control?
2. **PLACE** Describe the territories conquered by the Arabs by the year A.D. 661.
3. **CRITICAL THINKING** ***Making Connections*** Why do you think Muslim armies entered Europe from North Africa and not through Asia Minor?

V
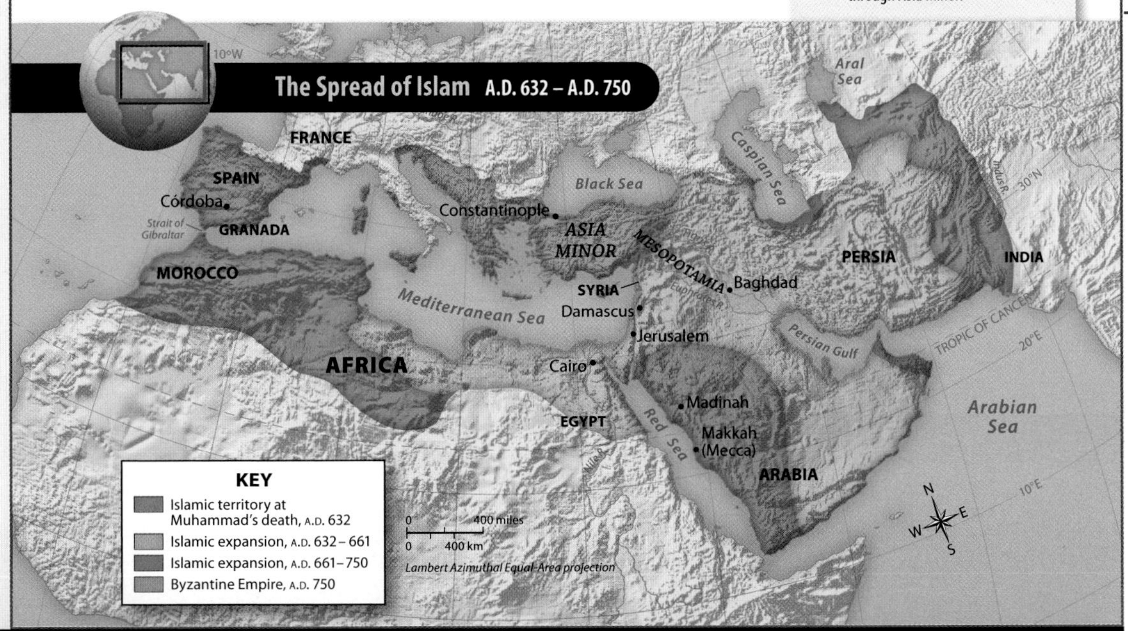

CHAPTER 14, Lesson 2
The Spread of Islam

V Visual Skills

Analyzing Maps Have students study the map on this page titled "The Spread of Islam, A.D. 632–A.D. 750." Discuss as a class what happened in Islam after Muhammad died. **Ask:** **What happened to the empire when the Umayyads took control?** *(They continued the expansion of the Arab Empire through conquest.)* **Based on this information, what do you predict will happen next in the spread of Islam?** *(It will continue to spread outward.)* **Visual/Spatial**

R Reading Skills

Listing Have students use details from the text to list the qualities of the Muslims that led them to create a large and powerful empire. *(They were experienced soldiers with good skills and believed that this was their religious duty. They let conquered people practice their own religion in comparison with opponents who treated people of other religions badly.)*
AL Verbal/Linguistic

W Writing Skills

Argument Ask students to consider the positive and negative consequences of the way the Muslims created their empire and spread their religion. Have students write an essay stating their opinions and supporting their arguments with evidence from the text. Have students share their essays with the class. Discuss different perspectives.

MAP

The Spread of Islam A.D. 632–A.D. 750

Analyzing Visuals Have students study the map showing the early spread of Islam. **Ask:** **The religion of Islam was being practiced in how many different countries by A.D. 750?** *(at least 10)* **Can you name them?** *(Persia, Arabia, Egypt, Syria, Morocco, Spain, Grenada, France, Mesopotamia, Asia Minor)*
Visual/Spatial

See page 395D for other online activities.

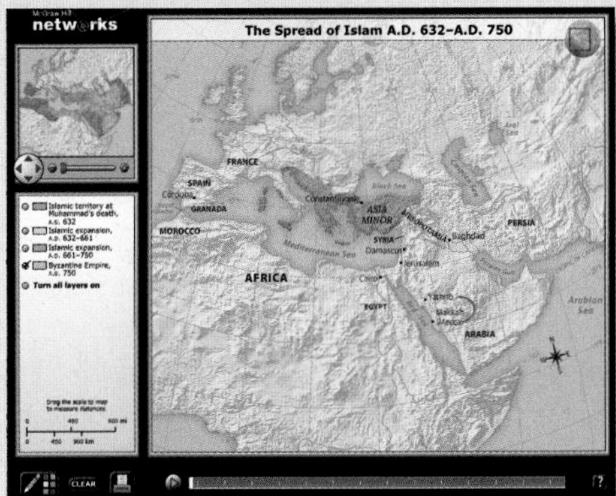

ANSWERS, p. 405

GEOGRAPHY CONNECTION

1. Spain came under Muslim control.
2. The territories were north, west, and east of Arab territory as of A.D. 632. They included the entire Arabian Peninsula, Egypt, Mesopotamia, and Persia.
3. **CRITICAL THINKING** The Byzantine Empire blocked access to Europe through Asia Minor.

The Spread of Islam

C Critical Thinking Skills

Comparing Show students the chart on the first four caliphs. **Ask:** What did the first four caliphs who ruled have in common? *(Each one was a close friend or relative of Muhammad.)* What were two common characteristics of the rule of the caliphs? *(They wanted to protect and spread Islam. They conquered lands beyond Arabia.)* ELL

R1 Reading Skills

Explaining Ask students to read the section about Muslims, Christians, and Jews in Spain. Then lead a discussion about the impact of Muslim expansion into Spain. **Ask:** How did Muslim expansion into Spain affect the Jews and Christians who lived there? *(Jews and Christians were accepted and often studied medicine and philosophy with Muslims.)* BL

R2 Reading Skills

Finding the Main Idea Read the section titled "Preachers and Traders" with students. Have students write the main idea of this section and two supporting details. AL
Verbal/Linguistic

ANSWERS, p. 406

CHART

1. Uthman's reign was the longest. Abu Bakr had the shortest reign.
2. CRITICAL THINKING Ali was a soldier and a writer rather than a merchant. He was also the first cousin of Muhammad.

THE FIRST FOUR CALIPHS

	Abu Bakr	Umar	Uthman	Ali
Relationship to Muhammad	father-in-law	friend	son-in-law, member of the Umayyad family	first cousin, son-in-law
Career	merchant	merchant	merchant	soldier, writer
Years as Caliph	A.D. 632–634	A.D. 634–644	A.D. 644–656	A.D. 656–661
Achievements as Caliph	spread Islam to all of Arabia; restored peace after death of Muhammad; created code of conduct in war; compiled Quran verses	spread Islam to Syria, Egypt, and Persia; redesigned government; paid soldiers; held a census; made taxes more fair; built roads and canals; aided poor	spread Islam into Afghanistan and eastern Mediterranean; organized a navy; improved the government; built more roads, bridges, and canals; distributed text of the Quran	reformed tax collection and other government systems; spent most of caliphate battling Muawiya, the governor of Syria

CHART

1. **IDENTIFYING** Which caliph ruled the longest? Whose rule was the shortest?
2. CRITICAL THINKING *Contrasting* How was Ali different from the other caliphs?

He is best known for his writings based on the works of the Greek philosopher Aristotle. Ibn Rushd's work influenced Christian and Jewish thinkers in Europe during the Middle Ages.

Muslims in Spain were generally tolerant, or accepting, of other cultures. In some schools, Muslims, Jews, and Christians studied medicine and philosophy together. In particular, the Jewish community in Córdoba flourished.

A Jewish scholar in Spain, Solomon ben Gabirol, wrote philosophy and poetry. His most famous book of philosophy, *The Well of Life*, shows the influence of the Greek philosophers. The book was translated from Arabic into Latin and influenced many philosophers in Christian Europe.

Another Jewish thinker called Moses Maimonides (my•MAHN•ih•deez) had to leave Spain at a very young age because it was conquered by an intolerant Muslim group. He later became a physician in the Muslim royal court in Egypt and wrote philosophy as well as a collection of Jewish laws.

Preachers and Traders

Muslim armies were not the only ones who spread Islam. Some Muslims used preaching to win followers to their religion. A group called Sufis (SOO•feez) won followers by teaching Islam.

Muslim merchants built trading posts throughout Southeast Asia and taught Islam to the people there. Today, the country of Indonesia (ihn•duh•NEE•zhuh) has more Muslims than any other nation in the world.

Reading HELPDESK CCSS

networks Online Teaching Options

CHART

The Four Caliphs

Categorizing Have students read the information on the interactive chart. Discuss the types of achievements each caliph had. Ask students to think of categories that would describe each type of achievement. Have students make a chart and place each achievement into a category? *(Categories could include spreading Islam, governing the people, education/religious practice, military conquest, and improving daily life and infrastructure.)* **Visual/Spatial**

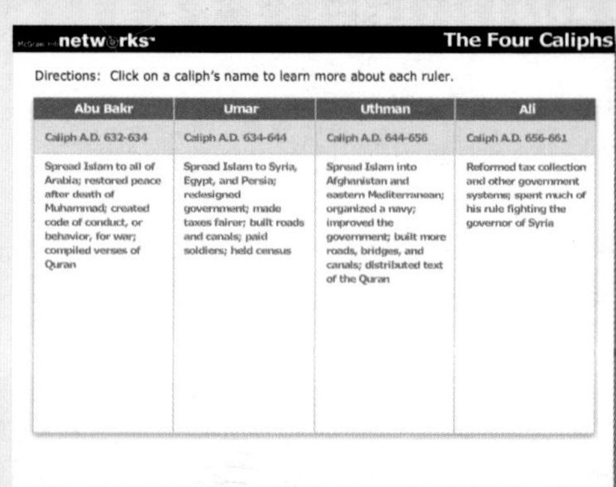

See page 395D for other online activities.

Some Muslim merchants crossed the Sahara to trade with powerful kingdoms in West Africa. In the 1300s, the West African city of Timbuktu (tihm•buhk•TOO) became a leading center of Muslim culture and learning.

✓ PROGRESS CHECK

Explaining Why was the Arab military successful?

Division and Growth

GUIDING QUESTION *How did the Arab Empire change after the Umayyads?*

While Arab Muslims created an empire, rival groups within Islam argued about who had the right to succeed Muhammad as caliph. Muslims divided into two groups, the **Sunni** (SU•nee) and the **Shia** (SHEE•ah). This split still divides Muslims today. Most Muslims are Sunni. Shia Muslims, however, make up most of the populations in present-day Iran and Iraq.

The Shia believed that Ali, Muhammad's son-in-law, was his rightful heir. They also believed that all future caliphs had to be Ali's descendants. According to the Shia, the Umayyad caliphs in Damascus had no right to rule. The Sunni, who outnumbered the Shia, disagreed. They recognized the Umayyad caliphs as rightful rulers, though they did not always agree with their actions.

The Shia and the Sunni agreed on the major **principles** of Islam. They both believed that there was only one God. They also believed in the Quran as Islam's holy book and the Five Pillars of Islam. In other ways, the two groups developed different religious practices and customs.

Muslim architecture can still be found in many parts of Spain today. The high interior arches, decorative columns, and bright colors are all details of Muslim design.

▶ CRITICAL THINKING

Drawing Conclusions Why was Spain home to many of Islam's great thinkers?

Fernando Fernandez/age fotostock

A New Dynasty

During the 700s, opposition to the Umayyad caliphs grew. Many non-Arab Muslims were angry that Arab Muslims had the best jobs and paid lower taxes. Discontent was especially strong in Mesopotamia and Persia, where Shia Islam was popular.

About 750, the Shia Muslims rebelled and won support from other Muslims throughout the empire. They overthrew the Umayyads, and the Abbasid (uh•BA•suhd) dynasty came to power. Abbasid caliphs ruled the Arab Empire until 1258.

Sunni group of Muslims who accepted the rule of the Umayyad caliphs

Shia group of Muslims who believed the descendants of Ali should rule

Academic Vocabulary (Tier 2 Words)

principle an important law or belief

C Critical Thinking Skills

Analyzing Text Read the section titled "Division and Growth" with students. **Ask:** What is the main way in which the text in this section is organized: sequence, compare and contrast, or cause and effect? *(compare and contrast)*

W Writing Skills

Informative/Explanatory Have students take notes from the text's explanation of the Sunni and Shia divisions and then supplement their knowledge by finding information on the Internet. Instruct students to write an explanatory essay to detail the similarities and differences of the Sunni and Shia Muslims. Ask pairs to critique each other's essays, looking for organization and clarity. BL **Verbal/Linguistic**

R Reading Skills

Explaining Before students read the text, encourage them to consider the factors and conditions that might cause a group of people to enter a rebellion. **Ask:** Why did the Shia Muslims rebel? *(They were angry that Arab Muslims had the best jobs and paid lower taxes, especially in Mesopotamia and Persia.)* What events did the rebellion of the Shia Muslims cause? *(the overthrowing of the Umayyads and the coming to power of the Abbasid dynasty)* **Verbal/Linguistic**

SLIDE SHOW

Islamic Architecture

Creating Visuals Have students look at the slide show and read the information. **Ask:** What lasting impact did Islam have on Spanish culture? *(Many buildings, especially those in Córdoba, have features of Islamic architecture.)* What are some features that characterize Muslim architecture? *(courtyards, columns, arches)* Have students use pencil and paper to design a building of their own with elements of Muslim architecture. **Visual/Spatial**

See page 395D for other online activities.

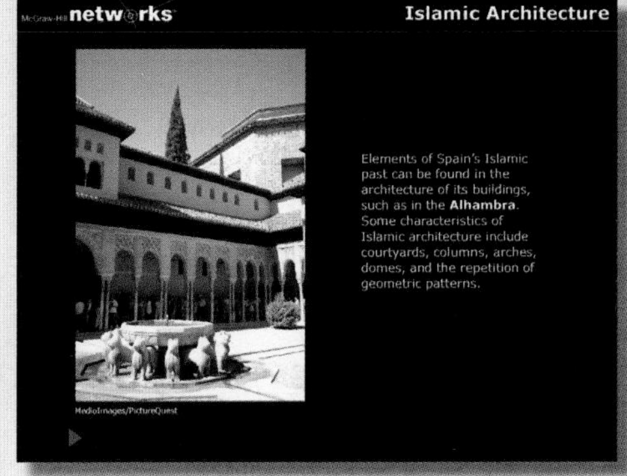

networks
Islamic Architecture
Elements of Spain's Islamic past can be found in the architecture of its buildings, such as in the Alhambra. Some characteristics of Islamic architecture include courtyards, columns, arches, domes, and the repetition of geometric patterns.

ANSWERS, p. 407

✓ PROGRESS CHECK Arab soldiers were good riders and warriors. They applied the skills they had used on tribal raids to fight large armies. They believed they had a religious duty to spread Islam.

CRITICAL THINKING Spain was home to many of Islam's great thinkers because the Muslim rulers of Spain created an atmosphere of religious tolerance where learning was encouraged.

V Visual Skills

Analyzing Images Have students study the map showing the Abbasid Empire in A.D. 800. Ask them to use what they've learned from the image and the text to identify factors that may have contributed to the fall of the Abbasid Empire. *(The region was very spread out, and the Abbasids may not have been able to keep control; this may have caused the Abbasids' followers to want to find their own rulers.)* **Visual/Spatial**

T Technology Skills

Making Presentations Using presentation software, have students create a time line with dates, pictures, and information they've found on the Internet, outlining the rule of the Abbasids, the breaking free of other territories, and the Seljuk Turks' seizing of Baghdad and coming to power. Have students share their time lines with the class. BL **Visual/Spatial**

C Critical Thinking Skills

Making Inferences Discuss the period when the Seljuk Turks moved into Abbasid territory. **Ask: Do you think the Seljuk Turks had more power, or did the Abbasids—who controlled religious matters—have more power?** *(Some students might mention the idea that the Seljuk Turks held more power, but other students might say the Abbasids—who controlled a religion that spread easily—had more power.)* Have students discuss what factors they took into account when making their inferences.

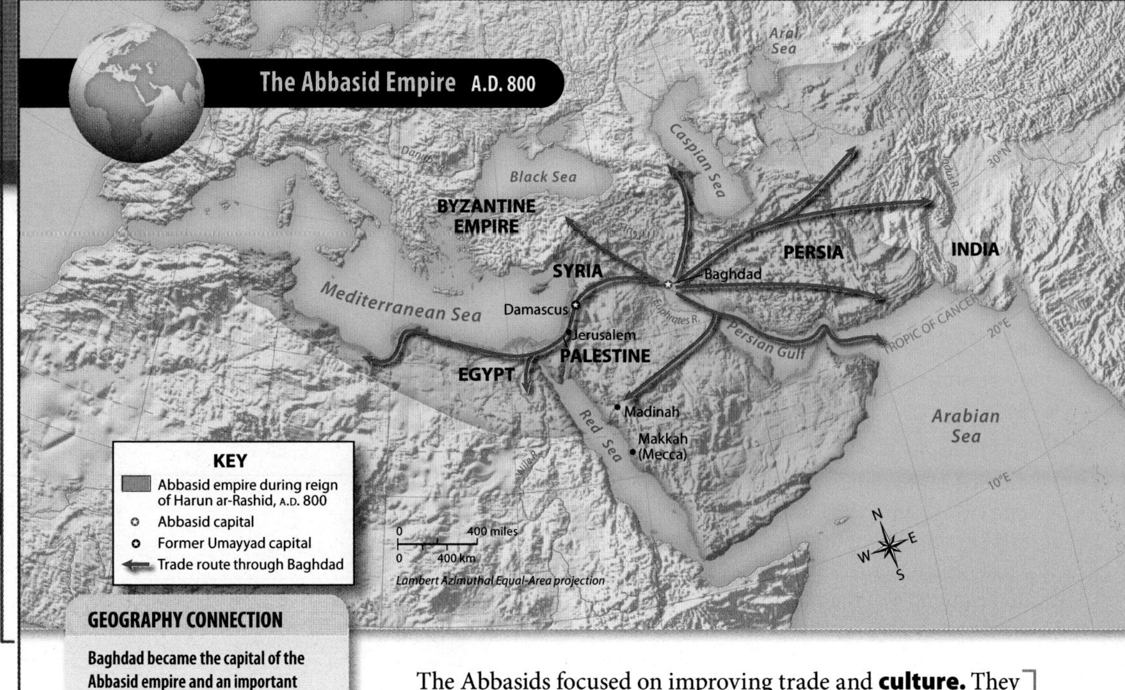

GEOGRAPHY CONNECTION

Baghdad became the capital of the Abbasid empire and an important center for trade.

1. **REGIONS** What blocked Abbasid expansion to the northwest?
2. **CRITICAL THINKING** *Evaluating* Does Baghdad appear to be well located for trade? Explain.

The Abbasids focused on improving trade and **culture.** They made Baghdad (BAG•dad) their capital city. Baghdad's location along the Tigris River was on trade routes that connected the Mediterranean Sea to East Asia. By the 900s, Baghdad was one of the world's most beautiful and prosperous cities.

Under Abbasid rule, the Arab Empire enjoyed a golden age. The Abbasids appreciated Persian culture and brought many Persian influences into the Arab Empire.

Who are the Seljuk Turks?

The Abbasids developed a rich culture, but they could not hold their empire together. Over time, many territories broke free from Abbasid rule. In Egypt and Spain, the Muslims set up their own caliphs. Rival rulers took over much of Persia. By the 1000s, the Abbasids ruled little more than the area around Baghdad.

Around this time, the Seljuk Turks of central Asia began moving into Abbasid territory. The Seljuk Turks were nomads and great warriors. In 1055, the Seljuks seized Baghdad. They took control of the government and army but allowed the Abbasid caliph to manage religious matters. The Seljuk ruler called himself **sultan** (SUHL•tuhn), or "holder of power."

Reading HELPDESK CCSS

sultan Seljuk leader

Academic Vocabulary (Tier 2 Words)

culture the customs, art, science, and learning of a group of people

networks Online Teaching Options

MAP

The Abbasid Empire A.D. 800

Analyzing Visuals Have students study the map of the Abbasid Empire. **Ask: Why do you think the Abbasids chose Baghdad as their capital? What is special about its location?** *(It is a central location.)* **Which cultures did the Abbasids strive to bring together?** *(Arabs, Muslims, and Persians)*

See page 395D for other online activities.

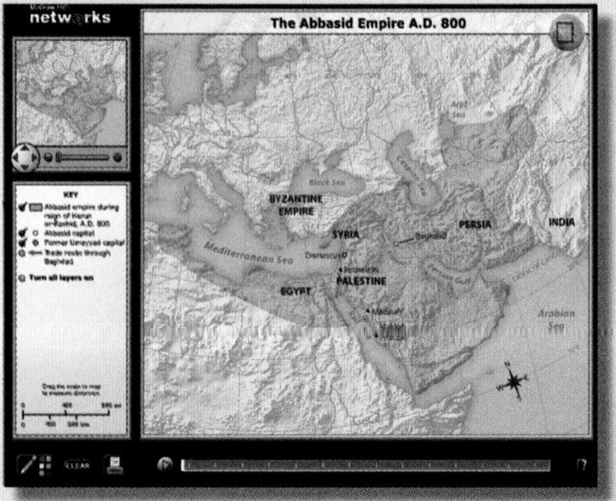

ANSWERS, p. 408

GEOGRAPHY CONNECTION

1. The Byzantine Empire blocked Abbasid expansion to the northwest.
2. **CRITICAL THINKING** Yes; Baghdad is centrally located and well positioned for the trade between Asia and the Mediterranean.

For 200 years, Seljuk sultans ruled with the Abbasid caliphs. Then, in the 1200s, people from central Asia, known as the Mongols, swept into the empire. In 1258 they stormed into Baghdad. There, the Mongols burned buildings and killed more than 50,000 people. This fierce attack brought an end to the Arab Empire. G1

✓ PROGRESS CHECK

Comparing and Contrasting How did the Sunni and Shia differ? What beliefs did they share?

Three Muslim Empires

GUIDING QUESTION *How did the Turks, Safavids, and Moguls rule their empires?*

After the Arab Empire ended, other Muslim groups created their own empires. These empires included the Ottoman Empire based in what is now Turkey, the Safavid (sah•FAH•weed) Empire in Persia, and the Mogul Empire in India.

The Ottomans

C2 During the late 1200s, Turkish clans settled part of Asia Minor. They called themselves Ottoman Turks, after their leader named Osman. The Ottomans conquered much of the Byzantine Empire. In 1453, the Ottoman ruler Mehmet II, known as "the Conqueror," seized the Byzantine capital, Constantinople. The Ottomans renamed the city Istanbul and made it their capital.

The Ottomans then pushed into southeastern Europe, Southwest Asia, and North Africa. The Ottomans controlled much of the Mediterranean region until the late 1500s.

The Ottoman leader was called a sultan, like the leader of the Seljuks. The most famous Ottoman sultan was Suleiman I (SOO•luh•mahn). He ruled during the 1500s. He was called "The Lawgiver" because he organized Ottoman laws. Suleiman also built many schools and mosques throughout the empire. W

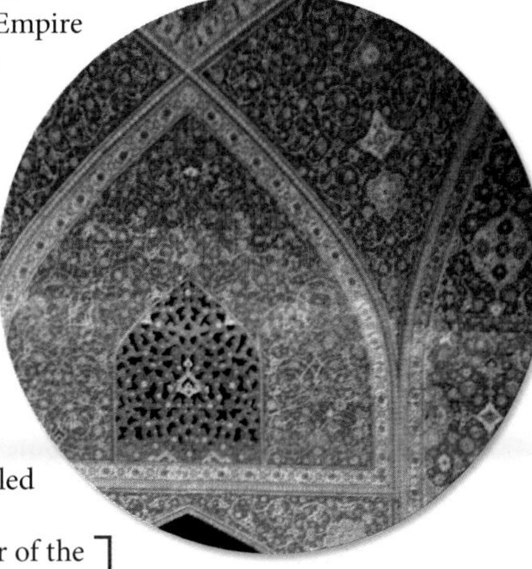

The Shah Mosque in Isfahan, Iran, shows traditional Muslim architecture. It is known for its internal design featuring mosaic tiles.

(l) James P. Blair/National Geographic (r) Arthur Thévenart/CORBIS

Lesson 2 409

CHAPTER 14, Lesson 2
The Spread of Islam

G1 Critical Thinking Skills

Identifying Cause and Effect Read about the period when the Seljuk sultans and Abbasid caliphs ruled Baghdad together. **Ask:** **What eventually happened to the joint rule of the empire?** *(Another group, the Mongols from central Asia, burned Baghdad and ended the Arab Empire in 1258.)* AL

C2 Critical Thinking Skills

Analyzing Read the section about the Ottomans. Ask students to analyze how the text develops the idea of the Ottoman rule. **Ask:** **How does the text tell us about the development of events? What style of organization does it use?** *(sequence)* **Does the text tell about things other than events?** *(yes)* **What?** *(important people)* **What type of information does it give us about the people?** *(who they are and what they were known for)* AL

W Writing Skills

Argument Review the paragraph about the Ottoman sultan, Suleiman, who was called "The Lawgiver." **Ask:** **What accomplishments was Suleiman known for?** *(organizing Ottoman laws, building many schools and mosques)* Have students write a short argument about what they can infer about the Sultan's goals for his empire. Have them cite evidence from the text to support their arguments. **Verbal/Linguistic**

IMAGE

The Shah Mosque

Drawing Conclusions Have students read the information about the Shah Mosque and study the picture. **Ask:** **When the Muslims built this mosque, what did they hope to achieve? Why did they take the time and expense to make it so elaborate?** *(They probably wanted to honor their God and to give the people a beautiful place to pray.)*

See page 395D for other online activities.

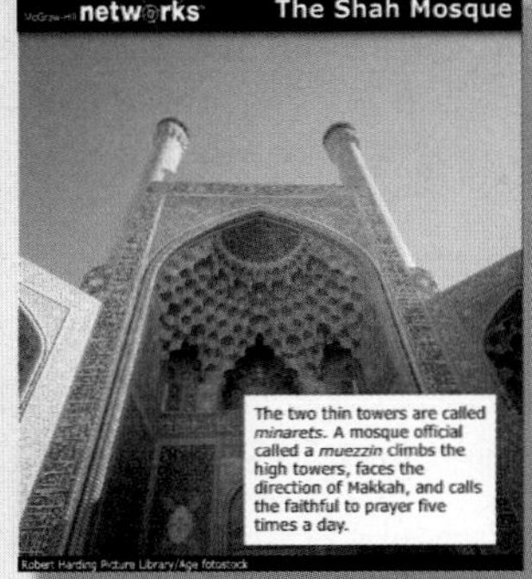

networks
The Shah Mosque
The two thin towers are called minarets. A mosque official called a muezzin climbs the high towers, faces the direction of Makkah, and calls the faithful to prayer five times a day.

ANSWER, p. 409

✓ PROGRESS CHECK The Sunni and Shia differed about who should lead Islam. They shared basic religious beliefs, such as the Five Pillars.

R Reading Skills

Explaining Have students read the section titled, "How Did Ottomans Rule?" Then ask the questions below. Encourage students to cite information from the text to support their answers. **Ask:** Why do you think non-Muslims stayed in the Ottoman Empire? *(Students should note that the Ottoman Empire was large and included many different peoples. Conquered peoples most likely wanted to remain in their homes. The Ottomans also allowed religious freedom as long as non-Muslims paid taxes.)* Do you think many people who lived in the Ottoman Empire chose to convert to Islam? Why? *(Some students might conclude that a number of people probably converted in order to enjoy the privileges that Muslims had. Other students might conclude that because non-Muslims had the freedom to practice their religion, they were less likely to convert to Islam.)* AL

W Writing Skills

Informative/Explanatory Have students write an essay that explains why not all Muslims are Arab. You may choose to have students write the essay for homework. Encourage students to share their essays with the class. ELL **Verbal/Linguistic**

Content Background Knowledge

Sikhism A teacher named Nanak founded Sikhism in the early 1500s in the Punjab region of India. Sikh religious leaders are called gurus. Sikh religious practice is based on the teachings of Nanak and of the nine gurus who came after him. Sikhs believe in one God and the equality of all human beings. Sikhism stresses doing good deeds, such as caring for the less fortunate. Today, Sikhism is the world's fifth-largest religion. It has 23 million followers around the world, but most Sikhs live in South Asia. About 500,000 Sikhs live in the United States today.

Have students complete the Lesson 2 Review.

CLOSE & REFLECT

Ask students why they think religion and government were so closely connected in Islamic countries. Have students give reasons for their ideas. Moderate the class discussion.

ANSWERS, p. 410

CRITICAL THINKING Suleiman was "magnificent" because he achieved military successes, expanded the territory of the Ottoman Empire, organized Ottoman law, and built many schools and mosques. His rule is considered the "Golden Age of the Ottoman Empire."

PROGRESS CHECK Urdu is a language spoken in Pakistan that is based on the Persian language.

BIOGRAPHY

Suleiman I (1494–1566)

In 1520, at the age of 26, Suleiman I became the sultan of the Ottoman Empire. His reign is known as the Golden Age of the Ottoman Empire. He is often referred to as "Suleiman the Magnificent" or "The Lawgiver." He achieved many military successes and expanded the territory of the empire. Suleiman was responsible for the empire's greatest achievements in law, art, architecture, and literature.

▶ CRITICAL THINKING
Defending Why was Suleiman "magnificent"?

Nakkas Osman/The Bridgeman Art Library/Getty Images

How Did the Ottomans Rule?

Because their empire was so large, the Ottomans ruled many peoples who practiced many religions. Islam was the empire's official religion, and Muslims enjoyed special privileges. The government passed different laws for non-Muslims. For example, non-Muslims had to pay a special tax. In return, they were free to practice their religion. R

After Suleiman, the Ottoman Empire began to break down. It lost lands to the Europeans. Local rulers and conquered people broke away. The empire finally crumbled in the early 1900s.

The Safavids

In 1501, a Shia leader named Ismail proclaimed himself shah, or king, of Persia. Ismail founded the Safavid dynasty, which ruled Persia until the 1700s. During this period, Persian spread as a language of culture and trade. Urdu, a language spoken in Pakistan today, is partly based on Persian.

India's Mogul Empire

During the 1500s, the Moguls (MOH•guhlz) set up a Muslim empire in India. Under Akbar (AHK•bar), the Mogul empire prospered. He allowed people to practice their religions. After Akbar, Mogul rulers were less tolerant. They persecuted Hindus and Sikhs (SEEKS). Sikhs believe in one God and stress doing good deeds. Today, Sikhism is the world's fifth-largest religion. W

During the late 1600s, Sikhs and Hindus rebelled against the Moguls. At the same time, Europeans arrived in India. Over time, the Moguls lost power, leaving the British in control.

PROGRESS CHECK
Identifying What is Urdu?

LESSON 2 REVIEW 

Review Vocabulary (Tier 3 Words)

1. How did the *Sunni* feel about the Umayyad *caliphs*? RH.6–8.2, RH.6–8.4
2. In addition to the Seljuks, who else used the title *sultan*? RH.6–8.2, RH.6–8.4

Answer the Guiding Questions

3. ***Identifying*** What area of Europe came under Muslim control at this time? RH.6–8.2
4. ***Describing*** What changes did Abbasid rulers bring to the world of Islam? RH.6–8.2
5. ***Determining Cause and Effect*** What effect did the burning of Baghdad in 1258 have on the Islamic Empire? RH.6–8.2, RH.6–8.5
6. ***Explaining*** What led to the downfall of the Ottoman Empire? RH.6–8.2
7. **INFORMATIVE/EXPLANATORY** Write a paragraph that compares how the Ottomans and Moguls each treated non-Muslims. WHST.6–8.2, WHST.6–8.10

410 *Islamic Civilization*

LESSON 2 REVIEW ANSWERS

1. The Sunni recognized the Umayyad caliphs as rightful rulers, although they sometimes disagreed with the caliphs' actions.
2. The Ottomans also called their rulers sultans.
3. Southwestern Europe and Spain came under Muslim control.
4. The Abbasids focused on improving trade and culture rather than conquering new lands.
5. The burning of Baghdad in 1258 marked the end of Arab leaders ruling the Islamic Empire.
6. After the rule of Suleiman I, the Ottoman Empire slowly declined. It lost territory to the Europeans. Conquered peoples rebelled and broke away from the empire. The Ottoman Empire dissolved in the early 1900s.
7. The Ottomans and the Moguls demonstrated some tolerance of non-Muslim groups. The Ottomans allowed non-Muslims to practice their religion if they paid a special tax, but Muslims were allowed special advantages. The Mogul leader Akbar also allowed people to practice their own religions. After Akbar, however, the Moguls were no longer tolerant of non-Muslims.

Life in the Islamic World

networks
There's More Online!
- CHART/GRAPH Shopping: Then and Now
- GRAPHIC ORGANIZER Muslim Contributions to Science
- SLIDE SHOW The Taj Mahal

Lesson 3
Life in the Islamic World

ESSENTIAL QUESTION *How do ideas change the way people live?*

It Matters Because
Muslim advances in mathematics, business, science, architecture, and the arts helped to create our modern society.

Daily Life and Trade

GUIDING QUESTION *How did people live and trade in the Islamic world?*

C Muslim merchants controlled trade in much of Asia and Africa from the A.D. 700s until the 1400s. Their caravans traveled from Egypt and Mesopotamia to China. Their ships sailed the Indian Ocean to East Africa, India, and Southeast Asia. Muslim traders set out on their journeys with spices, cloth, glass, and carpets from their homelands. They traded these items for rubies from India, silk from China, and spices from Southeast Asia. They also traded for gold, ivory, and enslaved people from Africa. In addition, Muslim merchants sold crops such as sugar, rice, oranges, cherries, and cotton.

Why Were Muslim Traders Successful?

R Muslim trade flourished for several reasons. Muslims spread the religion of Islam along with the Arabic language. As a result, Arabic became the language of business and trade in much of Asia and Africa. Muslim rulers also helped traders by providing them with coins to use for buying and selling goods. This was an easier trading method than bartering for goods.

Muslim merchants kept detailed records of their business dealings and their earnings. In time, these practices created a new industry—banking. Muslims respected merchants for their business skills and the wealth they created.

Reading HELPDESK (CCSS)

Taking Notes: *Organizing*
Draw a diagram like this one. Fill in details about Muslim contributions in the field of science. RH.6–8.2

Muslim Contributions to Science

Content Vocabulary (Tier 3 Words)
- mosque
- bazaar
- astrolabe
- minaret

ENGAGE

Bellringer Organize the class into pairs. Explain that you are going to ask a question and each student will write down his or her answer. Then each student shares with a partner. After they have had time to compare answers, pairs will share their answers with the class.

Tell students that Muslims have made many contributions to the world in the fields of mathematics, science, medicine, and literature. Ask students to think of one thing Muslims have contributed to the world. Moderate a class discussion of Muslim contributions.

TEACH & ASSESS

C Critical Thinking Skills

Determining Central Ideas After students read the first paragraph, ask them to determine the central idea and write it as a sentence. Have small groups share sentences and vote for the one that best expresses the central idea. *(Possible answer: Muslim merchants traveled by land and sea to countries in much of Asia and Africa to trade for goods.)* AL **Verbal/Linguistic**

R Reading Skills

Identifying After students have read the text, encourage them to identify reasons Muslims were so successful at trading. Record their answers in a list on the board. *(Answers: Most people spoke the same language—Arabic; Muslims developed a money system that eliminated bartering; they kept records of their transactions, which later developed into a banking system.)*

Making Connections

- Every country is known for certain goods that it produces and trades. These goods depend on the country's natural resources.
- Today, countries still specialize in certain products. The U.S. is very diverse, but some specialties include wheat, corn, cotton, beef, pork, poultry, and industry products such as high-technology items, electronics, petroleum, steel, lumber, and motor vehicles.

VIDEO

Islamic Scientific Advances

Giving Examples Have students watch this video, which shows how architecture, Islamic art, and music convey the breadth of early Islamic learning and scientific advances. Discuss the idea from the video that knowledge, beauty, science and art are not separate, but melded together. Ask students to give examples of how knowledge, beauty, science, and art meld in Islamic culture *(for example, the medical books with beautiful artwork).*

See page 395E for other online activities.

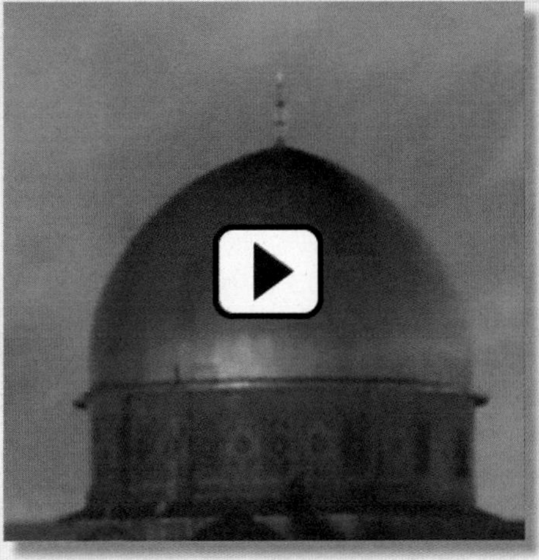

ANSWER, p. 411

TAKING NOTES: Answers could be any four: Astronomers accurately described the sun's eclipses and proved that the moon affects ocean tides. They perfected the astrolabe and used it to measure the size of and distance around Earth. Muslim scientists developed the concepts of chemistry, and al-Razi was the first to label chemical substances as animal, vegetable, or mineral.

Life in the Islamic World

C Critical Thinking Skills

Comparing and Contrasting Remind students that a bazaar, or marketplace for trading and shopping, was and is today a feature in all Muslim cities. Have students work in pairs to study the pictures on the page and compare and contrast an early city bazaar with a modern-day bazaar. AL Interpersonal

R Reading Skills

Explaining After students read this page, ask a volunteer to explain where people in the Islamic Empire lived. **Ask:** **Who owned and controlled most of the land?** *(Most of the land was owned and controlled by wealthy landowners.)* **How was Muslim society organized?** *(It was based on wealth and power. Government leaders, large landowners, and wealthy merchants held the greatest power.)*

T Technology Skills

Making Presentations Have students read the information about Muslim cities and farms. Ask them to use presentation software and pictures found on the Internet to create presentations that inform about the features of a Muslim city or farm. ELL Visual/Spatial

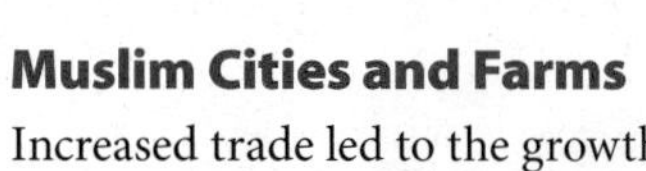

THEN

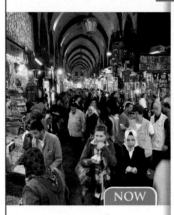

C The word "bazaar" is Persian and refers to the public market district in a town. These ancient markets with many stalls and shops sold both local and imported goods from all over the world. They were the forerunners of modern shopping centers that we know today.

NOW

▶ CRITICAL THINKING

Evaluating What are the advantages of having a central marketplace?

Muslim Cities and Farms

Increased trade led to the growth of cities throughout the Islamic world. Makkah, Baghdad, Cairo (KY•roh), and Damascus were located on major trade routes. Muslim cities, however, were more than places of trade. They also became centers of government, education, and culture.

Muslim cities generally had narrow streets separating closely packed buildings. The main buildings were mosques and palaces. **Mosques** (MAHSKS) are Muslim houses of worship. They also served as schools, courts, and centers of learning.

Another important feature of every Muslim city was the **bazaar** (buh•ZAHR), or marketplace. Like shopping malls today, bazaars were full of shops and stalls where goods were sold. They were often covered to protect merchants and customers from the scorching sun. Nearby inns provided travelers a place to eat and rest. T

Despite the importance of cities, most Muslims, however, lived in villages and farmed the land. The dry climate and the lack of rainfall, however, made farming difficult. Muslim farmers relied on irrigation to water their crops. They raised wheat, rice, beans, cucumbers, and melons in their fields. They planted orchards that provided almonds, apricots, figs, and olives. Farmers also grew flowers for use in perfume. R

Some Muslim villagers owned small farms. Most of the productive land, however, was owned by wealthy landowners. They had large estates and hired farmers from nearby villages or used enslaved people to farm the land.

How was Muslim Society Organized?

People in the Muslim world were divided into social groups based on their power and wealth. Government leaders, landowners, and wealthy merchants held the greatest power. Below them were artisans, farmers, and workers. Enslaved people held no power.

As in other civilizations, slavery was common in Muslim lands. Many enslaved people were prisoners of war. Although they faced hardships, enslaved people had some rights under Islamic law. For example, mothers and young children could not be separated, and enslaved people could buy their freedom.

Men and women had separate roles in the Muslim world. Men were in charge of government, society, and business. Women managed their families and households.

(t) Image Asset Management/World History Archive/Age fotostock
(b) Atlantide Phototravel/Corbis

Reading HELPDESK CCSS

mosque a Muslim house of worship

bazaar a marketplace

412 *Islamic Civilization*

networks Online Teaching Options

SLIDE SHOW

Mosques

Explaining Tell students that all Muslim cities and towns had mosques, and they still do today. **Ask:** **Besides being a house of worship, what else is located at a mosque?** *(Mosques are the location of schools and courts, and they are general centers of learning.)* **What are the most distinguishing features of a mosque?** *(Minarets, wells, courtyards, and domes are common features of mosques.)* Show students the slide show of mosques from around the world. AL ELL

See page 395E for other online activities.

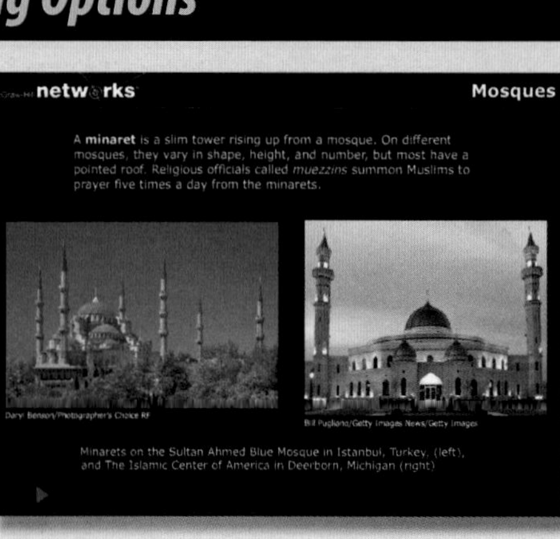

networks
Mosques
A minaret is a slim tower rising up from a mosque. On different mosques, they vary in shape, height, and number, but most have a pointed roof. Religious officials called muezzins summon Muslims to prayer five times a day from the minarets.
Daryl Benson/Photographer's Choice RF
Bill Pugliano/Getty Images News/Getty Images
Minarets on the Sultan Ahmed Blue Mosque in Istanbul, Turkey, (left), and The Islamic Center of America in Deerborn, Michigan (right)

ANSWER, p. 412

CRITICAL THINKING The advantages of having a central marketplace include being able to shop for and buy everything a person needs at the same place and, as a merchant, to access the largest number of customers in one location.

Women were also allowed to own property, invest in trade, and inherit wealth. Some upper-class women received an education and contributed to the arts. G1

☑ PROGRESS CHECK

Explaining Why were Muslim merchants successful?

Muslim Contributions

GUIDING QUESTION ***What were Muslim contributions in mathematics, science, and the arts?***

Arabic was the most widely spoken language in the Muslim world. The use of Arabic helped with the exchange of goods and ideas among the different Islamic peoples. For example, in A.D. 830 the Abbasid caliph Mamun (mah•MOON) founded the House of Wisdom in Baghdad. At this research center, Muslim, Jewish, and Christian thinkers translated Greek, Persian, and Indian works into Arabic.

C2 From the 700s to the 1400s, scholars in Muslim lands preserved learning of the ancient world. Europeans had lost many ancient Greek writings. In Spain, however, Jewish and Muslim scholars translated some Greek writings into Arabic. When these Arabic translations were translated into Latin, western Europeans learned about ancient Greek thinkers.

Science and Mathematics

At the Baghdad observatory founded by Mamun, Muslim astronomers studied the skies. These studies helped them create mathematical models of the universe. They correctly described the sun's eclipses and proved that the moon affects ocean tides. They gave many stars names that are still used today.

W Muslim astronomers improved the Greek **astrolabe** (AS•truh•layb). Sailors used this tool to determine their location at sea. Muslim scientists used the astrolabe to measure the distance around the Earth. Based on their measurements, they **confirmed** that the Earth is round.

Other Muslim scientists experimented with metals. As a result, Muslims are considered the founders of chemistry. One of the most famous Muslim chemists was al-Razi (ahl-RAH•zee). Al-Razi was the first scientist to label substances as animal, vegetable, or mineral. This type of labeling is still used today.

Connections to TODAY

Becoming a Doctor

Ancient Arab doctors had to attend medical school and pass a test before they could practice medicine. Today, doctors in the United States have similar requirements. To become a doctor, students must pass an exam to get into medical school and then complete four years of medical school. After completing those four years, medical students must pass another test to earn a license, or permit, to practice medicine. Without that license, they cannot be doctors.

Islamic civilization made important contributions to science, learning, and philosophy. This astrolabe advanced the Greek invention.

Michael Freeman/CORBIS

astrolabe a tool that helps sailors navigate by the positions of the stars

Academic Vocabulary (Tier 2 Words)

confirm to prove that something is true; to remove doubt

G1 Critical Thinking Skills

Analyzing Read with students the section of the textbook that compares the roles of men and women in the Muslim world. Then lead a discussion with students about the role of women in Muslim society. **Ask:** What kind of role did women have in Muslim society? How does this role compare to the roles of women in other cultures of this time period? Moderate the discussion, and encourage students to give reasons and evidence for their opinions. *(Answers will vary but should reflect information contained in the chapter.)*

C2 Critical Thinking Skills

Categorizing Have students categorize the many contributions Muslims have made. Ask them to identify Muslim contributions to science, architecture, art and literature, and economics. **Ask:** Can you think of any other contributions made by Muslims? *(Possible answers include the development of chemistry, the invention of algebra, and the discovery that the moon affects ocean tides.)* AL

W Writing Skills

Informative/Explanatory Discuss the section titled "Science and Mathematics." Ask students to formulate a question about one thing that they found interesting in this section. Have them research their questions on the Internet and write a short essay explaining what they learned. Have students cite the text and their research materials in their essays. BL

IMAGE

Abu Musa Jabir ibn Hayyan

Discussing Have students read the information in this interactive image and discuss the many contributions made by Abu Musa Jaber ibn Hayyan. Encourage students to pose questions during the discussion.

See page 395E for other online activities.

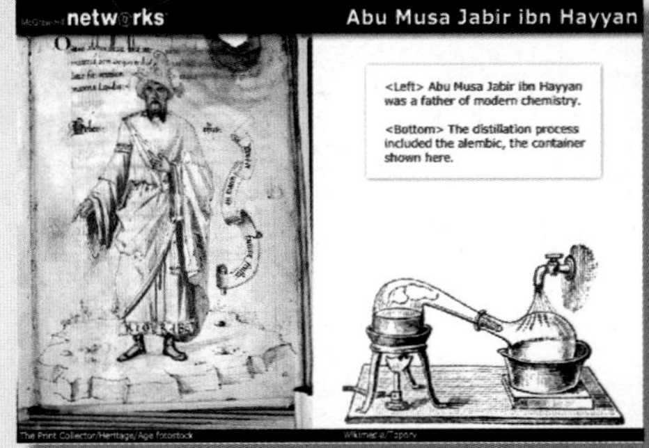

networks
Abu Musa Jabir ibn Hayyan
<Left> Abu Musa Jabir ibn Hayyan was a father of modern chemistry.
<Bottom> The distillation process included the alembic, the container shown here.

ANSWER, p. 413

☑ PROGRESS CHECK Muslim merchants were successful because they had support from Muslim rulers and kept detailed records.

V Visual Skills

Integrating Visual Information Have students look at the illustration of Omar Khayyam and read the text below it and at the bottom of the page. **Ask:** What do we know from the text and picture about the kind of man Omar Khayyam was? What might have been some of his character traits? *(Possible answers: smart, creative, focused, intense)* ELL Visual/Spatial

R Reading Skills

Summarizing Have students make an idea web with the words "Medical discoveries" in the middle. Have them fill in the Web with information from the "Medicine" section of the text. Ask students to write a summary of the section using their idea webs. ELL Visual/Spatial

C Critical Thinking Skills

Interpreting Discuss the section of the Rubaiyat quoted in the text. **Ask:** What is this poem saying? Have students write in their own words their interpretation of the poem and then share their ideas with the class. Discuss any differences in interpretation.

V Omar Khayyam—known for his poetry—was also a mathematician, philosopher, and astronomer.

Muslims also made contributions in mathematics. The Persian scholar al-Khawarizmi (ahl-khwa•RIHZ•meh) invented algebra. He and the Arab scholar al-Kindi borrowed the symbols 0 through 9 from Hindu scholars. These numbers were passed on to Europeans. Today, they are known as "Arabic numerals."

Medicine

Muslims made important medical discoveries too. Arab doctors discovered that blood circulates, or moves, to and from the heart. They also diagnosed certain diseases. Al-Razi wrote a book identifying the differences between smallpox and measles.

Muslim doctors shared their knowledge by **publishing** their findings. The Persian doctor Ibn Sina (ih•buhn SEE•nuh) produced the *Canon of Medicine*, which described how diseases spread and analyzed hundreds of different medicines. R

Unlike doctors in most other places, Arab doctors had to pass a test before they could practice medicine. The Arabs created the first medical schools and pharmacies. They also built medical clinics that gave care and medicine to the sick.

Literature

The Quran was the first and most important work written in Arabic. Muslims wrote non-religious literature as well. One of the best known works is *The Thousand and One Nights*, also called *The Arabian Nights*. It includes tales from India, Persia, and Arabia. Aladdin is one of the work's well-known characters.

Another Muslim, the Persian poet Omar Khayyam (OH•MAHR ky•YAHM), wrote the *Rubaiyat* (ROO•bee•aht). Many consider it one of the finest poems ever written. In a section of the poem, Khayyam describes the human being as a mystery:

PRIMARY SOURCE

C
"Man is a cup, his soul the wine therein,
Flesh is a pipe, spirit [give life to] the voice within;
O Khayyam, have you fathomed [figured out] what man is?
A magic lantern with a light therein!"

—from *The Rubaiyat* by Omar Khayyam, tr. E.H. Whinfield

Bettmann/CORBIS

Reading HELPDESK CCSS

minaret the tower of a mosque from which Muslims are called to prayer

Academic Vocabulary (Tier 2 Words)

publish to produce the work of an author, usually in print

networks Online Teaching Options

PRIMARY SOURCE

The Rubaiyat

Formulating Questions Have students read the information and the excerpts from the poem and formulate questions that they have. Ask students to share one of their questions with the class and discuss possible answers. AL

See page 395E for other online activities.

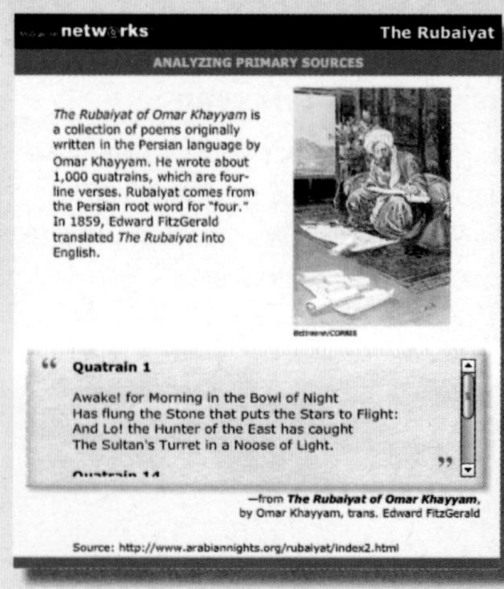

networks
The Rubaiyat
ANALYZING PRIMARY SOURCES
The Rubaiyat of Omar Khayyam is a collection of poems originally written in the Persian language by Omar Khayyam. He wrote about 1,000 quatrains, which are four-line verses. Rubaiyat comes from the Persian root word for "four." In 1859, Edward FitzGerald translated The Rubaiyat into English.
Quatrain 1
Awake! for Morning in the Bowl of Night
Has flung the Stone that puts the Stars to Flight:
And Lo! the Hunter of the East has caught
The Sultan's Turret in a Noose of Light.
—from The Rubaiyat of Omar Khayyam, by Omar Khayyam, trans. Edward FitzGerald
Source: http://www.arabiannights.org/rubaiyat/index2.html

Muslim scholars studied history. During the late 1300s, the Muslim historian Ibn Khaldun (IH•buhn KAL•DOON) looked for cause-and-effect relationships to explain historical events. He was one of the first historians to study how geography and climate shape human activities. **R**

Art and Architecture

Muslims developed forms of art based on Islam and the different cultures of the Muslim world. Opposed to idol worship, Muslim leaders discouraged artists from creating images of living creatures. Instead, Muslim art included designs entwined with flowers, leaves, stars, and beautiful writing. **C**

T Muslim cities were known for their beautiful buildings. Mosques dominated the skylines of Baghdad, Damascus, Cairo, and Istanbul. The most prominent features of a mosque are its **minarets** (mih•nuh•REHTS). These are towers from which an announcer calls Muslims to prayer five times each day.

Islamic rulers lived in large palaces with central courtyards. To cool the courtyards, architects added porches, fountains, and pools. To provide protection, they surrounded the palaces with walls. One famous example of a Muslim palace is the Alhambra (al•HAM•bruh) in Granada (gruh•NAH•duh), Spain.

Another famous Muslim building is the Taj Mahal in Agra (AH•gruh), India. The Mogul ruler Shah Jahan built it as a tomb for his wife. The Taj Mahal is made of marble and precious stones and is considered one of the world's most beautiful buildings.

It took Shah Jahan's workers and craftsmen more than 20 years to build the Taj Mahal.

▶ CRITICAL THINKING

Making Inferences What does the size and beauty of the Taj Mahal say about Shah Jahan's feelings for his wife?

Galen Rowell/CORBIS

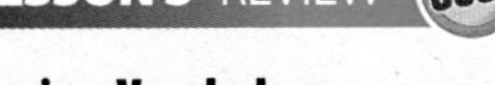

☑ PROGRESS CHECK

Listing What achievements were made by Muslims in medicine?

LESSON 3 REVIEW (CCSS)

Review Vocabulary (Tier 3 Words)

1. Why is a *minaret* an important feature of a *mosque*? RH.6–8.2, RH.6–8.4

Answer the Guiding Questions

2. ***Identifying*** What groups held the greatest power in Muslim society? RH.6–8.2
3. ***Explaining*** What did Muslim scientists discover once they improved the astrolabe? RH.6–8.2
4. ***Describing*** What are the defining features of Muslim art? RH.6–8.2
5. ***Summarizing*** Summarize the contributions that Muslim doctors made in the field of medicine. RH.6–8.2
6. **ARGUMENT** What Islamic invention or development do you think has had the greatest effect on our world today? Explain your choice. WHST.6–8.1, WHST.6–8.10

LESSON 3 REVIEW ANSWERS

1. Minarets are towers on a mosque from which an announcer calls the people to prayer five times a day.
2. Government leaders, landowners, and wealthy merchants held the greatest power in Muslim society.
3. In measuring Earth with the astrolabe, Muslim astronomers discovered the world is round.
4. Muslim art does not show people or animals. It shows flowers, leaves, and stars, and it sometimes includes beautiful writing.
5. Muslim doctor al-Razi wrote a book identifying the differences between smallpox and measles. Ibn Sina, a Muslim doctor, produced the Canon of Medicine, a work that tried to summarize all the medical knowledge of the time. Other doctors discovered that blood circulates to and from the heart. Muslims also established medical schools and required doctors to pass a test in order to practice medicine.
6. Students should choose the Islamic invention or development they think is the most significant and back up their choice with reasons. Their reasons should explain the benefits to the world today.

Life in the Islamic World

R Reading Skills

Stating Have students consider the various cultures that they have read about so far in the textbook and how those cultures arose. **Ask:** How do you think geography and climate can shape human activities? *(The weather and geographical type of area determine whether people may be farmers, nomads, etc.)* What other cause-and-effect relationships might come into play to explain historical events? *(Wars and exiles can explain the spread of religions.)*

C Critical Thinking Skills

Interpreting Explain to students that Muslims based their art on Islam and the various Muslim cultures. **Ask:** Why does Muslim art not depict living creatures? *(because Muslims are opposed to idol worship, and their leaders discouraged artists from creating images of living creatures)* Discuss with students the reasons and logic behind this decision.

T Technology Skills

Making Presentations Have students use the Internet to look up pictures and information about mosques around the world. Ask each student to find the three mosques that they find the most beautiful and use presentation software to develop a slide show. Have them share their presentations with the class. **Visual/Spatial**

Have students complete the Lesson 3 Review.

CLOSE & REFLECT

Discussing Discuss with students the major Muslim contributions. Ask students whether the contributions are evident today. **Ask:** Which contribution do you think is most important or has had the greatest impact? Have students provide supporting details for their answers.

ANSWERS, p. 415

CRITICAL THINKING The size and beauty of the Taj Mahal indicate that Shah Jahan felt great affection and admiration for his wife.

☑ PROGRESS CHECK They discovered circulation of the blood and were able to diagnose certain diseases. Muslims also established medical schools and pharmacies and required doctors to pass a test in order to practice medicine.

CHAPTER REVIEW ACTIVITY

Lead the class in a discussion of how Islam has changed things in the world. **Ask:**

- **How did Islam change life on the Arabian Peninsula?**
- **How did it change life in the countries that became part of Islamic empires?**
- **How did Islam become a source of unity?**
- **How did Islam change over time?**
- **What parts of Islam did not change?**

Create a graphic organizer like the one below in which to record student responses.

Changes Brought by Islam	Unifying Aspects of Islam

REVIEW THE ENDURING UNDERSTANDINGS

Review this chapter's Enduring Understandings with students:

- ***People, places, and ideas change over time.***
- ***Religion can influence a society's beliefs and values.***

Now pose the following questions in a class discussion to apply these to this chapter:

How did the Muslims change other cultures and places as the religion of Islam spread? *(The Muslims influenced the architecture, the ideas and thoughts and daily lives of the people who converted to Islam, and the way medicine was practiced.)*

How did the religion of Islam change over time? *(The Muslims divided themselves into sects based on whom they accepted as their leader, or caliph. The religion spread to other places and cultures, and in each place it combined with aspects of that place and culture.)*

What evidence do we see in the world today that shows the influence of Islam on society's beliefs and values? *(We see the big cities that were built by the Muslims and the mosques and unique architecture. We use the banking and medical practices they developed, as well as their artwork and their poetry.)*

CHAPTER 14 Activities CCSS

Write your answers on a separate piece of paper.

1 Exploring the Essential Question WHST.6–8.2, WHST.6–8.10

INFORMATIVE/EXPLANATORY How does the spread of a religion change the way people live? Write an essay that discusses how the influence of Islam changed the way people lived throughout the Islamic Empire. Include the influence of Islam in daily life as well as in trade, government, and culture.

2 21st Century Skills WHST.6–8.2, WHST.6–8.6, WHST.6–8.7, WHST.6–8.8, WHST.6–8.9, WHST.6–8.10

RECOGNIZE QUALITY SOURCES Using a computer word processing program, create a five-page report on the range of Islamic arts . Include arts that flourished in the Ottoman Empire during the reign of Suleiman I. Use primary source photos and information from reliable Internet sources such as the Metropolitan Museum of Art and national Turkish museums. Include secondary source information from encyclopedias.

3 Thinking Like a Historian RH.6–8.2, WHST.6–8.9

SEQUENCING EVENTS Create a time line. Place these four events in the correct order on the time line:

- Mongols burn Baghdad
- Abbasids replace the Umayyads
- Muhammad begins preaching
- Suleiman I rules the Ottoman Empire

4 GEOGRAPHY ACTIVITY

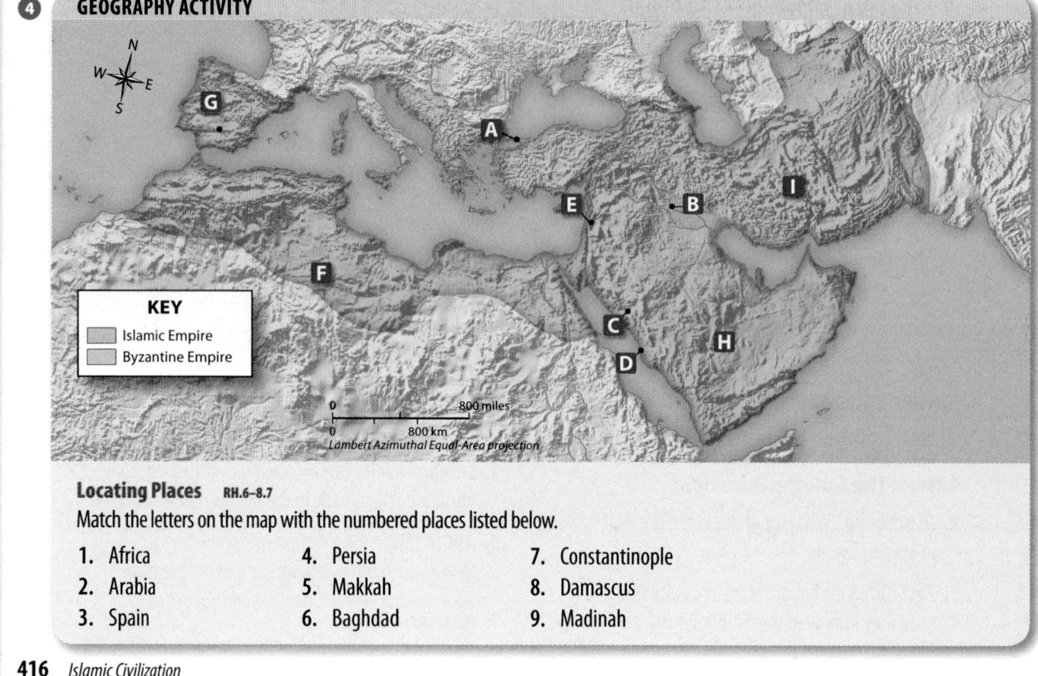

Locating Places RH.6–8.7

Match the letters on the map with the numbered places listed below.

1. Africa
2. Arabia
3. Spain
4. Persia
5. Makkah
6. Baghdad
7. Constantinople
8. Damascus
9. Madinah

416 *Islamic Civilization*

ACTIVITIES ANSWERS

Exploring the Essential Question

1 Students should note that religions often have a deep impact on culture and the way people live. They should compare life for the Arabs before Islam to life after people converted to Islam in categories such as daily life, trade, government, and overall culture. The development of Islam affected every aspect of people's lives.

21st Century Skills

2 Students should research carefully and use only reliable Internet sources in gathering photos and information for their reports on the development of the arts under the rule of Suleiman I. They should mention all of the arts that flourished but only focus on one or two. Students should be sure to cite references for their research.

Thinking Like a Historian

3 The time line should extend from A.D. 600 to 1600. The events should be placed on the time line in this order:

Muhammad begins preaching (A.D. 610)
Abbasids replace the Umayyads (A.D. 750)
Mongols burn Baghdad (1258)
Suleiman I rules the Ottoman Empire (1520–1566)

Locating Places

4 **1.** F, **2.** H, **3.** G, **4.** I, **5.** D, **6.** B, **7.** A, **8.** E, **9.** C

CHAPTER 14 Assessment CCSS

REVIEW THE GUIDING QUESTIONS

RH.6–8.2

1. The geography and climate that influenced the Arab way of life was
   A. a tropical rain forest.
   B. a cold and mountainous terrain.
   C. a hot desert and dry plains.
   D. a cool and rainy flat terrain.

RH.6–8.2

2. What main source provides guidance to Islam's followers?
   F. the Quran
   G. teachings in the Bible
   H. stories handed down by word-of-mouth
   I. teachings in the Vedas

RH.6–8.2

3. How did the Arab Empire change immediately after the Umayyads lost power?
   A. The Mongols ruled and focused on education.
   B. The Abbasids ruled and improved trade and culture.
   C. The Romans ruled and built a large army.
   D. The Safavids ruled and focused on religion.

RH.6–8.2

4. How did the Ottomans rule an empire with many different people and religions?
   F. Non-Muslims paid a special tax to practice their religions.
   G. Everyone paid a freedom-of-religion tax.
   H. No religious worship was allowed in the empire.
   I. Muslims paid an extra tax to practice their religion.

RH.6–8.2

5. How did trade spread throughout the Islamic world?
   A. Muslim soldiers ran trading companies.
   B. Throughout the Islamic Empire, Muslims built trading posts.
   C. Traders in the Islamic Empire didn't have to pay taxes.
   D. All schools in the empire taught trading skills.

RH.6–8.2

6. What contributions did Muslims make to astronomy?
   F. Muslim astronomers discovered the planet Mars.
   G. Muslims proved that the moon affects ocean tides.
   H. Muslim astronomers described the expanding universe.
   I. Astronomers in the Islamic Empire tracked the Earth's orbit.

ASSESSMENT ANSWERS

Review the Guiding Questions

1. **C** Choice C is the correct answer. The geography and climate that influenced the Arab way of life included hot deserts and dry plains. The area where Arabs lived was not a rain forest. It hardly rains in the deserts and dry plains. It was not cold and mountainous, like Viking countries, and although the geography was relatively flat, it was not cool and rainy.

2. **F** Choice F is the correct answer. The Quran, the holy book of Islam, is the primary teaching tool for the Islamic faith. Islam does not use the Christian Bible, and the Vedas are Hindu writings. Not all stories handed down by word-of-mouth are considered holy.

3. **B** Choice B is the correct answer. The Abbasids ruled the Arab Empire immediately after the Umayyads and focused on increasing trade and developing Arab culture. The Mongols did not rule until the 1200s. The Romans did not ever rule the Arab Empire, and the Safavids ruled after the Abbasids.

4. **F** Choice F is the correct answer. People in the Ottoman Empire were free to practice their own religion, but non-Muslims had to pay a special tax to do so.

5. **B** Choice B is the correct answer. Muslims increased trade throughout their empire by building trading posts in numerous places. Muslim soldiers did not operate trading companies wherever they were posted. Traders, like most people in the empire, had to pay taxes. Schools in the empire did not focus on teaching trading skills.

6. **G** Choice G is the correct answer. Muslim astronomers did not track Earth's orbit, describe the expanding universe, or discover the planet Mars. They did prove that the moon affects ocean tides.

Assessment Answers

Analyzing Documents

7 **D** Choice D is the correct answer. Students should use the word *splendid* as a clue to help them answer this question.

8 **F** Choice F is the correct answer. Students should note that marble is a more beautiful building material than stucco and mortar. If they are unsure of the words and their meanings, have them look up the words in a dictionary.

Short Response

9 Islamic rule gave Persians a new religion and changed their way of living.

10 Answers should include that enabling the Persians to maintain their culture would make the Persian people more accepting of being part of the Islamic empire. The Persian people would be less rebellious.

Extended Response

11 Students' diary entries should include the geography of the upcoming trading trip and the method of travel. Students might want to estimate how long the trip will take as well as mention the sights they will see.

CHAPTER 14 Assessment *(continued)*  

DBQ ANALYZING DOCUMENTS

Baghdad became a center of political and cultural power. A visitor, Yakut, describes the city after visiting it in A.D. 800.

"Baghdad formed two vast semi-circles on the right and left banks of the Tigris. . . . Baghdad was a veritable [true] City of Palaces, not made of stucco and mortar, but of [precious] marble."

—from *Readings in Ancient History,* edited by William Stearns Davis

RH.6–8.2, RH.6–8.6

7 **Summarizing** Which statement best summarizes Yakut's opinion about Baghdad?

A. Yakut is critical of Baghdad.
B. Yakut describes Baghdad as a small city on the Tigris River.
C. Yakut sees Baghdad as a poor city.
D. Yakut's description paints Baghdad as a splendid city of fine buildings.

RH.6–8.1, RH.6–8.6

8 **Comparing and Contrasting** Why does Yakut mention building materials?

F. All these materials were scarce throughout the Islamic Empire.
G. The building materials show how magnificent Baghdad was.
H. Stucco and mortar were unusual building materials.
I. Marble was a common building material throughout the Islamic Empire.

SHORT RESPONSE

"In the 7th century [600s] Persia fell to the conquering armies of Islam. ***Islamic*** *rule, under the* ***empire*** *of the caliphate, persisted for the next seven centuries. . . . Although Islam gave the Persians a wholly new religion and altered their way of living, Persian culture remained intact [unchanged]."*

—from "Islamic Dynasties" in *Encyclopedia Britannica Kids*

RH.6–8.2, RH.6–8.6

9 How did Islamic rule affect the Persians?

RH.6–8.2, RH.6–8.6

10 How did allowing Persian culture to remain unchanged strengthen the Islamic Empire?

EXTENDED RESPONSE

WHST.6–8.10

11 **Narrative** You are a merchant during the era of the Umayyads. You travel the empire buying and selling goods. Write a diary entry describing one of your travels.

Need Extra Help?

If You've Missed Question	1	2	3	4	5	6	7	8	9	10	11
Review Lesson	1	1	2	2	2	3	2	2	2	2	2

networks Online Teaching Options

More Assessment Resources

The *Assess* tab in the online Teacher Lesson Center includes resources to help students improve their test-taking skills. It also contains many project-based rubrics to help you assess students' work.

CHAPTER 15

African Civilizations Planner

UNDERSTANDING BY DESIGN®

Enduring Understanding

- *People, places, and ideas change over time.*

Essential Questions

- *Why do people trade?*
- *How does religion shape society?*
- *How do religions develop?*

Predictable Misunderstandings

Students may think:

- *Africa did not support many varied civilizations.*
- *European kingdoms grew larger and richer than African trading empires.*
- *The slave trade in Africa began with the arrival of the Europeans.*

Assessment Evidence

Performance Tasks:

- *Hands-On Chapter Project*

Other Evidence:

- *Responses to Interactive Whiteboard Activities*
- *Creation of an illustrated map*
- *Interactive Graphic Organizers*
- *21st Century Skills Activities*
- *Economics in History Activity*
- *Geography and History Activity*
- *Responses to classroom discussions*
- *Lesson Reviews*
- *Chapter Activities and Assessment*

SUGGESTED PACING GUIDE

Introducing the Chapter	1 Day	Lesson 3	1 Day
Lesson 1	2 Days	*What Do You Think?*	1 Day
Lesson 2	1 Day	Chapter Wrap-Up and Assessment	1 Day

TOTAL TIME 7 Days

Key for Using the Teacher Edition

SKILL-BASED ACTIVITIES

Types of skill activities found in the Teacher Edition.

V Visual Skills require students to analyze maps, graphs, charts, and photos.

R Reading Skills help students practice reading skills and master vocabulary.

W Writing Skills provide writing opportunities to help students comprehend the text.

C Critical Thinking Skills help students apply and extend what they have learned.

T Technology Skills require students to use digital tools effectively.

*Letters are followed by a number when there is more than one of the same type of skill on the page.

DIFFERENTIATED INSTRUCTION

All activities are written for the on-level student unless otherwise marked with the leveled labels below.

BL Beyond Level
AL Approaching Level
ELL English Language Learners

All students benefit from activities that utilize different learning styles. Many activities are marked as below when a particular learning style is highlighted.

Intrapersonal | **Naturalist**
Logical/Mathematical | **Kinesthetic**
Visual/Spatial | **Auditory/Musical**
Verbal/Linguistic | **Interpersonal**

NCSS STANDARDS covered in "African Civilizations"

Learners will understand:

1 CULTURE

1. "Culture" refers to the socially transmitted behaviors, beliefs, values, traditions, institutions, and ways of living together for a group of people

4. That the beliefs, values, and behaviors of a culture form an integrated system that helps shape the activities and ways of life that define a culture

2 TIME, CONTINUITY, AND CHANGE

6. The origins and influences of social, cultural, political, and economic systems

7. The contributions of key persons, groups, and events from the past and their influence on the present

9. The influences of social, geographic, economic, and cultural factors on the history of local areas, states, nations, and the world

3 PEOPLE, PLACES, AND ENVIRONMENTS

1. The theme of people, places, and environments involves the study of the relationships between human populations in different locations and geographic phenomena such as climate, vegetation, and natural resources

2. Concepts such as: location, region, place, migration, as well as human and physical systems

5. The concept of regions identifies links between people in different locations according to specific criteria (e.g., physical, economic, social, cultural, or religious)

6 POWER, AUTHORITY, AND GOVERNANCE

5. The ways in which governments meet the needs and wants of citizens, manage conflict, and establish order and society

7 PRODUCTION, DISTRIBUTION, AND CONSUMPTION

1. Individuals, government, and society experience scarcity because human wants and needs exceed what can be produced from available resources

3. The economic choices that people make have both present and future consequences

6. The economic gains that result from specialization and exchange as well as the trade-offs

7. How markets bring buyers and sellers together to exchange goods and services

CHAPTER OPENER PLANNER

Students will know:

- *how Africa's geography influenced trade in the region.*
- *what types of trade took place in Africa.*
- *how the African economy was dependent on trade.*
- *how Islam arrived in Africa.*
- *how ideas spread through trade.*
- *how African arts and music have influenced today's popular culture.*
- *the economic reasons behind the slave trade.*

Students will be able to:

- ***analyze** how trade affected Africa's development.*
- ***analyze** maps and visuals to interpret information about trade and Africa.*
- ***analyze** how trade affects the exchange of ideas.*
- ***demonstrate** understanding of Africa's influence on pop culture through classroom discussion.*
- ***compare and contrast** primary-source quotes on the slave trade.*

UNDERSTANDING BY DESIGN®

Print Teaching Options

V Visual Skills

- [ ] **P. 420** Students use a map to make predictions about settlement patterns.

C Critical Thinking Skills

- [ ] **P. 421** Students use the time line to make general inferences about ancient African kingdoms.

Online Teaching Options

V Visual Skills

- MAP **Geography and Climate Zones in Africa**—Students view the extent of climate zones and click to see descriptions and photos of the zones.
- TIME LINE **African Civilizations 400 B.C.–A.D. 1500**—Students learn about key events in African history during this time period.
- WORLD ATLAS Students can use this interactive map to identify regions of the world, learn about individual countries, locate political boundaries, measure distances, and much more.

Project-Based Learning

Hands-On Chapter Project

African Civilizations

Students working in small groups will create an illustrated children's story about a topic related to an African region, river, or people.

Technology Extension

edtechteacher 21st Century Learning

Children's Story eBook

- Find an additional activity online that incorporates technology for this project.
- Visit the EdTechTeacher Web sites (included in the Technology Extension for this chapter) for more links, tutorials, and other resources.

Print Resources

ANCILLARY RESOURCES

These ancillaries are available for every chapter and lesson.

- **Reading Essentials and Study Guide Workbook** AL ELL
- **Chapter Tests and Lesson Quizzes Blackline Masters**

PRINTABLE DIGITAL WORKSHEETS

These printable digital worksheets are available for every chapter and lesson.

- **Hands-On Chapter Projects**
- **What Do You Know? activities**
- **Chapter Summaries (English and Spanish)**
- **Vocabulary Builder activities**
- **Guided Reading activities**

More Media Resources

SUGGESTED READING

Grade 6 reading level:

- ***A Pride of African Tales,*** by Donna L. Washington

Grade 7 reading level:

- ***Africa for Kids: Exploring a Vibrant Continent,*** by Harvey Croze

Grade 8 reading level:

- ***Time's Memory,*** by Julius Lester

LESSON 1 PLANNER

THE RISE OF AFRICAN CIVILIZATIONS

Students will know:
- *how Africa's geography influenced trade in the region.*
- *what types of trade took place in Africa.*
- *how the African economy was dependent on trade.*

Students will be able to:
- ***analyze*** *how trade affected Africa's development.*
- ***analyze*** *maps and visuals to interpret information about trade and Africa.*

UNDERSTANDING BY DESIGN®

☑ Print Teaching Options

V Visual Skills

- ☐ **P. 423** Students integrate information from a map and photos. Visual/Spatial
- ☐ **P. 424** Students read a chart comparing Africa and the U.S. AL
- ☐ **P. 426** Students analyze a map of trade routes in Africa. ELL Visual/Spatial Kinesthetic
- ☐ **P. 428** Students answer questions about a map of African trading empires. AL

R Reading Skills

- ☐ **P. 422** Students calculate the time between first settlement and first civilizations. Logical/Mathematical
- ☐ **P. 425** Students list goods traded across the Sahara. AL
- ☐ **P. 426** Students find the main idea in a section about Ghana. AL
- ☐ **P. 427** Students name the most important figure in the founding of Mali.
- ☐ **P. 428** Students explain how Axum became an important trading empire.
- ☐ **P. 429** Students list traded goods in different parts of Africa. AL

W Writing Skills

- ☐ **P. 425** Students write a paragraph about the Sahara.

C Critical Thinking Skills

- ☐ **P. 422** Students draw conclusions about Africa's geography. AL
- ☐ **P. 423** Students determine the effects of the Sahel on the lives of inhabitants.
- ☐ **P. 424** Students make inferences about discoveries made in the Rift Valley.
- ☐ **P. 427** Students analyze a primary source about taxation. AL ELL
- ☐ **P. 429** Students speculate about the effects of Arab traders on African trade. BL

☑ Online Teaching Options

V Visual Skills

- ☐ VIDEO **Great African Queens**—Students view a video on the life of Mbande Nzinga, a seventeenth-century queen of Angola.
- ☐ MAP **Geography and Climate Zones in Africa**—Students view the extent of climate zones and click to see descriptions and photos of the zones.
- ☐ MAP **Trade Routes of North Africa c. 1050–1500**—Students click to reveal areas controlled by different groups and the trade routes they utilized.
- ☐ SLIDE SHOW **The Great Rift Valley**—Students examine modern scenes from the 6,000-mile long crack in Earth's crust.

R Reading Skills

- ☐ GRAPHIC ORGANIZER **Taking Notes: *Identifying:* West African Trading Kingdoms**—Students list the three major West African trading kingdoms and the products they traded.
- ☐ CHART **African Kingdoms**—Students click to reveal facts about five African kingdoms.

C Critical Thinking Skills

- ☐ WHITEBOARD ACTIVITY **How West Africa Changed Because of Trade**—Students drag and drop in order to sequence events related to West Africa and trade.
- ☐ DIAGRAM **Camels vs. Horses**—Students use a Venn diagram to compare and contrast camels and horses.
- ☐ SLIDE SHOW **Dhows**—Students analyze images that convey the importance of these wooden ships used for trade on the Indian Ocean.

T Technology Skills

- ☐ SELF-CHECK QUIZ **Lesson 1**—Students receive instant feedback on their mastery of lesson content.
- ☐ GAME **African Column Game**—Students identify countries colonized by England and France.
- ☐ GAME **Empire Building in Africa Concentration Game**—Students match terms and descriptions to review lesson concepts.
- ☐ GAME **Kingdoms and States of Africa Identification Game**—Students match kingdoms and states to their descriptors.

☑ Printable Digital Worksheets

W Writing Skills

- ☐ WORKSHEET **21st Century Skills Activity: Information Literacy: Find Cardinal and Intermediate Directions**—Students use cardinal and intermediate directions to write sentences that describe locations on maps.

LESSON **2 PLANNER**

AFRICA'S GOVERNMENTS AND RELIGIONS

Students will know:
- *how Islam arrived in Africa.*
- *how ideas spread through trade.*

Students will be able to:
- ***analyze** how trade affects the exchange of ideas.*

UNDERSTANDING BY DESIGN®

Print Teaching Options

V Visual Skills

- ☐ **P. 433** Students read a graph to determine the two religions most practiced in Africa today. AL **Visual/Spatial**

R Reading Skills

- ☐ **P. 430** Students cite text evidence to answer a question about Ghana and Mali. AL
- ☐ **P. 432** Students identify the most common religious belief in Africa.
- ☐ **P. 434** Students brainstorm adjectives to describe Mansa Musa's journey. ELL
- ☐ **P. 435** Students specify three ways Askia Muhammad encouraged the growth of Islam.

W Writing Skills

- ☐ **P. 431** Students work in a group to identify and write about key features of Ghana or Mali. AL **Interpersonal**

C Critical Thinking Skills

- ☐ **P. 430** Students evaluate African rulers' relationships with their subjects. BL
- ☐ **P. 431** Students contrast how Mali and Ghana ruled their provinces.
- ☐ **P. 433** Students evaluate the importance of the writings of Ibn Battuta. BL
- ☐ **P. 434** Students determine the main issues the Songhai had with Sunni Ali's son's rule. AL
- ☐ **P. 435** Students discuss the blending of Islamic and East African cultures. ELL

Online Teaching Options

V Visual Skills

- VIDEO **History and Traditions of Mali**—Students see the African savanna in the country of Mali, whose economy is based on agriculture.
- IMAGE **King of Benin**—Students analyze an image of an ancient carving of the king of Benin.
- MAP **Religion in Africa Today**—Students view a color-coded map showing concentrations of Christianity, traditional religions, and Islam in Africa today.

R Reading Skills

- GRAPHIC ORGANIZER **Taking Notes: *Organizing:* Leaders and Their Achievements**—Students record the achievements of three African leaders.
- BIOGRAPHY **Mansa Musa**—Students read of the life and accomplishments of this ruler of Mali.

C Critical Thinking Skills

- GRAPH **Religion in Africa**—Students interpret data on the percentages of Africans practicing various religions.
- SLIDE SHOW **Mosques in Africa**—Students compare and contrast the architecture and design of African mosques.

T Technology Skills

- SELF-CHECK QUIZ **Lesson 2**—Students receive instant feedback on their mastery of lesson content.
- GAME **Africa's Governments and Religion True or False Game**—Students determine whether statements about Africa's governments and religions are true or false.

Printable Digital Worksheets

C Critical Thinking Skills

- WORKSHEET **Economics of History Activity: The Value of Gold**—Students consider how the changing price of gold might affect a country's currency.

LESSON 3 PLANNER

AFRICAN SOCIETY AND CULTURE

Students will know:

- *how African arts and music have influenced today's popular culture.*
- *the economic reasons behind the slave trade.*

Students will be able to:

- ***demonstrate*** *understanding of Africa's influence on pop culture through classroom discussion.*
- ***compare and contrast*** *primary-source quotes on the slave trade.*

UNDERSTANDING BY DESIGN®

Print Teaching Options

V Visual Skills

- [ ] **P. 436** Students use a diagram to visualize what life was like in an early African village. **Visual/Spatial**
- [ ] **P. 437** Students analyze a map of Bantu migrations. **Visual/Spatial**

R Reading Skills

- [ ] **P. 437** Students explore the root of *matrilineal* and related words. **AL** **ELL**
- [ ] **P. 438** Students explain the roots of the slave trade.
- [ ] **P. 439** Students specify two events that caused the growth of the market for slaves.
- [ ] **P. 440** Students explain what historians might learn from early African art. **BL**

W Writing Skills

- [ ] **P. 438** Students write a paragraph from the point of view of an African woman.

C Critical Thinking Skills

- [ ] **P. 436** Students contrast lineage groups with extended families. **BL** **AL**
- [ ] **P. 439** Students analyze a primary source to determine point of view.
- [ ] **P. 440** Students generalize about the purposes of art in Africa. **AL**
- [ ] **P. 441** Students identify modern-day rites of passage that might be similar to ancient African life passages.

T Technology Skills

- [ ] **P. 441** Students research and report on traditional African music and instruments. **Interpersonal** **Auditory/Musical**

Online Teaching Options

V Visual Skills

- [ ] **VIDEO** **The History, Exploration, and Conquest of South Africa**—Students are introduced to the history of this southern-most African nation.
- [ ] **MAP** **Bantu Migrations**—Students view the Bantu migration routes from the Bantu homeland.
- [ ] **MAP** **The Slave Trade c. 1450–1800**— Students view the routes taken by slave traders, between slave-gathering areas and the Americas, Asia, and Europe.

R Reading Skills

- [ ] **GRAPHIC ORGANIZER** **Taking Notes: *Finding the Main Idea:* African Arts**—Students record important ideas about the different elements of African culture.
- [ ] **IMAGE** **The Great Zimbabwe and Bantu Migrations**—Students read about the ruins of massive stonewalls that cover almost 1,800 miles of what is now southeastern Zimbabwe.
- [ ] **PRIMARY SOURCE** **Traditional Story**—Students read a story that was originally passed down through oral tradition.

C Critical Thinking Skills

- [ ] **SLIDE SHOW** **African Artwork**—Students analyze examples of paintings, sculpture, weaving, and other art forms.

T Technology Skills

- [ ] **SELF-CHECK QUIZ** **Lesson 3**—Students receive instant feedback on their mastery of lesson content.
- [ ] **GAME** **African Society and Culture Concentration Game**—Students make matches to review lesson content.
- [ ] **GAME** **African Society and Culture Fill-In Game**—Students fill in the blanks to review lesson vocabulary.

Printable Digital Worksheets

W Writing Skills

- [ ] **WORKSHEET** **21st Century Skills Activity: Information and Communication Technologies: Use Presentation Software**—Students describe and depicting African art by designing slides with text and visuals.

Intervention and Remediation Strategies

LESSON 1 The Rise of African Civilizations

Reading and Comprehension

Creating Maps Provide students with a blank outline map of Africa. Tell them to label the locations of the places that they read about as they work through the lesson content.

Text Evidence

Argument Have students write a brief paragraph arguing which African civilization discussed in the lesson was the most important. Tell students to include facts and details from the text to support their argument.

LESSON 2 Africa's Governments and Religions

Reading and Comprehension

Summarizing Have students read the information about African governments. Then have them write a brief paragraph summarizing the key characteristics of these governments.

Text Evidence

Sequencing Have students create a sequence graphic organizer that shows events relating to the spread of Islam throughout Africa. Tell students to check their work using the content on pages 433–435 of the lesson.

LESSON 3 African Society and Culture

Reading and Comprehension

Defining Direct students to create flashcards showing the vocabulary words and definitions from this lesson. Encourage students to illustrate their flashcards to enhance their comprehension.

Text Evidence

Researching on the Internet Direct students to conduct online research to locate an image of a traditional African artwork. Tell them to write a few sentences to tell how this piece might have functioned in its creator's everyday life. Have students check their ideas by reviewing page 440 in their textbook

Online Resources

Approaching Level Reader

Use this online lower-level text that corresponds directly to the text in the Student Edition. It includes a Spanish version.

Guided Reading Activities

This resource uses graphic organizers and guiding questions to help students with comprehension.

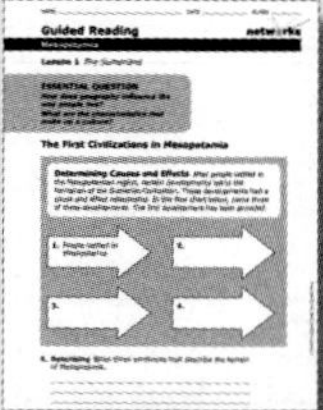

What Do You Know?

Use these worksheets to pre-assess student's background knowledge before they study the chapter.

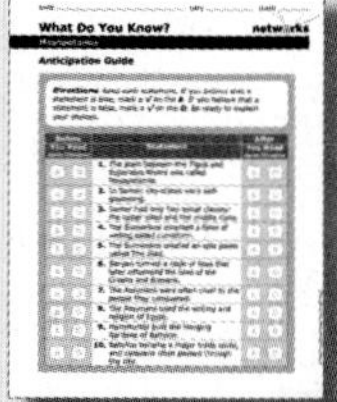

Reading Essentials and Study Guide Workbook

This resource offers writing and reading activities for the approaching-level student. Also available in Spanish.

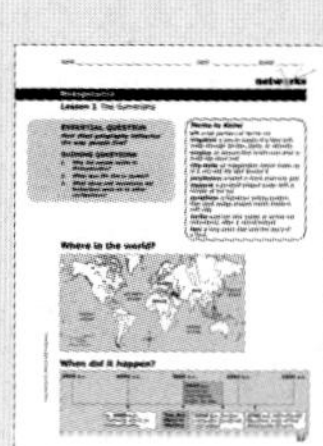

Self-Check Quizzes

This online assessment tool provides instant feedback for students to check their progress.

African Civilizations

400 B.C. to A.D. 1500

ESSENTIAL QUESTIONS • *Why do people trade?* • *How does religion shape society?* • *How do religions develop?*

networks

There's More Online about the beginnings and development of culture, government, and religion in Africa.

CHAPTER 15

Lesson 1
The Rise of African Civilizations

Lesson 2
Africa's Governments and Religions

Lesson 3
African Society and Culture

The Story Matters . . .

Around A.D. 1400 the steamy rain forests of Africa were home to the kingdom of Benin. The region's steamy climate and fertile soil allowed farmers to grow surpluses of crops. Over time, communities and societies developed.

As a result, arts became very important in Benin. The kingdom became well known for the ivory and wood carvings its artists produced. An example is this rare pendant carved in ivory in honor of Queen Idia. Other artists worked with metals to produce realistic-looking masks. Today, this surviving art allows historians to learn more about the rich history and culture of early African civilizations.

◄ *The African kingdom of Benin became well known for the detailed works of its artists, such as this ivory carving.*

Peter Horree/Alamy

419

Letter from the Author

Dear World History Teacher,

The mastery of agriculture gave rise to three early civilizations in Africa—Egypt, Kush, and Axum. Ghana, Mali, and Songhai were three flourishing trade states in West Africa. Zimbabwe played an important role in the southern half of Africa. In the fifteenth century, fleets from Portugal began to explore the coast of West Africa. At first, their sponsors searched for gold and slaves, but their goal soon changed to domination of trade in the Indian Ocean. The demands of the Europeans would soon pose a threat to the peoples of Africa.

Jackson J. Spielvogel

ENGAGE

Bellringer Ask a volunteer to read "The Story Matters . . ." aloud, or read it aloud in class for the students. Discuss with students the circumstances that allowed the arts to flourish in Benin. **Ask:** **What are some other early societies in which the arts held great importance?** Have students share examples with which they are familiar, such as ancient Greece. Then **ask:** **What can we learn about a culture by studying the works of art that its people produce?** Lead the class in a discussion of this question. Guide students to recognize that works of art often reflect the daily lives, traditions, hopes, and concerns of a cultural group. As a result, these works can provide clues about how people lived in the past. Inform them that they can learn more about Benin and African culture online.

Making Connections

Read the following information to students: What do you think of when you think of salt? Today, this is a common flavoring in foods. You might think of salty pretzels, for example. But salt is also often used in canned or packaged foods, such as green beans or pasta sauce. In the United States, a big box of salt might cost just a few dollars. However, in ancient Africa, salt was a valuable resource. Humans and animals need salt to live. Kingdoms in West Africa became very rich by controlling the salt trade. People in Ethiopia and in other parts of Africa and Europe even used cakes of salt as money.

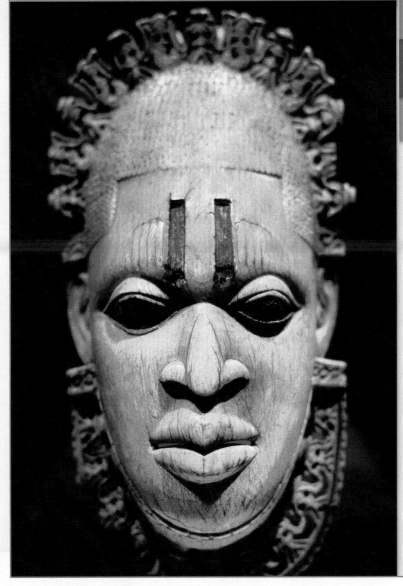

TEACH & ASSESS

Step Into the Place

V Visual Skills

Analyzing Maps Project the Interactive World Atlas on the whiteboard and show Africa. Direct students to take notice of the size of the continent, and point out important physical features. Discuss with students how Africa's location, size, and physical features might have influenced where people settled and traded. Ask students to predict where they think trading empires might have developed. Remind students to base their choices on their earlier observations about Africa's size and physical features, and on what they may already know about where people settle. Ask each volunteer to explain his or her choice.

Content Background Knowledge

Africa's geography has a large influence on where the continent's people live. Naturally, populations tend to cluster around water resources and, sometimes, in highlands. Traditionally, Africans have settled in widespread villages and small communities that may move to take advantage of better farmland. The onset of European colonialism during the nineteenth century contributed to the rise of numerous major cities. Today, Rwanda and Burundi in East Africa are the continent's two most densely populated nations. Desert areas in Mauritania, Libya, Botswana, and Namibia are among the continent's least densely populated zones.

ANSWERS, p. 420

Step Into the Place

1. The northern part of Africa, covered in desert, would be the most difficult land to farm.
2. Rain forest and savanna climate regions run along the Equator in Africa.
3. The Mediterranean climate occurs in the far northern and far southern portions of the continent.
4. CRITICAL THINKING The Great Rift Valley contains rivers and is accessible to the coast of the Indian Ocean. Because of this, it was a fertile and safe place to settle.

Step Into the Time

Answers will vary, but students should show understanding that the savanna and rain forest climate zones around Central and West Africa were the birthplaces of the earliest kingdoms in Africa

CHAPTER 15 CCSS

Place and Time: AFRICA 400 B.C. to A.D. 1500

The earliest civilizations in Africa emerged about five thousand years ago. These early kingdoms developed rich cultures that excelled at many art forms. Later African empires were affected by the arrival of Islam and then Europeans. All had an impact creating the Africa we know today.

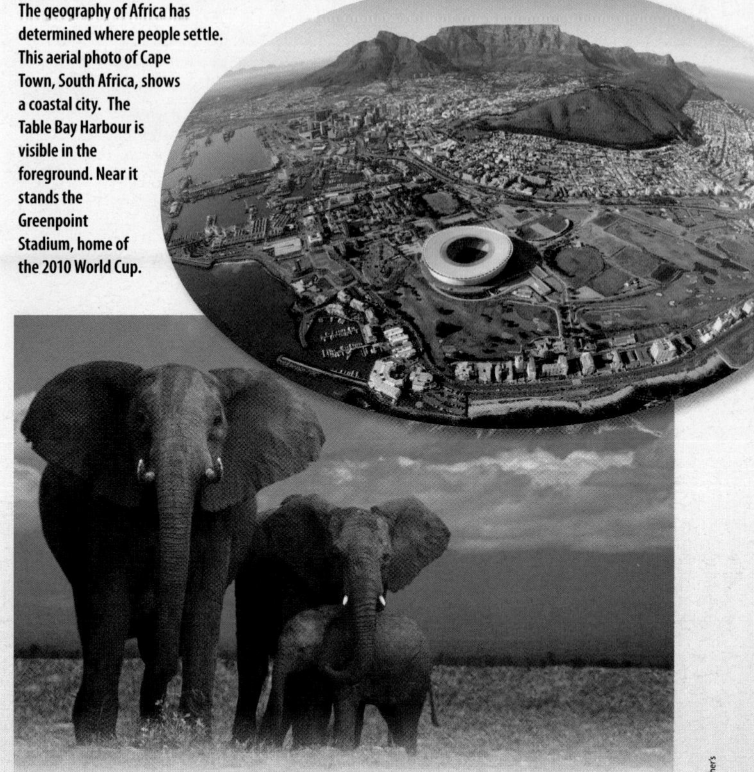

The geography of Africa has determined where people settle. This aerial photo of Cape Town, South Africa, shows a coastal city. The Table Bay Harbour is visible in the foreground. Near it stands the Greenpoint Stadium, home of the 2010 World Cup.

Wildlife abounds in Africa. Individual countries now have laws protecting their wildlife. These elephants, living near Kilimanjaro are one protected species. Other wildlife are a concern of environmentalists. All over the continent, animal life is recognized as one of Africa's most valuable resources.

Step Into the Place

MAP FOCUS The vast and varied landscape of Africa influenced the development of civilizations on the continent.

1. **REGION** In which part of Africa would you find the most land that is difficult to farm? RH.6–8.7
2. **PLACE** What climate region runs along the Equator in Africa? RH.6–8.7
3. **LOCATION** Describe the location of the Mediterranean climate in Africa. RH.6–8.7
4. CRITICAL THINKING
   Human-Environment Interaction What impact do you think the Great Rift Valley might have had on where people settled? RH.6–8.2

Step Into the Time

C **TIME LINE** A variety of climates are found in Africa. According to the time line, where and in what climate zone did the earliest kingdoms appear? RH.6–8.7

AFRICAN CIVILIZATIONS
- c. 250 B.C. Mali is West Africa's largest trading center
- c. A.D. 250 Bantu peoples settle south of Sahara

500 B.C. — A.D. 1 — A.D. 500

THE WORLD
- c. 312 B.C. Romans build Appian Way
- c. 44 B.C. Julius Caesar killed
- c. A.D. 400 Yamato control Japan

Project-Based Learning

Hands-On Chapter Project

African Civilizations

Students will create an illustrated children's story about a topic related to African civilization. Have students participate in a class discussion to review what they have learned about African civilizations. Then divide the class into small groups. Tell groups to choose a topic about an African region, river, or people, and then plan how they will plot, write, and illustrate their story. Next, students will research, write, and illustrate their stories. Student groups will present their stories to the rest of the class.

Technology Extension

Children's Story eBook

Students may transform their illustrated children's stories into eBooks. To do this, students may either write directly into an online eBook platform or upload their finished content into the platform. Students should share their books with younger children either in person or virtually.

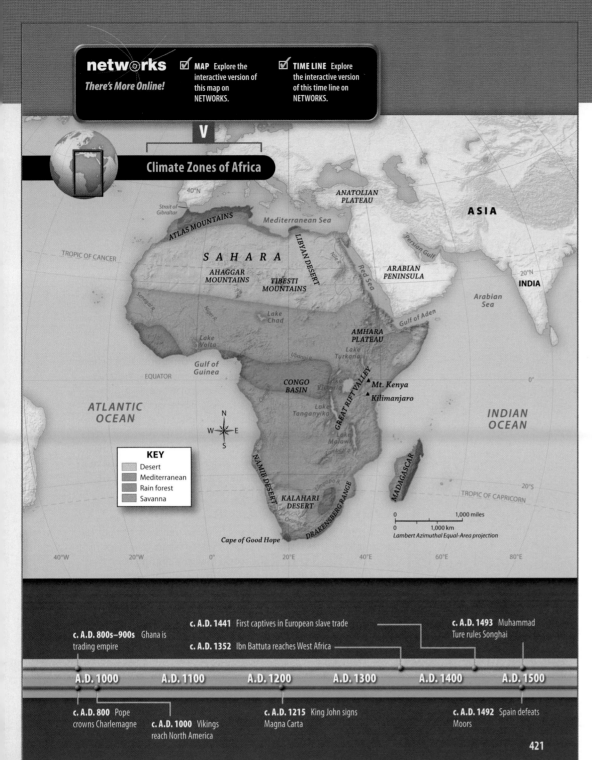

networks
There's More Online!

MAP Explore the interactive version of this map on NETWORKS.

TIME LINE Explore the interactive version of this time line on NETWORKS.

V

Climate Zones of Africa

40°N
Strait of Gibraltar
ATLAS MOUNTAINS
Mediterranean Sea
ANATOLIAN PLATEAU
ASIA
TROPIC OF CANCER
SAHARA
LIBYAN DESERT
Persian Gulf
Nile R.
Red Sea
AHAGGAR MOUNTAINS
TIBESTI MOUNTAINS
ARABIAN PENINSULA
20°N
INDIA
Arabian Sea
Senegal R.
Niger R.
Lake Chad
Gulf of Aden
AMHARA PLATEAU
Lake Volta
Lake Turkana
Ubangi R.
Gulf of Guinea
EQUATOR
CONGO BASIN
Lake Victoria
GREAT RIFT VALLEY
Mt. Kenya
Kilimanjaro
0°
ATLANTIC OCEAN
Lake Tanganyika
INDIAN OCEAN
N
W
E
S
Lake Malawi
Zambezi R.
KEY
Desert
Mediterranean
Rain forest
Savanna
NAMIB DESERT
MADAGASCAR
Limpopo R.
KALAHARI DESERT
DRAKENSBERG RANGE
20°S
TROPIC OF CAPRICORN
Orange R.
0 1,000 miles
0 1,000 km
Lambert Azimuthal Equal-Area projection
Cape of Good Hope
40°W 20°W 0° 20°E 40°E 60°E 80°E

c. A.D. 800s–900s Ghana is trading empire

c. A.D. 1441 First captives in European slave trade

c. A.D. 1352 Ibn Battuta reaches West Africa

c. A.D. 1493 Muhammad Ture rules Songhai

A.D. 1000 | A.D. 1100 | A.D. 1200 | A.D. 1300 | A.D. 1400 | A.D. 1500

c. A.D. 800 Pope crowns Charlemagne

c. A.D. 1000 Vikings reach North America

c. A.D. 1215 King John signs Magna Carta

c. A.D. 1492 Spain defeats Moors

421

CHAPTER 15

Place and Time

Step Into the Time

C Critical Thinking Skills

Making Inferences Have students review the time line for the chapter. Explain that they will be studying events from about 250 B.C. to A.D. 1500. **Ask:** Based on the information listed in the time line, what can you infer about the history of African civilizations during the period shown in the time line? *(During this time, the various empires were rising and falling.)*

Content Background Knowledge

Prince Henry the Navigator of Portugal sponsored a great deal of European exploration of the African coastline during the fifteenth century. He hoped to establish a sea route around Africa to the east. By doing this, Henry hoped that Portugal could gain control of the lucrative trade routes that were crossing both Asia as well as the Sahara, through North Africa—among other reasons. Portuguese navigator Vasco de Gama eventually rounded the southern tip of Africa in 1497. The interactions that resulted from European involvement in Africa from the fifteenth century onward greatly changed life in the West African region that students will study in this chapter.

CLOSE & REFLECT

Remind students that this era covers the same time period as the height of the rise of Islam in Southwest Asia as well as the Roman and—later—Byzantine empires. As a class, discuss how events taking place in these nearby places might have influenced life in Africa.

TIME LINE

Place and Time: African Civilizations 400 B.C. to A.D. 1500

Reading a Time Line Display the interactive time line. Remind students that the time line shows events that relate to the chapter content about Africa, and call out major events happening elsewhere around the world. Point out some pairs of events that took place in different parts of the world at about the same time. Invite students to suggest other world events that they could add to the time line.

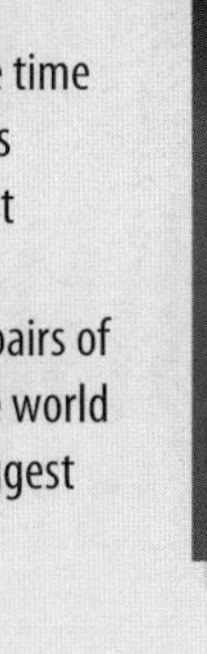

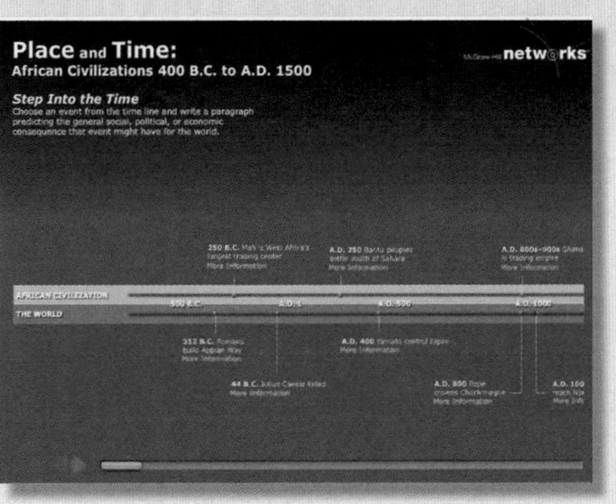

See page 419B for other online activities.

ENGAGE

Bellringer Present to students a physical map of Africa. Direct them to identify some of the major physical features they see. If necessary, guide students to point out features such as the Sahara or the Nile River. **Ask: How do you think these features might have affected trade in early Africa?** *(Answers will vary, but students should draw reasonable inferences about the effects of major physical features on trade. For instance, students might suggest that rivers and oceans may have benefited trade, while other features, such as mountains and deserts, could have made trade more difficult.)*

TEACH & ASSESS

R Reading Skills

Calculating After students have read the section titled "African Beginnings," discuss the early settlement of Africa with the class. Ask students to speculate about why humans transitioned from nomadic hunter-gatherer societies to settled villages to the first civilizations. **Ask: About how many years passed between the settlement of the first villages and the development of the first civilizations?** *(about 4,000 or 5,000 years)* **Logical/Mathematical**

C Critical Thinking Skills

Drawing Conclusions Point out that Africa is the world's second-largest continent. Make sure students understand that the continent has four different geographic zones and a wide variety of physical features and climates. **Ask: What is one reason that Africa has such varied geography?** *(Students should suggest that the continent's large size makes it highly diverse. It also spans much of two hemispheres.)* AL

ANSWER, p. 422

TAKING NOTES: Ghana: gold, salt; Mali: gold, salt; Songhai: gold, salt

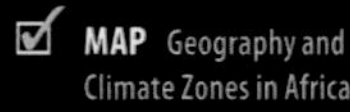

networks *There's More Online!*
- MAP Geography and Climate Zones in Africa
- SLIDE SHOW
  - Great Rift Valley
  - Dhows
  - Trade Routes of North Africa
- GRAPHIC ORGANIZER African Kingdoms
- VIDEO

Taghaza Timbuktu Gao Saleh

Lesson 1

The Rise of African Civilizations

ESSENTIAL QUESTION *Why do people trade?*

IT MATTERS BECAUSE

The geography of Africa affected the development and interaction of civilizations all over the huge continent.

African Beginnings

GUIDING QUESTION *How did early peoples settle Africa?*

People have lived in Africa for a very long time. Scientists believe that the first humans appeared in eastern and southern Africa between 150,000 and 200,000 years ago. Early human groups in Africa lived as hunters and gatherers. These early peoples moved from place to place to hunt and gather food.

About seven or eight thousand years ago, hunters and gatherers in Africa began to settle in villages. They learned to tame animals and grow crops. Around 3000 B.C., as farming villages became more widespread and organized, Africa's first civilizations developed. These early civilizations were Egypt and Kush.

A Vast and Varied Landscape

The people of Africa found opportunities and challenges in the geography of the continent. First of all, Africa is very large in size. After Asia, Africa is the world's largest continent.

Most of Africa lies in the tropics. However, this enormous continent is made up of four distinct geographic zones.

Rain forests stretch along the Equator, which slices through the middle of the continent. These forests make up about 10 percent of Africa's land **area**. The rain forest zone gets heavy rainfall, and it is warm there all year long. The dense growth of

Reading HELPDESK CCSS

Taking Notes: *Identifying*

On a chart like this one, list the three major West African trading kingdoms. Then add one product that each kingdom traded. RH.6–8.2

West African Kingdom	Product

Content Vocabulary (Tier 3 Words)
- savanna
- plateau
- griot
- dhow

networks Online Teaching Options

VIDEO

Great African Queens

Summarizing Play the video about African queens for the class. After viewing, ask students to identify some of the video's most important main ideas. Note these ideas on the board. Then work with students to summarize the main ideas into a few sentences that tell briefly about the lives of the various queens and their achievements.

See page 419C for other online activities.

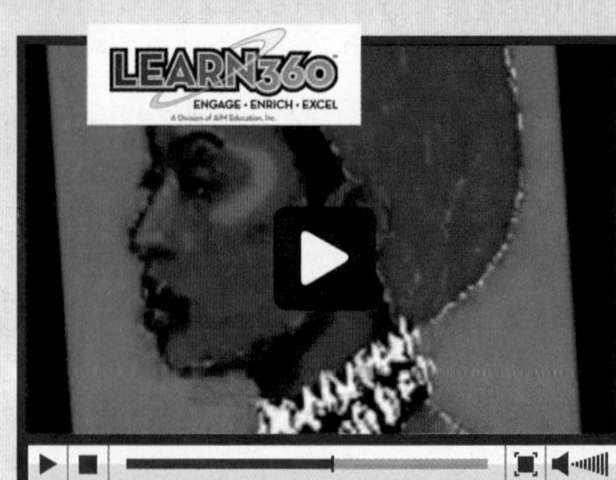

Geography and Climate Zones in Africa

trees and plants in the rain forest can make farming difficult. Farmers, however, clear some of the forestland to grow root crops, such as yams.

Grasslands and Deserts

Vast grasslands make up the second zone. They stretch north and south of the rain forest. **Savannas** (suh•VAN•uhs) are tropical grasslands dotted with small trees and shrubs. These flat or rolling plains cover about 40 percent of Africa's land area. The savannas have high temperatures and uneven rains. However, they get enough rainfall for farming and herding. Farmers grow grains, such as millet and sorghum (SAWR•guhm). Herders raise cattle and other animals.

In northern Africa, the savannas connect with an area of even drier grasslands known as the Sahel (SA•hil). Plants that grow there provide barely enough food for people and animals. The people of the Sahel were traditionally hunters and herders.

C

GEOGRAPHY CONNECTION

Differences in geographic features, such as climate, have had a strong influence on life in Africa's geographic zones.

1 **LOCATION** Which geographic feature covers most of East Africa?

2 **CRITICAL THINKING** ***Making Inferences*** How might the geographic zones of Africa have affected interaction between people from the northeastern and northwestern parts of the continent?

savanna tropical grasslands dotted with small trees and shrubs

Academic Vocabulary (Tier 2)
area the land included within a set of boundaries

Reading Strategy: *Contrasting*
When you contrast two things, you determine how they are different from each other. Read the information about savannas and the Sahel. On a separate sheet of paper, explain how these two areas differ.

V Visual Skills

Integrating Visual Information Point out the photographs and map to the class. Invite students to describe each of Africa's four major climate zones using the information given in the photographs. **Ask:** **Which zone do you think best supports human habitation? Why?** *(Students may suggest that the savannas or the Mediterranean regions, which show large grasslands and plant and animal life, are best for human habitation.)* **Ask:** **In which zone do you think it would be hardest for humans to live in? Why?** *(Students may suggest that the desert or rain forest regions would be the most challenging, since they do not appear to be good for farming.)* **Visual/Spatial**

C Critical Thinking Skills

Determining Cause and Effect Talk about the grasslands region of Africa with the class. Point out that grasslands are the most widespread geographic feature on the continent and cover more area than each of the other three geographic zones. Explain that the climate of the grasslands therefore varies across the continent. **Ask:** **How does the drier climate of the Sahel affect how people there live?** *(The people of the Sahel are traditionally hunters and herders rather than farmers because the dry grasslands make crops hard to grow.)*

LECTURE SLIDE

Geographic Zones of Africa

Identifying Show students the lecture slide on the geographic zones of Africa. Discuss the key differences among those zones. Help students understand the important characteristics of these areas, as well as how they differ. **Ask:** **How did the land area covered by deserts compare to that covered by rain forests?** *(The land area covered by deserts was much larger than that covered by rain forests.)* **In which geographic zone could people raise many crops?** *(mild climate zone)*

See page 419C for other online activities.

networks — African Beginnings

Geographic Zones of Africa

- **rain forest** the forests that grow along part of the Equator; they receive heavy rainfall, have an abundance of trees and plants, and make up about 10 percent of Africa's land area.
- **savanna** tropical grasslands dotted with small trees and shrubs; these plains have high temperatures and cover approximately 40 percent of Africa.
- **desert** make up about 40 percent of the land in Africa; the climate in this zone made travel difficult for many years.
- **mild climate** located along the northern coast and southern tip of Africa; these areas have moderate rainfall, warm temperatures, and fertile land for crops.

ANSWERS, p. 423

GEOGRAPHY CONNECTION

1 Savanna covers most of East Africa.

2 **CRITICAL THINKING** The difficulty of traveling across the desert zone probably would have limited interaction between people in these parts of Africa.

Reading Strategy Savannas are tropical grasslands dotted with small trees and shrubs. They have high temperatures and uneven rains. However, savannas do get enough rain to support farming and herding. The Sahel is drier than the savannas. It has different types of trees, thick shrubs, and grasses. These barely provide enough food for the people and animals that live there. For most of Africa's history, people living in this region were hunters and herders.

V Visual Skills

Reading a Chart Direct students' attention to the chart titled, "Comparing Africa to the U.S." Remind them that charts are organized into rows and columns to make it easier to find information. Model finding the size of Africa for students. **Ask:** **What is the largest desert in Africa?** *(Sahara)* **About how many square miles does this desert cover?** *(about 3,500,000 square miles)* AL

C Critical Thinking Skills

Making Inferences Tell students that, millions of years ago, geological changes shaped what the Africa continent looks like today. Invite a volunteer to read the information about the creation of the Great Rift Valley. Point out the sentence that tells about scientific discoveries there. **Ask:** **What do these discoveries suggest about human life in the Great Rift Valley?** *(It was most likely among the first places on Earth where humans lived.)*

ANSWERS, p. 424

INFOGRAPHIC

1. The longest river in Africa is the Nile River. The Missouri River is the longest river system in the United States.
2. **CRITICAL THINKING** Africa is more than three times larger than the United States in size and in population.

COMPARING AFRICA TO THE U.S.

V

	Africa	United States
Size	11,667,159 square miles (30,217,894 sq. km)	3,794,085 square miles (9,826,680 sq. km)
Population Today	about 1.03 billion people	about 308 million people
Longest River	Nile River 4,160 miles (6,693 km)	Missouri River 2,565 miles (4,130 km)
Largest Desert	Sahara 3,500,000 square miles (9,065,000 sq. km)	Mojave 15,000 square miles (38,850 sq. km)

UNITED STATES
AFRICA

Encyclopaedia Britannica OnLine s.v., "Africa," http://www.britannica.com/EBchecked/topic/7924/Africa

INFOGRAPHIC

Many areas of Africa remain mostly unpopulated. Africa's population represents only about 10 percent of the world's total population.

1. **IDENTIFYING** What are the longest rivers in Africa and the United States?
2. **CRITICAL THINKING** *Comparing and Contrasting* How do Africa and the United States compare in size and population?

Deserts are Africa's third zone. They are found north and south of the grasslands. About 40 percent of the land in Africa is desert. The world's largest desert—the Sahara—stretches across much of North Africa. The Kalahari (KA•luh•HAHR•ee), another desert region, lies in southwestern Africa. For many years, the deserts limited travel and trade. People had to move along the coastline to avoid these vast seas of sand.

Small areas of mild climate—the Mediterranean—make up the fourth zone. These areas are found along the northern coast and southern tip of Africa. In these areas, **adequate** rainfall, warm temperatures, and fertile land produce abundant crops. This food surplus can support large populations.

Africa's Landforms and Rivers

Most of Africa is covered by a series of plateaus. A **plateau** (pla•TOH) is an area of high and mostly flat land. In East Africa, mountains, valleys, and lakes cross the plateau. Millions of years ago, movements of the Earth's crust created deep cuts in the surface of the plateau. This activity created the Great Rift Valley. In recent years, scientists have found some of the earliest human fossils in the Great Rift Valley. C

Many large river systems are found in Africa. The civilizations of Egypt and Kush flourished along the banks of the Nile River in North Africa. The major river system in West Africa is found along the Niger (NY•juhr) River. Trade and farming led to the growth of villages and towns throughout the Niger River area.

Reading HELPDESK CCSS

plateau an area of high and mostly flat land

Academic Vocabulary (Tier 2 Words)

adequate enough to satisfy a need
transport to transfer or carry from one place to another

networks Online Teaching Options

SLIDE SHOW

The Great Rift Valley

Drawing Conclusions Direct students' attention to the information about plateaus and the Great Rift Valley in the section "Africa's Landforms and Rivers." Then have students view the interactive slide show about the Great Rift Valley to learn more about this area. **Ask:** **What does the information in the slide show suggest about the climate of the Great Rift Valley?** *(Answers will vary but may include that in some areas of the Great Rift Valley, the climate allows plants and animals to survive. The slide show reveals many different kinds of animals living in this area.)*

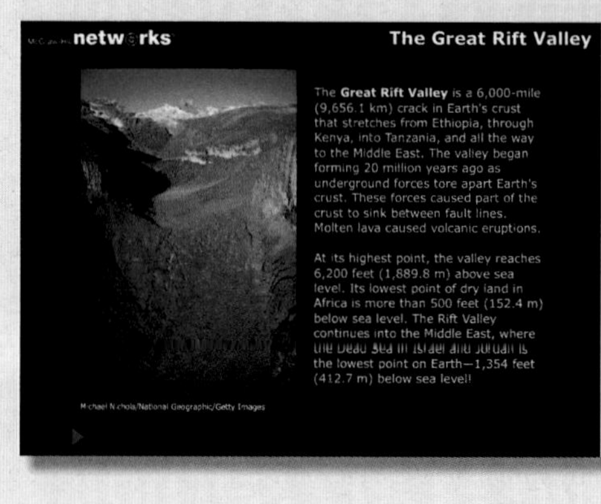

networks
The Great Rift Valley
The Great Rift Valley is a 6,000-mile (9,656.1 km) crack in Earth's crust that stretches from Ethiopia, through Kenya, into Tanzania, and all the way to the Middle East. The valley began forming 20 million years ago as underground forces tore apart Earth's crust. These forces caused part of the crust to sink between fault lines. Molten lava caused volcanic eruptions.

See page 419C for other online activities.

People living south of the Sahara also learned to make iron. This skill spread from East and Central Africa to West Africa. By 250 B.C., Djenné-jeno (jeh•NAY-JEH•noh) emerged as the largest trading center in West Africa. Its artisans produced iron tools, gold jewelry, copper goods, and pottery.

PROGRESS CHECK

Determining Cause and Effect How did Africa's climate zones affect people's ability to raise crops?

Trading Empires in Africa

GUIDING QUESTION *How did trade develop in Africa?*

For thousands of years, the hot, dry Sahara isolated North Africa from the rest of the continent. Then, about 400 B.C., the Berber people of North Africa found ways to cross the Sahara to West Africa. Trade soon opened between the two regions.

How Did the Sahara Trade Develop?

For hundreds of years, the Berbers carried goods across the Sahara on donkeys and horses. The animals often did not survive the desert heat. The Romans introduced the central Asian camel in A.D. 200. The use of camels greatly changed trade in Africa. Camels are well suited for the desert. Their humps store fat for food, and they can travel for many days without water. The Berbers quickly adopted camels, both as a source of food and as a way to travel. **W**

Berber traders formed caravans of many camels. These caravans crossed the Sahara between North Africa and West Africa. West African merchants sent gold mined in their region to towns bordering the Sahara. From there, caravans carried the gold northward. Some of this African gold reached Europe and Asia. Christian and Muslim rulers in these areas valued African gold.

Caravans from West Africa also carried ivory, spices, leather, and ostrich feathers. In addition, they **transported** enslaved people captured in wars. Merchants sent these captives to the Mediterranean area and Southwest Asia to serve as soldiers or servants. **R**

PROGRESS CHECK

Explaining Why were camels essential for the Sahara trade?

West African Kingdoms

GUIDING QUESTION *Why did West African trading empires rise and fall?*

Caravans also headed from North Africa to West Africa. They transported cloth, weapons, horses, paper, and books. Once in West Africa, they traded for salt from mines in the Sahara.

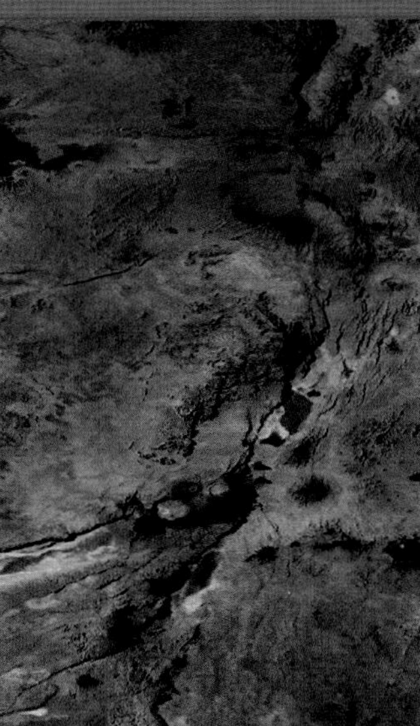

This satellite photo shows the Great Rift Valley, a deep crack in Earth's crust that is 6,000 miles (9,659 km) long. The valley began forming 20 million years ago.

W Writing Skills

Informative/Explanatory Tell students to consider what they have learned about the Sahara. Instruct them to reflect on how the desert influenced settlement and trade in early Africa. Students should write a short paragraph explaining their ideas. Encourage volunteers to share their work with a partner.

R Reading Skills

Listing After students read the text, discuss the importance of caravans to trade in North Africa. Then ask students to make a list of trade goods that these caravans transported across the Sahara. *(Lists should include goods such as gold, ivory, spices, leather, and ostrich feathers.)* After students have finished their lists, ask them to consider why these particular trade goods were carried. *(Students may note that many of these items had high value and low weight, such as spices and feathers. Others, such as salt, were needed for survival.)* AL

CHART

Camels versus Horses

Comparing and Contrasting Present to students the interactive chart comparing the use of camels and horses for trade. Tell students to consider what they have learned about trade, camels, and horses in the Sahara to complete the interactive Venn diagram featured in this activity.

See page 419C for other online activities.

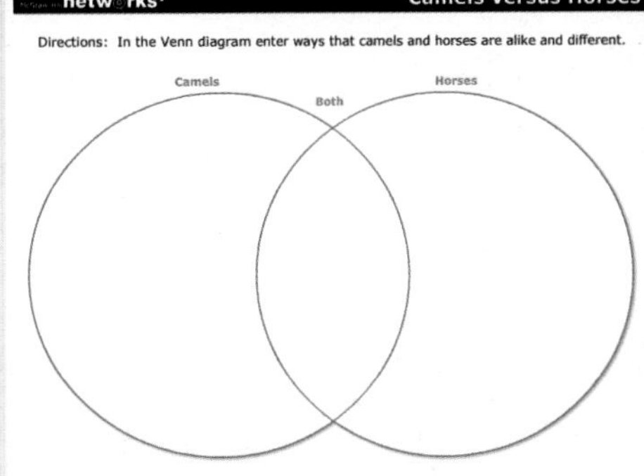

ANSWERS, p. 425

PROGRESS CHECK People could raise crops in Africa's rain forest, savanna, and mild climate zones. Growing crops was more difficult in the Sahel and desert zones.

PROGRESS CHECK Camels could survive the harsh conditions of the desert with minimal food and water. Their feet were also well-suited to walking in the sand.

V Visual Skills

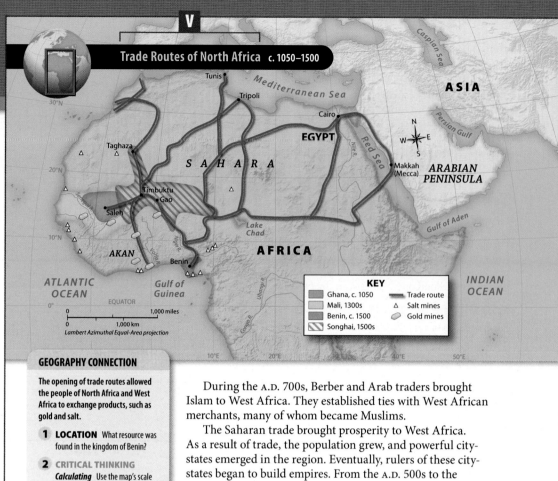

Analyzing Maps Review the map "Trade Routes of North Africa" with the class. Tell students to use their fingers to trace some of the North African trade routes from one end to another. Have volunteers offer words to describe the trade routes. *(Students may say words such as* long *or* indirect.*)*
Ask: **How did these trade routes probably affect the culture of North Africa?** *(Trade routes helped spread goods, people, and ideas among West Africa, North Africa, and Egypt because they encouraged people and goods to travel from place to place.)* ELL **Visual/Spatial Kinesthetic**

R Reading Skills

Finding the Main Idea Refer students to the section titled "How Did Ghana Begin?" Point out to students that Ghana became the first great trading empire in West Africa. **Ask:** **How did Ghana's location help it become a powerful trading empire?** *(Because Ghana was located between salt mines in the Sahara and gold mines near the West African rain forests, it became a crossroads of trade. Ghana's kings could tax traders passing through the kingdom. These taxes made Ghana wealthy.)* AL

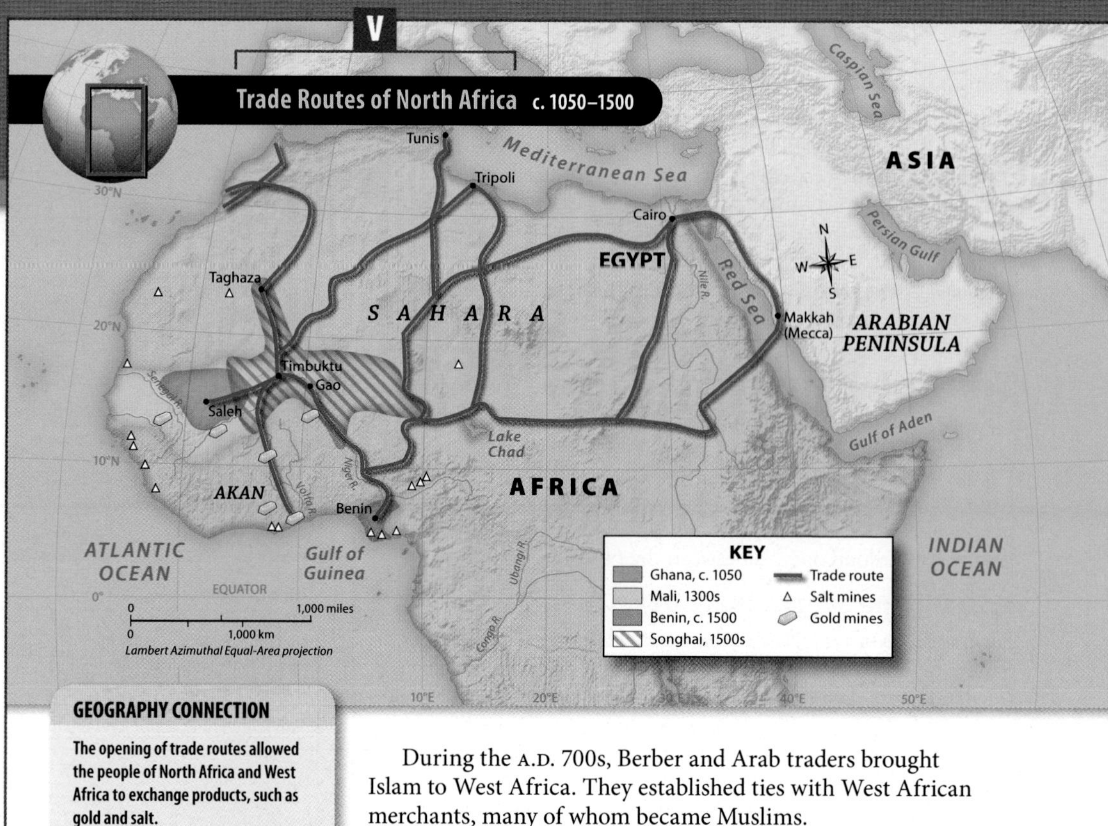

GEOGRAPHY CONNECTION

The opening of trade routes allowed the people of North Africa and West Africa to exchange products, such as gold and salt.

1. **LOCATION** What resource was found in the kingdom of Benin?
2. **CRITICAL THINKING** ***Calculating*** Use the map's scale to determine how many miles a caravan might travel along a route from Tunis to Benin.

During the A.D. 700s, Berber and Arab traders brought Islam to West Africa. They established ties with West African merchants, many of whom became Muslims.

The Saharan trade brought prosperity to West Africa. As a result of trade, the population grew, and powerful city-states emerged in the region. Eventually, rulers of these city-states began to build empires. From the A.D. 500s to the A.D. 1300s, these African empires were bigger than most European kingdoms in wealth and size.

How Did Ghana Begin?

R Ghana (GAH•nuh) was the first great trading empire in West Africa. It rose to power during the A.D. 400s. The kingdom of Ghana was located in the Sudan. This area was mostly grassland, stretching across north central Africa. Fertile soil and iron tools helped the farmers of Ghana produce enough food.

Ghana was located between the Sahara salt mines and gold mines near the West African coastal rain forests. As a result, Ghana became an important crossroads of trade. From Ghana, trade

Reading HELPDESK CCSS

Reading in the Content Area
When reading primary source quotes, note any words or phrases in brackets. The use of brackets provides you with additional words that help clarify the meaning of the quote.

griot traditional storytellers

networks Online Teaching Options

CHART

Tree Diagram

Organizing Display the tree-diagram chart for students. Add the heading "Saharan Trade" to the top box. With students, brainstorm possible characteristics or results of the Saharan trade that could be used to complete the graphic organizer. Then organize students into small groups to complete the tree diagram. Have them use the Jigsaw student graphic organizers to create a fuller picture of the Saharan trade. **Interpersonal**

See page 419C for other online activities.

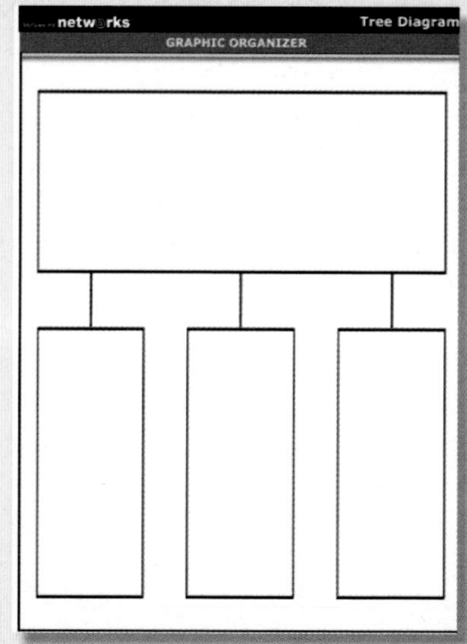

ANSWERS, p. 426

GEOGRAPHY CONNECTION

1. Salt was found in Benin.
2. **CRITICAL THINKING** A caravan would travel about 2,000 miles (3,219 km) along a trade route on this journey.

routes extended into North Africa and down the Niger River. They also linked to kingdoms in the Central African rain forest. Some routes reached all the way to Africa's eastern coast.

Traders interested in salt or gold had to pass through Ghana, which came at a price. Traders had no choice but to pay taxes to Ghana's kings. First, Ghana had iron ore and knew how to make iron weapons. Although Ghana owned no gold mines, it controlled the West Africans who did. Second, Ghana's kings had a well-trained army to enforce their wishes. Third, people were willing to pay any price for salt, a highly desired item used to flavor and preserve food. Berber traders wanted gold so they could buy goods from Arab countries and from Europe.

Abdullah Abu-Ubayd Al-Bakri (ehl•BEHK•ree), an Arab travelling writer in about A.D. 1067, described the way Ghana taxed merchants:

PRIMARY SOURCE

“The king [of Ghana] exacts the right of one dinar [of gold] on each donkey-load of salt that enters his country, and two dinars of gold on each load of salt that goes out.”

—from *Ghana in 1067*

C

Ghana reached the height of its trading power in the A.D. 800s and 900s. Muslim Arabs and Berbers involved in the salt and gold trade brought Islam to Ghana.

Rise of Mali

During the A.D. 1100s, invaders from North Africa disrupted Ghana's trade, and the empire fell. As Ghana weakened, local groups separated to form new trading states in West Africa.

R

In the A.D. 1200s, a small state named Mali (MAH•lee) conquered Ghana. Mali created a new empire. West African **griots** (GREE•ohz), or storytellers, credit a great king for Mali's rise. His name was Sundiata Keita (sun•dee•AH•tuh KY•tuh)—the "Lion Prince." Sundiata ruled from 1230 to 1255. He united the people of Mali.

Sundiata conquered territory extending from the Atlantic coast inland to the trading city of Timbuktu (TIHM•BUHK•TOO). His conquests put Mali in control of the gold mines in West Africa. As a result, Mali built its wealth and power on the gold and salt trade.

How did Songhai Begin?

Mali weakened after the death of king Mansa Musa (MAHN•sah moo•SAH) in 1337. One of the states that eventually broke away from Mali's control was Songhai (SAWNG•eye). In 1464, Sunni Ali (sun•EE ah•LEE) became the ruler of Songhai. He seized control of Timbuktu. Sunni Ali used Songhai's location along the Niger River to extend his territory.

Thinking Like a HISTORIAN

Researching on the Internet

Ghana became the first great trading empire in West Africa. In the A.D. 800s and 900s, Ghana was at the height of its trading power. Use the Internet to find reliable sources about what life was like in Ghana during this period. Write two or three sentences that summarize your findings and present your summary to the class. For more information about using the Internet for research, read *What Does a Historian Do?*

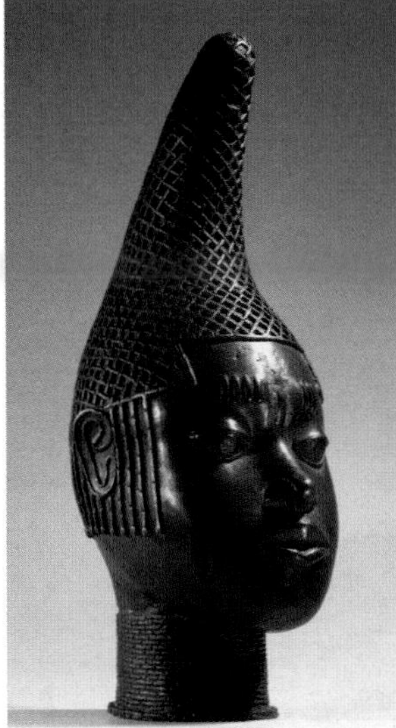

This West African sculpture is of the Queen Mother of Benin. Benin had great rulers. By the mid-1500s, the kingdom of Benin stretched from the Niger River delta to what is now Lagos.

C Critical Thinking Skills

Analyzing Primary Sources Read the primary-source excerpt about taxation with students. Make sure they understand that a *dinar* is a unit of money. **Ask:** What trade good does this excerpt suggest was the most important in Ghana? *(salt)* AL ELL

R Reading Skills

Naming Ask students to read the information under the heading "Rise of Mali." After students read the text, discuss the rise of the kingdom of Mali with them. Help them understand that Mali conquered the kingdom of Ghana during the 1200s and replaced it as the most important West African trading kingdom. **Ask:** Who was the most important person in the founding of Mali? *(Sundiata Keita)*

SLIDE SHOW

How to Find Resources on the Internet

Researching on the Internet Support students' online research on the West African kingdom of Ghana by having them complete the "How to Find Resources on the Internet" digital lesson. Encourage students to takes notes on the lesson to refer to as they perform research on the Internet in the future.

See page 419C for other online activities.

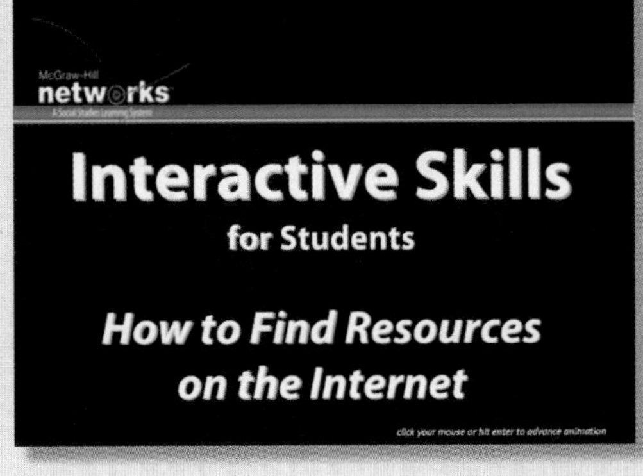

McGraw-Hill
networks
Interactive Skills
for Students
How to Find Resources
on the Internet

V Visual Skills

Interpreting Direct students' attention to the "African Trading Empires" infographic. Point out the location of each empire using the infographic maps. **Ask:** Which trading empire shown here flourished earliest? *(Axum)* Which trading empire shown here flourished latest? *(Songhai)* Which was the longest-lasting empire? *(Axum)* AL

R Reading Skills

Explaining Have students review the information about the kingdom of Axum. Note that this kingdom lay on the Red Sea far to the east of the trading kingdoms they have been studying. **Ask:** How did Axum's location help it become an important trading empire? *(Axum was located on the Red Sea, so it was in a spot that connected Africa, the Mediterranean, and India. This meant that many goods and enslaved peoples were transported through Axum.)*

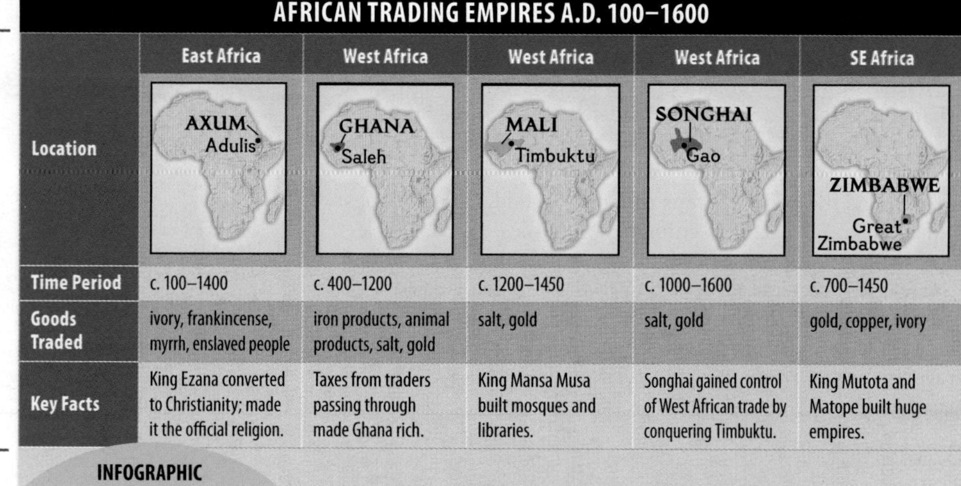

AFRICAN TRADING EMPIRES A.D. 100–1600

	East Africa	West Africa	West Africa	West Africa	SE Africa
Location	AXUM, Adulis	GHANA, Saleh	MALI, Timbuktu	SONGHAI, Gao	ZIMBABWE, Great Zimbabwe
Time Period	c. 100–1400	c. 400–1200	c. 1200–1450	c. 1000–1600	c. 700–1450
Goods Traded	ivory, frankincense, myrrh, enslaved people	iron products, animal products, salt, gold	salt, gold	salt, gold	gold, copper, ivory
Key Facts	King Ezana converted to Christianity; made it the official religion.	Taxes from traders passing through made Ghana rich.	King Mansa Musa built mosques and libraries.	Songhai gained control of West African trade by conquering Timbuktu.	King Mutota and Matope built huge empires.

INFOGRAPHIC

West African empires controlled trade for more than 1,000 years.

1. **IDENTIFYING** How long after the decline of Ghana did the Songhai Empire come to an end?
2. **CRITICAL THINKING** ***Comparing and Contrasting*** How were the goods traded by Ghana and Mali alike and different?

He took control of the river and then seized the salt mines. Songhai soon controlled the trade in salt from the Sahara and gold. By 1492, Songhai was the largest empire in West Africa. Invaders from North Africa ended the empire by A.D. 1600.

The West African kingdoms ruled the savannas. The rain forest, near the Equator, also had its own kingdoms. They included Benin, which arose in the Niger delta, and Kongo, which formed in the Congo River basin.

✓ **PROGRESS CHECK**

Identifying What were two valuable products traded through Ghana?

East African Kingdoms

GUIDING QUESTION *How did trade affect the development of East African kingdoms?*

In ancient times, powerful kingdoms also arose in East Africa. The kingdom of Kush thrived on the Nile River for hundreds of years. One of Kush's neighbors was the kingdom of Axum (AHK•SOOM) on the Red Sea.

Axum benefited from its location on the Red Sea. It was an important stop on the trade route linking Africa, the Mediterranean, and India. Axum exported ivory, incense, and enslaved people. It imported cloth, metal goods, and olive oil.

Reading HELPDESK CCSS

dhow sailboat using wind-catching, triangular sails

networks *Online Teaching Options*

WHITEBOARD ACTIVITY

How West Africa Changed Because of Trade

Categorizing Display the Interactive Whiteboard Activity for students. Have them complete the activity about the changes that trade brought to West Africa. Have students decide which of the effects in the item bank resulted from trade in West Africa. Help them place the effects they chose in the correct sequence on the chart. Remind students that trade did not affect only the economy of West Africa, but also areas such as government and culture.

See page 419C for other online activities.

ANSWERS, p. 428

INFOGRAPHIC

1. about 400 years
2. CRITICAL THINKING Ghana and Mali traded salt and gold. However, Ghana also traded iron products and animal products.

✓ PROGRESS CHECK Salt and gold were the two most valuable products to be traded by way of Ghana.

Axum fought Kush for control of trade routes to inland Africa. Around A.D. 300, King Ezana (ay•ZAHN•uh) conquered Kush. In A.D. 334, Ezana made Christianity the official religion of Axum. Islam was introduced to Axum later. Both religions had a major impact on Axum and other trading states.

Coastal States

C

In the early A.D. 600s, Arab traders from the Arabian Peninsula had reached East Africa. They sailed to Africa in boats called **dhows** (dowz). In the A.D. 700s, many Arab Muslim traders settled along the Indian Ocean in East Africa. They shared goods and ideas with Africans living there. By the 1300s, a string of key trading ports extended down the East African coast. They included Mogadishu (MAH•guh•DIH•shoo), Kilwa, Mombasa (mahm•BAH•suh), and Zanzibar (ZAN•zuh•BAHR).

A dhow usually had one or two sails. The bow, or front, of a dhow pointed sharply upward.

▶ CRITICAL THINKING

Making Inferences How do you think an invention such as the sails used on dhows might have benefited the Arab traders?

Mary Evans Picture Library

The Rise of Zimbabwe

R

The Indian Ocean trade reached far inland and led to the rise of wealthy states in Central and Southern Africa. These inland territories mined rich deposits of copper and gold. During the A.D. 900s, traders from the coastal cities of Africa began to trade with the inland states. The coastal traders brought silk, glass beads, carpets, and pottery. They traded for minerals, ivory, and coconut oil. They also obtained enslaved Africans for export to countries overseas.

An important trading state known as Zimbabwe (zihm•BAH•bway) arose in southeastern Africa. During the 1400s, this large empire reached from south of the Zambezi (zam•BEE•zee) River to the Indian Ocean.

✓ PROGRESS CHECK

Explaining Why did Axum become a prosperous trading center?

LESSON 1 REVIEW 

Review Vocabulary (Tier 3 Words)

1. How is a *savanna* different from a *plateau*? RH.6–8.2, RH.6–8.4

Answer the Guiding Questions

2. ***Explaining*** What are the four main geographic zones of Africa? RH.6–8.2
3. ***Identifying*** What role did the cities of Mogadishu and Mombasa play in the economic life of East Africa? RH.6–8.2
4. ***Naming*** What products did West Africans trade? RH.6–8.2
5. ***Describing*** What unique factors allowed the East African trading kingdoms to expand their trade? RH.6–8.2
6. **NARRATIVE** You live in ancient West Africa. Your family is traveling to East Africa. In a personal journal, describe what you might experience when you arrive in East Africa. Tell about the people, land, and weather. WHST.6–8.10

C Critical Thinking Skills

Speculating Refer students to the section titled "Coastal States." Review with them the information about the role of Arab traders in the settlement and trade along the coast of East Africa. **Ask:** What effects do you think the Arab traders had on African trade? *(Students might suggest that this gave African kingdoms access to new goods and new markets, as well as new ideas.)* BL

R Reading Skills

Listing After students have read the text, remind them that the most important trading goods of the West African kingdoms were salt and gold, but that these kingdoms also traded numerous other goods. Point out that the goods traded by inland and coastal Central and Southern African cities differed from those traded by their northern neighbors. **Ask:** What goods were traded by coastal African merchants? *(silk, glass beads, carpets, and pottery)* What goods were traded by inland African merchants? *(minerals, ivory, and coconut oil)* AL

Have students complete the Lesson 1 Review.

CLOSE & REFLECT

Ask students to sketch a rough outline map of Africa. Direct them to use the lesson content to shade in the areas in which West-African trading empires, rain forest kingdoms, and coastal city-states were located. Then lead the class in a discussion of how best to summarize the trade that took place in each region.

LESSON 1 REVIEW ANSWERS

1. A *savanna* is a tropical grassland dotted with small trees and shrubs. A *plateau* is an area of high and mostly flat land.
2. The four main geographic zones of Africa are rain forests, grasslands, deserts, and small areas of mild climate along the northern coast and southern tip of the continent.
3. Mogadishu and Mombasa were trading posts that played key roles in East Africa's trade across the Indian Ocean.
4. West Africans traded products such as gold, ivory, spices, leather, and ostrich feathers with other nations.
5. The climate of the East African trading kingdoms allowed them to grow products to trade that could not be produced in the empires of West Africa.
6. Answers will vary but should accurately use information from the lesson to describe the landscape, people, and climate of East Africa.

ANSWERS, p. 429

CRITICAL THINKING These sails might have helped the traders travel faster and more safely. This could have given them an advantage over other competing groups of traders.

✓ PROGRESS CHECK The location of Axum on the Red Sea made it an important trading center. It was located along a trade route connecting Africa, the Mediterranean world, and India.

ENGAGE

Bellringer Direct students' attention to the image of the king of Benin in the textbook. Use the critical-thinking question to prompt students' consideration of how this carving reflects the relationship between ruler and subjects that was discussed previously. Point out to students that the carving suggests this king is powerful but also has the respect and loyalty of his people. Tell students that in this lesson they will learn more about the governments of ancient Africa.

TEACH & ASSESS

C Critical Thinking Skills

Evaluating Direct students' attention to the text about rulers' relationships with their subjects. **Ask:** **How were African rulers' relationships with their subjects different from those of other rulers?** *(African rulers had closer relationships with common people than rulers in other civilizations.)* **How might this have helped these rulers govern more successfully?** *(By removing some of the distance between themselves and their subjects, African rulers may have won greater support from the people. This loyalty could have helped them govern more successfully.)* BL

R Reading Skills

Citing Text Evidence Invite student volunteers to read aloud the information about the strong central governments of Ghana and Mali. Point out that both rulers and everyday citizens benefited from this system of government. **Ask:** **What section of the text tells how the strong central governments of Ghana and Mali helped their subjects thrive?** *(Students should identify the sixth and seventh sentences of the paragraph under "Kings and the People.")* AL

ANSWER, p. 430

TAKING NOTES: Musa—ruled Mali and developed it into one of the world's largest empires; devoted to Islam; built many libraries and mosques; made famous pilgrimage to Makkah. Ture—created new dynasty; divided nation into provinces. Muhammad—ruled Songhai and developed it into the largest empire in West Africa.

networks
There's More Online!
- ☑ **BIOGRAPHY** Mansa Musa
- ☑ **SLIDE SHOW** Mosques in Africa
- ☑ **GRAPHIC ORGANIZER** Achievements of African Leaders
- ☑ **MAP** Religion in Africa Today
- ☑ **VIDEO**

Lesson 2

Africa's Governments and Religions

ESSENTIAL QUESTION *How does religion shape society?*

IT MATTERS BECAUSE

Ancient African societies showed the effects of government disputes, traditional religious beliefs, and Islam.

African Rulers and Society

GUIDING QUESTION *How did African rulers govern their territories?*

C In most ancient societies, rulers were isolated from their subjects. In Africa south of the Sahara, the distance between kings and the common people was not as great. Often, African rulers would hold meetings to let their people voice complaints. In Ghana, drums called the people to the king. Anybody with a concern could address him. Before talking, subjects demonstrated their respect. They poured dust over their heads or fell to the ground. Next, they bowed and stated their business. Then they waited for their king's reply.

Kings and the People

R Africans developed different ways to rule their territories. Powerful states, such as Ghana and Mali, favored strong central governments. Power rested with the rulers. They settled disputes, controlled trade, and defended the empire. They expected total loyalty from their people. Everyone benefited from the relationship. Merchants received favors from kings and paid the kings taxes in return. Local rulers held some power and gave the kings their support. This system allowed kingdoms to grow rich, control their lands, and keep the peace.

Reading HELPDESK CCSS

Taking Notes: *Organizing*

In a graphic organizer like this one, record at least one accomplishment of each of the leaders listed. RH.6–8.2

Leader	Accomplishments
Mansa Musa	
Muhammad Ture	
Askia Muhammad	

Content Vocabulary (Tier 3 Words)
- clan
- Swahili

networks ***Online Teaching Options***

VIDEO

History and Traditions of Mali

Classifying Play the video about the history and traditions of Mali. On the board, create a Web graphic organizer titled "History and Traditions of Mali." Have students suggest details from the video to complete the graphic organizer.

See page 419D for other online activities.

What Was Ghana's Government Like?

The kings of Ghana were strong rulers who played active roles in running the kingdom with the help of ministers and advisors. As the empire grew, the kings divided their territory into provinces. Lesser kings often governed the provinces, which were made up of districts and governed by district chiefs. Each district was composed of villages belonging to the chief's **clan**. A clan is a group of people descended from the same ancestor.

Ghana's government had a **unique** method of transferring power from one ruler to another. "This is their custom and their habit," stated an Arab writer, "that the kingdom is inherited only by the son of the king's sister." In Arab lands, property was inherited by a man's sons. In Ghana, leadership passed to the king's nephew.

The Government of Mali

Mali had a government like that of Ghana, but on a grander scale. Mali had more territory, more people, and more trade. As a result, royal officials had more responsibilities.

Mali's kings controlled a strong central government. The empire was divided into provinces, like those of Ghana. However, the kings put generals in charge of these areas. Many people supported the generals, because the generals protected Mali from invaders. Also, the generals often came from the provinces they ruled.

Mansa Musa, Mali's most powerful king, won the loyalty of his subjects by giving them gold, property, and horses. He gave military heroes the "National Honor of the Trousers." As one Arab writer said:

PRIMARY SOURCE

> "Whenever a hero adds to the lists of his exploits [adventures], the king gives him a pair of wide trousers. . . . [T]he greater the number of the knight's [soldier's] exploits, the bigger the size of his trousers."
>
> —from *Medieval West Africa: Views from Arab Scholars and Merchants*, excerpt by Ibn Fadl Allah al-'Umari

In Mali, only the king and his family could wear clothing that was sewn, like the clothes we wear today. Other people wore pieces of cloth wrapped around their bodies to form clothing. The trousers awarded to military heroes were truly a great honor.

This king of Benin was treated with respect by his subjects. This carving shows a public gathering.

▶ **CRITICAL THINKING**
Analyzing How does this carving show us that the people honored their king?

Werner Forman/Art Resource, NY

clan a group of people descended from the same ancestor

Academic Vocabulary (Tier 2 Words)
unique one of a kind

C Critical Thinking Skills

Contrasting Review the structure of the imperial governments of both Ghana and Mali with students.
Ask: **How did the rule of provinces differ in Ghana and Mali?** *(In Ghana, the provinces were usually ruled by lesser kings. In Mali, they were ruled instead by generals.)*

W Writing Skills

Informative/Explanatory Organize students into small groups. Tell student groups to select either Ghana or Mali. Have each group identify the key features of the empire's government and list those features. Then have students work on their own to write a short paragraph summarizing their group's information. Invite volunteers to share their work with the class. **AL** **Interpersonal**

WORKSHEET

Economics of History Activity: Africa's Governments and Religions: The Value of Gold

Discussing Remind students that empires expand through trade, and that trade played an especially important role in the growth of African empires. Inform students that they should understand the role of economics in the growth of empires. Display the Economics of History worksheet titled "The Value of Gold." Discuss which things are considered valuable—for example, gold, silver, money, diamonds, a college education. Then discuss why certain things are considered valuable and others are not. Point out that things can increase or decrease in value. Ask students for their ideas on why the value of something can change.

See page 419D for other online activities.

Economics of History Activity — networks
African Civilizations
Lesson 2 *Africa's Governments and Religions*
The Value of Gold

ANSWER, p. 431

CRITICAL THINKING The way people are gathered around the king in this carving suggests that African kings were powerful and held the loyalty of their people. The two people fanning the king also show a measure of their respect.

R Reading Skills

Identifying After students read the text, discuss traditional African religions with them. Have students list some of the attributes of the various religions discussed. Point out that most religions shared some common features. **Ask:** **What was one common religious belief of most African religions?** *(Most African religions believed in the existence of a single creator god.)*

Content Background Knowledge

Vodou Traditional West African religion, such as that practiced by the Yoruba people, had a great deal of influence over the modern religion called *vodou.* This belief system, practiced mostly in Haiti but also in the state of Louisiana, blends African beliefs in spirits with Christian ideas spread by missionaries among enslaved populations. One example of this blend is the honoring of certain traditional African spirits on Roman Catholic saints' feast days.

The kings of Ghana taxed gold. This tax helped to control the amount of gold produced.

Government in Songhai

Songhai built on the political traditions of Ghana and Mali. It reached the height of its power under Muhammad Ture. A general and a devout Muslim, Muhammad Ture seized power in 1493 and created a new dynasty. He was a capable administrator who divided Songhai into provinces. A governor, a tax collector, a court of judges, and a trade inspector ran each province. Muhammad Ture **maintained** the peace and security of his empire with a navy and soldiers on horseback.

✓ PROGRESS CHECK

Describing Why did many people in Mali support the generals who ruled the provinces?

Traditional African Religions

GUIDING QUESTION *How did traditional religions influence African life?*

Most African societies shared some common religious beliefs. One of these was a belief in a single creator god. Many groups, however, carried out their own religious practices. These practices differed from place to place. For example, the Yoruba lived in West Africa. They believed that their chief god sent his son from heaven in a canoe. The son then created the first humans. This religion was practiced by many of the enslaved people brought by Europeans to the Americas.

R

In some religions, the creator god was linked to a group of lesser gods. The Ashanti people of Ghana believed in a supreme god whose sons were lesser gods. Others held that the creator god had once lived on Earth but left in anger at human behavior. This god, however, was forgiving if people corrected their ways.

Even though Africans practiced different religions in different places, their beliefs served similar purposes. They provided rules for living and helped people honor their history and ancestors. Africans also relied on religion to protect them from harm and to **guarantee** success in life. A special group of people, called diviners, were believed to have the power to foretell events. Kings often hired diviners to guarantee good harvests and protect their kingdoms.

✓ PROGRESS CHECK

Explaining What was the role of diviners in African religion?

Reading HELPDESK CCSS

Academic Vocabulary (Tier 2 Words)

maintain to keep in the same state
guarantee to promise
challenge to present with difficulties
convert to accept a new belief

Reading in the Content Area

When you interpret a pie chart, or pie graph, remember that each slice or wedge represents a part of the whole. That is, a slice may stand for a fraction or a percentage—a smaller part of the whole.

networks Online Teaching Options

LECTURE SLIDE

Traditional African Religions

Hypothesizing Show students the lecture slide on traditional African religions. Note that although these religions varied from place to place, there were similarities. **Ask:** **Why might traditional religion have been a comfort to Africans?** *(It provided rules for living, and people believed it protected them from harm.)*

See page 419D for other online activities.

networks Traditional African Religions

African religion provided rules for living, protected people from harm, and guaranteed success in life. Traditional African religions shared the belief in a single creator god, but these beliefs varied across the continent.

- Some West Africans believed god sent his son from heaven in a canoe. Once on Earth, the son created humans.
- In other religions, people believed that the supreme god had sons. Those sons were lesser gods.
- Some Africans believed that the creator god was on Earth but left because he was disappointed with human behavior. People would be forgiven by this god if they corrected their ways.

ANSWERS, p. 432

✓ **PROGRESS CHECK** These generals protected the people from invaders. The generals also usually came from the province they ruled.

✓ **PROGRESS CHECK** Diviners were a special group of people who were believed to have the power to foretell events.

Islam Arrives in Africa

GUIDING QUESTION *How did Islam spread in Africa?*

Beginning in the A.D. 700s, traditional African religions were **challenged** by the arrival of Islam. Through trade, Berber and Arab merchants eventually introduced Muslim beliefs to West Africa. African rulers welcomed Muslim traders and allowed their people to **convert** to Islam. The rulers did not become Muslims themselves until the A.D. 1000s. By the end of the 1400s, much of the population south of the Sahara had converted to Islam.

Who Was Ibn Battuta?

Ibn Battuta (IH•buhn bat•TOO•tah) was a young Arab lawyer from Morocco. In 1325, he set out to see the Muslim world. He reached West Africa in 1352. There, he found that people had been following Islam for centuries. Yet not all West Africans were Muslims. People in rural areas still followed traditional African religions. Some rulers and traders accepted Islam only because it helped them trade with Muslim Arabs.

Ibn Battuta described in detail the people and places of West Africa. Some things amazed him. He was surprised that women did not cover their faces with a veil, as was the Muslim custom.

C

GEOGRAPHY CONNECTION

Today, people in Africa continue to practice a variety of religions.

1. **LOCATION** Which religion dominates the southern part of Africa?
2. CRITICAL THINKING
   Analyzing Use the graph to compare the percentages of Africans practicing traditional religions with those practicing Islam. How do they compare?

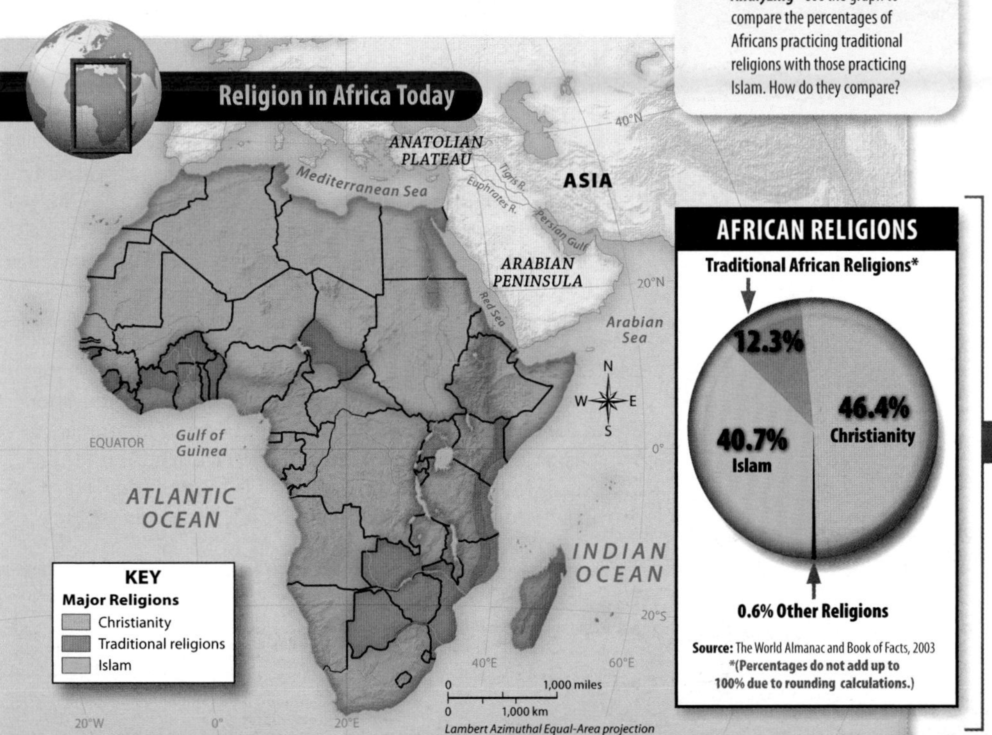

V

MAP

Religion in Africa Today

Analyzing Maps Show students the interactive map displaying the religions currently practiced in Africa. **Ask:** **Where do most African Muslims live?** *(in North Africa and along the eastern coast of Africa)* Ask students to recall what they learned in Lesson 1 about trade patterns in Africa. **How might trade have been tied to the spread of Islam?** *(Students might suggest that many Muslim traders and merchants brought their religious beliefs with them to their new locations.)*

See page 419D for other online activities.

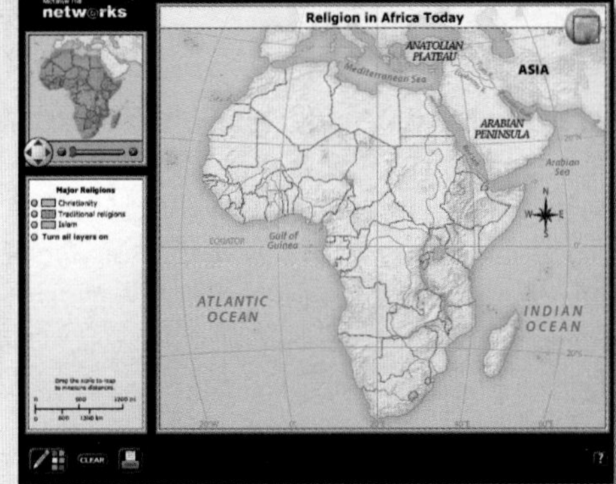

C Critical Thinking Skills

Evaluating Have students read the section titled "Who Was Ibn Battuta?" Ask volunteers to identify some of the observations that Ibn Battuta made about Islam in West Africa. Remind students that Ibn Battuta traveled throughout the Muslim world recording his observations about the people and places he visited. **Ask:** **Why do you think writings such as those of Ibn Battuta are so valuable to historians?** *(Answers will vary but may include that such writings provide historians with a firsthand account of a particular time in history. Observations such as the ones he made can give historians insight into a particular place or group of people.)* BL

V Visual Skills

Reading a Graph Explain that a circle graph shows all the parts of a whole. Point out each of the parts of the circle graph titled "African Religions." Make sure students understand that these four pieces together show all the religions practiced by modern Africans. **Ask:** **What are the two religions practiced by most of the people in Africa today?** *(Christianity and Islam)* AL Visual/Spatial

ANSWERS, p. 433

GEOGRAPHY CONNECTION

1. Christianity dominates the southern part of Africa.
2. CRITICAL THINKING The percentage of Africans practicing traditional African religions is less than one-third of the percentage of Africans practicing Islam.

R Reading Skills

Describing Discuss with students the information about Mansa Musa's journey to Makkah. Invite students to give details about his journey based on their reading in "The Journey of Mansa Musa." Have students brainstorm adjectives to describe the king's voyage. Record students' ideas on the board. ELL

C Critical Thinking Skills

Identifying Central Issues Remind students that traders and merchants helped Islam spread into West Africa. Point out that not all people in any given kingdom practiced Islam, however. Some people, even rulers, chose to follow traditional African religions. **Ask: What complaint did the people of Songhai have about the rule of Sunni Ali's son?** *(He refused to practice Islam.)* AL

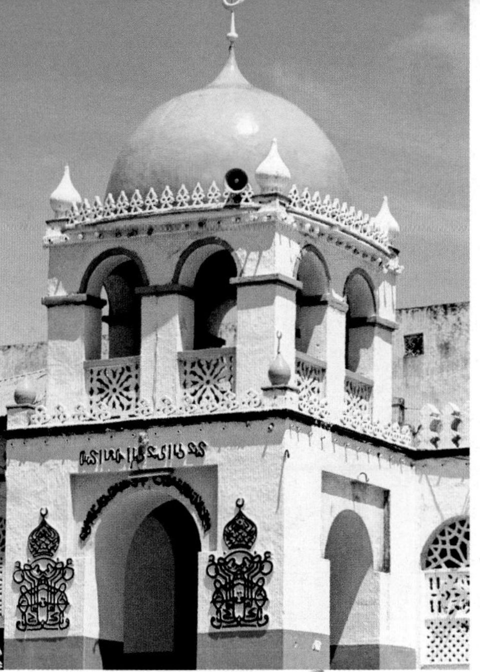

Muslim architecture, such as this mosque, demonstrates the lasting influence of Islam in Africa.

However, he did find that West African Muslims "zealously [eagerly] learned the Quran by heart" and faithfully performed their religious duties:

PRIMARY SOURCE

> "On Fridays, if a man does not go early to the mosque [a Muslim place of worship], he cannot
> find a corner to pray in, on account of the crowd.
> It is a custom of theirs to send each man his boy
> [to the mosque] with his prayer-mat; the boy spreads
> it out for his master in a place befitting him [and remains on it] until
> he comes to the mosque. Their prayer-mats are made of the leaves of a
> tree resembling a date-palm, but without fruit."
>
> —from *Travels in Asia and Africa*, by Ibn Battuta

The Journey of Mansa Musa

Ibn Battuta was impressed by Mansa Musa, Mali's most famous ruler. Mansa Musa let his subjects practice different religions. However, he was devoted to spreading Islam. Mansa Musa used his empire's wealth to build more mosques. In Timbuktu, Mansa Musa set up libraries with books from around the Muslim world.

In 1324, Mansa Musa increased the fame of Mali during a journey to Makkah (MAH•kuh). All Muslims are expected to travel to the Muslim holy city of Makkah. Mansa Musa made certain that people knew he was the ruler of a great empire. R

Mansa Musa traveled in grand style. Eighty camels carried two tons of gold. Mansa Musa gave away so much gold to the poor on his journey that the price of gold fell. While in Makkah, Mansa Musa met scholars of Islam. He convinced them to return with him to Mali. They helped spread Islam in West Africa.

Islam in Songhai

C Islam won followers among the Songhai people. Sunni Ali, the ruler, became a Muslim to keep the loyalty of merchants. After Sunni Ali died, his son refused to accept Islam. Muhammad Ture, a Songhai general, took over the government. With the backing of Muslim townspeople, he made himself king. He drove out Sunni Ali's family. He then took the name Askia.

Sylvain Grandadam / age fotostock

Reading HELPDESK CCSS

Swahili the unique culture of Africa's East Coast and the language spoken there

Academic Vocabulary (Tier 2 Words)

survive to continue to function or prosper

networks Online Teaching Options

SLIDE SHOW

Mosques in Africa

Analyzing Images Present the slide show on African mosques to the class. **Ask: Why do you think these mosques have different designs?** *(Students might suggest that the mosques were built in different parts of Africa and reflect different combinations of Muslim and African culture.)* Explain that African and Muslim cultures blended across Africa in different ways.

See page 419D for other online activities.

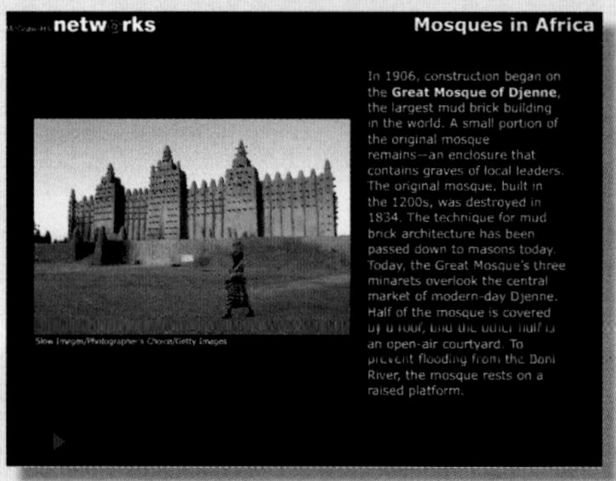

Under Askia Muhammad (moo•HAH•muhd), the Songhai created the largest empire in West Africa's history. He ordered local courts to follow Muslim laws. He also made Timbuktu an important center of Islamic learning. Askia Muhammad set up a famous university and opened schools to teach the Quran. **R**

The Songhai Empire **survived** disputes among royal family members. But it did not survive the guns of Moroccan invaders. This invasion in 1591 brought down the empire.

How Did Islam Develop in East Africa?

Islam spread slowly in East Africa. Islam arrived in the A.D. 700s, but the religion did not gain many followers until the 1100s and 1200s. A new society arose known as **Swahili** (swah•HEE•lee). It was based on a blend of African and Muslim cultures. The word Swahili comes from an Arabic word meaning "people of the coast." By 1331, however, it had come to mean both the culture of East Africa's coast and the language spoken there. **C**

The African influences on the Swahili culture came from the cultures of Africa's interior. Muslim influences came from Arab and Persian settlers. The Swahili culture and language still thrive in Africa.

Islam's Effect on Africa

Islam had a far-reaching effect on much of Africa. Africans who accepted Islam adopted Islamic laws and ideas. They also were influenced by Islamic learning. Muslim schools introduced the Arabic language to their students. In addition, Islam influenced African art and its buildings. Muslim architects built beautiful mosques and palaces in Timbuktu and other cities.

✓ **PROGRESS CHECK**

Determining Cause and Effect What caused a unique brand of Islam to develop in Africa?

BIOGRAPHY

Mansa Musa
(ruled 1312–1337)

Mansa Musa attracted the attention of many nations with his famous pilgrimage, or trip, to Makkah (Mecca). Countries in Europe, as well as kingdoms in North Africa and the Middle East, took notice. These nations hoped to trade with Mali and gain some of its wealth. Mansa Musa expanded his empire by capturing the cities of Gao (GAH • oh) and Timbuktu. During his reign, Mali was one of the world's largest empires. Mansa Musa once boasted that traveling from the empire's northern border to its southern border would take a year.

▸ **CRITICAL THINKING**

Identifying How did Mansa Musa's pilgrimage to Makkah benefit the kingdom of Mali?

LESSON 2 REVIEW (CCSS)

Review Vocabulary (Tier 3 Words)

1. What two meanings developed for the word *Swahili*? RH.6–8.2, RH.6–8.4

Answer the Guiding Questions

2. ***Comparing*** What did all the early governments of African kingdoms have in common? RH.6–8.2
3. ***Explaining*** How did the leaders of Mali manage the grand scale of their government? RH.6–8.2
4. ***Describing*** What similar purposes did traditional African religions share? RH.6–8.2
5. ***Summarizing*** What did Ibn Battuta observe about the different religious groups in West Africa? RH.6–8.2
6. **INFORMATIVE/EXPLANATORY** Write a brief paragraph in which you explain how Mansa Musa worked to spread Islam in West Africa. WHST.6–8.2, WHST.6–8.10

R Reading Skills

Specifying Have students read about the accomplishments of Askia Muhammad. **Ask:** **What were three ways in which Askia Muhammad encouraged the growth of Islam in Songhai?** *(He told local courts to follow Muslim laws, made Timbuktu a center of Islamic learning, and opened schools to teach the Quran.)*

C Critical Thinking Skills

Making Connections Refer students to the section titled "How Did Islam Develop in East Africa?" Point out that Ibn Battuta also visited East Africa. **Ask:** **What two meanings of the word Swahili had emerged in East Africa by 1331?** *(By 1331, the word* Swahili *had come to describe the unique culture of East Africa's coast and the language spoken there.)* Point out to students that the Swahili culture and language combine African and Muslim cultures. Then have students identify some other familiar examples in which two cultures have blended to produce a new form of culture. *(Students may identify examples of cultural blending in a wide range of areas, including language, music, or food.)* Invite English language learners either to identify words from their home languages that have been adopted into or taken on different meanings in English or to identify English words that have been adopted into their home language. **ELL**

Have students complete the Lesson 2 Review.

CLOSE & REFLECT

Point out to students that the Swahili culture and language combine African and Muslim cultures. Lead students in a discussion of what the emergence of the Swahili culture suggests about the spread of Islam in Africa, as well as the influence of religious beliefs on African society.

LESSON 2 REVIEW ANSWERS

1. *Swahili* came to describe the unique culture of East Africa's coast and the language spoken there.
2. These kingdoms had strong central governments with powerful kings. However, the distance between the kings and the people of the kingdoms was not as great as in other societies.
3. Royal officials took on extra responsibilities in the government of Mali. The kings also divided the empire into provinces. They placed generals in charge of these provinces to help them govern there.
4. These religions provided rules for living and helped people stay connected to their history. Africans also believed that these religions protected them from harm and guaranteed them success in life.
5. Upon his arrival in West Africa, Ibn Battuta observed that many people in rural areas continued to follow traditional African religions. He also observed that most Muslims in West Africa lived in the cities.
6. Sample response: Mansa Musa used his empire's wealth to build mosques. He also established libraries that housed books from across the Muslim world. During his pilgrimage to Makkah, he convinced many Muslim scholars to return with him to Mali and to help spread Islam in West Africa.

ANSWERS, p. 435

CRITICAL THINKING Mansa Musa's pilgrimage to Makkah helped bring the kingdom to the attention of other nations. Because these nations wanted to gain access to the wealth displayed during Mansa Musa's pilgrimage, the pilgrimage helped Mali establish new trading connections.

✓ **PROGRESS CHECK** At times, the beliefs and practices of Islam contrasted with those of traditional African societies. As Africans adopted new ideas from Islam, they changed them to fit traditional ways. This blending caused a unique brand of Islam to develop in Africa.

ENGAGE

Bellringer Lead students in a discussion of their favorite styles of music. Encourage students to suggest a variety of styles, and compile a list of students' suggestions. When this list is complete, inform students that many popular styles of music have developed from African music. These include ragtime, jazz, rock and roll, and rap. Inform students that they will learn more about Africa's culture in this lesson. Explain that in addition to music, they will also learn about elements of African culture such as family and lineage groups, education, slavery, and arts. AL ELL

TEACH & ASSESS

V Visual Skills

Visualizing Review the information about the composition of African villages and cities. Tell students to visualize the appearance of early rural villages. Then direct them to imagine those villages growing, first through the addition of walls and later through buildings that would house government and trade activities. Discuss students' visualizing as a class. Note the similarities among and differences between individuals' ideas about what these villages and cities looked like. **Visual/Spatial**

C Critical Thinking Skills

Contrasting Direct students' attention to the information about extended families and lineage groups. Point out that the family represented the basis of African society. **Ask:** **Who are the members of your extended family?** *(Students should correctly identify several members of their extended families.)* AL **How do extended families differ from lineage groups?** *(A lineage group is a larger social group than an extended family. The members of a lineage group share a common ancestor.)* BL

ANSWER, p. 436

TAKING NOTES: Art—Rock paintings were the earliest African art; Africans also made wooden masks and statues for religious ceremonies; they made fine metal and clay figures, and they wove cloth; **Music/Dance**—Music and dance were connected to everyday life; they were important to help ease the hard labors of daily life as well as to celebrate weddings and other milestones; **Storytelling**—Oral history played a vital role, as did griots, in passing down traditions and stories, especially of heroes.

networks *There's More Online!*

- MAP
  - Bantu Migrations
  - The Slave Trade c. 1450-1800
- PRIMARY SOURCE Traditional Story
- GRAPHIC ORGANIZER African Culture
- SLIDE SHOW African Art
- VIDEO

Lesson 3
African Society and Culture

ESSENTIAL QUESTION *How do religions develop?*

IT MATTERS BECAUSE

The people of early Africa formed complex societies with many common characteristics. They created artistic works that reflected their beliefs and built economies.

African Society

GUIDING QUESTION ***Why do people in different parts of Africa have similar traditions and cultures?***

V In early Africa, most people lived in rural villages. Their homes consisted of small, round dwellings made of packed mud. Villagers generally were farmers. Africa's urban areas often began as villages with protective walls. These villages grew into larger **communities**. African towns and cities were centers of government and trade. Traders and artisans thrived in these communities. Artisans were skilled in metalworking, woodworking, pottery making, and other crafts.

Family Ties

C The family formed the basis of African society. People often lived in **extended families**, or families made up of several generations. Extended families included parents, children, grandparents, and other relatives. These families ranged in size from a few individuals to hundreds of members.

Extended families were part of larger social groups known as lineage groups. Members of a lineage group could trace their family histories to a common ancestor. As in many other ancient

Reading **HELP**DESK CCSS

Taking Notes: *Finding the Main Idea*
Use a chart like this one to record and organize important ideas about the different elements of African culture. RH.6–8.2

Cultural Element	Main Idea
Art	
Music and Dance	
Storytelling	

Content Vocabulary (Tier 3 Words)
- **extended family**
- **matrilineal**
- **oral history**
- **sugarcane**
- **spiritual**

networks ***Online Teaching Options***

VIDEO

The History, Exploration, and Conquest of South Africa

Sequencing Play the video about South Africa for the class. Then invite volunteers to suggest some of the major turning points from the video. Record these ideas on the board. After collecting ideas, work with students to order these events chronologically.

See page 419E for other online activities.

societies, older members had more power than younger people. Members of a lineage group were expected to support and care for each other.

Bantu Migrations

Many of Africa's social practices are a result of migrations that began in West Africa about 3000 B.C. and lasted hundreds of years. The migrants, known as the Bantu (BAN•too), shared similar languages, cultures, and technologies. The Bantu migrated from West Africa to the south and east. They spread their farming and iron-working skills, along with their languages. Today, about 220 million Africans speak hundreds of Bantu languages.

Bantu villages were also **matrilineal** (ma•truh•LIH•nee•uhl). They traced their descent, or ancestry, through mothers, not fathers. When a woman married, however, she joined her husband's family. To make up for the loss, her family received presents from the husband's family. These gifts might include cattle, goats, cloth, or metal tools. R

How Did African Children Learn?

In Africa's villages, education was the duty of both the family and other villagers. Children learned the history of their people and the basic skills they would need as adults.

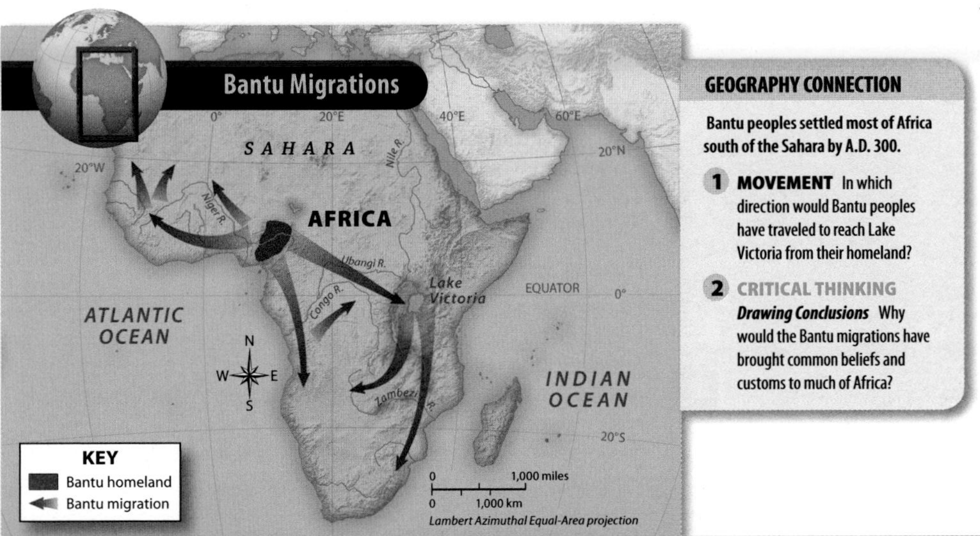

GEOGRAPHY CONNECTION

Bantu peoples settled most of Africa south of the Sahara by A.D. 300.

1. **MOVEMENT** In which direction would Bantu peoples have traveled to reach Lake Victoria from their homeland?
2. CRITICAL THINKING *Drawing Conclusions* Why would the Bantu migrations have brought common beliefs and customs to much of Africa?

V

extended family a family made up of several generations
matrilineal tracing family descent through mothers rather than fathers

Academic Vocabulary (Tier 2 Words)
community a large group with common values living in an area

R Reading Skills

Determining Word Meanings Model the pronunciation of the term *matrilineal.* Invite a volunteer to read aloud the definition of the term from the textbook. Explain that the term *matrilineal* is related to the Latin word *mater,* meaning "mother." Tell students that other English words—including *maternal,* which means "mother-like"—share the same Latin root. AL ELL

V Visual Skills

Analyzing Maps Point out to students the map showing Bantu migrations. Ask them to describe the overall direction and movement of the migrations. **Ask:** Which geographic feature stopped the Bantu migrations? *(the Sahara)* Why might this barrier have stopped the Bantu? *(Students will probably note that the Sahara was too harsh and dry for people to cross it easily.)* **Visual/Spatial**

IMAGE

The Great Zimbabwe and Bantu Migrations

Hypothesizing Show students the image on Bantu migrations. Point out that these migrations had a significant impact on African history, although historians do not know what caused the Bantu to begin these migrations. **Ask:** Why might historians be unable to determine the cause of the Bantu migrations? *(Answers will vary but may include that the Bantu might not have left any written records that could provide clues to the reasons for these migrations. There could also be few artifacts to help explain these migrations.)*

See page 419E for other online activities.

ANSWERS, p. 437

GEOGRAPHY CONNECTION

1. Bantu peoples would have traveled southeast to reach Lake Victoria from their homeland.
2. CRITICAL THINKING Bantu peoples traveled widely and settled throughout much of Africa during their migrations. By spreading their culture in the places they settled, they caused these beliefs to become common in many parts of the continent.

W Writing Skills

Narrative Review with students the information about the roles of African women. Point out that African women mostly filled roles as wives and mothers. **Ask:** **What are two examples of ways in which some women broke out of traditional roles in early African society?** *(Some women fought in the military or served as national leaders.)* Tell students to select the role of one African woman of either typical or unusual status. Then have them write a paragraph from the point of view of that person, giving their ideas about their role in African society.

R Reading Skills

Explaining After students have read the paragraph, ask them to explain the origin of the slave trade. **Ask:** **Did slavery originate with the arrival of Europeans?** *(Students should note that slavery already existed in Africa and many other places throughout the world.)* **How might enslaved people in Africa's slave trade gain their freedom?** *(Enslaved Africans could be set free for a payment. They could also gain their freedom through hard work or by marrying free people.)*

ANSWERS, p. 438

CRITICAL THINKING These explorers might have been surprised at these observations, because few women in Europe served in politics or as soldiers.

✓ **PROGRESS CHECK** In early Africa, people often lived in extended families. Families formed the basis of African society.

Some women in early Africa served as soldiers and political leaders. Queen Nzinga ruled in southern Africa.

▶ CRITICAL THINKING
Making Connections Why might European explorers have been surprised to observe women serving in these roles?

Mary Evans Picture Library

In West Africa, griots helped to teach the children. They vividly told their village's **oral history**. These stories were told and retold, and people passed them down from generation to generation. Many stories included a lesson about life. Lessons also were given through short proverbs. One Bantu proverb stated, "Patience is the mother of a beautiful child."

African Women

W

As in most other early societies, women in Africa acted mostly as wives and mothers. Men had more rights and supervised much of what women did. Visitors to Africa, however, noticed some exceptions. European explorers were amazed to learn that women served as soldiers in some African armies.

African women also served as rulers. In the A.D. 600s, Queen Dahia al-Kahina (dah•HEE•uh ahl•kah•HEE•nah) led an army against Arab invaders, who attacked her kingdom. Another woman ruler was Queen Nzinga (ehn•ZIHN•gah), who governed lands in southwestern Africa. She spent almost 30 years fighting Portuguese invaders and resisting the slave trade.

✓ **PROGRESS CHECK**

Describing What were families like in early Africa?

The Slave Trade

GUIDING QUESTION *How did the slave trade affect Africans?*

In 1441, a ship from the European nation of Portugal sailed down Africa's western coast. The ship captain's plan was to bring African captives back to Europe. During the voyage, the captain and crew seized 12 Africans—men, women, and boys. With its human cargo on board, the ship then sailed back to Portugal. These captives were the first Africans to be part of a slave trade that would involve millions of people.

How Was African Slavery Practiced?

R

Slavery was a common practice throughout the world. It had been practiced in Africa since ancient times. Bantu warriors raided nearby villages for captives to use as laborers, servants, or soldiers. Some were set free for a payment. Africans also enslaved their enemies and traded them for goods. The lives of enslaved Africans were hard, but they might win their freedom through work or by marrying a free person.

Reading HELPDESK (CCSS)

oral history stories passed down from generation to generation

sugarcane a grassy plant that is a natural source of sugar

Academic Vocabulary (Tier 2 Words)

contact interaction with other people
major great in rank or importance

networks Online Teaching Options

LECTURE SLIDE

African Education

Describing Show students the lecture slide on children's education in Africa. **Ask:** **In what way were children especially valued in African families?** *(African families especially valued children because they knew children guaranteed that the family would live on.)* Then discuss with students how education in African villages reflected the importance placed on family and passing knowledge from generation to generation.

See page 419E for other online activities.

networks — African Society

The education of children in Africa was the responsibility of the family and the village. Children would learn:

- The history of their people
- Basic skills they would use as adults
- Stories that were meant to give a lesson about life
- Proverbs that supported the lessons about life

African Society and Culture

The trade in humans grew as Africa's **contact** with the Muslim world increased. The Quran banned the enslavement of Muslims. Muslims, however, could enslave non-Muslims. Arab Muslim merchants, therefore, began to trade cotton and other goods for enslaved non-Muslim Africans.

When Europeans arrived in West Africa, a new market for enslaved Africans opened. Africans armed with European guns began raiding villages to seize captives to sell.

The European Slave Trade

In 1444, a Portuguese ship brought 235 enslaved Africans to a dock in Portugal. An official of the royal court saw the Africans being taken off the vessel. He was moved to ask:

R

PRIMARY SOURCE

> "What heart could be so hard as not to [be] pierced with . . . feeling . . . ? For some kept their heads low, and their faces bathed in tears. . . . Others stood groaning . . . crying out loudly, as if asking [for] help. . . . others struck their faces. . . . But to increase their sufferings still more, . . . was it then needful to part fathers from sons, husbands from wives, brothers from brothers?"
>
> —from Gomes Eannes de Zurara, as quoted in *The Slave Trade* by Hugh Thomas

C

This colorful blanket is made from Kente cloth. Its name comes from an African word that means "basket."

Portuguese merchants now sold humans. At first, most enslaved Africans worked as laborers in Portugal. Later, they were sent to the Atlantic islands of Madeira, the Azores, and Cape Verde. The Portuguese had settled these islands. The mild climate was ideal for growing **sugarcane** on plantations, or huge farms.

Harvesting sugarcane was hard work. Plantation owners could not pay high wages. Instead, they used enslaved Africans. Enslaved people received no wages. By 1500, Portugal had become the world's **major** supplier of sugar.

In the late 1400s, Europeans arrived in the Americas. They brought enslaved Africans across the Atlantic Ocean to grow sugar, tobacco, rice, and cotton.

Griots, such as this woman, often accompany themselves on a stringed instrument called a kora.

▶ CRITICAL THINKING

Evaluating How might the tradition of oral storytelling have affected African stories over time?

✓ PROGRESS CHECK

Analyzing How did increased contact with other parts of the world affect the slave trade in Africa?

C Critical Thinking Skills

Identifying Points of View Read aloud the primary-source excerpt with students. Discuss with students whether the speaker seems to support or oppose the institution of slavery. **Ask:** What practice does the speaker view as being particularly cruel to enslaved Africans? *(the splitting up of families)*

R Reading Skills

Specifying After students have read the text, ask a volunteer to review the information about the development of the slave trade. Point out that at first, merchants traded enslaved Africans mostly within Africa. **Ask:** What two events greatly grew the market for enslaved Africans? *(First, the Portuguese began purchasing and selling enslaved Africans. Later, Europeans began using enslaved workers on plantations in the Americas.)*

WORKSHEET

Guided Reading Activity: African Society and Culture

Organizing Direct students' attention to the section titled "The Slave Trade" on the Guided Reading worksheet. Have partners work together to complete the graphic-organizer activity. Then have students answer the Finding the Main Idea question on their own. Invite volunteers to share their answers. Assign the remainder of the worksheet for homework.

See page 419E for other online activities.

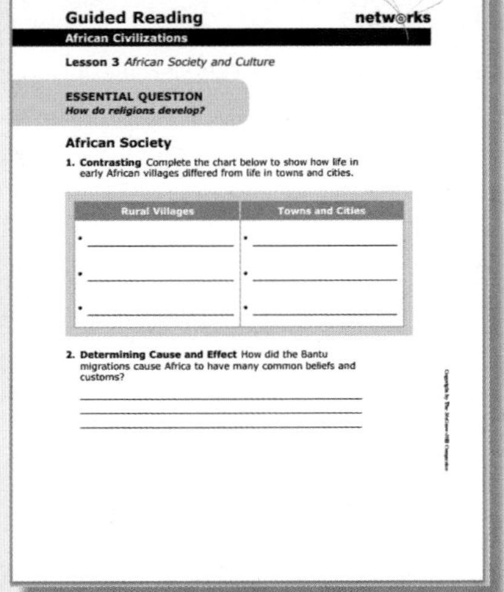

NAME ________ DATE ________ CLASS ________

Guided Reading networks

African Civilizations

Lesson 3 *African Society and Culture*

ESSENTIAL QUESTION
How do religions develop?

African Society

1. **Contrasting** Complete the chart below to show how life in early African villages differed from life in towns and cities.

Rural Villages	Towns and Cities
• ________	• ________
• ________	• ________
• ________	• ________

2. **Determining Cause and Effect** How did the Bantu migrations cause Africa to have many common beliefs and customs?

____

ANSWERS, p. 439

CRITICAL THINKING The tradition of oral storytelling might have caused these stories to change over time. Because the stories were not written down, storytellers may have gradually changed and adapted the stories as they retold them.

✓ **PROGRESS CHECK** The slave trade grew through increased contact with the Muslim world. Because Muslims could not enslave other Muslims, they began to trade goods for enslaved non-Muslim Africans. The arrival of Europeans in West Africa also opened a new market for the slave trade.

African Society and Culture

C Critical Thinking Skills

Making Generalizations Help students locate the information about the purposes that African art forms served. **Ask:** In general, what two purposes did African art forms serve? *(These art forms connected people to the gods, spirits, and ancestors. They also helped teach people about their community's history and folktales, since no written language had been developed.)* AL

R Reading Skills

Explaining Direct students to read the section on African art. Lead a class discussion about the significance and purposes of the various African art forms. **Ask:** What was the earliest art form in Africa? *(rock paintings)* What could historians learn from these works of art? *(Historians could learn about the daily lives of the early people who created these rock paintings. The paintings show people taking part in everyday tasks such as hunting and dancing.)* BL

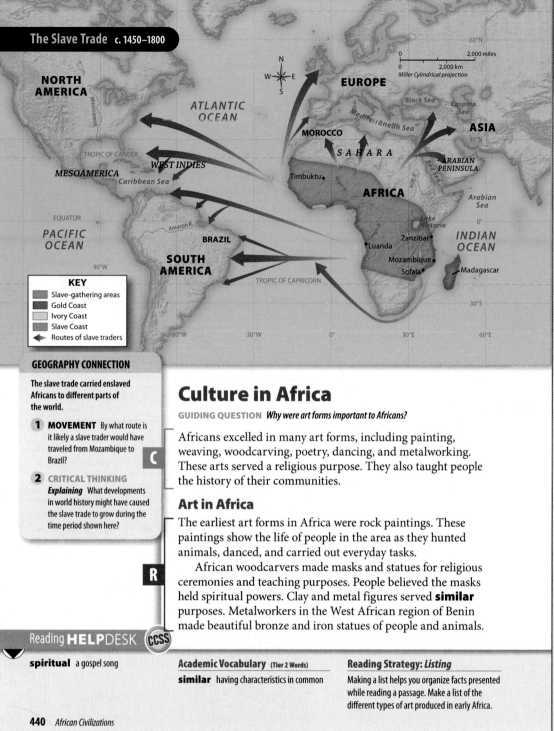

The Slave Trade c. 1450–1800

KEY
- Slave-gathering areas
- Gold Coast
- Ivory Coast
- Slave Coast
- Routes of slave traders

GEOGRAPHY CONNECTION

The slave trade carried enslaved Africans to different parts of the world.

1. **MOVEMENT** By what route is it likely a slave trader would have traveled from Mozambique to Brazil?
2. **CRITICAL THINKING** ***Explaining*** What developments in world history might have caused the slave trade to grow during the time period shown here?

Culture in Africa

GUIDING QUESTION *Why were art forms important to Africans?*

Africans excelled in many art forms, including painting, weaving, woodcarving, poetry, dancing, and metalworking. These arts served a religious purpose. They also taught people the history of their communities.

Art in Africa

The earliest art forms in Africa were rock paintings. These paintings show the life of people in the area as they hunted animals, danced, and carried out everyday tasks.

African woodcarvers made masks and statues for religious ceremonies and teaching purposes. People believed the masks held spiritual powers. Clay and metal figures served **similar** purposes. Metalworkers in the West African region of Benin made beautiful bronze and iron statues of people and animals.

Reading HELPDESK CCSS

spiritual a gospel song

Academic Vocabulary (Tier 2 Words)

similar having characteristics in common

Reading Strategy: *Listing*

Making a list helps you organize facts presented while reading a passage. Make a list of the different types of art produced in early Africa.

networks Online Teaching Options

SLIDE SHOW

African Art

Paraphrasing Have students view the interactive slide show about African artwork. Have them study each slide and read its corresponding caption. Then ask a volunteer to paraphrase the caption. Repeat this process for each slide.

See page 419E for other online activities.

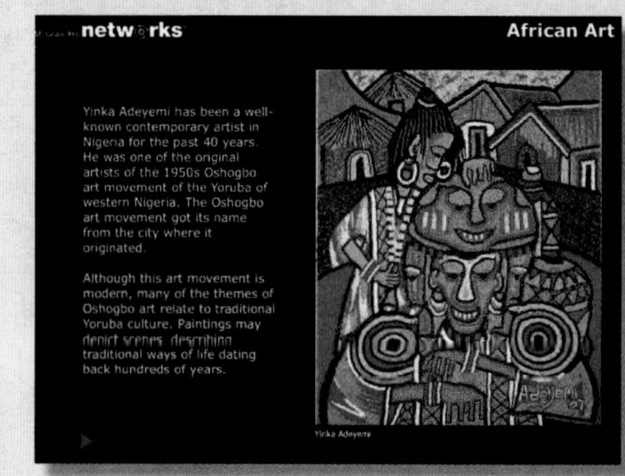

ANSWERS, p. 440

GEOGRAPHY CONNECTION

1. A slave trader would be likely to sail around the southern tip of Africa before heading northwest across the Atlantic Ocean toward Brazil.
2. **CRITICAL THINKING** The increase in European exploration and settlement might have caused the slave trade to grow during this period.

Reading Strategy Early African art included rock paintings, masks and statues for religious ceremonies, metal and clay figures, and woven cloth.

Early African Music and Dance

Music and dance were connected to everyday African life. People used these arts to express their religious feelings. They also used the arts to help ease an everyday task, such as planting a field. Music and dance also had a vital role in community activities.

African music included group singing. In many African songs, a singer calls out a line, then other singers repeat it. Musical instruments, such as drums, whistles, horns, flutes, or banjos, were used to keep the beat in early African music.

T

Enslaved Africans relied on music to remind them of their homeland. In America, songs of hardship eventually developed into a type of music called the blues. Songs of religious faith and hopes for freedom became **spirituals**, or gospel songs. Over time, other forms of African-based music developed, such as ragtime, jazz, rock and roll, and, more recently, rap.

C

For many Africans, dance was a way to communicate with the spirits and express the life of a community. Lines of dancers swayed and clapped their hands. In the background, drummers sounded out the rhythm. Many African peoples had dance rituals that marked particular stages of life, such as when young boys or girls became adults.

African Storytelling

In addition to music and dance, Africans also kept alive their storytelling tradition. A few enslaved Africans escaped and shared their stories. Those who heard these stories retold them. They also retold popular stories that focused on the deeds of famous heroes.

PROGRESS CHECK

Explaining What role did music and dance play in the everyday lives of early Africans?

Connections to TODAY

West African Music Today

West African music today rocks! Amadou and Miriam are a musical group from present-day Mali. In an unusual twist, both performers lost their eyesight at a young age. Eventually, they met at a school for the visually impaired. The duo first became well known in West Africa. They later grew in popularity in France before gaining worldwide acclaim. Their songs combine the music of West Africa with influences from rock and roll and the blues.

LESSON 3 REVIEW (CCSS)

Review Vocabulary (Tier 3 Words)

1. What made a Bantu village *matrilineal*? RH.6–8.2, RH.6–8.4

Answer the Guiding Questions

2. ***Explaining*** How did the Bantu spread their language, culture, and technology throughout Africa? RH.6–8.2
3. ***Describing*** What roles did women play in early African society? RH.6–8.2
4. ***Identifying*** Which European nation established the slave trade between Africa and Europe? RH.6–8.2
5. ***Sequencing*** How did art in Africa change over time? RH.6–8.2
6. **INFORMATIVE/EXPLANATORY** Describe your extended family. How might your extended family be similar to or different from extended families in early Africa? WHST.6–8.10

T Technology Skills

Researching on the Internet Organize students into small groups. Direct student groups to work together to research the origins of one type of music inspired by traditional African music, such as blues, jazz, or rap. Remind students to use reliable government, educational, or reference Web sites in their research. Have groups write a paragraph to summarize their findings. Then invite volunteer groups to share their paragraphs with the class. Encourage students to share audio clips of examples as part of their presentations. **Interpersonal Auditory/Musical**

C Critical Thinking Skills

Making Connections Point out that, in Africa, dance served as a way to communicate with spirits and as a way to express the life of the community. Guide students to understand that many African groups held special dances to mark important stages of life. Discuss with students examples of similar celebrations with which they are familiar. For instance, students might identify celebrations such as bar mitzvahs, high-school proms, or quinceañeras.

Have students complete the Lesson 3 Review.

CLOSE & REFLECT

Review with students the lesson content describing the ways in which enslaved Africans relied on music to remind them of their homeland. Lead students in a discussion about why people often turn to works of art or culture when facing difficult times or seeking comfort.

LESSON 3 REVIEW ANSWERS

1. Bantu villages were considered matrilineal because they traced their descent through mothers rather than fathers.
2. The Bantu traveled along Africa's waterways in small dugout canoes. They slowly spread across the continent. The Bantu would stop at a place to farm for a few years before moving on.
3. Women mostly acted as wives and mothers in African society. However, some women served as soldiers in African armies. Other women served as rulers.
4. Portugal established the slave trade between Africa and Europe.
5. The earliest forms of African art were rock paintings. In later centuries, artists made wood carvings and figures from clay and metal. By the 1200s and 1300s, metalworkers produced bronze and iron statues.
6. Answers will vary, but students should describe their extended families and use information from the lesson to identify potential similarities to and differences between early African extended families.

ANSWER, p. 441

PROGRESS CHECK Music and dance played a role in Expressing the religious beliefs of Africans. These art forms also played a role in community events such as weddings, ceremonies, and rituals.

ENGAGE

Bellringer Invite students to share what they know about where water comes from in the United States. Explain that cities usually offer a municipal water supply that citizens pay for through taxes or through usage fees. Point out that some people may use separate wells or systems that collect rain water. Discuss with students that, in Africa, the lack of a widespread infrastructure and the instability of local governments make it more difficult to get access to water than in the United States. Tell students that in this lesson they will consider two arguments about who should control Africa's water resources.

TEACH & ASSESS

R1 Reading Skills

Defining Make sure students understand the meaning of the term *privatization*. If needed, write the word on the board. Draw lines to divide the word into a base word and a suffix. Explain that the base word is private and that the two suffixes, *-ize* and *-ation*, change the root private into the noun privatization. ELL

R2 Reading Skills

Explaining Have students read the first excerpt. Discuss terms such as *oversight, management,* and *coverage* to make sure students understand the point being made. **Ask:** **Why does the author think poor people would be better off buying water from a private company than from a small vendor?** *(He argues that a private company charges much less money for the water than a small vendor does.)*

What Do You Think?

CCSS

Africa's Water Resources: Should Private Companies Control Them?

In ancient Africa, and today, the most precious natural resource is water. People worry about its availability. Many people cannot easily get clean water for daily use. Efforts are now underway to set up reliable water systems in Africa. Some local governments create their own water systems. Citizens are taxed according to their water use. Other governments cannot supply water. Then private companies agree to provide water to citizens for a fee. This system is known as *privatization*. Should control of water be left to governments or should private companies be allowed to control water? R1

Yes

PRIMARY SOURCE

R2 "During the 1990s, it also became apparent [clear] that private participation could bring better oversight and management. The most detailed studies . . . concluded [found] that well designed private schemes [systems] have brought clear benefits—but not perfection. For example, in water, the most difficult sector, in cities as diverse as . . . Abidjan and Conakry service coverage has increased significantly. . . . Extended coverage tends to bring the biggest benefits to households with lower incomes, as they previously had to pay much more for the service by small informal vendors."

—Klein, Michael. "Where Do We Stand Today with Private Infrastructure?" Development Outreach. March 2003. Washington D.C.: World Bank.

During the dry seasons, some areas of Africa are completely without natural water.

Image Source/Getty Images

networks Online Teaching Options

MAP

Geography and Climate Zones in Africa

Analyzing Show students the map of geography and climate zones in Africa. Point out the locations of major rivers and lakes. Have students identify the desert regions of Africa on the map. Remind students that the savanna climate zone covering much of Africa also receives low amounts of rainfall. **Ask:** **How might the climate of Africa make accessing freshwater difficult?** *(Students should note that much of Africa is desert, where water is scarce, and that the large savanna region does not receive a steady supply of rainfall.)*

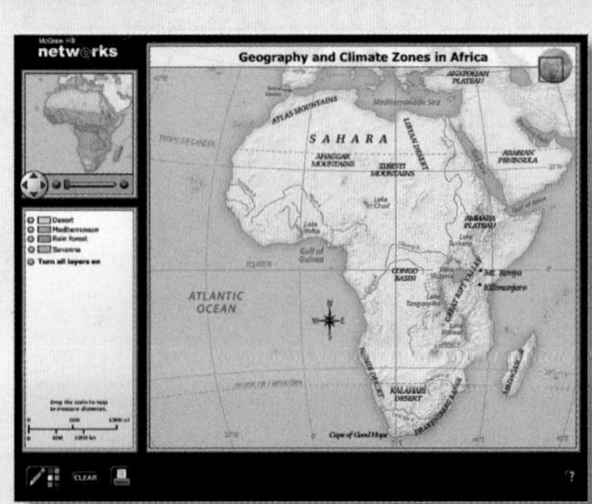

No

PRIMARY SOURCE

“Water is about life. The saying that 'water is life' cannot be more appropriate. Privatizing water is putting the lives of citizens in the hands of a corporate entity [business structure] that is accountable [responsible] only to its shareholders. Secondly, water is a human right and this means that any philosophy, scheme, or contract that has the potential to exclude [leave out] sections of the population from accessing water is not acceptable both in principal and in law. Privatization has that potential because the privateers are not charities: they are in for the profit. Price therefore becomes an important barrier to access by poor people. Water is the collective heritage of humanity and nature. . . . Water must remain a public good for the public interest.”

—Interview with Rudolf Amenga–Etego. "The rains do not fall on one person's roof. . ." *Pambazuka News*. 26 August 2004. Issue 171. *http://pambazuka.org/en/category/features/24190*

LYNN JOHNSON/National Geographic Stock

African governments are trying to find ways to provide clean drinking water for their people.

What Do You Think? DBQ

1. ***Describing*** What is privatization? RH.6–8.4
2. ***Identifying*** According to Michael Klein, where have private companies been most successful at providing water? RH.6–8.6

Critical Thinking

3. ***Analyzing*** What about Michael Klein's background would cause him to believe that privatization is the best solution? RH.6–8.6, RH.6–8.9
4. ***Analyzing Information*** Why does Amenga-Etego mean when he says that "water is a human right. . ."? RH.6–8.6, RH.6–8.9

Read to Write

5. ***Narrative*** Write a paragraph describing your feelings about whether private companies have the right to make a profit by providing water to citizens. WHST.6–8.10

C Critical Thinking Skills

Identifying Points of View Have students read the second excerpt. **Ask:** **What does the author mean when he says that "water is a human right"?** *(The author is arguing that water is so essential to life that every human being automatically should have a right to water.)* **Do you agree or disagree? Why?** *(Student answers will vary, depending upon whether they think the need for things like food, water, and air can be considered rights.)*

W Writing Skills

Argument Tell students to consider the argument presented in the excerpt. Then have them brainstorm two additional pieces of evidence that could support the author's argument. Direct students to write a few sentences in which they state these pieces of evidence and relate them to the author's argument. BL

CLOSE & REFLECT

Review with students the key points from the excerpts and the class discussion. Then have students complete the document-based questions. They may complete the Read to Write question as homework.

LECTURE SLIDE

What Do You Think?

Making Connections Ask students to think of the different ways in which they use water every day. *(Answers may include drinking, washing, and cooking.)* Then show students the lecture slide and discuss the importance of access to clean water. **Ask:** **Why is it important to have clean water?** *(Using unclean water can cause deadly diseases and infections; people will die of thirst quickly without it.)* **How would your daily life be different if you had to walk to collect water each day? What if you could use only 1/20th the amount of water you normally use?** *(Student answers will vary but should reflect an awareness of the challenges involved in using much less water or spending more time and effort to collect it.)*

networks — What Do You Think?

Should private companies control Africa's water?

- One individual thinks it is better to have people buy water from a private company.
- Another individual believes that water should not be privatized.

ANSWERS, p. 443

1. Privatization is when private companies, rather than the government, provide services to people for a fee.
2. They have been most successful in providing water to cities.
3. Klein is the vice president of the World Bank's Private Sector Development and Infrastructure division.
4. Amenga-Etego believes companies will exclude the poor because the companies will not make large enough profits in poor areas.
5. Paragraphs will vary but should include valid and logical arguments.

CHAPTER 15
Activities Answers

CHAPTER REVIEW ACTIVITY

Have a student volunteer write the heading "Effects of Trade in Africa" on the board. Create a web graphic organizer around the heading. Then ask students to work in small groups to brainstorm a list of the ways in which trade brought changes to early African civilizations. Ask a representative from each group to write one or two of their ideas in the web. When each group has recorded their responses, discuss with the class whether they agree or disagree with each response.

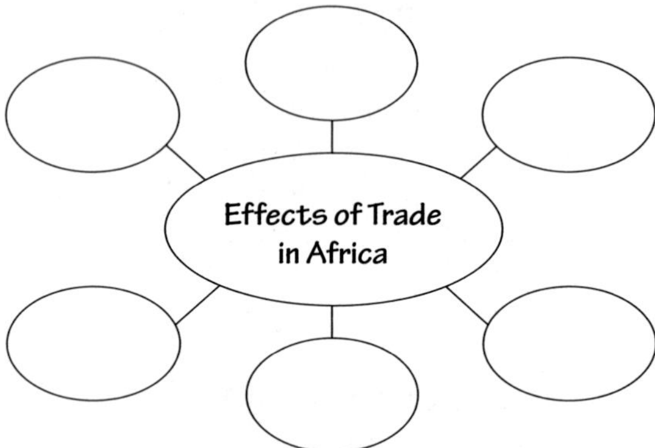

REVIEW THE ENDURING UNDERSTANDING

Review the chapter's Enduring Understanding with students.

- *People, places, and ideas change over time.*

Now pose the following questions in a class discussion to apply these to the chapter.

- **How did the kingdoms of West African both change and stay the same over time?** *(Students should note that all West African kingdoms were significant trading powers, primarily building their wealth through control of the lucrative trade in salt and gold. Over time, however, three different kingdoms covered roughly the same geographic territory. Later kingdoms such as Mali and Songhai also differed from Ghana in that they were influenced by Islamic ideas brought by traders from the north and east.)*
- **How did the arrival of Islam reshape the culture of Africa?** *(Students should understand Islam merged with local African cultures in different ways throughout the continent. In West Africa, Islamic influence contributed to the rise of Muslim scholarship based in the city of Timbuktu, for example. In East Africa, Swahili culture developed with a blend of African and Muslim influences. Varied styles of mosques and other buildings show this diversity.)*
- **How does traditional African culture and art influence U.S. life?** *(Students should connect traditional African art, storytelling, music, and dance with contemporary U.S. styles. These may include folk stories about heroes retold by enslaved Africans in the South, the use of music and dance in community life, and the modern popularity of music such as blues, rock, and rap.)*

CHAPTER 15 Activities CCSS

Write your answers on a separate piece of paper.

1. **Exploring the Essential Question** WHST.6–8.2, WHST.6–8.10
INFORMATIVE/EXPLANATORY How would you explain the ways in which trade affected the history of early African civilizations? Write a short essay in which you consider the parts of these civilizations that were affected by trade. You may choose to focus on aspects such as the civilizations' growth, government, religion, or culture.

2. **21st Century Skills** WHST.6–8.2, WHST.6–8.10
SUMMARIZING Write a paragraph summarizing what you have learned about one of the African civilizations discussed in this chapter. Your paragraph should describe why the civilization you chose is important in African and world history. It should also include significant events, people, and accomplishments related to this civilization.

3. **Thinking Like a Historian** RH.6–8.2
GEOGRAPHY AND CIVILIZATION Create a graphic organizer that lists at least three geographic features of Africa and explains their impact on the growth of civilizations there. For instance, you might write "Sahara" on the left side of your organizer. Then, on the opposite side, you could explain that for many years the Sahara limited travel and trade in Africa.

Feature → Impact on African Civilization

4. **GEOGRAPHY ACTIVITY**

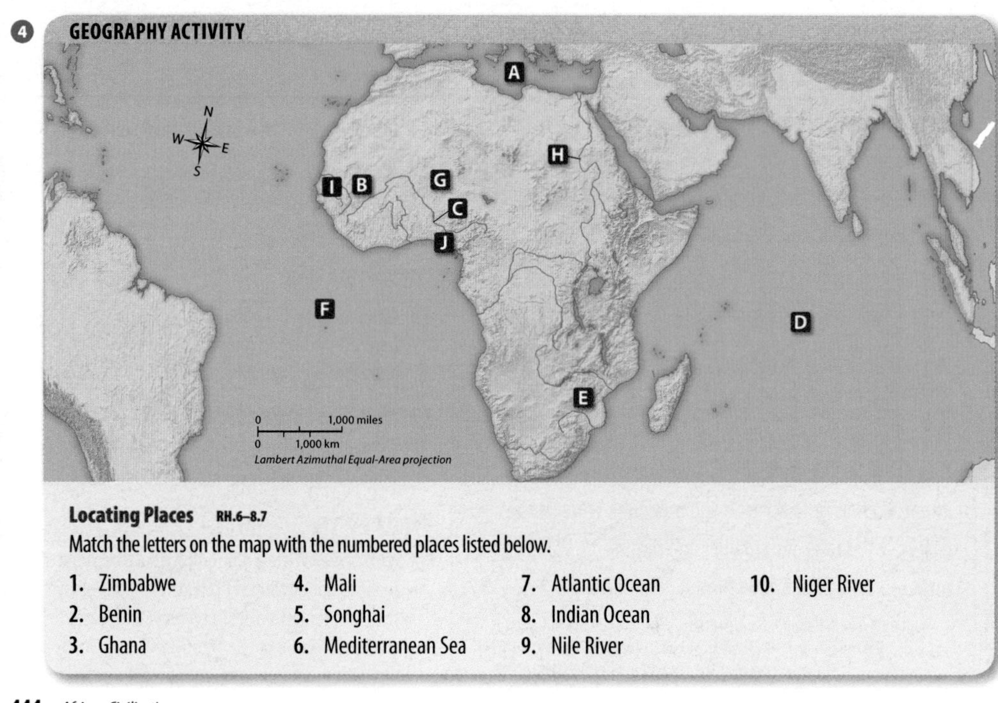

Locating Places RH.6–8.7
Match the letters on the map with the numbered places listed below.

1. Zimbabwe
2. Benin
3. Ghana
4. Mali
5. Songhai
6. Mediterranean Sea
7. Atlantic Ocean
8. Indian Ocean
9. Nile River
10. Niger River

444 *African Civilizations*

ACTIVITIES ANSWERS

Exploring the Essential Question

1. **EXPOSITORY WRITING** Students' essays will vary, but they should offer clear and accurate explanations of the ways in which trade affected various aspects of early African civilizations. For instance, they might point out that locations along trade routes helped empires such as Ghana expand, and the taxing of trade helped these civilizations become wealthy.

21st Century Skills

2. **SUMMARIZING** Students' paragraphs should provide an accurate overview of one of the civilizations discussed in the chapter. Paragraphs should give an overview of these civilizations' importance, as well as provide details about key events, historical figures, and achievements associated with the various civilizations.

Thinking Like a Historian

3. **GEOGRAPHY AND CIVILIZATION** Answers will vary, but students should select several geographic features, such as rivers, valleys, and climate, and accurately explain how these features affected the growth of civilization in Africa.

Locating Places

4. **1.** E; **2.** J; **3.** B; **4.** I; **5.** G; **6.** A; **7.** F; **8.** D; **9.** H; **10.** C

CHAPTER 15 Assessment CCSS

REVIEW THE GUIDING QUESTIONS

Directions: Choose the best answer for each question.

RH.6–8.2
1. About 40 percent of Africa's land area is covered by
   A. rain forests.
   B. plateaus.
   C. savannas.
   D. wetlands.

RH.6–8.2
2. Which of the following conquered the declining empire of Ghana and created a new empire?
   F. Mali
   G. Songhai
   H. Benin
   I. Axum

RH.6–8.2
3. Songhai reached the height of its power under the rule of
   A. Mansa Musa.
   B. Ibn Battuta.
   C. Sunni Ali.
   D. Muhammad Ture.

RH.6–8.2
4. African and Muslim cultures blended to form the ______ culture.
   F. Mogadishu
   G. Moroccan
   H. Swahili
   I. Timbuktu

RH.6–8.2
5. The migrations of which group brought common beliefs and practices to much of Africa?
   A. Kush
   B. Bantu
   C. Berbers
   D. Ashanti

RH.6–8.2
6. Early Africans created art because
   F. it supported their beliefs.
   G. they had nothing else to do.
   H. the Sun god ordered them to.
   I. it was how they voted for a ruler.

445

CHAPTER 15 Assessment Answers

Review the Guiding Questions

1. **C** Choice C is correct. Rain forests are found in central Africa and cover only about 10 percent of its surface. Savannas cover about 40 percent of Africa's surface. Plateaus are found throughout much of Africa. The continent has few wetlands.

2. **F** Choice F is correct. Mali conquered the declining empire of Ghana and created a new empire in the 1200s. Songhai arose when the Mali Empire began to break up. Benin was a rain forest civilization in a different part of Africa. The kingdom of Axum became part of Ethiopia.

3. **D** Choice D is correct. Songhai reached the height of its power under Muhammad Ture. He seized power in 1493 and built a new dynasty. Mansa Musa was a king of Mali. Battuta was an Arab lawyer and traveler.

4. **H** Choice H is correct. African and Muslim cultures blended to form the Swahili culture in East Africa. Mogadishu was a trading port along the Indian Ocean. The Moroccans helped bring about the end of the Songhai Empire. Timbuktu was the capital of Mali.

5. **B** Choice B is correct. By A.D. 300, the migrations of the Bantu had led them to settle most of Africa south of the Sahara. These migrations allowed them to spread their culture throughout this region. Kush was a land bordering Egypt. The Berbers were nomadic people in North Africa. The Ashanti lived in Ghana.

6. **F** Choice F is correct. Early Africans created art as part of how they worshiped and supported their beliefs. It did not relate to their leadership selection.

Analyzing Documents

7 **D** Choice D is correct. Ibn Battuta praises the people of Mali for their devotion to Islam. The passage does not address any criticism of leaders, policies, or government. The passage mentions parents bringing children to religious services, but it does not address education.

8 **H** Choice H is correct. Ibn Battuta's appreciative description of the people's behavior suggests that he views them with respect. Nothing in the passage indicates that Battuta is in awe of the people or that he is confused by their behavior. The passage does not indicate envy on the part of Battuta.

Short Response

9 Mansa Musa demonstrated his support for education in Mali by establishing a university for the study of Islam.

10 Answers will vary, but students should point out the leadership characteristics of Mansa Musa, such as his skills as an organizer and administrator, and his support of arts and education.

Extended Response

11 Students' essays should explain the key role various African art forms played in early African society. Examples could include rock paintings, clothing, sculpture, dancing, and music. Students should also note the lasting impact of early African arts. For instance, they could point to the continued use of brightly colored cloth from West Africa. They could also discuss the development of African-based musical forms such as jazz, ragtime, rock and roll, and rap. Students should provide supporting details based on the chapter content.

DBQ ANALYZING DOCUMENTS

Ibn Battuta wrote during his travels in Mali that

"[The people of Mali] are careful to observe the hours of prayer, and assiduous [always dutiful] in attending them in congregations, and in bringing up their children to them."

—from *Travels in Asia and Africa, 1325–1354*

RH.6–8.1, RH.6–8.6

7 **Drawing Conclusions** Which statement best describes Ibn Battuta's impressions of the people of Mali?

A. He praises their system for educating children.
B. He criticizes the policies of the leaders of Mali.
C. He criticizes the system of government used in Mali.
D. He praises their devotion to their religious beliefs.

RH.6–8.1, RH.6–8.6

8 **Making Inferences** From the passage, you can infer that Ibn Battuta likely views the people of Mali with

F. wonder.
G. confusion.
H. respect.
I. jealousy.

SHORT RESPONSE

"Mansa Musa was a skilled organizer and administrator who built Mali into one of the world's largest empires of the time. The empire was significant in both size and wealth. Mansa Musa encouraged the growth of trade in the empire. He also strongly supported the arts and education in Mali. He ordered the construction of mosques [Islamic temples] and established a university for Islamic studies."

—**EncyclopediaBritannica Online,** "Musa."
http://www.britannica.com/EBchecked/topic/398420/Musa

RH.6–8.1, RH.6–8.6

9 How did Mansa Musa show his support for education in Mali?

RH.6–8.1, RH.6–8.6

10 What traits do you think made Mansa Musa a successful ruler?

EXTENDED RESPONSE

WHST.6–8.2, WHST.6–8.10

11 **Informative/Explanatory** Write an essay in which you seek to explain the importance of the arts to early African society. What purposes did African art play in people's lives? How is the influence of early African art forms still felt today? Use details from the chapter to support your explanation.

Need Extra Help?

If You've Missed Question	1	2	3	4	5	6	7	8	9	10	11
Review Lesson	1	1	2	2	3	3	2	2	2	2	3

CHAPTER **16**

The Americas Planner

UNDERSTANDING BY DESIGN®

Enduring Understandings

- *People, places, and ideas change over time.*
- *Cultures are held together by shared beliefs and common practices and values.*

Essential Questions

- *How does geography affect the way people live?*
- *What makes a culture unique?*

Predictable Misunderstandings

Students may think:

- *All early Americans lived as nomads.*
- *All early Americans lived in tepees.*
- *All early Americans spoke the same language and had the same traditions.*

Assessment Evidence

Performance Task:

- *Hands-On Chapter Project*

Other Evidence:

- *Responses to Interactive Whiteboard activities*
- *Identification of geographic features that influenced where people settled*
- *Understanding of causes and effects of the growth of farming in the Americas*
- *Charting of the similarities and differences among native North Americans*
- *Understanding as to why farming was the anchor of a beginning civilization*
- *Interactive Graphic Organizers*
- *Geography and History Activity*
- *21st Century Skills Activity*
- *Written paragraphs*
- *Lesson Reviews*

SUGGESTED PACING GUIDE

Introducing the Chapter	1 Day	Lesson 2	2 Days
Lesson 1	1 Day	Chapter Wrap-Up and Assessment	1 Day

TOTAL TIME 5 Days

Key for Using the Teacher Edition

SKILL-BASED ACTIVITIES

Types of skill activities found in the Teacher Edition.

V Visual Skills require students to analyze maps, graphs, charts, and photos.

R Reading Skills help students practice reading skills and master vocabulary.

W Writing Skills provide writing opportunities to help students comprehend the text.

C Critical Thinking Skills help students apply and extend what they have learned.

T Technology Skills require students to use digital tools effectively.

*Letters are followed by a number when there is more than one of the same type of skill on the page.

DIFFERENTIATED INSTRUCTION

All activities are written for the on-level student unless otherwise marked with the leveled labels below.

BL Beyond Level

AL Approaching Level

ELL English Language Learners

All students benefit from activities that utilize different learning styles. Many activities are marked as below when a particular learning style is highlighted.

Intrapersonal	**Naturalist**
Logical/Mathematical	**Kinesthetic**
Visual/Spatial	**Auditory/Musical**
Verbal/Linguistic	**Interpersonal**

NCSS Standards covered in "The Americas"

Learners will understand:

1 CULTURE

1. "Culture" refers to the socially transmitted behaviors, beliefs, values, traditions, institutions, and ways of living together for a group of people

3. How culture influences the ways in which human groups solve the problems of daily living

4. That the beliefs, values, and behaviors of a culture form an integrated system that helps shape the activities and ways of life that define a culture

7. How people from different cultures develop different values and ways of interpreting experience

3 PEOPLE, PLACES, AND ENVIRONMENTS

1. The theme of people, places, and environments involves the study of the relationships between human populations in different locations and geographic phenomena such as climate, vegetation, and natural resources

2. Concepts such as: location, region, place, migration, as well as human and physical systems

4. The roles of different kinds of population centers in a region or nation

5. The concept of regions identifies links between people in different locations according to specific criteria (e.g., physical, economic, social, cultural, or religious)

7. Human modifications of the environment

CHAPTER OPENER PLANNER

Students will know:
- *how geography defined the ways people settled in the Americas.*
- *how early peoples arrived and settled in the Americas.*
- *what role farming played in civilizations.*
- *why the civilizations that developed in North America were so diverse.*
- *how the Maya created their civilization in the rain forests of Mesoamerica.*
- *how the Aztec built their society in central Mexico.*
- *how the Inca organized their government and society.*
- *how the different societies of North American peoples lived.*

Students will be able to:
- ***describe*** *how geography influenced migration from Asia to the Americas.*
- ***show and explain*** *how early peoples arrived and settled in the Americas.*
- ***compare*** *farming in the Americas with farming in the early river valley civilizations.*
- ***analyze*** *why farming was the basis of civilization.*
- ***identify*** *aspects of culture from the Maya, Aztec, and Inca civilizations.*
- ***describe*** *the cultures of the Maya, Aztec, and Inca civilizations.*
- ***analyze*** *how the different societies of North American peoples lived.*
- ***determine*** *whether a "typical" civilization existed in North America.*

UNDERSTANDING BY DESIGN®

☑ Print Teaching Options

V Visual Skills

- ☐ **P. 448** Students study a map of the Americas and answer questions about the climate and geography. **Visual/Spatial**
- ☐ **P. 449** Students review the chapter time line and use it to answer questions. **Visual/Spatial**

☑ Online Teaching Options

V Visual Skills

- **MAP** **Place and Time: North and South America 1500**—Students identify the locations of major civilizations and click to learn interesting facts.
- **TIME LINE** **Place and Time: The Americas 1500 B.C. to A.D. 1600**—Students learn about key events in the Americas during this time period.
- **WORLD ATLAS** Students can use this interactive map to identify regions of the world, learn about individual countries, locate political boundaries, measure distances, and much more.

Project-Based Learning

Hands-On Chapter Project

Native Peoples Journal Entries

Students will work together in groups to write journal entries from the point of view of native peoples living in the Americas.

Technology Extension

edtechteacher

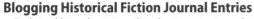

Blogging Historical Fiction Journal Entries
- Find an additional activity online that incorporates technology for this project.
- Visit the EdTechTeacher Web sites (included in the Technology Extension for this chapter) for more links, tutorials, and other resources.

Print Resources

ANCILLARY RESOURCES

These ancillaries are available for every chapter and lesson.
- **Reading Essentials and Study Guide Workbook** AL ELL
- **Chapter Tests and Lesson Quizzes Blackline Masters**

PRINTABLE DIGITAL WORKSHEETS

These printable digital worksheets are available for every chapter and lesson.
- **Hands-On Chapter Projects**
- **What Do You Know? activities**
- **Chapter Summaries (English and Spanish)**
- **Vocabulary Builder activities**
- **Guided Reading activities**

More Media Resources

SUGGESTED READING 

Grade 6 reading level:
- ***The Great Circle: A History of the First Nations,*** by Neil Philip

Grade 7 reading level:
- ***The Shaman's Nephew: A Life in the Far North,*** by Simon Tookoome with Sheldon Oberman

Grade 8 reading level:
- ***Who Came First? New Clues to Prehistoric Americans,*** by Patricia Lauber

LESSON 1 PLANNER

THE FIRST AMERICANS

Students will know:

- *how geography defined the ways people settled in the Americas.*
- *how early peoples arrived and settled in the Americas.*
- *what role farming played in civilizations.*
- *why the civilizations that developed in North America were diverse.*

Students will be able to:

- ***describe** how geography influenced migration from Asia to the Americas.*
- ***show and explain** how early peoples arrived and settled in the Americas.*
- ***compare** farming in the Americas with farming in the early river valley civilizations.*
- ***analyze** why farming was the basis of civilization.*

UNDERSTANDING BY DESIGN®

☑ Print Teaching Options

V Visual Skills

- ☐ **P. 453** Students examine the "Migration to America" map and answer questions about it. AL Visual/Spatial
- ☐ **P. 455** Students use a map and map key to analyze the coastlines of different early American civilizations. BL Logical/Mathematical Visual/Spatial
- ☐ **P. 457** Students analyze and discuss an image of Pueblo Bonito. BL Visual/Spatial

R Reading Skills

- ☐ **P. 450** Students define *isthmus* and locate an example on a map. ELL Visual/Spatial
- ☐ **P. 452** Students compare the plains in both North and South America. AL
- ☐ **P. 453** Students discuss different ideas about how people first came to the Americas and cite evidence to support each one.
- ☐ **P. 454** Students identify the different ways early people in each region of the Americas got their food.
- ☐ **P. 456** Students discuss the Moche people of Peru.

W Writing Skills

- ☐ **P. 451** Students write a narrative describing landforms they would encounter on a trip across the United States.

C Critical Thinking Skills

- ☐ **P. 450** Students discuss the geographic regions of North and South American and hypothesize how the geography affected the lifestyles of early inhabitants.
- ☐ **P. 452** Students discuss possible uses for large rivers in North and South America.
- ☐ **P. 454** Students discuss how life changed for early Americans when they began the practice of agriculture. BL
- ☐ **P. 458** Students compare and contrast the Mound Builders with the Hohokam and the Anasazi.

T Technology Skills

- ☐ **P. 456** Students use word processing software to create a time line of the major civilizations in Mesoamerica. BL Visual/Spatial

☑ Online Teaching Options

V Visual Skills

- ☐ VIDEO **Peru: A History**—Students get an overview of the peoples who have lived in this area.
- ☐ MAP **North and South America Groups**—Students identify the locations of major civilizations and click to learn interesting facts.
- ☐ MAP **Migration to America**—Students trace possible migration routes to the Americas.
- ☐ MAP **North America Physical**— Students identify aspects of the physical geography of North America.
- ☐ MAP **Civilizations of Mesoamerica**—Students identify the locations of major civilizations in Central America and hear audio of interesting facts.

R Reading Skills

- ☐ GRAPHIC ORGANIZER **Taking Notes: *Summarizing*: Climate and Mountain Ranges**—Students record the climates and mountain ranges of the four main areas of the Americas.
- ☐ SLIDE SHOW **Casa Grande, Mesa Verde, and Pueblo Bonito**—Students examine pueblos.
- ☐ SLIDE SHOW **Amazon Wildlife**—Extensive descriptions accompany photos of the rain forest.
- ☐ SLIDE SHOW **Native American Creation Stories**—Students analyze stories of Earth's beginnings from different cultures.
- ☐ IMAGE **Corn**—Students read about this important native plant.

C Critical Thinking Skills

- ☐ WHITEBOARD ACTIVITY **Dates in History**—Students sort important events in Zapotec, Teotihuacán, and Maya history.
- ☐ CHART **Highest Peaks in the United States**—Students compare heights of mountain peaks.
- ☐ SLIDE SHOW **Mound Builders**—Students compare and contrast mound shapes.
- ☐ IMAGE **Zapotec Writing**—Students examine stone carvings showing Stelae 12 and 13.

T Technology Skills

- ☐ SELF-CHECK QUIZ **Lesson 1**—Students receive instant feedback on their mastery of lesson content.
- ☐ GAME **Column Game: Moche, Toltec, and Zapotec**—Students sort characteristics of the Moche, Toltec, and Zapotec.

☑ Printable Digital Worksheets

C Critical Thinking Skills

- ☐ WORKSHEET **Geography and History Activity: Understanding Movement: Migration**—Students consider the paths people took from Asia to the Americas.

LESSON 2 PLANNER

LIFE IN THE AMERICAS

Students will know:

- *how the Maya created their civilization in the rain forests of Mesoamerica.*
- *how the Aztec built their society in central Mexico.*
- *how the Inca organized their government and society.*
- *how the different societies of North American peoples lived.*

Students will be able to:

- ***identify** aspects of culture from the Maya, Aztec, and Inca civilizations.*
- ***describe** the cultures of the Maya, Aztec, and Inca civilizations.*
- ***analyze** how the different societies of North American peoples lived.*
- ***determine** whether a "typical" civilization existed in North America.*

UNDERSTANDING BY DESIGN®

☑ Print Teaching Options

V Visual Skills

- ☐ **P. 460** Students draw their own interpretation of Chac and write a caption for their image. ELL **Visual/Spatial**
- ☐ **P. 464** Students draw mountains and answer questions about terraces. **Visual/Spatial**
- ☐ **P. 466** Students use the "People and Food Sources of North America" map to answer questions about early Native American peoples. AL ELL **Visual/Spatial**

R Reading Skills

- ☐ **P. 459** Students explain how the Maya were able to create a civilization in the rain forests of Mesoamerica.
- ☐ **P. 460** Students role play kings, nobles, priests, and working class members of Mayan society.
- ☐ **P. 461** Students identify achievements of the Maya. AL
- ☐ **P. 462** Students define a tribute and discuss the relationship between the Aztec ruler and the territories conquered by the Aztec empire. AL ELL
- ☐ **P. 464** Students make a diagram to illustrate the organization of Inca Society. AL ELL
- ☐ **P. 467** Students discuss the Native Americans who lived on the Great Plains and in the Eastern Woodlands.

W Writing Skills

- ☐ **P. 462** Students write a journal entry from the perspective of a noble, commoner, unskilled worker, or enslaved person who lived in Tenochtitlán. BL **Verbal/Linguistic**

C Critical Thinking Skills

- ☐ **P. 461** Students discuss possible reasons for the collapse of the Mayan culture.
- ☐ **P. 463** Students discuss how the Aztecs provided food for their community.

T Technology Skills

- ☐ **P. 465** Students work in small groups to research Machu Picchu or another Inca achievement and create a slide show presentation to share what they have learned. **Interpersonal**

☑ Online Teaching Options

V Visual Skills

- VIDEO **Aztec, Maya, and Inca Civilizations**—Students examine these three great empires that were overrun by Spanish conquistadors after centuries of flourishing civilizations.
- MAP **Civilizations of Mesoamerica**—Students identify the areas occupied by the Olmec, Maya, Toltec, and Aztec civilizations.
- MAP **The Inca Empire, 1532**—Students view the divisions of the Inca Empire
- IMAGE **Chac, Maya Rain God**—Students examine characteristics of this Maya deity.
- IMAGE **Maya Arts**—Students click to learn about the paper and books, sculpture, murals, carvings, and jewelry created by this group.
- SLIDE SHOW **Tenochtitlán**—Students view scenes from the Aztec city.
- IMAGE **Aztec Shield**—Students analyze the materials used to make an Aztec shield.

R Reading Skills

- GRAPHIC ORGANIZER **Taking Notes: *Organizing:* Aztec Social Classes**—Students use a pyramid diagram to order Aztec social classes.
- BIOGRAPHY **Pachacuti**—Students read about this Inca emperor.

C Critical Thinking Skills

- WHITEBOARD ACTIVITY **Think Like a Historian**—Students identify characteristics of Native American groups living in different areas.
- IMAGE **Machu Picchu, Hidden Inca City**—Students explore the ruins of this ancient Inca city.
- MAP **People and Food Sources of North America c. 1300–1500**—Students consider how people of North America provided for basic needs.
- SLIDE SHOW **Native American Groups**—Students compare and contrast three groups who lived in North America.

T Technology Skills

- SELF-CHECK QUIZ **Lesson 2**—Students receive instant feedback on their mastery of lesson content.

☑ Printable Digital Worksheets

C Critical Thinking Skills

- WORKSHEET **21st Century Skills: Critical Thinking and Problem Solving: Compare and Contrast**—Students write a paragraph comparing and contrasting the calendar used today in the United States with calendars of the Maya and Aztec.

INTERVENTION AND REMEDIATION STRATEGIES

LESSON 1 The First Americans

Reading and Comprehension

Have students describe the theories of how people first reached the Americas and how those early peoples shifted from hunting and gathering to agriculture.

Text Evidence

Ask students to make a three-column chart of the different civilizations that they have read about in this lesson. The first column should identify the civilization, the second should explain where the civilization lived, and the third should describe how each civilization lived and obtained its food. Information in the chart should come from the text.

LESSON 2 Life in the Americas

Reading and Comprehension

Have students work in small groups to discuss the similarities and differences among the Maya, Aztec, and Inca. Then have each group share what they have learned with the class.

Text Evidence

Have pairs of students choose one of the three civilizations described in this lesson and create a time line of major events and achievements of that civilization. Students should cite dates and events from the text.

Online Resources

Approaching Level Reader

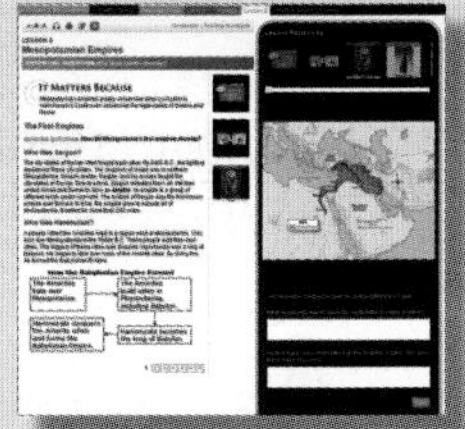

Use this online lower-level text that corresponds directly to the text in the Student Edition. It includes a Spanish version.

Guided Reading Activities

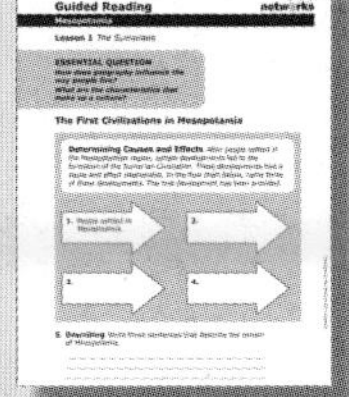

This resource uses graphic organizers and guiding questions to help students with comprehension.

What Do You Know?

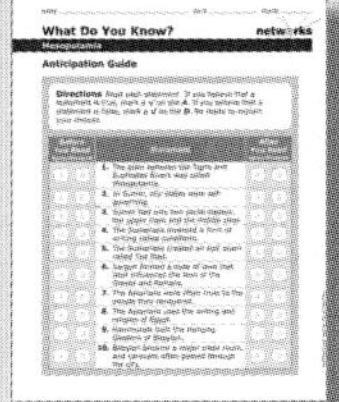

Use these worksheets to pre-assess student's background knowledge before they study the chapter.

Reading Essentials and Study Guide Workbook

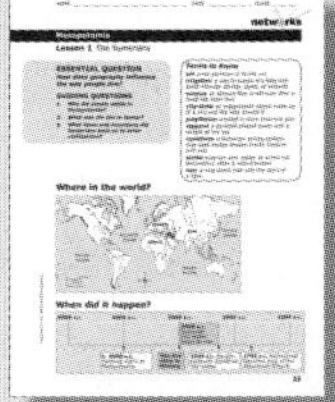

This resource offers writing and reading activities for the approaching-level student. Also available in Spanish.

Self-Check Quizzes

This online assessment tool provides instant feedback for students to check their progress.

How Do I Help With
Multimedia Presentations?

Students are quite comfortable operating computers and digital devices. They spend much of their time using these tools to consume entertainment and information. Not all students, however, are as familiar with how to effectively use computers as tools. In their professional life, they will often need to create digital presentations.

Tip 1 Don't focus on the platform. Focus on the content being presented.

- There are many different digital platforms that you can point students towards as the environment in which they build their online presentations. Do research and find the platform that you understand. This will allow you to clearly explain how to use the platform to your class.
- What you want your students to learn is the proper techniques required to build effective online presentations. Help them learn to consider the following design choices as they make their multimedia.
- **What sort of background image works best?** Encourage students to pick a background image that represents the content topic they are presenting, but one that is not too "busy" or distracting to the content, which should be the focal point.
- **How should they incorporate audio or video elements?** There is a temptation with online media to overload the presentation with audio or video that could not be used as easily in traditional two-dimensional presentations. But these dynamic content tools should be used sparingly to provide maximum impact. The presentation should not be "blinking" and "shouting" for attention.

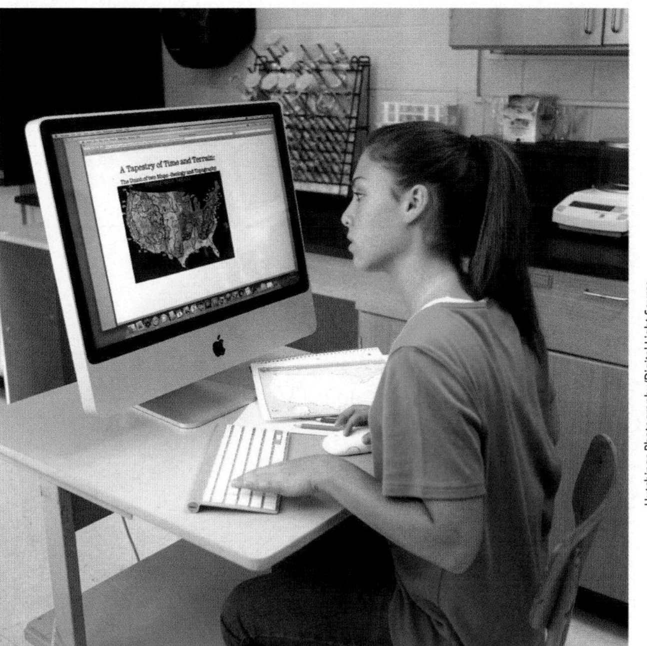

Hutchings Photography/Digital Light Source

Tip 2 Don't forget to do the research!

- Students must be careful that they don't get so involved in building their multimedia environment that they forget to spend an equal (or larger) amount of time researching the topic. This is especially true when learning a new platform with lots of tools and options. A presentation is no good if there is no content.

Tip 3 Show some examples of good models.

- Creating a multimedia presentation might seem overwhelming to students, especially ones that are focused on learning the content being presented or trying to learn how to use digital platforms. So, make it more understandable by displaying some models that show what you expect the students to create.
- Finding good models helps the students begin visualizing how to begin their own project. Also, take the time to explain details of the models that make them a good example. Allow time for students to review the models and ask you questions.

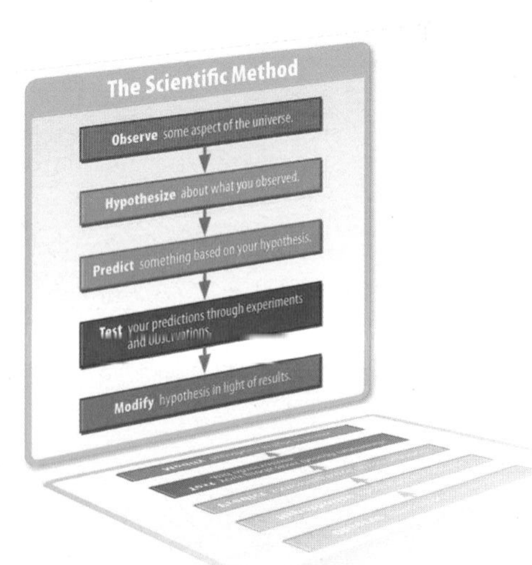

The Americas

1500 B.C. to A.D. 1600

ESSENTIAL QUESTIONS • *How does geography affect the way people live?* • *What makes a culture unique?*

networks

There's More Online about the civilizations and customs of the Americas.

CHAPTER 16

Lesson 1
The First Americans

Lesson 2
Life in the Americas

The Story Matters . . .

Why do the seasons change? What causes thunder? Today, we look to science to answer these questions. Ancient people told stories.

The native people of Central America told a story to explain the origin of the sun. According to the legend, Nanahuatzin (nah • nah • WAHT • zeen), an Aztec god, had warts, or bumps, all over his face. At the time the world was created, Nanahuatzin threw himself into a great fire. Rather than dying in the flames, Nanahuatzin arose and became the sun.

This mask was made in Mexico about 600 years ago. Some historians believe it is a mask of Nanahuatzin. Other historians believe this represents Xiuhtecuhtli (zhee • ooh • tay • COOT • lee), the Aztec god of fire.

◄ *Xiuhtecuhtli was also known as "The Turquoise Lord." This mask is made of wood and covered with turquoise mosaic. The teeth are made from shells.*

Letter from the Author

Dear World History Teacher,

About 10,000 years ago, farming settlements began to appear in Mesoamerica. Soon, communities along the Gulf of Mexico and in the central Andes began the ascent toward civilization. The Maya and Aztec built elaborate cities. Maya civilization collapsed about A.D. 900, and the Aztec fell to Spanish invaders in the sixteenth century. In the fifteenth century, the Inca flourished in South America, but also fell to Spain. While the Maya, Aztec, and Inca were rising, the peoples of North America were creating a remarkable number of different cultures.

Jackson J. Spielvogel

ENGAGE

Bellringer After students have read "The Story Matters . . .," ask them why people long ago told stories to explain why things in nature happened. *(They didn't have scientific explanations for why things happened, but they wanted to understand their environment.)*

Ask: **If you don't understand why something happens, where do you expect to find the answer? On the Internet? In a textbook?** Ask students where early Americans could look for answers to their questions. *(They might ask older people.)* **What topics might early people have known more about than you do?** *(Students might say that early people probably knew more about hunting than they do. Early Americans knew more about agriculture and probably knew more about the stars than many of us do.)* Discuss with students who would have a harder time surviving in the other's world: an early American transported into our world or a contemporary student transported to the world of early Americans.

Making Connections

Discuss with students whether they think there was a "typical" Native American culture. **Ask:** **What images come to mind when you think of early Native Americans?** *(Students may mention the image of a horseback rider hunting buffalo on the Great Plains or a similar image.)*

Display a map of the United States. Have students locate where they live on the map. Then have volunteers point out other places in the United States where they have lived or that they have visited. Have them describe the differences among the places named. **Ask:**

- **How was the climate different?**
- **Were there different kinds of geographical features nearby?**
- **Were houses there different from houses here?**
- **What other kinds of differences have you noticed?**

Help students recognize how different geographic locations lead to different ways of life.

Then explain to students that different Native American cultures lived in different regions of the Americas. Help students to understand that because the groups lived in different locations, there is no single, "typical" Native American culture.

TEACH & ASSESS

Step Into the Place

V1 Visual Skills

Analyzing Maps Have students look closely at the Chapter Opener map. Ask them what they know about the climates and geography of the Americas. As you point to various geographic areas of the map, have students identify them. Then **ask:** What native groups covered a large area of mid–North America? *(Mound Builders)* Then point to areas on the map that have different geographical features. What mountain range is located here? What South American group lived in the mountains? *(Inca)* Lead students to understand that the Americas form a vast region with many different climates and many different geographical features. **Visual/Spatial**

Content Background Knowledge

Many different terms are used to describe the Native peoples of the Americas. When Christopher Columbus arrived in the Americas, he used the term *indios,* which is Spanish for Indians, because he thought he had reached the Indies in South Asia. In the 1960s, many groups rejected this term and began used the term Native Americans. In Canada, native people began using the term First Nations around the same time. Today, many native people still refer to themselves as Indians.

V2

ANSWERS, p. 448

Step Into the Place

1. Cahokia is located north of the Amazon River.
2. The central location of Tenochtitlán allowed the Aztec to use a web of trade routes that reached throughout Mexico.
3. Cuzco is south and east of Cahokia.
4. CRITICAL THINKING Answers will vary but should emphasize that access to water, trade routes, and natural resources can strengthen an empire.

Step Into the Time

Answers will vary depending upon the event chosen but should be based on facts and reasonable arguments.

CHAPTER 16 CCSS

Place and Time: The Americas 1500 B.C. to A.D. 1600

Early people in the Americas depended on natural resources to survive. The development of farming and trade allowed them to build complex cultures. The Maya, Inca, and Aztec empires ruled over large parts of Mesoamerica and South America.

Early American mountain dwellers lived on wide plateaus such as this, found in mountain ranges. The level areas provided land for settlements and farming.

Step Into the Place

MAP FOCUS The geography and climates in North and South America influenced early people who lived there and caused them to develop different cultures.

1. **LOCATION** Look at the map. Is Cahokia located north or south of the Amazon River? RH.6–8.7
2. **PLACE** How did the location of Tenochtitlán affect Aztec trade? RH.6–8.7
3. **LOCATION** Use cardinal directions to locate Cuzco compared to Cahokia. RH.6–8.7
4. **CRITICAL THINKING** *Analyzing* How does location affect the strength of an empire? RH.6–8.1

The Navajo are known for their complex religious ceremonies. Many of these ceremonies take place within traditional buildings known as hogans. Hogans are built so that the entrance faces east—toward the rising sun. When a fire is built inside the hogan, the opening at the top allows smoke to escape.

Step Into the Time

TIME LINE Choose an event from the time line and write a paragraph predicting the general social, political, or economic consequence that event might have for the world. RH.6–8.7, WHST.6–8.10

THE AMERICAS
c. A.D. 500 Mayan cities flourish in Mesoamerica

A.D. 500 A.D. 600 A.D. 700 A.D. 800 A.D. 900

THE WORLD
c. A.D. 800 Pope crowns Charlemagne emperor
c. A.D. 830 Baghdad is center of Islamic learning

Project-Based Learning

Hands-On Chapter Project

Native Peoples Journal Entries

Students will write journal entries from the point of view of native peoples living in the Americas. They will first review what they have learned about the native peoples and civilizations of the Americas. Then, as a group, they will discuss ideas for their journal entries. After creating a plan, students will work individually to write journal entries. When they have finished, students will share their journal entries with the class.

Technology Extension

Blogging Historical Fiction Journal Entries

Students will create and publish blogs for historical fiction journal entries about native peoples in the Americas. They will choose a group to write about and then post several different blogs that are written from the perspective of someone in that group. Students can read and comment on each other's blog posts, and when they have finished, they will use an Assessment Rubric to evaluate their work.

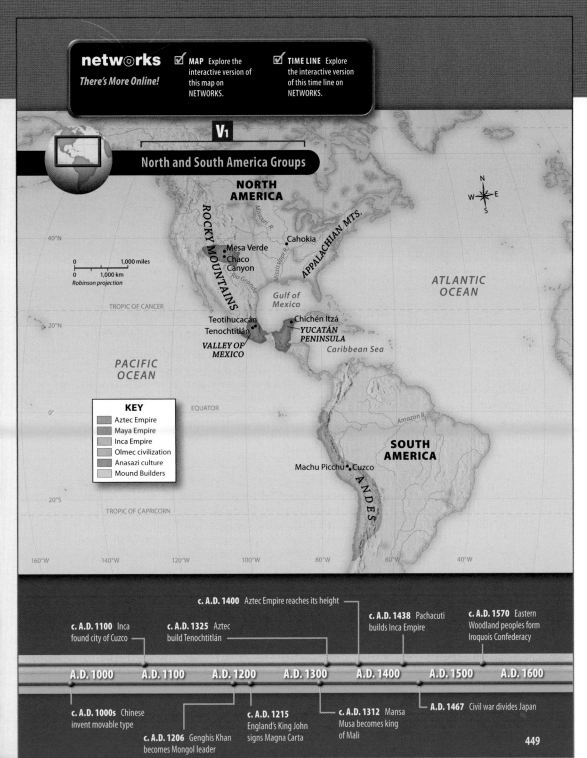

networks There's More Online!

☑ **MAP** Explore the interactive version of this map on NETWORKS.

☑ **TIME LINE** Explore the interactive version of this time line on NETWORKS.

V1

North and South America Groups

NORTH AMERICA
ROCKY MOUNTAINS
Missouri R.
APPALACHIAN MTS.
Cahokia
Mesa Verde
Chaco Canyon
Mississippi R.
Rio Grande
Gulf of Mexico
ATLANTIC OCEAN
TROPIC OF CANCER
Teotihuacán
Tenochtitlán
Chichén Itzá
YUCATÁN PENINSULA
VALLEY OF MEXICO
Caribbean Sea
PACIFIC OCEAN
EQUATOR
Amazon R.
SOUTH AMERICA
Machu Picchu
Cuzco
ANDES
TROPIC OF CAPRICORN
0 1,000 miles
0 1,000 km
Robinson projection
40°N 20°N 0° 20°S
160°W 140°W 120°W 100°W 80°W 60°W 40°W

KEY
- Aztec Empire
- Maya Empire
- Inca Empire
- Olmec civilization
- Anasazi culture
- Mound Builders

c. A.D. 1100 Inca found city of Cuzco

c. A.D. 1325 Aztec build Tenochtitlán

c. A.D. 1400 Aztec Empire reaches its height

c. A.D. 1438 Pachacuti builds Inca Empire

c. A.D. 1570 Eastern Woodland peoples form Iroquois Confederacy

A.D. 1000 | A.D. 1100 | A.D. 1200 | A.D. 1300 | A.D. 1400 | A.D. 1500 | A.D. 1600

c. A.D. 1000s Chinese invent movable type

c. A.D. 1206 Genghis Khan becomes Mongol leader

c. A.D. 1215 England's King John signs Magna Carta

c. A.D. 1312 Mansa Musa becomes king of Mali

A.D. 1467 Civil war divides Japan

449

CHAPTER 16

Place and Time

Step Into the Time

V2 Visual Skills

Analyzing Time Lines Have students read through both levels of events on the time line—those dealing with the Americas and those dealing with the rest of the world. Remind them that during the years covered by this time line, the Americas were separated from the rest of the world. To encourage students to analyze the time line more closely, pose questions such as these. **Ask:**

- What was happening in the Americas around A.D. 500? *(Maya cities in Mesoamerica were flourishing.)*
- What was happening in Europe around A.D. 500? *(The Roman Empire fell, and the period known as the Early Middle Ages was beginning.)*
- About how long after the Aztec built Tenochtitlán did their civilization reach its height? *(about 75 years later)* **Visual/Spatial**

Content Background Knowledge

- Cuzco, the capital of the Inca Empire, is one of the oldest continuously inhabited cities in the Americas. Today the city is in south-central Peru in the Andes and has an elevation of 11,150 feet. It is possible that at the height of the empire, 12,000 people lived in the city.
- Tenochtitlán, the capital of the Aztec empire, was located at the site of present-day Mexico City. Tenochtitlán was originally built on two small islands in Lake Texcoco. Over time, the Aztecs built artificial islands and a causeway to expand the size of the city. In 1519, about 400,000 people lived there.

TIME LINE

Place and Time: The Americas 1500 B.C. to A.D. 1600

Reading a Time Line Display the time line on the white board. Have students scroll through the time line and read each event. Remind them that they can click on the "more information" feature to learn more details about the events. After you have finished reviewing the time line, ask students which event in the Americas they are interested in learning more about and have them explain why. You may want to return to these comments as you progress through this chapter.

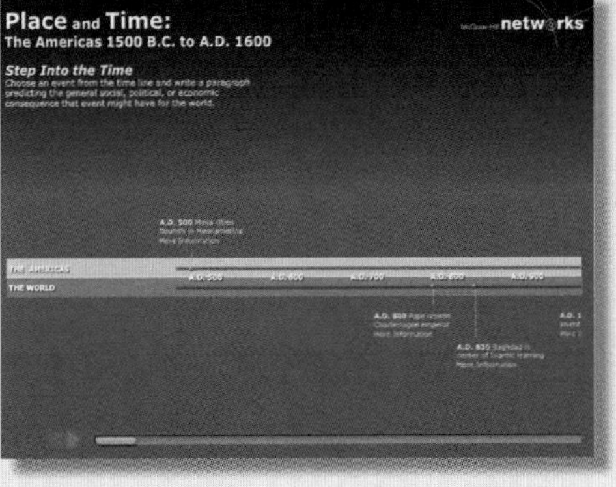

See page 447B for other online activities.

The First Americans

ENGAGE

Bellringer Before the beginning the lesson, ask students what they know about the geography of North and South America. Write their answers on the board so you can return to them. Then direct students to the physical map of North America on the facing page. Remind them that scientists have evidence that humans settled from north to south.

Ask: How do you think people first got to North America? Write students' ideas on the board. Explain to students that they will be learning about the early peoples who settled the Americas.

TEACH & ASSESS

C Critical Thinking Skills

Hypothesizing Point out that the Americas stretch for nearly 11,000 miles from north to south. Ask students to think about the different geographic regions of the continents. **Ask:** How do you think people's ways of living differed on different parts of these two continents? Students should explain that peoples' ways of living would have depended on the geography and resources of the region where they lived. Ask students to give specific examples to support this idea, such as fishing near the oceans or building shelters with available materials.

R Reading Skills

Determining Word Meanings Ask students locate the word *isthmus* in their text and to explain what an isthmus is. *(a narrow piece of land that connects two larger areas of land)* Have a volunteer point out on a map the large isthmus in the Western Hemisphere. *(Central America)* **ELL** **Visual/Spatial**

ANSWER, p. 450

TAKING NOTES:

	Climate	Mountains
North America	cold to tropical	Rocky Mountains, Pacific coastal ranges, Appalachians
South America	warm, rainy	Andes
Central America	warm, rainy	
Caribbean	warm, rainy	

networks *There's More Online!*

- GRAPHIC ORGANIZER Climates and Mountains
- SLIDE SHOW Peoples of the Southwest

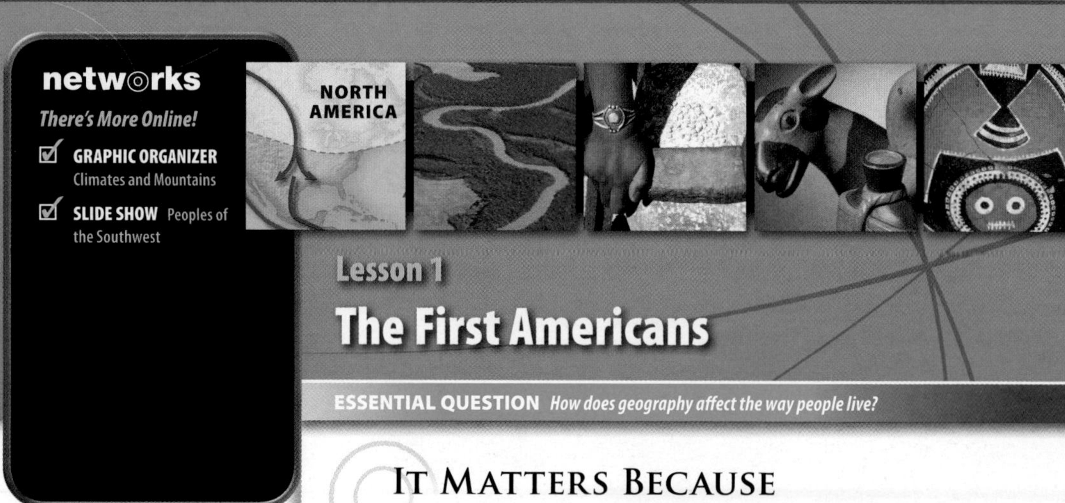

Lesson 1

The First Americans

ESSENTIAL QUESTION *How does geography affect the way people live?*

IT MATTERS BECAUSE

Early people in the Americas built the beginnings of several civilizations.

Geography of the Americas

GUIDING QUESTION *How did geography shape the ways people settled in the Americas?*

About 15,000 years ago, prehistoric hunters left northeastern Asia and arrived in what is today Alaska. They are believed to be among the first people to settle the region called the Americas. Their descendants are called Native Americans. Over the centuries, Native American groups adopted different ways of life. Each group's way of life was based on local resources.

A Diverse Region

C The Americas stretch north to south nearly 11,000 miles (almost 18,000 km). This vast region begins north at the Arctic Circle. It reaches south to Tierra del Fuego (tee•EHR•eh del FWAY•goh). Tierra del Fuego is a group of islands located off the coast of Chile and Argentina, at the southern tip of South America.

The four geographical areas of the Americas are North America, South America, Central America, and the Caribbean. R North America and South America are both continents. The two continents make up most of the Americas. Central America is an **isthmus** (IHS•muhs), a narrow piece of land that connects two larger areas of land. East of Central America is the Caribbean Sea. A string of islands spreads across the Caribbean Sea to the Atlantic Ocean. As a group, these islands are known as the Caribbean.

Reading HELPDESK (CCSS)

Taking Notes: ***Summarizing***

Use a chart like the one here to record the climates and mountain ranges of the four main areas of the Americas. RH.6–8.2

	Climate	Mountains
North America		
South America		
Central America		
Caribbean		

Content Vocabulary (Tier 3 Words)

- **isthmus**
- **maize**

isthmus a narrow piece of land linking two larger areas of land

networks Online Teaching Options

VIDEO

Peru: History

Finding the Main Idea Present the video on the history of Peru to students. As they watch, have them record at least three main ideas from the video on a sheet of paper. When they have finished watching the video, have them add at least one supporting detail to each main idea.

See page 447C for other online activities.

Within the vast expanse of the Americas you can find many different geographic features and climates. North America lies north of the Equator and has climates that range from cold to tropical.

Central America and the Caribbean islands are also north of the Equator. South America extends both north and south of the Equator. Most of these areas have a warm, rainy climate. A broad range of plants grows in the three areas.

Towering Mountains

In the west, rugged mountain chains run nearly the entire length of the Americas. They separate coastal plains near the Pacific Ocean from broad eastern plains that sweep toward the Atlantic Ocean.

The Andes are the world's longest mountain system. These mountains stretch along the Pacific coast of South America. Valleys and plateaus (plah•TOES) lie between the mountain chains. Plateaus are large areas of raised land that have a flat surface.

The Rocky Mountains and the Pacific coastal ranges are in western North America. These mountains contain passes, or low areas. Even with these passes, overland travel across the mountains could be difficult.

In eastern North America, a range of mountains—the Appalachians—runs near the Atlantic coast. The Appalachians are lower than the Rockies and Pacific coastal ranges. Early Americans had no difficulty traveling over the Appalachians.

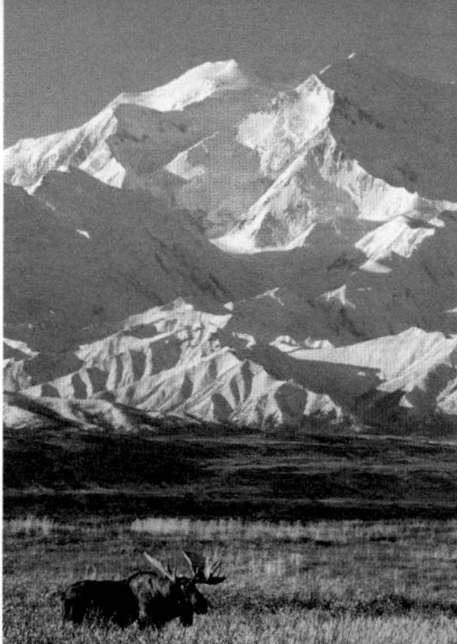

Mount McKinley is the tallest mountain in North America. It stands in Denali National Park, Alaska.

AlaskaStock/Corbis

W

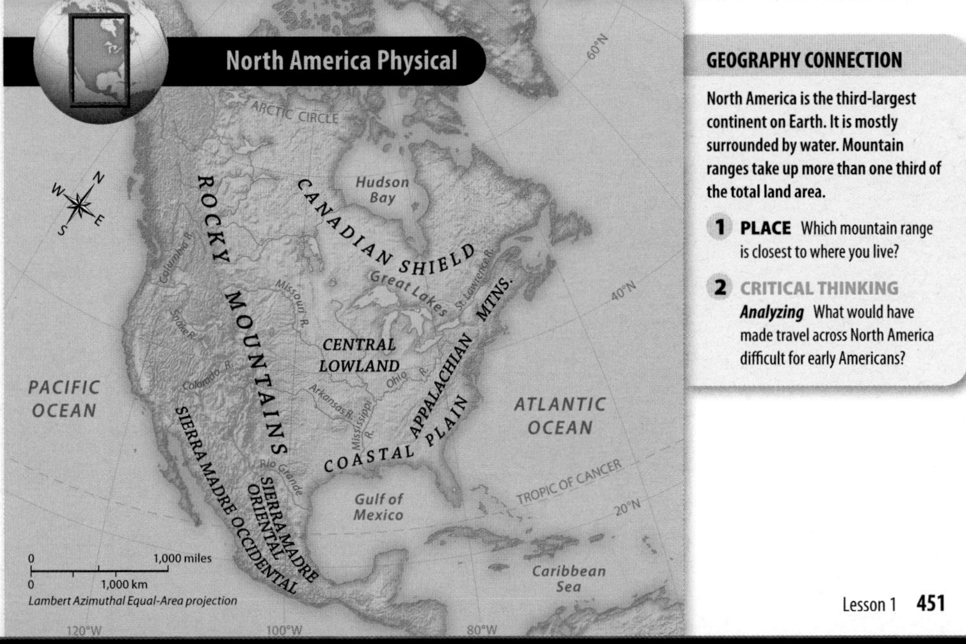

GEOGRAPHY CONNECTION

North America is the third-largest continent on Earth. It is mostly surrounded by water. Mountain ranges take up more than one third of the total land area.

1. **PLACE** Which mountain range is closest to where you live?
2. **CRITICAL THINKING** ***Analyzing*** What would have made travel across North America difficult for early Americans?

W Writing Skills

Informative/Explanatory Point out the map of North America at the bottom of the page. Ask students to imagine that they are taking a trip across the country from the Pacific Ocean to the Atlantic Ocean. Have them write a narrative describing the landforms and bodies of water they will travel through or across. *(Specific answers may vary depending on how far north or south students begin, but students should mention crossing the Rockies, then the Central Lowlands, then the Appalachian Mountains, then the coastal plain.)*

Content Background Knowledge

- North America is the third largest of the seven continents. It is more than 9,300,000 square miles, which is more than 16% of the world's land area.
- South America is about 6,876,000 square miles and covers about one-eighth, or 12.5%, of the world's land area. It is the fourth largest of the world's continents.
- The Rocky Mountains in North America and the Andes in South America are both part of the Cordilleras chain of mountains. They were formed when geologic forces pushed the bed of the Pacific Ocean up against the land masses of North America and South America.

MAP

North America: Physical

Analyzing Visuals Show the map of the North America on an interactive whiteboard. Ask students to locate North America, Central America, and the Caribbean and to circle these place names on the map. Then ask students to locate the Rocky Mountains and the Appalachians and circle them. Next, have a student find and circle the Mississippi River. **Ask:** **How do you think these geographical features influenced where people settled?** *(Students might say it is more likely that people first settled in river valleys and less likely that they settled in areas among high mountains.)* **Visual/Spatial**

See page 447C for other online activities.

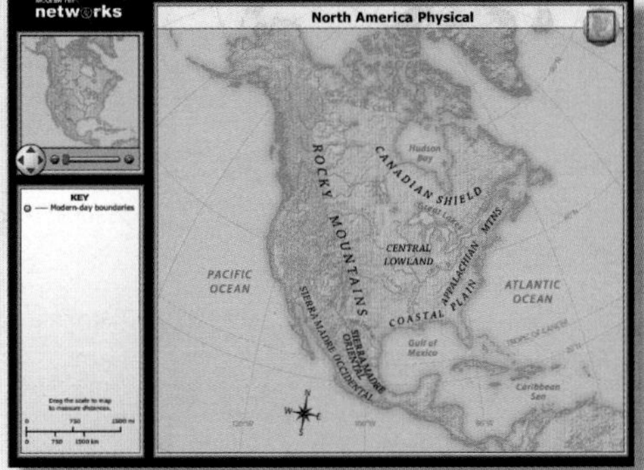

ANSWERS, p. 451

GEOGRAPHY CONNECTION

1. Students should accurately identify the mountain range closest to their community.
2. High mountains, long distances, possible bad weather, and the need to cross wide rivers would have made travel across North America difficult.

The First Americans

R Reading Skills

Specifying Have students read the section titled "Rolling Plains." Then ask students to compare and contrast the plains in North and South America. **Ask:** **Where are the plains in North and South America, and what are they called?** *(In North America, there is a large grasslands area in the center of the continent that is called the Great Plains. In South America, there are plains near the Amazon in the northeastern part of the continent, which are known as the Amazon Basin. There is a grassy plain in southern South America, which is called the Pampas.)* AL

C Critical Thinking Skills

Hypothesizing Remind students that the Mississippi River and the Amazon River are the largest rivers in North and South America, respectively. **Ask:** **How do you think these rivers are used?** *(Students should say that they are probably used for transporting goods and people. They may also suggest that the rivers are used for fishing and for hydroelectric power.)*

The land surrounding the Amazon is home to the greatest variety of plants on Earth. As many as 250 species of trees may grow in one acre of the Amazon River basin.

▶ CRITICAL THINKING

Analyzing How might early Americans have used the Amazon River?

Rolling Plains

North America has many coastal and inland plains. The rolling grasslands of central North America are known as the Great Plains. The Great Plains have fertile soil for farming and raising cattle.

South America also has large areas of plains. In the northeast, the tropical Amazon Basin covers about 2.7 million square miles (7.0 million sq km). It is home to the world's largest rain forest. R

Additional lowland plains are located north and south of the Amazon Basin. Tropical grasslands stretch across the northwest. Another area of plains called the Pampas lies in the south. The mild climate of the Pampas makes them a good place for growing grains. Many ranchers herd cattle there as well.

Rushing Rivers

Large river systems drain the Americas. They begin in the mountain ranges and flow through interior plains to the oceans. Today, the many waterways of the Americas transport people, goods, and ideas.

In North America, the largest river system is the Mississippi. It flows 2,350 miles (3,782 km), from present-day Montana and Minnesota to the Gulf of Mexico. The Mississippi is the major waterway for the central part of North America. C

The Amazon is South America's largest river system. It starts in the Andes and flows about 4,000 miles (6,437 km) to the Atlantic Ocean. The Amazon carries the highest **volume** of water of any river on Earth.

☑ PROGRESS CHECK

Describing Which four separate areas make up the Americas?

Reading **HELP**DESK CCSS

Academic Vocabulary (Tier 2 Words)

volume amount included within limits
link to connect

networks *Online Teaching Options*

CHART

Highest Peaks in the United States

Reading a Chart Have students click on the arrows at the bottom of the chart to see the highest peaks in North America. **Ask:**

- **What do all of these mountains have in common?** *(They are all in Alaska.)*
- **How much taller is Mount McKinley than South Peak?** *(159 feet taller)*
- **What is the difference in the heights of Churchill Peaks and Mount Sanford?** *(3,924 feet)*

Ask students to do research to find the heights of the highest peaks in your state and compare them to the mountains shown here. **Logical/Mathematical**

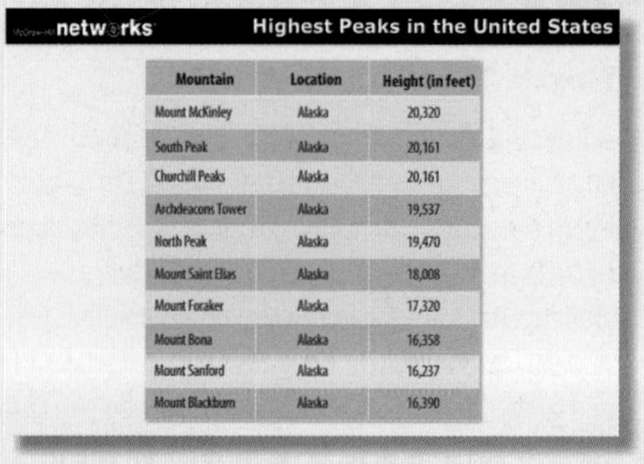

networks Highest Peaks in the United States

Mountain	Location	Height (in feet)
Mount McKinley	Alaska	20,320
South Peak	Alaska	20,161
Churchill Peaks	Alaska	20,161
Archdeacons Tower	Alaska	19,537
North Peak	Alaska	19,470
Mount Saint Elias	Alaska	18,008
Mount Foraker	Alaska	17,320
Mount Bona	Alaska	16,358
Mount Sanford	Alaska	16,237
Mount Blackburn	Alaska	16,390

See page 447C for other online activities.

ANSWERS, p. 452

CRITICAL THINKING Early Americans might have used the Amazon River as a waterway for trade and transportation. They also might have used it as a source of freshwater and for fishing.

☑ **PROGRESS CHECK** The four geographical areas that make up the Americas are North America, South America, Central America, and the Caribbean.

Settling the Americas

GUIDING QUESTION *How did prehistoric people reach the Americas and form settlements?*

How did prehistoric people come to the Americas? Today, the Americas are not **linked** to the world's other landmasses, but they were long ago.

Reaching the Americas

Some scientists think that people walked across a land bridge from Asia into the Americas during the last Ice Age. Evidence of ancient tools and other artifacts reveals that these first Americans were hunters following herds of animals.

Other scientists argue that the first Americans arrived by boat. They passed by Alaska and sailed south along the Americas' Pacific coast. The travelers first explored coastal areas. They then journeyed inland where they set up campsites.

Once they arrived, the first Americans did not stay in one place. They moved south and east. They travelled in boats to islands in the Caribbean. In time, there were people living in different groups in North, Central, and South America.

R

Hunters and Gatherers

How did the first Americans survive? Historians believe it is likely that the first people in the Americas lived in small groups. These early Americans moved from place to place to find food.

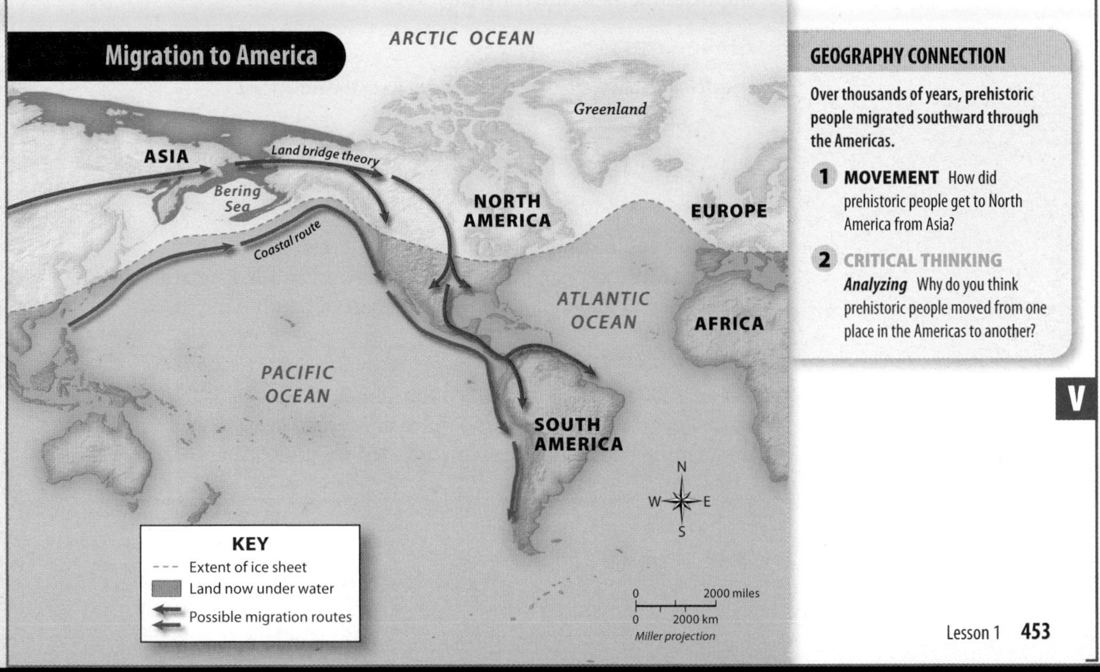

GEOGRAPHY CONNECTION

Over thousands of years, prehistoric people migrated southward through the Americas.

1. **MOVEMENT** How did prehistoric people get to North America from Asia?
2. **CRITICAL THINKING** ***Analyzing*** Why do you think prehistoric people moved from one place in the Americas to another?

V

WORKSHEET

Geography and History Activity: Understanding Movement: Migration

Explaining Present the Geography and History Activity, and have students work with a partner to complete it. BL

See page 447C for other online activities.

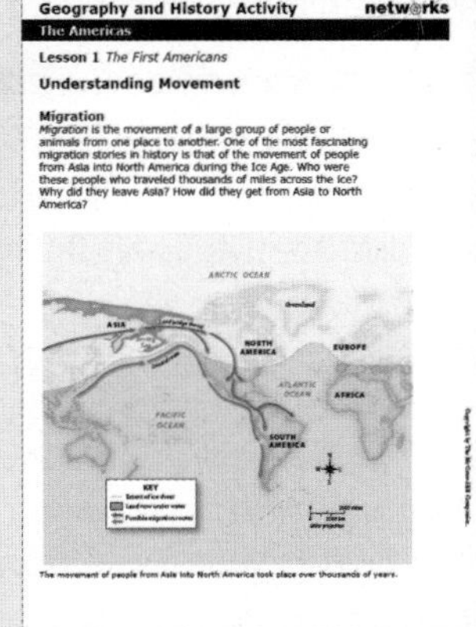

R Reading Skills

Citing Text Evidence Direct students to read the text. Ask students to cite the different ideas that scientists have about how people first came to the Americas. **Ask:** What evidence do scientists use to show that people who came to the Americas were following large herds of animals? *(Scientists have found tools and other artifacts that show that these people were hunters.)*

V Visual Skills

Analyzing Maps Direct students to the "Migration to America" map at the bottom of the page. **Ask:**

- According to the map, what are the two ways early people might have migrated to the Americas? *(over a land bridge between Asia and North America or by boat along the Pacific Coast of North America)*
- In the case of the migration of people to North America, what effect did geography have on history? *(The existence of a land bridge between Asia and North America made it easier for people to reach the Americas. Without the bridge, it might have taken much longer for people to settle in the Americas.)* Discuss the possible difficulties of the journey from Asia to North America.
- What do you think the journey from Asia to North America was like? What problems might early people have faced on the journey? *(Accept all reasonable responses.)* AL **Visual/Spatial**

ANSWERS, p. 453

GEOGRAPHY CONNECTION

1. Prehistoric peoples took a land bridge from Asia to North America or used boats to travel down along the coast of North America.
2. CRITICAL THINKING Students might mention the possibility that some places had harsh climates. They might realize that some locations might have become overpopulated and could no longer support the people who lived there. Students might also mention a desire for adventure and curiosity about new places. Accept all reasonable responses.

The First Americans

R Reading Skills

Identifying After students read the text, discuss how the earliest Americans lived. **Ask:** How did people in different regions get their food? *(Along the coast, people collected shellfish and snails. Inland, they fished in rivers and gathered plants in forests. Many people also hunted large animals for their meat, hides, and bones.)*

C Critical Thinking Skills

Making Inferences Discuss with students how life changed for early Americans when they began the practice of agriculture. *(They planted and harvested seeds and then developed more complex societies.)* **Ask:** Why do you think farming began in Mesoamerica rather than in some other part of the Americas? *(Farming probably began there because the geography was better. The region had a mild climate and rich volcanic soil, so it was probably easier to grow crops there than in any other part of the Americas.)* BL

Early Americans used corn in many forms. The corn grinding stone like this Anasazi tool developed out of necessity.

▶ CRITICAL THINKING
Predicting How do you think early Americans used ground corn?

Archaeologists have unearthed evidence of early American ways of life. This evidence includes heaps of shells, rounded grinding stones, and bone fishhooks.

Hunter-gatherers in the Americas used natural resources for food, clothing, and shelter. People living along seacoasts collected shellfish and snails. People who lived inland fished in rivers and gathered roots, nuts, and fruits in forests. Early Americans also hunted large animals, which provided meat, hides for clothing, and bones for tools. R

The Beginnings of Agriculture

As the last Ice Age ended, the climate grew warmer. People in the Americas learned to plant the seeds of grains and other plants. The seeds would grow into crops that could be eaten. This activity became the start of farming in the Americas.

Farming began in Mesoamerica (meh•zoh•uh•MEHR•ih•kuh) 9,000 to 10,000 years ago. *Meso* comes from the Greek word for "middle." This region includes lands stretching from central Mexico to Costa Rica in Central America. C

The geography of Mesoamerica was suited for farming. Much of the area had rich, volcanic soil and a mild climate. The first crops that early Americans grew included peppers, pumpkins, squash, gourds, beans, and potatoes. Corn, also known as **maize** (mayz), took longer to develop. However, it became the most important food in the Americas.

☑ PROGRESS CHECK

Describing What were the first crops grown in the Americas?

First American Societies

GUIDING QUESTION ***How did farming make civilization possible in the Americas?***

Growing and trading crops helped early Americans form more **complex** societies. The first American cultures emerged in Mesoamerica and along the western coast of South America.

Olmec Culture

About 1200 B.C., a people called the Olmec (OHL•mehk) built what may be the oldest culture in Mesoamerica. Based on farming and trade, the Olmecs lasted about 800 years.

Harald Sund

Reading HELPDESK CCSS

maize corn

Academic Vocabulary (Tier 2 Words)

complex made up of many related parts

networks Online Teaching Options

LECTURE SLIDE

The First American Civilizations

Speculating Ask for volunteers to read aloud the information about early agriculture that is shown on the slide. **Ask:** How do you think the development of agriculture led to building homes and temples, and having time for arts and crafts? *(Students should understand that planting and harvesting crops took less time than hunting and gathering, so people had time left over for arts and crafts. Agriculture also allowed people to stay in one place longer, which gave them time to build and use large structures.)*

See page 447C for other online activities.

networks — The First American Civilizations

Agriculture helped the development of early civilizations. It allowed people to
- grow crops such as beans, maize, pepper, squash, and cotton.
- build homes, temples, monuments, tombs, and palaces.
- specialize in pottery and metalwork.
- build canals to bring water from rivers.
- have time to create arts and crafts.

ANSWERS, p. 454

CRITICAL THINKING Students may mention that ground cornmeal might be used to make tortilla-like flatbread, or it could be boiled to make mush.

☑ PROGRESS CHECK The first crops grown in the Americas included peppers, pumpkins, squash, gourds, beans, and potatoes.

V

Civilizations of Mesoamerica

KEY
Olmec c. 500 B.C.
Maya c. A.D. 750
Toltec c. A.D. 1200
Aztec c. A.D. 1500

GEOGRAPHY CONNECTION

Mesoamerican societies developed in Mexico and Central America.

1. **PLACE** Which culture occupied the Yucatán Peninsula?
2. **CRITICAL THINKING** ***Making Inferences*** The Olmec built a pyramid of clay and sand at La Venta. Why do you think they did not use stone?

The Olmec set up farms in the tropical lowlands along the Gulf of Mexico. They grew beans and produced salt. The Olmec traded with people living inland. They exchanged salt and beans for jade and obsidian, or volcanic glass. Olmec artisans used the jade for jewelry. They made sharp knives from the obsidian.

The Olmec created centers for religious ceremonies. In these areas, they built pyramids and other stone monuments.

First Planned Cities

About 400 B.C., the Olmec culture collapsed. A group of inland peoples rose to power in central Mexico. This group built one of the first planned cities in the Americas, Teotihuacán (tay•oh•tee•wuh•KAHN), or "Place of the Gods." It lasted from about A.D. 250 to A.D. 800. Around 120,000 to 200,000 people lived in Teotihuacán. Temples and palaces lined its main street, which led to the Pyramid of the Sun.

A people called the Zapotec (ZAH•poh•tehk) built farms and cities in south central Mexico. Their magnificent capital, Monte Albán (MON•teh AL•bahn), had a main square surrounded by stone temples, monuments, and tombs. In addition to farming, the Zapotec created pottery and traded with Teotihuacán and other places in Mesoamerica. The Zapotec developed a writing system based on hieroglyphs (HIGH•roh•glifz).

Another people called the Maya (MY•uh) prospered in the steamy rain forests of the Yucatán Peninsula (yoo•kuh•TAN). Like the Zapotec, the Maya traded throughout Mesoamerica. From their central location, the Maya spread into southern Mexico and Central America.

One of the things the Olmecs are most famous for is colossal heads made out of rock. Some were more than seven feet high. How they managed to get them to the sites where they remain to this day is unknown.

De Agostini/Getty Images

V Visual Skills

Reading a Map Have students look at the map and find areas where each civilization lived. Ask them to use the key to estimate how much coastline each civilization had. *(Estimates can be rough, but should be similar to the following: Toltec: no coastline. Olmec: about 300 miles of coastline. Aztec: about 1,600 miles of coastline. Maya: about 2,000 miles of coastline.)*
BL **Logical/Mathematical Visual/Spatial**

Content Background Knowledge

Share with students the following information about the city of Teotihuacán.

- At its height, around 500 B.C.E., the city of Teotihuacán was about 8 square miles in area, and about 150,000 lived there. It was located near present-day Mexico City.
- The people who lived in the city are known as Teotihuacános, and it is believed that more than half of them were farmers. Others were merchants who traded with people in distant locations. The rulers of city were mostly priests.
- Teotihuacán contained large plazas, temples, palaces, and one-story apartment buildings.
- The Pyramid of the Sun is a large structure in the center of the city. It still exists today and is about 216 feet high, with a huge staircase on one side.

MAP

Civilizations of Mesoamerica

Reading a Map Have students click on the interactive key to see the locations of the four different Mesoamerican civilizations. Pose questions such as these. **Ask:**

- **Which two civilizations covered the largest areas?** *(the Maya and the Aztec)*
- **Which civilization existed the earliest?** *(the Olmec)*
- **Which civilization's location was later controlled by the Aztec people?** *(the Toltec)*

See page 447C for other online activities.

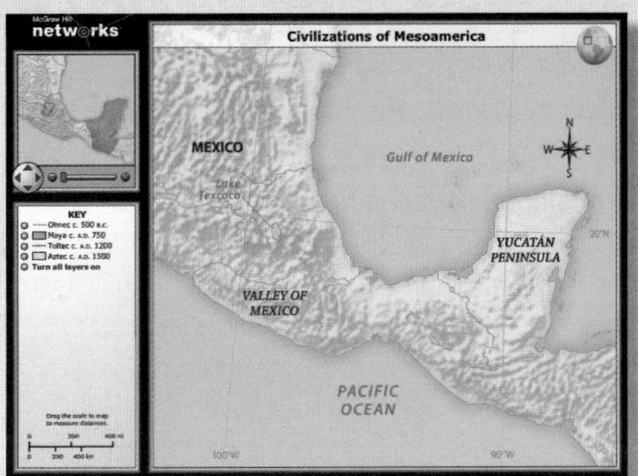

ANSWERS, p. 455

GEOGRAPHY CONNECTION

1. The Maya occupied the Yucatán Peninsula.
2. **CRITICAL THINKING** The Olmec probably used clay and sand because those materials were the most readily available to them. Stone had to be brought in from a long distance.

The First Americans

R Reading Skills

Finding the Main Idea Ask students to restate the main idea of the section about the Moche people. **Ask:**

- **What successes did the Moche have?** *(They built canals and were able to grow food in a dry climate. They also created arts and crafts.)*
- **What limits did the Moche face?** *(They did not succeed in building an empire.)*

T Technology Skills

Using Digital Tools Have students create a time line or an illustrated time line using word processing software. Students should use their textbooks to help them identify the major civilizations in Mesoamerica and the time periods in which they lived. BL **Visual/Spatial**

Teotihuacán and the Zapotec flourished between the A.D. 300s and A.D. 500s. Then, they declined. Historians are not sure why this happened. The causes for decline might have been a severe drought—a long period with little rainfall—or revolts by populations that had used up the natural resources of the area. Whatever the reason, the cities were **abandoned**.

Who Were the Toltec?

After the collapse of these cities, new groups rose to power in central Mexico. Most important were the Toltec (TOHL•tehk). The warlike Toltec conquered much of Mexico and northern Central America. Their empire reached the height of its power between A.D. 950 and A.D. 1150.

The Toltec grew crops of beans, maize, and pepper in irrigated fields. They also built pyramids and palaces. Toltec artisans introduced metalworking to Mesoamerica.

Around A.D. 1125, the Toltec Empire began to decline. Within a few decades, groups of invaders, including Aztec (AZ•tek) people, attacked and burned the Toltec city of Tollan (toh•lahn). For nearly 200 years, there was no ruling group in central Mexico. During the A.D. 1300s, the Aztec, a warrior people, gained control. T

Early Cultures in South America

In South America, several different early civilizations thrived along the Pacific coast. One of the earliest of these, the Moche (MOH•cheh), developed around A.D. 100 in the dry coastal desert of Peru. The Moche built canals to bring water from rivers in the Andes foothills to their desert homeland. This enabled them to grow enough food to feed a large part of the region. Much about Moche culture is known from their arts and crafts. R

In spite of everything they **achieved**, the Moche did not build an empire. The first empire in South America was built by another people called the Inca (IHNG•kuh). The Inca lived in the Andes mountain ranges of Peru. Their homeland was in the area of Cuzco (KOOS•koh). Cuzco was founded around A.D. 1100 and became the capital of the Inca Empire.

The story of the Moche culture is told through their artwork, such as this pottery figure of an alpaca.

▶ CRITICAL THINKING
Analyzing Visuals What can you tell about the Moche based on this example of art?

✓ **PROGRESS CHECK**

Explaining Why did early American cultures decline?

Reading HELPDESK (CCSS)

Academic Vocabulary (Tier 2 Words)

abandon to leave, often because of danger
achieve to successfully complete a task; to gain something by working for it

networks Online Teaching Options

GAME

Column Game: Moche, Toltec, and Zapotec

Identifying Have student play the game by reading the facts about the different civilizations and then placing them in the correct column, either the Moche, the Toltec, or the Zapotec. Students may time themselves or not, and they can play again several times if they place the fact in the wrong column. AL ELL

See page 447C for other online activities.

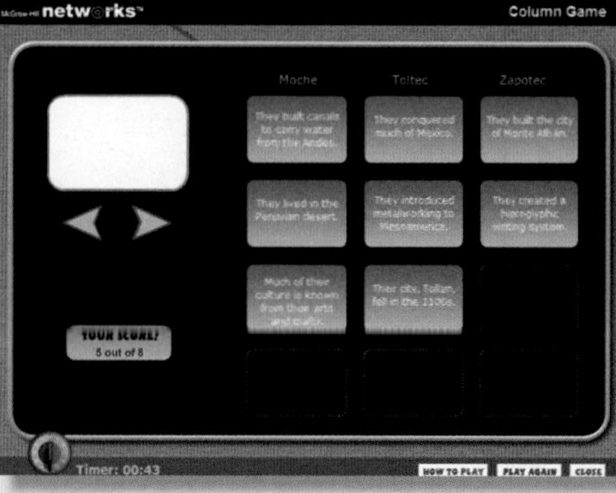

ANSWERS, p. 456

CRITICAL THINKING Students might mention that the Moche used animals, in this case llamas, to carry goods.

✓ **PROGRESS CHECK** Though the exact reasons are unknown, early American cultures might have declined because of a drain on resources due to overpopulation, a long drought, destructive revolts, or invasions.

V

Pueblo Bonito, located in present-day New Mexico, was a four-story sandstone village.

▶ CRITICAL THINKING

Analyzing Why do you think the ruins of this pueblo still remain?

Early Cultures in North America

GUIDING QUESTION ***Why did a large number of societies develop in North America?***

North of Mesoamerica, other early Americans developed their own ways of living. Despite their cultural differences, many of these groups learned the same farming methods as their Mesoamerican neighbors. Farming spread to the American Southwest and then along the coasts and up the Mississippi, Missouri, and Ohio Rivers. As farming developed in these areas, so did new cultures.

Peoples of the Southwest

The scorching desert of what is now Arizona was home to the Hohokam (hoh•hoh•KAHM). About A.D. 300, the Hohokam planted gardens on lands between the Salt and Gila rivers. They dug hundreds of miles of irrigation canals to carry river water to their fields. They grew corn, cotton, beans, and squash. The Hohokam also made pottery, carved stone, and etched shells.

Another group called the Anasazi (ah•nuh•SAH•zee) lived about the same time as the Hohokam. The Anasazi settled in the canyons and cliffs of the Southwest. Like the Hohokam, they practiced farming. To water their crops, they gathered the water that ran off cliffs and sent it through canals to their fields.

The Anasazi built large stone dwellings that the Spanish explorers later called pueblos (PWEH•blohs). They also built dwellings in the walls of steep cliffs. Cliff dwellings were easy to defend and offered protection from winter weather.

The Anasazi and the Hohokam both prospered until the early A.D. 1000s. At that time, they faced droughts that killed their crops. The two groups eventually abandoned their settlements.

The Anasazi were skilled at making pottery and jewelry.

Build Vocabulary: *Prefixes*

Meso is a prefix that means "middle." Another, more common prefix meaning middle is "mid." *Midterm* is the middle of the school term. *Midway* is halfway between two places. What other words with the prefix *mid* can you think of?

V Visual Skills

Analyzing Images Point out the image of Pueblo Bonito at the top of the page. Explain that this structure was built in the 10th century by the Anasazi people, who are also known as the Ancestral Pueblo people. **Ask:** **What does this structure tell you about the Anasazi?** *(Answers should include that they must have been capable of planning and carrying out large construction projects. Students may also offer reasons to explain why the Anasazi would have chosen to live in a single large structure like this, rather than in many smaller structures.)* **BL** **Visual/Spatial**

Making Connections

Explain to students that irrigation was an important part of life for the peoples of the Southwest. Today, the need for irrigation in that part of the United States remains a critical issue. The Colorado River is used to provide water to about 30 million people in seven states in the Southwest. Dams and other irrigation projects are used to move water from the river to farms, suburbs, and cities in the Southwest. However, people today worry that the growing population in that region, as well as climate change and increased water use, will lead to water shortages in the region in the future.

SLIDE SHOW

Casa Grande, Mesa Verde, and Pueblo Bonito

Analyzing Visuals Have students click on the arrows to learn more about the Hohokam and the Anasazi peoples and the structures they built. After students have looked at the images and read the accompanying text, ask them to describe the structures and what they tell about the peoples who built them. Then **ask:** **Who are some of the descendants of the Anasazi people today?** *(the Hopi, Zuni, and Acoma peoples, among others)* **Visual/Spatial**

McGraw-Hill networks
Casa Grande
National Park Service/U.S. Department of the Interior
The Hohokam people, who were farmers, built and occupied this Arizona pueblo between 600 and 800 years ago. It is called Casa Grande, which is Spanish for "Big House." Although it stands four stories high, the first floor of the clay building is useless. It is full of dirt. The dirt helps the building's walls stay standing. Twenty miles from the site, a Hohokam city called "Snaketown" is buried underground. Snaketown was once home to about 2,000 Hohokam.

See page 447C for other online activities.

ANSWERS, p. 457

CRITICAL THINKING The pueblo was built with strong materials and near cliffs for protection.

Build Vocabulary Students might identify the words midair and midday.

C Critical Thinking Skills

Comparing and Contrasting Discuss the Mound Builders's ways of life with students. Then **ask:**

- **How were the Hohokam, the Anasazi, and the Mound Builders similar?** *(They farmed and made impressive structures.)*
- **How were they different?** *(The Hohokam and the Anasazi lived in the Southwest and relied more on farming than the Mound Builders, who lived east of the Mississippi and were mainly hunters and gatherers.)*

Have students complete the Lesson 1 Review.

CLOSE & REFLECT

Summarizing To close the lesson, discuss with students the importance of agriculture to the early cultures of the Americas. Note that farming spread throughout many regions. **Ask:**

- **Where did farming begin in the Americas?** *(Mesoamerica)*
- **How did the introduction of farming change life for the peoples of the Americas?** *(Farming allowed people to settle in one place, create more complex societies, and in some cases build cities.)*

The Mound Builders

East of the Mississippi River, another early American civilization arose. It began about 1000 B.C. and lasted until about A.D. 400. Its founders built huge mounds of earth that were used as tombs or for ceremonies. These constructions gave these people their name—Mound Builders.

The Great Serpent Mound, made by the Mound Builders, still exists in southern Ohio. This mound may have been used in religious ceremonies. Why do you think it was named the Great Serpent Mound?

Richard A. Cooke/CORBIS

The Mound Builders were mostly hunters and gatherers, but they began to practice farming. Two major groups made up the culture—the Adena people and the Hopewell. Scientists believe that the Mound Builders domesticated many wild plants, such as sunflowers, gourds, and barley. Corn became another popular crop after it was introduced to the region about A.D. 100. C

Who Were the Mississippians?

By A.D. 700, a new people known as the Mississippians arose. Their name came from their location in the Mississippi River Valley. The Mississippians were able to produce enough corn, squash, and beans to become full-time farmers. They also built mounds and lived in cities.

Their largest city was Cahokia (kuh•HOH•kee•uh). It may have had 16,000 to 30,000 residents. Mississippian government was centered there between A.D. 850 and 1150. Cahokia was the site of the largest Mississippian mound. Cahokia and the Mississippian society collapsed during the A.D. 1200s.

✓ PROGRESS CHECK

Explaining How were early Americans able to grow crops in desert areas of the Southwest?

LESSON 1 REVIEW 

Review Vocabulary (Tier 3 Words)

1. Which main area of the Americas is an *isthmus*? RH.6–8.2, RH.6–8.4
2. How did *maize* help early people in the Americas? RH.6–8.2

Answer the Guiding Questions

3. ***Summarizing*** How did prehistoric people reach the Americas? RH.6–8.2
4. ***Explaining*** Why was Cuzco significant to the Inca? RH.6–8.2
5. ***Comparing*** What did early societies in North America have in common? RH.6–8.2
6. **INFORMATIVE/EXPLANATORY** Write a two-paragraph essay that describes the ways of life of the Olmec and the Toltec. WHST.6–8.2, WHST.6–8.10

LESSON 1 REVIEW ANSWERS

1. Central America is an isthmus.
2. Maize became the most important food in the Americas.
3. People from Asia might have used a land bridge to cross into the Americas. Another theory suggests that the first Americans arrived by boat, passing Alaska and then sailing south along the Pacific coast.
4. Cuzco was the capital of the Inca Empire, the largest territory in the ancient Americas.
5. Many of these groups learned how to farm from their Mesoamerican neighbors. As farming developed, so did new cultures.
6. Answers will vary. Answers should identify the importance of farming and trade in the Olmec and Toltec civilizations.

ANSWERS, p. 458

Caption: because it is in the shape of a snake

✓ **PROGRESS CHECK** Early Americans in desert areas of the Southwest dug irrigation canals to carry river water to their fields. They also collected water that ran off cliffs.

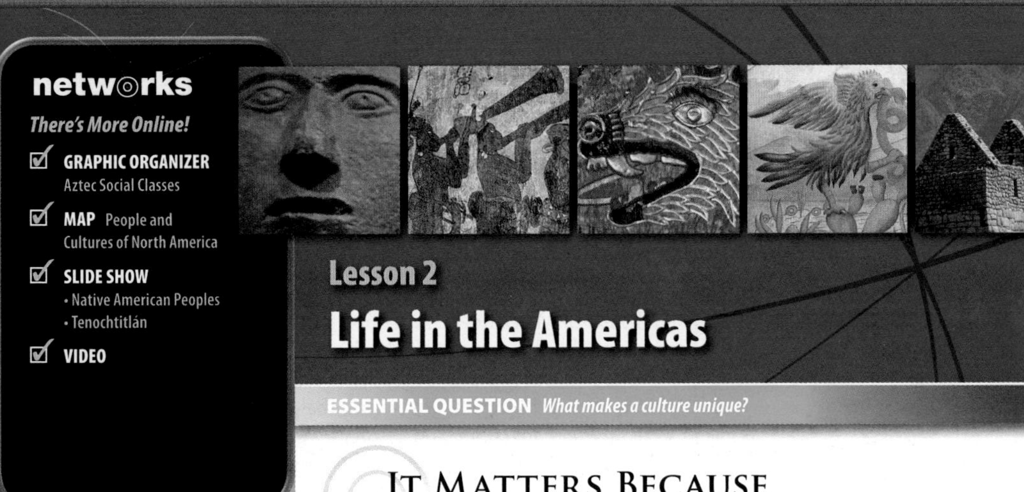

netw⊚rks
There's More Online!

- GRAPHIC ORGANIZER Aztec Social Classes
- MAP People and Cultures of North America
- SLIDE SHOW
  - Native American Peoples
  - Tenochtitlán
- VIDEO

Lesson 2
Life in the Americas

ESSENTIAL QUESTION *What makes a culture unique?*

IT MATTERS BECAUSE
Long before the arrival of Europeans, people in the Americas created complex societies.

The Maya

GUIDING QUESTION *How did the Maya live in the rain forests of Mesoamerica?*

In A.D. 1839, archaeologists John Lloyd Stephens and Frederick Catherwood discovered an ancient city, hidden for centuries by vines and trees. The people who had built the city were called the Maya. These early Americans were the ancestors of the millions of Maya who live in present-day Mexico, Guatemala, Honduras, El Salvador, and Belize.

Maya Communities

About A.D. 300, the Maya developed a complex culture in parts of southern Mexico and Central America. The ancient Maya faced many challenges in the area that they settled, which was called Petén (peh•TEHN). Thick forests nearly blocked out sunlight. Stinging insects filled the air. Yet, the ancient Maya prospered.

Swamps and sinkholes gave the Maya a year-round source of water. A **sinkhole** is an area where the soil has collapsed into a hollow or depression. Sinkholes gave the Maya access to a network of underground rivers and streams. R

The Maya began to develop a society. They worked together to clear forested areas. They planted fields of corn and other crops and built cities under government direction.

(l) Toño Labra/Age fotostock, (cl) Doug Stern & Enrico Ferorelli/National Geographic Society Image Collection, (c) Aztec/The Bridgeman Art Library/Getty Images, (cr) DEA / G. DAGLI ORTI, (r) Jeremy Horner/Getty Images

Reading **HELP**DESK (CCSS)

Taking Notes: *Organizing* RH.6–8.2

Use a pyramid like the one here to place the Aztec social classes in order. Begin at the top level of the pyramid and list classes from highest to lowest.

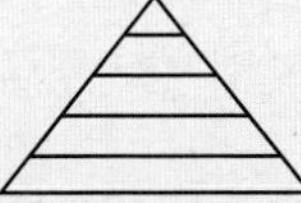

Content Vocabulary (Tier 3 Words)
- **sinkhole**
- **hogan**

ENGAGE

Bellringer Discuss with students the four geographic regions of the Americas: North America, Central America, South America, and the Caribbean. If necessary, refer students to the Chapter Opener map so they can identify these four regions.

Then ask students to list mountain ranges and major rivers of the Americas. *(mountain ranges: the Andes, the Rocky Mountains, and the Appalachians; rivers: the Amazon River and the Mississippi River)* **Ask:** How do you think the geography and climate contributed to the creation of many unique cultures in the Americas? *(Student answers will vary depending on their understanding of the many different geographic regions, such as far north, woodlands, desert, mountains, and so on, and the different climates experienced by each culture.)* Have students record their answers so they can refer to them at the end of the lesson.

TEACH & ASSESS

R Reading Skills

Explaining Have students read the text. Then ask students how the Maya were able to create a civilization in the rain forests of Mesoamerica. **Ask:** What challenges did the Maya face in the rain forest? *(Thick forests blocked the sun. Lots of insects lived there.)* After students have identified the key challenges faced by the Maya, **ask:** How did the Maya overcome these challenges? *(The Maya cleared the forests so they could plant crops and build cities.)*

VIDEO

Aztec, Maya, and Inca Civilizations

Discussing Play the video for the class. As they are watching, have students take notes on each of the different cultures that are described. Then have small groups discuss the most important achievements of each society.

See page 447D for other online activities.

ANSWERS, p. 459

TAKING NOTES: The Aztec social classes, from highest to lowest, were the emperor, nobles, commoners, unskilled workers, and enslaved people.

R Reading Skills

Depicting Have students read about Maya society, and then assign individual students the roles of the following people: the king, another noble, a priest, and a member of the working class—either a farmer, an artisan, or a hunter. Ask each member of the group to stand and describe his or her role in society to the rest of the group.

V Visual Skills

Analyzing Images Point out the carving of Chac at the bottom of the page. Remind students that the Maya believed that their gods controlled everything on Earth. Ask them to draw another image of Chac, doing something such as overseeing good harvests or watching and helping the Maya win a battle against an enemy. Have students write a one-sentence caption for their drawings. ELL Visual/Spatial

Connections to TODAY

The Maya Today

Modern-day descendants of the Maya speak about 70 different languages. They typically live on farms and grow corn, beans, and squash. As weaving and spinning have become less common, most present-day Maya, especially women, wear traditional clothing made of cloth produced in a factory.

The Maya set up more than 50 independent city-states. The Maya city-states were connected by culture, political ties, and trade. However, they often fought each other for control of territory.

What Was Maya Society Like?

Each Maya city-state was ruled by a king, who claimed he was descended from the sun god. As god-kings, Maya rulers expected people to serve them. The greatest Maya king was Pacal II. He ruled the city-state of Palenque (puh•LENGH•KAY) for 67 years in the A.D. 600s. Pacal II built many structures considered to be some of the best examples of Maya architecture.

The Maya city-states had a strict class system. Nobles and priests assisted kings in governing the city-states. Below them were farmers, artisans, and hunters. People of this class paid taxes and worked on large building projects.

The Maya believed that the gods controlled everything that happened on Earth. Priests performed ceremonies to please the gods. These ceremonies sometimes included human sacrifice.

When the Maya fought battles, they wanted captives and they wanted land. When drought came and threatened their crops, Maya priests tried to please Chac (CHOCK), the god of rain, by offering the lives of their captives.

Women played a significant role in the Maya city-states. In the city-state of Calakmul (kah•lahk•MOOL), at least two women served as ruling queens. One of them may have helped to found the city.

Royal Maya women often married into royal families in other Maya city-states. This practice increased trade. It also helped form alliances—political agreements between people or states to work together.

Maya artists often portrayed Chac seated, waiting to receive the arrival of captives.

Maya Achievements

Maya rulers turned to priests for advice. The priests thought the gods revealed their plans through movements of the sun, moon, and stars. By watching the sky, the priests learned about astronomy. They developed calendar systems to **predict** eclipses and to schedule religious festivals.

Reading HELPDESK (CCSS)

sinkhole a depression or hollow where soil has collapsed

Academic Vocabulary (Tier 2 Words)

predict to describe something that will happen in the future

networks Online Teaching Options

LECTURE SLIDE

The Maya

Identifying Show students the structure of the Maya Empire from the lecture slide. Remind students that the Maya did not create a single, unified empire. Instead, they founded many independent city-states that shared cultural characteristics. **Ask:** **What was Maya society like?** *(Answers may include the following: Each Maya city-state was ruled by a king who claimed he was descended from the sun god. The city-states had strict class systems, with nobles and priests at the top. Women played a significant role in Maya society.)* Point out to students that the Maya are well known for their creation of complex calendars.

networks
The Maya
Structure of the Maya Empire
• Each city-state had a king, who believed he was a descendant of the sun god.
• Royal Maya women played an important role in society and sometimes ruled as queens.
• Priests and nobles guided the kings.
• Farmers, artisans, and hunters paid taxes and worked on building projects.
• Captives taken in battle were used to work the land.

See page 447D for other online activities.

In Maya society, a birth in the royal family called for a musical celebration, such as the one depicted above.

▶ CRITICAL THINKING
Making Inferences Priests were almost as powerful as kings. Why do you think the Maya so honored their priests?

They also used calendars to decide when to plant and harvest crops. The Maya had two major calendars. They used a 260-day calendar for religious events. They used a 365-day calendar for events related to the seasons and agriculture.

The Maya developed a system of mathematics. They invented a method of counting based on 20, and they used the concept of zero. They also developed a written language to record numbers and dates. Like the Zapotec, they used hieroglyphics. They carved hieroglyphics on stone monuments and used them in books. **R**

About A.D. 900, the Maya culture collapsed. Historians do not know why this happened. Some evidence shows that conflict and warfare increased among city-states. Also, erosion and overuse of the soil may have caused a drop in food production. Too little food would have led to illnesses and starvation. **C**

☑ PROGRESS CHECK

Explaining How were the Maya governed?

The Aztec

GUIDING QUESTION *How did the Aztec establish their society in central Mexico?*

The Aztec came to power in Mesoamerica during the A.D. 1300s. The early Aztec were hunters and warriors. About A.D. 1200, they moved into central Mexico.

Rise of the Aztec

For many years, the Aztec had been searching for a home they believed had been promised to them by their sun god—the feathered serpent Quetzalcoatl (KWEHT•suhl•kuh•WAH•tuhl). In A.D. 1325, the Aztec took refuge on a swampy island in Lake Texcoco (tehs•KOH•koh). Although the land was hardly welcoming, the Aztec chose this site to be their new home.

Doug Stern & Enrico Ferorelli/National Geographic Society Image Collection

R Reading Skills

Identifying Ask students to read the text, and then to identify contributions by the Maya. **Ask:** **What were some of the significant achievements of the Maya?** *(Answers may include developing calendars, developing mathematical concepts, understanding and using the concept of zero, and developing a written language.)* AL

C Critical Thinking Skills

Determining Cause and Effect Have students review the text about possible reasons for the collapse of the Maya culture. For each cause given, ask a student volunteer to explain how it could have led to the collapse of the society.

IMAGE

Maya Arts

Analyzing Images Have students click on the buttons at the bottom of the image to learn more about the arts of the Maya. Then lead a class discussion about Maya artwork. **Ask:**

- **What were some forms of artwork created by the Maya?** *(sculptures, painted murals, stone carvings, and worked-metal jewelry)*
- **Why do you think the Maya created these works of art?** *(Answers will vary. Possible responses: to document their lifestyles, to honor special gods or leaders, to express themselves through images, to decorate their homes and villages)*

See page 447D for other online activities.

ANSWERS, p. 461

CRITICAL THINKING Answers will vary. Students should mention that priests advised kings and conducted ceremonies to please the gods. These duties gave them power over the rulers as well as over the rest of the population.

☑ PROGRESS CHECK Each Maya city-state was ruled by a king. Nobles and priests assisted kings in governing the city-states.

R Reading Skills

Defining After students have read the text, ask a volunteer to define the relationship between the Aztec ruler and the territories conquered by the Aztec Empire. **Ask:**

- What was a tribute? *(money paid by conquered peoples to their conquerors)* ELL
- What did the conquered peoples get in exchange for paying tribute? *(They were supported by the Aztec ruler.)* AL

W Writing Skills

Narrative Have each student choose either a noble, a commoner, an unskilled worker, or an enslaved person who lived in Tenochtitlán. Students should write a journal entry from the perspective of that person, describing a typical day in the person's life and identifying what the person thinks about his or her city. BL Verbal/Linguistic

This shield made of feathers most likely belonged to an Aztec emperor.

▶ CRITICAL THINKING

Analyzing What do you think the animal represented here is holding in its mouth?

Aztec priests declared that the gods demanded they build a great city upon this spot. Laborers worked around the clock. They built bridges to the mainland with soil dug from the lake bottom. Floating gardens dotted the surface of the lake. The wondrous city they built was Tenochtitlán (tay•nawch•teet•LAHN).

For the next 100 years, Aztec workers built temples, palaces, and homes in Tenochtitlán. The city eventually became the largest city in Mesoamerica. It was the center of a web of trade routes that reached throughout Mexico.

The Aztec **relied** on strong kings, or emperors, who claimed to be descended from the gods. A council of priests, nobles, and warriors usually named a new emperor from the ruling family. Council members wanted someone skilled in warfare who could lead troops into battle.

Montezuma I (MAHN•tuh•ZOO•muh) was perhaps the most powerful Aztec ruler. He governed from A.D. 1440 to A.D. 1469. Montezuma used his armies to expand the empire to the Gulf of Mexico. He also built temples, aqueducts, and roads.

R By A.D. 1500, Aztec armies had conquered much of what is today Mexico. The new empire was a collection of partly independent territories governed by local leaders. The Aztec ruler supported these leaders in return for tribute—goods or money paid by conquered peoples to their conquerors.

Aztec Life

W The emperor was at the top of Aztec society. There were four classes of people under the emperor. These were nobles, commoners, unskilled workers, and enslaved people. Most of the Aztec were commoners, who worked as farmers, artisans, or merchants.

From an early age, boys in Aztec society were taught to be warriors. Girls were trained to work at home, weave cloth, and prepare for motherhood. Although not equal to men, Aztec women could own and inherit property.

Priests played an important role in Aztec society. Some sacrificed captives to please the gods. Death was considered honorable. The Aztec believed that those sacrificed would be rewarded in the afterlife.

Aztec priests also worked to preserve the religion, history, and literature of their people. Priests recorded these in books that historians still refer to today. Like the Maya, the Aztec

Aztec/The Bridgeman Art Library/Getty Images

Reading **HELP**DESK CCSS

Academic Vocabulary (Tier 2 Words)

rely to depend on

networks Online Teaching Options

SLIDE SHOW

Tenochtitlán

Analyzing Visuals Present the digital slide show on the construction of Tenochtitlán. As students view the slides, note the size of the city and the types of buildings shown. **Ask:** What challenges did the Aztec overcome to build Tenochtitlán? *(Tenochtitlán was built on two small islands. The Aztec had to build artificial islands to allow the city to grow, as well as giant roads to connect it to the shore.)* What does studying the city of Tenochtitlán tell us about the Aztec? *(Answers may include the following: Religion was central to Aztec life; Aztec society had to be organized in order to build something so complex; the Aztec king was at the top of Aztec society. Accept other answers that are supported by the facts.)* BL

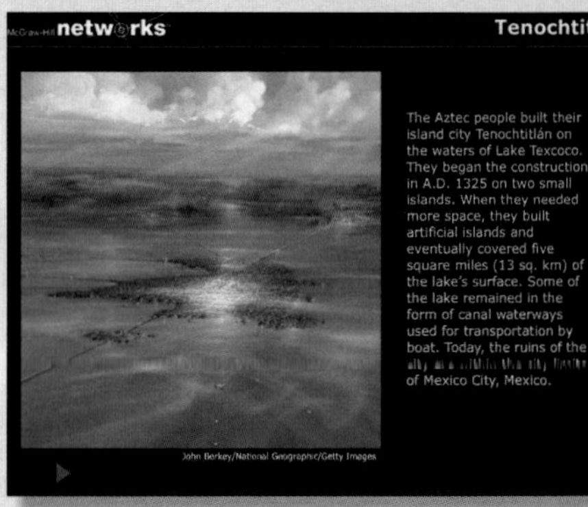

McGraw-Hill networks
Tenochtitlán
The Aztec people built their island city Tenochtitlán on the waters of Lake Texcoco. They began the construction in A.D. 1325 on two small islands. When they needed more space, they built artificial islands and eventually covered five square miles (13 sq. km) of the lake's surface. Some of the lake remained in the form of canal waterways used for transportation by boat. Today, the ruins of the
of Mexico City, Mexico.
John Berkey/National Geographic/Getty Images

See page 447D for other online activities.

ANSWER, p. 462

CRITICAL THINKING Answers will vary, but historians believe this shield shows a water beast, or a dragon, with a sacrificial knife in its mouth.

developed two different calendars. They used a religious calendar with 260 days to keep track of important ceremonies and festivals. They also had a 365-day calendar for everyday use and for marking the time for planting and harvesting crops.

Much of Mexico was not suited for farming. The Aztec overcame this difficulty by irrigating and fertilizing the land. Aztec crafts, as well as fruit, vegetables, and grain from Aztec farms, passed through markets and along trade routes. The trade in these goods and the tribute from conquered peoples helped make the Aztec Empire wealthy. C

✓ PROGRESS CHECK

Explaining Why did the Aztec develop two different calendars?

The Inca

GUIDING QUESTION *How did the Inca organize their government and society?*

In the late A.D. 1300s, the Inca were only one of many groups that fought over scarce fertile land in the valleys of the Andes Mountains. From their capital of Cuzco, the Inca raided nearby groups and seized territory. Within 100 years, the Inca had created a powerful empire.

Inca Rulers

A series of strong emperors helped build the Inca Empire. Pachacuti (PAH•chah•KOO•tee) was the first of these rulers. In the A.D. 1430s, he launched a campaign of conquest. The two emperors who followed continued this expansion, building the largest empire in the Americas.

DEA/G. DAGLI ORTI/Getty Images

According to Aztec legend, in 1325 an eagle was seen atop a cactus with a snake in its mouth. This event fulfilled an Aztec prediction. As a result, this location became the capital of the Aztec Empire, Tenochtitlán.

CHAPTER 16, Lesson 2
Life in the Americas

C Critical Thinking Skills

Identifying Problems Discuss how the Aztecs provided food for their community. **Ask:**

- **What problem did the Aztec have with the land where they lived?** *(The land was not well suited for farming.)*
- **How did they solve this problem?** *(They irrigated and fertilized their land.)*
- **What did they grow on their land?** *(fruit, vegetables, grains)*

Content Background Knowledge

Share with students the following information about the Inca.

- At its height, the Inca Empire extended along the west coast of South America in the Andes, from the northern border of modern-day Ecuador to the Maule River in central Chile.
- The Inca did not leave written records. Instead, they had official "memorizers," who shared their culture's history orally.
- The Inca are famous for the network of roads that they built throughout their empire. It was made up of two north-south roads and many east-west roads that connected them. One of these north-south roads ran along the Pacific coast for about 2,250 miles, and the other one, which was further inland, was similar in length.
- Today about 45% of the people of Peru are descendants of the Inca.

WORKSHEET

21st Century Skills Activity: Critical Thinking and Problem Solving: Compare and Contrast

Comparing and Contrasting Present the 21st Century Skills Activity comparing and contrasting the traits of the Maya, Aztec, and Inca.

On the interactive whiteboard, draw a Venn diagram similar to the one on the worksheet. After students have completed the activity, have a volunteer complete the Venn diagram.

See page 447D for other online activities.

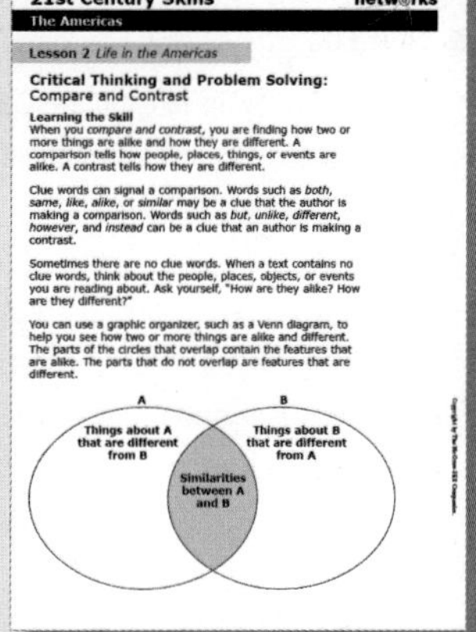

ANSWER, p. 463

✓ **PROGRESS CHECK** The Aztec used a religious calendar to keep track of important ceremonies and festivals and another calendar for everyday use.

V Visual Skills

Drawing Ask two volunteers to draw two images on the board: one showing a mountain in which terraces have been cut and the other showing a mountain without terraces. Have students look at the images and draw or describe where farming would have taken place on the terraces. **Ask: Why would building terraces be useful for farming in mountainous regions?** *(Answers should reflect that terraces create areas of small land for planting, and without terraces, there would be less land available for growing crops.)* **Visual/Spatial**

R Reading Skills

Identifying Direct students to read the selection, then discuss the organization of the Inca society. As a class, make a diagram on the board with the sun god at the top, and list the order of people in this society. *(Answers should reflect the following order: sun god; Inca emperors; head priest and commander of the army; regional army leaders; temple priests, local army commanders, skilled workers; farmers, herders, ordinary soldiers)* AL ELL

BIOGRAPHY

Pachacuti (ruled A.D. 1438–1471)

As emperor, Pachacuti concentrated on expanding the Inca Empire. When he wanted to conquer a kingdom, he first sent messengers to tell the local rulers all the benefits of being part of the Inca Empire. Pachacuti then asked the other rulers to join his empire. If they accepted willingly, they were treated with respect and given some rights. If they refused, the Inca attacked with brutal force.

▶ **CRITICAL THINKING**
Analyzing What do you think would be the advantages and disadvantages of joining the Inca Empire?

To hold the empire together, Inca rulers created a strong central government. They set up tax bureaus, legal courts, military posts, and other government offices. Inca emperors required people to learn Quechua (KEH•chuh•wuh), the language spoken by the Inca. People also had to work for the government for several weeks each year.

Inca Projects

The Inca had people work on projects such as a system of roads. When finished, these roads connected all parts of the empire. This large network helped the Inca overcome geographic barriers. The roads helped move soldiers, goods, and information quickly over the coastal deserts and high mountains.

V The Inca also used irrigation and fertilizers to improve the soil. Inca engineers developed terrace farming. Terrace farming uses a series of wide steps built into a mountainside. Each step creates level farmland. Inca farmers grew potatoes and quinoa, a protein-rich grain. Government officials stored food when there were good harvests and **distributed** it when harvests were poor.

How Was Inca Society Organized?

R The Inca believed their rulers had the protection of the sun god Inti (IHN•tee). As divine rulers, Inca emperors controlled the lives of their subjects. They owned all the land and set rules for growing crops and distributing food.

Below the emperor and his family were the head priest and the leading commander of the army. Next came regional army leaders. Below them were temple priests, local army commanders, and skilled workers. At the bottom were farmers, herders, and ordinary soldiers.

Like the Aztec Empire, the Inca Empire was built on war. All young men were required to serve in the army, which made it the largest and best armed military force in the region.

Culture of the Inca

The Inca believed in many gods. Unlike the Aztec, the Inca rarely sacrificed humans to honor their gods. They did, however, build large stone structures to please these dieties. They had no system of writing, no wheels, and no iron tools. Yet they built places like Machu Picchu (mah•choo PEE•choo), a retreat for Inca emperors. Constructed of white granite and thousands of feet high, Machu Picchu was located in the Andes.

Reading **HELP**DESK 

Academic Vocabulary (Tier 2 Words)
distribute to hand out or deliver, especially to members of a group

networks Online Teaching Options

BIOGRAPHY

Pachacuti

Explaining Display the biography of Pachacuti and have students read the accompanying text. Ask students to explain Pachacuti's method for expanding his empire. *(He sent messengers to local rulers explaining the benefits of being part of the Inca Empire.)* **Ask: Do you think this was an effective plan? Why or why not? How does this compare with other empires and rulers you know about?** *(Answers will vary; accept all reasonable answers.)*

See page 447D for other online activities.

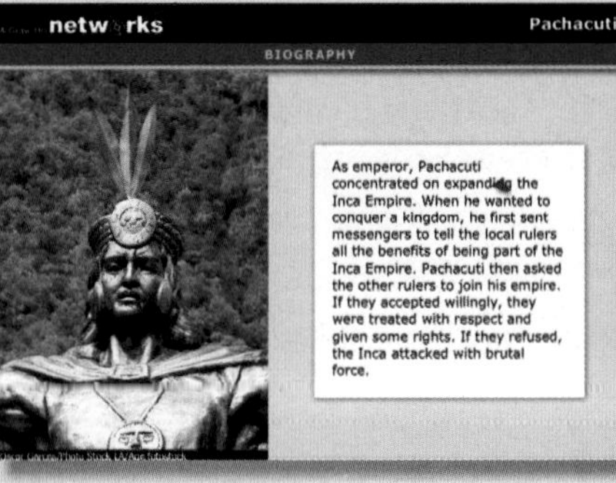

ANSWER, p. 464

CRITICAL THINKING Students may answer that one advantage would be avoiding being attacked by the Inca. Another possible advantage would be gaining wealth and prestige by being part of a large empire. A disadvantage would be the loss of independence.

Building enormous structures like Machu Picchu required the Inca to develop a method for doing mathematics. The Inca used a **quipu** (KEE•poo), a rope with knotted cords of different lengths and colors. This was a useful tool for both mathematics and for record keeping.

The Inca were also skilled engineers. Inca workers fit stones so tightly together that they needed no mortar. Because the stone blocks could slide up and down during earthquakes, many Inca structures have survived.

The ruins of Machu Picchu draw thousands of visitors. Research suggests that this monument was used as a home for the royal family and as a center for celebrations.

✓ PROGRESS CHECK

Describing What building projects did the Inca carry out?

North American Peoples

GUIDING QUESTION *What were the societies of North American peoples like?*

By A.D. 1500, many different groups of Native Americans lived north of Mesoamerica. They spoke about 300 languages and called themselves by thousands of different names. As they spread across North America, these peoples adapted to the different environments.

How Did People Live in the Far North?

The first people to reach the far northern areas of North America called themselves the Inuit (IH•new•weht), which means "the people." The Inuit settled along the coasts of the tundra (TUN•drah) region, the treeless land south of the Arctic.

The Inuit adapted well to their cold environment. They used dogsleds on land and seal-skin kayaks (KEYE•ackz) at sea. In winter, they built homes from stone and blocks of earth. When they traveled, they built igloos, **temporary** homes made from cut blocks of hard-packed snow.

The Inuit were skilled hunters. They used spears made from animal antlers or tusks to hunt seals, walruses, caribou, and polar bears. Blubber, or fat, from seals and whales was a food that provided needed calories and furnished oil for lamps.

Academic Vocabulary (Tier 2 Words)

temporary not permanent; lasting for a limited period

Visual Vocabulary

quipu a tool used in mathematics and as a system of historical record keeping. The quipu used knots to represent numbers and items.

T Technology Skills

Researching on the Internet Have students work in small groups to learn about Machu Picchu or another Inca achievement. Then have groups create a slide show that includes captioned images of what they have learned. When everyone is finished, have them share their presentations with the class. **Interpersonal**

Content Background Knowledge

- The Inuit have historically been known as Eskimos, but that term was given to them by the Cree Indians of Canada, and it has negative connotations. Today, the Inuit themselves use the term *Inuit.*
- Today, about 110,000 Inuit live in the Arctic region in northern Canada, Alaska, Greenland, and parts of Siberia. Many Inuit have left their traditional habitats and moved to towns and cities in Alaska and Canada, where they have assimilated into mainstream culture.
- In 1999, an Inuit homeland—called Nunavut—was created out of part of Canada's Northwest Territories. This new territory is about 770,000 square miles. The Inuit who live there govern themselves.

IMAGE

Machu Picchu, Hidden Inca City

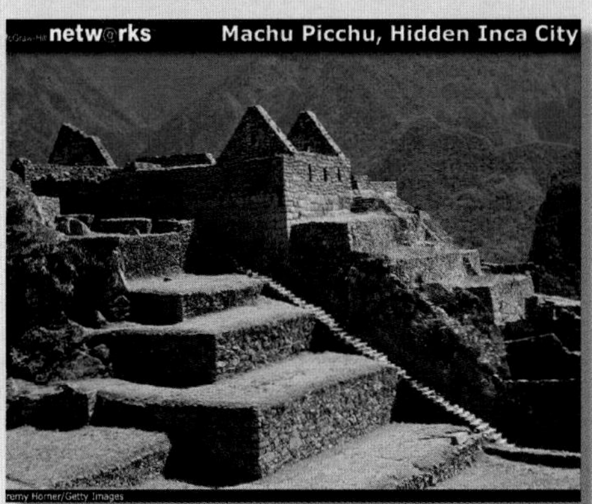

Analyzing Images Have students click on different parts of the image of Machu Picchu to learn more about the site. **Ask:**

- **The city was divided into how many different sections? What were they?** *(3; an agricultural district, a religious district, and a main square)* AL
- **What does the existence of a complex city such as Machu Picchu tell you about the Inca?** *(Answers should include that the Inca were an advanced, organized society. They must have been particularly good with mathematics and engineering in order to build a city such as this one.)* BL

See page 447D for other online activities.

ANSWER, p. 465

✓ PROGRESS CHECK The Inca built a system of roads for trade and travel. They also built large works of stone, such as Machu Picchu—a retreat for Inca emperors.

Life in the Americas

V Visual Skills

Analyzing Maps Direct students to the "People and Food Sources of North America" map. Point out that North America is divided into different regions. Explain that the Native Americans living in each of these regions often shared some cultural characteristics. Use the map key showing the different ways in which Native American peoples gathered food as an example of some of the similarities shared by groups living in the same regions. **Ask:**

- Which peoples lived on the Great Plains? *(Hidatsa, Mandan, and Pawnee)*
- Where did the Creek people live? *(in the Southeast)*
- What activity occurred in the largest region of North America? *(hunting)*
- Where was gathering the main way of getting food? *(in the West and in parts of modern-day Mexico)*
- Why do you think that is the case? *(Accept reasonable answers related to climate or geography.)* AL ELL **Visual/Spatial**

Making Connections

Ask students what they know about California and its economy today. Students may mention the state's large population, the importance of agriculture, or the state's role as a vacation destination. Explain that in the past, as today, California had a large and diverse population with over 500 early American cultures. In addition, the ocean and the climate provided good natural resources for the people who lived there, just as it does today.

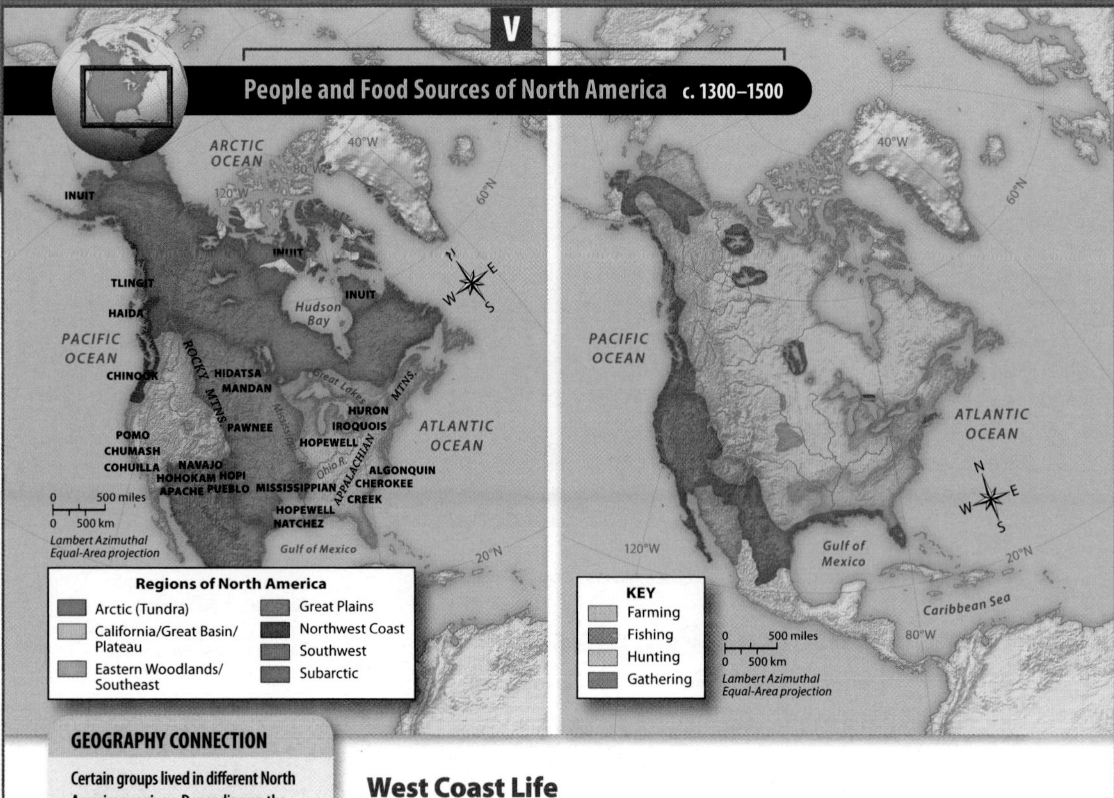

GEOGRAPHY CONNECTION

Certain groups lived in different North American regions. Depending on the geography of their region, North Americans found food in different ways.

1. **PLACE** What was the most common method for obtaining food on the Atlantic coast?
2. **CRITICAL THINKING** *Analyzing* Why do you think more groups did not live in the center of the California/Great Basin/Plateau?

West Coast Life

The Pacific coast of North America had a mild climate and reliable food sources. As a result, this was the most heavily populated region north of Mesoamerica.

In the Pacific Northwest, peoples such as the Tlingit (TLIHNG•kuht), Haida (HEYE•deh), and Chinook (shuh•NOOK) used cedar trees to build wooden houses and canoes. They hunted and fished for otters, seals, whales, and their main food—salmon.

More than 500 early American cultures thrived in the area that is now California, including the Chumash (choo•MASH), the Cahuilla (kuh•WEE•uh), and the Pomo (POH•moh).

In the Southwest, the Hopi (HOH•pee), the Acoma (AHK•eh•meh), and the Zuni (ZOO•nee) built apartment-like homes from sun-dried mud bricks called adobe (uh•DOH•bee). The Southwest peoples dug irrigation canals to bring water to their fields. Their major crops were corn, beans, squash, and melons. They developed a trade network that spread into Mesoamerica.

Reading HELPDESK CCSS

hogan a square wooden home

networks Online Teaching Options

SLIDE SHOW

Native American Groups

Analyzing Visuals Present the slide show about the Native Americans of North America.

After viewing each slide, **ask:** What does this picture tell us about the people of this region? What does it tell us about their society? *(Accept all reasonable answers that can be supported by references to the picture.)* AL BL

See page 447D for other online activities.

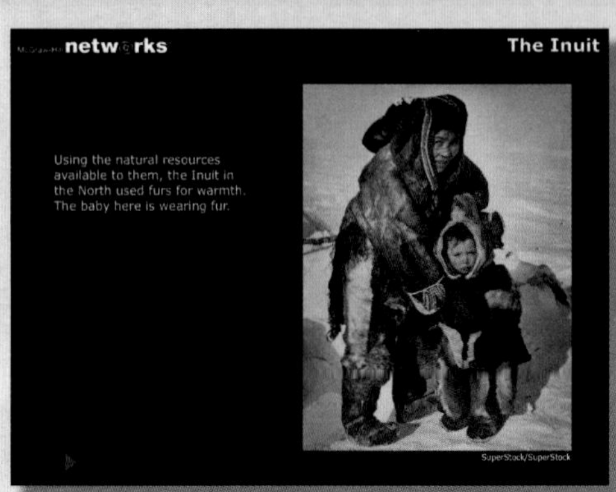

ANSWERS, p. 466

GEOGRAPHY CONNECTION

1. The most common method for obtaining food on the Atlantic coast was farming.
2. **CRITICAL THINKING** Students' answers will vary but may include that fish were more abundant along the Gulf of Mexico and in waters around Florida, or that the southern climate made it easier to fish throughout the year.

In the A.D. 1500s, two new groups—the Apache (uh•PAH•chee) and the Navajo (NAH•vah•hoe)—settled in the Southwest. The Apache and Navajo were hunters and gatherers. In time, the Navajo became farmers and settled in villages made up of square wooden homes called **hogans** (HOH•gahns). The Apache, however, remained hunters.

Life on the Great Plains

Native Americans living on the Great Plains were nomads. They set up temporary villages that lasted for only one or two growing seasons. Their homes were cone-shaped skin tents called tepees. Farming on the Great Plains was not easy. Peoples like the Mandan (MAHN•dahn) and Pawnee (paw•NEE), however, planted gardens in the fertile soil along rivers.

Plains women grew beans, corn, and squash. Before the arrival of the horse, men hunted by driving herds of antelope, deer, and buffalo over cliffs to their deaths. Plains peoples had many uses for the buffalo. They ate the meat, used the skins for clothing and tepees, and made tools from the bones.

How Did People Live in the Eastern Woodlands?

R

The land east of the Mississippi River was known as the Eastern Woodlands because of its dense forests. Farming was widely practiced in the southeast. The most important crops were corn, beans, and squash. In the cooler northeast, people depended more on hunting animals, such as deer, bear, rabbits, and beaver.

The people of the Eastern Woodlands formed complex societies with different kinds of governments. One plan was formed in the 1500s to end fighting among five groups. The Iroquois (IHR•uh•kwoy) Confederacy created the first constitution, or plan of government, in what is now the United States.

✓ PROGRESS CHECK

Explaining Why did the Iroquois form a confederacy?

Thinking Like a HISTORIAN

Comparing and Contrasting

Early Americans adapted to the environments in which they settled. As a result, many different cultures and ways of life developed. As you read, note the similarities and differences among Native Americans living in the far north, the Pacific Coast, the Southwest, the Great Plains, and the Eastern Woodlands. Share your findings with the class. For more information on comparing and contrasting, read the chapter *What Does a Historian Do?*

LESSON 2 REVIEW

Review Vocabulary (Tier 3 Words)

1. How did *sinkholes* help the Maya? RH.6–8.2, RH.6–8.4
2. How did a *hogan* differ from a tepee? RH.6–8.2, RH.6–8.4

Answer the Guiding Questions

3. ***Describing*** What role did Inca emperors play in the lives of their subjects? RH.6–8.2
4. ***Drawing Conclusions*** How did establishing a confederacy benefit Woodlands Native Americans? RH.6–8.2
5. ***Contrasting*** How did Native American groups on the Pacific Coast differ from those in the Southwest? RH.6–8.2
6. **NARRATIVE** Describe daily life in a Maya city-state from the point of view of a Maya priest. WHST.6–8.10

LESSON 2 REVIEW ANSWERS

1. Sinkholes connected the Maya with a huge network of underground rivers and streams and gave them a year-round source of water.
2. A hogan was a square, wooden home that was permanent; a tepee was a cone-shaped tent that was temporary.
3. Inca emperors controlled the lives of their subjects. They owned all the land and set rules for growing crops and distributing produce.
4. Answers will vary but should emphasize that federations connected several groups, promoting peace and protection.
5. Native Americans on the Pacific coast enjoyed a mild climate and reliable food sources. The Southwest peoples had to dig irrigation canals in order to water their fields and grow crops.
6. Students' writings should be consistent with lesson content describing Maya society.

R Reading Skills

Citing Text Evidence After students have read the text, ask them to describe the lives of the Native Americans who lived on the Great Plains. Remind students to cite evidence from the text in their discussion. **Ask:** **What animal was particularly important to the Plains peoples? Why?** *(The buffalo was important to the Plains peoples because it provided them with meat for food, skins for clothing and tepees, and bones for tools.)* Conclude the discussion of North American peoples with the people of the Eastern Woodlands region. **What was special about the organization of the Iroquois?** *(The Iroquois formed a confederacy of five different peoples that had a constitution.)*

Have students complete the Lesson 2 Review.

CLOSE & REFLECT

Summarizing Review with students the role that geography and climate played in the development of unique Native American cultures and civilizations. Have students return to the predictions they made in the beginning of the lesson about the possible effects of geography and climate. Discuss with students the differences between their earlier predictions and what they have learned from the lesson.

ANSWER, p. 467

✓ PROGRESS CHECK The Iroquois formed a confederacy to end fighting among the five groups.

CHAPTER REVIEW ACTIVITY

On the board, have a student volunteer create a three-column chart. Ask other students to copy the chart in their notebooks. Write "Mesoamerica" in the first column, "Peru/ Andes" in the second column, and "American Southwest" in the third column. Then have students come to the board and list the different Native American groups that lived in each area. Tell students to make sure they list the groups in chronological order. When the chart is finished, ask students what generalizations they can make based on the information in the chart. *(The people who live in an area change over time.)*

Mesoamerica	Peru/Andes	American Southwest

REVIEW THE ENDURING UNDERSTANDINGS

Review this chapter's Enduring Understandings with students:

- *People, places, and ideas change over time.*
- *Cultures are held together by shared beliefs and common practices and values.*

Now pose the following question in a class discussion to apply these to the chapter. **Ask:**

How did geography affect the development of early civilizations in the Americas? *(Answers may include examples such as the different crops grown in different regions, the use of different kinds of resources for shelter, food, and clothing, and the development of technology such as irrigation in places like the Southwest where there was a dry climate.)*

How did agriculture change life for early civilizations in the Americas? *(Once people started farming, they were able to stop moving around following large animals. They stayed in one place and developed more complex societies, which included governments, religions, and more complex social structures.)*

What were some of the achievements of the early civilizations such as the Maya, the Aztec, and the Inca? *(Answers may include Mayan understanding of astronomy and mathematics, Mayan calendars, and a Mayan writing system; the Aztec city of Tenochtitlán, Aztec calendars, and Aztec systems of irrigation; and Incan roads, irrigation projects, and terraced farms.)*

CHAPTER 16 Activities CCSS

Write your answers on a separate piece of paper.

1. **Exploring the Essential Question** WHST.6–8.2, WHST.6–8.10
INFORMATIVE/EXPLANATORY How did geography affect the societies and cultures that developed in the early Americas? Choose two early civilizations or cultures that developed in different parts of the Americas. Write an essay describing how each adapted to its environment. Describe their food, shelter, government, and religion.

2. **21st Century Skills** RH.6–8.1, RH.6–8.2
DEBATING Which society do you think had the greatest achievements—the Maya, the Aztec, or the Inca? Choose a culture and list its achievements as well as the reasons those achievements are important. Then, debate the issue with a fellow classmate who chose a different culture.

3. **Thinking Like a Historian** RH.6–8.2
SEQUENCING Create a time line like the one shown. Fill in significant events in the rise of the Aztecs.

A.D. 1200
Aztec move into central Mexico

4. 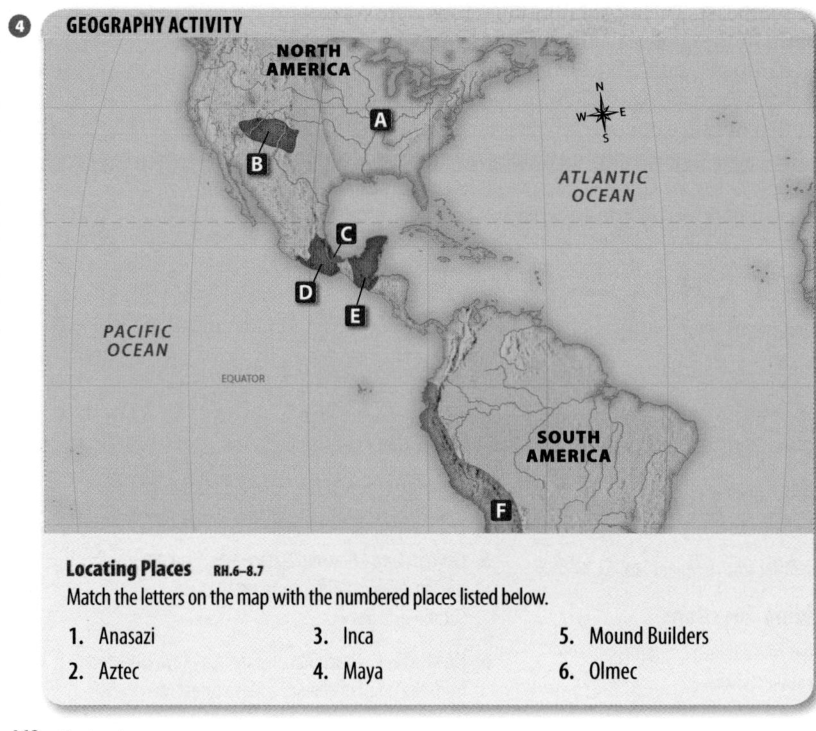

Locating Places RH.6–8.7
Match the letters on the map with the numbered places listed below.

1. Anasazi
2. Aztec
3. Inca
4. Maya
5. Mound Builders
6. Olmec

ACTIVITIES ANSWERS

Exploring the Essential Question

1. Answers will vary. Students should note that early peoples in the Americas fished, hunted, and farmed, depending on the climate and natural resources available to them. They also built homes out of animal skins, trees, mud, or other resources that were easily accessible. These factors affected the civilizations that developed—from the gods they worshiped to the roles of their leaders.

21st Century Skills

2. Answers will vary. Students should support their choices with evidence from the text, describing the achievements of their chosen civilization.

Thinking Like a Historian

3. Answers will vary but should include the following: Aztec begin to build Tenochtitlán (1325), Montezuma becomes ruler (1440), and Aztec armies conquer most of Mexico (1500).

Locating Places

4. **1.** B, **2.** D, **3.** F, **4.** E, **5.** A, **6.** C

REVIEW THE GUIDING QUESTIONS

Directions: Choose the best answer for each question.

RH.6–8.2
1. Pueblo Bonito was an important trade or religious center for
   A. the Inuit.
   B. the Anasazi.
   C. the Haida.
   D. the Navajo.

RH.6–8.2
2. Which of the following is the major waterway for the central part of North America?
   F. the Amazon River
   G. the Hudson River
   H. the Mississippi River
   I. the Red River

RH.6–8.2
3. Which of the following represents an achievement made by the Maya?
   A. calendar systems
   B. floating gardens
   C. quipu
   D. terrace farming

RH.6–8.2
4. Native Americans living on the Great Plains
   F. were part of the Iroquois League.
   G. set up temporary villages.
   H. hunted for walruses and caribou.
   I. built homes from stone and blocks of earth.

RH.6–8.2
5. Which was the most important food in the Americas?
   A. squash
   B. potatoes
   C. beans
   D. corn

RH.6–8.2
6. Early Americans living in which of the following areas dug irrigation canals to carry river water to their fields?
   F. the Southwest
   G. the Pacific coast
   H. the Great Plains
   I. the Eastern Woodlands

ASSESSMENT ANSWERS

Review the Guiding Questions

1. **B** The Anasazi built pueblos. The Inuit built their homes out of stone and turf or snow. The Haida used cedar trees to construct their homes. The Navajo lived in hogans.

2. **H** The Mississippi River is the major waterway for the central part of North America. The Amazon River flows in South America. The Hudson River flows from northeastern New York State to New York City. The Red River, a tributary of the Mississippi, flows from Texas to Louisiana, where it joins the Mississippi.

3. **A** The Maya developed a calendar for religious events and a calendar for events related to the seasons and agriculture. The Aztec created floating gardens. The Inca used the quipu and terrace farming.

4. **G** Native Americans living on the Great Plains were nomads, so they set up villages that lasted for one or two growing seasons. The Iroquois League was located in the Eastern Woodlands, not the Great Plains. The Inuit of the far north built homes from stones and blocks of earth and hunted caribou and walruses.

5. **D** Squash, potatoes, and beans were among the first crops grown in the Americas, but corn became the most important food in the Americas.

6. **F** Early Americans living in the scorching deserts of the Southwest dug irrigation canals to carry river water to their fields. Those living on the Pacific coast, on the Great Plains, or in the Eastern Woodlands did not experience the same irrigation problems.

Analyzing Documents

7 **D** Upper Cuzco was founded by the king, and Lower Cuzco was founded by the queen. Neither a council of elders nor invaders are mentioned in the myth. The citizens did not play a role in the separation.

8 **H** The inhabitants of Upper Cuzco were viewed as the elders because they had been brought together by a man. The myth does not mention the geography of the city, its founding dates, or any conflicts.

Short Response

9 Archaeologists probably want to know about rain to find out if the Maya experienced a drought. A drought could have caused the Maya to leave their cities.

10 When the author writes "the Maya world had too many people," he probably means there were more people than the environment could support with the technology of the time. There might not have been enough land to grow enough food for a large number of people or enough water for all the people living there.

Extended Response

11 Answers will vary. Students' writings should be consistent with chapter content. Students should note characteristics such as how people got food, what sort of buildings they created, how they dressed, what their beliefs were, and so forth.

CHAPTER 16 Assessment  

DBQ ANALYZING DOCUMENTS

The author of the following creation myth of the Inca is unknown:

"Thus our imperial city . . . was divided into two halves: . . . [Upper] Cuzco was founded by our king and . . . [Lower] Cuzco by our queen . . . There existed only one single difference between them, . . . that the inhabitants of Upper-Cuzco were to be considered as the elders . . . [they] had been brought together by the male, and those below by the female element."

RH.6–8.1, RH.6–8.6

7 **Analyzing** Which statement best describes how the imperial city was separated?

A. The citizens in Upper-Cuzco chose to be independent.

B. A council of elders decided to divide the city into four kingdoms.

C. Invaders captured the lower half of the city.

D. The king founded one half of the city and the queen founded the other.

RH.6–8.1, RH.6–8.6

8 **Evaluating** Why were the inhabitants of Upper-Cuzco considered to be elders?

F. They were located to the north.

G. They had founded their city first.

H. Their city was founded by a male.

I. They had defeated the citizens of Lower-Cuzco.

SHORT RESPONSE

"Recently, archaeologists have studied the Maya in many new ways . . . A big breakthrough was learning to read Maya writing.

"Archaeologists also look at layers of dirt in lake bottoms to see how the land has changed. . . . They even dig through the Maya's trash.

"All this work has given scientists new ideas . . . A big one was that the Maya world probably had too many people . . . ."

—Guy Gugliotta, "Maya Mystery," *National Geographic* 2007

RH.6–8.1, RH.6–8.6

9 Why do you think archaeologists think it is important to know about rain?

RH.6–8.1, RH.6–8.6

10 What does it mean, "the Maya world probably had too many people"?

EXTENDED RESPONSE

WHST.6–8.10

11 **Narrative** You are an early American. Write a journal entry describing an encounter with a Native American people in one of the regions described in the chapter. How would you describe their daily life?

Need Extra Help?

If You've Missed Question	1	2	3	4	5	6	7	8	9	10	11
Review Lesson	1	1	2	2	1	1	2	2	2	2	1, 2

470 *The Americas*

networks Online Teaching Options

Using eAssessment

Use eAssessment to access and assign the publisher-made Lesson Quizzes & Chapter Tests electronically. You can also use eAssessment to create your own quizzes and tests from hundreds of available questions. eAssessment helps you design assessments that meet the needs of different types of learners. Follow the link in the Assess tab of your Teacher Lesson Center.

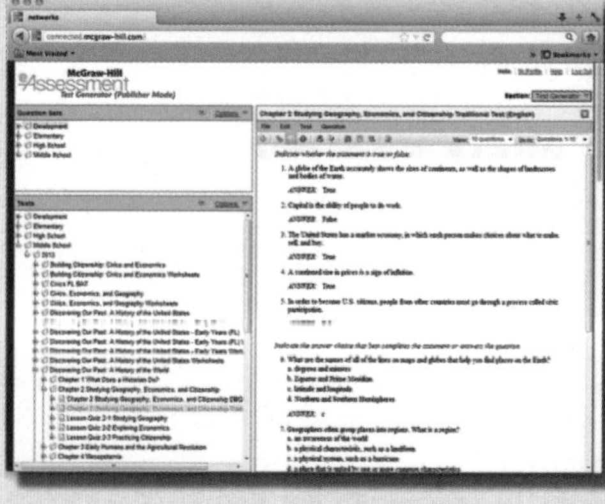

CHAPTER 17

Imperial China Planner

UNDERSTANDING BY DESIGN®

Enduring Understandings

- *People, places, and ideas change over time.*
- *Leaders can bring about change in a society.*

Essential Questions

- *How does geography influence the way people live?*
- *How do new ideas change the way people live?*
- *What are the characteristics of a leader?*

Predictable Misunderstandings

Students may think:

- *China has always been an isolated culture with no contact with the outside world.*
- *Imperial China was less culturally and technologically advanced than Western Europe.*

Assessment Evidence

Performance Tasks:

- *Hands-On Chapter Project*

Other Evidence:

- *Research activity*
- *Participation in class discussions*
- *Written activities*
- *Interactive Whiteboard Activities*
- *Graphic Organizer Activities*
- *Geography and History Activities*
- *Primary Sources Activity*
- *Economics of History Activity*
- *21st Century Skills Activity*
- *Lesson Reviews*
- *The World's Literature questions*

SUGGESTED PACING GUIDE

Introducing the Chapter	1 day	*The World's Literature*	1 day
Lesson 1	2 days	Lesson 4	1 day
Lesson 2	1 day	Chapter Wrap-Up and Assessment	1 day
Lesson 3	1 day		

TOTAL TIME 8 DAYS

Key for Using the Teacher Edition

SKILL-BASED ACTIVITIES

Types of skill activities found in the Teacher Edition.

V Visual Skills require students to analyze maps, graphs, charts, and photos.

R Reading Skills help students practice reading skills and master vocabulary.

W Writing Skills provide writing opportunities to help students comprehend the text.

C Critical Thinking Skills help students apply and extend what they have learned.

T Technology Skills require students to use digital tools effectively.

*Letters are followed by a number when there is more than one of the same type of skill on the page.

DIFFERENTIATED INSTRUCTION

All activities are written for the on-level student unless otherwise marked with the leveled labels below.

BL Beyond Level

AL Approaching Level

ELL English Language Learners

All students benefit from activities that utilize different learning styles. Many activities are marked as below when a particular learning style is highlighted.

Intrapersonal — **Naturalist**
Logical/Mathematical — **Kinesthetic**
Visual/Spatial — **Auditory/Musical**
Verbal/Linguistic — **Interpersonal**

NCSS Standards covered in "Imperial China"

Learners will understand:

1 **CULTURE**

4. That the beliefs, values, and behaviors of a culture form an integrated system that helps shape the activities and ways of life that define a culture

6. That culture may change in response to changing needs, concerns, social, political, and geographic conditions

7. How people from different cultures develop different values and ways of interpreting experience

8. That language, behaviors, and beliefs of different cultures can both contribute to and pose barriers to cross-cultural understanding

2 **TIME, CONTINUITY, AND CHANGE**

5. Key historical periods and patterns of change within and across cultures (e.g., the rise and fall of ancient civilizations, the development of technology, the rise of modern nation-states, and the establishment and breakdown of colonial systems)

7. The contributions of key persons, groups, and events from the past and their influence on the present

3 **PEOPLE, PLACES, AND ENVIRONMENTS**

8. Factors that contribute to cooperation and conflict among peoples of the nation and world, including language, religion, and political beliefs

5 **INDIVIDUALS, GROUPS, AND INSTITUTIONS**

9. That groups and institutions influence culture in a variety of ways

7 **PRODUCTION, DISTRIBUTION, AND CONSUMPTION**

1. Individuals, government, and society experience scarcity because human wants and needs exceed what can be produced from available resources

8 **SCIENCE, TECHNOLOGY, AND SOCIETY**

2. Society often turns to science and technology to solve problems

4. Science and technology have had both positive and negative impacts upon individuals, societies, and the environment in the past and present

5. Science and technology have changed peoples' perceptions of the social and natural world, as well as their relationship to the land, economy and trade, their concept of security, and their major daily activities

CHAPTER OPENER PLANNER

Students will know:

- *the accomplishments of the Sui, Tang, and Song dynasties.*
- *how neo-Confucianism influenced Chinese government.*
- *why civil service exams were important.*
- *how China's economy changed under the Tang and Song dynasties.*
- *the impact of technological advances developed during the Tang dynasty.*
- *how growth of the arts led to a golden age of Chinese culture.*
- *the characteristics of the Mongols and the extent of their conquest.*
- *changes that occurred in China as a result of the Mongol conquest.*
- *how the Ming dynasty restored China.*
- *the scope and purpose of Zheng He's travels.*
- *how the attitude of Chinese rulers toward exploration changed over time.*

Students will be able to:

- ***compare*** *concepts of leadership from imperial China with those of today.*
- ***analyze*** *the impact of neo-Confucian teachings.*
- ***evaluate*** *the effect of improvements in farming on population growth.*
- ***identify*** *three technological advances that brought changes to Chinese society.*
- ***recognize*** *artifacts of the golden age of Chinese culture.*
- ***analyze*** *a map of Mongol conquests.*
- ***determine*** *characteristics needed to rule a vast land.*
- ***explain*** *how the Mongol empire affected trade.*
- ***identify*** *how the Ming changed China.*
- ***interpret*** *a map showing Zheng He's travels.*
- ***describe*** *the factors that contributed to the fall of the Ming dynasty.*

UNDERSTANDING BY DESIGN®

Print Teaching Options

V Visual Skills

- ☐ **P. 472** Students identify features on the map. **Visual/Spatial**
- ☐ **P. 473** Students identify events located on the time line. **Visual/Spatial**

Online Teaching Options

V Visual Skills

- MAP **Imperial China, c. A.D. 1294**—Students view a map of the Mongol empire and identify the Great Wall, the Silk Road, and the route followed by Marco Polo.
- TIME LINE **Imperial China A.D. 600 to 1644**—Students learn about key events in China during this time period.
- WORLD ATLAS Students can use this interactive map to identify regions of the world, learn about individual countries, locate political boundaries, measure distances, and much more.

Project-Based Learning

Hands-On Chapter Project

Imperial China

Students will create an illustrated time line displaying key events and achievements of major Chinese dynasties of the period A.D. 581–1644.

Technology Extension

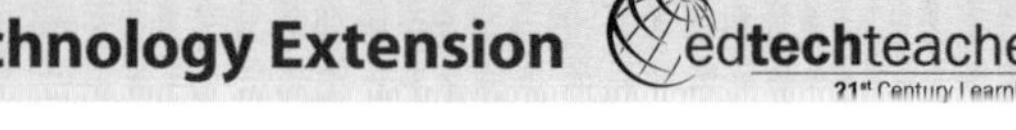

Online Interactive Time Line

- Find an additional activity online that incorporates technology for this project.
- Visit the EdTechTeacher Web sites (included in the Technology Extension for this chapter) for more links, tutorials, and other resources.

Print Resources

ANCILLARY RESOURCES

These ancillaries are available for every chapter and lesson.

- **Reading Essentials and Study Guide Workbook** AL ELL
- **Chapter Tests and Lesson Quizzes Blackline Masters**

PRINTABLE DIGITAL WORKSHEETS

These printable digital worksheets are available for every chapter and lesson.

- **Hands-On Chapter Projects**
- **What Do You Know? activities**
- **Chapter Summaries (English and Spanish)**
- **Vocabulary Builder activities**
- **Guided Reading activities**

More Media Resources

SUGGESTED READING

Grade 6 reading level:

- ***Chee-Lin: A Giraffe's Journey,*** by James Rumford

Grade 7 reading level:

- ***The Kite Rider,*** by Geraldine McCaughrean

Grade 8 reading level:

- ***Adventures of Marco Polo,*** by Russell Freedman

CHINA REUNITES

Students will know:
- *the accomplishments of the Sui, Tang, and Song dynasties.*
- *how neo-Confucianism influenced Chinese government.*
- *why civil service exams were important.*

Students will be able to:
- ***compare** concepts of leadership from imperial China with those of today.*
- ***analyze** the impact of neo-Confucian teachings.*

UNDERSTANDING BY DESIGN®

☑ Print Teaching Options

V Visual Skills

- ☐ **P. 479** Students analyze a picture of a colossal Buddha statue and answer questions. BL Visual/Spatial Logical/Mathematical

R Reading Skills

- ☐ **P. 474** Students discuss the state of China during the 300 years that followed the Han dynasty.
- ☐ **P. 475** Students summarize the major achievements of the Sui dynasty. AL
- ☐ **P. 476** Students explain the major accomplishments of the Tang dynasty.
- ☐ **P. 476** Students discuss the effects of prosperity and economic growth on imperial China. AL
- ☐ **P. 477** Students describe life in China during the Song dynasty. AL
- ☐ **P. 478** Students discuss how Buddhism came to China and its impact on the people. BL
- ☐ **P. 479** Students explain how Buddhism came to Japan. AL
- ☐ **P. 480** Students talk about the role Confucianism played in Chinese government.
- ☐ **P. 480** Students paraphrase a quotation. AL ELL

W Writing Skills

- ☐ **P. 477** Students do research and take notes to answer questions in a report about city life in Tang China. BL Verbal/Linguistic

C Critical Thinking Skills

- ☐ **P. 478** Students speculate on why early Tang rulers did not oppose Buddhism.
- ☐ **P. 480** Students draw conclusions about why Chinese rulers favored Confucianism over Buddhism.
- ☐ **P. 481** Students evaluate the usefulness of civil service examinations. BL

T Technology Skills

- ☐ **P. 475** Students do research to learn about the Three Gorges and prepare and deliver a presentation. Interpersonal

☑ Online Teaching Options

V Visual Skills

- ☐ VIDEO **Ming Dynasty**—Students view a video that explains how the northern capital city of China got the name Beijing.
- ☐ MAP **Song China c. A.D. 1200**—Students compare China's borders during the Song empire and today.
- ☐ MAP **Tang China c. A.D. 700**—Students examine the extent of China during this period and trace the route of the Grand Canal.

R Reading Skills

- ☐ GRAPHIC ORGANIZER **Taking Notes: *Identifying:* Accomplishments of Three Dynasties**—Students list the accomplishments of the Sui, Tang, and Song dynasties.
- ☐ IMAGE **Empress Wu**—Students read about the life and accomplishments of this Chinese ruler.

C Critical Thinking Skills

- ☐ CHART **Buddhists Around the World**—Students click to compare the percentage of Buddhists by country.
- ☐ SLIDE SHOW **The Tang Dynasty**—Students examine examples of musical instruments, pottery, and paintings from this time period.

T Technology Skills

- ☐ SELF-CHECK QUIZ **Lesson 1**—Students receive instant feedback on their mastery of lesson content.
- ☐ GAME **Dynasties, Buddhism, and Confucianism True or False Game**—Students identify statements as true or false to review lesson content.

☑ Printable Digital Worksheets

C Critical Thinking Skills

- ☐ WORKSHEET **Geography and History Activity: Imperial China: China Reunites: Understanding Location: Changan and Hangzhou**—Students compare and contrast the characteristics of these two capital cities.

CHINESE SOCIETY

Students will know:

- *how China's economy changed under the Tang and Song dynasties.*
- *the impact of technological advances developed during the Tang dynasty.*
- *how growth of the arts led to a golden age of Chinese culture.*

Students will be able to:

- ***evaluate*** *the effect of improvements in farming on population growth.*
- ***identify*** *three technological advances that brought changes to Chinese society.*
- ***recognize*** *artifacts of the golden age of Chinese culture.*

UNDERSTANDING BY DESIGN®

☑ *Print Teaching Options*

V Visual Skills

- ☐ **P. 487** Students analyze the style of a landscape painting. Visual/Spatial

R Reading Skills

- ☐ **P. 482** Students explain how farming improved during the Tang dynasty and how increased food production affected the general population. AL
- ☐ **P. 483** Students discuss China's trade and the different goods that were exported and imported. AL
- ☐ **P. 484** Students describe the invention of printing and how woodblock books were produced. AL
- ☐ **P. 486** Students identify the major themes of Chinese poets. AL
- ☐ **P. 488** Students clarify the meanings of unfamiliar terms used to discuss different types of art. AL ELL

W Writing Skills

- ☐ **P. 485** Students write two or three sentences summarizing a technology.

C Critical Thinking Skills

- ☐ **P. 483** Students hypothesize on how technological inventions travel from one society to another. BL
- ☐ **P. 484** Students make inferences about how steel changed the lives of people in China.
- ☐ **P. 485** Students discuss the effects that different technologies had on Chinese society. AL
- ☐ **P. 486** Students discuss the role Chinese rulers had in promoting the golden age of Chinese culture and explain how woodblock printing helped make literature popular.
- ☐ **P. 486** Students analyze a Li Bo poem.
- ☐ **P. 487** Students make inferences from landscape paintings about the values of the Chinese. BL
- ☐ **P. 488** Students compare and contrast the Chinese point of view about their place in nature with Americans' view of their place in nature today.

☑ *Online Teaching Options*

V Visual Skills

- VIDEO **Chinese History From the Grand Canal Waterway to Marco Polo**—Students examine the contributions of the Song dynasty and learn of Marco Polo's Chinese travels.
- SLIDE SHOW **Chinese Landscape Painting**—Students analyze two styles of landscape painting from the Song dynasty.
- SLIDE SHOW **Changan**—Students analyze scenes from this city, which served as the capital of China for over ten ruling dynasties.
- IMAGE **China Tableware**—Students click to learn about the development of fine tableware.

R Reading Skills

- GRAPHIC ORGANIZER **Taking Notes: *Categorizing:* Chinese Advancements**—Students identify advancements made in the Chinese economy, technology, and arts.
- PRIMARY SOURCE **The Poems of Li Bo**—Students read two of Li Bo's most famous poems.

C Critical Thinking Skills

- WHITEBOARD ACTIVITY **Traveling the Silk Road**—Students identify goods traded along the Silk Road.
- IMAGE **Movable Type**—Students examine blocks of movable type and consider the effect of this invention to the spread of knowledge.
- SLIDE SHOW **Silk-Making**—Students click to see the steps in making silk.

T Technology Skills

- SELF-CHECK QUIZ **Lesson 2**—Students receive instant feedback on their mastery of lesson content.
- GAME **Chinese Arts and Discoveries Concentration Game**—Students make matches to review lesson vocabulary and concepts.

☑ *Printable Digital Worksheets*

C Critical Thinking Skills

- WORKSHEET **Economics of History Activity: Imperial China: Chinese Society**—Students analyze the advantages and disadvantages of coins versus paper money.

THE MONGOLS IN CHINA

Students will know:
- *the characteristics of the Mongols and the extent of their conquest.*
- *changes that occurred in China as a result of the Mongol conquest.*

Students will be able to:
- ***compare*** *concepts of leadership.*
- ***analyze*** *a map of Mongol conquests.*
- ***determine*** *characteristics needed to rule vast lands.*
- ***explain*** *how the Mongol empire affected trade.*

UNDERSTANDING BY DESIGN®

☑ *Print Teaching Options*

V Visual Skills

- ☐ **P. 490** Students analyze a map and the campaigns Genghis Khan directed. Visual/Spatial
- ☐ **P. 491** Students analyze a map of the Mongol Empire and then compare it to a modern map. BL Visual/Spatial

R Reading Skills

- ☐ **P. 489** Students identify where the Mongols came from, how they lived, and what skills they had.
- ☐ **P. 490** Students explain the steps Genghis Khan took to prepare his nation for war. AL
- ☐ **P. 491** Students describe how the Mongols used terror to win territory.
- ☐ **P. 492** Students discuss events following the death of Genghis Khan and explain how the Mongols continued to expand their empire.
- ☐ **P. 493** Students explain why Kublai Khan's name for his dynasty was appropriate. AL
- ☐ **P. 495** Students list the items that Mongol China exported and imported. AL

W Writing Skills

- ☐ **P. 494** Students write and deliver a speech on whether or not Marco Polo actually traveled to China.

C Critical Thinking Skills

- ☐ **P. 493** Students evaluate Kublai Khan's strategy for ruling China. BL
- ☐ **P. 494** Students compare the Mongols' qualities as conquerors to their qualities as rulers. AL ELL
- ☐ **P. 495** Students discuss the point of view Europeans took to the stories that Marco Polo told about China.

☑ *Online Teaching Options*

V Visual Skills

- VIDEO **Marco Polo's Inspiration**—Students examine Marco Polo's early fascination with the Silk Road.
- IMAGE **Mongol Invasions of Japan**—Students click to learn of the typhoons, or *kamikazes,* that twice saved Japan.
- MAP **Mongol Empire Under Genghis Khan c. A.D. 1227**—Students compare the size of the Mongol homeland to the extent of Genghis Khan's empire.
- MAP **Mongol Empire c. A.D. 1294**—Students examine the extent of the Mongol empire at its height.

R Reading Skills

- GRAPHIC ORGANIZER **Taking Notes: *Sequencing:* Mongols in China**—Students sequence the events that led to Mongol control of China.
- IMAGE **Genghis Khan**—Students read about the life and accomplishments of this Mongol leader.

C Critical Thinking Skills

- WHITEBOARD ACTIVITY **Mongol Warriors**—Students identify characteristics of the Mongol warriors.
- IMAGE **Mongolian Literature**—Students click to learn of the earliest Mongol writings, which were later translated into Chinese.

T Technology Skills

- SELF-CHECK QUIZ **Lesson 3**—Students receive instant feedback on their mastery of lesson content.

☑ *Printable Digital Worksheets*

C Critical Thinking Skills

- WORKSHEET **Primary Source Activity: Imperial China: The Mongols in China**—Students analyze and respond to excerpts from two primary sources.

THE MING DYNASTY

Students will know:
- *how the Ming dynasty restored China.*
- *the scope and purpose of Zheng He's travels.*
- *how the attitude of Chinese rulers toward exploration changed over time.*

Students will be able to:
- ***identify** how the Ming changed China.*
- ***interpret** a map showing Zheng He's travels.*
- ***describe** the factors that contributed to the fall of the Ming dynasty.*

UNDERSTANDING BY DESIGN®

Print Teaching Options

V Visual Skills

- **P. 499** Students analyze a map of Ming China. Visual/Spatial
- **P. 501** Students analyze a map of Zheng He's voyages and determine where he went. Visual/Spatial

R Reading Skills

- **P. 499** Students explain what the name the Forbidden City says about the Ming rulers, why these rulers brought back civil service examinations, and why they carried out a census. BL
- **P. 500** Students identify the changes Ming rulers brought to China and how they helped China's economy grow.
- **P. 501** Students discuss the Ming emperors' motives for sponsoring the voyages of exploration.
- **P. 502** Students describe the trade items Zheng He carried on his voyages. AL
- **P. 502** Students identify the attitude the Chinese held toward the Portuguese.
- **P. 503** Students discuss the Chinese relationship with the Jesuits. AL

W Writing Skills

- **P. 502** Students write an essay defending the value of trade and contact with foreign lands.

C Critical Thinking Skills

- **P. 498** Students explain what caused the rise of the Ming dynasty. AL
- **P. 500** Students explain how the arts depend upon prosperity. BL AL ELL
- **P. 503** Students infer why the Portuguese were allowed to build a trading post despite China's official policy against it. BL

Online Teaching Options

V Visual Skills

- VIDEO **Chinese History From the Ming Dynasty to the Three Gorges Dam**—Students experience the overthrow of the Mongols and the rise of the Ming dynasty.
- MAP **The Voyages of Zheng He, 1405–1433**—Students trace the routes of this Chinese explorer.
- MAP **Ming China c. A.D. 1368–1644**—Students view the extent of the Ming dynasty and its northern border, the Great Wall.

R Reading Skills

- GRAPHIC ORGANIZER **Taking Notes: *Identifying Cause and Effect:* Voyages of Zheng He**—Students note the causes and effects of the voyages of Zheng He.
- SLIDE SHOW **The Forbidden City**—Students view images and read descriptions of this walled city where the emperors of China once lived.

C Critical Thinking Skills

- WHITEBOARD ACTIVITY **Dynasties and Eras**—Students categorize events by the dynasty in which they occurred.
- IMAGE **Ming Vases**—Students examine these highly prized porcelain pieces.

T Technology Skills

- SELF-CHECK QUIZ **Lesson 4**—Students receive instant feedback on their mastery of lesson content.
- GAME **Fill-in-the-Blank Game: Chinese Exploration**—Students review their understanding of lesson content.

Printable Digital Worksheets

W Writing Skills

- WORKSHEET **21st Century Skills Activity: Imperial China: The Ming Dynasty: Creativity and Innovation: Identify Problems and Solutions**—Students identify a problem and possible solutions and why the solution they chose is a good one.

C Critical Thinking Skills

- WORKSHEET **Geography and History Activity: Imperial China: The Ming Dynasty: Sailing the Western Oceans: The Voyages of Zheng He**—Students examine the routes traveled by this explorer on his seven voyages.

INTERVENTION AND REMEDIATION STRATEGIES

LESSON 1 China Reunites

Reading and Comprehension

Summarizing Have students review the three dynasties discussed in this lesson: the Sui, Tan, and Song. Ask them to write a paragraph for each dynasty, describing the challenges it faced and contributions it made to China's civilization.

Text Evidence

Researching on the Internet Have students work in pairs and do research into neo-Confucianism. Have them take notes on how the ideas of neo-Confucianism specifically counter the teachings of Buddhism. Ask them to share their findings in a class discussion.

LESSON 2 Chinese Society

Reading and Comprehension

Organizing Have students create an outline of Lesson 2. They can use the section headings to organize their outline. Have them write important main ideas and details for each heading.

Text Evidence

Citing Text Evidence Have students find evidence in Lesson 2 to support the statement that new technology promoted economic growth during the Tang and Sang dynasties. Have students list their facts and share them in small-group discussions.

LESSON 3 The Mongols in China

Reading and Comprehension

Summarizing Ask students to write a summary of either the Mongol empire or of the Mongol governance of China.

Text Evidence

Argument Have students write a two- or three-paragraph persuasive essay defending or opposing the statement that the Mongols helped advance civilization in the ancient world. Students should cite evidence from the text in their essays.

LESSON 4 The Ming Dynasty

Reading and Comprehension

Explaining Have students write and deliver a short presentation suitable for explaining the history of the Ming dynasty to a fourth-grade class.

Text Evidence

Informative/Explanatory Ask students to write an analysis of one of Zheng He's journeys. They should draw upon details in the text as well as on other research. They should include answers to these questions: *How did people respond to his visit? What did the voyage accomplish?*

Online Resources

Approaching Level Reader

Use this online lower-level text that corresponds directly to the text in the Student Edition. It includes a Spanish version.

Guided Reading Activities

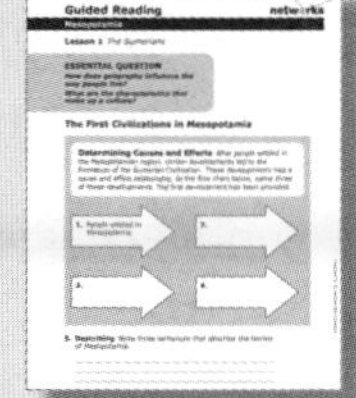

This resource uses graphic organizers and guiding questions to help students with comprehension.

What Do You Know?

Use these worksheets to pre-assess student's background knowledge before they study the chapter.

Reading Essentials and Study Guide Workbook

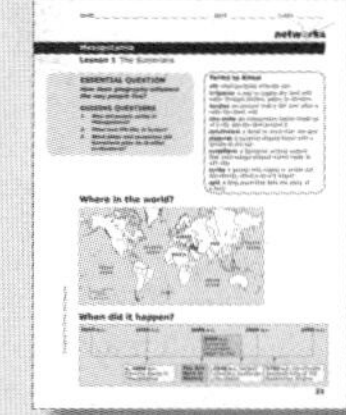

This resource offers writing and reading activities for the approaching-level student. Also available in Spanish.

Self-Check Quizzes

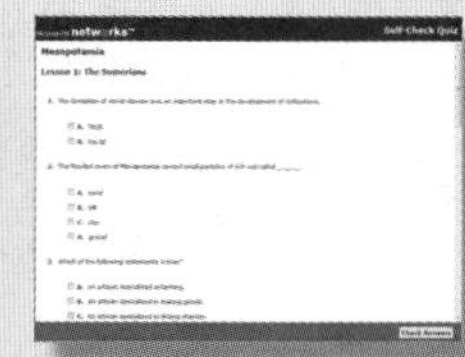

This online assessment tool provides instant feedback for students to check their progress.

How Do I Use
Primary Sources
in My Classroom?

A primary source is an oral or written account obtained from people who witnessed or experienced an event. Examples of primary sources can include official government documents; speeches, interviews, and oral histories; diaries; autobiographies; advertisements; physical historical objects; and songs or audio recordings.

Using primary sources transforms students into active participants in the examination of a subject. Students can use primary sources to think critically about events, issues, and concepts.

Step 1 How Do I Introduce Students to Primary Sources?

- Alert students to the fact that primary sources contain biases and prejudices and should be examined cautiously. Every primary source reflects the creator's point of view, which is only one interpretation of an event, a document, or an issue.
- Students can use questions such as *Who created the source? What was the purpose for doing so?*

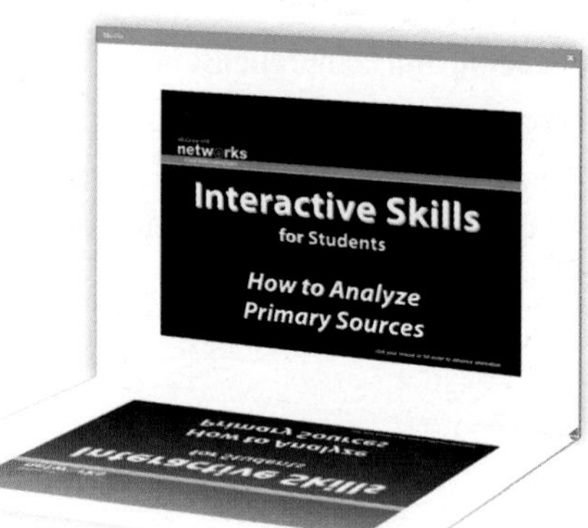

Step 2 Choosing Primary Sources

- Expose students to a variety of primary sources.
- Be aware that many documents include challenging vocabulary, or unfamiliar sentence structure. You may need to explain how to interpret these things before students can really begin to understand the source's content.

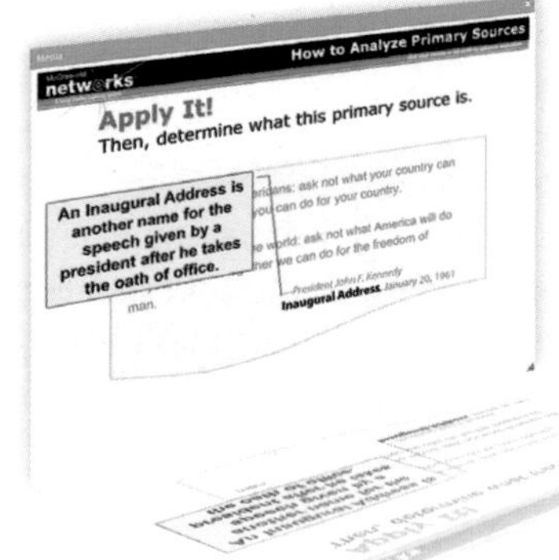

Step 3 Using Primary Sources in a Variety of Ways

- Use these types of sources in multiple ways to keep learners engaged.
- As a **prereading activity**, you can provide primary sources to introduce content at the start of the chapter or topic. Have students analyze the source and ask questions about it. Then ask students to make predictions about what they may learn when studying the main content.
- As an **evaluation activity**, ask students to compare what they learn in a primary source against the information provided by the textbook or in digital assets. Is the content the same? Does the primary source have a limited perspective of events that the narrative challenges or supports? Does the primary source increase student understanding on the human impact of the event, document, or issue?

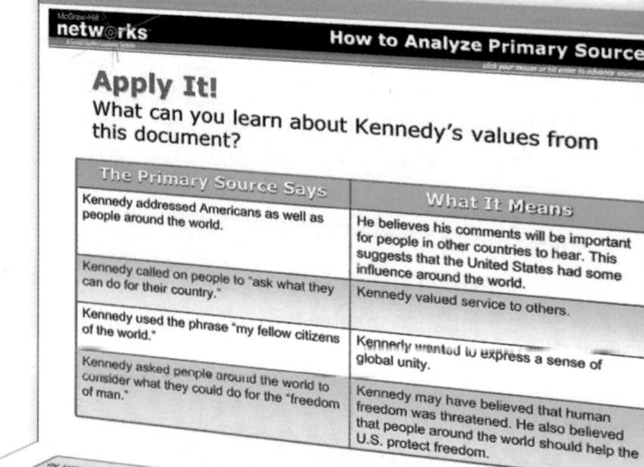

Imperial China

A.D. 600 to 1644

ESSENTIAL QUESTIONS *• How does geography influence the way people live? • How do new ideas change the way people live? • What are the characteristics of a leader?*

networks

There's More Online about the lives and customs of people in Imperial China.

CHAPTER 17

Lesson 1 *China Reunites*

Lesson 2 *Chinese Society*

Lesson 3 *The Mongols in China*

Lesson 4 *The Ming Dynasty*

The Story Matters . . .

The year is A.D. 683, and the Chinese Emperor Gaozong (GOW • ZUNG) has died from a crippling stroke. Who will rule China? His empress steps in and takes control of the government. Empress Wu at first places her sons on the throne, although she holds the real power. Then, in 690, she seized the throne for herself. Wu would be the only woman ever to rule China as emperor. She governed China using ruthless methods. Yet she is remembered for achieving prosperity, being fair to the people, and improving government services. Her long career outlasted many government officials who criticized her. Wu ruled China until her death at age 80.

◄ *Empress Wu showed no mercy to her enemies and demanded absolute acceptance of her rulings.*

Letter from the Author

Dear World History Teacher,

During the Sui, Tang, and Song dynasties, Chinese civilization blossomed. Then the Mongols overthrew the Song dynasty and established the Yuan dynasty in 1279. After Kublai Khan's death and a series of weak rulers, an uprising overthrew the Mongols and resulted in the establishment of the Ming dynasty. During the 1,000 years spanning these five dynasties, China's industrial, commercial, and agricultural sectors grew considerably. China's achievements were unsurpassed throughout the world and made it a civilization that was the envy of its neighbors.

Jackson J. Spielvogel

ENGAGE

Bellringer Read aloud "The Story Matters . . ." Make sure students understand any unfamiliar words in the passage, such as *ruthless, prosperity,* and *criticized.* Point out that the passage presents two opinions of Empress Wu. Have students identify the two opinions. **Ask: Is one opinion supported by more evidence than the other?** *(Students may say that the positive opinion of Empress Wu is more strongly supported.)*

Point out to students how Empress Wu is remembered. **Ask: Are all leaders remembered this way?** *(no)* **Why are some leaders remembered hundreds of years after their deaths but others are not?** *(Some leaders accomplish great feats or cause lasting changes.)*

Tell the class that the Chinese witnessed the rise and fall of five dynasties and several periods of civil war during the imperial period, which lasted more than 1,000 years. Yet with each new dynasty, China reunited itself, rebuilt its lands and economy, and rediscovered its culture and arts. Tell students they can explore to learn more about Chinese arts and culture online.

Making Connections

Tell students that Empress Wu was a strong leader who waged a war against traditional discrimination against women. She promoted the accomplishments of women by having scholars write biographies of successful Chinese women. She advanced her mother's clan by giving relatives leading political positions. She described the perfect ruler as one who ruled like a mother ruled her children.

TEACH & ASSESS

Step Into the Place

V1 Visual Skills

Analyzing Maps Help students identify the boundaries of Mongol-ruled China. Point out that China's borders later began to shrink when the Mongols lost power. Challenge students to draw on their knowledge of history and geography to indicate the areas of Asia that probably were always under Chinese rule. *(Students should indicate that the Chinese nearly always controlled the eastern part of the Asian continent, including the areas around Beijing, Changan, Guangzhou, and Hangzhou.)* **Visual/Spatial**

Content Background Knowledge

The Silk Road first came into use about 2,000 years ago, and it served to connect the two great civilizations of that period, Rome and China. The Silk Road was really a general route with multiple paths, and was about 4,000 miles long. Few caravans traveled the entire route. Goods were usually passed along in stages over the route. Many kinds of goods were carried, but most commonly silk was carried westward to Rome while gold, silver, and wool were the usual goods carried eastward to China. The Silk Road became unsafe as Rome's territory shrank ,and the road was rarely used. However, as the Mongols came to power around A.D. 1200, the use of the road was revived and it became a great trade route once more.

CHAPTER 17 CCSS

Place and Time: Imperial China A.D. 600 to 1644

In the late 1200s, the Mongol Empire stretched from Eastern Europe to the Pacific Ocean. China's borders expanded and contracted under Mongol rulers. For centuries, Mongols and other dynasties in China seized power, extended the territory, and developed trade routes. Eventually, they would collapse or be overthrown.

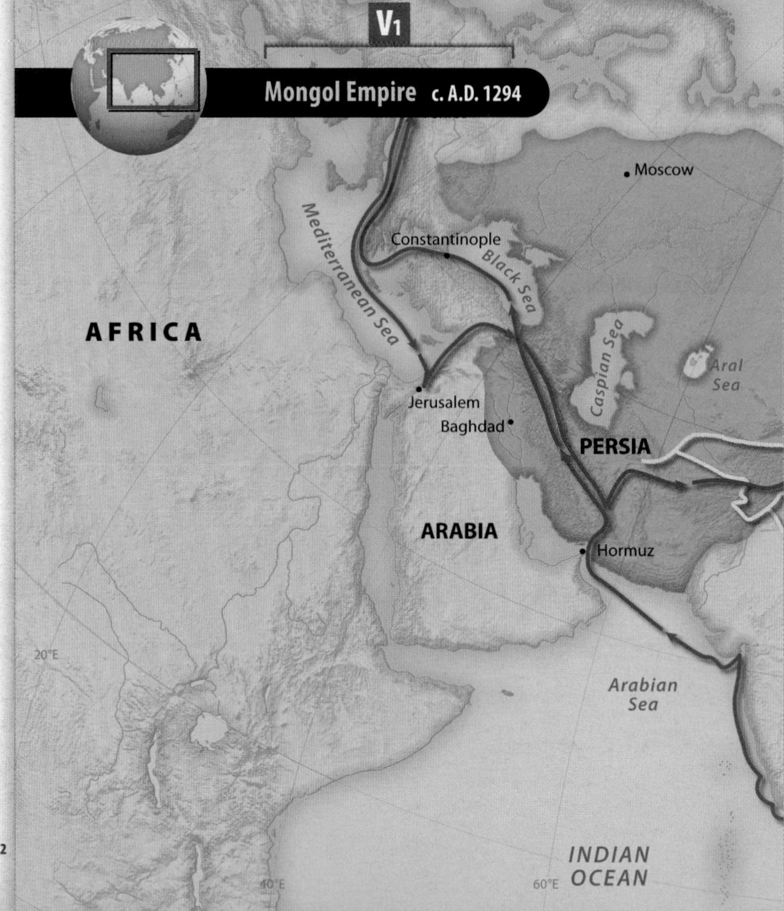

Step Into the Place

PLACE In A.D. 1200s, the Mongols conquered China. They set up a new dynasty and extended the empire south and west.

1. **PLACE** What challenges did the geography of the Mongol empire present for travelers? **RH.6–8.7**
2. **REGIONS** Describe the extent of the Silk Road. What were its farthest boundaries at either end? **RH.6–8.7**
3. **CRITICAL THINKING** *Analyzing* Identify two advantages and disadvantages of building and maintaining an enormous empire. **RH.6–8.2**

Step Into the Time

V2 **TIME LINE** Choose an event from the time line and write a paragraph predicting the general social, political, or economic consequence that event might have for the world. **RH.6–8.7, WHST.6–8.10**

IMPERIAL CHINA
- **c. A.D. 590** Grand Canal links northern and southern China
- **A.D. 690** Empress Wu begins rule
- **A.D. 898** Earliest known book printed

A.D. 450 — A.D. 600 — A.D. 750 — A.D. 900

THE WORLD
- **A.D. 496** Catholicism adopted by Franks
- **A.D. 631** Prince Shotoku creates Japan's constitution
- **c. A.D. 900** Islam spreads in Africa

ANSWERS, p. 472

Step Into the Place

1. The size of the region and the lack of waterways presented challenges for travelers.
2. The Silk Road extended from Persia in the west to the cities of Beijing and Hangzhou on China's east coast.
3. CRITICAL THINKING Advantages include access to large areas of land and unity among people for trade and travel. Disadvantages include difficulty communicating and maintaining order. Also, it is difficult to defend such a large empire.

Step Into the Time

Students might predict that the magnetic compass helped people travel long distances.

Project-Based Learning

Hands-On Chapter Project

Imperial China

Students will create an illustrated time line displaying key events and achievements of major Chinese dynasties of the period A.D. 581–1644. First, guide a discussion to review what students have learned about the Sui, Tang, Song, Yuan, and Ming dynasties. Then, students will discuss research ideas and plan their projects before creating their time lines. Have students share their time lines with the rest of the class. Finally, students will evaluate their research, presentation, and collaboration using an Assessment Rubric.

Technology Extension

Online Interactive Time Line

Students will individually or collaboratively develop online interactive time lines to see relationships among historical events. To add entries to the time line, students should identify an event, individual, or idea from imperial China, provide the date and a brief description, and then include images, media, and hyperlinks, depending on the platform. Once the time line is complete, facilitate sharing and publishing by embedding time lines into an existing Web site or by sharing the direct links.

networks *There's More Online!*

☑ **MAP** Explore the interactive version of this map on NETWORKS.

☑ **TIME LINE** Explore the interactive version of this time line on NETWORKS.

MONGOLIA
JAPAN
Khanbaliq (Beijing)
TIBET
CHINA
Hangzhou
HIMALAYA
INDIA
Tagaung
Bay of Bengal
East China Sea
South China Sea
PACIFIC OCEAN
Chang Jiang
Huang He
40°N
20°N
160°E
140°E
120°E
100°E
80°E
0°
EQUATOR

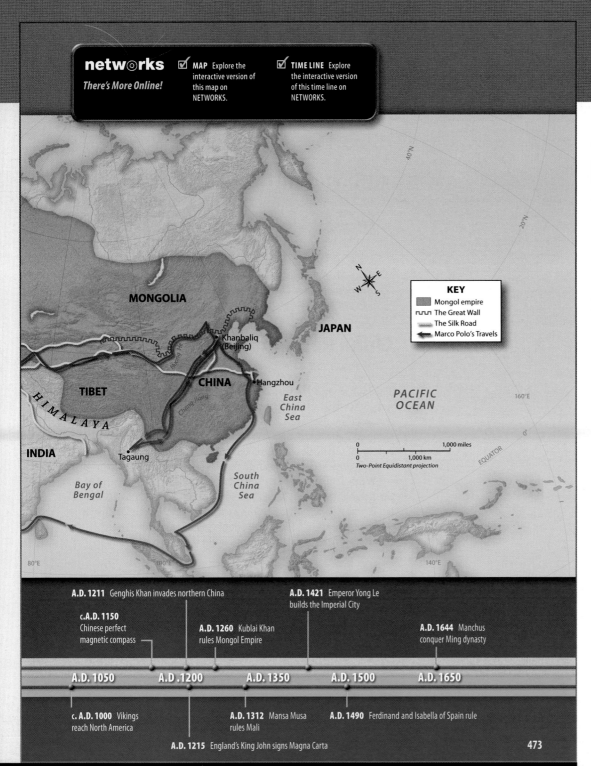

KEY
- Mongol empire
- The Great Wall
- The Silk Road
- Marco Polo's Travels

0 — 1,000 miles
0 — 1,000 km
Two-Point Equidistant projection

c.A.D. 1150 Chinese perfect magnetic compass

A.D. 1211 Genghis Khan invades northern China

A.D. 1260 Kublai Khan rules Mongol Empire

A.D. 1421 Emperor Yong Le builds the Imperial City

A.D. 1644 Manchus conquer Ming dynasty

A.D. 1050 | A.D. 1200 | A.D. 1350 | A.D. 1500 | A.D. 1650

c. A.D. 1000 Vikings reach North America

A.D. 1215 England's King John signs Magna Carta

A.D. 1312 Mansa Musa rules Mali

A.D. 1490 Ferdinand and Isabella of Spain rule

473

CHAPTER 17

Place and Time

Step Into the Time

V2 Visual Skills

Analyzing Time Lines Explain to students that this chapter covers events that took place in China between A.D. 590 and A.D. 1644. Call students' attention to the time line and **ask:** What questions do you have about events that occurred in imperial China? *(Students might wonder why the Grand Canal was important, what the first printed book was about, and so on.)* Write students' questions on the board so they are visible throughout instruction. Ask students to answer the questions as they progress through the chapter. **Visual/Spatial**

Content Background Knowledge

- The magnetic compass was invented almost simultaneously by the Chinese and Europeans during the twelfth century. They discovered that a piece of magnetite, or lodestone, could be placed on a stick and floated in water. It always turned to the north. The compass allowed the Chinese to navigate oceans and explore far from China.
- The Grand Canal was built by a succession of Chinese emperors. It is 1,085 miles long and was built to transport grain to the major cities, and to transport army troops when needed.

CLOSE & REFLECT

Have students review on their own the time line, map, and other material on these two pages. Ask them to write three questions based on these materials that they would like to find answers to as they study this chapter.

TIME LINE

Place and Time: Imperial China A.D. 600 to 1644

Describing By clicking on "More Information," students can read more information about events marked on the time line. Ask students to choose one event to learn more about. Have them do research and then share their findings with the class.

See page 471B for other online activities.

ENGAGE

Bellringer Lead students in a discussion of what China must have been like after centuries of civil war. Help students to understand that China had no centralized government, and many Chinese were struggling to survive because farmlands, canals, and roads were in ruins. Explain that the Sui, Tang, and Song dynasties provided stability and peace in China. Tell students that in this lesson they will be learning about the accomplishments of the Sui, Tang, and Song dynasties and the impact they had on China's land, economy, and population.

TEACH & ASSESS

R Reading Skills

Discussing After students have read the text, discuss with them the state of China during the 300 years that followed the end of the Han dynasty. **Ask:** How did the lack of a central government make China vulnerable to attacks by the nomads? *(Possible answers: The small kingdoms were not sufficiently strong to defend against the attacks. The warlords were rivals who were unwilling to cooperate against an outside threat.)*

ANSWER, p. 474

TAKING NOTES: Sui: unified China, rebuilt Great Wall, built Grand Canal; Tang: civil service exams, expanded China's borders, Buddhism became popular, supported neo-Confucianism; Song: moved capital to Hangzhou, supported neo-Confucianism

networks

There's More Online!

- **BIOGRAPHY** Empress Wu

- **GRAPHIC ORGANIZER** Accomplishments of Three Dynasties

- **MAP**
  - Tang China c. A.D. 700
  - Song China c. A.D. 1200

Lesson 1

China Reunites

ESSENTIAL QUESTION *How does geography influence the way people live?*

IT MATTERS BECAUSE

Ideas and innovations introduced during the Sui, Tang, and Song dynasties united China after centuries of chaos and helped it become a powerful empire.

China Rebuilds Its Empire

GUIDING QUESTION *How did China rebuild its empire after years of war?*

The Han dynasty of China came to an end in A.D. 220. For the next 300 years, China had no central government. The country collapsed into separate kingdoms, and the Chinese people suffered many hardships. Warlords—military leaders who rule local territories—fought each other. Meanwhile, groups of nomads attacked and captured parts of northern China. **R**

While China faced these challenges at home, it lost control of the neighboring lands it had previously conquered. One of these lands was Korea (kuh•REE•uh), located on the Korean Peninsula to the northeast of China. The people of Korea decided to free themselves from Chinese rule and build their own civilization.

The Sui

China eventually became more unified. In A.D. 581, a Chinese general named Wendi (WHEHN•dee) declared himself emperor. He won many battles and set up a new dynasty called the Sui (SWAY). The Sui dynasty again unified China under the rule of emperors.

Reading HELPDESK (CCSS)

Taking Notes: *Identifying*

Use a chart like this one to list important events and accomplishments during each Chinese dynasty. RH.6–8.2

Sui	Tang	Song

Content Vocabulary (Tier 3 Words)
- **neo-Confucianism**

networks ***Online Teaching Options***

VIDEO

Ming Dynasty

Integrating Visual Information Play the video about the Ming dynasty. Explain that this video provides an introduction to the everyday lives of the people and to the architecture of early Chinese civilization. Ask students to write questions as they view the video. Discuss the questions in class.

See page 471C for other online activities.

After Wendi died, his son Yangdi (YAHNG•dee) became emperor. Yangdi wanted to expand China's territory. He tried to regain lost lands. His army fought the Koreans, but it was badly defeated.

Within China, Yangdi had more success at expanding his dynasty. He wanted to bring back the glory of the Han dynasty. Yangdi repaired the Great Wall, which had fallen into ruins. He also rebuilt the magnificent Han capital city of Changan (CHAHNG•AHN).

Yangdi's most ambitious project was building the Grand Canal. This system of waterways connected China's two great rivers, the Huang He (HWAHNG HUH) (Yellow River) and the Chang Jiang (CHAHNG JYAHNG) (Yangtze River). The two rivers flowed east to west and were connected by the Grand Canal, which was built north to south. The Grand Canal made it easier to ship rice and other products between northern and southern China and united China's economy.

To rebuild China, Yangdi required help from the Chinese people. Farmers were forced to work on the Great Wall and the Grand Canal. They had to pay higher taxes to support these projects. Their taxes also paid for the emperor's luxurious way of life, which made the farmers angry. The farmers revolted and Yangdi was killed, bringing an end to the Sui dynasty.

Connections to TODAY

Three Gorges Dam

Construction of China's Three Gorges Dam began in 1994. Like the Grand Canal, the dam has had an effect on the Chinese economy. The dam controls flooding, produces electricity, and allows goods to be shipped inland. However, to create the dam, many towns were flooded. More than a million people lost their homes and farms, and historical and archaeological treasures were lost.

GEOGRAPHY CONNECTION

The Tang dynasty lasted about 300 years.

1. **PLACE** What two cities were connected by the Grand Canal?
2. **CRITICAL THINKING** ***Determining Cause and Effect*** How might these cities have been affected by the building of the Grand Canal?

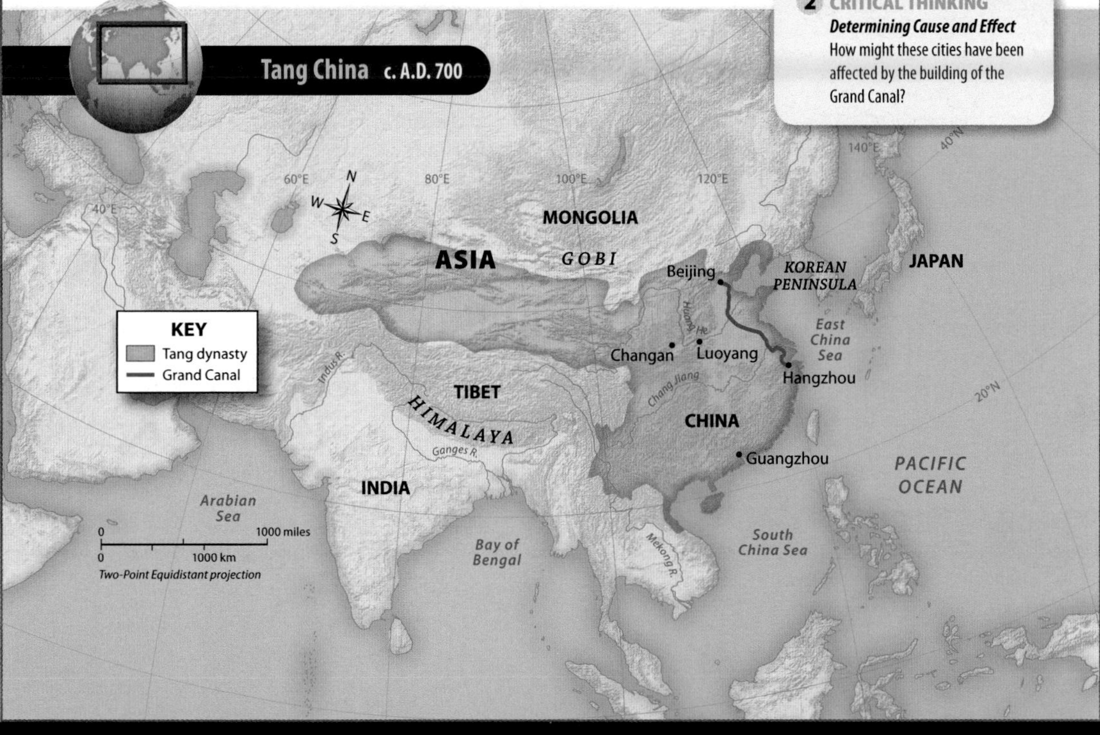

R Reading Skills

Summarizing After students have read the text, discuss the Sui dynasty with the class. **Ask:** **What were the major achievements of this dynasty?** *(It reunited China, rebuilt the Great Wall, and constructed the Grand Canal.)* Point out to students that reconstructing the Great Wall helped protect the empire against the invasion of the nomads that had been troubling northern China during the preceding 300 years. AL

Ask: **What were the benefits of the Grand Canal?** *(It made it easier to ship rice and other products and it united China's economy.)* **Why didn't Yangdi's successes make his subjects happy and proud of his accomplishments?** *(He forced them to work on his projects and taxed them heavily while he enjoyed a life of luxury.)*

T Technology Skills

Making Presentations Ask volunteers to work in pairs or in small groups and do Internet research to learn about what was lost as a result of the Three Gorges Dam. Have them read about the displacement of people, the drowning of towns and cities, and the archaeological treasures covered by the new lake. Have them download pictures and other materials and give a presentation to the class. **Interpersonal**

Making Connections

- The Grand Canal remains a major part of the Chinese transportation system.
- It was widened, deepened, and straightened in the 1950s and 1960s. New locks were added, and 40 more miles of canal were constructed.
- It can handle small ships and medium-size barges over its entire length.

MAP

Tang China c. A.D. 700

Analyzing Maps Have students explore the interactive map of Tang China on their own. Then discuss the geography of the Tang dynasty. Have students use the mileage scale and measure the size of the dynasty's territory. **Ask:** **About how far did it stretch from east to west at its widest point?** *(about 5,300 miles)* **How far did it stretch from north to south at its widest point?** *(about 2,900 miles)* Have students click on the Grand Canal in the key to highlight the canal on the map. **Ask:** **What two cities did it connect?** *(Beijing and Hangzhou)*

See page 471C for other online activities.

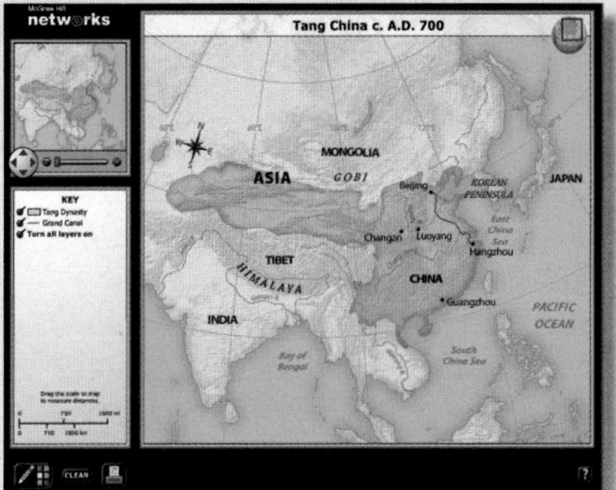

ANSWERS, p. 475

GEOGRAPHY CONNECTION

1. Beijing and Hangzhou
2. **CRITICAL THINKING** These cities could have seen population increases and economic growth.

China Reunites

R1 Reading Skills

Explaining Direct students to read the section titled "The Tang Dynasty." Then, ask for volunteers to explain the accomplishments of the Tang dynasty. **Ask:** How did a strong central government benefit the people? *(Possible answer: It helped ensure peace within the nation and security against outside threats, such as the nomads who had attacked China in previous centuries.)* In what other ways did the Tang rulers make life better for the people? *(They hired government officials based on civil service examinations to help ensure that new hires were competent. They gave land to farmers and brought peace and order.)* Students should cite evidence from the text to support their answers.

R2 Reading Skills

Discussing Ask a volunteer to read aloud the paragraph about the city of Changan in the section titled "Growth and Trade." Lead students in a discussion about the effects of prosperity and economic growth on the city of Changan and on imperial China. Guide students toward understanding that without the improvements to farming and the economy, Changan would not have been a thriving city. AL

Point out that nomad invaders were an ongoing problem for China's rulers through much of the nation's history. As a class, discuss how these invaders helped contribute to the downfall of the Tang dynasty.

BIOGRAPHY

Empress Wu (A.D. 624–705)

Chinese ruler Empress Wu did not come from an upper-class family. As a young woman, she joined the emperor's court, where she used her intelligence to influence important people. Emperor Gaozong (GOW • ZUNG) declared her his empress, and she ruled China in his name during his many illnesses. After the death of Emperor Gaozong, Empress Wu's sons were rulers. In A.D. 690, Empress Wu overthrew her second son. Wu won the respect of the people because of her ability to rule and her determination to make China stronger.

▶ CRITICAL THINKING

Explaining How did Empress Wu gain a great deal of support from the people?

The Tang Dynasty

R1 In A.D. 618, one of Yangdi's generals took over China. He made himself emperor and founded a new dynasty called the Tang (TAHNG). Unlike the short-lived Sui, the Tang dynasty lasted for nearly 300 years—from A.D. 618 to A.D. 907.

Tang rulers worked to **restore** a strong central government in China. They made many reforms, or changes, to improve the government. The most powerful Tang emperor was named Taizong (TY•DZUNG). He brought back the system of **civil** service examinations. Once again, government officials were selected based on how well they did on exams rather than on their family connections. Taizong also gave land to farmers and brought peace and order to the countryside.

During the late A.D. 600s, Empress Wu (WOO) ruled China. She was the only woman in Chinese history to rule the country on her own. Empress Wu was a powerful leader who added more officials to the government and strengthened the military.

Growth and Trade

Tang rulers worked to restore China's power in Asia. They expanded their rule westward to Tibet (tuh•BEHT), an area north of the Himalaya (HIH•muh•LAY•uh). The Chinese also took control of the Silk Road and northern Vietnam. They increased trade with other parts of Asia and forced neighboring states, such as Korea, to pay them tribute.

R2 As trade increased, Chinese cities became wealthy. Changan, the Tang capital, grew to be the world's largest city. About one million people lived there. Visitors were impressed by its wide avenues and large market squares. Merchants in Changan sold goods from places as far away as India and Southwest Asia.

By the mid-A.D. 700s, however, the Tang faced growing challenges to their rule. Turkish nomads drove Tang armies out of central Asia and won control of the Silk Road. Because Chinese merchants could not use the Silk Road safely, trade and the economy suffered.

Revolts by Chinese farmers further weakened the Tang. In response, the Tang rulers hired Uighurs (WEE•GURZ), a Turkish-speaking people in the northwest, to fight for them. However, it was too late. Continued unrest led to the fall of the Tang rule in A.D. 907.

Reading HELPDESK CCSS

Academic Vocabulary (Tier 2 Words)

restore to bring something back to an earlier or better condition

civil relating to the state or government

networks Online Teaching Options

SLIDE SHOW

The Tang Dynasty

Analyzing Images Show students the slide show of Tang art. **Ask:** What do you notice about these artifacts from the Tang dynasty? *(Students might notice the level of detail and the use of color in the artifacts.)* What skills and tools would have been needed to make these artifacts? *(Students might identify the need for precise cutting tools, paintbrushes, and metal stamps. They might also identify skills such as painting, carving, and sculpting.)*

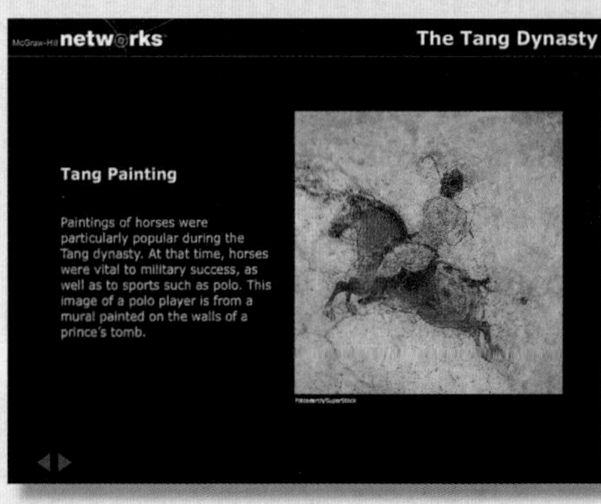

See page 471C for other online activities.

ANSWER, p. 476

CRITICAL THINKING She was an able ruler and was determined to make China stronger.

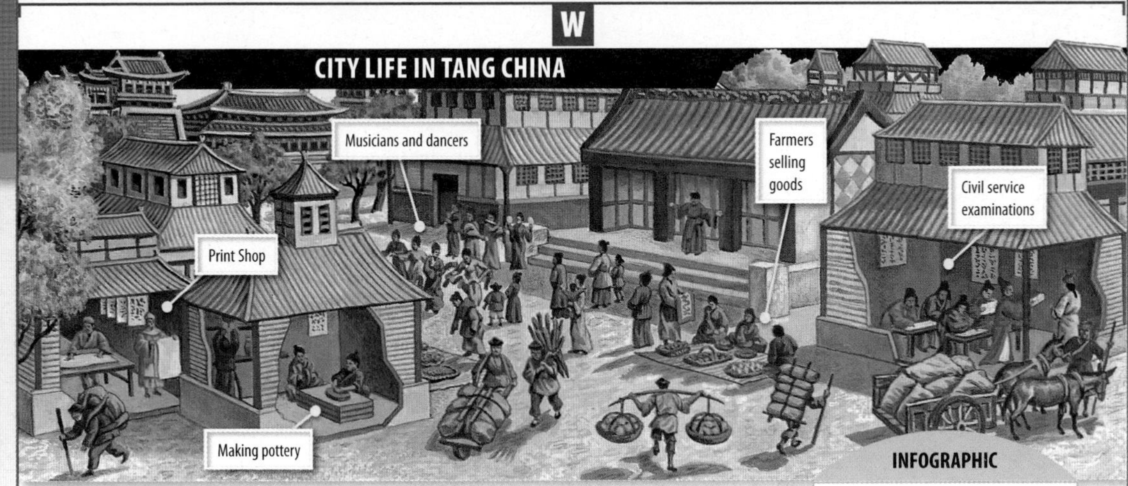

INFOGRAPHIC

Under the Tang, China grew wealthy. Its growing cities contained many shops and temples.

1 **DESCRIBING** What activities took place in the cities of Tang China?

2 **CRITICAL THINKING** ***Explaining*** How does producing a variety of goods make a country stronger?

The Song Dynasty

After the fall of the Tang, military leaders ruled China. Then in A.D. 960, one of the generals became emperor and founded the Song (SUNG) dynasty. The Song governed from A.D. 960 to A.D. 1279. During this time, the Chinese enjoyed economic prosperity and made many cultural achievements.

From the beginning, the Song emperors faced many challenges. They did not have enough military forces to protect their entire empire. In the north, groups of nomads took over parts of the country. For protection, the Song rulers moved their government south to the city of Hangzhou (HAHNG•JOH). Hangzhou was on the coast near the Chang Jiang delta.

R

✓ PROGRESS CHECK

Explaining How did the Grand Canal help China's economy?

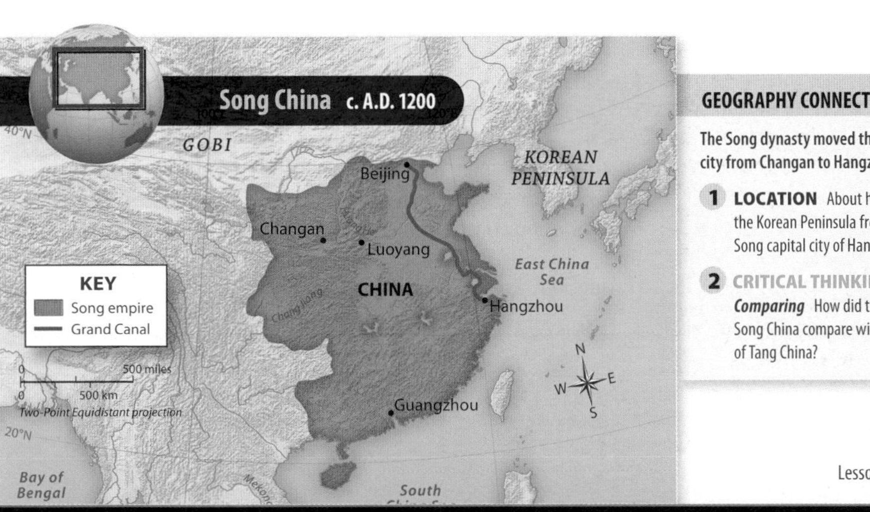

GEOGRAPHY CONNECTION

The Song dynasty moved the capital city from Changan to Hangzhou.

1 **LOCATION** About how far is the Korean Peninsula from the Song capital city of Hangzhou?

2 **CRITICAL THINKING** ***Comparing*** How did the size of Song China compare with the size of Tang China?

MAP

Song China c. A.D. 1200

Analyzing Maps Ask students to explore the map of Song China. Have them turn on all the layers. **Ask:** **What country lies to the north of China?** *(Mongolia)* **How does Song China compare in size to the modern Chinese nation?** *(Modern China is about three times larger than Song China.)* Remind students that nomads were raiding northern Song China and taking over parts of that area. **Ask:** **What nation controls that area today?** *(China)*

See page 471C for other online activities.

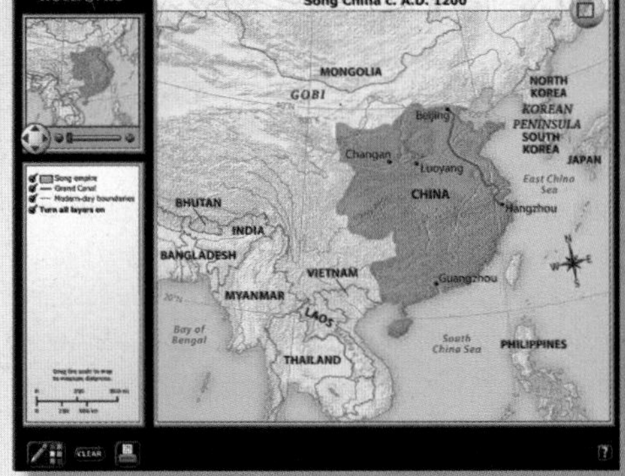

China Reunites

W Writing Skills

Informative/Explanatory Direct students' attention to the illustration of city life in Tang China. **Ask:** **What words describe Changan during the Tang era?** *(busy, thriving, growing, bustling, active)* Then suggest that students think of questions about life in Changan that their textbook does not answer. Prompt students by asking:

- **What kind of houses did people live in?**
- **What foods did they eat?**
- **How did people entertain themselves?**

Have students choose a question to research. Instruct students to take notes so they can write a brief report about their topic. You may choose to have students complete a bibliography to accompany their reports.

After the reports are completed, lead the class in a short discussion. **Ask:** **What was life like in Changan during the Tang dynasty?** *(Answers will vary depending upon student research.)* BL **Verbal/Linguistic**

R Reading Skills

Describing Have a student volunteer read the section aloud. Then, ask for another volunteer to describe life in China during the Song dynasty. **Ask:** **How long did the Song dynasty last?** *(319 years)* Point out that, like previous dynasties, the Song had problems with nomad invaders. **Ask:** **How did the Song respond to these invaders?** *(They moved their capital away from the northern border to Hangzhou.)* AL

ANSWERS, p. 477

INFOGRAPHIC

1. printing, making pottery, selling goods, shopping, test-taking, entertainment
2. **CRITICAL THINKING** Producing a variety of goods makes a country stronger because it will have more goods to sell and it will be better able to survive the loss of a crop or some other struggle.

✓ **PROGRESS CHECK** The Grand Canal connected two important rivers that run east to west. It allowed trade and travelers to move north and south. As a result, China's economy improved because more goods could be sent throughout the Chinese empire.

GEOGRAPHY CONNECTION

1. The Korean Peninsula is about 500 miles (805 km) from Hangzhou.
2. **CRITICAL THINKING** Song China was smaller than Tang China and did not extend as far to the north or west.

R Reading Skills

Discussing Direct students to read the first paragraph on this page. Then, as a class, discuss how Buddhism was brought to China. **Ask:** How would traders have brought Buddhism to China? *(They may not have brought it deliberately, but if they practiced it and talked about it, they would have introduced it.)* BL

Continue the discussion by reviewing the reasons why China was ripe for the teachings of the Buddha. **Ask:** What happened to people when the Han dynasty dissolved? *(The people suffered and died from fighting in the civil war, from hunger, and from lack of shelter.)* How did their sufferings lead them to Buddhism? *(Buddhism taught them that they could find peace and comfort by focusing on the search for truth and by giving up a desire for material things.)*

C Critical Thinking Skills

Speculating Discuss the response of the Tang dynasty to the practice of Buddhism. **Ask:** How did the Tang dynasty respond to Buddhism at first? *(They accepted it and allowed the building of temples and shrines.)* Why do you think the early Tang rulers did not oppose Buddhism? *(Answers will vary. Students may suggest that the country was just recovering from civil war and that the leaders may have thought Buddhism might bring calm and peace to the country.)*

Now guide a discussion of the Tang rulers' later reaction to Buddhism. **Ask:** Why did the Tang rulers later turn against Buddhism? *(They saw it as a threat; the monasteries were becoming very rich; many people may have become less willing to work, to support government projects, and to increase trade because they no longer believed in materialism.)*

ANSWER, p. 478

Reading Strategy At first, Tang rulers tolerated Buddhism. Later, they came to fear Buddhist influences so they destroyed Buddhist temples and shrines.

Buddhism in China

GUIDING QUESTION *Why did Buddhism become popular in Tang China?*

R Traders and missionaries from India brought Buddhism to China during the A.D. 100s. At the time, the Han dynasty was in decline, and civil war soon broke out in China. Many people died from the fighting, hunger, and lack of shelter. Buddhism taught that people could escape suffering by following its teachings. As a result, many Chinese seeking peace and comfort became Buddhists.

How Did Tang Rulers View Buddhism?

Early Tang rulers did not practice Buddhism, but they did not interfere with its following in China. They approved the building of new Buddhist temples and shrines.

Many Chinese Buddhists joined religious communities called monasteries, where they lived, worked, and worshipped. The men in these communities were monks, and the women were nuns. Buddhist monks and nuns helped local people by running schools and providing food and shelter for travelers. Monks also served as bankers and provided medical care.

C Although numerous Chinese became Buddhists, a large part of the population opposed the religion. Many believed that Buddhist temples and monasteries had grown too wealthy because of the donations they received. Others believed that monks and nuns weakened respect for family life because they were not allowed to marry.

Tang officials feared Buddhism's growing influence. They saw Buddhism as an enemy of China's Confucian (kuhn•FYOO•shuhn) traditions. Confucian traditions are customs related to the teachings of Confucius. In A.D. 845, the Tang government destroyed many Buddhist monasteries and temples. Buddhism in China never fully recovered from these attacks.

Buddhism in Korea

Korea broke free of Chinese rule when the Han dynasty fell in A.D. 220. For several hundred years afterward, Korea was divided into three distinct kingdoms.

In the A.D. 300s, Chinese Buddhists brought their religion to Korea. About A.D. 660, the three Korean kingdoms united to form one country. Because the new Korean government favored Buddhism, the religion attracted a large number of followers throughout Korea.

Reading HELPDESK CCSS

Reading Strategy: *Summarizing*

When you summarize, you restate important ideas in your own words. Read about how Tang rulers viewed Buddhism. On a separate sheet of paper, summarize what you read in one or two sentences.

networks Online Teaching Options

LECTURE SLIDE

Buddhism in China

Identifying Points of View Remind students that Buddhism teaches that the way to find truth is to give up all desires for things, such as fame and money. **Ask:** Why did many Chinese become Buddhists? *(Many had suffered during the civil wars. They wanted a religion that would help ease their suffering.)* Why do you think the Tang rulers at first encouraged the spread of Buddhism? *(It provided people with comfort.)* Why did China's rulers change their minds about Buddhism? *(They saw it as a threat to Chinese traditions.)* AL

networks — Buddhism in China

Buddhism:

- Teaches that the way to find truth is to give up all desires for things
- Brought to China by traders and missionaries
- Attracted many Chinese seeking comfort and peace
- Spread throughout China; many rulers feared Buddhism's growing influence and worried that Chinese traditions and customs would be lost.

See page 471C for other online activities.

Buddhism later spread from Korea to the nearby islands of Japan. In A.D. 552, a Korean king sent missionaries to the emperor of Japan. The missionaries brought Buddhist writings and a statue of the Buddha. They also brought a letter from the king meant to influence the emperor of Japan. As time passed, many people in Japan became Buddhists.

In a letter to the emperor, the Korean king wrote about Buddhism and its teachings:

PRIMARY SOURCE

> “This religion is the most excellent of all teachings. . . . It brings endless and immeasurable [countless] blessings . . . , even the attainment [achieving] of supreme enlightenment. . . . Moreover, the religion has come over to Korea far from India, and the peoples (in the countries between these two) are now ardent [eager] followers of its teaching.”
>
> —from *Nihonji* (Chronicles of Japan)

R

✓ PROGRESS CHECK

Describing How did Buddhist monks and nuns help the Chinese?

Ira Kirschenbaum/Stock Boston

This towering monument to the Buddha was carved in about A.D. 460 in the Yuan Kang caves of China.

▶ **CRITICAL THINKING**

Identifying Points of View Why might Buddhism appeal to people who had just experienced a civil war?

CHAPTER 17, Lesson 1
China Reunites

R Reading Skills

Explaining After students have read the text, explain the spread of Buddhism to Japan. **Ask: How did Buddhism arrive in Japan?** *(The Korean king sent missionaries to the Japanese empire.)* **What did the missionaries bring with them?** *(a statue of the Buddha and a letter to persuade the Japanese emperor of the benefits of Buddhism)* AL

V Visual Skills

Analyzing Images Tell students that this colossal Buddha statue is but one of many at this cave complex. Direct them to look at it carefully. **Ask: How tall do you think this statue is?** *(at least 55 feet)* **What do base your guess on?** *(The man sitting to the right of the statue is about five feet tall. The statue is at least ten times taller than he is.)* **What can you conclude about Buddhism in China by looking at this picture?** *(People must have been strong believers and the Buddhists must have had extraordinary wealth to be able to build such a place.)* BL **Visual/Spatial Logical/Mathematical**

V

Content Background Knowledge

- The Yuan Kang caves site extends for about one kilometer (two-thirds of a mile).
- There are 252 caves containing 51,000 statues.
- The site includes 20 large cave temples and many smaller ones.
- There are numerous massive figures of the Buddha, some measuring up to 55 feet tall.
- The caves were excavated by hand from a ridge of soft sandstone.
- The caves were designated a UNESCO World Heritage Site in 2001.

GRAPH

Buddhists Around the World

Analyze Graphs Have students view the empty graph. **Ask: Where are most of these countries located?** *(southeast Asia)* Guide a discussion of the text at the top of the graph. Have students click on the arrow to populate the graph. When they finish analyzing the data, **ask: Which two countries have the largest percentages of Buddhists?** *(Burma and Thailand)* Which two countries have the lowest percentages? *(the U.S. and Australia)* **What percentage of the Chinese practice Buddhism?** *(8.4 percent)*

See page 471C for other online activities.

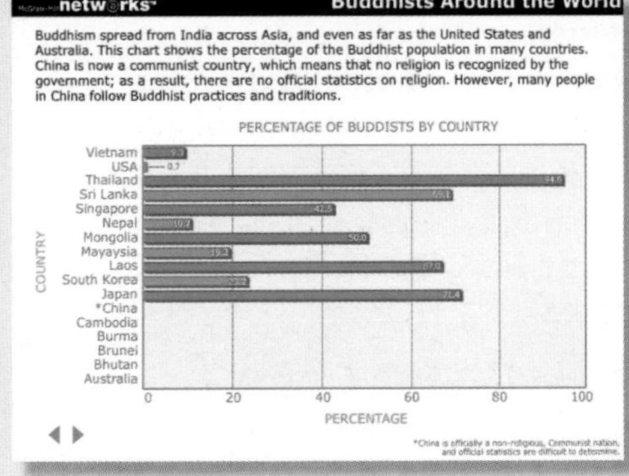

ANSWERS, p. 479

✓ PROGRESS CHECK Buddhist monks and nuns ran schools and provided food and shelter for travelers. The monks served as bankers and provided medical care.

CRITICAL THINKING Answers may vary. Possible answer: Buddhism offers a potential path to peace and truth, which people who had survived a civil war might find appealing.

R1 Reading Skills

Identifying Have students review the section about Confucian ideas and talk about the role Confucianism played in Chinese government. Then **ask:** **Why did Confucianism go into decline after the fall of the Han dynasty?** *(Without a central government to give civil service examinations, Confucianism lost influence and importance.)*

C Critical Thinking Skills

Drawing Conclusions Explain to students that Confucianism and Buddhism are very different. Buddhism teaches that people should give up their desire for worldly possessions while Confucianism teaches that people should be concerned about this life as well as the afterlife. **Ask:** **Why would the Chinese rulers have preferred that their people practice Confucianism over Buddhism?** *(People who practiced Confucianism would be more likely to work hard and to take an active role in society.)*

R2 Reading Skills

Paraphrasing Ask a volunteer to read the primary-source quotation aloud and discuss its meaning with the class. Then have students paraphrase the quotation and write their responses on the board. As a class, select the best paraphrase and have students copy it in their notebooks. AL ELL

Revival of Confucian Ideas

GUIDING QUESTION *How did Confucian ideas shape China's government?*

Confucius believed that a good government depended on having wise leaders. The civil service examinations begun by Han rulers were based on Confucian **principles.** The exams helped provide China's government with well-educated, talented officials.

After the fall of the Han dynasty, China had no central government to give civil service examinations. Confucianism went into decline, and Buddhism won many followers with its message of escape from suffering. Tang and Song rulers worked to return Confucianism to the respected position it had held previously in Chinese society.

Neo-Confucianism

The Tang and Song dynasties backed a new understanding of Confucianism called **neo-Confucianism** (NEE•oh-kuhn•FYOO•shuhn•ih•zuhm). One reason this new Confucianism was created was to stop the growing influence of Buddhism. Neo-Confucianism taught that people should be concerned about this world as well as the afterlife. Followers were expected to be active in society and to help others. A Confucian thinker named Han Yü (HAHN YOO) lived from A.D. 768 to A.D. 824. He encouraged the Chinese to remain faithful to the Confucian teachings of their ancestors:

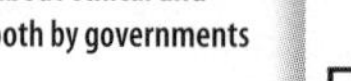

Confucius wrote about ethical and moral behavior, both by governments and individuals.

PRIMARY SOURCE

> “What were the teachings of our ancient kings? Universal love is called humanity. To practice this in the proper manner is called righteousness. To proceed according to these is called the Way. . . . They [ancestors] offered sacrifices to Heaven and the gods came to receive them. . . . What Way is this? I say: This is what I call the Way, and not what the Taoists [Daoists] and the Buddhists called the Way.”
>
> —from *An Inquiry on The Way*, by Han Yü

This new form of Confucianism also included some Buddhist and Daoist beliefs. Chinese culture was developing and changing at this time. For many Chinese, Confucianism became more than a set of rules for good behavior. It became

Reading HELPDESK (CCSS)

neo-Confucianism a new form of the ideas of the philosopher Confucius; included Buddhist and Daoist beliefs

Academic Vocabulary (Tier 2 Words)

principle a basic truth or belief

networks Online Teaching Options

GAME

True or False Game: Dynasties, Buddhism, and Confucianism

Summarizing Guide a review of the chapter. Then ask students to play the game. Challenge them to play against the clock. After students play, review the answers as a class.

See page 471C for other online activities.

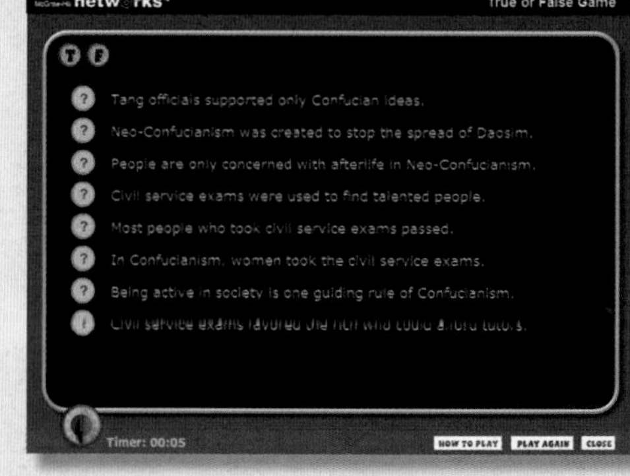

a religious tradition with beliefs about the spiritual world. Confucian thinkers taught that people would find peace of mind if they followed the teachings of Confucius.

The Civil Service

Tang and Song rulers saw neo-Confucianism and civil service examinations as a way to strengthen the government. They believed that a government run by educated people was less likely to become corrupt or weak.

The examinations tested candidates on their knowledge of Confucian writings. Only men were allowed to take the tests, and the examination system favored the rich. Few poor families could pay tutors to help their sons qualify for the tests.

Preparing for the tests was very difficult. At the age of four, boys began learning to write the characters of the Chinese language. Later, students had to memorize all the writings of Confucius. They had to recite the writings aloud. After years of preparing, the boys took the exams. Despite all the hard work, only one in five boys passed the tests. Those who did not pass usually found jobs teaching or helping government workers, but they were never given a government job. C

Over the years, the examination system created a new class of leaders in China. This group was made up of scholar-officials. Strict rules set the scholar-officials apart from the rest of society. One rule was that the scholar-officials could not perform any job that required physical work. These scholar-officials influenced Chinese thought and government well into modern times.

Connections to TODAY

Civil Service Examinations

As in imperial China, most people who apply for government jobs in the United States must take a civil service examination. Before the late 1800s, most government posts in the U.S. were appointed. Many people were placed in important jobs because of their political connections.

✓ **PROGRESS CHECK**

Determining Cause and Effect How did the civil service examinations affect Chinese society?

LESSON 1 REVIEW 

Review Vocabulary (Tier 3 Words)

1. How was *neo-Confucianism* different from Confucianism? RH.6–8.2, RH.6–8.4

Answer the Guiding Questions

2. ***Describing*** What actions did the emperors of the Sui and Tang dynasty take to unify China? RH.6–8.2
3. ***Identifying*** How did Chinese farmers react to the changes made during the Sui and Tang dynasties? RH.6–8.2
4. ***Explaining*** Why did Buddhism become widely adopted in China? RH.6–8.2
5. ***Comparaing and Contrasting*** How is Buddhism different from neo-Confucianism? RH.6–8.4
6. **ARGUMENT** You are a young Chinese man who has just passed the civil service examination. You will be given a government job. What opinion are you likely to have about neo-Confucianism? Write a short persuasive letter in which you explain how neo-Confucianism will help or hurt your career. WHST.6–8.1, WHST.6–8.10

C Critical Thinking Skills

Evaluating Discuss the civil service examinations during the Tang and Song dynasties. **Ask:** What did candidates have to go through to become civil servants? *(They had to learn to write the characters of the Chinese language, memorize all the writings of Confucius, and recite the writings aloud.)* Do you think the civil service examinations were a good way to find candidates for important positions? Why or why not? *(Students might point out that the exams did a good job of identifying those who were intelligent, educated, and willing to work hard to study Confucian principles carefully.)* BL

Have students complete the Lesson 1 Review.

CLOSE & REFLECT

Ask students to draw connections between themselves and the young imperial Chinese who studied for the civil service examinations. Have volunteers explain why they would or would not want to take the civil service examinations. Leave students with the impression that passing the examinations was probably the most important act in a young Chinese man's life. Ask students to identify equally important events in a young person's life today.

ANSWER, p. 481

✓ **PROGRESS CHECK** Tang and Song rulers used civil service examinations as the basis for hiring officials. The examinations evaluated a candidate's talent, not his social status. However, only the rich could afford to hire tutors to help their sons pass the exams.

LESSON 1 REVIEW ANSWERS

1. Neo-Confucianism added ideas from Buddhism and Daoism to the ideas of Confucius. Confucianism included only the ideas of Confucius.
2. The Sui emperors rebuilt the Great Wall and had the Grand Canal built to increase trade. The Tang emperors restored a strong central government and brought back civil service examinations. They also strengthened China's military forces.
3. Farmers were often angry about how they and their land were treated. Under the Sui, farmers grew angry about heavy taxes and having to build the Grand Canal. Under the Tang, farmers' revolts helped erode the power of the Tang dynasty.
4. Buddhism taught that people could escape suffering, and during hard times, many Chinese adopted the belief. The Chinese government allowed the spread of Buddhism because Buddhist monks and nuns helped the poor and served society as teachers, bankers, and doctors.
5. Buddhism is about following steps to escape suffering in this world. Followers of Neo-Confucianism believe it is important to be concerned about this world and to work to improve society and to help others.
6. Students' letters should be written from the point of view of a young Chinese man who has just passed the civil service exams. Letters should express and support an opinion about whether Confucianism will help or hurt a career in the civil service.

ENGAGE

Bellringer Have students consider the characteristics of these inventions: steel, movable type, gunpowder, paper money, and the navigational compass. Then have students meet with a partner to brainstorm what the inventions have in common. Explain that all the inventions were developed in China during the imperial period.

Tell students that in this lesson, they will learn how China's economy changed under the Tang dynasty and how important inventions were developed. They will also discover why the Tang and Song dynasties were a golden age of the arts, as well as a time of important economic growth and technological advances.

TEACH & ASSESS

R Reading Skills

Explaining Direct students to read the section on economic growth. Then, explain how farmers were affected by the fall of the Han dynasty and how conditions improved when the Tang rulers came to power. **Ask:** **Why did farming improve under the Tang dynasty?** *(The Tang rulers gave the farmers more land. The farmers made advances in farming, such as improving irrigation methods and developing new varieties of rice.)* **How did the availability of more food change China?** *(The population grew. The people settled in new areas. Groups of farmers moved from north to south.)* Encourage students to support their answers with evidence from the text. AL

networks *There's More Online!*

- GRAPHIC ORGANIZER Chinese Advancements
- SLIDE SHOW Silk-making

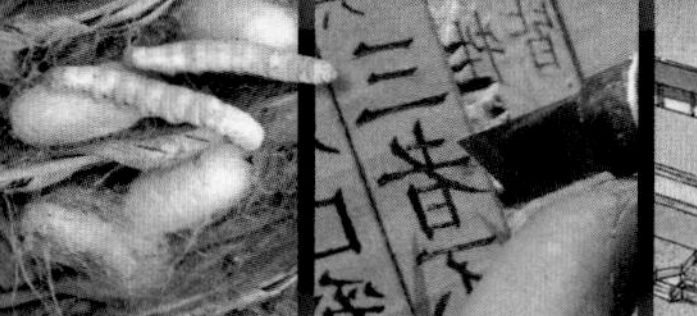

Lesson 2

Chinese Society

ESSENTIAL QUESTION *How do new ideas change the way people live?*

IT MATTERS BECAUSE

During the Tang and Song dynasties, the economy of China grew through trade and improvements in technology.

Economic Growth

GUIDING QUESTION *How did China's economy change under the Tang and Song dynasties?*

The fall of the Han dynasty in the A.D. 200s crippled the economy of China. Widespread fighting destroyed farms and cities. Farmers faced poor harvests. Artisans made fewer products, and merchants had fewer goods to trade. Under the Tang dynasty, China's economy recovered and even prospered.

Farming Improvements

R After taking power in A.D. 618, the Tang gave more land to farmers. Farmers made many advances in farming these large land plots. They improved irrigation methods, which increased the growth of their crops. They developed new kinds of rice that grew well in poor soil. The new varieties of rice produced more rice per acre and resisted disease. Farmers also began to grow tea, which became a popular drink.

Because more food was available, China's population increased as well. People began to settle in new areas, which then developed into cities. Groups of farmers moved from the north to southern China. They grew abundant amounts of rice in the Chang Jiang valley.

Reading **HELP**DESK (CCSS)

Taking Notes: *Categorizing* RH.6–8.2

Use a graphic organizer like the one here to identify Chinese advancements in the economy, technology, and the arts.

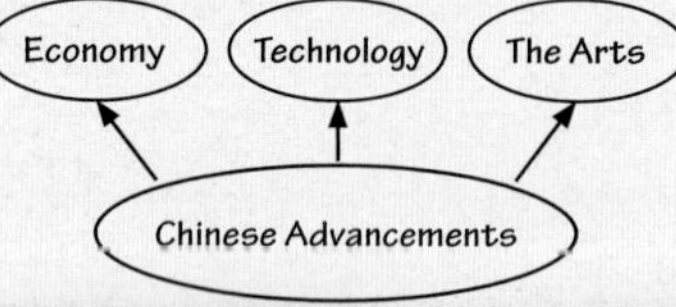

Content Vocabulary (Tier 3 Words)

- **porcelain**
- **calligraphy**

networks ***Online Teaching Options***

VIDEO

Chinese History From the Grand Canal Waterway to Marco Polo

Describing Explain to students that this video provides an overview of the growth of Chinese civilization from the time of the building of the Grand Canal in the A.D. 600s until the visit of Marco Polo around A.D. 1300. After students view the video, guide a discussion of how important developments of this period contributed to China's civilization.

See page 471D for other online activities.

ANSWER, p. 482

TAKING NOTES: Economy: new kinds of rice, greater crop yields, increased trade on new roads and waterways, paper money; Technology: steel, woodblock printing, movable type, gunpowder, ships, magnetic compass; The Arts: poetry, landscape painting, porcelain

Why Did China's Trade Grow?

Tang rulers built roads and waterways. As a result, travel within and outside of China became much easier. Chinese merchants increased trade with people in other parts of the world. After years of decline, the Silk Road reopened and thrived. Caravans traveled along it, carrying goods from China to other parts of Asia.

R Silk fabric was one of the goods traded by the Chinese. Silk was in high demand in areas west of China. In addition, China traded other products, such as tea, steel, paper, and porcelain. **Porcelain** (POHR•suh•luhn) is made of fine clay that is baked at high temperatures. It is used to make dishes, vases, and other items. In return for Chinese products, countries sent goods such as gold, silver, precious stones, and fine woods to China.

Other trade routes were also opened. Roads connected China to other parts of Asia. In addition, the Tang opened new seaports along China's coast to increase trade.

✔ PROGRESS CHECK

Determining Cause and Effect How did advancements in farming affect China's population?

Silk worms spin cocoons made of raw silk thread. Workers then collect and unravel the valuable cocoons by hand.

▶ CRITICAL THINKING

Making Inferences Why do you think silk is still expensive today?

Technological Advances

GUIDING QUESTION *How did new inventions change China's society?*

During the Tang and Song dynasties, new discoveries and inventions brought change to Chinese society. In time, these technological advancements spread to other parts of the world.

Coal and Steel

C Important changes took place in the use of fuels and metals. For most of their history, the Chinese burned wood to heat their homes and cook their food. By the A.D. 600s, less wood was available in China. The Chinese, however, discovered that coal could be used as a fuel. This discovery led to the development of a coal-mining industry.

porcelain a ceramic made of fine clay baked at very high temperatures

R Reading Skills

Listing After students have read the text, guide a discussion about the growth of trade in China. **Ask:** What did the Tang rulers do to stimulate an increase in trade? *(They built roads and waterways.)* Discuss how these improvements increased trade. **Ask:** What kinds of goods did China export using the Silk Road? *(silk, tea, steel, paper, porcelain)* What kinds of goods were brought into China? *(gold, silver, precious stones, fine woods)* AL

C Critical Thinking Skills

Hypothesizing Encourage students to talk about how technological advances made in one country get carried to other parts of the world. Guide students to understand that people everywhere are always looking for better ways of doing things and for ways to improve their lives. BL

Talk about the importance of coal. **Ask:** How is it possible that China began to run out of wood? *(China had a large population. Since everyone used wood for cooking and heating their homes, the available trees were rapidly used up.)*

Making Connections

Explain to students that technological advances have always brought change and, usually, improvement to people's lives. Point out how in the last 50 years some important advances have occurred in our society: cell phones, computers, the World Wide Web, advanced treatments for diseases such as cancer, DNA sequencing, and so on. Invite students to add to the list. Encourage students to discuss how these advances have changed our lives.

SLIDE SHOW

Silk-Making

Analyzing Visuals Have students view the slide show. They can see more images and read a description of the silk-making process by clicking on the arrow. After students view the slide show, lead a discussion of the process. Challenge students to summarize the process. Ask them to describe silk garments or other silk items they have seen.

See page 471D for other online activities.

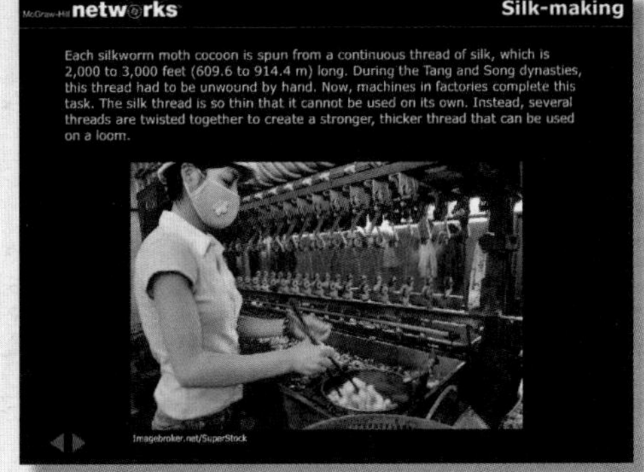

McGraw-Hill networks
Silk-making
Each silkworm moth cocoon is spun from a continuous thread of silk, which is 2,000 to 3,000 feet (609.6 to 914.4 m) long. During the Tang and Song dynasties, this thread had to be unwound by hand. Now, machines in factories complete this task. The silk thread is so thin that it cannot be used on its own. Instead, several threads are twisted together to create a stronger, thicker thread that can be used on a loom.

ANSWERS, p. 483

CRITICAL THINKING Answers may vary. Possible answers: Silk is so delicate that the process cannot be done by machines; silk is still expensive today because it is produced only by silkworms and is often still made by hand.

✔ PROGRESS CHECK Farming advances led to larger crop yields. With more food available, China's population grew.

C Critical Thinking Skills

Making Inferences Discuss the kinds of products that the Chinese were able to make out of steel. **Ask:** **How did the new steel armor, swords, and helmets change China?** *(Steel weapons would have been more deadly and steel helmets and armor would have protected soldiers better, giving Chinese armies an advantage over their enemies.)* **How did steel stoves, farm tools, drills, nails, and sewing needles change people's lives?** *(People could live more comfortably, build stronger homes, and farm faster and more easily.)*

R Reading Skills

Describing Have students read the section titled "The Invention of Printing." As a class, discuss the invention of printing and its effects on civilization. Ask a volunteer to describe how books were first created. *(each book was copied by hand)* **Ask:** **How were woodblock books produced?** *(Answers will vary, but students should understand that an entire page was carved onto a block of wood)* Have students compare woodblock printing with movable-type printing. Discuss the advantages of movable type. AL

The Chinese used coal to heat furnaces to high temperatures. This process led to another discovery. When iron was produced in coal-heated furnaces, the melted iron mixed with carbon from the coal. This mixing created a new, stronger metal known today as steel.

The Chinese used steel to make many different products. They made armor, swords, and helmets for their armies. They also produced stoves, farm tools, and drills. Nails and sewing needles were made from steel as well. C

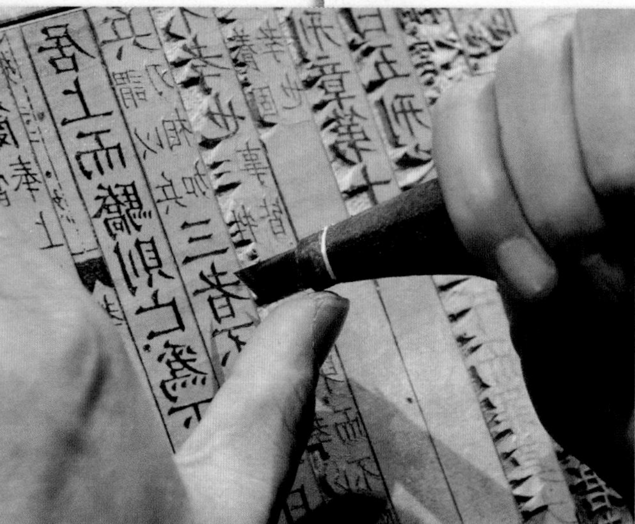

The Chinese invented movable type. It was necessary to carve individual symbols that could be moved and set into a printing press. Printing presses still use techniques pioneered by the Chinese.

▶ CRITICAL THINKING
Speculating What physical skill would a block printer need to have?

AFP/Getty Images

The Invention of Printing

Paper had been invented during the time of the Han dynasty. Under the Tang, paper was produced in large amounts.

The manufacture of paper led to another important Chinese invention: a **method** for printing books. Before printing, books were copied by hand and were very expensive.

Chinese Buddhist monks began woodblock printing in the A.D. 600s. In woodblock printing, printers used a wooden block for each page they needed to print. They carved the page's Chinese characters into the block. Then they put ink on the block and pressed a piece of paper onto it. The printers rubbed the sheet of paper to **transfer** the Chinese characters onto the page. Each wooden block could be used to make thousands of copies. R

The earliest known printed book dates from about A.D. 868. It is a Buddhist book called the *Diamond Sutra*. Even though woodblock printing was a major advancement, changes could not be made to a page once the wooden block was carved.

In the A.D. 1000s, a Chinese printer named Pi Sheng (PEE SHUHNG) solved this printing problem by inventing movable type. With movable type, each character is an individual piece. The pieces can be arranged to form sentences and used again and again. Pi Sheng made his pieces from clay and put them together to make book pages.

Reading HELPDESK CCSS

Academic Vocabulary (Tier 2 Words)
method a way of doing something
transfer to copy from one surface to another by contact

networks Online Teaching Options

IMAGE

Movable Type

Analyzing Visuals Have students view the interactive image. They can advance the text to read more about movable type by scrolling down. **Ask:** **How did woodblock printing affect life in China?** *(It made the printing of books easier, so ideas and information could spread throughout China.)*

See page 471D for other online activities.

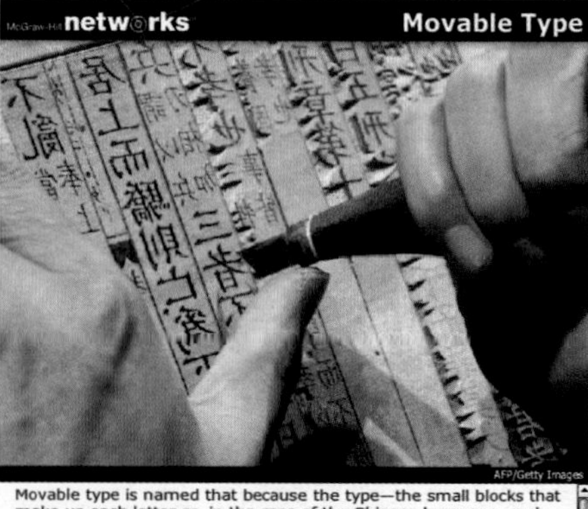

networks
Movable Type
AFP/Getty Images
Movable type is named that because the type—the small blocks that make up each letter or, in the case of the Chinese language, each word—is movable and reusable. Because the first movable type was made of clay, the pieces did not last long. Later, Chinese type was

ANSWER, p. 484

CRITICAL THINKING Sample answer: A block printer would need to be able to carve wood.

Printing also led to the invention of paper currency. During the Tang dynasty, both rice production and trade greatly increased. Chinese traders needed more money to carry out business. The Chinese already produced copper coins, but they could not make enough coins to support the empire's economy.

In A.D. 1024, during the Song dynasty, the Chinese began to print the world's first paper money as a way to benefit traders. It still had the value of coin money, and it was lighter to carry. The use of paper money helped both the economy and cities to grow.

Gunpowder and Ships

Gunpowder was another Chinese invention created during the Tang dynasty. Gunpowder was used in explosives and weapons, such as the fire lance. This invention worked somewhat like a gun. It could shoot a mix of flames and objects a distance of 40 yards (36.6 m). The fire lance helped make China's army a powerful fighting force. The Chinese also used gunpowder to make fireworks.

Different Chinese inventions helped increase long-distance trade. The Chinese built large ships with rudders and sails, which helped with steering. About A.D. 1150, Chinese inventors perfected the magnetic compass. This compass helped Chinese sailors navigate their ships' locations and sail farther from land. As a result of these inventions, the Chinese were able to sail to Southeast Asia, India, and other places to the west.

Thinking Like a **HISTORIAN**

Drawing Conclusions

Historians have concluded that technological developments expanded China's power during the Tang dynasty. Identify one technological advancement of the Tang dynasty. Then draw a conclusion about how the advancement affected China's economy, culture, or government. Share your conclusions with the class. For more information about drawing conclusions, read *What Does a Historian Do?*

The Tang capital city of Changan had a population of about one million people at its peak. The royal palace, shown below, was surrounded by park lands. It is thought to be one of the largest palaces ever built.

Chinese Society

W Writing Skills

Informative/Explanatory Have students work in pairs and assign each pair one of the technologies discussed on this page: paper currency, ships, or gunpowder. Ask students to write two or three sentences summarizing the technology.

Ask three volunteer pairs—one for each of the three technologies—to write their summary on the board as you prepare to discuss each technology.

C Critical Thinking Skills

Determining Cause and Effect Discuss the inventions of paper currency, gunpowder, and large ships with rudders and sails. Ask students to think about the effects each technology had on life in China. **Ask:**

- **Why was the invention of paper currency important?** *(It could be easily carried, and it encouraged trade and helped the economy and cities grow.)*
- **Why was gunpowder an important invention?** *(It transformed the way wars were fought and gave the army more power.)*
- **What effect did improvements in shipbuilding and navigation have in China?** *(These improvements enabled Chinese ships to travel overseas for trade and exploration.)* AL

Content Background Knowledge

How Gunpowder Works Gunpowder consists of saltpeter (or potassium nitrate), sulfur, and carbon. Saltpeter makes up about 75 percent of the mixture. It produces oxygen when lit. Oxygen is needed to fuel fire. The sulfur and carbon are combustible. Together, the ingredients in gunpowder create enough of a contained explosion to quickly propel shot from a gun barrel. Future improvements made gunpowder and firearms more efficient, but the basic formula developed by the Chinese is still effective.

WORKSHEET

Economics of History Activity: Imperial China: Chinese Society

Analyzing Information Help students understand the impact of printed paper money on the Chinese economy by having students read and complete the Economics of History Activity as homework for this lesson.

See page 471D for other online activities.

Economics of History Activity — networks
Imperial China
Lesson 2 *Chinese Society*
Chinese Currency
Background Information

Chinese Society

C1 Critical Thinking Skills

Determining Cause and Effect Discuss the golden age of Chinese culture. Encourage students to talk about what this means. **Ask:** **What role did Chinese rulers play in promoting this golden age?** *(They supported the artists and writers.)* Invite students to consider whether or how the arts would have succeeded without the support of the rulers. Then **ask:** **How did woodblock printing help to make literature popular?** *(Books could be printed more quickly and cheaply, so there were both more of them and more people who could afford them.)*

R Reading Skills

Identifying After students have read the text, discuss the poetry of China. **Ask:** **What were the major themes that poets wrote about?** *(the beauty of nature, the changes of the seasons, the joys of friendship, and the shortness of life)* AL

C2 Critical Thinking Skills

Analyzing Primary Sources Read the Li Bo poem aloud to students and discuss its meaning. Point out that the poem does not provide a lot of details about the scene it describes. Instead, it says very little but creates a strong impression through well-chosen words that create the outline of an idea that readers or listeners can fill in.

In time, many of these Chinese inventions would have a great effect on Europe. For example, printing made it possible to publish books in large quantities. Gunpowder changed how wars were fought. The magnetic compass enabled Europeans to explore the world.

✓ PROGRESS CHECK

Analyzing Why was the Chinese invention of printing important?

Literature and the Arts

GUIDING QUESTION ***Why were the Tang and Song dynasties a golden age of literature and the arts?***

The Tang and Song dynasties were a golden age of Chinese culture. The invention of woodblock printing helped make literature more available and popular. Art, especially landscape painting, flourished during this period. Chinese rulers supported artists and writers. They invited them to live and work in the capital city of Changan. C1

According to legend, Li Bo drowned after reaching for the moon's reflection in the water beside his boat. He most likely died, poor and out of favor, in eastern China.

An Age of Poetry

The Tang dynasty is regarded as the great age of poetry in China. The best known Chinese writers of this time are poets. Chinese poets often expressed a Daoist appreciation of the world. They wrote about the beauty of nature, the changes of the seasons, and the joys of friendship. They also expressed sadness at the shortness of life. R

Li Bo (LEE BWAW) was one of the most popular poets of the Tang dynasty. Known for leading a carefree life, Li Bo wrote poems about nature. His poem below is one of the best-known poems in China. For years, the Chinese have memorized it. Its title is "Alone Looking at the Mountain."

PRIMARY SOURCE C2

"All the birds have flown up and gone;
A lonely cloud floats leisurely by.
We never tire of looking at each other—
Only the mountain and I."

—from "Alone Looking at the Mountain," by Li Bo

Reading HELPDESK (CCSS)

calligraphy artistic handwriting

networks *Online Teaching Options*

PRIMARY SOURCE

The Poems of Li Bo

Expressing Read the poems aloud in an expressive voice. Then ask students to respond to your reading orally or in a quick-write. Have volunteers share their responses. **Ask:** **What did you feel as you listened to the poems? What did you picture in your mind as I read the poems aloud?** AL

See page 471D for other online activities.

networks
The Poems of Li Bo
ANALYZING PRIMARY SOURCES
Here are two of Li Bo's most famous poems.
The Art Archive/British Library
"Listening to a Flute in Yellow Crane Pavilion
I came here a wanderer thinking of home, remembering my faraway Ch'ang-an.
And then, from deep in Yellow Crane Pavilion, I heard a beautiful bamboo flute
It was late summer in a city by a river.
Song of the Forge
The forge-fire sets a glow in,"
—from "Listening to a Flute in Yellow Crane Pavilion" & "Song of the Forge", by Li Bo
Source: http://www.cscs.umich.edu/~crshalizi/Poetry/Li_Po/

ANSWER, p. 486

✓ PROGRESS CHECK The printing process made books readily available, which meant ideas could spread throughout China. The printing of paper money helped support China's growing economy.

Another favorite Tang poet was Du Fu (DOO FOO). He was a poor civil servant who faced many hardships. During Du Fu's lifetime, civil war raged throughout China. Food was scarce, and Du Fu nearly died of starvation. As a result, Du Fu often wrote about issues such as the problems of the poor, the unfairness of life, and the wastefulness of war. Du Fu wrote the poem below after an uprising left the capital city in ruins.

PRIMARY SOURCE

"Behind those red gates
meat and wine are left to spoil
outside lie the bones
of people who starved and froze."

—from "Five Hundred Words About My Journey to Fengxian," by Du Fu

Landscape Painting

C During the Song dynasty, many Chinese artists painted landscapes. However, they did not try to show the exact appearance of places. Instead they tried to portray the "idea" of mountains, lakes, and other scenes. They left empty spaces in their paintings on purpose. This style reflects the Daoist belief that a person cannot know the whole truth about something. Daoism is the belief that people should turn to nature and give up their worldly concerns.

This landscape (left)—painted in the 1100s—shows the Daoist love of nature. The lettering of the Chinese poems (right) is as delicate as the images in the art.

V

CHAPTER 17, Lesson 2
Chinese Society

C Critical Thinking Skills

Making Inferences Discuss the Chinese painters' attempt to portray the "idea" of the landscape. **Ask:** **What do the landscape paintings tell you about the values and beliefs of the Chinese during the Tang and Song dynasties?** *(Students should suggest that peace, calm, nature, and beauty were important to the Chinese.)* **BL**

Discuss the Daoist belief that people cannot know the whole truth about anything. Ask students to make the connection between painting the "idea" of a landscape and this Daoist belief. **BL**

V Visual Skills

Interpreting Discuss the landscape painting with students. Help them appreciate the stylistic nature of the painting that creates an "idea" of a calm and peaceful scene from nature. Ask them to notice the empty spaces on the painting, such as the foreground in the area where the two men are bowing to each other. Ask students to consider how this empty space affects the painting. **Ask:** **Does it change how you respond to the painting? Does it change its meaning? Do you like the effects or not?** *(Answers will vary. Encourage students to give reasons for their responses.)* **Visual/Spatial**

SLIDE SHOW

Chinese Landscape Painting

Making Inferences Have students view the slide show. By clicking on the arrows, they can see another landscape painting. **Ask:** **What do the landscape paintings tell you about the values and beliefs of the Chinese during the Tang and Song dynasties?** *(Students should suggest that peace, calm, nature, and beauty were important to the Chinese.)*

See page 471D for other online activities.

networks
Chinese Landscape Painting
Painting by Fan Kuan
The Song dynasty saw the rise of two different styles of landscape painting. Fan Kuan's art followed the style of Li Cheng, who followed the style of Jing Hao. Fan Kuan also branched out into his own unique style.
Asian Art & Archaeology, Inc./CORBIS

Chinese Society

C Critical Thinking Skills

Comparing and Contrasting Discuss the way landscape painters portrayed people in their paintings. Invite students to talk about what this says about the Chinese view of people's place in nature. Ask them to consider whether or not that view is similar to or different from how Americans view nature.

R Reading Skills

Defining Have a student volunteer read the section aloud. Then, clarify the terms used in discussing types of art. **Ask:** What is *calligraphy*? *(artistic handwriting)* What is *porcelain*? *(a ceramic made of fine clay baked at very high temperatures)* What are *figurines*? *(small models or figures, often of the human figure or animals)* Invite students to ask questions about other terms that may not be familiar to them. AL ELL

Have students complete the Lesson 2 Review.

CLOSE & REFLECT

Have students work in small groups to decide on the type of graphic organizer that would best help them identify and organize all the examples of China's cultural, technological, and economic advances during the Tang and Song dynasties. If necessary, ask leading questions to guide students. Have groups share their graphic organizers with the class.

ANSWER, p. 488

☑ PROGRESS CHECK Chinese poets often wrote about the themes of the beauty of nature, changes in seasons, the joys of friendship, and the shortness of life, as well as the problems of the poor and the wastefulness of war.

C

Daoism also influenced the way people are portrayed in landscape paintings. Humans are shown as very small figures in a natural landscape. The paintings express the idea that people are part of nature but do not control it. People are only one part of a much larger natural setting.

Chinese painters often wrote poems on their works. They used a brush and ink to write beautiful characters called **calligraphy** (kuh•LIH•gruh•fee).

Porcelain

R

During the Tang dynasty, Chinese artisans became skilled in making porcelain. As you may recall, porcelain is a ceramic made of fine clay baked at very high temperatures. Because porcelain later came from China to the West, people today sometimes call porcelain "china."

Porcelain can be made into figurines, vases, cups, and plates. An Arab traveler in A.D. 851 described Chinese porcelain:

PRIMARY SOURCE

"There is in China a very fine clay from which are made vases having the transparency [clearness] of glass bottles; water in these vases is visible through them, and yet they are made of clay."

—from *Account of Voyages Made by Arabs and Persians in India and China*

This bowl is Chinese porcelain. The word *porcelain* comes from French and Italian words for "shell," which the pottery resembles.

Henry Gan/Photodisc/Getty Images

Methods for making porcelain spread to other parts of the world. They finally reached Europe in the A.D. 1700s.

☑ PROGRESS CHECK

Identifying What themes did Chinese poets often write about?

LESSON 2 REVIEW CCSS

Review Vocabulary (Tier 3 Words)

1. What natural material do you need in order to make *porcelain*? RH.6–8.2, RH.6–8.4
2. How is *calligraphy* similar to painting? RH.6–8.2, RH.6–8.4

Answer the Guiding Questions

3. ***Describing*** How did the reopening of the Silk Road affect the economy and culture of China? RH.6–8.2
4. ***Explaining*** How did the printing of paper money help the economy of China? RH.6–8.2
5. ***Speculating*** Why did the rulers of the Tang and Song dynasties support the arts and literature? RH.6–8.2
6. ***Analyzing*** Which technological development had a greater impact on the Chinese empire—printing or gunpowder? Explain why. RH.6–8.2
7. **INFORMATIVE/EXPLANATORY** You are an imperial scholar-official. Your job is to report to the emperor about changes taking place. Which technological, economic, or cultural development do you think the emperor should know about? Write a short report that describes an important development. Support your ideas with at least two reasons. WHST.6–8.2, WHST.6–8.10

LESSON 2 REVIEW ANSWERS

1. Fine clay is used to make porcelain.
2. Calligraphy and painting both use brushes.
3. The reopening of the Silk Road made it easier for goods to travel between China and other parts of Asia. Because more goods were sold, the economy of China improved. Increased trade also meant that goods and ideas were exchanged with other places.
4. Because printed money was easier to make and carry than coins, more money became available for traders to use in business. As a result, the economy grew.
5. Students should suggest that the arts reflect the ideas and values of a culture. Rulers would have wanted poets and artists to create works that celebrated the Chinese landscape, people, and beliefs.
6. Students may suggest that printing had a greater impact because printed books helped spread ideas and educate people. Others may suggest that gunpowder was more important because it gave the Chinese an advantage in war. Students should give clear reasons for their answers.
7. Students' reports should identify one development and give at least two reasons why it was important. For example, students might focus on the use of coal to make steel. They should explain that coal made it possible to form steel, an important material for crafting strong tools and weapons. The stronger tools and weapons allowed China's workers and soldiers to be more efficient.

networks
There's More Online!
GRAPHIC ORGANIZER
Mongols in China
VIDEO

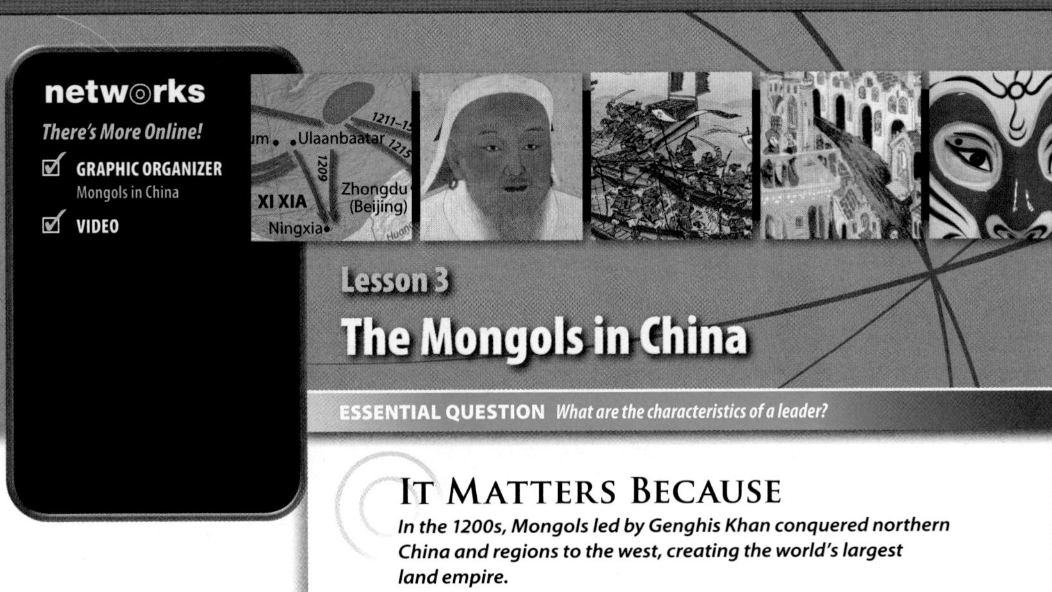

Lesson 3
The Mongols in China

ESSENTIAL QUESTION *What are the characteristics of a leader?*

IT MATTERS BECAUSE

In the 1200s, Mongols led by Genghis Khan conquered northern China and regions to the west, creating the world's largest land empire.

Mongol Expansion

GUIDING QUESTION ***Why were the Mongols able to build a vast empire so quickly?***

By the A.D. 1200s, Chinese civilization had made many achievements in government, technology, and the arts. However, enemies to the north were preparing to invade China. These people were the Mongols (MAHNG•guhlz), the dominant nomadic group in central Asia. They became the first non-Chinese people to rule all of China.

Who Were the Mongols?

R

The Mongols came from an area north of China called Mongolia (mahn•GOHL•yuh). The Mongols lived in movable tents called yurts and raised horses, sheep, and yaks, or long-haired oxen. Mongols were made up of clans, or groups of related families, that were loosely joined together. They followed their herds as the animals grazed the large **steppes** (STEHPS) of Mongolia. The steppes are wide, grassy plains that stretch from the Black Sea to northern China.

Early in their history, the Mongols developed skills that were necessary for nomadic living. The Mongols were excellent horseback riders. Their children learned to ride a horse at ages four or five and then they spent much of their lives on horseback.

Reading **HELP**DESK (CCSS)

Taking Notes: *Sequencing*

Use a graphic organizer like the one here to sequence the events that led to Mongol control of China. RH.6–8.2

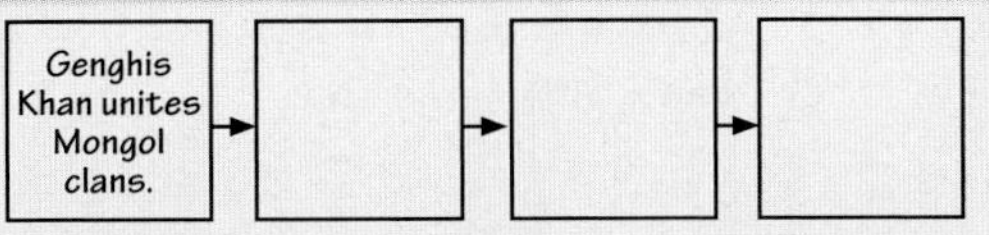

Content Vocabulary
- **steppe**
- **terror**

(Tier 3 Words)

ENGAGE

Bellringer Ask students to name some of the largest empires and countries they know about. Encourage suggestions such as the Roman Empire of ancient times or the Union of Soviet Socialist Republics or the United States in contemporary times. Then tell students that there is one empire they might not think about—the Mongol empire of the thirteenth century. Tell them that it was the largest land empire in all of history. Explain that they will be learning about the Mongols in this lesson.

TEACH & ASSESS

R Reading Skills

Identifying After students have read the "Mongol Expansion" section of the text, remind them that for hundreds of years, the Chinese had been under seemingly constant threat from nomads along their northern border. Tell students that the most dominant of these nomadic groups were the Mongols. **Ask:** **How did the Mongols live?** *(They lived in tents and followed their herds. They lived in clans.)* **Where did they come from?** *(Mongolia, a land of steppes north of China)* Then, discuss the riding skills of the Mongols. **Ask:** **How might these skills be useful in an invading army?** *(Horses would allow the warriors to travel and attack quickly.)*

VIDEO

Marco Polo's Inspiration

Discussing Have students watch the video about Marco Polo. Afterward, guide a discussion of the situation portrayed. **Ask:** **What is the narrator hinting at when he suggests that an imaginary journey is all he ever made?** *(that Marco Polo never really went to China)*

See page 471E for other online activities.

ANSWER, p. 489

TAKING NOTES: Box #1 Genghis Khan unites Mongol clans. Box #2 Mongols conquer northern China. Box #3 Kublai Khan establishes capital at Khanbaliq. Box #4 Kublai Khan conquers southern China.

The Mongols in China

V Visual Skills

Analyzing Maps Review the map key with students, pointing out that the arrows indicate the different Mongol campaigns and the dates they were undertaken. Ask them to observe the size of the Mongols' homeland. **Ask:** **In geographic terms, how did Genghis Khan expand the Mongol Empire?** *(He and his troops expanded the empire in nearly all directions, moving west, south, and southeast from the Mongol homeland.)* **In what directions were Gengis's early campaigns directed?** *(south, toward China)* **Where were his next campaigns directed?** *(east toward Liaoyang)* **In which direction did his last campaigns go?** *(west toward Samarkand)* **Visual/Spatial**

R Reading Skills

Explaining Ask students to read the section on Genghis Khan. Explain to the class that Genghis Khan was not this leader's real name, but a title given him by the other Mongol leaders. **Ask:** **What does Genghis Khan mean?** *(strong ruler)* **What steps did Genghis Khan take to prepare his nation for conquest?** *(created a legal code, formed a group of clan chiefs to plan military campaigns, created and trained an army of 100,000 warriors, organized them into units and placed skilled officers in charge)* AL

GEOGRAPHY CONNECTION

During the reign of Genghis Khan, the Mongols conquered many kingdoms in central Asia.

1. **MOVEMENT** In what direction did Genghis Khan launch his first campaign? What was the year?
2. **CRITICAL THINKING** *Contrasting* How would you describe the difference in size between Genghis Khan's empire and the Mongol homeland?

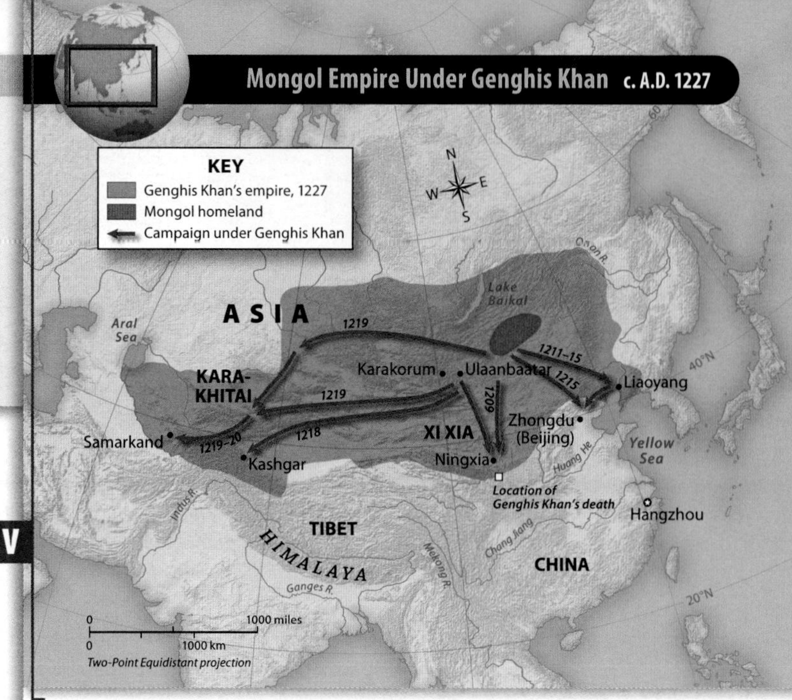

The Mongols also developed their fighting skills. Riding on their horses toward an enemy, the Mongols could accurately shoot arrows from far distances. As they got closer to their enemy, the Mongols attacked them with swords and spears.

Genghis Khan

In A.D. 1206, a meeting of Mongol leaders took place in the Gobi (GOH•BEE). This is a vast desert that covers parts of Mongolia and China. At that meeting, a warrior named Temujin (the• MOO•juhn) was elected Genghis Khan (jehng•guhs KAHN), which means "strong ruler."

Genghis Khan set out to **unify** the Mongol clans. He organized Mongol laws to create a new legal code. He also formed a group of clan chiefs to help him plan military campaigns. From the time of his election until the end of his life, Genghis Khan fought to conquer lands beyond Mongolia.

Genghis Khan created an army of more than 100,000 trained warriors. The soldiers were placed in groups called units. The units were then placed under the command of skilled officers.

Reading HELPDESK CCSS

steppe flat, dry grassland
terror violent acts that are meant to cause fear in people

Academic Vocabulary (Tier 2 Words)
unify to bring together as one

networks Online Teaching Options

MAP

Mongol Empire Under Genghis Khan c. A.D. 1227

Analyzing Maps Have students study the map. They can display or isolate different details by clicking on items in the map key. **Ask:** **When did Genghis Khan take his armies farthest to the west?** *(1219–1220)* **When did he capture Ningxia?** *(1209)* **In what part of Asia was Genghis Khan's homeland?** *(east-central Asia)*

See page 471E for other online activities.

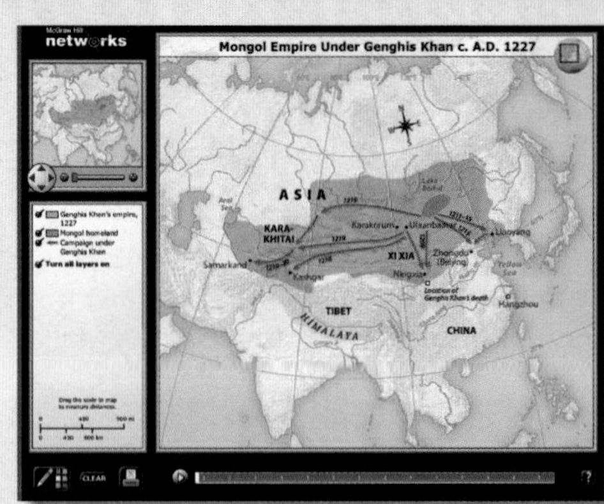

ANSWERS, p. 490

GEOGRAPHY CONNECTION

1. Genghis Khan launched his first campaign to the south in 1209.
2. **CRITICAL THINKING** Genghis Khan's empire was about nine times larger than the Mongol homeland.

The army officers were chosen for their abilities rather than their social position. These changes made the Mongols the most skilled fighting force in the world at that time.

Under Genghis Khan, Mongol forces first conquered other people of the steppes. These victories brought tribute money to the Mongol treasury. The victories also attracted new recruits to the army. Soon the Mongols were powerful enough to attack major civilizations. In A.D. 1211, thousands of Mongol horsemen invaded China. Within three years, they had taken control of all of northern China. They then turned west and invaded the kingdoms that controlled parts of the Silk Road. **R**

Genghis Khan and his Mongol warriors became known for their cruel fighting and use of **terror**. Terror refers to violent acts that are meant to cause fear. Mongol soldiers attacked, looted, and burned cities. Within a short time, many people began surrendering to the Mongols without even fighting them.

Empire Builders

After Genghis Khan died in A.D. 1227, his vast territory was split into several areas. Each area was ruled by one of his sons. The great Mongol fighting force was divided up.

Despite these divisions of troops, Mongol conquests continued. The ferocious warriors swept into parts of eastern and central Europe. They also conquered Persia located in Southwest Asia.

GEOGRAPHY CONNECTION

In less than 100 years, the Mongols created the largest land empire in the history of the world.

1. **REGIONS** What country to the east was attacked but not conquered by 1294?
2. **CRITICAL THINKING** ***Speculating*** What physical feature might have prevented the Mongols from conquering India?

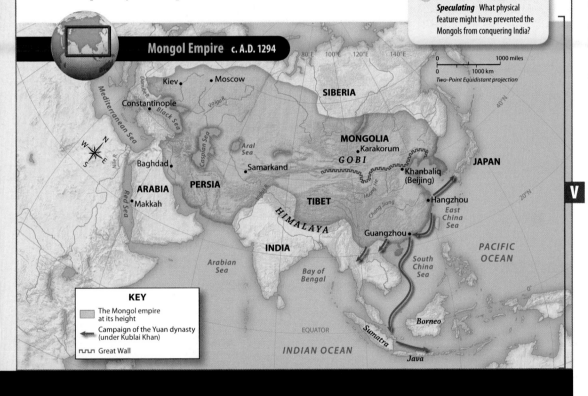

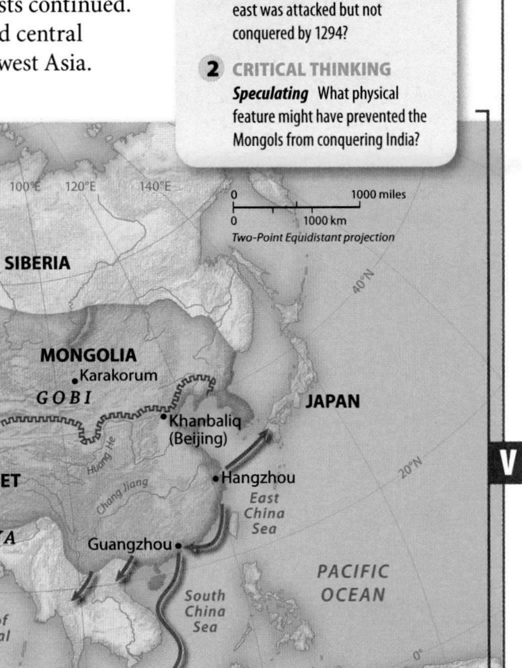

WHITEBOARD ACTIVITY

Mongol Warriors

Identifying Have students use the information in the lesson to complete the Interactive Whiteboard Activity "Mongol Warriors." Students may work alone or in pairs.

See page 471E for other online activities.

networks Mongol Warriors

Directions: Drag and drop the correct answer from the item bank.

Item Bank
- Strong Warrior
- steppes
- terror
- money and soldiers
- yurts
- Egypt
- clans
- Strong Ruler
- loyalty
- Russia
- horses and yaks

1. The Mongol groups were made up of
2. Genghis Khan means
3. Before attacking China, Genghis Khan needed
4. Some people surrendered to the Mongols out of
5. Where was the Mongols' western advance stopped?

The Mongols in China

R Reading Skills

Describing Have students read the text. Then, tell them that the Mongols had a large, well-organized, well-led, and well-trained army, but they used other strategies to win territory as well. **Ask: How did the Mongols get people to give up their lands?** *(They used terror; they were fierce fighters who burned and looted cities; they frightened people into giving up their lands.)*

V Visual Skills

Reading a Map Explain that the territory in the Mongolian empire was acquired over a period of about 50 years, between 1206 and 1260. Point out the major cities on the map. Explain that Khanbaliq is the site of China's modern capital, Beijing. To help students get a better sense of how large the Mongol empire was, provide a world map of modern Asia. Help them trace the Mongol empire's approximate boundaries on the modern map. Have students identify where some of the cities shown on the Mongol empire map are on the modern map. **BL Visual/Spatial**

Content Background Knowledge

Tell students that the Mongol army was usually described as quite large. In actuality, the Mongol army was often smaller than the armies they fought against. However, they used tactics to fool their enemies into thinking they had more soldiers than they did. The Mongol army was almost entirely cavalry. A group of 10,000 soldiers was a common size. Each soldier had three extra horses, or remounts. The Mongols made straw dummies to sit on the remounts. Sometimes they had captives ride on the horses, or they used captives as infantry, leading them into new cities or towns ahead of the cavalry. With these tricks, an army of 10,000 Mongols could look like 50,000.

ANSWERS, p. 491

GEOGRAPHY CONNECTION

1. The Mongols attacked but could not conquer Japan.
2. **CRITICAL THINKING** The Himalaya might have prevented the Mongols from conquering India.

The Mongols in China

R Reading Skills

Discussing Direct students to read the text. Then, talk about events following the death of Genghis Khan and explain how the Mongols continued to expand their empire. **Ask:** What brought an end to the conquests? *(The Mongols were stopped by Muslims when they attacked Egypt.)* Using geographic terms, how would you describe the Mongol empire? *(It extended from the Pacific Ocean in the east to eastern Europe in the west. It also extended from Siberia in the north to the Himalaya in the south. It covered almost all of Asia and parts of Eastern Europe.)*

Discuss the lands and people the Mongols conquered. **Ask:** What effects did the Mongols have on the lands they conquered? *(The Mongols caused great damage, but they also brought stability and peace to these lands. They opened up trade routes.)* Point out that unlike many other conquerors through history, the Mongols didn't try to destroy everything they found in the lands they came to rule. They learned and adopted ideas from these lands. **Ask:** What did the Mongols learn from the Chinese? *(They learned about gunpowder and the fire lance.)* How did these weapons aid the Mongols? *(They made the Mongols even more frightening and powerful.)*

ANSWERS, p. 492

CRITICAL THINKING Genghis Khan grew up poor, and his father was murdered. These experiences could have made Genghis Khan want the wealth and power that a ruler has.

✓ PROGRESS CHECK The Mongols sometimes adopted the technology and the customs of their opponents. For example, many Mongols accepted Islam and adopted Arab, Persian, and Turkish ways.

Reading Strategy Students' predictions and reflections should demonstrate accurate comprehension of the section's heads and content.

BIOGRAPHY

Genghis Khan (c. A.D. 1167–1227)

Genghis Khan's father, the Mongol chief Yisugei, named his son Temujin. According to folklore, Temujin had a large blood clot in his right hand, which meant he was destined to become a great warrior. In 1206, 40-year-old Temujin successfully took command of the Mongol forces in the Gobi. It is believed that he was inspired to rule because he grew up extremely poor, and his father was murdered by his enemies.

▶ **CRITICAL THINKING**
Determining Cause and Effect What about the personal life of Genghis Kahn would have led him to want to rule?

In A.D. 1258, the Mongols captured the Muslim city of Baghdad. The Mongols then moved into Syria and Palestine to Egypt. The Muslim leaders of Egypt stopped the Mongol's advance in A.D. 1260.

All of these different areas formed a vast Mongol empire. Mongol rule stretched from the Pacific Ocean in the east to eastern Europe in the west and from Siberia in the north to the Himalaya in the south. The Mongols created the largest land empire in history.

R The Mongols caused a great deal of damage to the lands they conquered, but they also brought stability. This stability encouraged trade and closer contact between Asia and Europe. Many of the great trade routes between Asia and Europe crossed Mongol lands. The Mongols grew wealthy because they taxed the products that were traded along these roads.

The Mongols admired the cultures they conquered, and sometimes they adopted their beliefs and customs. For example, the Mongols in Southwest Asia accepted Islam and adopted Arab, Persian, and Turkish ways.

The Mongols also learned from the Chinese. As they fought Chinese troops, the Mongols learned about gunpowder and its use as an explosive. They saw the Chinese use the fire lance, a weapon that the Chinese later developed into the gun and cannon. Adopting gunpowder and the fire lance from the Chinese, the Mongols became even more frightening to their opponents.

✓ PROGRESS CHECK

Determining Cause and Effect How were the Mongols influenced by their opponents?

Mongol Conquest of China

GUIDING QUESTION *How did the Mongols rule the Chinese?*

In A.D. 1260, the grandson of Genghis Khan, Kublai, became the new Mongol ruler. Kublai Khan (KOO•BLUH KAHN) continued the conquest of China that his grandfather had begun. In A.D. 1264, Kublai established his capital at Khanbaliq—the city of the khan—in northern China. Today, the modern city of Beijing (BAY•JIHNG) is located on the site of the former Mongol capital.

Reading HELPDESK (CCSS)

Reading Strategy: *Predicting*

When you predict, you use clues in the text and your own knowledge to make an educated guess. Skim the headings in "Mongol Conquest of China." What do you think you will learn? Now read the passages. Were your predictions correct?

networks Online Teaching Options

WORKSHEET

Primary Source Activity: Imperial China: The Mongols in China

Identifying Point of View Students will read two views of Mongol China that were written by Europeans. Ask students to read the introduction and the primary sources and then respond to the questions.

See page 471E for other online activities.

The Mongols invaded other areas after conquering China. Despite a fleet of warships built by the Koreans, the planned Mongol invasion of Japan ended in failure.

Mary Evans Picture Library

Mongols and Chinese

In 1271, Kublai Kahn decided he would control all of China. By A.D. 1279, Kublai Khan finished conquering southern China. He brought an end to the Song dynasty and declared himself emperor. Kublai Khan started the Yuan (YWAN) dynasty. The term *Yuan* means "beginning." The Yuan dynasty would last only about 100 years. Kublai Khan would rule for 30 of those years, until his death in A.D. 1294. **R**

To keep tight control of these new lands, Kublai appointed Mongol leaders to top jobs in China. He also kept some Chinese officials in positions of power.

The Mongol culture was quite different from the Chinese culture. The Mongols had their own language, laws, and customs. These characteristics separated them from the Chinese people they ruled. Mongols lived apart from the Chinese and did not mix with them socially. **C**

Government and Religion

In government affairs, the Yuan **regime** did not use civil service examinations as was previously done in China. Government jobs were open to non-Chinese people, including Mongols and Turks. However, the Yuan rulers respected Confucian writings and allowed Chinese scholar-officials to keep their posts.

The Mongols in China

R Reading Skills

Explaining Have a student volunteer read the first paragraph on this page aloud. As a class, discuss Kublai Khan's conquest of China. **Ask:** **How many years did it take him to conquer the remaining parts of China?** *(about 8 years)* AL **Why was Kublai Khan's name for his new dynasty—Yuan—appropriate?** *(Yuan means "beginning," and Kublai was beginning a new period in the history of China.)*

C Critical Thinking Skills

Evaluating Discuss Kublai Khan's strategy for ruling China: appointing many of his Mongol leaders to top jobs but also keeping some Chinese officials in place. **Ask:** **Do you think this was or was not a wise plan? Explain.** *(Most students will agree it was a wise plan. They may say Kublai Khan needed his own people in charge because he could trust them. He needed Chinese officials, too, because they knew the language, the culture, and how things worked in China. It would also foster goodwill among the Chinese.)* BL

Discuss the differences between the Mongols and the Chinese. Invite students to discuss the kinds of difficulties such differences would make for the Mongol rulers.

IMAGE

Mongol Invasions of Japan

Analyzing Images Have students view the image. By clicking on the bullets, they can read more about the Mongols' attempted invasion of Japan. Discuss with them the role that nature played in saving Japan.

See page 471E for other online activities.

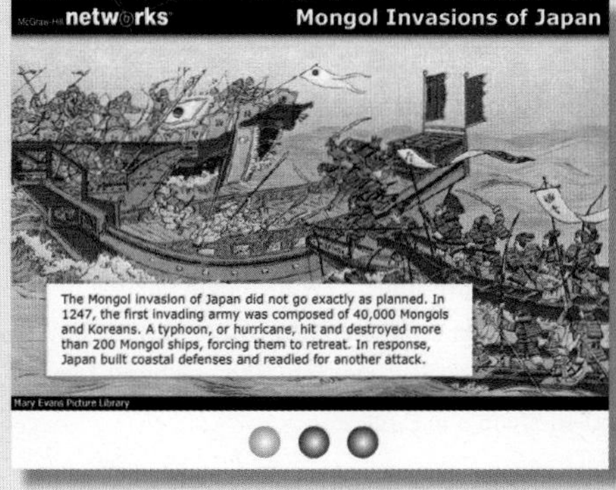

McGraw-Hill networks
Mongol Invasions of Japan
The Mongol invasion of Japan did not go exactly as planned. In 1247, the first invading army was composed of 40,000 Mongols and Koreans. A typhoon, or hurricane, hit and destroyed more than 200 Mongol ships, forcing them to retreat. In response, Japan built coastal defenses and readied for another attack.
Mary Evans Picture Library

The Mongols in China

C Critical Thinking Skills

Comparing and Contrasting Remind students that the Mongols were fierce and ruthless conquerors, but they proved to be different as rulers. **Ask:** **What kind of rulers were the Mongols? How did they treat their subjects?** *(They were tolerant of different religions and admired all cultures. They were peaceful rulers.)*

Lead students to understand that the Chinese and the Mongols seemed to respect each other even though they did not mix socially. Point out that the peace and prosperity the Mongols brought to China caused many Chinese to support the Mongol leaders. AL ELL

W Writing Skills

Argument Point out that while most historians believe Polo's account of his travels are mainly accurate, some question whether Polo ever actually made the journey to China. Challenge students to do research to learn more about this debate. Then ask them to take a position and to write and deliver a speech arguing for or against the truth of Marco Polo's journey.

ANSWER, p. 494

CRITICAL THINKING Marco Polo's travels were important to Europeans because he brought back stories and goods from China, the likes of which had not been seen before by Europeans of this period. He helped spark interest in acquiring Asian goods.

This colored lithograph was taken from a manuscript that described Marco Polo's journeys. It shows him leaving Venice in 1338.

▶ **CRITICAL THINKING**
Explaining Why were Marco Polo's travels important to Europeans?

North Wind/North Wind Picture Archives

Like many Chinese, the Mongols in China practiced Buddhism, but they were respectful of other religions. For example, Kublai Khan encouraged Christians, Muslims, and Hindus from outside China to practice their faiths.

C Under Mongol rule, China reached the height of its wealth and power. Foreigners were drawn to its capital city. Although they were foreigners, the Mongols gradually won the support of many Chinese people. Some Chinese appreciated the order and prosperity that the Mongols brought to the country. Foreign visitors were attracted to China and reached it by traveling along the Silk Road.

Marco Polo

W One of the most famous European travelers to reach China was Marco Polo. He came from the city of Venice in Italy. Polo lived in the capital of Khanbaliq during the reign of Kublai Khan. He wrote his impressions of the magnificent appearance of this city:

Reading **HELP**DESK (CCSS)

Academic Vocabulary (Tier 2 Words)

regime rulers during a given period of time

networks Online Teaching Options

GRAPHIC ORGANIZER

Taking Notes: *Sequencing:* Mongols in China

Sequencing Point out that the Mongol conquest of China did not happen all at once. Genghis Khan led the first invasions. Have students work independently to complete the graphic organizer by listing four major events in the Mongols' conquest. When students finish, discuss their ideas in class.

See page 471E for other online activities.

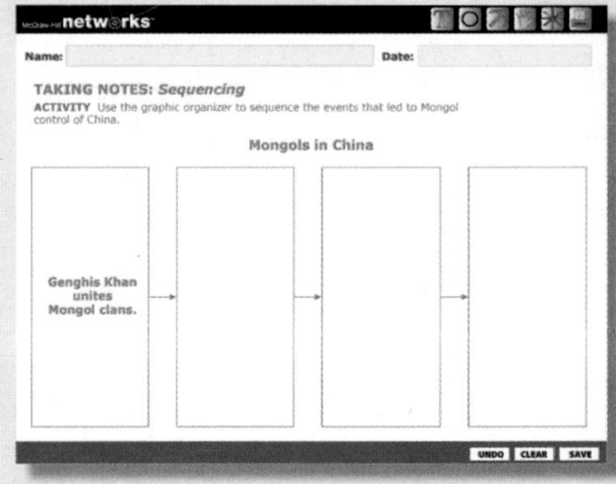

PRIMARY SOURCE

"The streets are so straight and wide that you can see right along them from end to end and from one gate to the other. And up and down the city there are beautiful palaces, and many great and fine hostelries [inns], and fine houses in great numbers."

—from "Concerning the City of Cambaluc [Khanbaliq]" by Marco Polo

C

Kublai was fascinated by Marco Polo's stories about his journeys. For about 16 years, Polo was a privileged resident of China. Kublai sent him on trips all over the region to gather information and carry out business. For some of those years, Polo ruled the Chinese city of Yangzhou. When Polo returned to Italy, he wrote a book about his adventures.

Trade and Empire

The Mongol empire stretched from China to eastern Europe. As a result, Mongol China prospered from increased overland trade with many parts of the world. The Yuan dynasty also built ships and expanded seagoing trade. China traded tea, silk, and porcelain in exchange for goods such as silver, carpets, cotton, and spices. Muslims and Europeans also took Chinese discoveries back to their homelands.

R

Mongol armies advanced into Vietnam and northern Korea. The rulers of Korea, called the Koryo (koh•RY•oh), remained in power because they agreed to Mongol control. The Mongols forced thousands of Koreans to build warships. The Mongols used these ships in two attempts to invade Japan. Both voyages ended in failure when huge storms destroyed much of the fleet.

☑ PROGRESS CHECK

Describing What was Marco Polo's reaction to seeing China's cities?

LESSON 3 REVIEW

Review Vocabulary (Tier 3 Words)

1. If you were to visit the Mongolian *steppes*, what would you likely see? RH.6–8.2, RH.6–8.4

Answer the Guiding Questions

2. ***Identifying*** Why did trading improve under Mongolian rule? Give examples of goods that were traded and how they were traded. RH.6–8.2
3. ***Analyzing*** How did the Mongols use terror in their conquests? RH.6–8.2
4. ***Summarizing*** How did the Chinese benefit from being ruled by the Mongols? RH.6–8.2
5. ***Evaluating*** Make a list of the leadership qualities of Genghis Khan and evaluate him as a leader. RH.6–8.2
6. **NARRATIVE** Imagine that you are Genghis Khan. You are concerned about how your empire will be ruled after your death. Write a journal entry in which you record advice that you want your family members to follow. WHST.6–8.2, WHST.6–8.10

The Mongols in China

C Critical Thinking Skills

Identifying Points of View Read aloud Polo's description of Khanbaliq in an expressive voice. Explain that Marco Polo's stories of imperial China provided many Europeans with their first glimpse of China and Chinese culture. To Europeans, Polo's tales of China would have sounded amazing. Point out that Polo's descriptions, and those of other later travelers, made China's wealth and achievements appear incredible. **Ask:** **Do you think the Europeans' tales of China's wealth were exaggerated or true?** *(Students might suspect that some of the details were exaggerated, but the tone of respect and awe seems real.)*

R Reading Skills

Listing Have students read the section "Trade and Empire." After they are done, point out that the size of the Mongol empire helped Mongol China increase trade with distant parts of the world. **Ask:** **What were important items that were traded between China and other parts of the world?** *(China exported tea, silk, and porcelain; China imported silver, carpets, cotton, and spices.)* AL

Have students complete the Lesson 3 Review.

CLOSE & REFLECT

As a class, have students suggest a list of leadership traits of the Mongols. Lead students in a discussion of the traits that Mongol leaders would have relied on most while ruling such a vast empire.

ANSWER, p. 495

☑ PROGRESS CHECK Marco Polo was amazed by the size, beauty, and organization of Chinese cities.

LESSON 3 REVIEW ANSWERS

1. You would see wide-open, grassy areas.
2. Trade improved because the territories ruled by Mongols stretched from China to Eastern Europe. As a result, all trade routes were under one rule and would not be blocked by enemies. Examples of goods that were traded from other areas of Asia include silver, cotton, and spices. Tea, silk, and porcelain as well as gunpowder, steel, and compasses were sent from China to Europe and elsewhere.
3. Mongols used violence and destruction (attacking, looting, and burning cities) to terrorize enemies and force them to surrender.
4. Although the Mongols were fierce conquerors, they established stability and safe trade routes. They ruled as a separate class but allowed many Chinese scholar-officials to keep their government posts. They also allowed those whom they conquered to practice their faiths.
5. Students should note that Genghis Khan was disciplined, tough, organized, and willing to take risks. He understood the value of loyalty and appreciated people for their abilities, not for their family ties. Students should understand that he was an effective leader.
6. Students should write from the perspective of Genghis Khan by using first-person pronouns to express his thoughts. Journal entries should include details that capture Khan's thoughts about conquering and ruling an empire. For example, as imagined by students, Khan might recommend using terror to conquer new lands and peoples.

ENGAGE

Bellringer Check online or in a book for images of the Monkey King. Explain to students that the Monkey King is a mythical figure that was the subject of stories shared orally for centuries. In the 1500s, a Ming dynasty scholar-official named Wu Cheng'en recorded them in a book. Tell students that the stories are about a Buddhist monk who discovers the Monkey King while traveling through a desert in India. The Buddha has imprisoned the Monkey King under a rock. Even though the Monkey King has magical powers, he cannot escape without the monk's help. This is part of the Buddha's plan. The monk will now serve as the Monkey King's assistant while they undergo a series of dangerous quests. Invite students to describe what they see in the illustrations.

TEACH & ASSESS

V Visual Skills

Analyzing Images Have students study the image of the Monkey King in the textbook. **Ask:** **Based on the images, what impression do you get of the Monkey King?** *(The Monkey King likes bright colors and wears armor like a soldier. He carries what looks like a weapon.)* **What characteristics do the images suggest that the Monkey King possesses?** *(Possible answers: He is intense and perhaps angry, but also playful. He is a fighter.)* Tell students that in this lesson, they will learn about allegories and read an excerpt from a Monkey King tale. **Visual/Spatial**

Content Background Knowledge

- Wu Cheng'en was a Chinese scholar with a Confucian education who spent all his working life in civil service as a district magistrate. He did not write seriously until he retired in his late sixties. His early stories and poems were written in the official, classical style.
- When Wu Cheng'en began writing the *Monkey* stories, he turned to the vernacular language, which was appropriate because the stories were based on folktales. Because he was an official scholar, however, Wu Cheng'en published the stories anonymously.

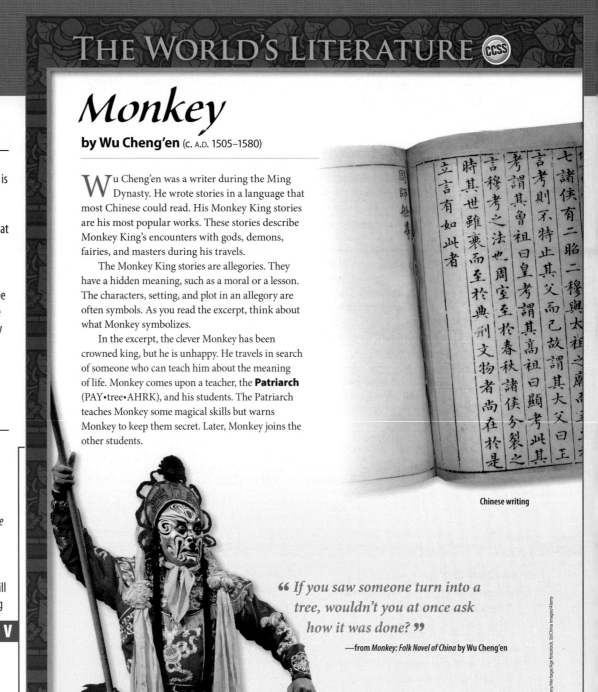

THE WORLD'S LITERATURE CCSS

Monkey

by Wu Cheng'en (c. A.D. 1505–1580)

Wu Cheng'en was a writer during the Ming Dynasty. He wrote stories in a language that most Chinese could read. His Monkey King stories are his most popular works. These stories describe Monkey King's encounters with gods, demons, fairies, and masters during his travels.

The Monkey King stories are allegories. They have a hidden meaning, such as a moral or a lesson. The characters, setting, and plot in an allegory are often symbols. As you read the excerpt, think about what Monkey symbolizes.

In the excerpt, the clever Monkey has been crowned king, but he is unhappy. He travels in search of someone who can teach him about the meaning of life. Monkey comes upon a teacher, the **Patriarch** (PAY•tree•AHRK), and his students. The Patriarch teaches Monkey some magical skills but warns Monkey to keep them secret. Later, Monkey joins the other students.

Chinese writing

"If you saw someone turn into a tree, wouldn't you at once ask how it was done?"

—from *Monkey: Folk Novel of China* by Wu Cheng'en

An actor playing the Monkey King searching for truth

networks Online Teaching Options

LECTURE SLIDE

The World's Literature

Defining Use the lecture slide to review the term *allegory*—a story in which the characters, settings, and events stand for or symbolize other ideas. Then ask students to brainstorm examples of allegories based on your definition. (Students might recognize that the books *The Lion, the Witch and the Wardrobe, Pilgrim's Progress,* the stories of Aesop's Fables, and the film *The Matrix* are allegories.) Finally, tell them that this Monkey King story is also an allegory.

networks — The World's Literature

allegory a story in which the characters, settings, and events stand for or symbolize other ideas

Monkey

PRIMARY SOURCE

R The **disciples** (dih • SY • puhls) clapped and burst into loud applause. "Bravo, Monkey, bravo," they cried. There was such a **din** that the **Patriarch** came running out. . . . "Who's making all this noise?" he asked. . . . Monkey changed himself back into his true form and slipped in among the crowd, saying, "Reverend Master, we are doing lessons out here. I assure you there was no noise in particular." "You were all bawling," said the Patriarch angrily. "It didn't sound in the least like people studying. I want to know what you were doing here, shouting and laughing." "To tell the truth," said someone, "Monkey was showing us a **transformation** (TRANS • fuhr • MAY • SHUHN) just for fun. We told him to change into a pine tree, and he did it so well that we were all applauding him." . . . "Go away, all of you!" the Patriarch shouted. "And you, Monkey, come here! . . . Did you think I taught you [magic] in order that you might show off in front of other people? If you saw someone turn into a tree, wouldn't you at once ask how it was done? If others see you doing it, aren't they certain to ask you? If you are frightened to refuse, you will give the secret away; and if you refuse, you're very likely to be roughly handled. You're putting yourself in grave danger." "I'm terribly sorry," said Monkey. "I won't punish you," said the Patriarch, "but you can't stay here." Monkey burst into tears. "Where am I to go to?" W

—From *Monkey: Folk Novel of China* by Wu Cheng'en

Vocabulary

disciples
students

din
loud noise

patriarch
an older male figure of authority, often within a religious community

transformation
a complete change

The mask of the adventurous Monkey King

Analyzing Literature DBQ

1. ***Describing*** What does Monkey do in front of the disciples? RH.6–8.1
2. ***Identifying Points of View*** Why is the Patriarch angry at Monkey after discovering what Monkey has done? RH.6–8.1, RH.6–8.6
3. ***Synthesizing*** Do you agree with the Patriarch that showing off can lead to great danger? Why or why not? RH.6–8.1, RH.6–8.6

R Reading Skills

Citing Text Evidence After students have read the excerpt, **ask:** **What evidence can you find that this story is an allegory?** *(Students should note that the Monkey King's magical powers, the lesson he learns at the end, and the fact that the Monkey King is not always what he seems all suggest that the story is an allegory.)* Write students' responses on the board. Point out that allegories work on more than one level—a literal level and a symbolic level.

Challenge students to find the hidden or symbolic meaning of the story. **Ask:** **What lesson might readers in imperial China have learned from the story?** *(Students should suggest that the point of the story is that people should not show off their talents or powers because others might misunderstand or become frightened or angry.)*

W Writing Skills

Narrative Have students write the next part of the story. Their writing should show what happens next to the Monkey King. It should also reflect students' understanding of what an allegory is. If students need help, have them work in groups to brainstorm what happens next in the story—where Monkey goes, whom he meets, and what other lessons he learns. BL **Verbal/Linguistic**

CLOSE & REFLECT

Ask volunteers to read aloud their story continuations. Ask the class to comment on the stories as allegories.

CHART

Chain-of-Events Flowchart

Sequencing Have students work individually to complete the chain-of-events flowchart showing the order of events in this excerpt from *Monkey.* Tell students to choose the three most important events to describe. When students complete their organizers, lead a class discussion of the story's plot.

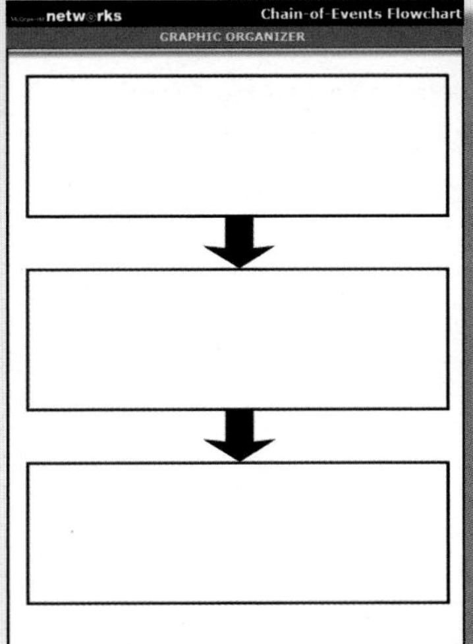

ANSWERS, p. 497

Analyzing Literature

1. He uses his powers to transform into a pine tree.
2. Monkey is showing off and putting himself in a dangerous situation.
3. Students' answers should suggest that showing off might have consequences. They should give an example from the excerpt. For instance, Monkey gained popularity by showing off, but he lost his home because the Patriarch was so angry at and disappointed in him.

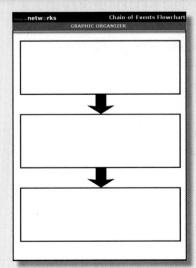

The Ming Dynasty

ENGAGE

Bellringer Tell students that in this lesson, they will learn about a period of great achievement in China brought about by the rise of the Ming dynasty. The Ming rulers restored and rebuilt China and created a thriving economy. A flourishing international trade brought new ideas and goods into China. The rulers sponsored the incredible voyages of one of the great explorers in all of history. This was one of China's most successful periods. Students will also learn why the Ming dynasty decided to end its exploration and international trade and to cut off contact with the outside world.

C Critical Thinking Skills

Determining Cause and Effect Discuss the events that led to the rise of the Ming dynasty. **Ask:** What brought about the rise of the Ming dynasty? *(Mongol rule went into decline; the government spent too much on foreign conquests; corrupt officials stole from the treasury; the people lost respect for the government. Unrest resulted, and a new emperor replaced the Yuan ruler.)* What does the word Ming mean? *(brilliant)* AL

ANSWER, p. 498

TAKING NOTES: CAUSES: desire for trade and tribute; Chinese ship-building. EFFECTS: introduction of foreign elements; closing of borders

networks *There's More Online!*

- **GRAPHIC ORGANIZER** Voyages of Zheng He
- **MAPS**
  - Ming China c. A.D. 1368–A.D. 1644
  - The Voyages of Zheng He A.D. 1405–A.D. 1433
- **SLIDE SHOW** The Forbidden City

Calicut
Bay of Bengal
Sri Lanka (Ceylon)

Lesson 4

The Ming Dynasty

ESSENTIAL QUESTION *How do new ideas change the way people live?*

IT MATTERS BECAUSE

The Ming dynasty's early emperors wanted to spread China's influence. By the late 1500s, however, China had limited its contact with the rest of the world.

The Ming Dynasty

GUIDING QUESTION *How did Ming rulers bring peace and prosperity to China?*

After Kublai Khan died in A.D. 1294, a series of weak emperors came to the throne. Mongol power in China began to decline, and problems increased for the Yuan dynasty. The government spent too many resources on foreign conquests. At the same time, many officials stole from the treasury and grew wealthy. Yuan rulers lost the respect of the people. As a result, many Chinese resented Mongol controls.

The Rise of the Ming

C Unrest swept through China and finally ended Mongol rule. In A.D. 1368, a military officer named Zhu Yuanzhang (JOO YWAHN•JAHNG) became emperor. Zhu reunited the country and then set up his capital at Nanjing (NAN•JIHNG) in southern China. There, he founded the Ming, or "Brilliant," dynasty. The Ming dynasty would rule China for the next 300 years.

As emperor, Zhu took the name Hong Wu (HAHNG WOO), or the "Military Emperor." He brought peace and order, but he was also a harsh leader. Hong Wu trusted few people and punished officials

Reading HELPDESK CCSS

Taking Notes: ***Identifying Cause and Effect***

Use this graphic organizer to note the causes and effects of the voyages of Zheng He. RH.6–8.2, RH.6–8.5

Voyages of Zheng He

Causes	Effects
1.	1.
2.	2.

Content Vocabulary (Tier 3 Words)
- **census**
- **barbarian**
- **novel**

networks ***Online Teaching Options***

VIDEO

Chinese History From the Ming Dynasty to the Three Gorges Dam

Analyzing Images Encourage students to take notes as they view the video. When they finish, have students meet in small groups and discuss the video. Ask them to list the three most important ideas they learned about the Ming dynasty.

See page 471F for other online activities.

that he suspected of treason, or disloyalty to the government. After Hong Wu died in A.D. 1398, his son became emperor and took the name of Yong Le (YUNG LEE).

Yong Le was determined to be a powerful ruler. In A.D. 1421, he moved the capital north to Beijing. There, he built the Imperial City, a large area of palaces and government buildings. The center of this area, known as the Forbidden City, was where the emperor and his family lived. Only top government officials were allowed to enter the Forbidden City.

The Forbidden City had beautiful gardens and palaces with thousands of rooms. China's emperor and court lived there in luxury for more than 500 years. The buildings of the Forbidden City still stand. You can visit them if you travel to China today. **R**

How Did the Ming Change China?

Ming emperors needed government officials to carry out their decisions. To make sure that officials took their jobs seriously, the emperors brought back the civil service examinations. As during the Tang and Song dynasties, the tests were extremely difficult and required years of preparation.

One responsibility of officials was to carry out a **census** (SEHN•suhs), or a count of the number of people in China. The census helped officials identify the people who owed taxes.

GEOGRAPHY CONNECTION

During the Ming dynasty, emperor Yong Le moved the capital to Beijing.

1. **PLACE** What feature forms the northern border of Ming China?
2. **PLACE** Along what river is the city of Nanjing?
3. **CRITICAL THINKING** *Speculating* Why might Yong Le have moved the capital to Beijing?

V

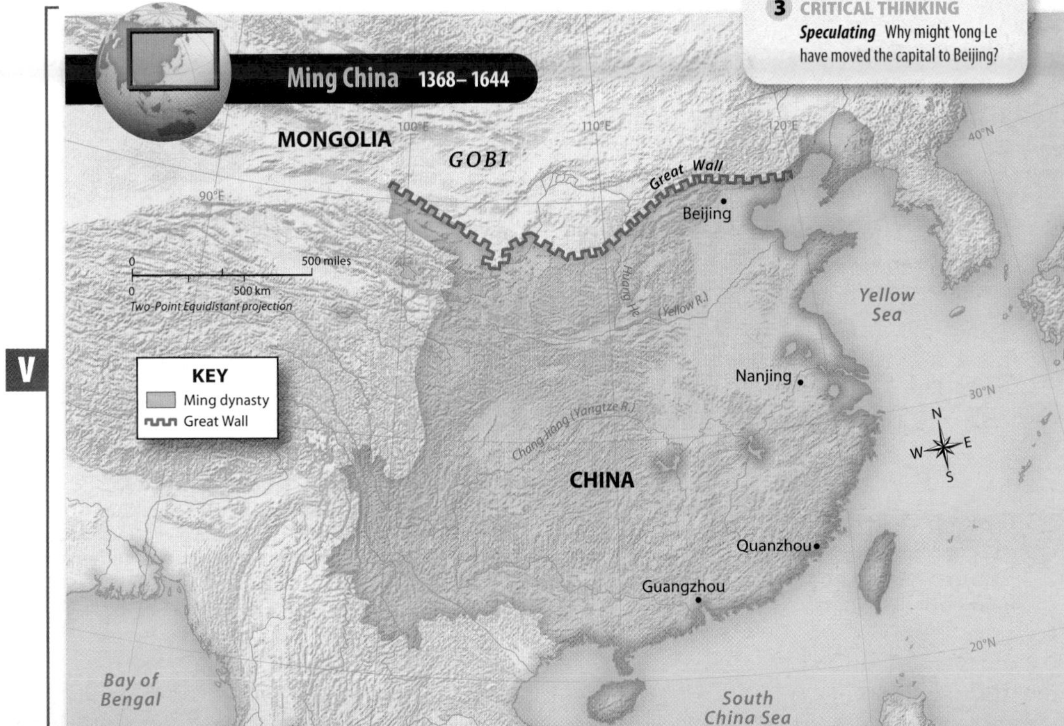

SLIDE SHOW

The Forbidden City

Analyzing Images Students can click on the arrows to see additional images and to read more about the Forbidden City. After viewing the slides, ask students to identify one feature of the city that interests them most and to write a paragraph or two describing that feature and telling what they find interesting about it.

See page 471F for other online activities.

networks
The Forbidden City
Beyond the Gate of Supreme Harmony is a huge courtyard large enough to hold tens of thousands of people. Here stands the largest building in the Forbidden City: the Hall of Supreme Harmony. The emperor's throne sits in this hall. Beyond the courtyard lies the Inner Court—the emperor's living quarters—as well as his private garden.

The Ming Dynasty

R Reading Skills

Explaining Direct the class to review this page. Then, ask students to explain what the Forbidden City is and have them describe it. **Ask:** What does the name of the city suggest about the Ming rulers? *(Possible answer: The rulers wanted to keep themselves apart from the common people. They may have mistrusted outsiders.)* BL

Guide a discussion of the changes the Ming rulers brought to China. **Ask:** Why did Ming emperors bring back civil service examinations? *(They wanted competent officials who would take their jobs seriously.)* Why did the Ming rulers carry out a census? *(to count how many people were in China and find out who owed taxes)*

V Visual Skills

Reading a Map Ask students to study the map of Ming China. **Ask:** Where did Yong Le establish his new capital? *(Beijing)* Have students find Beijing on the map. **Ask:** What forms the northern border of Ming China? *(the Great Wall)* Why might the Great Wall have been especially important to the Ming rulers living in Beijing? *(Beijing is located very near the northern border of China. Beyond are the steppes, where the Mongols and other nomadic groups lived.)* Visual/Spatial

ANSWERS, p. 499

GEOGRAPHY CONNECTION

1. The Great Wall forms the northern border of Ming China.
2. The city of Nanjing is along the Chang Jiang (Yangtze River).
3. CRITICAL THINKING Yong Le might have moved the capital to Beijing because Beijing was easier to defend or because it had been the capital under the Yuan (Mongol) dynasty.

The Ming Dynasty

R Reading Skills

Identifying Have students read the text to identify the changes the Ming rulers brought to China. **Ask:** How did these changes help China's economy grow? *(People trusted the government; good roads and canals helped them transport goods; better farmland and new types of rice allowed them to grow more crops.)*

C Critical Thinking Skills

Determining Cause and Effect Discuss the growth of the arts under the Ming rulers. Have students name the kinds of art that flourished. **Ask:** How do the arts depend on prosperity? *(People cannot buy art or go to plays if they do not have extra money, and without customers, artists cannot support themselves.)* BL

Discuss the literature of the period. **Ask:** What is a novel? *(a long fictional story)* What is the vernacular? *(everyday language)* What was one of the most popular novels of the period? *(The Romance of the Three Kingdoms)* How does writing in the vernacular affect stories and novels? *(It makes them sound more real and convincing.)* AL ELL

R

The strong government of the early Ming emperors provided peace and security. As a result, the Chinese economy began to grow. Hong Wu rebuilt many canals and farms. He also ordered that new roads be paved and new forests planted. Agriculture thrived as farmers worked on the new lands and grew more crops.

Ming rulers also repaired and expanded the Grand Canal. This allowed merchants to ship rice and other products between southern and northern China. Chinese traders introduced new types of rice from Southeast Asia that grew faster. More food was available to the growing number of people living in cities.

The Ming also supported the silk industry. They encouraged farmers to start growing cotton and weaving cloth. For the first time, cotton became the cloth worn by most Chinese.

This painting from a Ming vase shows Chinese farm workers collecting tea.

Arts and Literature

The arts flourished during the Ming dynasty. Newly wealthy merchants and artisans wanted entertainment and could afford to pay for printed books and trips to the theater. During the Ming period, Chinese writers produced **novels,** or long fictional stories. One of the most popular was *The Romance of the Three Kingdoms*. It described military rivalries at the end of the Han period. Many novels of the time were written in vernacular, or everyday language. Writers avoided formal language to tell their tales. Instead they tried to make their stories sound as if they had been told aloud by storytellers. Traditional Chinese dramas had been banned during the years of Mongol rule, but under the Ming they were restored to the stage. Actors in costumes performed stories of the day using words, music, dance, and symbolic gestures. C

✓ PROGRESS CHECK

Explaining What was the purpose of the Imperial City?

Chinese Exploration

GUIDING QUESTION *How did Chinese contact with the outside world change during the Ming dynasty?*

Early Ming emperors wanted to know more about the world outside of China and to expand Chinese influence abroad. Ming emperors built a large fleet of ships to sail to other countries. The ships, known as junks, usually traveled along the coast of

Reading HELPDESK CCSS

census a count of the number of people in a country
novel a long fictional story

networks Online Teaching Options

IMAGE

Ming Vases

Analyzing Images Have students click on "more information" to read about Ming vases and particularly about the one shown. Have them observe the fineness of the details and the delicacy of the vase. **Ask:** What is the design in the center of the vase? *(a vine with a flower)* What colors are used? *(copper-red on the white porcelain base)*

See page 471F for other online activities.

networks
Ming Vases
Today, original Ming vases are prized around the world for their masterful craftsmanship and delicate features.
During the Ming dynasty, pottery was mainly produced in the city of Jingdezhen in the south. The abundance of clay there, as well as the wood needed to heat the kilns, made Jingdezhen a suitable place for making pottery.
In the early 1300s, potters began to put a mark on the bottom of their pieces to identify the ruling family of the time. Some of the first pieces of Ming porcelain to be marked were those with copper-red designs under a transparent, or see-through, glaze. Created in this style, the vase shown here sold in 2006 for over $10 million!
BOBBY YIP/Reuters/Corbis

ANSWER, p. 500

✓ PROGRESS CHECK The Imperial City was the center of the government. The emperor and his family lived in the Forbidden City.

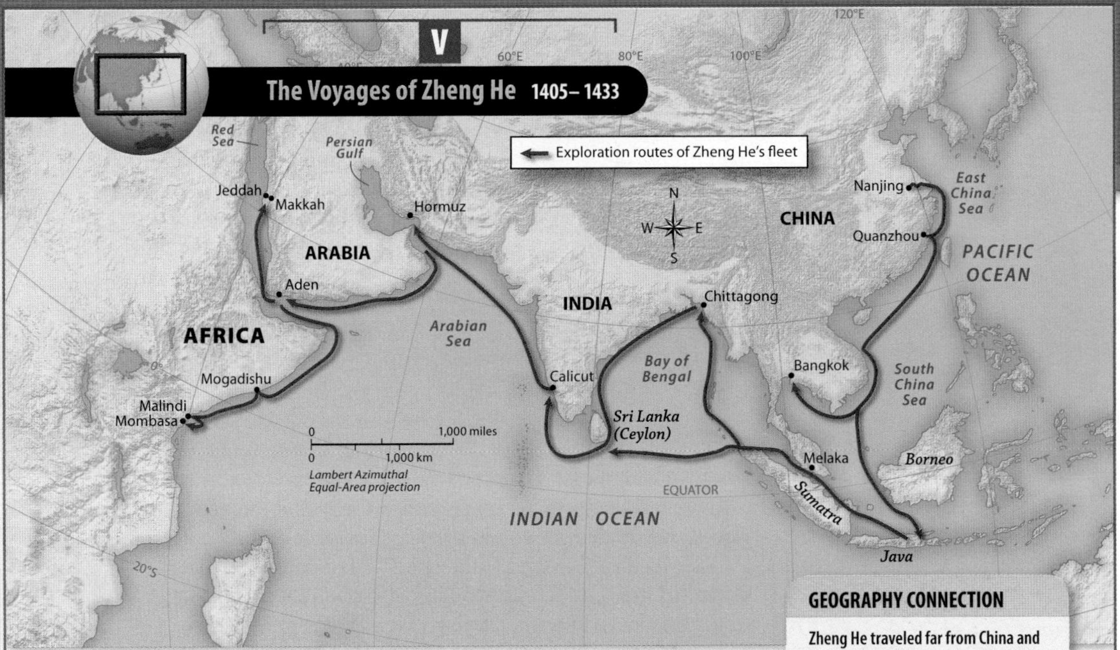

GEOGRAPHY CONNECTION

Zheng He traveled far from China and brought back many exotic items. He also spread Chinese culture.

1. **REGIONS** About how far is Nanjing from Chittagong?
2. **PLACE** Jeddah is on the coast of what body of water?
3. **CRITICAL THINKING** ***Making Connections*** Why were Zheng He's voyages important to the Chinese and other parts of the world?

China. They could also sail on the open sea. Between A.D. 1405 and A.D. 1433, Ming emperors sent the Chinese fleet on seven overseas voyages. They wanted to trade with other kingdoms and demonstrate Chinese power. They also wanted to demand that weaker kingdoms pay tribute to China.

The leader of these journeys was a Chinese Muslim and court official named Zheng He (JUNG HUH). The voyages of Zheng He were quite impressive. On the first voyage, nearly 28,000 men sailed on 62 large ships and 250 smaller ships. The largest ship was over 440 feet (134 m) long. That was more than five times as long as the Santa María that Christopher Columbus sailed almost 90 years later.

R

The Travels of Zheng He

Zheng He took his first fleet to Southeast Asia. In later voyages, he reached the western coast of India and the city-states of East Africa. Zheng He wrote about his travels:

PRIMARY SOURCE

> “We have traversed [traveled] more than 100,000 li [30,000 mi. or 50,000 km] of immense water spaces and have beheld in the ocean huge waves like mountains rising sky-high, . . . and we have set eyes on barbarian [foreign] regions far away, hidden in a blue transparency of light vapours, [fog] while our sails, loftily unfurled like clouds, day and night continued their course, rapid like that of a star, traversing [crossing] those savage waves.”
>
> —**from tablet erected in Fujian, China, by Zheng He**

V Visual Skills

Analyzing Maps Have students study the map. Ask them to describe where the voyages took Zheng He. Elicit that he explored almost the entire southern coast of Asia and the easternmost coast of Africa—almost everywhere he could reach via the ships of that time. **Ask: What was the southernmost point of his voyages?** *(Java)* **What cities did he visit in Arabia?** *(Jeddah, Makkah, Aden)* **What oceans did Zheng He travel on during his voyages?** *(Pacific and Indian oceans)* **Visual/Spatial**

R Reading Skills

Discussing After students have read the text, guide a discussion of the Ming emperors' motives for sponsoring these voyages of exploration. **Ask: Why do you think the Chinese sent such very large fleets on these voyages?** *(Possible answers: The voyages were trading expeditions as well as voyages of discovery, and they needed the ability to carry large amounts of trade goods. They wanted to impress the countries they visited with their sea power, to obtain tribute.)* **What do you find most interesting about Zheng He's voyages? Explain.** *(Students might remark upon the great distances he traveled, the size of his fleets, or the size of his ships.)* Ask students to support their answers with evidence from the text.

MAP

The Voyages of Zheng He, A.D. 1405–A.D. 1433

Analyzing Maps Have students click on the item in the map key and then click on Nanjing to activate Zhen He's exploration routes. **Ask: Where did Zheng He begin his voyages?** *(in the city of Nanjing)* **Where was his most distant stop?** *(Mombasa, Africa)* **What happened when Zheng He reached the northern tip of Sumatra?** *(He evidently divided his fleet, one part heading to Chittagong and one to Sri Lanka.)*

See page 471F for other online activities.

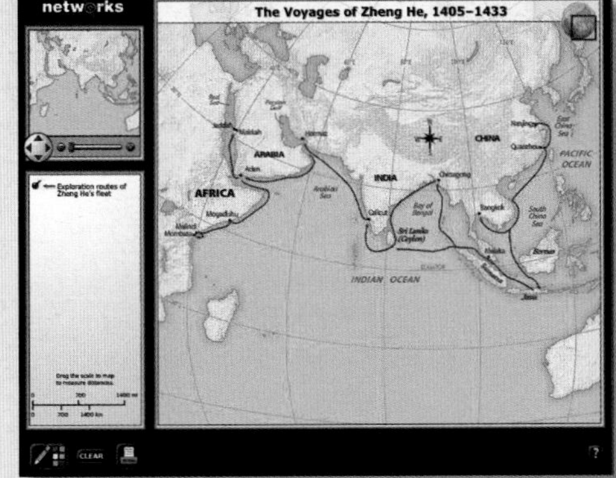

ANSWERS, p. 501

GEOGRAPHY CONNECTION

1. Nanjing is about 1,750 miles (2,815 km) from Chittagong.
2. Jeddah is on the coast of the Red Sea.
3. **CRITICAL THINKING** Zheng He's voyages spread Chinese culture to other parts of the world and also introduced foreign ideas to China. The voyages also helped increase trade between China and other parts of the world and demonstrated Chinese power.

R1 Reading Skills

Describing Have students review the section on Zheng He's voyages. As a class, discuss the results of his many voyages. Point out that Zheng He's travels opened many parts of Asia to trade with China. **Ask:** What Chinese trade goods did Zheng He take with him on his voyages? *(silk, paper, porcelain)* What exotic items did he return with? *(giraffes and other African animals; foreign visitors)* Why did Chinese merchants decide to settle in these distant locations? *(They realized that trade between China and these places would be profitable.)* AL

W Writing Skills

Argument Discuss the negative attitudes of some Chinese officials toward Zheng He's voyages. Invite student reactions to consider this point of view. Then ask students to write a short essay defending the value of trade and contact with foreign lands. Have students post their essays on the class or school Web site.

R2 Reading Skills

Identifying Ask students to read the section titled "Arrival of Europeans." Explain that despite the decision to cut themselves off from trade with the outside, the Chinese could not avoid the Portuguese. **Ask:** What was the Chinese attitude toward the Portuguese traders? *(They thought the Portuguese were uncivilized barbarians.)*

The Jesuits tried to convert the Chinese to Christianity. This image shows a Jesuit convent in China.

Bettmann/CORBIS

R1 At the different ports he visited, Zheng He traded Chinese goods, such as silk, paper, and porcelain. He returned with items unknown in China. For example, Zheng He brought giraffes and other animals from Africa, which fascinated Emperor Yong Le. Yong Le placed them in his imperial zoo in Beijing. Zheng He also brought back visitors from the outside world, including representatives from South and Southeast Asia. The voyages of Zheng He encouraged Chinese merchants to settle in Southeast Asia and India. In these places, they traded goods and spread Chinese culture.

W Despite these benefits, Chinese officials complained that the **ongoing** trips cost too much. They also said that these voyages would introduce unwanted foreign ideas. Some officials also believed that being a merchant was an unworthy and selfish occupation. A Confucian teaching said that people should place loyalty to society ahead of their own desires.

After Zheng He died in A.D. 1433, Confucian officials convinced the emperor to end the voyages. The fleet's ships were taken apart, and the construction of seagoing vessels was stopped. As a result, China's trade with other countries sharply declined. Within 50 years, the Chinese shipbuilding technology became outdated.

Arrival of Europeans

R2 Ming China was not able to cut off all contacts with the rest of the world. In A.D. 1514, ships from the European country of Portugal (POHR•chih•GUHL) arrived off the coast of southern China. It was the first direct contact between China and Europe since the journeys of Marco Polo.

The Portuguese wanted to trade with China and **convert** the Chinese to Christianity. At the time, the Ming government paid little attention to the arrival of the Portuguese. China was a powerful civilization and did not feel threatened by outsiders. To the Chinese, the Europeans were **barbarians** (bahr•BEHR•ee•uhnz), or uncivilized people.

Reading HELPDESK CCSS

barbarian an uncivilized person

Academic Vocabulary (Tier 2 Words)

ongoing continuously moving forward

convert to bring from one belief to another

networks Online Teaching Options

GAME

Fill in the Blank Game: Chinese Exploration

Applying Ask students to work in small groups and compete to see who answers the most questions correctly.

See page 471F for other online activities.

At first, local officials refused to trade with the Portuguese. The Chinese hoped the foreigners would give up and go home. By A.D. 1600, however, the Portuguese had built a trading post at the port of Macao (muh•KAU) in southern China. Portuguese ships carried goods between China and Japan. Trade between Europe and China, however, remained limited.

C

Despite limited contact, European ideas did reach China. Christian missionaries made the voyage to China on European merchant ships. Many of these missionaries were Jesuits, a group of Roman Catholic priests. The Jesuits were highly educated and hoped to establish Christian schools in China. Their knowledge of science impressed Chinese officials. However, the Jesuits did not convince many Chinese to accept Christianity.

R

The Fall of the Ming

After a long period of growth, the Ming dynasty began to weaken. Dishonest officials took over the country. They placed heavy taxes on farmers. The farmers objected to the taxes and began to revolt.

As law and order collapsed, a people—the Manchus—from the north prepared to invade a weakened China. Like the Chinese, the Manchus had been conquered by the Mongols. They had retreated to an area northeast of China's Great Wall, known today as Manchuria. The Manchus defeated the Chinese armies and captured Beijing. In A.D. 1644, they set up a new dynasty called the Qing (CHEENG) dynasty.

✓ PROGRESS CHECK

Analyzing Why did Chinese officials oppose overseas voyages?

LESSON 4 REVIEW 

Review Vocabulary (Tier 3 Words)

1. How would officials have taken a *census* of China's population? RH.6–8.2, RH.6–8.4
2. Why did the Chinese consider Europeans to be *barbarians*? RH.6–8.2, RH.6–8.4

Answer the Guiding Questions

3. ***Describing*** Describe the Imperial City and the Forbidden City. RH.6–8.2
4. ***Identifying*** How did the Ming dynasty change China? RH.6–8.2
5. ***Explaining*** Why did China's officials discourage the voyages of Zheng He? RH.6–8.2
6. ***Summarizing*** What effect did the arrival of the Jesuits have on the Chinese? RH.6–8.2
7. **ARGUMENT** Imagine that you are Zheng He, and government officials have threatened to stop supporting your voyages. Write a letter to persuade officials to let you continue traveling. Give at least three reasons why you should be allowed to continue. WHST.6–8.1, WHST.6–8.10

C Critical Thinking Skills

Making Inferences Discuss the ongoing relationship between the Portuguese and the Chinese. Point out that despite the Chinese desire to remain isolated, the Portuguese built a trading post in a southern Chinese city. **Ask: Why would the Chinese allow the Portuguese to build this trading post?** *(Elicit that the Chinese were not united in their opposition to foreign trade.)* BL

R Reading Skills

Discussing Direct students to read the text. As a class, discuss the other outsiders—the Jesuits—that entered China despite the official opposition to contact with foreigners. **Ask: What did the Chinese like about the Jesuits?** *(their knowledge of science)* **How successful were the Jesuits in converting the Chinese to Christianity?** *(not very)* AL

Have students complete the Lesson 4 Review.

CLOSE & REFLECT

Lead students in a discussion of how a society's beliefs affect the way its government operates. Ask students to draw examples from the lesson as well as from their understanding of U.S. politics and government.

ANSWER, p. 503

✓ PROGRESS CHECK Chinese officials thought the voyages were too expensive and that the trips would bring back unwanted foreign ideas to China. They also believed it was wrong for trading to benefit only the merchants instead of society as a whole.

LESSON 4 REVIEW ANSWERS

1. The officials would have counted the Chinese and recorded the numbers.
2. They thought the Europeans were uncivilized people.
3. The Imperial City was a large area filled with palaces and government buildings. At the center was the Forbidden City, where the emperor and his family lived. Many beautiful gardens and huge palaces were built in the Forbidden City.
4. The Ming dynasty brought order to China by bringing back civil service examinations, conducting censuses, rebuilding canals and farms, paving roads, planting forests, supporting the silk industry, and repairing the Grand Canal. These efforts helped improve trade and the economy. More food was available, and the population began to grow.
5. Chinese officials were convinced that the sea voyages were too expensive and that too many foreign ideas were entering China. They also considered trading to be an unworthy—even selfish—occupation. Traders gained wealth for themselves and did not contribute to improving Chinese society.
6. The Jesuits had little effect beyond some trading. European Jesuits who hoped to convert the Chinese to Christianity had little success.
7. Students' letters should point out that sea voyages demonstrated Chinese power, extended China's influence, and added to the wealth and prestige of China through trade. The voyages also exposed China to the ideas, information, and technologies in other places. In addition, the sea voyages meant China could maintain a high level of shipbuilding and sailing skills. To lose those skills would weaken China's power and influence in the world.

CHAPTER 17
Activities Answers

CHAPTER REVIEW ACTIVITY

Have students create a two-column chart like the one below. They should label one column "Empress Wu" and the other "Kublai Khan." Then lead the class in a discussion about how both leaders affected China's government, economy, and culture during their reigns. Have students write details from the discussion in their organizers. Challenge students to make a generalization about the impact of each ruler, based on their charts.

Empress Wu	Kublai Khan

REVIEW THE ENDURING UNDERSTANDINGS

Review this chapter's Enduring Understandings with students:

- ***People, places, and ideas change over time.***
- ***Leaders can bring about change in a society.***

Now pose the following questions in a class discussion to apply these to the chapter. **Ask:**

- **How did the Mongols change from being invaders and conquerors to being rulers?** *(The Mongols were some of the fiercest, most brutal of all conquerors. Apart from their skills at warfare, the Mongols struck terror in the hearts of people. They looted and burned cities and wreaked destruction everywhere as they swept through the land. But after the Mongols defeated their enemies and became rulers, their personalities changed. They organized government and provided safety for people. They respected the religions, culture, and society of the peoples they ruled.)*
- **How did Ming rulers bring change to Chinese society?** *(The Ming rulers took over from the Yuan rulers who had become corrupt and had lost the trust and respect of the Chinese people. The Ming restored that trust. The first ruler, Zhu Yuanzhang, brought peace and order to the society. His son, Yong Le, moved the capital to Beijing and built the magnificent Forbidden City. He brought back civil service examinations for public officials. Through efforts such as these, the Ming rulers provided peace and security. Roads were built. International trade grew through exploration. The economy grew and society prospered. Writing novels, making porcelain, writing and performing drama, and other arts flourished under the Ming rulers.)*

CHAPTER 17 Activities CCSS

Write your answers on a separate piece of paper.

1 Exploring the Essential Question WHST.6–8.2, WHST.6–8.10

INFORMATIVE/EXPLANATORY How would you describe imperial China's relations with other cultures through trade, travel, and war? Write an essay that summarizes how and why imperial China came into contact with groups outside its borders.

2 21st Century Skills RH.6–8.2, WHST.6–8.6, WHST.6–8.9

SEQUENCE EVENTS Review the chapter and identify at least 10 important events that took place during imperial China. Try to vary the types of events, including military as well as cultural and civic developments. Then create a time line that shows the sequence of the events or developments and explains their importance. Use presentation software or art supplies to create a time line that includes images and text. Present your work to the class.

3 Thinking Like a Historian RH.6–8.2

DRAWING CONCLUSIONS Think about the effects that an invention such as gunpowder had on imperial China. Then create a diagram like the one shown here. In the diagram, draw a conclusion about how that invention might have affected China.

Invention: ____________

Effects
1.
2.
3.

Conclusion: ____________

4 GEOGRAPHY ACTIVITY

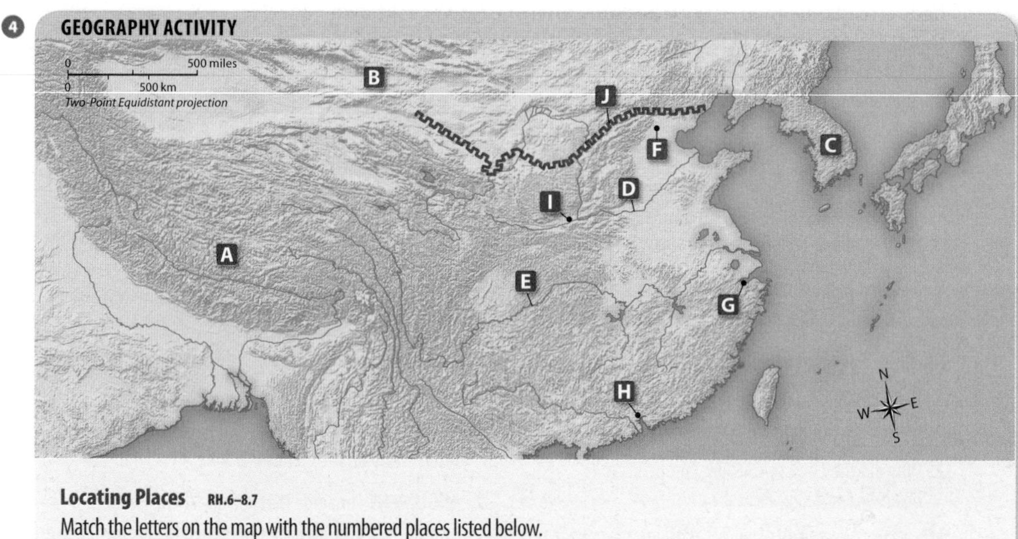

Locating Places RH.6–8.7

Match the letters on the map with the numbered places listed below.

1. Beijing
2. Hangzhou
3. Guangzhou
4. Changan
5. Great Wall
6. Tibet
7. Mongolia
8. Korean Peninsula
9. Huang He (Yellow River)
10. Chang Jiang (Yangtze River)

ACTIVITIES ANSWERS

Exploring the Essential Question

1 Students' essays should suggest that China had positive and negative interactions with outsiders. When the Chinese were openly trading on the Silk Road during the Tang dynasty, China benefited because its goods, ideas, and influence were spread throughout the world. In return, China obtained goods and wealth. Even after China was invaded by the Mongols, the Chinese eventually experienced peace, order, and prosperity. Travelers such as the Italian Marco Polo visited and sent reports of China's greatness and inventions back to Europe. During the Ming dynasty, however, government officials became mistrustful of influence from outsiders. They stopped all sea voyages, and they tried to limit the influence of Europeans, such as Portuguese missionaries.

21st Century Skills

2 Students should select 10 events from the chapter that they consider important to the development of China during the imperial period. They might select events such as the building of the Grand Canal, the restoration of civil service examinations, the invention of printing using movable type, the invasion of the Mongols, and the reading of novels. Students' time lines should clearly indicate the year the event happened. They should also provide a sentence or two that explains each event's significance. For example, the Grand Canal made it easier to transport goods to all areas of China.

CHAPTER 17 Assessment CCSS

REVIEW THE GUIDING QUESTIONS

Directions: Choose the best answer for each question.

RH.6–8.2
1. After years of war, what major construction project helped unify China during the Sui dynasty?
   A. the Forbidden City
   B. the Silk Road
   C. the Great Wall
   D. the Grand Canal

RH.6–8.2
2. The Chinese rulers preferred Confucianism over Buddhism because it taught
   F. how to escape suffering.
   G. how to pass the civil service examination.
   H. the importance of being active in society.
   I. the use of terror in conquering enemies.

RH.6–8.2
3. Which technological development immediately helped the Chinese economy during the Tang and Song dynasties?
   A. the use of coal for heating
   B. the printing process
   C. steel production
   D. shipbuilding

RH.6–8.2
4. Which idea would poets write about during China's "golden age of the arts"?
   F. Nature is beautiful.
   G. The people are happy.
   H. The emperor is cruel.
   I. Life lasts too long.

RH.6–8.2
5. Which of the following is the best description of the Mongols in China?
   A. disciplined fighters but lazy emperors
   B. fierce enemies but good rulers
   C. failed soldiers but respectful leaders
   D. loyal troops but selfish kings

RH.6–8.2
6. What was the main reason Ming emperors sent ships overseas?
   F. to conquer new territories
   G. to demonstrate China's power
   H. to escape invading Manchus
   I. to share new technologies with the West

505

Thinking Like a Historian

3. Students should select a technological invention discussed in the chapter, such as printing or gunpowder, and identify at least two effects of the invention. For example, printing allowed for the spread of Chinese ideas and the invention of paper currency. The conclusion that students may draw is that printing improved China's economy and communications.

Locating Places

4. **1.** F, **2.** G, **3.** H, **4.** I, **5.** J, **6.** A, **7.** B, **8.** C, **9.** D, **10.** E

ASSESSMENT ANSWERS

Review the Guiding Questions

1. **D** The Sui built the Grand Canal to connect two major rivers and make travel easier, thus unifying China. The Forbidden City was built by the Ming dynasty. The Great Wall was first built earlier in Chinese history. Thus, choice D is the correct answer.

2. **H** Leaders preferred Confucianism because it emphasized the importance of being active in this world. Buddhism taught people that they could escape suffering. Students had to understand Confucianism to pass civil service examinations, but the secret to passing was not among the principles. Confucianism emphasized living in harmony, not using terror. Choice H is the correct answer.

3. **B** Although the use of coal made the production of steel possible, it was the printing of paper money that gave an immediate boost to China's trade-based economy. Shipbuilding did not begin in earnest until the Ming dynasty. Therefore, choice B is the correct answer.

4. **F** Most poetry written during the "golden age" expressed the ideas that nature is beautiful and life is too short. Although poet Du Fu wrote about the hardships of the poor, no poet of the time would have criticized the emperor or complained that life was too long. Choice F is the correct answer.

5. **B** The Mongols used terror to conquer enemies and gain territory. However, they were organized and respectful rulers of the empire who tolerated different faiths and encouraged trade and prosperity. They were successful and loyal soldiers but also good leaders. Thus, choice B is the correct answer.

6. **G** One of the main reasons Ming emperors dispatched ships was to extend China's influence—as well as to increase trade and demand tribute from nearby regions. These were ways to demonstrate China's power. When the Ming dynasty collapsed, the Manchurians invaded Beijing; the emperor did not escape by ship. Choice G is the correct answer.

Assessment Answers

Analyzing Documents

7 **D** The details support the conclusion that the Mongols trained their children in riding and fighting skills from a very young age. The details do not suggest that Mongol children fought in battles or felt hatred. Mongol children might have been free to play, but they were taught skills while playing. Therefore, choice D is correct.

8 **H** Students should recall that Europeans like Marco Polo lived in China under the Mongols and would have observed Mongol traditions. A European was unlikely to be captured by Mongols or to be a Mongol fighter. It was also unlikely that there were many books about Mongols to read. Thus, choice H is correct.

Short Response

9 Empress Wu eliminated her opponents.

10 The empress was an effective ruler. She was efficient, decisive, brave, and willing to take action in order to rule China well.

Extended Response

11 Students should explain that the civil service examination is a written test that helps identify the most talented candidates for government jobs. The exam means that any good candidate, not just politically connected individuals, can obtain these jobs. These civil servants are more talented and better suited for their jobs; therefore, the government benefits. Students should note that civil service positions are prestigious and a good source of income.

CHAPTER 17 Assessment  

(continued)

DBQ ANALYZING DOCUMENTS

John of Plano Carpini explained why the Mongols were skilled warriors.

"Their children begin as soon as they are two or three years old to ride and manage horses and to gallop on them, and they are given bows to suit their stature [size] and are taught to shoot; they are extremely agile [able to move quickly] and also intrepid [fearless]."

—from *History of the Mongols*, by John of Plano Carpini

RH.6–8.1, RH.6–8.6

7 **Drawing Conclusions** Which statement best summarizes why the Mongols were skilled soldiers?

A. They believed that children should be free to play.
B. They made children fight their battles for them.
C. They taught their children to hate other people.
D. They were trained to ride horses and fight at a young age.

RH.6–8.1, RH.6–8.6

8 **Inferring** What can you infer about the author's experiences with the Mongols?

F. He read about them in a book.
G. He was captured by the Mongols.
H. He was a visitor to the Mongol empire.
I. He was a Mongol fighter.

SHORT RESPONSE

"[Empress Wu] continued to eliminate [get rid of] potential rivals, even when these were her own relatives, but she governed the empire with great efficiency, . . . Her great ability as an administrator, her courage, decisive [able to make judgments quickly] character, and readiness to use ruthless [unforgiving] means . . . won her the respect, if not the love, of the court."

—from "Wuhou," *Encyclopedia Britannica*

RH.6–8.1, RH.6–8.6

9 According to the reading, how did Empress Wu treat her opponents?

RH.6–8.1, RH.6–8.6

10 Why did the empress win the respect of the court?

EXTENDED RESPONSE

WHST.6–8.2, WHST.6–8.10

11 **Informative/Explanatory** You are studying for the civil service examination during the Tang dynasty. Write an essay to explain the examination and how it helps China. Tell why the examination is important to you and your family.

Need Extra Help?

If You've Missed Question	1	2	3	4	5	6	7	8	9	10	11
Review Lesson	1	1	2	2	3	4	3	3	1	1	1

506 *Imperial China*

networks Online Teaching Options

More Assessment Resources

The *Assess* tab in the online Teacher Lesson Center includes resources to help students improve their test-taking skills. It also contains many project-based rubrics to help you assess students' work.

CHAPTER 18

Civilizations of Korea, Japan, and Southeast Asia Planner

UNDERSTANDING BY DESIGN®

Enduring Understanding

- *People, places, and ideas change over time.*

Essential Questions

- *Why do people form governments?*
- *How does geography influence the way people live?*
- *How do new ideas change the way people live?*
- *What makes a culture unique?*

Predictable Misunderstandings

Students may think:

- *There is no difference between Korean culture and Chinese culture.*
- *Japan became a powerful nation only by going to war with its rivals.*
- *A shogun and a samurai are the same.*
- *No major religions other than Shinto are practiced in Southeast Asia.*

Assessment Evidence

Performance Task:

- *Hands-On Chapter Project*

Other Evidence:

- *Discussion answers to Korea as a bridge between China and Japan*
- *Identification of geographical features*
- *Answers from analyzing visuals*
- *Responses to Interactive Whiteboard Activities*
- *Geography and History Activity*
- *21st Century Skills Activities*
- *Economics and History Activity*
- *Lesson Reviews*
- *Analysis paper on why the Shinto religion may be followed today*
- *Illustration of one area of Southeast Asia*
- *Discussion answers on how the area was influenced by cultures of India, China, and Islam*

SUGGESTED PACING GUIDE

Introducing the Chapter	1 Day	Lesson 3	2 Days
Lesson 1	1 Day	Lesson 4	1 Day
Lesson 2	1 Day	Chapter Wrap-Up and Assessment	1 Day

TOTAL TIME 7 Days

Key for Using the Teacher Edition

SKILL-BASED ACTIVITIES

Types of skill activities found in the Teacher Edition.

V Visual Skills require students to analyze maps, graphs, charts, and photos.

R Reading Skills help students practice reading skills and master vocabulary.

W Writing Skills provide writing opportunities to help students comprehend the text.

C Critical Thinking Skills help students apply and extend what they have learned.

T Technology Skills require students to use digital tools effectively.

*Letters are followed by a number when there is more than one of the same type of skill on the page.

DIFFERENTIATED INSTRUCTION

All activities are written for the on-level student unless otherwise marked with the leveled labels below.

BL Beyond Level
AL Approaching Level
ELL English Language Learners

All students benefit from activities that utilize different learning styles. Many activities are marked as below when a particular learning style is highlighted.

Intrapersonal	**Naturalist**
Logical/Mathematical	**Kinesthetic**
Visual/Spatial	**Auditory/Musical**
Verbal/Linguistic	**Interpersonal**

NCSS Standards covered in "Civilizations of Korea, Japan, and Southeast Asia"

Learners will understand:

1 CULTURE

1. "Culture" refers to the socially transmitted behaviors, beliefs, values, traditions, institutions, and ways of living together for a group of people

2. Concepts such as beliefs, values, institutions, cohesion, diversity, accommodation, adaptation, assimilation, and dissonance

4. That the beliefs, values, and behaviors of a culture form an integrated system that helps shape the activities and ways of life that define a culture

5. How individuals learn the elements of their culture through interactions with others, and how individuals learn of other cultures through communication and study

7. How people from different cultures develop different values and ways of interpreting experience

8. That language, behaviors, and beliefs of different cultures can both contribute to and pose barriers to cross-cultural understanding

2 TIME, CONTINUITY, AND CHANGE

5. Key historical periods and patterns of change within and across cultures (e.g., the rise and fall of ancient civilizations, the development of technology, the rise of modern nation-states, and the establishment and breakdown of colonial systems)

6. The origins and influences of social, cultural, political, and economic systems

7. The contributions of key persons, groups, and events from the past and their influence on the present

3 PEOPLE, PLACES, AND ENVIRONMENTS

2. Concepts such as: location, region, place, migration, as well as human and physical systems

4. The roles of different kinds of population centers in a region or nation

5. The concept of regions identifies links between people in different locations according to specific criteria (e.g., physical, economic, social, cultural, or religious)

6. Patterns of demographic and political change, and cultural diffusion in the past and present (e.g., changing national boundaries, migration, and settlement, and the diffusion of and changes in customs and ideas)

8. Factors that contribute to cooperation and conflict among peoples of the nation and world, including language, religion, and political beliefs

4 INDIVIDUALS, GROUPS, AND INSTITUTIONS

6. That cultural diffusion occurs when groups migrate

7. That institutions may promote or undermine social conformity

CHAPTER OPENER PLANNER

Students will know:

- *the reasons Korea is described as a bridge between China and Japan.*
- *how Korea built a civilization.*
- *how geography affected ways of life in Japan and Southeast Asia.*
- *what caused military leaders to rise to power in Japan.*
- *why powerful kingdoms and empires developed in Southeast Asia.*

Students will be able to:

- ***explain** why Korea is considered a bridge between China and Japan.*
- ***describe** the ways in which Korea was influenced by China and Japan.*
- ***explain** how geography shaped Japan's society.*
- ***discuss** why nature was important to the Japanese.*
- ***describe** the influence of China during the Nara period.*
- ***explain** how military leaders became powerful in Southeast Asia.*
- ***explain** the flourishing of culture during the time of the shoguns.*
- ***identify** geographical features that affected settlement and early ways of life in Southeast Asia.*
- ***explain** why powerful kingdoms and empires developed in Southeast Asia.*

UNDERSTANDING BY DESIGN®

☑ Print Teaching Options

V Visual Skills

- ☐ **P. 508** Students analyze a map of Japan, Korea, and southeast Asia and locate strategic points for sea trade.
Visual/Spatial
- ☐ **P. 509** Students use a time line to answer questions.
Visual/Spatial

☑ Online Teaching Options

V Visual Skills

- **MAP** **Empires of Korea, Japan, and Southeast Asia**—Students locate the empires that existed in these areas on a map.
- **TIME LINE** **Civilizations of Korea, Japan, and Southeast Asia A.D. 300 to A.D. 1300s**—Students learn about key events in Korea, Japan, and Southeast Asia during this time period.
- **WORLD ATLAS** Students can use this interactive map to identify regions of the world, learn about individual countries, locate political boundaries, measure distances, and much more.

Project-Based Learning

Hands-On Chapter Project

Travel Itinerary

Student groups will create travel itineraries for a trip to view the historical and geographic highlights of Korea, Japan, or Southeast Asia.

Technology Extension

edtechteacher 21st Century Learning

Virtual Scrapbook

- Find an additional activity online that incorporates technology for this project.
- Visit the EdTechTeacher Web sites (included in the Technology Extension for this chapter) for more links, tutorials, and other resources.

Print Resources

ANCILLARY RESOURCES

These ancillaries are available for every chapter and lesson.

- **Reading Essentials and Study Guide Workbook** AL ELL
- **Chapter Tests and Lesson Quizzes Blackline Masters**

PRINTABLE DIGITAL WORKSHEETS

These printable digital worksheets are available for every chapter and lesson.

- **Hands-On Chapter Projects**
- **What Do You Know? activities**
- **Chapter Summaries (English and Spanish)**
- **Vocabulary Builder activities**
- **Guided Reading activities**

More Media Resources

SUGGESTED VIDEOS MOVIES

Watch clips of films set in medieval Japan, such as *The Men Who Tread on the Tiger's Tail* (1945) NR, directed by Akira Kurosawa.

(Note: Preview clips for age-appropriateness.)

SUGGESTED READING

Grade 6 reading level:

- ***Children of the Dragon: Selected Tales From Vietnam,*** by Sherry Garland

Grade 7 reading level:

- ***Project Mulberry,*** by Linda Sue Park

Grade 8 reading level:

- ***Cricket Never Does: A Collection of Haiku and Tanka,*** by Myra Cohn Livingston

KOREA: HISTORY AND CULTURE

Students will know:
- *the reasons Korea is described as a bridge between China and Japan.*
- *how Korea built a civilization.*

Students will be able to:
- ***explain** why Korea is considered a bridge between China and Japan.*
- ***describe** the ways in which Korea was influenced by China and Japan.*

UNDERSTANDING BY DESIGN®

Print Teaching Options

V Visual Skills

- [ ] **P. 511** Students create a time line that shows events that occurred during the Three Kingdoms period. **BL** **Visual/Spatial** **Interpersonal**
- [ ] **P. 511** Students discuss how natural barriers protected Korea. **Visual/Spatial**
- [ ] **P. 513** Students describe an image of a statue of Wang Kon. **AL** **ELL** **Visual/Spatial**

R Reading Skills

- [ ] **P. 510** Students discuss the legend of Tangun.
- [ ] **P. 512** Students list cultural influences that came to Korea from Japan and China during the Three Kingdoms period.
- [ ] **P. 512** Students use context clues to determine the meanings of unfamiliar **words.** **AL** **ELL**
- [ ] **P. 514** Students tell how the ruler Sejong and the Silla queen Sondok had similar interests.

W Writing Skills

- [ ] **P. 515** Students create and fill in a chart that describes the Chinese, Mongol, and Japanese invasions of Korea. **Verbal/Linguistic**

C Critical Thinking Skills

- [ ] **P. 510** Students make generalizations about Korean culture. **Verbal/Linguistic**
- [ ] **P. 512** Students discuss how the small Silla kingdom was able to conquer the larger kingdoms of Paekche and Koguryo. **BL**
- [ ] **P. 513** Students discuss what they know about Wang Kon and generate questions for further research.
- [ ] **P. 514** Students determine similarities between the Koryo/Yi governments and the Chinese government. **BL**

Online Teaching Options

V Visual Skills

- [ ] **VIDEO** **The Korean Landscape**—Students view a video that describes the geography of this country that lies on a peninsula and has both mountains and coastal plains.
- [ ] **MAP** **Three Kingdoms of Korea c. 400 A.D.**—Students learn of the influence of China and Japan on Korean kingdoms.
- [ ] **MAP** **Geography of Korea**—Students click to learn about Korea's highest peaks and its capital city.
- [ ] **SLIDE SHOW** **Yi Sun-shin & Hwarangdo**—Students learn about the philosophical and religious code followed by elite warriors.
- [ ] **IMAGE** **Korean Fan Dancers**—Students view an image of these traditional dancers who use fans to make butterfly-like effects.

R Reading Skills

- [ ] **GRAPHIC ORGANIZER** **Taking Notes: *Identifying*: Korean Kingdoms and Dynasties**—Students list details about the Korean kingdom and two dynasties that followed the Three Kingdoms period.

C Critical Thinking Skills

- [ ] **IMAGE** **Korean Alphabet**—Students analyze the phonetic alphabet the Koreans developed to replace Chinese characters.
- [ ] **SLIDE SHOW** **Silla Kingdom**—Students analyze artifacts of this Korean kingdom.

T Technology Skills

- [ ] **SELF-CHECK QUIZ** **Lesson 1**—Students receive instant feedback on their mastery of lesson content.
- [ ] **GAME** **Korea: History and Culture Identification Game**—Students match terms and definitions to review lesson vocabulary.

Printable Digital Worksheets

C Critical Thinking Skills

- [ ] **WORKSHEET** **Geography and History Activity: Understanding Borders: Korea**—Students analyze geographical features that form the borders of Korea.

EARLY JAPAN

Students will know:

- *how geography affected ways of life in Japan and Southeast Asia.*

Students will be able to:

- ***explain** how geography shaped Japan's society.*
- ***discuss** why nature was important to the Japanese.*
- ***describe** the influence of China during the Nara period.*

UNDERSTANDING BY DESIGN®

☑ *Print Teaching Options*

R Reading Skills

- ☐ **P. 516** Students analyze the geography of Japan.
- ☐ **P. 517** Students summarize the rise of the Yamato clans, including the emperor Jimmu.

W Writing Skills

- ☐ **P. 518** Students write a fictional story about a nature spirit. **BL** **Naturalist**

C Critical Thinking Skills

- ☐ **P. 516** Students talk about Japan's reliance on the sea. **BL**
- ☐ **P. 517** Students infer the significance of the Yayoi people.
- ☐ **P. 518** Students discuss the effects of Shinto on Japanese culture.
- ☐ **P. 519** Students discuss how Japanese life during the Nara period was similar to that of China.

☑ *Online Teaching Options*

V Visual Skills

- ☐ **VIDEO** **East Asian Religions and Other Cultural Traditions**—Students view a video that describes the many religions practiced in the regions and the cultural ideals shared by East Asians.
- ☐ **MAP** **Geography of Japan**—Students click to learn why Japan has many mountain peaks and is prone to earthquakes.

R Reading Skills

- ☐ **GRAPHIC ORGANIZER** **Taking Notes: *Identifying*: Chinese Cultural Influences on Japan**—Students show how Chinese culture influenced the early Japanese.

C Critical Thinking Skills

- ☐ **SLIDE SHOW** **Buddhist Temples**—Students analyze architectural aspects in the evolution of these religious sites.
- ☐ **IMAGE** **Chinese Calendar**—Students analyze the elements of the Chinese calendar.

T Technology Skills

- ☐ **SELF-CHECK QUIZ** **Lesson 2**—Students receive instant feedback on their mastery of lesson content.
- ☐ **GAME** **Early Japan Fill-in-the-Blank**—Students complete sentences to review lesson content.

☑ *Printable Digital Worksheets*

C Critical Thinking Skills

- ☐ **WORKSHEET** **21st Century Skills Activity: Information Literacy: Use Latitude and Longitude**—Students find and list the latitude and longitude of several Japanese cities.

LESSON 3 PLANNER

MEDIEVAL JAPAN

Students will know:

- *what caused military leaders to rise to power in Japan.*

Students will be able to:

- ***explain** how military leaders became powerful in Southeast Asia.*
- ***explain** the flourishing of culture during the time of the shoguns.*

UNDERSTANDING BY DESIGN®

Print Teaching Options

V Visual Skills

- [ ] **P. 521** Students interpret a painting of a samurai warrior. Visual/Spatial
- [ ] **P. 523** Students create a diagram that shows the sequence of events leading from the Ashikaga shogunate to the rise of the daimyo. AL Visual/Spatial

R Reading Skills

- [ ] **P. 520** Students identify the main idea and supporting details in a paragraph about the rise of nobles. AL ELL
- [ ] **P. 521** Students explain the Bushido code. ELL
- [ ] **P. 523** Students act out skits that show the structure of feudalism in Japan. BL Kinesthetic
- [ ] **P. 524** Students discuss the rise of the artisan class and the increase in trade in Japan.

W Writing Skills

- [ ] **P. 525** Students write an explanation of similarities and differences between Mahayana and Zen Buddhism.
- [ ] **P. 526** Students write a haiku poem.

C Critical Thinking Skills

- [ ] **P. 520** Students identify the advantages and disadvantages of the regents ruling Japan.
- [ ] **P. 522** Students predict what happened after the emperor made Yoritomo a shogun. AL
- [ ] **P. 522** Students infer why the Japanese named typhoons after divine spirits.
- [ ] **P. 523** Students analyze the reasons why wealth collected at the top of Japanese society.
- [ ] **P. 524** Students connect the warrior society in Japan with the loss of freedom among upper-class women. BL
- [ ] **P. 525** Students create a graphic organizer that compares and contrasts Shinto, Mahayana Buddhism, and Zen Buddhism. AL ELL
- [ ] **P. 526** Students hypothesize the problems with a pictographic writing system. BL
- [ ] **P. 527** Students contrast Shinto shrines and Buddhist temples.

T Technology Skills

- [ ] **P. 526** Students research plays, stories, and poems from the shogun period.

Online Teaching Options

V Visual Skills

- [ ] VIDEO **The Samurai**—Students view a video that describes the philosophy of these mighty warriors.
- [ ] IMAGE **Japanese Gardens**—Students examine the elements of these gardens and learn what they represent.
- [ ] SLIDE SHOW **Samurai Weapons**—Students view weapons and armor used by these warriors.

R Reading Skills

- [ ] GRAPHIC ORGANIZER **Taking Notes: *Showing Relationships*: Daimyo and Samurai**—Students show the relationship between daimyo and samurai.
- [ ] IMAGE **Shoguns**—Students learn of these top military commanders who eventually came to rule Japan.
- [ ] BIOGRAPHY **Murasaki Shikibu**—Students read of the life of this Japanese writer.

C Critical Thinking Skills

- [ ] WHITEBOARD ACTIVITY **Sequence of Events, Feudal Japan**—Students match events with the year they happened.
- [ ] CHART **Japanese Feudalism**—Students click to learn about feudal Japan's social strata.
- [ ] SLIDE SHOW **Japanese Art and Architecture**—Students compare examples of Japanese temples and gardens.

T Technology Skills

- [ ] SELF-CHECK QUIZ **Lesson 3**—Students receive instant feedback on their mastery of lesson content.
- [ ] GAME **Medieval Japan Tic-Tac-Toe**—Students capture squares by correctly identifying statements as true or false.

Printable Digital Worksheets

W Writing Skills

- [ ] WORKSHEET **21st Century Skills Activity: Communication: Writing a Poem**—Students learn about tanka poetry and then write their own tanka poem.

SOUTHEAST ASIA: HISTORY AND CULTURE

Students will know:

- *why powerful kingdoms and empires developed in Southeast Asia.*

Students will be able to:

- ***identify*** *geographical features that affected settlement and early ways of life in Southeast Asia.*
- ***explain*** *why powerful kingdoms and empires developed in Southeast Asia.*

UNDERSTANDING BY DESIGN®

☑ Print Teaching Options

V Visual Skills

☐ **P. 531** Students discuss what the design of the Angkor Wat suggests about the culture of southeast Asia. BL

R Reading Skills

☐ **P. 528** Students discuss the vocabulary term *archipelago.* AL ELL

☐ **P. 529** Students discuss the similarities between religion in early Japan and early southeast Asia. **Verbal/Linguistic**

☐ **P. 530** Students identify the main idea in a paragraph about southeast Asian art forms. AL ELL

☐ **P. 532** Students create a table that shows what elements became part of the Thai culture and where they originated.

W Writing Skills

☐ **P. 530** Students summarize how the arrival of Hindu traders ended cultural isolation in southeast Asia.

C Critical Thinking Skills

☐ **P. 528** Based on its geography, students theorize the kinds of cultures that might develop in southeast Asia.

☐ **P. 529** Students discuss why tsunamis pose a serious threat to southeast Asian nations.

☐ **P. 531** Students discuss a primary source that describes a Khmer king.

☐ **P. 532** Students make generalizations about the Sukhothai and Ayutthaya kingdoms.

☐ **P. 533** Students create a three-column chart that shows how India, China, and Arabia influenced the cultures of southeast Asia. AL ELL

☑ Online Teaching Options

V Visual Skills

☐ VIDEO **Religions of Southeast Asia**—Students learn about the predominant religions of the people of Southeast Asia.

☐ MAP **Southeast Asia Today**—Students view modern political boundaries in Southeast Asia.

R Reading Skills

☐ GRAPHIC ORGANIZER **Taking Notes: *Identifying*: Purposes of Angkor Wat**—Students identify the purposes of the temple of Angkor Wat.

☐ IMAGE **Angkor Wat**—Students click to reveal details of "the city that is a temple."

C Critical Thinking Skills

☐ IMAGE **The Strait of Malacca**—Students analyze the importance of this waterway that connects the Indian and Pacific oceans.

T Technology Skills

☐ SELF-CHECK QUIZ **Lesson 4**—Students receive instant feedback on their mastery of lesson content.

☐ GAME **Southeast Asia: History and Culture eFlashcards**—Students flip flashcards to review lesson vocabulary.

☑ Printable Digital Worksheets

C Critical Thinking Skills

☐ WORKSHEET **Economics of History Activity: The Rise of Angkor**—Students analyze how the building of Angkor both strengthened and weakened the Khmer empire.

INTERVENTION AND REMEDIATION STRATEGIES

LESSON 1 Korea: History and Culture

Reading and Comprehension

To ensure comprehension of the concepts in this lesson, organize students into small groups. Then have each group create a study guide by outlining the major periods of Korean history, with one or two important details under each.

Text Evidence

Have students review the meanings of the words *hierarchy* and *scholarly.* Have them explain how the sentences in which the words are used in the textbook give clues to their meanings. In pairs, have students list synonyms for each word and use each word in a sentence.

LESSON 2 Early Japan

Reading and Comprehension

In pairs, have students create a chart comparing and contrasting the roles of Jimmu and Prince Shotoku in early Japanese history.

Text Evidence

Ask students to review the section on Shinto in early Japanese culture. Then have them research the practice of Shinto in Japan today and prepare a short digital presentation.

LESSON 3 Medieval Japan

Reading and Comprehension

Have students write sentences using the new lesson vocabulary. Sentences should show an understanding of the meaning of each word and how it applies to the lesson content.

Text Evidence

Have students write a short paragraph explaining the relationships of samurai and the shogun.

LESSON 4 Southeast Asia: History and Culture

Reading and Comprehension

Help students create graphic organizers to collect details about each of the kingdoms discussed in the text. Tell them to fill in the organizers as they read and to review them when they are done.

Text Evidence

Direct students to choose one kingdom from this lesson and then select one important religion from that region. Have students research the way religion is practiced in that particular place. Remind them to be sure they are using reliable sources.

Online Resources

Approaching Level Reader

Use this online lower-level text that corresponds directly to the text in the Student Edition. It includes a Spanish version.

Guided Reading Activities

This resource uses graphic organizers and guiding questions to help students with comprehension.

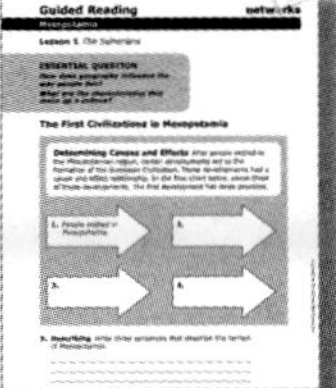

What Do You Know?

Use these worksheets to pre-assess student's background knowledge before they study the chapter.

Reading Essentials and Study Guide Workbook

This resource offers writing and reading activities for the approaching-level student. Also available in Spanish.

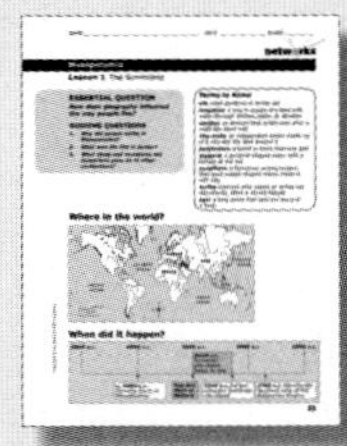

Self-Check Quizzes

This online assessment tool provides instant feedback for students to check their progress.

How Do I Teach
Geography Skills in the History Classroom?

Geography is an integral part of the study of history, which considers the human experience in terms of time and chronology. Geography focuses on the environment, and the interactions of physical and human systems within that environment. The five themes of geography—location, place, regions, movement, human-environment interaction—provide a framework to inform students' study of history.

Option 1 Human-Environment Interaction

- Review with the class how the climate of an area and the vegetation that grows there can influence population density.
- Ask students to think about how the climate and the vegetation of the area where they live may have influenced population density.
- Based on the map on this page, ask students where they think most of the world's people live. Why? What areas would they expect to be sparsely populated? Why?
- Ask students to explain whether the climate or the vegetation has more impact on an area's population density.

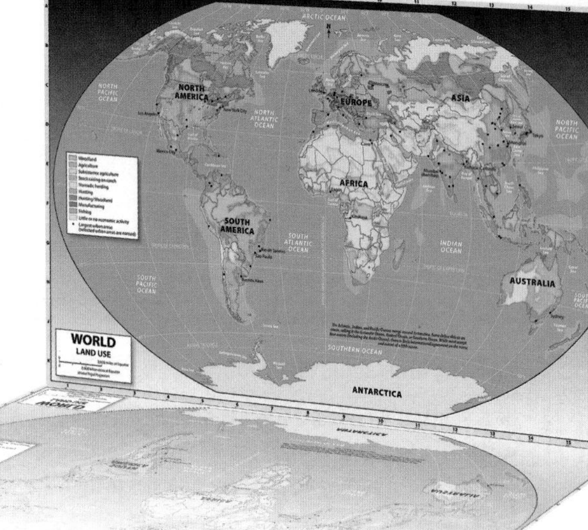

Option 2 Location

- Use what your students know about their school to make a connection with the five themes of geography. Write each theme on the board.
- Ask students how they would describe the location of your school. List student answers on the board.
- Then have students describe the physical and human characteristics that make the school unique.
- Continue until you have two or three student descriptions for each of the five themes of geography.

Option 3 Five Themes

- Explain that the way people have shaped a region changes over time. Organize the class into groups and assign each group a period of time in their local or state history.
- Have each group examine that time period through their understanding of the five geographic themes listed above.
- Students should consider the following: why this area was better suited for settlement than other nearby areas; patterns as to who came into or left the area; how people were employed; how the natural surroundings affected human action; and how human action affected the natural surroundings.

Civilizations of Korea, Japan, and Southeast Asia

A.D. 300 to A.D. 1300s

ESSENTIAL QUESTIONS • *Why do people form governments?* • *How does geography influence the way people live?* • *What makes a culture unique?*

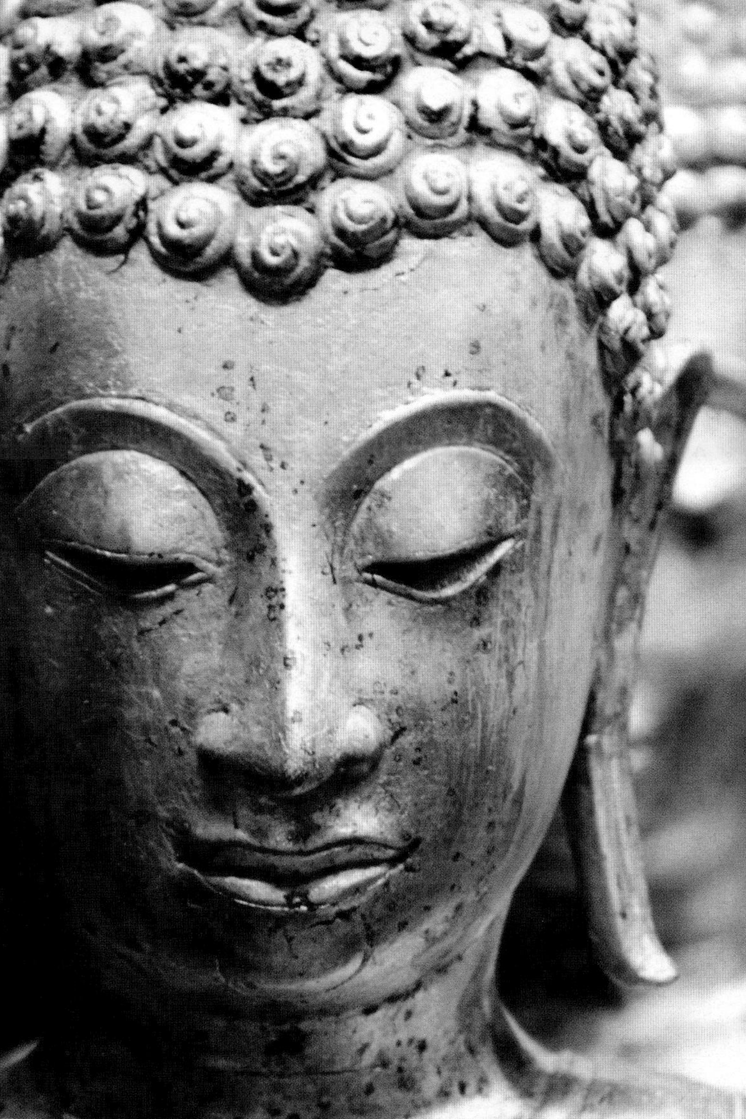

networks

There's More Online about the history and culture of Korea, Japan, and Southeast Asia.

CHAPTER 18

Lesson 1 *Korea: History and Culture*

Lesson 2 *Early Japan*

Lesson 3 *Medieval Japan*

Lesson 4 *Southeast Asia: History and Culture*

The Story Matters . . .

Buddhism began in India. By the A.D. 1200s, it was almost extinct there. The followers of the Buddha, however, carried his teachings to new lands. In time, Buddhism took firm root in Southeast Asia, China, Korea, and Japan. As Buddhism spread, it took on new forms and influenced the cultures of many nations in Asia.

Buddhism became more popular in countries outside of Asia in the second half of the twentieth century. Today more than 375 million people around the world practice some form of Buddhism.

◂ *Statues of the Buddha like this one were placed in temples throughout Korea, Japan, and Southeast Asia.*

507

Letter from the Author

Dear World History Teacher,

Situated at the crossroads of two oceans and two great civilizations, Southeast Asia has long served as a bridge linking peoples and cultures. Korea and Japan borrowed liberally from Chinese culture, but they also sought to maintain their political independence. As an island nation, Japan was the most successful in protecting its political sovereignty and its cultural identity. Korea was compelled on occasion to defend its independence through physical force. For Vietnam, years of conflict eventually led to Vietnam's conquest by China, ensuring that Chinese culture would profoundly affect the country.

Jackson J. Spielvogel

ENGAGE

Bellringer Read "The Story Matters . . ." aloud in class or ask a volunteer to read it aloud. Discuss with students the way in which Buddhism spread across Asia. **Ask:** **Through which country did Buddhism pass as it made its way from China to Japan?** *(Korea)* Then **ask:** **In the past, how did geography affect the spread of news from different areas of the world? What is its effect today?**

Lead the class in a discussion of this question. Point out that in modern times, we can learn about what is going on around us almost instantly, but before modern media, word traveled much more slowly. Encourage students to consider how different religions they have learned about might have spread before the age of modern communications.

Making Connections

Read the following information to students.

The exchange of ideas influences change in the world. Here are some things to think about that have changed the way you live.

- The United States is a democracy, which means that voters determine who serves in our government. Citizens can vote on laws and for the politicians who make them. The idea of democracy first arose in ancient Athens in the 5th century B.C. It took more than two thousand years for another successful democratic government to take root, but today, nearly 70 percent of the world's countries have at least some democratic institutions.
- In the 1970s, researchers in the United States and Europe developed a way to share computerized information through a series of connected satellites and computer terminals. This network grew and became the Internet.

TEACH & ASSESS

Step Into the Place

V1 Visual Skills

Location Direct students to the map in the book or project the Interactive World Atlas on the interactive whiteboard, focusing on the region of Korea, Japan, and Southeast Asia. Discuss with students the geographical features of the region.

Remind students that the region is made up of elongated peninsulas and many islands. Invite volunteers to suggest how trade was carried out among the many states. Have student volunteers analyze the map and locate strategic points for sea trade. Encourage them to consider why coastal cities were built where they were. **Visual/Spatial**

ANSWERS, p. 508
Step Into the Place **1.** India and China **2.** China and Japan **3.** the Sea of Japan, the East China Sea, and the Pacific Ocean **4.** **CRITICAL THINKING** through travel over land and by sea **Step Into the Time** Student answers will vary depending upon the event they choose.

CHAPTER 18 CCSS

Place and Time: Korea, Japan, and Southeast Asia A.D. 300 to A.D. 1300s

Korea, Japan, and Southeast Asia were greatly affected by China and India, their neighbors to the north and west. These influences first began between about 150 B.C. and A.D. 150. They lasted for almost a thousand years and greatly changed the regions.

Step Into the Place

MAP FOCUS Large bodies of water separate Korea, Japan, and Southeast Asia. As trade grew, however, those bodies of water formed a link between these regions and the outside world.

1. **PLACE** What are the largest two empires shown on the map? RH.6–8.7
2. **LOCATION** Between which two empires is Korea located? RH.6–8.7
3. **LOCATION** Which major bodies of water surround Japan? RH.6–8.7
4. **CRITICAL THINKING** ***Making Predictions*** How would ideas spread from China to Japan and Southeast Asia? RH.6–8.2

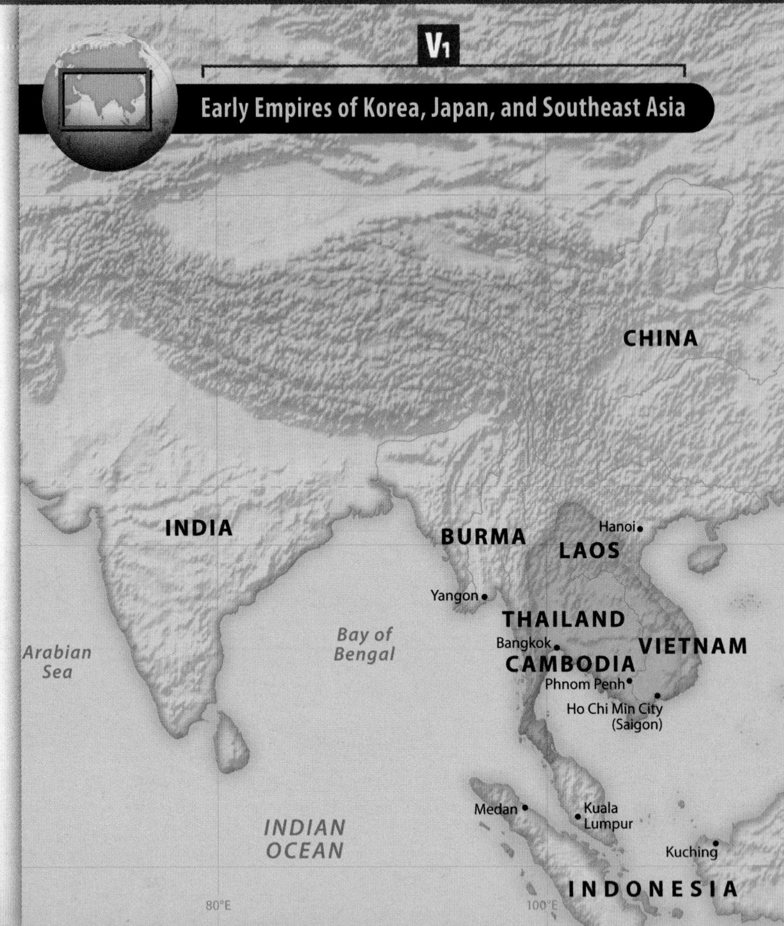

V2

Step Into the Time

TIME LINE Choose an event from the time line that happened in one region and write a paragraph predicting the effect of that event on the surrounding regions. RH.6–8.7, WHST.6–8.10

CIVILIZATIONS OF KOREA, JAPAN, AND SOUTHEAST ASIA

- **c. A.D. 300** Yayoi people organize in Japan
- **c. A.D. 400** Yamato control Japan
- **c. A.D. 604** Prince Shotoku writes Japanese constitution
- **c. A.D. 631** Taika reforms in Japan

A.D. 300 — A.D. 500 — A.D. 700

THE WORLD

- **c. A.D. 590** Grand Canal links northern and southern China
- **c. A.D. 610** Muhammad preaches Islam

Project-Based Learning

Hands-On Chapter Project

Travel Itinerary

Students will create travel itineraries for a trip to view the historical and geographic highlights of Korea, Japan, and Southeast Asia. Students will participate in a class discussion to review what they have learned about Korea, Japan, and Southeast Asia. Then students will divide into groups. Each group will use discussions and worksheets to plan their projects before creating their itineraries. Next, each group will complete its itinerary and share it with the rest of the class. Finally, students will evaluate their research, presentation, and collaboration using a class-developed Assessment Rubric.

Technology Extension

Virtual Scrapbook

Many people use photo storing and virtual scrapbook platforms to save, share, and document travels in their own lives. Virtual scrapbooks are an excellent medium for students to present images of and information about simulated trips to locations near and far. Most virtual scrapbooks can be embedded in existing Web pages or wikis and can be shared via social networking services. Students can collaborate online and help create content material for their classmates as well.

networks *There's More Online!*

☑ **MAP** Explore the interactive version of this map on NETWORKS.

☑ **TIME LINE** Explore the interactive version of this time line on NETWORKS.

Tonggu
Pyongyang
KOREA
Inchon
Kwangju
Kongju
Puyo
Kyongju
Kimhae
Sea of Japan (East Sea)
JAPAN
East China Sea
South China Sea
Manila
Davao
PACIFIC OCEAN
TROPIC OF CANCER
EQUATOR
40°N
20°N
0°
140°E
160°E

KEY

- Khmer Empire c. 1200
- Three Kingdoms: Koguryŏ c. 400
- Three Kingdoms: Silla c. 400
- Three Kingdoms: Kaya c. 400
- Three Kingdoms: Paekche c. 400
- Japan

0 500 miles
0 500 km
Miller projection

c. A.D. 918 Koryo unites Korea

c. A.D. 939 Chinese rule of Vietnam ends

c. A.D. 1113 Angkor Wat construction begins in Cambodia

c. A.D. 1231 Mongols invade northern Korea

A.D. 900 — A.D. 1100 — A.D. 1300

c. A.D. 800 Pope crowns Charlemagne emperor

c. A.D. 1000 Vikings reach North America

c. A.D. 1206 Genghis Khan becomes Mongol leader

c. A.D. 1215 England's King John signs Magna Carta

509

TIME LINE

Place and Time: Civilizations of Korea, Japan, and Southeast Asia A.D. 300 to A.D. 1300s

Display the time line on the whiteboard and have students propose an image or illustration that could accompany each event. Remind students that this is a brainstorming process, and they should generate as many ideas as they can. Then tell students that this is a process similar to the one they will use when they search for images for their digital presentations.

See page 507B for other online activities.

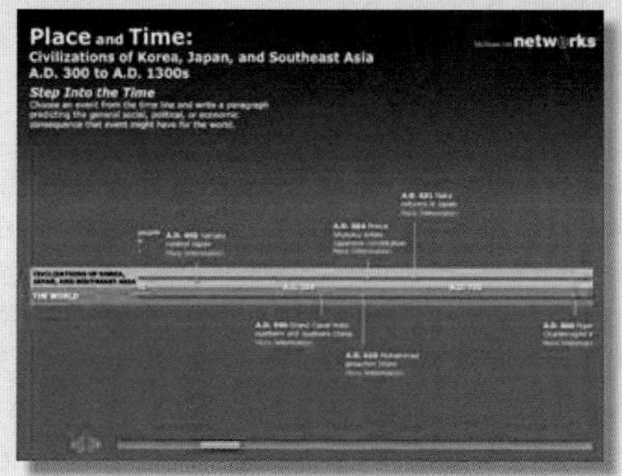

CHAPTER 18

Place and Time

Step Into the Time

V2 Visual Skills

Reading a Time Line Have students review the time line for the chapter. **Ask:**

- What two events happen around A.D. 900? *(Chinese rule of Vietnam ends and Koryo unites Korea.)*
- What was a world event that happened about a century before that? *(Charlemagne was crowned emperor of the Holy Roman Empire.)*
- According to the time line, how much time was there between when Genghis Kahn was chosen leader of the Mongols and when the Mongols invaded Korea? *(about 25 years)* **Visual/Spatial**

Content Background Knowledge

- Siddhartha Buddha, the founder of the Buddhist religion, was born in India. The date of his birth is uncertain, but tradition holds that it was sometime around 563 B.C.
- According to legend, Siddhartha's mother, Maya, conceived him while dreaming about a white elephant that pierced the right side of her body. This same legend states that, when Siddhartha was born, he came out of his mother's right side and proceeded to take seven steps.
- After Siddhartha's birth, an astrologer foretold that the child would become a king or a religious teacher.
- Siddhartha is thought to have died around age 80, after consuming tainted food. His body was cremated, the ashes dispersed to several groups of his followers.

CLOSE & REFLECT

Giving Examples Have each student give an example from either the map or the time line that supports the statement "Geography influences the way people live."

Korea: History and Culture

ENGAGE

Bellringer Before students begin the lesson, preview the text by looking at the geographic map of Korea. Tell students that China, Korea, and Japan have had a great influence on one another throughout history. **Ask:** **Why do you think China influenced Korea before Japan did?** *(The Chinese could enter Korea by land, but the Japanese had to access Korea by sea.)* Tell students they will be learning more about the relationship between China and Korea, and how Korea acted as a "bridge" between China and Japan. They will also learn about the geography, history, and culture of the Korean civilization.

TEACH & ASSESS

C Critical Thinking Skills

Making Generalizations Organize students into small groups and have each group take turns reading the first two paragraphs aloud. Then ask each group to come up with one or two sentences that make generalizations about Korean culture, based on what they have read. **Verbal/Linguistic**

R Reading Skills

Identifying Before students read the lesson, remind them that many cultures have founding legends. Ask students to identify founding legends from other cultures. **Ask:** **Who was the legendary founder of Korea?** *(Tangun, the son of a bear and a god)* **What do historians today believe about Korea's earliest people?** *(They were nomads who came to the area from northern and central Asia.)* If time permits, have students research more about Tangun to compare and contrast the Korean founding legend with those of other cultures.

ANSWER, p. 510

TAKING NOTES: Silla kingdom—built observatory; defeated other kingdoms to gain control of peninsula; time of peace and prosperity; opened up trade. Koryo dynasty—united Korean peninsula; lasted for about 400 years; increased spread of Buddhism; defeated by Mongols. Yi dynasty— defeated Mongols; lasted more than 500 years; influenced greatly by Chinese culture; greatest ruler was Sejong; did not support Buddhism; developed science and learning.

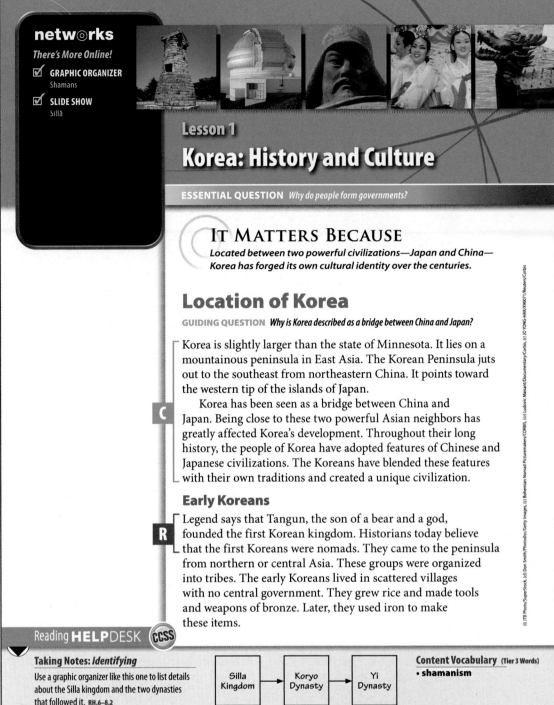

networks *There's More Online!*

- GRAPHIC ORGANIZER Shamans
- SLIDE SHOW Silla

Lesson 1

Korea: History and Culture

ESSENTIAL QUESTION *Why do people form governments?*

IT MATTERS BECAUSE

Located between two powerful civilizations—Japan and China—Korea has forged its own cultural identity over the centuries.

Location of Korea

GUIDING QUESTION *Why is Korea described as a bridge between China and Japan?*

Korea is slightly larger than the state of Minnesota. It lies on a mountainous peninsula in East Asia. The Korean Peninsula juts out to the southeast from northeastern China. It points toward the western tip of the islands of Japan.

Korea has been seen as a bridge between China and Japan. Being close to these two powerful Asian neighbors has greatly affected Korea's development. Throughout their long history, the people of Korea have adopted features of Chinese and Japanese civilizations. The Koreans have blended these features with their own traditions and created a unique civilization.

Early Koreans

Legend says that Tangun, the son of a bear and a god, founded the first Korean kingdom. Historians today believe that the first Koreans were nomads. They came to the peninsula from northern or central Asia. These groups were organized into tribes. The early Koreans lived in scattered villages with no central government. They grew rice and made tools and weapons of bronze. Later, they used iron to make these items.

Reading HELPDESK CCSS

Taking Notes: ***Identifying***

Use a graphic organizer like this one to list details about the Silla kingdom and the two dynasties that followed it. RH.6–8.2

Silla Kingdom → Koryo Dynasty → Yi Dynasty

Content Vocabulary (Tier 3 Words)
- **shamanism**

networks ***Online Teaching Options***

VIDEO

The Korean Landscape

Make Inferences Have students watch the video about the Korean landscape. Then ask them to make inferences based on what they have seen. For example, **ask:** **How might the mountainous terrain have contributed to the early Korean people being nomads?** *(Mountainous land makes farming and permanent settlements difficult.)*

See page 507C for other online activities.

Early Koreans believed in **shamanism** (SHAH•muh•nih•zuhm). They thought that certain people could communicate with spirits. These people, known as shamans, acted as a connection between humans and spirits. Many shamans were women. They carried out rituals—songs, dances, and chants—to convince the spirits to help people. Shamans were thought to have the ability to cure illnesses.

The Three Kingdoms

According to tradition, the earliest kingdom in Korea was founded in 2333 B.C. Historians know that the Chinese took over the northern part of the Korean Peninsula in 109 B.C. The Koreans drove them out in the A.D. 200s. Eventually, three kingdoms emerged: Koguryo (koh•goo•ryeoh) in the north, Paekche (payk•cheh) in the southwest, and Silla (sheel•lah) in the southeast. Historians call the years from about A.D. 300 to A.D. 700 the Three Kingdoms period.

Chinese culture spread from Koguryo to the other Korean kingdoms. The people of all three kingdoms used the Chinese writing system and adopted Buddhism and Confucianism.

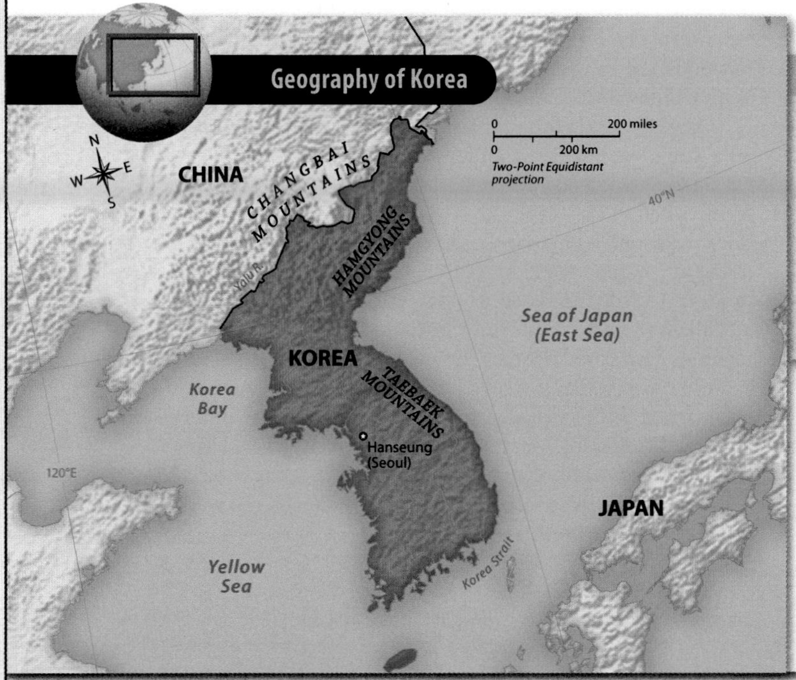

V1

Geography of Korea

V2

GEOGRAPHY CONNECTION

The Korean Peninsula extends from the northeastern part of the Chinese mainland.

1. **LOCATION** Between what two seas does Korea lie?
2. **CRITICAL THINKING** ***Analyzing*** Why would Korea have been seen as a bridge between China and Japan?

shamanism belief in gods and spirits

V1 Visual Skills

Creating a Time Line As a class, have students develop a timeline of the Three Kingdoms period. This can be done on the whiteboard or on a sheet of butcher paper. The time line should give information about each kingdom and, if possible, include other historical events that were happening at that time. Students may use Internet or library resources for their research
BL Visual/Spatial Interpersonal

V2 Visual Skills

Analyzing Maps Tell students that natural features can affect the development of a culture. **Ask:** What natural barriers offered Korea some protection from neighboring countries? *(the Changbai Mountains in the north and the Korean Strait in the South)* Visual/Spatial

WORKSHEET

Geography and History Activity: Understanding Borders: Korea

Locating Have students complete the Geography and History worksheet on the borders of Korea. **Ask:** Why was the Yalu River significant? *(It provided fishing and a means of transportation, and it served as a natural border between China and Korea.)* **AL**

See page 507C for other online activities.

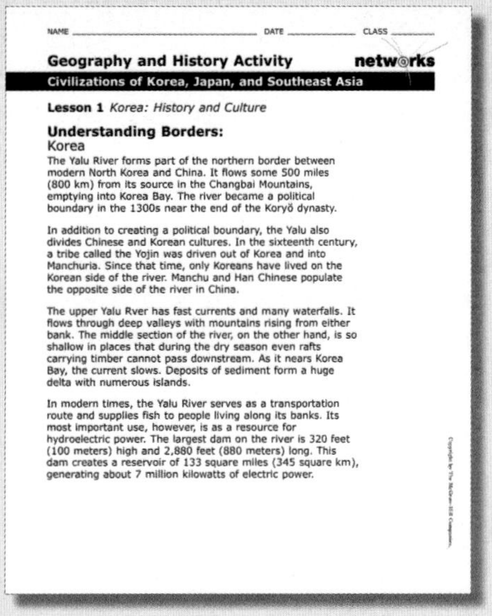

NAME ______ DATE ______ CLASS ______

Geography and History Activity **networks**

Civilizations of Korea, Japan, and Southeast Asia

Lesson 1 *Korea: History and Culture*

Understanding Borders:
Korea

The Yalu River forms part of the northern border between modern North Korea and China. It flows some 500 miles (800 km) from its source in the Changbai Mountains, emptying into Korea Bay. The river became a political boundary in the 1300s near the end of the Koryŏ dynasty.

In addition to creating a political boundary, the Yalu also divides Chinese and Korean cultures. In the sixteenth century, a tribe called the Yojin was driven out of Korea and into Manchuria. Since that time, only Koreans have lived on the Korean side of the river. Manchu and Han Chinese populate the opposite side of the river in China.

The upper Yalu Rver has fast currents and many waterfalls. It flows through deep valleys with mountains rising from either bank. The middle section of the river, on the other hand, is so shallow in places that during the dry season even rafts carrying timber cannot pass downstream. As it nears Korea Bay, the current slows. Deposits of sediment form a huge delta with numerous islands.

In modern times, the Yalu River serves as a transportation route and supplies fish to people living along its banks. Its most important use, however, is as a resource for hydroelectric power. The largest dam on the river is 320 feet (100 meters) high and 2,880 feet (880 meters) long. This dam creates a reservoir of 133 square miles (345 square km), generating about 7 million kilowatts of electric power.

ANSWERS, p. 511

GEOGRAPHY CONNECTION

1. Korea lies between the Yellow Sea and the Sea of Japan.
2. **CRITICAL THINKING** Korea could be described as a bridge because it connects to northeastern China and points toward Japan.

R1 Reading Skills

Listing Organize students in pairs. Have them use details from the text to list the cultural influences that came to Korea from both Japan and China during the Three Kingdoms period.

R2 Reading Skills

Determining Word Meanings After students have read about culture during the Three Kingdoms period, have them examine the words *astronomical* and *observatory* to determine their meaning. Students should list root words, synonyms, or related words for each one. AL ELL

C Critical Thinking Skills

Making Connections Tell students that Silla was the smallest of the three kingdoms. **Ask:** **How was Silla able to conquer Paekche and Koguryo?** *(with help from China)* **What did Silla have in common with China?** *(Answers may vary. Possible responses include: Buddhism, focus on the arts, system of Confucian government, education structure, and civil service examinations)* BL

THEN

The early Koreans built this astronomical observatory during the Silla era. Today, observatories around the world use high-powered telescopes to give scientists the best view of stars, planets, and even far away galaxies.

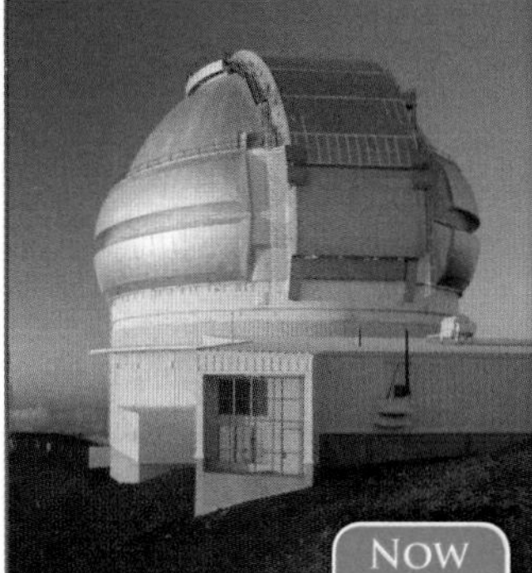

▶ CRITICAL THINKING

Speculating How would ancient astronomers from Silla have observed the movement of stars and other objects compared to astronomers today?

They began using Buddhist sacred writings in Chinese translation. They applied Confucian principles to political life. Each Korean kingdom modeled its government on China's government. In addition, each kingdom was ruled by a powerful monarch with the help of scholarly officials and noble families. R1

During the Three Kingdoms period, influences from Japan also reached the Korean Peninsula. Paekche in the southwest was located closer to Japan than the other two Korean kingdoms. As a result, it developed trade with the Japanese. Japanese merchants, artisans, and scholars settled in Paekche and introduced elements of Japanese culture there.

Although the Koreans adapted many outside ideas and practices, they also made their own unique contributions. For example, in the A.D. 300s, Koguryo artists created enormous cave art paintings. In Silla, a queen built an astronomical observatory that still stands today. This stone structure is considered the oldest observatory in Asia. R2

The Silla Kingdom

Despite their close cultural ties, the three Korean kingdoms were hostile to each other. In the A.D. 500s and 600s, they fought wars for control of the Korean Peninsula. In one conflict during the A.D. 660s, the Tang dynasty of China sided with the Silla kingdom. With Chinese help, Silla conquered Paekche and Koguryo.

The rise of Silla brought a time of peace to Koreans as the Silla kings tried to create an ideal Buddhist kingdom. Society was made up of a few nobles at the top and a large group of farmers below. However, the government made some vital improvements. It gave land to farmers and helped build irrigation systems for rice fields. As a result, more food was produced, trade increased, and the economy prospered. C

Silla kings also supported cultural advances. They wanted to employ educated people. To make that easier, they used an examination system to hire government officials. They also encouraged the arts, especially the building of many Buddhist temples. One temple was a nine-story wooden tower. This was perhaps the tallest structure in East Asia at the time. The printing of Buddhist sacred texts with wooden blocks was another Silla **achievement**.

✓ PROGRESS CHECK

Determining Cause and Effect How did outside influences affect early Korea?

Reading HELPDESK CCSS

Academic Vocabulary (Tier 2 Words)

achievement something gained by working for it

networks Online Teaching Options

SLIDE SHOW

Silla Kingdom

Determining Cause and Effect Present the interactive feature on the Silla kingdom. Discuss with students how the rise of Silla affected the lives of Koreans. **Ask:** **What were some of the key achievements of the Silla?** *(The Silla drove out the Chinese, created a Buddhist kingdom, brought peace, increased food production, helped the economy prosper, and encouraged education and the arts.)*

See page 507C for other online activities.

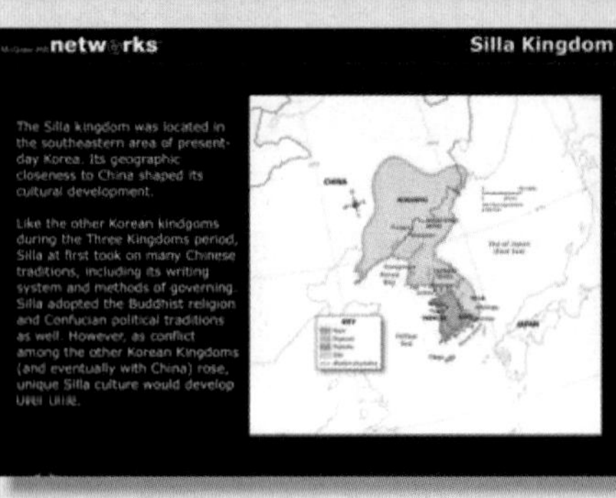

ANSWERS, p. 512

CRITICAL THINKING They would have had only the naked eye instead of telescopes.

✓ **PROGRESS CHECK** People adopted the Chinese writing system, adopted Buddhism and Confucianism, and applied the Chinese form of government.

Korea: History and Culture

Three Kingdoms of Korea c. 400 A.D.

CHINA
KOGURYO
Tonggu
Manpojin
HAMGYONG MTNS
Sea of Japan (East Sea)
Korea Bay
TAEBAEK MTNS
Kwangju
SILLA
Kyongju
Kongju
Puyo
PAEKCHE
KAYA
Kimhae
JAPAN
Yellow Sea
Korea Strait
Cheju
0 200 miles
0 200 km
Two-Point Equidistant projection
120°E
40°N

KEY
Kaya
Koguryŏ
Paekche
Silla
Modern boundary

GEOGRAPHY CONNECTION

During the Three Kingdoms period (c. 400 A.D.), Koguryo, Paekche, and Silla were the three main powers.

1. **REGION** Which kingdom was the smallest?
2. **CRITICAL THINKING** *Analyzing* Why might Buddhism and Confucianism have reached Koguryo before they reached the other Korean kingdoms?

Korean Civilization

GUIDING QUESTION *How did Korea build a civilization?*

After years of conflict, the Silla kingdom finally collapsed. Nobles in the north fought each other for power. By A.D. 935, a general named Wang Kon (wahng•keon) had won out over these rivals. He became the first Korean ruler to unite the entire Korean Peninsula. Wang Kon also founded a new dynasty known as Koryo (KAW•ree•oh). The English word "Korea" comes from the term *Koryo*.

The Silla used a combination of military might and diplomacy to secure the kingdom.

The Koryo Kingdom

Rulers of the Koryo kingdom followed the Chinese model of government that Silla had used. They were able to keep their territory united, and they remained in power for 400 years.

The Koryo rulers set up a code of laws. They also established a civil service system based on examinations. Under this leadership, Buddhism continued to grow and spread throughout the peninsula. Artisans developed movable metal type and produced the world's oldest book printed by this method.

Korean artisans also perfected the making of celadon pottery. This type of pottery is known for its green color and elegant shapes.

C Critical Thinking Skills

Formulating Questions Remind students that Korea changed from the time of the Silla kingdom to that of the Koryo kingdom. **Ask:** Who first united Korea? *(Wang Kon founded the Koryo dynasty, uniting Korea for the first time.)* On an index card, have students write "Wang Kon" at the top. Then have them list the facts that they know about him from the textbook. In pairs or small groups, have students brainstorm to generate questions for further research about this important early Korean ruler.

V Visual Skills

Analyzing Images Direct students to study the image of the statue of Wang Kon. Then **ask:** What adjectives come to mind when you look at this statue? *(Answers will vary. Possible responses include: strong, domineering, tough, controlling, authoritarian)* What do you think the artist was trying to convey about the ruler? *(Answers will vary. Possible response: The artist was trying to show that Wang Kon was a strong military leader.)* AL ELL **Visual/Spatial**

MAP

Three Kingdoms of Korea c. 400 A.D.

Describing Have students examine the layers of the map one at a time. For each layer, have them write one sentence that summarizes the information in that layer, such as the location and size of a particular kingdom and its relation to other countries or geographic features.

See page 507C for other online activities.

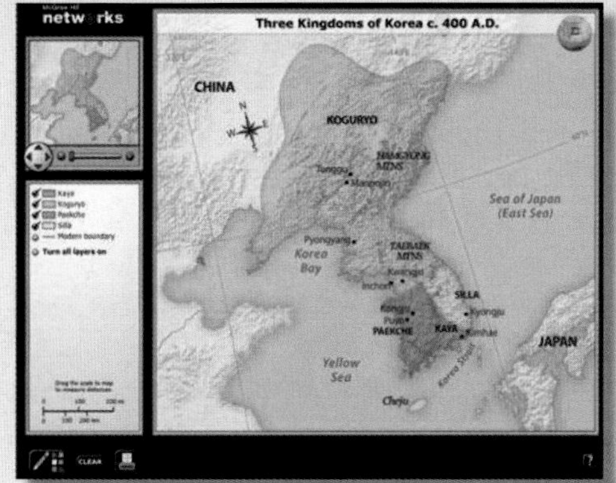

ANSWERS, p. 513

GEOGRAPHY CONNECTION

1. Silla
2. CRITICAL THINKING because Koguryo was physically closer to China

Korea: History and Culture

C Critical Thinking Skills

Comparing After reading about the fall of the Koryo kingdom, discuss with students how the people of Korea went from fighting against the Mongols from China to modeling their government after the Mongol model. **Ask: How were the Koryo and Yi governments similar to the Chinese government at the time?** *(Each of these governments was ruled by a powerful monarch. Each also used a civil service system based on examinations to select scholarly officials to help run the government. The Yi also introduced the Chinese beliefs of neo-Confucianism to Korea.)* BL

R Reading Skills

Specifying After students read the passage, ask them to identify the accomplishments of Sejong the Great during his rule. Students should note that Sejong was a leader in science and technology and that he was involved in producing globes that showed the position and motion of planets in the solar system. **Ask: In what way was Sejong similar to the Silla queen Sondok?** *(Both were interested in astronomy.)*

C Like other Korean kingdoms before it, Koryo faced internal disorders and outside threats. The Mongols who had taken over China were the main outside danger. In A.D. 1231, the Mongols invaded the northern part of Korea. They forced the Koryo king and royal family to flee to an island near the present-day city of Seoul. After 25 years of struggle, the royal family surrendered.

To remain in power, the Koryo dynasty agreed to accept Mongol rule. The Mongols brought much suffering to the Korean people. They forced thousands of Korean peasants and artisans to build ships for the Mongol ruler Kublai Khan's attempted invasion of Japan.

Mongol power eventually declined, and so did the rule of the Koryo. In 1392, a Korean general named Yi Song-gye (YEE sung•jay) overthrew the Koryo and founded a new dynasty. The Korean people were once again in charge of their country.

The Yi Dynasty

The dynasty that Yi Song-gye founded became known as the Yi. It lasted for over 500 years. The Yi dynasty was one of the world's longest ruling families. Yi rulers set up their capital at Hanseong, the site of Seoul, the modern capital of South Korea.

From Hanseong, Yi rulers strengthened their rule of Korea. Yi rulers still made use of Chinese ideas and practices. They named neo-Confucianism the state philosophy. They opened schools to teach Chinese classics to civil service candidates. However, at the same time, they refused to support Buddhism. The religion declined during this period. Despite the influences from China, the Koreans kept their own traditions and unique identity.

In the popular Korean fan dance, dancers in traditional robes hold brightly colored fans. They open and close and move the fans to make shapes of butterflies, flowers, and waves.

▶ CRITICAL THINKING
Drawing Conclusions Where do you think you would be most likely to see a traditional fan dance performance?

Ludovic Maisant/CORBIS

One of the greatest Yi kings was Sejong. He ruled from 1394 to 1450. Sejong was interested in science and technology. He used bronze to invent the first instruments for measuring rain. As a result, Korea has the world's oldest record of rainfall. Sejong was also involved in producing water clocks, sundials, and globes. These globes showed the position and motion of planets in the solar system. R

Sejong and his advisers worked to spread literacy, or the ability to read, among the Korean people. They made a great contribution by creating an alphabet called *hangul*. Chinese and Japanese use thousands of characters. Hangul is based on

Reading HELPDESK (CCSS)

tribute payment to a ruler as a sign of submission or for protection

networks Online Teaching Options

IMAGE

Korean Alphabet

Drawing Conclusions Present the interactive image on the hangul writing system. Discuss with students the writing systems of China, Korea, and Japan. **Ask: Why might hangul have been easier to read than Japanese or Chinese?** *(Possible answer: Japanese and Chinese required memorizing thousands of distinct characters. Hangul assigned a letter to each sound, reducing the amount of memorization needed.)* BL

See page 507C for other online activities.

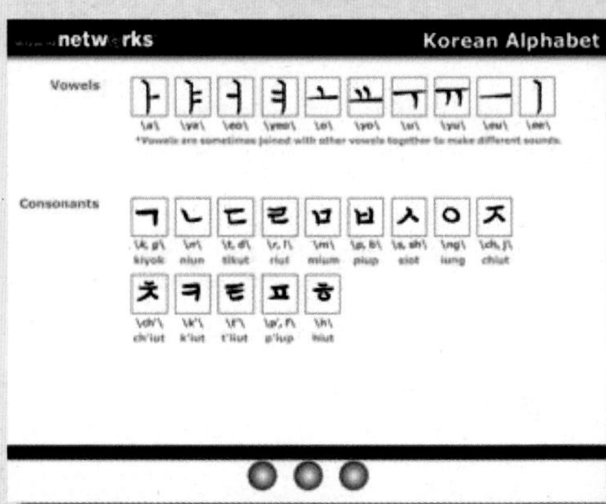

ANSWER, p. 514

CRITICAL THINKING A traditional fan dance is probably performed at patriotic celebrations or special performances with great pageantry.

symbols that represent sounds. It uses one letter for each sound, similar to the English alphabet. Hangul is still the standard writing system in present-day Korea.

War and Technology

In 1592, Japanese forces attacked Korea. Their goal was to cross the Korean Peninsula and conquer China. With Chinese help, the Koreans stopped the Japanese attack on land. At sea, the Koreans were also successful because of a new Korean invention: the world's first iron-covered ships.

W

Before fighting the Japanese, a Korean general named Yi Sun-shin and a team of workers had produced several ships. The vessels were known as turtle ships. Their plated armor looked like turtle shells. They had cannons on all sides and rows of spikes to keep attackers from boarding. These well-protected ships had strong firepower. The general used them to carry out fierce attacks on the Japanese fleet and they were the clear winners.

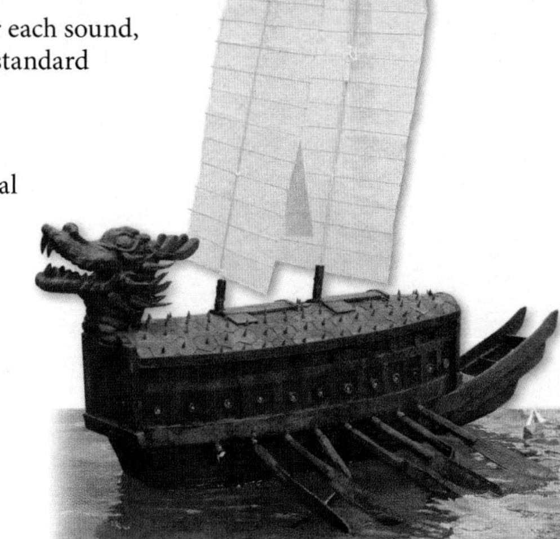

The dragon's head at the bow of the turtle ships could launch cannon fire or flames.

▶ CRITICAL THINKING
Explaining How did technology change warfare?

Korean Struggles

Although the Koreans were able to defeat the Japanese, their victory came at a high price. The fighting on land had destroyed Korean farms, villages, and towns. The Japanese had killed or kidnapped many Korean farmers and workers.

In the early 1600s, while still recovering from Japan's invasion, the Koreans were attacked by the Chinese. China at this time was ruled by a foreign dynasty known as the Manchus. The Yi dynasty was forced to surrender. They had to pay **tribute** to China's Manchu rulers. Korea's relations with its powerful neighbor remained tense for many centuries.

☑ PROGRESS CHECK

Explaining How did the building of turtle ships help the Koreans?

LESSON 1 REVIEW

Review Vocabulary (Tier 3 Words)

1. How was *shamanism* important to the Koreans? RH.6–8.2, RH.6–8.4

Answer the Guiding Questions

2. ***Identifying*** What is the physical location of Korea, and how did its location affect China and Japan? RH.6–8.2
3. ***Summarizing*** What did the first Koryo rulers do to establish a lasting civilization? RH.6–8.2
4. ***Explaining*** Why was the period of Silla rule considered a time of peace? RH.6–8.2
5. ***Describing*** Describe the achievements of Sejong that led him to be called one of the greatest Yi kings. RH.6–8.2
6. **NARRATIVE** Review the description of the Korean turtle ships. Write a letter to a friend describing the ships. WHST.6–8.10

LESSON 1 REVIEW ANSWERS

1. Shamanism was the religion of early Koreans. The shaman asked favors of the spirits for people and also cured physical and mental illness.
2. Korea is located between China and Japan. It served as a link of culture and development between the two countries.
3. The Koryo rulers set up a code of laws. They introduced a civil service system based on examinations. They encouraged the growth of Buddhism. Among their many cultural achievements were the invention of movable metal type and the creation of celadon pottery.
4. Silla rulers tried to create an ideal Buddhist kingdom, improve society, and create greater economic opportunities through farming and trade.
5. Sejong stressed science, technology, and literacy. He spread a system of writing across Korea.
6. Answers should include several descriptive details such as the following: The turtle ship is covered in iron, with oars and sails to allow movement.

W Writing Skills

Informative/Explanatory Using a whiteboard, create a three-column chart to compare and contrast the results of the Chinese, Mongol, and Japanese invasions of Korea. Pose the following questions, and have student volunteers summarize responses on the whiteboard. **Ask:**

- **What happened when the Mongols invaded Korea?** *(They seized control of the peninsula and brought much suffering to the Korean people before they were finally defeated.)*
- **What happened when the Japanese invaded Korea?** *(The Koreans defeated the Japanese but suffered a great loss in land and lives.)*
- **What happened when the Chinese invaded Korea?** *(Students should note that the Chinese invaded Korea more than once. At first, China controlled part of northern Korea. China later aided the Silla but were driven out. Finally, China's Manchu rulers invaded and forced the Yi dynasty to pay tribute.)* **Verbal/Linguistic**

Have students complete the Lesson 1 Review.

CLOSE & REFLECT

To close the lesson, ask students to reflect on how China and Japan influenced Korea's development. Ask students to consider whether foreign influences were more positive or negative for the Korean people. Discuss different answers to this question as a class. *(Students should note the hardships suffered by Koreans due to multiple foreign invasions as well as the political, technological, and cultural benefits that Korea received from contact with China and Japan.)*

ANSWERS, p. 515

CRITICAL THINKING The ironworking technology allowed warriors to have additional protection from harm.

☑ **PROGRESS CHECK** The ships were used to attack and defeat the Japanese fleet.

ENGAGE

Bellringer Before students begin the lesson, project the map of Japan on the interactive whiteboard. Have a volunteer find Japan. Ask students to list the four main Japanese islands from north to south. *(Hokkaido, Honshu, Shikoku, Kyushu)* AL

Also have students locate the Pacific Ocean and the Sea of Japan. Tell students they will be learning about the geography of Japan and how it influenced Japanese culture. They will also be learning about the first settlers in Japan and the development of religion in Japan.

TEACH & ASSESS

R Reading Skills

Analyzing After they have read the text, ask students to describe the topography of Japan. **Ask:** What effect did the mountainous terrain of Japan have on its early settlers? *(They fought over the little available farmland and turned to the sea for food.)*

C Critical Thinking Skills

Recognizing Relationships After students have read the text and studied the map on the next page, ask them to write two or three sentences that explain the relationship between Japan and the sea. Students should include that it was an important source of food and helped Japan develop as an independent civilization. BL

networks
There's More Online!
- GRAPHIC ORGANIZER China Influences Japanese Culture
- SLIDE SHOW Buddhist Temples

Heian-kyo (Kyoto) • Nara • Mt. Fuji • Shikoku

Lesson 2
Early Japan

ESSENTIAL QUESTION *How does geography influence the way people live?*

It Matters Because
Many of the characteristics of modern Japanese culture can be traced back to Shinto and to the samurai.

Geography and Settlement

GUIDING QUESTION *How did geography shape Japan's early society?*

Japan (juh•PAN) lies to the east of Korea and China. Japan is an **archipelago** (ahr•kuh•PEH•luh•goh), or a chain of islands, that runs north to south in the Pacific Ocean. For centuries, most Japanese have lived on the four largest islands: Hokkaido (haw•KY•doh), Honshu (HAHN•shoo), Shikoku (shee•KOH•koo), and Kyushu (KYOO•shoo).

R The islands of Japan are actually the tops of mountains that rise from the ocean floor. Earthquakes occur in Japan due to its position along an unstable part of the earth's crust. Because of the mountains, only a small amount of Japan's land can be farmed. Local armies have fought over this limited land for centuries.

C Many Japanese turned to the sea to make a living. They built villages along the coast and fished. The Japanese also traveled by ship among their many islands. Still, the seas around Japan kept the Japanese **isolated**, or separated, from the rest of Asia. As a result, Japan developed a strongly independent civilization.

The First Settlers

The first people to settle in Japan probably came from northeastern Asia around 20,000 years ago. About 300 B.C., a new group of people, the Yayoi (YAH•yoy), brought farming to Japan

Reading HELPDESK CCSS

Taking Notes: *Identifying*
Use a graphic organizer like the one here to show how Chinese culture influenced the early Japanese. RH.6–8.2

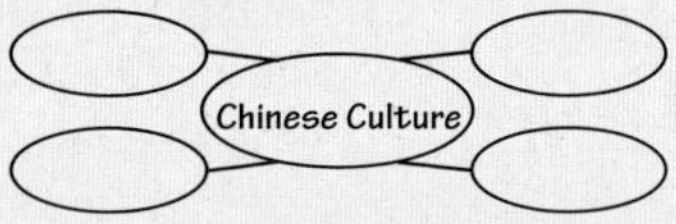

Chinese Culture

Content Vocabulary (Tier 3 Words)
- **archipelago**
- **animism**
- **constitution**

networks ***Online Teaching Options***

VIDEO

East Asian Religions and Other Cultural Traditions

Comparing Present the lesson video about East Asian religions and cultural traditions. Tell students that early religions in East Asia were based on nature and one's ancestors. East Asians also share many cultural ideals, which are evident in art, landscaping, architecture, music, and theater. Have students create a chart that compares religions and cultural traditions across East Asia.

See page 507D for other online activities.

ANSWER, p. 516

TAKING NOTES: Answers should include government, Confucianism, Buddhism, Chinese art, philosophy, and medicine.

Geography of Japan

GEOGRAPHY CONNECTION

Japan lies just 110 miles (204 km) east of Korea.

1. **LOCATION** Between what two bodies of water does Japan lie?
2. **CRITICAL THINKING** ***Analyzing*** How did Japan's geography affect its relationships with its neighbors?

and were the ancestors of the Japanese. They made pottery and grew rice and were skilled metalworkers. By A.D. 300, the Yayoi had organized themselves into clans, each headed by warrior chiefs. The clan's warrior chiefs protected the people. **C**

The Yamato

During the A.D. 500s, a clan called the Yamato (YAH•mah•taw) ruled most of Japan. Other clans had to give their loyalty to the Yamato chief. Yamato chiefs claimed that they were descended from a sun goddess who sent her grandson to rule over the people of Japan. Japanese legend states that a Yamato leader named Jimmu (jeem•moo) was the great-grandson of this goddess. This gave him the right to rule Japan. Jimmu took the title "emperor of heaven" and became the first emperor of Japan. **R**

PROGRESS CHECK

Identifying What skills did the Yayoi bring to Japan?

The skillfulness of the Yayoi people can be seen in their metalwork, such as this bronze bell.

Sakamoto Photo Research Laboratory/CORBIS

archipelago an expanse of water with many scattered islands

Academic Vocabulary (Tier 2 Words)
isolate to set apart from others

C Critical Thinking Skills

Making Inferences Discuss the Yayoi people with students. Prompt students to consider how the people were organized into groups and how this organization affected them. Ask students why these people were significant.

R Reading Skills

Identifying After students read the text, have them summarize the rise of the Yamato clans. **Ask:** What are historians certain of regarding the Yamato? *(During the A.D. 500s, the Yamato grew strong enough to rule most of Japan. The other clans had to give their loyalty to the Yamato chief.)* **Ask:** Why was Jimmu an important Yamato figure? *(He was the first emperor of Japan.)*

Content Background Knowledge

- The Yamato have left an enduring legacy in Japanese culture. The dominant ethnic group in Japan refers to themselves as "Yamato."
- A Yamato prince named Takeru is a Japanese folk hero known for his bravery. His stories have been told by Japanese writers over the centuries, similar to our stories of Paul Bunyan.
- A style of Japanese scroll painting popular in the 12th century is known as "e-Yamato." It incorporated strong colors and was often used to illustrate stories and poems.

WORKSHEET

21st Century Skills Activity: Information Literacy: Use Latitude and Longitude

Applying Introduce students to the 21st Century Skills worksheet on using latitude and longitude. Assign the questions on the worksheet as homework.

See page 507D for other online activities.

ANSWERS, p. 517

GEOGRAPHY CONNECTION

1. the Sea of Japan and the Pacific Ocean
2. **CRITICAL THINKING** As an island nation, Japan was isolated from its neighbors, allowing it to develop its own civilization. At the same time, the seas provided opportunities for trade and other contact with its neighbors.

PROGRESS CHECK They brought farming to Japan, especially the growing of rice in paddies. They also brought pottery making and metalworking.

C Critical Thinking Skills

Making Connections Discuss with students the effects of Shinto on Japanese customs and values. **Ask:** How did Shinto contribute to the early Japanese love of nature? *(Possible answer: The early Japanese believed in nature spirits, so they wanted to honor them by showing them respect.)* In what way did the Japanese honor the kami? *(They worshiped at shrines where priests, dancers, and musicians performed rituals.)*

W Writing Skills

Narrative Discuss the term *animism* with students and point out its meaning in the text. Next, have students choose an object that can be found in nature, such as an animal, flower, or specific kind of leaf. Then invite students to write a fictional story about a nature spirit associated with the object. When students have finished writing, have them share their narratives with the class. BL **Naturalist**

ANSWERS, p. 518

CRITICAL THINKING the respect for nature

✓ PROGRESS CHECK They worshiped at holy places.

Many Japanese still follow Shinto today and visit shrines such as the Kanda Myojin shrine in Tokyo. The design of this temple is similar to the temple built by Prince Shotoku hundreds of years before.

▶ CRITICAL THINKING

Explaining What about Shinto beliefs do you think appeals to modern people?

P. Narayan/Age fotostock

Shinto: Way of the Spirits

GUIDING QUESTION ***Why did the early Japanese believe that nature was important?***

The early Japanese believed that humans, animals, plants, rocks, and rivers all have their own spirits. This idea is known as **animism** (A•nuh•mih•zuhm). People believed they could call on the *kami* (KAH•mih), or the nature spirits for help. To show respect to the *kami*, the Japanese worshipped at holy places. W C

Early Japanese beliefs developed into a religion called Shinto. The word *Shinto* means "way of the spirits." Shinto later became linked to Japan's rulers. Their duties included taking part in Shinto rituals to **ensure** the well-being of Japan.

The practice of Shinto affects the Japanese people today. It has contributed to the Japanese love of nature. It also has influenced their striving for simplicity, cleanliness, and good manners.

✓ PROGRESS CHECK

Explaining How did the Japanese show respect to the *kami*?

Prince Shotoku

GUIDING QUESTION ***How did Prince Shotoku reform Japan's government?***

About A.D. 600, a Yamato prince named Shotoku (shoh•TOH•koo) ruled Japan on **behalf** of his aunt. He wanted to give Japan a strong, well-organized government, so Shotoku created a **constitution** (kahn•stuh•TOO•shuhn), or a plan of government. Shotoku's constitution stated that the emperor was an all-powerful ruler. The Japanese were expected to obey him. Specific rules in the constitution, based on the ideas of Confucius, stated how they should perform their duties.

Shotoku admired Chinese civilization and wanted the Japanese to learn from it. Officials and students studied Buddhism, as well as Chinese art, philosophy, and medicine.

After Shotoku's death, officials continued to use China as a model for Japan. In A.D. 646, the Yamato began the Taika (ty•kuh), or Great Change. Japan was divided into districts ruled by

Reading HELPDESK CCSS

animism belief in spirits that are outside of the body

constitution basic laws of a state that define the role of government and guarantee its obligation to the people

Academic Vocabulary (Tier 2 Words)

ensure to make sure; guarantee

behalf representing; in the place of

networks Online Teaching Options

IMAGE

Chinese Calendar

Identifying Present the interactive illustration on the zodiac calendar created by Prince Shotoku. **Ask:** How is time measured on the calendar? *(Time is measured based on the movements of the sun and the moon.)* How do animals play a part in the traditional zodiac calendar? *(Animal zodiac signs are paired with specific repeating years.)*

See page 507D for other online activities.

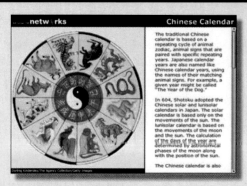

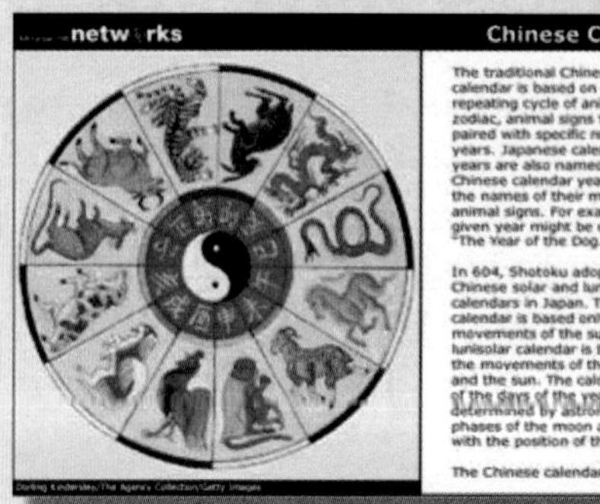

officials who reported to the emperor. All farmland was placed under the emperor's control. Clan leaders could oversee the farmers' work, but government officials now collected taxes. The Taika reforms created Japan's first strong central government.

✓ PROGRESS CHECK

Describing What was the goal of Shotoku's constitution?

The Nara Period

GUIDING QUESTION ***How did Chinese ways influence Japan during the Nara period?***

C

In the early A.D. 700s, Japanese emperors built a new capital city called Nara. It had broad streets, large public squares, Buddhist temples, and Shinto shrines. Nobles' families lived in large, Chinese-style homes. During the Nara period, the Japanese emperors ranked government officials into a hierarchy. However, they did not follow the Chinese practice of using examinations to hire officials. Instead, the emperor gave positions to nobles from powerful families. In return for their services, these officials received large farms. The emperor's control of the land gave him great power.

Buddhist teachings had reached Japan from Korea in the A.D. 500s. During the Nara period, Buddhism became powerful in Japan. In A.D. 770, a Buddhist monk tried to seize the throne. Shaken, the emperor decided to leave Nara for a new capital.

This grand statue of the Buddha stands in the Todaiji temple, which is one of the world's largest wooden buildings. This temple served as the major temple for Buddhism in Japan.

✓ PROGRESS CHECK

Explaining What was Nara?

LESSON 2 REVIEW (CCSS)

Review Vocabulary (Tier 3 Words)

1. How does a *constitution* benefit society? RH.6–8.2, RH.6–8.4

Answer the Guiding Questions

2. ***Explaining*** Why was early society in Japan isolated? RH.6–8.2, RH.6–8.7
3. ***Drawing Conclusions*** How did animism affect people's views about nature? RH.6–8.2
4. ***Identifying*** What was Prince Shotoku's main reform in government? RH.6–8.2
5. ***Contrasting*** How did the Japanese way of hiring officials differ from the Chinese during the Nara period? RH.6–8.2
6. **ARGUMENT** You are a Japanese worker under Prince Shotoku's rule. Write a persuasive plea to Prince Shotoku asking him to change his new constitution to give workers more rights. WHST.6–8.1, WHST.6–8.10

LESSON 2 REVIEW ANSWERS

1. A constitution offers a standard set of rules by which everyone in the country must live.
2. Japan is composed of islands and was therefore largely isolated from other nations.
3. The early Japanese believed that all things in nature are alive. If humans, animals, plants, rocks, and rivers had their own spirits, they would gain importance and merit greater respect.
4. He wrote Japan's first constitution.
5. The Chinese used a system of examinations to hire officials. In Japan, officials were appointed by the emperor.
6. Writing should focus on the idea that additional freedoms for the people would lead to innovations or creativity. Students may discuss the negative reactions that many workers have when they lack control over their work.

C Critical Thinking Skills

Comparing and Contrasting Remind students that China had a strong influence on neighboring countries such as Japan and Korea. **Ask:** **During the Nara period, how was Japanese life and government similar to that of China?** *(Responses might include the practice of Buddhism, similar layouts for cities and homes for nobles, and a hierarchy of officials under the emperor.)* **How was life in the Nara period different?** *(Nara emperors did not use civil service examinations to select officials.)*

Have students complete the Lesson 2 Review.

CLOSE & REFLECT

To close the lesson, ask students to explain what they learned about Japan. Have them summarize the changes from early Japan up to the Nara period of Japan's history. Have them use their own words to summarize their reading.

ANSWERS, p. 519

✓ PROGRESS CHECK to give Japan a strong, well-organized government

✓ PROGRESS CHECK Nara was a new capital city built in the early A.D. 700s.

ENGAGE

Bellringer Before students begin the lesson, ask what they may already know about the medieval period in Europe. Remind students that the word *medieval* shares a root meaning with the words *median* and *middle*. Discuss medieval times as times of transition between ancient and modern.

TEACH & ASSESS

R Reading Skills

Finding the Main Idea After students have read the section about the rise of nobles, ask them to find the sentence that best communicates the main idea of this section. Then ask for volunteers to restate the main idea in their own words.
AL ELL

C Critical Thinking Skills

Drawing Conclusions Discuss with students the rule of regents in Japan. **Ask:** What were the advantages and disadvantages of regents ruling in Japan? *(Possible answer: Regents provided stable rule when an emperor was too young or sick, but they didn't want to give up power when child emperors became adults.)*

networks *There's More Online!*

- **BIOGRAPHY**
  - Minamoto Yoritomo
  - Murasaki Shikibu c. A.D. 978–1014
- **CHART** Japanese Feudal Class System
- **SLIDE SHOW**
  - Samurai
  - Japanese Art

Lesson 3

Medieval Japan

ESSENTIAL QUESTION *How do new ideas change the way people live?*

IT MATTERS BECAUSE

Japanese society was transformed under the shoguns. The cultural influences from this time period still influence Japan and the world.

Samurai and Shoguns

GUIDING QUESTION *Why did military leaders rise to power in Japan?*

In A.D. 794, the emperor of Japan moved the capital from Nara to a new city called Heian-kyo (HAY•ahn kyoh). This city later became known as Kyoto (KYOH•toh). The city of Heian-kyo looked much like a major Chinese city.

Nobles Rise to Power

R During the A.D. 800s, emperors continued to rule Japan, but their power greatly weakened. Why did this happen? After a period of strong emperors, a number of weak emperors came to the throne. Court officials known as regents governed for them. A regent is a person who rules for an emperor who is too young or too sick to govern.

C The regents handled the city's day-to-day government, leaving the Japanese emperors to turn to learning and the arts. Emperors studied Buddhism or wrote poetry in their palace at Heian-kyo.

At the same time, other nobles took control in the outlying provinces of Japan. The government gave these nobles land in return for their support. It also let them stop paying taxes. It made the nobles responsible for governing the lands under their control. To pay for the local government, the nobles increased the taxes on the farmers working the land.

Reading **HELP**DESK CCSS

Taking Notes: *Showing Relationships*

Use a graphic organizer like the one here to show the relationship between daimyo and samurai. RH.6–8.2

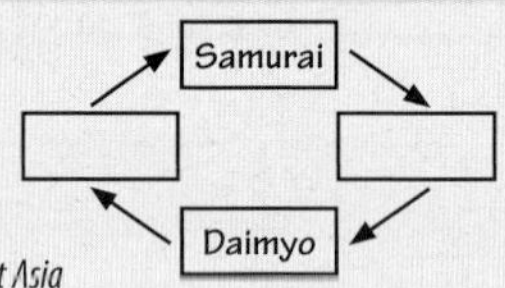

Content Vocabulary (Tier 3 Words)

- **samurai**
- **shogun**
- **vassal**
- **feudalism**
- **guild**
- **sect**
- **martial art**
- **meditation**

networks *Online Teaching Options*

VIDEO

The Samurai

Listing Direct students to watch the lesson video about samurai either in class or on their own. Then have them list all of the ways in which Bushido, the samurai code, affected the warriors' behavior.

See page 507E for other online activities.

ANSWER, p. 520
TAKING NOTES: Daimyo gave land to samurai. Samurai gave an oath of loyalty to serve daimyo.

The Samurai and Their Code

The nobles gave land to warriors who agreed to fight for them. These warriors became known as **samurai** (SA•muh•ry). In battle, samurai fought on horseback with swords, daggers, and bows and arrows. They wore armor made of leather or steel scales and helmets with horns or crests.

A few Japanese women were outstanding warriors. Perhaps the most famous was Tomoe. She fought in the A.D. 1100s during a time of civil war in Japan. One account from the A.D. 1200s describes her:

PRIMARY SOURCE

> “[S]he was a fearless rider whom neither the fiercest horse nor the roughest ground could dismay, and so dexterously [skillfully] did she handle sword and bow that she was a match for a thousand warriors and fit to meet either god or devil. . . . and so in this last fight, when all the others had been slain or had fled, among the last seven there rode Tomoe.”
>
> —from *Heike Monogatori (The Tale of Heike)*

R The word *samurai* means "to serve." The samurai lived by a strict code of conduct. This code was called Bushido (BU•shih•doh), or "the way of the warrior." It demanded that a samurai be loyal to his master. The samurai must also be brave and honorable. Samurai were not supposed to be concerned about riches. They viewed merchants as lacking in honor.

Bound to these principles, a samurai would rather die in battle than betray his master. He also did not want to suffer the disgrace of being captured in battle. The sense of loyalty that set apart the samurai lasted into modern times. During World War II, many Japanese soldiers fought to the death rather than accept defeat or capture. The Japanese have since turned away from the beliefs of the samurai.

Shoguns Assume Power

By the early 1100s, a period similar to the Middle Ages in Europe, noble families of Japan used their samurai armies to fight one another. They fought over land and to gain control of the emperor. In 1180, a civil war broke out between the two most powerful families: the Taira and the Minamoto. In a sea battle in 1185, the Taira were defeated. The commander of the Minamoto forces was Minamoto Yoritomo (mee•nah•MOH•toh yoh•ree•TOH•moh).

The samurai were warriors in Japan who followed a very strict code of behavior known as Bushido.

▶ CRITICAL THINKING
Explaining Why did samurai agree to fight for a noble?

V

samurai a warrior who served a Japanese lord and lived by a strict code of loyalty

R Reading Skills

Explaining After students have read the text, ask them to support the statement that Japan changed greatly with the rise of the samurai and shoguns. Have students explain the Bushido code in their own words. ELL Then **ask:** **Why did the samurai think merchants were lacking in honor?** *(Merchants were concerned about riches, which samurai considered beneath their dignity.)*

V Visual Skills

Interpreting Tell students to study the image of the samurai in conjunction with what they have read. Discuss with students the weapons and armor used by the samurai. **Ask:** **Which weapon that was commonly used by samurai is visible in this picture?** *(a sword or dagger)* **What might the flag symbolize?** *(Answers will vary. Possible response: It may be the symbol of the noble to whom the samurai is loyal.)* **Visual/Spatial**

IMAGE

Shoguns

Identifying Present the interactive feature on the shoguns in Japan. Point out that the shoguns established a strict class system within Japanese society with the samurai at the top. This system lasted for about 700 years. The last of the class system set up by the shoguns was dismantled in 1868. Elicit students' questions to check their understanding of shoguns. **Ask:** **What was a shogunate?** *(a military government in the Japanese Middle Ages)* AL

See page 507E for other online activities.

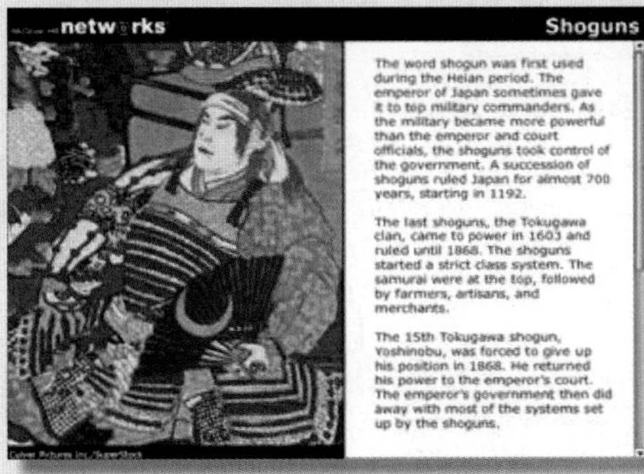

ANSWER, p. 521

CRITICAL THINKING The nobles gave land to the warriors who agreed to fight for them.

C1 Critical Thinking Skills

Reasoning After students have read the first paragraph, **ask:** Why did the emperor make Yoritomo a shogun? *(to reward him and keep him loyal to the throne)* AL What do you think will happen next? *(Responses will vary.)* Have students continue reading, and then ask them to assess how accurate their predictions were.

C2 Critical Thinking Skills

Making Inferences Remind students that China was a larger and more powerful country than Japan. Then **ask:** Why do you think the Japanese named the typhoon winds after divine spirits? *(because they were so thankful that the storms destroyed the Mongol ships and saved Japan)*

Minamoto Yoritomo, became the first shogun to rule Japan in 1185. One of his favorite pastimes was to release wild cranes on the beach near his castle. By this he believed he gained Buddhist merit.

▶ CRITICAL THINKING
Analyzing How did Minamoto Yoritomo come to power?

After Yoritomo won the civil war, the emperor feared that the Minamoto family would take the throne. To avoid this, he decided to reward Yoritomo to keep him loyal. In 1192, he gave Yoritomo the title of **shogun** (SHOH•guhn), or commander of the military forces. C1

This created two governments in Japan. The emperor remained in his palace at Heian-kyo with his advisers. He was Japan's official leader. Meanwhile, the shogun set up his own government in the small seaside town of Kamakura (kah•MAH•kuh•rah). This military government was known as a shogunate. For about the next 700 years, shoguns ran Japan's government.

Mongol Attacks

In the late 1200s, Japan was twice invaded by China's Mongol emperor. During both attempts, violent storms called typhoons destroyed many ships. The Mongols who made it to shore were defeated by the Japanese. C2

The victorious Japanese named the typhoons *kamikaze* (kah•mih•KAH•zee), or "divine wind," in honor of the spirits they believed had saved their islands. During World War II, Japanese pilots deliberately crashed their planes into enemy ships. They were named kamikaze pilots after the typhoons of the 1200s.

✓ PROGRESS CHECK

Identifying What is Bushido, and why was it important to the samurai?

A Divided Japan

GUIDING QUESTION *Why did Japan experience disunity from the 1300s to the 1500s?*

The Kamakura shogunate ruled Japan until 1333. At that time, a general named Ashikaga (ah•shee•KAH•gah) resisted the emperor and made himself shogun. A new government, the Ashikaga shogunate, began.

Reading HELPDESK CCSS

shogun a military governor who ruled Japan

Academic Vocabulary (Tier 2 Words)
labor work; the tasks that workers perform for pay

Reading Strategy: *Explaining*
Explaining means you give all the details of something. Why did the emperor make Minamoto Yoritomo shogun?

networks ***Online Teaching Options***

LECTURE SLIDE

A Divided Japan

Analyzing Show students the lecture slide on the rebellion in 1331 and the ensuing rise of the Ashikaga shogunate. **Ask:** Why did so many samurai turn against the Kamakura shogun? *(The samurai wanted to be given more land.)*

See page 507E for other online activities.

networks A Divided Japan

The Ashiga Shogunate:
- General Ashiga rebelled against the Kamakura shogunate and made himself shogun.
- Military lords called daimyo came to power and controlled small territories.
- Each daimyo had an army of samurai warriors.
- Samurai warriors were given land in return for their services.

ANSWERS, p. 522

CRITICAL THINKING He defeated the Taira in the civil war and was then named shogun by the emperor.

Reading Strategy to keep him loyal

✓ PROGRESS CHECK Bushido is a strict code of conduct. It set the standard of how a samurai must behave toward his master.

The Ashikaga shoguns turned out to be weak leaders. Uprisings swept Japan. The country soon divided into a number of small territories. These areas were headed by powerful military lords known as daimyo (DY•mee•oh).

The daimyo pledged to obey the emperor and the shogun. Still, they governed their lands as if they were independent states. To guard their lands, the daimyo used samurai warriors. They formed their own local armies.

V

Many samurai became **vassals** (VA•suhlz) of a daimyo. These samurai gave an oath of loyalty to their daimyo and pledged to serve him in battle. In return, each daimyo gave land to his samurai. This bond of loyalty between a lord and a vassal is known as **feudalism** (FYOO•duh•lih•zuhm). A similar form of feudalism existed in Europe between the fall of the Western Roman Empire and the early modern period.

R

With the collapse of central government, warriors battled one another throughout Japan. The violence finally ended the Ashikaga shogunate in 1567. By that time, only a few powerful daimyo were left. Each of these daimyo was eager to conquer his rivals—and rule all of Japan.

✓ PROGRESS CHECK

Analyzing Why did feudalism develop in Japan?

Society Under the Shoguns

GUIDING QUESTION ***How were the Japanese affected by their country's growing wealth?***

Under the shoguns, Japan produced more goods and grew richer. However, only the emperor and his family, noble families of the emperor's court, and leading military officials enjoyed this wealth. A small but growing class of merchants and traders also benefited from Japan's prosperity. Most Japanese, however, were farmers who remained poor.

C

Farmers, Artisans, and Trade

For the most part, Japan's wealth came from the hard **labor** of its farmers. Some farmed their own land, but most lived and worked on the estates of the daimyo. Rice, wheat, millet, and barley were their chief crops. Life improved for Japan's farmers during the 1100s, despite their many hardships.

The collapse of a shogunate often led to a period of civil war. This daimyo is one of the powerful military lords that took control and governed.

▶ CRITICAL THINKING

Contrasting What was the difference between the shoguns and the daimyo?

vassal a person under the protection of a lord to whom he has vowed loyalty

feudalism the system of service between a lord and the vassals who have sworn loyalty to the lord

WHITEBOARD ACTIVITY

Sequence of Events, Feudal Japan

Sequencing Use the Interactive Whiteboard Activity on feudal Japan to have students place key events in Japanese history in their proper sequence.

See page 507E for other online activities.

networks — Sequence of Events, Feudal Japan

Directions: Drag and drop events from the bank to the proper year.

Item Bank
- Ashikaga shogunate begins
- Taira are defeated
- Capital of Japan moved from Nara to Heian (modern Kyoto)
- Mongols attack Japan's Kamakura shogunate
- Power of emperors declines
- War breaks out between the Taira and the Minamoto
- Civil war devastates Heian
- Ashikaga shogunate ends
- Mongols attack Japan and are defeated for the second time
- Minamoto Yoritomo becomes the first shogun

Year	Event
794	
800s	
1180	
1185	
1192	
1272	
1281	
1333	
Late 1400s	
1567	

V Visual Skills

Diagramming Tell students to create a flowchart or another kind of diagram that shows the sequence of events leading from the Ashikaga shogunate to the rise of the daimyo. **AL** **Visual/Spatial**

R Reading Skills

Explaining After they have read the text, organize students into small groups. Then assign one student from each group to be the emperor, one to be the shogun, one to be the daimyo, and the remainder to be samurai. Then have students create and act out skits that show the structure of feudalism in Japan. Remind students to use details from the text in their skits. **BL** **Kinesthetic**

C Critical Thinking Skills

Analyzing After students have read about Japanese society under the shoguns, **ask:** **Why did most of the wealth collect at the top of Japanese society?** *(Answers will vary but may include the fact that the upper classes owned most of the land or collected tributes from those below them in the feudal hierarchy.)*

ANSWERS, p. 523

CRITICAL THINKING The shoguns were military leaders in the emperor's army, and the daimyo were wealthy landowners with their own armies.

✓ PROGRESS CHECK Feudalism developed because the Ashikaga shoguns were weak leaders and could not keep Japan united. Japan soon divided into a feudalistic system with a number of small territories headed by daimyo.

R Reading Skills

Discussing After students have read the text, lead the class in a discussion of the relationship between growing wealth and the rise of an artisan class in Japan. **Ask:**

- Whom did Japan trade with during the Shogun period? *(Korea, China, and Southeast Asia)*
- For which Chinese goods did the Japanese trade wooden goods, sword blades, and copper? *(silk, dyes, pepper, books, and porcelain)*
- Why do you think Asian cultures traded goods instead of exchanging money for them? *(Answers will vary. Possible response: The different Asian cultures did not have a common currency.)*

C Critical Thinking Skills

Making Connections Remind students that as Japan became more of a warrior society, upper-class women lost many of their freedoms. Ask students why they think this might have happened. BL

ANSWERS, p. 524

CRITICAL THINKING Improved irrigation helped farmers raise more crops with less labor.

PROGRESS CHECK Under the shoguns, skilled workers in Japan produced more goods. When combined with improved roads and increased farm production, this led to greater trade. Greater trade meant greater wealth.

In this painting, Japanese farmers are shown working their rice paddies.

▶ CRITICAL THINKING
Explaining How did improved irrigation practices help farmers?

A better irrigation process enabled them to plant more crops. This meant they could sell more food to the markets that were forming in the towns.

On the daimyo estates, other Japanese were producing a greater number of goods. Artisans made armor, weapons, and tools. These goods were sold by merchants in town markets throughout Japan. As trade increased, each region began to make certain goods that they were best at producing. These goods included pottery, paper, textiles, and lacquered ware. R

Heian-kyo, now called Kyoto, developed into a major center of production. It also benefited from trade with Korea, China, and Southeast Asia. Japanese merchants traded wooden goods, sword blades, and copper for silk, dyes, pepper, books, and porcelain. More and more artisans and merchants began to live in Kyoto. They set up groups called **guilds** (GIHLDZ), or *za* in Japanese, to protect their jobs and increase their earnings.

Women in Shogun Japan

During the time of the shoguns, the typical Japanese family included grandparents, parents, and children in the same household. A man was head of the family. He had complete control over family members.

C At the time of Prince Shotoku, wealthy Japanese women enjoyed a high standing in society. Several women were empresses, and women could own property. Wives who were abandoned could divorce and remarry. When Japan became a warrior society, upper-class women lost these freedoms.

In farming families, women had a greater say in choosing their husbands. However, they worked long hours in the fields. They also cooked, spun and wove cloth, and cared for their children. In the towns, the wives of artisans and merchants helped run the family businesses.

Despite the lack of freedom, some women were able to contribute to Japanese culture. These talented women gained fame as artists, writers, and entertainers.

PROGRESS CHECK

Explaining Why did Japan's wealth increase under the rule of the shoguns?

Reading HELPDESK (CCSS)

guild a group of merchants or craftspeople during medieval times

sect a religious group

martial arts sports that involve combat and self-defense

networks Online Teaching Options

CHART

Japanese Feudalism

Making Inferences Present the graphic organizer showing the social structure of feudal Japan. Allow students time to read the information and ask questions to clarify their understanding. AL **Ask:** How did the samurai help the daimyo stay in power? *(The samurai were warriors who served the daimyo and kept the other social groups in line.)*

See page 507E for other online activities.

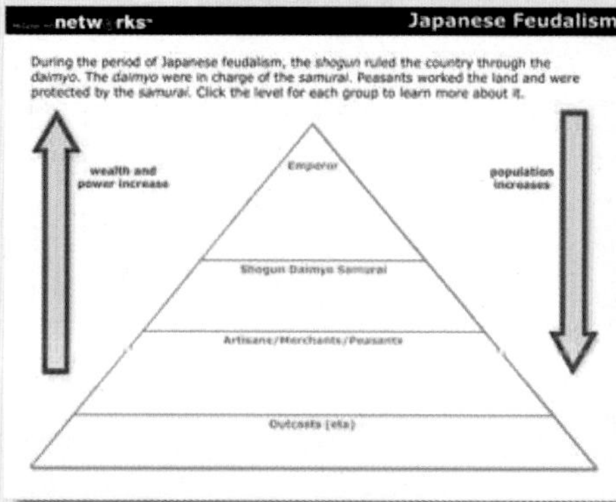

Religion and the Arts

GUIDING QUESTION *How did religion and the arts relate to each other under the shoguns?*

During the time of the shoguns, religion and the arts flourished in Japan. Many Japanese monks, artists, scribes, and traders visited China. This led to a borrowing of ideas and practices. Much of this borrowing from the Chinese exchange affected Japan in the areas of government and philosophy. The Chinese also influenced Japan's art, literature, science, and religion.

The Religions of Japan

Under the shoguns, religion influenced every part of daily life in Japan. Most Japanese came to believe in both Shinto and Buddhism. They worshipped at Shinto shrines and at Buddhist temples. To them, each religion met different needs. Shinto was concerned with daily life. It linked the Japanese to nature and their homeland. Buddhism promised spiritual rewards to the good. It prepared people for the life to come. In shogun Japan, religious ideas inspired many Japanese to write poems and plays and produce paintings. They also built shrines and temples.

C W Mahayana Buddhism, which teaches that the Buddha is a god, began in India and spread to China and Korea. By the time Buddhism reached Japan, it had formed into many different **sects** (SEHKTS), or small groups. One of the major sects in Japan was Zen. Buddhist monks brought Zen to Japan from China during the 1100s. Zen taught that people could find inner peace through self-control and a simple way of life. Followers of Zen disciplined their bodies through **martial arts** (MAHR•shuhl), or sports that involved combat and self-defense.

Zen Buddhists also practiced **meditation** (meh•duh•TAY•shuhn). A person who meditated sat cross-legged and motionless. The person tried to clear the mind of all worldly thoughts and desires. Meditation was considered a way for people to relax and find inner peace.

The Phoenix Hall was originally a single noble's home but was converted to a Buddhist temple in 1053.

C Critical Thinking Skills

Organizing Have students create a three-column graphic organizer that shows the three major religions in Japan under the shogun *(Shinto, Mahayana Buddhism, and Zen Buddhism).* Then have them fill in the organizer with information about each religion, including its core beliefs and common religious practices. AL ELL

W Writing Skills

Informative/Explanatory Have students write a paragraph explaining the similarities and differences between Mahayana Buddhism and Zen Buddhism.

SLIDE SHOW

Japanese Art and Architecture

Identifying Present the interactive feature on Japanese art and architecture during the time of the shoguns. As you present each slide, ask students to describe what they notice. **Ask:** **What do the architecture and the art of Japan reveal about Japanese culture?** *(Possible answer: their love of simplicity and beauty)* **How do the Japanese gardens compare or contrast with Western gardens?** *(Japanese gardens are similar to Western gardens because they use plants, rocks, and water to create beauty. The gardens may differ in their use of raked rocks as a garden feature to represent water.)*

See page 507E for other online activities.

C Critical Thinking Skills

Hypothesizing Remind students that Japan had a pictographic writing system, similar to the system used in China. Work with the class to have them hypothesize what some of the difficulties might be with such a system. BL

T Technology Skills

Researching on the Internet Explain to students that there are many surviving examples of plays, stories, and poems from the shogun period. Have students use the Internet to conduct research and identify one example from each genre. Remind students to make sure they are accessing reliable sources of information.

W Writing Skills

Narrative Have students write their own haiku. Remind them that these short poems usually express a mood or feeling.

BIOGRAPHY

Murasaki Shikibu (c. A.D. 978–1014)

In addition to *The Tale of Genji*, Lady Murasaki Shikibu wrote a diary and more than 120 poems. Her father was a scholar and a governor, and he broke with tradition by educating his daughter Murasaki in Chinese language and literature. Her family was noble but not rich. While serving as a lady-in-waiting in the royal court, Murasaki began writing her novel based on observations of life around her.

▶ **CRITICAL THINKING**
Explaining How did Murasaki herself break from tradition?

Writing and Literature

During the A.D. 500s, the Japanese adopted China's writing system. They used Chinese picture characters that represented whole words. The Japanese and Chinese languages were very different, so the Japanese found it difficult to use these characters. Then, in the A.D. 800s, they added symbols that stood for sounds, much like the letters of an alphabet. Reading and writing became much easier. **C**

The Japanese greatly admired calligraphy, or the art of writing beautifully. Every well-educated person was expected to practice it. Handwriting was believed to reveal much about a person's education, social standing, and character.

Under the shoguns, the Japanese wrote poems, stories, and plays. By the 1600s, a form of poetry called *haiku* (HY•koo) had emerged. A haiku consists of 3 lines of words with a total of 17 syllables. Haiku usually expresses a mood or feeling. The most noted writer of haiku was a man of samurai descent. Below are two of his most famous haiku. **W**

PRIMARY SOURCE

First snow
falling
on the half-finished bridge.

A field of cotton—
As if the moon
had flowered.

—tr. by Robert Hass

T Japan's first great prose literature was written around A.D. 1000 by women at the emperor's palace at Heian-kyo. Lady Murasaki Shikibu (mur•uh•SAH•kee shee•KEE•boo) wrote *The Tale of Genji*. This work describes the romances and adventures of a Japanese prince. Some people believe the work is the world's first novel, or long fictional story.

The Japanese also wrote plays. The oldest type of play is called Noh. Created during the 1300s, Noh plays developed out of religious dances and were used to teach Buddhist ideas. Many Noh plays are still performed in Japan today.

Architecture and Art

During the time of the shoguns, the Japanese adopted building and artistic ideas from China and Korea. They went on to develop their own styles. The architecture and art of Japan revealed the Japanese love of simplicity and beauty.

Reading **HELP**DESK (CCSS)

Visual Vocabulary

meditation mental exercise to reach a greater spiritual awareness

networks Online Teaching Options

BIOGRAPHY

Murasaki Shikibu

Identifying Evidence Have students read the biography of Murasaki Shikibu and cite evidence from her life that would have helped make it possible for her to write *Tale of the Genji*, considered the world's first novel.

See page 507E for other online activities.

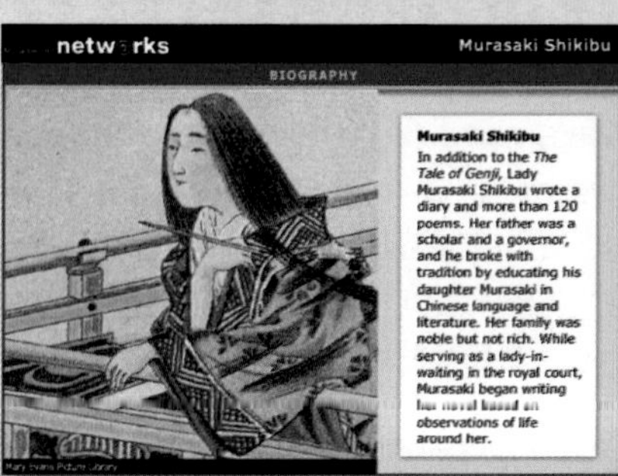

ANSWER, p. 526

CRITICAL THINKING She became a writer, something that few women of the time did because not even upper-class women had a lot of freedom.

Shinto shrines were built in the Japanese style, usually as a simple wooden building, with one room and a rice straw roof. Often they were built near a sacred tree or rock.

Unlike Shinto shrines, Buddhist temples were built in the Chinese style. They had massive tiled roofs held up by thick, wooden pillars. Inside, the temples were richly decorated. They had many altars, paintings, and statues.

Around buildings, the Japanese created gardens that copied nature on a small scale. Carefully placed large rocks served as symbols of mountains, while raked sand gave the sense of water flowing. They might contain only a few plants. The gardens were built this way to create a feeling of peace and calmness.

Creative Artisans

To create beauty inside buildings, Japan's artisans made wooden statues, furniture, and household items. They used a shiny black or red coating called lacquer on many decorative and functional objects. Other Japanese artists learned to do landscape painting from the Chinese. Using ink or watercolors, they painted scenes of nature or battles on paper scrolls or on silk. Japanese nobles at the emperor's palace learned to fold paper to make decorative objects. This art of folding paper is called origami. Buddhist monks and the samurai turned tea drinking into a beautiful ceremony.

The larger rocks in the Japanese garden are symbols of mountains. The raked white stones represent flowing water.

PROGRESS CHECK

Analyzing How did meditation play a part in Buddhism?

LESSON 3 REVIEW

Review Vocabulary (Tier 3 Words)

1. How did the *samurai* advisers serve the *shoguns*? RH.6–8.2, RH.6–8.4

Answer the Guiding Questions

2. ***Determining Cause and Effect*** How did regents affect the rise to power of military leaders in Japan? RH.6–8.2
3. ***Determining Cause and Effect*** What caused Japanese disunity from the 1300s to the 1500s? RH.6–8.2
4. ***Identifying*** What groups of Japanese benefited the most from the increasing wealth in Japan? RH.6–8.2
5. ***Analyzing*** What effect did religion have on the arts during the time of the shoguns? RH.6–8.2
6. **NARRATIVE** Write a narrative in which you describe an encounter with a samurai in the 1300s. This samurai tells you about the code of Bushido. Be sure to include how the samurai dresses and acts. WHST.6–8.10

C Critical Thinking Skills

Contrasting Remind students that different religions coexisted side by side in medieval Japan. **Ask:** **How were Shinto shrines and Buddhist temples different?** *(Shinto shrines were built in a Japanese style, as a simple, one-room building. Buddhist temples were built in a Chinese style, with many altars and statues.)* **Why do you think gardens were important in Japanese culture?** *(because nature was an important spiritual part of Japanese life)*

Have students complete the Lesson 3 Review.

CLOSE & REFLECT

To close the lesson, ask students to reflect on the contrast between the military society under the shoguns and the growth of religion and the arts. Encourage students to formulate questions and draw connections between these two seemingly contradictory facts of life.

LESSON 3 REVIEW ANSWERS

1. They controlled Japan's countryside, kept law and order, and fought in the armies of the shoguns.
2. The regents refused to give up power when the emperors were old enough to rule. This caused a division of power. As the emperors grew weaker, more nobles assumed power over smaller holdings.
3. Central power declined, and Japan was divided into a number of smaller territories ruled by the daimyo.
4. Those who benefited the most were the emperor and his family, a number of noble families, leading military officials, and a small but growing class of merchants and traders.
5. In shogun Japan, a period similar to the Middle Ages in Europe, Shinto and Buddhist ideas inspired many Japanese people. They wrote poems and plays, produced paintings, and built shrines and temples.
6. Narratives should include the key elements of Bushido: loyalty, courage, and honor. They should also have descriptions of weapons, clothing, and so on.

ANSWER, p. 527

PROGRESS CHECK Zen Buddhists practiced meditation to clear their minds and search for inner peace.

ENGAGE

Bellringer Before beginning the lesson, ask students to think about the different cultures that have influenced the area where they live. Explain to students that in this lesson they will learn about a number of different empires that rose and fell in Southeast Asia. They will see the similarities between these cultures as well as the aspects that made each culture unique.

TEACH & ASSESS

R Reading Skills

Determining Word Meanings Direct students' attention to the sentence about archipelagos. Explain that sometimes the definition of a word is presented set off by a comma, as it is here. Have students create a dictionary entry for the word, using the information in this text. Tell students to watch for these as they read, in order to help them understand new vocabulary. AL ELL

C Critical Thinking Skills

Theorizing Based on what students have read about the geography of Southeast Asia, ask them to make predictions about what kinds of cultures might develop there. *(Answers will vary. Students may predict that the cultures will develop independently, similar to the island of Japan, or that they will combine many influences, such as the Korean peninsula.)*

ANSWER, p. 528

TAKING NOTES: Hindu temple; Buddhist temple; royal tomb; astronomical observatory

networks *There's More Online!*
GRAPHIC ORGANIZER Angkor Wat

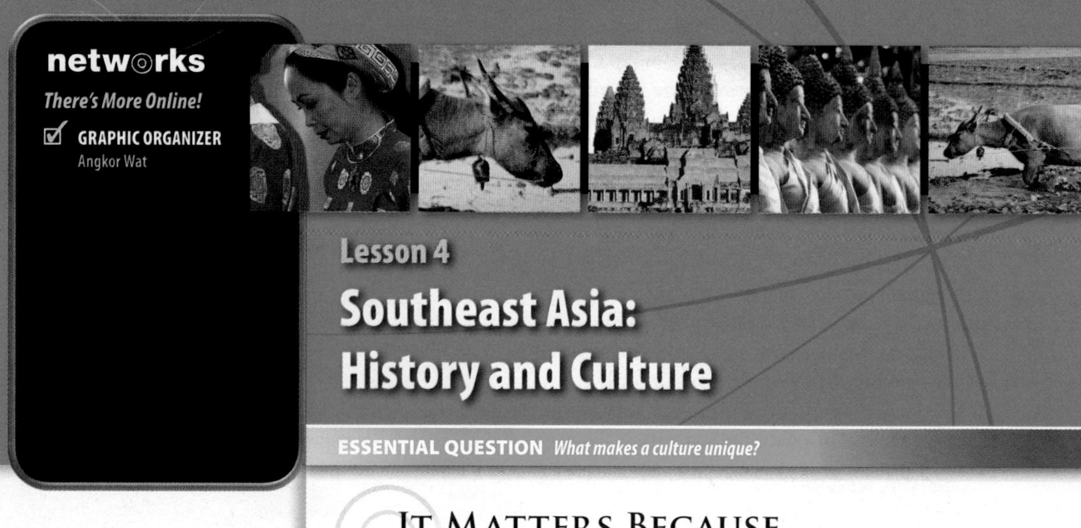

Lesson 4

Southeast Asia: History and Culture

ESSENTIAL QUESTION *What makes a culture unique?*

IT MATTERS BECAUSE

The varied cultures of Southeast Asia have been shaped by outside influences and, in turn, have shaped other cultures.

Early Civilization

GUIDING QUESTION *How did geography affect settlement and early ways of life in Southeast Asia?*

China, Korea, and Japan were not alone in developing civilizations along Asia's Pacific coast. Farther south, other civilizations arose in a region known today as Southeast Asia. Southeast Asians developed their own traditions, though they were influenced by India, China, and Islam.

The Geography of Southeast Asia

Southeast Asia has two major parts. One is a mainland area made up of long, winding peninsulas. The other is a large archipelago, or chain of islands.

Mountain ranges cross mainland Southeast Asia, running north to south. Between the ranges are narrow river valleys and broad coastal deltas. These lowlands are rich in fertile soil. They became prosperous farming and trading centers and home to most mainland Southeast Asians.

South and east of the region's mainland are thousands of mountainous islands. Part of a geographical area known for being unstable, these islands hold many active **volcanoes**. These

(l) STR/epa/Corbis, (cl) Juliet Coombe/Lonely Planet Images/Getty Images, (c) Glen Allison/Photodisc, (cr) Peter Adams/The Image Bank/Getty Images, (r) Juergen Ritterbach/The Image Bank/Getty Images

Reading **HELP**DESK CCSS

Taking Notes: ***Identifying***

Use a graphic organizer like this one to show what purposes the temple of Angkor Wat served. RH.6–8.2

Content Vocabulary (Tier 3 Words)
- **volcano**
- **tsunami**
- **maritime**

networks ***Online Teaching Options***

VIDEO

Religions of Southeast Asia

Identifying Present the lesson video and then discuss the significance of various religious beliefs of the peoples of Southeast Asia. **Ask:** **What religion did the early peoples of Southeast Asia follow?** *(animism)* **Which peoples adopted Buddhism as their main religion?** *(The Thai and Burmese people became Buddhist. Buddhism was also important to the Khmer.)* **Where in the region was Islam practiced?** *(primarily on the Malay Peninsula and on the islands of Indonesia)* AL

See page 507F for other online activities.

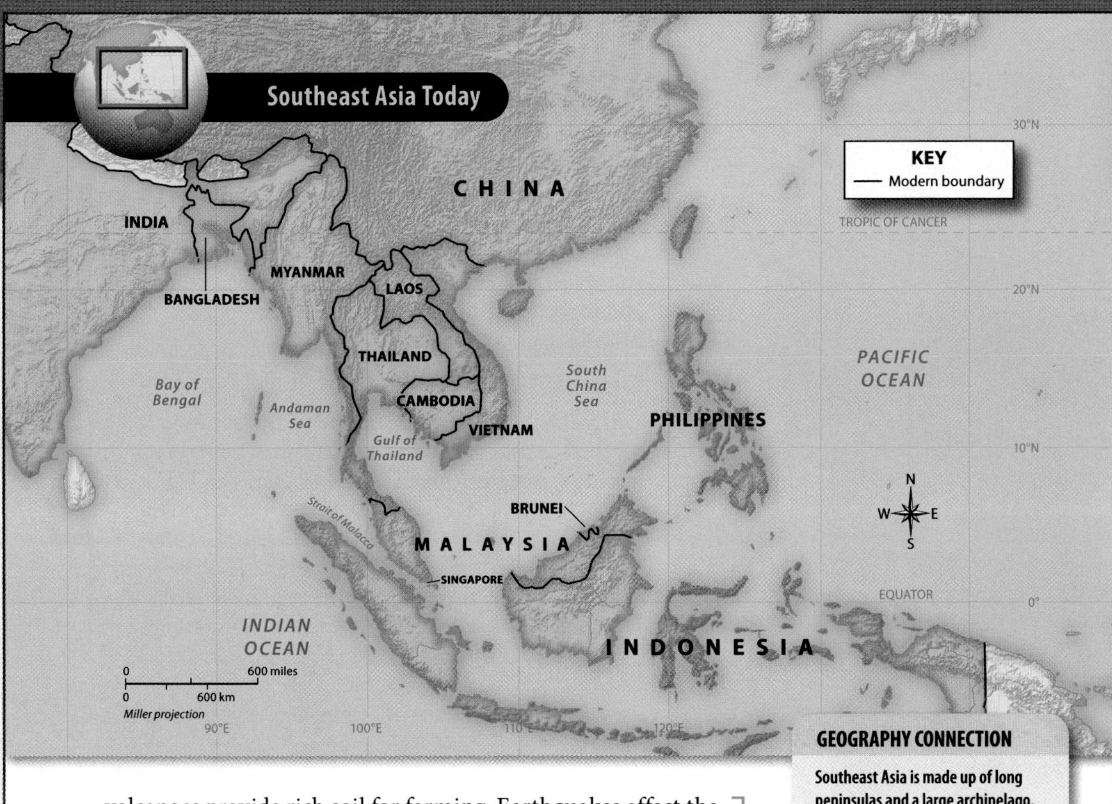

GEOGRAPHY CONNECTION

Southeast Asia is made up of long peninsulas and a large archipelago, or chain of islands.

1. **LOCATION** Between which five countries is Laos located?
2. **CRITICAL THINKING** ***Drawing Conclusions*** Looking at the map, why do you think a tsunami would be especially dangerous in this region?

volcanoes provide rich soil for farming. Earthquakes affect the island peoples of Southeast Asia. One particular danger comes from **tsunamis** (soo•NAH•meez). A tsunami is a huge ocean wave caused by an underwater earthquake. Tsunamis usually strike coastal lowlands, killing many people and destroying buildings. This happened in Japan in 2011. **C**

Sea trade and inland mountain barriers shaped Southeast Asia into a region of many ethnic groups, languages, and religions. As a result, Southeast Asia was never united under a single government. Instead, it was an area of separate territories.

Early Years

Early peoples in Southeast Asia grew rice, raised cattle and pigs, and made metal goods. These early people believed in animism, the idea that spirits exist in living and nonliving things. They practiced different rituals to honor their ancestors as well as animal and nature spirits. **R**

volcano a mountain that may release hot or melted rocks from inside the Earth
tsunami a huge ocean wave caused by an undersea earthquake

C Critical Thinking Skills

Drawing Conclusions After students have finished reading about the geography of Southeast Asia, **ask:** Why would tsunamis pose a particular threat in this region? *(The region is made up mainly of islands and archipelagos that are surrounded by water.)*

R Reading Skills

Discussing Direct students to read the text. Lead the class in a brief discussion of the similarities between religion in early Japan and in early Southeast Asia. Point out that both cultures believed in animism and honoring their ancestors. **Verbal/Linguistic**

Content Background Knowledge

In December 2004, a tsunami in the Indian Ocean hit the coast of Southeast Asia, causing massive amounts of destruction and loss of life. A large earthquake struck on the ocean floor, which created a series of enormous waves. Some of these waves were 30 feet high when they reached the shore. Nearly a quarter of a million people were killed.

MAP

Southeast Asia Today

Identifying Show students the map of Southeast Asia today. Have them identify key geographic features.
Ask: What kind of landforms make up Indonesia? *(It is made up of a series of mountainous islands.)*
Ask: Why would the soil in the valleys and deltas be fertile? *(Rainwater would wash soil from the mountains down into the valleys. The rivers would carry silt to the deltas on the coast.)*

See page 507F for other online activities.

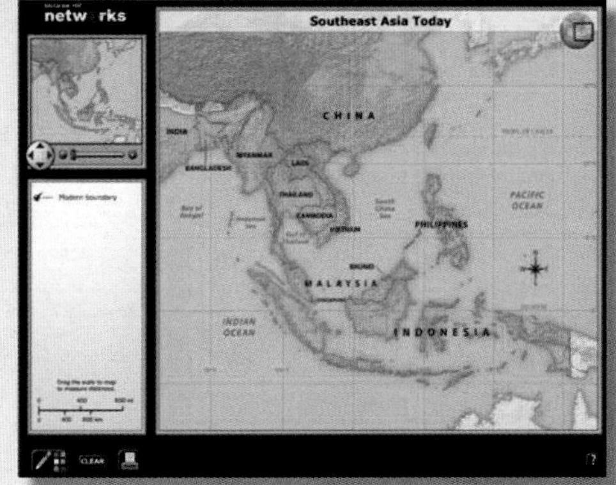

ANSWERS, p. 529

GEOGRAPHY CONNECTION

1. Thailand, Cambodia, Vietnam, Myanmar, and China
2. **CRITICAL THINKING** A tsunami would be especially dangerous in this area because it would sweep over many small islands. Also, on a small island, there is little room for people to move inland to escape the danger.

R Reading Skills

Finding the Main Idea Instruct students to read the paragraph about Southeast Asian art forms. Ask for volunteers to identify the main idea of that paragraph. Then ask for other students to identify the supporting details. AL ELL

W Writing Skills

Informative/Explanatory Remind students that the early cultures of Southeast Asia were isolated due to geography. Have students write a summary in two or three sentences that explains why the arrival of Hindu traders from India changed that.

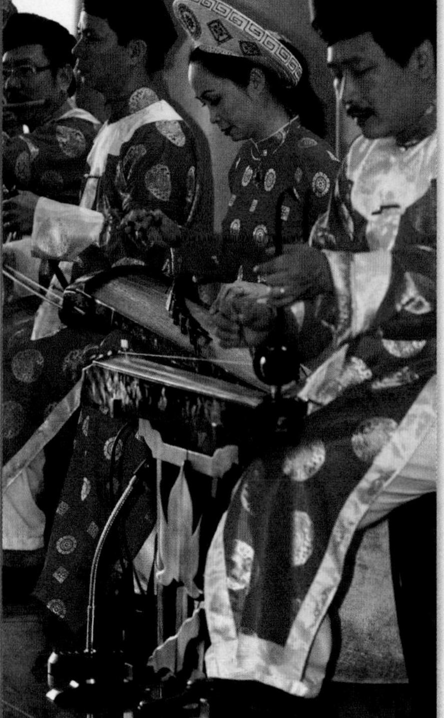

Musicians from Vietnam perform traditional music using string and wind instruments.

STR/epa/Corbis

Southeast Asians also developed their own forms of art. Artisans made a cloth of detailed patterns later called batik (buh•TEEK). Musicians played instruments including the *dan bau* (similar to a xylophone), the *dan day* (a type of guitar), and the *rammana* (a type of drum). Artists created a type of theater that used shadow puppets to tell stories. Performers holding long rods controlled the puppets behind a white screen, while audiences on the other side could see the puppets' moving shadows. R

Outside Contacts

During the A.D. 100s, Hindu traders from India reached coastal areas of Southeast Asia. They set up a trading **network** that exchanged goods and ideas among the peoples of Southeast Asia, India, and the Middle East. As these contacts increased, the cultures of other civilizations spread throughout Southeast Asia. Over time, the people of the region blended Hindu and Chinese ways with their own traditions. W

✓ PROGRESS CHECK

Analyzing Why did outside influences have a powerful effect on early Southeast Asia?

Kingdoms and Empires

GUIDING QUESTION *Why did powerful kingdoms and empires develop in Southeast Asia?*

From A.D. 500 to 1500, many kingdoms and empires thrived in Southeast Asia. States covering fertile inland areas drew their wealth from the land. States on the coast became **maritime** (MEHR•uh•tym), or seafaring, powers that controlled shipping.

Vietnam

Along the coast of the Indochinese Peninsula lies the present-day country of Vietnam. The ancient Viet were one of the first people in Southeast Asia to develop their own state and culture. During the 200s B.C., the Viet people ruled most of the Indochinese Peninsula.

During the early A.D. 900s, the Viet rebelled against China's weakened Tang dynasty. In A.D. 938, the Viet forces defeated a fleet of Chinese warships in the Battle of the Bach Dang River. The Viet had finally won independence.

Reading **HELP**DESK (CCSS)

maritime related to the sea or seafaring

Academic Vocabulary (Tier 2 Words)

network a system in which all parts are connected

style a distinctive form or type of something

networks Online Teaching Options

IMAGE

The Strait of Malacca

Analyzing Visuals Present the interactive image showing a map of the Strait of Malacca. **Ask: Why do you think the Strait of Malacca was important for shipping?** *(Possible answer: It provided a shortcut between the Indian Ocean and the South China Sea.)*

See page 507F for other online activities.

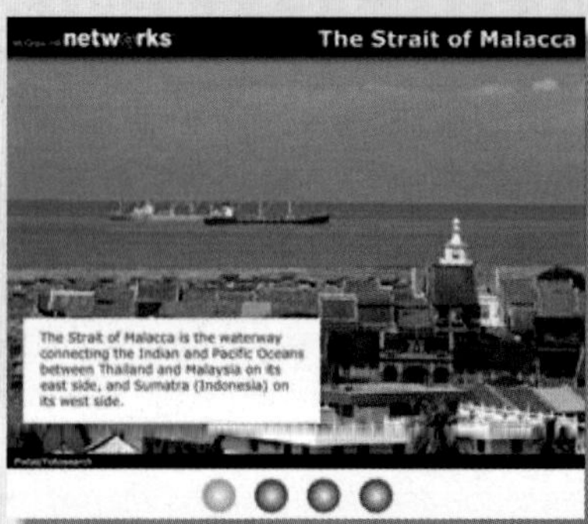

ANSWER, p. 530

✓ PROGRESS CHECK Outside influences linked Southeast Asians with other parts of the world, thus influencing cultural elements such as forms of government and religion.

The new state was modeled on the government of China and was known as Dai Viet, or Great Viet. Confucianism became its official religion. Viet emperors adopted Chinese court ceremonies. Just as in China, Viet government officials were selected through civil service examinations.

The Khmer Empire

West of Vietnam is the present-day country of Cambodia (kam•BOH•dee•uh). In ancient times, this region was the home of the Khmer (kuh•MEHR) people. During the A.D. 1100s, the Khmer founded an empire that covered much of mainland Southeast Asia. They became wealthy from growing rice.

Khmer kings based their rule on Hindu and Buddhist ideas from India. They increased their power by presenting themselves as god-kings to their people. A Chinese traveler once described the splendor, in dress and manner, of a Khmer king in about 1297:

PRIMARY SOURCE

> His crown of gold is high and pointed like those on the heads of the mighty gods. . . . His neck is hung with ropes of huge pearls; . . . his wrists and ankles are loaded with bracelets and on his fingers are rings of gold. . . . He goes barefoot—the soles of his feet, like the palms of his hands, are rouged [colored] with a red stuff. When he appears in public, he carries the Golden Sword.
>
> —from *A Record of Cambodia: The Land and Its People*, by Zhou Daguan, tr. by Peter Harris

C

Supported by Khmer kings, architects created a new **style** of building based on Indian and local designs. The most magnificent structure was Angkor Wat. It served as a religious temple, a royal tomb, and an astronomical observatory. Angkor Wat still stands today and attracts many visitors.

By the 1440s, building costs, high taxes, and internal revolts had weakened the Khmer Empire. In A.D. 1432, the Thai (TY), a neighboring Southeast Asian people, captured the capital city of Angkor. With this attack, the Khmer Empire faded into history.

Connections to TODAY

Saving Angkor Wat

Angkor Wat was overgrown by thick tropical plants and trees after its capture by the Thai in A.D. 1432. During the late 1900's the site was further damaged during various wars. Mostly, however, it suffered from neglect. In 1992, Angkor was named a UNESCO World Heritage site, a major step in protecting it for generations to come.

Glen Allison/Photodisc

Angkor Wat, the largest religious structure in the world, is a temple complex built in Cambodia. Built in the 1100's, it took nearly 40 years to complete.

▶ **CRITICAL THINKING**

Making Inferences Why do you think it took so long to build Angkor Wat?

V

C Critical Thinking Skills

Identifying Point of View Ask for volunteers to read aloud the primary source describing a Khmer king. Then lead a class discussion. **Ask:** **Who wrote this description?** *(a Chinese traveler)* **What might have been his purpose for writing it?** *(Responses will vary, but may include: to impress others in China, to flatter the Khmer king, to accurately report what he saw.)* Encourage students to discuss what this means about his point of view.

V Visual Skills

Interpreting Tell students to examine the image of the Angkor Wat temple complex. Explain that the site displays evidence of Buddhist and Hindu influences. **Ask:** **What does the design of Angkor Wat suggest about the cultures of Southeast Asia?** *(Students should note that the temple complex represents a blend of cultures, suggesting that Southeast Asia was a place where different cultures met and exchanged ideas.)* **BL**

WORKSHEET

Economics of History Activity: The Rise of Angkor

Determining Cause and Effect Show students the Economics of History worksheet on the rise and fall of the Khmer Empire. Have students complete the initial questions on the Khmer's rise to power; then assign the final questions as homework.

See page 507F for other online activities.

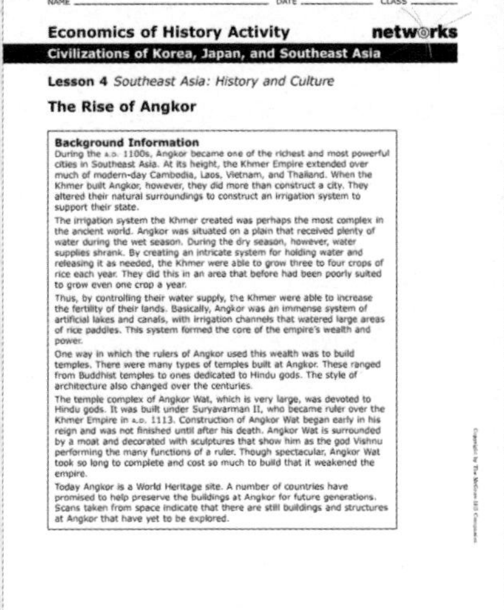

NAME ______ DATE ______ CLASS ______

Economics of History Activity **networks**

Civilizations of Korea, Japan, and Southeast Asia

Lesson 4 *Southeast Asia: History and Culture*

The Rise of Angkor

Background Information

During the A.D. 1100s, Angkor became one of the richest and most powerful cities in Southeast Asia. At its height, the Khmer Empire extended over much of modern-day Cambodia, Laos, Vietnam, and Thailand. When the Khmer built Angkor, however, they did more than construct a city. They altered their natural surroundings to construct an irrigation system to support their state.

The irrigation system the Khmer created was perhaps the most complex in the ancient world. Angkor was situated on a plain that received plenty of water during the wet season. During the dry season, however, water supplies shrank. By creating an intricate system for holding water and releasing it as needed, the Khmer were able to grow three to four crops of rice each year. They did this in an area that before had been poorly suited to grow even one crop a year.

Thus, by controlling their water supply, the Khmer were able to increase the fertility of their lands. Basically, Angkor was an immense system of artificial lakes and canals, with irrigation channels that watered large areas of rice paddies. This system formed the core of the empire's wealth and power.

One way in which the rulers of Angkor used this wealth was to build temples. There were many types of temples built at Angkor. These ranged from Buddhist temples to ones dedicated to Hindu gods. The style of architecture also changed over the centuries.

The temple complex of Angkor Wat, which is very large, was devoted to Hindu gods. It was built under Suryavarman II, who became ruler over the Khmer Empire in A.D. 1113. Construction of Angkor Wat began early in his reign and was not finished until after his death. Angkor Wat is surrounded by a moat and decorated with sculptures that show him as the god Vishnu performing the many functions of a ruler. Though spectacular, Angkor Wat took so long to complete and cost so much to build that it weakened the empire.

Today Angkor is a World Heritage site. A number of countries have promised to help preserve the buildings at Angkor for future generations. Scans taken from space indicate that there are still buildings and structures at Angkor that have yet to be explored.

ANSWER, p. 531

CRITICAL THINKING Angkor Wat was so large that it probably took a long time to build, because so many workers and materials were involved.

R Reading Skills

Identifying Remind students that Southeast Asia adopted practices from many cultures. Based on the readings in this text, have them create a table showing what elements became part of Thai culture and where they originated. *(writing system and porcelain from China; Buddhism and Hinduism from India)*

C Critical Thinking Skills

Making Generalizations After students have finished the reading, ask them to make a generalization about both the Sukhothai and Ayutthaya kingdoms. *(They were centers for learning and the arts; both kingdoms ruled for long periods of time.)*

Statues of the Buddha line a temple in Thailand. They are dressed in orange robes, which are the traditional garb for Buddhist monks.

▶ CRITICAL THINKING
Drawing Conclusions How did Buddhist monks from India influence the Thai people?

Peter Adams/The Image Bank/Getty Images

The Thai

The earliest Thai settlements arose along the border of China. Between A.D. 700 and 1100, Thai groups moved southward. They set up a kingdom at Sukhothai (SOO•kah•TY) in what is today north central Thailand.

The Thai developed a writing system and made the kingdom a center of learning and the arts. Artisans from China taught the making of porcelain. Buddhist monks from India converted many Thai to Buddhism. The Thai were influenced by Hinduism in their political practices, dance, and literature.

About A.D. 1350 a new Thai kingdom known as Ayutthaya (ah•yoo•TY•uh) arose. Its capital city was located where the city of Bangkok, the present Thai capital, stands today.

The Ayutthaya kingdom lasted for about 400 years. At its height, it held control over large areas of Southeast Asia. The Thai region was an important center of Buddhist learning and culture. Its merchants traded in teak wood, salt, spices, and hides with China and neighboring Asian kingdoms.

Burma

West of the Thai kingdom, a people known as the Burmese developed a civilization. In A.D. 849, they set up a capital city called Pagan (pah•GAHN). During the next 200 years, Pagan became a major influence in the western part of Southeast Asia.

Reading HELPDESK (CCSS)

Academic Vocabulary (Tier 2 Words)

institution a custom or practice that many people accept and use

networks Online Teaching Options

LECTURE SLIDE

Kingdoms and Empires

Sequencing Show students the lecture slide with a time line about the development of Thailand and Burma. Have a volunteer read aloud the details about each country. Discuss the similarities and differences that exist in the development of each country.

See page 507F for other online activities.

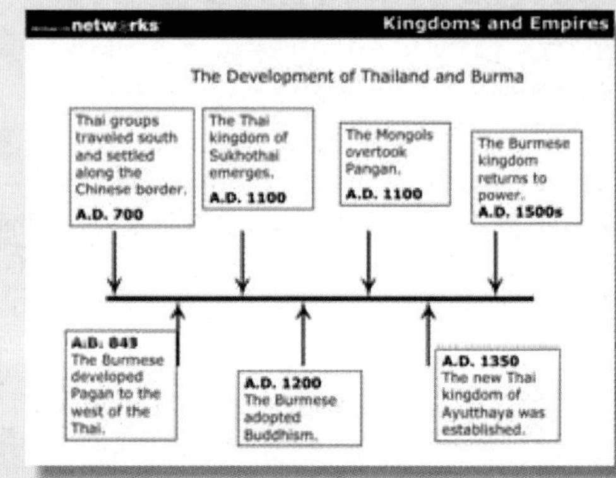

ANSWER, p. 532

CRITICAL THINKING The Buddhists from India converted many Thai people to Buddhism.

The city eventually became a center of Buddhist learning and culture. Like the Thai, the Burmese adopted Buddhism, as well as Indian political **institutions** and culture.

Attacks by the Mongols in the late 1200s weakened Pagan. To escape Mongol rule, many people in Burma moved south and built fortified towns along the rivers. Burmese culture was preserved, but the kingdom did not arise again until the 1500s.

The Malay States

On the Malay Peninsula and the islands of Indonesia, independent states developed around seaport cities. They traded porcelain, textiles, and silk, as well as Southeast Asian spices and wood.

Most of the people living on Southeast Asian islands were Malays. Despite common cultural ties, the Malays were divided into many separate communities by distance and trade rivalries. However, in the A.D. 700s, a Malay state arose on the islands of Java and Sumatra in present-day Indonesia. This state controlled the trade route passing through the Strait of Malacca.

Many Southeast Asian states continue to share common farming and trade ideas and practices.

Juliet Coombe/Lonely Planet Images/Getty Images

Islam in Southeast Asia

Muslim Arab traders and missionaries settled coastal areas of Southeast Asia during the A.D. 800s. Eventually, many people in these places converted to Islam. The first major Islamic center was Melaka, a trading port on the Malay Peninsula.

From Melaka, Islam spread throughout the Indonesian islands. Bali was the only island to remain outside of Muslim influence. Even today, Bali keeps its Hindu religion and culture. C

✓ PROGRESS CHECK

Summarizing How did the culture of China affect Southeast Asian states?

LESSON 4 REVIEW (CCSS)

Review Vocabulary (Tier 3 Words)

1. Why do *maritime* workers live along a seacoast? RH.6–8.2, RH.6–8.4

Answer the Guiding Questions

2. ***Identifying*** What separated early Southeast Asians? RH.6–8.2
3. ***Listing*** What were the most powerful kingdoms to develop on mainland Southeast Asia by A.D. 1500? RH.6–8.2
4. ***Contrasting*** Why did some Southeast Asian states rely mostly on trading while others relied on farming? RH.6–8.2
5. ***Explaining*** Why was Angkor Wat significant to the Khmer? RH.6–8.2
6. **INFORMATIVE/EXPLANATORY** Look at the photograph of Angkor Wat. Then write a paragraph describing its appearance to someone who has never seen it before. WHST.6–8.7, WHST.6–8.10

C Critical Thinking Skills

Comparing and Contrasting Create a three-column graphic organizer. Title the columns "India," "China," and "Arabia." Then hold a class discussion in which students identify key ways that each of these outside cultures influenced Southeast Asia. **Ask:**

- **What religions and other belief systems were introduced by each outside culture?** *(India introduced Buddhism and Hinduism to the region, and later it introduced Islam. China introduced Confucian ideas. Arabia brought Islam to the Malay Peninsula.)* AL
- **How did these outsiders influence government?** *(India influenced the Funan and Sukhothai kingdoms. The Viet based their government on the Chinese examination-system model. States based on Islam formed in the Southeast Asian islands.)*
- **What role did trade play in spreading ideas?** *(Indian merchants brought Hinduism and other ideas to Southeast Asia. Arabian merchants brought Islam to the Southeast Asian islands.)* AL ELL

Have students complete the Lesson 4 Review.

CLOSE & REFLECT

To close the lesson, lead the class in a discussion of how Southeast Asian nations developed in the same ways and how they developed in distinct, or different, ways. Ask students to consider the influence of trade, conquest, and religion on the region.

LESSON 4 REVIEW ANSWERS

1. *Maritime* refers to the sea or to seafaring, so workers in the fishing, shipbuilding, or other sea-related industries would need to live by the coast.
2. The vast mountain ranges and many seas separated the countries.
3. Dai Viet, Angkor, Sukhothai, Ayutthaya, Pagan, Melaka
4. From A.D. 500 to 1500, the different states of Southeast Asia developed economies based on either farming or trade. States covering large inland areas drew their wealth from farming the land. Other smaller, coastal states became maritime, or seafaring, powers that controlled shipping and trade.
5. Angkor Wat served as a temple and a cultural center for many years; today, it attracts visitors from around the world.
6. Students should include vivid descriptive details, such as size and composition, color, location on the water, and how it reflects on the water.

ANSWER, p. 533

✓ PROGRESS CHECK Answers should include that they affected government, architecture, and religion.

CHAPTER REVIEW ACTIVITY

Have students create a graphic organizer like the one below and label the center circle "Maintaining Control of a Dynasty." Then organize the class into groups to fill in the remaining circles. Have volunteers from each group list one key idea that they found to be necessary for founding and maintaining control of a specific government or dynasty in the region.

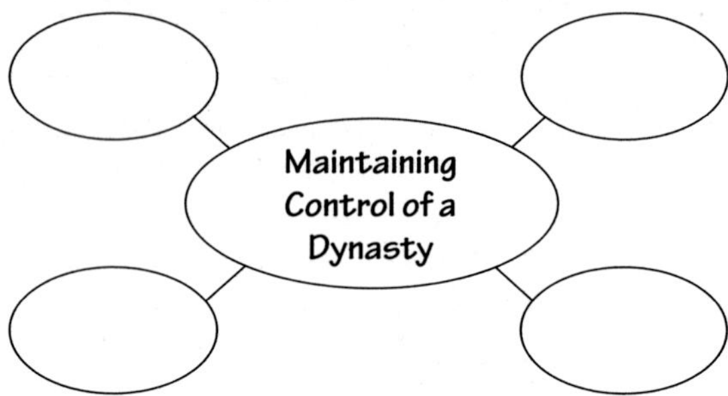

REVIEW THE ENDURING UNDERSTANDING

Review this chapter's Enduring Understanding with students:

- *People, places, and ideas change over time.*

Now pose the following questions in a class discussion to apply this to this chapter. **Ask:**

- Which period of Korean government was the strongest? *(Answers may include the Three Kingdoms period, Silla rule, the Koryo period, or the Yi Dynasty. Students should offer facts to support their answers.)*
- How was the Nara period different from the shogunate in Japan? *(Answers may include: The Nara period had a strong emperor who controlled the land. The shogunate was military rule under a weak emperor, with great wealth for the upper classes.)*

CHAPTER 18 Activities CCSS

Write your answers on a separate sheet of paper.

1. **Exploring the Essential Question** WHST.6–8.2, WHST.6–8.10
INFORMATIVE/EXPLANATORY Review the section about the first settlers in Japan. Then write a paragraph in which you discuss the Yayoi. How did they live? How were they organized? What kind of government did they have?

2. **21st Century Skills** RH.6–8.7, WHST.6–8.7, WHST.6–8.8, WHST.6–8.9
USING LATITUDE AND LONGITUDE Many Southeast Asian countries are linked by water. Notice where the Equator falls in the region on the map below. Do research to find out what effect living on the Equator can have on the lives of the people of Southeast Asia. How might this latitude influence their economies and lifestyle. Share your finding with the class, using the map as part of your presentation.

3. **Thinking Like a Historian** RH.6–8.2
UNDERSTANDING CAUSE AND EFFECT Create a diagram like the one to the right to identify what events caused shoguns to rise to power in Japan.

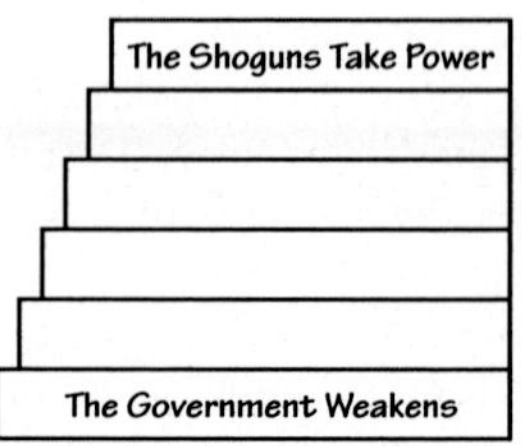

4. **GEOGRAPHY ACTIVITY**

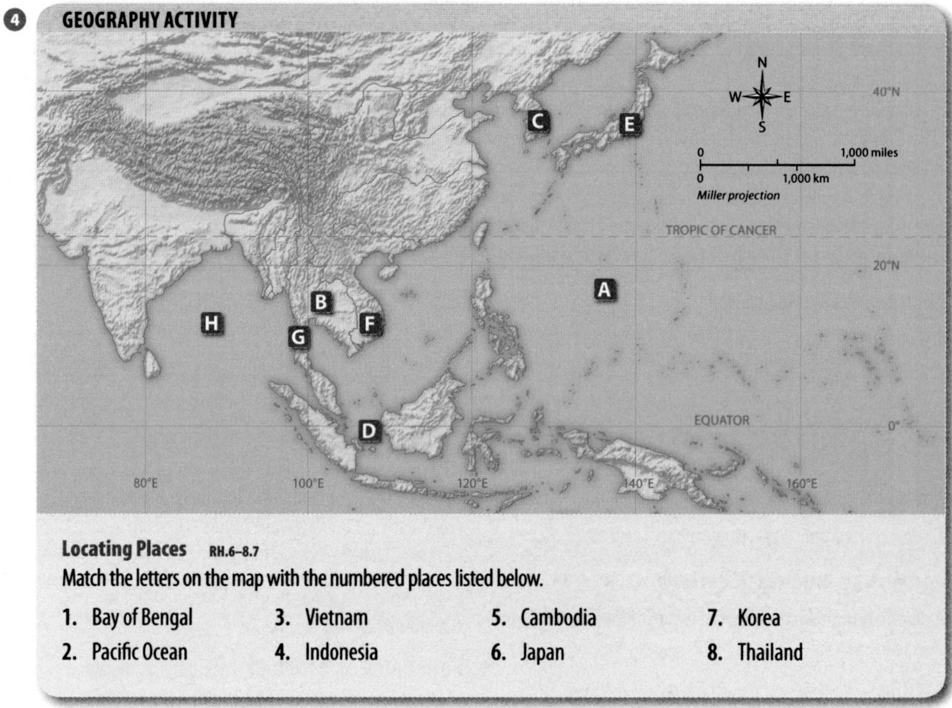

Locating Places RH.6–8.7
Match the letters on the map with the numbered places listed below.

1. Bay of Bengal
2. Pacific Ocean
3. Vietnam
4. Indonesia
5. Cambodia
6. Japan
7. Korea
8. Thailand

ACTIVITIES ANSWERS

Exploring the Essential Question

1. The early people hunted animals and gathered wild plants. They lived in pits dug into the ground. The Yayoi were farmers. They made pottery, iron tools, and bronze bells and weapons. They lived in clans headed by a small group of warriors.

21st Century Skills

2. Students may use the Internet, a wall map, or a globe to show the location of the countries of Southeast Asia in relation to the Equator. Presentations should include the effect of tropical rain forests on the types of crops grown and traded. They should also describe tropical-style housing and clothing.

Thinking Like a Historian

3. The Government Weakens—Regents Rule Japan—Nobles Take Control in Outlying Provinces—Nobles Form Their Own Armies—Civil War Breaks Out—Yoritomo Appointed Shogun by Emperor—The Shoguns Take Power

Locating Places

4. **1.** H, **2.** A, **3.** F, **4.** D, **5.** B, **6.** E, **7.** C, **8.** G

CHAPTER 18 Assessment CCSS

REVIEW THE GUIDING QUESTIONS

Directions: Choose the best answer for each question.

RH.6–8.2
1. Which group ruled Korea for 400 years?
   A. the Koryŏ
   B. the Silla
   C. the Tang
   D. the Confucians

RH.6–8.2, RH.6–8.4
2. What is *hangul*?
   F. an instrument for measuring rainfall
   G. the standard writing system in present-day Korea
   H. a globe that shows the position and motion of planets
   I. a turtle ship

RH.6–8.2, RH.6–8.4
3. Many samurai became
   A. daimyo.
   B. shoguns.
   C. vassals.
   D. Bushido.

RH.6–8.2
4. Why did the early Japanese turn to the sea for food?
   F. They preferred fishing to farming.
   G. There was little fertile land for farming.
   H. The seas around Japan left them isolated.
   I. Their crops were destroyed by volcanic eruptions.

RH.6–8.2
5. How did the Khmer Empire rulers increase their power?
   A. They opened schools.
   B. They built large temples.
   C. They presented themselves as god-kings.
   D. They traded goods with Hindu traders from India.

RH.6–8.2
6. Which city became a center of learning and trade in Burma?
   F. Sukhothai
   G. Pagan
   H. Sumatra
   I. Melaka

535

CHAPTER 18
Assessment Answers

ASSESSMENT ANSWERS
Review the Guiding Questions

1. **A** The correct choice is A. The Koryo kingdom united Korea and held it for 400 years. The earlier rulers of the Silla kingdom and the Tang dynasty fell after conflict with other rulers. Confucian teaching was part of the cultural literacy of the time but not a ruling group.

2. **G** The correct choice is G. Hangul was developed under Sejong the Great and is the standard writing system in present-day Korea.

3. **C** The correct choice is C. Many samurai became vassals of a powerful lord called a daimyo. They pledged loyalty to the daimyo in return for land. Very few samurai would rise to the status of daimyo or shogun. Bushido was the warrior code of the samurai.

4. **G** The correct choice is G. Little fertile land was available for farming, so the Japanese turned to fishing to meet their food needs.

5. **C** The correct choice is C. The Khmer rulers led their people to believe they were god-kings. Although they built Angkor Wat as a large temple, this was not the primary way they gained power.

6. **G** The correct choice is G. Pagan became a major center of Buddhist learning and culture in Burma. Melaka was the first major Islamic center.

Analyzing Documents

7 **D** The correct choice is D. According to the passage, individuals become master actors when they have perfected the skills of acting through study and practice and thus become "one with the art itself."

8 **I** The correct choice is I. Both practiced their skills to perfection. For the actor, this means he or she does not imitate the teacher, but perfects the skills of acting instead; for the samurai, this means perfecting the skills of fighting.

Short Response

9 Students should clearly point out that upper- and lower-class members were differentiated by their clothing, food, housing, and occupation.

10 Aristocrats were permitted to marry according to their social class. Their lives were supported by slaves.

Extended Response

11 Students should explain that animism is the belief that all living things as well as nonliving things such as rocks and rivers have a spirit, called a kami. Believers in animism show respect to the kami by praying at shrines and temples. They ask the kami for help. Over time, belief in animism developed into Shintoism, a religion practiced by Japan's rulers who took part in Shinto rituals in order to ensure the well-being of the Japanese people. Today, Shintoism still affects the Japanese people, who have a deep love of nature.

CHAPTER 18 Assessment *(continued)* 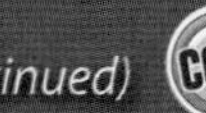

DBQ ANALYZING DOCUMENTS

A great Noh actor, explained how acting is mastered.

"As long as an actor is trying to imitate his teacher, he is still without mastery. . . . An actor may be said to be a master when, by means of his artistic powers, he quickly perfects the skills he has won through study and practice, and thus becomes one with the art itself."

—*The Book of the Way of the Highest Flower (Shikadō-Sho)* by Seami Jūokubushū Hyōshaku

RH.6–8.1, RH.6–8.6

7 **Analyzing** Which of the following best summarizes when actors become "masters"?

A. when they can imitate the teacher
B. when they begin to study and practice acting
C. when they learn artistic skills
D. when they become part of the art of acting

RH.6–8.1, RH.6–8.6

8 **Comparing and Contrasting** What might a master actor and a samurai have in common?

F. Both were well paid.
G. Both worked for shoguns.
H. Both owned land.
I. Both practiced their skills to perfection.

SHORT RESPONSE

"During the Three Kingdoms , . . . power in all three of the kingdoms was held by those who lived in the capital and by the aristocratic families who dominated a very rigid and hereditary social status system. Members of the upper and lower classes were differentiated in almost every aspect of their lives, including clothing, food, housing, and occupation. . . . The lifestyle of the aristocracy was supported by slaves, who led miserable lives."

—May Connor, editor, *The Koreas*

RH.6–8.1, RH.6–8.6

9 What factors differentiated members of the upper and lower classes?

RH.6–8.1, RH.6–8.6

10 What privileges did aristocrats have that the lower class didn't have?

EXTENDED RESPONSE

WHST.6–8.2, WHST.6–8.10

11 **Informative/Explanatory** Write a short essay in which you explain the concept of animism and its influence on the culture of the Japanese.

Need Extra Help?

If You've Missed Question	1	2	3	4	5	6	7	8	9	10	11
Review Lesson	1	1	3	2	3	4	3	2, 3	4	4	4

536 *Civilizations of Korea, Japan, and Southeast Asia*

networks Online Teaching Options

Help students use the Skills Builder resources

Your students can practice important 21st Century skills such as geography, reading, writing, and critical thinking by using resources found in the Skills Builder tab of the online Student Learning Center. Resources include templates, handbooks, and slide shows. These same resources are also available in the Resource Library of the Teacher Lesson Center.

CHAPTER 19

Medieval Europe Planner

UNDERSTANDING BY DESIGN®

Enduring Understandings

- *Religion can influence a society's beliefs and values.*
- *Cultures are held together by shared beliefs and common practices and values.*
- *Conflict can lead to change.*

Essential Questions

- *Why does conflict develop?*
- *What are the characteristics that define a culture?*
- *How do governments change?*
- *What is the role of religion in government?*

Predictable Misunderstandings

Students may think:

- *Society did not change during the Middle Ages.*
- *Feudalism is all about knights and castles, not everyday people.*
- *During the Crusades, one side was right and the other was wrong.*

Assessment Evidence

Performance Task:

- *Hands-On Chapter Project*

Other Evidence:

- *Geography and History Activity*
- *Primary Sources Activities*
- *21st Century Skills Activity*
- *Economics of History Activity*
- *Responses to Interactive Whiteboard Activities*
- *Class discussions about the structure of the Church*
- *Class discussions about the relationship between the pope and the king*
- *Listing activity about the rights guaranteed by the Magna Carta*
- *Class discussion and written assignment about problems in the Church and society in the late Middle Ages*
- *Lesson Reviews*
- *Chapter Activities and Assessment*

SUGGESTED PACING GUIDE

Introducing the Chapter	1 Day
Lesson 1	2 Days
Lesson 2	1 Day
Lesson 3	2 Days
Lesson 4	1 Day
Lesson 5	1 Day
Chapter Wrap-Up and Assessment	1 Day

TOTAL TIME 9 Days

Key for Using the Teacher Edition

SKILL-BASED ACTIVITIES

Types of skill activities found in the Teacher Edition.

V Visual Skills require students to analyze maps, graphs, charts, and photos.

R Reading Skills help students practice reading skills and master vocabulary.

W Writing Skills provide writing opportunities to help students comprehend the text.

C Critical Thinking Skills help students apply and extend what they have learned.

T Technology Skills require students to use digital tools effectively.

*Letters are followed by a number when there is more than one of the same type of skill on the page.

DIFFERENTIATED INSTRUCTION

All activities are written for the on-level student unless otherwise marked with the leveled labels below.

BL Beyond Level

AL Approaching Level

ELL English Language Learners

All students benefit from activities that utilize different learning styles. Many activities are marked as below when a particular learning style is highlighted.

Intrapersonal | **Naturalist**
Logical/Mathematical | **Kinesthetic**
Visual/Spatial | **Auditory/Musical**
Verbal/Linguistic | **Interpersonal**

NCSS Standards covered in "Medieval Europe"

Learners will understand:

1 CULTURE

3. How culture influences the ways in which human groups solve the problems of daily living

4. That the beliefs, values, and behaviors of a culture form an integrated system that helps shape the activities and ways of life that define a culture

6. That culture may change in response to changing needs, concerns, social, political, and geographic conditions

2 TIME, CONTINUITY, AND CHANGE

6. The origins and influences of social, cultural, political, and economic systems

7. The contributions of key persons, groups, and events from the past and their influence on the present

8. The history of democratic ideals and principles, and how they are represented in documents, artifacts, and symbols

9. The influences of social, geographic, economic, and cultural factors on the history of local areas, states, nations, and the world

3 PEOPLE, PLACES, AND ENVIRONMENTS

4. The roles of different kinds of population centers in a region or nation

5. The concept of regions identifies links between people in different locations according to specific criteria (e.g., physical, economic, social, cultural, or religious)

8. Factors that contribute to cooperation and conflict among peoples of the nation and world, including language, religion, and political beliefs

5 INDIVIDUALS, GROUPS, AND INSTITUTIONS

1. This theme helps us know how individuals are members of groups and institutions, and influence and shape those groups and institutions

5. That groups and institutions change over time

7. That institutions may promote or undermine social conformity

9. That groups and institutions influence culture in a variety of ways

6 POWER, AUTHORITY, AND GOVERNANCE

2. Fundamental ideas that are the foundation of American constitutional democracy (including those of the U.S. Constitution, popular sovereignty, the rule of law, separation of powers, checks and balances, minority rights, the separation of church and state, and Federalism)

3. Fundamental values of constitutional democracy (e.g., the common good, liberty, justice, equality, and individual dignity)

4. The ideologies and structures of political systems that differ from those of the United States

5. The ways in which governments meet the needs and wants of citizens, manage conflict, and establish order and society

7 PRODUCTION, DISTRIBUTION, AND CONSUMPTION

4. Economic incentives affect people's behavior and may be regulated by rules or laws

CHAPTER OPENER PLANNER

Students will know:

- *how the geography of Europe shaped the development of cultures.*
- *the achievements of European kings and emperors.*
- *the role of the Church in medieval Europe.*
- *what feudalism was and why it became an important social structure.*
- *why the Magna Carta is important.*
- *what the Crusades were and how they started.*
- *the role that architecture, education, literature, and religion played in medieval life.*
- *about the Black Death and its effect on medieval life.*
- *the conflicts experienced by the Catholic Church.*
- *the effects of the Hundred Years' War and the Reconquista.*

Students will be able to:

- ***discuss and analyze*** *the balance of power between the pope and Charlemagne.*
- ***draw conclusions*** *about Charlemagne's rule.*
- ***explain*** *feudalism.*
- ***compare and contrast*** *the lives of knights and peasants.*
- ***analyze*** *why the Magna Carta was needed.*
- ***explain*** *the causes and effects of the Crusades.*
- ***explain*** *how the rise of strong governments contributed to an increase in trade, banking, and business, and how this in turn affected building and learning.*
- ***analyze*** *the relationship between conformity and the Inquisition.*
- ***read*** *a map about the spread of the plague.*
- ***discuss*** *problems and changes during the late Middle Ages.*

UNDERSTANDING BY DESIGN®

☑ Print Teaching Options

V Visual Skills

- ☐ **P. 538** Students study a map and discuss the geography of medieval Europe. **Visual/Spatial**
- ☐ **P. 539** Students study a time line and use the information to discuss events related to medieval Europe. **Visual/Spatial**

☑ Online Teaching Options

V Visual Skills

- **MAP** **Place and Time: Medieval Europe, c. 950–1300**—Students click on European countries of the time to learn interesting facts.
- **TIME LINE** **Place and Time: Medieval Europe A.D. 500 to 1475**—Students learn about key events in Europe during this time period.
- **WORLD ATLAS** Students can use this interactive map to identify regions of the world, learn about individual countries, locate political boundaries, measure distances, and much more.

Project-Based Learning

Hands-On Chapter Project

A Day in the Life

Students working in groups will write and present a script about a day in the life of a lord, a vassal, a knight, or a peasant in medieval Europe.

Technology Extension

edtechteacher 21st Century Learning

Online Avatar

- Find an additional activity online that incorporates technology for this project.
- Visit the EdTechTeacher Web sites (included in the Technology Extension for this chapter) for more links, tutorials, and other resources.

Print Resources

ANCILLARY RESOURCES

These ancillaries are available for every chapter and lesson.

- **Reading Essentials and Study Guide Workbook** AL ELL
- **Chapter Tests and Lesson Quizzes Blackline Masters**

PRINTABLE DIGITAL WORKSHEETS

These printable digital worksheets are available for every chapter and lesson.

- **Hands-On Chapter Projects**
- **What Do You Know? activities**
- **Chapter Summaries (English and Spanish)**
- **Vocabulary Builder activities**
- **Guided Reading activities**

More Media Resources

SUGGESTED VIDEOS MOVIES

Watch clips of popular-culture films about medieval Europe, such as *Henry V*, *A Man for All Seasons*, *Becket*, or *The Adventures of Robin Hood.*

- **Ask:** **Do you think movies reflect what life was really like in the Middle Ages?**

(NOTE: Preview any clips for age-appropriateness.)

SUGGESTED READING

Grade 6 reading level:

- ***The Travels of Benjamin of Tudela: Through Three Continents of the Twelfth Century,*** by Uri Shulevitz

Grade 7 reading level:

- ***Eleanor of Aquitaine and the High Middle Ages,*** by Nancy Plain

Grade 8 reading level:

- ***Good Masters! Good Ladies!: Voices from a Medieval Village,*** by Laura Amy Schlitz

THE EARLY MIDDLE AGES

Students will know:

- *how the geography of Europe shaped the development of cultures.*
- *the achievements of European kings and emperors.*
- *the role of the Church in medieval Europe.*

Students will be able to:

- ***discuss and analyze*** *the balance of power between the pope and Charlemagne.*
- ***draw conclusions*** *about Charlemagne's rule.*

UNDERSTANDING BY DESIGN®

☑ Print Teaching Options

V Visual Skills

- ☐ **P. 541** Students examine the map of Europe's geography and people in A.D. 500. Visual/Spatial
- ☐ **P. 543** Students examine a modern map of Europe to better understand the extent of Charlemagne's empire. Visual/Spatial
- ☐ **P. 545** Students study a map of invasions of Europe and use the information to answer questions. AL Visual/Spatial

R Reading Skills

- ☐ **P. 540** Students examine the meanings of the words *middle* and *medieval.* AL ELL
- ☐ **P. 540** Students discuss the advantages of Paris being located on the Seine River.
- ☐ **P. 542** Students identify Frankish leaders and discuss the Battle of Tours. AL BL
- ☐ **P. 543** Students calculate how long Charlemagne had been king before his empire had grown to include most of Western Europe. Logical/Mathematical
- ☐ **P. 544** Students identify the different raiders of Europe in the 800s and 900s. AL
- ☐ **P. 545** Students discuss the events that resulted in the formation of the Holy Roman Empire.
- ☐ **P. 546** Students define and discuss missionaries. AL ELL
- ☐ **P. 547** Students discuss the disagreement between Pope Gregory VII and King Henry IV.

C Critical Thinking Skills

- ☐ **P. 541** Students contrast crossing geographical barriers during the Middle Ages with crossing them today. They also discuss the effects of these barriers on culture. AL
- ☐ **P. 543** Students consider whether a leader today could unify Europe as Charlemagne did. BL
- ☐ **P. 544** Students infer why Charlemagne did not want people to think the pope had the authority or power to crown kings. BL
- ☐ **P. 546** Students look at the structure of the Catholic Church. Visual/Spatial

T Technology Skills

- ☐ **P. 544** Students search online for photos of Scandinavian fjords and then create a presentation for the class.

☑ Online Teaching Options

V Visual Skills

- VIDEO **Castle Design**—Students are introduced to these structures, which dominated the European landscape for hundreds of years.
- MAP **Invasions of Europe c. A.D. 800–1000**—Students trace three waves of invaders: the Magyars, the Muslims, and the Vikings.
- IMAGE **The Vikings**—Students click to read about these Scandinavian raiders.

R Reading Skills

- GRAPHIC ORGANIZER **Taking Notes: *Identifying:* European Leaders**—Students identify the achievements of four European leaders.
- BIOGRAPHY **Gregory VII**—Students read of the life and accomplishments of this medieval pope.

C Critical Thinking Skills

- WHITEBOARD ACTIVITY **European Leaders**—Students identify characteristics of five European leaders.
- IMAGE **Charlemagne**—Students analyze an illumination from *The Coronation of Charlemagne.*
- MAP **Europe's Geography and People c. A.D. 500**—Students identify concentrations of various groups throughout Europe and relate those groups to physical geography.

T Technology Skills

- SELF-CHECK QUIZ **Lesson 1**—Students receive instant feedback on their mastery of lesson content.
- GAME **The Early Middle Ages Concentration Game**—Students make matches to review lesson content.
- GAME **The Early Middle Ages Crossword Puzzle**—Students solve clues to review lesson vocabulary.

☑ Printable Digital Worksheets

C Critical Thinking Skills

- WORKSHEET **Geography and History Activity: Medieval Europe: The Early Middle Ages: Location: How Christianity United Europe**—Students extract information from both a passage and a map to answer questions.

LESSON 2 PLANNER

FEUDALISM AND THE RISE OF TOWNS

Students will know:

- *what feudalism was and why it became an important social structure.*

Students will be able to:

- *explain feudalism.*
- *compare and contrast the lives of knights and peasants.*

UNDERSTANDING BY DESIGN®

☑ Print Teaching Options

V Visual Skills

- ☐ **P. 549** Students examine a graphic of class levels under feudalism. Visual/Spatial
- ☐ **P. 550** Students analyze an infographic of a castle. Visual/Spatial
- ☐ **P. 552** Students analyze an infographic of a medieval manor and use the information to answer questions. Visual/Spatial

R Reading Skills

- ☐ **P. 548** Students define and discuss feudalism. AL ELL
- ☐ **P. 551** Students define the terms *fief* and *manor* and discuss the basic makeup of a medieval manor. AL ELL
- ☐ **P. 553** Students identify three Italian cities and discuss why they were important trading centers.
- ☐ **P. 554** Students explain factors that created a middle class during the Middle Ages.
- ☐ **P. 555** Students list functions of medieval guilds. AL

W Writing Skills

- ☐ **P. 549** Students rewrite the oath from a vassal to his lord in modern language. Verbal/Linguistic
- ☐ **P. 551** Students write a diary entry from the point of view of a medieval peasant. Verbal/Linguistic
- ☐ **P. 554** Students work in groups to create advertisements for a medieval trade fair. Interpersonal

C Critical Thinking Skills

- ☐ **P. 548** Students consider the effects of feudalism.
- ☐ **P. 549** Students consider the benefits of feudalism for different levels of society. BL
- ☐ **P. 550** Students consider the defensive design features of a castle. BL ELL
- ☐ **P. 551** Students discuss why the manor system worked for many serfs. BL
- ☐ **P. 553** Students discuss reasons for the growth of the European population. AL

T Technology Skills

- ☐ **P. 552** Students search online for photos of European cities that retain a medieval character. Visual/Spatial

☑ Online Teaching Options

V Visual Skills

- ☐ VIDEO **Feudalism, Lords and Vassals Video Quiz**—Students test their knowledge of medieval social structure.
- ☐ SLIDE SHOW **The Manorial System**—Students examine aspects of this system that was set up to keep social order when governments were weak and invasions were common.

R Reading Skills

- ☐ GRAPHIC ORGANIZER **Taking Notes: *Summarizing:* Feudalism as a Social System**—Students summarize important features of feudalism.
- ☐ CHART **Serfs and Freemen**—Students read information about social classes and then click to see the information organized in a Venn diagram.

C Critical Thinking Skills

- ☐ CHART **Trade in Medieval Marketplaces**—Students click to compare goods traded in medieval marketplaces.
- ☐ CHART **Serfs and Freemen**—Students read information about social classes and then click to see the information organized in a Venn diagram.
- ☐ GRAPH **Classes Under Feudalism**—Students click the labels to learn more about the classes in feudal society.

T Technology Skills

- ☐ SELF-CHECK QUIZ **Lesson 2**—Students receive instant feedback on their mastery of lesson content.
- ☐ GAME **Feudalism and the Rise of Towns Column Game**—Students classify characteristics as belonging to lords, vassals, or both.

☑ Printable Digital Worksheets

C Critical Thinking Skills

- ☐ WORKSHEET **Primary Source Activity: Medieval Europe: Feudalism and the Rise of Towns: From Froissart's Chronicles**—Students analyze and respond to two excerpts from writings by this scholar, poet, and historian.

KINGDOMS AND CRUSADES

Students will know:
- *why the Magna Carta is important.*
- *what the Crusades were and how they started.*

Students will be able to:
- ***analyze*** *why the Magna Carta was needed.*
- ***explain*** *the causes and effects of the Crusades.*

UNDERSTANDING BY DESIGN®

☑ Print Teaching Options

V Visual Skills

- ☐ **P. 559** Students study a map of European kingdoms and use the information to answer questions. AL BL Visual/Spatial
- ☐ **P. 561** Students analyze the map of the growth of Moscow. Visual/Spatial
- ☐ **P. 562** Students study the map of the Crusades and use the information to answer questions. AL BL Visual/Spatial

R Reading Skills

- ☐ **P. 556** Students identify and discuss Alfred the Great and William the Conqueror. AL
- ☐ **P. 557** Students discuss how the Norman conquest made changes in English culture.
- ☐ **P. 558** Students explain the events that led to the signing of the Magna Carta.
- ☐ **P. 559** Students discuss the three estates in medieval France.
- ☐ **P. 561** Students define the word *cooperate* and discuss the cooperation between the rulers of Moscow and the Mongols. ELL

W Writing Skills

- ☐ **P. 563** Students write lyrics for a song about the Crusades. Auditory/Musical Interpersonal

C Critical Thinking Skills

- ☐ **P. 557** Students discuss the *Domesday Book* and infer how taking a census would help in levying taxes. BL
- ☐ **P. 558** Students consider how the nobles got King John to sign the Magna Carta and discuss the effects of the document on the king's rule. AL
- ☐ **P. 561** Students make inferences about the reasons for royal marriages. BL
- ☐ **P. 562** Students consider the causes and effects of the Crusades.
- ☐ **P. 563** Students discuss reasons why each side fought in the Crusades.

T Technology Skills

- ☐ **P. 560** Students use the Internet to research information about Vladimir the Great. BL Interpersonal

☑ Online Teaching Options

V Visual Skills

- ☐ VIDEO **Castles: The Center of Power**—Students learn that many of Europe's cities grew up around castles, which were military fortresses as well as administrative centers.
- ☐ SLIDE SHOW **The Crusades**—Students view images of the Christians' attempts to capture and hold Jerusalem.
- ☐ MAP **Europe c. 1160**—Students compare the boundaries of countries in the 12th century to those of today.
- ☐ MAP **The Crusades, 1096–1204**—Students trace the routes of three attempts of Christian crusaders to capture and hold Jerusalem.
- ☐ IMAGE **Batu and the Golden Horde**—Students read of the exploits of Genghis Khan's grandson.

R Reading Skills

- ☐ GRAPHIC ORGANIZER **Taking Notes: *Sequencing:* The Crusades**—Students identify causes and effects of the three Crusades.
- ☐ BIOGRAPHY **William the Conqueror**—Students read about the life and accomplishments of this fierce warrior.

C Critical Thinking Skills

- ☐ WHITEBOARD ACTIVITY **Monarchy in France**—Students sequence the events in the reigns of four French monarchs.
- ☐ CHART **The Magna Carta and the U.S. Bill of Rights**—Students compare aspects of these two documents.
- ☐ MAP **Growth of Moscow c. 1300–1505**—Students compare what today is a single city to the vast landholdings of the medieval kingdom.

T Technology Skills

- ☐ SELF-CHECK QUIZ **Lesson 3**—Students receive instant feedback on their mastery of lesson content.
- ☐ GAME **Kingdoms and Crusades True-or-False Game**—Students indicate the veracity of statements to review lesson content.

☑ Printable Digital Worksheets

R Reading Skills

- ☐ WORKSHEET **Primary Source Activity: Medieval Europe: Kingdoms and Crusades: The First Crusade**—Students analyze and respond to passages about the Crusades.

LESSON **4 PLANNER**

CULTURE AND THE CHURCH

Students will know:

- *the role that architecture, education, literature, and religion played in medieval life.*

Students will be able to:

- ***explain** how the rise of strong governments contributed to an increase in trade, banking, and business, and how this in turn affected building and learning.*
- ***analyze** the relationship between conformity and the Inquisition.*

UNDERSTANDING BY DESIGN®

☑ Print Teaching Options

V Visual Skills

- ☐ **P. 565** Students simulate flying buttresses. Visual/Spatial Kinesthetic

R Reading Skills

- ☐ **P. 564** Students determine the meaning of *secure* and discuss why medieval Europeans felt secure. AL ELL
- ☐ **P. 565** Students define *scholasticism.* ELL
- ☐ **P. 566** Students explain vernacular language and identify changes in European literature. AL ELL
- ☐ **P. 568** Students explain the terms *mass* and *sacrament.* AL ELL
- ☐ **P. 569** Students discuss the consequences of heresy.
- ☐ **P. 569** Students define anti-Semitism. ELL

W Writing Skills

- ☐ **P. 567** Students rewrite an excerpt from *The Song of Roland.* Verbal/Linguistic

C Critical Thinking Skills

- ☐ **P. 566** Students give examples of rights people have under the theory of natural law. BL
- ☐ **P. 567** Students assess how important the Church was for medieval peasants and rulers.
- ☐ **P. 567** Students discuss *The Song of Roland.*
- ☐ **P. 568** Students make a Venn diagram to organize information about Franciscans and Dominicans. Visual/Spatial

T Technology Skills

- ☐ **P. 564** Students find and present images of Romanesque and Gothic buildings. Visual/Spatial

☑ Online Teaching Options

V Visual Skills

- VIDEO **Religious Architecture**—Students view a collage of the gothic cathedrals of Europe.
- SLIDE SHOW **Medieval Architecture**—Students analyze elements of castles and medieval cathedrals.

R Reading Skills

- GRAPHIC ORGANIZER **Taking Notes: *Organizing Information:* Medieval Life**—Students list information about aspects of medieval life.
- SLIDE SHOW **Medieval Mystics**—Students explore the lives of Hildegard of Bingen and Julian of Norwich.

C Critical Thinking Skills

- WHITEBOARD ACTIVITY **Thomas Aquinas**—Students build a time line to sequence the events in Thomas Aquinas's life.
- CHART **Effects of Heresy Accusations**—Students identify three possible effects of being accused of heresy by leaders of the Inquisition.

T Technology Skills

- SELF-CHECK QUIZ **Lesson 4**—Students receive instant feedback on their mastery of lesson content.
- eFLASHCARDS **The Church and Society**—Students flip cards to review lesson vocabulary.

☑ Printable Digital Worksheets

C Critical Thinking Skills

- WORKSHEET **21st Century Skills Activity: Medieval Europe: Culture and the Church: Media Literacy: Understanding and Analyzing Media Messages**—Students analyze an early form of media—a troubadour's poem.

LESSON **5 PLANNER**

THE LATE MIDDLE AGES

Students will know:

- *about the Black Death and its effect on medieval life.*
- *the conflicts experienced by the Catholic Church.*
- *the effects of the Hundred Years' War and the Reconquista.*

Students will be able to:

- ***read** a map about the spread of the plague.*
- ***discuss** problems and changes during the late Middle Ages.*

UNDERSTANDING BY DESIGN®

☑ Print Teaching Options

V Visual Skills

- ☐ **P. 571** Students read a map of the Black Death in Europe. Visual/Spatial
- ☐ **P. 572** Students study a painting inspired by the Black Death. Visual/Spatial
- ☐ **P. 573** Students analyze a map of the Hundred Years' War. AL Visual/Spatial

R Reading Skills

- ☐ **P. 570** Students discuss and define *famine.* AL ELL
- ☐ **P. 573** Students write a bulleted list of challenges the Church faced in the Late Middle Ages. AL
- ☐ **P. 574** Students summarize the results of the Hundred Years' War.
- ☐ **P. 575** Students define and discuss the *Reconquista.* AL ELL

W Writing Skills

- ☐ **P. 575** Students write a letter from the perspective of a Muslim or Jew in Spain. Intrapersonal

C Critical Thinking Skills

- ☐ **P. 570** Students consider how the Black Death spread through Europe. ELL
- ☐ **P. 571** Students make a generalization about the spread of the Black Death.
- ☐ **P. 572** Students discuss the consequences of the spread of Black Death in medieval Europe. BL
- ☐ **P. 574** Students make inferences about the cross-bows the French soldiers used. BL

T Technology Skills

- ☐ **P. 572** Students use the Internet to find a full-sized image of a painting by Pieter Bruegel. Visual/Spatial

☑ Online Teaching Options

V Visual Skills

- VIDEO **History of Austria From the Late Middle Ages**—Students examine the history of Austria from the late Middle Ages until the 17th Century.
- MAP **The Hundred Year's War, 1346–1453**—Students view the effect of France's uniting to take back their lands from the English.
- MAP **The Black Death in Europe, 1350**—Students view the spread of the Black Death over a 100-year period.

R Reading Skills

- GRAPHIC ORGANIZER **Taking Notes: *Summarizing:* The Black Death in Europe**—Students use a circle graph to summarize the effects of the Black Death.
- BIOGRAPHY **Joan of Arc**—Students read of the life and accomplishments of this French heroine.

C Critical Thinking Skills

- WHITEBOARD ACTIVITY **Religious and Political Occurrences in Europe**—Students sort events as religious or political and then arrange the events in sequential order.
- GRAPH **European Population A.D. 1300–1500**—Students click to see the decrease and subsequent rebound in population over a 200-year period.

T Technology Skills

- SELF-CHECK QUIZ **Lesson 5**—Students receive instant feedback on their mastery of lesson content.

☑ Printable Digital Worksheets

C Critical Thinking Skills

- WORKSHEET **Economics of History Activity: Medieval Europe: The Late Middle Ages: Famine and Plague**—Students analyze how famine and plague had unexpected consequences for the economies of Europe.

INTERVENTION AND REMEDIATION STRATEGIES

LESSON 1 The Early Middle Ages

Reading and Comprehension

To ensure comprehension, have students rewrite the headings of the lesson in their own words. Tell students their new headings should reflect what they think is the main idea of the section.

Text Evidence

Ask students to do research to learn more about Charlemagne. Have them begin by rereading the primary source by Einhard and then finding out more from *The Life of Charlemagne.*

LESSON 2 Feudalism and the Rise of Towns

Reading and Comprehension

Have students write sentences using each of the lesson's new vocabulary words. Sentences should show an understanding of the words in the context of medieval Europe.

Text Evidence

Have students choose one class of people from medieval society—including nobles, knights, and peasants—and do research to find more about how that class lived during the Middle Ages.

LESSON 3 Kingdoms and Crusades

Reading and Comprehension

Have students make an outline of Lesson 3, using the larger heads as the first level and the smaller heads as the second level. They should use details from the lesson to support each head.

Text Evidence

Ask pairs of students to follow up on one of the leaders described in the lesson by researching more about that leader's life. Students should write two to three paragraphs of new information about the leader they selected.

LESSON 4 Culture and the Church

Reading and Comprehension

Have students skim the lesson to look for new or unfamiliar words. Have them use each word they find in a sentence about the culture of the Middle Ages.

Text Evidence

Organize students into small groups. Have each group create a list of cultural innovations from the Middle Ages that can still be seen today as influencing the culture of the modern world.

LESSON 5 The Late Middle Ages

Reading and Comprehension

Have students skim the lesson for new or unfamiliar words and then use dictionaries to look up definitions of these words. Then have them write down the definitions. When they are finished, pairs of students can quiz each other about the words they found.

Text Evidence

Have students do further research on the Black Death. Ask that they learn more information about the disease itself and also about how the epidemic affected medieval Europe.

Online Resources

Approaching Level Reader

Use this online lower-level text that corresponds directly to the text in the Student Edition. It includes a Spanish version.

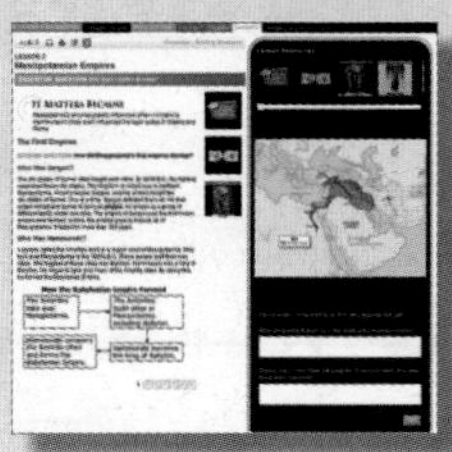

Guided Reading Activities

This resource uses graphic organizers and guiding questions to help students with comprehension.

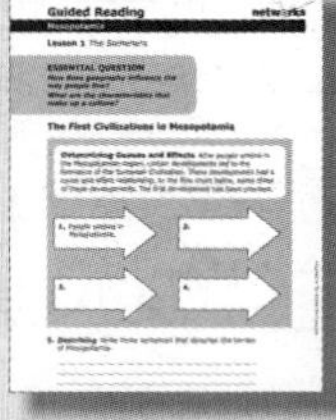

What Do You Know?

Use these worksheets to pre-assess student's background knowledge before they study the chapter.

Reading Essentials and Study Guide Workbook

This resource offers writing and reading activities for the approaching-level student. Also available in Spanish.

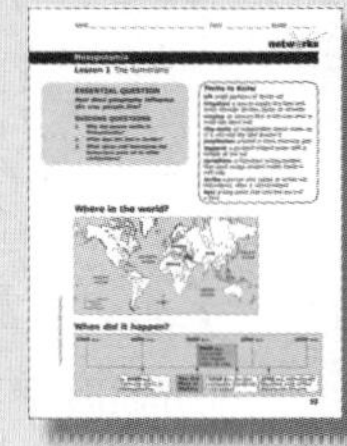

Self-Check Quizzes

This online assessment tool provides instant feedback for students to check their progress.

Medieval Europe

A.D. 500 to 1475

ESSENTIAL QUESTIONS • *Why does conflict develop?*
• *What is the role of religion in government?*
• *What are the characteristics that define a culture?* • *How do governments change?*

networks

There's More Online about the developing cultures of medieval Europe.

CHAPTER 19

Lesson 1 *The Early Middle Ages*

Lesson 2 *Feudalism and the Rise of Towns*

Lesson 3 *Kingdoms and Crusades*

Lesson 4 *Culture and the Church*

Lesson 5 *The Late Middle Ages*

The Story Matters . . .

Who would have predicted that a devout peasant girl, born in France in 1412, could help a prince become king? Yet Joan of Arc, shown in this painting, accomplished that for King Charles VII of France. She also helped defeat the English, whose armies occupied her native land.

The story of Joan of Arc reflects the history of medieval Europe in many ways. The Middle Ages were a time of struggle and conflict. They were also a period when the Catholic Church influenced almost every aspect of people's lives.

◄ *As a teenage girl in battle armor, Joan of Arc inspired the French army to defeat the English and rescue the French city of Orléans.*

Peter Willi/SuperStock/Getty Images

537

Letter from the Author

Dear World History Teacher,

A new European civilization began to emerge during the Early Middle Ages. Charlemagne's crowning as Holy Roman emperor in A.D. 800 represented the blending of Roman, Germanic, and Christian ways. After Charlemagne's empire collapsed, the feudal system put power into the hands of various ranks of nobles. Gradually, kings began to extend their power by bringing feudal territories under their direct control. European civilization began to flourish in the Middle Ages. In the 1300s, however, the Black Death killed millions of people, and warfare was constant.

Jackson J. Spielvogel

ENGAGE

Bellringer Read "The Story Matters . . ." aloud in class, or ask for a volunteer to read it aloud. Then lead students in a discussion about the qualities of a great leader. Tell students that Joan of Arc was an uneducated peasant girl who led an army against a powerful enemy. **Ask:** Would you have done what Joan of Arc did? Why or why not? Have a few students share their responses. Can you imagine what it was like for Joan of Arc—a young girl—to stand up to a grown man ready to fight? Is there a cause, idea, or other person you would stand up for? How difficult would that be?

Tell the class that during the Middle Ages, the local lord and the Catholic Church were the two most important institutions in a person's life. Most people worked in the lord's fields or fought in his armies, and almost everyone attended church daily. The Church was responsible for caring for the sick and poor, keeping historical records, and preserving knowledge. The lords were responsible for maintaining political and social order, which they did for hundreds of years.

Making Connections

- The Black Death, or plague, devastated Europe in the Middle Ages. The disease remains a problem. Most cases since the 1990s have occurred in Africa. In the United States, an average of seven cases are reported each year.
- A long historical debate has been waged over this question: Are the French or the Germans the true heirs of Charlemagne? His capital, Aachen, also known as Aix-la-Chapelle (ehks•lah•shah•PEHL) in French, sits just inside the German border near France, and German kings were crowned in the city's cathedral. On the other hand, the famous French military and political leader Napoleon called himself the successor of Charlemagne.

TEACH & ASSESS

Step Into the Place

V1 Visual Skills

Reading a Map Project the Chapter Opener map of Europe on the whiteboard. Make sure students recognize that Europe is a *peninsula*. Review the meaning of the word, if necessary. Ask a volunteer to identify key geographical features, such as rivers, mountains, and seas. Discuss as a class possible effects of geography on a culture. Encourage students to draw on prior knowledge. Have student volunteers analyze the map and circle regions that are set off by mountains or waterways. *(Britain, Ireland, France and Germany, Italy and the Mediterranean, Spain and Portugal, and Eastern Europe are separated from one another by mountains or waterways.)* As a class, discuss the Map Focus questions. **Visual/Spatial**

Content Background Knowledge

- The Volga River is the longest river in Europe, at about 2,300 miles long. The Danube River, at 1,770 miles long, is the second longest.
- Paris, France, is situated on the Seine River, about 233 miles upriver from the English Channel.
- The highest mountain in Western Europe is Mont Blanc in the Alps; it rises 15,771 feet high.

V2

ANSWERS, p. 538

Step Into the Place

1. Portugal, Spain, France, England, Scotland, and Ireland border the Atlantic Ocean.
2. Poland is the only inland country without access to a sea.
3. Rhine, Danube, Po, Oder
4. **CRITICAL THINKING** Goods can be moved easily to different places by boat.

Step Into the Time

Events that reflect the importance of religion are Charlemagne's coronation by the pope, the beginning of the First Crusade, the founding of the Franciscan Order, and the Spanish conquest of the Muslims.

CHAPTER 19 CCSS

Place and Time: Medieval Europe A.D. 500 to 1475

During the Middle Ages, Europeans lived in an ordered society of monarchs, nobles, and peasants. As trade and cities grew, the number of merchants and laborers rose. The Catholic Church greatly influenced all of these groups.

Step into the Place

MAP FOCUS Rivers, seas, and mountains provided both natural barriers and trade opportunities for medieval Europeans.

1. **PLACE** Look at the map. Which countries border the Atlantic Ocean? RH.6–8.7
2. **LOCATION** What is the only inland country without a coastal area link to a sea? RH.6–8.7
3. **PLACE** What major rivers flowed through the Holy Roman Empire? RH.6–8.7
4. **CRITICAL THINKING** *Drawing Conclusions* How does a location near a waterway contribute to the growth of trade? RH.6–8.2

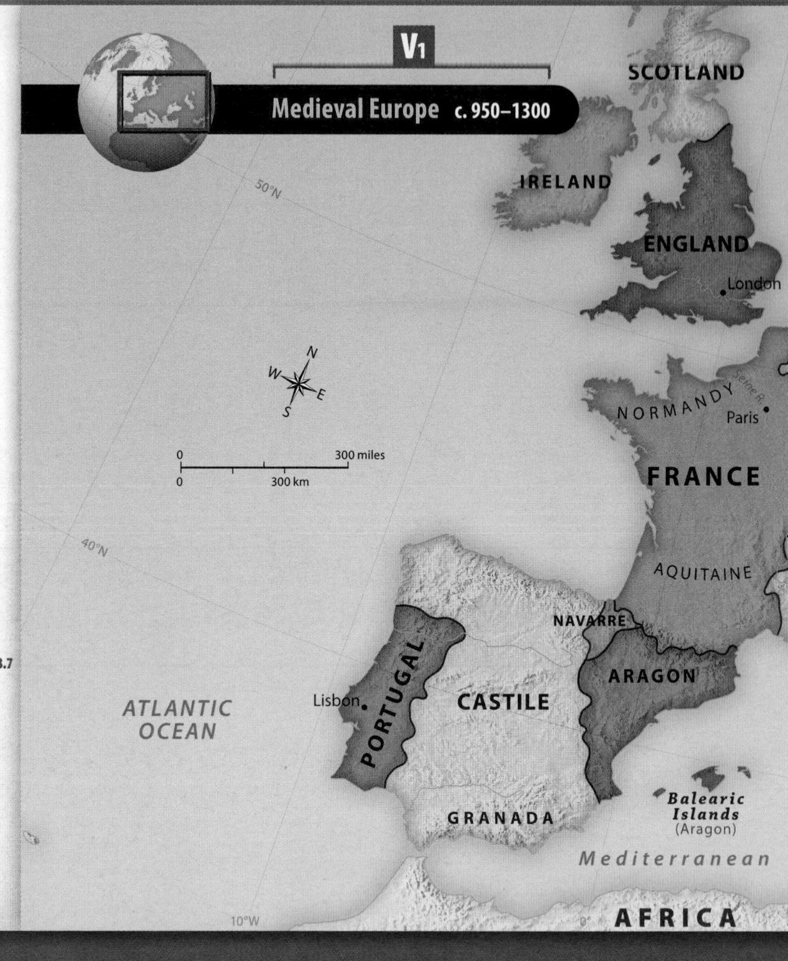

Step Into the Time

TIME LINE Choose an event from the time line and write a paragraph about the role religion played in that event. RH.6–8.7, WHST.6–8.2, WHST.6–8.10

MEDIEVAL EUROPE

THE WORLD

A.D. 500 — 700

496 Frankish King Clovis becomes Catholic

800 Pope crowns Charlemagne emperor

871 Alfred the Great is king of England

570 Muhammad is born

650 Cahokia culture begins in North America

Project-Based Learning

Hands-On Chapter Project

A Day in the Life

Students write a script about a day in the life of a lord, a vassal, a knight, or a peasant in medieval Europe. First, students will participate in a class discussion to review what they have learned about medieval European society. Then, students will divide into groups. Each group will use discussions and worksheets to plan their projects before researching and creating their scripts. Finally, each group will complete its script and share it with the rest of the class.

Technology Extension

Online Avatar

Students will develop an avatar of a person in feudal Europe and literally put words in the person's mouth. Students will develop a script that discusses the daily life of a chosen role—a lord, vassal, or peasant. When the script is complete and rehearsed, students should follow the instructions for the specific platform they are working with in order to create the avatar and narrate the script.

networks There's More Online!

MAP Explore the interactive version of this map on NETWORKS.

TIME LINE Explore the interactive version of this time line on NETWORKS.

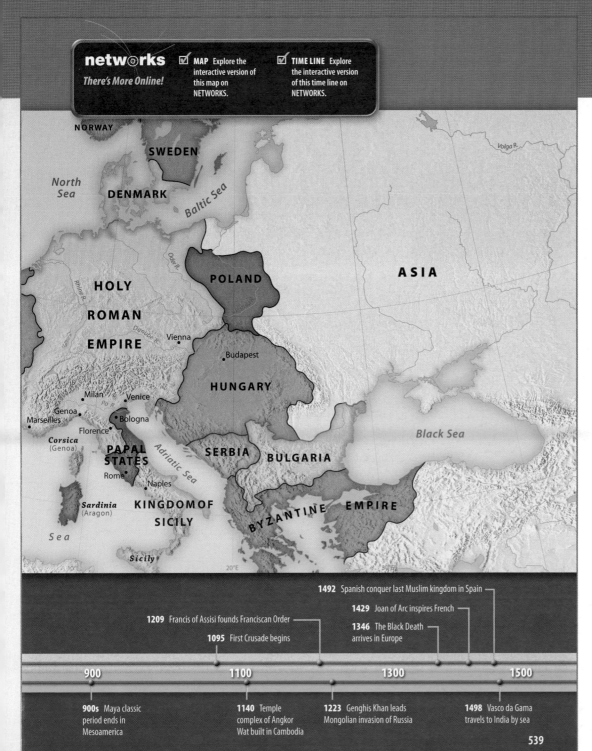

NORWAY
SWEDEN
North Sea
DENMARK
Baltic Sea
Volga R.
Oder R.
POLAND
ASIA
Rhine R.
HOLY ROMAN EMPIRE
Danube R.
Vienna
Budapest
HUNGARY
Milan
Venice
Po R.
Genoa
Marseilles
Bologna
Florence
Black Sea
Corsica (Genoa)
PAPAL STATES
Adriatic Sea
SERBIA
BULGARIA
Rome
Naples
Sardinia (Aragon)
KINGDOM OF SICILY
BYZANTINE EMPIRE
Sea
Sicily
10°E
20°E

1492 Spanish conquer last Muslim kingdom in Spain

1429 Joan of Arc inspires French

1209 Francis of Assisi founds Franciscan Order

1346 The Black Death arrives in Europe

1095 First Crusade begins

900 — 1100 — 1300 — 1500

900s Maya classic period ends in Mesoamerica

1140 Temple complex of Angkor Wat built in Cambodia

1223 Genghis Khan leads Mongolian invasion of Russia

1498 Vasco da Gama travels to India by sea

539

CHAPTER 19

Place and Time

Step Into the Time

V2 Visual Skills

Analyzing Time Lines Have students examine the time line for the chapter. Remind students that a time line is read from left to right. Make sure they understand that events related to the European Middle Ages are above the time line, while other world events of the same era are shown below the line. Explain that they will be studying events that occurred in Europe after the fall of the Western Roman Empire in A.D. 476 until the voyage of Christopher Columbus to the Americas in 1492.

Have students review the time line and then discuss the events listed on it as a class. **Ask:**

- Based on the dates in the time line, how long did the Middle Ages last? *(about 1,000 years)*
- What is the first event shown for medieval Europe on the time line? *(Frankish King Clovis becomes a Catholic.)*
- What happened in another part of the world in 570? *(Muhammad was born.)*
- When did the first Crusade begin? *(1095)*

As a class, complete the Step Into the Time activity and answer the question. **Visual/Spatial**

Content Background Knowledge

- In the twelve century, Charlemagne was canonized (made a saint) in the Catholic Church, but the modern Church no longer recognizes him as a saint.
- The Third Crusade ended in 1192 when Richard I of England—Richard the Lionheart—signed a truce with the Muslim leader Saladin.
- The plague that struck Europe in the 1300s was known as the *Black* Death because the symptoms of the disease included black boils that oozed blood.

TIME LINE

Place and Time: Medieval Europe A.D. 500 to 1475

Reading a Time Line Display the time line. Ask student volunteers to read each event as it is revealed. Then have students choose one event on the time line to research further on the Internet. Each student should create a more detailed time line that includes events that occurred near the same time as the event he or she chose.

See page 537B for other online activities.

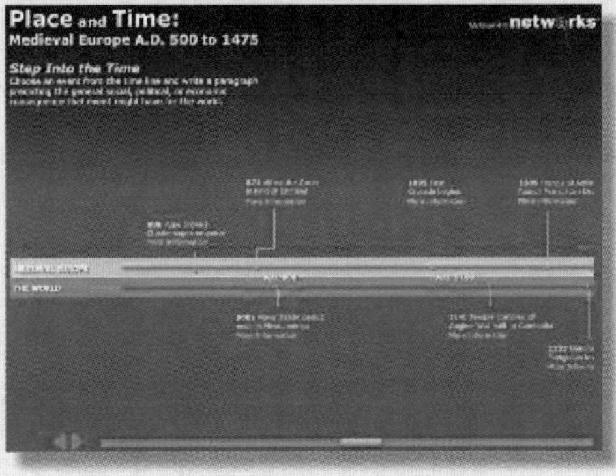

The Early Middle Ages

ENGAGE

Bellringer Before students begin the lesson, ask them to recall what they've learned about the Roman Empire and Western Europe. Remind students that Julius Caesar led Roman soldiers in Gaul. **Ask:** **Where was Gaul?** *(in the area of what is now France and Belgium)* **Who was the first Roman emperor to accept Christianity, and when did this happen?** *(Constantine in A.D. 312)* Remind students that there was a split in A.D. 395 between the Eastern Roman Empire and the Western Roman Empire. **What happened to the last Western Roman emperor?** *(He was overthrown by German invaders of Rome.)*

TEACH & ASSESS

R1 Reading Skills

Defining Explain to students that the time period they will study in this chapter is called the Middle Ages in Europe. **Ask:** **If this period is in the "middle," what periods came before and after?** *(ancient times and modern times)* Point out that the Middle Ages are often also called medieval times. *Medieval Europe* is a common term. Explain that the prefix *medi-* means "middle" and that the root word *eval* means "age." **What then does the term *medieval* mean?** *(middle age)* Emphasize that the Middle Ages and medieval times are two terms for the same thing. Have students pronounce *medieval.* AL ELL

R2 Reading Skills

Applying Have students read the section titled "Rivers and Seas." Explain to the class that rivers played an important role in the growth of Europe and point out that the city of Paris was built on the Seine River. **Ask:** **What advantages would there have been for medieval Paris to be situated on the Seine River?** *(The Seine, like Europe's other major rivers, flows from inland to the sea. The Seine is navigable, so people and goods could sail easily from Paris to the open sea and other parts of the world.)*

ANSWER, p. 540

TAKING NOTES: Answers may include the following: Clovis (won support of Roman citizens in his kingdom by becoming Catholic); Charles Martel (defeated Muslims at Tours); Charlemagne (crowned emperor by pope, encouraged education); Otto I of Germany (defeated Magyars, became emperor of Holy Roman Empire); Pope Gregory the Great (organized missionaries)

networks *There's More Online!*

- BIOGRAPHY Charlemagne (A.D. 742–814)
- GRAPHIC ORGANIZER Achievements of European Leaders
- PRIMARY SOURCE The Life of Charlemagne

Lesson 1

The Early Middle Ages

ESSENTIAL QUESTION *Why does conflict develop?*

IT MATTERS BECAUSE

Medieval European governments, religions, languages, and culture still influence the modern world.

Geography of Europe

GUIDING QUESTION *How did geography shape life in Europe after the fall of Rome?*

R1 During the 400s, Germanic groups invaded the Western Roman Empire. In A.D. 476, these groups overthrew the last emperor in Rome and brought the Empire to an end. Europe then entered a new era called the Middle Ages, or medieval times. This was a 1,000-year period between ancient and modern times. During the Middle Ages, Western Europe was divided into many kingdoms, and Catholic Christianity strongly influenced society.

Physical geography shaped Europe's development. The continent of Europe is a huge peninsula, with many smaller peninsulas branching out from it. As a result, most land in Europe lies within 300 miles (483 km) of a seacoast. This encouraged trade and helped the European economy to grow.

Rivers and Seas

R2 Rivers also played an important **role** in Europe's growth. Major rivers, such as the Rhine, Danube, Seine, and Po, flow from inland mountains into the oceans and seas surrounding the continent. These rivers are navigable, or wide and deep enough for ships to use. People and goods can sail easily from inland areas to the open sea and, from there, to other parts of the world.

(l) Florent Lamontagne/Age fotostock, (cl) Scala/Art Resource, NY, (c) Ted Spiegel/CORBIS, (cr) Elio Ciol/CORBIS, (r) The Gallery Collection/Corbis

Reading **HELP**DESK CCSS

Taking Notes: ***Identifying***

Choose four European leaders from this lesson. Use a diagram like this one to identify the achievements of each leader. RH.6–8.2

Content Vocabulary (Tier 3 Words)

- **fjord**
- **missionary**
- **concordat**

networks *Online Teaching Options*

VIDEO

Castle Design

Identifying Play the video about castle design in the Middle Ages, during which students will be introduced to the structures that dominated the land for hundreds of years. Then question students about major points in the video. **Ask:** **What was the common purpose for all castles?** *(keeping invaders out and protecting the people inside)* **Why were castles built on high ground?** *(to provide a lord with a good view of the surrounding countryside and a base to control the area)* **What were some architectural features of the castles that were designed to protect the inhabitants?** *(moats, drawbridges, small slit windows, spiral staircases, iron doors, high and thick walls)*

See page 537C for other online activities.

Europe's seas and rivers provided protection as well as possibilities for trade. The English Channel, for example, separated the islands of Britain and Ireland from the rest of Europe. As a result, these people were far enough away to be largely safe from the many wars fought on Europe's mainland. They were able to develop their own governments and societies. In mainland Europe, wide rivers like the Rhine also kept groups of people separated. Because of this separation and isolation, many different cultures developed.

Europe also has many mountain ranges. In the southwest, the Pyrenees isolated what is now Spain and Portugal from the rest of Europe. In the middle of the continent, the Alps separated Italy from central Europe. The Carpathians cut off what is now Ukraine and Russia from southeast Europe. The mountains, like the rivers, made it difficult for one group to control all of Europe and encouraged the growth of independent territories. **C**

✓ **PROGRESS CHECK**

Explaining Why were rivers important to the peoples of Europe?

GEOGRAPHY CONNECTION

After the Western Roman Empire came to an end, many different peoples lived throughout Europe.

1. **LOCATION** Where did the Celtic peoples live?
2. **CRITICAL THINKING** ***Speculating*** Why do you think there are no national boundaries on this map?

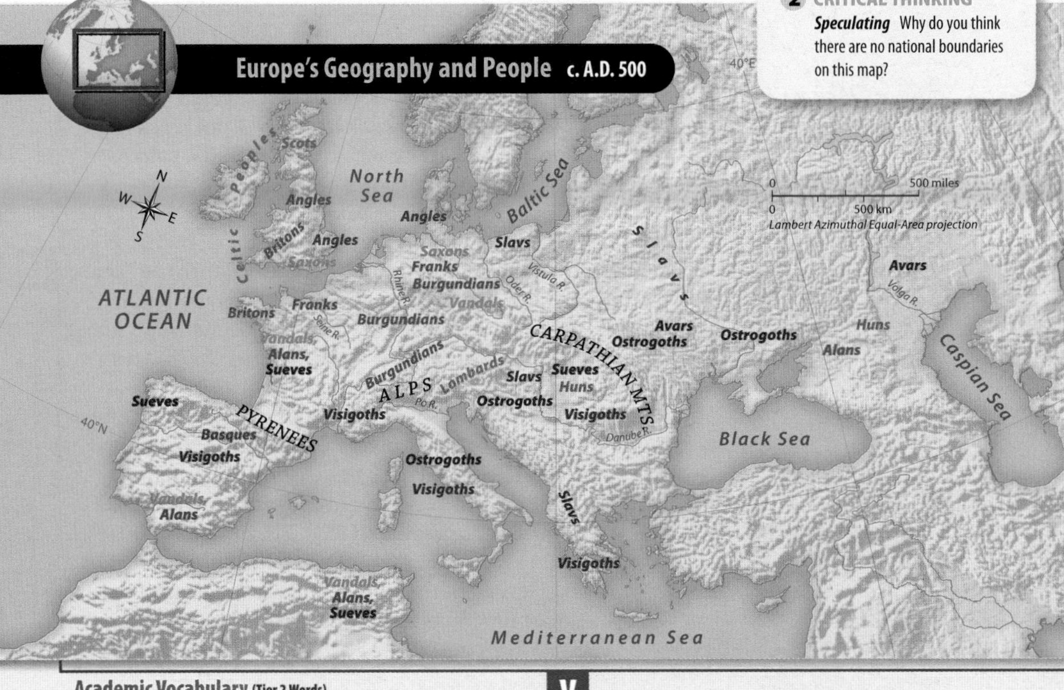

V

Academic Vocabulary (Tier 2 Words)

role something that plays a part in a process

MAP

Europe's Geography and People c. A.D. 500

Summarizing Show students the interactive map "Europe's Geography and People." **Ask:** **How did geographical features affect the development of Europe during the Middle Ages?** *(Mountains and rivers provided needed resources and protection that allowed different cultural groups to form. Rivers and seas provided transportation routes for trade and the development of a common European culture.)*

See page 537C for other online activities.

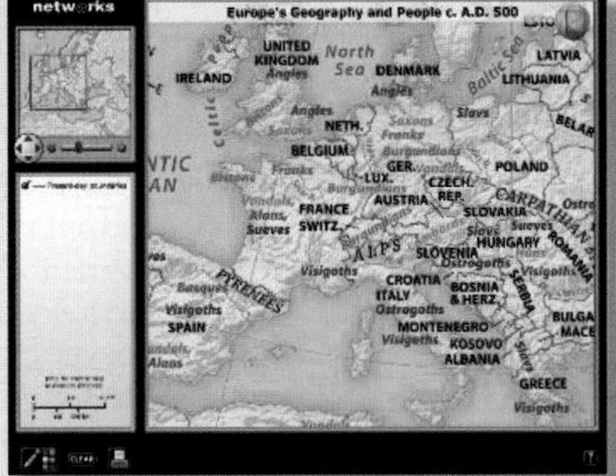

C Critical Thinking Skills

Contrasting Call on volunteers to describe wide rivers and high mountains they have crossed in their lives. **Ask:** **Did you have any trouble crossing these geographical barriers?** *(No. It's easy to fly over or drive across rivers or mountains.)* **How would crossing a wide river or high mountains have been different in the Middle Ages?** *(Answers will vary, but students should suggest that without modern transportation or roads and bridges, crossing rivers or mountains would have been very difficult.)* **How would this difficulty have affected the settlement of people on different sides of rivers or mountains?** *(Answers will vary, but students should understand that geographical barriers kept people and cultures apart.)* **AL**

V Visual Skills

Reading a Map Have students examine the map at the bottom of the page, including the title, the compass rose, and the scale. **Ask:** **What does this map show?** *(Answers will vary, though students should recognize that the map includes two basic kinds of information: Europe's geographic features and where different European groups lived in A.D. 500.)* As students study the map, **ask:**

- **What geographical barrier separated the Burgundians from the Ostrogoths?** *(the Alps)*
- **The Rhine River flows into which sea?** *(the North Sea)*
- **In what part of Europe did the Slavs live?** *(the eastern part of Europe)*
- **On which side of the Pyrenees did the Basques live?** *(the south side)*
- **Which group of people lived on the Seine River?** *(the Franks)* **Visual/Spatial**

ANSWERS, p. 541

✓ **PROGRESS CHECK** Rivers provided protection and enabled many different cultures to develop.

GEOGRAPHY CONNECTION

1. They lived on the islands off the west coast of Europe (Britain and Ireland).
2. **CRITICAL THINKING** Answers will vary, but students may say that no national boundaries exist because after the Western Roman Empire ended, so did national governments.

The Early Middle Ages

R Reading Skills

Identifying Have students read the section of the text about the Franks in Europe. Then have pairs of students work together to answer the following questions. **Ask:**

- Who was the first Germanic ruler to accept Catholic Christianity? *(King Clovis)*
- What was Charles Martel's nickname? *(Charles the Hammer)* AL
- Who fought the Battle of Tours? *(Charles Martel and his forces fought the Muslims.)* Who won? *(Charles Martel)* AL
- If Charles Martel hadn't won at the Battle of Tours, how might the history of Europe be different? *(Europe might have become Muslim instead of Christian.)* BL

Making Connections

Share the following information with students:

Many Americans are descendants of the Celtic peoples who were pushed into isolated areas of Great Britain by the invading Angles and Saxons. Today, millions of Americans can trace their roots to Ireland, Scotland, Wales, and the parts of England where Celtic peoples lived. Celtic tribes also lived on the fringes of the Roman Empire in Spain, France, Asia Minor, Switzerland, and other regions. Older Celtic settlements have even been discovered in Austria and Germany.

Kingdoms in Western Europe

GUIDING QUESTION *How did Germanic groups build kingdoms in Western Europe?*

By A.D. 500, Western Europe had divided into many Germanic kingdoms. Germanic people in Italy and Spain adopted many Roman ways. People farther from Rome held on to more of their Germanic traditions.

Roman influence was even weaker in Britain. After Roman armies abandoned the area that is today England, Germanic groups known as Angles and Saxons settled there. In time, they became the Anglo-Saxons.

The Anglo-Saxons pushed aside earlier settlers known as the Celts (KEHLTS). Some Celts fled north and west, while others crossed the sea to Ireland. The Scottish, Welsh, and Irish peoples today are largely descended from the Celts.

King Clovis won the support of Romans living in his kingdom when he accepted Christianity.

▶ CRITICAL THINKING

Speculating Why might the Romans in the kingdom have accepted Clovis more after he became a Christian?

Florent Lamontagne/Age fotostock

The Franks in Europe

The Franks were the strongest Germanic group. They settled what is now France and western Germany. In 481, Clovis (KLOH•vuhs) became king of the Franks. Fifteen years later, he became the first Germanic ruler to accept Catholic Christianity. Before long, nearly all of the Franks became Catholic.

After Clovis died, Frankish kings lost much of their power. By 700, power had passed from kings to government officials known as mayors of the palace.

In 714, Charles Martel (mahr•TEHL), or "Charles the Hammer," became mayor of the palace. The pope, who was the head of the Catholic Church, gave Martel his support. Martel and the pope wanted to restore order and strengthen Catholic Christianity in the lands of the old Western Roman Empire. R

Martel's first move was to halt the spread of Islam into Europe. By the early 700s, Muslims from North Africa had conquered Spain and entered France. In 732, Charles Martel defeated the Muslims at the Battle of Tours. This battle stopped the advance of Islam into Western Europe. It also ensured that Christianity would remain Western Europe's major religion.

After Charles Martel died, his son Pepin (PEH•puhn) became mayor of the palace. With the support and blessing of the pope, Pepin became king of the Franks. In return, Pepin was expected to help the

Reading HELPDESK CCSS

Reading Strategy: *Analyzing Primary Sources*

Why might Einhard—in his quote on the next page—have described Charlemagne's appearance in such positive terms?

networks Online Teaching Options

WHITEBOARD ACTIVITY

European Leaders

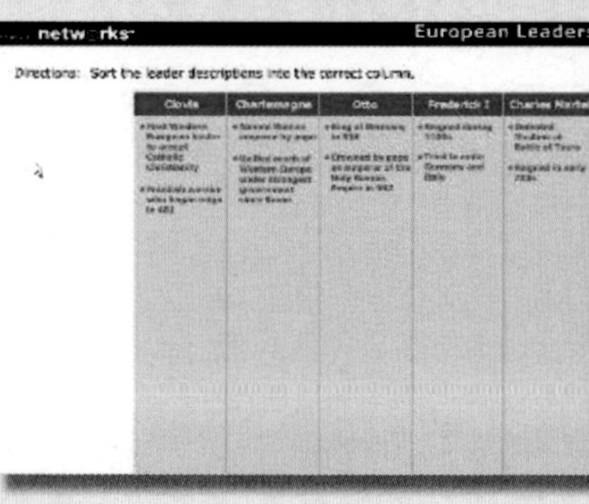

Summarizing Have students complete the interactive whiteboard activity for the lesson by clicking and dragging the descriptions of European leaders into the correct columns. If students have trouble sorting the facts, tell them to refer back to their notes and their graphic organizers. **Ask:** How did important kings like Clovis, Charlemagne, and Otto I affect European unity? *(Answers will vary. Students should note that Clovis helped spread Christianity, Charlemagne briefly united much of Western Europe in his empire, and Otto I helped unite the Germans and promote the power of the Holy Roman Empire.)*

See page 537C for other online activities.

ANSWER, p. 542

CRITICAL THINKING They might have felt that he was now more like then than he was before.

Reading Strategy Einhard understood that Charlemange was a powerful king and wanted to flatter him.

The Early Middle Ages

pope. In 754, Pepin forced a Germanic group called the Lombards to leave Rome. He then gave the pope a large strip of Lombard land in Italy. These lands became known as the Papal States.

Pope Leo III crowned Charlemagne "Emperor of the Romans."

▶ CRITICAL THINKING

Making Inferences Why was it important that the pope led the crowning ceremony?

The Emperor Charlemagne

After Pepin died in 768, his son Charles became king of the Franks. In the years that followed, Charles sent his armies into neighboring lands. He nearly doubled the size of his kingdom to include what is today Germany, France, northern Spain, and most of Italy.

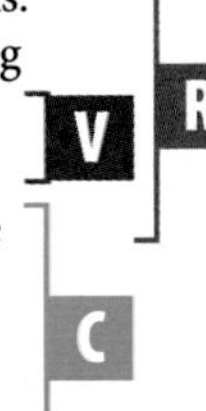

By 800, Charles's kingdom had grown into an empire. For the first time since the fall of Rome, most Western Europeans were ruled by one government. His conquests won Charles the name of Charlemagne (SHAHR•luh•MAYN), or Charles the Great. A monk named Einhard described Charlemagne this way:

PRIMARY SOURCE

> "Charles was large and strong, and of lofty stature [height] . . . [his] nose a little long, hair fair, and face laughing and merry. . . . He used to wear the . . . Frankish dress—next [to] his skin a linen shirt and linen breeches [pants], and above these a tunic fringed with silk. . . . Over all he flung a blue cloak, and he always had a sword girt [fastened] about him."
>
> —from *The Life of Charlemagne*, by Einhard

R Reading Skills

Calculating Have students use information from the text to answers the following questions. **Ask:**

- Who was Charlemagne's father? *(Pepin, king of the Franks)*
- When did Charlemagne become king? *(768)*
- By what year had Charlemagne's empire grown to include most of Western Europe? *(by 800)*
- How long had Charlemagne been king? *(32 years)*

Logical/Mathematical

V Visual Skills

Reading a Map To help students understand the extent of Charlemagne's empire, display on the board a map of Europe that shows current boundaries. **Ask:** When Charlemagne doubled the size of his empire, which areas did it include (using today's countries)? *(Germany, France, northern Spain, and most of Italy)* Ask a volunteer to indicate on the map where these countries are located. **Visual/Spatial**

C Critical Thinking Skills

Making Connections Ask students if they think Europe could be unified today under a single leader, like Charlemagne. Have students describe why they believe such a unification would or would not work in modern Europe. *(Students might recognize that such a unification would be difficult to accomplish because Europe's national identities have become much stronger today.)* BL

IMAGE

Charlemagne

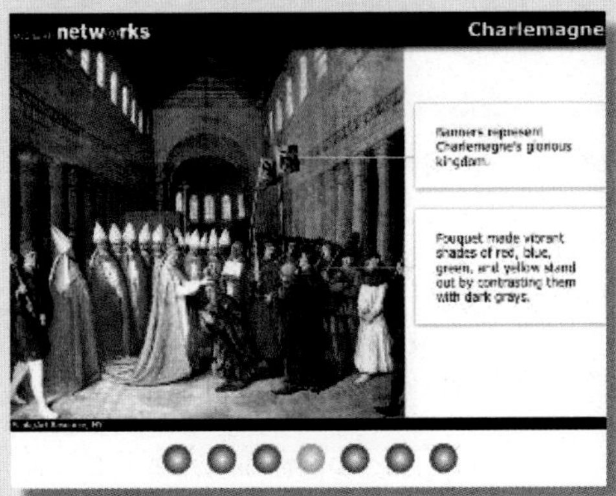

Analyzing Visuals Show students the interactive image of the coronation of Charlemagne. Read the description of Charlemagne that accompanies the image. **Ask:** What does this image suggest about the connection between the Catholic Church and political rulers during the Middle Ages? *(Students should note that the Church had a strong influence on political rulers such as kings.)* Note that Christianity could be a source of conflict as well as unity during the Middle Ages.

See page 537C for other online activities.

ANSWER, p. 543

CRITICAL THINKING It was important because of the great authority and power that the Catholic Church held in medieval life.

C Critical Thinking Skills

Making Inferences Explain to students that when they make inferences while reading, they make educated guesses based on information in the text. Point out the sentence in the textbook which explains that Charlemagne "did not want people to think the pope had the power to choose who was emperor." **Ask:** What can you infer about why Charlemagne cared what people thought as long as he was declared the new Roman emperor? *(Answers will vary, although students should suggest that if the pope had the power to choose who was emperor, then the pope was more powerful than the emperor. Also, Charlemagne may not have wanted to set the precedent in the future that the pope had the power to choose the emperor.)* BL

R Reading Skills

Identifying Have students review the text to identify the different raiders of the 800s and 900s. **Ask:** Who invaded eastern parts of France and Italy, and where were they from? *(Magyars, from Hungary)* Where did the Muslims from North Africa raid? *(France and Italy)* What were the raiders from Scandinavia called? *(Norsemen, or Vikings)* AL

T Technology Skills

Using Digital Tools Ask for volunteers to search online for photos of Scandinavian fjords. Students may want to search for images of fjords in Sweden, Norway, or Denmark. Ask them to choose several representative photos to present to the class, either with presentation software such as PowerPoint or simply by projecting the images onto the whiteboard. Students should be prepared to explain the location of each of the fjords they present.

Vikings sailed the northern seas in boats powered by oars and the wind. This longship is a replica of a Viking ship that carried explorers.

In 800, Charlemagne came to Rome and defended the pope against unruly Roman nobles. On Christmas day, Charlemagne was worshipping at the church of St. Peter in Rome. After the service, the pope placed a crown on Charlemagne's head and declared him the new Roman emperor. Charlemagne was pleased but also concerned. C He did not want people to think the pope had the power to choose who was emperor.

Despite this concern, Charlemagne accepted his duties as emperor and worked to strengthen the empire. The central government, located in the capital of Aachen (AH•kuhn), was small. As a result, Charlemagne relied on local officials called counts to help him govern. The counts ran local affairs and raised armies for Charlemagne. Royal messengers went on inspections and told the emperor how the counts were doing.

Charlemagne wanted to advance learning in his kingdom. He had tried late in life to learn to write and wanted his people to be educated too. He **established** a school for the children of government officials. Students at the school studied religion, Latin, music, literature, and arithmetic.

Waves of Invaders

More than anything else, Charlemagne's forceful personality held the empire together. After Charlemagne died in 814, his empire did not last long. It was soon divided into three kingdoms.

These Frankish kingdoms were prey to outside attacks. In the 800s and 900s, waves of invaders swept across Europe. Muslims from North Africa raided France and Italy. Fierce nomads called Magyars from Hungary invaded eastern parts of France and Italy. Vikings launched raids from their homeland in Scandinavia (SKAN•duh•NAY•vee•uh). R

Scandinavia is in northern Europe. Norway, Sweden, and Denmark are all part of modern Scandinavia. Much of Scandinavia has a long, jagged coastline. It has many **fjords** (fee•AWRDS), or narrow inlets of the sea. The fjords, T surrounded by steep cliffs or slopes, were carved by glaciers long ago. The Viking people, known as Norsemen or "north men," lived in villages near the fjords.

Scandinavia has little farmland, so the Vikings had to depend on the sea for food and trade. They became skilled sailors and traveled in sturdy longboats. These boats could survive the rough Atlantic and also navigate shallow rivers.

Ted Spiegel/CORBIS

Reading HELPDESK CCSS

fjord a narrow inlet of the sea between cliffs or steep slopes

Academic Vocabulary (Tier 2 Words)

establish to start; to bring into existence

networks Online Teaching Options

IMAGE

The Vikings

Discussing Display the interactive image and click to reveal the text next to the image. Ask a volunteer to read aloud the information about the Vikings. Then begin a class discussion by asking students to share the fact they found the most interesting. To conclude the discussion, have volunteers summarize the key points from the slide.

See page 537C for other online activities.

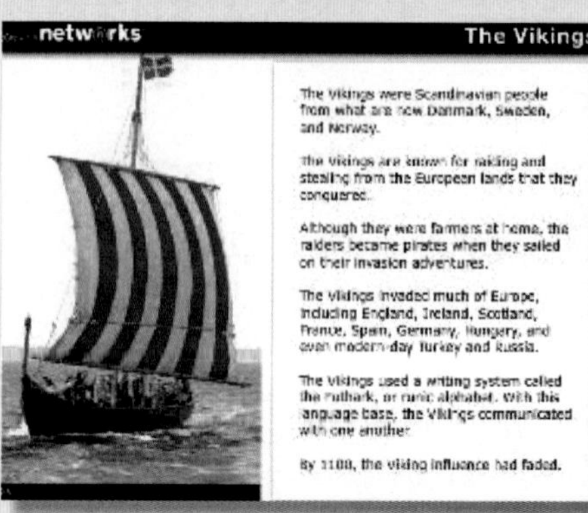

In the 700s and 800s, the Vikings left their crowded homeland and carried out raids along Europe's coasts. The word *viking* comes from their word for raiding. The Vikings attacked villages and churches, seizing grain, animals, and other valuable items. They burned whatever they could not steal.

The Vikings were more than just raiders. They were also explorers and settlers. They sailed across the Atlantic, settled the islands of Greenland and Iceland, and even landed in North America. For a short time, Viking groups also lived in England. They founded the territory of Normandy in northwestern France and settled in parts of what are now Russia and Ukraine.

Formation of the Holy Roman Empire

R

Muslim, Magyar, and Viking invaders brought much suffering to Europe's people. Their attacks also weakened the Frankish kingdoms. By the 900s, the eastern Frankish kingdom, known as Germany, became a collection of small territories ruled by nobles. In 911, a group of these nobles sought to unite Germany by electing a king.

In 936, Duke Otto of Saxony was elected king of Germany. Otto became a powerful ruler. Germanic forces defeated the Magyars and freed the pope from the control of Roman nobles. To reward Otto, the pope crowned him emperor of the Romans in 962. Otto's territory became known as the Holy Roman Empire. It included most of present-day Germany and northern Italy.

GEOGRAPHY CONNECTION

During the Early Middle Ages, several different groups invaded and settled in Europe.

1. **MOVEMENT** Which groups of invaders traveled by sea?
2. **CRITICAL THINKING** ***Speculating*** Why might an army have found it more difficult to invade Italy than Hungary?

V

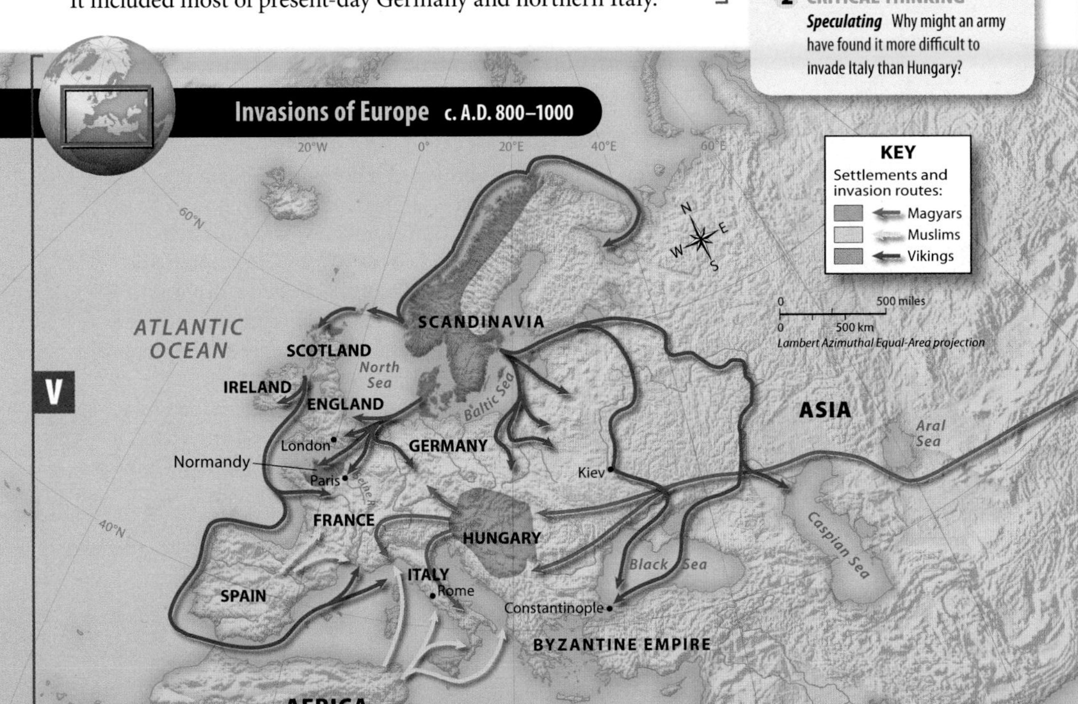

CHAPTER 19, Lesson 1
The Early Middle Ages

R Reading Skills

Explaining After students have read the text, make sure they understand the events that resulted in the formation of the Holy Roman Empire. **Ask:** By the 900s, why had Germany become a collection of small territories? *(Attacks from invaders had weakened Frankish kingdoms.)* Who elected Otto as the German king? *(a group of Frankish nobles)* What did King Otto do for the pope? *(Otto freed the pope from control of Roman nobles.)* What did the pope do for Otto in return? *(The pope crowned Otto as emperor of the Holy Roman Empire.)*

V Visual Skills

Reading a Map Have students study the map of Invasions of Europe at the bottom of this page. Then ask a series of questions about what the map shows. Ask:

- What period does this map cover? *(A.D. 800–1000)*
- Where did the Muslims come from that invaded Italy and France? *(northern Africa)*
- How did the Viking raiders reach southern France? *(They traveled on the Atlantic Ocean around Spain and into the Mediterranean Sea.)*
- Where did the Magyars come from? *(from the east, from Asia)* **AL** **Visual/Spatial**

MAP

Invasions of Europe c. A.D. 800–1000

Reading a Map Display the interactive map, and begin with all layers turned off. Click on the button below the map to activate an audio description of the three different invaders. As the narrator describes the invasions, the three layers will appear on the map—Vikings, Muslims, and then Magyars. After the audio, students can turn the three layers on and off to review the different invasion routes. As a class, discuss the pros and cons of each route.

See page 537C for other online activities.

ANSWERS, p. 545

GEOGRAPHY CONNECTION

1. Vikings and Muslims
2. **CRITICAL THINKING** Italy is a peninsula, surrounded on most sides by water and protected on the north by mountains; Hungary is inland and relatively protected by natural barriers.

R Reading Skills

Defining Ask for a student volunteer to read the paragraph aloud to the class. Remind students that important words in the text are often boldfaced and highlighted. **Ask:** What are missionaries? *(people who are sent out to teach their religion)* Explain that many religions send missionaries out today, to spread their religion. What effect did missionaries have on Western Europe? *(By 1050, most Western Europeans had become Catholic Christians.)* AL ELL

C Critical Thinking Skills

Recognizing Relationships On the whiteboard, have students help in making a concept map that shows relationships within the Catholic Church. Begin with a bubble for "Catholic Church." Draw a line down to a second bubble, and label the line "headed by." Elicit from students that "Pope" should be written in the second bubble. Continue the concept map by making a division between men and women. Men were monks who lived in monasteries headed by abbots. Women were nuns who lived in convents headed by abbesses. When the concept map has been completed on the whiteboard, have students copy it in their notebooks. **Visual/Spatial**

Content Background Knowledge

Saint Benedict of Nursia The man most responsible for the creation of Christian monasteries in the West was Saint Benedict of Nursia (A.D. 480–547). Benedict was an Italian who was famous for his piety. With a few followers, he founded a monastery south of Rome on a hilltop called Monte Cassino. This monastery became the source for the Benedictine Rule, a form of monastic life that has been the model for many Catholic institutions for 1,500 years. Benedict stressed simplicity, learning, the importance of community, and the goal of helping others. Because his influence was so widespread, in 1964 Pope Paul VI named Benedict one of Europe's patron saints.

ANSWERS, p. 546

✓ PROGRESS CHECK The defeat of the Muslims at Tours stopped the further advance of Islam into Western Europe. It also ensured that Christianity would remain Western Europe's major religion.

CRITICAL THINKING The actions of the kings threatened to weaken the pope's authority as head of the church..

After Otto, two important emperors, Frederick I and Frederick II, tried to bring Germany and Italy under a strong central government during the 1100s and 1200s. The popes did not want the emperor to control them. They joined with Italy's cities to resist the emperors' forces. Ongoing conflict kept Germany and Italy from becoming united countries until the 1800s.

✓ PROGRESS CHECK

Explaining What impact did the Battle of Tours have on European history?

The Church and Its Influence

GUIDING QUESTION *How did the Catholic Church influence life in early medieval Europe?*

The Roman Catholic Church played an important role in the growth of a new civilization in medieval Western Europe.

Christianity in Europe

At the time of Rome's fall, large areas of northwestern Europe practiced a variety of non-Christian religions. Ireland was different. In the 400s, a Christian priest named Patrick traveled to Ireland. There, Patrick spread Christianity and founded churches and monasteries, or religious houses.

R Patrick inspired Pope Gregory I, or Gregory the Great, to spread Christianity. Gregory asked monks to become **missionaries** (MIH•shuh•NEHR•eez)—people who are sent out to teach their religion. In 597, Gregory sent 40 monks to Britain to teach Christianity. Other monks spread Christianity, so that by 1050, most Western Europeans had become Catholic Christians.

This image shows Pope Gregory VII wearing his official vestments as head of the Church.

▶ CRITICAL THINKING

Drawing Conclusions Why do you think Pope Gregory VII wanted to stop kings from choosing Church officials?

The Contributions of Monks and Nuns

Monks and monasteries provided schools and hospitals. They taught carpentry and weaving, and they developed improvements in farming. Many monks copied Christian writings as well as Roman and Greek works. They also made illuminations, which are manuscripts decorated with beautiful lettering and miniature religious paintings. These monks helped preserve knowledge of the classical and early Christian worlds.

C Monks lived in communities headed by abbots (A•buhtz). Women called nuns lived in their own monasteries called convents. Convents were headed by abbesses (A•buhs•ihs).

Elio Ciol/CORBIS

Reading **HELP**DESK CCSS

missionaries people who are sent by a religious organization to spread the faith

concordat agreement between the pope and the ruler of a country

networks *Online Teaching Options*

BIOGRAPHY

Gregory VII

Identifying Central Issues Display the biography of Gregory VII, and scroll down the right side to read all the information. Ask a volunteer to read the biography to the class. **Ask:** What was the central issue for Gregory VII as he struggled for power with nobles and kings? *(that leaders of the papacy had control over local bishops)* What was the result for the Church during his papacy? *(The Catholic Church gained power, and the role of the pope increased in strength.)*

See page 537C for other online activities.

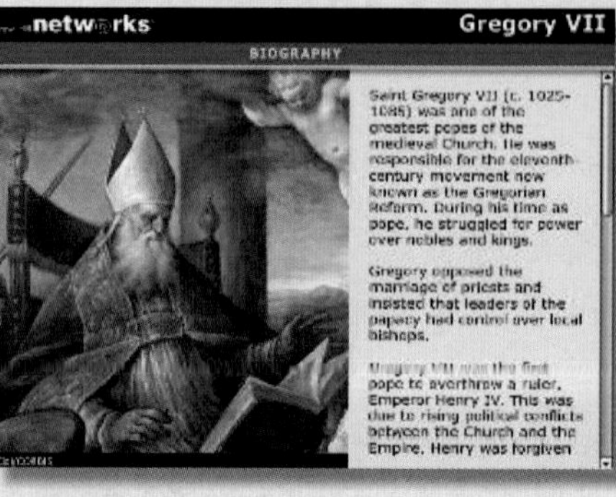

The Early Middle Ages

Church Authority

Many monasteries became wealthy. As their influence increased, abbots became active in political affairs. This caused disagreements. Kings wanted Church leaders to obey them. Popes, however, believed kings should obey the Church.

R

Elected pope in 1073, Gregory VII declared that only the pope had the power to appoint high-ranking Church officials. Pope Gregory's order angered Henry IV, the Holy Roman emperor. For many years, the Holy Roman emperor had chosen bishops in Germany. Henry insisted on naming his own bishops. Gregory then declared that Henry was no longer emperor and excommunicated him. This meant that he no longer had the rights of church membership and could not go to heaven.

When the German nobles supported the pope, Henry changed his mind. He traveled to Italy and begged the pope for forgiveness. Gregory forgave Henry, but the German nobles chose a new emperor. When Gregory accepted the new emperor, Henry seized Rome and named a new pope.

The struggle continued until 1122, when a new German king and a new pope agreed that only the pope could choose bishops, but only the king or emperor could give them government posts. This agreement, called the *Concordat of Worms*, was signed in the German city of Worms. A **concordat** (kuhn•KAWR•DAT) is an agreement between the pope and the ruler of a country.

In the days before printing presses, monks helped preserve knowledge by copying classical Greek and Roman writings as well as the Bible and other early Christian writings.

PROGRESS CHECK

Describing What major issue did kings and popes disagree on?

LESSON 1 REVIEW (CCSS)

Review Vocabulary (Tier 3 Words)

1. What is a *missionary* meant to do? RH.6–8.2, RH.6–8.4
2. What natural process created the *fjords*? RH.6–8.2, RH.6–8.4

Answer the Guiding Questions

3. ***Summarizing*** How did mountains and rivers make it difficult for one group to control all of Europe? RH.6–8.2
4. ***Explaining*** What happened in Britain after Roman armies abandoned the area during the 400s? RH.6–8.2
5. ***Identifying*** In what modern countries did the Franks settle? RH.6–8.2, RH.6–8.7
6. ***Analyzing*** What did Charlemagne do to advance education? RH.6–8.2
7. ***Analyzing*** What role did monasteries play in medieval Europe? RH.6–8.2
8. **INFORMATIVE/EXPLANATORY** Henry IV begged for the pope's forgiveness. If you were going to interview King Henry about this incident, what three questions would you ask him? Write your answer in a paragraph. WHST.6–8.2, WHST.6–8.10

Lesson 1 547

R Reading Skills

Discussing Direct students to read the text. Then, introduce the conflict between Pope Gregory VII and the Holy Roman Emperor Henry IV as an example of disagreements between political and religious leaders. **Ask:**

- What was the source of the conflict? *(The pope wanted to appoint the bishops, but Henry believed that he had the power to appoint them.)*
- What did the pope do to Henry? *(He excommunicated Henry.)*
- How did Henry respond? *(First, Henry asked for forgiveness, and when he did not receive forgiveness, he went to war.)*
- How was this issue resolved by a new German king and a new pope in 1122? *(In the agreement called the Concordat of Worms, the new pope and king agreed that only the pope could choose bishops but only the king or emperor could give bishops government posts.)*

Have students complete the Lesson 1 Review.

CLOSE & REFLECT

Analyzing Discuss the following questions and answers with students to review the lesson:

- What effect did geography have on the development of Europe during the Middle Ages? *(It both provided resources to and isolated people, allowing them to develop their own cultures.)*
- What effect did Germanic kings have on Europe's religion? *(They helped spread Christianity in Western Europe.)*
- How did the Church influence the Holy Roman emperors? *(The pope crowned kings and fought for the right to appoint bishops and make political decisions.)*

LESSON 1 REVIEW ANSWERS

1. Missionaries are meant to go out and teach their religion.
2. Retreating glaciers carved the fjords along the coast of Scandinavia.
3. Mountains and rivers were natural barriers that separated different groups of people.
4. Soon after the Romans left Britain, the Angles and the Saxons, who were Germanic groups from Denmark and northern Germany, moved in and settled there.
5. They settled in what is now France and western Germany.
6. He set up a school for the children of government officials and put the English scholar Alcuin in charge of it.
7. Answers will vary. Possible answer: Monasteries provided schools and hospitals and helped preserve written knowledge. They also owned land and made goods, allowing many monasteries to grow wealthy and influence politics.
8. Answers will vary, but paragraphs should mention at least three questions to ask Henry IV.

ANSWER, p. 547

PROGRESS CHECK Kings wanted to appoint their own bishops, but popes used the power of excommunication to force kings to accept papal appointees.

ENGAGE

Bellringer Display an image of medieval life that you find in a book or on the Internet. **Ask:** What was life probably like for people in the Middle Ages? *(Answers will vary. Accept any reasonable responses.)* Would you have wanted to live in medieval Europe? *(Answers will vary. Accept any reasonable responses.)* Write students' responses on the whiteboard. Then take a poll to see which students would like to have been a medieval knight and which students would like to have been a city merchant. Ask volunteers to explain their choices. Return to this poll at the end of the lesson to see if any students change their minds. Tell students that in this lesson they will learn about how most Europeans lived and worked during the Middle Ages.

TEACH & ASSESS

R Reading Skills

Determining Word Meanings Have students locate the word *feudalism* and then use clues from the text to determine its meaning. **Ask:** What did land-owning nobles offer to people living on their lands? *(protection and governance)* What did the people on the land offer the nobles in return? *(services such as fighting in the army or farming the land)* AL ELL

C Critical Thinking Skills

Determining Cause and Effect After students have read that feudalism developed after the fall of Charlemagne's empire, write the word *Causes* on the board. **Ask:** What were the causes of feudalism? *(the fall of Charlemagne's empire, the need for defense from enemies, the growing importance of local nobles)* Write the responses on the board. Discuss how feudalism improved life for Europeans. **Ask:** What benefits did feudalism provide for ordinary Europeans? *(It provided them with stability and protection from enemies.)*

There's More Online!

CHART/GRAPH
Pyramid of Classes

Lesson 2

Feudalism and the Rise of Towns

ESSENTIAL QUESTION *What are the characteristics that define a culture?*

IT MATTERS BECAUSE

The organization of society in medieval Europe affected nearly every aspect of people's lives.

The Feudal Order

GUIDING QUESTION *How did Europeans try to bring order to their society after the fall of Charlemagne's empire?*

After the fall of Charlemagne's empire, strong governments collapsed in Western Europe. Kings lost much of their power. Local land-owning nobles became increasingly important in political affairs. They raised armies. They also collected taxes and imposed laws on the people living on their lands.

When invaders swept through Europe, people turned to the nobles for protection. Nobles governed and protected the people in return for services, such as fighting in a noble's army or farming the land. This led to a new political and social order known as **feudalism** (FYOO•duh•LIH•zuhm).

By 1000, Europe's kingdoms were divided into hundreds of feudal territories. Most of these territories were small. A noble's castle was the center of each territory.

Lords, Vassals, and Knights

Feudalism was based on ties of loyalty and duty among members of the nobility. Nobles were both lords and vassals. A lord was a high-ranking noble who had power over others. A **vassal** (VA•suhl) was a lower-ranking noble who served a lord. In return, the lord protected the vassal.

Reading **HELP**DESK CCSS

Taking Notes: *Summarizing*

Use a cluster diagram like the one shown here to list important features of feudalism as a social system during the Middle Ages. RH.6–8.2

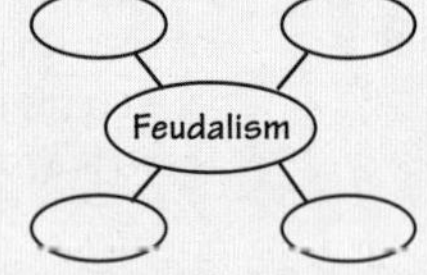

Content Vocabulary (Tier 3 Words)

- **feudalism**
- **knight**
- **chivalry**
- **vassal**
- **serf**
- **fief**
- **guild**

networks Online Teaching Options

VIDEO

Feudalism, Lords, and Vassals Video Quiz

Making Connections Play the video about the fanciful appearance of William the Conqueror in a modern-day classroom. Allow students to enjoy the silliness, but also explain that there is important factual information in the video. Have students take notes while watching the video. Then have small groups discuss what they learned from the video and what they would like to learn more about as they study this chapter.

See page 537D for other online activities.

ANSWER, p. 548

TAKING NOTES: Answers may include some of the following: ties of loyalty and duty; vassals and lords; fiefs; knights and code of chivalry; manorial system; serfs and freemen; nobles.

The tie binding a lord and his vassal was declared in a public ceremony. The vassal took an oath and placed his hands between those of his lord. Then the vassal swore:

PRIMARY SOURCE

> "Sir, I enter your homage [service] and faith and become your man by mouth and hands [that is, by taking the oath and placing his hands between those of the lord], and I swear and promise to keep faith and loyalty to you against all others."
>
> —from *A Source Book for Medieval History*, 1905

W

A vassal helped his lord in battle. In exchange for the vassal's **military** service, a lord gave his vassal land. The property granted to a vassal was known as a **fief** (FEEF).

Many lower-ranking vassals were known as **knights** (NYTS). They were armed warriors who fought on horseback. In early medieval times, warriors in Western Europe mostly fought on foot. In the 700s, knights began to use a foot piece called a stirrup. Stirrups allowed an armored warrior to sit on a horse and attack while he held a lance, or long, heavy spear.

V

Nobles and Knights in Medieval Society

C

During the Middle Ages, nobles were the most powerful people in Europe. Great lords had more land and wealth than ordinary knights. Yet, a shared belief in the feudal order united lords and knights in defending their society.

Knights followed the code of **chivalry** (SHIH•vuhl•ree). These rules stated that a knight was to be brave and obey his lord. A knight was also required to respect women of noble birth, honor the Church, and help people. Many of today's ideas about manners come from the **code** of chivalry.

feudalism political order; under feudalism, nobles governed and protected people in return for services
vassal a low-ranking noble under the protection of a feudal lord

fief a feudal estate belonging to a vassal
knight a mounted man-at-arms serving a lord

Academic Vocabulary (Tier 2 Words)
military relating to soldiers, arms, or war

W Writing Skills

Informative/Explanatory Call on a volunteer to read aloud the vassal's oath to his lord. Then ask each student to rewrite that oath in modern language, so that the oath would be easily understandable to someone hearing it today. After they have finished, call on a variety of students to share their rewrites. Discuss any differences in interpretation. **Verbal/Linguistic**

C Critical Thinking Skills

Interpreting Ask students what benefits feudalism provided for people at each of its levels. Have them offer suggestions regarding why those on the lower rungs generally accepted their roles. Then ask students to name similar situations in which all parties benefit from an arrangement, even though it might not be ideal for all participants. BL

V Visual Skills

Analyzing Images Have students study the graphic of the social order of classes under feudalism. **Ask:**

- **Which level represents the vassals in the feudal order?** *(the knights)*
- **What does the triangle shape of the graph indicate about the different classes in the feudal system?** *(The triangle shape indicates the number of people at each level. The greatest number of people made up the bottom level: the peasants and serfs.)* **Visual/Spatial**

GRAPH

Classes Under Feudalism

Categorizing Show students the interactive graph of the different social classes in the feudal system. **Ask: Which group had the most power in the feudal system? Which group had the least?** *(Students will note that kings and queens are at the top of the social pyramid. Peasants and serfs are at the bottom of feudal society.)*

See page 537D for other online activities.

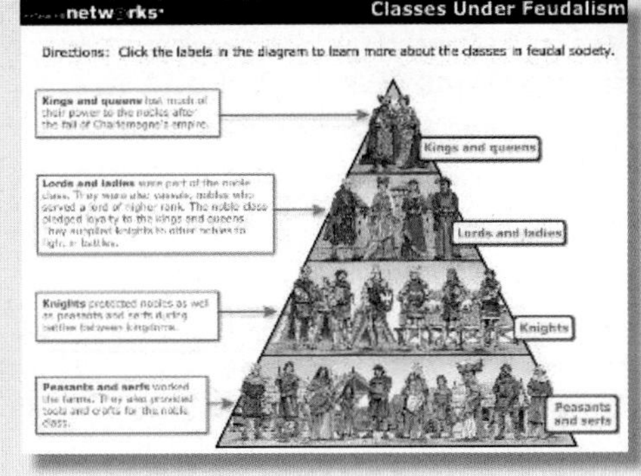

V Visual Skills

Analyzing Images Have students study the cut-away diagram of a castle. Then pose the following questions. **Ask:**

- What is the function and purpose of the drawbridge? *(The drawbridge allows people to cross the moat, or water, to enter the castle. The drawbridge is designed to be able to be pulled up so the castle can be closed in times of attack.)*
- Where are the bedrooms compared with the servants' quarters? What does that indicate? *(The bedrooms are at an upper level in a high tower, while the servants' quarters are at ground level above the storeroom. The difference indicates that the lords and ladies had much more protection than the servants in case invaders got inside the castle.)* **Visual/Spatial**

C Critical Thinking Skills

Making Inferences Point out that the castle keep, the central building, was constructed on the motte. **Ask:**

- What is a motte? *(a steep-sided hill)* ELL
- What was the purpose of building the keep on the motte? *(It was the best defense against invaders.)* BL
- Emphasize that castles were designed to provide good defenses. What other features were designed to help protect the castle and its residents? *(high walls, drawbridges, high towers)*

Content Background Knowledge

Medieval Tournaments One of the most famous activities of medieval knights was the tournament, a series of mock combats designed to showcase war skills. The earliest tournaments, probably held in France in the 1000s, featured a mock battle called a melee, between two groups of knights. The familiar joust, in which two riders charged each other and tried to knock an opponent off his horse with a long lance, came later.

By around 1300, steps were taken to prevent injury to the contestants, although serious injuries, and even death, sometimes occurred. In the 1500s, fighting on foot became popular, with knights striking each other across a barricade with swords and battle-axes.

ANSWER, p. 550

✓ PROGRESS CHECK A knight had to obey his lord, show bravery, respect women of noble birth, honor the Church, and help people. These rules were known as the code of chivalry.

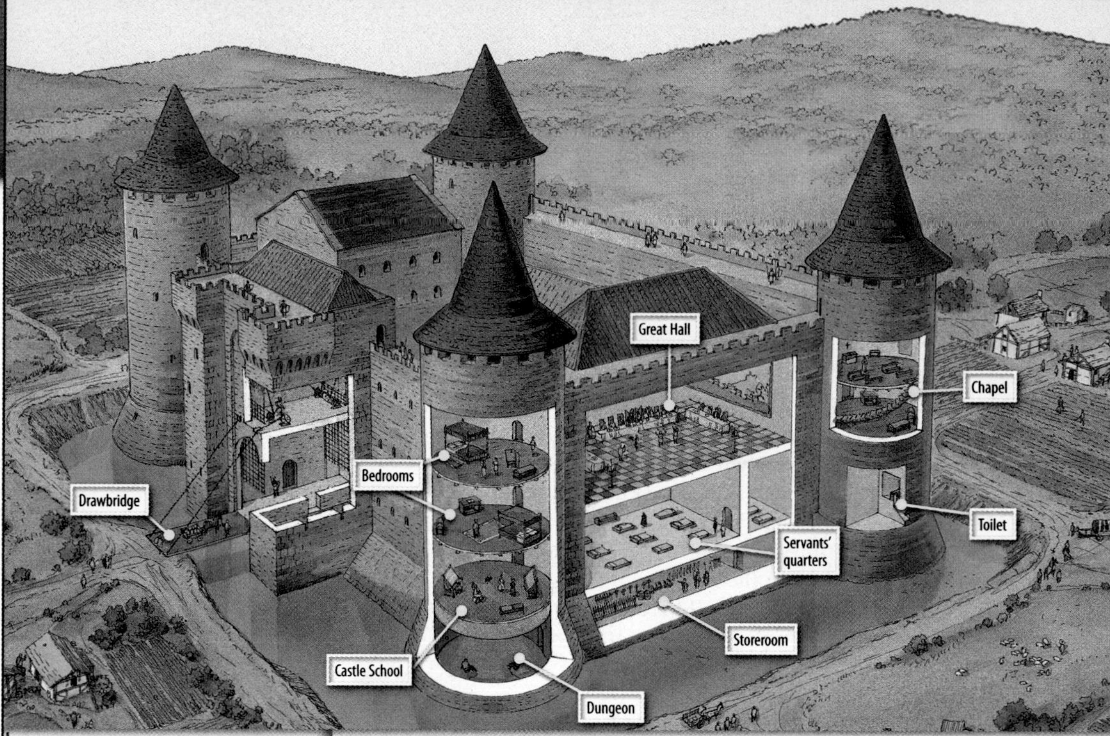

Castles in the Middle Ages were designed to provide good defenses for their owners. For example, castles often occupied high ground. High towers at each corner gave soldiers the chance to drive attackers away.

V Knights trained for war by fighting one another in tournaments, or special contests. The most popular event was the joust. Two knights on horseback carrying lances galloped toward each other and tried to knock each other off.

Nobles were often at war and away from their castles. In their absence, their wives or daughters ran the estates.

C The castle was at the center of the estate. Every castle had two parts. The first was a motte (MAHT), or steep-sided hill. The second part was the bailey, an open space next to the motte. Both parts were encircled by high walls. The castle keep, its central building, was constructed on the motte.

In the basement of the keep, tools and food were stored. On the ground floor were kitchens and stables. Above these was a great hall. The lord held court and met visitors here.

✓ PROGRESS CHECK

Identifying What were the rules of behavior that knights followed?

Reading HELPDESK (CCSS)

chivalry the system, spirit, or customs of medieval knighthood

serf a member of the peasant class tied to the land and subject to the will of the landowner

Academic Vocabulary (Tier 2 Words)

code a system of principles or rules

networks Online Teaching Options

GAME

Column Game: Feudalism and the Rise of Towns

Categorizing To reinforce students' understanding of the feudal order, have them play the Feudalism column game. A student can choose to be timed or not when playing the game. Once the game begins, the student clicks and drags various concepts related to feudalism to one of three columns: *lordship, vassalage, both.* Clicking on the Check Answers button tells the player how many items he or she placed in the correct column. Challenge students to complete the exercise as quickly as possible.

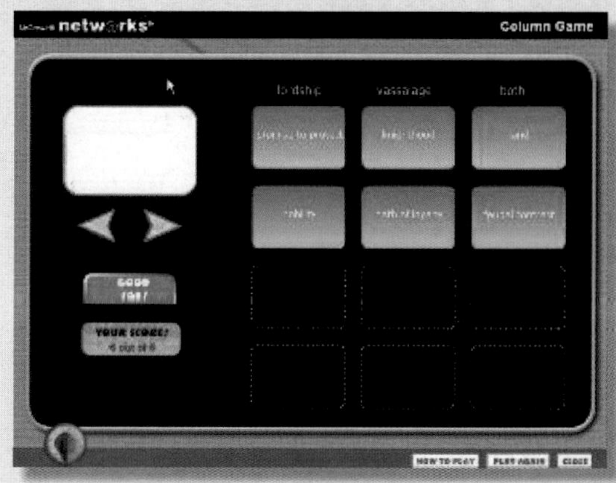

See page 537D for other online activities.

The Medieval Manor

GUIDING QUESTION *How did most Europeans live and work during the Middle Ages?*

Nobles, knights, and peasants (or farmers) depended on the land for everything they needed. The lands of a fief consisted of manors. A manor was a farming community that a noble ran and peasants worked. It usually consisted of the noble's castle, the surrounding fields, and a peasant village. **R**

Two Groups of Peasants

During the Middle Ages, the vast number of Europeans were peasants living and working on manors. There were two groups of peasants—freemen and serfs. Freemen paid the noble for the right to farm the land. They worked only on their own land and had rights under the law. They moved wherever and whenever they wished.

C Most peasants, however, were **serfs** (SUHRFS). Serfs and their descendants were tied to the manor. They could not own property, move to another area, or marry without the noble's permission. Serfs were not enslaved, however. Nobles could not sell them or take away the land they farmed to support themselves. Nobles were also expected to protect their serfs.

Serfs worked long hours in the fields and did many services for the nobles. They spent three days of the week working the noble's land and the rest of the week farming their own. However, they had to give part of their own crops to the noble. They also had to pay him for the use of the village's mill, bread oven, and winepress.

W It was not easy for serfs to gain their freedom. One way was to escape to the towns. If a serf was not caught and remained in a town for more than a year, he or she was considered free. By the end of the Middle Ages, serfs in many areas were allowed to buy their freedom.

Serfs had a busy life working in the fields growing the lord's crops and their own.

▶ CRITICAL THINKING
Differentiating What happened to the crops that serfs grew on their own land?

Limbourg Brothers/The Bridgeman Art Library/Getty Images

The Lives of the Peasants

Peasants—both freemen and serfs—lived in villages clustered around an open area called a village green. Their homes were simple cottages. The poorest peasants lived in a single room.

Peasants worked year round. In late winter and spring, they planted crops of beans, peas, barley, and oats. In early summer, they weeded fields and sheared sheep. In late summer, they harvested grain. They also slaughtered livestock and salted the meat for winter storage. Many peasants tended small vegetable gardens.

R Reading Skills

Defining Have students read the first paragraph on this page. Then, guide a class discussion about the basic makeup of a medieval manor. **Ask:**

- What made up the lands of a fief? *(manors)*
- What was a manor? *(a farming community that a noble ran and in which peasants worked)*
- What are three main parts of a medieval manor? *(the noble's castle, the surrounding fields, and a peasant village)* AL ELL

C Critical Thinking Skills

Reasoning As a class, discuss why the manor system worked for many serfs. **Ask:**

- What did a serf owe a noble for living on the noble's land? *(three days a week working on the noble's land, part of their own crops, and payment for use of the village's mill, bread oven, and winepress)*
- Why didn't most serfs just leave the noble's land? *(Answers will vary, though students should suggest that serfs gained protection and security by living on a manor.)* BL

W Writing Skills

Narrative Ask each student to write a diary entry for a peasant who lived in a medieval manor. Tell students that they can choose to write as a man or woman, old or young. Encourage them to write about a typical day in the life of the person they selected. Each diary entry should reflect what students have learned about the lives of peasants and their relationship to the lord of the manor. After allowing time for writing, invite volunteers to read their entries to the class. Lead a discussion of the typical lives of peasants of the era. **Verbal/Linguistic**

CHART

Serfs and Freemen

Comparing and Contrasting Display the Venn diagram on the whiteboard. Before clicking on the areas, ask a volunteer to read aloud the text material above the diagram. Then lead a discussion about the lives of serfs and freemen. Finally, click on each of the three areas to reveal the similarities among and differences between serfs and freemen. Encourage students to add any additional details that are not included on the graphic organizer.

See page 537D for other online activities.

ANSWER, p. 551

CRITICAL THINKING They gave part of the crops to the nobles and kept part for themselves.

T Technology Skills

Researching on the Internet Have interested students use Internet search engines to find photos of European cities, towns, and villages that retain a medieval character today. Have them look for preserved buildings, such as shops, castles, and churches, and unchanged rural and agricultural landscapes. Suggest that they begin by looking at the Cotswold region and the city of York in England; Assisi, Italy; or Rothenberg in Germany. After students do their research, they can share their results with the class by projecting the photos on the whiteboard. **Visual/Spatial**

V Visual Skills

Analyzing Images Have students study the infographic of a medieval manor. Point out that the illustration shows the three basic parts of a medieval manor: the castle, the surrounding fields, and the peasant village. Then ask a volunteer to read the caption aloud to the class. Continue with a class discussion about medieval manors. **Ask:**

- **What furniture did a serf's house contain?** *(a table made of boards stretched across benches; straw mattresses on the floor)*
- **What crops did serfs plant in the spring?** *(summer wheat, barley, oats, peas, beans)*
- **Would you like to live on a medieval manor? Why or why not?** *(Answers will vary, but students should be able to support their opinion with facts.)* **Visual/Spatial**

ANSWERS, p. 552

INFOGRAPHIC
CRITICAL THINKING the lord's castle, the peasant village, the fields, and the church

Reading Strategy The manor benefited peasants because they had enough to eat and were allowed to celebrate feast days and attend church.

A MEDIEVAL MANOR

INFOGRAPHIC

A medieval manor had several parts. At the center was the lord's castle or fortified manor house. Peasants usually lived in a small village nearby. The village contained cottages, huts, barns, gardens, and perhaps a small church. The peasants grew crops in the fields around the village. Manors were found not only in western Europe, but were also common in Russia and Japan.

▶ CRITICAL THINKING
Explaining What were the four areas of a medieval manor?

During times of leisure, peasant life centered on the church and the village green. Peasants took a break from work and went to church on Sunday and Catholic feast days. Certain feast days were celebrated with singing and dancing on the green. Peasant men took part in sports such as wrestling and archery.

Besides working in the fields, peasant women raised children and prepared the family's food. They made dark, heavy bread, which peasants ate with vegetables, milk, nuts, and fruits. They also ate eggs and meat, washed down with ale.

Improvements in Farming

Manors usually produced only enough food to support the peasants and the lord's household. However, over time, Europeans developed new ways to increase the number of crops they could grow, as well as how much the crops produced.

One major improvement was a heavy wheeled plow with an iron blade. The new plow made deeper cuts in the dense clay soil. The heavier plow meant peasant farmers spent less time

Reading HELPDESK (CCSS)

Reading Strategy: *Analyzing*
When you analyze a passage you have read, you think about how the facts lead to main conclusions. Reread the section about the medieval manor looking for facts. Then analyze how the manor was beneficial to peasants.

networks *Online Teaching Options*

SLIDE SHOW

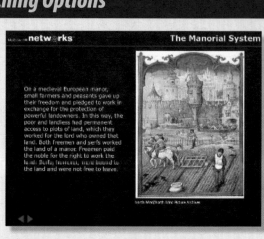

The Manorial System

Summarizing Show students the interactive slide show on manorial life. **Ask: What were the duties of medieval peasants?** *(to farm the nobles' land and maintain the manor)* Point out that there were two kinds of peasants—serfs and freemen. **How were freemen different from serfs?** *(Freemen had rights and were not tied to the land. Serfs had to stay on the land and ask permission to move or get married. At first, serfs could not buy their freedom. This changed later.)* **Who were the private warriors who helped nobles defend their land?** *(knights)*

See page 537D for other online activities.

in the fields. The horse collar was another important invention. The collar enabled a horse to pull a plow. Horses could pull plows faster than oxen could. This invention made it possible for peasants to produce more food.

Water and wind power also became important during the Middle Ages. Europe's rivers provided power for water mills to grind grain into flour. In places without rivers, windmills could be used for grinding grain, pumping water, and sawing wood.

Another improvement in agriculture was crop rotation. Peasants used three fields rather than two to keep the soil fertile. One field was planted in the fall, a second one in springtime, and the third field was left unplanted. With this system, only one-third of the land was left unused at a time, rather than one-half. More crops could be grown as a result. As food production increased, the population of Europe grew.

✓ PROGRESS CHECK

Comparing and Contrasting How did the lives of freemen and serfs differ?

The Growth of Towns and Cities

GUIDING QUESTION ***How did increased trade change life in medieval Europe?***

When the Roman Empire collapsed, trade throughout Europe sharply declined. Bridges and roads fell into ruin. Law and order largely disappeared. Most people spent their entire lives in the farming villages where they were born. They knew very little about the rest of the world.

C By 1100, feudalism had made Europe safer. Nobles repaired roads, arrested bandits, and enforced the law. Meanwhile, new technology enabled people to produce more food and goods. Europe's population grew for the first time since the fall of Rome.

Peasants began to make cloth and metal products. Nobles also sought luxury items, such as sugar, spices, silks, and dyes. These goods came from the East.

Wealthy Trading Centers

R As Europe's trade increased, towns grew larger. Several cities became wealthy from trade. The cities of Venice (VEH•nuhs), Pisa, and Genoa in Italy built fleets of trading ships. They became major trading centers. By 1200, these Italian cities controlled the profitable Mediterranean trade with the Byzantine Empire.

As Europe became more feudalistic, towns and cities grew. Tall stone buildings lining narrow streets were similar in England and France. This street is still in use in Blesle, France.

Robert Landau/Corbis

C Critical Thinking Skills

Determining Cause and Effect Discuss with students the growth of Europe's population for the first time since the fall of Rome. **Ask:**

- What are two main reasons why the population began to grow? *(Feudalism had made Europe safer, and new technology enabled people to produce more food and goods.)*
- What were some of the new forms of technology that resulted in more crops? *(heavier plows, horse collars, water power, windmills)* AL

R Reading Skills

Identifying After students have read about wealthy trading centers that developed as Europe's trade grew, ask students to identify the three major cities that are given as examples in the text. Then display a map of the Mediterranean region that shows these cities and have students locate them. **Ask:**

- What do these three Italian cities have in common? *(They are all seaports.)*
- What industry became successful in these cities? *(ship building)*
- As these cities grew, with whom did they often trade? *(the Byzantine Empire)*

WORKSHEET

Primary Source Activity: Medieval Europe: Feudalism and the Role of Towns: Froissart's *Chronicles*

Analyzing Primary Sources Display on the whiteboard the excerpts from *Chronicles* by Jean Froissart, and read the introduction to students. Ask volunteers to read each of the excerpts aloud. Answer any questions students have about the words and concepts of the excerpts. Then have students work individually or in pairs to answer the questions that follow.

See page 537D for other online activities.

ANSWER, p. 553

✓ PROGRESS CHECK Freemen paid nobles for the right to farm their land and could move around as they wished. Serfs were tied to the manor. Freemen had legal rights, while the rights of serfs were restricted. Freemen and serfs were below the lord in the social order.

W Writing Skills

Informative/Explanatory After students have read about trade fairs, have small groups design and write advertisements that merchants might use at a medieval European trade fair. Tell students their ads can be decorative and imaginative, but they also should be true to the age, with descriptions or pictures of products that might have been sold or services that might have been offered during this time period. Post the finished advertisements around the classroom. **Interpersonal**

R Reading Skills

Explaining Direct students to read the section titled "Government in Cities." Then, lead a class discussion about the rise of a middle class in medieval Europe. Explain to students that in the early Middle Ages, there were two main classes. **Ask:**

- **What were the two main classes in the early Middle Ages?** *(the land-owning lords and the peasants, including serfs and freemen)*
- **What factors created the new middle class in Europe?** *(The rise of trade and cities resulted in merchants, bankers, and artisans having some wealth.)*
- **Why did members of the new middle class try to break with the nobles who controlled towns under the feudal system?** *(The people in the towns didn't want to owe taxes and services to nobles. They wanted to be free to manage their own affairs without being ruled by lords of manors.)*

ANSWER, p. 554
CRITICAL THINKING mostly foodstuffs

Scala/Art Resource, NY

Trade was lively in medieval marketplaces with a variety of products for sale.

▶ **CRITICAL THINKING**
Analyzing Visuals What kinds of goods appear to be available at this market?

Meanwhile, Flanders—a region that is today part of Belgium—became a center of trade on Europe's northern coast. Towns in Flanders, such as Bruges and Ghent, were known for wool. Merchants from all over Western Europe traveled to these towns to trade their goods for woolen cloth.

W Trade fairs were established in northern France. At these fairs, northern European merchants bartered their products. They traded furs, tin, honey, and wool for swords and cloth from northern Italy and silks, sugar, and spices from Asia.

As trade increased, merchants demanded payment in gold and silver coins. People again began using money to buy goods. Some merchants set up banks.

Government in Cities

R The rise of trade and cities created a new middle class in medieval Europe. People in the middle class had some wealth as a result of their roles as merchants, bankers, or artisans. They became important leaders in the cities.

Eventually, medieval towns began to set up their own governments. Only males were considered citizens. In many cities, the citizens elected the members of a city council. These elected officials served as lawmakers and judges.

Under the feudal system, towns were often part of the territory belonging to a noble. As a result, nobles tried to control town affairs. Townspeople, however, disliked owing taxes and services to nobles. They wanted freedom to make their own

Reading HELPDESK (CCSS)

guild a group of merchants or craftspeople

networks *Online Teaching Options*

IMAGE

Trade in Medieval Marketplaces

Analyzing Images Display the image of a medieval marketplace on the whiteboard, and encourage students to look at the details in the painting. **Ask: Why types of items were being sold in the marketplace?** *(Answers will vary but may include the following: fruit, vegetables, bread, shoes, crafts)* **Today, what do we have that is similar to a Medieval Marketplace?** *(Answers will vary; students may suggest Farmer's Markets, Craft Fairs, or even grocery stores. Encourage them to support their idea with details from the images.)*

See page 537D for other online activities.

laws. As their wealth increased, townspeople forced nobles to grant them basic rights. These included the right to buy and sell property and the freedom from having to serve in the army.

What Did Guilds Do?

Trade encouraged townspeople to produce many different kinds of products. Craftspeople organized **guilds**, or business groups. Each craft had its own guild.

Guilds controlled business and trade in a town. The guild set the price for a product or service. Guilds also set and enforced standards of quality for products.

R

In addition, guilds decided who could join a trade. An apprentice, or trainee, learned a trade from a master artisan who provided room and board but no wages. After completing this training, the apprentice became a journeyman who worked under a master for a daily wage.

Life in a Medieval City

Medieval cities were surrounded by stone walls. Inside the walls, stone public buildings and wooden houses were jammed close together. Candles and fireplaces were used for light and heat.

Towns could be unhealthy places. Wood and coal fires in people's homes and shops filled the air with ashes and smoke. Sewers were open, and there was little concern for cleanliness.

City women kept house, cared for children, and managed the family's money. Wives often helped their husbands in their trade, sometimes carrying on the trade after their husbands' deaths.

✓ PROGRESS CHECK

Analyzing How did guilds affect the way medieval townspeople made a living?

Thinking Like a HISTORIAN

Researching Using Internet Resources

One of England's earliest historians was Bede. Bede (A.D. 673–735) was an educated monk who lived in northern England. He wrote the *Ecclesiastical History of the English People*, using the Latin language. Use the Internet to find reliable copies or selections from Bede's history. Choose three facts you discover about English history and present them to your class. For more information about using sources, review *What Does a Historian Do?*

LESSON 2 REVIEW CCSS

Review Vocabulary (Tier 3 Words)

1. What was a *fief*? RH.6–8.2, RH.6–8.4

Answer the Guiding Questions

2. ***Describing*** Draw a chart to show the major parts of a medieval manor. RH.6–8.2
3. ***Summarizing*** What impact did the code of chivalry have on knights during the Middle Ages? RH.6–8.2
4. ***Identifying Cause and Effect*** What explains the development of cities and towns during the Middle Ages? RH.6–8.2, RH.6–8.5
5. ***Drawing Conclusions*** If you were a person in business in medieval Europe, why would membership in a guild be important to you? RH.6–8.2
6. **INFORMATIVE/EXPLANATORY** What new inventions allowed people in Western Europe to grow more food during the Middle Ages? What was the result of this increase in food production? WHST.6–8.2, WHST.6–8.10

LESSON 2 REVIEW ANSWERS

1. A fief was a property granted to a vassal by a lord.
2. Charts should show the lord's manor house or castle at the center of the manor, the nearby village populated by freemen and serfs, and the surrounding fields, where crops were cultivated.
3. Chivalry had a great impact on knights because it was a code of behavior. For example, knights had to be brave, obey their lords, help people, respect women of noble birth, and honor the Church.
4. Growth in trade was the most important factor in the development of cities and towns during the Middle Ages. Increased trade allowed some townspeople to become wealthy and powerful enough to demand their rights from the nobles. Trade also was the reason many people left the farms to live and work in cities and towns.
5. Membership in a guild would be important because guilds, or trade and crafts associations, had a monopoly on the business of artisans and craftsmen. They controlled the setting of prices, the establishment of standards, and the rules by which apprentices were allowed to join the business.
6. Inventions included improved plows, the horse collar, and crop rotation. The effect of increased food production was growth in the population.

R Reading Skills

Listing Explain to students that making lists while reading can help them identify important ideas in a text, help show a sequence of events, or isolate supporting details. Have students review the text and ask them to list four functions that guilds performed in a medieval town. *(Guilds controlled business and trade, set the price for a product or service, set and enforced standards of quality, and decided who could join a trade.)* AL

Content Background Knowledge

Guilds Guilds in the Middle Ages were of two basic types: merchant guilds and craft guilds. Merchant guilds arose first. They were associations of most or all of the merchants in a town, including retailers, wholesalers, and importers/exporters. In most towns, the guild charged an entrance fee for merchants to join. Merchant guilds also limited membership to the inhabitants of the town. Historians believe they might have begun as a means of protecting traveling peddlers from bandits. They gradually evolved into broader associations as trade became centralized in towns.

Craft guilds developed in response to the gradual division of labor. Individuals or family workshops that did similar work joined together to improve distribution, working conditions, and profits. Craft guild members were organized into three groups: masters (at the highest level), journeymen (middle level), and apprentices (beginners). Journeymen and apprentices underwent long periods of training and learning. Once the craftspeople could produce a work that met the approval of guild masters, they could gain membership in the guild.

Have students complete the Lesson 2 Review.

CLOSE & REFLECT

Explaining To close the lesson, lead students in a discussion of life in a feudal society. Ask students to consider the answers they gave at the beginning of the lesson about whether they would want to have lived in medieval times. If they have changed their minds, ask them to explain why. Make sure students use the lesson's vocabulary words in their answers. Review the meanings of vocabulary words, if necessary.

ANSWER, p. 555

✓ PROGRESS CHECK Guilds controlled all business and trade. They decided the price for products and services, set standards for quality, and established who could join a trade and the steps that a new tradesman had to follow.

ENGAGE

Bellringer Project a map of medieval Europe on the whiteboard. Show students how the continent is divided into many different kingdoms, states, and empires. Point out that medieval France and England were not countries with strong unified governments, as they are today.

Ask: What would life be like if no central government and no laws existed? Allow students one or two minutes to quick write a response. Ask volunteers to share their answers. Make sure students understand how laws protect people. Laws guarantee that people with power do not take advantage of those with less power.

Tell students that in this lesson they will learn about important political developments in Europe, ones that established rights and laws.

TEACH & ASSESS

R Reading Skills

Identifying After students have read the text, lead a class discussion about the early rulers of England. **Ask:**

- Who united England? *(Alfred the Great)*
- Which European noble conquered England in 1066? *(William the Conqueror)*
- Which king of England halted the Viking advance? *(Alfred the Great)*
- Which English ruler was also the Duke of Normandy? *(William the Conqueror)*
- Which king of England came from France? *(William the Conqueror)* AL

ANSWER, p. 556

TAKING NOTES: Answers may include some or all of the following: Byzantine Empire is attacked by Turks; Pope agrees to help and calls for First Crusade; Pope promises salvation to those who die in battle; European Christians seize Jerusalem; Muslims conquer part of crusader states; Later crusades fail to recapture territory; Crusades result in a wider European worldview; Crusades help break down feudalism in Europe.

networks
There's More Online!

- GRAPHIC ORGANIZER Causes and Effects of the Crusades
- PRIMARY SOURCE Magna Carta

Lesson 3
Kingdoms and Crusades

ESSENTIAL QUESTION *How do governments change?*

IT MATTERS BECAUSE
The development of law and government during the Middle Ages in Europe still affects us today.

Royal Power in England

GUIDING QUESTION ***How was the king's power strengthened and then limited in medieval England?***

In the late 800s, Vikings from Scandinavia attacked Britain, where the Anglo-Saxons had founded many small kingdoms. King Alfred of Wessex, later known as Alfred the Great, united the Anglo-Saxons and halted the Viking advance. The kingdom that Alfred united became known as "Angleland," or England.

Alfred ruled England from A.D. 871 to 899. Unfortunately for England, the Anglo-Saxon kings who followed Alfred were generally weak rulers.

William the Conqueror

R In 1066, the last Anglo-Saxon king of England died without an heir. A noble named Harold Godwinson claimed the English throne. In France, a relative of the Anglo-Saxon kings, William, Duke of Normandy (NAWR•muhn•dee), said that he, not Harold, was the rightful king of England.

In the fall of 1066, William and his army of Norman knights landed in England. They defeated Harold and his foot soldiers at the Battle of Hastings. William was crowned king of England and became known as William the Conqueror.

Reading **HELP**DESK CCSS

Taking Notes: *Sequencing* RH.6–8.2
Complete a sequence diagram like this one to show the causes and effects of the Crusades.

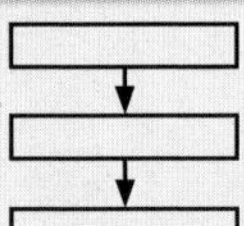

Content Vocabulary (Tier 3 Words)
- **grand jury**
- **trial jury**

networks ***Online Teaching Options***

VIDEO

Castles: The Center of Power

Discussing Before playing the video about European castles, explain that this video will show the importance of castles throughout Europe during the Middle Ages. Have students take notes while watching the video. Then organize students into small groups and have them discuss the information they found interesting. Then come back together for a whole-class discussion about medieval castles. Call on each group to read the points they identified during their discussion.

See page 537E for other online activities.

At first, the Anglo-Saxons resisted William's rule. To stop the Anglo-Saxon revolts, William seized the land of Anglo-Saxon nobles and divided it among his Norman knights.

William wanted to learn as much as possible about his new kingdom. To decide taxes, he carried out the first census since Roman times. Every person, and farm animal in England was counted and recorded in the *Domesday Book*. **C**

The Normans who ruled England kept many Anglo-Saxon laws and practices. However, they also brought many customs from mainland Europe. Under William's rule, officials and nobles in England spoke French, the language of Normandy. They built castles, cathedrals, and monasteries in the Norman style. Anglo-Saxons learned new skills from Norman weavers and artisans. Yet, they still spoke their own Anglo-Saxon language, which later became English. As more and more Normans and Anglo-Saxons married, their customs merged into a new English culture. **R**

Henry II

After the death of William, English kings further strengthened their power. From 1154 to 1189, King Henry II ruled England as well as most of Wales, and Ireland. He was also a feudal lord in France and Scotland. Some of the French lands belonged to his wife, Queen Eleanor of Aquitaine.

Henry set up a central royal court with lawyers and judges. Circuit judges, who traveled across the country to hear cases, brought the king's law to all parts of England.

Tom Lovell/National Geographic Society Image Collection

At the Battle of Hastings, William the Conqueror led Norman knights on horseback as well as infantry to attack the English foot soldiers.

▶ CRITICAL THINKING
Identifying Points of View Why did William believe that he was the rightful king of England?

C Critical Thinking Skills

Making Inferences Discuss with students the *Domesday Book* that William had compiled. **Ask:**

- **Why did William take the census?** *(to determine taxes)*
- **What information was recorded in the Domesday Book?** *(every person and farm animal in England)*
- **Why would taking a census help determine who paid taxes?** *(By collecting information about everyone in England, no one could escape paying taxes. Recording every farm animal was one way to determine each person's worth. With that information, authorities could collect taxes fairly.)* BL

R Reading Skills

Discussing Direct students to read the text. Then discuss the changes the Norman conquest made to English culture. **Ask:**

- **Under William's rule, what language did officials and nobles in England speak?** *(French)*
- **What types of buildings were built in the Norman style?** *(castles, cathedrals, and monasteries)*
- **How did French and English customs eventually merge into a new culture?** *(through the marriages of Normans and Anglo-Saxons)*

Content Background Knowledge

The Domesday Book The survey, or census, that resulted in the *Domesday Book* was carried out in 1086. The comprehensive nature of the survey led many to compare it to the Last Judgment as described in the Bible, commonly called "Doomsday" (*Domesday* in old English). The census collected information about the landowners, the land they owned, the people who lived on the land, the buildings on the land, the woodland, animals, fish, and plows on the land, and the value of the land. The census was carried out by royal commissioners, who were sent around England with a set of questions for representatives of each area. The collected information was then recorded in Latin. The final version of the *Domesday Book* was handwritten in Latin by one scribe. The main book, called the *Great Domesday*, is 413 pages long. A second book, with information from three English counties, is 475 pages long. The original *Domesday Book* is kept in the British National Archives in London.

BIOGRAPHY

William the Conqueror

Drawing Conclusions Project the biography of William the Conqueror onto the whiteboard, and ask a volunteer to read aloud the text beside the picture of William. Remind students that they can scroll down the right side to access the complete text. **Ask: At the Battle of Hastings, what advantage did the Norman knights have over the English foot soldiers?** *(The Norman knights were on horseback.)*

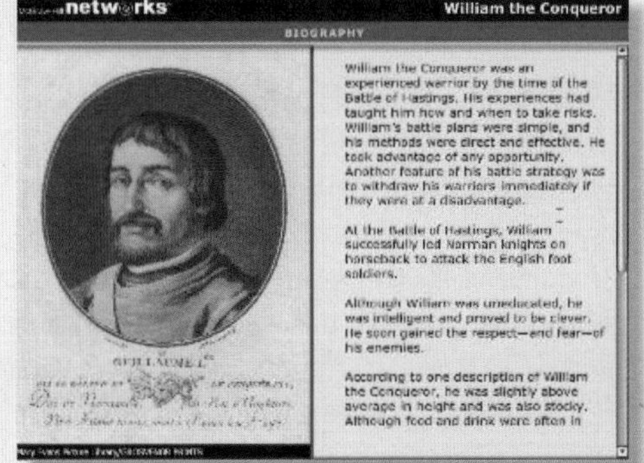

See page 537E for other online activities.

ANSWER, p. 557

CRITICAL THINKING The throne had been taken over by a nobleman, but William was related to the Anglo-Saxon kings.

R Reading Skills

Explaining Have students read the section titled "The Magna Carta and Parliament." Then, guide a class discussion about the events leading up to the signing of the Magna Carta. **Ask:**

- Why did English nobles rebel against King John? *(They did not like increased taxes or being punished without a trial.)*
- What do the words *Magna Carta* mean? *(Great Charter)*
- What did the Magna Carta do? *(limited the king's power)*
- Why was this important to the nobles? *(Students should suggest that the nobles did not want the king to have absolute power, and they wanted a voice in their government.)*

C Critical Thinking Skills

Determining Cause and Effect Explain that the Magna Carta placed limits on the English king's powers, and it forced the king to follow the same rules and laws as everyone else. **Ask:**

- How did the nobles get King John to sign the Magna Carta? *(They joined together. Together they had more power than the king.)*
- How did the Magna Carta change the way kings ruled England? *(They had to respect the rights of freemen and obey laws. They could not rule by whim.)* AL

Making Connections

The distinction between a grand jury and a trial jury set up in medieval England by Henry II holds today in the United States. In U.S. federal courts, a *grand jury* is composed of 23 members who listen to evidence presented by prosecutors and then determine whether a crime has been committed and whether someone should be charged. The charge against someone is called an *indictment*. A *trial jury*, also called a *petit jury*, hears cases in both criminal and civil cases. In criminal cases, the jury decides guilt or innocence. In the federal system, a grand jury is composed of 23 members, while a trial jury is composed of 6 to 12 members.

ANSWER, p. 558

PROGRESS CHECK The law courts of King Henry II helped create a body of common law, which replaced laws that differed from place to place.

The courts created a body of common law, or law that was the same throughout the whole kingdom. Common law helped unite England by replacing laws that differed from place to place.

Henry also set up juries of citizens to settle disputes. Traveling circuit judges met with a **grand jury.** It decided if people should be accused of a crime. Next came a **trial jury** to decide whether a person was innocent or guilty.

The Magna Carta and Parliament

Henry's son John became king of England in 1199. King John increased taxes in England and punished his enemies without trials. English nobles began to rebel against the king.

In 1215, the nobles met with King John at Runnymede, a nearby meadow. There they forced John to put his seal on a **document** called the Magna Carta, or the Great Charter. The Magna Carta placed limits on the king's power. The king could collect taxes only if a group of nobles called the Great Council agreed. R

The Magna Carta also forced the king to uphold the rights of freemen, including the right to fair trials by jury:

PRIMARY SOURCE

> "No free man shall be taken, imprisoned, disseised [seized], outlawed, banished [sent away], or in any way destroyed, nor will We proceed against or prosecute him, except by the lawful judgment of his peers [equals] and by the law of the land." C
>
> —from the *Magna Carta*, 1215

King John signed the Magna Carta, a document that brought significant change to England.

The Magna Carta relied on the feudal idea that the king and his noble vassals both had certain rights and duties. Over time, however, the Magna Carta helped strengthen the idea that all people, regardless of rank, have rights, and that the power of government should be limited.

Edward I, king of England in the late 1200s, increased the authority of his council. This group of lords, church leaders, knights, and townspeople became known as Parliament (PAHR•luh•muhnt). Parliament came to be divided into two groups—an upper house and lower house. The growth of Parliament marked an important step toward representative government.

PROGRESS CHECK

Explaining How did the common law help unite England?

Bettmann/CORBIS

Reading HELPDESK CCSS

grand jury a group of citizens that meets to decide whether people should be accused of a crime
trial jury a group of citizens that decides whether an accused person is innocent or guilty

Academic Vocabulary (Tier 2)
document an original or official paper used as the basis or proof of something

Building Vocabulary: *Word Origins*
The English word *Parliament* comes from the French word *parler*, meaning to talk or converse. Parliament was where people could talk about problems or concerns facing the kingdom.

networks Online Teaching Options

PRIMARY SOURCE

The Magna Carta and the U.S. Bill of Rights

Comparing and Contrasting Show students the table comparing the Magna Carta with the Bill of Rights in the U.S. Constitution. Ask a student to read aloud each section of the table. **Ask:** What do these documents say about religion? *(The Magna Carta says the English Church shall be free. The Bill of Rights says the government cannot create a state church, and it protects freedom of religion.)* What similar legal rights do they provide? *(Both require due process of law before a person can be convicted of a crime, both ban unreasonable seizures of property, and both prohibit excessive fines.)*

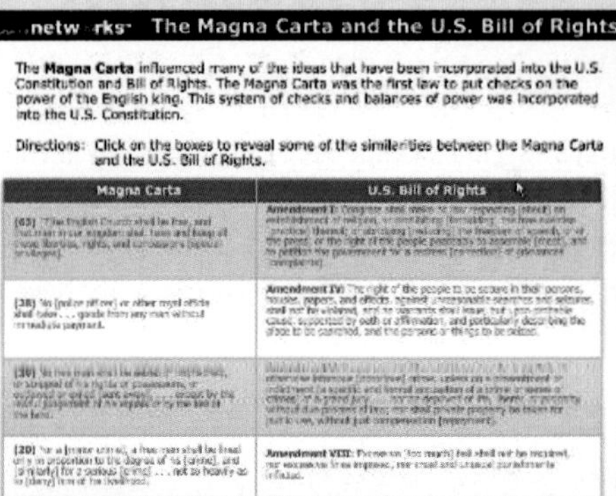
networks The Magna Carta and the U.S. Bill of Rights

The Magna Carta influenced many of the ideas that have been incorporated into the U.S. Constitution and Bill of Rights. The Magna Carta was the first law to put checks on the power of the English king. This system of checks and balances of power was incorporated into the U.S. Constitution.

Directions: Click on the boxes to reveal some of the similarities between the Magna Carta and the U.S. Bill of Rights.

Magna Carta	U.S. Bill of Rights
[illegible]	[illegible]
[illegible]	[illegible]
[illegible]	[illegible]
[illegible]	[illegible]

See page 537E for other online activities.

Monarchy in France

GUIDING QUESTION ***How did the kings of France increase their power?***

In 843, Charlemagne's empire was split into three parts. The western part became the kingdom of France. In 987, the west Frankish nobles made Hugh Capet their king. Hugh began the Capetian (kuh•PEE•shuhn) dynasty of French kings. Capetian kings controlled only the area around Paris, the capital. Many French nobles had more power than the kings did. This began to change when Philip II became the king of France in 1180.

Philip worked to expand the French monarchy's wealth and power. At the beginning of Philip's reign, the king of England ruled feudal lands in western France. Philip fought wars against the English and gained some of these territories.

Philip IV wanted to raise taxes to pay for his wars. In 1302, he gained approval for this plan from representatives of the three estates, or classes, of French society. The first estate was the clergy, or priests. Nobles made up the second estate, and townspeople and peasants were the third estate. This meeting began the Estates-General, France's first parliament. The Estates-General never became as powerful as Parliament in England. **R**

✓ PROGRESS CHECK

Comparing and Contrasting How was the Estates-General of France different from England's Parliament?

GEOGRAPHY CONNECTION

In 1160, Europe was divided into many small kingdoms and states.

1. **LOCATION** Which empire bordered Hungary to the south?
2. CRITICAL THINKING ***Analyzing*** What was the effect of having many small states ruled by French nobles?

V

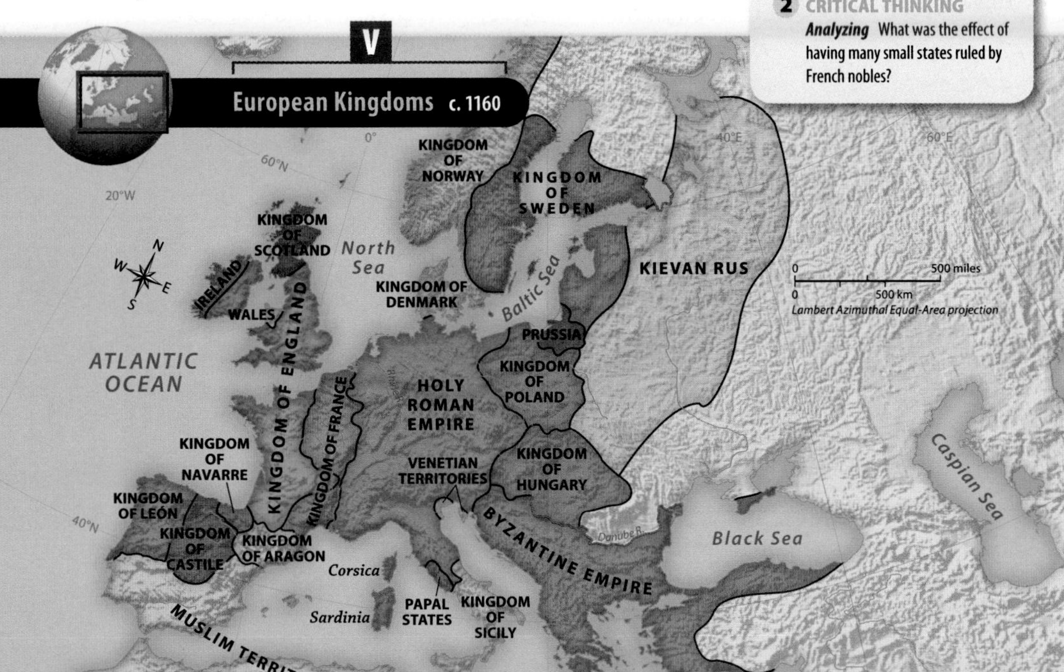

MAP

European Kingdoms c. 1160

Making Connections Display the interactive map on the whiteboard, unclicking the button for the modern-day boundaries so that only the medieval kingdoms show. Help students recognize the distinctions between the medieval kingdoms. Then click on the button to turn on the boundaries of modern-day countries. **Ask:** **What kingdoms extended into the area of modern-day France?** *(Kingdom of England, Kingdom of France, Holy Roman Empire)* **Which modern day country was home to the Kingdom of Castille?** *(Spain)* **Which territory was in both Europe and Africa?** *(Muslim Territory)*

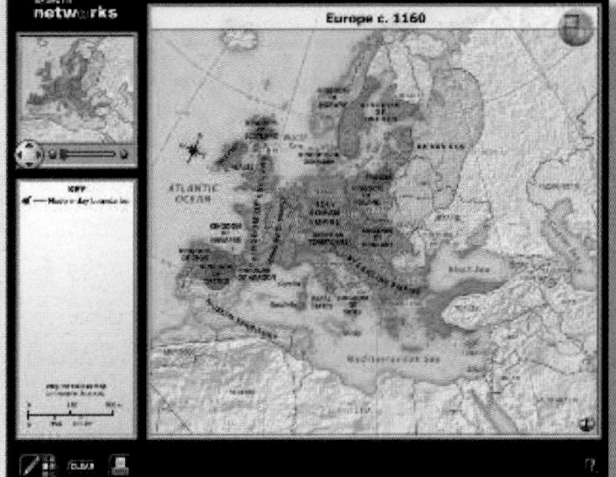

See page 537E for other online activities.

R Reading Skills

Stating Ask students to read the text about three estates of France. After discussing "Monarchy in France," **ask:** **What change in government did the Estates-General represent?** *(It was France's first parliament and the country's first step toward representative government.)* Tell students that the classification of the three estates is still sometimes referred to today. **Ask:** **In which of the three estates would you, as a student, be categorized? Why?** *(the third estate, because students are neither priests nor nobles)*

V Visual Skills

Reading a Map Have students study the map of European kingdoms at the bottom of the page. Make sure they notice the title, the compass rose, and the scale. Pose the following questions to help students interpret the information on the map. **Ask:**

- **How can you tell where one kingdom stops and another begins?** *(Each kingdom is shown in a different color.)* AL
- **Which European kingdom is in the most northern part of of the map?** *(Kingdom of Norway)*
- **Why does the Kingdom of England extend outside of the British Isles?** *(William the Conqueror from Normandy conquered England in 1066, and so the Kingdom of England included both England and Normandy.)* BL
- **What empire is the largest?** *(Keivan Rus)*

Visual/Spatial

ANSWERS, p. 559

GEOGRAPHY CONNECTION

1. The Byzantine Empire lies to the south of Hungary.
2. CRITICAL THINKING Many French nobles had more power than the kings did.

✓ PROGRESS CHECK France's Estates-General (made up of clergy, nobles, and townspeople and peasants) never became as powerful as England's Parliament did, because the kings of France ruled with a firm hand.

T Technology Skills

Researching on the Internet Ask small groups of students to use an Internet search engine to learn more about the life and accomplishments of Vladimir the Great, ruler of Kiev. Encourage the group to locate images and basic information about his life, such how long he ruled and how he is remembered today in Kiev. Have these students put together a short presentation to share with the rest of the class. **BL** **Interpersonal**

R Reading Skills

Identifying Have students refer to "Eastern States of the Slavs" in their textbooks. Then start a class discussion about this topic. **Ask:**

- **How were the groups of Slavs divided?** *(They were divided by the area they lived in—the southern, western, and eastern regions.)*
- **How did the city of Kiev become wealthy?** *(from trade with Scandanavia and the Byzantine Empire)*
- **What was the only Slavic city to be spared from attack by the Mongols?** *(Novgorod)*

Eastern States of the Slavs

GUIDING QUESTION ***How did the cities of Kiev and Moscow become centers of powerful Slavic states?***

In Eastern Europe, people called the Slavs established villages and towns along the rivers of that region. The Slavs consisted of three important groups: the southern Slavs, the western Slavs, and the eastern Slavs.

The Rise of Kiev

In the 800s, the eastern Slavs began to expand the city of Kiev (KEE•EHF). The medieval state of Kievan Rus grew wealthy from its river trade with Scandinavia and the Byzantine Empire.

In 988, the Rus ruler, Vladimir, married the sister of the Byzantine emperor. Vladimir became an Eastern Orthodox Christian. Soon, priests from Constantinople came to teach the people of Kievan Rus religious rituals and the art of painting icons.

Mongol Invaders

About 1240, Mongol warriors from Central Asia conquered Kievan Rus. The Slavic city of Novgorod was the only major city to be spared attack by the Mongols. However, Novgorod's rulers had to pay tribute to the khan, the Mongol leader, and accept the Mongols as their rulers.

Although the Mongols spared Novgorod, the city faced attacks from the west by Germans and Swedes. In 1240, Novgorod forces led by a prince named Alexander Nevsky (NEHV•skee) defeated these invaders.

Mongol warriors attacked towns and cities on horseback and had a reputation for being more hostile than previous invaders. The image below is from a film that recreated the Mongol invasions.

ANDREEVSKY FLAG FILM CO / KINOFABRIKA/KINOKOMPANIYA CTB/X-FILME CREATIVE POOL/Ronald Grant Arc/Mary Evans Picture Library

Reading HELPDESK (CCSS)

Academic Vocabulary (Tier 2 Words)

cooperate to work together with

Reading Strategy: *Making Connections*

As you read, try to link new information in your reading to what you already know.

networks *Online Teaching Options*

IMAGE

Batu and the Golden Horde

Explaining Project the interactive image on the whiteboard, and click on "more information" to display the text. Explain to students that the photo is from a recent movie about the Mongol invasions of Europe. Ask a volunteer to read the text about Batu to the class. Then discuss how the Mongol Rulers maintained power in Russia for more than 200 years. Tell students that they will learn more about the Black Death in Lesson 5.

See page 537E for other online activities.

networks
Batu and the Golden Horde
Batu was a Mongol ruler. He was Genghis Khan's grandson. Batu and his warriors invaded Europe starting in 1235, taking control of Russia, Hungary, Poland, and Bohemia. Batu then established the Golden Horde, which was a state in Russia. Mongol rulers remained in Russia as part of the Golden Horde for more than 200 years. The Black Death that swept Europe weakened the Golden Horde, and the Horde was destroyed completely in 1502.

V

Growth of Moscow 1300–1505

ARCTIC OCEAN
20°E 30°E 40°E 50°E 60°E 70°E 80°E
70°N
60°N

KEY
Moscow, 1300
Acquisitions:
Land added by 1340
Land added by 1389
Land added by 1425
Land added by 1462
Land added by 1505

Lake Ladoga
Lake Onega
Ustyug
Vologda
Novgorod
Galich
Volga R.
Vladimir
Volokolamsk
Moscow
Kasimov
Tula
0 200 miles
0 200 km
Lambert Azimuthal Equal-Area projection

GEOGRAPHY CONNECTION

Like Kievan Rus, Moscow grew in power and wealth because of its location along trade routes.

1. **LOCATION** Use the scale on the map. About how far is Novgorod from Moscow?
2. **CRITICAL THINKING** ***Analyzing Visuals*** During which period did Moscow add the greatest amount of land to its territory?

The Importance of Moscow

During the period of Mongol rule, many Slavs moved north from Kiev and built settlements in the area that is now Russia. One new settlement was Moscow (MAHS•KOH). Moscow became a large city that prospered because it was at the crossroads of several major trade routes.

R The rulers of Moscow learned to **cooperate** with the Mongols. In return, the Mongols gave them the right to collect taxes from other Slav territories. If a territory could not provide soldiers or tax money, Moscow's rulers took control of it. In this way, Moscow was able to gradually expand its territory.

Ivan III Becomes Czar

C Ivan III became the ruler of Moscow in 1462. He married Sophia, a niece of the Byzantine emperor. Ivan adopted the lavish style of Byzantine rulers and was referred to as czar. The Russian word *czar*, like *Caesar* in Latin, means "emperor."

By 1480, Ivan III had finally driven the Mongols from Moscow and Russian territory. He turned next to the north and west to add territory. By then, the people of Moscow, now known as Russians, had made great strides toward establishing a huge empire.

Ivan III's reign focused on expanding the Russian empire. During his rule, the Russian territory tripled in size.

✓ **PROGRESS CHECK**

Determining Cause and Effect Why did the rulers of Moscow work with the Mongols?

MAP

Growth of Moscow, 1300–1505

Reading a Map Display the interactive map on the whiteboard with only the red area turned on (Moscow, 1300). Have students briefly examine the map and then click on the arrow below the map to play the audio. **Ask:** **Whom did the leaders of Moscow cooperate with to expand their territory?** *(the Mongols)* Then click on the rest of the buttons in turn to display the growth of Moscow in stages between 1300 and 1505. **Ask:** **Is Moscow still in existence today?** *(Yes, but it is a single city, not a large empire.)*

See page 537E for other online activities.

V Visual Skills

Analyzing Maps Turn students' attention to the map of the growth of Moscow. **Ask:**

- **How many years does this map cover?** *(the 200 years from 1300 to 1500)*
- **What does the word *Acquisitions* mean in the key to the map?** *(land area gained)*
- **What natural barrier to the north of Moscow prevented the rulers of Moscow from gaining more land in that direction?** *(the Arctic Ocean)*
- **In what period of time did Moscow grow the most?** *(from 1462 to 1505)*
- **Why do you think most of the growth of Moscow was to the north?** *(Answers will vary. Students should infer that lands to the south were probably held by more powerful kingdoms than in the north.)* **Visual/Spatial**

R Reading Skills

Defining Direct students' attention to the term *cooperate* in their textbooks. Ask for a volunteer to define the word. *(to act or work with another or others)* ELL **Ask:** **Why did the rulers of Moscow cooperate with the Mongols?** *(so the Mongols would give them special privileges to collect taxes and acquire land)* **What happened to Moscow as a result of this cooperation?** *(The city expanded and flourished as it grew.)*

C Critical Thinking Skills

Making Inferences Explain that the royalty of Europe often married for political reasons. **Ask:** **What would Ivan III have gained for Moscow in marrying the niece of the Byzantine emperor?** *(Answers will vary, but students should suggest that such a marriage would help forge an alliance between Moscow and the larger Byzantine Empire to its south. Such a marriage might smooth relations between the two kingdoms and might also gain an ally for Moscow in the event of a war breaking out.)* BL

ANSWERS, p. 561

GEOGRAPHY CONNECTION

1. Novgorod is about 300 miles (500 km) northwest of Moscow.
2. **CRITICAL THINKING** Moscow acquired the greatest amount of land in the period 1462–1505.

✓ **PROGRESS CHECK** because in return for their cooperation, the Mongols gave the rulers of Moscow the right to collect taxes from other Slavic territories

Kingdoms and Crusades

V Visual Skills

Reading a Map Have students study the map of the Crusades at the top of the page. Then pose these questions to help students better understand the map. **Ask:**

- How close were the Christian lands to the Muslim lands? *(They bordered one another in Asia Minor.)* AL
- Who held more land during this time period, the Christians or the Muslims? *(the Christians)* AL
- All three Crusade routes pass near which river? *(the Danube)*
- Study the routes taken in each of the three Crusades. Which Crusade route was much different from the other two? In what way? *(In the first two Crusades, the Crusaders mostly traveled over land. The Third Crusade was different in that Crusaders mostly traveled on the seas.)* BL Visual/Spatial

C Critical Thinking Skills

Determining Cause and Effect Have students read how the Crusades began. Then **ask:**

- What were two causes of the Crusades? *(Muslim Turks attacked Byzantium, and the emperor asked for help. Muslims would not allow Christians to visit sites in the Holy Land.)*
- What did Pope Urban II hope for when he agreed to help the Byzantines and begin a crusade? *(He hoped that the Eastern Orthodox Church and the Roman Catholic Church would unite under his leadership.)*

V

The Crusades 1096–1204

KEY
- Christian lands, c. 1100
- Muslim lands, c. 1100
- First Crusade, 1096–1099
- Second Crusade, 1147–1149
- Third Crusade, 1189–1192

North Sea, Baltic Sea, ENGLAND, London, ATLANTIC OCEAN, Cologne, HOLY ROMAN EMPIRE, Rhine R., Paris, FRANCE, Clairvaux, Clermont, Venice, Marseille, Genoa, Pisa, SPAIN, ITALY, Rome, Danube R., Black Sea, Caspian Sea, Constantinople, ASIA MINOR, BYZANTINE EMPIRE, Sicily, Antioch, Cyprus, Crete, Tyre, Acre, Jerusalem, PALESTINE, Mediterranean Sea, 40°N, 20°E, 40°E

0 500 miles
0 500 km
Lambert Azimuthal Equal-Area projection

GEOGRAPHY CONNECTION

This map shows that the crusaders came from all over Europe. It also shows the land and sea routes that they took to the Holy Land.

1. **MOVEMENT** On the First Crusade, how did the crusaders from Cologne reach the Holy Land? In what direction did they travel?
2. **CRITICAL THINKING** *Comparing* Which crusade involved the most travel: the First, the Second, or the Third?

European Crusaders

GUIDING QUESTION *Why did Western Europeans go on crusades?*

C

During the 1000s, the Byzantine Empire in the east came under attack. In 1071, an army of Muslim Turks defeated the Byzantines and seized control of most of the Byzantine lands in Asia Minor.

The Byzantine emperor asked Pope Urban II for military aid to save his Christian empire from Muslim forces. The pope agreed to help the Byzantines. He hoped that, in return, the Eastern Orthodox Church would again unite with the Roman Catholic Church and accept him as its religious leader.

In 1095, the pope asked Europe's nobles to begin a crusade, or holy war, against the Muslim Turks. He urged them to capture Jerusalem and free the Holy Land, where Jesus had lived, from the Muslims.

The Crusades Begin

Thousands of European soldiers on horseback and on foot headed east on the First Crusade. They reached Jerusalem in 1099. In a fierce battle with Muslims, they stormed the city.

Reading **HELP**DESK CCSS

Academic Vocabulary (Tier 2 Words)

accurate correct and free from errors

networks ***Online Teaching Options***

SLIDE SHOW

The Crusades

Explaining Provide students with context by explaining that during the Middle Ages, people from every level of society went on pilgrimages, or journeys of faith. Pilgrims would travel from their homes in Europe to the Holy Land in the East. During the Middle Ages, many of these places were under Muslim control. Note that conflicts between Christians and Muslim Turks led to the Crusades. **Ask:** What stands out to you about the Crusades after seeing the slides? *(Student answers may include that the Crusades were bloody and violent.)*

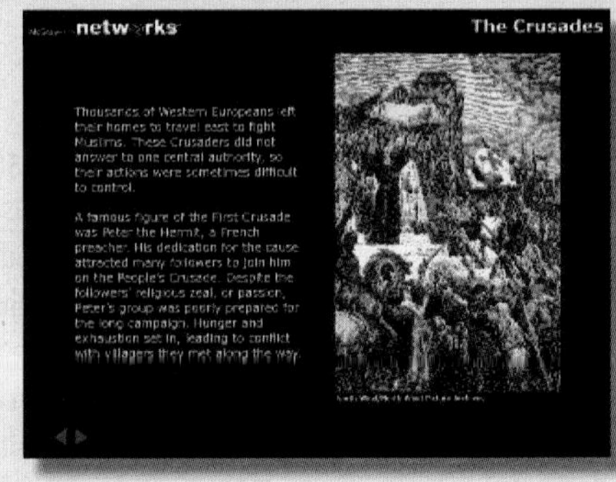

See page 537E for other online activities.

ANSWERS, p. 562

GEOGRAPHY CONNECTION

1. They traveled overland in a generally southeast direction.
2. **CRITICAL THINKING** The Third Crusade involved the most travel.

The crusaders conquered several regions. They set up four states controlled by Europe: the Kingdom of Jerusalem in the Holy Land, Edessa and Antioch in Asia Minor, and Tripoli in what is now Lebanon. These states were surrounded by Muslim territory. They depended on supplies from the Italian cities of Genoa, Pisa, and Venice.

W

Continued Conflicts

After Muslim forces retook Edessa, the Second Crusade began. This time, the Muslims easily defeated the Europeans. In 1174, led by a brilliant general named Saladin (SA•luh•DEEN), Muslims recaptured Jerusalem.

This action triggered the Third Crusade, which was also a failure. Throughout the 1200s, Europeans continued to organize crusades. They made few gains. By the end of the century, the Muslims had regained all the land conquered by the crusaders.

Many Crusaders wore red crosses on their tunics to show they were risking their lives in support of Christianity and the pope.

The Effects of the Crusades

C

The Crusades brought Western Europeans into contact with Byzantines and Muslims. As a result, Western Europeans gained new knowledge. In architecture, they learned how to build domes and create mosaics. They discovered how to build better ships and make more **accurate** maps. They also learned how to use the compass to tell direction. Wealthy people in Western Europe began to demand eastern goods such as spices, sugar, lemons, and silk.

The Crusades, however, weakened feudalism. Nobles who joined the Crusades sold their lands and freed their serfs. This reduced their power. Kings were able to build stronger central governments.

The Crusades lasted over a period of more than two hundred years. They caused bitter feelings between Christian Western Europe and the Islamic world.

PROGRESS CHECK

Determining Cause and Effect What was one way the Crusades changed Christian Europe?

LESSON 3 REVIEW

Review Vocabulary (Tier 3 Words)

1. How is a *grand jury* different from a *trial jury?* RH.6–8.2, RH.6–8.4

Answer the Guiding Questions

2. ***Explaining*** How did the Magna Carta limit the power of the king of England? RH.6–8.2
3. ***Describing*** How did royal power in England progress from William to Henry II to John to Edward I? RH.6–8.2
4. ***Describing*** How did the cities of Kiev and Moscow become centers of powerful Slavic states? RH.6–8.2
5. ***Identifying Cause and Effect*** Why did Western Europeans go on Crusades? RH.6–8.2, RH.6–8.5
6. **INFORMATIVE/EXPLANATORY** Write a paragraph discussing how the Crusades affected feudalism. WHST.6–8.2, WHST.6–8.10

W Writing Skills

Narrative Organize the class into small groups, and ask each group to compose new lyrics to a song they already know to tell a story about the Crusades. It could be a tune from the radio, a folk tune, a hymn, or even the school's fight song. The lyrics might be a call to action, a story about a battle, or a mournful remembrance of fallen comrades. Ask that members of each group write one or two verses. After groups have finished, invite students to share their songs with the class. Discuss how each song relates to the Crusades of the Middle Ages. **Auditory/ Musical Interpersonal**

C Critical Thinking Skills

Identifying Points of View Lead the class in a discussion about the Europeans' reasons for fighting in the Crusades. Then consider the Muslims' reasons for fighting the European crusaders. **Ask:**

- **Why was each side fighting?** *(Each side thought it was defending its religion. Both sides were also fighting over territory, including the Holy Land and the entire Byzantine Empire.)*
- **What were three effects of the Crusades?** *(Answers should include that Europeans gained a larger worldview, rediscovered lost knowledge, and began trade with the East. Also, feudalism broke down.)*

Have students complete the Lesson 3 Review.

CLOSE & REFLECT

Comparing and Contrasting To close the lesson, lead students in a discussion of the similarities and differences between the changes in government that took place in England, in France, and in the Eastern states. Ask them to consider who held power in each country and what rights the citizens of those countries possessed.

LESSON 3 REVIEW ANSWERS

1. A grand jury decides whether people should be accused of a crime. A trial jury decides whether an accused person is innocent or guilty.
2. In 1215, English nobles forced King John to sign the Magna Carta, which set limits on the king's power. It set limits on the king's ability to impose taxes and forced him to recognize the rights of the people.
3. William the Conqueror conquered England and created the Domesday Book; Henry II brought common law to England; John signed the Magna Carta; and Edward I established the English Parliament.
4. Kiev prospered from river trade between Scandinavia and the Byzantine Empire. Moscow was located at the crossroads of several major trade routes. In addition, Moscow cooperated with the Mongols, who gave the rulers of Moscow the right to collect taxes from other Slavic territories.
5. The pope agreed to help the Byzantines. He urged Western Europeans to liberate Jerusalem from Muslim rule. He promised those who might die in battle that they would gain immediate forgiveness for their sins.
6. Essays should mention that the Crusades weakened feudalism. Nobles who joined the Crusades sold their lands, thereby reducing their power, which allowed kings to build stronger central governments.

ANSWER, p. 563

PROGRESS CHECK Answers will vary. The split between Eastern and Western Christians became permanent. Western Europeans came into contact with cultured Byzantines and Muslims and developed a larger view of the world. They gained new knowledge of ancient texts and learned new building skills. The demand in Europe for luxury goods began to grow.

Culture and the Church

ENGAGE

Bellringer Show students an image of a medieval church, such as the Chartres Cathedral in France. Invite students to share their impressions. **Ask:** What words describe the building? *(Answers may include large, brick or stone, heavy, massive, or sharp-edged.)* Use the structure to illustrate the point that change and innovation occurred during the Middle Ages, although often slowly compared to today. Tell students that in this lesson, they will learn how European ideas about architecture and education changed. They will also learn about new institutions within the Catholic Church and how they affected Europeans.

TEACH & ASSESS

R Reading Skills

Determining Word Meanings Ask for a volunteer to read the first paragraph on this page aloud. Point out to the class that by the 1100s, Europeans were more confident and secure. Focus students' attention on the word *secure*. **Ask:**

- In this context, what does the word *secure* mean? *(Answers will vary, although students should mention that in this context, secure means "free from danger" or "free from risk or loss.")* AL ELL
- Why would the Crusades and strong governments have made medieval Europeans feel secure? *(Answers will vary. Students might suggest that the attacks against the Muslim armies in the Crusades made Europe safe from attack from the east and that strong governments brought law and order to Europe.)*

T Technology Skills

Making Presentations Ask students to use an Internet search engine to find and collect images of medieval European buildings in both the Romanesque style and the Gothic style. For each image that students collect, they should note the architectural style, the location of the building, and about when it was built. Ask these students to make a presentation to the class using PowerPoint or another presentation software. **Visual/Spatial**

ANSWER, p. 564

TAKING NOTES: Answers may include the following points: Cathedrals (Gothic architecture: flying buttresses, stained-glass windows); Universities (Paris and Bologna, Oxford and Cambridge; degrees); Theology (Scholasticism, St. Thomas Aquinas, and Aristotle); Literature (vernacular, songs of troubadours, heroic epics); Religious Orders (Cistercians, Franciscans, Dominicans)

networks *There's More Online!*

- GRAPHIC ORGANIZER Organizing Information: Medieval Life
- PRIMARY SOURCE The Song of Roland

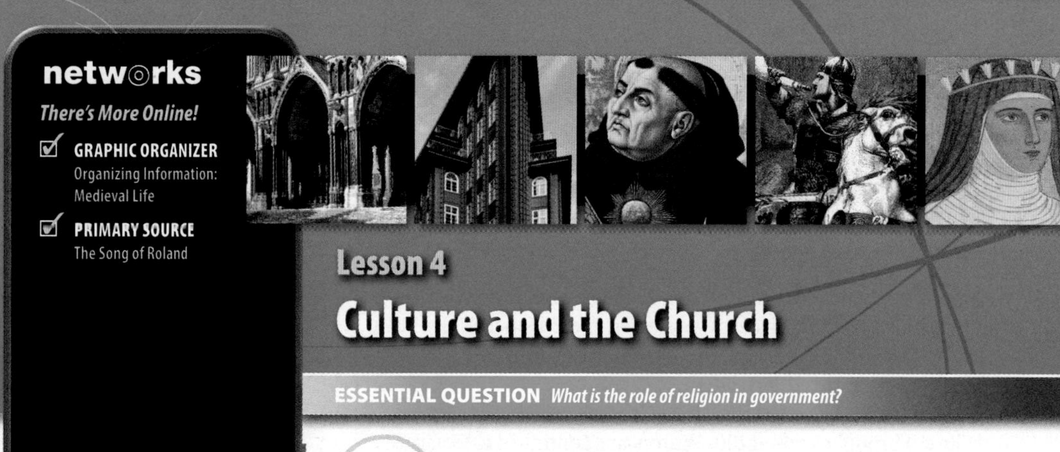

Lesson 4

Culture and the Church

ESSENTIAL QUESTION *What is the role of religion in government?*

IT MATTERS BECAUSE

Architecture, education, literature, and religion played very important roles in medieval life.

European Culture in the Middle Ages

GUIDING QUESTION ***What types of learning and art developed during the Middle Ages?***

R By the 1100s, the Crusades and the rise of strong governments made medieval Europeans more confident and **secure**. As a result, trade, banking, and businesses thrived. A better economy meant more money to spend on building and learning.

Styles in Architecture

In the 1000s and 1100s, Europeans began to construct many buildings. Because medieval society valued religion, many of the new buildings were churches and monasteries. Church leaders, wealthy merchants, and nobles supported the building of large churches called cathedrals. Soaring above the rooftops of medieval towns, cathedrals were built in either Romanesque (ROH•muh•NEHSK) or Gothic styles.

T Early medieval churches were Romanesque, a style that combined the features of Roman and Byzantine buildings. Romanesque churches were rectangular buildings with long, rounded ceilings called barrel vaults. These ceilings were supported by heavy walls and thick pillars set close together. The churches' small windows let in little light.

Reading **HELP**DESK CCSS

Taking Notes: *Organizing Information*

Use a table like the one shown here to list information about the parts of medieval life listed in the left-hand column. RH.6–8.2

Cathedrals	
Universities	
Theology	
Literature	
Religious Orders	

Content Vocabulary (Tier 3 Words)

- **mass**
- **heresy**
- **anti-Semitism**
- **theology**
- **scholasticism**
- **vernacular**

networks *Online Teaching Options*

VIDEO

Religious Architecture

Making Connections Before viewing the video, have students describe the features of various types of religious architecture they have seen, including temples, churches, and mosques. Write their descriptions on the board. Then lead the class in a discussion of how the features of these various centers of worship are alike and different. If desired, record students' ideas in a graphic organizer.

See page 537F for other online activities.

About 1150, builders began to construct churches in the Gothic style. They replaced Romanesque heavy walls with flying buttresses. These stone arches extended off the outside walls of the church and supported the weight of the building. They made it possible to build churches with thinner walls and large stained glass windows. Gothic churches were taller and had more space than Romanesque churches. **V**

Colorful stained glass windows often presented scenes from the life and teachings of Jesus. They also let in sunlight, which symbolized the divine light of God.

Development of Universities

The universities of today trace their origins to the Middle Ages. Two of the first medieval universities were in Bologna (buh•LOH•nyuh), Italy, and Paris, France. Universities also were founded in England at Oxford and Cambridge. By 1500, Europe had 80 universities.

Groups of students and teachers created the first universities to educate scholars. Medieval university students studied grammar, public speaking, logic, arithmetic, geometry, music, and astronomy. Teachers read from a text and discussed it, while students took notes on small, portable chalkboards called slates. Students did not have books because books were rare before the European printing press was created in the 1400s.

To get a degree, students took oral exams after four to six years. They could earn a bachelor of arts and later a master of arts. In about ten more years, a student could earn a doctor's degree in law, medicine, or **theology** (thee•AH•luh•jee)—the study of religion and God. People with doctor's degrees were officially able to teach but could also pursue other careers. For example, the monk Roger Bacon turned from teaching theology to studying the natural world. His interest in using experiments to test ideas helped pave the way for the rise of modern science.

What is Scholasticism?

By 1100, a new way of thinking called **scholasticism** (skuh•LAS•tuh•SIH•zuhm) was changing the study of theology. Its followers wanted to show that ideas accepted on faith did not have to contradict ideas developed by reason. The first scholastic thinker was Anselm, who served as archbishop of Canterbury in England from 1093 to 1109. Anselm became known for his reasoning about the existence of God. **R**

Advances in architecture enabled the French to build the great Gothic cathedral at Chartres. The Gothic style was revived in the 1700s. Today, architects still use this distinctive style of architecture. An example is this 1920s building in Hamburg, Germany.

▶ **CRITICAL THINKING**
Speculating Why do you think elements of the Gothic style might still be in use today?

(t) Adam Woolfitt/CORBIS, (b) Peter Eberts/dpa/Corbis

theology the study of religious faith, practice, and experience
scholasticism a way of thinking that combined faith and reason

Academic Vocabulary (Tier 2 Words)
secure free from danger

V Visual Skills

Simulating Discuss Gothic architecture with the class. **Ask:** How were the Gothic churches different than Romanesque churches? *(The Gothic churches were taller and had more space.)* What architectural innovation replaced the heavy walls of Romanesque buildings? *(flying buttresses)* Explain that a buttress is a structure that gives a wall or building support, and that the buttresses in Gothic buildings were called "flying" because they extended out from walls. To simulate flying buttresses, ask several students to line up a foot or so from a classroom wall, extend their arms over their heads, and then lean into the wall to "hold up" the wall with their hands. Explain that these students are like the flying buttresses in Gothic buildings, holding up the wall so that the wall doesn't need to be so thick and sturdy. **Visual/Spatial Kinesthetic**

R Reading Skills

Defining After students read the text, call on a volunteer to pronounce the word *scholasticism,* and then have the rest of the class repeat it. Explain that the root of the term comes from a Greek word for "school" and that the adjective *scholastic* is now used in a general sense for concepts related to school (as in *scholastic achievement*). **Ask:** What was the main idea behind scholasticism? *(that ideas accepted on faith did not have to contradict ideas developed by reason)* **ELL**

Content Background Knowledge

Chartres Cathedral One of the finest Gothic cathedrals is found in the French town of Chartres, southwest of Paris. Chartres Cathedral is recognized for the harmoniousness and quality of its architecture, stained glass, and sculpture. One reason for the cathedral's cohesiveness is that much of the structure was completed in a span of 26 years, a remarkably short time for the construction of a cathedral. Work on the present cathedral began in 1194, after the cathedral standing at the site burned down. The new cathedral used the façade and one of the towers from the burned church. This resulted in Chartres Cathedral's mismatched towers; the new tower is taller and much more ornate than the old one.

SLIDE SHOW

Medieval Architecture

Analyzing Images Display the slide show on the whiteboard, and use the arrows at the bottom left to move through the slides. For each slide, ask a student volunteer to read the text beside or underneath the image. Students will learn about Gothic architecture, with an emphasis on the Chartres Cathedral in France. When you have finished with the slide show, have the class discuss what traits of medieval architecture are still visible in buildings today. Encourage students to cite specific examples as they contribute to the conversation.

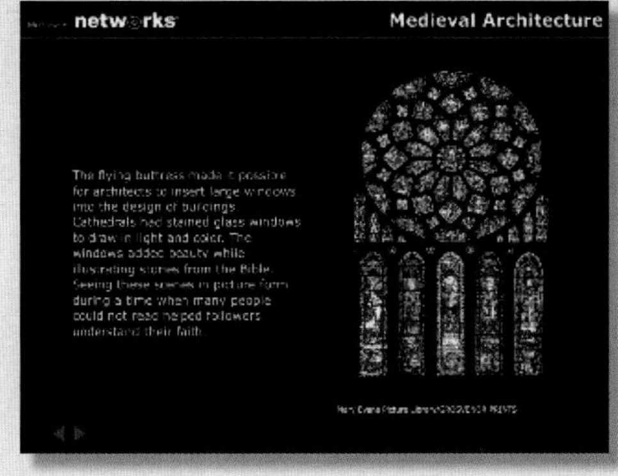

See page 537F for other online activities.

ANSWER, p. 565

CRITICAL THINKING Answers will vary but may include a sense of grandeur or history, and may note that the high ceilings and large windows make spaces feel large and airy.

Culture and the Church

C Critical Thinking Skills

Giving Examples Discuss the concept of natural law. **Ask:**

- What concept did Thomas Aquinas stress in his writings about government? *(natural law, or the idea that some laws have authority from nature)*
- According to Aquinas, what basic rights does natural law give to people? *(the right to live, to learn, to worship, and to marry)*

Lead a discussion of why the expression of these ideas may have seemed striking at the time. Have students recall, for example, that peasants on medieval manors had to ask the lord of the manor for permission to marry. **Ask:** Do you agree with Aquinas that people naturally have these rights? Why or why not? *(Answers will vary, but students should be able to support their thoughts with specific examples.)* BL

R Reading Skills

Identifying Have students read the subsection titled "Language and Literature." Explain to the class that Latin had been the language of educated people ever since the days of the Roman Empire. **Ask:**

- What is a vernacular language? *(the language people use in everyday life)*
- What modern-day languages were part of the vernacular languages in Europe? *(English, Italian, Spanish, French, and German)*
- Starting in the 1100s, how did literature change in Europe? *(Educated people began to write in the vernacular, as well as in Latin.)*
- What was a popular type of vernacular literature? *(troubadour poetry)* Guide students to understand that more people were becoming educated and able to express themselves during the 1000s and 1100s. Religion was an important concern of Europe's educated groups. AL ELL

Thomas Aquinas became one of the best-known scholars in the history of the Catholic Church.

▶ CRITICAL THINKING

Analyzing Visuals Why do you think Thomas Aquinas is shown with a church in one hand and a book in the other?

During the 1100s, the ideas of the ancient Greek philosopher Aristotle had a major influence on Europe. After the fall of Rome in the late 400s, Aristotle had been almost forgotten in Europe. Muslim libraries, however, had preserved copies of his books. In the 1100s, Muslim and Jewish scholars reintroduced Aristotle to Europe. The ancient philosopher's ideas disturbed some Christian thinkers. Aristotle used reason, rather than faith, to reach his conclusions.

In the 1200s, an Italian Dominican friar named Thomas Aquinas (uh•KWY•nuhs) became scholasticism's greatest thinker. His **goal** was to find agreement between Aristotle's teachings and Christian teachings. Aquinas taught that truths arrived at through reason could not conflict with truths arrived at through faith. Reason, unaided by faith, could discover truths about the physical universe but not spiritual truths.

Aquinas's major work was *Summa Theologica*, or a summary of knowledge on theology. In this book, Aquinas followed a logical order of scholarly investigation. First, he asked a question such as, "Does God exist?" Next, he quoted sources that offered opposing opinions and presented ways of reconciling these views. Finally, he drew his own conclusions.

In his writings about government, Thomas Aquinas stressed the concept of natural law. According to this idea, some laws have authority from human nature. Such laws do not have to be made by governments. Aquinas taught that natural law gives people certain basic rights. These include the right to live, to learn, to worship, and to marry. The ideas of Aquinas continue to influence human societies to the present day.

Language and Literature

In medieval times, Latin was the language of educated people, both for speaking and writing. Latin was also the language of the Church and of university teachers and scholars.

Besides Latin, each region in Europe had its own local language. People used this language, called the **vernacular** (vuhr•NA•kyuh•luhr), in everyday life. Among the vernacular languages in Europe were early versions of English, Italian, Spanish, French, and German.

Starting in the 1100s, writers created much new literature in the vernacular. Educated people became interested in this literature. One popular type of vernacular literature was troubadour (TROO•buh•DAWR) poetry. Troubadour poets often sang love poems, especially about the love of a knight for a lady.

Reading **HELP**DESK (CCSS)

vernacular the everyday spoken language of a region

Academic Vocabulary (Tier 2 Words)

goal something that a person works to achieve; aim

networks Online Teaching Options

CHART

Thomas Aquinas

Sequencing Display the time line on the whiteboard, and ask a volunteer to read all eight bulleted events to the class. Then have the class work together to sequence those events on the time line. When students are finished, click on each event to see where it belongs on the time line. At the end of the process, be sure to answer any remaining questions about the sequence of these events.

See page 537F for other online activities.

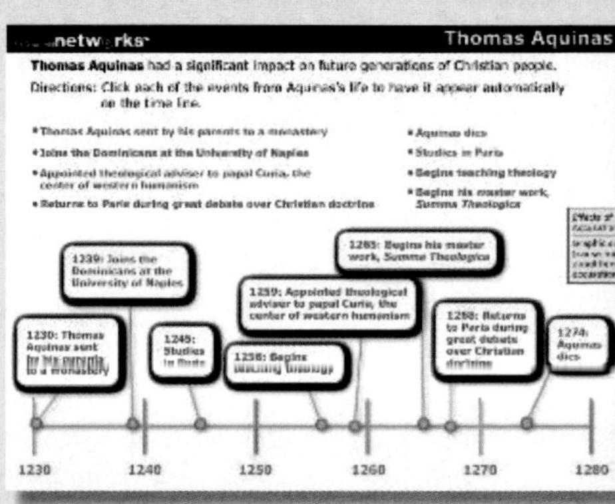

ANSWER, p. 566

CRITICAL THINKING He is probably shown this way because he found a way to reconcile truths arrived at through faith (represented by the Church) and through reason (represented by the book).

A second important type of vernacular literature was the heroic epic. Epics often tell the story of bold knights fighting in the service of kings and lords. *The Song of Roland* is an epic that was written in France about 1100. In this tale, a brave knight named Roland fights in the service of Charlemagne against the Muslims.

At a moment of crisis in the battle, Roland sounds his horn for Charlemagne to help him. For many the battle was over:

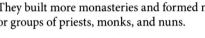

C1

> “Roland looks up on the mountains and slopes,
> sees the French dead, so many good men fallen,
> and weeps for them, as a great warrior weeps:
>
> Barons, my lords, may God give you his grace,
> may he grant Paradise [heaven] to all your souls,
> make them lie down among the holy flowers.
> I never saw better vassals than you.
> All the years you've served me, and all the times,
> the mighty lands you conquered for Charles our King!”
>
> —from *The Song of Roland*

W

PROGRESS CHECK

Explaining Why was it important that literature was written in everyday language?

In this illustration from *The Song of Roland*, Roland is sounding his horn for Charlemagne to help him.

Religion Affected Society

GUIDING QUESTION ***How did the Catholic Church affect the lives of medieval Europeans?***

During the Middle Ages, the Catholic Church became rich and powerful. Beginning in the 1000s, many Western Europeans became worried about the direction in which the Church was headed. They set out to return the Church to Christian ideals. They built more monasteries and formed new religious orders, or groups of priests, monks, and nuns.

C2

New Religious Orders

One of the most important new orders was the Cistercian (sihs•TUHR•shuhn) order. It was founded in 1098 by monks who were unhappy with wealthy monasteries and wanted a simpler, more spiritual way of life. Cistercian monks worshipped, prayed, and farmed the land. They developed new farming methods. Bernard of Clairvaux (klehr•VOH) was a famous Cistercian monk.

Culture and the Church

C1 Critical Thinking Skills

Making Connections Ask a volunteer to read aloud the excerpt from *The Song of Roland.* Then discuss the heroic nature of this excerpt. **Ask:** In this tale, who is Roland? *(a brave knight who fights in the service of Charlemagne against Muslims)* Remind students that Charlemagne's grandfather, Charles Martel, defeated a Muslim army at the Battle of Tours in 732 and that Charlemagne came to power in 768, hundreds of years before *The Song of Roland* was written. Explain that heroic tales that are written to inspire are often stories from the distant past. Ask students to think of heroic movies they have seen or books they have read that are also based on stories from the past.

W Writing Skills

Narrative Organize the class into small groups, and ask each group to rewrite the excerpt from *The Song of Roland* in language that would be used today. After students take time for writing, ask a member of each group to read the group's rewrite to the class dramatically. **Verbal/Linguistic**

C2 Critical Thinking Skills

Assessing Students should understand that the Church was a powerful institution. Its goal was to unify Europe as a Christian civilization or have everyone accept the Catholic Church's teachings. The Church tried to control Europe's rulers and had daily influence on ordinary people. **Ask:**

- On a scale of 1 to 10 (10 being highest), how important was the Church to Europe's peasants? *(10)*
- How important was the Church to Europe's rulers? *(10)*
- If the Church was so important, why did some people want to change it? *(Some believed the Church had gotten too worldly, and they wanted to make it more spiritual again.)*
- How did some people change the Church? *(They started new religious orders.)*

SLIDE SHOW

Medieval Mystics

Discussing Display the slide show on the whiteboard, and use the arrows at the bottom to move through the five slides. Ask volunteers to read the text of each slide to the class. **Ask:** What is a mystic? *(someone who gains spiritual knowledge through visions, meditation, or other mysterious means)* Then lead a class discussion about how religious mystics gain spiritual knowledge.

See page 537F for other online activities.

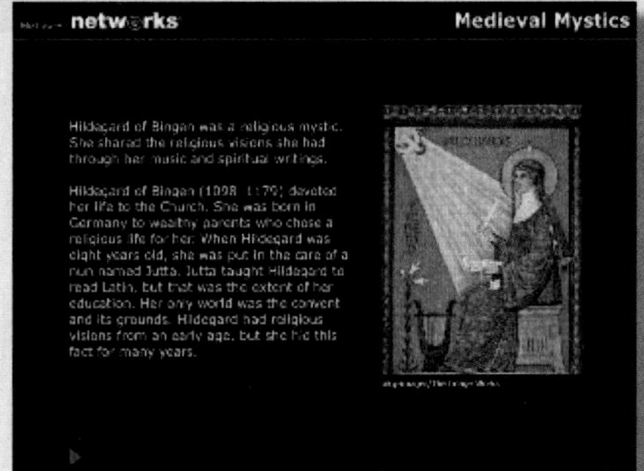

ANSWER, p. 567

PROGRESS CHECK Literature written in the vernacular could reach more people.

Culture and the Church

C Critical Thinking Skills

Organizing Draw a Venn diagram on the board, and label one side "Franciscans" and the other side "Dominicans." **Ask:**

- What information about the Franciscans can we write in that order's space? *(founded by St. Francis of Assisi; known for cheerfulness and love of nature)*
- What information about the Dominicans can we write in that order's space? *(founded by Dominic de Guzmán; chief goal: to defend the teachings of the church)*
- What are common to both orders that we can write in the overlapping middle? *(friars; lived a simple life; no personal wealth; aided the poor)* **Visual/Spatial**

R Reading Skills

Explaining Direct students' attention to the terms *mass* and *sacraments* in the text. Make sure students understand the meanings of both words. **Ask:** What is a mass? *(the Catholic worship service)* Explain that a religious ritual, such as attending mass, is an established form of a religious ceremony. What is a sacrament? *(a church ritual)* Explain that Holy Communion, which is a ritual in many Christian churches, is an example of a sacrament. AL ELL

Hildegard of Bingen composed music for the Catholic Church at a time when most church music was written by men.

▶ CRITICAL THINKING

Making Inferences What advantages would medieval nuns have had over other women that would have enabled them to create music, literature, or art?

Franz Waldhaeusl/Age fotostock

Bernard supported the Second Crusade, advised the pope, and took the side of the poor against the rich.

Between A.D. 1000 and 1200, many women joined female religious orders. Most of these women, called nuns, came from wealthy noble families. One famous nun of this period was Hildegard of Bingen. She was the abbess, or leader, of a convent in Germany and wrote music for the church. Most composers of church music at that time were men.

The Mission of Friars

Until the 1200s, most people in religious orders spent their time inside their monasteries in prayer or at work. They lived a simple life separate from the world. In the 1200s, several new religious orders were created. The men in these religious orders were called friars.

Friars were different from other monks. They left their monasteries and took Christianity to people in the towns. Friars preached, served as missionaries, and aided the poor. Friars could not own property or keep any personal wealth.

C

Two well-known orders of friars were the Franciscans (fran•SIHS•kuhns) and the Dominicans (duh•MIH•nih•kuhns). The Franciscan order was founded in 1209 by Francis of Assisi (uh•SIH•see). Franciscans were known for their cheerfulness and deep love of nature.

A Spanish monk named Dominic de Guzmán (DAH•muh•NIHK deh gooz•MAHN) started the Dominican order in 1216. Like the Franciscans, the Dominicans lived a life of poverty. Their chief goal was to defend the teachings of the Church.

The Role of Religion in Everyday Life

R

In medieval times, the Catholic Church affected almost every part of people's lives. On Sundays and holy days, most medieval Europeans gathered to attend **mass**, the Catholic worship service.

Medieval Christians also took part in church rituals called sacraments. The most important sacrament was Holy Communion during mass. People received bread and wine to remind them of the death of Jesus. Only clergy could give people the sacraments.

Saints also played an important role in the lives of medieval

Reading HELPDESK CCSS

mass religious worship service for Catholic Christians
heresy ideas that go against church teachings
anti-Semitism hostility toward or discrimination against Jews

networks Online Teaching Options

CHART

Effects of Heresy Accusations

Drawing Conclusions Show students the cause and effect chart on Church responses to heresy. **Ask:** What steps did the Church take to deal with heretics? *(It sent friars to preach. It also set up a court called the Inquisition to try heretics, or people suspected of heresy. Heretics could be sent to prison, excommunicated, or executed.)* Have volunteers fill in the blanks on the chart with their answers. Explain that people who were brought before the Inquisition did not have the rights that the accused have today. Thousands faced secret trials and suffered torture and punishment.

See page 537F for other online activities.

Effects of Heresy Accusations

Directions: Think about the possible effects of being accused of heresy by Church leaders of the Inquisition in the Middle Ages. Click the boxes to see three possible effects.

Heresy and the Inquisition → Excommunication; Punishment by going to prison or losing property; Execution

ANSWER, p. 568

CRITICAL THINKING Nuns had more education than other women. They also came from wealthy families, which had greater access to luxuries like music and art.

Christians. People prayed to the saints to ask for God's favor. Mary, the mother of Jesus, was the most honored of all the saints.

The Challenge of Heresy

Despite its power, the Church had to deal with **heresy** (HEHR•uh•see), or ideas that conflicted with church teaching. In the Middle Ages, heresy was regarded as a serious crime against the Church. In 1233, the pope set up a Church court called the Inquisition (IHN•kwuh•ZIH•shuhn). The Inquisition's task was to question and deal with people accused of heresy. R1

People who were found guilty by the Inquisition were allowed to confess their heresy and ask for forgiveness. Those who refused were excommunicated and punished. Punishment could mean going to prison, losing property, or being executed.

Anti-Semitism in the Middle Ages

In medieval Europe, Jews became scapegoats, or people blamed for other people's problems. Jews were often accused in times of trouble, such as famine, plague, or economic decline. Hostility toward Jews is called **anti-Semitism** (AN • tee • SEH • muh • TIH • zuhm).

In troubled times during the Middle Ages, anti-Semitism flared up. In towns and villages, Christians often discriminated against and even killed Jews. As a minority, Jews were often forced to live in separate neighborhoods called ghettos. Often, Jews were forbidden to own land and to practice certain trades. 

Beginning in the 1100s, rulers in England, France, and central Europe even drove out their Jewish subjects. Many of these Jews settled in Eastern Europe, especially Poland. Over the centuries, the Jews of Eastern Europe developed thriving communities.

✓ PROGRESS CHECK

Explaining Why did Church officials set up the Inquisition?

LESSON 4 REVIEW 

Review Vocabulary (Tier 3 Words)

1. What is *heresy*? RH.6–8.2, RH.6–8.4

Answer the Guiding Questions

2. ***Contrasting*** Contrast the chief characteristics of Romanesque and Gothic architecture. RH.6–8.2

3. ***Comparing and Contrasting*** How were monks and friars similar? How did they differ from each other? RH.6–8.2

4. ***Analyzing*** Why did the writings and ideas of Aristotle disturb some medieval Christians? RH.6–8.2

5. ***Identifying*** During the Middle Ages, what were two popular types of vernacular literature? Briefly describe each type. RH.6–8.2

6. **INFORMATIVE/EXPLANATORY** Write a brief announcement to attract students to a medieval university. In your announcement, include the location of the university, the subjects that students may study, and the degrees they can earn. WHST.6–8.2, WHST.6–8.10

LESSON 4 REVIEW ANSWERS

1. Heresy is the belief in ideas that conflict with Church teaching.
2. Romanesque features were found among Roman and Byzantine buildings. Romanesque buildings were rectangular and had barrel-vault ceilings, heavy walls, thick pillars, and small windows. Gothic architecture featured flying buttresses, thinner walls, tall and slender pillars, pointed arches, and large windows of stained glass.
3. Both monks and friars helped the poor. Monks, however, lived in monasteries while friars took Christianity to people in the towns.
4. Aristotle's writings were disturbing because the ancient Greek philosopher seemed to rely on reason, rather than faith, to reach his conclusions.
5. Two popular types of vernacular literature were heroic epics and the songs of troubadours. Troubadour songs often centered on the love of a knight for a lady, while heroic epics told the story of brave knights fighting in the service of their king or lord.
6. Announcements should identify the university's location (for example, Paris, Bologna, or Oxford). Announcements may mention the following subjects: grammar, public speaking, logic, arithmetic, geometry, music, and astronomy. Degrees include a bachelor of arts, a master of arts, and a doctorate.

Culture and the Church

R1 Reading Skills

Discussing After students have read the text, remind them that *heresy* refers to ideas that conflicted with church teaching. Point out that the Church, while trying to unify Europe under Christianity, felt threatened by heretics (former believers) and, to a lesser extent, nonbelievers (Jews and Muslims). **Ask:**

- **Why was heresy a problem for the Church?** *(Church leaders feared that if people stopped believing in Church teachings and became heretics, it would weaken the Church and endanger people's chances of getting into heaven.)*
- **What effect did Church policies have on Europe's non-Christian population?** *(Church leaders actively persecuted Jews, and Christian mobs often attacked and killed Jewish people.)*

R2 Reading Skills

Defining Ask students to read the section titled "Anti-Semitism in the Middle Ages." Then, lead a class discussion about anti-Semitism. **Ask:** **What is anti-Semitism?** *(hostility toward Jews)* Explain that the prefix *anti-* means "against," and that *Semitism* relates to people originally from the Middle East, mainly Jewish people. Explain that the terms *anti-Semitism* and *anti-Semitic* are still used today to characterize ideas and people that show hostility toward Jews. ELL

Have students complete the Lesson 4 Review.

CLOSE & REFLECT

Describing To close the lesson, have students think about the changes that came to medieval Europe beginning in the 1100s. Ask students to describe changes in architecture, universities, theology, language, literature, and religion.

ANSWER, p. 569

✓ PROGRESS CHECK They set up the Inquisition to end heresy.

ENGAGE

Bellringer Lead a discussion about what happens when a student becomes ill with a bacterial infection. **Ask:** **Normally, what does your doctor do for you?** *(Students probably will describe getting a prescription for an antibiotic.)* Point out that antibiotics usually end an infection in a few days. However, antibiotics weren't discovered until the 20th century. **What do you think might happen in a society that didn't have antibiotics or other modern medicines?** *(Students should suggest that infectious diseases could spread rapidly.)* Explain that in this lesson, they will learn about several catastrophes that medieval Europeans faced in the late Middle Ages, including famine, war, conflicts within the Catholic Church, and the spread of a disease called the plague.

TEACH & ASSESS

R Reading Skills

Discussing After students have read the text, guide a class discussion about the events that resulted in famine in northern Europe. **Ask:** **What caused crops to rot in the fields in the early 1300s?** *(very cold winters and rainy summers)* **What was the result of this agricultural disaster?** *(There was not enough food for the population, and there was a great famine.)* **What is a famine?** *(A famine is an extreme shortage of food.)* AL ELL

C Critical Thinking Skills

Determining Cause and Effect After students read about the Black Death in Europe, reinforce how the disease spread. Have students make a flowchart on the board. **Ask:**

- **What is a plague?** *(a disease that spreads quickly and kills large numbers of people)* ELL
- **What carried the disease-causing bacteria?** *(fleas)*
- **What animals had the fleas on them?** *(rats)*
- **How, then, did humans get the disease?** *(The fleas on the rats bit the humans, transferring the bacteria to people.)* Explain that at the time, no one understood this process, and so no one understood how the disease spread from person to person.

ANSWER, p. 570

TAKING NOTES: Answers may include the following: People did not know the causes of the plague, and many thought it was a punishment from God or the fault of the Jews; the economy was devastated and trade decreased; food prices fell sharply; the plague helped weaken the feudal system.

networks *There's More Online!*

- BIOGRAPHY Joan of Arc
- CHART/GRAPH The Black Death

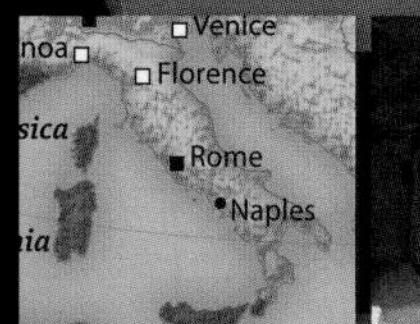

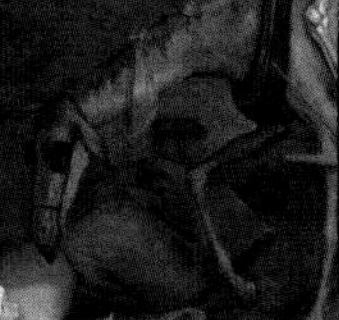

Lesson 5

The Late Middle Ages

ESSENTIAL QUESTION *How do governments change?*

IT MATTERS BECAUSE

During the Late Middle Ages, Europe experienced serious economic, political, and religious conflicts.

Famine and Plague

GUIDING QUESTION *How did the Black Death affect Europe during the Late Middle Ages?*

R Medieval Europe enjoyed prosperity and growth during the 1200s. Then, early in the next century, disaster struck. Extremely cold winters and rainy summers created miserable conditions. Crops rotted in the fields, and herds of livestock died from diseases. Soon, there was not enough food for Europe's growing population. The result was a great famine in northern Europe that lasted from about 1315 to 1322. During this time, many people died from starvation and epidemics.

The Plague Comes to Europe

C The great famine was only the beginning of troubles. During the 1300s, a **plague** (PLAYG) spread from Asia across Europe. A plague is a disease that spreads quickly and kills large numbers of people. The Black Death, as the disease was known, was probably bubonic plague. This illness is caused by a type of bacteria spread by fleas. Rats carry the fleas. The Black Death probably began in central Asia and spread to other places through trade. It first broke out in China in the 1330s. Between 40 and 60 million people eventually died, nearly half of the Chinese population.

Reading HELPDESK CCSS

Taking Notes: *Summarizing* RH.6–8.2

Use a pie chart like the one shown to summarize the effects of the Black Death in Europe in the mid-1300s.

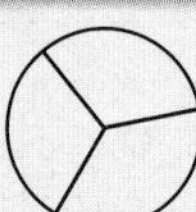

Content Vocabulary (Tier 3 Words)

- plague
- Reconquista

networks *Online Teaching Options*

VIDEO

History of Austria From the Late Middle Ages

Analyzing Information Have students watch the video about Austria. Tell students that this study of how one region changed during the Middle Ages will give them an example of the changes that many other regions saw during this period. After the video, discuss what they learned about Austria. **Ask:** **When did Vienna become the door to Western Europe?** *(in the 700s, during Charlemagne's rule)* Ask students what surprised them most about the history of Austria.

See page 537G for other online activities.

Trade between China, India, the Middle East, and Europe was greatly encouraged by the Mongols. Merchants used the Silk Road and other trade routes. Expanded trade also made it possible for the Black Death to spread quickly. More and more traders used the Silk Road and other routes linking Asia and Europe. As a result, rat-infested caravans and ships carried the disease from region to region. The plague then traveled to India and spread to Muslim territories.

C

In 1346, the Black Death reached the trading city of Caffa on the Black Sea. Italian ships carried the plague to the island of Sicily. From there, it spread to the Italian mainland and onto the continent of Europe. By the end of the 1340s, it had surfaced in France, Germany, and England. By 1351, the plague had reached Scandinavia, Eastern Europe, and Russia. Estimates of the dead in Europe between 1347 and 1351 range from 19 to 38 million people—nearly one out of every two Europeans.

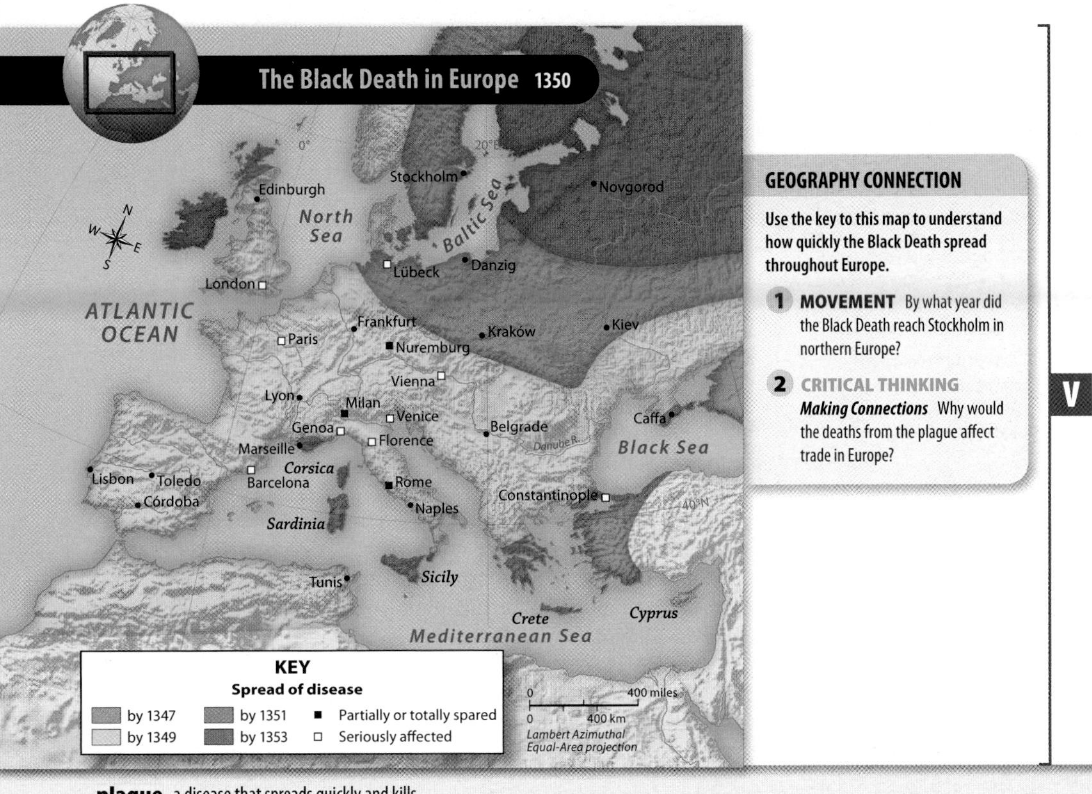

V

GEOGRAPHY CONNECTION

Use the key to this map to understand how quickly the Black Death spread throughout Europe.

1. **MOVEMENT** By what year did the Black Death reach Stockholm in northern Europe?
2. **CRITICAL THINKING** ***Making Connections*** Why would the deaths from the plague affect trade in Europe?

plague a disease that spreads quickly and kills many people

The Late Middle Ages

C Critical Thinking Skills

Making Generalizations Have students read about the spread of the Black Death into Europe. Point out that the trade between China, India, the Middle East, and Europe in the Middle Ages had made many regions wealthy and secure. Yet, it was through this activity that Europe suffered a great epidemic. **Ask:** **What generalization can you make about the spread of the Black Death?** *(It began in Asia and spread to Europe through trade routes.)* **About how many Europeans died from this disease?** *(between 19 and 28 million people)* **This figure made up about what percentage of Europe's population?** *(about 50 percent)*

V Visual Skills

Reading a Map Have students study the map of the Black Death in Europe at the bottom of the page. **Ask:**

- **According to the key, the brown area shows how far the plague had spread by what year?** *(1347)*
- **What does the pink area on the map show?** *(how far the plague had spread by 1353)*
- **In what direction did the plague spread?** *(southwest)* **Visual/Spatial**

Content Background Knowledge

The Black Death and a Nursery Rhyme Many folklorists believe the popular nursery rhyme "Ring Around the Rosie" is about the Black Death plague. The first line refers to the round pink rash that is an early sign of the disease. Posies, or bouquets of flowers, were worn to disguise the terrible smell of the infection. The third line refers to the burning of infected corpses. Finally, almost everyone who was infected with the plague eventually died, or fell down.

MAP

The Black Death in Europe, 1350

Identifying Cause and Effect Show students the interactive map of the Black Death in Europe. As a class, identify all the countries and areas the plague affected. *(Ireland, England, Sweden, Russia, France, Spain, Germany, Italy, Eastern Europe, Turkey, northern Africa)* **Ask:** **What happened to Europe's population as a result of the Black Death?** *(Overall, the population of Europe was cut in half, with greater percentages of people dying in some hard-hit areas and smaller percentages in other places.)*

See page 537G for other online activities.

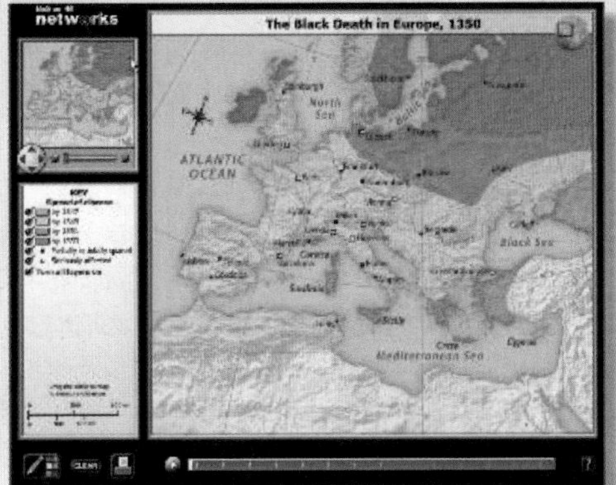

ANSWERS, p. 571

GEOGRAPHY CONNECTION

1. It reached Stockholm by 1351.
2. **CRITICAL THINKING** So many people died during the plague that few people were left to buy or sell goods.

V Visual Skills

Interpreting Have students study the painting inspired by the Black Death. **Ask:**

- Where do you see skeletons in this painting? *(Skeletons are shown on the cart, on the horse, and picking up the dead and dying.)*
- What do you think the skeletons in the cart symbolize? *(Answers may vary, but students should indicate that the skeletons represent those that have died from the plague.)*
- What do you think the inclusion of the dying king in the lower right corner symbolizes? *(Answers will vary. Students may suggest that including the king in this grisly scene shows that all classes of people experienced this horror.)* **Visual/Spatial**

T Technology Skills

Researching on the Internet The image inspired by the Black Death shown in the students' text is a detail from *El triunfo de la Muerta* ("The Triumph of Death"), painted by the Flemish painter Pieter Bruegel. Ask students to use an Internet search engine to find an image of the complete painting to show the class, either by projecting it on the whiteboard or by printing it out and passing it around. As a class, discuss what the title of the painting means. Then talk about how the image in the textbook fits into the larger painting, and the other details visible in the larger image. **Visual/Spatial**

C Critical Thinking Skills

Drawing Conclusions Discuss the consequences of the spread of plague throughout Europe. **Ask:** Why did the Black Death weaken the system of feudalism? *(With so many people dying, the number of workers was much smaller than before. As a result, landowners had to pay workers more money.)* BL

SuperStock/SuperStock

T **The Black Death inspired art and literature. This painting shows carts picking up those who had died to bury them quickly in mass graves.**

▶ CRITICAL THINKING

Analyzing Visuals Why do you think the artist portrayed skeletons collecting the bodies of the dead?

The Effects of the Plague V

People at the time did not know why the plague had happened. Some people thought God was punishing them for their sins. Others blamed the Jews. For this reason, the Germans expelled many Jews from some of their cities.

C The plague had an enormous effect on the **economy** of Europe. With so many deaths, trade declined. Wages rose steeply because of a high demand for workers. Fewer people, though, meant less demand for food, so food prices fell sharply.

Landlords now had to pay scarce workers more. Some peasants began to pay rent instead of providing services. Serfs gained more rights. Like the Crusades, the Black Death weakened feudalism.

✓ PROGRESS CHECK

Explaining How did the Black Death spread?

Reading **HELP**DESK CCSS

Academic Vocabulary (Tier 2 Words)

economy a country's system for the making, selling, and buying of goods and services

authority the power to influence or command thought, opinion, or behavior

networks Online Teaching Options

GRAPH

European Population A.D. 1300–1500

Analyzing Graphs Display the interactive graph on the whiteboard. With the first bar visible, **ask:** How many people lived in Europe in 1300? *(79 million people)* How many people died between 1300 and 1350? *(25 million)* With each successive bar, students will see how the population declined because of the Black Death and then rose again through the next century and a half. Between which years did Europe see the largest population growth? *(Between 1450 and 1500, the population grew by 10 million people.)* **Logical/Mathematical**

See page 537G for other online activities.

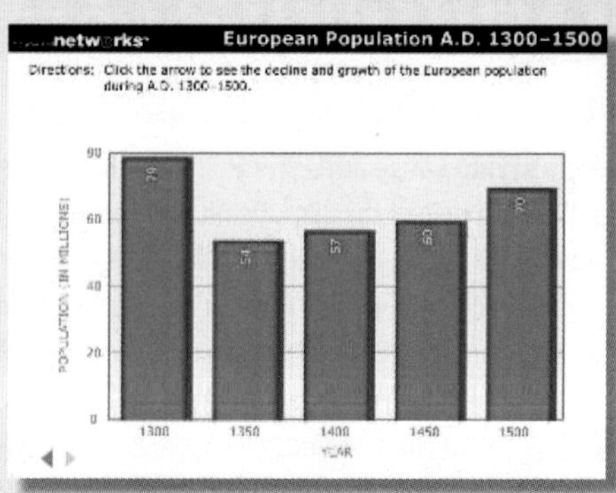

ANSWERS, p. 572

CRITICAL THINKING So many people were dying of the plague, no one was left once it passed through a town.

✓ PROGRESS CHECK Rats carrying fleas spread the plague. The fleas, in turn, carried a type of bacteria.

Divisions in Religion and Politics

GUIDING QUESTION *How did disputes and wars change societies in Europe during the Late Middle Ages?*

In addition to the bubonic plague, conflict swept through Europe during the Late Middle Ages. Disputes in the Church reduced its **authority**. English and French kings battled over territory in the Hundred Years' War. Christians in the Iberian Peninsula fought to drive out the Muslims who had conquered land there.

Conflict in the Church

From 1378 to 1417, a dispute called the Great Schism (SIH• zuhm) deeply divided the Church. During this time, two and even three church leaders claimed to be the rightful pope. This caused great confusion and doubt throughout Western Europe. In 1417, a council of bishops met at the German city of Constance. It finally ended the Great Schism with the election of a pope that all church members could accept.

The Great Schism was only one challenge the Church faced during the Late Middle Ages. Powerful European kings questioned the authority of popes. The kings of England and France would soon go to war. Many people criticized the growing wealth and corruption of the clergy. Reform leaders emerged who called on church leaders to return to a more spiritual form of Christianity. These reformers included John Wycliffe in England and Jan Hus in the Holy Roman Empire.

R

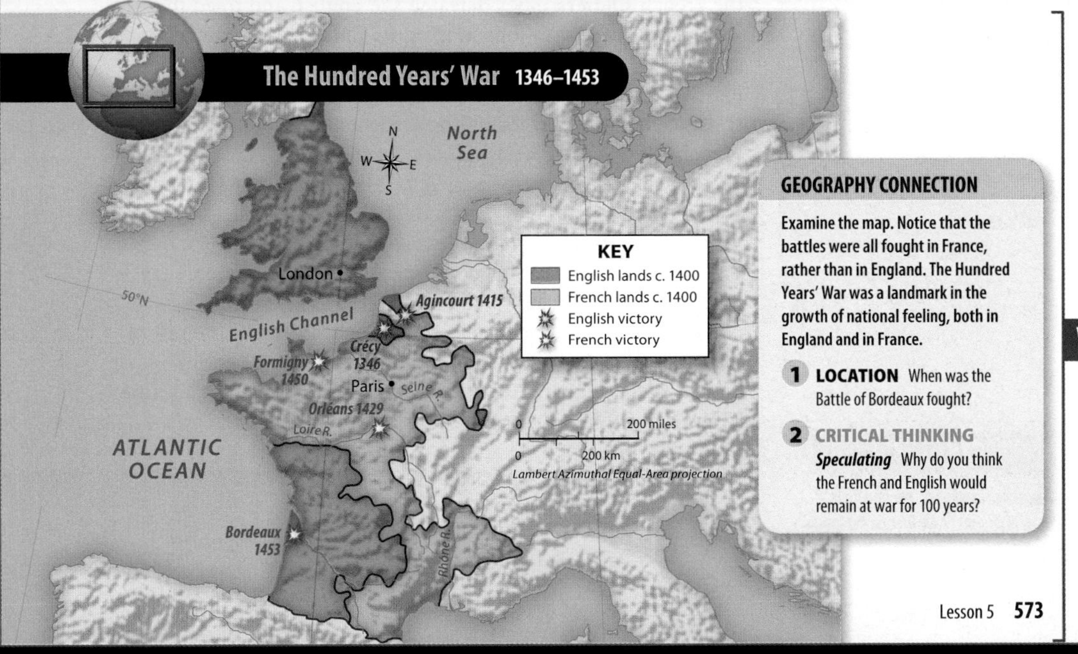

GEOGRAPHY CONNECTION

Examine the map. Notice that the battles were all fought in France, rather than in England. The Hundred Years' War was a landmark in the growth of national feeling, both in England and in France.

1. **LOCATION** When was the Battle of Bordeaux fought?
2. CRITICAL THINKING *Speculating* Why do you think the French and English would remain at war for 100 years?

V

R Reading Skills

Listing Direct students to read the section on conflict in the Church. Then, have pairs of students work together to make a bulleted list of challenges the Church faced in the late Middle Ages. *(the Great Schism; powerful European kings questioning the authority of popes; growing wealth and corruption of clergy)* After students have time for writing, call on pairs to read their points and explain each one. Invite discussion and debate when disagreements arise. AL

V Visual Skills

Analyzing Maps Have students turn their attention to the map of the Hundred Years' War at the bottom of the page. **Ask:**

- The Hundred Years' War was fought between which years? *(1346 to 1453)* AL
- What color are French lands on the map? *(green)*
- Where was the northernmost battle fought during this war? *(Agincourt)*
- Where did the last battle of this war take place? *(Bordeaux)* **Visual/Spatial**

MAP

The Hundred Years' War, 1346–1453

Sequencing Display the map on the whiteboard with all the layers turned off. Begin by clicking on the arrow below the map, which will activate a brief audio description. As the audio plays, the layers of the map will turn on automatically. As students watch the presentation, have them make a list of the battles in sequential order and which side won each battle. Then ask them what they can infer from this information. *(Answers will vary, but students should suggest that this sequence of battles is evidence that the French armies were growing stronger and were pushing the English out of France.)*

See page 537G for other online activities.

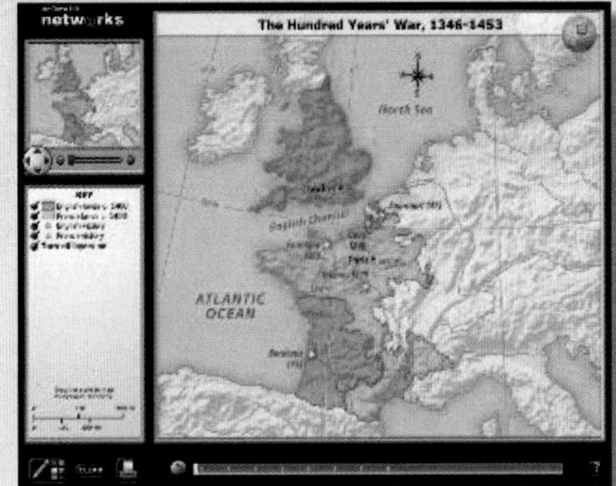

ANSWERS, p. 573

GEOGRAPHY CONNECTION

1. 1453
2. CRITICAL THINKING Answers will vary but should include something about how neither France nor England wanted to give up their land claims.

C Critical Thinking Skills

Making Inferences The English longbow had a crucial impact in the Hundred Years' War, allowing English archers to defeat a French feudal army with many mounted knights. Ask a volunteer to read the primary-source quotation to the class. **Ask:** Why didn't the French soldiers simply send arrows back with their cross-bows? *(Answers will vary, but most students will infer that cross-bows didn't have the range of the English longbows, so sending arrows back toward the English would have been pointless.)* BL

R Reading Skills

Summarizing Ask students to use evidence from the text to summarize the results of the Hundred Years' War. **Ask:**

- By 1453, what had happened to the English? *(They had been driven out of most of France.)*
- What happened to English lands in France? *(The English lost their French lands.)*
- What was the result of the war for the French? *(The French gained land area by driving the English out. The victory gave the French new confidence and strength.)*

BIOGRAPHY

Joan of Arc (1412–1431)

Joan of Arc was born in the village of Domrémy in eastern France. She was the daughter of a tenant farmer. In her teens, Joan felt herself guided by the voices of three saints. Joan traveled from her native village in France to ask to fight for Charles, the crown prince. She faced examination by church authorities about her faith and the voices she heard. Convinced, they allowed Joan to take part in a battle against the English at the town of Orléans. The French victory there unified France and led to the coronation of Charles as king. However, Joan was captured later by the English, tried for heresy, and executed.

CRITICAL THINKING
Speculating Why do you think a teenage girl like Joan of Arc was able to inspire the French troops and lead them into battle?

The Hundred Years' War

Western Europe at this time was torn apart by political as well as religious disputes. For centuries, England's monarchs had ruled areas of France. France's kings, however, wanted to unite these lands with their kingdom. Then King Edward III of England declared himself king of France and invaded that country. The conflict that followed lasted over 100 years.

C At first, the English were victorious—at Crécy (kray•SEE) in 1346 and Agincourt in 1415. The English had superior weapons: a longbow and an early form of the cannon. The longbow shot arrows that were able to pierce heavy armor at 300 yards (274 km). A French medieval writer described the effects of the longbow at Crécy:

PRIMARY SOURCE

> "Then the English archers stept forth one pace and let fly their arrows so wholly [together] and so thick, that it seemed snow. When the [French soldiers] felt the arrows piercing through heads, arms, and breasts, many of them cast down their cross-bows and did cut their strings and [retreated]."
>
> —from *The Chronicles of Froissart*, by Jean Froissart

Joan of Arc Aids the French

The French prince Charles wanted to take back French lands held by the English. In 1429, a 17-year-old French peasant girl named Joan came to his palace. Joan persuaded Charles to let her go with a French army to the city of Orléans. Joan's faith stirred the French soldiers. They defeated the English and freed the city.

Shortly after, with Joan at his side, Charles was crowned king. A few months later, however, the English army captured Joan. The English accused her of being a witch. Joan was burned at the stake for heresy. Later known as Joan of Arc, she became a French national hero and Catholic saint.

R Joan's courage led the French to rally around their king. By 1453, French armies had driven the English out of most of France. Victory gave the French a new sense of loyalty to their country. French kings used that loyalty to strengthen their power.

The Hundred Years' War also affected the English. England's nobles were bitter about the loss of French lands. For the rest of the 1400s, they fought over who should be king in a civil war known as the Wars of Roses. The winner, Henry Tudor, became King Henry VII of England.

Reading HELPDESK CCSS

Reconquista the Christian "reconquest" of the Iberian Peninsula

networks Online Teaching Options

BIOGRAPHY

Joan of Arc

Discussing Display the biography of Joan of Arc on the whiteboard. Click on the buttons below the picture to open the three boxes of information about Joan of Arc. Ask a student volunteer to read the information to the class. Then lead a discussion of Joan of Arc's life and her influence on the Hundred Years' War.

See page 537G for other online activities.

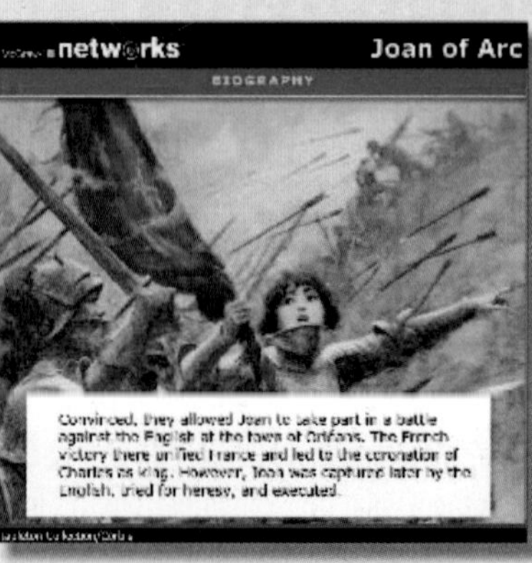

ANSWER, p. 574

CRITICAL THINKING She had great faith, courage, and confidence.

Jews and Muslims in Spain

During the Middle Ages, Muslims ruled much of the Iberian Peninsula. Today, the Iberian Peninsula is made up of Spain and Portugal. Medieval Muslims in this area developed a rich culture. They set up schools and built beautiful mosques and palaces, such as the Alhambra in Granada.

The Christians drove out the Muslims in a struggle called the **Reconquista** (ray•kohn•KEES•tuh), or "reconquest." By 1250, there were three Christian kingdoms: Portugal, Castile, and Aragon. The only remaining Muslim kingdom was Granada. In 1469, Prince Ferdinand of Aragon married Princess Isabella of Castile. They united their kingdoms into one Catholic country called Spain.

Under Muslim rule, Iberian Jews had lived freely for the most part. As Christians gained control, they sometimes mistreated the Jews. In order to avoid persecution by Christians, many Jews became Christian. Ferdinand and Isabella, however, believed that some of the Jews secretly practiced Judaism. To force obedience to the Catholic Church, the rulers put the Spanish Inquisition into place.

The Spanish Inquisition tried and tortured thousands of people who were accused of being disloyal to the Catholic Church in Spain. In 1492, Ferdinand and Isabella ordered Jews to convert or leave Spain. Most Jews left to avoid the charge of heresy. After Spain conquered Granada in 1492, Muslims were given the same choice. Rather than convert to Catholicism, most Muslims left for North Africa.

W

✓ PROGRESS CHECK

Determining Cause and Effect How did Ferdinand and Isabella treat those of Muslim and Jewish faiths?

LESSON 5 REVIEW

Review Vocabulary (Tier 3 Words)

1. What is a *plague*? RH.6–8.2, RH.6–8.4

Answer the Guiding Questions

2. ***Identifying*** After the Battle of Orléans, what happened to Joan of Arc? RH.6–8.2
3. ***Explaining*** How did the Black Death spread around the world? RH.6–8.2
4. ***Analyzing*** What was the major cause of the Hundred Years' War? RH.6–8.2
5. ***Explaining*** In what ways did the Muslims develop a rich culture in Spain and Portugal before they were forced out of those lands? RH.6–8.2
6. **INFORMATIVE/EXPLANATORY** You are King Charles of France. A young girl, Joan of Arc, has told you she believes the saints want her to help save France. Write three questions that you might ask Joan of Arc to determine if she is fit for battle. WHST.6–8.10

R Reading Skills

Defining After students read the text, ask a volunteer to pronounce *Reconquista,* and then have the class pronounce it together. Explain to students that this is the Spanish word for "reconquest," which means "conquering again." **Ask:**

- **Who was fighting during the Reconquista?** *(the Christians and the Muslims)*
- **Why was this struggle called the Reconquista?** *(All of Spain was once Christian, until the Muslims invaded from northern Africa and set up a Muslim kingdom. The Christians then worked to win back this land.)*
- **How many Christian kingdoms were there by 1250?** *(three: Portugal, Castile, and Aragon)* AL ELL

W Writing Skills

Narrative Ask students to imagine they are a Jew or Muslim living in Spain in the late 1400s. Have them individually write a letter to a friend describing what is occurring in his or her life. This letter should reflect the fear and turmoil in the lives of Muslims and Jews of this time. Encourage them to include as many details as possible in their writing. Ask volunteers to share their letters with the class. **Intrapersonal**

Have students complete the Lesson 5 Review.

CLOSE & REFLECT

Identifying Problems Have each student write a paragraph in which he or she states an opinion about the most important problem medieval Europeans faced during the late Middle Ages. Students should include at least two reasons to support their answers. Ask volunteers to share their ideas with the class.

LESSON 5 REVIEW ANSWERS

1. A plague is a disease that spreads quickly and kills many people.
2. The English captured her, accused her of heresy and being a witch, and then executed her. A subsequent investigation found her innocent of all the charges. Much later, she was declared a Catholic saint.
3. It originated in Asia and was spread by rats along trade routes to Europe.
4. The war was caused by a dispute between England and France. The king of England laid claim to large areas of France, but the French wanted the English to leave France.
5. The Muslims built beautiful palaces and mosques, and they established schools.
6. Answers will vary but should reflect students' understanding of the Hundred Years' War and Joan of Arc's role in the conflict.

ANSWER, p. 575

✓ PROGRESS CHECK They pressured Muslims and Jews to convert to Christianity. Most refused and left Spain.

CHAPTER REVIEW ACTIVITY

Have a student volunteer draw a three-column chart like the one below. Then lead a discussion in which students explain how the Catholic Church and feudalism affected daily life, the economy, and key political events in Europe during the Middle Ages. The volunteer should record answers in the chart.

	The Church	Feudalism
Daily Life		
Economy		
Political Events		

REVIEW THE ENDURING UNDERSTANDINGS

Review this chapter's Enduring Understandings with students:

- *Religion can influence a society's beliefs and values.*
- *Cultures are held together by shared beliefs and common practices and values.*
- *Conflict can lead to change.*

Now pose the following questions in a class discussion to apply these to the chapter. **Ask:**

- **What was feudalism? What ties bound a lord to his vassals and to the peasants on his manor?** *(Feudalism was a political and social order in which nobles governed and protected the people in return for services. Students should mention that a lord was a high-ranking noble who had power over others. Vassals were lower-ranking nobles who served a lord. Many lower-ranking vassals were knights, who were armed warriors loyal to their lords. Peasants, including serfs and freemen, lived on a lord's manor in exchange for services performed for the lord.)*
- **What was the Magna Carta, and what did it do for all people under the king of England?** *(Answers will vary but may include that the Magna Carta was a document signed by King John of England and by rebelling nobles that placed limits on the king's power. It allowed the king to collect taxes from nobles only if a Great Council agreed, forced the king to uphold rights of freemen, and helped strengthen the idea that all people, regardless of rank, have rights and that the power of government should be limited.)*
- **What was the Black Death, and how did it affect Europe?** *(Answers may include that the Black Death was a disease called a plague, caused by a type of bacteria. The disease was carried by fleas that lived on rats, and it spread through trade from Asia to Europe during the 1300s. The Black Death killed nearly one out of every two Europeans and had an enormous effect on the economy of Europe. With so many deaths, trade declined; landlords had to pay workers more, since healthy workers were scarce; and feudalism was weakened.)*

CHAPTER 19 Activities CCSS

Write your answers on a separate piece of paper.

1. **Exploring the Essential Question** WHST.6–8.2, WHST.6–8.10
INFORMATIVE/EXPLANATORY How would you describe the influence of religion on life in medieval Europe? In a summary essay, identify and evaluate the relationships between the Church and the government, as well as the ways in which religion influenced everyday life.

2. **21st Century Skills** RH.6–8.2, WHST.6–8.9, WHST.6–8.10
EVALUATING Consider the medieval order of feudalism. What strengths and weaknesses can you identify in feudalism? Do you think feudalism would work in modern society? Write your answer in a paragraph or two.

3. **Thinking Like a Historian** RH.6–8.2
COMPARING Describe the equipment that students in present-day universities might use and compare it to the equipment available to students in medieval universities. In particular, compare the role books in university education then and now.

4. **GEOGRAPHY ACTIVITY**

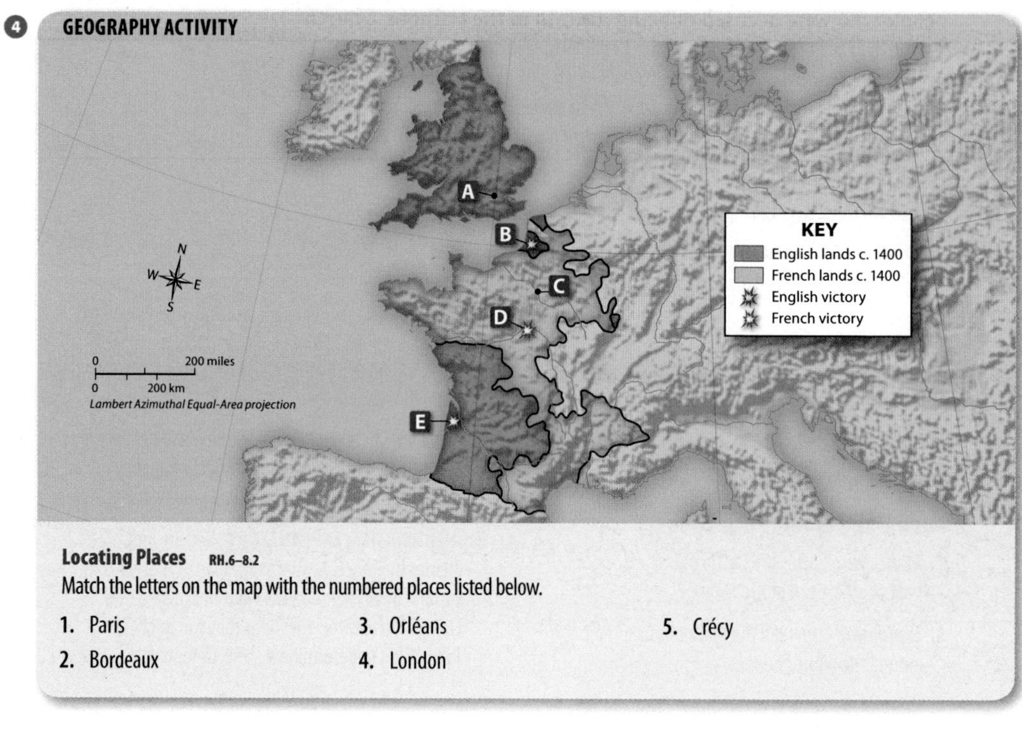

Locating Places RH.6–8.2
Match the letters on the map with the numbered places listed below.

1. Paris
2. Bordeaux
3. Orléans
4. London
5. Crécy

ACTIVITIES ANSWERS

Exploring the Essential Question

1. Essays should stress that religion had a major influence on almost everyone in medieval Europe, from kings to peasants. Kings and popes argued about who could appoint bishops; cities and towns built great churches and cathedrals, the clergy administered the sacraments, and religion was one of the main motivators of the Crusades.

21st Century Skills

2. Evaluations will vary. Students may mention that feudalism's strength was that the system valued virtues such as trust, loyalty, and bravery. It also involved a clear social hierarchy in which the nobles took care of the peasants in return for their service. Students might identify the following weaknesses: The nobles had all the power and wealth; the serfs were bound to the land; people in lower classes could not easily rise in society. Students might make a connection between how the medieval nobles took care of the peasants with the way modern governments provide social services for the poor or with how modern parents care for their children.

Thinking Like a Historian

3. Answers will vary, but students might mention that today's students have the use of computers and textbooks, but medieval students had only small, portable chalkboards. Without books, students had to rely on note-taking and memorization far more than students do today.

REVIEW THE GUIDING QUESTIONS

Directions: Choose the best answer for each question.

RH.6–8.2
1 The Danube and the Po in Europe are which of the following?
A. peninsulas
B. mountain ranges
C. rivers
D. islands

RH.6–8.2
2 In what way does the code of chivalry still affect people?
F. It provided a model for starting a business.
G. It formed the bases for our educational system.
H. Many of our ideas about social manners are based on it.
I. The code of chivalry did not have a lasting effect.

RH.6–8.2
3 King Henry II of England used which of the following to increase his power?
A. his serfs
B. the pope
C. courts of law
D. the Magna Carta

RH.6–8.2, RH.6–8.4
4 "Flying buttresses" are related to which of the following?
F. scholasticism
G. vernacular language
H. Romanesque architecture
I. Gothic architecture

RH.6–8.2
5 Why did Pope Urban II call for the First Crusade?
A. He hoped to reunite the Church.
B. He wanted to take over the Byzantine empire.
C. He wanted to convert the Turks to Christianity.
D. He was getting back at the Turks for an attack on Rome.

RH.6–8.2
6 From which of these European countries were Jews expelled in 1492?
F. Spain
G. Italy
H. England
I. France

ASSESSMENT ANSWERS

Review the Guiding Questions

1 **C** The Danube and the Po are rivers, not mountain ranges, peninsulas, or islands. Mountain ranges include the Pyrenees, the Alps, and the Carpathians; peninsulas include Spain and Italy; islands include England and Ireland.

2 **H** Chivalry is the knightly code of conduct. It had a lasting effect on most Western cultures and their belief systems today. It did not have an effect on business or education.

3 **C** Henry II increased his power using courts of law. Although Henry II had serfs, his peasant workers were not a source of increased power. Likewise, he did not rely on the pope, who was the head of the Catholic Church, or the Magna Carta, a document that limited the powers of the English king, to become more powerful.

4 **I** The flying buttress was a feature of Gothic architecture. Scholasticism was a philosophical worldview; the vernacular is everyday language; Romanesque architecture combined the features of Roman and Byzantine buildings.

5 **A** Urban II wanted to reunite the two Christian Churches. He did not want to take over the Byzantine Empire, convert the Turks to Christianity, or retaliate against the Turks.

6 **F** Jews were expelled in large numbers from Spain after Ferdinand and Isabella decided to make Roman Catholicism Spain's one religion. Jews were not expelled in large numbers from Italy, England, or France.

Locating Places

4 **1.** C, **2.** E, **3.** D, **4.** A, **5.** B

Analyzing Documents

7 **C** The relationship between king and vassal is part of the feudal system. The manorial system refers to the ways in which medieval communities grew crops and maintained a lifestyle centered on the manor. Scholasticism refers to a philosophical worldview. The guild system refers to organizations of craftspeople and artisans who controlled trade in medieval towns and cities.

8 **H** The fact that the king wrote down the rules for military service suggests that he intended to treat his vassals fairly by rewarding them for their service. It is unlikely that the vassals and knights would dare to rebel openly or overthrow the king or that the vassals and knights would become divided.

Short Response

9 The amount of farmland that could be cultivated was reduced substantially.

10 Without workers to work in the fields, the economy of Europe was greatly hurt.

Extended Response

11 Outlines will vary but may include the following: Architecture: construction of cathedrals and major features of the Romanesque and Gothic styles; Literature: use of the vernacular and major features of troubadour songs and heroic epics; Education: development of universities in cities such as Paris and Bologna, offering a variety of subjects and methods of study, examinations, and degrees.

 **Assessment** *(continued)* 

DBQ ANALYZING DOCUMENTS

Summarizing King Louis IX asked the following of his vassals:

"All vassals of the king are bound to appear before him when he shall summon [call] them, and to serve him at their own expense for forty days and forty nights, with as many knights as each one owes."

—King Louis IX, "Legal Rules for Military Service"

RH.6–8.1, RH.6–8.6

7 Which of the following best describes the obligations of the king's vassals?

A. manorial system
B. scholasticism
C. feudalism
D. guild system

RH.6–8.1, RH.6–8.6

8 **Making Inferences** Based on what you have learned about medieval Europe, which of the following best describes what would happen if the king needed vassals and knights for more than 40 days and nights?

F. The vassals and knights would overthrow the king.
G. The knights would rebel against the vassals.
H. The vassals and knights would continue serving at the king's expense.
I. The vassals and knights would withdraw to the manor.

SHORT RESPONSE

"A more lasting and serious consequence [of the plague] was the drastic reduction of the amount of land under cultivation [able to be farmed] due to the deaths of so many labourers. . . . The psychological effects of the Black Death were reflected . . . . by a preoccupation with death and the afterlife evinced [displayed] in poetry, sculpture, and painting."

—"Black Death," Encyclopaedia Britannica

RH.6–8.1, RH.6–8.6

9 According to the passage, what was one effect of the plague?

RH.6–8.1, RH.6–8.6

10 Why did the lack of labor have a negative effect on Europe?

EXTENDED RESPONSE

RH.6–8.2, WHST.6–8.2, WHST.6–8.10

11 **Informative/Explanatory** You have been asked to contribute to a reference article about the Middle Ages. You are responsible for these areas of medieval culture: architecture, literature, and education. Write an outline showing the specific facts and details you plan to cover in your article.

Need Extra Help?

If You've Missed Question	1	2	3	4	5	6	7	8	9	10	11
Review Lesson	1	2	3	4	3	5	2	2	3	5	5

networks Online Teaching Options

Using eAssessment

Use eAssessment to access and assign the publisher-made Lesson Quizzes & Chapter Tests electronically. You can also use eAssessment to create your own quizzes and tests from hundreds of available questions. eAssessment helps you design assessments that meet the needs of different types of learners. Follow the link in the *Assess* tab of your Teacher Lesson Center.

CHAPTER 20

Renaissance and Reformation Planner

UNDERSTANDING BY DESIGN®

Enduring Understandings

- *The movement of people, goods, and ideas causes societies to change over time.*
- *People, places, and ideas change over time.*
- *Religion can influence a society's beliefs and values.*
- *Countries have relationships with each other.*

Essential Questions

- *Why do people make economic choices?*
- *How do new ideas change the way people live?*
- *How do religions develop?*
- *Why does conflict develop?*

Predictable Misunderstandings

Students may think:

- *The Renaissance was only a period of time and not a way of thinking.*
- *Only painters, sculptors, and artists were a part of the Renaissance.*
- *There was only one Reformation.*

Assessment Evidence

Performance Tasks:

- *Hands-On Chapter Project*

Other Evidence:

- *Class discussion answers*
- *Class simulation participation*
- *Interactive Whiteboard Activity responses*
- *Geography and History Activity*
- *Economics of History Activities*
- *21st Century Skills Activities*
- *Lesson Reviews*
- *Evaluation of class simulation*
- *Writing activities*

SUGGESTED PACING GUIDE

Introducing the Chapter .... 1 day
Lesson 1 .... 1 day
Lesson 2 .... 2 days
The World's Literature .... 1 day
Lesson 3 .... 2 days
Lesson 4 .... 2 days
Chapter Wrap-Up and Assessment ...... 1 day

TOTAL TIME 10 DAYS

Key for Using the Teacher Edition

SKILL-BASED ACTIVITIES

Types of skill activities found in the Teacher Edition.

V Visual Skills require students to analyze maps, graphs, charts, and photos.

R Reading Skills help students practice reading skills and master vocabulary.

W Writing Skills provide writing opportunities to help students comprehend the text.

C Critical Thinking Skills help students apply and extend what they have learned.

T Technology Skills require students to use digital tools effectively.

*Letters are followed by a number when there is more than one of the same type of skill on the page.

DIFFERENTIATED INSTRUCTION

All activities are written for the on-level student unless otherwise marked with the leveled labels below.

BL Beyond Level

AL Approaching Level

ELL English Language Learners

All students benefit from activities that utilize different learning styles. Many activities are marked as below when a particular learning style is highlighted.

Intrapersonal **Naturalist**
Logical/Mathematical **Kinesthetic**
Visual/Spatial **Auditory/Musical**
Verbal/Linguistic **Interpersonal**

NCSS Standards covered in "Renaissance and Reformation"

Learners will understand:

2 TIME, CONTINUITY, AND CHANGE

5. Key historical periods and patterns of change within and across cultures (e.g., the rise and fall of ancient civilizations, the development of technology, the rise of modern nation-states, and the establishment and breakdown of colonial systems)

7. The contributions of key persons, groups, and events from the past and their influence on the present

3 PEOPLE, PLACES, AND ENVIRONMENTS

4. The roles of different kinds of population centers in a region or nation

6. Patterns of demographic and political change, and cultural diffusion in the past and present (e.g., changing national boundaries, migration, and settlement, and the diffusion of and changes in customs and ideas)

8. Factors that contribute to cooperation and conflict among peoples of the nation and world, including language, religion, and political beliefs

5 INDIVIDUALS, GROUPS, AND INSTITUTIONS

5. That groups and institutions change over time

6. That cultural diffusion occurs when groups migrate

8. That when two or more groups with differing norms and beliefs interact, accommodation or conflict may result

7 PRODUCTION, DISTRIBUTION, AND CONSUMPTION

4. Economic incentives affect people's behavior and may be regulated by rules or laws

7. How markets bring buyers and sellers together to exchange goods and services

8 SCIENCE, TECHNOLOGY, AND SOCIETY

2. Society often turns to science and technology to solve problems

5. Science and technology have changed people's perceptions of the social and natural world, as well as their relationship to the land, economy and trade, their concept of security, and their major daily activities

6. Values, beliefs, and attitudes that have been influenced by new scientific and technological knowledge (e.g., invention of the printing press, conceptions of the universe, applications of atomic energy, and genetic discoveries)

CHAPTER OPENER PLANNER

Students will know:

- *why the city-states of Italy became centers of culture during the Renaissance.*
- *how the city-states of Italy gained their power.*
- *how Renaissance writers developed new ideas.*
- *what methods Renaissance artists used to make their work natural and real.*
- *how the Renaissance changed as it moved from Italy into northern Europe.*
- *how the teachings of Protestant reformers shaped the western world.*
- *how the Reformation influenced England and its American colonies.*
- *how the Catholic Church responded to the spread of Protestantism.*
- *how wars of religion affected Europe.*

Students will be able to:

- ***discuss** who ruled the city-states of Italy and how they achieved that power.*
- ***describe** humanism.*
- ***analyze and identify** differences between a Middle Ages–style painting and a Renaissance–style painting.*
- ***describe** who Shakespeare was and his influence on literature.*
- ***explain** why the Church was pressured to reform.*
- ***identify** the three main differences between Lutheranism and the Catholic Church.*
- ***locate** European countries that were significant to the Reformation and explain why.*
- ***describe** how European monarchs used religion to their advantage.*
- ***explain** why France fought against Catholic countries in the Thirty Years' War.*

UNDERSTANDING BY DESIGN®

☑ *Print Teaching Options*

V Visual Skills

☐ **P. 580** Students analyze historical map of Renaissance Europe. Visual/Spatial

R Reading Skills

☐ **P. 581** Students identify important events on time line.

W Writing Skills

☐ **P. 581** Students complete Time Line activity.

☑ *Online Teaching Options*

V Visual Skills

MAP **Renaissance Europe, A.D. 1500**—Students view a map of Europe, identify the extent of the Holy Roman Empire, and learn about Bohemia.

TIME LINE **Renaissance and Reformation 1350–1650**—Students learn about key events during this time period.

WORLD ATLAS Students can use this interactive map to identify regions of the world, learn about individual countries, locate political boundaries, measure distances, and much more.

☑ *Printable Digital Worksheets*

R Reading Skills

GRAPHIC NOVEL **Welcome to Venice!**—In this graphic novel, a couple receives a brochure that describes Venetian government and trade, Venetian crafts, artists, and Carnival.

Project-Based Learning

Hands-On Chapter Project

Renaissance Interview

Students pairs will participate in an interview exercise in which they each get a chance to interview an important person from the Renaissance and be an interviewee.

Technology Extension

edtechteacher 21st Century Learning

Renaissance Online Chat

- Find an additional activity online that incorporates technology for this project.
- Visit the EdTechTeacher Web sites (included in the Technology Extension for this chapter) for more links, tutorials, and other resources.

Print Resources

ANCILLARY RESOURCES

These ancillaries are available for every chapter and lesson.

- **Reading Essentials and Study Guide Workbook** AL ELL
- **Chapter Tests and Lesson Quizzes Blackline Masters**

PRINTABLE DIGITAL WORKSHEETS

These printable digital worksheets are available for every chapter and lesson.

- **Hands-On Chapter Projects**
- **What Do You Know? activities**
- **Chapter Summaries (English and Spanish)**
- **Vocabulary Builder activities**
- **Guided Reading activities**

More Media Resources

SUGGESTED READING 

Grade 6 reading level:

- ***Leonardo: Beautiful Dreamer,*** by Robert Byrd

Grade 7 reading level:

- ***Elizabeth I, The Outcast Who Became England's Queen,*** by Simon Adams

Grade 8 reading level:

- ***Around the World in 1500,*** by Virginia Schomp

THE RENAISSANCE BEGINS

Students will know:
- *why the city-states of Italy became centers of culture during the Renaissance.*
- *how the city-states of Italy gained their power.*

Students will be able to:
- ***discuss** who ruled the city-states of Italy and how they achieved that power.*

UNDERSTANDING BY DESIGN®

☑ *Print Teaching Options*

V Visual Skills
- ☐ **P. 583** Students answer geography questions based on map of Italy. ELL Visual/Spatial
- ☐ **P. 586** Students study diagram of Il Duomo and answer questions. AL ELL

R Reading Skills
- ☐ **P. 582** Students answer questions about the Renaissance after reading the text.
- ☐ **P. 586** Students define key words from their reading. ELL
- ☐ **P. 587** Students answer questions based on what they learn about Lorenzo de' Medici. AL

W Writing Skills
- ☐ **P. 587** Students write an informative essay about the Italian city-states. Verbal/Linguistic

C Critical Thinking Skills
- ☐ **P. 583** Students write cause-and-effect sentences about how Italy's geographic location led to its key role in the Renaissance. BL
- ☐ **P. 585** Students analyze what they have read and make conclusions about the information. BL
- ☐ **P. 585** Students rank commonly traded goods in order of importance to them and explain their decisions.
- ☐ **P. 588** Students contemplate why diplomacy developed in Renaissance Italy. Intrapersonal
- ☐ **P. 588** Students read a selection of Machiavelli's *The Prince.* Verbal/Linguistic

T Technology Skills
- ☐ **P. 584** Student groups use the Internet to research an Italian city-state. Interpersonal

☑ *Online Teaching Options*

V Visual Skills
- VIDEO **Leonardo da Vinci**—Students explore how da Vinci defined the Renaissance.
- MAP **Italy, A.D. 1500**— Students view a map of Italy that shows all the city-states.
- SLIDE SHOW **Il Duomo**—Students view architectural aspects of this massive cathedral in Florence, Italy.

R Reading Skills
- GRAPHIC ORGANIZER **Taking Notes: *Identifying*: Wealth Grows in City-States**—Students list reasons why Italian city-states grew wealthy at the beginning of the Renaissance.
- PRIMARY SOURCES **Marco Polo**—Students analyze an excerpt from Polo's book.

C Critical Thinking Skills
- SLIDE SHOW **Venice**—Students analyze landmarks found in this Italian city.
- IMAGE **Gonzaga Family**—Students analyze a portrait of members of this family who played an important role in the Italian military and were sponsors of the arts.

T Technology Skills
- SELF-CHECK QUIZ **Lesson 1**—Students receive instant feedback on their mastery of lesson content.
- GAME **The Renaissance Begins Fill-in-the Blank Game**—Students complete sentences to review lesson content.

☑ *Printable Digital Worksheets*

C Critical Thinking Skills
- WORKSHEET **Economics of History Activity: The Role of Guilds**—Students analyze the role of guilds in Italian city-states.

LESSON 2 PLANNER

NEW IDEAS AND ART

Students will know:
- *how Renaissance writers developed new ideas.*
- *what methods Renaissance artists used to make their work natural and real.*
- *how the Renaissance changed as it moved from Italy into northern Europe.*

Students will be able to:
- ***describe*** *humanism.*
- ***analyze and identify*** *differences between a Middle Ages–style painting and a Renaissance–style painting.*
- ***describe*** *who Shakespeare was and his influence on literature.*

UNDERSTANDING BY DESIGN®

☑ Print Teaching Options

V Visual Skills

- ☐ **P. 589** Students create flowchart to illustrate how new ideas moved across Europe and the Middle East. Visual/Spatial

R Reading Skills

- ☐ **P. 589** Students list characteristics of humanism.
- ☐ **P. 590** Students explain the importance of Petrarch, Dante, and Chaucer. AL ELL
- ☐ **P. 592** Students explain the concept of perspective in their own words. Verbal/Linguistic
- ☐ **P. 593** Students analyze meaning of terms *chiaroscuro* and *fresco.*
- ☐ **P. 594** Students answer questions about Raphael based on what they have read in the text.

W Writing Skills

- ☐ **P. 590** Students write a poem or short story that uses vernacular slang. Verbal/Linguistic Intrapersonal

C Critical Thinking Skills

- ☐ **P. 591** Students compare difficulty of writing by hand with printing press and modern computers.
- ☐ **P. 592** Students use craft materials to build a model of a possible invention. Visual/Spatial Kinesthetic
- ☐ **P. 593** Students read a contemporary quote about the work of Michelangelo. BL
- ☐ **P. 595** Students consider why Shakespeare's plays continue to be popular today.

T Technology Skills

- ☐ **P. 591** Students type selection of text in word-processing program and alter font, color, size, and format. Visual/Spatial
- ☐ **P. 593** Student groups research a Renaissance artist and give a class presentation on the artist's life and work. BL Interpersonal

☑ Online Teaching Options

V Visual Skills

- VIDEO **Chaucer's England**—Medieval art, architecture, and poetry re-create the spirit of the Middle Ages with a focus on Chaucer's *Canterbury Tales.*
- IMAGE **Jan Van Eyck**—Students analyze one of Van Eyck's famous paintings.
- IMAGE **The Globe Theater**—Students click to reveal details about the structure of this London theater.
- SLIDE SHOW **Leonardo da Vinci**—Students view a selection of da Vinci's work.

R Reading Skills

- GRAPHIC ORGANIZER **Taking Notes: *Describing*: Renaissance Art**—Students describe how examples of Renaissance art reflect Renaissance ideas.
- IMAGE **Mona Lisa**—Students read about the history of what some consider to be the world's most famous painting.
- IMAGE **Michelangelo**—Students read of the life and accomplishments of this Italian sculptor.
- PRIMARY SOURCE **Petrarch**—Students read an excerpt from a sonnet by Petrarch.

C Critical Thinking Skills

- SLIDE SHOW **Gutenberg Press**—Students consider how Gutenberg's invention of movable metal type changed the dissemination of information.

T Technology Skills

- SELF-CHECK QUIZ **Lesson 2**—Students receive instant feedback on their mastery of lesson content.

☑ Printable Digital Worksheets

R Reading Skills

- GRAPHIC NOVEL **Renaissance Man**—Students examine the life of Leonardo da Vinci.

C Critical Thinking Skills

- WORKSHEET **21st Century Skills Activity: Critical Thinking and Problem Solving: Analyze Writing, Visuals, Communication**—Students read a paragraph, examine an image, and answer questions.

LESSON 3 PLANNER

THE REFORMATION BEGINS

Students will know:
- *how the teachings of Protestant reformers shaped the Western world.*
- *how the Reformation influenced England and its American colonies.*

Students will be able to:
- ***explain** why the Church was pressured to reform.*
- ***identify** the three main differences between Lutheranism and the Catholic Church.*
- ***locate** European countries that were significant to the Reformation and explain why.*

UNDERSTANDING BY DESIGN®

☑ Print Teaching Options

V Visual Skills

- ☐ **P. 600** Students create a time line of major events in Luther's life. Visual/Spatial
- ☐ **P. 602** Students answer questions based on a map of Europe during the Reformation. BL

R Reading Skills

- ☐ **P. 598** Students identify key facts about Martin Luther. AL ELL
- ☐ **P. 599** Students identify key details about the lives of John Wycliffe and Erasmus.
- ☐ **P. 601** Students paraphrase Luther's speech to the Diet of Worms in 1521. BL
- ☐ **P. 601** Students identify reasons why the Lutheran movement became tied to politics.
- ☐ **P. 603** Students identify key ideas about Calvanism. AL
- ☐ **P. 604** Students identify key details about Henry VIII of England from their reading.
- ☐ **P. 605** Students explain the origin of the name "Bloody Mary" for Mary I of England.

W Writing Skills

- ☐ **P. 598** Students write letter to the pope during Reformation arguing against a practice of the Church. BL Verbal/Linguistic Intrapersonal
- ☐ **P. 600** Students write a short essay about Luther's beliefs and his actions to reform the Church.
- ☐ **P. 604** Students write a newspaper article about the events surrounding Henry's battle with Rome. Verbal/Linguistic

C Critical Thinking Skills

- ☐ **P. 602** Students contemplate common reasons for conflict before compromise.
- ☐ **P. 603** Students will contrast Calvin's beliefs with those of Martin Luther. Students will consider the role Switzerland may have played in the dissemination of Protestant ideas. BL
- ☐ **P. 605** Students contrast the beliefs of Anglicans with Puritans.

☑ Online Teaching Options

V Visual Skills

- ☐ VIDEO **Martin Luther and the Reformation**—Students learn of the factors that led to the Reformation.
- ☐ MAP **Holy Roman Empire, 1520**—Students view the extent of the empire and the states that composed it.

R Reading Skills

- ☐ GRAPHIC ORGANIZER **Taking Notes: *Determining Cause and Effect*: Reasons for the Reformation**—Students identify reasons for the Reformation.
- ☐ BIOGRAPHY **John Calvin**—Students read of Calvin's life and accomplishments.
- ☐ IMAGE **Queen Elizabeth I**—Students read of Elizabeth's life and accomplishments.
- ☐ PRIMARY SOURCE **John Wycliffe**—Students read an excerpt from Wycliffe's Bible translation.

C Critical Thinking Skills

- ☐ WHITEBOARD ACTIVITY **Church Leaders of the Reformation**—Students identify actions of Luther, Wycliffe, and Erasmus.
- ☐ CHART **Martin Luther and the Reformation**—Students click to see the three main ideas of the Reformation.
- ☐ CHART **Sale of Indulgences**—Students click to see the prices that people of differing social status paid for an indulgence.
- ☐ PRIMARY SOURCE **Erasmus**—Students analyze a letter Erasmus wrote to convince a teacher to continue in his profession.

T Technology Skills

- ☐ SELF-CHECK QUIZ **Lesson 3**—Students receive instant feedback on their mastery of lesson content.
- ☐ GAME **The Reformation Begins True-or-False Game**—Students review lesson content by determining the veracity of several statements.

☑ Printable Digital Worksheets

C Critical Thinking Skills

- ☐ WORKSHEET **21st Century Skills Activity: Critical Thinking and Problem Solving: Determining Cause and Effect**—Students write cause-and-effect statements after analyzing a reading passage.

LESSON 4 PLANNER

CATHOLICS AND PROTESTANTS

Students will know:

- *how the Catholic Church responded to the spread of Protestantism.*
- *how wars of religion affected Europe.*

Students will be able to:

- ***describe** how European monarchs used religion to their advantage.*
- ***explain** why France fought against Catholic countries in the Thirty Years' War.*

UNDERSTANDING BY DESIGN®

Print Teaching Options

V Visual Skills

- [ ] **P. 608** Students answer questions based on a map of religions in Europe in the 1600s. **Visual/Spatial**

R Reading Skills

- [ ] **P. 606** Students state the two goals of the Catholic Reformation.
- [ ] **P. 607** Students state three reasons religious harmony ended in Spain.
- [ ] **P. 610** Students explain how Catherine de' Medici came to power in France.

W Writing Skills

- [ ] **P. 606** Students write a short essay arguing why one or two reforms made at the Council of Trent are positive ones. **Verbal/Linguistic Intrapersonal**

C Critical Thinking Skills

- [ ] **P. 610** Students consider causes of the conflict between Catholics and Protestants in France. Students determine how the Edict of Nantes offers an example for modern religious conflict. **BL**
- [ ] **P. 611** Students analyze France's role in the Thirty Years' War. **AL**

T Technology Skills

- [ ] **P. 609** Student groups choose a topic from the reading and use Internet resources to produce a research project. **Visual/Spatial Interpersonal**

Online Teaching Options

V Visual Skills

- **VIDEO** **Francis Drake**—Students view a video about this English sea captain who helped defeat the Spanish Armada.
- **IMAGE** **The Defenestration of Prague**—Students view an image and read about the event that led to the start of the Thirty Years' War.

R Reading Skills

- **GRAPHIC ORGANIZER** **Taking Notes: *Determining Cause and Effect*: Reform in the Catholic Church**—Students diagram the results of the Catholic Church's attempts at reform.
- **BIOGRAPHY** **Sir Francis Drake**—Students read of Drake's life and accomplishments.
- **IMAGE** **Catherine de' Medici**—Students read about this Italian supporter of the arts.
- **BIOGRAPHY** **Henry of Navarre**—Students read about the life and accomplishments of this leader who eventually became King of France.

C Critical Thinking Skills

- **CHART** **Effects of the Council of Trent**—Students click to reveal four reforms of the Catholic Church that resulted from the Council of Trent.
- **MAP** **Religions in Europe c. 1600**—Students draw parallels between a population's location and its religion.

T Technology Skills

- **SELF-CHECK QUIZ** **Lesson 4**—Students receive instant feedback on their mastery of lesson content.
- **GAME** **Catholics and Protestants Crossword Puzzle**—Students answer clues to review lesson content.

Printable Digital Worksheets

C Critical Thinking Skills

- **WORKSHEET** **Primary Source Activity: The Expulsion of the Jews From Spain**—Students analyze passages about the Inquisition and the expulsion of Jews from Spain.

INTERVENTION AND REMEDIATION STRATEGIES

LESSON 1 The Renaissance Begins

Reading and Comprehension

Hold a discussion with students about how power and influence are often tied to wealth. Discuss why students think this might be, and identify different types of wealth, such as financial wealth, property wealth, and wealth of knowledge.

- **Ask:** Do you think each type of wealth will gain someone the same amount of power and influence? If you answer "no," which type of wealth do you believe will give someone the most power and influence? Explain your answer.

Text Evidence

Place students into groups and assign an Italian state to each group. Have them use the textbook and do additional research on each Italian state during the Renaissance.

Then have group members perform skits that depict what life might have been like in that particular state. Students should pay particular attention to who held power in the state, how the state gained its wealth, and notable events that happened within the state.

LESSON 2 New Ideas and Art

Reading and Comprehension

Have students keep an "artist's notebook" during this lesson. In it, have students include information such as:

- artistic vocabulary terms that the students define in their own words.
- names of all artists discussed in the chapter (including Gutenberg, because type can be considered a form of art).
- brief summaries describing noted works discussed in the chapter, such as The Arnolfini Portrait, the Mona Lisa, and the Sistine Chapel.
- simple drawings or sketches that may illustrate artistic terms or an artist's style, or any information that relates to the chapter.

Text Evidence

Arrange a trip to a Renaissance art exhibit or a visit from a guest speaker who is an expert in Renaissance art. Have students prepare for the trip or the visit by writing questions for the expert or tour guide. Question topics should include queries about the artists mentioned in the chapter or about artistic terms, such as *chiaroscuro, fresco,* and *perspective.*

LESSON 3 The Reformation Begins

Reading and Comprehension

Hang a large sheet of colored butcher paper (or several large sheets side-by-side) in the classroom. Create a chart of information about each historical figure as you move through the chapter so that students are building a visual resource. The chart should include information such as names, locations, names of religions or beliefs, short summaries of those beliefs, and notable accomplishments during the Renaissance.

Text Evidence

Have students prepare oral presentations (that can include additional research other than the textbook) on any of the people mentioned in the chapter. Then have students speak as though they are their chosen person. They should tell the audience who they are, what they accomplished during the Renaissance, what they believe, and why they believe the audience should believe as they do.

LESSON 4 Catholics and Protestants

Reading and Comprehension

Discuss with students how this chapter focuses on dictating religious beliefs by rule, conflict, or intimidation and fear. Have students cite a specific example of each and tell the outcome of each action or event. Then have students hypothesize about how the use of such methods could affect the short- and long-term stability of a country.

Text Evidence

Have students research and discuss the history of conflict in Northern Ireland between Catholics and Protestants. Topics of study could include the Irish Republican Army, Sinn Fein, or the use of the colors green and orange to represent Catholics and Protestants, respectively.

Online Resources

Approaching Level Reader

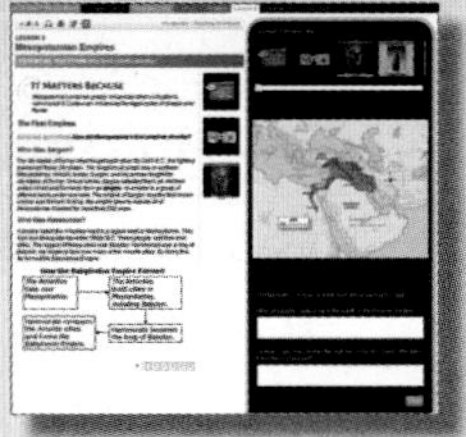

Use this online lower-level text that corresponds directly to the text in the Student Edition. It includes a Spanish version.

Guided Reading Activities

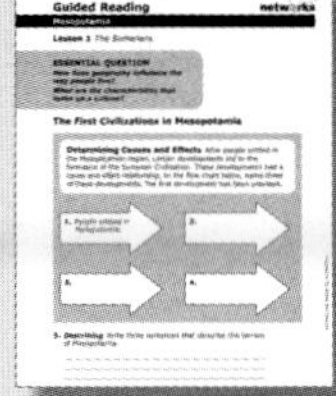

This resource uses graphic organizers and guiding questions to help students with comprehension.

What Do You Know?

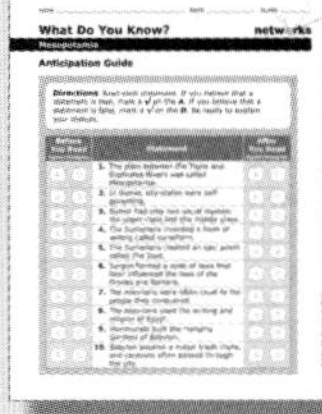

Use these worksheets to pre-assess student's background knowledge before they study the chapter.

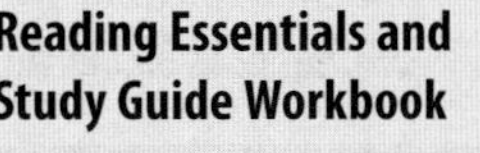

Reading Essentials and Study Guide Workbook

This resource offers writing and reading activities for the approaching-level student. Also available in Spanish.

Self-Check Quizzes

This online assessment tool provides instant feedback for students to check their progress.

How Do I Use Game-Based Learning?

Teachers are always looking for ways to speak to their students in ways that engage and excite the learner's imagination. Game-based learning strategies offer new, exciting ways to engage students in learning.

Strategy 1 Use a Pre-built Educational Game to Help You Teach Content

- There are many different companies and Web sites that offer educational games.
- For example, *iCivics.org,* provides many strategy games that offer fun ways to learn about our country's political process, legal system, and other civics and government-related topics. Lesson plans accompany each game.

FREDERICK FLORIN/Staff/AFP/Getty Images

Strategy 2 Correlate Existing Games to Your Own Learning Objectives.

- Research the wide variety of private company games available and incorporate them into your lesson plans.
- Use popular games, such as SimCity™, to help students learn more about the demands of city government and the decisions that need to be made by government leaders. Or use the game Civilization® to study topics that relate to ancient world history. Games like this can be used in group settings or as an individual learning tool.
- Browse the Internet to find lesson plans and strategies developed by other teachers.

Strategy 3 Create Your Own Game

- Think about how to turn one of your reliable teaching activities into a game-based scenario. Consider how to create a game's scoring system, appropriate game-based incentives, and content-driven gaming feedback.
- Use these questions to guide your planning strategy: What is your game player's motivation? What sort of game process or game mechanics do you need to design? What are the conditions for mastering the game?

To learn more about using games as teaching tools, visit McGraw-Hill Education's *btw* Current Events Web site (**blog.glencoe.com**) and use the search term EDUCATIONAL GAMES to learn more about the topic.

Renaissance and Reformation

1350 to 1650

ESSENTIAL QUESTIONS • *Why do people make economic choices?* • *How do new ideas change the way people live?* • *Why does conflict develop?*

networks

There's More Online about life during the Renaissance and Reformation.

CHAPTER 20

Lesson 1 *The Renaissance Begins*

Lesson 2 *New Ideas and Art*

Lesson 3 *The Reformation Begins*

Lesson 4 *Catholics and Protestants*

The Story Matters . . .

The Renaissance was a brilliant flowering of European culture from the 1300s to 1600s. During this time, the city-state of Florence in Italy became the center of business, art, and learning. It attracted many artists who are still famous today, including Michelangelo and Leonardo da Vinci.

This image is from a Renaissance painting of the three wise men traveling to see the baby Jesus. The painting was made to decorate the palace of the powerful Medici family. The Medicis ruled Florence during the Renaissance. Lorenzo de' Medici was the model for the wise man shown here.

◄ *Benozzo Gozzoli painted "The Procession of the Magi" (1459) for the Medici family.*

Letter from the Author

Dear World History Teacher,

Between 1350 and 1550, Italian intellectuals believed they were living in a new age based on rebirth of the culture of the Greeks and Romans. Intellectuals and artists proclaimed a new vision of humankind and raised questions about the value of the individual. The brilliant intellectual, cultural, and artistic accomplishments of the Renaissance were really products of and for the elite and did not have a broad base among the masses of the people. However, the intellectual revolution gave way to a religious reformation that touched the lives of all people in profound ways.

Jackson J. Spielvogel

ENGAGE

Bellringer Begin by telling students that the Renaissance was a specific time in Europe when the arts and new ideas were particularly important to people.

Read "The Story Matters . . ." aloud in class. Then discuss what it might have been like to live in Florence in the presence of so many famous artists and writers. **Ask:**

- **What is a famous work of art that you have seen in pictures or in person?** Have a few students give examples.
- **What would it be like to live at the time artists were creating these works? What would it be like to see these works when they were new instead of hanging in museums?** *(Answers will vary.)*

Tell the class that the citizens of Florence were surrounded by important art and artists because wealthy citizens paid for these works. **Ask: What stadiums, museums, or parks in America are named for well-known people?** Have students give examples of buildings that are named for well-known people. *(the Getty Museum, Wrigley Field, Kennedy Space Center, and so on)* Explain that these buildings are named for people who supported sports or the arts. These individuals are honored for their contributions by naming buildings after them. Tell students that modern examples of these contributors are like the Medicis of Florence during the Renaissance. The Medicis supported art and artists of their time. Similarly, people today support sports and a variety of art forms, such as music.

Making Connections

When Lorenzo de' Medici was seventeen, he prevented an ambush against his father. This act helped the family maintain its influence in Florence. Lorenzo was married and had seven children. He and his wife, Clarice, ensured that all seven of them were educated. Lorenzo also was a patron who supported the work of Botticelli, Leonardo da Vinci, Michelangelo, and other artists as well.

CHAPTER 20
Place and Time

Step Into the Place

V Visual Skills

Analyzing Maps Have students point out the locations of countries they have heard about or recognize on the Chapter Opener map of Renaissance Europe. Help them identify where major mountains, rivers, and oceans are located. Then point out the areas or countries on the map that have names that differ from what they are called today *(for example, Holy Roman Empire, Bohemia, Kingdom of the Two Sicilies)*. Explain that this is a historical map. Tell students that as the borders of countries have changed and developed throughout history, mountains, rivers, and oceans have played an important part in determining border locations. Next, as a class, discuss the Map Focus questions. **Visual/Spatial**

Content Background Knowledge

- Two members of the Medici family became popes of the Roman Catholic Church. Giovanni de' Medici was Pope Leo X and Giulio de' Medici was Pope Clement VII. The Medicis served as bankers for the Roman Catholic Church. Anyone who deposited funds in the Medici bank had to pay 10 percent of those earnings to the Church. If people couldn't pay this amount, they faced excommunication, or forced exile, from the Church. During the Renaissance, Roman Catholics believed that excommunication meant that one was destined for Hell upon death.
- In Italian, the city of Florence is known as *Firenze*. It is home to several famous art museums, such as the Pitti Palace. This was once a residence for the Medici family, and it now houses galleries, museums, and a garden. Many paintings that were collected by the Medicis hang in the Palatine Gallery, including works by Renaissance artists Raphael and Titian. The Boboli Gardens were designed for the enjoyment of the Medicis. People are now permitted to enjoy the natural setting, fountains, and statues of the area by taking a tour.

ANSWERS, p. 580

Step Into the Place

1. the Kingdom of the Two Sicilies, the Papal States, Florence, Bologna, Venice, and Milan
2. Venice, Naples, and Florence are located on the coast, which would allow for shipping.
3. **CRITICAL THINKING** Austria and Bohemia do not border the Mediterranean Sea. Ideas would not travel as quickly in those areas as they would in the Italian region because transportation and communication would be more difficult.

Step Into the Time

Answers will vary but may include Martin Luther's attempts to reform the Catholic Church, the Peace of Augsburg, and Henry of Navarre's need to change religion.

CHAPTER 20 CCSS

Place and Time: Renaissance and Reformation, 1350 to 1650

During the Renaissance, wealthy Italian states developed new ideas about art and learning. Meanwhile, a movement to reform the Church began in the Holy Roman Empire. As this Reformation spread, new Protestant churches arose in northern Europe. Southern Europe, however, remained Catholic.

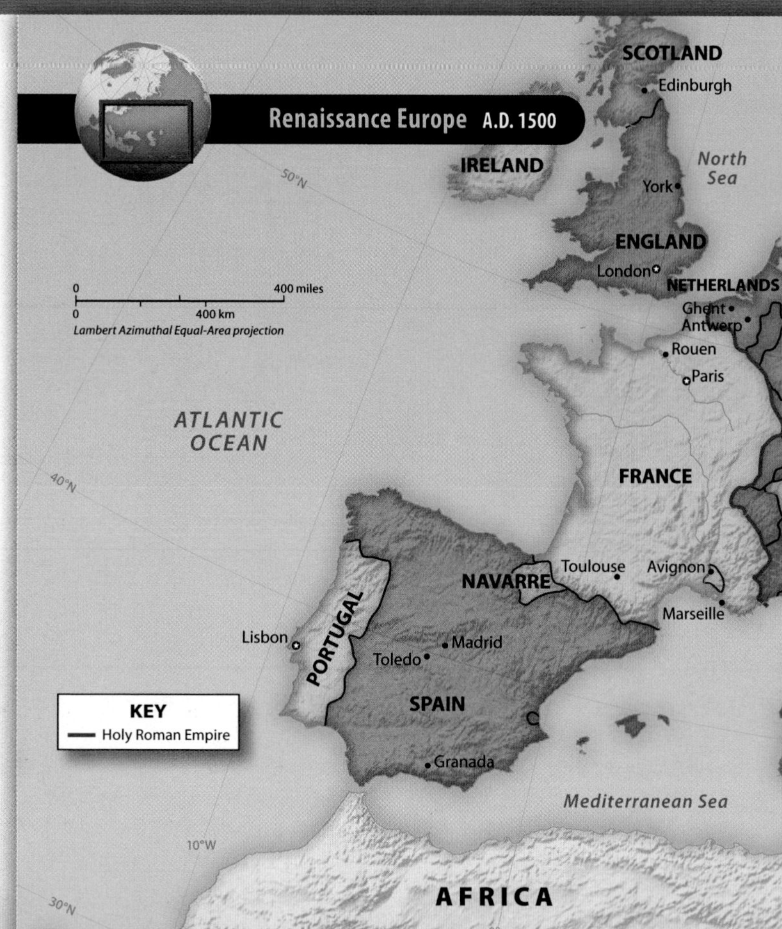

Step Into the Place

MAP FOCUS The states of the Italian peninsula became the center of the Renaissance.

1. **REGIONS** Look at the map. What territories are found on the Italian peninsula? RH.6–8.7
2. **PLACE** What physical features would make the cities of Venice and Naples important trade centers? RH.6–8.7
3. **CRITICAL THINKING** *Contrasting* Why might new ideas spread differently in the Italian region than in countries such as Austria and Bohemia? RH.6–8.2

Step Into the Time

TIME LINE Choose an event from the time line and write a paragraph predicting the religious, social, or political consequences that event might have for Europe. RH.6–8.7, WHST.6–8.10

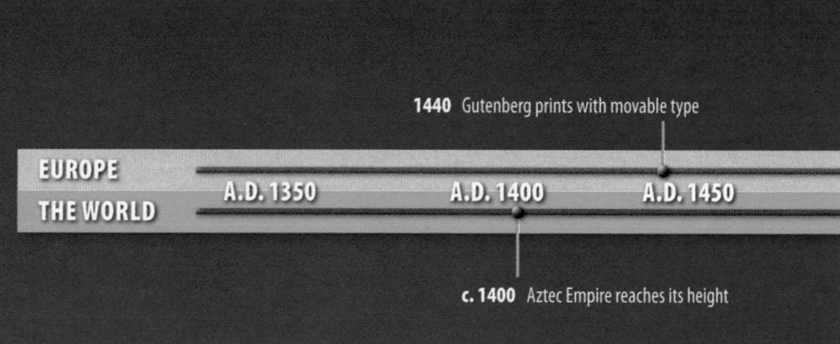

Project-Based Learning

Hands-On Chapter Project

Renaissance Interview

Student partners will participate in an exercise in which they will interview an important person from the Renaissance. Each student will conduct an interview and participate as an interviewee. Begin with a class discussion to review what students have learned about important people of the Renaissance. Then student pairs will choose a Renaissance figure for their project. Students will use discussions to help them prepare questions and answers for their interviews. Students will play both roles as they conduct their interviews for the rest of the class.

Technology Extension

Renaissance Online Chat

Students will participate in this activity to learn how to engage others in a synchronous online discussion, respond to questions thoroughly, and compose questions for the class.

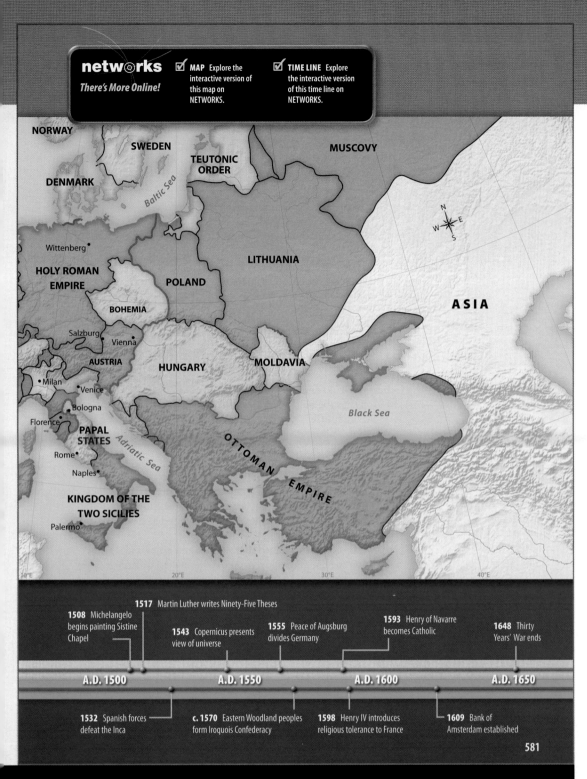

networks *There's More Online!*

☑ **MAP** Explore the interactive version of this map on NETWORKS.

☑ **TIME LINE** Explore the interactive version of this time line on NETWORKS.

NORWAY
SWEDEN
DENMARK
TEUTONIC ORDER
MUSCOVY
Baltic Sea
Wittenberg
HOLY ROMAN EMPIRE
LITHUANIA
POLAND
BOHEMIA
ASIA
Salzburg
Vienna
AUSTRIA
HUNGARY
MOLDAVIA
Milan
Venice
Bologna
Black Sea
Florence
PAPAL STATES
Adriatic Sea
OTTOMAN EMPIRE
Rome
Naples
KINGDOM OF THE TWO SICILIES
Palermo
10°E
20°E
30°E
40°E

1508 Michelangelo begins painting Sistine Chapel

1517 Martin Luther writes Ninety-Five Theses

1543 Copernicus presents view of universe

1555 Peace of Augsburg divides Germany

1593 Henry of Navarre becomes Catholic

1648 Thirty Years' War ends

A.D. 1500 — A.D. 1550 — A.D. 1600 — A.D. 1650

1532 Spanish forces defeat the Inca

c. 1570 Eastern Woodland peoples form Iroquois Confederacy

1598 Henry IV introduces religious tolerance to France

1609 Bank of Amsterdam established

581

CHAPTER 20

Place and Time

Step Into the Time

R Reading Skills

Locating Have students review the time line for the chapter. Explain that they will be studying events from about 1440 to 1648.

Have students locate two pieces of information on the time line that refer to the arts or new ideas in Europe. *(Possible answers: Gutenberg prints with movable type. Michelangelo begins painting Sistine Chapel. Martin Luther writes Ninety-five Theses. Copernicus presents view of universe.)*

W Writing Skills

Explanatory Have students write a paragraph to complete the Time Line activity.

Content Background Knowledge

- Humanism was one of the new ideas that developed during the Renaissance. Humanists believed that the Greek and Latin classics gave people the basis for leading a moral and effective life. Humanists created a new area of study in which the focus was on trying to understand the works of the Greeks and Romans. In several Italian cities, children from ruling or wealthy families were taught morality from a humanist perspective. They also wrote historical accounts and letters patterned after classical writing styles.
- Humanists convinced many popes that the Roman Catholic Church needed to adopt a more humanistic approach. Scholars knowledgeable in humanism were hired to write official correspondence for the Church. They also wrote a more classical form of the Mass. Humanistic popes wanted to create the impression that they were powerful rulers who were also enlightened and modern.

WORKSHEET

What Do You Know? Activity: Renaissance and Reformation

Determining Word Meanings Have students complete the What Do You Know? Four Square activity about the word *humanism* before they study the chapter. Help students create a definition of the word by examining the word parts. Then ask students to fill in the four squares with their best guesses. After students have read the chapter, have them use what they learned to add to or change their answers. ELL

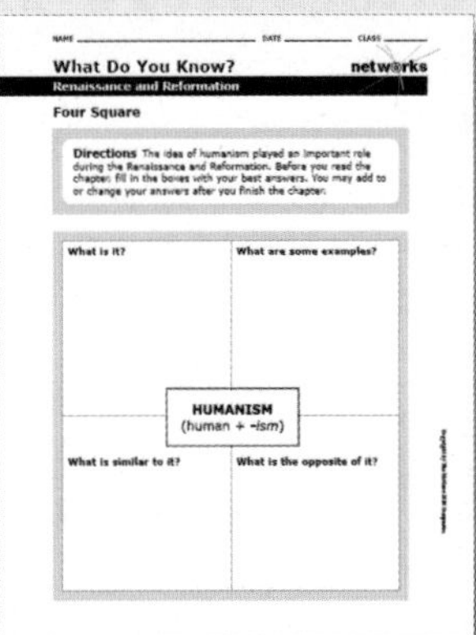
NAME ______ DATE ______ CLASS ______

What Do You Know? networks

Renaissance and Reformation

Four Square

Directions The idea of humanism played an important role during the Renaissance and Reformation. Before you read the chapter, fill in the boxes with your best answers. You may add to or change your answers after you finish the chapter.

What is it?	What are some examples?
What is similar to it?	What is the opposite of it?

HUMANISM (human + -ism)

The Renaissance Begins

ENGAGE

Bellringer Have students list five things that make them think of the country of Italy. *(Students may list foods such as spaghetti and pizza; a gondola; the colors red, white, and green; or famous sculptures or paintings.)*

Tell students they will be studying how Italy became a center in Europe for new types of architecture and methods of learning after the Middle Ages. Students will learn how classic Greek and Roman ideas influenced the artists and thinkers of Italy. Students will learn about city life and how society developed in Italy. They will also find out how developments in Europe's economy and government helped bring about these changes.

TEACH & ASSESS

R Reading Skills

Citing Text Evidence Ask students these six questions after they have read the opening paragraph in "The Renaissance in Italy" and "Rebirth of the Classics." **Ask:**

- Why did ways of thinking change greatly in Europe between 1350 and 1650? *(The Black Death eased. People became more confident about the future. Interest in learning and the arts was renewed.)*
- What was this new interest in culture called? *(the Renaissance)*
- What does this term mean? *(rebirth)*
- Which two ancient cultures did people become interested in during the Renaissance? *(the Greeks and the Romans)*
- What two things did Europeans begin to believe that people could do? *(make a difference and change the world for the better)*
- How are secular ideas and events different from religious ideas and events? *(Secular ideas and events are about the world, not religion.)*

Content Background Knowledge

Why the Renaissance Began in Italy

Due to numerous factors, the Renaissance began in Italy. These factors included but were not limited to:

- Italy was the center of the Roman Empire.
- Italy's cities had become wealthy and could afford to pay artists to produce new works.
- Italy was divided into smaller city-states that competed with one another to have artists make their city-state famous.
- Many people lived in cities in Italy, which allowed for a greater sharing of ideas.

ANSWER, p. 582

TAKING NOTES: The following contributed to the growth of wealth in the Italian city-states: Italy's long coastline and many ports made it an ideal location for trade; the Crusades brought Italian merchants into contact with Arab merchants; the rise of the Mongol Empire united almost all of Asia into one trade network.

networks *There's More Online!*
- GRAPHIC ORGANIZER Wealth Grows in City-States
- MAP Italy, c. 1500
- SLIDE SHOW
  - Il Duomo
  - Venice

Lesson 1

The Renaissance Begins

ESSENTIAL QUESTION *Why do people make economic choices?*

IT MATTERS BECAUSE

Renaissance developments helped shape today's arts, architecture, literature, and science.

The Renaissance in Italy

GUIDING QUESTION ***Why did the states of Italy become leading centers of culture during the Renaissance?***

Between 1350 and 1650, ways of thinking changed greatly in Europe. As the Black Death eased, people became more confident about the future. Their interest in learning and the arts was renewed. This new interest in culture is called the **Renaissance** (reh•nuh•SAHNTZ), from the French word for "rebirth."

Rebirth of the Classics

R The Renaissance sparked a renewed interest in ancient Greeks and Romans. European scholars improved their understanding of Greek and Latin languages, which they used to study ancient Greek and Roman writings.

Europeans also adopted many Greek and Roman ideas. They began to see that individual people could make a difference. They began to believe that people could change the world for the better.

During the Renaissance, most Europeans were still religious. However, they also began to value human efforts outside religion. As a result, people became more **secular** (SEH•kyuh•luhr). That is, they became more interested in worldly ideas and events, not just religious ones.

(l)Palazzo Ducale, Mantua, Italy/M. Magliani/Bridgeman Art Library, London/SuperStock, (cl)The Bridgeman Art Library, London/SuperStock, (cr)akg-images Philippe Michel/Age fotostock

Reading **HELP**DESK (CCSS)

Taking Notes: *Identifying* RH.6–8.2

Use a chart like this one to show the reasons Italian states grew wealthy.

Wealth Grows in Italian States		

Content Vocabulary (Tier 3 Words)
- **Renaissance**
- **secular**
- **urban**
- **mercenary**
- **diplomacy**

networks ***Online Teaching Options***

VIDEO

Leonardo da Vinci

Drawing Show students the video about the life and accomplishments of Leonardo da Vinci. Tell students that da Vinci was known to sketch and draw extensively. Have students make sketches or drawings that illustrate 3–5 significant accomplishments or events in da Vinci's life. If necessary, allow students to use one or two-word labels, but emphasize conveying information visually instead of in writing. **Visual/Spatial**

See page 579C for other online activities.

The Renaissance is Born

The birthplace of the Renaissance was Italy, the heart of the old Roman Empire. The ruins and statues were familiar to Italians. Because of this, Italians readily turned to ancient examples to inspire them in their own artistic efforts.

Art also flourished because by the 1300s, Italian cities had become very wealthy. Their leading citizens could pay painters, sculptors, and architects to produce many new works.

The powerful states of Italy encouraged the Renaissance. The population of Italy was becoming more **urban** (UHR•buhn). That is, more people were living in cities than in the country. In other parts of Europe, most people still lived in rural areas, including the nobles who owned estates.

As a result of its city life, Italy began to develop a different society. Large city populations meant more discussion among people. Strong economies developed. It also meant more customers for artists and more money for a new kind of art.

GEOGRAPHY CONNECTION

Many Italian states prospered during the Renaissance.

1 **LOCATION** In which territory was Rome located?

2 **CRITICAL THINKING** ***Drawing Conclusions*** By what mode of transportation would you probably travel from Naples to Venice?

V

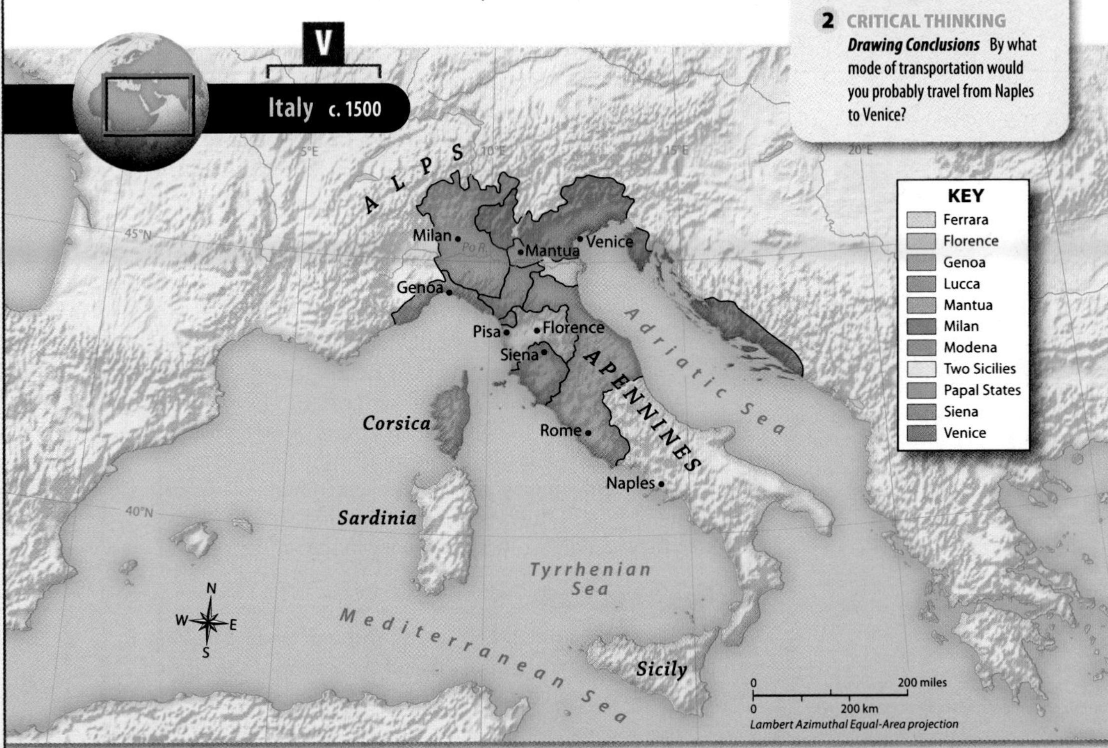

Renaissance a renewal or rebirth of interest in Greek and Roman arts

urban having to do with a town or city

secular related to worldly things

The Renaissance Begins

V Visual Skills

Reading a Map Have students look at the map of Italy from the lesson as you **ask:**

- According to the key, how many Italian states are shaded on the map? *(11)*
- Is Naples north, south, east, or west of Venice? *(south)*
- Venice sits on the coast of which sea? *(Adriatic Sea)*
- What are the names of the two islands off the west coast of Italy? *(Corsica and Sardinia)*
- Corsica was part of which Italian state? *(Genoa)*

ELL Visual/Spatial

C Critical Thinking Skills

Determining Cause and Effect Review the map of Italy and discuss how the region's geographic location could have helped launch the Renaissance. Have students use information from the map to help them write cause-and-effect sentences. *(Answers will vary. Sample answer: Because Italy has a long coastline, it had several coastal cities where ships could dock to trade goods and ideas.)* BL

C

GRAPHIC ORGANIZER

Taking Notes: *Identifying:* Wealth Grows in City-States

Identifying Display the Taking Notes graphic organizer. Guide students to complete it by thinking about how Italy's geographic location, its prominence as a center of trade and commerce, and the urbanization of cities could cause the effect of increased wealth.

See page 579C for other online activities.

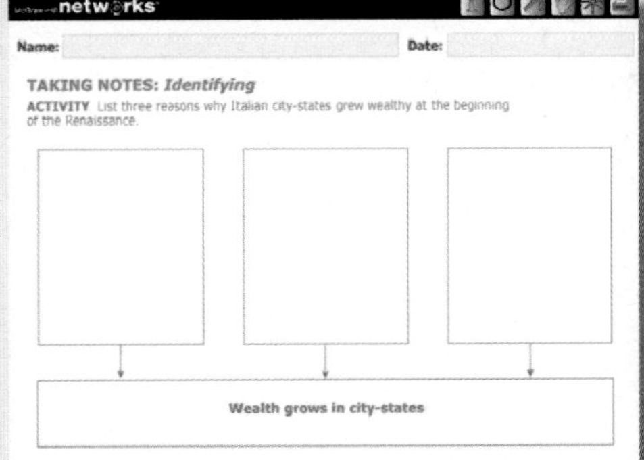

ANSWERS, p. 583

GEOGRAPHY CONNECTION

1 Papal States

2 CRITICAL THINKING by horseback over land

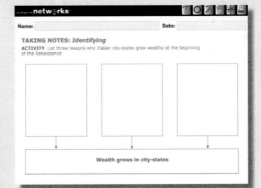

The Renaissance Begins

T Technology Skills

Researching on the Internet Divide the class into five groups and ask each group to research one of the cities of Florence, Genoa, Milan, Rome, or Venice. Each research project should include the following:

- A map (either drawn or found in a source) that shows the specific location of the city in Italy.
- One paragraph about what the geography of the city's location was like during the Renaissance.
- Two paragraphs that describe what life was like in the city during the Renaissance.

These paragraphs can include answers to such questions as:

- **Who had the most power in the city?**
- **Why did these people have it, or how did they get it?**
- **What were the sources of wealth in the city? What new ideas or teachings began in the city or were taught there?**
- **Who were two or three famous people who were either born in the city or lived there?**

Remind students to use two or three sources (with appropriate citations) other than the textbook. **Interpersonal**

Content Background Knowledge

A Summary of Italian Renaissance Cities

- **Florence** was the first major center of the Renaissance. It became a major trading post and made a great deal of wealth from the woolen-cloth trade.
- **Venice** was a city of canals. Venice was a center of trade and commerce and, in turn, a place where Renaissance ideas thrived. Marco Polo was from Venice, and the items that he brought back from China made Italians interested in exploring other parts of the world.
- **Genoa** was a major port city in Italy. It was also a powerful city in that it had gained control of Corsica and Sardinia following the Crusades. These colonial claims helped increase the wealth of Genoa.
- **Rome** was home to some of the greatest masterpieces that came from Renaissance artists, such as Michelangelo's painting on the ceiling of the Sistine Chapel as well as his *Pietá* in St. Peter's Cathedral; Raphael's *The School of Athens* in the Vatican; and Donato Bramante's architectural designs for St. Peter's.

ANSWERS, p. 584

PROGRESS CHECK Wealthy Italians competed with one another to bring fame to their cities. By having artists in their cities, they could help bring fame to those cities.

CRITICAL THINKING Wealth meant power in the Italian states. The Gonzaga family was extremely wealthy; thus, they had a lot of power.

Like the city-states of ancient Greece, Renaissance Italy's urban society and scholars produced many great works of art and literature.

PROGRESS CHECK

Explaining Why did wealthy Italians support artists during the Renaissance?

The States of Italy

GUIDING QUESTION *How did Italy's states become wealthy and powerful?*

During the Middle Ages, Italy remained a collection of states, many of which were independent city-states. There were several reasons for this. The states of Italy did not want emperors and kings to rule them. In addition, the Catholic Church did not want a united Italy. It did not want a powerful emperor or king to control the pope.

The independent states in Italy were equally strong. They fought many wars and often took land from each other. However, no state was able to rule the others. Florence (FLAWR•uhntz), Venice (VEH•nuhs), Genoa (JEH•nuh•wuh), Milan (mih•LAN), and Rome were some of the most important cities of the Italian Renaissance. The Renaissance began in Italy because city life was stronger than in other parts of Europe.

Above all, Italy's states were independent because of their riches. They used their wealth to build large fleets of ships. They also hired mercenaries to fight in their armies. A **mercenary** (MUHR•suh•nehr•ee) is a full-time soldier who fights in an army for money. Wealthy merchants and bankers in Italy's states also loaned money to the kings of Europe. The kings left the states alone so they could borrow more money in the future.

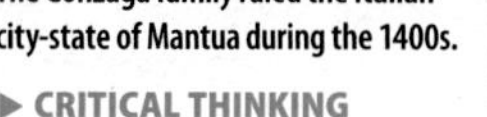

The Gonzaga family ruled the Italian city-state of Mantua during the 1400s.

► CRITICAL THINKING
Explaining Why was it possible for one family to become so powerful in Italy at this time?

Riches from Trade

The Italian states gained their wealth through trade. The long stretch of the Italian peninsula meant that many of the cities were port cities located on the coast.

Reading HELPDESK (CCSS)

mercenary a soldier who fights for money rather than loyalty to a country

networks Online Teaching Options

MAP

Italy, A.D. 1500

Narrative Use the interactive map of Italy to highlight Florence, Genoa, Milan, the Papal States (Rome), and Venice. Then have students write a short diary entry from the perspective of a wealthy merchant or a mercenary traveling between two of those cities. Encourage students to use the map to help them visualize the geography they might see as they traveled either by ship—from port to port—or overland on horseback. **BL Verbal/Linguistic Intrapersonal**

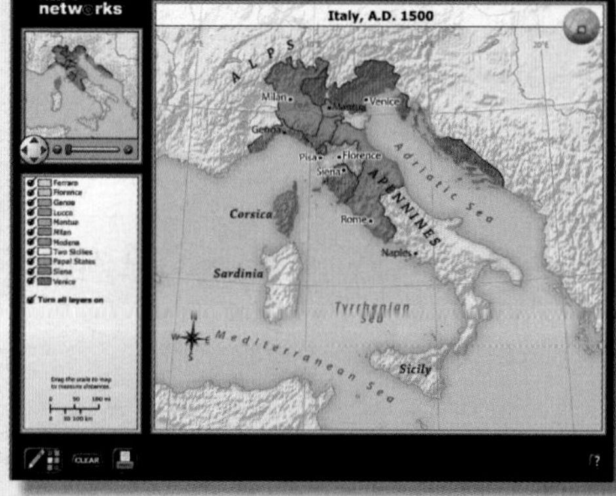

See page 579C for other online activities.

The Renaissance Begins

An illustrated book written by a Florence merchant named Marco Polo made many Europeans excited about Asia and its wealth. He wrote about the riches he found there.

The Italian peninsula was in the center of the Mediterranean world. The Byzantine and Ottoman Empires lay to the east, and Spain and France lay to the west. North Africa was only a short distance to the south. Italy's location made trade with these regions easier.

C2 In eastern ports like Constantinople, Italian merchants bought Chinese silk and Indian spices from Byzantine, Turkish, and Arab merchants. The Italians sold these goods in Italy and Western Europe for very high prices. Italian merchants bought wool, wine, and glass in Western Europe and sold them in the Middle East. Meanwhile, Italian artisans bought raw materials and made goods to sell abroad for high prices.

C1 In addition to geography, two important events helped the Italians succeed in trade. One event was the Crusades. These conflicts brought Italian merchants into contact with Arab merchants in the Middle East. The second event was the Mongol conquests, which united much of Asia into one large trading network.

The Mongols protected trade along the Silk Road. This made it easier and cheaper for caravans to carry goods between China and the Middle East. As more silk and spices were sent from Asia, the price of these goods fell. More Europeans could pay for the luxuries, and demand for the goods increased.

Who Was Marco Polo?

In the 1270s, the merchant Marco Polo, his father, and his uncle left their home in Venice and traveled to China. Their goal was to meet Kublai Khan (KUH•bluh KAHN), the Mongol emperor of China.

When the Polo family reached the Khan's court, the emperor was amazed by the stories that Marco Polo told of his travels. Kublai sent Marco Polo on fact-finding trips all over China. Polo learned more about Asia than any other European. After returning to Europe, Polo wrote a book about his adventures. His stories about life in China amazed Europeans, who then wanted to buy Chinese goods.

Florence: A Renaissance City

The city of Florence was the first major center of the Renaissance. Its wealth and central location attracted many artists, sculptors, writers, and architects. Florence lay on the banks of the Arno River in central Italy. The city was surrounded by walls with tall towers for defense. Soaring above the city was the dome of its cathedral. A local architect, Filippo Brunelleschi (fih•LEEP•oh broon•ehl•EHS•kee), completed the dome in 1436. The dome is considered to be the greatest engineering achievement of the time.

C1 Critical Thinking Skills

Analyzing Information Once students have read the text on this page, **ask:**

- **How important was the location of the city-states?** *(Location was important because city-states were both close to the sea and located in the center of the Mediterranean world.)*
- **Why do you think Kublai Khan might have been amazed by Marco Polo's stories?** *(People in China may have known very little about Europe.)*
- **How did the city-states' wealth affect the arts?** *(The wealth supported artists, architects, and writers, and the city-states flourished with new buildings, sculptures, paintings, and books.)* BL

C2 Critical Thinking Skills

Sequencing On the board, list the different goods traded by the Italian city-states:

- Chinese silk
- Indian spices
- wool
- wine
- glass
- goods made by Italian artisans

Have students rank these goods in order of personal preference. If they were wealthy adults during the Renaissance, which item would they buy first, second, third, and so on? Ask volunteers to share the reasons for their rankings.

PRIMARY SOURCE

Marco Polo

Analyzing Primary Sources Have students read the short selection from ***The Travels of Marco Polo*** that describes the strange and frightening animals that Marco Polo saw on his trip. As a class, discuss what these animals might have been (crocodiles). **Verbal/Linguistic**

See page 579C for other online activities.

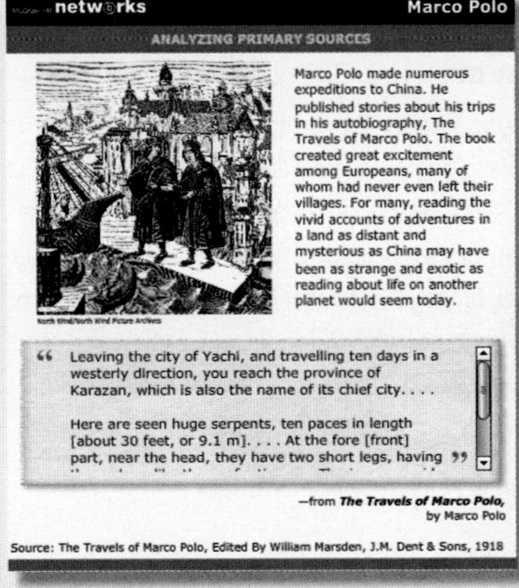

networks Marco Polo

ANALYZING PRIMARY SOURCES

Marco Polo made numerous expeditions to China. He published stories about his trips in his autobiography, The Travels of Marco Polo. The book created great excitement among Europeans, many of whom had never even left their villages. For many, reading the vivid accounts of adventures in a land as distant and mysterious as China may have been as strange and exotic as reading about life on another planet would seem today.

North Wind/North Wind Picture Archives

"Leaving the city of Yachi, and travelling ten days in a westerly direction, you reach the province of Karazan, which is also the name of its chief city. . . .

Here are seen huge serpents, ten paces in length [about 30 feet, or 9.1 m]. . . . At the fore [front] part, near the head, they have two short legs, having"

—from ***The Travels of Marco Polo,*** by Marco Polo

Source: The Travels of Marco Polo, Edited By William Marsden, J.M. Dent & Sons, 1918

The Renaissance Begins

V Visual Skills

Analyzing Images Have students study the diagram and photo titled "Florence Cathedral" and read the accompanying captions carefully. **Ask:**

- What is the cathedral's most impressive feature? *(the large dome)*
- What is the base of the dome called? *(the drum)*
- How would you describe the style of Il Duomo? *(grand, formal, impressive)*
- What does the cathedral show about the people who built it? *(The people who built it had strong technical skills. They valued beauty and style. They used new techniques.)* AL ELL

R Reading Skills

Defining After students have read the text on this page, have them define some of the words they have encountered. **Ask:**

- What is currency? *(money, in the form of coins or paper)*
- What was a florin? *(the gold coin of Florence used by Florentine bankers)* ELL

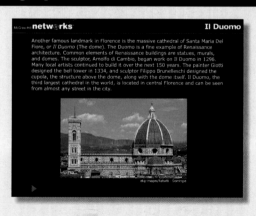

ANSWER, p. 586

CRITICAL THINKING Muslim civilization

FLORENCE CATHEDRAL

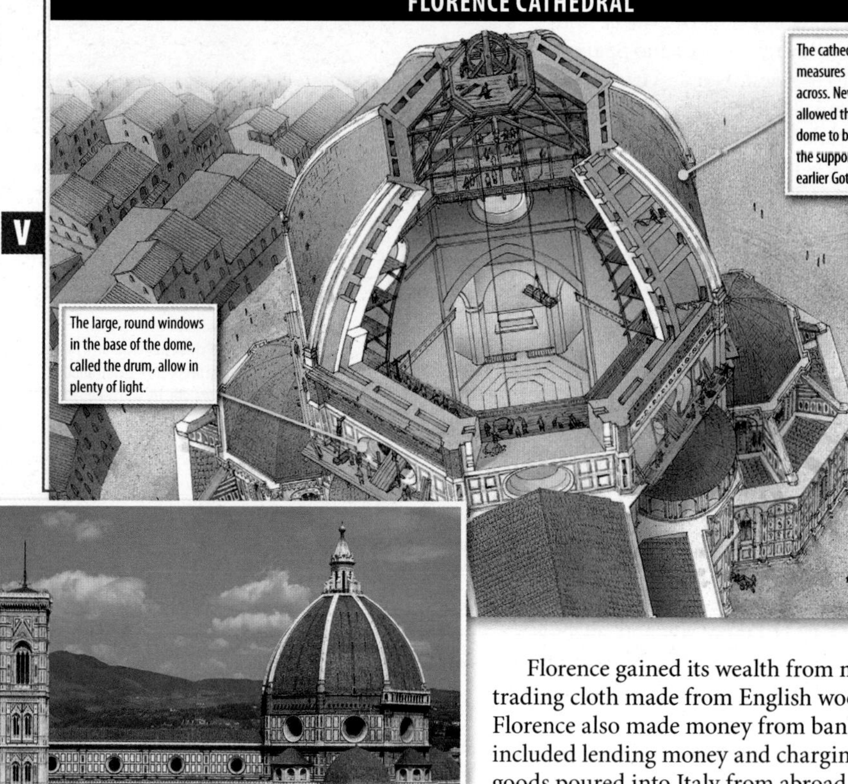

The cathedral's dome measures 140 feet (42.7m) across. New techniques allowed the tall, massive dome to be built without the supports used in earlier Gothic cathedrals.
The large, round windows in the base of the dome, called the drum, allow in plenty of light.

The dome of the cathedral in Florence, Italy, became a symbol of the city. It was considered a great architectural design of its time.

▶ CRITICAL THINKING

Making Connections What earlier civilization was known for building domes?

Florence gained its wealth from making and trading cloth made from English wool. Citizens of Florence also made money from banking, which included lending money and charging interest. As goods poured into Italy from abroad, merchants had to determine the value of **currency,** or money, from different countries. Florentine bankers used the florin, the gold coin of Florence, to measure the value of other money. The city's wealthiest family, the Medici (MEH•duh•chee), owned the largest bank in Europe during the 1400s. The Medici had branch banks, or other offices, as far away as Flanders.

Venice: A City of Canals

Another leading Renaissance city was Venice. Located on the northern coast of the Adriatic Sea in eastern Italy, Venice was built on many small islands. Venetians drove long wooden poles into mud to support their buildings. Instead of paving roads, the Venetians built canals and used boats for transportation around the city. Even today, Venice's canals and waterways serve as streets.

Reading HELPDESK (CCSS)

diplomacy the practice of conducting negotiations between countries

Academic Vocabulary (Tier 2 Words)

currency money, in the form of coins or paper
complex complicated

networks Online Teaching Options

SLIDE SHOW

Il Duomo

Analyzing Visuals Present the slide show of the cathedral of Santa Maria Del Fiore in Florence, Italy. Point out the doors by Lorenzo Ghiberti. Tell students that the doors are often called the Gates of Paradise and are made of gilded bronze. Explain that the doors contain reliefs of scenes from the Bible's Old Testament. Explain that some historians think the doors were the first ones to be built in the Renaissance style of architecture.

See page 579C for other online activities.

networks Il Duomo

Another famous landmark in Florence is the massive cathedral of Santa Maria Del Fiore, or *Il Duomo* (The dome). The Duomo is a fine example of Renaissance architecture. Common elements of Renaissance buildings are statues, murals, and domes. The sculptor, Arnolfo di Cambio, began work on Il Duomo in 1296. Many local artists continued to build it over the next 150 years. The painter Giotti designed the bell tower in 1334, and sculptor Filippo Brunelleschi designed the cupola, the structure above the dome, along with the dome itself. Il Duomo, the third largest cathedral in the world, is located in central Florence and can be seen from almost any street in the city.

During the Renaissance, Venice became an important link between Europe and Asia. Venetian merchants, such as Marco Polo, traveled abroad and made contacts with eastern civilizations. The city also was known as a major shipbuilding center. In a part of the city called the Arsenal, teams of workers built the wooden ships and also made the sails and oars.

✓ PROGRESS CHECK

Determining Cause and Effect How did the travels of Marco Polo affect Europeans?

A New Ruling Class

GUIDING QUESTION ***Who controlled the states of Italy?***

Wealthy merchants and bankers in the Italian city-states formed a new kind of leadership. Before the Renaissance, nobles in Europe gained their wealth from land, not trade.

In Italy, old noble families moved from the country to the cities. They became urban nobles. They formed ties of business and friendship with wealthy merchants.

Meanwhile, merchants began to adopt the customs of the nobles. Soon, the sons and daughters of nobles and rich merchants were marrying each other. These new families became the upper class of the city-states.

W

Who Ruled Italian City-States?

Many Italian city-states began as republics. A republic is a government in which power comes from its citizens. However, not all people in an Italian city-state were citizens. Citizenship belonged only to merchants and artisans.

In ancient Rome, power was often given to a dictator during a war or revolt. A dictator was a ruler who had absolute power. In many cases, the Italian city-states relied on a single powerful individual to run the government. Some of these leaders ruled harshly, using force to keep control. Others used a more gentle approach. To win support, these rulers improved city services.

In Venice, the ruler was the duke, or doge (DOHJ). He officially ran the city, but a council of wealthy merchants held the real power. This council passed laws and elected the doge.

In Florence, the powerful Medici family controlled the government for many years. Lorenzo de' Medici governed Florence from 1469 to 1492. He used his wealth to support artists, architects, and writers. As a result of Florence's prosperity and fame, Lorenzo was known as "the Magnificent."

R

Thinking Like a HISTORIAN

Drawing Conclusions

During the Renaissance, Venice's canals were avenues of transportation. The famous Grand Canal formed a large "S" shape winding through the city. Lining the canal were the homes of wealthy merchants. Many of these still stand today. Compare Venice with other Italian Renaissance cities. Then draw a conclusion about Renaissance Italy. For more information about drawing conclusions, read the chapter *What Does a Historian Do?*

The Venetians cut canals through the swampy land around the city's original islands. Today, gondolas—long, narrow boats—still carry people along these canals.

W Writing Skills

Informative/Explanatory Discuss as a class the development of business and trade. Remind students that trade made people wealthier while, at the same time, it helped increase people's knowledge of other parts of the world. Have students write an essay or paragraph about trade and commerce in the Italian city-states. Essays or paragraphs should discuss one of more of the following topics. **Ask:**

- How would an active trading business help a city grow? *(Students might write how trade encouraged people to move to cities. Trading would also encourage the growth of new ideas.)*
- Who controlled trade in the city-states? *(urban nobles, wealthy merchants)*
- How could the leaders of city-states govern their regions? *(Some individual leaders used force; others won the support of citizens by providing city services, arts, and entertainment.)*
- What was the role of the doge in Venice? *(He ruled the city, although a council of merchants had the real power.)*
- What might happen to a doge if he did not follow the wishes of the council of merchants? *(Students might write that the merchants would replace the doge with someone who supported them.)* **Verbal/Linguistic**

R Reading Skills

Citing Text Evidence After students have read the paragraph about Lorenzo de' Medici, **ask:**

- How did Lorenzo de' Medici use his wealth? *(He supported artists, architects, and writers.)*
- What name was Lorenzo de' Medici known by? *("the Magnificent")* AL

SLIDE SHOW

Venice

Speculating Have students look through the slide show on Venice to see images of people riding gondolas down the canals and waterways. Ask students to imagine if the streets of their community were waterways instead. Based on the distance between their home and school, ask them to predict how long it would take them to travel via gondola. *Would it be possible? How else could they commute to school if there were no roads?*

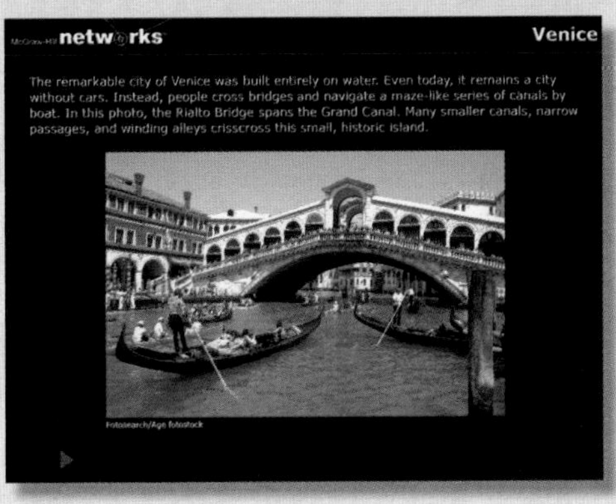

networks
Venice
The remarkable city of Venice was built entirely on water. Even today, it remains a city without cars. Instead, people cross bridges and navigate a maze-like series of canals by boat. In this photo, the Rialto Bridge spans the Grand Canal. Many smaller canals, narrow passages, and winding alleys crisscross this small, historic island.

See page 579C for other online activities.

ANSWER, p. 587

✓ PROGRESS CHECK The stories about China made Europeans want to buy the Chinese goods that Marco Polo described.

The Renaissance Begins

C1 Critical Thinking Skills

Assessing As a class, discuss the development of diplomacy in Renaissance Italy. **Ask:** **Why was it important for the Italians to develop diplomacy?** *(Students might say that Italians needed to make sure the city-states contributed equally and that no city-state became more powerful than the others. Italy was also close to other countries and had to keep good relations with bordering countries.)* **Intrapersonal**

C2 Critical Thinking Skills

Analyzing Primary Sources Have students read the quote from Machiavelli's *The Prince*. Then **ask:** **Why did Niccolò Machiavelli believe that it was better to be feared than loved?** *(It is difficult for one person to be both, so it is much safer for a ruler to be feared than loved.)* **Verbal/Linguistic**

Have students complete the Lesson 1 Review.

CLOSE & REFLECT

To close the lesson, ask students to identify the strengths of the Italian city-states and explain why they were successful. Student responses should summarize the lesson.

Keeping the Peace

Political affairs in Italy were **complex,** or complicated. Within each state, rulers had to put down revolts by the poor. They also had to prevent other wealthy people and city leaders from seizing control. At the same time, the rulers had to keep good relations with bordering states.

C1 To deal with the neighboring states, the Italians developed **diplomacy** (duh•PLOH•muh•see). Diplomacy is the art of making agreements with other countries. Italians worked to be sure that no single state had enough power to threaten the others.

How could a ruler keep his hold on power in the Italian states? Niccolò Machiavelli (nee•koh•LOH mah•kee•uh•VEH•lee), a diplomat in Florence, tried to answer this question. In 1513, he wrote *The Prince*, a book that took a critical look at politics in Renaissance Italy. In this work, Machiavelli stated that rulers should do whatever was necessary to keep power and protect their city, even if they had to lie and kill. Machiavelli gave leaders the following advice:

Lorenzo de' Medici had enough power to rule Florence by himself. He chose, however, to govern with the help of assemblies that represented the people of his city-state.

▶ CRITICAL THINKING

Theorizing Through what means do you think de' Medici would settle a dispute between nobles?

C2 PRIMARY SOURCE

> “Upon this a question arises: whether it is better to be loved than feared or feared than loved? It may be answered that one should wish to be both, but, because it is difficult to unite them in one person, it is much safer to be feared than loved.”
>
> —from *The Prince*, by Niccolò Machiavelli

Today when we say someone is being "Machiavellian," we mean that person is cunning or acting without a conscience.

✓ PROGRESS CHECK

Analyzing Why did the Italian states develop diplomacy?

LESSON 1 REVIEW (CCSS)

Review Vocabulary (Tier 3 Words)

1. What elements of Renaissance culture show *secular* ideas? RH.6–8.2, RH.6–8.4
2. How could a focus on *diplomacy* have helped the states of Italy? RH.6–8.2, RH.6–8.4

Answer the Guiding Questions

3. ***Explaining*** Why would ideas about art and culture develop faster in the city than in the countryside? RH.6–8.2
4. ***Identifying*** What was one reason Italian trade grew during the Renaissance? RH.6–8.2
5. ***Differentiating*** How were urban nobles different from nobles who lived in the country? RH.6–8.2
6. **INFORMATIVE/EXPLANATORY** Why did Renaissance ideas arise in the 1300s? Explain your answer in the form of a short essay. WHST.6–8.2, WHST.6–8.10

LESSON 1 REVIEW ANSWERS

1. The Renaissance focus on trade, diplomacy, and art provides examples of secular ideas.
2. A focus on diplomacy helped city-states form alliances and avoid wars. This would have improved the safety of people in city-states.
3. People in the city had more people to discuss ideas with than people who lived in rural areas. In addition, cities had wealth, which they could use to develop and support art and culture.
4. Italian trade grew during the Renaissance because people were becoming more aware of other countries' goods and were more open to trying different things than they were before the Renaissance.
5. Urban nobles were merchants who earned their money through trade. Nobles who lived in the country made their money from land, and they once thought of themselves as better than merchants.
6. Answers will vary but should include the idea that the rise of city-states and their wealth allowed the Renaissance to develop in the 1300s.

ANSWERS, p. 588

CRITICAL THINKING Students may say that de' Medici would have used his money to bring opposing sides together and help settle disputes between nobles.

✓ **PROGRESS CHECK** Italian city-states developed diplomacy to keep power balanced and to avoid conflicts.

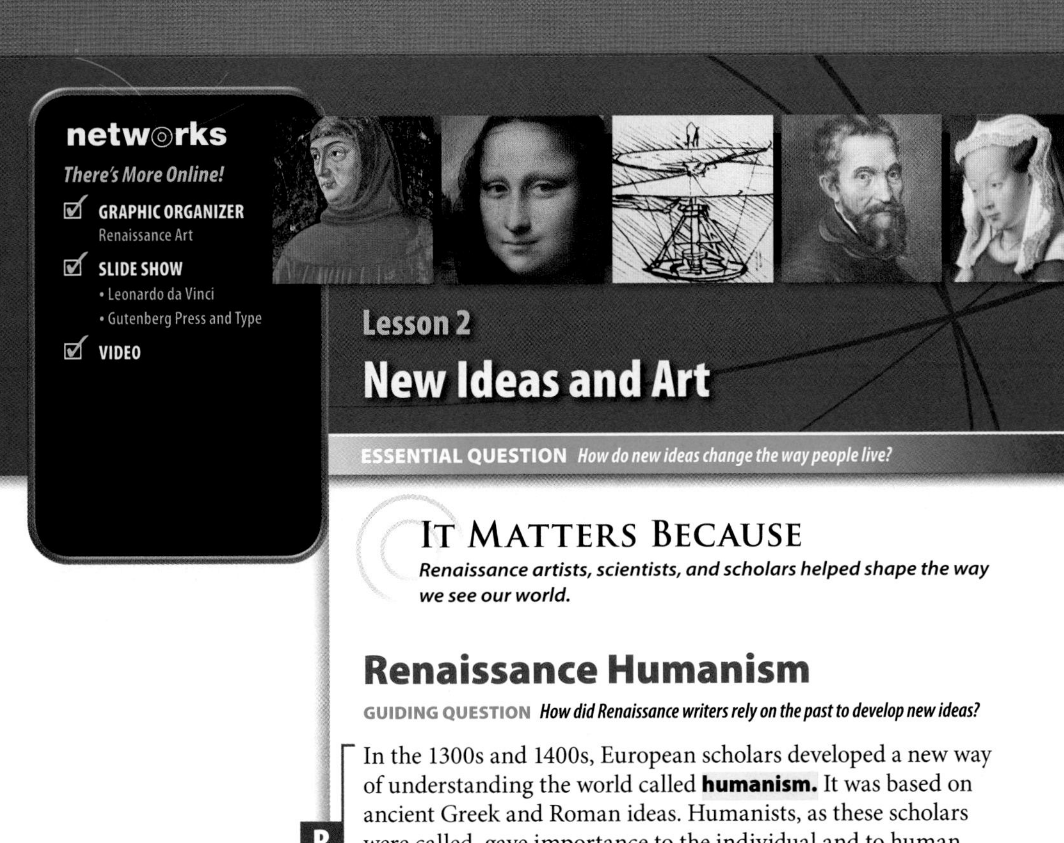

networks
There's More Online!
- ☑ GRAPHIC ORGANIZER
  Renaissance Art
- ☑ SLIDE SHOW
  • Leonardo da Vinci
  • Gutenberg Press and Type
- ☑ VIDEO

Lesson 2

New Ideas and Art

ESSENTIAL QUESTION *How do new ideas change the way people live?*

It Matters Because

Renaissance artists, scientists, and scholars helped shape the way we see our world.

Renaissance Humanism

GUIDING QUESTION *How did Renaissance writers rely on the past to develop new ideas?*

R In the 1300s and 1400s, European scholars developed a new way of understanding the world called **humanism.** It was based on ancient Greek and Roman ideas. Humanists, as these scholars were called, gave importance to the individual and to human society. They wanted to gain knowledge through reason, not just through religious faith. Humanism encouraged people to be active in their cities and to develop their talents.

Discovering Ancient Works

V In the 1300s, Italian scholars began to study ancient Roman and Greek works. For most of the Middle Ages, Western Europeans knew little about these writings. During the Crusades, however, they came into contact with the Middle East. Arab Muslim scholars there and in Spain knew the classic Greek and Roman writings. They passed on their knowledge to the Western Europeans. Byzantine scholars also brought classical works to Italy.

One famous humanist scholar was Petrarch (PEE•trahrk). Francesco Petrarch lived in Italy during the 1300s. He studied Roman writers such as Cicero (SIH•suh•roh) and wrote biographies of famous Romans.

Reading **HELP**DESK (CCSS)

Taking Notes: *Describing* RH.6–8.2

Create a word web to list examples of Renaissance art. For each type of art, describe how it reflects Renaissance ideas.

Renaissance Art → Literature | Painting | Sculpture

Content Vocabulary (Tier 3 Words)
- **humanism**

VIDEO

Chaucer's England

Contrasting Play the video for students. Discuss the ways that Chaucer's writing was different from other works of its time. *(Chaucer wrote in English, not Latin or French. He wrote for and about everyday people, not kings, rulers, nobles, or God. He also wrote about people who might have been considered immoral or nonreligious.)*

See page 579D for other online activities.

ENGAGE

Bellringer Have students write down some of the differences between the art of the Middle Ages and the art of the Renaissance. If possible, show students a painting from the Middle Ages next to one from the Renaissance and have them compare the different styles of painting. **Ask:** **How did art change during the Renaissance?** *(Answers should include that art became more realistic and natural in appearance.)* AL ELL

Tell students they will be learning some of the reasons Renaissance artists and writers began to change the methods they used to show and describe the world around them.

TEACH & ASSESS

R Reading Skills

Listing Have students read the opening paragraph on humanism. Then have them list details about humanism. **Ask:** **What are some characteristics of humanism?** *(It was based on ancient Greek and Roman ideas. Humanism gave importance to the individual and to human society. It was about gaining knowledge through reason, not just through religious faith. Humanism encouraged people to be active in their cities and to develop their talents.)*

V Visual Skills

Creating Charts Have students use the following four pieces of information to create a flowchart or a similar kind of graphic that shows how the Crusades altered the ways information and ideas were exchanged with Western Europe. The format and layout of the charts will vary, but students should use arrows and at least one type of line to connect the components.

- Byzantine scholars
- Western Europeans
- the Crusades
- Arab Muslim scholars from the Middle East and Spain

Visual/Spatial

ANSWER, p. 589

TAKING NOTES: Literature—can be written in the vernacular; Painting—can show realistic-looking people; Sculpture—artists studied human body.

R Reading Skills

Identifying After students have read about Petrarch, Dante, and Chaucer, **ask:** Who are each of these people, and what are they famous for doing during the Renaissance?

- Francesco Petrarch *(humanist scholar who lived in Italy; called the father of Italian Renaissance humanism)*
- Dante Alighieri *(poet from Florence; wrote* The Divine Comedy*)*
- Geoffrey Chaucer *(writer from England; wrote* The Canterbury Tales*)* AL ELL

W Writing Skills

Narrative Have students write a poem or short story that allows for the inclusion of common vernacular slang. Tell them that, while the use of slang is permissible for this assignment, conventional spellings should be present in their writing as well. **Verbal/Linguistic Intrapersonal**

Petrarch traveled to different monasteries to find old Latin manuscripts. Scholars throughout Europe followed Petrarch's example. In time, new libraries were built to hold the newly found manuscripts. The largest of these libraries was at the Vatican, the home of the pope in Rome.

Italians also began to value the ancient buildings and statues all around them. Throughout Rome, workers removed dirt and rubble from damaged columns and statues. Artists then eagerly studied the proportion of ancient works. For example, artists compared the length of a statue's arms to its height. They believed this comparison could tell them why the statue looked perfect. R

A New Literature

In addition to studying the classics, humanists in Italy and other parts of Europe made important achievements of their own. One of their contributions was new forms of literature.

During the Renaissance, educated Europeans wrote in the classical Latin used in ancient Rome. However, they also began writing in the vernacular, the everyday language people spoke in a region. Vernacular languages included Italian, French, and German. For example, Petrarch used Italian to write sonnets, or short poems, which expressed his love for a woman who died from the Black Death. Many more people could read works written in the vernacular instead of in Latin. W

Petrarch has been called the father of Italian Renaissance humanism.

Galleria degli Uffizi, Florence, Italy/Giraudon/Bridgeman Art Library

In the early 1300s, a poet from Florence named Dante Alighieri (DAHN•tay ah•lee•GYEHR•ee) wrote *The Divine Comedy.* It is known as one of the world's greatest poems. Written in the vernacular, it tells of a person's journey from hell to heaven. The poem describes the horrible punishments for different sins.

The English writer Geoffrey Chaucer (CHAW•suhr) also wrote popular vernacular literature. Chaucer wrote his famous work *The Canterbury* (KAN•tuhr•behr•ree) *Tales* in English. *The Canterbury Tales* is a collection of stories told by pilgrims on a religious journey to the town of Canterbury, England. In this work, Chaucer portrayed the entire **range** of English society. His work shows both nobles at the top of society and the poor at the bottom. The English we speak today comes from the form of English that Chaucer used in his writing.

Reading HELPDESK CCSS

humanism belief in the worth of the individual and that reason is a path to knowledge

Academic Vocabulary (Tier 2 Words)

range the limits between which something can change or differ

networks Online Teaching Options

WORKSHEET

21st Century Skills Activity: Renaissance and Reformation

Evaluating Write on the board the following bulleted ideas about humanism. Tell students to review these ideas when they begin the worksheet.

- Renaissance artists and writers used humanist ideas about art, culture, and education in creating their works.
- Petrarch was a Renaissance writer who used the ideas of ancient Romans.
- Renaissance writers and artists believed the ideas of individuals were important. AL

See page 579D for other online activities.

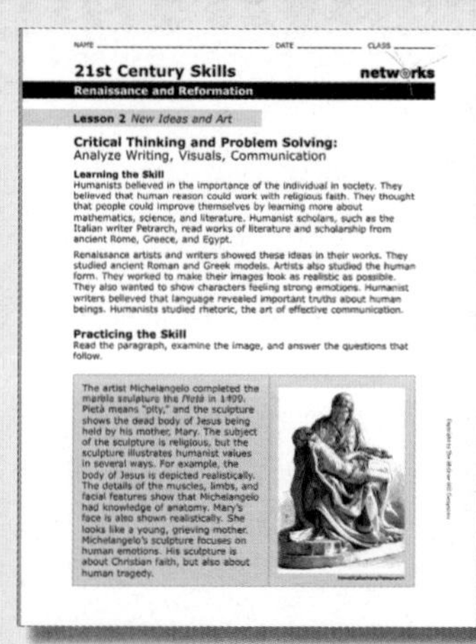

Gutenberg's Printing Press

The printing press helped spread humanist ideas throughout Europe. In the early 1450s, a German printer named Johannes Gutenberg (yoh•HAHN•uhs GOO•tuhn•buhrg) developed a printing press that used movable metal type. This new press held individual carved letters that could be arranged to form words and then could be used again. As a result, books could be quickly printed by machine rather than slowly written by hand.

C

The Chinese had already invented movable type. However, their written language had so many characters that the movable type system did not work well. For Europeans, the printing press was a great advance. It was easy to use with linen paper, another invention from China.

Gutenberg's printing press made many more books available to people. Its invention came at a time when many townspeople were learning to read and think for themselves. Scholars could read each other's works and discuss their ideas, often in letters. Ideas developed and spread more quickly than ever before in Europe.

T

In 1455, Gutenberg produced the first European printed book, the Christian Bible, on the new press. Soon, many books became available in Europe. In fact, more books were printed in the first 50 years of printing than were written by hand in the entire history of the world up to 1450. Half of the 40,000 books published by the year 1500 were religious works such as the Christian Bible or prayer books.

Gutenberg produced bibles on this printing press. Today, there are five complete, original Gutenberg Bibles in the United States.

What Effect Did Humanism Have on Society?

Humanist scholars were curious about such subjects as biology, medicine, and astronomy. Scholars' study of mathematics helped them in many areas of knowledge.

One of the leading Renaissance scientists was also a great artist, Leonardo da Vinci (lee•uh•NAHR•doh duh VIHN•chee). Da Vinci cut open dead bodies to learn more about the human body. He studied fossils to understand Earth's early history. Da Vinci was also an inventor and an engineer.

C Critical Thinking Skills

Making Connections After students have read about Gutenberg and the invention of the printing press, **ask:**

- **Why would a movable type system not work well with a language that has many characters or letters?** *(It would take a long time to arrange individual letters to form words.)*
- **Why was Gutenberg's printing press a better option than writing books by hand?** *(Books could be quickly printed by the printing press because it was a machine. Writing a book by hand was slow and took more time.)*
- **How are computers a better option than Gutenberg's printing press?** *(Answers will vary. Sample answers: You can correct mistakes easily when you use a computer. The printers that we use today aren't as messy as a printing press. You can read information on a computer screen without printing it on a piece of paper.)*

T Technology Skills

Using Digital Tools Have students type a paragraph of "Gutenberg's Printing Press" using a word processing program. Then have them change aspects of the paragraph's formatting to reflect the technological options that we use in printing today. Each student's paragraph should contain a change in the:

- type of font
- size of font
- color of font
- way the font looks (i.e., use of boldface, italics, or underlining) **Visual/Spatial**

SLIDE SHOW

Gutenberg Press

Explaining Show students the slide show on Gutenberg's printing press. Point out the different pieces of movable type and the parts of the press that are visible in the slide show. Discuss how these pieces and parts made it possible to print books. **Ask: How did the printing press help spread humanism throughout Europe?** *(The printing press made it easier and faster to print books, which helped spread humanist ideas.)*

See page 579D for other online activities.

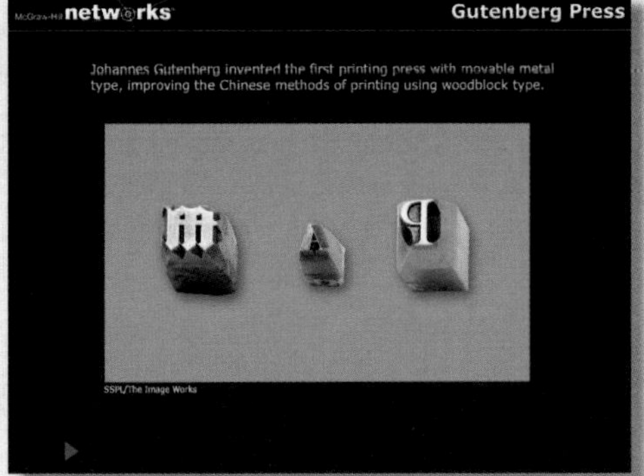

C Critical Thinking Skills

Problem-Solving Have students become engineers or inventors like Leonardo da Vinci by making an invention out of household items like boxes, cardboard tubes, milk cartons or jugs, garbage bags, and similar items. You may wish to give students the option of making their inventions operational like a machine. BL Otherwise, have student make a non-operational model. Allow students to present their inventions to the class and/or friends and family members. **Visual/Spatial Kinesthetic**

R Reading Skills

Paraphrasing Have students use details from the text to paraphrase how Renaissance artists used perspective in their work. *(Sample answer: Artists drew and painted people and things so that they appeared to be at different distances. They were able to give paintings a three-dimensional look so that they looked more realistic.)* **Verbal/Linguistic**

The *Mona Lisa* by Leonardo da Vinci is one of the most famous paintings from the Renaissance. It hangs today in the *Louvre*, a museum in Paris.

▶ CRITICAL THINKING
Speculating Why do you think people have been so fascinated by Mona Lisa's smile?

Most of what we know about da Vinci comes from his notebooks. Da Vinci filled the pages of his notebooks with notes and sketches of his scientific and artistic projects. These drawings often pictured parachutes, flying machines, and other mechanical inventions far ahead of his time. C

✓ PROGRESS CHECK

Explaining How did Gutenberg's printing press bring change to Europe?

Italy's Renaissance Artists

GUIDING QUESTION *How did Renaissance artists learn to make their art look natural and real?*

In Renaissance Italy, wealthy families and church leaders appreciated beautiful buildings and works of art. They hired talented people to construct beautiful buildings and to fill them with artwork. The pope funded works of art to decorate the Vatican, his headquarters in Rome.

Renaissance builders and artists carefully studied ancient Greek and Roman art, science, and mathematics. They also expressed the new humanist ideas. As one artist declared, human beings were "the center and measure of all things."

What New Styles Did Artists Develop?

Renaissance art was very different from medieval art. Artistic works of the Renaissance tried to show what people really looked like. They also tried to reveal people's feelings. An artist from Florence named Giotto (JAH•toh) was the first to show this change in the early 1300s. His series of wall paintings showed the life of Francis of Assisi. The paintings used gestures and facial expressions to reveal people's emotions.

Renaissance painters also used new methods that brought life, color, and action to their works. The most important was **perspective** (puhr•SPEHK•tihv), a way of showing people and things as they appear at different distances. Artists in the past had tried to use perspective, but Renaissance artists such as Leonardo da Vinci perfected it. Perspective, as used by these artists, gave paintings a realistic, three-dimensional look. R

Renaissance artists studied the human body to learn how to draw it accurately. They began to experiment with light, color, and shade. To make their paintings more realistic, artists used

Reading HELPDESK CCSS

Academic Vocabulary (Tier 2 Words)

perspective a way of drawing to show the relationship of objects in a drawing to give the look of depth or distance

networks *Online Teaching Options*

IMAGE

Mona Lisa

Evaluating a Web Site Have students look at the interactive image of Mona Lisa and read the story of the painting's theft in 1911. **Ask:** **Where was the Mona Lisa on display when it was stolen?** *(the Louvre Museum in Paris, France)*

networks
Mona Lisa
The Mona Lisa is considered by many to be the most famous painting in the world. On the night of August 21, 1911, a thief stole the Mona Lisa from the Louvre Museum in Paris, France. Then, in 1913, a man visited an art dealer in Florence, Italy, stating that he had found the Mona Lisa. He claimed the painting belonged in Florence and demanded a reward for returning the Mona Lisa to the Louvre. To the art dealer's surprise, after he inspected the painting, he realized that it was indeed the priceless Da Vinci portrait. Vincenzo Peruggia, the thief, was arrested, and the painting was returned to the Louvre. Today, thousands of tourists visit the Louvre every year to admire the woman with the mysterious smile.
Musee du Louvre, Paris/Giraudon, Paris/SuperStock

Allow students to visit the official Web site of the Louvre Museum at **www.louvre.fr/en** and ask them to search for the Mona Lisa. As a class, discuss how easy it is to find more information on the painting or to see it in more detail using the Louvre's Web site. What do they wish the Web site included that it did not have?

See page 579D for other online activities.

ANSWERS, p. 592

✓ PROGRESS CHECK The printing press made books available to many people and allowed ideas to spread more rapidly.

CRITICAL THINKING Students might note that the Mona Lisa's smile is mysterious and makes the viewer wonder what she was thinking when her portrait was painted.

a technique called chiaroscuro (kee•ahr•uh•SKYUR•oh). Chiaroscuro used light and shadows instead of stiff outlines to separate objects. In Italian, *chiaro* means "clear or light," and *oscuro* means "dark." Chiaroscuro created drama and emotion.

Many Renaissance artists painted on fresh wet plaster with watercolor paint. A painting done this way is called a fresco (FREHS•koh), which means "fresh" in Italian. Frescoes were painted in churches all over Italy.

Da Vinci was a great innovator. His drawing of a helicopter was very advanced for his time, and he is credited with having the first idea for a vehicle that could fly vertically.

Who Were Leading Renaissance Artists?

The period between 1490 and 1520 was the golden age of Italian Renaissance painting. Three of the most famous artists were Leonardo da Vinci, Michelangelo Buonarroti (MY•kuh•LAN•juh•loh bwah•nah•RAH•tee) and Raphael Sanzio (rah•feye•EHL SAHN•zee•oh).

Leonardo da Vinci was born in Florence. He is known for the *Mona Lisa*, a portrait of a young noblewoman. He gave her a smile that makes the viewer wonder what she is thinking. Da Vinci also painted *The Last Supper*, a wall painting of Jesus and his disciples. In this work, da Vinci showed human emotions through the way in which the apostles hold their heads or sit in relation to Jesus.

Another great Renaissance artist was Michelangelo. He began his career as a sculptor in Florence. In 1508, Pope Julius II hired Michelangelo to work at the Vatican. There, Michelangelo painted the ceiling of the Sistine Chapel with scenes from the Bible. These paintings are still famous today. A noted Renaissance biographer praised Michelangelo:

PRIMARY SOURCE

> The work [Sistine Chapel ceiling] has been, indeed, a light of our art, illuminating the world which had been so many centuries in darkness. Oh, truly happy age, and oh, blessed artists, who at such a fountain can purge [remove] away the dark films from your eyes. Give thanks to Heaven, and imitate Michael Angelo [Michelangelo] in all things.
>
> —from *Lives of the Artists* by Giorgio Vasari

All of Michelangelo's painted figures were like sculptures. They had muscular bodies that showed life and power. This scene of the creation of Adam appears on the ceiling of the Sistine Chapel in Rome.

SLIDE SHOW

Leonardo da Vinci's Flying Machine

Hypothesizing Project the slide show of Leonardo da Vinci's flying machine. Have students look at the image. Then ask them to write a paragraph hypothesizing how the machine might be able to fly. Encourage students to discuss the details that they see in the drawing as part of their hypotheses. BL

See page 579D for other online activities.

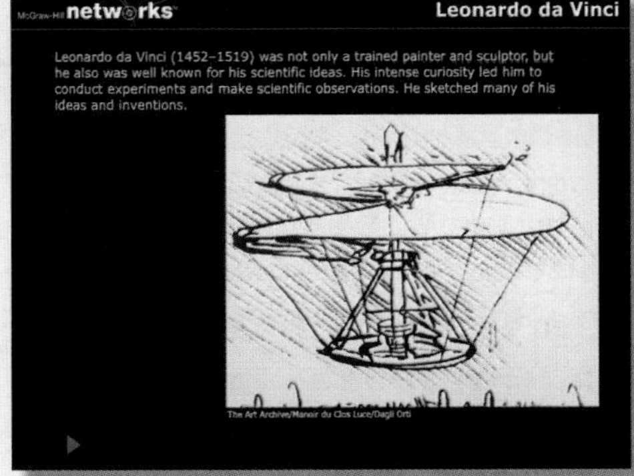

McGraw-Hill networks
Leonardo da Vinci
Leonardo da Vinci (1452–1519) was not only a trained painter and sculptor, but he also was well known for his scientific ideas. His intense curiosity led him to conduct experiments and make scientific observations. He sketched many of his ideas and inventions.

R Reading Skills

Determining Word Meanings After students have read the section on chiaroscuro and fresco, **ask:** What is the definition of the term *chiaroscuro*? *(the use of light and shadows instead of stiff outlines to separate objects)* What do the two parts of the word mean in Italian? *(*Chiaro *means "clear or light" and* oscuro *means "dark.")* What is the definition of the term *fresco*? *(a watercolor painting done on fresh, wet plaster)* What does the word mean in Italian? *("fresh")*

C Critical Thinking Skills

Analyzing Primary Sources Have a student volunteer read the Giorgio Vasari quote. Then **ask:** What does the Renaissance biographer seem to like best about the Sistine Chapel? *(It brings a sense of light to art and the world after the darkness of earlier centuries.)* BL What is the Renaissance biographer asking other artists to do? *(imitate Michelangelo)*

T Technology Skills

Making Presentations Have students work in groups to research a Renaissance artist. Students should research the artist's background, where he or she lived and worked, what media the artist worked in, and what some of the artist's most important works are. Ask each group to include visual aids in their research. As they are conducting their research, have students discuss the following questions within their groups:

- Why was this person an important Renaissance artist? *(Students might note that the artist's style was inherently that of the Renaissance, either in its subject matter or in the use of materials.)*
- What made the artist fit into the style of the Renaissance? *(Students may respond that the artist had a humanist style or that he or she wrote or painted in a way that was unique to the Renaissance style.)*
- Did the artist collaborate or work with any other Renaissance artists? *(Student answers will vary depending on the artist they choose.)*
- What was the artist's most important work? *(Student answers will vary depending on the artist they choose.)*
- Why are the artist's works still valued today by people around the world? *(Student answers will vary, but they might say that the works of a particular artist are timeless and can still be appreciated because they are such excellent examples of a certain style of writing or painting.)*
- How did this artist's work influence other artists? *(Student answers will vary depending on the artist they choose.)*

Have groups prepare presentations and take turns sharing information on their artist with the class. Students should include pictures of the artist's works in their presentation.

Encourage groups to use a computer and slide show presentation software to organize their research. Then groups can use the software during their presentations to the class. BL Interpersonal

R Reading Skills

Citing Text Evidence Together as a class, read the first paragraph on the page that describes the life of the artist Raphael. **Ask:**

- **What work did Raphael do at the Vatican?** *(He painted many frescoes for the palace of the pope.)*
- **What group of people is shown in Raphael's fresco *The School of Athens*?** *(Greek philosophers)*
- **Why did people admire Raphael's paintings of Mary, the mother of Jesus?** *(They were done in bright colors and showed the Renaissance ideals of grace and beauty.)*

Content Background Knowledge

- Jan van Eyck worked in the court of Philip the Good, duke of Burgundy. The Burgundian Netherlands were an area that included Belgium, the Netherlands, Luxembourg, and northern France during the fourteenth and fifteenth centuries. During this time period, the area was ruled by the dukes of Burgundy. Jan van Eyck went on several diplomatic missions for Philip the Good.
- In The *Arnolfini Portrait,* the mirror on the rear wall shows the reflection of two small figures entering the room. Experts suggest that one of the figures is probably van Eyck himself. This theory is supported by the signature above the mirror, which reads "Jan van Eyck has been here. 1434." The practice of signing and dating paintings was unusual at that time.
- Van Eyck's personal motto was "As well as I can."

ANSWERS, p. 594

PROGRESS CHECK Chiaroscuro uses light and shadow, rather than stiff outlines, to separate objects in a painting.

CRITICAL THINKING The Medicis' support of Michelangelo helped the young artist develop his talents.

Reading Strategy Student answers should accurately summarize the section on Northern European painters.

BIOGRAPHY

Michelangelo Buonarroti (1475–1564)

As a young artist, Michelangelo received support from Lorenzo de' Medici, the ruler of Florence. When he saw the young man's talent, de' Medici let Michelangelo study his art collection of ancient Roman statues. One of Michelangelo's first large sculptures was inspired by these statues. Michelangelo's most famous works, however, were based on Bible stories, such as "David and Goliath." He made his 13-foot-tall marble statue of David seem calm, yet ready for action. Most of Michelangelo's sculptures suggested strong but controlled emotions.

► **CRITICAL THINKING**
Assessing How important was the de' Medici family to Michelangelo?

R Like Michelangelo, the artist Raphael worked at the Vatican. He painted many frescoes for the palace of the pope. Perhaps his best-known fresco, the *School of Athens,* shows Greek philosophers. People also admired his paintings of Mary, the mother of Jesus. These works were done in bright colors and showed the Renaissance ideals of grace and beauty.

Renaissance women had few roles independent of men. Some women, though, contributed to the arts. These women were either the daughters of artists or the children of nobles. The most celebrated female artist was Artemisia Gentileschi (ahr•teh•MIHZ•ee•uh jehn•tih•LEHS•kee). She was one of the first women to paint major historical and religious scenes.

PROGRESS CHECK

Describing What is the technique of chiaroscuro?

The Northern Renaissance

GUIDING QUESTION *How did the Renaissance change as it moved from Italy into northern Europe?*

During the late 1400s, the Renaissance spread from Italy to northern Europe. War, trade, travel, and the printing press all spread humanist ideas. The people of northern Europe eagerly accepted Italian Renaissance style but changed it to suit their own tastes and needs.

Northern European Painters

The term "Northern Renaissance" refers to the cultural changes in what is today Belgium, the Netherlands, Luxembourg, and Germany. Like Italian artists, northern artists wanted more realism in their works. However, they used different methods to achieve it.

Northern artists began painting in oils rather than using water-based paints. Oils provided richer colors and allowed changes to be made on the painted canvas. Artists also used oils to show small surface details, such as the gold trim on a robe.

The Flemish painter Jan van Eyck (YAHN van EYEK) was skilled in using oils. One of his best-known paintings is *The Arnolfini* (ahr•nuhl•FEE•nee) *Portrait.* It shows a newly married couple standing together in a formal room. Van Eyck showed every fold in their richly colored clothes and every detail of the ceiling lamp above them.

CORBIS

Reading HELPDESK (CCSS)

Reading Strategy: *Finding the Main Idea*

Finding the main idea of a passage will help you understand what the passage is about. Read about the northern European painters. On a separate sheet of paper, write the main idea of that passage in your own words.

networks *Online Teaching Options*

IMAGE

Jan Van Eyck

Making Generalizations Display the image of Jan van Eyck's *The Arnolfini Portrait.* Explain that van Eyck was a Flemish artist, meaning he was from Flanders, an area that is now Belgium and the Netherlands. Ask students to make a list of five small details in the painting. Then **ask:**

- **What allowed van Eyck to paint such small details?** *(He worked in oil paints.)*
- **Why did artists from Northern Europe begin painting in oils instead of using water-based paints?** *(Oils provided richer colors and allowed changes to be made on the painted canvas.)*

See page 579D for other online activities.

networks
Jan Van Eyck
Jan Van Eyck's Arnolfini Marriage Portrait portrays a couple thought to be the Italian merchant Giovanni Arnolfini and Jeanne de Chenany, who married in Bruges in 1434. Look closely at the mirror in the back of the room. Strangely enough, the reflection does not show the married couple, but rather shows the painter and another person. Van Eyck painted with oil and used the technique of layering. Glazes used in the layering process enabled Van Eyck to add dimensions such as depth. Van Eyck and other Northern European Renaissance painters were also known for their use of darker colors in their works.
InterfotoScans/Age fotostock

Albrecht Dürer (AHL•brehkt DYUR•uhr) of Germany was another important artist of the Northern Renaissance. His work blended Italian Renaissance methods and medieval German traditions. Dürer was skilled in showing perspective and fine detail. He is best known for his engravings. An engraving is produced from an image carved on metal, wood, or stone. Ink is placed on the surface, and then the image is printed on paper.

Dürer's *Four Horsemen of the Apocalypse* (uh•PAH•kuh•lihpz) is an outstanding example of a woodcut, a print made from carved wood. His work shows four fierce riders who announce the end of the world.

The richly detailed objects in this van Eyck painting reflect the lives of the people portrayed, a merchant and his wife.

▶ CRITICAL THINKING

Analyzing Visuals What does this painting tell you about the lives of the people in it?

England's Theaters

The Renaissance reached its height in England during the rule of Elizabeth I in the late 1500s. The people of Renaissance England were especially fond of plays. About 1580, the first theaters in England were built. Their stages stood in the open air. Some wealthy people sat under a roof or covering. Admission was only one or two cents, so even the poor could attend. The poor stood in a large open area.

C

English playwrights, or authors of plays, wrote about people's strengths, weaknesses, and emotions. The greatest English playwright of that time was William Shakespeare (SHAYK•spihr). Shakespeare wrote all kinds of plays: histories, comedies, and tragedies. He drew ideas for his plays from the histories of England and ancient Rome. His plays often included Italian scenes, characters, and plots. Many of his plays were about loyalty, family, friendship, or justice. Some of Shakespeare's most famous works are *Hamlet, Macbeth, Romeo and Juliet,* and *Henry V.*

✔ PROGRESS CHECK

Comparing and Contrasting How did northern Renaissance painters differ from Italian Renaissance painters?

LESSON 2 REVIEW (CCSS)

Review Vocabulary (Tier 3 Words)

1. How could *humanism* help people solve problems? RH.6–8.2, RH.6–8.4

Answer the Guiding Questions

2. ***Explaining*** How were Renaissance scholars able to study ancient texts? RH.6–8.2
3. ***Determining Cause and Effect*** How did Gutenberg's printing press contribute to the spread of the ideas of scholars? RH.6–8.2
4. ***Making Inferences*** How might Renaissance scientific advances have helped artists to make more realistic art? RH.6–8.2, RH.6–8.5
5. ***Contrasting*** How did Renaissance ideas influence northern and southern European art differently? RH.6–8.2
6. **INFORMATIVE/EXPLANATORY** How do you think ancient Greek and Roman ideas have affected how people learn, relate to, or think about their place in the world? Explain your answer in a short paragraph. WHST.6–8.2, WHST.6–8.10

C Critical Thinking Skills

Drawing Conclusions Ask students what they might already know about William Shakespeare and his plays. **Ask: Why do you think Shakespeare's works continue to be popular?** *(Possible answers include: They are about universal themes, such as family relationships, jealousy, fear, love, and power; the comedies are funny; the words are eloquent, and many modern expressions come from his works; and popular actors continue to appear in them.)*

Have students complete the Lesson 2 Review.

CLOSE & REFLECT

Discuss with students some of the ideas from the Renaissance that still seem important to us today. Ask students to give several examples of Renaissance ideas and modern ideas that are similar. *(Answers will vary, but students may say that modern people value reason, appreciate the arts, and admire curiosity.)*

LESSON 2 REVIEW ANSWERS

1. Humanism helped people solve their problems using reason and logic.
2. Muslim scholars had access to ancient writings. Renaissance scholars from the West visited Muslim libraries to see these writings from ancient Greece and Rome.
3. The printing press made many more books available to many more people. Scholars could read each other's works and spread ideas much faster than before.
4. Artists who learned more about the human body and how it worked would have been able to depict people more accurately and realistically.
5. Northern Europeans painted in oils rather than in water-based paint. Southern Europeans based their art on ancient Greek and Roman models.
6. Answers will vary but should include the idea that humanism, which was based on ancient Greek and Roman ideas, encouraged people to use reason and knowledge to think for themselves as individuals. Humanism encouraged people to take responsibility for themselves and help their communities work for change.

ANSWERS, p. 595

CRITICAL THINKING that the people were wealthy

✔ PROGRESS CHECK Northern Renaissance painters painted in oils rather than in watercolors.

ENGAGE

Bellringer Begin by providing students with information about Shakespeare's background. Explain that Shakespeare was an enormously successful playwright in London, England. Shakespeare wrote plays about history, tragedies, and romance.

Ask: What is a live performance that you have seen? *(Students may share examples of theater, music, comedy, or skits performed in class.)* Share an example of a performance you have seen that was especially moving or funny. Tell students they will be learning about a great playwright who attracted huge audiences to see his plays performed live.

TEACH & ASSESS

V Visual Skills

Diagramming Ask students to study the diagram of the Globe theater and read the accompanying caption. Ask them to think about how this theater differs in shape and layout from other theaters they may have visited, either traditional theaters or even movie theaters. What features are the same?

Then have student volunteers attempt to diagram the Globe on the board from a top-down view, looking directly down into the open space in the roof. **Ask:**

- What shape was the Globe? *(round)*
- Why was there a round hole in the roof? *(Possible answers: to let in light or air.)* Visual/Spatial

THE WORLD'S LITERATURE 

Henry V

by William Shakespeare

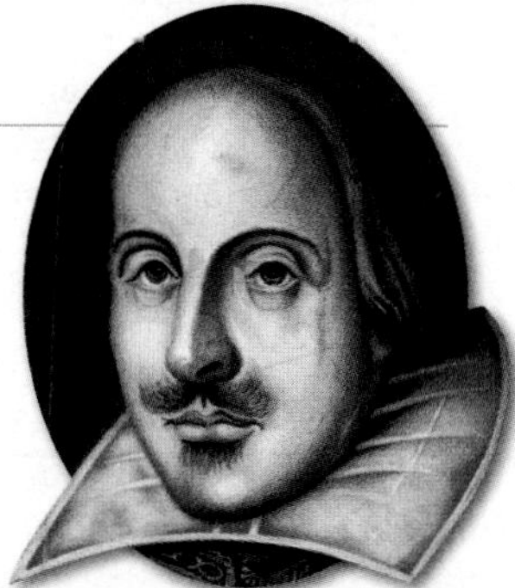

William Shakespeare

William Shakespeare, the greatest English playwright, was enormously successful. His theater company, the King's Men, employed London's best actor and playwright—Shakespeare himself.

Shakespeare's plays included histories of several British kings. In writing *Henry V,* Shakespeare drew on histories of the real King Henry V, who invaded France in 1415. The play *Henry V* tells how a small English army faces a much larger French force. Against all odds, the outnumbered Englishmen win.

Henry V is most famous for the king's uplifting speech to his men. Tired and outnumbered, the soldiers think they will be defeated in the next day's battle. Henry encourages them by describing their bravery, and how they will be remembered.

Henry V:
We few, we happy few, we band of brothers;
For he to-day that sheds his blood with me
Shall be my brother.

—From *Henry V,* Act IV, Scene iii, by William Shakespeare

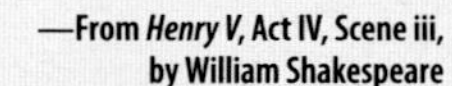

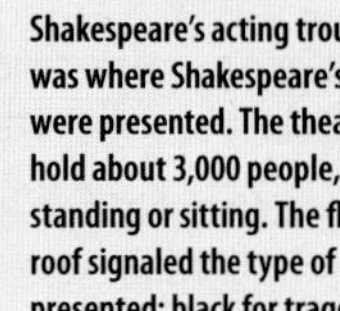

V The Globe theater was home to Shakespeare's acting troupe and was where Shakespeare's plays were presented. The theater could hold about 3,000 people, either standing or sitting. The flag on its roof signaled the type of play being presented: black for tragedies, white for comedies, and red for history plays.

Heritage Images/Corbis

networks Online Teaching Options

TIME LINE

Place and Time: Renaissance and Reformation 1350 to 1650

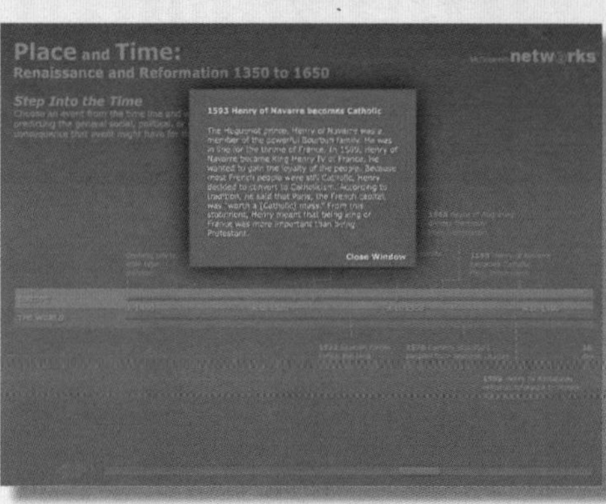

Analyzing Time Lines Project the Interactive Time Line from the Chapter Opener. **Ask:**

- What was going on at about the time Shakespeare was writing? *(King Henry IV of France was becoming Catholic to win the loyalty of the French people.)*
- Based on what you have read so far, what war or wars might Shakespeare have known about as he wrote this play? *(Shakespeare would have known that France was having a war between Protestants and Catholics.)* BL

PRIMARY SOURCE

Henry V:

“This day is called the feast of Crispian:
He that outlives this day, and comes safe home,
Will stand a tip-toe when the day is named,
And **rouse** him at the name of Crispian.

He that shall live this day, and see old age,
Will yearly on the **vigil** feast his neighbors,
R1 And say 'To-morrow is Saint Crispian:'
Then will he strip his sleeve and show his scars.
And say 'These wounds I had on Crispin's day.'

Old men forget: yet all shall be forgot,
But he'll remember with advantages
What **feats** he did that day: then shall our names.
Familiar in his mouth as household words
R2 Harry the king, Bedford and Exeter,
Warwick and Talbot, Salisbury and Gloucester,[1]
Be in their flowing cups freshly remember'd.

This story shall the good man teach his son;
And Crispin Crispian shall ne'er go by,
From this day to the ending of the world,
But we in it shall be remember'd; C
We few, we happy few, we band of brothers;
For he to-day that sheds his blood with me
Shall be my brother; be he ne'er so **vile**,
This day shall gentle his condition:
And gentlemen in England now a-bed
Shall think themselves **accursed** they were not here,
And hold their manhoods cheap whiles any speaks
That fought with us upon Saint Crispin's day.”

—From William Shakespeare's *Henry V*, Act IV, Scene iii

[1] Bedford, Exeter, Warwick, Talbot, Salisbury, and Gloucester were noblemen in Henry's army.

Vocabulary

rouse to stir up or excite
vigil the night before a religious feast
feats achievements, successes
vile morally low
accursed doomed, miserable

Analyzing Literature DBQ

1. ***Analyzing*** What is the purpose of King Henry's speech to his soldiers? What words show this purpose? RH.6–8.1, RH.6–8.6
2. ***Interpreting*** What does the king mean when he says, "For he to-day that sheds his blood with me / Shall be my brother; . . ."? RH.6–8.1, RH.6–8.4, RH.6–8.6
3. ***Assessing*** Would the king's speech persuade men to face death in battle? Why or why not? RH.6–8.1, RH.6–8.6

R1 Reading Skills

Explaining Read King Henry's monologue aloud slowly while students follow along in the text. Then ask student volunteers to read small sections aloud to the class. **Ask:** **Why does the king tell his soldiers what they will do in the future?** *(He is telling them they will survive the battle and win. He is telling them they will be heroes in the future because of their victory.)* **What do you think the king is doing as he speaks the names of the English nobles?** *(He might be pointing to them on the stage. He might be nodding at them and encouraging them.)* **BL** **Verbal/Linguistic**

C Critical Thinking Skills

Analyzing Primary Sources Write the following term on the board: *monologue*. Tell students that the excerpt they are reading is a monologue, which is a long speech spoken by a single person. **Ask:** **Do you think Henry was the only actor on the stage when he gave this speech?** *(No; he is addressing other people.)* **As a class, identify what Henry says his soldiers will do on Crispin's Day in the future.** *(They will stand "a tip-toe"; they will show their scars.)*

R2 Reading Skills

Using Context Clues Allow students to reread the selection one more time, then **ask:** **Who does King Henry say are the people who are "accursed"?** *(the people who are not fighting with him and his men)* **Why will they "hold their manhoods cheap"?** *(The men who fight with King Henry will be remembered by history as great heroes. The men who miss this battle will never receive such high honors.)*

CLOSE & REFLECT

Ask students to summarize why they think King Henry's speech would appeal to his men. *(Answers will vary but may include that the men would be encouraged when Henry says they are a "band of brothers." After Henry reminds them of their close ties, they will fight harder to help and protect one another.)*

MAP

Renaissance Europe, A.D. 1500

Argument Show students the Interactive Map of Renaissance Europe. Zoom in on England, the home of William Shakespeare. Then have students write a short speech or a note of encouragement that they might give to a family member, friend, or teammate before that person faced a difficult task or situation. **Verbal/Linguistic**

ANSWERS, p. 597

Analyzing Literature

1. King Henry wants to raise his soldiers' spirits and encourage them to fight. Phrases such as "we in it shall be remember'd; We few, we happy few, we band of brothers" promise soldiers that their bravery will be remembered and respected.
2. King Henry says the men who fight with him are noble, even though they might be peasants. He honors all the men who fight with him and says their bravery overcomes their humble status.
3. The king's speech is persuasive and stirring. Students might say that it appeals to men's sense of honor and would move them to fight for their country.

The Reformation Begins

ENGAGE

Bellringer Have students think about the qualities that our society expects people and groups to have when they are our leaders. **Ask:**

- What do we expect of these leaders? *(that they will be fair, that they will set good examples, and so on)*
- What do you think should happen when leaders decide things or allow things to happen that people don't like? *(Possible answers: People should tell their leaders they don't agree with their decisions. People should elect new leaders.)*

Explain that for centuries, the Catholic Church played the most important leadership role in Europe. Tell students they will be learning about the conditions that led people to challenge the authority of the Catholic Church during the Reformation.

TEACH & ASSESS

R Reading Skills

Identifying Instruct students to read the first section of this page. Write this information on the board as you **ask:**

- Who was Martin Luther? *(a German monk)*
- What did he want to do at first? *(reform the Catholic Church)*
- What new form of Christianity did he help produce? *(Protestantism)* AL ELL

W Writing Skills

Argument Have students imagine they are living during the early days of the Reformation, and ask them to write a letter to the pope at the Vatican. Students should describe what indulgences are and why they disagree with the practice of issuing them. Their letter should also discuss one additional situation that students disagree with, such as Church officials becoming wealthy from collecting taxes, bishops building palaces and acting like kings, bishops providing jobs for their relatives, or anything else they have learned from the reading. BL Verbal/Linguistic Intrapersonal

ANSWER, p. 598

TAKING NOTES: Answers may include: Martin Luther's Ninety-five Theses; the Church's focus on money; Luther's excommunication

networks *There's More Online!*

- **GRAPHIC ORGANIZER** Reasons for the Reformation
- **MAP** Holy Roman Empire, 1520
- **CHART/GRAPH**
  - Martin Luther and the Reformation
  - Sale of Indulgences

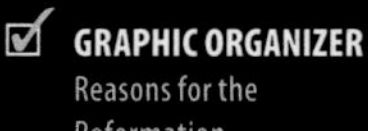
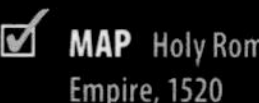

Lesson 3

The Reformation Begins

ESSENTIAL QUESTION *How do religions develop?*

IT MATTERS BECAUSE

Events during the Reformation led to the development of new Christian churches that still exist today.

Early Calls for Reform

GUIDING QUESTION *Why was the Church under pressure to reform itself?*

R Many educated Europeans were influenced by Renaissance humanism. They began to criticize the wealth and power of the Catholic Church. In 1517, a German monk named Martin Luther questioned the authority of the Church.

At first, Luther only wanted to reform the Catholic Church. This is why these events are called the **Reformation** (reh•fuhr•MAY•shuhn). The Reformation, however, produced a new form of Christianity called Protestantism (PRAH•tuhs•tuhnt•ih•zuhm). By 1600, many Protestant churches had risen in Europe.

John Wycliffe Speaks Out

W As early as the 1300s, many Europeans knew that the Catholic Church faced problems. Church officials had grown wealthy by collecting taxes. Some bishops acted like kings by building palaces and providing jobs for their relatives. Yet, in many villages, priests could barely read. In addition, churches began offering indulgences. An **indulgence** (ihn•DUHL•juhntz) was a certificate issued by the church. The certificate granted a pardon for a person's sins. Church members who performed "good works," such as giving money to build a church, could receive this pardon.

Reading HELPDESK CCSS

Taking Notes: *Determining Cause and Effect*

Use a diagram like this one to list some of the reasons for the Reformation. RH.6–8.2, RH.6–8.5

Reasons for the Reformation

Content Vocabulary (Tier 3 Words)
- **Reformation**
- **indulgence**
- **predestination**
- **annul**

networks ***Online Teaching Options***

VIDEO

Martin Luther and the Reformation

Defending Play the video for students. Then place students in pairs. Have one student play the role of Martin Luther and the other student play Pope Leo X. Give each pair 5–10 minutes to prepare. Then have them create a conversation that they think the two men might have had, based on the information in the video. Verbal/Linguistic

See page 579E for other online activities.

People were angry about the Church's focus on money. They also began to question the authority of the Church. Many years before, disputes within the Catholic Church had led to more than one leader claiming to be the rightful pope. Since then, respect for the pope had declined. In the 1370s, an English priest named John Wycliffe (WIH•klihf) preached that Christians needed only to recognize Jesus as head of the Church, not the pope.

R

Wycliffe also claimed that all religious truth came from the Christian Bible. He wanted everyone to read the Bible, so he translated many passages from Latin into English for his followers to use. After Wycliffe died, his followers finished the translation, creating the first Christian Bible in English.

Who Was Erasmus?

Renaissance humanism led to a new movement called Christian humanism. Christian humanists were loyal Catholics who wanted to restore the simple faith of the early Church. They believed that humanist learning and Bible study were the best ways to improve the church.

The best known Christian humanist was Desiderius Erasmus (DEHS•ih•DIHR•ee•uhs ih•RAZ•muhs). Erasmus believed that people should use their reason to become better Christians. He said that it was not enough to participate in religious activities like going to church on Sunday. He believed it was more important that Christians be good in their everyday lives. By improving themselves, they would be able to reform the Church and society.

In 1509, Erasmus wrote a book called *Praise of Folly*. In this work, he used humor to criticize Church corruption. He especially attacked the wealth of Renaissance popes. He said the popes were so concerned with luxury and pleasure that they no longer practiced Christianity.

Erasmus entered a monastery early in his life. His studies led him to criticize the wealth and power of Church leaders.

Scala/Art Resource, NY

✓ PROGRESS CHECK

Explaining What were the goals of the Christian humanists?

Reformation a religious movement that produced a new form of Christianity known as Protestantism
indulgence a pardon, or forgiveness, of a sin

R Reading Skills

Identifying After students have read the passage on John Wycliffe, **ask:**

- Who was John Wycliffe? *(an English priest)*
- What did he preach and claim? *(Wycliffe preached that Christians needed only to recognize Jesus as head of the Church, and that all religious truth came from the Christian Bible.)*
- What did he do for his followers? *(translated many Bible passages from Latin into English)*

After students have read the passage on Erasmus, **ask:**

- Who was Desiderius Erasmus? *(a Christian humanist)*
- What did he believe? *(Erasmus believe that people should use their reason to become better Christians, and that it was important for Christians to be good in their everyday lives.)*
- What was his book Praise of Folly about? *(criticism of Church corruption and the wealth of Renaissance popes)*

Content Background Knowledge

Erasmus of Rotterdam Desidarius Erasmus was a Dutch scholar and priest. He studied the Bible and early Christian writings for inspiration. He improved Greek and Latin translations of the New Testament. One of his goals was to translate the Bible into the vernacular language, or the language of ordinary people. He wanted farmers and workers as well as nobles to be able to read the Bible.

WHITEBOARD ACTIVITY

Church Leaders of the Reformation

Categorizing Work with the class to complete the Interactive Whiteboard Activity identifying details about Martin Luther, John Wycliffe, and Erasmus. Then **ask:**

- Why were many people angry with the Church? *(The Church's focus on money and power in the 1500s meant they were not acting like good religious leaders.)*
- What generalization can you make about why reformers thought Christians should be able to read the Bible for themselves? *(Reformers thought that Christians should be able to read their key religious document without having another person interpret it for them.)* BL

networks Church Leaders of the Reformation

Directions. Select phrases from the left and drag them to the correct column in the chart.

- Preached that Christians needed to recognize Jesus, not the pope, as the head of the Catholic Church
- Best known Christian humanist
- Claimed all religious truth came from the Christian Bible
- At first only wanted to reform the Catholic Church
- Believed that by doing good deeds, people could improve the Church and society
- Believed that salvation was a gift from God
- In his book, *In Praise of Folly*, he used humor to attack corrupt Church leaders and practices.
- Translated Bible passages from Latin to English
- His actions led to the rise of churches that were not under the authority of the pope.
- German monk who challenged the Church's authority

Martin Luther	John Wycliffe	Desiderius Erasmus

See page 579E for other online activities.

ANSWER, p. 599

✓ PROGRESS CHECK Christian humanists wanted to reform the Catholic Church. Some wanted to make the Bible available to people in the vernacular language.

The Reformation Begins

W Writing Skills

Informative/Explanatory Have students write paragraphs that describe and explain the concerns that Martin Luther had about the fate of his soul and the practices of the Roman Catholic Church. Students should include specific details about the Church actions that Luther objected to, and why he disagreed with those actions. Finally, have students identify the action that Luther took to publicly declare his displeasure with the Church.

V Visual Skills

Creating Time Lines Have students work in pairs or groups and use the information in "Who was Martin Luther?" to create time lines that show the progression of events in Luther's life and his thought processes as he moved toward reform. Students should follow the sequence in the textbook to place events that do not have specific dates. **Visual/Spatial**

Martin Luther's family wanted him to become a lawyer, but he decided on a career in the church.

Luther's Reformation

GUIDING QUESTION *How did Luther's reforms lead to a new form of Christianity?*

During the early 1500s, Martin Luther supported the cause of Church reform. Opposed by the pope, Luther broke away from many Catholic teachings. His rebellion led to a religious revolution that changed Europe.

Who was Martin Luther?

Born in 1483, Martin Luther became a monk and faithfully followed Church teachings and practices. However, he still worried about the fate of his soul. His concern about reaching heaven was not surprising. He had seen epidemics, famine, and war.

Luther's doubts grew after he visited Rome. He was shocked to find priests there made fun of Catholic rituals. They disobeyed Church rules. Some of them could not read the Bible. How could these disrespectful priests help people get to heaven?

Back in Wittenberg (VIH•tuhn•buhrg), Germany, Luther searched for answers. The Church taught that a person needed both faith and good works to go to heaven. His experiences in Rome caused Luther to question church policy.

In 1517, Luther became even angrier at Church leaders. Pope Leo X needed money to rebuild St. Peter's Basilica, a large church in Rome. To get that money, he sent monks out to sell indulgences. Local church leaders had offered, and even sold, indulgences for many years. Now the Pope was selling them, too. How could **W** Church leaders put a price on God's forgiveness? Luther thought the Church had moved too far away from the Bible in what they were teaching. **V**

Luther prepared a list of 95 arguments against the indulgences. He sent the list to his bishop. Some accounts say that Luther also nailed them to the door of Wittenberg Cathedral. The list became known as the Ninety-Five Theses. Thousands of copies were printed and read all across Germany.

A New Church

Luther began to openly attack other Catholic beliefs. He said that popes could make mistakes. He argued that the only true guide to religious truth was the Bible, which all Christians had a right to read. Finally, he stated that all Christians could confess their sins directly to God without the help of a priest.

Reading **HELP**DESK (CCSS)

Reading Strategy: ***Activating Prior Knowledge***

Martin Luther was concerned with salvation. You learned about the idea of salvation in an earlier chapter. What does the word *salvation* mean?

networks *Online Teaching Options*

CHART

Martin Luther and the Reformation

Determining Cause and Effect Show the interactive chart about Martin Luther and the Protestant Reformation. Have students predict the information that will appear in each column before you click on it. **Ask:**

- **What did Catholic Church leaders do that caused Luther to become angry?** *(The Catholic Church was abusing power, selling indulgences, and not getting rid of corrupt priests.)*
- **What did Luther do as a result of his beliefs?** *(posted the Ninety-five Theses, argued against the practices of the Catholic Church, helped start the Reformation)*

See page 579E for other online activities.

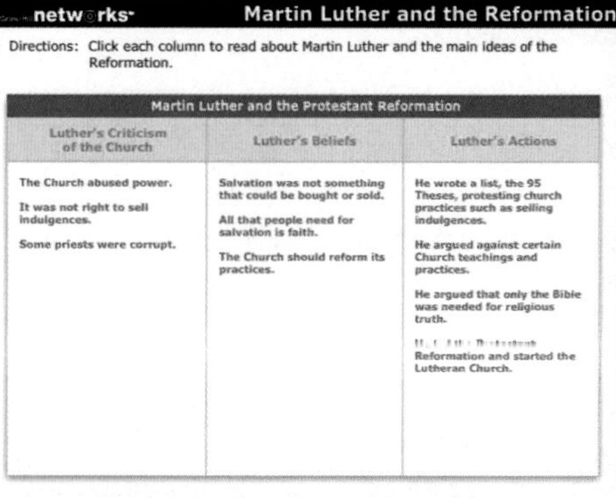

networks Martin Luther and the Reformation

Directions: Click each column to read about Martin Luther and the main ideas of the Reformation.

Martin Luther and the Protestant Reformation		
Luther's Criticism of the Church	Luther's Beliefs	Luther's Actions
The Church abused power. It was not right to sell indulgences. Some priests were corrupt.	Salvation was not something that could be bought or sold. All that people need for salvation is faith. The Church should reform its practices.	He wrote a list, the 95 Theses, protesting church practices such as selling indulgences. He argued against certain Church teachings and practices. He argued that only the Bible was needed for religious truth. [illegible] Reformation and started the Lutheran Church.

ANSWER, p. 600

Reading Strategy Salvation means "the act of being saved from the effects of sin."

Pope Leo X believed that Luther was dangerous. In 1521, he excommunicated Luther. A person who is excommunicated can no longer belong to the church. Then, a diet, or council, of German princes met in the city of Worms. The princes wanted Luther to change his ideas. Luther refused:

PRIMARY SOURCE

> "Unless I am convinced by Scripture and plain reason—I do not accept the authority of the popes and councils, for they have contradicted [spoken against] each other—my conscience is captive [loyal] to the Word of God. I cannot and will not recant [take back] anything for to go against conscience is neither right nor safe. God help me. Amen."
>
> —from Martin Luther's speech at the Diet of Worms, 1521

R1

Luther's ideas eventually led to the creation of the first Protestant church, known as Lutheranism (LOO•thuh•ruhn•ihzm). The new church was based on three main ideas. The first idea is that faith in Jesus, not good works, brings someone a place in heaven. The second is that the Bible is the final source for truth about God. Finally, Lutheranism said that the church was made up of all its believers, not just the clergy.

Revolts in Germany

Lutheranism gave rural peasants in Germany hope for a better life. During the 1520s, the peasants suffered as a result of poor crops and high taxes paid to noble landowners. The peasants thought that if Luther could rebel against the pope, then they could stand up to greedy nobles.

Huge revolts swept Germany. The peasants looked to Luther for support. At first, Luther agreed with their cause. In his sermons, Luther criticized nobles for their mistreatment of the peasants. However, Luther also feared violence. He told the peasants that God had set the government above them and they must obey it. The nobles soon defeated the peasants.

Rulers and Lutheranism

In the past, the Catholic Church could stop the spread of ideas that it opposed. Why was it unable to stop Protestantism in the 1500s? One reason is that Protestantism had the support of some European rulers. These rulers believed that they could increase their power by supporting Protestantism against the Catholic Church. The Lutheran movement became closely tied to politics.

R2

In this painting, indulgences are being sold at a village market.

R1 Reading Skills

Analyzing Primary Sources Ask students to paraphrase what Martin Luther said in his speech at the Diet of Worms in 1521. Students should use their own words. *(Sample answer: Martin Luther would only accept the authority of the pope and the Church unless he was convinced by Scripture and plain reason. He thought that the pope and councils had spoken against each other. Martin Luther felt that he was loyal to the Word of God. He could not and would not take back anything that he said because he believed it wasn't right or safe to go against his conscience.)* BL

R2 Reading Skills

Summarizing After students read the text, ask them to summarize the reason why the Lutheran movement became closely tied to politics. *(Protestantism had the support of some European rulers. These rulers thought they could become more powerful if they supported Protestantism instead of the Catholic Church.)* Have students list three main ideas that set Lutheranism apart from the Catholic Church. *(Faith in Jesus, not good works, brings salvation; the Bible is the source of truth about God; the Church is made up of all believers, not just clergy.)*

WORKSHEET

21st Century Skills Activity: Renaissance and Reformation—The Reformation Begins

Determining Cause and Effect Have students analyze the causes and effects of Martin Luther's call for reforms of the Catholic Church. Organize students into groups of four. Then have them complete the 21st Century Skills activity for this lesson.

See page 579E for other online activities.

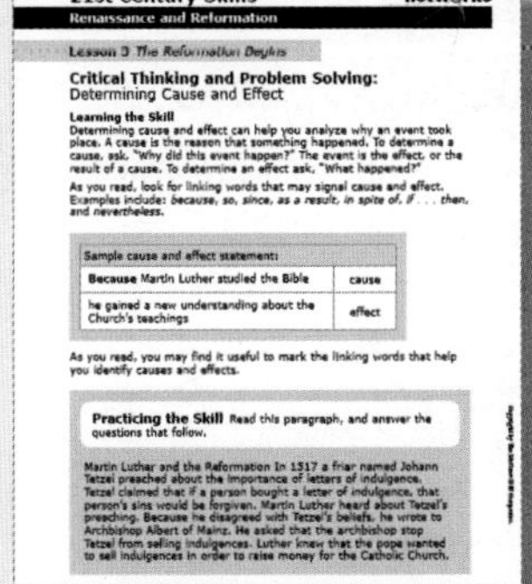

The Reformation Begins

V Visual Skills

Reading a Map Direct students to the map of the Holy Roman Empire. Have them locate England on the map. Then tell students that the German states were located in the part of the Holy Roman Empire north of Switzerland and east of the Netherlands. **Ask:**

- **In what part of Europe is England located?** *(northern Europe)*
- **How was England different politically from Germany?** *(England was not part of the Holy Roman Empire.)*
- **Why do you think the Holy Roman Empire was a Catholic region and not a Protestant one?** *(The Papal States were part of the Holy Roman Empire. The city of Rome was in the Papal States. Rome was where the Vatican was located.)* BL

C Critical Thinking Skills

Reasoning After students have read about the events leading up to the Peace of Augsburg, **ask:**

- **What would be a positive reason to sign the Peace of Augsburg?** *(Under its terms, each German ruler could decide the religion of his people.)*
- **What is one reason that conflict often happens before compromise?** *(Answers will vary. Students might say that people always think their opinion is the "right" one. At first, people don't want to talk to or listen to others or learn about other points of view.)*

ANSWERS, p. 602

GEOGRAPHY CONNECTION

1. Austria, Bohemia, Netherlands, Swiss Confederation, states in northern Italy
2. CRITICAL THINKING It was large.

GEOGRAPHY CONNECTION

In 1520, the Holy Roman Emperor ruled over a large part of Europe.

1. **REGIONS** What are some of the areas that made up the Holy Roman Empire?
2. **CRITICAL THINKING** *Drawing Conclusions* Why would it have been difficult for one ruler to control the Holy Roman Empire?

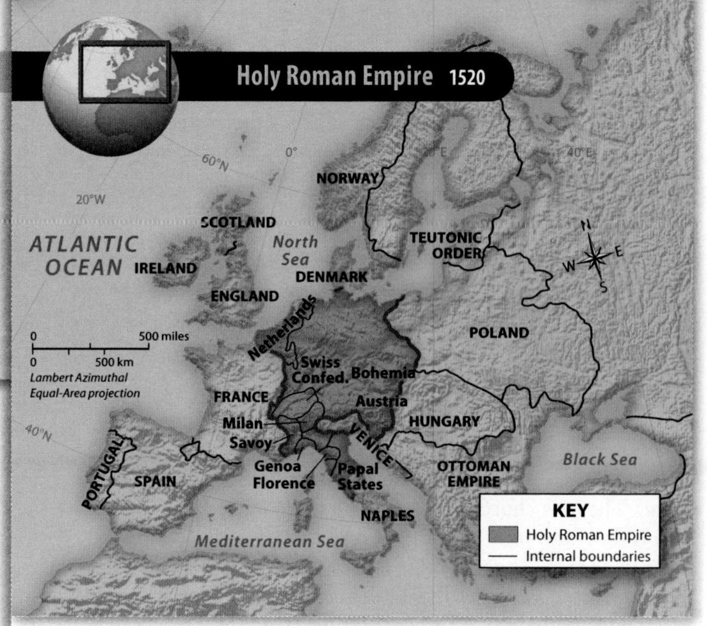

V

The Holy Roman Empire was Catholic and covered much of central Europe. It included about 300 German states. In 1519, Charles V became the Holy Roman Emperor. He also ruled Spain, the Netherlands, parts of Italy, and territories in the Americas.

Local German rulers worried about the growing power of Charles V. They wanted to keep their independence. Many of these leaders became Lutherans. By doing so, their states also became Lutheran. After breaking with the Catholic Church, these rulers took over Catholic lands in their territories. Now they, and not the Catholic Church, would earn income from those lands.

When rulers adopted Lutheranism, taxes no longer flowed to the pope in Rome. Rulers could **impose** their own church taxes and keep the money for themselves. This made Lutheran rulers stronger and the Catholic Church weaker.

C In order to regain control of these lands, Charles V went to war with the Lutheran rulers. However, he was not able to defeat them. In 1555, an agreement known as the Peace of Augsburg (AUGHZ•buhrg) ended the fighting. Under its terms, each German ruler—whether Catholic or Lutheran—could decide

Reading HELPDESK CCSS

predestination a religious belief that God has already decided who will go to heaven and who will not

Academic Vocabulary (Tier 2 Words)

impose to establish by force or authority

networks Online Teaching Options

MAP

Renaissance Europe, A.D. 1500

Interpreting Show students the interactive map of Renaissance Europe. **Ask:** **How do you think the size of Renaissance Europe helped the Reformation spread?** *(Sample answer: Not every country was close to Rome, and countries that were farther away developed different beliefs.)*

Continue by discussing how the number of countries in Europe and the travel routes to, from, and within the continent may have also helped to aid the growth of Protestantism. **Visual/Spatial**

See page 579E for other online activities.

the religion of his people. The Peace of Augsburg allowed the division of Germany into a Protestant north and a Catholic south. This division remains to this day.

✓ PROGRESS CHECK

Determining Cause and Effect How did the Ninety-Five Theses affect the Catholic Church in Germany?

The Reformation Spreads

GUIDING QUESTION *How did the teachings of Protestant reformers shape the western world?*

As the Reformation spread, different forms of Protestantism developed. Soon after Lutheranism began in Germany, many people in nearby Switzerland accepted Protestant ideas. They set up new reformed churches.

Who Was John Calvin?

John Calvin was born in France in 1509. Known for his sharp mind, Calvin studied law, humanism, and religion in Paris. He was especially interested in religion. He got up early and stayed up late to read books about it. The more Calvin read, the more he was convinced that Luther was right.

R

Eventually, Calvin fled from Paris because it became too dangerous to talk about Protestantism. He finally found safety in Geneva (juh•NEE•vuh), Switzerland. There, his powerful preaching convinced many people to follow him.

What Is Calvinism?

As he studied the Bible, Calvin developed his own ideas. He agreed with Luther that faith alone brought salvation, but he added other ideas. Calvin's main idea was that God decides the final outcome of all events in the universe. Therefore, God has already chosen who will go to heaven and who will not. This belief is called **predestination** (pree•dehs•tuh•NAY•shuhn).

Most of Calvin's followers believed that they were among the people who would be saved. To prove it, they worked hard, behaved well, and obeyed the laws of their towns. In this way, Calvinism became a powerful tool in society. It encouraged people to work hard at their business and watch their behavior.

Another idea of Calvinism is that church members, not kings or bishops, should choose the clergy. This idea influenced people in England, Scotland, and the Netherlands. Because of Calvinism, people began to think that they could elect government leaders.

C

✓ PROGRESS CHECK

Analyzing How did Calvinism influence ideas about government?

The writings of John Calvin helped Europeans accept Protestantism.

▶ CRITICAL THINKING

Explaining Why would followers of Calvin work to live a good life, even though they believed that God had already decided their fate?

Erich Lessing/Art Resource, NY

BIOGRAPHY

John Calvin

Integrating Visual Information Show students the interactive image of John Calvin. Read aloud the accompanying text. Review the meaning of the term predestination with students. ELL

See page 579E for other online activities.

networks
John Calvin
BIOGRAPHY
John Calvin
In Calvin's Institutes of the Christian Religion, he summarized the basic beliefs of Calvinism. At the center of these beliefs is the subject of predestination. (Pre = "before"; destined = "fated" or "meant to be") Calvin believed that there were certain people who were chosen to be called by God. In other words, certain religious outcomes in life were "meant to be."
Calvin's followers simplified some of the content in Institutes of the Christian Religion by using the acrostic TULIP. In an acrostic, the first letters of several sentences
Erich Lessing/Art Resource, NY

The Reformation Begins

R Reading Skills

Identifying Have students read the text. Then write this information on the board as you **ask:**

- Who was John Calvin? *(a Frenchman in Switzerland who was interested in religion)*
- Why did Calvin have to flee from Paris? *(It became too dangerous to talk about Protestantism in France.)*
- What is the main idea of Calvinism? *(God decides the final outcome of all events in the universe and has already chosen who will go to heaven and who will not.)* AL

C Critical Thinking Skills

Making Inferences Prompt students to further consider Calvinism, its origins, and the context in which it was developed. **Ask:** How does this view contrast with the beliefs of Martin Luther? *(Luther believed that salvation was available to all people.)* **Ask:** Why was Switzerland important in the development of the Reformation? *(Answers will vary, but students might say that Calvin developed his ideas in Switzerland, making the country a center of Reformation influence.)* BL

ANSWERS, p. 603

✓ PROGRESS CHECK The Ninety-five Theses began the Reformation, which led many people to leave the Catholic Church in Germany and begin Protestant churches.

CRITICAL THINKING Students may answer that because people didn't know what fate God had decided for them, they assumed they were among those who would be saved. Thus, they behaved well and obeyed the laws.

✓ PROGRESS CHECK Because of Calvinism, people thought of electing government officials, and that government leaders should not control the church.

The Reformation Begins

R Reading Skills

Identifying Ask students to read the text on this page, then ask:

- **Who was Henry VIII?** *(King of England)*
- **What did he ask the pope to do?** *(He asked the pope to annul, or declare invalid, his marriage to Queen Catherine.)*
- **What was the Act of Supremacy?** *(It was an act that made the king head of the new Church of England.)*

W Writing Skills

Informative/Explanatory Have students use the information in "The Break with Rome" to write an article as though they were reporting for an English newspaper during the time that Henry VIII was in conflict with Rome. In their articles, students should include as many details about specific events and people as possible. **Verbal/Linguistic**

Content Background Knowledge

Henry VIII

Henry VIII enjoyed sports, music, and literature, but he was also demanding and ruthless. He imprisoned and executed bishops and nobles for disagreeing with him. Henry married six times. He divorced his first wife (Catherine of Aragon, mother of Mary I) and beheaded his second wife (Anne Boleyn, mother of Elizabeth I). His third wife (Jane Seymour), mother of his only son Edward, died from complications of childbirth. Henry divorced his fourth wife (Anne of Cleves) and beheaded his fifth wife (Katherine Howard). Henry died while married to his last wife, Katherine Parr.

ANSWER, p. 604

CRITICAL THINKING because the Catholic Church did not allow divorce

The Reformation in England

GUIDING QUESTION ***How did the Reformation shape England and later its American colonies?***

The Reformation reached England about 10 years after it began in central Europe. In England, religious change at first did not come from church officials or the people. It started as a political quarrel between the king and the pope. Religious beliefs did not play a part until much later. **R**

Henry VIII challenged the Church to solve his own problems in England.

▶ **CRITICAL THINKING**
Explaining Why did the Pope refuse Henry's request to undo his marriage to Catherine?

The Break with Rome

Henry VIII ruled England from 1509 to 1547. He belonged to the Tudor family. Henry wanted to keep the Tudors on the throne. However, he had no son to follow him. Catherine, the first of Henry's six wives, had children. Only one of her children, Mary, survived. **W**

As Catherine grew older, Henry feared she could not have any more children. At the same time, he had fallen in love with Anne Boleyn (buh•LIHN), a young noblewoman. Henry asked the pope to **annul,** or declare invalid, his marriage to Catherine so that he could marry Anne. The Catholic Church did not allow divorce. If the pope granted an annulment, it would be as if Henry and Catherine had never married.

The pope refused Henry's request. Catherine was the daughter of King Ferdinand and Queen Isabella of Spain. Her nephew was Charles V, the Holy Roman Emperor. The pope did not want to anger Catherine's important family.

Henry had the Archbishop of Canterbury—the highest church official in England—end his marriage to Catherine. Henry then married Anne Boleyn. In response, the pope excommunicated Henry. Henry fought back. In 1534, he had Parliament pass the Act of Supremacy. The act made the king head of the new Church of England.

Henry ordered all bishops and priests in England to accept the Act of Supremacy. Some who refused were killed. Henry seized the land of the Catholic Church in England and gave some of it to his nobles. Giving the nobles this property made sure they remained loyal to Henry and his church.

Reading HELPDESK (CCSS)

annul to declare invalid

Academic Vocabulary (Tier 2 Words)

restore to bring back

networks Online Teaching Options

LECTURE SLIDE

The Reformation in England

Reading a Chart Show students the lecture slide on English rulers and the religion they practiced. **Ask:**

- **According to this chart, when did the Catholic ruler Mary rule England?** *(after Henry VIII and before Elizabeth)*
- **What is another name for the Church of England?** *(the Anglican Church)*
- **How did the change of rulers affect religion in England?** *(The country's religion changed every time the monarch changed. Henry made the country Anglican. Mary made it Catholic. Elizabeth made it a Protestant country again.)* AL

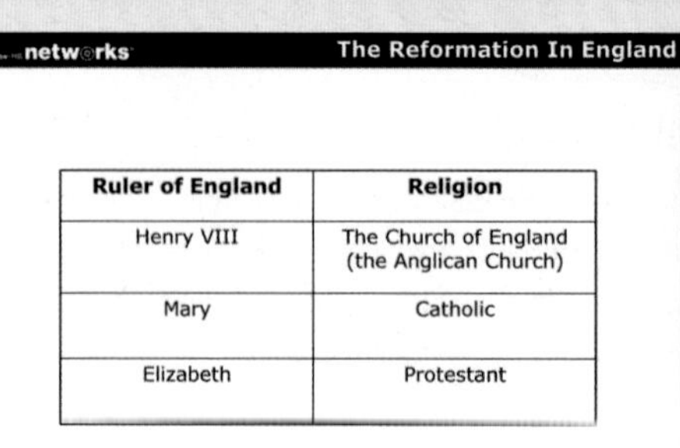

Ruler of England	Religion
Henry VIII	The Church of England (the Anglican Church)
Mary	Catholic
Elizabeth	Protestant

See page 579E for other online activities.

Who Was Bloody Mary?

The Church of England became known as the Anglican (AYN•glih•kuhn) Church. After Henry's death, the Anglican Church accepted some Protestant ideas, but it kept most Catholic rituals. Many English Catholics wanted more. They supported Henry's Catholic daughter Mary when she became queen.

R

As queen, Mary **restored** the Catholic Church in England and arrested Protestants who opposed her. More than 300 Protestants were burned at the stake. The English were horrified and turned against their queen, calling her "Bloody Mary."

Mary died in 1558. Her half-sister Elizabeth, the Protestant daughter of Henry VIII and Anne Boleyn, took the throne as Queen Elizabeth I. She restored the Anglican Church. Elizabeth became one of the greatest rulers in English history.

Elizabeth I succeeded her half-sister Mary as queen and halted the persecution of English Protestants.

Calvinism in England

Most English people were pleased with the Anglican Church. Some Protestants, however, had become Calvinists. These people became known as Puritans because they wanted to purify, or cleanse, the Anglican Church of Catholic ways. Puritan groups often refused to accept the authority of Anglican bishops.

C

Queen Elizabeth I tolerated the Puritans. When James I became king in 1603, however, the Puritans faced opposition. James believed that the Puritans threatened his power. He and later his son, King Charles I, closed Puritan churches and imprisoned Puritan leaders. Many Puritans left England and settled in North America to practice their religion freely.

Image Asset Management/World History Archive/Age fotostock

✓ PROGRESS CHECK

Explaining Why did Henry VIII seize Catholic Church lands in England?

LESSON 3 REVIEW 

Review Vocabulary (Tier 3 Words)

1. Why did Martin Luther want the *Reformation* of the Catholic Church? RH.6–8.2, RH.6–8.4
2. Why did the pope want to sell *indulgences*? RH.6–8.2, RH.6–8.4

Answer the Guiding Questions

3. ***Identifying*** Why did many Europeans criticize the Catholic Church at the time of the Reformation? RH.6–8.2
4. ***Generalizing*** What three types of reforms did Luther want for the Catholic Church? RH.6–8.2
5. ***Making Inferences*** Why was Germany's split between Protestants in the north and Catholics in the south important? RH.6–8.2
6. ***Determining Cause and Effect*** How did John Calvin's ideas take root in the American colonies? RH.6–8.2, RH.6–8.5
7. **ARGUMENT** Which argument for religious reform might be convincing to a priest, pope, or king? Choose one idea for reform and support it with evidence. Write a persuasive paragraph to one of these people that defends your idea. WHST.6–8.1, WHST.6–8.10

LESSON 3 REVIEW ANSWERS

1. Luther thought the Catholic Church was corrupt.
2. The pope wanted to sell indulgences to raise money to rebuild St. Peter's Basilica in Rome.
3. The Catholic Church angered its members by focusing on money and thereby losing its moral authority.
4. Luther wanted the Church to acknowledge that it could make mistakes, stop selling indulgences, and take responsibility away from priests and give it to Church members.
5. The split of Protestants and Catholics divided the continent and let rulers use religion to make their kingdoms stronger.
6. Some of John Calvin's followers wanted to "purify" the Anglican church. Because they did not accept the church's authority, many of these Puritans moved to the American colonies.
7. Students should support their ideas with different reformers' arguments and with their own opinions.

R Reading Skills

Explaining Direct students to read the text. Discuss Queen Mary's stance on religion. **Ask:** **How did "Bloody Mary" get her name?** *(Mary had more than 300 Protestants burned at the stake when she was queen. The English people were horrified by what she did. They turned against their queen by calling her "Bloody Mary.")*

C Critical Thinking Skills

Contrasting Once students have read about the development of Puritanism, **ask:** **What was the difference between an Anglican and a Puritan?** *(An Anglican accepted some Protestant ideas but followed most Catholic rituals. A Puritan wanted to purify the Anglican Church and get rid of Catholic ways.)*

Have students complete the Lesson 3 Review.

CLOSE & REFLECT

Discuss with students how reformers of the 1500s and 1600s changed well-established religious practices. Then ask students to think of other examples in ancient or modern times in which people started a movement to change a part of society. *(Answers will vary but may include the following: Gandhi challenged the use of violence to achieve a goal; Martin Luther King, Jr., challenged assumptions about racial inequalities; Susan B. Anthony challenged attitudes about women in the United States.)* BL

ANSWER, p. 605

✓ PROGRESS CHECK Henry seized the lands to gain the support of his nobles for the Church of England.

Catholics and Protestants

ENGAGE

Bellringer Have students brainstorm a list of reasons people in Europe left the Catholic Church. *(Answers may include the Church's corruption and focus on money.)* **Ask:** What would you do if you were a leader in the Catholic Church? How would you respond to the spread of Protestantism?

Tell students that in this lesson, they will learn how the Catholic Church responded to calls for reform and how the Church responded to other religions.

TEACH & ASSESS

R Reading Skills

Stating After students have read the introduction to the lesson, **ask:** What were the two goals of the Catholic Reformation? *(to improve the Catholic Church and to stop the spread of Protestant ideas)*

W Writing Skills

Argument Have students choose one or two reforms made at the Council of Trent and write about why they think those reforms would be positive ones for the Roman Catholic Church. Students should think about what they have already learned about the history of the Church to help them make their arguments. Verbal/Linguistic Intrapersonal

ANSWER, p. 606

TAKING NOTES: Answers may include: Council of Trent: set of strict rules for priests' behavior; made Catholic beliefs clear; set up seminaries; Society of Jesuits founded: fought heresy; taught; preached; ended the sale of indulgences

networks
There's More Online!

- CHART/GRAPH De' Medici Family Tree
- GRAPHIC ORGANIZER
  - Reform in the Catholic Church
  - Effects from the Council of Trent
- MAP Religion in Europe, c. 1600

Lesson 4

Catholics and Protestants

ESSENTIAL QUESTION *Why does conflict develop?*

It Matters Because

The struggle between Catholics and Protestants during the Reformation shaped the churches that we know today.

The Catholic Reformation

GUIDING QUESTION *How did the Catholic Church respond to the spread of Protestantism?*

R In the 1500s and 1600s, Catholics set out to improve their Church and to stop the spread of Protestant ideas. This effort was known as the Catholic Reformation. It helped the Church regain some of the areas in Europe it had lost to Protestantism.

Catholic Reforms

Catholics were dedicated to fighting Protestantism. They also knew they needed to reform their Church. Pope Paul III called a council of bishops. The council met at different times between 1545 and 1563 at Trent, Italy.

W The Council of Trent supported Catholic beliefs that had been challenged by the Protestants. However, it ended many Church abuses, such as the sale of indulgences. The Council also ordered bishops and priests to follow strict rules of behavior. The Church set up seminaries to train new priests. A **seminary** (SEH•muh•nehr•ee) is a special school for training and educating priests.

The Church also set out to win followers and to strengthen the spiritual life of Catholics. In 1540, Pope Paul III recognized a new order of priests, the Society of Jesus, known as the Jesuits. They taught and preached in an effort to bring Protestants back to the Catholic faith.

Reading **HELP**DESK (CCSS)

Taking Notes: ***Determining Cause and Effect***
Use a diagram like this one to show the results of the Catholic Church's attempts at reform. RH.6–8.2, RH.6–8.5

Reform in the Catholic Church → [ ] [ ] [ ]

Content Vocabulary (Tier 3 Words)
- **seminary**
- **heresy**

networks Online Teaching Options

VIDEO

Britain Arises: England Defeats the Spanish Armada

Listing Play the video for students. Have them list the ways in which the defeat of the Spanish Armada benefited Queen Elizabeth I and England. *(It was a way to prevent a civil war in England. It was a way for Elizabeth I to influence events but be able to deny doing so to Spain. It was a way to gain money to repay England's national debt. It helped England to be seen as a powerful country.)*

See page 579F for other online activities.

The man who founded the Jesuits was a Spanish noble, Ignatius (ihg•NAY•shuhs) of Loyola (loy•OH•luh). He was a soldier whose life changed when he was wounded in battle. While recovering, he read about the lives of the saints. Ignatius decided he would be a soldier for Jesus and the Church.

The Spanish nun Teresa of Avila (AH•vih•luh) was another reformer. Teresa founded an order of nuns and opened new convents throughout Spain. Teresa became known for her spiritual writings that rank among the classics of Christian writing.

Ferdinand and Isabella united the separate kingdoms of Aragon and Castile into the country of Spain.

Catholic Spain

Protestant ideas never became very popular in Spain. Still, when religious conflict began to divide Europe, Spain was affected. Spanish rulers distrusted Protestant countries and their own Protestant citizens.

When Luther called for reform in 1517, Spain was a united country. King Ferdinand of Aragon and Queen Isabella of Castile had married and joined their two kingdoms in 1469. They wanted to unite Spain and make all of their subjects be Catholic.

In the late 1400s, many Muslims lived in Spain. Muslims had ruled much of Spain during the Middle Ages. Under Muslim rule, Christians and Jews paid special taxes and had limited rights, but they were able to practice their religions. Muslims and non-Muslims lived in relative peace. This time period was a golden age for Jews in Spain. **R**

This age of religious harmony ended under Ferdinand and Isabella. Spain's rulers pressured Jews and Muslims to convert to Catholicism. But even those who converted were not safe. Spanish officials suspected them of secretly practicing their old religions. To ensure that their orders were being carried out, Ferdinand and Isabella began the Spanish Inquisition.

Spanish Inquisition

The Spanish Inquisition was a religious court. It was similar to the one that the Catholic Church had set up earlier in Europe to root out **heresy** (HEHR•uh•see), or beliefs that opposed Church teaching.

The Council of Trent is considered one of the most important councils in the history of the Catholic Church.

▶ CRITICAL THINKING
Identifying What do you think was the most important decision of the Council?

seminary a school for religious training
heresy a religious belief that contradicts what the church says is true

R Reading Skills

Identifying Ask students to name three reasons why the age of religious harmony ended in Spain. Students should support their answers with details from the text. *(King Ferdinand of Aragon and Queen Isabella of Castile married and joined their two kingdoms to unite Spain. They pressured Jews and Muslims to convert and become Catholic. Ferdinand and Isabella began the Spanish Inquisition.)*

Content Background Knowledge

- The trials held during the Spanish Inquisition were tribunals. In a tribunal, a judge (or more than one judge) tries the accused person and decides punishment. Anyone accused during the Spanish Inquisition was required to testify at a trial without a lawyer or any assistance. Any refusal to testify was considered to be proof of guilt. Any person could testify against someone who was accused, including relatives and criminals. Accused people also were not told who was testifying against them. Sometimes they didn't even know what charges were being leveled against them. Witnesses were often reluctant to testify on a person's behalf for fear of falling under suspicion themselves.
- The goal of the tribunal was to obtain a **confession.** Those accused of heresy could be imprisoned for years until they confessed. The inquisitors who questioned accused people were educated and also well versed in the Bible. They were also specifically trained to ask confusing or leading questions. It was often impossible to answer an inquisitor's questions and prove one's innocence.

GAME

Crossword Puzzle: Catholics and Protestants

Identifying Put students in pairs and have them play the interactive Catholics and Protestants crossword puzzle game. Tell students that they can use their textbooks or the Internet to research any answers they don't know. **Interpersonal**

See page 579F for other online activities.

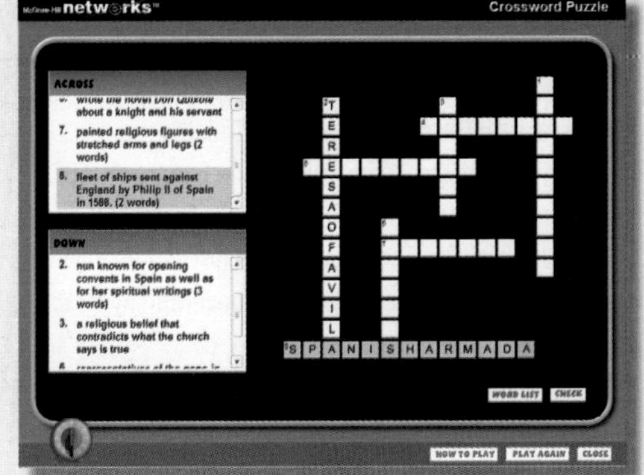

ANSWER, p. 607

CRITICAL THINKING Possible answer: The most important decision made by the Council of Trent was to make Catholic beliefs clear, because it helped people understand what the Catholic Church preached.

Catholics and Protestants

V Visual Skills

Reading a Map Guide students to look at the map "Religions in Europe." Have them name four Catholic countries *(Possible answers: Portugal, Spain, Italy, France, Ireland, Spanish Netherlands, Austria)*; name four Lutheran countries *(Possible answers: German States, Netherlands, Denmark, Norway, Sweden)*; name two Calvinist countries. *(Scotland and Switzerland).*

Then **ask:**

- **What was the minority religion in Hungary and Spain?** *(Muslim—Islam)*
- **Calvinists were the minority religious group in what countries?** *(France, Netherlands, and the Spanish Netherlands)*
- **What religions did people practice in Poland?** *(a mixture of Calvinist, Lutheran, and Roman Catholic religions)*
- **Lutherans lived along the coasts of what two seas?** *(Baltic Sea and North Sea)*
- **What religious groups lived in the area around the Black Sea?** *(Eastern Orthodox Christian and Muslim)* **Visual/Spatial**

V

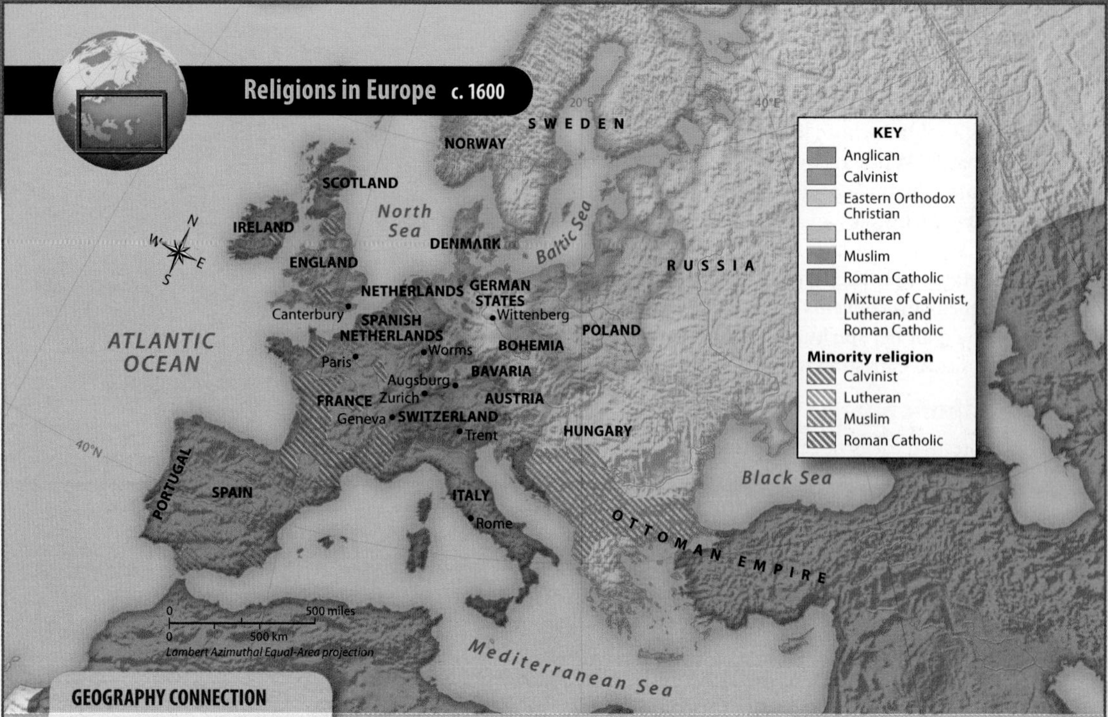

Religions in Europe c. 1600

GEOGRAPHY CONNECTION

By the late 1500s, many northern Europeans had become Protestants, and most southern Europeans had remained Catholic.

1. **PLACE** Which areas of Europe became mostly Calvinist?
2. **CRITICAL THINKING** ***Making Inferences*** Where in Europe was religious conflict most likely to take place?

The purpose of the Spanish Inquisition was to find and punish those guilty of heresy. Torture was used to force people to confess their guilt. The head of the Spanish Inquisition was Tomás de Torquemada (tawr • kay•MAH•duh). Even the pope could not stop him from eventually executing about 2,000 Spaniards.

In 1492, the Spanish monarchs ordered all Jews to become Catholic or leave the country. Ten years later, they gave Muslims the same order. Many people left in response to these orders.

Despite strong Church and government controls, literature and the arts flourished in Catholic Spain. The writer Miguel de Cervantes (mih•GEHL day suhr•VAHN•tehz) wrote the novel *Don Quixote* (dahn kee•HOH•tee), about a comical knight and his peasant servant. A Greek artist whom the Spanish called El Greco (ehl GREH•koh) painted religious figures with very long bodies, parts of which stretched beyond normal size.

PROGRESS CHECK

Explaining What was the goal of the Spanish Inquisition?

Reading HELPDESK CCSS

Academic Vocabulary (Tier 2 Words)

unify to join; to make into one group

networks *Online Teaching Options*

MAP

Religions in Europe c. 1600

Transferring Knowledge Show students the interactive map displaying religions in Europe in 1600. Have them identify which countries are Protestant and which are Catholic. Then lead a class discussion on why religion could influence a country's government. **Ask: How might a religion compete with a country's government for wealth and power?** Tell students that during this time period, rulers of countries used religion to unite and control their people.

See page 579F for other online activities.

ANSWERS, p. 608

GEOGRAPHY CONNECTION

1. Switzerland, Scotland
2. **CRITICAL THINKING** where there was a mixture of groups

PROGRESS CHECK The goal of the Spanish Inquisition was to identify and punish those people who were guilty of heresy.

Religious Wars

GUIDING QUESTION *How did wars of religion affect Europe?*

By the mid-1500s, most northern Europeans were Protestant, and most southern Europeans were Catholic. European monarchs had used religion to help **unify,** or unite, their people and to build powerful nations. The kings and queens of Europe expected their subjects to practice the religion of their ruler. People who did not join the churches of their monarchs were persecuted, or treated cruelly and unjustly. This led to bitterness among people of different faiths. Differences in religion led to wars between countries. Toward the end of the 1500s, Europe entered a period of religious wars that lasted until about 1650.

The Spanish Armada

T

Under the rule of Queen Elizabeth I, England became the leading Protestant power in Europe. At that time, Spain was the leading Catholic power. The Spanish king was Philip II, the son of Charles V and the great-grandson of Ferdinand and Isabella. King Philip at first supported Elizabeth as England's queen, against the wishes of the pope. However, during the 1560s, the Protestant Dutch rebelled against Spanish rule. Elizabeth helped the Dutch by letting Englishmen attack Spanish ships. Philip decided to get revenge against Elizabeth by invading England.

In 1588, Philip sent a huge fleet known as the Spanish Armada (ahr•MAH•duh) to England. To block the invasion, the English knew they had to make the Spanish ships break their formation. Their chance came when the Spanish fleet entered the English Channel, the narrow body of water between England and Europe. The huge Spanish ships had many guns, but they were hard to steer. The smaller English ships moved much more quickly in the tight channel. Their attacks forced the Armada to retreat. A great storm later broke up the mighty Spanish navy. The English throne was saved, and the English celebrated their victory.

Although Spain was still a powerful nation, England had shown that it could defend itself. The English gained respect throughout Europe as defenders of the Protestant faith.

A combination of bad decisions by the Spanish, faster English ships, and stormy weather sank the Spanish Armada.

Mary Evans Picture Library

T Technology Skills

Researching on the Internet Have students read the opening paragraph of "Religious Wars" and the section "The Spanish Armada." Then have student groups select a topic such as Queen Elizabeth I, Phillip II, the Spanish Armada, the naval battle between England and Spain, or England becoming known as defenders of the Protestant faith.

Ask student groups to research their topic and then create a visual that both shows what they have learned and uses technology in some way. This could take the form of

- a drawing of a person using a program like PowerPoint or Microsoft Paint and standard written research paragraphs (with citations of all sources) of information about them.
- a research report (with citations of all sources) that is typed with a word processing program and includes images or drawings imported from the Internet.
- a drawing of an event or object (such as a battle or a ship) that has been drawn using a graphics program and includes captions and labels (with a separate page of citations of all sources) to identify the important components or elements of the image.
- a collage of images found on the Internet (with a separate page of citations of all sources) that are related to a chosen topic. Collages should include images of people, events, and objects. **Visual/Spatial Interpersonal**

Content Background Knowledge

Queen Elizabeth I

Elizabeth I became queen of England upon the death of her half-sister Mary in 1558. Elizabeth's father, Henry VIII, became a leading figure in the Reformation in England when the Catholic Church excommunicated him in 1534. As a result, Elizabeth became a Protestant and brought her religion with her when she assumed the throne after her Catholic half-sister died. Elizabeth's religion was ever-present during her reign. As the primary Protestant power in the world, she encountered conflicts with the primary Catholic power, Spain. The English navy's famous defeat of the powerful Spanish Armada spoke to her abilities as a ruler as well as to her commitment to Protestantism.

BIOGRAPHY

Sir Francis Drake

Simulating Have students read the interactive biography of Sir Francis Drake, the great English explorer who wrote a first-hand account of the defeat of the Spanish Armada. Together as a class, research the route that Drake took when he became the first English explorer to sail around the world. Have students trace his journey using a globe or world map. **AL ELL**
Visual/Spatial

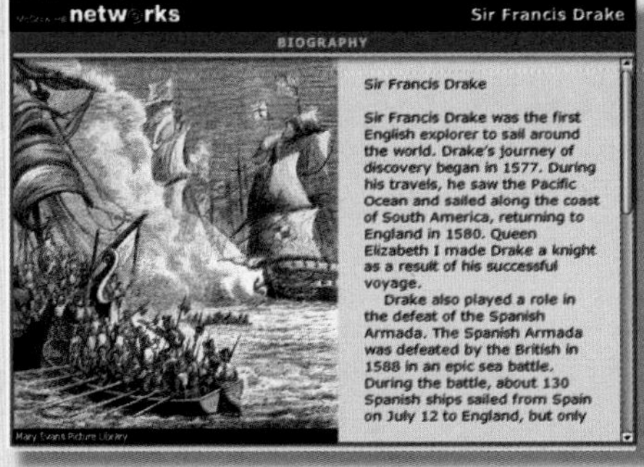

See page 579F for other online activities.

Catholics and Protestants

R Reading Skills

Explaining After students have read "Religious Conflict in France," **ask:**

- **Who were the Huguenots?** *(French Protestants who followed the teachings of John Calvin)*
- **How did Catherine de' Medici end up as the ruler of France?** *(King Francis II died in 1560. Charles, the younger brother of Francis, then became king of France at the age of 10. Charles was too young to rule, so his mother, Catherine de' Medici, ruled for him.)*

C Critical Thinking Skills

Determining Cause and Effect Explore the concept of religious tolerance with students in the context of a discussion about Catherine de' Medici's actions. **Ask: How did Catherine de' Medici's decision to allow Catholic nobles to kill the leading Huguenots in Paris cause conflict in France?** *(Catholics revolted in other parts of France. They formed mobs that killed Protestants and burned their homes. Many Protestants fled the country.)*

Prompt students to consider the consequences of an alternate course of action and to infer how policies of tolerance can be advantageous. **Ask: How could the Edict of Nantes offer an example for how countries could avoid religious conflicts?** *(Answers may include that the Edict of Nantes allowed Protestants to practice their religion in a Catholic country, and so showed religious tolerance. Students may say that policies of tolerance can help countries avoid religious conflicts.)* BL

ANSWER, p. 610

CRITICAL THINKING They would have liked having her as their queen, because she supported so many Renaissance ideas.

BIOGRAPHY

Catherine de' Medici (1519–1589)

The powerful de' Medici family was led by strong Italian men and women. Catherine de' Medici was a firm supporter of the arts. She promoted Renaissance ideas when she wed Prince Henry of France. She took Italian artists, dancers, musicians, and writers with her to the French court. Catherine supported the arts in France, also. She added to the royal library and sponsored a dance and theater presentation that is thought to be the first ballet performance.

▶ **CRITICAL THINKING**
Speculating How might the French people have felt about having Catherine de' Medici as their queen?

Religious Conflict in France

While England and Spain became rivals, a religious conflict divided France. During the 1500s, most people in France were Catholic. However, many wealthy people in France became Protestants. These Protestants, who were called Huguenots (HYU•guh•nahtz), followed the teachings of John Calvin.

R Many French nobles wanted to weaken the king, Henry II. The Huguenot nobles especially wanted the king weak so they could practice their religion freely. At the same time, Henry II wanted to build a strong central government.

Henry died in 1559, and his son Francis II died the next year. As a result, Charles, the younger brother of Francis, became king of France at the age of 10. Because Charles was too young to rule, his mother, Catherine de' Medici, ruled for him. She was the daughter of Lorenzo de' Medici, the powerful Italian leader of Florence.

Influential Rulers

Catherine was determined to keep the French kingdom strong for her son. When a civil war broke out, Catherine tried to keep the peace by supporting both Huguenots and Catholics. But in 1572, she allowed Catholic nobles to kill the leading Huguenots in Paris. Catholics in other parts of France also revolted. They formed mobs that killed Protestants and burned their homes. Many Protestants fled the country. The few who stayed were led by the Huguenot prince, Henry of Navarre (nuh•VAHR). Henry was a member of the powerful Bourbon family. He was in line for the throne of France.

C In 1589, Henry of Navarre became King Henry IV of France. He wanted to gain the loyalty of the people. Because most French people were still Catholic, Henry decided to convert to Catholicism. According to tradition, he said that Paris, the French capital, was "worth a [Catholic] mass." Henry meant that being king of France was more important than being Protestant.

As king, Henry worked to end the fighting between Catholics and Protestants in France. In 1598, he issued an edict, or order, while visiting the city of Nantes. The Edict of Nantes said Catholicism was the official religion of France. However, it also allowed Huguenots to worship freely.

Reading HELPDESK CCSS

networks Online Teaching Options

BIOGRAPHY

Henry of Navarre

Discussing Show students the interactive image of Henry of Navarre. Discuss how Henry, his mother Catherine de' Medici, the Huguenots, and the Edict of Nantes all were important to this period of French history.

See page 579F for other online activities.

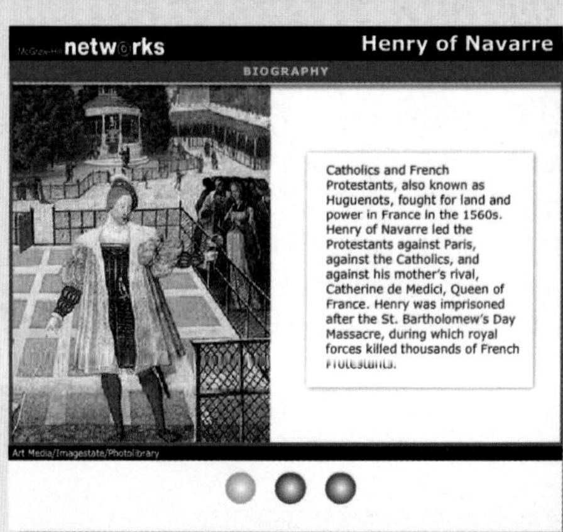

The Thirty Years' War

The most violent religious war of the Reformation period was fought in the Holy Roman Empire in the early 1600s. The war began in Bohemia, today known as the Czech Republic. Protestant nobles in Bohemia rebelled against their Catholic king. When other Protestant rulers in Germany joined the rebels, the war spread across the empire. C

The conflict grew into the Thirty Years' War that lasted from 1618 to 1648. Sweden and Denmark sent troops to help the Protestants. Spain and the Holy Roman Emperor supported the Catholics. Although France was Catholic, it wanted to gain power over neighboring states, so it entered the war on the Protestant side. As France fought against other Catholic countries, the war became a struggle for territory and wealth, not just religion.

The German people suffered great hardships during the war. A city official described the effects of the fighting on the German city of Magdeburg (MAHG•duh•burk):

The Thirty Years' War began when Protestant nobles threw two government officials out a window. The officials represented the Catholic Holy Roman Emperor.

> "Thus in a single day this noble and famous city, the pride of the whole country, went up in fire and smoke; and the remnant [remainder] of its citizens, with their wives and children, were taken prisoners and driven away by the enemy with a noise of weeping and wailing that could be heard from afar."
>
> —Otto von Guericke, from "Destruction of Magdeburg in 1631"

Finally, in 1643, the Holy Roman Emperor asked for peace. In 1648, the warring nations signed the Peace of Westphalia (wehst•FAYL•yuh). This treaty ended the conflict. The war had weakened Spain and the Holy Roman Empire, while France emerged as a stronger nation.

ullstein bild/Photolibrary

✓ PROGRESS CHECK

Analyzing Why was the Edict of Nantes important in the history of France?

LESSON 4 REVIEW 

Review Vocabulary (Tier 3 Words)

1. What kind of training might a priest receive in a *seminary*? RH.6–8.2, RH.6–8.4

Answer the Guiding Questions

2. ***Identifying*** Who were the Jesuits? RH.6–8.2

3. ***Making Inferences*** How did the spread of Protestantism in Europe threaten the Catholic Church? RH.6–8.2

4. ***Explaining*** Why did France fight against Catholic countries in the Thirty Years' War? RH.6–8.2

5. **NARRATIVE** You are visiting France and have friends who are both Catholic and Huguenot. Write a letter to a friend explaining the difficulties between the two religions and how the Edict of Nantes changes the situation. WHST.6–8.10

LESSON 4 REVIEW ANSWERS

1. A priest might learn about Catholic Church rules and policy, might study the Bible, or might learn biblical languages.

2. The Jesuits were a new order of priests recognized by the pope in 1540. They taught, preached, and won followers for the Catholic faith.

3. Protestants were leaving the Catholic Church. The Church was losing influence, members, and power.

4. France was a Catholic country, but it saw the war as a struggle for territory and power, not just religious beliefs.

5. Student responses should provide details about conflicts between Protestants and Catholics in France. Their responses should show an understanding of how the Edict of Nantes gave Protestants religious freedom in France.

C Critical Thinking Skills

Evaluating After reading "The Thirty Years' War", point out that France, a Catholic nation, sided with Protestants. **Ask:**

- **Why would you expect France to side with the Catholics?** *(France's king and most of the country's subjects were Catholic.)* AL
- **What does the outcome of the war show about France's decision?** *(France was a stronger country after the war, so its decision was a good one.)*
- **What does France's decision to side with the Protestants indicate about why countries go to war?** *(Answers may include that money and power can be more important than religion.)*

Have students complete the Lesson 4 Review.

CLOSE & REFLECT

Review with students the various conflicts that came about because of religion during the 1500s and 1600s. Ask students to think about why religion might cause such wars to happen.

Have students work in groups to discuss the various religious reasons countries would go to war. Have them discuss some of the conflicts we see around the world today that are fueled by people with diverse religious beliefs. Then have each group share what they discussed with the rest of the class.

ANSWER, p. 611

✓ PROGRESS CHECK The Edict declared Catholicism the country's official religion, but it gave Protestants the right to worship freely.

CHAPTER 20 Activities CCSS

Write your answers on a separate piece of paper.

1. **Exploring the Essential Question** WHST.6–8.10
   INFORMATIVE/EXPLANATORY How would you describe Renaissance ideas about humanism to a medieval person who knows nothing about them? Write a descriptive essay to explain humanism to a medieval person. Describe how these ideas will change this person's life.

2. **21st Century Skills** RH.6–8.7, WHST.6–8.6, WHST.6–8.7, WHST.6–8.9, WHST.6–8.10
   ANALYZING IMAGES Create a PowerPoint™ presentation that highlights art of the Renaissance. Use photos of the artwork from important artists such as Michelangelo and Leonardo da Vinci and point out important details in the artwork. Share your presentation with the class.

3. **Thinking Like a Historian** RH.6–8.2, RH.6–8.7, WHST.6–8.9
   SEQUENCING The Reformation of the Catholic Church was an important development in Europe's history. Create a time line that shows important events that led to the Reformation of the Catholic Church.

4. **GEOGRAPHY ACTIVITY**

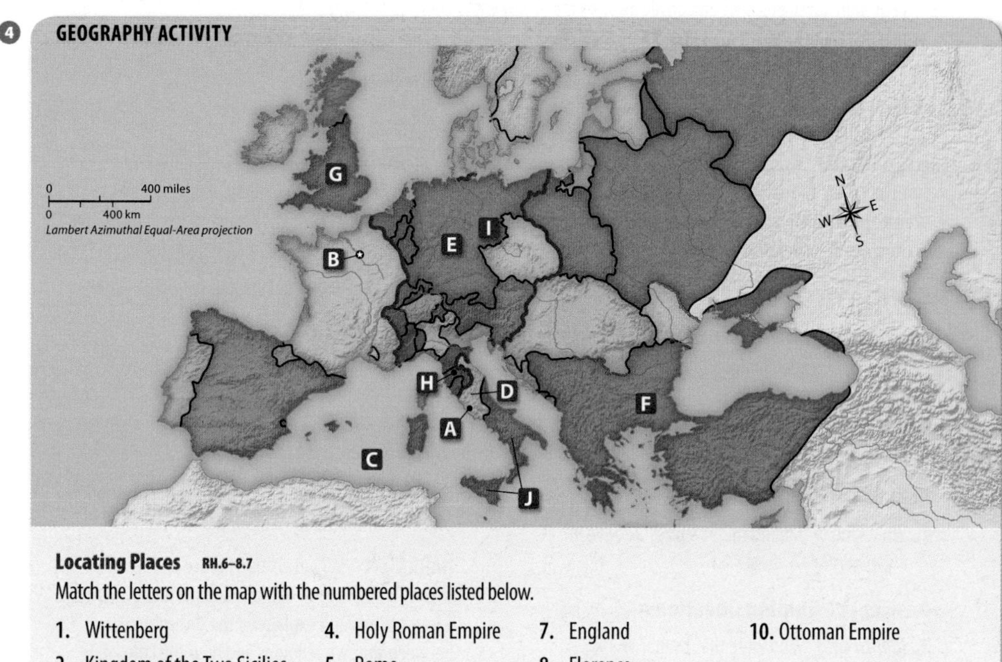

Locating Places RH.6–8.7
Match the letters on the map with the numbered places listed below.

1. Wittenberg
2. Kingdom of the Two Sicilies
3. Papal States
4. Holy Roman Empire
5. Rome
6. Paris
7. England
8. Florence
9. Mediterranean Sea
10. Ottoman Empire

CHAPTER REVIEW ACTIVITY

Analyzing Information Have students begin the review session by sharing and discussing any information from the chapter that surprised them. *(Students may share topics such as the Catholic Church allowing the sale of indulgences; an English queen being referred to as "Bloody Mary" by her people; Catherine de' Medici once ruling France for her ten-year-old son; or France fighting on the side of the Protestants during the Thirty Years' War.)*

Use the "surprise" topics shared by students as a guide for directing the session. Review the main ideas and details associated with each topic, including relevant people, places, events, and ideas. Then **ask:** **Why did this information surprise you?** *(Answers will vary.)*

On the board, have student volunteers create a two-column chart and write "Renaissance" at the top of one column and "Reformation" at the top of the other. Then lead a discussion that allows students to recall features and key events for each transformation. Student volunteers should record answers in the chart.

Renaissance	Reformation

REVIEW THE ENDURING UNDERSTANDINGS

Review this chapter's Enduring Understandings with students:

- *The movement of people, goods, and ideas causes societies to change over time.*
- *People, places, and ideas change over time.*
- *Religion can influence a society's beliefs and values.*
- *Countries have relationships with each other.*

Now pose the following questions in a class discussion to apply these to the chapter.

How did the emerging ideas of humanism change society for members of the elite class and for commoners and the poorer population? *(Answers may vary, but students should note that the brilliant intellectual, cultural, and artistic accomplishments of the Renaissance were really products of and for the elite. The ideas of the Renaissance did not have a broad base among the masses of the people.)*

What was significant about the challenge to the Catholic Church's sale of indulgences? *(Answers may vary, but students should note that the spread of Martin Luther's movement across Europe led to both the formation of new churches and changes within the Catholic church. Eventually Calvinism and Catholicism, both prepared to fight for their beliefs, would arrive at an age of religious passion soon to be followed by an age of religious warfare.)*

ACTIVITIES ANSWERS

Exploring the Essential Question

1. Descriptive essays should address how humanism will change medieval people's understanding of reason and logic. Essays also should include information about developments in art, literature, and science.

21st Century Skills

2. Student presentations should include representative images of artists discussed in the chapter, such as Michelangelo, da Vinci, or van Eyck. Presentations should point out examples of Renaissance style, such as the depiction of human emotion or the realistic depiction of the human body. Students should identify details, such as perspective, discussed in the text.

Thinking Like a Historian

3. Time lines may include the following information:
   1370s Wycliffe calls for reform of Catholic Church
   1509 Erasmus's Praise of Folly criticizes Catholic Church leaders
   1517 Luther writes Ninety-five Theses
   1521 Luther is excommunicated from Catholic Church
   1555 Peace of Augsburg allows rulers to decide the religion of their people

Locating Places

4. **1.** I, **2.** J, **3.** D, **4.** E, **5.** A, **6.** B, **7.** G, **8.** H, **9.** C, **10.** F

CHAPTER 20 Assessment CCSS

REVIEW THE GUIDING QUESTIONS

Directions: Choose the best answer for each question.

RH.6–8.2

1. The leaders of the city-states of Italy were
   A. landowners.
   B. merchants.
   C. bishops.
   D. artists.

RH.6–8.2, RH.6–8.4

2. The technique of *perspective* allowed Renaissance artists to
   F. place their work in cathedrals.
   G. charge more for their art.
   H. show details in their work.
   I. add dimension and depth to their art.

RH.6–8.2

3. Why did people such as Erasmus criticize the Catholic Church?
   A. They thought Church leaders were too concerned with money.
   B. They wanted Church services to be conducted in the vernacular.
   C. They thought indulgences should be more affordable.
   D. They wanted priests to provide an education to all children.

RH.6–8.2

4. Martin Luther believed that the Bible was
   F. less important than the words of the pope.
   G. equally important as the words of the pope.
   H. the best source of religious truth.
   I. the worst source of religious truth.

RH.6–8.2

5. The Catholic Church responded to the spread of Protestantism by
   A. selling more indulgences.
   B. allowing divorces.
   C. setting up seminaries.
   D. banning the Jesuits.

RH.6–8.2

6. In order to unite their kingdom, Queen Isabella and King Ferdinand
   F. supported Protestant ideas for reform.
   G. required their subjects to practice Catholicism.
   H. protected Jews and Muslims from abuse.
   I. increased religious freedom for all believers.

ASSESSMENT ANSWERS

Review the Guiding Questions

1. **B** The correct choice is B. The leaders of Italian city-states in the Renaissance were urban traders and bankers. Landowners were city leaders during the Middle Ages. Church leaders such as bishops focused on religious issues, not leading city-states. Leaders hired artists, but artists were not city leaders.

2. **I** The correct choice is I. Perspective could make artwork look three-dimensional. The technique, therefore, made Renaissance art appear more natural and realistic.

3. **A** The correct choice is A. Reformers were angry that the Catholic Church sold indulgences to make money. The money was used to build a cathedral, not for charity or education. The Catholic Church spent money for artwork, but nothing indicates that people objected to art.

4. **H** The correct choice is H. Martin Luther argued that the people should have access to the Bible and learn about its beliefs for themselves. He believed that people should be able to get their information from the Bible themselves without going through ministers.

5. **C** The correct choice is C. The Catholic Church established seminaries to improve the education of priests. Better-educated priests who could read, write, and preach well would help the Catholics win back people who had joined the Protestant church. It ended the practice of selling indulgences and made stricter rules for priests. The Jesuit order was another type of Catholic reform.

6. **G** The correct choice is G. The Spanish monarchy removed or punished residents who did not practice Catholicism. They rejected the beliefs of Protestants, Jews, and Muslims.

Analyzing Documents

7 **A** The correct choice is A. Luther says that Christians are forgiven if they ask for forgiveness. They do not need to ask a priest for indulgences or letters of pardon.

8 **G** The correct choice is G. Martin Luther thinks that anyone can be forgiven if he or she is truly sorry. He does not think people need to ask a pope or a priest for forgiveness.

Short Response

9 During the Thirty Years' War, many people in Marburg were killed, and their property was stolen or destroyed.

10 The statement from the Swedish general adds authority to the description. The general has seen war and destruction before, yet he finds the condition of northern Germany worse than any battlefield he has witnessed.

Extended Response

11 Students' responses should define and describe indulgences. Letters should show an understanding of how the indulgences raise money for the Catholic Church and why people object to selling forgiveness to the wealthy.

CHAPTER 20 Assessment *(continued)*

DBQ ANALYZING DOCUMENTS

RH.6–8.1, RH.6–8.6

7 **Summarizing** Martin Luther's Ninety-Five Theses included the following:

21. Therefore those [supporters] of indulgences are in error, who say that by the pope's indulgences a man is freed from every penalty, . . .

36. Every truly repentant Christian has a right to full remission of penalty [forgiveness] and guilt, even without letters of pardon.

—from "Disputation of Doctor Martin Luther on the Power and Efficacy of Indulgences," by Martin Luther, 1517

Which statement best summarizes Martin Luther's opinion?

A. Christians can be forgiven without indulgences.
B. Letters of pardon may be given by mistake.
C. All true Christians may receive letters of pardon.
D. Only the pope's indulgences are effective.

RH.6–8.1, RH.6–8.6

8 **Making Inferences** What do Luther's statements imply about forgiveness?

F. A pope can forgive only certain sins.
G. Forgiveness is available to all sinners.
H. Sinners should ask a priest for forgiveness.
I. All sinners will receive letters of pardon if they ask.

SHORT RESPONSE

" 'I would not believe a land could have been so despoiled [looted] had I not seen it with my own eyes,' reported the Swedish general Mortaigne . . . Marburg, which had been occupied 11 times, had lost half its population by 1648. When . . . imperial troops finally sacked [raided] . . . Magdeburg in 1631, it is estimated that only 5,000 of its 30,000 inhabitants survived . . ."

—from *Europe's Tragedy: A History of the Thirty Years' War*, by Peter H. Wilson

RH.6–8.1, RH.6–8.6

9 How did the Thirty Years' War affect the people of Marburg?

RH.6–8.1, RH.6–8.6

10 What does the statement from the Swedish general add to the description?

EXTENDED RESPONSE

WHST.6–8.10

11 **Narrative** You live in a village where people oppose the sale of indulgences. Write a letter to a friend in Rome and describe how people in your village feel about indulgences.

Need Extra Help?

If You've Missed Question	1	2	3	4	5	6	7	8	9	10	11
Review Lesson	1	2	3	3	4	4	3	3	4	4	3, 4

networks Online Teaching Options

More Assessment Resources

The *Assess* tab in the online Teacher Lesson Center includes resources to help students improve their test-taking skills. It also contains many project-based rubrics to help you assess students' work.

CHAPTER 21

Age of Exploration and Trade Planner

UNDERSTANDING BY DESIGN®

Enduring Understanding

- *The movement of people, goods, and ideas causes societies to change over time.*

Essential Questions

- *How does technology change the way people live?*
- *Why do civilizations rise and fall?*
- *Why do people make economic choices?*

Predictable Misunderstandings

Students may think:

- *Indigenous peoples had no influence on Europeans.*
- *The reasons for colonization were simple.*
- *The wealth that Europeans accumulated through colonization was not extraordinary.*
- *Mesoamerican civilizations were not very advanced.*

Assessment Evidence

Performance Task:

- *Hands-On Chapter Project*

Other Evidence:

- *Day-in-the life writing assignment*
- *Writing activity on why the Spanish conquered the Aztec and the Inca*
- *Answers to identifying the steps in creating an empire*
- *Graphic organizer activities*
- *Responses to Interactive Map discussion*
- *Economics of History Activities*
- *Geography and History Activity*
- *Primary Sources Activity*
- *Discussion answers about why Europeans explored the world*
- *Answers from analyzing visuals*
- *Interactive Whiteboard Activity responses*
- *Lesson Reviews*
- *Chapter Activities and Assessment*

SUGGESTED PACING GUIDE

Introducing the Chapter	1 Day
Lesson 1	1 Day
Lesson 2	1 Day
Lesson 3	2 Days
Chapter Wrap-Up and Assessment	1 Day
TOTAL TIME	**6 Days**

Key for Using the Teacher Edition

SKILL-BASED ACTIVITIES

Types of skill activities found in the Teacher Edition.

V Visual Skills require students to analyze maps, graphs, charts, and photos.

R Reading Skills help students practice reading skills and master vocabulary.

W Writing Skills provide writing opportunities to help students comprehend the text.

C Critical Thinking Skills help students apply and extend what they have learned.

T Technology Skills require students to use digital tools effectively.

*Letters are followed by a number when there is more than one of the same type of skill on the page.

DIFFERENTIATED INSTRUCTION

All activities are written for the on-level student unless otherwise marked with the leveled labels below.

BL Beyond Level

AL Approaching Level

ELL English Language Learners

All students benefit from activities that utilize different learning styles. Many activities are marked as below when a particular learning style is highlighted.

Intrapersonal	**Naturalist**
Logical/Mathematical	**Kinesthetic**
Visual/Spatial	**Auditory/Musical**
Verbal/Linguistic	**Interpersonal**

NCSS Standards covered in "Age of Exploration and Trade"

Learners will understand:

2 TIME, CONTINUITY, AND CHANGE

5. Key historical periods and patterns of change within and across cultures (e.g., the rise and fall of ancient civilizations, the development of technology, the rise of modern nation-states, and the establishment and breakdown of colonial systems).

7. The contributions of key persons, groups, and events from the past and their influence on the present.

3 PEOPLE, PLACES, AND ENVIRONMENTS

4. The roles of different kinds of population centers in a region or nation.

5 INDIVIDUALS, GROUPS, AND INSTITUTIONS

6. That cultural diffusion occurs when groups migrate.

8. That when two or more groups with differing norms and beliefs interact, accommodation or conflict may result

7 PRODUCTION, DISTRIBUTION, AND CONSUMPTION

1. Individuals, government, and society experience scarcity because human wants and needs exceed what can be produced from available resources

3. The economic choices that people make have both present and future consequences

5. That banks and other financial institutions channel funds from savers to borrowers and investors

6. The economic gains that result from specialization and exchange as well as the trade-offs

7. How markets bring buyers and sellers together to exchange goods and services

8 SCIENCE, TECHNOLOGY, AND SOCIETY

2. Society often turns to science and technology to solve problems

5. Science and technology have changed peoples' perceptions of the social and natural world, as well as their relationship to the land, economy and trade, their concept of security, and their major daily activities

CHAPTER OPENER PLANNER

Students will know:
- *the factors that led to Europeans being able to explore.*
- *what drove Europeans to explore.*
- *some of the discoveries of the earliest European explorers.*
- *the conquests of Spain in the Americas.*
- *where Europeans established colonies.*
- *how the Columbian Exchange affected Europe and the Americas.*
- *how economics influenced exploration.*
- *key features of the commercial revolution.*

Students will be able to:
- ***identify** new technologies and the establishments of stronger governments as factors that allowed exploration.*
- ***understand** why goods from Asia were a catalyst for exploration.*
- ***identify** the accomplishments of Magellan, Columbus, da Gama, and Verrazano.*
- ***Identify** the conquistadores who conquered Mexico and Peru, and the empires they vanquished.*
- ***analyze** Europe's cultural dominance as exhibited through colonization.*
- ***draw** conclusions about the advancements in economics that occurred due to trade and colonization.*

UNDERSTANDING BY DESIGN®

☑ Print Teaching Options

V Visual Skills

- ☐ **P. 616** Students observe the correspondence between the map key and the routes shown on the map and answer questions about the routes. **Visual/Spatial**
- ☐ **P. 617** Students examine the time line and answer questions that help them draw conclusions for the information presented. **AL** **Visual/Spatial**

☑ Online Teaching Options

V Visual Skills

- **MAP** **European Exploration of the World**—Students trace the routes of Dutch, English, French, Portuguese, and Spanish explorers.
- **TIME LINE** **Age of Exploration and Trade, 1400 to 1700**—Students learn about key events during this time period.
- **WORLD ATLAS** Students can use this interactive map to identify regions of the world, learn about individual countries, locate political boundaries, measure distances, and much more.

Project-Based Learning

Hands-On Chapter Project

Explorer Posters

Working independently, students will create a poster and a display honoring the achievements of a famous explorer as part of a "Hall of Explorers" presentation.

Technology Extension

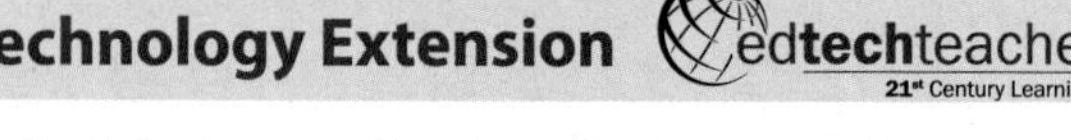

Hall of Explorers Multimedia Presentation
- Find an additional activity online that incorporates technology for this project.
- Visit the EdTechTeacher Web sites (included in the Technology Extension for this chapter) for more links, tutorials, and other resources.

Print Resources

ANCILLARY RESOURCES

These ancillaries are available for every chapter and lesson.
- **Reading Essentials and Study Guide Workbook** **AL** **ELL**
- **Chapter Tests and Lesson Quizzes Blackline Masters**

PRINTABLE DIGITAL WORKSHEETS

These printable digital worksheets are available for every chapter and lesson.
- **Hands-On Chapter Projects**
- **What Do You Know? activities**
- **Chapter Summaries (English and Spanish)**
- **Vocabulary Builder activities**
- **Guided Reading activities**

More Media Resources

SUGGESTED VIDEOS 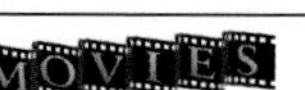

Watch clips of popular-culture films about *Christopher Columbus, such as Christopher Columbus: The Discovery* and *1492: Conquest of Paradise.* You can also view documentaries about the exploration of America, such as *The Explorers: The Spanish in America.*

(NOTE: Preview any clips for age-appropriateness.)

SUGGESTED READING 

Grade 6 reading level:
- ***Step Into the . . . Aztec and Maya Worlds,*** by Fiona MacDonald

Grade 7 reading level:
- ***If You Were There in 1492,*** by Barbara Brenner

Grade 8 reading level:
- ***Ferdinand Magellan and the Discovery of the World Ocean,*** by Rebecca Stefoff

LESSON 1 PLANNER

The Age of Exploration

Students will know:

- *the factors that led to Europeans being able to explore.*
- *what drove Europeans to explore.*
- *some of the discoveries of the earliest European explorers.*

Students will be able to:

- ***identify** new technologies and the establishments of stronger governments as factors that allowed exploration.*
- ***understand** why goods from Asia were a catalyst for exploration.*
- ***identify** the accomplishments of Magellan, Columbus, da Gama, and Verrazano.*

UNDERSTANDING BY DESIGN®

☑ Print Teaching Options

V Visual Skills

- ☐ **P. 620** Students examine a map showing da Gama's routes of discovery and use the scale of miles to determine the distance from Portugal to India. **Visual/Spatial**

R Reading Skills

- ☐ **P. 619** Students discuss the technologies that enabled exploration and discuss the state of mapmaking.
- ☐ **P. 620** Students discuss Portugal's explorations. **AL**
- ☐ **P. 622** Students describe how life changed for the Taino people after Columbus and his conquistadors arrived in the Americas. **AL**

W Writing Skills

- ☐ **P. 621** Students write a descriptive paragraph from the point of view of Christopher Columbus in the New World.

C Critical Thinking Skills

- ☐ **P. 618** Students determine the causes for the European voyages of exploration.
- ☐ **P. 621** Students discuss Columbus's plan to sail west and speculate about why no one wanted to support him. **AL**
- ☐ **P. 623** Students make inferences about European focus on finding the route to Asia rather than in developing the new continents. **BL**

T Technology Skills

- ☐ **P. 622** Students do research, write a script, and produce a multimedia presentation describing Magellan's expedition. **Verbal/Linguistic**

☑ Online Teaching Options

V Visual Skills

- **VIDEO** **Journey to the New World: Christopher Columbus**—Students view a video that explains how Portugal ignited a new age of exploration, spurred by desires to compete with Italy for goods from Asia.
- **MAP** **Portugal and da Gama**—Students trace the exploration routes da Gama followed between 1497 and 1499.
- **IMAGE** **The Santa María**—Students click to learn about Columbus's sailing ships.

R Reading Skills

- **GRAPHIC ORGANIZER** **Taking Notes: *Identifying:* European Explorers**—Students list Europeans who explored Asia and the Americas.
- **SLIDE SHOW** **The Madeira Islands**—Students learn about the history of this group of islands, which today are a self-governing region of Portugal.
- **BIOGRAPHY** **Ferdinand Magellan**—Students read of the life and accomplishments of this Portuguese explorer.

C Critical Thinking Skills

- **IMAGE** **GPS Technology**—Students consider how navigational technology has changed since 1500.
- **IMAGE** **The Taino**—Students consider this indigenous people of the Caribbean islands, who were decimated by contact with Europeans.

T Technology Skills

- **SELF-CHECK QUIZ** **Lesson 1**—Students receive instant feedback on their mastery of lesson content.

☑ Printable Digital Worksheets

C Critical Thinking Skills

- **WORKSHEET** **Geography and History Activity: Understanding Location: Europeans and the Known World**—Students analyze reasons why explorers followed the routes they did.

SPAIN'S CONQUESTS IN THE AMERICAS

Students will know:
- *the conquests of Spain in the Americas.*

Students will be able to:
- ***Identify** the conquistadores who conquered Mexico and Peru, and the empires they vanquished.*

UNDERSTANDING BY DESIGN®

☑ *Print Teaching Options*

R Reading Skills

- ☐ **P. 624** Students explain the motives and strategies of the conquistadors. AL
- ☐ **P. 626** Students discuss what Balboa found on his expedition and what Pizarro thought he would find in the Inca Empire. AL
- ☐ **P. 627** Students describe Pizarro's victory over the Inca. AL

W Writing Skills

- ☐ **P. 625** Students do research to answer questions about smallpox and then write a summary of what they learn. **Verbal/Linguistic**

C Critical Thinking Skills

- ☐ **P. 625** Student pairs order events in Cortés's conquest of the Aztec. AL **Interpersonal**
- ☐ **P. 626** Students discuss what happened after Cortés took control of the Aztec capital and infer his reasons for forbidding human sacrifice. BL

T Technology Skills

- ☐ **P. 627** Students research the Inca and their accomplishments and produce a multimedia presentation on the topic. **Visual/Spatial Interpersonal**

☑ *Online Teaching Options*

V Visual Skills

- ☐ VIDEO **Hernan Cortés**—Students learn of Cortés's adventures in the New World.
- ☐ MAP **Spanish Explorations, 1500–1600**—Students click to see land and sea routes followed by Spanish explorers.

R Reading Skills

- ☐ GRAPHIC ORGANIZER **Taking Notes: *Summarizing:* Methods Used to Conquer**—Students describe methods used by Cortés and Pizarro to conquer the people of Central and South America.
- ☐ BIOGRAPHY **Hernan Cortés**—Students read about the life of this conquistador.
- ☐ SLIDE SHOW **Atahualpa's Life**—Students read about the thirteenth and last emperor of the Inca.

C Critical Thinking Skills

- ☐ WHITEBOARD ACTIVITY **Spanish Conquest**—Students match people and descriptions to review players in the Spanish conquest of the New World.

T Technology Skills

- ☐ SELF-CHECK QUIZ **Lesson 2**—Students receive instant feedback on their mastery of lesson content.

☑ *Printable Digital Worksheets*

W Writing Skills

- ☐ WORKSHEET **Primary Source Activity: Cortés Arrives in Tenochtitlán**—Students compare and contrast European and Aztec accounts of the conquest of Mexico.

C Critical Thinking Skills

- ☐ WORKSHEET **Economics of History Activity: Quipu and Inca Society**—Students analyze the Inca system of accounting and record keeping.

LESSON 3 PLANNER

EXPLORATION AND WORLDWIDE TRADE

Students will know:
- *where Europeans established colonies.*
- *how the Columbian Exchange affected Europe and the Americas.*
- *how economics influenced exploration.*
- *key features of the commercial revolution.*

Students will be able to:
- ***analyze*** *Europe's cultural dominance as exhibited through colonization.*
- ***draw conclusions*** *about the advancements in economics that occurred due to trade and colonization.*

UNDERSTANDING BY DESIGN®

☑ Print Teaching Options

V Visual Skills
- ☐ **P. 632** Students analyze the map and answer questions about it. AL **Visual/Spatial**
- ☐ **P. 634** Students analyze a map showing the Columbian Exchange. **Visual/Spatial**

R Reading Skills
- ☐ **P. 628** Students discuss the Treaty of Tordesillas and describe the Spanish Empire in the New World. AL
- ☐ **P. 629** Students discuss the economies of the Portuguese and French colonies. AL
- ☐ **P. 630** Students give their classmates clues to help them identify and name important European explorers. **Interpersonal**
- ☐ **P. 631** Students discuss the English settlement of Jamestown and the importance of tobacco as a cash crop.
- ☐ **P. 632** Students discuss mercantilism and explain how colonies promote it. AL ELL
- ☐ **P. 633** Students define key terms. AL ELL
- ☐ **P. 634** Students define and explain the Columbian Exchange. AL ELL

W Writing Skills
- ☐ **P. 630** Students research the Black Robes, write a report, and answer specific questions. BL

C Critical Thinking Skills
- ☐ **P. 629** Students try to reconcile the contradiction in the Spanish purpose to both convert Native Americans to Catholicism and to enslave them. BL
- ☐ **P. 629** Students talk about the effects of the diseases that struck Native Americans.
- ☐ **P. 631** Students contrast the colonial goals of the Dutch to those of other European countries. BL
- ☐ **P. 633** Students discuss the risks of overseas trade and make generalizations about joint-stock companies. BL
- ☐ **P. 634** Students discuss the term *cottage industry* and brainstorm examples of modern-day cottage industries. **Interpersonal**
- ☐ **P. 635** Students discuss how the Columbian Exchange affected Europeans and Americans.

☑ Online Teaching Options

V Visual Skills
- ☐ VIDEO **Age of Discovery: English, French, and Dutch Explorers**—Students view a video that describes how England, France, and other European countries raced to find trade routes to Asia and to overcome Spain's dominance of the sea.
- ☐ MAP **The Columbian Exchange**—Students trace the goods and resources exchanged between North America and Europe.
- ☐ MAP **European Trade in Asia c. 1700**—Students click to identify Asian cities ruled by a variety of European nations.

R Reading Skills
- ☐ GRAPHIC ORGANIZER **Taking Notes: *Listing:* Crops and Workers in Colonies**—Students list the crops or products and the types of workers found in Spanish, Portuguese, and English colonies.
- ☐ CHART **Brazil's Cash Crops**—Students click to identify the cash crops produced by workers in Brazil.

C Critical Thinking Skills
- ☐ WHITEBOARD ACTIVITY **Explorers in the Americas**—Students match explorers with their accomplishments.
- ☐ IMAGE **The Virginia Company**—Students examine how this company, which established Jamestown in Virginia, functioned.
- ☐ SLIDE SHOW **Cottage Industry**—Students trace the steps in the production of wool cloth.

T Technology Skills
- ☐ SELF-CHECK QUIZ **Lesson 3**—Students receive instant feedback on their mastery of lesson content.
- ☐ GAME **Exploration and Worldwide Trade Crossword Puzzle**—Students solve clues to review lesson content.

☑ Printable Digital Worksheets

C Critical Thinking Skills
- ☐ WORKSHEET **Economics of History Activity: The Columbian Exchange**—Students consider the items involved in the Columbian Exchange, including the exchange of deadly diseases.

INTERVENTION AND REMEDIATION STRATEGIES

LESSON 1 The Age of Exploration

Reading and Comprehension

Ask students to work in small groups. Have each student in the group take the role of one of the early explorers. Tell them to review the relevant passage and then conduct a discussion comparing their expeditions and discoveries.

Text Evidence

Have students learn about one of the technological breakthroughs mentioned in the lesson. Then have them explain in greater detail how that breakthrough enabled the European explorers to sail the world's oceans.

LESSON 2 Spain's Conquests in the Americas

Reading and Comprehension

Have students create a compare-and-contrast graphic organizer and show how the campaigns of Cortés and Pizarro were alike and different.

Text Evidence

Have students work in pairs and do research to learn about Malintzin, the Native American ally who aided Cortés during his conquest of the Aztec people. Have them explain in a few paragraphs who Malintzin was and how her help enabled Cortés to conquer the Aztecs.

LESSON 3 Exploration and Worldwide Trade

Reading and Comprehension

List the Content Vocabulary words for Lesson 3 on the board. Ask students to write sentences using each of the terms correctly. The sentences should refer to the content of the lesson.

Text Evidence

Ask students whether they think Europe or the Americas benefited most from the Columbian Exchange. Have them write a short response to the question. Remind them to cite evidence from the text in their answers.

Online Resources

Approaching Level Reader

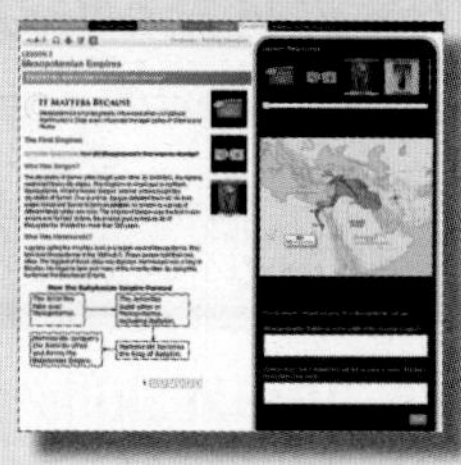

Use this online lower-level text that corresponds directly to the text in the Student Edition. It includes a Spanish version.

Guided Reading Activities

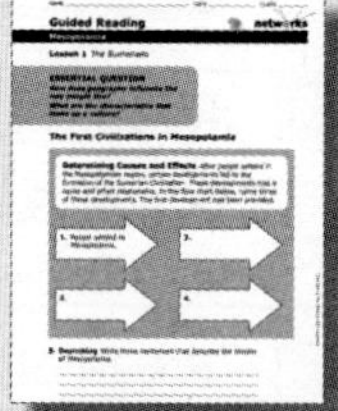

This resource uses graphic organizers and guiding questions to help students with comprehension.

What Do You Know?

Use these worksheets to pre-assess student's background knowledge before they study the chapter.

Reading Essentials and Study Guide Workbook

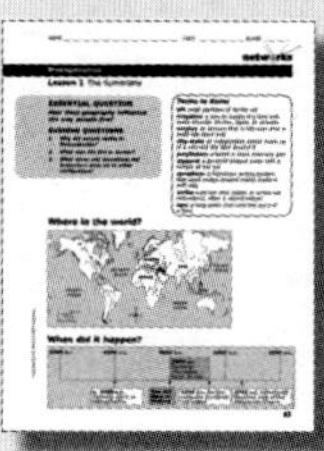

This resource offers writing and reading activities for the approaching-level student. Also available in Spanish.

Self-Check Quizzes

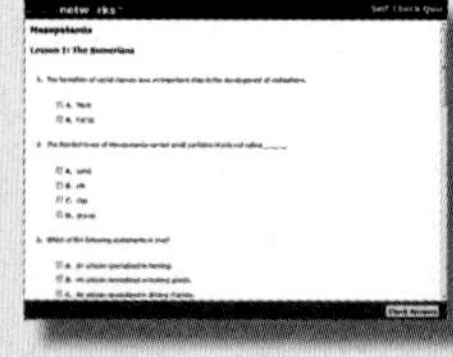

This online assessment tool provides instant feedback for students to check their progress.

Age of Exploration and Trade

1400 to 1700

ESSENTIAL QUESTIONS • *How does technology change the way people live?* • *Why do civilizations rise and fall?* • *Why do people make economic choices?*

networks

There's More Online about how civilizations changed during the Age of Exploration and Trade.

CHAPTER 21

Lesson 1
The Age of Exploration

Lesson 2
Spain's Conquests in the Americas

Lesson 3
Exploration and Worldwide Trade

The Story Matters . . .

Christopher Columbus lived in Genoa, Italy. He joined the Portuguese merchant marine and became a sailor. On trading voyages to Africa, he learned about navigation and wind currents. Columbus believed that if he sailed west, he would eventually reach Asia. He tried to convince various European rulers to help him test his idea.

Finally, Queen Isabella of Spain decided that Columbus could win glory and wealth for Spain. She and her husband Ferdinand supplied money for his voyage. When Columbus reached the Americas in 1492, he believed he had reached Asia. Instead, Columbus had opened up the Americas to Europeans.

◄ *The first voyage of Columbus in 1492 resulted in dramatic changes throughout the Americas, Europe, and the world.*

Letter from the Author

Dear World History Teacher,

At the end of the fifteenth century, Portuguese ships ventured along the West African coast bringing back gold and enslaving Africans. Spain had greater resources, and European expansion accelerated with the voyages of Christopher Columbus to the Americas and Vasco de Gama to the Indian Ocean in the 1490s. The European age of exploration changed the world. In some areas that exploration led to destruction of indigenous civilizations and establishment of European colonies. In others it left native regimes intact but had a strong impact on local societies and regional trade patterns.

Jackson J. Spielvogel

ENGAGE

Bellringer Read "The Story Matters . . ." aloud in class or ask for a volunteer to read it aloud. Then discuss with students what it might have been like to be a crew member on one of Columbus's ships. **Ask:** How would you feel trusting your captain to sail off across an ocean without knowing if you were ever going to find land? Have a few students share their opinions and feelings.

Then **ask:** Would you be willing to climb into a spaceship today that might be a one-way voyage to Mars? Have students explain how they would cope with that possibility.

Content Background Knowledge

Emphasize to students that Columbus was not the first European to visit America. The Vikings reached America in about A.D. 1000 and attempted unsuccessfully to settle there. Little is known about this early exploration. Still earlier visits to America by Europeans *may* have occurred, but historians lack solid evidence of them. Among them is the legend of an early people who were chased out of their homeland in Ireland by the Vikings and who sought refuge in the Americas. Proof of this migration is weak, but the idea is supported by conjecture and some limited evidence.

TEACH & ASSESS

Step Into the Place

V1 Visual Skills

Analyzing Maps Call students' attention to the map key and to the routes shown on the map. Point out that each of the colors represents the country that funded the exploration and that claimed the lands each explorer discovered. Ask volunteers to answer these questions:

- Which country sponsored the most explorations? *(Spain: four explorations)*
- Which country's route covered the most distance? *(Spain's: Magellan's round-the-world exploration)*
- Which countries led expeditions that entered the interior of North America? *(Spain, France, the Netherlands)* **Visual/Spatial**

Then have students answer and discuss the Map Focus questions.

CHAPTER 21 CCSS

Place and Time: Age of Exploration and Trade 1400 to 1700

In order to have direct access to Asia, Europeans wanted to find a water route that would bypass the Middle East. Using the new technology of the time, they searched for a southern route around Africa. In time, Europeans sailed across the Atlantic Ocean and encountered the Americas.

Step Into the Place

MAP FOCUS While searching for a new trade route to East Asia, Europeans came upon other parts of the world.

1. **LOCATION** In which directions did Europeans explore? **RH.6–8.7**
2. **LOCATION** Why did European explorers find the Americas first instead of Asia? **RH.6–8.7**
3. **MOVEMENT** What did Magellan's crew achieve, according to the map? What did that show to others about the world? **RH.6–8.7**
4. **CRITICAL THINKING** ***Drawing Conclusions*** How did the search for a new trade route to Asia affect the exploration of the Americas? **RH.6–8.2**

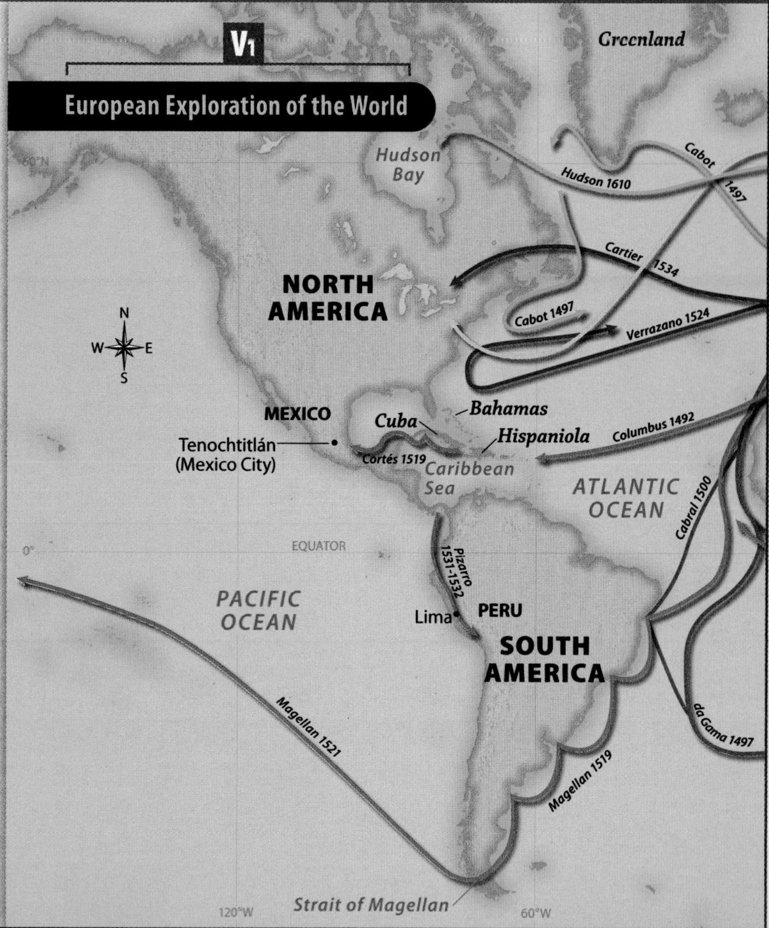

Step Into the Time

V2

TIME LINE Choose two events from the time line. Write a paragraph that explains the gap in time between related events. **RH.6–8.7, WHST.6–8.2, WHST.6–8.10**

AGE OF EXPLORATION AND TRADE

THE WORLD

1300 1400

1420 Portugal begins mapping coast of Africa

1271 Kublai Khan becomes emperor of China

1324 Mansa Musa travels to Makkah

1400 Aztec Empire reaches height

Project-Based Learning

Hands-On Chapter Project

Explorer Posters

Students will create a poster and a display honoring the achievements of a famous explorer. First, have students review what they have learned about the Age of Exploration. Then, working independently, each student will plan, research, and create a poster on an explorer. Students will present their posters in class and display them in a Hall of Explorers. Finally, have students evaluate their work using a class-developed assessment rubric.

Technology Extension

Hall of Explorers Multimedia Presentation

Successfully working with multimedia documentation tools is an important academic and work skill for the 21st century learner. Students will design, revise, and publish Famous Explorer slides in an authentic environment using web 2.0 tools. In this EdTechTeacher Technology Extension, students create Google Multimedia Presentation slides, combine them into a whole-class gallery, and finally share the gallery with an audience.

ANSWERS, p. 616

Step Into the Place

1. They sailed south, east, and west.
2. They didn't know the Americas existed, but they landed there while sailing west to Asia.
3. They proved that a water route can be used to travel around the world. It showed that the world is round.
4. **CRITICAL THINKING** As explorers traveled the continents' rivers and bays, they explored the interior of the Americas and eventually reached the Pacific Ocean.

Step Into the Time

Answers will vary, but students might suggest reasons for the time gaps that include new technology, better maps, an increase in competition between nations, and so on.

networks
There's More Online!

MAP Explore the interactive version of this map on NETWORKS.

TIME LINE Explore the interactive version of this time line on NETWORKS.

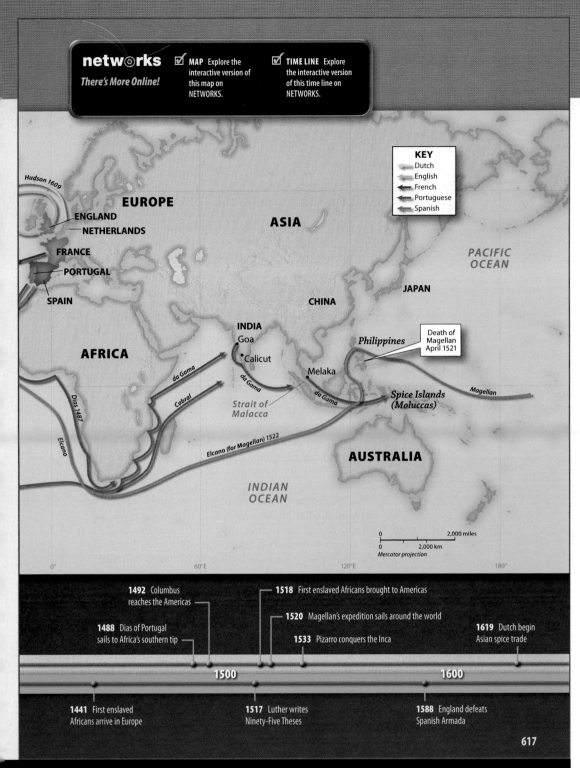

KEY
Dutch
English
French
Portuguese
Spanish

Hudson 1609
EUROPE
ENGLAND
NETHERLANDS
FRANCE
PORTUGAL
SPAIN
ASIA
PACIFIC OCEAN
JAPAN
CHINA
INDIA
Goa
Calicut
AFRICA
Philippines
Death of Magellan April 1521
Melaka
da Gama
da Gama
da Gama
Cabral
Dias 1487
Elcano
Strait of Malacca
Spice Islands (Moluccas)
Magellan
Elcano (for Magellan) 1522
AUSTRALIA
INDIAN OCEAN
0 2,000 miles
0 2,000 km
Mercator projection
0°
60°E
120°E
180°

1441 First enslaved Africans arrive in Europe

1488 Dias of Portugal sails to Africa's southern tip

1492 Columbus reaches the Americas

1500

1517 Luther writes Ninety-Five Theses

1518 First enslaved Africans brought to Americas

1520 Magellan's expedition sails around the world

1533 Pizarro conquers the Inca

1588 England defeats Spanish Armada

1600

1619 Dutch begin Asian spice trade

617

CHAPTER 21

Place and Time

Step Into the Time

V2 Visual Skills

Analyzing Time Lines Have students review the time line for the chapter. Point out that the Age of Exploration and Trade covers just 200 years, from 1420 to 1619. Explain that during this relatively short period, Europe went from almost no detailed knowledge of the world to a much more accurate understanding.

Ask students to consider the sequence of events shown on the time line. **Ask:** **When was Africa first explored, and what was the purpose of this voyage?** *(1420; to map the coast)* **What is the next event that occurs regarding Africa?** *(Enslaved Africans are brought to Europe.)* **What occurred next in the exploration of Africa?** *(Dias sails to Africa's southern tip in 1488.)* Guide a summation of these events, eliciting that each event built upon the discoveries of a previous one. Help students notice that this same sequence occurred with the exploration of the Americas, as each voyage brought in new information that was subsequently built upon by later expeditions. **AL Visual/Spatial**

Making Connections

Have students consider what they have already learned about explorers and the lands they encountered. **Ask:** **What were explorers looking for?** *(adventure, wealth, glory)* **What tools and technology would explorers need to be successful?** *(ships, maps, weapons, navigational equipment)* Discuss with students the differences between exploration then and now. Have students help you make a list on the board of the types of technology available today to scientists and others who explore mostly undiscovered areas of the world, such as Antarctica.

MAP

European Exploration of the World

Analyzing Maps Tell students that they can click on items in the key to reveal the route and direction of each of the voyages. After students explore the map, **ask:** **Why would Columbus's voyage sailing west across the Atlantic Ocean be the opposite of Portuguese sailors sailing south around the tip of Africa?** *(The Portuguese sailed east to find China. Columbus sailed west to find China.)*

See page 615B for other online activities.

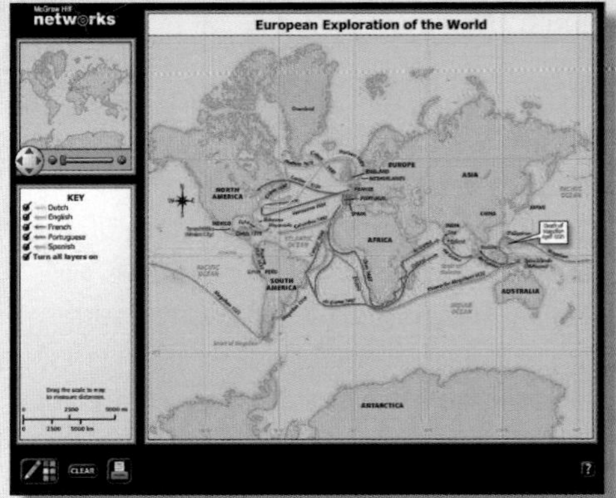

ENGAGE

Bellringer Explain to students that Columbus was part of the age of exploration in which Europeans traveled around the world. **Ask: Why do you think Europeans wanted to travel to distant lands?** *(Students may answer that Europeans wanted to trade for rare goods, to form colonies, or to gain knowledge.)* **What changes might this exploration have caused?** *(Student answers will vary. They may suggest that Europe could have grown wealthy, that new ideas would be spread, or that conquered peoples would suffer.)*

In this lesson, students will learn why Europeans began exploring and how profoundly this changed Europe as well as the rest of the world.

TEACH & ASSESS

C Critical Thinking Skills

Determining Cause and Effect Draw a cause-and-effect diagram on the board. Label the effect as "Europeans begin voyages of exploration." Have the class use information from their textbooks to provide the causes. *(the loss of the Silk Road, a desire for luxury goods, improved technology, a desire for wealth, strong central governments)*

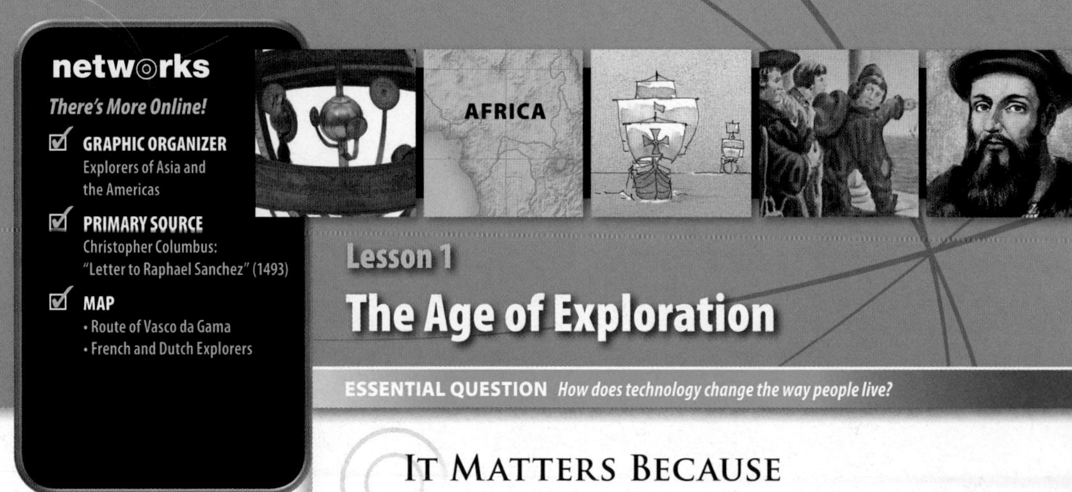

networks *There's More Online!*
- GRAPHIC ORGANIZER Explorers of Asia and the Americas
- PRIMARY SOURCE Christopher Columbus: "Letter to Raphael Sanchez" (1493)
- MAP
  - Route of Vasco da Gama
  - French and Dutch Explorers

Lesson 1
The Age of Exploration

ESSENTIAL QUESTION *How does technology change the way people live?*

IT MATTERS BECAUSE

The demand for goods from Asia as well as advances in technology helped start Europe's age of exploration.

Europe Gets Ready to Explore

GUIDING QUESTION *Why did Europeans begin to explore the world?*

In the 1400s and 1500s, Europeans gradually gained control of the Americas and parts of Asia. Many events came together to create the right time for **overseas** exploration.

Search for Trade Routes

C During the Middle Ages, Europeans began to buy silks, spices, and other luxury goods from Asia. Spices, such as pepper, cinnamon, and nutmeg were in great demand. Europeans used spices to preserve and flavor food, and for perfumes, cosmetics, and medicine.

A network of merchants controlled trade from Asia to Europe. Chinese and Indian traders sent spices by caravan over the Silk Road and other routes to the eastern Mediterranean region. From there, Arab and Byzantine traders shipped the spices to Europe. The Arabs earned huge profits selling luxury goods to Italian merchants. The Italians then sold the products to other Europeans.

Political changes eventually disrupted this trading network. However, merchants knew that if they could get goods directly and cheaply, they could make more profits. Also, if Europeans could reach Asia by sea, then they would not have to travel overland through the Middle East.

Reading HELPDESK (CCSS)

Taking Notes: ***Identifying***

Use a diagram like the one shown here to list the different Europeans who explored Asia and the Americas. RH.6–8.2

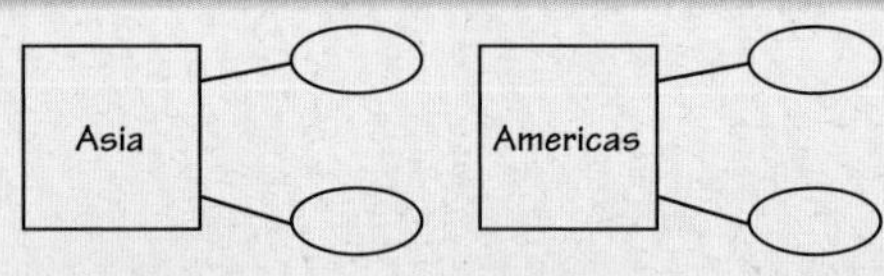

Content Vocabulary (Tier 3 Words)
- **circumnavigate**
- **conquistadors**

networks ***Online Teaching Options***

VIDEO

Journey to the New World: Christopher Columbus

Analyzing Visuals Show students the video and tell them to write questions that occur to them about Columbus and his journey. When the video ends, guide students in a discussion of the questions and their answers. You might additionally ask volunteers to research certain questions and share the answers with the class.

See page 615C for other online activities.

ANSWER, p. 618

TAKING NOTES: Answers may vary. Sample answer: ASIA: Vasco da Gama, Ferdinand Magellan; AMERICAS: Christopher Columbus, Ferdinand Magellan

Technology and Exploration

By the 1400s, a number of technological inventions became available to European explorers. These inventions helped them navigate vast oceans. Europeans learned about the astrolabe (AS•truh•layb) and the compass from the Arabs. The astrolabe was an ancient Greek instrument that was used to find latitude. Sailors used the compass to help determine the direction in which they were sailing.

European mapmakers also improved their skills. During the late Middle Ages, most educated Europeans were aware that the earth was round. The only maps that were available, however, were of Europe and the Mediterranean region. That changed during the Renaissance when people began to study ancient maps and books.

Europeans rediscovered the work of Ptolemy (TAH•luh•mee), a Greek geographer. Ptolemy had drawn maps of the world for his book, *Geography*. He recorded the latitude and longitude of over 8,000 locations. With the invention of the printing press, accurate maps became readily available to sailors and explorers.

R

European mapmakers also learned about the Indian Ocean by studying the works of the Arab geographer al-Idrisi (ehl-ah•DREE•see). Many Europeans concluded that sailing around Africa was the best way to get to Asia.

In addition, shipbuilders improved ships by using triangular sails developed by Arab traders. With these sails and other improvements, ships could now go in nearly every direction no matter where the wind blew.

Rise of Strong Kingdoms

Even with new sailing skills and tools, exploration was still expensive and dangerous. But by the 1400s, the rise of towns and trade had strengthened Europe's governments. By the end of the 1400s, four strong kingdoms had emerged in Europe: Portugal, Spain, France, and England. All of these kingdoms had ports on the Atlantic Ocean—and all were eager to find a sea route to Asia.

THEN

An astrolabe was made of brass or iron. It had discs with star maps and coordinate lines that rotated around a pin. The pin was in the position of the North Star. Today, navigation systems still look to the heavens. Computers use the positions of satellites in space to help drivers, pilots, sailors, and hikers know exactly where on Earth they are.

NOW

▶ CRITICAL THINKING

Contrasting What do you think are some of the differences between using an astrolabe and using a computerized system?

☑ PROGRESS CHECK

Explaining How did new technology make it possible for Europeans to make long ocean voyages?

Academic Vocabulary (Tier 2 Words)

overseas across the ocean or sea

R Reading Skills

Explaining Ask students to read the subsection titled "Technology and Exploration." Then, lead a class discussion about the various types of technology that benefited European explorers. Have students cite evidence from the text in their responses. **Ask:**

- **What is an astrolabe, and why was it so important?** *(It's an instrument used to find latitude. It helped sailors know how far north or south they had sailed.)*
- **Why were improvements in ship technology necessary?** *(so that explorers could sail greater distances)*
- **Why was the development of triangular sails helpful?** *(It allowed sailors to travel in almost any direction regardless of the direction of the wind.)*
- **Who was Ptolemy and how did he contribute to exploration?** *(He was a Greek geographer who drew maps of the world and who recorded the latitude and longitude of about 8,000 locations.)*

Content Background Knowledge

- Ptolemy's maps provide a detailed picture of the ancient world from the time when the Roman Empire was at its zenith.
- Ptolemy's maps no longer exist, but we do have his latitude and longitude data, from which the maps can be reconstructed.
- The latitude and longitude data place 8,000 locations on Earth from as far west as the Canary Islands off the northwest coast of Africa to China in the east, and from the Shetland Islands near Scotland to Egypt's Nile River.

IMAGE

GPS Technology

Making Connections Show students the interactive image on GPS technology. **Ask: How did technology help people learn about the world during the Age of Exploration, and how does it help in modern times?** *(Explorers used modern technology of the time to find their way around the world. Today we use GPS technology to help us find our way around streets and towns.)*

See page 615C for other online activities.

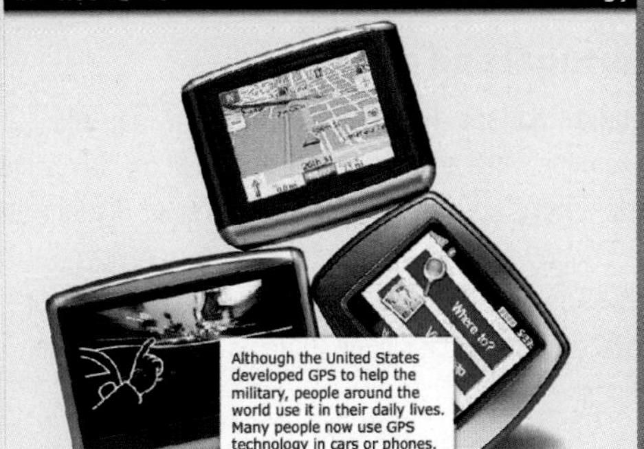

networks
GPS Technology
Although the United States developed GPS to help the military, people around the world use it in their daily lives. Many people now use GPS technology in cars or phones.

ANSWERS, p. 619

CRITICAL THINKING Answers may vary but could include: An astrolabe requires more skill to use; computers are more reliable; astrolabes don't need batteries or power; and computers work during the daytime while an astrolabe doesn't.

☑ **PROGRESS CHECK** Precise maps, new navigation equipment, and sturdy ships enabled Europeans to undertake long-distance voyages that were impossible before.

V Visual Skills

Analyzing Maps Have students examine the map, *Portugal and da Gama*. Emphasize that da Gama's route around the tip of Africa was a great breakthrough for European traders. It offered a sea route to India rather than a long, arduous, and dangerous land route. Point out that although the sea route was an improvement, it was still very long. **Ask:** **About how long was da Gama's sea route from Portugal to India?** *(about 25,000 miles)* Ask students to locate the first territories of the Portuguese Empire: the Azores, the Madeira, and the Cape Verde islands. **Visual/Spatial**

R Reading Skills

Discussing After student have read the text, engage them in a discussion about Portugal's explorations. Prompt them to cite the reading passage as they participate in the conversation. **Ask:**

- **Which European country was the first to begin voyages of exploration?** *(Portugal)*
- **Who was responsible for this?** *(Prince Henry the Navigator)* AL
- **How did Portugal benefit from these early voyages?** *(They gained new territories, including the Azores, Madeira, and Cape Verde islands; they obtained gold from African kingdoms.)*

GEOGRAPHY CONNECTION

Vasco da Gama followed the coastline of Africa to reach India.

1. **LOCATION** What is the southernmost point that da Gama reached?
2. **CRITICAL THINKING** ***Cause and Effect*** Why would sailors take a longer route along the coastline instead of the shortest distance between two points?

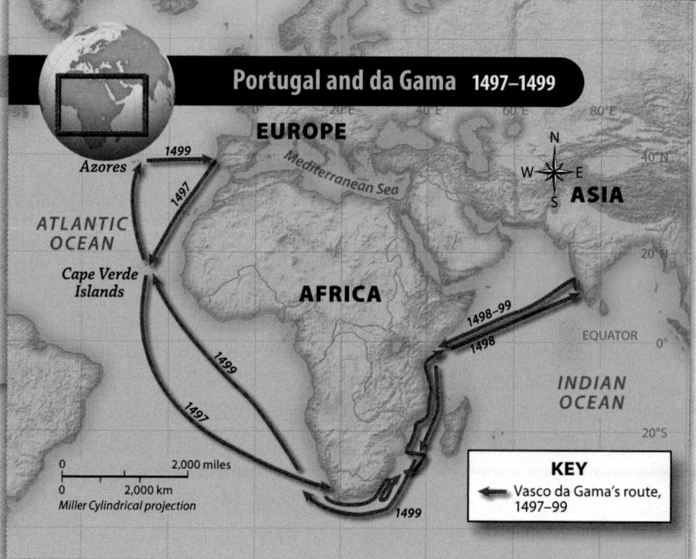

Early Voyages of Discovery

GUIDING QUESTION *Which leaders were responsible for European exploration of the world?*

During the early 1400s, England and France were still at war with each other, and Spain was still fighting the Muslims. This let Portugal take the lead in exploring new trade routes to Asia.

Portugal Leads the Way

Prince Henry of Portugal became known as "Henry the Navigator," even though he had never made an ocean voyage. Henry was eager for Portugal to explore the world, and he paid for many voyages of exploration. About 1420, Henry's adventurers sailed along Africa's west coast, mapping its features. They **obtained** gold from trade with African kingdoms. The explorers also traveled west into the Atlantic Ocean, where they seized the Azores (AY•zawrz), Madeira (muh•DIHR•uh), and Cape Verde (VUHRD) islands.

In 1488, the Portuguese explorer Bartolomeu Dias (bahr•tuh•luh•MEH•uh DEE•ahsh) sailed to the southern tip of Africa. Nine years later, Vasco da Gama (VAHS•koh dah GAM•uh) rounded the tip of Africa and landed on India's southwest coast. Europeans had at last found a water route to Asia.

During Prince Henry's lifetime, Portuguese sailors explored only about half of the west coast of Africa. Through Henry's efforts, other rulers knew that trade—and gold—could finance further exploration.

▶ **CRITICAL THINKING**
Drawing Conclusions How did Prince Henry contribute to European exploration?

Reading **HELP**DESK CCSS

Academic Vocabulary (Tier 2 Words)
obtain to take possession of

networks Online Teaching Options

MAP

Portugal and da Gama

Analyzing Maps Have students study the map and determine when and where da Gama went on his voyages. **Ask:** **Where are the Azores?** *(in the Atlantic Ocean, west of Portugal)* **About how far did da Gama sail to reach the Cape Verde Islands? In what direction?** *(about 2,300 miles south)* Challenge students to describe other locations.

See page 615C for other online activities.

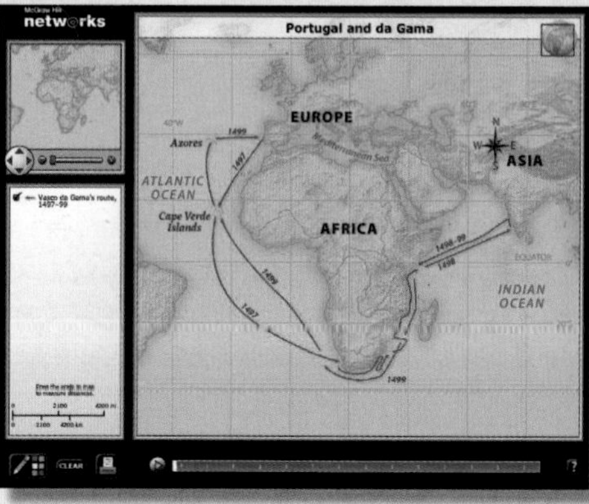

ANSWERS, p. 620

GEOGRAPHY CONNECTION

1. the southern tip of Africa
2. **CRITICAL THINKING** They tried to avoid the unknown and use the coastline as a guide.

CRITICAL THINKING Prince Henry paid for voyages of exploration and led other countries to begin exploring as well.

The First Voyage of Columbus

While the Portuguese explored Africa's western coast, an Italian navigator named Christopher Columbus formed a bold plan to reach Asia. He would sail west across the Atlantic Ocean.

C For years, Columbus had tried to convince various European rulers to pay for a voyage of exploration. Finally, in 1492, Ferdinand and Isabella of Spain agreed to support him. Earlier that year, the Spanish monarchs had defeated the Muslims in Spain. They were now able to pay for voyages seeking new trade routes.

W In August 1492, Columbus sailed west from Spain with three ships: the Santa María, the Niña, and the Pinta. As the weeks passed without sight of land, the sailors grew frightened. They wanted Columbus to sail back to Europe. Finally, the expedition sighted land. Columbus and his crew went ashore on San Salvador (sahn SAHL•vuh•dawr), an island in the Caribbean Sea.

Columbus claimed the island of San Salvador for Spain. He then traveled farther west in the Caribbean Sea. Eventually, his ships reached and explored the islands of Cuba and Hispaniola (hihs•puh•NYOH•luh). Today, the countries of Haiti and the Dominican Republic are located on the island of Hispaniola. Columbus began trading with the Taino (TEYE•noh) people.

INFOGRAPHIC

Columbus's flagship, the Santa María, was larger and slower than the other two ships on the voyage.

1. **TIME** What do the details of the ship reveal about the skills sailors at this time would need?
2. **CRITICAL THINKING** ***Making Generalizations*** Make a generalization about the hardships the crew probably faced on the long journey.

THE SANTA MARÍA

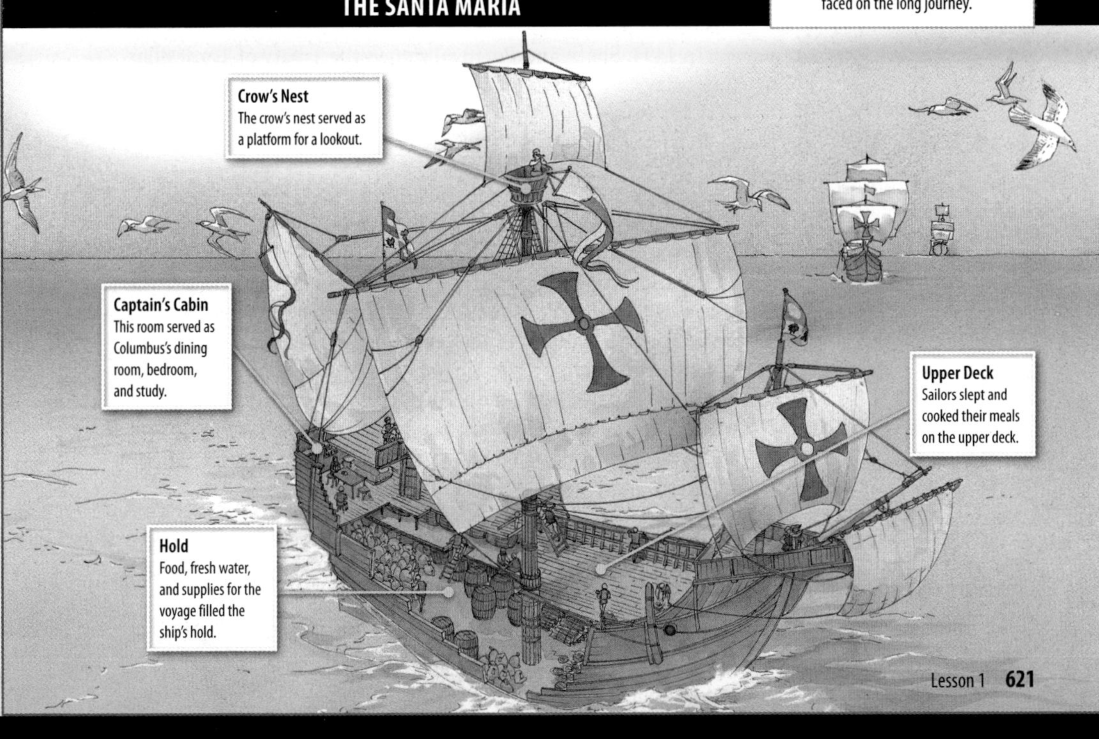

Crow's Nest
The crow's nest served as a platform for a lookout.
Captain's Cabin
This room served as Columbus's dining room, bedroom, and study.
Upper Deck
Sailors slept and cooked their meals on the upper deck.
Hold
Food, fresh water, and supplies for the voyage filled the ship's hold.

Lesson 1 621

W Writing Skills

Narrative Tell students to imagine that they are Christopher Columbus and have finally arrived in the Americas after a long and difficult voyage. Have them write a descriptive paragraph in which they tell how they feel about finally reaching land—and what they see and encounter in this strange, new place. Have students share their paragraphs with the class. Intrapersonal

C Critical Thinking Skills

Speculating Explain to the class that Columbus tried for years to convince European monarchs to support his plan to sail west to Asia. Invite students to consider the text and speculate why no one wanted to support him.

Ask: **Why do you think so many rulers turned Columbus down?** *(Answers will vary but may include that most rulers probably assumed Columbus would fail to discover new lands, or that his voyages were too dangerous to be successful.)* AL

Making Connections

Emphasize to students that war can be an enormous expense. The nine-year Iraq war that lasted from 2003 to 2011 cost $806 billion according to the Congressional Research Service and over $1 trillion according to President Obama. When nations spend so much money on war, they have little left over for other ventures, such as space exploration in the twenty-first century, or exploring what the world was like in the fifteenth century.

IMAGE

The Santa Maria

Analyzing Visuals Have students view the interactive image. **Ask:** **Why did the expedition need a cargo ship?** *(Possible answer: It was a long voyage and they needed to have room for plenty of supplies; Columbus wanted to bring goods back from India.)*

See page 615C for other online activities.

ANSWERS, p. 621

INFOGRAPHIC

1. Sailors needed to be able to climb and be strong to lift sails.
2. **CRITICAL THINKING** The crew probably faced hardships of bad weather and crowded conditions.

R Reading Skills

Describing Discuss with students how it must have felt to be a Taino on the day that Columbus and his conquistadors arrived in the Americas. **Ask:** What kind of life do you think the Taino people led before their land was discovered? *(They were most likely peaceful, independent people who lived off the land and rarely encountered outsiders.)* How did their lives change after Spain claimed their land? *(They became slaves. They may have been separated from loved ones. They were no longer independent.)* Why was the new world called the Americas? *(after Amerigo Vespucci, who explored the new world and realized it was a new continent and not Asia)* AL

T Technology Skills

Making Presentations Point out that Magellan's voyage was one of great hardship, courage, and tragedy. He left Spain with five ships and about 270 men. Only one ship and 17 men returned to Spain. Ask students to work in a group and research the voyage of Magellan. Have them assemble a multimedia presentation describing his epic exploration. **Verbal/Linguistic**

The Taino were the island's Native American people. Columbus returned to Spain with colorful parrots, some gold and spices, and several Taino as proof of his discovery.

Columbus, however, believed that he had been exploring the coast of Asia. He never realized that he had actually arrived in the Americas. It was not until 1502 that another Italian explorer, Amerigo Vespucci (ahm•uh•REE•goh veh•SPOO•chee), became convinced that Columbus had discovered a "new world." In 1507, early map makers labeled what is now the South American continent with the name *America*. Later, the name was applied to North America as well.

Amerigo Vespucci, explorer of the Americas, is believed to have influenced the naming of these lands with his name.

Spanish Conquerors

Columbus's success pleased the Spanish monarchs. Eager investors urgently, or quickly, organized a second return voyage. Columbus set out again in 1493. On this voyage, he took soldiers with him to conquer the people of these new lands. In November, the Spanish landed on Hispaniola.

R For the first time, the Taino saw the **conquistadors** (kahn•KEES•tuh•dawrz), the soldier-explorers that Spain sent to the Americas. The Taino became frightened by what they witnessed. Men in armor rode on powerful horses, with snarling dogs running alongside them. In a display of might, the soldiers fired guns that shot out flames and lead balls. The conquistadors claimed Hispaniola for Spain, and then they enslaved the Taino.

In 1494, Spain and Portugal signed the Treaty of Tordesillas (tawr•day•SEE•yahs). This agreement divided South America between Spain and Portugal.

Voyage of Magellan

During the 1500s, Spain continued to explore the Americas, but it was still interested in finding a western route to Asia. In 1518, Spain hired Ferdinand Magellan (muh•JEH•luhn) for an exploration voyage. Sailing west from Spain, Magellan's **primary** goal was to sail around the Americas and then on to Asia. T

Magellan traveled along South America's eastern coast, searching for a route to Asia. Near the southern tip of the continent, he reached a narrow water passage that is now called the Strait of Magellan. After passing through the stormy strait, the expedition entered a vast sea. It was so peaceful that Magellan named the sea the Pacific Ocean.

Reading **HELP**DESK 

conquistadors Spanish soldiers who conquered people in other lands
circumnavigate to go completely around something, such as the world

Academic Vocabulary (Tier 2 Words)
primary most important; first

networks Online Teaching Options

BIOGRAPHY

Ferdinand Magellan

Analyzing Images Have students read the biography of Magellan and explain the opening statements, which say that discovering trade and shipping routes led to greater economic and military power. Ask students to consider whether Magellan's motives for undertaking the voyage were related to economic and military power and, if not, what other motives he might have had.

See page 615C for other online activities.

Magellan then sailed west. Water and food ran out, and the crew had to eat leather, sawdust, and rats. Some sailors died. Finally, after four months at sea, the expedition reached the present-day Philippines. There, Magellan was killed in a battle between local groups. The remaining crew members continued west across the Indian Ocean, around Africa, and back to Spain. They became the first known people to **circumnavigate** (suhr•kuhm•NAV•uh•GAYT), or sail around, the world.

Early French and English Explorers

The Portuguese successes led England and France to begin their own overseas exploration. In 1497, Englishman John Cabot (KA•buht) explored the North American coasts of Newfoundland and Nova Scotia. He was unsuccessful in finding a waterway to Asia.

In 1524, France sent Giovanni da Verrazano (joh•VAH•nee dah ver•uh•ZAH•noh) to find a northern route to Asia. Verrazano explored and mapped much of the eastern coast of North America, but he did not find a route to Asia. In 1534, the French navigator Jacques Cartier (ZHAHK kahr•TYAY) sailed inland along the St. Lawrence River to present-day Montreal. Cartier claimed much of eastern Canada for France.

C

After these early expeditions, France and England had to focus their attention on religious conflicts and civil wars in their own countries. By the early 1600s, these countries renewed their overseas explorations. This time, the French and English began to establish their own settlements in the Americas. Since most of Spain and Portugal's territories were in South America, Mexico, and the Caribbean, France and England began to establish colonies in North America.

✓ PROGRESS CHECK

Sequencing Why was it important for the explorers of the Americas to use information they learned from earlier explorers?

Thinking Like a HISTORIAN

Predicting Consequences

Columbus was almost out of supplies when he reached land. Research how Columbus planned for his trip. What supplies did he take, and why? Then think about how his trip would be different today. What supplies would he take with him on a modern first voyage? Use library and Internet resources for your research. Then report your findings and predictions to your class. For more information about making predictions, read the chapter *What Does a Historian Do?*

Magellan, sailing for Spain, did not live to complete his voyage around the world.

LESSON 1 REVIEW (CCSS)

Review Vocabulary (Tier 3 Words)

1. How might sailors *circumnavigate* an island? RH.6–8.2, RH.6–8.4

Answer the Guiding Questions

2. ***Identifying*** Which European leaders most encouraged exploration of the world? RH.6–8.2
3. ***Explaining*** What prevented Europeans from exploring the world sooner, during the Middle Ages? RH.6–8.2
4. ***Differentiating*** Why did Portugal begin exploring before France, England, or Spain did? RH.6–8.2
5. ***Contrasting*** How did the second voyage of Columbus differ from the first? RH.6–8.2
6. **NARRATIVE** The crew of Magellan's voyage became the first people to sail all the way around the world. You are a crew member. Write a diary entry expressing your feelings after sailing around the world. WHST.6–8.10

LESSON 1 REVIEW ANSWERS

1. Sailors would circumnavigate an island by sailing all the way around it until they returned to where they started.
2. Prince Henry the Navigator, Christopher Columbus, Ferdinand and Isabella of Spain, Bartolomeu Dias, Vasco da Gama, and Ferdinand Magellan
3. A lack of central governments with wealth and power kept them from exploring.
4. France and England were at war, and Spain was still fighting the Muslims. This allowed Portugal under Prince Henry to explore first.
5. The first voyage was an exploration; the second was to conquer the lands he had discovered.
6. Answers will vary, but students should note that Magellan was trying to find a passage through the Americas and then go on to Asia. His crew would be excited and proud that they had accomplished something no one had ever done before. They also would be exhausted and extremely homesick.

C Critical Thinking Skills

Making Inferences Talk about the French and English exploration of the New World. Explain that many French and English explorers were seeking a sea route to Asia. **Ask: Why did the Europeans place so much emphasis on Asia when there was an unexplored and undeveloped continent available?** *(Possible answer: They were seeking wealth from trade for items that had a known value. At first, they weren't seeking to settle and build colonies, which would cost money to establish and might not bring profits.)* BL

Content Background Knowledge

Lasting Effects of Spanish and French Exploration

Spain and France established relatively few settlements in North America, yet they had a large impact on American culture. In the Southwest particularly, many geographic names come from the Spanish language. The Spanish influence on art, literature, music, and food have been a part of the culture of that region for centuries.

Communities such as St. Paul, St. Louis, and New Orleans include remnants of the French presence in America. They show a French influence in language, architecture, and cuisine. Food, for example, includes unmistakably French-inspired dishes such as baked goods like croissants and dishes with sauces, or etouffee.

Have students complete the Lesson 1 Review.

CLOSE & REFLECT

As a class, brainstorm a list of predictions that answer this question: **How did making contact with other lands and civilizations change Europeans and the cultures they contacted?** Guide the discussion so students consider the possibilities of conquest, cultural exchange, and the exchange of plants and animals. Write responses on the board.

ANSWER, p. 623

✓ **PROGRESS CHECK** The Western world was explored in steps, with each voyage going farther because it started with what was already known.

ENGAGE

Bellringer Explain to students that when the Spanish landed in the Americas, they did so with violence and ruthlessness. They brought heavily armed soldiers, cannons, and horses, which the Native Americans had never before seen. They sought to conquer the natives and did so brutally. **Ask:** How did the Spaniards' desire to find gold and other wealth lead to their treatment of Native Americans? *(Students may say that the Spanish thought any land or people they discovered could be used to make them rich.)*

Tell students that in this lesson they will learn how Spanish exploration of the Americas began with Columbus but evolved into conquest of the Native Americans and the destruction of the native empires of the Aztec and the Inca.

TEACH & ASSESS

R Reading Skills

Explaining After students have read this page, engage them in a conversation about the first conquistadors. Prompt them to refer to the passage as they discuss the following questions. **Ask:** Why did the New World attract poor nobles such as Hernán Cortés? *(They hoped to find gold and other wealth in America.)* Explain that the Spanish had relatively few soldiers and planned to attack many thousands of Native Americans. **Ask:** How could they expect to win such a confrontation? *(They intended to terrorize the Native Americans using cannons and horses, as Columbus and his soldiers had in Hispaniola.)* AL

ANSWER, p. 624

TAKING NOTES: Answers may include: Hernán Cortés—1. used his army's guns and horses to impress and frighten Native Americans, 2. relied on a Mayan woman named Malintzin to supply information about the Aztec, 3. took advantage of diseases weakening the Aztec, 4. attacked first and took Montezuma hostage; Francisco Pizarro—1. Shot at Inca villagers and raided their storehouses, 2. Used support from Native Americans who were hostile to Atahualpa, 3. took Atahualpa hostage, 4. failed to honor a deal to release Atahualpa for gold, 5. sentenced Atahualpa to death for crimes and installed a new ruler he controlled.

networks *There's More Online!*

- **BIOGRAPHY** Hernán Cortés (1485–1547)
- **GRAPHIC ORGANIZER** Conquests by Hernán Cortés and Francisco Pizarro
- **MAP** Spanish Conquests in North America

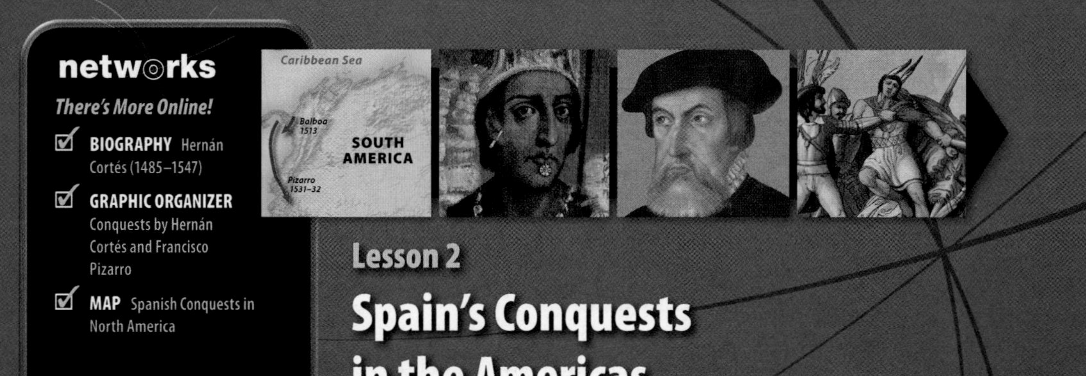

Lesson 2
Spain's Conquests in the Americas

ESSENTIAL QUESTION *Why do civilizations rise and fall?*

IT MATTERS BECAUSE

The Spanish conquest of Central and South America remains a dominant influence in the cultures and customs of these areas.

The Spanish Conquer Mexico

GUIDING QUESTION *How did Spain conquer Mexico?*

The voyages of Christopher Columbus inspired many poor Spanish nobles to become conquistadors. Their goal was to travel to the Americas and seek wealth. Nineteen-year-old Hernán Cortés (ehr•NAHN kawr•TEHZ) was one of these nobles. In 1504, he sailed to Hispaniola. Eleven years later, he took part in Spain's invasion of Cuba.

Cortés Arrives in Mexico

R While Cortés was in Cuba, he heard stories of Mexico's riches and the powerful Aztec Empire. In 1519, Cortés traveled to Mexico in search of gold and glory. He arrived near present-day Veracruz (vehr•uh•KROOZ) with about 508 soldiers, 100 sailors, 16 horses, and 14 cannons. How could such a small army expect to defeat the mighty Aztec?

Cortés used his army's guns and horses to frighten Native Americans. In a display of power, he forced thousands of them to surrender. Cortés also **relied** on a Maya woman named Malintzin (mah•LIHNT•suhn) for information about the Aztec.

Reading **HELP**DESK CCSS

Taking Notes: ***Summarizing***
Use a chart like this one to describe the methods used by Hernán Cortés and Francisco Pizarro to conquer the people of Central and South America. RH.6–8.2

Hernán Cortés	Francisco Pizarro

Content Vocabulary (Tier 3 Words)
- allies
- ambush
- smallpox
- hostage

networks ***Online Teaching Options***

VIDEO
Hernán Cortés

Analyzing Images Have students view the video. When they finish, draw a large circle on the board and label it *Hernán Cortés.* Then have students help you build a word web with words that describe the conquistador and include facts about his life.

See page 615D for other online activities.

Spanish Explorations 1500-1600

GEOGRAPHY CONNECTION

Spanish conquistadors explored during the 1500s.

1. **LOCATION** What is the northernmost point the Spanish explorers reached?
2. **CRITICAL THINKING** *Cause and Effect* What part of the world was affected by the Spanish conquests the most?

Malintzin spoke with Cortés through a Spanish translator who knew Mayan. She told Cortés that many people in her land resented the Aztec rulers. One reason for their anger was the Aztec practice of human sacrifices. Most often to please their gods, the Aztec killed people whom they had captured in war. Malintzin believed that people who were conquered by the Aztec would help Cortés. Malintzin helped Cortés find **allies** (AL•leyes), or other groups willing to battle the Aztec.

W Finally, another factor that helped Cortés defeat the Aztec was an invisible ally—germs that carried diseases such as the measles and **smallpox**. These diseases would eventually kill more Aztec people than Spanish weapons would.

Cortés Defeats the Aztec

C The Spanish traveled hundreds of miles inland to reach Tenochtitlán (TAY•NAWCH•teet•LAHN), the Aztec capital. Messengers reported their every move to the Aztec ruler, Montezuma II (MAHN•tuh•ZOO•muh). The Aztec believed in a light-skinned god named Quetzalcoatl (KWEHT•zuhl•kuh•WAH•tuhl). According to Aztec legend, this god, who opposed the practice of human sacrifice, had sailed away long ago but had promised to return someday to reclaim his land.

Montezuma II was the ninth Aztec emperor to rule the region of present-day Mexico.

allies those who support each other for some common purpose
smallpox a disease that causes a high fever and often death

Academic Vocabulary (Tier 2 Words)
rely to depend on; to count on for help

Spain's Conquests in the Americas

W Writing Skills

Informative/Explanatory Ask students to do research to learn about the effect of smallpox on Native Americans and why it killed so many of them. Have them answer these questions:

- What overall effect did smallpox have on Native Americans in North America?
- Why was smallpox such a deadly disease for the Native Americans?
- Where did the disease come from?
- Why didn't the disease affect the Europeans to the same degree that it affected the Aztec?

Have students summarize their findings in a two- or three-paragraph report. **Verbal/Linguistic**

C Critical Thinking Skills

Sequencing Have students read the section of the text titled "Cortés Defeats the Aztec." Next, organize students into pairs and give each pair several index cards. Have students record major events that occurred during Cortés's attempt to overtake the Aztec. Finally, have students mix up the cards and then put them in chronological order. **AL Interpersonal**

WORKSHEET

Primary Source Activity: Cortés Arrives in Tenochtitlán

Applying Have students read the introduction and then the two primary sources. Discuss the primary sources as necessary to clarify the meaning. Then have students answer the questions.

See page 615D for other online activities.

Primary Source Activity networks
Age of Exploration and Trade
Lesson 2 *Spain's Conquests in the Americas*
Cortés Arrives in Tenochtitlán
In November 1519, Hernán Cortés and his men entered the capital of the Aztec Empire, Tenochtitlán. The chief of the Aztec, Montezuma (referred to as Moctezuma or Motecuhzoma, below), had not attacked Cortés as he approached. The Aztec thought he might be a light-skinned god named Quetzalcoatl. Aztec legend maintained that this god who opposed human sacrifice would someday return to reclaim his land. An interpreter, a Native American woman named Malintzin (referred to below as La Malinche) assisted Cortés. The first account comes from a letter Cortés wrote to his king, Charles V, in 1520. The other retelling comes from accounts given by Aztec some time after the event.
Directions Read the following accounts of the arrival of Cortés.
Reading 1 Letter from Cortés to Charles V
After Cortés arrived in Aztec territory, he reported his findings to Charles V, the Holy Roman Emperor. This is part of the second letter that Cortés sent to the emperor.

ANSWERS, p. 625

GEOGRAPHY CONNECTION

1. Explorers almost reached the line of 40 degrees N latitude, north of present-day Santa Fe, New Mexico.
2. **CRITICAL THINKING** The areas that are modern-day Mexico, Florida, and northern South America were most affected by the Spanish conquests.

C Critical Thinking Skills

Making Inferences Discuss with students what happened after Cortés took control of the Aztec capital. **Ask: Why do you think Cortés decided to forbid the practice of human sacrifice?** *(Possible answers: The idea of human sacrifice may have horrified the Spanish; the Spanish may have wanted to weaken the Aztec religion.)* BL

R Reading Skills

Discussing Direct students to read the subsection "Spain Conquers Peru." Point out to the class that both Balboa and Pizarro were seeking a city of gold. Remind students that this was also one of Cortés's motivations. **Ask: What did Balboa actually find?** *(the Pacific Ocean)* **What do you think Pizarro thought he would find in the Inca Empire?** *(gold)* Encourage students to use evidence from the passage to justify their responses. AL

BIOGRAPHY

Hernán Cortés (1485–1547)

Assigned to lead troops in Mexico, Hernán Cortés forced his men to exercise and be disciplined. His well-trained forces acted quickly allowing Cortés to use their small numbers to outmaneuver a much larger Aztec force. He had also burned his ships so his men knew they had only one option—victory. After conquering Mexico, Cortés left in 1524 to explore Honduras. His two-year absence led to chaos in Mexico and ruined his reputation in Spain. He died in 1540, in debt and haunted by scandals.

▶ CRITICAL THINKING
Making Inferences What does it tell you about Cortés that he continued exploring even though he had conquered a great nation?

Montezuma was afraid Cortés was this god returning home. He was afraid to attack the Spanish right away. As Cortés marched closer, Montezuma changed his mind and decided to ambush the Spanish troops. Cortés, however, had already learned about the planned **ambush**.

In November 1519, Cortés took control of the Aztec capital. To prevent an Aztec uprising, Cortés took Montezuma **hostage** (HAHS•tihj), or prisoner. He then ordered the Aztec to stop sacrificing people. C

Cortés's orders angered the Aztec, who planned a rebellion. Fighting broke out, and the Spanish killed thousands of Aztec. However, there were far more Aztec, and Cortés had to fight his way out of the city. The Spanish took refuge in the nearby hills.

While Cortés prepared a second attack, smallpox broke out in Tenochtitlán. Many Aztec died of the disease, and the remaining Aztec could not fight off the Spanish and their allies. In June 1521, the Spanish destroyed the Aztec capital.

✓ PROGRESS CHECK

Explaining Why did the Aztec allow Cortés to remain in their lands?

Spain Conquers Peru

GUIDING QUESTION *How did Spanish conquistadors conquer the Inca?*

R Like Cortés, Vasco Núñez de Balboa (VAHS•koh NOON•yays day bal•BOH•uh) also sailed to the Americas. In 1513, he led a band of soldiers across the mountains of present-day Panama to look for a golden empire.

Balboa found a sea, known today as the Pacific Ocean, but he never found the golden empire he was looking for. A jealous Spanish official in Panama falsely charged Balboa with treason and had him beheaded.

Francisco Pizarro (fruhn•SIHS•koh puh•ZAHR•oh) had served as one of Balboa's soldiers. After Balboa was executed, Pizarro continued the search for gold. Even though Pizarro could not even write his own name, he knew how to fight. He longed to find the empire that Balboa had sought.

Pizarro Meets the Inca

The Inca ruled the empire that Balboa and Pizarro wanted to conquer. By the 1530s, the powerful Inca Empire had become **considerably** weaker. Despite their weaknesses, the Inca did

Reading **HELP**DESK CCSS

ambush a surprise attack
hostage someone held against his or her will in exchange for something

Academic Vocabulary (Tier 2 Words)
considerable large in size, quantity, or quality
global involving the entire Earth

networks Online Teaching Options

WHITEBOARD ACTIVITY

Spanish Conquest

Identifying Project the matching activity onto the whiteboard. Call on volunteers to match the name with the description. Discuss answers as they are given, whether they're right or wrong.

See page 615D for other online activities.

networks Spanish Conquest

Directions: Match items from the bank with the correct explanation.

Item Bank	
• Cortéz	• god the Aztecs believed in
• Montezume	• Maya woman who supplied Cortés with information about Aztecs
• Malintzin	• first European to discover the Pacific Ocean
• Quetzatcoatl	• a type of Spanish soldier who conquered Mexico and Peru
• Balboa	• Aztec ruler
• Pizarro	• Inca ruler
• Atahualpa	• became governor of Peru
• conquistador	• took Montezuma hostage

ANSWERS, p. 626

CRITICAL THINKING His skills and interests were in conquest and exploration, not in safer pursuits like administration, politics, or retirement.

✓ **PROGRESS CHECK** They believed he might be a returning god, and they were afraid to anger him.

not fear Pizarro and his troops. Pizarro had only 168 soldiers, one cannon, and 27 horses compared to the Inca army's 30,000 warriors. Still, Pizarro and his small army moved to attack the Inca homeland. In late 1532, Pizarro decided on a bold plan. T

The Inca Fall

R Spanish messengers invited the Inca ruler Atahualpa (ah•tuh•WAHL•puh) to meet with Pizarro. Atahualpa agreed and came to the meeting with just 4,000 unarmed bodyguards. At their meeting, Pizarro demanded that Atahualpa give up his gods. The emperor laughed at this, and Pizarro ordered an attack. The Spanish fired into the unarmed Inca crowd. Pizarro dragged Atahualpa from the battlefield.

Atahualpa tried to buy his freedom. He offered Pizarro an entire room full of gold and silver. Pizarro immediately accepted Atahualpa's offer. Atahualpa had his people bring Pizarro the precious metals. Pizarro, however, did not set Atahualpa free. Instead, he charged the emperor with plotting a rebellion, worshipping false gods, and other crimes. In 1533, a military court found the emperor guilty and sentenced him to death.

Pizarro betrayed Atahualpa. He set his soldiers to attack the Inca bodyguards.

The Spanish king rewarded Pizarro by making him governor of Peru. Pizarro chose a new emperor for the Inca, who had to follow Pizarro's orders. Still, the Spanish could not gain complete control of the Inca Empire. Even after Pizarro died in 1541, the Spanish were still fighting Inca rebels. Nonetheless, the conquest of Peru opened most of South America to Spanish rule. Spain would create the world's first **global** empire.

✓ PROGRESS CHECK

Evaluating How successful were the efforts of Atahualpa to free himself from Pizarro?

LESSON 2 REVIEW (CCSS)

Review Vocabulary (Tier 3 Words)

1. How did Pizarro's act of taking Atahualpa *hostage* force the Inca to do what Pizarro wanted? RH.6–8.2, RH.6–8.4

Answer the Guiding Questions

2. ***Describing*** Describe the troops and weapons that Hernán Cortés brought to Mexico. RH.6–8.2
3. ***Explaining*** What factors helped Cortés defeat the Aztec? RH.6–8.2
4. ***Differentiating*** How were the methods used by Cortés and Pizarro to conquer Native Americans different? RH.6–8.2
5. ***Inferring*** Why might Núñez de Balboa have believed that his expedition in Panama was a failure? RH.6–8.2
6. **INFORMATIVE/EXPLANATORY** Why do you think the Spanish conquered the Aztec and the Inca instead of trading with them for gold and other resources? Write a paragraph that explains your reasons. WHST.6–8.2, WHST.6–8.10

LESSON 2 REVIEW ANSWERS

1. Pizarro threatened his hostage Atahualpa with harm. This forced the Inca to do what Pizarro wanted out of fear that he would harm their emperor.
2. He commanded about 508 soldiers, 100 sailors, 16 horses, and 14 cannons.
3. He had the help of a local woman translator, diseases that killed the Aztec, and the Aztec belief that he was a returning light-skinned god.
4. Pizarro had fewer men and benefited from the Inca impression that he was not dangerous. Cortés attacked the Aztec first and used local translators.
5. He wanted to find a great empire filled with gold, but he found only the Pacific Ocean instead.
6. Answers will vary, but students might note that the Spanish were outnumbered, wanted to control the new lands they found and take the wealth for themselves, and forced the leaders of the Native Americans to give up their belief in gods.

R Reading Skills

Describing After students have read the text, point out that Pizarro was at an even greater disadvantage in his war with the Inca than Cortés was in attacking the Aztec. Invite volunteers to describe how Pizarro managed to defeat the Inca. *(He asked for a meeting with the Inca ruler. When Atahualpa showed up with 4,000 unarmed bodyguards, Pizarro attacked and took Atahaulpa prisoner.)* Discuss how Pizarro's victory led to Spain's dominance of South America and to Spain's becoming the first global empire. AL

T Technology Skills

Researching on the Internet Tell students that the Inca had created an amazing civilization that is known for many accomplishments, including their mathematical system, road network, and communications system. Ask students to use the Internet to research the Inca and then create a multimedia presentation that introduces the Inca and their accomplishments. **Visual/Spatial Interpersonal**

Have students complete the Lesson 2 Review.

CLOSE & REFLECT

As a class, discuss how Cortés and Pizarro were able to defeat much larger Native American forces. Have volunteers summarize the answers. *(Possible summary: Cortés and Pizarro tricked Montezuma and Atahualpa in order to imprison them and put them to death, leaving the Aztec and the Inca without their leaders. Also, Cortés and Pizarro got help from other Native Americans; Cortés was thought to be a returning god; disease weakened the Native Americans; the Spanish frightened people who had never seen guns and horses; the Spanish attacked the Native Americans first; and Pizarro, particularly, was not seen as a threat.)*

ANSWER, p. 627

✓ PROGRESS CHECK Atahualpa was not successful. When he tried to buy his freedom, Pizarro took his gold and then killed Atahualpa anyway.

ENGAGE

Bellringer Show students a map of European colonies in the Americas, such as the English colonies in North America or the Spanish colonies in North and South America.

Guide students toward understanding that, after exploration and conquest, making money from the colonies was the next goal of European nations.

Tell students that in this lesson they will be learning about how the colonies became moneymaking ventures for the Europeans. They will also learn about economic systems that used the areas the Europeans set up as colonies.

TEACH & ASSESS

R Reading Skills

Describing Ask students to read the the text. Then, lead a class discussion about the Treaty of Tordesillas, explaining that it was meant to settle a dispute between Spain and Portugal over their rights to lands in the New World. Then ask students to refer to the text as they describe Spain's American empire. *(Spain's holdings included much of South America and large parts of North America plus islands in the Caribbean.)* **Ask:** What were the two goals that Spanish rulers set for the American colonists? *(to send wealth back to Spain and to convert the Native Americans to Christianity)* AL

ANSWER, p. 628

TAKING NOTES: Spanish Colonies: sugarcane, gold, silver; Native Americans, enslaved Africans. Portuguese Colonies: sugarcane, tobacco, coffee, cotton; Native Americans, enslaved Africans. English Colonies: tobacco; enslaved Africans

There's More Online!

- **GRAPHIC ORGANIZER** Crops and Workers in Three Colonies
- **MAP**
  - European Trade in Asia
  - Columbia Exchange

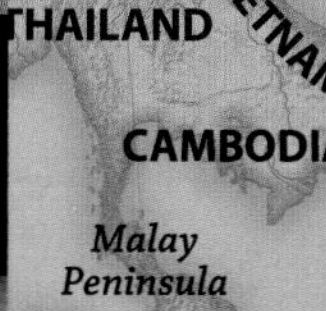

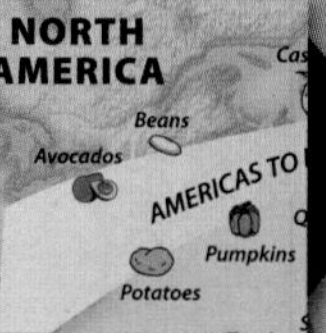

Lesson 3

Exploration and Worldwide Trade

ESSENTIAL QUESTION *Why do people make economic choices?*

IT MATTERS BECAUSE

European nations established colonies that produced great wealth, changing the Americas and other conquered lands forever.

Settling the Americas

GUIDING QUESTION *How did European nations build empires in the Americas?*

The Treaty of Tordesillas divided the Americas between Spain and Portugal. Other nations, however, did not accept this treaty. The Netherlands, France, and England soon joined Spain and Portugal in a race to gain wealth in new lands and to spread Christianity.

The Americas were the primary region where Europeans explored and established settlements. In the 1500s, the Spanish and the Portuguese had built empires in the Americas. Beginning in the 1600s, the French, English, and Dutch also began to establish their own settlements.

R

Spain's American Empire

By the 1600s, Spain's empire in the Americas had grown to include parts of North America and much of South America. The islands in the Caribbean Sea were also a part of this empire. Spanish rulers sent royal officials called viceroys to govern local areas. Councils of Spanish settlers also advised the viceroys.

The Spanish rulers set two goals for the colonists of their American empire: to bring wealth back to Spain and to convert Native Americans to Christianity. Spanish settlers grew crops of sugarcane on large farms known as **plantations** (plan•TAY•shuns).

Reading HELPDESK CCSS

Taking Notes: *Listing*

Use a diagram like the one here to list the crops or products and the type of workers found in each colony. RH.6–8.2

	Spanish Colonies	Portuguese Colonies	English Colonies
Crops or products			
Workers			

Content Vocabulary (Tier 3 Words)

- **plantations**
- **cash crops**
- **mercantilism**
- **commerce**
- **entrepreneur**
- **cottage industry**

networks ***Online Teaching Options***

VIDEO

Age of Discovery: English, French, and Dutch Explorations

Formulating Questions This video describes the motives, goals, and methods of the English, French, and Dutch in finding trade routes to Asia and establishing settlements in the New World. Ask students to write one question they have about the subject as they watch the video. Discuss their questions as a class.

See page 615E for other online activities.

Landowners also operated gold and silver mines. At the same time, Spanish priests established missions, or religious communities, to teach Christianity to the Native Americans.

G1

Spain permitted its settlers to use Native American labor to work the plantations. The Spanish, however, enslaved and mistreated the Native Americans. Also, the Spanish settlers unknowingly brought contagious diseases with them. Millions of Native Americans died from illness during the first 50 years of the arrival of Europeans. As the number of Native Americans declined, more laborers were needed. To solve this problem, the Spanish brought over enslaved Africans to work on the plantations and in the mines. In time, this mingling of Europeans, Native Americans, and Africans gave rise to a new **culture**.

C2

Portuguese Brazil

In 1500, the Portuguese explorer Pedro Álvares Cabral (PAY•droh AHL•vahr•ihs kuh•BRAHL) arrived in the region of South America that is now Brazil. He claimed this territory for Portugal. Settlers in Brazil grew **cash crops** such as sugarcane, tobacco, coffee, and cotton. A cash crop is a crop that is grown in large quantities to be sold for profit. With the help of enslaved Africans, Brazil became one of Portugal's most profitable overseas territories.

R

The French in North America

The fur trade was one of the main reasons the French settled in North America. By the 1600s, beaver fur was very popular in Europe. The French hoped they would become wealthy if they set up fur trading posts in North America. In 1608, French merchants hired explorer Samuel de Champlain (sham•PLAYN) to help them obtain furs in New France, which today is much of Eastern Canada. Champlain set up a trading post named Quebec (kwih•BEHK). Quebec became the capital of New France.

Sugarcane is a tall grassy plant. Its pulpy fibers are processed to create sugar as a final product.

plantation a large estate or farm that used enslaved people or hired workers to grow and harvest crops
cash crops crops grown in large amounts to be sold for profit

Academic Vocabulary (Tier 2 Words)
culture the customs, learning, and art of a civilization

G1 Critical Thinking Skills

Reasoning Point out that in some ways, the Spanish seemed concerned about the Native Americans—they wanted to convert them to Catholicism. However, they also enslaved and mistreated them. Invite students to reconcile these two actions. BL

C2 Critical Thinking Skills

Determining Cause and Effect Talk about the introduction of contagious diseases into the Americas. **Ask:** What effect did the diseases have on Native Americans? *(Millions died from them.)* What effect did the loss of so many Native American workers have on the European settlers? *(Because they had fewer workers, they had to import African slaves.)* Explain that the Spanish thus created a society made up of three races—Spanish, Native Americans, and Africans. **Ask:** What happened after these three races had been together for a while? *(They mingled, intermarried, and produced offspring that represented a new, fourth culture.)*

R Reading Skills

Discussing Have students read the text about the Portuguese and French colonies. Then lead a discussion about the economy in these colonies. Prompt students to include specific details from the text in their comments. **Ask:** How was Brazil's economy similar to that of Spain? *(Both grew sugarcane and used enslaved Africans as workers.)* What did the French find in their colonies that was as valuable as gold or silver? *(beaver furs)* AL

CHART

Brazil's Cash Crops

Identifying Have students read and discuss the introductory paragraph. Then ask them to click on the diagram to identify important cash crops of Brazil.

See page 615E for other online activities.

McGraw-Hill networks Brazil's Cash Crops

Portuguese ships brought settlers to Brazil in the early 1500s. At first, Portuguese colonists enslaved local Native Americans. Later, they brought enslaved Africans as additional sources of free labor to produce cash crops. Over the course of the Portuguese colonial period, millions of enslaved Africans came to Brazil. Enslaved people were treated harshly and worked in terrible conditions. The climate and geographic conditions in Brazil allowed for the production of a variety of crops on a large scale. The cash crops the enslaved laborers helped to produce played a major role in the development of Brazil's growing agricultural economy. Click the diagram to see the cash crops that were economically important in Brazil during the colonial period.

Brazil's Cash Crop

Content Background Knowledge

The Domesday Book The survey, or census, that resulted in the *Domesday Book* was carried out in 1086. William died before its completion. The comprehensive nature of the survey led many to compare it to the Last Judgment as described in the Bible, commonly called "Doomsday" (*Domesday* in old English). The census collected information about the landowners, the land they owned, the people who lived on the land, the buildings on the land, the woodland, animals, fish, and plows on the land, and the value of the land. The census was carried out by royal commissioners, who were sent around England with a set of questions for representatives of each area. The collected information was then recorded in Latin. The final version of the *Domesday Book* was handwritten in Latin by one scribe. The main book, called the *Great Domesday,* is 413 pages long. A second book, with information from three English counties, is 475 pages long. The original *Domesday Book* still exists and is kept in the British National Archives in London.

R Reading Skills

Naming Allow students time to study the infographic about important European explorers. Then invite five volunteers to the front of the classroom. Assign one of the five explorers to each volunteer. Have each volunteer take a turn giving the class a clue to his identity in the first person. For example, "I was the first European explorer to sail around the southern tip of Africa to reach India." Once a clue has been given, ask the rest of the class to identify the explorer being portrayed. **Interpersonal**

W Writing Skills

Informative/Explanatory Ask students to investigate the "Black Robes" and to write a brief report. Tell students that they should make sure to answer these questions in their writing: **Where did the Black Robes go? How did they live? What did the Black Robes learn about the Native Americans? What did they contribute to the exploration of the continent?** Have students share their reports informally with the class. BL

ANSWERS, p. 630

INFOGRAPHIC

1. Christopher Columbus
2. CRITICAL THINKING Henry Hudson

Reading Strategy Answers will vary but could include: merchants wanted trade; people sought religious freedom; there were economic troubles; people had been forced off their farms; people wanted to own their own lands.

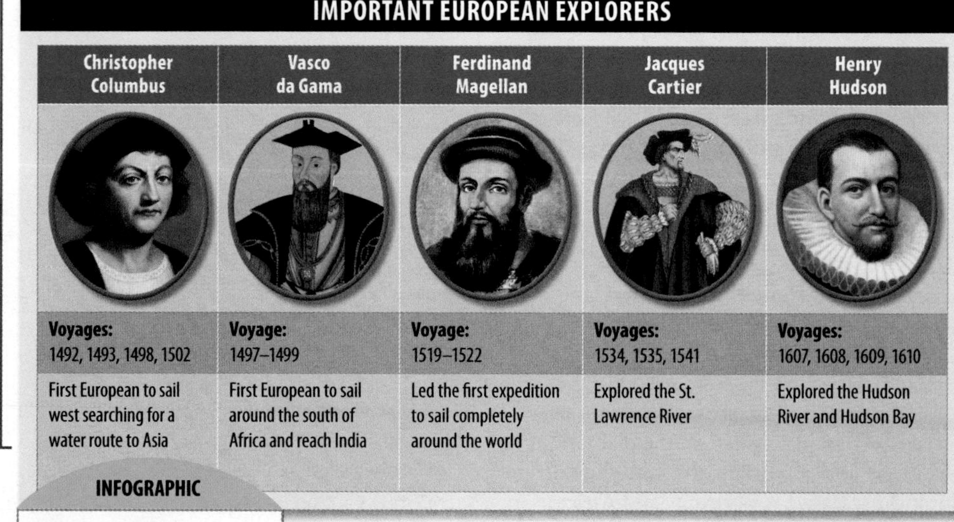

IMPORTANT EUROPEAN EXPLORERS

Christopher Columbus	Vasco da Gama	Ferdinand Magellan	Jacques Cartier	Henry Hudson
Voyages: 1492, 1493, 1498, 1502	**Voyage:** 1497–1499	**Voyage:** 1519–1522	**Voyages:** 1534, 1535, 1541	**Voyages:** 1607, 1608, 1609, 1610
First European to sail west searching for a water route to Asia	First European to sail around the south of Africa and reach India	Led the first expedition to sail completely around the world	Explored the St. Lawrence River	Explored the Hudson River and Hudson Bay

INFOGRAPHIC

For more than a hundred years, explorers searched for new trade routes.

1. **TIME** Who was the earliest European explorer?
2. **CRITICAL THINKING** ***Cause and Effect*** Which explorer gave his name to an important American river?

During the 1660s, the French king began sending political and military officials to rule New France. Jesuit and other Catholic missionaries also arrived. They taught Christianity to the Native Americans. The Native Americans called the Jesuits "Black Robes" because of the black clothes they wore.

From Quebec, French explorers, fur trappers, and missionaries spread out into the central part of New France. In 1673, the explorers Jacques Marquette (mar•KET) and Louis Joliet (joh•lee•EHT) reached the Mississippi River. Just nine years later, the French explorer La Salle (luh SAL) traveled south along the Mississippi to the Gulf of Mexico. He named the region Louisiana in honor of King Louis XIV. Like the Portuguese settlers, the French used enslaved Africans to work the fields.

England's Colonies in North America

During the early 1600s, England started to establish its own settlements in North America. The English government was interested in the natural **resources** from overseas territories.

English settlers sailed to North America for many reasons. Groups of merchants created settlements for trade. Others fled to North America to find religious freedom. Economic troubles in England also helped speed the growth of English settlements.

Academic Vocabulary (Tier 2 Words)

resource a ready supply of something valuable

Reading Strategy: *Identifying Cause and Effect*

As you read, look for key words to help you identify cause and effect, such as "because" and "since." Read about the English colonies in North America. What were the conditions—causes—that sent settlers to the New World?

networks ***Online Teaching Options***

WHITEBOARD ACTIVITY

Explorers in the Americas

Identifying Review the explorers mentioned in the lesson. Use a map to identify the region explored during each voyage. Then show students the Interactive Whiteboard Activity. Ask volunteers to match the name of the explorer to the voyage. Extend the activity by having students put the explorations in order from earliest to latest.

See page 615E for other online activities.

networks — Explorers in the Americas

Directions: Match the names to their correct descriptions.

Item Bank

• Henry Hudson	• claimed land along the Atlantic coast of North America for the Dutch
• Pedro Álvares Cabral	• explored the coasts of Newfoundland and Nova Scotia
• John Cabot	• first European to sail west in search of a route to Asia
• Giovanni de Verrazano	• explored and mapped much of the eastern coast of North America
• Jacques Cartier	• let the first expedition to circumnavigate the globe
• Christopher Columbus	• claimed much of eastern Canada for France
• Ferdinand Magellan	• claimed the region of South America now known as Brazil for Portugal

In 1606, a group of English merchants and nobles formed the Virginia Company. North America's first permanent English settlement was founded with the Virginia Company's support in 1607. The founders named it Jamestown after King James I. It was the first settlement in the new territory called Virginia.

At first, the early settlers in Virginia could barely find enough food to survive. During the winters, many of them starved to death. Others were killed in clashes with Native Americans.

In the early years, the merchants and nobles who invested in the settlement did not make any money. Jamestown needed to develop an economic activity in order to become profitable. Settlers discovered that tobacco grew well in Virginia.

Crops to Sell

Tobacco was very popular in Europe in the 1600s. Soon, the English settlers were producing and shipping it back to England in large amounts. Tobacco became the first cash crop of the English settlements. Eventually, it was grown on large plantations that needed many workers. Once again, enslaved Africans were brought in to work the land. **R**

Encouraged by its success in Virginia, England continued to establish settlements in North America that produced cash crops. South Carolina, for example, began growing rice and indigo, a dye-producing plant. The English established sugarcane plantations on Caribbean islands, such as Jamaica. Enslaved African people worked the lands on English plantations, as they did on French and Portuguese plantations.

Dutch Traders

Another European country, the Netherlands, was interested in overseas exploration and settlement. The Netherlands won its independence from Spain in the late 1500s. Its people, known as the Dutch, believed that trade was key to their survival.

The 1600s were a golden age for the Netherlands. Dutch ships were efficient. Compared with ships from other European countries, Dutch ships could transport more goods and be **C** operated by smaller crews.

Dutch trading ships sailed to the southern tip of Africa to the islands of Southeast Asia and soon set out for North America. An English navigator named Henry Hudson claimed land for the Dutch along the Atlantic coast of North America. In 1621, Dutch traders established settlements in the Americas, including one on Manhattan Island that they called New Amsterdam. Today, this region is part of New York City.

✓ PROGRESS CHECK

Summarizing Why did European colonists bring enslaved Africans to their plantations in the Americas?

Connections to **TODAY**

Blending Languages

Spanish and Portuguese settlers brought their languages to the Americas. Over time, Native Americans combined elements of Spanish and Portuguese with their own languages. Native American words such as "chocolate" and "coyote—words that we still use today—migrated into Spanish and later English. Another term--Hispanic--was originally used to describe a Spanish person in the Americas.

King James I (top) approved the creation of the Virginia Company. In 1619, the company created the House of Burgesses, America's first legislature. This seal is the king's official stamp put on important documents.

R Reading Skills

Paraphrasing Have students use information they have extracted from the passage to talk about the first English settlement in North America. **Ask:** **Why was it called Jamestown?** *(after James I, the king of England)* **What was life like for the early settlers of Jamestown?** *(It was harsh. Settlers didn't have enough food, and many starved to death; others were killed by Native Americans.)*

Elaborate on the importance of tobacco as a cash crop, pointing out that people had invested in the colony for the purpose of making money. **Ask:** **What other cash crops did England produce in its colonies?** *(rice, indigo, sugarcane)*

C Critical Thinking Skills

Contrasting Explain that the Netherlands is a very small country with few natural resources. **Ask:** **How did the Dutch differ from other European nations that explored and established colonies?** *(The Dutch made their money from trade as opposed to other Europeans, who made their money from establishing colonies where they could produce raw materials for other markets.)* **How did the ships they used reflect their interest in trade?** *(The ships could carry more trade goods and be operated by smaller crews.)* Elicit that these advantages made the ships more efficient and profitable for traders. BL

IMAGE

The Virginia Company

Discussing Have students view the image and read the text. When students finish reading, discuss the nature and purpose of the Virginia Company. **Ask:** **What is the difference between a planter and an adventurer?** *(A planter moves to the colony and settles. An adventurer buys shares in the company but stays at home.)*

See page 615E for other online activities.

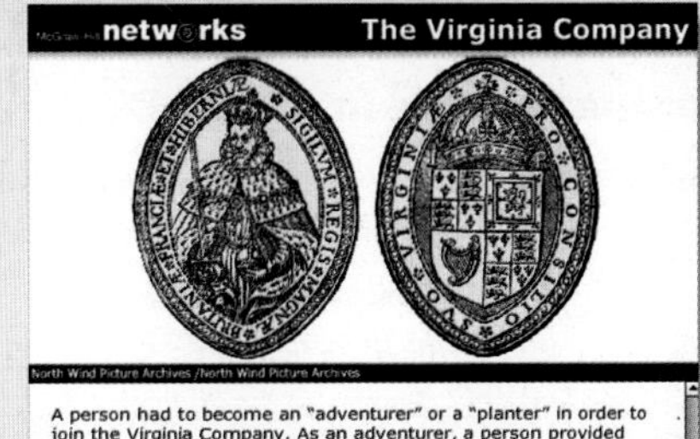

networks
The Virginia Company
North Wind Picture Archives /North Wind Picture Archives
A person had to become an "adventurer" or a "planter" in order to join the Virginia Company. As an adventurer, a person provided money by purchasing shares in the Virginia Company but stayed safe in England. As a planter, a person traveled to the new colony. In exchange for work settling the colony, a planter received food, clothing, and a place to live. At the end of a planter's term, he received a piece of land and a share of the company's profits.

ANSWER, p. 631

✓ PROGRESS CHECK Disease had reduced the number of Native Americans who were available to work, so enslaved Africans were brought in to do the labor on these plantations, which required large numbers of workers.

V Visual Skills

Analyzing Maps Ask students to study the map and notice where each of the European nations had their port cities. **Ask:** Which nation had a port city on the Malay Peninsula? *(the Netherlands)* Which nation had a port in China? *(Portugal)* Point out that the European nations had ports all over this part of Asia. AL **Ask:** How did having a network of colonies enhance trade? *(Traders in the settlements could trade locally, collect the goods, and then ship them in large lots back to the colonizing country.)* Visual/Spatial

R Reading Skills

Using Context Clues Direct students to read the subsection titled "What is Mercantilism?" Then, guide a discussion of mercantilism. Ensure that students have utilized the reading passage to understand the meaning of the term. **Ask:** What does a successful mercantile economy depend upon? *(A nation must have a greater amount of exports than imports in order to increase the country's supply of gold and silver.)* How do colonies help promote mercantilism? *(They are able to provide raw materials not found or made in the home country.)* AL ELL

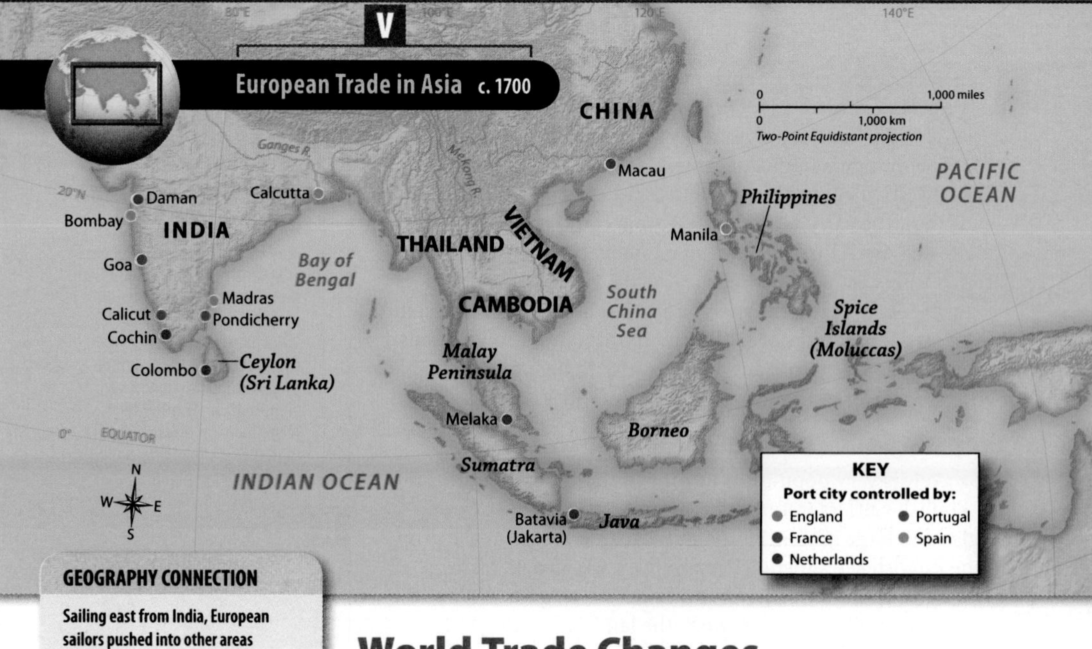

GEOGRAPHY CONNECTION

Sailing east from India, European sailors pushed into other areas of Asia.

1. **PLACE** Which countries had trading posts on the South China Sea?
2. **CRITICAL THINKING** ***Cause and Effect*** Why would the port cities shown on this map develop differently over time as compared to other cities in Asia?

World Trade Changes

GUIDING QUESTION *How did Europe's merchants change the world trade system?*

As Europeans created empires, profitable trade developed between their homelands and their overseas settlements. As a result, Europe's economy expanded. By the 1600s, European nations were competing for markets and trade goods.

What Is Mercantilism?

R Spain and Portugal took advantage of the gold and silver they gained from their empires. Other European countries wanted to do the same. This led to the theory of **mercantilism** (MUHR•kuhn•TEE•lih•zuhm). The key idea of mercantilism is that a country's power depends on its wealth. Countries can increase their wealth by owning more gold and silver. What is the best way for a country to get more gold and silver? According to mercantilism, a country must export, or sell to other countries, more goods than it imports, or buys from other countries.

According to mercantilism, countries should establish colonies. A colony is a settlement of people living in a territory controlled by their home country. Colonists provide raw materials that are not found or made in the home country.

Reading HELPDESK CCSS

mercantilism an economic theory that depends on a greater amount of exports than imports in order to increase a country's supply of gold and silver

networks ***Online Teaching Options***

MAP

European Trade in Asia c. 1700

Analyzing Maps Encourage students to explore the map. Clicking on items in the map key will reveal port cities that countries controlled. **Ask:** Which country controlled the most port cities? *(the Netherlands)* Where did Spain have its port city? *(Manila, in the Philippines)*

See page 615E for other online activities.

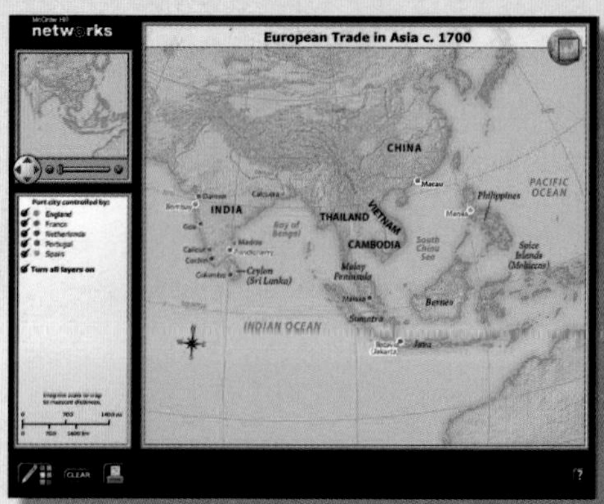

ANSWERS, p. 632

GEOGRAPHY CONNECTION

1. Spain and Portugal
2. **CRITICAL THINKING** The port cities would be affected by foreign influences from European trading. Goods and economic forces would change the development of the ports.

These materials are then shipped to the home country. In the home country, the raw materials are used to manufacture goods so that the home country does not have to buy these goods from other countries.

Europeans established trading posts and colonies in Asia and North America. By the end of the 1500s, Spain had a colony in the Philippines. In the 1600s, English and French merchants arrived in India. They began trading with the people there. In 1619, the Dutch built a fort on the island of Java, in what is now Indonesia. The Dutch became so powerful that they pushed the Portuguese out of the spice trade.

Guns and powerful ships helped Europeans defeat Arab fleets and Indian armies. Across Asia, Europeans forced local rulers to open their lands to trade. The arrival of the Europeans in Japan caused a dramatic change in that society. A new Japanese shogun used European-made guns and cannons to dominate his enemies. He was finally able to defeat the feudal lords and the daimyo and reunite Japan.

Creating Joint-Stock Companies

Europeans found that paying for overseas trading voyages was expensive. In the 1600s, however, Europeans developed new business **methods**. Historians call this the Commercial Revolution. **Commerce** (KAH•muhrs) is the buying and selling of goods in large amounts over long distances.

R

This type of commerce needed large amounts of money in order to be profitable. So, a new type of businessperson called an **entrepreneur** (AHN•truh•pruh•NUHR) emerged. Entrepreneurs **invest**, or put money into a project. Their goal is to make money from the success of the project.

C

As overseas trade increased in the 1600s, many projects were too large for one entrepreneur to pay for. If a voyage failed, for example, that individual would lose everything. As a result, groups of entrepreneurs began to form joint-stock companies. A joint-stock company is a business in which many people can invest. Groups or individuals, called investors, buy shares in the company. These shares are called stocks. By owning stock, investors would share the expenses, the risks—and the profits.

Bettmann/CORBIS

Henry Hudson lands in North America ready to establish trade with Native Americans. He was sent by the Netherlands to find a Northwest Passage to Asia.

▶ CRITICAL THINKING

Speculating What do you think Native Americans thought of Hudson and his crew?

commerce an exchange of goods; business
entrepreneur one who organizes, pays for, and takes on the risk of setting up a business

Academic Vocabulary (Tier 2 Words)

method a way of doing something; a process or procedure
invest to give money to a company in exchange for a return, or profit, on the money

R Reading Skills

Determining Word Meanings Ask for a volunteer to read the text aloud. Then, write the terms on the board that students will need to know to understand this section. **Ask:**

- What are business methods? *(ways of doing business)*
- What is commerce? *(the buying and selling of large amounts of goods over long distances)*
- What is an entrepreneur? *(someone who organizes, pays for, and takes on the risk of setting up a business)*
- What does it mean to invest? *(to give money to a company in exchange for profit on the money)*

Invite volunteers to record the meaning of each word on the board. AL ELL

C Critical Thinking Skills

Making Generalizations Guide a discussion of the risks that investors in overseas trade encountered. Help students understand that trade ships faced many dangers, from pirates to storms to unprofitable trades and competition.

Challenge students to make a generalization about how entrepreneurs tried to reduce the risk of losing money. Students should note how joint-stock companies shared this risk. **Ask:** Why did entrepreneurs create this way to invest in producing or trading goods? *(Students might say they were trying to lower their risk.)* Ask students to be as specific as possible. BL

GAME

Exploration and Worldwide Trade Crossword Puzzle

Defining Project the crossword puzzle onto the whiteboard. Invite volunteers to read the clues aloud and then type in the correct answer.

See page 615E for other online activities.

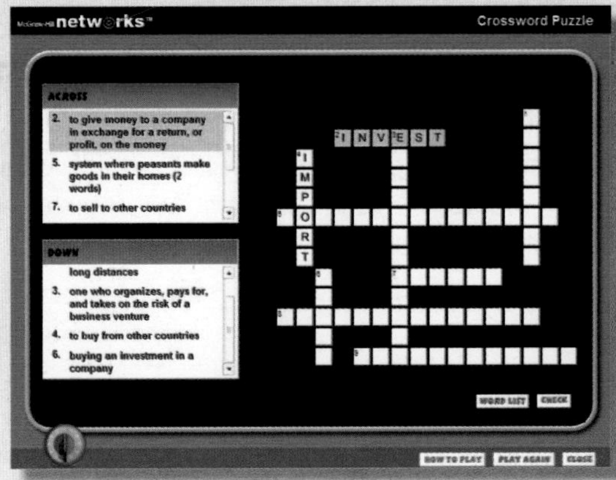

ANSWER, p. 633

CRITICAL THINKING Answers will vary but Native Americans were probably shocked, wary, and maybe afraid.

C Critical Thinking Skills

Making Connections Discuss the term *cottage industry* with students. **Ask:** **How was the term *cottage industry* first coined?** *(Peasants who were hired to make goods often worked in their small homes or cottages.)* Explain to students that cottage industries are still alive and well today, as many people choose to make and sell goods and other services right from their own homes. Ask students to brainstorm examples of modern-day cottage industries. Write their ideas on the board. **Interpersonal**

R Reading Skills

Explaining After students have read the text, talk about global exchange. **Ask:** **Why do historians call this flow of goods and ideas the Columbian Exchange?** *(It is named after Christopher Columbus.)* Ask students to define the Columbian Exchange. *(the purposeful and accidental flow of goods and ideas between Europe and the Americas during the Age of Exploration)* AL ELL

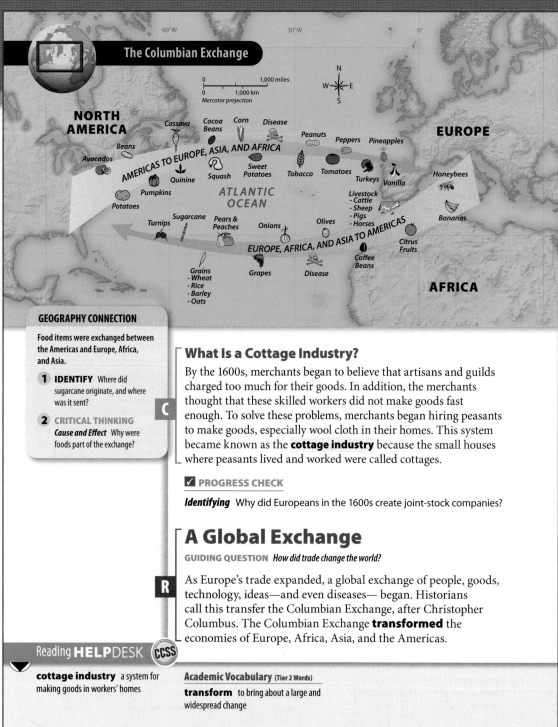

The Columbian Exchange

60°W 30°W 0°
0 1,000 miles
0 1,000 km
Mercator projection
N S W E
NORTH AMERICA
EUROPE
AFRICA
ATLANTIC OCEAN
30°N
AMERICAS TO EUROPE, ASIA, AND AFRICA
Avocados, Beans, Cassava, Cocoa Beans, Corn, Disease, Peanuts, Peppers, Pineapples, Quinine, Squash, Sweet Potatoes, Tobacco, Tomatoes, Turkeys, Vanilla, Pumpkins, Potatoes
EUROPE, AFRICA, AND ASIA TO AMERICAS
Honeybees, Bananas, Livestock - Cattle - Sheep - Pigs - Horses, Citrus Fruits, Coffee Beans, Olives, Onions, Pears & Peaches, Sugarcane, Turnips, Grains - Wheat - Rice - Barley - Oats, Grapes, Disease

GEOGRAPHY CONNECTION

Food items were exchanged between the Americas and Europe, Africa, and Asia.

1. **IDENTIFY** Where did sugarcane originate, and where was it sent?
2. **CRITICAL THINKING** *Cause and Effect* Why were foods part of the exchange?

What Is a Cottage Industry?

By the 1600s, merchants began to believe that artisans and guilds charged too much for their goods. In addition, the merchants thought that these skilled workers did not make goods fast enough. To solve these problems, merchants began hiring peasants to make goods, especially wool cloth in their homes. This system became known as the **cottage industry** because the small houses where peasants lived and worked were called cottages.

PROGRESS CHECK

Identifying Why did Europeans in the 1600s create joint-stock companies?

A Global Exchange

GUIDING QUESTION *How did trade change the world?*

As Europe's trade expanded, a global exchange of people, goods, technology, ideas—and even diseases— began. Historians call this transfer the Columbian Exchange, after Christopher Columbus. The Columbian Exchange **transformed** the economies of Europe, Africa, Asia, and the Americas.

Reading HELPDESK CCSS

cottage industry a system for making goods in workers' homes

Academic Vocabulary (Tier 2 Words)

transform to bring about a large and widespread change

networks Online Teaching Options

WORKSHEET

Economics of History Activity: The Columbian Exchange

Analyzing Have students read the introduction regarding the Columbian Exchange. Discuss any questions they have. Then assign students to complete the activity as homework.

See page 615E for other online activities

ANSWERS, p. 634

PROGRESS CHECK Joint-stock companies were a way for European businesses to increase the amount of money they had to invest in new ventures and decrease the risk of losing money. Investors bought shares in the business; the business used this money to buy or make new goods cheaply; from the sale of these goods at higher prices, the company hoped to make a profit, which was shared with the investors.

GEOGRAPHY CONNECTION

1. Sugarcane came from Europe, Africa, and Asia to the Americas.
2. **CRITICAL THINKING** They were either unique to one place or there was a demand for them in the place where they were sent.

Merchants introduced foods from the Americas to Europeans. Two of the most important crops were corn and potatoes. In Europe, these crops became essential to daily life. Corn was used to feed livestock, producing larger, healthier animals. This resulted in more meat, leather, and wool. Potatoes helped Europeans feed more people from their land.

Europeans acquired other foods from Native Americans, such as squash, beans, and tomatoes. Tomatoes greatly changed cooking in Italy, where tomato sauces became widely used. Chocolate was a popular food from Central America. By mixing chocolate with milk and sugar, Europeans made candy.

American settlers planted many European and Asian grains, such as wheat, oats, barley, rye, and rice. Coffee and tropical fruits, such as bananas, were brought to the Americas as well. Eventually, coffee and banana farms employed thousands of workers in Central America and South America.

Explorers and settlers also brought pigs, sheep, cattle, chickens, and horses to the Americas. Raising chickens changed the diet of many people in Central and South America.

The lives of Native Americans on the Great Plains changed when they acquired horses. Horses provided a faster way to travel. As a result, Native Americans became more efficient at hunting buffalo for food and at fighting enemies.

Europeans obtained sugarcane from Asia and began growing it in the Caribbean. This caused a migration, or movement of people. To plant and harvest the sugarcane, over time Europeans enslaved millions of Africans and moved them to the Americas.

In addition to slavery, the Columbian Exchange spread diseases from one area to another. When Europeans arrived in America, they were carrying viruses that were new to Native Americans. These diseases were deadly and eventually killed millions.

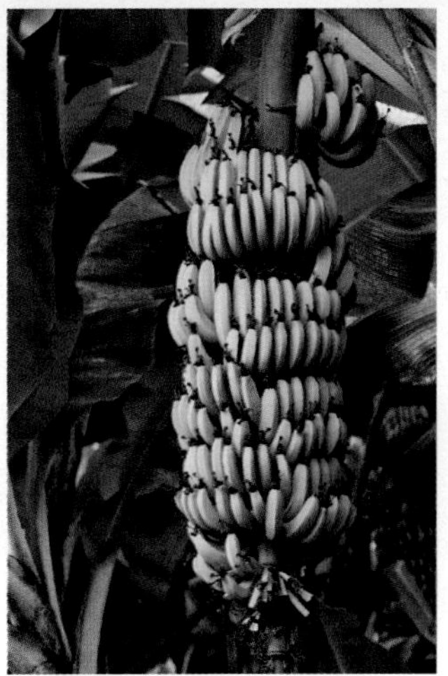

Bananas—a huge cash crop—grow on plantations in tropical locations such as Central America.

C

☑ PROGRESS CHECK

Evaluating Was the Columbian Exchange a benefit or a problem for the Americas?

LESSON 3 REVIEW (CCSS)

Review Vocabulary (Tier 3 Words)

1. How does *mercantilism* benefit the homeland more than the colony? RH.6–8.2, RH.6–8.4

Answer the Guiding Questions

2. ***Explaining*** Why was growing tobacco an important boost to help colonists trade? RH.6–8.2
3. ***Identifying*** Which group was brought in to replace Native American workers in American colonies? RH.6–8.2
4. ***Explaining*** Who receives the benefits and profits from a joint-stock company? RH.6–8.2
5. ***Identifying*** What was the Columbian Exchange? RH.6–8.2
6. **NARRATIVE** Write a paragraph describing how either Europeans or Native Americans might have reacted when they first tasted foods from another continent. Consider how chocolate, tomatoes, peanuts, and bananas must have puzzled people who were eating it for the first time. WHST.6–8.10

LESSON 3 REVIEW ANSWERS

1. The colony's purpose is to provide raw materials for manufacturing in the homeland. The majority of the profits are earned in the homeland, which is the purpose of mercantilism.
2. By trading items such as tobacco that had value in Europe, colonists provided income that supported the colonies in much the same way that mining gold and silver justified the expenses of establishing colonies elsewhere.
3. Enslaved Africans were brought in to work when the number of Native Americans declined.
4. stockholders
5. It was an interchange of goods, ideas, people, and diseases between Europe and the Americas.
6. Answers will vary, but students should describe how this exposure to something new would delight yet perplex someone from a culture that had never experienced it before.

C Critical Thinking Skills

Determining Cause and Effect Lead students in a discussion of how the Columbian Exchange permanently changed the cultures of Europe and the Americas. Guide students to understand that a new crop or a fruit or an animal that hasn't existed in that place before can meet a need or be used in a way that was not possible before.

Organize students into pairs and have them draw a cause-and-effect graphic organizer on a sheet of notebook paper. As they read the section on the Columbian Exchange, have them fill in the graphic organizer with examples from the text. Tell students to include at least five effects and their corresponding causes.

Have students complete the Lesson 3 Review.

CLOSE & REFLECT

Lead students in a discussion of the following question about contact between Europe and the places that explorers and conquerors encountered. **Ask:** **Who do you think benefited more from the contact between the Americas and the European nations? Why?** *(Answers will vary. Students may argue that Europeans gained many beneficial plants and animals from the Americas, as well as treasure. Or they may note that the Europeans transformed the people and cultures of the Americas.)*

ANSWER, p. 635

☑ PROGRESS CHECK Answers will vary, but students should discuss the devastation of Native American peoples from disease and how this made it easier for Europeans to conquer them. These ideas should be compared to the benefits introduced by Europeans.

Activities Answers

CHAPTER 21 Activities

Write your answers on a separate piece of paper.

1. **Exploring the Essential Question** WHST.6–8.2, WHST.6–8.10
   INFORMATIVE/EXPLANATORY When different cultures share technologies, the interchange can affect the lives of people on different continents. Write an expository essay about how sailing technologies led to changes in Europe and in the Americas.

2. **21st Century Skills** RH.6–8.2, WHST.6–8.6
   CREATING A BLOG Create a blog to share your thoughts on exploration. Discuss your observations about the positive and negative effects of the first encounters between Europeans and Native Americans. To encourage an exchange of ideas with other bloggers, ask discussion questions about how these two civilizations saw their contact in very different ways. Your questions should require bloggers to support their opinions with examples.

3. **Thinking Like a Historian** RH.6–8.2
   MAKING CONNECTIONS Create a diagram like the one shown here that traces the progress of European explorations. Start with the first attempts to seek a route to Asia by going around Africa to eventually sailing around the world.

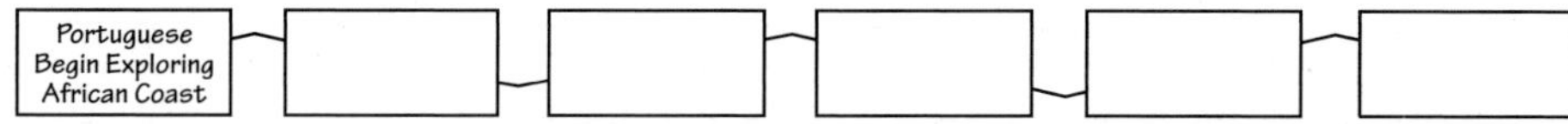

4. **GEOGRAPHY ACTIVITY**

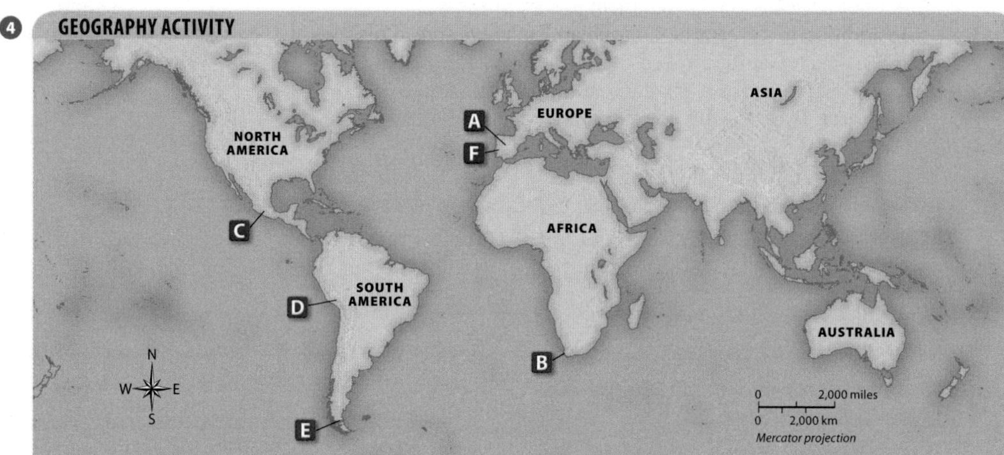

Locating Places RH.6–8.7
Match the letters on the map with the numbered places listed below.

1. Portugal
2. Aztec Empire
3. Inca Empire
4. Spain
5. Cape of Good Hope
6. Straights of Magellan

CHAPTER REVIEW ACTIVITY

Have students divide into debate teams. Their topic will be "Should the Europeans have conquered and occupied the Americas or merely traded and shared goods and ideas?" Have students argue both sides of the issue. Provide a Pros and Cons graphic organizer like the one shown to help record their ideas. Students' debates should consider alternatives to what actually did occur. Students could also debate whether the Native Americans should have tried to conquer Europe in the same way that Europeans took over the Americas. Lastly, students should propose how a more peaceful and creative interchange could have occurred between these very different civilizations, one of trade and cultural exchange, as well as mutual respect.

Pros	Cons

REVIEW THE ENDURING UNDERSTANDING

Review this chapter's Enduring Understanding with students:

- ***The movement of people, goods, and ideas causes societies to change over time.***

Now pose the following question in a class discussion to apply it to the chapter.

How did science and technology change people's lives during the period examined in this chapter? *(Answers may vary, but students should note that scientific and technological advances, such as the compass, astrolabe, improved maps, triangular sails, and better-designed ships, enabled explorers to travel the vast oceans. This capability led the nations of Europe to explore the world, conquer native groups, establish colonies, and build trade. The trade itself yielded more change, as the Columbian Exchange brought plants, animals, people, and ideas back and forth from Europe to the Americas. The exchange of crops fostered new industry and enabled people to feed themselves better than in the past. The exchange of disease from Europe to the Americas cost millions of lives, especially among Native Americans. The development of plantations to grow new cash crops created a need for slavery, and as a result, many people were enslaved.)*

ACTIVITIES ANSWERS

Exploring the Essential Question

1. Students' essays should correctly identify the technology that came from Arabic traders (astrolabe, triangular sails, ancient maps) and explain how this exchange fueled a larger exchange once the European explorers used these tools to extend their travels to unknown places. Students may discuss how the secondary exchange that occurred after Europeans began trading and conquering other civilizations was a benefit as well as a detriment to both parties.

21st Century Skills

2. Students should have a blog format or a bulletin board forum that clearly presents their opinions and observations and states how they feel about the positive and negative aspects of the interchange between cultures. Discussion questions should provoke reader reaction by offering differing viewpoints of the exchange but also require those making a response to support their opinions with examples.

Thinking Like a Historian

3. Graphic organizers should identify in sequence the various stages in the exploration of the world: Portuguese sail around Africa; Columbus sails to the Americas; Balboa discovers Pacific Ocean; French and Dutch explore North America; Magellan sails to Asia and back to Portugal.

Locating Places

4. **1.** F, **2.** C, **3.** D, **4.** A, **5.** B, **6.** E

REVIEW THE GUIDING QUESTIONS

Directions: Choose the best answer for each question.

RH.6–8.2

1. Europeans wanted to find a water route to Asia because
   A. the Italians cut off the flow of goods from Asia.
   B. the Ottoman Turks made spices less expensive.
   C. the Mongols lost power and overland trade was disrupted.
   D. the lack of road repairs blocked the Silk Road.

RH.6–8.2

2. Which advancement made by the Greeks did the Europeans adopt for overseas exploration?
   F. Ptolemy's maps
   G. triangular sails
   H. the astrolabe
   I. the compass

RH.6–8.2

3. Who first tried to help the Europeans to find a water route to Asia?
   A. Vasco da Gama
   B. Ferdinand of Spain
   C. Hernán Cortés
   D. Henry the Navigator

RH.6–8.2

4. Which of the following helped Europeans the most in conquering Native Americans?
   F. diseases
   G. gold
   H. improved ships
   I. horses

RH.6–8.2

5. Europeans used enslaved Africans to
   A. expand their conquering armies.
   B. explore unknown lands.
   C. work on farms in their colonies.
   D. form joint-stock companies.

RH.6–8.2

6. The key idea behind the concept of mercantilism is that countries
   F. did not need colonies.
   G. wanted to export more goods.
   H. wanted to import more goods.
   I. no longer needed entrepreneurs.

637

ASSESSMENT ANSWERS

Review the Guiding Questions

1. **C** The correct choice is C. When the Mongol Empire collapsed, local rulers could no longer protect people trading along the Silk Road. The Ottoman Turks took control of the spice trade with Europe and made Asian goods much more expensive. The Italians did not cut off the flow of goods from Asia, nor were road repairs related to the closing of the Silk Road.

2. **F** The correct choice is F. Ptolemy, a Greek, had prepared maps of the known world that European explorers used to venture into oceans and areas they knew little about. Triangular sails, the astrolabe, the compass, and the caravel were not Greek inventions.

3. **D** The correct choice is D. Henry the Navigator brought the finest minds of his time to advance the science of exploration. Although he wasn't an explorer himself, he helped Portugal begin the first explorations of Africa as a way to find a new route to Asia.

4. **F** The correct choice is F. The diseases the Europeans carried unintentionally caused vast loss of life in the Americas and weakened the empires there, allowing Europeans to take over. Caravels were useful for traveling to the Americas, and horses were useful in warfare, but they were smaller factors. Many Europeans came to the Americas seeking gold.

5. **C** The correct choice is C. Europeans brought enslaved Africans to their colonies to replace Native Americans who had been killed off by disease as well as by the Spanish conquest. Enslaved Africans were not employed as soldiers, explorers, or company investors.

6. **G** The correct choice is G. Countries need to export more goods than they import under the theory of mercantilism. They acquire raw goods cheaply from their colonies and convert these to manufactured goods, which they sell for wealth and power. If they had to purchase raw materials at high prices, they wouldn't profit as much by converting them into products.

Assessment Answers

Analyzing Documents

7 **B** The correct choice is B. Columbus wanted the Native Americans to trade with the Spanish so they could get goods and raw materials to bring back to Europe. He was not trying to protect his soldiers as much as he was preserving a relationship with the locals. B is the best answer.

8 **I** The correct choice is I. Europeans wanted products like cotton and gold that were valuable to them but were abundant or less expensive to the Native Americans.

Short Response

9 The description makes it clear that the Aztec Empire had a strong economy and a wide variety of goods for sale. The city was thriving with activity.

10 In the excerpt, the Aztec markets are compared to the silk market in Grenada.

Extended Response

11 Students' descriptive writing should provide details about how having new foods, guns, domestic animals, and fresh ideas would benefit Native Americans. They should also note how disease, being conquered, and being forced to work as enslaved people ruined the world they once knew.

CHAPTER 21 Assessment (continued)  

DBQ ANALYZING DOCUMENTS

Drawing Conclusions Columbus wrote about meeting Native Americans:

"Thus they bartered [traded], like idiots, cotton and gold for fragments of bows, glasses, bottles, and jars; which I forbad[e] as being unjust, and myself gave them many beautiful . . . articles which I had brought with me, taking nothing from them in return; I did this in order that . . . I might induce [persuade] them to take an interest in . . . delivering to us such things as they possessed in abundance, but which we greatly needed."

—Christopher Columbus, letter to Raphael Sanchez, March 14, 1493

RH.6–8.1, RH.6–8.6

7 Why did Columbus prevent his soldiers from trading items of little value with Native Americans?

A. to get more gold for himself
B. to encourage open and fair trading
C. to prevent any interchange between them
D. to avoid wasting their valuables on useless things

RH.6–8.1, RH.6–8.6

8 **Making Inferences** What were the "things as they possessed in abundance" which Columbus mentions?

F. bows and glasses
G. beautiful articles Columbus had brought
H. fragments of bottles and jars
I. gold and cotton

SHORT RESPONSE

Write your answers on a separate piece of paper.

"There are all kinds of green vegetables, . . . fruits, . . . honey and wax from bees . . . .Different kinds of cotton thread of all colors in skeins [loose balls] are exposed for sale in one quarter of the market, which has the appearance of the silk-market at Granada; . . . everything that can be found throughout the whole country is sold in the markets."

—from *The Second Letter to Charles V, 1520,* by Hernan Cortés

RH.6–8.1, RH.6–8.6

9 What can you tell about the economy of the Aztec empire from this description by Cortés?

RH.6–8.1, RH.6–8.6

10 What comparison does Cortés make to Granada, Spain?

EXTENDED RESPONSE

WHST.6–8.10

11 **Informative/Explanatory** Write a paragraph about how the Columbian Exchange presented advantages and disadvantages for Native Americans and Europeans.

Need Extra Help?

If You've Missed Question	1	2	3	4	5	6	7	8	9	10	11
Review Lesson	1	1	1	2	2	3	1	1	2	2	3

networks Online Teaching Options

Help students use the Skills Builder resources

Your students can practice important 21st Century skills such as geography, reading, writing, and critical thinking by using resources found in the Skills Builder tab of the online Student Learning Center. Resources include templates, handbooks, and slide shows. These same resources are also available in the Resource Library of the Teacher Lesson Center.

CHAPTER 22

The Scientific Revolution and the Enlightenment Planner

UNDERSTANDING BY DESIGN®

Enduring Understandings

- *Science and technology can change people's lives.*
- *The value that society places on individual rights is often reflected in that society's government.*

Essential Questions

- *How do new ideas change the way people live?*
- *How do governments change?*

Predictable Misunderstandings

Students may think:

- *Most people knew that Earth revolved around the sun before Copernicus.*
- *Most important scientific discoveries are recent.*
- *The English fought a war to gain democratic reforms.*
- *The monarchs in Europe were against any democratic reforms.*

Assessment Evidence

Performance Tasks:

- *Hands-On Chapter Project*

Other Evidence:

- *Responses to Interactive Whiteboard Activities*
- *Class discussion answers about the life and discoveries of Isaac Newton*
- *Organizing the steps in the scientific method*
- *Comparing and contrasting primary sources of Hobbes and Locke*
- *21st Century Skills Activity*
- *Primary Source Activity*
- *Interactive Graphic Organizers*
- *What Do You Think? questions*
- *Written paragraphs*
- *Lesson Reviews*
- *Chapter Activities and Assessment*

SUGGESTED PACING GUIDE

Introducing the Chapter	1 day	Lesson 2	1 day
Lesson 1	2 days	Chapter Wrap-Up and Assessment	1 day

TOTAL TIME 5 DAYS

Key for Using the Teacher Edition

SKILL-BASED ACTIVITIES

Types of skill activities found in the Teacher Edition.

V Visual Skills require students to analyze maps, graphs, charts, and photos.

R Reading Skills help students practice reading skills and master vocabulary.

W Writing Skills provide writing opportunities to help students comprehend the text.

C Critical Thinking Skills help students apply and extend what they have learned.

T Technology Skills require students to use digital tools effectively.

*Letters are followed by a number when there is more than one of the same type of skill on the page.

DIFFERENTIATED INSTRUCTION

All activities are written for the on-level student unless otherwise marked with the leveled labels below.

BL Beyond Level

AL Approaching Level

ELL English Language Learners

All students benefit from activities that utilize different learning styles. Many activities are marked as below when a particular learning style is highlighted.

Intrapersonal | **Naturalist**
Logical/Mathematical | **Kinesthetic**
Visual/Spatial | **Auditory/Musical**
Verbal/Linguistic | **Interpersonal**

NCSS Standards covered in "The Scientific Revolution and the Enlightenment"

Learners will understand:

2 TIME, CONTINUITY, AND CHANGE

5. Key historical periods and patterns of change within and across cultures (e.g., the rise and fall of ancient civilizations, the development of technology, the rise of modern nation-states, and the establishment and breakdown of colonial systems)

6. The origins and influences of social, cultural, political, and economic systems

7. The contributions of key persons, groups, and events from the past and their influence on the present

8. The history of democratic ideals and principles, and how they are represented in documents, artifacts and symbols

4 INDIVIDUAL DEVELOPMENT AND IDENTITY

1. The study of individual development and identity helps us know that individuals change physically, cognitively, and emotionally over time

5. That individuals' choices influence identity and development

6 POWER, AUTHORITY, AND GOVERNANCE

2. Fundamental ideas that are the foundation of American constitutional democracy (including those of the U.S. Constitution, popular sovereignty, the rule of law, separation of powers, checks and balances, minority rights, the separation of church and state, and Federalism)

3. Fundamental values of constitutional democracy (e.g., the common good, liberty, justice, equality, and individual dignity)

4. The ideologies and structures of political systems that differ from those of the United States

5. The ways in which governments meet the needs and wants of citizens, manage conflict, and establish order and society

8 SCIENCE, TECHNOLOGY, AND SOCIETY

1. Science is a result of empirical study of the natural world, and technology is the application of knowledge to accomplish tasks

2. Society often turns to science and technology to solve problems

4. Science and technology have had both positive and negative impacts upon individuals, societies, and the environment in the past and present

5. Science and technology have changed peoples' perceptions of the social and natural world, as well as their relationship to the land, economy and trade, their concept of security, and their major daily activities

6. Values, beliefs, and attitudes that have been influenced by new scientific and technological knowledge (e.g., invention of the printing press, conceptions of the universe, applications of atomic energy, and genetic discoveries)

8. Science and technology sometimes create ethical issues that test our standards and values

CHAPTER OPENER PLANNER

Students will know:

- *the Scientific Revolution generated much new knowledge.*
- *the scientific method represented a new way of studying the world.*
- *the Enlightenment influenced ideas about human rights and government.*

Students will be able to:

- ***describe*** *how science was practiced in ancient and medieval times.*
- ***describe*** *the theories of Ptolemy, Copernicus, and Newton.*
- ***identify*** *what instrument made the discovery of bacteria possible.*
- ***explain*** *why Descartes believed that mathematics is the source of scientific truth.*
- ***define*** *the scientific method.*
- ***compare and contrast*** *the ideas of Hobbes and Locke.*
- ***explain*** *why Voltaire criticized the Roman Catholic Church.*
- ***describe*** *the importance of Diderot's Encyclopedia.*
- ***explain*** *how Frederick the Great influenced the Enlightenment.*

UNDERSTANDING BY DESIGN®

☑ Print Teaching Options

C Critical Thinking Skills

- ☐ **P. 640** Students analyze a map that shows the Centers of Enlightenment.
- ☐ **P. 641** Students review a time line and make inferences about what was happening in Europe beginning around the 1500s.

☑ Online Teaching Options

V Visual Skills

- **MAP** **Centers of Enlightenment**—Students identify cities throughout Europe where ideas of the Enlightenment were developed.
- **TIME LINE** **The Scientific Revolution and the Enlightenment 1500 to 1800**—Students learn about key events during this time period.
- **WORLD ATLAS** Students can use this interactive map to identify regions of the world, learn about individual countries, locate political boundaries, measure distances, and much more.

☑ Printable Digital Worksheets

C Critical Thinking Skills

- **WORKSHEET** **What Do You Know? Activity: The Scientific Revolution and the Enlightenment: Cloze**—Students complete a paragraph about the Enlightenment using terms from a word bank.

Project-Based Learning

Hands-On Chapter Project

Scientific Revolution Newspaper Article

Student groups will write a newspaper article describing an important scientist's discovery during the Scientific Revolution.

Technology Extension

edtechteacher 21st Century Learning

Podcast or Role-Play Interview

- Find an additional activity online that incorporates technology for this project.
- Visit the EdTechTeacher Web sites (included in the Technology Extension for this chapter) for more links, tutorials, and other resources.

Print Resources

ANCILLARY RESOURCES

These ancillaries are available for every chapter and lesson.

- **Reading Essentials and Study Guide Workbook** AL ELL
- **Chapter Tests and Lesson Quizzes Blackline Masters**

PRINTABLE DIGITAL WORKSHEETS

These printable digital worksheets are available for every chapter and lesson.

- **Hands-On Chapter Projects**
- **What Do You Know? activities**
- **Chapter Summaries (English and Spanish)**
- **Vocabulary Builder activities**
- **Guided Reading activities**

More Media Resources

SUGGESTED VIDEOS 

Watch clips of movies about the Scientific Revolution, such as *Galileo*, and the documentaries *Genius: Galileo* and *Sir Isaac Newton: The Gravity of Genius.*

For the Enlightenment, have students watch the movie *Leonard Bernstein's Candide* and the documentary *Catherine the Great.*

(NOTE: Preview clips for age-appropriateness.)

SUGGESTED READING

Grade 6 reading level:

- ***Isaac Newton and Physics for Kids,*** by Kerrie Logan Hollihan

Grade 7 reading level:

- ***Catherine: The Great Journey, Russia, 1743,*** by Kristiana Gregory

Grade 8 reading level:

- ***1,000 Inventions and Discoveries,*** by Roger Bridgman

LESSON 1 PLANNER

THE SCIENTIFIC REVOLUTION

Students will know:

- *the Scientific Revolution generated much new knowledge.*
- *the scientific method represented a new way of studying the world.*

Students will be able to:

- ***describe*** *how science was practiced in ancient and medieval times.*
- ***describe*** *the theories of Ptolemy, Copernicus, and Newton.*
- ***identify*** *what instrument made the discovery of bacteria possible.*
- ***explain*** *why Descartes believed that mathematics is the source of scientific truth.*
- ***define*** *the scientific method.*

UNDERSTANDING BY DESIGN®

☑ *Print Teaching Options*

V Visual Skills

- ☐ **P. 644** Students chart branches of science and what Europeans in the 1400s contributed. **Visual/Spatial**
- ☐ **P. 645** Students use visuals to determine the main idea of a text feature. **Visual/Spatial**
- ☐ **P. 647** Students chart the Scientific Revolution and do research to add missing information. **Visual/Spatial**

R Reading Skills

- ☐ **P. 642** Students determine the main idea of an introductory paragraph. **AL**
- ☐ **P. 646** Students identify the structure used in the text to describe Galileo's achievements. **Verbal/Linguistic**
- ☐ **P. 647** Students use context clues to determine the meaning of the word *Principia*. **ELL**
- ☐ **P. 649** Students analyze the scientific method.

W Writing Skills

- ☐ **P. 643** Students compare attitudes of ancient Greeks and Romans with those of Europeans. **AL** **Verbal/Linguistic**
- ☐ **P. 648** Students write a paper arguing for or against Descartes's claim that mathematics is the source of scientific truth. **BL** **Intrapersonal**

C Critical Thinking Skills

- ☐ **P. 644** Students evaluate the reaction to Copernicus's theory of a heliocentric universe. **BL** **Verbal/Linguistic**
- ☐ **P. 645** Students discuss how Kepler's findings supported Copernicus's claim that Earth orbited the sun.
- ☐ **P. 646** Students make predictions about how the advances of Copernicus, Kepler, and Galileo influenced later scientists. **BL** **Verbal/Linguistic**
- ☐ **P. 648** Students hypothesize about how scientists proved that things needed oxygen to burn. **Verbal/Linguistic**
- ☐ **P. 649** Students evaluate whether Pascal's scientific and religious beliefs contradicted each other. **Intrapersonal**

T Technology Skills

- ☐ **P. 646** Students formulate a question about Galileo's achievements and do research on the Internet to answer it. **BL** **Interpersonal**

☑ *Online Teaching Options*

V Visual Skills

- **VIDEO** **Planetary Motion: Kepler's Three Laws**—Students observe how Kepler used the work of Copernicus and Tycho Brahe to inform his own study of planetary motion.
- **SLIDE SHOW** **Through a Microscope**—Students click to see magnified images of snowflakes, blood cells, and cotton fibers.
- **SLIDE SHOW** **Sir Isaac Newton**—Students see visual representations of some of Isaac Newton's important ideas.

R Reading Skills

- **GRAPHIC ORGANIZER** **Taking Notes: *Categorizing:* Scientists and Their Achievements**—Students record the names of scientists and their contributions.
- **BIOGRAPHY** **Galileo**—Students read a short biography of this scientist.

C Critical Thinking Skills

- **WHITEBOARD ACTIVITY** **Leaders of the Scientific Revolution**—Students match scientists with their accomplishments.
- **CHART** **Indian-Arabic and Roman Numerals**—Students click to reveal hints as to how to write a variety of Roman numerals.
- **CHART** **The Scientific Method**—Students click to properly order the steps in the scientific method.

T Technology Skills

- **SELF-CHECK QUIZ** **Lesson 1**—Students receive instant feedback on their mastery of lesson content.
- **GAME** **The Scientific Revolution Crossword Puzzle**—Students solve clues to review lesson content.
- **GAME** **Ptolemy and Copernicus Column Game**—Students categorize statements about Ptolemy and Copernicus.

☑ *Printable Digital Worksheets*

W Writing Skills

- **WORKSHEET** **21st Century Skills Activity: Communication: Write a Résumé**—Students analyze the parts of a résumé and then write a résumé for Isaac Newton.

THE ENLIGHTENMENT

Students will know:

- *the Enlightenment influenced ideas about human rights and government..*

Students will be able to:

- ***compare and contrast*** *the ideas of Hobbes and Locke.*
- ***explain*** *why Voltaire criticized the Roman Catholic Church.*
- ***describe*** *the importance of Diderot's Encyclopedia.*
- ***explain*** *how Frederick the Great influenced the Enlightenment.*

UNDERSTANDING BY DESIGN®

☑ Print Teaching Options

V Visual Skills

- ☐ **P. 653** Students depict consequences of combining different branches of government. **Visual/Spatial**
- ☐ **P. 654** Students analyze an image of people reading and discussing Voltaire's works. **AL** **Visual/Spatial**

R Reading Skills

- ☐ **P. 650** Students determine the meaning of the phrase *Age of Enlightenment.* **ELL**
- ☐ **P. 651** Students summarize England's government during Thomas Hobbes's time. **Verbal/Linguistic**
- ☐ **P. 653** Students identify the important ideas of the *philosophes* of France.
- ☐ **P. 655** Students paraphrase the section about France's Sun King. **AL** **Verbal/Linguistic**
- ☐ **P. 656** Students identify the text structures that help convey the information about Frederick II.
- ☐ **P. 657** Students explain why Peter the Great went to war with Sweden.

W Writing Skills

- ☐ **P. 652** Students write an essay explaining John Locke's idea that governments should answer to the people. **Intrapersonal**

C Critical Thinking Skills

- ☐ **P. 650** Students evaluate what political thinkers of this era used as the basis of thinking.
- ☐ **P. 652** Students compare and contrast the Glorious Revolution and the American Revolution. **BL**
- ☐ **P. 653** Students compare the ideas of Montesquieu with those of Hobbes and Locke. **AL**
- ☐ **P. 654** Students compare Voltaire's beliefs with those of thinkers with similar beliefs. **BL**
- ☐ **P. 656** Students analyze maps and the text to make inferences about German territories and states.
- ☐ **P. 657** Students discuss the main conflicts in the struggles between nobles and serfs.

T Technology Skills

- ☐ **P. 654** Students work in small groups to create a PowerPoint presentation about Voltaire. **Interpersonal**

☑ Online Teaching Options

V Visual Skills

- **VIDEO** **Reason and the Age of Enlightenment**—Students learn how ideas developed in the Enlightenment led thinkers to define "morality" as an individual trait that should form without guidance from the church or state.
- **MAP** **Growth of Prussia and Austria c. 1525–1720**—Students examine how these two German states expanded their lands over a 200-year period.

R Reading Skills

- **GRAPHIC ORGANIZER** **Taking Notes: *Identifying:* Thinkers and Their Ideas**—Students list the main thinkers of the Enlightenment and a major idea for each.
- **PRIMARY SOURCE** **Mary Wollstonecraft**—Students read a passage from *A Vindication of the Rights of Woman.*
- **PRIMARY SOURCE** **Voltaire**—Students read a passage from *Candide.*
- **IMAGE** **John Locke and His Ideas**—Students read about one of the fathers of the Enlightenment.

C Critical Thinking Skills

- **WHITEBOARD ACTIVITY** **Hobbs, Montesquieu, and Locke**—Students match statements with the thinker to which they belong.
- **PRIMARY SOURCE** **Catherine the Great**—Students analyze a passage from The Grand Instructions.
- **IMAGE** **Leviathan**—Students analyze Thomas Hobbes's use of the word *leviathan.*

T Technology Skills

- **SELF-CHECK QUIZ** **Lesson 2**—Students receive instant feedback on their mastery of lesson content.
- **GAME** **The Enlightenment Fill-in-the-Blank Game**—Students complete sentences to review lesson content.

☑ Printable Digital Worksheets

C Critical Thinking Skills

- **WORKSHEET** **Primary Source Activity: The Ideas of Hobbes and Locke**—Students analyze passages to determine points of view.

INTERVENTION AND REMEDIATION STRATEGIES

LESSON 1 The Scientific Revolution

Reading and Comprehension

Instruct students to summarize the events, ideas, and interests that led up to the Scientific Revolution. **Ask:** **How did these events lead up to the Scientific Revolution?**

Text Evidence

Ask students to work in pairs to list the major people, events, and ideas that were part of the scientific revolution. Have groups share their lists, citing where they found each name, event, and idea in the text.

LESSON 2 The Enlightenment

Reading and Comprehension

Have students explain how the beliefs of the thinkers of the Enlightenment conflicted with the thoughts and actions of the rulers who were in charge during this time in England, Europe, and Russia.

Text Evidence

Have students create a chart, listing the thinkers from England, France, and Switzerland and their main beliefs and accomplishments. They should cite evidence from the text to support their chart.

Online Resources

Approaching Level Reader

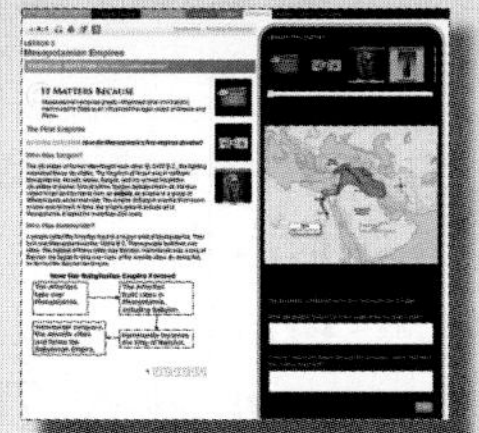

Use this online lower-level text that corresponds directly to the text in the Student Edition. It includes a Spanish version.

Guided Reading Activities

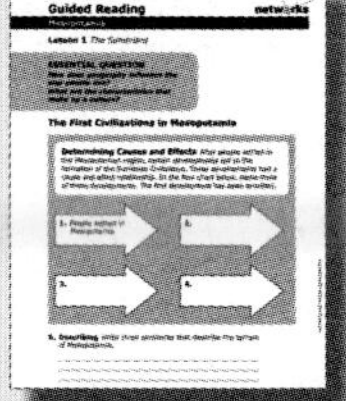

This resource uses graphic organizers and guiding questions to help students with comprehension.

What Do You Know?

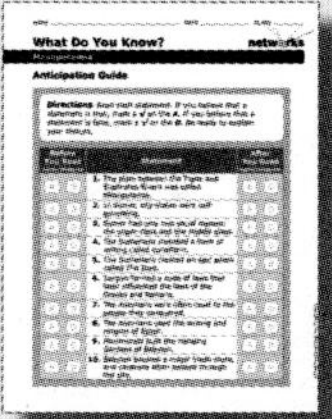

Use these worksheets to pre-assess student's background knowledge before they study the chapter.

Reading Essentials and Study Guide Workbook

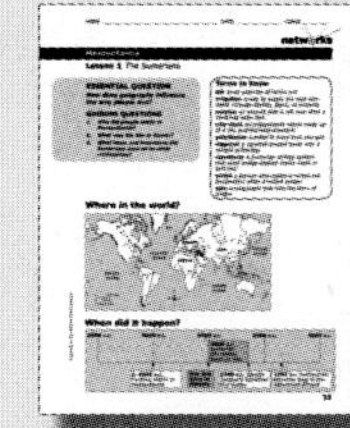

This resource offers writing and reading activities for the approaching-level student. Also available in Spanish.

Self-Check Quizzes

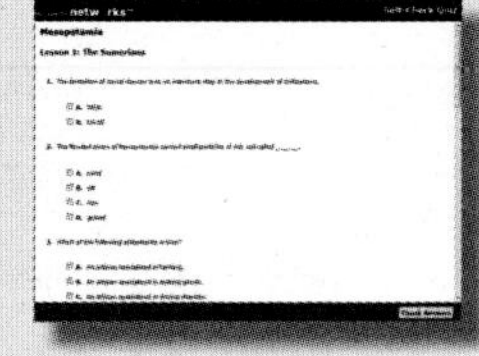

This online assessment tool provides instant feedback for students to check their progress.

How Do I Apply
Authentic Assessment?

Authentic assessment uses real-world challenges to help evaluate each student's knowledge and skills. Students rely on their analysis skills, creativity, presentation skills, and ability to work in groups to guide them through a process that leads to a final product or project. The role of the teacher in authentic assessment is to guide, provide models of excellence, and provide feedback for each step of the assessment process.

Teaching Strategy 1 Target Cooperative Learning and Group Work Skills

- If you normally like group assignments, consider turning one into an authentic assessment task.
- Remind and encourage students to be receptive to the various ideas of their group members—especially in the early planning phases of the assessment task.
- Emphasize to all groups that everyone gets an individual grade—not a single group grade. This helps to hold each student accountable for the work tasks they are given.

Teaching Strategy 2 Involve Community Participation with a Voting Guide Project

- Look for authentic assessment tasks that can lead students out of the classroom and into the community. For example, in an election year ask your class to conduct research on the local candidates running for office.
- Students' grades should be based on accuracy, objectivity, and serviceability as a tool for the voting public.

Teaching Strategy 3 Teach Self-Assessment

- One important skill that can result from an authentic assessment task is improvement in a student's ability to evaluate his or her own work prior to completion.
- To help students as they develop an assessment task or product, ask them to consider the following: What part of the product or process did they like best? Which tasks created the most roadblocks to completion? How would they evaluate their own work process?

INFORMATION PROBLEM SOLVING

ASK QUESTIONS

UNDERSTANDING THE TASK

- Select a reasonable and focused topic.
- Know the purpose of the product.
- Understand how the product will be presented.
- Identify the audience for the product.

SURVEY EXISTING KNOWLEDGE AND PREPARE FOR NEW LEARNING

- Summarize what is known.
- Outline what needs to be learned.
- Identify information sources.
- Prepare a task/time management plan.

RESEARCH THE SELECTED TOPIC

- Use a variety of quality information sources.
- Collect and organize information.

CONSTRUCT A PRODUCT

- Writing—Reports, Journal Entries, Scripts
- Oral Presentations—Monologues, Skits
- Visuals—Drawings, Models, Bulletin Boards, Maps, Graphs, Mass Media

ASSESS THE WHOLE PROCESS

1. Identify strengths and weaknesses of the process.
2. Identify strengths of the final product.
3. List goals to improve future work.

The Scientific Revolution and the Enlightenment

1500 to 1800

ESSENTIAL QUESTIONS • *How do new ideas change the way people live?* • *How do governments change?*

networks

There's More Online about the developments that led to the Scientific Revolution and the Enlightenment.

CHAPTER 22

Lesson 1 *The Scientific Revolution*

Lesson 2 *The Enlightenment*

The Story Matters . . .

Catherine the Great ruled Russia from 1762 to 1796. Catherine was born a German princess, but at the age of fifteen she married Russian Grand Duke Peter. Soon her husband became the emperor of Russia. Peter, however, was a weak leader. In contrast, Catherine was intelligent and also ambitious. She wanted to rule Russia herself. She used military support to remove her husband from the throne. Soon afterward, he was assassinated.

As empress, Catherine the Great made Russia into a world power. She could be a harsh ruler, especially toward the peasants whom she made serfs. However, she also supported advances in the sciences and culture. Indeed, new ideas were sweeping across most of Europe. Many of them, however, challenged the idea of monarchy.

◄ *Catherine II of Russia became known as Catherine the Great because she expanded her country's borders. This portrait hangs in the Museum of History in Moscow, Russia.*

639

Letter from the Author

Dear World History Teacher,

During the Scientific Revolution, the Western world overthrew the medieval Ptolemaic worldview and arrived at a new conception of the universe: the sun at the center, the planets as material bodies revolving around the sun in elliptical orbits, and an infinite rather than finite world. The development of a scientific method furthered the work of scientists. Highly influenced by the new worldview created by the Scientific Revolution, the philosophers of the eighteenth century believed education could create better human beings and a better human society.

Jackson J. Spielvogel

ENGAGE

Bellringer Read "The Story Matters . . ." aloud in class. Alternately, ask a volunteer to read it aloud. Then discuss what it might have been like to live in Russia during the time of Catherine the Great. **Ask:** Who are some kings and queens that are living today? Have you seen any television shows or news reports about these monarchs? Have a few students share their thoughts. Then **ask:** Why do you think some countries still have kings and queens? Do you think these monarchs have a great deal of power?

Tell the class that during the Scientific Revolution and the Enlightenment, most of the countries in Europe were ruled by monarchs. Tell interested students that they can find more online about Catherine the Great and other monarchs of the 1600s and 1700s.

Making Connections

Read the following information to students:

Catherine the Great had to make big changes in her path from German princess to Russian queen.

- Catherine's name when she was born was Sophie Friederike Auguste.
- Her marriage to Russian Grand Duke Peter was arranged by King Frederick II of Prussia to strengthen the relationship between Prussia (then part of Germany) and Russia.
- To prepare for the marriage, Sophie had to learn how to speak Russian, convert to the Russian Orthodox faith, change her name, and study Russian culture.
- Interestingly, in doing so, she became more overtly "Russian" than her husband, Grand Duke Peter, who liked German and Prussian ways and who was of the Protestant faith.

CHAPTER 22
Place and Time

TEACH & ASSESS

Step Into the Place

G1 Critical Thinking Skills

Analyzing Maps Direct students' attention to the Chapter Opener map that shows the Centers of Enlightenment. Remind students about the countries in Europe they already have studied in the chapter on the Renaissance. Discuss with the class how the locations of England, France, Germany, and Italy gave them access to the spread of ideas.

Have volunteers analyze the map of Europe and mark where they think new ideas about science and government might have started. **Ask:** What do you think are the things, geographically, that would most help the spread of ideas? *(having other countries nearby, or easy access to oceans or rivers)* What would be the things, geographically, which would be most likely to slow the spread of ideas? *(being far removed from other places, or blocked by a desert, mountains, or other barrier)*

As a class, discuss the Map Focus questions.

Content Background Knowledge

- Each of the Enlightenment centers contributed something different to the movement. Amsterdam and London were homes of the big publishers, and they printed many of the important books that helped spread the ideas of the Enlightenment.
- Paris was one of the main places where these books were read, and some circulated secretly.
- New public places emerged, such as salons and coffeehouses. People could gather there and share ideas.

ANSWERS, p. 640

Step Into the Place

1. Paris was the Enlightenment center of France.
2. Six Enlightenment centers were located either along the coast of the Baltic Sea or along a river.
3. St. Petersburg was the Enlightenment center that was the farthest away from Central Europe.
4. CRITICAL THINKING Answers will vary. Because many Enlightenment centers were located along waterways, people could easily spread ideas by ship to other lands.

Step Into the Time

Answers will vary but should demonstrate awareness of the level of scientific knowledge in Europe before the Enlightenment.

CHAPTER 22 CCSS
Place and Time: The Scientific Revolution and the Enlightenment 1500 to 1800

The Scientific Revolution and the Enlightenment began in Europe. Thinkers from various countries developed ideas about the world based on reason. These ideas gradually spread throughout Europe and beyond.

Step Into the Place

G1 **MAP FOCUS** Some cities in Europe were centers for Enlightenment ideas. Many of these cities were national capitals. Monarchs ruled them and supported these ideas.

1. **LOCATION** What was the Enlightenment center of France? RH.6–8.7
2. **REGION** How many Enlightenment centers were located along a river or coast? RH.6–8.7
3. **MOVEMENT** Which Enlightenment center was the farthest away from central Europe? RH.6–8.7
4. **CRITICAL THINKING** *Analyzing* Do you think the location of Enlightenment centers helped the spread of ideas? Explain. RH.6–8.2

Step Into the Time

G2 **TIME LINE** Choose an event from the time line for Europe, and write a paragraph that predicts the results of the event. RH.6–8.7, WHST.6–8.2, WHST.6–8.10

EUROPE
- **1543** Copernicus publishes theory that the sun is the center of the solar system
- **1632** Galileo writes book supporting Copernicus's theory

THE WORLD
- **1526** Mughal dynasty begins in India
- **1603** Tokugawa Ieyasu rules Japan

1500 · 1600

Project-Based Learning

Hands-On Chapter Project

Scientific Revolution Newspaper Article

Students will create a newspaper article describing an important scientist and discovery of the Scientific Revolution. Conduct a class discussion to review what students have learned about scientists and discoveries of the Scientific Revolution. Then students will divide into small groups, and each will choose a scientist and a discovery. Students will use discussions to help them plan, research, and write their newspaper articles. Next, each group will present their article to the class. Finally, students will evaluate their research, content, and presentation using an assessment rubric.

Technology Extension

Podcast or Role-Play Interview

Podcasts are audio files that can be downloaded and listened to. First, have groups write the dialogue for an interview of their historic figure. Then have students record their interview with a cell phone, a computer-based audio editing program, or a portable mp3 player with a microphone attachment. To learn more about podcasts, visit the Podcast page at EdTechTeacher's Teaching History with Technology site: http://thwt.org/historypodcasts.html.

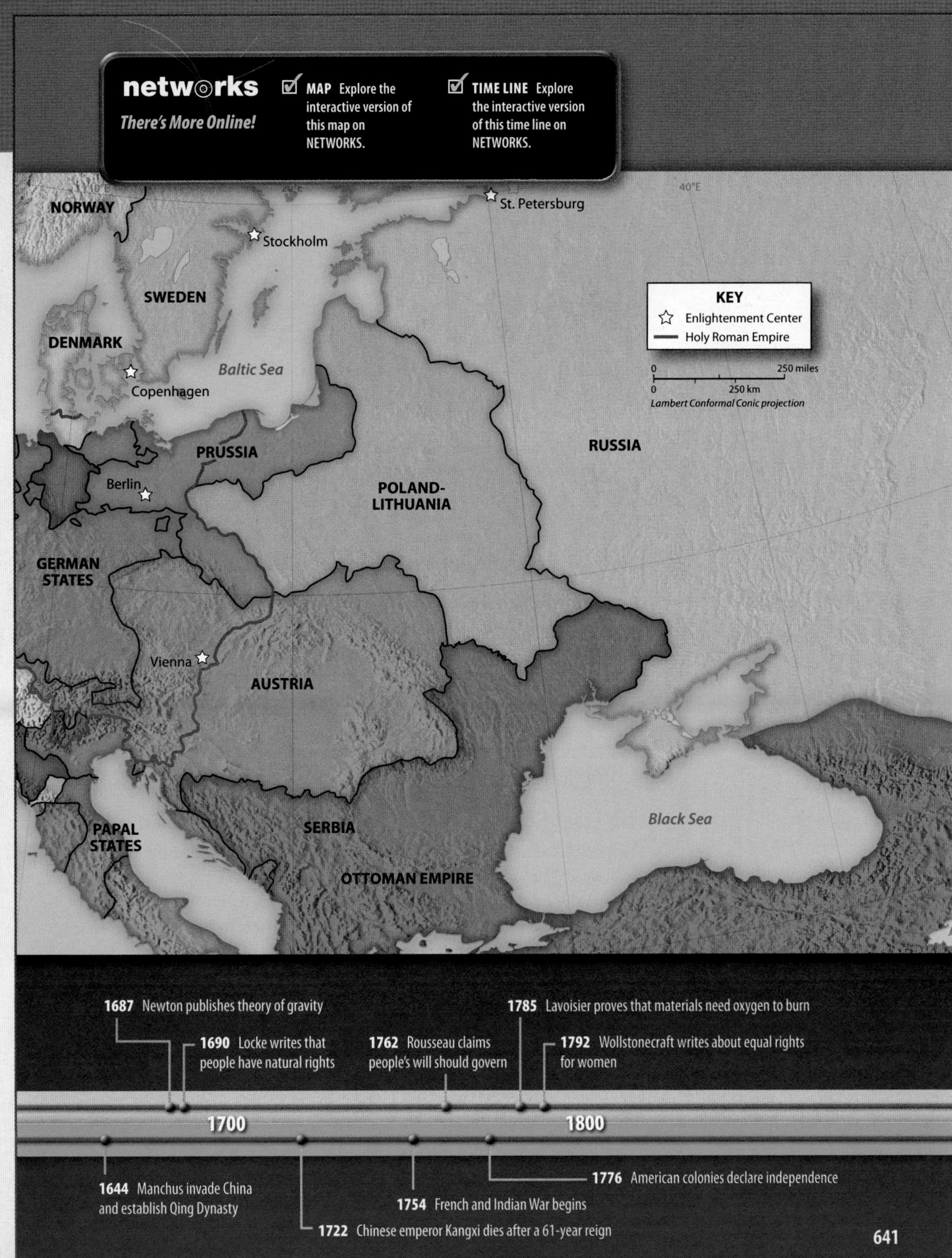

CHAPTER 22
Place and Time

Step Into the Time

C2 Critical Thinking Skills

Making Inferences Have students review the time line for the chapter. Explain that they will be studying events in Europe from about 1500 to 1800. **Ask:** **Based on the information in the time line, what can you infer about what was happening in Europe beginning around the 1500s?** *(Copernicus, Galileo, and Newton developed new ideas about the universe. Locke and Rousseau came up with new ideas about the nature of man. Wollstonecraft stressed that women should have equal rights with men. Lavoisier proved that materials need oxygen to burn.)*

Remind students to use the time lines in their books to help them keep in mind when each of these events took place in relation to the others.

CLOSE AND REFLECT

Discuss the map, time line, and other information presented in the Chapter Opener. Have students summarize what they've learned and predict what they may learn in the upcoming chapter.

WORKSHEET

What Do You Know? Activity: The Scientific Revolution and the Enlightenment: Cloze

Assessing Background Knowledge Direct students to read the paragraphs on the worksheet. Then have them fill in each blank with the correct term from the box. Next, take a poll for each blank to see how many students filled it in correctly. Use this information to tailor your lessons to focus on students' misconceptions. After students complete the chapter, have them reread the paragraphs and reevaluate their original answers. Ask students who changed their responses to explain why they did so. *(Students should cite facts from the chapter.)* AL

See page 639B for other online activities.

ENGAGE

Bellringer Point out to students that much of our modern technology relies on scientific concepts that were developed over time. Ask small groups of students to list as many branches of science as they can think of. Then challenge them to come up with scientific concepts that were developed within each branch of science. *(Example: astronomy—planets rotate around the sun.)* Have groups compare lists. Tell students that in this lesson, they will be learning about the development of scientific thought, with an emphasis on advances made in Europe.

TEACH & ASSESS

R Reading Skills

Finding the Main Idea After reading the introductory paragraph for "Early Science," have students determine the main idea and write it as a sentence. *(Possible answer: People have always studied the world to see how things work, and this is called science.)* Hold a class discussion about the concepts in this section. AL

C Critical Thinking Skills

Interpreting Read the section "The First Scientists." **Ask:**

- **What were some of the key advances made by the Greeks?** *(They used reason to study nature and develop theories. Aristotle classified living things. Ptolemy advanced the geocentric theory in astronomy.)*
- **How have these early scientists affected how we approach modern science?** *(We've built upon their knowledge, and we still classify things based on similarities and differences.)* **Verbal/Linguistic**

Content Background Knowledge

- The Greek philosopher Aristotle lived from 384–322 B.C.
- Aristotle's father was a physician in the royal court, and at an early age, Aristotle became interested in biology. The young Aristotle became a tutor for Alexander the Great.
- Aristotle grew up to develop a form of logic that he applied in the many books he wrote about science, philosophy, politics, ethics, and more. Aristotle is sometimes referred to as the founder of logic.

ANSWER, p. 642

TAKING NOTES: **Universe:** Copernicus forms the heliocentric theory of the universe; Kepler refines Copernicus's view of the universe; Galileo supports the heliocentric view of the universe; **Human Body:** Vesalius describes the internal structure of the human body; Hooke discovers cells; van Leeuwenhoek discovers bacteria.

networks
There's More Online!

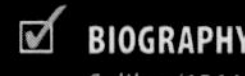

☑ **BIOGRAPHY**
Galileo (1564–1642)

☑ **CHART/GRAPH**
- Hindu-Arabic Numbers/ Roman Numerals
- Scientific Revolution
- Scientific Method

Lesson 1
The Scientific Revolution

ESSENTIAL QUESTION *How do new ideas change the way people live?*

IT MATTERS BECAUSE
The advances made during the Scientific Revolution laid the groundwork for modern science.

Early Science

GUIDING QUESTION ***How were the scientific ideas of early thinkers passed on to later generations?***

R During the Renaissance and the Age of Exploration, people developed new ways to learn about nature. However, humans have always shown an interest in the world around them. Thousands of years ago, people began watching plants and animals grow. Activities such as these represented the beginnings of science. Science is any organized study of the physical world. Scientists study the physical world to determine how things work.

The First Scientists

C The people of ancient civilizations developed science to solve problems. They used mathematics to keep records. People who studied the movement of the stars developed astronomy. This science helped people keep time and decide when to plant crops.

The ancient Greeks developed a large amount of scientific information. They believed that reason was a way to analyze nature. Their studies helped them develop theories. A **theory** is an explanation for how or why something happens. Theories are based on what people can observe about a thing or event. A theory may be incorrect, but it seems to explain the facts.

Reading HELPDESK CCSS

Taking Notes: *Categorizing*
Use a chart like this one to categorize the main advances of the Scientific Revolution concerning the universe or the human body. RH.6–8.2

Scientific Advances

Universe	Human Body

Content Vocabulary (Tier 3 Words)
- **geocentric**
- **Scientific Revolution**
- **heliocentric**

networks ***Online Teaching Options***

VIDEO

Planetary Motion: Kepler's Three Laws

Summarizing Have students watch this video about how Kepler used the work of Copernicus and Tycho Brahe to inform his study of planetary motion. Ask students to list the main points of the video and use them to write a short summary.

See page 639C for other online activities.

The ancient Greeks and Romans made many scientific advances. The Greek philosopher Aristotle (A•ruh•STAH•tuhl), for example, gathered facts about plants and animals. He then classified living things by arranging them into groups based on their similarities and differences. However, classical thinkers did not conduct scientific experiments. That means they did not test new ideas to find out whether they were true. Instead, they based their conclusions on "common sense," which led to many false beliefs. For instance, during Roman times, the Egyptian-born astronomer Ptolemy (TAH•luh•mee) stated that the sun and the planets moved around the Earth. His **geocentric** (JEE•oh•SEHN•trihk), or Earth-centered, theory was accepted in Europe for more than 1,400 years.

Medieval Science

During the Middle Ages, most Europeans were interested in religious ideas. Few people were interested in studying nature. Their ideas about science were based mostly on ancient classical writings. They did not think it was necessary to research the facts and draw their own conclusions. Many of the classical writings were poorly preserved. As people wrote out copies of the old texts, they sometimes made errors that changed the information.

C At the same time, Arabs and Jews in the Islamic empire preserved Greek and Roman science. They copied many Greek and Roman works into Arabic. They also came into contact with the Indian system of numbers that is used today. This system of numbers is now called Indian-Arabic.

W Arab and Jewish scientists made their own advances in mathematics, astronomy, and medicine. Even with these achievements, scientists in the Islamic world did not conduct experiments.

During the 1100s, European thinkers began to have more contact with Islamic peoples. As a result, they gained a renewed interest in science. Europeans began to read copies of Islamic works in Latin. After the Indian-Arabic system of numbers reached Europe, people adopted it in place of Roman numerals.

Thinkstock/Jupiterimages

In today's world, we use Indian-Arabic numbers. However, during the Middle Ages in Europe, Roman numerals were more common. The chart at the bottom of this page compares the two number systems.

▶ CRITICAL THINKING

Making Inferences How would the number 17 be written using Roman numerals?

Indian-Arabic Numbers	Roman Numerals
1	I
2	II
3	III
4	IV
5	V
6	VI
7	VII
8	VIII
9	IX
10	X
50	L
100	C
1,000	M

Content Vocabulary (Tier 3 Words)
- **ellipses**
- **gravity**
- **elements**
- **rationalism**
- **scientific method**

geocentric an earth-centered theory; having or relating to the earth as the center

Academic Vocabulary (Tier 2 Words)

theory an explanation for how or why something happens

Lesson 1 643

C Critical Thinking Skills

Drawing Conclusions Prompt students to consider the lasting contributions of the Greeks. **Ask:** Why were the Greeks important to later scientists? *(Greek ideas influenced Arab and Jewish scholars and were later rediscovered by Europeans, encouraging the development of new scientific ideas.)* AL Verbal/Linguistic

W Writing Skills

Informative/Explanatory Have students write a short essay comparing and contrasting the ancient Greek and Roman attitudes toward science with that of the Europeans in the Middle Ages. Ask students to cite the text to support their ideas. AL Verbal/Linguistic

CHART

Indian-Arabic and Roman Numerals

Analyzing Information Have students use this interactive chart to translate Indian-Arabic numbers into Roman numerals. Based on what they've learned from the chart, have students create a list of the most important Roman numerals, including 1, 5, 10, 50, and 100 *(I, V, X, L, C)*.

See page 639C for other online activities.

networks Indian-Arabic and Roman Numerals

Directions: Click the "Hint" and "Roman" columns to learn how to write each Indian-Arabic number in Roman numerals.

Indian-Arabic	Hint	Roman
12		
19	10 + (10 - 1)	XIX
25		
103	100 + 1 + 1 + 1	CIII
60		
15	10 + 5	XV
72		
90	100 - 10	XC

ANSWER, p. 643

CRITICAL THINKING The number 17 would be written as XVII using Roman numerals.

TEACH & ASSESS

V Visual Skills

Creating Charts Lead a class discussion about what the European explorations of the 1400s contributed to science. Have students each develop a chart in which they list branches of science such as geography, the study of plants, or the study of animals. Have students list under each category the types of things—such as size of oceans—that they believe the Europeans discovered and which added to the Europeans' scientific knowledge. **Visual/Spatial**

R Reading Skills

Determining Word Meanings Refer students to the portion of the text that contains the term *Scientific Revolution.* **Ask:** **Why is the word *revolution* used in referring to the advance of science?** Have students look up the definition of *revolution* in a dictionary. Lead a class discussion in which students examine the meaning of *revolution* in relation to the term *Scientific Revolution* and how it affects the meaning of the term. ELL

C Critical Thinking Skills

Determining Central Issues Read the section about Copernicus and the Church's reaction to his theory about a heliocentric universe. **Ask:**

- **Why do you think the publication of Copernicus's book was delayed?** *(His findings disagreed with Church teachings.)*
- **What were the central issues behind the negative reaction to Copernicus's theory?** *(These contradictory findings may have threatened the Church's authority or power over the people, and might have affected the trust that people had in the Church.)* RI **Verbal/Linguistic**

ANSWER, p. 644

✓ PROGRESS CHECK During ancient and medieval times, science was practiced by using "common sense." This method did not involve experimentation.

Thomas Aquinas (uh•KWY•nuhs) and other Christian thinkers showed that Christianity and reason could work together. Also, Europeans began building new universities. In these schools, teachers and students helped the growth of science.

Beginning in the 1400s, voyages of exploration added to scientific knowledge in Europe. Europeans began to create better charts and maps. These tools helped explorers reach different parts of the world. As more of the world was explored, people learned new information about the size of oceans and continents. Scientists gathered data about diseases, animals, and plants and organized the new information.

Gradually, scientific knowledge **expanded** in Europe. As this happened, a new understanding of the natural world developed.

✓ PROGRESS CHECK

Describing How was science practiced in ancient and medieval times?

New Ideas About the Universe

GUIDING QUESTION *Why did European ideas about the universe change during the 1500s and 1600s?*

In the 1500s, Europeans began to think differently about science. They began to realize that scientists had to use mathematics and experiments to make advances. This new way of thinking led to the **Scientific Revolution**. This revolution changed how Europeans understood science and how they searched for knowledge. The Scientific Revolution first affected astronomy, the science that studies the planets and stars of the universe. New discoveries in this field began to change European thinking about the universe. They challenged the traditional idea that God had made the Earth as the center of the universe.

Copernicus and Ptolemy

Nicolaus Copernicus (koh•PUHR•nih•kuhs) was a Polish astronomer. In 1491, he began his career at a university in Poland. A year later, Columbus reached the Americas. Like Columbus, Copernicus challenged old beliefs held by Europeans.

In 1543, Copernicus wrote a book called *On the Revolutions of the Heavenly Spheres.* He disagreed with Ptolemy's theory that the Earth was the center of the universe. Copernicus developed a **heliocentric** (HEE•lee•oh•SEHN•trihk), or sun-centered,

Reading HELPDESK (CCSS)

Scientific Revolution a period from the 1500s to the 1700s in which many scientific advances changed people's traditional beliefs

heliocentric having or relating to the sun as the center

ellipses ovals shapes

Academic Vocabulary (Tier 2 Words)

expand to increase in number, volume, or scope

networks Online Teaching Options

GAME

Ptolemy and Copernicus Column Game

Comparing and Contrasting Have students play this column game and then participate in a class discussion to compare and contrast Ptolemy and Copernicus.

See page 639C for other online activities.

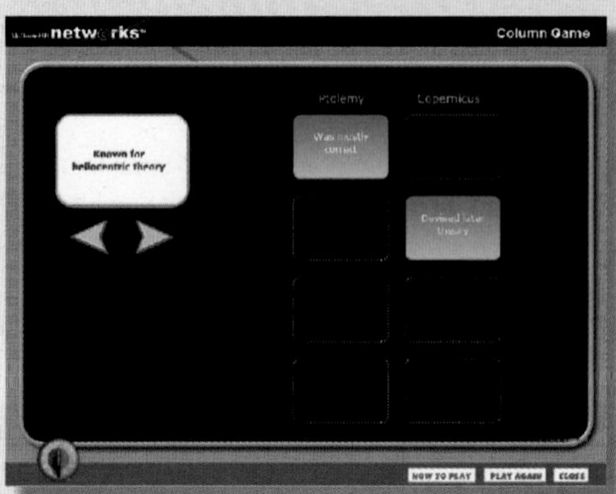

A NEW VIEW OF THE UNIVERSE

Ptolemy, a Greek astronomer of Egyptian descent, claimed that the planets and the sun revolved around Earth. His theory was accepted for more than a thousand years.

Ptolemaic Universe

Fixed Stars, Prime Mover, Saturn, Jupiter, Mars, Sun, Venus, Mercury, Earth, Moon

The theory of Copernicus gave a new perspective on the universe. He believed that the Earth and other planets orbit the sun. He also stated that Earth rotates daily on its axis. This new theory proved accurate in many ways.

Copernican Universe

Fixed Stars, Saturn, Jupiter, Moon, Mars, Earth, Venus, Sun, Mercury

V

theory of the universe. Copernicus believed that the sun was the center of the universe. Earth and the other planets followed a circular path around the sun.

Copernicus's theory disagreed with church teachings. As a result, publication of his book was delayed. He reportedly did not receive the first copy until he was dying.

Kepler's Ideas About Planets

C

A German astronomer named Johannes Kepler (KEH• pluhr) made more advances. He used mathematics to support Copernicus's theory that the planets revolve around the sun. His findings also made corrections to the theory. Kepler added the idea that the planets move in oval paths called **ellipses** (ih• LIHP•seez) instead of the circular paths in Copernicus's theory.

Also, Kepler stated that planets do not always travel at the same speed. Instead, they move faster as they approach the sun and slower as they move away from it. Kepler's theory provided a simpler explanation for the movements of the planets. In addition, it marked the beginning of modern astronomy.

▶ CRITICAL THINKING
Analyzing Study the diagrams. How did the theory of Copernicus differ from the theory of Ptolemy?

(t) Joos van Gent/The Bridgeman Art Library/Getty Images. (b) Bettmann/CORBIS

Lesson 1 645

V Visual Skills

Integrating Visual Information Have students look closely at the text and illustrations in the section "A New View of the Universe." **Ask:**

- What is the main idea of this section? *(a comparison of Copernicus's view of the universe with Ptolemy's)*
- How does this section achieve its goal to convey the main idea? *(through text explanations, diagrams of each view of the universe, and an illustration of each man)*
- Is the section effective in getting across the information? Why or why not? What new or extra information do the illustrations add? **Visual/Spatial**

C Critical Thinking Skills

Determining Central Ideas Have students study the section about Kepler. **Ask:**

- What is the central scientific idea around which this text is organized? *(the idea that the planets revolve around the sun)*
- How does the text develop the central idea? *(by telling how Kepler added to it)*

IMAGE

The Hubble Telescope

Analyzing Information Have students review this interactive image about the Hubble Telescope and relate what they learn from the image to the information about Kepler's discoveries from the text. **Ask:** How might Kepler's ideas and discoveries have led to some of the questions that scientists who came after him asked? *(They gave a basis for other scientists to build upon, and they marked the beginning of modern astronomy.)*

See page 639C for other online activities.

ANSWER, p. 645

CRITICAL THINKING Copernicus believed that Earth and other planets orbited the sun, which was contrary to Ptolemy's view that the sun revolved around Earth.

C Critical Thinking Skills

Predicting Consequences Remind students that the nature of scientific discovery is additive and constantly changing. **Ask: How do you think the advances of Copernicus, Kepler, and Galileo influenced later scientists?** *(Answers will vary, but students might mention that Newton probably supports a heliocentric view of the universe because of the advances made by previous scientists. Also, later scientists like Galileo will probably use experiments.)* Record their answers. **BL Verbal/Linguistic**

T Technology Skills

Researching on the Internet Have students formulate a question about one of Galileo's achievements. For example: *What was Galileo's telescope like?* Then have them do research on the Internet to find an answer to the question. Have students share their discoveries in small groups. **BL Interpersonal**

R Reading Skills

Identifying Ask students to consider the way in which the passage is written and identify the structure used in the text to describe Galileo's achievements. **Ask: Is the text organized in sequence, by cause and effect, or in a compare/contrast structure?** *(compare/contrast)* Have students cite evidence from the text to support their answers. **Verbal/Linguistic**

BIOGRAPHY

Galileo (1564–1642)

In 1632, Galileo, an Italian, published his ideas. Soon afterward, Catholic Church officials banned his book. They believed that the Christian Bible taught that the Earth was the center of the universe. Galileo's theory disagreed and stated the Earth revolved around the sun. Because of this, Galileo was ordered to stand trial for heresy. He was also forced to withdraw many of his statements.

▶ **CRITICAL THINKING**
Explaining Why did the Catholic Church want to stop the spread of Galileo's ideas?

Galileo's Achievements

An Italian scientist named Galileo Galilei (GA•luh•LEE•oh GA•luh•LY) made the next great discovery in the Scientific Revolution. He believed that conducting experiments was the correct way to achieve new scientific knowledge. His studies caused him to disagree with some long-held ideas. For example, Aristotle had thought that heavy objects fall to the ground faster than objects that weigh less. Galileo's experiments proved that was not correct. Objects fall at the same speed no matter what they weigh. **T**

Galileo also believed that scientific instruments could help people better explore the natural world. He heard about an early telescope and designed one of his own. With the telescope, Galileo found evidence that supported Copernicus's theory that Earth revolves around the sun. **R**

Galileo also improved the making of clocks. One day, Galileo was watching an overhead lamp swing back and forth from a cathedral ceiling. He timed each swing and discovered that all of the swings took the same amount of time. Galileo used this idea to make a clock that had a swinging pendulum. The pendulum made the clock more accurate.

C Galileo also developed new scientific instruments. In 1593, he invented a water thermometer. People could now measure changes in temperature. An assistant of Galileo then built the first barometer, an instrument that measures air pressure.

✓ **PROGRESS CHECK**

Comparing and Contrasting How did Galileo go about making scientific discoveries?

New Scientific Advances

GUIDING QUESTION *Which discoveries did scientists make during the 1600s and 1700s?*

During the 1600s and 1700s, scientists built on the advances of Copernicus, Kepler, and Galileo. These scientists made advances in medicine, astronomy, and physics.

Newton's Universe

Isaac Newton was an English mathematician. According to tradition, Newton was sitting in his garden one day when he saw an apple fall to the ground. The apple's fall led him to the

Reading **HELP**DESK 

gravity the attraction that the Earth has on an object on or near its surface

networks ***Online Teaching Options***

SLIDE SHOW

Sir Isaac Newton

Formulating Questions Have students view this slide show about Newton and his ideas and then formulate several questions about Newton and his scientific laws and discoveries. Have small groups share their questions and try to answer them. **Interpersonal**

See page 639C for other online activities.

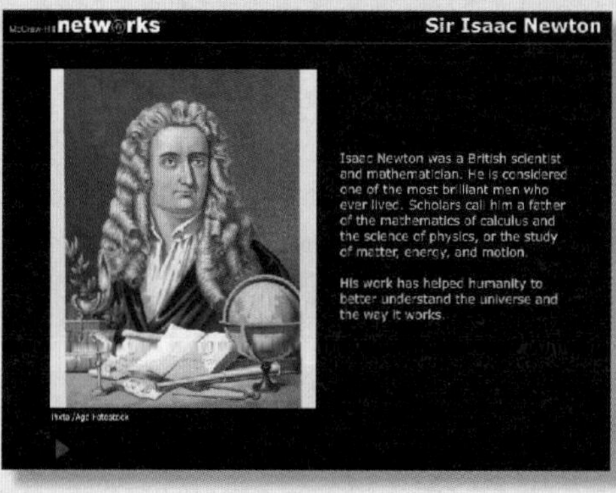

ANSWERS, p. 646

CRITICAL THINKING Galileo's ideas disagreed with the Catholic Church's view of the universe. Because of this, the Church felt threatened by Galileo. The Church might have feared that an increasing number of people would disagree with Church teachings.

✓ **PROGRESS CHECK** Galileo believed that conducting experiments was the correct way to go about making scientific discoveries.

idea of **gravity**. Gravity is the pull of the Earth or other bodies in space on objects that are on or near them.

R In 1687, Newton published a book called *Principia*. This was one of the most important books in the history of modern science. In *Principia,* Newton gave his laws, or well-tested theories, about the motion of objects on Earth and in space. The most important was the law of gravitation. It states that the force of gravity holds the solar system together. It does this by keeping the sun and the planets in their orbits. Newton's ideas greatly influenced the thinking of other scientists.

Isaac Newton analyzed rays of light. His experiments showed that light is made up of a wide band of colors called a spectrum.

▶ CRITICAL THINKING
Speculating Do you think Aristotle's scientific method could have been used to discover the spectrum? Explain your answer.

Studying the Human Body

C Many changes were made in medicine during the 1500s and 1600s. Since ancient times, the teachings of the Greek physician Galen had influenced European doctors. Galen wanted to study the human body, but he was not allowed to dissect, or cut open, dead human bodies. So, he dissected animals instead.

In the 1500s, the Flemish doctor Andreas Vesalius (vuh•SAY•lee•uhs) advanced medical research. He began dissecting dead human bodies. In 1543, he published *On the Structure of the Human Body.* In it, Vesalius described the internal structure of the human body. His account challenged many of Galen's ideas.

THE SCIENTIFIC REVOLUTION — INFOGRAPHIC

Scientist	Nation	Discoveries
Nicolaus Copernicus (1473–1543)	Poland	Earth orbits the Sun; Earth rotates on its axis
Galileo Galilei (1564–1642)	Italy	other planets have moons
Johannes Kepler (1571–1630)	Germany	planets have elliptical orbits
William Harvey (1578–1657)	England	heart pumps blood
Robert Hooke (1635–1703)	England	cells
Robert Boyle (1627–1691)	Ireland	matter is made up of elements
Isaac Newton (1642–1727)	England	gravity; laws of motion; calculus
Antoine Lavoisier (1743–1794)	France	how materials burn

During the Scientific Revolution, scientists made discoveries in many fields, such as astronomy and medicine. For example, William Harvey discovered that the heart pumps blood.

▶ CRITICAL THINKING
Comparing What other scientists worked with the same subject matter as Galileo?

V

R Reading Skills

Using Context Clues Refer students to the name of Newton's book, *Principia*. Point out that the full Latin title of the book was *Philosophiæ Naturalis Principia Mathematica*. **Ask:**

- **What do you think the word *Principia* means?** *(principles)*
- **Why would he call the book *Principles*? What principles is he referring to?** *(His laws and theories are types of principles.)* Discuss this with students and guide them to extract the full translation of the title: *Mathematical Principles of Natural Philosophy.* ELL

C Critical Thinking Skills

Drawing Conclusions Have students read the information about Galen and Vesalius. **Ask:**

- **What conclusions can you draw about scientific method based on the fact that Vesalius's dissection of dead human bodies led to different conclusions than Galen had come to, based on *his* dissection of animals?** *(that scientists keep trying to get better information to question and challenge old information, to make sure it's correct)*
- **Do scientists use this method today?** *(Yes, they continue to question and challenge and seek further information.)* BL **Verbal/Linguistic**

V Visual Skills

Creating Charts Ask students to study the chart about the Scientific Revolution. Have them create a chart in the same format in which they add the information about the Greek physician Galen and the Flemish doctor Andreas Vesalius. **Ask:**

- **Do you have enough information from the text to complete the chart?** *(no)*
- **Which information are you missing?** *(the birth and death dates of the doctors)*

Have students find this information on the Internet to complete their entries. **Visual/Spatial**

WHITEBOARD ACTIVITY

Leaders of the Scientific Revolution

Summarizing Show students the Interactive Whiteboard Activity on Bacon, Descartes, Newton, Copernicus, and Boyle. Have them identify the key accomplishments of each thinker.

See page 639C for other online activities.

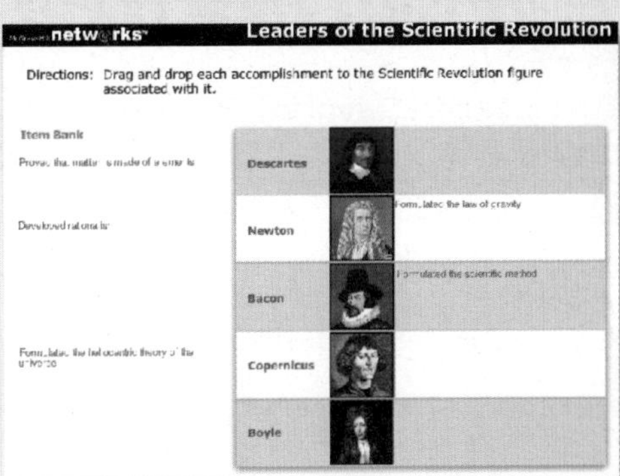

ANSWERS, p. 647

CRITICAL THINKING No; Aristotle's method was based on using "common sense." If a person just observes light, "common sense" tells the person that light is not made of many colors, because this fact is not easily seen with simple observation.

INFOGRAPHIC
CRITICAL THINKING Copernicus and Kepler worked with the same subject matter as Galileo.

R Reading Skills

Summarizing Have students read the first paragraph on the page and write a sentence summarizing the information. Challenge students to make their summaries as short and yet as complete as possible. Emphasize that practicing the ability to express a concise summary is a good way to better understand the reading material. **Verbal/Linguistic**

C Critical Thinking Skills

Hypothesizing Have students read about the scientists who proved that materials need oxygen in order to burn. **Ask:** How do you think that Antoine and Marie Lavoisier might have proved that things need oxygen to burn? What experiments might they have done? *(trying to burn things with and without oxygen present)* **Verbal/Linguistic**

W Writing Skills

Argument Have students read the section about Descartes. Tell them that Descartes claimed that mathematics is the source of scientific truth because it uses logic to move from simple principles to more complex truths. **Ask:** Do you agree with Descartes? Do believe this is the case? Have students write an essay arguing in favor of or against Descartes's claim. Ask students to support their arguments with as many details as possible from the text or from their experiences. BL **Intrapersonal**

ANSWER, p. 648

✓ PROGRESS CHECK According to Newton, the planets are held in orbit by gravity.

Early microscopes (left) were used to discover information about items too small to see, like bacteria and cells. Early telescopes (below) were used to learn about larger things in space, like planets and stars.

Other advances in medicine took place. In the early 1600s, an English scientist named Robert Hooke began using a microscope. He soon discovered cells, which are the smallest units of living matter. Then the Dutch merchant Antonie van Leeuwenhoek (LAY•vuhn•huk) improved the microscope by using more powerful lenses. He used this microscope to discover tiny organisms later called bacteria (bak•TIHR•ee•uh). **R**

In the mid-1600s, the Irish scientist Robert Boyle proved that all matter is made up of **elements**. Elements are basic materials that cannot be broken down into simpler parts.

During the 1700s, European scientists discovered gases such as hydrogen, carbon dioxide, and oxygen. By 1783, Antoine Lavoisier (AN•twahn luh•WAH•zee•AY) of France proved that materials need oxygen in order to burn. Marie Lavoisier, also a scientist, made contributions to her husband's work. **C**

✓ PROGRESS CHECK

Identifying According to Newton, how are the planets held in orbit?

The Triumph of Reason

GUIDING QUESTION ***How did Europeans of the 1600s and 1700s develop new ways of gaining knowledge?***

European thinkers soon began to apply the ideas of science to human society. These thinkers believed science revealed the natural laws of the universe. By using reason, people could study these laws and use them to solve many human problems.

Descartes and Pascal

France became a major center of scientific thought. In 1637, the French René Descartes (reh•NAY day•KAHRT) wrote a book called *Discourse on Method*. In this book, Descartes studied the problem of knowing what is true. To find truth, he decided to ignore everything he had learned and start over. However, one fact seemed to be beyond doubt. This fact was his own existence. To summarize this idea, Descartes wrote the phrase, "I think, therefore I am." **W**

In his work, Descartes claimed that mathematics is the source of scientific truth. In mathematics, he said, the answers are always true. His reasoning was that mathematics begins with

Reading HELPDESK (CCSS)

element a substance that consists of atoms of only one kind

rationalism the belief that reason and experience must be present for the solution of problems

scientific method the steps for an orderly search for knowledge

Academic Vocabulary (Tier 2 Words)

generation the time span between the birth of parents and the birth of their children

networks Online Teaching Options

GAME

The Scientific Revolution Crossword Puzzle

Expressing Have students complete the crossword puzzle and then express in their own words some of the pieces of information about the Scientific Revolution which were most interesting to them.

See page 639C for other online activities.

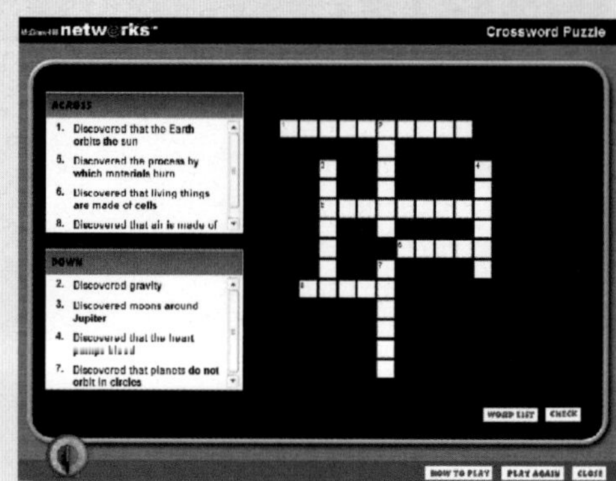

simple principles. It then uses logic, or reason, to move to more complex truths. Descartes is viewed as the founder of modern **rationalism** (RASH•uh•nuh•LIH•zuhm). This is the belief that reason is the main source of knowledge.

C

During the 1600s, another French thinker, Blaise Pascal (blehz pa•SKAL), studied science. At the age of 19, he invented a calculating machine. Pascal believed that reason and scientific ideas based on experiments could solve many practical problems. However, Pascal was also a religious man. He believed that the solutions to moral problems and spiritual truth could come only from faith in Christian teachings.

What Is the Scientific Method?

R

In the 1600s, the English thinker Francis Bacon influenced scientific thought. He believed that unproven ideas from earlier **generations** should be put aside. Bacon believed that to find the truth, you had to first find and examine the facts.

He developed the scientific method. This method is an orderly way of collecting and analyzing evidence. Its basic principles are still used in scientific research today.

The **scientific method** consists of several steps. First, scientists observe facts. Then, they try to find a hypothesis (hy•PAH•thuh•suhs), or an explanation of the facts. Scientists conduct experiments to test the hypothesis. These tests are done under all types of conditions. Repeated experiments may show that the hypothesis is true. Then it is considered a scientific law.

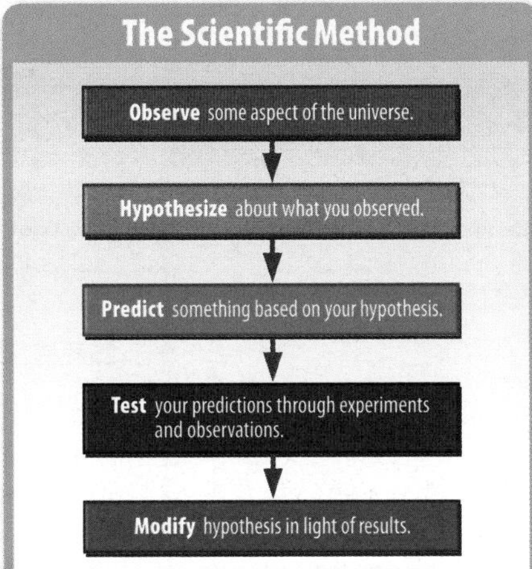

The Scientific Method
Observe some aspect of the universe.
Hypothesize about what you observed.
Predict something based on your hypothesis.
Test your predictions through experiments and observations.
Modify hypothesis in light of results.

The scientific method involves five steps. These steps build on each other.

▶ CRITICAL THINKING

Conjecturing Do you think scientists often have to do the fifth step? Explain.

☑ PROGRESS CHECK

Explaining Why did Descartes believe that mathematics is the source of scientific truth?

LESSON 1 REVIEW (CCSS)

Review Vocabulary (Tier 3 Words)

1. How is *rationalism* used in the *scientific method*? RH.6–8.2, RH.6–8.4

Answer the Guiding Questions

2. ***Identifying*** What was the heliocentric theory and who developed it? RH.6–8.2, RH.6–8.4
3. ***Summarizing*** How did the ancient Greeks study nature? RH.6–8.2
4. ***Explaining*** What instrument made the discovery of bacteria possible? Explain. RH.6–8.2
5. ***Defining*** What is the scientific method? RH.6–8.2, RH.6–8.4
6. **ARGUMENT** During the Scientific Revolution, advances were made in many scientific fields. Choose the step forward that you think is the most significant and explain your choice. WHST.6–8.1, WHST.6–8.10

LESSON 1 REVIEW ANSWERS

1. The scientific method involves a series of steps. Reason and experimentation are used to move from one step to another. The use of reason is called rationalism.
2. Copernicus developed the heliocentric theory, which states that the sun is the center of the universe.
3. The ancient Greeks used reason to study nature. They then developed theories based on their studies. However, they did not use experimentation.
4. The microscope magnified tiny materials, making it possible to see organisms such as bacteria.
5. The scientific method is an orderly way of collecting and analyzing evidence.
6. Answers will vary but should be supported by facts and logical arguments.

C Critical Thinking Skills

Judging Reliability Read the section about Blaise Pascal. **Ask:** What were Pascal's beliefs? Do you think that Pascal's scientific and religious beliefs ever contradicted each other? Why or why not? Discuss the students' opinions about Pascal's beliefs, and ask if they have personal experiences that they can use to support their opinions. **Intrapersonal**

R Reading Skills

Analyzing Information Refer students to the diagram of the steps involved in the scientific method and the text related to the topic. **Ask:**

- **Is it necessary to do the steps of the scientific method in a certain order? Explain.** *(Yes; the steps build on each other. Doing one step out of order would not be logical. A person could not hypothesize about what is observed without observing something first.)*
- **What is the goal of the scientific method?** *(to carefully gather data about the universe and use that data to form theories about how and why the universe looks and works as it does)*
- **Do you think following the scientific method always results in finding the truth?** *(Answers will vary. Some students will recognize that test results might be faulty because of a limited sample being tested or because of a limitation of the hypothesis.)*

Have students complete the Lesson 1 Review.

CLOSE & REFLECT

Review with students some of the key discoveries discussed in the lesson. Then conduct a debate about which discovery is the greatest. Have students form groups of four. Assign each group a discovery from the lesson.

Tell each group to discuss why its discovery is the greatest and to write down at least two reasons. Ask students to re-form into groups based on their opinions. Which discovery do students respond to the most, or are the groups evenly distributed? Did the discussion affect anyone's choice? Then have the students consider the effects these discoveries have had on people's lives. Students can use the whiteboard to record their reasons.

ANSWERS, p. 649

CRITICAL THINKING Yes; it is probably difficult to have predictions that are entirely accurate. Repeated experiments will most likely show some flaws in the prediction. As a result, the hypothesis will need to be modified.

☑ PROGRESS CHECK Mathematics uses reason or logic to move from simple truths to more complex truths. This process makes mathematics accurate. Because of this, Descartes believed that the mathematical process works well for science.

ENGAGE

Bellringer Review the introduction to the section "Reason and Politics." Tell students that thinkers during the Enlightenment started to use reason to determine the best type of government. **Ask:**

- What type of government do you think these thinkers decided was the best? Explain. *(Answers will vary. Students might say the thinkers decided democracy was the best, because it is reasonable to give people a say in the government.)*
- Do you think different thinkers came up with different ideas about the best type of government? *(Answers will vary. Some students might say that using reason will cause thinkers to decide on similar governments. Others will say that people think differently about what is reasonable, so the type of government they decide on could also be different.)*

TEACH & ASSESS

R Reading Skills

Determining Word Meanings Refer students to the phrase *Age of Enlightenment* in the text. Have them use context clues in the passage as they consider the following questions. **Ask:**

- Why is this era called the Age of Enlightenment? *(People were using reason as a "light" to show truth.)*
- What does *enlightenment* mean, and how does it relate to the ideas that were common in this period? *(Enlightenment means "knowledge or insight"; people thought that reason could provide knowledge or insight to people.)* ELL

C Critical Thinking Skills

Evaluating Launch a discussion in which you ask students to consider how they make decisions and what factors and processes are important in making good decisions. **Ask:** Like many scientists, what did political thinkers in this era decide to use as the basis of thinking? Guide students to go beyond the answer of "reason" by reminding them that the scientists based their conclusions on evidence.

ANSWER, p. 650

TAKING NOTES: Answers may vary but may include any of the following: Hobbes—developed the absolutism theory; Locke—thought government should be based on natural laws; Montesquieu—believed in the separation of powers for governments; Voltaire—had many criticisms of traditional beliefs; Diderot—supported religious freedom in a 28-volume encyclopedia; Wollstonecraft—supported equality for women; Rousseau—thought government should be based on a social contract.

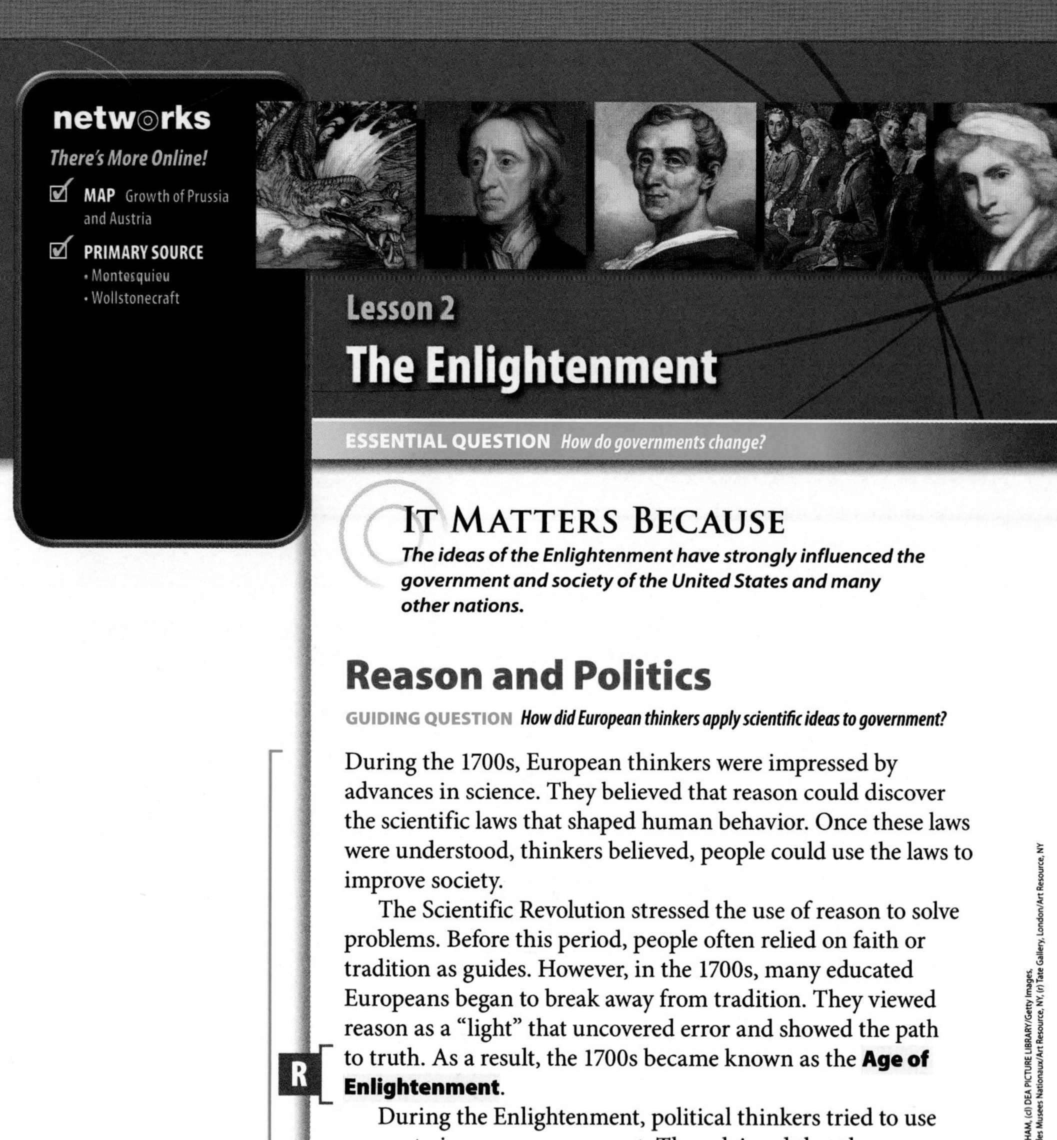

networks
There's More Online!
MAP Growth of Prussia and Austria
PRIMARY SOURCE
• Montesquieu
• Wollstonecraft

Lesson 2
The Enlightenment

ESSENTIAL QUESTION *How do governments change?*

IT MATTERS BECAUSE
The ideas of the Enlightenment have strongly influenced the government and society of the United States and many other nations.

Reason and Politics

GUIDING QUESTION ***How did European thinkers apply scientific ideas to government?***

During the 1700s, European thinkers were impressed by advances in science. They believed that reason could discover the scientific laws that shaped human behavior. Once these laws were understood, thinkers believed, people could use the laws to improve society.

The Scientific Revolution stressed the use of reason to solve problems. Before this period, people often relied on faith or tradition as guides. However, in the 1700s, many educated Europeans began to break away from tradition. They viewed reason as a "light" that uncovered error and showed the path to truth. As a result, the 1700s became known as the **Age of Enlightenment**.

During the Enlightenment, political thinkers tried to use reason to improve government. They claimed that there was a natural law, or a law that applied to everyone and could be understood by reason. This natural law was the key to making government work properly. As early as the 1600s, two English thinkers used natural law to develop very different ideas about government. The two men were Thomas Hobbes and John Locke.

Reading HELPDESK CCSS

Taking Notes: *Identifying*
On a chart like this one, list the main thinkers of the Enlightenment and a major idea for each one. RH.6–8.2

Thinker	Idea

Content Vocabulary (Tier 3 Words)
- Age of Enlightenment
- absolutism
- Glorious Revolution
- constitutional monarchy
- social contract
- separation of powers

650 *The Scientific Revolution and the Enlightenment*

networks Online Teaching Options

VIDEO

Reason and the Age of Enlightenment

Explaining Have students view the video about the Enlightenment, a period of intellectual and philosophical developments in the 18th Century. **Ask:**

- According to this video, what is morality, and how were people in the time of the Enlightenment expected to know how to be moral? *(Morality involves knowing right from wrong. In the time of the Enlightenment, people were supposed to use reason to know right from wrong.)*
- Do you agree with this philosophy? *(Answers will vary.)*

See page 639D for other online activities.

Who Was Thomas Hobbes?

English writer Thomas Hobbes wrote about England's government and society. At the time, England was torn apart by conflict. King Charles I wanted absolute power. Parliament, however, demanded a greater role in governing. The king's supporters fought those who supported Parliament.

Parliament already had some control over the king. In the 1620s, Parliament had forced Charles to sign the Petition of Right. It said the king could not tax the people without Parliament's approval. Also, he could not imprison anyone without a just reason. The Petition also stated that the king could not declare a state of emergency unless the country was at war.

Charles, however, ignored the Petition. His differences with Parliament led to civil war. The fighting finally forced Parliament's supporters to execute Charles. This event shocked Thomas Hobbes, who supported the monarchy.

In Hobbes's *Leviathan*, a sea serpent like the one below represents the powerful ruler necessary to running the most effective type of government—an absolute monarchy.

▶ CRITICAL THINKING
Analyzing How does the image of a serpent help make Hobbes's point about government?

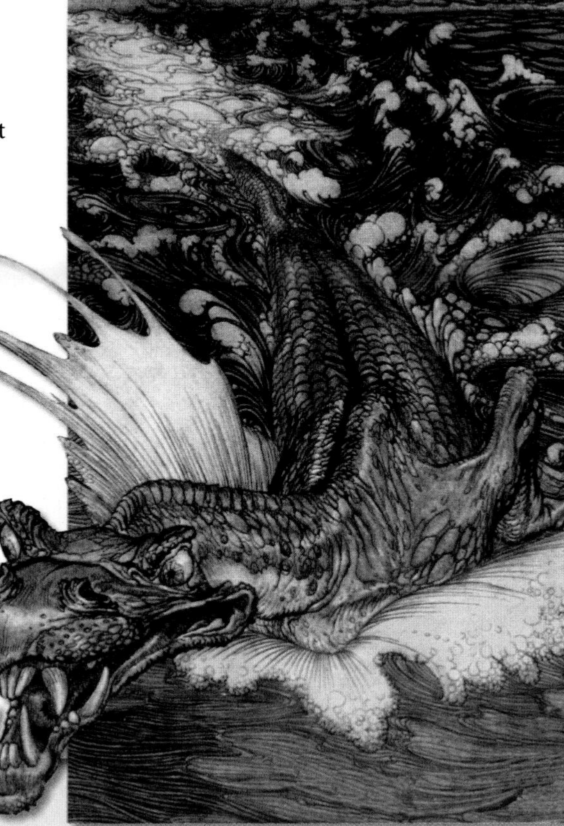

Mary Evans Picture Library/ARTHUR RACKHAM

Hobbes's Beliefs

In 1651, Hobbes wrote a book called *Leviathan*. In this work, Hobbes argued that natural law made absolute monarchy the best form of government. According to Hobbes, humans were naturally violent and selfish. They could not be trusted to make wise decisions on their own. Left to themselves, people would make life "nasty, brutish, and short."

Therefore, Hobbes said, people needed to obey a government that had the power of a leviathan (luh•VY•uh•thuhn), or sea monster. To Hobbes, this meant the rule of a powerful king, because only a strong ruler could give people direction. Under this ruler, people had to remain loyal. This political theory of Hobbes became known as **absolutism** (AB•suh•LOO•tih•zuhm), since it supported a ruler with absolute, or total, power.

Age of Enlightenment the time period in the 1700s during which many Europeans began to break away from tradition and rethink political and social norms
absolutism political system in which a ruler has total power

R Reading Skills

Summarizing Ask students to read the first section on the page and describe the state of England's government during Thomas Hobbes's time in a one-sentence summary. *(Possible summary: There was a struggle for power between King Charles I and Parliament.)* **Verbal/Linguistic**

C Critical Thinking Skills

Evaluating Read the section about Hobbes's beliefs. **Ask:** **Do you think Hobbes had evidence to support his conclusion about the best government?** *(Answers will vary. Some students might say yes, that Hobbes saw people constantly fighting each other in wars and in other ways, so he concluded that people are basically selfish.)*

Making Connections

- The term *absolutism* would become associated with many rulers of this period from England, Europe, and Russia.
- In an "absolutist" government, only the king got to make laws. New kings could even override the laws of the old kings. They could raise taxes whenever they wanted and often had big armies to enforce their power.
- Though "absolutism" refers to absolute power, it was rare that these rulers had total control over their subjects. Their effectiveness was limited by poor transportation, poor communication, and inadequate resources. Much of the king's time and energy was spent trying to satisfy the needs of the nobility.
- After some time, these "absolutist" governments weakened and disappeared.

IMAGE

Leviathan

Explaining Have students view the interactive image and read the text about Leviathan. Ask students to explain why they think Hobbes made the comparison between the biblical sea creature and a supreme ruler. *(Perhaps he thought the creature represented the idea of power and control by fear.)*

See page 639D for other online activities.

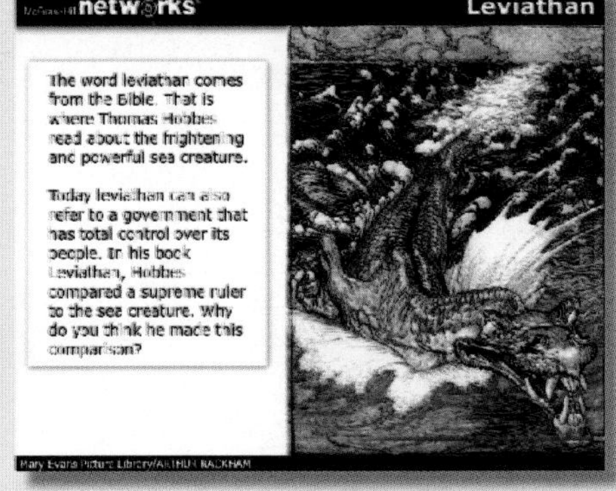

networks
Leviathan
The word leviathan comes from the Bible. That is where Thomas Hobbes read about the frightening and powerful sea creature.
Today leviathan can also refer to a government that has total control over its people. In his book Leviathan, Hobbes compared a supreme ruler to the sea creature. Why do you think he made this comparison?
Mary Evans Picture Library/ARTHUR RACKHAM

ANSWER, p. 651

CRITICAL THINKING The image of a serpent makes Hobbes's point by showing that an effective ruler needed to have the strength and power of a serpent.

John Locke wrote about many subjects, including education and religion. His ideas contributed to the U.S. Declaration of Independence.

▶ CRITICAL THINKING
Making Inferences Would Locke have supported freedom of religion? Explain.

DEA PICTURE LIBRARY/Getty Images

Locke and the Glorious Revolution

Another English thinker, John Locke, believed differently. He used natural law to support citizens' rights. He said the government had to answer to the people. During Locke's life, another English king, James II, wanted to be a strong ruler. Parliament again was opposed to the king's wishes. When civil war threatened in 1688, James fled the country. Parliament then asked Mary, the king's daughter, and her husband, William, to take the throne. This event became known as the "**Glorious Revolution**." **W** **C**

The Glorious Revolution eventually turned England into a **constitutional monarchy.** This is a form of government in which written laws limit the powers of the monarch. In return for the English throne, William and Mary agreed to a Bill of Rights. This document required William and Mary to obey Parliament's laws. The Bill of Rights also **guaranteed** all English people basic rights. For example, people had the right to a fair trial by jury and the right to freedom from cruel punishment for a crime. **R**

In 1690, John Locke wrote a book called *Two Treatises of Government.* His book explained many of the ideas of the Glorious Revolution. Locke stated that government should be based on natural law and natural rights. These rights included the right to life, the right to liberty, and the right to own property.

Locke believed that the purpose of government was to protect people's rights. He said that all governments were based on a **social contract.** This is an agreement between the people and their leaders. If rulers took away people's natural rights, the people had a right to rebel and set up a new government.

Montesquieu and Government

After the Glorious Revolution, many thinkers in France admired the government of England. They liked it better than the absolute monarchy that ruled France. In 1748, a French thinker, Baron Montesquieu (mahn•tuhs•KYOO), published a book called *The Spirit of the Laws.*

In this book, Montesquieu stated that England had the best government. He liked English government because it had a separation of powers. **Separation of powers** means that power should be equally divided among the branches of

Reading HELPDESK (CCSS)

Glorious Revolution the overthrow of King James II of England

constitutional monarchy a political system in which a king or queen rules according to a constitution

social contract an agreement between the people and their government

W Writing Skills

Explanatory Briefly discuss with students John Locke's idea that governments should answer to the people. Have students write an essay explaining what this idea means to them, how it differs from Hobbes's theory of absolutism, and which they feel is the best form of government. **Intrapersonal**

C Critical Thinking Skills

Comparing and Contrasting Ask students to compare and contrast the Glorious Revolution and the American Revolution. **Ask:**

- **How are the Glorious Revolution and the American Revolution different?** *(They happened in different countries and time periods; the American Revolution involved a war, but the Glorious Revolution did not; the American Revolution did away with monarchy, but the Glorious Revolution kept the monarchy.)*
- **How were these two revolutions similar?** *(Both established more liberty for the people; both resulted in a government with a separation of powers.)* BL

R Reading Skills

Determining Word Meanings Have students refer to the paragraph as they elaborate on the meaning of the term *constitutional monarchy.* **Ask: How did the constitutional monarchy guarantee more freedom for the British people?** *(It required the British monarchs to obey Parliament's laws; it gave people the right to a fair trial by jury; it gave people freedom from cruel punishment for a crime.)* ELL **Verbal/Linguistic**

networks Online Teaching Options

IMAGE

John Locke and His Ideas

Making Connections Have students view the interactive image and text about John Locke and his ideas. Ask students to explain which of his ideas are applied to the United States government today.

See page 639D for other online activities.

networks
John Locke and His Ideas
John Locke was a British political philosopher who is considered one of the fathers of the Enlightenment. His ideas greatly influenced the founders of the United States. He believed that people were born with natural rights that no government should deny. This idea influenced Thomas Jefferson's justification for the Declaration of Independence.
Locke rejected the absolutism of Hobbes. He believed in a "social contract" that was an agreement between citizens and rulers, clearly defining the rights of the citizens and the limits of the government's power. According to Locke, a just system of government was based on such an agreement between rulers and citizens.
National Portrait Gallery, London

ANSWER, p. 652

CRITICAL THINKING Yes, Locke claimed that people had a natural right to liberty. This implies that he thought people should have the freedom to choose their own religion.

government: legislative, executive, and judicial. The legislative branch makes the laws. The executive branch enforces the laws. The judicial branch interprets the laws and makes judgments when the laws are broken. By separating these powers, government could not become too powerful and threaten people's rights. As Montesquieu explained in the case of judges:

PRIMARY SOURCE

> "Again, there is no liberty, if the power of judging be not separated from the legislative and executive powers. Were it joined with the legislative, the life and liberty of the subject would be exposed to arbitrary [unreasonable] control, for the judge would be then the legislator. Were it joined to the executive power, the judge might behave with all the violence of an oppressor [cruel dictator]."
>
> —from *The Spirit of the Laws*, 1748

Montesquieu believed in the rights of individuals. His work influenced the writing of the constitutions of many countries, including the United States Constitution.

PROGRESS CHECK

Comparing and Contrasting How did Hobbes and Locke differ in their ideas about government and the people?

Baron Montesquieu traveled through Europe and compared governments. He wrote his conclusions in *The Spirit of Laws*.

▶ CRITICAL THINKING

Drawing Conclusions Why did so many scholars respect Montesquieu's ideas?

The Philosophes of France

GUIDING QUESTION ***How did French thinkers influence Europe during the Enlightenment?***

During the 1700s, France became the most active center of the Enlightenment. Thinkers in France and elsewhere became known by the French name *philosophe* (FEE•luh•ZAWF), which means "philosopher." Most philosophes were writers, teachers, and journalists who often discussed and debated new ideas at gatherings. These gatherings were held in the homes of wealthy citizens.

Philosophes wanted to use reason to improve society. They attacked superstition, or unreasoned beliefs, and disagreed with religious leaders who opposed new scientific discoveries. Philosophes believed in freedom of speech and claimed that each person had the right to liberty. Their ideas spread across Europe.

separation of powers a government structure that has three distinct branches: legislative, executive, and judicial

Academic Vocabulary (Tier 2 Words)

guarantee to make sure or certain; promise

TEACH & ASSESS

C Critical Thinking Skills

Comparing Ask students to consider the accomplishments of Montesquieu. Ask them to compare the ideas of Montesquieu with those of Hobbes and Locke. Which were most similar and why? *(Montesquieu's ideas were most like Locke's because both believed in preserving the rights of individuals.)* AL

V Visual Skills

Creating Visuals Ask students to read the primary-source quote and create a visual that they feel best depicts the negative consequences that would occur with each combination of legislative, executive, and judicial powers. **Visual/Spatial**

R Reading Skills

Finding the Main Ideas Refer students to the passage and prompt them to extract the main idea from the text. **Ask:** **What were the most important ideas of the *philosophes* of France?** *(They believed in individual freedom and in beliefs that were supported by reason.)* Have students write their answers as a one-sentence summary of the paragraph's main idea.

WHITEBOARD ACTIVITY

Hobbes, Montesquieu, and Locke

Recognizing Relationships Have students complete the Interactive Whiteboard Activity by dragging and dropping each fact into the box under the correct Enlightenment thinker. **Ask:** **How did these thinkers collectively help to advance thought during this period?** Facilitate a class discussion about this idea.

See page 639D for other online activities.

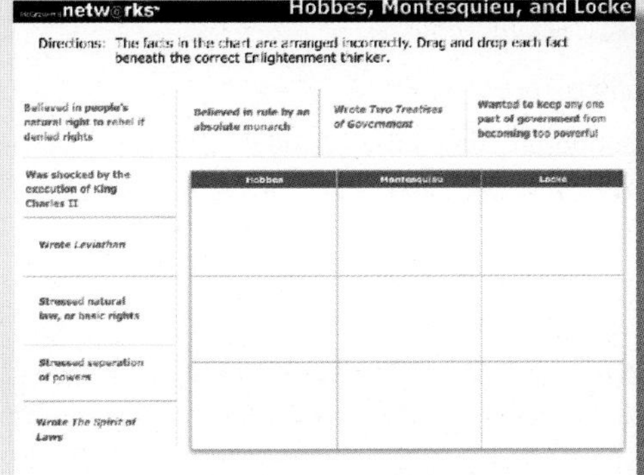

networks
Hobbes, Montesquieu, and Locke
Directions: The facts in the chart are arranged incorrectly. Drag and drop each fact beneath the correct Enlightenment thinker.
Hobbes
Montesquieu
Locke

ANSWERS, p. 653

PROGRESS CHECK Hobbes thought a government should be ruled by an absolute monarch. Locke believed that government should serve the people by protecting their rights.

CRITICAL THINKING Answers may vary, but responses should focus on the idea that Montesquieu wanted to compare the strengths and weaknesses of various governments before deciding which type was best.

The Enlightenment

C Critical Thinking Skills

Comparing Look at the text, which talks about Voltaire's beliefs about government, the Roman Catholic Church, and freedom of religion. Have students compare Voltaire with other thinkers whom they know of, from the past or present, who hold similar beliefs. How many similar thinkers can they think of? *(Possible answer: Current American political leaders believe in freedom of religion.)* BL

T Technology Skills

Making Presentations Have small groups of students work together to create a PowerPoint presentation about Voltaire. Ask each student in the group to choose one aspect of Voltaire's life, for which they will research and create informational slides. Then have the groups combine their parts into a single presentation. **Interpersonal**

V Visual Skills

Analyzing Images Have students study the illustration that shows the gathering in which people read and discussed Voltaire's works. **Ask:**

- **What can we tell about the French society by looking at this illustration. What do the people value?** *(art, wealth, beauty)*
- **What type of people are they?** *(They seem wealthy, civil, and sophisticated.)*
- **Are they fighting heatedly over issues or having an intellectual discussion?** *(It seems more like an intellectual discussion.)* AL **Visual/Spatial**

ANSWER, p. 654

Reading Strategy She thinks men will also become better and wise; "Make them free, and they will quickly become wise and virtuous, as men become more so; for the improvement must be mutual."

Who Was Voltaire?

In 1694, François-Marie Arouet (ahr•WEH) was born to a middle-class family in France. He became one of the greatest thinkers of the Enlightenment. Called just Voltaire (vohl•TAR), he wrote novels, plays, and essays that brought him wealth and fame.

Voltaire opposed the government's favoring one religion and forbidding others. He thought people should be free to choose their own beliefs. He often criticized the Roman Catholic Church for keeping knowledge from people in order to maintain the Church's power. C

Voltaire was a supporter of deism (DEE•ih•zuhm), a religious belief based on reason. Followers of deism believed that God created the universe and set it in motion. God then allowed the universe to run itself by natural law. T

Voltaire had opinions that caused a large amount of controversy. He was jailed for his viewpoints in France's Bastille prison.

Diderot's *Encyclopedia*

The French thinker Denis Diderot (duh•NEE dee•DROH) was also committed to spreading Enlightenment ideas. In the late 1700s, he produced a large, 28-volume encyclopedia that took him about 20 years to complete. The Encyclopedia covered a wide range of topics including religion, government,

V

During the Enlightenment, wealthy people held gatherings to discuss the ideas of the day. Here a group reads and discusses the works of Voltaire.

(t) Giraudon/Art Resource, NY; (b) Reunion des Musees Nationaux/Art Resource, NY

Reading HELPDESK CCSS

Reading Strategy: *Analyzing Primary Sources*

How does Mary Wollstonecraft think the advancement of women will affect men? What part in the quote on the next page supports your answer?

networks Online Teaching Options

PRIMARY SOURCE

Voltaire

Interpreting Have students read the information about Voltaire and the quotation from his book *Candide.* **Ask:** **What do you think Voltaire meant when he said that people had become wolves, and that there were millions of men on Earth more to be pitied than the Sultan?** *(Perhaps he meant that people are as aggressive as wolves, and that the Sultan and other nobility had lived better lives than most others.)*

See page 639D for other online activities.

networks — Voltaire

ANALYZING PRIMARY SOURCES

Voltaire is remembered today as a great French writer who often spoke out against tyranny. *Candide* is Voltaire's most famous written work. It is a novel about the upper class of the time. *Candide* uses sarcasm and satire, or humor and irony, to poke fun at many highly respected aspects of society, such as the upper classes, philosophy, government, and religion.

"If this is the best of all possible worlds, what are the others?

Men . . . must have corrupted [ruined] nature a little, for they were not born wolves, and they have become wolves. God did not give them twenty-four-pounder cannons or bayonets, and they have made bayonets and cannons to destroy each other.

All I presume is that there are millions of men on earth a hundred times more to be pitied than King Charles Edward, the Emperor Ivan, and the Sultan Achmet."

—from ***Candide*** by Voltaire, 1759

The Portable Voltaire by Ben Ray Redman, Penguin, 1977

the sciences, history, and the arts. The philosophes used it as a weapon in their fight against traditional ways. Many articles supported freedom of religion. Others called for changes to make society fairer for all people.

Women and the Enlightenment

Prior to the Enlightenment, women did not have equal rights with men. By the 1700s, a small number of women began to call for such rights. In 1792, the English writer Mary Wollstonecraft (WUL•stuhn•KRAFT) wrote a book called *A Vindication of the Rights of Woman*. In it, she states that women should have the same rights as men. Many consider Wollstonecraft to be the founder of the women's movement. G1

PRIMARY SOURCE

> “ In short, . . . reason and experience convince me that the only method of leading women to fulfil their peculiar [specific] duties, is to free them from all restraint [control] by allowing them to participate in the inherent [basic] rights of mankind. ”
>
> —from *A Vindication of the Rights of Woman*, by Mary Wollstonecraft, 1792

Who was Rousseau?

A Swiss thinker named Jean-Jacques Rousseau (roo•SOH) questioned Enlightenment ideas. In 1762 he published a book of political ideas called *The Social Contract*. This book states that government rests on the will of the people and is based on a social contract. This is an agreement in which everyone in a society accepts being governed by the general will. That is, what society as a whole wants should be law. G2

✓ PROGRESS CHECK

Describing What was Diderot's *Encyclopedia* ?

Absolute Monarchs

GUIDING QUESTION ***How did European monarchs model their countries on Enlightenment ideas?***

During the Enlightenment, thinkers called for controls on government. However, most of Europe was ruled by kings and queens who claimed to rule by divine right, or the will of God. Some absolute rulers used Enlightenment ideas to improve their societies—but they refused to give up any of their powers.

Who was France's Sun King?

During the 1600s and 1700s, France was one of Europe's most powerful nations. In 1643, Louis XIV, called the Sun King, came to the throne. He built the grand Versailles (vuhr•SY) palace. There, he staged large ceremonies to celebrate his power. R

Connections to TODAY

Women's Rights Around the World

Mary Wollstonecraft published *A Vindication of the Rights of Women* in 1792. Today, many organizations still work to advance and protect the social and political equality of women. In 2010, the United Nations voted unanimously to set up UN Women, an organization to promote gender equality around the world. UN Women is based in New York City.

Mary Wollstonecraft thought that women should have equal rights in education, the workplace, and political life.

▶ CRITICAL THINKING

Explaining How did Mary Wollstonecraft support her argument for women's equality?

TEACH & ASSESS

G1 Critical Thinking Skills

Reasoning Ask: Which concepts of the Enlightenment support the idea that women should have equal rights? *(The emphasis on individual rights and freedoms and on fairness means that everyone should have these rights, not just men.)*

G2 Critical Thinking Skills

Differentiating Read the section about Rousseau. Ask students to differentiate the idea of government by general will with the ideas of the Enlightenment, which called more for the rights and freedoms of individuals. **Ask:**

- When would these types of governments be similar? *(when the needs of the individual are the same as those of the larger group)*
- When would there be noticeable differences? *(when the needs of some individuals differ from the will of the larger group)* BL **Verbal/Linguistic**

R Reading Skills

Paraphrasing Have students read the section about France's Sun King and ask them to paraphrase the section, or express it in their own words. Then, **ask:** What do you feel is the most important thing to tell people about the Sun King? AL **Verbal/Linguistic**

GAME

The Enlightenment Fill-in-the-Blank Game

Comparing and Contrasting Have students play the fill-in-the-blank game about the ideas of the thinkers of the Enlightenment, then lead a class discussion about the similarities and differences between their ideas.

See page 639D for other online activities.

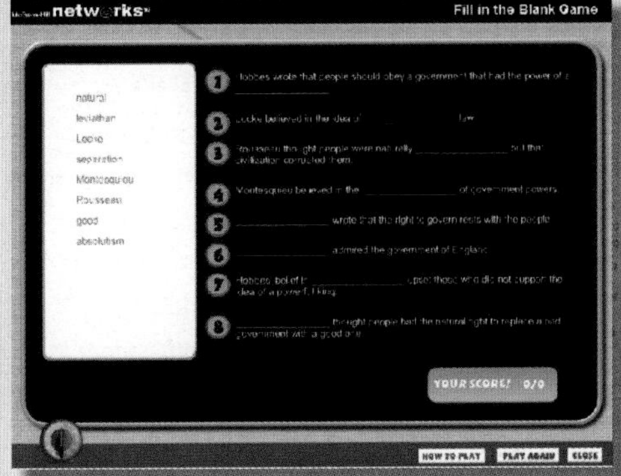

ANSWERS, p. 655

✓ PROGRESS CHECK It was a 28-volume encyclopedia that helped spread ideas about freedom of religion, including how to make society fairer throughout Europe.

CRITICAL THINKING Women possess the same capacity for reason as men, so they should have the same rights as men.

C Critical Thinking Skills

Analyzing Information Have students study the maps on this page and read the paragraph about German territories and states. **Ask:**

- What can you tell about the type of nation Germany is by analyzing the map and text? *(perhaps militant, based on wars and large land acquisitions)*
- What were some of Germany's goals? *(to gain more territory)*

Have students read the second paragraph, describing Frederick II's service to the people. **Ask:** Does this information surprise you? Why or why not? *(It may seem to contradict the militant feeling that is depicted in the other text and visuals.)*

R Reading Skills

Identifying Instruct students to reread the last paragraph on the page, describing Frederick II. **Ask:**

- What structure does the text use to develop the ideas that are conveyed in the first sentence? Is it sequence, compare and contrast, or cause and effect? *(compare and contrast)*
- What word or words do you see that show you that? *(although)*
- What text structure is used to convey the ideas in the last two sentences? *(cause and effect)*
- What word or words do you see which show you that? *(therefore)*

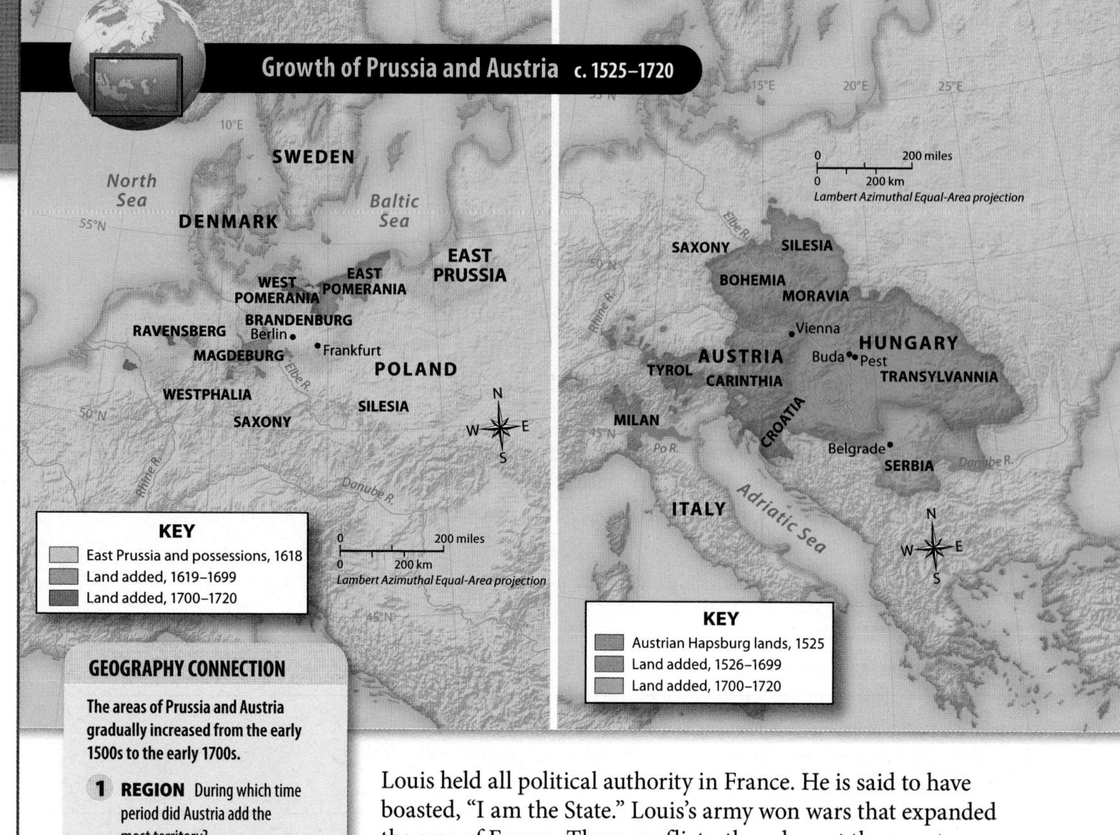

GEOGRAPHY CONNECTION

The areas of Prussia and Austria gradually increased from the early 1500s to the early 1700s.

1. **REGION** During which time period did Austria add the most territory?
2. **CRITICAL THINKING** *Analyzing Visuals* Which state had better access to the sea—Prussia or Austria? Explain.

Louis held all political authority in France. He is said to have boasted, "I am the State." Louis's army won wars that expanded the area of France. These conflicts, though, cost the country a large amount of money and soldiers. The king's constant wars and spending weakened France and the monarchy.

German Rulers

C Germany consisted of many territories during the 1600s and 1700s. The two most powerful German states were Prussia and Austria. The most famous Prussian ruler was Frederick II, also called Frederick the Great. He ruled Prussia from 1740 to 1786. Frederick strengthened the army and fought wars to gain new lands for Prussia.

Although Frederick was an absolute monarch, he saw himself as "first servant of the state." He therefore dedicated himself to the good of his people. Frederick permitted more freedom of speech and religious tolerance. R

Reading HELPDESK CCSS

Academic Vocabulary (Tier 2 Words)

military relating to the armed forces, such as the army, navy, and the air force

networks Online Teaching Options

MAP

Growth of Prussia and Austria c. 1525–1720

Comparing and Contrasting Have students explore the Interactive Map. **Ask:** When the audio clip says that Prussia and Austria "married strategically to expand their lands," what do you think that means? *(Their rulers marry royalty from other lands in order to gain the land.)*

See page 639D for other online activities.

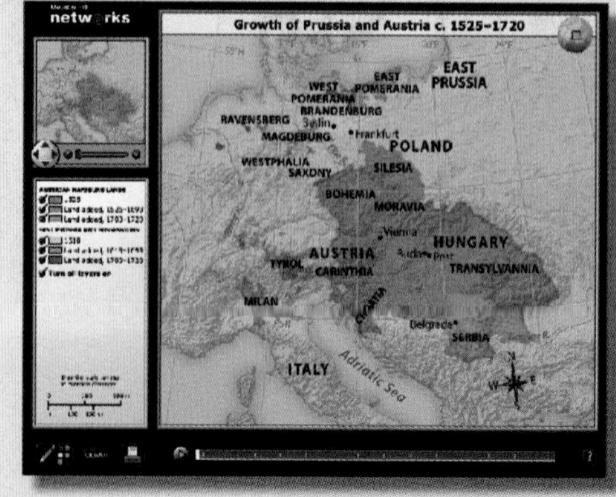

ANSWERS, p. 656

GEOGRAPHY CONNECTION

1. Austria acquired the most land from 1526 to 1699.
2. **CRITICAL THINKING** A large part of Prussia bordered the Baltic Sea, but only a small part of Austria bordered the Adriatic Sea. Prussia had better access to the sea.

The other German state, Austria, was ruled by the Hapsburg family. In 1740, a Hapsburg princess named Maria Theresa became the ruler of Austria. She introduced reforms. She set up schools and tried to improve the living conditions of the serfs, people who worked under the harsh rule of landowners.

After Maria Theresa died in 1780, her son, Joseph II, became ruler. He carried her reforms even further. He freed the serfs and made land taxes equal for nobles and farmers. The nobles opposed his reforms. As a result, Joseph was forced to back down.

Russia's Reforming Czars

C

East of Austria, the vast empire of Russia was ruled by czars. One of the most powerful czars was Peter I, also known as Peter the Great. Peter tried to make Russia a strong European power. He began reforms to help the government run more smoothly. Peter also improved Russia's **military** and created a navy.

R

Peter wanted Russia to have access to the Baltic Sea, but Sweden controlled the land. Peter went to war with Sweden in a conflict lasting 21 years. Russia won in 1721. Just three years after the war started, Peter founded the city of St. Petersburg (PEE•tuhrz•BUHRG). By 1712, this city was the Russian capital.

After Peter died, a series of weak monarchs governed Russia. Then, in 1762, a German princess named Catherine came to the throne. Catherine II expanded Russia's territory and became known as Catherine the Great. She supported the ideas of the Enlightenment and wanted to free the serfs. However, a serf revolt changed her mind. In the end, Catherine allowed the nobles to treat the serfs as they pleased.

In 1787, Catherine the Great and Joseph II traveled together through Southern Russia. An artist commemorated their trip with this oil painting.

▶ CRITICAL THINKING
Comparing What social reforms did both Joseph II and Catherine II seek for their countries?

☑ PROGRESS CHECK

Explaining How was Frederick the Great influenced by the Enlightenment?

LESSON 2 REVIEW (CCSS)

Review Vocabulary (Tier 3 Words)

1. How did the *Glorious Revolution* lead to a *constitutional monarchy* in England? RH.6–8.2, RH.6–8.4

Answer the Guiding Questions

2. ***Identifying*** Which monarch freed the serfs? RH.6–8.2
3. ***Summarizing*** What did the *Encyclopedia* created by Diderot contain? RH.6–8.2
4. ***Describing*** What type of government did John Locke support? RH.6–8.2
5. ***Explaining*** Why did Voltaire criticize the Roman Catholic Church? RH.6–8.2
6. **ARGUMENT** You are an Enlightenment thinker who opposes the views of Thomas Hobbes. Write a short letter to Hobbes that explains to him why you disagree with his ideas about government. WHST.6–8.1, WHST.6–8.10

LESSON 2 REVIEW ANSWERS

1. King James II of England was overthrown. Then the throne was offered to William and Mary under the condition that they allow their powers to be limited. William and Mary accepted the terms. This change of power is referred to as the Glorious Revolution. The result of this revolution was a new form of government called a constitutional monarchy.
2. Joseph II freed the serfs.
3. It contained 28 volumes with articles that covered religion, government, sciences, history, and the arts. Many of the articles in it called for religious freedom and a fairer society.
4. Locke supported a government based on a social contract between the government and its people. According to this contract, the government protects the rights of the people.
5. Voltaire criticized the Roman Catholic Church for keeping knowledge from the people to maintain its power.
6. Answers will vary but should be supported by logic and demonstrate an understanding of Hobbes's view of government—that natural law supported monarchy, and that monarchy would protect people from their selfish, violent nature. The letter should stress the importance of the rights of the people and the need for a government to support these rights.

C Critical Thinking Skills

Making Generalizations Have students read about the struggles between rulers and nobles on how to treat the serfs in Germany and in Russia. **Ask:**

- **What are some of the main conflicts that you see here?** *(whether the serfs should be given freedoms, rights, and better conditions or whether the power should be kept in the hands of the nobles)*
- **What is the main motivation of each group in their fight?** *(The serfs want better lives, but the nobles want to keep power over the serfs and keep the wealth for themselves. Some rulers want to help the serfs, but others want to please the nobles or keep the peace.)*
- **Why might the serf revolt in Russia have changed Catherine the Great's mind about granting freedom to the serfs?** *(Maybe she saw that they could be dangerous and needed to be controlled.)*

R Reading Skills

Specifying Instruct students to read the passage and then explain why Peter the Great went to war with Sweden. *(to give Russia access to the Baltic Sea)*

Have students complete the Lesson 2 Review.

CLOSE & REFLECT

Moderate a class discussion on the views of the political philosophers of the Enlightenment that they have studied. Ask students to choose the philosopher whose political ideas they believe are best, supported by evidence and argument. Allow students to explain their choices and reasoning.

ANSWERS, p. 657

☑ PROGRESS CHECK Frederick permitted more freedom of speech and religious tolerance.

CRITICAL THINKING They both wanted to free the serfs.

CHAPTER REVIEW ACTIVITY

On the board, have a student volunteer create a two-column chart like the one below, writing "Changes to European Society" as the title and, below it, "Science" at the top of one column and "Government" at the top of the other. Then lead a discussion that allows students to recall ways that the science and government of Europe changed during the Scientific Revolution and the Enlightenment. The student volunteer should record these features in the chart.

Changes to European Society	
Science	Government

REVIEW THE ENDURING UNDERSTANDINGS

Review this chapter's Enduring Understandings with students:

- *Science and technology can change people's lives.*
- *The value that society places on individual rights is often reflected in that society's government.*

Now pose the following questions in a class discussion to apply these understandings to this chapter. **Ask:**

- **How did the Scientific Revolution change the lives of the people who lived in Europe?** *(It helped them learn to use logic in their thinking and helped them to better understand the stars, the human body, and many other things.)*
- **Did the governments of Europe reflect the ideas of the enlightened thinkers?** *(Not many—most governments were still ruled by monarchs who were unwilling to give up their power.)*
- **How have the ideas of the major thinkers of the Enlightenment changed societies and governments that came after them?** *(One example is that many countries modeled the writing of their constitutions on Montesquieu's ideas about separation of powers.)*

CHAPTER 22 Activities

Write your answers on a separate piece of paper.

1. **Exploring the Essential Questions** WHST.6–8.2, WHST.6–8.10
INFORMATIVE/EXPLANATORY How did governments in Europe change during the 1600s and 1700s? Write a summary essay about how they changed during this period. Think about various Enlightenment ideas that influenced the formation of governments. Include the effects these ideas had on government structure and on rulers.

2. **21st Century Skills** RH.6–8.2, WHST.6–8.2, WHST.6–8.6, WHST.6–8.7, WHST.6–8.9, WHST.6–8.10
COMMUNICATION Create a presentation that explains the contributions of Galileo to the world of science. What do you think was his most important new idea? Do further research on the Internet. Write a short summary of Galileo's most important contribution to science. Include any diagrams or charts that will help support your argument. In your presentation, have the class ask you questions that require you to defend your opinion about Galileo.

3. **Thinking Like a Historian** RH.6–8.2
COMPARING AND CONTRASTING Create a diagram like the one on the right to compare and contrast the ideas and lives of Thomas Hobbes and John Locke.

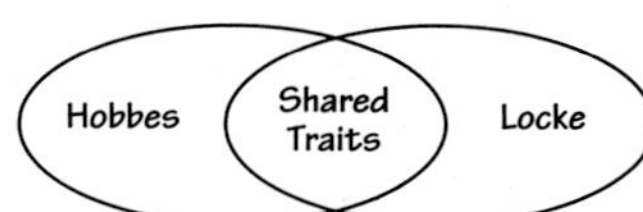

4. **GEOGRAPHY ACTIVITY**

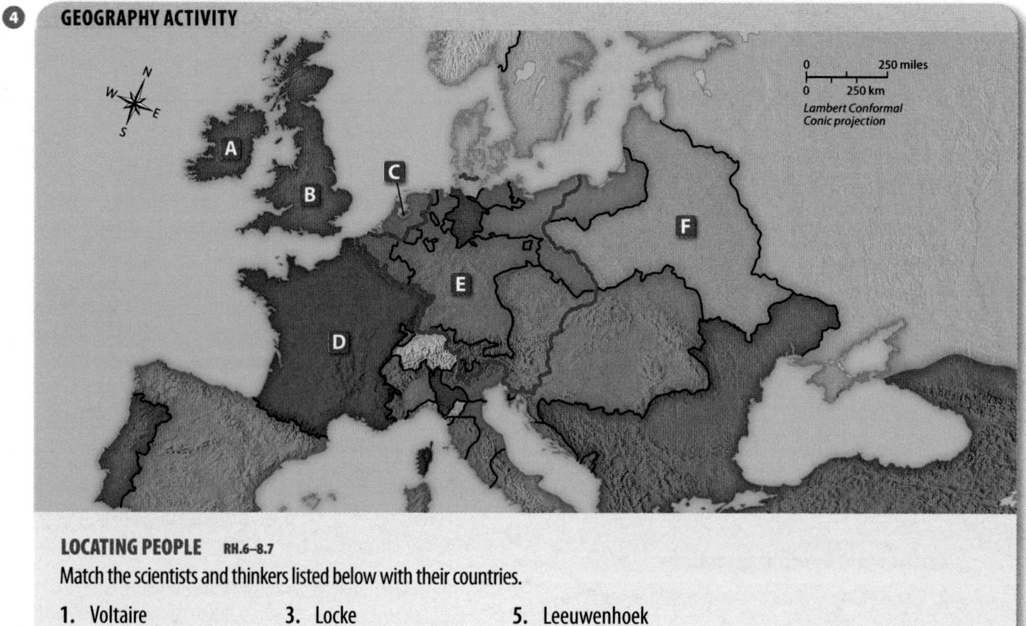

LOCATING PEOPLE RH.6–8.7
Match the scientists and thinkers listed below with their countries.

1. Voltaire
2. Copernicus
3. Locke
4. Kepler
5. Leeuwenhoek
6. Boyle

ACTIVITIES ANSWERS

Exploring the Essential Questions

1. Answers will vary, but students' answers should demonstrate an understanding of the ideas of Hobbes, Locke, Montesquieu, Diderot, and Rousseau and how these ideas affected the formation of a constitutional monarchy in England. They should also address the reforms attempted by other rulers in Europe.

21st Century Skills

2. Presentations will vary but should demonstrate an understanding of Galileo's view of the universe and provide reasons for this view. Students should also use a diagram to show a heliocentric universe.

Thinking Like a Historian

3. Hobbes: He thought government should have an absolute ruler. He did not trust the people to rule themselves. He thought people did not have the right to rebel against their ruler.

Shared traits: Both lived in England; both lived during the Enlightenment; both thought about politics.

Locke: He thought people had natural rights. He thought the power of the monarch should be limited. He thought government should be based on a social contract, in which the government agrees to protect the rights of the people. He thought the people had the right to overthrow an unjust ruler.

Locating People

4. **1.** D, **2.** F, **3.** B, **4.** E, **5.** C, **6.** A

CHAPTER 22 Assessment CCSS

REVIEW THE GUIDING QUESTIONS

Directions: Choose the best answer for each question.

RH.6–8.2
1. Which of the following best summarizes the ideas of Copernicus?
   A. The sun orbits the Earth.
   B. The Earth orbits the sun.
   C. The stars orbit the Earth.
   D. The moon orbits the sun.

RH.6–8.2
2. Which of the following discoveries did Antoine Lavoisier make?
   F. Matter needs oxygen to burn.
   G. Matter is made up of elements.
   H. Living matter contains cells.
   I. Matter on Earth obeys the laws of gravity.

RH.6–8.2
3. Descartes summarized his philosophy with the phrase
   A. "I am, therefore I think."
   B. "I think, therefore I am."
   C. "I am, therefore I have faith."
   D. "I have faith, therefore I am."

RH.6–8.2
4. The theory of Montesquieu was called separation of powers because it separated government
   F. into two branches, both with equal power.
   G. into two branches, with the judiciary being the more powerful.
   H. into three branches, all with equal power.
   I. into three branches, with the judiciary being the most powerful.

RH.6–8.2
5. Which of the following best summarizes the ideas of Rousseau?
   A. Reason is what people should rely on.
   B. People are naturally bad.
   C. The right to rule rests with a monarch.
   D. People should pay more attention to their feelings.

RH.6–8.2
6. During his reign, Frederick II
   F. thought about freeing the serfs.
   G. allowed freedom of speech and religion.
   H. built the palace of Versailles.
   I. made land taxes equal for nobles and farmers.

659

ASSESSMENT ANSWERS

Review the Guiding Questions

1. **B** Earth orbits the sun. The sun does not orbit anything. The stars do not orbit Earth, and the moon does not orbit the sun.

2. **F** Lavoisier showed that matter needs oxygen to burn. Robert Boyle proved that all matter is made up of elements. Robert Hooke showed that all living matter contains cells. Isaac Newton realized that matter on Earth obeys the laws of gravity.

3. **B** Descartes stated, "I think, therefore I am." He did not believe that "I am, therefore I think," "I am, therefore I have faith," or "I have faith, therefore I am." His beliefs had nothing to do with faith.

4. **H** Montesquieu wrote that the best form of government involved a split into three, not two, separate branches—executive, legislative, and judicial. None of the three branches was given more power than the other two.

5. **D** Rousseau believed people should pay more attention to their feelings and rely less on reason. He also thought people were naturally good. He did not think the right to rule rested with a monarch.

6. **G** Frederick II allowed freedom of speech and religion. Catherine II thought about freeing the serfs. Louis XIV built the palace of Versailles. Joseph II made land taxes equal for nobles and farmers.

Analyzing Documents

7 **A** Locke is supporting the idea that all men have freedom. He is not stating that all men should enforce laws. Also, he is not saying they should have equal wealth. In addition, he is not telling people to have limited possessions.

8 **H** The excerpt does not state that people must obey the laws of nature. Also, it does not claim that people will naturally form democracies. In addition, it is not specifically saying that people have the freedom to learn about nature.

Short Response

9 He meant that he is not only a ruler, but also a citizen who needs to obey the laws as other citizens do. He must set a good example for his citizens in order to be a just and effective ruler.

10 He would think that the king was not setting the proper example for his people and that it was inappropriate for the king to act so undignified.

Extended Response

11 Student responses should include dialogue for Voltaire, Rousseau, and Wollstonecraft. This dialogue should clearly present the ideas of each thinker and the reasons for these ideas. Also, a general description of the meeting should be included.

CHAPTER 22 Assessment *(continued)*

DBQ ANALYZING DOCUMENTS

Drawing Conclusions This excerpt was published by John Locke in 1690.

"To understand political power aright . . . we must consider what estate all [people] are naturally in, and that is, a state of perfect freedom . . ., within the bounds of the law of Nature. . . .

A state also of equality, wherein all the power and jurisdiction [enforcement of laws] is reciprocal [shared], no one having more than another."

—from *The Second Treatise of Government*, by John Locke

RH.6–8.1, RH.6–8.6

7 Which statement do you think Locke would agree with?

A. All people have freedom to do what they want.
B. All people should enforce laws.
C. All people should have equal wealth.
D. All people should have few possessions.

RH.6–8.1, RH.6–8.6

8 **Finding the Main Idea** Which of the following is the main idea of the excerpt?

F. People will naturally form democracies.
G. People must obey the laws of nature.
H. People are in a natural state of freedom and equality.
I. People have the freedom to learn about nature.

SHORT RESPONSE

"A sovereign [ruler] is not elevated to his high position . . . that he may live in lazy luxury. . . . The sovereign is the first servant of the state. He is well paid in order that he may sustain the dignity of his office, but one demands that he work efficiently for the good of the state,..."

—from the *Political Testament*, by Frederick II (the Great) of Prussia

RH.6–8.1, RH.6–8.6

9 What does Frederick mean when he says a ruler should be "the first servant of the state?"

RH.6–8.1, RH.6–8.6

10 What would Frederick think of a king who acted foolish in public?

EXTENDED RESPONSE

WHST.6–8.10

11 **Narrative** Write a description of a meeting in which Voltaire, Jean-Jacques Rousseau, and Mary Wollstonecraft discuss and argue their viewpoints. Include dialogue.

Need Extra Help?

If You've Missed Question	1	2	3	4	5	6	7	8	9	10	11
Review Lesson	1	1	1	2	2	2	2	2	1	1	2

networks Online Teaching Options

Using eAssessment

Use eAssessment to access and assign the publisher-made Lesson Quizzes & Chapter Tests electronically. You can also use eAssessment to create your own quizzes and tests from hundreds of available questions. eAssessment helps you design assessments that meet the needs of different types of learners. Follow the link in the *Assess* tab of your Teacher Lesson Center.

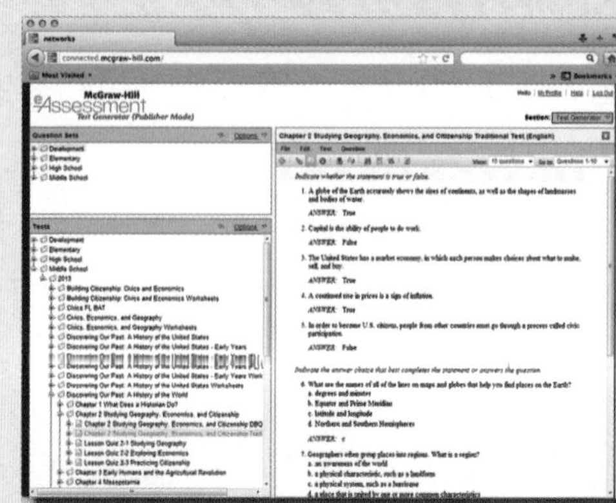

CHAPTER 23

Political and Industrial Revolutions Planner

UNDERSTANDING BY DESIGN®

Enduring Understandings

- *Conflict can lead to change.*
- *The social sciences help us understand history.*
- *The movement of people, goods, and ideas causes societies to change over time.*
- *Science and technology can change people's lives.*

Essential Questions

- *Why does conflict develop?*
- *Why is history important?*
- *How do governments change?*
- *How does technology change the way people live?*
- *How do new ideas change the way people live?*

Predictable Misunderstandings

Students may think:

- *The American Revolution had no influence on political change in Europe.*
- *The Magna Carta and the English Bill of Rights had no impact on the United States.*
- *The Industrial Revolution began in the United States.*

Assessment Evidence

Performance Task:

- *Hands-On Chapter Project*

Other Evidence:

- *Interactive Graphic Organizers*
- *Economics of History Activities*
- *21st Century Skills Activities*
- *Geography and History Activity*
- *Responses to Interactive Whiteboard Activities*
- *Participation in class discussion and debates*
- *Essay about nationalism*
- *Participation in class simulation*
- *Lesson Reviews*
- *Chapter Activities and Assessment*

SUGGESTED PACING GUIDE

Introducing the Chapter	1 Day	Lesson 3	2 Days
Lesson 1	2 Days	Lesson 4	1 Day
Lesson 2	1 Day	Lesson 5	2 Days
Feature: What Do You Think?	1 Day	Chapter Wrap-Up and Assessment	1 Day

TOTAL TIME 11 Days

Key for Using the Teacher Edition

SKILL-BASED ACTIVITIES

Types of skill activities found in the Teacher Edition.

V Visual Skills require students to analyze maps, graphs, charts, and photos.

R Reading Skills help students practice reading skills and master vocabulary.

W Writing Skills provide writing opportunities to help students comprehend the text.

C Critical Thinking Skills help students apply and extend what they have learned.

T Technology Skills require students to use digital tools effectively.

*Letters are followed by a number when there is more than one of the same type of skill on the page.

DIFFERENTIATED INSTRUCTION

All activities are written for the on-level student unless otherwise marked with the leveled labels below.

BL Beyond Level

AL Approaching Level

ELL English Language Learners

All students benefit from activities that utilize different learning styles. Many activities are marked as below when a particular learning style is highlighted.

Intrapersonal — **Naturalist**
Logical/Mathematical — **Kinesthetic**
Visual/Spatial — **Auditory/Musical**
Verbal/Linguistic — **Interpersonal**

NCSS Standards covered in "Political and Industrial Revolutions"

Learners will understand:

2 **TIME, CONTINUITY, AND CHANGE**

5. Key historical periods and patterns of change within and across cultures (e.g., the rise and fall of ancient civilizations, the development of technology, the rise of modern nation-states, and the establishment and breakdown of colonial systems)

7. The contributions of key persons, groups, and events from the past and their influence on the present

3 **PEOPLE, PLACES, AND ENVIRONMENTS**

4. The roles of different kinds of population centers in a region or nation

6. Patterns of demographic and political change, and cultural diffusion in the past and present (e.g., changing national boundaries, migration, and settlement, and the diffusion of and changes in customs and ideas)

7. Human modifications of the environment

8. Factors that contribute to cooperation and conflict among peoples of the nation and world, including language, religion, and political beliefs

5 **INDIVIDUALS, GROUPS, AND INSTITUTIONS**

4. That ways in which young people are socialized include similarities as well as differences across cultures

5. That groups and institutions change over time

6. That cultural diffusion occurs when groups migrate

7. That institutions may promote or undermine social conformity

8. That when two or more groups with differing norms and beliefs interact, accommodation or conflict may result

6 **POWER, AUTHORITY, AND GOVERNANCE**

1. Rights are guaranteed in the U.S. Constitution, the supreme law of the land

2. Fundamental ideas that are the foundation of American constitutional democracy (including those of the U.S. Constitution, popular sovereignty, the rule of law, separation of powers, checks and balances, minority rights, the separation of church and state, and Federalism)

3. Fundamental values of constitutional democracy (e.g., the common good, liberty, justice, equality, and individual dignity)

5. The ways in which governments meet the needs and wants of citizens, manage conflict, and establish order and society

7 **PRODUCTION, DISTRIBUTION, AND CONSUMPTION**

1. Individuals, government, and society experience scarcity because human wants and needs exceed what can be produced from available resources

2. How choices involve trading off the expected value of one opportunity gained against the expected value of the best alternative

3. The economic choices that people make have both present and future consequences

4. Economic incentives affect people's behavior and may be regulated by rules or laws

6. The economic gains that result from specialization and exchange as well as the trade-offs

8 **SCIENCE, TECHNOLOGY, AND SOCIETY**

1. Science is a result of empirical study of the natural world, and technology is the application of knowledge to accomplish tasks

2. Society often turns to science and technology to solve problems

3. Our lives today are media and technology dependent

4. Science and technology have had both positive and negative impacts upon individuals, societies, and the environment in the past and present

5. Science and technology have changed peoples' perceptions of the social and natural world, as well as their relationship to the land, economy and trade, their concept of security, and their major daily activities

6. Values, beliefs, and attitudes that have been influenced by new scientific and technological knowledge (e.g., invention of the printing press, conceptions of the universe, applications of atomic energy, and genetic discoveries)

8. Science and technology sometimes create ethical issues that test our standards and values

9. The need for laws and policies to govern scientific and technological applications

CHAPTER OPENER PLANNER

Students will know:

- *why the American colonies revolted against Britain.*
- *the ideas that shaped the Declaration of Independence and the U.S. Constitution.*
- *why France revolted against its monarchy.*
- *how Napoleon became the leader of France.*
- *the effects of nationalism on Europe.*
- *how the United States changed during the 1800s.*
- *how the countries of Latin America won independence.*
- *the advancements made during the Industrial Revolution and their impact on society.*
- *how changes in industry changed societal and political ideas.*
- *the art movements of romanticism, realism, and modernism.*
- *scientific advancements of the 1800s.*

Students will be able to:

- ***analyze** the role of economics in the American Revolution.*
- ***identify** ideas that shaped the Declaration of Independence and the U.S. Constitution.*
- ***identify** the reasons for the French Revolution.*
- ***explain** how Napoleon rose to power.*
- ***describe** changes in Europe due to nationalism.*
- ***describe** the causes and effects of the Civil War and westward expansion on the United States.*
- ***draw conclusions** as to why Latin American countries faced challenges after gaining independence.*
- ***compare** pre- and post-Industrial Revolution society.*
- ***identify** how the roles of women changed during the 1800s.*
- ***recognize** works of different art movements.*
- ***identify** some of the scientific advances made in the 1800s.*

UNDERSTANDING BY DESIGN®

Print Teaching Options

V **Visual Skills**

- **P. 662** Students analyze a map and explore political revolutions between 1775 and 1815.
- **P. 663** Students examine a time line to gather information about revolutions.

Online Teaching Options

V **Visual Skills**

- **MAP** **Political Revolutions, 1775–1815**—Students click on major world cities to read about the revolutions that took place in the surrounding areas.
- **TIME LINE** **Place and Time: Political and Industrial Revolution**—Students identify key events occurring in the Western Hemisphere and the world between 1620 and 1903.
- **WORLD ATLAS** Students can use this interactive map to identify regions of the world, learn about individual countries, locate political boundaries, measure distances, and much more.

Project-Based Learning

Hands-On Chapter Project

Create Political Cartoons

Student groups will create political cartoons that express a point of view about one of the events that took place during the political revolutions of the late eighteenth or early nineteenth century. Events might include the Boston Tea Party, the Stamp Act, the signing of the Declaration of Independence, or Napoleon's exile to Elba.

Technology Extension

Create Online Political Cartoons or Comics

- Find an additional activity online that incorporates technology for this project.
- Visit the EdTechTeacher Web sites (included in the Technology Extension for this chapter) for more links, tutorials, and other resources.

Print Resources

ANCILLARY RESOURCES

These ancillaries are available for every chapter and lesson.

- **Reading Essentials and Study Guide Workbook** AL ELL
- **Chapter Tests and Lesson Quizzes Blackline Masters**

PRINTABLE DIGITAL WORKSHEETS

These printable digital worksheets are available for every chapter and lesson.

- **Hands-On Chapter Projects**
- **What Do You Know? activities**
- **Chapter Summaries (English and Spanish)**
- **Vocabulary Builder activities**
- **Guided Reading activities**

More Media Resources

SUGGESTED VIDEOS MOVIES

Watch clips of popular-culture films about the French Revolution, such as *Marie Antoinette: A Film by David Grubin* (PBS Paramount).

- **Discuss: How did the royalty of the era perceive the revolution differently from the people of France?**

(NOTE: Preview any clips for age-appropriateness.)

SUGGESTED READING 

Grade 6 reading level:

- ***Odd Boy Out: Young Albert Einstein,*** by Don Brown

Grade 7 reading level:

- ***Something Out of Nothing: Marie Curie and Radium,*** by Carla Killough McClafferty

Grade 8 reading level:

- ***The Real Revolution: The Global Story of American Independence,*** by Marc Aronson

LESSON 1 PLANNER

THE AMERICAN REVOLUTION

Students will know:
- *why the American colonies revolted against Britain.*
- *the ideas that shaped the Declaration of Independence and the U.S. Constitution.*

Students will be able to:
- ***analyze*** *the role of economics in the American Revolution.*
- ***identify*** *ideas that shaped the Declaration of Independence and the U.S. Constitution.*

UNDERSTANDING BY DESIGN®

☑ Print Teaching Options

V Visual Skills

- ☐ **P. 665** Students analyze a map of the American colonies. BL Visual/Spatial
- ☐ **P. 668** Students interpret a map showing shipping routes. Visual/Spatial

R Reading Skills

- ☐ **P. 664** Students specify the motivations of the Europeans who colonized the Americas. AL
- ☐ **P. 666** Students define the terms *representative* and *burgess.* ELL
- ☐ **P. 670** Students list the challenges faced by the Patriots and the British during the Revolutionary War.
- ☐ **P. 671** Students summarize how the principle of popular sovereignty helped shape the new nation. BL

W Writing Skills

- ☐ **P. 669** Students write a speech arguing either in favor of or in opposition to fighting for independence from Great Britain. Verbal/Linguistic

C Critical Thinking Skills

- ☐ **P. 665** Students infer reasons why the relationship between Native Americans and settlers worsened over time.
- ☐ **P. 666** Students compare the House of Burgesses with the United States government today.
- ☐ **P. 667** Students examine the slogan "No taxation without representation!"
- ☐ **P. 669** Students use a cause-and-effect graphic organizer to evaluate the Battle of Lexington. Visual/Spatial
- ☐ **P. 669** Students determine whether the Revolutionary War was inevitable.

T Technology Skills

- ☐ **P. 668** Partners conduct research and write a paragraph about the events that occurred in Massachusetts that escalated tensions between colonists and the British. Verbal/Linguistic Interpersonal

☑ Online Teaching Options

V Visual Skills

- ☐ VIDEO **Making a Revolution**—Students view a video that explains the movement toward colonial unity.
- ☐ MAP **Europeans in North America, 1750**—Students view the parts of North America controlled by different European nations.
- ☐ MAP **Colonial Trade Routes, 1750**—Students view import and export routes between Europe, the colonies, and the Caribbean islands.
- ☐ IMAGE **The Boston Tea Party**—Students read about this act, which eventually led to war with the British.

R Reading Skills

- ☐ GRAPHIC ORGANIZER **Taking Notes: *Cause and Effect:* The American Revolution**—Students identify effects of actions taken during the Revolution.
- ☐ BIOGRAPHY **The Life of George Washington**—Students read about the life and accomplishments of the first president of the United States.
- ☐ PRIMARY SOURCE **The Declaration of Independence**—Students read the complete text of this document.

C Critical Thinking Skills

- ☐ WHITEBOARD ACTIVITY **The Bill of Rights**—Students match a summary and text for five amendments from the Bill of Rights.
- ☐ PRIMARY SOURCE **The Mayflower Compact**—Students analyze an excerpt from what is considered one of the first basic constitutions for self-rule in the Americas.

T Technology Skills

- ☐ SELF-CHECK QUIZ **Lesson 1**—Students receive instant feedback on their mastery of lesson content.
- ☐ GAME **The American Revolution Crossword Puzzle**—Students solve clues to review lesson content.

☑ Printable Digital Worksheets

C Critical Thinking Skills

- ☐ WORKSHEET **Economics of History Activity: Tariffs in the American Colonies**—Students consider the role of tariffs as a way to influence how people buy goods.

LESSON 2 PLANNER

THE FRENCH REVOLUTION AND NAPOLEON

Students will know:
- *why France revolted against its monarchy.*
- *how Napoleon became the leader of France.*

Students will be able to:
- ***identify** the reasons for the French Revolution.*
- ***explain** how Napoleon rose to power.*

UNDERSTANDING BY DESIGN®

☑ Print Teaching Options

V Visual Skills

- ☐ **P. 673** Students analyze circle graphs showing statistics related to French class structure. **Visual/Spatial**
- ☐ **P. 674** Students create posters or banners that show the views of peasants and rebels after the fall of the Bastille.
- ☐ **P. 678** Students analyze a map showing France and surrounding states during the Napoleonic Wars and use a map scale to determine how far Napoleon's troops marched into Russia. **Visual/Spatial Logical/Mathematical**

R Reading Skills

- ☐ **P. 674** Students compare and contrast the systems of government that France had during the late 1700s.
- ☐ **P. 675** Students discuss the Reign of Terror.
- ☐ **P. 675** Students debate whether Robespierre was justified in enforcing his violent laws during the Reign of Terror. **Verbal/Linguistic**
- ☐ **P. 677** Students list the changes Napoleon made to the French government.
- ☐ **P. 679** Students discuss the Congress of Vienna.

W Writing Skills

- ☐ **P. 676** Students write a paragraph explaining how the policies of the Directory differed from the policies of earlier groups that were in charge of France's government during the Revolution.
- ☐ **P. 677** Students write a dialogue that two French people might have had on the day after Napoleon crowned himself emperor in 1804. **BL**

C Critical Thinking Skills

- ☐ **P. 672** Students discuss the role of taxes in modern-day economies and in France in the late 1700s.
- ☐ **P. 673** Students put the events that led to the French Revolution in chronological order. **Interpersonal**
- ☐ **P. 676** Students discuss how Napoleon came to power.
- ☐ **P. 677** Students discuss how Napoleon's achievements differed from the ideals of the French Revolution.

T Technology Skills

- ☐ **P. 675** Students research Marie Antoinette on the Internet and present their findings to the class. **BL Visual/Spatial**

☑ Online Teaching Options

V Visual Skills

- **VIDEO** **Napoleon**—Students view a video that describes this military leader.
- **IMAGE** **Napoleon's Europe**—Students analyze a map of Europe to determine the extent of land controlled by France during Napoleon's reign.
- **IMAGE** **The Guillotine**—Students view this symbol of political violence in the French Revolution.
- **SLIDE SHOW** **The Bastille**—Students learn the story of the storming of the Bastille through images and text.

R Reading Skills

- **GRAPHIC ORGANIZER** **Taking Notes: *Sequencing:* Events of the French Revolution**—Students use a time line to keep track of the major events of the French Revolution.
- **BIOGRAPHY** **Marie Antoinette**—Students read a biography of the last French queen while viewing an image of a guillotine.

C Critical Thinking Skills

- **WHITEBOARD ACTIVITY** **Revolution and Empire in France**—Students correlate dates to events in France.
- **SLIDE SHOW** **The Estates-General**—Students analyze graphs and text to understand the makeup of the Estates-General, which had helped govern France since the Middle Ages.

T Technology Skills

- **SELF-CHECK QUIZ** **Lesson 2**—Students receive instant feedback on their mastery of lesson content.
- **GAME** **The French Revolution and Napoleon Concentration Game**—Students match vocabulary and definitions to review lesson content.

☑ Printable Digital Worksheets

W Writing Skills

- **WORKSHEET** **21st Century Skills Activity: Leadership and Responsibility: Citizenship**—Students list ways that governments serve the needs of people and then write paragraphs in which they explain the interactions they have with government organizations in their daily lives.

NATIONALISM AND NATION-STATES

Students will know:

- *the effects of nationalism on Europe.*
- *how the United States changed during the 1800s.*
- *how the countries of Latin America won independence.*

Students will be able to:

- ***describe** changes in Europe due to nationalism.*
- ***describe** the causes and effects of the Civil War and westward expansion on the United States.*
- ***draw conclusions** as to why Latin American countries faced challenges after gaining independence.*

UNDERSTANDING BY DESIGN®

☑ Print Teaching Options

V Visual Skills

- ☐ **P. 685** Students analyze a map showing territorial expansion in Europe in the 1800s. **Visual/Spatial**
- ☐ **P. 687** Students identify Confederate and Union states on a map. **Visual/Spatial**
- ☐ **P. 688** Students analyze a photograph of women marching for the right to vote.

R Reading Skills

- ☐ **P. 682** Students describe the political situation in Britain in the early 1800s.
- ☐ **P. 683** Students paraphrase a quotation.
- ☐ **P. 684** Students examine the actions of Czar Alexander II.
- ☐ **P. 686** Students define "Manifest Destiny." **ELL**
- ☐ **P. 687** Students discuss how the differences between states contributed to the Civil War. **AL**
- ☐ **P. 688** Students discuss the early independence movements in Latin America in the early 1800s. **AL** **BL**

W Writing Skills

- ☐ **P. 683** Students write a paragraph about the reforms passed in the early 1900s that improved workers' lives. **Verbal/Linguistic**

C Critical Thinking Skills

- ☐ **P. 685** Students discuss the gradual unification of Italy. **BL**
- ☐ **P. 686** Students create a cause-and-effect chart to illustrate the formation of Germany. **Visual/Spatial**
- ☐ **P. 689** Students draw conclusions about Simón Bolívar's struggle against the Spanish. **BL**

T Technology Skills

- ☐ **P. 687** Students conduct research on the Internet about a specific Civil War battle and present their findings to the class. **Interpersonal**

☑ Online Teaching Options

V Visual Skills

- **VIDEO** **Napoleon's Early Military Career**—Students view a video that explains how a combination of hard work, bravery, political connections, and being born in a turbulent age impacted Napoleon's early successes.
- **MAP** **The Rise of Italy and Germany**—Students view the expansion of lands claimed by these countries in the 1800s.
- **MAP** **U.S. Expansion, 1783–1898**—Students view the steady growth of the country during these years.
- **IMAGE** **Life at the Beginning of the 20th Century: Role of Women and Suffragettes**—Students view an image of American women marching for voting rights.

R Reading Skills

- **GRAPHIC ORGANIZER** **Taking Notes: *Organizing:* Uprisings in Different Countries**—Students organize information about uprisings in different countries.
- **IMAGE** **British Parliament**—Students read a description of the two houses of Parliament while viewing an image of the exterior of the building.
- **BIOGRAPHY** **Simón Bolívar**—Students read a short biography of the "George Washington of South America."

C Critical Thinking Skills

- **WHITEBOARD ACTIVITY** **The American Civil War**—Students compare the Northern and Southern states at the outbreak of the American Civil War.
- **PRIMARY SOURCE** **Blood and Iron**—Students analyze an excerpt from a well-known speech by Otto von Bismarck, Prime Minister of Prussia.

T Technology Skills

- **SELF-CHECK QUIZ** **Lesson 3**—Students receive instant feedback on their mastery of lesson content.
- **GAME** **Nationalism and Nation-States Fill-in-the-Blank Game**—Students complete sentences to review lesson content.

☑ Printable Digital Worksheets

C Critical Thinking Skills

- **WORKSHEET** **Geography and History Activity: Human/Environment Interaction: Crossing the Andes Mountains**—Students analyze how geography aided and hindered Bolívar's attack on the Spanish army at the Battle of Boyacá.

THE INDUSTRIAL REVOLUTION

Students will know:
- *the advancements made during the Industrial Revolution and their impact on society.*

Students will be able to:
- ***compare** pre- and post-Industrial Revolution society.*

UNDERSTANDING BY DESIGN®

☑ Print Teaching Options

V Visual Skills
- ☐ **P. 691** Students examine a map of Europe during the Industrial Revolution. **Visual/Spatial**

R Reading Skills
- ☐ **P. 690** Students discuss the meaning of the term *revolution.*
- ☐ **P. 692** Students use a two-column chart to organize information about important inventions of the late 1700s.
- ☐ **P. 694** Students define the word *corporation.* **AL** **ELL**
- ☐ **P. 695** Students use a three-column chart to help them classify inventions by type. **Visual/Spatial**

W Writing Skills
- ☐ **P. 692** Students write a paragraph either supporting or opposing the statement "Great Britain's geography was the most important factor in the rise of industry in that nation." **BL** **Verbal/Linguistic**

C Critical Thinking Skills
- ☐ **P. 691** Students draw cause-and-effect chains to show how changes in land ownership laws in Britain helped bring about the Industrial Revolution. **Visual/Spatial**
- ☐ **P. 693** Students illustrate the difference between factory work and cottage industry by making paper airplanes. **AL** **ELL** **Kinesthetic**

☑ Online Teaching Options

V Visual Skills
- **VIDEO** **The Wright Brothers**—Students view a video that describes the mechanical genius the brothers used to make aviation history with the first recorded flight of a heavier-than-air powered machine.
- **IMAGE** **Locomotive**—Students analyze a diagram to learn the parts of an engine.
- **MAP** **Industrial Revolution, 1870**—Students note that industrial centers are located near population centers and sources of fuel.

R Reading Skills
- **GRAPHIC ORGANIZER** **Taking Notes: *Sequencing:* Industrial Revolution**—Students list events that led to the Industrial Revolution.
- **BIOGRAPHY** **Thomas Edison**—Students learn of the life of one of the greatest inventors of all time.
- **BIOGRAPHY** **The Wright Brothers**—Students view an image of one of the Wright Brothers' planes as they learn about how the brothers developed their flying machine.

C Critical Thinking Skills
- **SLIDE SHOW** **Industrial Revolution Inventions**—Students analyze the evolution of inventions that revolutionized the textile industry.

T Technology Skills
- **SELF-CHECK QUIZ** **Lesson 4**—Students receive instant feedback on their mastery of lesson content.

☑ Printable Digital Worksheets

T Technology Skills
- **WORKSHEET** **21st Century Skills Activity: Research on the Internet**—Students research information on inventors and identify reliable and unreliable sites.

LESSON 5 PLANNER

SOCIETY AND INDUSTRY

Students will know:
- *how changes in industry changed societal and political ideas.*
- *the art movements of romanticism, realism, and modernism.*
- *scientific advancements of the 1800s.*

Students will be able to:
- ***Identify** how the roles of women changed during the 1800s.*
- ***recognize** works of different art movements.*
- ***identify** some of the scientific advances made in the 1800s.*

UNDERSTANDING BY DESIGN®

☑ Print Teaching Options

R Reading Skills

- ☐ **P. 696** Students discuss how industrialization led to urbanization.
- ☐ **P. 698** Students discuss the rise of liberalism. AL BL
- ☐ **P. 702** Students describe Darwin's theory of evolution. AL

W Writing Skills

- ☐ **P. 697** Students write journal entries describing a day in the life of a worker in a factory or a mine. Intrapersonal
- ☐ **P. 700** Students write "incendiary speeches" to convince someone in the mid-1800s to support workers or to support a strike. Verbal/Linguistic

C Critical Thinking Skills

- ☐ **P. 697** Students use a Venn diagram to compare and contrast the effects of the Industrial Revolution on middle class and professional workers with industrial workers who labored in factories and mines.
- ☐ **P. 698** Students discuss why women started demanding equal rights in the nineteenth century.
- ☐ **P. 699** Students use a Venn diagram to compare and contrast the terms *liberalism, utilitarianism,* and *socialism.* AL ELL BL Visual/Spatial
- ☐ **P. 700** Students discuss the basic ideas of Marxism and socialism.
- ☐ **P. 701** Students distinguish the artistic movements of the nineteenth century.
- ☐ **P. 703** Students select and discuss a scientist and evaluate his or her impact on society. Interpersonal

T Technology Skills

- ☐ **P. 702** Students conduct research on the Internet to find examples of impressionist painting or impressionist music. Auditory/Musical Visual/Spatial

☑ Online Teaching Options

V Visual Skills

- VIDEO **The Industrial Revolution**—Students examine the impact of the Industrial Revolution on modern society and explore the beginnings of labor unions.
- IMAGE **Darwin and the *Beagle***—Students view a map that shows the route of Charles Darwin's journey of natural discovery aboard the *HMS Beagle,* from 1831 to 1836.
- SLIDE SHOW **Monet's Paintings**—Students view various paintings by this impressionist.

R Reading Skills

- GRAPHIC ORGANIZER **Taking Notes: *Explaining:* Social Advances During the Industrial Revolution**—Students identify four ways in which the Industrial Revolution affected society.
- BIOGRAPHY **Albert Einstein**—Students learn about Einstein's life before he moved to the United States.
- PRIMARY SOURCE ***A Tale of Two Cities***—Students analyze text from this Dickens novel set at the time of the French Revolution.
- IMAGE **Robert Owen**—Students read about New Lanark, a model industrial community created by Robert Owen.

C Critical Thinking Skills

- CHART **Marxism, Socialism, and Communism**—Students compare and contrast the basic beliefs of these three theories of social organization.
- SLIDE SHOW **Working Conditions**—Students view images of factories and working conditions during the Industrial Revolution.

T Technology Skills

- SELF-CHECK QUIZ **Lesson 5**—Students receive instant feedback on their mastery of lesson content.
- GAME **Society and Industry Crossword Puzzle**—Students solve clues to review lesson content.

☑ Printable Digital Worksheets

C Critical Thinking Skills

- WORKSHEET **Economics of History Activity: Specialization and the Industrial Revolution**—Students learn how specialization can make a business more competitive.

INTERVENTION AND REMEDIATION STRATEGIES

LESSON 1 The American Revolution

Reading and Comprehension

Determining Cause and Effect Have students identify the causes and effects of the events leading to the American Revolution. Then ask them to summarize the most important effect of the entire Revolution.

Text Evidence

Stating Have students write a dialogue that would have taken place between a leader of the Revolution and a member of Britain's Parliament. In the dialogue, the Patriot should state reasons for independence and the member of Parliament should give reasons for the colonies to remain part of Britain.

LESSON 2 The French Revolution and Napoleon

Reading and Comprehension

Determining Word Meanings To ensure comprehension of this lesson, have students write sentences using new vocabulary and highlighted words in the lesson. Sentences should show an understanding of word meanings and how they apply to the lesson.

Text Evidence

Creating Time Lines Have pairs of students work together to create a timeline of the major events of the French Revolution and Napoleon's rule. Time lines should include dates of major events and at least a single sentence about each one.

LESSON 3 Nationalism and Nation-States

Reading and Comprehension

Finding the Main Idea For each of the four main headings in the lesson (Nationalism and Reform, New Nations in Europe, Growth of the United States, Independence in Latin America), have students write the main idea and at least two supporting details.

Text Evidence

Integrating Visual Information On an outline map of the world, have students shade in countries or regions where nationalism led to significant political changes in the late 1700s or early 1800s. Have students write a caption describing what happened in each location.

LESSON 4 The Industrial Revolution

Reading and Comprehension

Summarizing Have students summarize the effects of the Industrial Revolution in these different areas: manufacturing, farming, transportation, and communication.

Text Evidence

Creating Visuals Have students choose an innovation that occurred in the 1800s as part of the Industrial Revolution. Ask them to create a poster showing what the innovation was, who developed it, and what the effects of this innovation were.

LESSON 5 Society and Industry

Reading and Comprehension

Organizing Have students keep track of new vocabulary in this lesson using word webs. In one web, the central phrase should be "new political ideas." In another web the central phrase should be "artistic movements and ideas."

Text Evidence

Identifying Points of View Have students work in small groups to act out a dialogue among workers in the 18th century. The characters should describe their jobs, their living conditions, and a new development in society or the arts that has captured their attention.

Online Resources

Approaching Level Reader

Use this online lower-level text that corresponds directly to the text in the Student Edition. It includes a Spanish version.

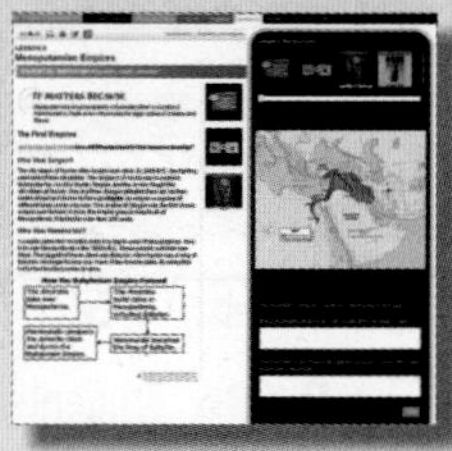

Guided Reading Activities

This resource uses graphic organizers and guiding questions to help students with comprehension.

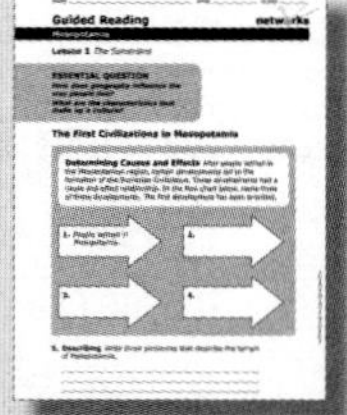

What Do You Know?

Use these worksheets to pre-assess student's background knowledge before they study the chapter.

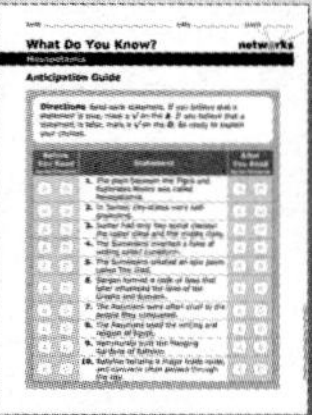

Reading Essentials and Study Guide Workbook

This resource offers writing and reading activities for the approaching-level student. Also available in Spanish.

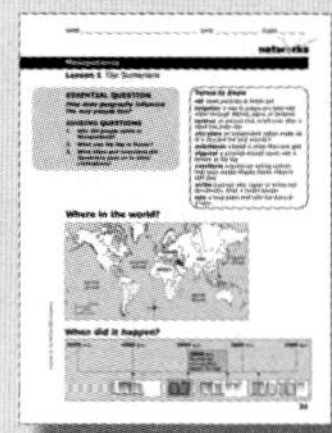

Self-Check Quizzes

This online assessment tool provides instant feedback for students to check their progress.

Political and Industrial Revolutions

1775 to 1850

ESSENTIAL QUESTIONS • *Why does conflict develop?* • *How do new ideas change the way people live?* • *How do governments change?*

networks

There's More Online about how revolutions changed Europe and the United States.

CHAPTER 23

Lesson 1 *The American Revolution*

Lesson 2 *The French Revolution and Napoleon*

Lesson 3 *Nationalism and Nation-States*

Lesson 4 *The Industrial Revolution*

Lesson 5 *Society and Industry*

The Story Matters . . .

The people of France have risen up. They have stormed prisons, seized property, and set nobles on the run. In Paris, the capital, crowds fill the streets, thrilled with their power. Yet, problems remain. The poor are hungrier than ever. It may be a long time before there will be work to do or safe places to set up markets. As you read this chapter, note how revolution can lead to great joy and great tragedy.

◄ *French artist Jacques Louis David became famous for his paintings about the French Revolution. He painted ordinary people, such as this poor woman of Paris, and leaders, such as the Emperor Napoleon.*

ENGAGE

Bellringer Start a class discussion by asking students to share what they know about social classes. Explain that in the United States today, class differences do exist, but they are different from those in other places of the world and at other times in history. Explain that in the 18th century, when a person was born into a social class, he or she was unlikely to ever move up or down to another class. Tell students that this was the case in France at the time of the French Revolution.

Have a volunteer read "The Story Matters . . ." aloud. You may want to explain that the phrase "the people" is used in this context to refer to ordinary people, or the working class. Then tell students that this episode took place during a revolution in France. **Ask:**

- **The text says the revolution will lead to great joy and great tragedy. Based on the details of the paragraph, what is the great joy? What tragedy do you predict will occur as a result of the revolt?** Have students use the details from the paragraph to make their predictions.
- **Why do you think the artist sees ordinary people as interesting artistic subjects? What message is the artist sending about life during this time period? How is this message sad, happy, or troubling?** Tell students that some artists wanted to show the world as it truly was. They painted scenes of real life and real people, such as in this painting. Explain that students will learn more about the artistic movements that emerged during the periods of revolution covered in this chapter.

Letter from the Author

Dear World History Teacher,

The revolutionary era of the late eighteenth century brought dramatic changes. Revolutions in North America and in France produced movements in which the people, not individuals, became the source of political power. The revolutions were based on the principles of liberty and equality. In 1815, a conservative order was reestablished in Europe that the great powers worked to maintain. However, waves of revolution showed that nationalism and liberalism were still alive and active. Between 1850 and 1871, the nation-state became the focus of people's loyalty. Wars were fought to create unified nation-states, while reforms served to strengthen them.

Jackson J. Spielvogel

TEACH & ASSESS

Step Into the Place

V1 Visual Skills

Analyzing a Map Point out the map on these two pages. Have students explore the political revolutions that occurred between 1775 and 1815. Encourage students to think about the impact on the world of the many revolutions within this 40-year time period. **Ask:** How many years passed between the American Revolution and the French Revolution? *(13 years)* Explain to students that although the American Revolution was about gaining independence, the language of the Declaration of Independence also talked about equality and individual rights, which became important issues in the French Revolution as well.

Remind students that communication was slow during the late 1700s and that news of a revolt might have taken months to travel between continents. Explain that in spite of slow communications, the early revolutions inspired the later ones. **Ask:** How would you feel if you lived in a place that was a colony of a European country and you learned that another colony had revolted and gained its independence? *(Students may suggest that they would be inspired to fight for their own independence.)*

Content Background Knowledge

Share with students the following information about the Mexican independence movement.

- In 1810, Miguel Hidalgo y Costilla, a priest from the town of Dolores, rang his church's bells and called to local Native Americans to take back their land from the Spanish. This action is seen as the beginning of the Mexican Independence movement. V2
- In 1813, Mexican leaders declared themselves independent, but they did not defeat Spain and become independent until 1821.
- In 1821, Mexican leaders created a new government, a constitutional monarchy. Agustin de Iturbide, who had been one of the leaders of the revolution, crowned himself emperor in 1822. Two years later, in 1824, Iturbide was overthrown and Mexico became a republic.

ANSWERS, p. 662

Step Into the Place

1. five
2. United States (1776)
3. CRITICAL THINKING Possible answers: These revolutions might frighten the rest of the Western Hemisphere. These revolutions might inspire revolutions in other parts of the Western Hemisphere.

Step Into the Time

Students may say this was a time period of great change.

CHAPTER 23 CCSS
Place and Time: Europe and the Americas 1775 to 1850

Between 1775 and 1815, conflict erupted throughout Europe and the Americas. New ideas led to the overthrow of kings and nobles. New governments favoring citizens' rights were created. Revolutions in one country spread to other countries. At the same time, revolutions in politics were accompanied by advances in economics and technology. Everything seemed to be changing.

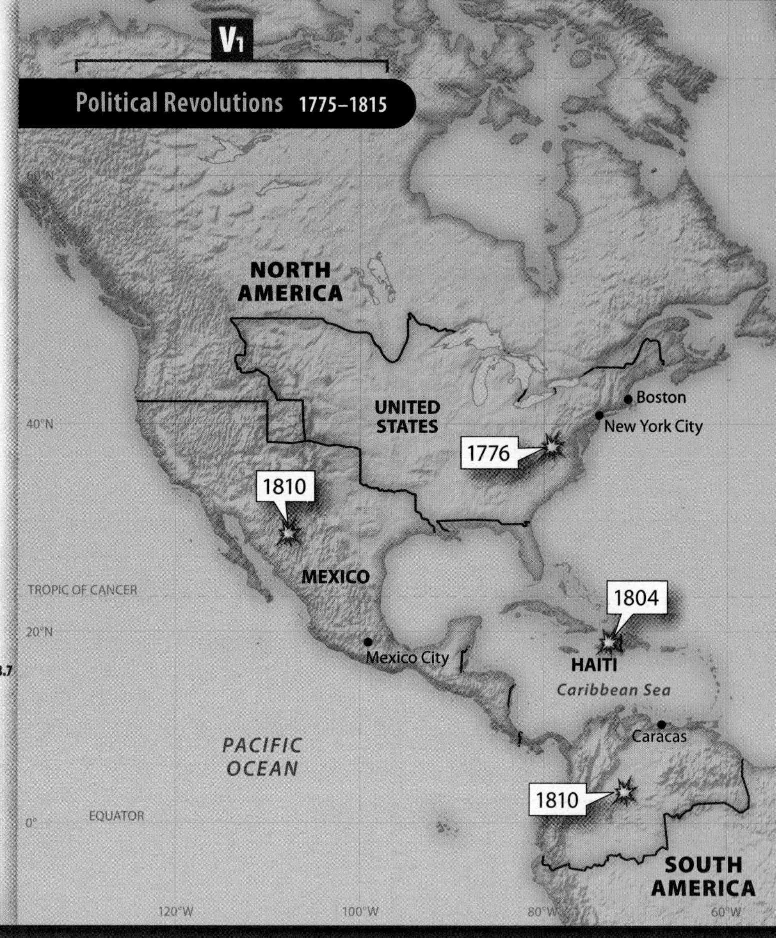

Step Into the Place

MAP FOCUS Between 1775 and 1815, political revolutions took place in Europe and the Americas.

1. **REGIONS** How many revolutions occurred between 1775 and 1815? **RH.6–8.7**
2. **PLACE** Where did revolution happen first? **RH.6–8.7**
3. **CRITICAL THINKING** *Predicting* Make a prediction about how these revolutions might influence the rest of the world. **RH.6–8.2**

Step Into the Time

TIME LINE Choose an event from the time line and use this information to make a generalization about world events during this time period. **RH.6–8.7**

THE WESTERN HEMISPHERE
THE WORLD
1600 1650 1700

1620 Pilgrims establish colony in Massachusetts

1632 Galileo publishes ideas

1652 Dutch settle at Cape Town in South Africa

Project-Based Learning

Hands-On Chapter Project

Create Political Cartoons

Students will create a political cartoon that expresses a point of view about an event from the political revolutions of the late eighteenth or early nineteenth century. Students will discuss events such as the Boston Tea Party, the Stamp Act, the signing of the Declaration of Independence, or Napoleon's exile to Elba. Then small groups will each choose an event and create a political cartoon for it. Students will use worksheets and discussions to help plan their cartoons. Next, each group will present its cartoon to the class. Finally, students will evaluate their research, content, and presentation using an Assessment Rubric.

Technology Extension

Create Online Political Cartoons or Comics

Students will create online comics or cartoons about one of the events that took place during the revolutions of the late eighteenth or early nineteenth century. They will work in groups to choose an event and then use online tools to create the cartoon. They can also add video or audio to their cartoon. Groups can share their work by printing it and displaying it, or they can share it on a class Web site or blog, or via email.

networks *There's More Online!*

☑ **MAP** Explore the interactive version of this map on NETWORKS.

☑ **TIME LINE** Explore the interactive version of this time line on NETWORKS.

ARCTIC CIRCLE
GREAT BRITAIN
London
GERMANY
Paris
FRANCE
Vienna
EUROPE
1789
Rome
ITALY
ATLANTIC OCEAN
Mediterranean Sea
AFRICA

KEY
Revolution
• Major city

0 1,000 miles
0 1,000 km
Miller projection

20°W 0° 20°E

1750 1800 1850 1900

- **1704** John Locke dies
- **1776** U.S. Declaration of Independence signed
- **1788** First British colony in Australia
- **1789** French Revolution begins
- **1804** Haiti wins independence
- **1821** Mexico wins independence
- **1857** Revolt against British rule in India
- **1868** Meiji Era begins in Japan
- **1876** Alexander Graham Bell invents the telephone
- **1900** Boxer Rebellion sweeps China
- **1903** Wright Brothers make first airplane flight

663

CHAPTER 23

Place and Time

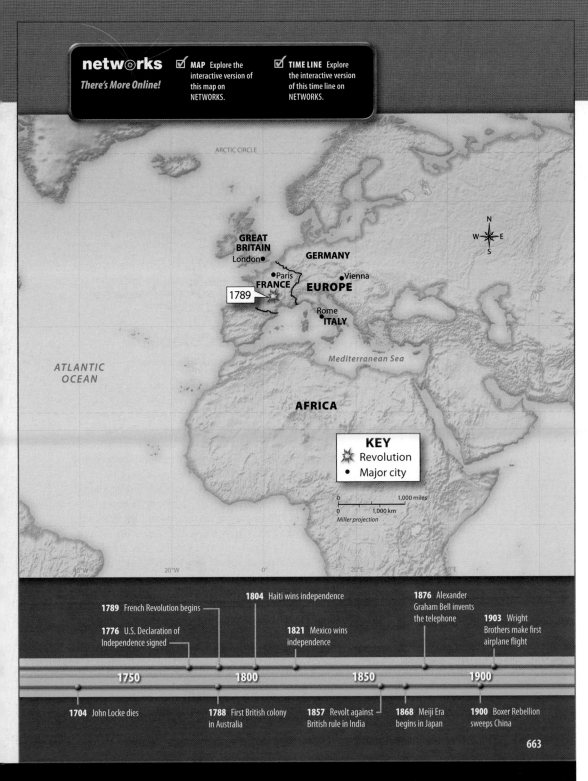

Step Into the Time

V2 Visual Skills

Reading a Time Line Have students review the time line for the chapter. Point out the events that represent a revolution. Have students identify the nations in which the revolutions took place. Have them evaluate how many years passed between each major revolution. **Ask:**

- Which events on the time line are probably part of the Industrial Revolution? *(1876—Alexander Graham Bell invents the telephone; 1903—Wright Brothers make first airplane flight.)*
- Haiti was a French colony. How long after the French Revolution did Haiti win its independence? *(15 years)*
- What possible connection might there have been between all these events? *(Accept reasonable answers, but point out that if people in France are demanding their rights, and gaining them, people in France's colony might have believed that they could also gain rights or freedom.)*

Content Background Knowledge

- Although nations in the western hemisphere were gaining independence in the late 1700s and early 1800s, parts of Asia and Africa were being colonized during these same years. For example, beginning in the mid-1700s, the British East India Company took over large parts of India. In the mid-1800s, a rebellion known as the Indian Mutiny occurred, which led to the British government's taking control of India. In 1877, Queen Victoria of Britain was crowned empress of India.
- Beginning in the 1880s, residents of India organized to work for self-government, and throughout the first half of the twentieth century, the independence movement grew stronger through the leadership of Mohandas Gandhi and Jawaharlal Nehru. After years of protests, most of which were nonviolent, India became an independent country in 1947.

TIME LINE

Place and Time: Political and Industrial Revolution

Analyzing Time Lines Have students scroll through the time line and click on each event to learn more about it. Then ask individual students to describe each event and offer a hypothesis about how that event might have affected people in other parts of the world.

See page 661B for other online activities.

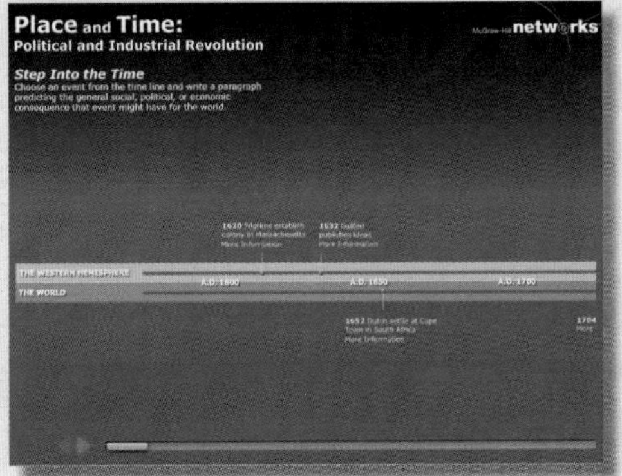

The American Revolution

ENGAGE

Bellringer Write the word *pilgrim* on the board. Remind students that although the term has broad usage, students are to think about it in relation to American history.

Ask: What do you think of when I say the word pilgrim? *(Possible answers: Thanksgiving, Plymouth Rock, black and white clothing, the Mayflower)*

Record answers on the board. Tell students they will learn how the first English settlers served as role models in many ways for generations to come. AL ELL

TEACH & ASSESS

R Reading Skills

Specifying After students have read the passage, ask them to specify, citing evidence from the text, why people chose to leave Europe to establish colonies in the Americas. **Ask:**

- What are two reasons why Europeans wanted to establish new colonies? *(to make money and to escape religious persecution)*
- For which of those two reasons did the Pilgrims create the settlement of Plymouth? *(to escape religious persecution)* AL

ANSWERS, p. 664

TAKING NOTES: Possible answers include: ROW 1: Colonists settle in North America, balancing self-government with British rule. ROW 2: Conflict between Britain and colonists escalates, leading to acts of rebellion such as the Boston Tea Party and, eventually, war. ROW 3: The nation's leaders agree to form a new Constitution based on a federal model, with a stronger central government.

networks *There's More Online!*

- BIOGRAPHY George Washington
- GRAPHIC ORGANIZER The American Revolution
- PRIMARY SOURCE The Declaration of Independence

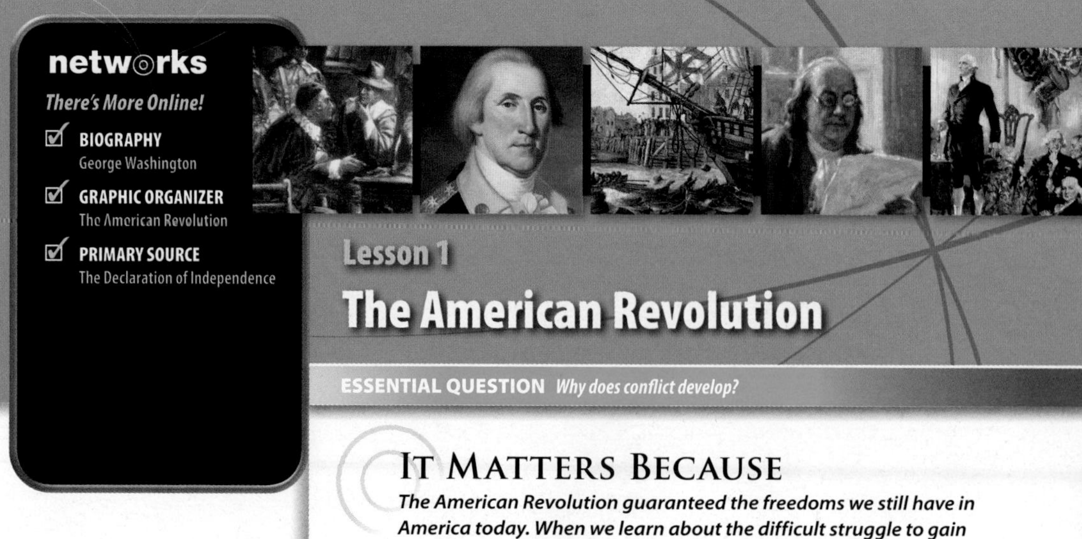

Lesson 1

The American Revolution

ESSENTIAL QUESTION *Why does conflict develop?*

IT MATTERS BECAUSE

The American Revolution guaranteed the freedoms we still have in America today. When we learn about the difficult struggle to gain independence, we value and protect our freedoms.

Britain's American Colonies

GUIDING QUESTION ***Why did England found colonies in North America?***

The first permanent English colony in North America was set up by the Virginia Company in the area that is now Virginia. The company owners wanted riches and planned to make money from the colony. People who wanted religious freedom, such as the Puritans, established other colonies in North America.

R During the early 1600s, Puritans in England were **persecuted** (PUR•seh•kyoo•tehd) for their beliefs. When a group is persecuted, its members are punished and made to suffer. People sometimes persecute others because of religious differences.

In 1620, a group of Puritans known as the Pilgrims left Britain for America so they could worship freely. They sailed across the Atlantic Ocean in a ship called the *Mayflower* and landed in what is today the state of Massachusetts. Their settlement was called Plymouth.

Founding Colonies

The success of Plymouth may have influenced other Puritans to come to America. In 1630, about 1,000 Puritans founded the Massachusetts Bay Colony. Others soon followed. By the mid-1640s, more than 20,000 Puritans had settled in America.

Reading HELPDESK (CCSS)

Taking Notes: ***Cause and Effect***

As you read, keep track of the events on a cause-and-effect chart. For each event, note what happened as a result of the event. RH.6–8.2, RH.6–8.5

The American Revolution

Cause	Effect
Puritans were persecuted.	
The Stamp Act	
The Articles of Confederation	

networks ***Online Teaching Options***

VIDEO

Making a Revolution

Discussing Play the video about the events leading up to the American Revolution. Encourage students to take notes while the experts explain their points of view. Then have a class discussion about the events that unified the American colonists and the idea that the revolution was inevitable.

See page 661C for other online activities.

Other people seeking religious freedom set up colonies elsewhere along the Atlantic coast. For example, English Catholics founded Maryland in 1634. The Quakers, a religious group that had also been persecuted in England, established Pennsylvania in 1680.

When the first English settlers arrived in North America, they came into contact with Native Americans. At first the two groups lived peacefully. The English learned Native American farming skills. Settlers began eating local foods, such as corn and beans. As more English settlers arrived, however, the relationship worsened. Native Americans often died of diseases brought by the English or in battles with the settlers over land.

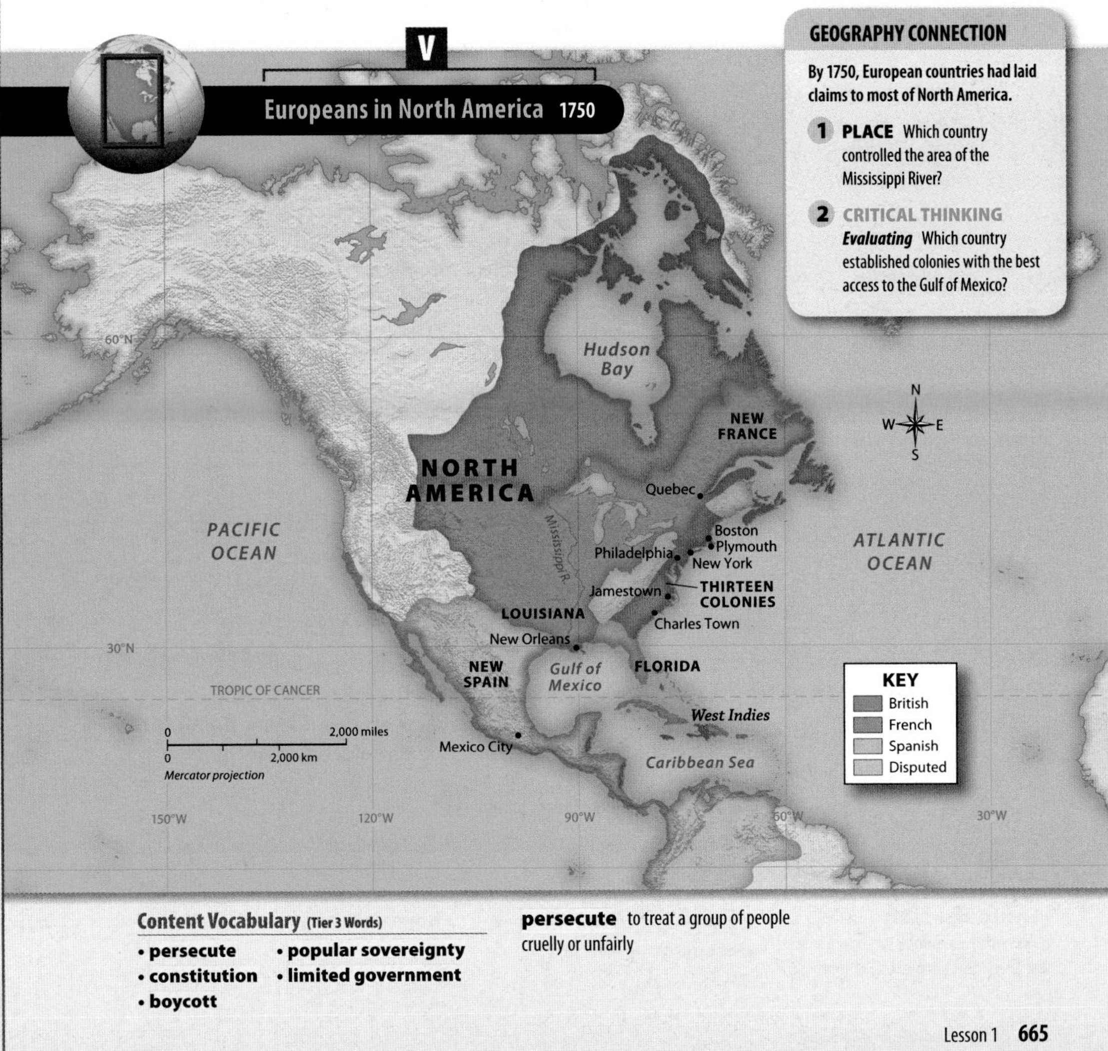

GEOGRAPHY CONNECTION

By 1750, European countries had laid claims to most of North America.

1. **PLACE** Which country controlled the area of the Mississippi River?
2. **CRITICAL THINKING** *Evaluating* Which country established colonies with the best access to the Gulf of Mexico?

Content Vocabulary (Tier 3 Words)

- persecute
- popular sovereignty
- constitution
- limited government
- boycott

persecute to treat a group of people cruelly or unfairly

V Visual Skills

Analyzing Maps Explain to students that European countries competed with each other for the resources and benefits that came from the American colonies. **Ask:**

- In 1750, which part of North America was still unclaimed? *(the west)*
- Which country owned the land in what is present-day Florida? *(Spain)*
- How did the location of the 13 British colonies make those colonies beneficial to Great Britain? *(They were near the coast, so it would be easier to reach them for trade and settlement.)* **BL Visual/Spatial**

C Critical Thinking Skills

Making Inferences Discuss with students how relations between Native Americans and English settlers changed over time. **Ask:**

- Why do you think settlers and Native Americans lived peacefully at first? *(The numbers of settlers may have been so small that they were not a threat to the Native Americans. Also, the settlers may have been accommodating because they desperately needed the Native Americans' help.)*
- Why do you think the relationship between the two groups became worse over time? *(As more settlers arrived, they might have wanted to take over more land from Native Americans. Also, if settlements became stronger, the Europeans had less need for help from Native Americans and did not treat them as well as they did previously.)*

MAP

Europeans in North America, 1750

Drawing Conclusions Display the interactive map, and have students click on the different symbols in the map key to see which areas of North America were claimed by the different European countries. **Ask:** Given the location of the disputed territory, which two countries do you think disputed it? *(France and Great Britain)* How do you think those European powers will settle this dispute? *(Accept reasonable answers. Students may suggest that the two countries will fight for the land.)* Although other groups are not shown on this map, what other groups of people lived in the Americas at this time? *(Native Americans)* **Visual/Spatial**

See page 661C for other online activities.

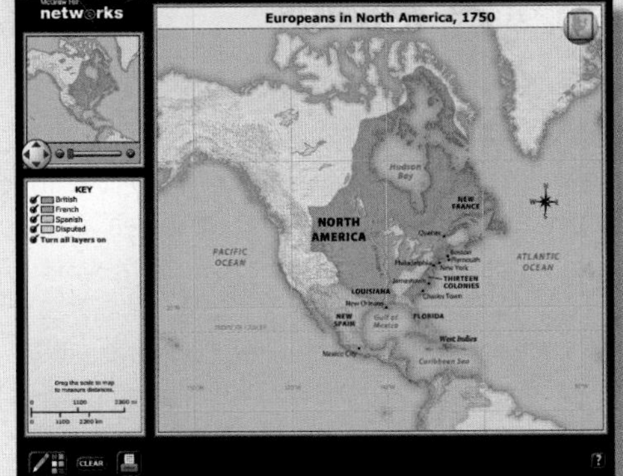

ANSWERS, p. 665

GEOGRAPHY CONNECTION

1. France controlled the area along the Mississippi River.
2. CRITICAL THINKING Spain established colonies with the best access to the Gulf of Mexico.

R Reading Skills

Determining Word Meanings Have students use context clues from the text and consult a dictionary as needed to verify their understanding of the meaning of the terms *representative* and *burgess*. **Ask:** What is a representative? *(someone who represents, or acts for, others)* ELL Students should be able to clearly express that *representative* is a general term and that a *burgess* was a specific term for representatives in colonial Virginia's government.

C Critical Thinking Skills

Making Comparisons Have a class discussion in which students compare the House of Burgesses with the organization of the United States government today. **Ask:**

- What was the House of Burgesses modeled after? *(English Parliament)*
- How is our Congress today similar to the House of Burgesses? *(Both are groups of people elected by others to make laws.)*
- Instead of *burgesses,* what are our representatives in Congress called today? *(Senators, Congressmen, Congresswomen, representatives)*

ANSWER, p. 666

✓ PROGRESS CHECK The colonists wrote constitutions, and they elected their own representatives to organize the colonies.

By the early 1700s, the English had thirteen colonies along the Atlantic coast of North America. Settlers in northern colonies found a cool or moderate climate and rocky soil. The land was more suitable for smaller farms than the warmer, more fertile southern colonies. In the South, large plantations worked by enslaved African people grew crops for export.

In 1620, before stepping off the *Mayflower*, the Pilgrims signed the Mayflower Compact. The Mayflower Compact was a document that called for the signers to follow any laws that would be established.

Self-Government in the Colonies

Self-government began early in England's American colonies. To attract more settlers, the Virginia Company gave colonists in Virginia the right to elect burgesses, or representatives. The elected burgesses formed the first House of Burgesses, modeled on England's Parliament. The House of Burgesses first met in 1619. R

The House of Burgesses set an example of representative government, or a government in which people elect representatives to make laws. Other colonies soon set up their own legislatures. C

The Puritans in Massachusetts also wanted to govern themselves. Before leaving the *Mayflower*, the Pilgrims signed an agreement called the Mayflower Compact. They agreed that they would choose their own leaders and make their own laws:

PRIMARY SOURCE

We, whose names are underwritten . . . Having undertaken for the glory of God, and Advancement of the Christian Faith . . . a Voyage to plant [a] colony . . . do . . . enact, constitute, and frame, such just and equal Laws . . . as shall be thought most meet [acceptable] and convenient for the general good of the Colony . . . .

—from the *Mayflower Compact*

Over the years, most of the English colonies developed **constitutions,** or written plans of government. These **documents** let the colonists elect assemblies and protected their rights.

SuperStock/Getty Images

✓ PROGRESS CHECK

Explaining What steps did the colonists take to govern themselves?

Reading HELPDESK (CCSS)

constitution a document that describes how a country will be governed and guarantees people certain rights

Academic Vocabulary (Tier 2 Words)

document a piece of writing

boycott to protest by refusing to do something

networks Online Teaching Options

LECTURE SLIDE

Britain's American Colonies

Identifying Points of View Show students the lecture slide with the excerpt from the Mayflower Compact. Invite a volunteer to read the excerpt to the class. Then, ask other students to put this excerpt into their own words. **Ask:** Why did the Puritans create such a document? *(They wanted to govern themselves, and a written document was the best way to start doing that.)* Why do you think it is important for a group of people to be led by a written list of rules? *(When all people in a group agree to live by the rules of one document, the group is more likely to get along.)* Explain that the Mayflower Compact and the U.S. Declaration of Independence have some similarities. Help students identify some of those similarities.

networks — Britain's American Colonies

"We, whose names are underwritten...Having undertaken for the glory of God, and Advancement of the Christian Faith...a Voyage to plant [a] colony...do...enact, constitute, and frame, such just and equal Laws...as shall be thought most meet [acceptable] and convenient for the general good of the Colony...."

—from the *Mayflower Compact*

See page 661C for other online activities.

Road to Revolt

GUIDING QUESTION *How did conflict develop between Britain and its American colonies?*

During the 1700s, many changes came to England and its colonies. In 1707, England united with Scotland to form Britain. The term *British* came to mean both the English and the Scots. Meanwhile, the colonies came to depend on Britain for trade and defense.

Trade and the Colonies

The American colonies shipped their raw materials to Britain. In return, they received British manufactured products as well as tea and spices from Asia. To control this trade, Britain passed the Navigation Acts. Under these laws, the colonists had to sell their products to Britain even if they could get a better price elsewhere. Any goods bought from other countries had to go to Britain first and be taxed before going to the Americas.

The colonists at first accepted the trade laws because Britain was a guaranteed buyer of their raw materials. Later, as the colonies grew, colonists wanted to produce their own manufactured goods. They also wanted to sell their products elsewhere if they could get higher prices. Many colonial merchants began smuggling goods in and out of the colonies. Smuggling is shipping products without paying taxes or getting government permission.

Britain Tightens Its Controls

Between 1756 and 1763, Britain and France fought a war for control of North America. When Britain won, it gained nearly all of France's North American empire. The conflict, however, left Britain deeply in debt. Desperate for money, the British made plans to tax the American colonists and tighten trade rules.

In 1765, Parliament passed the Stamp Act, which taxed newspapers and other printed material. These items had to bear a stamp showing that the tax was paid. The colonists were outraged. They responded by boycotting British goods. **Boycotting** is refusing to buy specific products in protest.

Finally, nine colonies sent delegates to a Stamp Act Congress in New York City. The Congress declared that Parliament could not tax the colonies because the colonies did not have representatives in Parliament. The colonists united under the slogan, "No taxation without representation!" They believed that only colonial legislatures had the right to tax them. The British government backed down for a while, but it still needed money. In 1767, Parliament placed taxes on glass, lead, paper, paint, and tea. **C**

George Washington at first tried to peacefully settle the Americans' differences with Britain. What do you think changed his mind about going to war?

C Critical Thinking Skills

Identifying Central Issues Write the slogan "No taxation without representation!" on the board. Have volunteers define the words in the slogan. **Ask:** Who used the slogan? *(the colonists)* What does it mean? *(It means the colonists wanted to participate in the decisions about who and what would be taxed. They wanted a say in the process.)*

Confirm that students understand the importance of taxes to support society. Students should evaluate, however, whether the colonists' demand is reasonable. Have students create a list of reasons to demonstrate their understanding of whether the demand was fair.

Making Connections

Ask students if they are familiar with any modern-day or twentieth-century boycotts. Explain that throughout history, people have used boycotts to protest social and political conditions that they believed were unfair. In 1955–1956, African Americans refused to ride buses in Montgomery, Alabama, to protest segregation on city buses. In the late 1960s, Cesar Chavez led a nationwide boycott of grapes grown in California to protest working conditions for migrant farm workers. Both of these boycotts allowed people to voice their opinions and eventually led to significant social changes.

WORKSHEET

Economics of History Activity: Tariffs in the American Colonies

Evaluating Assign the Economics of History worksheet for homework. Tell students that they will learn how governments use tariffs to control trade. This activity will also help students understand why the colonists objected to Britain's effort to control trade.

See page 661C for other online activities.

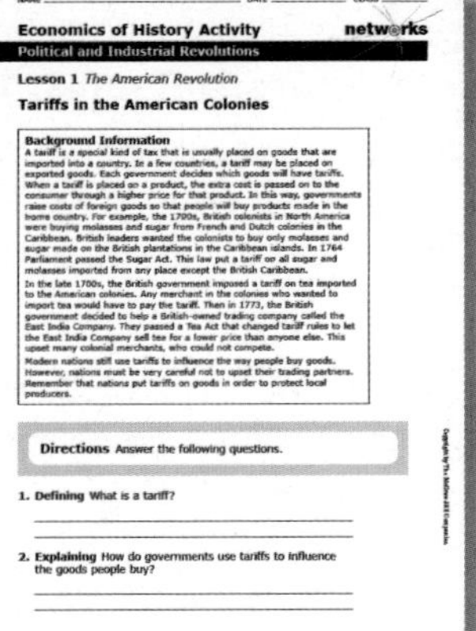

Economics of History Activity
Political and Industrial Revolutions

Lesson 1 The American Revolution
Tariffs in the American Colonies

Background Information

Directions Answer the following questions.

1. Defining What is a tariff?

2. Explaining How do governments use tariffs to influence the goods people buy?

ANSWER, p. 667

Caption Students might say that the fighting at Lexington and Concord changed George Washington's mind or that he was convinced by the arguments of those who were for independence, such as Samuel Adams.

V Visual Skills

Reading a Map Help students understand that the raw materials that were exported from one location were often used to make manufactured goods that were then shipped out of the next location. For example, the sugar that was exported from the Caribbean islands to the Northern colonies was used to make the rum that was then shipped from the Northern colonies to West Africa. **Visual/Spatial** **Ask:**

- **What kinds of good were shipped from Britain to the colonies?** *(manufactured goods)*
- **What goods were shipped from Boston to Britain?** *(furs, fish, fruit)*
- **What was shipped from West Africa to North America?** *(enslaved persons and gold dust)*

T Technology Skills

Researching on the Internet Have pairs of students choose one of the events that took place in Massachusetts, such as the Boston Massacre , the Boston Tea Party, or the Intolerable Acts. Then have them research this event on the Internet and write a brief paragraph explaining what happened and how it increased tensions between the colonists and the British government. **Verbal/Linguistic** **Interpersonal**

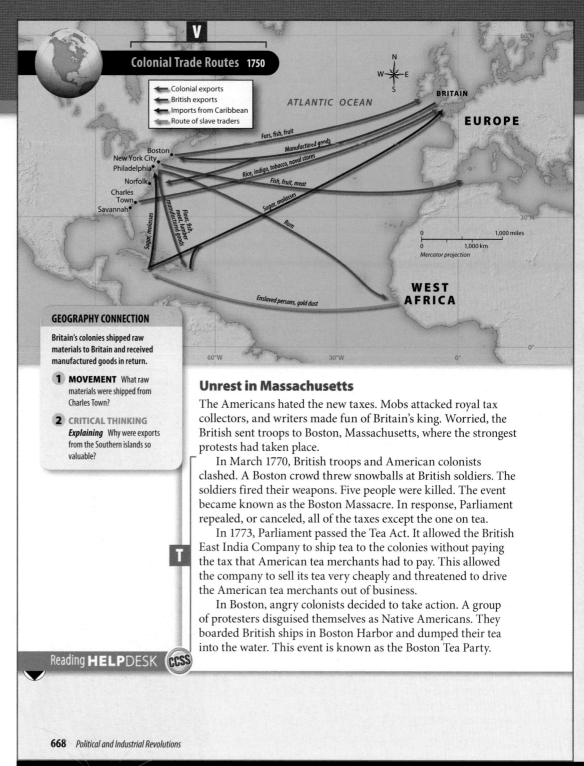

ANSWERS, p. 668

GEOGRAPHY CONNECTION

1. Rice, indigo, and tobacco were shipped from Charles Town.
2. **CRITICAL THINKING** because they could not be found in Europe

V

Colonial Trade Routes 1750

Colonial exports
British exports
Imports from Caribbean
Route of slave traders

ATLANTIC OCEAN
BRITAIN
EUROPE
WEST AFRICA
Boston
New York City
Philadelphia
Norfolk
Charles Town
Savannah
Furs, fish, fruit
Manufactured goods
Rice, indigo, tobacco, naval stores
Fish, fruit, meat
Sugar, molasses
Rum
Flour, fish, meat, lumber, manufactured goods
Sugar, molasses
Enslaved persons, gold dust
0 1,000 miles
0 1,000 km
Mercator projection

GEOGRAPHY CONNECTION

Britain's colonies shipped raw materials to Britain and received manufactured goods in return.

1. **MOVEMENT** What raw materials were shipped from Charles Town?
2. **CRITICAL THINKING** ***Explaining*** Why were exports from the Southern islands so valuable?

Unrest in Massachusetts

The Americans hated the new taxes. Mobs attacked royal tax collectors, and writers made fun of Britain's king. Worried, the British sent troops to Boston, Massachusetts, where the strongest protests had taken place.

In March 1770, British troops and American colonists clashed. A Boston crowd threw snowballs at British soldiers. The soldiers fired their weapons. Five people were killed. The event became known as the Boston Massacre. In response, Parliament repealed, or canceled, all of the taxes except the one on tea.

T

In 1773, Parliament passed the Tea Act. It allowed the British East India Company to ship tea to the colonies without paying the tax that American tea merchants had to pay. This allowed the company to sell its tea very cheaply and threatened to drive the American tea merchants out of business.

In Boston, angry colonists decided to take action. A group of protesters disguised themselves as Native Americans. They boarded British ships in Boston Harbor and dumped their tea into the water. This event is known as the Boston Tea Party.

Reading HELPDESK CCSS

networks Online Teaching Options

MAP

Colonial Trade Routes, 1750

Calculating Display the map of Colonial Trade Routes, and ask students to identify the products that traveled on the different routes. Then have students work in small groups to calculate distances, such as the following:

- **The distance that slaves traveled from West Africa to the Caribbean** *(about 3,000 miles)*
- **The distance that sugar and molasses traveled from the Caribbean to the ports of New York and Philadelphia** *(about 1,000 miles)*
- **The distance that manufactured goods traveled from Britain to Norfolk** *(about 3,300 miles)*

Logical/Mathematical

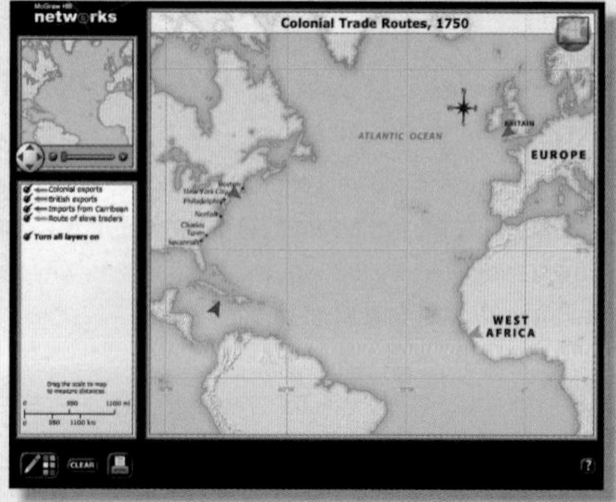

See page 661C for other online activities.

To punish the colonists, Parliament passed laws that shut down Boston Harbor and placed Massachusetts under military control. It also required colonists to house and feed British soldiers. The colonists called these laws the Intolerable Acts, or laws they could not accept. The Acts made the colonies realize that they had to work together to defend their liberties. In September 1774, delegates from twelve colonies met in Philadelphia at the First Continental Congress. They demanded that the Intolerable Acts be repealed. Colonial leaders, however, could not agree about what to do. Some, such as George Washington of Virginia, hoped to settle the dispute with Britain. Others, like Samuel Adams of Massachusetts and Patrick Henry of Virginia, wanted the colonies to declare independence. W

✓ PROGRESS CHECK

Identifying Cause and Effect What were the Intolerable Acts? How did the colonists respond to them?

A War for Independence

GUIDING QUESTION *How did war between Britain and the American colonies lead to the rise of a new nation—the United States of America?*

While colonial leaders debated, fighting began in Massachusetts. British soldiers set out to destroy colonial weapons being stored in the town of Concord. On April 19, 1775, they met armed colonists at Lexington and fought the first battle of the American Revolution. C1

News of the conflict spread throughout the colonies. In May 1775, the Second Continental Congress met in Philadelphia. It created an army with George Washington as commander. The Congress, however, tried one last time to settle differences with the British. Members sent an appeal to King George III, but he refused to listen. C2

North Wind/North Wind Picture Archives

Over 100 people, mostly young artisans and laborers, took part in the Boston Tea Party. Nearly 45 tons of tea—about equal in value to a million dollars today—were tossed into Boston Harbor.

▶ CRITICAL THINKING

Explaining Why did the protesters dress up as Native Americans?

W Writing Skills

Argument Remind students that many people opposed the idea of declaring or fighting for independence from Great Britain. Have them each write a brief speech that would have been given by either someone who initially opposed declaring independence, such as George Washington, or someone who wanted to declare independence, such as Patrick Henry. Students' speeches should include evidence from the text to support their arguments. **Verbal/Linguistic**

C1 Critical Thinking Skills

Cause and Effect Draw a cause-and-effect graphic organizer on the board, and have students evaluate the following important developments. **Visual/Spatial Ask:**

- **What was the immediate cause of the first battle of the war?** *(The British set out to destroy colonial weapons in Concord, Massachusetts. This led to the first battle, which was fought in nearby Lexington.)*
- **What was the effect of the first battle?** *(The Second Continental Congress met and organized an army. It also sent an appeal to the king to settle their differences.)*

C2 Critical Thinking Skills

Drawing Conclusions Ask students to reflect on the sequence of events leading to the war between Great Britain and the Colonies. **Ask: Based on the events of the spring of 1775, do you think war between Great Britain and the colonies was inevitable?** *(Accept reasonable answers, but make sure students understand that the battle at Lexington did not automatically lead to war.)*

BIOGRAPHY

The Life of George Washington

Identifying/Evaluating Have students read the biography of George Washington, sliding the bat at the side of the text to see additional information. Ask volunteers to identify Washington's achievements and then to state which achievement they think was the most important, giving factual reasons for their answers.

See page 661C for other online activities.

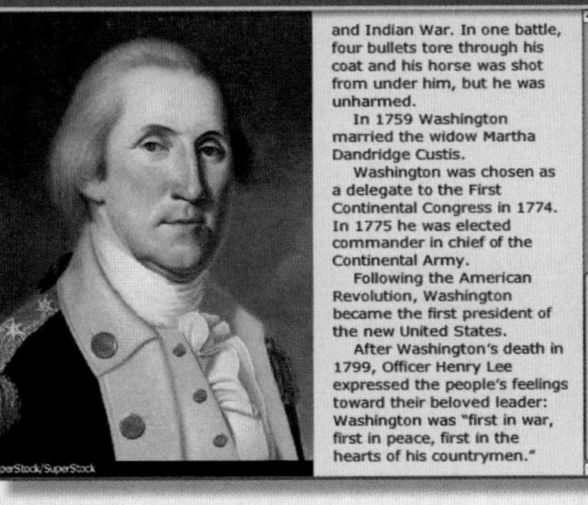

networks
The Life of George Washington
BIOGRAPHY
and Indian War. In one battle, four bullets tore through his coat and his horse was shot from under him, but he was unharmed.
In 1759 Washington married the widow Martha Dandridge Custis.
Washington was chosen as a delegate to the First Continental Congress in 1774. In 1775 he was elected commander in chief of the Continental Army.
Following the American Revolution, Washington became the first president of the new United States.
After Washington's death in 1799, Officer Henry Lee expressed the people's feelings toward their beloved leader: Washington was "first in war, first in peace, first in the hearts of his countrymen."
SuperStock/SuperStock

ANSWERS, p. 669

✓ PROGRESS CHECK The Intolerable Acts was the name given by the colonists to a series of laws imposed by the British and designed to punish the colonists. These acts included laws to shut down Boston Harbor, to place Massachusetts under military control, and to require the colonists to house and feed British soldiers. In response, the colonists agreed to work together to protect their rights. The colonists' displeasure with the Acts led to the First Continental Congress.

CRITICAL THINKING Protesters dressed up as Native Americans to disguise their identities and to make the British think Native Americans were responsible for the Tea Party.

The American Revolution

R Reading Skills

Listing After students have read the selection, hold a class discussion about challenges that Patriots and the British faced during the Revolutionary War. Have students list advantages and disadvantages for each side, citing evidence from the text. *(Possible answers: PATRIOTS: Advantages include fighting on home soil, fighting for a cause they believed in, willingness to use nontraditional tactics in battle; disadvantages include having a smaller and weaker army and navy. BRITISH: Advantages include having a much stronger military; disadvantages include having to fight far from Britain, needing to defeat the opposition in many different colonies, and facing foreign allies of America.)*

Ask: **Could the American forces have defeated the British without foreign help?** *(Answers will vary but should demonstrate comprehension of the reading.)*

Content Background Knowledge

The Declaration of Independence

When writing the Declaration of Independence, Thomas Jefferson drew on historical as well as contemporary ideas. The Declaration drew from earlier English documents, such as the Magna Carta and the English Bill of Rights. Both documents established the idea that government powers have limits. They also say that rulers have to obey the laws and treat citizens fairly.

The document also cited newer ideas from the Enlightenment, most significantly the ideas of English philosopher John Locke. Locke stated that all people are born with certain natural rights: the rights to life, liberty, and property. Jefferson borrowed this idea but changed the list of inalienable rights to life, liberty, and the pursuit of happiness.

Locke also believed in the concept of a social contract. According to Locke, this contract was an agreement between the people and their government stating that the government would protect the people's rights. If the government failed to do so and it violated the social contract, the people had the right and the responsibility to overthrow that government and replace it with leadership that would abide by the social contract.

This argument formed the crux of the Declaration of Independence: King George III had abused the rights of the colonists, and so the colonists were obliged to rebel against him.

ANSWER, p. 670

CRITICAL THINKING so that they would be taken seriously by the British crown

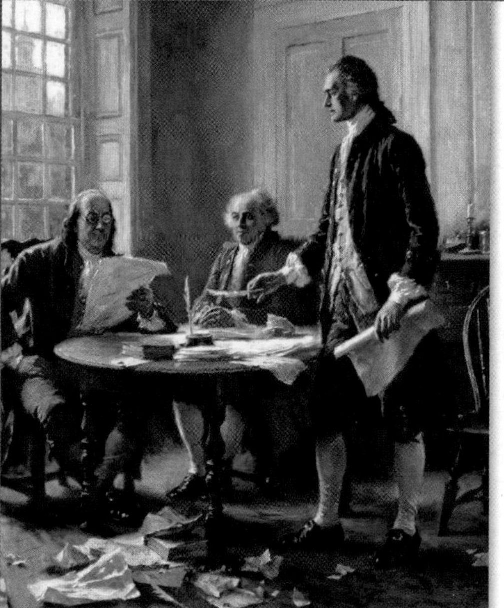

Benjamin Franklin, John Adams, and Thomas Jefferson worked together to write the Declaration of Independence.

▶ **CRITICAL THINKING**
Speculating Why do you think Americans needed an official document to declare independence?

More and more Americans began to think that independence was the only answer. In January 1776, in a pamphlet called *Common Sense*, writer Thomas Paine called on the colonists to break away from Britain.

The Declaration of Independence

On July 4, 1776, the Congress issued the Declaration of Independence. Written by Thomas Jefferson of Virginia, the Declaration stated that the colonies were separating from Britain and forming a new nation—the United States of America.

In the Declaration, Jefferson explained why the Americans were creating a new nation. He referred to John Locke's idea that people can overthrow a government that ignores their rights. The Declaration stated that "all men are created equal" and have certain God-given rights. King George III had violated colonists' rights, and so the colonists had the right to rebel.

An American Victory

R

The Declaration turned the conflict into a war for independence. The struggle was long and bitter. The American Continental Army had fewer and less-disciplined soldiers than the British. However, they had a skilled general in Washington. The British had the disadvantage of trying to fight a war a long way from home. Also, they had to conquer the whole country to win. The Americans only had to hold out until the British accepted defeat.

The turning point came in October 1777 when the Americans won the Battle of Saratoga in New York. France, Britain's old enemy, realized that the colonists might win and agreed to help the Americans.

The final victory came in 1781 at the Battle of Yorktown in Virginia. American and French forces surrounded and trapped the British. The British surrendered. Peace talks began, and two years later, the Treaty of Paris ended the war. Britain finally accepted American independence.

The United States Constitution

The United States at first was a confederation, or a loose union of independent states. Its plan of government was called the Articles of Confederation. The Articles created a national government,

Reading HELPDESK (CCSS)

popular sovereignty the idea that government is created by the people and must act according to people's wishes

limited government a government whose powers are restricted through laws or a document such as a constitution

Academic Vocabulary (Tier 2 Words)

federal referring to an organized union of states under one government

networks Online Teaching Options

GAME

The American Revolution Crossword Puzzle

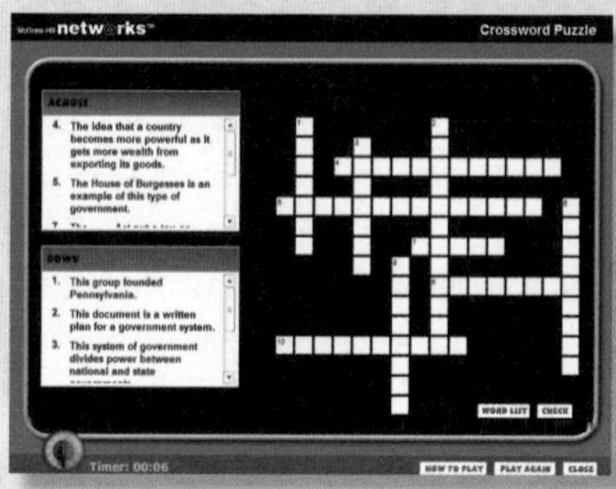

Identifying Have students work individually or in pairs to complete the crossword puzzle. If they need help, encourage them to review the lesson, or they can click on the "Word List" box for a word bank of possible answers. You may wish to organize the class into small groups and challenge students to see who can solve the puzzle the fastest.

See page 661C for other online activities.

The American Revolution

but the states held most powers. It soon became clear that the Articles were too weak to deal with the new nation's problems.

To change the Articles, 55 delegates met in Philadelphia in 1787. They decided instead to write a constitution for an entirely new national government. The new United States Constitution set up a **federal** system, which divided powers between the national government and the states. The delegates divided power in the national government between executive, legislative, and judicial branches. A system called checks and balances enabled each branch to limit the powers of the other branches.

The American leaders who met in Philadelphia in 1787 and wrote the U.S. Constitution were some of the nation's best political minds. What sort of government did the Constitution create?

SuperStock/SuperStock

The Constitution made the United States a republic with an elected president. In 1789, George Washington was elected the first president of the United States. That same year, a Bill of Rights was added to the Constitution. The Bill of Rights guaranteed certain rights to citizens that the government could not violate. These rights included freedom of religion, speech, and press, and the right to trial by jury.

The U.S. Constitution was shaped by Enlightenment principles. One of these is **popular sovereignty**, or the idea that government receives its powers from the people. Another principle is **limited government**, or the idea that a government may use only those powers given to it by the people. **R**

PROGRESS CHECK

Explaining What kind of government did the Americans set up after the American Revolution?

LESSON 1 REVIEW 

Review Vocabulary (Tier 3 Words)

1. Use the words *persecute* and *boycott* in a sentence about the American colonies. RH.6–8.2, RH.6–8.4
2. What is meant by *popular sovereignty* and why was it important? RH.6–8.2, RH.6–8.4

Answer the Guiding Questions

3. ***Evaluating*** Why did the success of the Pilgrims influence others to settle in the Americas? RH.6–8.2
4. ***Making Connections*** What types of British laws did American colonists protest the most? RH.6–8.2
5. ***Drawing Conclusions*** Why do you think it was important for the authors of the Constitution to create a Bill of Rights? RH.6–8.2
6. **ARGUMENT** Write a short essay from the viewpoint of Thomas Paine in which you try to persuade American colonists to declare independence from Britain. WHST.6–8.1, WHST.6–8.10

R Reading Skills

Summarizing From the reading, ask students to explain the meaning of the term *popular sovereignty.* Ask them to express how this principle led to the Declaration of Independence, and also how it shaped the government that was created by the Declaration of Independence. Use the discussion to cultivate student understanding that the colonists believed in popular sovereignty, but they did not have it under British rules, so they fought the American Revolution. When writing the Constitution, leaders put in place systems that allowed the people to elect their leaders at both the state and national levels, which gave them popular sovereignty. BL

Have students complete the Lesson 1 Review.

Content Background Knowledge

The U.S. Constitution Like the Declaration, the Constitution draws upon the ideas of the social contract and natural rights. The first line of the document ("We the People of the United States of America . . .") makes it plain that the people are the source of government power. The Bill of Rights enforces the idea that all people are guaranteed certain rights. The Constitution also draws on other Enlightenment ideals, such as Montesquieu's separation of powers. Although the Founders may have agreed on the broad principles of the Constitution, heated arguments occurred over the details. Larger states wanted to make sure they had power proportionate to their size. Smaller states wanted to make sure they had power equal to that of larger states. In the end, a compromise was reached: a bicameral (two-house) legislature. In the House of Representatives, states with larger populations would have greater representation and, therefore, greater power. In the Senate, every state would have an equal number of representatives and, therefore, equal power.

LESSON 1 REVIEW ANSWERS

1. Sample answer: American colonists felt persecuted by British tax policies, so they boycotted British goods.
2. Popular sovereignty is the idea that government receives its powers from the people. It is significant because it determines the source of power in a government: the people.
3. The success of the Pilgrims set an example for other groups seeking religious freedom, such as the Quakers and the Catholics.
4. The colonists protested most against British laws that restricted colonial businesses or impacted the colonial economy.
5. The Bill of Rights spelled out the laws held by the citizens of the nation that could not be taken away by the national government.
6. Essays should include a coherent argument in favor of declaring independence. Examples and concrete details should be included to support the argument.

CLOSE & REFLECT

Speculating Point out to students that the U.S. Constitution was developed after the Articles of Confederation was determined to be too weak to govern the nation effectively. Have students speculate about what might have happened if the Articles had not been revised. **Ask: How might the nation have fared under a weaker constitution?** *(Conflict would have developed; the government might have fallen apart.)*

ANSWERS, p. 671

Caption: The Constitution set up a representative government.

PROGRESS CHECK After the American Revolution, the Americans set up a national government under the Articles of Confederation. This confederation, or loose union of states, gave most power to the states.

ENGAGE

Bellringer Write the word *bourgeoisie* on the board. Have students brainstorm a list of jobs they would like to hold when they are adults. ELL

After writing these jobs on the board, cross out any government jobs or jobs in the church. Tell students that the remaining workers would be considered part of the French bourgeoisie.

Explain that students will learn how the bourgeoisie solved some of their problems in this lesson.

TEACH & ASSESS

C Critical Thinking Skills

Making Connections Discuss with students the role of taxes in modern-day economies. **Ask:**

- Who pays taxes in the United States today? *(almost everyone)*
- What are taxes used for? *(Accept reasonable answers such as schools, the military, public services, etc.)*
- In France in the late 1700s, which groups of people did not have to pay taxes? *(the nobles and the clergy)*
- How do you think the rest of society felt about that? *(Accept reasonable answers.)*

networks *There's More Online!*

- GRAPHIC ORGANIZER Time Line
- MAP Napoleon's Empire
- SLIDE SHOW • The Estates General • The Bastille
- VIDEO

Lesson 2

The French Revolution and Napoleon

ESSENTIAL QUESTION *Why is history important?*

IT MATTERS BECAUSE

The French Revolution drew on some of the ideas of the American Revolution.

The Revolution Begins

GUIDING QUESTION *Why did revolution break out in France?*

The American Revolution had an immediate effect on many people in France. They also wanted political changes based on the ideas of freedom and equality. The French Revolution began in 1789. It dramatically changed France and all of Europe.

The Causes of the French Revolution

In the 1700s, France was one of the most powerful countries in Europe. French kings ruled with absolute power. Nobles lived in great wealth and enjoyed many privileges. Most of France's people, however, were poor. They had little education and struggled to make a living.

The French people were divided into three **estates,** or classes. This system determined a person's legal rights and social standing. It also created great inequality in French society.

C The First Estate was the Catholic clergy, or church officials. They did not pay taxes, and they received money from church lands. The Second Estate was the nobles. They held the highest posts in the military and in government. Like the clergy, the nobles paid no taxes. They lived in luxury at the king's court or in their country houses surrounded by large areas of land.

Reading **HELP**DESK CCSS

Taking Notes: ***Sequencing***

As you read, use a time line to keep track of when events happened. Note the date and a word or two about the event. RH.6–8.2

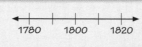

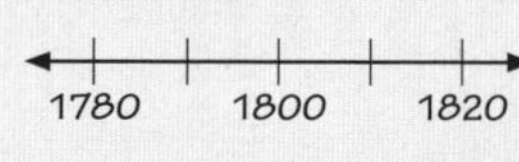

Content Vocabulary (Tier 3 Words)

- **estate**
- **bourgeoisie**
- **coup d'etat**

networks ***Online Teaching Options***

VIDEO

Napoleon

Listing Have students take notes about Napoleon's life and achievements while watching the video titled *Napoleon.* Then organize the class into small groups and have them create a list of the important events and achievements in Napoleon's life. After they have shared their lists with the class, have a class discussion to explore why Napoleon was a successful leader.

See page 661D for other online activities.

ANSWERS, p. 672

TAKING NOTES:
1789 French Revolution Begins
1791 National Assembly makes France a constitutional monarchy; Marie Antoinette imprisoned
1792 Louis XVI executed
1793 Reign of Terror begins
1794 Reign of Terror ends; the Directory is created
1799 Napoleon takes power in coup d'état
1804 Empire of Napoleon established

Everyone else in France belonged to the Third Estate. At the top of this group were members of the middle class, known as the **bourgeoisie** (burzh•wah•ZEE). Merchants, bankers, doctors, lawyers, and teachers were members of the bourgeoisie. Next were the city workers—artisans, day laborers, and servants. At the bottom were the peasants, who made up more than 80 percent of the French people. Although the members of the Third Estate paid taxes to the king, they had no voice in governing the country.

As the middle class learned more about Enlightenment ideas, they began to resent the privileges of the nobles and clergy. An Englishman traveling in France discovered how **widespread** the unrest had become:

PRIMARY SOURCE

"Walking up a long hill . . . I was joined by a poor woman who complained of the times, and that it was a sad country; . . . she said her husband had but a morsel [small piece] of land, one cow, and a poor little horse, yet they had [42 lbs.] of wheat and three chickens to pay as rent to one [lord], and [4 lbs.] of oats, one chicken, and 1s. [a coin] to pay to another, besides very heavy tallies [land taxes] and other taxes."

—from *Travels*, by Arthur Young, 1789

V

The National Assembly

In 1788, food shortages and rising prices caused great discontent throughout France. At the same time, the French government was almost bankrupt because of costly wars and rising expenses for the court of King Louis XVI (LOO•ee). French banks became reluctant to lend money to the government. The king, desperate for funds, asked the nobles and clergy to pay taxes. When these groups refused, Louis called a meeting of the country's legislature, the Estates-General. This group was made up of representatives from all three estates. If the Estates-General agreed, Louis could impose new taxes.

C

In the Estates-General, the nobles and clergy refused to give up their privileges, including not paying taxes. Frustrated, the delegates of the Third Estate decided to meet separately. They formed a new group—the National Assembly—and agreed not to break up until they wrote a constitution for France.

The people of Paris celebrated this victory, but they worried that the king's troops would shut down the National Assembly. They got ready to fight. On July 14, 1789, a large crowd stormed a prison called the Bastille (ba•STEEL).

THE THREE ESTATES IN PREREVOLUTIONARY FRANCE

Population

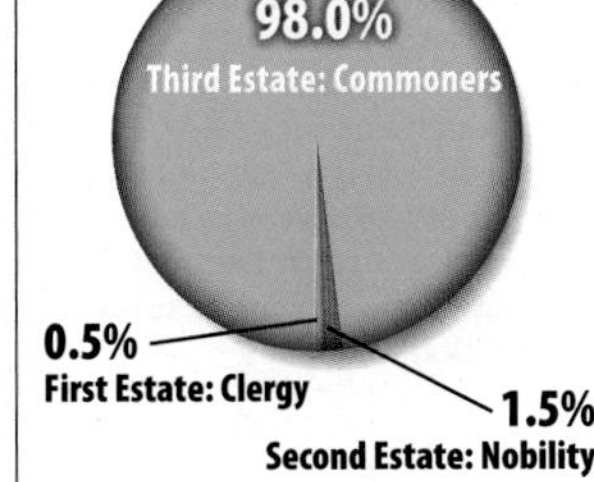

Land Ownership

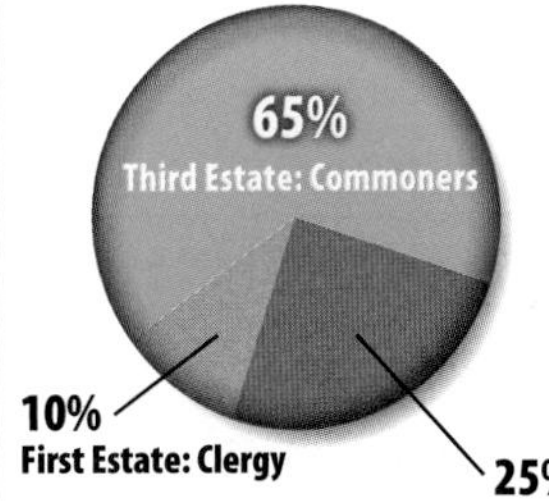

Taxation

Ninety-eight of every 100 people in France were members of the Third Estate.

▶ **CRITICAL THINKING**

Drawing Conclusions Upon which estate in France did the government depend for its income?

estate a social class in France before the French Revolution

bourgeoisie the middle class in France

Academic Vocabulary (Tier 2 Words)

widespread frequent in many places; common

SLIDE SHOW

The Estates-General

Identifying Problems Have students view the slide show, clicking on the arrows at the bottom left of the screen to move to new slides. Then have small groups choose one of the three estates and write a short speech as a member of that estate, telling what problems, if any, they see in the current social and economic structure.

See page 661D for other online activities.

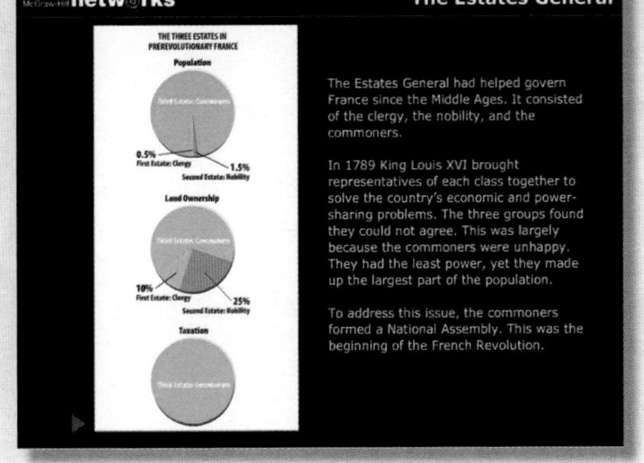

networks
The Estates General
THE THREE ESTATES IN PREREVOLUTIONARY FRANCE
Population
Land Ownership
Taxation
The Estates General had helped govern France since the Middle Ages. It consisted of the clergy, the nobility, and the commoners.
In 1789 King Louis XVI brought representatives of each class together to solve the country's economic and power-sharing problems. The three groups found they could not agree. This was largely because the commoners were unhappy. They had the least power, yet they made up the largest part of the population.
To address this issue, the commoners formed a National Assembly. This was the beginning of the French Revolution.

V Visual Skills

Analyzing Graphs Direct students' attention to the circle graphs on the right side of the page. After providing time for students to review the graphs, **ask:**

- **Which estate made up the largest part of the population?** *(the third)* **The smallest?** *(the first)*
- **What percentage of land did the Nobles own?** *(25%)*
- **Who paid all the taxes?** *(the commoners or the Third Estate)*
- **Based on this infographic, why do you think the members of the Third Estate were unhappy?** *(They made up the largest part of the population and paid taxes, but they had no voice in the government.)* **Visual/Spatial**

C Critical Thinking Skills

Sequencing After reading "The National Assembly" section in the textbook, write the following events on the board:

- The nobles and clergy refused to pay taxes or give up privileges.
- The National Assembly was formed.
- There were food shortages and rising discontent.
- French banks did not want to lend money to the government.
- A new constitution was written for France.
- King Louis called a meeting of the Estates-General.

Have students work in small groups to put these events in the correct chronological order. *(There were food shortages and rising discontent. French banks did not want to lend money to the government. King Louis called a meeting of the Estates-General. The nobles and clergy refused to pay taxes or give up privileges. The National Assembly was formed. A new constitution was written for France.)* **Interpersonal**

Content Background Knowledge

During the Enlightenment, also known as the Age of Reason, philosophers in England and France developed theories about government and individual rights. Jean-Jacques Rousseau wrote *Of the Social Contract,* in which he said that government should be a contract between the people and their rulers and that if the government did not serve the people's needs, the people had the right to rebel. Rousseau also wrote that people should not have to follow laws that they had no part in making. This was one of the ideas that influenced members of France's Third Estate when they wrote the "Declaration of the Rights of Man and of the Citizen" during the French Revolution.

ANSWER, p. 673

CRITICAL THINKING the Third Estate

V Visual Skills

Creating Visuals Have students create posters or banners that reflect the views of peasants and rebels after the fall of the Bastille. Posters should use words and images to show what people believed and why they wanted their government to change.

R Reading Skills

Comparing and Contrasting After students have read the selection, have them describe and differentiate the types of government in France during the late 1700s. **Ask:**

- **What is a constitutional monarchy?** *(It is a form of government in which a monarch has some powers, but those powers are limited by a written constitution.)*
- **How did that differ from the form of government France had before?** *(Until this time, France had a monarchy that was not limited by a written constitution.)*
- **What type of government did the National Convention create?** *(It created a republic, which is a government in which the people elect leaders to represent them.)*

ANSWERS, p. 674

✓ **PROGRESS CHECK** The National Assembly issued the Declaration of the Rights of Man and the Citizen, which guaranteed freedom of speech, the press, and religion, and protected against unjust arrest and punishment.

Caption: The French celebrate a day of violence because it marks the start of their revolution.

Connections to TODAY

Political Left and Right

When the National Assembly met in 1789, those who supported far-reaching political changes sat on the left side of the meeting room. The people who favored little or no change sat on the right side. Today we still use the terms *left* and *right* to describe these two political viewpoints.

V News of the fall of the Bastille spread to the countryside, where the peasants rose up against the nobles. To satisfy the people, the National Assembly ended the privileges of the clergy and nobles. It also issued the Declaration of the Rights of Man and the Citizen. Based on Enlightenment ideas, the declaration stated that the government's powers came from the people, not the king. All people, it said, were equal under the law.

In 1791, the National Assembly made France a constitutional monarchy. France was to be ruled by an elected legislature. Louis, however, refused to accept these changes and tried to flee Paris. As Europe's kings threatened to crush France's revolution, some leaders in Paris pushed for greater change. In 1792, they set up a new government called the National Convention.

✓ **PROGRESS CHECK**

R ***Identifying*** What political reforms did the National Assembly adopt?

A Republic in France

GUIDING QUESTION ***How did supporters of France's revolution enforce their reforms?***

The National Convention ended the monarchy and made France a republic. It wrote a new constitution giving the vote to every man, whether or not he owned property. Meanwhile, two

The people of Paris demonstrated against the king by violently attacking the hated Bastille prison. Today, the French celebrate the day of attack—July 14—as Bastille Day, their national holiday. Why do you think the French celebrate a day of violence?

SuperStock/SuperStock

Academic Vocabulary (Tier 2 Words)

radical extreme or far-reaching

networks Online Teaching Options

SLIDE SHOW

The Bastille

Comparing Have students view the slide of *The Bastille.* After they have read all the information, have the class compare the Declaration of the Rights of Man and the Citizen to the Declaration of Independence. Encourage students to cite specific examples as they contribute to the discussion. BL

See page 661D for other online activities.

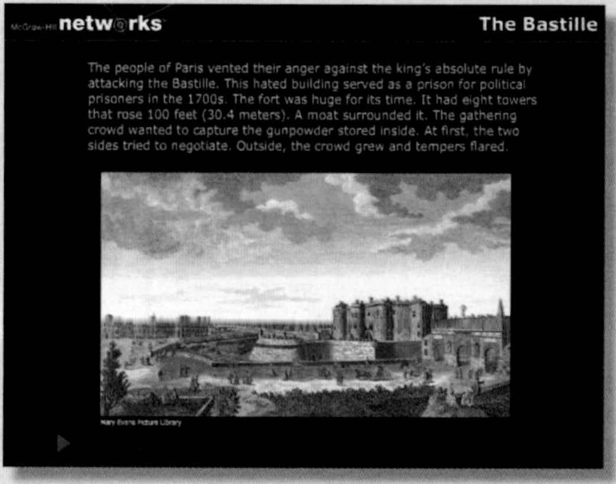

groups fought for control of the Convention. One group, called Girondists, believed the revolution had gone far enough. The other group, known as Jacobins, favored more **radical** change. The Jacobins finally won and took power.

Toward the Future

In late 1792, the National Convention put King Louis XVI on trial and found him guilty of aiding France's enemies. A month later, Louis was beheaded on the guillotine (GEE•oh•teen)—a new machine designed to quickly execute people.

Louis's execution alarmed Europe's ruling monarchs. The rulers of Austria and Prussia were already at war with France. In early 1793, Britain, Spain, the Netherlands, and Sardinia joined them in battle against France's revolutionary army.

As the threat of foreign invasions rose, many French people rushed to defend the revolution. The people of Paris were dedicated supporters, shopkeepers, artisans, and workers who saw themselves as heroes and heroines and demanded respect from the upper classes. They addressed each other as "citizen" or "citizeness" rather than "mister" or "madame."

The Reign of Terror

Despite widespread support, the revolution had many enemies within France. To deal with growing unrest, the National Convention set up the Committee of Public Safety to run the country. The Committee took harsh steps against anyone they felt opposed the revolution. Revolutionary courts sentenced to death by guillotine anyone believed to be disloyal. This included Girondists, clergy, nobles, and even women and children. To blend in, wealthy people adopted the simple clothing of the lower classes. About 40,000 people died, including Queen Marie Antoinette. This period, from July 1793 to July 1794, became known as the Reign of Terror.

During this time, the Committee came under the control of a lawyer named Maximilien Robespierre (mak•see•meel•ya ROHBZ•pyehr). Robespierre wanted to create a "Republic of Virtue." By this he meant a democratic society made up of good citizens. Under Robespierre's lead, the Committee opened new schools, taught the peasants new farming skills, and worked to keep prices under control. Robespierre even created a new national religion that worshipped a "Supreme Being." This attempt to replace France's traditional Catholic faith, however, did not last.

With France facing pressure from foreign invasions, the Committee decided to raise a new army. All single men between the ages of 18 and 25 were required to join this new army.

BIOGRAPHY

Marie Antoinette (1755–1793)

As the wife of King Louis XVI, Queen Marie Antoinette ruled over a court of luxury. Her many expenses were partly to blame for France's large debt. As problems and debts mounted, many French people turned against her. Public anger rose when the queen was claimed to have said, "Let them eat cake!" in response to the cry that the peasants had no bread. Later, during the Revolution, Louis and Marie Antoinette tried to flee to Austria, where the queen's brother ruled. They did not get far. Soldiers arrested the royal couple and returned them to Paris. In August 1792, the queen was held in prison until she was executed more than a year later.

▶ CRITICAL THINKING

Speculating Would Marie Antoinette have been treated differently if she had not fled Paris?

R1 Reading Skills

Specifying After students have read the passage, ask them to specify how the Reign of Terror occurred. Pose questions such as the following to guide the discussion. **Ask:**

- What was the Committee of Public Safety? *(It was a committee that was chosen by the National Convention to run the country.)*
- What positive actions did the Committee take? *(It opened new schools, taught the peasants new farming skills, and tried to keep prices low.)*
- What negative actions did the Committee take? *(It oversaw the killing of about 40,000 people who were believed to be disloyal to the Revolution.)*

R2 Reading Skills

Expressing Review the section titled "The Reign of Terror." Hold a brief debate in which students argue for and against the following statement: *Robespierre was justified in enforcing his violent laws during the Reign of Terror.* Have students take a position and justify it with facts from the text. **Verbal/Linguistic**

T Technology Skills

Researching on the Internet Ask a small group of students to discuss Marie Antoinette's roles in France during the revolution. Then ask interested students to use an Internet search engine to find images of her and basic information about her life. Give this group a limited amount of time to find and save a few images and to gather basic information such as how long she lived, how she treated the people in France, and how she is remembered today. Have these students put together a short presentation to share with the class about what they learned. BL **Visual/Spatial**

WORKSHEET

21st Century Skills Activity: Leadership and Responsibility: Citizenship

Evaluating Explain to students that the nobles and the monarchy of France were not meeting the needs of their people. This situation led to a bloody revolt and the downfall of the government. Assign the 21st Century Skills worksheet on citizenship for homework. Tell students that they will focus on the relationship between the government and the people of a nation.

See page 661D for other online activities.

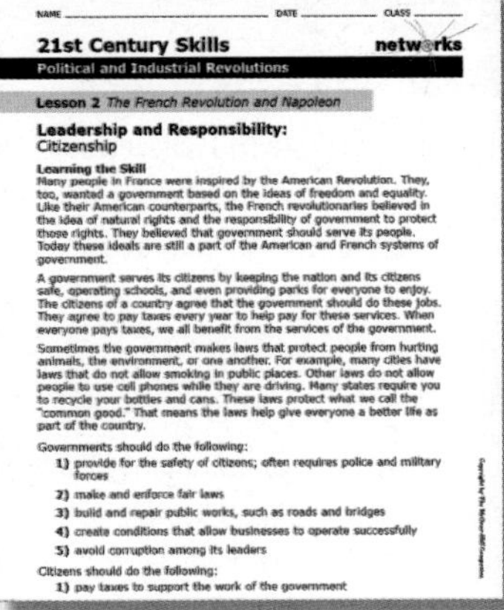

NAME ______ DATE ______ CLASS ______

21st Century Skills networks

Political and Industrial Revolutions

Lesson 2 *The French Revolution and Napoleon*

Leadership and Responsibility: Citizenship

Learning the Skill

Many people in France were inspired by the American Revolution. They, too, wanted a government based on the ideas of freedom and equality. Like their American counterparts, the French revolutionaries believed in the idea of natural rights and the responsibility of government to protect those rights. They believed that government should serve its people. Today these ideals are still a part of the American and French systems of government.

A government serves its citizens by keeping the nation and its citizens safe, operating schools, and even providing parks for everyone to enjoy. The citizens of a country agree that the government should do these jobs. They agree to pay taxes every year to help pay for these services. When everyone pays taxes, we all benefit from the services of the government.

Sometimes the government makes laws that protect people from hurting animals, the environment, or one another. For example, many cities have laws that do not allow smoking in public places. Other laws do not allow people to use cell phones while they are driving. Many states require you to recycle your bottles and cans. These laws protect what we call the "common good." That means the laws help give everyone a better life as part of the country.

Governments should do the following:

1) provide for the safety of citizens; often requires police and military forces
2) make and enforce fair laws
3) build and repair public works, such as roads and bridges
4) create conditions that allow businesses to operate successfully
5) avoid corruption among its leaders

Citizens should do the following:

1) pay taxes to support the work of the government

ANSWER, p. 675

CRITICAL THINKING Students might say that Marie Antoinette probably would not have been treated any differently if she had stayed in Paris. As queen, she was the symbol of the monarchy, and the people of France were angry at the monarchy. Also, the rumor that she told people to eat cake probably made the French even angrier with her.

W Writing Skills

Informative/Explanatory Have students write a paragraph explaining how the policies of the Directory differed from the policies of earlier groups that were in charge of France's government during the Revolution. Students should correctly use the terms *radical* and *moderate* in their paragraphs.

C Critical Thinking Skills

Determining Cause and Effect Discuss with students how Napoleon came to power—through a coup d'état. **Ask:** **Why do you think many people accepted Napoleon as the leader of France after his military takeover of the government?** *(Accept reasonable answers, but help students understand that people wanted order after all the years of turmoil, and Napoleon appeared to be a strong leader who could restore this order.)*

Content Background Knowledge

The Guillotine

Along with the Bastille, the guillotine remains one of the enduring symbols of the French Revolution. In 1789 a member of the National Assembly by the name of Dr. Joseph-Ignace Guillotin proposed sweeping legal reforms. Among the tenets of his reform bill were the ideas that death as punishment for a crime should be without torture and that the best way to achieve this kind of painless death was by decapitation by machine. At the time of the proposal, such a machine did not exist. The National Assembly did not take action on Dr. Guillotin's proposal for two years, but his idea was dubbed the "guillotine."

The guillotine was meant to fulfill the Enlightenment ideals of individual dignity and humanitarianism, as well as the revolutionary ideal of equality. Before the French Revolution, a person's social status determined his or her punishment. Commoners were subjected to more brutal forms of punishment than nobles, but all punishments included some element of torture. With the guillotine, all convicts faced the same punishment: a quick, "humane" death.

The Reign of Terror transformed the symbolism of the guillotine. Thousands of often innocent people were beheaded by the machine. At times, the guillotine resembled an assembly line of death. The bloodshed turned a symbol of equality and dignity into a symbol of fear and power run amok. France continued to use the guillotine as a form of capital punishment into the twentieth century.

ANSWER, p. 676

✓ PROGRESS CHECK The Reign of Terror was the period after the French Revolution in which harsh steps were used to end unrest within France. Anyone believed to be disloyal to the revolution was sentenced to death by revolutionary courts. This period lasted from July 1793 to July 1794.

The guillotine was designed by Dr. Joseph Guillotine to make executions quick and more humane. Instead, the guillotine came to represent harshness and fear during the French Revolution.

With this new force of almost a million soldiers, France halted the threat from abroad. Revolutionary generals gained confidence from their military victories. They soon became important in French politics.

With the republic out of danger, people in France wanted to end the Reign of Terror. Robespierre lost his influence, and his enemies ordered him to be executed without trial. Wealthy middle-class leaders then came to power.

W France's new leaders tried to follow more moderate policies. They wrote a new constitution that allowed only men with property to vote. In 1795, a five-man council known as the Directory was created to run the country. The Directory, however, was unable to handle food shortages, rising prices, government bankruptcy, and attacks by other countries. By 1799, the Directory had lost much support. The French people began to look for a strong leader who could restore order.

✓ PROGRESS CHECK

Identifying What was the Reign of Terror?

Napoleon Leads France

GUIDING QUESTION *How was Napoleon able to take over France's government?*

As the Directory weakened at home, the French army won victories in the war with Europe's monarchies. One battle front was in Italy, where the French were fighting against Austrian troops. In those battles, a young French general captured public attention. His name was Napoleon Bonaparte (nuh•POH•lee•uhn BOH•nuh•pahrt).

Born on the Mediterranean island of Corsica in 1769, Napoleon Bonaparte went to military school and became an officer. He supported the revolution. His great talent for military work helped him rise to the rank of general by the time he was 24 years old. After his successes in Italy, Napoleon attacked the British in Egypt in 1799. While in Egypt, he heard of the political troubles back home. He immediately returned to France. There, he opposed the Directory and took part in a **coup d'état** (koo day • TAH). This is when a group seeking power uses force to suddenly replace top government officials. Napoleon took the title of First Consul and became the strong leader many French people believed they needed. C

Fotosearch

Reading HELPDESK CCSS

coup d'état a change of government in which a new group of leaders seize power by force

networks Online Teaching Options

LECTURE SLIDE

Napoleon Leads France

Defining Show students the lecture slide defining the term *coup d'état*. Then ask for a volunteer to pronounce the term correctly and define it in his or her own words. ELL **Ask:** **What group did Napoleon overthrow?** *(the Directory)* **What title did he take?** *(First Consul)*

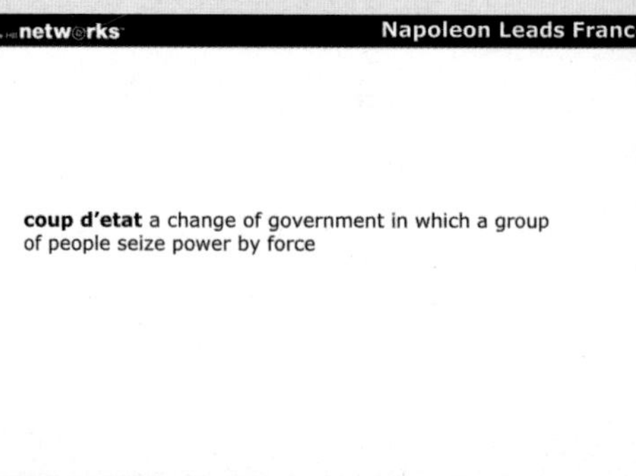

networks
Napoleon Leads France
coup d'etat a change of government in which a group of people seize power by force

Hold a class discussion about the idea of a coup d'état, asking students if they think this a good way to make changes to the government. Encourage them to support their opinions with specific examples.

See page 661D for other online activities.

Napoleon quickly reorganized the government to strengthen his control. He changed France's finances and tax system. He appointed local officials and created many new schools. In addition, he created a new legal system known as the Napoleonic Code. This code of laws was based on Enlightenment ideas. Finally, Napoleon established a more peaceful relationship with the Catholic Church, which had opposed the revolution. **R**

Napoleon did not carry out all of the French Revolution's ideas. People were equal under the law, but freedom of speech and the press were restricted. A new class of nobles was created, based on ability rather than wealth or family. **C** Then, in 1804, Napoleon crowned himself emperor, and France became an empire. Now his dream could be fulfilled. **W**

This famous portrait of Napoleon shows him riding to battle. It was painted by Jacques-Louis David.

▶ CRITICAL THINKING

Analyzing How did the artist show that Napoleon was a powerful leader?

✓ PROGRESS CHECK

Explaining How did Napoleon strengthen his control after becoming First Consul?

The Creation of an Empire

GUIDING QUESTION ***How did Napoleon build and then lose an empire?***

Napoleon wanted to do more than govern France. He wanted to build a great empire. Beginning in 1803, Napoleon won a number of military battles that helped him reach his goal. By 1807, Napoleon controlled an empire that stretched across Europe from the Atlantic Ocean to Russia.

Many different territories were part of Napoleon's empire. Napoleon directly ruled France and parts of Germany and Italy. He named relatives to govern other lands in his empire, such as Spain and the Netherlands. Outside the empire, independent countries, such as Prussia, Austria, and Sweden, were forced to ally with France.

Two forces, however, helped to bring Napoleon's empire to an end. One was nationalism, or the desire of a people for self-rule. The nations conquered by Napoleon's army rejected his rule and the French practices forced on them. The other force was the combined strength of Britain and Russia working against him.

Napoleon Meets Defeat

Napoleon hoped to cross the English Channel and invade Britain. He never achieved this goal. A major French defeat took place off the coast of Spain. There, in 1805, the British admiral Lord Horatio Nelson defeated the French navy in the Battle of Trafalgar.

R Reading Skills

Listing After students have read the passage, ask them to detail the changes Napoleon made to the French government after becoming the First Consul. Ask students to create a two-column chart with the headings "Change" and "Benefits." Have them list each of Napoleon's changes in the first column and then describe in the second column how this change would benefit the people of France.

C Critical Thinking Skills

Speculating Discuss how Napoleon's achievements differed from the ideals of the French Revolution. **Ask:** How do you think people who supported the Revolution felt about Napoleon? Have students cite evidence from the text to defend their answers. *(Accept reasonable answers. Make sure students understand that Napoleon made all people equal under the law, but that he also created new groups of nobles and took great power for himself when he crowned himself emperor.)*

W Writing Skills

Narrative Have pairs of students write a dialogue that two French people might have had on the day after Napoleon crowned himself emperor in 1804. In the dialogue, the two people should state their views of the new ruler and explain why they have those views. BL

GAME

The French Revolution and Napoleon Concentration Game

Identifying Have students play the game to correctly match the terms and people from this lesson to their descriptions. Allow time at the end of the activity for students to ask any questions they may have about these terms or people. AL ELL

See page 661D for other online activities.

ANSWERS, p. 677

✓ PROGRESS CHECK He reorganized the government, created many new schools, and appointed local officials. He reorganized the country's finances and tax system. He created a new legal system and made peace with the Catholic Church.

CRITICAL THINKING Napoleon is in uniform and riding a horse. He is pointing forward as if to say "Let's go." Students might notice the disproportionate scale of the image, such as Napoleon being bigger than his horse and as big as the mountain.

V Visual Skills

Reading a Map Direct students' attention to the map on this page. **Ask:**

- Which European powers allied themselves against Napoleon? *(Russia, Sweden, Portugal, and the United Kingdom)*
- Which states were dependent on Napoleon? *(Spain, the Kingdoms of Italy and Naples, Switzerland, the Grand Duchy of Warsaw, and the Confederation of the Rhine)*
- Where was the northernmost battle fought? *(Borodino)* Who won this battle? *(the French)*
Visual/Spatial

Remind students that the Russian troops led Napoleon's troops deep into Russia. **Ask:**

- Use the map scale to calculate how far a soldier who marched from Kovno to Moscow would have traveled. *(more than 500 miles)*
- How many soldiers in the Grand Army died in Russia? *(500,000)*
- Why did Napoleon lose so many soldiers? *(The soldiers were unprepared to face the harsh Russian winters.)*
Logical/Mathematical

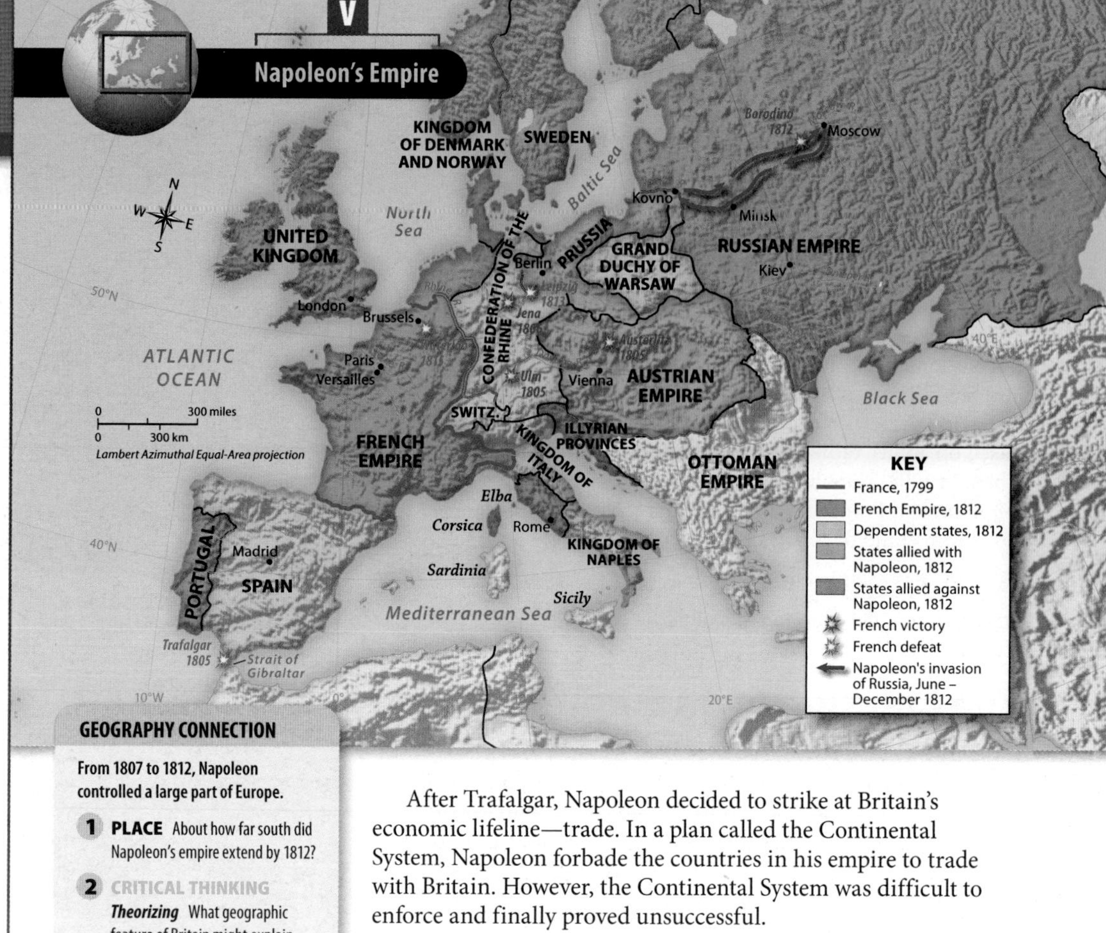

GEOGRAPHY CONNECTION

From 1807 to 1812, Napoleon controlled a large part of Europe.

1. **PLACE** About how far south did Napoleon's empire extend by 1812?
2. **CRITICAL THINKING** ***Theorizing*** What geographic feature of Britain might explain why the British navy was able to defeat Napoleon's attempts at invasion?

After Trafalgar, Napoleon decided to strike at Britain's economic lifeline—trade. In a plan called the Continental System, Napoleon forbade the countries in his empire to trade with Britain. However, the Continental System was difficult to enforce and finally proved unsuccessful.

Napoleon next decided to invade Russia. He organized the Grand Army, a force of about 600,000 soldiers from all over Europe. Napoleon led the Grand Army into Russia in the summer of 1812. Except for one battle, the Russians refused to fight. Instead, they drew Napoleon's army deeper into Russia. When the harsh Russian winter arrived, Napoleon's soldiers were unprepared, helpless, and far from home. Their retreat proved to be a disaster. Fewer than 100,000 soldiers returned alive.

France's enemies then captured Napoleon and exiled him to Elba, an island off the coast of Italy. Napoleon escaped and returned to France in the spring of 1815. He easily won public

Reading HELPDESK (CCSS)

Academic Vocabulary (Tier 2 Words)

overseas across an ocean

networks Online Teaching Options

WHITEBOARD ACTIVITY

Revolution and Empire in France

Sequencing Show students the time line covering the periods in France's revolution. Have them work in pairs to place each date or range of dates in the correct spot in the Events and People columns.

See page 661D for other online activities.

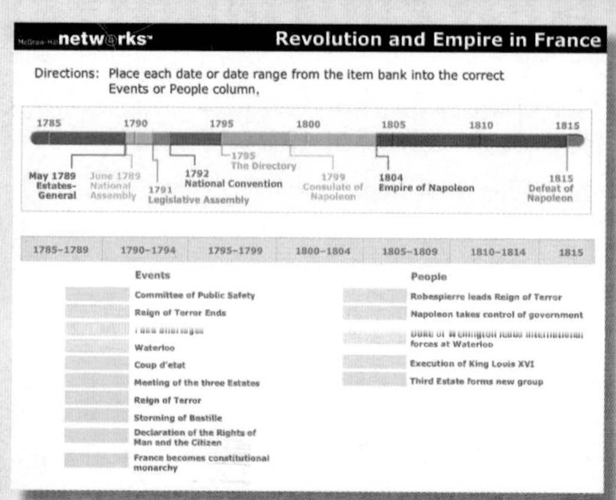

ANSWERS, p. 678

GEOGRAPHY CONNECTION

1. His empire extended to the south of Rome.
2. Great Britain is made up of islands. Islands require a strong navy for protection from invasion.

support and assembled his old army. At Waterloo in Belgium, an international force led by Britain's Duke of Wellington finally defeated Napoleon. This time, Napoleon was sent to the island of St. Helena in the southern Atlantic Ocean, where he died in 1821.

What Was the Congress of Vienna?

In September 1814, European leaders gathered in Vienna, Austria. Their goal was to return peace and stability to Europe. This meeting, called the Congress of Vienna, was led by Austria's foreign minister, Klemens von Metternich (MEH•tuhr•nihk).

Metternich and the other leaders were conservative. That is, they opposed changes that threatened traditional ways. Today, conservatives in the U.S. believe in traditional ways but also support self-rule. European conservatives of the early 1800s supported powerful monarchies. They opposed individual liberties and the right of self-rule. Hoping to crush revolutionary ideas, the conservative leaders at the Congress restored the royal families who had ruled in Europe before Napoleon.

R

European leaders at Vienna also redrew Europe's borders. France lost the lands won by Napoleon. It also had to pay other countries for war damages. At the same time, Russia, Prussia, Austria, and Great Britain expanded in size. Russia increased its share of Poland, Prussia gained more German lands, and Austria acquired territory in Italy. Adding to its **overseas** empire, Britain won colonies in Asia, Africa, and the Caribbean.

The Congress above all wanted to create a balance of power, or equal strength among their countries. They hoped that such a balance would prevent any one nation from controlling Europe. To keep the peace, the leaders agreed to meet from time to time. These meetings were called the Concert of Europe.

PROGRESS CHECK

Analyzing Why did the Congress of Vienna support rule by powerful monarchs?

Austria's foreign minister Klemens Von Metternich led the Congress of Vienna. This was a gathering of European leaders who shared the goal of returning Europe to a time of unity and stability.

LESSON 2 REVIEW (CCSS)

Review Vocabulary (Tier 3 Words)

1. Use the word *bourgeoisie* in a sentence about the Third Estate in French society. RH.6–8.2, RH.6–8.4
2. Explain how a *coup d'etat* is different from an election. RH.6–8.2, RH.6–8.4

Answer the Guiding Questions

3. ***Differentiating*** What were the three estates in France before the revolution, and how were their tax responsibilities different? RH.6–8.2
4. ***Assessing*** What was the result of Napoleon's invasion of Russia in 1812? RH.6–8.2
5. ***Evaluating*** What happened at the Battle of Trafalgar, and why was it significant? RH.6–8.2
6. **INFORMATIVE/EXPLANATORY** Explain the results of the Congress of Vienna in a short paragraph. WHST.6–8.2, WHST.6–8.10

R Reading Skills

Stating Have students read the passage and then cite evidence from the text as they respond to the following questions about the Congress of Vienna. **Ask:**

- What was the main goal of the Congress of Vienna? *(to bring peace and stability back to Europe)*
- What did Metternich and the other leaders at the Congress do to achieve these goals? *(They restored royal families who had ruled in Europe before Napoleon and redrew Europe's borders to take land away from France.)*
- How do you think people in Europe felt about these actions? *(Accept all reasonable answers that are supported by text evidence.)*

Have students complete the Lesson 2 Review.

CLOSE & REFLECT

Evaluating Ask students to discuss whether Napoleon's rule was good or bad for the nation of France. Then ask students to consider whether Napoleon's rule was good or bad for *Europe* as a whole. *(Accept answers that are well supported by evidence.)*

LESSON 2 REVIEW ANSWERS

1. Sample answer: The bourgeoisie was part of the Third Estate and included merchants, bankers, lawyers, and teachers.
2. A coup d'état is a change of government by force. An election is peaceful.
3. The three estates were the clergy, the nobles, and a group made up of the bourgeoisie, urban workers, and peasants. The nobles and the clergy did not pay taxes, so the remaining group, which comprised the largest part of the population, had the burden of the cost of governing the nation.
4. Napoleon's invasion of Russia was a disaster because his forces were not prepared for the harsh Russian winter.
5. Napoleon was defeated by Lord Nelson of Britain, whose forces defeated the French navy. It was significant because it weakened Napoleon's power in Europe.
6. Paragraphs should explain how the Congress of Vienna redrew the borders of European nations, created a balance of power in Europe, and created regular meetings called the Concert of Europe.

ANSWER, p. 679

PROGRESS CHECK At the Congress of Vienna, Europe's leaders wanted to return to traditional ways and a firm social order. They wanted royal families to return to power. In this way, their own power would increase and the power of the lower classes would decrease.

ENGAGE

 **Bellringer** Tell students that this feature deals with the relationship between governments and citizens.

Ask: Do you think government leaders should get paid more than other people? Do you think those in government should have more luxurious lifestyles? Do you think all citizens should pay taxes or just some citizens? *(Students should show some understanding of the complexity of the relationship between citizens and their government leaders.)*

TEACH & ASSESS

R Reading Skills

Summarizing Have a volunteer read the primary-source quote on this page aloud to the class. After reviewing any challenging words in the passage with students, ask for volunteers to summarize the main argument of the passage. To help get the summary started, you may want to **ask:** What does the member of the Third Estate believe happens during wartime? *(The nobles lead the army, but the common people are the ones who are killed.)* **Auditory**

Content Background Knowledge

- The Estates-General was the governing body of France that was made up of the three estates: the nobles (First Estate), the clergy (Second Estate), and the ordinary people (Third Estate).
- The Estates-General did not have the power to pass laws. Its role was to vote to levy taxes that would provide money to the king. The Estates-General was not even called into session at all between the years 1614 and 1788.
- King Louis XVI called the Estates-General to meet in 1788 because he needed money. At this meeting, the Third Estate refused to vote in the way that it had in the past, where each estate received one vote. They insisted on giving each individual a vote, and since the Third Estate was the largest, it had the power to create the new National Assembly.

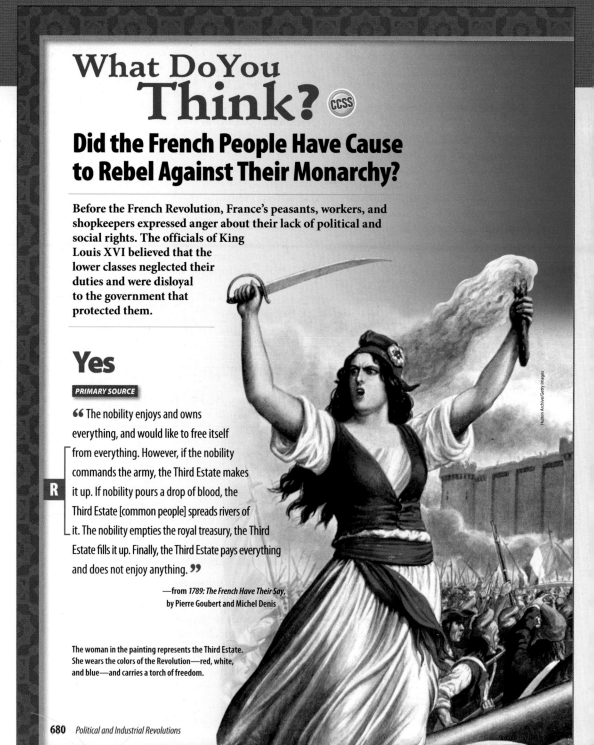

What Do You Think? CCSS

Did the French People Have Cause to Rebel Against Their Monarchy?

Before the French Revolution, France's peasants, workers, and shopkeepers expressed anger about their lack of political and social rights. The officials of King Louis XVI believed that the lower classes neglected their duties and were disloyal to the government that protected them.

Yes

PRIMARY SOURCE

R "The nobility enjoys and owns everything, and would like to free itself from everything. However, if the nobility commands the army, the Third Estate makes it up. If nobility pours a drop of blood, the Third Estate [common people] spreads rivers of it. The nobility empties the royal treasury, the Third Estate fills it up. Finally, the Third Estate pays everything and does not enjoy anything."

—from *1789: The French Have Their Say,* by Pierre Goubert and Michel Denis

The woman in the painting represents the Third Estate. She wears the colors of the Revolution—red, white, and blue—and carries a torch of freedom.

Hulton Archive/Getty Images

networks Online Teaching Options

SLIDE SHOW

Interactive Skills: How to Distinguish Fact from Opinion

Analyzing Review the lesson on distinguishing fact from opinion. Then have students use what they have learned to identify the sentences in each quotation that are facts and those that are opinions. After discussing their responses, reinforce the skill by having students write their own statements—one fact and one opinion—about the French Revolution. AL

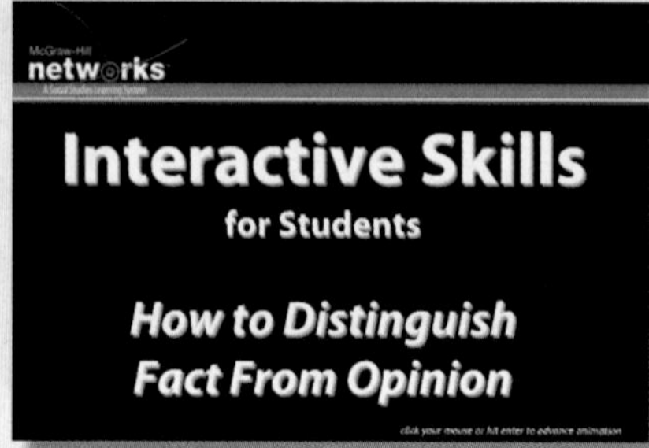

Marie Antoinette

King Louis XVI

No

PRIMARY SOURCE

“[The] districts [of the country] are made up of a certain number of towns and villages, which are in turn inhabited by families. To them belong the lands which yield products, provide for the livelihood of the inhabitants, and furnish the revenues [money] from which salaries are paid to those without land and taxes are levied to meet public expenditures . . . .

Families themselves scarcely know that they depend on this state, of which they form a part: . . . They consider the . . . taxes required for the maintenance of public order as nothing but the law of the strongest; and they see no other reason to obey than their powerlessness to resist. As a result, everyone seeks to cheat the authorities and to pass social obligations on to his neighbors.”

—from *The Works of Turgot*, ed. by Gustave Schelle

What Do You Think? DBQ

1. ***Explaining*** What were conditions like for the Third Estate in France before the Revolution? RH.6–8.1, RH.6–8.9
2. ***Identifying Central Issues*** What was the position of the ruling class on taxes? Do you think its attitude was fair or unfair? Why? RH.6–8.1, RH.6–8.9
3. ***Making Inferences*** Who does the Third Estate think enjoys the benefits from government money? Why? RH.6–8.1, RH.6–8.9

What Do You Think?

R Reading Skills

Paraphrasing Have a volunteer read the “No” position quotation aloud to the class. Then **ask:** **What government services does the public official believe the citizens are not aware of?** *(maintaining public order)* **Why does the public official think the king cannot enforce his tax laws by using force?** *(He believes the king would be seen as a brute if he enforced the tax laws and that it would cause war to break out.)*

Making Connections

Point out that the debate over who should pay taxes and how much they should pay continues today. Explain that some taxes are charged on goods, such as the taxes you pay when you buy a television or a book at a bookstore.

Have students reflect on whether the French citizens would object to these taxes as well, or if the French citizens' objections had more to do with who had to pay taxes and who did not.

CLOSE & REFLECT

Defending Hold a debate over the issue of how the government should tax its citizens. Organize the class into two groups, and assign a position on the issue to each group.

Then have students prepare their arguments. Encourage them to use details from their reading, examples from other periods of history, or their own experiences to support their positions.

Finally, allow each side to make an opening statement, ask a question of the other side, and present a closing statement that supports its position.

BIOGRAPHY

Marie Antoinette

Identifying Points of View Have students examine the biography of Marie Antoinette and discuss how differing attitudes of the classes contribute to conflict in society.

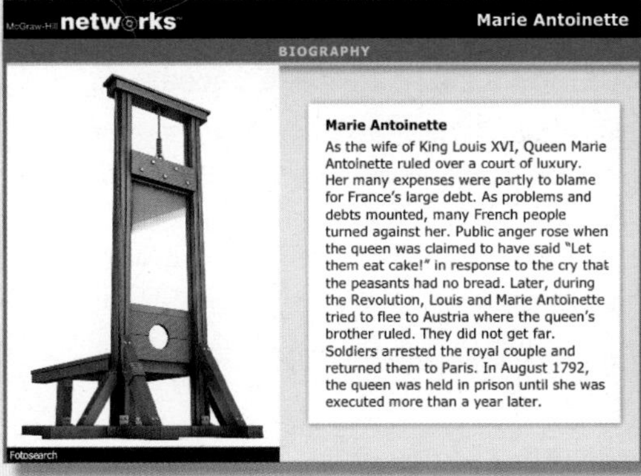

McGraw-Hill networks
Marie Antoinette
BIOGRAPHY
Marie Antoinette
As the wife of King Louis XVI, Queen Marie Antoinette ruled over a court of luxury. Her many expenses were partly to blame for France's large debt. As problems and debts mounted, many French people turned against her. Public anger rose when the queen was claimed to have said "Let them eat cake!" in response to the cry that the peasants had no bread. Later, during the Revolution, Louis and Marie Antoinette tried to flee to Austria where the queen's brother ruled. They did not get far. Soldiers arrested the royal couple and returned them to Paris. In August 1792, the queen was held in prison until she was executed more than a year later.
Fotosearch

ANSWERS, p. 681

1. The members of the Third Estate were the laborers, and they supported the lifestyle of the nobles and the monarchy. They did not enjoy the same privileges as the other two estates.
2. The ruling class argued that the people of the state received services from the state and should pay for them. Students might agree with this idea, or they might disagree and say that everyone, including the ruling class, needs to pay a fair share.
3. The Third Estate believes the nobility benefits the most from government money. The passage, for example, says that “the nobility empties the royal treasury; the Third Estate fills it up.” Before the revolution, the nobility had special privileges that exempted them from paying taxes. The government was built on taxes paid by the Third Estate.

Nationalism and Nation-States

ENGAGE

Bellringer Write the word *nationalism* on the board. Have volunteers define the term. *(an attitude of common identity of people and desire for self-determination)* ELL

Next, discuss examples of nationalism that students have already learned about. **Ask:** How were the American colonies and France changed by feelings of nationalism? *(Nationalism contributed to the American colonies' fight for independence and to France's revolution and support for Napoleon.)*

Tell students that in this lesson they will be learning about the effects of nationalism around the world.

TEACH & ASSESS

R Reading Skills

Describing Have students read the passage and then describe their understanding of the political situation in Britain in the early 1800s with the class, citing details from the text. **Ask:**

- Who had the right to vote in Britain in the early 1800s? *(only nobles)*
- How did that change in 1832? *(A law was passed that gave most middle-class men the right to vote.)*
- At that point, who was still excluded from voting? *(Workers and women)*
- Was the working class happy with this rule? *(no)* What did they do? *(They sent a petition to Parliament demanding the right to vote and other reforms.)*

ANSWERS, p. 682

TAKING NOTES: Possible answers: Britain: gave more people the right to vote; France: elected Louis Napoleon, became an empire again, and then returned to being a republic; Germany: became a united country; Italy: became a united country; Haiti: became independent.

networks
There's More Online!
- ☑ GRAPHIC ORGANIZER Uprisings and Outcomes
- ☑ MAP The Rise of Italy and Germany
- ☑ PRIMARY SOURCE *Blood and Iron*

Lesson 3
Nationalism and Nation-States

ESSENTIAL QUESTION *How do governments change?*

IT MATTERS BECAUSE
The demands of peasants and workers can make changes in a nation's government.

Nationalism and Reform

GUIDING QUESTION ***What political ideas shaped Europe during the 1800s and early 1900s?***

Nationalism means the desire of people with the same history, language, and customs for self-rule. During the 1800s, nationalism, along with demands for political reform, led to dramatic and far-reaching changes in Europe and the Americas.

Political Reform in Britain

R While war and revolution raged in most of Europe, change came peacefully to Britain. In the early 1800s, nobles ran Britain's government, and the middle and working classes could not vote. Groups having no voice in government began demanding change. In 1832, the British government passed a law that gave voting rights to most middle-class men. New and growing cities gained more seats in Parliament.

As industry continued to grow, dissatisfied workers began to speak out and protest for additional rights. Workers still did not have the right to vote and felt they were being unfairly represented by the government. In 1838, supporters of the working class, known as Chartists, demanded a fully democratic Parliament and reforms, including the vote for all men. They sent a petition to Parliament, stating:

Reading HELPDESK CCSS

Taking Notes: *Organizing* RH.6–8.2
As you read about the uprisings in each country, keep a list of the nations and the events of each revolt. Write down the outcome in each case.

Country	Uprising and Its Outcome

Content Vocabulary (Tier 3 Words)
- **nationalism**
- **guerrilla warfare**
- **kaiser**
- **abolitionism**

networks ***Online Teaching Options***

VIDEO

Napoleon's Early Military Career

Summarizing Play *Napoleon's Early Military Career* for the class and encourage students to take notes while they are watching it. Have a class discussion to summarize the important events in Napoleon's life. Then discuss how political life changed in France under his rule.

See page 661E for other online activities.

PRIMARY SOURCE

> "May it please your Honourable House . . . to use your utmost endeavors [efforts] . . . to have a law passed, granting to every male of lawful age, sane mind, and unconvicted of crime, the right of voting for members of Parliament; and directing all future elections . . . to be in the way of secret ballot; . . . ."
>
> —from *The Life and Struggles of William Lovett*

The government would not accept the Chartists' demands. By the late 1800s, however, Britain's leaders were willing to make some changes. William Gladstone led the Liberal Party, which was supported by many middle-class voters. After Gladstone became prime minister in 1868, he had Parliament grant the vote to many rural workers and reorganize districts to give more equal representation.

Benjamin Disraeli, the leader of the Conservative Party, was Gladstone's main rival. Disraeli worked to maintain British traditions but cautiously adopted reforms. In 1867, Disraeli's Conservative government gave the vote to many urban workers.

In 1900, a new political group—the Labour Party—formed. It claimed to represent the working class. Labour Party supporters backed a Liberal government elected in 1906. Liberal and Labour members of Parliament tried to improve workers' lives. They passed laws that provided workers with retirement pensions, a minimum wage, unemployment aid, and health insurance.

In the early 1900s, British women known as suffragettes pushed for women to have the right to vote. They marched in protest and went on hunger strikes. In 1918, Parliament gave women over the age of 30 the right to vote. Ten years later, it gave the vote to all women over age 21.

Irish Demands for Self-Rule

During the 1800s, Britain had difficulty ruling its neighbor, Ireland. British and Irish Protestants owned most of Ireland's wealth. Yet, most Irish people were Catholic and poor. By 1830, their protests had won them the right to vote and to sit in Britain's Parliament. Still, British leaders refused to grant the Irish their main goal—self-rule.

The Palace at Westminster, which includes London's famous Big Ben, also houses the British Parliament. In 1870, the two houses of Parliament—House of Lords and House of Commons—established headquarters there.

nationalism the desire of people with the same customs and beliefs for self-rule

Build Vocabulary: *The Suffix –ism*

Throughout this chapter, you will read many words with the suffix *–ism*. The suffix *–ism* means "belief in." Nationalism, for example, can mean "belief in nations."

R Reading Skills

Paraphrasing Direct students' attention to the primary source quotation at the top of the page. After reading it, ask students to put this quotation in their own words. Then have them explain how and when this goal was achieved in Britain. *(The goal was partially achieved in 1867 when many urban male workers got the vote—and more thoroughly achieved the following year, in 1868, when many rural workers got the vote.)*

W Writing Skills

Informative/Explanatory Discuss with students the reforms passed in the early 1900s that improved workers' lives. Have students do research, if needed, to learn more about each one. Then have them write a paragraph explaining one of the reforms and why workers felt that reform was necessary.
Verbal/Linguistic

IMAGE

British Parliament

Making Connections Project the interactive image of the British Parliament on the board. As you click on different parts of the image, have students volunteer to read the information aloud. After you have reviewed all the information presented, have a class discussion about how some traditions from the early days of the Parliament are still in place today—such as the green benches, or the mace being in the chamber. Ask students why it is important to protect traditions.

networks
British Parliament
The British Parliament has two houses, or parts. The lower house is called the House of Commons. It has 650 elected representatives. The upper house is called the House of Lords. The number of members in this chamber varies. In 2010 there were 738 Lords. Members of Parliament are called MPs. The upper

See page 661E for other online activities.

Nationalism and Nation-States

R Reading Skills

Identifying Central Issues Direct students' attention to the beginning of the paragraph, and have them describe the position that Czar Alexander II was in after Russia lost the war. *(He realized that the wealth of his country was far behind that of other European countries.)* **Ask:**

- **What did he think would correct this problem?** *(more factories and improved farming)*
- **What did Alexander do for the serfs?** *(He gave them their freedom.)* **Was this successful?** *(No; they felt that they didn't get enough land, so they were still unhappy.)*
- **How do his actions compare with the way rulers in other countries treated the working class?** *(He gave them freedom, which many countries did not do. However, he did not give them the power or land they wanted. In this way, he was similar to the rulers in Britain, France, and Austria.)*

Content Background Knowledge

Austria-Hungary had gained power in the early 1800s, at the Congress of Vienna. It was ruled by the Hapsburg family, and it was second in size only to Russia. It included territory that is today the countries of Austria, Hungary, the Czech Republic, Slovakia, Croatia, Bosnia and Herzegovina, and parts of Ukraine and Romania.

When Hungarians protested for self-rule in the 1860s, the emperor was forced to divide the empire in half and give Hungary control of its domestic affairs. This satisfied the Magyar people, but the Slavic peoples, who made up the majority of the empire, were still unhappy. Their unhappiness at a lack of self-rule would later be a factor in the events that led to World War I.

Irish hatred of British rule increased when a severe famine hit Ireland in the 1840s. The British government did not send enough aid. At least one million Irish died of starvation and disease. Millions more left for the United States and other lands.

After this tragedy, pressure rose for Irish home rule, or Ireland's right to its own legislature to handle Irish affairs. Gladstone tried to pass home rule, but Parliament did not support him. Many British and Irish Protestants opposed home rule, fearing it would lead to Irish independence.

After defeat in the Austro-Prussian War, Russian ruler Czar Alexander II introduced reforms in hopes of making Russia the strongest country in Europe.

Chris Hellier/CORBIS

Political Changes in France

In 1848, nationalist and reforming revolts swept Europe. Most of them failed, but revolution was somewhat successful in France. There, King Louis-Philippe was overthrown and a republic declared. Louis Napoleon, nephew of Napoleon Bonaparte, soon was elected president and later emperor. Under Napoleon III, France enjoyed prosperity, but its government was not democratic.

In 1870, Napoleon III declared war on Prussia, the most powerful German state. Prussia won, and Napoleon's government fell. France faced civil war when workers took control of Paris. The upper-class government sent troops to crush the workers. By 1875, France was again a republic. However, distrust between upper classes and workers remained strong.

Monarchies in Austria and Russia

During the late 1800s, monarchs in Austria and Russia tried to block reform. However, bitter defeats in war forced both empires to make some changes.

In 1867, Austria made a deal with the Hungarians, who were part of the Austrian Empire. Hungary became a separate kingdom linked to Austria, called Austria-Hungary. The Hungarians were satisfied, but other national groups were not. Their demands for self-rule increased.

R In Russia, defeat in war made Czar Alexander II realize that his country was far behind other European powers. He decided to build factories and improve farming. In 1861, Alexander freed the serfs—peasants tied to the land, which they farmed for landlords. The peasants did not get enough land, however, and they remained discontented.

PROGRESS CHECK

Inferring Why might the people of France have voted for Louis Napoleon?

Reading HELPDESK CCSS

guerrilla warfare a form of war in which soldiers make surprise attacks on the enemy

Reading Strategy: *Activating Prior Knowledge*

You read about Napoleon Bonaparte in the previous lesson. Who was he? What did he do?

networks *Online Teaching Options*

LECTURE SLIDE

Nationalism and Reform

Evaluating Show students the slide that lists reforms in Britain. Ask students how each set of political reforms might have made it easier to enact later reforms. Note that as more people were allowed to vote, it became easier for them to express their concerns in Parliament. *(Students should note that as the workers and middle class elected politicians to represent their interests, it became easier for new reforms to be brought up in and passed by Parliament.)* Then discuss with students how British treatment of the Irish differed from treatment of people at home. *(Although the British government was willing to create reforms at home, it was not willing to allow Irish independence or even to grant home rule, because they feared it would strengthen the independence movement.)*

networks
Nationalism and Reform
British Political Reforms
The British government gave most middle-class men the right to vote in 1832.
Rural workers gained the right to vote in 1868.
Many urban workers could vote in 1867.
The Labour Party formed in 1900 and tried to pass laws that improved the lives of workers.
British women, called suffragettes, argued for the right to vote. Women over the age of 30 gained the right to vote in 1918. Later, the age was changed to 21.
Irish Catholics won the right to vote but were denied self-rule and suffered during the famine in the 1840s.

See page 661E for other online activities.

ANSWERS, p. 684

PROGRESS CHECK Louis Napoleon's name reminded people of Napoleon Bonaparte, and they hoped Louis Napoleon would be like his uncle.

Reading Strategy Napoleon Bonaparte was a general who became emperor of France. He established a French empire, reformed French law, and restored order after the chaos of the French Revolution.

New Nations in Europe

GUIDING QUESTION *Why did new nations arise in Europe during the mid-1800s?*

In the early 1800s, Germany and Italy as we know them today did not exist. They were made up of many territories. After 1850, their peoples began to form united countries.

How Did Italy Unite?

In 1848, Austria controlled most of Italy's small territories. In the north, the kingdom of Piedmont was independent. Piedmont's rulers were King Victor Emmanuel and the prime minister, Camillo di Cavour (kah•MEEL•loh dee kuh•VUR). Both leaders wanted to unite all of Italy into one nation.

C

In 1854, Piedmont sided with Britain and France in a war with Russia. In return for Piedmont's support, France helped Piedmont drive Austria out of Italy in 1859. Piedmont's victory was the first step toward uniting Italy. Soon, other parts of northern Italy overthrew their rulers and united with Piedmont.

At the same time, nationalist leader Giuseppe Garibaldi (joo•ZEHP•pay gar•uh•BAWL•dee) led uprisings in southern Italy. In 1860, his forces gained control of the island of Sicily. Garibaldi was skilled in **guerrilla warfare** (guh•RIH•luh WAWR•fehr), a type of fighting in which soldiers make surprise attacks on the enemy. Garibaldi's army won Italy's mainland. People in the south then voted to join a united Italy.

GEOGRAPHY CONNECTION

Both Italy and Germany unified their nations in the mid-1800s.

1. **PLACE** What was the effect of adding the North German Confederation to Prussia?
2. **CRITICAL THINKING** ***Drawing Conclusions*** How did nationalism influence the rise of Italy?

V

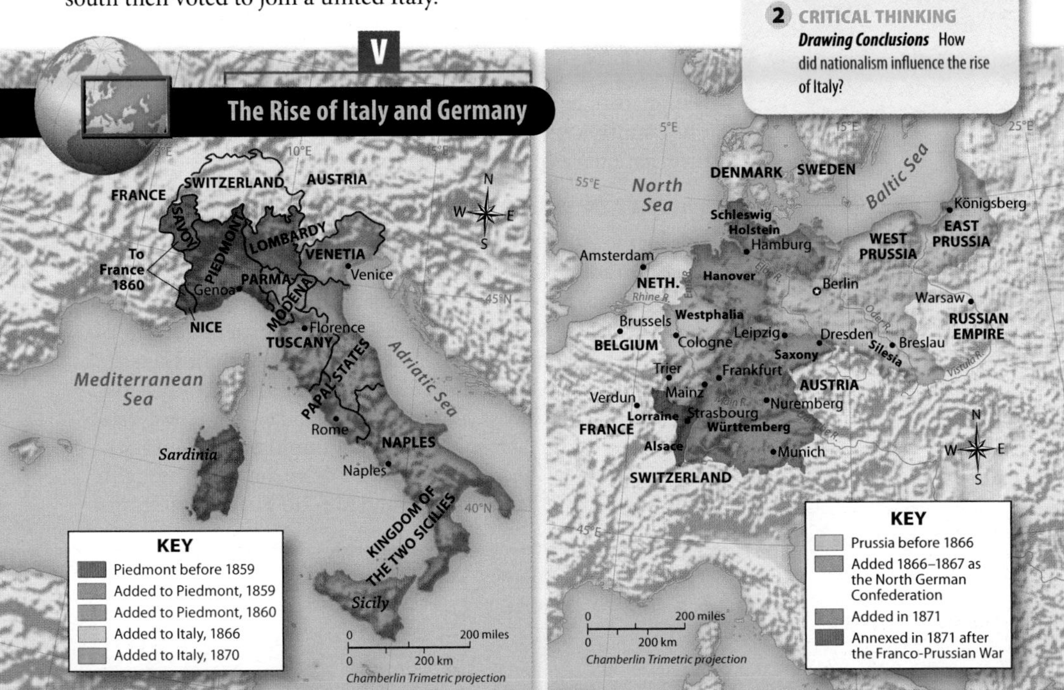

C Critical Thinking Skills

Speculating Discuss the gradual unification of Italy. **Ask:**

- What event had to occur before Italy could begin to unite? *(Austria had to be driven out of Italy.)*
- Why do you think France was willing to help Piedmont drive Austria out of Italy? *(Accept reasonable answers; students should point out that powerful nations such as France were probably interested in preventing other empires from becoming too strong. France might have been willing to accept a united Italy if it helped weaken Austria.)* BL

V Visual Skills

Reading a Map Direct students' attention to the map of Italy at the bottom of the page. **Ask:**

- In what year was the most land added to Piedmont? *(1860)*
- What territories were given to France in 1860? *(Nice and Savoy)*
- What was the last territory that was added to Italy? *(the Papal States/Rome)*
- What does this map tell you about Italy from 1859 to 1870? *(Answers will vary, but students should suggest it was growing and becoming more powerful.)* Visual/Spatial

Making Connections

Write the term guerilla warfare on the board and ask for a volunteer to pronounce the term correctly. Then tell the class that this is a type of fighting in which soldiers make surprise attacks on the enemy. ELL Explain that this tactic helped Garibaldi's army win Italy's mainland. Then, as a class, discuss some examples of guerrilla warfare from more recent wars or current events.

MAP

The Rise of Italy and Germany

Simulating Display the interactive map and have students click on the symbols in the key to see when territory was added by both Italy and Germany. To help reinforce the strength that each new nation gained, assign students to "role-play" the different states or regions of Italy and Germany. For each nation, call out dates beginning with the first date shown on the map. Each year that a new region joined the nation, have that student go stand in a particular section of the room. By the end of the activity, the Italian states and the German states should all be standing together. **Kinesthetic**

See page 661E for other online activities.

networks
The Rise of Italy and Germany

ANSWERS, p. 685

GEOGRAPHY CONNECTION

1. Adding the North German Confederation unified two separate areas of Prussia.
2. **CRITICAL THINKING** Answers will vary, but students should show understanding of the concept of nationalism and that the various parts of Italy joined together during a period when nationalism was part of the culture.

C Critical Thinking Skills

Determining Cause and Effect Have students review the series of events in the formation of Germany. Create a cause-and-effect chart on board. Have small groups of students copy and complete it with details from the text. **Ask:** What convinced the German kingdoms to join the nation under Bismarck? *(Prussia was rich and powerful. It had defeated Denmark, Austria, and France. The German kingdoms wanted to avoid war with Bismarck.)* After completing the chart, ensure that students understand how nationalism played a role in the way the nations united. Visual/Spatial

R Reading Skills

Determining Word Meanings Point out the term "Manifest Destiny" in the section on Westward Expansion at the bottom of the page. **Ask:**

- What does *manifest* mean? *(obvious or clear)*
- What does *destiny* mean? *(Destiny means "fate or something that is meant to happen.")* ELL
- How do these words relate to the idea that the United States should stretch from coast to coast? *(Many people believed that it was the obvious fate of the United States to expand, to take over territory and reach from the Atlantic Ocean to the Pacific Ocean.)*

ANSWERS, p. 686

CRITICAL THINKING Bismarck's "iron fist" made him a successful prime minister because he was willing to do what was necessary to make his country strong and to achieve his goals.

☑ PROGRESS CHECK Bismarck fought against the neighboring countries to form a united Germany.

Otto von Bismarck was a firm leader. He decided to govern with an iron fist rather than win people over with speeches.

▶ CRITICAL THINKING
Analyzing How did Bismarck's "iron fist" make him a successful prime minister?

In 1861, Italy became a constitutional monarchy. Two areas remained outside the new kingdom. One was Rome, and the other was Venice. By 1870, wars had brought both areas into Italy.

A New German Empire

During the mid-1800s, nationalism grew stronger in the German states. Many people wanted a united Germany under a strong monarchy. They gained Prussia's support. In 1862, Prussia's King William I named Otto von Bismarck (AHT•oh fawn BIHZ•mahrk) as his prime minister.

Bismarck was a deeply conservative Junker (YUN•kuhr), or wealthy landowner. He vowed to govern Prussia by "blood and iron" rather than by votes and speeches. Bismarck quickly strengthened Prussia's army. He used the army to defeat Denmark, Austria, and France. As a result of Bismarck's victories, other German states agreed to unite with Prussia. On January 18, 1871, William was proclaimed **kaiser** (KY•zuhr), or emperor, of a united Germany. C

☑ PROGRESS CHECK

Explaining What role did Bismarck play in uniting Germany?

Growth of the United States

GUIDING QUESTION *How did the United States change during the 1800s?*

Nationalism helped shape the United States during the 1800s. The country's size steadily grew. Many Americans believed that their nation was destined to be rich and powerful.

Westward Expansion

R During the 1800s, the United States pushed westward. Many Americans came to believe in "Manifest Destiny," the idea that their country should stretch from the Atlantic Ocean to the Pacific Ocean.

In 1845, the United States annexed Texas, which had declared independence from Mexico. This led to war between the United States and Mexico. The United States won in 1848 and gained the area that today includes California and several other western states.

Settlers set up farms, **founded** communities, and created states in the new lands. The westward drive, however, brought suffering—loss of land, culture, and life—to Native Americans.

Reading HELPDESK CCSS

kaiser emperor of Germany
abolitionism movement to end slavery

Academic Vocabulary (Tier 2 Words)
found to establish; to bring into being

networks Online Teaching Options

PRIMARY SOURCE

Blood and Iron

Identifying Points of View Display the primary source excerpt from the "Blood and Iron" speech given by Otto von Bismarck in 1862. Give students a chance to read it quietly to themselves. Then ask a volunteer to read the speech aloud as Bismarck might have done. When he or she has finished, have others respond, in similarly formal language, saying whether they agree with this philosophy and giving reasons for their opinions. Verbal/Linguistic

See page 661E for other online activities.

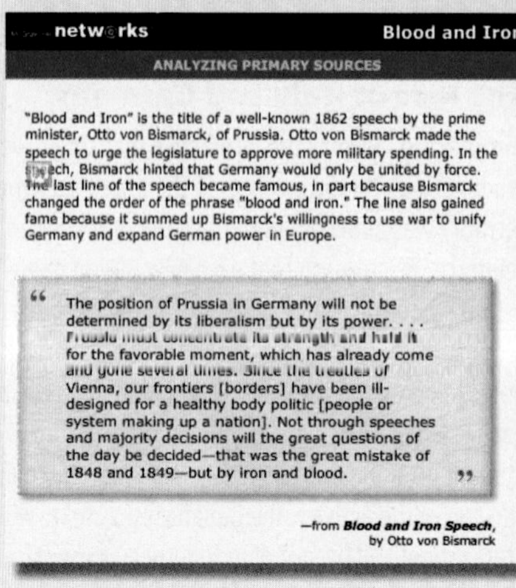

networks — Blood and Iron
ANALYZING PRIMARY SOURCES

"Blood and Iron" is the title of a well-known 1862 speech by the prime minister, Otto von Bismarck, of Prussia. Otto von Bismarck made the speech to urge the legislature to approve more military spending. In the speech, Bismarck hinted that Germany would only be united by force. The last line of the speech became famous, in part because Bismarck changed the order of the phrase "blood and iron." The line also gained fame because it summed up Bismarck's willingness to use war to unify Germany and expand German power in Europe.

"The position of Prussia in Germany will not be determined by its liberalism but by its power. . . . Prussia must concentrate its strength and hold it for the favorable moment, which has already come and gone several times. Since the treaties of Vienna, our frontiers [borders] have been ill-designed for a healthy body politic [people or system making up a nation]. Not through speeches and majority decisions will the great questions of the day be decided—that was the great mistake of 1848 and 1849—but by iron and blood."

—from ***Blood and Iron Speech***, by Otto von Bismarck

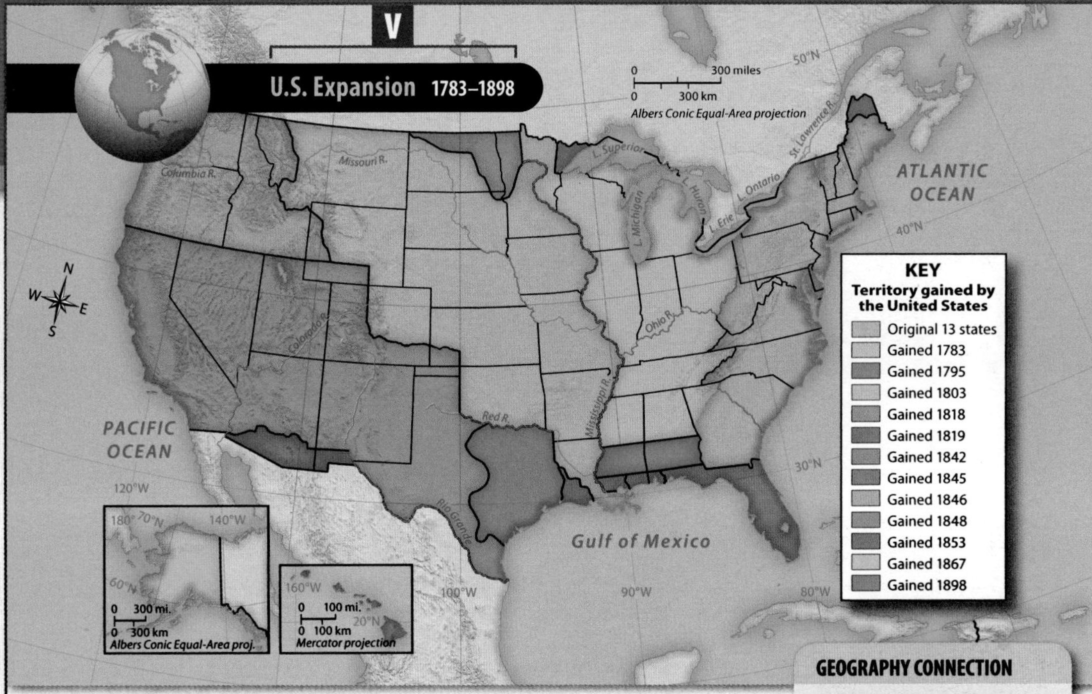

GEOGRAPHY CONNECTION

Because of continued expansion, the United States reached across the middle of the North American continent by 1848.

1. **LOCATION** What present-day state was gained in 1819?
2. **CRITICAL THINKING** ***Theorizing*** Why might Americans have wanted the country to expand all the way to the Pacific Coast?

The American Civil War

Over time, the Northern and Southern states developed different ways of life. The South had an agricultural economy based on raising cotton. Cotton growing depended on the labor of enslaved African Americans. In the North, industries created a manufacturing economy. Some Northerners believed in **abolitionism** (a•buh•LIH•shuhn•ih•zuhm), a movement to end slavery.

The disagreement over slavery grew more heated. In 1860, Abraham Lincoln, an opponent of slavery, was elected president. Southern states feared that he would end slavery. Eleven states seceded, or left, the United States. They formed the Confederate States of America. Fighting erupted between this group and the United States in April 1861. The American Civil War had begun.

The North had more people and more industries than the South. In spite of this, skilled military leaders such as Robert E. Lee led Confederate forces to many early victories. Later, the North threw all of its resources against the South. The conflict ended in a Northern victory. More than 600,000 Americans died in the war.

The North's victory reunited the country. Millions of African Americans were freed from slavery and became citizens. Factories, railroads, and cities were built at increasing speeds. Millions of immigrants from Europe and Asia contributed to the country's growth during the late 1800s.

V Visual Skills

Analyzing Maps Direct students to the map of westward expansion in the United States. Note the territories possessed by the United States before 1867. Then help students identify the states shown on the map that became part of the Union and the Confederacy during the Civil War. **Visual/Spatial**

R Reading Skills

Summarizing After students have read the passage, moderate a class discussion about the role that westward expansion played in helping to cause a conflict between the North and the South. Make sure students articulate the different views on slavery in the North and the South. *(Students should note that as the United States expanded to the west, northern and southern states began to argue over whether new states formed from western territories would allow slavery.)* **Ask: How did the differences between the states contribute to the outcome of the war?** *(The more industrialized North was able to supply its troops better than the South could supply its troops.)* AL

T Technology Skills

Researching on the Internet Have interested students work in small groups and use the Internet to learn more about a specific Civil War battle. Allow them to choose a battle, research it, and prepare a short slide to explain the battle to the rest of the class. **Interpersonal**

WHITEBOARD ACTIVITY

The American Civil War

Contrasting Present the Interactive Whiteboard Activity about the Northern and Southern states at the outbreak of the American Civil War. Have students drag and drop each characteristic of the group into the correct area.

See page 661E for other online activities.

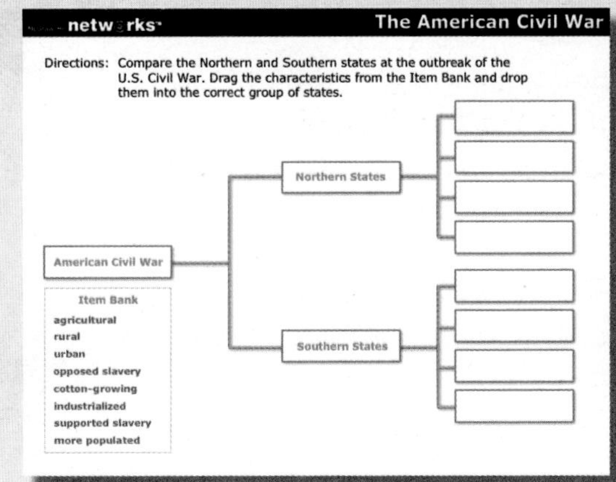

ANSWERS, p. 687

GEOGRAPHY CONNECTION

1. The present-day state of Florida was gained in 1819.
2. **CRITICAL THINKING** Answers will vary but may include national pride, greed, to protect their borders, and to seek new trading ports.

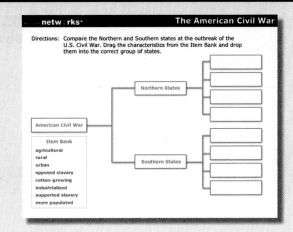

V Visual Skills

Analyzing Images Point out the photograph of women marching for the right to vote in Washington, D.C., in 1913. **Ask:** How does this demonstration compare or contrast with marches and demonstrations that take place in the United States today? *(Accept reasonable answers.)* Point out the sign that the woman near the front is carrying, and explain that earlier in U.S. history, married women were not allowed to own property and, in some places, to earn wages.

R Reading Skills

Making Inferences After they have read the section, ask students to identify the early independence movements in Latin America in the early 1800s. **Ask:** Which country gained its independence from France in 1804? *(Haiti)* Which Catholic priests sparked the independence movement in Mexico? *(Miguel Hidalgo and José María Morelos)* AL

Then ask students to infer the possible connections between the French and American Revolutions and those in Latin America. **Ask:** How do you think the American and French revolutions inspired revolutions in Latin America? *(People in Latin America may have felt that if others could overthrow unfair rulers, they could too. They may also have been inspired by the idea that all people had the right to self-rule.)* BL

Women suffragists marched in Washington D.C. the day before President Woodrow Wilson's inauguration in 1913. Though Wilson did not support woman suffrage at first, in the years following he helped pass the Nineteenth Amendment, which gave all women the right to vote.

North Wind/North Wind Picture Archives

America Rebounds

During the 1800s, the United States became more democratic. President Andrew Jackson's election in 1828 was called a victory for the "common people." It was made possible by the spread of voting rights to almost all adult white men.

In the 1800s, women also began to demand equality. Women suffragists fought hard for the right to vote. Finally, in 1920, the Nineteenth Amendment to the Constitution was ratified, or approved. This guaranteed women in all states the right to vote.

PROGRESS CHECK

Comparing and Contrasting How were the economies of the North and the South different before the American Civil War?

Independence in Latin America

GUIDING QUESTION *How did the countries of Latin America win independence?*

During the 1700s, Spain and Portugal did not face serious challenges to their rule in Latin America. In the early 1800s, the situation changed. Latin Americans, inspired by the American and French revolutions, wanted independence.

Winning Independence

The first successful revolt against European rule took place in Haiti, an island territory in the Caribbean Sea. There, Toussaint L'Ouverture (TOO•sahn LOO•vehr•toor) led enslaved Africans in a revolt that **eventually** threw off French rule in 1804.

People in the Spanish colonies of Latin America were also ready to revolt. In Mexico in 1810, two Catholic priests, Miguel Hidalgo and José María Morelos, urged Mexican peasants to fight for freedom. Mexico finally won its independence in 1821.

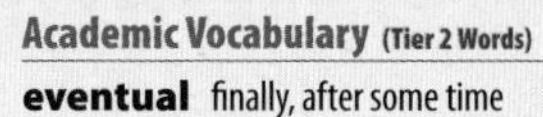

Academic Vocabulary (Tier 2 Words)

eventual finally, after some time

networks Online Teaching Options

GAME

Nationalism and Nation-States Fill-in-the-Blank Game

Identifying Have students' check their understanding of the content of this lesson by placing the words on the left of the screen into the appropriate sentences at the right of the screen.

See page 661E for other online activities.

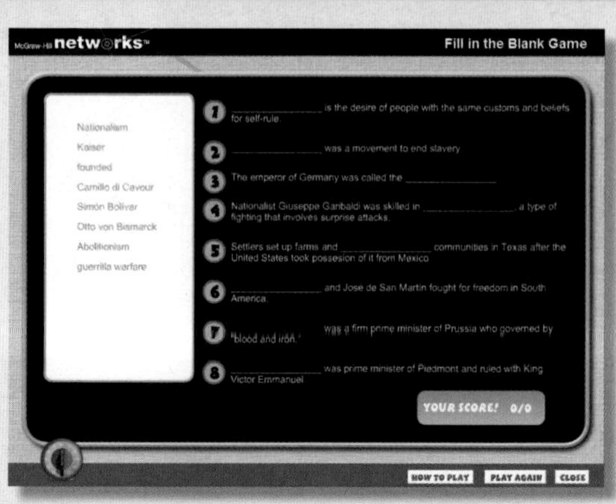

ANSWER, p. 688

PROGRESS CHECK Before the Civil War, the economy of the North depended on industry and small farms. The economy of the South was agricultural and depended on the labor of enslaved Africans.

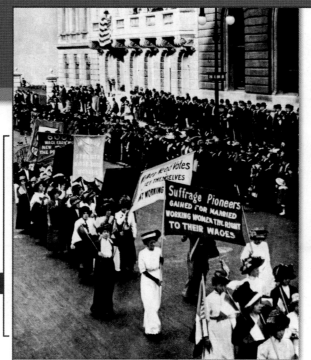

In 1823, Central America declared its independence from Mexico. During the next decade, it divided into the republics of Guatemala, Honduras, Nicaragua, El Salvador, and Costa Rica.

In the northern part of South America, a wealthy military leader named Simón Bolívar (see•MAWN boh•LEE•vahr) started a revolt in 1810. Bolívar's forces finally crushed the Spanish at the 1819 Battle of Boyacá in Colombia. It took another 20 years, but Bolívar won freedom for the present-day countries of Venezuela, Colombia, Bolivia, Ecuador, Peru, and Panama. **C**

As Bolívar fought in the north, a soldier named José de San Martín (hoh•SAY day san mahr•TEEN) led the struggle in the south. In 1817, San Martín led his army from Argentina across the Andes Mountains into Chile. The crossing was difficult, but San Martín took the Spanish by surprise. A few years later, San Martín and Bolívar together defeated the Spanish in Peru.

Many places have been named after Simón Bolívar to honor his revolutionary spirit, including the South American nation of Bolivia.

Challenges to Growth

Latin Americans wanted their new countries to become stable and prosperous. Their hopes, however, were not realized and these new countries faced many challenges. Political parties quarreled over the role of the Catholic Church. Border disagreements led to wars between countries. Tensions developed between rich and poor.

PROGRESS CHECK

Contrasting How did Haiti's revolution differ from those of other Latin American countries?

LESSON 3 REVIEW (CCSS)

Review Vocabulary (Tier 3 Words)

1. Use the following terms in a sentence about revolutions in South America: *guerrilla warfare, nationalism.* RH.6–8.2, RH.6–8.4

Answer the Guiding Questions

2. ***Comparing*** How were the political reforms that took place in Britain similar to the reforms that took place in France? RH.6–8.2
3. ***Evaluating*** How did nationalism play a part in the rise of Italy and Germany? RH.6–8.2
4. ***Determining Cause and Effect*** How did the expansion of settlers in the United States affect Native Americans? RH.6–8.2
5. ***Identifying Points of View*** Why were Americans divided over abolitionism? RH.6–8.2
6. ***Assessing*** What factors led to continued discontent after Latin American countries had won their freedom? RH.6–8.2
7. **INFORMATIVE/EXPLANATORY** Write a short essay in which you explain how José de San Martín and Simón Bolívar changed life in South America. WHST.6–8.2, WHST.6–8.10

C Critical Thinking Skills

Drawing Conclusions Point out that it took about 20 years for Simón Bolívar and his forces to defeat the Spanish and gain independence for many modern-day countries in South America. **Ask:** **What advantages do you think the Spanish would have had in this struggle? What advantages do you think the South Americans would have had?** *(Accept reasonable answers, but help students understand that the Spanish troops were well organized and that the Spanish had more money. However, the South Americans were fighting for something they strongly believed in—self-government. They were also more familiar with the geography of the places where they were fighting, which would give them an advantage over the Spanish troops.)* BL

Have students complete the Lesson 3 Review.

CLOSE & REFLECT

Explaining Have students write a one-page essay defining *nationalism.* Tell them to provide at least three examples that illustrate the effects of nationalism on Europe and the Americas in the 1800s and 1900s.

LESSON 3 REVIEW ANSWERS

1. Sentences should show an understanding that a feeling of nationalism led to fighting, much of which was guerrilla warfare.
2. The political reforms in Britain and France were similar because they were driven by feelings of nationalism.
3. In both countries, nationalists wanted to unite their regions under one ruling government.
4. Native Americans suffered from loss of their land, their culture, and their lives.
5. Abolitionists believed that slavery should be ended. Those against ending slavery depended on enslaved Africans for their agricultural economy.
6. Political parties quarreled over the role of the Catholic Church in society. Individual countries went to war over boundary disputes. Tensions developed between rich and poor.
7. Students should understand that the two revolutionaries, Simón Bolívar and José de San Martín, led revolutions that caused the overthrow of the Spanish colonial government in South America.

ANSWER, p. 689

PROGRESS CHECK Haiti's revolution was led by enslaved Africans against French rule. The other Latin American revolutions were led by priests or soldiers against Spanish rule.

ENGAGE

Bellringer Ask students to list the different types of technology and machinery they use in their homes and at school. *(Answers will vary but may include cars, computers, kitchen appliances, cell phones, iPods, etc.)* Then ask volunteers to share which item they think has the greatest impact on their lives. Explain that in this lesson, they will learn about the impact of technologies that were new about 200 years ago.

TEACH & ASSESS

R Reading Skills

Determining Word Meanings Instruct students to use context clues from the reading and a dictionary if necessary to determine the meaning of the term *revolution*. After students demonstrate understanding of the term, clarify that, in addition to referring to a violent change in government, such as the American Revolution or the French Revolution, a revolution can be any change that is rapid and significant. **Ask:** What do you think will be the effects of the Industrial Revolution? *(Accept reasonable answers, but help students to see that the changes in technology and invention of machinery changed how people everywhere worked and lived.)*

Content Background Knowledge

Child Labor During the Industrial Revolution The Industrial Revolution created a huge demand for child labor. Children were needed in the factories to help maintain the machines, but they were also needed for other odd jobs that were unique to the new urban environment. In addition to working in factories and mines, children earned money as rat catchers or chimney sweeps. Sometimes children were paid for collecting dog and horse droppings. These droppings were sold to local tanneries for use in curing hides to make leather.

Living Conditions and the Spread of Disease The crowded, unclean living conditions of the working class were a breeding ground for diseases. Cholera, which had a 50 percent death rate, spread through contaminated water. Typhus, which was caused by lice, was also common in crowded, dirty living quarters. The most common disease of the era was tuberculosis. In 1838, it caused one out of every six deaths in Britain.

ANSWERS, p. 690

TAKING NOTES: enclosure laws; changes in farming; entrepreneurship

networks *There's More Online!*

- DIAGRAM Locomotive
- GRAPHIC ORGANIZER Causes of the Industrial Revolution
- MAP The Industrial Revolution, 1870
- SLIDE SHOW Industrial Revolution Inventions
- VIDEO

Lesson 4

The Industrial Revolution

ESSENTIAL QUESTION *How does technology change the way people live?*

IT MATTERS BECAUSE

Small steps in industrial development led to big changes over time.

Birth of Industry

GUIDING QUESTION ***Why did the Industrial Revolution begin in Britain?***

While political change affected much of Europe and the Americas, a new economic system known as **industrialism** began in Britain. There, people began to use machines to do work that had been performed by animals or humans. Over the next 200 years, industrialism affected life so dramatically that historians call the changes it brought the Industrial Revolution. **R**

Before the rise of industrialism, most people lived in small farming villages. Cloth was made by village people working in their homes. Merchants went from cottage to cottage, bringing the workers raw wool and cotton. The workers used hand-powered wheels to spin the wool and cotton into thread. They worked on looms to weave the thread into cloth. The merchants then sold the finished cloth for the highest possible price.

The Industrial Revolution began in the woven cloth, or textile, industry. Merchants could make a great deal of money from textiles, so they began to look for ways to produce cloth better and faster. By the 1700s, changes in Britain made this possible.

What Caused the Industrial Revolution?

Britain led the way in the Industrial Revolution for many reasons. One important reason was a change in the way British landowners used their land. For hundreds of years, landowners

Reading **HELP**DESK CCSS

Taking Notes: *Sequencing*

Use a diagram like the one shown here to list events that led to the Industrial Revolution. RH.6–8.2

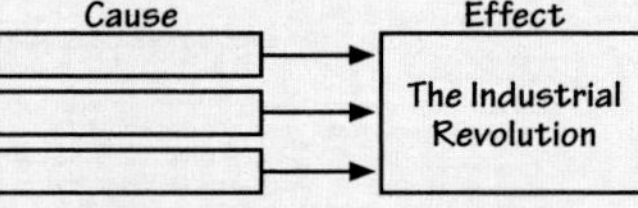

Content Vocabulary (Tier 3 Words)
- **industrialism**
- **corporation**

networks ***Online Teaching Options***

VIDEO

The Wright Brothers

Analyzing Play *The Wright Brothers* video for the class. Then, discuss how the Industrial Revolution impacted their work and their discoveries. **Ask:** What might have happened if the Wright Brothers gave up after their first attempt at flying? *(Answers will vary, but students should indicate an understanding of the idea that inventors need to accept failure and learn from their mistakes in order to become successful.)* Continue the discussion by creating a list of the traits of successful inventors and entrepreneurs.

See page 661F for other online activities.

rented land to villagers, who divided it into strips. Different families worked different strips of land. In addition, villagers could keep livestock on public lands.

In the 1700s, new enclosure laws allowed landowners to combine and fence off the strips and public lands. This created large farms where the same crop could be grown on large areas. This meant larger harvests and greater profits. Often the landowners used the land as pasture for sheep. The landowners could then sell wool to the textile industry. **C**

Successful farming provided landowners with more money to spend. Many chose to invest, or put money into new businesses. Money invested in businesses is called capital. A growing middle class of merchants and shopkeepers also began to invest capital in new industries.

GEOGRAPHY CONNECTION

The Industrial Revolution spread throughout Europe in the 1800s.

1. **HUMAN-ENVIRONMENT INTERACTION** In what areas do most of the coal mining and ironworking symbols appear?
2. **CRITICAL THINKING** ***Making Generalizations*** What generalization can you make about the location of railroads and manufacturing and industrial areas?

V

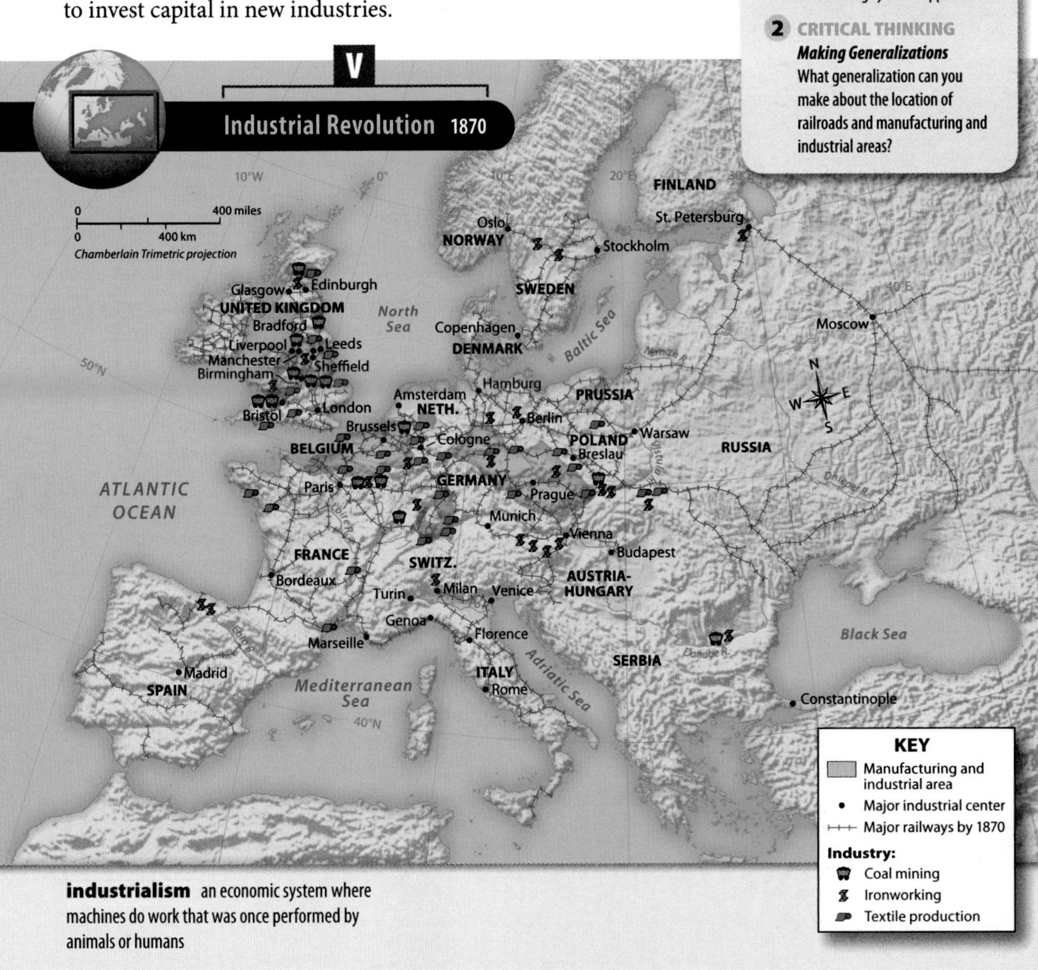

industrialism an economic system where machines do work that was once performed by animals or humans

C Critical Thinking Skills

Determining Cause and Effect Ask pairs of students to draw cause-and-effect chains to show how changes in land ownership laws in Britain helped bring about the Industrial Revolution. *(Laws allowed people to own larger farms > farmers had greater harvests and profits > farmers were able to use the land as pasture for sheep > farmers produced more wool > farmers sold the wool to the textile industry for a profit.)* **Visual/Spatial**

V Visual Skills

Reading a Map Have students look closely at the map. Have each student choose a city on the map and identify the industries that were located near it. Then **ask:** **How do you think a map showing this information would have looked in 1840? How do you think it would have looked in 1900?** *(Answers will vary but should reflect the idea that there was less industry in 1840 and more industry in 1900. Students should suggest that rapid changes were taking place in industry in Europe in the nineteenth century.)* **Visual/Spatial**

MAP

Industrial Revolution, 1870

Locating Have students click on the different symbols in the map key to see where different industries and railroads were located in Europe in 1870. Have small groups choose an industry—coal, iron, or textiles—and make a list of the regions or cities where this industry was predominantly located. **Visual/Spatial**

See page 661F for other online activities.

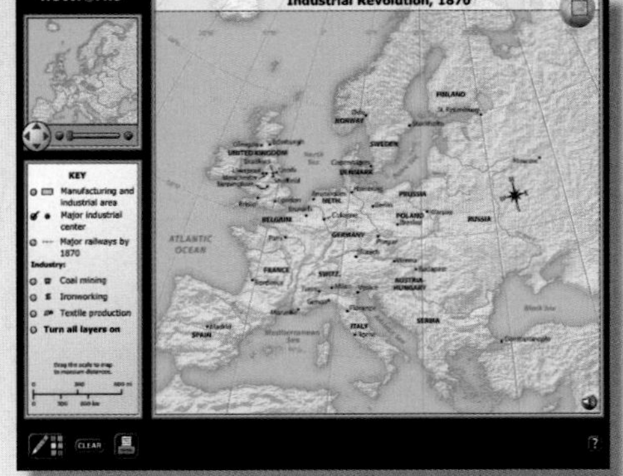

ANSWERS, p. 691

GEOGRAPHY CONNECTION

1. The northern part of Western Europe is home to more coal mining and ironworks operations.
2. **CRITICAL THINKING** The railroads appear more frequently in the industrial and manufacturing areas.

W Writing Skills

Argument Write the following sentence on the board: "Great Britain's geography was the most important factor in the rise of industry in that nation." After reading it aloud, have students write a paragraph either supporting or opposing the statement, with evidence from the text. *(Students who support the statement will mention the pasture land for raising sheep, the large network of rivers, and large supplies or coal and iron. Students who oppose the statement may refer to changes in population and the role of inventors as more important than geography.)* BL Verbal/Linguistic

R Reading Skills

Listing After reading the segment, have students identify the many inventions that were created in the late 1700s. Then ask students to create a three-column chart with the headings "Inventor," "Invention," and "Purpose." Have students list the inventors in the first column, the inventions in the second column, and explain what each did in the third column.

Henry Bessemer invented the first method of mass-producing steel. This process revolutionized the development of industry and machinery.

Stock Montage/Archive Photos/Getty Images

Increased Population

Still another cause of the Industrial Revolution was the growing workforce. Britain's population grew rapidly in the 1700s. People now had more and better food. They were healthier, lived longer, and had larger families. At the same time, changes in farming helped increase the supply of industrial workers. New machines, such as the steel plow, meant that farms needed fewer workers. Workers forced off the land often went to work in new industries.

Britain's rich supply of natural resources also helped in the rise of industry. The country had fine harbors and a large network of rivers that flowed year-round. Britain's earliest cotton mills were powered by the flow of river water. Britain also had large supplies of coal and iron. Coal, which replaced wood as a fuel, helped to run machines. Iron was used to build machinery. W

Inventors Make Advances

In the late 1700s, cloth merchants were looking for new ways to increase production. A textile weaver named James Hargreaves (HAHR•greevz) invented a machine called a spinning jenny that could spin cotton into thread very quickly. Richard Arkwright developed a way to power a spinning machine with water. Edmund Cartwright created a new powered loom. This machine could weave the thread into cloth as fast as the spinning machines produced it.

As industry developed, machines required more power than water could provide. Steam power answered this need. In 1769, the Scottish mathematician James Watt **designed** a steam engine that could power the new machines. Steam soon replaced water as the major source of power. R

As the need for machines grew, iron was needed to make machine parts. In 1753, Henry Cort discovered a way to use coal to turn iron ore into pure iron. As a result, iron production grew. Coal mining became a major industry. In 1856, Henry Bessemer, an engineer, invented a less costly way to make large amounts of iron into steel. Steel was excellent for making machinery, because it was stronger than iron. Soon mining towns and steel centers grew in areas with supplies of iron ore and coal.

Reading HELPDESK CCSS

Academic Vocabulary (Tier 2 Words)

design to skillfully plan or create something

networks Online Teaching Options

SLIDE SHOW

Industrial Revolution Inventions

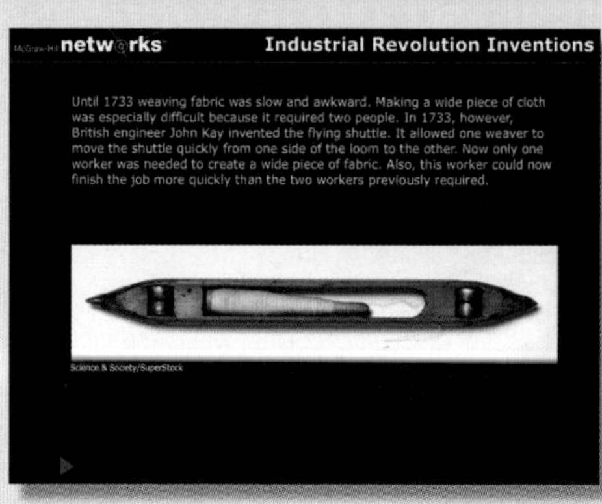

networks
Industrial Revolution Inventions
Until 1733 weaving fabric was slow and awkward. Making a wide piece of cloth was especially difficult because it required two people. In 1733, however, British engineer John Kay invented the flying shuttle. It allowed one weaver to move the shuttle quickly from one side of the loom to the other. Now only one worker was needed to create a wide piece of fabric. Also, this worker could now finish the job more quickly than the two workers previously required.

Making Connections Show the slide show on the inventions of the textile industry. Have volunteers read the captions. Have students respond to the images by listing and describing inventions that have changed how people work today. Then ask students to consider how these inventions affect society and business. Compare these changes to some of the changes described in the slide show. For example, new technologies made production more efficient, but many workers were afraid that the new machines would put them out of work. Ask students to evaluate whether technology is helpful or harmful in their lives. *(Student answers will vary, but most are likely to say technological changes benefit their lives in many areas.)* AL ELL

See page 661F for other online activities.

A LOCOMOTIVE

INFOGRAPHIC

The steam-powered locomotive made trains the fastest way to travel during much of the 1800s.

1. **IDENTIFYING** What natural resource was used to power the locomotive?
2. **CRITICAL THINKING** ***Assessing*** In addition to speed, what other advantages did a locomotive provide?

Factories and Railroads

Faster modes of transportation and new business successes fueled enormous economic growth. In 1807, Robert Fulton, an American inventor, developed a boat powered by a steam engine.

Then came the railroad—the biggest improvement in land transportation. By the mid-1800s, trains pulled by steam-powered locomotives were faster and cheaper than any other kind of transportation. Railroads soon connected major cities all across Europe. They completely changed the amount of time and money spent on the transport of goods to market. Trains carried raw materials and finished goods, as well as passengers, faster than horses.

Ambitious entrepreneurs, or people who took risks to start businesses, set up and ran Britain's growing industries. They created industries by bringing together capital, labor, and new industrial inventions. Their efforts led to the building of factories, the major centers of the Industrial Revolution.

Why did factories develop? Machines became too large and expensive for home use. Workers and machines were brought together in one place in factories, working under managers. Workers could share skills. Factories provided a better organized and less costly way to produce large amounts of goods. C

C Critical Thinking Skills

Simulating To illustrate the difference between factory work and cottage industry, organize the class into two groups. One group will be the cottage industry group. The other will be the factory group.

Provide simple instructions for making a paper airplane. The members of the cottage industry group get the instructions, and each individual makes airplanes. They can modify the design or decorate the airplanes any way they want. Meanwhile, the factory team chooses a boss who positions the team in a line with each member making one fold or performing one action, per the instructions. The team makes airplanes on an assembly line. ELL

Have students work for a set period of time. Then compare the number and quality of the airplanes that were made by each group. AL

Ask: What were the advantages and disadvantages of each method? *(Factory groups produced a higher quantity with more consistency, although the factory airplanes might not have been as unique or as high in quality as those produced by the cottage industry group.)*

Allow students a predesignated period of time for flying the airplanes after the lesson. **Kinesthetic**

Making Connections

Review the word *entrepreneur* with students. Explain that just as there were entrepreneurs during the Industrial Revolution, there are many entrepreneurs today. Ask students to give some examples of people they consider to be modern-day entrepreneurs. *(Answers will vary, but students should suggest people who are modern-day business leaders who have taken risks and started new businesses. Students may be most familiar with entrepreneurs in the high-tech or entertainment industries.)*

IMAGE

Locomotive

Describing Display the interactive image of the locomotive and have students form groups of ten. Have each group member pull a number (1–10) out of a hat and then describe the role of the part of the locomotive that corresponds with his or her number.

See page 661F for other online activities.

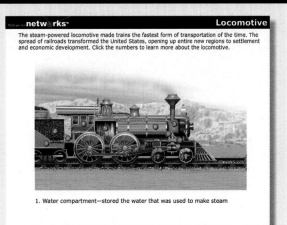

networks — Locomotive

The steam-powered locomotive made trains the fastest form of transportation of the time. The spread of railroads transformed the United States, opening up entire new regions to settlement and economic development. Click the numbers to learn more about the locomotive.

1. Water compartment—stored the water that was used to make steam

ANSWERS, p. 693

INFOGRAPHIC

1. The locomotive was powered by steam, which was created by burning coal.
2. **CRITICAL THINKING** In addition to speed, the locomotive could move larger quantities of goods over longer distances than a horse or a human being could. Locomotives also allowed goods to be moved farther inland, which was an advantage over using boats.

R Reading Skills

Defining Instruct students to determine the definition of the word *corporation* from the text and to compare it with the definition they look up in the dictionary. Have students express the definition to verify their comprehension. *(a company that raises money by selling shares, or partial ownership, in the company to investors)* ELL **Ask:**

- **Why did people create corporations?** *(in order to raise large amounts of money, known as capital)*
- **Why did people running these businesses need so much money?** *(To be more productive—they wanted to build larger factories and hire more workers.)* AL

Content Background Knowledge

The beginnings of the American textile industry is credited to Samuel Slater, who violated the English laws against exporting information about textile factories when he disguised himself as a farmer and sailed to New York. Slater had worked in textile factories and had completely memorized the plans for the spinning frame that had been invented in England by Richard Arkwright. Once in New York, Slater sold his knowledge to Moses Brown, a Quaker merchant in Pawtucket, Rhode Island. Together they built the first successful water-powered textile mill in America, which began operating in 1793. Later, Slater opened other factories in Rhode Island and Massachusetts.

Ask students to consider whether Slater did the right thing by breaking the English laws. Hold a class discussion about the fairness of the English laws and the benefits of spreading the Industrial Revolution.

Edison's electric lightbulb took about two years to develop and allowed people to use electric lighting in their homes and businesses. How would nighttime be different in your city without this invention?

akg-images/The Image Works

One British writer described the changes brought by factory organization, especially in weaving cloth:

PRIMARY SOURCE

> “In 1818, there were in Manchester, Stockport, Middleton, . . .and their vicinities, fourteen factories, containing about two thousand Looms. In 1821, there were in the same neighbourhoods thirty-two factories, containing five thousand seven hundred and thirty-two Looms. Since 1821, their number has still farther increased, and there are at present not less than ten thousand Steam Looms at work in Great Britain.”
>
> —from *Compendious History of the Cotton Manufacture* by Richard Guest

As the Industrial Revolution developed, entrepreneurs looked for different ways to raise money. One way was to form a partnership in which two or more people owned the business and pooled their own money. Another way was to create a **corporation** (kor•puh•RAY•shuhn). A corporation raises money by selling shares, or partial ownership, in the company to investors. Creating a corporation allowed entrepreneurs to have the capital to build large factories with hundreds of workers. R

✓ **PROGRESS CHECK**

Understanding Cause and Effect How did successful farming and a growing population influence the Industrial Revolution in Britain?

Growth of Industry

GUIDING QUESTION *How did new inventions help advance the growth of industry?*

Britain's early start in the Industrial Revolution made it the richest and most productive country in the world. To protect this dominant position, Parliament passed laws restricting the flow of ideas, machines, and skilled workers out of the country. Despite these laws, many inventors and entrepreneurs left Britain. They carried their industrial knowledge with them. As a result, the Industrial Revolution soon spread to other areas.

Reading HELPDESK CCSS

corporation a type of company that sells shares in the company to investors

Reading Strategy: *Comparing and Contrasting*

When you compare and contrast, you look for similarities and differences between two things as you read. Read the section about the growth of industry in Britain and America. Note one or two similarities between the two countries. Then identify one difference.

networks *Online Teaching Options*

BIOGRAPHY

Thomas Edison

Formulating Questions Have pairs of students read the biography of Thomas Edison together, scrolling down the right side to read all of the information. Then have them use what they have learned to write three to four interview questions and answers that a reporter might have asked Edison near the end of his life.

See page 661F for other online activities.

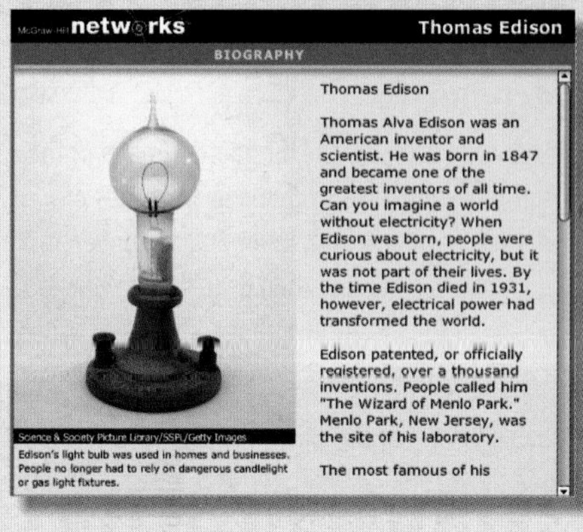

ANSWERS, p. 694

Caption Without the invention of the light bulb, people could not drive at night. They would have to use fires, torches, and candles to see by, which means they could do less at night and would be more likely to cause a house fire.

✓ **PROGRESS CHECK** Successful farming meant people ate better and were healthier. Because people were living longer, there were enough people to provide a workforce for factories.

Reading Strategy Similarities: abundant natural resources, access to waterways. Difference: The United States is much larger than Britain, so it had to build more roads, canals, and railways.

Industry Grows in Europe and America

The Industrial Revolution spread from Britain to other European countries. European governments helped build factories, railroads, canals, and roads. The Industrial Revolution also took hold in the United States. British investors and American engineers built factories and ironworks in New England.

Like Britain, the United States had many natural resources. Americans quickly built roads and canals across the vast nation. Fulton's steamboats provided transportation on inland waterways. Railroads soon crisscrossed the country.

New Scientific Advances

During the 1800s, inventors found many ways to use electricity. In the 1830s, Samuel Morse developed the telegraph. It sent coded messages through wires. Soon telegraph lines linked most European and North American cities.

R Alexander Graham Bell developed the telephone in 1876. The telephone used tiny electrical wires to carry sound. For the first time, telephones allowed people to speak to each other over long distances. Finally, in 1895, Guglielmo Marconi put together a wireless telegraph, which was later developed into the radio.

Inventors found more ways to use electric power. In 1877, Thomas Edison developed the lightbulb. As demand for electricity rose, investors in Europe and the United States funded the first power plants. These were powered by coal or oil.

Major breakthroughs also took place in transportation. In the 1880s, Rudolf Diesel and Gottlieb Daimler invented internal combustion engines. These engines produced power in autos by burning oil-based fuels. In 1903, Orville and Wilbur Wright successfully tested the world's first airplane.

Hulton Archive/Getty Images

PROGRESS CHECK

Identifying How did electricity change communications?

BIOGRAPHY

The Wright Brothers
(Wilbur Wright 1867–1912; Orville Wright 1871–1948)

The brothers Orville and Wilbur Wright were bicycle mechanics. They also were fascinated with the idea of human flight. It took them years of study to develop a flying machine. In their local library, they researched everything they could find on the subject of flight. Finally, when they could learn no more from other experts, they began experimenting with their own airplane models. The brothers eventually built a flying machine that would support a human being. Their research and experiments formed the basis of the modern airplane industry.

▶ **CRITICAL THINKING**

Theorizing How would the Wright Brothers' knowledge of bicycles have helped them build an airplane?

LESSON 4 REVIEW (CCSS)

Review Vocabulary (Tier 3 Words)

1. How does a *corporation* raise money? RH.6–8.2, RH.6–8.4
2. Write a sentence to explain how *industrialism* changed the lives of workers. RH.6–8.2, RH.6–8.4

Answering the Guiding Questions

3. ***Finding the Main Idea*** Why do historians consider this time of industrial development a revolution? RH.6–8.2
4. ***Determining Cause and Effect*** What inventions had an effect on the textile industry? RH.6–8.2
5. ***Analyzing*** Why were the telegraph and telephone important inventions at this time? RH.6–8.2
6. **INFORMATIVE/EXPLANATORY** Explain how the Industrial Revolution spread from Britain to other places in the world. WHST.6–8.2, WHST.6–8.10

R Reading Skills

Classifying Ask students to make a three-column chart with the headings "Transportation," "Communication" and "Other." Then have them list the inventions described on this page in the correct columns. *(Transportation: railroads, canals, roads, steamboats, autos, airplanes. Communication: telegraph, telephone, radio. Other: factories, ironworks, electricity, power plants)* **Visual/Spatial**

Have students complete the Lesson 4 Review.

CLOSE & REFLECT

Evaluating Review the key advancements made during the Industrial Revolution. Note to the class that some of these advancements involved new types of machines, while others involved new ways of organizing workers. **Ask: What were the most important advancements in the Industrial Revolution?** *(Students may suggest individual inventions or processes, such as the assembly line.)* Encourage students to explain their choice and to support it with facts and details from the text. AL

LESSON 4 REVIEW ANSWERS

1. A corporation raises money by selling shares in the company to investors.
2. Because of industrialism, workers moved from working on farms to working in factories.
3. Industry affected life so dramatically that historians call the changes it brought the Industrial Revolution.
4. Inventions such as the spinning jenny and the industrial loom changed the textile industry.
5. The telegraph and the telephone were important inventions because they allowed people who were separated by great distances to communicate much faster.
6. Students should show an understanding that information about building machines and mechanizing factories spread as entrepreneurs moved to new countries and as nations encouraged the growth of industry.

ANSWERS, p. 695

CRITICAL THINKING Knowing about bicycles taught the Wright brothers certain principles of motion and mechanics, which they could then apply to airplanes.

PROGRESS CHECK The telegraph, the telephone, and later the radio were advances in communications that used electricity.

ENGAGE

Bellringer Explain that the Industrial Revolution brought many changes, both positive and negative, to society. Have students work in pairs to develop a list of changes that they think the Industrial Revolution would have created for them if they were alive at the time. After volunteers have shared their lists, ask students if they think they would have preferred living during this time period, and discuss their responses.

Tell students that in this lesson they will learn more about how the Industrial Revolution changed people's daily lives and ideas about politics, art, and science.

TEACH & ASSESS

R Reading Skills

Determining Cause and Effect Ask students to use the text to define the term *urbanization. (the movement of people from the countryside to the cities)* Lead a discussion that requires students to demonstrate understanding of how industrialization led to urbanization. **Ask:** **How did new farm machines lead to the growth of cities?** *(As farmers began using machines to do work, they needed fewer laborers. People who used to work on farms left rural areas and moved to cities to look for new jobs in factories.)*

ANSWERS, p. 696

TAKING NOTES: Workers moved from the farm to cities, women found new opportunities, the arts blossomed in new directions, and scientific discoveries advanced medicine.

networks
There's More Online!
- **CHART** Marxism, Socialism, & Communism
- **GRAPHIC ORGANIZER** Social Advances during the Industrial Revolution
- **PRIMARY SOURCE** *A Tale of Two Cities* by Charles Dickens
- **SLIDE SHOW** Impressionism

Lesson 5

Society and Industry

ESSENTIAL QUESTION *How do new ideas change the way people live?*

IT MATTERS BECAUSE
Today's society is largely driven by powerful industry and the movement of goods around the world.

A New Society

GUIDING QUESTION ***How did industry change society in Europe and North America during the 1800s and early 1900s?***

By the 1860s, the Industrial Revolution brought sweeping changes to Europe and North America. During the next 100 years, industrialism also changed other regions of the world.

The Growth of Cities

One important change was the rapid growth in the population of cities. **Urbanization** (uhr•buh•nuh•ZAY•shuhn) is the movement of people from the countryside to cities. A nation is urbanized when many of its people live in cities.

R Why did cities grow so rapidly? Farms were using more machines. This meant there were fewer jobs for farm workers. To find employment, many rural workers headed to nearby cities. They hoped to find jobs in the new factories.

A New Industrial Society

Before the rise of industry, there were fewer job opportunities. The Industrial Age, however, brought new jobs and a new way of life. The middle class grew as more people took advantage of these new opportunities.

Reading HELPDESK CCSS

Taking Notes: *Explaining*

Use a web diagram like this one to list ways that the Industrial Revolution affected society. RH.6–8.2

Content Vocabulary (Tier 3 Words)
- **urbanization**
- **liberalism**
- **utilitarianism**
- **socialism**
- **proletariat**
- **labor union**

networks *Online Teaching Options*

VIDEO

The Industrial Revolution

Determining Cause and Effect After watching the *Industrial Revolution* video, have students work in small groups to create a list of effects of the Industrial Revolution. After they have finished, have each group share their list with the class. If time permits, you may wish to continue the discussion by talking about which of these effects are still visible today.

See page 661G for other online activities.

Industrial growth expanded not just the size of the middle class, but also its power and wealth. The middle class had once been made up of a small number of bankers, lawyers, doctors, and merchants. Now it included the successful owners of factories, mines, and railroads. Professional workers such as clerks, managers, and teachers added to the growing number.

Industrial growth also created a much larger working class. The members of this group were people who labored in the factories and mines. Their lives were often hard, and they had few of the luxuries enjoyed by the new middle class.

Working-Class Families

Entire working-class families—children as well as adults—had to work to make enough money to live. Working conditions ranged from barely acceptable to dreadful. Workers did the same tasks over and over again. People worked up to 16 hours a day, 6 days a week. Factories and mines were hot and dirty. Diseases spread quickly. The machinery often was unsafe. As a result, many workers lost fingers, limbs, or even their lives.

Living conditions in the cities were often miserable. However, rural workers continued to look for urban factory jobs. Despite low pay and long hours, most city workers had more money than when they lived in the country. Cities also offered many leisure-time opportunities. These included parks, sports, libraries, and education.

As time passed, working conditions improved. Workers organized to demand changes. Middle-class reformers tried to better the lives of workers. As a result, factories were made safer. Working hours for women and children were reduced. New laws were passed that reduced pollution and unclean food and water in the cities.

C

W

Women's Lives

During the 1800s, women of all classes had fewer legal rights than men. It was believed that a woman's place was in the home. At this time, women worked to improve their position and find new roles. Women found jobs in businesses and in government service. There were also more opportunities for education.

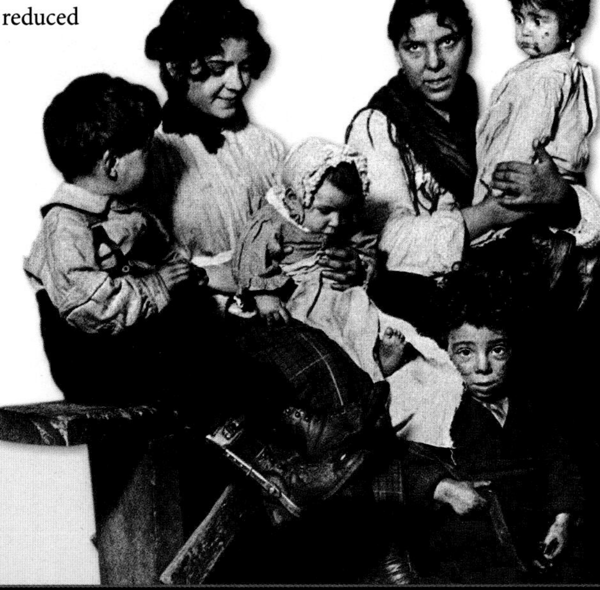

National Media Museum/SSPL/The Image Works

City life was often hard, but it was usually better than life as a farm worker. Often several families lived together and shared what they had.

▶ CRITICAL THINKING
Analyzing Why did people living in cities face hardships?

urbanization the increase in the proportion of people living in cities rather than rural areas

CHAPTER 23, Lesson 5
Society and Industry

C Critical Thinking Skills

Comparing and Contrasting Have students compare and contrast the effects of the Industrial Revolution on middle class and professional workers with industrial workers who labored in factories and mines.

Create a Venn diagram on the board to help students organize the answers they provide during class discussion. *(Students should note that the Industrial Revolution led to the growth of the middle class and the number of industrial workers. However, working conditions and pay were much better for the middle class than for the majority of the working class.)*

Then ask students to compare how conditions for these two groups changed over time. *(In class discussion, students should note that middle-class reformers and organized workers both pushed for changes that improved working conditions in factories and living conditions in the cities.)*

W Writing Skills

Narrative Have students write journal entries describing a day in the life of a worker in a factory or a mine. Entries should include details from the text about both working and living conditions for workers. **Intrapersonal**

SLIDE SHOW

Working Conditions

Analyzing Visuals Show students the slide show on working conditions in the textile mills. Explain that the Industrial Revolution brought many changes to society. Some changes were positive, and others were negative. **Ask:** **Who were working in these mills and factories?** *(mostly women and children)* **Why do you think factory owners wanted to hire these groups?** *(because they had fewer opportunities to find work and so they would agree to work for less money)* **Would you want to work under these conditions?** *(Accept reasonable answers that are supported by text evidence.)*

See page 661G for other online activities.

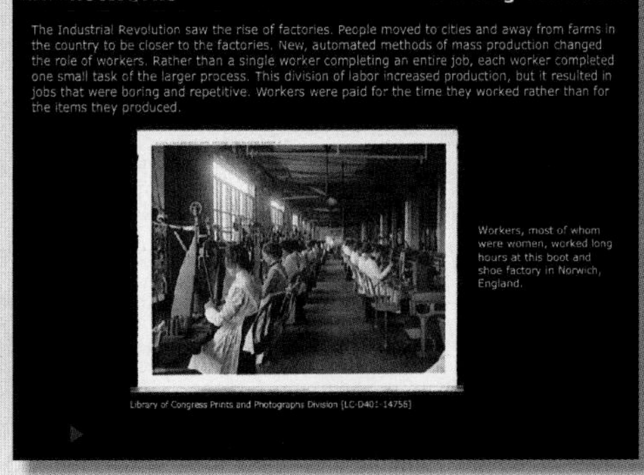

ANSWER, p. 697

CRITICAL THINKING People living in cities faced hardships because they lived in crowded areas and worked long hours for low pay.

C Critical Thinking Skills

Making Inferences Point out to students that in the nineteenth century, women began demanding equal rights in industrialized countries. **Ask:** Why do you think women began asking for equal rights at this time? How is the movement related to the Industrial Revolution? *(Answers will vary but should suggest that some women were now holding jobs outside the home, and this may have led them to see themselves as equal to men. Additionally, more women were being educated, which may have led them to want to be treated as equally as men.)*

R Reading Skills

Discussing Ask students to use details from the text to summarize the political philosophy of liberalism. Then facilitate a class discussion about the rise of liberalism in the 1800s. **Ask:**

- What were some views of the liberals during this time? *(They believed in equality under the law, freedom of speech and press, limiting government through written constitutions, and having elected legislatures write the laws.)* AL
- Why do you think people believed that these political ideas could improve the problems created by the Industrial Revolution? *(The idea of equality for all meant that workers' rights and safety would be protected. If individuals had political rights and a voice in their government, they could elect leaders who could protect them and improve their lives.)* BL

For its time, New Lanark, Scotland, was a socially progressive industrial community. Workers here enjoyed better than average conditions.

▶ CRITICAL THINKING
Explaining How did industrialization improve the lives of the working class?

Image Asset Management/World History Archive/Age fotostock

C Women began to demand equal rights with men. In the United States, Britain, and other countries, women challenged the long-standing idea that politics was a man's world. They demanded the rights to vote and to hold public office.

✓ PROGRESS CHECK

Describing What were working conditions like for early industrial workers?

Industrialization Changes Political Ideas

GUIDING QUESTION *What new political ideas arose as a result of industrial society?*

The Industrial Revolution brought many changes, both good and bad. Starting in the early 1800s, people looked for ways to solve the problems that industry had created. They developed different ideas to address these concerns.

What Is Liberalism?

One of these new ideas was **liberalism.** Liberalism is a political philosophy based on the ideas of the Enlightenment and the French Revolution.

R Liberals in the 1800s believed that all people have individual rights. These include equality under the law and freedom of speech and the press. Liberals also believed that government power should be limited by written constitutions. They felt that elected legislatures should make the laws. Most liberals believed that only men who owned property should be allowed to vote.

Reading HELPDESK CCSS

liberalism a political philosophy based on the Enlightenment ideas of equality and individual rights
utilitarianism the idea that society should promote the greatest happiness for the largest number of people
socialism the idea that the means of production should be owned and controlled by the people, through their government

Academic Vocabulary (Tier 2 Words)
cooperate to work together for the good of all

networks Online Teaching Options

IMAGE

Robert Owen

Explaining Have students read the text below the interactive image of New Lanark, the community created by Robert Owen. **Ask:** What was unique about New Lanark? *(There was a minimum wage, a reduced workday, good housing for workers, and day care for workers' children.)* What conditions was Owen responding to when he created this community? *(He was responding to low wages and poor, dangerous working and living conditions for factory workers.)* Would you like to have lived in New Lanark? Why or why not? *(Answers will vary; students should support their opinions with examples from the interactive image.)*

See page 661G for other online activities.

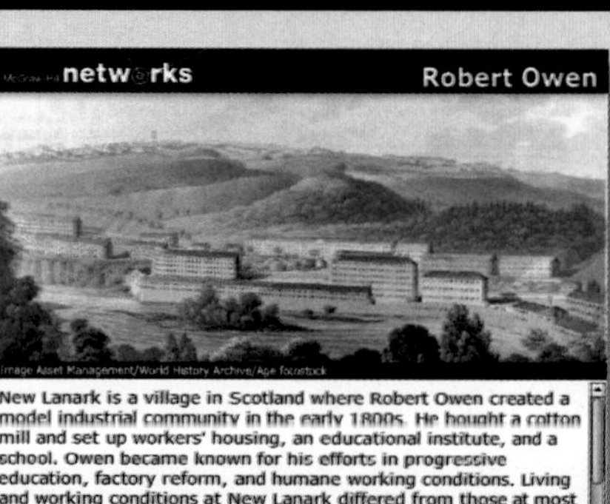

networks
Robert Owen
New Lanark is a village in Scotland where Robert Owen created a model industrial community in the early 1800s. He bought a cotton mill and set up workers' housing, an educational institute, and a school. Owen became known for his efforts in progressive education, factory reform, and humane working conditions. Living and working conditions at New Lanark differed from those at most factory towns in Britain. The belief in creating an ideal community was known as utopianism. A utopia is a kind of perfect place or

ANSWERS, p. 698

CRITICAL THINKING Industrialization improved the lives of the working class by leading to reforms such as expanded voting rights, safer working conditions, and better treatment of workers.

✓ PROGRESS CHECK Working conditions were unhealthful, with long hours and polluted air and water. However, factory work paid higher wages than farm labor.

The new middle class adopted liberalism. Middle class businesspeople believed that government should not interfere with business or society. British economist Adam Smith supported this idea. In a book called *The Wealth of Nations*, Smith wrote that government should stay out of the economy and let businesses compete. This idea was known as "laissez-faire," a French word meaning "to let be."

Two other liberal thinkers in Britain, however, believed that government should step in to make society better. Jeremy Bentham (BEHN•thuhm) and John Stuart Mill promoted an idea known as **utilitarianism** (yoo•tih•luh•TEHR•ee•uh•nih•zuhm). As utilitarians, Bentham and Mill believed society should promote the greatest happiness for the most people. They supported ideas like full rights for women and improved health services. They also promoted better education.

C

What Is Socialism?

Not all thinkers in the 1800s agreed with the ideas of liberalism. Some supported an idea known as **socialism.** Socialists believed that the people should own and control all factories, land, capital, and raw materials. They believed that the government should manage these means of production for the people. In this way, wealth could be distributed equally among all citizens.

Some early socialists set up communities where workers could share equally in the profits. Robert Owen, a wealthy British factory owner, was one of these socialists. Owen believed that if people **cooperated,** they could create a better society.

In 1800, Owen made the Scottish mill town of New Lanark into a model industrial community. He did not turn the mill over to the workers. However, he did greatly improve living and working conditions.

The Socialism of Karl Marx

Other socialists thought Owen's work was impractical. They believed it would do little to change society. One of these socialists was Karl Marx.

Marx believed that history was a continual struggle between social classes. According to Marx, the ruling class controlled production. They also held on to most of the wealth. The working class were the actual makers of goods, therefore they should share in the profits. However, they were not paid enough.

Karl Marx believed in equality and a classless society. He also supported a government controlled by the workers. Why might Marx have been thought of as a rebel?

C Critical Thinking Skills

Comparing and Contrasting Write the terms *liberalism, utilitarianism,* and *socialism* on the board. Work with students to write definitions for each term. AL ELL

Ask students to compare and contrast the views of these different theories about how society should operate. *(Students should note that utilitarianism and liberalism supported the idea of individual rights. However, liberals argued for little or no government involvement in the economy, utilitarians argued for government involvement to improve society, and socialists argued that the government should play a major role in running the economy.)* BL

As a class, create a Venn diagram on the board. Have volunteers suggest information to include in each part of the diagram. **Visual/Spatial**

CHART

Marxism, Socialism, and Communism

Analyzing Show students the interactive chart that compares Marxism, socialism, and communism. After students read the chart, ask them to restate each organization's slogan or basic belief in their own words. Have a class discussion comparing and contrasting the three different theories.

See page 661G for other online activities.

McGraw-Hill networks™ **Marxism, Socialism, and Communism**

Karl Marx believed in equality and a classless society. According to his social theory, socialism was a stage in the multi-step process of transition from free-market capitalism to communism.

Directions: Click on each heading in the chart to learn more about each of the basic beliefs of these three theories of social organization.

Marxism	Socialism	Communism
• System of social organization in which all means of production are commonly owned	• System of social organization in which the government controls private property and the distribution of income	• System of social organization in which the community as a whole or the state holds property, rather than individuals
• Predicts that after a period of dictatorship by the working class, no class divisions in society should remain	According to Marxist theory: • Socialism is a temporary stage of change from capitalism to communism. • Ownership of the economy by the working class has not yet been fully achieved.	• System of government in which the state plans and controls the economy, NOT individuals. • A single party holds power, claiming to make progress toward a society in which all goods are equally shared.
• States all people should enjoy the fruits of their labor	• Slogan: "From each according to his ability, to each according to his work." • Income distributed according to work rather than need	• Slogan: "From each according to his ability, to each according to his needs."

ANSWER, p. 699

Caption Karl Marx might have been considered a rebel because his socialist theories proposed overthrowing the current industrial system.

Society and Industry

C Critical Thinking Skills

Contrasting Discuss the basic ideas of Marxism and socialism with students. **Ask:** **How were socialist ideas different from Marxist ideas?** *(Socialists believed that they could use democratic processes to elect leaders who would help workers. Marxists believed that change would not come from democratic practices, but instead from a revolution in which the workers—the proletariat—would rise up against the middle and ruling classes.)*

W Writing Skills

Argument Point out the phrase "incendiary speeches" in the primary-source quotation. Explain that union leaders often gave speeches describing poor working conditions and proposing improvements or other changes in society. The passionate speeches were often given in hopes of inspiring action to bring about change. Have students write their own "incendiary speeches" to convince someone in the mid-1800s to support workers or to support a strike. Then ask volunteers to give their speeches to the rest of the class. **Verbal/Linguistic**

Marx stated that eventually the working class, which he called the **proletariat** (proh•luh•TEHR•ee•uht), would revolt and create a communist society. Under communism, social classes would end. People would be equal and share the wealth.

Marx's ideas, later called Marxism, were very influential. His ideas were the basic principles of socialist political parties in Germany, Britain, and other countries. These socialist parties encouraged government control of industry. However, instead of calling for revolution, many of these parties adopted the democratic process. Their supporters elected representatives to national legislatures, where they worked to pass laws that helped workers.

The growth of labor unions was another response to the horrors of factory life. A **labor union** is an organization of workers who unite to improve working conditions. Union leaders used strikes, or work stoppages, to force owners to bargain with the unions. One woman who worked in a textile mill wrote about a strike led by factory women in the 1830s:

PRIMARY SOURCE

> "The mills were shut down, and the girls . . . listened to incendiary [angry] speeches from some early labor reformers. One of the girls stood on a pump, and gave vent [release] to the feelings of her companions in a neat speech, declaring that it was their duty to resist all attempts at cutting down wages. . . . [The] event caused . . . consternation [dismay]."
>
> —from "Early Factory Labor in New England" by Harriet H. Robinson

The realistic characters in Charles Dickens's novels such as *Oliver Twist* and *Great Expectations* were the everyday people of England. This painting shows a scene from Dickens's *A Christmas Carol.*

✓ PROGRESS CHECK

Describing What did Adam Smith believe about government and business?

Revolution in the Arts

GUIDING QUESTION *How did artists and writers describe the new industrial society?*

The growth of industry also sparked new movements in art, literature, and music. The often ugly appearance of industrial society caused some artists to turn away from it. Others, however, chose to portray it.

Reading HELPDESK (CCSS)

proletariat the working class

labor union an organization of those employed who work together to improve wages and working conditions

Academic Vocabulary (Tier 2 Words)

symbol something that stands for or suggests something else

networks Online Teaching Options

PRIMARY SOURCE

A Tale of Two Cities

Using Context Clues Have students read the introduction to the primary source and the paragraphs that begin the book *A Tale of Two Cities.* Ask students to think about the first paragraph, which describes the contrasts of that time period. **Ask:** **What two groups might Dickens have been thinking of when he wrote "It was the best of times, it was the worst of times . . ."?** *(Answers will vary, but students might suggest that he might have been writing about the nobles and the common people and pointing out how different their lives were.)*

See page 661G for other online activities.

networks — A Tale of Two Cities

ANALYZING PRIMARY SOURCES

The characters in Charles Dickens' novels, such as *A Tale of Two Cities*, were everyday people. *A Tale of Two Cities* is set at the time of the French Revolution. The book is best known for its famous opening lines, which describe England and France in 1775. In the book, the rulers of both countries live a good life. As the book soon reveals, the rulers are unaware of the terrible way the common people are forced to live.

> "It was the best of times, it was the worst of times, it was the age of wisdom, it was the age of foolishness, it was the epoch [era] of belief, it was the epoch of incredulity [disbelief], it was the season of Light, it was the season of Darkness, it was the spring of hope, it was the winter of despair, we had everything before us, we had nothing before us, we were all going direct to Heaven, we were all going direct the other way. . . .
>
> There were a king with a large jaw and a queen with a plain face, on the throne of England; there were a king with a large jaw and a queen with a fair face, on"
>
> —from *A Tale of Two Cities*, by Charles Dickens

Source: http://www.online-literature.com/dickens/twocities/1/

ANSWER, p. 700

✓ PROGRESS CHECK Smith believed that if government stayed out of the economy and let businesses compete, prosperity and a better society would result.

What Is Romanticism?

By the late 1700s, artists and writers known as the romantics began to react against the Enlightenment's stress on order and reason. Their movement, called romanticism, valued feelings and the imagination as the best way to find the truth.

Poets, such as Britain's William Wordsworth and Germany's Johann von Goethe (yoh•HAHN fawn GUH•tuh), chose nature, the past, and the unusual as their subjects. They wrote poems to express their inner feelings. Romantic painters, such as Eugène Delacroix (yoo•JEEN deh•luh•KWAH) of France, chose historical or legendary subjects. Their paintings were meant to stir the emotions. The first great romantic musician was Ludwig van Beethoven (LOOD•wihg vahn BAY•toh•vuhn). This German composer's music expressed strong emotions.

What is Realism?

By the mid-1800s, some artists and writers began to reject the romantic emphasis on feelings. Known as the realists, they wanted to portray life as it actually was.

Novelists like Britain's Charles Dickens, France's Honoré de Balzac (AHN•uh•ray day BAWL•zak), and Russia's Leo Tolstoy focused on ordinary people in everyday settings. Painters like France's Gustave Courbet (GUS•tahv kur•BAY) and Honoré Daumier (AHN•uh•ray doh•MYAY) also portrayed life in the city and countryside.

C Beethoven remains one of Germany's most famous composers. At age 49, Beethoven was completely deaf but continued to compose music. This sculpture stands in his honor in Bonn, Germany.

Dawn of Modernism

The late 1800s saw the rise of modernism. Modernist artists and writers experimented with new subjects and styles. One group of modernists studied social problems of the day.

Novelists such as Émile Zola of France and American Theodore Dreiser explored issues such as crime, alcoholism, and women's rights. Norwegian Henrik Ibsen also dealt with social issues in his plays. Another modernist group took a different approach. Symbolist artists and writers believed that the outer world was a reflection of an individual's inner reality. They studied dreams and **symbols** and used them in their works.

The soft sunlight sparkles off the water in Claude Monet's impressionist painting.

C Critical Thinking Skills

Differentiating Discuss how the artistic movements of the time were related to one another. **Ask:**

- **How was the romantic movement a reaction to earlier philosophical movements?** *(The Enlightenment had stressed order and rational thought. Romanticism was a reaction against this emphasis on reason and instead focused on feelings and imagination.)*
- **In what way was realism a reaction against romanticism?** *(People rejected the emphasis on feelings and wanted to show life as it really was.)*

Making Connections

Help students connect the romantic and realistic styles of the nineteenth century with the popular art and music of today. Then have students work in pairs to select three modern works—books or songs—and classify them as realistic or romantic. Have them support their answers with factual information about the books or songs and details about the two artistic styles.

SLIDE SHOW

Monet's Paintings

Interpreting Show students the slide show about Claude Monet's impressionist paintings. Point out that the famous paintings in the slide show were significant for their use of color and outdoor subjects.

Ask: What emotions do the paintings make the viewer feel? *(Possible answers: peacefulness, gentleness, appreciation of nature or the outdoors)* AL ELL

See page 661G for other online activities.

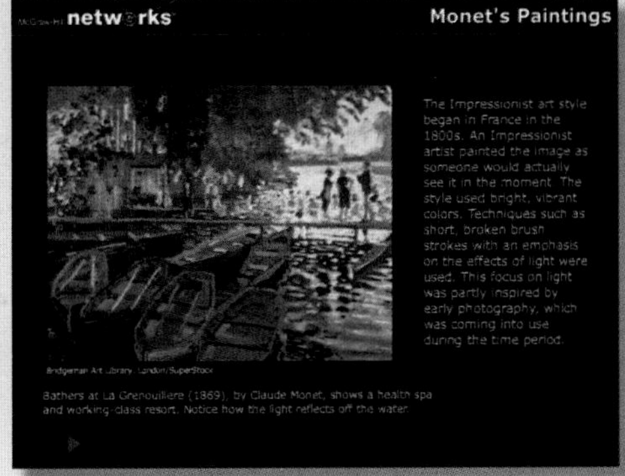

T Technology Skills

Researching on the Internet Have students use the Internet to find examples of impressionist painting or impressionist music. Ask them to work in pairs to create a slide show of the paintings or a collection of recordings (mp3s) of the songs and then share them with the rest of the class. Student should include a written sentence about each painting or song they present, naming the artist and the date the work was created. **Auditory/Musical Visual/Spatial**

R Reading Skills

Describing Direct students' attention to the section about diversity and Charles Darwin. Have them refer to the text for support in their answers to the following questions. **Ask:**

- **What was Darwin's theory of evolution?** *(that living things adapt to their environment and that humans evolved over time from animal species)*
- **Why were his ideas controversial?** *(People believed they contradicted the creation story in the Bible and could lead to a world without morals.)* AL

BIOGRAPHY

Albert Einstein (1879–1955)

Albert Einstein was born in Germany in 1879. He struggled to do well at school and had trouble finding work after graduation. After attending technical school, Einstein worked as a clerk in a government office. The job was simple for him, and it left him plenty of time to pursue his interest in physics. Einstein's research earned him a job as a professor at a university. When Hitler came to power in Germany, Einstein moved to the United States and continued his work in physics. His ideas about the physical universe eventually led to the development of the atomic bomb and the nuclear reactor.

▶ **CRITICAL THINKING**
Making Inferences Why might Einstein have struggled to find work after graduation?

Bettmann/Corbis

T During the 1870s, a group of artists developed a style called impressionism. The impressionists were interested in color and the effects of light on outdoor subjects. The French impressionists included Claude Monet (moh•NAY), Pierre-Auguste Renoir (REN•wahr), and Edgar Degas (duh•GAH). Mary Cassatt of the United States was also a famous impressionist painter. Composers, led by France's Claude Debussy, created impressionist music. They layered sound upon sound to create a dreamy, shimmering effect.

✓ PROGRESS CHECK

Describing What did the romantics emphasize in their works?

The New Science

GUIDING QUESTION ***What advances made in science in the mid-1800s have transformed life today?***

During the 1800s, scientists expanded knowledge about life and the universe. Their work also led to medical advances that cured deadly diseases and lengthened life spans.

The Diversity of Life

During the 1800s, many people wondered why the world has so many kinds of plants and animals. Charles Darwin set out to find an answer. His research led him to develop a theory of evolution: plants and animals change very slowly over time.

In a book called *On the Origin of Species,* Darwin stated that plant and animal populations increase faster than the food supply. As a result, they are constantly struggling to survive. Those that survive are better adapted to their environment. They produce offspring that have the same successful characteristics.

R Darwin believed that humans evolved, or developed, from animal species. His ideas were controversial. Some people believed that his theory contradicted the biblical story of creation. Others believed it opened the door to a world without moral values. Many people, however, accepted Darwin's theory.

In the 1860s, Gregor Mendel discovered how characteristics were passed to the next generation. From his studies of pea plants, Mendel concluded that offspring receive their traits from their parents. He developed rules to explain what traits parents pass on. Today, Mendel is known as the father of genetics.

Reading **HELP**DESK CCSS

Reading Strategy: *Making Inferences*

As you read, you can put together clues to gain information the author doesn't tell you directly. This is called making inferences. Read about Jenner and Pasteur. Make an inference about what it would have been like for someone who became sick in the early 1800s.

networks Online Teaching Options

MAP

Darwin and the *Beagle*

Analyzing Maps Display the map and have students click on different locations to learn the details of Darwin's journey. Then discuss what he learned at each of these locations that might have contributed to his theory of evolution.

See page 661G for other online activities.

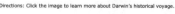

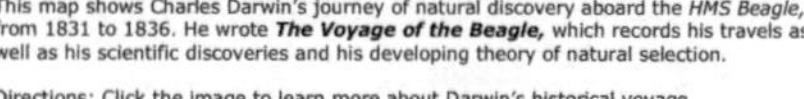

This map shows Charles Darwin's journey of natural discovery aboard the *HMS Beagle,* from 1831 to 1836. He wrote ***The Voyage of the Beagle,*** which records his travels as well as his scientific discoveries and his developing theory of natural selection.

Directions: Click the image to learn more about Darwin's historical voyage.

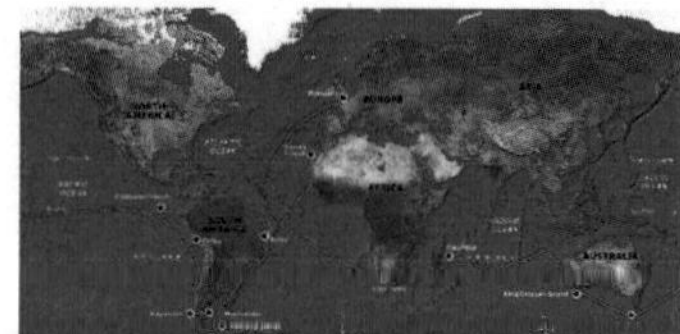

ANSWERS, p. 702

✓ PROGRESS CHECK The romantics valued feelings and the imagination as the best way to find truth. Their work focused on subjects that were meant to stir the emotions, not the intellect.

CRITICAL THINKING Einstein might have struggled to find work after graduation because he did not do well in school.

Reading Strategy It was dangerous to become sick in the early 1800s because doctors did not know much about the causes or spread of diseases.

What Did Pasteur Discover?

During the 1800s, scientists made advances that gave people longer, healthier lives. One of the first breakthroughs was the discovery of vaccines. In 1796, Edward Jenner noticed that workers who caught a disease called cowpox never caught the deadly smallpox. Jenner found that vaccinating people with cowpox made them immune, or resistant, to smallpox.

About 50 years later, Louis Pasteur learned why Jenner's vaccination worked. In the 1850s, Pasteur discovered bacteria, or germs. He proved that they cause infectious diseases. Pasteur also showed that killing bacteria prevented many diseases.

C The discovery of anesthesia, or pain-deadening drugs, was another great step forward. It enabled patients to sleep through their operations. British surgeon Joseph Lister provided another advance. He developed ways to sterilize medical instruments. Before Lister, many patients died after surgery due to infection.

Einstein and Physics

New ideas also changed the way people understood the world. Expanding the work of Galileo and Newton, scientists developed the atomic theory. This is the idea that all matter is made up of tiny particles called atoms.

Albert Einstein then overturned long-held ideas about the universe. His theory of relativity stated that space and time could not be measured in an absolute sense. Instead, they depended on the relative motion of bodies in space. For example, the speed of two trains appears differently to people on the station platform than it does to passengers on the train.

Darwin's observations led him to develop his theory of natural selection. This is the idea that the animals best adapted to their environment would multiply. Poorly adapted members of a species would die off.

Bettmann/CORBIS

☑ PROGRESS CHECK

Explaining How did Louis Pasteur extend the work of Edward Jenner?

LESSON 5 REVIEW (CCSS)

Review Vocabulary (Tier 3 Words)

1. Use the word *socialism* in a sentence about working conditions in the Industrial Revolution. RH.6–8.2, RH.6–8.4
2. Explain the significance of *urbanization* in the context of the Industrial Revolution. RH.6–8.2, RH.6–8.4

Answer the Guiding Questions

3. ***Determining Cause and Effect*** How did the lives of women change during the Industrial Revolution? RH.6–8.2
4. ***Analyzing*** What effect did labor unions have on the working conditions in factories? RH.6–8.2
5. ***Contrasting*** How were the realists different from the romantics? RH.6–8.2
6. ***Assessing*** What was the importance of Gregor Mendel's work? RH.6–8.2
7. **ARGUMENT** Choose a style of art from the lesson. In a paragraph, describe your personal reaction to that style. WHST.6–8.10

Lesson 5 703

LESSON 5 REVIEW ANSWERS

1. The horrid working conditions of the Industrial Revolution led some leaders to look for a better way of governing, called socialism, in which the people of a nation share the wealth equally.
2. Urbanization occurred as a result of the Industrial Revolution. Cities grew when workers moved there from the countryside to get factory jobs.
3. Women began to work outside the home. They earned higher wages and had more opportunities for education.
4. Labor unions forced owners to bargain with union members for better working conditions.
5. The realists examined industrialized society closely, while the romantics turned away from it.
6. Gregor Mendel conducted experiments that proved traits are passed from one generation to the next.
7. Answers will vary, but students should identify an artistic style and recognize how it appeals to them on a personal level.

C Critical Thinking Skills

Collaborating Have students choose a scientist from their reading, such as Charles Darwin, Gregor Mendel, Edward Jenner, Louis Pasteur, Joseph Lister, or Albert Einstein.

In small groups, have students discuss their chosen scientist and evaluate his or her impact on society. Have the members of the group choose the one scientist they believe has made the greatest impact. Ask each group to share the scientist they chose and explain why they selected him, citing specific evidence from the text to defend their choices. **Interpersonal**

Have students complete the Lesson 5 Review.

CLOSE & REFLECT

Making Generalizations Wrap up the lesson by asking students to make generalizations about how society has or has not benefited from the scientific progress of the Industrial Revolution.

Ask volunteers to explain how artistic movements impact society and how the impact of art on society is different from the impact of science.

ANSWER, p. 703

☑ PROGRESS CHECK Louis Pasteur discovered the reason that Jenner's research was correct. He discovered bacteria, and this discovery was the basis of Jenner's successful vaccine.

Activities Answers

CHAPTER REVIEW ACTIVITY

Draw the following table on the board. Then organize the class into four groups and assign each group one of the Enduring Understandings for this chapter. Have each group list details and examples of their understanding from this chapter. Then have them come to the board and write their Enduring Understanding and their examples in the table. After all groups have finished, challenge the class to add more examples from the world today.

Enduring Understanding	Example from Chapter

REVIEW THE ENDURING UNDERSTANDINGS

Review this chapter's Enduring Understandings with students:

- *Conflict can lead to change.*
- *The social sciences help us understand history.*
- *The movement of people, goods, and ideas causes societies to change over time.*
- *Science and technology can change people's lives.*

Now pose the following questions in a class discussion to apply these understandings to the chapter. **Ask:**

- **How did nationalism affect different regions of the world in the nineteenth century?** *(Answers should include the unification of Italy and Germany, expansion of the United States, and independence movements in the western hemisphere, such as in Mexico and South America.)*
- **How do you think ideas from one revolution affected people in other parts of the world?** *(Answers may include: The Enlightenment ideas from Europe influenced leaders of the American Revolution, and these ideas in turn influenced the French Revolution. In addition, independence movements in the Western Hemisphere spread as people in one region learned of successful revolutions in other places.)*
- **Were the overall results of the Industrial Revolution positive or negative? Support your answer with evidence from the chapter.** *(Answers may vary but should include the changes such as increased productivity, urbanization, poor working conditions, and political reform movements in response to the changes.)*
- **How did movements in arts and literature reflect changes in society in the nineteenth century?** *(Answers will vary but should include details about the Romantic, Realistic, and Impressionistic art movements.)*

CHAPTER 23 Activities CCSS

Write your answers on a separate piece of paper.

1. **Exploring the Essential Question** WHST.6–8.2, WHST.6–8.10
   INFORMATIVE/EXPLANATORY How do new ideas change the way people live? Write an essay that explains how inventions in the textile industry led to changes in the way British people lived in the nineteenth century.

2. **21st Century Skills** RH.6–8.2, WHST.6–8.6, WHST.6–8.10
   BUILD A WEB SITE Plan a Web site with a home page and three linking pages on either the French Revolution or the American Revolution. On the page, identify the important events you will include, the documents you will link to, and the images that will help tell the story. On your home page, set up a logical list of categories to help a visitor navigate your pages.

3. **Thinking Like a Historian** RH.6–8.2, WHST.6–8.6, WHST.6–8.9
   IDENTIFYING POINTS OF VIEW Think about the views of a nineteenth century person who believed in liberalism and one who believed in socialism. Using a Venn diagram compare and contrast the viewpoints of these two belief systems.

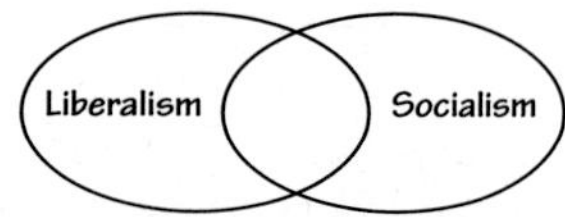

4. **GEOGRAPHY ACTIVITY**

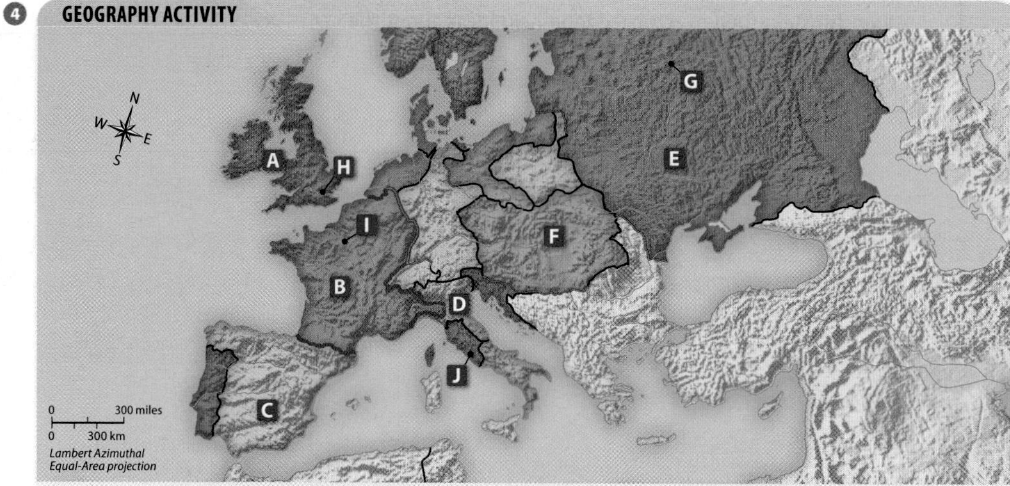

Locating Places RH.6–8.7
Match the letters on the map with the numbered places listed below.

1. Britain	4. Kingdom of Italy	7. Moscow	10. Rome
2. France	5. Russian Empire	8. London	
3. Spain	6. Austrian Empire	9. Paris	

ACTIVITIES ANSWERS

Exploring the Essential Question

1. Answers may include the concept that ideas can spark people to take actions that change the world. Inventions such as the spinning jenny led to a change in the way British people lived.

21st Century Skills

2. Student plans should show logical connections of events of either the French Revolution or the American Revolution. Plans should also demonstrate an understanding of how Web pages are designed and navigated.

Thinking Like a Historian

3. Graphic organizers should contain information indicating that liberals and socialists wanted reform. Liberals, however, wanted limited reform and wanted government to stay away from businesses. Socialists wanted broad reforms and for government to take over the means of production from businesses.

Locating Places

4. **1.** A, **2.** B, **3.** C, **4.** D, **5.** E, **6.** F, , **6.** F, **7.** G, **8.** H, **9.** I, **10.** J

CHAPTER 23 Assessment

Directions: Choose the best answer for each question.

RH.6–8.2

1. The slogan "No taxation without representation" is associated with which revolution?
   A. the French Revolution
   B. the Revolution in Haiti
   C. the Industrial Revolution
   D. the American Revolution

RH.6–8.2

2. Why was the Napoleonic Code created?
   F. Napoleon wanted to control his military leaders.
   G. The Catholic Church demanded that Napoleon create the code.
   H. Napoleon created the code of laws to control the people of France.
   I. Napoleon created it when he planned to rule all of Europe.

RH.6–8.2

3. Which two men led the South American fight for independence?
   A. Miguel Hidalgo and José María Morelos
   B. Simón Bolívar and José de San Martín
   C. Toussaint L'Ouverture and Giuseppe Garibaldi
   D. Camillo di Cavour and Otto von Bismarck

RH.6–8.2, RH.6–8.4

4. What was Manifest Destiny?
   F. the idea that America should hold all lands from east to west on the North American continent
   G. the idea that industry should grow fastest in the north
   H. the idea that enslaved Africans should be free
   I. the idea that all people should be represented by a fair government

RH.6–8.2

5. Why do historians call the period of industrialization the "Industrial Revolution"?
   A. because it was bloody and terrible
   B. because it dramatically changed life in many places
   C. because it led to the overthrow of leaders
   D. because it stopped scientific advances

RH.6–8.2

6. Which of the following best describes a laissez-faire approach to government?
   F. Government should stay out of the way and let businesses compete.
   G. Federal government should have more control than states.
   H. Businesses should have more control of laws than government.
   I. Business is better able to run a government.

705

CHAPTER 23

Assessment Answers

ASSESSMENT ANSWERS

Review the Guiding Questions

1. **D** The correct choice is D. This slogan was associated with the American Revolution. Colonists in North America objected to being taxed by King George III without a chance to represent themselves in Parliament. The slogan of the French Revolution involved liberty for the masses. The Industrial Revolution was not involved with taxation, and the revolution in Haiti was fought to get rid of a colonial power.

2. **H** The correct choice is H. Napoleon made many changes in France as consul and later as emperor. One such change was to create the Napoleonic Code—a code of laws to enforce the rules of his empire. As emperor, Napoleon did not take orders from the Catholic Church, and he had other means of controlling his military leaders.

3. **B** The correct choice is B. Símon Bolívar and José de San Martín led the movements for South American independence. Miguel Hidalgo and José María Morelos sparked the revolution in Mexico. Toussaint L'Ouverture led the Haitian revolution. Giuseppe Garibaldi and Camillo di Cavour united Italy, and Otto von Bismarck united Germany.

4. **F** The correct choice is F. As the United States expanded into the Louisiana Territory, Florida, California, and the Oregon Territory, many people began to believe that U.S. occupation of all the lands from east to west was destined to occur. Although many reformers worked on freeing enslaved Africans or on policies of fair government and growth of industry, Manifest Destiny involved the simple concept of the U.S. right to expand from coast to coast.

5. **B** The correct choice is B. The Industrial Revolution changed the way people worked, lived, communicated, and enjoyed their culture. The changes were so profound that historians think of this period as revolutionary. The Industrial Revolution was neither bloody nor terrible. It did not overthrow any government leaders. The revolution was a result of scientific advances rather than the stopping of those advances.

6. **F** The correct choice is F. Adam Smith believed that government should stay out of the economy and let businesses compete, and that this system would lead to prosperity and a better society. The concept did not involve a business takeover of government or allow businesses to make new laws. The idea that the federal government should have more control than states was the opposite of laissez-faire policies.

Assessment Answers

Analyzing Documents

7 **D** The correct choice is D. The most adaptable species can find ways to survive even when their habitats change or when other influences impact their lives. Darwin saw how strong creatures, as well as those with great or little intelligence, were equally likely to become extinct, while those that could adapt were likely to survive changes in their environment.

8 **I** The correct choice is I. Darwin's quotation makes it clear that the ability to change is more important in determining which creatures will survive. This ability is more important than being strong or intelligent.

Short Response

9 Answers should use details and descriptive language to describe the features of the image. They should recognize dangerous working conditions and note the presence of women and children in the factory.

10 Karl Marx believed that such working conditions would cause workers to rebel and overthrow the ruling class. The workers would then create a communist society based on equality.

Extended Response

11 Students' editorials should make a convincing argument for or against declaring independence from England. They should include specific details and a clear call to action.

CHAPTER 23 Assessment *(continued)*

DBQ ANALYZING DOCUMENTS

Drawing Conclusions Charles Darwin sums up his research on how animals in nature survive.

"It is not the strongest of the species [group] that survives, nor the most intelligent that survives. It is the one that is the most adaptable to change."

—from *Psyography: Charles Darwin* by Shayla Porter

RH.6–8.1, RH.6–8.6

7 According to Darwin's theory, which species are the most likely to survive?

A. the strongest
B. the most intelligent
C. the least intelligent
D. the most adaptable to change

RH.6–8.1, RH.6–8.6

8 **Analyzing** According to Darwin, which of the following is correct?

F. The ability to change is not as important as being strong.
G. The ability to change is not as important as being intelligent.
H. The ability to change is as important as being strong and intelligent.
I. The ability to change is more important than being strong or intelligent.

SHORT RESPONSE

RH.6–8.7

9 In one or two sentences, describe the working conditions shown in the image of the textile factory in England during the Industrial Revolution.

RH.6–8.2, RH.6–8.6, WHST.6–8.9

10 Explain what Karl Marx would say about these conditions.

EXTENDED RESPONSE

WHST.6–8.1, WHST.6–8.10

11 **Argument** You have read Thomas Paine's *Common Sense* and you know American colonists who object to the Intolerable Acts. But the choice to declare independence from England will mean bitter war. Write a letter to the editor in which you take a position on whether the American colonies should declare their independence from England.

Need Extra Help?

If You've Missed Question	1	2	3	4	5	6	7	8	9	10	11
Review Lesson	1	2	3	3	4	5	5	5	4	5	1

networks Online Teaching Options

More Assessment Resources

The *Assess* tab in the online Teacher Lesson Center includes resources to help students improve their test-taking skills. It also contains many project-based rubrics to help you assess students' work.

GLOSSARY/GLOSARIO

- Content vocabulary words are words that relate to world history content.
- Words that have an asterisk (*) are academic vocabulary. They help you understand your school subjects.
- All vocabulary words are **boldfaced** or **highlighted in yellow** in your textbook.

A

ENGLISH	ESPAÑOL
***abandon** to leave and not return; to leave, often because of danger (p. 252; p. 456)	***abandonar** salir y no regresar; dejar, con frecuencia debido al peligro (pág. 252; pág. 456)
abolitionism movement to end slavery (p. 687)	**abolicionismo** movimiento para poner fin a la esclavitud (pág. 687)
absolutism a political system in which a ruler has total power (p. 651)	**absolutismo** sistema político en el cual un gobernante tiene poder total (pág. 651)
***accompany** to go with someone as a companion (p. 200)	***acompañar** ir con alguien como compañero (pág. 200)
***accurate** free from errors; in agreement with truth (p. 239; pp. 562–563)	***exacto** sin errores; que se ajusta a la verdad (pág. 239; págs. 562–563)
accursed doomed, miserable (p. 597)	**maldito** condenado, miserable (pág. 597)
***achieve** to succeed; to gain something as the result of work; to successfully complete a task (p. 187; p. 456)	***lograr** tener éxito; obtener algo como resultado del trabajo; completar una tarea con éxito (pág. 187; pág. 456)
***achievement** something gained by working for it (p. 512)	***logro** algo que se obtiene trabajando por ello (pág. 512)
***acquire** to get possession of something; to get as one's own (p. 124; p. 310)	***adquirir** tomar posesión de algo; tomar como propio (pág. 124; pág. 310)
acupuncture originally, a Chinese practice of inserting fine needles through the skin at specific points to treat disease or relieve pain (pp. 296–297)	**acupuntura** práctica originaria de la China que consiste en insertar agujas delgadas a través de la piel en puntos específicos para tratar una enfermedad o aliviar el dolor (págs. 296–297)
***adequate** enough for a particular requirement (p. 424)	***adecuado** suficiente para un requisito en particular (pág. 424)
***administer** to be lawfully in charge of (p. 342)	***administrar** estar legalmente a cargo (pág. 342)
***affect** influence; to cause a change (p. 179)	***afectar** influir; ocasionar un cambio (pág. 179)
agora a gathering place; marketplace in ancient Greece (p. 180)	**ágora** sitio de reunión; plaza de la Grecia antigua (pág. 180)
allies those who support each other for some common purpose (pp. 624–625)	**aliados** quienes se apoyan entre sí para un propósito en común (págs. 624–625)
alphabet a set of letters or other characters used to write a language (pp. 144–145)	**abecedario** conjunto de letras o de otros caracteres usados en la lengua escrita (págs. 144–145)

ambush a surprise attack (p. 626)	**emboscada** ataque sorpresivo (pág. 626)
anatomy the study of the body's structure (p. 344)	**anatomía** estudio de la estructura del cuerpo (pág. 344)
ancestor a person that someone is descended from (p. 282)	**ancestro** persona de la cual alguien desciende (pág. 282)
animism belief in spirits that are outside of the body (p. 518)	**animismo** creencia en espíritus que están fuera del cuerpo (pág. 518)
annul to declare invalid (p. 604)	**anular** declarar inválido (pág. 604)
anthropology the study of human culture and how it develops over time (pp. 8–9)	**antropología** estudio de la cultura humana y su desarrollo a lo largo del tiempo (págs. 8–9)
anti-Semitism hostility toward or discrimination against Jews (pp. 568–569)	**antisemitismo** hostilidad o discriminación hacia los judíos (págs. 568–569)
apostle Christian leader chosen by Jesus to spread his message (pp. 377)	**apóstol** líder cristiano elegido por Jesús para difundir su mensaje (pág. 377)
archaeology the study of objects to learn about past human life (p. 8)	**arqueología** estudio de objetos para conocer el pasado de la vida humana (pág. 8)
archipelago many scattered islands surrounded by an expanse of water (pp. 516–517)	**archipiélago** muchas islas dispersas rodeadas por una extensión de agua (págs. 516–517)
***area** the land included within a set of boundaries (pp. 422–423)	***área** terreno incluido dentro de un conjunto de límites (págs. 422–423)
aristocrat a member of an upper class of society, usually made up of hereditary nobility (p. 282)	**aristócrata** miembro de la clase alta de la sociedad o de la nobleza, por lo general formada por la nobleza hereditaria (pág. 282)
artifact an object made by people (pp. 8–9)	**artefacto** objeto elaborado por las personas (págs. 8–9)
***assume** to take for granted to be true (p. 316)	***suponer** dar por hecho que algo es cierto (pág. 316)
astrolabe a tool that helps sailors navigate using the positions of the stars (p. 413)	**astrolabio** instrumento que ayuda a los marineros a navegar mediante la ubicación de las estrellas (pág. 413)
astronomer a person who studies planets and stars (p. 92)	**astrónomo** persona que estudia los planetas y las estrellas (pág. 92)
***authority** the right or power to give orders, make decisions, or control people; power over thoughts, opinions, and behavior (p. 125; pp. 400–401; pp. 572–573)	***autoridad** derecho o facultad de dar órdenes, tomar decisiones o controlar a las personas; poder sobre los pensamientos, las opiniones y el comportamiento (pág. 125; págs. 400-401; págs. 572–573)
***available** ready to be used (p. 56)	***disponible** listo para usarse (pág. 56)
***awareness** the state of having understanding or knowledge (p. 32)	***conciencia** tener comprensión o conocimiento (pág. 32)

B

barbarians uncivilized people (p. 502)

bárbaros personas no civilizadas (pág. 502)

bard someone who writes or performs epic poems or stories about heroes and their deeds (p. 178)

bardo alguien que escribe o relata poemas épicos o historias sobre héroes y sus hazañas (pág. 178)

barter to trade by exchanging one good or service for another; to exchange goods without using money (p. 42)

hacer trueque comerciar intercambiando un bien o servicio por otro; intercambiar productos sin usar dinero (pág. 42)

bazaar a marketplace (p. 412)

bazar mercado (pág. 412)

***behalf** representing; in the place of (p. 518)

***en nombre** en representación; en lugar de (pág. 518)

***benefit** to receive help; to gain (p. 310)

***beneficiarse** recibir ayuda; obtener (pág. 310)

Bhagavad Gita a section of the Indian epic *The Mahabharata* (p. 269)

Bhagavad Gita sección de la epopeya india el Mahabharata (pág. 269)

bias an unreasoned, emotional judgment about people or events (p. 12)

parcialidad juicio emotivo o que no tiene fundamento racional acerca de personas o eventos (pág. 12)

bourgeoisie the middle class in France (p. 673)

burguesía clase media francesa (pág. 673)

boycott to protest by refusing to do something (pp. 666–667)

boicotear protestar negándose a hacer algo (págs. 666–667)

Brahman the universal spirit worshiped by Hindus (pp. 257–258)

Brahmán espíritu universal adorado por los hindúes (págs. 257–258)

Bronze Age the period in ancient human culture when people began to make and use bronze (p. 67)

Edad del Bronce periodo de la cultura humana antigua en el cual las personas comenzaron a fabricar y usar el bronce (pág. 67)

Buddhism a religion founded in ancient India by the religious teacher the Buddha (p. 260)

budismo religión fundada en la antigua India por el maestro religioso Buda (pág. 260)

bureaucracy a group of non-elected government officials (p. 284)

burocracia grupo de funcionarios del gobierno que no son elegidos (pág. 284)

bureaucrat a government official (p. 109)

burócrata funcionario del gobierno (pág. 109)

C

caliph a Muslim leader (p. 404)

califa líder musulmán (pág. 404)

***calligraphy** artistic handwriting (p.486; p. 488)

***caligrafía** letra artística (pág. 486; pág. 488)

***capable** able, competent (p. 331)

***capaz** hábil, competente (pág. 331)

capital money and goods used to help people make or do things (pp. 38–39)

capital dinero y bienes usados para ayudar a las personas a hacer cosas (págs. 38–39)

caravan a group of merchants traveling together for safety, usually with a large number of camels; a group of traveling merchants and animals (p. 92; p. 400)

caravana grupo de mercaderes que viajan juntos por seguridad, usualmente con un gran número de camellos; grupo de mercaderes y animales que viajan (pág. 92; pág. 400)

cardinal directions north, south, east, and west (p. 35)

puntos cardinales norte, sur, este y oeste (pág. 35)

cash crops crops grown in large amounts to be sold for profit (p. 629)

cultivo comercial cultivo producido en grandes cantidades para venderlo y obtener ganancias (pág. 629)

caste an Indian social class whose members are restricted in the jobs they may take and in their association with others (p. 254; p. 256)

casta clase social de la India a cuyos miembros se les restringen los trabajos que pueden desempeñar y su relación con miembros de otras castas (pág. 254; pág. 256)

cataract a waterfall or rapids in a river (p. 102)

catarata cascada o rápidos de un río (pág. 102)

cavalry part of an army in which the soldiers ride horses (p. 232)

caballería división de un ejército en la cual los soldados montan a caballo (pág. 232)

censor an official who watches others for correct behavior (p. 293)

censor funcionario que vigila el correcto comportamiento de otros (pág. 293)

census a count of the number of people in a country (pp. 499–500)

censo conteo del número de personas de un país (págs. 499–500)

***challenge** to invite the start of a competition; to present with difficulties (p. 130; pp. 432–433)

***desafiar** invitar para que se dé inicio a una competencia; presentarse con dificultades (pág. 130; págs. 432–433)

***channel** a straight or narrow sea between two land masses; a canal; narrow body of water between two land masses (p. 196; p. 280)

***canal** mar recto o estrecho que se encuentra entre dos masas continentales; masa de agua estrecha que se encuentra entre dos masas continentales (pág. 196; pág. 280)

checks and balances a system in which each branch of government limits the power of another branch (pp. 44–45)

equilibrio de poderes sistema en el cual cada rama del gobierno limita el poder de otra (págs. 44–45)

chivalry the system, spirit, or customs of medieval knighthood (pp. 549–550)

caballerosidad sistema, espíritu o costumbres de los caballeros medievales (págs. 549–550)

choropleth a special-purpose map that uses color to show population density (p. 36)

mapa de coropletas mapa temático que mediante colores muestra la densidad de población (pág. 36)

circumference the outer border of a circle; the measurement of that border (p. 239)

circunferencia borde externo de un círculo; medida de ese borde (pág. 239)

circumnavigate to go completely around something, such as the world (pp. 622–623)

circunnavegar rodear por completo algo, como por ejemplo el mundo (págs. 622–623)

city-state a city that governs itself and its surrounding territory (pp. 78–79)

ciudad-estado ciudad que se gobierna a sí misma y el territorio que la rodea (págs. 78–79)

civic duty the idea that citizens have a responsibility to help their country (p. 315)

deber cívico idea según la cual los ciudadanos tienen la responsabilidad de ayudar a su país (pág. 315)

***civil** of or relating to citizens; relating to the state or government (p. 324; p. 476)

***civil** relativo a los ciudadanos; relativo al Estado o al Gobierno (pág. 324; pág. 476)

civil service the administrative service of a government (p. 294)

servicio civil servicio administrativo de un gobierno (pág. 294)

clan a group of people descended from the same ancestor (p. 431)

clan grupo de personas que descienden el mismo ancestro (pág. 431)

clergy church officials (p. 383)

clero funcionarios de la Iglesia (pág. 383)

***code** a set of official rules; a system of principles or rules (p. 87; pp. 549–550)

***código** conjunto de leyes oficiales; sistema de principios o reglas (pág. 87; págs. 549–550)

collapse to break down; to lose effectiveness (p. 194)

colapsar derrumbarse; perder efectividad (pág. 194)

colony a group of people living in a new territory who have ties to their homeland; a new territory (p. 179)

colonia grupo de personas que viven en un nuevo territorio y mantienen vínculos con su tierra natal; territorio nuevo (pág. 179)

comedy a play or film that tells a humorous story (p. 217)

comedia obra de teatro o película que cuenta una historia humorística (pág. 217)

command economy an economic system in which a central government decides what goods will be made and who will receive them (p. 40)

economía planificada sistema económico en el cual un gobierno central decide qué bienes se producirán y quién los recibirá (pág. 40)

commandment a rule that God wanted the Israelites to follow (p. 143)

mandamiento regla que Dios quería que los israelitas cumplieran (pág. 143)

commerce an exchange of goods; business (p. 633)

comercio intercambio de bienes; negocio (pág. 633)

***commit** to carry out or do (p. 261)

***cometer** llevar a cabo o hacer (pág. 261)

***communicate** to share information with someone; to exchange knowledge or information (p. 58; p. 156)

***comunicar** compartir información con alguien; intercambiar conocimientos o información (pág. 58; pág. 156)

***community** a group of people with common interests and values living in an area; people living in a particular area; an area (p. 157; pp. 174–175; p. 238; p. 381; pp. 436–437)

***comunidad** grupo de personas con intereses y valores comunes que viven en un área; personas que viven en un área en particular; un área (pág. 157; págs. 174–175; pág. 238; pág. 381; págs. 436–437)

***complex** having many parts, details, or ideas; made up of many related parts; complicated (pp. 90–91; p. 454; p. 586; p. 588)

***complejo** que tiene muchas partes, detalles o ideas; que consta de muchas partes relacionadas (págs. 90–91; pág. 454; pág. 586; pág. 588)

***conclude** to reach an understanding; to make a decision (p. 176)

***concluir** llegar a un acuerdo; tomar una decisión (pág. 176)

conclusion a decision reached after examining evidence (p. 14)

conclusión decisión que se toma luego de examinar evidencias (pág. 14)

concordat agreement between the pope and the ruler of a country (pp. 546–547)

concordato acuerdo entre el papa y el gobernante de un país (págs. 546–547)

***confirm** to prove that something is true; to remove doubt (p. 413)

***confirmar** demostrar que algo es verdadero; despejar dudas (pág. 413)

***conflict** a battle or war; a fight or disagreement; a fight or battle (p. 203; pp. 218–219)

***conflicto** batalla o guerra; lucha o desacuerdo; lucha o batalla (pág. 203; págs. 218–219)

Confucianism a system of beliefs based on the teachings of Confucius (pp. 286–287)	**confucianismo** sistema de creencias basado en las enseñanzas de Confucio (págs. 286–287)
conquistadors Spanish soldiers who conquered people in other lands (p. 622)	**conquistadores** soldados españoles que conquistaron pueblos en otras tierras (pág. 622)
***consider** to give careful thought (pp. 183–184)	***considerar** pensar detenidamente (págs. 183–184)
***considerable** large in size, quantity, or quality (p. 626)	***considerable** de gran tamaño, cantidad o calidad (pág. 626)
***consist** to be made up of (p. 80)	***constar** estar formado de (pág. 80)
***constant** always happening (p. 58)	***constante** que siempre sucede (pág. 58)
constitution basic laws of a state that define the role of government and guarantee its obligation to the people; a document that describes how a country will be governed and guarantees people certain rights (p. 518; p. 666)	**constitución** leyes básicas de un Estado que definen la función del Gobierno y garantizan su obligación con el pueblo; documento que describe cómo será gobernado un país y garantiza a las personas algunos derechos (pág. 518; pág. 666)
constitutional monarchy a political system in which the head of state is a king or queen who rules according to a constitution (p. 652)	**monarquía constitucional** sistema político en el cual el jefe de Estado es un rey o una reina que gobierna de acuerdo con una Constitución (pág. 652)
***construct** to build by putting parts together; to build; to create (pp. 56–57; p. 115; p. 188; pp. 214–215)	***construir** formar uniendo las partes; edificar; crear (págs. 56-57; pág. 115; pág. 188; págs. 214–215)
consul head of a government, usually with a limited term in office (p. 313)	**cónsul** jefe de un gobierno, por lo general durante un tiempo limitado en el cargo (pág. 313)
***contact** communication or connection; interaction with other people (p. 344; pp. 438–439)	***contacto** comunicación o conexión; interacción con otras personas (pág. 344; págs. 438–439)
***contrast** the act of comparing by looking at differences (p. 330)	***contrastar** acción de comparar observando diferencias (pág. 330)
***contribute** to give or donate something (p. 269)	***contribuir** dar o donar algo (pág. 269)
***convert** to accept a new belief; to bring from one belief to another (pp. 432–433; p. 502)	***convertir** (se) aceptar una nueva creencia; llevar de una creencia a otra (págs. 432–433; pág. 502)
***cooperate** to work together for the good of all (pp. 560–561; pp. 698–699)	***cooperar** trabajar juntos para el bien de todos (págs. 560–561; págs. 698–699)
***cooperation** working together (p. 163)	***cooperación** trabajar juntos (pág. 163)
corporation a type of company that sells shares in the company to investors (p. 694)	**sociedad anónima** tipo de compañía que vende acciones en la compañía a inversionistas (pág. 694)
cottage industry making goods in workers' homes (p. 634)	**industria casera** fabricación de bienes en casa de los trabajadores (pág. 634)
coup d'état a change of government in which a new group of leaders seize power by force (p. 676)	**golpe de Estado** cambio de gobierno en el cual un nuevo grupo de líderes se hace al poder por medio de la fuerza (pág. 676)

covenant an agreement with God (p. 142)

alianza acuerdo con Dios (pág. 142)

***create** to make or produce something; to bring something into existence; to produce by a course of action (pp. 230–231; p. 374)

***crear** hacer o producir algo; hacer que algo exista; producir mediante una serie de acciones (págs. 230-231; pág. 374)

credentials something that gives confidence that a person is qualified for a task (p. 19)

credenciales algo que brinda confianza con respecto a las cualificaciones de una persona para una tarea (pág. 19)

***crucial** important or significant (p. 110)

***crucial** importante o relevante (pág. 110)

***culture** the set of beliefs, behaviors, and traits shared by a group of people (pp. 36–37; pp. 140–141; p. 408; p. 629)

***cultura** conjunto de creencias, comportamientos y características que comparte un grupo de personas (págs. 36–37; págs. 140–141; pág. 408; pág. 629)

cuneiform writing developed by the Sumerians that used wedge-shaped marks made in soft clay (p. 82)

cuneiforme sistema de escritura desarrollado por los sumerios que consta de marcas en forma de cuña hechas sobre arcilla blanda (pág. 82)

***currency** something, such as coins or paper money, that is used as a medium of exchange; money in the form of coins or paper (p. 293; p. 586)

***moneda** algo que se usa como medio de intercambio, como las monedas o el papel moneda; dinero en forma de o monedas billetes (pág. 293; pág. 586)

D

Dao Chinese system of beliefs which describes the way a person must rule (pp. 284–285)

Tao sistema chino de creencias que describe la manera en que una persona debe gobernar (págs. 284–285)

Daoism a Chinese philosophy concerned with obtaining long life and living in harmony with nature (p. 288)

taoísmo filosofía china que se interesa en la forma de obtener larga vida y vivir en armonía con la naturaleza (pág. 288)

***data** information, usually facts and figures (p. 20)

***datos** información, por lo general hechos y cifras (pág. 20)

***decade** a group or set of 10; period of 10 years (p. 5; p. 202)

***década** grupo o conjunto de diez; periodo de diez años (pág. 5; pág. 202)

***decline** to become weaker; to move toward a weaker condition (pp. 126–127; p. 177; p. 268)

***decaer** debilitarse; moverse hacia una condición de mayor fragilidad (págs. 126–127; pág. 177; pág. 268)

delta a fan-shaped area of silt near where a river flows into the sea (p. 102)

delta área cenagosa en forma de abanico cercana al punto donde un río desemboca en el mar (pág. 102)

demand the amount of something that a consumer wants to buy (p. 39)

demanda cantidad de algo que los consumidores quieren comprar (pág. 39)

democracy a government by the people (p. 184)

democracia gobierno del pueblo (pág. 184)

descendant future member of a family (p. 349)

descendiente miembro futuro de una familia (pág. 349)

***design** to skillfully plan or create something (p. 692)

***diseñar** planear o crear algo con destreza (pág. 692)

***despite** in spite of; regardless of (p. 222)

***a pesar de** pese a que, sin tener en cuenta (pág. 222)

***devote** to give one's time, effort, or attention earnestly (p. 309)	***dedicar** brindar tiempo, esfuerzo o atención sinceramente (pág. 309)
***devotion** dedication, a strong commitment (p. 163)	***devoción** dedicación, compromiso sólido (pág. 163)
dharma a person's personal duty, based on the individual's place in society (pp. 258–259)	**darma** deber individual de una persona, de acuerdo con su lugar en la sociedad (págs. 258–259)
dhow sailboat using wind-catching, triangular sails (pp. 428–429)	**dhow** velero que usa velas triangulares para atrapar el viento (págs. 428–429)
Diaspora groups of Jews living outside of the Jewish homeland (pp. 160–161)	**diáspora** grupos de judíos que viven fuera de su territorio natal (págs. 160–161)
dictator a person with absolute power to rule (p. 314)	**dictador** persona con poder absoluto para gobernar (pág. 314)
din loud noise (p. 497)	**bulla** ruido alto (pág. 497)
diplomacy conducting negotiations between countries (p. 586; p. 588)	**diplomacia** realizar negociaciones entre países (pág. 586; pág. 588)
direct democracy a form of democracy in which all citizens can participate firsthand in the decision-making process (pp. 198–199)	**democracia directa** forma de democracia en la cual todos los ciudadanos pueden participar directamente en el proceso de toma de decisiones (págs. 198–199)
disciple student (p. 497)	**discípulo** estudiante (pág. 497)
***display** to place an object where people can view it (p. 387)	***exponer** colocar un objeto donde las personas puedan verlo (pág. 387)
***distort** to twist out of shape or change the size of (pp. 30–31)	***distorsionar** deformar o cambiar el tamaño de algo (págs. 30–31)
***distribute** to divide into shares and deliver the shares to different people; to give or deliver to members of a group (p. 109; p. 330; p. 464)	***distribuir** dividir en partes y repartirlas entre diferentes personas; dar o repartir a los miembros de un grupo (pág. 109; pág. 330; pág. 464)
doctrine official church teaching (p. 384)	**doctrina** enseñanza oficial de la Iglesia (pág. 384)
***document** an official paper used as proof or support of something; an original or official paper used as the basis or proof of something; a piece of writing (p. 166; p. 558; p. 666)	***documento** texto oficial que se usa como prueba o respaldo de algo; papel original u oficial que se usa como base o prueba de algo; escrito (pág. 166; pág. 558; pág. 666)
domesticate to adapt an animal to live with humans for the advantage of the humans (pp. 62–63)	**domesticar** adaptar a un animal para que viva con los seres humanos para provecho de estos (págs. 62–63)
***dominate** control or influence something or someone (pp. 174 – 175)	***dominar** controlar o ejercer influencia sobre algo o alguien (págs. 174–175)
downtrodden people who are poor or suffering (p. 349)	**oprimidos** personas pobres o que están sufriendo (pág. 349)
drama a story written in the form of a play (p. 217)	**drama** historia escrita en forma de obra de teatro (pág. 217)
dynasty a line of rulers from one family (pp. 106–107)	**dinastía** línea de gobernantes de una familia (págs. 106–107)

E

***economic** the system in a country that involves making, buying, and selling goods (p. 176)

***económico** sistema de un país que implica la elaboración, compra y venta de productos (pág. 176)

***economy** the system of economic life in an area or country; an economy deals with the making, buying, or selling of goods and services (p. 64; p. 572)

***economía** sistema de la vida económica en un área o un país; la economía se relaciona con la elaboración, compra y venta de productos o servicios (pág. 64; pág. 572)

.edu the ending of an Internet URL of a Web site for an educational institution (p. 20)

.edu parte final del URL (por sus siglas en inglés) del sitio web de una institución educativa (pág. 20)

elements substances that consist of atoms of only one kind (p. 648)

elementos sustancias formadas por átomos de un solo tipo (pág. 648)

ellipses shapes like stretched circles; ovals (pp. 644–645)

elipses figuras semejantes a círculos estirados; óvalos (págs. 644–645)

embalming the process of treating a body to prevent it from decaying (p. 111)

embalsamamiento proceso que consiste en tratar un cuerpo para evitar que se descomponga (pág. 111)

embrace to hug someone (p. 85)

abrazar estrechar entre los brazos a alguien (pág. 85)

***emerge** to come into being or become known (p. 252; pp. 278–279)

***surgir** llegar a ser o darse a conocer (pág. 252; págs. 278–279)

***emphasize** attach a sense of importance to something; express the importance of something (p. 203)

***poner énfasis** dar importancia a algo; expresar la importancia de algo (pág. 203)

empire a large territory or group of many territories governed by one ruler (pp. 86–87)

imperio gran territorio o grupo de muchos territorios a cargo de un gobernante (págs. 86–87)

***enable** to make possible (p. 326)

***permitir** hacer posible (pág. 326)

***ensure** to make certain or make sure of (pp. 146–147; p. 518)

***asegurar** tener certeza o garantizar (págs. 146–147; pág. 518)

entrepreneur one who organizes, pays for, and takes on the risk of setting up a business (p. 633)

empresario persona que organiza, paga y asume el riesgo de establecer un negocio (pág. 633)

entrepreneurship the act of running a business and taking on the risks of that business (pp. 38–39)

espíritu empresarial acción de dirigir un negocio y asumir los riesgos de ese negocio (págs. 38–39)

envoy a government representative to another country (p. 123)

enviado representante de un gobierno ante otro país (pág. 123)

ephor a high-ranked government official in Sparta who was elected by the council of elders (p. 186)

éforo funcionario del gobierno de alto rango en Esparta a quien elegía el consejo de ancianos (pág. 186)

epic a long poem that records the deeds of a legendary or real hero (pp. 82–83)

epopeya poema largo que registra las hazañas de un héroe legendario o real (págs. 82–83)

Epicureanism the philosophy of Epicurus, stating that the purpose of life is to look for happiness and peace (p. 238)

epicureísmo filosofía instaurada por Epicuro, la cual afirmaba que el propósito de la vida es la búsqueda de la felicidad y la paz (pág. 238)

era a large division of time (p. 5)

era gran división de tiempo (pág. 5)

***establish** to start; to bring into existence (p. 544)

***establecer** iniciar; hacer que exista (pág. 544)

estate a social class in France before the French Revolution (pp. 672–673)

estado una de las clases sociales en Francia antes de la Revolución francesa (págs. 672–673)

***estimate** to determine an approximate value, size, or nature of something (p. 262)

***estimar** determinar el valor, el tamaño o la naturaleza aproximados de algo (pág. 262)

***eventual** taking place at an unnamed later time; later; final or ultimate; (p. 266; p. 308; p. 688)

***final** que ocurre en un tiempo futuro indeterminado; posterior o último (pág. 266; pág. 308; pág. 688)

evidence something that shows proof or an indication that something is true (pp. 10–11)

evidencia algo que proporciona pruebas o indicios de que algo es cierto (págs. 10–11)

excommunicate to declare that a person or group is no longer a member of the church (p. 389)

excomulgar declarar que una persona o un grupo ya no son miembros de la Iglesia (pág. 389)

executive branch the part of government that enforces laws (pp. 44–45)

poder ejecutivo rama del gobierno que hace cumplir las leyes (págs. 44–45)

extended family a family made up of several generations (pp. 436–437)

familia extendida familia compuesta por varias generaciones (págs. 436–437)

Exodus the departure of the Israelites out of slavery in Egypt (p. 142)

éxodo salida de los israelitas de Egipto que puso fin a su esclavitud (pág. 142)

exile a forced absence from one's home or country (pp. 152–153)

exilio ausencia obligada del propio hogar o país (págs. 152–153)

***expand** to enlarge; to spread out; to increase the number, volume, or scope (p. 162; pp. 352–353; p. 644)

***expandir** agrandar; extender; aumentar el número, el volumen o el alcance (pág. 162; págs. 352–353; pág. 644)

***expert** a skilled person who has mastered a subject (p. 41)

***experto** persona cualificada que domina una materia (pág. 41)

export a good that is sent from one country to another in trade (p. 42)

exportación producto enviado de un país a otro para comercializarlo (pág. 42)

***extract** to remove by a physical or chemical process (p. 145)

***extraer** eliminar mediante un proceso físico o químico (pág. 145)

F

fable a story meant to teach a lesson (p. 216)

fábula historia que busca enseñar una lección (pág. 216)

feat achievement, success (p. 597)

hazaña logro, éxito (pág. 597)

***federal** referring to an organized union of states under one government (pp. 670–671)

***federal** relativo a una unión organizada de estados bajo un gobierno (págs. 670–671)

federal system a government which divides power between central and state governments (pp. 44–45)

sistema federal gobierno en el cual el poder está dividido entre el gobierno central y los gobiernos estatales (págs. 44–45)

feudalism the system of service between a lord and the vassals who have sworn loyalty to the lord; political order; under feudalism, nobles governed and protected people in return for services (p. 523; pp. 548–549)

feudalismo sistema de servicio entre un señor y los vasallos que le han jurado lealtad; orden político; en el feudalismo, los nobles gobernaban y protegían a las personas a cambio de sus servicios (pág. 523; págs. 548–549)

fief a feudal estate belonging to a vassal (p. 549)

feudo propiedad feudal perteneciente a un vasallo (pág. 549)

filial piety the responsibility of children to respect, obey, and care for their parents (pp. 290–291)

piedad filial responsabilidad que tienen los hijos de respetar, obedecer y cuidar a sus padres (págs. 290–291)

***finite** limited; having boundaries (p. 14)

***finito** limitado; que tiene límites (pág. 14)

fjord a narrow inlet of the sea between cliffs or steep slopes (p. 544)

fiordo entrada estrecha del mar entre acantilados o pendientes empinadas (pág. 544)

***focus** to place all of one's attention on something (p. 260)

***enfocar** poner toda la atención en algo (pág. 260)

fossil plant or animal remains that have been preserved from an earlier time (pp. 8–9)

fósil restos vegetales o animales que se han preservado desde una época anterior (págs. 8–9)

***found** to create or set up something such as a city; to set up or establish; established or took the first steps in building; (p. 6; p.151; p. 307; p. 686)

***fundar** crear o instituir algo, como una ciudad; establecer o formar; establecer o dar los primeros pasos en la construcción (pág. 6; pág. 151; pág. 307; pág. 686)

G

***generation** a group of individuals born and living at the same time; the time span between the birth of parents and the birth of their children (p. 295; pp. 648–649)

***generación** grupo de individuos que nacen y viven en la misma época; periodo de tiempo entre el nacimiento de los padres y el nacimiento de sus hijos (pág. 295; págs. 648–649)

geocentric an Earth-centered theory; having or relating to the Earth as the center (p. 643)

geocéntrico teoría centrada en la Tierra; que tiene o se relaciona con la Tierra como el centro (pág. 643)

gladiator in ancient Rome, a person who fought people or animals for public entertainment (p. 341)

gladiador en la antigua Roma, alguien que se enfrentaba a una persona o a un animal para entretener al público (pág. 341)

***global** involving the entire Earth (pp. 626–627)

***global** que implica toda la Tierra (págs. 626–627)

globalization the growth in free trade between countries (pp. 42–43)

globalización crecimiento del libre comercio entre los países (págs. 42–43)

Glorious Revolution the overthrow of King James II of England (p. 652)

Revolución Gloriosa derrocamiento del rey Jacobo II de Inglaterra (pág. 652)

***goal** something that a person works to achieve; aim (p. 566)

***meta** algo que una persona se esfuerza por alcanzar; objetivo (pág. 566)

gospel the accounts that apostles wrote of Jesus' life (pp. 384–385)

evangelio relato que los apóstoles escribieron sobre la vida de Jesús (págs. 384–385)

.gov the ending of a URL of a government Web site (p. 20)

.gov parte final del URL (por sus siglas en inglés) de un sitio web del gobierno (pág. 20)

grand jury a group of citizens that meets to decide whether people should be accused of a crime (p. 558)

gran jurado grupo de ciudadanos que se reúne para decidir si se debe acusar a una persona de un crimen (pág. 558)

gravity the attraction that the Earth or another celestial body has on an object on or near its surface (pp. 646–647)

gravedad atracción que la Tierra u otro cuerpo celeste ejerce sobre un objeto que se encuentra en su superficie o cerca de esta (págs. 646–647)

griot traditional storyteller (pp. 426–427)

griot narrador tradicional (págs. 426–427)

guarantee to promise (p. 432)

garantizar prometer (pág. 432)

***guarantee** something that is assured or certain (pp. 652–653)

***garantía** algo que se asegura o es cierto (págs. 652–653)

guerrilla warfare a form of war in which soldiers make surprise attacks on the enemy (pp. 684–685)

guerra de guerrillas forma de guerra en la cual los soldados lanzan ataques sorpresivos al enemigo (págs. 684–685)

guild a group of merchants or craftsmen during medieval times; a group of merchants or craftspeople (p. 524; pp. 554–555)

gremio grupo de mercaderes o artesanos durante la Edad Media; grupo de mercaderes o artesanos (pág. 524; págs. 554–555)

guru a teacher (p. 254; p. 256)

gurú maestro (pág. 254; pág. 256)

H

heliocentric having or relating to the sun as the center of the solar system (p. 644)

heliocéntrico que tiene o se relaciona con el Sol como centro del sistema solar (pág. 644)

Hellenistic Era the time period following the death of Alexander during which Greek culture spread through the known world (pp. 234–235)

Época helenística periodo posterior a la muerte de Alejandro, durante el cual la cultura griega se difundió por todo el mundo conocido (págs. 234–235)

helot enslaved person in ancient Sparta (p. 185)

ilota persona esclavizada de la antigua Esparta (pág. 185)

hemisphere a "half sphere," used to refer to one-half of the globe when divided into North and South or East and West (p. 29)

hemisferio "media esfera"; término usado para referirse a la mitad del planeta al dividirlo en Norte y Sur, o en Este y Oeste (pág. 29)

hereditary having title or possession by reason of birth (p. 284)

hereditario que tiene el título o la posesión debido a su nacimiento (pág. 284)

heresy ideas that go against Church teachings; a religious belief that contradicts what the Church says is true (pp. 568–569; p. 607)

herejía ideas que van en contra de las enseñanzas de la Iglesia; creencia religiosa que contradice lo que la Iglesia dice que es cierto (págs. 568-569; pág. 607)

***hierarchy** an organization with different levels of authority; a classification into ranks (p. 383; pp. 518–519)

***jerarquía** organización con diferentes niveles de autoridad; clasificación en categorías (pág. 383; págs. 518–519)

hieroglyphics a writing system made up of a combination of pictures and sound symbols (p. 105)

jeroglíficos sistema de escritura formado por una combinación de imágenes y símbolos que representan sonidos (pág. 105)

Hinduism a major religion that developed in ancient India (pp. 257–258)

hinduismo religión de gran importancia que se desarrolló en la antigua India (págs. 257–258)

Hippocratic Oath a set of promises about patient care that new doctors make when they start practicing medicine (pp. 226–227)

Juramento Hipocrático conjunto de promesas acerca del cuidado de los pacientes que los nuevos médicos hacen cuando empiezan a ejercer su profesión (págs. 226–227)

hogan a square wooden home of Native Americans (pp. 466–467)

hogan casa cuadrada de madera de indígenas americanos (págs. 466–467)

hostage someone held against his or her will in exchange for something (p. 626)

rehén alguien retenido en contra de su voluntad a cambio de algo (pág. 626)

humanism an emphasis on worldly concerns; belief in the worth of the individual and that reason is the path to knowledge (pp. 589–590)

humanismo énfasis en las preocupaciones terrenales; creencia de que la razón es el camino al conocimiento, y en el valor del individuo (págs. 589–590)

I

Ice Age a time when glaciers covered much of the land (p. 60)

Era de Hielo tiempo en el cual los glaciares cubrían la mayor parte de la Tierra (pág. 60)

icon a representation of an object of worship (p. 387)

ícono representación de un objeto de adoración (pág. 387)

iconoclast originally: a person who destroys icons; today: a person who criticizes traditional beliefs (p. 387)

iconoclasta originalmente, persona que destruye íconos; hoy, persona que critica las creencias tradicionales (pág. 387)

ideograph a symbol in a writing system that represents a thing or idea (p. 282)

ideograma símbolo en un sistema escrito que representa un objeto o una idea (pág. 282)

import a good brought into a country from another country (p. 42)

importación producto que entra a un país procedente de otro (pág. 42)

***impose** to establish by force or authority (p. 602)

***imponer** establecer mediante la fuerza o la autoridad (pág. 602)

incense a material that produces a pleasant smell when burned (p. 123)

incienso material que produce un aroma agradable al quemarlo (pág. 123)

***individual** a single human being; human being; person (pp. 40–41; p. 223; p. 287)

***individuo** un solo ser humano; ser humano; persona (págs. 40–41; pág. 223; pág. 287)

indulgence a pardon, or forgiveness, of a sin (pp. 598–599)

indulgencia perdón, o exoneración, de un pecado (págs. 598–599)

industrialism an economic system where machines do work that was once performed by animals or humans (pp. 690–691)

industrialismo sistema económico en el cual las máquinas realizan el trabajo que antes realizaban los animales o las personas (págs. 690–691)

inflation a continued rise in prices or the supply of money; a period of rapidly increasing prices (p. 41)

inflación aumento continuo de los precios o de la oferta de dinero; periodo de rápido aumento de los precios (pág. 41)

***innovation** the introduction of something new (pp. 316–317)

***innovación** introducción de algo nuevo (págs. 316–317)

***inspect** to look over carefully (p. 329)

***inspeccionar** examinar de una manera cuidadosa (pág. 329)

institution a custom or practice that many people accept and use (pp. 532–533)

institución costumbre o práctica que muchas personas aceptan y usan (págs. 532–533)

***integral** essential, necessary (pp. 4–5)

***integral** esencial, necesario (págs. 4-5)

***intensify** to become stronger (pp. 316–317)

***intensificar** hacerse más fuerte (págs. 316-317)

***interpret** to explain the meaning of (p. 375)

***interpretar** explicar el significado de algo (pág. 375)

***interpretation** an explanation of the meaning of something (pp. 14–15)

***interpretación** explicación del significado de algo (págs. 14–15)

***invest** to give money to a company in exchange for a return, or profit, on the money; to put money in new businesses or other money-making projects (p. 633; p. 691)

***invertir** dar dinero a una compañía a cambio de rendimientos, o ganancias, sobre el dinero; colocar dinero en nuevas empresas y otros proyectos lucrativos (pág. 633; pág. 691)

***investigate** to observe or study by examining closely and questioning systematically (pp. 224–225)

***investigar** observar o estudiar examinando detenidamente y formulando preguntas de manera sistemática (págs. 224–225)

***involve** to include (p. 307)

***involucrar** incluir (pág. 307)

irrigation a system that supplies dry land with water through ditches, pipes, or streams (p. 77)

irrigación sistema que abastece de agua los terrenos secos mediante zanjas, tuberías o corrientes (pág. 77)

Islam a religion based on the teachings of Muhammad (pp. 398–399)

islam religión basada en las enseñanzas de Mahoma (págs. 398–399)

***isolate** to separate from others; to separate from other populated areas; to set apart from others (p. 102; p. 399; pp. 516–517)

***aislar** separar de otros; separar de otras áreas pobladas; apartar de otros (pág. 102; pág. 399; págs. 516–517)

***issue** a concern or problem that has not yet been solved (p. 46)

***asunto** inquietud o problema que aún no se ha resuelto (pág. 46)

isthmus a narrow piece of land linking two larger areas of land (p. 450)

istmo porción estrecha de tierra que une dos áreas más grandes de tierra (pág. 450)

J

Jainism a religion of ancient India that does not believe in a supreme being, but emphasizes nonviolence and respect for all living things (p. 263)

jainismo religión de la antigua India que no cree en un ser supremo sino que enfatiza en la no violencia y el respeto a todos los seres vivos (pág. 263)

judicial branch part of government that interprets laws (p. 45)

poder judicial rama del gobierno que interpreta las leyes (pág. 45)

***jury** a group of people sworn to make a decision in a legal case (pp. 45–46)

***jurado** grupo de personas que prestan juramento para tomar una decisión en un caso legal (págs. 45–46)

K

kaiser emperor of Germany (p. 686)

káiser emperador de Alemania (pág. 686)

karma a force that decides the form that people will be reborn into in their next lives (pp. 258–259)

karma fuerza que decide la forma en que las personas renacerán en sus próximas vidas (págs. 258–259)

knight a mounted man-at-arms serving a feudal superior (p. 549)

caballero hombre armado que cabalga y sirve a un superior feudal (pág. 549)

kosher prepared according to Jewish dietary law (p. 158)

kosher preparado de acuerdo con la ley judía sobre la alimentación (pág. 158)

L

***labor** the ability of people to do work; work; the tasks that workers perform (pp. 38–39; pp. 112–113; pp. 522–523)

***mano de obra** capacidad de las personas para trabajar; tareas que los trabajadores realizan (págs. 38–39; págs. 112–113; págs. 522–523)

labor union an organization of those employed who work together to improve wages and working conditions (p. 700)

sindicato organización de empleados que trabajan juntos para mejorar sus salarios y condiciones laborales (pág. 700)

laity regular church members (p. 383)

laicado miembros regulares de la Iglesia (pág. 383)

language family a group of similar languages (p. 253)

familia lingüística grupo de idiomas semejantes (pág. 253)

latifundia large farming estates (p. 321)

latifundios propiedades agrícolas de gran tamaño (pág. 321)

latitude imaginary lines that circle the Earth parallel to the Equator (p. 30)

latitud líneas imaginarias que rodean la Tierra en dirección paralela al ecuador (pág. 30)

***legal** of or relating to the law (p. 362)

***legal** relativo a la ley (pág. 362)

legalism a Chinese philosophy that stressed the importance of laws (p. 289)

***legalismo** filosofía china que resaltaba la importancia de las leyes (pág. 289)

legion large groups of Roman soldiers (p. 310)

legion grupos numerosos de soldados romanos (pág. 310)

legislative branch the part of government that passes laws (pp. 44–45)

poder legislativo rama del gobierno que aprueba las leyes (págs.44–45)

***legislature** a group of people who make the laws (p. 313)

***asamblea legislativa** grupo de personas que hace las leyes (pág. 313)

liberalism a political philosophy based on the Enlightenment ideas of equality and individual rights (p. 698)

liberalismo filosofía política basada en la Ilustración y en las ideas de igualdad y derechos individuales (pág. 698)

limited government a government whose powers are restricted through laws or a constitution (pp. 670–671)

gobierno limitado gobierno cuyos poderes los restringen las leyes o la constitución (págs. 670–671)

***link** a connecting element or factor; to connect; to join (p. 298; pp. 452–453)

***vínculo** elemento o factor que conecta; el término en inglés "link" también significa "conectar"; "unir" (pág. 298; págs. 452–453)

***locate** set up in a particular place (p. 65)

***localizarse** establecerse en un lugar en particular (pág. 65)

longitude imaginary lines that circle the Earth from the North Pole to the South Pole, measuring distance east or west of the Prime Meridian (p. 30)

longitud líneas imaginarias que rodean la Tierra desde el Polo Norte hasta el Polo Sur, que mide la distancia al este o al oeste del meridiano principal (pág. 30)

M

***maintain** to keep in the same state (p. 432)

***mantener** conservar en el mismo estado (pág. 432)

maize corn (p. 454)

maíz elote (pág. 454)

***major** great in rank or importance (pp. 438-439)

***principal** de gran rango o importancia (págs. 438-439)

Mandate of Heaven the belief that the Chinese king's right to rule came from the gods (p. 284)

mandato divino creencia de que el derecho de gobernar del emperador chino venía de los dioses (pág. 284)

***manual** involving physical effort; work done by hand (p. 118; p. 254; p. 256)

***manual** que implica esfuerzo físico; trabajo elaborado a mano (pág. 118; pág. 254; pág. 256)

maritime related to the sea or seafaring (p. 530)

marítimo relacionado con el mar o los marineros (pág. 530)

martial arts sports that involve combat and self-defense (pp. 524–525)

artes marciales deportes que implican combate y defensa personal (págs. 524–525)

martyr a person who is willing to die for his or her beliefs (p. 382)

mártir persona dispuesta a morir por sus creencias (pág. 382)

mass religious worship service for Catholic Christians (p. 568)

misa culto religioso de los cristianos católicos (pág. 568)

matrilineal tracing descent through mothers rather than fathers (p. 437)

matrilineal linaje que se traza teniendo en cuenta la línea materna, no la paterna (pág. 437)

***medical** relating to the practice of medicine (p. 344)

***médico** relativo al ejercicio de la medicina (pág. 344)

***meditate** to focus one's thoughts to gain a higher level of spiritual awareness (p. 260)

***meditar** enfocar los pensamientos para alcanzar un nivel más elevado de conciencia espiritual (pág. 260)

mercantilism an economic theory that depends on a greater amount of exports than imports in order to increase a country's supply of gold and silver (p. 632)

mercantilismo teoría económica que depende de una mayor cantidad de exportaciones que de importaciones para aumentar la oferta de oro y plata de un país (pág. 632)

mercenary a soldier who fights for money rather than loyalty to a country (p. 584)

mercenario soldado que combate por dinero y no por lealtad a un país (pág. 584)

***method** a way of doing something; a procedure or process (p. 56; p. 239; p. 484; p. 633)

***método** manera de hacer algo; procedimiento o proceso (pág. 56; pág. 239; pág. 484; pág. 633)

***migrate** to move from one place to another (p. 252)

***migrar** desplazarse de un luqar a otro (páq. 252)

migration the movement of people from one place to settle in another place (p. 36)

migración desplazamiento de personas de un lugar a otro (pág. 36)

***military** of or relating to soldiers, arms, or war; relating to the armed forces (p. 87; p. 185; p. 281; p. 549; pp. 656–657)

***militar** relativo a los soldados, las armas o la guerra; relativo a las fuerzas armadas (pág. 87; pág. 185; pág. 281; pág. 549; págs. 656–657)

minaret the tower of a mosque from which Muslims are called to pray (pp. 414–415)

alminar torre de una mezquita desde la cual se convoca a los musulmanes a orar (págs. 414–415)

missionaries people who are sent by a religious organization to spread the faith (p. 546)

misioneros personas enviadas por una organización religiosa a difundir la fe (pág. 546)

monarchy a government whose ruler, a king or queen, inherits the position from a parent (p. 68)

monarquía gobierno cuyo jefe, un rey o una reina, hereda el cargo de uno de sus padres (pág. 68)

monastery a religious community (p. 389)

monasterio comunidad religiosa (pág. 389)

monotheism a belief in one God (pp. 140–141)

monoteísmo creencia en un solo Dios (págs. 140–141)

monsoon seasonal wind, especially in the Indian Ocean and southern Asia (p. 249)

monzón viento estacional, especialmente en el océano Índico y el sur de Asia (pág. 249)

mosaics motifs or images created by an arrangement of colored glass or stone (p. 364)

mosaicos motivos o imágenes creadas con vidrios o piedras de colores (pág. 364)

mosque a Muslim house of worship (p. 412)

mezquita casa musulmana de culto (pág. 412)

myth a traditional story that explains the practices or beliefs of a people or something in the natural world (pp. 212–213)

mito historia tradicional que explica las prácticas o creencias de un pueblo, o algo en el mundo natural (págs. 212–213)

N

nationalism the desire of people with the same customs and beliefs for self-rule (pp. 682–683)

nacionalismo deseo de autogobierno de las personas con las mismas costumbres y creencias (págs. 682–683)

neo-Confucianism a new form of the ideas of the philosopher Confucius; included Buddhist and Daoist beliefs (p. 480)

neoconfucianismo nueva forma de las ideas del filósofo Confucio; incluía las creencias budistas y taoístas (pág. 480)

Neolithic Age relating to the latest period of the Stone Age (pp. 62–63)

Era Neolítica relativo al último periodo de la Edad de Piedra (págs. 62–63)

***network** a connected group or system; a system where all parts are connected (p. 297; p. 530)

***red** grupo o sistema conectado; sistema donde todas las partes están conectadas (pág. 297; pág. 530)

nirvana in Buddhism, a state of perfect happiness and peace (p. 261)

nirvana en el Budismo, estado de felicidad y paz perfecta (pág. 261)

nomads people who move from place to place as a group to find food (pp. 54–55)

nómadas personas que viajan de un lugar a otro en búsqueda de alimento (págs. 54–55)

novel a long fictional story (p. 500)

novela historia de ficción larga (pág. 500)

O

oasis a green area in a desert fed by underground water (pp. 398–399)

oasis área verde en el desierto que se alimenta de agua subterránea (págs. 398–399)

obstacle something that stands in the way (p. 85)

obstáculo algo que se interpone en el camino (pág. 85)

***obtain** to gain something through a planned effort; to acquire or receive something; to take possession of (p. 118; p. 191; p. 620)	***obtener** conseguir algo mediante un esfuerzo planificado; adquirir o recibir algo; tomar posesión de (pág. 118; pág. 191; pág. 620)
***occur** to happen (p. 308)	***ocurrir** suceder (pág. 308)
ode a lyric poem that expresses strong emotions about life (pp. 346–347)	**oda** poema lírico que expresa fuertes emociones acerca de la vida (págs. 346–347)
oligarchy a government in which a small group has control (p. 184)	**oligarquía** gobierno en el cual un grupo pequeño tiene control (pág. 184)
ongoing continuously moving forward (p. 502)	**en curso** que se mueve continuamente hacia delante (pág. 502)
opportunity cost what is given up, such as time or money, to make or buy something (p. 40)	**costo de oportunidad** lo que se entrega, como tiempo o dinero, para hacer o comprar algo (pág. 40)
oracle a sacred shrine where a priest or priestess spoke for a god or goddess (p. 214)	**oráculo** templo sagrado donde un sacerdote o una sacerdotisa hablaba en nombre de un dios o una diosa (pág. 214)
oral history stories passed down from generation to generation (p. 438)	**historia oral** historias transmitidas de generación en generación (pág. 438)
oral tradition the custom of passing along stories by speech (pp. 216–217)	**tradición oral** costumbre de transmitir historias verbalmente (págs. 216–217)
orator a public speaker (p. 349)	**orador** persona que habla en público (pág. 349)
.org the ending of an Internet URL for an organization (p. 20)	**.org** parte final del URL (por sus siglas en inglés) de una organización (pág. 20)
***overseas** across the ocean or sea (pp. 618–619; pp. 678–679)	***ultramar** cruzando el océano o el mar (págs. 618–619; págs. 678–679)

P

Paleolithic relating to the earliest period of the Stone Age (pp. 54–55)	**Paleolítico** relativo al periodo más antiguo de la Edad de Piedra (págs. 54–55)
paleontology the study of fossils (pp. 8–9)	**paleontología** estudio de los fósiles (págs. 8–9)
papyrus a reed plant that grows wild along the Nile River (pp. 104–105)	**papiro** planta hueca que crecía a lo largo del río Nilo (págs. 104–105)
parable a short story that teaches moral lesson (p. 375)	**parábola** historia corta que enseña una lección moral (pág. 375)
***parallel** moving or lying in the same direction and the same distance apart (p. 77)	***paralelo** que se mueve o se extiende en la misma dirección y a la misma distancia (pág. 77)
***participate** to take part (p. 356)	***participar** tomar parte (pág. 356)

patriarch an older male figure of authority, often within a religious community (p. 497)

patriarca figura masculina de edad mayor que representa la autoridad, con frecuencia dentro de una comunidad religiosa (pág. 497)

patricians the ruling class of ancient Rome (pp. 312–313)

patricios clase gobernante de la antigua Roma (págs. 312–313)

Pax Romana Roman peace (pp. 328–329)

Pax Romana paz romana (págs. 328–329)

peninsula a piece of land nearly surrounded by water (pp. 174–175)

península espacio de tierra casi completamente rodeado por agua (págs. 174–175)

***period** a division of time that is shorter than an era (p. 150)

***periodo** división de tiempo más corta que una era (pág. 150)

persecute to treat a group of people cruelly or unfairly (pp. 664–665)

perseguir tratar a un grupo de personas de manera cruel o injusta (págs. 664–665)

***perspective** a way of showing the relationship between objects in a drawing to give the look of depth or distance (p. 592)

***perspectiva** modo de mostrar la relación entre los objetos en un dibujo para dar un aspecto de profundidad o distancia (pág. 592)

phalanx a group of armed foot soldiers in ancient Greece arranged close together in rows (p. 182)

falange grupo de infantería armada en la Grecia antigua que se organizaba en filas muy cerradas (pág.182)

pharaoh ruler of ancient Egypt (pp. 108–109)

faraón emperador del antiguo Egipto (págs. 108–109)

philosopher a person who searches for wisdom or enlightenment (p. 199)

filósofo persona que busca la sabiduría o la iluminación (pág. 199)

***philosophy** the study of the basic ideas about society, education, and right and wrong; basic beliefs, concepts, and attitudes (pp. 286–287; p. 344)

***filosofía** estudio de las ideas básicas sobre la sociedad, la educación y el bien y el mal; creencias, conceptos y actitudes básicas (págs. 286–287; pág. 344)

physical map a map that shows land and water features (p. 34)

mapa físico mapa que muestra los accidentes geográficos terrestres y marítimos (pág. 34)

pictograph a symbol in a writing system based on pictures (p. 282)

pictograma símbolo usado en un sistema de escritura que se basa en imágenes (pág. 282)

pilgrim a person who travels to holy sites (p. 268)

peregrino persona que viaja a lugares santos (pág. 268)

plagiarize to present someone's work as your own without giving that person credit (pp. 20–21)

plagiar presentar el trabajo de otra persona como propio sin darle ningún crédito a esa persona (págs. 20–21)

plague a disease that spreads quickly and kills many people (p. 570)

plaga enfermedad que se extiende rápidamente y mata a muchas personas (pág. 570)

plane geometry a branch of mathematics centered around measurement and relationships of points, lines, angles, and surfaces of figures on a plane (p. 240)

geometría plana rama de las matemáticas que estudia las medidas, las propiedades y las relaciones entre los puntos, las rectas, los ángulos y las superficies de las figuras en un plano (pág. 240)

plantation a large estate or farm that used enslaved people or hired workers to grow and harvest crops (pp. 628–629)

plantación gran propiedad o granja en la cual los esclavos o personas contratadas cultivaban y recolectaban las cosechas (págs. 628–629)

plateau an area of high and mostly flat land (p. 424)	**meseta** área alta y en su mayoría plana (pág. 424)
plebeians ordinary citizens in ancient Rome (pp. 312–313)	**plebeyos** ciudadanos comunes en la Roma antigua (págs. 312–313)
point of view a personal attitude about people or life (p. 12)	**punto de vista** actitud personal acerca de la vida o las personas (pág. 12)
polis a Greek city-state (p. 180)	**polis** ciudad-Estado griega (pág. 180)
political map a map that shows the names and borders of countries (p. 34)	**mapa político** mapa que muestra los nombres y las fronteras de los países (pág. 34)
polytheism a belief in more than one god (pp. 78–79)	**politeísmo** creencia en uno o más dioses (págs. 78–79)
pope the title given to the Bishop of Rome (pp. 384–385)	**papa** título dado al obispo de Roma (págs. 384–385)
popular sovereignty the idea that government is created by the people and must act according to people's wishes (pp. 670–671)	**soberanía popular** la idea de que el gobierno es creado por el pueblo y debe actuar de acuerdo con sus deseos (págs. 670–671)
porcelain a ceramic made of fine clay baked at very high temperatures (p. 483)	**porcelana** cerámica elaborada con arcilla fina cocida a temperaturas muy elevadas (pág. 483)
praetors Roman government officials who interpreted the law and judged (p. 313)	**pretores** funcionarios del gobierno romano que interpretaban la ley y actuaban como jueces (pág. 313)
***precise** exact (p. 6)	***preciso** exacto (pág. 6)
predestination a religious belief that God has already decided who will go to heaven and who will not (pp. 602–603)	**predestinación** creencia religiosa según la cual Dios ya ha decidido quién irá al Cielo y quién no (págs. 602–603)
***predict** to describe something that will happen in the future (p. 460)	***predecir** describir algo que sucederá en el futuro (pág. 460)
***primary** most important; first (p. 622)	***principal** lo más importante; primero (pág. 622)
primary source firsthand evidence of an event in history (pp. 10–11)	**fuente primaria** evidencia de primera mano de un hecho histórico (págs. 10–11)
***principle** an important law or belief; rules or a code of conduct (p. 407; p. 480)	***principio** ley o creencia importante; reglas o código de conducta (pág. 407; pág. 480)
proconsul a governor (p. 329)	**procónsul** gobernador (pág. 329)
***professional** relating to a type of job that usually requires training and practice (p. 322)	***profesional** relativo a un tipo de trabajo que por lo general exige capacitación y práctica (pág. 322)
projection a way of showing the round Earth on a flat map (pp. 30–31)	**proyección** manera de mostrar la forma redonda de la Tierra sobre un planisferio (págs. 30–31)
proletariat the working class (p. 700)	**proletariado** clase obrera (pág. 700)
***promote** to encourage the doing of something (pp. 266–267)	***promover** estimular la realización de algo (págs. 266–267)

prophet a messenger sent by God to share God's word with people (pp. 140–141)

profeta mensajero enviado por Dios para compartir su palabra con las personas (págs. 140–141)

***protect** to defend from trouble or harm (pp. 342–343)

***proteger** defender de problemas o daños (págs. 342-343)

proverb a wise saying (p. 150)

proverbio refrán sabio (pág. 150)

province a territory governed as a political district of a country or empire (p. 88)

provincia territorio gobernado como distrito político de un país o imperio (pág. 88)

psalm a sacred song or poem used in worship (p. 149)

salmo canción o poema sagrado que se usa en el culto (pág. 149)

***publish** to produce the work of an author, usually in print (p. 414)

***publicar** producir la obra de un autor, por lo general de manera impresa (pág. 414)

***pursue** to follow in order to capture or defeat (pp. 232–233)

***perseguir** seguir para capturar o derrotar (págs. 232–233)

pyramid great stone tomb for an Egyptian pharaoh (pp. 112–113)

pirámide gran tumba de piedra para los faraones egipcios (págs. 112–113)

Q

quipu a tool with a system of knots used for mathematics (p. 465)

quipu instrumento con un sistema de nudos usado para las matemáticas (pág. 465)

Quran the holy book of Islam (pp. 402–403)

Corán libro sagrado del islam (págs. 402–403)

R

rabbi the official leader of a Jewish congregation (p. 166)

rabino líder oficial de una congregación judía (pág. 166)

***radical** extreme or far-reaching (pp .674–675)

***radical** extremo o de largo alcance (págs. 674–675)

raja an Indian prince (p. 254)

rajá príncipe indio (pág. 254)

***range** the limits between which something can change or differ (p. 590)

***intervalo** límites entre los cuales algo puede cambiar o diferir (pág. 590)

rationalism the belief that reason and experience must be present for the solution of problems (pp. 648–649)

racionalismo creencia en que la razón y la experiencia son necesarias para la solución de problemas (págs. 648–649)

recession a period of slow economic growth or decline (p. 41)

recesión periodo de crecimiento económico lento o descendente (pág. 41)

Reconquista the Christian effort to take back the Iberian Peninsula (pp. 574–575)

Reconquista esfuerzo cristiano por recuperar la Península Ibérica (págs. 574–575)

Reformation a religious movement that created a new form of Christianity known as Protestantism (pp. 598–599)

***Reforma** movimiento religioso que creó una nueva forma de cristianismo conocida como protestantismo (págs. 598–599)

reforms changes to bring about improvement (p. 352)

reformas cambios para obtener mejoras (pág. 352)

***regime** rulers during a given period of time (pp. 493–494)	***régimen** gobernantes durante un periodo determinado (págs. 493–494)
***region** a broad geographic area (p. 90; pp. 380–381)	***región** área geográfica amplia (pág. 90; págs. 380–381)
reincarnation the rebirth of the soul (p. 258)	**reencarnación** renacimiento del alma (pág. 258)
***reinforce** to strengthen (p. 352)	***reforzar** fortalecer (pág. 352)
***reject** to refuse to accept or consider (p. 221; p. 387)	***rechazar** negarse a aceptar o considerar (pág. 221; pág. 387)
***reluctantly** hesitantly or unwillingly (p. 315)	***a regañadientes** con vacilación o de mala gana (pág. 315)
***rely** to depend on someone or something; to be dependent; to count on for help (pp. 128–129; p. 281; p. 462; pp. 624–625)	***confiar** depender de alguien o de algo; ser dependiente; contar con la ayuda de alguien (págs. 128–129; pág. 281; pág. 462; págs. 624-625)
Renaissance a renewal or rebirth of interest in Greek and Roman arts (pp. 582–583)	**Renacimiento** renacer del interés en las artes griegas y romanas (págs. 582–583)
representative democracy a form of democracy in which citizens elect officials to govern on their behalf (pp. 198–199)	**democracia representativa** forma de democracia en la cual los ciudadanos eligen a los funcionarios para que gobiernen en su nombre (págs. 198–199)
representative government government in which citizens elect officials who administer its policies (pp. 44–45)	**gobierno representativo** gobierno en el cual los ciudadanos eligen a los funcionarios que administran sus políticas (págs. 44–45)
republic a form of government in which citizens elect their leaders (p. 310)	**república** forma de gobierno en la cual los ciudadanos eligen a sus líderes (pág. 310)
***reside** to be present continuously or have a home in a particular place; to live (p. 111; p. 252)	***residir** estar presente de manera continua o tener un hogar en un lugar determinado; vivir (pág. 111; pág. 252)
***resource** something that is useful; a ready supply of something valuable (pp. 38–39; p. 630)	***recurso** algo que es útil; una provisión constante de algo valioso (págs. 38–39; pág. 630)
***restore** to bring something back to an original state; to bring something back to an earlier or better condition (p. 362; p. 476; pp. 604–605)	***restaurar** volver a dejar algo en su estado original; volver a dejar algo en una condición anterior o mejor (pág. 362; pág. 476; págs. 604–605)
resurrection the act of rising from the dead (p. 377)	**resurrección** acción de levantarse de entre los muertos (pág. 377)
***reveal** to make information public; to tell a secret; to make known (p. 221)	***revelar** hacer pública una información; contar un secreto; dar a conocer (pág. 221)
rhetoric the art of public speaking and debate (p. 221)	**retórica** arte de hablar y debatir en público (pág. 221)
ritual words or actions that are part of a religious ceremony (p. 213)	**ritual** palabras o acciones que forman parte de una ceremonia religiosa (pág. 213)
***role** the function or part an individual fills in society; something that plays a part in the process (p. 116; pp. 540–541)	***rol** función o papel que un individuo cumple en la sociedad; algo que desempeña un papel en el proceso (pág. 116; págs. 540–541)

rouse to stir up or excite (p. 597)

despertar provocar o suscitar (pág. 597)

S

Sabbath a weekly day of worship and rest (pp. 154–155)

sabbat día semanal de culto y descanso (págs. 154–155)

saints people considered holy by followers of the Christian faith (p. 364)

santos personas que los seguidores de la fe cristiana consideran sagradas (pág. 364)

salvation the act of being saved from the effects of sin (pp. 378–379)

salvación acción de salvarse de los efectos del pecado (págs. 378–379)

samurai a warrior who served a Japanese lord and lived by a strict code of loyalty (p. 521)

samurái guerrero que servía a un señor japonés y vivía de acuerdo con un estricto código de lealtad (pág. 521)

Sanskrit the first written language of India (p. 254)

sánscrito primera lengua escrita de la India (pág. 254)

satrap the governor of a province in ancient Persia (p. 191)

sátrapa gobernador de una provincia en la antigua Persia (pág. 191)

satrapy the territory governed by an official known as a satrap (p. 191)

satrapía territorio gobernado por un funcionario llamado sátrapa (pág. 191)

satire verse or prose that pokes fun at human weakness (pp. 346–347)

sátira verso o prosa que se burla de la debilidad humana (págs. 346–347)

savanna a flat grassland, sometimes with scattered trees, in a tropical or subtropical region (pp. 128–129; p. 423)

sabana pradera llana en una región tropical o subtropical, algunas veces con árboles dispersos (págs. 128-129; pág. 423)

scale a measuring line that shows the distances on a map (p. 35)

escala línea de medición que muestra las distancias en un mapa (pág. 35)

scarcity the lack of a resource (p. 40)

escasez falta de un recurso (pág. 40)

schism a separation or division from a church (p. 389)

cisma separación o división de una Iglesia (pág. 389)

scholarly concerned with academic learning or research (p. 14)

erudito relacionado con el aprendizaje académico o la investigación (pág. 14)

scholasticism a way of thinking that combined faith and reason (p. 565)

escolasticismo forma de pensar que combinaba la fe y la razón (pág. 565)

scientific method the steps for an orderly search for knowledge (pp. 648–649)

método científico pasos para una búsqueda de conocimiento ordenada (págs. 648–649)

Scientific Revolution a period from the 1500s to the 1700s in which many scientific advances changed people's traditional beliefs about science (p. 644)

revolución científica periodo entre los siglos XVI y XVIII en el cual muchos avances científicos cambiaron las creencias tradicionales de las personas sobre la ciencia (pág. 644)

scribe a person who copies or writes out documents; often a record keeper (p. 82)

escriba persona que copia o escribe documentos; con frecuencia, quien lleva los archivos (pág. 82)

scroll a long document made from pieces of parchment sewn together (p. 155)

rollo documento largo elaborado con pedazos de pergamino unidos (pág. 155)

secondary source a document or written work created after an event (p. 11)	**fuente secundaria** documento o trabajo que se escribe después de que ocurre un evento (pág. 11)
sect a religious group (pp. 524–525)	**secta** grupo religioso (págs. 524–525)
secular related to worldly things (pp. 582–583)	**secular** relacionado con las cosas terrenales (págs. 582–583)
***secure** free from danger (pp. 564–565)	***seguro** libre de peligro (págs. 564–565)
***seek** to look for or try to achieve; to search for (pp. 45–46; p. 237)	***buscar** indagar o tratar de alcanzar; investigar (págs. 45–46; pág. 237)
seminary a school for religious training (pp. 606–607)	**seminario** escuela para la formación religiosa (págs. 606–607)
separation of powers the division of power among the branches of government; a government structure that has three distinct branches: legislative, executive, and judicial (pp. 44–45; pp. 652–653)	**separación de poderes** división del poder entre las ramas del gobierno; estructura de gobierno que tiene tres ramas distintas: legislativa, ejecutiva y judicial (págs. 44–45; págs. 652–653)
serf a member of the peasant class tied to the land and subject to the will of the landowner (pp. 550–551)	**siervo** miembro de la clase campesina atado a la tierra y sujeto a la voluntad del terrateniente (págs. 550–551)
shadoof a bucket attached to a long pole used to transfer river water to storage basins (p. 104)	**cigoñal** cubeta atada a una pértiga larga que se usa para pasar agua del río a vasijas de almacenamiento (pág. 104)
shamanism belief in gods, demons, and spirits (p. 511)	**chamanismo** creencia en dioses, demonios y espíritus (pág. 511)
shari'ah Islamic code of law (pp. 402–403)	***sharia*** código jurídico islámico (págs. 402–403)
Shia group of Muslims who believed the descendants of Ali should rule (p. 407)	**chiíta** grupo musulmán que creía que los descendientes de Alá debían gobernar (pág. 407)
sheikh the leader of an Arab tribe (p. 399)	**jeque** líder de una tribu árabe (pág. 399)
shogun a military governor who ruled Japan (p. 522)	**sogún** gobernante militar que reinaba en Japón (pág. 522)
shrine a place where people worship (p. 66)	**templo** lugar donde la gente rinde culto (pág. 66)
silt fine particles of fertile soil (p. 77)	**limo** partículas finas de suelo fértil (pág. 77)
***similar** having things in common; having characteristics in common (p. 287; p. 440)	***similar** que tiene cosas en común; que tiene características en común (pág. 287; pág. 440)
sinkhole a depression or hollow where soil has collapsed (pp. 459–460)	**sumidero** depresión u hoyo donde el suelo ha colapsado (págs. 459–460)
smallpox a disease that causes a high fever and often death (p. 625)	**viruela** enfermedad que produce fiebre alta y con frecuencia, la muerte (pág. 625)
smith craftsperson who works with metal (p. 349)	**herrero** artesano que trabaja los metales (pág. 349)
***social class** a group of people who are at a similar cultural, economic, or educational level (p. 289)	***clase social** grupo de personas con un nivel cultural, económico o educativo similar (pág. 289)

Socratic method philosophical method of questioning to gain truth (p. 221)

método socrático método filosófico que consiste en hacer preguntas para conocer la verdad (pág. 221)

social contract an agreement between the people and their government (p. 652)

contrato social acuerdo entre el pueblo y su gobierno (pág. 652)

socialism the means of production are owned and controlled by the people, through their government (pp. 698–699)

socialismo medios de producción de propiedad de las personas y controlados por ellas a través de su gobierno (págs. 698–699)

solid geometry a branch of mathematics about measurement and relationships of points, lines, angles, surfaces, and solids in three-dimensional space (p. 240)

geometría sólida rama de las matemáticas que estudia las medidas, las propiedades y las relaciones entre los puntos, las líneas, los ángulos, las superficies y los sólidos en el espacio tridimensional (pág. 240)

Sophists Greek teachers of philosophy, reasoning, and public speaking (p. 221)

sofistas maestros griegos de filosofía, razonamiento y retórica (pág. 221)

***source** a document or reference work (pp. 10–11)

***fuente** documento u obra de referencia (págs. 10–11)

special-purpose map a map that shows themes or patterns such as climate, natural resources, or population (pp. 34–35)

mapa temático mapa que muestra temas o patrones como el clima, los recursos naturales o la población (págs. 34–35)

specialization the act of training for a particular job (p. 66)

especialización acción de capacitarse para un trabajo específico (pág. 66)

species a class of individuals with similar physical characteristics (pp. 8–9)

especie clase de individuos con características físicas semejantes (págs. 8–9)

spiritual a gospel song (pp. 440–441)

espiritual canción de música gospel (págs. 440–441)

***stability** the condition of being steady and unchanging (p. 186)

***estabilidad** cualidad de estar fijo o ser inalterable (pág. 186)

***status** a person's rank compared to others (pp. 258–259)

***estatus** posición de una persona en comparación con otras (págs. 258–259)

steppe flat, dry grassland (pp. 489–490)

estepa sabana plana y seca (págs. 489–490)

Stoicism the philosophy of the Stoics who believed that people should not try to feel joy or sadness (p. 238)

estoicismo filosofía de los estoicos, quienes creían que las personas no debían tratar de sentir alegría ni tristeza (pág. 238)

***stress** to focus on or emphasize (p. 701)

***destacar** enfocarse o poner énfasis en algo (pág. 701)

***structure** a building or other built object (p. 270)

***estructura** edificio u otro tipo de construcción (pág. 270)

stupa a Buddhist shrine, usually dome-shaped (pp. 266–267)

estupa templo budista, por lo general en forma de domo (págs. 266–267)

stutter an uneven repetition of sounds and words (p. 85)

tartamudeo repetición irregular de sonidos y palabras (pág. 85)

***style** a distinctive form or type of something (pp. 218–219; pp. 530–531)

***estilo** forma o tipo característicos de algo (págs. 218–219; págs. 530–531)

subcontinent a large landmass that is smaller than a continent (pp. 248–249)

subcontinente gran masa continental más pequeña que un continente (págs. 248–249)

***successor** one that comes after (p. 332)	***sucesor** persona que sucede a otra (pág. 332)
***sufficient** enough (p. 202)	***suficiente** bastante (pág. 202)
sugarcane a grassy plant that is a natural source of sugar (pp. 438–439)	**caña de azúcar** planta herbácea que es una fuente natural de azúcar (págs. 438–439)
sultan Seljuk leader (p. 408)	**sultán** líder seléucida (pág. 408)
Sunni group of Muslims who accepted the rule of the Umayyad caliphs (p. 407)	**sunita** grupo musulmán que solo acepta el mandato de los califas Umayyad (pág. 407)
supply the amount of a good or service that a producer wants to sell (p. 39)	**oferta** cantidad de un producto o servicio que un productor quiere vender (pág. 39)
surplus an amount that is left over after a need has been met (p. 78)	**excedente** cantidad que queda luego de satisfacer una necesidad (pág. 78)
***survive** to continue to live; to live through a dangerous event; to continue to function or prosper (p. 152; pp. 434–435)	***sobrevivir** seguir viviendo; vivir luego de haber tenido una experiencia peligrosa; continuar funcionando o prosperar (pág. 152; págs. 434–435)
Swahili the unique culture of Africa's East Coast and the language spoken there (pp. 434–435)	**swahili** cultura exclusiva de la costa este de África y lengua que se habla allí (págs. 434–435)
***symbol** a sign or image that stands for something else; something that stands for or suggests something else (p. 35; p. 701)	***símbolo** signo o imagen que representa otra cosa; algo que representa o sugiere algo más (pág. 35; pág. 701)
synagogue a Jewish house of worship (pp. 154–155)	**sinagoga** casa judía de culto (págs. 154–155)
systematic agriculture the organized growing of food on a regular schedule (pp. 62–63)	**agricultura sistemática** cultivo organizado de alimentos de acuerdo con un calendario habitual (págs. 62–63)

T

***technology** the use of advanced methods to solve problems; an ability gained by the practical use of knowledge (pp. 38–39; p. 56)	***tecnología** uso de métodos avanzados para solucionar problemas habilidad obtenida mediante el uso práctico del conocimiento (págs. 38–39; pág. 56)
***temporary** not permanent; lasting for a limited period (pp. 464–465)	***temporal** que no es permanente; que dura un periodo limitado (págs. 464–465)
tenant farmer a farmer who works land owned by someone else and pays rent in cash or as a share of the crop (p. 295)	**agricultor arrendatario** agricultor que trabaja la tierra que pertenece a otro y le paga una renta ya sea en efectivo o con parte de sus cosechas (pág. 295)
***tensions** opposition between individuals or groups; stress (p. 164)	***tensiones** oposición entre individuos o grupos; presión (pág. 164)
terror violent acts that are meant to cause fear in people (pp. 490–491)	**terror** actos violentos que buscan atemorizar a las personas (págs. 490–491)

***text** words written down in a particular form, such as a book (p. 254)

***texto** palabras escritas en un formato específico, como un libro (pág. 254)

textile woven cloth (pp. 132–133)

textil tela tejida (págs. 132–133)

***theme** a topic that is studied or a special quality that connects ideas (p. 32)

***tema** materia que se estudia o cualidad especial que conecta ideas (pág. 32)

theocracy a government of religious leader(s) (pp. 108–109)

teocracia gobierno de uno o más líderes religiosos (págs. 108–109)

theology the study of religious faith, practice, and experience (p. 565)

teología estudio de la fe, la práctica y la experiencia religiosas (pág. 565)

***theory** an explanation of how or why something happens (pp. 642–643)

***teoría** explicación de cómo o por qué sucede algo (págs. 642–643)

Torah teachings that Moses received from God; later became the first part of the Hebrew Bible (p. 143)

Tora enseñanza que recibió Moisés de Dios; llegó a ser la primera parte de la Biblia hebrea (pág. 143)

***tradition** a custom, or way of life, passed down from generation to generation (pp. 154–155)

***tradición** costumbre, o forma de vida, que se transmite de una generación a otra (págs. 154–155)

traditional economy an economic system in which custom decides what people do, make, buy, and sell (p. 40)

economía tradicional sistema económico en el cual la costumbre decide lo que las personas hacen, producen, compran y venden (pág. 40)

tragedy a play or film in which characters fail to overcome serious problems (p. 217)

tragedia obra de teatro o película en la cual los personajes no pueden superar problemas graves (pág. 217)

***transfer** to copy from one surface to another by contact (p. 484)

***transferir** copiar de una superficie a otra por contacto (pág. 484)

***transform** to change the structure of; to bring about a large and widespread change (p. 322; p. 634)

***transformar** cambiar la estructura; provocar un cambio grande y generalizado (pág. 322; pág. 634)

transformation a complete change (p. 497)

transformación cambio total (pág. 497)

transport to transfer or carry from one place to another (pp. 424–425)

***transportar** transferir o llevar de un lugar a otro (págs. 424–425)

trial jury a group of citizens that decides whether an accused person is innocent or guilty (p. 558)

jurado grupo de ciudadanos que decide si un acusado es inocente o culpable (pág. 558)

tribe a social group made up of families or clans (p. 142)

tribu grupo social conformado por familias o clanes (pág. 142)

tribune an elected Roman official who protects the rights of ordinary citizens (p. 313)

tribuno funcionario romano elegido que protege los derechos de los ciudadanos comunes (pág. 313)

tribute payment made to a ruler or state as a sign of surrender; payment to a ruler as a sign of submission or for protection (p. 88; pp. 514–515)

tributo pago hecho a un gobernante o Estado en señal de rendición; pago a un gobernante como señal de sumisión o para obtener protección (pág. 88; págs. 514–515)

triumvirate three rulers who share equal political power (p. 323)

triunvirato tres gobernantes que comparten el mismo poder político (pág. 323)

tsunami a huge ocean wave caused by an undersea earthquake (p. 529)

tsunami enorme ola oceánica causada por un sismo subacuático (pág. 529)

tyrant an absolute ruler unrestrained by law; harsh ruler (pp. 183–184; p. 719)

tirano gobernante absoluto que actúa sin control por parte de la ley; gobernante cruel (págs. 183–184; pág. 719)

U

***unify** to bring together in one unit; to join; to make into one group (pp. 106–107; pp. 292–293; pp. 608–609)

***unificar** juntar en una unidad; unir; formar un grupo (págs. 106–107; págs. 292–293; págs. 608–609)

***unique** one of a kind; different from all others (pp. 100–101; p. 431)

***exclusivo** único en su clase; diferente de los demás (págs. 100–101; pág. 431)

urban having to do with a town or city rather than a rural area (p. 583)

urbano relativo a un pueblo o una ciudad, no a un área rural (pág. 583)

urbanization the increase in the proportion of people living in cities rather than rural areas (pp. 696–697)

urbanización aumento en la proporción de personas que viven en las ciudades y no en áreas rurales (págs. 696–697)

utilitarianism belief that society should provide the greatest happiness for the largest number of people (p. 699)

utilitarismo creencia de que la sociedad debe brindar la mayor felicidad al mayor número de personas (pág. 699)

URL the abbreviation for uniform resource locator; the address of an online resource (p. 20)

URL abreviatura de uniform resource locator (localizador uniforme de recursos); dirección de un recurso en línea (pág. 20)

V

vassal a person under the protection of a lord to whom he has vowed loyalty; a low-ranking noble under the protection of a feudal lord (p. 523; pp. 548–549)

vasallo persona bajo la protección de un señor a quien ha jurado lealtad; noble de baja categoría bajo la protección de un señor feudal (pág. 523; págs. 548–549)

vault a curved ceiling made of arches (p. 345)

bóveda techo curvo compuesto por arcos (pág. 345)

Vedas ancient sacred writings of India (p. 254)

Vedas antiguos escritos sagrados de la India (pág. 254)

vernacular the everyday spoken language of a region (p. 566)

vernácula lengua hablada en una región (pág. 566)

***version** a different form or edition; a translation of the Bible (p. 161)

***versión** formato o edición diferentes; traducción de la Biblia (pág. 161)

veto to reject (p. 313)

vetar rechazar (pág. 313)

vigil the night before a religious feast (p. 597)

vigilia la noche anterior a una fiesta religiosa (pág. 597)

vile morally low (p. 597)

vil de baja moral (pág. 597)

***violate** to disobey or break a rule or law (pp. 20–21)

***violar** desobedecer o incumplir una regla o ley (págs. 20-21)

volcano a mountain that releases hot or melted rocks from inside the Earth (pp. 528–529)

volcán montaña que libera rocas calientes o fundidas desde el interior de la Tierra (págs. 528–529)

***volume** amount included within limits (p. 452)

***volumen** cantidad incluida dentro de los límites (pág. 452)

***voluntarily** by choice or free will; willingly (p. 231)

***voluntariamente** por elección o voluntad propia, con gusto (pág. 231)

W

warlord a military commander exercising civil power by force, usually in a limited area (p. 281)

caudillo comandante militar que ejerce el poder civil por la fuerza, usualmente en un área limitada (pág. 281)

widespread frequent in many places, common (p. 673)

***generalizado** frecuente en muchos lugares, común (pág. 673)

Z

ziggurat a pyramid-shaped structure with a temple at the top (p. 80)

zigurat estructura en forma de pirámide, en cuya punta se encuentra un templo (pág. 80)

Zoroastrianism a Persian religion based on the belief of one god (p. 192)

zoroastrismo religión persa que se basaba en la creencia en un dios (pág. 192)

The following abbreviations are used in the index: *m=map, c=chart, p=photograph or picture, g=graph, crt=cartoon, ptg=painting, q=quote*

A

Abbasid dynasty, 407–08, *m408,* 413
abolitionism, 689
Abraham, *c138,* 141, *ptg141,* 150, 403; in Canaan, *c138*
absolute monarchy, 651, 655–57, 672
absolutism, 651
Abu Bakr, *c406*
Academy, Plato's, 222, *p223*
Achilles, 234
acropolis, 180–81
Actium, Battle of, 326
Act of Supremacy, 604
actors, 217–19, *p217, p496,* 500, 526, 536, *q536,* 596, *p596*
acupuncture, 296, *p297*
Adams, Samuel, 671
adobe, 466
Adriatic Sea, *m366,* 586
Aegean Sea, *c172,* 174, 176, 177, 178, 179, *m206*
Aelius Aristides, *q358*
Aeneas, 307, 348, *ptg348*
***Aeneid* (Virgil),** 307, 346, *q346,* 348–49, *q348, q349*
Aesop's fables, 216–17
Africa, *m334, m416,* 419–21, *m421,* 422–29, 430–35, 436–43, *c472,* 502, 615, 616, *c616–17,* 631; architecture, 435; art, 419, *p419,* 420, 435, 439–41, *p439, q446;* Central, 64; cities and city-states, 426, 436, 501; Christianity in, 429, *c428;* civilizations of, 419–21, 422–29, 430–35, 436–43; culture of, 439–41; early humans, 51, 422, 424; East, 51, *c173,* 428–29, 435, 501; economy, 634; education, 435, 437–38, *q446;* exploration of, 620, *m620;* family, 436–37; farming, 64, 419, 422, 423, 424, 426, 436, 437; geography, 419, 420, *p420, m421,* 422–25, *m423, p423, c424;* gods and goddesses, 432; gold, 425, 426–27, *q427, c428,* 429, *p432,* 434, 442, 620; government, 430–32, 442, 443; iron-making, *c173,* 425, 427, 437, 440; Islam in, 420, 426, 427, 429, 432–35, *q434;* life in, 436–443; military, 431, *q431,* 432, 438; North, 364, *m366,* 385, *m392,* 396, 404, 405, 409, 435, 575; poetry, 440; privatization, 442–43; religions of, 428–29, 432, 433, *m433,* 440–41; salt, 425, 426–27, *q427, c428,* 442; slavery, 411, 420, *c421,* 425, 428, *c428,* 429, 432,438–39, *q439, m440,* 441, *c617,* 629, 630, 635, 666; storytelling, 427, 438, 439, *p439,* 441; trade, *c420-21,* 424, 425–29, *m426, q427, c428,* 429, 430, 431, 432, 433, 436, 441, 444, *q446,* 502, 615, 620, *m634;* water resources, 442–43, *q442, q443;* West, 406–07, 419, *c421,* 425–28, 433–35, 437–39, 441; women, 433, 437–38. *See also individual country listings.*
African Americans, 264, 687; civil rights, 264; slavery, 687
agora, 181, *ptg181*
Agricultural Revolution, 62–69, *m70*
agriculture, 454, 552–53, 567; crop rotation, 553; development of new crops, 482; food surpluses, 66, 78, 106, 178, 251, 424, 482; in early civilizations, *m70, q72,* 77–81, 454; in Korea, 512; irrigation, 77–78, *p77, p79,* 91, 104, 106, 109, 120, 147, 254, 285, 412, 457, 466, 482, 512, 524; Mongolian, 489; Roman, 358, *q358;* Spartan, 185, 187. *See also* Agricultural Revolution; farming.
ahimsa, 264
Ahmose, prince of Egypt, 121, 122
Akbar, ruler of Mogul Empire, 410
Akhenaton, pharaoh of Egypt, 125
Akkadians, 86, 87; Sargon, 86, 87, *p87;* Sumer and, 86, 87
Alaric, Visigoth leader, 354
Al-Bakri, Abdullah Abu-Ubayd, 427, *q427*
Aldrete, Gregory, 368
Alexander II, czar of Russia, 684; frees serfs, 684
Alexander the Great, *c139,* 160–61, *c173,* 209, *p209, c211, ptg223,* 231–35, *ptg233, q233, c304;* conquers Persia, *c173,* 197, 210, 265, *c277;* empire of, *m34,* 161, 231–35, *m232,* 236; invasion of India, 233, 265
Alexandria, Egypt, 210, *m210,* 233, 235, *ptg235,* 236, 239, 240, *m242, q244,* 327, *m366,* 344; library of, 210, 235, 236, 239; lighthouse of, 210, 235, *ptg235*
Alfred the Great, king of England, *c538,* 556
Alhambra palace, 415, 575
Ali, *c406,* 407
al-Idrisi, 619
Alighieri, Dante, 590
al-Khawarizmi, 414
al-Kindi, 414
Allah, 400, 401, *q401,* 403
alphabets, 105, 145, *c145,* 148, 282–83, *c390,* 515; Cyrillic, *c390;* English, 515; hangul, 514, 515; Hebrew, *c145;* Greek, 145, *c145,* 178, *c178,* 308, *c390;* Latin, 356; Nubian, 129; Phoenician, 123, 145, *c145;* Roman, 145, *c145*
Alps, 66, 307, 318
al-Razi, *c397,* 413–14
Amazon, 452, *p452*
Amenga-Etego, Rudolf, 443
Amenhotep IV, pharaoh of Egypt, 125
American Revolution, 315, 662–63, *c662–63, m662–63;* 664–71, 672
Americas, 447–49, *c448–49, m449,* 450–58, 459–67, 602, 615–17, *c617, m616–17,* 618, 622–23, 624–27, 628–35; colonies in, 620, 623, 628–31, *p629,* 632–33, 664–71; culture, 448, 629; early civilizations of, 453–58, 459–67; economy, 634; exploration of, 615–17, *c617, m616–17,* 618–23, 624–27, 628–35; farming, 64, 65, 448, 454–58, 460, 461, 467; geography, 448, *p448,* 450–52, *m451, p452,* 454, 455–56; gods and goddesses, 456, 460, *p460,* 461, 625; migration to and settlement of, 450, 453–54, *m453, p457;* political revolutions, 662–63, *c662–63, m662–63;* slavery, 432, 439, *c617,* 622, 629–30, 635, 688; trade, 448, 454–56, 460, 466, 628–35, *m634, q638. See also* Anasazi civilization; Aztec Empire; Inca; Maya; Native Americans; Central America; North America, South America.
Amon-Re, 131, *p131, q131,* 132
Amos, 153
Amsterdam, 631
***Analects* (Confucius),** 287, *q287*
Anasazi civilization, *m449,* 457, *p457, m468;* artifacts, *p457;* cliff dwellings, 457; decline of, *c448;* farming, 457; pueblos, *p457,* 457
Anatolia, 174, 178, 191, 193, 202, 204, *m206*
anatomy, 344
Andes, 451, 456
Angkor Wat, *c509,* 531, *p531, c539*
Anglican Church. *See* Church of England.
Anglo-Saxons, 391, 542, 556–57, *ptg557*
animism, 518, 529

Anselm, archbishop of Canterbury, 565–66
anthropology, 9
Antigone **(Sophocles),** 217–18
Antiochus IV, king of the Seleucids, 161
anti-Semitism, 569
Antoinette, Marie, queen of France, 675, *ptg675;* biography, 675
Antony, Mark, 326, *p326;* biography, 326
Anyang, China, 281
Apache, 467
Aphrodite, 213, 343
Apollo, 213, 214, 237; Oracle of, 214
apostles, 377–78, 380, 384–85
Appian Way, *c420*
Appolonius of Rhodes, 237
aqueducts: Roman, 332, 344–45
Aquinas, Thomas, 566, *ptg566*
Arab Empire, *m396–397,* 404–09; fall of, 409
Arabia, *m300,* 398–403, *m416;* geography, 398–400, *m399*
Arabian Sea, 249, *m272*
archaeology, 8–9, 11, 16, 77, 125, 146, 164, 176, 177, 252, 276, 280, 281, 282, 285, 303, 308, 424; digs, 10; early humans and, 9, 51, 424, 454, 457, 458, 459, *q470;* ruins, *p5,* 91, 101, 147, 176, *p176,* 177, 241, *p241,* 252, 281, 340, 447, 583. *See also* artifacts.
archbishops, 384, *c384*
Archimedes, 240, *ptg240;* inventions of, 240; scientific contributions, *c239;* solid geometry and, 240;
architecture, 146, 176, *p192, p241,* 270, 356, 357; African, 435; American, 219, *p219,* 357, *p357;* Byzantine, 363, *p363,* 564; Doric, Ionic, and Corinthian columns, *c218;* Egyptian, *c74,* 113–15, *p113, ptg114, p115,* 117–18, 121, *p122, q136,* 147; Gothic, 564–65, *p565;* Greek, 176, *p176,* 177, *ptg181, c201,* 218, *c218,* 219, 236–37, 241, 344, 345; Harappan, 251–52; Indian, 270, 415, *p415;* Islamic, 407, *p407,* 409, *p409,* 415, *p415;* Japanese, 527; Khmer, 531, *p531;* Korean, 512; Maya, 460; Mohenjo-Daro, 251–52, *c251;* modern, 565; of medieval Europe, 564–65, *p565,* 585, 590; Roman, 241, 340–41, 344, 345, *p345, p351,* 356, 357, 564; Romanesque, 564–65
Argentina: art, *p58;* early humans, *p58*
Argonautica **(Appolonius),** 237
Aristarchus, 238, 239; scientific contributions, *c239*
aristocrats: Chinese, 281, 284–85, 287, 289, 290, 293, 294, 295, 299
Aristophanes, 217–18
Aristotle, 209, *c211,* 222–23, *ptg223, c224, c247,* 405, 565–66, 643, 646; founds Lyceum in Athens, *c211,* 222–23; "golden mean," 223, *c224;* ideas and influence of, 223, *c224,* 565–66
Ark of the Covenant, *p143,* 147, 150
Arkwright, Richard, 692
Arnolfini Portrait, The **(van Eyck),** 594, *p595*
art, 10, 16–17, *p192, p246,* 460, *p460, p461,* 530, 532, 701–02; African, 419, *p419,* 420, 435, 439–41, *p439, q446;* as a source of information, 10; Assyrian, *p73;* Buddhist, 479, *p479, p507,* 510; Byzantine, *p361,* 363-63, *p363, ptg387;* chiaroscuro, 593; Chinese, *p1, p11,* 283, *p283, p285,* 290, 295, *p487,* 487–88, 500, *ptg500,* 518; Egyptian, *p16, q16, p97,* 107, *p107, p109, ptg110, ptg111, p117, ptg118,* 121, *p121, ptg121, p123, p125, p126, p130;* Etruscan, 308–09, *ptg309;* French, 58, *p59,* 610, 661, *ptg661,* 701–02; fresco, 309, *ptg309,* 592, 593; Greek, 171, *p171,* 172, *p172,* 176, 177, *p177, p186,* 189, *p189,* 236–37, *p237,* 344, 345, 592; Hindu, 270, *p270;* Indian, *p246,* 270; Islamic, 415; Japanese, 520, 525, 527; modernism, 701–02; of early humans and early civilizations, *p13,* 58–59, *p58, p59,* 66, 69, *p72, c74;* of Kush, 131, *p131,* 132; of medieval Europe, 579, 580, 583, *p584,* 584, 587, 590, 591–95, *ptg592, ptg593, p594, ptg595,* 608, 610; perspective, 592, 594; realism, 701; Roman, 303, *p303,* 321, *p321,* 333, *p344,* 345, *p352,* 592; romanticism, 701; Sumerian, 80, *p80, p81,* symbolism, 701–02. *See also* artisans.
artifacts, 2, 8–9, 10–11, 13, 16–17, 77, *p81,* 126, 129, 303, 308, 415, 447; Anasazi, *p457;* Assyrian, 88, *p88;* Byzantine, *p365;* Chinese, 280, 282, *p282, q302;* Egyptian, *p16, q16, p97, p98,* 126, *p126;* Greek, 172, *p172;* Harappan, 252, *p252;* Italian, *p17, q17;* Mohenjo-Daro, 250, *p250;* of early humans, 9, *p13, p56,* 66, *p67,* 68, *p72, c74,* 276, 453, 457, *p457, q536*
artisans, 66, 92, 252, 412, 425, 436, 512, 513, 514, 524, 530, 554, 555, 557, 575, 585, 586, 587, 633, 673, 675; Chinese, 282, 283, 290, 296, 482, 488, 500, 532; Egyptian, 106, 114, 116, 117, 121, 129, 131; Greek, 177, 179, 183, 200, 201; in the Americas, 455, 460; Roman, 308, 312, 333; Sumerian, 78, 81, 83. *See also* art.
Aryabhata, 270
Aryans, 252–54, 257; caste system, 246; development of Sanskrit, 254; farming, 254; Hinduism, *c7,* 246, *c247,* 257; India and, *c7,* 37, 246, 252–54, 257; language, 252–53, 254, *p254,* 257; literature, 254; migration of, 252–53, *m253;* nomadic life of, 250, 253–54; religion, 254, *q254,* 257; trade, 254; warriors, 253
Ashanti, 432
Ashikaga Takauji, 522
Ashoka, emperor of India, 246, 266–68, *p267, q267,* 270; Buddhism and, 266–67; laws and public works of, 266–67, *q267;* religious tolerance, 267
Ashurnasirpal II, king of Assyria, 73, *p73*
Asia, 507–09, 510–15, 516–19, 520–27, 528–33, 570–71, 585, 587, *c617,* 618–23, 633, 635; Central, 15, 253, 489, 560; disease and Black Death in, 365, 570–71, *m571;* East, 15, 260, 262, 278, 408, 510, 512, 616, 618; economy, 634; search for a sea route to, 618–23, *m620;* South, 193, 279, 410, 494, 502; trade, 512, 524, 528–30, 532, 533, *c617,* 618, *m632,* 633, *m634;* West, 67. *See also* China; India; Japan; Korea; Mongol Empire; Silk Road; Southeast Asia; Southwest Asia.
Asia Minor, *c139,* 201, 232, *m232, m334, m392,* 409, 562–63
Askia Muhammad. *See* Ture, Muhammad.
Aspasia, 201, *p201;* biography, 201
Assyria, 73, *p73,* 87–89, *q96;* cities, 73, 88; geography, 87, 88, 89; library of Nineveh, 88; life in, 88–89; *See also* Assyrians.
Assyrians, *c74,* 87–90, 92, 127, 132, *c139,* 151–53; art and artifacts, 88, *p88;* Chaldeans and, 89–90, control of Mesopotamia, *c74,* 87–90; empire of, 87–89, *m89, q96,* 151–52; farming, 89; government, 88; iron-making, 88; law, 88; military, 87–88; religion and gods, 88; trade, 89; tribute to, 88, 151; weapons, 88, 89, 132; writing, 88
astrolabe, 413, *p413,* 619, *p619*
astronomy, 325, 413, 531, 565, 591, 642, 643, 644–45, *c645,* 646–47, *c647;* Chaldean, 92; Egyptian, 114; geocentrism, 643, 644–46, *c645;* Greek, 177, 223, 226, 238–40, *p238, c239,* 344, 643, *c645;* heliocentrism, 644–46, *c645;* Indian, 271; Korean, 512, *p512,* 514 ; Maya, 461; modern, 512, *p512;* Sumerian, 83; telescopes, 646, *p646*
Atahualpa, 627
Athena, 171, *p171,* 188, 213, *c218;* Parthenon and, *c218*
Athens, 172, 181, *ptg181,* 182, 184, *m184,* 187–89, 190, 193–95, 197, 198–205, *m206,* 221, 222, 225, *q226,* 228, *q229,* 230, 236, 237, 238; art and architecture, *ptg181,* 189, *p189, c201;* burned by Persians, 197; citizenship, 188, 189, 198–200, *c200,* 203, 228, *q229;* civil rights, 203, 228; constitution, 188, 202; democracy, 189, 198–99, *c200, q203;* economy, 188, 202; education, 187–88, *ptg187,* 200; empire of, 202–05; farming, 188, 200, 201, 202; law, *q182,* 188, *p188p,* 189, 199, *c200,* 222; lottery system, 189; military, 182, *q182,* 193–94, 202–04; modern Olympics, 214; politics and government, 183–184, 188–89, 198–99, *ptg199, c200,* 203; reforms, 188–89; religion, 188; roles of men and women, 187–88, 189, 200–201, *c200;* ships,

Index

202, 204; slavery, 188, 189, 200, 201; trade, 188, 202

Atlantic Ocean, *m334,* 439, *m444,* 451, 452, *m453,* 544, 615, 616, *m616–17,* 619, 620, 664, 686

Aton, 125

Augustine, 385, *ptg385,* 389, *ptg389*

Augustus, emperor of Rome, 343, 348, *c370,* 372

Australia, *c663*

Austria, 656–57, *m656,* 685, 686; Austrian Empire, 685; demands for self-rule, 685; formation of Austria-Hungary, 684; Italy and, 686

Austria-Hungary, 684

automobile, 4

Axum, 133, *c339,* 428–29, *c428;* defeats Kush, 133, *c339,* 428; religion, 429; trade, *c428*

Aztec Empire, *m449,* 461–63, *p462, m468, c580, c616,* 624–26, *q638;* defeated by Cortés, 625–26; human sacrifices, 625; gods, 447, 625; smallpox epidemic, 625, 626

B

Babylon, 87, 90–92, 152, 154, 156, 234; artisans, 92; empire of, *c74,* 87, 90–93, *q96,* 123, *c172;* exile of Jews to, 153, *q153,* 154, 156, 160, 190; fall of, 93; Hanging Gardens, 90–91, *p91, ptg91*

Bacon, Francis, 649; development of the scientific method, 649, *c649*

Bacon, Roger, 565

Baghdad, *c396–97,* 408–09, *m408,* 412, 413, 415, *m416,* 418, *q418,* 492

Balboa, Vasco Núñez de, 626

Bali, 533, *p533*

Balkan Peninsula, 174

Baltic Sea, 657

Balzac, Honoré de, 701

Bank of Amsterdam, *c581*

Bantu, *c420,* 437, *m437,* 438; migrations, 437, *m437*

Ban Zhao, 295, *p295;* biography, 295

barter, 42, 351, 411, 554, *q638*

Basil, 389

Basilian Rule, 389–90

Bastille, 661, 673, *ptg674,* 674, *ptg680;* Bastille Day, 673

Bay of Bengal, *m272*

bazaar, 412, *p412, ptg412*

Bay of Bengal, *m534*

Bede, 555

Bedouin, 399–400, *p400*

Beethoven, Ludwig von, 701

Beijing, China, 492, 499, *m499,* 503, *m504;* Forbidden City, 499; Imperial City, 499;

Belgium, 594, 695

Bell, Alexander Graham, *c663*

Benedict, 389, *q390*

Benedictine Rule, 389

Benin, 419, 431, 440; art, 419, *p419, p431,* 440, *m444;* farming, 419; geography, 419

Bentham, Jeremy, 699

Berbers, 425–26, 427, 433

Bernard of Clairvaux, 567

Bessemer, Henry, 692

Bethlehem, 157

Bhagavad Gita, 269–70

Bible, 149, 374, *q374, c375,* 377, 379, 384–85, 387, 389, 546, 591, 593, 599, 600–01, 603, 646, 702; Beatitudes, 375, *c375;* conflict with the theory of evolution, 702; first printed book, 591; gospels, 384–85; New Testament, 385; Old Testament, 141, 385. *See also* Hebrew Bible; Psalms, Book of.

Bill of Rights: United States, *c27*

bishops, 383–84, *c384,* 385, 387, 389

Bismarck, Otto von, 686, *ptg686;* rule by "blood and iron," 686

Black Death, *c539,* 569, 570–72, *m571, q578,* 582, 590, 600; impact on global population, 570–71; spread of, 570–71, *m571, p572*

blacks. *See* African Americans.

Black Sea, 179, *m366,* 571

Bodhisattvas, 262

Bohemia, 611; Thirty Years' War, 611, *ptg611*

Boleyn, Anne, 604, 605

Bonaparte, Napoleon, 661, 676–79, *ptg676;* as First Consul and emperor, 677; Continental System of trade, 678; defeat at Waterloo, 679; defeated by Britain and Russia, 678–79; empire of, 677–79, *m678;* exile of, 679; Grand Army, 678–71; Napoleonic Code, 677

Book of the Dead, 111, *q111*

Bordeaux, *m573, m576*

Boston, Massachusetts, 669, 671

Boston Massacre, 668

Boston Tea Party, *ptg669,* 668

Bourbon family, 610

bourgeoisie, 673

Boxer Rebellion, *c663*

Boyle, Robert, *c647,* 648

Brahmaputra River, 248

Brahma, 258, *ptg258*

Brahman, 257–58

Brahmins, 255, *c255,* 257

Brazil, 629; cash crops, 629

Britain, 332, *c371,* 541, 542, 546, 550, *c663,* 664–71, 678, 690–95, *q694,* 698–701, Chartists, 682–83, *q683;* Christianity in, *c371,* 391; colonies, *c663,* 664–71; economy, 695; empire of, 669; enclosure movement, 691–92; English Channel, 541, 609, 677; India and, 264, *c663;* Industrial Revolution, 690–95, *q694;* inventions in, 692–93, *p692;* law, 694; Labour party, 683; literature, 701; medicine, 703; military, 678; Parliament, 682; political reform in, 682–84; trade, 668–69, *m668,* 670, 678. *See also* British Empire; England.

British East India Company, 668

British Empire. *See* Britain.

Bronze Age, *c53,* 67, 68, 69; art, 69; development of cities, 68; discovery of copper and bronze, 67; emergence of river valley civilizations, 68; government, 68; invention of writing, 69; military, 68; religion, 69; slavery, 69; social classes, 69; trade, 68

Brunelleschi, Filippo, 585–86; dome of cathedral in Florence, 585–86, *ptg586, p586*

Brutus, 325

Buddha, the, 7, *c7,* 246, *p246, c247,* 260–62, *p260,* 267, 270, *c277,* 507, 525; biography, 260; reincarnations of, 262

Buddhism, 262, 274, *c277,* 532, 533; art of, 479, *p479, p507,* 493, 511; Eightfold Path, 261, 262; "Enlightened One," 260; Four Noble Truths, 261; in China, *c247,* 262, *c277,* 299, *c338, c370,* 478-80, *p479,* 484, 494, 525; in India, *c139,* 246, *c247,* 260–62, 266–67, *c277, c338, c370, q479,* 507, 525, 530, 531, 532; in Japan, 262, 479, 519, *p519,* 520, 522, 525–26, *p525,* 527; in Korea, 262, 478–79, 510–11, 512, 514, 525; Mahayana, 262, 525; monks, 259, 260, 261, *p261,* 263, *p263,* 519, 525, 527, 532; reincarnation, 261, 262; spread of, *c247,* 261, 262, 267, *c277,* 299, *c338,* 477, 478–79, *q479,* 507, 525; stupas, 267, *p267;* Tibetan, 262, 263, *p263;* Theravada, 262; Zen, 525

bureaucracy, 282–83

Burma, 532–33; Buddhism in, 533

Bushido, 521, 522

Business: capital investment in, 692–95; corporations, 694; partnerships, 694

Byzantine Empire, 360–65, 386–88, 409, 553, 560, 561, 563, 589; architecture, 363, *p363,* 564; art and artifacts, *p361,* 363–64, *p364, ptg387;* conquered by Ottoman Turks, 409; creation of, *g355,* 356; cultural influences on, 361; geography, 360–61, 364; government, 361, 362; Justinian, emperor of, 360, 362–65, *p362, m364;* law, 361, 362, 363; military, 362, 365, *p365, m364;* religion, 386–90; trade, 561; women, 362

Byzantium, 352, 353, 360, 362. *See also* Constantinople.

C

Cabot, John, 623

Cabral, Pedro Álvares, 629

Caesar Augustus, 327, 328–30, 336, *q336,* 343; reforms, 328–30. *See also* Octavian, emperor of Rome.

Caesar, Julius, 6, 322–26, *p323, ptg324, q336, c420;* development of Julian calendar, 6, 325, *p325*
Cahokia, 458, *p458, c538*
Cairo, Egypt, 16, 115, 412, 415; Cairo Museum, 16
calendar, 6–7, 83, 148,; Chinese, 6; Egyptian, 6, 114; Gregorian, 6–7, 325; Hebrew, 6–7; Julian, 6, 325, *p325;* leap year, 6; Mayan, 461; Minoan, 7, *p7;* Muslim, 402; Sumerian, 83
California, 686
Caligula, emperor of Rome, 330
caliphs, 404–05, *c406,* 407–08
calligraphy, 488, 526
Calvinism, 603, 605; predestination as a belief of, 603
Calvin, John, 603, *ptg603,* 610
Cambodia, 262, *c509, m534;* Buddhism in, 262. *See also* Khmer Empire.
Canaan, 126, 141–47, 148; architecture, 146; life in, 147; Promised Land, 141. *See also* Canaanites.
Canaanites, 144; farming, 144; trade, 144. *See also* Canaan; Philistines; Phoenicians.
Canada, 623, 629, 666
***Canon of Medicine* (Ibn Sina),** 414
Canterbury, England, 391, 590, 604; Archbishop of, 604
***Canterbury Tales, The* (Chaucer),** 590
Capet, king of France, 559
Cape Town, South Africa, 420, *p420, c662*
caravans, 92, *p92–93,* 106, 130, 400, 401, 411, 483, 571
Caribbean, 450, 451, 621, 628, 631, 635; exploration of, 621–22; slavery, 622; trade, 621–22
Caribbean Sea, 450, 621, 628
Carter, Howard, 126
Carthage, 145, *c173,* 316–19, 320, *m334;* colonies on Sicily, 317; as a trading empire, 316, 319; Hannibal, 318–19, *ptg318;* navy, 317, 318; Punic Wars, 316–19; Spain and, 318
Cartier, Jacques, 623
Cartwright, Edmund, 692
Cassius, 325
caste system, *c173,* 246, 255–56, *c255, p255;* Hinduism and, 246
catacombs, 381, 382, *p382*
Çatalhüyük, *c53,* 65–66, *p65,* 67
cataracts, 102, *p102,* 132, *c134*
Catherine the Great, queen of Russia, 639, *ptg639,* 657; reforms of, 639
Catherine, queen of England, 604
Catherwood, Frederick, 459
Catholic Church. *See* Christian Church; Christianity; Roman Catholic Church.
Catholic Reformation, 606–08
Celts, 391, 542
censors, government, 293
census, 12, 499, 557; Domesday Book, 12, 557
Central America, 447, 450, 451, 453, 454, *m455,* 456, 459, 635; art, *c74;* farming, 64. *See also* Maya; Mesoamerica; *individual country listings*.
Central powers. *See* World War I.
Cervantes, Miguel de, 608
Chac, 460, *p460*
Chaeronea, battle of, 231
Chaldeans, *c75,* 89–93, *c139,* 154–55; Assyrians and, 89–90; Babylon, 90–93, 154; defeat and rule by Persians, *c74,* 93, 154–55, 160; destruction of Jerusalem, *c139,* 154–55; empire of, 90–93, *m90,* 151, 152; government of, 92; Nebuchadnezzar, 90–93; religion and gods, 91, 92; science, 92; taxes, 92; trade, 92, 93; tribute to, 92
Champlain, Samuel de, 629
Chandra Gupta I, 268
Changan, China, 475–76, *m477, ptg485, m504*
Chang Jiang (Yangtze River), 279, 292, 293, 475, 477, 482, *ptg493, m504*
Charlemagne, emperor of Rome, 388, 389, *ptg389, c396, c421, c448, c509, c538,* 543–44, *ptg543, q543,* 548, 558, 567; advancements in education, 544; empire and government of, 543–44; military conquests, 543
Charles I, king of England, 605, 651; execution of, 651
Charles V, Holy Roman Emperor, 602, 604, 609
Charles VII, king of France, 537, 574
Chaucer, Geoffrey, 590
Cherokee, *m466*
child labor, 697
China, *c98, c139, c210,* 275–77, *c276–77, m276–77,* 278–85, 292–99, *m300, c371,* 400, 471–73, *c472–73, m472–73,* 474–81, *m475, m477,* 482–88, 489–97, 507, 508, 510, 525, 527, 528, 532, 570, 585, *c663;* arrival of Europeans, 502–03; art and artisans, *p1, p11,* 283, *p283, p285,* 290, 295, *p487,* 487–88, 500, *ptg500,* 503, *p503,* 518; artifacts, 280, 282, *p282, q302;* Black Death in, 570–71, *m571;* Buddhism in, *c247,* 262, *c277,* 299, *c338, c370,* 478-80, *p479,* 484, 494, 525; census, 499; Christianity in, 502–03; cities, 281, 298, 475–76, 477, *ptg477,* 482, 485, 500, 519, 520; civil service, 287, 294–96, 481; civil service examinations, 287, 294–95, 476, *ptg477,* 480, 481, 493, 499; civil war, 299, 474, 478, 487; culture, 11, 275, 280, 286–91, 295–96, 477, *ptg477,* 482–88, 495, 499–500, 502; 510, 511–12, 514, 518, 525, 530; development of the gun and cannon, 492; discovery of coal and steel, 483–84; drama, 500; early, 275–302, *m276–77;* economy, 476, 477, 482–83, 485, 500; education, 295, 478; emergence of civilization, 68, *m68,* 74, 276, 278–80; expansion of, *m294,* 295, 476; family, *c290,* 291, 296; farmers and farming, *c53,* 64, 65, 276, 278–80, *p280,* 282, 283, 285, 289–90, *c290,* 291, 293, 295, 296, 299, 475, 476, *ptg477,* 482, 484, 500, *ptg500,* 503; geography, 278–80, *m279, p280,* 472, *m472–73,* 475, 476, 482, *m504;* gods and goddesses, 282, 284, *q480,* 496; government, 282, 283–84, 287, 291, 292–93, 294–95, 299, 471–78, 480–81, 498–500, 503, 512, 513, 531; Grand Canal, *c472,* 475, *m475, m477,* 500, *c508;* Great Wall, 293, 475, 503, *m504;* inventions, *c26,* 285, 296, 297, *c449, c473,* 484–85, 486, 492; Korea and, 295, 474–75, 476, 478–79, 510, 511–515, 519; language, 282–83, 481, 496, 515, 526; law, *c288,* 289; life in, 289–91, *c290,* 296; literature and poetry, 486–88, *ptg486, p487,* 496–97, *q496, q497,* 500; Mandate of Heaven, 284; medicine, 296, *p297,* 478, 518; military, 290, 474–77, 484, 485, 498; Mongol invasion and rule, 472, *c473,* 489–95, 498, 500, 503; myths and legends, 280, 282, 283; nomads, 293, 295, 474, 476, 477, 489; "Period of the Warring States," 285, 286, 292; philosophy, 286–89, *c288,* 518; population increase, 295, 482; revolts against the government, 299, 475, 476; rivers, 278–79, 280, 292, 293, 475, *m475,* 477, 482, *ptg493, m504;* roles of men and women, 291, *p291,* 295; scholar-officials, 481, 494; ships and shipping, 296, 475, 485, 500–02; Silk Road, 476, 483, 491, 493, *ptg494,* 571, 585; silk weaving and manufacturing, *c74,* 283, 290, 296, 483, *p483,* 500; social classes, 289–92, 296; technology, 285, 483–85, 483; trade, 268, 285, 290–91, 296, 297–98, *m298,* 472, 476, 478, 482, 483, *p483,* 484–85, 500, 501–02, 524, 571; tribute to, 476, 501, 515; Vietnam and, *c509,* 530–31; writing, *c172,* 282–83, 293, 510, 526. *See also* Chinese dynasties; Mongol Empire.
Chinese dynasties, 472, 474; Han, *c277, m294,* 294–97, 299, 474–75, 478, 480, 482, 484, 500; Manchu, 503, 515, *c641;* Ming, 293, 496, 498–503; Qin, 11, *c277,* 292–93, *m294, c305;* Qing, 503, *c641;* Shang, *c276,* 280–83, *m281, q302;* Song, 474, 477, *m477,* 480, 481, 482, 483, 485–87, 493, 499; Sui, 474–75; Tang, *c396,* 474, *m475,* 476, *ptg477,* 478, 480, 481, 482–88, 499, 512, 530; Xia, 280–81; Yuan, 493, 495, 498; Zhou, *c277,* 283–85, *m284,* 290, 292. *See also* individual dynasties.
chivalry, 549
Christian Church, 377–78, 382–85, *c384,* 386–89; archbishops, 384, *c384;* bishops, 383–84, *c384,* 385, 387, 389; Church Fathers, 385; Church of England, 604–05, 664, 684; clergy, 383–84, *c384,* 601, 603, 672, 673; diocese, 384; doctrine, 384; early, 377–78, 383–84,

Index

c384; Eastern Orthodox Church, 385, 386–89, 560, 561; gospels, 384–85; hierarchy, 383–84, *c384;* organization of, 383–84; patriarchs, 384, *c384;* priests, 383, *c384;* schism in, 387–89, 573; women, 384. *See also* Christianity; Jesus of Nazareth; religion; Roman Catholic Church.

Christianity, 138, *c139,* 141, 153, 156, 257, 356, 357, 361, 368, 369–71, *c370–71,* 372–79, 380–85, 386–91, 406, 428, *c428,* 429, 494, 502–03, 644, 649, *q666;* beliefs of, 379, 381, 384–85; Calvinism, 603, 605; Crusades, *c397,* 562–63, *m562,* 564, 567, 572, 578, 585, 589; Dominican order, 566, 568; Franciscan order, *c539,* 568; humanism and, 599; in medieval Europe, 386–91; legalization of, 337, *c371;* Lutheranism, 601–02; martyrs, 382; outlawed by Romans and, 337, 356, 357, 370, *c370, c371,* 372–73, 380–85; persecution of Christians, 337, 381–82; Puritans, 605, 664–67; spread of, 361, 369, 370, *m370–71,* 377–78, 379, 380–81, *m381, m388,* 388–91, 628–29; Trinity, 379. *See also* Christian Church; Jesus of Nazareth; missionaries; Protestantism; religion; Roman Catholic Church.

***Christmas Carol, A* (Dickens),** 700, *ptg701*

***Chronicles of Froissart* (Froissart),** 574, *q574*

Church of England, 604–05, 664

Cicero, 327, 589

Cincinnatus, dictator of Rome, 314–15, *ptg315*

Circus Maximus, 341

Cistercian Order, 567

cities, 68, 458, *q470,* 696–97; growth of, 696; African, 426, 436, 501; Assyrian, 73, 88; Chinese, 281, 298, 475–76, 477, *ptg477,* 482, 485, 500, 519, 520; development of, 68; Egyptian, 107, 108, 119, 125; in Kush, 130, 132; in the Roman Empire, 320, 321, 332, 333, 352–53, *g355;* Islamic, 412, 415; Italian, 579, 580, 583–88, *m583;* Japanese, 519, 520; life in, 696–97, *p697;* Maya, *c339, c371, c397, c448,* 459–61; medieval, 553–55, 619; Mesoamerican, *c448,* 455–56; Sumerian, 78–80, 81, 86; urbanization, 696. *See also* city-states.

citizens, 25, *c26–27,* 44–47, *q50,* 554, 557, 558, 587; citizen soldiers, 182; duties of, 46–47; global citizens, 47; Greek, *c173,* 181–82, 183, 184, 185, 186, 188, 189, 192, 193, 198–200, *c200,* 203; Roman, 310, 312, 314, 315, 328, 329, 333, *q336,* 342, 350, *q356,* 356, *q359. See also* citizenship.

citizenship, 25, 44–47, *q50,* 181–82, *p181,* 587; Greek, 181–82, 188, 228, *q229;* jury duty, 558; Oath of Allegiance, 25, 47, *p47;* naturalization, 46, 47; Roman, 311, 325. *See also* citizens.

***City of God, The* (Augustine),** 378

city-states, 79–80, 81, 460–61, 501; Greek, 172, 180–82, 183–89, 202–05, 212–14, 218, 219, 222, 223, 230–32, 241, 584; Italian, 582–88, *m583;* Mayan, *c339, c371, c397, c448,* 459–61; Mesopotamian, 79–80, 81, 180; Sumerian, 79–80, 81, 86. *See also* Athens; Sparta.

civics, 26, 315. *See also* citizenship.

civil rights, 44, 45–46, 80, 181–82, *c200,* 203, 228, 256, 264, 312, 313, 314, 316, 329, 356, 438, 551, 555, 558, *q558,* 608, 652, 653, 667, 674, *q673,* 687, 699; Bill of Rights, *c27,* 652; Declaration of the Rights of Man, 674, *q673;* Greek, 181–82; human rights, 47, 443, 566; of enslaved persons, 124, 412; of women, 21, 80, 87, 118, 182, 186, 222, 256, 314, 342, 362, *c641,* 655, *q655,* 655, 683–84, 698, 699, 701; Roman, 312, 313, 314, 316, 328, 347. *See also* Magna Carta; voting.

clans, 64, 409, 431, 489, 490, 517, 519

Claudius Augustus, 343

Claudius, emperor of Rome, 330

Cleisthenes, 189

Cleopatra, queen of Egypt, 326, *p326;* biography, 326

clergy, 383–84, *c384,* 601, 603, 672, 673

Clovis, king of the Franks, *c538,* 542

coal, 483–84, 692, 693, 695; coal-mining industry, 483, 692, 695; mixed with iron to make steel, 483–84, 692

Code of Hammurabi, *p83,* 87, *p88*

Code of Justinian. *See* Justinian Code.

colonies, 316, 317, *q336,* 620, 623, 628–31, *p629,* 632–33, *c663,* 664–71, *m665, p666;* British, 620, 623, 630, *c663,* 664–71, *m665;* Dutch, 631; French, 623, 629–30, 663, 656, 670; Greek, 172, *c172,* 179, *m180,* 193, 202, 204; in ancient Greece, 172, *c172,* 179, 193, 202, 204; in the Americas, 620, 623, 628–31, *p629,* 632–33, 664–71; Portuguese, 629, *p629,* 631; relationship with home country, 632–33; Spanish, 628–29, 633, *c663,* 666; United States's colonies, 605, *c641,* 664–71, *m665*

Colosseum, 330, *c338,* 341, 345

Columbian Exchange, 634–35, *m634*

Columbus, Christopher, 501, 615, *ptg615,* *c617,* 621–22, 624, 634, *q638,* 644; Santa María, 501, 621, *c621*

comedy, Greek, 217, 237; Greek New Comedy, 237

Commercial Revolution, 633

***Common Sense* (Paine),** 670

compass, *c473,* 485, 563, 619; compass rose on maps, 35

computers, 2, *p2,* 270, 619; Internet, 19–20, *p19*

Concordat of Worms, 547

concrete, 345, 357

Confucius, *c139, c210,* 275, *ptg275, c277,* 286–87, *p287, q287,* 288, *c288,* 291, 296, 299, 478, 480, *ptg480,* 518; Analects, 287, *q287*

Confucianism, 275, 286–87, 288, *c288,* 291, 478, 480, 493, 502, 511–12, 531; spread of, 275, 287, 511–12. *See also* neo-Confucianism.

Congress of Vienna, 679

conquistadors, 622, 624–27, *m625*

Constantine, emperor of Rome, 337, *p337,* 352, *p352,* 353, 360, *c371,* 382, *ptg383;* acceptance of Christianity, *c371,* 382, 383

Constantinople, 352, 353, *g355,* 360-61, 362, 363, *m366,* 409, *m416;* renamed Istanbul, 409. *See also* Istanbul.

constitutional monarchy, 652, 674, 686

constitutions, 467, *c472,* 653, 667, 674, 675, 676, 698; Athenian, 188, 203; Japanese, *c508,* 518; United States, 25, *c27,* 44–46, 224, 327, 653, 666

consul, 313–14, 322, 327; proconsul, 329

convents, 389, 546, 567, 607

Copernicus, *c581, c640,* 644–45, *c645, p645,* 646, *c647, m658*

Cort, Henry, 692

Cortés, Hernán, 624–26, *p626;* biography, 626; defeats Aztecs, 625–26

Council of Trent, 606–07, *ptg607*

Courbet, Gustave, 701

covenant, 142–43, *p143;* Ark of the Covenant, *p143,* 147, 150

Crassus, 323

Crécy, 574, *m576*

Creek, *m466*

Crete, 176, *m206*

Croesus, 214

crucifixion, 343, 377

Crusades, *c397,* 562–63, *m562,* 564, 568, 572, 585, 589; First, *c397, c539, m562;* Second, 562, *m562,* 568; Third, *m562, p563*

Cuba, 40, 621, 624; economy, 40; Spanish invasion of, 621

cultural diffusion. *See* culture(s).

culture(s), 4, 9, 36–37, 148, 448, 557; African, 440–41; changes over time, 21; Chinese, 11, 275, 280, 286–91, 295–96, 477, *ptg477,* 482–88, 495, 499–500, 502; 510, 511–12, 514, 518, 525, 530; Egyptian, 122, 123, 131; European, 557, 564–69; Greek, 171, 178–79, 185–87, 212–19, 306, 361, 582; Indian, 245, 254–56, 264, 269–71, 532–33; in the Americas, 448, 629; in the Renaissance, 589–97; Japanese, 512, 517–19, 523–527; Jewish, 155, 156–59; Korean, 510–15; Maya, 447, 460-61, *p461;* Mongol Empire, 15, 492, 493; of Kush, 129, 131; of medieval Europe, 557, 564–69; Roman, *q17,* 303, 306, 340–49, 350, 582; spread of, 37, 86, 87, 88, 106, 122, 123, 129, 131, 145, 152,

160–61, 171, 177, 178–79, 197, 209, 210, 234–35, 251, 253, 270–71, 297, 306, 492, 501–03; 510–12, 530, 563; storytelling, 82, 179, 218, 427, 437, 438, *p439*, 441
cuneiform writing, *c74*, 81–82, *p83*, 87, *c172*, 461
Cuno, James, *q17*
Cuzco, *q470*
Cyril, 390, *c390*, *ptg390;* Cyrillic alphabet, *c390*
Cyrus II, king of Persia, 154, 190–91, 193

D

da Gama, Vasco, *c539*, 620, *m620*
Dahia al-Kahina, queen of Africa, 438
daimyo, 523–24, 633
Dalai Lama, 262
Damascus, *c396*, 404, 407, 412, 415
Daniel, 156, *ptg156*, 157
Dao (Tao), 284, 288, *c288*, *q302*
Daoism, 286, 288, *c288*, 299, 302, *q302*, 480, 487–88
Darius I, king of Persia, 191–93, *p193*, *q193*, *c211*
Darius III, king of Persia, 233
Dark Age, of Greece, 178–79, 182, 185
Darwin, Charles, *p703*, 706, *q706*
Daumier, Honoré, 701
da Verrazano, Giovanni, 623
David, Jacques-Louis, 661, *ptg661*, 677, *p677*
David, king of Israel, 137, *ptg137*, *c139*, 149–50, *ptg149;* and Goliath, 149; Psalms of, 137, 149, *q149;* unites the tribes of Israel, 137, 149
***David* (Michelangelo),** 594
da Vinci, Leonardo, 378, 579, 591–592, 593; inventions of, 591, *p593; Mona Lisa, ptg592*, 593, notebooks of, 592
Dead Sea Scrolls, 162–163, *p164*, 166
Deborah, 146
Debussy, Claude, 702
Deccan Plateau, 249, *m272*
Declaration of Independence, *c641*, *c663*
Declaration of the Rights of Man, 674
Degas, Edgar, 702
de Guzmán, Dominic, 568
Delacroix, Eugène, 701
Delhi, 271
Delian League, 202–03
Delos, 202–203, *p202*
Delphi, 214, 237; Oracle of Apollo, 214
delta, 102, *m134*
democracy, 143, 184, 189, 198–99, *c200*, *q203;* direct, 198, *c200;* democratic republic, 356; representative, *q50*, 198, *c200;* 310, 327, 356
democratic republic, 356
Demosthenes, 231, *p231*, *q231*, 244, *q244*
Denis, Michel, *q680*
Denmark, 544, 611
depressions, 41
Descartes, René, 648–49
***Destruction of Magdeburg in 1631* (von Guericke),** *q611*
***Destruction of the Temple in Jerusalem, The* (Poussin),** *q359*
dharma, 259, 261
dhow, 429, *ptg429*
Diamond Sutra, 484
Dias, Bartholomeu, *c617*, 620
Diaspora, 160–61, *m161*
Dickens, Charles, 700, *ptg700*, 701
dictators, 314–15, 322, 323–24, 327, 587
Diderot, Denis, 654; encyclopedia of, 654
Diet of Worms, 601, *q601*
diocese, 384
Diocletian, emperor of Rome, *c339*, 352, *g355*, 382
diplomacy, 588
direct democracy, 198, *c200*
disciples, 374, 376–78, *ptg378*
***Discourse on Method* (Descartes),** 648
discoveries. *See* inventions.
Disraeli, Benjamin, 683
***Divine Comedy, The* (Alighieri),** 590
Djenné-jeno, 425
doctrine, 384
Domesday Book, 11–12, 13, 557
Dominican order, 566, 568
Dominican Republic, 621
***Don Quixote* (Cervantes),** 608
Dorians, 178, 185
drama, 500, 608, 610; Greek, 217–19, *p217*, 237; Japanese, 525, 526–27; Shakespearean, 595, 596–97, *p596*, *q596*, *q597;* Southeast Asian, 530, *p530*. *See also* actors; Noh; theater.
Dreiser, Theodore, 701
Du Fu, 487, *q487*
Dürer, Albrecht, 595
Dutch. *See* Netherlands.
dynasties, 190, 432; Abbasid, 407–08, *m408*, 412; Capetian, 558–59; Egyptian, 107, 120, 122, 123, 130; Indian, *c211*, 265, *m266*, 268, *m269*, *c304;* Korean, 513–15. *See also* Chinese dynasties.

E

***Early Factory Labor in New England* (Robinson),** *q700*
East China Sea, 279
Eastern desert, 102
Eastern Orthodox Church, 385, 386–89, 560, 562; icons in, 387, *p387*
Eastern Woodland peoples, *c449*, 467, *c581;* farming, 467; government and law, 467
***Ecclesiastical History of the English People* (Bede),** 555
economics, 26, 38–43, 47, 50, 571, 633–34, 642, 699; African, 634; American economy, *c27*, 40, 42–43, 689; barter, 42, 351, 554, *q638;* boom, 41; British economy, 695; business cycle, 41, *g41;* capital, 692–95; Chinese economy, 476, 477, 482–83, 485, 500; command economy, 40; cost of living, 41; depressions, 41; devaluation of money, 351, 553; Egyptian economy, 40, 106; entrepreneurs, 633, 693, 694–95; European economy, 630, 634, 695; free market, 39, 43; French economy, 673, 684; Great Depression, 41, 42; Greek economy, 188, 202; Indian economy, 254; inflation, 41, 351; investments, 694; Korean economy, 512; "laissez-faire," 699; market economy, 40; medieval European economy, 540, 541, 544, 564, 569, 571; mercantilism, 632–33, 668; mixed economy, 41; profits, 39, 351, 633; Roman economy, 320–22, 331, 351, *p351*, 352; Russian economy, 684; shares, 694; specialization, 66; stocks and stock market, *c27*, 633; Sumerian economy, 81; supply and demand, 39–40, *g39*, 42, 571; recession, *c27*, 41; traditional economy, 40; wages, 572
Edict of Milan, 382
Edict of Nantes, 610
Edison, Thomas, *p694*, 695
education, 697, 699; African, 435, 437–38, *q446;* Chinese, 295, 478; Egyptian, 119; Greek, 187–88, *ptg187*, 200, 208, *q208;* Indian, 256; Islamic, 412, 413–15, 435, 575, 589, 643; Jewish, 157; Korean, 514; medieval European , 546, 565, 579, 580, 589–91; Roman, 331, *c331*, 342, 350; universities, 565, 566, 644
Edward I, king of England, 558
Edward III, king of England, 574
Egypt: population density, *m37*
Egypt, ancient, *q16*, 40, 97–99, *c98–99*, *m99*, *m101*, 100–07, 108–19, 120–27, 233, 234, 235, 236, *m300*, *m392*, 398, 422, 424, 492; Alexandria, 210, *m210*, 233, 235, *ptg235*, *m242*, *q244*, 327, *m366*, 344; art and architecture, *q16*, *p16*, *c74*, 107, *p107*, *p109*, *ptg110*, *ptg111*, 113–15, *p113*, *c114*, *p115*, 117–18, *p117*, *ptg118*, 121, *p121*, *ptg121*, *p122*, *p123*, *p125*, *p126*, *ptg130*, *q136;* artifacts, *p16*, *q16*, *p97*, *p98*, 126, *p126;* astronomy, 114; calendar, 6, 114; cities, 107, 108, 119, 125; civil rights, 181; culture, 122, 123, 131; dynasties, 107, 120, 122, 123, 130; economy, 40, 106; education, 119; emergence of civilization, 68, *m68*, 74, 250, 278; empire of, 98, 120–27, 141; fall of, 126–27; families, 118–19; farming, *c53*, 64, 65, 100, 101, 104–05, *p104*, *ptg104*, 106, 109, 110, 113, 116, 117, 119, 120; geography, 98, 100, *m101*, 102, *p102*, *p103*, 107; gods and goddesses, 97, *p97*, 109–12, *p111*, 121, 125, 129, 131, *p131*, *q131*,

Index

132; government, 106–07, 108–09; Hyksos and, 121, 123; isolation of, 102; Israelites and, *c75, c138,* 157, *c277;* Kush and, *c99,* 100, 127, 128–32, *c210;* law, 108–09; life in, 116–19, *c116, p117, ptg118;* Lower Egypt, 107, *m134;* mathematics, *c74,* 104, 114–15; medicine, 112; Middle Kingdom, 98, 107, 120–21, *m124,* 130, *c246;* military, 120, 121, *ptg121,* 124, 126, 127, 129, 142; New Kingdom, 98, *c99, m99,* 107, 122–27, *m124;* Old Kingdom, *c98,* 107, 108; politics, 123, *m124;* population, 116; religion, 97, 98, 108–13, *ptg110, ptg111,* 118, 121, 126–27; roles of men and women, 118–19; slavery, 117, 118, 124, 142; social class, 116–18, *c116,* 125; tools, 104; trade, 102, 106, *m106,* 108, 116, 121, 122, 123, 126, 130, 178; tribute to, 120; unification of kingdoms, *c98,* 106–07, 108; Upper Egypt, 107, 114, *m134;* women, 117, *p117,* 118–19, 122–24; writing, 105, 123. *See also* mummies; Nile River valley.

Einhard, 543, *q543*

Einstein, Albert, 703; biography, 702; theory of relativity, 703

Eleanor of Aquitaine, 557

***Elements* (Euclid),** 240

El Greco, 369, 608

Elizabeth I, queen of England, 595, 605, 609

enclosure movement, 691

***Encyclopedia* (Diderot),** 654

England, *c538,* 545, 550, 556–558, 571, 574, 595, 596, 603–05, 609, *m612, c617,* 618, 620, 623, 628, 630, 631, 633, 640, 651, 664–71; Bill of Rights, 652; Calvinism, 605; citizens, 558; civil rights, 558, *q558;* colonies and settlers, 620, 623, 630, 664–71, *m665;* culture, 557; economy, 630; English Channel, 541, 609; Enlightenment in, 640, 650; exploration by, 623, 628; government, 558, 651; Great Council, 558; Hundred Years' War, 573, 574; law, 557–58, *q558;* life in ancient, 11-12, 13; literature and drama, 590, 596–97, *q596, q597;* military, 537, 609; Norman rule of, 556–57; Parliament, 558, 559, 604, 652–53, 667, 669, 682–84, *p683, q683,* 694; Petition of Right, 651; Puritans, 605; Reformation in, 603–05; religion, 630; Renaissance in, 595; ships, 609, *ptg609;* slavery, 630; trade, 630, 633; unites with Scotland to become the United Kingdom, 667; War of Roses, 574. *See also* Anglo-Saxons; Britain; Church of England.

Enlightenment, 639–41, *m640–41,* 650–57, 673, 674, 677, 698, 701; natural law, 650–52, 654; political thought, 650–53, *q652–53;* spread of ideas, 639, 640; use of reason, 650; women, 655

entrepreneurs, 693, 694–95

environment, the, 33, 60, 420, *q470;* human-environment interaction, 32, 33, 47, 60, 67, 415

ephors, 186

***Epic of Gilgamesh*,** 82–83, 84–85, *p84, ptg84, q84, q85*

epics, 83, 84–85, 215–16, 234, 269, 566–67, *q567*

Epicureanism, 238

Epicurus, 238

Erasmus, Desiderius, 599, *ptg599*

Eratosthenes, 239; scientific contributions, *c239*

Essenes, 163

Ethelbert, King of Kent, 391

Ethiopia, 9

Etruria, Italy, 308

Etruscans, 308–09; art, 308–09, *ptg309;* influence on Roman civilization, 308–09, 345; military, 309; religion, 309; trade, 309

Euclid, 239, 240, *ptg239;* plane geometry and, 240; scientific contributions, *c239*

Euphrates River, 74, *m75,* 76–78, 87, 91, *m94,* 103, 124

Euripides, 217–18

Europe, *c99,* 618–23, 624–27, 628–35, 639–41, 642–49, 650–57, 664–71, *m665,* 682–87, 696; economy, 630, 634, 695; farming, *c53,* 64, 65; government and politics, 557–58, 587–88, 610, 650–53, 655–57, 672–81, 682–84, 686–87, 695; military, *c99;* political revolutions, 661–63, *c662–63, m662–63,* 684, 686; religion, 610; science, 642–49; trade, 618–22, 628–35, *m632, m634;* world exploration and colonization, 618–23, 624–27, 628–35, 664–71, *m665. See also* Europe, medieval; *individual country listings.*

Europe, medieval, 386–91, 396, 409, 435, 521, 523, 537–39, *c538–39, m538–39,* 540–47, 548–55, 556–63, *m559,* 564–69, 570–75, *m573,* 578, 582–88, 589–97, 598–605, 606–11, 615–17, *c616–17, m616–17;* architecture, 415, 564–65, *p565,* 585–86, 590; art, 579, 580, 583, *p584,* 584, 587, 590, 591–95, *ptg592, ptg593, p594, ptg594,* 608, 610; castle, *d550;* central, 602; Christianity in, 386–91; cities and towns, 553–55, 619; citizens, 554; culture, 557, 564–69; disease in, 364, *c539,* 569, 570–72, *m571;* Eastern, 361, 560–61, 569, 571; economy, 540, 541, 544, 564, 569, 571; education and scholarship, 546, 565, 579, 580, 589–91; farming, 546, 567, 570; geography, *m538–39,* 540–41, *m541,* 553, *m583,* 585; government, 543, 547, 554, 558, 563, 564, 566, 587–88, 610, 619; invasions of, 544, *m545,* 546, 548; iron-making, *c173;* kingdoms of, 542–47, *m559,* 571, 619; language, 566; law, 548, 553, 554, 557–58, *q558,* 565; literature, poetry, and drama, 566–67, *q567,* 584, 590–91, 593, *q593,* 596–97, *q596, q597,* 607, 608, 610; medicine, 565; military, 537, 548, 573, 574, 584, 588, 609, 610; philosophy, 565–66; politics, 546–47, 574, 602; population, 553; religion, 405–07, 415, 537, 538, *c538,* 540, 542, 546–47, 549, 552, 562–63, 564–69, 572–75, 580, *c581,* 582, 584, 598–602, 603–05, 606–11, *m608;* religious wars, 609–11; rivers, 540–41, 553; Roman influence in, 542; science, 565, 643–44; ships, 540–41, 553, 584, 586, 587, *p587,* 609, *ptg609, c617;* slavery, *c617;* Spanish Inquisition, 568–69, 575, 607–08; trade, 540, 553–54, *ptg554,* 555, 564, 570–71, 575, 584–86, 587, 588; universities, 565, 566, 643; Western, 542–47, 548–55, 556–59, 561–63, 564–69, 570–75. *See also* Black Death; Crusades; feudalism; guilds; Reformation; Renaissance; *individual country listings.*

Evans, Arthur, 176

excommunication, 389, 547, 569, 601, 604

exile, 153; Jewish exile from Judah, 153, *q153,* 154, 159, 160, 190

Exodus, 142, 159

exploration, *c26,* 28, 37, 297, *c473, c539,* 544, 615–17, *c616–17, m616–17,* 618–23, *m620,* 624–27, *m625,* 628, 629–30, 635, 642, 643–44; age of, 618–23; Chinese, 500–02, *m501;* conquistadors, 622, 624–27, *m625;* of Africa, 620, *m620,* 621; of Mexico, 623, 624–26; quest for gold, 624, 626, 627, *ptg627,* 632, *q638;* search for sea route to Asia, 618–23, *m620;* smallpox and other diseases, 625, 626, 629, 635; spread of Christianity during, 628–29, *q638;* technology and, 619, *p619*

Ezana, king of Axum, 429

Ezra, 155

F

fables, 216–17; Aesop's, 216–17

factories, 692, 693–94, *q694,* 695, 696–97, 700, *q700;* working conditions in, 697, *p706*

families, 64, 80, 87; African, 436–37; Chinese, *c290,* 291, 296; Egyptian, 118–19; Greek, 186; Indian, 256; in hunter-gatherer societies, 56, Japanese, 521, 524; Jewish, 157–58, *p157;* Roman, 342; working-class, 697

famine, 569, 570

farming, 39, 40, 42–43, 52, *c53,* 56, 62–67, *m63,* 69, *m70, q72,* 144, 230, 306, 412, 642, 686; African, 64, 419, 422, 423, 424, 426, 436, 437; Aryan, 254; Assyrian, 89; Athenian, 188, 200, 201, 202; Chinese, *c53,* 64, 65, 276, 278–80, *p280,* 282, 283, 285, 289–90, *c290,* 291, 293, 295, 296, 299, 475, 476, *ptg477,* 482, 484, 500, *ptg500,* 503; early humans and, 52, *c53,* 62–67, *m63, m70, q72,* 448, 454–58, 460, 461, 467, 642; Egyptian, *c53,* 64, 65, 100, 101, 104–05, *p104, ptg104,* 106, 109, 110, 113, 116, 117, 119, 120; European, *c53,* 64, 65, 308, 546, 567, 570, 676, 691–92; Greek, 174–75, 177, 178, 179, 181, 183, 205, 308; in ancient Israel, 147, 150; Indian, 64, 65, 248, 250, 252; in Kush, 128, 132; in the

Americas, 64, 65, 448, 454–58, 460, 461, 467, 666; Japanese, 516–17, 519, 523–524; Korean, *c74,* 495, *m504,* 510, 512; Mesopotamian, 77–81, *p77, p79,* 87, 103; Roman, 320–21, *p321,* 322, 331, 333; Southeast Asian, 500, 528–29; spread of, 64; Sumerian, 79–81, *ptg79;* tenant farmers, 295. *See also* agriculture.

Ferdinand and Isabella of Spain, 575, 604, 607–08, *p607,* 609, 621

Fertile Crescent, 74, *m75,* 77

feudalism, 523, 548–55, *c549, c550,* 557, 558, 559, 563, 572; castles, 548, 550, 551, *c550;* civil rights, 551, 554; farming, 551–53, *p551, c552;* freemen, 551, 552, ; in Japan, 523, 549, 633; knights and military action, 549–50, *c549,* 551, 556–58, *ptg557,* 566, *q578;* manors, 551–53, *c552;* nobles, 519, 521, 523, 526, 527, 548–51, *c549,* 553, 554, 557–65, 564, 567, 574; politics and government, 548, 554; religion, 549, *c552,* 552; serfs and peasants, *c549,* 551–53, *c551, p552,* 553, 557, 559, 563, 572; vassals, 548–49, *c549,* 554, 558, *q567,* 578, *q578;* women, 550, 552, 555

fief, 549, 550, 551

Fifteenth Amendment, *c27*

filial piety, 291, 296

First Continental Congress, 669

Five Pillars of Islam, 403, 407

Flanders, 553, 586

floods, 77, 103–04, 113, 128, *m134,* 278–79, 280

Florence, 579, 583, 585–86, 587, 588, 590, 592, 593, 610, *m612;* art and architecture, 585, 592; banking, 586; cathedral, 585–86; cloth industry, 586; importance during the Renaissance, 586; trade, 585–86. *See also* Medici family.

Florida, *m665, m687*

Forum, the, *p5,* 315, 340, 352

fossils, 9, *p9,* 51, *p51,* 424, 591; Lucy, 9, *p9*

***Four Horsemen of the Apocalypse* (Dürer),** 595

Four Noble Truths, 261

France, 537, *c539,* 542, 544, 553, 559, 567, *m571,* 573, 574, 586, 596, 610, 611, 618, 620, 628, 629–30, 633, *m640,* 670, 672–81, 684, 695; art, 59, *p59,* 610, 661, *ptg661,* 701–02; becomes a republic, 674–75, 684; civil war, 684; colonies and settlers, 623, 629–30, 663, 667, 670; constitution, 674, 676; Directory, 676; early humans, 59, *p59;* economy, 673, 684; Enlightenment in, 640, 652–55, 673, 674, 677; Estates-General, 559, 673; exploration by, 623, 628, 629–30; farming, 676; Franco-Prussian War, *m685;* government and politics, 610, 672–81, *q674,* 684; Huguenots, 610; Hundred Years' War, 573, *m573,* 574; Jacobin club, 675; literature, 701; military, 672, 676–79, 684; monarchy, 559, 655–56, 672–74; Napoleonic Code, 677; National Convention, 674–76; philosophes, 653–55, *ptg654;* Reign of Terror, 675–76; slavery, 630; theater, 610; trade, 553–54, 633; War of Roses, 574. *See also* Europe, medieval; French Revolution.

Franciscan order, *c539,* 568

Francis of Assisi, *c539,* 568, 592

Franco-Prussian War, *m685*

Franks, 388, 542–43, 544, 559; government, 542; kingdoms of, 544, 545

Frederick I, emperor of Holy Roman Empire, 546

Frederick II, emperor of Holy Roman Empire, 546

Frederick the Great, king of Prussia, 656

French and Indian War, *c641*

French Empire, 677–79, *m678, m704*

French Revolution, 661, *c663,* 672–74, 677, 680–81, *ptg680, ptg681,* 698; Declaration of the Rights of Man, 674; guillotine, 675, *p676;* National Assembly, 673–74; three estates, 672–74, *g673, q680*

fresco, 309, *ptg309,* 592, 593, 594

friars, 566, 568

Froissart, Jean, 574, *q574*

Fulton, Robert, 693, 695

Gabirol, Solomon ben, 406

Galen, 344, 647; influence on European doctors, 647

Galilee, *c338,* 372, 374, 377, 378

Galileo (Galilei), *c640,* 646, *c647,* 703; biography, 646, *p646;* designs pendulum clock, 646; designs telescope, 646, *p646;* invents thermometer, 646

Gandhi, Mohandas K., 264, *p264*

Ganges River, 248, 254, 259, *p259, m272*

Gansser, August, *q58*

Gaozong, emperor of China, 471, 476

Garibaldi, Giuseppe, 685

Gaul, 318, 323, 333, 354

Gentileschi, Artemisia, 594

geography, 26, 28–37, 42, 415, 619; African, 419, 420, *p420, m421,* 422–25, *m423, p423, c424;* Arabian, 398–400, *m399,* 619; Assyria, 87, 88, 89; Byzantine, 360-61, 364; China, 278–80, *m279, p280,* 472, *m472–73,* 475, 476, 482, *m504;* Egypt, 98, 100, *m101,* 102, *p102, p103,* 107; Equator, 29–30, 31; European, *m538–39,* 540–41, *m541,* 553, *m583,* 585; Greece, 174–76, *m175,* 180, *m334, m366; Guide to Geography, c26;* hemispheres of Earth, 29, *p29;* India, 248–50, *m249;* influence of on settlement patterns and development, 33, 56, 60, 62, 76, 420, 422, 529, 540–41, 692; Italy, 306–07; Japanese, 516, *m517;* Korean, 510, *m511;* Kush, 128; latitude and longitude, 30, *p30,* 36; Mesopotamia, 74, *m74–75,* 76–77; of the Americas, 448, *p448,* 450–52, *m451, p452,* 454, 455–56; Persia, 190–91, *m191;* physical systems, 32; Prime Meridian, 29–30, Roman Empire, 338, *m338–39, m346,* 353–54; Rome, 306–07; Southeast Asia, 528–29, *m529;* Sumer, 78–79; using charts, graphs, and diagrams, 35–36; *See also* environment, the; glaciers; hurricanes; maps; volcanoes.

geometry, 239–40, *c239,* 565; plane geometry, 240; solid geometry, 240

George III, king of England, 669, 670

Germanic kingdoms, 347, 351–52, 353–56, *m354,* 391, 540, 542, 545; mercenaries, 351–52. *See also* Franks.

Germany, 542, 544–45, 547, 568, 571, *c581,* 594, 600–02, 640, 685, *m685,* 687, 695, 701, 702; demands for self-rule, 684; Enlightenment in, 640; government, 547, 686; literature, 701; Lutheranism, 601–02; nationalism in, 686; revolt of the peasants, 601; Thirty Years' War, 611, *ptg611;. See also* Europe, medieval.

Ghana, *c421,* 426–27, *q427, c428,* 430–31, 432, *m444;* farming, 426; government, 430–31; military, 427; trade, *c421,* 426–27, *c428*

Gilgamesh: A Verse Narrative. *See Epic of Gilgamesh.*

Giotto, 592

Giza, Egypt, 113, 115, *m134, c276*

glaciers, 32, 60; in the Ice Ages, 60, 453, *m453*

gladiators, 341, 343

Gladstone, William, 683, 684

globalization, 43, 47; global citizens, 47

Gobi, 279, 293, 490, 492; nomads of, 293

God, 140–44, 146–47, 148, 152, 153, 154–59, *q156,* 162, 163, 164, *q166, q229,* 337, 372, 374, *c375,* 379, 382, 386–87, 389, 401–03, 407, 565–66, *q567,* 569, 572, 600, 601, *q601,* 603, 654, 655, *q666; The City of God* (Augustine), 385

gods and goddesses, 129, 140, 144, 157, 517; African, 432; Arabian, 400, 401; Chinese, 282, 284, *q480,* 496; Egyptian, 97, *p97,* 109–12, *p111,* 121, 125, 129, 131, *p131, q131,* 132; Greek, 161, 162, 171, *p171,* 188, 189, 192, 212–14, *c218,* 237, 343; in India, 245, *p245,* 246, 258, 259, 268, 269–70, *p270;* in the Americas, 455, 460, *p460,* 461, 625; Mesopotamian, 79–80, 82, 84, 87, 88, 91, 92; of early humans, 66, 69; Roman, 303, 307, 312, 342, 343, 345, *q349,* 381; Sumerian, 79–80, 82, 87. *See also* Buddha, the; God.

Goethe, Johann von, 701

Gojoseon, 510

Gonzaga family, 584, *ptg584*

Good Samaritan, parable of, 375, *ptg376*

gospel, 384–85

Goubert, Pierre, *q680*

government, 40, 41, 44–46, 68, 356, 529; absolutism, 651; African, 430–32, 442, 443; Assyrian, 88; branches of, 652–53; Byzantine, 361, 362; censors, 293; centralized (federal), 40, 44, 430, 431, 476, 519, 523, 543, 548, 563, 610; Chaldean, 92; Chinese, 282, 283–84, 287, 291, 292–93, 294–95, 299, 471–78, 480–81, 498–500, 503, 512, 513, 531; democracy, *q50,* 143, 184, 189, 198–99, *c200, q203,* 224, 310, 327, 356; early civilizations and, 68, 76, 80, 92, 458, 460, 467; Egyptian, 106–07, 108–09; European, 558–59, 610, 650–53, 655–57, 672–81, 682–84, 685–86, 695; federations, 467; German, 547, 686; Greek, 176–77, 183–184, 186, 188–89, 198–99, *ptg199, c200,* 203, 235; Indian, 265; in the American colonies, 667–71, *q667;* Islamic, 402; Italian, 587–88, 685–86; Japanese, 518–19, 520, 522, 523, 525; Korean, 478, 512, 513; limited powers of, 558, 699; Mayflower Compact, 666, *q666;* monarchy, 68, 80, 224, 559, 651–52, 655–57, 658–59, 672–74, 685–87; of city-states, 79, 80; of ancient Israel, 151; of medieval Europe, 543, 547, 554, 558, 563, 564, 566, 587–88, 610; oligarchy, 184, 186, 224; Persian, 191, 197; representative, 44, 667, 670, 682–83, 700; representative democracy, *q50,* 198, *c200;* 310, 327, 356; republics, 310, 327, 356, 587, 675, 684; role in economics, 40, 41; Roman, 310–11, 312–16, *p313,* 320–22, 324–25, 327, 329, 350–55, *q355,* 356; Russian, 657, 686; separation of powers, 652, *q652–53;* social contracts, 652, 655; Sumerian, 80, 82; theocracy, 108–09, 192–93; United States, 43, 44–46, *q45,* 199, *c200,* 313; Vietnamese, 531. *See also* constitutions; law; politics.

Gozzoli, Benozzo, 579

Gracchus, Gaius and Tiberius, 321–22, *ptg322*

Grand Canal, *c472,* 475, *m475, m477,* 500, *c508*

Granicus, battle of, 232

Great Britain. *See* Britain; England.

Great Depression, 41, 43

***Great Expectations* (Dickens),** 700

Great Plains, 452, 635

Great Pyramid, *c98,* 115, *c138, c276*

Great Rift Valley, 424, *p425*

Great Wall of China, 293, 475, 503, *m504*

Greece, ancient, 8, 171–73, *c172–73, m173,* 174–82, 183–89, 190–97, 198–205, 209–11, *c210–11,* 212–19, 220–29, 230–35, 236–41, *m242, m334,* 343–46, *m366, m392,* 399, alphabet, 178–79, *c178,* 308; art and architecture, 171, *p171,* 172, *p172,* 176, *p176,* 177, *p177, ptg181, p186,* 189, *p189, c201,* 218, *c218,* 219, 236–37, *p237,* 241, 344, *p344,* 345; astronomy, 177, 223, 226, 238–40, *p238, c239,* 344, 643, *c645;* citizens and citizenship, *c173,* 181–82, 183, 184,185, 186, 188, 189, 192, 193, 198–200, *c200,* 203, 228, *q229;* city-states, 172, 180–82, 183–89, 194–97, 202–05, 212–14, 218, 219, 222, 223, 230–32, 241, 548, 584; civilization, 209–241; civil rights, 181–82; classical, *see* Golden Age of; colonies, 172, *c172,* 179, 193, 202, 204; culture, 171, 178–79, 212–19, 306, 361, 582; Dark Age of, 178–79, 180; drama, 217–19, *p217,* 237; farming, 174–75, 177, 178, 179, 180, 183, 205, 308; geography, 174–76, *m175,* 180, *m366;* gods and goddesses, 161, 162, 171, *p171,* 188, 189, 192, 212–14, *c218,* 237, 343; Golden Age of, 217, 220, 237; history, 225–26; influence in the modern world, 171, 209, 215, *c224,* 226, 237, 239, 240, 344, *p345;* iron-making,178; language, 160, 171, 212, 234, 235, 377, 380, 385; law, 181; literature, 215–17, 234, 237, 345–47, 348, 390, 413, 546, 582, 589; mathematics, 220, 221, 226, 238–40, *c239,* 345; medicine, 226–27, 344, *p345,* 647; military, *c173,* 181, 182, *ptg182,* 184, 192, 194–97; mythology, 171, 176, 212–14, *c213;* philosophy, 209, 220–23, 238, 240, *q240,* 344, 406, 413; Persia and, *c173,* 190–97, *c211,* 230, 231–34, *c304;* politics, 180–81, 183–84, 205; religion, 171, *p171,* 180, 188, 192, 212–14, 218, 219, 343; Roman Empire and, 171, 241, 319; science, 223, 226, 238–40, *p238, c239,* 306, 344, 592, 642–43, *c645,* 647; slavery, 177, 179, 183, 185, 188, 189, 200, 201, 343; spread of culture by Alexander the Great, 160–61, 197, 209, 210, 234–35; storytelling, 178, 218; trade, 174, 176, 177, 178, 179, *m180,* 183, 187, 188, 202; tyrants, 183–84; women, 181, 222; writing, 178. *See also* Athens; Greece, modern; Minoans; Mycenaeans; Sparta.

Gregorian calendar, 6–7

Gregory I, Pope, 355, *q355–56,* 391, *p391,* 394, *q394,* 546

Gregory VII, Pope, *ptg546,* 547

Gregory XIII, Pope, 6, *p6;* Gregorian calendar, 6–7, 325

griots, 427, 438, 439, *p439*

Guangzhou, China, 293, *m504*

guerrilla warfare, 162

***Guide to Geography* (Ptolemy),** *c26*

guilds, 524, 555, 634

gunpowder, 485, 492

Gupta Empire, 246, *c247,* 268, 269–71, *m269, c339, c371;* Gupta dynasty, 268, *m269;* Hinduism and, 268; trade, 268

Gupta, Samudra, *c247,* 268

guru, 256

Gutenberg, Johannes, *c580,* 591

H

Hadrian, emperor of Rome, 331, *c331,* 332

Hagia Sophia, 337, 363, *p363*

Haiti, 621, *c663*

Hammurabi, king of Babylon, *c74,* 87, *c172;* code of, 87, *p88, c246*

Han dynasty, *c277, m294,* 294–297, 299, 474–75, 478, 480, 482, 484, 500; art, 295; civil service, 294–96; culture, 295–96; fall of, 299; government, 294–95; Han Wudi, 294–95, 297, 299; inventions, 296, 297; papermaking, 296, *p296;* trade, 296, 297–98, *m298*

Hanfeizi, *c288,* 289; legalism and, *c288,* 289

Hanging Gardens of Babylon, 90–91, *p91, ptg91;* as one of the Seven Wonders of the Ancient World, 91

hangul, 514, 515

Hangzhou, China, 477, *m477, m504*

Hannibal, 318–19, *ptg318*

Hanukkah, 162

Han Wudi, emperor of China, 294–95, 297, 299

Han Yü, 480, *q480*

Hapi, 110

Hapsburgs, 656–57; reforms of, 656–57

Harappa, *c7, c246,* 251, 252, *m272;* architecture, 251–52; artifacts, 252, *p252*

Hargreaves, James, 692

Harvey, William, 647, *c647*

Hastings, Battle of, 556, 557, *ptg557*

Hatshepsut, queen of Egypt, *c99,* 122–24, *p123, c172;* biography, 123; tomb of, 122, *p122*

Hebrew Bible, 141–44, 146–47, *q146,* 148–50, 153, *q153,* 155–56, *q156,* 157, *q158,* 161, 166, 377, 379. *See also* Torah.

Hebrews, ancient, calendar, 6–7. *See also* Israelites, ancient.

Heian-kyo (Kyoto), 520, 522, 524, 526

Heike Monogatori, *q521*

Helena, 382

Hellenistic Era, 234–35, *m234,* 236–41. *See also* Greece, ancient.

Hellenistic kingdoms, 235, 236, 240, 241; governments of, 235

helots, 185, 186

Henry II, king of England, 557–58; court and laws of, 557–58

Henry II, king of France, 610

Henry IV, emperor of Holy Roman Empire, 547; excommunication of, 547

Henry IV, king of France (Henry of Navarre), *c581,* 610; brings religious tolerance to France, *c581;* conversion to Catholicism, 610; Edict of Nantes, 610

***Henry V* (Shakespeare),** 596–97, *q596, q597*

Henry VII, king of England, 574

Henry VIII, king of England, 604–05, *p604*

Henry, Patrick, 669

Henry, prince of Portugal (Henry the Navigator), 620
heresy, 384, 569, 574, 607, 646
Herod, king of Judaea, 162, 163
Herodotus, 195, *q195, c211,* 225, *p225,* 347
hieroglyphics, *c98,* 105, 129, 455, 461
Hildegard of Bingen, 568, *ptg568*
Himalaya, 246, 248–49, *m249,* 260, *m272,* 279, *m300,* 476
Hinduism, *c173,* 245, 267, 268, 410, 494, 532, 533; art and architecture, 270, *p270;* Aryans and, *c7,* 246, *c247,* 257; caste system and, 246; epics, 269; in India, 245, *p245, c247,* 257–59, 260, 267, 268, 410, 529, 530, 531; reincarnation, 258–59, *q258*
Hipparchus: scientific contributions, *c239*
Hippocrates, 227; "Father of Medicine," 227, *c239;* scientific contributions, *c239*
Hippocratic Oath, 227
Hippodrome, 361
Hispaniola, 621, 622, 624
historians, 1–3, *p3,* 4–9, 10–17, 18–21, *q24,* 36–37, 41, 54, 59, 63, 77, 79, 88, 163–64, 176, 178, 216, 252, 276, 295, *p295,* 336, 385, 419, 447, 453, 456, 458, 461, 510, 690; Arabic, 414–15; Christian, 385; English, 550; Greek, 92, 203, 224–25, *p225,* 347; Roman, 307–08, 318, *q319,* 336, 346–47
***History of Rome* (Livy),** *q308,* 347
***History of the Peloponnesian War* (Thucydides),** 225, *q226*
Hittites, 88, 123, 126, 136, *q136;* iron-making, 88
Hobbes, Thomas, 650–51
hogans, 448, *p448,* 467
Hohokam civilization, 457; farming, 457
Holy Roman Empire, 545, 573, 602, 604, *m602,* 611, *m612*
Homer, *c210,* 215–16, *q216,* 234, 346, 348
Honduras, 626
Hooke, Robert, *c647,* 648; discovery of cells, 648
hoplites, 182, 184
Horace, 347, 357
House of Wisdom, 413
Huang He (Yellow River), 278–79, 280, 292, 475, *m504;* "China's Sorrow," 279; floods, 278–79, 280
Huang He Valley, 276, 278–81
Hudson, Henry, 631
Huguenots, 610, *ptg610*
humanism, 589–91, 592, 594, 598, 599, 603; Christian humanism, 598; spread of, 594
human rights, 47, 443, 566
humans, early, 9, 51–53, *c52–53, m52–53,* 54–61, 62–69, *m68,* 422, 453–58, 459–67; art and adaptations to the environment, 56–57, 60–61, 67, 465, 467; Agricultural Revolution, 62–69, *m70;* archaeology and, 9, 51, 454, 457, 457, 458, 459, *q470;* artifacts, 9, *p9, p13, p51, p56,* 58–59, *p58, p59,* 66, *p67,* 69, *p72, c74,* 276, 453, *p458,* 457; development of spoken language, 58–59; discovery and use of fire, 57, 60, 61, *ptg61;* economic specialization, 66; emergence of civilizations, *c53,* 68–69, *m68,* 76–83, 422, 454–58, 459–67; farming, 52, *c53,* 62–67, *m63, m70, q72,* 422, 448, 454–58, 460, 461, 467; gods and goddesses, 66, 69; homes, 61, *ptg61,* 64, 65–66, 67, *ptg64,* 454–58, 466–67; in Africa, 51, 422, 424; invention of and use of writing, 69, 293, 461, *q470;* metalworking, 67; migration, 51, 60, *m60;* nomadic life, 54, 62, 453, 454; religion, 66, 69, 448, 455; roles of men and women, 55–56, 67; settlements, *m52–53,* 422, *c449, p457,* 458, *p458,* 459–60; 465–67; technology, 52, 56, 60, 67; tools and weapons, 52, 54, *ptg55,* 55, *p56,* 56, 57, 60, 67, 453; trade, 66, 68, 448, 454–55, 456, 466. *See also* Bronze Age; hunter-gatherers; Ice Ages; Mesolithic Age, Neolithic Age; Paleolithic Age; Stone Ages.
Hundred Years' War, 573, *m573,* 574
Hungary: demands for self-rule, 684; becomes a separate kingdom from Austria, 684
Huns, 353
hunter-gatherers, 40, *p40,* 54–61, *ptg55, p58, p59, m60,ptg61,* 62, 63, 100, 422, 453–54, 458, 467, artifacts, 9, *p9, p13, p51, p56,* 58–59, *p58, p59,* 66, *p67,* 68, *p72, c74,* 276, 453, *p458,* 457; art, 58–59, *p58, p59;* discovery and use of fire, 57, 60, 61, *ptg61;* language, 58; migration, 60, *m60;* nomadic life, 54, 62, 453, 454; roles of men and women, 55–56; technology, 56, 60; tools and weapons, 54, 55, *ptg55,* 56, *p56,* 57, 61. *See also* humans, early; Mound Builders.
hurricanes, 32
Hus, Jan, 573
Hyksos, 121, 123
Hypatia, 240, *q240;* scientific contributions, *c239*

I

Ibn Battuta, *c421,* 433–34, *q434,* 446, *q446*
Ibn Fadl Allah al-'Umari, 431
Ibn Khaldun, 415
Ibn Rushd, 405–06
Ibn Sina, 414
Ibsen, Henrik, 701
Ice Ages, *c52–53,* 60–61, *m60, ptg61,* 62, *q72,* 453–54; homes, 61, *ptg61;* migration after, 453, *m453;* technology, 60; tools and weapons, 60; use of fire, 60, 61, *ptg61*
Iceman (Ötzi), 66, *p66,* 67; biography, 66
iconoclast, 387
icons, 387, *ptg387*
ideographs, 282–83, *p283*
Idia, 419
***Iliad* (Homer),** *c210,* 215–16, *q216*
Imhotep, 114
immigration. *See* migration.
Immortals, 192
impressionism, *ptg701,* 702
Inca, *m449,* 462–65, *m468, q470, c581, c617,* 626–27; cities, *q470;* Cuzco, *q470;* gods, 627; myths, *q470;* Pizarro and, *c617,* 626–27; roles of men and women, *q470*. *See* Machu Picchu.
India, *c7, c211,* 233, 235, 245–47, *c246–47, m247,* 248–56, *m249,* 257–64, 265–71, 295, *m300,* 396, 501, 502, 508, 528, *c539,* 571, 620, *m620, m632,* 633; art and architecture, *p246,* 270, 415, *p415;* Aryans and, *c7,* 37, 246, *c247,* 252–54, 257; astronomy, 271; Britain and, 264, *c663;* Buddhism, *c139,* 246, *c247,* 260–62, 266–67, *c277, c338, c370, q479,* 507, 525, 530, 531, 532; caste system, *c173,* 246, 255–56, *c255, p255;* civil rights, 256; culture, 245, 254–56, 264, 269–71, 532–33; dynasties, *c211,* 265, *m266,* 268, *m269, c304;* early, 248–56; economy, 254; education, 256; emergence of civilization, 68, *m68,* 76, *c98,* 246, 278; family, 256; farming, 64, 65, 248, 250, 252; geography, 248–50, *m249;* gods and goddesses, 245, *p245,* 246, 258, 259, 268, 269–70, *p270;* government, 265; Gupta Empire, 246, *c247,* 268, 269–71, *m269, c339;* Hinduism, 245, *p245, c247,* 257–59, 267, 268, 410, 529, 530, 531; independence from Britain, 264; invasion by Alexander the Great, 233, 265; Jainism, 263–64, 274; literature, 245, 269–70; mathematics, 270–71; Mauryan Empire, *c7,* 246, *c247,* 265–68, 269, *m266;* medicine, 271; Mogul Empire, 409, 410, 415, *c640;* politics, 264; roles of men and women, 256; science, 271; subcontinent of, 248, *m249, m253;* Taj Mahal, 415, *p415;* trade, 248, 252, 267, 268, 296, 297, 530, 571, *m632,* 633; varnas, 255–56, *c255, p255,* 259, 261
Indian Ocean, *m300,* 429, *m444,* 533, 619, 623, *m620;* trading ports, 429
Indians. *See* Native Americans; *see also individual Native American Nations*.
Indonesia, 406, 533, *m534,* 633
indulgences, 598, 600, *ptg601,* 606, *q614*
Indus River, *c74,* 248, 250, 252, *m272;* settlements on, *c74,* 250
Indus River valley, 246, 265; civilization of, 250–52, 253; spread of culture, 252, 253. *See also* India.
industrialism, 696–700; changes in political ideas due to, 698–700; growth of middle class and working class due to, 696–97
Industrial Revolution, 690–95, *m691;* entrepreneurs, 693, 694; factories, 692, 693–94, *q694,* 695; farming, 690–91; inventions, 692–95, *p692, p693, p694;* railroads, 693, *p693,* 695; science, 695; spread of ideas, 695; steam power, 692–93; textile industry, 585–86, 634,

Index

690; women and children in, 692; working conditions, *p706*
industry, 690–95, 696–700; airplane, 695; banking, 411, 554, 564, *c581,* 584, 586, 587; cloth and textiles, 585–86, 634, 690, *p706;* coal, 483–84, 692, 693, 695; cottage, 634, 690; growth of, 696–97; Industrial Age, 696; silk weaving and manufacturing, *c74,* 283, 290, 296, 483, *p483,* 500. *See also* Industrial Revolution.
Intolerable Acts, 669
Inuit, 465, *m466*
inventions: algebra, 414; anesthesia, 703; automobile, 4; barometer, 646; calculating machine, 649; cannon, 492; cart, 83; chariot, 83; chemistry, 413; Chinese, *c26,* 285, 296, 297, *c449,* 484–85, 486, 492, 591; chronometer (sailing), *c27;* compass, *c473,* 485, 619; concrete, 345, 357; discovery of bacteria, 648, 703; discovery of cells, 648; discovery of coal and steel, 483–84; discovery of copper and bronze, 67, 83; discovery of fire, 57, 60, 61, *ptg61;* discovery of gases, 648; drill bits, 296; during the Industrial Revolution, 692–95, *p693, p694;* GPS navigation system, *c27;* gun, 492; gunpowder, 485; horse collar, 552–53; Korean, 514–15; light bulb, 694–95, *p694*; loom, 692; map projection, *c26;* microscope, *p648;* movable type, *c449,* 484, 512, *c580,* 591; number symbols, 270–71; of Archimedes, 240; of Galileo, 646; of Leonardo da Vinci, 592, *p592;* paper and paper currency, *c26,* 296, 484–85, 591; pendulum clock, 646; plow, 83, 296, 552; potter's wheel, 83; printing press, 484, *p484, ptg591,* 591, 594, 619; rainfall measures, 514; rudder, 296; saddle and stirrup, 285; sailboat, 83; steel, 484; spinning jenny, 692; steam engine, 692, *p693,* 693; Sumerian, *c74,* 82–83; sundial, 92; telephone, *c663;* telescope, 646, 648; thermometer, 646; waterwheel, 296; wheel, 4, 83; wheelbarrow, 296; writing, 5, 8, 69, 74, 81 82, 104, 123, 254, 455, 461; zero, 270, 461. *See also* technology.
Ionian Sea, *m206*
Iran, 407
Iraq, 76, 87, 407
Ireland, 391, 542, 546, 557, 683–84; Christianity in, 391, 546, 683–84; demands for self-rule, 684; English Channel, 541; famine, 684
iron, 88, 131–32, 145, *c173,* 178, 510, 515, 692, 693, 695; in Africa, *c173,* 425, 427, 437, 440; in shipbuilding, 515; mixed with coal to make steel, 483–84, 692
Iroquois Confederacy, *c449,* 467, *c581;* constitution, 467
Isaac, 142, 150
Isabella, queen of Spain, 615. *See also* Ferdinand and Isabella of Spain.
Isis, 110, *ptg111*
Islam, 138, 141, 153, 257, 398, 401–403, *q401,* 409, 415, 420, 433–35, *q446, c472,* 492, 528, 533; beliefs and practices of, 403, 415, 434; First Four Caliphs, *c406;* Five Pillars of Islam, 403, 407; Hijrah, 402; in Africa, 420, 425, 427, 429, 433–35, *q434;* in Spain, 405–06, 407, *p407,* 415, *c539,* 542, 572, 575, 607–08, 621; spread of, 404–10, *m405,* 411, 425, 427, 428, 432–35, 533, 542; Shia, 407, 410; Sufis, 406; sunna, 403; Sunni, 407, 410. *See also* Allah; Islamic civilization; Muhammad; Muslims; Quran.
Islamic civilization, 395–97, *m396–397,* 398–403, 404–410, 411–15, *q418,* 563, 571, 575, 618, 633; Abbasid dynasty, 407–08, *m408,* 413; architecture, 407, *p407,* 409, *p409,* 415, *p415, p434,* 435; art and artifacts, 395, 415; bedouin, 399–400, *p400;* cities, 412, 415; education and scholarship, 412, 413–15, 435, 575, 589, 643; farming, 412; geographers, 619; gods and goddesses, 400, 401; government, 402; historians, 414–15; law (shari'ah), 402, 403, 434, 435; life in, 411–13; literature and poetry, 400, *q400,* 414, *q414;* mathematics, 413–14, 643; medicine, 406, 413, 414; military, 402, 404–05, *q418,* 542; minarets, 415; Mogul Empire, 409, 410, 415; Muslim calendar, 402; philosophy, 405–06; religious tolerance, 405, 406; roles of men and women, 412–13; Ottoman Empire, 363, 395, *c397,* 409–10; Safavid Empire, 409, 410; science, 413, 643; Seljuk Turks, 408–09; ships, 411, 429, 619; slavery, 411, 412, 438–39; social classes, 412–13; trade, 400, 401, 406–07, 411–12, 413, 429, 433, 533; tribes, 399–400, 401, 402; Umayyads, *c396,* 404–05, *c406,* 407. *See also* Arab Empire; Arab–Israeli conflict; Arabia; Islam.
Israel, 151; fall of ancient, 151; kingdom of ancient, 151–52, *m151,* 372; *See also* Arab-Israeli conflict; Israelites, ancient.
Israelites, ancient, 137–39, *c138–39, m138–39,* 140–47, 149–53, *m151,* 399; alphabet, 148; culture, 148; calendar, 148; division of the kingdom, 150–51, in Egypt, *c75, c138,* 142, 159, *c277;* farming, 147, 150; government, 151; kingdom of Israel, 151–52, *m151,* 372; laws, 155; role of kings, 148–50, 152; military, 146–47, 148–49; slavery, 142; tabernacle, 147, *p147;* trade, 141, 150. *See also* Jews; Judah; Judaism.
Issus, battle of, 233
Istanbul, 337, 353, *p353,* 409. *See also* Constantinople.
Italian Papal States, 542–43, *m612*
Italy, *m334,* 365, 387–88, *m392,* 540, 542, 545, 546, 553, 571, 579, 580, 582–88, *m583,* 602, 635, 676–77, *m685,* 685–86; architecture, 585, 590; art, 579, 580, 583, *p584,* 584, 587, 590, 591–95, *ptg592, ptg593, p594, ptg595;* Austria and, 686; banking, 584, 586, 587; cities and city-states, 579, 580, 584–88, *m583;* citizenship, 587; demands for self-rule, 685; diplomacy, 588; education and scholarship, 579, 580; farming, 308; first settlers, 308; geography, 306–07, *m583,* 585; government and politics, 587–88, 685–86; Kingdom of, *m704;* literature, 584, 590–91, 595; military, 584, 588; ships, 553, 584, 586, 587, *p587;* trade, 553, 571, 584–86, 587, 588; unification of, 685–87
Ivan III, czar of Russia, 561

J

Jacob, 142, 149; Twelve Tribes of Israel, 142, 149
Jainism, 263–64, 274
Jamaica, 631
James I, king of England, 605, 631, *p631*
James II, king of England, 652
Jamestown, 631
Japan, 42, *c339, c472,* 495, 507–509, *c508, m508–509,* 516–19, *m517,* 520–27, *m534,* 633, *c640, c663;* architecture, 526–27; arrival of Europeans, 633; art, 520, 525, 527; Buddhism in, 262, 479, 519, *p519,* 520, 522, 525, *p525,* 527; cities, 519, 520; civil war, 521–22, 523; constitution, *c508,* 518; culture, 512, 517–19, 523–527; daimyo, 523–24, 633; European influence, 42, 633; family, 521, 524; farming, 516–17, 518, 519, 523–524; feudalism in, 523, 549, 633; geography, 516, *m517;* gods and goddesses, 517; government, 518–19, 520, 522, 523, 525; Korea and, 510, 512, 514, 515; life in, 523–527; literature, *q521,* 525, 526; medieval, 520–27; Meiji Era, *c663;* military, 516, 517, 522; Mongol invasion of, 522; philosophy, 525; poetry, 520, 525, 526, *q526,* 527; religion, 525; science, 525; samurai, 521, *p521,* 523, 526, 527, 549; settlement of, 516–17; Shinto, 518, *p518,* 519; ships, 516; shoguns, 520–27, 633; trade, 42, 512, 523–524, 525; women, 524, *ptg524,* 526
Jefferson, Thomas, 670
Jenner, Edward, 703
Jeremiah, 152
Jericho, 65, 146, *p146;* farming, 65
Jerome, 389
Jerome, Saint, 368, *q368*
Jerusalem, 138, *c139, m139,* 147, 149, 150, 151, 152, *q153,* 154, 162, 163, 164–65, 166, *c247,* 330, *c370,* 372, 373, 374, 376, 378, 382, 562–63
Jesuits, *p502,* 503, 602–07, 630; "Black Robes," 630
Jesus of Nazareth, 6, 7, 325, *c338,* 369, 370, *c370,* 374–79, *q374, ptg378,* 380, 384, 387, 403, 562, 565, 568, 579, 593, 599, 601, 607; death of, 369, *c370,* 377–78, 568; miracles of, 375; resurrection of, 377
***Jewish War, The* (Josephus),** *q359*

Jews, 141, 142, 150, 154–59, 160–67, 372–74, 375–79, 406, *c539,* 566, 569, 572, 575; anti-semitism, 569; culture, 155, 156–59; daily life, 157–59; diet of, 157–59, *p158, p159;* education and scholarship, 157, 406, 566; exile from Judah, 153, *q153,* 154, 159, 160, 190; family, 157–58, *p157;* ghettos, 569; in Spain, 607–08; in the Roman Empire, *c139,* 162–65, *m168, c277, c305,* 330, *c338, q359,* 370, *c370,* 372–74, 375–79; law, 406; persecution of in medieval Europe, 569, 572, 575
Joan of Arc, 537, *ptg537, c539,* 574, *ptg574;* biography, 574
John, king of England, *c421, c449, c473, c509,* 558
John of Plano Carpini, 506, *q506*
joint-stock companies, 633
Joliet, Louis, 630
Joseph II, king of Austria, 656–57; reforms of, 657
Josephus (Flavius): *The Jewish War, q359*
Joshua, 144, 146
Judaea, 162–65, *m164,* 330, *c338,* 372, 374, 377, 378, *m392;* Jewish return to, 154–55; renamed as Palestine, 165; Roman rule of, 162–65, 330, *c370. See also* Judah.
Judah, 151–53, *m151,* 154–55, 372; fall of, 152; Greek rule of, 160–62; renamed as Judaea, 162, 372; tribes of, *q170. See also* Judaea.
Judaism, 138, 140–41, 152, 154–59, 160–67, 372–74, 575; destruction of Temple, *c139,* 152, 154–55, 164, 165, 330, *q359,* 373; myth of creation, 7, 155; roles of men and women, 157; Rome and, 162–65, *c168, q359,* 370, *c370,* 372–74, 375–79; spread of, 160–61. *See also* Hebrew Bible; Torah.
Julius II, Pope, 593
jury system, 557, 558, 652
Justinian Code, 363
Justinian I, emperor of Byzantine Empire, 360, 362-65, *p362, m364;* biography, 362; "Justinian's Plague," 365

K

Kaaba, 400, *ptg401,* 402, *p402*
Kalahari, 424
Kamakura, 522–23
Kangxi, emperor of China, *c641*
karma, 258–59
Karnak, 126, *p127*
Kashta, king of Kush, 130
Kazakhstan, 297
Kepler, Johannes, 645, 646, *c647*
Kerma, kingdom of, 128–29
Khan, Genghis, 15, *p15, c449, c473,* 490–91, *m490,* 492, *p492, c509, c539;* biography, 492
Khan, Kublai, *c473,* 492–94, 498, 514, 585, *c616*
Khanbaliq, China, 492, 493–94, *q494*
Khayyam, Omar, 414, *ptg414, q414*
Khmer Empire, 531; Angkor Wat, *c509,* 531, *p531, c539;* architecture, *c509,* 531, *p531;* religion, 531; Koguryo, 511, 512, *m513*
Khufu, king of Egypt, 115
Kiev, 560
Kilimanjaro, 420, *p420*
Kingdom of the Two Sicilies, *m612*
King, Dr. Martin Luther Jr., 153, 264
King's Men, 596
Klein, Michael, 442
knights, 549–50, *c549,* 551, 556–57, *ptg557, q578;* code of chivalry, 549–50
Knossos, 176, *p176, m206*
Korea, 507–509, *c509, m508–509,* 510–515, *m513,* 526, *m534;* agriculture and farming, 495, *m504,* 510, 512; animism, 518; architecture, 512; art, 512, 513–14; Buddhism in, 262, 478–79, 510–11, 513, 514, 519, 525; China and, 295, 474–75, 476, 478–79, 510, 511–515, 518; civil service examinations, 512, 513, 514; Confucianism in, 510–11; culture, 510–15; economy, 512; education, 514; geography, 510, *m511;* government, 478, 512, 513; Japan and, 510, 512, 514, 515; kingdoms of, 478, 511–512, *m513;* Koryo dynasty, 495, *c509,* 513–14; law, 513; literacy, 514–15; military, 513, *p513,* 515, *p515;* Mongols and, 514; printing, *c477,* 512, 513; science and technology, 514; shamanism, 511; ships, 515, *p515,* 516; Three Kingdoms period, 511–12; trade, 524; unified, 478, 513–14; women, *p514*
Koryo dynasty, 495, *c509,* 513–14
kosher foods, 158
Krishna, 245, 269–70, *ptg270*
Kshatriyas, 255, *c255*
Kush, civilization of, 97–99, *c99,* 128–33, *m131, c305,* 422; art, 131, *p131,* 132, 424, 428; cities, 130, 132; conquered by Axum, 133, *c339;* culture, 129, 131; Egypt and, *c99,* 100, 127, 128–32, *c210;* farming, 128, 133; geography, 128; Kerma, 128–29; Meroë, 132–33, *p133, m134;* military, 128–29, 130, 132; religion, 129, 131, *q131;* slavery, 129, 133; trade, 129, 130, 132–33; use of iron, 131–32. *See also* Nubia.

L

labor: child labor, 697; labor unions, 700; working conditions, 697–700, *p706*
labor unions, 700
laity, 383, *c384*
lamas, 262
language, 5, 37, 155, 347, 356, 460, 465, 565, 631; Arabic, 401, 405, 406, 411, 413, 414, 435, 643; Aryan, 252–53, 254, *p254,* 257; Bantu, 437; Chinese, 282–83, 481, 496, 515, 526; development of spoken language, 58; early humans and, 58; English, 253, 356, 557, 566, 599; French, 347, 357, 557, 566, 590; German, 566, 590; Greek, 160, 171, 212, 234, 235, 361, 377, 380, 385, 582; Hindi, 253, 254; Indo-European, 252–53; Italian, 347, 357, 566, 590; Japanese, 515, 526; Latin, 7, 347, 357, 361, 380, 385, 390, 406, 413, 550, 566, 582, 590, 599; Native American, 630; Persian, 410; Portuguese, 357, 631; Romanian, 356; Sanskrit, 254, *p254,* 257, 269; Slavic, 390; Spanish, 347, 356, 566, 631; spread of, 160, 171, 234–35, 410; Swahili, 435; Urdu, 410; vernacular, 500, 566–67, 590
Laos, 262; Buddhism in, 262
Laozi, 288, *c288, p289;* Daoism and, 288, *c288*
latifundia, 320–22
Last Supper, 376, 377, *ptg378*
Last Supper, The **(da Vinci),** 593
Latin, 7, 347, 356, 361, 380, 385, 390, 406, 413, 542, 550, 566, 582, 590, 599; alphabet, 356
Lavoisier, Antoine, *c641, c647,* 648
law, 697, 699, 700; Assyrian, 88; British, 694; Byzantine, 361, 362, 363; Chinese, *c288,* 289; Code of Hammurabi, *p83,* 87, *p88;* copyright, 21; Egyptian, 110; Greek, 181, *q182,* 186, 188, *p188p,* 189, 199, *c200,* 222; in ancient Israel, 151; Indian, 266–67, *q267;* influence of religion on, 143; in medieval Europe, 548, 553, 554–55, 557–58, *q558,* 565; in the Americas, 467; in the Torah, 156–57, 162–63, 166; Islamic (shari'ah), 403; Korean, 513; Jewish, 406; Mesopotamian, 87; Mongolian, 15, 490; Napoleonic Code; natural law, 566; Roman, 313, 314, 315–16, 322, 329, 331, *c331,* 333, 342, 356, 361; Sumerian, 79, 80, 87; United States, 44–45, 46, *c200,* 316, 667
Lee, Robert E., 687
Leeuwenhoek, Antonie van, 648
legalism, 286, *c288,* 289
legionaries, Roman, 310, *p310, ptg311;* armor and weapons, 310, *p310*
legions, 310
Leo III, Emperor of Byzantine Empire, 387
Leo III, Pope, 543, *ptg543*
Leo X, Pope, 600–01
Leonidas, king of Sparta, 194–95
Lepidus, Marcus, 326
Leviathan **(Locke),** 651, *p651*
Lewis and Clark: expeditions, *m22*
liberalism, 682, 698–99
Li Bo, 486, *ptg486, q486*
libraries, 88, *c98,* 164, 166, 210, 235, 236, 239, 434, 566, 590, 610
Libya, 127

Index

Libyan Desert, 102
***Life of Charlemagne, The* (Einhard),** *q543*
Lincoln, Abraham, 687
Lister, Joseph 703
literature, 10, 701; as a source of information, 10; Aryan, 254; Chinese, 295, *ptg486, p487,* 486–88, 496–97, *q496, q497,* 500; French, 701; Greek, 215–17, 234, 237, 345–47, 348, 390, 413, 546, 589; Indian, 245, 269–70; Islamic, 401, *q401,* 414, *q414;* Japanese, *q521,* 525, 526; modernism, 701; realism, 701; Roman, 345–49, 390, 546, 589; romanticism, 701; Russian, 701; symbolism, 701–02; vernacular, 500, 566–67, *q567,* 590. *See also* poetry.
Liu Bang, emperor of Han, 294
***Lives of the Artists* (Vasari),** 593
Livia Augustus, 343, *p343;* biography, 343
Livy, 307–08, 347, 357
Locke, John, *c641,* 650, 652, *ptg652, m658, q660*
London, *m576,* 595, 596, *m704*
Louis IX, king of France, 578, *q578*
Louis XIV, king of France, 630, 655; Sun King, 655
Louis XVI, king of France, 673–75; French Revolution and, 672–75
Louis-Philippe, king of France, 684
Louvre, 209
Loyola, Ignatius, 607
Lucy, 9, *p9*
Luoyang, *c277,* 299
Lutheranism, 600–03; creation of, 601; in Germany, 601–02; politics and, 601–02. *See also* Luther, Martin.
Luther, Martin, 580, *c581,* 598, 600–03, *ptg600, q601, ptg603,* 607, *q614, c617;* creation of Lutheranism, 601; Ninety-Five Theses as beginning of Reformation, 600
Luxembourg, 594
Lyceum, *c211,* 222–23

M

Maccabees: revolt of, *c139,* 161–62
Maccabeus, Judas, 161–62, *ptg162;* biography, 162
Macedonia, 205, 209, *c211,* 230–32, 235, *m242;* conquers Greece, 230–31, 241; farming, 230; military, 230–31
Machiavelli, Niccolò, 588, *q588*
Machu Picchu, 464–65, *p465*
Madinah, 7, *c396,* 402, *m416*
Magdeburg, 611, *q611, q614*
Magellan, Ferdinand, *c617,* 622–23, *ptg623;* circumnavigation of the world, 623
Magna Carta, *c421, c449, c473, c509,* 558, *q558*
Magyars, 544, *m545*
Mahabharata, 269
Mahavira, 263
Mahayana Buddhism, 262
Maimonides, Moses, 406
Makkah, 7, 400–401, 402, *m416,* 434, 435; Kaaba, 401, *ptg401,* 402, *p402,* 412
Malay states, 533; trade, 533
Mali, *c420,* 427, *c428,* 431, 434, 435, *m444, q446;* government, 431; military, 431, *q431;* trade, *c420,* 427, *c428,* 431, 441, *q446*
Malintzin, 624–25
Mamun, 413
Manchu dynasty, 503, 515, *c641*
Mandate of Heaven, 284
manors, 551–53, *p551,* 557
Mansa Musa, king of Mali, 427, 431, 434, 435, *q446, c449, c473, c616;* biography, 435; journey to Makkah, 434, 435, *c616*
Mantua, 584
maps, 12, *p12, p22,* 28–35, *p494,* 563, 619, 644; globes, 28–31; map projections, *c26, m30,* 31, *m31;* mapmakers, 31, 35, 619, 620, 622, 623. *See also* Mercator, Gerardus.
Marathon, Battle of, 193–94
Marius, consul of Rome, 322
Marquette, Jacques, 630
Mars, god of war, 307
Martel, Charles, 542
martyrs, 382
Marxism, 700
Marx, Karl, 699–700, *p699*
Maryland, 665
Mary Magdalene, 377, *p377;* biography, 377
Mary I, queen of England, 605; "Bloody Mary," 605
Mary II, queen of England, 652; "Glorious Revolution," 652
Masada, Israel, 163, *p163,* 373, *p373, q394*
Massachusetts, *c662,* 664–65, 668–69
mathematics, 565, 591, 642, 643, 644, 645, 646, 648; algebra, 270; Arabic, 413–14, 643; Egyptian, *c74,* 104, 114–15; Greek, 220, 221, 226, 238–40, *c239,* 345, 592; Indian, 270–71; infinity, 270; invention and use of zero and number symbols, 270–71, 414, 461, 643, *c643;* map projections and, 30; Maya, 461; Roman, 345, 592; Sumerian, 83; value of *pi,* 240. *See also* geometry; numbering systems.
Matsuo Basho, 526, *q526*
Maurya, Chandra Gupta, 265–66; government of, 265; founder of India's first empire, 265; postal system, 265
Mauryan Empire, *c7,* 246, *c247,* 265–68, *m266,* 269; decline of, 268; Golden Age of, *c247;* Mauryan dynasty, *c211,* 265, *m266, c304*
Maya, *c397, c448–49, m449,* 456, 459–61, *p460, p461, m468, q470, c539,* 624; architecture, 460; art and artisans, 460, *p460, p461;* artifacts, 447, *p447;* astronomy, 447, 461; calendars, 461; cities and city-states, *c339, c371, c397, c448,* 459–61; culture, 460–61, *p461;* empire, *c448, m449, m468;* farming, 460, 461; gods, 460, *p460,* 461; government and politics, 460; mathematics, 461; modern-day Maya, 460; Petén, 459; social classes, 460; trade, 455, 460; women, 460; writing and hieroglyphics, 461, *q470*
Mayapán, *c397*
Mayflower, 664, 666
Mayflower Compact, 666, *q666*
McNeill, William H., *q24*
Medes, *c75,* 90
Medici, Catherine de', 610, *ptg610;* biography, 610
Medici family, 579, 586, 587, 610
Medici, Lorenzo de', 579, 587, 588, *ptg588,* 594, 610
medicine, 591, 618, 647, 703; Arabic, 406, 413, 414; British, 703; *Canon of Medicine,* 414; Chinese, 297, *p296,* 478, 518; discovery of anesthesia, 703; discovery of bacteria, 703; Egyptian, 112; European, 565, 647; Greek, 226–27, 344, *p345,* 647; Hippocrates, 226–27; Indian, 271; infection, 703; Roman, 344, *p345;* vaccines, 703
Mediterranean Sea, *m94,* 102, 123, *m134,* 144, 160–67, *m168,* 172, 174, 176, 179, 241, *m242,* 267, 297, *m300,* 307, *m314,* 319, 333, *m334, m366,* 408, *m444, m612*
Mehmet II, 409
Meiji Era, *c663*
Memphis, Egypt, 107, 110, 120, *m124*
Menander, 237; influence on later writers, 237
Mendel, Gregor, 702
Mercator, Gerardus, *c26,* 35, *p35;* biography, 36; Mercator projection map, 31, *m31,* 36
mercenaries, 584; Germanic, 351; in Kush, 129; Turkish, 476
Meroë, Kush, 132–33, *p133, m134*
Mesoamerica, *c339, c371, c448,* 454–56, *m455,* 466, *c539;* cities of, *c448,* 455–56; farming, 454, 455–56; geography, 454, 455–56; Moche, 456, *p456;* Olmec, 454–55, *m468;* Teotihuacán, *c448,* 455–56, *m468;* trade, 466; Zapotec, 455–56, 461. *See also* Maya.
Mesolithic Age (Middle Stone Age), 63
Mesopotamia, 40, 73–75, *m74–75,* 76–85, 86–93, *q96,* 100, 103, 105, 106, 110, 141, 180, 233, 332, 398, 400, 407; civil rights, 181; economy, 40; emergence of civilization, 68, *m68,* 74, 250, 278; farming, 77–81, *p77, p79,* 87, 103; flooding, 77, 103; geography, 74, *m74–75,* 76–77; laws, 87; library, *c98;* military, 86–90; poetry, 95, *q95;* religion and gods, 79–80, 82, 84, 87, 88, 91, 92; trade, 86, 106, 252; women

in, 87; *See also* Akkadians, Assyria; Chaldeans; Epic of Gilgamesh; Sumer.
metalworking, 67, 81, 132–133, 271, *q358,* 436, 439, 440, 517, 529, 553. *See also* iron.
Methodius, 390, *ptg390*
Metternich, Klemens von, 679
Mexico, 64, 65, *c99,* 447, 454, *m455,* 455, 459, 623, 624–26, 630, *m662,* 688; conquered by Spain, 624–26, 666; exploration of, 623, 624–26; farming, 64, 65; first settlements, *c99;* independence of, *c663;* war with the United States, 688
Michelangelo (Buonarroti), 579, *c581,* 583, 593, *Sistine Chapel, q593, ptg593;* biography, 594
***Micrographia* (Hooke),** 648
Middle Ages, *c3,* 6, 406, 521, 537–39, *c538–59, m538–39,* 540–47, 548–55, 556–63, 564–69, 570–75, 582–88, 589–97, 598–605, 606–11, 618; early, 540–47; late, 570–75, 619; middle class, 554; science, 643–44; wind and water power, 553. *See also* Europe, medieval.
middle class, 696–97, 699; growth of, 696–97
migration, 36–37, 51, 60, *m60,* 100, 252–53, *m253, m354,* 437, *m437,* 450, 453, *m453,* 635; immigration, 684, 689
military, *c99;* African, 431, *q431,* 432, 438; Arabic, 402, 404–05, *q418,* 542; Assyrian, 87–88; British, 679; Byzantine, 362, 365, *p365, m364;* Chinese, 281, 284, 285, 290, 474–77, 484, 485, 498; Egyptian, 120, 121, *ptg121,* 124, 126, 127, 129, 142; Etruscan, 309; French, 672, 676–79, 684; Greek, 172, *c173,* 177, 181, 182, *ptg182, q182,* 184, 185–87, *ptg185, q185,* 192, 194–97, *q195,* 202–04; guerrilla warfare, 685; in ancient Israel, 146–47, 148–49; in early civilizations, 68; in Kush, 128–29, 130, 132; in medieval Europe, 537, 548, 572, 574, 584, 588, 609, 610; Italian, 584, 588; Japanese, 516, 517, 522, 523; Korean, 513, *p513,* 515, *p515;* Macedonian, 230–31; Mesopotamian, 86–90; Mongol, 472, 489–95, *ptg493;* Persian, 190–97, *q195,* 205, 351; Philistine, 145; Roman, 240, 310, *p310,* 312, 313, 314–15, 317–19, 320, 322–24, 328, 333, *q336,* 343, 344, 350–55, *q359, q368,* 381, 382, *ptg383*
Mill, John Stuart, 699
Minamoto Yoritomo, 521–22, *ptg522*
minarets, 415
Ming dynasty, 293, 496, 498–503, *m499*
Minoans, 7, *p7,* 172, *c172,* 176, 177; art and architecture, 176, *p176;* calendar, 7, *p7;* collapse of civilization, 176; gods and goddesses, 177; ships, 176; spread of culture, 177; trade, 176, 177
Minos, king of Crete, 176
missionaries, 389–91, 478, 479, 503, 533, 546, 568, 630. *See also* friars.
Mississippians, *c396,* 458; cities, 458; collapse of civilization, 458; farming, 458; government, 458; mounds, 458; social classes, 458
Mississippi River, 452, 458, 630
Missouri River, *c424*
Mittani, 123
modernism, 701–02
Mogul Empire, 409, 410, 415, *c640;* military, 410; Shah Jahan, 415; Taj Mahal, 415, *p415*
Mohenjo-Daro, *c7, c246,* 250, 251, *m272;* architecture, 251–52, *c251;* artifacts, 250, *p250*
***Mona Lisa* (da Vinci),** *ptg592,* 593
monasteries, 389, 391, *q394,* 478, 546, 557, 564, 567–68, 599
Monet, Claude, 701, *ptg701,* 702
money, 42, 187, 293, 333, 484–85, 553, 554, 586, 633; banks, 411, 554, 564, 572, *c581,* 584, 586, 587, 588; coins, 179, *p179,* 187, *q298, p326,* 351, *p351,* 411, 485, 554; florin, 586; invention of paper currency, *c26,* 484–85
Mongol Empire, 15, *c397,* 409–10, 489–97, *m490, m491, c509,* 533, 560–61, 571, 585; agriculture, 489; Black Death and, Black Death in, 571, *m571;* Buddhism, 494; culture, 15, 492, 493; division of, 491; invasion and rule in China and Asia, 408–09, 472, *c473,* 489–95, 498, 500, 503, 514, 522, *c539,* 585; Japan and, 522; Korea and, 514; law, 15, 490; nomadic life, 489–90; Persia and, 491; shipbuilding, 494, 495, 515; trade, 492, 494, 571, 585; tribute to, 491, 560; use of terror, 491; warriors, 15, 490, *ptg493, q506. See also* Khan, Genghis; Khan, Kublai.
Mongolia, 489, *m504. See also* Mongol Empire.
***Monkey* (Wu Cheng'en),** 496–97, *p496, q496, q497*
monks, *c7,* 274, 394, *q394, c371,* 389–90, 391, 478, 484, 546, 565, 567–69, 598, 699; Buddhist, 259, 260, 261, *p261,* 263, *p263,* 519, 525, 527, 532
monotheism, 140, 143, *c143,* 403
monsoons, 249–50, *m249*
Montesquieu, 652–53, *ptg652, q653*
Montezuma II, 625–26, *ptg625*
Moors, *c421*
Morell, Virginia, 136
mosaics, 303, *p303,* 337, *p337,* 358, *p358, p362,* 364, 409, 563
Moscow, 561, *m561,* 639, *m704*
Moses, *c75, c138,* 142, *ptg142, c143,* 144, *c277,* 403; biography, 142; leads Israelites from Egypt, *c138,* 142–44, 277
mosques, 337, 409, *p409,* 412, 415, 434, *p434,* 435, *q446,* 575
Mound Builders, *m449,* 458, *p458, m468;* cities, 458; farming, 458; Hopewell, 458; Mississippians, *c396,* 458, *c538*
Mount Everest, 248
Mount McKinley, *p451*
Mount Olympus, 212–13
Mount Sinai, 143, *c143*
Mount St. Helens, 33, *p33*
Mount Vesuvius, 14, 303, 330, *p330, c370;* eruption, 14, 303, 330, *c370*
Muhammad, 7, *c396,* 401–03, 404, *c406,* 407, *c508, c538;* biography, 401
mummies, 98, *p98,* 101, 111–12, *ptg112;* of animals, 112
Murasaki Shikibu, 526, *ptg526;* biography, 526; *The Tale of Genji,* 526
Muslims, 7, 156, 402–03, 409, 426, 427, 432, 433–35, 439, 492, 494, 501, 533, 542, 545, *m545,* 562–63, 566, 567, 571, 575, 607, 620, 621
Myanmar, 262; Buddhism in, 262
Mycenae, 177, *m206;* ruins of, 177
Mycenaeans, 172, *c172,* 176–77, 178, 187; art, 177, *p177;* adoption of Minoan culture, 177; decline of, *c172,* 177; farming, 177; gods and goddesses, 177; kingdoms and government of, 176–77; military, 177; ships, 177; slavery, 177
mythology: Chinese, 280; Greek, 171, 176, 212–14, *c213;* Jewish, 7, 155; Incan: *q470*

N

NAFTA. *See* North American Free Trade Agreement.
Nanjing, China, 498, *m499*
Naomi, 157, *ptg158*
Napata, Kush, 130
Napoleon. *See* Bonaparte, Napoleon.
Napoleon III, emperor of France, 684
Napoleonic Code, 677
Nara, 519, 520
Nardo, Don, *q96 c581*
Narmer, *c98,* 107, *p107*
nationalism, 677–78, 682–89
Native Americans, 450, 453–54, 465–67, 624–27, 629, 630, 635, *q638,* 665–66, 668, 686; Acoma, 466; along the Pacific Ocean, 467; Apache, 467; Aztec, *c580, c616,* 624–26, *q638;* Cahuilla, 466; Cherokee, 466; Chinook, 466; Chumash, 466; during westward expansion of the United States, 686; Eastern Woodland peoples, *c449,* 467, *c581;* effects of smallpox and other diseases on, 625, 626, 629, 635, 665; farming, 466–67; Great Plains, 467; Haida, 466; Hohokam, 457; Hopi, 466; Inca, *m468, q470, c581,* 626–27; Inuit, 465; Iroquois League, *c449,* 467, *c581;* Mandan, 467; Mississippians, *c396,* 458, *c538;* Mound Builders, 458, *p458, m468;* Navajo, 448, 467; Pawnee, 467; Pomo, 466; slavery of, 629; Taino, 621–22; tepees, 467; Tlingit, 466; trade, 466, 635, *q638;* use of adobe, 466; women, 466; Zuni, 466. *See also* individual Native American Nations.

Index

NATO. *See* North Atlantic Treaty Organization.
natural law, 650–52, 654
natural wonders, 26, m26–27
Navajo, 448, 467; hogans, 448, p448, 467; religion, 448; settlements, 467
Navigation Acts, 667
Nazareth, 374
Nebuchadnezzar, 90–93, 152, c247
Nefertiti, queen of Egypt, 125
Nelson, Lord Horatio, 677
neo-Confucianism, 480–81, 514
Neolithic Age (New Stone Age), c53, 62–67, 308; art and artifacts, 66, p67; economic specialization, 66; farming, 62–67, m63; homes, 64, 65–66, 67, ptg64, metalworking, 67; Ötzi, 66, p66; religion, 66; roles of men and women, 67; technology, 67; tools and weapons, 67; trade, 66
Nero, emperor of Rome, 330, 382
Netherlands, c581, 586, 594, 602, 603, c617, 628, 633, c662; colonies and settlers, 631; economy, 631, c662; exploration by, 628, 631; independence from Spain, 631; ships, 631; trade, 631
New Lanark, Scotland, 698, ptg698, 699
New Testament, 385
Newton, Isaac, c641, 646–47, c647, p647, 703; law of gravity, 647
New York, New York, 33, p33, 631, 666
Niger River, 424, m444
Nihonji, q479
Nile River valley, m94, 97, 98, 100–07, m101, 110, 113, 114, 116, 117, 120, 121, 123,124, 127, 128, 130, 132, c134, m134, 142, 279, 424, 428, m444; emergence of civilization, 68, m68, 74, 100, 424, c424; farming, c53, 64, 100, 101, 104–05, p104, ptg104, 106; flooding, 103–04, 113, 128; geography, 100, m101, 102, p102, p103
Nineteenth Amendment, c27
Ninety-Five Theses, c581, 600, ptg603, c617
nirvana, 261, 262
Noah, 155
nobles, 519, 521, 523, 526, 527, 548–51, c549, 553, 554, 557–63, 564, 567, 574
Noh, 526–27, 536, q536
nomads, 144, 408, 467, 510, 544; Aryan, 250, 253–54; Bedouin, 399–400, p400; early humans, 54, 62, 453, 454; in China, 293, 295, 474, 476, 477, 489–90; Mongol, 489–90
Norman conquest, 556–57, ptg557
Normandy, 556, 557
North America, c397, c421, 448, m449, 450–51, m451, 453, 457–58, 465–67, c473, c509, c538, 545, c580, 622, 623, 628–31, 633, 664–71, m665, 696; civilizations of, 457–58, c396, 465–67; colonial government, 667–71; establishment of colonies, 620, 623, 628–31, p629, 632–33, 664–71, m665; exploration of, 622, 623, 628–31, 633; farming, 457, 666, m665; trade 628–35, 667–69, m668, 670. *See also* Americas; Mexico; Native Americans; United States.
Norway, 544, 701; art, 701
Nubia, c99, 106, 120, 124, 128–29, m134; alphabet, 129. *See also* Kush, civilization of.
numbering systems: Arabic numerals, 414; Indian-Arabic, 270–71, 414, 643, c643; Roman, 643, c643
nuns, 274, 389–90, 478, 546, 567–68, ptg568, 607
***Nympheas* (Monet),** 701, ptg701
Nzinga, queen of Africa, 438, p438

Octavian, emperor of Rome, c305, 325–27, p327
Odoacer, 354–55
Odysseus, 215
***Odyssey* (Homer),** c210, 215–16, 346
Old Testament, 141, 384
oligarchy, 184, 186, 224
***Oliver Twist* (Dickens),** 700
Olmec, c211, 454–55, m449, m468; artisans, 455; collapse of, c211, 455; farming, 454–55; religion, 455; trade, 454–55
Olympic Games, c75, 189, 195, c210, 214, c247, c277
***On the Origin of Species* (Darwin),** 702
***On the Revolutions of the Heavenly Spheres* (Copernicus),** 644
oracles, 214, ptg214, 282, p282, q302; Oracle of Apollo at Delphi, 214
oral tradition, *See* storytelling.
***Oresteia* (Aeschylus),** 217
Orléans, 537, 574, m576
Osiris, 97, p97, 110, p111, 111
Osman, 395, 409
Otto, emperor of Holy Roman Empire, 545–46
Ottoman Empire, 395, c397, 409–10, m612; captures Constantinople, 409; conquers Byzantine Empire, 409; fall of, 410; Golden Age, 410; laws, 409
Ötzi (the Iceman), 66, p66, 67; biography, 66
Owen, Robert, 699

Pacal II, 460
Pachacuti, biography, 464
Pacific Ocean, 451, m451, 453, 456, 466, 516, m534, 622, 626, 688; named by Magellan, 622
Paekche, 511, 512, m513; trade, 512
Paine, Thomas, 670
Palenque, 460
Paleolithic Age (Old Stone Age), 52, c52, 54–61, ptg55; art and artifacts, p13, p56, 58–59, p58, p59, p72; discovery and use of fire, 57, 60, 61, ptg61; language, 58; migrations, 51, 60, m60; nomadic life, 54, 62; roles of men and women, 55–56; technology, 52, 56, 60; tools and weapons, 52, 54, 55, ptg55, 56, p56, 57, 60
paleontology, 9
Palestine, 165, 492
Panama, 626
Panchen Lama, 262
Papal States. *See* Italian Papal States.
papermaking: Chinese, 296, p296, 484–85; Egyptian, 105, p105, ptg105; modern, 296, p296.
papyrus, 105, p105, ptg105, 112, 296
parables, 375, ptg376
Paris, 559, 565, m576, 610, m612, 661, 673, 674, ptg674, 675, 684
Parliament, 558, 559, 604, 651–52, 667, 669, 682–84, p683, q683, 694
Parthenon, c218, 219
Pascal, Blaise, 649
Passover, celebration of, 142, 158–59, 376, 378
Pasteur, Louis, 703
patricians, 312–14, 315, 320, 322
Patrick, 391, 546
Paula, 389
Paul III, Pope, 606–07
Paul of Tarsus, c139, 378, 379, p379, 384
Pax Romana, c305, 328, 330–33, c331, 350
Peace of Augsburg, c581, 602–03
Peace of Westphalia, 611
Peisistratus, 188–89
Peloponnesian War, c173, 203–05, m204, c206, 221, 225, 228, 230
Peloponnesus Peninsula, 185, 203, m206
Pennsylvania, 665
Pepin, king of the Franks, 542–43
Pergamum, 235
Pericles, 198–99, 201, 203–04, p203, q203; funeral oration, 203, q203, q208
Persepolis, 192, p192
Persia, m242, m300, 360, m366, 406, 410, m416, q418; conquered by Mongol Empire, 491; Safavid Empire, 409, 410. *See also* Persian Empire.
Persian Empire, c139, 172, 190–97, m191, 204, 230, 231–35, 265, 360, 399, q418; art and architecture, p192; conquered by Alexander the Great, c173, 197, 210, 265, c277; defeat and rule of Chaldeans, c75, 93, 154–55, 160; decline of, 197; expansion of, 190–91; geography, 190–91, m191; government, 191, 197; Greece and, c173, 190–97, 214, 230, 231–34, c304; language, 410; military, 190–97, q195, 205, 351; religion,

Index

192–93; roads, 191, *m191;* trade, 191, 410. *See also* Persian Wars.
Persian Wars, 193–97, *m194,* 198, 199, 202, *c206, c211,* 225
Peru, 626–27; conquered by Spain, 626–27
Peter, emperor of Russia, 639, 657; overthrown by Catherine the Great, 639, 657
Peter, the Apostle, 369, *ptg369,* 374, *p374,* 378, 387; biography, 374
Peter the Great, czar of Russia, 657; reforms of, 657
Petrarch, Francesco, 589–90, *p590*
pharaohs, 108–14, *ptg109,* 116, 120–27, 129, 130, *p130,* 142; Tutankhamen, 16, *p16, c99*
Pharisees, 162–63
Philadelphia, Pennsylvania, 670–71
Philip II, king of France, 559
Philip II, king of Macedonia, *c211,* 230–32, *q231, q244*
Philip II, king of Spain, 609
Philippines, 623, 633
Philistines, 144, 145, 148–49, 165; iron-making, 145; military, 145; towns, 145
philosophes, 653–55, *ptg654*
***Philosophiae Naturalis Principia Mathematica* (Newton),** 647
philosophy: Chinese, 286–89, *c288,* 518; Greek, 209, 220–23, *q229,* 238, 240, *q240,* 344, 406, 413; in medieval Europe, 565–66; Islamic, 405–06; Japanese, 525; philosophes, 653–55, *ptg654;* Roman, 238, 343–44
Phoenicians, 123, 144–45, *p144,* 178, 316; alphabet, 145, *c145,* 178; Carthage, 145, 316; settlements, 123, 145; ships, *p144,* 144–45; trade, 123, 144–45
physics, *c239*
pictographs, 282–83, *p283*
Pilgrims, *c662,* 664, 666
pilgrims and pilgrimages, 268, 400, 402, *p402,* 403, 434, 435, 590
pirates, 176, 307, 333
Pi Sheng, 484
Piye, king of Kush, 130
Pizarro, Francisco, *c617,* 626–27, *ptg627;* defeats Inca and becomes governor of Peru, 627
plague. *See* Black Death.
plane geometry, 240
Plataea, 197
plateaus, 424, *p448*
Plato, 201, 222, *p222,* 223, *q229;* Academy of, 222, 223, *c224;* biography, 222
plebeians, 312–14, *p313,* 315; Council of the Plebs, 313–14, 320; strike against the government, 313, *p313*
Plutarch, 185, *q185,* 336, *q336*
Plymouth, 664–65
poetry, 137, 254, 269–70, 271, 440, 566–67, 590, 701; Arab, 400, *q400,* 414, *q414;* Chinese, 486–88, *p487;* Egyptian, 126, *q126;* Greek, 237, 345–46, 348; Japanese, 520, 525, 526, *q526,* 527; Mesopotamian: 95, *q95;* Roman, 346–47, *q346,* 348–49, *q348, q349;* troubador, 566. *See also* epics.
Poland, 569, 608, 640, 644; Enlightenment in, 640
polis, 180–82, 221
***Politics* (Aristotle),** 223
politics, political ideas, political systems, 512, 618, 661–63, 679, 682–89, 698–700; alliances, 460; American, 679; Aristotle's *Politics,* 223; conservatives, 679; diplomacy, 588; during the Enlightenment, 650–53, *q653;* French, 672–74, *q673,* 675–76; Greek, 180–81, 183–84, 205; in city-states, 79, 80, 180–81, 183–184, 460; in ancient Egypt, 123, *m124;* Indian, 264; in medieval Europe, 546–47, 574, 602; liberalism, 683, 698–99; Lutheranism and, 602; Maya, 460; nationalism, 677–78, 682–89; provinces as political districts, 319, 431, 432; revolutions, 652, 661–63, *c662–63, m662–63,* 664–71, 672–74, 677, 680–81, 682, 686, 698; Roman, 322, 350; separation of powers, 44–45, *g45;* socialism, 699–700; women in, 698. *See also* government.
Polo, Marco, 472, 494–95, *ptg494, q495,* 502, 585, *ptg585,* 586
Polybius, 318, *q319*
Pompeii, 14, 303, 330, *p330,* 340, *c370*
Pompey, 323–24, 326
pope, 6, *p6,* 355, *q355–56,* 385, 386, 387–88, *c421, c448, c509, c538,* 542, 544, 546–47, 562, 568, 573, 584, 590, 592, 599–604, *q601,* 606, 608, 609, *q614;* Gregory I, 355, *q355–56,* 391, *p391,* 394, 546; Gregory VII, 547, *ptg546;* Gregory XIII, 6, *p6;* Julius II, 593; Leo III, 543, *ptg543;* Leo X, 600–01; Paul III, 606–07; Urban II, *c397*
population, 35, 36, 63, 116, *c424,* 553; density, 36, *m37,* 116; shifts, 36, 63, 66, 67, 265, 482, 553. *See also* migration.
porcelain, 483, 488, *p488,* 495
Portugal, 438–39, 502, *c616, c617,* 619, 620, *m620,* 622–23, 628, 629–630, 632–33; colonies and settlers, 629, *p629,* 630; exploration by, 620, *m620,* 622–23, 629; ships, 502; slavery, 438–39, 629; trade, 502, 633
Poseidon, 213
postal system, 265
Poussin, Nicholas: *The Destruction of the Temples in Jerusalem,* *q359*
Praetorian Guard, 328, 330
praetors, 313
***Praise of Folly* (Erasmus),** 599
predestination, 603
Prehistory, *c2,* 4, 5, 8–9; Greek, 8
***Prince, The* (Machiavelli),** 588, *q588*
printing, *c371, c472,* 479, *p484,* 484–85, 486; first book printed, *c371, c472;* invention of movable type, *c449,* 484, 513, *c580,* 591; in Korea, 479, 512, 513; invention of paper currency, 484–85; invention of printing press, 484, *p484, ptg591,* 591, 594, 619
privatization, 442–43
***Procession of the Magi, The* (Gozzoli),** *ptg579*
proconsul, 329. *See also* consul.
Procopius, *q362*
Prodigal Son, parable of, 375, *ptg376*
proletariat, 700
prophets, 140, 142, 152, *c152,* 153, 401, 402, 403, 404
Protestantism, 580, *c581,* 598, 601, 602–03, 605, 606–11, 664, 684; Calvinism, 603, 605; Lutheranism, 600–03. *See also* Puritans.
proverbs, 150, *q150*
Prussia, 656, *m656,* 684, 686; military, 686; rule by Otto von Bismarck, 686; Franco-Prussian War, 686
Psalms, Book of, 137, 149, *q149,* 153, *q153*
Ptolemy, *c26,* 344, 619, 643, 644, *c645*
pueblos, *p457,* 457; Pueblo Bonito, *p457,* 457
Punic Wars, *c173, c305,* 316–319, *m317, ptg319*
Puritans, 605, 664–67; immigration to North America, 605, 664; persecution of, 664
pyramids, 101, 113–15, *ptg114, p115,* 118, 131, *p132, q136, c138,* 455, 456; Great Pyramid, *c98,* 115, *c138, c276;* in the Americas, 455, 456; Pyramid of the Sun, 455
Pythagoras, 226; Pythagorean Theorem, 226; scientific contributions, *c239*

Q

Quakers, 665
Quebec, 629
Quetzalcoatl, 625
Qin dynasty, 11, *c277,* 292–93, *m294, c305;* government, 292–93
Qing dynasty, 503, *c641*
Qin Shihuangdi, emperor of China, 292–93, *ptg293;* government, 292–93
quipu, 465, *p465*
Quran, *q401,* 403, 407, 434, 435, 439

R

rabbis, 166–67, *p167*
Radha, 245, *p245*
railroad, 693; locomotive, *c693*
rain forests, 419, *m421,* 422–23, *m423,* 426, 452
raja, 254
Ramayana, 270

Index

Ramses II, pharaoh of Egypt, 126, *p126,* 127, 136, *q136*

Raphael (Sanzio), *p187, p239,* 593

Re, 109, 110

realism, 701

Reconquista, 575

Record of Cambodia: The Land and its People, A **(Zhou),** 531

Red Sea, 102, 120–21, *m134,* 142, 296, 398, 400, 428; parting of the, 142

Reformation, 580, *c581,* 598–605; English, 603–05; spread of, 603–05. *See also* Catholic Reformation; Luther, Martin.

Reign of Terror, 675–76

reincarnation, 258–59, *q258;* 261, 262

relativity, theory of, 703

religion, 6–7, 88, 152, 282, 284, 309, 529, 531; African, 428–29, 432, 433, *m433,* 440–41; Aryan, 254, *q254,* 257; calendars and, 6–7; Chaldean, 91, 92; common beliefs of Judaism, Christianity, and Islam, 141, 156, 402; Egyptian, 97, 98, 108–13, *ptg110, p111, ptg112,* 118, 125, 126–27; Greek, 171, *p171,* 180, 188, 192, 212–14, 218, 219, 343; influence on modern law, 143; in Kush, 129, 131, *q131;* in the Americas, 448, 455; in medieval Europe, 405–07, 415, 542, 546, 564, 565–66, 567–69, 572–75, 582, 605, 607–11, *m608;* Japanese, 525; Mesopotamian, 79–80, 82, 84, 87, 88, 91, 92; monotheism, 140, 141, 192, 379; of early humans and civilizations, 66, 68–69, 448, 455; Persian, 192–93; polytheism, 79, 140, 192, 282, 284; Reformation, 580, *c581,* 598–605; Roman, 303, 307, 312, 343–44, 345, 347, 356, *q359,* 380–82; Sikhism, 410; spread of, 37, 261, 404–10, *c472;* Sumerian, 79–80; theocracy, 108–09, 192–93. *See also* Buddhism; Christian Church; Christianity; gods and goddesses; Hinduism; Islam; Jainism; Judaism; missionaries; Roman Catholic Church; Zoroastrianism.

Remus, 307–08, *p307, q308*

Renaissance, 237, 579–81, *m580-81,* 582–88, 589–97, 598, 599, 619, 642; art, 579, 580, 583, *p583,* 584, 587, 590, 591–95, *ptg592, ptg593, p594, ptg595;* comedy during, 237; education and scholarship, 579, 580, 589–91, 619; Northern Renaissance, 594–95; religion, 591; shipbuilding, 619; women, 593–94

Renoir, Pierre-Auguste, 702

representative democracy, *q50,* 198, *c200;* 310, 327, 356

republic, 310, 327, 356, 587, 674–75, 684; Plato's *Republic,* 222. *See also* Roman Republic.

Republic **(Plato),** 222

resurrection, 377

revolutions, 652, 661–63, *c662–63, m662–63,* 664–71, 672–74, 677, 680–81, 684, 686, 698

rhetoric, 221

rice, 64, *q72,* 500, 510, 512, 517, 524, 529, 531, 631, 635; in China, 64, 290, 475, 482, 485, 500

rights. *See* civil rights.

Robespierre, Maximilien, 675

Robinson, Harriet H., 700

Roman Catholic Church, 378, 385, 386–89, *c472,* 503, 537, 538, *c538,* 540, 542, 546–47, 550, 552, 562–63, 564–69, 572–73, 575, 580, *c581,* 584, 598–602, 604–05, 606–11, 644, 646, 654, 664, 665, 672, 673, 677, 685; annulment of marriage, 604; Catholic Reformation, 606–08; excommunication, 389, 547, 569, 601, 604; heresy, 384, 569, 574, 607, 646; Holy Communion, 568; divorce, 604; Henry VIII breaks with, 604; Inquisition, 569, 575; literature, 607; Mary, mother of Jesus, 568; mass, 568; restored to England by Mary, 605; sacraments, 568; saints, 568-69; schism in, 387–89, 573; seminaries, 606; Spanish Inquisition, 569, 575, 607–08. *See also* Christian Church; Christianity; pope; Reformation.

Romance of the Three Kingdoms, The, 500

Roman civilization, 303–05, *c304–05,* 306–11, 312–19, 320–27, 328–33, 337–39; 340–49, *m346,* 350–59, 399, *c420;* agriculture, 358, *q358;* art and architecture, 241, 303, *p303,* 321, *p321,* 333, 340–41, 344, *p344,* 345, *p345, p351, p352,* 356, 357, 564, 592; Byzantine Empire, *g355,* 356; citizens and citizenship, 310, 311, 312, 314, 315, 325, 328, 329, 333, *q336,* 342, 350, *q356,* 356, *q359;* civil rights, 328, 347; culture, *q17,* 303, 306, 340–49, 350, 582; education, 331, *c331,* 342, 350; emperors, 340, 342, 343, 347, 350, *p351,* 357, 380, 381; Etruscan influence on, 308–09; family, 342; gods and goddesses, 303, 307, 312, 342, 343, 345, *q349,* 381; Greek influence on, 236, 238, 306, 308, 343–46, 348; historians, 307–08, 318, *q319,* 336, 346–47; Latin, 7, 347, 356, 380, 385; law, 329, 331, *c331,* 333, 342, 356; life in, 303, *q331,* 340–49; literature and theater, 237, 345–49, 390, 546, 582, 589; mathematics, 345, 592; medicine, 344, *p345;* philosophy, 238, 343–44; religion, 303, 307, 312, 343–44, 345, 347, 356, *q359,* 380–82; science, 344, 592, 643; women, *ptg342,* 342–43

Roman Confederation, 311

Roman Empire, *q17,* 241, 298, *q298, c304–05, m304–05,* 325–27, 328–33, 337–39, *c338–39,* 340, 342, 343, 344, *m346,* 350–59, 360, 361, 365, 425, 583; agriculture, 358, *q358;* cities, 332, 333, 352–53, *g355;* Christianity, 337, 356, 357, 361, 370, *c370, c371,* 372–74, 380–85; civil wars, 350, 351; colonies, *q336;* corruption, 338, 350, *g355;* Diocletian's reforms, *c339,* 352, *g355;* division of, 338, *c339,* 353, *g355, c371;* Eastern Roman Empire, 353, *m354, g355,* 356, 389; economy, 331, 351, *p351,* 352; expansion of, 162, 332, 343, 368; fall of, 350–59, *m354, g355, q355–56, q368,* 546, 553, 566; farming, 331, 333; "Five Good Emperors," 331, *c331;* geography, 338, *m338–39, m346,* 353–54; Germanic invasion, 338, 351, 353–56, *m354;* government, 313, *p313,* 329, 350–55, *g355,* 356; Greece and, 171, 241, 319; influence in the modern world, 6, 340, *p345,* 344–47, 356–57; Jewish revolt against, *c139,* 164–65, *c277, c305,* 330, *c338,* 373; Judaism and, 162–65, *c168, q359,* 370, *c370,* 372–74, 375–79; Julio-Claudian emperors, 330; military, 240, 328, 333, *q336,* 343, 344, 350–55, *q359,* 368, 381, 382, *ptg383,* 391; *Pax Romana, c305,* 328, 330–33, *c331,* 350; Persian invasion, 351; road system, 311, 333, 343, 344, *m346,* 357, 358, 368, 380, *c420;* rule of Judaea, 162–65, 330, *c370;* slavery, 333, *c338,* 341, 342, 343, 350, 353; trade, 331, *m332,* 333, 344, *p344, m346,* 347, 351, 358, *q358,* 368; Visigoths, *ptg353,* 353–54, 355; Western Roman Empire, 353, *m354,* 355–56, *g355,* 357, 386, 389, 523, 540, 541, 542

Roman Republic, *c211, c304,* 309–11, 312–19, *m314,* 320–27, 342, 344, 356; art, 321, *p321,* 587, 675; Assembly of Centuries, 313; cities, 320, 321; civil rights, 312, 313, 314, 316; civil war, 324, 325–27; Council of the Plebs, 313–14; court system, 316, *ptg316;* economy, 320–22; expansion of, 310, *m314,* 316; fall of, 326; farming, 320–21, *p321,* 322; government, 310–11, 312–16, 320–22, 324–25, 327; influence in the modern world, 304, 315, 316; Julius Caesar, 6, 322–26, *p323, ptg324, q336, c420;* Law of Nations, 316; laws, 313, 314, 315–16, 322; marriage, 312, 314; military, 310, *p310,* 312, 313, 314–15, 317–19, 320, 322–24; patricians, 312–14, 315, 320, 322; plebeians, 312–14, *p313,* 315; reforms, 321–22, 323, 324; ships, 317; slavery, 321, 325; women, 314

romanticism, 701

Rome, *p5,* 133, *c139,* 162, *c173,* 241, 303, *c304–05, m305,* 306–11, 312–19, 320–27, 329, *ptg329, m334,* 337–47, *m346,* 348, 350–59, *m366,* 368, 369, 379, 382, 386, 583, 600, *m612,* 686, *m704;* capture of, 354, *g355;* founding of, 6, 307–08, 346, 348–49, *q349;* geography, 306–07; life in ancient, 340–47, *p341;* rise to power, 347; Senate, 313, 315, 319, *q319,* 320, 321, 322, 323–25, 327, 329, 330, 343; trade, 307

Romulus, 307–08, *p307, q308, q349*

Rousseau, Jean-Jacques, *c641,* 655

Royal Road, 191, *m191*

Rubaiyat **(Khayyam),** 414, *q414*

Rubicon River, 323; Caesar's crossing, 323–24, *ptg324, q324;* "crossing the Rubicon," 324

Rule of Good Emperors, *c305*

Index

Russia, 541, 561, 571, 639, 657, 678–79, 685–86; economy, 684; farming, 686; government and politics, 657, 686; literature, 701; military, 657, 678, 686; Mongols and, *c539*, 560–61
Ruth, 157, *q158*, *ptg158*

S

Sabbath, *c143*, 154, 157, *p157*
Sadducees, 163
Safavid Empire, 409, 410
Sahara, 102, 128, *c420*, 424, 425–26, 428, 430, 433
Saladin, 563
Salamis, 195–96; battle of, 195, *ptg195*, *ptg196*; strait of, 196
salvation, 379
Samaria, 151
Samaritans, 152, 375; Good Samaritan parable, 375, *p376*; religion, 152
Samuel, 148–49, *ptg149*
samurai, 521, *p521*, 523, 526, 527, 549; Bushido, 521; women, 521, *q521*
San Salvador, 621
Sargon, king of Akkad, *c74*, 86, 87, *p87*; biography, 87
satrapies, 191
satraps, 191
Saul, king of Israelites, 148, *c172*
savannas, 128, *p129*, 423
Scandinavia, 544, *m545*, 556, 560, 571; trade, 544, 560. *See also* Vikings.
schism, 387–89, 573; between the Catholic and Eastern Orthodox Churches, 387–89
Schliemann, Heinrich, 8, *ptg8*, 177; biography, 8
Schoenberg, Shira, *q170*
scholasticism, 652–65
***School of Athens* (Raphael),** 187, *ptg187*, 239, *ptg239*, 594
science, 8–9, 51, 64, 66, 92, 271, 413, 514, 525, 565, 639–41, 642–49, 695, 702–03; anatomy, 344; anthropology, 9; atomic theory, 703; evolution, 702; genetics, 702; Greek, 223, 226, 238–40, *p238*, *c239*, 306, 344, 592, 642–43, *c645*, 647; Islamic, 413, 643; modern, 227, *p227*, 591, *p591*; paleontology, 9; physics, *c239*, 702; reasoning and rationalism, 648–49; relativity, 703; Roman, 344, 592, 643; scientific method, 649, *c649*; theories about the universe, 644–45, *c645*, 646, 647, 703; use of microscopes, 648
scientific method, 649, *c649*
Scientific Revolution, 639–41, 642–49, 650
Scipio, 319
Scotland, 542, 557, 603, 667, 698
scribes, 82, 105, 116, 117, 155, 163, 525
Second Continental Congress, 669
***Second Treatise of Government, The* (Locke),** 660, *q660*
Sejong, king of Korea, 514; inventions of, 514–15
Seleucids, 161–62, 235; empire of, 235
Seljuk Turks, 408–09
seminaries, 606
separation of powers, 652–53, *q653*
serfs, 551–53, *c552*, *p551*, 563, 572; freedom and, 551, 563
Sermon on the Mount, 374, *c375*
***Seven Books on the Structure of the Human Body, The* (Vesalius),** 647
Seven Wonders of the Ancient World, 91, 235, *ptg235*
Shah Jahan, 415
Shakespeare, William, 214, 325, 595, 596–97, *p596*, *q596*, *q597*; Globe theater, 596, *p596*; plays of, 595, 596–97
shamanism, 511
Shang dynasty, *c276*, 280–283, *m281*, *q302*; art, 283; farming, 282; government, 282; importance of ancestors, 282, 283; language and writing, 282–83; military, 281; oracles, 282, *p282*, *q302*; religion, 282; slavery, 282; social structure, 281–82
shari'ah, 403
sheikh, 399
Shia, 407, 410
Shinto, 518, *p518*, 519, 525, 527
ships and shipping, 42, 43, *p43*, 102, 103, *p102*, 121, *p144*, 144–45, 176, 177, 193–97, *ptg195*, *ptg196*, 202, 204, 296, 317, *q358*, 411, *ptg428*, 429, 438–39, 475, 485, 494, *ptg494*, 495, 500–02, 514, 515, *p515*, 516, 530, 540–41, 544, 553, 563, 571, 584, 586, 587, *p587*, 609, *ptg609*, 615–17, *c617*, *m616–17*, 618–23, *c621*, 630, 631, 633, *m668*, 668–69, 670; in exploration, 615–17, *m616–17*, 618–23, *c621*; circumnavigation of the world, 623; in the slave trade, 438–39; *Mayflower*, 664, 666; *Santa Maria*, 501, 620, *c620*; smuggling, 667
Shiva, 258
Shoguns, 520–27, 633; Kamakura, 522–23; Ashikaga, 522–23
Shotoku, prince of Japan, *c508*, 518, 524
Sicily, 241, 317–18, 571, 685; architecture, *p241*
Siddhartha Gautama, prince, 260, *p260*, 263. *See also* Buddha, the.
Sikhism, 410
Silk Road, *c211*, *c247*, *c277*, 297–99, *m298*, *c305*, 476, 483, 491, 494, *ptg494*, 571, 585
Silla, 511, 512–13, *m513*
Sistine Chapel, *c581*, 593, *ptg593*, *q593*
slavery, 80, 142, 177, 179, 183, 185, 282; African Americans and, 687; Arabic, 411, 412; Egyptian, 117, 118, 124, 142; Europe and, 432, 438–39, *c617*, 622, 629–30, 635; Greek, 177, 179, 183, 185, 188, 189, 200, 201, 343; in Africa, 411, 420, *c421*, 425, 428, *c428*, 429, 432,438–39, *q439*, *m440*, 441, *c617*, 629, 630, 635, 666; in early civilizations, 69, 80; in Islamic civilizations, 411, 412, 438–39; in Kush, 129, 133; in the Americas, 432, 439, *c617*, 622, 629–30, 635, 687; rights of enslaved persons, 124, 412; Roman, 319, 321, 325, 333, *c338*, 341, 342, 343, 350, 353; *The Slave Trade*, 439
***Slave Trade, The* (Thomas),** 439
Slavs, 390, 560–61; Christianity and, 390; languages, 390; Mongol invasion of, 560; rivers, 560; trade, 560
Smith, Adam, *c27*, 50, *q50*, 699
***Social Contract, The* (Rousseau),** 655
socialism, 699–700
Socrates, *c211*, 221–22, *p221*, *c224*, 228–29, *q228*, *ptg*, *229*, *q229*
Socratic method, 221, *c224*
solid geometry, 240
Solomon, king of the Israelites, 150–51, *q170*; proverbs, 150; temple of (First Temple), 150, *ptg150*
Solon, 188, *p188*; biography, 188; reforms of, 188
Song dynasty, 474, 477, *m477*, 480, 481, 482, 483, 485–87, 493, 499
Songhai, 427–28, *c428*, 432, *m444*; government, 432; Islam in, 434–35; military, 432; trade, 432
Song of Roland, 566–67, *q567*
Sophists, 221, *c224*
Sophocles, 217–18
Source Book for Medieval History, A, *q549*
South America, 448, *m449*, 450, 451, 452, 453, 454, 456, 622, 623, 628–29, 631, 635 civilizations of, 456; exploration of, 622, 623, 626–27; farming, 454; gods, 455, 627; Treaty of Tordesillas, 622, 628. *See also* Americas; Inca; *individual country listings.*
South China Sea, *m300*
Southeast Asia, 64, 260, 262, 268, 295, 396, 406, 501, 502, 507–509, *m508–509*, 524, 528–33, *m529*, *q536*, 631; art, 530; farming, 500, 528–29; geography, 528–29, *m529*; government, 529; Islam in, 528, 533; kingdoms and empires, 530–33; religion, 529, 531; shipping, 530; trade, 500, 528–30, 532, 533. *See also individual country listings.*
Southwest Asia, 52, *c53*, 64, 65, 78, 123, 140, 154, 161, 190, 235, 236, 396, 398, *m399*, 404, 408–09, 491
Spain, *m48*, 318, 323, 333, *m334*, 364, 405–06, 413, 415, *m416*, *c473*, *c539*, 542, 575, 602, 607–09, 611, 619, 620, 621-22, 623, 624–27, 628–29, 631, 633–34; American empire, 628–29, 632; architecture, 415; art, 58, 608; Armada, 609, *ptg609*, *c617*; Catholicism in,

607–09; colonies and settlers, 628–29, 633, *c663, m665;* conquers Mexico, 624–26; conquers Peru, 626–27; conquistadors, 622, 624–27, *m625;* early humans, 58; exploration by, *c26,* 28, *c581,* 619, 621–22, 623, 624–27, *m625;* Inquisition, 568–69, 575, 607–08; Islam in, 405–06, 407, *p407,* 415, *c539,* 542, 571, 575, 607–08, 621; literature, 608; trade, 633. *See also* Europe, medieval.

Spanish Armada, 609, *ptg609, c617*

Spanish Inquisition, 569, 575, 607–08

Sparta, 172, 184–87, *m184,* 194–96, 203–05, *m206,* 225, *q225,* 241; agriculture, 185, 187; art and artifacts, 172, *p172, p186;* citizens, 185, 186; culture, 185–87; education, 208, *q208;* family, 186; government, 186; invasion of city-states, 185; law, 186; military, 172, 185–87, *ptg185, q185, q195;* roles of men and women, 172, 185–86, *q185, p186;* slavery, 185; trade, 187; women, 186

Spartacus, *c338,* 342, 343

Sphinx, 101, 113, *p113*

***Spirit of the Laws, The* (Montesquieu),** 652–53, *q653*

Sri Lanka: Buddhism in, 262

Stamp Act, 669; Stamp Act Congress, 669

Stearns, Peter N., *q24*

steel, 484

Stephens, John Lloyd, 459

steppes, 489, 491

Stoicism, 238, 344

stoics, 238

Stone Ages, 54, 61, *ptg61,* 62–63; homes, 61, *ptg61; See also* Mesolithic Age (Middle Stone Age); Neolithic Age (New Stone Age), Paleolithic Age (Old Stone Age).

Stonehenge, *c99*

storytelling, 82, 178, 218, 427, 437, 438, *p439,* 441

St. Peter's Basilica, 600

St. Petersburg, 657

stupas, 267, *p267;* "Great Stupa," 267

subcontinent, 248, *m249, m253*

Sudras, 255, *c255*

Suetonius, 324

Sufis, 406

Sui dynasty, 474–75, 476

Suleiman I, *c397,* 409, 410; biography, 410; Golden Age of Ottoman Empire, 410

Suleiman II, 395, *ptg395*

Sulla, 322, 323

sultan, 395, 408, 409, 410

Sumer, 74, *c74,* 76–85; Akkad and, 86, 87; art and artisans, 78, 80, *p80,* 81, *p81,* 83; artifacts, *p81;* astronomy, 83; calendar, 83; cities and city-states, 78–80, 81, 86; "cradle of civilization," 81; cuneiform writing, *c74,* 81–82, 87; development of civilization, 74, 76–83; economy, 81; farming, 79–81, *ptg79;* geography, 78–79; government, 80, 82; influence on history, 81; inventions, *c74,* 82–83; law, 79, 80, 87; life in, *p80,* 82; mathematics, 83; religion and gods, 79–80, 82, 87; roles of men and women, 80; slavery, 80; social classes, 76, 80; storytelling, 82; trade, 78, 79, 81, *p81*

***Summa Theologica* (Aquinas),** 566

Sundiata Keita, king of Mali, 427

Sunni, 407

Sunni Ali, 427, 434

Sushruta, 271

Swahili, 435

Sweden, 544, 611, 657

Switzerland, 603, 655

symbolism, 701–02

synagogues, 154–55, 165

Syracuse, 240; Roman attack of, 240

Syria, 86, 323, 400, 492; trade, *c99*

T

Tacitus, 347, 357

Taika reforms, *c508,* 518–19

Taino people, 621–22; slavery, 622

Taizong, emperor of China, 476

Taj Mahal, 415, *p415*

***Tale of Genji, The* (Murasaki),** 526

Talmud, 166–67, *p166, q167*

Tang dynasty, *c396,* 474, *m475,* 476, *ptg477,* 478, 480, 481, 482–88, 499, 512, 530

Tangun, 510

Taoism. *See* Daoism.

Tarquin the Proud, king of Etruscans, 310

taxes and taxation, 39, 42–43, 46, 88, 92, 109, 150, 155, *q170,* 177, 186, 191, 197, 203, 264, 268, 290, 311, 312, 313, 329, *c331,* 350, 352, 362, 376, 382, 406, 410, 427, *c428,* 430, 432, 460, 475, 492, 503, 519, 520, 531, 548, 554, 557, 558, 559, 561, 598, 601, 602, 607, 651, 657, 667–69, 672–73, *q673,*675, 677, *q681*

Tea Act, 668

technology, 19–20, 32, 38, 76, 82–83, 88, 271, 483–85, 502, 512, *p512,* 514, 552–53, 616, 619, 642, 690–95; changes over time, 4, 32, 56, 512, 619, 648, 692; Chinese, 285, 483–85, 486; computers, 2, *p2,* 270, 619; electricity, 694, 695; exploration and, 619, *p619;* geographic information systems (GIS), 32; Global Positioning System (GPS), *c27,* 32, 619, *p619;* Internet, 19–20, *p19;* of early humans, 52, 56, 60, 67; spread of, 37, 88, 483, 485–86, 488, 492; windmills and water mills, 553

Temple Mount, 150

Temujin. *See* Khan, Genghis.

Ten Commandments, 143, *c143, p143,* 147, *c170*

Tenochtitlán, *c449,* 625–26

Teotihuacán, 455–56; as first planned city, 455–56; decline of, 455–56

Teresa of Avila, 607

Terra-cotta warriors, 1, *p1*

terror, 491; Mongol use of, 491

Tertullian, *q331*

Texas, 686

Thailand, *m534,* 531–32; art, 532; Buddhism in, 262, 532; Hinduism in, 532; writing, 532

Thales, 226, *p226*

theater, 500, 595, 596, 610; Greek, 176, *ptg181,* 217–19, *p217,* 236, 237, 345; Globe theater, 596, *p596;* modern, 217, *p217;* Roman, 345, 347; Southeast Asian, 530, *p530. See also* drama.

Thebes, 120, *m124,* 126, *m134,* 205, 231

Themistocles, 195–96

theocracy, 108–09, 192–93, 531

Theocritus, 237

Theodosius, emperor of Rome, 352–53, 382

Theodora, Empress of Byzantine Empire, 362, *p362, q362;* biography, 362

theology, 565, 566

Theravada Buddhism, 262

Thermopylae, 195

Thirty Years' War, *c581,* 611, *ptg611, q614*

Thomas, Hugh, 439

Thoth, 110

Three Kingdoms period (Korea), 511–12

Thucydides, 203, 225, *q226*

Thutmose III, pharaoh of Egypt, 124

Tiberius, emperor of Rome, 330

Tiber River, 304, 307, *m334, m366*

Tibet, *m300,* 476, *m504;* Buddhism in, 262, 263, *p263;* lamas, 262

Tigris River, 74, *m75,* 76–78, 87, 88, *m94,* 103, 233, 408, *q418*

Timbuktu, 407, 427, *c428,* 434, 435

time lines, *c2–3,* 7; Africa, *c420-21;* Age of Exploration and Trade, *c616–17;* Americas, *c448–49;* Ancient Greece, *c172–73, c210–11;* Ancient India, *c7, c246–47;* Ancient Rome, *c304–05;* Early China, *c276–77;* Early Christianity *c370-72;* Early Civilizations, *c52–53;* Egypt and Kush, *c98–99;* Imperial China, *c472–73;* Islamic civilization, *c396-97;* Israelites, *c138–39;* Korea, Japan, and Southeast Asia, *c508–09;* Medieval Europe, *c538–39;* Mesopotamia, *c74–75;* Political Revolutions, *c662–63;* Renaissance and Reformation, *c580–81;* Roman Empire, *c338–39;* Scientific Revolution and the Enlightenment, *c640–41;* United States Voting Rights, *c26–27*

Titus, emperor of Rome, 330

Tokugawa Ieyasu, *c640*
Tolstoy, Leo, 701
Tomoe Gozen, 521, *q521*
Torah, 142–43, 152, 155, *p155,* 156–57, 162–63, 166; teachings of, 156–57, 162–63, 166; the Prophets, 155; the Writings, 155
Torquemada, Tomás de, 608
Tours, Battle of, 542
trade, 37, 39,41–43, 89, *c99,* 191, 254, 308, 478, 570, 575, 628–35; African, *c420-21,* 424, 425–29, *m426, q427, c428,* 429, 430, 431, 432, 433, 436, 441, 444, *q446,* 502, 615, 620, *m634;* Arabic, 400, 401, 406–07, 411–12, 413, 429, 433, 533; Asian, 500, 512, 524, 528–30, 532, 533, *c617,* 618, *m632,* 633, *m634;* barriers to, 42; British, 668–69, 670, *m668,* 678; boycotts, 669; camels and, 400, 425; Chaldean, 92, 93; Chinese, 268, 285, 290–91, 296, 297–98, *m298,* 472, 476, 478, 482, 483, *p483,* 484–85, 500, 501–02, 524, 571; Columbian Exchange, 634–35, *m634;* Commercial Revolution, 633; cottage industries, 634; early humans and, 66, 68, 448, 454, 466; Egyptian, 102, 106, *m106,* 108, 116, 121, 122, 123, 126, 130, 178; European, 540, 553–54, *ptg554,* 555, 564, 570–71, 575, 584–86, 587, 588, 618–22, 628–35, *m632, m634,* 668–69, 670, *m668;* exports, 42, *g42,* 632; global, 43; Greek, 174, 176, 177, 178, 179, *m180,* 183, 187, 188, 202; imports, 42, *g42,* 43, 632; in ancient Israel, 141, 150; Indian, 248, 252, 267, 268, 296, 297, 530, 571, *m632,* 633; in Kush, 129, 130, 132–33; in the Americas, 42–43, 448, 454–55, 460, 466, 628–35, *m634, q638,* 668–69, 670, *m668;* Japanese, 42, 512, 523–524, 525; joint-stock companies, 633; Korean, 524; limits and bans, 42; mercantilism, 632–33, 668; Mesopotamian, 86, 106, 252; Mongolian, 492, 494; Native American, 466, 635, *q638;* Phoenician, 123, 144–45; Portuguese, 502, 633; Roman, 307, 331, *m332,* 333, 344, *p344, m346,* 347, 351, 358, *q358,* 368; shipping, 144–45, *p144;* Sumerian, 78, 79, 81, *p81;* trade routes, 81, 87, 92, *c99, m106,* 123, 151, 268, 297, *m298, m332, m346,* 360–61, 407, *m408,* 412, 425–27, *m426,* 428, *m440,* 472, *m472–73,* 483, 492, 533, 561, 571, 618–23, *m668;* United States, 42–43, 668–69, *m668,* 670
Trafalgar, Battle of, 677
tragedy, Greek, 217
Trajan, emperor of Rome, 331, *c331,* 332
***Travels* (Young),** *q673*
***Travels in Asia and Africa* (Ibn Battuta),** *p434, q446*
treaties, 150, 622, 628
Treaty of Tordesillas, 622, 628
tribes, 40, 142, 144, 146–47, *q170,* 254, 318, 510; Arab, 399–400, 401, 402. *See also* Twelve Tribes of Israel.
Tribonian, 363
tribunes, 313, 327
tribute, 88, 92, 120, 151, 476, 491, 501, 515, 561
triumvirate, 323; First Triumvirate, 323; Second Triumvirate, 326
Trojan horse, 215, *ptg215*
Trojan War, 8, 177, 215, 217
Troy, 8, 177, *m206,* 215, 307; battle of, 215, 348; people of, 307, *q349*
Tudor family, 604–05
Ture, Muhammad, *c421,* 432, 434–35
Tutankhamen, Pharoah of Egypt, 16; gold mask of, *p16, c99,* 125–26, *p125*
Twelve Tables, *c304,* 315
Twelve Tribes of Israel, 142, 148, 149, *p149, q170*
Twenty-sixth Amendment, *c27*
***Two Treatises of Government* (Locke),** 652
tyrants, 183–84, 188

U

Uighurs, 476
Umar, *c406*
Umayyads, *c396,* 404–05, *c406,* 407
United Kingdom, *m704. See also* Britain; England; Ireland; Scotland.
United Nations, 655; UN Women, 655
United States, 687–89, *m687,* 695, 698; abolitionism, 687; Capitol Building, 357, *p357;* Civil War, 687; colonies of, 605, *c641,* 664–71, *m665;* Confederate States of America, 687; Congress, *c27,* 44, *g45, c200;* Continental Army, 315; Constitution and amendments, 25, *c27,* 44–46, 224, 327, 653; Declaration of Independence, *c641, c663;* economy, *c27,* 40, 42–43, 689; expansion of, *m687;* exploration of, *m22;* geography, *c424;* government, 42–43, 44–46, *g45,* 199, *c200,* 313, 666–71, *q667;* Great Depression, 41, 43; House of Burgesses, 631; immigrants, 684, 687; industry, 689, 695; inventions in, 693; laws, 44–45, 46, *c200,* 316; Library of Congress, 89; literature, 701; "Manifest Destiny," 686; nationalism, 686–89; politics, 679; Puritans, 605; recession, *c27,* 41; recreation, 33; slavery, 687; Supreme Court, 45, *q50;* trade, 42–43, 668–69, *m668,* 670; war with Mexico, 688; westward expansion, 686, *m688*
universities, 565, 566, 643; development of, 565
Untouchables, 256, 262
Upanishads, 257–58, *p258, q258*
Urban II, Pope, *c397,* 561
urbanization, 696
Uthman, *c406*
utilitarianism, 699

V

Vaisyas, 255, *c255, p255*
Valley of the Kings, 121, 122
Vandals, 354
van Eyck, Jan, 594, *ptg595*
varnas, 255–56, *c255, p255,* 259, 261
vassals, 548–49, *c549,* 554, 558, *q567,* 578, *q578*
Vatican, 239, 590, 592, 593; art, 592, 593; library, 590
Vedas, 254, *q254,* 257, 269
Venice, Italy, 494, 583, 585, 586, 587, 686; canals of, 586, *p587;* doge; 587; importance during the Renaissance, 586; ships, 586, 587, *p587*
***Vergil's Aeneid: Hero, War, Humanity* (tr. G.B. Cobbold),** *q249*
Versailles, 655
Vesalius, Andreas, 647
Vespasian, emperor of Rome, 330
Vespucci, Amerigo, 622
veto, 313
Victor Emmanuel, king of Italy, 685
Vienna, 679; Congress of Vienna, 679
Vietnam, 476, 495, *m534,* 530–31; China and, *c509,* 530–31; civil service examinations, 531; government, 531; independence, 530
Vikings, *c397, c421, c473, c509,* 544, *m545,* 556; longboats, 544
***Vindication of the Rights of Women, A* (Wollstonecraft),** 655, *q655*
Virgil, 307, 346, *q346,* 348–49, *p348, q348, q349,* 357
Virginia, 664, 666, 670; House of Burgesses, 631, 666; law, 666
Virginia Company, 631, 664, 666
Vishnu, 258
Visigoths, *ptg353,* 353–54, 355
Vladimir, 560
volcanoes, 32, 528–29; Mount St. Helens, 33, *p33;* Mount Vesuvius, 14, 303, 330, *p330, c370;*
Voltaire, 653, *ptg654, m658;* deism, 654
von Guericke, Otto, 611, *q611*
voting: electoral districts, 683; rights, *c26–27,* 46, 189, *c200,* 203, 311, 312, 356, 675, 682–84, *q683,* 698, 699

W

Wales, 542, 557
Wang Kŏn, 513
War of Roses, 574
warlords, 474
Washington, D.C., 219
Washington, George, 315, *ptg667,* 671
Waterloo, Battle of, 679
Watt, James, 692

Wealth of Nations, The **(Smith),** 699
Wellington, Duke of, 679
Well of Life, The **(Gabirol),** 406
Wendi, emperor of China, 474
West Bank, 65
Western Wall, 165, *p165*
William I, emperor of Germany, 686
William I, king of England (William the Conqueror), 11–12; 556–57, *ptg557*
William III, king of England, 652; "Glorious Revolution," 652
Wittenberg, Germany, 600
Wollstonecraft, Mary, *c641,* 655, *q655, ptg655*
women, 87, 295, 362, 383, 412–13, 460, 467, 511, 521, *q521,* 655, 695, 697, 698, 700, *q700;* African, 433, 437–38; as soldiers, 438, 521, *q521;* discrimination against, 481; early humans, 55–56, 67; Greek, 172, 181, 185–86, *p186,* 187–88, 189, 200–201, *c200,* 222; in ancient Egypt, 117, *p117,* 118–19, 122–24; Japanese, 524, *ptg524,* 526; rights of, 21, 80, 87, 118, 181, 186, 222, 256, 314, 342, 362, *c641,* 655 *q655,* 683–84, 698; roles of men and women, 55–56, 67, 80, 118–19, 157, 172, 185–86, *q185, p186,* 187–88, 189, 200–201, *c200,* 256, 291, *p291,* 295, 412–13, *q470,* 654, 698, 699, 701; Roman, 314, *ptg342,* 342–43; rulers and leaders, 122–24, 125, 342,362, 438, *p438,* 460, 471, 476, *q470,* 512, 524; suffrage, *p688*
woodblock printing, *c397,* 484, *p484,* 512, 591, *p591*
working class, 697, 699; growth of, 697
Works of Turgo, The **(ed. Schelle),** *q681*
World War I, *p14*
World War II, 521, 522
Wright, Orville and Wilbur, *c663,* 695; biography, 695
writing: Chinese, *c172,* 282–83, 293, 511, 526; cuneiform, *c74,* 81–82, *p83,* 87, *c172,* 178, 461; hieroglyphics, *c98,* 105, 129, 455, 461; in early civilizations, 69, 74, 81–82, 88, 123, 282–83, 293, 455, 461, *q470;* invention and development of, 6, 8, 69, 74, 81–82, 104–05, 123, 254, 455, 461, 544; Thai, 532
Wu, empress of China, 471, *ptg471, c472,* 476, *ptg476, q506;* biography, 476
Wu Cheng'en, 496–97, *p496, q496, q497*
Wu Wang, 283
Wycliffe, John, 573, 598–99

X

Xenophon, 228
Xerxes, king of Persia, *c173,* 194, 196, *ptg196*
Xia dynasty, 280–81
Xiongnu, 293, 295, 297
Yamato, *c339, c371, c420, c508,* 517, 518

Y

Yangdi, emperor of China, 474–75; revolt against, 475, 476
Yayoi, *c508,* 516–17
Yi dynasty, 514–15
Yi Song-gye, 514
Yong Le, *c473,* 499, 502
Yoruba, 432
Young, Arthur, 673, *q673*
Yuan dynasty, 493, 494, 498
Yü the Great, 280

Z

Zaccai, Yohanan ben, 166
Zapotec, 455–56, 461; cities, 455–56; decline of, 456; development of hieroglyphic writing, 455, 461; farming, 455; trade, 455
Zealots, 164, 373, *q394*
Zeno, 238
Zeus, 189, 213–14, 343
Zhang Qian, 297
Zheng He, 501–02, *m501, q501*
Zhou Daguan, 531, *q531*
Zhou dynasty, *c277,* 283–85, *m284,* 290, 292; artisans, 290; farming, 285; fall of, 285; government, 283–84; inventions, 285; Mandate of Heaven, 284; military, 284, 285; religion, 284; trade, 285
Zhu Yuanzhang, 498
ziggurat, 79–80, *ptg81,* 90
Zimbabwe, *c428,* 429, *m444;* trade, *c428,* 429
Zola, Émile, 701
Zoroaster, 192
Zoroastrianism, 192–93, *p192, q193*

McGraw-Hill Networks™ A Social Studies Learning System. Meets you anywhere—takes you everywhere. Go online at connected.mcgraw-hill.com.

1. Go to connected.mcgraw-hill.com.
2. Get your User Name and Password from your teacher and enter them.
3. Click on your **Networks** book.
4. Select your chapter and lesson.